Hoover's MasterList of U.S. Companies

2022

Hoover's MasterList of U.S. Companies is intended to provide readers with accurate and authoritative information about the enterprises covered in it. The information contained herein is as accurate as we could reasonably make it. In many cases we have relied on third-party material that we believe to be trustworthy but were unable to independently verify. We do not warrant that the book is absolutely accurate or without error. Readers should not rely on any information contained herein in instances where such reliance might cause financial loss.

The publisher, the editors, and their data suppliers specifically disclaim all warranties, including the implied warranties of merchantability and fitness for a specific purpose. This book is sold with the understanding that neither the publisher, the editors, nor any content contributors are engaged in providing investment, financial, accounting, legal, or other professional advice.

Mergent Inc., provided financial data for most public companies in this book. For private companies and historical information on public companies prior to their becoming public, we obtained information directly from the companies or from third-party material that we believe to be trustworthy. Hoover's, Inc., is solely responsible for the presentation of all data.

Many of the names of products and services mentioned in this book are the trademarks or service marks of the companies manufacturing or selling them and are subject to protection under U.S. law. Space has not permitted us to indicate which names are subject to such protection, and readers are advised to consult with the owners of such marks regarding their use. Hoover's is a trademark of Hoover's, Inc.

Copyright © 2022 by Hoover's, Inc. All rights reserved. No part of this book may be reproduced or transmitted in any form or by any means, electronic or mechanical, including by photocopying, facsimile transmission, recording, rekeying, or using any information storage and retrieval system, without permission in writing from Hoover's, except that brief passages may be quoted by a reviewer in a magazine, in a newspaper, online, or in a broadcast review.

10 9 8 7 6 5 4 3 2 1

Publishers Cataloging-in-Publication Data

Hoover's MasterList of U.S. Companies 2021,

    Includes indexes.

    ISBN: 978-1-64972-827-2

    ISSN 1549-6457

    1. Business enterprises — Directories. 2. Corporations — Directories.

HF3010 338.7

U.S. AND WORLD BOOK SALES

Mergent Inc.
28 Liberty ST
58th Floor
New York, NY 10005
Phone: 704-559-6961

e-mail: skardon@ftserussell.com
Web: www.mergentbusinesspress.com

Mergent Inc.

Executive Managing Director: John Pedernales

Managing Director of Print Products and Publisher: Thomas Wecera

Director of Print Products: Charlot Volny

Quality Assurance Editor: Wayne Arnold

Production Research Assistant: Davie Christna

Data Manager: Allison Shank

MERGENT CUSTOMER SERVICE-PRINT PRODUCTS
Support and Fulfillment Manager: Stephanie Kardon
Phone: 704-559-6961
e-mail: skardon@ftserussell.com
Web: www.mergentbusinesspress.com

ABOUT MERGENT, INC.

For over 100 years, Mergent, Inc. has been a leading provider of business and financial information on public and private companies globally. Mergent is known to be a trusted partner to corporate and financial institutions, as well as to academic and public libraries. Today we continue to build on a century of experience by transforming data into knowledge and combining our expertise with the latest technology to create new global data and analytical solutions for our clients. With advanced data collection services, cloud-based applications, desktop analytics and print products, Mergent and its subsidiaries provide solutions from top down economic and demographic information, to detailed equity and debt fundamental analysis. We incorporate value added tools such as quantitative Smart Beta equity research and tools for portfolio building and measurement. Based in the U.S., Mergent maintains a strong global presence, with offices in New York, Charlotte, San Diego, London, Tokyo, Kuching and Melbourne. Mergent, Inc. is a member of the London Stock Exchange plc group of companies. The Mergent business forms part of LSEG's Information Services Division, which includes FTSE Russell, a global leader in indexes.

Abbreviations

AFL-CIO – American Federation of Labor and Congress of Industrial Organizations
AMA – American Medical Association
AMEX – American Stock Exchange
ARM – adjustable-rate mortgage
ASP – application services provider
ATM – asynchronous transfer mode
ATM – automated teller machine
CAD/CAM – computer-aided design/computer-aided manufacturing
CD-ROM – compact disc – read-only memory
CD-R – CD-recordable
CEO – chief executive officer
CFO – chief financial officer
CMOS – complementary metal oxide silicon
COO – chief operating officer
DAT – digital audiotape
DOD – Department of Defense
DOE – Department of Energy
DOS – disk operating system
DOT – Department of Transportation
DRAM – dynamic random-access memory
DSL – digital subscriber line
DVD – digital versatile disc/digital video disc
DVD-R – DVD-recordable
EPA – Environmental Protection Agency
EPROM – erasable programmable read-only memory
EPS – earnings per share
ESOP – employee stock ownership plan
EU – European Union
EVP – executive vice president
FCC – Federal Communications Commission
FDA – Food and Drug Administration
FDIC – Federal Deposit Insurance Corporation
FTC – Federal Trade Commission
FTP – file transfer protocol
GATT – General Agreement on Tariffs and Trade
GDP – gross domestic product
HMO – health maintenance organization
HR – human resources
HTML – hypertext markup language
ICC – Interstate Commerce Commission
IPO – initial public offering
IRS – Internal Revenue Service
ISP – Internet service provider
kWh – kilowatt-hour
LAN – local-area network
LBO – leveraged buyout
LCD – liquid crystal display

LNG – liquefied natural gas
LP – limited partnership
Ltd. – limited
mips – millions of instructions per second
MW – megawatt
NAFTA – North American Free Trade Agreement
NASA – National Aeronautics and Space Administration
NASDAQ – National Association of Securities Dealers Automated Quotations
NATO – North Atlantic Treaty Organization
NYSE – New York Stock Exchange
OCR – optical character recognition
OECD – Organization for Economic Cooperation and Development
OEM – original equipment manufacturer
OPEC – Organization of Petroleum Exporting Countries
OS – operating system
OSHA – Occupational Safety and Health Administration
OTC – over-the-counter
PBX – private branch exchange
PCMCIA – Personal Computer Memory Card International Association
P/E – price to earnings ratio
RAID – redundant array of independent disks
RAM – random-access memory
R&D – research and development
RBOC – regional Bell operating company
RISC – reduced instruction set computer
REIT – real estate investment trust
ROA – return on assets
ROE – return on equity
ROI – return on investment
ROM – read-only memory
S&L – savings and loan
SCSI – Small Computer System Interface
SEC – Securities and Exchange Commission
SEVP – senior executive vice president
SIC – Standard Industrial Classification
SOC – system on a chip
SVP – senior vice president
USB – universal serial bus
VAR – value-added reseller
VAT – value-added tax
VC – venture capitalist
VP – vice president
VoIP – Voice over Internet Protocol
WAN – wide-area network
WWW – World Wide Web

CONTENTS

Volume 1

About Hoover's MasterList of
U.S. Companies 2022 vii

Company Lists 2a-21a
   Top 500 Companies By Sales 2a
   Top 500 Companies By Employer 7a
   Top 500 Companies by Net Profit 12a
   Mergent Top 500 Global Companies . . . 17a

Company Listings A – L 2

Volume 2

Company Listings M – Z 854

Indexes 1535
   By Company 1537
   By Headquarters Location 1575

Hoover's MasterList
of U.S. Companies

Company Rankings

Top 500 Companies by Sales
Hoover's MasterList of U.S. Companies 2022

Rank	Company	Headquarters	Sales ($ Mil)
1	Walmart Inc	AR	$559,151
2	Amazon.com Inc	WA	$469,822
3	Apple Inc	CA	$365,817
4	CVS Health Corp	RI	$292,111
5	UnitedHealth Group Inc	MN	$287,597
6	Exxon Mobil Corp	TX	$285,640
7	Alphabet Inc	CA	$257,637
8	Berkshire Hathaway Inc	NE	$245,510
9	McKesson Corp	TX	$238,228
10	AmerisourceBergen Corp.	PA	$213,989
11	Costco Wholesale Corp	WA	$195,929
12	AT&T Inc	TX	$168,864
13	Microsoft Corporation	WA	$168,088
14	Cardinal Health, Inc.	OH	$162,467
15	Cigna Corp (New)	CT	$160,401
16	Anthem Inc	IN	$138,639
17	Ford Motor Co. (DE)	MI	$136,341
18	Verizon Communications Inc	NY	$133,613
19	Walgreens Boots Alliance Inc	IL	$132,509
20	Kroger Co (The)	OH	$132,498
21	Home Depot Inc	GA	$132,110
22	JPMorgan Chase & Co	NY	$127,202
23	General Motors Co	MI	$127,004
24	Centene Corp	MO	$125,982
25	Meta Platforms Inc	CA	$117,929
26	Comcast Corp	PA	$116,385
27	Phillips 66	TX	$114,852
28	Valero Energy Corp	TX	$113,977
29	Federal Reserve System	DC	$104,976
30	Fannie Mae	DC	$101,543
31	United Parcel Service Inc	GA	$97,287
32	Chevron Corporation	CA	$94,692
33	Dell Technologies Inc	TX	$94,224
34	Bank of America Corp	NC	$93,851
35	Johnson & Johnson	NJ	$93,775
36	Target Corp	MN	$93,561
37	Lowe's Companies Inc	NC	$89,597
38	Citigroup Inc	NY	$88,839
39	Archer Daniels Midland Co.	IL	$85,249
40	FedEx Corp	TN	$83,959
41	Humana, Inc.	KY	$83,064
42	Wells Fargo & Co (New)	CA	$82,407
43	T-Mobile US Inc	WA	$80,118
44	PepsiCo Inc	NY	$79,474
45	Intel Corp	CA	$79,024
46	Procter & Gamble Co (The)	OH	$76,118
47	General Electric Co	MA	$74,196
48	MetLife Inc	NY	$71,080
49	Prudential Financial Inc	NJ	$70,934
50	Albertsons Companies Inc	ID	$69,690
51	Marathon Petroleum Corp.	OH	$69,032
52	Disney (Walt) Co. (The)	CA	$67,418
53	Lockheed Martin Corp	MD	$67,044
54	Freddie Mac	VA	$65,898
55	Raytheon Technologies Corp	MA	$64,388
56	HP Inc	CA	$63,487
57	Boeing Co.	IL	$62,286
58	HCA Healthcare Inc	TN	$58,752
59	International Business Machines Corp.	NY	$57,350
60	AbbVie Inc	IL	$56,197
61	Dow Inc	MI	$54,968
62	Federal Reserve Bank Of New Y	NY	$54,640
63	Tesla Inc	TX	$53,823
64	Goldman Sachs Group Inc	NY	$53,498
65	American International Group Inc	NY	$52,057
66	Morgan Stanley	NY	$52,047
67	Charter Communications Inc (New)	CT	$51,682
68	Sysco Corp	TX	$51,298
69	Caterpillar Inc.	IL	$50,971
70	Allstate Corp	IL	$50,588
71	Cisco Systems Inc	CA	$49,818
72	ConocoPhillips	TX	$48,349
73	Merck & Co Inc	NJ	$47,994
74	Best Buy Inc	MN	$47,262
75	Tyson Foods Inc	AR	$47,049
76	Bristol Myers Squibb Co.	NY	$46,385
77	Publix Super Markets, Inc.	FL	$45,204
78	NIKE Inc	OR	$44,538
79	Deere & Co.	IL	$44,024
80	American Express Co.	NY	$43,663
81	Abbott Laboratories	IL	$43,075
82	Progressive Corp. (OH)	OH	$42,658
83	StoneX Group Inc	NY	$42,443
84	Pfizer Inc	NY	$41,908
85	Oracle Corp	TX	$40,479
86	Energy Transfer LP	TX	$38,954
87	Coca-Cola Co (The)	GA	$38,655
88	General Dynamics Corp	VA	$38,469
89	CHS Inc	MN	$38,448
90	Northrop Grumman Corp	VA	$35,667
91	3M Co	MN	$35,355
92	Travelers Companies Inc (The)	NY	$34,816
93	Arrow Electronics, Inc.	CO	$34,477
94	Honeywell International Inc	NC	$34,392
95	Dollar General Corp	TN	$33,747
96	Qualcomm Inc	CA	$33,566
97	Exelon Corp	IL	$33,039
98	Thermo Fisher Scientific Inc	MA	$32,218
99	TJX Companies, Inc.	MA	$32,137
100	Capital One Financial Corp	VA	$31,643
101	TD SYNNEX Corp	CA	$31,614
102	Philip Morris International Inc	NY	$31,405
103	Performance Food Group Co	VA	$30,399
104	Delta Air Lines Inc (DE)	GA	$29,899
105	American Airlines Group Inc	TX	$29,882
106	Netflix Inc	CA	$29,698
107	US Foods Holding Corp	IL	$29,487
108	Danaher Corp	DC	$29,453
109	Jabil Inc	FL	$29,285
110	Starbucks Corp.	WA	$29,061
111	Mondelez International Inc	IL	$28,720
112	Paramount Global	NY	$28,586
113	Eli Lilly & Co	IN	$28,318
114	Hewlett Packard Enterprise Co	TX	$27,784
115	DR Horton Inc	TX	$27,774
116	Molina Healthcare Inc	CA	$27,771
117	Micron Technology Inc.	ID	$27,705
118	Broadcom Inc (DE)	CA	$27,450
119	Gilead Sciences Inc	CA	$27,305
120	PBF Energy Inc	NJ	$27,253

Top 500 Companies by Sales
Hoover's MasterList of U.S. Companies 2022 continued)

Rank	Company	Headquarters	Sales ($ Mil)
121	Enterprise Products Partners L.P.	TX	$27,200
122	Lennar Corp	FL	$27,131
123	United Natural Foods Inc.	RI	$26,950
124	Altria Group Inc	VA	$26,153
125	Kraft Heinz Co (The)	PA	$26,042
126	Amgen Inc	CA	$25,979
127	AutoNation, Inc.	FL	$25,844
128	Penske Automotive Group Inc	MI	$25,555
129	Dollar Tree Inc	VA	$25,509
130	PayPal Holdings Inc	CA	$25,371
131	United Airlines Holdings Inc	IL	$24,634
132	Visa Inc	CA	$24,105
133	Rite Aid Corp.	PA	$24,043
134	Cummins, Inc.	IN	$24,021
135	Duke Energy Corp	NC	$23,868
136	CBRE Group Inc	TX	$23,826
137	U.S. Bancorp (DE)	MN	$23,714
138	Paccar Inc.	WA	$23,522
139	Plains GP Holdings LP	TX	$23,290
140	Plains All American Pipeline LP	TX	$23,290
141	Southern Co.	GA	$23,113
142	Robinson (C.H.) Worldwide, Inc.	MN	$23,102
143	Applied Materials, Inc.	CA	$23,063
144	Freeport-McMoRan Inc	AZ	$22,845
145	Lithia Motors Inc	OR	$22,832
146	Truist Financial Corp	NC	$22,715
147	Hartford Financial Services Group Inc.	CT	$22,390
148	AFLAC Inc.	GA	$22,106
149	Whirlpool Corp	MI	$21,985
150	Union Pacific Corp	NE	$21,804
151	Salesforce.Com Inc	CA	$21,252
152	ManpowerGroup	WI	$20,724
153	Lumen Technologies Inc	LA	$20,712
154	PG&E Corp (Holding Co)	CA	$20,642
155	Carrier Global Corp	FL	$20,613
156	Baker Hughes Company	TX	$20,502
157	Baker Hughes Holdings LLC	TX	$20,502
158	Cleveland-Cliffs Inc (New)	OH	$20,444
159	World Fuel Services Corp.	FL	$20,358
160	United States Steel Corp.	PA	$20,275
161	Becton Dickinson And Co	NJ	$20,248
162	Nucor Corp.	NC	$20,140
163	Sherwin-Williams Co (The)	OH	$19,945
164	Marsh & McLennan Companies Inc.	NY	$19,820
165	Avnet Inc	AZ	$19,535
166	Tenet Healthcare Corp.	TX	$19,485
167	Kimberly-Clark Corp.	TX	$19,440
168	International Paper Co	TN	$19,363
169	Kyndryl Holdings Inc	NY	$19,352
170	Lear Corp.	MI	$19,263
171	Lincoln National Corp.	PA	$19,230
172	McDonald's Corp	IL	$19,208
173	Carmax Inc.	VA	$18,950
174	Mastercard Inc	NY	$18,884
175	Genuine Parts Co.	GA	$18,871
176	WestRock Co	GA	$18,746
177	Cognizant Technology Solutions Corp.	NJ	$18,507
178	CDW Corp	IL	$18,468
179	Texas Instruments, Inc.	TX	$18,344
180	PNC Financial Services Group (The)	PA	$18,262
181	Emerson Electric Co.	MO	$18,236
182	L3Harris Technologies Inc	FL	$18,194
183	General Mills Inc	MN	$18,127
184	Macy's Inc	NY	$18,097
185	Rocket Companies Inc	MI	$18,029
186	Waste Management, Inc. (DE)	TX	$17,931
187	DXC Technology Co	VA	$17,729
188	Exelon Generation Co LLC	PA	$17,603
189	Constellation Energy Corp	MD	$17,603
190	Goodyear Tire & Rubber Co.	OH	$17,478
191	Colgate-Palmolive Co.	NY	$17,421
192	Murphy USA Inc	AR	$17,361
193	Stryker Corp	MI	$17,108
194	NextEra Energy Inc	FL	$17,069
195	Bank of New York Mellon Corp	NY	$16,940
196	Western Digital Corp	CA	$16,922
197	PPG Industries Inc	PA	$16,802
198	NVIDIA Corp	CA	$16,675
199	DuPont de Nemours Inc	DE	$16,653
200	Kinder Morgan Inc.	TX	$16,610
201	Jones Lang LaSalle Inc	IL	$16,590
202	Advanced Micro Devices Inc	CA	$16,434
203	Occidental Petroleum Corp	TX	$16,261
204	Lauder (Estee) Cos., Inc. (The)	NY	$16,215
205	BlackRock Inc	NY	$16,205
206	Regeneron Pharmaceuticals, Inc.	NY	$16,072
207	Kohl's Corp.	WI	$15,955
208	Southwest Airlines Co	TX	$15,790
209	Adobe Inc	CA	$15,785
210	Synchrony Financial	CT	$15,752
211	Fluor Corp.	TX	$15,668
212	Stanley Black & Decker Inc	CT	$15,617
213	DISH Network Corp	CO	$15,493
214	BJs Wholesale Club Holdings Inc	MA	$15,430
215	Tenneco Inc	IL	$15,379
216	Halliburton Company	TX	$15,295
217	Automatic Data Processing Inc.	NJ	$15,005
218	DTE Energy Co	MI	$14,964
219	American Electric Power Co Inc	OH	$14,919
220	Fiserv Inc	WI	$14,852
221	BorgWarner Inc	MI	$14,838
222	Pilgrims Pride Corp.	CO	$14,777
223	Loews Corp.	NY	$14,657
224	Pioneer Natural Resources Co	TX	$14,643
225	AutoZone, Inc.	TN	$14,630
226	Lam Research Corp	CA	$14,626
227	Reinsurance Group of America, Inc.	MO	$14,596
228	Illinois Tool Works, Inc.	IL	$14,455
229	Parker-Hannifin Corp	OH	$14,348
230	Otis Worldwide Corp	CT	$14,298
231	Omnicom Group, Inc.	NY	$14,289
232	Principal Financial Group Inc	IA	$14,263
233	Kellogg Co	MI	$14,181
234	Qurate Retail Inc - Com Ser B	CO	$14,177
235	Qurate Retail Inc	CO	$14,177
236	Dominion Energy Inc (New)	VA	$14,172
237	Wayfair Inc	MA	$14,145
238	Jacobs Engineering Group, Inc.	TX	$14,093
239	Corning Inc	NY	$14,082
240	LabCorp	NC	$13,979

Top 500 Companies by Sales
Hoover's MasterList of U.S. Companies 2022 (continued)

Rank	Company	Headquarters	Sales ($ Mil)
241	PulteGroup Inc	GA	$13,927
242	Fidelity National Information Serv	FL	$13,877
243	IQVIA Holdings Inc	NC	$13,874
244	Marriott International, Inc.	MD	$13,857
245	Berry Global Group Inc	IN	$13,850
246	Ball Corp	CO	$13,811
247	Gap Inc	CA	$13,800
248	Leidos Holdings Inc	VA	$13,737
249	Consolidated Edison Inc	NY	$13,676
250	Edison International	CA	$13,578
251	Southern California Edison C	CA	$13,546
252	Xcel Energy Inc	MN	$13,431
253	AECOM	TX	$13,341
254	Toyota Motor Credit Corp.	TX	$13,165
255	Unum Group	TN	$13,162
256	Grainger (W.W.), Inc.	IL	$13,022
257	Discover Financial Services	IL	$12,953
258	Fox Corp	NY	$12,909
259	Markel Corp (Holding Co)	VA	$12,846
260	XPO Logistics, Inc.	CT	$12,806
261	Baxter International Inc	IL	$12,784
262	Tractor Supply Co.	TN	$12,731
263	Federal Reserve Bank of San F	CA	$12,679
264	Ross Stores Inc	CA	$12,532
265	CSX Corp	FL	$12,522
266	Equitable Holdings Inc	NY	$12,415
267	Henry Schein Inc	NY	$12,401
268	Textron Inc	RI	$12,382
269	Community Health Systems, Inc.	TN	$12,368
270	Mosaic Co. (The)	FL	$12,357
271	Wesco International, Inc.	PA	$12,326
272	Thor Industries, Inc.	IN	$12,317
273	Devon Energy Corp.	OK	$12,206
274	Charles Schwab Corp	TX	$12,109
275	Aramark	PA	$12,096
276	State Street Corp.	MA	$12,030
277	Santander Holdings USA Inc.	MA	$11,970
278	Coupang Inc		$11,967
279	Viatris Inc	PA	$11,946
280	CNA Financial Corp	IL	$11,908
281	Ameriprise Financial Inc	MN	$11,899
282	Boston Scientific Corp.	MA	$11,888
283	Bath & Body Works Inc	OH	$11,847
284	Ecolab Inc	MN	$11,790
285	VMware Inc	CA	$11,767
286	Florida Power & Light Co.	FL	$11,662
287	LKQ Corp	IL	$11,629
288	DaVita Inc	CO	$11,619
289	Keurig Dr Pepper Inc	MA	$11,618
290	O'Reilly Automotive, Inc.	MO	$11,604
291	Crown Holdings Inc	PA	$11,575
292	Universal Health Services, Inc.	PA	$11,559
293	Newmont Corp	CO	$11,497
294	Vistra Corp	TX	$11,443
295	Hormel Foods Corp.	MN	$11,386
296	Sempra	CA	$11,370
297	Republic Services Inc	AZ	$11,295
298	Quanta Services, Inc.	TX	$11,203
299	Mohawk Industries, Inc.	GA	$11,201
300	Conagra Brands Inc	IL	$11,185
301	HollyFrontier Corp	TX	$11,184
302	Norfolk Southern Corp	GA	$11,142
303	Uber Technologies Inc	CA	$11,139
304	FirstEnergy Corp	OH	$11,132
305	EOG Resources, Inc.	TX	$11,032
306	Advance Auto Parts Inc	NC	$10,998
307	Biogen Inc	MA	$10,982
308	Booking Holdings Inc	CT	$10,958
309	Amphenol Corp.	CT	$10,876
310	Group 1 Automotive, Inc.	TX	$10,852
311	Ally Financial Inc	MI	$10,780
312	Fidelity National Financial Inc	FL	$10,778
313	Nordstrom, Inc.	WA	$10,715
314	Sunoco LP	TX	$10,710
315	Discovery Inc	NY	$10,671
316	Consolidated Edison Co. of N	NY	$10,647
317	Newell Brands Inc	GA	$10,589
318	Tennessee Valley Authority	TN	$10,503
319	Air Products & Chemicals Inc	PA	$10,323
320	Molson Coors Beverage Co	Quebec	$10,280
321	eBay Inc.	CA	$10,271
322	Interpublic Group of Companies Inc.	NY	$10,241
323	Weyerhaeuser Co	WA	$10,201
324	Assurant Inc	NY	$10,188
325	Expeditors International of Washing	WA	$10,116
326	Entergy Corp. (New)	LA	$10,114
327	Altice USA Inc	NY	$10,091
328	Jones Financial Companies LL	MO	$10,063
329	Raymond James Financial, Inc.	FL	$9,910
330	Eversource Energy	MA	$9,863
331	Yum China Holdings Inc	TX	$9,853
332	Sonic Automotive, Inc.	NC	$9,767
333	United Rentals Inc	CT	$9,716
334	ODP Corp (The)	FL	$9,710
335	Ryder System, Inc.	FL	$9,663
336	AES Corp	VA	$9,660
337	Hunt (J.B.) Transport Services, Inc.	AR	$9,637
338	Intuit Inc	CA	$9,633
339	Public Service Enterprise Gr	NJ	$9,603
340	Steel Dynamics Inc.	IN	$9,601
341	Dick's Sporting Goods, Inc	PA	$9,584
342	Huntington Ingalls Industries, Inc.	VA	$9,524
343	Block Inc	CA	$9,498
344	Quest Diagnostics, Inc.	NJ	$9,437
345	Insight Enterprises Inc.	AZ	$9,436
346	Liberty Media Corp (DE)	CO	$9,363
347	News Corp (New)	NY	$9,358
348	Cheniere Energy Inc.	TX	$9,358
349	SpartanNash Co	MI	$9,348
350	Avis Budget Group Inc	NJ	$9,313
351	Alcoa Corporation	PA	$9,286
352	Georgia Power Co	GA	$9,260
353	VF Corp.	CO	$9,239
354	Bed, Bath & Beyond, Inc.	NJ	$9,233
355	Seaboard Corp.	KS	$9,229
356	First American Financial Corp	CA	$9,221
357	Intercontinental Exchange Inc	GA	$9,168
358	AGCO Corp	GA	$9,150
359	NRG Energy Inc	TX	$9,093
360	Hershey Company (The)	PA	$8,971

Top 500 Companies by Sales
Hoover's MasterList of U.S. Companies 2022 (continued)

Rank	Company	Headquarters	Sales ($ Mil)	Rank	Company	Headquarters	Sales ($ Mil)
361	NVR Inc.	VA	$8,970	421	Brighthouse Life Insurance Co	NC	$7,552
362	Alleghany Corp. (New)	NY	$8,897	422	Foot Locker, Inc.	NY	$7,548
363	Reliance Steel & Aluminum Co.	CA	$8,812	423	Chipotle Mexican Grill Inc	CA	$7,547
364	EMCOR Group, Inc.	CT	$8,797	424	Cincinnati Financial Corp.	OH	$7,536
365	Toll Brothers Inc.	PA	$8,790	425	Arconic Corp	PA	$7,504
366	Carlyle Group Inc (The)	DC	$8,782	426	Westlake Corp	TX	$7,504
367	Casey's General Stores, Inc.	IA	$8,707	427	Autoliv Inc		$7,447
368	Sirius XM Holdings Inc	NY	$8,696	428	UGI Corp.	PA	$7,447
369	Genworth Financial, Inc. (Holding Co)	VA	$8,658	429	Avantor Inc	PA	$7,386
370	Constellation Brands Inc	NY	$8,615	430	Clorox Co (The)	CA	$7,341
371	Expedia Group Inc	WA	$8,598	431	CMS Energy Corp	MI	$7,329
372	CommScope Holding Co Inc	NC	$8,587	432	Analog Devices Inc	MA	$7,318
373	Builders FirstSource Inc.	TX	$8,559	433	Qwest Corp	LA	$7,313
374	ONEOK Inc	OK	$8,542	434	Delek US Holdings Inc (New)	TN	$7,302
375	Celanese Corp (DE)	TX	$8,537	435	Graybar Electric Co., Inc.	MO	$7,266
376	Global Payments Inc	GA	$8,524	436	WEC Energy Group Inc	WI	$7,242
377	Brighthouse Financial Inc	NC	$8,503	437	Darden Restaurants, Inc. (US)	FL	$7,196
378	Owens Corning	OH	$8,498	438	Old Republic International Corp.	IL	$7,166
379	Owens & Minor, Inc. (New)	VA	$8,480	439	Graphic Packaging Holding Co	GA	$7,156
380	Campbell Soup Co	NJ	$8,476	440	Frontier Communications Parent Inc	CT	$7,155
381	Eastman Chemical Co	TN	$8,473	441	Chewy Inc	FL	$7,146
382	Huntsman Corp	TX	$8,453	442	PVH Corp	NY	$7,133
383	Franklin Resources Inc	CA	$8,426	443	Asbury Automotive Group Inc	GA	$7,132
384	Avery Dennison Corp	CA	$8,408	444	Cintas Corp	OH	$7,116
385	Fifth Third Bancorp (Cincinnati, OH)	OH	$8,402	445	Dana Inc	OH	$7,106
386	Masco Corp.	MI	$8,375	446	Science Applications International	VA	$7,056
387	CenterPoint Energy, Inc	TX	$8,352	447	Zimmer Biomet Holdings Inc	IN	$7,025
388	Global Partners LP	MA	$8,322	448	Xerox Holdings Corp	CT	$7,022
389	S&P Global Inc	NY	$8,297	449	Consumers Energy Co.	MI	$7,021
390	Univar Solutions Inc	IL	$8,265	450	Duke Energy Carolinas LLC	NC	$7,015
391	Targa Resources Corp	TX	$8,260	451	Rockwell Automation, Inc.	WI	$6,997
392	Gallagher (Arthur J.) & Co.	IL	$8,209	452	Citizens Financial Group Inc (New)	RI	$6,986
393	Andersons Inc	OH	$8,208	453	KLA Corp	CA	$6,919
394	Polaris Inc	MN	$8,198	454	Ingredion Inc	IL	$6,894
395	Jefferies Financial Group Inc	NY	$8,185	455	HanesBrands Inc	NC	$6,801
396	Motorola Solutions Inc	IL	$8,171	456	Federal Reserve Bank of Richm	VA	$6,792
397	Zillow Group Inc	WA	$8,147	457	Williams Sonoma Inc	CA	$6,783
398	WR Berkley Corp	CT	$8,099	458	Sanmina Corp	CA	$6,757
399	Organon & Co	NJ	$8,096	459	ON Semiconductor Corp	AZ	$6,740
400	Activision Blizzard, Inc.	CA	$8,086	460	Commercial Metals Co.	TX	$6,730
401	American Tower Corp (New)	MA	$8,042	461	Packaging Corp of America	IL	$6,658
402	Liberty Com SiriusXM Group	CO	$8,040	462	Regions Financial Corp	AL	$6,655
403	Smucker (J.M.) Co.	OH	$8,003	463	Beacon Roofing Supply Inc	VA	$6,642
404	Southern Copper Corp	AZ	$7,985	464	Equinix Inc	CA	$6,636
405	GXO Logistics Inc	CT	$7,940	465	Yum! Brands Inc	KY	$6,584
406	APA Corp	TX	$7,928	466	Landstar System, Inc.	FL	$6,540
407	American Financial Group Inc	OH	$7,909	467	Sprouts Farmers Market Inc	AZ	$6,469
408	Dover Corp	IL	$7,907	468	Half Robert International Inc.	CA	$6,461
409	Booz Allen Hamilton Holding Corp.	VA	$7,859	469	Hasbro, Inc.	RI	$6,420
410	Wabtec Corp.	PA	$7,822	470	Alabama Power Co	AL	$6,413
411	Zoetis Inc	NJ	$7,776	471	Ameren Corp	MO	$6,394
412	Virginia Electric & Power Co	VA	$7,763	472	O-I Glass Inc	OH	$6,357
413	Oshkosh Corp (New)	WI	$7,737	473	Veritiv Corp	GA	$6,346
414	Williams Cos Inc (The)	OK	$7,719	474	Chemours Co (The)	DE	$6,345
415	Federal Reserve Bank Of Atlan	GA	$7,677	475	Crown Castle International Corp (New)	TX	$6,340
416	Voya Financial Inc	NY	$7,649	476	MasTec Inc. (FL)	FL	$6,321
417	A-Mark Precious Metals, Inc	CA	$7,613	477	Avangrid Inc	CT	$6,320
418	Vertex Pharmaceuticals, Inc.	MA	$7,574	478	Agilent Technologies, Inc.	CA	$6,319
419	MPLX LP	OH	$7,569	479	McCormick & Co Inc	MD	$6,318
420	KeyCorp	OH	$7,561	480	DCP Midstream LP	CO	$6,302

Top 500 Companies by Sales
Hoover's MasterList of U.S. Companies 2022 (continued)

Rank	Company	Headquarters	Sales ($ Mil)
481	Northern Trust Corp	IL	$6,301
482	Protective Life Insurance Co	AL	$6,297
483	Live Nation Entertainment Inc	CA	$6,268
484	ABM Industries, Inc.	NY	$6,229
485	Post Holdings Inc	MO	$6,227
486	Realogy Holdings Corp	NJ	$6,221
487	Realogy Group LLC	NJ	$6,221
488	Moody's Corp.	NY	$6,218
489	NCR Corp.	GA	$6,207
490	T Rowe Price Group, Inc.	MD	$6,207
491	Big Lots, Inc.	OH	$6,199
492	Alaska Air Group, Inc.	WA	$6,176
493	Cheniere Energy Partners L P	TX	$6,167
494	Ulta Beauty Inc	IL	$6,152
495	Amkor Technology Inc.	AZ	$6,138
496	Taylor Morrison Home Corp (Hold Co)	AZ	$6,129
497	Icahn Enterprises LP	FL	$6,123
498	RPM International Inc (DE)	OH	$6,106
499	M & T Bank Corp	NY	$6,106
500	Blackstone Inc	NY	$6,102

Top 500 Companies by Employees
Hoover's MasterList of U.S. Companies 2022

Rank	Company	Headquarters	Employees
1	Walmart Inc	AR	2,300,000
2	Amazon.com Inc	WA	1,608,000
3	United Parcel Service Inc	GA	534,000
4	Home Depot Inc	GA	504,800
5	Kroger Co (The)	OH	465,000
6	Target Corp	MN	409,000
7	Starbucks Corp.	WA	383,000
8	Berkshire Hathaway Inc	NE	360,000
9	Kelly Services, Inc.	MI	354,500
10	UnitedHealth Group Inc	MN	350,000
11	Lowe's Companies Inc	NC	340,000
12	Cognizant Technology Solutions Corp.	NJ	330,600
13	TJX Companies, Inc.	MA	320,000
14	Walgreens Boots Alliance Inc	IL	315,000
15	PepsiCo Inc	NY	309,000
16	International Business Machines Corp.	NY	307,600
17	CVS Health Corp	RI	300,000
18	Albertsons Companies Inc	ID	300,000
19	Concentrix Corp	CA	290,000
20	FedEx Corp	TN	289,000
21	Costco Wholesale Corp	WA	288,000
22	HCA Healthcare Inc	TN	284,000
23	Jabil Inc	FL	280,000
24	JPMorgan Chase & Co	NY	271,025
25	Aramark	PA	248,300
26	Wells Fargo & Co (New)	CA	247,848
27	Publix Super Markets, Inc.	FL	227,000
28	Citigroup Inc	NY	210,153
29	Bank of America Corp	NC	208,000
30	AT&T Inc	TX	203,000
31	McDonald's Corp	IL	200,000
32	Dollar Tree Inc	VA	199,327
33	Half Robert International Inc.	CA	191,600
34	Disney (Walt) Co. (The)	CA	190,000
35	Comcast Corp	PA	189,000
36	Ford Motor Co. (DE)	MI	183,000
37	Microsoft Corporation	WA	181,000
38	Raytheon Technologies Corp	MA	174,000
39	General Electric Co	MA	168,000
40	Lear Corp.	MI	160,100
41	Dell Technologies Inc	TX	158,000
42	Dollar General Corp	TN	158,000
43	General Motors Co	MI	157,000
44	Darden Restaurants, Inc. (US	FL	156,883
45	Alphabet Inc	CA	156,500
46	Apple Inc	CA	154,000
47	Johnson & Johnson	NJ	144,300
48	Boeing Co.	IL	142,000
49	Hilton Worldwide Holdings Inc	VA	142,000
50	Tyson Foods Inc	AR	137,000
51	DXC Technology Co	VA	134,000
52	Oracle Corp	TX	132,000
53	ABM Industries, Inc.	NY	124,000
54	American Airlines Group Inc	TX	123,400
55	Intel Corp	CA	121,100
56	Marriott International, Inc.	MD	120,000
57	GXO Logistics Inc	CT	120,000
58	Verizon Communications Inc	NY	118,400
59	Gap Inc	CA	117,000
60	Barrett Business Services, Inc.	WA	115,075
61	Lockheed Martin Corp	MD	114,000
62	Abbott Laboratories	IL	113,000
63	Kohl's Corp.	WI	110,000
64	Caterpillar Inc.	IL	107,700
65	General Dynamics Corp	VA	103,100
66	Best Buy Inc	MN	102,000
67	Tenet Healthcare Corp.	TX	101,100
68	Procter & Gamble Co (The)	OH	101,000
69	CBRE Group Inc	TX	100,000
70	AutoZone, Inc.	TN	100,000
71	Tesla Inc	TX	99,290
72	Honeywell International Inc	NC	99,000
73	Anthem Inc	IN	98,200
74	Chipotle Mexican Grill Inc	CA	97,660
75	Humana, Inc.	KY	96,900
76	3M Co	MN	95,000
77	Charter Communications Inc (New)	CT	93,700
78	Ross Stores Inc	CA	93,700
79	Bath & Body Works Inc	OH	92,300
80	Jones Lang LaSalle Inc	IL	90,800
81	Kyndryl Holdings Inc	NY	90,000
82	Amphenol Corp.	CT	90,000
83	Universal Health Services, Inc.	PA	89,000
84	Northrop Grumman Corp	VA	88,000
85	Emerson Electric Co.	MO	86,700
86	United Airlines Holdings Inc	IL	84,100
87	Delta Air Lines Inc (DE)	GA	83,000
88	Marsh & McLennan Companies Inc.	NY	83,000
89	Stanley Black & Decker Inc	CT	81,700
90	Thermo Fisher Scientific Inc	MA	80,000
91	Danaher Corp	DC	80,000
92	Cisco Systems Inc	CA	79,500
93	Coca-Cola Co (The)	GA	79,000
94	Mondelez International Inc	IL	79,000
95	IQVIA Holdings Inc	NC	79,000
96	Pfizer Inc	NY	78,500
97	O'Reilly Automotive, Inc.	MO	77,827
98	Bloomin' Brands Inc	FL	77,000
99	Brinks Co (The)	VA	76,500
100	McKesson Corp	TX	76,000
101	Macy's Inc	NY	75,711
102	Deere & Co.	IL	75,550
103	T-Mobile US Inc	WA	75,000
104	Becton Dickinson And Co	NJ	75,000
105	Merck & Co Inc	NJ	74,000
106	Cigna Corp (New)	CT	73,700
107	NIKE Inc	OR	73,300
108	Tenneco Inc	IL	73,000
109	Centene Corp	MO	72,500
110	LabCorp	NC	72,400
111	Goodyear Tire & Rubber Co.	OH	72,000
112	Meta Platforms Inc	CA	71,970
113	Omnicom Group, Inc.	NY	71,700
114	Otis Worldwide Corp	CT	70,000
115	Cracker Barrel Old Country Store Inc	TN	70,000
116	Philip Morris International Inc	NY	69,600
117	Whirlpool Corp	MI	69,000
118	DaVita Inc	CO	69,000
119	U.S. Bancorp (DE)	MN	68,796
120	Morgan Stanley	NY	68,000

Top 500 Companies by Employees in
Hoover's MasterList of U.S. Companies 2022 (continued)

Rank	Company	Headquarters	Employees	Rank	Company	Headquarters	Employees
121	Advance Auto Parts Inc	NC	68,000	181	Freeport-McMoRan Inc	AZ	46,900
122	Autoliv Inc		68,000	182	Vail Resorts Inc	CO	46,300
123	Community Health Systems, Inc.	TN	66,000	183	Stryker Corp	MI	46,000
124	Western Digital Corp	CA	65,600	184	Tractor Supply Co.	TN	46,000
125	Fidelity National Information Servic	FL	65,000	185	Qualcomm Inc	CA	45,000
126	American Express Co.	NY	64,000	186	Kimberly-Clark Corp.	TX	45,000
127	Exxon Mobil Corp	TX	63,000	187	Illinois Tool Works, Inc.	IL	45,000
128	Conduent Inc	NJ	63,000	188	Viatris Inc	PA	45,000
129	Lauder (Estee) Cos., Inc. (The)	NY	62,000	189	Las Vegas Sands Corp	NV	44,700
130	Nordstrom, Inc.	WA	62,000	190	Fiserv Inc	WI	44,000
131	Sherwin-Williams Co (The)	OH	61,626	191	Ecolab Inc	MN	44,000
132	Texas Roadhouse Inc	KY	61,600	192	LKQ Corp	IL	44,000
133	Corning Inc	NY	61,200	193	Huntington Ingalls Industries, Inc.	VA	44,000
134	TTEC Holdings Inc	CO	61,000	194	Genesis Healthcare Inc	PA	44,000
135	Hewlett Packard Enterprise Co	TX	60,400	195	Hyatt Hotels Corp	IL	44,000
136	Baxter International Inc	IL	60,000	196	Fluor Corp.	TX	43,717
137	Cummins, Inc.	IN	59,900	197	Progressive Corp. (OH)	OH	43,326
138	Brinker International, Inc.	TX	59,491	198	Encompass Health Corp	AL	43,178
139	Pilgrims Pride Corp.	CO	59,400	199	MetLife Inc	NY	43,000
140	HanesBrands Inc	NC	59,000	200	Micron Technology Inc.	ID	43,000
141	Sysco Corp	TX	58,000	201	Leidos Holdings Inc	VA	43,000
142	Carrier Global Corp	FL	58,000	202	Mohawk Industries, Inc.	GA	43,000
143	Marathon Petroleum Corp.	OH	57,900	203	Ryder System, Inc.	FL	42,800
144	HireQuest Inc	SC	57,040	204	Cheesecake Factory Inc. (The)	CA	42,500
145	Salesforce.Com Inc	CA	56,606	205	Acadia Healthcare Company Inc.	TN	42,200
146	Automatic Data Processing Inc.	NJ	56,000	206	AmerisourceBergen Corp.	PA	42,000
147	Burlington Stores Inc	NJ	55,959	207	XPO Logistics, Inc.	CT	42,000
148	Interpublic Group of Companies Inc.	NY	55,600	208	MGM Resorts International	NV	42,000
149	ASGN Inc	VA	55,200	209	Aveanna Healthcare Holdings Inc	GA	42,000
150	Southwest Airlines Co	TX	55,100	210	StarTek, Inc.	CO	42,000
151	Jacobs Engineering Group, Inc.	TX	55,000	211	Epam Systems, Inc.	PA	41,168
152	Allstate Corp	IL	54,700	212	Archer Daniels Midland Co.	IL	41,000
153	Parker-Hannifin Corp	OH	54,640	213	Boston Scientific Corp.	MA	41,000
154	Baker Hughes Company	TX	54,000	214	Prudential Financial Inc	NJ	40,916
155	Baker Hughes Holdings LLC	TX	54,000	215	Goldman Sachs Group Inc	NY	40,500
156	Caesars Entertainment Inc (New)	NV	54,000	216	Halliburton Company	TX	40,000
157	Truist Financial Corp	NC	52,641	217	Quest Diagnostics, Inc.	NJ	40,000
158	Genuine Parts Co.	GA	52,000	218	VF Corp.	CO	40,000
159	GameStop Corp	TX	52,000	219	Cintas Corp	OH	40,000
160	Capital One Financial Corp	VA	51,985	220	Healthcare Services Group Inc.	PA	39,200
161	PNC Financial Services Group (The)	PA	51,257	221	Lumen Technologies Inc	LA	39,000
162	Foot Locker, Inc.	NY	51,252	222	Gallagher (Arthur J.) & Co.	IL	39,000
163	HP Inc	CA	51,000	223	State Street Corp.	MA	38,784
164	AECOM	TX	51,000	224	International Paper Co	TN	38,200
165	Cedar Fair LP	OH	50,700	225	Dana Inc	OH	38,200
166	Dick's Sporting Goods, Inc	PA	50,100	226	Bed, Bath & Beyond, Inc.	NJ	37,600
167	Rite Aid Corp.	PA	50,000	227	Casey's General Stores, Inc.	IA	37,205
168	AbbVie Inc	IL	50,000	228	ODP Corp (The)	FL	37,000
169	Coupang Inc		50,000	229	Big Lots, Inc.	OH	37,000
170	Jones Financial Companies LL	MO	50,000	230	Ulta Beauty Inc	IL	37,000
171	WestRock Co	GA	49,900	231	American Eagle Outfitters, Inc.	PA	37,000
172	Select Medical Holdings Corp	PA	49,600	232	Laureate Education Inc	MD	37,000
173	PPG Industries Inc	PA	49,300	233	American International Group Inc	NY	36,600
174	BorgWarner Inc	MI	49,300	234	Kraft Heinz Co (The)	PA	36,000
175	Waste Management, Inc. (DE)	TX	48,500	235	Avery Dennison Corp	CA	36,000
176	Bank of New York Mellon Corp	NY	48,500	236	Yum! Brands Inc	KY	36,000
177	L3Harris Technologies Inc	FL	48,000	237	NCR Corp.	GA	36,000
178	Chevron Corporation	CA	47,736	238	Quanta Services, Inc.	TX	35,800
179	Cardinal Health, Inc.	OH	47,300	239	MAXIMUS Inc.	VA	35,800
180	Berry Global Group Inc	IN	47,000	240	Dow Inc	MI	35,700

Top 500 Companies by Employees in Hoover's MasterList of U.S. Companies 2022 (continued)

Rank	Company	Headquarters	Employees
241	Addus HomeCare Corp	TX	35,139
242	Eli Lilly & Co	IN	35,000
243	General Mills Inc	MN	35,000
244	Republic Services Inc	AZ	35,000
245	Sanmina Corp	CA	35,000
246	VMware Inc	CA	34,000
247	Abercrombie & Fitch Co	OH	34,000
248	Colgate-Palmolive Co.	NY	33,800
249	ON Semiconductor Corp	AZ	33,300
250	Textron Inc	RI	33,000
251	Crown Holdings Inc	PA	33,000
252	EMCOR Group, Inc.	CT	33,000
253	PVH Corp	NY	33,000
254	Sprouts Farmers Market Inc	AZ	33,000
255	Brookdale Senior Living Inc	TN	33,000
256	Exelon Corp	IL	32,340
257	Bristol Myers Squibb Co.	NY	32,200
258	Union Pacific Corp	NE	32,124
259	Mattel Inc	CA	32,100
260	BJs Wholesale Club Holdings Inc	MA	32,000
261	Charles Schwab Corp	TX	32,000
262	Newell Brands Inc	GA	32,000
263	Yellow Corp (New)	TN	32,000
264	ExlService Holdings Inc	NY	31,900
265	Texas Instruments, Inc.	TX	31,000
266	Kellogg Co	MI	31,000
267	Thor Industries, Inc.	IN	31,000
268	Six Flags Entertainment Corp	TX	30,950
269	PayPal Holdings Inc	CA	30,900
270	Travelers Companies Inc (The)	NY	30,800
271	Amkor Technology Inc.	AZ	30,400
272	Hunt (J.B.) Transport Services, Inc.	AR	30,309
273	ManpowerGroup	WI	30,000
274	CommScope Holding Co Inc	NC	30,000
275	Life Time Group Holdings Inc	MN	30,000
276	AMERCO	NV	29,800
277	KBR Inc	TX	29,000
278	Dillard's Inc.	AR	29,000
279	Sally Beauty Holdings Inc	TX	29,000
280	Paccar Inc.	WA	28,500
281	Cinemark Holdings Inc	TX	28,500
282	United Natural Foods Inc.	RI	28,300
283	US Foods Holding Corp	IL	28,000
284	DuPont de Nemours Inc	DE	28,000
285	LHC Group Inc	LA	27,959
286	Victorias Secret & Co	OH	27,900
287	Newmont Corp	CO	27,800
288	Booz Allen Hamilton Holding Corp.	VA	27,700
289	Duke Energy Corp	NC	27,535
290	Syneos Health Inc	NC	27,525
291	Fortune Brands Home & Security, Inc.	IL	27,500
292	JOANN Inc	OH	27,500
293	Wynn Resorts Ltd	NV	27,500
294	TaskUs Inc	TX	27,500
295	Southern Co.	GA	27,300
296	Paramount Global	NY	27,265
297	Petco Health & Wellness Co Inc	CA	27,081
298	Fidelity National Financial Inc	FL	27,058
299	NOV Inc	TX	27,043
300	TD SYNNEX Corp	CA	27,000
301	Applied Materials, Inc.	CA	27,000
302	Keurig Dr Pepper Inc	MA	27,000
303	Carmax Inc.	VA	26,889
304	Bright Horizons Family Solutions, Inc	MA	26,800
305	Qurate Retail Inc - Com Ser B	CO	26,508
306	Carrols Restaurant Group Inc	NY	26,500
307	Qurate Retail Inc	CO	26,424
308	Nucor Corp.	NC	26,400
309	PG&E Corp (Holding Co)	CA	26,000
310	Cleveland-Cliffs Inc (New)	OH	26,000
311	Builders FirstSource Inc.	TX	26,000
312	Science Applications International	VA	26,000
313	Ingles Markets Inc	NC	26,000
314	Adobe Inc	CA	25,988
315	Ensign Group Inc	CA	25,900
316	Cerner Corp.	MO	25,150
317	AMC Entertainment Holdings Inc.	KS	25,019
318	Penske Automotive Group Inc	MI	25,000
319	Global Payments Inc	GA	25,000
320	Dover Corp	IL	25,000
321	Wabtec Corp.	PA	25,000
322	Graphic Packaging Holding Co	GA	25,000
323	lululemon athletica inc	British Columbia	25,000
324	Analog Devices Inc	MA	24,700
325	Xerox Holdings Corp	CT	24,700
326	JELD-WEN Holding Inc	NC	24,700
327	Service Corp. International	TX	24,658
328	SS&C Technologies Holdings Inc	CT	24,600
329	United States Steel Corp.	PA	24,540
330	Rockwell Automation, Inc.	WI	24,500
331	Ball Corp	CO	24,300
332	Amgen Inc	CA	24,200
333	Grainger (W.W.), Inc.	IL	24,200
334	Mastercard Inc	NY	24,000
335	News Corp (New)	NY	24,000
336	O-I Glass Inc	OH	24,000
337	Hertz Global Holdings Inc (New)	FL	24,000
338	Iron Mountain Inc (New)	MA	24,000
339	Weis Markets, Inc.	PA	24,000
340	Icahn Enterprises LP	FL	23,800
341	Old Dominion Freight Line, Inc.	NC	23,663
342	Performance Food Group Co	VA	23,000
343	II-VI Inc. (Two-Six Inc.)	PA	23,000
344	Regal Rexnord Corp	WI	23,000
345	Knight-Swift Transportation Holdin	AZ	22,900
346	S&P Global Inc	NY	22,850
347	Alaska Air Group, Inc.	WA	22,833
348	Uber Technologies Inc	CA	22,800
349	Cooper-Standard Holdings Inc	MI	22,600
350	First American Financial Corp	CA	22,233
351	AutoNation, Inc.	FL	22,200
352	CACI International Inc	VA	22,000
353	Academy Sports & Outdoors Inc	TX	22,000
354	Diebold Nixdorf AG	OH	22,000
355	R1 RCM Inc	UT	22,000
356	BGSF Inc	TX	21,900
357	Henry Schein Inc	NY	21,600
358	Vishay Intertechnology, Inc.	PA	21,600
359	Visa Inc	CA	21,500
360	AGCO Corp.	GA	21,400

Top 500 Companies by Employees in Hoover's MasterList of U.S. Companies 2022 (continued)

Rank	Company	Headquarters	Employees	Rank	Company	Headquarters	Employees
361	Red Robin Gourmet Burgers Inc	CO	21,374	421	Align Technology Inc	AZ	18,070
362	Lithia Motors Inc	OR	21,150	422	Synchrony Financial	CT	18,000
363	Avis Budget Group Inc	NJ	21,000	423	Wesco International, Inc.	PA	18,000
364	Williams Sonoma Inc	CA	21,000	424	SpartanNash Co	MI	18,000
365	Tetra Tech Inc	CA	21,000	425	MasTec Inc. (FL)	FL	18,000
366	Amedisys, Inc.	LA	21,000	426	American Axle & Manufacturing Hold	MI	18,000
367	Krispy Kreme Inc	NC	21,000	427	Timken Co. (The)	OH	18,000
368	Vertiv Holdings Co	OH	20,972	428	Carter's Inc	GA	18,000
369	CSX Corp	FL	20,900	429	Marriott Vacations Worldwide Corp.	FL	18,000
370	Northern Trust Corp	IL	20,900	430	Cinemark USA Inc	TX	18,000
371	Air Products & Chemicals Inc	PA	20,875	431	Mettler-Toledo International, Inc.	OH	17,800
372	Arrow Electronics, Inc.	CO	20,700	432	Sanderson Farms Inc	MS	17,662
373	Fastenal Co.	MN	20,507	433	KeyCorp	OH	17,654
374	ADT Inc (DE)	FL	20,500	434	Discover Financial Services	IL	17,600
375	BrightView Holdings Inc	PA	20,500	435	M & T Bank Corp	NY	17,569
376	United Rentals Inc	CT	20,400	436	Under Armour Inc	MD	17,500
377	Markel Corp (Holding Co)	VA	20,300	437	ModivCare Inc	CO	17,500
378	Booking Holdings Inc	CT	20,300	438	Expeditors International of Washing	WA	17,480
379	Leggett & Platt, Inc.	MO	20,300	439	Citizens Financial Group Inc (New)	RI	17,463
380	Ralph Lauren Corp	NY	20,300	440	Dominion Energy Inc (New)	VA	17,300
381	Cornerstone Building Brands Inc	NC	20,230	441	Catalent Inc	NJ	17,300
382	Raymond James Financial, Inc.	FL	20,021	442	Party City Holdco Inc	NY	17,298
383	Broadcom Inc (DE)	CA	20,000	443	Agilent Technologies, Inc.	CA	17,000
384	Hormel Foods Corp.	MN	20,000	444	Fortive Corp	WA	17,000
385	Owens Corning	OH	20,000	445	Littelfuse Inc	IL	17,000
386	Masco Corp.	MI	20,000	446	FirstCash Holdings Inc	TX	17,000
387	Zimmer Biomet Holdings Inc	IN	20,000	447	BJ's Restaurants Inc	CA	17,000
388	Sonoco Products Co.	SC	20,000	448	ServiceNow Inc	CA	16,881
389	Charles River Laboratories Intern	MA	20,000	449	Robinson (C.H.) Worldwide, Inc.	MN	16,877
390	GEO Group Inc (The) (New)	FL	20,000	450	American Electric Power Co Inc	OH	16,787
391	Universal Corp	VA	20,000	451	Xylem Inc	NY	16,700
392	SPAR Group, Inc.	MI	20,000	452	TTM Technologies Inc	CA	16,700
393	Howmet Aerospace Inc	PA	19,900	453	Papa John's International, Inc.	KY	16,700
394	Fifth Third Bancorp (Cincinnati, OH)	OH	19,872	454	Graham Holdings Co.	VA	16,661
395	Microchip Technology Inc	AZ	19,500	455	Levi Strauss & Co.	CA	16,600
396	JetBlue Airways Corp	NY	19,466	456	Gartner Inc	CT	16,600
397	Regions Financial Corp	AL	19,406	457	BlackRock Inc	NY	16,500
398	Roper Technologies Inc	FL	19,300	458	Sealed Air Corp.	NC	16,500
399	Plexus Corp.	WI	19,200	459	Tapestry Inc	NY	16,400
400	Urban Outfitters, Inc.	PA	19,000	460	Synopsys Inc	CA	16,361
401	Five Below Inc	PA	19,000	461	Molson Coors Beverage Co	Quebec	16,300
402	Genesco Inc.	TN	19,000	462	Unisys Corp	PA	16,300
403	Exela Technologies Inc	TX	19,000	463	Americold Realty Trust	GA	16,300
404	AlerisLife Inc	MA	19,000	464	Frontier Communications Parent Inc	CT	16,200
405	Hershey Company (The)	PA	18,990	465	Colfax Corp	DE	16,200
406	NVIDIA Corp	CA	18,975	466	Wayfair Inc	MA	16,122
407	Owens & Minor, Inc. (New)	VA	18,800	467	Spirit AeroSystems Holdings Inc	KS	16,100
408	TravelCenters of America Inc	OH	18,724	468	Schneider National Inc (WI)	WI	16,050
409	Motorola Solutions Inc	IL	18,700	469	Polaris Inc	MN	16,000
410	Principal Financial Group Inc	IA	18,600	470	Greif Inc	OH	16,000
411	Conagra Brands Inc	IL	18,600	471	Flowserve Corp	TX	16,000
412	Brunswick Corp.	IL	18,582	472	Ingersoll Rand Inc	NC	15,900
413	Norfolk Southern Corp	GA	18,500	473	Coca-Cola Consolidated Inc	NC	15,800
414	Chewy Inc	FL	18,500	474	Quad/Graphics, Inc.	WI	15,800
415	AMETEK Inc	PA	18,500	475	Edwards Lifesciences Corp	CA	15,700
416	Huntington Bancshares Inc	OH	18,442	476	Santander Holdings USA Inc.	MA	15,698
417	Penn National Gaming Inc	PA	18,321	477	Rollins, Inc.	GA	15,616
418	Hubbell Inc.	CT	18,300	478	Assurant Inc	NY	15,600
419	Gannett Co Inc (New)	VA	18,141	479	MercadoLibre Inc		15,546
420	Hartford Financial Services Group Inc.	CT	18,100	480	Chemed Corp	OH	15,544

Top 500 Companies by Employees in Hoover's MasterList of U.S. Companies 2022 (continued)

Rank	Company	Headquarters	Employees	Rank	Company	Headquarters	Employees
481	Advanced Micro Devices Inc	CA	15,500	491	DENTSPLY SIRONA Inc	NC	15,000
482	Parsons Corp (DE)	VA	15,500	492	Change Healthcare Inc	TN	15,000
483	Travel + Leisure Co	FL	15,500	493	Stericycle Inc.	IL	15,000
484	RPM International Inc (DE)	OH	15,490	494	TPI Composites Inc	AZ	14,900
485	Volt Information Sciences Inc	CA	15,400	495	Expedia Group Inc	WA	14,800
486	SkyWest Inc.	UT	15,205	496	Sempra	CA	14,706
487	Packaging Corp of America	IL	15,200	497	Murphy USA Inc	AR	14,615
488	Vectrus Inc	CO	15,200	498	Pactiv Evergreen Inc	IL	14,600
489	Oshkosh Corp (New)	WI	15,000	499	Cannae Holdings Inc	NV	14,509
490	Paychex Inc	NY	15,000	500	Avnet Inc	AZ	14,500

Top 500 Companies by Net Profit in Hoover's MasterList of U.S. Companies 2022

Rank	Company	Headquarters	Net Income	Rank	Company	Headquarters	Net Income
1	Apple Inc	CA	$94,680,000	61	Thermo Fisher Scientific Inc	MA	$6,375,000
2	Alphabet Inc	CA	$76,033,000	62	Lockheed Martin Corp	MD	$6,315,000
3	Microsoft Corporation	WA	$61,271,000	63	Dow Inc	MI	$6,311,000
4	JPMorgan Chase & Co	NY	$48,334,000	64	Gilead Sciences Inc	CA	$6,225,000
5	Berkshire Hathaway Inc	NE	$42,521,000	65	Anthem Inc	IN	$6,104,000
6	Meta Platforms Inc	CA	$39,370,000	66	Deere & Co.	IL	$5,963,000
7	Amazon.com Inc	WA	$33,364,000	67	3M Co	MN	$5,921,000
8	Bank of America Corp	NC	$31,978,000	68	Amgen Inc	CA	$5,893,000
9	Exxon Mobil Corp	TX	$23,040,000	69	Applied Materials, Inc.	CA	$5,888,000
10	Fannie Mae	DC	$22,176,000	70	Micron Technology Inc.	ID	$5,861,000
11	Verizon Communications Inc	NY	$22,065,000	71	Lowe's Companies Inc	NC	$5,835,000
12	Wells Fargo & Co (New)	CA	$21,548,000	72	International Business Machines Corp.	NY	$5,743,000
13	Johnson & Johnson	NJ	$20,878,000	73	NIKE Inc	OR	$5,727,000
14	AT&T Inc	TX	$20,081,000	74	Progressive Corp. (OH)	OH	$5,704,600
15	Intel Corp	CA	$19,868,000	75	eBay Inc.	CA	$5,667,000
16	Ford Motor Co. (DE)	MI	$17,937,000	76	Eli Lilly & Co	IN	$5,581,700
17	UnitedHealth Group Inc	MN	$17,285,000	77	Honeywell International Inc	NC	$5,542,000
18	Procter & Gamble Co (The)	OH	$14,306,000	78	Tesla Inc	TX	$5,519,000
19	Comcast Corp	PA	$14,159,000	79	FedEx Corp	TN	$5,231,000
20	Oracle Corp	TX	$13,746,000	80	Netflix Inc	CA	$5,116,228
21	Walmart Inc	AR	$13,510,000	81	Costco Wholesale Corp	WA	$5,007,000
22	United Parcel Service Inc	GA	$12,890,000	82	BlackRock Inc	NY	$4,932,000
23	Home Depot Inc	GA	$12,866,000	83	Adobe Inc	CA	$4,822,000
24	Visa Inc	CA	$12,311,000	84	McDonald's Corp	IL	$4,730,500
25	Freddie Mac	VA	$12,109,000	85	Charter Communications Inc (New)	CT	$4,654,000
26	AbbVie Inc	IL	$11,542,000	86	Paramount Global	NY	$4,543,000
27	Citigroup Inc	NY	$11,047,000	87	Ford Motor Credit Company LLC	MI	$4,521,000
28	Morgan Stanley	NY	$10,996,000	88	Altria Group Inc	VA	$4,467,000
29	Cisco Systems Inc	CA	$10,591,000	89	Lennar Corp	FL	$4,430,111
30	General Motors Co	MI	$10,019,000	90	Target Corp	MN	$4,368,000
31	Coca-Cola Co (The)	GA	$9,771,000	91	NVIDIA Corp	CA	$4,332,000
32	Pfizer Inc	NY	$9,616,000	92	AFLAC Inc.	GA	$4,325,000
33	Goldman Sachs Group Inc	NY	$9,459,000	93	Freeport-McMoRan Inc	AZ	$4,306,000
34	American International Group Inc	NY	$9,388,000	94	Mondelez International Inc	IL	$4,300,000
35	Philip Morris International Inc	NY	$9,109,000	95	Bio-Rad Laboratories Inc	CA	$4,245,902
36	Qualcomm Inc	CA	$9,043,000	96	Synchrony Financial	CT	$4,221,000
37	Mastercard Inc	NY	$8,687,000	97	Starbucks Corp.	WA	$4,199,300
38	Cigna Corp (New)	CT	$8,458,000	98	DR Horton Inc	TX	$4,175,800
39	ConocoPhillips	TX	$8,079,000	99	United States Steel Corp.	PA	$4,174,000
40	Regeneron Pharmaceuticals, Inc.	NY	$8,075,300	100	PayPal Holdings Inc	CA	$4,169,000
41	American Express Co.	NY	$8,060,000	101	Salesforce.Com Inc	CA	$4,072,000
42	U.S. Bancorp (DE)	MN	$7,963,000	102	Intercontinental Exchange Inc	GA	$4,058,000
43	CVS Health Corp	RI	$7,910,000	103	loanDepot Inc	CA	$4,026,220
44	Texas Instruments, Inc.	TX	$7,769,000	104	Publix Super Markets, Inc.	FL	$3,971,838
45	Prudential Financial Inc	NJ	$7,724,000	105	Sempra	CA	$3,933,000
46	PepsiCo Inc	NY	$7,618,000	106	Lam Research Corp	CA	$3,908,458
47	PNC Financial Services Group (The)	PA	$7,517,000	107	Raytheon Technologies Corp	MA	$3,864,000
48	Abbott Laboratories	IL	$7,071,000	108	CSX Corp	FL	$3,781,000
49	Merck & Co Inc	NJ	$7,067,000	109	Enterprise Products Partners L.P.	TX	$3,775,600
50	Northrop Grumman Corp	VA	$7,005,000	110	Travelers Companies Inc (The)	NY	$3,662,000
51	Bristol Myers Squibb Co.	NY	$6,994,000	111	Bank of New York Mellon Corp	NY	$3,617,000
52	HCA Healthcare Inc	TN	$6,956,000	112	NextEra Energy Inc	FL	$3,573,000
53	Broadcom Inc (DE)	CA	$6,736,000	113	Hewlett Packard Enterprise Co	TX	$3,427,000
54	MetLife Inc	NY	$6,554,000	114	Charles Schwab Corp	TX	$3,299,000
55	Union Pacific Corp	NE	$6,523,000	115	General Dynamics Corp	VA	$3,257,000
56	HP Inc	CA	$6,503,000	116	Dell Technologies Inc	TX	$3,250,000
57	Caterpillar Inc.	IL	$6,489,000	117	Advanced Micro Devices Inc	CA	$3,162,000
58	DuPont de Nemours Inc	DE	$6,467,000	118	Marsh & McLennan Companies Inc.	NY	$3,143,000
59	Truist Financial Corp	NC	$6,440,000	119	Tyson Foods Inc	AR	$3,047,000
60	Danaher Corp	DC	$6,433,000	120	T-Mobile US Inc	WA	$3,024,000

Top 500 Companies by Net Profit in Hoover's MasterList of U.S. Companies 2022 (continued)

Rank	Company	Headquarters	Net Income	Rank	Company	Headquarters	Net Income
121	S&P Global Inc	NY	$3,024,000	180	Corning Inc	NY	$1,906,000
122	Prologis LP	CA	$3,021,515	181	Public Service Enterprise Gr	NJ	$1,905,000
123	Norfolk Southern Corp	GA	$3,005,000	182	Celanese Corp (DE)	TX	$1,890,000
124	Cleveland-Cliffs Inc (New)	OH	$2,988,000	183	Hologic Inc	MA	$1,871,500
125	Carlyle Group Inc (The)	DC	$2,974,700	184	Sherwin-Williams Co (The)	OH	$1,864,400
126	Cooper Companies, Inc.	CA	$2,944,700	185	M & T Bank Corp	NY	$1,858,746
127	Prologis Inc	CA	$2,939,723	186	Paccar Inc.	WA	$1,852,100
128	Humana, Inc.	KY	$2,933,000	187	Franklin Resources Inc	CA	$1,831,200
129	TPG Partners LLC	TX	$2,877,864	188	Waste Management, Inc. (DE)	TX	$1,816,000
130	Lauder (Estee) Cos., Inc. (The)	NY	$2,870,000	189	Kimberly-Clark Corp.	TX	$1,814,000
131	Newmont Corp	CO	$2,829,000	190	Best Buy Inc	MN	$1,798,000
132	Devon Energy Corp.	OK	$2,813,000	191	Cannae Holdings Inc	NV	$1,786,200
133	Capital One Financial Corp	VA	$2,714,000	192	Kinder Morgan Inc.	TX	$1,784,000
134	Archer Daniels Midland Co.	IL	$2,709,000	193	Whirlpool Corp	MI	$1,783,000
135	Illinois Tool Works, Inc.	IL	$2,694,000	194	Align Technology Inc	AZ	$1,775,888
136	State Street Corp.	MA	$2,693,000	195	DISH Network Corp	CO	$1,762,673
137	Macquarie Infrastructure Holdings LLC	NY	$2,683,868	196	O'Reilly Automotive, Inc.	MO	$1,752,302
138	Dollar General Corp	TN	$2,655,050	197	International Paper Co	TN	$1,752,000
139	Florida Power & Light Co.	FL	$2,650,000	198	Parker-Hannifin Corp	OH	$1,746,100
140	KeyCorp	OH	$2,625,000	199	Principal Financial Group Inc	IA	$1,710,600
141	Weyerhaeuser Co	WA	$2,607,000	200	Qwest Corp	LA	$1,707,000
142	Automatic Data Processing Inc.	NJ	$2,598,500	201	Intuitive Surgical Inc	CA	$1,704,600
143	Kroger Co (The)	OH	$2,585,000	202	American Tower Corp (New)	MA	$1,690,600
144	Walgreens Boots Alliance Inc	IL	$2,542,000	203	Stanley Black & Decker Inc	CT	$1,689,200
145	Markel Corp (Holding Co)	VA	$2,425,003	204	Jefferies Financial Group Inc	NY	$1,674,352
146	Southern Co.	GA	$2,408,000	205	Carrier Global Corp	FL	$1,664,000
147	Annaly Capital Management Inc	NY	$2,389,896	206	Federal Reserve System	DC	$1,662,000
148	T Rowe Price Group, Inc.	MD	$2,372,700	207	Continental Resources Inc.	OK	$1,660,968
149	Hartford Financial Services Group Inc.	CT	$2,365,000	208	PennyMac Financial Services Inc	CA	$1,646,884
150	Vertex Pharmaceuticals, Inc.	MA	$2,342,100	209	Mosaic Co. (The)	FL	$1,630,600
151	General Mills Inc	MN	$2,339,800	210	Fortive Corp	WA	$1,613,300
152	Citizens Financial Group Inc (New)	RI	$2,319,000	211	Allstate Corp	IL	$1,599,000
153	Emerson Electric Co.	MO	$2,303,000	212	Xcel Energy Inc	MN	$1,597,000
154	Moody's Corp.	NY	$2,214,000	213	Amphenol Corp.	CT	$1,590,800
155	American Electric Power Co Inc	OH	$2,200,100	214	Loews Corp.	NY	$1,578,000
156	Activision Blizzard, Inc.	CA	$2,197,000	215	Yum! Brands Inc	KY	$1,575,000
157	AutoZone, Inc.	TN	$2,170,314	216	Southern Copper Corp	AZ	$1,570,400
158	Colgate-Palmolive Co.	NY	$2,166,000	217	LabCorp	NC	$1,556,100
159	Organon & Co	NJ	$2,160,000	218	Biogen Inc	MA	$1,556,100
160	Fox Corp	NY	$2,150,000	219	AmerisourceBergen Corp.	PA	$1,539,932
161	Cognizant Technology Solutions Corp.	NJ	$2,137,000	220	Ameriprise Financial Inc	MN	$1,534,000
162	Cummins, Inc.	IN	$2,131,000	221	Tennessee Valley Authority	TN	$1,512,000
163	Pioneer Natural Resources Co	TX	$2,118,000	222	Edwards Lifesciences Corp	CA	$1,503,100
164	Silicon Laboratories Inc	TX	$2,117,399	223	Skyworks Solutions Inc	CA	$1,498,300
165	CME Group Inc	IL	$2,105,200	224	Kellogg Co	MI	$1,488,000
166	Air Products & Chemicals Inc	PA	$2,099,100	225	CenterPoint Energy, Inc	TX	$1,486,000
167	Becton Dickinson And Co	NJ	$2,092,000	226	Hershey Company (The)	PA	$1,477,512
168	KLA Corp	CA	$2,078,292	227	UGI Corp.	PA	$1,467,000
169	Intuit Inc	CA	$2,062,000	228	Halliburton Company	TX	$1,457,000
170	VMware Inc	CA	$2,058,000	229	Mr Cooper Group Inc	TX	$1,454,000
171	Zoetis Inc	NJ	$2,037,000	230	PPG Industries Inc	PA	$1,439,000
172	Toyota Motor Credit Corp.	TX	$2,017,000	231	Quest Diagnostics, Inc.	NJ	$1,431,000
173	KKR & Co Inc	NY	$2,002,509	232	Fidelity National Financial Inc	FL	$1,427,000
174	Constellation Brands Inc	NY	$1,998,000	233	Fifth Third Bancorp (Cincinnati, OH)	OH	$1,427,000
175	Disney (Walt) Co. (The)	CA	$1,995,000	234	Monster Beverage Corp (New)	CA	$1,409,594
176	Stryker Corp	MI	$1,994,000	235	Omnicom Group, Inc.	NY	$1,407,800
177	Exelon Corp	IL	$1,963,000	236	Entergy Corp. (New)	LA	$1,406,653
178	Public Storage	CA	$1,953,263	237	Lincoln National Corp.	PA	$1,405,000
179	PulteGroup Inc	GA	$1,946,320	238	Raymond James Financial, Inc.	FL	$1,403,000

Top 500 Companies by Net Profit in Hoover's MasterList of U.S. Companies 2022 (continued)

Rank	Company	Headquarters	Net Income
239	Analog Devices Inc	MA	$1,390,422
240	TransUnion	IL	$1,387,100
241	United Rentals Inc	CT	$1,386,000
242	ERP Operating L.P.	IL	$1,378,750
243	Duke Energy Corp	NC	$1,377,000
244	Louisiana-Pacific Corp	TN	$1,377,000
245	AutoNation, Inc.	FL	$1,373,000
246	Assurant Inc	NY	$1,372,400
247	Rockwell Automation, Inc.	WI	$1,358,100
248	CMS Energy Corp	MI	$1,353,000
249	Centene Corp	MO	$1,347,000
250	Consolidated Edison Inc	NY	$1,346,000
251	Dollar Tree Inc	VA	$1,341,900
252	Equity Residential	IL	$1,332,850
253	Keurig Dr Pepper Inc	MA	$1,325,000
254	Phillips 66	TX	$1,317,000
255	Federal Reserve Bank Of New Y	NY	$1,317,000
256	Sirius XM Holdings Inc	NY	$1,314,000
257	OneMain Holdings Inc	IN	$1,314,000
258	OneMain Finance Corp	IN	$1,314,000
259	Conagra Brands Inc	IL	$1,298,800
260	Huntington Bancshares Inc	OH	$1,295,000
261	Republic Services Inc	AZ	$1,290,400
262	Jones Financial Companies LL	MO	$1,285,000
263	Avis Budget Group Inc	NJ	$1,285,000
264	Baxter International Inc	IL	$1,284,000
265	FirstEnergy Corp	OH	$1,283,000
266	CoBank, ACB	CO	$1,263,001
267	American Water Works Co, Inc.	NJ	$1,263,000
268	Alabama Power Co	AL	$1,253,000
269	Otis Worldwide Corp	CT	$1,246,000
270	Motorola Solutions Inc	IL	$1,245,000
271	First American Financial Corp	CA	$1,241,000
272	NVR Inc.	VA	$1,236,719
273	Eversource Energy	MA	$1,220,527
274	Discovery Inc	NY	$1,219,000
275	Cincinnati Financial Corp.	OH	$1,216,000
276	Agilent Technologies, Inc.	CA	$1,210,000
277	Northern Trust Corp	IL	$1,209,300
278	SVB Financial Group	CA	$1,208,368
279	Autodesk Inc	CA	$1,208,200
280	Qurate Retail Inc - Com Ser B	CO	$1,204,000
281	Qurate Retail Inc	CO	$1,204,000
282	CNA Financial Corp	IL	$1,202,000
283	WEC Energy Group Inc	WI	$1,201,100
284	Penske Automotive Group Inc	MI	$1,187,800
285	Nasdaq Inc	NY	$1,187,000
286	Consolidated Edison Co. of N	NY	$1,185,000
287	Cheniere Energy Partners L P	TX	$1,183,000
288	Comerica, Inc.	TX	$1,168,000
289	Booking Holdings Inc	CT	$1,165,000
290	Roper Technologies Inc	FL	$1,152,600
291	Discover Financial Services	IL	$1,141,000
292	Dover Corp	IL	$1,123,818
293	L3Harris Technologies Inc	FL	$1,119,000
294	Simon Property Group, Inc.	IN	$1,112,564
295	Cintas Corp	OH	$1,110,968
296	Arrow Electronics, Inc.	CO	$1,108,197
297	Marriott International, Inc.	MD	$1,099,000
298	Paychex Inc	NY	$1,097,500
299	Crown Castle International Corp (New)	TX	$1,096,000
300	Regions Financial Corp	AL	$1,094,000
301	Ally Financial Inc	MI	$1,085,000
302	Entergy Louisiana LLC (New)	LA	$1,082,352
303	First Republic Bank (San Francisco,	CA	$1,064,151
304	Lithia Motors Inc	OR	$1,060,100
305	Blackstone Inc	NY	$1,045,363
306	Huntsman Corp	TX	$1,045,000
307	Grainger (W.W.), Inc.	IL	$1,043,000
308	Boston Scientific Corp.	MA	$1,041,000
309	Old Dominion Freight Line, Inc.	NC	$1,034,375
310	CDK Global Inc	IL	$1,034,300
311	Mohawk Industries, Inc.	GA	$1,033,159
312	Virginia Electric & Power Co	VA	$1,021,000
313	Teradyne, Inc.	MA	$1,014,589
314	Kraft Heinz Co (The)	PA	$1,012,000
315	ON Semiconductor Corp	AZ	$1,009,600
316	Molson Coors Beverage Co	Quebec	$1,005,700
317	Campbell Soup Co	NJ	$1,002,000
318	Kimco Realty Corp	NY	$1,000,833
319	Tractor Supply Co.	TN	$997,114
320	Owens Corning	OH	$995,000
321	Boston Properties L.P.	MA	$990,479
322	Altice USA Inc	NY	$990,311
323	AMETEK Inc	PA	$990,053
324	Yum China Holdings Inc	TX	$990,000
325	Ameren Corp	MO	$990,000
326	DaVita Inc	CO	$978,450
327	Southwest Airlines Co	TX	$977,000
328	APA Corp	TX	$973,000
329	IQVIA Holdings Inc	NC	$966,000
330	Global Payments Inc	GA	$965,460
331	Credit Acceptance Corp (MI)	MI	$958,300
332	Fiserv Inc	WI	$958,000
333	Duke Energy Carolinas LLC	NC	$956,000
334	Interpublic Group of Companies Inc.	NY	$952,800
335	Incyte Corporation	DE	$948,581
336	Marathon Oil Corp.	TX	$946,000
337	Universal Health Services, Inc.	PA	$943,953
338	Southern California Edison C	CA	$942,000
339	Copart Inc	TX	$936,495
340	Valero Energy Corp	TX	$930,000
341	Fastenal Co.	MN	$925,000
342	Tenet Healthcare Corp.	TX	$914,000
343	Hormel Foods Corp.	MN	$908,839
344	DTE Energy Co	MI	$907,000
345	Gallagher (Arthur J.) & Co.	IL	$906,800
346	Brown-Forman Corp.	KY	$903,000
347	Genuine Parts Co.	GA	$898,790
348	Keysight Technologies Inc	CA	$894,000
349	VICI Properties Inc	NY	$891,674
350	SLM Corp.	DE	$880,690
351	Ball Corp	CO	$878,000
352	Smucker (J.M.) Co.	OH	$876,300
353	Boston Properties Inc	MA	$872,727
354	Consumers Energy Co.	MI	$868,000
355	DTE Electric Company	MI	$866,000
356	BioMarin Pharmaceutical Inc.	CA	$859,100

Top 500 Companies by Net Profit in
Hoover's MasterList of U.S. Companies 2022 (continued)

Rank	Company	Headquarters	Net Income
357	Duke Realty Corp	IN	$852,895
358	Albertsons Companies Inc	ID	$850,200
359	First Horizon Corp	TN	$845,000
360	Robinson (C.H.) Worldwide, Inc.	MN	$844,245
361	Bath & Body Works Inc	OH	$844,000
362	Arista Networks Inc	CA	$840,854
363	WestRock Co	GA	$838,300
364	Electronic Arts	CA	$837,000
365	Zebra Technologies Corp.	IL	$837,000
366	Tapestry Inc	NY	$834,200
367	Toll Brothers Inc.	PA	$833,627
368	AvalonBay Communities, Inc.	VA	$827,630
369	Church & Dwight Co Inc	NJ	$827,500
370	MidAmerican Energy Co.	IA	$826,000
371	Stifel Financial Corp	MO	$824,858
372	Western Digital Corp	CA	$821,000
373	Snap-On, Inc.	WI	$820,500
374	Magellan Midstream Partners LP	OK	$816,965
375	National Rural Utilities Coo	VA	$811,667
376	Nexstar Media Group Inc	TX	$811,441
377	Service Corp. International	TX	$802,939
378	Gartner Inc	CT	$793,560
379	Unum Group	TN	$793,000
380	Phillips 66 Partners LP	TX	$791,000
381	CDW Corp	IL	$788,500
382	Verisign Inc	VA	$784,830
383	New Residential Investment Corp	NY	$772,226
384	Duke Energy Florida LLC	FL	$771,000
385	Mettler-Toledo International, Inc.	OH	$768,985
386	Goodyear Tire & Rubber Co.	OH	$764,000
387	Illumina Inc	CA	$762,000
388	Synopsys Inc	CA	$757,516
389	McCormick & Co Inc	MD	$755,300
390	Leidos Holdings Inc	VA	$753,000
391	CBRE Group Inc	TX	$751,989
392	Carmax Inc.	VA	$746,919
393	Textron Inc	RI	$746,000
394	Idexx Laboratories, Inc.	ME	$744,845
395	Western Union Co	CO	$744,300
396	Avery Dennison Corp	CA	$740,100
397	Edison International	CA	$739,000
398	Pacificorp	OR	$739,000
399	Meritage Homes Corp	AZ	$737,444
400	Qorvo Inc	NC	$733,611
401	Berry Global Group Inc	IN	$733,000
402	American Financial Group Inc	OH	$732,000
403	Globe Life Inc	TX	$731,773
404	Netapp Inc	CA	$730,000
405	PerkinElmer, Inc.	MA	$727,887
406	MSCI Inc	NY	$725,983
407	Crocs Inc	CO	$725,694
408	Worthington Industries, Inc.	OH	$723,795
409	Nucor Corp.	NC	$721,470
410	Oncor Electric Delivery Co	TX	$713,000
411	John Deere Capital Corp.	NV	$710,600
412	Clorox Co (The)	CA	$710,000
413	Quidel Corp.	CA	$704,226
414	FleetCor Technologies Inc	GA	$704,216
415	Martin Marietta Materials, Inc.	NC	$702,500
416	Allscripts Healthcare Solutions, Inc.	IL	$700,407
417	Expeditors International of Washing	WA	$696,140
418	Jabil Inc	FL	$696,000
419	Cadence Design Systems Inc	CA	$695,955
420	Williams Sonoma Inc	CA	$680,714
421	TransDigm Group Inc	OH	$680,000
422	Alliant Energy Corp	WI	$674,000
423	Zoom Video Communications Inc	CA	$672,316
424	American Equity Investment Life Hoo	IA	$671,460
425	Chimera Investment Corp	NY	$670,114
426	Verisk Analytics Inc	NJ	$666,200
427	Atmos Energy Corp.	TX	$665,563
428	West Pharmaceutical Services, Inc.	PA	$661,800
429	Thor Industries, Inc.	IN	$659,872
430	Molina Healthcare Inc	CA	$659,000
431	Chipotle Mexican Grill Inc	CA	$652,984
432	Amkor Technology Inc.	AZ	$642,995
433	LKQ Corp	IL	$638,423
434	Vistra Corp	TX	$636,000
435	Henry Schein Inc	NY	$631,232
436	Darden Restaurants, Inc. (Us	FL	$629,300
437	Big Lots, Inc.	OH	$629,191
438	Kilroy Realty Corp.	CA	$628,144
439	SS&C Technologies Holdings Inc	CT	$625,200
440	Evergy Inc	MO	$618,300
441	Ubiquiti Inc	NY	$616,584
442	Advance Auto Parts Inc	NC	$616,108
443	ONEOK Inc	OK	$612,809
444	Cardinal Health, Inc.	OH	$611,000
445	AMERCO	NV	$610,856
446	Booz Allen Hamilton Holding Corp.	VA	$608,958
447	Chemours Co (The)	DE	$608,000
448	Hovnanian Enterprises, Inc.	NJ	$607,817
449	Home Point Capital Inc	MI	$607,003
450	Sage Therapeutics Inc	MA	$606,073
451	Half Robert International Inc.	CA	$598,626
452	PSEG Power LLC	NJ	$594,000
453	Brunswick Corp.	IL	$593,300
454	Exelon Generation Co LLC	PA	$589,000
455	Constellation Energy Corp	MD	$589,000
456	lululemon athletica inc	British Columbia	$588,913
457	Take-Two Interactive Software, Inc.	NY	$588,886
458	Atkore Inc	IL	$587,857
459	Brown & Brown Inc	FL	$587,104
460	Catalent Inc	NJ	$585,000
461	NiSource Inc. (Holding Co.)	IN	$584,900
462	Vulcan Materials Co (Holding Com	AL	$584,480
463	Georgia Power Co	GA	$584,000
464	Avangrid Inc	CT	$581,000
465	Crown Holdings Inc	PA	$579,000
466	M.D.C. Holdings, Inc.	CO	$573,657
467	Avantor Inc	PA	$572,600
468	Newell Brands Inc	GA	$572,000
469	Alexandria Real Estate Equities Inc	CA	$571,247
470	Seaboard Corp.	KS	$570,000
471	Essex Property Trust Inc	CA	$568,870
472	Arizona Public Service Co.	AZ	$568,028
473	East West Bancorp, Inc	CA	$567,797
474	Affiliated Managers Group Inc.	FL	$565,700

Top 500 Companies by Net Income in
Hoover's MasterList of U.S. Companies 2022 (continued)

Rank	Company	Headquarters	Net Income
475	KB HOME	CA	$564,746
476	Old Republic International Corp.	IL	$558,600
477	Wabtec Corp.	PA	$558,000
478	Akamai Technologies Inc	MA	$557,054
479	Cerner Corp.	MO	$555,596
480	NortonLifeLock Inc	AZ	$554,000
481	CHS Inc	MN	$553,952
482	Levi Strauss & Co.	CA	$553,541
483	Fortune Brands Home & Security, Inc.		$553,100
484	FMC Corp.	PA	$551,500
485	Terminix Global Holdings Inc	TN	$551,000
486	Steel Dynamics Inc.	IN	$550,822
487	Pinnacle West Capital Corp	AZ	$550,559
488	Generac Holdings Inc	WI	$550,494
489	Broadridge Financial Solutions Inc	NY	$547,500
490	SEI Investments Co	PA	$546,593
491	Huntington Ingalls Industries, Inc.	VA	$544,000
492	Shell Midstream Partners LP	TX	$543,000
493	Encore Wire Corp.	TX	$541,422
494	Zions Bancorporation, N.A.	UT	$539,000
495	Flagstar Bancorp, Inc.	MI	$538,000
496	BorgWarner Inc	MI	$537,000
497	MAA	TN	$533,791
498	WR Berkley Corp	CT	$530,670
499	Dick's Sporting Goods, Inc	PA	$530,251
500	Cboe Global Markets Inc	IL	$529,000

Hoover's MasterList
of U.S. Companies

Company
Listings
---

1 SOURCE CONSULTING INC.

1250 H St. NW Ste. 575
Washington DC 20005
Phone: 202-624-0800
Fax: 202-624-0810
Web: www.1-sc.com

CEO: William Teel Jr
CFO: Kimberly Logan
HR: Brandon Teele
FYE: December 31
Type: Private

1 Source Consulting isn't the only company to provide information technology and strategic consulting services to the US government but it would like to be at the top of the list. The company offers IT systems design development and integration services as well as security management program management infrastructure and operations consulting and systems development. 1 Source has served federal agencies such as the departments of Homeland Security Energy Transportation as well as the ATF and SEC. The company operates from offices in Germantown Maryland and Washington D.C. 1 Source was founded in 1999 by CEO William R. Teel Jr.

1105 MEDIA INC.

9121 Oakdale Ave. Ste. 101
Chatsworth CA 91311
Phone: 818-734-1520
Fax: 818-734-1522
Web: www.101com.com

CEO: –
CFO: Richard Vitale
HR: –
FYE: December 31
Type: Private

1105 Media has a myriad of ways to distribute business-to-business information. The company covers markets such as IT and computing office technology home medical equipment and the public sector. Its products and operations include publications (Redmond Magazine for the Microsoft IT community) e-newsletters (Federal Employees News Digest) websites (CampusTechnology.com) and conferences and events (The Defense Systems Conference). Its 1105 Government Information Group subsidiary covers the government information technology market. 1105 Media was founded in 2006 by Nautic Partners Alta Communications and publishing and marketing executive Neal Vitale.

1-800 CONTACTS INC.

66 E. Wadsworth Park Dr. 3rd Fl.
Draper UT 84020
Phone: 801-924-9800
Fax: 801-924-9905
Web: www.1800contacts.com

CEO: John Graham
CFO: Brett Gappmayer
HR: Max Neves
FYE: December 31
Type: Private

Lose a contact? If you can still find your telephone or computer you can get replacement lenses from 1-800 CONTACTS. Through its website and over the phone the company offers contact lenses from major manufacturers and distributors. Its most popular brands include Acuvue Air Optix Biomedics Focus FreshLook and Proclear. To ensure order accuracy 1-800 CONTACTS verifies prescription information with eye doctors. The company was founded in 1995 by entrepreneurs Jonathan Coon and John Nichols. It was bought by WellPoint for an undisclosed amount in mid-2012 as the health insurance giant looks to grow its direct-to-consumer operations.

180 DEGREE CAPITAL CORP

7 N. Willow Street, Suite 4B
Montclair, NJ 07042
Phone: 973 746-4500
Fax: –
Web: www.180degreecapital.com

NMS: TURN
CEO: Kevin Rendino
CFO: Daniel Wolfe
HR: –
FYE: December 31
Type: Public

Harris & Harris Group likes to think small. The business development company invests mostly in startup firms developing so-called "tiny technology" — microsystems microelectromechanical systems and nanotechnology used in applications in such sectors as electronics medical devices pharmaceuticals semiconductors telecommunications and clean technology. The company seeks out small thinly capitalized firms lacking operating history or experienced management. Harris & Harris has made more than 80 venture capital investments since 1983; its current portfolio consists of interests in some 30 firms including Nanosys and NeoPhotonics.

	Annual Growth	12/16	12/17	12/18	12/19	12/20
Sales ($ mil.)	17.9%	1.8	1.2	0.7	0.9	3.5
Net income ($ mil.)	–	(16.4)	(3.6)	(2.4)	(4.8)	(0.5)
Market value ($ mil.)	12.6%	14.3	20.4	18.2	22.3	23.0
Employees	–	8				

1-800 FLOWERS.COM, INC.

Two Jericho Plaza, Suite 200
Jericho, NY 11753
Phone: 516 237-6000
Fax: –
Web: www.1800flowers.com

NMS: FLWS
CEO: Christopher McCann
CFO: William Shea
HR: –
FYE: June 27
Type: Public

1-800-FLOWERS.COM sells fresh-cut flowers floral arrangements and plants through its toll-free number and websites; it also markets gifts via catalogs TV and radio ads and online affiliates. Through subsidiaries the company offers gourmet foods (Harry & David) popcorn (The Popcorn Factory) baked goods (Cheryl's) fruit arrangements (FruitBouquets.com) and a host of other products. Its BloomNet service provides products and services to florists. 1-800-FLOWERS operates primarily in the US. Founder and chairman James McCann launched the company in 1976. In 2020 the company has completed its acquisition of PersonalizationMall.com.

1MAGE SOFTWARE INC.

384 Inverness Pkwy. Ste. 206
Englewood CO 80112
Phone: 800-844-1468
Fax: 303-796-0587
Web: www.1mage.com

CEO: David R Deyoung
CFO: –
HR: –
FYE: December 31
Type: Private

For 1mage Software images are everything. 1mage helps organizations manage their paper and electronic files by providing software that captures stores and displays documents as electronic images. The company's software handles a wide range of documents including e-mails scanned forms memos letters spreadsheets databases multimedia documents faxes and maps. Add-on modules include tools for faxing printing workflow searching reporting and remote access. 1mage licenses its software to a wide range of clients including energy manufacturing transportation and real estate firms as well as government agencies and organizations.

	Annual Growth	07/17	07/18*	06/19	06/20	06/21
Sales ($ mil.)	15.5%	1,193.6	1,151.9	1,248.6	1,489.6	2,122.2
Net income ($ mil.)	28.1%	44.0	40.8	34.8	59.0	118.7
Market value ($ mil.)	36.3%	633.8	815.8	1,227.3	1,291.6	2,189.3
Employees	0.9%	4,633	4,785	4,095	4,300	4,800

*Fiscal year change

1ST CENTURY BANCSHARES, INC.   NAS: FCTY

1875 Century Park East, Suite 1400   CEO: –
Los Angeles, CA 90067   CFO: –
Phone: 310 270-9500   HR: –
Fax: –   FYE: December 31
Web: www.1cbank.com   Type: Public

Where would Jesus bank? Probably at 1st Century Bank the operating subsidiary of 1st Century Bancshares. Not to be confused with First Century Bank of West Virginia 1st Century Bank is a one-branch commercial bank located in western Los Angeles near Beverly Hills. It caters to small businesses entrepreneurs and high-net-worth professionals. 1st Century Bank offers checking money market accounts CDs trusts debit and credit cards and online banking to more than 2300 account holders. Commercial loans make up about half of its loan portfolio with real estate loans accounting for most of the rest. 1st Century Bancshares was founded in 2004 not the 1st century.

	Annual Growth	12/10	12/11	12/12	12/13	12/14
Assets ($ mil.)	17.4%	308.4	405.3	499.2	538.1	585.2
Net income ($ mil.)	–	(2.0)	1.0	2.9	6.9	2.4
Market value ($ mil.)	11.5%	41.6	35.9	46.8	72.5	64.4
Employees	14.7%	41	49	56	63	71

1ST COLONIAL BANCORP INC   NBB: FCOB

210 Lake Drive East, Suite 300, Woodland Falls Corporate Park   CEO: Robert B White
Cherry Hill, NJ 08002   CFO: Robert Faix
Phone: 877 785-8550   HR: –
Fax: 856 321-8272   FYE: December 31
Web: www.1stcolonial.com/   Type: Public

1st Colonial Bancorp is the holding company for 1st Colonial National Bank. Founded in 2000 the bank serves Camden County in southern New Jersey through branches in the communities of Cinnaminson Collingswood and Westville. With an emphasis on personalized service it caters to small and midsized businesses professional practices and local government entities as well as consumers. The bank provides traditional deposit products such as checking savings and money market accounts and certificates of deposit. Additional services include check cards online banking and safe deposit boxes.

	Annual Growth	12/16	12/17	12/18	12/19	12/20
Assets ($ mil.)	6.9%	487.8	540.1	543.9	575.2	636.1
Net income ($ mil.)	6.8%	3.7	4.0	5.2	3.2	4.8
Market value ($ mil.)	(4.9%)	47.1	57.0	61.0	51.8	38.5
Employees	–	–	–	–	–	–

1ST CONSTITUTION BANCORP   NMS: FCCY

2650 Route 130, P.O. Box 634   CEO: –
Cranbury, NJ 08512   CFO: –
Phone: 609 655-4500   HR: –
Fax: –   FYE: December 31
Web: www.1stconstitution.com   Type: Public

In order to "secure the blessings of liberty" the founding fathers established the US Constitution. As for promoting the general welfare some banks share the same dedication to "We the people." 1st Constitution Bancorp is the parent of 1st Constitution Bank which serves consumers small businesses and not-for-profits through more than a dozen branches in Middlesex Mercer and Somerset counties in New Jersey. Services and products include demand savings and time deposits as well as loans and mortgages. Commercial mortgages business loans and construction loans make up more half of the bank's lending portfolio.

	Annual Growth	12/15	12/16	12/17	12/18	12/19
Assets ($ mil.)	13.1%	968.0	1,038.2	1,079.3	1,177.8	1,586.3
Net income ($ mil.)	12.0%	8.7	9.3	6.9	12.0	13.6
Market value ($ mil.)	14.5%	131.2	190.6	186.5	203.1	225.5
Employees	4.8%	183	206	185	197	221

1ST FRANKLIN FINANCIAL CORP.

135 East Tugalo Street, Post Office Box 880   CEO: Virginia Herring
Toccoa, GA 30577   CFO: A. Roger Guimond
Phone: 706 886-7571   HR: –
Fax: –   FYE: December 31
Web: www.1ffc.com   Type: Public

Benjamin Franklin was known for doling out sage financial advice to "common folk." Today 1st Franklin Financial is known for doling out direct cash loans and first and second home mortgages to a similar demographic. Secured direct cash loans make up the lion's share of the company's lending activity; finance charges on loans account for the majority of its revenues. 1st Franklin also offers credit insurance to borrowers and supplements its business by purchasing and servicing sales finance contracts from retailers. The firm operates through about 250 branch offices in the Southeast. Chairman and CEO Ben Cheek III and his family own 1st Franklin which was founded by his father in 1941.

	Annual Growth	12/16	12/17	12/18	12/19	12/20
Assets ($ mil.)	10.7%	674.0	718.2	796.4	939.2	1,013.7
Net income ($ mil.)	97.5%	1.0	14.9	17.3	13.3	15.9
Market value ($ mil.)	–	–	–	–	–	–
Employees	2.1%	1,360	1,439	1,488	1,513	1,476

1ST SOURCE CORP   NMS: SRCE

100 North Michigan Street   CEO: Christopher Murphy
South Bend, IN 46601   CFO: Brett Bauer
Phone: 574 235-2000   HR: –
Fax: –   FYE: December 31
Web: www.1stsource.com   Type: Public

1st Source Corporation parent of 1st Source Bank provides commercial and consumer banking services through its lending operations retail branches and fee based businesses. 1st Source Corporation has about 80 banking centers locations in 18 counties in Indiana and Michigan and Sarasota County in Florida. The bank provides commercial small business agricultural and real estate loans to private owned business clients and traditional banking services include checking and savings accounts certificate of deposits and individual retirement accounts. Its specialty finance group provides financing for aircraft automobile fleets trucks and construction and environmental equipment new construction equipment new and used aircraft auto and light trucks and medium and heavy-duty trucks.

	Annual Growth	12/17	12/18	12/19	12/20	12/21
Assets ($ mil.)	8.3%	5,887.3	6,293.7	6,622.8	7,316.4	8,096.3
Net income ($ mil.)	14.9%	68.1	82.4	92.0	81.4	118.5
Market value ($ mil.)	0.1%	1,223.4	998.0	1,283.5	997.0	1,227.1
Employees	0.1%	1,125	1,150	1,175	1,175	1,130

1ST UNITED BANCORP, INC.   NMS: FUBC

One North Federal Highway   CEO: –
Boca Raton, FL 33432   CFO: –
Phone: 561 362-3400   HR: –
Fax: 561 362-3439   FYE: December 31
Web: www.1stunitedbankfl.com   Type: Public

1st United Bancorp is the holding company for 1st United Bank a community-based retail bank with 15 branches in the greater Miami area of Broward Brevard Indian River Miami-Dade and Palm Beach counties plus another handful of branches in Central Florida. 1st United Bank offers checking savings money market and NOW accounts as well as debit and credit cards. It caters mostly to professionals entrepreneurs and high-net-worth individuals. 1st United Bancorp has a mortgage-heavy loan portfolio; some 75% consists of commercial and residential real estate loans. 1st United Bancorp was founded in 2000 as Advantage Bancorp the holding company for Advantage Bank.

	Annual Growth	12/08	12/09	12/10	12/11	12/12
Assets ($ mil.)	26.2%	617.8	1,015.6	1,267.8	1,421.2	1,566.8
Net income ($ mil.)	–	(1.4)	4.7	2.2	3.7	4.7
Market value ($ mil.)	1.0%	204.4	243.3	235.4	189.1	212.9
Employees	18.1%	153	229	301	291	298

1SYNC INC.

Princeton Pike Corporate Center 1009 Lenox Dr. Ste. 115
Lawrenceville NJ 08648
Phone: 312-463-4000
Fax: 609-620-4601
Web: www.1sync.org

CEO: Steven Sivitter
CFO: Gary Lo
HR: –
FYE: December 31
Type: Subsidiary

1SYNC hopes to help you synchronize all sorts of trading relationships and product information. The company provides collaborative software used to synchronize data in multiple locations formats and languages. 1SYNC's products are used for functions such as supply chain management business intelligence collaborating with trading partners and managing catalog and pricing information. The company also offers services such as consulting implementation maintenance support and training. Its customers include manufacturers membership organizations and retailers. The company was formed in 2005 when the operations of Transora and UCCnet were combined. 1SYNC is a not-for-profit subsidiary of GS1 US.

21ST CENTURY NORTH AMERICA INSURANCE COMPANY

3 Beaver Valley
Wilmington DE 19803
Phone: 800-443-3100
Fax: 330-668-7204
Web: www.aschulman.com

CEO: Bruce W Marlow
CFO: –
HR: –
FYE: December 31
Type: Subsidiary

Cutting out the middleman — that's how 21st Century Insurance grew in the 20th century. The company's primary subsidiaries provide inexpensive auto and personal umbrella insurance for customers by selling directly rather than through brokers which eliminates the cost of agents and commissions. 21st Century Insurance limits sales of its auto policies to preferred-risk applicants (good drivers). The company has historically been most active in California but has been actively expanding into other states including Texas. 21st Century Insurance is part of the Farmers Group of Zurich Financial Services.

24/7 REAL MEDIA INC.

132 W. 31st St.
New York NY 10001
Phone: 212-231-7100
Fax: 212-760-1774
Web: www.247realmedia.com

CEO: Brian Lesser
CFO: Christina Van Tassell
HR: –
FYE: December 31
Type: Subsidiary

Keeping it real — 24/7. 24/7 Real Media provides key elements in the rapidly changing Internet advertising arena: search marketing services software to host and manage digital ads (including mobile Web ads) and a network of websites that run the ads. The company's Advertiser Solutions segment provides advertisers access to its network of websites and permission-based e-mail marketing database. 24/7 also offers search engine optimization services. Technology offerings revolve around its ad delivery and management software which allows advertisers to plan manage and measure their online campaigns. Operating through 18 offices across 12 countries 24/7 is a subsidiary of communications conglomerate WPP.

30DC INC

NBB: TDCH

80 Broad Street, 5th Floor
New York, NY 10004
Phone: 212 962-4400
Fax: –
Web: www.30dcinc.com

CEO: Henry Pinskier
CFO: Theodore A Greenberg
HR: –
FYE: June 30
Type: Public

30DC offers digital marketing platforms tools services and training through four business units. Its original product was a free 30 day challenge (30DC) training program for Internet marketers. The company also offers digital publishing and marketing tools with MagCast a platform that enables online content to be published and delivered via Apple's Newsstand application and Market ProMax a comprehensive online marketing platform that aids in the creation of digital products and e-commerce sites. Formerly a business development company named Infinity Capital Group the company completed a reverse merger with 30DC in 2010 and adopted its name business and management team.

	Annual Growth	06/11	06/12	06/13	06/14	06/15
Sales ($ mil.)	(21.0%)	1.9	2.9	2.0	2.8	0.7
Net income ($ mil.)	–	(1.4)	0.0	(0.4)	0.1	(1.6)
Market value ($ mil.)	(50.3%)	13.1	7.7	4.6	10.0	0.8
Employees	2.4%	10	10	14	11	11

360I LLC

1 Peachtree Pointe 1545 Peachtree St. Ste. 450
Atlanta GA 30309
Phone: 404-876-6007
Fax: 404-876-9097
Web: www.360i.com

CEO: Sarah Hofstetter
CFO: –
HR: –
FYE: March 31
Type: Subsidiary

If you are ready for a revolution in your online marketing campaign keep this company on your short list. 360i provides search engine optimization paid placement management and performance analytics services for US and international clients including H&R Block NBCUniversal and Office Depot. In addition to turning Web searches into marketing opportunities (through optimization and paid placement) the company provides development and management services for targeted marketing campaigns using banner ads e-mails and websites. A subsidiary of Innovation Interactive 360i got off the ground in 1998. In 2010 Innovation Interactive was acquired by Japanese advertising conglomerate Dentsu.

374WATER INC

NBB: SCWO

701 W Main Street, Suite 410
Durham, NC 27701
Phone: 919 888-8194
Fax: –
Web: www.powerverdeenergy.com

CEO: Richard Davis
CFO: John Hofmann
HR: –
FYE: December 31
Type: Public

PowerVerde (formerly known as Vyrex) has abandoned its quest for a molecular fountain of youth. These days it's only interested in power. The development-stage biotech company had been researching antioxidants to develop cures for respiratory cardiovascular and neurodegenerative diseases and other conditions related to aging. Unable to continue funding its activities however Vyrex executed a reverse merger with PowerVerde which has designed a power system that generates electricity with zero emissions. The system created by the company's founders George Konrad and Fred Barker uses solar-heated water to power an environmentally friendly motor.

	Annual Growth	12/16	12/17	12/18	12/19	12/20
Sales ($ mil.)	(48.9%)	0.6	0.9	0.2	0.0	0.0
Net income ($ mil.)	–	(0.1)	0.4	(0.7)	(0.5)	(0.5)
Market value ($ mil.)	59.7%	3.6	3.3	1.4	2.5	23.4
Employees	(15.9%)	2	1	1	1	1

3D SYSTEMS CORP. (DE) — NYS: DDD

333 Three D Systems Circle
Rock Hill, SC 29730
Phone: 803 326-3900
Fax: –
Web: www.3dsystems.com

CEO: Jeffrey Graves
CFO: Jagtar Narula
HR: –
FYE: December 31
Type: Public

3D Systems' stereolithography apparatuses (SLAs) and other machines create 3D prototypes of everything from toys to airplane parts. The company provides comprehensive 3D printing and digital manufacturing solutions including 3D printers for plastics and metals materials software on demand manufacturing services and digital design tools. The company's solutions support advanced applications in a wide range of industries and verticals including healthcare dental aerospace automotive and durable goods. The company also offers several 3D printing technologies such as selective laser sintering direct metal printing Multi Jet printing and ColorJet printing. Its brands include Figure 4 NextDent DuraForm and VisiJet. The company generates approximately half of its sales domestically.

	Annual Growth	12/16	12/17	12/18	12/19	12/20
Sales ($ mil.)	(3.1%)	633.0	646.1	687.7	629.1	557.2
Net income ($ mil.)	–	(38.4)	(66.2)	(45.5)	(69.9)	(149.6)
Market value ($ mil.)	(5.8%)	1,649.7	1,072.5	1,262.4	1,086.2	1,300.9
Employees	(5.0%)	2,445	2,666	2,620	2,472	1,995

3M CO — NYS: MMM

3M Center
St. Paul, MN 55144-1000
Phone: 651 733-1110
Fax: 651 733-9973
Web: www.3m.com

CEO: Michael Roman
CFO: Monish Patolawala
HR: Kristen Ludgate
FYE: December 31
Type: Public

3M is a diversified company that operates four segment categories: Safety & Industrial Transportation & Electronics Health Care and Consumer. 3M boasts some of the world's most recognizable consumer brands including Post-it notes Scotch tapes Scotchgard fabric protectors Scotch-Brite scouring pads Filtrete home air filters and ACE bandages. 3M sells products directly to users and through numerous e-commerce and traditional wholesalers retailers distributors and dealers worldwide. The company generates about 50% of its sales outside the US. 3M was founded in 1902 as a small mining venture in Northern Minnesota called Minnesota Mining and Manufacturing Company.

	Annual Growth	12/17	12/18	12/19	12/20	12/21
Sales ($ mil.)	2.8%	31,657.0	32,765.0	32,136.0	32,184.0	35,355.0
Net income ($ mil.)	5.1%	4,858.0	5,349.0	4,570.0	5,384.0	5,921.0
Market value ($ mil.)	(6.8%)	134,595.3	108,959.4	100,885.0	99,952.9	101,576.9
Employees	0.9%	91,536	93,516	96,163	95,000	95,000

3M COGENT INC.

639 N. Rosemead Blvd.
Pasadena CA 91107
Phone: 626-325-9600
Fax: 626-325-9700
Web: www.cogentsystems.com

CEO: –
CFO: –
HR: –
FYE: December 31
Type: Subsidiary

3M Cogent knows security. The company provides Automated Fingerprint Identification Systems (AFIS) that governments law enforcement agencies and companies use to capture analyze and compare fingerprints. 3M Cogent's offerings include proprietary biometrics access control software hardware (including mobile systems) system maintenance and services that include consulting implementation and systems integration. It also enjoys an alliance with Northrop Grumman for design development and sale of biometric ID systems. 3M Cogent operates in Austria Canada China Taiwan the UK and the US where the Department of Homeland Security is a core customer. In 2010 3M purchased the company for $943 million.

3M PURIFICATION INC.

400 Research Pkwy.
Meriden CT 06450
Phone: 203-237-5541
Fax: 203-238-8977
Web: www.3mpurification.com

CEO: Mike Roman
CFO: Frederick Flynn Jr
HR: –
FYE: October 31
Type: Subsidiary

3M Purification looks at liquids and gases through rose-colored filters. The company a unit of 3M's Industrial and Transportation segment makes a full line of filtration products for the health care fluid-processing and potable-water markets. Its filters remove contaminants as small as molecules and particles as large as sand from liquids and gases. They are used to purify drugs paints and resins oil and gas and home drinking water. 3M Purification assigns its own scientists to work with customers when creating new products. The company which was known as CUNO until 2009 operates sales offices worldwide and eight manufacturing plants in Australia Europe Japan South America and the US.

454 LIFE SCIENCES

20 Commercial St.
Branford CT 06405
Phone: 203-871-2300
Fax: 203-481-2075
Web: www.454.com

CEO: Christopher K Mc Leod
CFO: –
HR: –
FYE: December 31
Type: Subsidiary

454 Life Sciences wants to give drug developers and other gene researchers the 411 on entire genomes. The company has developed computer-controlled instruments and related software that enable scientists to analyze whole genomes in one fell swoop rather than a few hundred genes at a time. Parent company Roche Diagnostics distributes 454 Life Sciences' Genome Sequencing systems (GS Junior and GS FLX) to clinical laboratories medical research institutes drugmakers and other scientific customers worldwide. Research fields include cancer infectious disease drug discovery agriculture and paleontology.

4LICENSING CORP — NBB: FOUR

5 Penn Plaza
New York, NY 10001
Phone: 646 931-1022
Fax: –
Web: www.4kidsentertainment.com

CEO: –
CFO: –
HR: –
FYE: December 31
Type: Public

If your kids are into Yu-Gi-Oh! thank (or blame) 4Kids Entertainment. The company licenses the rights to third-party entertainment properties for use in cartoons games toys and apparel. It also uses those properties to produce TV shows videos films music and websites for kids. Its youth-oriented portfolio includes Chaotic Yu-Gi-Oh! Cabbage Patch Kids Dinosaur King and Viva Pi ±ata. 4Kids also handles licensing for the American Kennel Club the Cat Fanciers' Association and the UK's Royal Air Force. It has a five-year partnership with The CW Network (ending in 2013) to program its Saturday morning The CW4Kids lineup. In 2011 4Kids voluntarily filed for Chapter 11 bankruptcy protection.

	Annual Growth	12/10	12/11	12/12	12/13	12/14
Sales ($ mil.)	(46.7%)	14.5	12.3	3.3	1.2	1.2
Net income ($ mil.)	–	(27.2)	(15.2)	9.5	(3.2)	(0.9)
Market value ($ mil.)	4.2%	–	–	–	9.5	9.9
Employees	(49.0%)	89	71	16	10	6

5LINX HOLDINGS INC.

400 ANDREWS ST STE 400 # 400　　　　　　　　CEO: Nelson Gerard
ROCHESTER, NY 146041429　　　　　　　　　　CFO: –
Phone: 585-359-2922　　　　　　　　　　　　　HR: –
Fax: –　　　　　　　　　　　　　　　　FYE: December 31
Web: www.5linx.com　　　　　　　　　　　　Type: Private

You won't see 5LINX stores popping up anytime soon but the telecommunications company is still a fast growing enterprise. Relying on a network of independent marketing representatives to sell its products (similar to the model employed by Mary Kay) 5LINX provides an array of telecommunications products and services. Among these are cellular phones and plans from major US carriers; satellite TV service from DISH Network and DIRECTV; and broadband Internet and home security services. Representatives also sell GLOBALINX VoIP services for residential and business customers; a subsidiary of 5LINX GLOBALINX products include Wi-Fi phones and digital phone services.

	Annual Growth	12/08	12/09	12/10	12/11	12/12
Sales ($ mil.)	43.9%	–	–	50.0	81.4	103.6
Net income ($ mil.)	76.3%	–	–	1.2	1.5	3.8
Market value ($ mil.)	–	–	–	–	–	–
Employees	–	–	–	–	–	35

7-ELEVEN INC.

1722 Routh St. Ste. 1000 1 Arts Plz　　　　　　CEO: Joseph Depinto
Dallas TX 75201　　　　　　　　　　　　CFO: Stanley Reynolds
Phone: 972-828-7011　　　　　　　　　　　　　HR: –
Fax: 972-828-7848　　　　　　　　　　　FYE: December 31
Web: www.7-eleven.com　　　　　　　　　　Type: Subsidiary

"If convenience stores are open 24 hours why the locks on their doors?" If anyone knows it's 7-Eleven. The North American subsidiary of Seven-Eleven Japan 7-Eleven operates more than 7200 company-owned or franchised stores in the US and Canada under the 7-Eleven name. Globally 7-Eleven licenses more than 24000 stores in about a dozen countries mostly in the Asia Pacific and Nordic regions. Its stores range from 2400 to 3000 sq. ft. and sell about 2500 items. The world's leading convenience store company is owned by the Japanese retail conglomerate Seven & i Holdings which is the holding company for Seven-Eleven Japan Ito-Yokado Denny's restaurants and other businesses.

800-JR CIGAR INC.

301 Rte. 10 East　　　　　　　　　　　　CEO: Lew Rothman
Whippany NJ 07981　　　　　　　　　CFO: Michael E Colleton
Phone: 973-884-9555　　　　　　　　HR: Karen Dallesondro
Fax: 973-884-9556　　　　　　　　　　　FYE: December 31
Web: www.jrcigars.com　　　　　　　　　　Type: Subsidiary

800-JR Cigar would like to give that man (or woman) a cigar. Doing business as JR Cigars the company that began as a small Manhattan cigar shop is now a leading distributor and retailer of premium cigars. It also sells pipe tobacco lighters humidors and other smoking accessories as well as coffee. JR Cigars' retail operations include three discount outlet stores in North Carolina a catalog and an e-commerce site. The company's website also features regular auctions and a section called JR Cigar University where tobacco aficionados can read up on all things stogie related. 800-JR Cigar is a subsidiary of Altadis itself owned by Imperial Tobacco Group.

84 LUMBER COMPANY

1019 Rte. 519　　　　　　　　　　　　　　CEO: Joe Hardy
Eighty Four PA 15330-2813　　　　　　　　　CFO: Paul Lentz
Phone: 724-228-8820　　　　　　　　　　　　HR: –
Fax: 310-319-0310　　　　　　　　　　　FYE: December 31
Web: www.amark.com　　　　　　　　　　　Type: Private

With its utilitarian stores (most don't have heat or A/C) 84 Lumber has built itself up to be a leading low-cost provider of lumber building materials and related services. Through about 250 stores in 30 states the company (which is the nation's largest privately held building materials retailer) sells lumber siding drywall windows and other supplies as well as plans to construct decks garages and houses. Its 84 Components subsidiary operates plants that make floor and roof trusses and wall panels. In addition 84 Lumber provides insurance travel and professional installation services. CEO Joseph Hardy Sr. founded 84 Lumber in 1956.

8X8 INC　　　　　　　　　　　　　　　　　NYS: EGHT

675 Creekside Way　　　　　　　　　　　　CEO: Dave Sipes
Campbell, CA 95008　　　　　　　　　　CFO: Samuel Wilson
Phone: 408 727-1885　　　　　　　　　　　　　HR: –
Fax: 408 980-0432　　　　　　　　　　　　FYE: March 31
Web: www.8x8.com　　　　　　　　　　　　　Type: Public

8x8 is transforming the future of business communications as a leading Software-as-a-Service (SaaS) provider of voice video chat contact center and enterprise-class API solutions powered by one global cloud communications platform. 8x8 empowers workforces worldwide by connecting individuals and teams so they can collaborate faster and work smarter. 8x8 provides real-time business analytics and intelligence giving its customers unique insights across all interactions and channels on its platform so they can delight their end-customers and accelerate their business. 8x8 has approximately 1.8 million global business users. About 75% its total sales comes from its US customers.

	Annual Growth	03/17	03/18	03/19	03/20	03/21
Sales ($ mil.)	20.4%	253.4	296.5	352.6	446.2	532.3
Net income ($ mil.)	–	(4.8)	(104.5)	(88.7)	(172.4)	(165.6)
Market value ($ mil.)	20.8%	1,664.3	2,035.4	2,204.5	1,512.6	3,540.3
Employees	13.6%	1,019	1,225	1,497	1,675	1,696

99 CENTS ONLY STORES　　　　　　　　　　NYSE: NDN

4000 Union Pacific Ave.　　　　　　　　　　CEO: Barry J Feld
Los Angeles CA 90023　　　　　　　　　　CFO: Ashok Walia
Phone: 323-980-8145　　　　　　　　　　　　　HR: –
Fax: 323-980-8160　　　　　　　　　　　　FYE: March 31
Web: www.99only.com　　　　　　　　　　　Type: Private

Pass the buck get a penny back. 99 Cents Only Stores sells closeout and regular general merchandise for 99 cents or less. With about 300 stores the company sells name-brand and private-label food and beverages (more than 50% os sales) health and beauty aids household and seasonal goods hardware toys and more. Nearly three-quarters of its stores are in California; other stores are located in Arizona Nevada and Texas. The company's Bargain Wholesale unit distributes discounted merchandise to retailers distributors and exporters. Founded in 1982 99 Cents Only Stores was taken private by Ares Management Canada Pension Plan Investment and the Gold/Schiffer family in 2012.

A & H SPORTSWEAR CO. INC.

500 William St.
Pen Argyl PA 18072
Phone: 610-863-4176
Fax: 630-467-3010
Web: www.necdisplay.com

CEO: Mark Waldman
CFO: Mark Greenberg
HR: –
FYE: October 31
Type: Private

When swimsuit season rolls around Houdini has nothing on A & H Sportswear. The company's Miraclesuit makes 10 pounds disappear! The Miraclesuit bathing suits suck in that tummy using three times as much Lycra as most other swimwear. The firm also makes shapewear jeans and other casual apparel using its patented Miratex fabric. A & H Sportswear's clothing and swimsuits are sold in the US through finer retailers (such as Bloomingdale's Nordstrom Saks Fifth Avenue) catalogs (Eddie Bauer Norm Thompson and Spiegel) and online. A & H Sportswear's offerings are also marketed internationally through independent dealers.

A & K RAILROAD MATERIALS, INC.

1505 S REDWOOD RD
SALT LAKE CITY, UT 841045106
Phone: 801-974-5484
Fax: –
Web: www.akrailroad.com

CEO: –
CFO: Jeff Galyean
HR: –
FYE: December 31
Type: Private

You won't find A & K Railroad next to B&O Railroad on a Monopoly board but you will find the company's pieces all over the railroad. A & K Railroad Materials sells a multitude of new and used railroad supplies including steel and wood railroad ties and tie plugs landscaping railroad ties (reclaimed) frogs (plates used to guide rail wheels at crossings) guard rails switches and components (braces clips and plates) rails and rail tools. Services offered by A & K Railroad Materials include track removal/salvage and custom rail welding. Its lineup is used for railroads as well as mines and cranes in North and South America. About 90% of the company is owned by its founder and chairman Kern Schumacher.

	Annual Growth	01/01	01/02	01/03	01/04*	12/14
Sales ($ mil.)	7.8%	–	60.9	67.8	59.7	150.2
Net income ($ mil.)	–	–	(3.2)	0.3	0.4	16.9
Market value ($ mil.)	–	–	–	–	–	–
Employees	–	–	–	–	–	255

*Fiscal year change

A&E TELEVISION NETWORKS LLC

235 E. 45th St.
New York NY 10017
Phone: 212-210-1400
Fax: 212-210-1308
Web: www.aetn.com

CEO: –
CFO: –
HR: –
FYE: December 31
Type: Joint Venture

You might say this company gives viewers a lifetime dose of television. A&E Television Networks (AETN) owns and operates a portfolio of ten cable TV channels including Lifetime Television the flagship network of AETN subsidiary Lifetime Entertainment that targets women with a variety of lifestyle and entertainment content. Its A&E network offers a mix of reality-based programming and documentaries while its HISTORY channel airs original programs on historical topics. The company also operates sister networks such as Crime & Investigation Network and The Biography Channel. AETN is a joint venture between Hearst Walt Disney and NBCUniversal (NBCU).

A&R LOGISTICS INC.

8440 S. Tabler Rd.
Morris IL 60450
Phone: 815-941-5200
Fax: 800-406-5703
Web: www.artransport.com

CEO: Chris Ball
CFO: –
HR: –
FYE: December 31
Type: Private

Through its subsidiaries A&R Logistics offers a diverse menu of transportation and logistics services. A&R Transport is a bulk plastic and dry flowable transportation provider with about 25 terminals and 10 warehouses throughout the US; its fleet includes 770 tractors and about 1100 trailers. A&R Global Logistics arranges freight transportation (mostly bulk shipments of dry plastic pallets in hopper trucks for chemical companies) through a network of independent carriers and A&R Packaging & Distribution operates warehouses and provides packaging services. UTC Overseas provides freight-forwarding and door-to-door services in Europe.

A&W RESTAURANTS INC.

1648 McGrathiana Pkwy.
Lexington KY 40511
Phone: 859-219-0019
Fax: 770-448-7726
Web: www.presidio.com/presidio_tech_cap

CEO: Kevin Bazner
CFO: –
HR: –
FYE: December 31
Type: Private

The old-fashioned root beer stand lives on thanks to this business. A&W Restaurants franchises more than 1200 quick-service restaurants in the US and unaffiliated restaurants in about 15 other countries. The eateries many of which still offer drive-up service in addition to dine-in seating offer a menu featuring hamburgers hot dogs onion rings and fries along with its signature root beer. A&W traces its roots back to a California root beer stand business started by Roy Allen in 1919. It belonged to YUM! Brands the world's largest fast-food franchisor until late 2011 when a group of franchisees purchased it.

A. B. BOYD COMPANY

600 S. McClure Rd.
Modesto CA 95357
Phone: 209-236-1111
Fax: 209-236-0154
Web: www.boydcorp.com

CEO: –
CFO: Eric Struik
HR: –
FYE: December 31
Type: Private

A. B. Boyd Company puts a little zip in rubber manufacturing. Initially a zipper distributor the company has evolved to operate as Boyd Corporation and manufacture rubber plastic and fiber products that offer environmental sealing and energy-efficient solutions. The custom-designed and manufactured products meet requirements for acoustic thermal shock and shielding systems among others. Boyd uses a range of specialized materials from silicone to Mylar polypropylene copper and aluminum foils and coated fabrics to deliver a low-cost engineered lineup. It caters to OEMs in aerospace electronics medical equipment telecommunications and transportation. Boyd is held by Stonebridge Partners Management.

A. DUIE PYLE INC.

650 Westtown Rd.
West Chester PA 19381-0564
Phone: 610-696-5800
Fax: 610-696-3768
Web: www.aduiepyle.com

CEO: Peter Latta
CFO: –
HR: –
FYE: December 31
Type: Private

A. Duie Pyle has piled up a collection of transportation-related businesses. The company's services include less-than-truckload (LTL) and truckload freight hauling warehousing third-party logistics and equipment leasing. (LTL carriers consolidate freight from multiple shippers into a single trailer.) A. Duie Pyle's LTL business operates primarily in the Northeast US and in Canada from a network of more than 15 service depots. The LTL unit maintains a fleet of about 790 tractors and 1800 trailers; another 325 tractors for heated truckload hauling. The company offers service outside its core region through alliances with other carriers. A. Duie Pyle maintains about 2 million sq. ft. of warehouse space.

A. EICOFF & COMPANY

401 N. Michigan Ave.
Chicago IL 60611
Phone: 312-527-7100
Fax: 312-527-7192
Web: www.eicoff.com

CEO: Bill McCabe
CFO: Pat Sacony
HR: –
FYE: December 31
Type: Subsidiary

This firm's business is getting couch potatoes to take action. A. Eicoff & Company is a leading advertising agency specializing in direct response television marketing. It helps create TV spots and campaigns that not only highlight a product or brand but also urge consumers to call write or log onto the Internet for more information. In addition to creative work A. Eicoff provides monitoring and measuring services to track the effectiveness of its campaigns and it offers planning services to help its clients target specific consumer groups. The company was founded in 1965 by Alvin Eicoff and now operates as part of OgilvyOne the marketing services arm of global advertising agency network Ogilvy & Mather.

A. FINKL & SONS COMPANY

2011 N. Southport Ave.
Chicago IL 60614
Phone: 773-975-2510
Fax: 773-348-5347
Web: www.finkl.com

CEO: Bruce C Liimatainen
CFO: Joseph E Curci
HR: –
FYE: January 31
Type: Private

Thanks to Mrs. O'Leary's cow A. Finkl & Sons has chiseled a niche for itself in the steel industry. The company was founded in 1879 when Anton Finkl developed a chisel to clean bricks rescued from buildings destroyed in the Great Chicago Fire. Since then Finkl has forged ahead to become a leading global supplier of forging die steels. (A forging die is a steel block used in a hammer or press for shaping metal.) The firm also produces plastic mold steels die casting tool steels and custom open-die forging. German steel company SCHMOLZ+BICKENBACH owns Finkl.

A. P. HUBBARD WHOLESALE LUMBER CORPORATION

1027 ARNOLD ST
GREENSBORO, NC 274057101
Phone: 336-275-1343
Fax: –
Web: www.hubbardlumber.com

CEO: –
CFO: –
HR: –
FYE: March 31
Type: Private

A.P. Hubbard Lumber manufactures lumber and lumber products for the construction industry. Its offerings include air- and kiln-dried lumber made from cypress hardwoods softwoods and eastern white pine as well as engineered wood products such as glue-laminated timber rim board wood deckinh sheathing and framing lumber. The company distributes its products in the Carolinas Virginia and Maryland. A.P. Hubbard Lumber was founded in Greensboro North Carolina in 1952.

	Annual Growth	03/08	03/09	03/10	03/11	03/12
Sales ($ mil.)	20.2%	–	8.8	8.8	11.7	15.3
Net income ($ mil.)	96.7%	–	–	0.0	0.0	0.1
Market value ($ mil.)	–	–	–	–	–	–
Employees	–	–	–	–	–	5

A.C. MOORE ARTS & CRAFTS INC.

130 A.C. Moore Dr.
Berlin NJ 08009
Phone: 856-768-4930
Fax: 856-753-4723
Web: www.acmoore.com

NASDAQ: ACMR
CEO: Adolph Pipeno
CFO: David Stern
HR: –
FYE: December 31
Type: Private

Some are content to collect and dust their tchotchkes but others are compelled to make them. A.C. Moore Arts & Crafts is eager to serve them all (focusing on women 35 and older). The chain's 130-plus superstores (up from 17 in 1997) sell crafts and art and scrapbooking supplies which account for about 60% of sales as well as yarn seasonal items fashion crafts home decor and picture frames and everything else needed to glue paint or arrange. A.C. Moore also offers in-store arts-and-crafts classes. Its stores are located in more than a dozen states along the East Coast. Founded in 1985 A.C. Moore was acquired in late 2011 by affiliates of arts and crafts distributor Sbar's Inc. for about $41 million.

A.V. THOMAS PRODUCE, INC.

3900 SULTANA AVE
ATWATER, CA 953019605
Phone: 209-394-7514
Fax: –
Web: www.avthomasproduce.com

CEO: –
CFO: Dana Miller
HR: –
FYE: December 31
Type: Private

A.V. Thomas Produce knows a sweet potato is not just a yam by another name. The California grower produces packages and sells several varieties of yams and the yam's sweeter cousin the sweet potato. (Though the names are used interchangeably in this country most US-grown "yams" are actually sweet potatoes.) With 1700 acres in production its brands include Best West Court House Nature's Pride Oriental Beauty Royal Flush Sweetie Pie Thomas and Winner; it is also a major US producer of organic sweet potatoes which it sells under the Natural Beauty label. Founded in 1960 by Antonio Vieira Tomas an immigrant from the Azores Islands A.V. Thomas is owned and run by Tomas's nephew CEO Manuel Vieira.

	Annual Growth	12/10	12/11	12/12	12/13	12/14
Sales ($ mil.)	11.9%	–	60.8	65.5	69.7	85.1
Net income ($ mil.)	(3.6%)	–	10.6	9.0	14.5	9.5
Market value ($ mil.)	–	–	–	–	–	–
Employees	–	–	–	–	–	8

A2D TECHNOLOGIES

2345 Atascocita Rd.
Humble TX 77396
Phone: 281-319-4944
Fax: 281-319-4945
Web: www.tgsnopec.com

CEO: –
CFO: Fredrik Amundsen
HR: –
FYE: December 31
Type: Subsidiary

Less talkative than Star Wars' R2-D2 A2D Technologies nevertheless communicates well by providing digital well log data interpretive software and data management services. A2D's LOG-LINE system allows geoscientists to access and download well log data from their workstations. Customers use its well log data to calibrate seismic data to known geologic conditions in well bores. A2D Technologies has data coverage worldwide including the US Canada the Gulf of Mexico offshore Northwest Europe Russia West Africa and Madagascar. Parent TGS-NOPEC Geophysical is one of the largest owners of digital well log data in North America.

AAA COOPER TRANSPORTATION

1751 KINSEY RD
DOTHAN, AL 363035877
Phone: 334-793-2284
Fax: –
Web: www.aaacooper.com

CEO: Reid Dove
CFO: J Steven Roy
HR: Renee Lingo
FYE: January 01
Type: Private

AAA Cooper Transportation (ACT) is a trucking company offering freight hauling services primarily in the Southwest Southeast and Midwest along with carriers with coverage into Puerto Rico Canada and Mexico. ACT offers less-than-truckload (LTL) truck load international services freight brokerage services dedicated contract carriage and fleet maintenance services through 40 locations. The company's International Services division offers cross-border services to Canada and Mexico. ACT can also facilitate transportation in Puerto Rico. The company's fleet includes 3000 tractors and 6500 trailers.

	Annual Growth	12/12	12/13	12/14*	01/16	01/17
Sales ($ mil.)	0.9%	–	–	576.9	595.4	592.0
Net income ($ mil.)	(4.3%)	–	–	20.1	14.1	17.7
Market value ($ mil.)	–	–	–	–	–	–
Employees	–	–	–	–	–	4,933

*Fiscal year change

AAC GROUP HOLDING CORP.

7211 Circle S Rd.
Austin TX 78745
Phone: 512-444-0571
Fax: 512-443-5213
Web: www.cbi-rings.com

CEO: –
CFO: Kris G Radhakrishnan
HR: –
FYE: August 31
Type: Subsidiary

School spirit tops the shopping list of customers of AAC Group. Doing business as American Achievement the company manufactures and supplies class rings yearbooks and letter athletic jackets as well as graduation items such as caps and gowns diplomas and announcements for the US elementary through high school and college markets. Its ring and accessory brands include ArtCarved Balfour and Keepsake. Although scholastic products account for most of its sales AAC Group also makes commemorative jewelry for families bridal jewelry personalized rings for the military bowling tournaments and pro sports such as World Series Super Bowl and Stanley Cup. The memorabilia maker is owned by Fenway Partners.

AAMCO TRANSMISSIONS INC.

201 Gibraltar Rd.
Horsham PA 19044
Phone: 215-643-5885
Fax: 215-956-0340
Web: www.aamco.com

CEO: Keith A Morgan
CFO: Jim Gregory
HR: –
FYE: December 31
Type: Private

AAMCO Transmissions is geared for transmission repair. The company is a leading franchiser of transmission fix-it facilities with about 900 independently owned and operated shops throughout the US Canada and Puerto Rico. In addition to transmission work AAMCO locations provide automotive cooling and electrical system repairs as well as other general maintenance services. The company was established in 1963 by Robert Morgan and MAACO founder Anthony Martino. Today it operates alongside sister franchiser Cottman Transmission under holding company American Driveline Systems itself a subsidiary of investment firm American Capital.

AAON, INC.   NMS: AAON

2425 South Yukon Ave.
Tulsa, Oklahoma 74107
Phone: 918 583-2266
Fax: –
Web: www.aaon.com

CEO: Gary Fields
CFO: Rebecca Thompson
HR: –
FYE: December 31
Type: Public

AAON is the world's leading manufacturer of premium HVAC equipment creating comfortable and healthy indoor environments. Operating through subsidiaries the company makes and markets air conditioning and heating equipment for commercial and industrial buildings primarily in the US. AAON's products include rooftop units air-handling and make-up air units chillers and energy recovery units as well as condensing units and geothermal/water-source heat pumps and coils. The company sells to property owners and contractors in both the new construction and replacement markets looking for a higher quality and more options than offered by standardized manufacturers.

	Annual Growth	12/16	12/17	12/18	12/19	12/20
Sales ($ mil.)	7.6%	384.0	405.2	433.9	469.3	514.6
Net income ($ mil.)	10.3%	53.4	54.5	42.6	53.7	79.0
Market value ($ mil.)	19.2%	1,726.0	1,916.6	1,831.0	2,580.4	3,479.7
Employees	8.8%	1,619	1,991	2,221	2,290	2,268

AAR CORP   NYS: AIR

One AAR Place, 1100 N. Wood Dale Road
Wood Dale, IL 60191
Phone: 630 227-2000
Fax: 630 227-2019
Web: www.aarcorp.com

CEO: John Holmes
CFO: Sean Gillen
HR: –
FYE: May 31
Type: Public

AAR provides a wide variety of aviation services and technology products primarily for the commercial aviation and defense industries. The company sells and leases new and overhauled aircraft engines and airframe parts to commercial aviation military and government customers. AAR provides supply chain management services parts and MRO (aircraft maintenance repair and overhaul) services. The company also supplies government agencies and non-governmental organizations (NGOs) with transportation pallets containers shelters mobility systems and control systems used in support of military deployments and humanitarian activities. About four-fifths of AAR's revenue comes from North America. The company traces its historical roots to 1951 when Allen Eichner began selling aircraft radios and instruments.

	Annual Growth	05/17	05/18	05/19	05/20	05/21
Sales ($ mil.)	(1.7%)	1,767.6	1,748.3	2,051.8	2,072.0	1,652.3
Net income ($ mil.)	(10.8%)	56.5	15.6	7.5	4.4	35.8
Market value ($ mil.)	4.6%	1,236.0	1,580.9	1,064.4	713.5	1,476.9
Employees	(2.1%)	5,350	5,775	6,550	5,400	4,920

AARON AND COMPANY, INC.

30 TURNER PL
PISCATAWAY, NJ 088543839
Phone: 732-752-8200
Fax: –
Web: www.aaronco.com

CEO: Barry Portnoy
CFO: Victor De Rosa
HR: –
FYE: December 31
Type: Private

Aaron & Company knows a thing or two about staying cool. Catering primarily to contractors in New Jersey and eastern Pennsylvania the wholesaler offers plumbing and HVAC supplies through more than five locations in the Garden State. Three of these outlets house Aaron Kitchen & Bath Design Galleries which feature complete kitchen and bathroom set-ups to help customers with building and remodeling plans. Aaron & Company is served by a single 120000-sq.-ft. distribution center that is stocked with more than 15000 items.

	Annual Growth	12/13	12/14	12/15	12/16	12/17
Sales ($ mil.)	3.0%	–	81.4	83.4	86.6	89.0
Net income ($ mil.)	23.7%	–	1.0	0.4	(0.4)	1.9
Market value ($ mil.)	–	–	–	–	–	–
Employees	–	–	–	–	–	188

AARP

601 E ST NW
WASHINGTON, DC 200490003
Phone: 202-434-2277
Fax: –
Web: www.aarp.org

CEO: Jo Ann Jenkins
CFO: –
HR: –
FYE: December 31
Type: Private

AARP is a nonprofit nonpartisan organization with a membership of nearly 38 million current members. With staffed offices in all 50 states the District of Columbia Puerto Rico and the US Virgin Islands AARP works to strengthen communities and promote the issues that matter most to families such as healthcare security financial security and personal fulfillment. AARP also advocates for individuals in the marketplace by selecting products and services of high quality and value to carry the AARP name. It also produces the world's largest circulation magazine AARP The Magazine and AARP Bulletin. The company was founded in 1999.

	Annual Growth	12/11	12/12	12/13	12/14	12/16
Sales ($ mil.)	3.7%	–	–	1,439.0	1,399.0	1,605.0
Net income ($ mil.)	(29.8%)	–	–	408.8	84.5	141.2
Market value ($ mil.)	–	–	–	–	–	–
Employees	–	–	–	–	–	1,800

AASTRA INTECOM INC.

2811 Internet Blvd.
Frisco TX 75034
Phone: 469-365-3237
Fax: 469-365-3533
Web: www.aastraintecom.com

CEO: –
CFO: –
HR: –
FYE: December 31
Type: Subsidiary

Aastra Intecom also known as Aastra USA is the US division of Canada's Aastra Technologies. The company provides IP telephony systems and contact center services to enterprise and government customers. Its products include the Clearspan line of IP communications equipment as well as its Centergy virtual contact center for managing agents across multiple sites. The company also offers professional services such as project management system installation and technical support. It targets such industry sectors as education government health care and insurance. Aastra USA represents less than 15% of its parent's overall sales.

ABATIX CORP.

2400 SKYLINE DR STE 400
MESQUITE, TX 751491990
Phone: 214-381-0322
Fax: –
Web: www.abatix.com

CEO: Terry W Shaver
CFO: Frank J Cinatl IV
HR: Elisabeth Parker
FYE: December 31
Type: Private

Following a huff and a puff Abatix cleans up. The company distributes more than 30000 personal protection and safety equipment products to environmental contractors as well as construction and industrial safety companies. Abatix's lineup is used by workers involved in cleanup projects such as asbestos and lead abatement and natural disasters. Products include sheeting and bags dehumidifiers air scrubbers and filters and germicidals and fire retardant and disposable protective clothing. Abatix serves some 6000 customers located throughout the US. It operates a dozen sales and distribution centers in Texas Arizona Georgia Louisiana Nevada California Washington and Florida.

	Annual Growth	12/06	12/07	12/11	12/13	12/14
Sales ($ mil.)	5.3%	–	69.0	69.3	84.5	99.1
Net income ($ mil.)	17.3%	–	1.3	1.7	2.7	3.9
Market value ($ mil.)	–	–	–	–	–	–
Employees	–	–	–	–	–	180

ABAXIS, INC.

3240 WHIPPLE RD
UNION CITY, CA 945871217
Phone: 510-675-6500
Fax: –
Web: www.abaxis.com

CEO: Clinton H Severson
CFO: Ross Taylor
HR: –
FYE: March 31
Type: Private

The genesis of the Abaxis technology took place at the Oak Ridge National Laboratory where under contract to the National Aeronautics and Space Administration scientists sought to develop and manufacture a small biochemical analyzer for use in space laboratories. Founded in 1989 Abaxis licenses and manufactures reagents utilizing the Orbos technology to other companies. It introduces Piccolo and VETSCAN analyzer in the market. The company covers more than 90% of the general chemistry tests normally used in medical and veterinary diagnostics. Abaxis sells to primary care physicians pediatric caregivers hospitals managed care organizations and the military.

	Annual Growth	03/14	03/15	03/16	03/17	03/18
Sales ($ mil.)	6.5%	–	202.6	218.9	227.2	244.7
Net income ($ mil.)	(0.2%)	–	27.3	31.6	32.7	27.2
Market value ($ mil.)	–	–	–	–	–	–
Employees	–	–	–	–	–	656

ABBOTT LABORATORIES

NYS: ABT

100 Abbott Park Road
Abbott Park, IL 60064-6400
Phone: 224 667-6100
Fax: –
Web: www.abbottinvestor.com

CEO: Robert Ford
CFO: Robert Funck
HR: Mary Moreland
FYE: December 31
Type: Public

Abbott Laboratories develop manufacture and sell a broad and diversified line of health care products. Abbott has product lines of branded generic pharmaceuticals diagnostic systems and tests pediatric and adult nutritional products (including well-known brands such as Similac and PediaSure) and medical devices for the treatment of cardiovascular diseases including diabetes care products for people with diabetes neuromodulation devices for chronic pain and movement disorder management. The US accounts for about 40% of company's total sales. Abbott was founded in 1888 by physician and drug store proprietor Dr. Wallace C. Abbott.

	Annual Growth	12/17	12/18	12/19	12/20	12/21
Sales ($ mil.)	12.0%	27,390.0	30,578.0	31,904.0	34,608.0	43,075.0
Net income ($ mil.)	96.2%	477.0	2,368.0	3,687.0	4,495.0	7,071.0
Market value ($ mil.)	25.3%	100,676.2	127,596.1	153,228.2	193,149.4	248,276.9
Employees	3.4%	99,000	103,000	107,000	109,000	113,000

ABBVIE INC
NYS: ABBV

1 North Waukegan Road
North Chicago, IL 60064-6400
Phone: 847 932-7900
Fax: -
Web: www.abbvie.com

CEO: Richard Gonzalez
CFO: Robert Michael
HR: -
FYE: December 31
Type: Public

AbbVie is a global research-based biopharmaceutical company. The company has a portfolio of products that include a broad line of therapies that address some of the world's most complex and serious diseases. Its primary product is Humira best known as a rheumatoid arthritis drug; it accounts for some 40% of the company's total net revenues. Other key products include cancer treatment Imbruvica and hepatitis C drug Mavyret. Products are sold globally but the US is AbbVie's largest market accounting for more than 75% of total sales. In mid-2020 the company completed the acquisition of Allergan.

	Annual Growth	12/17	12/18	12/19	12/20	12/21
Sales ($ mil.)	18.8%	28,216.0	32,753.0	33,266.0	45,804.0	56,197.0
Net income ($ mil.)	21.4%	5,309.0	5,687.0	7,882.0	4,616.0	11,542.0
Market value ($ mil.)	8.8%	171,015.9	163,023.1	156,568.6	189,477.4	239,432.9
Employees	14.6%	29,000	30,000	30,000	47,000	50,000

ABC APPLIANCE INC.

1 Silverdome Industrial Park
Pontiac MI 48343-6001
Phone: 248-335-4222
Fax: 248-335-2568
Web: www.abcwarehouse.com

CEO: -
CFO: -
HR: Bernadette Brdak
FYE: October 31
Type: Private

When customers have to buy retail they turn to ABC Appliance for "the closest thing to wholesale." The company sells audio equipment electronics computers home appliances and other products at more than 60 stores in Michigan Ohio and Indiana as well as online. ABC Appliance's inventory includes products from manufacturers such as LG General Electric Sony and Whirlpool. The company's retail stores operate under the ABC Warehouse Mickey Shorr (mobile electronics) and Hawthorne Appliance banners. US-Appliance.com is the firm's online-only consumer electronics and appliance sales business. CEO Gordy Hartunian founded ABC Appliance in 1964 and the chain remains owned by his family.

ABC CABLE NETWORKS GROUP

3800 W. Alameda Ave.
Burbank CA 91505
Phone: 818-569-7500
Fax: +972-9-956-1610
Web: www.onsettechnology.com

CEO: Gary K Marsh
CFO: -
HR: -
FYE: September 30
Type: Subsidiary

ABC Cable Networks Group wants to work a little magic on the television dial. The unit of Disney/ABC Television Group owns and operates a portfolio of cable television networks including entertainment channels ABC Family. It also owns Disney Channels Worldwide which operates kids' networks the Disney Channel and Disney XD; other kids' programming is distributed under Disney Junior (launched in 2012) and Jetix. (Through ABC Family ABC Cable Networks owns animation distributor Jetix Europe.) In addition ABC Cable Networks holds a 42% stake in A&E Television. Disney/ABC Television Group oversees the television broadcasting production and distribution operations of media giant Walt Disney.

ABC INC.

77 W. 66th St.
New York NY 10023-6298
Phone: 212-456-7777
Fax: 212-456-1424
Web: abc.go.com

CEO: -
CFO: -
HR: -
FYE: September 30
Type: Subsidiary

Some Desperate Housewives a Modern Family and a group of doctors schooled in Grey's Anatomy call this network home. ABC operates the #3 television network in the US (behind CBS and FOX) with more than 230 affiliates (including 10 corporate-owned stations). ABC also owns an 80% stake in ESPN a leader in cable sports broadcasting with a stable of channels including ESPN2 ESPN Classic and ESPN News as well as its flagship channel. (Publisher Hearst owns the remaining 20% of ESPN.) In addition the company operates mass-market publisher Hyperion. ABC is the cornerstone of Disney-ABC Television Group the TV division of parent Walt Disney.

ABDON CALLAIS OFFSHORE, LLC

1300 N ALEX PLISANCE BLVD
GOLDEN MEADOW, LA 703572612
Phone: 985-475-7111
Fax: -

CEO: -
CFO: Lionel Largared
HR: -
FYE: December 31
Type: Private

Abdon Callais Offshore provides freight and passenger transportation services to the offshore oil and gas industry. The company operates its fleet of about 75 supply vessels utility vessels and crew boats in the Gulf of Mexico serving coastal shelf and deepwater projects. It counts both production companies and service companies among its customers. The company was founded in 1945 by Abdon Callais grandfather of president and CEO Peter Callais. The Callais family controls the company; other backers have included private equity firm Stonehenge Capital.

	Annual Growth	12/07	12/08	12/09	12/10	12/12
Sales ($ mil.)	15.8%	-	-	-	75.5	101.2
Net income ($ mil.)	65.1%	-	-	-	14.4	39.3
Market value ($ mil.)	-	-	-	-	-	-
Employees	-	-	-	-	-	430

ABEONA THERAPEUTICS INC
NAS: ABEO

1330 Avenue of the Americas, 33rd Floor
New York, NY 10019
Phone: 646 813-4701
Fax: -
Web: www.abeonatherapeutics.com

CEO: Vishwas Seshadri
CFO: Edward Carr
HR: -
FYE: December 31
Type: Public

Abeona Therapeutics (formerly PlasmaTech Pharmaceuticals) is developing treatments to tap into the cancer therapy market. The company makes pharmaceutical products based on nanopolymer chemistry and other drug delivery technologies. Its FDA-approved MuGard is a prescription oral rinse for the treatment of mucositis or mouth ulceration a common side effect of chemotherapy or radiation. MuGard has marketing approval in the US and it is available in Europe through partner SpePharm. Other Abeona products include ovarian cancer treatments and drug delivery technologies for solid tumors and diabetes.

	Annual Growth	12/14	12/15	12/16	12/17	12/18
Sales ($ mil.)	34.2%	0.9	1.0	0.9	0.8	3.0
Net income ($ mil.)	-	(26.8)	(14.5)	(21.9)	(27.3)	(56.7)
Market value ($ mil.)	19.9%	165.4	161.1	232.5	759.9	342.3
Employees	85.6%	7	15	19	42	83

ABERCROMBIE & FITCH CO
NYS: ANF

6301 Fitch Path
New Albany, OH 43054
Phone: 614 283-6500
Fax: –
Web: www.abercrombie.com

CEO: Fran Horowitz
CFO: Scott Lipesky
HR: –
FYE: January 30
Type: Public

Abercrombie & Fitch (A&F) is a global multi-brand omnichannel specialty retailer that sells upscale men's women's and kids' casual clothes and accessories. A&F trades under two main brands the eponymous Abercrombie & Fitch and Hollister which targets teens and is actually the larger of the two; it also sells intimates under the Gilly Hicks brand and kids clothing under Abercrombie kids. The company's approximately 735 stores are found mainly in the US but also in Europe the Asia Pacific region and the Middle East while A&F ships globally online. The US is its largest market accounting for nearly 70% of total revenue.

	Annual Growth	01/17*	02/18	02/19	02/20*	01/21
Sales ($ mil.)	(1.5%)	3,326.7	3,492.7	3,590.1	3,623.1	3,125.4
Net income ($ mil.)	–	4.0	7.1	74.5	39.4	(114.0)
Market value ($ mil.)	19.4%	708.9	1,281.7	1,333.5	1,020.8	1,439.5
Employees	(5.7%)	43,000	38,000	42,000	44,000	34,000

*Fiscal year change

ABF FREIGHT SYSTEM INC.

3801 Old Greenwood Rd.
Fort Smith AR 72903
Phone: 479-785-6000
Fax: 800-599-2810
Web: www.abfs.com

CEO: –
CFO: –
HR: –
FYE: December 31
Type: Subsidiary

ABF Freight System knows the ABCs of freight transportation. The largest subsidiary of Arkansas Best ABF Freight System offers national and regional less-than-truckload (LTL) transportation of general commodities such as apparel appliances chemicals food furniture metal plastics and textiles. LTL carriers generally combine freight from multiple shippers into a single truckload. The company operates a fleet of more than 17000 trailers and about 1600 tractors from a network of some 275 terminals. It ships throughout the US and to Canada Mexico Guam and Puerto Rico. Beyond its core LTL business ABF is expanding with end-to-end supply chain management services.

ABILENE CHRISTIAN UNIVERSITY INC

1600 CAMPUS CT
ABILENE, TX 796013761
Phone: 325-674-2000
Fax: –
Web: www.acu.edu

CEO: –
CFO: –
HR: –
FYE: May 31
Type: Private

Abilene was once the home where the buffalo roamed but now it's where the Abilene Christian University Wildcats play. The private Church of Christ-affiliated university which requires Bible study courses and daily chapel attendance has an enrollment of about 4600 students. By 2020 the school intends to be the world's premier Christ-centered university. It offers some 70 baccalaureate majors that include more than 125 areas of study in addition to about 25 graduate academic programs one doctoral program and study abroad programs in Oxford England; Montevideo Uruguay; and Leipzig Germany. The student-teacher ratio is 15:1. Abilene Christian was founded in 1906.

	Annual Growth	05/16	05/17	05/18	05/20	05/21
Sales ($ mil.)	2.2%	–	131.6	135.6	139.3	143.8
Net income ($ mil.)	65.7%	–	33.8	44.6	11.2	254.9
Market value ($ mil.)	–	–	–	–	–	–
Employees	–	–	–	–	–	675

ABINGTON MEMORIAL HOSPITAL INC

1200 OLD YORK RD
ABINGTON, PA 190013788
Phone: 215-481-2000
Fax: –
Web: www.abingtonhealth.org

CEO: Laurence M Merlis
CFO: –
HR: –
FYE: June 30
Type: Private

Abington Hospital?Jefferson Health (formerly Abington Memorial Hospital) brings health care to residents of southeastern Pennsylvania. The not-for-profit community hospital has some 800 beds. In addition to general medical and surgical care the hospital offers specialized care centers for cancer and cardiovascular conditions operates high-tech orthopedic and neurological surgery units and serves as a regional trauma care facility. With approximately 126000 inpatient admissions 499000 Emergency Department visits and four million outpatient visits annually it also runs an inpatient pediatric unit in affiliation with The Children's Hospital of Philadelphia. Abington?Jefferson Health operates the neighboring 140-bed Lansdale Hospital?Jefferson Health and range of inpatient and outpatient facilities.

	Annual Growth	06/12	06/13	06/14	06/15	06/16
Sales ($ mil.)	1.5%	–	708.5	697.3	697.7	740.9
Net income ($ mil.)	19.2%	–	20.9	0.7	28.5	35.3
Market value ($ mil.)	–	–	–	–	–	–
Employees	–	–	–	–	–	4,018

ABIOMED, INC.
NMS: ABMD

22 Cherry Hill Drive
Danvers, MA 01923
Phone: 978 646-1400
Fax: 978 777-8411
Web: www.abiomed.com

CEO: Michael Minogue
CFO: Todd Trapp
HR: –
FYE: March 31
Type: Public

ABIOMED gives weary hearts a rest. The medical device maker has developed a range of cardiac assist devices and is developing a self-contained artificial heart. Its Impella micro heart pumps can temporarily take over blood circulation during surgery or catheterization. Its Impella CP device provides blood flow of approximately one liter more per minute than the Impella 2.5 device and is primarily used by either interventional cardiologists to support patients in the cath lab or by cardiac surgeons in the heart surgery suite. ABIOMED markets its products through both a direct sales force and distributors. About 85% of the company's revenue is generated from the US.

	Annual Growth	03/17	03/18	03/19	03/20	03/21
Sales ($ mil.)	17.5%	445.3	593.7	769.4	840.9	847.5
Net income ($ mil.)	44.2%	52.1	112.2	259.0	203.0	225.5
Market value ($ mil.)	26.3%	5,667.9	13,173.4	12,928.9	6,571.5	14,429.2
Employees	17.4%	908	1,143	1,371	1,536	1,725

ABM INDUSTRIES, INC.
NYS: ABM

One Liberty Plaza, 7th Floor
New York, NY 10006
Phone: 212 297-0200
Fax: –
Web: www.abm.com

CEO: Scott Salmirs
CFO: Earl Ellis
HR: Andrea Newborn
FYE: October 31
Type: Public

ABM Industries is a leading provider of integrated facility solutions. The company primarily offers janitorial services to owners and operators of office buildings hospitals manufacturing plants schools shopping centers catering logistics parking and transportation facilities. ABM also provides maintenance of mechanical air cabin facilities engineering electrical and plumbing systems and it operates parking services and garages mainly at airports across all 50 states. ABM makes most of its revenue in the US. The company's history dates back to 1909.

	Annual Growth	10/17	10/18	10/19	10/20	10/21
Sales ($ mil.)	3.4%	5,453.6	6,442.2	6,498.6	5,987.6	6,228.6
Net income ($ mil.)	140.1%	3.8	97.8	127.4	0.3	126.3
Market value ($ mil.)	1.2%	2,824.7	2,069.6	2,453.8	2,336.7	2,962.0
Employees	(3.0%)	140,000	140,000	140,000	114,000	124,000

ABM SECURITY SERVICES

7324 Southwest Fwy. Ste. 1400 — CEO: –
Houston TX 77074 — CFO: –
Phone: 713-926-4453 — HR: –
Fax: 713-926-2435 — FYE: October 31
Web: www.abm.com/services/security/pages/commercial — Type: Subsidiary

ABM Security Services keeps its eagle eyes on guard. The company provides uniformed security officers security systems monitoring and consulting services through a variety of subsidiaries and brand names such as Security Services of America (SSA) Silverhawk Security and Elite Protection. All told the company maintains about 70 branch offices in more than 30 states. Its guards protect high-rise buildings high-tech computer facilities financial institutions data centers and other commercial and industrial locations. ABM Security is a subsidiary of ABM Industries. The parent company also provides parking janitorial and engineering services.

ABP CORPORATION

1 Au Bon Pain Way — CEO: Susan Morelli
Boston MA 02210 — CFO: –
Phone: 617-423-2100 — HR: –
Fax: 617-423-7879 — FYE: September 30
Web: www.aubonpain.com — Type: Private

To make dough in the bistro business it helps to start with good bread. ABP Corporation operates the Au Bon Pain bakery cafe chain with more than 250 company-owned and franchised locations in the US Kuwait Japan Thailand South Korea and Taiwan. The bistros offer a wide range of sandwiches soups salads and baked goods as well as coffee and other cafe beverages. Most of the restaurants are located in urban areas but ABP also has on-site locations in airports shopping malls and on university campuses. The company also does catering and sells gift baskets. The Au Bon Pain chain was started in 1978 by Louis Kane. ABP is controlled by LNK Partners a Boston-based private equity firm.

ABRA INC.

6601 Shingle Creek Pkwy. Ste. 200 — CEO: Steve Grimshaw
Brooklyn Center MN 55430 — CFO: Brent A Moen
Phone: 763-561-7220 — HR: –
Fax: 763-561-7433 — FYE: December 31
Web: www.abraauto.com — Type: Private

ABRA Auto Body & Glass offers more than just an incantation to get your wrecked car back on the road. Through more than 105 company-owned and franchised shops in a dozen states the company provides collision repair services as well as paintless dent removal and glass repair. The majority of ABRA's stores are in Colorado Georgia and Minnesota. Almost all of the company's services are paid for by insurance companies. Insurance agents can earn continuing education credits for ABRA's classes on issues relating to car repair. Founded in 1984 ABRA Auto Body & Glass is owned by investors and employees.

ABRAXAS PETROLEUM CORP. NBB: AXAS

18803 Meisner Drive — CEO: Robert Watson
San Antonio, TX 78258 — CFO: Steven Harris
Phone: 210 490-4788 — HR: –
Fax: – — FYE: December 31
Web: www.abraxaspetroleum.com — Type: Public

Abraxas Petroleum Corporation (Abraxas) an independent energy company based in San Antonio Texas engages in acquisition exploration development and production of oil NGLs and gas in the US. Raven Drilling is a fully owned subsidiary. The company grows through acquisitions mostly by redeveloping old fields. It has primary operating areas in the Rocky Mountains South Texas Powder River Basin and Permian Basin. Abraxas was founded in 1977.

	Annual Growth	12/16	12/17	12/18	12/19	12/20
Sales ($ mil.)	(6.6%)	56.6	86.3	149.2	129.1	43.0
Net income ($ mil.)	–	(96.4)	16.0	57.8	(65.0)	(184.5)
Market value ($ mil.)	(2.8%)	21.6	20.7	9.2	3.0	19.3
Employees	(21.3%)	–	–	100	65	62

ABS CAPITAL PARTNERS L.P.

400 E. Pratt St. Ste. 910 — CEO: –
Baltimore MD 21202-3116 — CFO: –
Phone: 410-246-5600 — HR: –
Fax: 410-246-5606 — FYE: December 31
Web: www.abscapital.com — Type: Private

ABS Capital Partners seeks out companies that have learned their business ABCs. The firm typically invests $10 million to $30 million per transaction in late-stage (but growing) US companies in the business services health care media and communications and technology sectors. It provides capital for expansions acquisitions management buyouts and recapitalizations. In addition to taking a seat on the boards of its portfolio companies the firm also provides strategic and financial advice to them but usually does not get involved with their day-to-day operations. ABS Capital Partners has interests in more than two dozen companies including Liquidity Services Rosetta Stone and Vibrant Media.

ABT ASSOCIATES INC.

55 Wheeler St. — CEO: Kathleen L Flanagan
Cambridge MA 02138-1168 — CFO: Noel N Samuel
Phone: 617-492-7100 — HR: Jessen Carroll
Fax: 617-492-5219 — FYE: March 31
Web: www.abtassociates.com — Type: Private

Abt Associates offers a wide array of research-based consulting services to government agencies businesses and other organizations worldwide. The firm specializes in issues related to social economic and health policy; clinical research; and international development. Its services include consulting implementation and technical assistance; research and evaluation; survey data collection management and analysis (through Abt SRBI); and strategy planning and policy. Abt Associates has served the US Departments of Agriculture Education and Defense and does business from four US offices and from 40 project sites around the globe. Employees own the company which was founded in 1965 by Clark Abt.

ACACIA RESEARCH CORP   NMS: ACTG

767 3rd Aveneue, Suite 602
New York, NY 10017
Phone: 949 480-8300
Fax: 949 480-8301
Web: www.acaciaresearch.com

CEO: Clifford Press
CFO: Richard Rosenstein
HR: –
FYE: December 31
Type: Public

Acacia Research provides protection under its canopy for intellectual property. The company acquires develops licenses and protects patented technologies for individual inventors and small companies that have limited resources to protect against infringement. The company and its partners owns or controls the rights to over 1200 licensing agreements with many of the world's largest companies. Acacia Research partners with disenfranchised patent owners including individual inventors universities and large multi-national corporations in the technology medical technology energy and industrial industries which includes Table Rock Technologies Newscolor LLC and PricePlay Inc.

	Annual Growth	12/16	12/17	12/18	12/19	12/20
Sales ($ mil.)	(33.5%)	152.7	65.4	131.5	11.2	29.8
Net income ($ mil.)	–	(54.1)	22.2	(105.0)	(17.1)	113.4
Market value ($ mil.)	(11.8%)	320.3	199.6	146.9	131.1	194.2
Employees	(7.2%)	27	13	13	17	20

ACACIA TECHNOLOGIES LLC

500 Newport Center Dr. 7th Fl.
Newport Beach CA 92660
Phone: 949-480-8300
Fax: 949-480-8301
Web: www.acaciatechnologies.com

CEO: Paul R Ryan
CFO: –
HR: –
FYE: December 31
Type: Subsidiary

Acacia Technologies offers shade to more than 150 patent portfolios. The company (which is the primary subsidiary of Acacia Research) acquires and licenses patent rights to various technologies related to digital audio-on-demand and video-on-demand transmission. It markets many of these patents under the DMT brand to makers of electronics gear who incorporate the technologies into applications for cable satellite and Internet distribution of digital content. Acacia Technologies has reached licensing agreements with Fujitsu Pioneer Sony and Union Pacific among other companies.

ACADEMY LTD.

1800 N. Mason Rd.
Katy TX 77449
Phone: 281-646-5200
Fax: 281-646-5000
Web: www.academy.com

CEO: Ken Hicks
CFO: Michael Arnett
HR: –
FYE: January 31
Type: Private

Academy is near the head of the class among sporting goods retailers. It's one of the leading full-line sporting goods chains in the US with more than 150 Academy Sports + Outdoors stores in Texas and about a dozen other southeastern states. Academy's low-frills stores carry clothing shoes and equipment for almost any sport and outdoor activity including camping golf hunting fishing and boating. The company which also operates a catalog and e-commerce site dates back to a San Antonio tire shop opened by Max Gochman in 1938. The business moved into military surplus items and during the 1980s began focusing on sports and outdoor goods. Academy was acquired by the investment firm KKR in 2011.

ACADEMY OF MOTION PICTURE ARTS & SCIENCES

8949 WILSHIRE BLVD
BEVERLY HILLS, CA 902111907
Phone: 310-247-3000
Fax: –
Web: www.oscars.org

CEO: Dawn Hudson
CFO: Andy Horn
HR: –
FYE: June 30
Type: Private

And the Oscar goes to … the Academy of Motion Picture Arts and Sciences (AMPAS). The not-for-profit organization promotes the movie industry by recognizing excellence fostering cultural progress providing a forum for various crafts and cooperating in technical research. It is best known for the annual Academy Awards in which Britannia metal trophies (known as the Oscars) are awarded for outstanding achievements in the motion picture industry. The more than 6000 AMPAS members (who pick the Oscar winners) represent 15 branches of the industry including actors directors producers and executives. The organization was founded in 1927 and is governed by seven officers and a board of governors.

	Annual Growth	06/14	06/15	06/19	06/20	06/21
Sales ($ mil.)	9.3%	–	123.6	147.9	158.4	210.7
Net income ($ mil.)	18.7%	–	37.4	44.1	32.7	104.6
Market value ($ mil.)	–	–	–	–	–	–
Employees	–	–	–	–	–	174

ACADEMY OF TELEVISION ARTS & SCIENCES INC.

5220 Lankershim Blvd.
North Hollywood CA 91601-3109
Phone: 818-754-2800
Fax: 818-761-2827
Web: www.emmys.org

CEO: Dick Askin
CFO: –
HR: –
FYE: December 31
Type: Private - Not-for-Pr

And the award for best organization that honors the television industry goes to: the Academy of Television Arts & Sciences (ATAS). ATAS which has more than 13000 members presents the annual Emmy Awards and sponsors various television-related conferences and activities. The organization also oversees the Daytime and L.A. Area Emmy Awards publishes "emmy" magazine manages archival and educational programs through its ATAS Foundation and operates Web sites such as emmys.tv and emmys.com. The Emmy statuette features a winged woman holding an atom aloft to symbolize the melding of art and science. The award's name is a deviation of "Immy" an early television camera. ATAS was founded in 1946.

ACADIA HEALTHCARE COMPANY INC.   NMS: ACHC

6100 Tower Circle, Suite 1000
Franklin, TN 37067
Phone: 615 861-6000
Fax: –
Web: www.acadiahealthcare.com

CEO: Debra K Osteen
CFO: David Duckworth
HR: –
FYE: December 31
Type: Public

Acadia Healthcare is a leading pure-play provider of behavioral health services. Acadia operates over 570 behavioral health facilities with approximately 18100 licensed beds in some 40 US states the UK and Puerto Rico. Its specialty treatment facilities include residential recovery facilities eating disorder facilities and CTCs which include detoxification partial hospitalization and outpatient programs. The majority of its specialty treatment services are provided to patients who abuse addictive substances such as alcohol illicit drugs or opiates including prescription drugs. Some of our facilities also treat other addictions and behavioral disorders such as chronic pain sexual compulsivity compulsive gambling mood disorders emotional trauma and abuse. . Its UK facilities were discontinued in 2020.

	Annual Growth	12/16	12/17	12/18	12/19	12/20
Sales ($ mil.)	(7.1%)	2,810.9	2,836.3	3,012.4	3,107.5	2,089.9
Net income ($ mil.)	–	6.1	199.8	(175.8)	108.9	(672.1)
Market value ($ mil.)	11.0%	2,913.6	2,872.2	2,263.1	2,924.2	4,424.1
Employees	1.1%	40,400	40,600	42,100	42,800	42,200

ACADIA PHARMACEUTICALS INC
NMS: ACAD

12830 El Camino Real, Suite 400
San Diego, CA 92130
Phone: 858 558-2871
Fax: –
Web: www.acadia-pharm.com

CEO: Stephen Davis
CFO: Mark Schneyer
HR: –
FYE: December 31
Type: Public

ACADIA Pharmaceuticals develops small molecule drugs for the treatment of central nervous system disorders. The biopharmaceutical company's pimavanserin (Nuplazid) was approved by the FDA in 2016 as a treatment for Parkinson's disease psychosis a common development with the disease. Two other clinical-stage candidates are being developed in collaboration with Allergan to treat patients with chronic pain. The company's pipeline also includes pre-clinical candidates in development for chronic pain and Parkinson's disease. All candidates are birthed from ACADIA's own R-SAT drug discovery platform.

	Annual Growth	12/16	12/17	12/18	12/19	12/20
Sales ($ mil.)	124.7%	17.3	124.9	223.8	339.1	441.8
Net income ($ mil.)	–	(271.4)	(289.4)	(245.2)	(235.3)	(281.6)
Market value ($ mil.)	16.7%	4,604.0	4,806.7	2,581.3	6,829.3	8,534.2
Employees	12.9%	370	425	430	503	601

ACADIA REALTY TRUST
NYS: AKR

411 Theodore Fremd Avenue, Suite 300
Rye, NY 10580
Phone: 914 288-8100
Fax: –
Web: www.acadiarealty.com

CEO: Kenneth Bernstein
CFO: John Gottfried
HR: –
FYE: December 31
Type: Public

Acadia Realty acquires redevelops and manages retail properties in the Northeast Mid-Atlantic and Midwest. The self-managed real estate investment trust (REIT) specializes in community shopping centers and mixed-use properties in urban areas. It owns about 185 properties — mostly shopping centers anchored by a grocery store drug store or big box store — sporting about 13 million sq. ft. of leasable space. The REIT's largest tenants include Target H & M Walgreens TJX Companies Royal Ahold and LA Fitness. Acadia Realty owns joint venture interests in another 60 similar properties with investments in self-storage units mortgage loans and other real estate investments.

	Annual Growth	12/16	12/17	12/18	12/19	12/20
Sales ($ mil.)	7.7%	189.9	250.3	262.2	295.3	255.5
Net income ($ mil.)	–	72.8	61.5	31.4	53.0	(8.8)
Market value ($ mil.)	(18.8%)	2,819.2	2,360.3	2,049.7	2,236.9	1,224.1
Employees	(0.4%)	122	118	112	118	120

ACADIAN AMBULANCE SERVICE, INC.

130 E KALISTE SALOOM RD
LAFAYETTE, LA 705088308
Phone: 337-291-3333
Fax: –
Web: www.acadianambulance.com

CEO: Richard Zuschlag
CFO: David L Kelly
HR: –
FYE: December 31
Type: Private

Acadian Ambulance Service is one of the nation's largest privately-held medical transportation companies. The company covers over 70 parishes and counties that are home to more than 24 million residents in Louisiana Mississippi Tennessee and Texas. Along with its ground ambulances the company also operates a handful of helicopter ambulances and fixed-wing airplanes. Its services include emergency transportation air services non-emergency transportation special services mobile healthcare medical education offshore & industrial health and medical alert systems. Established in 1971 Acadian Ambulance Service is owned by its employees through a private stock option plan.

	Annual Growth	12/07	12/08	12/09	12/10	12/11
Sales ($ mil.)	14.4%	–	–	290.8	358.3	380.6
Net income ($ mil.)	39.5%	–	–	4.8	7.2	9.3
Market value ($ mil.)	–	–	–	–	–	–
Employees	–	–	–	–	–	4,000

ACCEL PARTNERS

428 University Ave.
Palo Alto CA 94301
Phone: 650-614-4800
Fax: 650-614-4880
Web: www.accel.com

CEO: –
CFO: Jonathan Biggs
HR: –
FYE: December 31
Type: Private

How fast can you make money? Venture capital and growth equity investment firm Accel Partners hopes to accelerate that. Founded in 1983 the firm which has more than $6 billion under management makes early-stage investments mostly in software and networking companies. Accel also targets more established companies in IT internet digital media mobile networking software and services. After making an investment Accel typically provides its companies with strategic financing recruiting and business development among other services. Its strategy has helped grow some of the most powerful and influential tech companies in the world including Macromedia Riverbed Groupon and Facebook.

ACCELERATE DIAGNOSTICS INC
NAS: AXDX

3950 South Country Club Road, Suite 470
Tucson, AZ 85714
Phone: 520 365-3100
Fax: –
Web: www.acceleratediagnostics.com

CEO: John Phillips
CFO: Steve Reichling
HR: –
FYE: December 31
Type: Public

Accelerate Diagnostics (formerly Accelr8 Technology) wants to speed up your lab results. Using its ID/AST system the company is working on quicker methods for identifying bacterial infections. The system is being designed for use in clinical settings to provide bacterial identification within hours instead of days. If successful it will be an improvement over existing methods that depend upon identifying bacteria in a culture grown over two to three days from a patient sample. Instead ID/AST will look directly at the sample itself sort thousands of bacterial cells to identify any pathogenic bacteria and determine if any are resistant to antibiotics.

	Annual Growth	12/16	12/17	12/18	12/19	12/20
Sales ($ mil.)	159.6%	0.2	4.2	5.7	9.3	11.2
Net income ($ mil.)	–	(66.4)	(64.0)	(88.3)	(84.3)	(78.2)
Market value ($ mil.)	(22.3%)	1,195.4	1,509.3	662.5	973.6	436.7
Employees	3.8%	193	239	287	275	224

ACCELERON PHARMA, INC.
NMS: XLRN

128 Sidney Street
Cambridge, MA 02139
Phone: 617 649-9200
Fax: –
Web: www.acceleronpharma.com

CEO: Habib J Dable
CFO: Kevin F McLaughlin
HR: –
FYE: December 31
Type: Public

Acceleron Pharma is ready to accelerate the treatment of cancer. The biopharmaceutical company is developing protein therapies to treat certain types of cancer and rare diseases such as the blood diseases beta-thalassemia and myelodysplastic syndromes (MDS). The company have focused and prioritized its research and development activities within three key therapeutic areas: hematology pulmonary and neuromuscular. It has collaboration agreements with pharmaceutical giants Alkermes Shire and Bristol-Myers Squibb but its work with Bristol-Myers Squibb shows the most promise. The two companies are developing sotatercept and ACE-083 is designed for the treatment of focal muscle disorders.

	Annual Growth	12/15	12/16	12/17	12/18	12/19
Sales ($ mil.)	42.2%	18.1	27.8	13.5	14.0	74.0
Net income ($ mil.)	–	(63.9)	(57.0)	(108.5)	(118.9)	(124.9)
Market value ($ mil.)	2.1%	2,590.4	1,355.7	2,254.6	2,313.5	2,816.6
Employees	23.5%	102	121	139	173	237

ACCELPATH INC
NBB: ACLP

137 National Plaza, Suite 300
National Harbor, MD 20745
Phone: 240 273-3295
Fax: –

CEO: –
CFO: –
HR: –
FYE: June 30
Type: Public

Technest Holdings can help you get a better picture of your security efforts or better diagnose your patients. The company makes 3-D modeling and imaging software and equipment primarily for the security and health care industries. Technest's products include intelligent surveillance 3-D facial recognition and 3-D imaging devices and systems. The company's customers have included the Department of Defense and the National Institute of Health.

	Annual Growth	06/10	06/11	06/12	06/13	06/14
Sales ($ mil.)	(21.7%)	–	0.4	0.6	0.3	0.2
Net income ($ mil.)	–	(0.3)	(2.9)	(2.1)	(2.0)	(2.5)
Market value ($ mil.)	–	0.8	1.3	0.2	0.0	0.0
Employees	(55.0%)	–	11	5	1	1

ACCELRYS INC
NMS: ACCL

5005 Wateridge Vista Drive
San Diego, CA 92121
Phone: 858 799-5000
Fax: –
Web: www.accelrys.com

CEO: Max Carnecchia
CFO: Michael Piraino
HR: –
FYE: December 31
Type: Public

Accelrys feels strongly that nothing speeds up research like good software. The company develops business intelligence applications used in the development of new drugs and medical technologies. Its software is designed to enable and automate the collection aggregation and analysis of scientific data and include tools for reporting documentation modeling database access and collaboration. Accelrys also offers consulting software integration contract research and training services. While its customers come primarily from the pharmaceutical life sciences and biotech industries Accelrys also serves clients in industries with significant R&D efforts such as aerospace consumer packaged goods and energy.

	Annual Growth	03/09	03/10*	12/10	12/11	12/12
Sales ($ mil.)	26.1%	81.0	83.0	80.2	144.3	162.5
Net income ($ mil.)	–	0.1	1.2	(20.6)	1.8	(10.4)
Market value ($ mil.)	31.5%	222.4	344.2	463.8	375.5	505.7
Employees	21.1%	364	362	580	601	647

*Fiscal year change

ACCENTIA BIOPHARMACEUTICALS INC
NBB: ABPI

324 South Hyde Park Avenue, Suite 350
Tampa, FL 33606
Phone: 813 864-2554
Fax: –
Web: www.accentia.net

CEO: –
CFO: Garrison J Hasara
HR: –
FYE: September 30
Type: Public

Accentia Biopharmaceuticals is accentuating its positives and eliminating its negatives. The drug development company is focused on two development-stage drugs multiple sclerosis drug Revimmune and BiovaxID a possible vaccine for non-Hodgkin's lymphoma being developed by majority-owned subsidiary BioVest International. BioVest also sells cell growth instruments and offers contract manufacturing of cell cultures. The company and its subsidiaries (including BioVest) filed for Chapter 11 bankruptcy protection in late 2008 and emerged in late 2010.

	Annual Growth	09/08	09/09	09/10	09/11	09/12
Sales ($ mil.)	(29.0%)	15.9	10.6	10.5	4.0	4.1
Net income ($ mil.)	–	(60.8)	(5.3)	(47.8)	(11.6)	(9.2)
Market value ($ mil.)	(26.6%)	47.9	18.6	89.5	40.7	13.9
Employees	(16.3%)	110	80	67	68	54

ACCENTIA BIOPHARMACEUTICALS INC.
PINK SHEETS: ABPIQ

324 S. Hyde Park Ave. Ste. 350
Tampa FL 33606
Phone: 813-864-2554
Fax: 813-258-6912
Web: www.accentia.net

CEO: –
CFO: Garrison J Hasara
HR: –
FYE: September 30
Type: Public

Accentia Biopharmaceuticals is accentuating its positives and eliminating its negatives. The drug development company is focused on two development-stage drugs multiple sclerosis drug Revimmune and BiovaxID a possible vaccine for non-Hodgkin's lymphoma being developed by majority-owned subsidiary BioVest International. BioVest also sells cell growth instruments and offers contract manufacturing of cell cultures. The company and its subsidiaries (including BioVest) filed for Chapter 11 bankruptcy protection in late 2008 and emerged in late 2010.

ACCESS BUSINESS GROUP LLC

7575 FULTON ST E
ADA, MI 493550001
Phone: 616-787-6000
Fax: –
Web: www.accessbusinessgroup.com

CEO: –
CFO: –
HR: –
FYE: December 31
Type: Private

Somehow all those Amway products have to get from factories to the sales floor and that's where Access Business Group (ABG) comes in. The company manufactures and distributes cosmetics nutritional supplements home care and personal care products for its sister company Amway. (Both companies are units of Alticor.) It also offers contract manufacturing services for third-party consumer goods companies but to a lesser extent. Other offerings include product packaging services as well as catalog and direct mail printing services. In addition the company operates R&D labs that develop and test products for Amway. Alticor is the parent company of Access Business Group as well as Amway and is a holding company for Amway's non-direct selling companies.

	Annual Growth	12/11	12/12	12/13	12/14	12/15
Sales ($ mil.)	(5.7%)	–	–	1,135.5	1,068.1	1,009.9
Net income ($ mil.)	–	–	–	0.0	0.0	0.0
Market value ($ mil.)	–	–	–	–	–	–
Employees	–	–	–	–	–	3,000

ACCESS NATIONAL CORP
NMS: ANCX

1800 Robert Fulton Drive, Suite 300
Reston, VA 20191
Phone: 703 871-2100
Fax: –
Web: www.accessnationalbank.com

CEO: –
CFO: –
HR: –
FYE: December 31
Type: Public

Enabling easy access to your money is Access National's aim. The holding company owns Access National Bank a thrift founded in 1999 that serves the suburbs of Washington DC in northern Virginia through about five branches. The bank offers credit deposit mortgage services and wealth management services to middle market commercial businesses and associated professionals primarily in the greater Washington D.C. area. Commercial real estate loans make up some 40% of the company's portfolio; the bank also writes residential real estate and commercial loans. Access National is merging with Middleburg Financial Corporation in a $233 million deal.

	Annual Growth	12/12	12/13	12/14	12/15	12/16
Assets ($ mil.)	13.4%	863.9	847.2	1,052.9	1,178.5	1,430.7
Net income ($ mil.)	(1.9%)	17.7	13.2	13.9	15.4	16.4
Market value ($ mil.)	20.9%	138.3	159.0	180.0	217.6	295.3
Employees	(2.5%)	305	215	220	249	276

ACCESS SYSTEMS AMERICAS INC.

1188 E. Arques Ave.
Sunnyvale CA 94085-4602
Phone: 408-400-3000
Fax: 408-400-1500
Web: www.access-company.com

CEO: Kiyo Oishi
CFO: Jeanne Seeley
HR: –
FYE: May 31
Type: Private

ACCESS Systems Americas wants to help you step away from your desk. The company develops software for mobile products and the networking infrastructure needed to support them. Its software makes it possible for netbook computers laptops and notebooks and smartphones to access the Internet through wireless communications systems. Along with its IP Infusion subsidiary ACCESS also develops software to run the networks and servers in the wireless infrastructure. The company provides the Garnet operating system the successor to the OS that powered the Palm Pilot PDA and a commercial-grade platform based on the open-source Linux OS for mobile phones. ACCESS Systems Americas is a subsidiary of Japan's ACCESS Co. Ltd.

ACCOR NORTH AMERICA

4001 International Pkwy.
Carrollton TX 75007
Phone: 972-360-9000
Fax: 703-834-3593
Web: www.airbusnorthamerica.com

CEO: Rob Palleschi
CFO: Didier Bosc
HR: –
FYE: December 31
Type: Business Segment

This company is keeping the light on for North American travelers. A division of global hotel giant Accor Accor North America operates a total of 17 upscale Sofitel and midscale Novotel hotels in the US and Canada. In order to reduce its debt and fund international expansion parent Accor sold Accor North America's economy division which included 1100 US and Canadian hotels under the Motel 6 and Studio 6 brands to private equity giant Blackstone Group for $1.9 billion in October 2012. Accor North America has operational and development teams in Dallas and New York.

ACCIDENT FUND HOLDINGS INC.

200 N. Grand Ave.
Lansing MI 48901
Phone: 517-342-4200
Fax: 480-609-6520
Web: www.peterpiperpizza.com

CEO: Lisa Corless
CFO: Frank H Freund
HR: –
FYE: December 31
Type: Subsidiary

Accident Fund Holdings wants to keep your workplace safe. Founded in 1912 the company is the largest non-governmental specialty writer of workers' compensation insurance in the US; it serves more than 50000 businesses nationwide. Its main subsidiary Accident Fund Insurance Company of America does business with small and midsized companies but also provides third-party administration (TPA) and loss prevention services. Three other subsidiaries — CompWest Third Coast Underwriters and United Heartland provide regional coverage. Accident Fund sells its products through a network of independent agents. Formerly state-owned Accident Fund operates as a for-profit subsidiary of Blue Cross Blue Shield of Michigan.

ACCREDO HEALTH INCORPORATED

1640 Century Center Pkwy.
Memphis TN 38134
Phone: 901-385-3688
Fax: 901-385-3689
Web: www.accredo.com

CEO: David D Stevens
CFO: Joel Kimbrough
HR: –
FYE: December 30
Type: Subsidiary

Accredo Health doesn't stock aspirin in its medicine cabinet. As part of the specialty pharmacy segment of pharmacy benefits manager Express Scripts Accredo dispenses high-tech injectable and infusion drugs for chronic and serious illnesses such as cancer multiple sclerosis hemophilia pulmonary arterial hypertension (PAH) and certain autoimmune disorders. Under contracts with managed care organizations and drugmakers it delivers drugs and related supplies in temperature-controlled packaging to patient homes or clinics. It also provides consulting and monitoring services to make sure patients are complying with their drug regimens and it files claims on behalf of patients and doctors.

ACCO BRANDS CORP

NYS: ACCO

Four Corporate Drive
Lake Zurich, IL 60047
Phone: 847 541-9500
Fax: –
Web: www.accobrands.com

CEO: Boris Elisman
CFO: Neal Fenwick
HR: –
FYE: December 31
Type: Public

ACCO Brands is one of the world's largest designers marketers and manufacturers of branded academic consumer and business products. The company makes office school and consumer products under a host of brand names recognizable to anyone who has shopped for school or office supplies including Mead Five-Star AT-A-GLANCE and Rexel. It offers items for storage and organization laminating and binding and shredding as well as writing instruments whiteboards notebooks calendars and computer accessories. ACCO sells mostly through retail superstores mass merchandisers commercial stationers wholesalers e-tailers and warehouse clubs. It operates worldwide with approximately 50% of sales coming from the US.

ACCUCODE INC.

6886 S. Yosemite St. Ste. 100
Centennial CO 80112
Phone: 303-639-6111
Fax: 303-639-6178
Web: www.accucode.com

CEO: Kevin Price
CFO: Michael Kleinberg
HR: –
FYE: December 31
Type: Private

AccuCode designs and installs customized asset-tracking systems that combine mobile computing with automated data collection tools such as bar codes and radio-frequency identification (RFID). The company's offerings include hardware from manufacturers such as Datalogic Scanning Intermec Motorola Solutions and Psion Teklogix as well as proprietary software. Its customers — which include airlines delivery service providers retail stores manufacturers and health care providers — use AccuCode's systems to track warehouse inventory and corporate assets monitor patients and manage assembly-line efficiency. The company counts British Airways Corporate Express DHL and Kroger among its clients.

	Annual Growth	12/16	12/17	12/18	12/19	12/20
Sales ($ mil.)	1.5%	1,557.1	1,948.8	1,941.2	1,955.7	1,655.2
Net income ($ mil.)	(10.2%)	95.5	131.7	106.7	106.8	62.0
Market value ($ mil.)	(10.3%)	1,239.0	1,158.3	643.7	888.7	802.3
Employees	4.9%	5,040	6,620	6,700	7,000	6,100

ACCURAY INC (CA)   NMS: ARAY

1310 Chesapeake Terrace   CEO: Joshua Levine
Sunnyvale, CA 94089   CFO: Shigeyuki Hamamatsu
Phone: 408 716-4600   HR: –
Fax: –   FYE: June 30
Web: www.accuray.com   Type: Public

Accuray gets an A not a C for accuracy. Its radiosurgery CyberKnife system uses precisely aimed high-dose radiation and improves upon older radiosurgery systems that have limited mobility and are mostly used to treat brain tumors. Doctors can use CyberKnife to treat tumors anywhere in the body; the system tracks and adjusts for movement in real time allowing for patient and tumor movement. Accuray also offers the TomoTherapy systems which allow doctors to change the intensity of the radiation beam to adapt to the shape location and size of a tumor. The company's sales and distribution channels cover more than 90 countries. Accuracy generates most of its sales internationally.

	Annual Growth	06/17	06/18	06/19	06/20	06/21
Sales ($ mil.)	0.8%	383.4	404.9	418.8	382.9	396.3
Net income ($ mil.)	–	(29.6)	(23.9)	(16.4)	3.8	(6.3)
Market value ($ mil.)	(1.2%)	431.4	372.4	351.5	184.4	410.5
Employees	1.3%	944	998	947	932	995

ACCURIDE CORP   NYS: ACW

7140 Office Circle   CEO: Robin Kendrick
Evansville, IN 47715   CFO: Michael A Hajost
Phone: 812 962-5000   HR: –
Fax: –   FYE: December 31
Web: www.accuridecorp.com   Type: Public

If you're driving a big rig Accuride offers the goods to keep you rolling — or to stop you in your tracks. The company is a leading manufacturer of steel and forged aluminum wheels for commercial trucks and trailers pickups and military vehicles. It also makes truck body and chassis parts brake systems seating assemblies aftermarket components and non-powered farm equipment. Customers include commercial vehicle OEM Navistar trailer manufacturers (Great Dane and Wabash National) and automaker General Motors. Accuride's brands include Accuride AOT Brillion Gunite and Accuride Wheel end Solutions.

	Annual Growth	12/10	12/11	12/12	12/13	12/14
Sales ($ mil.)	1.7%	659.9	936.1	929.8	642.9	705.2
Net income ($ mil.)	–	(126.5)	(17.0)	(178.0)	(38.3)	(2.3)
Market value ($ mil.)	(27.7%)	757.8	339.8	153.2	178.0	207.1
Employees	(6.4%)	2,927	3,280	2,752	2,056	2,247

ACCURIDE INTERNATIONAL INC.

12311 Shoemaker Ave.   CEO: Scott E Jordan
Santa Fe Springs CA 90670   CFO: –
Phone: 562-903-0200   HR: –
Fax: 562-903-0208   FYE: December 31
Web: www.accuride.com   Type: Private

Business at Accuride International is on a finely crafted roll. The company is the world's largest manufacturer of ball bearing slides. Its lineup makes it easy every time to open and close drawers in residential and office furniture or the doors of appliances and electronic enclosures or rack mounts. The company's slides are also made for automotive accessories including storage units and arm rests and industrial equipment such as cash registers and assembly lines. Accuride International builds and maintains its own tools and machinery for manufacturing its products. Its operations dot China Germany Japan Mexico the UK and the US. Founded in 1962 by Fred Jordan the company remains family owned.

ACCUVANT INC.

1125 17th St. Ste. 1700   CEO: –
Denver CO 80202   CFO: –
Phone: 303-298-0600   HR: –
Fax: 303-298-0868   FYE: December 31
Web: www.accuvant.com   Type: Private

Data security consultant Accuvant likes to get it right for its customers. The company helps businesses assess risk improve regulatory compliance and protect data and network infrastructure through needs assessment systems design and compliance management. Accuvant identifies vulnerabilities in enterprise applications and tests network security after which it procures and implements the necessary technology to protect digital assets. The company also provides managed security services training and consulting. Accuvant operates nationwide from more than 30 offices. Customers have included Piper Jaffray BSML and Union Bank. The company was founded in 2002 by CEO Dan Burns COO Scott Walker and SVP Dan Wilson.

ACE HARDWARE CORPORATION

2200 KENSINGTON CT   CEO: John Venhuizen
OAK BROOK, IL 605232100   CFO: William Guzik
Phone: 630-990-6600   HR: –
Fax: –   FYE: December 30
Web: www.acehardware.com   Type: Private

In an age of big-box home improvement centers (Home Depot Lowes) wholesaler Ace makes the case for the local hardware store. By sales it is the leading hardware cooperative in the US. Ace Hardware is a retailer-owned hardware cooperative in the world with more than 5300 locally owned and operated hardware stores in approximately 70 countries. The overall home improvement industry is consists of a broad range of products and services including lawn and garden products paint and sundries certain building supplies and general merchandise. Ace also provides value-added services such as advertising market research merchandising assistance and store location and design services. Ace was founded in 1924 by a group of Chicago hardware store owners.

	Annual Growth	01/14	01/15	01/16*	12/16	12/17
Sales ($ mil.)	6.8%	–	–	5,045.0	5,125.5	5,388.4
Net income ($ mil.)	(5.6%)	–	–	156.2	161.2	147.4
Market value ($ mil.)	–	–	–	–	–	–
Employees	–	–	–	–	–	4,500

*Fiscal year change

ACE PARKING MANAGEMENT INC.

645 Ash St.   CEO: John Baumgardner
San Diego CA 92101   CFO: Charles Blottin
Phone: 619-233-6624   HR: –
Fax: 619-233-0741   FYE: December 31
Web: www.aceparking.com   Type: Private

When you're betting on finding a convenient parking spot in the western US your chances of drawing an Ace are pretty good. Controlling about 70% of the San Diego parking market Ace Parking Management oversees more than 450 parking locations in eight states including Arizona California Oregon Texas and Washington. The company manages facilities at locations such as airports hospitals hotels medical centers office and retail buildings and stadiums. It serves almost 200000 customers per day including Bank of America and the San Diego Padres baseball team. Chairman Scott Jones owns Ace Parking which was founded in San Diego by his father in 1950.

ACE RELOCATION SYSTEMS, INC.

5608 EASTGATE DR
SAN DIEGO, CA 921212816
Phone: 858-677-5500
Fax: –
Web: www.acerelocation.com

CEO: Lawrence Lammers
CFO: –
HR: –
FYE: December 31
Type: Private

Hoping to trump the kings and queens of the moving industry Ace Relocation Systems provides corporate and household relocation services. The family owned company operates from more than half a dozen offices spread throughout the US. Ace Relocation Systems is an agent of Atlas Van Lines; as an agent Ace Relocation Systems operates within its assigned geographic territories and cooperates with other Atlas agents on interstate moves. In addition the company can arrange international moves and provide transportation of items such as trade show exhibits through the Atlas network. Ace Relocation Systems was founded in 1968.

	Annual Growth	12/12	12/13	12/14	12/15	12/16
Sales ($ mil.)	7.8%	–	53.8	58.5	65.1	67.3
Net income ($ mil.)	(25.5%)	–	2.2	2.1	1.3	0.9
Market value ($ mil.)	–	–	–	–	–	–
Employees	–	–	–	–	–	255

ACENTO ADVERTISING INCORPORATED

2254 S. Sepulveda Blvd.
Los Angeles CA 90064
Phone: 310-943-8300
Fax: 310-943-8330
Web: www.acento.com

CEO: Donnie Broxson
CFO: Roberto Orci
HR: Brenda Galo-Sanchez
FYE: December 31
Type: Private

Founded in 1983 Acento Advertising offers advertising and marketing services geared toward the Hispanic market. Acento provides such services as creative development in broadcast print and interactive media as well as TV production facilities in the US and Latin America. The agency also offers expertise in market research public relations and direct marketing. The company's clients have included Alaska Airlines Wells Fargo and Staples.

ACE USA

436 Walnut St.
Philadelphia PA 19106-3703
Phone: 215-640-1000
Fax: 215-640-2489
Web: www.aceusa.com

CEO: –
CFO: –
HR: –
FYE: December 31
Type: Subsidiary

ACE USA's deck is stacked with insurance cards. The company is the US retail operating division of Swiss insurance firm ACE Limited. ACE USA provides a comprehensive range of property/casualty risk management accident disaster professional lines workers' compensation and health insurance products to individuals and businesses throughout the US. It sells these through licensed insurance brokers. ACE USA has dedicated efforts to tailor its services to four specialized industries: construction health care energy and public entities. It also has an arm dedicated to merger and acquisition underwriting practices.

ACER AMERICA CORPORATION

333 W. San Carlos St. Ste. 1500
San Jose CA 95110
Phone: 408-533-7700
Fax: 408-533-4555
Web: www.acer.us

CEO: Greg Prendergast
CFO: Ming Wang
HR: –
FYE: December 31
Type: Subsidiary

Whether it's laptops in Los Angeles or servers in Saskatchewan Acer America has North America covered. The company a subsidiary of Taiwanese computer giant Acer sells to businesses government agencies schools and consumers. Its core products are desktop and portable PCs with consumer models sold under the Aspire brand and professional models marketed under the Veriton banner. Acer America also supports the eMachines Gateway and Packard Bell PC brands. Other Acer products include smartphones network servers LCD monitors data storage systems and video projectors. Acer's sales in North America account for less than one quarter of its total revenue. Acer America was established in 1976.

ACELRX PHARMACEUTICALS INC   NMS: ACRX

25821 Industrial Boulevard, Suite 400
Hayward, CA 94545
Phone: 650 216-3500
Fax: –
Web: www.acelrx.com

CEO: Vincent Angotti
CFO: Raffi Asadorian
HR: –
FYE: December 31
Type: Public

For patients with acute pain a slip of the tongue could be a useful thing. AcelRx is developing the Sufentanil NanoTab PCA System which administers pain medication sublingually or under the tongue. Designed for patients with post-operative pain the system administers measured doses of the opioid sufentanil in the form of tiny tablets which quickly dissolve and are absorbed into the body through the lining under the tongue. Currently in late-stage of development its NanoTab system is also being developed to treat cancer-related pain or provide sedation and pain relief to patients having procedures at doctors' offices. Founded in 2005 AcelRx went public in 2011 through a $40 million IPO.

	Annual Growth	12/16	12/17	12/18	12/19	12/20
Sales ($ mil.)	(25.3%)	17.4	8.0	2.2	2.3	5.4
Net income ($ mil.)	–	(43.2)	(51.5)	(47.1)	(53.2)	(40.4)
Market value ($ mil.)	(16.9%)	256.9	200.1	228.3	208.5	122.5
Employees	8.5%	39	41	61	99	54

ACER THERAPEUTICS INC   NAS: ACER

222 Third Street, Suite #2240
Cambridge, MA 02142
Phone: 844 902-6100
Fax: –
Web: www.opexatherapeutics.com

CEO: Christopher Schelling
CFO: Harry Palmin
HR: –
FYE: December 31
Type: Public

Biopharmaceutical company Opexa Therapeutics wants to develop chronic remedies for chronic diseases. Specializing in autologous treatments (those which use the patient's own tissue and cells) Opexa is developing Tovaxin a T-cell vaccine used for the treatment of multiple sclerosis which is caused when the body's immune system (T-cells) attacks the nervous system. Currently in late stages of development Tovaxin works by lowering the levels of harmful T-cells in the body. Opexa was also researching its adult stem cell technology with the goal of developing treatments for diabetes and other chronic diseases but it sold rights to the stem cell technology to Novartis in 2009. Opexa is being acquired by Acer Therapeutics; the combined firm will focus on developing treatments for serious rare diseases.

	Annual Growth	12/12	12/13	12/14	12/15	12/16
Sales ($ mil.)	31.9%	–	1.3	1.3	2.6	2.9
Net income ($ mil.)	–	(8.9)	(16.7)	(15.1)	(12.0)	(8.0)
Market value ($ mil.)	(68.4%)	–	–	–	1.9	0.6
Employees	(47.3%)	26	38	39	26	2

ACETO CORP

4 Tri Harbor Court
Port Washington, NY 11050
Phone: 516 627-6000
Fax: –
Web: www.aceto.com

NMS: ACET
CEO: Gilles Cottier
CFO: Rebecca Roof
HR: –
FYE: June 30
Type: Public

Distributor Aceto (pronounced "a-seat-o") is getting bigger through chemicals — primarily specialty chemicals and pharmaceuticals. It sources and distributes more than 1100 chemical products through three segments. Its largest segment is Performance Chemicals which sources and distributes specialty chemicals and agricultural protection products. Aceto's other business segments include Pharmaceutical Ingredients (active pharmaceutical ingredients or APIs and pharmaceutical intermediates) and Human Health (generic drugs and nutraceutical products). Aceto sources about two-thirds of its products from Asia mostly China and India and turns around to sell more than half of them in the US.

	Annual Growth	06/14	06/15	06/16	06/17	06/18
Sales ($ mil.)	8.7%	510.2	547.0	558.5	638.3	711.4
Net income ($ mil.)	–	29.0	33.5	34.8	11.4	(316.1)
Market value ($ mil.)	(34.5%)	558.5	758.3	673.9	475.7	103.1
Employees	3.9%	270	270	270	286	315

ACF INDUSTRIES LLC

101 Clark St.
St. Charles MO 63301
Phone: 636-949-2399
Fax: 636-949-2825
Web: www.acfindustries.com

CEO: James E Bowles
CFO: –
HR: –
FYE: December 31
Type: Private

After more than a century ACF Industries is still on track making railcars and railcar components. ACF (originally The American Car and Foundry Co.) manufactures and fabricates an array of transportation equipment for the new railcar and repair railcar markets as well as custom steel parts for non-rail customers. Operations include facilities in Pennsylvania and West Virginia which churn out related products such as weld sub-assemblies pressure vessels and wheel and axle machining and mounting. ACF is owned by financier Carl Icahn who serves as chairman. Icahn is a major stockholder and chairman of American Railcar Industries and American Railcar Leasing trade affiliates of ACF railcar components.

ACH FOOD COMPANIES INC.

7171 Goodlett Farms Pkwy.
Memphis TN 38016
Phone: 901-381-3000
Fax: 901-381-2968
Web: www.achfood.com

CEO: Imad Bazzi
CFO: Stephen Zaruba
HR: John Smith
FYE: September 30
Type: Subsidiary

ACH Food Companies is ACH-ing to help the cook. The company markets sells and produces a variety of cooking oils and other food ingredients such as cornstarch syrup spices and sauces. Its lineup is led by well-known brands including Mazola (the #1 corn oil brand in North America) Argo corn starch Fleischmann's yeast Karo corn syrup and Spice Islands seasonings. The company also offers private-label and custom manufacture services. Operating through two divisions consumer products and commercial products it caters to the retail and industrial food and foodservice industries in the US Canada and Mexico. ACH is a subsidiary of UK food giant Associated British Foods which purchased ACH in 1995.

ACHILLION PHARMACEUTICALS INC

300 George Street
New Haven, CT 06511
Phone: 203 624-7000
Fax: –
Web: www.achillion.com

NMS: ACHN
CEO: –
CFO: –
HR: –
FYE: December 31
Type: Public

Achillion Pharmaceuticals is looking for the Achilles heel of infectious disease. The firm is developing treatments for infectious diseases including antiviral treatments for HIV infection and hepatitis C as well as antibacterials for fighting drug-resistant hospital-based infections. Achillion is focused on the development of three hepatitis C treatments. It has out-licensed elvucitabine a late-stage treatment of HIV and hepatitis B to GCA Therapeutics and sent its eye and skin infection treatment to Ora Inc. Achillion has other candidates aimed at combating drug-resistant staph. The company was formed in 1998 and went public in 2006.

	Annual Growth	12/12	12/13	12/14	12/15	12/16
Sales ($ mil.)	54.9%	2.6	–	–	66.1	15.0
Net income ($ mil.)	–	(47.1)	(58.9)	(69.0)	(5.0)	(61.7)
Market value ($ mil.)	(15.3%)	1,095.1	453.8	1,674.8	1,475.2	564.7
Employees	9.2%	57	62	69	80	81

ACI WORLDWIDE INC

600 Brickell Avenue, Suite 1500, PMB #11
Miami, FL 33131
Phone: 305 894-2200
Fax: –
Web: www.aciworldwide.com

NMS: ACIW
CEO: Odilon Almeida
CFO: Scott W Behrens
HR: –
FYE: December 31
Type: Public

ACI Worldwide develops markets installs and supports a broad line of software products and solutions primarily focused on facilitating real-time digital payments. The company provides enterprise payments capabilities that target any channel any network and any payment type and its solutions empower customers to regain control choice and flexibility in today's complex payments environment get to market more quickly and reduce operational costs. In addition the company products and services are used globally by banks intermediaries merchants and billers such as third-party digital payment processors payment associations and a wide range of transaction-generating endpoints including automated teller machines (ATM) merchant point-of-sale (POS) terminals bank branches corporations and more. The company was founded in 1975.

	Annual Growth	12/16	12/17	12/18	12/19	12/20
Sales ($ mil.)	6.5%	1,005.7	1,024.2	1,009.8	1,258.3	1,294.3
Net income ($ mil.)	(13.5%)	129.5	5.1	68.9	67.1	72.7
Market value ($ mil.)	20.6%	2,125.6	2,654.9	3,240.5	4,436.8	4,500.6
Employees	(2.2%)	4,111	3,979	3,807	4,018	3,768

ACMAT CORP.

30 South Road
Farmington, CT 06032-2418
Phone: 860 415-8400
Fax: –
Web: www.acmatcorp.com

NBB: ACMT A
CEO: Henry Nozko
CFO: Michael Cifone
HR: –
FYE: December 31
Type: Public

ACMAT does its part to wipe out asbestos. Originally a contracting firm focused on asbestos abatement the company moved into the insurance industry when it was dropped by its own insurer. Through its ACSTAR Insurance subsidiary the company handles liability insurance and supply bonds to customers such as general specialty trade environmental and asbestos and lead abatement contractors. ACMAT's insurance products are sold nationwide. AMCAT still provides design and construction contracting services for commercial and government customers through its ACMAT Contracting division.

	Annual Growth	12/16	12/17	12/18	12/19	12/20
Sales ($ mil.)	(8.1%)	4.2	3.7	2.8	4.0	3.0
Net income ($ mil.)	(2.4%)	0.8	0.3	0.7	1.5	0.7
Market value ($ mil.)	12.2%	16.8	15.5	22.4	25.0	26.6
Employees		–	–	–	–	–

ACME COMMUNICATIONS INC — NBB: ACME

2101 E. Fourth Street, Suite 202
Santa Ana, CA 92705
Phone: 714 245-9499
Fax: 714 245-9494
Web: www.acmecommunications.com

CEO: Jamie Kellner
CFO: Thomas Allen
HR: –
FYE: December 31
Type: Public

ACME Communications' relationship with Warner Bros. has nothing to do with a wily coyote rockets or any other explosives. The company owns and operates three television stations in midsized markets (KWBQ and KASY in Albuquerque/Santa Fe New Mexico and WBUW in Madison Wisconsin) most of which are affiliated with The CW Network a joint venture between Time Warner's Warner Bros. Entertainment and CBS Corporation. In addition to its stations ACME Communications produces a syndicated morning program called The Daily Buzz that airs on about 150 TV stations throughout the country.

	Annual Growth	12/09	12/10	12/11	12/12	12/13
Sales ($ mil.)	(61.0%)	26.8	14.6	12.9	14.7	0.6
Net income ($ mil.)	–	(8.7)	(8.5)	12.4	4.9	0.3
Market value ($ mil.)	(50.0%)	8.0	18.0	10.8	2.2	0.5
Employees	–	–	–	–	–	–

ACME MARKETS INC.

75 Valley Stream Pkwy.
Malvern PA 19355
Phone: 610-889-4000
Fax: 610-889-3039
Web: www.acmemarkets.com

CEO: –
CFO: –
HR: –
FYE: February 28
Type: Subsidiary

Wile E. Coyote has nothing to fear from this Acme company. Regional grocery chain Acme Markets operates about 115 supermarkets under the Acme and Acme Sav-on banners in Delaware Maryland New Jersey and Pennsylvania. It's the #2 food and drug retailer (behind Wakefern Food-owned ShopRite) in the competitive Philadelphia market where it competes with local chains including A&P-owned Pathmark and Giant. In addition to its bricks-and-mortar operations Acme offers online grocery ordering for its customers in and around Philadelphia. Founded in 1891 Acme Markets is a division of grocery-retailer-and-wholesaler SUPERVALU.

ACME UNITED CORP. — ASE: ACU

1 Waterview Drive
Shelton, CT 06484
Phone: 203 254-6060
Fax: –
Web: www.acmeunited.com

CEO: Walter Johnsen
CFO: Paul Driscoll
HR: –
FYE: December 31
Type: Public

Acme United has the goods for measuring twice and cutting once ... even if you cut yourself in the process. The company supplies measuring instruments (including rulers protractors tape measures) cutting devices (scissors paper trimmers) and safety items (first-aid kits personal protection products) under the Westcott Camillus Clauss PhysiciansCare and Pac-Kit brands as well as under private labels. Acme's products are sold to stationery and industrial supply distributors office supply stores drugstores hardware chains mass merchants and florists. Its operations span Canada Germany Hong Kong China and the US (its biggest market). Chairman and CEO Walter Johnsen owns about 15% of the company.

	Annual Growth	12/16	12/17	12/18	12/19	12/20
Sales ($ mil.)	7.1%	124.6	130.6	137.3	142.5	164.0
Net income ($ mil.)	8.5%	5.9	4.1	4.6	5.5	8.1
Market value ($ mil.)	4.2%	85.4	78.1	47.6	79.4	100.6
Employees	8.4%	400	421	435	441	552

ACNB CORP — NAS: ACNB

16 Lincoln Square
Gettysburg, PA 17325
Phone: 717 334-3161
Fax: –
Web: www.acnb.com

CEO: James Helt
CFO: David Cathell
HR: –
FYE: December 31
Type: Public

Seven score and a few years ago ACNB Corporation's fathers brought forth a small-town bank. Now ACNB is dedicated to the proposition of being the holding company for Adams County National Bank operating more than 20 branches in the Gettysburg and Newville areas of Pennsylvania. It is altogether fitting and proper that the bank offers traditional retail banking services. The world may long note and remember that the bank also provides residential mortgage (about 60% of the portfolio) commercial real estate consumer and business loans. In addition ACNB gives a full measure of devotion to insurance products; provides trust services; and hopes that community banking shall not perish from the earth.

	Annual Growth	12/16	12/17	12/18	12/19	12/20
Assets ($ mil.)	20.6%	1,206.3	1,595.4	1,647.7	1,720.3	2,555.4
Net income ($ mil.)	14.1%	10.9	9.8	21.7	23.7	18.4
Market value ($ mil.)	(5.4%)	272.2	257.4	341.8	329.4	217.7
Employees	6.9%	303	358	361	374	396

ACO HARDWARE INC.

23333 Commerce Dr.
Farmington Hills MI 48335
Phone: 248-471-0100
Fax: 248-615-2696
Web: www.acohardware.com

CEO: –
CFO: –
HR: –
FYE: February 28
Type: Private

ACO Hardware can provide both the food and the supplies if you want to get your floor clean enough to eat off. Michigan's largest independent hardware chain sells automotive supplies electrical goods food and beverages hardware housewares paint lawn and garden necessities apparel furniture and tools. It also sharpens knives refills propane tanks and rents equipment for carpet cleaning plumbing and home maintenance. ACO Hardware operates about 70 stores in southeastern Michigan primarily in the Detroit area. Customers can view weekly specials and find hardware tips on the company's Web site. Founded in 1946 by Ted Traskos and his four brothers ACO Hardware is still owned by the Traskos family.

ACORDA THERAPEUTICS INC — NMS: ACOR

420 Saw Mill River Road
Ardsley, NY 10502
Phone: 914 347-4300
Fax: 914 347-4560
Web: www.acorda.com

CEO: Ron Cohen
CFO: Michael Gesser
HR: –
FYE: December 31
Type: Public

Acorda Therapeutics is a biopharmaceutical company focused on developing prescription drugs that aim to restore neurological function for patients with central nervous system disorders. The company's marketed drugs include Ampyra which enhances conduction in nerves damaged from multiple sclerosis (MS); and Inbrija treatment for OFF periods in people with Parkinson's disease. Acorda's other drug candidates include therapies for MS and other central nervous system disorders as well as cardiac conditions. Acorda markets its product in the US through its own specialty sales force and being distributed primarily through a network of specialty pharmacies.

	Annual Growth	12/16	12/17	12/18	12/19	12/20
Sales ($ mil.)	(26.3%)	519.6	588.3	471.4	192.4	153.0
Net income ($ mil.)	–	(34.6)	(223.4)	33.7	(273.0)	(99.6)
Market value ($ mil.)	(56.3%)	178.0	203.1	147.5	19.3	6.5
Employees	(27.2%)	597	484	484	344	168

ACORN ENERGY INC   NBB: ACFN

1000 N West Street, Suite 1200 — CEO: Jan Loeb
Wilmington, DE 19801 — CFO: Tracy Clifford
Phone: 410 654-3315 — HR: –
Fax: – — FYE: December 31
Web: www.acornenergy.com — Type: Public

Acorn Energy is hopeful that its seedling energy technology companies might one day grow into big trees. The company has controlling or equity positions in four energy infrastructure firms — Energy & Security Sonar Solutions GridSense Systems OmniMetrix US Sensor Systems (USSI). Its largest company Israel-based Energy & Security Sonar Solutions offers underwater acoustic and sonar security systems for the military and offshore oil rigs through 84%-owned DSIT Solutions. GridSense makes electronic monitoring systems for utility companies and USSI designs fiber optic sensing systems for energy companies. OmniMetrix is engaged in remote monitoring of emergency back-up power generation systems.

	Annual Growth	12/16	12/17	12/18	12/19	12/20
Sales ($ mil.)	(9.1%)	8.7	4.4	5.1	5.5	5.9
Net income ($ mil.)	(16.9%)	0.1	(1.2)	(2.0)	(0.6)	0.1
Market value ($ mil.)	20.4%	6.8	8.9	10.0	14.4	14.3
Employees	(27.2%)	82	21	22	23	23

ACOSTA INC.

6600 Corporate Center Pkwy. — CEO: Brian Wynne
Jacksonville FL 32216 — CFO: Chandra McCormack
Phone: 904-281-9800 — HR: –
Fax: 904-281-9966 — FYE: October 31
Web: www.acosta.com — Type: Private

Acosta spends a lot of time thinking about which products are top-shelf. The company (which does business as Acosta Sales and Marketing Company) offers sales and marketing services that reach consumers from the shelves of North American retail food service and grocery businesses. Major consumer products manufacturers call on Acosta to help them position their products in grocery and convenience stores drug stores and mass merchandisers. The company which operates through 75 locations in the US and Canada specializes in inventory and merchandising services and business consulting for promotions marketing campaigns and sales. Established in 1927 Acosta is owned by Thomas H. Lee Partners.

ACQUITY GROUP L.L.C.   NYSE: AQ

500 W. Madison St. Ste. 2200 — CEO: Chris Dalton
Chicago IL 60661 — CFO: –
Phone: 312-427-2470 — HR: –
Fax: 403-266-6259 — FYE: December 31
Web: www.crewenergy.com — Type: Public

Acquity Group thinks the digital sphere is the best place to get a brand name out into the world. A marketing and e-commerce company Acquity offers digital marketing services primarily to multinational companies operating in the US and Asia. It provides digital marketing analysis and strategy as well as marketing services targeted to Internet mobile devices and social media channels. In addition Acquity designs and implements e-commerce websites such as online stores and other points of sale for its clients. Its core clients have included Adobe Systems Inc. Allstate American Express GM and HTC. Acquity Group went public in 2012.

ACRE REALTY INVESTORS INC   ASE: AIII

c/o Avenue Capital Group, 399 Park Avenue, 6th Floor — CEO: –
New York, NY 10022 — CFO: –
Phone: 212 878-3504 — HR: –
Fax: – — FYE: December 31
Web: www.acrerealtyinvestors.com — Type: Public

Roberts Realty Investors really wants to get it REIT. A self-administered real estate investment trust (REIT) Roberts Realty owns and operates commercial real estate and land primarily in metropolitan Atlanta. The company sold a 400-unit apartment community in 2008; it followed that sale with a handful of other property divestitures. The REIT now owns about five retail and office assets and approximately 150 acres of land which it plans to develop into residential and mixed-use properties. Roberts Realty Investors operates through its majority-owned Roberts Properties Residential partnership.

	Annual Growth	12/11	12/12	12/13	12/14	12/15
Sales ($ mil.)	(86.4%)	1.3	1.4	0.0	0.0	0.0
Net income ($ mil.)	–	(9.1)	(6.9)	(0.5)	(2.4)	(1.5)
Market value ($ mil.)	(0.4%)	25.7	23.5	18.1	21.3	25.3
Employees	–	1	1	1	1	–

ACRES COMMERCIAL REALTY CORP   NYS: ACR

390 RXR Plaza — CEO: Mark Fogel
Uniondale, NY 11556 — CFO: David Bryant
Phone: 516 535-0015 — HR: –
Fax: – — FYE: December 31
Web: www.exantas.com — Type: Public

Exantas (formerly Resource Capital) is looking to pump some capital into real estate resources. The real estate investment trust (REIT) was launched in 2005 and invests in originating holding and managing commercial real estate or CRE mortgage loans and other commercial real estate-related debt investments. To a lesser extent the REIT invests in commercial finance assets such as syndicated corporate loans and direct financing leases. CRE loans account for more than 80% of the REIT's portfolio. The firm's investments are managed by Resource Capital Manager a subsidiary of Resource America.

	Annual Growth	12/16	12/17	12/18	12/19	12/20
Sales ($ mil.)	(1.8%)	116.4	101.4	122.9	145.0	108.3
Net income ($ mil.)	–	(30.4)	33.5	27.4	36.0	(197.7)
Market value ($ mil.)	(16.8%)	84.7	95.2	101.8	120.0	40.5
Employees	–	–	–	–	–	–

ACSIS INC.

9 E. Stow Rd. — CEO: Jeremy Coote
Marlton NJ 08053 — CFO: Stephanie Seibel
Phone: 856-673-3000 — HR: –
Fax: 856-810-3597 — FYE: December 31
Web: www.acsisinc.com — Type: Private

Acsis connects the shop floor with the top floor by helping customers keep track of their products. The company provides supply chain software and services to help large manufacturers make the most of their SAP-based supply chain systems. Its products and services improve data collection and help users integrate supply chain and enterprise resource planning (ERP) systems. Acsis's ProducTrak software makes supply chain data accessible throughout an organization; its online TrakExchange service lets customers share information with trading partners. Clients have included BASF Coca Cola and Wyeth. The company has partnered with Cisco Systems (hardware) Accenture (systems integration) and WaveLink (software).

ACT, INC.

500 ACT DR
IOWA CITY, IA 522439003
Phone: 319-337-1000
Fax: –
Web: www.act.org

CEO: Marten Roorda
CFO: Thomas J Goedken
HR: –
FYE: August 31
Type: Private

A C and T... three little letters that can strike fear in the hearts of high school students across the US. ACT most notably develops and administers the ACT national college admission exam with nearly 1.8 million high school seniors taking the test each year. The not-for-profit organization was founded in 1959 by E. F. Lindquist and Ted McCarrel who sought to create an exam to measure potential college students' capacity for critical thinking.

	Annual Growth	08/02	08/03	08/05	08/14	08/16
Sales ($ mil.)	6.7%	–	151.1	179.3	328.8	350.1
Net income ($ mil.)	1.2%	–	15.4	208.4	9.9	18.0
Market value ($ mil.)	–	–	–	–	–	–
Employees	–	–	–	–	–	1,202

ACTAVIS U.S.

60 Columbia Rd. Bldg. B
Morristown NJ 07960
Phone: 973-993-4500
Fax: 973-993-4303
Web: www.actavis.us

CEO: –
CFO: R Todd Joyce
HR: –
FYE: December 31
Type: Subsidiary

As its name implies the Actavis U.S. is the US manufacturing and marketing unit of global generics firm Actavis. The company makes some 150 generic equivalents of both prescription and OTC drugs in a number of forms including liquids tablets creams and suppositories. Actavis U.S. has manufacturing and distribution facilities in Florida Maryland New Jersey and North Carolina. The group also provides contract manufacturing services to third parties. Actavis U.S. accounts for a quarter of its parents revenues. The parent has agreed to be acquired by US rival Watson Pharmaceuticals. Following the acquisition Watson will likely integrate Actavis U.S.' products and pipeline into its existing operations.

ACTELIS NETWORKS INC.

6150 Stevenson Blvd.
Fremont CA 94538
Phone: 510-545-1045
Fax: 510-545-1075
Web: www.actelis.com

CEO: –
CFO: Stephen Cordial
HR: –
FYE: December 31
Type: Private

Actelis Networks prefers copper over glass. The company's transmission equipment enables carriers and telecommunications providers to deliver Ethernet services over copper wires. Its products are intended to increase the data-carrying capacity of the copper lines and eliminate the need for installing fiber optics in the "last mile" between service providers' networks and their subscribers. Actelis targets regional Bell telephone companies independent and competitive local exchange carriers and alternative carriers worldwide. The company has received financial backing from investors including The Carlyle Group Innovacom Venture Capital and New Enterprise Associates.

ACTION FOR BOSTON COMMUNITY DEVELOPMENT, INC.

178 TREMONT ST
BOSTON, MA 021111006
Phone: 617-357-6000
Fax: –
Web: www.bostonabcd.org

CEO: –
CFO: Marjorie Lombard
HR: –
FYE: August 31
Type: Private

Action For Boston Community Development (ABCD) strives to make helping others as easy as 1-2-3. The not-for-profit serves more than 100000 low-income people in New England in areas such as advocacy child care consumer services education health and housing. The group operates through a decentralized model that utilizes a citywide network of Area Planning Action Councils Neighborhood Service Centers and Family Service Centers. It partners with more than a dozen programs like SUMMERWORKS (work experience for low-income teens) Foster Grandparents Urban College of Boston and another 10 or so government agencies. ABCD was established in 1962 as one of several national programs to combat poverty.

	Annual Growth	08/09	08/10	08/14	08/15	08/16
Sales ($ mil.)	1.8%	–	151.5	157.2	176.0	168.9
Net income ($ mil.)	–	–	(0.0)	0.1	0.2	(0.1)
Market value ($ mil.)	–	–	–	–	–	–
Employees	–	–	–	–	–	1,000

ACTIONET, INC.

2600 PARK TWR DR STE 1000
VIENNA, VA 22180
Phone: 703-204-0090
Fax: –
Web: www.actionet.com

CEO: Ashley W Chen
CFO: –
HR: Nancy Graves
FYE: December 31
Type: Private

ActioNet is an IT engineering service firm with strong qualifications and expertise in cloud-based solutions cyber security and Agile software engineering. It provides cybersecurity cloud solutions as well as managed services. Customers have included US Agencies such as Army Navy Air Force Department of Transportation and more. ActioNet was founded in 1998 by president and CEO Ashley Chen.

	Annual Growth	12/12	12/13	12/14	12/15	12/16
Sales ($ mil.)	12.5%	–	298.5	352.6	411.5	425.5
Net income ($ mil.)	11.3%	–	23.8	25.3	32.0	32.8
Market value ($ mil.)	–	–	–	–	–	–
Employees	–	–	–	–	–	1,400

ACTIONTEC ELECTRONICS, INC.

2445 AUGUSTINE DR STE 501
SANTA CLARA, CA 950543033
Phone: 408-752-7700
Fax: –
Web: www.actiontec.com

CEO: Dean Chang
CFO: Brian Paul
HR: –
FYE: December 31
Type: Private

Actiontec Electronics aims to broaden your approach to networking. The company makes gateways routers modems and other broadband connection equipment used to create wireless home networks. Its fiber optic routers allow broadband television and other content to be distributed to multiple devices throughout the home over coaxial cables. Actiontec sells its equipment through partnerships with broadband service providers and equipment makers such as Qwest Verizon& Cisco and Entropic. It also sells directly through retailers including Amazon.com Best Buy and Wal-Mart.

	Annual Growth	12/04	12/05	12/06	12/07	12/10
Sales ($ mil.)	2.8%	–	–	145.6	183.1	162.3
Net income ($ mil.)	–	–	–	0.0	0.0	1.8
Market value ($ mil.)	–	–	–	–	–	–
Employees	–	–	–	–	–	350

ACTIVE DAY INC.
400 Redland Ct. Ste. 114　　　　　　　　　　　CEO: Robert Creamer
Owings Mills MD 21117　　　　　　　　　　　　CFO: Linda Chen
Phone: 443-548-2200　　　　　　　　　　　　　HR: –
Fax: 443-548-2280　　　　　　　　　　　　　　FYE: December 31
Web: www.activeday.com　　　　　　　　　　　Type: Private

From dawn to dusk and back again Active Day sees no rest until it has cared for the needs of its elderly and disabled clients. The company operates about 50 adult day care centers in more than half a dozen states. Visitors to its centers participate in social gatherings crafts exercise and other activities. The centers also provide medical care (such as physical therapy and nursing care) and assistance with personal care including feeding and bathing. Active Day offers its patients transportation to and from home as well. It also provides therapeutic services to independent clients and operates home health agencies. Active Day is a subsidiary of Senior Care Centers of America.

ACTIVEVIDEO NETWORKS INC.
333 W. San Carlos St. Ste. 400　　　　　　　　CEO: Jeff Miller
San Jose CA 95110　　　　　　　　　　　　　　CFO: Matt Andrade
Phone: 408-931-9200　　　　　　　　　　　　　HR: –
Fax: 408-931-9100　　　　　　　　　　　　　　FYE: December 31
Web: www.avnetworks.com　　　　　　　　　　Type: Private

ActiveVideo Networks bridges the gap between the TV and the Internet. The company creates software that allows cable system operators to offer advanced interactive services to their subscribers. Its technology delivers new applications to digital set-top boxes eliminating the need for costly equipment upgrades. ActiveVideo Networks also provides a variety of professional services such as consulting planning deployment implementation maintenance support and training. Customers include Cablevision Systems and Time Warner Cable. The company's majority investor is Lauder Partners an investment fund managed by the Estee Lauder family.

ACTIVE MEDIA SERVICES INC.
1 Blue Hill Plaza　　　　　　　　　　　　　　CEO: –
Pearl River NY 10965　　　　　　　　　　　　CFO: –
Phone: 845-735-1700　　　　　　　　　　　　HR: –
Fax: 845-735-0717　　　　　　　　　　　　　FYE: June 30
Web: www.activeinternational.com　　　　　Type: Private

Take a pawn shop cross it with a factoring service and you have Active Media Services. Doing business as Active International the corporate trading firm acquires underperforming assets including surplus inventory capital equipment real estate and receivables. It exchanges these for cash and/or trade credit which is used to offset expenses or purchase such services as advertising freight printing shipping event planning and travel. Clients may barter future manufacturing capacity for services including advertising across all mediums. Active International also provides traditional marketing services. Alan Elkin and Art Wagner founded the employee-owned company in 1984.

ACTIVIDENTITY CORPORATION
6623 Dumbarton Cir.　　　　　　　　　　　　CEO: –
Fremont CA 94555　　　　　　　　　　　　　CFO: –
Phone: 510-574-0100　　　　　　　　　　　　HR: –
Fax: 510-574-0101　　　　　　　　　　　　　FYE: September 30
Web: www.actividentity.com　　　　　　　　Type: Subsidiary

ActivIdentity isn't passive about data security. The company provides a variety of authentication and user management products including smart cards biometric readers tokens and USB keys. Its products are used to control and monitor access to intranets extranets and the Internet enabling businesses to digitally authenticate and manage the identities of employees customers and trading partners. The company's commercial customers have included Citibank Novell and Oracle; the US Department of Defense is also a client. About half of ActivIdentity's business is done outside of North America. It also offers services such as consulting support and training. The company is a subsidiary of ASSA ABLOY.

ACTIVECARE INC　　　　　　　　　　　　　NBB: ACAR
1365 West Business Park Drive, Suite 100　　CEO: James J Dalton
Orem, UT 84058　　　　　　　　　　　　　　CFO: Jeffrey S Peterson
Phone: 877 219-6050　　　　　　　　　　　　HR: –
Fax: 855 864-2511　　　　　　　　　　　　　FYE: September 30
Web: www.activecare.com　　　　　　　　　Type: Public

ActiveCare (formerly known as Volu-Sol Reagents) deals in two very different areas of the health care industry. The company manufactures diagnostic products for use by clinical laboratories; it also provides personal emergency response products and services for consumers. The company's diagnostic business develops and manufactures chemical reagents stains and related equipment used by hematology and microbiology laboratories to detect certain properties in biological samples. The company's ActiveOne services employ biosensors cell phone and GPS technology to remotely monitor a client's vital signs and provide assistance.

	Annual Growth	09/12	09/13	09/14	09/15	09/16
Sales ($ mil.)	35.2%	2.2	21.1	6.1	6.6	7.5
Net income ($ mil.)	–	(12.4)	(25.6)	(13.5)	(11.5)	(9.1)
Market value ($ mil.)	–	0.0	0.3	0.1	0.0	0.0
Employees	(28.8%)	148	65	49	37	38

ACTIVISION BLIZZARD, INC.　　　　　　　NMS: ATVI
3100 Ocean Park Boulevard　　　　　　　　　CEO: Robert Kotick
Santa Monica, CA 90405　　　　　　　　　　CFO: Armin Zerza
Phone: 310 255-2000　　　　　　　　　　　　HR: –
Fax: –　　　　　　　　　　　　　　　　　　FYE: December 31
Web: www.activisionblizzard.com　　　　　　Type: Public

Activision Blizzard is a leading global developer and publisher of interactive entertainment content and services. The company is the biggest producer of video games including some of the most durable franchises: World of Warcraft Overwatch Candy Crush and Call of Duty. Users play Activision Blizzard's games on PCs game consoles and mobile devices. Activision Blizzard also operates esports league and offer digital advertising within their content. The company generates some 55% of its revenue in the Americas. The company was founded in 1979.

	Annual Growth	12/16	12/17	12/18	12/19	12/20
Sales ($ mil.)	5.2%	6,608.0	7,017.0	7,500.0	6,489.0	8,086.0
Net income ($ mil.)	22.8%	966.0	273.0	1,813.0	1,503.0	2,197.0
Market value ($ mil.)	26.6%	27,957.4	49,024.2	36,055.9	46,004.7	71,887.2
Employees	(0.3%)	9,600	9,800	9,900	9,200	9,500

ACTS RETIREMENT-LIFE COMMUNITIES, INC.

375 MORRIS RD
WEST POINT, PA 19486
Phone: 215-699-3204
Fax: –
Web: www.acts-retirement.org

CEO: Gerald Grant
CFO: –
HR: –
FYE: December 31
Type: Private

No acting here! ACTS is serious about providing seniors with the opportunity to live independently but with a helping hand when needed. ACTS develops owns and operates continuing-care retirement communities (CCRSs) in nine US states along the Eastern Seaboard. The company's properties feature resort-style amenities in Christian environments (ACTS comes from a Biblical reference). One of the largest not-for-profit operators of CCRCs in the US ACTS serves about 8500 older adults at about 25 communities from Pennsylvania to Florida. The not-for-profit organization was founded as Open Door Estates by a group of Pennsylvania church members in 1971.

	Annual Growth	12/12	12/13	12/14	12/15	12/16
Sales ($ mil.)	3.1%	–	–	363.0	373.0	386.1
Net income ($ mil.)	–	–	–	9.0	1.4	(6.0)
Market value ($ mil.)	–	–	–	–	–	–
Employees	–	–	–	–	–	5,375

ACTUA CORP

NBB: ACTA

555 East Lancaster Ave., Suite 640
Radnor, PA 19087
Phone: 610 727-6900
Fax: –
Web: www.actua.com

CEO: –
CFO: –
HR: –
FYE: December 31
Type: Public

Actua Corporation (formerly ICG Group) actually invests in companies in the business-to-business (B2B) market working with its holdings to develop strategy. It owns stakes in roughly a handful of cloud-based companies involved in technology-enabled business process outsourcing cloud-based software and software as a service (SaaS) including government-focused communications provider GovDelivery wealth management platform FolioDynamix EHS compliance software provider MSDSonline and property/casualty insurance distribution platform Bolt Solutions. Actua works closely with its companies often helping in day-to-day management.

	Annual Growth	12/12	12/13	12/14	12/15	12/16
Sales ($ mil.)	(10.0%)	166.6	59.2	84.8	133.4	109.3
Net income ($ mil.)	32.1%	23.0	209.1	(23.6)	(96.1)	70.1
Market value ($ mil.)	5.2%	399.3	650.9	645.3	400.0	489.1
Employees	(36.2%)	1,125	551	761	867	186

ACTUATE CORP.

NMS: BIRT

951 Mariners Island Boulevard
San Mateo, CA 94404
Phone: 650 645-3000
Fax: –
Web: www.actuate.com

CEO: Mark J Barrenechea
CFO: John Doolittle
HR: –
FYE: December 31
Type: Public

Actuate accentuates reporting. The company provides enterprise reporting and analytics software that corporations use to analyze business data and design publish and distribute content over company networks and the Internet. Actuate's customers which include HSBC Johnson Controls State Street Bank and PNC Bank use the company's software to publish financial statements performance metrics manufacturing and distribution reports and customer account information; that information is pulled from databases and displayed in easily digestible interactive Web pages Excel spreadsheets and other formats. Founded in 1993 Actuate operates in North America Europe and the Asia Pacific region.

	Annual Growth	12/08	12/09	12/10	12/11	12/12
Sales ($ mil.)	1.5%	131.0	119.3	131.5	134.9	138.8
Net income ($ mil.)	(6.7%)	13.6	12.2	10.6	12.0	10.3
Market value ($ mil.)	17.3%	142.7	206.4	274.9	282.6	270.0
Employees	3.9%	533	497	569	553	622

ACUATIVE CORPORATION

695 RTE 46 W STE 305
FAIRFIELD, NJ 070041561
Phone: 862-926-5600
Fax: –
Web: www.acuative.com

CEO: Vincent Sciarra
CFO: Patrick J Danna
HR: –
FYE: December 31
Type: Private

This company helps businesses stay in touch. Acuative builds and manages voice and data networks for business clients. It provides network integration and field engineering services using equipment from third-party vendors such as Aruba Networks Cisco Systems and HP. The company also offers managed services including network administration performance monitoring and security. Its areas of focus include data security unified communications and infrastructure. Acuative serves customers in financial services insurance retail and manufacturing among other sectors.

	Annual Growth	12/14	12/15	12/16	12/17	12/18
Sales ($ mil.)	(6.5%)	–	120.2	112.4	95.8	98.2
Net income ($ mil.)	–	–	0.3	0.8	(1.2)	(2.0)
Market value ($ mil.)	–	–	–	–	–	–
Employees	–	–	–	–	–	325

ACUITY A MUTUAL INSURANCE COMPANY

2800 S. Taylor Dr.
Sheboygan WI 53082
Phone: 920-458-9131
Fax: 920-458-1618
Web: https://www.acuity.com

CEO: –
CFO: –
HR: Jamie Van Dyck
FYE: December 31
Type: Private - Mutual Com

For Acuity A Mutual Insurance Company keeping its eye on the prize means meeting its customers' insurance needs. The company writes a variety of personal and commercial property/casualty insurance plans for policyholders in 20 states primarily in the Midwest. Its products include automobile homeowners liability marine umbrella and workers' compensation coverage. Acuity provides policies for such businesses as construction contractors manufacturers trucking and small service businesses. Some 1000 independent agencies sell the company's policies. Acuity was founded in 1925 as Mutual Auto Insurance Company of the Town of Herman. As a mutual insurance firm the company is owned by its policyholders.

ACUITY BRANDS INC (HOLDING COMPANY)

NYS: AYI

1170 Peachtree Street, N.E., Suite 2300
Atlanta, GA 30309-7676
Phone: 404 853-1400
Fax: 404 853-1300
Web: www.acuitybrands.com

CEO: Neil Ashe
CFO: Karen Holcom
HR: –
FYE: August 31
Type: Public

Acuity Brands is a market-leading industrial technology company. It technology to solve problems in spaces and light and uses designs manufactures and brings to market products and services that make the world more brilliant productive and connected. Its products ? marketed under brands like Lithonia Holophane Peerless Mark Architectural and Gotham include luminaires lighting controls controls for building systems as well as an integrated lighting systems for indoor and outdoor applications. The company serves customers such as electrical distributors retail home improvement centers electric utilities national accounts system integrators digital retailers lighting showrooms and energy service companies. Majority of the company's sales are generated domestically.

	Annual Growth	08/17	08/18	08/19	08/20	08/21
Sales ($ mil.)	(0.3%)	3,505.1	3,680.1	3,672.7	3,326.3	3,461.0
Net income ($ mil.)	(1.2%)	321.7	349.6	330.4	248.3	306.3
Market value ($ mil.)	1.1%	6,221.7	5,378.8	4,413.5	3,846.2	6,494.0
Employees	1.0%	12,500	13,000	12,000	11,500	13,000

ACUMEN SOLUTIONS INC.

1660 International Dr. Ste. 500   CEO: David Joubran
McLean VA 22102   CFO: –
Phone: 703-600-4000   HR: –
Fax: 703-600-4001   FYE: December 31
Web: www.acumensolutions.com   Type: Private

Acumen Solutions has keen insight into IT services. The company offers such services as enterprise architecture systems integration program management data warehousing and application development. Acumen also offers services focused on customer relationship management including salesforce.com optimization and customer analytics. Its clients include companies in the communications media consumer products and financial services industries as well as schools and government agencies. Customers have included American Express Comcast Sprint Nextel and the SEC. Acumen was founded by David Joubran and Stacy Reed in 1999.

ACURA PHARMACEUTICALS INC   NBB: ACUR

616 N. North Court, Suite 120   CEO: Robert Jones
Palatine, IL 60067   CFO: Peter Clemens
Phone: 847 705-7709   HR: –
Fax: –   FYE: December 31
Web: www.acurapharm.com   Type: Public

Acura Pharmaceuticals is working to provide accurate dosages of powerful drugs while preventing drug abuse. The company has developed a technology to add abuse-deterring agents to commonly abused pharmaceuticals. If a drug with these agents (what Acura calls Aversion Technology) is crushed and inhaled certain ingredients will cause nasal irritation and if an abuser attempts to dissolve the powder it will form a non-injectable gel. Its Impede Technology works with pseudoephedrine to disrupt the process used to turn the decongestant into meth. Acura's approved products include prescription Aversion oxycodone and over-the-counter Nexafed (pseudoephedrine with Impede ingredients).

	Annual Growth	12/16	12/17	12/18	12/19	12/20
Sales ($ mil.)	(5.4%)	4.5	3.0	0.4	2.7	3.6
Net income ($ mil.)	–	(7.4)	(5.7)	(3.8)	(3.8)	(1.2)
Market value ($ mil.)	(27.8%)	16.6	8.7	2.5	5.0	4.5
Employees	(3.5%)	15	14	13	13	13

ACUSHNET COMPANY

333 Bridge St.   CEO: David Maher
Fairhaven MA 02719-0965   CFO: –
Phone: 508-979-2000   HR: –
Fax: 508-979-3927   FYE: December 31
Web: www.acushnet.com   Type: Subsidiary

Acushnet stays teed off all the time. The company is a top maker of golf balls clubs shoes gloves and other golfing equipment and accessories. Its Titleist golf balls and FootJoy golf shoes and gloves are #1 sellers in the US. Acushnet also makes value-priced Pinnacle golf balls Titleist golf clubs Scotty Cameron putters and Vokey Design wedges as well as golf bags and outerwear. Products are sold worldwide through golf pro shops specialty sporting goods stores and mass merchants. PGA players who have used Acushnet's equipment include Adam Scott Davis Love III Geoff Ogilvy and Mark O'Meara. Global Fila brand owner Fila Korea bought Acushnet from spirits maker Beam Inc. (formerly Fortune Brands) for $1.2 billion in mid-2011.

ADA-ES INC.   NASDAQ: ADES

8100 SouthPark Way Unit B   CEO: Greg Marken
Littleton CO 80120-4527   CFO: –
Phone: 303-734-1727   HR: –
Fax: 303-734-0330   FYE: December 31
Web: www.adaes.com   Type: Public

ADA-ES wants to make "clean coal" more than just a marketing term. The company makes environmental technology systems and specialty chemicals to reduce emissions at coal-burning power plants. It offers integrated mercury control systems as well as flue gas conditioning and combustion aid chemicals. ADA-ES provides consulting and testing services and mercury measurement equipment. It also has a joint venture with NexGen Refined Coal to market technology that reduces emissions of nitrogen oxides and mercury from some treated coals. The company has withdrawn plans to reorganize its operations under the name Advanced Emissions Solutions in 2012. ADA-ES was created after being spun off from Earth Sciences in 2003.

ADAC PLASTICS, INC.

5690 EAGLE DR SE   CEO: Jim Teets
GRAND RAPIDS, MI 495122057   CFO: –
Phone: 616-957-0311   HR: –
Fax: –   FYE: December 31
Web: www.adacautomotive.com   Type: Private

ADAC Plastics which does business as ADAC Automotive has a handle on what automakers need. The company (privately owned by the Teets and Hungerford families) supplies automakers and tier 1 suppliers worldwide with door handles and components exterior trim and marker lighting. Other products include cowl vent grilles and fuel filler doors. Services provided by ADAC Automotive include design molding painting and assembly. Its ADAC Technologies subsidiary is a leading supplier of plastic moldings subassemblies and decorative finishes. It is part of the VAST (Vehicle Access Systems Technology) Alliance along with fellow automotive suppliers STRATTEC SECURITY and WITTE Automotive of Velbert Germany.

	Annual Growth	12/03	12/04	12/05	12/06	12/07
Sales ($ mil.)	–	–	–	(1,820.3)	177.2	177.2
Net income ($ mil.)	32691.6%	–	–	0.0	3.8	25.8
Market value ($ mil.)	–	–	–	–	–	–
Employees	–	–	–	–	–	800

ADAMIS PHARMACEUTICALS CORP.   NAS: ADMP

11682 El Camino Real, Suite 300   CEO: Dennis Carlo
San Diego, CA 92130   CFO: David Benedicto
Phone: 858 997-2400   HR: –
Fax: –   FYE: December 31
Web: www.adamispharmaceuticals.com   Type: Public

Adamis Pharmaceuticals adamantly develops and markets specialty prescription drugs for respiratory ailments allergies viral infections and other medical conditions. Subsidiary Adamis Labs develops and markets allergy respiratory and pediatric prescription medicines to physicians in the US. Its products include a pre-filled epinephrine syringe for severe allergic reactions dubbed Epi PFS. Adamis Viral Therapies is developing vaccine technologies for ailments such as influenza and hepatitis. The company is also developing other specialty pharmaceutical product candidates for the potential treatment of asthma and chronic obstructive pulmonary disease bronchospasms and allergic rhinitis.

	Annual Growth	12/16	12/17	12/18	12/19	12/20
Sales ($ mil.)	26.4%	6.5	13.1	15.1	22.1	16.5
Net income ($ mil.)	–	(19.4)	(25.5)	(39.0)	(29.3)	(49.4)
Market value ($ mil.)	(37.4%)	295.6	412.9	211.1	65.7	45.5
Employees	72.9%	16	126	231	171	143

ADAMS FAIRACRE FARMS, INC.

765 DUTCHESS TPKE
POUGHKEEPSIE, NY 126032000
Phone: 845-454-4330
Fax: –
Web: www.adamsfarms.com

CEO: –
CFO: –
HR: –
FYE: January 31
Type: Private

From seeds to seafood and fertilizer to fencing Adams Fairacre Farms has a few things covered. The company's four locations in New York's Hudson River Valley offer groceries including fresh produce power equipment (John Deere tractors and mowers chippers chain saws) fencing supplies landscaping materials and gifts and gardening supplies (plants seeds soil pest control). Adams Fairacre Farms was founded in 1919 by Ralph Adams Sr. as a roadside produce stand where the Adams family sold the excess from its 50-acre farm. The company added other items as customers requested them. Descendants of Adams including some third-generation members own and run the family business.

	Annual Growth	01/07	01/08	01/09	01/11	01/12
Sales ($ mil.)	2.4%	–	–	113.7	115.6	122.1
Net income ($ mil.)	(23.5%)	–	–	1.8	1.6	0.8
Market value ($ mil.)	–	–	–	–	–	–
Employees	–	–	–	–	–	550

ADAMS GOLF INC.

2801 E. Plano Pkwy.
Plano TX 75074
Phone: 972-673-9000
Fax: 972-398-8818
Web: www.adamsgolf.com

NASDAQ: ADGF
CEO: –
CFO: –
HR: –
FYE: December 31
Type: Public

Like any golfer Adams Golf says the problem isn't in the swing it's in the clubs. The company's Speedline fairway woods are designed to lift a golf ball from any lie — even bunkers rough or divots — and send it farther. Adams Golf also develops drivers wedges irons putters and accessories (golf bags and hats). A Women's Golf Unlimited subsidiary caters to women golfers with irons in various colors clubs balls and other gear. Specialty retailers mass merchants pro shops and sporting goods stores account for about 80% of Adams' sales. In addition to endorsing Adams Golf's products pro golfer Tom Watson assists in design and testing. The company was founded by chairman Barney Adams in 1987.

ADAMS MEDIA

57 Littlefield St.
Avon MA 02322
Phone: 508-427-7100
Fax: 508-427-6790
Web: www.adamsmedia.com

CEO: –
CFO: –
HR: –
FYE: December 31
Type: Business Segment

Adams Media publishes everything. The company publishes trade paperback books including titles in its Everything series (Everything Parenting Everything Pets Everything Health). Adams Media primarily covers non-fiction topics such as cooking pets health careers parenting and travel. Other imprints include Platinum Press (business) Polka Dot Press (for women) and Provenance Press (new age). The company publishes some 140 new titles per year with a total catalog of about 700 titles. Other series include "Streetwise Cup of Comfort Small Miracles" and Knock 'Em Dead. Adams Media is a unit of niche magazine publisher F+W Media.

ADAMS RESOURCES & ENERGY, INC.

17 South Briar Hollow Lane, Suite 100
Houston, TX 77027
Phone: 713 881-3600
Fax: –
Web: www.adamsresources.com

ASE: AE
CEO: Kevin Roycraft
CFO: Tracy E Ohmart
HR: Shayla Gann
FYE: December 31
Type: Public

Adams Resources & Energy (AE) markets transports and stores crude oil across the US Mexico and Canada. Based in Houston the company owns terminals in the Gulf Coast region of the US and provides liquid chemicals dry bulk and tank truck transportation services through its two wholly-owned subsidiaries GulfMark and Service Transport. AE reports approximately 691000 barrels of crude oil storage capacity. The company is a publicly traded Delaware corporation organized in 1973.

	Annual Growth	12/16	12/17	12/18	12/19	12/20
Sales ($ mil.)	(1.8%)	1,099.5	1,322.1	1,750.2	1,811.2	1,022.4
Net income ($ mil.)	(20.7%)	2.5	(0.5)	2.9	8.2	1.0
Market value ($ mil.)	(11.7%)	168.3	184.6	164.3	161.6	102.3
Employees	3.0%	645	575	703	664	726

ADAMS-COLUMBIA ELECTRIC COOPERATIVE

401 E LAKE ST
FRIENDSHIP, WI 539348050
Phone: 800-831-8629
Fax: –
Web: www.acecwi.com

CEO: Martin Hillard Jr
CFO: John West
HR: Bill Gneiser
FYE: December 31
Type: Private

With a name that harkens back to Christopher Columbus and the Founding Fathers Adams-Columbia Electric Cooperative provides power to more than 36000 member-owners in 12 counties in central Wisconsin. The rural distribution cooperative operates nearly 5300 miles of transmission and distribution lines. Adams-Columbia Electric was formed through the merger of Adams-Marquette Electric Cooperative and Columbus Rural Electric Cooperative in 1987. The utility expanded further through its 1992 acquisition of Waushara Electric Cooperative. The cooperative covers a 2500 sq. ml. geographic service area.

	Annual Growth	12/13	12/14	12/15	12/16	12/17
Sales ($ mil.)	(0.3%)	–	69.0	65.6	65.9	68.3
Net income ($ mil.)	99.7%	–	0.8	0.4	5.6	6.2
Market value ($ mil.)	–	–	–	–	–	–
Employees	–	–	–	–	–	115

ADB AIRFIELD SOLUTIONS LLC

977 Gahanna Pkwy.
Columbus OH 43230
Phone: 614-861-1304
Fax: 614-864-2069
Web: www.adb-airfield.com

CEO: –
CFO: –
HR: Kelly Pfeiffer
FYE: September 30
Type: Business Segment

ADB Airfield Solutions (formerly Siemens Airfield Solutions) can shed some light on landings takeoffs and other aircraft endeavors. The company makes products that illuminate approach zones aprons main runways and taxiways. From the largest freight hub in the world to small regional airports ADB's products can be found in virtually any airport. Other products include externally lighted wind cones guidance and control monitoring systems and cables and connectors. ADB also acts as a turnkey contractor for a variety of airport projects. Montagu Private Equity acquired ADB in November 2009 for E45 million ($60 million) from German giant Siemens AG which had owned the airfield lighting business since 1987.

ADDUS HOMECARE CORP   NMS: ADUS

6303 Cowboys Way, Suite 600 — CEO: R. Dirk Allison
Frisco, TX 75034 — CFO: Brian Poff
Phone: 469 535-8200 — HR: –
Fax: – — FYE: December 31
Web: www.addus.com — Type: Public

Addus HomeCare doing business through subsidiary Addus HealthCare it serves the elderly and disabled. Its home and community unit provides long-term non-medical social services such as bathing grooming housekeeping meal preparation and transportation. State and county government payors generate most of its revenues. Operating from 215 offices Addus provides its services in about 20 states primarily in the Midwestern and western US with its largest markets in Illinois New York and New Mexico.

	Annual Growth	12/16	12/17	12/18	12/19	12/20
Sales ($ mil.)	17.5%	400.7	425.7	518.1	648.8	764.8
Net income ($ mil.)	28.8%	12.0	13.6	17.5	25.2	33.1
Market value ($ mil.)	35.2%	554.7	550.7	1,074.3	1,538.6	1,853.1
Employees	11.1%	23,070	26,097	33,153	33,238	35,139

ADDVANTAGE TECHNOLOGIES GROUP, INC.   NAS: AEY

1430 Bradley Lane, Suite 196 — CEO: Joseph Hart
Carrollton, TX 75007 — CFO: Michael Rutledge
Phone: 918 251-9121 — HR: –
Fax: – — FYE: September 30
Web: www.addvantagetechnologies.com — Type: Public

ADDvantage Technologies provides turn-key wireless infrastructure services for wireless carriers tower companies and equipment manufacturers and distributes and services a comprehensive line of electronics and hardware for the telecommunications industry. For its telecommunications subsidiaries it sells new surplus-new and refurbished equipment that it purchases in the market as a result of telecommunications system upgrades or overstock supplies. It maintains one of the industry's largest inventories of new and used equipment which allows it to expedite the delivery of system-critical products to its customers. ADDvantage gets most of its sales in the US with a small portion in Central America and South America.

	Annual Growth	09/17	09/18	09/19	09/20	09/21
Sales ($ mil.)	6.3%	48.7	47.4	55.1	50.2	62.2
Net income ($ mil.)	—	(0.1)	(7.3)	(5.3)	(17.3)	(6.5)
Market value ($ mil.)	14.4%	17.4	17.8	25.2	24.2	29.8
Employees	(0.9%)	176	141	188	124	170

ADELPHI UNIVERSITY

1 SOUTH AVE — CEO: –
GARDEN CITY, NY 115304299 — CFO: –
Phone: 516-877-3000 — HR: –
Fax: – — FYE: August 31
Web: www.adelphi.edu — Type: Private

It may not house an oracle but Adelphi University hopes to provide answers to students' questions about their future. Founded in 1896 the university has about 7700 students enrolled at its four campuses located in New York (Garden City Hauppage Manhattan and the Hudson Valley). Adelphi University a private institution offers graduate undergraduate and continuing education programs in areas including business management education nursing and social work. Its Swirbul Library contains about 600000 books and documents and 33000 audiovisual materials. The school counts Nextel co-founder Brian McAuley US Chamber of Commerce CEO Thomas Donahue and author Alice Hoffman among its alumni.

	Annual Growth	08/16	08/17	08/18	08/19	08/20
Sales ($ mil.)	8.0%	–	196.6	232.8	233.6	247.5
Net income ($ mil.)	324.3%	–	0.2	16.3	8.8	15.4
Market value ($ mil.)	–	–	–	–	–	–
Employees	–	–	–	–	–	1,400

ADENA HEALTH SYSTEM

272 HOSPITAL RD STE 4 — CEO: Jeffrey J Graham
CHILLICOTHE, OH 456019031 — CFO: Lisa Carlson
Phone: 740-779-7500 — HR: –
Fax: – — FYE: December 31
Web: www.adena.org — Type: Private

Adena Health System serves the residents of about a dozen counties in south and south-central Ohio centered on the city of Chillicothe. Its main facility is the 261-bed Adena Regional Medical Center which provides general medical and surgical care as well as specialty care in a number of areas including cardiology women's health oncology and rehabilitation. The not-for-profit health system also features two smaller hospitals six regional clinics surgery centers and a counseling center among other facilities. The history of the Adena Health System goes back to 1895 when a group of local women established an emergency hospital in the wake of a fatal train wreck.

	Annual Growth	12/13	12/14	12/15*	03/17*	12/17
Sales ($ mil.)	6.0%	–	394.9	393.4	112.0	470.6
Net income ($ mil.)	26.6%	–	14.5	11.7	10.8	29.5
Market value ($ mil.)	–	–	–	–	–	–
Employees	–	–	–	–	–	3,000

*Fiscal year change

ADEONA PHARMACEUTICALS INC.   NYSE AMEX: AEN

3930 Varsity Dr. — CEO: Steven Shallcross
Ann Arbor MI 48108 — CFO: Steven A Shallcross
Phone: 734-332-7800 — HR: –
Fax: 775-358-4458 — FYE: December 31
Web: www.alliednevada.com — Type: Public

Adeona Pharmaceuticals is developing drugs for the treatment of serious central nervous system disorders. In its pipeline are a prescription medical food — specifically an oral tablet of zinc and an amino acid called cysteine — for Alzheimer's disease and drugs for age-related macular degeneration (loss of vision) fibromyalgia (arthritis-related muscle pain) multiple sclerosis and rheumatoid arthritis. The company generally prefers to in-license product candidates that have already shown certain clinical efficacy and then either develop them to commercialization or attract development partners such as it did with Meda which holds rights to complete development of Adeona's fibromyalgia drug Effirma.

ADEPT TECHNOLOGY INC.   NAS: ADEP

5960 Inglewood Drive — CEO: Rob Cain
Pleasanton, CA 94588 — CFO: Seth Halio
Phone: 925 245-3400 — HR: –
Fax: 925 960-0590 — FYE: June 30
Web: www.adept.com — Type: Public

Within 25-plus years Adept Technology has evolved from making industrial robots to a lineup of intelligent automation products. Its robots are designed to handle assemble test inspect and package goods in the electronics food processing automotive component packaging and pharmaceutical industries. Adept Technology's robots can replicate the movements of human shoulders elbows and wrists. The company also makes vision guidance and inspection systems as well as software that allows operators to control robots from a PC. Adept Technology targets a diverse group of Global 1000 companies including Procter & Gamble Johnson & Johnson Seagate Boeing and General Motors.

	Annual Growth	06/10	06/11	06/12	06/13	06/14
Sales ($ mil.)	2.7%	51.6	57.5	66.2	46.8	57.5
Net income ($ mil.)	—	(1.4)	(6.8)	(3.7)	(10.0)	(0.3)
Market value ($ mil.)	20.1%	65.8	52.9	56.8	50.8	136.9
Employees	(1.7%)	163	183	183	139	152

ADEXA INC.

5933 W. Century Blvd. 12th Fl.
Los Angeles CA 90045
Phone: 310-642-2100
Fax: 310-338-9878
Web: www.adexa.com

CEO: Khosrow Cyrus Hadavi
CFO: Mario A Disandro
HR: –
FYE: January 31
Type: Private

Adexa gives businesses a bit more digital dexterity. The company's Enterprise Global Planning System (eGPS) software includes components designed to help manufacturers manage a wide range of operations including costs factory scheduling sales inventory and materials management and supply chain planning. The application suite also includes tools for managing product information and collaborating with suppliers distributors and customers. Adexa targets clients in the semiconductor aerospace soft goods industrial automotive electronics chemicals and consumer packaged goods industries; its customers have included Advanced Micro Devices Boeing General Motors and Samsung.

ADIRONDACK PARK AGENCY

PO Box 99 1133 NYS Rte. 86
Ray Brook NY 12977
Phone: 518-891-4050
Fax: 518-891-3938
Web: www.apa.state.ny.us

CEO: –
CFO: –
HR: –
FYE: December 31
Type: Government Agency

In the Northeastern corner of New York state campers hikers and nature lovers of all sorts flock to Adirondack Park. The park is the largest publicly protected area in the lower 48 bigger than Yellowstone Glacier Everglades and Grand Canyon National Parks combined. New York's Adirondack Park Agency (APA) oversees the 2.6 million acres that belong to the state; the total acreage is 6 million acres and includes more than 3000 lakes and 30000 miles of rivers and streams. The agency develops long-range plans for use of the entire area protects the public land and manages the development of private lands within the park. The New York State Legislature created the APA in 1971.

ADHERA THERAPEUTICS INC   NBB: ATRX

8000 Innovation Parkway Drive
Baton Rouge, LA 70820
Phone: 919 518-3748
Fax: –
Web: www.adherathera.com

CEO: Andrew Kucharchuk
CFO: –
HR: –
FYE: December 31
Type: Public

Marina Biotech is a biopharmaceutical with a focus on arthritis pain oncology and hypertension therapies. In addition to developing and commercializing non-addictive pain medicines the company also studies combination therapies of approved drugs. Its pipeline includes next-generation versions of non-steroidal anti-inflammatory drug (NSAID) celecosib which due to dangerous side effect of swelling is currently limited in its usage. The company's Prestalia drug is commercially available for the treatment of hypertension. Formerly dedicated to gene-silencing treatments the struggling Marina Biotech altered its course with the late 2016 merger with IthenaPharma.

	Annual Growth	12/15	12/16	12/17	12/18	12/19
Sales ($ mil.)	(22.0%)	0.7	–	–	0.1	0.3
Net income ($ mil.)	–	3.3	(0.8)	(6.2)	(16.8)	(12.0)
Market value ($ mil.)	(32.6%)	2.9	1.6	17.9	3.0	0.6
Employees	18.9%	1	4	7	24	2

ADM INVESTOR SERVICES INC.

141 W. Jackson Blvd. Suite 1600A
Chicago IL 60604
Phone: 312-242-7000
Fax: 312-242-7045
Web: www.admis.com

CEO: –
CFO: Richy Macanip
HR: –
FYE: June 30
Type: Subsidiary

ADM Investor Services is a sprout off of agribusiness giant Archer Daniels Midland. The commodities brokerage offers market research and trade clearing and execution services to retail commercial and institutional customers for trading conducted on all major commodities exchanges. It also performs business consulting marketing and investment analysis. The company's ADM Derivatives division provides foreign exchange services via an electronic trading platform. ADM Investor Services serves international markets through affiliates in Hong Kong London and Taiwan. Through a joint venture the company also operates in Mumbai India.

ADHEREX TECHNOLOGIES INC.   PINK SHEETS: ADHXF

501 Eastowne Dr. Ste. 140
Chapel Hill NC 27514
Phone: 919-636-4530
Fax: 604-689-9022
Web: www.pacificgeoinfo.com

CEO: Rostislav Raykov
CFO: Robert Andrade
HR: –
FYE: December 31
Type: Public

Working nimbly with a very sticky subject Adherex Technologies researches and develops cancer treatments. One of its lead drug candidates targets a tumor's blood supply and makes those blood vessels weak and leaky by disrupting a key protein. Other potential therapies could make cancer cells more vulnerable to anti-cancer drugs or help prevent hearing loss in children undergoing certain types of chemotherapy. Adherex Technologies' pipeline is strongly based on compounds that disrupt cadherins proteins that adhere similar molecules together in cell adhesion. Southpoint Capital Advisors owns a controlling stake in the company.

ADM TRONICS UNLIMITED, INC.   NBB: ADMT

224-S Pegasus Avenue
Northvale, NJ 07647
Phone: 201 767-6040
Fax: 201 784-0620
Web: www.admtronics.com

CEO: Andre' Dimino
CFO: Andre Dimino
HR: –
FYE: March 31
Type: Public

ADM Tronics has had its own Industrial Revolution. While the company previously focused on the making of medical devices ADM has shifted its main focus to water-based chemical products for industrial use. These products include coatings resins primers and additives primarily for the printing and packaging industries. The firm licenses many of its medical products which include the Sonotron line of devices (used to treat osteoarthritis and inflammatory joint ailments with radio waves). Its Pros-Aide unit makes adhesives used in professional makeup products. ADM spun off Ivivi Technologies in 2006 but still owns about a third of the company. The founding DiMino family owns nearly half of ADM Tronics.

	Annual Growth	03/17	03/18	03/19	03/20	03/21
Sales ($ mil.)	(12.5%)	5.3	3.8	3.0	3.5	3.1
Net income ($ mil.)	–	1.2	0.1	(0.3)	(0.1)	(0.6)
Market value ($ mil.)	(9.7%)	12.2	13.5	10.7	10.8	8.1
Employees	5.4%	27	22	30	–	–

ADOBE INC
NMS: ADBE

345 Park Avenue
San Jose, CA 95110-2704
Phone: 408 536-6000
Fax: –
Web: www.adobe.com

CEO: Shantanu Narayen
CFO: Dan Durn
HR: Gloria Chen
FYE: December 03
Type: Public

Adobe is one of the largest and most diversified software companies in the world. It has been known for brands such as Acrobat Photoshop and Marketing Cloud. Adobe serves customers such as content creators and web application developers with its digital media products and marketers advertisers publishers and others with its digital marketing business. Its creative cloud offering is a cloud-based subscription offering that enables creative professionals and enthusiasts alike to express themselves with apps and services for video design photography and the web that connect across devices platforms and geographies. Subscriptions account for some 90% of revenue. The company was founded in 1982.

	Annual Growth	12/17*	11/18	11/19	11/20*	12/21
Sales ($ mil.)	21.3%	7,301.5	9,030.0	11,171.3	12,868.0	15,785.0
Net income ($ mil.)	29.9%	1,694.0	2,590.8	2,951.5	5,260.0	4,822.0
Market value ($ mil.)	36.1%	85,272.0	119,172.8	147,026.8	226,589.3	292,851.8
Employees	9.7%	17,973	21,357	22,634	22,516	25,988

*Fiscal year change

ADT CORP
NYS: ADT

1501 Yamato Road
Boca Raton, FL 33431
Phone: 561 988-3600
Fax: –
Web: www.adt.com

CEO: James D Devries
CFO: Michael Geltzeiler
HR: –
FYE: September 25
Type: Public

Burglar at your window? ADT wants you to be armed and calm with its alarms. The company provides products and services used for fire protection access control alarm monitoring medical alert system monitoring video surveillance and intrusion detection. It divides its security operations across four disciplines: Residential Security (provides burglar fire carbon dioxide alarms) Small Business (intruder detection and cameras) ADT Pulse (allows users to access and control security systems remotely) and Home Health (emergency response in the case of medical emergencies).

	Annual Growth	09/11	09/12	09/13	09/14	09/15
Sales ($ mil.)	3.5%	3,110.0	3,228.0	3,309.0	3,408.0	3,574.0
Net income ($ mil.)	(5.8%)	376.0	394.0	421.0	304.0	296.0
Market value ($ mil.)	(13.7%)	–	–	6,843.0	5,905.9	5,091.6
Employees	2.2%	–	16,000	17,000	17,500	17,100

ADTALEM GLOBAL EDUCATION INC
NYS: ATGE

500 West Monroe Street
Chicago, IL 60661
Phone: 866 374-2678
Fax: –
Web: www.adtalem.com

CEO: Lisa Wardell
CFO: Robert Phelan
HR: Nancy Johnson
FYE: June 30
Type: Public

Adtalem Global Education is in the big leagues of health care business law and financial education. The for-profit educational company offers professional undergraduate and graduate degrees. Adtalem offers health care education through Chamberlain University American University of the Caribbean School of Medicine and the Ross University Schools of Medicine and Veterinary Medicine. Schools of finance include the Association of Certified Anti-Money Laundering Specialists Becker Professional Education OnCourse Learning and EduPristine. Adtalem is divesting its business degree division Educacional do Brasil. Chamberlain had approximately 29000 students enrolled in the July 2019 term in more than 20 campuses and online. Amgen operates in more than 180 countries.

	Annual Growth	06/17	06/18	06/19	06/20	06/21
Sales ($ mil.)	(11.5%)	1,809.8	1,231.2	1,239.7	1,052.0	1,112.4
Net income ($ mil.)	(10.9%)	122.3	33.8	95.2	(85.3)	76.9
Market value ($ mil.)	(1.6%)	1,869.2	2,369.1	2,218.8	1,534.2	1,755.4
Employees	(27.9%)	16,363	18,018	11,356	4,299	4,426

ADTRAN, INC.
NMS: ADTN

901 Explorer Boulevard
Huntsville, AL 35806-2807
Phone: 256 963-8000
Fax: –
Web: www.adtran.com

CEO: Thomas Stanton
CFO: Michael Foliano
HR: –
FYE: December 31
Type: Public

ADTRAN turns copper and fiber into gold. The company offers more than 1700 network access products and systems used to enable Internet access telephony data transport and video over voice and data networks from traditional copper wire to optical. ADTRAN sells its switches routers multiplexing systems and other carrier-grade equipment to wireline and wireless service providers such as AT&T and CenturyLink. Its enterprise networking equipment ranges from modems to larger integrated access devices for multiple users access routers multiplexers firewalls and radio equipment. ADTRAN sells directly and through a network of distributors to a mostly US-based clientele.

	Annual Growth	12/16	12/17	12/18	12/19	12/20
Sales ($ mil.)	(5.6%)	636.8	666.9	529.3	530.1	506.5
Net income ($ mil.)	(49.0%)	35.2	23.8	(19.3)	(53.0)	2.4
Market value ($ mil.)	(9.8%)	1,078.2	933.5	518.1	477.1	712.5
Employees	(8.8%)	2,033	2,060	1,900	1,790	1,405

ADVANCE AMERICA CASH ADVANCE CENTERS INC.
NYSE: AEA

135 N. Church St.
Spartanburg SC 29306
Phone: 864-342-5600
Fax: 864-342-5612
Web: www.advanceamerica.net

CEO: Patrick O'Shaughnessy
CFO: James A Ovenden
HR: –
FYE: December 31
Type: Subsidiary

Advance America Cash Advance Centers is one of the largest payday advance firms in the US. Active in nearly 30 states it operates more than 2100 locations under the Advance America brand and more than 400 more under the National Cash Advance Check Advance First American Cash Advance First American Cash Loans Purpose Financial and Purpose Money banners; California Florida and Texas are its largest markets. At its branches or online customers provide proof of identification source of income bank account and references and Advance America loans them from $50 to $1000 (plus fees and interest) to cover unexpected expenses. Grupo Elektra acquired Advance America in 2012 for some $780 million.

ADVANCE AUTO PARTS INC
NYS: AAP

4200 Six Forks Road
Raleigh, NC 27609
Phone: 540 362-4911
Fax: –
Web: www.advanceautoparts.com

CEO: Tom Greco
CFO: Jeffrey Shepherd
HR: Natalie Schechtman
FYE: January 01
Type: Public

Serving both the do-it-yourself (DIY) and professional installer markets Advance Auto Parts (AAP) operates more than 4800 stores under the Advance Auto Parts Autopart International (AI) Carquest and Worldpac banners in the US and Canada. Its stores carry brand-name and private-label replacement parts batteries maintenance items and automotive chemicals for individual car and truck owners. AAP's Carquest AI and Worldpac stores cater to commercial customers including garages service stations and auto dealers.

	Annual Growth	12/17	12/18	12/19*	01/21	01/22
Sales ($ mil.)	3.2%	9,373.8	9,580.6	9,709.0	10,106.3	10,998.0
Net income ($ mil.)	5.3%	475.5	423.8	486.9	493.0	616.1
Market value ($ mil.)	19.2%	6,181.7	9,639.9	9,819.1	9,767.0	14,874.7
Employees	(0.9%)	71,000	71,000	67,000	68,000	68,000

*Fiscal year change

ADVANCE DISPLAY TECHNOLOGIES INC.

7334 S. Alton Way Ste. F
Centennial CO 80112-2320
Phone: 303-267-0111
Fax: 303-267-0330

CEO: –
CFO: –
HR: –
FYE: June 30
Type: Private

Advance Display Technologies (ADTI) develops large-screen fiber-optic video displays. The company plans to license or sell its intellectual property assets. After a brief foray into theater operations ADTI is looking to raise capital and restructure its debt in order to continue development of its displays. It acquired the rights to light-emitting diode (LED) display technologies that are patented as SkyNet. Affiliate ADTI Media agreed to pay ADTI a 20% royalty on revenues from the patents after ADTI's lender foreclosed on its assets. In 2010 a group of stockholders including majority owner Lawrence DeGeorge formed GLSD Holdings and acquired the company in a going private transaction.

ADVANCE MAGAZINE PUBLISHERS INC.

4 Times Square
New York NY 10036
Phone: 212-286-2860
Fax: 952-944-7869
Web: www.datalink.com

CEO: Charles Townsend
CFO: David Geithner
HR: –
FYE: December 31
Type: Subsidiary

While being Wired may hold a certain Allure traditional publishing will always be in Vogue at Advance Magazine Publishers doing business as Conde Nast. Owned by newspaper publisher Advance Publications Conde Nast publishes one of the most recognizable magazine portfolios in the industry including fashion bible Vogue and cybermag Wired as well as stalwarts GQ The New Yorker and Vanity Fair and newer shopping title "Lucky". Conde Nast Digital runs websites such as Epicurious (food) and Concierge (travel) while Conde Nast International produces foreign versions of its titles for readers across the globe. In addition Conde Nast oversees fashion and trade magazine unit Fairchild Fashion Group.

ADVANCE PUBLICATIONS INC.

950 Fingerboard Rd.
Staten Island NY 10305
Phone: 718-981-1234
Fax: 718-981-1456
Web: www.advance.net

CEO: –
CFO: Thomas Summer
HR: –
FYE: December 31
Type: Private

The drumbeat urging this company forward is the drone of printing presses. Advance Publications is a leading newspaper and magazine publisher with several dozen titles. Its portfolio of about 25 newspapers includes The Star-Ledger (New Jersey) The Cleveland Plain Dealer and namesake Staten Island Advance as well as more than 40 weekly titles published by American City Business Journals. Through Advance Magazine Publishers (DBA Conde Nast) the company owns magazines including The New Yorker Vanity Fair and Wired. Other operations and interests include online content and cable television. Patriarch Sam Newhouse started the family-owned business with the purchase of the Staten Island Advance in 1922.

ADVANCED ANALOGIC TECHNOLOGIES INCORPORATED   NASDAQ: AATI

3230 Scott Blvd.
Santa Clara CA 95054
Phone: 408-330-1400
Fax: 408-737-4611
Web: www.analogictech.com

CEO: Richard K Williams
CFO: Ashok Chandran
HR: –
FYE: December 31
Type: Subsidiary

Advanced Analogic Technologies tries to take an advanced approach to its chip technology. The company known as AnalogicTech provides specialized power management semiconductors for use in a variety of computing communications and consumer electronics applications. AnalogicTech's chips go into portable media players digital cameras netbook and notebook computers smartphones and wireless handsets. The company's customers include Samsung Electronics and LG Electronics. AnalogicTech gets most of its revenues from the Asia/Pacific region; South Korea makes up about two-thirds of sales. In 2012 the company was acquired by Skyworks Solutions in a deal valued at about $260 million in cash.

ADVANCED EMISSIONS SOLUTIONS INC   NMS: ADES

8051 E. Maplewood Ave, Suite 210
Greenwood Village, CO 80111
Phone: 720 598-3500
Fax: –
Web: www.advanceemissionssolutions.com

CEO: Greg Marken
CFO: Morgan Fields
HR: –
FYE: December 31
Type: Public

Advanced Emissions Solutions wants to make "clean coal" more than just a marketing term. The company makes environmental technology systems and specialty chemicals to reduce emissions at coal-burning power plants. It offers integrated mercury control systems as well as flue gas conditioning and combustion aid chemicals. Advanced Emissions Solutions provides consulting and testing services and mercury measurement equipment. It also has a joint venture with NexGen Refined Coal to market technology that reduces emissions of nitrogen oxides and mercury from some treated coals. The company has three reportable segments: Refined Coal Emission Control and CO2 Capture.

	Annual Growth	12/16	12/17	12/18	12/19	12/20
Sales ($ mil.)	5.0%	50.6	35.7	23.9	70.1	61.6
Net income ($ mil.)	–	97.7	27.9	35.5	35.5	(20.3)
Market value ($ mil.)	(12.2%)	171.2	178.9	195.4	194.5	101.9
Employees	52.7%	25	29	128	133	136

ADVANCED ENERGY INDUSTRIES INC   NMS: AEIS

1595 Wynkoop Street, Suite 800
Denver, CO 80202
Phone: 970 407-6626
Fax: –
Web: www.advancedenergy.com

CEO: Stephen Kelley
CFO: Paul Oldham
HR: –
FYE: December 31
Type: Public

Advanced Energy Industries tames electricity for its high-tech clients. The company's power conversion products transform raw electricity making it uniform enough to ensure consistent production in high-precision manufacturing. Semiconductor and solar manufacturing equipment maker Applied Materials is its top customer. Advanced Energy's gear also is used in the production of solar panels and other thin-film products such as cell phones computers cars and glass panels for windows and electronic devices. The company gets about half of its sales from the US. The company strengthened its portfolio of industrial products in 2019 with the $400 million acquisition of Artesyn Embedded Technologies.

	Annual Growth	12/16	12/17	12/18	12/19	12/20
Sales ($ mil.)	30.8%	483.7	671.0	718.9	788.9	1,415.8
Net income ($ mil.)	1.4%	127.5	137.9	147.0	64.9	134.7
Market value ($ mil.)	15.4%	2,096.5	2,584.0	1,643.9	2,726.5	3,713.3
Employees	59.2%	1,558	1,876	2,259	10,917	10,000

ADVANCED ENVIRONMENTAL RECYCLING TECHNOLOGIES, INC.

914 JEFFERSON ST
SPRINGDALE, AR 727643400
Phone: 479-756-7400
Fax: –

CEO: –
CFO: –
HR: –
FYE: December 31
Type: Private

It may not turn straw into gold but Advanced Environmental Recycling Technologies (AERT) does turn recycled waste into building materials. The company specializes in processing and converting scrap plastic and wood fiber waste into outdoor decking and fencing systems and window and door components. Its products are mainly used in residential renovation and remodeling by homeowners homebuilders and contractors as a greener alternative to traditional wood and plastic products. AERT markets its products under such names as ChoiceDek and MoistureShield; ChoiceDek is sold to home improvement retailers such as Lowe's through an agreement with distributor BlueLinx. H.I.G. Capital acquired 80% of AERT in 2011.

	Annual Growth	12/12	12/13	12/14	12/15	12/16
Sales ($ mil.)	7.5%	–	68.8	76.0	82.7	85.3
Net income ($ mil.)	–	–	–	(0.1)	0.4	0.7	3.9
Market value ($ mil.)	–	–	–	–	–	–
Employees	–	–	–	–	–	428

ADVANCED HEALTH MEDIA LLC

300 Somerset Corporate Blvd.
Bridgewater NJ 08807
Phone: 908-393-8700
Fax: 908-393-8701
Web: www.ahmdirect.com

CEO: Christine Croft
CFO: Frank Spender
HR: –
FYE: December 31
Type: Private

Advanced Health Media (AHM) keeps biotech and pharma companies' operations from going astray. The company provides hosted sales force logistics and compliance management tools that clients use to manage their interactions with healthcare professionals. Its offerings are focused on logistics (venue management travel meeting coordination) finances (budgeting travel reimbursement reporting) and compliance (attendee tracking healthcare provider eligibility). It also serves venues through its VenueVantage program. Chairman Kevin McMurtry and founding partner Joseph Luzi formed the company in 1999.

ADVANCED LIGHTING TECHNOLOGIES INC.

32000 Aurora Rd.
Solon OH 44139
Phone: 440-519-0500
Fax: 440-519-0501
Web: www.adlt.com

CEO: –
CFO: Michael Knight
HR: Stephanie Ferguson
FYE: June 30
Type: Private

And then there was light the metal halide kind. Made by Advanced Lighting Technologies (ADLT) metal halide simulates sunlight more closely and efficiently than other technologies. ADLT subsidiary Venture Lighting produces metal halide lamps and ballast systems. Its lineup includes lamp components power supplies and lamp-making equipment for commercial and industrial markets. ADLT's APL Engineered Materials business makes the metal halide salts used in its products as well as sells the salts to other manufacturers. Via Deposition Sciences ADLT also produces durable thin-film optical coatings for industrial medical and biological sciences instrumentation. ADLT is owned by private equity Saratoga Partners.

ADVANCED MICRO DEVICES INC

NMS: AMD

2485 Augustine Drive
Santa Clara, CA 95054
Phone: 408 749-4000
Fax: –
Web: www.amd.com

CEO: Lisa Su
CFO: Devinder Kumar
HR: –
FYE: December 25
Type: Public

Advanced Micro Devices (AMD) produces microprocessors as standalone devices or as incorporated into an accelerated processing unit (APU) chipsets discrete and integrated graphics processing units (GPUs) data center and professional GPUs and development services and servers and embedded processors semi-custom System-on-Chip (SoC) products development services and technology for game consoles. In recent years the company has armed itself with new product families: Radeon for graphics and Ryzen for computing to strengthen its position against longtime rival and market leader Intel. Majority of AMD's sales comes from international customers.

	Annual Growth	12/17	12/18	12/19	12/20	12/21
Sales ($ mil.)	32.5%	5,329.0	6,475.0	6,731.0	9,763.0	16,434.0
Net income ($ mil.)	192.8%	43.0	337.0	341.0	2,490.0	3,162.0
Market value ($ mil.)	94.2%	12,408.0	21,508.7	55,739.3	110,814.7	176,391.0
Employees	14.9%	8,900	10,100	11,400	12,600	15,500

ADVANCED MP TECHNOLOGY INC.

1010 CALLE SOMBRA
SAN CLEMENTE, CA 92673-6227
Phone: 949-492-3113
Fax: –
Web: www.advancedmp.com

CEO: Homayoun Shorooghi
CFO: –
HR: –
FYE: December 31
Type: Private

Advanced MP Technology advances the cause of global electronic components distribution services for high-tech manufacturers. The company distributes linear and digital integrated circuits such as logic devices; DRAMs static random-access memories (SRAMs) and flash memories; and microprocessors. It also distributes passive components such as capacitors. The company which was founded by CEO Jeff Yassai in 1978 offers inventory management services including inventory reduction programs designed to keep customers from getting stuck with excess inventory during industry downturns. Yassai owns half of the company while president Homey Shorooghi owns the other half.

	Annual Growth	12/98	12/99	12/00	12/01	12/11
Sales ($ mil.)	(3.0%)	–	167.0	455.0	227.0	115.7
Net income ($ mil.)	(15.6%)	–	21.7	147.0	31.0	2.8
Market value ($ mil.)	–	–	–	–	–	–
Employees	–	–	–	–	–	274

ADVANCED PHOTONIX, INC.

ASE: API

2925 Boardwalk Drive
Ann Arbor, MI 48104
Phone: 734 864-5600
Fax: –
Web: www.advancedphotonix.com

CEO: –
CFO: –
HR: –
FYE: March 31
Type: Public

Advanced Photonix Inc. (API) senses more with light. The company makes devices that detect light and radiation including photodiodes photo detectors and optoelectronic assemblies which are used by manufacturers in analysis and imaging equipment for applications ranging from missile guidance and satellite positioning to baggage scanning and blood analysis. API's large-area avalanche photodiodes (LAAPDs) are used to sense low levels of light and radiation. Its FILTRODE technology applies optical coatings to photodiode chips to filter out bright background light. About 25% of its sales are to federal government contractors.

	Annual Growth	03/10	03/11	03/12	03/13	03/14
Sales ($ mil.)	8.3%	21.1	28.8	29.5	23.6	29.0
Net income ($ mil.)	–	(3.7)	(1.9)	(2.1)	(4.4)	(4.3)
Market value ($ mil.)	2.7%	17.5	62.7	20.8	14.7	19.5
Employees	(5.5%)	153	185	157	134	122

ADVANCED PROTEOME THERAPEUTICS INC.   TSX VENTURE: APC

650 Albany St. Ste. 113 — CEO: –
Boston MA 02118 — CFO: –
Phone: 617-638-0340 — HR: –
Fax: 617-638-0341 — FYE: July 31
Web: www.advancedproteome.com — Type: Public

Advanced Proteome Therapeutics (APT) has the technology to help biopharmaceutical developers place their therapeutic proteins in exactly the right spot. However it's taking a while to find those developers and those right spots. One of its applications will enhance the usefulness of existing polyethylene glycol-based drug delivery technology. The company is housed with other research firms on the campus of Boston University but is technically a Canadian company. APT's technology is based upon the work of its founder and CEO Dr. Allen Krantz.

ADVANTAGE SALES AND MARKETING LLC

18100 Von Karman Ave. Ste. 900 — CEO: Tanya Domier
Irvine CA 92612 — CFO: Brian Stevens
Phone: 949-797-2900 — HR: –
Fax: 949-797-9112 — FYE: December 31
Web: www.asmnet.com — Type: Private

Making consumer products is one thing but selling them is another and that's where Advantage Sales & Marketing (ASM) comes in. The company provides outsourced sales merchandising and marketing services to consumer goods and food product manufacturers and suppliers. It works to win optimal placement of clients' products at retail locations throughout the US and Canada and it offers a variety of promotional programs aimed at boosting sales. Owning more than 65 offices in the US and Canada ASM does merchandising for 1200 clients — including Johnson & Johnson Mars Unilever Energizer. Investment group Apax Partners owns a controlling stake in the company which was established in 1987.

ADVANCEPIERRE FOODS INC.

9990 Princeton Rd. — CEO: Tom Hayes
Cincinnati OH 45246 — CFO: Dennis Leatherby
Phone: 513-874-8741 — HR: –
Fax: 513-874-8395 — FYE: February 28
Web: www.pierrefoods.com — Type: Private

AdvancePierre Foods takes the prep out of preparing a meal. The company is a top US supplier of packaged sandwiches fully-cooked chicken and beef items veggie patties breaded meats and bakery products. It caters to several sectors such as schools vending wholesale clubs and grocery and convenience stores. As part of its business it operates meat processing plants sandwich assembly facilities and bakeries across five mostly Midwestern states. AdvancePierre Foods was formed by the 2010 merger of Pierre Foods Advance Food Company and Advance Brands. The company is owned by Oaktree Capital Management along with shareholders and managers of its predecessor companies.

ADVANTEGO CORP   NBB: ADGO

3801 East Florida Ave., Suite 400 — CEO: Robert Ferguson
Denver, CO 80210 — CFO: Tracy A Madsen
Phone: 949 627-8977 — HR: –
Fax: – — FYE: December 31
— Type: Public

In search of gold and copper Golden Eagle International has spread its wings in Bolivia. The company is exploring prospects in the Tipuani-Cangalli area north of La Paz and in eastern Bolivia's Precambrian Shield area. Gold production on the company's Cangalli claims was halted in 2004 because of a farmers' strike and has not yet restarted; the company has yet to produce minerals on its other properties. Golden Eagle has generated no revenue since late 2004.

	Annual Growth	12/14	12/15	12/16	12/17	12/18
Sales ($ mil.)	973.8%	–	–	–	0.0	0.2
Net income ($ mil.)	–	(0.1)	(0.1)	(0.2)	(0.6)	(1.3)
Market value ($ mil.)	132.1%	0.1	0.1	0.4	1.4	2.9
Employees	59.7%	2	2	3	4	13

ADVANT-E CORPORATION   NBB: ADVC

2434 Esquire Dr. — CEO: Jason Wadzinski
Beavercreek, OH 45431 — CFO: James Lesch
Phone: 937 429-4288 — HR: –
Fax: – — FYE: December 31
Web: www.advant-e.com — Type: Public

Advant-e makes B2B e-commerce EZ. Through subsidiaries Edict Systems and Merkur Group the holding company offers Electronic Data Interchange (EDI) and electronic document management software for small and midsized businesses. More than half of Advant-e's sales come from Edict Systems' GroceryEC.com which helps suppliers such as Associated Grocers do business with retailers by automating invoices and purchase orders. Merkur Group which accounts for less than 20% of sales sells document management software that works within a company's Oracle SAP or Microsoft application. President and CEO Jason Wadzinski who founded Edict System when he was 25 controls more than 54% of Advant-e's stock.

	Annual Growth	12/08	12/09	12/10	12/11	12/12
Sales ($ mil.)	3.3%	8.9	8.6	9.3	9.6	10.1
Net income ($ mil.)	17.1%	1.1	1.2	1.6	1.7	2.0
Market value ($ mil.)	(34.4%)	81.1	16.2	13.2	13.3	15.0
Employees	4.4%	59	66	65	68	70

ADVANZEON SOLUTIONS INC   NBB: CHCR

2901 W. Busch Blvd., Suite 701 — CEO: Clark Marcus
Tampa, FL 33618 — CFO: Arnold Finestone
Phone: 813 517-8484 — HR: –
Fax: – — FYE: December 31
Web: www.advanzeonshareholders.com — Type: Public

It's not comprehensive health care if doesn't cover body and mind. That's why Comprehensive Care helps commercial and government-run health plans nationwide offer behavioral health care services. Through its Comprehensive Behavioral Care subsidiary (CompCare for short) the company manages behavioral health care including psychiatric and substance abuse services through a network of about 21000 health care providers in 39 states and Puerto Rico. For the most part it operates under capitation agreements in which the plans pay CompCare a fixed monthly fee for each member.

	Annual Growth	12/15	12/16	12/17	12/18	12/19
Sales ($ mil.)	(9.0%)	0.4	0.2	0.6	0.5	0.3
Net income ($ mil.)	–	(3.6)	(4.5)	(5.9)	4.8	(3.3)
Market value ($ mil.)	35.6%	8.5	4.7	9.1	6.9	28.7
Employees	7.5%	9	12	12	9	12

ADVAXIS INC

NBB: ADXS

9 Deer Park Drive, Suite K-1
Monmouth Junction, NJ 08852
Phone: 609 452-9813
Fax: –
Web: www.advaxis.com

CEO: Kenneth Berlin
CFO: –
HR: –
FYE: October 31
Type: Public

Advaxis is making a bad bacteria do well. A clinical-stage biotechnology firm that focused on the development and commercialization of proprietary Lm Technology antigen delivery products based on a platform technology that utilizes live attenuated Listeria monocytogenes or Lm bioengineered to secrete antigen/adjuvant fusion proteins. Advaxis' lead candidate axalimogene filolisbac targets HPV-associated cancers and is being tested for the treatment of cervical head and neck and anal cancer. Other candidates in development target prostate cancer and solid tumors.

	Annual Growth	10/17	10/18	10/19	10/20	10/21
Sales ($ mil.)	(28.0%)	12.0	6.1	20.9	0.3	3.2
Net income ($ mil.)	–	(93.4)	(66.5)	(16.6)	(26.5)	(17.9)
Market value ($ mil.)	(38.6%)	495.2	81.7	46.1	49.2	70.6
Employees	(39.0%)	108	58	35	18	15

ADVENT INTERNATIONAL CORPORATION

75 State St.
Boston MA 02109
Phone: 617-951-9400
Fax: 617-951-0566
Web: www.adventinternational.com

CEO: –
CFO: Eileen Sivolella
HR: –
FYE: December 31
Type: Private

Buyout firm Advent International invests in mid-market companies in the Americas Europe and Japan. The active investor focuses on business and financial services health care industrial consumer and technology and media. Advent provides its portfolio companies with capital infusions (up to $1.25 billion) for international expansion restructuring or to fuel growth. In developing markets in Central Europe and Latin America Advent finances companies with up to $200 million per transaction. Founded in 1984 Advent has backed more 500 companies and has raised some $26 billion in capital. Investors include pension funds funds of funds financial institutions university endowments and foundations.

ADVENT SOFTWARE, INC.

NMS: ADVS

600 Townsend Street
San Francisco, CA 94103
Phone: 415 543-7696
Fax: –
Web: www.advent.com

CEO: David Peter Hess Jr
CFO: James Cox
HR: –
FYE: December 31
Type: Public

Advent Software manages investments from beginning to end. A provider of investment management software for advisers brokers funds and other financial firms Advent offers applications for managing everything from client relationships to trade order executions. The company's products (marketed under the APX Geneva Black Diamond and Tamale brands among others) are used to manage portfolio accounting trading and order execution hedge and venture fund allocation reconciliation and other functions. Advent also offers services such as consulting hosting support and maintenance. More than 80% of sales come from customers in the US including TIAA CREF Merrill Lynch and Wells Capital Management.

	Annual Growth	12/09	12/10	12/11	12/12	12/13
Sales ($ mil.)	10.2%	259.5	283.5	326.2	358.8	383.0
Net income ($ mil.)	(6.0%)	36.9	24.2	30.2	30.4	28.8
Market value ($ mil.)	(3.8%)	2,087.7	2,968.9	1,248.6	1,095.9	1,791.6
Employees	3.6%	998	1,051	1,201	1,222	1,151

ADVENTIST HEALTH SYSTEM/SUNBELT, INC.

900 HOPE WAY
ALTAMONTE SPRINGS, FL 327141502
Phone: 407-357-1000
Fax: –
Web: www.adventhealth.com

CEO: –
CFO: Terry D Shaw
HR: –
FYE: December 31
Type: Private

Adventist Health System Sunbelt (AdventHealth) provides full system care from everyday wellness and preventive health care to life-saving diagnostic services and innovative medical treatments in cancer heart failure and more. It works with the world's brightest medical minds and innovators. Its integrated network of health care serves neighbors across more than 130 facilities nationwide including hospital campuses urgent-care centers home-health and hospice agencies and nursing homes across roughly 10 states. Extend the Healing Ministry of Christ its Christian mission shared vision common values and focus on whole-person health is its commitment to making communities healthier with a unified system with nearly 50 hospital campuses and hundreds of care sites in diverse markets.

	Annual Growth	10/07	10/08*	12/09	12/19	12/20
Sales ($ mil.)	45.1%	–	145.3	0.0	11,892.3	12,623.2
Net income ($ mil.)	–	–	(8.2)	0.0	1,607.3	951.4
Market value ($ mil.)	–	–	–	–	–	–
Employees	–	–	–	–	–	46,960

*Fiscal year change

ADVENTIST HEALTH SYSTEM/SUNBELT, INC.

900 HOPE WAY
ALTAMONTE SPRINGS, FL 327141502
Phone: 407-357-1000
Fax: –
Web: www.adventhealth.com

CEO: –
CFO: –
HR: –
FYE: December 31
Type: Private

Florida Hospital Heartland Medical Center provides care to residents of central Florida. The not-for-profit 160-bed medical center is the flagship facility of the Florida Hospital Heartland division of Adventist Health System. Other facilities in the Heartland system include Florida Hospital Lake Placid (a 50-bed community hospital) Florida Hospital Wauchula (25 beds) various fitness centers medical clinics and counseling agencies. Together the facilities provide primary and acute care as well as specialty medical services including diagnostics obstetrics cardiac care and cancer treatment. The Florida Hospital Heartland Medical Center opened in 1997.

	Annual Growth	12/07	12/08	12/14	12/15	12/16
Sales ($ mil.)	6.7%	–	126.5	167.2	193.7	212.5
Net income ($ mil.)	189.3%	–	0.0	(14.1)	(6.1)	7.3
Market value ($ mil.)	–	–	–	–	–	–
Employees	–	–	–	–	–	1,200

ADVENTIST HEALTH SYSTEM/WEST, CORPORATION

1 ADVENTIST HEALTH WAY
ROSEVILLE, CA 956613266
Phone: 844-574-5686
Fax: –
Web: www.adventisthealth.org

CEO: Kerry Heinrich
CFO: John Beaman
HR: –
FYE: December 31
Type: Private

Not content to wait around for the advent of good health Adventist Health System/West o is a faith-based nonprofit integrated health system serving more than 80 communities on the West Coast and Hawaii as well as others across the US through its Blue Zones company a pioneer in taking a systemic and environmental approach to improving the health of entire cities and communities. Annually Adventist Health System/West has nearly 135000 admissions 757000 emergency department visits 208000 home health visits 2.2 million clinic visits and 1.5 million outpatient visits. Adventist Health maintains strong ties to the Seventh-day Adventist Church but is independently owned. A sister organization Adventist Health System operates in the central and southern parts of the country.

	Annual Growth	12/14	12/15	12/16	12/17	12/18
Sales ($ mil.)	160.3%	–	251.5	3,945.9	4,114.5	4,434.0
Net income ($ mil.)	267.8%	–	10.9	185.4	200.0	544.0
Market value ($ mil.)	–	–	–	–	–	–
Employees	–	–	–	–	–	19,512

ADVENTIST HEALTHCARE, INC.

820 W DIAMOND AVE STE 600
GAITHERSBURG, MD 208781469
Phone: 301-315-3030
Fax: –
Web: www.adventisthealthcare.com

CEO: –
CFO: James Lee
HR: Patrise Prather
FYE: December 31
Type: Private

Adventist HealthCare is the first and largest provider of healthcare in Montgomery County Maryland. The not-for-profit system with nearly 1950 physicians and medical providers is home to five acute care hospitals and more than 423540 outpatient visits. Its hospitals are Adventist HealthCare Shady Grove Medical Center (Rockville) White Oak Medical Center (Silver Spring) Fort Washington Medical Center (Fort Washington) Germantown Emergency Center and Adventist Rehabilitation (Rockville). Among its specialized medical services include heart and vascular car mental health care pregnancy care and birth and radiology and diagnostic imaging. Adventist HealthCare which is affiliated with the Seventh-day Adventist Church has been in operation since 1907.

	Annual Growth	12/16	12/17	12/18	12/19	12/20
Sales ($ mil.)	10.5%	–	723.2	820.6	862.5	974.9
Net income ($ mil.)	9.8%	–	31.9	21.4	32.8	42.1
Market value ($ mil.)	–	–	–	–	–	–
Employees	–	–	–	–	–	5,236

ADVENTRX PHARMACEUTICALS INC.

6725 Mesa Ridge Rd. Ste. 100
San Diego CA 92121
Phone: 858-552-0866
Fax: 858-552-0876
Web: www.adventrx.com

NYSE AMEX: ANX
CEO: Matthew Pauls
CFO: David Lowrance
HR: –
FYE: December 31
Type: Public

Mast Therapeutics (formerly ADVENTRX Pharmaceuticals) steers its R&D ship towards investigational drug treatments for genetic disease and cancer. The company is focused on developing a late-stage treatment for sickle-cell disease patients. The drug aims to reduce tissue and organ damage by repairing microvascular function and is being explored as a treatment for other inflammatory and circulatory disorders. The company also has some candidates in development to treat cancer. To reflect its focus on its MAST (molecular adhesion and sealant technology) platform the company changed its name to Mast Therapeutics in 2013.

ADVENTURELAND PARK

305 34th NW
Altoona IA 50009
Phone: 515-266-2121
Fax: 515-266-9831
Web: www.adventureland-usa.com

CEO: –
CFO: –
HR: –
FYE: December 31
Type: Private

Adventureland is indeed a land within itself. The 180-acre family resort boasts an amusement park with more than 100 attractions (Adventureland Park) an inn (Adventureland Inn) and a full-service campground (Adventureland Campground). Rides range from roller coasters to kiddie-sized fun and shows include live music magic and musicals. The Adventureland Inn features a tropical themed pool and free shuttle service to and from the amusement park. Adventureland Campground offers its own pool along with RV and tent camping spots. The company opened a new water area Adventure Island in 2008. Former CEO John Krantz founded Adventureland in 1974. Krantz died in 2006.

ADVISORY BOARD COMPANY (THE)

2445 M Street N.W.
Washington, DC 20037
Phone: 202 266-5600
Fax: –
Web: www.advisory.com

NMS: ABCO
CEO: Robert W Musslewhite
CFO: –
HR: –
FYE: December 31
Type: Public

The Advisory Board Company specializes in providing best practices consulting to member-clients in the health care and education industries. Members include some 4500 hospitals pharmaceutical and insurance companies universities and related organizations. The Advisory Board offers more than 60 programs across three key areas: best practices research software tools and management and advisory services. Members buy subscriptions to its programs and participate in research efforts. Programs typically include research studies seminars customized reports and decision-support tools. The firm was founded in 1979 as the Research Council of Washington.

	Annual Growth	03/12	03/13	03/14*	12/14	12/15
Sales ($ mil.)	27.5%	370.3	450.8	520.6	436.2	768.3
Net income ($ mil.)	–	25.3	22.1	24.6	4.6	(119.0)
Market value ($ mil.)	(17.6%)	3,684.2	2,183.4	2,671.0	2,036.2	2,062.4
Employees	23.7%	1,850	2,400	2,800	3,100	3,500

*Fiscal year change

ADVIZEX TECHNOLOGIES LLC

6480 Rockside Woods Blvd. South Ste. 190
Independence OH 44131
Phone: 216-901-1818
Fax: 216-901-1447
Web: www.advizex.com

CEO: Fred Traversi
CFO: Mark Woelke
HR: –
FYE: December 31
Type: Private

AdvizeX Technologies marks the spot where hardware meets IT. The value-added reseller provides information technology (IT) products including servers enterprise storage systems workstations and database applications. It works with such vendors as EMC Hewlett-Packard Cisco Systems Microsoft Oracle and VMware. The company's services range from implementation and support to business process consulting and performance management. AdvizeX serves clients in banking and financial services education government health care manufacturing and retail sectors. Its offices are located primarily in the Midwest and East Coast regions of the US.

ADVOCATE HEALTH AND HOSPITALS CORPORATION

1775 DEMPSTER ST
PARK RIDGE, IL 600681143
Phone: 847-723-6610
Fax: –
Web: www.care.advocatehealth.com

CEO: –
CFO: –
HR: –
FYE: December 31
Type: Private

Advocate Lutheran General Hospital also known simply as Lutheran General provides acute and long-term medical and surgical care to the residents of Park Ridge Illinois and the surrounding northern suburban Chicago area. As one of the largest hospitals in the region Lutheran General boasts nearly 640 beds and a Level I trauma center. Its operations also include a complete children's hospital and pediatric critical care center. Lutheran General serves as a teaching hospital and its specialized programs include oncology cardiology women's health emergency medicine and hospice care. Lutheran General is part of the Advocate Health Care network.

	Annual Growth	12/13	12/14	12/15	12/16	12/17
Sales ($ mil.)	2.1%	–	741.8	752.1	785.3	790.5
Net income ($ mil.)	(9.6%)	–	107.4	104.8	118.4	79.3
Market value ($ mil.)	–	–	–	–	–	–
Employees	–	–	–	–	–	4,818

AEA INVESTORS LP

65 E. 55th St.
New York NY 10022
Phone: 212-644-5900
Fax: 212-888-1459
Web: www.aeainvestors.com

CEO: John Garcia
CFO: –
HR: –
FYE: December 31
Type: Private

AEA Investors is in business to make its group of rich investors even richer by buying midsized companies improving their operations and eventually selling them at a profit if all goes to plan. With an exclusive club-like reputation the company has interests in some two dozen firms in the consumer products specialty chemicals and industrial sectors in the US Asia and Europe. It seeks out established enterprises with strong management and competitive position. Holdings include roofing products manufacturer Henry Company and industrial insulation maker Unifrax.

AEARO TECHNOLOGIES LLC

5457 W. 79th St.
Indianapolis IN 46268
Phone: 317-692-6666
Fax: 317-692-6772
Web: www.aearo.com

CEO: –
CFO: –
HR: –
FYE: December 31
Type: Subsidiary

When the sparks fly it helps to be under the aegis of Aearo Technologies. The company manufactures and sells a slew of personal protection and energy-absorbing equipment to the do-it-yourself retail market in more than 70 countries. Sold under brand names such as AOSafety E-A-R Peltor and SafeWaze its products include earplugs goggles face shields respirators hard hats safety clothing first-aid kits and communication headsets. Aearo also supplies safety prescription eyewear and makes energy-absorbing foams that control noise vibration and shock. The company operates as part of 3M Company's Safety Security and Protection Services business segment.

AECOM

13355 Noel Road
Dallas, TX 75240
Phone: 972 788-1000
Fax: –
Web: www.aecom.com

NYS: ACM
CEO: W. Troy Rudd
CFO: Gaurav Kapoor
HR: –
FYE: September 30
Type: Public

AECOM is one of the world's top engineering and design groups. The company provides planning consulting architectural and engineering design services for civil and infrastructure construction to public and private clients. The company also offers other services including logistics and consulting in a range of end markets that include transportation facilities environmental energy water and government. Some of AECOM's major projects include World Trade Center Port of Los Angeles Waterfront Mercedes Benz Stadium Golden 1 Center and Warner Bros. World Abu Dhabi. AECOM generates 40% of sales in the Americas region.

	Annual Growth	09/17	09/18	09/19	09/20	09/21
Sales ($ mil.)	(7.5%)	18,203.4	20,155.5	20,173.3	13,240.0	13,340.9
Net income ($ mil.)	(15.5%)	339.4	136.5	(261.1)	(186.4)	173.2
Market value ($ mil.)	14.4%	5,270.0	4,675.9	5,377.4	5,990.2	9,041.1
Employees	(12.5%)	87,000	87,000	86,000	54,000	51,000

AEGERION PHARMACEUTICALS INC

One Main Street, Suite 800
Cambridge, MA 02142
Phone: 617 500-7867
Fax: –
Web: www.aegerion.com

NMS: AEGR
CEO: Joe Wiley
CFO: Gregory Perry
HR: –
FYE: December 31
Type: Public

Bad cholesterol beware! Aegerion Pharmaceuticals is hot on your trail. The biopharmaceutical company develops cholesterol-lowering drugs for the treatment of cardiovascular and metabolic disease specifically targeting elevated LDL (low-density lipoprotein also known as "bad" cholesterol) levels. Aegerion's first approved drug is Juxtapid (lomitapide branded Lojuxta in Europe) a protein inhibitor that blocks cholesterol production in the liver and intestine. The company is working on getting Juxtapid an oral once-daily medication approved in Japan and for children and teens. Aegerion also markets Myalept a treatment for leptin deficiency.

	Annual Growth	12/10	12/11	12/12	12/13	12/14
Sales ($ mil.)	226.2%	–	–	–	48.5	158.4
Net income ($ mil.)	–	(14.3)	(39.5)	(62.3)	(63.4)	(39.4)
Market value ($ mil.)	10.3%	403.3	476.5	722.4	2,019.9	596.1
Employees	107.2%	16	33	98	217	295

AEGERION PHARMACEUTICALS INC.

101 Main St. Ste. 1850
Cambridge MA 02142
Phone: 617-500-7867
Fax: 908-541-1155
Web: www.aegerion.com

NASDAQ: AEGR
CEO: Joe Wiley
CFO: Gregory Perry
HR: –
FYE: December 31
Type: Public

Bad cholesterol beware! Aegerion Pharmaceuticals is hot on your trail. The biopharmaceutical company develops cholesterol-lowering drugs for the treatment of cardiovascular and metabolic disease specifically targeting elevated LDL (low-density lipoprotein also known as "bad" cholesterol) levels. Cutting LDL levels may add years to patients' lives and reduce the risk of cardiovascular events. Aegerion's lead development candidates are protein inhibitors that aim to block cholesterol production in the liver and intestine. The company filed to go public (for the second time) in 2010. It began trading late in the year after raising about $42 million through its IPO.

AEGION CORP

17988 Edison Avenue
Chesterfield, MO 63005-1195
Phone: 636 530-8000
Fax: –
Web: www.aegion.com

NMS: AEGN
CEO: –
CFO: –
HR: –
FYE: December 31
Type: Public

Aegion owns a legion of companies that aim to rehabilitate and strengthen the world's pipeline infrastructure primarily for the wastewater water energy mining and refining industries. The company's flagship product ? Insituform CIPP ? utilizes a trenchless seamless cure-in-place method which places a pipe within a pipe to minimize excavation activities. Other products for pipe rehabilitation are a patented Fusible PVC pipe its Tyfo reinforced polymer system for larger diameter pipes and pipe coatings for corrosion protection. Through its Energy Services segment Aegion offers maintenance and turnaround services for oil and gas facilities. Aegion operates in over 90 countries across six continents although about 75% of total revenue comes from the US.

	Annual Growth	12/15	12/16	12/17	12/18	12/19
Sales ($ mil.)	(2.3%)	1,333.6	1,221.9	1,359.0	1,333.6	1,213.9
Net income ($ mil.)	–	(8.1)	29.5	(69.1)	2.9	(20.9)
Market value ($ mil.)	3.7%	593.1	728.0	781.1	501.3	687.1
Employees	(5.7%)	6,200	5,150	5,820	5,350	4,900

AEGIS AEROSPACE, INC.

18050 SATURN LN STE 300
HOUSTON, TX 770584502
Phone: 281-283-6200
Fax: –
Web: www.meitechinc.com

CEO: David Cazes
CFO: –
HR: –
FYE: December 31
Type: Private

MEI Technologies helps companies with high aspirations. The engineering and IT services firm serves government agencies such as NASA and the Department of Defense with cyber services space access engineering services and solutions and simulation and modeling. Other high-tech services include launch vehicle and shuttle payload integration and operations mission safety satellite development and 3D food printing. Furthermore the company currently has about 35 free flying satellites and more than 120 payloads flown. MEI Technologies was founded in 1992 as Muñiz Engineering Inc. (MEI) by former CEO Edelmiro Muñiz. MEI Technologies also serves commercial sectors across seven states.

	Annual Growth	12/05	12/06	12/07	12/08	12/12
Sales ($ mil.)	3.4%	–	–	116.1	118.9	137.2
Net income ($ mil.)	15.4%	–	–	2.3	(0.9)	4.8
Market value ($ mil.)	–	–	–	–	–	–
Employees	–	–	–	–	–	721

AEGIS COMMUNICATIONS GROUP INC.

8201 Ridgepoint Dr.
Irving TX 75063
Phone: 972-830-1800
Fax: 972-868-0220
Web: www.aegiscomgroup.com

CEO: –
CFO: –
HR: –
FYE: December 31
Type: Subsidiary

This is not a pre-recorded message. Aegis Communications Group (which does business as Aegis BPO) provides outsourced telemarketing and customer care services through about 50 facilities in Africa the Asia/Pacific Costa Rica India and the US. Through its operations (which includes Aegis PeopleSupport) it handles both inbound and outbound calling services order provisioning and multilingual communications programs. Besides teleservices Aegis offers online customer services such as e-mail responses real-time chat and data collection. Major clients have included AT&T Qwest Communications and Western Union. India-based conglomerate Essar Group owns Aegis which was established in 1985.

AEGON USA LLC

4333 Edgewood Rd. NE
Cedar Rapids IA 52499
Phone: 319-398-8511
Fax: 319-369-2209
Web: www.aegonins.com

CEO: –
CFO: –
HR: –
FYE: December 31
Type: Subsidiary

If AEGON USA were an Argonaut its quest would be to conquer the US insurance market. The company a subsidiary of Dutch insurance giant AEGON that operates under the AEGON Americas moniker provides life insurance and accident and health insurance (such as cancer and long-term care policies) to some 30 million customers throughout the US. Its products include traditional whole life universal life variable universal life and term life insurance for individuals and groups. AEGON USA also offers annuity and investment products such as mutual funds as well as asset management services. Subsidiaries include Monumental Life Transamerica Life and Western Reserve Life.

AEHR TEST SYSTEMS

NAS: AEHR

400 Kato Terrace
Fremont, CA 94539
Phone: 510 623-9400
Fax: 510 623-9450
Web: www.aehr.com

CEO: Gayn Erickson
CFO: Kenneth Spink
HR: –
FYE: May 31
Type: Public

Aehr Test Systems' products don't test air but rather silicon. Aehr (pronounced "air") makes gear that tests logic and memory semiconductors to weed out defective devices. Its burn-in systems test chips' reliability under stress by exposing them to high temperatures and voltages. Aehr also makes massively parallel test systems for handling thousands of chips simultaneously die carriers for testing unpackaged chips custom-designed fixtures for test equipment and other memory test products. Top customers include Spansion (about 80% of sales) and Texas Instruments. Aehr gets more than one-third of its business outside the US.

	Annual Growth	05/17	05/18	05/19	05/20	05/21
Sales ($ mil.)	(3.2%)	18.9	29.6	21.1	22.3	16.6
Net income ($ mil.)	–	(5.7)	0.5	(5.2)	(2.8)	(2.0)
Market value ($ mil.)	(16.3%)	108.7	61.7	41.5	39.1	53.4
Employees	0.0%	79	86	79	71	79

AEOLUS PHARMACEUTICALS INC

NBB: AOLS

26361 Crown Valley Parkway, Suite 150
Mission Viejo, CA 92691
Phone: 949 481-9825
Fax: –
Web: www.aolsrx.com

CEO: John McManus
CFO: David Cavalier
HR: –
FYE: September 30
Type: Public

Aeolus Pharmaceuticals wants to put an end to free radicals' free-wheeling cell-damaging fun. The development-stage company is focusing its attention on developing catalytic antioxidant drugs which can neutralize free radicals. Aeolus' drug candidates could battle amyotrophic lateral sclerosis (ALS better known as Lou Gehrig's disease) stroke Parkinson's disease and other neurodegenerative conditions. The company is also developing antioxidant drugs to treat respiratory conditions and protect healthy tissue from cancer-fighting radiation. Chairman David Cavalier controls about half of the company through investment company XMark Asset Management.

	Annual Growth	09/12	09/13	09/14	09/15	09/16
Sales ($ mil.)	(27.0%)	7.3	3.9	9.6	3.1	2.1
Net income ($ mil.)	–	1.7	(3.2)	(0.1)	(2.6)	(3.6)
Market value ($ mil.)	(15.4%)	56.3	42.6	38.0	36.6	28.9
Employees	(5.4%)	5	4	4	4	4

AEON GLOBAL HEALTH CORP

NBB: AGHC

2225 Centennial Drive
Gainesville, GA 30504
Phone: 888 661-0225
Fax: –
Web: www.authentidate.com

CEO: Hanif A Roshan
CFO: –
HR: Julia Anglin
FYE: June 30
Type: Public

AuthentiDate Holding wants to leave its technological stamp of approval on the US health care industry. Through its subsidiaries the company provides secure workflow management software and remote patient monitoring technology to health care companies and government entities. Its hosted Inscrybe platform facilitates administrative functions like electronic signing identity management and content authentication while its ExpressMD Solutions subsidiary makes in-home patient vital signs monitoring systems. Other offerings include Inscrybe Office which extends its Web-based workflow management software to personal and business customers. Major customers include the US Department of Veterans Affairs.

	Annual Growth	06/15	06/16	06/17	06/18	06/19
Sales ($ mil.)	36.8%	3.7	34.6	20.2	16.3	12.9
Net income ($ mil.)	–	(9.7)	5.3	(32.1)	(8.0)	(8.0)
Market value ($ mil.)	11.2%	1.9	30.2	15.9	9.4	2.9
Employees	20.1%	25	76	137	108	52

AERO SYSTEMS ENGINEERING INC.

358 E. Fillmore Ave.
St. Paul MN 55107-1289
Phone: 651-227-7515
Fax: 651-227-0519
Web: www.aerosysengr.com

CEO: Thomas G Moll
CFO: Steven R Hedberg
HR: –
FYE: December 31
Type: Private

But will it fly? Aero Systems Engineering (AeroSystems) answers that question by designing and building engine and aerodynamic testing components and facilities. Besides its turbine and wind-tunnel facilities AeroSystems makes test equipment for turbine engines and aircraft control and instrumentation systems. Customers can buy the equipment or test at the company's Minnesota lab. AeroSystems also offers design installation and engineering support as well as acoustic measurement processes to measure noise levels; it serves OEMs MROs (maintenance repair and overhaul) the military and researchers. Investment firms Tonka Bay Equity Partners and Centerfield Capital Partners own AeroSystems.

AEROGROUP INTERNATIONAL LLC

201 Meadow Rd.
Edison NJ 08817
Phone: 732-985-6900
Fax: 732-985-3697
Web: www.aerosoles.com

CEO: Denise Incandela
CFO: –
HR: –
FYE: June 30
Type: Private

Aerogroup International wants ladies to feel like they're walking on air or at least feel like buying a pair of its Aerosoles. The company designs and peddles women's footwear sold under the Aerosoles What's What A2 Aerology Sole A and Flexation brands. Aerogroup's shoes are sold in more than 100 Aerosoles stores in the US located mostly in New York and California and abroad. The shoe maker also sells shoes by catalog website and through thousands of department and specialty stores (such as Kohl's Macy's and Boscov's). Originally a division of Kenneth Cole CEO Jules Schneider got together a group of investors and took the business private in 1987.

AEROCENTURY CORP.

3000 El Camino Real, Bldg. 4, Suite 200
Palo Alto, CA 94306
Phone: 650 340-1888
Fax: –
Web: www.aerocentury.com

ASE: ACY
CEO: Yucheng Hu
CFO: Qin Wang
HR: –
FYE: December 31
Type: Public

With a high-flyin' inventory AeroCentury leases used turboprop aircraft and engines to domestic and foreign regional airlines and other commercial customers. The company buys equipment from an airline and then either leases it back to the seller buys assets already under lease and assumes the obligations of the seller or makes a purchase and then immediately enters into a new lease with a third-party lessee (when it has a customer committed to a lease). Typically lessees are responsible for any maintenance costs. AeroCentury owns over 40 aircraft mainly deHavilland and Fokker models. Almost 90% of the company's lease revenues come from airlines headquartered outside the US.

	Annual Growth	12/16	12/17	12/18	12/19	12/20
Sales ($ mil.)	(13.4%)	28.7	35.6	27.1	43.6	16.2
Net income ($ mil.)	–	1.2	7.4	(8.1)	(16.7)	(42.2)
Market value ($ mil.)	3.3%	14.6	23.6	14.8	7.0	16.6
Employees	–	–	–	12	10	9

AEROGROW INTERNATIONAL, INC.

5405 Spine Road
Boulder, CO 80301
Phone: 303 444-7755
Fax: –
Web: www.aerogrow.com

NBB: AERO
CEO: J Michael Wolfe
CFO: –
HR: –
FYE: March 31
Type: Public

No time or space for a garden? AeroGrow may be able to cultivate your inner indoor gardener self. The company develops and manufactures a line of indoor gardening products and seed kits for both amateur and experienced gardeners. Using a self-contained light source and hydroponics technologies (water in place of soil) AeroGrow's products are capable of growing a variety of vegetables herbs and flowers. It offers more than 15 garden models and 50 seed kits which are sold in the US through retailers such as Target Kohl's and Bed Bath & Beyond as well as through its own website. Aerogrow was founded in 2002 by former CEO and chairman Michael Bissonnette.

	Annual Growth	03/16	03/17	03/18	03/19	03/20
Sales ($ mil.)	18.9%	19.6	23.6	32.3	34.4	39.2
Net income ($ mil.)	–	(0.6)	(2.6)	(0.4)	(0.3)	0.1
Market value ($ mil.)	(12.5%)	76.6	102.6	80.0	53.9	45.0
Employees	7.5%	30	30	34	40	40

AEROFLEX HOLDING CORP.

35 South Service Road, P.O. Box 6022
Plainview, NY 11803-0622
Phone: 516 694-6700
Fax: –
Web: www.aeroflex.com

NYS: ARX
CEO: Leonard Borow
CFO: John Adamovich Jr
HR: –
FYE: June 30
Type: Public

Aeroflex flexes its high-tech muscle with aerospace and communications components. Its Aeroflex Microelectronic Solutions (AMS) division offers integrated circuits radio-frequency (RF) components and microwave assemblies for use in military aircraft satellites and wireless communications networks. The company also provides test and measurement equipment used in avionics military and mobile radio applications through its Aeroflex Test Solutions (ATS) unit. Customers include the US government and such blue-chip clients as Boeing Cisco Alcatel Lucent and Lockheed Martin. It generates most of its sales in the US.

	Annual Growth	06/09	06/10	06/11	06/12	06/13
Sales ($ mil.)	1.9%	599.3	655.0	729.4	673.0	647.1
Net income ($ mil.)	–	(76.7)	(12.3)	(34.7)	(53.6)	(104.2)
Market value ($ mil.)	(34.1%)	–	–	1,541.6	513.9	670.1
Employees	(2.9%)	–	2,950	2,900	2,800	2,700

AEROJET ROCKETDYNE HOLDINGS INC

222 N. Pacific Coast Highway, Suite 500
El Segundo, CA 90245
Phone: 310 252-8100
Fax: –
Web: www.aerojetrocketdyne.com

NYS: AJRD
CEO: Eileen Drake
CFO: Daniel Boehle
HR: –
FYE: December 31
Type: Public

Aerojet Rocketdyne is a world-recognized technology-based engineering and manufacturing company that develops and produces specialized power and propulsion systems as well as armament systems. These propulsion systems are used in missile defense interceptors tactical missiles and hypersonic systems. Principal customers include the US Department of Defense and NASA. The company also has a much smaller business segment that deals in real estate. In late 2020 Aerojet Rocketdyne announced that it has agreed to acquire by Lockheed Martin for $5 billion.

	Annual Growth	12/17	12/18	12/19	12/20	12/21
Sales ($ mil.)	3.9%	1,877.2	1,895.9	1,981.5	2,072.5	2,188.0
Net income ($ mil.)	–	(9.2)	137.3	141.0	137.7	143.7
Market value ($ mil.)	10.6%	2,499.1	2,821.9	3,657.4	4,233.3	3,745.5
Employees	(0.8%)	5,157	5,004	4,814	4,969	5,000

AEROJET-GENERAL CORPORATION

2001 Aerojet Rd.
Rancho Cordova CA 95742-6418
Phone: 916-355-4000
Fax: 916-351-8667
Web: www.aerojet.com

CEO: Eileen Drake
CFO: Paul Landstrom
HR: –
FYE: November 30
Type: Subsidiary

They say it doesn't take a rocket scientist to figure this out. But in the case of Aerojet-General it actually did. Founded by a professor and his colleagues at Caltech the company today develops and manufactures propulsion systems for defense and space applications including tactical missiles and space launch vehicles. It is the largest provider of propulsion systems in the US serving the likes of the US Army the Missile Defense Agency (MDA) and NASA. Aerojet in fact is the only domestic supplier of all four propulsion types: solid liquid air-breathing and electric. The company is the primary operating subsidiary of GenCorp.

AEROKOOL AVIATION CORPORATION

1495 SE 10TH AVE
HIALEAH, FL 330105916
Phone: 305-887-6912
Fax: –
Web: www.aerokool.com

CEO: Jon Silva
CFO: Steven Favazza
HR: –
FYE: December 31
Type: Private

Aero Kool makes sure aircraft pilots are not left out in the cold. The aircraft maintenance company which has its own engineering and manufacturing departments, provides airframe and engine accessory repair and overhaul services. Aero Kool works on a wide range of equipment including air cycle machines air starters fuel heaters heat exchangers oil tanks and coolers refrigeration packs valves (both electro mechanical and electro pneumatic) and water separators. The company also sells airframe and engine accessories and designs and manufactures replacement parts. Aero Kool, was founded in 1959.

	Annual Growth	12/04	12/05	12/06	12/08	12/09
Sales ($ mil.)	(75.7%)	–	–	642.6	9.5	9.2
Net income ($ mil.)	1335.8%	–	–	0.0	0.4	0.3
Market value ($ mil.)	–	–	–	–	–	–
Employees	–	–	–	–	–	50

AERONET, INC.

42 CORP PARK STE 100
IRVINE, CA 92606
Phone: 949-474-3000
Fax: –
Web: www.aeronet.com

CEO: Anthony Pereira
CFO: –
HR: –
FYE: April 30
Type: Private

Aeronet is casting a wide net for its logistics business. The company provides a full range of logistics services both in the US and overseas. Offerings include time-guaranteed domestic freight delivery (ranging from same-day to five-day) air and ocean freight forwarding customs brokerage shipment tracking supply chain management and warehousing and distribution. As a freight forwarder the company purchases transportation capacity from carriers and resells it to customers. Aeronet maintains 10 offices near major trade gateways throughout the US and operates through agents in other regions.

	Annual Growth	04/14	04/15	04/16	04/17	04/18
Sales ($ mil.)	6.1%	–	69.0	62.0	64.5	82.4
Net income ($ mil.)	(29.1%)	–	0.7	0.5	0.6	0.2
Market value ($ mil.)	–	–	–	–	–	–
Employees	–	–	–	–	–	140

AEROTEK, INC.

7301 PARKWAY DR
HANOVER, MD 210761159
Phone: 410-694-5100
Fax: –
Web: www.aerotek.com

CEO: –
CFO: Thomas B Kelly
HR: –
FYE: December 31
Type: Private

Aerotek a unit of staffing powerhouse Allegis Group offers commercial and technical staffing services throughout North America Europe and Asia Pacific. Through several divisions Aerotek staffs workers such as engineers mechanics scientists and technical professionals as well as administrative staff members general laborers and tradespeople. The company also provides training and support services. Along with aerospace auto and engineering companies Aerotek's clients include companies from the construction energy manufacturing health care and finance industries.

	Annual Growth	12/16	12/17	12/18	12/19	12/20
Sales ($ mil.)	(1.2%)	–	6,070.1	6,586.3	6,662.1	5,859.1
Net income ($ mil.)	–	–	0.0	0.0	0.0	0.0
Market value ($ mil.)	–	–	–	–	–	–
Employees	–	–	–	–	–	4,200

AEROVIRONMENT, INC.

241 18th Street, Suite 415
Arlington, VA 22202
Phone: 805 520-8350
Fax: –
Web: www.avinc.com

NMS: AVAV
CEO: Wahid Nawabi
CFO: Kevin Mcdonnell
HR: –
FYE: April 30
Type: Public

AeroVironment (AV) designs develops produces delivers and supports a technologically-advanced portfolio of intelligent multi-domain robotic systems and related services for government agencies and businesses. The company designs and manufactures a line of small unmanned aircraft systems (UAS) tactical missile systems (TMS) unmanned ground vehicles (UGV) and related services primarily for the Department of Defense (DoD). The business addresses the increasing economic and security value of distributed network-centric intelligence surveillance and reconnaissance (ISR) communications remote sensing and effects delivery with innovative UAS and tactical missile system solutions. AeroVironment was founded in 1971. The company generates around 60% of total sales domestically.

	Annual Growth	04/17	04/18	04/19	04/20	04/21
Sales ($ mil.)	10.5%	264.9	271.1	314.3	367.3	394.9
Net income ($ mil.)	16.9%	12.5	20.1	47.4	41.1	23.3
Market value ($ mil.)	40.2%	707.9	1,350.4	1,698.7	1,493.1	2,734.7
Employees	15.5%	661	697	699	828	1,177

AERUS LLC

5956 Sherry Ln.
Dallas TX 75225
Phone: 214-378-4000
Fax: 214-378-4053
Web: www.aerusonline.com

CEO: Joseph Urso
CFO: Bret Holland
HR: Kathy Greene
FYE: December 31
Type: Private

A pioneer in the vacuum business Aerus has been dirt's worst enemy since 1924. The company manufactures and sells vacuums air and water purification systems cleansers and allergy-control products. Its brands include Guardian Lux and Epic. Aerus' products are marketed through in-home demonstrations more than 500 Aerus sales centers in the US and Canada and online. The company formerly named Electrolux sold the brand's North American rights to AB Electrolux in 2000. Aerus is a subsidiary of Aerus Holdings. It is owned by investment firm Engles Urso Follmer Capital.

AES CORP
NYS: AES

4300 Wilson Boulevard
Arlington, VA 22203
Phone: 703 522-1315
Fax: 703 528-4510
Web: www.aes.com

CEO: Andres R Gluski
CFO: Stephen Coughlin
HR: –
FYE: December 31
Type: Public

The AES Corp. is a world power producer. The US-based company has about 110 generation facilities in nearly 15 countries throughout the Americas(NorthCentral-South) Asia and Europe. AES sells electricity to utilities industrial users and intermediaries. The company also sells power directly to end-users such as homes and businesses mainly in Latin America and the US. Non regulated generates the biggest share of electricity while regulated generate about 30%. The US supplies more than 30% of AES' revenue. Overall AES provides power to about 2.5 million customers.

	Annual Growth	12/16	12/17	12/18	12/19	12/20
Sales ($ mil.)	(8.2%)	13,586.0	10,530.0	10,736.0	10,189.0	9,660.0
Net income ($ mil.)	–	(1,130.0)	(1,161.0)	1,203.0	303.0	46.0
Market value ($ mil.)	19.3%	7,731.6	7,206.0	9,621.3	13,240.9	15,636.2
Employees	(18.9%)	19,000	10,500	9,000	–	8,200

AETEA INFORMATION TECHNOLOGY INC.

1445 RES BLVD STE 300
ROCKVILLE, MD 20850
Phone: 301-721-4200
Fax: –
Web: www.aetea.com

CEO: –
CFO: Charles V Brown III
HR: –
FYE: December 31
Type: Private

AETEA knows information technology backward and forward. The company provides systems integration enterprise resource management software consulting and other IT services. It also offers IT staffing services to a variety of customers ranging from large global enterprises to small and midsized companies. Industries served include financial services pharmaceuticals and health care. AETEA also has a unit devoted to public sector clients which targets the US Department of Defense as well as civilian agencies. Clients have included ADP BNP Paribas and Bristol-Myers Squibb. The company operates from offices in Maryland New Jersey New York Pennsylvania and Washington. AETEA was established in 1979.

	Annual Growth	12/02	12/03	12/04	12/06	12/07
Sales ($ mil.)	(2.6%)	–	–	74.2	73.8	68.5
Net income ($ mil.)	(20.2%)	–	–	7.7	0.6	3.9
Market value ($ mil.)	–	–	–	–	–	–
Employees	–	–	–	–	–	350

AETERNA ZENTARIS INC
NAS: AEZS

315 Sigma Drive
Summerville, SC 29486
Phone: 843 900-3223
Fax: –
Web: www.aezsinc.com

CEO: Klaus Paulini
CFO: Giuliano La Fratta
HR: –
FYE: December 31
Type: Public

Æterna Zentaris formerly Æterna Laboratories knows seriously ill patients can't wait an eternity for new drugs so the firm is working to take lead drug candidates through trials and to approvals as quickly as possible. The company's pipeline got a boost from the purchase of Zentaris which has drugs on the market and a dozen others in development for the treatment of cancer and endocrinology disorders. The firm's flagship drug Centrotide is an endocrine therapy used for in vitro fertilization. It is approved in 80 countries and is marketed worldwide (except for Japan) by Merck Serono; Shionogi and Nippon Kayaku market the drug in Japan.

	Annual Growth	12/16	12/17	12/18	12/19	12/20
Sales ($ mil.)	41.5%	0.9	0.9	26.9	0.5	3.7
Net income ($ mil.)	–	(25.0)	(16.8)	4.2	(6.0)	(5.1)
Market value ($ mil.)	(41.3%)	225.6	147.9	184.3	57.0	26.7
Employees	(30.4%)	47	34	22	11	11

AETNA INC.
NYS: AET

151 Farmington Avenue
Hartford, CT 06156
Phone: 860 273-0123
Fax: –
Web: www.aetna.com

CEO: Mark Bertolini
CFO: –
HR: –
FYE: December 31
Type: Public

Life death health or injury — Aetna's got an insurance policy to cover it. The company one of the largest health insurers in the US also offers life and disability insurance as well as retirement savings products. Its health care division offers HMO PPO point of service (POS) health savings account (HSA) and traditional indemnity coverage along with dental vision behavioral health and Medicare and Medicaid plans to groups and individuals. The health care segment covers some 23 million medical members. Aetna's group insurance segment (which it is selling to The Hartford) sells life and disability insurance nationwide and its large case pensions segment offers pensions annuities and other retirement savings products. In what would be the largest health insurance deal in history retail pharmacy giant CVS plans to buy Aetna for $69 billion.

	Annual Growth	12/12	12/13	12/14	12/15	12/16
Assets ($ mil.)	13.6%	41,494.5	49,871.8	53,402.1	53,424.1	69,146.0
Net income ($ mil.)	8.2%	1,657.9	1,913.6	2,040.8	2,390.2	2,271.0
Market value ($ mil.)	27.9%	16,287.2	24,123.1	31,241.5	38,025.8	43,614.3
Employees	9.1%	35,000	48,600	48,800	50,100	49,500

AFFILIATED COMPUTER SERVICES INC.

2828 N. Haskell Ave.
Dallas TX 75204
Phone: 214-841-6111
Fax: 732-205-8237
Web: www.mack-cali.com

CEO: Robert Zapfel
CFO: Brian Walsh
HR: –
FYE: December 31
Type: Subsidiary

Affiliated Computer Services (ACS) handles jobs its clients would rather hand off. The company provides business process outsourcing (BPO) services for commercial enterprises and government agencies focusing on markets such as communications health care and transportation. As an outsourcer ACS handles functions such as administration including health care claims processing; finance and accounting; human resources; payment processing; sales marketing and customer care call centers; and supply chain management. BPO services account for most of the company's sales. ACS also offers information technology and systems integration services. In early 2010 ACS was acquired by printing equipment giant Xerox.

AFFILIATED FOODS MIDWEST COOPERATIVE, INC.

1301 W OMAHA AVE
NORFOLK, NE 687015872
Phone: 402-371-0555
Fax: –
Web: www.afmidwest.com

CEO: –
CFO: –
HR: –
FYE: June 26
Type: Private

Affiliated Foods Midwest Cooperative is a wholesale food distribution cooperative that supplies more than 800 independent grocers in some 15 states in the Midwest. From its handful of distribution centers in Kansas Nebraska and Wisconsin the co-op distributes fresh produce meats deli items baked goods dairy products and frozen foods as well as general merchandise and equipment. It distributes goods under the Shurfine brand (from Topco Associates) and IGA labels. Additionally Affiliated Foods Midwest provides marketing merchandising and warehousing support services for its members. The cooperative was formed in 1931 to make wholesale purchases for a group of retailers in Nebraska.

	Annual Growth	06/11	06/12	06/13	06/14	06/15
Sales ($ mil.)	0.9%	–	1,486.3	1,391.7	1,477.5	1,527.3
Net income ($ mil.)	(19.5%)	–	2.8	2.7	2.8	1.5
Market value ($ mil.)	–	–	–	–	–	–
Employees	–	–	–	–	–	850

AFFILIATED FOODS, INC.

1401 W FARMERS AVE
AMARILLO, TX 791186134
Phone: 806-372-3851
Fax: –
Web: www.afiama.com

CEO: Randy Arceneaux
CFO: Noman Burr
HR: –
FYE: October 03
Type: Private

This company helps keep pantries stocked in the Texas Panhandle and elsewhere. Affiliated Foods is a leading wholesale distribution cooperative that supplies grocery stores and restaurants in about a half a dozen states including Texas New Mexico and Oklahoma. It distributes fresh produce meat and non-food products as well as dairy products and beverages through its Plains Dairy unit. Its Tri State Baking Company supplies bread and other baked goods. In addition Affiliated Foods owns a stake in private-label products supplier Western Family Foods. The company was founded in 1946 as Panhandle Associated Grocers which merged with South Plains Associated Grocers to form Affiliated Foods in 1968.

	Annual Growth	10/15	10/16*	09/17	09/19*	10/20
Sales ($ mil.)	2.0%	–	1,440.3	1,421.5	1,450.9	1,556.9
Net income ($ mil.)	21.2%	–	0.7	1.2	2.0	1.6
Market value ($ mil.)	–	–	–	–	–	–
Employees	–	–	–	–	–	1,200

*Fiscal year change

AFFILIATED MANAGERS GROUP INC.   NYS: AMG

777 South Flagler Drive
West Palm Beach, FL 33401
Phone: 800 345-1100
Fax: –
Web: www.amg.com

CEO: Jay Horgen
CFO: Thomas Wojcik
HR: –
FYE: December 31
Type: Public

Affiliated Managers Group Inc. is a leading partner to independent active investment management firms globally. AMG's affiliates manage about $716 billion in assets across a broad range of active return-oriented strategies. Through its affiliates the company provides a comprehensive and diverse range of active return-oriented strategies designed to assist institutional and retail investors as well as high net worth clients. AMG offers centralized capabilities including strategy marketing and distribution and product development. Affiliates currently manage assets for investors in more than 50 countries including all major developed markets. Majority of the company's sales were generated in the US.

	Annual Growth	12/17	12/18	12/19	12/20	12/21
Sales ($ mil.)	1.1%	2,305.0	2,378.4	2,239.6	2,027.5	2,412.4
Net income ($ mil.)	(4.8%)	689.5	243.6	15.7	202.2	565.7
Market value ($ mil.)	(5.4%)	8,251.1	3,917.1	3,406.5	4,088.3	6,613.3
Employees	(2.1%)	4,400	4,450	4,000	3,900	4,050

AFFINIA GROUP HOLDINGS INC.

1101 Technology Dr.
Ann Arbor MI 48108
Phone: 734-827-5400
Fax: 814-278-7286
Web: www.rexenergy.com

CEO: –
CFO: –
HR: –
FYE: December 31
Type: Private

Affinia Group caters to car drivers with a natural affinity for parts. The company is a leading designer manufacturer and distributor of aftermarket vehicular components. The aftermarket comprises a global network of suppliers that sell automotive goods intended to replace a manufacturer's stock parts. Affinia's slew of products — primarily brake filtration and chassis parts — are made for passenger cars; SUVs; light medium and heavy trucks; and off-highway vehicles. Its well-known brand names including AIMCO McQuay-Norris Nakata Raybestos and WIX are sold in 70-plus countries. The Cypress Group and OMERS Administration are Affinia's largest stakeholders. In mid-2010 Affinia filed to go public.

AFFIRMATIVE INSURANCE HOLDINGS INC   NBB: AFFM Q

4450 Sojourn Drive, Suite 500
Addison, TX 75001
Phone: 972 728-6300
Fax: –

CEO: –
CFO: –
HR: –
FYE: December 31
Type: Public

If you've got an iffy driving record or let your insurance lapse can you still get auto coverage? This company answers in the Affirmative. Affirmative Insurance Holdings through its subsidiaries writes nonstandard auto insurance policies — that is coverage for drivers in high-risk categories due to their age driving records and other factors. It sells its policies through about 5300 independent agents in seven southern and mid-western states. Affirmative sold its nearly 200 company-owned retail locations (including A-Affordable Driver's Choice InsureOne and USAgencies stores) in late 2013. Investment firm J.C. Flowers controls more than half of the company.

	Annual Growth	12/10	12/11	12/12	12/13	12/14
Assets ($ mil.)	(18.0%)	745.7	444.8	338.4	386.8	337.7
Net income ($ mil.)	–	(88.9)	(164.2)	(51.9)	30.7	(32.2)
Market value ($ mil.)	(17.5%)	43.1	8.6	2.3	41.2	20.0
Employees	(21.2%)	1,268	1,078	949	522	489

AFFYMAX INC   NBB: AFFY

19200 Stevens Creek Blvd. Suite 240
Cupertino, CA 95014
Phone: 650 812-8700
Fax: –
Web: www.affymax.com

CEO: Jonathan Couchman
CFO: Mark Thompson
HR: –
FYE: December 31
Type: Public

Affymax is training peptides to give red blood cells a pep talk. The biotechnology firm is researching and developing drugs based upon peptides which can help regulate biological processes. Its leading drug candidate Omontys (peginesatide) was approved by the FDA in 2012 as a treatment for anemia due to chronic kidney disease. Affymax believes Omontys which was developed and commercialized through a partnership with Japan's Takeda Pharmaceutical will prove to be cheaper and longer lasting than the EPO stimulants currently used on dialysis patients. However the product was recalled in 2013 due to adverse reactions to the drug.

	Annual Growth	12/09	12/10	12/11	12/12	12/13
Sales ($ mil.)	(67.0%)	114.9	112.5	47.7	94.4	1.4
Net income ($ mil.)	–	(76.5)	(14.1)	(61.4)	(93.4)	(14.4)
Market value ($ mil.)	(57.9%)	927.5	249.3	247.8	711.9	29.2
Employees	(59.1%)	143	140	130	304	4

AFFYMETRIX, INC.

3380 CENTRAL EXPY
SANTA CLARA, CA 950510704
Phone: 408-731-5000
Fax: –
Web: www.thermofisher.com

CEO: –
CFO: –
HR: –
FYE: December 31
Type: Private

Affymetrix microarray solutions are now branded Applied Biosystems and include all necessary components for a microarray experiment from arrays and reagents to instruments and software. Its solutions enable scientists and clinicians to understand underlying disease mechanisms identify biomarkers for personalized medicine create novel molecular diagnostic tests and improve genetic marker-assisted breeding programs in agriculture thereby translating research results into biology for a better world. Its popular products have included Clariom D Assay Axiom Precision Medicine Research Array and CarrierScan Assay. Its key applications have also included Transcriptome Analysis Human Genotyping for Precision Medicine Research Cytogenetics Analysis miRNA Profiling Large-scale Biobank Genotyping and Plant and Animal Genotyping.

	Annual Growth	12/10	12/11	12/12	12/13	12/14
Sales ($ mil.)	8.7%	–	–	295.6	330.4	349.0
Net income ($ mil.)	–	–	–	(10.7)	(16.3)	(3.8)
Market value ($ mil.)	–	–	–	–	–	–
Employees	–	–	–	–	–	1,100

AFLAC INC   NYS: AFL

1932 Wynnton Road
Columbus, GA 31999
Phone: 706 323-3431
Fax: 706 596-3488
Web: www.aflac.com

CEO: Daniel Amos
CFO: J. Todd Daniels
HR: –
FYE: December 31
Type: Public

Aflac sells supplemental health and life insurance products including first sector insurance coverage and third sector insurance coverage for cancer hospitalization and income support in Japan; and cancer accident critical illness and short-term disability insurance in the US. Aflac Japan is the largest insurer in Japan in terms of cancer and medical (third sector insurance products) policies in force. Aflac US is expanding its product offerings to network dental and vision and employer paid group life and disability. Aflac which is marketed through — and is an acronym for — American Family Life Assurance Company sells policies that pay cash benefits to more than 50 million people worldwide.

	Annual Growth	12/17	12/18	12/19	12/20	12/21
Assets ($ mil.)	3.5%	137,217.0	140,406.0	152,768.0	165,086.0	157,542.0
Net income ($ mil.)	(1.6%)	4,604.0	2,920.0	3,304.0	4,778.0	4,325.0
Market value ($ mil.)	(9.7%)	57,244.1	29,711.1	34,497.8	29,000.3	38,078.0
Employees	(13.0%)	11,318	11,390	11,729	6,239	6,492

AG INTERACTIVE INC.

1 American Rd.
Cleveland OH 44144
Phone: 216-889-5000
Fax: 216-889-5371
Web: www.aginteractive.com

CEO: –
CFO: Michael Waxman-Lenz
HR: –
FYE: February 28
Type: Subsidiary

This company has just the thing for those special occasions when an e-mail just won't do. AG Interactive represents the electronic greetings and other digital content of its parent company American Greetings. The subsidiary offers e-cards to nearly 4 million subscribers through a variety of electronic channels including websites Internet portals instant messaging services and mobile devices. AG Interactive's portfolio of e-card websites includes AmericanGreetings.com BlueMountain.com Egreetings.com. In addition the company operates Kiwee.com (graphics animations emoticons text generators) Cardstore.com (custom physical greeting cards) and Webshots.com (photo sharing).

AG MORTGAGE INVESTMENT TRUST INC   NYS: MITT

245 Park Avenue, 26th Floor
New York, NY 10167
Phone: 212 692-2000
Fax: –
Web: www.agmit.com

CEO: David N Roberts
CFO: Anthony Rossiello
HR: –
FYE: December 31
Type: Public

AG Mortgage Investment Trust invests in acquires and manages a diverse portfolio of residential mortgage assets as well as other real estate-related securities and financial assets. Residential mortgage-backed securities backed by US government agencies including Fannie Mae Freddie Mac and Ginnie Mae known as "Agency RMBS" make up more than 50% of the mortgage real estate investment trust's (REIT) portfolio. Credit assets including RMBS not issued or backed by the government account for most of the rest. Formed in 2011 by executives of investment adviser Angelo Gordon looking to profit from a recovery in the US mortgage bond market the mortgage REIT is managed by a subsidiary of Angelo Gordon.

	Annual Growth	12/16	12/17	12/18	12/19	12/20
Assets ($ mil.)	(14.6%)	2,628.6	3,789.3	3,548.9	4,347.8	1,400.0
Net income ($ mil.)	–	63.7	118.6	1.6	92.9	(420.9)
Market value ($ mil.)	(35.6%)	236.3	262.6	220.0	213.0	40.7
Employees	–	–	–	–	–	–

AG PROCESSING INC A COOPERATIVE

12700 W DODGE RD
OMAHA, NE 681546102
Phone: 402-496-7809
Fax: –
Web: www.agp.com

CEO: John Keith Spackler
CFO: Scott Simmelink
HR: –
FYE: August 31
Type: Private

Soy far soy good for Ag Processing (AGP) the largest farmer-owned soybean processor in the world and roughly the fourth-largest soybean processor in the US based on capacity. It purchases and processes more than 5.5 million acres of members' soybeans per year. The farmer-owned cooperative is also a leading supplier of refined vegetable oil in the US. It procures processes markets and transports grains and grain products ranging from human food ingredients to livestock feed to renewable fuels. AGP is owned by about 180 local and regional cooperatives and represents more than 250000 farmers in 15 states throughout the US.

	Annual Growth	08/04	08/05	08/06*	12/10*	08/16
Sales ($ mil.)	3.7%	–	–	2,360.5	3.3	3,411.0
Net income ($ mil.)	7.9%	–	–	62.7	0.0	134.4
Market value ($ mil.)	–	–	–	–	–	–
Employees	–	–	–	–	–	1,456

*Fiscal year change

AG&E HOLDINGS INC   NBB: AGNU

223 Pratt Street, Hammonton
Hammonton, NJ 08037
Phone: 609 704-3000
Fax: –
Web: www.agegaming.com

CEO: Anthony R Tomasello
CFO: Francis X McCarthy
HR: –
FYE: December 31
Type: Public

After selling assets and losing a key contract AG&E Holdings formerly known as Wells-Gardner Electronics is resetting its business as a distributor of electronic parts to the casino and gaming markets. The company sells parts for video gaming machines to some 700 casinos in the US. In 2014 the company sold its LCD business and in 2015 it lost a contract with GTech to supply video lottery terminals for the Illinois Lottery. In 2016 AG&E bought Advanced Gaming Associates (AGA) which services slot machines in the US. AG&E changed its name from Wells-Gardner in 2014.

	Annual Growth	12/12	12/13	12/14	12/15	12/16
Sales ($ mil.)	(41.0%)	51.1	57.9	21.9	13.9	6.2
Net income ($ mil.)	–	0.2	0.7	(5.5)	(0.5)	(2.7)
Market value ($ mil.)	(38.9%)	30.2	30.2	12.0	8.3	4.2
Employees	(1.0%)	75	69	28	20	72

AGAR SUPPLY CO. INC.

Myles Standish Industrial Park 225 John Hancock Rd.
Taunton MA 02780-7318
Phone: 508-821-2060
Fax: 617-880-5113
Web: www.agarsupply.com

CEO: –
CFO: –
HR: –
FYE: September 30
Type: Private

Agar Supply is a leading independent wholesale foodservice supplier serving restaurants and other hospitality operators in New England. Recognized for its assortment of meats poultry and seafood the company also distributes a variety of produce dairy items and herbs as well as non-food products (such as kitchenware and cleaning supplies). In addition Agar Supply provides retailers with grocery goods. Karl Bressler founded the family-owned business in 1940.

AGC AMERICA INC.

11175 Cicero Dr. Ste. 400
Alpharetta GA 30022
Phone: 404-446-4200
Fax: 404-446-4295
Web: us.agc.com

CEO: –
CFO: Toshihiko Uchida
HR: –
FYE: December 31
Type: Subsidiary

AGC America is a wholly owned subsidiary of Asahi Glass the world's #1 maker of flat glass. AGC America is the holding company for more than 10 of Asahi's major subsidiaries in North America that manufacture products for the automotive chemicals glass and electronics industries. It makes architectural automotive flat float figured solar and other processed glass. AGC Chemicals Americas manufactures and markets fluorochemicals caustic soda specialty chemicals and soda ash for glass production. AGC Electronics America makes high-purity silicon carbide and synthetic quartz glass for semiconductors and glass substrates for LCDs.

AGC FLAT GLASS NORTH AMERICA INC.

11175 Cicero Dr. Ste. 400
Alpharetta GA 30022
Phone: 404-446-4200
Fax: 404-446-4221
Web: www.na.agc-flatglass.com

CEO: Kazuhiko Ishimura
CFO: Jackie Beverly
HR: –
FYE: December 31
Type: Subsidiary

In this company's line of work if the boss catches you staring out the window you can say that you're doing research. AGC Flat Glass North America (formerly AFG Industries) is one of North America's largest manufacturers of construction/specialty glass and the continent's second-largest maker of flat glass. AGC North America offers its coated insulated solar laminated store-front and fire-rated glass products to customers in the residential/commercial building products specialty solar and automotive glass markets. AFG Industries was formed via the 1978 merger of Fourco Glass and ASG. AGC North America is a subsidiary of AGC America which is a subsidiary of Japan's glass-making giant Asahi Glass.

AGCO CORP.

NYS: AGCO

4205 River Green Parkway
Duluth, GA 30096
Phone: 770 813-9200
Fax: –
Web: www.agcocorp.com

CEO: Eric Hansotia
CFO: Andrew Beck
HR: –
FYE: December 31
Type: Public

AGCO makes tractors combines hay and forage tools sprayers grain storage and protein production systems seeding and tillage implements and replacement parts for agricultural end uses. It sells through a global network of almost 3300 dealers and distributors spanning about 140 countries. It also builds diesel engines gears and generators through its power engines unit. Core brands include Massey Ferguson GSI Challenger Valtra (Finland-based) and Fendt (Germany). AGCO Finance offers financing services to retail customers and dealers via a venture with Rabobank a Dutch bank specializing in agricultural loans. Europe accounts for nearly 60% of AGCO's sales.

	Annual Growth	12/16	12/17	12/18	12/19	12/20
Sales ($ mil.)	5.4%	7,410.5	8,306.5	9,352.0	9,041.4	9,149.7
Net income ($ mil.)	27.8%	160.1	186.4	285.5	125.2	427.1
Market value ($ mil.)	15.5%	4,337.3	5,354.6	4,173.1	5,790.8	7,727.9
Employees	2.0%	19,800	20,500	21,200	21,000	21,400

AGE GROUP LTD.

2 PARK AVE FL 18
NEW YORK, NY 100165675
Phone: 212-213-9500
Fax: –

CEO: –
CFO: Mark Goldberg
HR: –
FYE: December 31
Type: Private

People like to be comfy under there no matter what their age group. Age Group makes and markets sleepwear lingerie and underwear under the brand name Of the Moment as well as apparel and accessories under licensed names including Hello Kitty Disney Roca Wear and American Tourister and others. A leading wholesaler Age Group also manufactures and designs pet accessories including an exclusive line of pet apparel bedding and grooming supplies under the Martha Stewart brand for sale in PetSmart stores. The company's products are distributed through large-scale department stores nationwide. Age Group's age? The company has been in the design and manufacturing business for more than 25 years.

	Annual Growth	12/00	12/01	12/02	12/04	12/09
Sales ($ mil.)	–	–	–	0.0	60.0	69.8
Net income ($ mil.)	–	–	–	0.0	5.8	5.1
Market value ($ mil.)	–	–	–	–	–	–
Employees	–	–	–	–	–	65

AGEAGLE AERIAL SYSTEMS INC (NEW)

ASE: UAVS

8863 E. 34th Street North
Wichita, KS 67226
Phone: 620 325-6363
Fax: –
Web: www.ageagle.com

CEO: Barrett Mooney
CFO: Nicole Fernandez-McGovern
HR: –
FYE: December 31
Type: Public

When other oil companies have given up EnerJex Resources steps in and injects some capital. The oil and gas exploration and production company works primarily in Eastern Kansas buying producing properties that it feels are undervalued or that were abandoned by other oil companies when oil prices were below $10 a barrel. The company which has proved reserves of 1.2 million barrels of oil equivalent holds full or partial interest in half a dozen oil gas and oil and gas projects across Kansas. It uses enhanced drilling techniques to recover additional oil and gas from already explored fields.

	Annual Growth	12/16	12/17	12/18	12/19	12/20
Sales ($ mil.)	(15.0%)	2.5	1.3	0.1	0.3	1.3
Net income ($ mil.)	–	(13.2)	8.3	(2.1)	(2.5)	(4.9)
Market value ($ mil.)	113.3%	17.0	12.9	33.1	26.4	351.8
Employees	(4.1%)	13	1	6	10	11

AGENT INFORMATION SOFTWARE INC

NBB: AIFS

10535 Foothill Blvd., Suite 200
Rancho Cucamonga, CA 91730
Phone: 800 776-6939
Fax: –
Web: www.auto-graphics.com

CEO: –
CFO: –
HR: –
FYE: December 31
Type: Public

Agent Information Software (AIS) seeks to organize information on your behalf. A holding company AIS owns two niche information management software subsidiaries: Auto-Graphics and AgentLegal. Auto-Graphics which primarily serves public libraries offers hosted software used to manage share (e.g. interlibrary loans) and search library resources. On the other hand AgentLegal's software caters to law firm professionals including firm CFOs looking to manage the cost of search resources; law librarians and IT departments who manage and protect information; and researchers who gather information. AIS was formed in 2009 to take over Auto-Graphics' stock.

	Annual Growth	12/16	12/17	12/18	12/19	12/20
Sales ($ mil.)	3.0%	4.8	5.0	5.2	5.6	5.4
Net income ($ mil.)	19.0%	0.2	0.3	0.5	0.5	0.4
Market value ($ mil.)	63.0%	1.6	5.1	3.6	10.1	11.3
Employees						

AGENUS INC
NAS: AGEN

3 Forbes Road
Lexington, MA 02421
Phone: 781 674-4400
Fax: –
Web: www.agenusbio.com

CEO: Garo Armen
CFO: –
HR: –
FYE: December 31
Type: Public

Agenus is a clinical-stage immuno-oncology (I-O) company advancing an extensive pipeline of immune checkpoint antibodies adoptive cell therapies and neoantigen cancer vaccines to fight cancer. Its patient-specific vaccines work on the theory that each person's cancer has a unique signature that can be derived from the tumor after it has been removed. The company refers to these vaccines as its Prophage Series the lead drug candidate in the series its most advanced antibody candidates are balstilimab (an anti-PD-1 antibody) and zalifrelimab (an anti-CTLA-4 antibody) which are in Phase 2 trials of balstilimab monotherapy and balstilimab/zalifrelimab combination for patients with second-line cervical cancer. Agenus is also developing viral vaccines and QS-21 Stimulon an improved vaccine adjuvant to make vaccines more effective. Vast Majority of its revenue comes from its domestic operations.

	Annual Growth	12/16	12/17	12/18	12/19	12/20
Sales ($ mil.)	40.6%	22.6	42.9	36.8	150.0	88.2
Net income ($ mil.)	–	(127.0)	(120.7)	(159.7)	(107.7)	(180.9)
Market value ($ mil.)	(6.3%)	807.9	639.3	466.7	798.1	623.6
Employees	8.9%	255	255	294	328	359

AGFIRST FARM CREDIT BANK

1901 MAIN ST
COLUMBIA, SC 292012443
Phone: 803-799-5000
Fax: –
Web: www.agfirst.com

CEO: Tim Amerson
CFO: Charl Butler
HR: –
FYE: December 31
Type: Private

AgFirst Farm Credit Bank is a member of the Farm Credit System the largest agricultural lending organization in the United States and one of the four banks in the Farm Credit Systems and provides funding to about 20 affiliated associations and provides services to 20 associations in 18 states and Puerto Rico. Boasting $30 billion in assets the bank provides financing to about 20 farmer-owned agricultural credit associations. The associations in turn offer mortgages and loans to some 80000 farmers agribusinesses and rural homeowners in 15 Eastern states and Puerto Rico. The company also offers credit and credit-related services to qualified borrowers. AgFirst raises money by selling bonds and notes on the capital markets. AgFirst Farm Credit Bank was founded in 1916.

	Annual Growth	12/12	12/13	12/14	12/15	12/17
Assets ($ mil.)	3.0%	–	–	–	30,620.6	32,487.5
Net income ($ mil.)	1.2%	–	–	–	336.8	344.7
Market value ($ mil.)	–	–	–	–	–	–
Employees	–	–	–	–	–	530

AGILENT TECHNOLOGIES, INC.
NYS: A

5301 Stevens Creek Blvd.
Santa Clara, CA 95051
Phone: 800 227-9770
Fax: 408 345-8474
Web: www.agilent.com

CEO: Michael McMullen
CFO: Robert McMahon
HR: Dominique Grau
FYE: October 31
Type: Public

Agilent Technologies is a leading maker of scientific testing equipment. Agilent supplies a slew of analytical and measurement instruments including gas and liquid chromatographs mass spectrometers spectroscopy software and informatics lab automation and robotics vacuum technology and cell analysis. Its operations include products used in the pharmaceutical biotechnology academic and government chemical and energy food and environment and forensics markets. The company's domestic sales accounts for about a third of total revenue.

	Annual Growth	10/17	10/18	10/19	10/20	10/21
Sales ($ mil.)	9.0%	4,472.0	4,914.0	5,163.0	5,339.0	6,319.0
Net income ($ mil.)	15.3%	684.0	316.0	1,071.0	719.0	1,210.0
Market value ($ mil.)	23.3%	20,559.2	19,580.1	22,892.3	30,852.4	47,594.7
Employees	5.9%	13,500	14,800	16,300	16,400	17,000

AGILYSYS INC
NMS: AGYS

1000 Windward Concourse, Suite 250
Alpharetta, GA 30005
Phone: 770 810-7800
Fax: –
Web: www.agilysys.com

CEO: Ramesh Srinivasan
CFO: William Wood
HR: –
FYE: March 31
Type: Public

Agilysys is a leading provider of IT services and software to customers across the hospitality industry. Its areas of expertise include point-of-sale (POS) systems payment reservation and table management property management inventory and procurement business analytics and guest loyalty programs. The company's primary product suites include rGuest (a complete hospitality platform) InfoGenesis (POS) Eatec (inventory and procurement) and Visual One (activities management). Serving clients of all sizes in gaming resorts and restaurants among other sectors. Organized in 1963 as Pioneer-Standard Electronic the company began operations as a distributor of electric components.

	Annual Growth	03/17	03/18	03/19	03/20	03/21
Sales ($ mil.)	1.8%	127.7	127.4	140.8	160.8	137.2
Net income ($ mil.)	–	(11.7)	(8.4)	(13.2)	(34.1)	(21.0)
Market value ($ mil.)	50.1%	226.9	286.2	508.3	401.0	1,151.6
Employees	22.7%	596	841	936	1,275	1,350

AGIOS PHARMACEUTICALS INC
NMS: AGIO

88 Sidney Street
Cambridge, MA 02139
Phone: 617 649-8600
Fax: –
Web: www.agios.com

CEO: Jacqualyn Fouse
CFO: Jonathan Biller
HR: –
FYE: December 31
Type: Public

Agios Pharmaceuticals wants to say " adios " to cancer. The biopharmaceutical company is developing metabolic treatments for certain types of cancer and rare genetic diseases. Its lead drug candidates AG-221 and AG-120 are oral tablets that apply cellular metabolism to treat patients with cancers that harbor certain mutations. Agios has a development collaboration agreement with Celgene for its cancer metabolism program. Another drug candidate AG-348 would treat a form of hemolytic anemia known as pyruvate kinase deficiency or PK deficiency. Agios went public in 2013 raising about $106 million in its IPO which it plans to use to further fund clinical development for its drug candidates.

	Annual Growth	12/16	12/17	12/18	12/19	12/20
Sales ($ mil.)	30.6%	69.9	43.0	94.4	117.9	203.2
Net income ($ mil.)	–	(198.5)	(314.7)	(346.0)	(411.5)	(327.4)
Market value ($ mil.)	0.9%	2,891.6	3,961.5	3,195.1	3,308.8	3,002.5
Employees	18.3%	287	382	482	536	562

AGL RESOURCES INC.
NYS: GAS

Ten Peachtree Place N.E.
Atlanta, GA 30309
Phone: 404 584-4000
Fax: –
Web: www.aglresources.com

CEO: Kimberly Greene
CFO: David P Poroch
HR: –
FYE: December 31
Type: Public

AGL Resources brings its resources to customers in seven states through its fleet of utilities. Its Nicor Gas unit has 2.2 million customers in Illinois; Atlanta Gas Light 1.5 million natural gas customers in Georgia. AGL also distributes natural gas to 4.5 million customers in half a dozen states. Through its nonregulated subsidiaries AGL markets natural gas to retail and wholesale customers stores and transports gas and offers asset and risk management services. The company serves 628000 energy customers and 1.2 million service contracts across through its SouthStar unit. In 2015 the company agreed to be bought by Southern Company for $8 billion.

	Annual Growth	12/11	12/12	12/13	12/14	12/15
Sales ($ mil.)	13.9%	2,338.0	3,922.0	4,617.0	5,385.0	3,941.0
Net income ($ mil.)	19.7%	172.0	271.0	313.0	482.0	353.0
Market value ($ mil.)	10.9%	5,087.1	4,811.5	5,685.4	6,561.7	7,681.2
Employees	(5.0%)	6,400	6,121	6,094	5,165	5,203

AGNC INVESTMENT CORP   NMS: AGNC

2 Bethesda Metro Center, 12th Floor — CEO: Peter Federico
Bethesda, MD 20814 — CFO: Bernice Bell
Phone: 301 968-9315 — HR: –
Fax: 301 968-9301 — FYE: December 31
Web: www.agnc.com — Type: Public

AGNC Investment (formerly American Capital Agency) is taking on the rocky real estate market. The real estate investment trust (REIT) was created in 2008 to invest in securities backed by single-family residential mortgages and collateralized mortgage obligations guaranteed by government agencies Fannie Mae Freddie Mac and Ginnie Mae. The Maryland-based REIT is externally managed and advised by American Capital AGNC Management a subsidiary of US publicly traded alternative asset manager American Capital which spun off American Capital Agency in 2008 but retained about a 33% stake in the REIT.

	Annual Growth	12/16	12/17	12/18	12/19	12/20
Assets ($ mil.)	9.5%	56,880.0	70,376.0	109,241.0	113,082.0	81,817.0
Net income ($ mil.)	–	623.0	771.0	129.0	688.0	(266.0)
Market value ($ mil.)	(3.7%)	9,781.1	10,892.5	9,462.8	9,538.4	8,416.2
Employees	(1.9%)	54	56	56	51	50

AGNES SCOTT COLLEGE, INC.

141 E COLLEGE AVE — CEO: Elizabeth Kiss
DECATUR, GA 300303797 — CFO: John Hegman
Phone: 404-471-6000 — HR: –
Fax: – — FYE: June 30
Web: www.agnesscott.edu — Type: Private

Great Scott Agnes it's a liberal arts college for women! Agnes Scott College (ASC) offers bachelor of arts degrees in 33 majors and 27 minors with pre-law and pre-medicine programs and dual degree programs in architecture engineering and nursing as well as post-baccalaureate programs. The school also grants master of arts in teaching degrees in English biology chemistry physics and mathematics. Enrollment in 2008 was about 850 students. Founded in 1889 ASC is affiliated with the Presbyterian Church and has an endowment of about $300 million. Tuition fees room and board cost $39000 per year. The 100-acre campus rated one of the most beautiful in the country is in Decatur Georgia.

	Annual Growth	06/10	06/11	06/14	06/15	06/16
Sales ($ mil.)	(1.1%)	–	62.2	70.3	62.2	58.8
Net income ($ mil.)	–	–	(3.6)	1.7	(8.5)	(16.5)
Market value ($ mil.)	–	–	–	–	–	–
Employees	–	–	–	–	–	350

AGREE REALTY CORP.   NYS: ADC

70 E. Long Lake Road — CEO: Joel Agree
Bloomfield Hills, MI 48304 — CFO: Peter Coughenour
Phone: 248 737-4190 — HR: –
Fax: 248 737-9110 — FYE: December 31
Web: www.agreerealty.com — Type: Public

Shopping sprees really agree with Agree Realty. The self-managed real estate investment trust (REIT) owns develops and manages retail real estate. It owns around 820 retail properties spanning approximately 14.6 million square feet of leasable space across 45-plus states. Most of its tenants are national retailers with its largest tenants being Sherwin-Williams Wal-Mart and TJX Companies. The REIT typically acquires either property portfolios or single-asset net lease retail properties worth approximately $702.9 million with creditworthy tenants. It was founded in 1971 by CEO Richard Agree.

	Annual Growth	12/16	12/17	12/18	12/19	12/20
Sales ($ mil.)	28.4%	91.5	116.6	148.2	187.5	248.6
Net income ($ mil.)	19.3%	45.1	58.1	58.2	80.1	91.4
Market value ($ mil.)	9.7%	2,764.0	3,087.5	3,548.5	4,211.7	3,996.2
Employees	19.5%	24	32	36	41	49

AGRI-MARK INC.

100 Milk St. — CEO: –
Methuen MA 01844-4665 — CFO: –
Phone: 978-689-4442 — HR: –
Fax: 978-794-8304 — FYE: November 30
Web: www.agrimark.net — Type: Private - Cooperativ

Cheese lovers who make a habit of Cabot ought to know about Agri-Mark. The northeastern US dairy cooperative makes Cabot-brand Vermont cheddar cheese butter and cultured dairy products as well as McCadam-branded and European cheeses. The co-op boasts more than 1200 member-owners who operate farms throughout New England and New York producing 300 million gallons of milk a year. Agri-Mark also sells milk to bottlers and manufacturers in the eastern US and dairy ingredients to foodservice and industrial clients. It owns processing plants in Vermont Massachusetts and New York. The co-op was formed in 1916 as the New England Milk Producers Association and became Agri-Mark in 1980.

AGRIBANK FCB

30 E. 7th St. Ste. 1600 — CEO: Jeffrey Swanhorst
St. Paul MN 55101 — CFO: Jeff Moore
Phone: 651-282-8800 — HR: –
Fax: 651-282-8666 — FYE: December 31
Web: www.agribank.com — Type: Private - Cooperativ

AgriBank puts the "green" in green acres. The borrower-owned bank provides wholesale lending and business services to Farm Credit System (FCS) associations in America's heartland. Established by Congress in 1916 the FCS is a nationwide network of cooperatives that provide loans and financial services for farmers ranchers agribusiness timber producers and rural homeowners. The co-ops write loans for homes land equipment and other farm operating costs. AgriBank also provides credit to rural electric water and telephone systems. The largest bank in the FCS its footprint includes more than half of the cropland in the US covering 15 states from Ohio to Wyoming and Minnesota to Arkansas.

AGRITECH WORLDWIDE INC   NBB: FBER

1120 Avenue of the Americas, Suite 1514 — CEO: Edward Smith III
New York, NY 10036 — CFO: Donald Wittmer
Phone: 847 549-6002 — HR: –
Fax: – — FYE: December 31
Web: www.ztrim.com — Type: Public

Z Trim Holdings is trying to cut the fat while at the same time allowing users to chew the fat. Its core product Z Trim developed and licensed by the USDA is a zero-calorie fiber ingredient typically made from corn or oats that is manufactured into gel and powdered form to replace fat gums starches and carbohydrates in foods. Z Trim sells its fat-replacement products as ingredients to food manufacturers and foodservice companies. Founder and former CEO Gregory Halpern owns about 13% of Z Trim Holdings; individual investor Nurieel Akhamzadeh owns 5%.

	Annual Growth	12/12	12/13	12/14	12/15	12/16
Sales ($ mil.)	(2.0%)	1.3	1.4	1.0	1.2	1.2
Net income ($ mil.)	–	(9.6)	(13.4)	(5.6)	(24.0)	(3.2)
Market value ($ mil.)	(72.2%)	269.7	86.8	58.1	6.5	1.6
Employees	(7.4%)	19	21	13	14	14

AGTEGRA COOPERATIVE

908 LAMONT ST S
ABERDEEN, SD 574015515
Phone: 605-225-5500
Fax: –
Web: www.agtegra.com

CEO: –
CFO: Robert Porter
HR: –
FYE: July 31
Type: Private

Who loves you a bushel and a peck? South Dakota Wheat Growers may; it is an agricultural co-op comprising some 6800 member-farmers. It provides a grain warehouse along with grain marketing services intended to compete with big food and ag companies. In addition to storage and drying Wheat Growers offers agronomy spreading and spraying and transportation. It supplies feed fertilizer chemicals and other farm-related provisions for members in and around counties in North and South Dakota. Wheat Growers generates more than half of its revenues through marketing some 160 million bushels of grain (corn wheat and soybeans) each year. Remaining revenues are made through agronomy and retail sales and services.

	Annual Growth	07/15	07/16	07/17	07/18	07/19
Sales ($ mil.)	7.7%	–	1,209.2	1,275.6	1,544.3	1,509.7
Net income ($ mil.)	–	–	6.7	22.8	32.5	(6.0)
Market value ($ mil.)	–	–	–	–	–	–
Employees	–	–	–	–	–	638

AGY HOLDING CORP.

2556 Wagener Rd.
Aiken SC 29801
Phone: 803-648-8351
Fax: 803-643-1180
Web: www.agy.com

CEO: Patrick J Burns
CFO: Jay W Ferguson
HR: –
FYE: December 31
Type: Private

Glass and yarns usually go together in a pub frequented by sailors but AGY Holding Corp. (formerly Advanced Glassfiber Yarns and its subsidiaries) brings them together in a business. The company produces glass yarns (thin filaments of glass twisted together to form advanced yarn or fiber) which are used in myriad aerospace automotive construction defense electronics industrial and recreational applications. The US military for example reinforces Humvees and other armored vehicles with AGY's proprietary glass fiber. AGY products are differentiated by glass chemistry coating technology and form; brands include L Glass S-2 Glass and S-1 HM Glass. Private equity Kohlberg & Co. owns AGY Holding.

AHOLD U.S.A. INC.

1149 Harrisburg Pike
Carlisle PA 17013
Phone: 717-249-4000
Fax: 801-569-6045
Web: www.kennecott.com

CEO: –
CFO: –
HR: –
FYE: December 31
Type: Subsidiary

Ahold USA is the American arm of Netherlands-based Royal Ahold — one of the world's leading grocery retailers. The subsidiary oversees some 750 supermarkets in about 10 states — from Massachusetts to Virginia. Ahold USA's four divisions include: Stop & Shop New England Stop & Shop Metro New York Giant-Landover and Giant-Carlisle each with its own support business. Its online grocery ordering and delivery service Peapod serves Giant Food and Stop & Shop customers in select markets. Ahold USA accounts for about 60% of its Dutch parent's group sales. After nearly a decade of retrenchment Royal Ahold is growing again on both sides of the Atlantic.

AHS HILLCREST MEDICAL CENTER, LLC

1120 S UTICA AVE
TULSA, OK 741044012
Phone: 918-579-1000
Fax: –
Web: www.hillcrestmedicalcenter.com

CEO: Kevin Gross
CFO: Joseph Mendoza
HR: –
FYE: June 30
Type: Private

Hillcrest Medical Center as part of the Hillcrest HealthCare System provides a helping hand to health care patients in northeastern Oklahoma. The medical center operates health care facilities in Tulsa and surrounding areas. The main hospital facility has about 730 beds and offers emergency cancer cardiology neurology rehabilitation and other acute and specialty care services. Hillcrest Medical Center also operates outpatient and extended care facilities including general health and specialty clinics and provides home health foster care and hospice services. The health care organization is part of Ardent Health Services.

	Annual Growth	06/12	06/13	06/14	06/15	06/16
Sales ($ mil.)	7.5%	–	–	–	472.5	508.0
Net income ($ mil.)	89.4%	–	–	–	7.7	14.7
Market value ($ mil.)	–	–	–	–	–	–
Employees	–	–	–	–	–	2,126

AHS MEDICAL HOLDINGS LLC

1 Burton Hills Blvd. Ste. 250
Nashville TN 37215
Phone: 615-296-3000
Fax: 615-296-6351
Web: www.ardenthealth.com

CEO: –
CFO: –
HR: –
FYE: December 31
Type: Private

AHS Medical Holdings (doing business as Ardent Health Services) is passionate about healing the body. The company operates about 10 acute care hospitals a rehab hospital a heart hospital and a number of specialty care facilities through health systems in the southern US. Its facilities are primarily located in New Mexico where it operates as the Lovelace Health System and in Oklahoma where it operates as Hillcrest HealthCare System. Ardent Health Services' operations also include physician practices about a dozen pharmacies and the Lovelace Health Plan which serves some 240000 members in New Mexico. Welsh Carson Anderson & Stowe owns a controlling stake in Ardent Health Services.

AIADVERTISING INC

321 Sixth Street
San Antonio, TX 78215
Phone: 805 964-3313
Fax: –

NBB: AIAD
CEO: Andrew Van Noy
CFO: Isabel Gongora
HR: –
FYE: December 31
Type: Public

Warp 9 (formerly Roaming Messenger) hopes to get all sorts of messages across. The company provides software used for e-commerce applications such as product presentation online catalogs and store management. Warp 9 also offers a Web-based e-mail and list management system that can be used for marketing and customer loyalty campaigns. Former chairman president and CFO Jonathan Lei owns about 48% of the company.

	Annual Growth	06/17*	12/17	12/18	12/19	12/20
Sales ($ mil.)	49.2%	2.9	4.5	11.8	9.2	9.7
Net income ($ mil.)	–	(2.0)	(2.5)	(2.9)	(10.1)	(1.3)
Market value ($ mil.)	(13.5%)	6.8	27.3	9.5	1.3	4.4
Employees	(23.4%)	69	64	65	49	31

*Fiscal year change

AIKIDO PHARMA INC
NAS: AIKI

One Rockefeller Plaza, 11th Floor
New York, NY 10020
Phone: 703 992-9325
Fax: –
Web: www.spherix.com

CEO: Anthony Hayes
CFO: Anthony Hayes
HR: –
FYE: December 31
Type: Public

Spherix is sweet on health. The company's BioSpherix division is developing products from tagatose a low-calorie sweetener with possible applications for improving health. Approved for use in foods the company sold the food-use rights for tagatose to Arla Foods but hung onto the non-food rights which it then branded Naturlose. The product is in clinical trials as a possible treatment for Type 2 diabetes although patient recruitment has been slower than expected. Spherix reported it will likely need a development partner to see the product through to market. To supplement its income Spherix launched a Health Sciences division to provide regulatory and technical consulting services to other biotech firms.

	Annual Growth	12/15	12/16	12/17	12/18	12/19
Sales ($ mil.)	(27.7%)	0.0	0.9	1.2	0.0	0.0
Net income ($ mil.)	–	(51.5)	(6.5)	(3.3)	1.7	(4.2)
Market value ($ mil.)	73.9%	0.7	5.0	6.8	3.1	6.4
Employees	(6.9%)	4	5	3	6	3

AIM IMMUNOTECH INC
ASE: AIM

2117 SW Highway 484
Ocala, FL 34473
Phone: 352 448-7797
Fax: –
Web: www.aimimmuno.com

CEO: Thomas Equels
CFO: Ellen Lintal
HR: –
FYE: December 31
Type: Public

Targeting chronic viral diseases and immune disorders Hemispherx Biopharma hopes to do a world of good with its RNA (ribonucleic acid) and other drugs. The company has acquired the rights to Alferon N an FDA-approved drug for genital warts that the company is developing to fight other viral diseases such as West Nile virus. Hemispherx also is developing Ampligen an intravenously administered RNA drug that is in clinical trials to treat HIV and chronic fatigue syndrome (CFS). Ampligen is also being tested as an adjuvant for vaccines conditions including seasonal flu and bird flu. The compound has received orphan status from the FDA for kidney cancer melanoma CFS and HIV.

	Annual Growth	12/16	12/17	12/18	12/19	12/20
Sales ($ mil.)	15.4%	0.1	0.4	0.4	0.1	0.2
Net income ($ mil.)	–	(7.5)	(8.3)	(9.8)	(9.5)	(14.4)
Market value ($ mil.)	26.9%	29.1	14.6	7.6	22.9	75.5
Employees	(9.3%)	34	27	33	26	23

AIMCO PROPERTIES, L.P.

4582 S ULSTER ST STE 1100
DENVER, CO 802372662
Phone: 303-757-8101
Fax: –

CEO: Terry Considine
CFO: Ernest M Freedman
HR: –
FYE: December 31
Type: Private

AIMCO Properties' aim is true. The company is the operating arm of multifamily real estate giant Apartment Investment and Management Company (AIMCO) which owns and/or manages some 500 apartment properties (with nearly 94000 individual units) throughout the US. AIMCO Properties holds most of AIMCO's assets and manages its day-to-day operations including property management and asset management. Its portfolio includes suburban apartment communities urban high-rise properties and government-subsidized affordable housing properties. Investment management operations include management of its own portfolio as well as services for affiliated partnerships. AIMCO controls more than 90% of AIMCO Properties.

	Annual Growth	12/12	12/13	12/14	12/15	12/16
Assets ($ mil.)	0.8%	–	6,079.4	6,097.0	6,144.2	6,232.8
Net income ($ mil.)	26.7%	–	237.8	356.1	272.0	483.3
Market value ($ mil.)	–	–	–	–	–	–
Employees	–	–	–	–	–	15,301

AINOS INC
NBB: AIMD

8880 Rio San Diego Drive, Suite 800
San Diego, CA 92108
Phone: 858 869-2986
Fax: –
Web: www.amarbio.com

CEO: Stephen Chen
CFO: Tsai Chun-Hsien
HR: –
FYE: December 31
Type: Public

Amarillo — home to cattlemen prairies and...interferon? Amarillo Biosciences hopes its low-dose interferon alpha (IFNa) which modulates the immune system will help those suffering from a range of maladies including viral and autoimmune diseases. The company's interferon technology which uses a low-dose dissolving tablet potentially offers effective treatment with fewer side effects than injectable forms of the drug. Amarillo Biosciences is developing its interferon technology as a treatment for flu oral warts in HIV patients and chronic cough. Through research partners it is also investigating the drug in relation to Behcet's disease (a severe inflammatory disorder) and hepatitis C.

	Annual Growth	12/16	12/17	12/18	12/19	12/20
Sales ($ mil.)	(59.6%)	–	0.3	0.1	0.0	0.0
Net income ($ mil.)	–	(0.7)	(0.6)	(1.3)	(1.6)	(1.5)
Market value ($ mil.)	(10.9%)	11.4	11.8	11.4	12.6	7.2
Employees	0.0%	4	4	6	4	4

AIR LEASE CORP
NYS: AL

2000 Avenue of the Stars, Suite 1000N
Los Angeles, CA 90067
Phone: 310 553-0555
Fax: –
Web: www.airleasecorp.com

CEO: John Plueger
CFO: Gregory Willis
HR: –
FYE: December 31
Type: Public

Air Lease doesn't really lease air unless of course you include the air inside the cabins of its fleet of airplanes. An aircraft leasing company Air Lease buys new and used commercial aircraft from manufacturers and airlines and then leases to airline carriers in Europe the Asia-Pacific region and the Americas. It owns a fleet of almost 240 aircraft comprised of 181 single-aisle narrowbody jet aircraft 40 twin-aisle widebody jet aircraft and 19 turboprop aircraft. In addition to leasing Air Lease also offers fleet management services such as lease management and sales.

	Annual Growth	12/17	12/18	12/19	12/20	12/21
Sales ($ mil.)	8.3%	1,516.4	1,679.7	2,016.9	2,015.4	2,088.4
Net income ($ mil.)	(12.8%)	756.2	510.8	587.1	516.3	436.6
Market value ($ mil.)	(2.1%)	5,481.6	3,443.6	5,416.7	5,063.3	5,041.7
Employees	10.3%	87	97	117	120	129

AIR METHODS CORPORATION

5500 S QUEBEC ST STE 300
GREENWOOD VILLAGE, CO 801111926
Phone: 303-792-7400
Fax: –
Web: www.airmethods.com

CEO: Jaelynn Williams
CFO: Peter Csapo
HR: –
FYE: December 31
Type: Private

With a fleet of more than 450 medically equipped aircraft mainly helicopters Air Methods is one of the largest providers of emergency medical air-transportation services in the US. The company operates through three divisions. A community-based operating company Air Methods also provides tourism operations around Hawaiian Islands through Blue Hawaiian Helicopters. The smallest division United Rotorcraft designs manufactures and installs aircraft medical-transport products. Air Methods was founded in 1980 by Roy Morgan.

	Annual Growth	12/11	12/12	12/13	12/14	12/15
Sales ($ mil.)	11.0%	–	–	881.6	1,004.8	1,085.7
Net income ($ mil.)	32.7%	–	–	62.1	95.5	109.3
Market value ($ mil.)	–	–	–	–	–	–
Employees	–	–	–	–	–	5,133

AIR PRODUCTS & CHEMICALS INC — NYS: APD

1940 Air Products Boulevard
Allentown, PA 18106-5500
Phone: 610 481-4911
Fax: 610 481-5900
Web: www.airproducts.com

CEO: Seifollah Ghasemi
CFO: Melissa Schaeffer
HR: –
FYE: September 30
Type: Public

Air Products and Chemicals produces and distributes atmospheric process and specialty gases in the US and across the world. It is a leading hydrogen supplier as well as helium and liquefied natural gas (LNG) process technology and equipment. Air Products and Chemicals which generates more than 60% revenue outside the US also provides related equipment and services (air separation hydrocarbon recovery natural gas liquefaction etc.) to customers in the refining gasification electronics chemicals metals manufacturing and food and beverage industries.

	Annual Growth	09/17	09/18	09/19	09/20	09/21
Sales ($ mil.)	6.0%	8,187.6	8,930.2	8,918.9	8,856.3	10,323.0
Net income ($ mil.)	(8.5%)	3,000.4	1,497.8	1,760.0	1,886.7	2,099.1
Market value ($ mil.)	14.1%	33,479.6	36,984.3	49,119.1	65,945.2	56,701.9
Employees	8.1%	15,300	16,300	17,700	19,275	20,875

AIR T INC — NMS: AIRT

5930 Balsom Ridge Road
Denver, NC 28037
Phone: 828 464-8741
Fax: –
Web: www.airt.net

CEO: Nicholas Swenson
CFO: Brian Ochocki
HR: –
FYE: March 31
Type: Public

Air T helps FedEx deliver the goods. The company owns two overnight air cargo subsidiaries — Mountain Air Cargo (MAC) and CSA Air — which operate under contracts with FedEx. MAC and CSA Air fly mainly in the Eastern and Midwest regions of the US as well as the Caribbean and South America. Its combined fleet consists of about 80 turboprop Cessna aircraft most of which are leased from FedEx. Air Cargo Services accounts for about half of its sales. Air T's Aircraft Ground Service Equipment and Service business comprises Global Ground Support (GGS; de-icing and scissor-lift equipment used at airports) and Global Aviation Services (GAS; provides related maintenance services).

	Annual Growth	03/17	03/18	03/19	03/20	03/21
Sales ($ mil.)	4.2%	148.5	194.5	249.8	236.8	175.1
Net income ($ mil.)	–	(3.2)	2.3	1.3	7.7	(7.3)
Market value ($ mil.)	4.2%	58.1	72.9	87.0	36.1	68.5
Employees	(10.6%)	708	775	769	478	452

AIR TRANSPORT SERVICES GROUP, INC. — NMS: ATSG

145 Hunter Drive
Wilmington, OH 45177
Phone: 937 382-5591
Fax: –
Web: www.atsginc.com

CEO: Richard Corrado
CFO: Quint Turner
HR: –
FYE: December 31
Type: Public

Air Transport Services Group (ATSG) leases aircraft and provides airline operations ground handling services aircraft modification and maintenance services and other support services to the air transportation and logistics industries. It is a leading provider of aircraft leasing and air cargo transportation services in the United States and internationally. In addition it is a provider of passenger charter service to the United States Department of Defense ("DoD"). The company has segments ACMI Services provides aircraft crew maintenance and insurance operations to the company's customers DHL and the US military through airline subsidiaries Ohio-based ABX Air Inc. and Arkansas-based ATI. ATSG's Cargo Aircraft Management (CAM) subsidiary leases Boeing 777 767 and 757 aircraft and aircraft engines.. The company was founded in 1980.

	Annual Growth	12/16	12/17	12/18	12/19	12/20
Sales ($ mil.)	19.6%	768.9	1,068.2	892.3	1,452.2	1,570.6
Net income ($ mil.)	8.1%	23.5	18.5	69.3	61.2	32.1
Market value ($ mil.)	18.4%	950.6	1,378.2	1,358.6	1,397.3	1,866.6
Employees	13.2%	3,230	3,010	3,830	4,380	5,305

AIR2WEB INC.

3424 Peachtree Rd. NE Ste. 400
Atlanta GA 30326
Phone: 404-942-5300
Fax: 202-692-2901
Web: www.peacecorps.gov

CEO: –
CFO: –
HR: –
FYE: December 31
Type: Private

Air2Web believes that marketers should take a flying leap. The company provides mobile markeing software and related managed services under the AirCARE banner which are used by customers to wirelessly reach potential clients on the go. Other products include customer service-oriented messaging applications (DirectTEXT) and mobile and Web accessible customer data access tools (Enterprise Agent). Air2Web targets industries such as insurance financial services food and retail. Customers include enterprises phone companies marketing agences and content providers such as Office Depot Dominos and Axciom. Mobile marketing and advertising technology firm Velti acquired Air2Web for $19 million in 2011.

AIRBAND COMMUNICATIONS HOLDINGS INC.

14800 Landmark Pkwy. Ste. 500
Dallas TX 75254
Phone: 469-791-0000
Fax: 469-374-0741
Web: www.airband.com

CEO: Michael Ruley
CFO: Timothy Kinnear
HR: –
FYE: December 31
Type: Private

There are no air guitarists in this band. Wireless communications provider airBand Communications offers broadband Internet and data services as well as computer telephony connections to businesses in about 14 US cities. The company's fixed-wireless services include data colocation Internet access virtual private networks wireless private lines and Web hosting. airBand operates networks in select cities in Arizona California Georgia Maryland North Carolina Pennsylvania and Texas. The company serves clients in such industries as financial services and health care; customers have included CoStar Group Medifast and WakeMed.

AIRCASTLE LTD. — NYS: AYR

c/o Aircastle Advisor LLC, 201 Tresser Blvd., Suite 400
Stamford, CT 06901
Phone: 203 504-1020
Fax: 203 504-1021
Web: www.aircastle.com

CEO: Michael Inglese
CFO: Aaron Dahlke
HR: –
FYE: December 31
Type: Public

Not to be confused with the inflatable palaces that parents rent for kids' birthday parties Aircastle Limited is an aircraft leasing concern. The company owns a lineup of utility jet aircraft that it adds to leases and sells to passenger and cargo markets. Aircastle touts a portfolio of nearly 160 aircraft which are leased to about 50 customers located in roughly 30 countries. Lessees of Aircastle's aircraft maintain the planes as well as pay operating and insurance expenses. Aircastle also invests in industry-related assets such as financing vehicles secured by commercial aircraft.

	Annual Growth	12/14	12/15	12/16	12/17	12/18
Sales ($ mil.)	2.1%	818.6	819.2	773.0	796.6	890.4
Net income ($ mil.)	25.2%	100.8	121.7	151.5	147.9	247.9
Market value ($ mil.)	–					
Employees	3.0%	97	103	102	111	109

AIRCRAFT SERVICE INTERNATIONAL INC.

201 S. Orange Ave. Ste. 1100-A
Orlando FL 32801
Phone: 407-648-7373
Fax: 407-206-5391
Web: www.asig.com
CEO: –
CFO: Benjamin Adam Weaver
HR: –
FYE: December 31
Type: Subsidiary

Rather than soaring through the skies the company (dba Aircraft Service International Group or "ASIG") offers flight support services to commercial planes on the ground. It provides refueling as well as ground handling services including baggage and cargo handling and transfer cabin and lounge cleaning and other related services. Technical services include de-icing and jetway maintenance. ASIG operates at about 70 airports worldwide primarily in the US and the UK but also in Europe Central America and Asia/Pacific. Sister company Signature Flight Support serves the general aviation community as a leading fixed-base operator (FBO). ASIG was founded in 1947 and acquired by UK-based BBA Aviation in 2001.

AIRGAS, INC.

259 N RADNOR CHESTER RD # 100
RADNOR, PA 190875240
Phone: 610-687-5253
Fax: –
Web: www.airgas.com
CEO: Marcelo Fioranelli
CFO: –
HR: –
FYE: March 31
Type: Private

Airgas safely and reliably provides products services and expertise to industries through its more than 18500 associates in more than 1400 locations robust e-Business platform and Airgas Total Access telesales channel. Airgas distributes argon carbon dioxide hydrogen nitrogen oxygen and a variety of specialty gases as well as welding products tools and equipment dry ice and protective equipment (hard hats goggles). The company serves more than 1 million customers in various industries. The company is owned by Air Liquide SA.

	Annual Growth	03/10	03/11	03/12	03/13	03/15
Sales ($ mil.)	3.4%	–	–	–	4,957.5	5,304.9
Net income ($ mil.)	3.9%	–	–	–	340.9	368.1
Market value ($ mil.)	–	–	–	–	–	–
Employees	–	–	–	–	–	17,000

AIRTRAN AIRWAYS INC.

9955 AirTran Blvd.
Orlando FL 32827
Phone: 407-318-5600
Fax: 407-318-5900
Web: www.airtran.com
CEO: –
CFO: –
HR: –
FYE: December 31
Type: Subsidiary

Need to be transported by air with a low fare? AirTran Airways offers low-cost passenger transportation to almost 70 cities mainly in the eastern US but also in Aruba the Bahamas Jamaica Mexico and Puerto Rico. The airline operates from a primary hub in Atlanta and secondary hubs in Baltimore; Milwaukee; and Orlando Florida. AirTran maintains a fleet of about 140 Boeing aircraft (717s and 737s). It is a leading carrier in the Atlanta market behind Delta which handles the largest share of the traffic at Hartsfield-Jackson Atlanta International Airport. AirTran Airways was acquired by Southwest Airlines in 2011.

AIRVANA INC.

19 Alpha Rd.
Chelmsford MA 01824
Phone: 978-250-3100
Fax: 978-250-3910
Web: www.airvana.com
CEO: –
CFO: –
HR: –
FYE: December 31
Type: Private

Airvana makes a technology called femtocells which are basically 3G network cell phone transmitters that improve weak signal reception indoors. Airvana's femtocell products sold under the HubBub brand bring better voice service and speed up data downloads and uploads for 3G network users in homes and small offices. The company has partnered with several telecommunications and IT manufacturers to integrate femtocell technology with their equipment. These companies include Alcatel-Lucent Ericsson Freescale Semiconductor and Hitachi. Sprint Nextel and KDDI provide service powered by Airvana femtocells.

AK STEEL HOLDING CORP.   NYS: AKS

9227 Centre Pointe Drive
West Chester, OH 45069
Phone: 513 425-5000
Fax: 513 425-5220
Web: www.aksteel.com
CEO: –
CFO: –
HR: –
FYE: December 31
Type: Public

Automobile sales help AK Steel's business keep rolling though it also has operations in the infrastructure and manufacturing industries. The company manufactures carbon stainless and electrical steel. It sells hot- and cold-rolled carbon steel to construction companies steel distributors and service centers and automotive and industrial machinery producers. AK Steel also sells cold-rolled and aluminum-coated stainless steel to automakers. The company produces electrical steels (iron-silicon alloys with unique magnetic properties) for makers of power transmission and distribution equipment.

	Annual Growth	12/14	12/15	12/16	12/17	12/18
Sales ($ mil.)	1.2%	6,505.7	6,692.9	5,882.5	6,080.5	6,818.2
Net income ($ mil.)	–	(96.9)	(509.0)	(7.8)	6.2	186.0
Market value ($ mil.)	(21.5%)	1,874.3	706.8	3,221.6	1,785.9	710.0
Employees	4.4%	8,000	8,500	8,500	9,200	9,500

AKAL SECURITY, INC.

3 RAM DAS GURU PL
ESPANOLA, NM 875328213
Phone: 505-692-6600
Fax: –
Web: www.akalglobal.com
CEO: –
CFO: –
HR: –
FYE: December 31
Type: Private

Unarmed? Akal Security provides contract security guard services for customers in the US and abroad. Akal's Judicial Security division specializes in security services for protecting federal courthouses in approximately 40 states. It also transports prisoners and illegal aliens for homeland security efforts. In addition Akal supplies security officers for detention facilities and military installations and offers electronic security surveillance and access control system design installation and integration. The company serves federal agencies as well as commercial clients and state and local government facilities.

	Annual Growth	12/07	12/08	12/09	12/10	12/11
Sales ($ mil.)	(1.9%)	–	–	479.6	466.2	461.5
Net income ($ mil.)	11.2%	–	–	2.9	2.5	3.6
Market value ($ mil.)	–	–	–	–	–	–
Employees	–	–	–	–	–	15,000

AKAMAI TECHNOLOGIES INC

NMS: AKAM

145 Broadway
Cambridge, MA 02142
Phone: 617 444-3000
Fax: 617 444-3001
Web: www.akamai.com

CEO: F. Thomson Leighton
CFO: Edward McGowan
HR: –
FYE: December 31
Type: Public

Akamai Technologies provides solutions for securing and delivering content and business applications over the internet. The company's cloud services help its customers ? corporations and government agencies ? deliver digital content over the internet at optimal speeds and security. It also offers applications that supply network data feeds and website analytics to customers. With its software working from a network of more than 325000 servers in some 130 countries Akamai analyzes and manages web traffic transmitting content from servers that are geographically closest to end users. Customers include Toshiba the Coca-Cola Company and PayPal. About 55% of the company's total revenue comes from US.

	Annual Growth	12/16	12/17	12/18	12/19	12/20
Sales ($ mil.)	8.1%	2,340.0	2,503.0	2,714.5	2,893.6	3,198.1
Net income ($ mil.)	15.2%	316.1	218.3	298.4	478.0	557.1
Market value ($ mil.)	12.0%	10,849.5	10,582.6	9,938.3	14,054.9	17,082.9
Employees	6.6%	6,490	7,650	7,519	7,724	8,368

AKELA PHARMA INC.

TORONTO: AKL

11501 Domain Dr. Ste. 130
Austin TX 78758
Phone: 512-834-0449
Fax: 512-834-2105
Web: akelapharma.com

CEO: Rudy Emmelot
CFO: –
HR: –
FYE: December 31
Type: Private

Drug developer Akela Pharma is hoping to be there before the last dose of pain meds wears off and the next dose kicks in. The company's lead product candidate is Fentanyl Taifun an inhaled formulation of cancer pain fighter fentanyl to be used in conjunction with other drugs to manage severe pain. Akela Pharma is also working on research in areas not related to pain relief; it is developing a growth hormone stimulator to help treat frailty and malnutrition in patients with kidney failure. Akela Pharma's subsidiary PharmaForm provides contract drug development services and specializes in controlled-release drug delivery technology.

AKERS BIOSCIENCES INC.

LONDON: AKR

201 Grove Rd.
Thorofare NJ 08086
Phone: 856-848-8698
Fax: 856-848-0269
Web: www.akersbiosciences.com

CEO: Chris Chapman
CFO: Ian Rhodes
HR: –
FYE: December 31
Type: Public

When there's no time to send a sample off to the lab Akers Biosciences (ABI) steps up. The company manufactures a variety of point-of-care rapid diagnostic tests. In addition to tests for such diseases as malaria it has produced screening tools to detect drug and enzyme levels in blood. ABI has also developed sniffing devices to detect breath alcohol as well as diseases such as lung disease and diabetes through breath analysis. Another product whiffs for biological warfare agents in the air. Its Tri-Cholesterol product is a home-use test kit. ABI customers include healthcare facilities (hospitals physicians' offices) as well as the US military and aid organizations.

AKIBIA INC.

4 Technology Dr.
Westborough MA 01581
Phone: 508-621-5100
Fax: 508-621-5205
Web: www.akibia.com

CEO: Thomas Tucker
CFO: Thomas Tucker
HR: –
FYE: March 31
Type: Private

Akibia provides information technology (IT) consulting systems integration and technical support services for a variety of computing environments. Its areas of specialty include data security data storage and infrastructure design and maintenance. The company also offers consulting related to customer relationship management (CRM) software installation and customization as well as network planning and support. Akibia's outsourced services include technical support and training for corporate call centers. It serves such industries as financial services consumer electronics and retail. Clients have included Bose Atmel and Egenera. Founded in 1988 Akibia is a subsidiary of India-based Zensar Technologies.

AKORN INC

NMS: AKRX

1925 W. Field Court, Suite 300
Lake Forest, IL 60045
Phone: 847 279-6100
Fax: –
Web: www.akorn.com

CEO: Douglas S Boothe
CFO: Duane A Portwood
HR: –
FYE: December 31
Type: Public

Akorn makes and sells generic drugs in alternative dosage forms including ophthalmics injectables liquids and inhalants. Products include diagnostic and therapeutic injections eye drops and pain medicines. Akorn also has a portfolio of branded prescription drugs for ophthalmic and respiratory ailments including Akten AzaSite Cosopt and Xopenex. The Akorn Consumer Health division sells over-the-counter products such as TheraTears Zostrix and MagOx while Akorn Animal Health makes branded and generic companion animal medicines. Akorn has manufacturing facilities in the US (Illinois New Jersey and New York) Switzerland and India. Most of its revenue is generated in the US.

	Annual Growth	12/14	12/15	12/16	12/17	12/18
Sales ($ mil.)	4.0%	593.1	985.1	1,116.8	841.0	694.0
Net income ($ mil.)	–	35.3	150.8	184.2	(24.6)	(401.9)
Market value ($ mil.)	(44.7%)	4,542.8	4,682.1	2,739.5	4,044.6	425.4
Employees	4.2%	1,881	2,172	2,388	2,308	2,220

AKRON GENERAL MEDICAL CENTER INC

1 AKRON GENERAL AVE
AKRON, OH 443072432
Phone: 330-344-6000
Fax: –
Web: www.my.clevelandclinic.org

CEO: –
CFO: –
HR: –
FYE: December 31
Type: Private

Akron General Medical Center the flagship hospital of Akron General Health System is a not-for-profit teaching hospital that boasts more than 530 acute care beds. The hospital serves the residents of Northeast Ohio as a regional referral center in a number of medical specialties including cardiovascular disease heart surgery cancer care women's health orthopedics sports medicine and trauma care. Akron General Medical also operates Edwin Shaw Rehab the area's only rehabilitation hospital. Edwin Shaw has 35 beds and treats patients who have experienced stroke head trauma and other critical injuries. Akron General Medical was founded in 1914 as Peoples Hospital.

	Annual Growth	12/03	12/04	12/12	12/13	12/14
Sales ($ mil.)	–	–	0.0	486.3	507.3	544.5
Net income ($ mil.)	–	–	0.0	10.7	22.3	47.4
Market value ($ mil.)	–	–	–	–	–	–
Employees	–	–	–	–	–	875

ALABAMA FARMERS COOPERATIVE, INC.

121 SOMERVILLE RD NE
DECATUR, AL 356012659
Phone: 256-353-6843
Fax: –

CEO: –
CFO: Thomas Hallin
HR: Susana Salcido
FYE: July 31
Type: Private

Alabama Farmers Cooperative (AFC) provides farmers in the Yellowhammer state with a range of agricultural supplies and services. The co-op offers animal feed crop fertilizer and home-gardening items such as seed and hand tools as well as grain storage and hardware. AFC comprises 37 member associations including about 90 retail locations. Expanding through joint ventures it boasts one of the largest farmer-owned agriculture businesses in the southeastern US. Its Bonnie Plants is one of the biggest suppliers of vegetable and herb plants for home gardeners. Bio-Logic makes forage products for wild game. AFC supplies the foodservice industry with fresh fish through its SouthFresh Farms catfish farm.

	Annual Growth	07/07	07/08	07/09	07/10	07/11
Sales ($ mil.)	(53.5%)	–	–	2,088.8	401.0	450.8
Net income ($ mil.)	22830.8%	–	–	0.0	8.1	9.2
Market value ($ mil.)	–	–	–	–	–	–
Employees	–	–	–	–	–	3,000

ALABAMA POWER CO

600 North 18th Street
Birmingham, AL 35203
Phone: 205 257-1000
Fax: –
Web: www.alabamapower.com

NYS: ALP PRQ
CEO: Mark Crosswhite
CFO: Philip Raymond
HR: –
FYE: December 31
Type: Public

Founded in 1906 Alabama Power a wholly-owned subsidiary of the Southern Company is a vertically integrated utility that provides electric service to retail customers in three Southeastern states and to wholesale customers in the Southeast region. It owns or operates more than 75 electric generating units with total nameplate capacity of more than 12 million kilowatts. These generating units are located at 25 facilities. Alabama Power owns coal reserves near its Plant Gorgas site and uses their output in its generating plants. In addition Alabama Power sells and cooperates with dealers in promoting the sale of electric appliances and products and also markets and sells outdoor lighting services.

	Annual Growth	12/17	12/18	12/19	12/20	12/21
Sales ($ mil.)	1.5%	6,039.0	6,032.0	6,125.0	5,830.0	6,413.0
Net income ($ mil.)	9.7%	866.0	945.0	1,085.0	1,165.0	1,253.0
Market value ($ mil.)	(0.7%)	824.0	735.9	839.5	866.5	801.0
Employees	(2.0%)	6,613	6,650	6,324	6,200	6,100

ALABAMA STATE PORT AUTHORITY

250 N WATER ST
MOBILE, AL 366024000
Phone: 251-441-7200
Fax: –
Web: www.asdd.com

CEO: James Lyons
CFO: Larry R Downs
HR: –
FYE: September 30
Type: Private

Offering a gateway to the Gulf of Mexico the Alabama State Port Authority (ASPA) a government agency operates the deepwater port facilities in Mobile. The port complex includes facilities for handling general cargo such as containers forest products and metals as well as liquid bulk and dry bulk cargo such as chemicals coal iron ore and steel. The port complex features more than 4 million sq. ft. of warehouse space and open yards and almost 40 berths. A 75-mile rail line links Port of Mobile facilities and provides connections to major freight railroads. The ASPA began operations in 1928.

	Annual Growth	09/15	09/16	09/17	09/18	09/19
Sales ($ mil.)	12.2%	–	–	125.9	134.9	158.4
Net income ($ mil.)	170.2%	–	–	1.2	4.7	8.5
Market value ($ mil.)	–	–	–	–	–	–
Employees	–	–	–	–	–	495

ALACRA INC.

100 Broadway Ste. 1101
New York NY 10005
Phone: 212-363-9620
Fax: 212-363-9630
Web: www.alacra.com

CEO: Steve Goldstein
CFO: Craig Kissel
HR: –
FYE: December 31
Type: Private

Those who lack business knowledge may want to consult Alacra. The company gathers business and financial information from about 200 sources (such as Thomson Reuters Dow Jones and LexisNexis) and feeds it to some 400 knowledge-hungry clients including investment and commercial banks management consulting firms law firms and other corporations. The company's Alacra Book searches for and collects company and industry information relevant to the customer's query and publishes it for the customer as a single PDF or Word file. The firm was founded in 1996 by former Knight-Ridder execs Steven Goldstein (chairman and CEO) and Michael Angle (president and COO).

ALAMEDA CORRIDOR TRANSPORTATION AUTHORITY

3760 KILROY AIRPORT WAY
LONG BEACH, CA 908062443
Phone: 310-233-7480
Fax: –
Web: www.acta.org

CEO: –
CFO: Kevin Scott
HR: –
FYE: June 30
Type: Private

There's nothing illicit about the underground activities of the Alameda Corridor Transportation Authority; in fact the agency's mission — to facilitate efficient rail transportation of containerized cargo in Southern California — is strictly aboveboard. The Alameda Corridor Transportation Authority maintains 20 miles of freight rail lines between the ports of Long Beach and Los Angeles and the main rail terminals near downtown Los Angeles. The agency's system known as the Alameda Corridor includes the Mid-Corridor Trench a 10-mile section of railroad constructed 30 feet underground.

	Annual Growth	06/14	06/15	06/16	06/17	06/18
Sales ($ mil.)	9.5%	–	–	–	107.7	117.9
Net income ($ mil.)	–	–	–	–	(28.5)	(18.6)
Market value ($ mil.)	–	–	–	–	–	–
Employees	–	–	–	–	–	15

ALAMO COMMUNITY COLLEGE DISTRICT

201 W SHERIDAN
SAN ANTONIO, TX 782041450
Phone: 210-485-0000
Fax: –
Web: www.alamo.edu

CEO: –
CFO: –
HR: –
FYE: August 31
Type: Private

San Antonio Texas high school students are encouraged to remember the Alamo ... the Alamo Community College District that is. The district oversees five schools — Northeast Lakeview College Northwest Vista College Palo Alto College St. Philip's College and San Antonio College — all of which serve the post-secondary education needs of the greater San Antonio area. The colleges offer 325 degree and certificate programs. Classes are available during the day in the evening and on weekends through six campuses the Internet and at various off-campus sites. The Alamo Community College District serves more than 52000 students about half of whom are Hispanic.

	Annual Growth	12/07	12/08*	08/12	08/16	08/17
Sales ($ mil.)	59.5%	–	1.4	96.9	90.9	93.9
Net income ($ mil.)	–	–	0.0	11.9	25.6	30.0
Market value ($ mil.)	–	–	–	–	–	–
Employees	–	–	–	–	–	2,134

*Fiscal year change

ALAMO GROUP, INC.   NYS: ALG

1627 East Walnut   CEO: Jeffery Leonard
Seguin, TX 78155   CFO: Richard Wehrle
Phone: 830 379-1480   HR: Janet Pollock
Fax: 830 372-9683   FYE: December 31
Web: www.alamo-group.com   Type: Public

Alamo Group is a leader in the design and manufacture of high quality agricultural equipment and infrastructure maintenance equipment for governmental and industrial use. Its branded lines Alamo Industrial and Tiger hydraulically powered tractor-mounted mowers serve US government agencies. Rhino Products and M&W Gear subsidiaries sell rotary cutters and other equipment to farmers for pasture upkeep. UK McConnel and Bomford and France's S.M.A. subsidiaries market vegetation maintenance equipment such as hydraulic boom-mounted hedge and grass mowers. The company generates majority of revenue domestically.

	Annual Growth	12/16	12/17	12/18	12/19	12/20
Sales ($ mil.)	8.3%	844.7	912.4	1,008.8	1,119.1	1,163.5
Net income ($ mil.)	9.0%	40.0	44.3	73.5	62.9	56.6
Market value ($ mil.)	16.0%	898.7	1,333.0	913.1	1,482.7	1,629.2
Employees	8.3%	2,900	3,280	3,470	4,270	3,990

ALANCO TECHNOLOGIES INC   NBB: ALAN

7950 E. Acoma Drive, Suite 111   CEO: Steven Oman
Scottsdale, AZ 85260   CFO: Danielle L Haney
Phone: 480 607-1010   HR: –
Fax: –   FYE: June 30
Web: www.alanco.com   Type: Public

Having failed to strike gold and feeling lost Alanco Technologies is looking for a new business venture. The company once made pollution control systems owned gold mines and made unsuccessful forays into both the data storage and restaurant fryer businesses. It also made radio-frequency ID (RFID) tracking devices for correctional facilities through its TSI PRISM subsidiary until that line of business was sold in 2010 to Alabama-based Black Creek Integrated Systems for about $2 million in cash. Alanco then offered subscription-based GPS tracking data services for the refrigerated transport industry through StarTrak Systems (acquired for $15 million in 2006) but sold that business to ORBCOMM in 2011.

	Annual Growth	06/12	06/13	06/14	06/15	06/16
Sales ($ mil.)	(21.0%)	–	0.4	0.6	0.8	0.2
Net income ($ mil.)	–	(0.6)	(0.7)	(0.1)	(0.9)	(1.6)
Market value ($ mil.)	(37.9%)	7.4	2.2	2.4	1.4	1.1
Employees	–	–	2	1	5	3

ALASKA AIR GROUP, INC.   NYS: ALK

19300 International Boulevard   CEO: Benito Minicucci
Seattle, WA 98188   CFO: Shane Tackett
Phone: 206 392-5040   HR: –
Fax: –   FYE: December 31
Web: www.alaskaair.com   Type: Public

The fifth-largest airline in the US Alaska Air Group offers unparalleled guest service connectivity and schedules from its hub markets along the West Coast. With its regional partners Alaska Air flies to over 115 destinations through the US and North America. Alaska operates a fleet of narrowbody passenger jets on primarily longer stage-length routes and contracts primarily with Horizon and SkyWest Airlines Inc. (SkyWest) for shorter-haul capacity such that Alaska receives all passenger revenue from those flights. Alaska Airlines' fleet is comprised of over 210 aircraft.

	Annual Growth	12/17	12/18	12/19	12/20	12/21
Sales ($ mil.)	(6.1%)	7,933.0	8,264.0	8,781.0	3,566.0	6,176.0
Net income ($ mil.)	(17.5%)	1,034.0	437.0	769.0	(1,324.0)	478.0
Market value ($ mil.)	(8.2%)	9,255.3	7,661.4	8,530.1	6,547.1	6,559.7
Employees	(0.4%)	23,156	23,376	24,134	21,997	22,833

ALASKA COMMUNICATIONS SYSTEMS GROUP INC   NMS: ALSK

600 Telephone Avenue   CEO: William H Bishop
Anchorage, AK 99503-6091   CFO: Laurie M Butcher
Phone: 907 297-3000   HR: –
Fax: –   FYE: December 31
Web: www.alsk.com   Type: Public

Alaska Communications Systems Group keeps customers in the largest US state connected. Through subsidiaries the telecom carrier operates the leading local-exchange network in the state providing wired local and long-distance voice and data services mostly to enterprise customers. It also offers wireless phone service through a joint venture with GCI that offers mobile devices from Apple HTC and Samsung. The company has about 130000 wired phone lines in service about 110000 wireless subscribers and about 55000 Internet customers. Alaska Communications sells to consumers in part through its network of retail stores.

	Annual Growth	12/15	12/16	12/17	12/18	12/19
Sales ($ mil.)	(0.1%)	232.8	226.9	226.9	232.5	231.7
Net income ($ mil.)	(21.5%)	13.0	2.4	(6.1)	9.1	4.9
Market value ($ mil.)	0.3%	92.9	87.1	142.3	76.4	94.0
Employees	(3.3%)	664	642	589	596	581

ALASKA CONSERVATION FOUNDATION

441 W. 5th Ave. Ste. 402   CEO: –
Anchorage AK 99501-2340   CFO: –
Phone: 907-276-1917   HR: –
Fax: 907-274-4145   FYE: June 30
Web: www.akcf.org   Type: Private - Not-for-Pr

Whales and otters and bears oh my! The Alaska Conservation Foundation strives to protect the environment (and all its inhabitants) in Alaska as well as help the state's native people retain their cultural connections to the land. The foundation has awarded more than $22 million in grants to about 200 organizations. Its projects include the Alaska Coalition (national parks wildlife refuges and other federal lands) Alaska Oceans Program (conservation and sustainable fishing) Alaska Conservation for the Majority (finding common ground between conservationists and state residents) and Climate Change Program (minimizing individual impact). The Alaska Conservation Foundation was formed in 1980.

ALASKA NATIVE TRIBAL HEALTH CONSORTIUM

4000 AMBASSADOR DR   CEO: –
ANCHORAGE, AK 995085909   CFO: –
Phone: 907-729-1900   HR: –
Fax: –   FYE: September 30
Web: www.anthc.org   Type: Private

The Alaska Native Tribal Health Consortium (ANTHC) brings good health to Alaska Natives. The company is a not-for-profit statewide health care organization managed by regional tribal governments and their respective regional health organizations. The organization connects disparate medical providers by providing a range of health programs and services including community health care public health advocacy and education initiatives health research (including water and sanitation) and medical supply distribution. The nearly 175-bed Alaska Native Medical Center (ANMC) a native-owned hospital is jointly managed by ANTHC and Southcentral Foundation a regional health corporation based in the Cook Inlet region.

	Annual Growth	09/12	09/13	09/14	09/15	09/16
Sales ($ mil.)	(2.6%)	–	–	618.6	511.9	587.0
Net income ($ mil.)	(31.2%)	–	–	154.1	3.3	72.9
Market value ($ mil.)	–	–	–	–	–	–
Employees	–	–	–	–	–	1,850

ALASKA PACIFIC BANCSHARES, INC. OTC: AKPB

2094 Jordan Avenue CEO: –
Juneau, AK 99801 CFO: –
Phone: 907 789-4844 HR: –
Fax: – FYE: December 31
Web: www.alaskapacificbank.com Type: Public

If you hail from Alaska Juneau about Alaska Pacific Bancshares. It is the holding company for Alaska Pacific Bank which serves the communities of Juneau Ketchikan and Sitka through about a half-dozen branches. The bank offers deposit products including checking and savings accounts CDs IRAs and check cards. Single- to four-family residential mortgages and commercial real estate loans each account for about a quarter of the company's loan portfolio. The bank also originates construction business and consumer loans. Alaska Pacific Bank was founded in 1935.

	Annual Growth	12/08	12/09	12/10	12/11	12/12
Assets ($ mil.)	(1.2%)	190.9	178.3	174.4	172.1	182.1
Net income ($ mil.)	–	(2.3)	(2.2)	0.8	0.9	0.5
Market value ($ mil.)	18.9%	2.9	2.9	3.9	4.0	5.8
Employees	0.0%	70	66	64	63	70

ALASKA RAILROAD CORPORATION

327 W SHIP CREEK AVE CEO: William G O'Leary
ANCHORAGE, AK 995011671 CFO: Barbara Amy
Phone: 907-265-2494 HR: –
Fax: – FYE: December 31
Web: www.alaskarailroad.com Type: Private

Alaska Railroad operates freight and passenger trains that run between Anchorage near the Gulf of Alaska up through scenic Denali National Park and north to Fairbanks. Known as the railbelt the area between Anchorage and Fairbanks is home to 70% of Alaska's population. Cargo carried by the railroad includes chemicals coal consumer goods gravel oil field and mining supplies and petroleum products. The company's rail network spans some 465 miles of main line track 80 miles of branch line and 110 miles of rail siding (auxiliary track used to store cars waiting to load or unload). The Alaska Railroad Corporation also owns more than 35000 acres of land about half of which is leased.

	Annual Growth	12/16	12/17	12/18	12/19	12/20
Sales ($ mil.)	(7.7%)	–	165.2	163.4	177.6	129.9
Net income ($ mil.)	–	–	22.4	18.0	21.6	(7.8)
Market value ($ mil.)	–	–	–	–	–	–
Employees	–	–	–	–	–	775

ALASKA USA FEDERAL CREDIT UNION

4000 Credit Union Dr. CEO: William B Eckhardt
Anchorage AK 99503 CFO: Norman P West
Phone: 907-563-4567 HR: –
Fax: +44-1962-867-037 FYE: December 31
Web: www.basepoint.co.uk Type: Private - Not-for-Pr

Alaska USA is no half-baked financial institution. The member-owned credit union provides financial services to more than 435000 members from about 65 branch locations in Alaska Washington and California. Serving consumers and small businesses Alaska USA offers deposit accounts loans credit cards insurance and trust and investment management services. Loans for automobiles and RVs account for nearly two-thirds of the credit union's lending portfolio; it also originates real estate consumer and commercial loans. Alaska USA was founded in 1948 as the Alaskan Air Depot Federal Credit Union.

ALBANY COLLEGE OF PHARMACY AND HEALTH SCIENCES

106 NEW SCOTLAND AVE CEO: –
ALBANY, NY 122083425 CFO: –
Phone: 518-459-1975 HR: –
Fax: – FYE: June 30
Web: www.acphs.edu Type: Private

Students with a prescription for medical and pharmaceutical training get their fill at Albany College of Pharmacy and Health Sciences (ACPHS). The college offers health care degree programs including pharmacy pre-med clinical laboratory sciences cytotechnology and biomedical technology. The school also is home to the Pharmaceutical Research Institute and Center for NanoPhamaceuticals which focuses on drug discovery and development. A satellite campus in Vermont offers doctor of pharmacy degrees. ACPHS enrolls more than 1500 students and was founded in 1881. The school changed its name to include "Health Sciences" in 2008. The change was made to better reflect the school's range of offerings.

	Annual Growth	06/13	06/14	06/15	06/16	06/17
Sales ($ mil.)	5.4%	–	50.2	61.8	58.3	58.7
Net income ($ mil.)	(42.9%)	–	7.7	5.3	1.7	1.4
Market value ($ mil.)	–	–	–	–	–	–
Employees	–	–	–	–	–	310

ALBANY INTERNATIONAL CORP NYS: AIN

216 Airport Drive CEO: A. William Higgins
Rochester, NH 03867 CFO: Stephen Nolan
Phone: 603 330-5850 HR: Alice McCarvill
Fax: – FYE: December 31
Web: www.albint.com Type: Public

Albany International's products look good on paper and on papermaking machines. The company makes machine clothing (MC custom-made fabrics and belts that move paper stock through each phase of production). It markets these products to paper mills worldwide through a direct sales staff and also provides woven/nonwoven fabrics for paper/tannery/textile industries and building products. Its other business segment Albany Engineered Composites (AEC) makes engineered composite parts for the aerospace industry and high-tech applications. Over the years the company has been selling off former units and operations to focus on its MC and AEC segments. About 55% of the company's sale comes from the US.

	Annual Growth	12/16	12/17	12/18	12/19	12/20
Sales ($ mil.)	3.7%	779.8	863.7	982.5	1,054.1	900.6
Net income ($ mil.)	16.9%	52.7	33.1	82.9	132.4	98.6
Market value ($ mil.)	12.2%	1,497.5	1,987.4	2,019.1	2,455.4	2,374.6
Employees	(2.4%)	4,400	4,400	4,400	4,600	4,000

ALBANY MED HEALTH SYSTEM

43 NEW SCOTLAND AVE CEO: James J Barba
ALBANY, NY 122083412 CFO: William C Hasselbarth
Phone: 518-262-3125 HR: –
Fax: – FYE: December 31
Web: www.amc.edu Type: Private

Albany Medical Center (AMC) provides medical care in upstate New York. Serving residents of northeastern New York and western New England the health system has at its heart the 730-bed Albany Medical Center Hospital. The general medical-surgical facility also provides specialty care in such areas as oncology rehabilitation and organ transplantation. AMC also features a children's hospital an outpatient surgery center and a group medical practice. It employs some 400 full-time physicians. Its Albany Medical College is one of the nation's first private medical schools. It offers undergraduate and graduate medical degrees and residency programs as well as fellowships and continuing medical education.

	Annual Growth	12/12	12/13	12/15	12/16	12/17
Sales ($ mil.)	(9.3%)	–	980.6	1,167.2	317.8	664.8
Net income ($ mil.)	23.4%	–	115.1	5.4	78.0	267.0
Market value ($ mil.)	–	–	–	–	–	–
Employees	–	–	–	–	–	8,760

ALBANY MOLECULAR RESEARCH INC
NMS: AMRI

26 Corporate Circle
Albany, NY 12203
Phone: 518 512-2000
Fax: -
Web: www.amriglobal.com

CEO: John Ratliff
CFO: Felicia I Ladin
HR: -
FYE: December 31
Type: Public

Albany Molecular Research dba AMRI pushes drug development efforts along from start to finish. The company provides contract research and manufacturing services to pharmaceutical and biotechnology firms. The company's services run the gamut — from compound screening and other drug discovery services to the contract manufacturing of existing and experimental drugs and drug ingredients for clinical trials and commercial sale. The company has R&D locations and manufacturing plants in the US Europe and Asia. Historically AMRI has leveraged its drug-discovery expertise to conduct some of its own research with the goal of licensing its compounds to other firms for further development.

	Annual Growth	12/11	12/12	12/13	12/14	12/15
Sales ($ mil.)	18.0%	207.6	226.7	246.6	276.6	402.4
Net income ($ mil.)	-	(32.3)	(3.8)	12.7	(3.3)	(2.3)
Market value ($ mil.)	61.3%	104.4	188.1	359.0	579.9	707.0
Employees	12.4%	1,389	1,329	1,282	1,668	2,220

ALBEMARLE CORP.
NYS: ALB

4250 Congress Street, Suite 900
Charlotte, NC 28209
Phone: 980 299-5700
Fax: -
Web: www.albemarle.com

CEO: Jerry Masters
CFO: Scott Tozier
HR: -
FYE: December 31
Type: Public

Albemarle develops makes and sells specialty chemicals for a wide range of markets including automotive construction consumer electronics crop protection lubricants pharmaceuticals plastics and refining. It is a major producer of lithium compounds used in batteries for consumer electronics; thermoplastic elastomers for car tires rubber soles and plastic bottles; and catalysts for chemical reactions. Albemarle also makes catalysts and fine chemicals used primarily in refining and bromine and bromine-based products for flame resistance and other specialty applications. About 75% of the company's revenue are generated outside the US.

	Annual Growth	12/17	12/18	12/19	12/20	12/21
Sales ($ mil.)	2.0%	3,072.0	3,375.0	3,589.4	3,128.9	3,328.0
Net income ($ mil.)	22.5%	54.9	693.6	533.2	375.8	123.7
Market value ($ mil.)	16.3%	14,965.1	9,018.4	8,546.8	17,262.1	27,354.7
Employees	2.7%	5,400	5,900	6,000	5,900	6,000

ALBERICI CORPORATION

8800 PAGE AVE
SAINT LOUIS, MO 631146106
Phone: 314-733-2000
Fax: -
Web: www.alberici.com

CEO: -
CFO: -
HR: -
FYE: December 31
Type: Private

Alberici helped shape the St. Louis skyline; it now sets its sights — or its construction sites — across North America. As the parent company of Alberici Constructors the company encompasses a group of enterprises with a presence in North America Central America South America and Europe. Operations include construction services building materials and steel fabrication and erection units. Alberici offers general contracting design/build construction management demolition and specialty contracting services while also offering facilities management. Founded in 1918 the Alberici family still holds the largest share of the employee-owned firm.

	Annual Growth	12/13	12/14	12/15	12/16	12/17
Sales ($ mil.)	(0.0%)	-	1,532.2	1,886.0	1,742.7	1,532.0
Net income ($ mil.)	-	-	0.0	0.0	0.0	0.0
Market value ($ mil.)	-	-	-	-	-	-
Employees	-	-	-	-	-	2,080

ALBERTSON'S LLC

250 Parkcenter Blvd.
Boise ID 83706
Phone: 208-395-6200
Fax: 208-395-6349
Web: albertsonsmarket.com

CEO: -
CFO: Robert Dimond
HR: -
FYE: February 28
Type: Private

Call it the incredible shrinking grocery chain. Albertson's LLC runs about 190 Albertsons supermarkets in Arizona Arkansas Colorado Florida Louisiana New Mexico and Texas. That's all that remains of what was once the nation's #2 supermarket operator with about 2500 stores. Stung by competition the firm sold itself to a consortium that included rival grocer SUPERVALU drugstore chain CVS investment firm Cerberus Capital Management and Kimco Realty for about $9.7 billion in 2006. SUPERVALU and CVS cherry-picked the company's best supermarket and drugstore assets. Subsequent closings and divestments including 132 stores in Northern California and most of its Florida locations further shrunk the firm.

ALBERTSONS COMPANIES, INC.

250 E PARKCENTER BLVD
BOISE, ID 837063999
Phone: 208-395-6200
Fax: -
Web: www.albertsonscompanies.com

CEO: Vivek Sankaran
CFO: Sharon McCollam
HR: -
FYE: February 29
Type: Private

Albertsons Companies is one of the biggest supermarket retailers in the US with more than 2275 stores in about 35 states and the District of Columbia. In addition to traditional grocery items many of the stores offer pharmacies and coffee shops and over 400 include adjacent gas stations. The company operates under some 20 banners including Albertsons Vons Pavilions Randalls Tom Thumb Carrs Jewel-Osco Shaw's Star Market Safeway Market Street Haggen and United Supermarkets. It also owns meal kit company Plated. Albertsons which traces its roots to 1939 owned by Cerberus Capital Management went public in mid-2020.

	Annual Growth	02/16	02/17	02/18	02/19	02/20
Sales ($ mil.)	2.1%	-	-	59,924.6	60,534.5	62,455.1
Net income ($ mil.)	217.4%	-	-	46.3	131.1	466.4
Market value ($ mil.)	-	-	-	-	-	-
Employees	-	-	-	-	-	210,000

ALBIREO PHARMA INC
NAS: ALBO

10 Post Office Square, Suite 1000
Boston, MA 02109
Phone: 857 254-5555
Fax: -
Web: www.albireopharma.com

CEO: Ron Cooper
CFO: Simon Harford
HR: -
FYE: December 31
Type: Public

Albireo Pharma (formerly Biodel) is a clinical-stage biopharmaceutical with a focus on orphan pediatric liver diseases. The company is developing novel bile acid modulators to treat liver diseases and gastrointestinal disorders where the body doesn't process bile correctly. Its lead product candidate A4250 is being studied for the treatment of children with life-threatening cholestatic liver disease. Headquartered in Boston the company's research and development facilities are located in Sweden. Spun out of AstraZeneca in 2008 Albireo went public in a reverse merger with biotech firm Biodel in November 2016.

	Annual Growth	12/16	12/17	12/18	12/19	12/20
Sales ($ mil.)	(7.5%)	11.4	0.0	12.7	9.6	8.3
Net income ($ mil.)	-	(16.4)	(24.4)	(46.1)	(62.7)	(107.6)
Market value ($ mil.)	20.6%	338.8	489.1	468.7	485.7	716.7
Employees	62.2%	13	22	39	55	90

ALCATEL-LUCENT USA INC.

600 Mountain Ave.
Murray Hill NJ 07974
Phone: 908-582-6173
Fax: 908-508-2576
Web: www.usa.alcatel.com

CEO: Pekka Lundmark
CFO: -
HR: -
FYE: December 31
Type: Subsidiary

Alcatel-Lucent USA may be headquartered in New Jersey but that doesn't mean it's not as technologically sophisticated as its Parisian parent. The US subsidiary of France-based Alcatel-Lucent designs develops and builds wireline wireless and converged communications networks. It supplies equipment software applications and related services to telecom carriers and network service providers such as 360networks AT&T and Verizon as well as enterprise customers. Government customers are served through DC-based subsidiary LGS Innovations which works with federal agencies including the US Army and major contractors such as Raytheon. Alcatel-Lucent USA accounts for almost 30% of its parent's overall revenues.

ALDAGEN INC.

2810 Meridian Pkwy. Ste. 148
Durham NC 27713
Phone: 919-484-2571
Fax: 919-484-8792
Web: www.aldagen.com

CEO: -
CFO: -
HR: -
FYE: December 31
Type: Subsidiary

Aldagen's work stems from the need for tissue repair. The biopharmaceutical company develops cell regeneration therapies using adult stem cells. It uses a proprietary technology that isolates an enzyme known as aldehyde dehydrogenase or ALDH which it believes can target a number of diseases. Aldagen hopes its products will be used to treat ailments such as cardiovascular conditions hereditary metabolic diseases in children and leukemia; all its drugs are in the development stage. The company does its own manufacturing and plans to do its own marketing. The company was acquired by Cytomedix in 2012.

ALCO STORES INC

751 Freeport Parkway
Coppell, TX 75019
Phone: 469 322-2900
Fax: -
Web: www.alcostores.com

NBB: ALCS Q
CEO: -
CFO: -
HR: -
FYE: February 02
Type: Public

Some retailers prize locations where they can battle competitors toe-to-toe; ALCO Stores (formerly Duckwall-ALCO) covets locations big national discounters such as Wal-Mart and Target won't even consider. The retailer runs some 200 ALCO and ALCO Market Place discount stores in small towns in some two dozen states primarily in the central US. Situated in towns with populations of 5000 or fewer ALCO stores offer a broad line of merchandise that includes automotive apparel consumables crafts electronics fabrics furniture hardware health and beauty aids toys and more. The company closed all of its smaller Duckwall stores to focus on growing its larger and more profitable ALCO chain.

	Annual Growth	01/10	01/11	01/12*	02/13	02/14
Sales ($ mil.)	(0.8%)	488.7	465.2	482.8	492.6	474.1
Net income ($ mil.)	-	3.0	(4.6)	1.7	1.3	(26.4)
Market value ($ mil.)	(7.1%)	39.7	44.2	28.3	27.6	29.6
Employees	(5.6%)	4,150	3,460	3,700	3,400	3,300

*Fiscal year change

ALDRIDGE ELECTRIC, INC.

844 E ROCKLAND RD
LIBERTYVILLE, IL 600483358
Phone: 847-680-5200
Fax: -
Web: www.aldridgegroup.com

CEO: Alex Aldridge
CFO: Gene Huebner
HR: -
FYE: March 31
Type: Private

Aldridge Electric powers up the Windy City and other parts of the Midwest. The electrical contractor divides its business into six main areas: airport industrial power drilling highway and transit. It works on projects ranging from Chicago's subway system to its airport runways. Additional activities include services for street lighting traffic signals high-voltage cabling and splicing and foundation drilling. Aldridge Electric has worked for clients such as Commonwealth Edison Company and Exelon Corporation. It sister companies in the family-owned AldridgeGroup include Aldridge Construction GFS Construction and Woodward Brothering.

	Annual Growth	03/08	03/09	03/10	03/11	03/17
Sales ($ mil.)	6.3%	-	-	272.2	208.9	417.2
Net income ($ mil.)	-	-	-	10.5	2.1	0.0
Market value ($ mil.)	-	-	-	-	-	-
Employees	-	-	-	-	-	850

ALDA OFFICE PROPERTIES INC.

315 S. Beverly Dr. Ste. 211
Los Angeles CA 90212
Phone: 310-734-2300
Fax: 925-474-2599
Web: www.coolsculpting.com

CEO: -
CFO: -
HR: -
FYE: December 31
Type: Private

California just may be the land of opportunity for ALDA Office Properties. The real estate company is focused on acquiring owning and operating office properties primarily in Northern and Southern California. Having formed as a new business in 2011 it filed to go public that same year with the intent of acquiring office properties that are 300000 sq. ft. or smaller in such markets as Los Angeles Orange County and San Francisco. Upon completion of its $18 million IPO ALDA Office Properties' initial portfolio will consist of a leasehold interest in a property in Beverly Hills California totaling 68000 sq. ft. The company intends to eventually qualify as an office real estate investment trust (REIT).

ALERE INC.

51 Sawyer Road, Suite 200
Waltham, MA 02453
Phone: 781 647-3900
Fax: 781 647-3939
Web: www.alere.com

NYS: ALR
CEO: -
CFO: -
HR: -
FYE: December 31
Type: Public

Alere offers both professional and consumer diagnostic health tests. Its professional diagnostic products include tests for cancers cardiovascular disease drugs of abuse infectious diseases and women's health including pregnancy tests and fertility monitors. Alere also makes consumer diagnostics including First Check drug tests through a venture with Procter & Gamble. Branded products include Cholestech (lipid and cholesterol testing) and Determine (HIV tuberculosis hepatitis B and syphilis detection). Abbott Laboratories is buying Alere for $5.8 billion.

	Annual Growth	12/11	12/12	12/13	12/14	12/15
Sales ($ mil.)	0.8%	2,386.5	2,818.8	3,029.4	2,586.7	2,463.3
Net income ($ mil.)	-	(133.5)	(78.2)	(71.3)	9.9	206.4
Market value ($ mil.)	14.1%	1,994.1	1,597.7	3,126.4	3,281.8	3,376.0
Employees	(10.8%)	14,500	17,400	17,600	9,800	9,200

ALERIS CORP
NL:

25825 Science Park Drive, Suite 400
Cleveland, OH 44122-7392
Phone: 216 910-3400
Fax: –
Web: www.aleris.com

CEO: Sean M Stack
CFO: Eric M Rychel
HR: –
FYE: December 31
Type: Public

Aleris is a global leader in the manufacture of aluminum products. The company's rolled products unit supplies product to manufacturers in most major industries but particularly the automotive building and construction transportation and consumer durables industries. It has manufacturing sites in North America Europe and Asia that turn out almost 863300 tons of finished product each year. Aleris diversified customer base includes a number of industry-leading companies such as Airbus Audi Boeing Bombardier Daimler Embraer Ford General Motors and Volvo. More than 55% of Aleris' revenue comes from US. Aleris is majority owned by Oaktree Capital.

	Annual Growth	12/15	12/16	12/17	12/18	12/19
Sales ($ mil.)	3.7%	2,917.8	2,663.9	2,857.3	3,445.9	3,375.9
Net income ($ mil.)	–	48.7	(75.6)	(210.6)	(91.6)	(11.8)
Market value ($ mil.)	–	–	–	–	–	–
Employees	1.9%	5,200	5,400	5,400	5,500	5,600

ALERISLIFE INC
NAS: ALR

400 Centre Street
Newton, MA 02458
Phone: 617 796-8387
Fax: –

CEO: Katherine Potter
CFO: Jeffrey Leer
HR: Ada Omejia
FYE: December 31
Type: Public

Five Star Senior Living runs about 250 senior living communities with more than 29270 living units across more than 30 states. Most of its properties are independent- and assisted-living communities that include independent living apartments assisted living suites and nursing homes. The rest of its properties are skilled nursing facilities involving Alzheimer's and memory care healthcare centers with skilled nursing and rehabilitation centers and continuing care retirement communities. Most of the company's senior living facilities are leased from DHC.

	Annual Growth	12/16	12/17	12/18	12/19	12/20
Sales ($ mil.)	(4.1%)	1,378.1	1,396.1	1,390.4	1,415.1	1,163.7
Net income ($ mil.)	–	(21.8)	(20.9)	(74.1)	(20.0)	(7.6)
Market value ($ mil.)	26.5%	85.5	47.5	15.2	117.5	218.6
Employees	(6.2%)	24,500	24,800	24,700	23,600	19,000

ALEX LEE, INC.

120 4TH ST SW
HICKORY, NC 286022947
Phone: 828-725-4424
Fax: –
Web: www.alexlee.com

CEO: –
CFO: Andrew Almquist
HR: –
FYE: October 03
Type: Private

The Alex Lee family of companies includes Lowes Foods and Merchants Distributors (MDI). Alex Lee grew out of Merchants Produce Company which was founded in 1931 by Alex and Lee George. MDI supplies food and general merchandise to more than 600 retailers with food and non-food items in over 10 Eastern states. The company's Consolidation Services supplies an array of warehousing and logistics services. As part of its business Alex Lee also operates Lowes Food Stores a chain of approximately 75 grocery stores located in the Carolinas and Virginia. The George family continues to control Alex Lee.

	Annual Growth	09/16	09/17	09/18	09/19*	10/20
Sales ($ mil.)	12.2%	–	2,261.7	2,239.0	2,286.1	3,192.2
Net income ($ mil.)	130.8%	–	4.6	14.7	25.2	56.4
Market value ($ mil.)	–	–	–	–	–	–
Employees	–	–	–	–	–	9,550

*Fiscal year change

ALEXANDER & BALDWIN INC (REIT)
NYS: ALEX

Post Office Box 3440
Honolulu, HI 96801
Phone: 808 525-6611
Fax: –
Web: www.alexanderbaldwin.com

CEO: Christopher Benjamin
CFO: James E Mead
HR: –
FYE: December 31
Type: Public

Alexander & Baldwin (A&B) is a fully integrated real estate investment trust which focuses in its real estate and agribusiness operations in Hawaii. The company has been operating ever since 1870. The company operated through its segments; Commercial Real Estate Land operation and Materials & Construction. The company's portfolio includes about 3.9 million square feet of gross leasable area as well as about 154 acres of land. In addition the company also owns more than 28000 acres of land in Hawai'i primarily conservation- and agriculture-zoned but also urban-zoned land.

	Annual Growth	12/16	12/17	12/18	12/19	12/20
Sales ($ mil.)	(5.8%)	387.5	425.5	644.4	435.2	305.3
Net income ($ mil.)	–	(10.2)	228.3	(72.0)	(36.4)	5.6
Market value ($ mil.)	(21.3%)	3,248.6	2,008.4	1,330.7	1,517.5	1,243.8
Employees	(6.4%)	806	836	875	793	618

ALEXANDER'S INC
NYS: ALX

210 Route 4 East
Paramus, NJ 07652
Phone: 201 587-8541
Fax: –
Web: www.alx-inc.com

CEO: Steven Roth
CFO: Matthew Iocco
HR: –
FYE: December 31
Type: Public

Alexander's is a real estate investment trust (REIT) that owns manages and leases more than five properties in metropolitan New York City. Once a department store chain Alexander's held on to its property interests including the site of its erstwhile flagship store — an entire block on Manhattan's Lexington Avenue. The REIT leases space at the mixed-use site to tenants such as Bloomberg The Home Depot and The Container Store. The Lexington site is also home to about 105 condominiums. In total Alexander's has about 2.7 million sq. ft. of leasable space. Vornado Realty Trust manages the company and leases and develops its properties.

	Annual Growth	12/17	12/18	12/19	12/20	12/21
Sales ($ mil.)	(2.8%)	230.6	232.8	226.4	199.1	206.1
Net income ($ mil.)	13.4%	80.5	32.8	60.1	41.9	132.9
Market value ($ mil.)	(9.9%)	2,021.7	1,556.4	1,687.2	1,416.5	1,329.4
Employees	(2.4%)	77	70	69	70	70

ALEXANDRIA EXTRUSION COMPANY

401 COUNTY ROAD 22 NW
ALEXANDRIA, MN 563084974
Phone: 320-762-7657
Fax: –
Web: www.alexandriaindustries.com

CEO: –
CFO: –
HR: –
FYE: December 31
Type: Private

Alexandria Extrusion Company (doing business as Alexandria Industries) makes precision aluminum extruded products such as custom front panels and heat sinks. The company's services include assembly CNC (computerized numerical control) machining finishing stretch forming and welding. Alexandria Industries markets its products to companies in a variety of industries such as electronics medical equipment power tools telecommunications and transportation. The company has expanded its offerings through acquisitions including those of aluminum specialty extruder M&M Metals and precision component maker Doege Precision Machining both in 2008. CEO Tom Schabel owns the company which was founded in 1966.

	Annual Growth	12/08	12/09	12/10	12/11	12/12
Sales ($ mil.)	(64.7%)	–	–	685.3	72.2	85.3
Net income ($ mil.)	–	–	–	0.0	0.0	0.0
Market value ($ mil.)	–	–	–	–	–	–
Employees	–	–	–	–	–	600

ALEXANDRIA INOVA HOSPITAL

4320 SEMINARY RD
ALEXANDRIA, VA 223041535
Phone: 703-504-3000
Fax: –
Web: www.alexandriaradiology.com

CEO: Jennifer McCarthy
CFO: Thomas Knight
HR: Bernardine Dunn
FYE: December 31
Type: Private

Inova Alexandria Hospital provides medical surgical and therapeutic services in northeastern Virginia. The hospital was founded in 1872 and became part of the not-for-profit Inova Health System in 1997. Inova Alexandria Hospital has about 320 beds. The hospital offers specialty services such as heart and cancer treatment women's and children's health care emergency medicine vascular procedures interventional radiology and sleep disorder and heartburn treatment services. The Inova Health System provides health care services in northern Virginia through a network of hospitals clinics assisted living centers and other provider facilities.

	Annual Growth	12/13	12/14	12/15	12/17	12/18
Sales ($ mil.)	2.8%	–	361.4	369.3	387.4	403.1
Net income ($ mil.)	(0.2%)	–	56.5	63.4	52.3	56.0
Market value ($ mil.)	–	–	–	–	–	–
Employees	–	–	–	–	–	1,750

ALEXANDRIA REAL ESTATE EQUITIES INC

NYS: ARE

26 North Euclid Avenue
Pasadena, CA 91101
Phone: 626 578-0777
Fax: –
Web: www.are.com

CEO: Stephen Richardson
CFO: Dean Shigenaga
HR: –
FYE: December 31
Type: Public

Alexandria Real Estate Equities owns develops and operates offices and labs to life science tenants including biotech and pharmaceutical companies universities research institutions medical office developers and government agencies. A real estate investment trust (REIT) Alexandria owns approximately 340 specialized properties with more than 35.1 million sq. ft. of rentable space in the US and Canada. Its portfolio is largely located in high-tech hotbeds such as Boston greater New York City the San Francisco Bay area San Diego Seattle and Research Triangle.

	Annual Growth	12/17	12/18	12/19	12/20	12/21
Sales ($ mil.)	17.0%	1,128.1	1,327.5	1,531.3	1,885.6	2,114.2
Net income ($ mil.)	35.6%	169.1	379.3	363.2	771.0	571.2
Market value ($ mil.)	14.3%	20,639.0	18,213.0	25,536.7	28,166.6	35,237.5
Employees	14.7%	323	386	439	470	559

ALEXIAN BROTHERS HEALTH SYSTEM

2601 NAVISTAR DR BLDG 4
LISLE, IL 605323697
Phone: 847-437-5500
Fax: –
Web: www.ascensionliving.org

CEO: Keith Parrott
CFO: –
HR: –
FYE: June 30
Type: Private

O brother can you spare some health care? Alexian Brothers Health System — which follows the principles set forth by St. Alexius of Rome the patron of beggars and pilgrims — runs two acute care medical centers a psychiatric hospital and a rehabilitation hospital. It also operates numerous occupational health and community health clinics in the northwestern suburbs of Chicago as well as home health and hospice agencies. With some 800 beds Alexian Brothers Health System's hospitals emphasize such specialties as cardiology obstetrics orthopedics and oncology. The health system was acquired by Catholic hospital operator Ascension Health in 2012.

	Annual Growth	06/10	06/11	06/12	06/13	06/14
Sales ($ mil.)	61.8%	–	–	–	61.6	99.7
Net income ($ mil.)	14.6%	–	–	–	6.9	8.0
Market value ($ mil.)	–	–	–	–	–	–
Employees	–	–	–	–	–	8,000

ALEXION PHARMACEUTICALS INC.

NMS: ALXN

121 Seaport Boulevard
Boston, MA 02210
Phone: 475 230-2596
Fax: –
Web: www.alexion.com

CEO: Ludwig N Hantson
CFO: Aradhana Sarin
HR: –
FYE: December 31
Type: Public

Alexion Pharmaceuticals develops drugs that inhibit immune system functions that cause rare hematology nephrology neurology metabolic disorders and cardiology. Its primary product monoclonal antibody Soliris treats two rare genetic blood disorders: paroxysmal nocturnal hemoglobinuria (PNH) and atypical hemolytic uremic syndrome (aHUS). Soliris was also approved in Europe Japan and the US to treat the rare refractory generalized myasthenia gravis (gMG) in adults. Other products include enzyme replacement therapies Strensiq the first approved treatment for hypophosphatasia in children Kanuma a treatment for lysosomal acid lipase deficiency and Ultomiris a new treatment option for adult patients with PNH in the U.S. International sales make up more than half of Alexion's revenue.

	Annual Growth	12/15	12/16	12/17	12/18	12/19
Sales ($ mil.)	17.7%	2,604.0	3,084.0	3,551.1	4,131.2	4,991.1
Net income ($ mil.)	102.0%	144.4	399.0	443.3	77.6	2,404.3
Market value ($ mil.)	(13.2%)	42,213.0	27,076.1	26,465.3	21,545.8	23,933.6
Employees	1.3%	2,924	3,121	2,525	2,656	3,082

ALEXZA PHARMACEUTICALS INC

NAS: ALXA

2091 Stierlin Court
Mountain View, CA 94043
Phone: 650 944-7000
Fax: –
Web: www.alexza.com

CEO: –
CFO: –
HR: Rhonda Ryan
FYE: December 31
Type: Public

Alexza Pharmaceuticals has found that its inhalation technologies can lead to swifter drug absorption. That is the basis for the company's primary product Staccato inhalers which it is developing to treat central nervous system (CNS) disorders. The inhalers contain a heating element coated with a thin layer of medicine. Before use the patient triggers the heating element which vaporizes the medicine allowing the patient to inhale it. The medicine is then rapidly absorbed through the lungs at a rate typically faster than oral and intravenous applications. Alexza Pharmaceuticals targets neurological disorders including addiction and anxiety.

	Annual Growth	12/10	12/11	12/12	12/13	12/14
Sales ($ mil.)	(40.0%)	42.9	5.7	4.1	47.8	5.6
Net income ($ mil.)	–	(1.5)	(40.5)	(28.0)	(39.6)	(36.7)
Market value ($ mil.)	4.4%	24.3	16.1	96.1	91.8	28.9
Employees	(4.4%)	97	44	63	90	81

ALFA CORPORATION

2108 E. South Blvd.
Montgomery AL 36116
Phone: 334-288-3900
Fax: 334-613-4709
Web: www.alfains.com

CEO: Jerry A Newby
CFO: Stephen G Grutledge
HR: –
FYE: December 31
Type: Private

Alfa Corporation wants to be top dog in Alabama's insurance pack. As part of the Alfa Mutual group of companies (Alfa Mutual Insurance Alfa Mutual Fire Insurance and Alfa Mutual General Insurance) Alfa Corporation primarily provides auto homeowners and other personal property/casualty insurance in about a dozen central and southeastern states. It also offers life insurance policies in its core markets of Alabama Georgia and Mississippi. The company which has nearly 400 office locations enjoys a pooling arrangement between all of the Alfa companies.

ALFRED UNIVERSITY

1 SAXON DR
ALFRED, NY 148021232
Phone: 607-871-2111
Fax: –
Web: www.alfred.edu

CEO: –
CFO: –
HR: –
FYE: June 30
Type: Private

Alfred University was a progressive bastion of learning from the start. A private university in Western New York the small non-sectarian school serves about 2400 students. Its academic programs range from the liberal arts and sciences to engineering business and art and design with degrees from a bachelor's to a Ph.D. The school also houses the New York State College of Ceramics. The student-faculty ratio is 12-to-1. The university was founded as the Select School in 1836 providing a coeducational environment from the school's beginnings. Alfred University (and the village it's in) is named for Alfred the Great ninth-century ruler of southern England. Its mascot is of course the Saxons.

	Annual Growth	06/12	06/13	06/14	06/15	06/16
Sales ($ mil.)	24.5%	–	64.2	63.5	67.3	123.9
Net income ($ mil.)	25.5%	–	12.5	11.1	4.0	24.7
Market value ($ mil.)	–	–	–	–	–	–
Employees	–	–	–	–	–	530

ALICO, INC.

NMS: ALCO

10070 Daniels Interstate Court, Suite 200
Fort Myers, FL 33913
Phone: 239 226-2000
Fax: –
Web: www.alicoinc.com

CEO: John Kiernan
CFO: Richard Rallo
HR: Johany Rosario
FYE: September 30
Type: Public

Alico is bullish on cattle but citrus generates more revenue. The agribusiness company which owns approximately 111000 acres of farm land in Florida dabbles in citrus and sod and native plant production as well as land leasing and conservation. Alico is one of the largest citrus producers in the United States of America. It has a breeding herd of approximately 8700 cows and bulls and it sells stock primarily to meat packing and processing plants.

	Annual Growth	09/17	09/18	09/19	09/20	09/21
Sales ($ mil.)	(4.4%)	129.8	81.3	122.3	92.5	108.6
Net income ($ mil.)	–	(9.5)	13.1	37.8	23.7	34.9
Market value ($ mil.)	0.1%	257.0	254.4	256.0	215.4	257.7
Employees	(5.9%)	283	233	235	251	222

ALIENWARE CORPORATION

14591 SW 120th St.
Miami FL 33186-8638
Phone: 305-251-9797
Fax: 305-259-9874
Web: www.alienware.com

CEO: –
CFO: –
HR: –
FYE: December 31
Type: Subsidiary

Aliens have landed in Florida and they're spreading! Relax they come in peace. Based in Miami Alienware caters to consumer video game enthusiasts in the market for high-performance gaming PCs with striking case designs. Sporting names like Area-51 and Aurora the company's colorfully appointed systems utilize processors video cards and storage components optimized for gaming applications. Its PC's are further differentiated by customized cases upgraded power supplies and multiple cooling fans. The company has branch facilities in Australia Costa Rica and Ireland. Alienware is a subsidiary of Dell.

ALIGN AEROSPACE LLC

21123 Nordhoff St.
Chatsworth CA 91311
Phone: 818-727-7800
Fax: 818-773-5493
Web: www.alignaero.com

CEO: –
CFO: –
HR: –
FYE: December 31
Type: Private

Align Aerospace (formerly Anixter Aerospace Hardware) isn't deploying any troops just scads of aircraft fasteners. The company distributes threaded fasteners for Airbus Boeing and military planes and related components such as bolts nuts screws and studs. In addition to distribution services the company also offers testing supply chain management inventory management kitting assembly and related services. Its customers are primarily aerospace and military manufacturers. The company has distribution hubs in Canada France and the US and a sales office in the UK. Former parent Anixter International sold the company to investment firm Greenbriar Equity Group in 2011.

ALIGN TECHNOLOGY INC

NMS: ALGN

410 North Scottsdale Road, Suite 1300
Tempe, AZ 85281
Phone: 602 742-2000
Fax: –
Web: www.aligntech.com

CEO: Joseph Hogan
CFO: John Morici
HR: Stuart Hockridge
FYE: December 31
Type: Public

Align Technology is a global medical device company engaged in the design manufacture and marketing of Invisalign clear aligners and iTero intraoral scanners and services for dentistry and exocad computer-aided design and computer-aided manufacturing (CAD/CAM) software for dental laboratories and dental practitioners. Its products are intended primarily for the treatment of malocclusion or the misalignment of teeth and are designed to help dental professionals achieve the clinical outcomes that they expect and the results patients' desire. To date over 9.6 million people worldwide have been treated with Invisalign System. Most of the company's revenues come from the US.

	Annual Growth	12/16	12/17	12/18	12/19	12/20
Sales ($ mil.)	23.0%	1,079.9	1,473.4	1,966.5	2,406.8	2,471.9
Net income ($ mil.)	74.9%	189.7	231.4	400.2	442.8	1,775.9
Market value ($ mil.)	53.5%	7,580.8	17,521.9	16,515.6	22,005.1	42,141.2
Employees	31.4%	6,060	8,715	11,660	14,530	18,070

ALIMERA SCIENCES INC

NMS: ALIM

6120 Windward Parkway, Suite 290
Alpharetta, GA 30005
Phone: 678 990-5740
Fax: –
Web: www.alimerasciences.com

CEO: Richard Eiswirth
CFO: J. Phillip Jones
HR: –
FYE: December 31
Type: Public

Alimera Sciences wants to see clear into the future. The biopharmaceutical develops prescription ophthalmic medicines particularly those aimed at treating ocular diseases affecting the retina. Alimera's first commercialized product Iluvien is an injectable insert — smaller than a grain of rice — that slowly releases a corticosteroid to the back of the eye to treat diabetic macular edema (DME). DME a retinal disease affecting diabetics can lead to severe vision loss and blindness. Iluvien is approved in the US (where it became commercially available in 2015) and in about 20 nations in Europe. Alimera is investigating another group of drugs as potential treatments for macular degeneration and diabetic retinopathy.

	Annual Growth	12/16	12/17	12/18	12/19	12/20
Sales ($ mil.)	10.3%	34.3	35.9	47.0	53.9	50.8
Net income ($ mil.)	–	(33.2)	(22.0)	(16.4)	(10.4)	(5.3)
Market value ($ mil.)	40.4%	6.2	7.6	4.1	43.4	24.1
Employees	2.9%	125	126	124	127	140

ALION SCIENCE AND TECHNOLOGY CORPORATION

1750 Tysons Blvd. Ste. 1300
McLean VA 22102
Phone: 703-918-4480
Fax: 703-714-6508
Web: www.alionscience.com

CEO: Bahman Atefi
CFO: Kevin Cook
HR: –
FYE: September 30
Type: Private

Alion creates alliances between science and big government. Alion Science and Technology is an employee-owned development and research company that provides scientific engineering and information technology research and consulting services primarily to federal agencies. More than 90% of its revenue comes from contracts with the US Department of Defense (DOD) especially the Navy. Focusing on national defense homeland security energy and the environment Alion specializes in naval architecture and marine engineering defense operations modeling and simulations technology integration and wireless communications.

ALIXPARTNERS LLP

2000 Town Center Ste. 2400
Southfield MI 48075
Phone: 248-358-4420
Fax: 248-358-1969
Web: www.alixpartners.com

CEO: Simon Freakley
CFO: Lisa Carnoy
HR: –
FYE: October 1/
Type: Private

Company headed in the wrong direction? AlixPartners would like to try to help you turn things around. The consulting firm provides operational and financial advisory services to underperforming companies worldwide. Specialties include assistance with bankruptcy reorganizations and litigation. AlixPartners also offers performance improvement and strategic consulting services for healthy companies. The firm operates from more than a dozen offices not only in the US but also in Europe and the Asia/Pacific region. Private equity firm Hellman & Friedman together with AlixPartners employees owns a controlling stake in the turnaround firm.

ALJ REGIONAL HOLDINGS INC

244 Madison Avenue, PMB #358
New York, NY 10016
Phone: 888 486-7775
Fax: –
Web: www.aljregionalholdings.com

NMS: ALJJ
CEO: Jess Ravich
CFO: Brian Hartman
HR: –
FYE: September 30
Type: Public

ALJ Regional Holdings owns a steel mini-mill in Kentucky which it acquired in 2005. The mill is operated by Kentucky Electric Steel which produces bar flat products that it sells to service centers as well as makers of truck trailers steel springs and cold drawn bars. Kentucky Electric Steel produces steel in both Merchant Bar Quality and Special Bar Quality. The company also recycles steel from scrap to produce steel. Kentucky Electric Steel operates mainly in the US Canada and Mexico.

	Annual Growth	09/17	09/18	09/19	09/20	09/21
Sales ($ mil.)	7.8%	326.7	369.8	355.0	389.1	440.9
Net income ($ mil.)	–	15.7	(7.3)	(16.0)	(67.7)	(4.6)
Market value ($ mil.)	(25.6%)	146.7	72.5	58.9	30.7	45.0
Employees	668.1%	2	2	6,322	8,407	6,963

ALL AMERICAN CONTAINERS, LLC

9330 NW 110TH AVE
MEDLEY, FL 331782519
Phone: 305-887-0797
Fax: –
Web: www.allamericancontainers.com

CEO: –
CFO: –
HR: –
FYE: December 31
Type: Private

It has become an All American pastime to put liquid consumer products (everything from beer to honey to cleaning products) in safe sturdy and attractive containers. All American Containers supports this tradition by making containers for the beverage chemical cosmetic food liquor perfume and pharmaceutical industries. The manufacturer's range of products includes glass plastic and metal tubes and dispensers and plastic and metal closures. The company exports its products to more than 50 countries around the world. Major customers include Coca-Cola McCormick PepsiCo and Seven-Up. All American Containers was founded by female Floridian and CEO Remedios Diaz-Oliver in 1991.

	Annual Growth	12/01	12/02	12/03	12/06	12/07
Sales ($ mil.)	2.7%	–	96.0	104.0	102.1	109.7
Net income ($ mil.)	9.4%	–	2.6	2.3	5.9	4.0
Market value ($ mil.)	–	–	–	–	–	–
Employees	–	–	–	–	–	260

ALL AMERICAN GROUP INC.

2831 Dexter Dr.
Elkhart IN 46514
Phone: 574-266-2500
Fax: 574-266-2559
Web: www.allamericangroupinc.com

CEO: Richard M Lavers
CFO: Colleen A Zuhl
HR: –
FYE: December 31
Type: Private

All American Group makes modular housing and other structures. The company's residential housing segment includes the All American Homes and Mod-U-Kraf Homes subsidiaries which build one-story ranch homes and two-story colonials. Its Ameri-Log Homes brand makes log homes and a line of energy-efficient houses are sold under the Solar Village banner. Subsidiary Innovative Design and Building Serives specializes in larger-scale housing projects such as apartments hotels and military and student housing. All American Group also sells a line of wheelchair-accessible buses through a joint venture with ARBOC Mobility. H.I.G. Capital acquired All American Group in 2011.

ALL AMERICAN SEMICONDUCTOR LLC

16115 NW 52nd Ave.
Miami FL 33014-9317
Phone: 305-621-8282
Fax: 305-620-7831
Web: www.allamerican.com

CEO: –
CFO: –
HR: –
FYE: December 31
Type: Private

They couldn't be more patriotic at All American Semiconductor. They take pride in distributing electronic components from more than 55 suppliers. The company primarily sells active semiconductor components such as transistors diodes integrated circuits microprocessors and memory products; it also offers passive components including capacitors resistors and switches. After filing for Chapter 11 protection from creditors All American sold substantially all of its assets to Rock River Capital for about $15 million. In 2008 Rock River Capital brought in new management to run the company.

ALL POINTS COOPERATIVE

120 8TH ST
GOTHENBURG, NE 691381006
Phone: 308-537-7141
Fax: –
Web: www.allpoints.coop

CEO: –
CFO: –
HR: –
FYE: September 30
Type: Private

All Points Cooperative provides agricultural support services to farmers and ranchers in central Nebraska. The cooperative offers seed energy fuel agronomy storage and purchasing services along with financial credit marketing and purchasing assistance for its member/farmers. Its agronomy services include fertilizer application soil sampling and crop planning and management. Its energy division offers bulk fuel bulk oil heating oil and propane delivery. It also operates retail outlets including two Ampride Convenience Stores and the Trustworthy Feed and Hardware Store. In addition to its headquarters in Gothenburg Nebraska All Points has cooperative operations in 12 other communities.

	Annual Growth	09/04	09/05	09/06	09/08	09/12
Sales ($ mil.)	–	–	0.0	91.7	192.9	236.1
Net income ($ mil.)	–	–	0.0	0.0	10.8	7.6
Market value ($ mil.)	–	–	–	–	–	–
Employees	–	–	–	–	–	150

ALL-AMERICAN SPORTPARK INC.

NBB: AASP

6730 South Las Vegas Boulevard
Las Vegas, NV 89119
Phone: 702 317-7301
Fax: 702 896-9754

CEO: Ronald Boreta
CFO: –
HR: –
FYE: December 31
Type: Public

If golf is your sport then this company has a park for you. All-American SportPark operates Callaway Golf Center (CGC) a 42-acre golf practice facility located at the end of the famous Las Vegas Strip. Amenities include 110 driving stations in two tiers and a lighted nine-hole par-three golf course called the Divine Nine. The center also features a restaurant and St. Andrews Golf Shop where customers can buy golf equipment and related merchandise. The founding Boreta family owns more than 20% the company. Tennis pro Andre Agassi and partner Perry Rogers together also own almost 20% of All-American SportPark.

	Annual Growth	12/11	12/12	12/13	12/14	12/15
Sales ($ mil.)	(1.3%)	2.1	2.1	2.1	2.1	2.0
Net income ($ mil.)	–	(0.7)	(0.9)	(0.9)	(0.7)	(0.7)
Market value ($ mil.)	(3.8%)	0.7	0.5	4.7	3.7	0.6
Employees	(38.5%)	35	30	30	31	5

ALLAN MYERS, INC.

1805 BERKS RD
WORCESTER, PA 19490
Phone: 610-222-8800
Fax: –
Web: www.allanmyers.com

CEO: A Ross Myers
CFO: –
HR: –
FYE: December 31
Type: Private

American Infrastructure provides heavy civil construction services for projects in the Mid-Atlantic. Operating as Allan A. Myers in Pennsylvania and Delaware and as American Infrastructure in Maryland and Virginia the family-run business builds and reconstructs highways water treatment plants medical facilities and shopping centers and offers site development for homebuilders. Its quarries and asphalt plants operate under the Independence Construction Materials (ICM) subsidiary which supplies aggregates asphalt and ready-mixed concrete to its construction companies. The company is ranked by Engineering News-Record as 25th on the country's Top 50 list of heavy civil contractors.

	Annual Growth	12/15	12/16	12/17	12/19	12/20
Sales ($ mil.)	7.9%	–	756.3	751.0	989.3	1,025.7
Net income ($ mil.)	22.2%	–	15.0	21.1	49.0	33.6
Market value ($ mil.)	–	–	–	–	–	–
Employees	–	–	–	–	–	2,000

ALLEGHANY CORP.

NYS: Y

1411 Broadway, 34th Floor
New York, NY 10018
Phone: 212 752-1356
Fax: –
Web: www.alleghany.com

CEO: Joseph Brandon
CFO: Kerry Jacobs
HR: –
FYE: December 31
Type: Public

Alleghany is a holding company with a focus on property/casualty reinsurance and insurance. Its subsidiaries include Transatlantic Holdings (TransRe) which offers property/casualty reinsurance globally through Transatlantic Reinsurance. The group also issues specialty property/casualty insurance policies through RSUI Group and CapSpecialty. CapSpecialty underwrites specialty lines of property and casualty insurance and professional lines of business. Alleghany Corporation was founded in 1929.

	Annual Growth	12/16	12/17	12/18	12/19	12/20
Assets ($ mil.)	5.0%	23,756.6	25,384.3	25,344.9	26,931.6	28,927.0
Net income ($ mil.)	(31.3%)	456.9	90.1	39.5	857.8	101.8
Market value ($ mil.)	(0.2%)	8,538.7	8,369.8	8,752.1	11,226.9	8,476.5
Employees	32.1%	3,420	4,402	9,300	10,786	10,407

ALLEGHENY COLLEGE

520 N MAIN ST
MEADVILLE, PA 163353902
Phone: 814-332-3100
Fax: –
Web: www.allegheny.edu

CEO: –
CFO: David McInally
HR: –
FYE: June 30
Type: Private

Allegheny College ranks among the oldest colleges and universities in the US. The private co-educational liberal arts school was founded in 1815 with a class of just four students. Today approximately 2100 enrolled students can pursue Bachelor of Arts and Bachelor of Science degrees in more than 50 academic programs including art biology communications computer science English history math music philosophy psychology and religious studies. It also offers accelerated master's and doctorate programs in partnership with other universities. Though the college is non-sectarian it maintains a historic affiliation with the United Methodist Church.

	Annual Growth	06/13	06/14	06/15	06/17	06/18
Sales ($ mil.)	(9.7%)	–	119.9	123.4	79.9	79.6
Net income ($ mil.)	–	–	(0.1)	0.6	21.5	6.9
Market value ($ mil.)	–	–	–	–	–	–
Employees	–	–	–	–	–	479

ALLEGHENY GENERAL HOSPITAL INC

320 E NORTH AVE
PITTSBURGH, PA 152124772
Phone: 412-359-3131
Fax: –
Web: www.ahn.org

CEO: Gregory Burfitt
CFO: –
HR: –
FYE: June 30
Type: Private

If there is a critical trauma anywhere near Pittsburgh Allegheny General Hospital (AGH) is ready to take it on. The roughly 630-bed hospital is the Level I Shock Trauma Center for the five-state region surrounding Steel City. AGH offers traditional medical and surgical services as well as cardiology care and organ transplants. The hospital also is engaged in research in areas such as neuroscience oncology trauma and genetics. AGH which treats nearly 22000 patients each year has about 800 physicians on its staff. The hospital which is affiliated with Philadelphia's Drexel University College of Medicine is a subsidiary of Allegheny Health System which itself is owned by Highmark Inc.

	Annual Growth	06/12	06/13	06/14	06/15	06/16
Sales ($ mil.)	2.8%	–	–	–	700.5	720.3
Net income ($ mil.)	(31.7%)	–	–	–	107.5	73.4
Market value ($ mil.)	–	–	–	–	–	–
Employees	–	–	–	–	–	5,064

ALLEGHENY TECHNOLOGIES, INC NYS: ATI

1000 Six PPG Place
Pittsburgh, PA 15222-5479
Phone: 412 394-2800
Fax: –
Web: www.atimetals.com

CEO: Robert Wetherbee
CFO: Donald Newman
HR: –
FYE: December 31
Type: Public

Allegheny Technologies Incorporated (ATI) is a global manufacturer of technically advanced specialty materials and complex components. In 2020 ATI revised its operating segment to High Performance Materials & Components (HPMC) and Advanced Alloys & Solutions (AA&S). The company's HPMC segment produces a wide range of high performance specialty materials parts and components for several major end markets including aerospace & defense medical and energy. The AA&S segment produces nickel-based alloys specialty alloys titanium and titanium-based alloys and stainless steel in a variety of forms including plate sheet and PRS products. The US customers generate about 60% of company's total revenue.

	Annual Growth	12/16	12/17	12/18	12/19	12/20
Sales ($ mil.)	(1.2%)	3,134.6	3,525.1	4,046.6	4,122.5	2,982.1
Net income ($ mil.)	–	(640.9)	(91.9)	222.4	257.6	(1,572.6)
Market value ($ mil.)	1.3%	2,020.2	3,061.4	2,760.8	2,620.1	2,126.7
Employees	(6.5%)	8,500	8,600	8,800	8,100	6,500

ALLEGIANT TRAVEL COMPANY NMS: ALGT

1201 North Town Center Drive
Las Vegas, NV 89144
Phone: 702 851-7300
Fax: –
Web: www.allegiant.com

CEO: Maurice Gallagher
CFO: Gregory Anderson
HR: –
FYE: December 31
Type: Public

Allegiant Travel pledges to serve the vacation needs of US residents in about 45 states. The company provides nonstop flights to tourist destinations such as Las Vegas Los Angeles and Orlando Florida Phoenix and other routes. Besides providing scheduled air transportation which sells travel on more than 575 routes to nearly 130 cities the company also supply unbundled air-related services and products as well as offering third party travel products such as hotel rooms and shuttle rental cars to its passengers. Allegiant Travel was founded in 1997.

	Annual Growth	12/16	12/17	12/18	12/19	12/20
Sales ($ mil.)	(7.7%)	1,362.8	1,503.8	1,667.4	1,841.0	990.1
Net income ($ mil.)	–	219.6	194.9	161.8	232.1	(184.1)
Market value ($ mil.)	3.3%	2,729.9	2,538.8	1,644.2	2,855.2	3,104.6
Employees	3.2%	3,589	3,951	4,159	4,697	4,068

ALLEGIS GROUP, INC.

7301 PARKWAY DR
HANOVER, MD 210761159
Phone: 410-579-3000
Fax: –
Web: www.allegisgroup.com

CEO: –
CFO: David Standeven
HR: –
FYE: December 31
Type: Private

Allegis Group is one of the world's largest staffing and recruitment firms. Among its group of staffing companies are Aerotek (engineering automotive and scientific professionals) Aston Carter (recruitment for accounting finance and professional skills) and TEKsystems (information technology staffing and consulting). Other Allegis Group units include sales support outsourcer MarketSource. Allegis Group operates through more than 500 locations worldwide. Chairman Jim Davis helped found the company (originally known as Aerotek) in 1983 to provide contract engineering personnel to two clients in the aerospace industry.

	Annual Growth	12/16	12/17	12/18	12/19	12/20
Sales ($ mil.)	(0.1%)	–	12,296.8	13,402.8	13,583.4	12,269.4
Net income ($ mil.)	–	–	0.0	0.0	0.0	0.0
Market value ($ mil.)	–	–	–	–	–	–
Employees	–	–	–	–	–	85,000

ALLEGRO MICROSYSTEMS, LLC

955 PERIMETER RD
MANCHESTER, NH 031033353
Phone: 603-626-2300
Fax: –
Web: www.allegromicro.com

CEO: Ravi Vig
CFO: Mark A Feragne
HR: –
FYE: March 30
Type: Private

Allegro MicroSystems is a leading global designer developer fabless manufacturer and marketer of sensor integrated circuits (ICs) and application-specific analog power ICs enabling critical technologies in the automotive and industrial markets. Its solutions are based on its monolithic Hall effect and xMR technology that allows customers to develop contactless sensor solutions that reduce mechanical wear and provide greater measurement accuracy and system control. The company went public after it closed its initial public offering in 2020.

	Annual Growth	03/12	03/13	03/16	03/17	03/18
Sales ($ mil.)	6.0%	–	489.9	526.3	600.1	654.9
Net income ($ mil.)	9.7%	–	45.8	43.7	65.5	72.6
Market value ($ mil.)	–	–	–	–	–	–
Employees	–	–	–	–	–	3,500

ALLEN & COMPANY LLC

711 5th Ave. 9th Fl.
New York NY 10022
Phone: 212-832-8000
Fax: 212-832-8023

CEO: –
CFO: –
HR: –
FYE: November 30
Type: Private

For Allen & Company there's no business like financing show business. The investment bank serves variously as investor underwriter and broker to some of the biggest names in entertainment technology and information. Viewed as something of a secret society the firm has had a quiet hand in such hookups as Seagram (now part of Vivendi) and Universal Studios Hasbro and Galoob Toys and Disney and Capital Cities/ABC. The notoriously secretive firm's famous annual retreat in Sun Valley Idaho attracts more moguls than a double-black ski run (Warren Buffett Bill Gates Rupert Murdoch and Oprah Winfrey have attended). Brothers Herbert and Charles Allen founded the company in 1922.

ALLEN COMMUNICATION LEARNING SERVICES INC.

55 W 900 S
SALT LAKE CITY, UT 841012931
Phone: 801-537-7800
Fax: –
Web: www.allencomm.com

CEO: Ron Zamir
CFO: Paul Zackrison
HR: –
FYE: December 31
Type: Private

Allen Communication Learning Services helps improve organizations' performance and productivity by developing customized training offerings. Founded in 1981 the employee-owned company provides systems like e-learning courseware and multimedia instruction (i.e. combining electronic courseware with Web meetings podcasts and e-mail) as well as related consulting presentation preparation and technical support services. The company's training courses address issues such as compliance ethics safety and management effectiveness. Catering to a variety of industries Allen has served clients such as Deutsche Bank Avon American Express Rockwell Collins Northrop Grumman and Pfizer.

	Annual Growth	12/08	12/09	12/10	12/12	12/13
Sales ($ mil.)	11.7%	–	6.4	7.5	9.9	10.0
Net income ($ mil.)	(16.3%)	–	–	1.0	0.9	0.6
Market value ($ mil.)	–	–	–	–	–	–
Employees	–	–	–	–	–	53

ALLEN HARIM FOODS LLC

126 N. Shipley St.
Seaford DE 19973
Phone: 302-629-9163
Fax: 541-608-4519
Web: www.asante.org

CEO: Joseph Moran
CFO: Brian G Hildreth
HR: –
FYE: March 31
Type: Private

The Allen family counts its chickens before and after they hatch. Allen Harim Foods (formerly Allen Family Foods) is a vertically-integrated poultry operation that includes breeding hatching feed milling and processing of its chickens. It operates nearly 30 of its own "growout" farms and contracts with about 270 independent farms to raise the rest of its chickens. Allen Harim offers whole frying roasting and rotisserie chickens chicken parts and tray packs. It sells 600 million pounds of chicken a year to food retailers in the US and throughout the rest of the world. Founded in 1919 Allen Family Foods filed for Chapter 11 bankruptcy protection in 2011 and sold its assets to Korea's Harim Group.

ALLEN-EDMONDS SHOE CORPORATION

201 E. Seven Hills Rd.
Port Washington WI 53074-0998
Phone: 262-235-6000
Fax: 262-268-7427
Web: www.allenedmonds.com

CEO: Paul D Grangaard
CFO: Jay Schauer
HR: –
FYE: December 31
Type: Private

Allen-Edmonds' shoes stand their ground in the US. Maker of high-end men's dress and casual shoes boots belts leather care goods and hosiery Allen-Edmonds makes most of its shoes in Maine and Wisconsin resisting the trend of moving production abroad. Its shoes are handmade by skilled craftsmen and Allen-Edmonds is known for its full range of shoe sizes for men. Its footwear is sold in more than 25 company-owned stores in the US Belgium and Italy as well as in department stores (Nordstrom) and specialty shops in more than 20 countries in Europe and Latin America and online and by catalog. Founded by Elbert Allen in 1922 the iconic American shoemaker is owned by Goldner Hawn Johnson & Morrison.

ALLEN LUND COMPANY, LLC

4529 ANGELES CREST HWY
LA CANADA FLINTRIDGE, CA 910113247
Phone: 818-790-8412
Fax: –
Web: www.allenlund.com

CEO: –
CFO: –
HR: –
FYE: December 31
Type: Private

The Allen Lund Company (ALC) knows loads; it matches shippers' loads with a network of truckload and less-than-truckload (LTL) carriers. (LTL carriers collect consolidate and haul freight from multiple shippers.) The brokerage firm arranges the transport of dry refrigerated (predominantly produce) and flatbed cargo. It operates from 30 offices throughout more than 20 US states. ALC Logistics ALC Perishable Logistics and ALC International (an international division) assist shippers in managing transportation costs tracking and tracing shipments managing appointments and executing freight forward management services overseas. The company was founded in 1976 by Allen Lund and his wife Kathie Lund.

	Annual Growth	12/14	12/15	12/16	12/17	12/18
Sales ($ mil.)	13.1%	–	457.5	426.3	516.0	661.8
Net income ($ mil.)	15.1%	–	13.2	12.4	10.3	20.1
Market value ($ mil.)	–	–	–	–	–	–
Employees	–	–	–	–	–	310

ALLERGAN, INC

2525 Dupont Drive
Irvine, CA 92612
Phone: 714 246-4500
Fax: –
Web: www.allergan.com

NYS: AGN
CEO: –
CFO: –
HR: –
FYE: December 31
Type: Public

Vanity thy true name be Profits — at least for Allergan. The company is a leading maker of eye care skin care and aesthetic products including best-selling pharmaceutical Botox. Originally used to treat muscle spasms (as well as eye spasms and misalignment) Botox found another more popular application in diminishing facial wrinkles. Allergan's eye care products include medications for glaucoma allergic conjunctivitis and chronic dry eye. Skin care products include treatments for acne wrinkles and psoriasis. Allergan also sells breast augmentation implants and other surgical devices. Its products are sold in more than 100 countries. Pharmaceutical giant Actavis is buying Allergan in a $66 billion deal.

	Annual Growth	12/09	12/10	12/11	12/12	12/13
Sales ($ mil.)	8.8%	4,503.6	4,919.4	5,419.1	5,806.1	6,300.4
Net income ($ mil.)	12.2%	621.3	0.6	934.5	1,098.8	985.1
Market value ($ mil.)	15.2%	18,752.2	20,436.7	26,112.0	27,299.5	33,058.2
Employees	8.3%	8,300	9,200	10,000	10,800	11,400

ALLEN ORGAN COMPANY

150 Locust St.
Macungie PA 18062-0036
Phone: 610-966-2202
Fax: 610-965-3098
Web: www.allenorgan.com

CEO: Steven Markowitz
CFO: Maggie Bova
HR: Teresa Omalley
FYE: December 31
Type: Private

Allen Organ's musical instruments may inspire hymns of praise but the company has faith in technology too. The company which introduced the world's first commercially available electronic organ in 1939 makes electronic keyboards including digital organs and accessories for use in churches theaters and other venues. Subsidiary Allen Integrated Assemblies performs contract manufacturing of electronic assemblies while Allen Audio makes PA systems for churches or social halls. Allen Organ sold its Eastern Research subsidiary to Sycamore Networks a provider of optical switching products in 2006. Allen Organ was founded by the late Jerome Markowitz (father of president Steven) in 1937.

ALLETE INC

30 West Superior Street
Duluth, MN 55802-2093
Phone: 218 279-5000
Fax: –
Web: www.allete.com

NYS: ALE
CEO: Bethany Owen
CFO: Robert Adams
HR: –
FYE: December 31
Type: Public

ALLETE provides light to the northern climes. Most of its business is classified within its regulated operations which include electric gas and water utilities located in northeastern Minnesota and northwestern Wisconsin. Those operations are conducted through subsidiaries Minnesota Power (approximately 145000 retail customers) and Superior Water Light and Power (some 15000 electric nearly 15000 gas and some 10000 water customers). ALLETE's other segment includes coal mining operations emerging technologies related to electric utilities and a real estate business (large land tracts in Florida). Subsidiary BNI Energy operates a mine in North Dakota that supplies primarily two generating co-ops Minnkota Power and Square Butte. In 2019 the company sold US Water Services to a subsidiary of Kurita Water Industries Ltd.

	Annual Growth	12/17	12/18	12/19	12/20	12/21
Sales ($ mil.)	(0.0%)	1,419.3	1,498.6	1,240.5	1,169.1	1,419.2
Net income ($ mil.)	(0.4%)	172.2	174.1	185.6	174.2	169.2
Market value ($ mil.)	(2.8%)	3,957.4	4,056.6	4,319.9	3,296.5	3,531.1
Employees	(9.3%)	2,017	1,889	1,339	1,342	1,365

ALLEY-CASSETTY COMPANIES, INC.

2 OLDHAM ST
NASHVILLE, TN 372131107
Phone: 615-244-7077
Fax: –
Web: www.alley-cassetty.com

CEO: Fred Cassetty
CFO: –
HR: –
FYE: April 30
Type: Private

Some build with blood sweat and tears; Alley-Cassetty Companies do it with trucks bricks and coal. The company's trucking division specializes in hauling liquid- and dry-bulk cargo including hazardous materials while the Alley-Cassetty Truck Center sells and services commercial trucks. The building supply division which operates in Georgia Kentucky and Tennessee produces and distributes bricks and other masonry products. Alley-Cassetty also provides coal to commercial and industrial users arranging its transportation via barge train and truck. Originally a coal company Alley-Cassetty was formed in 1964 through the merger of two Nashville residential coal delivery companies dating to the 1880s.

	Annual Growth	03/06	03/07	03/08	03/09*	04/10
Sales ($ mil.)	(28.5%)	–	–	–	114.0	81.5
Net income ($ mil.)	–	–	–	–	1.0	(0.3)
Market value ($ mil.)	–	–	–	–	–	–
Employees	–	–	–	–	–	180

*Fiscal year change

ALLIANCE BANCORP INC. OF PENNSYLVANIA   NASDAQ: ALLB

541 Lawrence Rd.
Broomall PA 19008
Phone: 610-353-2900
Fax: 610-359-6908
Web: www.allianceanytime.com

CEO: –
CFO: –
HR: –
FYE: December 31
Type: Public

Alliance Bancorp Inc. of Pennsylvania is the holding company for Alliance Bank (formerly Greater Delaware Valley Savings Bank). The bank has about 10 branch offices that serve individuals and local businesses in suburban Philadelphia's Delaware and Chester counties. It offers standard deposit products such as checking and savings accounts money market accounts CDs and IRAs. Commercial real estate loans (more than 45% of the company's loan portfolio) and residential mortgages (more than 40%) comprise most of the bank's lending activities. Alliance Bancorp was formed in 2007 when the bank converted from mutual ownership to a mid-tier stock holding company structure.

ALLIANCE DATA SYSTEMS CORP.   NYS: ADS

3075 Loyalty Circle
Columbus, OH 43219
Phone: 614 729-4000
Fax: –
Web: www.alliancedata.com

CEO: Ralph Andretta
CFO: Perry Beberman
HR: –
FYE: December 31
Type: Public

Alliance Data Systems a leading provider of data-driven marketing loyalty and payment solutions serving large consumer-based industries. Clients includes major retailers like Signet IKEA and Victoria's Secret as well as banks and brands in other large consumer-based industries. The company also develops and operates customer loyalty programs such as its Canadian-focused AIR MILES program and Netherlands-based BrandLoyalty a provider of tailor-made loyalty programs for grocers. Dependent on domestic business more than 80% of Alliance Data's revenue comes from the US.

	Annual Growth	12/16	12/17	12/18	12/19	12/20
Sales ($ mil.)	(10.8%)	7,138.1	7,719.4	7,791.2	5,581.3	4,521.4
Net income ($ mil.)	(19.8%)	515.8	788.7	963.1	278.0	213.7
Market value ($ mil.)	(24.5%)	11,356.5	12,598.0	7,459.0	5,576.3	3,682.8
Employees	(17.2%)	17,000	20,000	20,000	8,500	8,000

ALLIANCE ENTERTAINMENT LLC

4250 Coral Ridge Dr.
Coral Springs FL 33065
Phone: 954-255-4000
Fax: 954-255-4078
Web: www.aent.com

CEO: Jeff Walker
CFO: John Kutch
HR: –
FYE: January 31
Type: Private

Alliance Entertainment rolls out the rock 'n' roll to retailers colleges and public libraries. The company is a distributor of some 400000 CDs DVDs videogames and related products to some 3000 merchants including Target Best Buy Barnes and Noble and Borders Group as well as Internet retailers such as Amazon.com. Alliance also provides fulfillment e-commerce and related support services through its AEC Direct division. Its NCircle Entertainment unit licenses and distributes family entertainment titles based on such characters as Super Mario Bros. and My Little Pony. Alliance Entertainment founded in 1990 is owned by investment firms Platinum Equity and The Gores Group.

ALLIANCE FIBER OPTIC PRODUCTS INC.   NMS: AFOP

275 Gibraltar Drive
Sunnyvale, CA 94089
Phone: 408 736-6900
Fax: 408 736-4882
Web: www.afop.com

CEO: Peter C Chang
CFO: Anita K Ho
HR: –
FYE: December 31
Type: Public

Alliance Fiber Optic Products (AFOP) is no light weight in light waves. Communications equipment designers and manufacturers plug AFOP's fiber-optic components into products used to build networks that connect cities regions within cities and telecommunications service providers with their individual customers. Its optical path integration and optical fiber amplifier components which include attenuators couplers depolarizers multiplexers and splitters account for most of sales. The company sells directly to telecom equipment makers primarily in North America where it gets about half of sales. AFOP has more than 200 customers.

	Annual Growth	12/10	12/11	12/12	12/13	12/14
Sales ($ mil.)	17.3%	45.4	42.0	46.6	76.1	86.0
Net income ($ mil.)	24.6%	6.0	4.4	9.6	18.8	14.5
Market value ($ mil.)	(1.9%)	281.3	137.4	215.7	270.0	260.3
Employees	5.3%	1,137	1,037	1,063	1,514	1,397

ALLIANCE HEALTHCARE SERVICES INC   NMS: AIQ

100 Bayview Circle, Suite 400
Newport Beach, CA 92660
Phone: 949 242-5300
Fax: –
Web: www.alliancehealthcareservices-us.com

CEO: Rhonda Longmore-Grund
CFO: –
HR: –
FYE: December 31
Type: Public

Alliance HealthCare Services has a lead apron ready for you. Through its Alliance Imaging division the company operates some 500 diagnostic imaging systems for more than 1000 hospitals and other health care providers throughout the US. For most customers the company provides imaging systems and the staff to run and maintain them as well as marketing and billing support. In addition to MRI equipment and services (its largest revenue source) Alliance offers positron emission tomography (PET) computed tomography (CT) combination scanning X-rays and ultrasound among other imaging services. The company's Alliance Oncology unit runs about 30 cancer centers that provide radiation therapy.

	Annual Growth	12/11	12/12	12/13	12/14	12/15
Sales ($ mil.)	(1.1%)	493.7	472.3	448.8	436.4	473.1
Net income ($ mil.)	–	(160.1)	(11.9)	(21.5)	10.6	6.7
Market value ($ mil.)	64.2%	13.4	67.7	262.7	222.8	97.5
Employees	6.2%	1,909	1,720	1,504	1,582	2,430

ALLIANCE HOLDINGS GROUP LP   NMS: AHGP

1717 South Boulder Avenue, Suite 400   CEO: Joseph W Craft III
Tulsa, OK 74119   CFO: Brian L Cantrell
Phone: 918 295-1415   HR: –
Fax: –   FYE: December 31
Web: www.ahgp.com   Type: Public

When it comes to coal mining it takes more than one company to make this Alliance work. Alliance Holdings GP owns Alliance Resource Management GP the managing general partner of major coal mining company Alliance Resource Partners L.P. The latter manages some eight coal mining complexes in Illinois Indiana Kentucky and Maryland plus other coal interests in Pennsylvania and West Virginia. The company has coal reserves totaling 1.76 billion tons. Alliance Holdings GP generates all of its revenues from its general partnership interest and its ownership stake in Alliance Resource Partners L.P.

	Annual Growth	12/12	12/13	12/14	12/15	12/16
Sales ($ mil.)	(1.3%)	2,033.9	2,205.2	2,300.3	2,273.3	1,931.0
Net income ($ mil.)	(1.3%)	196.1	233.9	284.4	211.3	185.9
Market value ($ mil.)	(12.3%)	2,848.3	3,509.8	3,651.0	1,208.0	1,682.2
Employees	(6.5%)	4,345	4,313	4,439	4,243	3,324

ALLIANCE LAUNDRY HOLDINGS LLC

221 SHEPARD ST   CEO: Michael Schoeb
RIPON, WI 549711390   CFO: Bruce Rounds
Phone: 920-748-3121   HR: –
Fax: –   FYE: December 31
Web: www.alliancelaundry.com   Type: Private

Laundry day can't come often enough for Alliance Laundry Holdings (ALH). Through its wholly owned subsidiary Alliance Laundry Systems the company designs makes and markets commercial laundry equipment used in Laundromats multi-housing laundry facilities (such as apartments dormitories and military bases) and on-premise laundries (hotels hospitals and prisons). Its washers and dryers are sold under the brands Speed Queen UniMac Huebsch IPSO and Cissell. They're sold primarily in the US and Canada but also overseas. Investment firm BDT Capital Partners controls the company which was founded in 1908.

	Annual Growth	12/07	12/08	12/09	12/12	12/14
Sales ($ mil.)	13.1%	–	–	393.2	505.5	726.3
Net income ($ mil.)	12.3%	–	–	16.6	16.4	29.6
Market value ($ mil.)	–	–	–	–	–	–
Employees	–	–	–	–	–	2,100

ALLIANCE OF PROFESSIONALS & CONSULTANTS, INC.

8200 BROWNLEIGH DR   CEO: –
RALEIGH, NC 276177411   CFO: –
Phone: 919-510-9696   HR: –
Fax: –   FYE: December 31
Web: www.apc-services.com   Type: Private

Alliance of Professionals & Consultants (APC) provides information technology and other technical staffing services for clients in the telecommunications financial manufacturing e-commerce pharmaceutical and health care industries. The company offers temp-to-hire and permanent placement — as well as total outsourcing arrangements — in such areas as application development quality assurance and testing network engineering and security and project management. It also operates staffing and consulting practices in engineering and business services. APC which was founded in 1993 uses subcontractors to supply its clients with personnel for some projects.

	Annual Growth	12/13	12/14	12/15	12/16	12/17
Sales ($ mil.)	6.8%	–	58.1	58.9	63.1	70.7
Net income ($ mil.)	7.7%	–	1.2	1.3	1.1	1.5
Market value ($ mil.)	–	–	–	–	–	–
Employees	–	–	–	–	–	735

ALLIANCE RESOURCE PARTNERS LP   NMS: ARLP

1717 South Boulder Avenue, Suite 400   CEO: Joseph Craft
Tulsa, OK 74119   CFO: Brian Cantrell
Phone: 918 295-7600   HR: –
Fax: –   FYE: December 31
Web: www.arlp.com   Type: Public

Coal is the main resource of Alliance Resource Partners which operates in the Illinois Basin Central Appalachia and Northern Appalachia. The company has 11 underground coal mining complexes in Illinois Indiana Kentucky Maryland Pennsylvania and West Virginia. Alliance controls about 650 million tons of reserves. Approximately 205 million tons of these reserves located in Hamilton County Illinois are leased to independent coal company White Oak Resources. Alliance produces about 32 million tons of coal annually nearly all of which is sold to electric utilities.

	Annual Growth	12/16	12/17	12/18	12/19	12/20
Sales ($ mil.)	(8.9%)	1,931.5	1,796.2	2,002.9	1,961.7	1,328.1
Net income ($ mil.)	–	339.4	303.6	366.6	399.4	(129.2)
Market value ($ mil.)	(33.2%)	2,855.5	2,505.7	2,205.6	1,376.3	569.8
Employees	(3.3%)	3,324	3,321	3,599	3,602	2,902

ALLIANCEBERNSTEIN HOLDING LP   NYS: AB

501 Commerce Street   CEO: –
Nashville, TN 37203   CFO: –
Phone: 615 622-0000   HR: –
Fax: –   FYE: December 31
Web: www.alliancebernstein.com   Type: Public

The raison d'etre of AllianceBernstein Holding is its more than 35% stake in investment manager AllianceBernstein. (French insurer AXA through its AXA Financial unit owns a majority of the subsidiary.) AllianceBernstein which has more than $420 million of client assets under management administers about 200 mutual funds invested in growth and value equities fixed-income securities and index and blended strategies. The subsidiary also offer separately managed accounts closed-end funds structured financial products and alternative investments such as hedge funds. It mainly serves institutional clients such as pension funds corporations and not-for-profits in addition to retail investors.

	Annual Growth	12/17	12/18	12/19	12/20	12/21
Sales ($ mil.)	15.7%	232.4	270.6	266.3	308.4	416.1
Net income ($ mil.)	16.8%	207.4	242.4	238.6	279.4	385.8
Market value ($ mil.)	18.2%	2,486.8	2,712.1	3,004.0	3,352.4	4,848.4
Employees	4.4%	3,466	3,641	3,811	3,929	4,118

ALLIANT CREDIT UNION

11545 W. Touhy Ave.   CEO: –
Chicago IL 60666   CFO: Mona Leung
Phone: 773-462-2000   HR: –
Fax: 773-462-2095   FYE: December 31
Web: www.alliantcreditunion.org   Type: Private - Not-for-Pr

Members fly high with Alliant Credit Union. Though its branch total may be small — about 15 locations in or near major US airports — Alliant is one of the largest credit unions in the country with some $8 billion in assets and more than 275000 members. Its financial products and services include checking and savings accounts credit cards investments and insurance. Alliant also offers mortgages as well as home equity auto and student loans. Membership is open to all residents of the Chicago area as well as current and retired employees (and their family members) of firms such as United Airlines Google Kaiser Permanente and more than a hundred other qualifying companies and organizations.

ALLIANT ENERGY CORP
NMS: LNT

4902 N. Biltmore Lane
Madison, WI 53718
Phone: 608 458-3311
Fax: 608 458-4824
Web: www.alliantenergy.com

CEO: John Larsen
CFO: Robert Durian
HR: –
FYE: December 31
Type: Public

The spark of Alliant Energy's business is keeping the lights on and stoves lit for its upper Midwest customers. Alliant is the parent of two regulated utility companies Interstate Power and Light (IPL) and Wisconsin Power and Light (WPL) which together serve approximately 970000 electricity customers and approximately 420000 natural gas customers in Iowa and Wisconsin. In addition to providing retail energy the utilities sell wholesale electricity in Iowa Illinois and Minnesota.

	Annual Growth	12/17	12/18	12/19	12/20	12/21
Sales ($ mil.)	2.1%	3,382.2	3,534.5	3,647.7	3,416.0	3,669.0
Net income ($ mil.)	9.6%	467.5	522.3	567.4	624.0	674.0
Market value ($ mil.)	9.6%	10,672.7	10,582.5	13,706.0	12,907.0	15,396.7
Employees	(4.5%)	3,989	3,885	3,597	3,375	3,313

ALLIANT INTERNATIONAL UNIVERSITY, INC.

10455 POMERADO RD
SAN DIEGO, CA 921311799
Phone: 415-955-2000
Fax: –
Web: www.alliant.edu

CEO: Andy Vaughn
CFO: Tarun Bhatia
HR: –
FYE: June 30
Type: Private

Alliant International University churns out mental health professionals lawyers teachers businessmen and forensic specialists. The university prepares students (graduates and undergraduates who've completed at least two years of college) for careers in psychology and applied social sciences. Alliant International University consists of five graduate schools specializing in psychology business management forensics law and education. It also operates two undergraduate educational centers and has an affiliation with the Presidio Graduate School which focuses on sustainable management. It serves more than 4000 students from its seven campus locations in California as well as three satellite locations overseas.

	Annual Growth	06/07	06/08	06/09	06/10	06/14
Sales ($ mil.)	–	–	–	0.0	78.3	76.3	71.7
Net income ($ mil.)	–	–	–	0.0	8.5	1.9	(5.2)
Market value ($ mil.)	–	–	–	–	–	–
Employees	–	–	–	–	–	471

ALLIANZ LIFE INSURANCE COMPANY OF NORTH AMERICA

5701 Golden Hills Dr.
Minneapolis MN 55416
Phone: 763-765-6500
Fax: 212-771-9884
Web: www.cit.com/products-and-services/corporate-fi

CEO: Walter White
CFO: Bill Gaumond
HR: –
FYE: December 31
Type: Subsidiary

There's more to Allianz Life than life. The subsidiaries and affiliates of Allianz Life Insurance Company of North America (Allianz Life) offer a range of insurance investment and savings products to individuals throughout the US. Allianz Life boasts a network of more than 100000 independent agents and financial planners selling such products as life insurance variable and fixed life annuity products and long-term care insurance. It offers mutual funds and other broker-dealer services through its Questar Capital affiliate. Allianz Life operates in New York through its Allianz Life Insurance Company of New York unit. Allianz Life became a subsidiary of Allianz SE in 1979.

ALLIED BUILDING PRODUCTS CORP.

15 E. Union Ave.
East Rutherford NJ 07073
Phone: 201-507-8400
Fax: 201-507-3842
Web: www.alliedbuilding.net

CEO: Bob Feury Jr
CFO: –
HR: –
FYE: December 31
Type: Subsidiary

Allied Building Products counts home builders and contractors as part of its circle of friends. Serving the commercial and residential construction markets the company distributes exterior and interior building materials including roofing siding drywall and acoustical tile from major manufacturers. Allied also markets products under its own Cutting Edge and Tri-Bilt brands. The firm operates about 180 branches in 30 states and it maintains a fleet of more than 2700 vehicles including cranes and delivery trucks. Allied is a subsidiary of Oldcastle (itself a subsidiary of CRH). The company was founded in 1950 as a family-operated roofing and custom sheet metal fabrication business.

ALLIED HEALTHCARE INTERNATIONAL INC.

245 Park Ave.
New York NY 10167
Phone: 212-750-0064
Fax: 212-750-7221
Web: www.alliedhealthcare.com

CEO: –
CFO: –
HR: –
FYE: September 30
Type: Subsidiary

Allied Healthcare International offers temporary staffing services to the UK health care industry. The company operates through a network of about 110 branches across the UK. Allied Healthcare places its staff which includes more than 10000 nurses nurses aides and home health aides in hospitals nursing homes care homes and private homes. Customers affiliated with the British government such as the UK National Health Service and local social service departments account for a sizeable portion of the company's sales each year. Allied Healthcare International was established in 1981. In late 2011 it was acquired by Saga Group Limited.

ALLIED HEALTHCARE PRODUCTS INC
NAS: AHPI

1720 Sublette Avenue
St. Louis, MO 63110
Phone: 314 771-2400
Fax: –
Web: www.alliedhpi.com

CEO: Joseph Ondrus
CFO: Daniel Dunn
HR: –
FYE: June 30
Type: Public

Allied Healthcare Products helps medical workers get oxygen flowing. The medical equipment maker produces respiratory equipment used in hospitals surgery centers ambulances and other medical facilities as well as in patient homes. Its products include anesthesia equipment oxygen cylinders and nebulizers used in home respiratory therapy as well as emergency resuscitation products. It also makes medical gas system components installed in hospital walls during construction as well as spine immobilization backboards and other items used in trauma situations. Allied Healthcare sells directly to hospitals and through equipment dealers in the US and abroad.

	Annual Growth	06/17	06/18	06/19	06/20	06/21
Sales ($ mil.)	2.0%	33.5	33.8	31.4	31.9	36.3
Net income ($ mil.)	–	(2.1)	(2.2)	(2.1)	(3.0)	1.7
Market value ($ mil.)	9.5%	11.6	9.7	7.5	47.3	16.7
Employees	(3.5%)	218	202	181	218	189

ALLIED INTERNATIONAL CORPORATION OF VIRGINIA

101 DOVER RD NE STE 2
GLEN BURNIE, MD 210606561
Phone: 410-424-4003
Fax: –
Web: www.alliedint.com

CEO: –
CFO: –
HR: Heather Adkins
FYE: December 31
Type: Private

Allied International imports packed food products from more than 35 countries for distribution to grocery retailers throughout the US. Its product portfolio includes breakfast cereals candy condiments cookies and crackers as well as pasta products oils and salad dressings. It distributes such brands as Forrelli Smith & Johnson and Sunrise Valley. In addition Allied International imports and distributes kosher products and general merchandise including cleaning products and personal care items. The family-owned company was formed in 1980.

	Annual Growth	12/05	12/06	12/07	12/08	12/09
Sales ($ mil.)	(99.2%)	–	–	302,448.6	17.4	17.5
Net income ($ mil.)	(83.5%)	–	–	16.4	0.4	0.4
Market value ($ mil.)	–	–	–	–	–	–
Employees	–	–	–	–	–	19

ALLIED MOTION TECHNOLOGIES INC NMS: AMOT

495 Commerce Drive
Amherst, NY 14228
Phone: 716 242-8634
Fax: –
Web: www.alliedmotion.com

CEO: Richard Warzala
CFO: Michael Leach
HR: –
FYE: December 31
Type: Public

Allied Motion Technologies is a global company that designs manufactures and sells precision and specialty controlled motion components and systems. The company makes specialized brush and brushless DC (BLDC) motors and brushless drives used in broad range of industries. Its products are incorporated into a number of end products including high-definition printers scanners surgical tools and equipment surgical robots diagnostic equipment test equipment patient mobility and rehabilitation equipment hospital beds and mobile equipment carts. Allied Motion's target markets include vehicle aerospace and defense industrial and medical. The company was incorporated in 1962. The US was responsible for about 60% of the total sales.

	Annual Growth	12/16	12/17	12/18	12/19	12/20
Sales ($ mil.)	10.5%	245.9	252.0	310.6	371.1	366.7
Net income ($ mil.)	10.7%	9.1	8.0	15.9	17.0	13.6
Market value ($ mil.)	24.3%	313.0	484.1	653.9	709.6	747.6
Employees	9.7%	1,220	1,250	1,600	1,700	1,770

ALLIED NEVADA GOLD CORP ASE: ANV

9790 Gateway Drive, Suite 200
Reno, NV 89521
Phone: 775 358-4455
Fax: 775 358-4458
Web: www.alliednevada.com

CEO: –
CFO: –
HR: –
FYE: December 31
Type: Public

All that glitters is not gold; some of it's silver. That's the story at Allied Nevada Gold a mining company that produces gold primarily and silver as a by-product from its property in Nevada. Its wholly owned Hycroft Mine sitting on 96 sq. mi. has proven and probable mineral reserves of about 3 million ounces of gold and nearly 50 million ounces of silver. The company is conducting feasibility studies for a mill on the property that would process sulfide and other high oxide ores. Allied Nevada Gold also explores for gold silver and other minerals on more than 100 properties in the state. The company was spun off from Vista Gold in 2007 when it acquired its former parent's Nevada mining operations.

	Annual Growth	12/09	12/10	12/11	12/12	12/13
Sales ($ mil.)	57.8%	43.2	130.9	152.0	214.6	267.9
Net income ($ mil.)	(36.1%)	8.5	34.1	36.7	47.7	1.4
Market value ($ mil.)	(30.3%)	1,569.0	2,737.4	3,150.4	3,134.8	369.4
Employees	24.7%	177	231	291	742	428

ALLIED RESOURCES INC NBB: ALOD

1403 East 900 South
Salt Lake City, UT 84105
Phone: 801 232-7395
Fax: –
Web: www.alliedresourcesinc.com

CEO: Ruairidh Campbell
CFO: Ruairidh Campbell
HR: –
FYE: December 31
Type: Public

Allied Resources has allied with Allstate Energy to get the most out of its Appalachian energy resources. The company is an oil and natural gas exploration and production enterprise with primary operations in West Virginia (in Calhoun and Ritchie counties). Allied Resources produces oil and natural gas from 145 wells which are maintained and operated by Allstate Energy. The depth at which the wells produce ranges from 1730 feet to more than 5470 feet. The company also owns 13 gross wells in Goliad Edwards and Jackson counties Texas. In 2008 Allied Resources reported proved reserves of 18950 barrels of oil and 1.4 billion cu. ft. of natural gas. CEO Ruairidh Campbell owns 27% of the company

	Annual Growth	12/16	12/17	12/18	12/19	12/20
Sales ($ mil.)	(16.9%)	0.3	0.3	1.1	0.9	0.1
Net income ($ mil.)	–	(0.3)	(0.2)	0.6	0.3	(0.2)
Market value ($ mil.)	15.8%	1.0	1.1	0.8	1.1	1.8
Employees	–	–	–	–	–	–

ALLIED SECURITY HOLDINGS LLC

161 WASHINGTON ST STE 600
CONSHOHOCKEN, PA 194282083
Phone: 484-351-1300
Fax: –
Web: www.aus.com

CEO: William C Whitmore Jr
CFO: –
HR: –
FYE: December 31
Type: Private

Better than a blanket Allied Security Holdings gives customers a sense of security. One of the largest private contract security firms in the US it does business as AlliedBarton Security Services. It recruits and employs trained security guards to serve thousands of customers (some of which are large FORTUNE 500 companies) and their facilities. They include government facilities hospitals offices ports residential communities shopping centers and universities. The firm also provides employment and background screening services through its HR Plus subsidiary. In mid-2016 AlliedBarton merged with Universal Services of America to create Allied Universal North America's largest security services group.

	Annual Growth	12/10	12/11	12/12	12/13	12/14
Sales ($ mil.)	5.7%	–	–	1,923.9	2,042.4	2,149.2
Net income ($ mil.)	(25.0%)	–	–	43.8	51.7	24.7
Market value ($ mil.)	–	–	–	–	–	–
Employees	–	–	–	–	–	53,760

ALLIED SYSTEMS HOLDINGS INC.

2302 Parklake Dr. Bldg. 15 Ste. 600
Atlanta GA 30345
Phone: 404-373-4285
Fax: 404-370-4206
Web: www.alliedholdings.com

CEO: Mark J Gendregske
CFO: Thomas H King
HR: –
FYE: December 31
Type: Private

Allied Systems Holdings is busting to "get a move on." Carrying millions of cars trucks and SUVs every year Allied Systems Holdings leads the North American vehicle-hauling market. Through subsidiary Allied Automotive Group Allied Systems moves approximately 9 million vehicles annually with a fleet of about 4000 tractor-trailer rigs which it operates from about 90 terminals in the US and Canada. Assembled vehicles are transported from manufacturing plants railway distribution points ports and auctions to auto dealers and car rental companies. Customers have included major auto OEMs Chrysler Ford General Motors Honda and Toyota. In mid-2012 Allied Systems filed for Chapter 11 bankruptcy protection.

ALLINA HEALTH SYSTEM

2925 CHICAGO AVE
MINNEAPOLIS, MN 554071321
Phone: 612-262-5000
Fax: -
Web: www.allinahealth.org

CEO: Tom Lindquist
CFO: Duncan Gallagher
HR: -
FYE: December 31
Type: Private

Allina Health System is a not-for-profit health care system that works to protect people's #1 asset — their good health. The system owns and operates a dozen hospitals a network of nearly 100 clinics and specialty centers and a whole bunch of pharmacies. It has licensed bed capacity of 2451 acute care beds. Its vast system of provider locations serve residents throughout Minnesota and western Wisconsin providing disease prevention programs along with specialized inpatient and outpatient services. Allina's Aspen Medical Group division also operates a range of outpatient clinics providing primary and specialty care.

	Annual Growth	12/13	12/14	12/15	12/16	12/17
Sales ($ mil.)	8.4%	-	-	-	3,947.7	4,279.1
Net income ($ mil.)	131.3%	-	-	-	74.9	173.1
Market value ($ mil.)	-	-	-	-	-	-
Employees	-	-	-	-	-	26,400

ALLIS-CHALMERS ENERGY INC.

11125 Equity Dr. Ste. 200
Houston TX 77041
Phone: 713-856-4222
Fax: 713-856-4246
Web: www.alchenergy.com/profiles/investor/fullpage.

CEO: -
CFO: -
HR: -
FYE: December 31
Type: Subsidiary

This company knows the drill. Allis-Chalmers Energy provides drilling and oil field services to oil and gas exploration companies operating primarily Argentina and in the western and southern US. It operates in three segments: Drilling and Completion; Oilfield Services (underbalanced drilling directional drilling tubular services and production services); and Rental Services. Its Strata Directional Technology subsidiary offers directional drilling services to clients in conventional and unconventional hydrocarbon plays. In 2011 Archer Limited (formerly Seawell) acquired debt-laden Allis-Chalmers for some $890 million including assumed debt.

ALLISON TRANSMISSION HOLDINGS INC
NYS: ALSN

One Allison Way
Indianapolis, IN 46222
Phone: 317 242-5000
Fax: -
Web: www.allisontransmission.com

CEO: David Graziosi
CFO: G. Bohley
HR: -
FYE: December 31
Type: Public

Allison Transmission is the world's largest manufacturer of fully-automatic transmissions for on- and off-highway commercial vehicles and US military vehicles. Its products are used in vehicles such as medium- and heavy-duty trucks transit buses motorhomes and mining and construction equipment. Allison's customers include original equipment manufacturers (OEMs) as well as the US Department of Defense. The company also makes electric drives for transit buses and shuttles and its ReTran remanufactured transmissions for aftermarket customers. The US accounts for most of the company's revenue but Allison also serves customers in Europe the Middle East Africa Asia and South America. The company traces its historical roots back to 1915.

	Annual Growth	12/17	12/18	12/19	12/20	12/21
Sales ($ mil.)	1.5%	2,262.0	2,713.0	2,698.0	2,081.0	2,402.0
Net income ($ mil.)	(3.2%)	504.0	639.0	604.0	299.0	442.0
Market value ($ mil.)	(4.2%)	4,275.3	4,358.6	4,796.4	4,281.2	3,608.2
Employees	5.9%	2,700	2,900	3,700	3,300	3,400

ALLOS THERAPEUTICS INC.
NASDAQ: ALTH

11080 CirclePoint Rd. Ste. 200
Westminster CO 80020
Phone: 303-426-6262
Fax: 303-426-4731
Web: www.allos.com

CEO: -
CFO: -
HR: -
FYE: December 31
Type: Public

Drug developer Allos Therapeutics has worked to make a big breakthrough in the fight against cancer. The company's first FDA-approved drug Folotyn (pralatrexate) was launched commercially in the US in 2010 to treat a relatively rare blood cancer called peripheral T-cell lymphoma (PTCL). Allos Therapeutics is also investigating the compound as a potential treatment in other oncology applications including additional forms of lymphoma. Spectrum Pharmaceuticals acquired Allos Therapeutics in 2012.

ALLOY INC.

151 W. 26th St. 11th Fl.
New York NY 10001
Phone: 212-244-4307
Fax: 212-244-4311
Web: www.alloy.com

CEO: -
CFO: -
HR: -
FYE: January 31
Type: Subsidiary

Alloy has its eye on the next generation. Through its Alloy Media + Marketing division the company provides advertising and marketing services for online and print media designed to help customers reach the attractive yet elusive youth market of people between the ages of 10 and 24. Its Alloy Entertainment develops TV shows (Gossip Girl) while its Alloy Digital broadcasts content online including original sponsored Web series (Private). In addition the company's Channel One TV network broadcasts daily newscasts and educational videos at junior and senior high schools across the country. Investment firm ZelnickMedia Corporation owns Alloy. Warner Bros. Television Group is buying Alloy Entertainment.

ALLSCRIPTS HEALTHCARE SOLUTIONS, INC.
NMS: MDRX

222 Merchandise Mart, Suite 2024
Chicago, IL 60654
Phone: 800 334-8534
Fax: -
Web: www.allscripts.com

CEO: Paul Black
CFO: Richard Poulton
HR: -
FYE: December 31
Type: Public

Allscripts Healthcare Solutions provides information technology ("IT") solutions and service to help healthcare organizations around the world achieve optical clinical financial and operational results. The company provides electronic health record ("EHR") from financial management population health management and precision medicine and consumer solutions. In additions built in on an open integrated platform which enables to streamline the workflows leverage functionality from other software vender and exchange date. . The US accounts for more than 95% of revenue. The company was founded in 1986.

	Annual Growth	12/16	12/17	12/18	12/19	12/20
Sales ($ mil.)	(0.8%)	1,549.9	1,806.3	1,750.0	1,771.7	1,502.7
Net income ($ mil.)	294.8%	2.9	(152.6)	412.3	(182.2)	700.4
Market value ($ mil.)	9.1%	1,428.8	2,036.2	1,349.0	1,373.5	2,020.8
Employees	2.9%	7,500	8,900	9,500	9,600	8,400

ALLSTATE CORP
NYS: ALL

2775 Sanders Road
Northbrook, IL 60062
Phone: 847 402-5000
Fax: –
Web: www.allstate.com

CEO: Don Civgin
CFO: Mario Rizzo
HR: –
FYE: December 31
Type: Public

Serving more than 175.9 million policies in force Allstate is one of the top overall property/casualty insurers. Its Allstate Protection segment sells auto homeowners and other property/casualty insurance products in Canada and the US. Other divisions provide life insurance voluntary benefits such as short-term disability and critical illness policies and consumer protection plans. In early 2021 Allstate agreed to sell its Allstate Life Insurance Company and certain affiliates for $2.8 billion to Antelope US Holdings Company an affiliate of an investment fund associated with The Blackstone Group Inc.

	Annual Growth	12/17	12/18	12/19	12/20	12/21
Assets ($ mil.)	(3.0%)	112,422.0	112,249.0	119,950.0	125,987.0	99,440.0
Net income ($ mil.)	(15.9%)	3,189.0	2,252.0	4,847.0	5,576.0	1,599.0
Market value ($ mil.)	3.0%	29,423.5	23,219.0	31,598.5	30,890.3	33,059.7
Employees	6.3%	42,900	45,700	46,290	42,160	54,700

ALLSTEEL INC.

2210 2nd Ave.
Muscatine IA 52761
Phone: 563-262-4800
Fax: 563-272-7812
Web: www.allsteeloffice.com

CEO: –
CFO: –
HR: –
FYE: December 31
Type: Subsidiary

Allsteel believes that the best offices are filled with Energy. The company makes office systems desks seating storage products tables and accessories under names such as Energy Stride Align Concensys Scout and Terrace. Allsteel sells its products through dealers and its own sales force. Its customers originate in the corporate government and educational markets. The company operates about 10 showrooms in the US and Canada. Founded in 1912 as All-Steel-Equip Allsteel invented the lateral file in 1967. The company is a subsidiary of HNI.

ALLWAYS HEALTH PARTNERS, INC.

399 REVOLUTION DR
SOMERVILLE, MA 021451484
Phone: 617-772-5500
Fax: –
Web: www.nhp.org

CEO: Deborah Enos
CFO: Garrett Parker
HR: –
FYE: December 31
Type: Private

AllWays Health Partners previously known as Neighborhood Health Plan (NHP) packages and delivers innovative products and programs that improve the experience of accessing care and coverage and health outcomes. AllWays Health Partners offers health plans for small businesses large groups and families and individuals. The company offers Value HMO for Boston employees and retirees ensuring access to the highest quality care. The Value HMO networks include Massachusetts General Hospital Brigham and Women's Hospital Beth Israel Deaconess Medical Center Lahey Clinic Spaulding Rehab Mass Eye and Ear and more.

	Annual Growth	12/11	12/12	12/13	12/14	12/15
Sales ($ mil.)	25.6%	–	–	1,380.1	1,743.7	2,178.2
Net income ($ mil.)	–	–	–	(68.1)	(108.7)	(22.8)
Market value ($ mil.)	–	–	–	–	–	–
Employees	–	–	–	–	–	340

ALLY BANK

6985 S UNION PARK CTR # 435
MIDVALE, UT 840474177
Phone: 801-790-5005
Fax: –
Web: www.ally.com

CEO: Diane E Morais
CFO: James N Young
HR: –
FYE: December 31
Type: Private

Ally Bank is on your side when it comes to banking. Formerly known as GMAC Bank Ally Bank (which is a subsidiary of government-backed Ally Financial) offers savings and money market accounts as well as traditional and no-penalty CDs. The online bank also offers interest checking accounts. The bank offers its services online and over the phone; it operates no physical branch locations. Clients also can use any ATM in the US and Ally will reimburse any fees charged by other banks. Ally Bank was revamped and renamed in 2009 in the midst of GM's (very public) financial difficulties. Predecessor GMAC Bank had been in operation since 2001.

	Annual Growth	06/04	06/05	06/06*	12/07	12/16
Assets ($ mil.)	42.5%	–	–	3,586.2	28,472.5	123,547.7
Net income ($ mil.)	131.3%	–	–	0.3	291.4	1,273.3
Market value ($ mil.)	–	–	–	–	–	–
Employees	–	–	–	–	–	42

*Fiscal year change

ALLY COMMERCIAL FINANCE LLC

3000 Town Center Ste. 280
Southfield MI 48075
Phone: 248-356-4622
Fax: 248-350-2733
Web: www.allycf.com

CEO: –
CFO: –
HR: Rebecca King
FYE: December 31
Type: Subsidiary

In the market for some cash for your business? Ally Commercial Finance provides funding to large and middle-market businesses in a variety of industries. The company's product menu includes term loans letters of credit working capital asset-based lending equipment finance and leasing import/export financing equity co-investments and recapitalizations. Target industries include automotive business services consumer goods health care manufacturing and retail. Ally Commercial typically lends from $5 million to $250 million per transaction. Its portfolio entails approximately $4 billion in financing to some 125 corporate clients. A subsidiary of auto lender Ally Financial the firm has five US offices.

ALLY FINANCIAL INC
NYS: ALLY

Ally Detroit Center, 500 Woodward Ave., Floor 10
Detroit, MI 48226
Phone: 866 710-4623
Fax: –
Web: www.ally.com

CEO: Jeffrey Brown
CFO: Jennifer LaClair
HR: –
FYE: December 31
Type: Public

Ally Financial is one of the leading online banks in the US Ally operates its digital direct bank Ally Bank which offers deposit mortgage (through Ally Home) auto and investing products. Ally also provides auto financing for auto dealerships (mostly GM and Chrysler) and their customers. The company sells both consumer finance protection and insurance products to automotive dealers and commercial insurance products directly to dealers. Additionally the company offers securities-brokerage and investment-advisory services through Ally Invest. Ally's robust corporate-finance business offers capital for equity sponsors and middle-market companies.

	Annual Growth	12/16	12/17	12/18	12/19	12/20
Assets ($ mil.)	2.7%	163,728.0	167,148.0	178,869.0	180,644.0	182,165.0
Net income ($ mil.)	0.4%	1,067.0	929.0	1,263.0	1,715.0	1,085.0
Market value ($ mil.)	17.0%	7,126.3	10,925.5	8,490.1	11,450.1	13,360.9
Employees	5.7%	7,600	7,900	8,200	8,700	9,500

ALMOST FAMILY, INC.

9510 ORMSBY STATION RD # 300　　　　　　　　　　　　　CEO: –
LOUISVILLE, KY 402235016　　　　　　　　　　　　　　　CFO: –
Phone: 502-891-1000　　　　　　　　　　　　　　　　　　HR: –
Fax: –　　　　　　　　　　　　　　　　　　　　FYE: December 29
Web: www.almostfamily.com　　　　　　　　　　　　Type: Private

Almost Family steps in when you're more than an arm's reach from family members with health needs. With its home health nursing services Almost Family offers senior citizens in 26 states (including Florida) an alternative to institutional care. Its Visiting Nurse unit provides skilled nursing care and therapy services at home under a variety of names including Apex Caretenders Community Home Health and Mederi-Caretenders. Its Personal Care Services segment operating under the Almost Family banner offers custodial care such as housekeeping meal preparation and medication management. Almost Family operates 175 Visiting Nurse agencies and about 65 Personal Care Services locations. The company is merging with LHC Group.

	Annual Growth	12/13	12/14*	01/16*	12/16	12/17
Sales ($ mil.)	17.1%	–	495.8	532.2	623.5	797.0
Net income ($ mil.)	14.7%	–	13.5	19.5	18.2	20.4
Market value ($ mil.)	–	–	–	–	–	–
Employees						14,200

*Fiscal year change

ALNYLAM PHARMACEUTICALS INC　　　　　　NMS: ALNY

675 West Kendall Street, Henri A. Termeer Square　　　　CEO: Yvonne Greenstreet
Cambridge, MA 02142　　　　　　　　　　　　　　　　CFO: Jeffrey Poulton
Phone: 617 551-8200　　　　　　　　　　　　　　　　　HR: –
Fax: 617 551-8101　　　　　　　　　　　　　　FYE: December 31
Web: www.alnylam.com　　　　　　　　　　　　　　Type: Public

Like a genetic linebacker Alnylam Pharmaceuticals runs interference with RNA to prevent the forward progress of disease. RNA interference (RNAi) technology developed by the biotech firm can selectively shut off harmful genes. The company is developing a pipeline of candidates both individually and through collaborations with other drugmakers. Its disease targets include neurological ailments hypercholesterolemia and hemophilia. In mid-2018 the FDA approved the firm's patisiran drug for the treatment of neuropathy (nerve damage); it was the first RNAi-based therapy to gain approval in the US. Alnylam has additional partner-based programs in clinical or development stages including candidates targeting respiratory syncytial virus (RSV) infection and liver cancers.

	Annual Growth	12/17	12/18	12/19	12/20	12/21
Sales ($ mil.)	75.1%	89.9	74.9	219.8	492.9	844.3
Net income ($ mil.)	–	(490.9)	(761.5)	(886.1)	(858.3)	(852.8)
Market value ($ mil.)	7.5%	15,269.1	8,762.5	13,841.4	15,620.1	20,380.5
Employees	22.1%	749	1,065	1,323	1,453	1,665

ALOHA PETROLEUM LTD.

1132 Bishop St. Suite 1700　　　　　　　　　　　　　　CEO: –
Honolulu HI 96813-2820　　　　　　　　　　　　　　　CFO: –
Phone: 808-522-9700　　　　　　　　　　　　HR: Beverly Dumond
Fax: 808-522-9707　　　　　　　　　　　　　FYE: December 31
Web: www.alohagas.com　　　　　　　　　　　　　Type: Private

Aloha Petroleum has focused on fueling its convenience store business through its longtime island heritage. The company provides fuel to its customers through 30-plus company-operated convenience store and gasoline facilities that operate under the Aloha Petroleum and Island Mini-Mart banners. Overall Aloha Petroleum counts about 50 retail fuel locations among its retail portfolio on the Big Island and on Oahu. As part of its business the retail and gas company also provides fuel storage and transportation services between its locations. Aloha Petroleum was established in the early 1900s as Associated Oil a division of Tidewater Oil which was then owned by J. Paul Getty.

ALON USA ENERGY INC　　　　　　　　　　　　NYS: ALJ

12700 Park Central Dr., Suite 1600　　　　　　　　CEO: Ezra Uzi Yemin
Dallas, TX 75251　　　　　　　　　　　　　　　　　　　CFO: –
Phone: 972 367-3600　　　　　　　　　　　　　　　　　HR: –
Fax: –　　　　　　　　　　　　　　　　　　　　FYE: December 31
Web: www.alonusa.com　　　　　　　　　　　　　　Type: Public

Alon USA Energy is the driving force behind Alon (formerly FINA)-branded marketing and refining operations throughout the US Southwest. The Delek US Holdings unit provides fuel to 633 Alon-branded retail sites. It owns or operates 309 convenience stores under the 7-Eleven and Alon brands. It also sub-licenses the Alon brand to distributors supplying other locations. Alon USA Energy's refineries in California (two) Louisiana (one) and Oregon (one) have a combined throughput capacity of 144000 barrels per day. It also indirectly owns a 73000 barrels-per-day refinery in Texas and is a top asphalt producer. In 2016 the company agreed to buy all of Alon USA Energy.

	Annual Growth	12/11	12/12	12/13	12/14	12/15
Sales ($ mil.)	(11.9%)	7,186.3	8,017.7	7,046.4	6,779.5	4,338.2
Net income ($ mil.)	4.8%	43.7	90.6	48.1	38.5	52.8
Market value ($ mil.)	14.2%	618.1	1,283.7	1,173.7	899.1	1,053.1
Employees	0.3%	2,824	2,824	2,740	2,745	2,860

ALON USA PARTNERS LP　　　　　　　　　　　NYS: ALDW

12700 Park Central Drive, Suite 1600　　　　　　　　CEO: Alan Moret
Dallas, TX 75251　　　　　　　　　　　　　　　　CFO: Shai Even
Phone: 972 367-3600　　　　　　　　　　　　　　　　　HR: –
Fax: –　　　　　　　　　　　　　　　　　　　　FYE: December 31
Web: www.alonpartners.com　　　　　　　　　　　Type: Public

The crude oil refinery of Alon USA Partners doesn't exactly stand alone seeing as how it's situated right in the middle of the West Texas oil patch. Located in Big Spring with a capacity of 70000 barrels per day it powers the company's petroleum products refining and marketing business. The refinery mainly produces gasoline and diesel and jet fuel along with asphalt and petrochemicals and the company markets them in Arizona New Mexico Oklahoma and Texas. In 2012 Alon USA Partners was spun off by Alon USA Energy which in turn is majority-owned by Alon Israel Oil. The same year the company went public through an IPO that raised $184 million.

	Annual Growth	12/11	12/12	12/13	12/14	12/15
Sales ($ mil.)	(9.4%)	3,208.0	3,476.8	3,430.3	3,221.4	2,157.2
Net income ($ mil.)	(14.6%)	294.4	37.1	136.2	169.1	156.9
Market value ($ mil.)	(1.1%)	–	1,504.6	1,041.4	807.0	1,453.4
Employees		–	–	–	–	–

ALORICA INC.

5 Park Plaza Ste. 1100　　　　　　　　　　　　　　　CEO: Andy Lee
Irvine CA 92614　　　　　　　　　　　　　　CFO: Max Schwendner
Phone: 949-527-4600　　　　　　　　　　　　　　　　　HR: –
Fax: 301-874-5685　　　　　　　　　　　　　　FYE: December 31
Web: www.canam-steeljoists.ws　　　　　　　　　Type: Private

Alorica is here to remedy your front- and back-office ailments. The company provides outsourced customer service operations through about 40 call centers located in the US India and the Philippines. Its contact center services include technical support customer service help desk billing and sales (inbound and outbound). The company also offers fulfillment and service logistics including returns management warranty support management and field service dispatch. Alorica caters to customers in the automotive consumer products energy and utilities financial services health care media and entertainment retail technology telecommunications and travel sectors. It was founded in 1999 by Andy Lee.

ALPHA ASSOCIATES INC.

2 Amboy Ave.
Woodbridge NJ 07095
Phone: 732-634-5700
Fax: 732-634-1430
Web: www.alphainc.com

CEO: Christopher J Avallone
CFO: –
HR: –
FYE: December 31
Type: Private

Alpha Associates would like to be seen as the alpha and omega of high-performance industrial fabrics composites and elastomers. The company makes and markets coated fabrics and laminates for a myriad of products from marine insulation welding fabrics outdoor jacketing to acoustical baffles. Alpha Associates also develops and manufactures specialty materials for high temperature insulation. Within its high performance elastomer (HPE) line goods include flexible expansion joints for flue gas ducting industrial belting and gasket sheeting. Alpha Associates' plants are setup in South Carolina Nevada and New Jersey. The family-owned company is led by its co-founder chairman and CEO A. Louis Avallone.

ALPHA NATURAL RESOURCES INC   NBB: ANRZ Q

One Alpha Place, P.O. Box 16429
Bristol, VA 24209
Phone: 276 619-4410
Fax: –
Web: www.alphanr.com

CEO: David Stetson
CFO: Andy Eidson
HR: –
FYE: December 31
Type: Public

The alpha and omega of Alpha Natural Resources is coal mining. One of the top coal producers in the US the company produces steam and metallurgical coal at 60 active mines and 22 coal preparation plants primarily in central and northern Appalachia and the Powder River Basin in Wyoming. Alpha's sales are split between low-sulfur steam coal used mainly for electricity generation and metallurgical coal used primarily for steelmaking. The company produces about 84 million tons of coal per year. Alpha controls about 4 billion tons of proved and probable coal reserves. Faced with increasing debt and tightening federal regulations the company entered into Chapter 11 bankruptcy protection in August 2015.

	Annual Growth	12/10	12/11	12/12	12/13	12/14
Sales ($ mil.)	2.3%	3,917.2	7,109.2	6,974.9	4,953.5	4,287.1
Net income ($ mil.)	–	95.6	(677.4)	(2,437.1)	(1,113.5)	(875.0)
Market value ($ mil.)	(59.2%)	13,302.6	4,527.3	2,158.4	1,582.2	370.1
Employees	8.2%	6,500	14,500	12,400	10,500	8,900

ALPHA-EN CORPORATION   OTC: ALPE

120 White Plains Rd.
Tarrytown NY 10591
Phone: 914-631-5265
Fax: +41-58-158-88-89
Web: www.jetaviation.com

CEO: Sam Pitroda
CFO: Thomas Suppanz
HR: –
FYE: December 31
Type: Public

alpha-En Corporation (formerly Avenue Entertainment) once brought entertainment to the street where you live. The company produced films such as Closer and The Merchant of Venice and made-for-TV and cable movies including Angels in America and Path To Paradise: The Untold Story of the World Trade Center Bombing both for HBO. Its Wombat Productions created one-hour profiles of Hollywood celebrities shown on networks such as PBS A&E and Bravo. The company halted production activities and sold its assets in 2007. It is seeking another business to acquire.

ALPHABET INC   NMS: GOOG L

1600 Amphitheatre Parkway
Mountain View, CA 94043
Phone: 650 253-0000
Fax: –
Web: www.abc.xyz

CEO: Sundar Pichai
CFO: Ruth Porat
HR: –
FYE: December 31
Type: Public

Google is a search engine. Core to Google's business is its ubiquitous Search product; other key products and platforms include Android Chrome Gmail Google Drive Google Maps Google Play and YouTube. The firm generates revenue through ad sales in two categories: Performance Advertising creates and delivers relevant ads that users click on and Brand Advertising lets businesses run ad campaigns to promote brand awareness. In addition Google Display Network allows advertisers to build a custom network of sites utilizing a wide range of targeting technologies. Google is owned by Alphabet Inc. a holding company that also includes emerging businesses such as Calico and about life sciences. The Google story begins in 1995 at Stanford University.

	Annual Growth	12/17	12/18	12/19	12/20	12/21
Sales ($ mil.)	23.5%	110,855.0	136,819.0	161,857.0	182,527.0	257,637.0
Net income ($ mil.)	56.5%	12,662.0	30,736.0	34,343.0	40,269.0	76,033.0
Market value ($ mil.)	28.8%	697,478.3	691,890.0	886,838.2	1,160,459.7	1,918,191.0
Employees	18.2%	80,110	98,771	118,899	135,301	156,500

ALPHATEC HOLDINGS INC   NMS: ATEC

1950 Camino Vida Roble
Carlsbad, CA 92008
Phone: 760 431-9286
Fax: –
Web: www.atecspine.com

CEO: Patrick Miles
CFO: J. Todd Koning
HR: –
FYE: December 31
Type: Public

Alphatec Holdings aims to help people stand up straight and keep moving. The company develops and manufactures products used to treat spinal disorders including stenosis compression fractures and degenerating discs. Through its Alphatec Spine subsidiary the company makes a variety of FDA-approved products for the spinal fusion market in the US the world's largest spinal fusion market. Its spinal implant products include screws plates fixation systems grafting materials and surgical instruments. Alphatec markets its products to surgeons through a network of independent but exclusive distributors as well as a direct sales force. The company develops its products through its manufacturing facilities in California and France.

	Annual Growth	12/16	12/17	12/18	12/19	12/20
Sales ($ mil.)	4.8%	120.2	101.7	91.7	113.4	144.9
Net income ($ mil.)	–	(29.9)	(2.3)	(29.0)	(57.0)	(79.0)
Market value ($ mil.)	45.8%	263.6	218.4	188.0	582.5	1,192.2
Employees	16.3%	162	138	195	227	296

ALPINE AIR EXPRESS INC.   OTC: APNX

1177 Alpine Air Way
Provo UT 84601
Phone: 801-373-1508
Fax: 801-377-3781
Web: www.alpine-air.com

CEO: Michael Dancy
CFO: Rick Wood
HR: –
FYE: October 31
Type: Public

Alpine Air Express flies the western skies to cart cargo for its customers. The air cargo company provides scheduled transportation of mail packages and other time-sensitive freight to more than 25 cities in the western half of the US mainland and in Hawaii. Its primary customers the United States Postal Service and United Parcel Service together account for more than 85% of sales. Alpine Air operates a fleet of about 25 Beechcraft turboprop planes from bases in Hawaii Montana and Utah. Along with its cargo operations the company provides pilot training and aircraft maintenance services. CEO Eugene Mallette owns a controlling stake in Alpine Air.

ALPS HOLDINGS INC.

1290 Broadway Ste. 1100
Denver CO 80203
Phone: 303-623-2577
Fax: 303-623-7850
Web: www.alpsinc.com

CEO: –
CFO: –
HR: –
FYE: December 30
Type: Subsidiary

ALPS Holdings wants to make sure fund managers can attain peak performance by keeping their focus on their investments and letting ALPS handle the rest. Through various subsidiaries the company performs a range of back-office functions for mutual funds closed-end funds hedge funds and exchange-traded funds (ETFs). Its offerings encompass fund administration and accounting shareholder servicing and legal marketing tax distribution and transfer agency services. Clients include Cohen & Steers Macquarie Group and exchange-traded Standard & Poor's Depositary Receipts (SPDR) sector funds. DST Systems acquired ALPS from Lovell Minnick Partners in 2011.

ALSERES PHARMACEUTICALS INC   NBB: ALSE

275 Grove Street Suite 2-400
Auburndale, MA 02466
Phone: 508 497-2360
Fax: –

CEO: –
CFO: –
HR: –
FYE: December 31
Type: Public

Unlike most people the folks at Alseres Pharmaceuticals (formerly Boston Life Sciences) want to get on your nerves. The biotechnology company is developing therapies and diagnostics related to nervous system conditions such as spinal cord injury Parkinson's disease and attention deficit hyperactivity disorder (ADHD). Its lead candidate is Altropane a molecular imaging agent for diagnosing Parkinson's disease and ADHD. Another candidate Cethrin aims to repair nerve damage caused by spinal cord injury; Alseres licensed Cethrin from Canadian firm BioAxone Therapeutic in 2006.

	Annual Growth	12/09	12/10	12/11	12/12	12/13
Sales ($ mil.)	(10.7%)	–	–	–	0.5	0.5
Net income ($ mil.)	–	(10.8)	0.5	(2.9)	(1.6)	(0.9)
Market value ($ mil.)	–	0.0	0.0	0.0	0.0	0.0
Employees	(12.0%)	5	4	3	3	3

ALRO STEEL CORPORATION

3100 E HIGH ST
JACKSON, MI 492036413
Phone: 517-787-5500
Fax: –
Web: www.alrosteel.com

CEO: Alvin Glick
CFO: Steve Laten
HR: –
FYE: May 31
Type: Private

Alro Steel runs its service centers like a grocery store for metals keeping what customers need in easy reach. The service center operator which has a dozen facilities in the US Northeast Midwest and Southeast provides processing services such as aluminum circle cutting CNC flame cutting forming and machining. The company carries an extensive inventory of steel products along with industrial tools and supplies. It also offers plastic sheet rod tube and film through its Alro Plastics division and distributes industrial tools and materials through subsidiary Alro Industrial Supplies.

	Annual Growth	05/16	05/17	05/18	05/19	05/20
Sales ($ mil.)	(1.2%)	–	–	1,989.0	2,213.2	1,941.4
Net income ($ mil.)	(5.1%)	–	–	165.8	198.5	149.3
Market value ($ mil.)	–	–	–	–	–	–
Employees	–	–	–	–	–	2,400

ALSTON & BIRD LLP

1 Atlantic Center 1201 W. Peachtree St.
Atlanta GA 30309-3424
Phone: 404-881-7000
Fax: 404-881-7777
Web: www.alston.com

CEO: –
CFO: Richard Levinson
HR: –
FYE: December 31
Type: Private - Partnershi

One of the South's leading law firms Alston & Bird groups its 80-plus practices into four main areas: corporate and finance intellectual property litigation and tax. The firm's intellectual property practice group is one of the nation's largest. Overall Alston & Bird has more than 800 attorneys policy advisers and patent agents. The firm serves a wide range of domestic and international clients which have included Bank of America Duke University General Electric Mohawk Industries New Frontier Media PSS World Medical Qualstar Corporation and UPS. Alston & Bird traces its roots to a law practice founded in 1893.

ALSCO INC.

505 E 200 S STE 101
SALT LAKE CITY, UT 841022053
Phone: 801-328-8831
Fax: –
Web: www.alsco.com

CEO: –
CFO: –
HR: Bettie Wicks
FYE: December 31
Type: Private

Alsco is a global leader in uniform and linen rental services. Operating from more than 180 branches in about 15 countries worldwide the company rents and sells uniforms linens towels napkins and soft blankets to more than 355000 customers worldwide. It also manages janitorial services provides washroom supplies and soap and sanitizer services. In addition Alsco provides professional textile rental services and offers First aid that is fresh and budget friendly. The company was founded in 1889 by George Steiner and is still owned and operated by the Steiner family. It is headquartered in Utah and has locations in Australia Brazil Canada China Germany Italy New Zealand Singapore Malaysia Thailand and the US.

	Annual Growth	12/13	12/14	12/15	12/16	12/17
Sales ($ mil.)	14.3%	–	–	683.4	704.3	892.3
Net income ($ mil.)	45.2%	–	–	30.6	38.5	64.6
Market value ($ mil.)	–	–	–	–	–	–
Employees	–	–	–	–	–	16,000

ALSTON CONSTRUCTION COMPANY, INC.

8775 FOLSOM BLVD STE 201
SACRAMENTO, CA 958263725
Phone: 916-340-2400
Fax: –
Web: www.alstonco.com

CEO: Paul Little
CFO: Adam Nickerson
HR: –
FYE: December 31
Type: Private

Alston Construction (formerly Panattoni Construction) offers a broad platform of general contracting construction management design-build services and virtual design management construction. The company serves a diverse array of industries including healthcare food and beverage industrial office athletic facilities and retail among others. Refurbishing and extending buildings from its network of offices throughout the US Alston Construction provides construction management services for such clients as Amazon.com Bridgestone Caterpillar Clorox FedEx Petco Helen of Troy Under Armour and Whirlpool. Completed approximately 6010 projects Alston Construction started in 1986.

	Annual Growth	12/14	12/15	12/17	12/18	12/19
Sales ($ mil.)	18.6%	–	642.5	865.5	909.9	1,271.4
Net income ($ mil.)	28.4%	–	6.9	13.7	14.2	18.7
Market value ($ mil.)	–	–	–	–	–	–
Employees	–	–	–	–	–	200

ALTA BATES SUMMIT MEDICAL CENTER

2450 Ashby Ave.
Berkeley CA 94705
Phone: 510-204-4444
Fax: 510-869-8980
Web: www.altabates.com

CEO: –
CFO: Robert Petrina
HR: –
FYE: December 31
Type: Subsidiary

Alta Bates Summit Medical Center operates a private non-profit hospital system spanning three campuses in Berkeley and Oakland California. Specializing in clinical and community outreach Alta Bates offers advanced medical care services through 30 different programs located in the East Bay including behavioral health oncology orthopedics rehabilitation cardiovascular diabetes neuroscience and women's services. Its facilities have a combined capacity of more than 1000 beds and are staffed with more than 1100 physicians. The company is a Sutter Health affiliate and was formed in 1999 through the merging of Alta Bates Herrick Merritt Peralta and Providence hospitals.

ALTA MESA HOLDINGS LP

15415 Katy Fwy. Ste. 800
Houston TX 77094-1813
Phone: 281-530-0991
Fax: +44-0161-455-4079
Web: www.odeonanducicinemasgroup.com

CEO: –
CFO: –
HR: –
FYE: December 31
Type: Private

If Alta Mesa Holdings were your dinner companion it'd ask "Are you going to finish that?" The company goes over established oil and natural gas fields looking for what's left behind. It exploits mature fields originally developed by the big boys — Shell Chevron and Exxon — using enhanced oil recovery techniques that boost the amount of extractable oil and gas. Its properties are located in South Louisiana Oklahoma the Deep Bossier resource play of East Texas Eagle Ford Shale play and Indian Point field in South Texas the Blackjack Creek field in Florida and the Marcellus Shale in West Virginia. The company reports proved reserves of 325 billion cu. ft. of natural gas and about 250 producing wells.

ALTADIS U.S.A. INC.

5900 N. Andrews Ave. Ste. 1100
Fort Lauderdale FL 33309-2369
Phone: 954-772-9000
Fax: 954-267-1198
Web: www.altadisusa.com

CEO: Gary R Ellis
CFO: –
HR: –
FYE: December 31
Type: Subsidiary

When the smoke clears connoisseur puffers may find themselves holding a cigar crafted by Altadis USA. Created in 2000 from the consolidation of HavaTampa Inc. and Consolidated Cigar Holdings Altadis USA has grown to rival the world's largest cigar makers and generate a considerable share of parent Altadis S.A.'s global cigar sales. Altadis USA manufactures markets and sells both premium and mass-market cigars under such well-known brand names as Montecristo Romeo y Julieta H. Upmann and Trinidad. It also sells little cigars under the Dutch Treats and Supre Sweets brands as well as humidors and cigar cases. Altadis USA's Spanish parent company was acquired by Britain's Imperial Tobacco Group in 2008.

ALTAIR NANOTECHNOLOGIES INC

NL:

204 Edison Way
Reno, NV 89502-2306
Phone: 775 856-2500
Fax: –
Web: www.altairnano.com

CEO: Guohua Sun
CFO: Karen Werner
HR: –
FYE: December 31
Type: Public

When Altair Nanotechnologies paints the town its pigment of choice is titanium dioxide (TiO 2). The company produces titanium dioxide particles used in paints coatings and sensors. Altair intends to create new applications and products with its nanocrystalline technology. Its major development thus far has been its nano lithium-titanate battery materials which offer superior performance the company says to other rechargeable batteries. In 2011 Canon Investment Holdings through a subsidiary purchased a 49% share in Altair for $57.5 million. The deal includes the transfer of Altair's lithium-titanate manufacturing process for producing battery cells to Canon's Energy Storage Technology (China) Group.

	Annual Growth	12/12	12/13	12/14	12/15	12/16
Sales ($ mil.)	143.8%	1.5	8.2	6.7	14.3	54.7
Net income ($ mil.)	–	(18.0)	(14.6)	(16.0)	(19.5)	(3.6)
Market value ($ mil.)	(77.1%)	25.0	45.5	12.9	0.3	–
Employees	88.0%	90	–	–	631	1,125

ALTARUM INSTITUTE

3520 GREEN CT STE 300
ANN ARBOR, MI 481051566
Phone: 734-302-4600
Fax: –
Web: www.altarum.org

CEO: Michael Monson
CFO: Mark Kielb
HR: –
FYE: December 31
Type: Private

The Altarum Institute is a not-for-profit organization that provides health care research and consulting services primarily to government agencies. Altarum's services include policy analysis program development and management business operations planning and finance clinical research support strategic communications and event design and management. Key customers include the US Department of Health and Human Services the US Department of Defense Military Health System and the US Department of Veterans Affairs. Altarum operates in California Georgia Maine Michigan Texas and the Washington DC area.

	Annual Growth	12/09	12/10	12/11	12/12	12/13
Sales ($ mil.)	2.6%	–	73.2	84.7	87.1	79.0
Net income ($ mil.)	–	–	–	(4.6)	0.1	(1.8)
Market value ($ mil.)	–	–	–	–	–	–
Employees	–	–	–	–	–	455

ALTEC LANSING LLC

535 Rte. 6 and 209
Milford PA 18337-0277
Phone: 570-296-4434
Fax: 570-296-6887
Web: www.alteclansing.com

CEO: Ross Gatlin
CFO: Richard P Horner
HR: –
FYE: March 31
Type: Private

Altec Lansing (formerly Altec Lansing Technologies) is in the business of selling sound. The company is a leading manufacturer and marketer of speaker systems for consumer PCs as well as sound accessories such as headsets headphones and docking stations for personal digital media. It also makes home entertainment systems and scales its units to accommodate large venues. Altec Lansing traces its name back to audio pioneer James B. Lansing who founded a company devoted to theater sound systems in the 1920s. Headset specialist Plantronics which acquired Altec in 2005 to strengthen its position in the PC speaker market sold the company in December 2009 to a private equity firm.

ALTEGRITY INC.

7799 Leesburg Pike Ste. 1100 North
Falls Church VA 22043-2413
Phone: 703-448-0178
Fax: 703-448-1422
Web: www.altegrity.com

CEO: Guy Abramo
CFO: Thomas Spaeth
HR: –
FYE: September 30
Type: Private

It doesn't take a great detective to determine that Altegrity is a leader in security services. The holding company owns Kroll Kroll Ontrack HireRight and USIS. Kroll is a risk management company offers a range of security and technology services. Kroll Ontrack provides legal technologies data recovery and information management services while HireRight specializes in employment background and drug testing services for the private sector. USIS (formerly US Investigations Services) is the largest provider of background investigations and employment screening to the federal government. Altegrity and its subsidiaries have operations in 30 countries. The company is controlled by Providence Equity Partners.

ALTERA CORP.   NMS: ALTR

101 Innovation Drive
San Jose, CA 95134
Phone: 408 544-7000
Fax: –
Web: www.altera.com

CEO: John P Daane
CFO: Ronald J Pasek
HR: –
FYE: December 31
Type: Public

Altera is a fabless semiconductor company that specializes in high-density programmable logic devices (PLDs) — integrated circuits (ICs) that OEMs can program to perform logic functions in electronic systems. PLDs are an alternative to custom-designed ICs and offer a quick reduced-cost chip. The company's products are used by its more than 13000 customers worldwide in communications network gear consumer electronics medical systems and industrial equipment. Altera outsources fabrication of the devices to top silicon foundry Taiwan Semiconductor Manufacturing Company. Customers outside the US represent most of the company's sales.

	Annual Growth	12/10	12/11	12/12	12/13	12/14
Sales ($ mil.)	(0.3%)	1,954.4	2,064.5	1,783.0	1,732.6	1,932.1
Net income ($ mil.)	(11.9%)	782.9	770.7	556.8	440.1	472.7
Market value ($ mil.)	0.9%	10,760.5	11,220.2	10,400.6	9,832.3	11,171.8
Employees	3.8%	2,666	2,884	3,129	3,094	3,091

ALTERNET SYSTEMS INC.   OTC: ALYI

1 Glen Royal Pkwy. Ste. 401
Miami FL 33125
Phone: 786-265-1840
Fax: 786-513-2887
Web: www.alternetsystems.com/

CEO: –
CFO: –
HR: –
FYE: December 31
Type: Public

Alternet Systems turns your mobile phone into a virtual wallet. The company provides mobile payment services to consumers as well as banks and financial processing institutions merchants and retailers public transportation and utilities providers telecommunications operators and government customers throughout North America Latin America and the Caribbean. Its mobile commerce and e-ticketing products and services allow for cashless transactions such as transferring and withdrawing funds receiving overseas payments and making point-of-sale purchases. Alternet Systems restructured its operations in 2008 after acquiring VoIP telecom company TekVoice Communications.

ALTEVA   ASE: ALTV

401 Market Street, 1st Floor
Philadelphia, PA 19106
Phone: 877 258-3722
Fax: –
Web: www.alteva.com

CEO: William J Fox III
CFO: Matthew G Conroy
HR: –
FYE: December 31
Type: Public

Alteva (formerly Warwick Valley Telephone) provides communications services from its quiet niche. The independent facilities-based telecom company was established in 1902 and has about 20000 access lines in operation. It provides local and long-distance services to consumers and businesses in a mostly rural area in southeastern New York (Warwick Wallkill and Goshen) and northwestern New Jersey (Vernon and West Milford). The company's Warwick Online unit offers dial-up and DSL Internet access digital video and a VoIP computer telephony service that is sold under the VoiceNet brand. Alteva's services for business customers include hosted conferencing and wholesale voice access.

	Annual Growth	12/09	12/10	12/11	12/12	12/13
Sales ($ mil.)	5.9%	23.9	24.4	25.9	27.9	30.1
Net income ($ mil.)	–	6.8	2.9	(2.9)	(9.5)	(0.6)
Market value ($ mil.)	(11.1%)	80.4	85.7	80.4	64.1	50.2
Employees	2.3%	113	112	143	155	124

ALTEX INDUSTRIES, INC.   NBB: ALTX

700 Colorado Blvd #273
Denver, CO 80206
Phone: 303 265-9312
Fax: –

CEO: –
CFO: –
HR: –
FYE: September 30
Type: Public

More OilRockies than AllTex(as) Altex Industries buys and sells oil and gas properties participates in drilling exploratory wells and sells oil and gas production to refineries pipeline operators and processing plants. The oil and gas exploration and production independent owns interests in two gross productive oil wells and 200 gross developed acres in Utah and Wyoming. Over the last few years Altex Industries has been forced to sell most of its oil and gas assets in order to pay down debt. CEO Steven Cardin holds a majority stake in the company.

	Annual Growth	09/17	09/18	09/19	09/20	09/21
Sales ($ mil.)	(7.8%)	0.1	0.1	0.1	0.0	0.0
Net income ($ mil.)	–	(0.1)	(0.1)	(0.0)	(0.1)	(0.1)
Market value ($ mil.)	11.7%	0.9	0.9	0.9	1.0	1.4
Employees	(15.9%)	2	1	1	1	1

ALTICOR INC.

7575 FULTON ST E
ADA, MI 493550001
Phone: 616-787-1000
Fax: –
Web: www.amway.com

CEO: –
CFO: Michael Cazer
HR: –
FYE: December 31
Type: Private

Where there's a will (and an army of independent sales representatives) there's Amway. Operated through holding company Alticor Amway is the world's top direct-selling company with millions of individual ABOs (Amway Business Owners) pitching everything from air filters to vitamins. The company makes some 450 unique products across the categories of nutrition (which generates about half of sales) beauty and personal care and home. It is active in more than 100 countries across the globe with Asia (led by China) its largest market. Alticor is controlled by the families of Rich DeVos and Jay Van Andel who founded Amway in 1959.

	Annual Growth	12/11	12/12	12/13	12/14	12/15
Sales ($ mil.)	(10.3%)	–	–	11,754.2	10,804.5	9,459.8
Net income ($ mil.)	–	–	–	0.0	0.0	0.0
Market value ($ mil.)	–	–	–	–	–	–
Employees	–	–	–	–	–	14,000

ALTIGEN COMMUNICATIONS INC

NBB: ATGN

670 N. McCarthy Blvd., Suite 200
Milpitas, CA 95035
Phone: 408 597-9000
Fax: –
Web: www.altigen.com

CEO: Jeremiah Fleming
CFO: Philip McDermott
HR: –
FYE: September 30
Type: Public

AltiGen Communications helps businesses find their calling on the Internet. The company provides Microsoft brand voice-over-IP (VoIP) telephone systems and administration software to small and midsized businesses and call centers. Its phone systems utilize both the Internet and public telephone networks to transmit voice signals. Its MaxCommunications Server (MaxCS) systems include voicemail auto attendant menus and other features of traditional business PBX systems; its AltiContact Manager product adds advanced call center functionality. AltiGen deals primarily through resellers and distributors counts thousands of customers most of them in the US.

	Annual Growth	09/17	09/18	09/19	09/20	09/21
Sales ($ mil.)	7.0%	8.4	10.0	10.6	11.8	11.0
Net income ($ mil.)	–	0.4	9.8	1.9	1.4	(0.5)
Market value ($ mil.)	68.7%	6.6	12.1	26.4	54.6	53.4
Employees	14.1%	36	51	53	64	61

ALTIMMUNE INC

NMS: ALT

910 Clopper Road, Suite 201S
Gaithersburg, MD 20878
Phone: 240 654-1450
Fax: –
Web: www.altimmune.com

CEO: Vipin Garg
CFO: Richard Eisenstadt
HR: –
FYE: December 31
Type: Public

Anthrax beware Altimmune is out to get you and your brethren. Formerly known as PharmAthene the clinical-stage immunotherapeutics firm develops medical products that protect against biological and chemical threats. Treatments under development include SparVax an antigen anthrax vaccine; NasoVAX a single-dose influenza vaccine; and HepTcell an immunotherapeutic for chronic hepatitis B. Altimmune has two proprietary platforms (RespirVec and Densigen) which activate the body's immune system differently than traditional vaccines. Pharmathene merged with private firm Altimmune in May 2017.

	Annual Growth	12/16	12/17	12/18	12/19	12/20
Sales ($ mil.)	11.8%	5.2	10.7	10.3	5.8	8.2
Net income ($ mil.)	–	193.9	(46.4)	(39.2)	(20.5)	(49.0)
Market value ($ mil.)	36.5%	120.7	73.9	76.5	70.2	419.0
Employees	34.9%	13	30	27	25	43

ALTO INGREDIENTS INC

NAS: ALTO

1300 South Second Street
Pekin, IL 61554
Phone: 916 403-2123
Fax: 916 446-3937
Web: www.pacificethanol.com

CEO: Michael Kandris
CFO: Bryon McGregor
HR: –
FYE: December 31
Type: Public

Alto Ingredients (formerly Pacific Ethanol) is the leading producer and marketer of specialty alcohols and essential ingredients and the largest producer of specialty alcohols in the US. The company sells co-products such as wet distillers grain (WDG) a nutritional animal feed dried distillers grains with solubles (DDGS) wet and dry corn gluten feed condensed distillers solubles corn gluten meal corn germ corn oil dried yeast and CO2. Serving integrated oil companies and gasoline marketers who blend ethanol into gasoline Alto Ingredients provides transportation storage and delivery of ethanol through third-party service providers in the Western US. On an annualized basis the company markets over 500 million gallons combined of its own alcohols and nearly 1.5 million tons of essential ingredients on a dry matter basis.

	Annual Growth	12/16	12/17	12/18	12/19	12/20
Sales ($ mil.)	(13.8%)	1,624.8	1,632.3	1,515.4	1,424.9	897.0
Net income ($ mil.)	–	1.4	(35.0)	(60.3)	(88.9)	(15.1)
Market value ($ mil.)	(13.0%)	688.6	329.8	62.4	47.1	393.6
Employees	(7.3%)	500	560	510	500	370

ALTRA INDUSTRIAL MOTION CORP

NMS: AIMC

300 Granite Street, Suite 201
Braintree, MA 02184
Phone: 781 917-0600
Fax: –
Web: www.altramotion.com

CEO: Carl R Christenson
CFO: Christian Storch
HR: –
FYE: December 31
Type: Public

Altra Industrial Motion manufactures mechanical power transmission and motion control products for virtually any industrial application. It specializes in industrial clutches and brakes couplings and gear drives for diverse applications from elevator braking systems to lawnmowers. The company serves industries like energy aerospace general industrial metals mining transportation and turf and garden. Its products are marketed under multiple brands such as TB Wood's and Warner Electric and sold directly to OEMs and through a network of more than 3000 distributors. North America accounts for about 55% of sales. The company was founded in 2004.

	Annual Growth	12/16	12/17	12/18	12/19	12/20
Sales ($ mil.)	24.9%	708.9	876.7	1,175.3	1,834.1	1,726.0
Net income ($ mil.)	–	25.1	51.4	35.3	127.2	(25.5)
Market value ($ mil.)	10.7%	2,386.6	3,259.7	1,626.6	2,341.9	3,585.0
Employees	18.8%	4,564	4,850	9,300	9,200	9,100

ALTRIA GROUP INC

NYS: MO

6601 West Broad Street
Richmond, VA 23230
Phone: 804 274-2200
Fax: –
Web: www.altria.com

CEO: William Gifford
CFO: Salvatore Mancuso
HR: Charlie Whitaker
FYE: December 31
Type: Public

The house the Marlboro Man built Altria Group owns the largest cigarette company in the US. Altria operates through subsidiary Philip Morris USA which sells Marlboro — the world's #1-selling cigarette brand. Altria manufactures cigarettes under the Parliament Virginia Slims and Basic brands among many others. Altria however has diversified from solely a cigarette maker to a purveyor of cigars and pipe tobacco through John Middleton Co. and Nat Sherman; smokeless tobacco products through UST; and wine through Ste. Michelle Wine Estates. The company's investments in equity securities consisted of AB InBev Cronos Group and JUUL Labs.

	Annual Growth	12/16	12/17	12/18	12/19	12/20
Sales ($ mil.)	0.4%	25,744.0	25,576.0	25,364.0	25,110.0	26,153.0
Net income ($ mil.)	(25.2%)	14,239.0	10,222.0	6,963.0	(1,293.0)	4,467.0
Market value ($ mil.)	(11.8%)	125,666.3	132,709.7	91,787.3	92,753.7	76,195.2
Employees	(3.8%)	8,300	8,300	8,300	7,300	7,100

ALTRU HEALTH SYSTEM

1200 S COLUMBIA RD
GRAND FORKS, ND 582014044
Phone: 701-780-5000
Fax: –
Web: www.altru.org

CEO: Dave Molmen
CFO: Craig Faerber
HR: –
FYE: December 31
Type: Private

Altru Health System provides medical care to over 200000 residents throughout northeastern North Dakota and northwestern Minnesota. The integrated health care network administers everything from primary care to inpatient medical and surgical care through its Altru Hospital (with more than 255 beds) and some 45 specialty centers. It also operates a cancer center a rehabilitation center dialysis facilities and home health providers. For area seniors Altru Health operates Parkwood Place a senior living facility that provides several levels of care to residents depending on need. A community of approximately 3800 health professionals and support staff the not-for-profit center was formed in 1997 by the integration of Grand Forks Clinic and United Health Services.

	Annual Growth	12/16	12/17	12/18	12/19	12/20
Sales ($ mil.)	2.7%	–	549.4	566.7	589.2	595.3
Net income ($ mil.)	31.4%	–	20.2	(13.2)	10.5	45.8
Market value ($ mil.)	–	–	–	–	–	–
Employees	–	–	–	–	–	3,800

ALTUM INCORPORATED

12100 SUNSET HILLS RD # 101
RESTON, VA 201903233
Phone: 703-657-8299
Fax: –
Web: www.altum.com

CEO: Steve Pinchotti
CFO: Wendy Fyock
HR: –
FYE: December 31
Type: Private

Altum hopes to provide alternatives to old fashioned data management solutions such as filing cabinets paper and pen. The company provides software and services that clients use to access analyze and manage enterprise data. Altum's software products include applications for data collection collaboration reporting and text searches as well as tools that enable grant-making organizations to analyze and manage their grant programs. The company also offers services such as consulting training support and maintenance. Altum was founded in 1997.

	Annual Growth	03/05	03/06	03/07	03/08*	12/12
Sales ($ mil.)	38.4%	–	–	–	2.3	8.4
Net income ($ mil.)	(47.3%)	–	–	–	2.1	0.2
Market value ($ mil.)	–	–	–	–	–	–
Employees	–	–	–	–	–	39

*Fiscal year change

ALVAREZ & MARSAL HOLDINGS LLC

600 Lexington Ave. 6th Fl.
New York NY 10022
Phone: 212-759-4433
Fax: 212-759-5532
Web: www.alvarezandmarsal.com

CEO: Bryan Marsal
CFO: Steven Cohn
HR: –
FYE: December 31
Type: Private

A&M specializes in M&A along with restructuring right-sizing and other corporate turnaround processes. Alvarez & Marsal provides advisory and consulting services related to mergers and acquisitions (M&A) restructuring turnaround situations crisis and interim management divestitures performance improvement dispute resolution and strategic planning. The firm is becoming increasingly involved in private equity investing. It possesses expertise in the financial services healthcare real estate retail and public sectors. Alvarez & Marsal has some 40 offices around the world. Co-CEOs Bryan Marsal and Tony Alvarez II started the firm in 1983.

ALVERNIA UNIVERSITY

400 SAINT BERNARDINE ST
READING, PA 196071737
Phone: 610-796-8200
Fax: –
Web: www.alvernia.edu

CEO: –
CFO: Joshua E Hoffman
HR: –
FYE: June 30
Type: Private

Alvernia University (formerly Alvernia College) is a private Catholic Franciscan liberal arts college. It offers about 40 undergraduate majors and about 20 undergraduate minors as well as associate of science degrees in business and computer information systems six master's degrees programs and a doctor of philosophy program. Its main campus is located in Reading Pennsylvania with additional courses taught in Pottsville and Philadelphia. The university has a total enrollment of some 3000 students. Alvernia was founded in 1958 by the Bernardine Franciscan Sisters. The institution gained university status in 2008.

	Annual Growth	06/10	06/11	06/13	06/14	06/15
Sales ($ mil.)	3.8%	–	63.3	69.1	70.8	73.4
Net income ($ mil.)	(27.7%)	–	5.6	4.0	1.6	1.5
Market value ($ mil.)	–	–	–	–	–	–
Employees	–	–	–	–	–	293

ALYESKA PIPELINE SERVICE COMPANY

900 E. Benson St.
Anchorage AK 99519
Phone: 907-787-8700
Fax: 907-787-8240
Web: www.alyeska-pipe.com

CEO: –
CFO: –
HR: Karen Anderson
FYE: December 31
Type: Private - Consortium

Named after the Aleut word for mainland The Alyeska Pipeline Service Company operates the 800-mile-long 48-inch-diameter pipeline that transports crude oil and natural gas liquids from Alaska's North Slope to the marine oil terminal of Valdez in Prince William Sound. Founded in 1970 to make the newly discovered finds in Prudhoe Bay commercially accessible the company was assigned the task of designing building operating and maintaining the Trans-Alaska Pipeline System (TAPS). TAPS is owned by a consortium of oil and gas firms including BP (47%) ConocoPhillips (28%) Exxon Mobil (20%) Koch (3%) and Chevron (Unocal Pipeline 1%).

ALZHEIMER'S DISEASE AND RELATED DISORDERS ASSOCIATION, INC.

225 N MICHIGAN AVE FL 17
CHICAGO, IL 606017652
Phone: 312-335-8700
Fax: –
Web: www.alz.org

CEO: Harry Johns
CFO: –
HR: –
FYE: June 30
Type: Private

Alzheimer's Association wants you to "maintain your brain". The charitable organization is working to prevent treat and ultimately cure Alzheimer's a progressive brain disorder that destroys memory and the ability to learn reason and do other daily activities. The group has more than 80 local chapters throughout the US and numerous service programs including a 24-hour helpline support groups information libraries public advocacy an online community and a registration program so wandering Alzheimer patients can be returned home safely. Alzheimer's Association also funds research and hosts national and international conferences for scientists and caregivers. Its annual fund raiser is the Walk to End Alzheimer's.

	Annual Growth	06/14	06/15	06/16	06/19	06/20
Sales ($ mil.)	136.7%	–	5.4	1.8	389.7	403.1
Net income ($ mil.)	124.7%	–	0.3	0.1	3.1	15.3
Market value ($ mil.)	–	–	–	–	–	–
Employees	–	–	–	–	–	200

AM-MEX PRODUCTS INC.

3801 W. Military Hwy.
McAllen TX 78503-8810
Phone: 956-631-7916
Fax: 956-631-7999
Web: www.ammexproducts.com

CEO: –
CFO: –
HR: –
FYE: December 31
Type: Private

Am-Mex Products helps companies set up maquiladora operations in the McAllen Texas and Reynosa Mexico border region. The maquiladora program allows US firms and other foreign companies to import raw materials into Mexico duty-free for assembly there by lower-wage Mexican workers. The program also offers faster startup lower shipping costs and central distribution. Its services include contract manufacturing engineering factory management warehousing and distribution cross-border trucking training and other services required for international trade. Am-Mex has been in business since 1990 and has around 1 million sq. ft. of manufacturing and warehouse space in Mexico in addition to its US operation.

AMAG PHARMACEUTICALS, INC. NMS: AMAG

1100 Winter Street
Waltham, MA 02451
Phone: 617 498-3300
Fax: –
Web: www.amagpharma.com

CEO: Michael Porter
CFO: Ozgur Kilic
HR: –
FYE: December 31
Type: Public

It's rare when the illness and cure are one in the same; but in AMAG Pharmaceuticals' case iron is the problem and the solution. The biopharmaceutical company is focused on the development and commercialization of an iron compound to treat iron deficiency anemia (IDA). Its primary money maker is Makena a drug a drug to reduce the risk of pre-term births. Another product Feraheme Injection treats IDA in patients with chronic kidney disease (CKD). AMAG sells Feraheme in the US and Canada through its own sales force. Another product MuGard Mucoadhesive Oral Wound Rinse is used in the management of oral mucositis; it is also marketed in the US.

	Annual Growth	12/14	12/15	12/16	12/17	12/18
Sales ($ mil.)	39.7%	124.4	418.3	532.1	609.9	474.0
Net income ($ mil.)	–	135.8	32.8	(2.5)	(199.2)	(65.8)
Market value ($ mil.)	(22.7%)	1,474.9	1,044.8	1,204.3	458.5	525.7
Employees	16.1%	257	552	545	762	467

AMALGAMATED LIFE INSURANCE COMPANY

333 Westchester Ave.
White Plains NY 10604-2910
Phone: 914-367-5000
Fax: 404-872-0457
Web: www.arthritis.org

CEO: David J Walsh
CFO: Vinecsa Castro
HR: –
FYE: December 31
Type: Private

Amalgamated Life Insurance has combined a variety of life insurance products and services to aid the working man and woman. The company provides life insurance retirement plans voluntary benefits and other products to members of some 30 different labor unions and other moderate income individuals. In addition to its group and individual products (life accident and disability) Amalgamated Life Insurance and its affiliates offer third party administration (TPA) and medical cost management to self-insured groups. The company is licensed in over 40 states and has offices nationwide. It provides coverage to some 800000 customers.

AMAZON.COM INC NMS: AMZN

410 Terry Avenue North
Seattle, WA 98109-5210
Phone: 206 266-1000
Fax: 206 266-1821
Web: www.amazon.com

CEO: Andrew Jassy
CFO: Brian Olsavsky
HR: –
FYE: December 31
Type: Public

Amazon.com designs its stores to enable hundreds of millions of unique products to be sold by the company and by third parties across dozens of product categories. Customers access its offerings through its websites mobile apps Alexa devices streaming and physically visiting its stores. In terms of electronics Amazon manufactures and sells electronic devices including Kindle Fire tablet Fire TV Echo Ring and other devices and develops and produces media content. Amazon serve consumers sellers developers enterprises content creators advertisers and employees. Amazon acquired MGM for approximately $8.45 billion in 2021. Majority of sales were generated in US.

	Annual Growth	12/17	12/18	12/19	12/20	12/21
Sales ($ mil.)	27.5%	177,866.0	232,887.0	280,522.0	386,064.0	469,822.0
Net income ($ mil.)	82.1%	3,033.0	10,073.0	11,588.0	21,331.0	33,364.0
Market value ($ mil.)	29.9%	595,260.2	764,502.7	940,550.6	1,657,777.4	1,697,179.1
Employees	29.8%	566,000	647,500	798,000	1,298,000	1,608,000

AMB FINANCIAL CORP NBB: AMFC

7880 Wicker Avenue, Suite 101
St. John, IN 46373
Phone: 219 365-6700
Fax: 219 365-9106
Web: www..acbanker.com

CEO: Michael Mellon
CFO: Steven Bohn
HR: –
FYE: December 31
Type: Public

AMB Financial is the holding company for American Savings a thrift serving Lake County Indiana near the southern tip of Lake Michigan. It operates four offices in Dyer Hammond Munster and Schererville. Catering to local families and businesses the bank offers checking and savings accounts money market accounts certificates of deposit and IRAs. It mainly uses these deposit funds to originate real estate construction consumer commercial land and other loans. One- to four-family residential mortgages account for approximately three-quarters of its loan portfolio. American Savings offers financial planning services through its American Financial Services division.

	Annual Growth	12/15	12/16	12/18	12/19	12/20
Assets ($ mil.)	6.7%	189.9	205.1	226.6	228.6	262.3
Net income ($ mil.)	16.0%	1.3	1.6	1.3	1.3	2.8
Market value ($ mil.)	7.9%	10.6	14.5	17.4	16.5	15.5
Employees	–	–	–	–	–	–

AMBAC FINANCIAL GROUP, INC. NYS: AMBC

One World Trade Center
New York, NY 10007
Phone: 212 658-7470
Fax: 212 208 3414
Web: www.ambac.com

CEO: Claude LeBlanc
CFO: David Trick
HR: –
FYE: December 31
Type: Public

Ambac has scaled back in a major way. Holding company Ambac Financial operates through subsidiaries including its flagship unit Ambac Assurance Everspan Financial Guarantee and Ambac Assurance UK. The businesses offered financial guarantees and related services to customers around the world. Ambac Assurance guaranteed public finance structured finance and international finance obligations. Its US account is the highest premiums which accounts for about 75%.

	Annual Growth	12/16	12/17	12/18	12/19	12/20
Assets ($ mil.)	(12.6%)	22,635.7	23,192.4	14,588.7	13,320.0	13,220.0
Net income ($ mil.)	–	74.8	(328.7)	267.4	(216.0)	(437.0)
Market value ($ mil.)	(9.1%)	1,030.7	732.0	789.7	988.1	704.5
Employees	(5.1%)	154	124	113	104	125

AMBARELLA, INC. NMS: AMBA

3101 Jay Street
Santa Clara, CA 95054
Phone: 408 734-8888
Fax: –
Web: www.ambarella.com

CEO: Feng-Ming Wang
CFO: Kevin C Eichler
HR: –
FYE: January 31
Type: Public

Ambarella's technology helps capture crisp clear digital images in cameras designed for sports autos drones and security. The company designs and markets video processing semiconductors for taking high-definition video and still images. It combines its system-on-a-chip semiconductor designs with proprietary software to create both industry and consumer products. The hardware/software combo helps cameras compensate for motion as a skier swoops downhill or a drone sweeps over a mountain. In security applications Amabarella's video chips can gather high-def images in low light. The company designs its chips which are made by contractors for small form factors and to run on low power. It sells its products through distributors and serves leading OEMs including Avigilon Corporation Dahua Technology Garmin Ltd. and Nest Labs.

	Annual Growth	01/17	01/18	01/19	01/20	01/21
Sales ($ mil.)	(7.9%)	310.3	295.4	227.8	228.7	223.0
Net income ($ mil.)	–	57.8	18.9	(30.4)	(44.8)	(59.8)
Market value ($ mil.)	–	–	–	–	–	–
Employees	4.1%	669	706	750	761	786

AMBASSADORS GROUP INC

NMS: EPAX

Dwight D. Eisenhower Building, 2001 South Flint Road
Spokane, WA 99224
Phone: 509 568-7800
Fax: –
Web: www.ambassadorsgroup.com

CEO: Philip B Livingston
CFO: –
HR: –
FYE: December 31
Type: Public

Ambassadors Group provides students and professionals with opportunities to meet their counterparts overseas. It organizes trips under contracts with the People to People organization which was founded by President Eisenhower to promote world peace. Ambassadors Group markets trips using the People to People name and makes travel arrangements for participants which include student athletes and leaders as well as professionals. It also offers international adventure travel services to students through its World Adventures Unlimited subsidiary. Outside the travel industry the firm operates BookRags.com a research website with more than 8 million pages of educational content for students and teachers.

	Annual Growth	12/09	12/10	12/11	12/12	12/13
Sales ($ mil.)	(15.1%)	98.6	76.1	66.4	58.1	51.2
Net income ($ mil.)	–	20.3	8.1	3.0	1.7	(7.1)
Market value ($ mil.)	(23.1%)	226.0	196.0	76.9	72.6	79.2
Employees	(3.5%)	251	221	240	238	218

AMBIENT CORP.

NBB: AMBT Q

7 Wells Avenue
Newton, MA 02459
Phone: 617 332-0004
Fax: –
Web: www.ambientcorp.com

CEO: –
CFO: –
HR: –
FYE: December 31
Type: Public

Ambient hopes its smart grid technology will stand out not blend in. The company develops technology that allows power lines to serve as high-speed data communications networks. Ambient's products — including nodes couplers and network management software — utilize Broadband over Power Line (BPL) and other technologies to create advanced power grids (also known as smart grids) with two-way communication capabilities. Its systems are designed to be used by utility companies for such applications as demand management direct load control meter reading and real-time pricing. Ambient has landed deals with Con Ed and Duke Energy to develop and deploy its technology.

	Annual Growth	12/09	12/10	12/11	12/12	12/13
Sales ($ mil.)	50.8%	2.2	20.4	62.3	42.8	11.4
Net income ($ mil.)	–	(14.2)	(3.2)	4.8	(5.4)	(17.7)
Market value ($ mil.)	105.9%	2.5	1.7	78.1	50.8	44.9
Employees	(1.7%)	44	59	88	105	41

AMC ENTERTAINMENT HOLDINGS INC.

NYS: AMC

One AMC Way, 11500 Ash Street
Leawood, KS 66211
Phone: 913 213-2000
Fax: –
Web: www.amctheatres.com

CEO: Adam Aron
CFO: Sean Goodman
HR: –
FYE: December 31
Type: Public

AMC Entertainment is one of the largest theater operators around the world. The world's largest theatrical exhibition company and an industry leader in innovation and operational excellence owns partially owns or operates approximately 950 theaters with around 10545 screens worldwide most of which are in megaplexes (units with more than 10 screens and stadium seating). It also has a significant presence in Europe through London-based subsidiary Odeon & UCI Cinemas Group. Most of its revenue were generated from the US. The company was founded in 1920.

	Annual Growth	12/16	12/17	12/18	12/19	12/20
Sales ($ mil.)	(21.3%)	3,235.8	5,079.2	5,460.8	5,471.0	1,242.4
Net income ($ mil.)	–	111.7	(487.2)	110.1	(149.1)	(4,589.1)
Market value ($ mil.)	(49.9%)	7,548.8	3,387.4	2,754.8	1,624.2	475.6
Employees	(11.8%)	41,373	39,843	39,802	38,862	25,019

AMC NETWORKS INC

NMS: AMCX

11 Penn Plaza
New York, NY 10001
Phone: 212 324-8500
Fax: –
Web: www.amcnetworks.com

CEO: Matthew Blank
CFO: Christina Spade
HR: –
FYE: December 31
Type: Public

AMC Networks is a global entertainment company known for its ground-breaking and award-winning original content. The company owns and operates a suite of focused and targeted video entertainment products that are delivered to viewers on an ever-expanding array of platforms. These include: linear TV channels carried by traditional and virtual multi-channel video programming distributors (MVPD); streaming services consisting of AMC+ as well as targeted streaming services; and various social media platforms. Each of its networks reach between 60 million and 80 million Nielsen subscribers. The company also produces original programming and licenses program rights worldwide. It distributes independent films through IFC Films. AMC operates worldwide but more than 80% of its sales come from the US.

	Annual Growth	12/17	12/18	12/19	12/20	12/21
Sales ($ mil.)	2.3%	2,805.7	2,971.9	3,060.3	2,815.0	3,077.6
Net income ($ mil.)	(14.6%)	471.3	446.2	380.5	240.0	250.6
Market value ($ mil.)	(10.7%)	2,291.7	2,325.6	1,673.9	1,515.8	1,459.4
Employees	(2.1%)	2,205	3,214	3,062	2,357	2,026

AMCOL INTERNATIONAL CORP.

NYS: ACO

2870 Forbs Avenue
Hoffman Estates, IL 60192
Phone: 847 851-1500
Fax: 847 851-1699
Web: www.amcol.com

CEO: Ryan F McKendrick
CFO: Donald W Pearson
HR: –
FYE: December 31
Type: Public

AMCOL International is nothing if not diverse with operations in minerals environmental services oilfield services and transportation. Its performance materials segment is a global supplier of bentonite products used in cat litter laundry detergent metal casting paper manufacturing and as a plastic additive. Its construction services segment provides building materials and construction services to concrete waterproofing drilling flood control and site remediation projects. AMCOL's energy services unit offers water treatment and well testing to the oil and gas industry. The company's transportation business provides long-haul trucking and freight brokerage services to AMCOL units and third parties in the US and Canada.

	Annual Growth	12/08	12/09	12/10	12/11	12/12
Sales ($ mil.)	2.8%	883.6	703.2	852.5	942.4	985.6
Net income ($ mil.)	26.6%	25.3	34.8	30.3	59.1	65.1
Market value ($ mil.)	10.0%	674.3	914.7	997.7	864.1	987.4
Employees	4.3%	2,388	2,211	2,383	2,563	2,824

AMCON DISTRIBUTING COMPANY

ASE: DIT

7405 Irvington Road
Omaha, NE 68122
Phone: 402 331-3727
Fax: 402 331-4834
Web: www.amcon.com

CEO: Christopher Atayan
CFO: Charles Schmaderer
HR: –
FYE: September 30
Type: Public

AMCON Distributing enjoys a healthy meal but the company is not without its vices. A leading consumer products wholesaler AMCON distributes more than 16000 different consumer products including cigarettes and other tobacco products as well as candy beverages groceries paper products and health and beauty aids. AMCON serves about 4500 convenience stores supermarkets drugstores tobacco shops and institutional customers in the Great Plains and Rocky Mountain regions. Throughout the Midwest and Florida the company also operates a growing chain of health food stores under the Chamberlin's Natural Foods and Akin's Natural Foods Market banners.

	Annual Growth	09/17	09/18	09/19	09/20	09/21
Sales ($ mil.)	7.0%	1,275.0	1,322.3	1,392.4	1,521.3	1,672.4
Net income ($ mil.)	51.5%	2.9	3.6	3.2	5.5	15.5
Market value ($ mil.)	12.7%	50.9	47.9	42.0	35.6	82.1
Employees	4.3%	790	919	912	929	934

AMEDISYS, INC.   NMS: AMED

3854 American Way, Suite A   CEO: Paul B Kusserow
Baton Rouge, LA 70816   CFO: Scott Ginn
Phone: 225 292-2031   HR: –
Fax: –   FYE: December 31
Web: www.amedisys.com   Type: Public

Through approximately 515 home health care agencies located throughout the US Amedisys provides skilled nursing and home health services primarily to geriatric patients covered by Medicare. It is also a post-acute care partner to over 2900 hospitals and about 78000 physicians across the country. Its range of services includes disease-specific programs that help patients recovering from stroke as well as assistance for those coping with emphysema or diabetes. In addition to home health services Amedisys owns or manages about 180 hospice centers that offer palliative care to terminally ill patients. Amedisys provides home health hospice care and personal care services to more than 418000 patients annually.

	Annual Growth	12/16	12/17	12/18	12/19	12/20
Sales ($ mil.)	10.0%	1,437.5	1,533.7	1,662.6	1,955.6	2,105.9
Net income ($ mil.)	49.0%	37.3	30.3	119.3	126.8	183.6
Market value ($ mil.)	62.0%	1,398.9	1,729.6	3,842.9	5,477.4	9,625.4
Employees	7.0%	16,000	17,900	21,000	21,300	21,000

AMEN PROPERTIES INC   NBB: AMEN

P.O. Box 835451   CEO: Jon Morgan
Richardson, TX 75080   CFO: Kris Oliver
Phone: 972 999-0494   HR: –
Fax: –   FYE: December 31
Web: www.amenproperties.com   Type: Public

AMEN Properties is hoping that the answer to its prayers are power and energy and a little property thrown in for good measure. The company's Priority Power subsidiary provides energy management and consulting services. This unit has current or previous business activities in Texas and 21 other states and serves more than 1200 clients (including a large number of oil and gas companies.) These activities include electricity load aggregation natural gas and electricity procurement energy risk management and energy consulting. AMEN Properties also invests in commercial real estate in secondary markets and in oil and gas royalties.

	Annual Growth	12/16	12/17	12/18	12/19	12/20
Sales ($ mil.)	(0.4%)	1.2	2.7	4.6	2.7	1.1
Net income ($ mil.)	–	2.2	2.4	5.1	0.0	(0.5)
Market value ($ mil.)	(4.8%)	25.7	25.8	36.7	39.9	21.1
Employees		–	–	–	–	–

AMERALIA INC.   PINK SHEETS: AALA

9233 Park Meadows Dr. Ste. 431   CEO: –
Lone Tree CO 80124   CFO: Bill H Gunn
Phone: 720-876-2373   HR: –
Fax: 970-878-5866   FYE: June 30
Web: www.naturalsoda.com   Type: Public

AmerAlia is sold on soda. Through subsidiary Natural Soda Inc. AmerAlia owns sodium bicarbonate leases in the region of Colorado's Piceance Creek Basin. AmerAlia can produce about 110000 tons of various grades of sodium bicarbonate per year. Sodium bicarbonate (baking soda) is used in animal feed food and pharmaceuticals. Byproducts such as soda ash and caustic soda are used to make glass detergents and chemicals. Investment group Sentient USA Resources Fund owns about three-quarters of AmerAlia. The company's operations are handled through 18%-owned subsidiary Natural Soda Holdings which itself owns Natural Soda Inc. outright.

AMERAMEX INTERNATIONAL INC.   PINK SHEETS: AMMX

3930 Esplanade   CEO: –
Chico CA 95973   CFO: Hope Stone
Phone: 530-895-8955   HR: –
Fax: 530-895-8959   FYE: December 31
Web: www.ammx.net/index.htm   Type: Public

Let AmeraMex take care of the heavy stuff. The company sells leases services and maintains heavy equipment to businesses such as heavy construction surface mining infrastructure logging shipping and transportation. AmeraMex has four business units: Hamre Equipment Hamre Heavy Haul Industry Hamre Parts and Service and John's Radiator. Its inventory includes front-end loaders excavators container handlers and trucks and trailers; manufacturers represented include Taylor Machine Works Terex Heavy Equipment and Barko Hydraulics. The firm is active in the Americas Europe the Middle East and Asia. AmeraMex also provides heavy hauling services throughout the US.

AMERCO   NMS: UHAL

5555 Kietzke Lane, Suite 100   CEO: Edward Shoen
Reno, NV 89511   CFO: Jason Berg
Phone: 775 688-6300   HR: –
Fax: 775 688-6338   FYE: March 31
Web: www.amerco.com   Type: Public

AMERCO is North America's largest "do-it-yourself" moving and storage operator through nearly 21100 independent dealers and more than 2100 company-owned centers across the US and Canada. Operating through its principal subsidiary U-Haul International the company serves customers through rentals of its ubiquitous orange-and-white trucks trailers and towing devices as well as sales of packing supplies. U-Haul's websites offer equipment reservations and moving information. AMERCO owns U-Haul-managed self-storage facilities and provides property and casualty insurance to U-Haul customers through Repwest. Its Oxford Life unit provides annuities Medicare supplement and life insurance coverage. Most of its revenue are generated in the US.

	Annual Growth	03/17	03/18	03/19	03/20	03/21
Sales ($ mil.)	7.3%	3,421.8	3,601.1	3,768.7	3,978.9	4,542.0
Net income ($ mil.)	11.3%	398.4	790.6	370.9	442.0	610.9
Market value ($ mil.)	12.6%	7,474.3	6,766.6	7,284.5	5,697.0	12,011.7
Employees	1.3%	28,300	29,000	30,000	30,000	29,800

AMEREN CORP   NYS: AEE

1901 Chouteau Avenue   CEO: Warner Baxter
St. Louis, MO 63103   CFO: Michael Moehn
Phone: 314 621-3222   HR: –
Fax: –   FYE: December 31
Web: www.ameren.com   Type: Public

Missouri-based Ameren is a public utility holding company whose primary assets are its equity interests in its subsidiaries. As the sole distributor in its service region the holding company distributes electricity to 1.2 million customers and natural gas to 0.1 million customers. Ameren has generating capacity of around 5.1 million net kilowatt of primarily coal-fired power most of which is owned by Ameren Missouri. About 97% of Ameren Missouri's coal is purchased from the Powder River Basin in Wyoming which has a limited number of suppliers. The remaining coal is typically purchased from the Illinois Basin.

	Annual Growth	12/17	12/18	12/19	12/20	12/21
Sales ($ mil.)	0.9%	6,177.0	6,291.0	5,910.0	5,794.0	6,394.0
Net income ($ mil.)	17.3%	523.0	815.0	828.0	871.0	990.0
Market value ($ mil.)	10.8%	15,201.7	16,809.8	19,791.4	20,116.1	22,937.9
Employees	1.4%	8,615	8,838	9,323	9,183	9,116

AMEREN ILLINOIS CO
NBB: AILI M

10 Executive Drive
Collinsville, IL 62234
Phone: 618 343-8150
Fax: –

CEO: Richard Mark
CFO: Michael L Moehn
HR: –
FYE: December 31
Type: Public

Ameren Illinois brings gas and electric services to customers across the Land of Lincoln. The Ameren subsidiary operates a rate-regulated electric and natural gas transmission and distribution business in Illinois serving more than 1.2 million electricity and 806000 natural gas customers in 85 of Illinois' 102 counties. The multi-utility has a service area of 43700 square miles. Ameren Illinois operates 4500 miles of transmission lines 45400 miles of power distribution lines and 18000 miles of gas transmission and distribution mains. It also has 12 underground natural gas storage fields.

	Annual Growth	12/16	12/17	12/18	12/19	12/20
Sales ($ mil.)	0.4%	2,490.0	2,528.0	2,576.0	2,527.0	2,535.0
Net income ($ mil.)	10.6%	255.0	271.0	307.0	346.0	382.0
Market value ($ mil.)	0.1%	2,537.5	2,504.1	2,422.5	2,511.8	2,550.0
Employees	(0.9%)	3,429	3,423	3,458	3,476	3,304

AMERESCO INC
NYS: AMRC

111 Speen Street, Suite 410
Framingham, MA 01701
Phone: 508 661-2200
Fax: –
Web: www.ameresco.com

CEO: George Sakellaris
CFO: Spencer Doran Hole
HR: –
FYE: December 31
Type: Public

Primarily serving commercial and industrial customers along with municipal and federal government agencies Ameresco provides designing engineering and installation services to clients seeking to upgrade and improve the efficiency of their heating and air conditioning ventilation lighting and other building systems. Other services include developing and constructing small-scale on-site (or near-site) renewable energy plants for customers as well as installing solar panels wind turbines and other alternative energy sources. Ameresco operates through more than 70 regional offices in the US Canada and the UK. The US accounts for about 95% of company's revenues.

	Annual Growth	12/16	12/17	12/18	12/19	12/20
Sales ($ mil.)	12.2%	651.2	717.2	787.1	866.9	1,032.3
Net income ($ mil.)	45.6%	12.0	37.5	38.0	44.4	54.1
Market value ($ mil.)	75.6%	265.2	414.7	680.0	843.9	2,519.3
Employees	2.4%	1,038	1,049	1,116	1,127	1,141

AMERIANA BANCORP
NAS: ASBI

2118 Bundy Avenue
New Castle, IN 47362-1048
Phone: 765 529-2230
Fax: 765 529-2232
Web: www.ameriana.com

CEO: –
CFO: –
HR: –
FYE: December 31
Type: Public

Ameriana Bancorp may sound merry but it takes business seriously. It's the parent of Ameriana Bank which has about a dozen offices in central Indiana. The bank offers standard deposit products including checking savings and money market accounts; CDs; and IRAs. It focuses on real estate lending: Residential mortgages account for about half of its loan portfolio and commercial real estate loans represent about 30%. The company sells auto home life health and business coverage through its Ameriana Insurance Agency subsidiary. Another unit Ameriana Investment Management provides brokerage and investment services through an agreement with LPL Financial.

	Annual Growth	12/09	12/10	12/11	12/12	12/13
Assets ($ mil.)	1.0%	441.6	429.7	429.8	445.8	458.6
Net income ($ mil.)	–	(0.3)	0.6	1.1	1.8	2.2
Market value ($ mil.)	49.2%	8.0	12.1	11.8	24.6	39.6
Employees	–	–	–	–	–	–

AMERICA CHUNG NAM (GROUP) HOLDINGS LLC

1163 FAIRWAY DR
CITY OF INDUSTRY, CA 917892846
Phone: 909-839-8383
Fax: –
Web: www.acni.net

CEO: Teresa Cheung
CFO: Kevin Zhao
HR: –
FYE: December 31
Type: Private

America Chung Nam (ACN) sells recovered fiber sources to Chinese paper mills where it can be converted into fiberboard cardboard and packaging. It also collects and exports a number of grades of post-consumer plastics. The company sources its materials through exclusive relationships with recycling facilities. Founder Yan Cheung and Ming Chung Liu own the company. It was founded in 1990.

	Annual Growth	12/07	12/08	12/09	12/18	12/19
Sales ($ mil.)	(6.3%)	–	1,363.3	1,125.2	1,711.7	664.5
Net income ($ mil.)	23.9%	–	7.9	16.9	216.3	83.6
Market value ($ mil.)	–	–	–	–	–	–
Employees	–	–	–	–	–	200

AMERICA FIRST CREDIT UNION

1344 W. 4675 South
Riverdale UT 84405
Phone: 801-627-0900
Fax: 801-778-8079
Web: www.americafirst.com

CEO: –
CFO: Rex Rollo
HR: –
FYE: December 31
Type: Private - Not-for-Pr

If saving your money makes you feel like doing a little flag-waving could there be a more appropriate place for it than America First Credit Union? The institution offers deposits loans credit cards investments and other financial services to both business and consumer customers through more than 100 branches in Utah and Nevada. With more than 597000 members America First ranks among the nation's top 10 credit unions by membership and is one of the 15 largest by assets. Membership is open to residents of certain counties in Utah and Nevada food service workers in Utah employees of selected companies and family members of America First members.

AMERICA'S BODY COMPANY INC.

939 E. Starr Ave.
Columbus OH 43201
Phone: 614-299-1136
Fax: 614-299-2314
Web: www.abctruck.com

CEO: –
CFO: –
HR: –
FYE: December 31
Type: Private

America's Body Company (ABC) is one business that really wants you to get carried away with its product. Operating through some seven facilities in Florida Kentucky Ohio Oregon Maryland and Texas ABC customizes trucks with equipment and accessories for several industries including landscaping contracting distribution and manufacturing. The company also customizes trucks for special needs. ABC sells to vehicle dealers fleet operators and end users. Its products include aerial lift devices dump bodies for pickup trucks liftgates and water tanks. ABC was founded in 1976 as Great Lakes Truck Equipment. It was owned by Leggett & Platt until September 2008 when The Reading Group acquired the company.

AMERICA'S CAR-MART INC

NMS: CRMT

1805 North 2nd Street, Suite 401
Rogers, AR 72756
Phone: 479 464-9944
Fax: –
Web: www.car-mart.com

CEO: Jeffrey Williams
CFO: Vickie Judy
HR: –
FYE: April 30
Type: Public

No Credit? Bad Credit? No problem. America's Car-Mart targets car buyers with poor or limited credit histories. The company's subsidiaries operate about 150 used car dealerships in more than 10 states primarily in smaller urban and rural markets throughout the US South Central region. Dealerships focus on selling basic and affordable transportation with an average selling price of about $11795 in 2020. It has facilities in Alabama Tennessee and Mississippi among others. While the company's business plan has focused on cities with up to 50000 in population (about 75% of sales) it sees better collection results among the smaller communities it serves. America's Car-Mart was founded in 1981 as the Crown Group. Most of the company's stores are located in Arkansas.

	Annual Growth	04/17	04/18	04/19	04/20	04/21
Sales ($ mil.)	11.8%	587.8	612.2	669.1	744.6	918.6
Net income ($ mil.)	50.7%	20.2	36.5	47.6	51.3	104.1
Market value ($ mil.)	41.8%	247.1	353.2	656.3	437.0	999.4
Employees	6.1%	1,460	1,504	1,600	1,750	1,850

AMERICA'S HOME PLACE, INC.

2144 HILTON DR
GAINESVILLE, GA 305016172
Phone: 770-532-1128
Fax: –
Web: www.americashomeplace.com

CEO: Barry G Conner
CFO: –
HR: –
FYE: December 31
Type: Private

America's Home Place builds custom homes on its customers' land. The company builds single-family detached houses with more than 100 custom floor plans and designs. Its two- to five-bedroom cabin chalet ranch two-story and split-level houses range in price from about $80000 to more than $300000. Sizes start at about 900 sq. ft. and go up to to 4000 sq. ft. America's Home Place operates nearly 40 home building and model centers in the southeastern US. Buyers typically already own their land from a single lot to many acres. The company also assists buyers who are not landowners in locating available property. President Barry Conner owns the company he founded in 1972.

	Annual Growth	12/05	12/06	12/07	12/11	12/15
Sales ($ mil.)	–	–	–	0.0	173.4	125.6	175.2
Net income ($ mil.)	–	–	–	0.0	8.4	4.6	5.3
Market value ($ mil.)	–	–	–	–	–	–	–
Employees	–	–	–	–	–	–	320

AMERICAN ACADEMY OF PEDIATRICS

345 PARK BLVD
ITASCA, IL 601432644
Phone: 847-228-5005
Fax: –
Web: www.aap.org

CEO: Mark Del Monte
CFO: John Miller
HR: –
FYE: June 30
Type: Private

The American Academy of Pediatrics (AAP) is a membership group of some 64000 pediatricians pediatric specialists and pediatric surgeons dedicated to improving the health and well-being of infants children teenagers and young adults. The not-for-profit organization executes research on a number of topics including school health common childhood illnesses and immunizations and acts as an advocate on behalf of children's health needs. It also provides continuing education for its members through courses scientific meetings and publications such as Pediatrics and Pediatrics in Review . The organization is funded by membership dues grants gifts and its own activities. AAP was founded in 1930.

	Annual Growth	06/12	06/13	06/14	06/15	06/17
Sales ($ mil.)	4.6%	–	105.8	117.3	111.2	126.5
Net income ($ mil.)	6.5%	–	4.6	7.6	(0.2)	6.0
Market value ($ mil.)	–	–	–	–	–	–
Employees	–	–	–	–	–	400

AMERICAN AGIP COMPANY INC.

485 Madison Ave.
New York NY 10022
Phone: 646-264-2100
Fax: 646-264-2222
Web: www.americanagip.com

CEO: Walter D'Ankeli
CFO: –
HR: –
FYE: December 31
Type: Subsidiary

You might say that American Agip is as slick as a whistle. Formed in 1987 the subsidiary of Italian energy heavyweight Eni operates three major petrochemical businesses: the manufacturing and marketing of lubricants; the marketing and trading of MTBE and methanol; and the trading of refined petroleum products. American Agip supplies bulk and package customers throughout the eastern US and across Canada. It has a manufacturing center in Cabot Pennsylvania (where it has more than 1 million gallons of lubricant storage) and distribution centers located in New Jersey New York Ohio Pennsylvania and West Virginia as well as in Quebec Canada.

AMERICAN AIR LIQUIDE INC.

2700 Post Oak Blvd. Ste. 1800
Houston TX 77056
Phone: 713-624-8000
Fax: 713-624-8085
Web: www.us.airliquide.com

CEO: Pierre Dufour
CFO: Scott Krapf
HR: –
FYE: December 31
Type: Subsidiary

American Air Liquide builds up its liquid assets through the supply of gas in the US. The company supplies industrial gases (oxygen nitrogen CO2 argon etc.) to companies in the automotive chemicals food and beverage and health care industries. The US distribution arm of industrial gas provider Air Liquide the company can depending on its customers' needs it can manufacture onsite ship its product in cylinders or through more than 2000 miles of pipeline. It operates 200 locations throughout the US including 140 industrial gas plants. American Air Liquide also fulfills semiconductor companies' gas and liquid chemical requirements from its own fabrication plants.

AMERICAN AIRLINES FEDERAL CREDIT UNION

4151 Amon Carter Blvd.
Fort Worth TX 76155
Phone: 817-963-6000
Fax: 817-963-6108
Web: https://www.aacreditunion.org

CEO: Angie Owens
CFO: –
HR: –
FYE: December 31
Type: Private - Not-for-Pr

American Airlines Federal Credit Union won't hassle you about the position of your seatback or tray table. The member-owned institution (aka AA Credit Union) operates more than 40 branches in or near airports in about 20 cities in the US and Puerto Rico. It provides standard retail financial services such as checking and savings accounts loans credit cards and investments to some 237000 members who also have access to more than 6600 shared locations and 30000 ATMs. Its lending program consists of home mortgages and vehicle education and other personal loans as well as real estate equipment and vehicle loans and lines of credit for small businesses.

HOOVER'S MASTERLIST OF U.S. COMPANIES 2022

AMERICAN AIRLINES GROUP INC — NMS: AAL

1 Skyviwe Drive
Fort Worth, TX 76155
Phone: 682 278-9000
Fax: 817 967-9641
Web: www.aa.com

CEO: William Parker
CFO: Derek Kerr
HR: –
FYE: December 31
Type: Public

American Airlines Group (AAG) is one of the largest airline in the world. The company's primary business activity is the operation of a major network air carrier providing scheduled air transportation along with its group of regional subsidiaries and third-party regional carriers operating as American Eagle. It also offers freight and mail services through its cargo division. In all American operates an average of nearly 6700 flights daily to some 365 destinations in about 50 countries. It operates some 865 mainline aircraft and over 565 regional aircraft. American Airlines Group is also a founding member of oneworld alliance where member carriers share airport lounge facilities and offer interconnected loyalty programs. Over 80% of passenger sales of American Airlines Group is generated from the US.

	Annual Growth	12/17	12/18	12/19	12/20	12/21
Sales ($ mil.)	(8.3%)	42,207.0	44,541.0	45,768.0	17,337.0	29,882.0
Net income ($ mil.)	–	1,919.0	1,412.0	1,686.0	(8,885.0)	(1,993.0)
Market value ($ mil.)	(23.3%)	33,701.3	20,798.5	18,576.8	10,214.7	11,633.2
Employees	(0.6%)	126,600	128,900	133,700	102,700	123,400

AMERICAN APPAREL, INC. — ASE: APP

747 Warehouse Street
Los Angeles, CA 90021
Phone: 213 488-0226
Fax: –
Web: www.americanapparel.com

CEO: Chelsea Grayson
CFO: –
HR: –
FYE: December 31
Type: Public

American Apparel wants you to be hip and comfortable inside and out. It designs and makes logo-free T-shirts tanks yoga pants and more for men women and children — and does it all from its California factory rather than exporting labor overseas. Brands include Classic Girl Standard American Classic Baby and Sustainable Edition among others. American Apparel runs 250-plus retail stores in 20 countries. Known for its no-sweat factory and for paying up to $19-an-hour for manufacturers American Apparel was teetering on the brink of insolvency until it received strategically timed funding. In mid-2014 the board replaced controversial CEO Dov Charney who founded American Apparel in 1998.

	Annual Growth	12/09	12/10	12/11	12/12	12/13
Sales ($ mil.)	3.2%	558.8	533.0	547.3	617.3	633.9
Net income ($ mil.)	–	1.1	(86.3)	(39.3)	(37.3)	(106.3)
Market value ($ mil.)	(20.6%)	345.1	184.8	80.2	112.4	136.9
Employees	0.0%	10,000	11,300	10,000	10,000	10,000

AMERICAN ARBITRATION ASSOCIATION INC

120 BROADWAY FL 21
NEW YORK, NY 102710016
Phone: 212-716-5800
Fax: –
Web: www.adr.org

CEO: India Johnson
CFO: Francesco Rossi
HR: –
FYE: December 31
Type: Private

The American Arbitration Association (AAA) wants to keep things civil. The organization provides arbitration mediation and other forms of alternative dispute resolution services — alternatives that is to going to court. It maintains a panel of more than 7000 arbitrators and mediators who can be engaged to hear cases and supports their work. Every year more than 185000 cases are filed with AAA in a full range of matters including commercial construction labor employment insurance international and claims program disputes. The association's services include development of alternative dispute resolution (ADR) systems for corporations unions government agencies law firms and the courts.

	Annual Growth	12/05	12/06	12/08	12/09	12/13
Sales ($ mil.)	(36.9%)	–	1,929.9	70.7	67.9	77.2
Net income ($ mil.)	–	–	–	(23.0)	8.9	8.5
Market value ($ mil.)	–	–	–	–	–	–
Employees	–	–	–	–	–	750

AMERICAN ASSETS TRUST, INC.

3420 CARMEL MOUNTAIN RD # 100
SAN DIEGO, CA 921211069
Phone: 858-350-2600
Fax: –
Web: www.americanassetstrust.com

CEO: Ernest Rady
CFO: Robert Barton
HR: –
FYE: December 31
Type: Private

American Assets Trust is a self-administered real estate investment trust (REIT) that owns develops and operates upscale retail office and residential property mostly in Northern and Southern California but also in Oregon Washington Texas and Hawaii. Its approximately 3.1 million square foot portfolio includes more than 10 shopping centers about 10l of office buildings a 369-room hotel and retail complex and more than five multi-family residential properties. Its tenants include SalesForce Autodesk the Veterans Benefits Administration and well-known retailers such as Kmart Lowe's Sports Authority Old Navy and Vons. Formed in 1967 as American Assets the firm went public in 2011.

	Annual Growth	12/13	12/14	12/15	12/16	12/17
Assets ($ mil.)	5.2%	–	1,941.8	1,978.4	1,986.9	2,259.9
Net income ($ mil.)	8.8%	–	31.1	53.9	45.6	40.1
Market value ($ mil.)	–	–	–	–	–	–
Employees	–	–	–	–	–	113

AMERICAN ASSOCIATION FOR THE ADVANCEMENT OF SCIENCE

1200 NEW YORK AVE NW
WASHINGTON, DC 200053928
Phone: 202-326-6730
Fax: –
Web: www.aaas.org

CEO: Sudip Parikh
CFO: Colleen Strusss
HR: –
FYE: December 31
Type: Private

The American Association for the Advancement of Science (AAAS) likes to think of itself as the voice of science. Founded in 1848 AAAS is a nonprofit that promotes scientific research and technology through educational and international programs policy support and the publication of books newsletters and weekly magazine Science (available to AAAS members and institutional subscribers). It also runs science news website EurekAlert! The association includes about 250 affiliated societies and academies of science reaching some 10 million individuals. AAAS has advised policymakers on such topics as global climate change and stem cell research and has rallied for more US research and development funding.

	Annual Growth	12/06	12/07	12/08	12/09	12/13
Sales ($ mil.)	3.2%	–	88.6	89.7	87.8	107.0
Net income ($ mil.)	8.9%	–	7.3	(14.4)	3.6	12.2
Market value ($ mil.)	–	–	–	–	–	–
Employees	–	–	–	–	–	475

AMERICAN AXLE & MANUFACTURING HOLDINGS INC — NYS: AXL

One Dauch Drive
Detroit, MI 48211-1198
Phone: 313 758-2000
Fax: –
Web: www.aam.com

CEO: David Dauch
CFO: Christopher May
HR: Terri Kemp
FYE: December 31
Type: Public

American Axle & Manufacturing (AAM) is a global Tier 1 supplier to the automotive industry. AAM manufactures engineers and designs axles driveshafts and transmission shafts mainly for light trucks and SUVs but also for cars and crossover vehicles. The Tier 1 supplier gets about 40% of its business from GM. Other customers include Ford FCA US Chrysler Pacifica and Lincoln Nautilus. AAM operates nearly 80 manufacturing facilities in more than 15 countries around the world and generates more than 75% of its revenue from North America.

	Annual Growth	12/17	12/18	12/19	12/20	12/21
Sales ($ mil.)	(4.8%)	6,266.0	7,270.4	6,530.9	4,710.8	5,156.6
Net income ($ mil.)	(63.6%)	337.1	(57.5)	(484.5)	(561.3)	5.9
Market value ($ mil.)	(14.0%)	1,941.4	1,265.4	1,226.6	950.8	1,063.6
Employees	(7.9%)	25,000	25,000	20,000	20,000	18,000

AMERICAN BANK INC (PA)   NBB: AMBK

4029 West Tilghman Street   CEO: Mark Jaindl
Allentown, PA 18104   CFO: Harry Birkhimer
Phone: 610 366-1800   HR: –
Fax: 610 366-1900   FYE: December 31
Web: www.ambk.com   Type: Public

American Bank Incorporated is the holding company for American Bank which operates a single branch in Allentown Pennsylvania. It serves customers throughout the US via its pcbanker.com Web site. The bank's products and services include checking and savings accounts money market accounts CDs credit cards and discount brokerage. It primarily originates real estate loans although it also offers commercial mortgages and residential mortgages. The Jaindl family including company president and CEO Mark Jaindl owns a majority of American Bank Incorporated.

	Annual Growth	12/16	12/17	12/18	12/19	12/20
Assets ($ mil.)	7.1%	557.1	580.8	621.9	641.6	734.3
Net income ($ mil.)	18.3%	4.4	5.6	6.8	7.9	8.7
Market value ($ mil.)	(0.8%)	69.1	63.8	69.7	66.9	66.9
Employees	–	–	–	–	–	–

AMERICAN BANKERS ASSOCIATION INC

1120 CONNECTICUT AVE NW # 600   CEO: Rob Nichols
WASHINGTON, DC 200363959   CFO: –
Phone: 202-663-5000   HR: –
Fax: –   FYE: August 31
Web: www.aba.com   Type: Private

The American Bankers Association (ABA) brings together banks of various types and sizes. Its members include bank holding companies savings associations savings banks trust companies and community regional and money center banks. The ABA serves as an advocate for its members in legislative and regulatory arenas. It also engages in consumer education research and training efforts. The ABA's BankPac the banking industry's largest political action committee provides financial support to candidates for the US Senate and House of Representatives. The ABA was founded in 1875 and claims to represent more than 95% of banking assets. The group merged with the America's Community Bankers association in 2007.

	Annual Growth	08/06	08/07	08/08	08/09	08/10
Sales ($ mil.)	(42.0%)	–	–	239.7	64.0	80.7
Net income ($ mil.)	612.2%	–	–	0.0	(22.3)	0.8
Market value ($ mil.)	–	–	–	–	–	–
Employees	–	–	–	–	–	354

AMERICAN BAR ASSOCIATION

321 N CLARK ST STE LL2   CEO: –
CHICAGO, IL 606547598   CFO: Bill Phelan
Phone: 312-988-5000   HR: –
Fax: –   FYE: August 31
Web: www.americanbar.org   Type: Private

The world's largest voluntary professional organization American Bar Association (ABA) promotes improvements in the American justice system and develops guidelines for the advancement of the legal profession and education. The association provides law school accreditation continuing education legal information and other services to assist legal professionals. The ABA's roster of about 400000 members includes lawyers judges court administrators law librarians and law school professors and students. The organization cannot discipline lawyers nor enforce its rules; it can only develop guidelines. The ABA was founded in 1878.

	Annual Growth	08/11	08/12	08/13	08/14	08/15
Sales ($ mil.)	1.2%	–	146.3	206.0	204.4	151.7
Net income ($ mil.)	–	–	9.1	39.4	35.9	(7.4)
Market value ($ mil.)	–	–	–	–	–	–
Employees	–	–	–	–	–	900

AMERICAN BILTRITE INC.   NBB: ABLT

57 River Street, Suite 302   CEO: Roger S Marcus
Wellesley Hills, MA 02481-2097   CFO: Howard N Feist III
Phone: 781 237-6655   HR: –
Fax: –   FYE: December 31
Web: www.ambilt.com   Type: Public

American Biltrite (ABI) which makes and distributes commercial flooring and industrial rubber has its hand in several different pots some of which are sticky. Its Tape division makes adhesive-coated pressure-sensitive tapes and films used to protect materials during handling and storage as well as for applications in the heating ventilation and air conditioning automotive and electrical industries. ABI also designs and distributes wholesale jewelry and accessories to stores through its K&M subsidiary while its AB Canada subsidiary makes floor tile and rubber products. The founding Marcus family controls ABI.

	Annual Growth	12/16	12/17	12/18	12/19	12/20
Sales ($ mil.)	(3.1%)	184.3	200.5	202.6	204.8	162.5
Net income ($ mil.)	–	1.3	5.0	8.3	(4.6)	(14.1)
Market value ($ mil.)	5.1%	6.8	16.6	16.6	13.1	8.3
Employees	–	–	–	–	–	–

AMERICAN BIO MEDICA CORP.   NBB: ABMC

122 Smith Road   CEO: Melissa Waterhouse
Kinderhook, NY 12106   CFO: Melissa A Waterhouse
Phone: 518 758-8158   HR: –
Fax: –   FYE: December 31
Web: www.abmc.com   Type: Public

There's a thin line between employment and unemployment and that line might just be on one of American Bio Medica's drug-testing kits. The company's Rapid Drug Screen products indicate within minutes the presence in a urine sample of such illegal substances as marijuana cocaine amphetamines and opiates. Used by employers law enforcement agencies hospitals schools and other institutions the tests offer up to 10-panel options (each panel tests for different substances). The company's Rapid One is a line of single-drug specific tests; its Rapid Tec and Rapid TOX products detect multiple drug classes on one panel. American Bio Medica also offers saliva-based tests for law enforcement customers.

	Annual Growth	12/16	12/17	12/18	12/19	12/20
Sales ($ mil.)	(7.3%)	5.6	4.9	3.9	3.7	4.1
Net income ($ mil.)	–	(0.3)	(0.5)	(1.0)	(0.7)	(0.8)
Market value ($ mil.)	5.2%	4.0	3.8	2.6	2.6	4.9
Employees	(7.4%)	57	53	43	48	42

AMERICAN BUILDINGS COMPANY

1150 State Docks Rd.   CEO: –
Eufaula AL 36027   CFO: –
Phone: 334-687-2032   HR: –
Fax: 334-688-2185   FYE: December 31
Web: www.americanbuildings.com   Type: Subsidiary

American Buildings Company can put a roof over your head quite literally. It manufactures metal buildings and roofing products for industrial institutional and commercial construction applications. From multi-story buildings to customized self-storage units to metal roof and wall panels the company's buildings and components are marketed through a network of more than 1000 authorized builders and dealers in the US and Canada. Its heavy fabrication capabilities include building custom-engineered steel mills sports stadiums and large aircraft maintenance hangars. American Buildings Company and its former parent MAGNATRAX were acquired by steelmaker Nucor Corporation in 2007.

AMERICAN BUREAU OF SHIPPING

1701 CITY PLAZA DR
SPRING, TX 773891878
Phone: 281-877-6000
Fax: -
Web: www.eagle.org

CEO: -
CFO: -
HR: -
FYE: December 31
Type: Private

One of the world's largest ship classification societies American Bureau of Shipping (ABS) offers inspection and analysis services to verify that vessels are mechanically and structurally fit. The not-for-profit company's surveyors examine ships in major ports throughout the world assessing whether the vessels comply with ABS rules for design construction and maintenance. Additionally its engineers consult with shipbuilders on proposed designs and repairs. The not-for-profit company operates from more than 150 offices in about 70 countries. For-profit subsidiaries ABS Group offers risk management consulting services while ABS Nautical Systems provides fleet management software. ABS was founded in 1862.

	Annual Growth	12/08	12/09	12/11	12/12	12/17
Sales ($ mil.)	(3.6%)	-	648.8	726.7	1,134.3	484.4
Net income ($ mil.)	(12.5%)	-	180.8	143.6	155.3	62.2
Market value ($ mil.)	-	-	-	-	-	-
Employees	-	-	-	-	-	3,000

AMERICAN CAMPUS COMMUNITIES INC   NYS: ACC

12700 Hill Country Blvd., Suite T-200
Austin, TX 78738
Phone: 512 732-1000
Fax: -
Web: www.americancampus.com

CEO: William Bayless
CFO: Daniel Perry
HR: -
FYE: December 31
Type: Public

American Campus Communities (ACC) is a fully integrated self-managed and self-administered real estate investment trust (REIT) with expertise in the acquisition design financing development construction management leasing and management of student housing properties. The company leases the ground for on-campus properties from the schools which in turn receive about half of the net cash flow from these properties. ACC also works with schools to develop new properties and renovate existing housing and provides third-party leasing and management services for other student housing owners. In all the REIT manages more than 200 properties (with more than 141000 beds) at some 95 schools in the US and Canada.

	Annual Growth	12/16	12/17	12/18	12/19	12/20
Sales ($ mil.)	2.6%	786.4	796.4	880.8	943.0	870.6
Net income ($ mil.)	(7.4%)	99.1	69.0	117.1	85.0	72.8
Market value ($ mil.)	(3.7%)	6,845.4	5,643.3	5,692.8	6,468.5	5,882.6
Employees	(1.5%)	3,170	3,183	3,098	3,096	2,988

AMERICAN CANNABIS CO INC   NBB: AMMJ

2590 Walnut Street #6
Denver, CO 80205
Phone: 303 974-4770
Fax: -

CEO: Ellis Smith
CFO: David Michael Godfrey
HR: -
FYE: December 31
Type: Public

NatureWell hopes to offer relief out of the mist to migraine sufferers in a fog. The company has developed its MICROMIST technology to deliver homeopathic and natural remedies under the tongue. Currently the company's only product is over-the-counter migraine treatment MigraSpray which can be used both as a preventative measure and to relieve the acute pain of migraines. It is only available through healthcare professionals and by mail order. NatureWell outsources manufacturing distribution and customer service functions. It is exploring new product offerings for arthritis and general pain including Arthrispray PMS Spray and Allerspray.

	Annual Growth	12/16	12/17	12/18	12/19	12/20
Sales ($ mil.)	0.1%	1.6	2.4	1.0	2.1	1.6
Net income ($ mil.)	-	(0.6)	(1.5)	(1.0)	(0.3)	(0.5)
Market value ($ mil.)	(47.3%)	64.7	83.5	21.2	6.9	5.0
Employees	(8.1%)	7	8	6	9	5

AMERICAN CAPITAL LTD.   NASDAQ: ACAS

2 Bethesda Metro Center 14th Fl.
Bethesda MD 20814
Phone: 301-951-6122
Fax: 301-654-6714
Web: www.americancapital.com

CEO: R Kipp Deveer
CFO: -
HR: Kasey Reisman
FYE: December 31
Type: Public

Whether you make musical instruments or mints salon appliances or safes this company has a strategy for you. Founded in 1986 American Capital invests in a diverse selection of middle-market companies both directly and through its global asset management business. It typically provides up to $300 million per transaction to companies for management and employee buyouts and private equity buyouts. The firm also directly provides capital to companies. Other investments include financial products such as commercial mortgage-backed securities and collateralized loan obligations. American Capital's portfolio consists of stakes in more than 150 companies and has a focus on manufacturing services and distribution.

AMERICAN CARESOURCE HOLDINGS INC   NBB: GNOW

55 Ivan Allen Jr. Blvd., Suite 510
Atlanta, GA 30308
Phone: 404 465-1000
Fax: -
Web: www.americancaresource.com

CEO: -
CFO: -
HR: -
FYE: December 31
Type: Public

American CareSource owns and operates a chain of about a dozen urgent and primary care centers (branded GoNow and Medac) in the Southeast US. However the firm has found itself in high levels of debt. In early 2017 the company sold subsidiary Ancillary Care Services which negotiates contracts with specialty health care providers with (i.e. outpatient surgery rehabilitation hospice laboratory and other services). It is also exploring the sale of its urgent care assets. American CareSource's clients have included preferred provider organizations (PPOs) health maintenance organizations (HMOs) third-party administrators and self-insured employers. The firm's roots go back to the mid-1990s.

	Annual Growth	12/11	12/12	12/13	12/14	12/15
Sales ($ mil.)	(32.7%)	48.9	34.9	26.8	27.1	10.0
Net income ($ mil.)	-	(7.2)	(3.1)	(3.8)	(6.8)	(13.3)
Market value ($ mil.)	(1.1%)	7.1	23.7	27.2	48.1	6.8
Employees	35.4%	56	56	52	141	188

AMERICAN CHARTERED BANCORP INC.

1199 E. Higgins Rd.
Schaumburg IL 60173
Phone: 847-517-5400
Fax: 415-675-6701
Web: www.wideorbit.com

CEO: -
CFO: -
HR: -
FYE: December 31
Type: Private

American Chartered Bancorp helps customers stay the course in the oft-choppy waters of money management. The holding company owns American Chartered Bank a commercial and retail bank that primarily serves small to midsized businesses and individuals in the Chicago area. Through about 15 branches it offers standard deposit products such as checking and savings accounts and credit cards as well as loans and leases treasury management and merchant services. American Chartered Bancorp was founded in 1987 and is locally owned and operated.

AMERICAN CHEMICAL SOCIETY

1155 16TH ST NW
WASHINGTON, DC 200364892
Phone: 202-872-4600
Fax: –
Web: www.acs.org

CEO: –
CFO: –
HR: –
FYE: December 31
Type: Private

With more than 151000 members the American Chemical Society (ACS) is the world's largest scientific society. The not-for-profit organization provides information career services engagement programs and educational resources to members and scientists. The company also publishes magazines journals and books. Its Chemical Abstract Service provides the most comprehensive repository of research in chemistry and related sciences. ACS also serves as an advocate for its members on public policy issues. The ACS Member Insurance Program provides insurance plans to its members. The company was founded in 1876.

	Annual Growth	12/03	12/04	12/05	12/08	12/13
Sales ($ mil.)	4.1%	–	–	411.7	451.5	568.7
Net income ($ mil.)	11.3%	–	–	26.4	(38.4)	62.3
Market value ($ mil.)	–	–	–	–	–	–
Employees	–	–	–	–	–	2,000

AMERICAN CITY BUSINESS JOURNALS INC.

120 W. Morehead St. Ste. 400
Charlotte NC 28202
Phone: 704-973-1000
Fax: 704-973-1001
Web: www.acbj.com

CEO: Whitney R Shaw
CFO: George B Guthinger
HR: –
FYE: December 31
Type: Subsidiary

Cities big and small can turn to this company for coverage of US metropolitan business news. American City Business Journals (ACBJ) is a leading newspaper publisher that serves more than 500000 subscribers with local business news through more than 40 publications. Its bizjournals subsidiary also publishes news and information online for about 4 million registered users. In addition ACBJ owns The Sporting News one of the top sports magazines in the US and Hemmings Motor News a publisher of collectible-car books and magazines. Its Street & Smith's Sports Group publishes several sports publications including SportsBusiness Journal. ACBJ is a unit of newspaper and magazine publisher Advance Publications.

AMERICAN COMMERCE SOLUTIONS INC   NBB: AACS

1400 Chamber Drive
Bartow, FL 33830
Phone: 863 533-0326
Fax: –
Web: www.aacssymbol.com

CEO: Daniel Hefner
CFO: Frank Puissegur
HR: –
FYE: February 29
Type: Public

Holding company American Commerce Solutions (ACS) through its International Machine and Welding subsidiary provides specialized machining and repair services for heavy equipment used in the agricultural construction forestry mining and scrap industries. Its Chariot Manufacturing Company subsidiary (which includes Chariot Trailers) manufactures open and enclosed trailers to carry motorcycles. ACS also sells aftermarket repair parts. The company also has a strategic relationship with American Fiber Green Products. The Mosaic Company generates about 36% of sales.

	Annual Growth	02/12	02/13	02/14	02/15	02/16
Sales ($ mil.)	(4.3%)	2.4	2.4	2.7	2.2	2.1
Net income ($ mil.)	–	0.0	(0.0)	(0.2)	(0.1)	(0.2)
Market value ($ mil.)	22.5%	1.2	2.9	3.9	2.4	2.7
Employees	22.1%	18	19	21	20	40

AMERICAN COMMERCIAL LINES INC.

1701 E. Market St.
Jeffersonville IN 47130
Phone: 812-288-0100
Fax: 812-288-1766
Web: www.aclines.com

CEO: Mark K Knoy
CFO: Thomas R Pilholski
HR: –
FYE: December 31
Type: Private

One of the mightiest on the mighty Mississippi barge operator American Commercial Lines (ACL) navigates the inland waterways of the US. ACL moves dry bulk commodities including grain cement fertilizer salt coal steel and pig iron. It also transports bulk liquid cargo such as chemicals ethanol and petroleum products. ACL's fleet comprises more than 2000 dry cargo barges and some 330 tank barges powered by 125 towboats. In addition to transportation its Jeffboat subsidiary designs and manufactures inland and ocean service vessels for ACL and other customers and its Elliott Bay Design Group (EBDG) provides marine engineering. ACL was acquired by an affiliate of Platinum Equity in late 2010.

AMERICAN COMMUNITY MUTUAL INSURANCE COMPANY

39201 Seven Mile Rd.
Livonia MI 48152-1094
Phone: 734-591-9000
Fax: 734-591-4628
Web: www.american-community.com

CEO: –
CFO: –
HR: –
FYE: December 31
Type: Private - Mutual Com

American Community Mutual Insurance worked to maintain the health and wellbeing of America's communities but failed to keep itself robust. American Community provided group and individual health care plans and life insurance plans in over a dozen states throughout the Midwest and Southwest. The company's offerings included PPO short-term health dental vision and prescription plans. Focusing largely on the small to midsized employer group market the company insured more than 165000 individuals. The company distributes its products through a force of 14000 independent agents. American Community was founded in 1938. Due to financial troubles the company entered into rehabilitation in 2010.

AMERICAN CRYSTAL SUGAR COMPANY

101 3RD ST N
MOORHEAD, MN 565601990
Phone: 218-236-4400
Fax: –
Web: www.crystalsugar.com

CEO: David Berg
CFO: Thomas Astrup
HR: –
FYE: August 31
Type: Private

Sugarbeet cooperative American Crystal Sugar is owned by some 2800 growers in the Red River Valley of North Dakota and Minnesota who farm approximately 425000 acres of cropland. The company has sugar packaging facilities located at the Moorhead Hillsboro Crookston East Grand Forks and Sidney factories. The cooperative's products are sold in the US and other markets to industrial users and retail and wholesale customers under the Crystal name as well as under private labels through marketing co-ops United Sugars and Midwest Agri-Commodities. American Crystal Sugar owns some 50% of a corn wet-milling plant leased to agriculture giant Cargill. It was founded by Henry Oxnard in 1890.

	Annual Growth	08/15	08/16	08/17	08/18	08/19
Sales ($ mil.)	5.8%	–	1,290.8	1,420.0	1,515.1	1,528.2
Net income ($ mil.)	3.6%	–	561.7	511.9	650.9	624.4
Market value ($ mil.)	–	–	–	–	–	–
Employees	–	–	–	–	–	1,365

AMERICAN DEFENSE SYSTEMS INC.   NYSE AMEX: EAG

420 McKinney Pkwy.
Lillington NC 27546
Phone: 910-514-9701
Fax: 910-514-9702
Web: www.adsi-armor.com

CEO: Dale Scales
CFO: Gary Sidorsky
HR: –
FYE: December 31
Type: Public

American Defense Systems Inc. (ASDI) does a bang-up job of supporting our troops. The company makes custom bulletproof steel plates and glass panes that provide protection to US military vehicles in combat. It also manufactures bullet- and blast-resistant transparent armor walls and doors to protect buildings as well as barriers steel gates and bollards to keep vehicles from crashing into them. ASDI earns all of its revenues from the Departments of Defense and Homeland Security and branches of the US military. In addition the company runs the American Institute for Defense and Tactical Studies which offers tactical training courses. CEO Tony Piscitelli owns almost three-quarters of the company's stock.

AMERICAN DENTAL ASSOCIATION

211 E CHICAGO AVE
CHICAGO, IL 606112637
Phone: 312-440-2500
Fax: –
Web: www.ada.org

CEO: –
CFO: Paul Sholty
HR: –
FYE: December 31
Type: Private

Four out of five dentists recommend the ADA to their peers who join organizations. The American Dental Association is the world's oldest and largest dental association representing some 158000 dentists. The ADA provides information on oral health promotes dental science and conducts research development and testing on dental products and materials. If products are up to the organization's standards they are allowed to carry the ADA Seal of Acceptance. The group's Professional Product Review (PPR) evaluates and reports on products used by dental professionals. The ADA was founded in 1859 by 26 representatives from dental societies around the country.

	Annual Growth	12/07	12/08	12/14	12/16	12/19
Sales ($ mil.)	1.9%	–	110.0	132.9	123.5	134.8
Net income ($ mil.)	–	–	4.1	24.5	6.4	(0.5)
Market value ($ mil.)	–	–	–	–	–	–
Employees	–	–	–	–	–	475

AMERICAN DENTAL PARTNERS INC.   NASDAQ: ADPI

401 Edgewater Place Ste. 430
Wakefield MA 01880
Phone: 781-224-0880
Fax: 781-224-4216
Web: www.amdpi.com

CEO: Kevin Trexler
CFO: Breht T Feigh
HR: –
FYE: December 31
Type: Private

Helping dentists focus on drilling (and not billing) is the mission of American Dental Partners. The company provides management and support services for the growing group practice segment of the dental care industry. Through long-term service agreements the company manages about 25 general and specialty dental practice groups operating some 275 dental facilities in 22 states mainly in the eastern and midwestern US. Its services include planning and budgeting facilities development and management scheduling training recruiting economic analysis financial reporting and quality assurance. American Dental Partners was acquired by private equity firm JLL Partners in 2012.

AMERICAN DG ENERGY INC   ASE: ADGE

45 First Avenue
Waltham, MA 02451
Phone: 781 522 6000
Fax: –
Web: www.americandg.com

CEO: John N Hatsopoulos
CFO: Bonnie Brown
HR: –
FYE: December 31
Type: Public

Doggone tired of high utility bills? American DG Energy wants to put an end to that. The company provides DG or distributed generation energy by installing electricity generating equipment on-site to save on energy loss during transmission. The equipment which the company owns and maintains uses clean natural gas to generate power and for heating and cooling; it captures waste heat for water chilling and heating. While the technology is in wide use by consumers of more than 10 MW of power American DG Energy targets smaller users one MW and less. The Hatsopoulos family including chairman George Hatsopoulos and CEO John Hatsopoulos control about 25% of the company.

	Annual Growth	12/11	12/12	12/13	12/14	12/15
Sales ($ mil.)	9.2%	6.0	5.6	7.5	8.6	8.6
Net income ($ mil.)	–	(3.8)	(6.5)	(4.9)	(5.9)	(5.4)
Market value ($ mil.)	(30.8%)	73.5	117.1	86.2	30.4	16.9
Employees	(9.6%)	24	27	27	26	16

AMERICAN DIABETES ASSOCIATION

2451 CRYSTAL DR STE 900
ARLINGTON, VA 222024804
Phone: 703-549-1500
Fax: –
Web: www.diabetes.org

CEO: Kevin Hagan
CFO: Charlotte Carter
HR: –
FYE: December 31
Type: Private

The American Diabetes Association (ADA) lives for the day when it has no customers but for now seeks to serve the some 30 million children and adults in the US who have the disease. It is a nonprofit research information and advocacy organization that works to prevent and cure diabetes while also focusing on improving the lives of people affected by diabetes. The ADA has a number of fundraising programs Step Out: Walk to Fight Diabetes is the group's main fundraiser; others include the Tour de Cure (cycling); School Walk for Diabetes; and Kiss-A-Pig which honors the pig for its role in discovering the effectiveness of insulin in controlling diabetes.

	Annual Growth	12/11	12/12	12/13	12/14	12/15
Sales ($ mil.)	447.1%	–	–	–	33.3	182.3
Net income ($ mil.)	–	–	–	–	1.5	(1.0)
Market value ($ mil.)	–	–	–	–	–	–
Employees	–	–	–	–	–	838

AMERICAN EAGLE OUTFITTERS, INC.   NYS: AEO

77 Hot Metal Street
Pittsburgh, PA 15203-2329
Phone: 412 432-3300
Fax: –
Web: www.ae.com

CEO: Jay Schottenstein
CFO: Michael Mathias
HR: –
FYE: January 30
Type: Public

Once a purveyor of outdoor gear American Eagle Outfitters now feathers its nest with jeans and polos. The mall-based retailer is a powerhouse in denim and sells other casual apparel and accessories — aimed at men and women — under its American Eagle Outfitters and fast-growing Aerie brands; top product categories include intimates apparel active wear and swim collections. It also has two emerging brands: Tailgate (vintage sports-inspired apparel) and Todd Snyder New York (premium menswear). The company operates or licenses over 1300 stores worldwide of which about 1080 were company-owned; it generates the majority of its sales in the US. It was founded in 1977.

	Annual Growth	01/17*	02/18	02/19	02/20*	01/21
Sales ($ mil.)	1.0%	3,609.9	3,795.5	4,035.7	4,308.2	3,759.1
Net income ($ mil.)	–	212.4	204.2	261.9	191.3	(209.3)
Market value ($ mil.)	11.5%	2,440.1	2,920.8	3,481.4	2,395.2	3,774.1
Employees	(1.1%)	38,700	40,700	45,000	46,000	37,000

*Fiscal year change

AMERICAN ELECTRIC POWER CO INC NMS: AEP

1 Riverside Plaza
Columbus, OH 43215-2373
Phone: 614 716-1000
Fax: 614 223-1823
Web: www.aep.com

CEO: Nicholas Akins
CFO: Julie Sloat
HR: –
FYE: December 31
Type: Public

Serving markets in Ohio Michigan Indiana and other midwestern states American Electric Power (AEP) is one of the largest power generators and distributors in the US. The holding company owns the nation's largest electricity transmission system and distribution lines comprising a network of more than 227000 miles. AEP's electric utilities boasts 5.4 million customers in about 10 states and has about 21100 megawatts of largely coal-fired generating capacity although it is adding renewable sources to its generation portfolio. AEP is also a top wholesale energy company.

	Annual Growth	12/16	12/17	12/18	12/19	12/20
Sales ($ mil.)	(2.3%)	16,380.1	15,424.9	16,195.7	15,561.4	14,918.5
Net income ($ mil.)	37.8%	610.9	1,912.6	1,923.8	1,921.1	2,200.1
Market value ($ mil.)	7.2%	31,266.2	36,535.2	37,116.2	46,934.1	41,352.2
Employees	(1.2%)	17,634	17,666	17,582	17,408	16,787

AMERICAN EQUITY INVESTMENT LIFE HOLDING CO NYS: AEL

6000 Westown Parkway
West Des Moines, IA 50266
Phone: 515 221-0002
Fax: –
Web: www.american-equity.com

CEO: Anant Bhalla
CFO: Axel André
HR: –
FYE: December 31
Type: Public

American Equity Investment Life Holding (American Equity Life) helps middle-income investors plan for a cushier retirement. The company issues and administers fixed-rate and indexed annuities through subsidiaries American Equity Investment Life Insurance Eagle Life Insurance Company and American Equity Investment Life Insurance Company of New York. Licensed in all 50 states and the District of Columbia the company sells its products through various channels including nearly 25100 independent agents and some 40 national marketing associations.

	Annual Growth	12/16	12/17	12/18	12/19	12/20
Assets ($ mil.)	6.2%	56,053.5	62,030.7	61,625.6	69,696.6	71,389.7
Net income ($ mil.)	68.5%	83.2	174.6	458.0	246.1	671.5
Market value ($ mil.)	5.3%	2,157.5	2,941.5	2,674.4	2,864.9	2,647.6
Employees	5.5%	530	515	554	608	657

AMERICAN EUROCOPTER CORPORATION

2701 Forum Dr.
Grand Prairie TX 75052-7099
Phone: 972-641-0000
Fax: 972-641-3550
Web: www.eurocopterusa.com

CEO: Marc Paganini
CFO: Francois Bordes
HR: –
FYE: December 31
Type: Subsidiary

You've heard of An American In Paris? Well how about a Eurocopter in America? American Eurocopter is the US-based arm of European helicopter giant Eurocopter itself a subsidiary of aerospace conglomerate EADS. American Eurocopter's primary offerings include Eurocopter helicopter repair and overhaul services spares and parts support technical publications and maintenance training services. It also provides manufacturing completion and final assembly for A-Star AS350 helicopters and provides customization services for Eurocopter EC120 EC135 EC145 and EC155 helicopter models among others. American Eurocopter keeps more than 1800 helicopters flying across the US and caters to 600 customers.

AMERICAN EXPRESS CO. NYS: AXP

200 Vesey Street
New York, NY 10285
Phone: 212 640-2000
Fax: 212 640-0404
Web: www.americanexpress.com

CEO: Stephen Squeri
CFO: Jeffrey Campbell
HR: –
FYE: December 31
Type: Public

American Express is a globally integrated payments company that provides our customers with access to products insights and experiences that enrich lives and build business success. The company is also one of the world's largest providers of travel services. And yes the company still issues traveler's checks. Still the company's charge and credit cards are its bread and butter; American Express boasts about $870 billion in worldwide proprietary billed business and has about 70 million proprietary cards-in-force worldwide. Nearly 80% of company's total sales comes from US.

	Annual Growth	12/17	12/18	12/19	12/20	12/21
Assets ($ mil.)	1.0%	181,159.0	188,602.0	198,321.0	191,367.0	188,548.0
Net income ($ mil.)	31.0%	2,736.0	6,921.0	6,759.0	3,135.0	8,060.0
Market value ($ mil.)	13.3%	75,574.9	72,538.5	94,736.9	92,012.5	124,499.6
Employees	3.9%	55,000	59,000	64,500	63,700	64,000

AMERICAN EXPRESS PUBLISHING CORPORATION

1120 Avenue of the Americas
New York NY 10036
Phone: 212-382-5600
Fax: 212-768-1568
Web: www.amexpub.com

CEO: Edward F Kelly Jr
CFO: Paul Francis
HR: –
FYE: December 31
Type: Subsidiary

American Express Publishing targets readers who enjoy the high life in their travel and culinary adventures. A division of American Express the company publishes magazines such as "Food & Wine Travel + Leisure" "Departures" Black Ink and Executive Travel. It also publishes a number of books (100 Greatest Trips) produces events (Food & Wine Classic in Aspen) and has custom publishing operations (magazines newsletters and other publications for corporate clients). American Express Publishing uses the credit card publisher's database to cull customers. The business is managed by Time Inc.; Time and American Express share its profits. American Express has been in the magazine business since 1968.

AMERICAN FEDERATION OF LABOR & CONGRESS OF INDUSTRIAL ORGANZATION

815 16TH ST NW
WASHINGTON, DC 200064101
Phone: 202-637-5000
Fax: –

CEO: –
CFO: –
HR: –
FYE: June 30
Type: Private

Talk about spending a long time in labor: The AFL-CIO (American Federation of Labor and Congress of Industrial Organizations) has been focused on the task for more than a century. The AFL-CIO is an umbrella organization for more than 55 autonomous national and international unions. Altogether the AFL-CIO represents more than 12 million workers — from actors and airline pilots to marine engineers and machinists. It fights to improve wages and working conditions. The organization charters 50-plus state federations and about 500 central labor councils. Union members generally receive about 30% higher pay and more benefits than nonmembers. The AFL-CIO was created in 1955 by the merger of the AFL and the CIO.

	Annual Growth	06/13	06/14	06/15	06/16	06/19
Sales ($ mil.)	(4.5%)	–	159.0	152.1	154.8	126.3
Net income ($ mil.)	46.2%	–	1.5	(3.9)	5.8	9.9
Market value ($ mil.)	–	–	–	–	–	–
Employees	–	–	–	–	–	380

AMERICAN FEDERATION OF STATE COUNTY & MUNICIPAL EMPLOYEES

1625 L ST NW
WASHINGTON, DC 200365665
Phone: 202-429-1000
Fax: -
Web: www.afscme.org

CEO: -
CFO: -
HR: -
FYE: December 31
Type: Private

American Federation of State County and Municipal Employees AFL-CIO (AFSCME) finds strength in its numbers. The 1.6 million member labor union represents public sector employees in industries such as health care education social services transportation and public works. The group advocates and seeks legislative change for issues relating to social and economic justice in the workplace. AFSCME has more than 3400 local unions in some 45 states the District of Columbia and Puerto Rico. The union is a member of The American Federation of Labor-Congress of Industrial Organizations (AFL-CIO). AFSCME began in 1932 as the Wisconsin State Administrative Clerical Fiscal and Technical Employees Association.

	Annual Growth	12/10	12/11	12/12	12/15	12/17
Sales ($ mil.)	2.1%	-	-	160.2	168.3	177.7
Net income ($ mil.)	-	-	-	(15.8)	27.8	47.5
Market value ($ mil.)	-	-	-	-	-	-
Employees	-	-	-	-	-	450

AMERICAN FIBER GREEN PRODUCTS INC

NBB: AFBG

4209 Raleigh Street
Tampa, FL 33619
Phone: 813 247-2770
Fax: -
Web: www.americanfibergreenproducts.com

CEO: Daniel Hefner
CFO: Frank Puissegur
HR: -
FYE: December 31
Type: Public

The recycled fiberglass molding to be made by American Fiber Green Products will come in more colors than green. American Fiber Green Products announced plans in 2008 to build the first fiberglass recycling plant in the US. Its subsidiaries including American Leisure Products and Chariot Manufacturing will incorporate the recycled resin products into their manufacturing process to build such products as picnic tables park benches trailers boats and vehicle bodies for replicas of vintage cars. American Fiber Green Products is working on other uses to circumvent fiberglass away from landfills. Company president and CEO Dan Hefner also holds those positions for American Commerce Solutions.

	Annual Growth	12/11	12/12	12/13	12/14	12/15
Sales ($ mil.)	47.8%	0.1	0.3	0.3	0.4	0.5
Net income ($ mil.)	-	(0.1)	(0.2)	(0.1)	(0.3)	(0.2)
Market value ($ mil.)	(14.3%)	8.9	3.5	5.3	2.8	4.8
Employees	0.0%	3	3	3	3	3

AMERICAN FIDELITY ASSURANCE COMPANY

2000 N. Classen Blvd.
Oklahoma City OK 73106-6013
Phone: 405-523-2000
Fax: 405-523-5421
Web: www.afadvantage.com

CEO: -
CFO: -
HR: -
FYE: December 31
Type: Private

American Fidelity Assurance (AFA) puts its faith in the American people and insurance policies. It provides voluntary supplemental life and health insurance products and related services to more than 1 million customers primarily in the US and in about 23 other countries. The company's insurance plans include disability life cancer long term care and hospitalization insurance. The company also provides tax deferred annuity and flexible spending programs. It has tailored units to serve primary and secondary education employees and trade association members. Products and services are sold via worksite marketing by the company's sales force and a network of insurance brokers.

AMERICAN FINANCIAL GROUP INC

NYS: AFG

301 East Fourth Street
Cincinnati, OH 45202
Phone: 513 579-2121
Fax: -
Web: www.afginc.com

CEO: Carl Lindner
CFO: Brian Hertzman
HR: -
FYE: December 31
Type: Public

American Financial Group (AFG) insures American businessmen in pursuit of the Great American Dream. Through the operations of Great American Insurance Company AFG offers commercial property/casualty insurance and in the sale of traditional fixed and indexed annuities in the retail financial institutions broker-dealer and registered investment advisor markets. AFG's property and casualty insurance operations provide a wide range of commercial coverages through approximately 35 insurance businesses that make up the Great American Insurance Group. The company also provides surety and fidelity coverage and risk management services. It was founded in 1959 but its insurance roots started in 1872.

	Annual Growth	12/16	12/17	12/18	12/19	12/20
Assets ($ mil.)	7.5%	55,072.0	60,658.0	63,456.0	70,130.0	73,566.0
Net income ($ mil.)	3.1%	649.0	475.0	530.0	897.0	732.0
Market value ($ mil.)	(0.1%)	7,608.7	9,371.9	7,816.8	9,467.8	7,565.6
Employees	106.7%	400	600	7,600	7,700	7,300

AMERICAN FOODS GROUP LLC

500 So. Washington St.
Green Bay WI 54301-4219
Phone: 920-436-4229
Fax: 920-436-6466
Web: www.americanfoodsgroup.com

CEO: -
CFO: -
HR: -
FYE: December 31
Type: Subsidiary

American Foods Group is a bona fide Green Bay packer. With facilities in that Wisconsin city and cities in four other Midwestern states the company slaughters cattle to process four-plus million pounds of beef a day. Its lineup comprises an assortment of ground beef and specialty cuts such as bone-in tenderloin boneless beef roast and consumer-ready variety meats as well as specialty brands including Halal Meats and America's Heartland Organic Ground Beef. The group supplies beef to the US retail grocery and foodservice markets federal school lunch programs and American soldiers worldwide. It also exports to markets in some 38 countries. American Foods is owned by holding company Rosen's Diversified.

AMERICAN FRUIT & PRODUCE CORP.

12805 NW 42ND AVE
OPA LOCKA, FL 33054-4401
Phone: 305-681-1880
Fax: -

CEO: Hugo J Acosta
CFO: -
HR: -
FYE: December 31
Type: Private

American Fruit & Produce's (AFP) patriotic duty is to distribute fresh fruits and vegetables. The company supplies everything from apples to zucchini to US wholesale foodservice and retail customers. AFP also exports fresh fruits and vegetables from Florida ports to locations in the Americas and Europe. It is the largest US supplier of fresh produce to Caribbean countries. Hugo Acosta and his uncle Delio Medina opened their small produce outfit in Miami in 1983. The company has grown to include some 300000 sq. ft. of floor space situated on 32 acres in South Florida. American Fruit & Produce is still owned and operated by the its founders and their families.

	Annual Growth	12/06	12/07	12/08	12/09	12/11
Sales ($ mil.)	0.9%	-	-	-	83.2	84.8
Net income ($ mil.)	(9.5%)	-	-	-	1.9	1.6
Market value ($ mil.)	-	-	-	-	-	-
Employees	-	-	-	-	-	100

AMERICAN FURNITURE MANUFACTURING INC.

604 Pontotoc County Industrial Park Rd. — CEO: Randy Spak
Ecru MS 38841 — CFO: Todd Campbell
Phone: 662-489-2633 — HR: –
Fax: 662-488-9558 — FYE: December 31
Web: americanfurn.net — Type: Private

American Furniture Manufacturing (AFM) does most of its business at home. The company makes low-cost upholstered home furnishings including sofas chairs and recliners as well as accent tables. Its products are distributed to independent furniture stores in the US. AFM can ship most furniture within 48 hours and delivery is handled by its American Furniture Trucking division which maintains a fleet of trucks. The furniture maker sources wood and fabrics from the Asia/Pacific region which has also helped to keep costs down. AFM is owned by investment firm Compass Diversified Holdings.

AMERICAN FURNITURE WAREHOUSE CO INC

8820 AMERICAN WAY — CEO: Jacob Jabs
ENGLEWOOD, CO 801127056 — CFO: –
Phone: 303-799-9044 — HR: Cathy Steffes
Fax: – — FYE: March 31
Web: www.afw.com — Type: Private

Tony the Tiger hawking home furnishings might give some marketers pause but the combination seems to work for American Furniture Warehouse. American Furniture's television commercials often spotlight white-haired president and CEO Jake Jabs (who has become a well-known personality in the state as well as in the home furnishings industry) accompanied by baby exotic animals mostly tigers. The company sells furniture electronics and decor at discounted prices. It boasts about a dozen retail locations in Colorado and Arizona and sells through its website which also features bridal and gift registries. The company has built a reputation as a home-spun local furniture retailer. Jabs bought the company in 1975.

	Annual Growth	03/17	03/18	03/19	03/20	03/21
Sales ($ mil.)	7.9%	–	673.2	694.5	740.8	845.0
Net income ($ mil.)	21.3%	–	28.3	29.8	21.2	50.4
Market value ($ mil.)	–	–	–	–	–	–
Employees	–	–	–	–	–	3,500

AMERICAN GENERAL LIFE INSURANCE COMPANY

2727 Allen Pkwy. — CEO: Ronald H Ridlehuber
Houston TX 77019 — CFO: Robert Frank Herbert Jr
Phone: 713-522-1111 — HR: –
Fax: 713-620-6653 — FYE: December 31
Web: www.aigag.com — Type: Subsidiary

A-ten-schun! American General Life Insurance is still among the top brass of US life insurance and financial services firms. It anchors the domestic life insurance operations of American International Group under the AIG Life and Retirement umbrella. Serving some 13 million policyholders American General Life offers clients a variety of products to build their nest eggs including fixed and deferred annuities. Life insurance offerings include individual and group policies for families businesses and affiliation groups. Other products include accident and supplemental health insurance income protection and retirement planning programs.

AMERICAN GOLF CORPORATION

2951 28th St. — CEO: Jim Hinckley
Santa Monica CA 90405 — CFO: Mike Moecker
Phone: 310-664-4000 — HR: –
Fax: 310-664-4386 — FYE: December 31
Web: www.americangolf.com — Type: Private

You might say this company knows to stay out of the rough. American Golf Corporation (AGC) is one of the largest golf course management firms in the world with more than 110 public private and resort properties in more than 25 states. Its portfolio of courses includes such country clubs as The Golf Club at Mansion Ridge (Monroe New York) Oakhurst Country Club (Clayton California) and Palm Valley Country Club (Palm Desert California). The company also runs the American Golf Foundation which helps promote the game through charity and education. AGC is owned by investment firms Goldman Sachs and Starwood Capital.

AMERICAN HERITAGE LIFE INSURANCE COMPANY

1776 American Heritage Life Dr. — CEO: –
Jacksonville FL 32224 — CFO: –
Phone: 904-992-1776 — HR: –
Fax: 904-992-2658 — FYE: December 31
Web: https://www.ahlcorp.com — Type: Subsidiary

American Heritage Life Insurance Company doing business as Allstate Workplace Division offers voluntary supplemental insurance products — the ones you might pay a little extra for in addition to basic employee benefits. A wholly-owned subsidiary of Allstate American Heritage Life Insurance offers individual and group life and health insurance products including dental cancer stroke accident disability income and hospital indemnity. Its products are sold by more than 29000 exclusive and independent workplace enrollment agents to more than 20000 businesses. The company is licensed to operate in all US states as well as in Washington DC Guam Puerto Rico and the US Virgin Islands.

AMERICAN HOMEPATIENT INC.

5200 Maryland Way Ste. 400 — CEO: Kristen Hoefer
Brentwood TN 37027-5018 — CFO: Stephen Clanton
Phone: 615-221-8884 — HR: –
Fax: 615-373-9932 — FYE: December 31
Web: www.ahom.com — Type: Private

American HomePatient is making sure no one is home alone when it comes to health care. American HomePatient provides home health services from some 250 locations in the US. The company provides respiratory therapy and equipment including oxygen therapy sleep apnea systems and nebulizers. It also offers home infusion therapy services including feeding and intravenous drug administration. American HomePatient also rents and sells durable hospital equipment including beds and wheelchairs. Mostly it operates independently but also provides home care in a few areas through joint ventures with hospitals. Founded in 1983 American HomePatient is owned by funds of investment firm Highland Capital Management.

AMERICAN HOMESTAR CORPORATION

2450 S SHORE BLVD STE 300
LEAGUE CITY, TX 775732997
Phone: 281-334-9700
Fax: –
Web: www.americanhomestar.com

CEO: Finis F Teeter
CFO: Craig A Reynolds
HR: Katherine Santos
FYE: June 30
Type: Private

American Homestar shines brightly in the manufactured housing industry. The company produces factory-built modular multi-section and single-section manufactured homes and commercial structures under the Oak Creek and Platinum brand names. Its homes which typically range from about 1200 to 2600 sq. ft. have average prices comparable to site-built homes. Its multi-section homes have as many as six bedrooms. American Homestar sells its homes through company-owned home centers and franchised retail centers in the South and the Southeast. Other operations include insurance and mortgage financing services.

	Annual Growth	06/13	06/14*	07/15	07/16*	06/17
Sales ($ mil.)	8.7%	–	108.8	120.4	125.5	139.9
Net income ($ mil.)	102.6%	–	0.4	0.2	1.5	3.4
Market value ($ mil.)	–	–	–	–	–	–
Employees	–	–	–	–	–	568

*Fiscal year change

AMERICAN HONDA FINANCE CORPORATION

1919 TORRANCE BLVD
TORRANCE, CA 905012722
Phone: 310-972-2239
Fax: –
Web: www.hondafinancialservices.com

CEO: Hideo Tamaka
CFO: John Weisickle
HR: –
FYE: March 31
Type: Private

If you're fonda the idea of driving a Honda you might want to call on American Honda Finance. Operating as Honda Financial Services the company provides retail financing in the US for Honda and Acura automobiles motorcycles all-terrain vehicles power equipment and outboard motors. Its American Honda Service division administers service contracts while Honda Lease Trust offers leases on new and used vehicles. Honda Financial Services also offers dealer financing and related dealer services. Ancillary services include servicing loans and securitizing and selling loans into the secondary market. A subsidiary of American Honda Motor the company began as a wholesale motorcycle finance provider in 1980.

	Annual Growth	03/06	03/07	03/08	03/16	03/17
Assets ($ mil.)	5.4%	–	41,431.2	50,526.6	66,653.0	69,854.0
Net income ($ mil.)	6.7%	–	394.9	(45.2)	910.0	753.0
Market value ($ mil.)	–	–	–	–	–	–
Employees	–	–	–	–	–	1,000

AMERICAN HOSPITAL ASSOCIATION

155 N WACKER DR STE 400
CHICAGO, IL 606061719
Phone: 312-422-3000
Fax: –
Web: www.aha.org

CEO: Richard J Pollack
CFO: Christina Fisher
HR: Lisa Allen
FYE: December 31
Type: Private

The American Hospital Association (AHA) represents some 5000 hospitals and other health care providers and some 43000 individuals from various health care fields. The AHA acts as an advocate in national health care policy development and provides services to its members such as helping hospitals and other health care providers form networks for patient care conducting research and development projects on the structuring and delivery of health care services and producing educational programs and publications. The AHA Resource Center maintains an extensive collection of books and documents relating to hospitals and health care. The AHA was founded in 1898.

	Annual Growth	12/09	12/10	12/11	12/13	12/19
Sales ($ mil.)	3.2%	–	107.8	113.0	124.4	142.8
Net income ($ mil.)	0.1%	–	6.5	7.8	7.4	6.6
Market value ($ mil.)	–	–	–	–	–	–
Employees	–	–	–	–	–	508

AMERICAN HOTEL REGISTER COMPANY

100 S. Milwaukee Ave.
Vernon Hills IL 60061-4305
Phone: 847-564-4000
Fax: 847-743-2098
Web: www.americanhotel.com

CEO: Angela Korompila
CFO: –
HR: –
FYE: December 31
Type: Private

Delighted by the embossed soaps and sundries offered during your hotel visit? Thank American Hotel Register. The company distributes more than 50000 products in 20-plus categories including toiletries cleaning products appliances furniture carpeting drapery and linens to hotels of all sizes. It also caters to funeral homes health care facilities government offices and military institutions. American Hotel Register sells products through its 2150-page catalog and website. It operates distribution centers in the US Puerto Rico Canada and Mexico. Founded in 1865 to sell hotel guest registers the company was acquired by Thomas Leahy in the early 1900s. It is owned and operated by his descendants.

AMERICAN INDEPENDENCE CORP

NAS: AMIC

485 Madison Avenue
New York, NY 10022
Phone: 212 355-4141
Fax: –
Web: www.americanindependencecorp.com

CEO: Roy T K Thung
CFO: Teresa A Herbert
HR: –
FYE: December 31
Type: Public

Since the name American Independence tells you nothing about the company we'll help you out. What sounds like a lone bold ideal is really a holding company which through its subsidiaries provides reinsurance and insurance coverage specializing in medical stop-loss insurance for self-insured employers. It also offers group and individual health and short-term medical insurance policies. Subsidiary Independence American is licensed to provide property/casualty insurance throughout most of the US. American Independence is majority-owned by Independence Holding which also owns Madison National Life Insurance and Standard Security Life Insurance.

	Annual Growth	12/10	12/11	12/12	12/13	12/14
Sales ($ mil.)	16.5%	89.4	88.0	101.9	153.3	164.9
Net income ($ mil.)	25.8%	2.1	2.5	9.6	3.4	5.3
Market value ($ mil.)	20.6%	39.2	31.3	40.4	97.1	82.9
Employees	38.1%	52	50	74	123	189

AMERICAN INSTITUTE OF ARCHITECTS, INC

1735 NEW YORK AVE NW
WASHINGTON, DC 200065209
Phone: 202-626-7300
Fax: –
Web: www.aia.org

CEO: Robert Ivy Jr
CFO: Tracy Harris
HR: –
FYE: December 31
Type: Private

The American Institute of Architects (AIA) knows how to raise the roof. The group represents the interests of some 83000 professional architects through more than 300 chapters in every state in the US and in Asia Europe and South America. Members adhere to a code of ethics and the AIA disciplines members who break the rules with censure admonition suspension of membership or permanent termination of membership. The organization's member benefits include educational programs referrals discounted contract documents and job search assistance. It also lobbies government bodies on behalf of its members and provides media relations support.

	Annual Growth	12/07	12/08	12/10	12/13	12/15
Sales ($ mil.)	1.5%	–	59.5	57.3	60.5	66.1
Net income ($ mil.)	1.6%	–	2.3	2.6	0.9	2.6
Market value ($ mil.)	–	–	–	–	–	–
Employees	–	–	–	–	–	200

AMERICAN INSTITUTE OF CERTIFIED PUBLIC ACCOUNTANTS

220 LEIGH FARM RD
DURHAM, NC 277078110
Phone: 919-402-0682
Fax: –
Web: www.aicpa.org

CEO: Barry C Melancon
CFO: Scott H Spiegel
HR: –
FYE: December 31
Type: Private

When you add it all up the American Institute of Certified Public Accountants (AICPA) makes perfect sense. One of the nation's leading nonprofit professional associations the AICPA has more than 431000 members from some 130 countries who are involved in public accounting business education law and government. The group promotes awareness of the accounting profession; identifies financial trends; sets certification licensing and professional standards; and provides information and advice to CPAs. The AICPA distributes its information through websites conferences and forums and publications. The group was founded in 1887.

	Annual Growth	07/08	07/09	07/13	07/15*	12/17
Sales ($ mil.)	3.7%	–	199.8	219.9	247.5	266.8
Net income ($ mil.)	–	–	(13.6)	15.2	(7.2)	13.5
Market value ($ mil.)	–	–	–	–	–	–
Employees	–	–	–	–	–	800

*Fiscal year change

AMERICAN INSTITUTE OF PHYSICS INCORPORATED

1 PHYSICS ELLIPSE
COLLEGE PARK, MD 20740-3841
Phone: 301-209-3100
Fax: –
Web: www.aip.org

CEO: Michael Moloney
CFO: Catherine Swartz
HR: –
FYE: December 31
Type: Private

Who says scientists don't know how to get physical? The American Institute of Physics (AIP) publishes magazines (Physics Today) journals (Journal of Applied Physics) conference proceedings online products and other publications in the sciences of physics and astronomy. The company provides publishing services for its own publications as well as for its member societies and other publishers. Scitation AIP's online publishing platform hosts 1.6 million articles from 190 sources. AIP was founded in New York in 1931 by a group of American physical science societies. It was chartered as a membership corporation to advance and diffuse knowledge of the science of physics and its applications to human welfare.

	Annual Growth	12/08	12/09	12/10	12/11	12/12
Sales ($ mil.)	(2.3%)	–	77.4	76.0	73.1	72.3
Net income ($ mil.)	(4.5%)	–	23.0	8.6	(8.3)	20.0
Market value ($ mil.)	–	–	–	–	–	–
Employees	–	–	–	–	–	273

AMERICAN INSTITUTES FOR RESEARCH IN THE BEHAVIORAL SCIENCES

1400 CRYSTAL DR FL 10
ARLINGTON, VA 222023289
Phone: 202-403-5000
Fax: –
Web: www.air.org

CEO: David Myers
CFO: Marijo Ahlgrimm
HR: –
FYE: December 31
Type: Private

The American Institutes for Research (AIR) lives and breathes to enhance human performance. The not-for-profit organization conducts behavioral and social science research on topics related to education and educational assessment health international development and work and training. Clients including several federal agencies use AIR's research in developing policies. As a major ongoing initiative the organization provides tools to improve education both in the US and internationally particularly in disadvantaged areas. John C. Flanagan who developed the Critical Incident Technique personnel-selection tool to identify human success indicators in the workplace founded the organization in 1946.

	Annual Growth	12/14	12/15	12/16	12/17	12/19
Sales ($ mil.)	14.2%	–	488.3	474.1	497.6	829.6
Net income ($ mil.)	72.5%	–	45.1	43.6	55.1	398.6
Market value ($ mil.)	–	–	–	–	–	–
Employees	–	–	–	–	–	1,500

AMERICAN INTERNATIONAL INDUSTRIES INC

NBB: AMIN

601 Cien Street, Suite 235
Kemah, TX 77565-3077
Phone: 281 334-9479
Fax: 281 334-9508
Web: www.americanii.com

CEO: Daniel Dror
CFO: Charles Zeller
HR: –
FYE: December 31
Type: Public

Nothing says Texas like oil and real estate. American International Industries (AII) covers those bases — and more — from its home in the Houston metro area. The company typically takes a controlling interest in undervalued companies; it holds investments in oil wells real estate and various industrial manufacturers. AII owns Delta Seaboard International (formerly Hammonds Industries) which operates technical services fuel additives and water treatment systems divisions. Its Northeastern Plastics subsidiary makes automotive after-market products. International Diversified Corporation (a firm connected with the brother of chairman and CEO Daniel Dror) owns 27% of the firm.

	Annual Growth	12/10	12/11	12/12	12/13	12/14
Sales ($ mil.)	(80.8%)	24.3	21.7	8.0	7.2	0.0
Net income ($ mil.)	–	0.1	(3.3)	(2.1)	(1.8)	(2.4)
Market value ($ mil.)	6.1%	1.5	0.6	5.8	4.2	1.9
Employees	(22.9%)	51	60	18	18	18

AMERICAN ITALIAN PASTA COMPANY

4100 N. Mulberry Dr. Ste. 200
Kansas City MO 64116
Phone: 816-584-5000
Fax: 816-584-5100
Web: www.aipc.com

CEO: –
CFO: –
HR: –
FYE: September 30
Type: Subsidiary

American Italian Pasta Company (AIPC) uses its noodle in many ways. The company is one of the biggest makers of dry pasta in North America by volume offering some 300 different pasta shapes and 3100 stock-keeping units or SKUs from angel hair to ziti. Its name brands such as Golden Grain Heartland and Mueller's are staples on retail shelves in the US and overseas. The company's regional private-label customers include most major US grocers and club stores. It also serves the institutional market comprising foodservice operators that supply restaurants and schools and food manufacturers that use pasta as an ingredient. AIPC is owned by private-label giant Ralcorp which acquired the company in 2010.

AMERICAN JEWISH WORLD SERVICE, INC.

45 W 36TH ST FL 10
NEW YORK, NY 100187641
Phone: 212-792-2900
Fax: –
Web: www.ajws.org

CEO: –
CFO: –
HR: –
FYE: April 30
Type: Private

The American Jewish World Service (AJWS) helps poor people around the globe in areas such as health nutrition education housing and women's issues. It offers grants technical assistance advocacy and emergency relief through hundreds of organizations in more than 35 developing nations worldwide. Projects include antisexual exploitation clinics building orphanages helping street children entrepreneur programs for women HIV/AIDS education and intervention and sustainable agriculture programs. AJWS was founded in 1985 to help American Jews do tzedakah or good deeds which is part of a Jewish obligation to help the world.

	Annual Growth	04/13	04/14	04/15	04/16	04/17
Sales ($ mil.)	7.0%	–	–	58.2	69.0	66.6
Net income ($ mil.)	–	–	–	(3.3)	3.5	(0.4)
Market value ($ mil.)	–	–	–	–	–	–
Employees	–	–	–	–	–	112

AMERICAN LAFRANCE LLC

1090 Newton Way
Summerville SC 29483
Phone: 843-486-7400
Fax: 843-486-7417
Web: www.americanlafrance.com

CEO: -
CFO: -
HR: -
FYE: December 31
Type: Subsidiary

The flashing lights in your rear-view mirror just might be an American LaFrance product. The company manufactures emergency vehicle equipment for fire medical and rescue services. Signals of public safety its custom and commercial red offerings include fire trucks tankers ambulances tractor drawn aerial ladders fire pumps and fire rescue boats. A former subsidiary of DaimlerChrysler's Freightliner American LaFrance has roots that date back to 1832 and has operated under the management of private equity group Patriarch Partners since 2005.

AMERICAN LAND LEASE INC.

380 Park Place Blvd. Ste. 200
Clearwater FL 33759
Phone: 727-726-8868
Fax: 727-725-4391
Web: www.americanlandlease.com

CEO: Terry Considine
CFO: Shannon E Smith
HR: -
FYE: December 31
Type: Private

American Land Lease wants to make the American Dream an American Reality especially during the golden years. The self-managed real estate investment trust (REIT) owns develops renovates and manages manufactured housing communities for active adults. It owns about 35 communities in Arizona and Florida; properties include some 9000 leased developed and undeveloped homesites and RV parks. In light of growing senior demographics American Land Lease operates its properties primarily as retirement communities. The REIT's communities often feature swimming pools golf courses and clubhouses. American Land Lease was acquired by Chicago private equity firm Green Courte Partners in 2009.

AMERICAN LEATHER

4501 Mountain Creek Pkwy.
Dallas TX 75236
Phone: 972-296-9599
Fax: 972-296-8859
Web: www.americanleather.com

CEO: Robert Duncan
CFO: -
HR: -
FYE: December 31
Type: Private

It may not be as American as apple pie but American Leather hopes to make itself into a household name. The company a manufacturer of custom-made leather and upholstered furniture offers furnishing pieces such as sofas sleepers beds recliners chairs and ottomans in more than a dozen styles (including traditional transitional and contemporary) and nearly 300 colors and textures. American Leather sells its products through independent retailers located throughout the US and has showrooms in Dallas San Francisco and High Point North Carolina. It also makes exclusive styles for Crate & Barrel Design Within Reach and Room & Board. CEO Bob Duncan has a controlling interest in the company.

AMERICAN LICORICE COMPANY

2796 NW Clearwater Dr.
Bend OR 97701
Phone: 541-617-0800
Fax: 541-617-0224
Web: www.americanlicorice.com

CEO: John R Kretchmer
CFO: -
HR: Karen Kopka
FYE: October 31
Type: Private

American Licorice makes candy concoctions using one of America's favorite flavorings — licorice. The company manufactures licorice twists pieces and ropes in various flavors (including original red original black strawberry and cherry). It also makes sour hard candies and drinking straws packed with sour candy. American's brand names include Red Vines Natural Vines (sweetened with brown rice syrup instead of high-fructose corn syrup) Snaps Super Ropes Sour Punch Sip-n-Chew and Extinguisher. The company's products can be purchased at retail food outlets grocery chains club dollar and drug stores and specialty venues throughout the US as well as online through its CandyCabinet.com division.

AMERICAN LIFE INSURANCE COMPANY

1 ALICO Plaza 600 King St.
Wilmington DE 19899
Phone: 302-594-2000
Fax: 408-428-3732
Web: www.ss8.com

CEO: Marlene Debel
CFO: -
HR: -
FYE: December 31
Type: Subsidiary

Belying its moniker American Life Insurance Company (ALICO) provides life and health insurance only "outside" the US. (Fairness dictates noting that ALICO was named Asia Life Insurance Company for its first three decades dating from its 1921 founding in Shanghai.) The company operates in more than 50 countries worldwide; Japan is ALICO's largest single market. ALICO sells such individual and group products as life insurance and annuities accident and health coverage and pensions. The company markets its products through a network of some 40000 agents and brokers and banks. US insurance giant American International Group (AIG) sold ALICO to MetLife in 2010.

AMERICAN LOCKER GROUP, INC.

2701 Regent Blvd., Suite 200
DFW Airport, TX 75261
Phone: 817 329-1600
Fax: -
Web: www.americanlocker.com

NBB: ALGI
CEO: -
CFO: -
HR: -
FYE: December 31
Type: Public

Ever carried around one of those orange plastic-capped locker keys at the theme park? That's American Locker Group. The company sells and rents coin- key- and electronically controlled lockers used by health clubs amusement parks ski resorts bus stations and employee locker rooms. Customers include SeaWorld Vail Resorts Walt Disney World The UPS Store and the University of Colorado. Postal mailboxes such as those used by apartment complexes make up about a third of sales. Besides the US American Locker Group serves customers in Canada Chile Greece India Mexico and the UK (less than 20% of sales in 2009). The company was founded in 1958.

	Annual Growth	12/09	12/10	12/11	12/12	12/13
Sales ($ mil.)	4.0%	12.5	12.1	13.4	13.7	14.6
Net income ($ mil.)	-	(0.4)	0.1	0.0	(0.6)	(2.8)
Market value ($ mil.)	5.1%	2.7	1.9	2.5	2.9	3.3
Employees	(3.3%)	137	103	110	108	120

AMERICAN MANAGEMENT ASSOCIATION INTERNATIONAL

1601 BROADWAY FL 7
NEW YORK, NY 100197420
Phone: 212-586-8100
Fax: –
Web: www.amacombooks.org

CEO: Manos Avramidis
CFO: Vivianna Guzman
HR: Barbara Zung
FYE: March 31
Type: Private

American Management Association (AMA) is a not-for-profit membership association that provides a variety of educational and management development services to businesses government agencies and individuals. The associations is engaged in professional development advancing the skills of individuals. AMA offers more than 140 training seminars in more than 25 subject areas of business management and workforce development. It also sponsors conferences and workshops and provides webcasts podcasts and books in such areas as communication leadership project management sales and marketing human resources and finance and accounting.

	Annual Growth	03/09	03/10	03/11	03/13	03/14
Sales ($ mil.)	0.2%	–	83.9	87.9	90.8	84.5
Net income ($ mil.)	–	–	(2.9)	(3.7)	1.2	(2.1)
Market value ($ mil.)	–	–	–	–	–	–
Employees	–	–	–	–	–	500

AMERICAN MANAGEMENT SERVICES WEST LLC

Pier 70 2801 Alaskan Way Ste. 200
Seattle WA 98121
Phone: 206-215-9700
Fax: 206-215-9777
Web: www.pinnaclerealty.com

CEO: –
CFO: –
HR: –
FYE: December 31
Type: Private

American Management Services (which operates as Pinnacle) makes sure investment properties are in top form. Pinnacle provides property management and brokerage services for real estate investors such as financial institutions foreign investors government housing agencies pension funds and private partnerships. Its portfolio of properties — worth around $20 billion — spans 250 cities across the US as well as Asia and Canada. Its assets under management include about 175000 apartment units as well as military housing and industrial retail and office space. Pinnacle also offers such services as customized financial reporting risk management recruitment and technology planning.

AMERICAN MEDICAL ALERT CORP.   NASDAQ: AMAC

3265 Lawson Blvd.
Oceanside NY 11572
Phone: 516-536-5850
Fax: 516-536-5276
Web: www.amacalert.com

CEO: Oscar Meyer
CFO: –
HR: –
FYE: December 31
Type: Subsidiary

It's like having a guardian angel hovering above but without the wings. American Medical Alert Corp (AMAC) provides health care communication and monitoring services. The company's Health Safety and Monitoring Services (HSMS) unit markets remote patient monitoring systems including personal emergency response systems health management and medication management systems and safety monitoring systems. Its Telephony Based Communication Services (TBCS) unit provides telephone answering services and operates clinical trial recruitment call centers. In late 2011 UK health care services company Tunstall Healthcare Group acquired AMAC for an estimated $82 million.

AMERICAN MEDICAL ASSOCIATION INC

330 N WABASH AVE # 39300
CHICAGO, IL 606115885
Phone: 312-464-5000
Fax: –

CEO: James Madera
CFO:
HR:
FYE: December 31
Type: Private

The AMA knows whether there's a doctor in the house. The American Medical Association (AMA) prescribes the standards for the medical profession. The membership group's activities include advocacy for physicians promoting ethics standards in the medical community and improving health care education. Policies are set by the AMA's House of Delegates comprised of elected representatives. The AMA is also a publisher of books for physicians and provides an online physician network through a partnership with Medfusion sells medical malpractice insurance and helps doctors fight legal claims. Founded in 1847 by a physician to establish a code of medical ethics AMA has nearly 225000 members.

	Annual Growth	12/07	12/08	12/13	12/14	12/15
Sales ($ mil.)	90.1%	–	3.2	258.5	261.4	284.3
Net income ($ mil.)	–	–	(0.3)	(7.0)	29.1	30.0
Market value ($ mil.)	–	–	–	–	–	–
Employees	–	–	–	–	–	1,150

AMERICAN MEDICAL RESPONSE AMBULANCE SERVICE INC.

6200 S. Syracuse Way #200
Greenwood Village CO 80111
Phone: 303-495-1200
Fax: 303-495-1295
Web: www.amr.net

CEO: Edward Van Horne
CFO: Timothy Dorn
HR: –
FYE: December 31
Type: Subsidiary

Because driving yourself to the emergency room isn't always the best plan there is American Medical Response (AMR). With thousands of vehicles in some 40 states AMR is the largest contract provider of emergency and non-emergency ambulance services in the US. Non-emergency services include transportation for medically unstable patients and such non-medical transport services as transfers to and from health care facilities. The company provides around 3 million transports annually for customers that also include hospitals and local government agencies. AMR is a subsidiary of Emergency Medical Services Corporation (EMSC).

AMERICAN MEDICAL SYSTEMS HOLDINGS INC.

10700 Bren Rd. West
Minnetonka MN 55343
Phone: 952-930-6000
Fax: 952-930-6373
Web: www.americanmedicalsystems.com

CEO: –
CFO: Mark A Heggestad
HR: –
FYE: December 31
Type: Subsidiary

Purchasing American Medical Systems' products could make a few of us blush but they are important nonetheless. AMS is a leading maker of urological devices including products to help with erectile dysfunction such as inflatable penile implants as well as urinary incontinence devices for men and women. Its other products treat such conditions as menorrhagia (excessive uterine bleeding) enlarged prostate and fecal incontinence. AMS has around 80 independent distributors in addition to a global sale and marketing force of about 500 employees. Marketing efforts target urologists gynecologists and colorectal surgeons. The company was acquired by Endo Pharmaceuticals in 2011 for $2.9 billion.

AMERICAN MIDSTREAM PARTNERS LP
NYS: AMID

2103 CityWest Boulevard, Building #4, Suite 800
Houston, TX 77042
Phone: 346 241-3400
Fax: -
Web: www.americanmidstream.com
CEO: Matthew W Rowland
CFO: -
HR: -
FYE: December 31
Type: Public

If natural gas exploration and production companies are hunters then American Midstream Partners is a gatherer. Serving oil and gas companies American Midstream gathers treats processes and transports natural gas through a network of 1400 miles of pipeline stretching across Alabama Louisiana Mississippi Tennessee and Texas. Its owned and operated assets include eight interstate or intrastate pipelines nine gathering systems and three processing facilities. The company has counted Exxon ConocoPhillips and Dow Hydrocarbons as customers. Formed in 2009 American Midstream went public in 2011 through a $73 million IPO. In 2016 it agreed to merge with JP Energy Partners LP.

	Annual Growth	12/13	12/14	12/15	12/16	12/17
Sales ($ mil.)	22.1%	292.7	308.4	236.4	232.7	651.4
Net income ($ mil.)	-	(34.0)	(98.0)	(127.5)	(3.5)	(223.0)
Market value ($ mil.)	(16.2%)	1,453.5	1,058.0	434.2	976.9	716.6
Employees	-	-	-	-	-	-

AMERICAN MUNICIPAL POWER, INC.

1111 SCHROCK RD STE 100
COLUMBUS, OH 432291155
Phone: 614-540-1111
Fax: -
Web: www.amppartners.org
CEO: -
CFO: Robert W Trippe
HR: -
FYE: December 31
Type: Private

Power to the Public is the motto of American Municipal Power (AMP). The nonprofit membership organization supplies wholesale power to more than 80 community-owned distribution utilities in Ohio 30 in Pennsylvania 6 in Michigan 5 in Virginia 3 in Kentucky 2 in West Virginia 1 in Indiana and 1 in Delaware (a joint action agency). AMP and its members own and operate plants that generate more than 1500 MW of power. The company also handles projects on behalf of the Ohio Municipal Electric Generating Agency (OMEGA) Joint Ventures program (jointly owned generation and transmission projects). The power generation company is owned by its member municipalities. AMP member utilities serve some 635000 customers.

	Annual Growth	12/13	12/14	12/15	12/19	12/20
Sales ($ mil.)	0.8%	-	1,039.9	1,128.0	1,170.0	1,091.4
Net income ($ mil.)	(0.5%)	-	2.6	5.8	5.3	2.5
Market value ($ mil.)	-	-	-	-	-	-
Employees	-	-	-	-	-	229

AMERICAN NATIONAL BANKSHARES, INC. (DANVILLE, VA)
NMS: AMNB

628 Main Street
Danville, VA 24541
Phone: 434 792-5111
Fax: -
Web: www.amnb.com
CEO: Jeffrey Haley
CFO: Jeffrey Farrar
HR: -
FYE: December 31
Type: Public

American National Bankshares with total assets of around $2.5 billion is the holding company for American National Bank and Trust. Founded in 1909 the bank operates some 30 branches that serve southern and central Virginia and north central North Carolina. Operating through two segments — Community Banking and Trust and Investment Services — it offers checking and savings accounts CDs IRAs and insurance. Lending activities primarily consist of real estate loans: Commercial mortgages account for about 40% of its loan portfolio while residential mortgages bring in another 20%. American National Bankshares' trust and investment services division manages nearly $610 million in assets.

	Annual Growth	12/16	12/17	12/18	12/19	12/20
Assets ($ mil.)	16.1%	1,678.6	1,816.1	1,862.9	2,478.6	3,050.0
Net income ($ mil.)	16.5%	16.3	15.2	22.6	20.9	30.0
Market value ($ mil.)	(6.8%)	382.2	420.6	321.9	434.6	287.8
Employees	1.7%	320	328	305	355	342

AMERICAN NATIONAL GROUP INC
NMS: ANAT

One Moody Plaza
Galveston, TX 77550-7999
Phone: 409 763-4661
Fax: -
Web: www.americannational.com
CEO: James E Pozzi
CFO: Timothy A Walsh
HR: -
FYE: December 31
Type: Public

American National Group (formerly American National Insurance Company) offers agricultural commercial and personal property/casualty insurance as well as life insurance annuities limited health corporate and other and other types of insurance throughout the US Puerto Rico and other territories. Its subsidiaries include Garden State Life Insurance Standard Life and Accident Insurance and Farm Family Casualty Insurance Company and United Farm Family Insurance. Also known as American National the company markets its products through independent insurance agents broker-dealers employee benefit firms financial institutions and large marketing organizations. In 2021 Brookfield Reinsurance will acquire American National in an all-cash transaction valued at approximately $5.1 billion.

	Annual Growth	12/16	12/17	12/18	12/19	12/20
Assets ($ mil.)	4.7%	24,533.2	26,386.8	26,912.4	28,597.6	29,467.8
Net income ($ mil.)	26.8%	181.0	493.7	159.0	620.4	467.5
Market value ($ mil.)	(6.3%)	3,350.4	3,448.3	3,421.1	3,164.1	2,584.4
Employees	0.0%	4,597	4,621	4,640	-	4,600

AMERICAN NATURAL ENERGY CORP.
TVX: ANR U

One Warren Place, 6100 South Yale, Suite2010
Tulsa, OK 74136
Phone: 918 481-1440
Fax: 918 481-1473
Web: www.annrg.com
CEO: Michael K Paulk
CFO: Steven P Ensz
HR: -
FYE: December 31
Type: Public

American Natural Energy Corp. is not selling organic food and dietary supplements to boost metabolism it is tapping into that other American natural energy source — hydrocarbons. Doing business as ANEC the company is an oil and natural gas exploration and production company which focuses its operations on a property in St. Charles Parish Louisiana. ANEC works in tandem with partner Exxon Mobil to develop this Louisiana project. In 2007 the company sold 75% of ANEC's development rights in this project to Dune Energy.

	Annual Growth	12/09	12/10	12/11	12/12	12/13
Sales ($ mil.)	32.3%	1.1	2.6	2.0	2.1	3.3
Net income ($ mil.)	-	24.0	(2.1)	(0.9)	(3.3)	(3.1)
Market value ($ mil.)	(26.9%)	0.7	6.3	2.2	2.0	0.2
Employees	0.0%	6	7	7	7	6

AMERICAN NUTRITION INC.

2813 Wall Ave.
Odgen UT 84401
Phone: 801-394-3477
Fax: 801-394-3674
Web: www.anibrands.com
CEO: -
CFO: -
HR: -
FYE: June 30
Type: Private

American Nutrition (ANI) is looking out for your canine and feline friends — er family members. The company makes more than 300000 tons of dry and wet food and snacks for dogs and cats annually. Its products are sold under such brand names as Atta Boy Atta Cat Basic Plus Natural Harmony and Vita Bone. ANI also produces premium biodegradable cat litter. In addition to making its own products for dogs and cats the company provides contract pet food manufacturing services. It operates production facilities in Arizona Utah and Washington. ANI was founded in 1972 by the late Jack Behnken.

AMERICAN OIL & GAS INC.

1050 17th St. Ste. 2400
Denver CO 80265
Phone: 303-991-0173
Fax: 303-595-0709
Web: www.americanoilandgasinc.com

CEO: –
CFO: –
HR: –
FYE: December 31
Type: Subsidiary

Deep in the heart of the North American continent lie untapped natural gas deposits and American Oil & Gas is searching for them. The exploration and production company is focusing its efforts on the Rocky Mountains a region with one of the largest underdeveloped natural gas fields in the US (the Bakken Shale formation). American Oil & Gas in 2009 reported that it had estimated proved reserves of about 64420 barrels of oil and 645.3 million cu. ft. of natural gas. The company is developing its position in the Bakken and Three Forks plays in the Williston Basin in North Dakota. In 2010 American Oil & Gas was acquired by Hess in a $450-million stock deal that grew Hess' Bakken holdings.

AMERICAN PACIFIC CORP.

NMS: APFC

3883 Howard Hughes Parkway, Suite 700
Las Vegas, NV 89169
Phone: 702 735-2200
Fax: –
Web: www.apfc.com

CEO: Hal Murdock
CFO: –
HR: –
FYE: September 30
Type: Public

American Pacific (AMPAC) manufactures and markets a potent mix of Specialty Chemicals and Fine Chemicals mainly for pharmaceutical uses. Its largest unit makes and supplies active pharmaceutical ingredients and advanced intermediates to the pharmaceutical industry. AMPAC's specialty chemicals also include sodium azide an airbag deployment chemical also used in pharmaceuticals; and Halotron an ozone-friendly fire suppressant. The company also makes and environmental protection products including electro-chemical equipment for the water treatment.

	Annual Growth	09/09	09/10	09/11	09/12	09/13
Sales ($ mil.)	2.2%	197.1	176.2	209.7	185.6	215.1
Net income ($ mil.)	–	(6.0)	(3.3)	(7.2)	25.3	23.2
Market value ($ mil.)	63.6%	60.8	35.1	58.3	95.0	435.3
Employees	(2.6%)	589	595	653	494	530

AMERICAN PETROLEUM INSTITUTE INC

200 MSSCHSTTS AVE NW STE
WASHINGTON, DC 20001
Phone: 202-682-8000
Fax: –
Web: www.api.org

CEO: Jack N Gerard
CFO: –
HR: –
FYE: December 31
Type: Private

The American Petroleum Institute (API) is a trade association for the oil and natural gas industry. The group represents more than 625 corporate members including such industry giants as BP and Exxon Mobil as well as small independent companies with offices in more than 20 state capitals and overseas. Besides serving as an advocate in legislative regulatory and media arenas the API compiles data on industry operations. The organization's members come from several segments of the petroleum industry including upstream (exploration and production) downstream (refining and marketing) pipeline operations marine transportation and oil field service. The API was founded in 1919.

	Annual Growth	12/06	12/07	12/08	12/09	12/13
Sales ($ mil.)	1.9%	–	–	204.2	197.4	224.4
Net income ($ mil.)	–	–	–	(10.4)	19.0	1.0
Market value ($ mil.)	–	–	–	–	–	–
Employees	–	–	–	–	–	250

AMERICAN PLASTIC TOYS INC.

799 LADD RD
WALLED LAKE, MI 483903025
Phone: 248-624-4881
Fax: –
Web: www.americanplastictoys.com

CEO: –
CFO: –
HR: –
FYE: December 31
Type: Private

If your child spends hours applying pretend makeup at her Enchanted Beauty Salon or hammering away at his Build & Play Tool Bench or digging in the sand with her Castle Pail of Toys you can thank American Plastic Toys for the much-needed break. The company manufactures plastic toys including doll accessories (strollers nurseries) children's furniture role-playing items (kitchen sets tool benches) riding toys (trikes wagons) seasonal toys (pail and shovel sets) and vehicles (dump trucks airplanes). Products are sold by such retailers as Wal-Mart Kmart and Toys "R" Us across the US as well as in Canada the Caribbean Central and South America and Mexico. The company was founded in 1962.

	Annual Growth	12/09	12/10	12/11	12/12	12/13
Sales ($ mil.)	(1.7%)	–	51.1	45.4	51.0	48.5
Net income ($ mil.)	–	–	–	(1.5)	5.2	3.0
Market value ($ mil.)	–	–	–	–	–	–
Employees	–	–	–	–	–	300

AMERICAN POP CORN COMPANY

1 Fun Place
Sioux City IA 51108
Phone: 712-239-1232
Fax: 712-239-1268
Web: www.jollytime.com

CEO: –
CFO: –
HR: Rosa Bailey
FYE: December 31
Type: Private

Settle down with a bowl of Jolly Time a bottle of pop and prepare yourself for a jolly popping-good time. Founded in 1914 when Cloid Smith and his son Howard set up shop in their basement the American Pop Corn Company still makes the traditional American treat in bagged unpopped kernel form for the purists among us. For those with less time than purists it makes microwave popcorn in lots of varieties and flavors. American's brands include AMERICAN'S BEST (kernals) and Jolly Time (microwave and kernals). The family-owned company is run by Carlton (chairman) and Garrett (president) Smith the great-grandsons of Cloid. Jolly Time popcorn is distributed throughout the US and overseas.

AMERICAN POWER GROUP CORP

NBB: APGI

2503 East Poplar St
Algona, IA 50511
Phone: 781 224-2411
Fax: –
Web: www.americanpowergroupinc.com

CEO: Charles Coppa
CFO: Charles E Coppa
HR: –
FYE: September 30
Type: Public

Wish your engine ran on natural gas instead of diesel? American Power Group Corporation (formerly GreenMan Technologies) makes and sells dual-fuel energy technology that allows for the easy conversion of diesel engines to liquid and compressed natural gas as well as well-head gas or biomethane. This technology is specifically designed for aftermarket vehicular and diesel engines and diesel generators. The former GreenMan Technologies changed its name to American Power Group Corporation in mid-2012 after acquiring American Power Group in mid-2009.

	Annual Growth	09/12	09/13	09/14	09/15	09/16
Sales ($ mil.)	(8.3%)	2.6	7.0	6.3	3.0	1.9
Net income ($ mil.)	–	(4.6)	(2.0)	(2.3)	0.5	(7.6)
Market value ($ mil.)	(28.1%)	48.0	51.0	45.0	21.8	12.8
Employees	9.3%	14	20	21	19	20

AMERICAN PSYCHOLOGICAL ASSOCIATION, INC.

750 1ST ST NE STE 605
WASHINGTON, DC 200028009
Phone: 202-336-5500
Fax: –
Web: www.apa.org

CEO: Norman B Anderson
CFO: Archie L Turner
HR: –
FYE: December 31
Type: Private

The American Psychological Association (APA) works to advance mental health: yours and that of its members. The APA is the largest scientific and professional organization representing psychology in the US as well as the world's largest association of psychologists. The association seeks to advance the study and practice of psychology in the US. It is also vocal about the role of psychological services in health care reform. It offers members career resources insurance and financial and other services. The APA has more than 134000 members including researchers educators clinicians consultants and students as well some 55 professional divisions.

	Annual Growth	12/12	12/13	12/14	12/15	12/17
Sales ($ mil.)	0.1%	–	127.5	130.4	117.8	128.0
Net income ($ mil.)	(46.2%)	–	8.4	2.9	(12.2)	0.7
Market value ($ mil.)	–	–	–	–	–	–
Employees						550

AMERICAN PUBLIC EDUCATION INC

NMS: APEI

111 West Congress Street
Charles Town, WV 25414
Phone: 304 724-3700
Fax: –
Web: www.apei.com

CEO: Angela Selden
CFO: Richard Sunderland
HR: –
FYE: December 31
Type: Public

American Public Education (APEI) promotes military intelligence. The firm offers online post-secondary education to those in the military and other public servants such as police and firefighters. Its American Military University and American Public University make up the American Public University System which offers around 120 degree programs and around 110 certificate programs in such disciplines as business administration criminal justice intelligence technology liberal arts and homeland security. Enrollment in the university consists of more than 83680 students from all 50 states and about 20 foreign countries. Meanwhile its National Education Seminars (Hondros College of Nursing) offers nursing education.

	Annual Growth	12/16	12/17	12/18	12/19	12/20
Sales ($ mil.)	0.7%	313.1	299.2	297.7	286.3	321.8
Net income ($ mil.)	(6.0%)	24.2	21.1	25.6	10.0	18.8
Market value ($ mil.)	5.6%	363.6	371.0	421.5	405.6	451.4
Employees	(2.1%)	3,200	1,280	2,900	1,910	2,940

AMERICAN RAILCAR INDUSTRIES INC

NMS: ARII

100 Clark Street
St. Charles, MO 63301
Phone: 636 940-6000
Fax: –
Web: www.americanrailcar.com

CEO: John O'Bryan
CFO: Luke M Williams
HR: –
FYE: December 31
Type: Public

American Railcar Industries (ARI) doesn't make the little engine that could but it does make the cars that the engine pulls. A North American manufacturer of railcars and railcar components the company also provides maintenance and fleet management services to freight shippers railcar leasing companies and railroads. Its two Arkansas manufacturing facilities make several types of railcars including covered hoppers for grains cement and other dry bulk and tank cars for liquid and gas commodities. The company also serves non-rail industries with industrial products such as steel and aluminum casting machining stamping welding and fabrication.

	Annual Growth	12/12	12/13	12/14	12/15	12/16
Sales ($ mil.)	(2.7%)	711.7	750.6	733.0	889.3	639.1
Net income ($ mil.)	3.3%	63.8	86.9	99.5	133.5	72.7
Market value ($ mil.)	9.3%	605.5	873.1	982.8	883.2	864.3
Employees	(4.9%)	2,643	2,663	2,865	2,407	2,159

AMERICAN REALTY CAPITAL TRUST INC.

NASDAQ: ARCT

106 York Rd.
Jenkintown PA 19046
Phone: 215-887-2189
Fax: +66-2-661-6664
Web: www.indorama.net

CEO: –
CFO: –
HR: –
FYE: December 31
Type: Public

American Realty Capital Trust (ARCT) isn't afraid to stand alone. The self-administered and self-advised real estate investment trust (REIT) owns a portfolio of more than 480 single-tenant free-standing commercial properties (as opposed to strip malls or shopping centers with multiple tenants) located in 43 states and Puerto Rico. Almost half of its properties are leased by top tenants Bridgestone CVS Dollar General FedEx PNC Bank and Walgreens. Formed by American Realty Capital in 2007 the REIT went public via an initial public offering in February 2012. Later that year Realty Income Corporation arranged to acquire ARCT for nearly $3 billion in cash stock and debt.

AMERICAN REALTY INVESTORS, INC.

NYS: ARL

1603 LBJ Freeway, Suite 800
Dallas, TX 75234
Phone: 469 522-4200
Fax: 469 522-4299
Web: www.amrealtytrust.com

CEO: Bradley Muth
CFO: Erik Johnson
HR: –
FYE: December 31
Type: Public

American Realty Investors (ARI) invests in develops and operates commercial properties and land in growing suburban markets. The company's portfolio includes approximately 60 apartment communities about 20 office buildings and about five each of industrial retail and hotel properties. It also owns a trade show and exhibit hall as well as undeveloped land. ARI has properties in about 20 states but most of its holdings are located in Texas. The company is part of a complex web of ownership that includes Prime Income Asset Management which manages ARI and owns about 15% of it. Through various entities Texas real estate mogul Gene Phillips and his family control around three-quarters of ARI.

	Annual Growth	12/16	12/17	12/18	12/19	12/20
Sales ($ mil.)	(16.2%)	119.7	126.2	121.0	48.0	59.0
Net income ($ mil.)	–	(2.7)	(8.4)	173.7	(16.0)	9.0
Market value ($ mil.)	20.5%	83.5	207.6	195.0	276.7	176.1
Employees	–	–	–	–	–	–

AMERICAN RESIDENTIAL SERVICES L.L.C.

965 Ridge Lake Blvd. Ste. 201
Memphis TN 38120
Phone: 901-271-9700
Fax: 703-873-2100
Web: www.lcc.com

CEO: Don Karnes
CFO: James McMahon
HR: Angela Carpenter
FYE: December 31
Type: Private

For those whose home maintenance skills don't rival Bob Vila's there's American Residential Services (operating as ARS/Rescue Rooter). The company is an amalgamation of some 100 firms combined to create a national home improvement services company specializing in heating ventilation air-conditioning plumbing sewer and rain services and electricity as well as major home appliance installation maintenance repair and replacement. With some more than 60 locations across the US ARS/Rescue Rooter services homes as well as small commercial buildings. The company is owned by CI Capital Partners Royal Palm Capital Partners and its management.

AMERICAN RESTAURANT GROUP INC.

4410 El Camino Real Ste. 201 — CEO: –
Los Altos CA 94022 — CFO: –
Phone: 650-949-6400 — HR: –
Fax: 650-917-9207 — FYE: December 31
Web: www.blackangus.com — Type: Private

As far as this company is concerned Angus beef is as American as apple pie. American Restaurant Group owns and operates the Black Angus Steakhouse chain with about 45 locations in half a dozen western states. The upscale casual dinnerhouses offer a menu of Black Angus steaks and prime rib along with chicken seafood and pasta dishes. Some locations also offer happy hour specials. In addition to dine-in seating the chain provides drive-up take-out service at many of its units. Rancher and entrepreneur Stuart Anderson opened the first Black Angus restaurant in Seattle in 1964. The chain was acquired in 2009 by affiliates of private equity firm Versa Capital Management.

AMERICAN RIVER BANKSHARES — NMS: AMRB

3100 Zinfandel Drive, Suite 450 — CEO: –
Rancho Cordova, CA 95670 — CFO: –
Phone: 916 851-0123 — HR: –
Fax: – — FYE: December 31
Web: www.americanriverbank.com — Type: Public

American River Bankshares' family is growing. The holding company is the parent of American River Bank which has about a dozen branches in Central California. About half of the bank's offices are operating under the North Coast Bank or Bank of Amador names. The bank serves area small to midsized businesses and individuals offering traditional deposit products such as checking and savings accounts and CDs. It offers commercial and residential mortgages as well as business construction and consumer loans and lease financing for business equipment.

	Annual Growth	12/15	12/16	12/17	12/18	12/19
Assets ($ mil.)	3.2%	634.6	651.5	655.6	688.1	720.4
Net income ($ mil.)	1.1%	5.3	6.4	3.2	4.9	5.5
Market value ($ mil.)	8.9%	62.4	89.1	89.9	82.3	87.7
Employees	0.5%	100	97	91	101	102

AMERICAN SAVINGS BANK FSB

1001 Bishop St. — CEO: Richard Wacker
Honolulu HI 96813 — CFO: Heather Schwarm
Phone: 808-523-6844 — HR: –
Fax: 808-531-7292 — FYE: December 31
Web: www.asbhawaii.com — Type: Subsidiary

You might say this bank is a real powerhouse — American Savings Bank is owned by Hawaiian Electric Industries which supplies power to almost all of the state's residents. Hawaii's third-largest financial institution (behind Bankoh and First Hawaiian Bank) the bank operates more than 50 branches across the state's five main islands; many of its locations have extended hours and are open on weekends. In addition to traditional products such as deposit accounts mortgages credit cards and business and consumer loans the bank also offers insurance investments and financial planning. Residential mortgages secured by Hawaiian real estate comprise the majority of its loan portfolio.

AMERICAN SCIENCE & ENGINEERING INC — NMS: ASEI

829 Middlesex Turnpike — CEO: Charles P Dougherty
Billerica, MA 01821 — CFO: Diane J Basile
Phone: 978 262-8700 — HR: –
Fax: – — FYE: March 31
Web: www.as-e.com — Type: Public

You can't hide from American Science and Engineering (AS&E). The company makes X-ray detection systems for inspection and security at airports border stations military situations shipping ports high-security facilities and law enforcement scenarios. Using a lower radiation dose than typical systems AS&E's Z Backscatter technology detects organic materials such as illegal drugs plastic explosives and plastic weapons. AS&E also makes scanning equipment for detecting contraband on persons in aircraft vehicles and in luggage and packages. About 40% of sales are to the US government and its contractors; top customers include Al Hamra Group Sal Offshore and US Customs and Border Protection.

	Annual Growth	03/11	03/12	03/13	03/14	03/15
Sales ($ mil.)	(17.9%)	278.6	203.6	186.7	190.2	126.8
Net income ($ mil.)	(61.1%)	42.8	21.4	17.5	15.1	1.0
Market value ($ mil.)	(14.7%)	664.4	482.3	438.7	483.2	351.5
Employees	(7.2%)	420	415	347	344	311

AMERICAN SEAFOODS GROUP LLC

Marketplace Tower 2025 1st Ave. Ste. 900 — CEO: Mikel Durham
Seattle WA 98121-3119 — CFO: Kevin McMenimen
Phone: 206-374-1515 — HR: –
Fax: 206-374-1516 — FYE: December 31
Web: www.americanseafoods.com — Type: Private

With operations in the northern Pacific (i.e. in the Bering Sea and Aleutian Islands) American Seafoods Group casts a bountiful net. The vertically integrated company offers frozen and processed fish such as Alaska pollock Pacific whiting Pacific cod sea and bay scallops haddock sole and farm-raised tilapia and catfish. It operates its own fleet of ships that process and freeze the catch while at sea as well as a fleet of transport trucks. American Seafoods' land-based operation in Massachusetts makes breaded seafood products. The company sells its fish under the American Pride brand name in North America Asia and Europe.

AMERICAN SHARED HOSPITAL SERVICES — ASE: AMS

Two Embarcadero Center, Suite 410 — CEO: Raymond Stachowiak
San Francisco, CA 94111 — CFO: Craig Tagawa
Phone: 415 788-5300 — HR: –
Fax: – — FYE: December 31
Web: www.ashs.com — Type: Public

Business is brain surgery for American Shared Hospital Services (ASHS). The company owns 81% of GK Financing (GKF) which installs finances and services the Leksell Gamma Knife a noninvasive surgical device that uses gamma rays to destroy brain tumors without harming surrounding tissue. Sweden-based Elekta which makes the Gamma Knife owns the other 19% of GKF. GKF usually leases the Gamma Knife units on a per-use basis to major urban medical centers; it has contracts for units installed in about 20 hospitals in the US; it markets the product in the US and Brazil.

	Annual Growth	12/16	12/17	12/18	12/19	12/20
Sales ($ mil.)	(1.2%)	18.7	19.6	19.7	20.6	17.8
Net income ($ mil.)	–	0.9	1.9	1.0	0.7	(7.1)
Market value ($ mil.)	(9.7%)	19.4	15.0	13.8	14.1	12.9
Employees	23.6%	9	9	12	14	21

AMERICAN SNUFF COMPANY LLC

813 Ridge Lake Blvd. #100
Memphis TN 38120
Phone: 901-761-2050
Fax: 901-767-1302
Web: https://www.americansnuff.com

CEO: –
CFO: –
HR: –
FYE: January 31
Type: Subsidiary

American Snuff Company loves a bear market when it comes to moist snuff and other smokeless tobacco products. It makes the Grizzly Kodiak Hawken and Cougar brands of moist tobacco and is the second-largest manufacturer of smokeless tobacco products in the US. American Snuff also makes loose-leaf tobacco (including Morgan's Levi Garrett and Taylor's Pride brands) snuff (Garrett and Dental brands) and a variety of other smokeless tobacco (including twist moist and plug). Its Lane unit sold in 2011 made little cigars and roll-your-own tobacco. Purchased by Reynolds American for $3.5 billion in 2006 the firm generates about 8% of its parent's annual revenue and took its existing name in 2010.

AMERICAN SOCIETY FOR TESTING AND MATERIALS

100 BARR HARBOR DR
CONSHOHOCKEN, PA 194282951
Phone: 610-832-9500
Fax: –
Web: www.astm.org

CEO: –
CFO: –
HR: –
FYE: December 31
Type: Private

The American Society for Testing and Materials — which does business as ASTM International — is a not-for-profit standards organization focused on developing voluntary codes and regulations for technical materials products systems and services. Established in 1898 to set standards for railroad steel the organization also works in such areas as petroleum medical devices consumer products and environmental assessment. ASTM International publishes its technical specifications in the Annual Book of ASTM Standards a more than 70-volume set. Its income is derived from selling its publications and through annual administrative fees. The organization has more than 30000 members in over 120 countries.

	Annual Growth	12/12	12/13	12/14	12/15	12/17
Sales ($ mil.)	7.7%	–	63.1	68.9	84.7	84.7
Net income ($ mil.)	(10.5%)	–	67.5	(9.0)	20.8	43.3
Market value ($ mil.)	–	–	–	–	–	–
Employees	–	–	–	–	–	230

AMERICAN SOFTWARE INC

NMS: AMSW A

470 East Paces Ferry Road, N.E.
Atlanta, GA 30305
Phone: 404 261-4381
Fax: –
Web: www.amsoftware.com

CEO: H. Allan Dow
CFO: Vincent Klinges
HR: –
FYE: April 30
Type: Public

American Software delivers an innovative technical platform that enables enterprises to accelerate their digital supply chain optimization from product concept to customer availability. The company's cloud-based and on-premise supply chain management and enterprise resource planning (ERP) software is used by manufacturers and distributors to manage back-office operations. Its Logility subsidiary makes collaborative applications that connect buyers with suppliers and help in planning transportation and logistics. It also provides IT staffing and consulting services. The company's customers come from a wide range of industries worldwide generating about 85% of its revenue from the US.

	Annual Growth	04/17	04/18	04/19	04/20	04/21
Sales ($ mil.)	1.2%	106.3	112.7	108.7	115.5	111.4
Net income ($ mil.)	(13.8%)	14.6	12.1	6.8	6.7	8.1
Market value ($ mil.)	17.2%	360.5	419.3	425.6	541.6	679.9
Employees	3.3%	372	462	424	428	424

AMERICAN SOIL TECHNOLOGIES INC

NBB: SOYL

9018 Balboa Ave., #558
Northridge, CA 91325
Phone: 818 899-4686
Fax: –
Web: www.americansoiltech.com

CEO: Carl P Ranno
CFO: Carl P Ranno
HR: –
FYE: September 30
Type: Public

American Soil Technologies works to make sure your farmland isn't dirt poor. The company manufactures agricultural chemicals that help retain water in soil the direct benefit of which is manifold. In addition to minimizing the frequency of irrigation the chemicals also decrease the likelihood of erosion and reduce other damage. Its products are used by agricultural residential and recreational clients. Subsidiary Smart World Organics gives American Soil entrance to the organic turf and horticultural markets. Though primarily operating in the US it also distributes internationally to the Middle East North Africa and China. The family of the late chairman Louie Visco controls 30% of the company.

	Annual Growth	09/11	09/12	09/13	09/14	09/15
Sales ($ mil.)	(61.5%)	0.1	0.1	0.1	0.0	0.0
Net income ($ mil.)	–	(0.7)	(0.6)	(0.5)	0.1	(0.6)
Market value ($ mil.)	(29.3%)	1.2	0.3	1.5	0.8	0.3
Employees	0.0%	3	3	3	3	3

AMERICAN SPECTRUM REALTY, INC.

ASE: AQQ

2401 Fountain View, Suite 750
Houston, TX 77057
Phone: 713 706-6200
Fax: –
Web: www.americanspectrum.com

CEO: William Carden
CFO: –
HR: –
FYE: December 31
Type: Public

American Spectrum Realty invests in and manages commercial real estate primarily multitenant office and industrial space. The company and its subsidiaries own manage or lease 90 properties valued at more than $1 billion. Most properties are located in Texas but it also owns assets in California and 20 other states. Since 2010 subsidiary American Spectrum Realty Management has owned the property and asset management assets of Evergreen Realty Group. The deal brought contracts for 80 properties ranging from storage units to student housing and has helped American Spectrum expand its third-party management and leasing capabilities across the US. CEO William Carden controls about 40% of the company.

	Annual Growth	12/09	12/10	12/11	12/12	12/13
Sales ($ mil.)	6.4%	33.3	55.6	69.4	55.1	42.7
Net income ($ mil.)	–	(8.3)	(8.0)	4.0	1.4	(13.8)
Market value ($ mil.)	(46.6%)	82.5	64.9	18.0	12.7	6.7
Employees	(12.6%)	283	219	183	180	165

AMERICAN STANDARD ENERGY CORP

NBB: ASEN

4800 North Scottsdale Road, Suite 1400
Scottsdale, AZ 85251
Phone: 480 371-1929
Fax: –
Web: www.asenergycorp.com

CEO: –
CFO: –
HR: –
FYE: December 31
Type: Public

Famous Uncle Al's Hot Dogs & Grille operates a chain of about 10 franchised quick-service restaurants in Arizona Connecticut Florida Nevada and Virginia that specialize in hot dogs and sausage sandwiches. The eateries also serve a variety of Italian-style sandwiches burgers and fries. CEO Paul Esposito and president Dean Valentino together control more than 30% of the company.

	Annual Growth	12/08	12/09	12/10	12/11	12/12
Sales ($ mil.)	259.6%	0.1	0.0	1.4	12.4	19.7
Net income ($ mil.)	–	(0.6)	(0.1)	(5.5)	(13.7)	(93.7)
Market value ($ mil.)	73.9%	2.6	0.3	194.0	162.9	23.8
Employees	(9.6%)	3	1	5	5	2

AMERICAN STATES WATER CO   NYS: AWR

630 E. Foothill Boulevard   CEO: Robert Sprowls
San Dimas, CA 91773-1212   CFO: Eva Tang
Phone: 909 394-3600   HR: –
Fax: –   FYE: December 31
Web: www.aswater.com   Type: Public

American States Water Company (AWR) is the parent company of GSWC Bear Valley Electric Service Inc. (BVESI) and American States Utility Services Inc. (ASUS) serving over 1 million consumer in nine states. Through its water utility subsidiary GSWC the company provides water service to approximately 261000 customer connections located within more than 80 communities in Northern Coastal and Southern California. Through its electric utility subsidiary BVESI the company distributes electricity to approximately 24000 customer connections in the City of Big Bear Lake and surrounding areas in San Bernardino County California. Through its contracted services subsidiary ASUS the provides operations maintenance/construction management services for water distribution and wastewater collection and treatment facilities located on eleven military bases throughout the country under 50-year privatization contracts with the government.

	Annual Growth	12/16	12/17	12/18	12/19	12/20
Sales ($ mil.)	2.9%	436.1	440.6	436.8	473.9	488.2
Net income ($ mil.)	9.7%	59.7	69.4	63.9	84.3	86.4
Market value ($ mil.)	14.9%	1,680.7	2,136.2	2,473.0	3,196.1	2,933.1
Employees	3.4%	736	758	817	841	841

AMERICAN SUPERCONDUCTOR CORP.   NMS: AMSC

114 East Main Street   CEO: Daniel Mcgahn
Ayer, MA 01432   CFO: John Kosiba
Phone: 978 842-3000   HR: –
Fax: –   FYE: March 31
Web: www.amsc.com   Type: Public

American Superconductor (AMSC) gets a charge out of carrying a heavy load. The company provides designs and technologies for building and operating wind turbines and connecting them to the power grid. Its wind segment licenses highly engineered wind turbine designs and supplies wind turbine makers with advanced power electronics and control systems. The grid segment offers grid interconnection systems for wind farms solar power plants and transmission cable systems. Subsidiary AMSC Windtec designs wind turbines. Customers inside the US account for more than half of sales. Major customers include Department of Homeland Security Vestas and Inox Wind Limited.

	Annual Growth	03/17	03/18	03/19	03/20	03/21
Sales ($ mil.)	3.8%	75.2	48.4	56.2	63.8	87.1
Net income ($ mil.)	–	(27.4)	(32.8)	26.8	(17.1)	(22.7)
Market value ($ mil.)	28.9%	189.3	160.6	354.9	151.2	523.2
Employees	(10.7%)	354	247	233	242	225

AMERICAN SYSTEMS CORPORATION

14151 PK MADOW DR STE 500   CEO: Peter L Smith
CHANTILLY, VA 20151   CFO: –
Phone: 703-968-6300   HR: –
Fax: –   FYE: December 31
Web: www.americansystems.com   Type: Private

American Systems provides government and commercial clients with IT management and consulting services including custom engineering and application development. Its consulting division advises clients on such issues as network access and identity management data security and process optimization. The company also provides managed technical support and staffing. American Systems works with government customers to develop systems related to command and control logistics and national security functions. Its commercial-focused operations serve the energy financial services retail and telecom industries among others.

	Annual Growth	12/16	12/17	12/18	12/19	12/20
Sales ($ mil.)	18.0%	–	275.0	0.0	373.9	451.5
Net income ($ mil.)	59.0%	–	4.4	0.0	10.8	17.8
Market value ($ mil.)	–	–	–	–	–	–
Employees	–	–	–	–	–	1,500

AMERICAN TECHNICAL CERAMICS CORP.

1 Norden Ln.   CEO: John Lawing
Huntington Station NY 11746   CFO: –
Phone: 631-622-4700   HR: –
Fax: 631-622-4748   FYE: June 30
Web: www.atceramics.com   Type: Subsidiary

American Technical Ceramics (ATC) isn't into pottery. The company makes ceramic and porcelain single- and multilayer capacitors that store and discharge precise amounts of electrical current. The company's radio-frequency (RF) microwave and millimeter-wave capacitors are key components in mobile phones instruments radar and navigation systems and broadcast satellites. Its high-reliability products are used in critically sensitive military and aerospace applications. ATC also makes resistors as well as custom thin-film substrates for microwave and fiber-optic telecommunications devices. In 2007 rival AVX acquired ATC for about $231 million in cash.

AMERICAN TERRAZZO COMPANY LTD.

309 GOLD ST   CEO: –
GARLAND, TX 750426648   CFO: Juliana Filippi
Phone: 972-272-8084   HR: –
Fax: –   FYE: December 31
Web: www.americanterrazzo.com   Type: Private

If you walk all over American Terrazzo's handiwork well that's really kind of the point. The company installs mural-like terrazzo flooring in public commercial and residential facilities. Terrazzo derived from the word for terraces in Italian is made from discarded marble remnants or cement and is used in a wide range of applications including sidewalks plazas terraces and stairways. American Terrazzo does most of its business in Texas primarily in Dallas. The company's handiwork can be found anywhere from homes schools and churches to offices airports and arenas. Mattia "Mike" Flabiano founded the family-owned firm in 1931.

	Annual Growth	12/05	12/06	12/07	12/08	12/12
Sales ($ mil.)	(46.8%)	–	666.0	9.2	8.0	15.1
Net income ($ mil.)	61.0%	–	–	0.1	0.3	1.5
Market value ($ mil.)	–	–	–	–	–	–
Employees	–	–	–	–	–	133

AMERICAN TIRE DISTRIBUTORS HOLDINGS, INC.

12200 HERBERT WAYNE CT # 150   CEO: Stuart Schuette
HUNTERSVILLE, NC 280786335   CFO: Jason Yaudes
Phone: 704-992-2000   HR: –
Fax: –   FYE: December 28
Web: www.atd-us.com   Type: Private

American Tire Distributors (ATD) is the largest independent tire and service distributor in North America. Its offerings include flagship brands Yokohama Hankook Continental Pirelli and Michelin as well as budget brands and private-label tires. ATD also markets custom wheels and tire service equipment. Its network of nearly 145 distribution centers and mixing warehouses serve independent tire dealers retail chains and auto service centers across the US and Canada and has approximately 1400 deliver vehicles on the road across the nation. In addition to some 40 million delivery miles annually the company provides access to over 4 million tires in every style and size from the top global brands in the industry.

	Annual Growth	12/09	12/10	12/11	12/12	12/13
Sales ($ mil.)	12.2%	–	–	3,050.2	3,455.9	3,839.3
Net income ($ mil.)	–	–	–	0.1	(14.3)	(6.4)
Market value ($ mil.)	–	–	–	–	–	–
Employees	–	–	–	–	–	1,072

AMERICAN TOWER CORP (NEW)

116 Huntington Avenue
Boston, MA 02116
Phone: 617 375-7500
Fax: -
Web: www.americantower.com

NYS: AMT
CEO: Thomas Bartlett
CFO: Rodney Smith
HR: -
FYE: December 31
Type: Public

Growth in wireless communications is taking American Tower to new heights. The company rents space on towers and rooftop antenna systems to wireless carriers and radio and TV broadcasters who use the infrastructure to enable their services. It owned more than 27200 towers in North America some 74700 in India and about 62600 throughout the rest of the world. Its portfolio additionally includes approximately 1780 Distributed Antenna System networks. American Tower also offers tower-related services such as site application structural analysis to determine support for additional equipment and zoning and permitting management services.

	Annual Growth	12/16	12/17	12/18	12/19	12/20
Sales ($ mil.)	8.6%	5,785.7	6,663.9	7,440.1	7,580.3	8,041.5
Net income ($ mil.)	15.3%	956.4	1,238.9	1,236.4	1,887.8	1,690.6
Market value ($ mil.)	20.7%	46,956.8	63,392.6	70,288.6	102,115.9	99,734.3
Employees	5.7%	4,507	4,752	5,026	5,454	5,618

AMERICAN TRANSMISSION COMPANY, LLC

W234N2000 RDGVIEW PKY CT
WAUKESHA, WI 531881022
Phone: 262-506-6700
Fax: -
Web: www.atcllc.com

CEO: Patricia Kampling
CFO: -
HR: -
FYE: December 31
Type: Private

American Transmission Company is an entrepreneur in the US power grid business — a for-profit multi-state transmission-only utility. Connecting electricity producers to distributors American Transmission owns operates monitors and maintains 9480 miles of high-voltage electric transmission lines and 529 substations in portions of Illinois Michigan Minnesota and Wisconsin. The company a member of the Midwest Independent Transmission System Operator (MISO) regional transmission organization operates the former transmission assets of some of its shareholders. About 30 utilities municipalities electric companies and cooperatives in its service area have an ownership stake in American Transmission.

	Annual Growth	12/14	12/15	12/16	12/17	12/18
Sales ($ mil.)	3.7%	-	615.8	650.8	714.3	687.4
Net income ($ mil.)	(5.0%)	-	200.4	147.4	172.6	172.1
Market value ($ mil.)	-	-	-	-	-	-
Employees	-	-	-	-	-	547

AMERICAN TRIM LLC

1005 W. Grand Ave.
Lima OH 45801-3429
Phone: 419-228-1145
Fax: 419-996-4850
Web: www.amtrim.com

CEO: Jeffrey A Hawk
CFO: Dana Morgan
HR: -
FYE: December 31
Type: Private

American Trim is not a new fad diet but a company that manufactures metal components for the automotive appliance and furniture industries. American Trim's automotive products include bumper beams frame members and interior and exterior trim. Other products include office furniture doors and shelves appliance handles and hinges support members and decorative metal tiles. The company also provides services such as product design tooling and process development metal forming metal finishing and assembly. The company has manufacturing facilities in Alabama Ohio and Pennsylvania as well as in Mexico. Founded in 1948 by the Hawk family American Trim is a subsidiary of Superior Metal Products.

AMERICAN TV & APPLIANCE OF MADISON INC.

2404 W. Beltline Hwy.
Madison WI 53713
Phone: 608-271-1000
Fax: 608-275-7339
Web: www.americantv.com

CEO: -
CFO: -
HR: -
FYE: June 30
Type: Private

American TV & Appliance of Madison is happy to outfit your entire house including your upscale kitchen. The company sells appliances electronics and furniture in Illinois Iowa Michigan and Wisconsin. Its 11 plus retail outlets offer such products as recliners dining room sets mattresses car stereos CD players dishwashers refrigerators personal computers digital cameras plasma and LCD TVs and DVD players. The company also has a distribution center and a service center offering parts and repairs. American TV even makes house calls to fix large appliances regardless of where they were purchased. Ferd Mattioli founded the company in 1954.

AMERICAN UNIVERSITY

4400 MASSACHUSETTS AVE NW
WASHINGTON, DC 200168200
Phone: 202-885-1000
Fax: -
Web: www.american.edu

CEO: -
CFO: -
HR: -
FYE: April 30
Type: Private

Fulfilling the vision of George Washington for a national university in the country's capital American University was chartered by an Act of Congress in 1893 as a private independent co-educational institution under the auspices of the United Methodist Church. Today the school offers a broad range of undergraduate and graduate degree programs to more than 12000 students from more than 120 countries. Its student-teacher ratio is 12:1. American University has schools devoted to arts and sciences business communications international service public affairs and law. It is one of the top producers of Peace Corps volunteers serving overseas. Nine US presidents have served on American University's Board of Trustees.

	Annual Growth	04/07	04/08	04/09	04/12	04/18
Sales ($ mil.)	4.3%	-	398.1	54.2	605.3	608.1
Net income ($ mil.)	14.1%	-	23.8	(108.7)	55.1	88.7
Market value ($ mil.)	-	-	-	-	-	-
Employees	-	-	-	-	-	2,000

AMERICAN VANGUARD CORP.

4695 MacArthur Court
Newport Beach, CA 92660
Phone: 949 260-1200
Fax: -
Web: www.american-vanguard.com

NYS: AVD
CEO: Eric Wintemute
CFO: David Johnson
HR: -
FYE: December 31
Type: Public

American Vanguard Corporation (AVD) is a specialty chemical manufacturer that develops and markets products for agricultural commercial and consumer uses. This California-based specialty chemical manufacturer sells products to protect crops turf and ornamental plants as well as human and animal health. Products include insecticides fungicides herbicides molluscicides growth regulators and soil fumigants. Through its subsidiary AMVAC Chemical Corporation the company pursues new product acquisitions and licensing for US domestic sales and worldwide product distribution. Its products are sold across the US and about 55 countries around the world. The company generates about 60% of sales from the US.

	Annual Growth	12/16	12/17	12/18	12/19	12/20
Sales ($ mil.)	10.1%	312.1	355.0	454.3	468.2	458.7
Net income ($ mil.)	4.5%	12.8	20.3	24.2	13.6	15.2
Market value ($ mil.)	(5.1%)	591.0	606.4	468.8	600.9	479.0
Employees	18.2%	395	605	624	671	771

AMERICAN WATER WORKS CO, INC. NYS: AWK

1 Water Street
Camden, NJ 08102-1658
Phone: 856 955-4001
Fax: –
Web: www.amwater.com

CEO: –
CFO: Linda G Sullivan
HR: Melanie Kennedy
FYE: December 31
Type: Public

American Water Works is the largest publicly traded water utility in the US providing water and wastewater services to some 15 million people in about 45 states through its regulated utilities. It also has market-based operations that include complementary home services primarily to residential and smaller commercial customers and water and wastewater services to the US government on military installations as well as municipalities utilities and industrial customers. Regulated operations account for over 85% of sales. Subsidiary American Water Works Service provides support and operational services to the company and its affiliates.

	Annual Growth	12/17	12/18	12/19	12/20	12/21
Sales ($ mil.)	4.0%	3,357.0	3,440.0	3,610.0	3,777.0	3,930.0
Net income ($ mil.)	31.2%	426.0	567.0	621.0	709.0	1,263.0
Market value ($ mil.)	19.9%	16,615.6	16,484.8	22,310.9	27,871.9	34,299.1
Employees	(1.9%)	6,900	7,100	6,800	7,000	6,400

AMERICAN WOODMARK CORP. NMS: AMWD

561 Shady Elm Road
Winchester, VA 22602
Phone: 540 665-9100
Fax: –
Web: www.americanwoodmark.com

CEO: M. Scott Culbreth
CFO: Paul Joachimczyk
HR: –
FYE: April 30
Type: Public

American Woodmark offers a wide variety of products that fall into product lines including kitchen cabinetry bath cabinetry office cabinetry home organization and hardware. Its cabinetry products are available in a variety of designs finishes and finish colors and door styles. Styles vary by finish (oak cherry hickory maple as well as laminate) and door design. Brands include American Woodmark Shenandoah Cabinetry Timberlake and Waypoint. Targeting the remodeling and new home construction markets American Woodmark sells its lineup through home centers and independent dealers and distributors; it also sells directly to major builders. American Woodmark was established through a leveraged buyout of Boise Cascade's cabinet division.

	Annual Growth	04/17	04/18	04/19	04/20	04/21
Sales ($ mil.)	14.1%	1,030.2	1,250.3	1,645.3	1,650.3	1,744.0
Net income ($ mil.)	(4.7%)	71.2	63.1	83.7	74.9	58.8
Market value ($ mil.)	2.0%	1,544.0	1,381.1	1,510.9	863.7	1,671.0
Employees	14.5%	5,808	9,400	9,300	9,900	10,000

AMERICARES FOUNDATION, INC.

88 HAMILTON AVE STE 1
STAMFORD, CT 069023100
Phone: 203-658-9500
Fax: –
Web: www.americares.org

CEO: Christine Squires
CFO: –
HR: –
FYE: June 30
Type: Private

AmeriCares Foundation provides emergency medical aid around the world. The not-for-profit charitable organization helps victims of natural disasters and supports long-term humanitarian programs by collecting medical supplies in the US and overseas and delivering them to places where they are needed. AmeriCares has provided aid in more than 90 countries worldwide. In the US the organization offers medical assistance runs a camp for kids with HIV/AIDS and conducts HomeFront a program that renovates housing for the needy in parts of Connecticut and New York. Robert C. Macauley founded AmeriCares in 1982.

	Annual Growth	06/13	06/14	06/15	06/19	06/20
Sales ($ mil.)	17.0%	–	560.2	742.0	976.3	1,440.8
Net income ($ mil.)	–	–	(4.5)	101.5	(101.3)	192.8
Market value ($ mil.)	–	–	–	–	–	–
Employees	–	–	–	–	–	231

AMERICO LIFE INC.

300 West 11th Street
Kansas City MO 64105
Phone: 937-492-6129
Fax: 937-498-4554
Web: peoplesfederalsandl.com

CEO: –
CFO: Mark K Fallon
HR: –
FYE: December 31
Type: Private

Americo Life sells insurance to cover American lives. The holding company sells life insurance and annuities to individuals families and groups mainly through its Americo Financial Life and Annuity Insurance unit. Americo Life companies also offer insurance policies that cover funeral expenses and mortgages. Policies are distributed through 13000 independent agents nationwide to about 800000 policyholders. The firm is a wholly owned subsidiary of Financial Holding Corporation which the family of chairman Michael Merriman controls. Other Financial Holding business interests include real estate ventures in the Southeast and a 50% stake in Argus Health Systems a processor of prescription drug claims.

AMERICUS MORTGAGE CORPORATION

6110 PINEMONT DR STE 215
HOUSTON, TX 770923216
Phone: 713-684-0725
Fax: –
Web: www.alliedhomenet.com

CEO: –
CFO: James Hagen
HR: –
FYE: June 30
Type: Private

Need someone on your side while seeking a home loan? Americus Mortgage (formerly Allied Home Mortgage Capital) wants to be your ally. The company is a privately held mortgage banker and broker with offices and representatives located throughout the US and the Virgin Islands. Through its history it has brokered a variety of mortgages including conventional loans jumbo loans reverse mortgages FHA loans and VA loans. At its peak (in 2003) Americus Mortgage originated more than $15 billion in loans in a single year; however the company has had trouble in recent years following the housing crisis of 2008.

	Annual Growth	06/05	06/06	06/07	06/08	06/09
Assets ($ mil.)	0.7%	–	–	16.4	15.6	16.6
Net income ($ mil.)	–	–	–	(2.5)	0.2	0.1
Market value ($ mil.)	–	–	–	–	–	–
Employees	–	–	–	–	–	2,500

AMERIFLIGHT LLC

Burbank-Glendale-Pasadena Airport Hangar #1 4700 W. Empire Ave.
Burbank CA 91505-1098
Phone: 818-980-5005
Fax: 818-980-5105
Web: www.ameriflight.com

CEO: Brian Randow
CFO: David W Moore
HR: –
FYE: December 31
Type: Private

Ameriflight takes flight across the Americas delivering time-sensitive packages for banks and for other air cargo carriers. The company serves some 200 communities primarily in the western US but also elsewhere in the US and in Canada and Mexico. Managing 75000 packages a day it operates a fleet of about 170 aircraft consisting of small jets and turboprops from several manufacturers from about a dozen hubs. The company serves other air cargo carriers by meeting their larger air freighters at major airports and distributing cargo to markets not easily served by big aircraft. Ameriflight is owned by its management team.

AMERIGAS PARTNERS LP
NYS: APU

460 North Gulph Road
King of Prussia, PA 19406
Phone: 610 337-7000
Fax: –
Web: www.amerigas.com

CEO: Hugh J Gallagher
CFO: Ann P Kelly
HR: –
FYE: September 30
Type: Public

America has a gas with AmeriGas Partners. Purveying propane has propelled the company to its position as the top US retail propane marketer (besting Ferrellgas). It serves more than 2 million residential commercial industrial agricultural motor fuel and wholesale customers from 2000 locations in 50 states. AmeriGas also sells propane-related supplies and equipment and exchanges prefilled portable tanks for empty ones. The company stores propane in Arizona California and Virginia and distributes its products through an interstate carrier structure that runs across the US and in Canada.

	Annual Growth	09/14	09/15	09/16	09/17	09/18
Sales ($ mil.)	(6.6%)	3,712.9	2,885.3	2,311.8	2,453.5	2,823.0
Net income ($ mil.)	(10.0%)	289.9	211.2	207.0	162.1	190.5
Market value ($ mil.)	(3.5%)	4,241.6	3,861.3	4,245.3	4,178.4	3,673.5
Employees	(2.2%)	8,400	8,500	8,300	8,100	7,700

AMERIGROUP CORPORATION
NYSE: AGP

4425 Corporation Ln.
Virginia Beach VA 23462
Phone: 757-490-6900
Fax: +33-1-49-02-27-41
Web: www.coface.com

CEO: James G Carlson
CFO: James W Truess
HR: –
FYE: December 31
Type: Public

AMERIGROUP looks after the health of America's needy. The managed health care provider targets people eligible for Medicaid the State Children's Health Insurance Program (SCHIP) FamilyCare and other government special needs plans. Its top Medicaid plans include a product for families receiving temporary assistance to needy families (TANF) benefits and one for aged blind or disabled (ABD) persons receiving supplemental income. AMERIGROUP's SCHIP programs cover uninsured kids ineligible for Medicaid. The company contracts with about 135000 primary care doctors and specialists as well as 800 hospitals to serve some 2.7 million members in more than a dozen states. The company is owned by WellPoint.

AMERIPATH INC.

7111 Fairway Dr. Ste. 400
Palm Beach Gardens FL 33418
Phone: 561-712-6200
Fax: 561-845-0129
Web: www.ameripath.com

CEO: –
CFO: –
HR: –
FYE: December 31
Type: Subsidiary

Pickled organs and preserved tissues are AmeriPath's favorite things. The firm provides anatomic pathology dermatopathology and esoteric testing services to hospitals doctors clinics and clinical laboratories in about 20 states across the US. Some 400 pathologists in AmeriPath's network diagnose conditions such as cancer and kidney disease by examining tissue samples; work is performed in more than 70 outpatient labs and in about 200 hospitals. The company's esoteric testing operations involve complex specialized clinical tests (including DNA analysis and molecular diagnostics) that doctors use to diagnose and treat disease. AmeriPath is a subsidiary of Quest Diagnostics.

AMERIPRISE FINANCIAL INC
NYS: AMP

1099 Ameriprise Financial Center
Minneapolis, MN 55474
Phone: 612 671-3131
Fax: –
Web: www.ameriprise.com

CEO: James Cracchiolo
CFO: Walter Berman
HR: Kelli Hunter Petruzillo
FYE: December 31
Type: Public

Ameriprise Financial provides solutions to help clients confidently achieve their financial objectives. It does so through its various brands and affiliates — which include Ameriprise Financial Services Columbia Threadneedle and RiverSource. Ameriprise manages some $1.1 trillion in assets for individual and institutional clients. It markets and administers its products primarily through a network of over 10000 financial advisors. Founded in 1893 Ameriprise Financial was spun off from American Express in 2005.

	Annual Growth	12/16	12/17	12/18	12/19	12/20
Sales ($ mil.)	0.4%	11,696.0	12,027.0	12,835.0	12,967.0	11,899.0
Net income ($ mil.)	3.9%	1,314.0	1,480.0	2,098.0	1,893.0	1,534.0
Market value ($ mil.)	15.0%	12,954.0	19,788.3	12,186.8	19,450.8	22,691.1
Employees	(1.4%)	13,000	13,000	14,000	12,500	12,300

AMERIQUEST TRANSPORTATION SERVICES INC.

457 Haddonfield Rd. Ste. 220
Cherry Hill NJ 08002
Phone: 856-773-0600
Fax: 856-773-0609
Web: www.ameriquestcorp.com

CEO: Douglas Clark
CFO: Mark Joyce
HR: –
FYE: December 31
Type: Private

AmeriQuest Transportation Services makes money helping its clients save on transportation costs. AmeriQuest offers fleet management services touted for cost-savings and expertise to the commercial trucking industry. Through its primary businesses of AmeriQuest Transportation Services NationaLease CURE and Corcentric it offers supply and asset management truck rental and leasing fleet maintenance materials handling purchasing programs and logistics services. It also arranges dedicated contract carriage where drivers and equipment are assigned to a customer long-term. Founded in 1996 AmeriQuest offers more than 600 facilities and 700000 vehicles in the US and Canada.

AMERIS BANCORP
NMS: ABCB

3490 Piedmont Rd N.E., Suite 1550
Atlanta, GA 30305
Phone: 404 639-6500
Fax: –
Web: www.amerisbank.com

CEO: H. Palmer Proctor
CFO: Nicole Stokes
HR: –
FYE: December 31
Type: Public

Ameris Bancorp is a financial holding company whose business is conducted primarily through its wholly owned banking subsidiary Ameris Bank which provides a full range of banking services to its retail and commercial customers who are primarily concentrated in select markets in in Alabama Georgia South Carolina and northern Florida. It operates nearly 165 full-service domestic banking offices. Loans secured by commercial real estate and farmland accounted for over 35% of the company's loan portfolio. Ameris Bank opened its doors as American Banking company on 1971.

	Annual Growth	12/16	12/17	12/18	12/19	12/20
Assets ($ mil.)	31.2%	6,892.0	7,856.6	11,443.5	18,242.6	20,438.6
Net income ($ mil.)	38.1%	72.1	73.5	121.0	161.4	262.0
Market value ($ mil.)	(3.3%)	3,032.0	3,351.9	2,202.4	2,958.3	2,647.4
Employees	19.8%	1,298	1,460	1,804	2,722	2,671

AMERISAFE INC   NMS: AMSF

2301 Highway 190 West   CEO: Gerry Frost
DeRidder, LA 70634   CFO: Neal Fuller
Phone: 337 463-9052   HR: –
Fax: –   FYE: December 31
Web: www.amerisafe.com   Type: Public

AMERISAFE has what it takes to insure roughnecks and truckers. AMERISAFE specializes in providing workers' compensation insurance for businesses in hazardous industries including agriculture manufacturing construction logging and lumber oil and gas maritime and trucking. Through its subsidiaries American Interstate Insurance Silver Oak Casualty and American Interstate Insurance Company the company writes coverage for more than 8000 policyholders (mainly small and midsized firms). In addition AMERISAFE offers worksite safety reviews loss prevention and claims management services. AMERISAFE sells its products in more than 45 states and the District of Columbia and the US Virgin Islands in which Florida accounts for the highest premiums.

	Annual Growth	12/16	12/17	12/18	12/19	12/20
Assets ($ mil.)	(0.8%)	1,518.9	1,518.2	1,515.9	1,492.9	1,470.9
Net income ($ mil.)	2.7%	77.9	46.2	71.6	92.7	86.6
Market value ($ mil.)	(2.0%)	1,205.3	1,190.8	1,095.9	1,276.4	1,110.2
Employees	(2.6%)	439	438	429	434	395

AMERISERV FINANCIAL INC.   NMS: ASRV

Main & Franklin Streets, P.O. Box 430   CEO: James Huerth
Johnstown, PA 15907-0430   CFO: Michael Lynch
Phone: 814 533-5300   HR: –
Fax: –   FYE: December 31
Web: www.ameriserv.com   Type: Public

AmeriServ Financial offers up a smorgasbord of banking services for Pennsylvanians. The company owns AmeriServ Financial Bank which primarily serves the southwestern portion of the state through some 20 branches. Targeting individuals and local businesses the bank offers standard services such as deposits credit cards and loans. Commercial mortgages account for more than half of its loan portfolio; other real estate loans including residential mortgage and construction loans make up about 30%. One of a handful of unionized banks in the US AmeriServ also manages union pension funds through its AmeriServ Trust and Financial Services subsidiary which provides trust and wealth management services as well.

	Annual Growth	12/16	12/17	12/18	12/19	12/20
Assets ($ mil.)	2.6%	1,153.8	1,167.7	1,160.7	1,171.2	1,279.7
Net income ($ mil.)	18.8%	2.3	3.3	7.8	6.0	4.6
Market value ($ mil.)	(4.1%)	63.1	70.8	68.8	71.7	53.4
Employees	(0.9%)	326	321	321	328	314

AMERISOURCEBERGEN CORP.   NYS: ABC

1 West First Avenue   CEO: Steven Collis
Conshohocken, PA 19428-1800   CFO: James Cleary
Phone: 610 727-7000   HR: –
Fax: 610 647-0141   FYE: September 30
Web: www.amerisourcebergen.com   Type: Public

AmerisourceBergen is the source for many of North America's pharmacies and health care providers. Operating primarily in the US it distributes generic branded and over-the-counter pharmaceuticals as well as medical supplies and other products using its network of facilities. The company serves acute care hospitals and health systems independent and chain retail pharmacies mail order pharmacies medical clinics long-term care and alternate site pharmacies among others. Its specialty distribution unit focuses on sensitive and complex biopharmaceuticals. Other operations include pharmaceutical packaging commercialization and consulting services and animal health product distribution. In 2021 AmerisourceBergen completed the acquisition of the majority of Walgreens Boots Alliance's Alliance Healthcare businesses for $6.275 billion in cash.

	Annual Growth	09/17	09/18	09/19	09/20	09/21
Sales ($ mil.)	8.7%	153,143.8	167,939.6	179,589.1	189,893.9	213,988.8
Net income ($ mil.)	43.4%	364.5	1,658.4	855.4	(3,408.7)	1,539.9
Market value ($ mil.)	9.6%	17,219.4	19,190.0	17,132.0	20,168.0	24,856.3
Employees	20.4%	20,000	21,000	22,000	22,000	42,000

AMERISURE MUTUAL INSURANCE COMPANY

26777 Halsted Rd.   CEO: Gregory J Crabb
Farmington Hills MI 48331-3586   CFO: Matt Simon
Phone: 248-615-9000   HR: –
Fax: 248-615-8548   FYE: December 31
Web: www.amerisure.com   Type: Private - Mutual Com

This company wants to help all businesses rest Amerisured. Amerisure Mutual Insurance Company provides a range of commercial property/casualty products with a special focus on the manufacturing health care and construction contracting industries. Coverage includes general and employee benefits liability workers compensation property auto inland marine and equipment insurance. The mutual firm is licensed in all US states and operates out of about a dozen offices across the nation. It uses a network of independent agents and brokers to distribute its products. Amerisure was founded as Michigan Workmen's Compensation Mutual Insurance in 1912.

AMERITAS MUTUAL HOLDING COMPANY

5900 O St.   CEO: Joann M Martin
Lincoln NE 68510   CFO: –
Phone: 402-467-1122   HR: –
Fax: 402-467-7335   FYE: December 31
Web: www.ameritas.com   Type: Private - Mutual Com

Ameritas Mutual Holding takes the task of providing life insurance to its members seriously. The company primarily operates through Ameritas Life Insurance and Ameritas Life Insurance of New York which provide life insurance and annuity products to about 430000 policyholders nationwide. In addition to managing some $80 billion in life insurance policies in force its subsidiaries also offer such services as financial planning and workplace investing. Ameritas' investment firms boast more than $30 billion of assets under management. Other companies under its umbrella include mutual fund manager Calvert Group.

AMERITRANS CAPITAL CORPORATION   NASDAQ: AMTC

830 3rd Ave. Ste. 830   CEO: –
New York NY 10022   CFO: –
Phone: 212-355-2449   HR: –
Fax: 212-759-3338   FYE: June 30
Web: www.ameritranscapital.com   Type: Public

Ameritrans Capital Corporation has switched off the meter on its taxi cab medallion business. The company previously provided financing to taxicab drivers in Boston Chicago Miami and New York City to acquire medallions or city-granted operating licenses. Medallion loans accounted for about half of Ameritrans' lending portfolio. However in 2008 it sold its portfolio of medallion loans held by subsidiary Elk Associates Funding to Medallion Financial for $31 million. Since then Ameritrans has focused on real estate mortgages corporate loans and equity investments in real estate while Elk Associates originates small business loans.

AMERITYRE CORPORATION   NBB: AMTY

1501 Industrial Road
Boulder City, NV 89005
Phone: 702 293-1930
Fax: –
Web: www.amerityre.com

CEO: Michael Sullivan
CFO: Lynda Keeton-Cardno
HR: –
FYE: June 30
Type: Public

Amerityre makes polyurethane foam tires which are unable to go flat for the bicycle and lawn equipment industries. The company also offers composite tires pneumatic tires and solid tires along with tire-filling materials. Central Purchasing accounts for one-fifth of Amerityre's sales. In 2008 the company acquired the manufacturing assets of a competitor KIK Technology International and KIK went out of business.

	Annual Growth	06/17	06/18	06/19	06/20	06/21
Sales ($ mil.)	7.6%	3.6	3.6	3.6	3.9	4.9
Net income ($ mil.)	66.9%	0.0	(0.0)	0.0	0.0	0.3
Market value ($ mil.)	37.9%	1.8	1.7	1.4	1.8	6.5
Employees	(1.3%)	19	14	16	14	18

AMERON INTERNATIONAL CORPORATION

245 S. Los Robles Ave.
Pasadena CA 91101-3638
Phone: 626-683-4000
Fax: 626-683-4060
Web: www.ameron.com

CEO: Clay C Williams
CFO: Jeremy Thigten
HR: –
FYE: November 30
Type: Subsidiary

Oil water and other liquids need a place to flow and that's where Ameron International comes in. The firm designs makes and markets fiberglass-composite pipes for transmitting oil chemicals corrosive liquids and other specialty materials. Ameron also makes and sells concrete and fabricated steel products used for water transmission and wind towers. Additionally its infrastructure unit supplies ready-mix concrete and aggregates box culverts and sand for construction projects in Hawaii. The firm's pole products division makes concrete and steel poles for lighting and traffic signals. Oilfield equipment maker National Oilwell Varco bought Ameron for some $777 million in 2011.

AMES CONSTRUCTION, INC.

2500 COUNTY ROAD 42 W
BURNSVILLE, MN 553376911
Phone: 952-435-7106
Fax: –
Web: www.amesconstruction.com

CEO: –
CFO: Michael J Kellen
HR: –
FYE: November 30
Type: Private

Ames Construction aims right for the heart of heavy construction. The company is a general contractor providing heavy civil and industrial construction services to the transportation mining and power industries mainly in the West and Midwest. The family-owned company works on highways airports bridges rail lines mining facilities power plants and other infrastructure projects. Ames also performs flood control environmental remediation reclamation and landfill work. Additionally the firm builds golf courses and undertakes commercial and residential site development projects. Ames typically partners with other companies to perform the engineering and design portion of construction jobs.

	Annual Growth	11/14	11/15	11/16	11/19	11/20
Sales ($ mil.)	4.1%	–	1,068.2	845.3	1,248.8	1,308.8
Net income ($ mil.)	52.5%	–	5.1	2.4	61.3	42.2
Market value ($ mil.)	–	–	–	–	–	–
Employees		–	–	–	–	2,500

AMES NATIONAL CORP.   NAS: ATLO

405 5th Street
Ames, IA 50010
Phone: 515 232-6251
Fax: 515 663-3033
Web: www.amesnational.com

CEO: John Nelson
CFO: John Pierschbacher
HR: –
FYE: December 31
Type: Public

This company aims to please citizens of Ames... and central Iowa. Ames National Corporation is the multi-bank holding company for flagship subsidiary First National Bank Ames Iowa as well as Boone Bank & Trust Reliance State State Bank & Trust and United Bank & Trust. Boasting over $1 billion in assets and 15 branches the banks provide area individuals and businesses with standard services such as deposit accounts IRAs and credit and debit cards. Commercial-related loans account for about 50% of Ames' loan portfolio while agricultural loans make up another 20%. The banks also write residential construction consumer and business loans and offer trust and financial management services.

	Annual Growth	12/16	12/17	12/18	12/19	12/20
Assets ($ mil.)	9.7%	1,366.5	1,375.1	1,455.7	1,737.2	1,975.6
Net income ($ mil.)	4.6%	15.7	13.7	17.0	17.2	18.9
Market value ($ mil.)	(7.6%)	301.1	254.1	231.9	256.0	219.1
Employees	7.0%	202	221	138	133	265

AMES TRUE TEMPER INC.

465 Railroad Ave.
Camp Hill PA 17011
Phone: 717-737-1500
Fax: 717-730-2552
Web: www.ames.com

CEO: –
CFO: Marcus Hamilton
HR: –
FYE: September 30
Type: Subsidiary

It could be said that Ames True Temper is at the root of all lawn and garden tool manufacturers in the US. Tracing its history to 1774 the firm was founded as a shovel maker by John Ames. Today it's one of the largest suppliers of non-powered yard equipment in North America. Its product portfolio includes long-handle tools planters pruning and striking tools wheelbarrows hoses and hose reels and snow tools. Products are marketed under the Ames True Temper Hound Dog Jackson Professional Razor-Back and Union Tools brand names. They are sold in North America Europe and Australia via mass merchandisers wholesalers and distributors. Ames True Temper is owned by plastics maker Griffon Corporation.

AMETEK INC   NYS: AME

1100 Cassatt Road
Berwyn, PA 19312-1177
Phone: 610 647-2121
Fax: 610 647-0211
Web: www.ametek.com

CEO: David Zapico
CFO: William Burke
HR: –
FYE: December 31
Type: Public

AMETEK is a leading global manufacturer of electronic instruments and electro-mechanical devices. Its Electronic Instruments Group (EIG) makes monitoring metering and analytic devices for the aerospace heavy equipment and power generation markets among others. Its Electromechanical Group (EMG) makes air-moving electric motors for vacuum cleaners and other floor care equipment blowers and heat exchangers connectors for moisture-proof applications and specialty metals for the aerospace mass transit medical and office products markets. AMETEK has some 150 manufacturing facilities throughout the world; about half its sales are to customers outside the US.

	Annual Growth	12/17	12/18	12/19	12/20	12/21
Sales ($ mil.)	6.6%	4,300.2	4,845.9	5,158.6	4,540.0	5,546.5
Net income ($ mil.)	9.8%	681.5	777.9	861.3	872.4	990.1
Market value ($ mil.)	19.3%	16,788.6	15,683.5	23,106.0	28,017.2	34,063.6
Employees	2.3%	16,900	18,200	18,100	16,500	18,500

AMEXDRUG CORP.   NBB: AXRX

6465 Corvette Street   CEO: Jack Amin
Commerce, CA 90040   CFO: Jack Amin
Phone: 323 725-3100   HR: –
Fax: 323 725-3133   FYE: December 31
Web: www.amexdrug.com   Type: Public

Amexdrug through subsidiaries Allied Med and Dermagen is a wholesale distributor of pharmaceuticals nutritional supplements and beauty products to pharmacies and other retailers. The company allows small pharmacies to get the lower prices that large pharmaceutical chains such as Walgreen and CVS enjoy. Its customers are primarily located in California. Part of Allied Med's growth strategy includes increasing its online traffic so it is increasing its name recognition and branding efforts. Top executive Jack Amin and his wife own more than 90% of the company.

	Annual Growth	12/16	12/17	12/18	12/19	12/20
Sales ($ mil.)	(9.0%)	9.3	10.4	10.5	7.7	6.4
Net income ($ mil.)	27.7%	0.1	0.1	0.2	0.2	0.2
Market value ($ mil.)	(1.4%)	14.2	40.7	18.8	9.8	13.4
Employees	–	–	–	–	–	–

AMGEN INC   NMS: AMGN

One Amgen Center Drive   CEO: Robert Bradway
Thousand Oaks, CA 91320-1799   CFO: Peter Griffith
Phone: 805 447-1000   HR: Lori Johnston
Fax: 805 447-1010   FYE: December 31
Web: www.amgen.com   Type: Public

Amgen is among the biggest of the biotechs. The company is committed to unlocking the potential of biology for patients suffering from serious illnesses. Its principal products which have the most significant annual commercial sales are ENBREL Prolia Neulasta Otezla XGEVA Aranesp KYPROLIS and Repatha Amgen focuses on six commercial areas: inflammation oncology/hematology bone health CV disease nephrology and neuroscience and it conducts discovery research primarily in three therapeutic areas: inflammation oncology/hematology and CV/metabolic diseases Amgen's products are marketed worldwide with the US market accounting for over 70% of sales.

	Annual Growth	12/17	12/18	12/19	12/20	12/21
Sales ($ mil.)	3.3%	22,849.0	23,747.0	23,362.0	25,424.0	25,979.0
Net income ($ mil.)	31.4%	1,979.0	8,394.0	7,842.0	7,264.0	5,893.0
Market value ($ mil.)	6.6%	97,088.4	108,684.3	134,589.4	128,364.3	125,600.8
Employees	3.9%	20,800	21,500	23,400	24,300	24,200

AMICUS THERAPEUTICS INC   NMS: FOLD

3675 Market Street   CEO: John Crowley
Philadelphia, PA 19104   CFO: Daphne Quimi
Phone: 215 921-7600   HR: –
Fax: –   FYE: December 31
Web: www.amicusrx.com   Type: Public

Amicus Therapeutics develops drugs that treat rare genetic diseases known as lysosomal storage disorders. Unlike other treatments which replace defective enzymes Amicus' lead drug Galafold is an oral small molecule pharmacological chaperone that is designed to bind to and stabilize a patient's own endogenous target protein. The drug is a treatment for adults with a confirmed diagnosis of Fabry disease and an amenable galactosidase alpha gene (GLA) variant based on in vitro assay data. Other candidates are in development to treat Pompe disease. The company is also researching treatments for neurodegenerative diseases. The company generates about 70% of its revenue in Ex-US.

	Annual Growth	12/16	12/17	12/18	12/19	12/20
Sales ($ mil.)	169.3%	5.0	36.9	91.2	182.2	260.9
Net income ($ mil.)	–	(200.0)	(284.0)	(349.0)	(356.4)	(276.9)
Market value ($ mil.)	46.8%	1,302.5	3,771.1	2,510.6	2,552.5	6,051.0
Employees	16.4%	263	325	508	584	483

AMKOR TECHNOLOGY INC.   NMS: AMKR

2045 East Innovation Circle   CEO: Giel Rutten
Tempe, AZ 85284   CFO: Megan Faust
Phone: 480 821-5000   HR: –
Fax: –   FYE: December 31
Web: www.amkor.com   Type: Public

Amkor Technology Inc. is one of the world's leading providers of outsourced semiconductor packaging and test services making sure that chips are ready to go for smartphones tablets computers high-performance gaming systems automobiles IoT wearable and network systems. The company's some 250 customers worldwide include many of the largest semiconductor companies around the world. Although Amkor is a public company founder and chairman James Kim and his family control the firm. More than 45% of revenue is from US customers. The company traces its roots back to 1935.

	Annual Growth	12/17	12/18	12/19	12/20	12/21
Sales ($ mil.)	10.0%	4,186.5	4,316.5	4,052.7	5,050.6	6,138.3
Net income ($ mil.)	25.3%	260.7	127.1	120.9	338.1	643.0
Market value ($ mil.)	25.3%	2,455.4	1,602.7	3,176.1	3,684.3	6,056.6
Employees	0.9%	29,300	30,850	29,650	29,050	30,400

AML COMMUNICATIONS INC.

1000 Avenida Acaso   CEO: –
Camarillo CA 93012   CFO: –
Phone: 805-388-1345   HR: –
Fax: 805-484-2191   FYE: March 31
Web: www.amlj.com   Type: Subsidiary

AML Communications wants to pump up the volume with its microwave amplifiers for wireless communications. The amplifiers support defense-related radar satellite and surveillance systems as well as commercial wireless applications. AML also makes higher-power microwave amplifiers for the defense market through subsidiary Microwave Power. AML's customers include defense equipment manufacturers (such as Raytheon and Boeing) systems integrators and commercial wireless operators (AT&T Mobility and Verizon Wireless). In 2011 AML was acquired by Microsemi for about $28 million in cash to complement its existing defense-related product portfolio and to expand its wireless communications business.

AMN HEALTHCARE SERVICES INC   NYS: AMN

8840 Cypress Waters Boulevard, Suite 300   CEO: Susan Salka
Dallas, TX 75019   CFO: Jeffrey Knudson
Phone: 866 871-8519   HR: –
Fax: –   FYE: December 31
Web: www.amnhealthcare.com   Type: Public

Operating under such brands as American Mobile Healthcare NurseChoice NursesRx Med Travelers Staff Care and O'Grady-Peyton International AMN Healthcare Services is one of the leading talent solutions for the healthcare sector in the US. It places nurses technicians and therapists for 13-week stints at hospitals clinics and schools across the US. AMN total talent solutions include managed services programs clinical and interim healthcare leaders temporary staffing executive search solutions vendor management systems recruitment process outsourcing predictive modeling language interpretation services revenue cycle solutions credentialing and other services. The majority of temporary assignments for its clients are at acute-care hospitals. The company generated all of its revenue in US.

	Annual Growth	12/16	12/17	12/18	12/19	12/20
Sales ($ mil.)	5.9%	1,902.2	1,988.5	2,136.1	2,222.1	2,393.7
Net income ($ mil.)	(9.6%)	105.8	132.6	141.7	114.0	70.7
Market value ($ mil.)	15.4%	1,809.2	2,317.4	2,666.0	2,931.9	3,211.4
Employees	0.1%	2,990	2,980	2,920	3,236	3,000

AMNEAL PHARMACEUTICALS INC — NYS: AMRX

400 Crossing Boulevard
Bridgewater, NJ 08807
Phone: 908 947-3120
Fax: –
Web: www.amneal.com

CEO: –
CFO: –
HR: –
FYE: December 31
Type: Public

Impax Laboratories is betting that its pharmaceuticals will make a positive impact on the world's health. The company makes specialty generic pharmaceuticals which it markets through its Impax Generics division and through marketing alliances with other pharmaceutical firms. It concentrates on controlled-release versions of various generic versions of branded and niche pharmaceuticals that require difficult-to-obtain raw materials or specialized expertise. Additionally the company's branded pharmaceuticals business (Impax Specialty Pharma) is developing and improving upon previously approved drugs that target Parkinson's disease multiple sclerosis and other central nervous system disorders. In 2018 Impax merged with Amneal Pharmaceuticals to create a top generics firm.

	Annual Growth	12/16	12/17	12/18	12/19	12/20
Sales ($ mil.)	24.7%	824.4	775.8	1,663.0	1,626.4	1,992.5
Net income ($ mil.)	–	(472.0)	(469.3)	(169.7)	(361.9)	91.1
Market value ($ mil.)	(41.9%)	–	–	4,056.2	1,445.0	1,370.0
Employees	41.5%	1,495	1,257	6,000	5,500	6,000

AMOS PRESS INC.

911 Vandemark Rd.
Sidney OH 45365
Phone: 937-498-2111
Fax: 937-498-0812
Web: www.amospress.com

CEO: Bruce Boyd
CFO: Jane Volland
HR: Harry Haberer
FYE: December 31
Type: Private

Amos Press (also known as Amos Publishing) is something of a hobby horse. The company publishes more than 15 niche titles that provide news information and entertainment pieces for collectors. Initially a daily newspaper publishing company Amos expanded into the collectibles business in 1960 with its launch of Coin World a weekly national news magazine for coin collectors. It later acquired Linn's Stamp News a weekly periodical serving stamp collectors and Cars & Parts a publication designed for automotive fans with a focus on authentic collector cars. In 1984 Amos bought Scott Publishing Company another publisher of content for stamp collectors. Amos Press was founded by James Amos in 1876.

AMPACET CORPORATION

660 White Plains Rd.
Tarrytown NY 10591
Phone: 914-631-6600
Fax: 914-631-7278
Web: www.ampacet.com

CEO: –
CFO: Joel Slutsky
HR: –
FYE: December 31
Type: Private

Ampacet helps manufacturers of plastic products show their true hues with custom color and additive concentrates. Using polyethylene polypropylene polyamide and polyester resins Ampacet makes compounds concentrates and masterbatches that enable those manufacturers to produce consistent colors and chemical characteristics for their extruded and molded products. Globally the company competes with firms such as BASF and Clariant in the color concentrates market. Its additives are used in food and industrial packaging pipe and conduit wire and cable and other plastic products.

AMPCO SERVICES, L.L.C.

16945 NORTHCHASE DR # 1950
HOUSTON, TX 770602135
Phone: 281-872-8324
Fax: –
Web: www.atlanticmethanol.com

CEO: –
CFO: –
HR: –
FYE: December 31
Type: Private

Atlantic Methanol Production Company (AMPCO) must have adopted "Waste not want not" as its motto. It tries not to waste the natural gas that is a by-product of its parent companies' production processes. A joint venture between Noble Energy (45% ownership) Marathon Oil (45%) and SONAGAS the National Gas Company of Equatorial Guinea (10%) the company operates one of the largest methanol plants in the world. The plant off the coast of Equatorial Guinea produces about 1 million tons of methanol annually — 2% of the global market. AMPCO also distributes using three vessels and five terminals in Europe and US where it sells most of its production.

	Annual Growth	12/05	12/06	12/07	12/08	12/10
Sales ($ mil.)	(43.4%)	–	–	1,405.6	341.1	254.2
Net income ($ mil.)	10372.8%	–	–	0.0	122.0	65.5
Market value ($ mil.)	–	–	–	–	–	–
Employees	–	–	–	–	–	500

AMPCO-PITTSBURGH CORP. — NYS: AP

726 Bell Avenue, Suite 301
Carnegie, PA 15106
Phone: 412 456-4400
Fax: 412 456-4404
Web: www.ampcopittsburgh.com

CEO: J. Brett McBrayer
CFO: Michael McAuley
HR: –
FYE: December 31
Type: Public

Steel giant Ampco-Pittsburgh keeps its worth by never losing its temper. Among the leaders in steel producers the company divides its work in two segments: The Forged and Engineered Cast Products segment — comprising subsidiaries Union Electric Steel and Union Electric Steel UK — makes forged hardened-steel rolling mill rolls and cast rolls for steel and aluminum manufacturers. The Air and Liquid Processing unit has three divisions: Buffalo Pumps which makes centrifugal pumps for refrigeration marine defense and power generation industries; Aerofin highly-engineered heat-exchange coils and Buffalo Air Handling air-handling systems for defense power generation and construction customers.

	Annual Growth	12/16	12/17	12/18	12/19	12/20
Sales ($ mil.)	(0.3%)	331.9	432.4	419.4	397.9	328.5
Net income ($ mil.)	–	(79.8)	(12.1)	(69.3)	(21.0)	8.0
Market value ($ mil.)	(24.4%)	306.7	227.1	56.8	55.1	100.3
Employees	(5.4%)	1,915	1,943	1,922	1,673	1,533

AMPHENOL CORP. — NYS: APH

358 Hall Avenue
Wallingford, CT 06492
Phone: 203 265-8900
Fax: 203 265-8746
Web: www.amphenol.com

CEO: Richard Norwitt
CFO: Craig Lampo
HR: David Silverman
FYE: December 31
Type: Public

Amphenol Corp. is a manufacturer of connector and interconnect products for the communications industrial automotive aerospace military mobile networks and devices. In addition it designs manufactures and markets electrical electronic and fiber optic connectors and interconnect systems antennas sensors and sensor-based products and coaxial and high-speed specialty cable. It is also used for electrical and optical signals in wire bundling and cable management networking equipment vehicles aircraft and airframe power distribution and energy applications. Amphenol also makes high-speed and specialized coaxial cable. Nearly 70% of its sales come from outside the US. Certain predecessor businesses of the company were founded in 1932.

	Annual Growth	12/17	12/18	12/19	12/20	12/21
Sales ($ mil.)	11.6%	7,011.3	8,202.0	8,225.4	8,598.9	10,876.3
Net income ($ mil.)	25.1%	650.5	1,205.0	1,155.0	1,203.4	1,590.8
Market value ($ mil.)	(0.1%)	52,601.0	48,539.1	64,840.6	78,344.3	52,397.3
Employees	6.5%	70,000	73,600	74,000	80,000	90,000

AMPIO PHARMACEUTICALS INC
ASE: AMPE

373 Inverness Parkway, Suite 200
Englewood, CO 80112
Phone: 720 437-6500
Fax: –
Web: www.ampiopharma.com

CEO: Michael Martino
CFO: Daniel Stokely
HR: –
FYE: December 31
Type: Public

With hopes one day of taking in revenues somewhere between ample and copious Ampio Pharmaceuticals is a development-stage company that focuses on repositioning existing drugs for new uses. Drugs in formulation for new indications include candidates for treating eye and kidney disorders inflammatory conditions and metabolic disease. In addition the company is working on diagnostic devices for measuring levels of oxidation in the bloodstream. Ampio is conducting clinical trials for two drugs: Ampion (for osteoarthritis of the knee) and Optina (for diabetic macular edema). In late 2013 it announced plans to spin off its sexual dysfunction business (Zertane and Zertane-ED).

	Annual Growth	12/11	12/12	12/13	12/14	12/15
Sales ($ mil.)	180.6%	0.0	0.1	0.1	0.1	1.2
Net income ($ mil.)	–	(18.4)	(11.6)	(24.0)	(38.1)	(32.0)
Market value ($ mil.)	(4.8%)	222.0	186.7	370.7	178.4	182.0
Employees	15.0%	12	13	16	23	21

AMPLIFY ENERGY CORP (NEW)
NYS: AMPY

500 Dallas Street, Suite 1700
Houston, TX 77002
Phone: 713 490-8900
Fax: –
Web: www.amplifyenergy.com

CEO: Martyn Willsher
CFO: Jason Mcglynn
HR: –
FYE: December 31
Type: Public

Midstates Petroleum Company knows there's much more to Louisiana than Creoles crawfish and alligators. An independent oil and gas exploration and production company Midstates operates on some 64700 net acres in the central Louisiana portion of the Upper Gulf Coast Tertiary. The company's assets consist primarily of mature oilfields discovered in the 1940s and '50s that continue to show production potential when developed with modern techniques. The company routinely uses such techniques and technologies to produce oil including hydraulic fracturing and 3D seismic data. In 2013 Midstates reported proved reserves of 127.8 million barrels of oil equivalent. If filed for bankruptcy protection in 2016.

	Annual Growth	12/16	12/17	12/18	12/19	12/20
Sales ($ mil.)	42.9%	48.5	228.8	208.6	275.6	202.1
Net income ($ mil.)	–	9.9	(85.1)	49.8	(35.2)	(464.0)
Market value ($ mil.)	(49.9%)	781.1	624.5	282.9	249.0	49.3
Employees	11.1%	124	129	85	230	189

AMPLIPHI BIOSCIENCES CORP
ASE: APHB

3579 Valley Centre Drive, Suite 100
San Diego, CA 92130
Phone: 858 829-0829
Fax: –
Web: www.ampliphibio.com

CEO: Brian Varnum
CFO: Steven Martin
HR: –
FYE: December 31
Type: Public

AmpliPhi Biosciences (formerly called Targeted Genetics) is amping up the fight against bacterial infections. The drug developer focuses on anti-bacterial (bacteriophage) therapeutics. It was after the 2011 acquisition of Biocontrol that AmpliPhi reorganized itself; going from being focused on developing DNA-based gene therapies to encourage (or sometimes inhibit) the production of proteins associated with disease to its current focus of treatments for antibiotic-resistant bacterial infections. The field for anti-infective treatments is receiving great attention these days with the spread of antibiotic-resistant infections such as the deadly methicillin-resistant Staphylococcus aureus aka MRSA.

	Annual Growth	12/13	12/14	12/15	12/16	12/17
Sales ($ mil.)	(22.9%)	0.3	0.4	0.5	0.3	0.1
Net income ($ mil.)	–	(58.4)	23.1	(0.5)	(18.8)	(12.8)
Market value ($ mil.)	19.5%	4.7	1.9	37.8	4.2	9.6
Employees	29.7%	12	23	30	33	34

AMREIT INC.
NYSE: AMRE

8 Greenway Plaza Ste. 1000
Houston TX 77046
Phone: 713-850-1400
Fax: 713-850-0498
Web: www.amreit.com

CEO: –
CFO: –
HR: –
FYE: December 31
Type: Private

AmREIT is tuned in to its own shopping network. A self-managed real estate investment trust (REIT) the company invests in develops and manages retail properties primarily lifestyle centers grocery store-anchored strip centers and single-tenant retail properties. It owns some 30 properties with more than 1 million sq. ft. of leasable space; more than half are located in Texas. The company's preferred assets are located in dense high-traffic areas in the suburbs of Houston Dallas and San Antonio. The REIT's largest tenants are Kroger H-E-B and CVS Care; together they account for about 20% of its rental revenues. After a brief stint off the public markets AmREIT went public again in 2012.

AMREP CORP.
NYS: AXR

850 West Chester Pike, Suite 205
Havertown, PA 19083
Phone: 610 487-0905
Fax: –
Web: www.amrepcorp.com

CEO: Christopher Vitale
CFO: –
HR: –
FYE: April 30
Type: Public

Mailing magazines and developing land in New Mexico keep AMREP hopping. About 80% of the company's sales come from newsstand distribution and subscription and product fulfillment services it provides through its Kable Media Services and Palm Coast Data subsidiaries. The units serve about 200 publishing clients by managing subscriptions and mailing 900-plus magazine titles. Through its AMREP Southwest subsidiary the company develops its Rio Rancho property (roughly 17300 acres) as well as certain parts of Sandoval County outside Albuquerque New Mexico. AMREP was founded in 1961. Its largest shareholder in 2010 scrapped plans to take AMREP private and merge it with another firm.

	Annual Growth	04/17	04/18	04/19	04/20	04/21
Sales ($ mil.)	(1.4%)	42.4	40.2	12.8	18.8	40.1
Net income ($ mil.)	–	(0.0)	0.2	1.5	(5.9)	7.4
Market value ($ mil.)	15.5%	42.7	51.5	39.6	34.4	75.9
Employees	(52.8%)	404	420	11	16	20

AMRON INTERNATIONAL, INC.

1380 ASPEN WAY
VISTA, CA 920818349
Phone: 760-208-6500
Fax: –
Web: www.amronintl.com

CEO: Debra L Ritchie
CFO: –
HR: –
FYE: December 31
Type: Private

Talk about being under pressure. Amron International is a manufacturer and supplier of specialized diving and hyperbaric equipment. Its underwater products include helium unscramblers oxygen treatment panels and hoods chamber conditioning systems diver communication systems and vulcanized rubber dry suits. The company also distributes tactical and outdoor gear from such brands as Patagonia Slumberjack and Suunto. Amron International is a prime vendor for the US military. Other customers include commercial business with many in the oil industry. The company has facilities in Vista California and in Virginia Beach Virginia. Amron International was founded in 1978 by Norma Ockwig.

	Annual Growth	12/04	12/05	12/06	12/07	12/08
Sales ($ mil.)	–	–	–	(1,073.2)	63.4	79.4
Net income ($ mil.)	20730.4%	–	–	0.0	3.1	4.6
Market value ($ mil.)	–	–	–	–	–	–
Employees	–	–	–	–	–	75

AMS HEALTH SCIENCES INC.

4000 N. Lindsay
Oklahoma City OK 73105
Phone: 405-842-0131
Fax: 405-843-4935
Web: www.amsonline.com

CEO: –
CFO: –
HR: –
FYE: December 31
Type: Private

Combine green algae ionized silver shark cartilage and pomegranate juice and you might find the fountain of youth or at least the ingredients for a multi-level marketing company like AMS Health Sciences. The company's 60 products consist of dietary supplements weight management products and hair and skin care products — all of which are manufactured by third parties. A network of 7000 independent distributors sell the products in Canada and the US. Its products are sold under the Advantage AMS Prime One and ToppFast brands. The company also markets and sells promotional material to its distributors. AMS has restructured and emerged from Chapter 11 bankruptcy protection.

AMSCAN HOLDINGS INC.

80 Grasslands Rd.
Elmsford NY 10523
Phone: 914-345-2020
Fax: 541-774-7617
Web: www.lithiainvestorrelations.com

CEO: –
CFO: –
HR: –
FYE: December 31
Type: Private

Amscan Holdings caters to the party animal in all of us. The vertically-integrated company operates a wholesale business Amscan Inc. that manufactures and distributes party goods such as balloons invitations pi?atas favors stationery and tableware. It also sells its party supplies to its own growing chain of retail stores including nearly 500 Party City superstores as well as those operated by rival party chains discount and grocery stores dollar stores and gift shops. Amscan has production and distribution facilities in North America Europe and the Asia/Pacific region. It is a subsidiary of Party City Holdingswhich is owned by Berkshire Partners Weston Presidio and Advent International.

AMSTED INDUSTRIES INCORPORATED

2 Prudential Plaza 180 N. Stetson St. Ste. 1800
Chicago IL 60601
Phone: 312-645-1700
Fax: 312-819-8494
Web: www.amsted.com

CEO: Steven R Smith
CFO: Tomas Bergmann
HR: Diane Orland
FYE: September 30
Type: Private

Wilbur and Orville Wright's first flight might never have succeeded without an assist from Amsted Industries' Diamond Chain subsidiary. A maker of bicycle and industrial roller chains Diamond produced the propeller chain for the Wright brothers' aircraft. Amsted Industries' three different segments manufacture highly engineered industrial components for locomotive and railcar makers automotive OEMs and construction and building suppliers. It is a major force in making freight car undercarriages too. Main subsidiaries include ASF-Keystone Griffin Pipe Products Griffin Wheel and Means Industries. Employee-owned Amsted Industries runs about 50 plants in 11 countries.

AMSURG CORP

NMS: AMSG

1A Burton Hills Boulevard
Nashville, TN 37215
Phone: 615 665-1283
Fax: –
Web: www.amsurg.com

CEO: –
CFO: –
HR: –
FYE: December 31
Type: Public

It's not quite an assembly line but AmSurg aims to make outpatient surgeries more efficient cost effective and up to date. The company operates ambulatory surgery centers that specialize in a few high-volume low-risk procedures with no overnight stays. Its specialties include gastroenterology (colonoscopy and endoscopy) orthopedics (knee scopes and carpal tunnel repair) ophthalmology (cataracts and laser eye surgery) otolaryngology (earn nose and throat) and urology. It also provides multi-specialty services primarily in anesthesiology children's services radiology and emergency medicine to health care facilities. Each of its centers are affiliated with a physicians practice group.

	Annual Growth	12/10	12/11	12/12	12/13	12/14
Sales ($ mil.)	22.9%	710.4	786.9	928.5	1,079.3	1,621.9
Net income ($ mil.)	1.9%	49.8	50.0	62.6	72.7	53.7
Market value ($ mil.)	27.1%	1,008.0	1,252.9	1,443.9	2,209.3	2,633.2
Employees	35.7%	3,100	5,500	6,100	6,200	10,500

AMTEC PRECISION PRODUCTS INC.

1875 Holmes Rd.
Elgin IL 60123-1298
Phone: 847-622-2686
Fax: 847-695-8295
Web: www.amtecprecision.com

CEO: –
CFO: –
HR: –
FYE: May 31
Type: Private

Liking neither Dr. Seuss' Sam-I-am nor green eggs and ham AMTEC would like precision components here or there. Its products include precision-machined metals injection-molded plastics and mechanical electromechanical and electronic assemblies. Clients for its precision products include Bosch Caterpillar Copeland Ford and General Motors. Its clients for molded plastics include Barber Coleman Bergstrom Ecolab and Kysor Westran. The company maintains three manufacturing plants in Illinois. AMTEC Precision Products was founded in 1954. Since 2005 the company has operated as a subsidiary of India-based Ucal Fuel Systems Ltd.

AMTECH SYSTEMS, INC.

NMS: ASYS

131 South Clark Drive
Tempe, AZ 85281
Phone: 480 967-5146
Fax: –
Web: www.amtechsystems.com

CEO: Michael Whang
CFO: Lisa Gibbs
HR: –
FYE: September 30
Type: Public

Amtech Systems furnishes fabs with furnaces and more. The company operates through four subsidiaries: Tempress Systems makes diffusion furnaces for semiconductor and solar cell fabrication as well as for precision thermal processing (annealing brazing silvering sealing and soldering) of electronic devices including optical components and photovoltaic (PV) solar cells. P.R. Hoffman Machine Products makes equipment used to polish items such as silicon wafers precision optics ceramic components and disk media. Bruce Technologies makes horizontal diffusion furnace systems and R2D Automation makes wafer automation and handling equipment for the solar and semiconductor sectors and is based in France.

	Annual Growth	09/17	09/18	09/19	09/20	09/21
Sales ($ mil.)	(15.2%)	164.5	176.4	85.0	65.5	85.2
Net income ($ mil.)	(36.3%)	9.1	5.3	(5.2)	(15.7)	1.5
Market value ($ mil.)	(1.2%)	171.4	76.4	75.8	69.9	163.5
Employees	(10.2%)	455	468	415	296	296

AMTRUST FINANCIAL SERVICES INC — NMS: AFSI

59 Maiden Lane, 43rd Floor
New York, NY 10038
Phone: 212 220-7120
Fax: –
Web: www.amtrustgroup.com

CEO: Barry D Zyskind
CFO: Adam Karkowsky
HR: –
FYE: December 31
Type: Public

Insurance holding company AmTrust Financial Services likes a mix of businesses on its plate. Its subsidiaries offer a range of commercial property/casualty insurance products for small and midsized customers including workers' compensation products auto and general liability workplace and agricultural coverage and extended service and warranty coverage of consumer and commercial goods. It also provides a small amount of personal auto reinsurance. AmTrust operates in Bermuda Ireland the UK and the US and distributes its products through brokers agents and claims administrators. Customers include restaurants retailers physicians' offices auto and electronics manufacturers and trucking operations.

	Annual Growth	12/12	12/13	12/14	12/15	12/16
Assets ($ mil.)	32.1%	7,417.2	11,257.4	13,847.4	17,111.6	22,614.7
Net income ($ mil.)	23.3%	178.0	290.9	447.0	503.6	411.0
Market value ($ mil.)	(1.2%)	4,891.9	5,573.9	9,591.1	10,499.9	4,668.5
Employees	39.7%	2,100	3,238	5,100	6,200	8,000

AMWAY INTERNATIONAL INC.

7575 Fulton St. East
Ada MI 49355-0001
Phone: 616-787-6000
Fax: 616-682-4000
Web: www.amway.com

CEO: –
CFO: –
HR: –
FYE: August 31
Type: Subsidiary

Selling makeup and vitamins to friends and family is a way of life at Amway International. One of the world's largest direct-sales businesses Amway boasts more than 3 million independent consultants who sell its catalog of more than 450 personal care household nutrition and cleaning products. It also sells the products and services of other companies in 80-plus markets worldwide. Revival-like techniques are used to motivate distributors (mostly part-timers) to sell products and find new recruits to build the multi-level marketing platform. Operations outside of the US generate about 80% of sales mainly in Asia. Founder Richard DeVos and the Van Andel family own Amway and its parent company Alticor.

AMX LLC

3000 Research Dr.
Richardson TX 75082
Phone: 469-624-8000
Fax: 469-624-7153
Web: www.amxcorp.com

CEO: Rashid Skap
CFO: C Chris Apple
HR: –
FYE: December 31
Type: Subsidiary

Like a football fan on Sunday AMX really knows how to work the remote control. The company designs and sells systems that control devices such as lights audio and video equipment and security cameras from a common remote interface. Its systems are used in corporate educational entertainment industrial and government settings. AMX also offers residential systems that control security systems lighting and electronic devices. The company sells through distributors and manufacturers including Tech Data and Dell; it also has partnerships with a number of Asian vendors including Fujitsu Hitachi NEC Samsung and Sony. Founded in 1982 AMX is a subsidiary of The Duchossois Group.

AMY'S KITCHEN INC.

Corporate Circle Ste. 200
Petaluma CA 94954
Phone: 707-578-7270
Fax: 310-752-4444
Web: www.thephelpsgroup.com

CEO: Xavier Unkovic
CFO: Andrew Koprel
HR: –
FYE: June 30
Type: Private

Amy's Kitchen helps you stock your own with lots of vegetarian options. The company makes and markets more than 170 frozen and pre-packaged vegetarian meals and other food products using all-natural and organic ingredients. Foods from Amy's Kitchen are also a popular option for non-vegetarian health-conscious consumers. The company's products include more than 88 frozen entrees including pizzas pocket sandwiches pot pies snacks toaster pops and veggie burgers as well as canned soups beans chili jarred pasta sauces and salsa. Founded in 1987 Amy's Kitchen distributes specialty foods in North America through supermarkets natural food and grocery stores warehouse stores and college campuses.

AMYLIN PHARMACEUTICALS INC. — NASDAQ: AMLN

9360 Towne Centre Dr.
San Diego CA 92121
Phone: 858-552-2200
Fax: 858-552-2212
Web: www.amylin.com

CEO: –
CFO: –
HR: –
FYE: December 31
Type: Public

Amylin Pharmaceuticals helps diabetics gain the upper hand in their battle with the disease. The company makes and markets injectable diabetes drugs Byetta and Symlin which are approved as adjunct therapies to other diabetes treatments such as metformin and insulin. Byetta is also approved as a stand-alone diabetes therapy. Amylin gained FDA approval for Bydureon a once-weekly version of Byetta in 2012 and it is developing additional drugs for metabolic conditions. The company's US sales force markets its products to patients and physicians; development partner Eli Lilly markets Byetta internationally although Amylin and Lilly are ending their partnership. Amylin was acquired by Bristol-Myers Squibb in 2012.

AMYRIS INC — NMS: AMRS

5885 Hollis Street, Suite 100
Emeryville, CA 94608
Phone: 510 450-0761
Fax: –
Web: www.amyris.com

CEO: John Melo
CFO: Han Kieftenbeld
HR: –
FYE: December 31
Type: Public

Amyris is a science and technology leader in the research development and production of sustainable ingredients for the Clean Health & Beauty and Flavors & Fragrances markets. Amyris uses an impressive array of exclusive technologies including state-of-the-art machine learning robotics and artificial intelligence. Its ingredients are included in over 3000 products from the world's top brands reaching more than 200 million consumers. Amyris is proud to own and operate a family of consumer brands - all built around its No Compromise promise of clean ingredients: Biossance clean beauty skincare Pipette clean baby skincare and Purecane a zero-calorie sweetener naturally derived from sugarcane. Around 60% of its sales are generated internationally.

	Annual Growth	12/16	12/17	12/18	12/19	12/20
Sales ($ mil.)	26.7%	67.2	143.4	63.6	152.6	173.1
Net income ($ mil.)	–	(97.3)	(72.3)	(230.2)	(242.8)	(331.0)
Market value ($ mil.)	70.5%	178.8	918.6	818.1	756.9	1,512.6
Employees	7.8%	440	414	503	561	595

ANACOR PHARMACEUTICALS INC   NMS: ANAC

1020 East Meadow Circle
Palo Alto, CA 94303-4230
Phone: 650 543-7500
Fax: –
Web: www.anacor.com

CEO: –
CFO: –
HR: –
FYE: December 31
Type: Public

Anacor is hardcore about curing skin conditions. The company is developing boron-based drug compounds for use as topical treatments of bacterial fungal and inflammatory conditions. Its lead candidates aim to treat onychomycosis (a kind of toenail fungus) psoriasis and hospital-acquired bacterial infections. Anacor has focused on topical treatments for the time being because they are relatively easy to develop and market but it believes its boron chemistry can produce drugs in therapeutic fields such as viral and parasitic infections and rare infectious diseases. The company went public in 2010.

	Annual Growth	12/10	12/11	12/12	12/13	12/14
Sales ($ mil.)	(7.1%)	27.8	20.3	10.7	17.2	20.7
Net income ($ mil.)	–	(10.1)	(47.9)	(56.1)	84.8	(87.1)
Market value ($ mil.)	56.5%	232.4	268.3	225.0	726.1	1,395.6
Employees	11.4%	65	80	85	79	100

ANADARKO PETROLEUM CORP   NYS: APC

1201 Lake Robbins Drive
The Woodlands, TX 77380-1046
Phone: 832 636-1000
Fax: –
Web: www.anadarko.com

CEO: R A Walker
CFO: Benjamin M Fink
HR: –
FYE: December 31
Type: Public

Anadarko Petroleum has ventured beyond its original area of operation — the Anadarko Basin — to explore for develop produce and market oil natural gas natural gas liquids and related products worldwide. The company boasts reported proved reserves (90% of which is located in the US) of 1.7 billion barrels of oil equivalent. Additional assets include coal trona (natural soda ash) and other minerals. Anadarko operates a handful of gas-gathering systems in the Mid-Continent. Internationally the company has substantial oil and gas interests in Algeria. It also has holdings in Brazil Mozambique and West Africa.

	Annual Growth	12/13	12/14	12/15	12/16	12/17
Sales ($ mil.)	(4.9%)	14,581.0	18,470.0	8,698.0	7,869.0	11,908.0
Net income ($ mil.)	–	801.0	(1,750.0)	(6,692.0)	(3,071.0)	(456.0)
Market value ($ mil.)	(9.3%)	42,103.1	43,791.0	25,786.3	37,012.7	28,472.1
Employees	(6.3%)	5,700	6,100	5,800	4,500	4,400

ANADIGICS INC   NAS: ANAD

141 Mt. Bethel Road
Warren, NJ 07059
Phone: 908 668-5000
Fax: –
Web: www.anadigics.com

CEO: –
CFO: –
HR: –
FYE: December 31
Type: Public

ANADIGICS makes chips that cook with GaAs. The company makes gallium arsenide (GaAs) radio-frequency integrated circuits for cellular wireless WiFi and infrastructure applications. GaAs ICs may be costlier than silicon but their physical properties allow the compound materials to be used for chips that are smaller and faster or more energy-efficient than silicon chips. ANADIGICS' power amplifiers switches and other chips can be found in the cable modems set-top boxes wireless devices and other gear of companies including Samsung Huawei and ZTE. The majority of customers come from Asia. In late 2015 ANADIGICS agreed to be acquired by GaAs Labs a venture capital firm.

	Annual Growth	12/10	12/11	12/12	12/13	12/14
Sales ($ mil.)	(20.6%)	216.7	152.8	112.6	134.2	86.3
Net income ($ mil.)	–	1.3	(49.3)	(69.9)	(54.0)	(38.9)
Market value ($ mil.)	(42.6%)	601.3	190.0	218.6	159.6	65.1
Employees	(16.1%)	590	540	504	477	293

ANADIGICS, INC.   NMS: ANAD

141 Mt. Bethel Road
Warren, NJ 07059
Phone: 908 668-5000
Fax: –
Web: www.anadigics.com

CEO: –
CFO: –
HR: –
FYE: December 31
Type: Public

ANADIGICS makes chips that cook with GaAs. The company makes gallium arsenide (GaAs) radio-frequency integrated circuits for cellular wireless WiFi and infrastructure applications. GaAs ICs may be costlier than silicon but their physical properties allow the compound materials to be used for chips that are smaller and faster or more energy-efficient than silicon chips. ANADIGICS' power amplifiers switches and other chips can be found in the cable modems set-top boxes wireless devices and other gear of companies including Samsung Huawei and ZTE. The majority of customers come from Asia.

	Annual Growth	12/09	12/10	12/11	12/12	12/13
Sales ($ mil.)	(1.1%)	140.5	216.7	152.8	112.6	134.2
Net income ($ mil.)	–	(57.1)	1.3	(49.3)	(69.9)	(54.0)
Market value ($ mil.)	(18.7%)	355.8	584.4	184.7	212.5	155.2
Employees	(4.1%)	564	590	540	504	477

ANADYS PHARMACEUTICALS INC.   NASDAQ: ANDS

5871 Oberlin Dr. Ste. 200
San Diego CA 92121
Phone: 858-530-3600
Fax: 858-527-1540
Web: www.anadyspharma.com

CEO: –
CFO: –
HR: –
FYE: December 31
Type: Public

Anadys Pharmaceuticals has hepatitis and cancer in the crosshairs. The biotechnology company is developing new therapeutic treatments for those infected with hepatitis C (HCV) and other bacterial infections as well as for applications in oncology. Anadys is exploring compounds that either act as direct antivirals or that stimulate the body's immune system responses to fight disease. In addition Anadys Pharmaceuticals explores potential strategic alliances with other pharmaceutical firms for collaborative development or licensing arrangements. In late 2011 the company agreed to be acquired by Roche Holding in a deal worth about $230 million.

ANALOG DEVICES INC   NMS: ADI

One Analog Way
Wilmington, MA 01887
Phone: 781 935-5565
Fax: –
Web: www.analog.com

CEO: Vincent Roche
CFO: Prashanth Mahendra-Rajah
HR: –
FYE: October 30
Type: Public

Analog Devices Inc. (ADI) is a leading maker of mixed-signal analog and digital integrated circuits (ICs) that convert real-world phenomena such as pressure temperature and sound into digital signals. Its devices include converters amplifiers power management products and digital signal processors (DSPs). The company's chips are used in industrial process controls medical and scientific instruments defense/aerospace communications gear computers automobiles and consumer electronics. ADI claims around 125000 customers around the world with around two-thirds of its revenue from customers outside the US.

	Annual Growth	10/17*	11/18	11/19*	10/20	10/21
Sales ($ mil.)	9.4%	5,107.5	6,200.9	5,991.1	5,603.1	7,318.3
Net income ($ mil.)	17.6%	727.3	1,495.4	1,363.0	1,220.8	1,390.4
Market value ($ mil.)	17.4%	47,915.4	45,798.3	57,455.4	62,267.4	91,139.6
Employees	12.7%	15,300	15,800	16,400	15,900	24,700

*Fiscal year change

ANALOGIC CORP
NMS: ALOG

8 Centennial Drive
Peabody, MA 01960
Phone: 978 326-4000
Fax: –
Web: www.analogic.com

CEO: Fred B Parks
CFO: Will Rousmaniere
HR: –
FYE: July 31
Type: Public

Analogic provides evidence of things unseen (or at least hard to see) in health care and airport security. The company's data acquisition conversion and signal processing gear converts analog signals such as pressure temperature and X-rays into digital computer data. Its medical image processing systems and security imaging products are used in equipment such as CT and MRI scanners and other diagnostic screeners as well as luggage inspection systems. The company also makes ultrasound systems under the brands BK Medical and Sonix for the surgery anesthesia and general imaging markets among others. Analogic has facilities in Asia Europe and North America and generates more than 60% of its sales outside the US.

	Annual Growth	07/13	07/14	07/15	07/16	07/17
Sales ($ mil.)	(3.0%)	550.4	517.5	540.3	508.8	486.4
Net income ($ mil.)	–	31.1	34.5	33.5	12.1	(74.2)
Market value ($ mil.)	(0.4%)	890.1	896.6	1,004.3	1,047.5	875.2
Employees	(2.9%)	1,700	1,700	1,679	1,577	1,510

ANCESTRY.COM INC.
NASDAQ: ACOM

360 W. 4800 North
Provo UT 84604
Phone: 801-705-7000
Fax: 801-705-7001
Web: corporate.ancestry.com

CEO: Timothy Sullivan
CFO: Howard Hochhauser
HR: –
FYE: December 31
Type: Private

For those with the urge to unearth and discover their roots Ancestry.com helps people research and share family histories as well as create family trees. Users can search through a variety of documents photographs maps and newspapers on its website. In addition to this data Ancestry.com relies on user-generated content and social networking activities — including uploading and sharing family trees photographs and documents and written stories — to encourage collaboration among users. Ancestry.com also provides family-history desktop software Family Tree Maker and offers research services. Ancestry.com was taken private in late 2012 by Permira.

ANCHIN BLOCK & ANCHIN LLP

1375 Broadway
New York NY 10018
Phone: 212-840-3456
Fax: 212-840-7066
Web: www.anchin.com

CEO: –
CFO: –
HR: –
FYE: September 30
Type: Private - Partnershi

Einstein knew that logic will get you from A to B and Anchin Block & Anchin is no exception. The regional accounting and consulting firm concentrates on serving privately held businesses in a number of industries. It offers audits financial statements reviews and compilations tax preparation and other advisory services. Its Anchin Wealth Management unit serves wealthy clients with investment estate and other financial services while Anchin Capital Advisors specializes in mergers and acquisitions. Anchin Block & Anchin which was founded in 1923 as a three-man partnership has grown to number more than 50 partners and principals.

ANCHOR BANCORP WISCONSIN INC (DE)
NMS: ABCW

25 West Main Street
Madison, WI 53703
Phone: 608 252-8700
Fax: 608 252-8783
Web: www.anchorbank.com

CEO: Chris M Bauer
CFO: Thomas G Dolan
HR: –
FYE: December 31
Type: Public

Anchor BanCorp Wisconsin is the holding company for AnchorBank which has more than 50 branches across the Badger State. The thrift courts individuals and local businesses offering checking and savings accounts credit cards CDs and IRAs as well as insurance and investment products. Founded in 1919 AnchorBank is predominantly a real estate lender with residential and commercial mortgages and construction and land loans accounting for the majority of its loan portfolio. Like many other banks though AnchorBank is struggling with its capital levels due to real estate-related losses. The company has sold some of its branches to raise capital.

	Annual Growth	03/11	03/12	03/13*	12/13	12/14
Assets ($ mil.)	(15.0%)	3,394.8	2,789.5	2,367.6	2,112.5	2,082.4
Net income ($ mil.)	–	(41.2)	(36.7)	(34.2)	111.6	14.6
Market value ($ mil.)	–	–	–	–	–	328.8
Employees	(7.1%)	817	738	690	693	656

*Fiscal year change

ANCHOR GLASS CONTAINER CORPORATION

401 E. Jackson St. Ste. 2800
Tampa FL 33602
Phone: 813-884-0000
Fax: 212-549-2646
Web: www.aclu.org

CEO: Nipesh Shah
CFO: –
HR: –
FYE: December 31
Type: Private

In a sea of options Anchor Glass Container anchors its business on manufacturing sustainable safe attractive glass packaging. One the leading glass container-makers in the US — it ranks behind Owens-Illinois and Saint-Gobain Containers Anchor Glass Container serves primarily manufacturers of beverages beer and liquor and foods and other consumer goods. It produces clear and colored-glass containers in a myriad of sizes via eight glassmaking plants and one for making moulds. For years the company's largest customer has included beer giant Anheuser-Busch. Anchor Glass Container's lineup also caters to Snapple LiDestri Foods and High Falls Brewing. The company is controlled by Wayzata Investment Partners.

ANCHORAGE, MUNICIPALITY OF (INC)

632 W 6TH AVE STE 810
ANCHORAGE, AK 995016312
Phone: 907-343-6610
Fax: –
Web: www.muni.org

CEO: –
CFO: –
HR: –
FYE: December 31
Type: Private

Anchorage is Alaska's largest city in both size and population. The city encompasses almost 2000 sq. mi. of land — almost the size of Delaware. Anchorage had a 2010 population of about 290000 residents or about a quarter of the state's population. Anchorage is located in the south central part of the state and sits on the Gulf of Alaska.

	Annual Growth	12/16	12/17	12/18	12/19	12/20
Sales ($ mil.)	5.4%	–	816.9	740.2	800.8	956.5
Net income ($ mil.)	–	–	(33.6)	26.4	21.7	272.3
Market value ($ mil.)	–	–	–	–	–	–
Employees	–	–	–	–	–	3,680

ANDALAY SOLAR INC

NBB: WEST

2721 Shattuck Avenue, #305
Berkeley, CA 94705
Phone: 408 402-9400
Fax: –
Web: www.andalaysolar.com

CEO: Edward Bernstein
CFO: Margaret Randazzo
HR: –
FYE: December 31
Type: Public

Ask anyone at Akeena about their company's name and they'll tell you Akeena was the mistress of the Greek sun god Apollo. The company (which does business under the Westinghouse Solar name as the result of a 2010 partnership agreement) designs markets and sells solar power systems for residential and small commercial customers. Akeena was founded in 2001 and by early 2009 had installed more than 3000 solar power systems at schools wineries restaurants housing developments and other locations. However the company exited the installation business in 2009 to concentrate on manufacturing and distribution. Previously limited to six states the company now distributes in some 34 states and in Canada.

	Annual Growth	12/10	12/11	12/12	12/13	12/14
Sales ($ mil.)	(37.9%)	8.7	11.4	5.2	1.1	1.3
Net income ($ mil.)	–	(12.9)	(4.6)	(8.6)	(2.8)	(1.9)
Market value ($ mil.)	(55.9%)	131.9	89.4	12.6	6.1	5.0
Employees	(26.4%)	34	31	7	9	10

ANDEAVOR

NYS: ANDV

19100 Ridgewood Pkwy.
San Antonio, TX 78259-1828
Phone: 210 626-6000
Fax: –
Web: www.tsocorp.com

CEO: Gary R Heminger
CFO: Steven M Sterin
HR: –
FYE: December 31
Type: Public

Andeavor Corporation does its best to turn crude oil into something useful for its customers. The independent oil refiner and marketer operates seven US refineries that produce nearly 900000 barrels per day of gasoline jet fuel diesel fuel fuel oil liquid asphalt and other fuel products. It has refineries in Alaska California (two) North Dakota (two) Utah and Washington. Andeavor markets fuel to nearly 25000 branded retail gas stations (including Shell and USA Gasoline brands) primarily in Alaska and the Western US. It owns 36% of Andeavor Logistics LP (ALLP). In 2017 Andeavor (then called Tresoro) acquired all segments of Western Refining except its logistics arm in a $6.4 billion deal. The combined Tesoro-Western company changed its name to Andeavor.

	Annual Growth	12/12	12/13	12/14	12/15	12/16
Sales ($ mil.)	(7.1%)	32,974.0	37,601.0	40,633.0	28,711.0	24,582.0
Net income ($ mil.)	(0.3%)	743.0	412.0	843.0	1,540.0	734.0
Market value ($ mil.)	18.7%	5,149.4	6,838.6	8,691.5	12,317.7	10,222.9
Employees	2.5%	5,700	7,000	5,600	6,000	6,300

ANDEAVOR LOGISTICS LP

NYS: ANDX

200 East Hardin Street
Findlay, OH 45840
Phone: 419 421-2414
Fax: –
Web: www.tesorologistics.com

CEO: Gregory J Goff
CFO: Steven Sterin
HR: –
FYE: December 31
Type: Public

Andeavor Logistics was created to serve its parent. The company a spinoff of oil refiner Andeavor Corporation owns and operates US crude oil gathering transportation and storage facilities. Its trucks and 700 miles of Montana and North Dakota pipeline serve Andeavor's Mandan refinery while eight refined product terminals hold petroleum in California Utah Washington Alaska and North Dakota. Andeavor Logistics' primary storage facility in Salt Lake City holds 880000 barrels of crude and refined petroleum. In 2016 it announced plans to invest $1.1 billion to beef up its midstream business. That year it agreed to buy two natural gas processing plants in North Dakota from Whiting Petroleum for $700 million.

	Annual Growth	12/13	12/14	12/15	12/16	12/17
Sales ($ mil.)	80.1%	305.5	600.0	1,112.0	1,220.0	3,213.0
Net income ($ mil.)	44.7%	79.7	99.0	272.0	339.0	349.0
Market value ($ mil.)	(3.1%)	11,478.2	12,905.8	11,035.2	11,142.6	10,129.5
Employees	50.6%	470	853	965	1,088	2,418

ANDERSEN CONSTRUCTION COMPANY

6712 N CUTTER CIR
PORTLAND, OR 972173933
Phone: 503-283-6712
Fax: –
Web: www.andersen-const.com

CEO: David L Andersen
CFO: Bill Eckhardt
HR: –
FYE: January 31
Type: Private

Andersen Construction Company focuses on commercial and industrial construction in the Western US. The group which introduced concrete tilt-up construction to the Pacific Northwest builds everything from parking structures to medical facilities manufacturing plants and industrial complexes. It also works on institutional projects for the government and education markets. Other projects include tenant improvements seismic upgrades and remediation construction. The company provides construction management (which accounts for 80% of its work) as well as general contracting and design/build delivery. It also offers startup and commissioning services. Chairman and CEO Andy Andersen founded the company in 1950.

	Annual Growth	01/10	01/11	01/14	01/15	01/16
Sales ($ mil.)	15.9%	–	279.0	329.5	392.6	582.3
Net income ($ mil.)	(1.4%)	–	1.0	0.5	0.2	1.0
Market value ($ mil.)	–	–	–	–	–	–
Employees	–	–	–	–	–	150

ANDERSEN CORPORATION

100 4th Ave. North
Bayport MN 55003-1096
Phone: 651-264-5150
Fax: 651-264-5107
Web: www.andersenwindows.com

CEO: Jay Lund
CFO: Philip E Donaldson
HR: –
FYE: December 31
Type: Private

Windows of opportunity abound for Andersen a maker of wood-clad windows and patio doors in North America. Andersen offers window designs from hinged bay and double-hung to skylight gliding and picture windows. Its Renewal by Andersen subsidiary provides start-to-finish window renewal services in more than 100 markets in the US. Anderson Storm Doors makes storm and screen doors. Through independent and company-owned distributorships (including its Andersen Logistics division) Andersen sells to homeowners architects builders designers and remodelers. The company which builds some 12 million doors and windows each year at more than 15 factories is owned by the Andersen family and company employees.

ANDERSON AND DUBOSE, INC.

5300 TOD AVE SW
WARREN, OH 444819767
Phone: 440-248-8800
Fax: –
Web: www.a-d.us

CEO: –
CFO: –
HR: –
FYE: December 27
Type: Private

You might say this company keeps the Big Mac big and the Happy Meals happy. Anderson-DuBose Pittsburgh is a leading wholesale distributor that supplies food and non-food items to McDonald's and Chipotle fast-food restaurants in Ohio Pennsylvania New York and West Virginia. It serves about 500 Golden Arches locations with frozen meat and fish dairy products and paper goods and packaging as well as toys for Happy Meals. One of the largest black-owned companies in the US Anderson-DuBose was started in 1991 by Warren Anderson and Stephen DuBose who purchased control of a McDonald's distributorship from Martin-Brower. Anderson became sole owner in 1993 when he bought out his partner's stake in the business.

	Annual Growth	12/14	12/15	12/16	12/18	12/19
Sales ($ mil.)	2.3%	–	546.8	518.2	577.7	599.0
Net income ($ mil.)	16.1%	–	2.4	2.1	3.9	4.4
Market value ($ mil.)	–	–	–	–	–	–
Employees	–	–	–	–	–	100

ANDERSON KILL & OLICK P.C.

1251 Avenue of the Americas
New York NY 10020
Phone: 212-278-1000
Fax: 212-278-1733
Web: www.andersonkill.com

CEO: Robert M Horkovich
CFO: –
HR: –
FYE: December 31
Type: Private - Partnershi

Law firm Anderson Kill & Olick is well known for representing policyholders in recovery claims against insurance companies. Other practice areas include anti-counterfeiting bankruptcy business litigation financial services employment and labor law and real estate and construction. The firm represents businesses governmental entities nonprofits and personal estates. Its 100 attorneys practice from offices in Greenwich Connecticut; Newark New Jersey; New York; Philadelphia; Ventura California; and Washington DC. Anderson Kill was founded in 1969.

ANDERSON TRUCKING SERVICE INC.

725 Opportunity Dr.
St. Cloud MN 56301
Phone: 320-255-7400
Fax: 320-255-7438
Web: www.atsinc.com

CEO: Rollie Anderson
CFO: Paul Pfeiffer
HR: –
FYE: December 31
Type: Private

Anderson Trucking Service (ATS) moves cargo that ranges from cranes to chairs. The company's ATS Specialized unit transports heavy equipment and other cargo requiring flatbed trailers; an offshoot concentrates on wind energy equipment. Its ATS Van Solutions unit offers dry van truckload transportation and other operations transport new furniture for manufacturers. Overall the company's trucking units operate a fleet of some 2400 tractors and 8600 trailers. ATS also offers logistics services including international freight forwarding. Harold Anderson established the family-owned business in 1955.

ANDERSONS INC   NMS: ANDE

1947 Briarfield Boulevard
Maumee, OH 43537
Phone: 419 893-5050
Fax: –
Web: www.andersonsinc.com

CEO: Patrick Bowe
CFO: Brian Valentine
HR: –
FYE: December 31
Type: Public

Agribusiness giant The Andersons operates in a variety of areas including trade ethanol and plant nutrients and rail. It generates some three-quarters of its sales from trading ? primarily corn soybeans and wheat ? via grain elevators located in the US and Canada. The company purchases and sells ethanol offers facility operations risk management and ethanol and corn oil marketing services to the ethanol plants it invests in and operates. The Anderson's Plant Nutrient Group makes and sells fertilizers crop protection chemicals and related products and the company leases repairs and sells railcars locomotives and barges through its Rail Group. It operates primarily in the US where over 75% of the company's total revenue is generated from.

	Annual Growth	12/16	12/17	12/18	12/19	12/20
Sales ($ mil.)	20.3%	3,924.8	3,686.3	3,045.4	8,170.2	8,208.4
Net income ($ mil.)	(9.7%)	11.6	42.5	41.5	18.3	7.7
Market value ($ mil.)	(13.9%)	1,499.9	1,045.2	1,002.9	848.2	822.4
Employees	(5.8%)	2,998	1,843	1,858	2,320	2,359

ANDREA ELECTRONICS CORP.   NBB: ANDR

620 Johnson Avenue, Suite 1B
Bohemia, NY 11716
Phone: 631 719-1800
Fax: –

CEO: Douglas Andrea
CFO: Corisa Guiffre
HR: –
FYE: December 31
Type: Public

Andrea Electronics wants to make a big noise with its Anti-Noise technology. The company's Anti-Noise products include software that increases voice clarity and reduces background noise plus headsets that enhance audio in high-noise environments. Andrea Electronics also offers voice recognition products for voice-activated computing applications such as word processing. The company designs its products for audio- and videoconferencing call centers in-vehicle communications and personal computing. Andrea Electronics sells directly and through distributors software publishers ISPs and other resellers. The company gets most of its sales in the US.

	Annual Growth	12/16	12/17	12/18	12/19	12/20
Sales ($ mil.)	(21.6%)	3.6	6.9	1.5	1.9	1.4
Net income ($ mil.)	–	(1.3)	(1.2)	(0.9)	(0.5)	(0.8)
Market value ($ mil.)	(15.0%)	4.8	3.4	3.9	1.4	2.5
Employees	0.0%	9	9	8	9	9

ANGELICA CORPORATION

1105 Lakewood Pkwy. Ste. 210
Alpharetta GA 30009
Phone: 678-823-4100
Fax: 678-823-4165
Web: www.angelica.com

CEO: Cary B Wood
CFO: –
HR: –
FYE: January 31
Type: Private

Hospitals don't have to move heaven and earth to get clean sheets — Angelica will do it for them. The firm provides laundry services and rents linens to more than 4200 health care providers including dentists medical clinics hospitals and nursing homes. It rents and cleans scrubs bed sheets towels gowns and surgical linens. Angelica also provides mops mats sterile surgical packs and on-site linen room management. The firm operates about 30 laundry service centers across the US. Angelica traces its roots back to 1878 when it was established as a uniform manufacturer. It is owned by private equity firm Trilantic Capital Partners.

ANGELO IAFRATE CONSTRUCTION COMPANY

26300 SHERWOOD AVE
WARREN, MI 480914168
Phone: 586-756-1070
Fax: –
Web: www.iafrate.com

CEO: –
CFO: –
HR: –
FYE: December 31
Type: Private

Angelo Iafrate Construction Company spends most of its time on the road. The company specializes in highway and road construction and is qualified by the US Department of Transportation to work in more than half of the states across the country. Angelo Iafrate provides preconstruction construction and project management services for both the public and private sector. The heavy construction contractor targets clients in the commercial transportation utilities manufacturing health care and education industries. Angelo Iafrate also sells used equipment. The company is owned and managed by the Iafrate family.

	Annual Growth	12/10	12/11	12/12	12/13	12/14
Sales ($ mil.)	167.1%	–	–	–	34.4	92.0
Net income ($ mil.)	372.9%	–	–	–	0.7	3.1
Market value ($ mil.)	–	–	–	–	–	–
Employees	–	–	–	–	–	350

ANGELO STATE UNIVERSITY

2601 W AVENUE N
SAN ANGELO, TX 769095099
Phone: 325-942-2555
Fax: –
Web: www.angelo.edu

CEO: –
CFO: Angela Wright
HR: –
FYE: August 31
Type: Private

Out in the West Texas town of San Angelo (a community of 100000) more than 6000 students attend Angelo State University (ASU). The school offers approximately 45 undergraduate programs of study at its College of Liberal and Fine Arts College of Education College of Business and College of Sciences. ASU also has a School of Graduate Studies that offers nearly 30 master's degree programs. It also offers one doctorate program. With more than 330 faculty members its student-teacher ratio is 20:1. ASU is part of the Texas Tech University System.

	Annual Growth	08/10	08/11	08/12	08/13	08/14
Sales ($ mil.)	0.2%	–	60.6	64.0	64.7	60.9
Net income ($ mil.)	164.8%	–	–	0.7	12.1	5.2
Market value ($ mil.)	–	–	–	–	–	–
Employees	–	–	–	–	–	550

ANGELS BASEBALL LP

2000 Gene Autry Way
Anaheim CA 92806
Phone: 714-940-2000
Fax: 714-940-2001
Web: www.angelsbaseball.com

CEO: –
CFO: –
HR: –
FYE: December 31
Type: Private

Los Angeles' other baseball team actually resides in Anaheim California. Angels Baseball owns and operates the Los Angeles Angels of Anaheim professional baseball franchise. The team originally owned by cowboy actor Gene Autry joined Major League Baseball as an expansion franchise in 1960 and has boasted such Hall of Fame talent as Rod Carew and Nolan Ryan. However Angels fans had to wait until 2002 for the team to win its first American League pennant and World Series title. Phoenix businessman Arturo Moreno who has owned the team since 2003 was the first Hispanic to own a major sports franchise in the US.

ANGIE'S LIST INC.   NMS: ANGI

1030 E. Washington Street
Indianapolis, IN 46202
Phone: 888 888-5478
Fax: –
Web: www.angieslist.com

CEO: Christopher Terrill
CFO: –
HR: –
FYE: December 31
Type: Public

Better not get on Angie's bad side — she's got a list. Angie's List provides consumer ratings on companies in the service industry. Consumers rate local providers in more than 550 business service categories including roofing plumbing home remodeling and doctors. The company has amassed a collection of some 2.2 million reviews receiving about 40000 new reviews each month from consumers in 175 markets across the US. Revenues come from ads and subscription fees. Angie's List has more than 1 million paying members who access ratings and reviews via AngiesList.com and Angie's List Magazine. The firm was founded by Angie Hicks and Bill Oesterle in 1995. It filed to go public in 2011.

	Annual Growth	12/11	12/12	12/13	12/14	12/15
Sales ($ mil.)	39.8%	90.0	155.8	245.6	315.0	344.1
Net income ($ mil.)	–	–	(49.0)	(52.9)	(33.0)	(12.1)	10.2
Market value ($ mil.)	(12.7%)	943.5	702.7	887.9	365.1	548.0
Employees	49.2%	349	1,158	1,637	1,852	1,730

ANGIODYNAMICS INC   NMS: ANGO

14 Plaza Drive
Latham, NY 12110
Phone: 518 795-1400
Fax: –
Web: www.angiodynamics.com

CEO: James Clemmer
CFO: Stephen Trowbridge
HR: Marna Bronfenmoore
FYE: May 31
Type: Public

AngioDynamics Inc. designs manufactures and sells a wide range of medical surgical and diagnostic devices used by professional healthcare providers for the treatment of peripheral vascular disease vascular access and for use in oncology and surgical settings. Its devices are generally used in minimally invasive image-guided procedures. Products include laser systems that ablate varicose veins angiographic catheters that deliver drugs and contrast agents for imaging dialysis catheters for those with renal failure abscess drainage devices and radiofrequency ablation devices that help destroy tumors. The US market accounts about 80% of total revenue. AngioDynamics was founded in 1988.

	Annual Growth	05/17	05/18	05/19	05/20	05/21
Sales ($ mil.)	(4.5%)	349.6	344.3	270.6	264.2	291.0
Net income ($ mil.)	–	5.0	16.3	61.3	(166.8)	(31.5)
Market value ($ mil.)	11.3%	581.3	810.7	724.4	393.6	891.3
Employees	(10.6%)	1,250	1,145	750	800	800

ANGSTROM GRAPHICS INC.

2025 McKinley St.
Hollywood FL 33020
Phone: 954-920-7300
Fax: 212-613-9565
Web: www.redcats.com

CEO: Wayne R Angstrom
CFO: Rachel Malakoff
HR: –
FYE: July 31
Type: Private

Angstrom Graphics loves it when its customers get graphic. The company provides prepress printing finishing and fulfillment services for catalogs magazines and newspapers. It also prints annual reports brochures and marketing materials. Angstrom Graphics also offers graphic arts and digital photography production services including redesigns copywriting and image retouching. The firm operates facilities in Ohio and Florida. In 2009 Angstrom Graphics formerly named St Ives US Division was sold by European printing group St Ives through a management-led buyout.

ANHEUSER-BUSCH COMPANIES INC.

1 Busch Place
St. Louis MO 63118-1852
Phone: 314-577-2000
Fax: 314-577-2900
Web: www.anheuser-busch.com

CEO: Carlos Brito
CFO: W Randolph Baker
HR: –
FYE: December 31
Type: Subsidiary

Anheuser-Busch (A-B) has brewed up a billion-dollar business with its Buds. The company is best known for brewing Budweiser one of the world's largest-selling beers by volume. Other A-B labels include Bud Light Busch Michelob O'Doul's and Kirin under license. As part of its business the company also owns a 50% stake in Mexico's GRUPO MODELO maker of beers under the Corona and Negra Modelo names. Besides beer A-B produces distilled beverages energy drinks and non-alcoholic malt beverages. The company has operated as a subsidiary of Anheuser-Busch InBev (AB InBev) the world's largest beer maker since the Belgium brewer acquired A-B for $52 billion in 2008.

ANI PHARMACEUTICALS INC
NMS: ANIP

210 Main Street West
Baudette, MN 56623
Phone: 218 634-3500
Fax: -
Web: www.anipharmaceuticals.com

CEO: Nikhil Lalwani
CFO: Stephen Carey
HR: -
FYE: December 31
Type: Public

ANI Pharmaceuticals wants to stabilize hormonal ups and downs. The firm is an integrated specialty pharmaceutical company focused on developing and manufacturing branded and generic prescription pharmaceuticals. It focuses on areas including anti-cancers hormones and steroids and complex formulations. It produces oral solid dose products as well as semi-solids liquids and topicals potent products and controlled substances. Products have include menopause treatment Esterified Estrogen with Methyltestosterone (EEMT); Hydrocortisone Enema (for ulcerative colitis) Methazolamide (for ocular conditions) and Opium Tincture (diarrhea). ANI also performs contract manufacturing. The US market accounts the largest for more than 95% of total sales.

	Annual Growth	12/16	12/17	12/18	12/19	12/20
Sales ($ mil.)	12.8%	128.6	176.8	201.6	206.5	208.5
Net income ($ mil.)	-	3.9	(1.1)	15.5	6.1	(22.5)
Market value ($ mil.)	(16.8%)	749.6	796.9	556.7	762.6	359.1
Employees	26.7%	143	173	299	338	369

ANIKA THERAPEUTICS INC.
NMS: ANIK

32 Wiggins Avenue
Bedford, MA 01730
Phone: 781 457-9000
Fax: -
Web: www.anika.com

CEO: Cheryl Blanchard
CFO: Michael Levitz
HR: Thomas Finnerty
FYE: December 31
Type: Public

Founded in 1992 Anika Therapeutics Inc. is a global joint preservation company that creates and delivers meaningful advancements in early intervention orthopedic care. Anika Therapeutics uses hyaluronic acid (HA) a natural polymer extracted from rooster combs and other sources to make products that treat bone cartilage and soft tissue. Anika's Orthovisc treats osteoarthritis of the knee and other joints and is available in the US and overseas. The company also makes and sells ophthalmic products use in surgical procedures such as cataract extraction and intraocular lens implantation. Other items include surgical anti-adhesive products veterinary osteoarthritis therapies and dermatology products. The US accounts for about 80% of sales.

	Annual Growth	12/16	12/17	12/18	12/19	12/20
Sales ($ mil.)	6.0%	103.4	113.4	105.6	114.6	130.5
Net income ($ mil.)	-	32.5	31.8	18.7	27.2	(24.0)
Market value ($ mil.)	(1.9%)	701.5	772.5	481.6	743.0	648.5
Employees	22.8%	122	123	133	154	277

ANIXA BIOSCIENCES INC
NAS: ANIX

3150 Almaden Expressway, Suite 250
San Jose, CA 95118
Phone: 408 708-9808
Fax: -

CEO: Amit Kumar
CFO: Michael Catelani
HR: -
FYE: October 31
Type: Public

CopyTele has an original take on display and communications technology. The company licenses technology used in thin low-voltage phosphor displays. A licensing agreement with Videocon Industries allows the India-based consumer electronics company to develop televisions utilizing CopyTele's technology. CopyTele also provides secure communications products. Its stand-alone devices provide encryption for secure voice fax and data communication. Boeing the exclusive distributor for many of the company's security products uses CopyTele's encryption products on the Thuraya satellite communications network which is employed by the US military.

	Annual Growth	10/15	10/16	10/17	10/18	10/19
Sales ($ mil.)	(59.5%)	9.3	0.3	0.4	1.1	0.3
Net income ($ mil.)	-	(1.4)	(5.0)	(5.0)	(14.0)	(11.6)
Market value ($ mil.)	1.0%	75.6	129.1	41.7	82.3	78.7
Employees	7.5%	6	7	7	8	8

ANN & ROBERT H. LURIE CHILDREN'S HOSPITAL OF CHICAGO

225 E CHICAGO AVE
CHICAGO, IL 606112991
Phone: 312-227-4000
Fax: -
Web: www.luriechildrens.org

CEO: Thomas Shanley
CFO: Paula Noble
HR: -
FYE: August 31
Type: Private

When it comes to caring for kids Ann & Robert H. Lurie Children's Hospital of Chicago has the Windy City covered. Founded in 1882 the not-for-profit hospital provides a full range of pediatric services with acute and specialty care. Lurie Children's provides services through its main hospital campus with about 300 beds and outpatient centers in Chicago's Lincoln Park neighborhood and through more than a dozen suburban outpatient centers and outreach partner locations in the greater Chicago area. A leader in pediatric research the hospital operates the Children's Hospital of Chicago Research Center and is the pediatric teaching facility of Northwestern University's Feinberg School of Medicine.

	Annual Growth	08/07	08/08	08/09	08/10	08/13
Sales ($ mil.)	6.8%	-	-	534.0	599.3	694.2
Net income ($ mil.)	-	-	-	(5.2)	53.0	28.8
Market value ($ mil.)	-	-	-	-	-	-
Employees	-	-	-	-	-	2,800

ANN INC
NYS: ANN

7 Times Square
New York, NY 10036
Phone: 212 541-3300
Fax: -
Web: www.anntaylor.com

CEO: Katherine L Krill
CFO: Michael J Nicholson
HR: -
FYE: February 01
Type: Public

ANN: a name favored by royalty and commoners as well as a company recognized for its aspirational luxury and feminine wear-to-work style. The national retailer specializes in women's clothing shoes and accessories designed and sold exclusively under its Ann Taylor and LOFT monikers. The Ann Taylor brand targets fashion-conscious career women through about 375 namesake stores (about 110 of which are "Factory" outlets) while the LOFT brand offers moderate-to-more priced casual apparel through some 650 stores (110 of which are outlets). ANN also moves merchandise for both brands through its fast-growing online business. ANN has favored its own name since changing from AnnTaylor Stores Corporation in 2011.

	Annual Growth	01/10	01/11	01/12*	02/13	02/14
Sales ($ mil.)	8.1%	1,828.5	1,980.2	2,212.5	2,375.5	2,493.5
Net income ($ mil.)	-	(18.2)	73.4	86.6	102.6	102.4
Market value ($ mil.)	26.7%	580.5	1,009.9	1,129.1	1,426.8	1,494.7
Employees	1.3%	18,800	19,400	19,900	19,600	19,800

*Fiscal year change

ANNALY CAPITAL MANAGEMENT INC
NYS: NLY

1211 Avenue of the Americas
New York, NY 10036
Phone: 212 696-0100
Fax: 212 696-9809
Web: www.annaly.com

CEO: David Finkelstein
CFO: Serena Wolfe
HR: -
FYE: December 31
Type: Public

A real estate investment trust (REIT) Annaly Capital Management invests in and finances residential and commercial assets. It primarily manages a portfolio of mortgage-backed securities including mortgage pass-through certificates collateralized mortgage obligations issued or guaranteed by the likes of Freddie Mac Fannie Mae and Ginnie Mae and backed by single-family residential mortgages. The REIT has four investment groups ? Annaly Agency Annaly Residential Credit Annaly Real Estate and Annaly Middle Market Lending Group. Founded in 1996 as Annaly Mortgage Management Inc. and became public in 1997.

	Annual Growth	12/17	12/18	12/19	12/20	12/21
Assets ($ mil.)	(6.8%)	101,760.1	105,787.5	130,295.1	88,455.1	76,764.1
Net income ($ mil.)	11.1%	1,569.6	54.4	(2,162.9)	(891.2)	2,389.9
Market value ($ mil.)	(9.9%)	17,356.3	14,334.6	13,750.7	12,334.8	11,415.1
Employees	3.0%	152	170	175	180	171

ANNIE'S INC   NYS: BNNY

1610 Fifth Street
Berkeley, CA 94710
Phone: 510 558-7500
Fax: -
Web: www.annies.com

CEO: John Foraker
CFO: Kelly J Kennedy
HR: -
FYE: March 31
Type: Public

While doing what it loves Annie's also wouldn't mind taking a bite out of Kraft's business. An organic and natural food producer Annie's makes about 125 products consisting of pastas cereals dressings condiments and snacks through its Annie's Homegrown and Annie's Naturals units. Annie's Homegrown banner includes boxed organic macaroni and cheese breakfast cereals (Cinna Bunnies) fruit snacks (Bunny Fruit) organic granola bars and organic ready meals. Under the Annie's Naturals name the company offers organic and natural salad dressings condiments (marinades sauces mustard ketchup) and olive oil. Annie's which began trading in 2012 is 63%-owned by private equity firm Solera Capital.

	Annual Growth	03/09	03/10	03/11	03/12	03/13
Sales ($ mil.)	16.1%	93.6	96.0	117.6	141.3	170.0
Net income ($ mil.)	-	(1.0)	6.0	20.2	9.6	11.6
Market value ($ mil.)	9.8%	-	-	-	587.0	644.6
Employees	15.1%	-	-	86	93	114

ANOMATIC CORPORATION

1650 Tamarack Rd.
Newark OH 43055
Phone: 740-522-2203
Fax: 740-522-3339
Web: www.anomatic.com

CEO: William B Rusch
CFO: -
HR: Dixie N Moore
FYE: December 31
Type: Private

Anomatic has made anodizing aluminum into an art form. The company anodizes stamps and packages small aluminum parts which are made into such products as cosmetics containers and packaging hand tools jewelry musical instruments and plumbing fittings. Its Anomatic anodizing process (by which an oxide coating is formed on aluminum to provide a corrosive resistant and decorative finish) was the first automated belt conveyor system built for high speed high volume anodizing of small aluminum parts. Anomatic operates eight anodizing lines which run two shifts per day and generate a monthly production of 80 million anodized components. Customers include Estee Lauder Mary Kay and Revlon.

ANR PIPELINE COMPANY

700 LOUISIANA ST STE 700 # 700
HOUSTON, TX 770022873
Phone: 832-320-2000
Fax: -
Web: www.anrpl.com

CEO: Lee Hobbs
CFO: -
HR: -
FYE: December 31
Type: Private

ANR Pipeline keeps natural gas in line a pipeline that is. The company operates one of the largest interstate natural gas pipeline systems in the US. A subsidiary of TransCanada Corp. ANR controls about 10350 miles of pipeline and delivers more than 1 trillion cu. ft. of natural gas per year. The company primarily serves customers in the Midwest but through its network is capable of connecting to all major gas basins in North America. In tandem with its ANR Storage and Blue Lake Gas Storage subsidiaries ANR Pipeline also provides natural gas storage services and has ownership interests in more than 250 billion cu. ft. of underground natural gas storage capacity.

	Annual Growth	12/04	12/05	12/06	12/16	12/17
Sales ($ mil.)	2.7%	-	548.0	540.0	686.3	758.2
Net income ($ mil.)	(0.4%)	-	147.0	152.0	54.7	139.9
Market value ($ mil.)	-	-	-	-	-	-
Employees	-	-	-	-	-	1,000

ANSCHUTZ COMPANY

555 17th St. Ste. 2400
Denver CO 80202
Phone: 303-298-1000
Fax: 303-298-8881

CEO: Phillip Anschutz
CFO: -
HR: -
FYE: December 31
Type: Private

Denver multibillionaire Philip Anschutz is a man of varied interests. His holding company includes an eclectic stable of entertainment media and sports businesses in addition to telecom and energy development. Through Anschutz Entertainment Group (AEG) Anschutz promotes concerts and other events and owns 120 sports and entertainment centers such as Staples Center and Best Buy Theater. It also owns soccer and other pro teams in the US and Europe (including the NHL's Los Angeles Kings and a stake in the Los Angeles Lakers). Other Anschutz holdings include movie chain Regal Entertainment Group the family-oriented Anschutz Film Group and the San Francisco Examiner newspaper.

ANSEN CORPORATION

100 Chimney Point Dr.
Ogdensburg NY 13669-2289
Phone: 315-393-3573
Fax: 315-393-7638
Web: www.ansencorp.com

CEO: James Kingman
CFO: -
HR: -
FYE: March 31
Type: Private

Ansen offers electronics design and manufacturing services to makers of microelectronics systems and components. Ansen provides services such as printed circuit board surface mounting and assembly from manufacturing facilities in China Hong Kong and the US. It also offers design prototyping and engineering services as well as packaging distribution warranty and support. The company's products are used in medical instruments computers telecommunications gear and industrial controls. Ansen was taken private by management in 2003 and then combined with fellow EMS firm InnerStep in 2004. Ansen divested two US plants in 2005 in favor of expanding Chinese operations.

ANSYS INC.   NMS: ANSS

2600 ANSYS Drive
Canonsburg, PA 15317
Phone: 844 462-6797
Fax: -
Web: www.ansys.com

CEO: Ajei Gopal
CFO: Nicole Anasenes
HR: -
FYE: December 31
Type: Public

ANSYS develops and globally markets engineering simulation software and services widely used by engineers designers researchers and student across a broad spectrum of industries and academia including aerospace and defense automotive electronics semiconductors energy consumer products healthcare and more. The company focus on development and flexible solutions that enable users to analyze and designs directly to desktop providing a common platform for fast efficient and cost-conscious product development from design concept to final-stage testing and validation. The company products consist of Platform Structures Fluids Electronics Semiconductors Embedded Software and more The company distribute simulation technologies through direct sales offices in strategic global locations and independent resellers and distributors (collectively channel partners).

	Annual Growth	12/17	12/18	12/19	12/20	12/21
Sales ($ mil.)	14.9%	1,095.3	1,293.6	1,515.9	1,681.3	1,906.7
Net income ($ mil.)	15.1%	259.3	419.4	451.3	433.9	454.6
Market value ($ mil.)	28.4%	12,852.0	12,447.1	22,415.0	31,679.3	34,929.1
Employees	15.2%	2,900	3,400	4,100	4,800	5,100

ANTARES PHARMA INC.   NAS: ATRS

100 Princeton South, Suite 300 — CEO: Robert Apple
Ewing, NJ 08628 — CFO: Fred Powell
Phone: 609 359-3020 — HR: Peter Graham
Fax: – — FYE: December 31
Web: www.antarespharma.com — Type: Public

Antares Pharma understands antagonism towards needles. The company develops needle-free systems for administering injectable drugs. Its Medi-Jector Vision system for instance injects a thin high-pressure stream of liquid eliminating the need for a needle. The Vision system is used primarily for the delivery of insulin and of human growth hormones (hGH) and Vibex disposable pen injectors carry epinephrine and other products. The products are available in the US and overseas. In addition to its needle-free systems the company develops other drug-delivery platforms including topical gels orally administered disintegrating tablets and mini-needle injection systems.

	Annual Growth	12/16	12/17	12/18	12/19	12/20
Sales ($ mil.)	30.1%	52.2	54.5	63.6	123.9	149.6
Net income ($ mil.)	–	(24.3)	(16.7)	(6.5)	(2.0)	56.2
Market value ($ mil.)	14.4%	388.7	332.0	453.8	784.1	665.7
Employees	13.9%	110	111	165	178	185

ANTERO RESOURCES CORP   NYS: AR

1615 Wynkoop Street — CEO: Paul Rady
Denver, CO 80202 — CFO: Michael Kennedy
Phone: 303 357-7310 — HR: –
Fax: – — FYE: December 31
Web: www.anteroresources.com — Type: Public

It shares a name with a Coloradan mountain but digs under the Appalachian crust. Antero Resources explores for and produces natural gas natural gas liquids (NGLs) and oil across more than 540000 acres in the Marcellus and Utica Shale formations in West Virginia and Ohio's Appalachian Basin. It reports proved reserves of almost 19 trillion cu. ft. of natural gas equivalent. The largest producer of NGLs in the US and among the largest natural gas producers the company maintains its daily output of 3.2 billion cu. ft. of natural gas equivalent by deploying horizontal drilling and advanced fracturing stimulation technologies. It focuses on unconventional reservoirs typically fractured shale formations. Subsidiary Antero Midstream owns operates and develops Antero's energy infrastructure.

	Annual Growth	12/17	12/18	12/19	12/20	12/21
Sales ($ mil.)	6.0%	3,655.6	4,139.6	4,408.7	3,491.7	4,619.4
Net income ($ mil.)	–	615.1	(397.5)	(340.1)	(1,267.9)	(186.9)
Market value ($ mil.)	(2.0%)	5,964.7	2,947.8	894.7	1,710.9	5,493.8
Employees	(3.3%)	593	623	547	522	519

ANTHELIO HEALTHCARE SOLUTIONS INC.

5400 LBJ Fwy. Ste. 200 — CEO: –
Dallas TX 75240 — CFO: –
Phone: 214-257-7000 — HR: –
Fax: 214-257-7042 — FYE: September 30
Web: www.antheliohealth.com — Type: Private

Anthelio (formerly PHNS) provides IT consulting and cloud computing services to hospitals private physicians and other health care businesses across the US. Its offerings provide assistance with admission/registration medical records management and electronic medical records implementations coding and transcription and revenue cycle management. The company also provides data center services network security protection disaster recovery and electronic data backup and recovery. Anthelio counts Symantec Healthland and Microsoft among its technology partners. Clients include Fairfield California-based NorthBay Healthcare and Plano Texas-based Legacy Hospital Partners.

ANTHEM INC   NYS: ANTM

220 Virginia Avenue — CEO: Gail Boudreaux
Indianapolis, IN 46204 — CFO: John Gallina
Phone: 800 331-1476 — HR: –
Fax: – — FYE: December 31
Web: www.antheminc.com — Type: Public

Health benefits provider Anthem through a number of subsidiaries provides health coverage to approximately 45 million members in the US. One of the nation's largest health insurers Anthem is a Blue Cross and Blue Shield Association licensee in more than a dozen states (where it operates as Anthem Empire and BCBS) and provides non-BCBS plans under the Unicare Amerigroup CareMore Simply Healthcare HealthSun HealthLink and other brands in numerous states across the US. Plans include PPO HMO POS indemnity and hybrid plans offered to employers individuals and Medicare and Medicaid recipients. Anthem also provides administrative services to self-insured groups as well as specialty insurance.

	Annual Growth	12/17	12/18	12/19	12/20	12/21
Sales ($ mil.)	11.4%	90,039.4	92,105.0	104,213.0	121,867.0	138,639.0
Net income ($ mil.)	12.3%	3,842.8	3,750.0	4,807.0	4,572.0	6,104.0
Market value ($ mil.)	19.8%	54,400.8	63,496.3	73,022.0	77,630.2	112,070.4
Employees	15.1%	56,000	63,900	70,600	83,400	98,200

ANTHERA PHARMACEUTICALS INC   NAS: ANTH

25801 Industrial Boulevard, Suite B — CEO: J. Craig Thompson
Hayward, CA 94545 — CFO: –
Phone: 510 856-5600 — HR: –
Fax: – — FYE: December 31
Web: www.anthera.com — Type: Public

Anthera Pharmaceuticals is involved in some very complicated sounding (not to mention hard to say) drug development. Its lead product varespladib methyl is in late stage clinical trials to treat acute coronary syndrome. Other candidates include A-623 to treat lupus and varespladib sodium to treat acute chest syndrome. Varespladib is designed to inhibit an enzyme called sPLA 2 that is implicated in a variety of acute inflammatory conditions such as cardiovascular disease sickle cell disease and coronary artery disease. Since its founding in 2004 Anthera's operations have consisted primarily of research and development activities. The company went public in early 2010 in an IPO worth about $37 million.

	Annual Growth	12/12	12/13	12/14	12/15	12/16
Sales ($ mil.)	(95.4%)	–	–	–	3.2	0.1
Net income ($ mil.)	–	(59.4)	(30.9)	(29.6)	(35.2)	(55.5)
Market value ($ mil.)	0.7%	3.6	17.6	9.1	26.7	3.7
Employees	9.4%	23	25	20	25	33

ANTHONY & SYLVAN POOLS CORPORATION

Mt. Vernon Sq. 6690 Beta Dr. Ste. 300 — CEO: Stuart D Neidus
Mayfield Village OH 44143 — CFO: Matthew Chiappa
Phone: 440-720-3301 — HR: –
Fax: 440-720-3303 — FYE: December 31
Web: www.anthonysylvan.com — Type: Private

Pooling resources is second nature to Anthony & Sylvan Pools Corporation. The company created through the 1996 union of industry leaders Anthony Pools and Sylvan Pools installs custom in-ground concrete swimming pools for private residences. The company has roots dating back to 1946 and has installed more than 360000 pools during its history. It operates a network of more than 35 company-owned locations consisting of sales and design centers pool and spa renovation centers and retail service centers that sell pool accessories such as chemicals heaters filters pumps and pool toys. The company is active in Texas Nevada and 10 East Coast states.

ANTHONY FOREST PRODUCTS COMPANY, LLC

309 N WASHINGTON AVE
EL DORADO, AR 717305614
Phone: 870-862-3414
Fax: –
Web: www.anthonyforest.com

CEO: Aubra H Anthony Jr
CFO: –
HR: Kim Winfrey
FYE: April 24
Type: Private

Anthony Forest Products first logged on well before the computer age. The company which began in 1916 obtains its timber from more than 90000 acres maintained according to Sustainable Forestry Initiative policy in Arkansas Louisiana and Texas. Anthony Forest Products then processes the timber into lumber and wood chips at mills located in the same three states. The company operates engineered wood laminating plants in Arkansas and Georgia and through a joint venture with Domtar it produces I-joists under the Power Joist name at a plant in Canada. Anthony's Power Log products are used for log-home construction. Anthony Forest Products is owned by the fourth generation of the Anthony family.

	Annual Growth	04/06	04/07	04/08	04/09	04/10
Sales ($ mil.)	–	–	–	(1,423.0)	91.4	98.3
Net income ($ mil.)	31511.1%	–	–	0.0	(5.8)	49.3
Market value ($ mil.)	–	–	–	–	–	–
Employees	–	–	–	–	–	470

ANTS SOFTWARE INC.

OTC: ANTS

71 Stevenson St. Ste. 400
San Francisco CA 94105
Phone: 650-931-0500
Fax: 650-931-0510
Web: www.ants.com

CEO: –
CFO: –
HR: –
FYE: December 31
Type: Public

ANTs software hopes to help your data march about in perfect order with no locking up. The company develops and markets software used to improve the performance of database-driven enterprise applications. ANTs' technology is designed to process and manipulate data with no database locking. Its primary product is its ANTs Compatibility Server which enables customers to move software applications from one company's database product to another. ANTs markets its products to information technology departments application developers and database architects. The company also provides professional services such as consulting training support implementation and maintenance.

ANVIL INTERNATIONAL INC.

110 Corporate Dr. Ste. 10
Portsmouth NH 03802-6822
Phone: 603-422-8000
Fax: 603-422-8033
Web: www.anvilint.com

CEO: Jason Hild
CFO: –
HR: –
FYE: December 31
Type: Subsidiary

In the hot red glow of industrial competition Anvil International hammers out its profits by making a comprehensive range of pipe fittings pipe hangers and related products and services. Anvil International (Anvil) manufactures cast iron fittings couplings pipe fittings pipe hangers seamless pipe nipples and valves. The company also provides basic design services such as fabrication drawings to extended design services for air handling units commercial piping oilfield piping and single-line routing systems. Anvil has 11 manufacturing facilities in the US and Canada. The company is a subsidiary of Atlanta-based Mueller Water Products which was spun off by Walter Industries in 2006.

ANWORTH MORTGAGE ASSET CORP.

NYS: ANH

1299 Ocean Avenue, 2nd Floor
Santa Monica, CA 90401
Phone: 310 255-4493
Fax: 310 434-0070
Web: www.anworth.com

CEO: Thomas E Capasse
CFO: –
HR: –
FYE: December 31
Type: Public

What's an Anworth? Depends on the mortgage market. An externally managed real estate investment trust (REIT) Anworth Mortgage invests in finances and manages residential mortgage-related assets primarily mortgage-backed securities (MBS) guaranteed by the US government or federally sponsored entities Fannie Mae Freddie Mac and Ginnie Mae. As a REIT the trust is exempt from paying federal income tax so long as it distributes dividends back to shareholders. Anworth were incorporated in Maryland in 1997.

	Annual Growth	12/15	12/16	12/17	12/18	12/19
Assets ($ mil.)	(7.1%)	6,636.3	5,395.8	5,765.5	5,037.9	4,938.6
Net income ($ mil.)	–	14.7	22.5	54.4	(6.5)	(55.4)
Market value ($ mil.)	(5.2%)	430.0	511.1	537.7	399.4	347.9
Employees	–	–	–	–	–	–

ANXEBUSINESS CORP.

2000 Town Center Ste. 2050
Southfield MI 48075
Phone: 248-263-3400
Fax: 248-356-9380
Web: www.anx.com

CEO: Rich Stanbaugh
CFO: Mike Mahoney
HR: Lisa Moore
FYE: January 31
Type: Private

ANXeBusiness provides secure business-to-business network management and security services to companies worldwide. The company specializes in building and maintaining virtual private networks (VPN) for customers who want to outsource their data and security management operations in order to cut costs. It also implements networking software and offers managed services related to data translation business-to-business transactions and e-commerce systems under the ANXVelocity brand. ANXeBusiness is a subsidiary of equity investor One Equity Partners.

AOL ADVERTISING INC.

1020 Hull St. Ivory Bldg.
Baltimore MD 21230
Phone: 410-244-1370
Fax: 410-244-1699
Web: advertising.aol.com

CEO: Scott Ferber
CFO: Don Neff
HR: –
FYE: December 31
Type: Subsidiary

AOL Advertising (formerly Platform-A) offers a host of digital marketing and advertising services including display video mobile contextual and search marketing. Its sponsored listing network allows advertisers to target an ad's placement whether it be by site section or page. Its flagship product ADTECH is an ad serving platform enabling users to manage campaigns across various mediums including display video and mobile. As a whole AOL Advertising reaches more than 180 million consumers and its Advertising.com network is comprised of 6000 sites. Operating as a wholly owned subsidiary of AOL the company operates from a dozen offices in the US the UK and Japan.

AOL INC.   NYS: AOL

770 Broadway   CEO: Jim Lanzone
New York, NY 10003   CFO: Karen Dykstra
Phone: 212 652-6400   HR: –
Fax: –   FYE: December 31
Web: www.corp.aol.com   Type: Public

Though it's no longer a part of Time Warner AOL is still serving America online. The Web portal serves users with an array of content and communication tools including sites for news (TheHuffingtonPost.com) maps (MapQuest) entertainment (Moviephone) local information (Patch) and technology (Engadget and TechCrunch). AOL primarily earns revenues through display search and contextual advertising (AOL Advertising) sales. It sells ads on AOL Properties as well as its Third Party Network (third-party sites). Search is provided through a deal with Google. AOL still offers dial-up Internet access to 3.3 million subscribers in the US. Time Warner spun off AOL to shareholders at the tail end of 2009.

	Annual Growth	12/09	12/10	12/11	12/12	12/13
Sales ($ mil.)	(8.1%)	3,257.4	2,416.7	2,202.1	2,191.7	2,319.9
Net income ($ mil.)	(21.9%)	248.8	(782.5)	13.1	1,048.4	92.4
Market value ($ mil.)	19.0%	1,843.8	1,877.8	1,195.9	2,345.1	3,692.3
Employees	(6.6%)	6,700	5,860	5,660	5,600	5,100

AON BENFIELD INC.

200 E. Randolph St.   CEO: –
Chicago IL 60601   CFO: –
Phone: 312-381-5300   HR: –
Fax: 312-381-0160   FYE: December 31
Web: www.aonbenfield.com   Type: Subsidiary

Aon Benfield is ensuring that those who are insuring won't go broke. The company is one of the world's leading reinsurance brokerages. It operates in more than 50 countries placing reinsurance coverage (protection for insurance companies against excessive losses on traditional insurance policies) as well as providing investment banking risk management consulting and catastrophe information forecasting services. The company's client services unit also offers accounting market security contract writing and claims processing services. Aon Benfield is a subsidiary of top global insurance broker Aon Corporation.

AOXING PHARMACEUTICAL CO INC   NBB: AOXG

1098 Foster City Blvd., Suite 106-810   CEO: –
Foster City, CA 94404   CFO: –
Phone: 646 367-1747   HR: –
Fax: –   FYE: June 30
Web: www.aoxingpharma.com   Type: Public

Narcotics are the name of the game for Aoxing Pharmaceutical which makes Naloxone and oxycodone products. Opioids are relatively new to China and the company has one of the only government-sanctioned manufacturing facilities; it is also the largest. Like many pharma companies Aoxing operates through many joint ventures and partnerships including a JV with pharmaceutical ingredient maker Johnson Matthey Plc and strategic alliances with American Oriental Bioengineering QRxPharma and Phoenix PharmaLabs. In addition to narcotics the company offers OTC pain relievers some based on traditional Chinese medicine. Aoxing which traces its roots to 1600 became a public company in 2006 through a reverse merger.

	Annual Growth	06/12	06/13	06/14	06/15	06/16
Sales ($ mil.)	41.2%	8.1	10.8	12.7	25.5	32.3
Net income ($ mil.)	–	(15.8)	(16.8)	(8.2)	5.5	2.1
Market value ($ mil.)	18.9%	24.8	16.4	24.4	133.4	49.5
Employees	(2.0%)	375	589	481	339	346

APA CORP   NMS: APA

One Post Oak Central, 2000 Post Oak Boulevard, Suite 100   CEO: John Christmann
Houston, TX 77056-4400   CFO: Stephen Riney
Phone: 713 296-6000   HR: –
Fax: –   FYE: December 31
Web: www.apachecorp.com   Type: Public

Apache Corporation an oil and gas exploration and production company has onshore and offshore operations in major oil patches around the world including in the US Egypt and the UK's North Sea oil fields. In the US it is active in the Permian Basin in West Texas and New Mexico including the Permian sub-basins: Midland Basin Central Basin Platform/Northwest Shelf and Delaware Basin. The company boasts worldwide estimated proved reserves of about 874 million barrels of oil equivalent. Most of the company's sales is generated in the US at about 45%. In 2021 Apache and APA announced completion of the previously announced holding company structure making APA the parent holding company of Apache. APA replaces Apache as the public company trading on the Nasdaq stock market under the ticker symbol "APA."

	Annual Growth	12/17	12/18	12/19	12/20	12/21
Sales ($ mil.)	5.4%	6,423.0	7,424.0	6,411.0	4,308.0	7,928.0
Net income ($ mil.)	(7.1%)	1,304.0	40.0	(3,553.0)	(4,860.0)	973.0
Market value ($ mil.)	(10.7%)	14,647.4	9,106.9	8,878.0	4,922.9	9,329.0
Employees	(9.5%)	3,356	3,420	3,163	2,272	2,253

APAC CUSTOMER SERVICES INC.

2201 Waukegan Rd. Ste. 300   CEO: –
Bannockburn IL 60015   CFO: –
Phone: 847-374-4980   HR: –
Fax: 847-374-4989   FYE: December 31
Web: www.apaccustomerservices.com   Type: Private

The telephone isn't the instrument of choice for APAC Customer Services anymore. The company provides outsourced customer-management and acquisition services using the telephone and the Internet. APAC's customer management services include customer retention help-line information direct mail response training recruitment and order entry services. Clients include companies in the communications government health care insurance retail technology utility and education sectors. Through its affiliation with sister company NCO Group the company operates through more than 100 facilities around the globe. In late 2011 APAC was acquired by investment firm One Equity Partners.

APACHE DESIGN SOLUTIONS INC.

2645 Zanker Rd.   CEO: Andrew T Yang
San Jose CA 95134   CFO: Emily Chang
Phone: 408-457-2000   HR: –
Fax: 408-428-9569   FYE: December 31
Web: www.apache-da.com   Type: Subsidiary

Apache Design Solutions makes sure new semiconductor designs have integrity — power and signal integrity that is. Its physical design and verification software packages enable engineers to design integrated circuits (ICs) that use less power ensure reliable power delivery and reduce signal interference or noise that can lead to poor performance in mobile electronics. Clients have included Intel Texas Instruments Toshiba STMicroelectronics and Samsung Electronics. The company gets more than half of its sales from customers in the US. Apache Design was acquired by rival ANSYS for $310 million in mid-2011 following an IPO filing earlier that year.

APARTMENT INVESTMENT & MANAGEMENT CO   NYS: AIV

4582 South Ulster Street, Suite 1450 — CEO: Wesley Powell
Denver, CO 80237 — CFO: H. Lynn Stanfield
Phone: 303 224-7900 — HR: –
Fax: 303 759-3226 — FYE: December 31
Web: www.aimco.com — Type: Public

Apartment Investment and Management Company (Aimco) is a self-administered and self-managed real estate investment trust (REIT) specializes in buying managing and redeveloping multi-family residential homes in top rental markets. Through a wholly-owned subsidiary Aimco is the general partner and directly is the special limited partner of the Aimco Operating Partnership. It conducts all of its business and owns all of its assets through the Aimco Operating Partnership. With more than 6340 apartment homes its portfolio of operating properties includes garden style mid-rise and high-rise apartment communities located in more than 10 states and the DC. In late 2020 Aimco completed the previously announced separation of its business into two separate and distinct publicly traded companies Aimco and AIR.

	Annual Growth	12/16	12/17	12/18	12/19	12/20
Sales ($ mil.)	(37.6%)	995.9	1,005.4	972.4	914.3	151.5
Net income ($ mil.)	–	430.4	315.8	666.2	474.1	(5.0)
Market value ($ mil.)	(41.6%)	6,773.7	6,514.4	6,539.7	7,697.7	786.9
Employees	(56.5%)	1,456	1,350	1,050	950	52

APELON INC.

100 Danbury Rd. — CEO: Stephen F Coady
Ridgefield CT 06877 — CFO: –
Phone: 203-431-2530 — HR: –
Fax: 203-431-2523 — FYE: December 31
Web: www.apelon.com — Type: Private

If it sometimes sounds like your doctor is speaking a foreign language Apelon is trying to make sure that she's at least speaking the same language as all the other doctors. Founded in 1999 Apelon provides software and services that health care providers use to create maintain and standardize medical terminology. The company offers medical terminology databases concept-based indexing and retrieval applications vocabulary information authoring applications and tools for integrating standard vocabularies into health care software products. Apelon's technologies have been used by the American Medical Association and the College of American Pathologists to create consistent terminology.

APEX GLOBAL BRANDS INC   NBB: APEX

5990 Sepulveda Boulevard — CEO: Henry Stupp
Sherman Oaks, CA 91411 — CFO: Steven Brink
Phone: 818 908-9868 — HR: –
Fax: – — FYE: February 01
Web: www.apexglobalbrands.com — Type: Public

Apex Global Brands (formerly Cherokee Global Brands) owns several trademarks including Cherokee Liz Lange Sideout Tony Hawk and Everyday California and licenses them to retailers and wholesalers of apparel footwear and accessories. The main idea behind Apex's business is that large retailers can source merchandise more efficiently than individual brand owners and that licensed brands can sell better for retailers than private labels. In addition to licensing its own brands Apex helps other brand owners gain licensing contracts. Target the company's largest customer accounts for more than half of Apex's revenue; other licensees include Tesco (in Europe) and TJ Maxx. The company changed its name from Cherokee Global Brands to Apex Global Brands in 2019 to reflect its expanded brand portfolio marketing and design services.

	Annual Growth	01/16	01/17*	02/18	02/19	02/20
Sales ($ mil.)	(11.7%)	34.7	40.6	29.4	24.4	21.0
Net income ($ mil.)	–	8.4	(7.9)	(56.0)	(12.3)	(11.5)
Market value ($ mil.)	(54.2%)	9.1	5.2	0.8	0.5	0.4
Employees	(7.7%)	51	123	60	43	37

*Fiscal year change

APEX TOOL GROUP LLC

14600 York Rd. Ste. A — CEO: James J Roberts
Sparks MD 21152 — CFO: –
Phone: 800-688-8949 — HR: –
Fax: 800-234-0472 — FYE: December 31
Web: www.apextoolgroup.com — Type: Joint Venture

Apex Tool Group is near the top of the heap among global producers of hand power and electronic tools. Geared at industrial commercial and do-it-yourself (DIY) markets the group manufactures and markets more than 30 leading tool brands including Crescent wrenches Jobox storage boxes Lufkin measuring tools and Weller soldering equipment. Directly and through subsidiaries Apex serves a range of markets including automotive aerospace electronics energy industrial and consumer retail. Apex Tool Group was formed in 2010 as a joint venture between Danaher and Cooper Industries (now Eaton). In February 2013 Danaher and Eaton sold Apex to global private investment firm Bain Capital for about $1.6 billion.

API GROUP, INC.

1100 OLD HIGHWAY 8 NW — CEO: Russell A Becker
NEW BRIGHTON, MN 551126447 — CFO: Thomas A Lydon
Phone: 651-636-4320 — HR: –
Fax: – — FYE: December 31
Web: www.apigroupinc.com — Type: Private

Holding company APi Group has a piece of the action in two main sectors: fire protection systems and industrial and specialty construction services. APi boasts about 40 subsidiaries which operate as independent companies across the US (nearly half of them in Minnesota) the UK and Canada. Services provided by the company's construction subsidiaries include HVAC and plumbing system installation; electrical industrial and mechanical contracting; industrial insulation; and garage door installation. Safety-focused units install a host of fire sprinkler detection security and alarm systems. The family-owned company was founded in 1926 by Reuben Anderson father of chairman Lee Anderson.

	Annual Growth	12/14	12/15	12/16	12/17	12/18
Sales ($ mil.)	15.1%	–	2,448.7	2,608.5	3,046.1	3,730.3
Net income ($ mil.)	5.0%	–	106.2	104.0	112.7	122.9
Market value ($ mil.)	–	–	–	–	–	–
Employees	–	–	–	–	–	4,237

API TECHNOLOGIES CORP   NAS: ATNY

4705 S. Apopka Vineland Rd., Suite 210 — CEO: Terrence Hahn
Orlando, FL 32819 — CFO: Mark McClanahan
Phone: 855 294-3800 — HR: –
Fax: – — FYE: November 30
Web: www.apitech.com — Type: Public

API Technologies is good at defense. Through various operating subsidiaries the company designs and manufactures highly-engineered electronic components and robotics as well as secure communications systems for military and aerospace applications. It develops products for missile electronic warfare flight control and range finder systems as well as devices that remotely manage critical IT and communications systems. With manufacturing facilities in North America and the UK API maintains a direct sales and marketing team and primarily sells to defense prime contractors and contract manufacturers. Roughly half of its revenues are generated by US Department of Defense subcontractors.

	Annual Growth	05/11*	11/11	11/12	11/13	11/14
Sales ($ mil.)	28.0%	108.3	144.3	280.8	244.3	226.9
Net income ($ mil.)	–	(26.2)	7.9	(148.7)	(7.2)	(18.9)
Market value ($ mil.)	(32.6%)	380.6	181.7	145.7	210.5	116.6
Employees	43.5%	630	2,140	2,234	1,975	1,862

*Fiscal year change

APOGEE ENTERPRISES INC
NMS: APOG

4400 West 78th Street, Suite 520
Minneapolis, MN 55435
Phone: 952 835-1874
Fax: –
Web: www.apog.com

CEO: Ty Silberhorn
CFO: Nisheet Gupta
HR: Audrey Hyland
FYE: February 27
Type: Public

Apogee Enterprises goes to great panes for its glass customers. The company designs and develops value-added glass products primarily for the US market. Its architectural products and services segment fabricates and installs glass that features specialized colors or coatings and aluminum framing systems for commercial institutional and institutional buildings. Customers include architects general contractors glazing subcontractors and building owners. Its large-scale optical (LSO) technologies segment manufactures anti-reflective UV-protected glass and acrylic under the Tru Vue brand for custom picture framing. Tru Vue products are sold through independent distributors and retail chains. Its Architectural framing systems segment accounts for nearly half of its revenue.

	Annual Growth	03/17	03/18	03/19*	02/20	02/21
Sales ($ mil.)	2.5%	1,114.5	1,326.2	1,402.6	1,387.4	1,230.8
Net income ($ mil.)	(34.9%)	85.8	79.5	45.7	61.9	15.4
Market value ($ mil.)	(10.5%)	1,496.3	1,130.6	926.5	776.3	961.7
Employees	2.6%	5,511	6,700	7,000	7,200	6,100

*Fiscal year change

APOLLO COMMERCIAL REAL ESTATE FINANCE INC.
NYS: ARI

c/o Apollo Global Management, LLC, 9 West 57th Street, 43rd Floor
New York, NY 10019
Phone: 212 515-3200
Fax: –
Web: www.apolloreit.com

CEO: Stuart Rothstein
CFO: Anastasia Mironova
HR: –
FYE: December 31
Type: Public

Apollo Commercial Real Estate Finance thinks the sky is the limit for commercial property loans. The New York-based mortgage real estate investment trust (REIT) originates buys and manages performing US commercial real estate loans subordinate loans commercial mortgage-backed securities (CMBS) and other commercial real estate debt investments. About 40% of its $2.6 billion investment portfolio is made up of commercial mortgage loans while another 35% is made up of subordinate loans. Formed in 2009 by Apollo Global Management the REIT is externally managed by ACREFI Management (an indirect subsidiary of Apollo Global Management).

	Annual Growth	12/13	12/14	12/15	12/16	12/17
Sales ($ mil.)	44.6%	77.5	123.3	192.2	264.4	338.5
Net income ($ mil.)	38.5%	52.5	82.7	103.3	157.9	193.0
Market value ($ mil.)	3.2%	1,740.7	1,752.5	1,845.7	1,780.4	1,976.4
Employees	–	–	–	–	–	–

APOLLO EDUCATION GROUP, INC.
NMS: APOL

4025 S. Riverpoint Parkway
Phoenix, AZ 85040
Phone: 480 966-5394
Fax: 480 929-7499
Web: www.apollo.edu

CEO: Gregory W Cappelli
CFO: Gregory J Iverson
HR: –
FYE: August 31
Type: Public

Apollo's creed could be that we all deserve the chance to advance. The for-profit Apollo Education Group provides educational programs through a number of subsidiaries including online stalwart University of Phoenix. The largest private university in the US the University of Phoenix accounts for about 85% of Apollo's sales and has an enrollment of more than 900000 students in degree programs ranging from associate's to doctoral. Other schools include Western International University (graduate and undergraduate courses) South Africa's MBA-grantor Milpark Education and UK-based BPP Holdings a provider of legal and financial professional training. Apollo is going private in a $1.1 billion transaction.

	Annual Growth	08/11	08/12	08/13	08/14	08/15
Sales ($ mil.)	(14.2%)	4,733.0	4,253.3	3,681.3	3,024.2	2,566.3
Net income ($ mil.)	(52.3%)	572.4	422.7	248.5	209.3	29.8
Market value ($ mil.)	(30.2%)	5,075.8	2,910.5	2,013.0	3,010.3	1,204.3
Employees	(12.0%)	56,743	49,992	44,000	39,000	34,000

APOLLO GLOBAL MANAGEMENT INC (NEW)
NYS: APO

9 West 57th Street, 43rd Floor
New York, NY 10019
Phone: 212 515-3200
Fax: –

CEO: Marc Rowan
CFO: Martin Kelly
HR: –
FYE: December 31
Type: Public

Apollo Global Management invests across a range of industries including consumer services financial services manufacturing and media on behalf of institutions and individuals. Apollo has some $455.5 billion of assets under management spread among credit private equity and real assets. It specializes in buying distressed businesses and believes that the long-term capital it manages also leaves it well-positioned during economic downturns. The firm has offices in the US Europe and Asia and is run by billionaire Leon Black Joshua Harris and Marc Rowan.

	Annual Growth	12/16	12/17	12/18	12/19	12/20
Sales ($ mil.)	4.5%	1,970.4	2,610.2	1,093.1	2,931.8	2,354.0
Net income ($ mil.)	(21.0%)	402.9	629.1	(10.4)	843.2	156.6
Market value ($ mil.)	26.1%	4,431.0	7,660.4	5,616.6	10,919.6	11,210.2
Employees	15.1%	986	1,047	1,143	1,421	1,729

APOLLO RESIDENTIAL MORTGAGE, INC.
NYS: AMTG

c/o Apollo Global Management, LLC, 9 West 57th Street, 43rd Floor
New York, NY 10019
Phone: 212 515-3200
Fax: –
Web: www.apolloresidentialmortgage.com

CEO: –
CFO: –
HR: –
FYE: December 31
Type: Public

The gods at Apollo Global Management are trying their luck with the residential mortgage market. The alternative asset manager formed Apollo Residential Mortgage to invest in residential mortgage-backed securities (MBS) and collateralized mortgage obligations (CMOs) guaranteed by Fannie Mae Freddie Mac and Ginnie Mae. A real estate investment trust the company is externally managed by ARM Manager an indirect subsidiary of Apollo Global Management. Formed in March 2011 Apollo Residential Mortgage went public later that year via a $205 million initial public offering (IPO).

	Annual Growth	12/10	12/11	12/12	12/13	12/14
Sales ($ mil.)	–	0.0	10.7	94.4	154.7	154.2
Net income ($ mil.)	–	0.0	4.5	172.8	(47.2)	96.1
Market value ($ mil.)	–	0.0	489.7	647.9	474.3	506.0
Employees	–	–	–	–	2	2

APPALACHIAN POWER CO.

1 Riverside Plaza
Columbus, OH 43215-2373
Phone: 614 716-1000
Fax: –
Web: www.aep.com

CEO: Nicholas Akins
CFO: Brian Tierney
HR: –
FYE: December 31
Type: Public

When they're not out enjoying the scenery Virginians and West Virginians count on Appalachian Power to keep indoor temperatures stable. A subsidiary of American Electric Power Appalachian Power serves about 960000 residential and business customers in southwestern Virginia and southern West Virginia and a small portion of northwestern Tennessee. The electric utility operates about 53300 miles of distribution and transmission lines. It operates coal-fired gas-fired and hydroelectric plants that give it about 8020 MW of capacity and it markets power to wholesale customers in the region.

	Annual Growth	12/16	12/17	12/18	12/19	12/20
Sales ($ mil.)	(1.8%)	3,001.2	2,934.2	2,967.5	2,924.7	2,796.2
Net income ($ mil.)	0.0%	369.1	331.3	367.8	306.3	369.7
Market value ($ mil.)	–	–	–	–	–	–
Employees	(2.7%)	1,845	1,817	1,797	1,699	1,652

APPALACHIAN REGIONAL HEALTHCARE, INC.

2260 EXECUTIVE DR
LEXINGTON, KY 405054808
Phone: 859-226-2440
Fax: -
Web: www.arh.org

CEO: Jerry W Haynes
CFO: Christopher Ellington
HR: -
FYE: June 30
Type: Private

Under-the-weather coal miners (and their daughters) can turn to Appalachian Regional Healthcare (ARH) for medical services. The not-for-profit health system serves residents of eastern Kentucky and southern West Virginia through a dozen hospitals with more than 1000 beds as well as dozens of clinics home health care agencies HomeCare Stores and retail pharmacies. Its largest hospital in Hazard Kentucky has 310 beds and features an inpatient psychiatric unit that serves as the state mental health facility. Several of the system's hospitals are Critical Access Hospitals a federal government designation for rural community hospitals that operate in medically underserved areas.

	Annual Growth	06/16	06/17	06/18	06/19	06/20
Sales ($ mil.)	9.7%	-	657.3	689.1	760.3	868.6
Net income ($ mil.)	(18.9%)	-	43.6	65.1	1.2	23.2
Market value ($ mil.)	-	-	-	-	-	-
Employees	-	-	-	-	-	4,520

APPALACHIAN STATE UNIVERSITY INC

438 ACADEMY ST RM 340
BOONE, NC 286080001
Phone: 828-262-2000
Fax: -
Web: www.appstate.edu

CEO: -
CFO: -
HR: -
FYE: June 30
Type: Private

Appalachian State University located in the heart of North Carolina's Blue Ridge Mountains has a student enrollment of about 17000 graduate and undergraduate students. The school has a student-teacher ratio of 17:1. Part of the University of North Carolina system the university offers roughly 140 degree programs and 1500 courses. Appalachian State was founded in 1899 as Watauga Academy by Blanford B. Dougherty and his brother Dauphin D. Dougherty to educate teachers for the mountains of northwestern North Carolina. It became known as Appalachian State Teachers College in 1929 and adopted its current name in 1967.

	Annual Growth	06/14	06/15	06/16	06/17	06/18
Sales ($ mil.)	4.3%	-	194.6	204.6	217.0	220.5
Net income ($ mil.)	100.3%	-	7.3	20.7	21.1	58.5
Market value ($ mil.)	-	-	-	-	-	-
Employees	-	-	-	-	-	3,390

APPLABS INC.

3170 Fairview Park Dr.
Falls Church VA 22042
Phone: 703-876-1000
Fax: +47-24-13-47-01
Web: www.birdstep.com

CEO: -
CFO: -
HR: -
FYE: December 31
Type: Private

AppLabs made its living by getting more than a little testy when it comes to computer software. The software testing firm provided a variety of software testing third-party validation and custom application development services for customers in such industries as information technology life sciences financial services and health care. AppLabs largely US customer base has included Avis. The vast majority of its employees worked at the company's offices in India. AppLabs was acquired by Computer Sciences Corporation (CSC) in 2011 for $171 million.

APPLE AMERICAN GROUP LLC

6200 OAK TREE BLVD # 250
INDEPENDENCE, OH 441316943
Phone: 216-525-2775
Fax: -
Web: www.appleamerican.com

CEO: -
CFO: -
HR: Jennifer Zika
FYE: December 27
Type: Private

This company must really enjoy casual dining in its neighborhood. Apple American Group is the largest franchisee of Applebee's with about 450 Applebee's Neighborhood Grill & Bar locations in about two dozen states. The #1 casual dining chain in the US Applebee's restaurants offer a full-service menu of beef chicken and seafood entrees along with a wide selection of appetizers. Apple American's restaurants are found from coast to coast with large concentrations in the Midwest (Ohio Indiana Pennsylvania) and on the West Coast (California Washington). Founded in 1998 by CEO Greg Flynn Apple American is controlled by private equity firm Weston Presidio Service.

	Annual Growth	12/05	12/06	12/07	12/08	12/09
Sales ($ mil.)	19.0%	-	-	339.0	431.1	479.8
Net income ($ mil.)	13783.8%	-	-	0.0	9.9	19.3
Market value ($ mil.)	-	-	-	-	-	-
Employees	-	-	-	-	-	5,500

APPLE FINANCIAL HOLDINGS INC.

122 E. 42nd St. 9th Fl.
New York NY 10168
Phone: 212-224-6400
Fax: 212-224-6589
Web: www.theapplebank.com

CEO: -
CFO: -
HR: -
FYE: December 31
Type: Private

Helping customers manage their money is at the core of Apple Financial Holdings. It is the holding company of Apple Bank for Savings which serves the New York metropolitan area from about 50 branches throughout New York City Long Island and Westchester County. Catering to retail and commercial customers the bank offers savings checking amd retirement accounts certificates of deposit and credit cards. Subsidiary ABS Associates markets life insurance products and fixed annuities to bank customers. Apple Bank traces its roots back to 1863.

APPLE INC

One Apple Park Way
Cupertino, CA 95014
Phone: 408 996-1010
Fax: 408 974-2483
Web: www.apple.com

NMS: AAPL
CEO: Tim Cook
CFO: Luca Maestri
HR: -
FYE: September 25
Type: Public

Apple designs manufactures and markets smartphones personal computers tablets wearables and accessories. The company also offers and sells a variety of related services. Apple products include its famous iPhone which is the company's line of smartphones bases on its iOS operating system. The company recently released its iPhone 13 product line last year. Other apple products also include Mac computers and iPad tablets Apple Music the Apple Watch and other wearable devices. Its' services include AppleCare Cloud Services Digital content and Payment services (Apple-Pay). Apple has entered entertainment with the Apple TV+ streaming service. More than 60% of Apple's revenue comes from outside the Americas.

	Annual Growth	09/17	09/18	09/19	09/20	09/21
Sales ($ mil.)	12.4%	229,234.0	265,595.0	260,174.0	274,515.0	365,817.0
Net income ($ mil.)	18.3%	48,351.0	59,531.0	55,256.0	57,411.0	94,680.0
Market value ($ mil.)	-	0.0	0.0	0.0	0.0	0.0
Employees	5.8%	123,000	132,000	137,000	147,000	154,000

APPLETON COATED LLC

569 Carter Ct.
Kimberly WI 54136
Phone: 920-968-3999
Fax: 920-968-3950
Web: www.appletoncoated.com

CEO: –
CFO: –
HR: –
FYE: December 31
Type: Subsidiary

Curious paper buyers may find that Appleton Coated has the ticket to Utopia. The company manufactures and markets coated free-sheet carbonless paper products under brands names including Altima Curious and Utopia. The company's products are used to make such goods as books magazines corporate annual reports and consumer product packaging. Its Curious products include metallic tactile and translucent sheets. Appleton Coated primarily serves printers and paper merchants and produces about 400000 tons of paper per year. The company is a subsidiary of France-based paper manufacturer ArjoWiggins which is in turn owned by Sequana Capital.

APPLIED CONCEPTS INC.

2609 Technology Dr.
Plano TX 75074-7467
Phone: 972-398-3750
Fax: 972-398-3751
Web: www.stalkerradar.com

CEO: Alan Mead
CFO: Darlene Stoneham
HR: Sandra Nietche
FYE: December 31
Type: Private

Your Speed Is: Below the posted speed limit we hope for your own safety. Applied Concepts (dba Stalker Radar) makes radar speed detectors and in-car video camera systems used largely by law enforcement agencies. The branded Stalker Radar Speed Sensor garners about 40% of the law enforcement market. The company also caters to sports and OEM testing applications making laser-based speed measuring devices and display equipment (including roadside signs that signal vehicle speed) and accessories (cables and power supplies). Stalker Radar products are marketed in the US and more than 100 countries. Co-founders CEO Alan Mead and president Stan Partee started the company in 1977; they are its majority owners.

APPLETON PAPERS INC.

825 E. Wisconsin Ave.
Appleton WI 54912-0359
Phone: 920-734-9841
Fax: 972-830-2619
Web: www.tm.com

CEO: –
CFO: –
HR: –
FYE: December 31
Type: Private

Paper is the apple of Appleton Papers' eye. The company manufactures specialty coated paper products including carbonless and security papers and thermal papers. It is the world's #1 producer of carbonless paper. Sold under the NCR Paper brand carbonless paper is used in multi-part business forms (such as invoices). Appleton makes security papers for government documents and coated products for point-of-sale displays. Its thermal papers are used in coupons gaming and transportation tickets and medical charts. The company's Encapsys segment makes microencapsulation (the process of inserting a microscopic wall around a substance) materials.

APPLIED DISCOVERY INC.

13427 NE 16th St. Ste. 200
Bellevue WA 98005-2307
Phone: 425-467-3000
Fax: 425-467-3010
Web: www.applieddiscovery.com

CEO: –
CFO: –
HR: –
FYE: December 31
Type: Subsidiary

This firm helps you find that information and apply it to the real world. Applied Discovery (aka LexisNexis Applied Discovery) provides electronic discovery services to law firms and corporate clients. A division of information provider LexisNexis the company offers document management services such as data collection legacy media restoration data processing and format conversion as well as document production and reporting. Applied Discovery has worked with such big name law firms as Akin Gump Clifford Chance and Morrison & Foerster. Its corporate clients have included 3M Honeywell and Pfizer. Founded in 1998 Applied Discovery was acquired in 2003 by LexisNexis a unit of Reed Elsevier Group.

APPLIED CARD SYSTEMS INC.

5401 BROKEN SOUND BLVD NW
BOCA RATON, FL 334873512
Phone: 561-995-8820
Fax: –
Web: www.appliedcard.com

CEO: Rocco A Abessinio
CFO: –
HR: –
FYE: December 31
Type: Private

Applied Card Systems is the servicing arm for Applied Bank a subprime consumer lender that issues secured and unsecured credit cards to customers with little or no credit history. Applied Card Systems processes payments from and provides customer service to more than 500000 holders of subprime Visa and MasterCard accounts. Applied Card Systems also services credit card accounts for third-party issuers primarily small and midsized financial institutions. Rocco Abessinio is the founder of both Applied Card Bank and Applied Card Systems which was formed in 1987. The company has offices in Florida and Pennsylvania.

APPLIED DNA SCIENCES INC   NAS: APDN

50 Health Sciences Drive
Stony Brook, NY 11790
Phone: 631 240-8800
Fax: –
Web: www.adnas.com

CEO: James Hayward
CFO: Beth Jantzen
HR: –
FYE: September 30
Type: Public

Counterfeiters needn't apply here. Applied DNA Sciences makes anti-counterfeiting and product authentication solutions. Its products are encoded with botanical DNA sequences that can distinguish counterfeits from the genuine article. The DNA markers (which hold the SigNature DNA brand) can be employed in ink glue holograms microchips and paint and are then used to tag documents currency event tickets and clothing labels. The company applies its SigNature markers to art and collectibles fine wine consumer products digital recording media pharmaceuticals and homeland security products.

	Annual Growth	12/05	12/06	12/07	12/08	12/09
Sales ($ mil.)	(24.3%)	–	–	282.4	251.2	162.0
Net income ($ mil.)	(61.1%)	–	–	144.0	145.4	21.8
Market value ($ mil.)	–	–	–	–	–	–
Employees	–	–	–	–	–	126

	Annual Growth	09/17	09/18	09/19	09/20	09/21
Sales ($ mil.)	17.4%	4.8	3.9	5.4	1.9	9.0
Net income ($ mil.)	–	(12.9)	(11.7)	(8.6)	(13.0)	(14.3)
Market value ($ mil.)	17.1%	21.5	11.2	1.7	57.9	40.4
Employees	15.4%	57	59	51	61	101

APPLIED ENERGETICS INC — NBB: AERG

2480 W. Ruthrauff Road, Suite 140 Q — CEO: Gregory J Quarles
Tucson, AZ 85705 — CFO: –
Phone: 520 628-7415 — HR: –
Fax: – — FYE: December 31
Web: www.appliedenergetics.com — Type: Public

Bullets?!! We don't need no stinkin' bullets — not with the Buck Rogers technology of Applied Energetics. The company is developing Laser Guided Energy and Laser Induced Plasma Channel directed-energy weapons for sale to the US government. In plain English? Laser-guided man-made lightning! Applied Energetics is developing more compact laser sources and field testing its technology for mobile platforms such as tanks Humvees and personnel carriers. Depending on the military situation the charge can be set to stun or kill people or to disable vehicles. Applied Energetics also develops technology for neutralizing car bombs and other explosives.

	Annual Growth	12/10	12/11	12/12	12/13	12/14
Sales ($ mil.)	(78.0%)	13.1	5.1	1.3	0.0	0.0
Net income ($ mil.)	–	–	(2.9)	(6.4)	(3.5)	(1.4)	(0.7)
Market value ($ mil.)	(75.1%)	78.1	6.7	2.6	0.9	0.3
Employees	(51.5%)	54	27	10	4	3

APPLIED INDUSTRIAL TECHNOLOGIES, INC. — NYS: AIT

One Applied Plaza — CEO: Neil Schrimsher
Cleveland, OH 44115 — CFO: David Wells
Phone: 216 426-4000 — HR: Mary Lekan
Fax: – — FYE: June 30
Web: www.applied.com — Type: Public

Applied Industrial Technologies distributes millions of industrial parts made by manufacturers. Its lineup short-list includes bearings power transmission components specialty flow control solutions industrial rubber products and tools. Customers are concentrated across the maintenance repair and operations (MRO) and original equipment manufacturer (OEM) markets. The company markets its products with a set of service solutions including inventory management engineering design repair and systems integration as well as customized mechanical fabricated rubber and shop services. Applied Industrial Technologies traces its historical roots back to 1923. Its largest market is the US which generates more than 85% of revenue.

	Annual Growth	06/17	06/18	06/19	06/20	06/21
Sales ($ mil.)	5.7%	2,593.7	3,073.3	3,472.7	3,245.7	3,235.9
Net income ($ mil.)	2.0%	133.9	141.6	144.0	24.0	144.8
Market value ($ mil.)	11.4%	2,274.4	2,701.9	2,369.9	2,403.0	3,507.3
Employees	1.7%	5,554	6,634	6,650	6,200	5,947

APPLIED MATERIALS, INC. — NMS: AMAT

3050 Bowers Avenue, P.O. Box 58039 — CEO: Gary Dickerson
Santa Clara, CA 95052-8039 — CFO: Bob Halliday
Phone: 408 727-5555 — HR: –
Fax: – — FYE: October 31
Web: www.appliedmaterials.com — Type: Public

Applied Materials is the leading producer of machines for semiconductor display and related industries. The company's semiconductor systems segment handles the complex processes of making chips from laying down patterns on silicon at the beginning to packaging them for shipment at the end. Its display business produces equipment for manufacturing liquid crystal displays (LCDs) organic light-emitting diodes (OLEDs) and other display technologies for TVs personal computers and smart phones. The services business offers manufacturing consulting and automation software. Asian customers account for about 85% of revenue.

	Annual Growth	10/17	10/18	10/19	10/20	10/21
Sales ($ mil.)	12.2%	14,537.0	17,253.0	14,608.0	17,202.0	23,063.0
Net income ($ mil.)	14.4%	3,434.0	3,313.0	2,706.0	3,619.0	5,888.0
Market value ($ mil.)	24.6%	50,567.5	28,865.1	49,702.2	54,367.4	121,891.8
Employees	10.1%	18,400	21,000	22,000	24,000	27,000

APPLIED MICRO CIRCUITS CORP. — NMS: AMCC

4555 Great America Parkway, 6th Floor — CEO: Paramesh Gopi
Santa Clara, CA 95054 — CFO: Martin S McDermut
Phone: 408 542-8600 — HR: –
Fax: 408 542-8601 — FYE: March 31
Web: www.apm.com — Type: Public

For Applied Micro Circuits X marks the spot for its chips. The company's lines of chips bearing the "X" are aimed at data centers scientific and high-performance computing and enterprise applications. The X-Gene and X-Weave families of chips based on the ARM architecture provide computing power and high-speed connectivity for telecommunications applications while operating on a low-level of energy. The company outsources manufacturing to TSMC and UMC. Its top customers include Avnet (26% of sales) and Wintec (20%). Applied Micro gets 57% of its sales from outside the US.

	Annual Growth	03/11	03/12	03/13	03/14	03/15
Sales ($ mil.)	(9.7%)	247.7	230.9	195.6	216.2	165.0
Net income ($ mil.)	–	(1.0)	(82.7)	(134.1)	(5.7)	(52.1)
Market value ($ mil.)	(16.3%)	838.9	560.9	599.7	800.1	412.2
Employees	(6.8%)	672	728	649	591	507

APPLIED MINERALS INC — NBB: AMNL

1200 Silver City Road, P.O. Box 432 — CEO: Christopher Carney
Eureka, UT 84628 — CFO: –
Phone: 435 433-2059 — HR: –
Fax: – — FYE: December 31
Web: www.appliedminerals.com — Type: Public

Applied Minerals (formerly Atlas Mining) develops the Dragon mine in Utah. The 230-acre site contains a deposit of halloysite clay a substance used as an intermediate ingredient in chemicals manufacturing as well as in making bone china fine china and porcelain. The mine is believed to be the only source of halloysite clay in the Western Hemisphere suitable for large-scale commercial production. In addition to halloysite the Dragon mine contains other clays including kaolinite ilite and smectite as well as iron oxide ores such as hematite goethite and manganese. The Dragon property contains a measured resource of nearly 600000 tons of clay and more than 2 million tons of iron ore.

	Annual Growth	12/16	12/17	12/18	12/19	12/20
Sales ($ mil.)	(31.6%)	4.0	2.4	4.9	0.5	0.9
Net income ($ mil.)	–	(7.6)	(14.9)	(3.3)	(6.0)	(3.3)
Market value ($ mil.)	(24.7%)	21.2	10.1	9.2	1.2	6.8
Employees	(25.2%)	32	13	13	11	10

APPLIED MOLECULAR EVOLUTION INC.

10300 Campus Point Dr. Ste. 200 — CEO: –
San Diego CA 92121 — CFO: –
Phone: 858-597-4990 — HR: –
Fax: 858-597-4950 — FYE: December 31
Web: www.amevolution.com — Type: Subsidiary

Natural selection doesn't happen fast enough for Applied Molecular Evolution (AME). The biotech firm uses its AMEsystem technology to customize antibodies and proteins for medical uses. Employing what AME calls directed evolution the company adjusts a protein's amino acids one at a time until the protein acquires the desired therapeutic characteristics. AME's biopharmaceuticals have increased the potency of MedImmune's anti-tumor drug Vitaxin (which AME helped developed). The system has also been used to customize a protein which may ultimately help lymphoma patients who otherwise don't respond to Rituxin. The company is a subsidiary of Eli Lilly

APPLIED OPTOELECTRONICS INC
NMS: AAOI

13139 Jess Pirtle Blvd.
Sugar Land, TX 77478
Phone: 281 295-1800
Fax: –
Web: www.ao-inc.com

CEO: Chih-Hsiang Lin
CFO: Stefan Murry
HR: –
FYE: December 31
Type: Public

Applied Optoelectronics is a leading vertically integrated provider of fiber-optic networking products primarily for four networking end-markets: internet data center cable television (CATV) telecommunications (telecom) and fiber-to-the-home (FTTH). The company designs and manufacture a range of optical communications products at varying levels of integration from components subassemblies and modules to complete turn-key equipment. Applied Optoelectronics designs manufactures and integrates its own analog and digital lasers using proprietary Molecular Beam Epitaxy (MBE) and Metal Organic Chemical Vapor Deposition (MOCVD) fabrication process. Customers include Cisco Systems Amazon and Microsoft. Over 90% of sales are generated from customers in Taiwan and China.

	Annual Growth	12/16	12/17	12/18	12/19	12/20
Sales ($ mil.)	(2.6%)	260.7	382.3	267.5	190.9	234.6
Net income ($ mil.)	–	31.2	74.0	(2.1)	(66.0)	(58.5)
Market value ($ mil.)	(22.4%)	588.6	949.7	387.4	298.3	213.7
Employees	(0.9%)	2,776	3,054	2,956	3,115	2,682

APPLIED RESEARCH ASSOCIATES, INC.

4300 SAN MATEO BLVD NE
ALBUQUERQUE, NM 871101229
Phone: 505-883-3636
Fax: –
Web: www.ara.com

CEO: Robert H Sues
CFO: –
HR: –
FYE: September 30
Type: Private

Applied Research Associates (ARA) has defense down to a science. The research and engineering contractor develops tests and manages software and equipment for the defense technologies civil engineering computer software and simulation systems analysis environmental technologies and blast testing and measurement. With offices laboratories and testing and manufacturing facilities primarily in the US ARA provides expertise in system analysis blast testing environmental site characterization pavement evaluation robotic vehicles and other technologies and technical fields. Founded in 1979 the company is owned by its employees.

	Annual Growth	09/09	09/10	09/11	09/12	09/13
Sales ($ mil.)	(4.0%)	–	–	232.1	226.8	213.7
Net income ($ mil.)	1.3%	–	–	6.0	2.8	6.1
Market value ($ mil.)	–	–	–	–	–	–
Employees	–	–	–	–	–	1,235

APPLIED SYSTEMS INC.

200 Applied Pkwy.
University Park IL 60484
Phone: 708-534-5575
Fax: 708-534-8016
Web: www.appliedsystems.com

CEO: Taylor Rhodes
CFO: Graham Blackwell
HR: –
FYE: December 31
Type: Private

Applied Systems applies technology to automate the insurance industry — from lone agent to large agency. The company helps independent insurance agents become more efficient by minimizing paperwork streamlining workflows and improving access to information. Its main product The Agency Manager (TAM) system assists with client management policy pricing electronic data interchange policy and claims servicing and office administration. Its Vision system provides large carriers with automated billing policy and claims processing and reports. DORIS provides small brokers with a hosted system. Applied Systems is owned by chairman and CEO James Kellner and Bain Capital.

APPLIED UV INC
NAS: AUVI

150 N. Macquesten Parkway
Mount Vernon, NY 10550
Phone: 914 665-6100
Fax: –
Web: www.applieduvinc.com

CEO: –
CFO: –
HR: –
FYE: December 31
Type: Public

Yucaipa has a hungry eye for picking out ripe bargains in different industries but made its name with grocery stores. The private equity and venture capital firm which was formed in 1986 forged its reputation as the ultimate grocery shopper executing a series of grocery chain mergers and acquisitions involving such companies as Fred Meyer Ralphs and Jurgensen's that put the company on the supermarket map. It currently owns stakes in about 35 companies including grocery chains A&P and Whole Foods. Yucaipa's chairman billionaire and former grocery store bag boy Ron Burkle is a prominent Democratic activist and fundraiser. He owns a significant stake in the NHL's Pittsburgh Penguins as well.

	Annual Growth	12/16	12/17	12/18	12/19	12/20
Sales ($ mil.)	–	0.0	0.0	7.6	9.3	5.7
Net income ($ mil.)	–	0.0	0.0	0.7	2.8	(3.4)
Market value ($ mil.)	–	0.0	0.0	–	–	36.5
Employees	42.3%	–	–	–	26	37

APPLIED VISUAL SCIENCES INC.
OTC: APVS

250 Exchange Place Ste. H
Herndon VA 20170
Phone: 703-464-5495
Fax: 703-464-8530
Web: www.guardiantechintl.com

CEO: William J Donovan
CFO: Gregory Hare
HR: –
FYE: December 31
Type: Public

Applied Visual Sciences sees a new future for itself. Formerly Guardian Technologies the company changed its name and restructured its operations in July 2010. It primarily operates through two subsidiaries: Guardian Technologies (homeland security and defense technology) and Signature Mapping Medical Sciences (health care technology). Its security and defense products include threat identification and screening software for airlines while its health care offerings include medical image processing applications.

APPRISS INC.

10401 Linn Station Rd. Ste. 200
Louisville KY 40223-3842
Phone: 502-561-8463
Fax: 502-561-1825
Web: www.appriss.com

CEO: Michael D Davis
CFO: Jeffrey S Byal
HR: –
FYE: December 31
Type: Private

Appriss aptly observes offenders. The company's flagship product Victim Information & Notification Everyday or VINE makes information about offenders' custody or court status available to victims of crime as well as the general public. It also offers automated notification services to victims of federal crimes in partnership with AT&T and the US Department of Justice. Appriss' ancillary products include JusticeXchange a tool that enables law enforcement officials to track offenders in jail and investigate crimes; MethCheck a program that helps track and report pseudoephedrine purchases; and AlertXpress which enables government agencies to deliver mass notifications to via phone fax or e-mail.

APPROACH RESOURCES INC
NBB: AREX Q

One Ridgmar Centre, 6500 West Freeway, Suite 800
Fort Worth, TX 76116
Phone: 817 989-9000
Fax: –
Web: www.approachresources.com

CEO: Sergei Krylov
CFO: –
HR: –
FYE: December 31
Type: Public

Approach Resources takes a different approach to natural gas and oil exploration development and production. Specializing in finding and exploiting unconventional reservoirs the company operates primarily in West Texas' Permian Basin. It also has operations in East Texas. The company's unconventional designation results from a focus on developing natural gas reserves in tight gas sands and shale areas necessitating a reliance on advanced completion fracturing and drilling techniques. In 2012 Approach Resources reported proved reserves of 95.5 million barrels of oil equivalent.

	Annual Growth	12/14	12/15	12/16	12/17	12/18
Sales ($ mil.)	(18.5%)	258.5	131.3	90.3	105.3	114.0
Net income ($ mil.)	–	56.2	(174.1)	(52.2)	(112.4)	(19.9)
Market value ($ mil.)	(39.2%)	607.2	174.9	318.4	281.3	82.9
Employees	(8.6%)	142	102	100	97	99

APPTECH CORP
NAS: APCX

5876 Owens Ave, Suite 100
Carlsbad, CA 92008
Phone: 760 707-5959
Fax: –

CEO: Luke D'Angelo
CFO: Gary Wachs
HR: –
FYE: December 31
Type: Public

When nutritional supplements didn't transform its fortunes AppTech decided to apply itself elsewhere. Formerly known as Natural Nutrition the company it lost its primary customer in 2009 and switched its focus to mobile device applications. AppTech plans to create an online marketplace for not just Apple apps but apps that will run on Motorola Mobility's Android the BlackBerry Palm smartphones and China Mobile's new OPhone. The company plans to act a middleman for US-based app developers and mobile users in the emerging markets of Brazil China India. The company will translate English-based apps and sell them to wireless carriers overseas.

	Annual Growth	12/16	12/17	12/18	12/19	12/20
Sales ($ mil.)	4.0%	0.3	0.3	0.3	0.3	0.3
Net income ($ mil.)	–	(2.2)	(1.5)	(2.1)	(1.3)	(4.2)
Market value ($ mil.)	–	–	–	–	–	–
Employees	(62.5%)	–	–	–	8	3

APPTIS INC.

4800 Westfields Blvd.
Chantilly VA 20151
Phone: 703-745-6016
Fax: 210-366-4722
Web: www.mysiriuszone.com

CEO: Albert Notini
CFO: Francis Meyer
HR: –
FYE: December 31
Type: Subsidiary

Apptis — 'tis an appropriate name for a company that provides many apps for its customers. The company offers a wide range of information technology services including network engineering software development and systems integration for US federal agencies and commercial clients. It also distributes and integrates equipment from such vendors as Cisco Dell and Hewlett-Packard. Apptis provides such other services as maintenance support and training. Clients have included the FAA and the Department of Defense (DOD). Apptis has several offices in its home state of Virginia and several more in five other states. The company was acquired by URS Corporation in 2011 for about $260 million.

APRIA HEALTHCARE GROUP INC.

26220 Enterprise Ct.
Lake Forest CA 92630
Phone: 949-639-2000
Fax: 516-593-7039
Web: www.biospecifics.com

CEO: Daniel J Stark
CFO: Debra L Morris
HR: –
FYE: December 31
Type: Private

When an apple a day doesn't keep the illness away perhaps Apria Healthcare Group can help. With about 540 branches nationwide Apria is one of the country's largest home health firms. The company provides supplemental oxygen ventilators nebulizers and sleep monitoring equipment and medication to patients with emphysema sleep apnea and other respiratory conditions. Its infusion therapy nurses administer intravenous or injectable therapies — including pain drugs chemotherapy and parenteral nutrition — at home or in one of the company's outpatient infusion clinics. Apria also delivers home medical equipment such as walkers and hospital beds. The company is owned by the Blackstone Group.

APRICUS BIOSCIENCES INC
NAS: APRI

11975 El Camino Real, Suite 300
San Diego, CA 92130
Phone: 858 222-8041
Fax: –
Web: www.apricusbio.com

CEO: Raj Mehra
CFO: Michael Golembiewski
HR: –
FYE: December 31
Type: Public

Apricus Biosciences (formerly NexMed) wants you to rub it in. The drug development company uses its NexACT technology to deliver drugs through the skin; it is developing topical formulations with improved absorption rates using already-proven drug ingredients. One of the company's products is a treatment for erectile dysfunction Vitaros that is sold in select international markets. Another offering Totect works to detoxify tissue that has been accidentally exposed to chemotherapy agents. Apricus Biosciences is also working on a topical product called Femprox that treats female sexual arousal disorder as well as a topical nail fungus treatment called MycoVa.

	Annual Growth	12/12	12/13	12/14	12/15	12/16
Sales ($ mil.)	(9.0%)	8.4	2.5	9.3	4.8	5.8
Net income ($ mil.)	–	(31.8)	(16.9)	(21.8)	(19.0)	(7.4)
Market value ($ mil.)	(10.0%)	15.4	20.5	7.7	7.7	10.1
Employees	(39.8%)	114	21	23	24	15

APRISO CORPORATION

301 E. Ocean Blvd. Ste. 1200
Long Beach CA 90802
Phone: 562-951-8000
Fax: 562-951-9000
Web: www.apriso.com

CEO: James Henderson
CFO: Carey Tokirio
HR: –
FYE: December 31
Type: Private

Apriso helps companies size up their manufacturing activities. The company's FlexNet product which works with languages and currencies from around the world is a suite of manufacturing operations management applications. The FlexNet suite addresses plant activities such as production supply chain warehousing labor and maintenance. In more than 40 countries spread across the Americas Europe Africa and Asia Apriso's more than 200-strong client list includes British American Tobacco General Motors Lockheed Martin and Microsoft. The company was founded in 1992.

APS HEALTHCARE INC.

44 S. Broadway Ste. 1200　　　　　　　　　　CEO: Greg Scott
White Plains NY 10601　　　　　　　　　　CFO: John McDonough
Phone: 800-305-3720　　　　　　　　　　　　　　　　　HR: –
Fax: +44-2079227789　　　　　　　　　　　FYE: December 31
Web: www.northernandshell.com　　　　　　　　　Type: Private

At APS Healthcare attitude is everything. What started out as a behavioral health services provider has morphed into a full-service health management firm aiming to reduce health care costs and improve wellness through lifestyle changes. APS provides disease and care management wellness and prevention clinical quality reviews and mental health services to Medicaid agencies state and local governments health plans and employers. The company which serves some 17 million members in 25 US states plus Puerto Rico also provides employee assistance and work-life programs. APS which was previously owned by private equity firm GTCR Goldner Rauner was acquired by Medicare provider Universal American in 2012.

APTIFY

1850 K St. NW 3rd Fl.　　　　　　　　　　CEO: Amith Nagarajan
Washington DC 20006-1605　　　　　　　　CFO: Chris Frederick
Phone: 202-223-2600　　　　　　　　　　　　　　　　　HR: –
Fax: 202-223-8800　　　　　　　　　　　　FYE: December 31
Web: www.aptify.com　　　　　　　　　　　　　　Type: Private

Aptify hopes to help the disorganized masses. The company develops data management software used by customers for the automation of a variety of back-office functions such as accounting order entry fundraising marketing membership renewal and polling and surveying. Aptify serves a range of industries including education health care and manufacturing. It also has products tailored for religious groups and other non-profit organizations. Clients have included Publishing Technology and The Catholic Health Association of the United States. The company has additional offices in California Illinois and Pennsylvania. Chairman and CEO founded Aptify in 1993.

APTALIS PHARMA INC.

22 Inverness Center Pkwy. Ste. 310　　　　　　　CEO: John Fraher
Birmingham AL 35242　　　　　　　　　　　　　　　　　CFO: –
Phone: 205-991-8085　　　　　　　　　　　　　　　　　HR: –
Fax: 604-688-7168　　　　　　　　　　　　FYE: September 30
Web: www.ivanhoe-energy.com　　　　　　　　　Type: Private

Aptalis Pharma knows its ABCs when it comes to treating CF and GI ailments. The company formerly named Axcan Intermediate Holdings develops and sells drugs mainly to treat cystic fibrosis (CF) and gastrointestinal (GI) conditions. Its Urso line treats liver disease; Carafate and Sulcrate treat ulcers; and Canasa and Salofalk offer relief for inflammatory bowel diseases. In addition Aptalis Pharma markets Zenpep a digestive aids for patients with exocrine pancreatic insufficiency a condition associated with cystic fibrosis. The firm's products are primarily sold in North America and the European Union. Aptalis Pharma is a subsidiary of Axcan Holdings which is controlled by TPG Capital.

APTIMUS INC.

199 Fremont St. Ste. 1800　　　　　　　　　　　　　CEO: –
San Francisco CA 94105　　　　　　　　　　　　　　　CFO: –
Phone: 415-896-2123　　　　　　　　　　　　　　　　　HR: –
Fax: 415-896-2561　　　　　　　　　　　　FYE: December 31
Web: www.aptimus.com　　　　　　　　　　　　Type: Subsidiary

Aptimus thinks it's the most qualified to bring you online shopping deals. The company whose name is derived from the Latin words "aptus" (unusually qualified) and "optimus" (most beneficial) operates an ad network that showcases free trial and promotional offers from a variety of corporate clients. Serving primarily the education sector Aptimus provides banner ads hyper-links and pop-ups across its network of sites as part of its clients' marketing campaigns and coordinates mailings using its database of e-mail addresses of people who have opted to receive promotional offers. Owning offices in Seattle and San Francisco Aptimus is a subsidiary of education services company Apollo Group.

APTARGROUP INC.　　　　　　　　　　　　　　NYS: ATR

265 Exchange Drive, Suite 100　　　　　　　　CEO: Stephan Tanda
Crystal Lake, IL 60014　　　　　　　　　　　　CFO: Robert Kuhn
Phone: 815 477-0424　　　　　　　　　　　　　　　　　HR: –
Fax: 815 477-0481　　　　　　　　　　　　FYE: December 31
Web: www.aptar.com　　　　　　　　　　　　　　　Type: Public

AptarGroup pumps out products all over the world. Also known as Aptar the company manufactures pump dispensers that are used for fragrances and cosmetics food and pharmaceuticals and a myriad of other personal care items. Aptar makes dispensing closures for plastic-capped squeezable containers holding toiletries and to a lesser extent food and beverage and household goods. The company also offers aerosol valves in both continuous-spray and metered-dose options (such as inhalers). Majority of the company's sales are generated internationally.

APTINA LLC

3080 N. 1st St.　　　　　　　　　　　　　　　　　　　CEO: –
San Jose CA 95134　　　　　　　　　　　　　　　　　CFO: –
Phone: 408-660-2699　　　　　　　　　　　　　　　　　HR: –
Fax: 408-660-2674　　　　　　　　　　　　FYE: December 31
Web: www.aptina.com　　　　　　　　　　　　　　Type: Private

For Aptina image is everything. The company is a leader in CMOS (complementary metal-oxide-semiconductor) imaging technology. Its digital image sensor components and processors are used in standard digital still and video cameras as well as cameras built into mobile phones PCs and surveillance equipment. The company also makes sensors for medical imaging scopes (used in colonoscopies for example) and automobile cameras that enable rear view images. Aptina partners with mobile handset makers and camera component designers and distributes its products from offices in North America Europe and Asia. Memory chip maker Micron Technology formed Aptina in 2008 and spun it off in 2009.

	Annual Growth	12/17	12/18	12/19	12/20	12/21
Sales ($ mil.)	6.9%	2,469.3	2,764.8	2,859.7	2,929.3	3,227.2
Net income ($ mil.)	2.6%	220.0	194.7	242.2	214.0	244.1
Market value ($ mil.)	9.2%	5,651.3	6,161.6	7,573.1	8,966.3	8,022.4
Employees	(0.4%)	13,200	14,100	14,000	13,000	13,000

APTIUM ONCOLOGY INC.

8201 Beverly Blvd.   CEO: –
Los Angeles CA 90048-4505   CFO: –
Phone: 323-966-3400   HR: –
Fax: 323-966-3685   FYE: December 31
Web: www.aptiumoncology.com   Type: Subsidiary

The side effects of cancer treatment can be nearly as devastating as the disease itself but Aptium Oncology offers treatment variations to make the best of a bad situation for patients. Aptium Oncology manages hospital-based outpatient and comprehensive cancer treatment centers for patients with all types of cancer. It operates a network of 24-hour cancer treatment centers in hospitals in California Florida New York and New Jersey. Aptium Oncology provides consulting management information technology and research coordination services to its clients. The company is a subsidiary of UK-based AstraZeneca a top maker of cancer drugs.

APYX MEDICAL CORP   NMS: APYX

5115 Ulmerton Road   CEO: Charles Goodwin
Clearwater, FL 33760   CFO: Tara Semb
Phone: 727 384-2323   HR: –
Fax: –   FYE: December 31
Web: www.apyxmedical.com   Type: Public

Surgeons don't think about Bovie Medical during surgery but Bovie thinks about them. Bovie makes electrosurgical generators and disposable electrosurgical products (including desiccators electrodes electrosurgical pencils and other devices) for cutting and cauterizing tissue. These are mainly used for outpatient surgical procedures in doctors' offices surgery centers and hospitals. Bovie also makes battery-operated cauteries (to stop bleeding) physician penlights and other medical lighting instruments and nerve locator simulators (used in hand and facial reconstruction) to identify motor nerves. Bovie markets and distributes worldwide under its own Aaron ICON and IDS brands and under private labels.

	Annual Growth	12/16	12/17	12/18	12/19	12/20
Sales ($ mil.)	(6.7%)	36.6	38.9	16.7	28.2	27.7
Net income ($ mil.)	–	(4.0)	(5.1)	64.0	(19.7)	(11.9)
Market value ($ mil.)	(14.9%)	–	–	–	290.1	246.9
Employees	5.2%	217	211	222	266	266

ARAMARK   NYS: ARMK

2400 Market Street   CEO: John Zillmer
Philadelphia, PA 19103   CFO: Thomas Ondrof
Phone: 215 238-3000   HR: Lynn McKee
Fax: –   FYE: October 01
Web: www.aramark.com   Type: Public

Founded in 1959 ARAMARK is a leading global provider of food facilities and uniform services to education healthcare business & industry and sports leisure & corrections clients. The company offers corporate dining services and operates concessions at sports arenas and other entertainment venues. The firm is the third top companies in the food and facilities services and second in uniform services in North America. Through ARAMARK Uniform and Career Apparel the company supplies uniforms for manufacturing transportation construction restaurant and hotel healthcare and pharmaceutical industries. The US customers generate about three-quarters of the company's revenue.

	Annual Growth	09/17	09/18	09/19*	10/20	10/21
Sales ($ mil.)	(4.6%)	14,604.4	15,789.6	16,227.3	12,829.6	12,096.0
Net income ($ mil.)	–	373.9	567.9	448.5	(461.5)	(90.8)
Market value ($ mil.)	(3.1%)	10,396.1	11,013.0	11,013.0	7,052.7	9,159.6
Employees	(1.2%)	260,500	274,400	283,500	247,900	248,300

*Fiscal year change

ARAMARK REFRESHMENT SERVICES LLC

ARAMARK Tower 1101 Market St.   CEO: –
Philadelphia PA 19107-2934   CFO: –
Phone: 215-238-3000   HR: –
Fax: 215-238-3333   FYE: September 30
Web: www.aramarkrefreshments.com   Type: Subsidiary

You might say this company facilitates water cooler discussions and break-room meetings. ARAMARK Refreshment Services is a leading supplier of vending machines and office coffee and water services. The subsidiary of foodservices firm ARAMARK Corporation serves its customers through about 90 distribution facilities that cater to more than 100000 locations in North America. Its "Complete Breaktime Experience" offers an array of coffee and brewing systems along with water dispensing equipment and other supplies. In addition the firm's vending unit stocks and maintains vending machines mainly in workplaces. In 2011 it picked up Van Houtte US Coffee Service or Filterfresh from Green Mountain Coffee Roasters.

ARAMARK UNIFORM AND CAREER APPAREL LLC

115 N. 1st St.   CEO: –
Burbank CA 91502   CFO: –
Phone: 818-973-3700   HR: Lydia Leong
Fax: 818-973-2848   FYE: September 30
Web: www.aramark-uniform.com   Type: Subsidiary

What do butchers chefs municipal workers nurses and supermarket clerks have in common? Their uniforms may all be provided by ARAMARK Uniform and Career Apparel. The company makes rents and sells professional uniforms and workplace apparel to businesses in 45 US states Puerto Rico and Ontario Canada. ARAMARK Uniform and Career Apparel also sells or leases workplace supplies including floor mats mops towels and dispensers. Divisions of the company include ARAMARK Uniform Services Galls and WearGuard and Crest. A subsidiary of the world's third-largest food service provider ARAMARK ARAMARK Uniform and Career Apparel is the #2 uniform rental company in the US (behind rival Cintas).

ARATANA THERAPEUTICS, INC   NMS: PETX

11400 Tomahawk Creek Parkway, Suite 340   CEO: Craig Tooman
Leawood, KS 66211   CFO: Rhonda Hellums
Phone: 913 353-1000   HR: –
Fax: –   FYE: December 31
Web: www.aratana.com   Type: Public

If you can't teach old dogs new tricks you can at least ease their stiff joints with medications by Aratana Therapeutics. The company is developing biopharmaceuticals for dogs and cats by licensing pharmaceutical compounds already approved for human consumption and reformulating them for animal use. Aratana has three products on the market: ENTYCE to stimulate appetite in dogs NOCITA to alleviate post-operative pain in cats and dogs and Galliprant to treat osteoarthritis pain and inflammation in dogs. The company's pipeline includes a weight-loss therapeutic for cats with chronic kidney disease and a feline herpes virus.

	Annual Growth	12/13	12/14	12/15	12/16	12/17
Sales ($ mil.)	279.7%	0.1	0.8	0.7	38.6	25.6
Net income ($ mil.)	–	(4.3)	(38.8)	(84.1)	(33.6)	(47.5)
Market value ($ mil.)	(27.6%)	812.4	757.9	237.3	305.4	223.7
Employees	17.9%	44	57	58	88	85

ARBELLA MUTUAL INSURANCE COMPANY

1100 Crown Colony Dr.
Quincy MA 02169
Phone: 617-328-2800
Fax: 617-328-2970
Web: www.arbella.com

CEO: –
CFO: –
HR: –
FYE: December 31
Type: Private

The ship Arbella carried the Puritan settlers of the Massachusetts Bay Colony but Arbella Mutual Insurance would insure their worldly goods. The New England company provides consumer and personal property/casualty insurance in Massachusetts and is one of the state's top auto insurers. Operating through Arbella Mutual and Commonwealth Mutual it underwrites auto homeowners and other personal insurance products in Massachusetts. The group also provides business insurance products (auto fleet coverage and workers' compensation for instance) in its home state New Hampshire and Rhode Island. Arbella's Covenant Insurance affiliate writes personal insurance policies in Connecticut.

ARBINET CORPORATION

460 Herndon Parkway
Herndon VA 20170
Phone: 703-456-4100
Fax: 703-456-4123
Web: www.arbinet.com

CEO: Shawn F O'Donnell
CFO: Gary G Brandt
HR: –
FYE: December 31
Type: Subsidiary

Arbinet makes communications capacity a tradable commodity. The company operating as PTGi International Carrier Services created and operates the leading electronic marketplace for communications trading. Used by roughly 1100 members primarily communications services providers its automated platform offers anonymous buying and selling of wholesale voice and data traffic capacity. The company targets customers in the Americas Asia Europe and the Middle East. Arbinet was acquired by Primus Telecommunications (PTGi) in 2011. Primus integrated Arbinet's business brand and technology into a division called PTGi International Carrier Services (PTGi ICS).

ARBITECH, LLC

64 FAIRBANKS
IRVINE, CA 926181602
Phone: 949-376-6650
Fax: –
Web: www.arbitech.com

CEO: –
CFO: David Walker
HR: –
FYE: December 31
Type: Private

There's nothing arbitrary about Arbitech's business model. Arbitech sells a variety of new and used computer equipment made by such companies as Avaya Cisco Systems Hewlett-Packard IBM Microsoft Nortel and VMware. The company's wide range of products include PCs networking equipment servers storage systems components memories and software. In addition to new equipment the company deals in open-box discontinued and refurbished inventory a niche typically not served by other large distributors and resellers of computer products. Arbitech was co-founded in 2000 by CEO Torin Pavia and one of the company's partners William Poovey.

	Annual Growth	12/03	12/04	12/05	12/08	12/09
Sales ($ mil.)	5.7%	–	–	153.3	180.3	191.4
Net income ($ mil.)	–	–	–	8.4	0.0	0.0
Market value ($ mil.)	–	–	–	–	–	–
Employees	–	–	–	–	–	74

ARBOR COMMERCIAL MORTGAGE LLC

333 Earle Ovington Blvd. Ste. 900
Uniondale NY 11553
Phone: 516-832-8002
Fax: 516-832-8045
Web: www.arbor.com

CEO: Ivan Kaufman
CFO: Paul Elenio
HR: –
FYE: December 31
Type: Private

Countless borrowers have sought shelter in this arbor. Arbor Commercial Mortgage originates underwrites and services real estate loans with an emphasis on multifamily housing as well as commercial health care industrial office and retail properties. It services more than 600 loans totaling about $3.5 billion for investors including Fannie Mae institutional and corporate investors and private mortgage holders. The company operates about a dozen sales and origination support offices throughout the US. CEO Ivan Kaufman founded Arbor in 1983.

ARBOR NETWORKS INC.

6 Omni Way
Chelmsford MA 01824
Phone: 978-703-6600
Fax: 978-250-1905
Web: www.arbornetworks.com

CEO: Matthew Moynahan
CFO: Donald W Pratt Jr
HR: –
FYE: December 31
Type: Private

Arbor Networks provides network security software and related computing equipment intended to help businesses grow healthy secure networks. The company's Peakflow and Pravail systems are designed to recognize and respond to network threats such as denial of service attacks. Its eSeries products enable network traffic monitoring and routing among other tasks. Arbor's customers come from such industries as financial services education health care and telecommunications. Clients include Cox Communications Comerica and Tata Communcations. Arbor has international sales offices in Europe and Asia. In 2010 the company was acquired by Tektronix.

ARBOR REALTY TRUST INC

333 Earle Ovington Boulevard, Suite 900
Uniondale, NY 11553
Phone: 516 506-4200
Fax: –
Web: www.arbor.com

NYS: ABR
CEO: Ivan Kaufman
CFO: Paul Elenio
HR: –
FYE: December 31
Type: Public

Money doesn't grow on trees so Arbor Realty Trust invests in real estate-related assets. The real estate investment trust (REIT) buys structured finance assets in the commercial and multifamily real estate markets. It primarily invests in bridge loans (short-term financing) and mezzanine loans (large and usually unsecured loans) but also invests in discounted mortgage notes and other assets. The REIT targets lending and investment opportunities where borrowers seek interim financing until permanent financing is attained. Arbor Realty Trust is managed by financing firm Arbor Commercial Mortgage though in early 2016 the REIT agreed to buy Arbor Commercial Mortgage for $250 million to expand into the government-sponsored multi-family real estate loan origination business.

	Annual Growth	12/17	12/18	12/19	12/20	12/21
Sales ($ mil.)	23.2%	346.7	484.9	535.8	603.7	799.2
Net income ($ mil.)	29.2%	121.6	180.2	128.6	170.9	339.3
Market value ($ mil.)	20.7%	1,307.8	1,524.2	2,172.0	2,146.3	2,773.0
Employees	6.8%	445	468	532	522	579

ARBORGEN INC.

180 Westvaco Rd.
Summerville SC 29483
Phone: 843-851-4129
Fax: 843-832-2164
Web: www.arborgen.com

CEO: Andrew Baum
CFO: John Radak
HR: –
FYE: March 31
Type: Private

ArborGen's seedlings are a chip off the ol' bioengineering block. The company produces and markets genetically enhanced eucalyptus and pine tree seedlings designed to grow quickly and resist frigid temperatures and disease. The company which also offers conventional seedlings typically markets to customers in the US New Zealand and Australia. While sold directly to core customers like large land owners and managers its trees are ultimately used by pulp and paper products producers and companies in the biopower charcoal and biofuels industries. ArborGen operates a dozen nurseries 15 orchards three R&D facilities and several distribution centers. In mid-2011 the company shelved its plans to go public.

ARBUTUS BIOPHARMA CORP   NMS: ABUS

701 Veterans Circle
Warminster, PA 18974
Phone: 267 469-0914
Fax: 604 419-3201
Web: www.arbutusbio.com

CEO: William Collier
CFO: David Hastings
HR: –
FYE: December 31
Type: Public

Tekmira Pharmaceuticals is giving diseases the silent treatment. The biopharmaceutical company is attempting to develop therapies that inhibit or "silence" certain disease-causing genes through ribonucleic acid interference (RNAi) a mechanism that disrupts the production of proteins that can lead to cancer metabolic and infectious diseases. Tekmira's lead candidates are being developed to treat tumors and high cholesterol. It also partners with other pharmaceutical companies such as Alnylam Pharmaceuticals and Pfizer to advance additional RNAi products using Tekmira's stable nucleic acid-lipid particles (SNALP) RNAi drug delivery technology.

	Annual Growth	12/16	12/17	12/18	12/19	12/20
Sales ($ mil.)	46.7%	1.5	10.7	5.9	6.0	6.9
Net income ($ mil.)	–	(384.2)	(84.4)	(57.1)	(153.7)	(63.7)
Market value ($ mil.)	9.7%	219.7	452.9	343.5	249.3	318.4
Employees	(10.6%)	122	130	80	80	78

ARC DOCUMENT SOLUTIONS, INC.   NYS: ARC

12657 Alcosta Blvd., Suite 200
San Ramon, CA 94583
Phone: 925 949-5100
Fax: –
Web: www.e-arc.com

CEO: Kumarakulasingam Suriyakumar
CFO: Jorge Avalos
HR: –
FYE: December 31
Type: Public

This "arc" keeps builders from being flooded with too much paper. ARC Document Solutions also known as ARC provides large-format document reproduction services mainly to architectural engineering building owner/operator and construction firms. It operates about 175 service centers under a variety of local brands and offers on-site document management services at some 10900 customer locations. Adapting to the shift to digital the company offers a number of applications such as SKYSITE Planwell and Abacus that offer digital documentation management. ARC's network of facilities extends beyond the US into Canada China India Hong Kong UAE and the UK. The company generates more than 85% of sales in the US.

	Annual Growth	12/16	12/17	12/18	12/19	12/20
Sales ($ mil.)	(8.1%)	406.3	394.6	400.8	382.4	289.5
Net income ($ mil.)	–	(47.9)	(21.5)	8.9	3.0	6.2
Market value ($ mil.)	(26.5%)	217.4	109.1	87.7	59.5	63.3
Employees	(9.4%)	2,600	2,500	2,400	2,300	1,750

ARC GROUP WORLDWIDE INC   NBB: ARCW

810 Flightline Blvd.
Deland, FL 32724
Phone: 386 736-4890
Fax: –
Web: www.arcw.com

CEO: Alan Quasha
CFO: Aaron Willman
HR: –
FYE: June 30
Type: Public

ARC Group puts a modern twist on making old-fashioned parts. The company makes industrial parts for aerospace automotive and medical uses with a 3D manufacturing process. The 3D process reduces times to prototype and make a part and helps the customer get its product to market faster. ARC offers more traditional manufacturing processes such as metal injection molding plastic injection molding and metal stamping. Those processes are ARC's biggest moneymaker accounting for more than four-fifths of revenue. The US is by far the company's biggest market. It has added to its portfolio of manufacturing processes through a series of acquisitions.

	Annual Growth	06/17	06/18	06/19	06/20	06/21
Sales ($ mil.)	(11.0%)	99.1	82.4	60.1	48.5	62.2
Net income ($ mil.)	–	(10.2)	(13.2)	(24.0)	(5.3)	4.6
Market value ($ mil.)	(16.0%)	69.0	60.0	11.0	7.3	34.3
Employees	(8.0%)	576	530	–	–	–

ARC LOGISTICS PARTNERS LP   NYS: ARCX

725 Fifth Avenue, 19th Floor
New York, NY 10022
Phone: 212 993-1290
Fax: –
Web: www.arcxlp.com

CEO: Jeffrey R Armstrong
CFO: Carlos Ruiz
HR: –
FYE: December 31
Type: Public

Arc Logistics Partners owns more than a dozen fuel storage terminals in 10 states that can hold almost 5 million barrels of oil ethanol and other types of petroleum products. It also owns two rail transloading facilities in Alabama that can move 23000 barrels per day and a liquefied natural gas storage facility in Mississippi. Customers include oil and gas companies refineries marketers distributors and other industrial manufacturers. Arc Logistics Partners was formed by Lightfoot Capital Partners (which is majority owned by GE). Organized as a limited partnership Arc is exempt from paying corporate income tax as long as it distributes quarterly dividends to shareholders. The partnership went public in 2013.

	Annual Growth	12/11	12/12	12/13	12/14	12/15
Sales ($ mil.)	40.4%	21.0	22.9	47.8	54.9	81.8
Net income ($ mil.)	19.0%	5.4	5.4	12.8	1.3	10.7
Market value ($ mil.)	(22.2%)	–	–	421.7	328.5	255.5
Employees	11.5%	–	80	83	95	111

ARCA BIOPHARMA INC.   NASDAQ: ABIO

8001 Arista Place Ste. 200
Broomfield CO 80021
Phone: 720-940-2200
Fax: 720-208-9261
Web: www.arcabiopharma.com

CEO: Michael Bristow
CFO: C. Jeffrey Dekker
HR: –
FYE: December 31
Type: Public

ARCA biopharma is using genes to treat your heart. The biopharmaceutical company's lead candidate Gencaro is a beta-blocker being developed to treat chronic heart failure and other cardiovascular diseases. Having identified common genetic variations in the cardiac nervous system ARCA biopharma believes those variations may help predict how well patients will respond to Gencaro. Pending regulatory approval Gencaro may be marketed directly by the company or through partnerships. If approved it will be the first genetically-targeted heart failure treatment. ARCA biopharma is also collaborating with LabCorp to develop a companion genetic diagnostic test for Gencaro.

ARCBEST CORP
NMS: ARCB

8401 McClure Drive
Fort Smith, AR 72916
Phone: 479 785-6000
Fax: 479 785-6004
Web: www.arkbest.com

CEO: Judy McReynolds
CFO: David Cobb
HR: –
FYE: December 31
Type: Public

ArcBest knows what's best when it comes to moving freight. Subsidiary ABF Freight System specializes in long-haul less-than-truckload (LTL) shipments of general commodities (no hazardous waste or dangerous explosives). LTL carriers combine freight from multiple shippers into a single truckload. It also offers ground expedite solutions under Panther Premium Logistics household moving via U-Pack and vehicle maintenance under FleetNet America. ArcBest was founded in Arkansas in 1923 (its name was shortened from Arkansas Best in 2014) and has grown to serve all US states plus Canada and Puerto Rico through more than 240 service/distribution centers.

	Annual Growth	12/16	12/17	12/18	12/19	12/20
Sales ($ mil.)	2.2%	2,700.2	2,826.5	3,093.8	2,988.3	2,940.2
Net income ($ mil.)	39.7%	18.7	59.7	67.3	40.0	71.1
Market value ($ mil.)	11.5%	702.0	907.6	869.8	700.7	1,083.3
Employees	0.0%	13,000	13,000	13,000	13,000	13,000

ARCH CHEMICALS INC.

501 Merritt 7
Norwalk CT 06856-5204
Phone: 203-229-2900
Fax: 519-888-7884
Web: www.rim.com

CEO: –
CFO: –
HR: –
FYE: December 31
Type: Subsidiary

Arch Chemicals and its line of pool-cleaning products may make it safe to go back in the water but the company is after bigger (smaller) fish — dangerous microbes in the environment. Arch "The Biocides Company" makes products designed to destroy and control the growth of harmful microbes in several areas. In addition to products for the pool Arch sells chemicals for hair and skin care wood treatment preservation and protection applications for paints and building products and health and hygiene applications. The company operates two business segments: biocides products and performance products. In 2011 Swiss biopharmaceutical company Lonza Group acquired Arch in a $1.2 billion cash tender offer.

ARCH VENTURE PARTNERS

8725 W. Higgins Rd. Ste. 290
Chicago IL 60631
Phone: 773-380-6600
Fax: 773-380-6606
Web: www.archventure.com

CEO: –
CFO: –
HR: –
FYE: December 31
Type: Private

ARCH Venture Partners wants to catch companies on the upward curve of their development. The firm invests in startup and seed-stage companies particularly those concentrating on information technology life sciences and physical sciences. The company also specializes in the commercialization of technologies originating from academic and research institutions. ARCH launched its first fund in 1989 and now manages seven funds totaling some $1.5 billion. It has invested in more than 130 companies since its founding. Portfolio holdings include AmberWave Systems Impinj Nanosys Surface Logix and Xtera Communications.

ARCHEMIX CORP.

300 Third St.
Cambridge MA 02142
Phone: 617-621-7700
Fax: 617-621-9300
Web: www.archemix.com

CEO: Kenneth M Bate
CFO: –
HR: –
FYE: December 31
Type: Private

Monoclonal antibodies and small molecules? Feh! Archemix is focused on aptamers a type of synthetic oligonucleotide that the drug discovery company believes will trump those other cutting edge biotech tools in treating acute and chronic diseases. Aptamers bind to molecular targets much like antibodies but are more easily reproduced. It has R&D programs for potential treatments for cancers rheumatoid arthritis and multiple sclerosis. The company has partnered with larger firms including Merck Serono GlaxoSmithKline and Elan Pharmaceuticals.

ARCH RESOURCES INC (DE)
NYS: ARCH

One CityPlace Drive, Suite 300
St. Louis, MO 63141
Phone: 314 994-2700
Fax: –
Web: www.archcoal.com

CEO: Paul Lang
CFO: Matthew Giljum
HR: –
FYE: December 31
Type: Public

Arch Resources (formerly Arch Coal) is one of the world's largest coal producers by volume selling approximately 63 million tons of coal including some 0.9 million tons of coal it purchased from third parties coming from seven active mining complexes spread across all the major coal-producing regions of the US. The company sells its metallurgical coal to five North American customers and exports to nearly 25 customers overseas in about 15 countries. Arch's main properties are in the Powder River Basin in southeast Montana and northeast Wyoming.

	Annual Growth	12/17	12/18	12/19	12/20	12/21
Sales ($ mil.)	(1.3%)	2,324.6	2,451.8	2,294.4	1,467.6	2,208.0
Net income ($ mil.)	9.1%	238.5	312.6	233.8	(344.6)	337.6
Market value ($ mil.)	(0.5%)	1,434.0	1,277.5	1,104.3	673.8	1,405.7
Employees	(3.4%)	3,790	3,822	3,700	3,200	3,300

ARCHER DANIELS MIDLAND CO.
NYS: ADM

77 West Wacker Drive, Suite 4600
Chicago, IL 60601
Phone: 312 634-8100
Fax: –
Web: www.adm.com

CEO: Juan Luciano
CFO: Ray Young
HR: Jennifer Weber
FYE: December 31
Type: Public

Archer-Daniels-Midland (ADM) forges every link in the food chain from field to processing to store. One of the world's largest processors of agricultural commodities the company converts corn oilseeds and wheat into products for food animal feed industrial and energy uses at more than 300 processing plants worldwide. The company is also a leading manufacturer of protein meal vegetable oil corn sweeteners flour biodiesel ethanol and other value-added food and feed ingredients. ADM operates an extensive US grain elevator and global transportation network that buys stores transports and resells feed commodities for the agricultural processing industry connecting crops with markets on six continents. About 40% of its sales comes from US.

	Annual Growth	12/17	12/18	12/19	12/20	12/21
Sales ($ mil.)	8.8%	60,828.0	64,341.0	64,656.0	64,355.0	85,249.0
Net income ($ mil.)	14.2%	1,595.0	1,810.0	1,379.0	1,772.0	2,709.0
Market value ($ mil.)	14.0%	22,444.8	22,943.2	25,956.0	28,229.6	37,850.4
Employees	7.0%	31,300	31,600	38,100	39,000	41,000

ARCHIE COMIC PUBLICATIONS INC.

325 Fayette Ave.
Mamaroneck NY 10543-2306
Phone: 914-381-5155
Fax: 914-381-2335
Web: www.archiecomics.com

CEO: –
CFO: –
HR: –
FYE: December 31
Type: Private

Throw on your letterman jacket grab Veronica and Betty (really who can choose between them?) and head to Riverdale home to Archie and friends. Archie Comic Publications (ACP) publishes the family-friendly comic book Archie in addition to titles featuring cat-suited rockers Josie and the Pussycats and Sabrina the Teenage Witch. The company's Archie Comics Entertainment division produces and distributes original projects for TV film home video music live events and the Internet and also represents ACP's licensing and merchandising. All total ACP publishes more than 10 million comics per year in a dozen languages worldwide.

ARCHIPELAGO LEARNING INC.

3232 McKinney Ave. Ste. 400
Dallas TX 75204
Phone: 800-419-3191
Fax: 877-592-1357
Web: www.archipelagolearning.com

NASDAQ: ARCL
CEO: Tim J McEwen
CFO: James Walburg
HR: –
FYE: December 31
Type: Public

Archipelago Learning is a subscription-based online education company that provides instruction assessment and productivity tools to improve student and teacher performance. Its products Study Island and EducationCity are used by more than 37000 elementary and secondary schools in the US Canada and the UK to improve student performance on standardized tests. The company's Northstar Learning products offer adult education study and exam prep services. It also distributes Reading Eggs an online reading program for younger children. Providence Equity Partners owns nearly half of the company's stock. Archipelago Learning has agreed to be acquired by PLATO Learning.

ARCHON CORPORATION

4336 Losee Rd. Ste. 5
North Las Vegas NV 89030
Phone: 702-732-9120
Fax: 702-658-4331

OTC: ARHN
CEO: Paul Lowden
CFO: –
HR: –
FYE: September 30
Type: Public

Archon is banking on gamblers to follow the trail of the Pioneer. Formerly Santa Fe Gaming the embattled company owns and operates one casino the Pioneer Hotel & Gambling Hall in Laughlin Nevada. The Pioneer features some 400 guest rooms and gaming operations that consist of approximately 730 slot machines six blackjack tables one craps table one roulette wheel and five other gaming tables. The hotel includes two restaurants and bars a special events area banquet rooms and a swimming pool and spa. Gaming accounts for more than half of revenues. Chairman and CEO Paul Lowden owns about 75% of the company.

ARCHON GROUP L.P.

6011 Connection Dr.
Irving TX 75039
Phone: 972-368-2200
Fax: 972-368-2290
Web: www.archongroup.com

CEO: –
CFO: –
HR: –
FYE: November 30
Type: Subsidiary

Archon Group keeps it real ... real estate that is. Archon provides portfolio management and financing services to commercial property owners and investors around the world. Its offerings include accounting legal consultation and IT services. The group also provides mortgage origination and specialty financing. Archon manages a property portfolio worth nearly $60 billion in North America Europe and Asia; property types include office buildings industrial facilities multifamily residences and retail spaces. Archon was established in 1996 by Goldman Sachs; its primary client is Whitehall Street Real Estate Funds also part of the Goldman Sachs family.

ARCHROCK INC

9807 Katy Freeway, Suite 100
Houston, TX 77024
Phone: 281 836-8000
Fax: –
Web: www.archrock.com

NYS: AROC
CEO: Douglas Childers
CFO: Douglas Aron
HR: –
FYE: December 31
Type: Public

Archrock has a rock solid compression game going. The US based company is a leading natural gas contract operator and compression service provider to the oil & gas producers and midstream companies. In addition the company provides aftermarket services to compression equipment owners. The company owns some 6430 compression units providing an aggregate roughly 4.4 million horsepower.

	Annual Growth	12/16	12/17	12/18	12/19	12/20
Sales ($ mil.)	2.0%	807.1	794.7	904.4	965.5	875.0
Net income ($ mil.)	–	(54.6)	19.0	21.1	97.3	(68.4)
Market value ($ mil.)	(10.0%)	2,019.1	1,606.1	1,145.7	1,535.7	1,324.7
Employees	(7.4%)	1,700	1,700	1,700	1,700	1,250

ARCHROCK PARTNERS LP

9807 Katy Freeway, Suite 100
Houston, TX 77024
Phone: 281 836-8000
Fax: –
Web: www.archrock.com

NMS: APLP
CEO: Douglas Childers
CFO: Raymond Guba
HR: –
FYE: December 31
Type: Public

Archrock Partners (formerly Exterran Partners) is the largest operator of contract compression equipment in the US. Its services include designing installing operating repairing and maintaining compression equipment. The company operates a fleet of more than 3950 compressor units comprising almost 1.6 million horsepower. Archrock a global leader in full-service natural gas compression equipment and services controls Archrock Partners. Archrock Partners and Archrock (formerly Exterran Holdings) manage their respective US compression fleets as one pool of compression equipment in order to more easily fulfill their respective customers' needs.

	Annual Growth	12/12	12/13	12/14	12/15	12/16
Sales ($ mil.)	9.8%	387.5	466.2	581.0	656.8	562.4
Net income ($ mil.)	–	10.5	64.0	61.7	(84.0)	(10.8)
Market value ($ mil.)	(5.7%)	1,355.0	2,020.8	1,445.2	822.9	1,072.2
Employees						

ARCHWAY MARKETING SERVICES INC.

19850 S. Diamond Lake Rd.
Rogers MN 55374
Phone: 763-428-3300
Fax: 763-428-3302
Web: www.archway.com
CEO: Doug Mann
CFO: Tom Smith
HR: –
FYE: December 31
Type: Private

Archway Marketing Services provides marketing information management and customer service for clients primarily residing in the business-to-business sector. It offers such marketing services as program management for rebates sweepstakes and other promotions; fulfillment and distribution; merchandising; and customer relationship management through a dozen facilities throughout North America. It also helps clients hit by the slumping economy by providing cost-saving ideas integrating marketing programs and consolidating a number of outsourced services as they relate to marketing and merchandising. Archway traces its roots to 1952 when it began offering mailing services in Minnesota.

ARCSIGHT LLC

5 Results Way
Cupertino CA 95014
Phone: 408-864-2600
Fax: 408-342-1615
Web: www.arcsight.com
CEO: –
CFO: –
HR: –
FYE: April 30
Type: Subsidiary

ArcSight keeps a watchful eye on business risk. The company provides security and compliance management products used to identify prioritize and respond to corporate policy violations and cyber attacks. Its business software tools and network devices handle such security functions as compliance automation event collection and management (ESM) identity monitoring (IdentityView) and log management (Logger). The company also provides consulting implementation support and training services. ArcSight markets to the aerospace and defense energy and utilities financial services food production and health care industries among others. The company is a subsidiary of Hewlett-Packard.

ARCTIC CAT INC   NMS: ACAT

500 North 3rd Street
Minneapolis, MN 55401
Phone: 612 350-1800
Fax: –
Web: www.arcticcat.com
CEO: Christopher T Metz
CFO: Christopher J Eperjesy
HR: –
FYE: March 31
Type: Public

Prowling over hard ground or snow Arctic Cat offers drivers a purrfect ride. The company manufactures and markets about 30 types of all-terrain vehicles (ATVs) and about 60 snowmobile models. Its four-wheel recreational and utility ATVs and snowmobiles are marketed under the Arctic Cat name. Arctic Cat also supplies replacement parts and Cat-branded protective clothing and riding gear to foster its drivers' experience and loyalty. The company produces and outsources parts to other vehicle OEMs too. Products are sold through a network of independent dealers throughout North America and through representatives of dealers worldwide. The US accounts for roughly 60% of Arctic Cat's sales.

	Annual Growth	03/12	03/13	03/14	03/15	03/16
Sales ($ mil.)	2.0%	585.3	671.6	730.5	698.8	632.9
Net income ($ mil.)	–	29.9	39.7	39.4	4.9	(9.2)
Market value ($ mil.)	(20.9%)	558.6	569.8	623.1	473.5	219.0
Employees	3.5%	1,369	1,508	1,611	1,670	1,573

ARCTIC SLOPE REGIONAL CORPORATION

3900 C ST STE 801
ANCHORAGE, AK 995035963
Phone: 907-339-6000
Fax: –
Web: www.asrc.com
CEO: Rex A Rock Sr
CFO: Kristin Mellinger
HR: –
FYE: December 31
Type: Private

The Inupiat-owned Arctic Slope Regional Corporation (ASRC) is a locally owned and operated business in Alaska. It gets the bulk of its sales from energy services (ASRC Energy Services) and petroleum refining and marketing unit (Petro Star). Other operations include construction (ASRC Construction Holding) governmental services (ASRC Federal Holding) economic development (Alaska Growth Capital BIDCO) local services (Eskimos Inc.) and tourism (Tundra Tours).

	Annual Growth	12/04	12/05	12/06	12/07	12/08
Sales ($ mil.)	13.6%	–	1,566.5	1,700.5	1,777.5	2,297.3
Net income ($ mil.)	5.8%	–	127.5	206.3	207.7	151.2
Market value ($ mil.)	–	–	–	–	–	–
Employees	–	–	–	–	–	6,700

ARCTURUS THERAPEUTICS HOLDINGS INC   NMS: ARCT

10628 Science Center Drive, Suite 250
San Diego, CA 92121
Phone: 858 900-2660
Fax: –
Web: www.arcturusrx.com
CEO: –
CFO: –
HR: –
FYE: December 31
Type: Public

If it were that easy to treat ADHD Alcobra would wave a magic wand and say "Abracadabra!" Instead the Israeli company is developing a new type of drug to treat ADHD (Attention Deficit Hyperactivity Disorder). The drug candidate MG01CI differs from traditional pharmaceuticals prescribed to manage ADHD in that it is not a stimulant like its well-known counterparts Adderall and Ritalin. MG01CI aims to be a safer alternative for patients who cannot tolerate the side effects such as insomnia and high blood pressure associated with stimulants Alcobra plans to merge with private biotech Arcturus Therapeutics the combined firm will focus on developing RNA medicines to treat rare liver diseases non-alcoholic steatohepatitis (NASH) cystic fibrosis infectious diseases and other therapeutic areas.

	Annual Growth	12/16	12/17	12/18	12/19	12/20
Sales ($ mil.)	(9.8%)	–	13.0	15.8	20.8	9.5
Net income ($ mil.)	–	(24.6)	(10.9)	(21.8)	(26.0)	(72.1)
Market value ($ mil.)	113.2%	55.0	208.2	118.6	284.7	1,136.2
Employees	57.9%	19	60	72	88	118

ARDEA BIOSCIENCES INC.   NASDAQ: RDEA

4939 Directors Place
San Diego CA 92121
Phone: 858-652-6500
Fax: 858-625-0760
Web: www.ardeabiosciences.com
CEO: –
CFO: John W Beck
HR: –
FYE: December 31
Type: Public

Ardea Biosciences wants to end the ordeal painful conditions. The biotechnology company discovers and develops therapies for the treatment of ailments such as cancer gout and inflammatory diseases. The company which focuses on the development of small-molecule therapies (named as such because the molecular compounds weigh less than 1000 Daltons) has drug candidates in clinical and preclinical stages of development. The company's most advanced candidate lesinurad is in Phase III clinical development as a treatment to manage hyperuricaemia — the build up of uric acid in the bloodstream otherwise known as gout. The company was acquired by AstraZeneca for $1.26 billion in 2012.

ARDEN GROUP, INC. NMS: ARDN A

2020 South Central Avenue
Compton, CA 90220
Phone: 310 638-2842
Fax: –
Web: www.ardengroupinc.com
CEO: Bernard Briskin
CFO: Laura J Neumann
HR: –
FYE: December 29
Type: Public

Glitz meets groceries at Arden Group's 18 supermarkets in Southern California (primarily in the Los Angeles area). Through its wholly-owned subsidiary Arden-Mayfair the company operates Gelson's Markets (18000 - 40000 sq. ft.) which carry traditional grocery items as well as imported foods and unusual deli selections. Most also feature coffee and gelato bars fresh pizza sushi and bakeries. While some house in-store banks and pharmacies most are too small to accommodate additional services. The company converted its last Mayfair Markets store to the Gelson's banner in 2009. Arden Group owns a shopping center in Calabasas California that houses a Gelson's supermarket.

	Annual Growth	01/09	01/10	01/11*	12/11	12/12
Sales ($ mil.)	(2.9%)	479.1	431.2	417.1	429.5	439.0
Net income ($ mil.)	(8.5%)	24.7	21.6	18.1	17.0	18.9
Market value ($ mil.)	(10.8%)	390.0	293.6	253.4	276.4	276.4
Employees	(3.0%)	2,291	2,134	2,082	2,134	2,088

*Fiscal year change

ARENA PHARMACEUTICALS INC NMS: ARNA

136 Heber Avenue, Suite 204
Park City, UT 84060
Phone: 858 453-7200
Fax: –
Web: www.arenapharm.com
CEO: Amit Munshi
CFO: Laurie Stelzer
HR: –
FYE: December 31
Type: Public

Arena Pharmaceuticals is a biopharmaceutical company focused on delivering novel transformational medicines with optimized pharmacology and pharmacokinetics to patients globally. Its most advanced clinical programs include etrasimod (APD334) for ulcerative colitis a program for Crohn's disease and a program for atopic dermatitis. Its Olorinab (APD371) is being evaluated for a broad range of visceral pain conditions associated with gastrointestinal diseases. It has partnered with various companies including United Therapeutics (a program for pulmonary arterial hypertension) Everest Medicines (etrasimod in development in Greater China) and Beacon Discovery (research platform for GPCR targets).

	Annual Growth	12/16	12/17	12/18	12/19	12/20
Sales ($ mil.)	(77.5%)	124.0	21.3	18.0	806.4	0.3
Net income ($ mil.)	–	(22.5)	(91.4)	(29.4)	397.6	(404.7)
Market value ($ mil.)	171.2%	83.2	1,991.0	2,282.9	2,662.1	4,503.1
Employees	36.0%	106	159	194	320	363

ARES CAPITAL CORPORATION NASDAQ: ARCC

280 Park Ave. 44th Fl.
New York NY 10167
Phone: 212-750-7300
Fax: +91-20-2747-7380
Web: www.bajajfinserv.in
CEO: Robert deVeer
CFO: Penelope Roll
HR: –
FYE: December 31
Type: Public

Targeting US middle-market companies Ares Capital invests in senior debt loans (secured loans that receive repayment priority over other types of debt) and mezzanine debt; it also makes equity investments. The firm which typically invests between $20 and $250 million per transaction manages a portfolio of more than 140 middle-market companies representing the health care education food service beverage financial services industries among others. Founded in 2004 Ares Capital is externally managed by Ares Capital Management a subsidiary of Ares Management LLC. Arees Capital is one of the larest development companies in the US with some $52 billion of capital under management.

ARES COMMERCIAL REAL ESTATE CORP NYS: ACRE

245 Park Avenue, 42nd Floor
New York, NY 10167
Phone: 212 750-7300
Fax: –
Web: www.arescre.com
CEO: Bryan Donohoe
CFO: Tae-Sik Yoon
HR: –
FYE: December 31
Type: Public

Ares Commercial Real Estate Corporation is primarily engaged in commercial real estate loans and related investments. The company is externally managed by Ares Commercial Real Estate Management LLC (ACREM) a subsidiary of Ares Management Corporation a leading global alternative investment manager with approximately $165 billion of assets under management. The company target borrowers whose capital needs are not being suitably met by traditional bank or capital markets sources by offering these borrowers customized financing solutions. The company was formed in late 2011.

	Annual Growth	12/17	12/18	12/19	12/20	12/21
Assets ($ mil.)	10.4%	1,770.2	1,603.3	1,784.1	1,929.5	2,631.8
Net income ($ mil.)	18.7%	30.4	38.6	37.0	21.8	60.5
Market value ($ mil.)	3.0%	608.2	614.8	746.8	561.5	685.5
Employees	20.4%	1,000	1,075	1,200	1,450	2,100

ARGAN INC NYS: AGX

One Church Street, Suite 201
Rockville, MD 20850
Phone: 301 315-0027
Fax: –
Web: www.arganinc.com
CEO: Rainer Bosselmann
CFO: David Watson
HR: –
FYE: January 31
Type: Public

Argan makes sure its customers stay all juiced up. The holding company owns subsidiaries that provide power services and products for the government telecommunications power and personal health care industries. Its main subsidiary Gemma Power Systems designs builds and maintains power plants including traditional and alternate fuel plants. The company's Southern Maryland Cable unit provides inside-premise wiring and also performs splicing and underground and aerial telecom infrastructure construction services to carriers government entities service providers and electric utilities. Argan's power industry segment accounts for more than 95% of its total revenues.

	Annual Growth	01/17	01/18	01/19	01/20	01/21
Sales ($ mil.)	(12.7%)	675.0	892.8	482.2	239.0	392.2
Net income ($ mil.)	(23.7%)	70.3	72.0	52.0	(42.7)	23.9
Market value ($ mil.)	(12.5%)	1,158.1	684.6	663.0	661.3	678.8
Employees	3.5%	1,286	1,552	1,487	1,154	1,473

ARGO INTERNATIONAL CORPORATION

125 CHUBB AVE FL 1
LYNDHURST, NJ 070713504
Phone: 212-431-1700
Fax: –
Web: www.argointl.com
CEO: –
CFO: –
HR: –
FYE: December 31
Type: Private

Argo International is naut about Jason and the Golden Fleece but it does have a stimulating story to tell. The company distributes electrical (fuses generators motors) mechanical (cable reels pumps thrusters) and marine (controls gauges valves) equipment to industrial users in the mining oil utility marine petroleum and refining industries. Argo has more than 20 offices and warehouses throughout Asia Europe the Middle East and North and South America. The company which was established in 1952 is a subsidiary of New York-based Delcal Enterprises Inc.

	Annual Growth	12/00	12/01	12/02	12/12	12/13
Sales ($ mil.)	–	–	0.0	73.4	81.7	59.0
Net income ($ mil.)	11.6%	–	–	1.0	0.7	3.3
Market value ($ mil.)	–	–	–	–	–	–
Employees	–	–	–	–	–	150

ARGO-TECH CORPORATION

23555 Euclid Ave.
Cleveland OH 44117
Phone: 216-692-6000
Fax: 216-692-5293
Web: www.argo-tech.com

CEO: Craig Arnold
CFO: John S Glover
HR: –
FYE: October 31
Type: Subsidiary

Argo-Tech makes Fantasy Island's "De plane Boss de plane!" a reality; the company keeps commercial and military aircraft aloft with its high-performance fuel-flow devices. It builds main engine fuel pumps and systems airframe fuel pumps and various ground fuel distribution products. Through its Carter Ground Fueling division Argo-Tech also makes ground refueling equipment. Customers have included the US Army and Air Force; engine and airframe makers such as Airbus Boeing GE Aircraft Engines and Lockheed Martin; and aerospace distributor Upsilon International. In 2007 investment concerns Greenbriar Equity Group and Vestar Capital Partners sold AT Holdings Corp. the parent of Argo-Tech to Eaton.

ARGON ST INC.

12701 Fair Lakes Circle Ste. 800
Fairfax VA 22033
Phone: 703-322-0881
Fax: 703-322-0885
Web: www.argonst.com

CEO: –
CFO: John Holt
HR: –
FYE: September 30
Type: Subsidiary

Argon ST has the five C's of defense down: command control communications computers and combat. It also develops systems for intelligence reconnaissance and surveillance. Together these areas are known as C5ISR. Electronic systems tailored for these purposes track intercept and interpret data needed to make mission decisions on land at sea or in the air. Argon ST's portfolio includes sensors that detect hostile signals and radar; ISR force protection geo-location navigation and threat warning systems; integrated communications networks; and engineering integration and training services. The Boeing subsidiary primarily serves the US defense and homeland security markets from about a dozen US offices.

ARGOSY EDUCATION GROUP INC.

2 First National Plaza 20 S. Clark St. Fl. 3
Chicago IL 60603
Phone: 312-201-0200
Fax: 312-424-7282
Web: www.argosy.edu

CEO: –
CFO: –
HR: –
FYE: August 31
Type: Subsidiary

It's never too late for school at Argosy Education Group. Geared toward working people the for-profit school offers bachelor's master's and doctoral degrees in fields such as psychology and behavioral sciences education and human development business and information technology and the health sciences. Created with the 2001 merger of the American Schools of Professional Psychology the Medical Institute of Minnesota and the University of Sarasota the company operates nearly 20 Argosy University campuses throughout the US in more than a dozen US states. It also offers some classes on the Internet and others through intensive week-long programs.

ARI NETWORK SERVICES, INC.   NAS: ARIS

10850 West Park Place, Suite 1200
Milwaukee, WI 53224
Phone: 414 973-4300
Fax: –
Web: www.arinet.com

CEO: Roy W Olivier
CFO: William A Nurthen
HR: –
FYE: July 31
Type: Public

ARI Network Services helps some very manly industries attract smart shoppers. The company makes and sells software for creating electronic catalogs and e-commerce websites (together more than 80% of sales) in industries such as outdoor power equipment power sports motorcycles marine and agricultural equipment. Dealers manufacturers and distributors use its applications including its PartSmart software which allows companies to access product information for their suppliers and dealers who can use the database. In addition the company's e-commerce and communication applications process orders product registrations and warranty claims and perform search engine optimization.

	Annual Growth	07/12	07/13	07/14	07/15	07/16
Sales ($ mil.)	20.7%	22.5	30.1	33.0	40.4	47.7
Net income ($ mil.)	13.4%	1.1	(0.8)	(0.1)	1.1	1.7
Market value ($ mil.)	67.3%	11.3	11.3	51.4	55.0	88.6
Employees	31.4%	139	270	248	397	415

ARIA HEALTH

10800 KNIGHTS RD
PHILADELPHIA, PA 191144299
Phone: 215-612-4000
Fax: –
Web: www.northeast.jeffersonhealth.org

CEO: Kathleen Kinslow
CFO: –
HR: –
FYE: June 30
Type: Private

Aria Health wants to get you back to singing arias in no time flat. Aria Health provides medical care from two acute care hospitals in Philadelphia (Frankford Campus and Torresdale Campus) as well as the Bucks County Campus in Langhorne Pennsylvania. Combined the three facilities boast about 480 beds and offer a full range of specialty care from anesthesiology and pain management to women's care and invasive oncology as well as cardiac and surgical procedures. Aria Health also operates primary care and specialty outpatient facilities throughout its service area. In 2016 Aria announced plans to rejoin forces with Thomas Jefferson University Hospitals eight years after the systems separated.

	Annual Growth	06/11	06/12	06/13	06/15	06/19
Sales ($ mil.)	1.5%	–	–	460.0	432.0	501.7
Net income ($ mil.)	(29.4%)	–	–	52.0	31.7	6.4
Market value ($ mil.)	–	–	–	–	–	–
Employees	–	–	–	–	–	4,000

ARIAD PHARMACEUTICALS, INC.   NMS: ARIA

26 Landsdowne Street
Cambridge, MA 02139-4234
Phone: 617 494-0400
Fax: –
Web: www.ariad.com

CEO: Harvey J Berger
CFO: Manmeet S Soni
HR: –
FYE: December 31
Type: Public

ARIAD Pharmaceuticals is exploring the myriad possibilities for new cancer treatments. The firm has a handful of candidates being studied for the treatment of various types of cancer. Its drug Iclusig (ponatinib) a treatment for two rare forms of leukemia is already approved in the US and Europe though the company is seeking approvals for additional indications. ARIAD is also developing ridaforolimus with Merck for the treatment of soft tissue and bone cancers. Other drug candidates aim to treat maladies including lung cancer and lymphoma. ARIAD's drug candidates are in varying stages of preclinical research and clinical trials.

	Annual Growth	12/10	12/11	12/12	12/13	12/14
Sales ($ mil.)	(12.4%)	179.0	25.3	0.6	45.6	105.4
Net income ($ mil.)	–	85.2	(123.6)	(220.9)	(274.2)	(162.6)
Market value ($ mil.)	7.7%	955.2	2,294.4	3,592.3	1,277.3	1,286.7
Employees	32.8%	122	150	300	307	379

ARIBA INC.

NASDAQ: ARBA

910 Hermosa Ct.
Sunnyvale CA 94085
Phone: 650-390-1000
Fax: 317-392-6208
Web: www.shelbycountybank.com

CEO: Alex Atzberger
CFO: Marc Malone
HR: Els Van Den Bussche
FYE: September 30
Type: Public

Ariba helps ensure that your supplies arrive in a timely fashion. The company provides spend management software and consulting services used by manufacturers retailers and distributors to connect with suppliers and to manage procurement. Its applications automate buying help target preferred suppliers and manage enterprise sourcing. Companies use its tools to procure such services as equipment repair temporary staffing and travel. Ariba works with more than 150 million suppliers. The company gets the majority of its revenues in North America. Customers have included Bank of America Chevron FedEx Heinz and TE Connectivity. Ariba was acquired by SAP in 2012 for about $4.3 billion.

ARIVA DISTRIBUTION INC.

50 RiverCenter Blvd. Ste. 260
Covington KY 41011
Phone: 859-292-5000
Fax: 859-261-9777
Web: www.arivanow.com

CEO: –
CFO: –
HR: –
FYE: December 31
Type: Subsidiary

Ariva Distribution formerly known as RIS Paper doesn't mind being called a paper pusher. With approximately 20 branches dotting the US Northeast Mid-Atlantic and Midwest regions the company is a giant merchant of paper and packaging. Ariva purchases warehouses sells and distributes fine printing papers and communication products such as magnetic media copier laser and computer papers. Its lineup includes industrial and packaging products from films and tapes to corrugated strapping and packaging equipment. A branch-based sales force markets to a diverse mix of small to large commercial printers and publishing houses catalog and retail businesses and institutional and government organizations.

ARINC INCORPORATED

2551 Riva Rd.
Annapolis MD 21401
Phone: 410-266-4000
Fax: 410-266-2329
Web: www.arinc.com

CEO: Robert K Ortberg
CFO: Patrick E Allen
HR: Tara Wigglesworth
FYE: December 31
Type: Subsidiary

ARINC is a high flyer in communications and systems integration. Commercial aviation US defense and government customers rely on its communications products IT know-how and engineering expertise to make their operations run smoothly. The company's broad range of products and services cover airport security air traffic management aircraft and satellite testing modeling and simulation network design passenger and baggage processing voice and data communications and weather reporting. ARINIC operates from more than 50 offices in the US and it does business in about 100 other countries from facilities in Europe Latin America and Asia. ARINC is owned by private investment firm The Carlyle Group.

ARIZONA CHEMICAL HOLDINGS CORPORATION

4600 Touchton Rd. East Bldg. 100 Ste. 1500
Jacksonville FL 32246
Phone: 904-928-8700
Fax: 904-928-8779
Web: www.arizonachemical.com

CEO: Kevin M Fogarty
CFO: –
HR: –
FYE: December 31
Type: Private

Arizona Chemical is pining for more business. The company is among the world's largest fractionators (separators) of crude tall oil (from the Swedish talloja or pine oil). (It claims to be the world's largest producer of pine chemicals). Arizona Chemical manufactures such pine tree-based chemicals as fatty acids rosin esters and terpenes. Those chemicals are used to manufacture a wide variety of products including adhesives household cleaners hydraulic fluids inks paints personal care products and plastics. Investment firm American Securities LLC acquired a 75% stake in Arizona Chemical in 2010 though former majority owner Rhone Capital maintained a 25% stake in the company.

ARISTOCRAT TECHNOLOGIES INC.

7230 Amigo St.
Las Vegas NV 89119
Phone: 702-270-1000
Fax: 702-270-1001
Web: www.aristocrat.com.au/company/about/pages/amer

CEO: Trevor Croker
CFO: Toni Korsanos
HR: –
FYE: December 31
Type: Subsidiary

Aristocrat Technologies helps casino managers tell if the house is ahead. The company is the North America Latin America and Caribbean operations of Australian gaming machine manufacturer Aristocrat Leisure. It designs manufactures and markets casino management tools and software to monitor gaming machine use and control payouts. The information systems can also monitor table games and offer additional tools for marketing and accounting. In addition the company makes a variety of gaming machines including reel slot machines video gaming systems and progressive payout machines. Aristocrat Technologies has sales and support centers in Argentina and the US (Minnesota Mississippi New Jersey and Nevada).

ARIZONA INSTRUMENT LLC

3375 N. Delaware St.
Chandler AZ 85225
Phone: 602-470-1414
Fax: 480-804-0656
Web: www.azic.com

CEO: George G Hays
CFO: –
HR: –
FYE: December 31
Type: Private

Undaunted by their amorphous character Arizona Instrument (AZI) puts the predictable in liquids and gases. The company designs manufactures and sells automated instruments for analyzing moisture content and detecting and monitoring the presence of toxic gas. The equipment is used in a range of industrial environmental and quality control applications. AZI's Jerome handheld analyzer detects toxic substances such as mercury and hydrogen sulfide while its Computrac Vapor Pro moisture analyzer spies moisture levels key to quality control in producing cookie dough to tobacco adhesives paints and plastics. The privately held company is owned by CEO George Hays his father James Hays and Harold Schwartz.

ARIZONA PROFESSIONAL BASEBALL LP

401 E JEFFERSON ST
PHOENIX, AZ 850042438
Phone: 602-462-3430
Fax: –
Web: www.mlb.com

CEO: –
CFO: –
HR: –
FYE: December 31
Type: Private

These serpents strike at the baseball diamond. Arizona Professional Baseball owns and operates the Arizona Diamondbacks baseball franchise. The team joined Major League Baseball as a National League expansion franchise in 1998 and enjoyed early success reaching the postseason in its second year and winning the World Series in 2001. The Diamondbacks play host at the state-of-the-art Chase Field which features a retractable roof air-conditioning and a swimming pool in the outfield stands. A group led by former computer industry executive and Datatel founder Ken Kendrick has controlled the team since 2004.

	Annual Growth	12/14	12/15	12/16	12/17	12/18
Sales ($ mil.)	1.0%	–	–	–	233.1	235.4
Net income ($ mil.)	–	–	–	–	77.9	(44.1)
Market value ($ mil.)	–	–	–	–	–	–
Employees	–	–	–	–	–	150

ARIZONA PUBLIC SERVICE CO.

400 North Fifth Street, P.O. Box 53999
Phoenix, AZ 85072-3999
Phone: 602 250-1000
Fax: –
Web: www.apsc.com

CEO: Donald Brandt
CFO: Theodore Geisler
HR: –
FYE: December 31
Type: Public

Arizona Public Service (APS) a subsidiary of Pinnacle West Capital distributes power to about 1.3 million customers in about 10 of 15 Arizona counties making it the largest electric utility in the state. Its transmission facilities consist of 5730 pole miles of overhead lines and some 75 miles of underground lines. APS's distribution facilities consist of some 11225 miles of overhead lines and over 22450 miles of underground primary cable all of which are located in Arizona. It owns and leases around 6320 MW of regulated generation capacity and holds a mix of both long-term and short-term purchased power agreements for additional capacity including a variety of agreements for the purchase of renewable energy.

	Annual Growth	12/16	12/17	12/18	12/19	12/20
Sales ($ mil.)	0.7%	3,489.8	3,554.1	3,688.3	3,471.2	3,587.0
Net income ($ mil.)	5.3%	462.1	504.3	570.3	565.3	568.0
Market value ($ mil.)	–	–	–	–	–	–
Employees	(1.3%)	6,244	6,196	6,158	6,111	5,933

ARIZONA STATE UNIVERSITY

300 E UNIVERSITY DR # 410
TEMPE, AZ 852812061
Phone: 480-965-2100
Fax: –
Web: www.asu.edu

CEO: –
CFO: Carol Campbell
HR: –
FYE: June 30
Type: Private

Arizona State University (ASU) offers more than 800 degree programs for undergraduate and degree pursuing a master's degree or doctoral program. The university offers nearly 300 undergraduate and graduate degree programs and certificates are also offered 100% online. It has 54000 students enrolled. ASU was founded in 1885.

	Annual Growth	06/16	06/17	06/18	06/19	06/20
Sales ($ mil.)	7.0%	–	1,782.2	1,915.8	2,048.6	2,180.6
Net income ($ mil.)	(59.4%)	–	99.4	63.1	85.4	6.7
Market value ($ mil.)	–	–	–	–	–	–
Employees	–	–	–	–	–	8,000

ARK RESTAURANTS CORP

NMS: ARKR

85 Fifth Avenue
New York, NY 10003
Phone: 212 206-8800
Fax: 212 206-8845
Web: www.arkrestaurants.com

CEO: Michael Weinstein
CFO: Anthony Sirica
HR: –
FYE: October 02
Type: Public

You might say this company floats the boat of fine dining fans. Ark Restaurants owns and manages about 20 chic eateries in New York City Las Vegas and Washington DC including the Bryant Park Grill Center Caf © and V-Bar. It also operates locations under the names America and Sequoia. In addition Ark Restaurants manages food courts banquet facilities and room services at several casino resorts including the New York-New York Hotel & Casino (owned by MGM Resorts International) the Venetian Casino Resort (Las Vegas Sands) and the Foxwoods Resorts Casino (Mashantucket Pequot Tribal Nation). Founder and CEO Michael Weinstein owns about 30% of the company.

	Annual Growth	09/17	09/18	09/19*	10/20	10/21
Sales ($ mil.)	(3.8%)	153.9	160.0	162.4	106.5	131.9
Net income ($ mil.)	33.7%	4.0	4.7	2.7	(4.7)	12.9
Market value ($ mil.)	(10.7%)	86.5	82.7	72.3	40.9	55.0
Employees	(3.8%)	2,034	2,102	2,145	1,262	1,741

*Fiscal year change

ARKANSAS CHILDREN'S HOSPITAL

1 CHILDRENS WAY
LITTLE ROCK, AR 722023500
Phone: 501-364-1100
Fax: –
Web: www.archildrens.org

CEO: –
CFO: Gena G Wingfield
HR: –
FYE: June 30
Type: Private

As the only pediatric medical center in the state Arkansas Children's Hospital (ACH) serves the youngest Razorbacks from birth to age 21. The not-for-profit hospital with its about 335 beds specializes in childhood cancer pediatric orthopedics and neonatology. Besides acute care services a staff of approximately 505 physicians and over 200 residents it operates more than 80 specialty clinics and outpatient centers. One of the US's largest pediatric hospitals ACH is also engaged in teaching and medical research through its affiliation with the University of Arkansas for Medical Sciences. Its Arkansas Children's Hospital Research Institute focuses on biological mechanisms underlying birth defects diabetes-related complications and childhood diseases.

	Annual Growth	06/16	06/17	06/18	06/19	06/20
Sales ($ mil.)	1.7%	–	615.1	660.4	703.3	646.4
Net income ($ mil.)	(5.2%)	–	59.7	57.4	93.4	51.0
Market value ($ mil.)	–	–	–	–	–	–
Employees	–	–	–	–	–	3,700

ARKANSAS ELECTRIC COOPERATIVE CORPORATION

1 COOPERATIVE WAY
LITTLE ROCK, AR 722095493
Phone: 501-570-2200
Fax: –
Web: www.aecc.com

CEO: –
CFO: –
HR: Sarah Littleton
FYE: October 31
Type: Private

Having access to power is the natural state in the Natural State thanks to Arkansas Electric Cooperative Corporation (AECC) the sole wholesale power provider for 17 Arkansas electric distribution cooperatives. The company operates power plants with 3418 MW of generating capacity owns transmission assets and buys wholesale power to meet its members' demands. Affiliate Arkansas Electric Cooperatives Inc. (AECI) provides administrative and maintenance services to the distribution companies. The distribution utilities serve about 500000 customers in more than 60% of Arkansas. AECC and AECI along with the state's 17 electric distribution cooperatives are known as the Electric Cooperatives of Arkansas.

	Annual Growth	12/13	12/14	12/15*	10/18	10/19
Sales ($ mil.)	11.7%	–	455.3	462.4	827.5	790.7
Net income ($ mil.)	(3.8%)	–	30.0	35.4	38.9	24.7
Market value ($ mil.)	–	–	–	–	–	–
Employees	–	–	–	–	–	220

*Fiscal year change

ARKANSAS HEART HOSPITAL LLC

1701 S SHACKLEFORD RD
LITTLE ROCK, AR 722114335
Phone: 501-219-7000
Fax: –
Web: www.arheart.com

CEO: Bruce Murphy
CFO: –
HR: –
FYE: September 30
Type: Private

You won't be leaving your heart in Little Rock. At least not with help of Arkansas Heart Hospital which specializes in the diagnosis and treatment of heart disease. With more than 110 beds the hospital provides inpatient and outpatient cardiac care as well as 24-hour emergency services. Arkansas Heart Hospital also has six catheterization labs and offers pharmacy radiology and respiratory services. The hospital also offers advanced wound healing services through its Wound Care and Hyperbaric Oxygen Therapy Clinic. Former parent MedCath held 70% of the Arkansas Heart Hospital before selling its stake to another shareholder physician-owned entity AR-MED in 2011.

	Annual Growth	09/14	09/15	09/16	09/17	09/18
Sales ($ mil.)	11.0%	–	144.8	150.6	184.0	197.8
Net income ($ mil.)	12.9%	–	11.5	(3.9)	12.1	16.5
Market value ($ mil.)	–	–	–	–	–	–
Employees	–	–	–	–	–	414

ARKANSAS STATE UNIVERSITY

2105 AGGIE RD
JONESBORO, AR 72401
Phone: 870-972-2400
Fax: –
Web: www.astate.edu

CEO: –
CFO: –
HR: –
FYE: June 30
Type: Private

Arkansas State University (A-State) is home to more than 14000 students or Red Wolves. The university has more than 10 colleges that offer more than 140 undergraduate and graduate academic programs; classes are also offered at technical sites and in partnership with community colleges. It offers doctoral degrees in educational leadership environmental science heritage studies and molecular biosciences. In additional to its flagship campus in Jonesboro the ASU system offers courses at regional campuses in Beebe Mountain Home and Newport. The university has a 17:1 student-teacher ratio; and approximately 600 international students came from more than 60 countries. A-State was founded in 1909.

	Annual Growth	06/16	06/17	06/18	06/19	06/20
Sales ($ mil.)	0.9%	–	136.0	137.9	135.7	139.7
Net income ($ mil.)	50.4%	–	6.5	(2.6)	12.2	22.1
Market value ($ mil.)	–	–	–	–	–	–
Employees	–	–	–	–	–	13

ARKANSAS TECH UNIVERSITY

1605 COLISEUM DR
RUSSELLVILLE, AR 728018819
Phone: 479-968-0300
Fax: –
Web: www.arkansastechnews.com

CEO: –
CFO: –
HR: –
FYE: June 30
Type: Private

Technically Arkansas Tech University is more than a tech college. The state-supported four-year institution of higher education offers undergraduate and graduate degrees in a variety of disciplines including science business arts and humanities engineering and computer science. The school employs more than 400 faculty members and has an average enrollment of more than 11000 students. Based in Russellville Arkansas it also operates a small satellite campus in the town of Ozark. Arkansas Tech was founded in 1909 as the Second District Agricultural School. The school's purpose and name were changed in 1925 when it became Arkansas Polytechnic College; it was renamed Arkansas Tech University in 1976.

	Annual Growth	06/13	06/14	06/15	06/16	06/17
Sales ($ mil.)	3.6%	–	73.0	77.4	80.7	81.2
Net income ($ mil.)	(41.8%)	–	10.2	7.4	5.1	2.0
Market value ($ mil.)	–	–	–	–	–	–
Employees	–	–	–	–	–	1,039

ARLINGTON ASSET INVESTMENT CORP

NYS: AAIC

6862 Elm Street, Suite 320
McLean, VA 22101
Phone: 703 373-0200
Fax: –
Web: www.arlingtonasset.com

CEO: J. Rock Tonkel
CFO: Richard Konzmann
HR: –
FYE: December 31
Type: Public

Arlington Asset Investment invests mostly in residential mortgage-backed securities (MBS) to provide funds in the mortgage market for institutions such as commercial banks savings and loans associations mortgage banking companies seller/servicers securities dealers and other investors. More than 85% of the securities in the financial firm's $4 billion-plus MBS portfolio are backed by the US government through agencies such as Freddie Mac and Fannie Mae. The remainder of Arlington's MBS portfolio consists of private-label funds issued by private organizations. Arlington Asset Investment was founded as Friedman Billings Ramsey in 1989.

	Annual Growth	12/16	12/17	12/18	12/19	12/20
Sales ($ mil.)	–	36.0	127.1	7.1	126.0	(32.2)
Net income ($ mil.)	–	(41.3)	17.4	(91.8)	13.7	(67.7)
Market value ($ mil.)	(28.9%)	496.7	394.8	242.7	186.7	126.7
Employees	2.2%	11	12	12	11	12

ARLINGTON INDUSTRIES, INC.

1 STAUFFER INDUSTRIAL PAR
SCRANTON, PA 185179620
Phone: 570-562-0270
Fax: –
Web: www.aifittings.com

CEO: –
CFO: –
HR: –
FYE: December 31
Type: Private

Thank goodness for zinc's abundance; the element has enabled Arlington Industry's dominance in manufacturing individual zinc die-cast line items. Arlington manufactures and distributes a slew of metallic and non-metallic fittings and connectors. Its lineup includes bushings cable connectors concrete pipe sleeves conduit bodies gaskets and screw couplings used in the electrical and construction markets. The company operates a sole plant in Scranton Pennsylvania. Since 2003 the privately-held manufacturing company has introduced more than 400 new products.

	Annual Growth	12/08	12/09	12/11	12/12	12/17
Sales ($ mil.)	–	–	(2,130.4)	99.0	109.0	171.9
Net income ($ mil.)	–	–	0.0	0.0	0.0	0.0
Market value ($ mil.)	–	–	–	–	–	–
Employees	–	–	–	–	–	320

ARMANINO FOODS OF DISTINCTION, INC.

NBB: AMNF

30588 San Antonio St.
Hayward, CA 94544
Phone: 510 441-9300
Fax: –
Web: www.armaninofoods.com

CEO: Timothy Anderson
CFO: Edgar Estonina
HR: –
FYE: December 31
Type: Public

Armanino Foods would tell us: "You're too skinny! Eat!" Armanino Foods of Distinction makes upscale frozen and refrigerated Italian-style food. Its flagship product is pesto and it makes half a dozen varieties. The company also manufactures frozen filled pastas and frozen meatballs. It counts other US food manufacturers restaurants and foodservice vendors among its customers as well as club stores and major retail food chains. Near its headquarters in Hayward California Armanino Foods operates pesto and pasta production facilities. The firm processes its meat in nearby Stockton California. It has branch offices in San Francisco Sacramento Los Angeles Las Vegas Boston and Sioux City Iowa.

	Annual Growth	12/16	12/17	12/18	12/19	12/20
Sales ($ mil.)	(2.8%)	35.7	39.0	41.8	42.6	31.8
Net income ($ mil.)	(16.8%)	4.2	5.1	6.3	6.5	2.0
Market value ($ mil.)	3.2%	71.8	82.1	91.4	112.2	81.4
Employees	(5.3%)	46	45	42	42	37

ARMCO METALS HOLDINGS INC
ASE: AMCO

1730 S Ampheltt Blvd, #230
San Mateo, CA 94402
Phone: 650 212-7620
Fax: –
Web: www.armcometals.com

CEO: –
CFO: –
HR: –
FYE: December 31
Type: Public

Steel is important to China's growth and iron ore is important to steel. That's where China Armco Metals comes in. The company imports ores for sale to steel mills and other heavy industry. Its iron copper chrome and nickel ore as well as coal come from South America and Asia. Armco's largest customers include Lianyungang Jiaxin Resources Import & Export Sundial Metals and Minerals and China-Base Ningbo Foreign Trade together about two-thirds of sales. The company also imports and recycles scrap metal a cheaper replacement for iron ore in steel production. Armco was incorporated in 2001 in China as Armco & Metawise; it went public in 2008 through a reverse merger with US firm Cox Distributing.

	Annual Growth	12/10	12/11	12/12	12/13	12/14
Sales ($ mil.)	15.9%	68.8	106.2	106.6	128.7	124.2
Net income ($ mil.)	–	(2.2)	(3.3)	(2.6)	(4.1)	1.9
Market value ($ mil.)	(50.6%)	21.8	1.6	2.7	1.7	1.3
Employees	(20.2%)	131	115	98	58	53

ARMED FORCES BENEFIT ASSOCIATION

909 N WASHINGTON ST # 767
ALEXANDRIA, VA 223141555
Phone: 703-549-4455
Fax: –
Web: www.afba.com

CEO: –
CFO: –
HR: A Jeanine Hoover
FYE: December 31
Type: Private

Taking risks that might scare off other commercial insurance companies Armed Forces Benefit Association (AFBA) provides group life insurance products for military personnel government employees police officers and firefighters and defense department contractors. The not-for-profit membership association was established in 1947 and has some 300000 members; its policies contain no war or terrorism restrictions. It sells property/casualty policies through affiliate Armed Forces Insurance. AFBA's for-profit 5Star Financial division founded in 1989 sells to the general public offering individual life insurance supplemental health insurance and other financial services such as banking and mutual funds.

	Annual Growth	12/02	12/03	12/04	12/05	12/13
Sales ($ mil.)	(4.0%)	–	154.6	141.1	129.4	102.5
Net income ($ mil.)	–	–	31.0	10.0	1.7	(6.3)
Market value ($ mil.)	–	–	–	–	–	–
Employees	–	–	–	–	–	210

ARMOUR RESIDENTIAL REIT INC.
NYS: ARR

3001 Ocean Drive, Suite 201
Vero Beach, FL 32963
Phone: 772 617-4340
Fax: –
Web: www.armourreit.com

CEO: Scott Ulm
CFO: James Mountain
HR: –
FYE: December 31
Type: Public

ARMOUR Residential hopes to protect its investments with the strength of the US government. A real estate investment trust or REIT ARMOUR Residential invests in single-family residential mortgage-backed securities issued or guaranteed by Fannie Mae Freddie Mac and Ginnie Mae. The company's investments include fixed-rate adjustable-rate and hybrid adjustable-rate mortgages (hybrid mortgages start off with fixed rates that may eventually increase as the loan matures). To a lesser extent the company also invests in government-issued bonds unsecured notes and other debt. Formed in 2008 ARMOUR Residential is externally managed by ARMOUR Residential Management LLC.

	Annual Growth	12/17	12/18	12/19	12/20	12/21
Assets ($ mil.)	(12.3%)	8,928.9	8,464.6	13,272.4	5,524.5	5,277.3
Net income ($ mil.)	(46.0%)	181.2	(106.0)	(249.9)	(215.1)	15.4
Market value ($ mil.)	(21.4%)	2,421.6	1,930.1	1,682.5	1,015.9	923.6
Employees	–	–	–	–	–	–

ARMSTRONG ENERGY INC.

7733 Forsyth Blvd. Ste. 1625
St. Louis MO 63105
Phone: 314-721-8202
Fax: 510-632-2169
Web: www.laborbank.com

CEO: –
CFO: –
HR: –
FYE: December 31
Type: Private

Armstrong Energy is strong on coal. The company produces coal from Kentucky's Illinois Basin with proved and probable reserves of 319 million tons; it sells about 7 million tons of coal per year to utilities. In addition to six mines the company also owns three coal processing plants along the Green River with access to river rail and truck transportation. Armstrong Energy uses a variety of coal seams and processing techniques to deliver custom blends to its energy plant customers. The company leases the land its mine are on from its sister firm real estate management company Armstrong Resource Partners. Both are owned by investors Yorktown Partners which filed in late 2011 for both to trade publicly.

ARMSTRONG WORLD INDUSTRIES INC
NYS: AWI

2500 Columbia Avenue
Lancaster, PA 17603
Phone: 717 397-0611
Fax: –
Web: www.armstrong.com

CEO: Victor Grizzle
CFO: Brian MacNeal
HR: Ellen Romano
FYE: December 31
Type: Public

Armstrong World Industries (AWI) is a leading producer of ceiling systems for use in the construction and renovation of commercial and residential buildings. It designs manufactures and sells ceiling and wall systems (primarily mineral fiber fiberglass wool metal wood wood fiber glass-reinforced-gypsum and felt). Among the company's brands are Armstrong Calla Cirrus Dune HumiGuard Total Acoustics and WoodWorks. AWI makes its products in around 15 plants in the US and Canada. Most of AWI's sales are to distributors. The US accounts for over 90% of the company's sales. The company was founded in 1860.

	Annual Growth	12/17	12/18	12/19	12/20	12/21
Sales ($ mil.)	5.5%	893.6	975.3	1,038.1	936.9	1,106.6
Net income ($ mil.)	4.3%	154.8	185.9	214.5	(99.1)	183.2
Market value ($ mil.)	17.7%	2,864.2	2,753.5	4,445.0	3,518.8	5,492.7
Employees	(8.0%)	3,900	4,000	2,500	2,700	2,800

ARMY & AIR FORCE EXCHANGE SERVICE

3911 S WALTON WALKER BLVD
DALLAS, TX 752361598
Phone: 214-312-2011
Fax: –

CEO: –
CFO: –
HR: –
FYE: February 03
Type: Private

Paraphrasing the Army's longtime recruiting slogan buy all that you can buy at the PX (Post Exchange). The Army and Air Force Exchange Service (AAFES) runs about 3100 facilities including PXs and BXs (Base Exchanges) at US Army and Air Force bases in 30-plus countries all 50 US states and five US territories. Its presence includes some 180 retail stores and more than 1000 fast-food outlets (brands like Burger King and Taco Bell) as well as convenience stores/gas stations movie theaters and beauty shops. AAFES — which serves active-duty military personnel reservists retirees and their families — also sells goods online. Although it's a government agency under the DOD it receives less than 5% of its funding from the department.

	Annual Growth	01/14	01/15	01/16	01/17*	02/18
Sales ($ mil.)	3.7%	–	–	–	6,952.5	7,210.8
Net income ($ mil.)	2.5%	–	–	–	292.4	299.9
Market value ($ mil.)	–	–	–	–	–	–
Employees	–	–	–	–	–	35,000

*Fiscal year change

ARNOLD & PORTER LLP

555 12th St. NW
Washington DC 20004-1206
Phone: 202-942-5000
Fax: 202-942-5999
Web: www.arnoldporter.com

CEO: -
CFO: -
HR: -
FYE: December 31
Type: Private - Partnershi

A tourist might go to Washington DC to see the Smithsonian's museums but an executive's agenda might include a visit to Arnold & Porter. The law firm's wide-ranging practice areas center on business transactions and public policy; its specialties include antitrust bankruptcy and corporate restructuring white collar criminal defense international trade intellectual property and litigation. The firm is also known for its strong pro bono work. Arnold & Porter has about 825 lawyers at seven offices in the US and two in Europe. The firm was established in 1946 as Arnold Fortas & Porter; Abe Fortas later a Supreme Court justice was a founding partner.

ARNOLD MACHINERY COMPANY

2975 W 2100 S
SALT LAKE CITY, UT 841191273
Phone: 801-972-4000
Fax: -
Web: www.arnoldmachinery.com

CEO: -
CFO: Jon Pugmire
HR: -
FYE: September 25
Type: Private

Arnold Machinery helps keep construction on the move. Through its many divisions the company distributes construction mining industrial and material handling equipment as well as farm machinery throughout the US. Arnold Machinery also offers used equipment and provides repair and maintenance rebuild exchange and rental services. The company's divisions include General Implement Distributors Mining Equipment Construction Equipment and Material Handling. Arnold Machinery operates about 20 branch facilities covering more than 15 states in the Western US.

	Annual Growth	09/16	09/17	09/18	09/19	09/20
Sales ($ mil.)	9.3%	-	306.3	363.5	367.0	399.5
Net income ($ mil.)	19.9%	-	11.8	18.1	18.3	20.4
Market value ($ mil.)	-	-	-	-	-	-
Employees	-	-	-	-	-	450

ARNOLD WORLDWIDE LLC

101 Huntington Ave.
Boston MA 02199
Phone: 617-587-8000
Fax: 617-587-8004
Web: www.arnoldworldwide.com

CEO: George Sargent
CFO: -
HR: -
FYE: December 31
Type: Business Segment

A partnership with this Arnold will get your brand promoted not terminated. Arnold Worldwide is a full-service advertising agency that offers creative ad development campaign planning and brand management services. Responsible for creating those ubiquitous "Progressive Flo" ads for Progressive Insurance its vast advertising agency network spans 15 offices in Amsterdam Canada China Italy the Czech Republic London Lisbon Spain the UK and the US. The agency's primary three East Coast offices in the US have served such brands as Titleist McDonald's Levi's and Volvo. Arnold Worldwide is a unit of Paris-based advertising conglomerate Havas.

ARO LIQUIDATION INC

NBB: AROP Q

112 W. 34th Street
New York, NY 10120
Phone: 646 485-5410
Fax: -
Web: www.aeropostale.com; www.ps4u.com

CEO: -
CFO: David J Dick
HR: -
FYE: January 30
Type: Public

Despite it name A⊙ropostale is more mall-based than mail-based. It operates more than 800 mostly mall-based stores under the A⊙ropostale and P.S. from A⊙ropostale (for kids) banners in 50 US states Puerto Rico and Canada. It stocks the usual teen outerwear (jeans T-shirts accessories) mostly under the A⊙ropostale and A⊙ro names. The retailer designs and sources its own merchandise so that it can quickly respond to trends but has been struggling in a competitive environment in the aftermath of the US recession. In 2016 A⊙ropostale filed for Chapter 11 bankruptcy protection.

	Annual Growth	01/12*	02/13	02/14*	01/15	01/16
Sales ($ mil.)	(10.4%)	2,342.3	2,386.2	2,090.9	1,838.7	1,506.9
Net income ($ mil.)	-	69.5	34.9	(141.8)	(206.5)	(136.9)
Market value ($ mil.)	(64.6%)	1,320.4	1,081.6	564.9	195.5	20.8
Employees	(5.8%)	25,766	26,279	29,337	21,007	20,330

*Fiscal year change

AROTECH CORP

NMS: ARTX

1229 Oak Valley Drive
Ann Arbor, MI 48108
Phone: 800 281-0356
Fax: -
Web: www.arotech.com

CEO: Dean M Krutty
CFO: Kelli L Kellar
HR: -
FYE: December 31
Type: Public

Arotech has broadened its horizon from making batteries and chargers in 1990 to military training simulators and aviation and vehicle armor. Subsidiary FAAC supplies simulators related software and training for the US military and various government and private industry clients. MDT Protective Industries and MDT Armor produce lightweight armor and ballistic glass for vehicles as well as aircraft armor kits under the Armour of America name. Arotech also makes lithium batteries and charging systems for military and homeland security markets via Electric Fuel Battery and Epsilor Electronic Industries. The US government (through its military branches) is Arotech's #1 customer representing about 40% of sales.

	Annual Growth	12/13	12/14	12/15	12/16	12/17
Sales ($ mil.)	2.7%	88.6	103.6	96.6	93.0	98.7
Net income ($ mil.)	15.5%	2.2	3.5	(2.9)	(2.8)	3.8
Market value ($ mil.)	0.4%	92.1	61.2	53.8	92.4	93.7
Employees	7.0%	373	531	523	514	489

ARQULE INC.

NMS: ARQL

One Wall Street
Burlington, MA 01803
Phone: 781 994-0300
Fax: -
Web: www.arqule.com

CEO: -
CFO: -
HR: -
FYE: December 31
Type: Public

ArQule is pursuing drug research in the molecular biology field with a focus on cancer cell termination. The biotechnology firm works independently and with other drugmakers to discover new potential drug compounds based on its cancer-inhibiting technology platform. ArQule is developing a portfolio of oncology drugs with a handful of anti-cancer compounds undergoing clinical trials. Its lead product candidate in Phase 2 and Phase 3 clinical development together with development and commercialization partner Daiichi Sankyo is tivantinib an oral selective inhibitor of the c-MET receptor tyrosine kinase.

	Annual Growth	12/12	12/13	12/14	12/15	12/16
Sales ($ mil.)	(40.0%)	36.4	15.9	11.3	11.2	4.7
Net income ($ mil.)	-	(10.9)	(24.6)	(23.4)	(13.8)	(22.7)
Market value ($ mil.)	(18.0%)	198.5	153.0	86.8	154.4	89.6
Employees	(22.5%)	97	63	40	36	35

ARRAY BIOPHARMA INC.

NMS: ARRY

3200 Walnut Street
Boulder, CO 80301
Phone: 303 381-6600
Fax: –
Web: www.arraybiopharma.com

CEO: –
CFO: –
HR: –
FYE: June 30
Type: Public

Array BioPharma wants to offer cancer sufferers a multitude of treatment options. The development-stage biopharmaceutical company has a handful of programs in its development pipeline including three late-stage cancer candidates. Clinical trials in progress include cancer drugs binimetinib encorafenib and selumetinib as well as hematology drug filanesib (for multiple myeloma) and ARRY-797 for Lamin A/C-related dilated cardiomyopathy. Commercial partners include AstraZeneca and Genentech. The company also has R&D or commercialization agreements with ASLAN Cascadian Therapeutics Loxo Pierre Fabre VentiRx and Roche. Array grants distribution rights when it partners with other companies.

	Annual Growth	06/14	06/15	06/16	06/17	06/18
Sales ($ mil.)	42.6%	42.1	51.9	137.9	150.9	173.8
Net income ($ mil.)	–	(85.3)	9.4	(92.8)	(116.8)	(147.3)
Market value ($ mil.)	38.5%	963.5	1,523.4	752.2	1,768.5	3,545.4
Employees	10.8%	198	156	177	209	298

ARRIS GROUP INC. (NEW)

NMS: ARRS

3871 Lakefield Drive
Suwanee, GA 30024
Phone: 678 473-2000
Fax: –
Web: www.arrisi.com

CEO: –
CFO: –
HR: –
FYE: December 31
Type: Public

ARRIS brings the idea of broadband home. The company makes communications equipment and components used to enable broadband voice and data transmission and to build television broadcast networks. Products include cable network head-end gear Internet protocol switching systems modems and other consumer premises products. It also sells such related hardware as cable connectors and other supplies used for mounting and installation. ARRIS primarily markets to large cable-network operators. The company added cable set-top boxes digital video and Internet TV distribution systems and other products to its portfolio in 2013 with the acquisition of Motorola Mobility's Home business which more than triples its size.

	Annual Growth	12/09	12/10	12/11	12/12	12/13
Sales ($ mil.)	34.5%	1,107.8	1,087.5	1,088.7	1,353.7	3,620.9
Net income ($ mil.)	–	90.8	64.1	(17.7)	53.5	(48.8)
Market value ($ mil.)	20.8%	1,624.2	1,594.4	1,537.5	2,123.0	3,458.7
Employees	36.3%	1,884	1,942	2,211	2,175	6,500

ARROW ELECTRONICS, INC.

NYS: ARW

9201 East Dry Creek Road
Centennial, CO 80112
Phone: 303 824-4000
Fax: –
Web: www.arrow.com

CEO: Michael J Long
CFO: Christopher Stansbury
HR: –
FYE: December 31
Type: Public

Arrow Electronics hits its target markets with a quiver of thousands of electronic products. The company is a global distributor of electronic components and enterprise computing solutions. It sells semiconductors passive components interconnect products computing and memory and computer peripherals to more than 180000 equipment and contract manufacturers resellers and other commercial customers. The company's Global ECS' portfolio of computing solutions includes data-center cloud security and analytics solutions. Arrow Electronics which generates about 65% of revenue outside the US serves over 85 countries.

	Annual Growth	12/17	12/18	12/19	12/20	12/21
Sales ($ mil.)	6.5%	26,812.5	29,676.8	28,916.8	28,673.4	34,477.0
Net income ($ mil.)	28.9%	402.0	716.2	(204.1)	584.4	1,108.2
Market value ($ mil.)	13.7%	5,473.2	4,693.2	5,767.9	6,622.8	9,139.2
Employees	2.4%	18,800	20,100	19,300	19,600	20,700

ARROW FINANCIAL CORP.

NMS: AROW

250 Glen Street
Glens Falls, NY 12801
Phone: 518 745-1000
Fax: –
Web: www.arrowfinancial.com

CEO: Thomas Murphy
CFO: Edward Campanella
HR: –
FYE: December 31
Type: Public

Arrow Financial has more than one shaft in its quiver. It's the holding company for two banks: $2 billion-asset Glens Falls National Bank operates 30 branches in eastern upstate New York while $400 million-asset Saratoga National Bank and Trust Company has around 10 branches in Saratoga County. Serving local individuals and businesses the banks offer standard deposit and loan products as well as retirement trust and estate planning services and employee benefit plan administration. Its subsidiaries include: McPhillips Insurance Agency and Upstate Agency which offer property and casualty insurance; Capital Financial Group which sells group health plans; and North Country Investment Advisors which provides financial planning services.

	Annual Growth	12/16	12/17	12/18	12/19	12/20
Assets ($ mil.)	9.1%	2,605.2	2,760.5	2,988.3	3,184.3	3,688.6
Net income ($ mil.)	11.4%	26.5	29.3	36.3	37.5	40.8
Market value ($ mil.)	(7.3%)	647.2	542.6	511.7	604.1	478.0
Employees	(0.3%)	524	533	516	520	517

ARROW FINANCIAL SERVICES L.L.C.

5996 W. Touhy Ave.
Niles IL 60714
Phone: 847-557-1100
Fax: 847-647-9526
Web: www.arrow-financial.com

CEO: –
CFO: –
HR: –
FYE: December 31
Type: Subsidiary

Sallie Mae giveth what Arrow Financial Services taketh back with interest. The collection services company which is majority owned by student loan provider SLM (Sallie Mae) performs contingency collection services on past-due consumer accounts. Arrow Financial works on behalf of its parent as well as credit card issuers; telecommunications providers; utility companies; and auto education and other consumer lenders. The company also purchases and services performing and nonperforming consumer debt. It has about a half-dozen call centers and other offices around the nation. Sallie Mae acquired a majority stake in Arrow Financial in 2004.

ARROWHEAD PHARMACEUTICALS INC

NMS: ARWR

177 E. Colorado Blvd., Suite 700
Pasadena, CA 91105
Phone: 626 304-3400
Fax: –
Web: www.arrowheadpharmaceuticals.com

CEO: Christopher Anzalone
CFO: Kenneth Myszkowski
HR: –
FYE: September 30
Type: Public

Arrowhead Pharmaceuticals develops drugs that silence disease-causing genes in the body. Its RNA interference (RNAi) platform named Targeted RNAi Molecule or TRiM utilizes ligand-mediated delivery and is designed to enable tissue-specific targeting while being structurally simple. The company's JNJ-3989 (formerly ARO-HBV) drug is in clinical trials for the treatment of hepatitis B. Arrowhead has other RNA assets that are being explored to work in combination with ARO-HBV to treat various diseases. In late 2016 the company stopped developing its intravenously delivered dynamic polyconjugate delivery vehicle programs in order to focus on its TRiM technology. Arrowhead was originally incorporated in 1989.

	Annual Growth	09/17	09/18	09/19	09/20	09/21
Sales ($ mil.)	44.9%	31.4	16.1	168.8	88.0	138.3
Net income ($ mil.)	–	(34.4)	(54.5)	68.0	(84.6)	(140.8)
Market value ($ mil.)	94.9%	451.7	1,999.9	2,939.9	4,492.3	6,513.1
Employees	37.1%	93	95	109	232	329

ARROWHEAD REGIONAL MEDICAL CENTER

400 N PEPPER AVE
COLTON, CA 923241819
Phone: 909-580-1000
Fax: –
Web: www.arrowheadregional.org

CEO: –
CFO: –
HR: –
FYE: June 30
Type: Private

Find yourself dehydrated after searching the Inland Empire deserts for arrowheads? Arrowhead Regional Medical Center (ARMC) can fix you up. The San Bernardino County owned and operated hospital provides a range of health services from general medical and surgical care to emergency services rehabilitation inpatient psychiatric care pediatric and women's health services. It also serves as a Level II trauma center a regional burn center and medical training facility. ARMC with some 460 beds (370 inpatient and 90 behavioral) opened in 1999 to replace the aging San Bernardino County Hospital. The hospital also offers outpatient services on its main campus and at area clinics.

	Annual Growth	06/02	06/03	06/04	06/09	06/15
Sales ($ mil.)	3.4%	–	313.5	439.1	225.0	469.0
Net income ($ mil.)	–	–	(1.1)	3.7	25.4	74.3
Market value ($ mil.)	–	–	–	–	–	–
Employees	–	–	–	–	–	2,500

ART CENTER COLLEGE OF DESIGN INC

1700 LIDA ST
PASADENA, CA 911031999
Phone: 626-396-2200
Fax: –
Web: www.artcenter.edu

CEO: –
CFO: Gina Luciffino
HR: Dave Di Raddo
FYE: June 30
Type: Private

Art Center College of Design (ACCD) is designing a future of creativity for its students. The college offers undergraduate and graduate degrees in such fields as advertising film fine art media graphic design illustration photography industrial design product design and transportation design. Degrees offered include 11 Bachelor of Fine Arts and Bachelor of Science programs and six Master of Fine Arts and Master of Science programs. ACCD which has an enrollment of about 1700 full-time students is ranked among top design schools in the US.

	Annual Growth	06/10	06/11	06/14	06/15	06/20
Sales ($ mil.)	2.7%	–	107.1	121.1	94.1	136.2
Net income ($ mil.)	–	–	5.6	2.8	(5.5)	(0.6)
Market value ($ mil.)	–	–	–	–	–	–
Employees	–	–	–	–	–	400

ARTECH INFORMATION SYSTEMS L.L.C.

240 Cedar Knolls Rd. Ste. 100
Cedar Knolls NJ 07927
Phone: 973-998-2500
Fax: 973-998-2599
Web: www.artechinfo.com

CEO: –
CFO: –
HR: –
FYE: December 31
Type: Private

Artech Information Systems comes to the rescue for the technically unsavvy. The minority- and woman-owned company specializes in providing IT staffing and consulting project management and business process outsourcing (BPO) services. Artech Information Systems serves clients in the financial services pharmaceutical telecommunications and technology industries among others. The company which operates from more than 20 locations in China India Mexico and the US also works with federal and state government agencies. It provides its services 24 hours a day seven days a week.

ARTESIAN RESOURCES CORP.   NMS: ARTN A

664 Churchmans Road
Newark, DE 19702
Phone: 302 453-6900
Fax: –
Web: www.artesianresources.com

CEO: Dian Taylor
CFO: David Spacht
HR: –
FYE: December 31
Type: Public

All's well that ends in wells for Artesian Resources. Operating primarily through regulated utility Artesian Water the company provides water in parts of Delaware Maryland and Pennsylvania (about 76300 metered customers). It serves residential commercial industrial municipal and utility customers; residential customers account for about 55% of the utility's water sales. Artesian pumps nearly 2 billion gallons of water annually from its wells then sends it to customers through approximately 1300 miles of mains. The company also provides wastewater services in Delaware Pennsylvania and Maryland.

	Annual Growth	12/16	12/17	12/18	12/19	12/20
Sales ($ mil.)	2.7%	79.1	82.2	80.4	83.6	88.1
Net income ($ mil.)	6.7%	13.0	14.0	14.3	14.9	16.8
Market value ($ mil.)	3.8%	298.9	360.8	326.3	348.2	347.0
Employees	1.1%	225	233	241	239	235

ARTHROCARE CORP.   NMS: ARTC

7000 W. William Cannon, Building One
Austin, TX 78735
Phone: 512 391-3900
Fax: 512 391-3901
Web: www.arthrocare.com

CEO: David Fitzgerald
CFO: Todd Newton
HR: –
FYE: December 31
Type: Public

With the wave of a wand ArthroCare can make tissue disappear. The company's proprietary Coblation technology (one of several of its technologies) uses bipolar radiofrequency energy to remove and shape cartilage and tendons and other soft tissues. Its specialized wands focus the energy and minimize damage to nearby healthy tissue simultaneously sealing small bleeding vessels. First used in arthroscopic procedures to repair joints the electrosurgery system line now includes equipment used in a wide range of minimally invasive surgeries. The company also makes ligament repair spinal stabilization and wound-care products.

	Annual Growth	12/08	12/09	12/10	12/11	12/12
Sales ($ mil.)	4.1%	314.2	331.6	355.4	354.9	368.5
Net income ($ mil.)	–	(34.7)	(5.8)	37.1	(0.9)	46.4
Market value ($ mil.)	64.1%	133.5	663.1	869.0	886.3	967.7
Employees	38.4%	463	1,363	1,407	1,600	1,700

ARTISAN PARTNERS ASSET MANAGEMENT INC   NYS: APAM

875 E. Wisconsin Avenue, Suite 800
Milwaukee, WI 53202
Phone: 414 390-6100
Fax: –
Web: www.artisanpartners.com

CEO: Eric Colson
CFO: Charles Daley
HR: –
FYE: December 31
Type: Public

These artisans are into making bread. Artisan Partners Asset Management is an institutional investment manager with $64 billion in assets under management. The firm manages a dozen funds from small- and mid-cap growth and value funds to foreign and emerging markets funds. It acts as the investment adviser to Artisan Funds mutual funds which account for about 55% of its assets under management. The remainder is made up of separate accounts for institutional investors including pension plans trusts endowments foundations not-for-profit organizations government entities and private companies. Founded in 1994 Artisan Partners Asset Management went public in 2013.

	Annual Growth	12/16	12/17	12/18	12/19	12/20
Sales ($ mil.)	5.7%	720.9	795.6	828.6	799.0	899.6
Net income ($ mil.)	30.6%	73.0	49.6	158.3	156.5	212.6
Market value ($ mil.)	14.1%	2,337.5	3,103.6	1,737.2	2,539.5	3,955.3
Employees	4.5%	380	400	425	440	453

ARTISANAL BRANDS INC.

NBB: AHFP

483 Tenth Avenue
New York, NY 10018
Phone: 212 871-3150
Fax: –
Web: www.artisanalcheese.com

CEO: Daniel W Dowe
CFO: –
HR: –
FYE: May 31
Type: Public

American Home Food Products which does business as Artisanal Cheese aspires to be the big cheese. Formerly a building supply marketing firm the company is now active in the marketing of private-label foods. In 2007 it acquired specialty food company Artisanal Premium Cheese for about $4.5 million. At the same time the company sold its building material assets for approximately $1 million. Artisanal Cheese markets and sells specialty and handmade cheeses to upscale restaurants and retailers. In addition to wholesale and foodservice distribution the company sells products in supermarkets through catalogs and on its Web site.

	Annual Growth	05/08	05/09	05/10	05/11	05/12
Sales ($ mil.)	–	0.0	5.7	4.2	4.6	3.6
Net income ($ mil.)	–	0.0	(1.6)	(2.3)	(2.5)	(4.3)
Market value ($ mil.)	–	0.0	8.1	3.4	4.8	1.3
Employees	21.6%	–	–	23	30	34

ARTIVION INC

NYS: CRY

1655 Roberts Boulevard N.W.
Kennesaw, GA 30144
Phone: 770 419-3355
Fax: 770 426-0031
Web: www.cryolife.com

CEO: James Mackin
CFO: D. Ashley Lee
HR: Matthew Getz
FYE: December 31
Type: Public

CryoLife preserves lives by conserving the tissues that sustain them. The company is a leader in the manufacturing processing and distribution of medical devices and implantable human tissues used in cardiac and vascular surgical procedures for patients with aortic disease. It takes human heart valves and blood vessels from deceased volunteer donors processes them and stores them in liquid nitrogen freezers (a process called cryopreservation). For some preserved tissue the company uses its proprietary SynerGraft technology which reduces the presence of donor cells and makes the tissue more compatible with the recipient. CryoLife also develops BioGlue an adhesive used to seal internal surgical wounds. Majority of its sales were generated in the US.

	Annual Growth	12/16	12/17	12/18	12/19	12/20
Sales ($ mil.)	8.9%	180.4	189.7	262.8	276.2	253.2
Net income ($ mil.)	–	10.8	3.7	(2.8)	1.7	(16.7)
Market value ($ mil.)	5.4%	745.1	745.1	1,104.2	1,054.0	918.6
Employees	15.9%	665	1,000	1,100	1,200	1,200

ARTS WAY MANUFACTURING CO INC

NAS: ARTW

5556 Highway 9
Armstrong, IA 50514
Phone: 712 864-3131
Fax: 712 864-3154
Web: www.artsway-mfg.com

CEO: David King
CFO: Michael Woods
HR: –
FYE: November 30
Type: Public

Sinatra did it his way but farmers have been doing it Art's way since 1956. Art's-Way Manufacturing makes an assortment of machinery under its own label and its customers' private labels. Art's-Way equipment includes custom animal-feed processing machines high-bulk mixing wagons mowers and stalk shredders and equipment for harvesting sugar beets and potatoes. Its private-label OEM customers include CNH Global for whom Art's-Way makes and supplies hay blowers. Equipment dealers throughout the US sell Art's-Way products. Steel truck bodies are also manufactured under the Cherokee Truck Bodies name. Art's-Way owns subsidiaries Art's-Way Vessels and Art's-Way Scientific.

	Annual Growth	11/16	11/17	11/18	11/19	11/20
Sales ($ mil.)	1.0%	21.6	20.7	19.7	22.9	22.4
Net income ($ mil.)	–	(0.8)	(1.6)	(3.4)	(1.4)	(2.1)
Market value ($ mil.)	(6.5%)	14.4	12.0	10.6	8.2	11.0
Employees	(0.6%)	129	119	132	103	126

ARUBA NETWORKS INC

NMS: ARUN

1344 Crossman Ave.
Sunnyvale, CA 94089-1113
Phone: 408 227-4500
Fax: –
Web: www.arubanetworks.com

CEO: –
CFO: Jon Faust
HR: –
FYE: July 31
Type: Public

Aruba Networks wants to turn your business into a wireless paradise. The company offers network access equipment and software for mobile enterprise networks. Its Mobile Virtual Enterprise (MOVE) architecture unifies access between wired and wireless network infrastructures for employees both at and away from the office. Products include controllers access points and concentrators as well as operating system and management software. Aruba also provides professional and support services. It targets the corporate education and government sectors. Aruba outsources most manufacturing to partners such as Flextronics and Sercomm. The US is the company's largest market.

	Annual Growth	07/10	07/11	07/12	07/13	07/14
Sales ($ mil.)	28.6%	266.5	396.5	516.8	600.0	728.9
Net income ($ mil.)	–	(34.0)	70.7	(8.9)	(31.6)	(29.0)
Market value ($ mil.)	1.3%	1,826.3	2,468.4	1,525.2	1,912.4	1,921.0
Employees	26.7%	681	1,057	1,223	1,473	1,754

ARUP LABORATORIES INC.

500 Chipeta Way
Salt Lake City UT 84108
Phone: 801-583-2787
Fax: 800-522-2706
Web: www.aruplab.com

CEO: Edgar Eraenele
CFO: Andy Theurer
HR: –
FYE: June 30
Type: Private

The good folks at ARUP Laboratories don't grow pale at the sight of blood. The clinical reference lab performs tens of thousands of tests daily on blood body fluids and tissue for health care clients including teaching hospitals hospital groups clinics government entities and other labs across the US. Its test menu includes thousands of assays ranging from routine screenings (such as allergy and infectious diseases tests) to highly complex genetic and molecular tests. The organization also offers consulting and information services including online access to test results. ARUP Laboratories is owned by the University of Utah.

ARVEST BANK GROUP INC.

125 W. Central Ste. 218
Bentonville AR 72712
Phone: 479-750-1400
Fax: 614-716-1823
Web: www.aeptexas.com

CEO: –
CFO: Karla Payne
HR: –
FYE: December 31
Type: Private

Arvest Bank Group operates more than 240 locations in Arkansas Kansas Missouri and Oklahoma. Through Arvest Bank it provides traditional services such as checking and savings accounts CDs and credit cards. The bank's lending activities mainly consist of commercial real estate loans residential mortgages and business construction and consumer loans. The group maintains a decentralized structure of about 15 individually chartered banks; local managers and directors control lending decisions and deposit rates in many communities. Descendants of Wal-Mart founder Sam Walton (including bank CEO Jim Walton a son of Sam and one of the richest men in America) control Arvest Bank Group.

ARXAN TECHNOLOGIES INC.

6903 Rockledge Dr. Ste. 910
Bethesda MD 20817
Phone: 301-968-4290
Fax: 301-968-4291
Web: www.arxan.com

CEO: Joe Sander
CFO: Charlie Velasquez
HR: –
FYE: December 31
Type: Private

Arxan Technologies doesn't mind being defensive when it comes to security. The company provides network security software and services for protecting computer systems from piracy and unauthorized access. Businesses in a variety of industries used its GuardIT and EnsureIT software suites to control access to their data and applications. Its TransformIT product provides cryptographic key security and BindIT application safeguards against HostID spoofing. Arxan's professional services include needs and risk assessment as well as technical consulting. The company serves clients in such industries as publishing media and telecommunications services. Arxan has satellite offices in San Francisco and London.

ASAHI/AMERICA INC.

35 Green St.
Malden MA 02148-0134
Phone: 781-321-5409
Fax: 781-321-4421
Web: www.asahi-america.com

CEO: Hidetoshi Hashimoto
CFO: Stephen Harrington
HR: –
FYE: March 31
Type: Subsidiary

Asahi/America has made it its mission in life to keep track of the ebb and flow. A subsidiary of Japan-based Asahi Organic Chemicals Industry Asahi/America makes and distributes corrosion-resistant products for fluid and gas flow such as thermoplastic valves tubing and piping systems filtration equipment flow meters and components used in mining pulp and paper chemical/petrochemical water treatment aquarium and semiconductor manufacturing applications. Asahi/America's revenues come from the distribution of valves made by its parent company pipe made by Asahi partner Austrian firm Alois-Gruber and from the sale of its own products (flow meters actuators valve controls filtration equipment).

ASARCO LLC

5285 E. Williams Cir. Ste. 2000
Tucson AZ 85711
Phone: 520-798-7500
Fax: 520-798-7780
Web: www.asarco.com

CEO: –
CFO: –
HR: –
FYE: December 31
Type: Subsidiary

Copper is king for ASARCO. A subsidiary of diversified mining firm Grupo Mexico ASARCO (American Smelting and Refining Company) operates mining and copper smelting activities primarily in the Southwestern US. Each year its mines produce from 350 million to 400 million pounds of copper as well as silver and gold as byproducts of copper production. It produces copper cathode rod and cake. The company's three mines and a 720000 tons per year smelter are located in Arizona. It also operates a copper refinery with a 279.5 million pounds per year production capacity in Amarillo Texas. ASARCO was founded in 1899.

ASB FINANCIAL CORP.

503 Chillicothe Street
Portsmouth, OH 45662
Phone: 740 354-3177
Fax: –
Web: www.bankwithasb.com

NBB: ASBN
CEO: –
CFO: –
HR: –
FYE: June 30
Type: Public

ASB Financial is the holding company for American Savings Bank. Operating since 1892 the bank serves Scioto and Pike counties in southern Ohio as well as communities across the Ohio River in northern Kentucky. From about five offices the thrift originates a variety of loans more than half of which are one- to four-family mortgages. Other loan products include commercial real estate construction business consumer and land loans. American Savings' deposit products include traditional checking and savings accounts NOW and money market accounts CDs IRAs and health savings accounts. The thrift also provides access to financial planning services.

	Annual Growth	06/11	06/12	06/13	06/14	06/15
Assets ($ mil.)	2.2%	229.3	238.1	260.6	252.1	250.5
Net income ($ mil.)	(3.0%)	2.0	1.7	1.6	1.3	1.7
Market value ($ mil.)	1.8%	23.9	23.9	26.7	25.2	25.7
Employees	–	–	–	–	–	–

ASBURY AUTOMOTIVE GROUP INC

2905 Premiere Parkway N.W., Suite 300
Duluth, GA 30097
Phone: 770 418-8200
Fax: –
Web: www.asburyauto.com

NYS: ABG
CEO: David Hult
CFO: Michael Welch
HR: –
FYE: December 31
Type: Public

Car dealership giant Asbury Automotive Group oversees more than 110 new vehicle franchises representing about 90 dealership locations in about 10 states including the Carolinas Florida Texas and Virginia. The dealerships sell more than 30 different brands of US-made and imported new and used vehicles. Asbury also offer parts servicing and collision repair from about 25 repair centers as well as financing insurance and warranty and service contracts. The auto dealer has grown by acquiring large locally-branded dealership groups as well as smaller groups and individually-owned dealerships throughout the US. Honda vehicles account for approximately 20% of Asbury's new car sales.

	Annual Growth	12/16	12/17	12/18	12/19	12/20
Sales ($ mil.)	2.2%	6,527.8	6,456.5	6,874.4	7,210.3	7,131.8
Net income ($ mil.)	11.1%	167.2	139.1	168.0	184.4	254.4
Market value ($ mil.)	24.0%	1,189.9	1,234.3	1,285.6	2,155.9	2,810.6
Employees	0.0%	7,900	8,000	8,200	8,500	7,900

ASCENA RETAIL GROUP INC

933 MacArthur Boulevard
Mahwah, NJ 07430
Phone: 551 777-6700
Fax: 845 369-8001
Web: www.ascenaretail.com

NBB: ASNA Q
CEO: –
CFO: –
HR: –
FYE: August 01
Type: Public

Ascena Retail Group operates approximately 3400 specialty stores throughout the US Puerto Rico and Canada. Its largest chain Justice courts "tweens" at nearly 850 stores and online. The company offers premium women's clothing through about 300 Ann Taylor stores and about 670 LOFT stores. It also offers plus-size wear through more than 700 Lane Bryant stores and more than 300 Catherines stores. Ascena also operates about a dozen Lou & Grey clothing stores which target younger women. The company sold its women's clothing chain Maurices Inc. to an affiliate of OpCapita LLP in 2019. Ascena has announced it is closing its 730 dressbarn stores which courted working women. The Company's operations are largely concentrated in the United States and Canada.

	Annual Growth	07/16	07/17*	08/18	08/19	08/20
Sales ($ mil.)	(14.6%)	6,995.4	6,649.8	6,578.3	5,493.4	3,718.1
Net income ($ mil.)	–	(11.9)	(1,067.3)	(39.7)	(661.4)	(1,141.8)
Market value ($ mil.)	(45.4%)	82.0	23.4	40.5	3.3	7.3
Employees	(14.7%)	66,000	64,000	63,000	53,000	35,000

*Fiscal year change

ASCENA RETAIL GROUP INC.

NASDAQ: ASNA

30 Dunnigan Dr.
Suffern NY 10901
Phone: 845-369-4500
Fax: 914-428-4581
Web: www.drewindustries.com

CEO: -
CFO: -
HR: -
FYE: July 31
Type: Public

Ascena Retail Group (formerly Dress Barn Inc.) has left the farm for greener — but not leaner — retail pastures. The apparel and accessories retailer operates more than 3800 specialty stores throughout the US Puerto Rico and Canada. Its 825 Dress Barn stores cater to women ages 35 to 55. Maurices with some 830 locations targets 17-to-34-year-old females in small towns with populations between 25000 and 100000. Its Justice chain courts "tweens" at 940 stores and online. Its newly-acquired Charming Shoppes subsidiary operates the plus-size Lane Bryant and Catherines Plus Sizes apparel chains. Founded as Dress Barn in 1962 the company changed its name to Ascena Retail Group in 2011.

ASCEND HOLDINGS LLC

450 E. 1000 N.
North Salt Lake UT 84054
Phone: 801-299-6400
Fax: 801-299-6401
Web: www.ascendhr.com

CEO: -
CFO: -
HR: -
FYE: December 31
Type: Private

If moving up means moving human resources away then this is the company for you. Ascend HR Solutions a professional employer organization provides off-site human resources employee benefits administration and payroll services so clients can focus on their core business. The company also offers computer maintenance consulting and support services for clients of any size. The company's services include skills testing employee handbook development recruiting 401K plan administration tax filing and insurance. Ascend HR Solutions was founded in 1995.

ASCENSION BORGESS HOSPITAL

1521 GULL RD
KALAMAZOO, MI 490481640
Phone: 269-226-7000
Fax: -
Web: www.healthcare.ascension.org

CEO: -
CFO: -
HR: -
FYE: June 30
Type: Private

Borgess Medical Center is part of the Borgess Health Alliance which is a member of the Ascension Health network. The general acute care facility which serves residents of southwestern Michigan houses more than 420 beds. It has a comprehensive offering of medical and surgical services including specialty care in areas such as cancer heart disease neuroscience and orthopedics. Borgess Medical Center also serves as a Level II trauma center and features a research institute a sleep disorders clinic a weight loss surgery center no-wait emergency room and outpatient facilities. The hospital was founded in 1889 by a local priest.

	Annual Growth	06/13	06/14	06/15	06/16	06/19
Sales ($ mil.)	1.9%	-	449.3	382.8	394.2	492.6
Net income ($ mil.)	(3.8%)	-	64.3	28.2	60.7	53.0
Market value ($ mil.)	-	-	-	-	-	-
Employees	-	-	-	-	-	2,200

ASCENSION GENESYS HOSPITAL

1 GENESYS PKWY
GRAND BLANC, MI 484398065
Phone: 810-606-5000
Fax: -
Web: www.healthcare.ascension.org

CEO: Christopher J Palazzolo
CFO: David Carrol
HR: -
FYE: June 30
Type: Private

Genesys Regional Medical Center generates health care services for residents of a six-county region in eastern Michigan. The integrated medical center features a 410-bed hospital providing general medical and surgical care as well as specialty care in areas such as heart disease (through the Genesys Heart Institute). Additionally Genesys Regional includes family medicine outpatient diagnostic and rehabilitative care centers. It also operates a women and children's center and in cooperation with Flint's Hurley Medical Center it runs the Genesys Hurley Cancer Institute. Genesys Regional is a member the Genesys Health System which is part of Catholic hospital operator Ascension Health.

	Annual Growth	06/08	06/09	06/10	06/13	06/14
Sales ($ mil.)	(2.0%)	-	-	452.9	415.1	417.6
Net income ($ mil.)	(62.7%)	-	-	11.5	1.8	0.2
Market value ($ mil.)	-	-	-	-	-	-
Employees	-	-	-	-	-	3,739

ASCENSION HEALTH

4600 EDMUNDSON RD
SAINT LOUIS, MO 631343806
Phone: 314-733-8000
Fax: -
Web: www.healthcare.ascension.org

CEO: Joseph R Impicciche
CFO: Anthony J Speranzo
HR: Tandala Cook
FYE: June 30
Type: Private

As one of the leading non-profit and Catholic health systems in the US Ascension provided $2.4 billion in care of persons living in poverty and other community benefit programs. Ascension includes more than 160000 associates and 40000 aligned providers. Ascension provide variety of services including clinical and network services venture capital investing investment management biomedical engineering facilities management risk management and contracting through Ascension's own group purchasing organization. Ascension Health was created in 1999 from a union of the Daughters of Charity National Health System and the Sisters of St. Joseph Health System.

	Annual Growth	06/06	06/07	06/08	06/10	06/15
Sales ($ mil.)	(44.2%)	-	-	13,489.3	14,773.3	227.8
Net income ($ mil.)	-	-	-	351.0	1,230.9	(18.0)
Market value ($ mil.)	-	-	-	-	-	-
Employees	-	-	-	-	-	109,000

ASCENSION PROVIDENCE HOSPITAL

16001 W 9 MILE RD
SOUTHFIELD, MI 480754818
Phone: 248-849-3000
Fax: -
Web: www.providenceobgynresidency.com

CEO: Brant Russell
CFO: -
HR: -
FYE: June 30
Type: Private

Providence Hospital and Medical Centers provides health care in the Motor City and surrounding areas. The main Providence Hospital is a 408-bed teaching facility that has been recognized for its cardiology program and clinical expertise in behavioral medicine. It offers a variety of other services ranging from cancer treatment and neurosurgery to orthopedics and women's health. The network also includes dozens of affiliated general practice and specialty health clinics. The not-for-profit medical center founded in 1845 as St. Vincent's Hospital in Detroit by the Daughters of Charity is part of Catholic health ministry St. John Health (itself a subsidiary of Ascension Health).

	Annual Growth	06/10	06/11	06/14	06/15	06/16
Sales ($ mil.)	(0.1%)	-	706.6	659.5	654.1	703.6
Net income ($ mil.)	(4.9%)	-	27.8	53.2	25.5	21.6
Market value ($ mil.)	-	-	-	-	-	-
Employees	-	-	-	-	-	4,700

ASCENSION PROVIDENCE ROCHESTER HOSPITAL

1101 W UNIVERSITY DR
ROCHESTER, MI 483071863
Phone: 248-652-5000
Fax: –
Web: www.healthcare.ascension.org

CEO: Terry Hamilton
CFO: Donna Kopinski
HR: –
FYE: June 30
Type: Private

Crittenton Hospital Medical Center treats patients in the western counties of the suburban Detroit area. The not-for-profit hospital has 290 beds for acute care but also provides primary and specialist care. Crittenton offers such services as urgent pediatric care rehabilitative therapy inpatient psychiatric care joint replacement and sleep analysis. It is a fully accredited teaching campus and partners with area universities and medical providers. It also operates outpatient facilities including surgery imaging and therapy centers. With a heritage that reaches back to the early 1900s Crittenton Hospital Medical Center opened its doors in 1967.

	Annual Growth	12/13	12/14	12/15*	06/19	06/20
Sales ($ mil.)	(0.5%)	–	230.4	188.3	212.6	223.9
Net income ($ mil.)	8.4%	–	5.9	(48.2)	4.0	9.7
Market value ($ mil.)	–	–	–	–	–	–
Employees	–	–	–	–	–	1,515

*Fiscal year change

ASCENSION VIA CHRISTI HEALTH, INC

2622 W CENTRAL AVE # 200
WICHITA, KS 672034972
Phone: 316-858-4900
Fax: –
Web: www.viachristi.org

CEO: –
CFO: –
HR: Marianne Moore
FYE: June 30
Type: Private

How do the sick become well? Via Christi Health of course. Via Christi Health is a Catholic not-for-profit health care system that provides a range of medical services to residents of Kansas and northern Oklahoma through a network of hospitals medical centers and health service organizations. The system's facilities include four hospitals about a dozen senior living communities nearly 20 medical clinics and specialized facilities for behavioral health and rehabilitative care. The system is affiliated with Marian Health System and Ascension Health. Via Christi Health was formed in 1995 when the Sisters of the Sorrowful Mother and the Sisters of St. Joseph of Wichita merged their health care ministries.

	Annual Growth	06/11	06/12	06/13	06/14	06/15
Sales ($ mil.)	13.7%	–	–	–	131.6	149.6
Net income ($ mil.)	–	–	–	–	(23.5)	(31.0)
Market value ($ mil.)	–	–	–	–	–	–
Employees	–	–	–	–	–	11,970

ASCENT HEALTHCARE SOLUTIONS INC.

10232 S. 51st St.
Phoenix AZ 85044
Phone: 480-763-5300
Fax: 480-763-0101
Web: ascenths.com

CEO: Kevin A Lobo
CFO: Tim Einwechter
HR: Christi Garner
FYE: December 31
Type: Subsidiary

Ascent Healthcare Solutions is banking on the idea that one doctor's trash could be another doctor's treasure. The company is out to help hospitals with the three "R"s — reduce reuse and recycle. Ascent focuses on reprocessing disposable medical devices for health care facilities (from small rural providers to surgery centers and group purchasing organizations). Its OR-based systems permit the collection of thousands of tons of devices marketed as "single-use" as well as a range of recyclable materials. After collecting the used devices it cleans sterilizes tests and then returns them from its centers in Florida and Arizona. The company is part of the MedSurg division of medical products maker Stryker.

ASCENT SOLAR TECHNOLOGIES INC
NBB: ASTI D

12300 Grant Street
Thornton, CO 80241
Phone: 720 872-5000
Fax: –
Web: www.ascentsolar.com

CEO: Kong Hian Lee
CFO: Michael Gilbreth
HR: –
FYE: December 31
Type: Public

As long as that sun keeps ascending in the eastern skies every day there will be ventures trying to tap its enormous energy resources. Ascent Solar Technologies is a development-stage company working on photovoltaic modules for use in consumer applications as well as satellites and spacecraft. The firm aspires to make such gear smaller lighter and more flexible than existing solar cells for use in space by utilizing a thin-film absorbing layer on top of a polyimide substrate. The thin-film layer on top of the high-temperature plastic is made up of copper indium gallium and selenium which is why the technology is called CIGS. Norsk Hydro has a 39% stake in the company.

	Annual Growth	12/16	12/17	12/18	12/19	12/20
Sales ($ mil.)	(55.8%)	1.7	0.6	0.9	0.6	0.1
Net income ($ mil.)	–	(38.9)	(18.6)	(16.0)	(4.9)	1.6
Market value ($ mil.)	–	0.0	0.0	0.1	0.0	0.0
Employees	(23.8%)	86	71	22	21	29

ASG TECHNOLOGIES GROUP, INC.

708 GOODLETTE RD
NAPLES, FL 341025644
Phone: 239-435-2200
Fax: –
Web: www.asg.com

CEO: Charles Sansbury
CFO: Dilip Upmanyu
HR: –
FYE: December 31
Type: Private

ASG Technologies Group Inc. (ASG) is a Global Enterprise Software vendor providing solutions for some of the world's largest businesses. ASG is the only solutions provider for both Information Management and IT Systems Management. Its information management solutions capture manage govern and enable companies to understand and support all types of information while its IT systems management solutions ensure that the systems and infrastructure supporting that information lifecycle are always available and performing as expected. Customers have included Oney Clemson Postbank and Primerica.

	Annual Growth	12/06	12/07	12/08	12/09	12/17
Sales ($ mil.)	(1.9%)	–	–	300.1	276.5	252.4
Net income ($ mil.)	–	–	–	(12.6)	(11.5)	15.7
Market value ($ mil.)	–	–	–	–	–	–
Employees	–	–	–	–	–	5,664

ASGN INC
NYS: ASGN

4400 Cox Road, Suite 110
Glen Allen, VA 23060
Phone: 888 482-8068
Fax: –
Web: www.asgn.com

CEO: Theodore Hanson
CFO: Edward Pierce
HR: –
FYE: December 31
Type: Public

ASGN Incorporated (formerly known as On Assignment) is a specialist staffing agency that places professionals from IT consultants to lab assistants with clients in need of temporary (or permanent) help. The firm operates through several divisions: Apex (IT and engineering staffing for temporary temp-to-hire and permanent placements); Oxford (engineering and specialized high-end IT consultants); and ECS (cloud cybersecurity and software). ASGN brands include CyberCoders Cyrus Lab Support Oxford Oxford Global Resources and among other. The company generated majority of its sales in domestic operations.

	Annual Growth	12/16	12/17	12/18	12/19	12/20
Sales ($ mil.)	12.8%	2,440.4	2,625.9	3,399.8	3,923.9	3,950.6
Net income ($ mil.)	19.8%	97.2	157.7	157.7	174.7	200.3
Market value ($ mil.)	17.3%	2,336.1	3,399.9	2,883.1	3,754.3	4,418.7
Employees	(0.3%)	55,880	59,200	66,200	67,700	55,200

ASHFORD HOSPITALITY TRUST INC   NYS: AHT

14185 Dallas Parkway, Suite 1100 — CEO: J. Robison Hays
Dallas, TX 75254 — CFO: Deric Eubanks
Phone: 972 490-9600 — HR: –
Fax: 972 980-2705 — FYE: December 31
Web: www.ahtreit.com — Type: Public

A self-administered real estate investment trust (REIT) Ashford Hospitality Trust owns more than 100 hotel properties representing more than 22620 rooms throughout the US. It holds some 90 condominium units at WorldQuest Resort in Orlando Florida and 17.5% ownership in OpenKey with a carrying value of $2.8 million. Most of its properties operate under the upscale and upper upscale Hilton Marriott Hyatt and Intercontinental Hotels Group brands. Ashford Hospitality Trust also provides other products and services including project management services debt placement and related services audio visual services real estate advisory services insurance claims services hypoallergenic premium rooms investment management services broker-dealer services and mobile key technology. Ashford Hospitality Trust is based in Dallas TX and went public in 2003.

	Annual Growth	12/16	12/17	12/18	12/19	12/20
Sales ($ mil.)	(23.6%)	1,492.0	1,439.3	1,430.8	1,502.8	508.2
Net income ($ mil.)	–	(46.3)	(67.0)	(127.0)	(113.6)	(543.9)
Market value ($ mil.)	(23.9%)	49.9	43.3	25.7	18.0	16.7
Employees	–	–	103	102	116	116

ASHLAND INC   NYS: ASH

50 E. RiverCenter Boulevard, P.O. Box 391 — CEO: William Wulfsohn
Covington, KY 41012-0391 — CFO: J Willis
Phone: 859 815-3333 — HR: –
Fax: – — FYE: September 30
Web: www.ashland.com — Type: Public

Ashland's three business units are built on chemicals and cars. Ashland Performance Materials makes specialty resins polymers and adhesives. Specialty Ingredients makes cellulose ethers vinyl pyrrolidones and biofunctionals. It offers industry-leading products technologies and resources for solving formulation and product-performance challenges. Consumer Markets led by subsidiary Valvoline runs an oil-change chain in the US and sells Valvoline oil and Zerex antifreeze. The company's Ashland Specialty Ingredients unit produces polymers and additives for the food personal care pharmaceutical and other industries. In 2015 Ashland announced plans to spin off Valvoline.

	Annual Growth	09/11	09/12	09/13	09/14	09/15
Sales ($ mil.)	(4.6%)	6,502.0	8,206.0	7,813.0	6,121.0	5,387.0
Net income ($ mil.)	(7.1%)	414.0	26.0	683.0	233.0	309.0
Market value ($ mil.)	22.9%	2,957.4	4,797.2	6,196.2	6,974.7	6,741.5
Employees	(8.5%)	15,000	15,000	15,000	11,000	10,500

ASI COMPUTER TECHNOLOGIES INC

48289 FREMONT BLVD — CEO: Christine Liang
FREMONT, CA 945386510 — CFO: –
Phone: 510-226-8000 — HR: –
Fax: – — FYE: December 31
Web: www.asipartner.com — Type: Private

ASI offers an extensive line of products components and services and also provides ISO-9001 compliant system integration and value add contract assembly. ASI Computer Technologies is a national distributor of IT software and hardware products. It offers more than 15000 products including PCs scanners security surveillance and data storage devices. The company has rapidly grown to become the partner of choice for over 20000 VARs throughout North America. Its vendor partners include companies the likes of AMD Intel Microsoft and Western Digital. ASI's services include custom systems integration. It also markets PCs and notebooks under its own brands: Pegatron and Nspire. Furthermore it caters to various industries such as retail and the SMB market The company was established in 1987 by president and owner Cristine Liang.

	Annual Growth	12/01	12/02	12/03	12/04	12/13
Sales ($ mil.)	6.6%	–	865.6	982.5	1,057.1	1,746.9
Net income ($ mil.)	4.9%	–	10.4	13.1	12.2	17.6
Market value ($ mil.)	–	–	–	–	–	–
Employees	–	–	–	–	–	76

ASICS AMERICA CORPORATION

29 Parker Ste. 100 — CEO: –
Irvine CA 92618 — CFO: Kenji Sakai
Phone: 949-453-8888 — HR: –
Fax: 949-453-0292 — FYE: March 31
Web: www.asicsamerica.com — Type: Subsidiary

With ASICS America you don't have to earn your stripes you just have to purchase them. ASICS America is the North American arm of Japanese athletic footwear apparel and accessories maker ASICS Corporation. Its shoe collection — featuring a trademarked stripe design — includes footwear for basketball racing and running track and field volleyball walking and wrestling. ASICS products which were introduced in the US in 1977 are sold at regional and national retailers throughout the country as well as through online vendors such as Zappos.com. ASICS opened its first freestanding store in the US in fall 2009.

ASK.COM

555 12th St. Ste. 500 — CEO: Doug Leeds
Oakland CA 94607 — CFO: Steven J Sordello
Phone: 510-985-7400 — HR: –
Fax: 510-985-7412 — FYE: December 31
Web: www.ask.com — Type: Subsidiary

Ask and you shall receive especially when it comes to the Internet. Ask.com (formerly Ask Jeeves) operates an online question-and-answer service. The site solicits users to ask questions as well as answer questions from other users. Results reveal answers from a variety of sources. Previously the operator of a search engine Ask.com switched gears in 2010. While it still offers search on its site it no longer compiles an index of billions of Web pages. Instead it delivers results via an agreement with search partner Google. Ask.com operates alongside websites such as CityGrid Media's Citysearch.com and Lexico Publishing Group's Dictionary.com as part of the Search holdings of IAC/InterActiveCorp (IAC).

ASPEN MARKETING SERVICES INC.

1240 North Ave. — CEO: –
West Chicago IL 60185 — CFO: –
Phone: 630-293-9600 — HR: –
Fax: 630-293-7584 — FYE: December 31
Web: www.aspenms.com — Type: Business Segment

Need marketing services? Ask Aspen. The company provides integrated marketing services with particular expertise in serving the automotive and telecommunications industries. Aspen Marketing Services blends strategic planning public relations and brand promotion as well as event and direct marketing to provide clients in a wide range of industries unified marketing for greater results. Its digital marketing capabilities utilize Web design e-mail marketing database processing and online loyalty marketing services. Aspen was founded in 1986 and operates about 10 offices spanning North America. In mid-2011 it was acquired by Alliance Data Systems and integrated into its Epsilon Data Management unit.

ASPEN TECHNOLOGY INC
NMS: AZPN

20 Crosby Drive
Bedford, MA 01730
Phone: 781 221-6400
Fax: -
Web: www.aspentech.com

CEO: Antonio Pietri
CFO: Chantelle Breithaupt
HR: -
FYE: June 30
Type: Public

Aspen Technology (AspenTech) helps its customers scale mountains of supply chain and engineering challenges. It provides supply chain manufacturing and engineering process optimization software to some 2400 companies in the energy chemical construction and pharmaceutical industries among others. The company's software ? which includes supplier collaboration inventory management production planning and collaborative engineering functions ? is offered under its aspenONE subscription service. AspenTech which generates most of its sales outside the US also provides related technical and professional services such as technical support training and systems implementation and integration.

	Annual Growth	06/17	06/18	06/19	06/20	06/21
Sales ($ mil.)	10.1%	482.9	499.5	598.3	598.7	709.4
Net income ($ mil.)	18.5%	162.2	148.7	262.7	229.7	319.8
Market value ($ mil.)	25.6%	3,752.8	6,298.2	8,440.1	7,036.4	9,340.6
Employees	7.5%	1,419	1,466	1,600	1,710	1,897

ASPIRUS, INC.

2200 WESTWOOD DR
WAUSAU, WI 544017806
Phone: 715-847-2121
Fax: -
Web: www.aspirus.org

CEO: Matthew Heywood
CFO: Sidney Sczygelski
HR: Hannah Brabec
FYE: June 30
Type: Private

Aspirus is a non-profit community-directed health system based in Wausau Wisconsin. The health system provides a comprehensive range of health and medical services to communities through four hospitals in Upper Michigan and about 15 hospitals in Wisconsin some 75 clinics home health and hospice care pharmacies critical care and air-medical transport medical goods nursing homes and a broad network of physicians. In addition to its four hospitals in Michigan Aspirus operates the Aspirus Wausau Hospital a 325-bed and staffed by 350 physicians in 35 specialties. With approximately 15000 admissions per year outpatient visits exceed 50000 and there are also more than 24000 annual emergency department visits.

	Annual Growth	06/12	06/13	06/18	06/19	06/20
Sales ($ mil.)	10.7%	-	536.9	911.4	996.5	1,090.7
Net income ($ mil.)	19.7%	-	48.0	78.2	102.7	169.1
Market value ($ mil.)	-	-	-	-	-	-
Employees	-	-	-	-	-	7,100

ASPLUNDH TREE EXPERT CO.

708 Blair Mill Rd.
Willow Grove PA 19090
Phone: 215-784-4200
Fax: 215-784-4493
Web: www.asplundh.com

CEO: Scott Asplundh
CFO: Joseph P Dwyer
HR: -
FYE: December 31
Type: Private

How much wood would a woodchuck chuck if a woodchuck could chuck wood? A lot if the woodchuck were named Asplundh. One of the world's leading tree-trimming businesses Asplundh clears tree limbs from power lines for utilities and municipalities throughout the US and in Canada Australia and New Zealand. Asplundh also offers utility-related services such as line construction meter reading and pole maintenance; in addition the company has branched out into fields such as billboard maintenance traffic signal and highway lighting construction and vegetation control for railroads and pipelines. The Asplundh family owns and manages the company which was founded in 1928.

ASRC ENERGY SERVICES

3900 C St. Ste. 701
Anchorage AK 99503
Phone: 907-339-6200
Fax: 907-339-6219
Web: www.asrcenergy.com

CEO: Doug Smith
CFO: -
HR: -
FYE: December 31
Type: Subsidiary

Alaska's slippery slopes have led to financial success for ASRC Energy Services. A subsidiary of Arctic Slope Regional Corp. ASRC Energy Services provides oil and gas and other engineering services to customers operating in the North Slope region of Alaska and to other energy and communications companies around the world. The company's services include well drilling and completion well testing facilities engineering geophysical services demolition pipeline construction and maintenance module fabrication and assembly and offshore construction and maintenance.

ASSEMBLY BIOSCIENCES INC
NMS: ASMB

331 Oyster Point Blvd., Fourth Floor
South San Francisco, CA 94080
Phone: 833 509-4583
Fax: -
Web: www.assemblybio.com

CEO: John McHutchison
CFO: Michael Samar
HR: -
FYE: December 31
Type: Public

Assembly Biosciences is a development-stage drug company focused specifically on anal disorders (such as difficile-associated diarrhea or CDAD) and the treatment of hepatitis B infections. Its primary product is a diltiazem cream for pain associated with anal fissures while a secondary product is a phenylephrine gel for fecal incontinence. Assembly has licensed intellectual property associated with an oral drug delivery system that targets sites within the intestines. Assembly Biosciences is the result of a 2014 merger between Ventrus Biosciences and Assembly Pharmaceuticals.

	Annual Growth	12/16	12/17	12/18	12/19	12/20
Sales ($ mil.)	106.2%	-	9.0	14.8	16.0	79.1
Net income ($ mil.)	-	(44.3)	(42.8)	(90.8)	(97.6)	(62.2)
Market value ($ mil.)	(16.0%)	413.4	1,539.7	769.7	696.2	205.9
Employees	19.1%	69	79	95	115	139

ASSERTIO HOLDINGS INC
NAS: ASRT

100 South Saunders Road, Suite 300
Lake Forest, IL 60045
Phone: 224 419-7106
Fax: -
Web: www.assertiotx.com

CEO: Daniel Peisert
CFO: Paul Schwichtenberg
HR: Marni Luchsinger
FYE: December 31
Type: Public

Assertio Therapeutics (formerly Depomed) is a pharmaceutical firm with a focus on neurology orphan and specialty medicines. The company works to discover develop and license new drugs; it has three products on the market in the US. Gralise is used to treat nerve pain CAMBIA is a non-steroidal anti-inflammatory drug for the acute treatment of migraine attacks in adults and Zipsor is used for pain relief in adults. In late 2017 the firm granted Collegium Pharmaceutical the commercialization rights for its Nucynta franchise of pain medications for which it will receive royalty payments. In mid-2018 Depomed changed its name to Assertio in reference to its confident assertive and entrepreneurial activities.

	Annual Growth	12/16	12/17	12/18	12/19	12/20
Sales ($ mil.)	(30.5%)	455.9	380.7	311.8	229.5	106.3
Net income ($ mil.)	-	(88.7)	(102.5)	36.9	(217.2)	(28.1)
Market value ($ mil.)	(62.4%)	511.6	228.6	102.5	35.5	10.2
Employees	(51.6%)	490	434	116	125	27

ASSET PROTECTION & SECURITY SERVICES, LP

5502 BURNHAM DR
CORPUS CHRISTI, TX 784133855
Phone: 361-906-1552
Fax: –
Web: www.asset-security-pro.com

CEO: –
CFO: Thelma Mandel
HR: –
FYE: December 31
Type: Private

Asset Protection & Security Services is a leading provider of patrol and security guard services in the US. It offers both armed and unarmed guard services as well as specialized services such as executive protection movie production security and mobile command centers. In addition Asset Protection provides investigative services (computer security internal investigations loss prevention) and electronic surveillance and security as well as security consulting and training services. The company was founded in 1994 by CEO Charles Mandel.

	Annual Growth	12/04	12/05	12/06	12/07	12/14
Sales ($ mil.)	–	–	0.0	31.2	51.8	84.4
Net income ($ mil.)	–	–	0.0	3.3	10.7	5.0
Market value ($ mil.)	–	–	–	–	–	–
Employees	–	–	–	–	–	800

ASSOCIATED BANC-CORP
NYS: ASB

433 Main Street
Green Bay, WI 54301
Phone: 920 491-7500
Fax: –
Web: www.associatedbank.com

CEO: Andrew Harmening
CFO: Christopher Del Moral-Niles
HR: –
FYE: December 31
Type: Public

One of the largest banks based in Wisconsin Associated Banc-Corp operates more than 225 branches in that state as well as in Illinois and Minnesota. Catering to consumers and local businesses it offers deposit accounts loans mortgage banking credit and debit cards and leasing. The bank's wealth management division offers investments trust services brokerage insurance and employee group benefits plans. Commercial loans including construction and real estate loans make up more than 60% of bank's loan portfolio. The bank also writes residential mortgages consumer loans and home equity loans.

	Annual Growth	12/17	12/18	12/19	12/20	12/21
Assets ($ mil.)	3.6%	30,483.6	33,647.9	32,386.5	33,419.8	35,104.3
Net income ($ mil.)	11.2%	229.3	333.6	326.8	306.8	351.0
Market value ($ mil.)	(2.9%)	3,793.3	2,955.5	3,291.5	2,546.3	3,373.7
Employees	(2.3%)	4,388	4,655	4,669	4,100	4,000

ASSOCIATED CATHOLIC CHARITIES INC.

320 CATHEDRAL ST
BALTIMORE, MD 212014421
Phone: 410-561-6363
Fax: –
Web: www.catholiccharities-md.org

CEO: –
CFO: –
HR: –
FYE: June 30
Type: Private

Catholic Charities of Baltimore (CCB) provides people in the greater Baltimore area including about a dozen Maryland counties with a wide variety of social services. The not-for-profit religious organization runs 80 programs that focus on children and families the elderly and people with developmental disabilities; offerings include adoption services child abuse prevention food immigration assistance residential facilities and services for homeless people. It serves more than 160000 people of all religions each year. Money for its operations comes mainly from government contracts and grants. In addition CCB relies on a network of about 15000 volunteers. CCB was founded in 1923.

	Annual Growth	06/04	06/05	06/06	06/08	06/09
Sales ($ mil.)	6.6%	–	92.3	108.6	115.8	119.4
Net income ($ mil.)	–	–	0.0	9.7	(8.0)	(11.0)
Market value ($ mil.)	–	–	–	–	–	–
Employees	–	–	–	–	–	2,000

ASSOCIATED ELECTRIC COOPERATIVE, INC.

2814 S GOLDEN AVE
SPRINGFIELD, MO 658073213
Phone: 417-881-1204
Fax: –
Web: www.aeci.org

CEO: David Tudor
CFO: David W McNabb
HR: Becca Stapleton
FYE: December 31
Type: Private

Associated Electric Cooperative makes the connection between power and cooperatives. The utility provides transmission and generation services to its six member/owner companies which in turn provide power supply services to 51 distribution cooperatives in three Midwest states. (The distribution cooperatives have a combined customer count of about 875000 member homes farms and businesses.) Associated Electric operates 9937 miles of power transmission lines and has about 5895 MW of generating capacity from interests in primarily coal- and gas-fired power plants and from wholesale energy transactions with other regional utilities.

	Annual Growth	12/10	12/11	12/12	12/13	12/14
Sales ($ mil.)	1.8%	–	1,083.7	1,081.9	1,129.8	1,142.3
Net income ($ mil.)	(5.1%)	–	46.9	50.4	41.8	40.1
Market value ($ mil.)	–	–	–	–	–	–
Employees	–	–	–	–	–	600

ASSOCIATED ENTERTAINMENT RELEASING

4401 Wilshire Blvd.
Los Angeles CA 90010
Phone: 323-556-5600
Fax: 323-556-5610
Web: www.associatedtelevision.com

CEO: –
CFO: Murray Dreschler
HR: –
FYE: December 31
Type: Private

You might say this company has a close association with the small screen. Associated Entertainment Releasing which does business as Associated Television International (ATI) produces and distributes television programming mostly for the syndication market. Its shows include American Adventurer and reality crime program Crime Strike as well as specials such as Masters of Illusion: Impossible Magic and World Magic Awards. The company also distributes a library of TV programming to the home entertainment market and it produces some radio content. ATI began producing television programming in 1967.

ASSOCIATED ESTATES REALTY CORP.
NYS: AEC

1 AEC Parkway
Richmond Hts., OH 44143-1550
Phone: 216 261-5000
Fax: 216 289-9600
Web: www.associatedestates.com

CEO: –
CFO: –
HR: –
FYE: December 31
Type: Public

The estates this corporation associates with house the multitudes. Associated Estates Realty is a self-administered real estate investment trust (REIT) that specializes in apartment communities in the Midwest Mid-Atlantic and Southeast. It invests in develops builds operates and manages multifamily real estate. More than half of the company's properties are located in Ohio and Michigan its largest markets. The REIT's portfolio includes more than 50 residential communities containing around 14000 individual units; it also owns a handful of properties under development and land. Subsidiary Merit Enterprises performs in-house general contracting and construction management services.

	Annual Growth	12/09	12/10	12/11	12/12	12/13
Sales ($ mil.)	8.6%	130.4	153.7	175.9	174.9	181.5
Net income ($ mil.)	77.2%	6.2	(8.6)	5.3	30.6	61.3
Market value ($ mil.)	9.2%	647.8	878.8	916.7	926.5	922.5
Employees	2.7%	360	390	400	410	400

ASSOCIATED FOOD STORES, INC.

1850 W 2100 S
SALT LAKE CITY, UT 841191304
Phone: 801-973-4400
Fax: –
Web: www.afstores.com

CEO: Neil Berube
CFO: –
HR: –
FYE: March 31
Type: Private

This business makes sure there's plenty of grub for the Wild West. Associated Food Stores (AFS) is a leading regional cooperative wholesale distributor that supplies groceries and other products to some 500 independent supermarkets in about eight Western states. It also offers support services for its member-owners including market research real estate analysis store design technology procurement and training. In addition AFS owns a stake in Western Family Foods a grocery wholesalers' partnership that produces Western Family private-label goods. The co-op formed in 1940 also operates 40-plus corporate stores in Utah under five different banners including Fresh Market.

	Annual Growth	03/08	03/09	03/10	03/11	03/12
Sales ($ mil.)	6.1%	–	–	1,785.6	1,954.0	2,011.3
Net income ($ mil.)	–	–	–	(2.1)	(6.5)	5.9
Market value ($ mil.)	–	–	–	–	–	–
Employees	–	–	–	–	–	300

ASSOCIATED GROCERS OF NEW ENGLAND, INC.

11 COOPERATIVE WAY
PEMBROKE, NH 032753251
Phone: 603-223-6710
Fax: –
Web: www.agne.com

CEO: Mike Violette
CFO: Steven N Murphy
HR: –
FYE: March 28
Type: Private

AGNE gets the products you want on to grocers' shelves. Associated Grocers of New England (AGNE) is a leading wholesale grocery distributor. The retailer-owned organization supplies more than 650 independent grocers and convenience stores in six New England states and the Upstate New York and Albany area. AGNE supplies customers with baked goods fresh produce and meat as well as general grocery items and other merchandise. The grocery distributor also offers such retail support services as advertising marketing and merchandising. AGNE's retail arm operates about a half a dozen supermarkets under the Harvest Market Sully's Superette and Vista Foods banners. The cooperative was formed in 1946.

	Annual Growth	03/05	03/06	03/07	03/08	03/09
Sales ($ mil.)	–	–	–	(1,996.9)	315.8	340.3
Net income ($ mil.)	3701.4%	–	–	0.0	0.2	0.7
Market value ($ mil.)	–	–	–	–	–	–
Employees	–	–	–	–	–	625

ASSOCIATED MATERIALS LLC

3773 State Rd.
Cuyahoga Falls OH 44223
Phone: 330-929-1811
Fax: 330-922-2354
Web: www.associatedmaterials.com

CEO: Brian C Strauss
CFO: Scott F Stephens
HR: –
FYE: December 31
Type: Private

Vinyl has never gone out of style at Associated Materials (AM). The company makes and distributes vinyl aluminum and steel exterior building products as well as siding windows fencing decking and railing. Products are marketed under the brand names Alpine Alside Gentek Preservation Revere and UltraGuard. Its products are also sold through about 275 independent distributors in North America under brands such as Alside Revere and Gentek. The company's customer base includes contractors remodelers and architects. Private equity firm Hellman & Friedman owns a majority stake of the company.

ASSOCIATED MILK PRODUCERS INC.

315 N. Broadway
New Ulm MN 56073
Phone: 507-354-8295
Fax: 507-359-8651
Web: www.ampi.com

CEO: Donn Develder
CFO: Patricia Radloff
HR: –
FYE: December 31
Type: Private - Cooperativ

Associated Milk Producers Inc. (AMPI) might wear a cheesy grin but it churns up solid sales. The dairy cooperative transforms (a record) about 5.8 billion pounds of milk into butter cheese fluid milk and other dairy products each and every year. A regional co-op with some 2800 member/farmers in six states across the Midwest AMPI operates about a dozen manufacturing plants. In addition to its State Brand and Cass-Clay brand Associated Milk Producers also makes private-label products for food retailers fast-food restaurants (including McDonald's) and other food service operators. It also makes dairy ingredients for food manufacturers.

ASSOCIATED WHOLESALE GROCERS, INC.

5000 KANSAS AVE
KANSAS CITY, KS 661061135
Phone: 913-288-1000
Fax: –
Web: www.awginc.com

CEO: –
CFO: –
HR: –
FYE: December 31
Type: Private

Associated Wholesale Grocers (AWG) knows its customers can't live on bread and milk alone. The one of -largest retailer-owned grocery cooperative in the US AWG supplies more than 3800 grocery retail outlets in more than half of the US states from 10 distribution centers which collectively have some 7 million square feet of space. In addition to its wholesale grocery operation AWG offers a variety of business services to its members including print and digital marketing services and health beauty care general merchandise specialty/International foodsand pharmaceutical products. . AWG was founded by a group of independent grocers in 1924.

	Annual Growth	12/12	12/13	12/14	12/15	12/17
Sales ($ mil.)	3.7%	–	8,380.2	8,934.2	8,935.9	9,703.8
Net income ($ mil.)	0.8%	–	192.5	226.9	198.9	199.1
Market value ($ mil.)	–	–	–	–	–	–
Employees	–	–	–	–	–	2,997

ASSOCIATION OF UNIVERSITIES FOR RESEARCH IN ASTRONOMY, INC.

1331 PENN AVE NW STE 1475
WASHINGTON, DC 200041752
Phone: 202-483-2101
Fax: –
Web: www.aura-astronomy.org

CEO: –
CFO: –
HR: –
FYE: September 30
Type: Private

There is nothing quasi-scientific about this aura. The Association of Universities for Research in Astronomy (AURA) is a consortium of universities and not-for-profit organizations devoted to the study of space. The organization was founded to create astronomical observing facilities for use by qualified researchers and to serve the community by offering public outreach education and dissemination of information. AURA was founded in 1957 and operates astronomical observatories at 34 US institutions and six international affiliates including Harvard University Ohio State University and the University of Toronto.

	Annual Growth	09/09	09/10	09/13	09/14	09/19
Sales ($ mil.)	7.2%	–	197.2	238.4	264.4	369.9
Net income ($ mil.)	–	–	(2.4)	2.1	1.0	1.8
Market value ($ mil.)	–	–	–	–	–	–
Employees	–	–	–	–	–	1,000

ASSURANT INC
NYS: AIZ
55 Broadway, Suite 2901
New York, NY 10006
Phone: 212 859-7000
Fax: –
Web: www.assurant.com
CEO: Keith Demmings
CFO: Richard Dziadzio
HR: –
FYE: December 31
Type: Public

From appliance protection to trailer park coverage Assurant aims to give its customers peace of mind. The company provides a diverse range of specialty insurance products such as extended service contracts for electronics appliances and vehicles; mobile device protection; manufactured home coverage; renters insurance; creditor-placed homeowners insurance; and pre-need funeral policies. Assurant's products are distributed through sales offices and independent agents across North America and in Latin America Europe and the Asia/Pacific region. The US accounts for about 80% of sales.

	Annual Growth	12/17	12/18	12/19	12/20	12/21
Assets ($ mil.)	1.6%	31,843.0	41,089.3	44,291.2	44,649.9	33,911.5
Net income ($ mil.)	27.5%	519.6	251.0	382.6	441.8	1,372.4
Market value ($ mil.)	11.5%	5,622.2	4,986.6	7,308.2	7,594.8	8,689.8
Employees	1.4%	14,750	14,750	14,200	14,100	15,600

ASTA FUNDING, INC.
NMS: ASFI
210 Sylvan Avenue
Englewood Cliffs, NJ 07632
Phone: 201 567-5648
Fax: –
Web: www.astafunding.com
CEO: Gary Stern
CFO: Bruce R Foster
HR: –
FYE: September 30
Type: Public

Say Hasta luego to unpaid receivables. Asta Funding buys services and collects unpaid credit card debts and consumer loans. The company buys delinquent accounts at a discount directly from the credit grantors as well as indirectly through auctions brokers and other third parties. It targets credit card charge-offs from banks finance companies and other issuers of Visa MasterCard and private-label cards as well as telecom and other industry charge-offs. The company then collects on its debt balances either internally or through an outsourced agency. Asta Funding also invests in semi-performing and non-delinquent receivables. Subsidiary VATIV Recovery Solutions services bankrupt and deceased accounts.

	Annual Growth	09/15	09/16	09/17	09/18	09/19
Sales ($ mil.)	(14.6%)	44.2	58.7	21.3	26.1	23.4
Net income ($ mil.)	37.4%	2.0	7.9	(13.0)	4.1	7.2
Market value ($ mil.)	(4.8%)	56.0	69.0	49.6	25.9	46.0
Employees	(21.7%)	149	188	86	60	56

ASTAR USA LLC
1200 Brickell Ave. 16th Flr.
Miami FL 33131
Phone: 305-982-0500
Fax: 305-416-9564
Web: www.astaraircargo.us
CEO: John Dasburg
CFO: Stephen Dodd
HR: –
FYE: December 31
Type: Private

ASTAR USA helps DHL take on delivery giants FedEx and UPS on their own turf. Hiring the carrier's fleet of some 8 aircraft enables DHL and other customers including the US Air Force Department of Defense and the United States Postal Service to achieve overnight delivery of virtually any kind of cargo. ASTAR's service includes scheduled as well as chartered flights. In early 2009 ASTAR suffered a blow to its business when — in order to cut costs — DHL was forced to shut down its US express delivery operations. ASTAR and other carriers continue to operate DHL's international shipping services to and from the US albeit at a reduced level. An investment group led by CEO John Dasburg controls ASTAR.

ASTEA INTERNATIONAL, INC.
NBB: ATEA
240 Gibraltar Road
Horsham, PA 19044
Phone: 215 682-2500
Fax: –
Web: www.astea.com
CEO: Marne Martin
CFO: Fredric Etskovitz
HR: –
FYE: December 31
Type: Public

Astea International keeps employees in the field connected to the home office. The company's field service management software Astea Alliance is used to automate sales and service processes manage contracts and warranties logistics and distribute information to employees customers and suppliers. FieldCentrix offers mobile workforce management. Altogether it counts more than 650 customers including API Group ARX Brains II and Centric from a range of industries. Most of its revenue comes from services. Founder and CEO Zack Bergreen owns about 54% of Astea.

	Annual Growth	12/13	12/14	12/15	12/16	12/17
Sales ($ mil.)	6.7%	20.3	20.7	23.0	25.8	26.3
Net income ($ mil.)	–	(3.0)	(3.4)	(4.4)	0.4	0.1
Market value ($ mil.)	2.6%	9.2	6.3	8.1	6.3	10.2
Employees	2.0%	161	159	171	189	174

ASTEC INDUSTRIES, INC.
NMS: ASTE
1725 Shepherd Road
Chattanooga, TN 37421
Phone: 423 899-5898
Fax: 423 899-4456
Web: www.astecindustries.com
CEO: Barry Ruffalo
CFO: Rebecca Weyenberg
HR: Reuben Srinivasan
FYE: December 31
Type: Public

Astec Industries design engineers manufactures and markets equipment and components used primarily in road building and related construction activities. Its products are used in each phase of road building from quarrying and crushing the aggregate to application of the road surface for both asphalt and concrete. The company is comprised of two segments: Infrastructure Solutions and Materials Solutions. Customers are highway and heavy equipment contractors as well as utility and government agencies and mine and quarry operators. Its largest market is the US which accounts for some 80%. The company was founded in 1972. In 2020 the company acquired two premier full-line concrete batch plant manufacturers.

	Annual Growth	12/16	12/17	12/18	12/19	12/20
Sales ($ mil.)	(2.8%)	1,147.4	1,184.7	1,171.6	1,169.6	1,024.4
Net income ($ mil.)	(4.0%)	55.2	37.8	(60.4)	22.3	46.9
Market value ($ mil.)	(3.8%)	1,525.4	1,322.8	682.7	949.7	1,308.8
Employees	20.4%	1,681	1,712	1,626	3,866	3,537

ASTELLAS PHARMA US INC.
1 Astellas Way
Northbrook IL 60062
Phone: 847-317-8800
Fax: 248-435-1120
Web: www.axletech.com
CEO: Masao Yoshida
CFO: Shinichiro Katayanagi
HR: –
FYE: March 31
Type: Subsidiary

Astellas Pharma US pilots pharma efforts that are outta this world. The company conducts research development and marketing efforts focused on therapeutic areas including cardiology dermatology immunology infectious disease neurology oncology urology and metabolism. The company's primary products include transplant rejection therapy Prograf overactive bladder treatment Vesicare and vascular dilator Adenoscan as well as antifungals Mycamine and AmBisome and enlarged prostate treatment Flomax. Astellas Pharma US which is a subsidiary of Japan-based pharmaceutical firm Astellas Pharma uses a direct sales force to market its products to consumers and health professionals in the US market.

ASTORIA FINANCIAL CORP.

NYS: AF

One Astoria Bank Plaza
Lake Success, NY 11042-1085
Phone: 516 327-3000
Fax: 516 327-7860
Web: www.astoriabank.com

CEO: –
CFO: –
HR: –
FYE: December 31
Type: Public

Astoria Financial is the holding company for Astoria Bank (formerly Astoria Federal) one of the largest thrifts in New York with deposits totaling $9.7 billion. The bank has more than 85 branches in and around New York City and on Long Island in addition to a network of third-party mortgage brokers spanning more than a dozen states and Washington DC. It offers standard deposit products such as CDs and checking savings and retirement accounts. With these funds Astoria Bank primarily writes loans and invests in mortgage-backed securities. Subsidiary AF Insurance Agency sells life and property/casualty coverage to bank customers. New York Community Bancorp agreed to acquire Astoria in late 2015.

	Annual Growth	12/11	12/12	12/13	12/14	12/15
Assets ($ mil.)	(3.0%)	17,022.1	16,496.6	15,793.7	15,640.0	15,076.2
Net income ($ mil.)	7.0%	67.2	53.1	66.6	95.9	88.1
Market value ($ mil.)	16.9%	855.1	942.8	1,393.0	1,345.6	1,596.4
Employees	(1.9%)	1,730	1,614	1,603	1,649	1,601

ASTORIA SOFTWARE INC.

300 Broadway St. Ste. 8
San Francisco CA 94133
Phone: 650-357-7477
Fax: 650-357-7677
Web: www.astoriasoftware.com

CEO: Michael Rosinski
CFO: –
HR: –
FYE: December 31
Type: Subsidiary

Astoria Software is a disciplinarian when it comes to content — all your documents need is a little structure. Astoria provides a content management system that enables companies to collect and manage their data and then to use that data to create and publish documents including charts images and tables. Astoria maintains partnerships with software providers including Innodata Isogen. Customers include ABB Cessna Aircraft Honeywell Lockheed Martin Nokia Texas Instruments the US Armed Forces and Xerox. In 2010 Astoria Software was acquired by TransPerfect Translations International.

ASTRAL HEALTH & BEAUTY INC.

3715 Northside Pkwy. NW Bldg. 200 Ste. 200
Atlanta GA 30327
Phone: 678-303-3088
Fax: 858-625-3010
Web: www.enterpriseinformatics.com

CEO: Robert K Cohen
CFO: Stephen E Merrick
HR: –
FYE: December 31
Type: Private

Astral Health & Beauty believes in natural beauty. The company owns three cosmetics and skin care lines that use nature-based ingredients — Aloette CosMedix and Pur Minerals. Aloette's aloe vera-based skin care products and cosmetics are sold mainly through home parties held by Aloette's direct sales network of more than 10000 consultants in some 40 franchises across the US and Canada. CosMedix is a line of premium skin care products sold only at professional spas while Pur Minerals' mineral makeup is sold at major retailers such as Dillard's Duane Reade and Ulta. All three brands are also sold online and on television shopping channels such as QVC.

ASTRAZENECA PHARMACEUTICALS LP

1800 Concord Pike
Wilmington DE 19850-5437
Phone: 302-886-3000
Fax: 302-886-2972
Web: www.astrazeneca-us.com

CEO: Pascal Soriot
CFO: David V Elkins
HR: Annet Van Geen
FYE: December 31
Type: Subsidiary

AstraZeneca Pharmaceuticals (which does business as AstraZeneca US) can help with a full alphabet of ailments. The company a subsidiary of global drugmaker AstraZeneca is one of the largest pharma companies in the US. Its sales represent about 5% of all the drugs sold in the US and about 40% of its parent company's revenues. AstraZeneca US' treatments focus on several therapeutic areas: cardiovascular and metabolic gastrointestinal neuroscience oncology respiratory and infection. Its best-known products include Crestor (high cholesterol) Seroquel (anti-psychotic) Nexium (acid reflux) Symbicort (asthma) and Zoladex (cancer treatment).

ASTRONAUTICS CORPORATION OF AMERICA

135 W FOREST HILL AVE
OAK CREEK, WI 531542901
Phone: 414-449-4000
Fax: –
Web: www.astronautics.com

CEO: Dr Ronald E Zelazo
CFO: Stephen Givant
HR: –
FYE: May 31
Type: Private

Astronautics Corporation of America is a global leader in the design and manufacture of avionics equipment and systems for commercial and military aerospace. The company's key product areas include electronic primary flight displays engine displays mission computers electronic flight bags and certified servers for airborne applications. Its customers have included Commercial Transport Defense and Helicopter markets. It also provides system integration and custom software for critical applications. The company was founded in 1959 by Nathaniel Zelazo and Norma Paige.

	Annual Growth	05/04	05/05	05/06	05/07	05/08
Sales ($ mil.)	8.2%	–	–	201.2	233.0	235.7
Net income ($ mil.)	12.8%	–	–	15.4	20.7	19.6
Market value ($ mil.)	–	–	–	–	–	–
Employees	–	–	–	–	–	1,550

ASTRONICS CORP

NMS: ATRO

130 Commerce Way
East Aurora, NY 14052
Phone: 716 805-1599
Fax: –
Web: www.astronics.com

CEO: Peter Gundermann
CFO: David C Burney
HR: –
FYE: December 31
Type: Public

Astronics Corporation is a leading provider of advanced technologies to the global aerospace defense and other mission-critical industries. Its products and services include advanced high-performance electrical power generation distribution and seat motion systems lighting and safety systems avionics products systems and certification aircraft structures and automated test systems for commercial general aviation and military defense aircraft. Astronics operates subsidiaries including Astronics Advanced Electronic Systems Corp. Ballard Luminescent Systems and DME Corporation. Approximately three-quarters of the sales were generated from the US.

	Annual Growth	12/16	12/17	12/18	12/19	12/20
Sales ($ mil.)	(5.6%)	633.1	624.5	803.3	772.7	502.6
Net income ($ mil.)	–	48.4	19.7	46.8	52.0	(115.8)
Market value ($ mil.)	(20.9%)	1,045.5	1,281.2	940.7	863.5	408.7
Employees	(1.1%)	2,300	2,500	2,700	2,800	2,200

ASTRONOVA INC
NMS: ALOT

600 East Greenwich Avenue
West Warwick, RI 02893
Phone: 401 828-4000
Fax: –
Web: www.astronovainc.com

CEO: Gregory Woods
CFO: David Smith
HR: Megan Herne
FYE: January 31
Type: Public

AstroNova (formerly Astro-Med) designs develops manufactures and distributes a broad range of specialty printers and data acquisition and analysis systems including both hardware and software. Its target markets are apparel automotive avionics chemicals computer peripherals and communications. Its Test & Measurement (T&M) division focuses on aerospace flight deck cabin printers and test and measurement data acquisition systems. The company's Product Identification includes specialty printing systems and related supplies sold under the brand names Quick-Label GetLabels and TrojanLabel. AstroNova generates around 60% of total sale from its home country the US. The company was founded in 1969 by Albert W. Ondis and Everett V. Pizzuti.

	Annual Growth	01/17	01/18	01/19	01/20	01/21
Sales ($ mil.)	4.2%	98.4	113.4	136.7	133.4	116.0
Net income ($ mil.)	(25.8%)	4.2	3.3	5.7	1.8	1.3
Market value ($ mil.)	(6.2%)	98.8	96.2	142.4	88.7	76.6
Employees	1.2%	312	352	374	365	327

ASTROTECH CORP
NAS: ASTC

2105 Donley Drive, Suite 100
Austin, TX 78758
Phone: 512 485-9530
Fax: –
Web: www.astrotechcorp.com

CEO: Thomas B Pickens III
CFO: Eric N Stober
HR: –
FYE: June 30
Type: Public

Astrotech is the muscle on the ground prior to satellite launch countdown. Formerly SPACEHAB the company offers services and products that aid the US government and commercial customers in preparing satellites and cargo payloads for space launch. Its Astrotech Space Operations (ASO) business unit is a contractor that provides such services as ground transportation hardware integration fueling and launch pad delivery. It also fabricates launch equipment and hardware. Astrotech's much smaller Spacetech unit is focused on using space-based technologies to develop commercial products in the chemical and biotechnology sectors. About 75% of Astrotech's revenues are made from NASA and US government contracts.

	Annual Growth	06/17	06/18	06/19	06/20	06/21
Sales ($ mil.)	(38.5%)	2.3	0.1	0.1	0.5	0.3
Net income ($ mil.)	–	(11.6)	(13.3)	(7.5)	(8.3)	(7.6)
Market value ($ mil.)	10.0%	45.0	153.3	123.6	140.9	65.8
Employees	(26.9%)	42	33	30	27	12

ASURE SOFTWARE INC.
NAS: ASUR

3700 N. Capital of Texas Hwy., Suite 350
Austin, TX 78746
Phone: 512 437-2700
Fax: –
Web: www.asuresoftware.com

CEO: Patrick Goepel
CFO: John Pence
HR: Emily Henkes
FYE: December 31
Type: Public

Asure Software wants to guaranty a more organized workplace. The company develops Web-based business administration software through its NetSimplicity and iEmployee divisions. NetSimplicity's offerings include Meeting Room Manager which lets users reserve meeting rooms and schedule equipment and resources. NetSimplicity also provides an asset management tool called Visual Asset Manager that tracks and manages fixed and mobile IT assets. The company's iEmployee division offers tools for managing time and attendance benefits payroll and expense information. Asure primarily sells its products directly in North America; it uses resellers for customers outside the US and for federal government sales.

	Annual Growth	12/16	12/17	12/18	12/19	12/20
Sales ($ mil.)	16.5%	35.5	54.4	89.0	73.2	65.5
Net income ($ mil.)	–	(1.0)	(5.7)	(7.5)	30.0	(16.3)
Market value ($ mil.)	(4.4%)	161.4	267.9	96.4	155.2	134.7
Employees	28.1%	179	324	564	423	482

ASURION CORPORATION

648 Grassmere Park Dr. Ste. 300
Nashville TN 37211
Phone: 615-837-3000
Fax: 615-837-3001
Web: www.asurion.com

CEO: Bret Comolli
CFO: Mark Gunning
HR: –
FYE: December 31
Type: Private

Dead battery? Would that be the battery on your car or cell phone? Either way Asurion assures that you won't be stranded. A global leader in wireless and technology insurance Asurion replaces defunct cell phones and other tech equipment but also provides specialty services such as roadside assistance to stranded motorists via their wireless phones. The firm serves about 80 million end users through partnerships with wireless carriers including Cricket T-Mobile and AT&T Mobility. In 2008 Asurion merged with extended service plan provider N.E.W. Customer Service Companies. Both companies continue to operate independently.

AT&T INC
NYS: T

208 S. Akard St.
Dallas, TX 75202
Phone: 210 821-4105
Fax: –
Web: www.att.com

CEO: Jeffery McElfresh
CFO: Pascal Desroches
HR: Angela Santone
FYE: December 31
Type: Public

AT&T is a leading provider of telecommunications media and technology services globally. The company offers wireless wireline and satellite as well as strategic data services including Virtual Private Networks (VPN) AT&T Dedicated Internet (ADI) and Ethernet and broadband services. It is one of the biggest wireline and wireless providers in the US with more than 182 million subscribers. It offers digital TV voice and internet service through its U-verse brand and satellite Pay-TV through DIRECTV. The US supplies the majority of the company's revenue.

	Annual Growth	12/17	12/18	12/19	12/20	12/21
Sales ($ mil.)	1.3%	160,546.0	170,756.0	181,193.0	171,760.0	168,864.0
Net income ($ mil.)	(9.1%)	29,450.0	19,370.0	13,903.0	(5,176.0)	20,081.0
Market value ($ mil.)	–	0.0	0.0	0.0	0.0	0.0
Employees	(5.3%)	252,000	268,000	246,000	230,000	203,000

AT&T MOBILITY LLC

1025 Lenox Park Blvd.
Atlanta GA 30319
Phone: 866-662-4548
Fax: 914-666-2188
Web: www.curtisinst.com

CEO: Thaddeus Arroyo
CFO: Peter A Ritcher
HR: –
FYE: December 31
Type: Subsidiary

The second-largest wireless voice and data carrier in the US by subscribers (after Verizon) AT&T Mobility serves about 100 million mobile users over a nationwide network that spans all major metropolitan areas. The subsidiary which accounts for about half of parent AT&T's business provides a full range of wireless voice messaging and data services to consumer and enterprise customers. AT&T Mobility's services for businesses government agencies and educational institutions include e-mail wireless Internet access and private wireless networking. The company provides international network coverage for its subscribers in more than 200 countries through partnerships with other carriers.

HOOVER'S MASTERLIST OF U.S. COMPANIES 2022

ATALANTA CORPORATION

1 ATALANTA PLZ
ELIZABETH, NJ 072062186
Phone: 908-351-8000
Fax: –
Web: www.atalantacorp.com

CEO: –
CFO: Tom Decarll
HR: –
FYE: December 31
Type: Private

Atalanta Corporation helps customers outfit any wine and cheese soir ©e. The company is a top specialty food importer that markets 3000 different products such as gourmet cheeses deli and canned meats and frozen seafood. Its menu of products also includes pastas rices and grains as well as coffee and a line of kosher foods. Atalanta's brands include Casa Diva Celebrity Zerto Del Destino Maria Brand Martel and Atalanta. Importing products from Europe Asia and South America Atalanta sells primarily to restaurants and other foodservice operators grocery stores and specialty food retailers. Founded in 1945 the company is controlled by the Gellert family and led by CEO George Gellert.

	Annual Growth	12/04	12/05	12/06	12/07	12/09
Sales ($ mil.)	–	–	–	(1,092.3)	348.8	384.9
Net income ($ mil.)	14310.1%	–	–	0.0	10.8	9.0
Market value ($ mil.)	–	–	–	–	–	–
Employees	–	–	–	–	–	220

ATALIAN US NORTHEAST, LLC

525 WSHINGTON BLVD STE 25
JERSEY CITY, NJ 07310
Phone: 212-889-6353
Fax: –
Web: www.atalian.us

CEO: Christopher Hughes
CFO: –
HR: –
FYE: September 30
Type: Private

Temco Service Industries provides temps trees and tidiness. The company offers facility management services including building management cleaning maintenance landscaping and temporary personnel staffing. It also provides temperature control HVAC systems mechanical equipment building automation systems lighting fire and security services. To address varied client needs the company runs its business through three divisions that offer support services to commercial properties; education facilities including public school systems and universities; and corporate manufacturing and industrial properties. Temco was founded in 1917.

	Annual Growth	09/96	09/97	09/98	09/05	09/07
Sales ($ mil.)	7.7%	–	–	172.3	306.3	334.7
Net income ($ mil.)	47.8%	–	–	1.2	1.2	40.7
Market value ($ mil.)	–	–	–	–	–	–
Employees	–	–	–	–	–	2,000

ATHENAHEALTH INC

311 Arsenal Street
Watertown, MA 02472
Phone: 617 402-1000
Fax: –
Web: www.athenahealth.com

NMS: ATHN
CEO: Robert E Segert
CFO: Luis Borgen
HR: –
FYE: December 31
Type: Public

athenahealth knows that managing physician practices can result in a splitting headache especially when patients are late paying bills or miss appointments. The company provides health care organizations with online software for cloud-based electronic health record (EHR) practice management and patient communication services. Offerings include revenue cycle management (athenaCollector) medical record automation (athenaClinicals) and patient relations and referral systems (athenaCommunicator and athenaCoordinator). Its services help health care providers streamline workflow data and billing and collection tasks. athenahealth's programs are managed through its cloud-based athenaNet network.

	Annual Growth	12/13	12/14	12/15	12/16	12/17
Sales ($ mil.)	19.7%	595.0	752.6	924.5	1,082.9	1,220.3
Net income ($ mil.)	112.7%	2.6	(3.1)	14.0	21.0	53.1
Market value ($ mil.)	(0.3%)	5,393.5	5,842.6	6,454.9	4,217.3	5,334.9
Employees	14.8%	2,966	3,676	4,668	5,305	5,156

ATHENS BANCSHARES CORP

106 Washington Avenue
Athens, TN 37303
Phone: 423 745-1111
Fax: –
Web: www.athensfederal.com

NBB: AFCB
CEO: –
CFO: –
HR: –
FYE: December 31
Type: Public

Athens Bancshares Corporation is the holding company for Athens Federal Community Bank an eight-branch bank in Athens Tennessee. Athens is located in the southeast corner of the state halfway between Knoxville and Chattanooga. The town is home to major manufacturers such as DENSO Heil Johnson Controls and Thomas & Betts where many of the bank's customers are employed. Athens Federal offers checking and savings accounts including NOW and money market accounts as well as debit and credit cards and online banking services. Through Florida-based INVEST Financial Corporation (a subsidiary of Prudential) it offers mutual funds variable and fixed annuities and discount brokerage services.

	Annual Growth	12/12	12/13	12/14	12/15	12/16
Assets ($ mil.)	10.8%	291.6	294.8	302.4	323.8	439.9
Net income ($ mil.)	5.1%	2.6	2.3	2.7	2.9	3.2
Market value ($ mil.)	20.5%	29.4	35.3	45.3	44.1	62.0
Employees	1.0%	104	109	106	–	–

ATHEROTECH INC.

201 London Pkwy.
Birmingham AL 35211
Phone: 205-871-8344
Fax: 205-871-8392
Web: www.atherotech.com

CEO: –
CFO: –
HR: –
FYE: December 31
Type: Private

The Good the Bad and the VAP. Atherotech makes the Vertical Auto Profile (VAP) Cholesterol test a cholesterol level diagnostic that directly measures both low-density lipoprotein (LDL the "good cholesterol") and high-density lipoprotein (HDL the "bad cholesterol"). At its clinical laboratory site in Birmingham the company performs the tests on blood samples collected at doctors' offices hospitals clinics and other labs around the US. In addition to the VAP test Atherotech makes other diagnostics used to detect cardiovascular disease and is developing new tests based on its VAP technology. The company was acquired by private equity firm Behrman Capital in 2010.

ATHERSYS INC

3201 Carnegie Avenue
Cleveland, OH 44115-2634
Phone: 216 431-9900
Fax: –
Web: www.athersys.com

NAS: ATHX
CEO: –
CFO: Ivor Macleod
HR: –
FYE: December 31
Type: Public

Biotechnology is all the RAGE at Athersys. The development-stage company uses its Random Activation of Gene Expression (RAGE) technology to scan the human genome identify proteins with specific biological functions and link those protein functions with gene structures (functional genomics). It is also developing therapies for oncology and vascular applications based on its MultiStem technology which uses stem cells from adult bone marrow. The firm plans to leverage its technologies by partnering with other biotechs and drugmakers but it also aims to develop its own proprietary drugs. It counts Bristol-Myers Squibb and Angiotech Pharmaceuticals among its partners.

	Annual Growth	12/16	12/17	12/18	12/19	12/20
Sales ($ mil.)	(46.3%)	17.3	3.7	24.3	5.6	1.4
Net income ($ mil.)	–	(15.3)	(32.2)	(24.3)	(44.6)	(78.8)
Market value ($ mil.)	3.4%	309.0	365.6	290.8	248.4	353.5
Employees	12.8%	60	66	75	83	97

ATI LADISH LLC

5481 S. Packard Ave.
Cudahy WI 53110
Phone: 414-747-2611
Fax: 414-747-2963
Web: www.ladishco.com

CEO: Gary J Vroman
CFO: -
HR: Nicole Murray
FYE: December 31
Type: Subsidiary

ATI Ladish started in 1905 when Herman Ladish bought a 1500-lb. steam hammer; the company's been swinging ever since. ATI Ladish (formerly Ladish Co. Inc.) designs and manufactures high-strength forged and cast metal components for aerospace and industrial markets. Complex jet engine parts missile components landing gear helicopter rotors and other aerospace products generate about 85% of company sales; general industrial components account for the remainder. Rolls-Royce (26%) United Technologies (17%) and GE (13%) collectively account for more than half of its sales. In 2011 Allegheny Technologies (ATI) acquired and renamed Ladish and joined its operations with ATI's High Performance Metals segment.

ATI TITANIUM LLC

1600 NE Old Salem Rd.
Albany OR 97321
Phone: 541-926-4211
Fax: 541-967-6994
Web: www.atimetals.com/businesses/business-units/wa

CEO: -
CFO: -
HR: -
FYE: December 31
Type: Subsidiary

ATI Titanium (doing business as ATI Wah Chang which in part means "great development") creates specialty metals and chemicals. Wah Chang principally makes zirconium mill products as well as other corrosion-resistant specialty metals such as hafnium niobium titanium and vanadium. Its products are used in industries including aerospace chemical processing energy production medical and consumer goods. It also provides laboratory services for metal testing and analysis. Its Ti Wire division makes titanium bar and wire products while business unit Midwest Laboratory performs radiological monitoring. The company now a subsidiary of Allegheny Technologies dates back to a trading company founded in 1916.

ATLANTA CLARK UNIVERSITY INC

223 JAMES P BRAWLEY DR SW
ATLANTA, GA 303144385
Phone: 404-880-8000
Fax: -
Web: www.cau.edu

CEO: Dr Colton Brown
CFO: Lucille Mauge
HR: -
FYE: June 30
Type: Private

Clark Atlanta University (CAU) is a historically African-American liberal arts college that enrolls about 3500 students. The private school which is affiliated with the United Methodist Church offers undergraduate and graduate degrees through its four schools: Arts and Sciences Business Administration Education Social Work. It also offers professional programs and certificates. CAU is a member of the Atlanta University Center a consortium of educational institutions that includes Spelman College and Morehouse College. Clark Atlanta University was formed by the 1988 merger of two colleges founded in the 1860s — Clark College and Atlanta University.

	Annual Growth	06/13	06/14	06/15	06/17	06/18
Sales ($ mil.)	(0.6%)	-	114.6	116.6	103.5	111.9
Net income ($ mil.)	39.8%	-	6.1	8.1	17.4	23.3
Market value ($ mil.)	-	-	-	-	-	-
Employees	-	-	-	-	-	1,150

ATLANTA FALCONS FOOTBALL CLUB LLC

4400 Falcon Pkwy.
Flowery Branch GA 30542
Phone: 770-965-3115
Fax: 770-965-2766
Web: www.atlantafalcons.com

CEO: -
CFO: -
HR: -
FYE: February 28
Type: Private

These birds keep Atlanta flapping about the gridiron all year round. The Atlanta Falcons Football Club is a professional football franchise that joined the National Football League in 1966. First awarded to businessman Rankin Smith the team has made the playoffs just nine different seasons and counts only one conference championship in 1998. (Atlanta lost that year to the Denver Broncos in Super Bowl XXXIII.) The Georgia Dome has played host to Falcons games since 2002 the same year Home Depot co-founder Arthur Blank acquired the franchise from Smith's family.

ATLANTA HARDWOOD CORPORATION

5596 RIVERVIEW RD SE
MABLETON, GA 301262914
Phone: 404-792-2290
Fax: -
Web: www.hardwoodweb.com

CEO: James W Howard Jr
CFO: Paul Harris
HR: -
FYE: December 31
Type: Private

Atlanta Hardwood Corporation, carves out, its living from the trees of the Appalachian Mountains. Through its various divisions Atlanta Hardwood supplies hardwood products including lumber plywood veneer, moulding and flooring made from some, 75 varieties of wood., It, specializes in processing distributing and exporting products, made from Appalachian wood including Ash Maple Poplar and White Oak. It also imports Mahogany Teak European Beech and several other types of wood from international sources. Other offerings include custom product services that cater to architects designers and fabricators. Founded in 1952 by James Howard Sr. Atlanta Hardwood is today headed by Howard's son Jim Howard.

	Annual Growth	12/04	12/05	12/06	12/07	12/08
Sales ($ mil.)	(82.5%)	-	-	761.0	27.3	23.3
Net income ($ mil.)	-	-	-	0.0	0.6	(0.3)
Market value ($ mil.)	-	-	-	-	-	-
Employees	-	-	-	-	-	243

ATLANTA NATIONAL LEAGUE BASEBALL CLUB INC.

755 Hank Aaron Dr. SW
Atlanta GA 30315
Phone: 404-522-7630
Fax: 303-312-2116
Web: www.coloradorockies.com

CEO: -
CFO: Chip Moore
HR: -
FYE: December 31
Type: Subsidiary

America may be the land of the free but Atlanta is the home of these baseball Braves. Atlanta National League Baseball Club owns and operates the Atlanta Braves Major League Baseball franchise which boasts three World Series championships its last in 1995. A charter member of the National League the team was formed as the Boston Red Stockings in 1871 (it became the Braves in 1912) and moved to Milwaukee in the 1950s before settling in Atlanta in 1966. Under the ownership of media mogul Ted Turner the Braves won five pennants during the 1990s. The Braves play host at Turner Field. John Malone's Liberty Media has owned the team since 2007.

ATLANTIC AMERICAN CORP.   NMS: AAME

4370 Peachtree Road, N.E.   CEO: Hilton Howell
Atlanta, GA 30319   CFO: J. Ross Franklin
Phone: 404 266-5500   HR: –
Fax: –   FYE: December 31
Web: www.atlam.com   Type: Public

Baseball apple pie and... insurance! Atlantic American sells a mix of property/casualty health and life insurance throughout the US. Its Bankers Fidelity Life Insurance subsidiary provides life and supplemental health insurance offerings with income primarily coming from sales of Medicare supplement policies. Its American Southern subsidiary offers commercial and personal property/casualty products including automobile insurance products targeted at large motor pools and fleets owned by local governments. The unit also offers general commercial liability coverage and surety bonds catering to niche markets such as school bus transportation and subdivision construction.

	Annual Growth	12/16	12/17	12/18	12/19	12/20
Assets ($ mil.)	6.2%	318.6	343.2	344.3	377.6	405.2
Net income ($ mil.)	46.6%	2.6	4.5	(0.7)	(0.4)	12.2
Market value ($ mil.)	(15.8%)	83.7	69.4	49.2	40.2	42.1
Employees	(1.7%)	164	159	161	155	153

ATLANTIC CITY ELECTRIC CO

500 North Wakefield Drive   CEO: David M Velazquez
Newark, DE 19702   CFO: Frederick J Boyle
Phone: 202 872-2000   HR: –
Fax: –   FYE: December 31
Web: www.atlanticcityelectric.com   Type: Public

Atlantic City Electric makes America's favorite playground shine in the nighttime. The Pepco Holdings' utility generates transmits and distributes electricity to 547000 homes and businesses in southern New Jersey. Atlantic City Electric operates more than 11000 miles of transmission and distribution lines in its 2700 sq. ml. 8-county service area. Atlantic City Electric's electricity delivery operations are regulated by the New Jersey Board of Public Utilities. As part of the 2016 acquisition of Pepco Holdings Atlantic City Electric joined the Exelon family of utilities.

	Annual Growth	12/16	12/17	12/18	12/19	12/20
Sales ($ mil.)	(0.2%)	1,257.0	1,186.0	1,236.0	1,240.0	1,245.0
Net income ($ mil.)	–	(42.0)	77.0	75.0	99.0	112.0
Market value ($ mil.)	–	–	–	–	–	–
Employees	2.2%	595	647	612	639	650

ATLANTIC COAST FINANCIAL CORP   NMS: ACFC

4655 Salisbury Road, Suite 110   CEO: –
Jacksonville, FL 32256   CFO: –
Phone: 800 342-2824   HR: –
Fax: –   FYE: December 31
Web: www.atlanticcoastbank.net   Type: Public

Atlantic Coast Financial Corporation (formerly Atlantic Coast Federal Corporation) is the holding company for Atlantic Coast Bank which operates about a dozen branches and 900 ATMs in southeastern Georgia and the Jacksonville Florida area. The bank offers standard deposit lending and investment services. Residential mortgages make up around half of its loan portfolio. Atlantic Coast Bank was established in 1939 as a credit union that served Atlantic Coast Line Railroad employees. Formerly mutually owned Atlantic Coast Federal Corporation converted to a stock form of ownership in 2011 changed its name and moved its headquarters to Jacksonville where the company is focusing its growth strategy.

	Annual Growth	12/12	12/13	12/14	12/15	12/16
Assets ($ mil.)	4.1%	772.6	733.6	706.5	857.2	907.5
Net income ($ mil.)	–	(6.7)	(11.4)	1.3	7.7	6.4
Market value ($ mil.)	35.6%	31.2	67.2	61.6	90.9	105.5
Employees	0.0%	147	135	172	190	147

ATLANTIC DIVING SUPPLY, INC.

621 LYNNHVEN PKWY STE 160   CEO: Jason Wallace
VIRGINIA BEACH, VA 23452   CFO: Kiran Rai
Phone: 757-481-7758   HR: –
Fax: –   FYE: December 31
Web: www.adsinc.com   Type: Private

Atlantic Diving Supply (doing business as ADS) is geared toward gearing up the military. Serving agencies in the Federal Government the company specializes in helping customers procure tactical and operational military equipment. The Company is serving the local and military diving community and Defense Logistics Agency (DLA) as a prime vendor for marine and lifesaving diving and search and rescue equipment. The Company holds more than 50 Indefinite Delivery Indefinite Quantity (IDIQ) contracts and Blanket Purchase Agreement (BPAs) and has grown to be a top 5 DLA Supplier and Top 50 Federal Government Contractor.

	Annual Growth	12/06	12/07	12/08	12/09	12/10
Sales ($ mil.)	42.8%	–	–	650.8	938.9	1,327.2
Net income ($ mil.)	38.7%	–	–	40.2	54.4	77.3
Market value ($ mil.)	–	–	–	–	–	–
Employees	–	–	–	–	–	360

ATLANTIC HEALTH SYSTEM INC.

475 SOUTH ST   CEO: Brian Gragnolati
MORRISTOWN, NJ 079606459   CFO: –
Phone: 973-660-3100   HR: –
Fax: –   FYE: December 31
Web: www.atlantichealth.org   Type: Private

The not-for-profit Atlantic Health System (AHS) operates about dozen urgent care hospital providing general medical and surgical services to residents of northern New Jersey. Its flagship Morristown Medical Center is a nationally-recognized leader in cardiology orthopedics nursing critical care and geriatrics.. The system's Overlook Medical Center houses the Atlantic Neuroscience Institute; home to the Comprehensive Stroke Center. Its smaller Newton Medical Center serves patients in two New Jersey counties as well as counties in Pennsylvania and New York.

	Annual Growth	12/14	12/15	12/16	12/17	12/19
Sales ($ mil.)	8917.8%	–	–	–	0.4	3,163.4
Net income ($ mil.)	–	–	–	–	(0.5)	476.1
Market value ($ mil.)	–	–	–	–	–	–
Employees	–	–	–	–	–	3,100

ATLANTIC POWER CORP   NYS: AT

3 Allied Drive, Suite 155   CEO: James J Moore Jr
Dedham, MA 02026   CFO: Terrence Ronan
Phone: 617 977-2400   HR: –
Fax: 617 977-2410   FYE: December 31
Web: www.atlanticpower.com   Type: Public

Atlantic Power a Canadian independent power producer owns 21 power generation projects in eleven US states and two provinces of Canada. The company has a generation capacity of more than 1300 MW about 85% of which is generated in the US. Its primarily sells natural gas biomass and hydro-power under long-term fuel supply agreements to utilities and other parties. The company also partners with Heorot Power Management and Purenergy LLC to provide operations maintenance and repair services. Nearly three-quarters of Atlantic Power's revenue comes from the US.

	Annual Growth	12/15	12/16	12/17	12/18	12/19
Sales ($ mil.)	(9.5%)	420.2	399.2	431.0	282.3	281.6
Net income ($ mil.)	–	(62.4)	(122.4)	(98.6)	36.8	(42.6)
Market value ($ mil.)	4.3%	214.1	271.7	255.4	235.8	253.2
Employees	(2.2%)	291	277	246	230	266

ATLANTIC PREMIUM BRANDS LTD.

1033 Skokie Blvd. Ste. 600
Northbrook IL 60062
Phone: 847-412-6200
Fax: 516-327-7461
Web: www.astoriafederal.com

CEO: Thomas M Dalton
CFO: Thomas M Dalton
HR: –
FYE: December 31
Type: Private

Atlantic Premium Brands doesn't operate along the Atlantic Ocean but it does have a boatload of premium regional meat brands. The company processes and distributes packaged value-added meats under names such as J.C. Potter Blue Ribbon Texas Traditions Richard's Cajun Foods Carlton and Cajun Favorites. It also offers its customers private-label products and services. Atlantic Premium's meats include smoked and breakfast sausages ham bacon and meat-based entrees. The Northbrook Illinois-headquartered company distributes its products to US supermarkets and discount stores.

ATLANTIC RECORDS GROUP

1290 Avenue of the Americas
New York NY 10104
Phone: 212-707-2000
Fax: 212-405-5475
Web: www.atlanticrecords.com

CEO: Ahmet M Ertegun
CFO: –
HR: –
FYE: September 30
Type: Business Segment

This record company makes sure there's music to please fans from sea to shinning sea. Atlantic Records Group is one of the top purveyors of pop music in the US promoting such artists as Southern rapper T. I. and the rock band Death Cab for Cutie. It distributes such imprints as Elektra Records as well as the venerable Atlantic Records label. Music industry mogul Ahmet Ertegun and partner Herb Abramson started Atlantic in 1947. Atlantic Records and Elektra Records merged in 2004 to form The Atlantic Records Group. Along with Warner Bros. Records today the company is one of the two flagship recorded music operations of Warner Music Group.

ATLANTIC SOUTHEAST AIRLINES INC.

A-Tech Center 990 Toffie Terrace
Atlanta GA 30354
Phone: 404-856-1000
Fax: 404-856-1203
Web: www.flyasa.com

CEO: –
CFO: –
HR: –
FYE: December 31
Type: Subsidiary

It's all about connections for Atlantic Southeast Airlines (ASA). Operating as a Delta Connection regional carrier ASA flies to smaller markets on behalf of Delta Air Lines primarily from Delta's hubs in Atlanta and Cincinnati. The carrier serves about 110 destinations mainly east of the Mississippi in the US but also in western states and in Canada Mexico and the Caribbean. ASA maintains a fleet of about 160 aircraft all of which are Canadair regional jets (CRJs) made by Bombardier. Founded in 1979 ASA is a subsidiary of SkyWest which bought the company from Delta in 2005. In late 2010 SkyWest boosted its capacity by acquiring rival ExpressJet via ASA establishing ExpressJet as a subsidiary of ASA.

ATLANTIC UNION BANKSHARES CORP   NMS: AUB

1051 East Cary Street, Suite 1200
Richmond, VA 23219
Phone: 804 633-5031
Fax: –
Web: www.bankatunion.com

CEO: John Asbury
CFO: Robert Gorman
HR: –
FYE: December 31
Type: Public

Union Bankshares Corporation is a community bank that provides fill retail commercial municipal banking and asset management. The bank also provides trust services through about 20 banking offices less than 5 loan centers and several ATMs across northern Vermont and northern New Hampshire. The bank serves individuals and commercial banking services to small and medium sized corporations partnerships and sole proprietorships as well as nonprofit organizations local municipalities and school districts.

	Annual Growth	12/16	12/17	12/18	12/19	12/20
Assets ($ mil.)	23.5%	8,426.8	9,315.2	13,765.6	17,563.0	19,628.4
Net income ($ mil.)	19.5%	77.5	72.9	146.2	193.5	158.2
Market value ($ mil.)	(2.0%)	2,813.8	2,847.6	2,222.5	2,956.3	2,593.3
Employees	7.3%	1,416	1,149	1,609	1,989	1,879

ATLANTICARE HEALTH SYSTEM INC.

2500 ENGLISH CREEK AVE
EGG HARBOR TOWNSHIP, NJ 082345549
Phone: 609-407-2300
Fax: –
Web: www.atlanticare.org

CEO: David Tilton
CFO: –
HR: –
FYE: December 31
Type: Private

AtlantiCare Health System won't gamble with your health. The not-for-profit health system operates AtlantiCare Regional Medical Center (ARMC) home to roughly 570 beds at two campuses (Atlantic City and Mainland). The hospital's specialty departments include a Level II Trauma center heart institute center for childbirth weight loss clinic cancer center and joint and spine institutes. Other facilities include child care centers (AtlantiCare Kids) behavioral health facilities and urgent care centers. The company also operates a PPO (AtlantiCare Health Plans) and offers home health and hospice services.

	Annual Growth	12/04	12/05	12/06	12/14	12/15
Sales ($ mil.)	21.7%	–	9.1	11.7	66.4	65.0
Net income ($ mil.)	1.3%	–	1.1	(0.6)	0.4	1.2
Market value ($ mil.)	–	–	–	–	–	–
Employees	–	–	–	–	–	5,000

ATLANTICUS HOLDINGS CORP   NMS: ATLC

Five Concourse Parkway, Suite 300
Atlanta, GA 30328
Phone: 770 828-2000
Fax: –
Web: www.atlanticus.com

CEO: Jeffrey Howard
CFO: William Mccamey
HR: –
FYE: December 31
Type: Public

Suffering from a fiscal near-death experience? Let Atlanticus Holdings help resuscitate you. Subprime is the strategy for this company. Formerly named CompuCredit until November 2012 it traditionally issued unsecured Visa and MasterCard credit cards to customers with low credit scores and charged them more for the risk. The economic downturn compelled the firm to close most of its active credit card accounts. However Atlanticus continues to collect on portfolios of credit card receivables underlying now-closed credit card accounts. The company current portfolio offers Credit and Other Investments; and Auto Finance.

	Annual Growth	12/16	12/17	12/18	12/19	12/20
Sales ($ mil.)	49.2%	113.6	135.4	233.5	458.2	563.4
Net income ($ mil.)	–	(6.3)	(40.8)	7.9	26.4	94.1
Market value ($ mil.)	71.6%	45.8	38.7	58.7	145.2	396.9
Employees	2.9%	292	297	310	319	327

ATLANTICUS HOLDINGS CORPORATION
NASDAQ: CCRT

5 Concourse Pkwy. Ste. 400
Atlanta GA 30328
Phone: 770-828-2000
Fax: 770-870-5183
Web: atlanticusholdings.net

CEO: –
CFO: J Paul Whitehead III
HR: –
FYE: December 31
Type: Public

Suffering from a fiscal near-death experience? Let Atlanticus Holdings resuscitate you. Subprime was the strategy for this company. Formerly named CompuCredit until November 2012 it traditionally issued unsecured Visa and MasterCard credit cards to customers with low credit scores and charged them more for the risk; however the economic downturn compelled the firm to close most of its active accounts. Subsidiary Jefferson Capital Systems collects on debt other companies have written off. Atlanticus sold its 300 US microloan retail locations — which provided payday loans under such banners as First American Cash Advance and First Southern Cash Advance — to Advance America for more than $46 million in 2011.

ATLAS AIR WORLDWIDE HOLDINGS, INC.
NMS: AAWW

2000 Westchester Avenue
Purchase, NY 10577
Phone: 914 701-8000
Fax: –
Web: www.atlasairworldwide.com

CEO: John Dietrich
CFO: Spencer Schwartz
HR: –
FYE: December 31
Type: Public

Atlas Air Worldwide Holdings (AAWW) is a global leader in outsourced aircraft and aviation operating services. It leases cargo planes to customers mainly airlines under long-term ACMI (aircraft crew maintenance and insurance) contracts. AAWW operates the world's largest fleet of Boeing 747 freighters and offers its customers a broad array of 747 777 767 and 737 aircraft for domestic regional and international cargo and passenger applications. It also offers dry leasing (aircraft and engines only) via its Titan division. In addition affiliates Atlas Air and 51% economic interest and 75% voting interest in Polar Air Cargo.

	Annual Growth	12/17	12/18	12/19	12/20	12/21
Sales ($ mil.)	16.9%	2,156.5	2,677.7	2,739.2	3,211.1	4,030.8
Net income ($ mil.)	21.9%	223.5	270.6	(293.1)	360.3	493.3
Market value ($ mil.)	12.6%	1,713.5	1,232.6	805.5	1,593.4	2,749.8
Employees	9.0%	2,870	3,275	3,587	4,061	4,056

ATLAS COPCO USA HOLDINGS INC.

34 Maple Ave.
Pine Brook NJ 07058
Phone: 973-439-3400
Fax: 973-439-9455
Web: www.atlascopco.com

CEO: –
CFO: –
HR: –
FYE: May 31
Type: Subsidiary

With businesses both Swedish and American you may not think of construction and mining equipment. But you should. Atlas Copco USA Holdings operates throughout the US Canada and Mexico as an arm of Swedish manufacturing giant Atlas Copco AB. The US-based business manufactures a slew of compressors and generators construction and mining equipment and power tools. Its power tool lineup includes air assembly devices grinders drills air motors hoists and trolleys and related services. Demolition equipment rock drills blast hole drilling rigs and exploration drilling tools are part of the list of mining and construction offerings. North America generates about 18% of the parent company's total sales.

ATLAS PIPELINE PARTNERS LP
NYS: APL

Park Place Corporate Center One, 1000 Commerce Drive, 4th Floor
Pittsburgh, PA 15275-1011
Phone: 877 950-7473
Fax: –

CEO: Eugene N Dubay
CFO: Matthew Jones
HR: –
FYE: December 31
Type: Public

Atlas Pipeline Partners shoulders the burden of getting natural gas from wellheads to major gas utilities such as Peoples Natural Gas National Fuel Gas and East Ohio Gas. The midstream company is engaged in the transmission gathering and processing of natural gas in the Appalachia and Mid-Continent regions. Atlas Pipeline Partners operates about 9700 miles of active intrastate gas gathering and processing pipelines in Kansas Oklahoma Tennessee and Texas. It also owns and operates five natural gas processing plants. Atlas Pipeline Partners' general partner is owned by Atlas Energy L.P (formerly Atlas Pipeline Holdings L.P.) In 2014 the company agreed to be acquired by Targa Resources Partners.

	Annual Growth	12/09	12/10	12/11	12/12	12/13
Sales ($ mil.)	23.5%	904.2	935.6	1,302.7	1,246.0	2,106.8
Net income ($ mil.)	–	62.7	280.4	295.4	68.1	(91.6)
Market value ($ mil.)	37.5%	790.5	1,988.0	2,993.7	2,544.1	2,824.5
Employees	9.8%	310	270	280	350	450

ATLAS WORLD GROUP, INC.

1212 SAINT GEORGE RD
EVANSVILLE, IN 477112364
Phone: 812-424-2222
Fax: –
Web: www.atlasvanlines.com

CEO: John P Griffin
CFO: Donald R Breivogel Jr
HR: –
FYE: December 31
Type: Private

Willing to carry the weight of a moving world agent-owned Atlas World Group is the holding company for Atlas Van Lines one of the largest moving companies in the US. Atlas Van Lines' more than 500 agents transport household goods domestically and between the US and Canada; it also offers specialized transportation of items such as trade show exhibits fine art and electronics. Atlas Van Lines International provides international corporate relocation and freight forwarding services. Its Atlas Canada unit moves household goods in that country while American Red Ball International specializes in military relocations and serves van lines outside Atlas' network.

	Annual Growth	12/16	12/17	12/18	12/19	12/20
Sales ($ mil.)	(1.5%)	–	842.1	900.5	906.4	806.0
Net income ($ mil.)	19.0%	–	4.8	10.0	9.6	8.0
Market value ($ mil.)	–	–	–	–	–	–
Employees	–	–	–	–	–	726

ATMEL CORPORATION

1600 TECHNOLOGY DR
SAN JOSE, CA 951101382
Phone: 408-735-9110
Fax: –
Web: www.microchip.com

CEO: –
CFO: –
HR: –
FYE: December 31
Type: Private

Atmel is a leading maker of microcontrollers which are used in a wide range of products from computers and mobile devices (smartphones tablets e-readers) to automobile motor control systems television remote controls and solid-state lighting. In addition the company offers touchscreen controllers and sensors non-volatile memory devices and radio frequency (RF) and wireless components. Its chips are used worldwide in consumer communications industrial military and networking applications. Most of Atmel's sales come from customers outside the US. In mid-2016 the company was bought by Microchip a chip maker for $3.6 billion.

	Annual Growth	12/10	12/11	12/12	12/13	12/14
Sales ($ mil.)	(0.7%)	–	–	1,432.1	1,386.4	1,413.3
Net income ($ mil.)	7.5%	–	–	30.4	(22.1)	35.2
Market value ($ mil.)	–	–	–	–	–	–
Employees	–	–	–	–	–	5,200

ATMI, INC.   NMS: ATMI

7 Commerce Drive   CEO: Douglas A Neugold
Danbury, CT 06810   CFO: Timothy C Carlson
Phone: 203 794-1100   HR: Kathleen G Mincieli
Fax: 203 792-8040   FYE: December 31
Web: www.atmi.com   Type: Public

ATMI's original name — Advanced Technology Materials Inc. — is a pretty good summary of its business. The company provides ultrapure materials and related packaging and delivery systems used by semiconductor and flat-panel display manufacturers during copper integration deposition ion implantation photolithography and surface preparation production processes. It also offers single-use disposable storage systems mixers and bioreactors along with flexible film and cleanroom packaging to the biotechnology cell therapy laboratory and pharmaceutical industries. (This life sciences segment is being sold to Pall Corporation.) Most of its business comes from customers located in the Asia/Pacific region.

	Annual Growth	12/08	12/09	12/10	12/11	12/12
Sales ($ mil.)	4.7%	339.1	254.7	367.3	390.1	407.4
Net income ($ mil.)	6.2%	33.3	(6.7)	39.5	(20.0)	42.3
Market value ($ mil.)	7.9%	493.5	595.5	637.7	640.6	667.8
Employees	1.8%	761	693	773	814	817

ATMOS ENERGY CORP.   NYS: ATO

1800 Three Lincoln Centre, 5430 LBJ Freeway   CEO: John Akers
Dallas, TX 75240   CFO: Christopher Forsythe
Phone: 972 934-9227   HR: John Robbins
Fax: 972 855-3075   FYE: September 30
Web: www.atmosenergy.com   Type: Public

Atmos Energy is one of the country's leading natural gas distributors. The company safely delivers reliable affordable efficient and abundant natural gas through regulated sales and transportation arrangements to over three million residential commercial public authority and industrial customers in eight states located primarily in the South. It also manages one of the largest intrastate pipeline operations in Texas. All told Atmos Energy has a network of more the 75000 miles of transmission and distribution lines.

	Annual Growth	09/17	09/18	09/19	09/20	09/21
Sales ($ mil.)	5.4%	2,759.7	3,115.5	2,901.8	2,821.1	3,407.5
Net income ($ mil.)	13.8%	396.4	603.1	511.4	601.4	665.6
Market value ($ mil.)	1.3%	11,102.1	12,435.5	15,081.3	12,658.0	11,679.4
Employees	0.6%	4,565	4,628	4,776	4,694	4,684

ATN INTERNATIONAL INC   NMS: ATNI

500 Cummings Center, Suite 2450   CEO: Michael Prior
Beverly, MA 01915   CFO: Justin Benincasa
Phone: 978 619-1300   HR: –
Fax: –   FYE: December 31
Web: www.atni.com   Type: Public

ATN is a holding company that directly and through its subsidiaries owns and operates telecommunications businesses in North America the Caribbean and Bermuda as well as a renewable energy business in India. The company look for businesses that offer growth opportunities or potential strategic benefits but require additional capital investment in order to execute on their business plans. Within its telecommunication operations ATN globally owns nearly 300 towers. In addition its renewable energy operations own 52MW commercial solar projects at five sites. About 25% of the company's revenue comes from US Telecom.

	Annual Growth	12/16	12/17	12/18	12/19	12/20
Sales ($ mil.)	(0.1%)	457.0	481.2	451.2	438.7	455.4
Net income ($ mil.)			12.1	31.5	(10.8)	(14.1)
Market value ($ mil.)	(15.0%)	1,273.9	878.5	1,137.2	880.6	663.9
Employees	(1.4%)	1,800	1,800	1,700	1,700	1,700

ATRIA SENIOR LIVING INC.

401 S. 4th St. Ste. 1900   CEO: John A Moore
Louisville KY 40202   CFO: –
Phone: 502-779-4700   HR: Angelica Ybarra
Fax: 502-779-4701   FYE: December 31
Web: www.atriaseniorliving.com   Type: Private

Atria Senior Living is breathing new life as a senior living management company. It was formed in 2011 as a spinoff of Atria Senior Living Group (ASLG) formerly an owner and operator of about 120 independent and assisted living communities throughout the US. After those assets were acquired for $3.1 billion by health care real estate investment trust Ventas Atria Senior Living signed a long-term contract to manage that portfolio of communities for Ventas. Atria Senior Living also manages communities for other owners. In addition to long-term care its facilities offer temporary and short-term stay options as well as specialized assistance for residents with Alzheimer's.

ATRICURE INC   NMS: ATRC

7555 Innovation Way   CEO: Michael Carrel
Mason, OH 45040   CFO: Angela Wirick
Phone: 513 755-4100   HR: –
Fax: –   FYE: December 31
Web: www.atricure.com   Type: Public

AtriCure Inc. provides innovative technologies for the treatment of Afib and related conditions. Afib affects more than 33 million people worldwide. The medical device maker markets the Synergy Ablation System used in the treatment of atrial fibrillation (AFib) a common type of heart arrhythmia. Cardiothoracic surgeons use the AtriCure Synergy Ablation System in conjunction with elective surgical ablation procedures to treat patients through minimally invasive procedures. AtriCure also sells reusable and disposable cryoablation devices (probes using extreme cold) to ablate cardiac tissue. Additionally the company offers the AtriClip Left Atrial Appendage System or AtriClip system designed to help surgeons exclude the left atrial appendage. Its US markets accounts for about 80% of revenues.

	Annual Growth	12/17	12/18	12/19	12/20	12/21
Sales ($ mil.)	11.9%	174.7	201.6	230.8	206.5	274.3
Net income ($ mil.)	–	(26.9)	(21.1)	(35.2)	(48.2)	50.2
Market value ($ mil.)	39.7%	839.3	1,408.1	1,496.0	2,561.7	3,199.5
Employees	11.3%	570	620	730	750	875

ATRION CORP.   NMS: ATRI

One Allentown Parkway   CEO: David Battat
Allen, TX 75002   CFO: Jeffery Strickland
Phone: 972 390-9800   HR: –
Fax: –   FYE: December 31
Web: www.atrioncorp.com   Type: Public

While Atrion is a comparatively small company in the medical products industry it is the leading US manufacturer of products in several market niches including soft contact lens disinfection cases clamps for IV sets vacuum relief valves surgical loops used in minimally invasive surgery and check valves. As an extension of its expertise in valve design and manufacturing Atrion also is the leading manufacturer of valves and inflation devices for the marine and aviation markets supplying valves used in safety products such as life vests and inflatable boats. About 60% of company's revenue comes from US customers.

	Annual Growth	12/16	12/17	12/18	12/19	12/20
Sales ($ mil.)	0.7%	143.5	146.6	152.4	155.1	147.6
Net income ($ mil.)	3.9%	27.6	36.6	34.3	36.8	32.1
Market value ($ mil.)	6.1%	926.1	1,151.5	1,353.2	1,372.2	1,172.7
Employees	5.2%	520	528	570	616	636

ATRIUS HEALTH, INC.

275 GROVE ST STE 3300
AUBURNDALE, MA 024662274
Phone: 617-559-8444
Fax: –
Web: www.atriushealth.org

CEO: Steven Strongwater
CFO: Leland J Stacy
HR: –
FYE: December 31
Type: Private

Atrius Health an innovative nonprofit healthcare leader delivers an effective system of connected care for adult and pediatric patients at some 30 medical practice locations in eastern Massachusetts. Atrius Health's physicians and primary care providers along with additional clinicians work in close collaboration with hospital partners community specialists and skilled nursing. Atrius Health provides high-quality patient-centered coordinated cost effective care to every patient it serves. Atrius Health was founded in 2004 by medical groups including Dedham Medical Associates and Harvard Vanguard Medical Associates; Granite Medical Group joined a short time later in 2005.

	Annual Growth	12/13	12/14	12/15	12/17	12/19
Sales ($ mil.)	137.6%	–	28.6	1,577.0	1,873.0	2,167.7
Net income ($ mil.)	–	–	(0.2)	(28.5)	39.5	5.7
Market value ($ mil.)	–	–	–	–	–	–
Employees	–	–	–	–	–	3,906

ATRIX INTERNATIONAL INC.

1350 Larc Industrial Blvd.
Burnsville MN 55337-1412
Phone: 952-894-6154
Fax: 952-894-6256
Web: www.atrix.com

CEO: Steven Reidel
CFO: –
HR: –
FYE: June 30
Type: Private

Atrix International manufactures fine particulate vacuum cleaners and related products and accessories for use in industrial hospital office restaurant and HAZ-MAT applications. Atrix also makes copier control management and tracking products. Its Omega vacuum cleaner can be used to make cleanrooms for manufacturing semiconductors and other precision components even cleaner. The Omega line guards against electrostatic discharges (ESD) and is shielded against electromagnetic and radio-frequency interference. The company also offers the Windows-based ATRAX network monitoring software. Atrix was established in 1981. Steve Riedel the company's president is the majority shareholder.

ATRM HOLDINGS INC

NBB: ATRM

5215 Gershwin Avenue N.
Oakdale, MN 55128
Phone: 651 704-1800
Fax: –
Web: www.atrmholdings.com

CEO: Daniel Koch
CFO: Stephen Clark
HR: –
FYE: December 31
Type: Public

Aetrium can attribute whatever success it reaps to its semiconductor testing equipment. The company makes systems used in testing integrated circuits (ICs) and other electronic components. Its main products are test handlers which work with testers to thermally condition and sort ICs. Other product lines include automated IC handling products reliability test systems and gear for adapting test handlers to different types of IC packages. Aetrium's customers include analog chip maker Maxim Integrated Products (more than half of sales). The company gets about three-quarters of its sales outside the US mostly in Asian nations.

	Annual Growth	12/12	12/13	12/14	12/15	12/16
Sales ($ mil.)	45.7%	6.2	2.7	33.1	25.6	28.2
Net income ($ mil.)	–	(6.1)	(2.9)	(8.3)	(3.3)	(6.5)
Market value ($ mil.)	35.1%	1.2	15.8	6.9	7.1	4.0
Employees	50.2%	36	19	210	140	183

ATS CORPORATION

NYSE AMEX: ATSC

7925 Jones Branch Dr.
McLean VA 22102
Phone: 571-766-2400
Fax: 571-766-2401
Web: www.atsc.com

CEO: Pamela A Little
CFO: Gerry Beard
HR: –
FYE: October 31
Type: Public

ATS Corporation knows that the key to technological success lies in the right mix of services. Doing business as ATSC the company provides a variety of IT services to the federal government and commercial organizations including consulting systems integration network design and support. ATSC which was founded in 1978 as Advanced Technology Systems went public in 2010. In April 2012 the company was bought by Salient Federal Solutions in an all-stock transaction and taken private. ATSC is now part of Salient's Civilian Mission Critical Solutions division and its System and Software Engineering Solutions division.

ATTORNEY GENERAL, TEXAS

300 W 15TH ST
AUSTIN, TX 787011649
Phone: 512-475-4375
Fax: –
Web: www.texasattorneygeneral.gov

CEO: –
CFO: Greg Herbert
HR: –
FYE: August 31
Type: Private

The Office of the Attorney General of Texas defends the state Constitution represents the state in litigation and approves public bond issues. The office is legal counsel to state government boards and agencies and issues legal opinions when requested by the Governor and agency heads. The Attorney General also sits as an ex-officio member of state committees and commissions and defends state laws and suits against agencies and state employees. Other roles include enforcing health safety and consumer regulations; protecting elderly and disabled residents' rights; collecting court-ordered child support; and administering the Crime Victims' Compensation Fund. Greg Abbott was elected Attorney General in 2002.

	Annual Growth	08/05	08/06	08/14	08/15	08/16
Sales ($ mil.)	–	–	0.0	571.1	561.5	659.7
Net income ($ mil.)	–	–	0.0	(7.0)	8.7	45.1
Market value ($ mil.)	–	–	–	–	–	–
Employees	–	–	–	–	–	4,200

ATTRONICA COMPUTERS, INC.

15867 GAITHER DR
GAITHERSBURG, MD 208771403
Phone: 301-417-0070
Fax: –
Web: www.attronica.com

CEO: Atul Thakkar
CFO: –
HR: –
FYE: December 31
Type: Private

Attronica hopes to offer an alternative to chunking your old outdated computers out the window. The company provides a variety of information technology (IT) services including network and systems integration product consulting and hardware procurement to middle-market businesses in the mid-Atlantic states. Attronica also offers such services as network security support inventory management and training. The company's customers come from a wide range of industries including financial services health care manufacturing retail consumer goods and transportation. It operates from four offices in Maryland and Virginia. Attronica was co-founded by CEO Atul Tucker in 1983.

	Annual Growth	12/11	12/12	12/13	12/16	12/17
Sales ($ mil.)	0.0%	–	61.4	62.1	61.7	61.5
Net income ($ mil.)	(20.8%)	–	0.4	0.5	0.5	0.1
Market value ($ mil.)	–	–	–	–	–	–
Employees	–	–	–	–	–	70

ATWELL, LLC

2 TOWNE SQ STE 700
SOUTHFIELD, MI 480763737
Phone: 248-447-2000
Fax: –
Web: www.atwell-group.com

CEO: Brian Wenzel
CFO: Roderick Petschauer
HR: –
FYE: December 31
Type: Private

Atwell provides real estate and development consulting encompassing civil engineering land planning surveying and environmental services. Spanning the commercial residential corporate real estate and institutional development markets the company helps clients manage real estate development projects and navigate local regulations and planning requirements. The company's consulting services include feasibility studies and economic viability analysis. Atwell's more technical services consist of surveying civil engineering landscape architecture as well as expertise covering environmental impact water and wastewater systems and water resource management.

	Annual Growth	12/11	12/12	12/13	12/15	12/17
Sales ($ mil.)	19.4%	–	36.6	64.7	86.3	88.9
Net income ($ mil.)	(23.4%)	–	5.4	2.2	2.0	1.4
Market value ($ mil.)	–	–	–	–	–	–
Employees	–	–	–	–	–	421

ATWOOD OCEANICS, INC.

15011 Katy Freeway, Suite 800
Houston, TX 77094
Phone: 281 749-7800
Fax: 281 492-7871
Web: www.atwd.com

NYS: ATW
CEO: –
CFO: –
HR: –
FYE: September 30
Type: Public

Atwood Oceanics is at work in oceans all over the world. An offshore oil and gas drilling contractor the firm owns about a dozen drilling rigs including six semisubmersible rigs five jack-ups and one semisubmersible tender assist vessel (which places drilling equipment on permanent platforms). Its rigs operate in the Gulf of Mexico offshore Southeast Asia offshore West Africa offshore Australia and in the Mediterranean. Atwood Oceanics serves a limited number of customers at one time and generates nearly all of its sales internationally.

	Annual Growth	09/12	09/13	09/14	09/15	09/16
Sales ($ mil.)	6.7%	787.4	1,063.7	1,174.0	1,395.9	1,020.6
Net income ($ mil.)	(0.6%)	272.2	350.2	340.8	432.6	265.3
Market value ($ mil.)	(33.9%)	2,945.1	3,566.5	2,831.1	959.7	563.1
Employees	(10.5%)	1,460	1,830	1,905	1,868	938

ATX GROUP INC.

8550 Freeport Pkwy.
Irving TX 75063-2547
Phone: 972-753-6200
Fax: 972-753-6226
Web: www.atxg.com

CEO: Michael Rodriguez
CFO: –
HR: –
FYE: December 31
Type: Private

ATX Group takes its business in every direction. The company provides telematics services to automobile manufacturers primarily in North America including BMW Toyota Motor Sales and Rolls-Royce; in Europe it provides services for PSA Group Peugeot. Drivers of telematics-enabled vehicles can utilize ATX's collision notification emergency assistance navigation roadside diagnostics stolen vehicle tracking and traffic information services. In addition to managing a telematics service network and response centers ATX provides dealer support remote activation services and maintenance. A division of Cross Country Automotive Services the company operates from offices in Texas France and Germany.

AUBURN NATIONAL BANCORP, INC.

100 N. Gay Street
Auburn, AL 36830
Phone: 334 821-9200
Fax: –
Web: www.auburnbank.com

NMS: AUBN
CEO: Robert Dumas
CFO: David Hedges
HR: –
FYE: December 31
Type: Public

War Eagle! Auburn National Bancorporation is the holding company for AuburnBank which operates about 10 branches and a handful of loan offices in and around its headquarters in the eastern Alabama home of Auburn University. With offices in area grocery stores and Wal-Mart locations AuburnBank offers traditional retail banking services such as checking and savings accounts and CDs. It uses funds from deposits to fund residential mortgages and other loans for individuals and businesses. Auburn Bank was founded in 1907.

	Annual Growth	12/16	12/17	12/18	12/19	12/20
Assets ($ mil.)	3.6%	831.9	853.4	818.1	827.9	956.6
Net income ($ mil.)	(2.2%)	8.2	7.8	8.8	9.7	7.5
Market value ($ mil.)	7.4%	111.7	138.7	112.9	189.0	148.7
Employees	(1.0%)	158	156	159	158	152

AUBURN UNIVERSITY

107 SAMFORD HALL
AUBURN, AL 368490001
Phone: 334-844-4650
Fax: –
Web: www.auburn.edu

CEO: –
CFO: Kelli Shomaker
HR: –
FYE: September 30
Type: Private

Most of us bleed red but students and alumni of this university bleed auburn. One of the largest schools in the South Auburn University has an enrollment of more than 30000 students on two campuses and offers bachelors master's and doctoral degrees in more than 140 different fields of study through about a dozen colleges and schools. Fields of study include agriculture business education construction forestry and mathematics and science as well as medical fields including nursing pharmacy and veterinary medicine. Auburn has 1200 faculty members and a student-to-teacher ratio of 18:1.

	Annual Growth	09/15	09/16	09/17	09/18	09/19
Sales ($ mil.)	5.0%	–	775.1	805.2	876.1	897.5
Net income ($ mil.)	(15.3%)	–	130.0	79.3	78.9	79.0
Market value ($ mil.)	–	–	–	–	–	–
Employees	–	–	–	–	–	6,000

AUDACY INC

2400 Market Street, 4th Floor
Philadelphia, PA 19103
Phone: 610 660-5610
Fax: –
Web: www.entercom.com

NYS: AUD
CEO: David Field
CFO: Richard Schmaeling
HR: –
FYE: December 31
Type: Public

The signals from Entercom Communications come through loud and clear. The company is among the largest radio broadcasters in the US about 25 markets including Austin Boston Denver Kansas City New Orleans San Francisco and Seattle. Operating a number of stations in one market allows the company to combine such back office functions as finance and accounting as well as advertising sales and marketing. Its stations program a variety of formats including oldies country and adult contemporary as well as talk sports and news. The Field family including founder and chairman Joseph Field control Entercom.

	Annual Growth	12/16	12/17	12/18	12/19	12/20
Sales ($ mil.)	23.2%	460.2	592.9	1,462.6	1,489.9	1,060.9
Net income ($ mil.)	–	–	38.1	233.0	(362.6)	(420.2)	(242.2)
Market value ($ mil.)	(36.6%)	2,156.7	1,522.4	804.9	654.0	348.2
Employees	20.9%	2,828	7,614	7,626	7,055	6,037

AUDIBLE INC.

1 Washington Park
Newark NJ 07102
Phone: 973-820-0400
Fax: 973-820-0505
Web: www.audible.com

CEO: Donald R Katz
CFO: William H Mitchell
HR: –
FYE: December 31
Type: Subsidiary

Audible has a story to tell. The subsidiary of online retail giant Amazon.comsells downloadable audio versions of books as well as radio broadcasts speeches stand-up comedy and other spoken word performances via its Audible website. Some 85000 audiobooks are available. Users can listen to programs on their computer or via wireless mobile device (iPad iPhone or Kindle to name a few) or burn to CD. Audible has distribution rights to content from some 1000 content providers including The New York Times The Wall Street Journal and Forbes. Audible also provides audiobooks for Apple's iTunes store. The company has international versions of its site for consumers in the UK France and Germany.

AUDIENCESCIENCE INC.

1110 112th Ave. NE Ste. 300
Bellevue WA 98004
Phone: 425-216-1700
Fax: 425-216-1777
Web: www.audiencescience.com

CEO: Jeff Pullen
CFO: –
HR: –
FYE: December 31
Type: Private

AudienceScience (formerly Revenue Science) has a vested interest in your behavior. The company provides behavioral targeting services that help clients determine prime audiences for specific campaigns. AudienceScience primarily serves Web publishers (such as Dow Jones FT.com and The Wall Street Journal Online) that can then offer advertisers and ad agencies with behaviorally targeted audiences. It provides search-based and rules-based targeting and segments audiences based on search terms used or other criteria such as geographic location or how often they visit a certain portion of the site. The company was established in 2000.

AUGUSTANA COLLEGE

639 38TH ST
ROCK ISLAND, IL 612012296
Phone: 309-794-3377
Fax: –
Web: www.augustana.edu

CEO: –
CFO: David English
HR: –
FYE: June 30
Type: Private

Augustana College is a private liberal arts college located near the Mississippi River in northwestern Illinois. The school offers undergraduate degrees in some 50 areas of study plus pre-professional programs in fields including dentistry law medicine and veterinary medicine. It enrolls approximately 2500 students. The Swenson Center a national archive dedicated to the study of Swedish immigration to the US is housed on the Augustana campus. Augustana College is associated with the Evangelical Lutheran Church.

	Annual Growth	06/14	06/15	06/16	06/17	06/18
Sales ($ mil.)	1.5%	–	75.2	75.1	76.4	78.5
Net income ($ mil.)	29.2%	–	7.4	(2.5)	29.9	16.0
Market value ($ mil.)	–	–	–	–	–	–
Employees	–	–	–	–	–	650

AUNTIE ANNE'S INC.

48-50 W. Chestnut St. Ste. 200
Lancaster PA 17603
Phone: 717-435-1435
Fax: 717-435-1436
Web: www.auntieannes.com

CEO: –
CFO: –
HR: –
FYE: December 31
Type: Private

You don't have to be twisted to enjoy one of these pretzels. Auntie Anne's is a leading franchisor of snack outlets with about 1150 pretzel stores located in some 45 states and 20 other countries. The stores offer a variety of pretzel flavors including original cinnamon sugar garlic almond and sesame as well as the popular pretzel-wrapped hot dog. They are primarily found in high-traffic areas such as malls airports train stations and stadiums. Anne Beiler started the company in 1988 to help fund a faith-based family assistance foundation. Roark Capital company FOCUS Brands acquired Auntie Anne's in 2010.

AURA MINERALS INC (BRITISH VIRGIN ISLANDS)   TSX: ORA

78 SW 7th Street, Suite # 7144
Miami, FL 33130
Phone: 305 239-9499
Fax: –
Web: www.auraminerals.com

CEO: –
CFO: Joao Cardoso
HR: –
FYE: December 31
Type: Public

Aura Minerals digs deep to make a profit. The mid-tier producer of gold and copper owns operating projects in Honduras Mexico and Brazil. The company's diversified portfolio of precious metal assets include the San Andres producing gold mine in Honduras the Sao Francisco producing gold mine in Brazil and the copper-gold-silver Aranzazu mine in Mexico (where operations were temporarily suspended in late 2015 due to disruptions caused by unauthorized persons entering the company mine). Aura Minerals' core development asset is the copper-gold-iron Serrote project in Brazil. In early 2018 the company acquired fellow gold miner Rio Novo.

	Annual Growth	12/16	12/17	12/18	12/19	12/20
Sales ($ mil.)	19.7%	146.2	157.7	157.7	226.2	299.9
Net income ($ mil.)	37.7%	19.0	10.2	52.0	24.9	68.5
Market value ($ mil.)	–	–	–	–	–	–
Employees	(1.5%)	1,170	783	863	863	1,102

AURA SYSTEMS INC   NBB: AUSI

20431 North Sea Circle
Lake Forest, CA 92630
Phone: 310 643-5300
Fax: –
Web: www.aurasystems.com

CEO: –
CFO: David Mann
HR: –
FYE: February 28
Type: Public

Aura Systems is charging ahead with its AuraGen electric generator which can produce 8500 watts of power from an idling car engine. Companies in the telecommunications utilities and oil and gas industries use the AuraGen to generate mobile power; the military version of the AuraGen is marketed as the VIPER. RV maker Country Coach announced plans in 2004 to install the AuraGen on its Prevost model. Aura Systems also is entitled to royalties from Daewoo Electronics for use of electro-optical technology found in projection TVs. The company gets about 80% of its sales in the US.

	Annual Growth	02/17	02/18	02/19	02/20	02/21
Sales ($ mil.)	71.1%	–	–	0.0	0.8	0.1
Net income ($ mil.)	–	(7.7)	1.7	(4.5)	(2.6)	0.8
Market value ($ mil.)	30.8%	8.5	48.4	36.3	14.2	24.9
Employees	73.2%	1	4	5	7	9

AURARIA HIGHER EDUCATION CENTER

1068 9TH STREET PARK
DENVER, CO 80204
Phone: 303-556-3291
Fax: –

CEO: Dean W Wolf
CFO: –
HR: –
FYE: June 30
Type: Private

The Auraria Higher Education Center supports high learning in the Mile High City. On its campus the company offers non-academic services such as facilities management child care and human resources support for the Community College of Denver Metropolitan State College of Denver and the University of Colorado at Denver and Health Sciences Center's Downtown Denver Campus. It runs the student union events center childcare facilities and all parking facilities. The combined enrollment for all three institutions on the Auraria campus totals about 40000 students.

	Annual Growth	06/04	06/05	06/06	06/16	06/17
Sales ($ mil.)	2.2%	–	49.0	49.8	63.1	63.6
Net income ($ mil.)	–	–	(2.3)	(3.5)	8.8	(17.0)
Market value ($ mil.)	–	–	–	–	–	–
Employees	–	–	–	–	–	380

AURORA CAPITAL PARTNERS L.P.

10877 Wilshire Blvd. Ste. 2100
Los Angeles CA 90024
Phone: 310-551-0101
Fax: 310-277-5591
Web: www.auroracap.com

CEO: –
CFO: –
HR: –
FYE: December 31
Type: Private

Aurora Capital Partners (or Aurora Capital Group) focuses on buyouts of midsized companies in the energy health care industrial services software manufacturing and transportation industries. It typically invests in companies with values between $100 million and $1 billion. Employing a buy-and-build strategy the investor works with existing management to create organic growth then adds on acquisitions to increase the value of its portfolio companies. Aurora's Resurgence Fund invests in companies that face operational or financial troubles. Holdings include Mitchell International and ADCO Global. Aurora Capital which has completed more than 100 acquisitions has some $2 billion of assets under management.

AURORA CASKET COMPANY INC.

10944 Marsh Rd.
Aurora IN 47001
Phone: 812-926-1111
Fax: 800-457-1112
Web: www.auroracasket.com

CEO: Michael Quinn
CFO: –
HR: Terry Brogan
FYE: December 31
Type: Private

Aurora Casket Company won't meet you at the Pearly Gates but it will get you there in style. One of the nation's largest casket and cremation urn makers it sells its products directly to licensed funeral homes via 60 US service centers. Known for its stainless-steel line Aurora Caskets makes caskets in a variety of woods and metals. Its cremation items extend beyond urns to include memorial markers tablets and plaques. It provides online advice on funeral planning and grief support and offers consulting software and website design services to funeral homes. Aurora Casket was owned and managed by the Backman and Barrott families for more than 120 years. In mid-2012 Kohlberg & Co. acquired the company.

AURORA DIAGNOSTICS INC.

11025 RCA Center Dr. Ste. 300
Palm Beach Gardens FL 33410
Phone: 561-626-5512
Fax: 561-626-4530
Web: www.auroradx.com

CEO: Daniel D Crowley
CFO: Michael Grattendick
HR: –
FYE: December 31
Type: Private

Doctors turn to Aurora Diagnostics when they need help making a diagnosis. The company performs anatomical pathology services studying organ samples and tissue biopsies to diagnose cancer and other diseases. Through a network of almost 20 labs it specializes in women's health urology gastrointestinal pathology hematopathology and dermatopathology services. The company performs more than 1.5 million tests a year and has a network of 10000 referring physicians. While the majority of its clients are clinics and doctor's offices the company does have contracts with more than 35 hospitals. Aurora Diagnostics also offers a Web-based system to report its findings. The company filed to go public in 2010.

AURORA FLIGHT SCIENCES CORP

9950 WAKEMAN DR
MANASSAS, VA 201102702
Phone: 703-369-3633
Fax: –
Web: www.aurora.aero

CEO: Per Beith
CFO: Christopher Decker
HR: Ashley McElwain
FYE: September 30
Type: Private

Pilots? For most of its products Aurora Flight Sciences doesn't need pilots (at least not ones who sit in a cockpit of a plane). The company makes unmanned aerial vehicles (UAVs aka drones) and composite structures for aircraft with both military and scientific applications. It also provides flight operations and testing services for a variety of aircraft. Customers include major aerospace contractors such as Raytheon and US government agencies. Aurora Flight Sciences along with Georgia Institute of Technology is developing next-generation distributed controllers for turbine engines for the Air Force Research Laboratory.

	Annual Growth	09/06	09/07	09/08	09/09	09/10
Sales ($ mil.)	–	–	–	(1,111.2)	65.1	62.7
Net income ($ mil.)	1064.5%	–	–	0.0	(1.6)	0.1
Market value ($ mil.)	–	–	–	–	–	–
Employees	–	–	–	–	–	292

AURORA NETWORKS INC.

5400 Betsy Ross Dr.
Santa Clara CA 95054
Phone: 408-235-7000
Fax: 408-845-9043
Web: www.aurora.com

CEO: –
CFO: –
HR: –
FYE: December 31
Type: Private

Aurora Networks wants to lighten up the atmosphere of digital broadband networks. The company manufactures optical transport systems used by cable companies to build fiber-optic networks and upgrade older hybrid fiber/coax (HFC) networks. Its products include optical nodes and headend equipment such as amplifiers transmitters receivers and switches. The company also provides engineering and field services as well as equipment repair. Aurora chief scientist Dr. Charles Barker VP Krzysztof Pradzynski and CEO Guy Sucharczuk founded the company in 1999. It counts Battery Ventures Castile Ventures Sprout Group TA Associates and Velocity Interactive Group among its backers and shareholders.

AURORA ORGANIC DAIRY CORP.

1919 14TH ST STE 300
BOULDER, CO 803025350
Phone: 720-564-6296
Fax: –
Web: www.auroraorganic.com

CEO: Scott McGinty
CFO: –
HR: –
FYE: December 31
Type: Private

Aurora Organic Dairy suspects you've never heard of its herd. That's why the cow-to-carton company is aiming to change that situation by becoming a leader in the US organic dairy market. Aurora Organic specializes in private-label and store-brand milk and butter cream and non-fat dry milk for large grocery retailers and natural food stores. It also supplies industrial customers with bulk milk cream butter and non-fat dry milk. The company has agreements with Colorado and Texas farmers who operate 50000 acres of organic farmland and supply Aurora with organic feed and pasture for its cows. With its clean-living herds Aurora works to make organic dairy products widespread and affordable.

	Annual Growth	12/05	12/06	12/07	12/08	12/09
Sales ($ mil.)	16.2%	–	77.5	111.3	125.9	121.6
Net income ($ mil.)	183.5%	–	0.8	(12.4)	(1.8)	18.1
Market value ($ mil.)	–	–	–	–	–	–
Employees	–	–	–	–	–	300

AURORA WHOLESALERS LLC

31000 AURORA RD
SOLON, OH 441392769
Phone: 440-248-5200
Fax: –
Web: www.themazelcompany.com

CEO: –
CFO: –
HR: Rich Reedy
FYE: December 31
Type: Private

Aurora Wholesalers (dba The Mazel Company) buys a broad range of name-brand closeout consumer products from some 700 global suppliers and sells the items at below-wholesale prices. It also offers such proprietary goods as candles party goods tableware batteries and light bulbs. The company operates from offices and a warehouse distribution facility in Solon Ohio. It has buyers in Solon and in New York City and sales and marketing representation in Boston Chicago New York Philadelphia and in Solon and Columbus Ohio. CEO Reuven Dessler and EVP Jacob "Jake" Koval founded The Mazel Company as a wholesaler of closeout merchandise in 1975.

	Annual Growth	12/07	12/08	12/09	12/12	12/13
Sales ($ mil.)	(0.5%)	–	65.3	70.8	61.2	63.7
Net income ($ mil.)	(19.9%)	–	–	2.8	0.0	1.1
Market value ($ mil.)	–	–	–	–	–	–
Employees	–	–	–	–	–	100

AUSTIN COLLEGE

900 N GRAND AVE
SHERMAN, TX 750904400
Phone: 903-813-2000
Fax: –
Web: www.austincollege.edu

CEO: –
CFO: –
HR: –
FYE: June 30
Type: Private

Located in the North Texas city of Sherman rather than in Austin Austin College is a small private liberal arts college. The educational institution sits on an 85-acre campus and draws an enrollment of about 1350 full-time undergraduate students including graduate students working on a Master of Arts in Teaching. It's nationally known for its focus on international education pre-professional training and leadership studies. Tuition and fees at Austin College run about $26500 and housing costs are typically $8600 per year. Affiliated with the Presbyterian Church Austin College was founded in 1849 by missionary Daniel Baker. It plans to open its new IDEA Center in fall 2013.

	Annual Growth	06/10	06/11	06/12	06/13	06/16
Sales ($ mil.)	12.0%	–	40.7	41.6	39.6	71.8
Net income ($ mil.)	14.0%	–	0.7	(4.2)	5.5	1.3
Market value ($ mil.)	–	–	–	–	–	–
Employees	–	–	–	–	–	325

AUSTIN COMMUNITY COLLEGE

5930 MIDDLE FISKVILLE RD
AUSTIN, TX 787524390
Phone: 512-223-7000
Fax: –
Web: www.austincc.edu

CEO: Richard M Rhodes
CFO: –
HR: –
FYE: August 31
Type: Private

It may not be the most well known school in Austin Texas but Austin Community College (ACC) does have its fans. ACC provides technical certificate programs (50 fields) associate's degrees (30 university transfer majors) and continuing education courses to central Texas students through about a dozen campuses. The school which has an enrollment of more than 70000 students also offers honors programs college prep classes for high school students and Tech-Prep courses that allow high school students to earn credits toward an ACC technical certificate. The school serves as a primary feeder for students transferring to the University of Texas one of the nation's largest universities. ACC was founded in 1973.

	Annual Growth	08/13	08/14	08/15	08/16	08/17
Sales ($ mil.)	6.2%	–	78.5	88.5	92.1	94.0
Net income ($ mil.)	–	–	(6.1)	7.3	17.7	26.9
Market value ($ mil.)	–	–	–	–	–	–
Employees	–	–	–	–	–	4,200

AUSTIN INDUSTRIES INC.

3535 Travis St. Ste. 300
Dallas TX 75204-1466
Phone: 214-443-5500
Fax: 806-364-3842
Web: www.aztx.com

CEO: David B Walls
CFO: Jt Fisher
HR: –
FYE: December 31
Type: Private

Austin Industries is actually based in Dallas rather than its namesake Live Music Capital of the World. The company provides civil commercial and industrial construction services in the southern half of the US. Its oldest subsidiary Austin Bridge & Road provides road bridge and parking lot construction across Texas. (It built the longest bridge in Texas the Queen Isabella Causeway.) Subsidiary Austin Commercial builds office buildings technology sites hospitals and other commercial projects. The group's Austin Industrial arm provides construction maintenance and electrical services for the chemical refining power and manufacturing industries. The employee-owned company was founded in 1918.

AUSTIN POWDER COMPANY

25800 Science Park Dr.
Cleveland OH 44122
Phone: 216-464-2400
Fax: 216-464-4418
Web: www.austinpowder.com

CEO: David M Gleason
CFO: –
HR: –
FYE: December 31
Type: Subsidiary

Austin Powder has the original boom box. The company was founded in 1833 to manufacture black powder used to blast rocks mine coal create canals and generally move mountains. Today Austin Powder's commercial explosives are used primarily for construction mining quarrying and seismic exploration. Products include detonating cord detonator-sensitive emulsions cast boosters and high-explosive emulsions. It also makes electric and non-electric detonators. Austin International through joint ventures and partnerships provides explosives for projects outside the US mostly in other parts of the Americas.

AUSTIN RIBBON & COMPUTER SUPPLIES INC.

9211 Waterford Centre Blvd. Ste. 202	CEO: Laura Grant
Austin TX 78758	CFO: –
Phone: 512-452-0651	HR: –
Fax: 512-452-0691	FYE: December 31
Web: www.arc-texas.com	Type: Private

Nothing as archaic as ribbons and typewriters adorn the shelves at ARC (Austin Ribbon & Computer). The old-school name belies a modern firm offering IT products and services to state government education and health care customers throughout Texas. It sells more than 400 brands of computers tablets and peripherals — including Dell HP EMC Lenovo and Cisco. (The company is the largest supplier of Dell computers to Texas government.) ARC also provides IT services from single computer fixes to office-wide system design installation and maintenance. Customers have included the Texas Lottery Commission City of Dallas The University of Texas at Austin and University Health Systems San Antonio.

AUTHENTEC INC. NASDAQ: AUTH

100 Rialto Place Ste. 100	CEO: –
Melbourne FL 32901	CFO: –
Phone: 321-308-1300	HR: –
Fax: 321-308-1430	FYE: December 31
Web: www.authentec.com	Type: Public

AuthenTec is good at fingering out who's using your electronic gear. The company designs biometric fingerprint sensor chips a way to digitally verify identity and to allow only authorized users to access the equipment. Electronics makers incorporate its TruePrint devices into a variety of goods such as automotive subsystems PCs and wireless devices. With most of sales made in the Asia/Pacific region the company's top three customers (Fujitsu Lenovo and Edom Technology) together account for one third of revenues. The technology was originally developed within Harris Semiconductor; AuthenTec was spun out of Harris Corporation in 1998.

AUTO-OWNERS INSURANCE COMPANY

6101 Anacapri Blvd.	CEO: Jeffrey Franci Harrold
Lansing MI 48917	CFO: Eileen Kay Fhaner
Phone: 517-323-1200	HR: –
Fax: 517-323-8796	FYE: December 31
Web: www.auto-owners.com	Type: Private

There's more to Auto-Owners Insurance Group than the name implies. In addition to auto coverage the company provides a range of personal property/casualty and life insurance products to more than 3 million policyholders. Auto-Owners Insurance Group operates through subsidiaries including Auto-Owners Life Insurance Home-Owners Insurance and Property-Owners Insurance Company. Its Southern-Owners Insurance subsidiary offers property/casualty insurance in Florida. Auto-Owners Insurance also sells commercial auto liability and workers' compensation policies. Established in 1916 the company operates in 26 states nationwide and is represented by more than 6000 independent agencies.

AUTOALLIANCE INTERNATIONAL INC.

1 International Dr.	CEO: –
Flat Rock MI 48134-9401	CFO: –
Phone: 734-782-7800	HR: –
Fax: 734-783-8216	FYE: December 31
Web: media.ford.com/plant_display.cfm?plant_id=62	Type: Joint Venture

Two heads are better than one at AutoAlliance International (AAI). A 50/50 joint venture between Ford Motor and Mazda the company is a contract manufacturer of the Mazda6 and Ford Mustang. AutoAlliance's history traces back to 1984 when Mazda built a plant in Michigan to make the Mazda MX-6 and called the new company Mazda Motor Manufacturing (USA) Corporation (MMUC). In 1992 MMUC teamed up with Ford and the name of the company took its present form. In addition to its current model lineup AutoAlliance International produces the Mazda 626 and Mustang GT500. Ford and Mazda are considering (in 2011) the dissolution of AAI due to low capacity and sluggish sales.

AUTOCAM CORPORATION

4436 Broadmoor SE	CEO: –
Kentwood MI 49512	CFO: Warren A Veltman
Phone: 616-698-0707	HR: –
Fax: 616-698-6876	FYE: December 31
Web: www.autocam.com	Type: Private

Members of both the UAW and the AMA are fans of Autocam. The company manufactures precision components and assemblies for the automotive as well as the medical device industries. Its automotive components are used in brake fuel and power steering systems. Customers include Bosch Hitachi and Delphi. Autocam also makes electric motors and offers machined parts for power tools. Its medical arm specializes in surgical devices implants and hand pieces which serve a range of surgical applications. Customers include Abbott Medtronic Stryker and others. Founded in 1988 the company is owned by a group of investors led by its founder and CEO John Kennedy who holds a 60% stake.

AUTODESK INC NMS: ADSK

111 McInnis Parkway	CEO: Andrew Anagnost
San Rafael, CA 94903	CFO: Deborah Clifford
Phone: 415 507-5000	HR: –
Fax: –	FYE: January 31
Web: www.autodesk.com	Type: Public

Autodesk is a global leader in 3D design engineering and entertainment software and services offering customers productive business solutions through powerful technology products and services. The AutoCAD and Revit software programs are used by architects engineers and structural designers to design draft and make models of products buildings and other objects. The company also provides product and manufacturing software for manufacturers in automotive transportation industrial machinery consumer products and building product industries with comprehensive digital design engineering manufacturing and production solutions. The company's digital media and entertainment products provide tools for digital sculpting modeling animation effects rendering and compositing for design visualization visual effects and games production. Customers in the US account for nearly 35% sales.

	Annual Growth	01/17	01/18	01/19	01/20	01/21
Sales ($ mil.)	16.9%	2,031.0	2,056.6	2,569.8	3,274.3	3,790.4
Net income ($ mil.)	–	(582.1)	(566.9)	(80.8)	214.5	1,208.2
Market value ($ mil.)	35.9%	17,862.3	25,390.2	32,325.1	43,228.3	60,923.6
Employees	6.3%	9,000	8,800	9,600	10,100	11,500

AUTOGRILL GROUP INC.

6905 Rockledge Dr.
Bethesda MD 20817
Phone: 240-694-4100
Fax: 240-694-4790
Web: www.hmshost.com

CEO: Steve Johnson
CFO: –
HR: –
FYE: December 31
Type: Subsidiary

Autogrill Group knows some travelers hunger for more than just transportation. Operating as HMSHost the company is a leading contract foodservice operator focused on the travel market. It has restaurant operations in more than 100 airports in North America Europe and parts of the Asia Pacific. Its eateries operate under such licensed brands as Burger King Chili's Too California Pizza Kitchen Quiznos and Starbucks as well as proprietary names Fresh Attractions Deli and Flatbreadz. HMSHost also has service operations at more than 80 highway rest areas and runs newsstands and other retail locations in addition to restaurants. HMSHost is a unit of Italian contract foodservices giant Autogrill.

AUTOMOBILE PROTECTION CORPORATION

6010 Atlantic Blvd.
Norcross GA 30071
Phone: 678-225-1000
Fax: 770-246-2468
Web: www.easycare.com

CEO: –
CFO: John Marks
HR: –
FYE: December 31
Type: Private

For those sweet cars that turn out to be sour lemons Automobile Protection Corporation (APCO) sells lemon aid. The company offers extended-care warranties (under the EasyCare brand) and service contracts for new and used vehicles including cars pickups and recreational vehicles. It has some 1.7 million active contracts which are insured by XL Capital. The warranties provide bumper-to-bumper mechanical coverage and offer rental car and towing reimbursements. The company has agreements with auto manufacturers such as Honda Jaguar Land Rover Mazda and Volvo. It sells its contracts through more than 3000 car dealers in the US and Canada.

AUTOLIV ASP INC.

3350 Airport Rd.
Ogden UT 84405
Phone: 801-625-4800
Fax: 801-625-4964
Web: www.autoliv.com

CEO: –
CFO: William Campbell
HR: –
FYE: December 31
Type: Subsidiary

Autoliv ASP the North American subsidiary of Sweden-based Autoliv Inc. designs and manufactures automobile safety restraint systems such as airbags and airbag inflators (the highest-cost item in making an airbag module) seatbelts night vision systems radar sensors gas generators and other airbag modules. It is credited with the invention of the side-impact airbag the Inflatable Curtain (for head protection) the Anti-Whiplash Seat and night vision systems. It also provides testing of automotive safety products for vehicle manufacturers as well as engineering design of products at its technical center and test laboratory. Autoliv ASP with 10 locations across the US was founded in 1996.

AUTOMOTIVE FINANCE CORPORATION

13085 H CROINING BLVD 3
CARMEL, IN 46032
Phone: 317-815-9645
Fax: –
Web: www.afcdealer.com

CEO: John Hammer
CFO: –
HR: –
FYE: December 31
Type: Private

Automotive Finance Corp. (AFC) is where auto dealers go to make a deal. The firm finances floor planning or inventory purchases for independent used car dealers that buy vehicles from sister company ADESA Auctions as well as independent auctions auctions affiliated with other networks and non-auction purchases. Through more than 80 North American offices (about half of which are located at ADESA sites) AFC provides short-term (30- to 60-day) loans; it sells most of its finance receivables to subsidiary AFC Funding Corp. which then sells them to a bank conduit facility. Proceeds from the revolving sale of receivables are used to fund new loans. AFC is a subsidiary of KAR Auction Services.

	Annual Growth	12/04	12/05	12/06	12/07	12/08
Assets ($ mil.)	2704.9%	–	–	0.9	975.2	720.2
Net income ($ mil.)	–	–	–	0.0	41.9	(149.0)
Market value ($ mil.)	–	–	–	–	–	–
Employees	–	–	–	–	–	488

AUTOMATIC DATA PROCESSING INC.   NMS: ADP

One ADP Boulevard
Roseland, NJ 07068
Phone: 973 974-5000
Fax: 973 974-5390
Web: www.adp.com

CEO: Carlos Rodriguez
CFO: Kathleen Winters
HR: Alexander Quevedo
FYE: June 30
Type: Public

Automatic Data Processing (ADP) is one of the largest payroll and tax filing processors in the world serving over 920000 clients and pay more than 38 million workers in approximately 140 countries and territories. Employer services (payroll services benefits administration talent management HR management workforce management compliance services insurance services and retirement services) account for the majority of the company's sales and its PEO (Professional Employer Organization) services are provided through ADP TotalSource. Other offerings include HR management benefits administration payroll background checking services. The US accounts for more than 85% of the company's revenue.

	Annual Growth	06/17	06/18	06/19	06/20	06/21
Sales ($ mil.)	4.9%	12,379.8	13,325.8	14,175.2	14,589.8	15,005.4
Net income ($ mil.)	10.7%	1,733.4	1,620.8	2,292.8	2,466.5	2,598.5
Market value ($ mil.)	18.0%	43,412.3	56,835.1	70,050.3	63,084.7	84,155.3
Employees	(0.9%)	58,000	57,000	58,000	58,000	56,000

AUTONATION, INC.   NYS: AN

200 SW 1st Avenue
Fort Lauderdale, FL 33301
Phone: 954 769-6000
Fax: –
Web: www.autonation.com

CEO: Mike Manley
CFO: Joseph Lower
HR: –
FYE: December 31
Type: Public

The brainchild of entrepreneur Wayne Huizenga (Waste Management Blockbuster) AutoNation is the #1 auto dealer in the US. It owns approximately 315 new-vehicle franchises in about 15 states and conducts online sales through AutoNation.com and individual dealer websites. The company sells more than 30 brands of new vehicles. In addition to auto sales AutoNation provides automotive repair and maintenance services (it owns about 75 AutoNation-branded collision centers five AutoNation USA used vehicle stores four AutoNation-branded automotive auction operations and three parts distribution centers) wholesale parts and collision businesses automotive finance and insurance.

	Annual Growth	12/17	12/18	12/19	12/20	12/21
Sales ($ mil.)	4.7%	21,534.6	21,412.8	21,335.7	20,390.0	25,844.0
Net income ($ mil.)	33.3%	434.6	396.0	450.0	381.6	1,373.0
Market value ($ mil.)	22.8%	3,213.8	2,235.2	3,044.8	4,369.6	7,316.0
Employees	(3.9%)	26,000	26,000	25,000	21,600	22,200

AUTOSCOPE TECHNOLOGIES CORP   NAS: AATC

Spruce Tree Centre, Suite 400, 1600 University Avenue West | CEO: Chad Stelzig
St. Paul, MN 55104 | CFO: Frank Hallowell
Phone: 651 603-7700 | HR: –
Fax: – | FYE: December 31
Web: www.imagesensing.com | Type: Public

If you're stuck in traffic you can't blame Image Sensing Systems (ISS). ISS's Autoscope vehicle detection system converts video images into digitized traffic data for traffic management. Unlike traditional embedded wire loop detectors which are buried in the pavement Autoscope enables wide-area detection using video cameras a microprocessor software and a PC. The systems help users to design roads manage traffic signals and determine the environmental impact of gridlock. Royalty income from traffic management company Econolite Control Products accounts for nearly half of sales. The company gets three-quarters of its sales in North America.

	Annual Growth	12/16	12/17	12/18	12/19	12/20
Sales ($ mil.)	(1.8%)	14.1	14.5	14.6	14.7	13.2
Net income ($ mil.)	11.5%	0.7	2.1	1.9	7.0	1.1
Market value ($ mil.)	4.9%	19.8	15.8	24.1	24.3	24.0
Employees	(4.8%)	56	59	53	55	46

AUTOTRADER GROUP INC.

3003 Summit Blvd. Ste. 200 | CEO: Victor A Perry IV
Atlanta GA 30319 | CFO: –
Phone: 404-568-8000 | HR: –
Fax: 404-568-3060 | FYE: December 31
Web: www.autotradergroup.com | Type: Subsidiary

AutoTrader Group gives the Internet its very own Motor Mile. The company operates the AutoTrader.com and KBB.com websites which work to connect online buyers with those who have cars to sell. AutoTrader.com draws an average of about 29 million visitors a month who browse its extensive listings and popular features such as vehicle reviews warranty information insurance and financing. In addition to used cars and trucks the site offers listings for motorcycles and classic cars for collectors (at AutoTrader Classics) as well as some new cars. Its kbb.com website provides consumers with a ballpark car value when they set out to shop. Majority-owned by Cox Enterprises AutoTrader Group withdrew an IPO in 2013.

AUTOWEB INC   NAS: AUTO

400 North Ashley Drive, Suite 300 | CEO: Jared Rowe
Tampa, FL 33602 | CFO: J Hannan
Phone: 949 225-4500 | HR: –
Fax: – | FYE: December 31
Web: www.autoweb.com | Type: Public

AutoWeb (formerly Autobytel) puts cars on the information superhighway. Using the company's websites a potential car buyer can research make model fuel efficiency and more than complete an online request form for the desired new or used car. The form is forwarded to local auto dealers and manufacturers who contact the shopper within 24 hours. Car buyers can also research insurance financing and other related services. AutoWeb generates 80% of its revenue through lead generation it charges dealers and manufacturers (car buyers pay no fees). However the company also operates digital advertising-driven consumer website autoweb.com which offers many of the same services.

	Annual Growth	12/16	12/17	12/18	12/19	12/20
Sales ($ mil.)	(16.4%)	156.7	142.1	125.6	114.0	76.6
Net income ($ mil.)	–	3.9	(65.0)	(38.8)	(15.2)	(6.8)
Market value ($ mil.)	(34.5%)	177.1	118.7	40.2	32.5	32.5
Employees	(12.5%)	254	228	199	171	149

AUTOZONE, INC.   NYS: AZO

123 South Front Street | CEO: William Rhodes
Memphis, TN 38103 | CFO: Jamere Jackson
Phone: 901 495-6500 | HR: Richard Smith
Fax: – | FYE: August 28
Web: www.autozone.com | Type: Public

With more than 6050 stores in the US AutoZone is one of the nation's leading auto parts chains. It also has more than 660 stores in Mexico and more than 52 in Brazil. AutoZone stores carry an extensive product line for cars sport utility vehicles vans and light trucks including new and remanufactured automotive hard parts maintenance items accessories and non-automotive products. AutoZone stores sell failure parts (alternators engines batteries) maintenance items (oil antifreeze) and discretionary merchandise and accessories (car stereos floor mats) under brand names and private labels. AutoZone's commercial sales program provides credit and distributes parts and other products to garages dealerships and other businesses. The company operates an electronic parts catalog Z-net that provides a wide range of information on parts for employees and customers.

	Annual Growth	08/17	08/18	08/19	08/20	08/21
Sales ($ mil.)	7.7%	10,888.7	11,221.1	11,863.7	12,632.0	14,629.6
Net income ($ mil.)	14.1%	1,280.9	1,337.5	1,617.2	1,733.0	2,170.3
Market value ($ mil.)	30.8%	11,180.9	16,287.3	23,287.5	25,135.6	32,732.0
Employees	3.5%	87,000	90,000	96,000	100,000	100,000

AUVIL FRUIT COMPANY INC.

21902 STATE HIGHWAY 97 | CEO: –
ORONDO, WA 988439759 | CFO: Josh Weldy
Phone: 509-784-1033 | HR: –
Fax: – | FYE: March 31
Web: www.auvilfruit.com | Type: Private

Auvil Fruit Company's products are "auvilly" tasty. The company grows apples in the US's cool misty Northwest whose climate would do Johnny Appleseed proud. Auvil markets its crops under the brand names Elite Gee Whiz and Topaz. Granny Smith Fuji Gala and Pink Lady apples are grown on one of three Auvil ranches (some 1350 acres) and sold at grocery stores throughout the US and Canada. Auvil also sells Rainier and Bing cherries. Its retail food customers include Raley's and Stop & Shop. The company was founded in 1928 by Grady Auvil who introduced the Granny Smith apple to state of Washington.

	Annual Growth	03/08	03/09	03/10	03/11	03/12
Sales ($ mil.)	16.6%	–	32.6	36.0	40.6	51.6
Net income ($ mil.)	70.7%	–	–	5.4	7.2	15.8
Market value ($ mil.)						
Employees	–	–	–	–	–	575

AUXILIUM PHARMACEUTICALS INC   NMS: AUXL

640 Lee Road | CEO: Adrian Adams
Chesterbrook, PA 19087 | CFO: Andrew Saik
Phone: 484 321-5900 | HR: –
Fax: – | FYE: December 31
Web: www.auxilium.com | Type: Public

Auxilium Pharmaceuticals wants to be the wingman for patients suffering from ailments including hormonal imbalances or tissue conditions. The biopharmaceutical developer markets products that include Testim a topical testosterone gel used to treat hypogonadism (low testosterone production) and XIAFLEX an injectable enzyme approved to treat Dupuytren's contracture (a progressive disease which causes a person's fingers to permanently contract). Auxilium added several testosterone replacement and erectile dysfunction drugs through the 2013 acquisition of Actient. The company's pipeline of candidates includes potential treatments for unusual soft tissue conditions and pain.

	Annual Growth	12/08	12/09	12/10	12/11	12/12
Sales ($ mil.)	33.3%	125.4	164.0	211.4	264.3	395.3
Net income ($ mil.)	–	(46.3)	(53.5)	(51.2)	(32.9)	85.9
Market value ($ mil.)	(10.1%)	1,401.6	1,477.5	1,039.9	982.2	913.7
Employees	11.5%	340	540	565	530	526

AV HOMES INC
NMS: AVHI

8601 N. Scottsdale Rd., Suite 225
Scottsdale, AZ 85253
Phone: 480 214-7400
Fax: –
Web: www.avatarholdings.com

CEO: –
CFO: –
HR: –
FYE: December 31
Type: Public

AV Homes (formerly Avatar Holdings) aspires to be the embodiment of stylish retirement living. The company develops active adult and primary residential communities and builds homes in Florida Arizona and North Carolina. Its Joseph Carl Homes unit builds homes for people of all ages in Florida and Phoenix. AV Homes owns some 23000 acres of developed and developable land. AV Homes also operates a title insurance agency and manages the day-to-day operations of its communities' amenities. The company gets nearly 90% of its revenue from homebuilding developments while the remainder comes from land sales.

	Annual Growth	12/12	12/13	12/14	12/15	12/16
Sales ($ mil.)	64.1%	107.5	143.7	285.9	517.8	779.3
Net income ($ mil.)	–	(90.2)	(9.5)	(1.9)	12.0	147.1
Market value ($ mil.)	2.7%	320.1	409.1	328.0	288.4	355.7
Employees	31.2%	112	133	214	308	332

AVALON HOLDINGS CORP.
ASE: AWX

One American Way
Warren, OH 44484-5555
Phone: 330 856-8800
Fax: –
Web: www.avalonholdings.com

CEO: Ronald Klingle
CFO: Bryan Saksa
HR: –
FYE: December 31
Type: Public

The magical promise of this Avalon is waste management services and golf courses. Through its American Waste Management Services subsidiary Avalon Holdings helps customers manage and dispose of wastes. Services include hazardous and nonhazardous waste brokerage and management services and captive landfill management services — management of landfills used exclusively by their owners. The company also operates two golf courses near its headquarters. The golf operations include the management of dining and banquet facilities and a travel agency. Chairman Ronald Klingle controls a 67% voting stake in Avalon Holdings.

	Annual Growth	12/16	12/17	12/18	12/19	12/20
Sales ($ mil.)	(1.1%)	61.4	55.8	62.2	68.4	58.7
Net income ($ mil.)	–	(0.1)	(0.3)	(1.1)	(0.5)	0.0
Market value ($ mil.)	(3.2%)	11.5	7.8	10.3	7.5	10.1
Employees	(0.8%)	498	423	455	521	482

AVALONBAY COMMUNITIES, INC.
NYS: AVB

4040 Wilson Blvd, Suite 1000
Arlington, VA 22203
Phone: 703 329-6300
Fax: 703 329-9130
Web: www.avalonbay.com

CEO: Benjamin Schall
CFO: Kevin O'shea
HR: –
FYE: December 31
Type: Public

Real estate investment trust (REIT) AvalonBay Communities buys develops renovates and operates multifamily residential properties in the US. It specializes in upscale properties in high barrier-to-entry markets such as Boston Los Angeles New York City San Francisco Seattle and Washington DC. AvalonBay operates its apartment communities under three core brands Avalon AVA and Eaves by Avalon. The REIT holds direct or indirect ownership interests in more than 270 active apartment communities with about 79800 units. It also has about 15 properties under construction and owns rights to develop some 25 additional communities.

	Annual Growth	12/16	12/17	12/18	12/19	12/20
Sales ($ mil.)	3.0%	2,045.3	2,158.6	2,284.5	2,324.6	2,301.3
Net income ($ mil.)	(5.4%)	1,034.0	876.9	974.5	786.0	827.6
Market value ($ mil.)	(2.4%)	24,717.1	24,893.0	24,284.6	29,258.7	22,384.3
Employees	0.2%	3,071	3,112	3,087	3,122	3,090

AVANADE INC.

818 Stewart St. Ste. 400
Seattle WA 98101
Phone: 206-239-5600
Fax: 206-239-5605
Web: www.avanade.com

CEO: Adam Warby
CFO: Ken Guthrie
HR: –
FYE: September 30
Type: Subsidiary

Avanade tries to give its customers a fresh view into their own operations. A subsidiary of Dublin-based information technology services provider Accenture the company provides IT consulting services centered mostly around Microsoft products. With offices worldwide Avanade helps large corporations with the design implementation and support of the software systems related to communications operations management resource planning and customer relationship management (CRM). A large portion of Avanade's business comes from subcontracting services provided to its parent company and minority shareholder Microsoft. The company's other clients have included European electricity company Vattenfall and EMI Music.

AVANIR PHARMACEUTICALS, INC.
NMS: AVNR

20 Enterprise, Suite 200
Aliso Viejo, CA 92656
Phone: 949 389-6700
Fax: 858 453-5845
Web: www.avanir.com

CEO: Rohan Palekar
CFO: –
HR: –
FYE: September 30
Type: Public

AVANIR Pharmaceuticals doesn't have anything against tears it just wants them to be triggered by emotions instead of central nervous system disorders. Its drug NUEDEXTA has been approved as a treatment for pseudobulbar affect — the involuntary crying or laughing experienced by some people with neurological disorders such as multiple sclerosis or following brain injury or stroke. NUEDEXTA is also in late-stage trials for diabetic neuropathic pain. AVANIR had an earlier success with its development of OTC cold sore cream Abreva which GlaxoSmithKline Consumer Healthcare markets in North America. The company receives royalty revenues from GSK and other licensees around the world.

	Annual Growth	09/09	09/10	09/11	09/12	09/13
Sales ($ mil.)	106.1%	4.2	2.9	10.5	41.3	75.4
Net income ($ mil.)	–	(22.0)	(26.7)	(60.6)	(59.7)	(75.5)
Market value ($ mil.)	19.4%	316.3	485.1	434.1	486.6	643.2
Employees	91.1%	20	128	188	225	267

AVANTAIR INC
NBB: AAIR

4311 General Howard Drive
Clearwater, FL 33762
Phone: 727 539-0071
Fax: –
Web: www.avantair.com

CEO: –
CFO: –
HR: –
FYE: June 30
Type: Public

Rather than fly commercial Avantair offers a little privacy. The company sells fractional ownership interests in piloted aircraft coupled with fleet maintenance. Pricier than commercial flights but cheaper than owning a jet a fractional interest allows travelers to schedule their own flights generally from smaller airports. Ownership can be purchased in increments beginning with a 1/16th share equating to 50 hours of flight time a year. Avantair also sells charter flight-cards for 15 or 25 hours and an Axis Club membership for a three-year term. Its fleet includes 55 aircraft which operate on the East and West coasts. Service extends across the US as well as Canada Mexico and the Bahamas and Caribbean.

	Annual Growth	06/08	06/09	06/10	06/11	06/12
Sales ($ mil.)	10.8%	115.6	136.8	143.0	149.0	174.0
Net income ($ mil.)	–	(18.9)	(4.5)	(4.0)	(10.8)	(6.6)
Market value ($ mil.)	(23.9%)	51.4	30.5	79.5	49.8	17.2
Employees	6.8%	403	445	450	530	525

AVAYA GOVERNMENT SOLUTIONS INC.

12730 Fair Lakes Cir. — CEO: -
Fairfax VA 22033 — CFO: -
Phone: 703-653-8000 — HR: -
Fax: 703-653-8001 — FYE: December 31
Web: www.avayagov.com — Type: Subsidiary

Avaya Government Solutions is delighted when the feds come calling. The subsidiary of business communications systems maker Avaya has developed communications and networking systems for a number of government agencies including the Department of Defense the FAA and the US Treasury; other clients come from the homeland security and criminal justice sectors among others. Its services include technology consulting systems engineering and integration of older legacy systems with newer technology as well as consulting training and support. The subsidiary specializes in designing and implementing large-scale telecom systems and call centers using Avaya's extensive selection of enterprise communications products.

AVAYA HOLDINGS CORP.

2605 MERIDIAN PKWY # 200 — CEO: James Chirico
DURHAM, NC 277135253 — CFO: Kieran McGrath
Phone: 908-953-6000 — HR: -
Fax: - — FYE: September 30
Web: www.avaya.com — Type: Private

Avaya Holdings Corp. is the holding company that owns enterprise communications equipment and services provider Avaya Inc.. Spun off from Lucent Technologies in 2000 Avaya was a publicly traded company until 2007 when it was taken private by Silver Lake Partners and TPG Capital for more than $8 billion. After four years of unprofitable private ownership its investors are looking for an exit and Avaya Holdings Corp. was created to make a second bid for listing on a US stock exchange filing for an initial public offering in 2011. The IPO is on hold however and Avaya has been expanding its business and product line through acquisitions.

	Annual Growth	09/10	09/11	09/13	09/14	09/15
Sales ($ mil.)	(7.4%)	-	5,547.0	4,708.0	4,371.0	4,081.0
Net income ($ mil.)	-	-	(863.0)	(376.0)	(253.0)	(168.0)
Market value ($ mil.)	-	-	-	-	-	-
Employees	-	-	-	-	-	8,266

AVAYA INC.

211 Mt. Airy Rd. — CEO: James M Chirico
Basking Ridge NJ 07920 — CFO: Kieran McGrath
Phone: 908-953-6000 — HR: -
Fax: 908-953-7609 — FYE: September 30
Web: www.avaya.com — Type: Subsidiary

Avaya helps to tie the corporate world together. The company's communication equipment and software integrate voice and data services for customers including large corporations government agencies and small businesses. Its office phone systems incorporate Internet protocol (IP) and Session Initiation protocol (SIP) telephony messaging Web access and interactive voice response. Avaya also offers a wide array of consulting integration and other managed IT services. The company sells directly and through distributors resellers systems integrators and telecommunications service providers; more than three-quarters of its sales are made indirectly. Parent company Avaya Holdings filed for an IPO in 2011.

AVEO PHARMACEUTICALS INC   NAS: AVEO

30 Winter Street — CEO: Michael Bailey
Boston, MA 02108 — CFO: Erick Lucera
Phone: 857 400-0101 — HR: -
Fax: - — FYE: December 31
Web: www.aveooncology.com — Type: Public

AVEO Pharmaceuticals' models don't pout strut or even turn heads — unless you're a cancer drug researcher. Operating as AVEO Oncology the biotech firm develops cancer models to uncover how genes mutate into tumors and how tumors progress through additional mutations. AVEO then builds genetic profiles of such tumors and applies them to antibody (protein) drug candidates in preclinical and clinical development to help predict actual human responses. In addition to its own pipeline of potential drugs AVEO has partnered with other pharmaceutical developers to apply its Human Response Platform to their drug candidates.

	Annual Growth	12/16	12/17	12/18	12/19	12/20
Sales ($ mil.)	24.4%	2.5	7.6	5.4	28.8	6.0
Net income ($ mil.)	-	(26.9)	(65.0)	(5.3)	9.4	(35.6)
Market value ($ mil.)	80.8%	14.5	75.0	43.0	16.8	155.1
Employees	25.1%	20	19	17	19	49

AVERA HEALTH

3900 W AVERA DR STE 100 — CEO: -
SIOUX FALLS, SD 571085721 — CFO: -
Phone: 605-322-4700 — HR: -
Fax: - — FYE: June 30
Web: www.avera.org — Type: Private

Avera Health provides health care services to eastern South Dakota as well as parts of Iowa Minnesota Nebraska and North Dakota. The health care system operates an extensive network of facilities across approximately 315 locations including community hospitals primary care clinics nursing homes hospices urgent care clinics and home health offices. The Avera Medical Group Primary Care Service Line developed Healthy Weight with Avera an order providers can click in the AveraChart electronic medical record. Avera Health is sponsored by the Benedictine Sisters and Presentation Sisters. The Avera Health Plans and DAKOTACARE cover more than 95000 members.

	Annual Growth	06/12	06/13	06/14	06/15	06/20
Sales ($ mil.)	13.1%	-	125.0	134.8	169.4	295.6
Net income ($ mil.)	(3.6%)	-	37.4	15.4	19.3	28.9
Market value ($ mil.)	-	-	-	-	-	-
Employees	-	-	-	-	-	2,450

AVERA ST. MARYS

801 E SIOUX AVE — CEO: Paul Ebmeier
PIERRE, SD 575013323 — CFO: Tom Wagner
Phone: 605-224-3100 — HR: -
Fax: - — FYE: June 30
Web: www.avera.org — Type: Private

St. Mary's Healthcare Center consisting of a 60-bed acute-care hospital a 105-bed long-term-care hospital and 58-unit senior-living apartments provides health care services in central South Dakota. The health care center offers both inpatient and outpatient care including surgery children's health home and hospice care and rehabilitation services. St. Mary's got its start in the nineteenth century; in the 1920s it became one of the first hospitals in South Dakota to become accredited.

	Annual Growth	06/12	06/13	06/14	06/15	06/16
Sales ($ mil.)	3.0%	-	-	-	77.7	80.1
Net income ($ mil.)	-	-	-	-	(2.3)	(2.8)
Market value ($ mil.)	-	-	-	-	-	-
Employees	-	-	-	-	-	450

AVERITT EXPRESS, INC.

1415 NEAL ST
COOKEVILLE, TN 385014328
Phone: 931-526-3306
Fax: –
Web: www.averittexpress.com

CEO: Gary Sasser
CFO: George Johnson
HR: –
FYE: December 31
Type: Private

Small loads add up at Averitt Express. The company provides less-than-truckload (LTL) freight transportation service. (LTL carriers combine freight from multiple shippers into a single trailer.) . Averitt Express directly serves the southern US and Mexico and it provides service elsewhere in North America through partnerships with other carriers such as Lakeville Motor Express and DATS. The company also offers truckload and expedited freight transportation along with logistics warehousing and international freight forwarding.

	Annual Growth	12/14	12/15	12/16	12/18	12/20
Sales ($ mil.)	2.0%	–	1,091.8	1,088.4	1,292.7	1,204.9
Net income ($ mil.)	11.5%	–	44.8	45.0	77.0	77.3
Market value ($ mil.)	–	–	–	–	–	–
Employees	–	–	–	–	–	8,208

AVERY DENNISON CORP

207 Goode Avenue
Glendale, CA 91203
Phone: 626 304-2000
Fax: –
Web: www.averydennison.com

NYS: AVY
CEO: Mitchell Butier
CFO: Gregory Lovins
HR: –
FYE: January 01
Type: Public

Avery Dennison is a world-leader in sticky labels used by businesses to add their branding to products such as drinks food personal care items and pharmaceuticals. It also makes RFID tags for individual products. Its adhesives extend to vinyl wraps and specialty materials designed for digital imaging screen printing and sign-cutting applications. Under the Avery Dennison and Fasson brands it makes papers films and foils coated with adhesive. It also makes retail branding and security tags printer systems and fasteners as well as medical adhesive products. The California-based company gets about 75% of its revenue from international customers.

	Annual Growth	12/17	12/18	12/19*	01/21	01/22
Sales ($ mil.)	4.9%	6,613.8	7,159.0	7,070.1	6,971.5	8,408.3
Net income ($ mil.)	21.3%	281.8	467.4	303.6	555.9	740.1
Market value ($ mil.)	13.5%	9,488.1	7,337.9	10,871.8	12,813.0	17,890.0
Employees	3.7%	30,000	30,000	30,000	32,000	36,000

*Fiscal year change

AVERY WEIGH-TRONIX LLC

1000 Armstrong Dr.
Fairmont MN 56031-1439
Phone: 507-238-4461
Fax: 507-238-8258
Web: www.wtxweb.com

CEO: –
CFO: –
HR: –
FYE: December 31
Type: Subsidiary

Avery Weigh-Tronix puts the whole weight of its being into its work. The company makes a full slate of industrial and retail weighing systems from bench scales to conveyor scales counting scales floor scales truck scales and weigh bars. It also produces accessories such as printers remote displays signal processors and wireless transceivers. Clients come from such sectors as transportation and logistics as well as public safety. The company operates globally through regional sales offices; much of its revenue comes from outside North America. It has about 500 locations worldwide with about half of those in the US. The company is a subsidiary of Illinois Tool Works (ITW).

AVI SYSTEMS, INC.

9675 W 76TH ST STE 200
EDEN PRAIRIE, MN 553443707
Phone: 952-949-3700
Fax: –
Web: www.avisystems.com

CEO: Jeff Stoebner
CFO: Christopher Mounts
HR: –
FYE: March 31
Type: Private

AVI Systems is an employee-owned company that delivers next-generation visual collaboration solutions built with a people-first approach. Its unique four-step planning process delivers better adoption. Its PRO Development phase lays the foundation for exceptional user adoption. Its PRO Design applies engineering best practices to develop the standards that help organizations scale its workflows and optimize its investment. Its PRO Integration ensures that the project is completed on time on budget and meets high expectations. Its PRO Support supplements IT departments enabling customers' team to focus on more strategic priorities. AVI runs around 30 regional business units with local delivery in over 50 countries. AVI was founded in 1974 by Joe Stoebner.

	Annual Growth	03/14	03/15	03/16	03/17	03/18
Sales ($ mil.)	9.8%	–	–	182.1	196.5	219.6
Net income ($ mil.)	17.8%	–	–	6.5	9.7	9.0
Market value ($ mil.)	–	–	–	–	–	–
Employees	–	–	–	–	–	650

AVI-SPL INC.

6301 Benjamin Rd. Ste. 101
Tampa FL 33634
Phone: 813-884-7168
Fax: 813-882-9508
Web: www.splis.com

CEO: John Zettel
CFO: Steve Palmer
HR: –
FYE: December 31
Type: Private

AVI-SPL wants to win the eyes and ears of its clients. The company designs and installs videoconferencing systems and integrated multimedia audio and video systems. Customers include corporations universities and government agencies. It serves commercial clients in such industries as health care hospitality and financial services. Projects have included upgrading the audiovisual systems of the Budget Hearing Room of the US House of Representatives and the sound system at Gillette Stadium in Massachusetts. AVI-SPL also sells and rents equipment and offers event management and production through its Creative Show Services. The company has more than 30 locations across the US with an international office in Dubai.

AVIALL INC.

2750 Regent Blvd.
DFW Airport TX 75261-9048
Phone: 972-586-1000
Fax: 972-586-1361
Web: www.aviall.com

CEO: Eric Strafel
CFO: Colin M Cohen
HR: –
FYE: December 31
Type: Subsidiary

When it comes to aviation Aviall has all the right parts. The Boeing subsidiary is one of the top global distributors of commercial aircraft parts and aftermarket services. Through its primary operating unit Aviall Services the company markets and distributes aviation parts for 240 manufacturers and offers related aftermarket supply chain services to the aerospace and defense sectors. Its supply chain and logistics services include order processing and inventory management. Other services include repair and maintenance of components such as batteries brakes and hose assemblies. Aviall has some 40 service centers located in North America Europe the Middle East and other regions.

AVIAT NETWORKS, INC.
NMS: AVNW

200 Parker Drive, Suite C100A
Austin, TX 78728
Phone: 408 941-7100
Fax: –
Web: www.aviatnetworks.com

CEO: Peter Smith
CFO: David Gray
HR: –
FYE: July 02
Type: Public

Aviat Networks designs manufactures and sells wireless networking products solutions and services. Its products utilize microwave and millimeter wave technologies to create point to point wireless links for short medium and long-distance interconnections. It also provides software tools and applications to enable deployment monitoring network management and optimization of its systems as well as to automate network design and procurement. It sources qualifies supplies and supports third party equipment such as antennas routers optical transmission equipment and other equipment necessary to build and deploy a complete telecommunications transmission network. Aviat's customers include mobile network operators public safety agencies private network operators and utility and transportation companies. The company gets over 65% of its sales in North America.

	Annual Growth	06/17	06/18	06/19*	07/20	07/21
Sales ($ mil.)	3.3%	241.9	242.5	243.9	238.6	274.9
Net income ($ mil.)	–	(0.8)	1.8	9.7	0.3	110.1
Market value ($ mil.)	16.3%	194.1	182.6	152.8	207.3	355.6
Employees	(2.8%)	769	736	738	674	687

*Fiscal year change

AVID BIOSERVICES INC
NAS: CDMO

2642 Michelle Drive, Suite 200
Tustin, CA 92780
Phone: 714 508-6100
Fax: –
Web: www.avidbio.com

CEO: Nicholas Green
CFO: Daniel Hart
HR: –
FYE: April 30
Type: Public

Peregrine Pharmaceuticals is spreading its wings and taking flight to attack and kill its prey: cancer and viral infections. While nearly all its revenue comes from its Avid Bioservices subsidiary which provides contract antibody and protein manufacturing to drug companies Peregrine is focused on shepherding its own candidates through clinical trials. Up first is bavituximab a monoclonal antibody candidate being tested to treat lung pancreatic and liver cancers as well as for other oncology and infectious disease applications. Next is Cotara being tested to treat glioblastoma multiforme a deadly brain cancer. The company also has development programs for potential diagnostic imaging agents.

	Annual Growth	04/17	04/18	04/19	04/20	04/21
Sales ($ mil.)	13.6%	57.6	53.6	53.6	59.7	95.9
Net income ($ mil.)	–	(28.2)	(21.8)	(4.2)	(10.5)	11.2
Market value ($ mil.)	142.8%	37.6	224.1	292.5	372.5	1,307.2
Employees	(5.6%)	323	186	215	227	257

AVID TECHNOLOGY, INC.
NMS: AVID

75 Network Drive
Burlington, MA 01803
Phone: 978 640-6789
Fax: –
Web: www.avid.com

CEO: Jeff Rosica
CFO: Kenneth Gayron
HR: –
FYE: December 31
Type: Public

Avid Technology is a leading technology provider that powers the media and entertainment industry. The company develops markets sells and supports software and integrated solutions for video and audio content creation management and distribution. Products include its Media Composer video editing systems and its Pro-Tools professional audio recording and editing systems and are used by music and film studios post-production facilities radio broadcasters and TV stations as well as independent professionals and amateurs. With sales offices in about 15 countries some 60% of revenue comes from outside the US.

	Annual Growth	12/16	12/17	12/18	12/19	12/20
Sales ($ mil.)	(8.4%)	511.9	419.0	413.3	411.8	360.5
Net income ($ mil.)	(30.8%)	48.2	(13.6)	(10.7)	7.6	11.1
Market value ($ mil.)	37.8%	195.4	239.4	211.0	381.1	704.9
Employees	(4.4%)	1,945	1,763	1,446	1,429	1,625

AVIENT CORP
NYS: AVNT

33587 Walker Road
Avon Lake, OH 44012
Phone: 440 930-1000
Fax: –

CEO: Robert Patterson
CFO: Jamie Beggs
HR: –
FYE: December 31
Type: Public

Avient Corporation (formerly PolyOne Corporation) a top North American plastics compounder and resins distributor has a single focus ? providing specialized polymer products and services. Its products include specialty engineered materials advanced composites color and additive systems and polymer distribution. The company is also a highly specialized developer and manufacturer of performance enhancing additives liquid colorants and fluoropolymer and silicone colorants. The company is one of the biggest formulator of plastic materials and color and additive systems in both the US and Europe with a growing presence in Asia and South America. The US accounts for approximately 50% of sales.

	Annual Growth	12/16	12/17	12/18	12/19	12/20
Sales ($ mil.)	(0.7%)	3,339.8	3,229.9	3,533.4	2,862.7	3,242.1
Net income ($ mil.)	(5.5%)	165.2	(57.7)	159.8	588.6	131.6
Market value ($ mil.)	5.9%	2,925.3	3,971.6	2,611.2	3,358.9	3,677.6
Employees	4.7%	7,000	6,300	6,600	5,600	8,400

AVIS BUDGET GROUP INC
NMS: CAR

6 Sylvan Way
Parsippany, NJ 7054
Phone: 973 496-4700
Fax: –
Web: www.avisbudgetgroup.com

CEO: Joseph Ferraro
CFO: Brian Choi
HR: –
FYE: December 31
Type: Public

Avis Budget Group (ABG) has a car rental brand for you. The company's core brands include: Avis Rent A Car Budget Rent A Car Payless Car Rental and Zipcar a car-sharing service. The company and their licensees operate their brands in approximately 180 countries in North America Europe Australia and New Zealand. Their rental fleet totaled approximately 530000 vehicles and it completed approximately 22 million vehicle rental transactions worldwide. Their brands and mobility solutions have an extended global reach with more than 11000 rental locations including approximately 4100 locations operated by their licensees. Avis's Budget Truck is one of the leading truck rental businesses in the US.

	Annual Growth	12/17	12/18	12/19	12/20	12/21
Sales ($ mil.)	1.3%	8,848.0	9,124.0	9,172.0	5,402.0	9,313.0
Net income ($ mil.)	37.4%	361.0	165.0	302.0	(684.0)	1,285.0
Market value ($ mil.)	47.4%	2,452.9	1,256.6	1,802.2	2,085.1	11,592.0
Employees	(9.3%)	31,000	30,000	30,000	20,000	21,000

AVIS RENT A CAR SYSTEM LLC

6 Sylvan Way
Parsippany NJ 07054
Phone: 973-496-3500
Fax: 408-990-4040
Web: www.quicklogic.com

CEO: F Robert Salerno
CFO: –
HR: –
FYE: December 31
Type: Subsidiary

A major player in the car rental industry Avis Rent A Car System maintains some 2200 locations primarily in the US and Canada but also in Australia New Zealand Latin America and the Caribbean. The company owns about 1275 of its locations; franchisees operate the rest. Together with sister company Budget Rent A Car System Avis Rent A Car System has a fleet of more than 350000 rental cars. Business travelers account for 60% of Avis' sales with leisure renters making up the rest. The company is a wholly-owned subsidiary of Avis Budget Group which is seeking to acquire UK-based Avis Europe a separately owned company with operations in Europe Africa the Middle East and parts of Asia.

AVISTA CORP
NYS: AVA

1411 East Mission Avenue
Spokane, WA 99202-2600
Phone: 509 489-0500
Fax: 509 482-4361
Web: www.avistacorp.com

CEO: Dennis Vermillion
CFO: Mark Thies
HR: Bryan Cox
FYE: December 31
Type: Public

Avista enjoys quite a wide vista when it comes to its service area. This electric and natural gas utility primarily serves the Pacific Northwest through Avista Utilities and some customers in Juneau Alaska through electric utility AEL&P (Alaska Electric Light and Power). Through its subsidiaries Avista also engages in sheet metal fabrication venture fund investments real estate and capital investments. The company has a net capability of more than 1880 MW of which over 55% come from hydroelectric and about 45% is thermal. It serves more than 600000 electric and natural gas customers.

	Annual Growth	12/16	12/17	12/18	12/19	12/20
Sales ($ mil.)	(2.2%)	1,442.5	1,445.9	1,396.9	1,345.6	1,321.9
Net income ($ mil.)	(1.4%)	137.2	115.9	136.4	197.0	129.5
Market value ($ mil.)	0.1%	2,768.9	3,565.1	2,941.3	3,329.7	2,779.2
Employees	(1.1%)	1,982	1,948	2,026	1,920	–

AVISTAR COMMUNICATIONS CORPORATION
PINK SHEETS: AVSR

1875 S. Grant St. 10th Fl.
San Mateo CA 94402
Phone: 650-525-3300
Fax: 650-525-1360
Web: www.avistar.com

CEO: Robert Kirk
CFO: Elias MurrayMetzger
HR: –
FYE: December 31
Type: Public

If geography prevents you from concluding business with a firm handshake Avistar Communications is ready to furnish the next-best thing. The company provides communication software and hardware used to equip communications networks with video capabilities. Its systems enable videoconferencing content creation video broadcasting and data sharing between users over telephony networks and the Internet. Avistar markets its products primarily to corporations in the financial services industry including UBS Investment Bank Deutsche Bank and JPMorgan Chase. Chairman Gerald Burnett owns about 42% of the company.

AVIV REIT INC.

303 W. Madison St. Ste. 2400
Chicago IL 60606
Phone: 312-855-0930
Fax: 312-855-1684
Web: www.avivreit.com/

CEO: –
CFO: –
HR: –
FYE: December 31
Type: Private

Aviv REIT sees a healthy future in health care-related real estate. The self-administered real estate investment trust (REIT) invests in and owns nursing homes that provide post-acute (short-term stays) and long-term assisted living care. Its portfolio includes more than 250 properties in some 30 states. (Texas is home to about 60 facilities and California about 35.) Aviv REIT doesn't run the facilities — it leases them to more than 35 local regional and national operators including Daybreak Venture Saber Healthcare and Sun Healthcare. Aviv REIT is trying its hand at the IPO market again. It first filed an IPO back in 2008 but withdrew it a year later. The company then filed a second IPO in December 2012.

AVNET INC
NMS: AVT

2211 South 47th Street
Phoenix, AZ 85034
Phone: 480 643-2000
Fax: –
Web: www.avnet.com

CEO: Phil Gallagher
CFO: Thomas Liguori
HR: –
FYE: July 03
Type: Public

If you need an electronic component Avnet probably has it. The company is one of the world's top distributors of electronic components (including connectors and semiconductors) Inductors and storage products and software with competitors Arrow Electronics and World Peace Group. It works with more than 1400 suppliers to provide some 2.1 million customers with parts and services. Customers include startups small and mid-sized businesses and big companies that produce electronics. Avnet has about 115 locations around the world and makes most of its sales to international customers with Asia/Pacific generating roughly 40% of revenue. Semiconductors and related products comprise about three quarters of Avnet's revenue.

	Annual Growth	07/17*	06/18	06/19	06/20*	07/21
Sales ($ mil.)	2.9%	17,440.0	19,036.9	19,518.6	17,634.3	19,534.7
Net income ($ mil.)	(22.1%)	525.3	(156.4)	176.3	(31.1)	193.1
Market value ($ mil.)	0.7%	3,872.5	4,271.9	4,509.0	2,593.6	3,987.0
Employees	(2.0%)	15,700	15,400	15,500	14,600	14,500

*Fiscal year change

AVNET TECHNOLOGY SOLUTIONS

8700 S. Price Rd.
Tempe AZ 85284
Phone: 480-794-6500
Fax: 480-794-6890
Web: www.ats.avnet.com

CEO: –
CFO: –
HR: –
FYE: June 30
Type: Business Segment

Avnet Technology Solutions (ATS) distributes everything under the technology sun. A unit of electronic components and computer products distribution giant Avnet ATS sells servers networking gear data storage and software to independent software vendors equipment makers systems integrators and resellers worldwide. ATS accounts for about 40% of Avnet's revenues through two main groups. Its Enterprise Solutions unit provides resellers with computing systems and software as well as financing logistics marketing sales and technical support. Its Embedded Solutions group offers design and integration services to developers of application-specific computing systems used in medical telecom and industrial settings.

AVSTAR AVIATION GROUP INC.
PINK SHEETS: AAVG

9801 Westheimer Ste. 302
Houston TX 77042
Phone: 713-706-6350
Fax: 713-706-6351
Web: avstargroup.com

CEO: Clayton Gamber
CFO: Robert Wilson
HR: –
FYE: December 31
Type: Public

AvStar Aviation Group is making the switch from searching for oil and gas to investing in the aviation sector. Once known as Pangea Petroleum the company formerly specialized in oil and natural gas exploration and production in the US Gulf Coast region. In 2009 however Pangea Petroleum was acquired by AvStar Aviation Services which redirected the company's focus as a service provider to the general aviation industry. Now known as AvStar Aviation Group the company plans to acquire fixed base operations (FBOs) at airports. Its San Diego Airmotive subsidiary provides maintenance repair and overhaul services for aircraft.

AVX CORP.   NYS: AVX

1 AVX Boulevard
Fountain Inn, SC 29644
Phone: 864 967-2150
Fax: –
Web: www.avx.com

CEO: John Sarvis
CFO: Michael Hufnagel
HR: –
FYE: March 31
Type: Public

AVX proves that tiny parts can add up to big business. The company's largest segment passive components makes passive electronic components for automotive braking systems copiers hearing aids locomotives and wireless phones. The KED Resale segment specializes in products made by Kyocera (which owns a controlling stake in the company) such as ceramic and tantalum capacitors that store filter and regulate electrical energy in electronic devices. The interconnect segment makes electronic connectors for automotive and medical electronics applications. Asia is its largest market.

	Annual Growth	03/15	03/16	03/17	03/18	03/19
Sales ($ mil.)	7.3%	1,353.2	1,195.5	1,312.7	1,562.5	1,791.8
Net income ($ mil.)	4.7%	225.9	101.5	125.8	4.9	271.8
Market value ($ mil.)	5.0%	2,409.1	2,122.1	2,765.4	2,794.1	2,927.4
Employees	9.8%	10,400	10,200	10,800	14,920	15,100

AWARE INC. (MA)   NMS: AWRE

40 Middlesex Turnpike
Bedford, MA 01730
Phone: 781 276-4000
Fax: –
Web: www.aware.com

CEO: Robert Eckel
CFO: David Barcelo
HR: –
FYE: December 31
Type: Public

Aware is mindful of both the physical and intellectual aspects of its business. The company provides biometrics and imaging software to capture and verify fingerprint facial and iris images for identification purposes. The software is primarily used in law enforcement border control access control and national defense applications. Aware also offers imaging software used to process and display medical images and data. While DSL service assurance systems were once its largest product line Aware discontinued its DSL hardware business opting to focus on DSL software used by broadband service providers to manage DSL networks. The company also has a small intellectual property (IP) licensing business.

	Annual Growth	12/16	12/17	12/18	12/19	12/20
Sales ($ mil.)	(14.9%)	21.6	16.3	16.1	12.2	11.3
Net income ($ mil.)	–	4.1	1.3	1.2	(8.3)	(7.6)
Market value ($ mil.)	(13.0%)	130.4	96.2	77.2	71.8	74.8
Employees	69.1%	11	68	67	71	90

AXA EQUITABLE LIFE INSURANCE COMPANY

1290 Avenue of the Americas
New York NY 10104
Phone: 212-554-1234
Fax: 716-823-6454
Web: www.sorrentocheese.com

CEO: Mark Pearson
CFO: Anders Malmstrom
HR: Salvatore Piazzolla
FYE: December 31
Type: Subsidiary

This company definitely has what it takes to be equitable. AXA Equitable Life Insurance is the US life insurance and annuities underwriting arm of its globe-spanning ultimate parent AXA. The company has some 2.3 million life insurance policies in force and is licensed throughout the US and Puerto Rico. Policies are sold through affiliates AXA Advisors (retail brokerage) and AXA Distributors (wholesale brokerage that sells to independent brokers and advisors) as well as corporate sales representatives. AXA Equitable a subsidiary of AXA Financial offers investment management services through affiliate Alliance Bernstein; together the firms have about $500 billion in assets under management.

AXA FINANCIAL INC.

1290 Avenue of the Americas
New York NY 10104
Phone: 212-554-1234
Fax: 212-314-4480
Web: www.axa-equitable.com/axa/axa-financial.html

CEO: Mark Pearson
CFO: Richard S Dziadzio
HR: –
FYE: December 31
Type: Subsidiary

A US-based subsidiary of French insurance giant AXA AXA Financial provides financial advisory and insurance services through subsidiaries such as AXA Equitable AXA Advisors and AXA Distributors. These businesses offer life insurance annuities mutual funds separate accounts and other investment products. It caters to individuals small businesses and professional organizations. AXA Financial's investment management business is anchored by majority-owned affiliate AllianceBernstein and serves institutional and retail clients including individuals with high net worth. AXA Financial and its subsidiaries have approximately $575 billion in assets under management most of it at AllianceBernstein.

AXA ROSENBERG INVESTMENT MANAGMENT LLC

4 Orinda Way Bldg. E
Orinda CA 94563
Phone: 925-254-6464
Fax: 925-253-0141
Web: www.axarosenberg.com

CEO: –
CFO: –
HR: –
FYE: December 31
Type: Subsidiary

No need for rose-colored glasses; AXA Rosenberg Group prefers a more analytical approach to equity investing. The unit of insurance giant AXA manages investment portfolios for institutional clients such as corporations pension funds endowments foundations and government entities. It also acts as a manager or subadvisor for several mutual funds with holdings in global equities; such funds are available to retail customers as well. AXA Rosenberg operates a handful of offices in financial centers around the globe and has more than $30 billion of assets under management. Established in 1985 the company became part of AXA in 1999.

AXCELIS TECHNOLOGIES INC   NMS: ACLS

108 Cherry Hill Drive
Beverly, MA 01915
Phone: 978 787-4000
Fax: 978 787-3000
Web: www.axcelis.com

CEO: Mary G Puma
CFO: Kevin J Brewer
HR: –
FYE: December 31
Type: Public

Axcelis Technologies designs manufactures and services ion implantation and other processing equipment used in the fabrication of semiconductor chips. Axcelis Technologies manufactures its ion implantation devices in house at its plant in Beverly Massachusetts. In addition to equipment it offers aftermarket service and support including used tools spare parts equipment upgrades and maintenance services. While the company sells its products around the world the US accounts for some third-quarter of sales. Axcelis' business commenced in 1978.

	Annual Growth	12/16	12/17	12/18	12/19	12/20
Sales ($ mil.)	15.5%	267.0	410.6	442.6	343.0	474.6
Net income ($ mil.)	46.0%	11.0	127.0	45.9	17.0	50.0
Market value ($ mil.)	18.9%	489.4	965.3	598.7	810.4	979.4
Employees	4.4%	845	985	1,079	1,009	1,004

AXCESS INTERNATIONAL INC.
OTC: AXSI

16650 Westgrove Dr.
Addison TX 75001
Phone: 972-407-6080
Fax: 972-407-9085
Web: www.axcessinc.com

CEO: Allan Griebenow
CFO: Allan L Frank
HR: –
FYE: December 31
Type: Public

Axcess International can watch the door and mind the store. The company's Active-Tag radio-frequency identification (RFID) system is for tracking people vehicles inventory and equipment. Axcess International's Online Supervisor system integrates RFID data and digital video to a standard Web browser. The company has also developed a micro-wireless technology platform called Dot a small low-cost battery powered wireless computer for the automatic identification location tracking protecting and monitoring of personnel physical assets and vehicles; applications include airport school and military installations. Customers include security systems integrators and distributors in the US.

AXEL JOHNSON INC.

155 SPRING ST FL 6
NEW YORK, NY 100125254
Phone: 646-291-2445
Fax: -
Web: www.axeljohnson.com

CEO: –
CFO: –
HR: –
FYE: December 31
Type: Private

The Johnson family of Stockholm Sweden has an investment arm that stretches across the ocean. Axel Johnson owns and operates North American businesses on behalf of the Johnson dynasty. The investment firm focuses on several industries such as energy medical device manufacturing and water treatment. Its portfolio includes Sprague Energy Parkson Corp. and Kinetico Incorporated. Axel Johnson's companies boast about $4 billion in annual revenues. Axel Johnson along with Axel Johnson AB and AXFast are all affiliated with Sweden-based Axel Johnson Group but are independent. Established in 1873 the Johnson family of companies is in its fourth generation of family ownership.

	Annual Growth	12/06	12/07	12/08	12/09	12/10
Sales ($ mil.)	(16.8%)	–	–	4,312.8	2,598.3	2,982.1
Net income ($ mil.)	35.5%	–	–	8.2	11.9	15.0
Market value ($ mil.)	–	–	–	–	–	–
Employees	–	–	–	–	–	1,200

AXESSTEL INC
NBB: AXST

6815 Flanders Drive, Suite 210
San Diego, CA 92121
Phone: 858 625-2100
Fax: –

CEO: Patrick Gray
CFO: Patrick Gray
HR: –
FYE: December 31
Type: Public

Axesstel can soup up that old phone on your desk. The company designs and manufactures fixed wireless voice and broadband data systems that link stationary office phones to the communications network via cellular connections. Axesstel's products include fixed wireless telephones transmission terminals and wireless modems. The company mostly sells its products to telecommunications companies in developing countries that then resell the products to consumers. Axesstel has shifted its engineering and design operations to China in an effort to reduce operating expenses.

	Annual Growth	12/08	12/09	12/10	12/11	12/12
Sales ($ mil.)	(14.1%)	109.6	50.8	45.4	54.1	59.7
Net income ($ mil.)	32.1%	1.4	(10.1)	(6.3)	1.1	4.3
Market value ($ mil.)	50.4%	8.5	3.1	2.4	7.5	43.5
Employees	(11.8%)	71	22	34	39	43

AXIALL CORP
NYS: AXLL

1000 Abernathy Road, Suite 1200
Atlanta, GA 30328
Phone: 770 395-4500
Fax: –
Web: www.axiall.com

CEO: Albert Chao
CFO: M Steven Bender
HR: –
FYE: December 31
Type: Public

Axiall's business revolves around the axis of commodity chemicals. The company makes chlorovinyls and aromatics used by the construction and housing plastics pulp and paper and pharmaceutical industries. Its primary chlorovinyl products are PVC (polyvinyl chloride) caustic soda and chlorine; this segment also makes vinyl chloride monomer (VCM) used to make PVC resins. Aromatics include phenol acetone (for makers of acrylic resins) and cumene (used to make phenol and acetone). Its building products unit makes extruded vinyl window and door profiles and moldings products. In 2016 Axiall rejected a $1.4 billion buyout from rival Westlake Chemical.

	Annual Growth	12/10	12/11	12/12	12/13	12/14
Sales ($ mil.)	12.8%	2,818.0	3,222.9	3,325.8	4,666.0	4,568.7
Net income ($ mil.)	2.1%	42.7	57.8	120.6	165.3	46.3
Market value ($ mil.)	15.3%	1,688.9	1,368.1	2,897.7	3,330.1	2,981.2
Employees	11.1%	3,932	3,744	6,000	6,000	6,000

AXION INTERNATIONAL HOLDINGS INC
NBB: AXIH Q

4005 All American Way
Zanesville, OH 43701
Phone: 740 452-2500
Fax: –
Web: www.axih.com

CEO: –
CFO: –
HR: –
FYE: December 31
Type: Public

Axion International Holdings surveyed the landscape and decided to shift into a new line of business. Formerly operating as Analytical Surveys the company completed a reverse merger with Axion in 2008 and adopted that company's name and line of business. Axion is a licensee of technology regarding the manufacture of plastic composites used for structural applications such as railroad crossties bridge infrastructure marine pilings. and bulk headings. While the company is initially targeting the railroad industry it has yet to generate any significant revenues.

	Annual Growth	12/10	12/11	12/12	12/13	12/14
Sales ($ mil.)	54.7%	–	3.9	5.3	6.6	14.4
Net income ($ mil.)	–	(2.3)	(8.1)	(5.4)	(24.2)	(16.3)
Market value ($ mil.)	(19.9%)	68.7	51.0	24.8	70.8	28.3
Employees	125.8%	6	12	28	120	156

AXIS CONSTRUCTION CORP.

125 LASER CT
HAUPPAUGE, NY 117883911
Phone: 631-243-5970
Fax: –
Web: www.theaxisgroup.com

CEO: –
CFO: Andrew Meyerson
HR: John Buongiorno
FYE: December 31
Type: Private

Axis Construction revolves around building health care facilities from operating suites and emergency rooms to outpatient treatment centers and medical imaging facilities. About 80% of the company's business comes from the health care industry but Axis also constructs commercial and retail buildings modular structures and educational and intuitional facilities. The company provides general contracting construction management design/build consulting and renovation services to clients throughout New York. Its list of clients include Brookhaven National Lab Northrop Grumman and Est ©e Lauder. Axis Construction was founded in 1993 by company leaders Robert Wihlborg and Roy and Ralph Lambert.

	Annual Growth	12/03	12/04	12/05	12/07	12/08
Sales ($ mil.)	13.4%	–	31.9	43.2	47.5	52.8
Net income ($ mil.)	(25.9%)	–	–	0.9	0.5	0.4
Market value ($ mil.)	–	–	–	–	–	–
Employees	–	–	–	–	–	45

AXOGEN INC
NAS: AXGN

13631 Progress Blvd., Suite 400
Alachua, FL 32615
Phone: 386 462-6800
Fax: -
Web: www.axogeninc.com

CEO: Karen Zaderej
CFO: Peter Mariani
HR: -
FYE: December 31
Type: Public

AxoGen formerly known as LecTec is an intellectual property licensing and holding company. It licenses topical patches that deliver over-the-counter drugs through the skin. Its patents used by pharmaceutical companies include adhesive patches wound dressings and inhalation therapies. AxoGen licenses its technology to Novartis for that company's Triaminic Vapor Patch a cough suppressant for adults and children and is pursuing additional licensing agreements with Novartis. After acquiring AxoGen Corporation in 2011 LecTec changed its name to AxoGen Inc. and became the parent of AxoGen Corporation which develops and sells peripheral nerve reconstruction and regeneration products.

	Annual Growth	12/16	12/17	12/18	12/19	12/20
Sales ($ mil.)	28.6%	41.1	60.4	83.9	106.7	112.3
Net income ($ mil.)	-	(14.4)	(10.4)	(22.4)	(29.1)	(23.8)
Market value ($ mil.)	18.8%	365.6	1,149.5	829.8	726.7	727.1
Employees	26.0%	146	199	297	394	368

AXON ENTERPRISE INC
NMS: AXON

17800 North 85th Street
Scottsdale, AZ 85255
Phone: 480 991-0797
Fax: -
Web: www.axon.com

CEO: Patrick Smith
CFO: Jawad Ahsan
HR: -
FYE: December 31
Type: Public

Axon Enterprise's weapons aim to take perps down but not out. The company formerly known as TASER International is well known for designing and manufacturing various non-lethal TASER lines of stun guns including its best-selling TASER X26. These conducted energy devices (CEDs) are geared at the law enforcement corrections military and private security markets as well as consumers. The company also offers AXON wearable video cameras for officers and a hosted product called Evidence.com that allows digital evidence to be viewed shared and managed from a Web browser. Products are sold worldwide through a direct sales force distribution partners and online store and third-party resellers. The US generates about 85% of the company's total revenue.

	Annual Growth	12/16	12/17	12/18	12/19	12/20
Sales ($ mil.)	26.2%	268.2	343.8	420.1	530.9	681.0
Net income ($ mil.)	-	17.3	5.2	29.2	0.9	(1.7)
Market value ($ mil.)	49.9%	1,545.7	1,689.8	2,789.8	4,672.8	7,813.3
Employees	29.7%	901	1,095	1,386	1,916	2,548

AXOS FINANCIAL INC
NYS: AX

9205 West Russell Road, STE 400
Las Vegas, NV 89148
Phone: 858 649-2218
Fax: -
Web: www.axosfinancial.com

CEO: Gregory Garrabrants
CFO: Derrick Walsh
HR: -
FYE: June 30
Type: Public

Formerly BofI Holding Axos Financial is the holding company for Axos Bank which provides consumers and businesses a variety of deposit and loan products via the internet. It has designed its online banking platform and its workflow processes to handle traditional banking functions with elimination of duplicate and unnecessary paperwork and human intervention. Most of its business originates in its home state of California though its operations attract customers from every US state. Founded in 2000 the company holds over $14 billion in assets and a total portfolio of net loans and leases of about $12 billion.

	Annual Growth	06/17	06/18	06/19	06/20	06/21
Assets ($ mil.)	13.8%	8,501.7	9,539.5	11,220.2	13,851.9	14,265.6
Net income ($ mil.)	12.5%	134.7	152.4	155.1	183.4	215.7
Market value ($ mil.)	18.3%	1,407.0	2,426.7	1,616.4	1,309.7	2,751.8
Employees	14.4%	681	801	1,007	1,099	1,165

AXSUN TECHNOLOGIES INC.

1 Fortune Dr.
Billerica MA 01821
Phone: 978-262-0049
Fax: 978-262-0035
Web: www.axsun.com

CEO: -
CFO: -
HR: -
FYE: December 31
Type: Subsidiary

AXSUN Technologies takes the ax to bulky optoelectronic subsystems. Its Axsun Packaging Platform is a suite of components and manufacturing techniques that reduce the size of photonic assemblies used in optical networking systems. The platform combines specialized lenses microelectromechanical system devices and other components into packages much smaller than the usual printed circuit boards; these units can be tailored for many combinations of active and passive optical chips. The company was founded in 1999 by optical industry veterans. In early 2009 Volcano Corp. acquired AXSUN for $21.5 million in cash.

AXT INC
NMS: AXTI

4281 Technology Drive
Fremont, CA 94538
Phone: 510 438-4700
Fax: -
Web: www.axt.com

CEO: Morris Young
CFO: Gary Fischer
HR: -
FYE: December 31
Type: Public

For applications in which plain silicon would get the ax AXT offers fancier fare. AXT makes semiconductor substrates from compounds such as gallium arsenide (GaAs) and indium phosphide (InP) and from single elements such as germanium. Manufacturers use AXT's substrates to make high-performance semiconductors for products — including fiber-optic devices satellite solar cells and wireless handset — for which standard silicon microchips are not adequate. Most of its customers — and its employees — are in China. International customers include Soitec of France and IQE Group of the UK.

	Annual Growth	12/16	12/17	12/18	12/19	12/20
Sales ($ mil.)	4.1%	81.3	98.7	102.4	83.3	95.4
Net income ($ mil.)	(12.9%)	5.6	10.1	9.7	(2.6)	3.2
Market value ($ mil.)	18.8%	201.4	365.1	182.6	182.6	401.6
Employees	(5.8%)	994	694	1,080	731	784

AZEK CO INC (THE)
NYS: AZEK

1330 W. Fulton Street, Suite 350
Chicago, IL 60607
Phone: 877 275-2935
Fax: -
Web: www.azekco.com

CEO: Jesse Singh
CFO: Ralph Nicoletti
HR: -
FYE: September 30
Type: Public

When it comes to CPG's building products appearance is key. Through its AZEK Scranton and Vycom operating segments CPG is a leading manufacturer of synthetic building products and other materials used in residential remodeling and construction as well as by commercial and industrial clients in the US and Canada. Its core AZEK unit manufactures PVC-based residential products such as trim deck rail moulding and porch materials made to look like wood and other natural materials. CPG's Scranton unit makes polyurethane bathroom partitions and lockers for commercial and institutional end-users while Vycom makes PVC plastic sheeting for industrial uses. CPG's TimberTech unit makes decking and railings.

	Annual Growth	09/17	09/18	09/19	09/20	09/21
Sales ($ mil.)	-	0.0	681.8	794.2	899.3	1,179.0
Net income ($ mil.)	-	0.0	6.7	(20.2)	(122.2)	93.2
Market value ($ mil.)	-	0.0	-	-	5,390.9	5,657.3
Employees	16.0%	-	-	1,540	1,663	2,072

AZENTA INC
NMS: AZTA

15 Elizabeth Drive
Chelmsford, MA 01824
Phone: 978 262-2400
Fax: –
Web: www.brooks.com

CEO: Stephen Schwartz
CFO: Lindon Robertson
HR: William Montone
FYE: September 30
Type: Public

Azenta formerly Brooks Automation is a leading provider of life sciences solutions worldwide. The company provides precision robotics integrated automation systems and contamination control solutions to semiconductor fabrications plants and original equipment manufacturers worldwide. In the life sciences market it offers a full suite of services and solutions for analyzing managing and storing biological and chemical compound samples to advance research and development for clinical pharmaceutical and other scientific endeavors. Azenta has sales operations in more than 80 countries and generates around 65% from its domestic customers.

	Annual Growth	09/17	09/18	09/19	09/20	09/21
Sales ($ mil.)	(7.2%)	692.9	631.6	780.8	897.3	513.7
Net income ($ mil.)	15.3%	62.6	116.6	437.4	64.9	110.7
Market value ($ mil.)	35.5%	2,257.2	2,604.4	2,753.1	3,439.3	7,609.4
Employees	13.9%	1,661	1,548	2,984	3,159	2,800

AZURE MIDSTREAM PARTNERS LP
NBB: AZUR Q

12377 Merit Drive, Suite 300
Dallas, TX 75251
Phone: 972 674-5200
Fax: –
Web: www.marlinmidstream.com

CEO: –
CFO: –
HR: –
FYE: December 31
Type: Public

Marlin Midstream Partners knows how to capture and prepare the biggest of energy fish. An oil and gas company Marlin gathers transports and processes natural gas and crude oil for energy companies. It operates two natural gas facilities in East Texas with an aggregate 65 miles of natural gas pipelines a gathering capacity of 200 million cu. ft. of gas per day (MMcf/d) and a 300 MMcf/d processing capacity. It also operates crude oil transloading facilities in Wyoming and Colorado. Marlin's core customer base comprises Anadarko and Associated Energy Services. The company was formed in 2013 and went public that year using its $137.5 million in proceeds to repay debt.

	Annual Growth	12/11	12/12	12/13	12/14	12/15
Sales ($ mil.)	5.2%	65.8	51.0	52.9	75.2	80.6
Net income ($ mil.)	–	–	8.5	(4.3)	1.2	22.1	(222.4)
Market value ($ mil.)	(56.7%)	–	–	–	372.9	403.6	69.9
Employees	–	–	–	–	–	111

AZUSA PACIFIC UNIVERSITY

901 E ALOSTA AVE
AZUSA, CA 917022701
Phone: 626-969-3434
Fax: –
Web: www.apu.edu

CEO: Jon R Wallace
CFO: Joan Singleton
HR: –
FYE: June 30
Type: Private

An evangelical Christian institution Azusa Pacific University (APU) has an enrollment of more than 9000 undergraduate graduate and doctoral students. It offers about 70 bachelor's degrees more than 45 master's degrees nearly 20 certificates nine credentials and nine doctoral programs. APU also maintains seven off-site regional locations throughout Southern California including in the High Desert Inland Empire Los Angeles Monrovia Murrieta Orange County and San Diego as well as many online programs. With nearly 980 teaching faculty the university has a 12:1 student-to-faculty ratio. APU traces its roots to 1899 and the Training School for Christian Workers the West Coast's first bible college.

	Annual Growth	06/15	06/16	06/18	06/19	06/20
Sales ($ mil.)	4.7%	–	248.5	265.9	239.2	298.1
Net income ($ mil.)	–	–	0.4	(5.7)	5.5	(6.5)
Market value ($ mil.)	–	–	–	–	–	–
Employees	–	–	–	–	–	1,545

AZZ GALVANIZING SERVICES

3100 W. 7th St. Ste. 500
Fort Worth TX 76107
Phone: 817-810-0095
Fax: 817-336-5354
Web: www.azzgalvanizing.com

CEO: Tom Ferguson
CFO: –
HR: Lisa Baeza
FYE: December 31
Type: Subsidiary

AZZ Galvanizing Services (formerly North American Galvanizing & Coatings) is glad that rust never sleeps. Operations include hot-dip galvanizes fabricated structural iron and steel components to provide protection against corrosion. The company galvanizes its metal products by submerging them in molten zinc. Typical galvanizing customers work in the petrochemical irrigation food processing highway and transportation wastewater treatment telecommunications energy and utilities industries. It operates facilities in eight states and sells its services directly to customers primarily in the US. Texas-based galvanizer AZZ paid more than $125 million to acquire North American Galvanizing & Coatings in 2010.

AZZ INC
NYS: AZZ

One Museum Place, Suite 500, 3100 West 7th Street
Fort Worth, TX 76107
Phone: 817 810-0095
Fax: –
Web: www.azz.com

CEO: Thomas Ferguson
CFO: Philip Schlom
HR: –
FYE: February 28
Type: Public

AZZ's products act as a shield for steel. The company has two business segments: Energy and Metal Coatings. To protect steel from environmental corrosion galvanizing services dip steel products into baths of molten zinc. The process is vital for steel fabricators who serve highway construction electrical utility transportation and water-treatment firms. Through subsidiaries AZZ makes electrical power distribution systems industrial lighting switchgear motor control centers bus duct systems and tubular goods. Industrial petrochemical and power generation and transmission companies use the company's products. Its larger segment Energy accounts for more than half of sales around 80% of which comes from its domestic market.

	Annual Growth	02/17	02/18	02/19	02/20	02/21
Sales ($ mil.)	(0.6%)	858.9	810.4	927.1	1,061.8	838.9
Net income ($ mil.)	(10.2%)	60.9	45.2	51.2	48.2	39.6
Market value ($ mil.)	(3.4%)	1,472.6	1,025.7	1,155.5	926.2	1,282.8
Employees	(1.8%)	4,183	3,650	3,884	4,343	3,883

B&G FOODS INC
NYS: BGS

Four Gatehall Drive
Parsippany, NJ 07054
Phone: 973 401-6500
Fax: –
Web: www.bgfoods.com

CEO: Kenneth Keller
CFO: Bruce Wacha
HR: Eric Hart
FYE: January 02
Type: Public

Peter Piper picks more than a peck of peppers from B&G Foods. The company makes markets and distributes a wide variety of shelf-stable foods frozen foods and household goods. Many of B&G's products are regional or national best-sellers including B&M and B&G (beans condiments) Clabber Girl (baking) Green Giant (frozen and canned foods) Spice Islands (seasonings) McCann's (oatmeal) Ortega (Mexican foods) Grandma's and Brer Rabbit (molasses) Snackwell's (snacks) and Underwood (meat spread). They are sold through B&G's subsidiaries to supermarkets mass merchants warehouse clubs and drug store chains as well as institutional and food service operators in the US Canada and Puerto Rico.

	Annual Growth	12/16	12/17	12/18	12/19*	01/21
Sales ($ mil.)	7.2%	1,391.3	1,668.1	1,700.8	1,660.4	1,967.9
Net income ($ mil.)	3.8%	109.4	217.5	172.4	76.4	132.0
Market value ($ mil.)	(8.7%)	2,814.3	2,258.5	1,925.0	1,170.7	1,781.7
Employees	4.4%	2,590	2,680	2,675	2,899	3,207

*Fiscal year change

B&R STORES INC.

4554 W. St.
Lincoln NE 68503-2831
Phone: 402-464-6297
Fax: 402-434-5733
Web: www.brstores.com

CEO: –
CFO: Kipp Utemark
HR: –
FYE: December 31
Type: Private

B&R Stores operates about 20 supermarkets in six cities across Nebraska and Iowa that operate under the Super Saver Russ's Market and ALPS (an acronym for Always Low Price Store) banners. The stores offer the usual grocery selections as well as carpet cleaner and video rentals. Other specialties include smoked meat products produced by in-store smokehouses at all Super Saver stores. The regional grocery chain was founded in 1962 by Russ Raybould (father of company president Pat Raybould) and Clayton Burnett. The Raybould family owns a majority stake in B&R Stores; employees own the rest.

B&W TECHNICAL SERVICES Y-12 LLC

Y-12 National Security Complex 301 Bear Creek Rd.
Oak Ridge TN 37830
Phone: 865-576-5454
Fax: 865-576-3806
Web: www.y12.doe.gov

CEO: –
CFO: –
HR: –
FYE: December 31
Type: Subsidiary

B&W Technical Services Y-12 (formerly BWXT Y-12) manages the Y-12 National Security Complex for the Department of Energy and the National Nuclear Security Administration (NNSA). The Y-12 National Security Complex (built as part of the Manhattan Project during WWII) makes dismantles refurbishes stores and manages nuclear weapons and weapon components; removes and secures nuclear material and equipment from foreign sources and provides fuel for research and Naval reactors; and works with the Department of Defense and Homeland Security on national security projects such as the Future Medical Shelter System and the Vulnerability Assessment Resource Center. Y-12 is a unit of Babcock & Wilcox Technical Services.

B. BRAUN MEDICAL INC.

824 12th Ave.
Bethlehem PA 18018-3524
Phone: 610-691-5400
Fax: 610-691-6249
Web: www.bbraunusa.com

CEO: –
CFO: Bruce Heugel
HR: Carol Monheim
FYE: December 31
Type: Subsidiary

B. Braun Medical is the US arm of German medical supply firm B. Braun Melsungen. The company's products and services include a wide range of traditional and needleless IV systems and accessories pharmaceutical devices dialysis machines critical care products and vascular access and interventional product lines as well as continuing education and training programs. B. Braun's customers include hospitals outpatient surgery centers and home care services companies. Its network of CAPS (Central Admixture Pharmacy Services) compounding pharmacies provides IV admixtures and solutions to hospitals clinics and home care providers throughout the US.

B.L. HARBERT INTERNATIONAL, L.L.C.

820 SHADES CREEK PKWY # 3000
BIRMINGHAM, AL 352094564
Phone: 205-802-2800
Fax: –
Web: www.blharbert.com

CEO: Billy Harbert
CFO: R Alan Hall
HR: –
FYE: December 31
Type: Private

My way or the highway? For Harbert it's my way and the highway. B. L. Harbert International Group provides highway and heavy construction services for commercial industrial and public projects throughout the world but primarily in the Southeast US. The design/build company's portfolio includes commercial and institutional buildings research facilities hotels and condominiums water and wastewater treatment plants dams and highways and pipelines. B. L. Harbert International has offices in the US and Dubai. CEO Billy Harbert Jr. leads the family-owned company which traces its roots to the 1949 founding of Harbert Construction by brothers Bill and John Harbert.

	Annual Growth	12/05	12/06	12/07	12/08	12/14
Sales ($ mil.)	6.5%	–	–	–	554.1	807.6
Net income ($ mil.)	9.7%	–	–	–	33.2	57.8
Market value ($ mil.)	–	–	–	–	–	–
Employees						1,400

B/E AEROSPACE, INC

NMS: BEAV

1400 Corporate Center Way
Wellington, FL 33414-2105
Phone: 561 791-5000
Fax: 561 791-7900
Web: www.beaerospace.com

CEO: Kelly Ortberg
CFO: Patrick Allen
HR: –
FYE: December 31
Type: Public

A leading maker of cabin components for commercial business jets and military aircraft B/E Aerospace makes aircraft seats coffeemakers lighting refrigeration equipment galley structures and emergency oxygen systems. B/E aftermarket operations represent about 40% of its revenue. Operating through two business segments (commercial aircraft and business jet) B/E sells its products to most major airlines and aviation OEMs. The company also provides oil field equipment and services. In late 2016 B/E Aerospace agreed to be acquired by rival Rockwell Collins in a transaction valued at $6.4 billion plus the assumption of $1.9 billion in debt.

	Annual Growth	12/11	12/12	12/13	12/14	12/15
Sales ($ mil.)	2.2%	2,499.8	3,085.3	3,483.7	2,599.0	2,729.6
Net income ($ mil.)	5.8%	227.8	233.7	365.6	104.3	285.7
Market value ($ mil.)	2.3%	3,952.7	5,044.2	8,886.7	5,924.4	4,326.4
Employees	6.9%	7,700	9,500	10,825	9,617	10,057

BAB INC

NBB: BABB

500 Lake Cook Road, Suite 475
Deerfield, IL 60015
Phone: 847 948-7520
Fax: –

CEO: Michael Evans
CFO: Geraldine Conn
HR: –
FYE: November 30
Type: Public

Bagels muffins and coffee are fueling this company. BAB operates a chain of about 110 franchised coffee and baked goods outlets under the brand names Big Apple Bagels and My Favorite Muffin. The stores offer several varieties of bagels and spreads muffins sandwiches soups salads and gourmet coffee. The company also markets a proprietary java brand Brewster's Coffee. BAB has coffee shops in more than 25 states as well as in the United Arab Emirates. An investment group controlled by CEO Michael Evans and VP Michael Murtaugh owns nearly 40% of the company.

	Annual Growth	11/16	11/17	11/18	11/19	11/20
Sales ($ mil.)	(0.2%)	2.4	2.2	2.2	3.1	2.4
Net income ($ mil.)	–	0.4	0.5	0.5	0.4	(0.1)
Market value ($ mil.)	(9.6%)	6.0	5.1	4.9	6.0	4.0
Employees	(6.9%)	16	13	13	13	12

BABSON COLLEGE

231 FOREST ST
BABSON PARK, MA 02457
Phone: 781-235-1200
Fax: –
Web: www.babson.edu

CEO: –
CFO: Philip Shapiro
HR: –
FYE: June 30
Type: Private

Babson students could babble on and on about business management. With an enrollment of more than 3000 students Babson College is lauded as one of the nation's leading business schools. The school's undergraduate programs combine liberal arts with business curriculum; it also grants master's degrees in business administration entrepreneurship and other fields. Babson students in their first year receive the practical experience of creating for-profit ventures. Babson's entrepreneurship program has been ranked at the top of such programs in publications including Entrepreneur and U.S. News & World Report.

	Annual Growth	06/09	06/10	06/11	06/13	06/15
Sales ($ mil.)	3.5%	–	–	202.8	177.6	232.5
Net income ($ mil.)	(4.7%)	–	–	14.5	43.3	11.9
Market value ($ mil.)	–	–	–	–	–	–
Employees	–	–	–	–	–	750

BABYCENTER L.L.C.

163 Freelon St.
San Francisco CA 94107
Phone: 415-537-0900
Fax: 415-537-0909
Web: www.babycenter.com

CEO: –
CFO: –
HR: –
FYE: December 31
Type: Subsidiary

If the parenting information you're getting from other sources is a bit too infantile turn to BabyCenter. The company operates websites for parents of infants and young children. Its BabyCenter.com Baby.com and Pregnancy.com sites contain content for parents of offspring from pre-conception through age eight. The sites also include the BabyCenter Community feature for interactive communication advice and support. BabyCenter additionally has international sites and a retail partnership with Quidsi's Diapers.com to sell clothing and baby products online. Johnson & Johnson owns BabyCenter which was founded in 1997 by Matt Glickman and Mark Selcow. The firm was acquired by Johnson & Johnson in 2001.

BACK YARD BURGERS INC.

500 Church St. Ste. 200
Nashville TN 37219
Phone: 615-620-2300
Fax: 615-620-2301
Web: www.backyardburgers.com

CEO: Scott Shotter
CFO: –
HR: –
FYE: December 31
Type: Private

Back Yard Burgers offers diners the chance to eat a charbroiled burger without having to slave over hot coals. The company operates and franchises about 120 quick service restaurants in Tennessee Mississippi and more than 15 other states in the Southeast and Midwest. The eateries are known for their made-to-order charbroiled hamburgers made from 100% Black Angus beef. Back Yard Burgers' menu also includes chicken sandwiches chili milkshakes salads and cobbler. The company's "Grills on the Go" team caters events by grilling food on location. The firm was ounded by Lattimore Michael in 1987. Back Yard Burgers filed for bankruptcy in 2012.

BACKUS CORPORATION

326 Washington St.
Norwich CT 06360
Phone: 860-889-8331
Fax: 860-886-1219
Web: www.backushospital.org

CEO: –
CFO: –
HR: –
FYE: September 30
Type: Private

Backus Corporation is a real part of the backbone of Norwich and its environs. Backus Corporation is the parent company of The William W. Backus Hospital which was founded in 1893 and serves eastern Connecticut. The hospital has some 210 medical surgical and critical care beds. It provides specialty services such as trauma care cancer care neurology obstetrics urology and cardiology. The Backus Corporation network also includes several community health clinics outpatient and rehabilitation centers medical labs and a hospice. The Backus Foundation is a not-for-profit affiliate that solicits and receives contributions on behalf of the hospital. Backus has agreed to join Hartford Health Care.

BACTOLAC PHARMACEUTICAL INC.

7 Oser Ave. Unit 14
Hauppauge NY 11788-3808
Phone: 631-951-4908
Fax: 631-951-4749
Web: www.bactolac.com

CEO: Gregory Pusey
CFO: Renee Reynolds
HR: Casey Nunn
FYE: September 30
Type: Private

Bactolac Pharmaceutical (formerly Advanced Nutraceuticals) makes private-label vitamins minerals herbs and other over-the-counter nutritional supplement products. The company's encapsulated and tablet-based products are available already packaged and branded or sold in bulk to customers who repackage them for private-label sale. Customers include distributors retailers and multi-level marketing companies. Its services include product formulation sample runs and product testing. Chairman and CEO Pailla Reddy holds a majority of the company.

BADGER METER INC

NYS: BMI

4545 W. Brown Deer Road
Milwaukee, WI 53233
Phone: 414 355-0400
Fax: –
Web: www.badgermeter.com

CEO: Kenneth Bockhorst
CFO: Robert Wrocklage
HR: Sheryl Hopkins
FYE: December 31
Type: Public

Badger Meter is a leading innovator manufacturer and marketer of products incorporating flow measurement quality control and other system solutions serving markets worldwide. Badger is a major manufacturer of water meters and automatic meter reading (AMR) and advanced metering infrastructure (AMI) products which are mainly sold to municipalities(both residential and commercial). Its flow instrumentation business is made up of metering technologies for industrial markets including HVAC water and wastewater and heating. Established in 1905 Badger's product line includes meters valves and other sensing instruments. Majority of its sales come from the US.

	Annual Growth	12/16	12/17	12/18	12/19	12/20
Sales ($ mil.)	2.0%	393.8	402.4	433.7	424.6	425.5
Net income ($ mil.)	11.2%	32.3	34.6	27.8	47.2	49.3
Market value ($ mil.)	26.3%	1,077.0	1,393.3	1,434.4	1,892.6	2,741.6
Employees	0.6%	1,562	1,632	1,531	1,567	1,602

BADGERLAND MEAT AND PROVISIONS LLC

1849 Wright St.
Madison WI 53704
Phone: 608-244-1934
Fax: 608-244-9162
Web: www.badgerlandmeats.com

CEO: –
CFO: John Fueling
HR: –
FYE: December 31
Type: Private

All those University of Wisconsin sports fans have a place to buy meat. Badgerland Meat and Provisions stores wholesales and distributes beef pork and poultry products in its home state as well as parts of Illinois and Michigan. It sells to grocery chains meat markets restaurants and warehouses stores. The company gets its meat from producers such as American Foods Excel Farmland Foods Gold Kist and Iowa Turkey. Badgerland also operates a case-ready business for which the company cuts packs and distributes more than 300000 pounds of pre-packaged and pre-priced pork products every week.

BAE SYSTEMS INC.

1101 Wilson Blvd. Ste. 2000
Arlington VA 22209-2444
Phone: 703-312-6100
Fax: 703-312-6111
Web: www.baesystems.com

CEO: Thomas A Arseneault
CFO: –
HR: –
FYE: December 31
Type: Subsidiary

BAE Systems takes care of business in North America for UK-based parent BAE SYSTEMS plc — the largest foreign player in the US defense market. BAE Systems' military operations include the design manufacture and maintenance of armored combat vehicles weapons munitions and other defense systems. Affiliate BAE Systems also provides security information technology (IT) systems for defense commercial and law enforcement applications. It is a top supplier to the US Department of Defense (DoD) and adheres to the Pentagon's Special Security Agreement to ensure control of sensitive technology. The US division has operations in 38 states and in Germany Israel Mexico South Africa Sweden and the UK.

BAE SYSTEMS NORFOLK SHIP REPAIR INC.

750 W. Berkley Ave.
Norfolk VA 23523
Phone: 757-494-4000
Fax: 757-494-4184
Web: www.baesystems.com/productsservices/bae_eis_sh

CEO: –
CFO: –
HR: Mary Sharp
FYE: December 31
Type: Subsidiary

A giant white whale is no match for contractor BAE Systems Norfolk Ship Repair. The company is a leading non-nuclear ship repair modernization conversion and overhaul facility which operates at one of the US Navy's principal ports at Norfolk Virginia the home of the Atlantic Fleet. Parent company UK-based BAE SYSTEMS plc a defense security and aerospace company also has ship repair operations in San Diego (home of the Pacific Fleet). BAE Systems Norfolk Ship Repair is a full-service repair facility that focuses on dry dock and ship repair for the US Navy and other defense agencies as well as commercial customers such as cruise ship owners liquefied natural gas tankers ferries and cargo ships.

BAER'S FURNITURE CO., INC.

1589 NW 12TH AVE
POMPANO BEACH, FL 330691734
Phone: 954-946-8001
Fax: –
Web: www.baers.com

CEO: Jerome Baer
CFO: –
HR: –
FYE: December 31
Type: Private

Having assembled a furniture portfolio full of big-name brands Baer's Furniture counts the likes of Lexington Home Brands and Bernhardt as family. Family-owned Baer's Furniture operates about 15 mid-priced to high-end retail furniture showrooms and two warehouses in South Florida. The company offers furnishings (living room dining room bedroom and office furniture) bedding rugs and accessories made by popular manufacturers that are designed to fit the budgets of shoppers who have a little cash tucked away. The chain was founded in 1945 by Melvin and Lucile Baer in South Bend Indiana. Their sons Robert now the company's CEO and Allan company president moved the business to Florida in 1968.

	Annual Growth	12/11	12/12	12/13	12/15	12/16
Sales ($ mil.)	7.3%	–	143.2	160.8	196.8	189.8
Net income ($ mil.)	7.1%	–	9.5	10.6	16.6	12.5
Market value ($ mil.)	–	–	–	–	–	–
Employees	–	–	–	–	–	437

BAIN CAPITAL LLC

111 Huntington Ave.
Boston MA 02199
Phone: 617-516-2000
Fax: 617-516-2010
Web: www.baincapital.com

CEO: –
CFO: –
HR: –
FYE: December 31
Type: Private

If you want to make a big deal out of it chances are Bain Capital will get involved. The private equity and venture capital investor acquires and owns interests in companies in the business services retail and consumer products communications health care hospitality and technology sectors. The firm has made private equity investments in more than 250 companies since its 1984 founding. Its diverse portfolio currently includes stakes in such well-known companies as American Standard Burlington Coat Factory Clear Channel Communications Dunkin' Brands SunGard Data Systems Warner Music Group The Weather Channel and HD Supply the former wholesale construction supply business of The Home Depot.

BAIRD & WARNER HOLDING COMPANY

120 S. LaSalle
Chicago IL 60603
Phone: 312-368-1855
Fax: 312-368-1490
Web: www.bairdwarner.com

CEO: Stephen W Baird
CFO: Warren Habib
HR: Audra Lapointe
FYE: December 31
Type: Private

Baird & Warner knows its Chicagoland history. It has been around to witness events from the Great Fire in 1871 to the the Cubbies' last World Series win. Illinois' largest independent real estate brokerage offers residential sales financial services and title services in the Chicago area through more than 25 branch offices and some 1600 sales agents. Its listings include foreclosed properties ultra-luxury homes and some commercial properties. The firm also maintains a directory of vetted home services providers (cleaning repair landscaping etc.) to help sellers prepare their homes for sale. Baird & Warner was founded in 1855 and has been family-owned and operated for five generations.

BAKEMARK USA LLC

7351 Crider Ave.
Pico Rivera CA 90660
Phone: 562-949-1054
Fax: 562-948-5506
Web: www.yourbakemark.com

CEO: –
CFO: –
HR: Robert Braden
FYE: December 31
Type: Subsidiary

When it comes to baking BakeMark USA has the secret ingredient. The company makes a slew of ingredients and bakery goods such as cake and cookie mixes pie and pastry fillings various flours and yeast as well as pre-baked goods and paper supplies. Its lineup is sold under brand names: Produits Marguerite (nut pastes mousses custards for French pastries); Trigal Dorado (mixes and fillings for Mexican pastries); Westco (baked good mixes and dough). Customers are mainly US retail wholesale and in-store bakeries and bakery chains. BakeMark USA and sister subsidiary BakeMark Canada are part of Dutch ingredient maker CSM's Bakery Supplies North America business which generates about half of all CSM sales.

BAKER & HOSTETLER LLP

PNC Center 1900 E. 9th St. Ste. 3200
Cleveland OH 44114-3482
Phone: 216-621-0200
Fax: 216-696-0740
Web: www.bakerlaw.com

CEO: –
CFO: Kevin L Cash
HR: –
FYE: December 31
Type: Private - Partnershi

Like Major League Baseball a longtime client law firm Baker & Hostetler has players from coast to coast. The firm's more than 800 lawyers practice from about a dozen offices in the US from New York to Los Angeles. Besides baseball and other sports and entertainment enterprises the firm's roster of clients has included leading companies in the automotive energy health care hospitality and media industries. Among Baker & Hostetler's major practice groups are teams devoted to intellectual property business employment and labor and tax and litigation.

BAKER & MCKENZIE LLP

300 E. Randolph St. Ste. 5000
Chicago IL 60601
Phone: 312-861-8000
Fax: 312-861-2899
Web: www.bakermckenzie.com

CEO: –
CFO: –
HR: –
FYE: June 30
Type: Private

Baker & McKenzie believes big is good and bigger is better. One of the world's largest law firms it has about 4000 attorneys practicing from more than 70 offices — from Bangkok to Berlin to Buenos Aires — in almost 45 countries. It offers expertise in a wide range of practice areas including antitrust intellectual property international trade mergers and acquisitions project finance and tax law. Baker & McKenzie's client list includes big companies from numerous industries including banking and finance construction and technology as well as smaller enterprises.

BAKER BOOK HOUSE COMPANY

6030 FULTON ST E
ADA, MI 493019156
Phone: 616-676-9185
Fax: –
Web: www.bakerpublishinggroup.com

CEO: Dwight Baker
CFO: –
HR: –
FYE: April 30
Type: Private

Baker Publishing Group has a spirit in its step. The Christian publisher publishes books through seven market-focused divisions: Baker Books Baker Academic Bethany House Publishers Brazos Press Cambridge University Press Chosen Books and Revell. Its Baker Books division includes titles for pastors and church leaders featuring books on worship preaching counseling and leadership. Its Cambridge division focuses on bible publishing. Other imprints publish Christian fiction and self-help titles as well as books on subjects such as theology discipleship and Christian living. The company was founded in 1939 by Herman Baker.

	Annual Growth	04/12	04/13	04/14	04/15	04/16
Sales ($ mil.)	4.0%	–	53.2	56.4	54.5	59.9
Net income ($ mil.)	5.3%	–	4.0	4.7	1.4	4.7
Market value ($ mil.)	–	–	–	–	–	–
Employees		–	–	–	–	215

BAKER BOTTS L.L.P.

1 Shell Plaza 910 Louisiana St.
Houston TX 77002-4995
Phone: 713-229-1234
Fax: 713-229-1522
Web: www.bakerbotts.com

CEO: –
CFO: Lydia Companion
HR: –
FYE: December 31
Type: Private - Partnershi

Baker Botts is a Lone Star legal legend. The law firm's history stretches back to 1840 when founding partner Peter Gray was admitted to the bar of the Republic of Texas. The firm became Baker & Botts after Walter Browne Botts and James Addison Baker (great-grandfather of former US Secretary of State and current partner James A. Baker III) joined the partnership. The firm has some 725 lawyers in about a dozen offices worldwide. Over the years Baker Botts has represented numerous clients from the energy industry including Exxon Mobil and Halliburton. The firm practices in such areas as corporate intellectual property and tax law.

BAKER BOYER BANCORP

7 W. Main St.
Walla Walla WA 99362
Phone: 509-525-2000
Fax: 509-525-1034
Web: www.bakerboyer.com

OTC: BBBK
CEO: Mark Kajita
CFO: Jolene Riggs
HR: –
FYE: December 31
Type: Public

For Baker Boyer Bancorp it "is" personal. The holding company for Baker Boyer National Bank takes pride in the personal touch it applies to its services which include standard deposit products loans financial planning and insurance services. One- to four-family residential mortgages account for the largest portion of the bank's loan portfolio. Through Baker Boyer Wealth Management Services the company offers investments private banking brokerage and trust services. Baker Boyer National Bank serves individual and business customers through about 10 branches in southern Washington and northern Oregon. Founded in 1869 the family-owned company is the oldest bank in Washington State

BAKER CAPITAL

540 Madison Ave. 29th Fl.
New York NY 10022
Phone: 212-848-2000
Fax: 212-848-0660
Web: www.bakercapital.com

CEO: -
CFO: Joseph Saviano
HR: -
FYE: December 31
Type: Private

Cream puffs and tarts need not apply at Baker Capital. This Madison Avenue private equity firm is instead looking to take controlling or significant minority stakes in mainly later-stage communication and technology companies. In addition to providing funding Baker Capital also offers post-investment consulting services in such areas as strategy executive and board recruitment and international expansion. It typically exits its investments through a sale or an IPO within five years. The firm which has approximately $1.5 billion of funds under management owns stakes in about 20 companies in the US and Europe.

BAKER COMMODITIES INC.

4020 Bandini Blvd.
Los Angeles CA 90023
Phone: 323-268-2801
Fax: 323-268-5166
Web: www.bakercommodities.com

CEO: -
CFO: -
HR: -
FYE: December 31
Type: Private

This Baker is somewhere between a butcher and a candlestick maker. Baker Commodities is a rendering company that takes unused animal byproducts from meat processing plants supermarkets restaurants and butcher shops and produces animal fats and oils poultry and bone meal and tallow. These products then can be used to make candles cosmetics paints plastics organic detergents livestock feed pet food and biodiesel. It is one of the nation's largest rendering companies with 21 plants in about a dozen US states including four in California four in New York and one in Hawaii.

BAKER DONELSON BEARMAN CALDWELL & BERKOWITZ PC

First Tennessee Bldg. Ste. 2000 165 Madison Ave.
Memphis TN 38103
Phone: 901-526-2000
Fax: 901-577-2303
Web: www.bakerdonelson.com

CEO: Timothy M Lupinacci
CFO: -
HR: -
FYE: January 31
Type: Private - Partnershi

Law firm Baker Donelson Bearman Caldwell & Berkowitz has grown beyond its southern roots to represent clients with stakes in national and international issues as well as local and regional matters. The firm boasts more than 630 attorneys and public policy advisers in about 15 offices which are concentrated in the southeastern US; it also operates out of Washington DC and London. Baker Donelson's practice areas focus on real estate and construction contract drafting and licensing mediation dispute resolution intellectual property financial services and tax advisory issues among others. The law firm traces its roots back to 1888 when James F. Baker established his law firm in Tennessee.

BAKER HUGHES HOLDINGS LLC

17021 Aldine Westfield Road
Houston, TX 77073-5101
Phone: 713 439-8600
Fax: 713 439-8699
Web: www.bakerhughes.com

CEO: Lorenzo Simonelli
CFO: Brian Worrell
HR: -
FYE: December 31
Type: Public

Baker Hughes is a leading provider of services and equipment for drilling extracting moving processing and refining oil and natural gas. Its offerings range from tools for drilling wells and producing hydrocarbons to deepwater drilling equipment subsea production systems flexible pipe systems and mechanical-drive compression and power-generation applications as well as hardware and software for digitizing some operations. The company has worldwide reach operating in more than 120 countries. About 70% of Baker Hughes' revenue is from international customers. In 2019 General Electric sold its controlling interest in the company making Baker Hughes a majority publicly held company.

	Annual Growth	12/17	12/18	12/19	12/20	12/21
Sales ($ mil.)	4.4%	17,259.0	22,877.0	23,838.0	20,705.0	20,502.0
Net income ($ mil.)	-	(350.0)	120.0	241.0	(15,825.0)	(372.0)
Market value ($ mil.)	-	-	-	-	-	-
Employees	(4.2%)	64,000	66,000	68,000	55,000	54,000

BAKER MICHAEL INTERNATIONAL INC

500 GRANT ST STE 5400
PITTSBURGH, PA 152192523
Phone: 412-269-6300
Fax: -
Web: www.mbakerintl.com

CEO: Brian A Lutes
CFO: -
HR: -
FYE: December 31
Type: Private

Michael Baker Jr. is the first-born subsidiary of engineering and construction consulting group Michael Baker. Michael Baker Jr. focuses on engineering design for civil infrastructure and transportation projects which include highways bridges airports busways corporate headquarters data centers correctional facilities and educational facilities. The unit also provides planning geotechnical and environmental services in the water/wastewater pipeline emergency and consequence management resource management and telecommunications markets. Recent projects include facilities for the US government.

	Annual Growth	12/04	12/05	12/06	12/07	12/09
Sales ($ mil.)	8.3%	-	-	329.2	351.9	418.5
Net income ($ mil.)	-	-	-	(12.4)	10.2	15.5
Market value ($ mil.)	-	-	-	-	-	-
Employees	-	-	-	-	-	3,200

BALCHEM CORP.

52 Sunrise Park Road
New Hampton, NY 10958
Phone: 845 326-5600
Fax: -
Web: www.balchem.com

NMS: BCPC
CEO: Theodore Harris
CFO: Martin Bengtsson
HR: -
FYE: December 31
Type: Public

Balchem developed a technology that encapsulates ingredients used in food and animal health products; the microencapsulation improves nutritional value and shelf life and allows for controlled time release. Balchem also provides specialty gases such as ethylene oxide (used to sterilize medical instruments) propylene oxide (used to reduce bacteria in spice treating and chemical processing) and ammonia. The company is engaged in the development manufacture and marketing of specialty performance ingredients and products for the food nutritional feed pharmaceutical medical sterilization and industrial markets. Balchem presently has three reportable segments: Human Nutrition & Health; Animal Nutrition & Health; and Specialty Products.

	Annual Growth	12/16	12/17	12/18	12/19	12/20
Sales ($ mil.)	6.2%	553.2	594.8	643.7	643.7	703.6
Net income ($ mil.)	10.9%	56.0	90.1	78.6	79.7	84.6
Market value ($ mil.)	8.2%	2,716.7	2,609.2	2,536.4	3,290.0	3,730.0
Employees	6.1%	1,060	1,165	1,135	1,424	1,342

BALDOR ELECTRIC COMPANY

5711 R. S. Boreham Jr. St.
Fort Smith AR 72901
Phone: 479-646-4711
Fax: 479-648-5792
Web: www.baldor.com

CEO: Ronald E Tucker
CFO: George E Moeschner
HR: –
FYE: December 31
Type: Subsidiary

Electricity drives Baldor Electric's sales — and its products. The company manufactures industrial AC and DC electric motors controls and speed drives that power products ranging from material handling conveyors to fluid handling pumps. Other products include industrial grinders buffers polishing lathes and generators. Baldor Electric sells to OEMs primarily in the agricultural and semiconductor equipment industries and to independent distributors for resale as replacement parts. It has about two dozen plants in Canada China Mexico the UK and the US. Baldor Electric a subsidiary of ABB gets most of its sales in the US although it has customers in some 70 countries.

BALDWIN FILTERS INC.

4400 E. Hwy. 30
Kearney NE 68848-6010
Phone: 308-234-1951
Fax: 800-828-4453
Web: www.baldwinfilter.com

CEO: –
CFO: –
HR: Heather Kirk
FYE: November 30
Type: Subsidiary

Baldwin Filters wants to clear the air — and the fuel and the oil and a lot more. A key subsidiary of manufacturing group CLARCOR Baldwin Filters makes thousands of different products designed for the filtration of air fuel hydraulic and transmission fluid coolant and oil for all types of off-road heavy-duty and light trucks; locomotives; industrial mining and marine equipment; heavy-duty construction and agricultural equipment; as well as for passenger cars and SUVs. Baldwin Filters sells its products through a worldwide network of distributors. Founded in 1936 the company has operations in North America and throughout the world.

BALDWIN PIANO INC.

309 Plus Park Blvd.
Nashville TN 37217
Phone: 615-871-4500
Fax: 615-889-5509
Web: www.baldwinpiano.com

CEO: Henry Juszkiewicz
CFO: –
HR: –
FYE: December 31
Type: Subsidiary

The keys to success for Baldwin alternate in color — black and white. One of the top piano manufacturers in the US Baldwin Piano is best known for making concert and upright pianos under the Baldwin Howard Hamilton Chickering and Wurlitzer names. The company also makes ConcertMaster computerized player pianos. Its custom models feature hand-painted designs including gold-leaf scrollwork and pinstripes marble finishes and exotic leopard spots and zebra stripes. Gibson Guitar which has been working to breathe new life into Baldwin bought the ailing piano maker from GE Capital in 2001. Dwight Hamilton Baldwin established the company as Baldwin Piano & Organ in 1862.

BALDWIN RICHARDSON FOODS CO.

20201 S. LaGrange Rd. Ste. 200
Frankfort IL 60423
Phone: 815-464-9994
Fax: 815-464-9995
Web: www.brfoods.com

CEO: Eric Johnson
CFO: Evelyn White
HR: –
FYE: December 31
Type: Private

Baldwin Richardson is sweet on foods. The company started out in in 1916 making dessert toppings. Today it makes many kinds of liquid products for the food industry including condiments sauces syrups and fruit fillings. Baldwin Richardson Foods sells its products such as Mrs. Richardson's toppings and Nance's condiments to retail food customers. Its consumer offerings also include Baldwin ice cream Mrs. Richardson's ice cream toppings and Nance's mustards and condiments. In addition the company has customers in the food manufacturing and foodservice sectors. Baldwin Richardson offers private-label co-packing and contract-manufacturing services.

BALDWIN TECHNOLOGY COMPANY INC.

NYSE AMEX: BLD

2 Trap Falls Rd. Ste. 402
Shelton CT 06484-0941
Phone: 203-402-1000
Fax: 203-402-5500
Web: www.baldwintech.com

CEO: Joe Kline
CFO: Ivan R Habibe
HR: –
FYE: June 30
Type: Private

Baldwin Technology has pressing business. The company supplies an array of process automation technologies for commercial printing and newspaper publishing. It manufactures printing press equipment and control systems (such as for press cleaning ink control drying water-regulation and paper flow). Baldwin products are marketed as a premium technology via subsidiaries and distributors in about a dozen countries. Customers include printing press OEMs who bolt the products onto their own systems for sale to printers. The company also sells directly to printers wanting to upgrade their presses. Baldwin Technology was acquired by Forsyth Capital Investors in 2012.

BALFOUR BEATTY CONSTRUCTION GROUP, INC.

3100 MCKINNON ST FL 10
DALLAS, TX 752017007
Phone: 214-451-1000
Fax: –
Web: www.balfourbeattyus.com

CEO: Mark Layman
CFO: Richard Jaggers
HR: –
FYE: December 31
Type: Private

Balfour Beatty Construction is deep in the heart of Texas — and beyond. The company provides start-to-finish project management pre-construction and related services for commercial construction projects. Offerings include site evaluation and analysis general contracting cost consulting process equipment installation turnkey medical facility development capital equipment planning and closeout services. The company works on a range of facilities including hotels office buildings civic centers airports hospitals schools public buildings and retail locations. UK firm Balfour Beatty plc acquired the company then named Centex Construction from Centex Corp. in 2007.

	Annual Growth	12/11	12/12	12/13	12/14	12/15
Sales ($ mil.)	3.7%	–	3,459.0	3,816.9	3,933.0	3,852.8
Net income ($ mil.)	–	–	19.2	24.8	17.5	(14.7)
Market value ($ mil.)	–	–	–	–	–	–
Employees	–	–	–	–	–	2,495

BALFOUR BEATTY INFRASTRUCTURE, INC.

600 GALLERIA PKWY SE # 15
ATLANTA, GA 303395994
Phone: 707-427-8900
Fax: –
Web: www.balfourbeattyus.com

CEO: Ray Bond
CFO: Mark Birch
HR: –
FYE: December 31
Type: Private

Balfour Beatty is an industry-leading provider in the US of general contracting at-risk construction management and design-build services for public and private sector clients across the nation. Performing heavy civil and vertical construction it builds the unique structures and infrastructure that play an important role in how people live work learn and play in their communities. Consistently ranked among the nation's largest building contractors by Engineering News-Record its US business is a subsidiary of London-based Balfour Beatty plc. Its portfolio have included buildings rails highways and bridges and water. Beyond stand-alone projects it is involved in multiple joint ventures and works on some of the nation's largest public works projects including the design and construction of the $1.1 billion Texas State Highway 130 toll road.

	Annual Growth	12/11	12/12	12/13	12/14	12/15
Sales ($ mil.)	0.8%	–	–	509.3	555.6	517.8
Net income ($ mil.)	–	–	–	9.5	9.9	(3.4)
Market value ($ mil.)	–	–	–	–	–	–
Employees	–	–	–	–	–	1,100

BALKAMP INC.

2601 S. Holt Rd.
Indianapolis IN 46241
Phone: 317-244-7241
Fax: 317-381-2200
Web: www.balkamp.com

CEO: –
CFO: –
HR: –
FYE: December 31
Type: Subsidiary

A majority-owned subsidiary of Genuine Parts Balkamp distributes parts and accessories for cars trucks motorcycles and farm equipment to repair shops and retail members of the National Automotive Parts Association (NAPA). The company also provides diagnostics equipment cleaning supplies chemicals and other service-related items. Balkamp offers some 45000 items from about 600 domestic and foreign suppliers. It operates distribution centers in Indianapolis and Plainfield Indiana and West Jordan Utah. Balkamp was formed in 1936 by the NAPA board of directors. Its moniker blends the surnames of the company's first managers John Baldwin and Bob Leercamp.

BALL CORP

9200 West 108th Circle
Westminster, CO 80021
Phone: 303 469-3131
Fax: –
Web: www.ball.com

NYS: BLL
CEO: John Hayes
CFO: Scott Morrison
HR: –
FYE: December 31
Type: Public

The Ball Corporation is one of the world's leading suppliers of aluminum packaging for the beverage personal care and household products industries. Its largest product line is aluminum beverage containers and it also produces extruded aluminum aerosol containers aluminum slugs and aluminum cups. Its aerospace business produces spacecraft instruments and sensors radio frequency systems and components data exploitation solutions and a variety of advanced technologies and products. Ball Corporation operates in 100-plus locations with the US its largest market at approximately 55% of the total sales. The company was founded in 1880.

	Annual Growth	12/17	12/18	12/19	12/20	12/21
Sales ($ mil.)	5.9%	10,983.0	11,635.0	11,474.0	11,781.0	13,811.0
Net income ($ mil.)	23.8%	374.0	454.0	566.0	585.0	878.0
Market value ($ mil.)	26.3%	12,143.9	14,752.4	20,749.0	29,896.2	30,887.6
Employees	7.3%	18,300	17,500	18,300	21,500	24,300

BALL HORTICULTURAL COMPANY

622 Town Rd.
West Chicago IL 60185-2698
Phone: 630-231-3600
Fax: 630-231-3605
Web: www.ballhort.com

CEO: –
CFO: Todd Billings
HR: –
FYE: June 30
Type: Private

Flower power still reigns at Ball Horticultural. One of the nation's largest sellers of commercial seed for flowers and ornamental crops Ball Horticultural develops produces and distributes seeds young plants and cuttings to professional growers landscapers wholesalers and retailers. It operates in more than 20 countries through subsidiaries and joint ventures including PanAmerican Seed and Ball Seed. The firm sells through its own sales force and online. It also publishes FloraCulture International Green Profit and "GrowerTalks" magazines. Founded in 1905 by George Ball Ball Horticultural remains family owned. The Ball clan also owns W. Atlee Burpee a major seed seller to home gardeners.

BALL STATE UNIVERSITY

2000 W UNIVERSITY AVE
MUNCIE, IN 473060002
Phone: 765-289-1241
Fax: –
Web: www.bsu.edu

CEO: –
CFO: –
HR: –
FYE: June 30
Type: Private

Ball State University (BSU) has an enrollment of around 22540 undergraduate and graduate students. It offers approximately 120 undergraduate majors more than 100 graduate programs in seven academic colleges. It has a Teachers College as well as colleges of health; architecture and planning; business; communication information and media; fine arts; and sciences and humanities. BSU has a student-to-faculty ratio of 16:1. Notable alumni include late night talk show host David Letterman Garfield comic strip creator Jim Davis and John Schnatter the founder of Papa John's.

	Annual Growth	06/03	06/04	06/05	06/06	06/07
Sales ($ mil.)	3.4%	–	–	209.7	219.7	224.1
Net income ($ mil.)	35.6%	–	–	23.6	24.5	43.4
Market value ($ mil.)	–	–	–	–	–	–
Employees	–	–	–	–	–	6,426

BALLANTYNE STRONG, INC.

4201 Congress Street, Suite 175
Charlotte, NC 28209
Phone: 704 994-8279
Fax: –
Web: www.ballantynestrong.com

ASE: BTN
CEO: Mark Roberson
CFO: Todd Major
HR: –
FYE: December 31
Type: Public

Ballantyne Strong projects a lot of images. The company is an international supplier of motion picture theater equipment used by major theater chains such as AMC Entertainment and Regal Entertainment. Primary offerings include its digital projectors and accessories which it distributes through an agreement with NEC Solutions. The company also operates a cinema screen manufacturing business and offers specialty lighting equipment and services. Ballantyne Strong has international operations in Canada Hong Kong Beijing and China. The company exited the analog projector manufacturing business in early 2012.

	Annual Growth	12/16	12/17	12/18	12/19	12/20
Sales ($ mil.)	(27.2%)	76.7	72.6	64.7	62.6	21.5
Net income ($ mil.)	–	0.3	(3.6)	(12.3)	(10.1)	(0.3)
Market value ($ mil.)	(29.2%)	118.4	68.8	17.0	48.0	29.8
Employees	(7.7%)	320	335	294	296	232

BALLARD SPAHR LLP

1735 Market St. 51st Fl.
Philadelphia PA 19103-7599
Phone: 215-665-8500
Fax: 215-864-8999
Web: www.ballardspahr.com

CEO: -
CFO: -
HR: -
FYE: December 31
Type: Private - Partnershi

As a law firm Ballard Spahr employs more than 475 attorneys and operates 12 offices throughout the West and Mid-Atlantic. Ballard Spahr represents individuals and companies as well as other entitles globally in nearly 40 practice areas including construction franchise and distribution intellectual property and zoning and land use. The firm has particular expertise in climate change health care reform economic stabilization and recovery and legal guidance for distressed real estate projects. Clients have included Aetna Comcast the Philadelphia Phillies and The John Hopkins University. The firm was founded in 1886. In 2009 it shortened its name from Ballard Spahr Andrews & Ingersoll.

BALTIMORE ORIOLES L.P.

333 W. Camden St.
Baltimore MD 21201
Phone: 410-685-9800
Fax: 410-547-6277
Web: baltimore.orioles.mlb.com

CEO: -
CFO: -
HR: -
FYE: June 30
Type: Private

These birds are partial to Louisville timber. The Baltimore Orioles baseball team is a storied franchise of Major League Baseball boasting seven American League pennants and three World Series titles (its last in 1983). Organized as the Milwaukee Brewers in 1901 the team became the St. Louis Browns the next year and moved to Baltimore in 1954. The team's roster has boasted such Hall of Fame talent as Jim Palmer Cal Ripken Jr. and Brooks Robinson. The Orioles organization also has a controlling interest in Mid-Atlantic Sports Network a regional cable sports channel. Peter Angelos has controlled the team since 1993.

BALLY TECHNOLOGIES INC

6601 S. Bermuda Rd.
Las Vegas, NV 89119
Phone: 702-584-7700
Fax: 702-263-5636
Web: www.ballytech.com

NYS: BYI
CEO: -
CFO: -
HR: -
FYE: June 30
Type: Public

Bally Technologies helps keep the casinos buzzing. The firm is a leading manufacturer and supplier of casino gaming machines gaming operations and gaming information systems. Its gaming equipment segment includes both video and mechanical-reel slot machines used in gambling casinos in the US and abroad. Bally Technologies' gaming operations segment rents gaming devices and content and provides systems for linking slot machines together so players can gamble for progressively increasing jackpots. In addition the company's systems segment includes software and hardware that helps gaming operator customers with marketing player bonusing data management accounting player tracking and security services.

	Annual Growth	06/09	06/10	06/11	06/12	06/13
Sales ($ mil.)	3.1%	883.4	778.2	758.2	879.8	997.0
Net income ($ mil.)	2.9%	126.3	137.5	98.3	101.1	141.4
Market value ($ mil.)	17.2%	1,162.5	1,258.5	1,580.6	1,813.0	2,192.2
Employees	4.3%	2,907	2,620	2,827	3,146	3,443

BALTIMORE RAVENS LIMITED PARTNERSHIP

1 Winning Dr.
Owings Mills MD 21117
Phone: 410-701-4000
Fax: 410-654-6239
Web: www.baltimoreravens.com

CEO: -
CFO: -
HR: -
FYE: January 31
Type: Private

Named in honor of the Edgar Allan Poe poem the Baltimore Ravens Limited Partnership owns and operates Baltimore's National Football League franchise which won its first Super Bowl following the 2000 season and its second championship after the 2012 campaign. The team was created in 1996 when former Cleveland Browns owner Art Modell relocated his franchise to Maryland. As part of the deal Modell agreed to give up all rights to the Browns' name colors and history. The team plays host at M&T Bank Stadium. Stephen Bisciotti a local businessman who founded staffing firm Allegis Group acquired control of the team from Modell in 2004.

BALTIC TRADING LIMITED

299 Park Ave. 20th Fl.
New York NY 10171
Phone: 646-443-8550
Fax: 541-386-7316
Web: www.fullsailbrewing.com

NYSE: BALT
CEO: John C Wobensmith
CFO: Apostolos D Zafolias
HR: -
FYE: December 31
Type: Public

Baltic Trading swims against the current in international shipping. While most cargo carriers look for long-term contracts to fill their holds Baltic Trading operates in the spot market immediate charters that are usually single voyages. The company was formed in 2009 by parent Genco Shipping & Trading to serve the dry bulk industry. Its initial fleet of six drybulk vessels (two Capesize and four Supramax) will have an aggregate carrying capacity of 566000 deadweight tons (DWT). Genco is providing strategic and administrative services and establishing a link to companies like Cargill COSCO and Louis Dreyfus. Baltic Trading completed an IPO in 2010 with Genco investing $75 million for majority control.

BANC OF AMERICA MERCHANT SERVICES LLC

1231 Durrett Ln.
Louisville KY 40213-2008
Phone: 502-315-2000
Fax: 502-315-3535
Web: corp.bankofamerica.com/public/merchant/index.j

CEO: -
CFO: David E Fountain
HR: -
FYE: December 31
Type: Joint Venture

The next time you swipe your card and it clears you might thank Banc of America Merchant Services. A 2009 joint venture between Bank of America and First Data it is one of the largest processors of electronic payments in the US. The firm handles more than 7 billion check and credit debit stored value payroll and electronic benefits transfer card transactions (worth a total of some $250 billion) annually. Its clients are small businesses and large corporations including retailers restaurants hotels supermarkets utilities gas stations convenience stores and government entities. First Data owns 51% of Banc of America Merchant Services while Bank of America owns 49%.

BANC OF CALIFORNIA INC   NYS: BANC

3 MacArthur Place   CEO: Jared M Wolff
Santa Ana, CA 92707   CFO: Lynn M Hopkins
Phone: 855 361-2262   HR: -
Fax: -   FYE: December 31
Web: www.bancofcal.com   Type: Public

Banc of California delivers comprehensive products and solutions for businesses business owners and individual through about 30 branches from San Diego to Santa Barbara. Customers enjoy checking savings and money market accounts as well as mobile online and card payment services telephone banking automated bill payment safe deposit boxes direct deposit and wire transfers. In addition to its branches the $9 billion-asset Banc of California operates around loan production offices.

	Annual Growth	12/16	12/17	12/18	12/19	12/20
Assets ($ mil.)	(8.1%)	11,029.9	10,327.9	10,630.1	7,828.4	7,877.3
Net income ($ mil.)	(42.5%)	115.4	57.7	45.5	23.8	12.6
Market value ($ mil.)	(4.0%)	871.7	1,037.6	668.8	863.2	739.1
Employees	(23.6%)	1,797	738	741	660	611

BANCFIRST CORP. (OKLAHOMA CITY, OKLA)   NMS: BANF

101 N. Broadway   CEO: Darryl Schmidt
Oklahoma City, OK 73102-8405   CFO: Kevin Lawrence
Phone: 405 270-1086   HR: -
Fax: 405 270-1089   FYE: December 31
Web: www.bancfirst.com   Type: Public

This Oklahoma bank wants to be more than OK. It wants to be super. BancFirst Corporation is the holding company for BancFirst a super-community bank that emphasizes decentralized management and centralized support. BancFirst operates more than 100 branches in more than 50 Oklahoma communities. It serves individuals and small to midsized businesses offering traditional deposit products such as checking and savings accounts CDs and IRAs. Commercial real estate lending (including farmland and multifamily residential loans) makes up more than a third of the bank's loan portfolio while one-to-four family residential mortgages represent about 20%. The bank also issues business construction and consumer loans.

	Annual Growth	12/16	12/17	12/18	12/19	12/20
Assets ($ mil.)	7.0%	7,019.0	7,253.2	7,574.3	8,565.8	9,212.4
Net income ($ mil.)	9.0%	70.7	86.4	125.8	134.9	99.6
Market value ($ mil.)	(10.9%)	3,044.6	1,673.6	1,632.7	2,043.0	1,920.7
Employees	3.5%	1,773	1,782	1,906	1,948	2,036

BANCINSURANCE CORPORATION

250 E. Broad St. 10th Fl.   CEO: John S Sokol
Columbus OH 43215   CFO: Matthew C Nolan
Phone: 614-220-5200   HR: -
Fax: 614-228-5552   FYE: December 31
Web: www.bancins.com   Type: Private

Insurance holding company Bancinsurance Corporation underwrites niche insurance products through its subsidiary Ohio Indemnity Company. Operating throughout the US it provides coverage to protect auto dealers banks and other lenders by insuring collateralized personal property against damage and theft. It also bonds employers that elect not to pay unemployment taxes and provides waste management coverage. Policies are sold directly to lenders through subsidiary Ultimate Services Agency; Bancinsurance also sells insurance through independent agents. CEO John Sokol (son of founder Si Sokol) and his family own a controlling stake in the firm.

BANCO POPULAR NORTH AMERICA INC.

9600 W. Bryn Mawr Ave.   CEO: -
Rosemont IL 60018   CFO: -
Phone: 847-994-5400   HR: -
Fax: 847-994-6969   FYE: December 31
Web: www.bancopopular.com   Type: Subsidiary

Banco Popular North America (BPNA) is the mainland subsidiary of Puerto Rican bank Popular. Through Popular Community Bank (formerly Banco Popular) the company provides commercial banking products and services including deposit accounts loans and mortgages and insurance and investment products from approximately 100 branches in New York California Florida Illinois and New Jersey. (It exited Texas in 2008.) Faced with losses in the global financial downturn the company sold its Popular Equipment Financing leasing portfolio and stripped down the offerings of its online unit E-LOAN in 2009.

BANCORP OF NEW JERSEY, INC.   ASE: BKJ

1365 Palisade Avenue   CEO: -
Fort Lee, NJ 07024   CFO: -
Phone: 201 944-8600   HR: -
Fax: 201 944-8618   FYE: December 31
Web: www.bonj.net   Type: Public

Bancorp of New Jersey caters to individuals and small businesses on the west side of the Hudson River. It is the holding company for the Bank of New Jersey a community bank with about a half-dozen branches in Bergen County. The Bank of New Jersey offers personal and business checking and savings accounts as well as interest-bearing money market accounts CDs and IRAs. The bank's loan portfolio primarily consists of residential and commercial mortgages secured by real estate located in Bergen County. The holding company and the Bank of New Jersey were formed in 2006.

	Annual Growth	12/13	12/14	12/15	12/16	12/17
Assets ($ mil.)	9.8%	610.8	743.7	802.9	822.4	887.4
Net income ($ mil.)	(6.4%)	4.7	3.8	4.8	4.0	3.6
Market value ($ mil.)	8.0%	97.5	83.3	81.0	98.3	132.8
Employees	4.9%	66	71	74	75	80

BANCTEC INC.

2701 E. Grauwyler Rd.   CEO: Ronald Cogburn
Irving TX 75061-3414   CFO: -
Phone: 972-821-4000   HR: -
Fax: 972-821-4823   FYE: December 31
Web: www.banctec.com   Type: Private

Through its outsourced work BancTec keeps tabs on all sorts of financial transactions. The company offers electronic processing systems business process outsourcing (BPO) software hardware and services for government agencies banks utility and telecommunications companies. It serves other organizations too that do high-volume financial transactions. BancTec's systems and software capture and process checks bills and other documents. Products include digital archiving systems workflow software and scanners. Services include cost estimates and contingency planning. As part of its business BancTec operates more than 20 BPO centers globally.

BANCWEST CORPORATION

180 Montgomery St.
San Francisco CA 94104
Phone: 415-765-4800
Fax: 765-747-1473
Web: www.firstmerchants.com

CEO: Robert Harrison
CFO: Ralph Mesick
HR: –
FYE: December 31
Type: Subsidiary

BancWest knows which direction it's heading. The subsidiary of French banking group BNP Paribas is the holding company for Bank of the West and First Hawaiian Bank. On the US mainland Bank of the West founded in 1874 has more than 700 locations in some 20 states west of the Mississippi River. Founded in 1858 First Hawaiian has about 60 branches in Hawaii Guam and Saipan. The banks' services include residential and commercial real estate lending commercial banking (with expertise in niche lending such as agricultural loans church loans and loans to RV and boat dealers) consumer finance credit cards insurance investments private banking and wealth management. BNP Paribas acquired BancWest in 2001.

BAND-IT-IDEX INC.

4799 Dahlia St.
Denver CO 80216-0307
Phone: 303-320-4555
Fax: 303-333-6549
Web: www.band-it-idex.com

CEO: –
CFO: –
HR: –
FYE: December 31
Type: Subsidiary

It's not daylight robbery but Band-It-Idex's BAND-IT brand products are a steal when it comes to holding up other equipment and components. Band-It-Idex a subsidiary of IDEX Corporation makes a wide range of stainless steel clamping bundling fastening and identification products for a variety of industrial applications. The company's fasteners include clamps buckles hose fittings and mounting hardware. It also makes related manual and power installation tools. Band-It-Idex sells its clamps and other products worldwide to the aerospace/defense agricultural automotive communications construction manufacturing mining utilities oil and gas and transportation industries among others.

BANDAI AMERICA INCORPORATED

5551 Katella Ave.
Cypress CA 90630
Phone: 714-816-9500
Fax: 714-816-6710
Web: www.bandai.com

CEO: Masayuki Matsuo
CFO: –
HR: –
FYE: March 31
Type: Subsidiary

Confused as to who Ben Tennyson Loula and Lion-O are? Bandai America the North American marketing arm of Japanese toy maker Namco Bandai is happy to help clear up any game character and/or action figure confusion you may have. The company's portfolio of licensed and original toy and video game brands include Ben 10 ThunderCats Dragon Ball Z Harumika Pocoyo Power Rangers Tamagotchi and Teeny Little Families. Bandai America's operations consist of toy distribution Japanese animated video distribution (through Bandai Entertainment) video game production and the development of wireless technology and content that works with existing mobile phones.

BANK LEUMI USA

579 5th Ave.
New York NY 10017
Phone: 917-542-2343
Fax: 917-542-2254
Web: www.leumiusa.com

CEO: Avner Mendelson
CFO: –
HR: Julie Malyn
FYE: December 31
Type: Subsidiary

Bank Leumi USA is a subsidiary of Bank Leumi le-Israel one of Israel's largest banks. It specializes in commercial and international banking services to large and midsized corporations (particularly import and export lending) as well as lending to businesses in such industries as textiles and apparel real estate diamonds technology food and entertainment. The bank which also acts as an intermediary for American firms and individuals with investments in Israel has more than a dozen offices in California Florida Illinois New York and the Cayman Islands. The bank was established in New York in 1954.

BANK MUTUAL CORP

NMS: BKMU

4949 West Brown Deer Road
Milwaukee, WI 53223
Phone: 414 354-1500
Fax: –
Web: www.bankmutualcorp.com

CEO: –
CFO: –
HR: –
FYE: December 31
Type: Public

Bank Mutual Corporation wants to be the place America's Dairyland put its moo-la. Bank Mutual Corp. is the holding company for Bank Mutual which serves consumers and businesses through about 75 branches in Wisconsin and one in Minnesota. Founded in 1892 the bank offers standard products such as checking and savings accounts CDs and credit cards. The bank mainly uses funds gathered from deposits to originate a variety of loans and to invest in mortgage-backed securities and US government securities. Bank subsidiary BancMutual Financial and Insurance Services offers mutual funds annuities insurance and brokerage and investment advisory services.

	Annual Growth	12/11	12/12	12/13	12/14	12/15
Assets ($ mil.)	0.0%	2,498.5	2,418.3	2,347.3	2,328.4	2,502.2
Net income ($ mil.)	–	(47.6)	6.8	10.8	14.7	14.2
Market value ($ mil.)	25.2%	144.5	195.4	318.6	311.7	354.5
Employees	(2.0%)	719	720	722	715	663

BANK OF AMERICA CORP

NYS: BAC

Bank of America Corporate Center, 100 N. Tryon Street
Charlotte, NC 28255
Phone: 704 386-5681
Fax: –
Web: www.bankofamerica.com

CEO: Brian Moynihan
CFO: Alastair Borthwick
HR: –
FYE: December 31
Type: Public

Among the United States' largest banks by assets (alongside JPMorgan Chase and Citigroup) ubiquitous Bank of America Corporation operates one of the country's most extensive branch networks with nearly 4500 locations and roughly 17000 ATMs. The bank's core services include consumer and small and middle-market businesses institutional investors large corporations and governments with a full range of banking investing asset management and other financial and risk management products and services. Its online banking operation counts nearly 40 million active users and about 30 million mobile users. Bank of America acquired Merrill Lynch in 2009 making it one of the world's leading wealth managers with about $2.5 trillion assets under management and boasting a beefed up trading and international businesses. Its US operations account for the vast majority of sales.

	Annual Growth	12/17	12/18	12/19	12/20	12/21
Assets ($ mil.)	8.6%	2,281,234.0	2,354,507.0	2,434,079.0	2,819,627.0	3,169,495.0
Net income ($ mil.)	15.1%	18,232.0	28,147.0	27,430.0	17,894.0	31,978.0
Market value ($ mil.)	–	0.0	0.0	0.0	0.0	0.0
Employees	(0.1%)	209,000	204,000	208,000	213,000	208,000

BANK OF COMMERCE HOLDINGS (CA)
NMS: BOCH

555 Capitol Mall, Suite 1255
Sacramento, CA 95814
Phone: 800 421-2575
Fax: –
Web: www.bankofcommerceholdings.com

CEO: –
CFO: –
HR: –
FYE: December 31
Type: Public

Bank of Commerce Holdings provides traditional banking services through subsidiary Redding Bank of Commerce and its Roseville Bank of Commerce and Sutter Bank of Commerce divisions. It targets small to midsized businesses and medium-to high-net-worth individuals in the northern California communities of Redding Roseville and Yuba City. Through more than five branches the banks offer checking and savings accounts CDs IRAs and money market accounts. Commercial mortgages and business and industrial loans account for more than two-thirds of the company's loan portfolio.

	Annual Growth	12/15	12/16	12/17	12/18	12/19
Assets ($ mil.)	9.9%	1,015.4	1,141.0	1,269.4	1,307.1	1,479.6
Net income ($ mil.)	14.9%	8.6	5.3	7.3	15.7	15.0
Market value ($ mil.)	14.7%	121.2	172.3	208.6	198.8	209.8
Employees	6.2%	168	191	189	197	214

BANK OF HAWAII CORP
NYS: BOH

130 Merchant Street
Honolulu, HI 96813
Phone: 888 643-3888
Fax: –
Web: www.boh.com

CEO: Peter Ho
CFO: Dean Shigemura
HR: –
FYE: December 31
Type: Public

Bank of Hawaii Corporation is the holding company for Bank of Hawaii (familiarly known as Bankoh) which has about 70 branches and 380-plus ATMs in its home state plus an additional dozen in American Samoa Guam Palau and Saipan. Founded in 1897 the bank operates through four business segments: retail banking for consumers and small businesses in Hawaii; commercial banking including property/casualty insurance for middle-market and large corporations (this segment also includes the bank's activities beyond the state); investment services such as trust asset management and private banking; and treasury which performs corporate asset and liability management services.

	Annual Growth	12/16	12/17	12/18	12/19	12/20
Assets ($ mil.)	5.7%	16,492.4	17,089.1	17,144.0	18,095.5	20,603.7
Net income ($ mil.)	(4.0%)	181.5	184.7	219.6	225.9	153.8
Market value ($ mil.)	(3.6%)	3,558.2	3,438.2	2,700.8	3,817.8	3,073.9
Employees	(1.2%)	2,122	2,132	2,122	2,124	2,022

BANK OF KENTUCKY FINANCIAL CORP.
NMS: BKYF

111 Lookout Farm Drive
Crestview Hills, KY 41017
Phone: 859 371-2340
Fax: –
Web: www.bankofky.com

CEO: –
CFO: –
HR: –
FYE: December 31
Type: Public

The Bank of Kentucky Financial Corporation is the holding company for The Bank of Kentucky which provides a variety of personal and commercial banking services from more than 30 branches in northern portions of the Bluegrass State. It attracts deposits by offering checking and savings accounts CDs and IRAs. Commercial real estate loans make up about 30% of the bank's loan portfolio while residential mortgage loans account for more than 20%. Real estate loans account for about 80% of the bank's total loan portfolio. The Bank of Kentucky also offers business and consumer loans as well as credit cards investments and trust services.

	Annual Growth	12/09	12/10	12/11	12/12	12/13
Assets ($ mil.)	4.4%	1,565.0	1,664.9	1,744.7	1,844.1	1,857.5
Net income ($ mil.)	22.6%	8.8	11.7	16.5	18.1	19.8
Market value ($ mil.)	18.4%	143.1	147.9	152.8	188.4	281.2
Employees	1.3%	352	370	387	389	371

BANK OF MARIN BANCORP
NAS: BMRC

504 Redwood Boulevard, Suite 100
Novato, CA 94947
Phone: 415 763-4520
Fax: –
Web: www.bankofmarin.com

CEO: Timothy Myers
CFO: Tani Girton
HR: Robert Gotelli
FYE: December 31
Type: Public

Bank of Marin supports the wealthy enclave of Marin County north of San Francisco. The bank operates more than 20 branches in the posh California counties of Marin Sonoma and Napa as well as in San Francisco and Alameda counties. Targeting area residents and small to midsized businesses the bank offers standard retail products as checking and savings accounts CDs credit cards and loans. It also provides private banking and wealth management services to high net-worth clients. Commercial mortgages account for the largest portion of the company's loan portfolio followed by business construction and home equity loans.

	Annual Growth	12/16	12/17	12/18	12/19	12/20
Assets ($ mil.)	9.5%	2,023.5	2,468.2	2,520.9	2,707.3	2,911.9
Net income ($ mil.)	6.9%	23.1	16.0	32.6	34.2	30.2
Market value ($ mil.)	(16.2%)	941.7	918.0	556.8	608.2	463.6
Employees	2.6%	262	313	305	306	290

BANK OF NEW YORK MELLON CORP
NYS: BK

240 Greenwich Street
New York, NY 10286
Phone: 212 495-1784
Fax: –
Web: www.bnymellon.com

CEO: Thomas Gibbons
CFO: Emily Portney
HR: Jolen Anderson
FYE: December 31
Type: Public

The Bank of New York Mellon (BNY Mellon) is a New York state-chartered bank which houses the Investment Services businesses including Asset Servicing Issuer Services Treasury Services Clearance and Collateral Management as well as the bank-advised business of Asset. The firm boasts $37.1 trillion in assets under custody and administration and some $1.9 trillion in assets under management. BNY Mellon N.A. also offers wealth management services. Alexander Hamilton a founding father of the US and icon of the US $10 bill helped establish in 1784. The Bank of New York which merged in 2007 with Pittsburgh's Mellon Financial to form BNY Mellon.

	Annual Growth	12/16	12/17	12/18	12/19	12/20
Assets ($ mil.)	8.9%	333,469.0	371,758.0	362,873.0	381,508.0	469,633.0
Net income ($ mil.)	0.5%	3,547.0	4,090.0	4,266.0	4,441.0	3,617.0
Market value ($ mil.)	(2.7%)	42,014.9	47,761.5	41,740.0	44,630.8	37,634.2
Employees	(1.7%)	52,000	52,500	51,300	48,400	48,500

BANK OF SOUTH CAROLINA CORP
NAS: BKSC

256 Meeting Street
Charleston, SC 29401
Phone: 843 724-1500
Fax: –
Web: www.banksc.com

CEO: Fleetwood Hassell
CFO: Eugene Walpole
HR: –
FYE: December 31
Type: Public

What were you expecting something different? The Bank of South Carolina Corporation is the holding company for The Bank of South Carolina which was founded in 1987. It operates four branches in and around Charleston. Targeting individuals and small to midsized business customers the bank offers such standard retail services as checking and savings accounts credit cards and money market and NOW accounts. Real estate loans make up more than 70% of the The Bank of South Carolina's loan portfolio which also includes commercial loans (around 20%) and to a lesser extent personal loans. President and CEO Hugh Lane and his family control about 12% of the company.

	Annual Growth	12/16	12/17	12/18	12/19	12/20
Assets ($ mil.)	6.5%	413.9	446.6	429.1	445.0	532.5
Net income ($ mil.)	5.3%	5.2	4.9	6.9	7.3	6.5
Market value ($ mil.)	(6.4%)	115.4	106.6	100.5	103.7	88.5
Employees	0.7%	74	77	79	79	76

BANK OF THE CAROLINAS CORP
NBB: BCAR

135 Boxwood Village Drive
Mocksville, NC 27028
Phone: 336 751-5745
Fax: –
Web: www.bankofthecarolinas.com

CEO: –
CFO: –
HR: –
FYE: December 31
Type: Public

It would be more accurate to call it Bank of the North Carolina. Bank of the Carolinas Corporation was formed in 2006 to be the holding company for Bank of the Carolinas which provides traditional deposit and lending services to individuals and businesses through about 10 branches in central North Carolina. Deposit services include checking savings and money market accounts; IRAs; and CDs. Commercial real estate loans account for the largest portion of the company's loan portfolio; the bank's lending activities also include business construction and consumer loans residential mortgages and home equity lines of credit.

	Annual Growth	12/09	12/10	12/11	12/12	12/13
Assets ($ mil.)	(8.6%)	610.4	535.0	486.0	437.4	426.7
Net income ($ mil.)	–	(3.1)	(2.7)	(28.3)	(4.6)	(0.4)
Market value ($ mil.)	(36.0%)	17.3	9.7	1.1	0.8	2.9
Employees	(4.2%)	120	108	112	105	101

BANK OF THE JAMES FINANCIAL GROUP INC
NAS: BOTJ

828 Main Street
Lynchburg, VA 24504
Phone: 434 846-2000
Fax: –
Web: www.bankofthejames.com

CEO: Robert Chapman
CFO: J. Todd Scruggs
HR: –
FYE: December 31
Type: Public

Bank of the James Financial Group is the holding company for Bank of the James a financial institution serving central Virginia from about 10 branch locations. Catering to individuals and small businesses the bank offers standard retail products and services including checking and savings accounts CDs and IRAs. Funds from deposits are mainly used to originate residential mortgages which make up about half of the bank's loan portfolio and commercial and consumer loans. Subsidiary BOTJ Investment Group offers bank customers brokerage services annuities and related investment products through a third-party broker-dealer.

	Annual Growth	12/16	12/17	12/18	12/19	12/20
Assets ($ mil.)	10.3%	574.2	626.3	674.9	725.4	851.4
Net income ($ mil.)	11.0%	3.3	2.9	5.3	5.6	5.0
Market value ($ mil.)	(5.4%)	72.4	71.3	62.1	72.9	57.9
Employees	2.4%	133	143	158	160	146

BANK OF THE WEST

180 Montgomery St.
San Francisco CA 94104
Phone: 415-765-4800
Fax: 925-943-1224
Web: www.bankofthewest.com

CEO: J Michael Shepherd
CFO: Dan Beck
HR: –
FYE: December 31
Type: Subsidiary

Bank of the West can't "bear" the thought of customers banking elsewhere. The bank (which uses a bear as its logo) has more than 700 offices in some 20 states in the western and Midwestern US. Catering to consumers and small to midsized companies Bank of the West offers deposit accounts credit cards insurance investment products trust services and financial planning. It focuses its lending on residential mortgages and consumer loans which together make up about half of its loan portfolio. Parent company BancWest is owned by French bank BNP Paribas.

BANK OF VIRGINIA
NASDAQ: BOVA

11730 Hull Street Rd.
Midlothian VA 23112
Phone: 804-774-7576
Fax: 804-774-2306
Web: www.bankofva.com

CEO: –
CFO: –
HR: –
FYE: December 31
Type: Public

Bank of Virginia helps put the Rich in Richmond. The bank serves Chesterfield and Henrico counties from a handful of branches in Richmond Chester and Midlothian. It offers standard retail and commercial deposit services such as checking and savings accounts CDs IRAs and money market accounts. Commercial mortgages account for more than half of the bank's loan portfolio which also includes business loans one-to-four-family residential mortgages and construction loans. Consumer lending accounts for less than 1% of its portfolio. Washington DC-based Cordia Bancorp bought a majority of Bank of Virginia in 2010 and plans to buy the rest.

BANK OZK
NMS: OZK

18000 Cantrell Road
Little Rock, AR 72223
Phone: 501 978-2265
Fax: 501 978-2224
Web: www.bankozarks.com

CEO: –
CFO: –
HR: –
FYE: December 31
Type: Public

Bank of the Ozarks is the holding company for the bank of the same name which has about 260 branches in Alabama Arkansas California the Carolinas Florida Georgia New York and Texas. Focusing on individuals and small to midsized businesses the $12-billion bank offers traditional deposit and loan services in addition to personal and commercial trust services retirement and financial planning and investment management. Commercial real estate and construction and land development loans make up the largest portion of Bank of the Ozarks' loan portfolio followed by residential mortgage business and agricultural loans. Bank of the Ozarks grows its loan and deposit business by acquiring smaller banks and opening branches across the US.

	Annual Growth	12/16	12/17	12/18	12/19	12/20
Assets ($ mil.)	9.5%	18,890.1	21,275.6	22,388.0	23,555.7	27,162.6
Net income ($ mil.)	2.0%	270.0	421.9	417.1	425.9	291.9
Market value ($ mil.)	(12.2%)	6,802.5	6,267.0	2,953.1	3,945.8	4,044.8
Employees	3.5%	2,315	2,400	2,563	2,774	2,652

BANKERS FINANCIAL CORPORATION

11101 Roosevelt Blvd. North
St. Petersburg FL 33716
Phone: 727-823-4000
Fax: 727-823-6518
Web: www.bankersfinancialcorp.com

CEO: Dr John A Strong
CFO: Jim D Albert
HR: –
FYE: December 31
Type: Private

Bankers Financial Corporation has more to do with extended warranties and hurricanes than it does with checking and savings accounts. The holding company operates two primary arms: Bankers Insurance Group and Bankers Business Group. The insurance group offers commercial and personal lines through a handful of property/casualty carriers an annuity company and an insurance outsourcing services provider. The business group offers a range of services from bail bonds to new-home warranties to medical plans through a handful of companies in Florida. Its diverse portfolio even includes a private hunting and sporting club in the Florida woodlands called the Gilchrist Club and a parolee monitoring company.

BANKFINANCIAL CORP
NMS: BFIN

60 North Frontage Road
Burr Ridge, IL 60527
Phone: 800 894-6900
Fax: –

CEO: Frank Gasior
CFO: Paul Cloutier
HR: –
FYE: December 31
Type: Public

If you need a BankNow to handle your BankBusiness try BankFinancial. The bank serves individuals and businesses through about 20 branches in Cook DuPage Lake and Will counties in northeastern Illinois including parts of Chicago. It offers standard products such as checking and savings accounts credit cards and loans; services such as account management are available online. Multifamily residential mortgage loans make up 40% of its loan portfolio while another 40% is made up of commercial leases and non-residential mortgage loans. The bank also writes one-to-four family residential mortgages and home equity loans and lines of credit business loans and construction and land loans.

	Annual Growth	12/16	12/17	12/18	12/19	12/20
Assets ($ mil.)	(0.4%)	1,620.0	1,625.6	1,585.3	1,488.0	1,596.8
Net income ($ mil.)	5.1%	7.5	9.0	19.3	11.7	9.2
Market value ($ mil.)	(12.3%)	218.9	226.6	220.8	193.2	129.7
Employees	(3.4%)	264	259	260	242	230

BANKRATE INC (DE)
NYS: RATE

1675 Broadway, 22nd Floor
New York, NY 10019
Phone: 917 368-8600
Fax: –
Web: www.bankrate.com

CEO: Scott Kim
CFO: Ken Stelzer
HR: –
FYE: December 31
Type: Public

Bankrate knows there's life after budget-cutting. The firm's online network including flagship Bankrate.com provides information (including rate data and reviews) on more than 300 personal finance products including mortgages credit cards money market accounts and car and home equity loans. Bankrate culls information from about 4800 institutions covers nearly 600 local markets across the US and distributes content to about 175 media partners. Other Bankrate sites include InsureMe.com and NetQuote which sell leads to insurance agents and carriers and CreditCardGuide.com a credit card comparison website. Bankrate in 2011 filed to go public.

	Annual Growth	12/11	12/12	12/13	12/14	12/15
Sales ($ mil.)	(3.3%)	424.2	457.2	457.4	544.9	370.5
Net income ($ mil.)	–	(13.4)	29.3	(10.0)	5.2	(13.3)
Market value ($ mil.)	(11.3%)	2,081.1	1,205.1	1,736.5	1,203.1	1,287.4
Employees	4.2%	438	452	488	552	517

BANKUNITED INC.
NYS: BKU

14817 Oak Lane
Miami Lakes, FL 33016
Phone: 305 569-2000
Fax: –
Web: www.bankunited.com

CEO: Rajinder Singh
CFO: Leslie Lunak
HR: –
FYE: December 31
Type: Public

BankUnited is a bank holding company with one direct wholly-owned subsidiary BankUnited. BankUnited a national banking association provides a full range of commercial lending and both commercial and consumer deposit services through banking centers located in Florida and the New York metropolitan area. The Bank also provides certain commercial lending and deposit products through national platforms and certain consumer deposit products through an online channel. Deposit offerings include checking and savings accounts treasury management services and certificates of deposit. Commercial loans including multi-family residential mortgages account for some 80% of the bank's lending portfolio.

	Annual Growth	12/16	12/17	12/18	12/19	12/20
Assets ($ mil.)	5.9%	27,880.2	30,347.0	32,164.3	32,871.3	35,010.5
Net income ($ mil.)	(3.2%)	225.7	614.3	324.9	313.1	197.9
Market value ($ mil.)	(2.0%)	3,507.7	3,789.7	2,786.4	3,402.5	3,236.9
Employees	(3.2%)	1,706	1,763	1,790	1,511	1,495

BANNER CORP.
NMS: BANR

10 South First Avenue
Walla Walla, WA 99362
Phone: 509 527-3636
Fax: –
Web: www.bannerbank.com

CEO: Mark Grescovich
CFO: Peter Conner
HR: Kayleen Kohler
FYE: December 31
Type: Public

Flagging bank accounts? See Banner Corporation. Banner is the holding company for Banner Bank which serves the Pacific Northwest through about 100 branches and 10 loan production offices in Washington Oregon and Idaho. The company also owns Islanders Bank which operates three branches in Washington's San Juan Islands. The banks offer standard products such as deposit accounts credit cards and business and consumer loans. Commercial loans including business agriculture construction and multifamily mortgage loans account for about 90% of the company's portfolio. Bank subsidiary Community Financial writes residential mortgage and construction loans.

	Annual Growth	12/16	12/17	12/18	12/19	12/20
Assets ($ mil.)	11.3%	9,793.7	9,763.2	11,871.3	12,604.3	15,031.6
Net income ($ mil.)	7.9%	85.4	60.8	136.5	146.3	115.9
Market value ($ mil.)	(4.4%)	1,962.2	1,938.0	1,880.3	1,989.7	1,638.1
Employees	(0.2%)	2,137	2,128	2,187	2,198	2,116

BANNER PHARMACAPS INC.

4100 Mendenhall Oaks Pkwy Ste 301
High Point NC 27265
Phone: 336-812-3442
Fax: 336-812-7030
Web: www.banpharm.com

CEO: –
CFO: –
HR: –
FYE: December 31
Type: Subsidiary

Skip the spoonful of sugar Banner Pharmacaps uses gelatin to help the medicine go down. The company develops and makes a range of softgels for convenient oral dosage and delivery of prescription over-the-counter (OTC) and nutritional medicines and supplements. Its soft gelatin technologies are used in both branded and private-label OTC products such as pain and cold medicines. Banner also works with prescription drugmakers to enhance solubility and delivery methods for existing products as well as for compounds in clinical trial stages. It specializes in softgel technologies that control release rate and enhance performance of certain compounds. Parent company VION has agreed to sell Banner to Patheon.

BANNER-UNIVERSITY MEDICAL CENTER TUCSON CAMPUS LLC

1501 N CAMPBELL AVE
TUCSON, AZ 857240001
Phone:
Fax: –
Web: www.uahealth.ixt.com

CEO: –
CFO: –
HR: –
FYE: June 30
Type: Private

Banner - University Medicine (formerly The University of Arizona Health Network) heals Arizonans and trains Wildcats. It operates three academic medical centers in Phoenix and Tucson serving as the primary teaching hospital for the University of Arizona (UA) and offering medical treatment research and education services. The not-for-profit center provides cancer cardiology geriatric respiratory transplant and dialysis care as well as general practice and home health services. Specialty services include burn care behavioral health integrative medicine sports medicine and level I trauma care. The network merged with Banner Healthcare in 2015.

	Annual Growth	06/03	06/04	06/05	06/08	06/09
Sales ($ mil.)	(6.5%)	–	–	708.8	512.2	541.5
Net income ($ mil.)	–	–	–	0.0	27.1	0.0
Market value ($ mil.)	–	–	–	–	–	–
Employees	–	–	–	–	–	3,000

BAPTIST HEALTH

9601 BAPTIST HEALTH DR # 109
LITTLE ROCK, AR 722056323
Phone: 501-202-2000
Fax: -
Web: www.baptist-health.com

CEO: -
CFO: -
HR: -
FYE: December 31
Type: Private

For those seeking medical salvation Baptist Health may be the answer to their prayers. The organization provides health services through about 175 points of care scattered throughout in Arkansas. Its facilities include seven hospitals and a number of rehabilitation facilities family clinics and therapy and wellness centers. Arkansas Health Group a division of Baptist Health runs more than 20 physician clinics across the state. Specialized services include cardiology women's health orthopedics rehabilitation and home and hospice care. Baptist Health's Parkway Village is a 90-acre retirement community for active seniors located close to Baptist Health Medical Center - Little Rock.

	Annual Growth	12/08	12/09	12/17	12/18	12/20
Sales ($ mil.)	5.4%	-	924.0	875.4	1,215.9	1,650.6
Net income ($ mil.)	8.3%	-	64.5	49.4	(45.1)	155.2
Market value ($ mil.)	-	-	-	-	-	-
Employees	-	-	-	-	-	7,000

BAPTIST HEALTH CARE

1000 W. Moreno St.
Pensacola FL 32501
Phone: 850-434-4011
Fax: 850-469-2307
Web: www.ebaptisthealthcare.org

CEO: -
CFO: Joseph Felkner
HR: -
FYE: September 30
Type: Private - Not-for-Pr

Baptist Health Care strives for coastal health excellence. The firm operates hospitals clinics and a home health agency in northern and western Florida as well as southern Alabama. Founded in 1951 the Pensacola Florida-based not-for-profit health care system operates four acute-care hospitals including the 490-bed Baptist Hospital and 65-bed Gulf Breeze Hospital. Baptist Health Care in conjunction with its affiliates provides a wide variety of services such as home health care rehabilitation services and behavioral health services. Its Baptist Manor in Pensacola provides sub-acute care and long-term care and the Andrews Institute provides sports medicine services.

BAPTIST HEALTH SOUTH FLORIDA, INC.

6855 S RED RD
SOUTH MIAMI, FL 331433647
Phone: 305-596-1960
Fax: -
Web: www.baptisthealth.net

CEO: Alexandra Villoch
CFO: Ralph E Lawson
HR: -
FYE: September 30
Type: Private

Faith-based non-for-profit Baptist Health South Florida (BHSF) is the largest healthcare organization in the region With more than 1.5 million patient visits every year. Baptist Hospital is its flagship facility that offers a full range of medical and technological services and home to three Centers of Excellence ? Miami Cardiac & Vascular Institute Miami Neuroscience Institute and Miami Cancer Institute. Baptist Children's Hospital provides neonatal intensive care inpatient pediatric oncology services and pediatric care among other services.

	Annual Growth	09/08	09/09	09/15	09/17	09/19
Sales ($ mil.)	7.7%	-	616.1	846.4	608.3	1,294.0
Net income ($ mil.)	17.3%	-	121.3	137.4	244.3	598.5
Market value ($ mil.)	-	-	-	-	-	-
Employees	-	-	-	-	-	16,000

BAPTIST HEALTH SYSTEM, INC.

841 PRUDENTIAL DR # 1802
JACKSONVILLE, FL 322078329
Phone: 904-202-2000
Fax: -
Web: www.baptistjax.com

CEO: Michael Mayo
CFO: Michael Lukaszewski
HR: -
FYE: September 30
Type: Private

Founded in 1955 Baptist Health serves the Jacksonville Florida area through four acute care hospitals and a children's hospital with a combined total of more than 1200 physicians in about 90 specialties. Baptist MD Anderson Cancer Center is a regional destination for world-renowned cancer care which is clinically integrated with MD Anderson Cancer Center in Houston Across the street Wolfson Children's Hospital also cares for the city's youngest residents. The system's satellite acute-care facilities include Baptist Medical Center Beaches Baptist Medical Center Nassau and Baptist Medical Center South.

	Annual Growth	09/16	09/17	09/18	09/19	09/20
Sales ($ mil.)	7.4%	-	1,630.4	1,736.3	1,923.2	2,022.2
Net income ($ mil.)	(32.0%)	-	304.5	252.4	176.8	95.8
Market value ($ mil.)	-	-	-	-	-	-
Employees	-	-	-	-	-	7,000

BAPTIST HEALTHCARE SYSTEM, INC.

2701 EASTPOINT PKWY
LOUISVILLE, KY 402234166
Phone: 502-896-5000
Fax: -
Web: www.baptisthealth.com

CEO: Gerard Colman
CFO: Stephen R Oglesby
HR: -
FYE: August 31
Type: Private

Baptist Health owns eight acute-care hospitals in Kentucky with a total capacity of more than 2700 beds. The not-for-profit health system's largest facility is Baptist Health Louisville a 519-bed hospital in Louisville that provides a wide range of health services with special expertise in cardiology rehabilitation and women's health. In addition to its owned facilities Baptist Health manages Baptist Health Lexington a 434-bed tertiary care facility and Baptist Health Richmond with approximately 105 beds. The growing Baptist Health was founded as a single hospital in Louisville in 1924.

	Annual Growth	08/16	08/17	08/18	08/19	08/20
Sales ($ mil.)	3.7%	-	2,688.0	2,725.1	2,878.7	2,994.6
Net income ($ mil.)	224.5%	-	5.8	149.9	122.0	199.5
Market value ($ mil.)	-	-	-	-	-	-
Employees	-	-	-	-	-	12,601

BAPTIST HOSPITAL OF MIAMI, INC.

8900 N KENDALL DR
MIAMI, FL 331762197
Phone: 786-596-1960
Fax: -
Web: www.baptisthealth.net

CEO: -
CFO: Ralph Lawson
HR: -
FYE: September 30
Type: Private

Baptist Hospital of Miami can treat many vices for Miami residents. The flagship facility of the Baptist Health South Florida health system provides residents of the city with a full range of health care services including pediatric cancer home health rehabilitation neurology and cardiovascular care. The hospital has more than 680 beds and includes the Baptist Children's Hospital which offers a pediatric emergency room and a neonatal intensive care unit. Baptist Hospital of Miami also includes the Baptist Cardiac & Vascular Institute a regional cancer program and a diabetes care center. Baptist Hospital of Miami was founded in 1960.

	Annual Growth	09/15	09/16*	12/17*	09/18	09/19
Sales ($ mil.)	25.6%	-	867.8	1,004.3	1,169.4	1,717.7
Net income ($ mil.)	92.6%	-	39.5	73.2	143.7	282.2
Market value ($ mil.)	-	-	-	-	-	-
Employees	-	-	-	-	-	4,200

*Fiscal year change

BAPTIST MEMORIAL HEALTH CARE SYSTEM, INC.

350 N HUMPHREYS BLVD
MEMPHIS, TN 381202177
Phone: 901-227-5117
Fax: –
Web: www.bmhcc.org

CEO: Jason Little
CFO: –
HR: –
FYE: September 30
Type: Private

Serving portions of Tennessee Mississippi and Arkansas Baptist Memorial Health Care consists of 21 acute care and specialty hospitals and a network of urgent care clinic home health care and hospice operations. The health system has more than 2300 beds more than half of which are located in the greater Memphis area. Its flagship facility is Baptist Memorial Hospital-Memphis which offers advanced care in numerous medical specialties including cardiovascular disease and oncology. Through an affiliation with Baptist College of Health Sciences the organization provides undergraduate education in a number of health care fields including nursing and medical radiography.

	Annual Growth	09/08	09/09	09/10	09/12	09/15
Sales ($ mil.)	8.2%	–	124.1	136.2	161.9	199.5
Net income ($ mil.)	–	–	(3.5)	(1.5)	1.3	(10.0)
Market value ($ mil.)	–	–	–	–	–	–
Employees	–	–	–	–	–	9,877

BAPTIST MEMORIAL HOSPITAL

6019 WALNUT GROVE RD
MEMPHIS, TN 381202113
Phone: 901-226-5000
Fax: –
Web: www.baptistonline.org

CEO: Jason Little
CFO: Don Pounds
HR: Larry Braughton
FYE: September 30
Type: Private

When most of us think of Memphis we think of Elvis Presley. When doctors think of Memphis they think of Elvis and Baptist Memorial Hospital-Memphis. As the flagship facility of Baptist Memorial Health Care the 710-bed hospital often simply called Baptist Memphis offers patients the full spectrum of health care services including cancer treatment orthopedics surgical services and neurology. The campus also features the Baptist Heart Institute for cardiovascular care and research a pediatric emergency room a skilled nursing facility and the Plaza Diagnostic Pavilion for outpatient health care. Baptist Memphis established in 1979 is one of the state's highest volume hospitals.

	Annual Growth	09/11	09/12	09/13	09/14	09/15
Sales ($ mil.)	(0.3%)	–	697.3	504.3	663.5	691.0
Net income ($ mil.)	–	–	15.1	17.4	(47.8)	(1.2)
Market value ($ mil.)	–	–	–	–	–	–
Employees	–	–	–	–	–	6,000

BAR HARBOR BANKSHARES

P.O. Box 400, 82 Main Street
Bar Harbor, ME 04609-0400
Phone: 207 288-3314
Fax: –
Web: www.barharbor.bank

ASE: BHB
CEO: Curtis Simard
CFO: Josephine Iannelli
HR: –
FYE: December 31
Type: Public

Bar Harbor Bankshares which holds Bar Harbor Bank & Trust is a Maine -stay. Boasting $1.6 billion in assets the bank offers traditional deposit and retirement products trust services and a variety of loans to individuals and businesses through 15 branches in the state's Hancock Knox and Washington counties. Commercial real estate and residential mortgages loans make up nearly 80% of the bank's loan portfolio though it also originates business construction agricultural home equity and other consumer loans. About 10% of its loans are to the tourist industry which is associated with nearby Acadia National Park. Subsidiary Bar Harbor Trust Services offers trust and estate planning services.

	Annual Growth	12/16	12/17	12/18	12/19	12/20
Assets ($ mil.)	20.7%	1,755.3	3,565.2	3,608.5	3,669.1	3,725.8
Net income ($ mil.)	22.1%	14.9	26.0	32.9	22.6	33.2
Market value ($ mil.)	(16.9%)	706.0	402.9	334.6	378.7	337.0
Employees	30.0%	186	423	445	460	531

BARAN TELECOM INC.

2355 Industrial Park Blvd.
Cumming GA 30041
Phone: 678-513-1501
Fax: 678-513-1501
Web: www.barantelecom.com

CEO: Eyal Cohen
CFO: Talli Shechter
HR: –
FYE: December 31
Type: Subsidiary

Baran Telecom provides network infrastructure development services to the global wireless telecommunications industry. The company specializes in the planning design deployment and maintenance of mobile phone and other wireless and broadband networks. It has undertaken projects at more than 50000 communication facilities in all states of the US and in more than 35 countries in Europe Africa and Asia. Baran Telecom primarily serves mobile phone operators and other telecom carriers tower operators and equipment vendors. Clients have included Ericsson Nokia Orange and Vodafone. It is a subsidiary of Israel's engineering construction and technology giant Baran Group.

BARCELO CRESTLINE CORPORATION

3950 University Dr. Ste. 301
Fairfax VA 22030
Phone: 571-529-6000
Fax: 571-529-6050
Web: www.barcelocrestline.com

CEO: James A Carroll
CFO: –
HR: –
FYE: December 31
Type: Subsidiary

Though some of its hotels are upscale Barcelo Crestline Corporation's clientele includes more than just the upper crust. The company primarily operates through its Crestline Hotels & Resorts hotel management subsidiary which oversees a portfolio of about 50 hotels resorts and conference centers in nearly a dozen US states and Washington DC. Properties include leading hotel brands such as Marriott Hilton and Sheraton. Barcelo Crestline also has equity interests in several upscale hotels. The company was formed in 2002 when the Spanish hotel operator Barcelo Group acquired the American hotel operator Crestline Capital the parent company of Crestline Hotels & Resorts to set up an American branch.

BARCLAYS BANK DELAWARE

100 S WEST ST
WILMINGTON, DE 198015015
Phone: 302-255-8000
Fax: –
Web: www.cards.barclaycardus.com

CEO: Barry Rodrigues
CFO: –
HR: –
FYE: December 31
Type: Private

Spending money is a rewarding experience for holders of Barclays Bank Delaware cards. With co-branded credit cards from Barclays Bank Delaware (aka Barclays US) customers accumulate points that can be redeemed for air travel hotel stays and other perks. The company a division of Barclays issues Visa and MasterCard credit cards in addition to co-branded credit cards through partnerships with over 25 top companies including Priceline Choice Privileges Carnival World and JetBlue. Founded as Juniper Financial in 2000; it became a part of Barclays in 2004.

	Annual Growth	12/06	12/07	12/08	12/13	12/14
Assets ($ mil.)	18.8%	–	7,470.3	12,418.3	19,055.5	25,012.7
Net income ($ mil.)	–	–	0.0	20.6	331.6	239.8
Market value ($ mil.)	–	–	–	–	–	–
Employees	–	–	–	–	–	349

BARD (CR) INC

730 Central Avenue
Murray Hill, NJ 07974
Phone: 908 277-8000
Fax: -
Web: www.crbard.com

NYS: BCR
CEO: Timothy Ring
CFO: Christopher Holland
HR: Betty Larson
FYE: December 31
Type: Public

C. R. Bard has been in the medical device business for more than a century — it introduced the Foley urological catheter (still one of its top sellers) in 1934. Its products fall into four general therapeutic categories: vascular oncology urology and surgical specialties. Among other things the company makes stents catheters and guidewires used in angioplasties and other vascular procedures; catheters for delivering chemotherapy treatments; and urology catheters and products used to treat urinary incontinence. Its line of specialty surgical tools made by subsidiary Davol includes devices used in laparoscopic and orthopedic procedures and for hernia repair.

	Annual Growth	12/12	12/13	12/14	12/15	12/16
Sales ($ mil.)	5.9%	2,958.1	3,049.5	3,323.6	3,416.0	3,714.0
Net income ($ mil.)	0.1%	530.1	689.8	294.5	135.4	531.4
Market value ($ mil.)	23.1%	7,125.2	9,764.1	12,146.5	13,810.0	16,377.5
Employees	7.5%	12,200	13,000	13,900	14,900	16,300

BARD COLLEGE

30 CAMPUS RD
ANNANDALE ON HUDSON, NY 125049800
Phone: 845-758-7518
Fax: -
Web: www.bard.edu

CEO: -
CFO: -
HR: -
FYE: June 30
Type: Private

Although Shakespeare might appreciate the curriculum Bard College is not named for the Bard of Avon but for founder John Bard. The institution of higher learning is an independent nonsectarian residential coeducational four-year college of the liberal arts and sciences. Bard's total enrollment of 1900 includes some 600 graduate students. First-year students are required to take a three-week Workshop in Language and Thinking that emphasizes the connection between expression and thought. Students must also complete a year-long senior project that is reviewed by faculty members.

	Annual Growth	06/13	06/14	06/16	06/17	06/18
Sales ($ mil.)	(3.4%)	-	227.0	189.6	184.9	197.8
Net income ($ mil.)	-	-	(17.9)	(21.6)	18.9	(11.2)
Market value ($ mil.)	-	-	-	-	-	-
Employees	-	-	-	-	-	525

BARE ESCENTUALS INC.

71 Stevenson St. 22nd Fl.
San Francisco CA 94105
Phone: 415-489-5000
Fax: 877-963-3329
Web: www.bareescentuals.com

CEO: Leslie A Blodgett
CFO: Mike Gray
HR: -
FYE: December 31
Type: Subsidiary

When it comes to keeping its customers looking naturally pretty Bare Escentuals has a mineral interest. The company which rolled out its bareMinerals makeup brand in 1976 along with its first retail shop develops markets and sells natural cosmetics skin care and body care items. Brand names include bareMinerals Buxom md formulations RareMinerals and its namesake line. Bare Escentuals sells its products in the US through about 120 company-owned shops 880 beauty product retailers and 1500 spas and salons. It also has distributors in Canada Japan and the UK and other European countries. Japanese cosmetics company Shiseido acquired Bare Escentuals for about $1.8 billion in 2010.

BARKLEY INC.

1740 Main St.
Kansas City MO 64108
Phone: 816-842-1500
Fax: 830-788-7279
Web: www.jbfoods.com

CEO: Jeff King
CFO: Greg Trees
HR: -
FYE: December 31
Type: Private

Barkley (formerly known as Barkley Evergreen & Partners) is an employee-owned agency that integrates advertising and marketing services across such disciplines as public relations relationship marketing event marketing and interactive services. It has provided marketing communication services for such clients as Weight Watchers Sonic CITGO NASCAR and the Kansas Lottery. The agency serves national clientele through full-service offices in Kansas City Missouri and Pittsburgh with field offices located across the country. Units within Barkley include Barkley Blacktop and BarkleyREI.

BARNES & NOBLE COLLEGE BOOKSELLERS LLC

120 Mountain View Blvd.
Basking Ridge NJ 07920
Phone: 908-991-2665
Fax: 908-991-2846
Web: www.bncollege.com/

CEO: Max J Roberts
CFO: -
HR: -
FYE: April 30
Type: Subsidiary

Barnes & Noble College Booksellers is the scholastic subsidiary of Barnes & Noble (B&N) the nation's #1 bookstore chain. Established in 1965 the company operates some 645 bookstores serving more than 4 million students on college campuses nationwide selling textbooks (new used rental and electronic) trade books school supplies collegiate clothing and emblematic merchandise. It also offers merchandise through campus bookstores' websites. Universities medical and law schools and community colleges hire B&N College to replace traditional campus cooperatives. Some of its well-known campus bookstores include Boston University and Yale. B&N College accounts for nearly 25% of its parent company's sales.

BARNES & NOBLE, INC.

122 5TH AVE FL 2
NEW YORK, NY 100115634
Phone: 212-633-3300
Fax: -
Web: www.barnesandnobleinc.com

CEO: James Daunt
CFO: Allen W Lindstorm
HR: -
FYE: April 28
Type: Private

Barnes & Noble is one of the largest bookstore chains in the US operating more than 600 Barnes & Noble superstores in all 50 states and Washington DC. Carrying about 5500 magazine titles and nearly 1000 newspaper titles the company sold approximately 190 million physical books between its retail stores and online operations annually. In addition Barnes & Noble has approximately 1 million unique physical book titles sold per year. The company's NOOK brand develops supports and creates digital content and products for the digital reading and digital education markets. Founded in 1971 by bookseller Leonard Riggio Barnes & Noble is now owned by Elliott Advisors (UK) Limited.

	Annual Growth	04/14	04/15	04/16	04/17	04/18
Sales ($ mil.)	(6.2%)	-	-	4,163.8	3,894.6	3,662.3
Net income ($ mil.)	-	-	-	(24.4)	22.0	(125.5)
Market value ($ mil.)	-	-	-	-	-	-
Employees	-	-	-	-	-	24,000

BARNES & THORNBURG LLP

11 S. Meridian St.
Indianapolis IN 46204-3535
Phone: 317-236-1313
Fax: 317-231-7433
Web: www.btlaw.com

CEO: -
CFO: -
HR: -
FYE: December 31
Type: Private - Partnershi

Barnes & Thornburg's more than 550 attorneys counsel clients ranging from individuals to multinational corporations. With particular expertise in serving clients in the technology sector the law firm offers experience in more than 50 practice areas and industry specializations including health care intellectual property global logistics and taxation. Deeply seeded in the Midwest it also owns offices in Delaware and Washington DC. To increase its international footprint the firm is a part of TerraLex a global network of more than 150 law firms in about 100 jurisdictions. Barnes & Thornburg was founded in 1940 as Barnes Hickam Pantzer & Boyd.

BARNEYS NEW YORK INC.

575 5th Ave. 11th Fl.
New York NY 10017
Phone: 212-339-7300
Fax: 212-450-8489
Web: www.barneys.com

CEO: Mark Lee
CFO: Steven Feldman
HR: -
FYE: December 31
Type: Subsidiary

Barneys New York is no purple dinosaur even if it did have a brush with extinction. The luxury department store chain sells designer apparel for men women and children; shoes; accessories; and home furnishings. It operates more than 40 locations including 10 full-size Barneys New York flagship stores in New York City Beverly Hills Boston Chicago Dallas and other major cities; more than 15 smaller Barneys Co-Op shops; and about a dozen outlet stores. Founded in 1923 by Barney Pressman Barneys New York is owned by an affiliate of Istithmar PJSC an investment firm owned by the Dubai government. After a tough couple of years for luxury retailers Barneys has a new leader and is looking to recover.

BARNES GROUP INC.   NYS: B

123 Main Street
Bristol, CT 06010
Phone: 860 583-7070
Fax: -
Web: www.bginc.com

CEO: Patrick Dempsey
CFO: Julie Streich
HR: Dawn Edwards
FYE: December 31
Type: Public

Barnes Group is a global provider of highly engineered products differentiated industrial technologies and innovative solutions serving a wide range of end markets and customers. The aerospace and industrial components provide highly-engineered high-quality precision components products and systems for critical applications serving a diverse customer base in end-markets such as transportation industrial equipment automation personal care packaging electronics and medical devices as well as fabricated components and assemblies for turbine engines and airframes. Its customers include transportation industrial equipment automation personal care packaging electronics and medical devices located worldwide. Barnes Group generates about half of sales from the Americas.

	Annual Growth	12/17	12/18	12/19	12/20	12/21
Sales ($ mil.)	(3.2%)	1,436.5	1,495.9	1,491.1	1,124.4	1,258.8
Net income ($ mil.)	13.9%	59.4	166.2	158.4	63.4	99.9
Market value ($ mil.)	(7.4%)	3,206.8	2,717.7	3,140.4	2,569.2	2,361.4
Employees	(1.3%)	5,375	5,908	5,749	4,952	5,100

BARNHILL CONTRACTING COMPANY

2311 N. Main St.
Tarboro NC 27886
Phone: 252-823-1021
Fax: 252-823-0137
Web: www.barnhillcontracting.com

CEO: Robert E Barnhill Jr
CFO: William F Davis
HR: -
FYE: March 31
Type: Private

Barnhill Contracting Company provides general construction site development and heavy highway construction services throughout the Carolinas and Virginia. Barnhill's building division provides construction services in the industrial biotech office retail mixed-use hospitality correctional and institutional markets. The unit offers general construction construction management design/build and fast-track services. Barnhill Contracting also operates asphalt plants and has one of the largest construction equipment divisions in the US Southeast. The family-owned firm was founded in 1949 by Robert E. Barnhill Sr; it is headed by his son Robert Barnhill Jr.

BARNESANDNOBLE.COM LLC

76 9th Ave. 9th Fl.
New York NY 10011
Phone: 212-414-6000
Fax: 212-414-6140
Web: www.barnesandnoble.com

CEO: -
CFO: -
HR: -
FYE: January 31
Type: Subsidiary

barnesandnoble.com (BN.com) wants to be the Internet bookshelf's best seller. A subsidiary of the nation's #1 bookstore chain Barnes & Noble the online retailer sells books textbooks magazines music software videos toys and games and more. BN.com also features author interviews as well as book reviews from in-house editors customers and contributors to such sources as The Boston Globe The Wall Street Journal and The New Yorker. Other offerings include rare and out-of-print books and online book clubs. BN.com attracts bookworms from more than 230 countries. Under pressure from shareholders parent Barnes & Noble put itself up for sale in mid-2010.

BARNWELL INDUSTRIES, INC.   ASE: BRN

1100 Alakea Street, Suite 2900
Honolulu, HI 96813-2840
Phone: 808 531-8400
Fax: -
Web: www.brninc.com

CEO: Alexander Kinzler
CFO: Russell Gifford
HR: -
FYE: September 30
Type: Public

Barnwell Industries has more than a barnful of assets which range from oil and gas production contract well drilling and Hawaiian land and housing investments. Barnwell Industries explores for and produces oil and natural gas primarily in Alberta. In 2009 it reported proved reserves of 1.3 million barrels of oil and 20.6 billion cu. ft. of gas. Subsidiary Water Resources International drills water and geothermal wells and installs and repairs water pump systems in Hawaii. The company also owns a 78% interest in Kaupulehu Developments which owns leasehold rights to more than 1000 acres in Hawaii and is engaged in other real estate activities.

	Annual Growth	09/17	09/18	09/19	09/20	09/21
Sales ($ mil.)	8.6%	13.0	9.4	12.1	18.3	18.1
Net income ($ mil.)	52.0%	1.2	(1.8)	(12.4)	(4.8)	6.3
Market value ($ mil.)	13.9%	17.0	16.8	4.9	8.1	28.6
Employees	5.6%	29	31	43	43	36

BARRACUDA NETWORKS INC — NYS: CUDA

3175 S. Winchester Blvd.
Campbell, CA 95008
Phone: 408 342-5400
Fax: –
Web: www.barracuda.com

CEO: Hatem Naguib
CFO: Dustin Driggs
HR: –
FYE: February 29
Type: Public

Barracuda Networks hunts down network threats. The company provides firewalls that combine computer network hardware and software to protect enterprises from e-mail spam viruses and spyware. Other products include appliances for e-mail archiving Web filtering and load balancing. It serves businesses in industries such as consumer goods financial services manufacturing retail technology and utilities. Barracuda also provides professional services such as support consulting and implementation. Its extensive customer list has included Coca-Cola FedEx IBM and Toshiba. The company went public in 2013.

	Annual Growth	02/12	02/13	02/14	02/15	02/16
Sales ($ mil.)	18.8%	160.9	198.9	233.8	277.4	320.2
Net income ($ mil.)	–	0.6	(7.4)	(3.6)	(67.5)	(4.4)
Market value ($ mil.)	(40.2%)	–	–	1,874.3	1,985.8	670.5
Employees	10.4%	–	1,108	1,122	1,365	1,491

BARRETT (BILL) CORP — NYS: BBG

1099 18th Street, Suite 2300
Denver, CO 80202
Phone: 303 293-9100
Fax: –
Web: www.billbarrettcorp.com

CEO: Scot R Woodall
CFO: William M Crawford
HR: –
FYE: December 31
Type: Public

Bill Barrett Corp. (named after a veteran oil industry wildcatter) is hoping for a Rocky Mountain high as it digs down deep for oil and gas. The company focuses its exploration and development activities in the Wind River Uinta Piceance Big Horn Denver-Julesburg and Paradox Basins and the Montana Overthrusts. Bill Barrett holds almost 1.1 million net undeveloped leasehold acres. The bulk of its properties are unconventional resources such as shale gas. In 2012 the company had net working interests in more than 1360 wells and had estimated net proved reserves of more than 1 trillion cu. ft. of natural gas equivalent. Natural gas accounts for the bulk of its reserves.

	Annual Growth	12/12	12/13	12/14	12/15	12/16
Sales ($ mil.)	(28.9%)	700.2	568.1	472.3	207.9	178.8
Net income ($ mil.)	–	0.6	(192.7)	15.1	(487.8)	(170.4)
Market value ($ mil.)	(20.8%)	1,347.1	2,027.8	862.5	297.6	529.3
Employees	(24.6%)	344	258	202	139	111

BARRETT BUSINESS SERVICES, INC. — NMS: BBSI

8100 NE Parkway Drive, Suite 200
Vancouver, WA 98662
Phone: 360 828-0700
Fax: 360 828-0701
Web: www.barrettbusiness.com

CEO: Gary Kramer
CFO: Anthony Harris
HR: Jason Jocson
FYE: December 31
Type: Public

Barrett Business Services (BBSI) is employed in helping businesses. BBSI offers professional employment organization (PEO) services to some 7200 small and mid-sized businesses and their approximately 200000 employees. Its PEO services business provides outsourced human resource services such as payroll management benefits administration and other administrative functions. The company also offers temporary and long-term staffing services such as on-demand or short-term staffing on-site management contract staffing direct placement. Established in 1965 BBSI operates through about 65 branch offices in more than 10 US states. More than 75% of revenue comes from clients in California.

	Annual Growth	12/16	12/17	12/18	12/19	12/20
Sales ($ mil.)	1.2%	840.6	920.4	940.7	942.3	880.8
Net income ($ mil.)	15.8%	18.8	25.2	38.1	48.3	33.8
Market value ($ mil.)	1.6%	485.0	487.9	433.2	684.4	516.1
Employees	(0.1%)	115,746	124,212	122,958	127,085	115,075

BARRY (R.G.) CORP. — NMS: DFZ

13405 Yarmouth Road N.W.
Pickerington, OH 43147
Phone: 614 864-6400
Fax: –
Web: www.rgbarry.com

CEO: Greg Tunney
CFO: Jose Ibarra
HR: Yvonne Kalucis
FYE: June 29
Type: Public

R.G. Barry would be perfectly happy if women and men would scuff around everywhere in their slippers. As the world's leading maker and marketer of comfort footwear and slippers the company specializes in manufacturing soft slippers and casual footwear for men women and children. They're sold under such brands as Angel Treads Dearfoams EZfeet My College Footwear Terrasoles Soluna and Snug Treds as well as licensed names which account for most of its revenue. R.G. Barry sells its footwear through department stores nationwide. In 2011 the company added insoles and handbags to its lineup by acquiring a pair of non-shoe makers: Foot Petals and Baggallini.

	Annual Growth	06/09*	07/10	07/11*	06/12	06/13
Sales ($ mil.)	6.6%	113.8	123.8	129.6	155.9	147.0
Net income ($ mil.)	17.3%	7.0	9.4	7.5	14.5	13.3
Market value ($ mil.)	20.8%	86.2	127.6	129.2	153.4	183.4
Employees	(1.0%)	160	154	163	138	154

*Fiscal year change

BARRY UNIVERSITY, INC.

11300 NE 2ND AVE
MIAMI, FL 331616695
Phone: 305-899-3000
Fax: –
Web: www.barry.edu

CEO: –
CFO: –
HR: –
FYE: June 30
Type: Private

Barry University is a Catholic institution of Dominican heritage based in South Florida. With a student-faculty ratio of about 14:1 the liberal arts university annually enrolls about 3000 undergraduate students and some 4000 graduate students. The university's academic division includes two colleges (the College of Arts and Sciences and the College of Health Sciences) and seven schools. It offers more than 100 specializations and programs for undergraduate graduate and doctoral studies. Barry University also offers about 35 non-degree and certificate programs. Barry University was founded by the Adrian Dominican Sisters in 1940.

	Annual Growth	06/13	06/14	06/15	06/19	06/20
Sales ($ mil.)	(1.1%)	–	215.7	211.9	192.7	201.3
Net income ($ mil.)	(18.9%)	–	5.7	7.9	(0.4)	1.6
Market value ($ mil.)	–	–	–	–	–	–
Employees	–	–	–	–	–	1,407

BARRY-WEHMILLER GROUP, INC.

8020 FORSYTH BLVD
SAINT LOUIS, MO 631051707
Phone: 314-862-8000
Fax: –
Web: www.barrywehmiller.com

CEO: Robert H Chapman
CFO: –
HR: –
FYE: September 30
Type: Private

With Barry-Wehmiller you get the whole package. The company manufactures and supplies packaging corrugating paper converting filling and labeling automation equipment for a broad range of industries. It conducts business around the world through nine operating companies that together own more than 90 subsidiaries such as Accraply (labeling machinery) Design Group (automation and control systems) Winkler and Dunnebier (postage systems and tissue and hygiene) and Synerlink (ultra-clean packaging for milk products and desserts). Other divisions manufacture paper converting machinery and offer engineering/IT consulting services. Berry-Wehmiller is privately owned by the Chapman family who took over from Fred Wehmiller in 1963.

	Annual Growth	09/09	09/10	09/11	09/18	09/19
Sales ($ mil.)	11.2%	–	1,097.5	1,241.0	3,037.9	2,856.3
Net income ($ mil.)	–	–	0.0	0.0	85.0	77.9
Market value ($ mil.)	–	–	–	–	–	–
Employees	–	–	–	–	–	4,500

BARTON MALOW COMPANY

26500 AMERICAN DR
SOUTHFIELD, MI 480342252
Phone: 248-436-5000
Fax: –
Web: www.bartonmalow.com

CEO: –
CFO: Lars Luedeman
HR: –
FYE: March 31
Type: Private

Barton Malow scores by building end zones and home plates. The construction management and general contracting firm which has built its share of sporting facilities also focuses on projects such as schools hospitals offices and plants. Across the eastern US and Mexico the company offers design/build and program management services ranging from the pre-planning stage to completion. Projects have included the Detroit Institute of Arts and Cultural Center and the Baltimore Orioles stadium. Affiliate Barton Malow Design provides architecture and engineering services while Barton Malow Rigging installs process equipment and machinery. Carl Osborn Barton founded the employee-owned firm as C.O. Barton Company in 1924.

	Annual Growth	03/16	03/17	03/18	03/19	03/20
Sales ($ mil.)	(5.8%)	–	2,361.9	2,502.2	1,634.1	1,971.7
Net income ($ mil.)	202.9%	–	0.4	11.1	8.2	11.0
Market value ($ mil.)	–	–	–	–	–	–
Employees		–	–	–	–	1,600

BASF CATALYSTS LLC

25 Middlesex/Essex Tpke.
Iselin NJ 08830-0770
Phone: 732-205-5000
Fax: 732-321-1161
Web: www.catalysts.basf.com

CEO: –
CFO: –
HR: –
FYE: December 31
Type: Subsidiary

BASF Catalysts converts base materials into wealth — but no alchemy is involved. Part of chemicals giant BASF it makes chemical catalysts and adsorbents used in pharmaceutical steel and packaging products as well as other chemicals at some 30 sites worldwide. BASF Catalysts produces catalysts used in emission-control systems such as catalytic converters for automobiles. The unit holds leading global positions in making mobile emission catalysts process catalysts for the chemicals industry and fluid catalytic cracking catalysts for refineries. It also sources precious and base metals as raw materials for manufacturers. Its battery materials unit serves cell and battery manufacturers worldwide.

BASHAS' INC.

22402 S. Basha Rd.
Chandler AZ 85248
Phone: 480-895-9350
Fax: 480-895-5371
Web: www.bashas.com

CEO: Edward N Basha III
CFO: –
HR: –
FYE: December 31
Type: Private

Bashas' is working up a sweat standing its ground in the Southwest. The regional grocery chain operates about 130 stores (down from more than 160 in 2008) all but two of which are located in Arizona. (The other locations are in California and New Mexico.) Its holdings include Bashas' traditional supermarkets AJ's Fine Foods (gourmet-style supermarkets) and about a dozen Food City supermarkets (which cater to Hispanics in southern Arizona). It also runs a handful of Dine Markets in the Navajo Nation ("dine" means "the people" in Navajo) and Phoenix wine retailer Sportsman's Fine Wine and Spirits. Founded in 1932 family-owned Bashas' emerged from Chapter 11 bankruptcy in mid-2010 after closing stores.

BASIC AMERICAN INC.

2121 North California Blvd. Ste. 400
Walnut Creek CA 94596
Phone: 925-472-4000
Fax: 925-472-4360
Web: www.baf.com

CEO: Bryan Reese
CFO: James Collins
HR: –
FYE: December 31
Type: Private

Basic American Foods caters to your basic meat-and-potatoes kind of person. The company makes dehydrated potato products under such brands as Hungry Jack Nana's Own Potato Pearls Nature's Own Redi-Shred and WHIPP. Its portfolio includes a variety of potato products such as au gratin hash brown mashed and scalloped. It also produces Santiago brand refried and black beans as well as Quick-Start chili mixes. Basic American Foods has processing plants across the US and international operations in Mexico City and Hong Kong. The company's customers include foodservice distributors and operators industrial food manufacturers wholesale clubs and supermarkets.

BASIC ENERGY SERVICES INC

801 Cherry Street, Suite 2100
Fort Worth, TX 76102
Phone: 817 334-4100
Fax: –
Web: www.basices.com

NBB: BASX Q

CEO: Robert Reeb
CFO: –
HR: –
FYE: December 31
Type: Public

Basic Energy Services make wells flow. It provides onshore well-site services to the domestic oil & natural gas industry across the US. This includes completion and remedial services water logistics well servicing and manufacturing and rig servicing was realigned with Well Servicing segment. The company has significant presence in liquids-rich basins including the Permian Basin and the Bakken Eagle Ford Haynesville and Denver-Julesburg. Customers include a motley of some 2000 oil and gas companies.

	Annual Growth	12/16	12/17	12/18	12/19	12/20
Sales ($ mil.)	(6.9%)	547.5	864.0	964.7	567.3	411.4
Net income ($ mil.)	–	(123.4)	(96.7)	(144.6)	(181.9)	(268.2)
Market value ($ mil.)	(76.7%)	880.2	584.4	95.6	6.6	2.6
Employees	(7.4%)	3,800	4,100	4,100	3,000	2,800

BASIN ELECTRIC POWER COOPERATIVE

1717 E INTERSTATE AVE
BISMARCK, ND 585030564
Phone: 701-223-0441
Fax: –
Web: www.basinelectric.com

CEO: Paul M Sukut
CFO: Steve Johnson
HR: –
FYE: December 31
Type: Private

Ranges at home on the range depend on Basin Electric Power Cooperative as do other electric-powered items in nine states from Montana to Iowa to New Mexico. The consumer-owned power generation and transmission co-op provides power to 138 rural electric member systems which serve about 2.8 million people. It had generating capacity of 5478 MW (mostly coal-fired) in 2014. Basin Electric's subsidiaries include Dakota Gasification (which produces natural gas from coal) Dakota Coal (markets lignite and limestone) Basin Telecommunications (Internet access) Basin Cooperative Services (property management) PrairieWinds (wind power) and Souris Valley Pipeline (CO2 pipeline).

	Annual Growth	12/15	12/16	12/17	12/18	12/19
Sales ($ mil.)	13.0%	–	1,561.6	2,112.4	2,436.7	2,253.5
Net income ($ mil.)	12.0%	–	54.6	72.3	64.5	76.6
Market value ($ mil.)	–	–	–	–	–	–
Employees		–	–	–	–	1,579

BASIS TECHNOLOGY CORPORATION

150 CambridgePark Dr.
Cambridge MA 02140
Phone: 617-386-2000
Fax: 617-386-2020
Web: www.basistech.com

CEO: -
CFO: -
HR: -
FYE: December 31
Type: Private

Speaking only one language isn't a good basis for global growth. Basis Technology provides software for companies that want to establish multilingual Web sites products and sales channels. The company's Rosette Linguistics Platform includes text analysis tools for Arabic Asian European and other languages as well as data extraction tools that searches unstructured e-mail Web and other documents. Rosette allows developers to add Unicode (an international standard for software code) compliance to their products. Service offerings include project management engineering and globalization services. Customers have included Cisco L.L. Bean and US defense and intelligence agencies.

BASS PRO INC.

2500 E. Kearney
Springfield MO 65898
Phone: 417-873-5000
Fax: 308-254-4800
Web: www.cabelas.com

CEO: Johnny Morris
CFO: -
HR: Jane Gillard
FYE: December 31
Type: Private

Bass Pro knows how to reel in shoppers. The company operates about 60 Bass Pro Shops Outdoor World stores in the US and Canada that sell boats firearms equipment and apparel for most outdoor activities. Stores feature archery ranges fish tanks bowling lanes billiards tables and dining areas. Bass Pro also lures shoppers at home with its catalogs online store and TV and radio programs. Its first Outdoor World store (in Missouri) has been one of the state's biggest tourist attractions since it opened in 1981. Bass Pro owns Tracker Marine (boat manufacturing) and American Rod & Gun (sporting goods wholesale) and runs an 850-acre resort in the Ozark Mountains. Founder John Morris owns Bass Pro.

BASSETT FURNITURE INDUSTRIES, INC
NMS: BSET

3525 Fairystone Park Highway
Bassett, VA 24055
Phone: 276 629-6000
Fax: 276 629-6332
Web: www.bassettfurniture.com

CEO: Robert Spilman
CFO: John Daniel
HR: -
FYE: November 27
Type: Public

Bassett Furniture Industries is a leading retailer manufacturer and marketer of branded home furnishings. The company founded in 1902 makes wooden and upholstered furniture for home use featuring bedroom and dining suites furniture. Bassett sells through nearly 65 company-owned stores. Texas is the largest market among some 25 states in which Bassett operates. The company's logistics unit handles getting goods from factories and warehouses to stores; it has more than 940 vehicles on the road.

	Annual Growth	11/17	11/18	11/19	11/20	11/21
Sales ($ mil.)	1.8%	452.5	456.9	452.1	385.9	486.5
Net income ($ mil.)	(0.3%)	18.3	8.2	(1.9)	(10.4)	18.0
Market value ($ mil.)	(19.1%)	382.2	197.9	148.6	161.8	163.9
Employees	(5.3%)	2,754	2,735	2,579	2,071	2,219

BATESVILLE TOOL & DIE INC.

177 Six Pine Ranch Rd.
Batesville IN 47006
Phone: 812-934-5616
Fax: 812-934-5828
Web: www.btdinc.com

CEO: Jody Fledderman
CFO: -
HR: -
FYE: November 30
Type: Private

Carving its own niche in the metal stampings industry Batesville Tool & Die manufactures deep drawn stamping and motor housings using cutting edge design and stamping equipment and systems such as CAD systems Wire EDM CNC vertical machining centers and CNC horizontal lathes. Batesville primarily serves the automotive industry; customers include Ford General Motors and Honda. At its two facilities in Batesville Indiana and Queretaro Mexico the company makes a range of 500 metal stampings and assemblies. It also offers prototyping resistance welding and drilling. Batesville Tool & Die operates 40 presses at its US plant and four at its facility in Mexico.

BATH & BODY WORKS INC
NYS: BBWI

Three Limited Parkway
Columbus, OH 43230
Phone: 614 415-7000
Fax: -
Web: www.lb.com

CEO: Andrew Meslow
CFO: Wendy C Arlin
HR: -
FYE: January 30
Type: Public

L Brands (formerly Limited Brands) is as much of a shopping-mall mainstay as food courts and teenagers. The company operates about 2670 specialty stores in the US Canada and China primarily under the Victoria's Secret PINK and Bath & Body Works (BBW) banners as well as corresponding websites and catalogs. Originally focused on apparel the company turned into a segment leader focused on women's intimate and other apparel personal care and beauty and home fragrance products. L Brands also owns apothecary C.O. Bigelow and The White Barn.

	Annual Growth	01/17*	02/18	02/19	02/20*	01/21
Sales ($ mil.)	(1.5%)	12,574.0	12,632.0	13,237.0	12,914.0	11,847.0
Net income ($ mil.)	(7.6%)	1,158.0	983.0	644.0	(366.0)	844.0
Market value ($ mil.)	(8.8%)	16,404.8	13,207.8	7,547.7	6,438.5	11,331.3
Employees	(0.3%)	93,600	93,200	88,900	94,400	92,300

*Fiscal year change

BATH & BODY WORKS LLC

7 Limited Pkwy.
Reynoldsburg OH 43068
Phone: 614-856-6000
Fax: 614-856-6013
Web: www.bathandbodyworks.com

CEO: Nicholas Coe
CFO: Tom Fitzgerald
HR: -
FYE: January 31
Type: Subsidiary

Women turn to Bath & Body Works (BBW) to help wash away the daily stresses of life. A subsidiary of Limited Brands BBW operates more than 1650 stores throughout North America and an online shop. The company sells shower gels lotions antibacterial soaps home fragrance and accessories under its own BBW brand as well as the C.O. Bigelow and White Barn Candle Co. brands. Customers in need of rejuvenation can also find a line of aromatherapy and at-home spa treatments and in some stores extra indulgences such as massages and pedicures. The BBW brand has had an image makeover from country-inspired to a modern-day apothecary of beauty. BBW accounts for about a quarter of Limited Brands' sales.

BATH IRON WORKS CORPORATION

700 Washington St.
Bath ME 04530
Phone: 207-442-3311
Fax: 207-442-1567
Web: www.gdbiw.com

CEO: –
CFO: –
HR: –
FYE: December 31
Type: Subsidiary

Rub-a-dub-dub Bath Iron Works builds some really high-tech tubs. The company which is part of the Marine Systems group of parent company General Dynamics constructs surface ships for the US Navy. BIW is the lead designer and builder for the Arleigh Burke class AEGIS guided-missile destroyer and is building the next-generation Zumwalt class DDG-1000 land attack destroyer and the LPD-17 amphibious assault ship. BIW's Surface Ship Support Center offers design and engineering upgrades logistics manpower management fleet services and other support services. Among the largest private-sector employers in the state of Maine BIW built its first ship for the US Navy the gunboat "USS Machias" in the 1890s.

BATTALIA WINSTON INTERNATIONAL

555 Madison Ave.
New York NY 10022
Phone: 212-308-8080
Fax: 212-308-1309
Web: www.battaliawinston.com

CEO: Dale Winston
CFO: –
HR: –
FYE: December 31
Type: Private

Battalia Winston International provides senior-level executive searches in a variety of industries including the technology industrial products professional services consumer health care financial services and not-for-profit sectors. Founded in 1963 the company has locations in Boston; Chicago; Edison New Jersey; Los Angeles; and New York City. It has international capabilities through partnerships with search firms overseas that allow Battalia Winston to service clients in Asia Canada Europe and Latin America.

BATON ROUGE GENERAL MEDICAL CENTER

3600 FLORIDA ST
BATON ROUGE, LA 708063889
Phone: 225-387-7000
Fax: –
Web: www.brgeneral.org

CEO: Milton Sietman
CFO: –
HR: –
FYE: September 30
Type: Private

The first hospital founded in Louisiana's capital Baton Rouge General Medical Center is a not-for-profit full-service community hospital offering patients general medical and surgical care. Through the hospital's two locations Bluebonnet and Mid City Baton Rouge General also provides specialty services for cancer heart and neonatal care. In addition the nearly 530-bed health care facility provides services in areas such as burn treatment diabetes sleep disorders and behavioral health. Baton Rouge General Medical Center is the flagship facility of General Health System.

	Annual Growth	12/04	12/05*	09/08	09/09	09/15
Sales ($ mil.)	(14.9%)	–	2,026.2	281.9	304.6	403.1
Net income ($ mil.)	280.1%	–	0.0	2.5	0.8	20.8
Market value ($ mil.)	–	–	–	–	–	–
Employees	–	–	–	–	–	394

*Fiscal year change

BATTALION OIL CORP

3505 West Sam Houston Parkway North, Suite 3
Houston, TX 77043
Phone: 832 538-0300
Fax: –
Web: www.battalionoil.com

ASE: BATL
CEO: Richard Little
CFO: R. Kevin Andrews
HR: Katie Weingardt
FYE: December 31
Type: Public

The company changed its corporate name from Halcon Resources Corporation to Battalion Oil Corporation an independent energy company focused on the acquisition production exploration and development of onshore oil and gas properties in the US. After a string of asset sell-offs the company is focusing on the Delaware Basin in Texas. It has just about 140 net wells with oil and gas reserves at about 65 MMBoe beyond half of which is proved developed. The company has working interests in about 41675 net acres in the Delaware Basin in Pecos Reeves Ward and Winkler Counties Texas.

	Annual Growth	12/17	12/18*	10/19*	12/19	12/20
Sales ($ mil.)	(26.8%)	378.0	226.6	159.1	65.6	148.3
Net income ($ mil.)	–	535.7	46.0	(1,156.1)	(10.5)	(229.7)
Market value ($ mil.)	–	–	–	–	–	134.5
Employees	(20.4%)	119	116	–	69	60

*Fiscal year change

BATSON-COOK COMPANY

817 4th Ave.
West Point GA 31833
Phone: 706-643-2500
Fax: 706-643-2199
Web: www.batson-cook.com

CEO: Randall Hall
CFO: –
HR: –
FYE: October 31
Type: Subsidiary

Batson-Cook is well prepped in commercial construction. The firm offers general contracting construction management program management and design/build services throughout the Southeastern US. It has worked on a wide variety of projects including aerospace facilities courtrooms hospitals hotels industrial plants offices parking structures places of worship retail stores and schools. Clients have included Lockheed Martin Target and the University of Tampa. Batson-Cook began in West Point Georgia in 1915. It operates from a handful of regional offices in Georgia and Florida. Construction and development firm Kajima U.S.A. acquired Batson-Cook in 2008.

BATTELLE MEMORIAL INSTITUTE INC

505 KING AVE
COLUMBUS, OH 432012681
Phone: 614-424-6424
Fax: –
Web: www.battelle-japan.com

CEO: Lewis Von Thaer
CFO: –
HR: –
FYE: September 30
Type: Private

When you use a copier hit a golf ball or listen to a CD you're using technologies developed by Battelle Memorial Institute. The not-for-profit is one of the world's largest research enterprises with more than 22000 scientists engineers and staff serving corporate and government clients. Research areas include national security energy and health and life sciences. Battelle owns facilities in the US Asia and Europe and manages six Department of Energy-sponsored labs: Brookhaven National Laboratory Oak Ridge National Laboratory Idaho National Laboratory and Pacific Northwest National Laboratory. The institute was established by the family of steel industry pioneer Gordon Battelle in 1929.

	Annual Growth	09/12	09/13	09/14	09/15	09/16
Sales ($ mil.)	0.1%	–	4,796.0	4,769.9	4,783.6	4,810.7
Net income ($ mil.)	–	–	(7.3)	(111.9)	(63.1)	(19.3)
Market value ($ mil.)	–	–	–	–	–	–
Employees	–	–	–	–	–	7,457

BATTLE CREEK FARMERS COOPERATIVE, NON-STOCK

83755 HIGHWAY 121
BATTLE CREEK, NE 687155004
Phone: 402-675-2375
Fax: –

CEO: Dean Thernes
CFO: –
HR: –
FYE: November 30
Type: Private

From crop aggregation to fuel supply Battle Creek Farmers Cooperative provides its members with an arsenal of farm supplies and services. The co-op serves some 900 northeastern Nebraskan farmers. Its offerings include grain marketing soil nutrient inputs pest-control products seed animal feed transportation and energy (gasoline ethanol diesel kerosene propane and lubricants). The co-op processes soybeans and offers soybean meal and oil under the NewMaSoy brand. In addition to its administrative offices in Battle Creek Nebraska it operates 10 service centers. Battle Creek Farmers Cooperative was established in 1929.

	Annual Growth	11/08	11/09	11/10	11/11	11/12
Sales ($ mil.)	29.0%	–	–	120.6	188.5	200.8
Net income ($ mil.)	2.9%	–	–	6.2	7.5	6.5
Market value ($ mil.)	–	–	–	–	–	–
Employees	–	–	–	–	–	90

BAUER BUILT, INC.

1111 W PROSPECT ST
DURAND, WI 547361061
Phone: 715-672-8300
Fax: –
Web: www.bauerbuilt.com

CEO: Jerome M Bauer
CFO: Sean P Brant
HR: –
FYE: December 31
Type: Private

Bauer Built ensures its customers are well-treaded. The company owns about 30 automotive tire and service centers throughout the Midwest more than 10 wholesale distribution centers seven tire retread plants and three rim and wheel reconditioning centers. It delivers petroleum products (including gasoline ethanol biodiesel and kerosene) throughout eastern Minnesota and western Wisconsin as well as operates a car wash in Durand Wisconsin. Bauer Built was founded in 1944 by Sam Bauer the father of president Jerome "Jerry" Bauer as Bauer Oil Co. It got into the retread business in 1950. Employees own about 30% of the company; the Bauer family holds the remainder.

	Annual Growth	12/03	12/04	12/05	12/06	12/08
Sales ($ mil.)	4.3%	–	161.7	182.1	171.8	191.0
Net income ($ mil.)	6.7%	–	2.7	2.9	2.6	3.5
Market value ($ mil.)	–	–	–	–	–	–
Employees	–	–	–	–	–	450

BAUER PUBLISHING USA

270 Sylvan Ave.
Englewood Cliffs NJ 07632-2521
Phone: 201-569-6699
Fax: 201-510-3297
Web: www.bauerpublishing.com/

CEO: Hubert Boehle
CFO: –
HR: –
FYE: December 31
Type: Subsidiary

Feeling out of touch? Turn to Bauer Publishing USA publisher of celebrity and style magazines In Touch Weekly and Life & Style Weekly women's magazines "First" and "Woman's World" soap magazine Soaps in Depth and teen magazines "TWIST" M and "J-14". Bauer Publishing USA uses a European approach to publishing which includes a focus on newsstand not subscription sales. The company is owned by German parent company Bauer Verlagsgruppe (also known as The Bauer Publishing Group). The Bauer Publishing Group operates in the UK through Bauer Publishing USA sister companies H. Bauer Publishing and Bauer Consumer Media.

BAUSCH & LOMB INCORPORATED

1 Bausch & Lomb Place
Rochester NY 14604-2701
Phone: 585-338-6000
Fax: 585-338-6007
Web: www.bausch.com

CEO: –
CFO: Robert Bertolini
HR: –
FYE: December 31
Type: Private

The eyes are the windows to profit for Bausch & Lomb. Operating as Bausch + Lomb the eye care company is best known as a leading maker of contact lenses and lens care solutions (including the PureVision and ReNu brands). Along with its contact lens products Bausch + Lomb makes prescription ophthalmic drugs Alrex Lotemax and Zylet. It also makes over-the-counter vitamins and drops through its pharmaceuticals division. Its surgical unit makes instruments and equipment for cataract vitreoretinal and other ophthalmic surgeries. Bausch + Lomb markets its products in more than 100 countries worldwide. The company is owned by private equity firm Warburg Pincus.

BAXANO SURGICAL INC

NMS: BAXS

110 Horizon Drive, Suite 230
Raleigh, NC 27615
Phone: 919 800-0020
Fax: –

CEO: Kenneth Reali
CFO: Timothy M Shannon
HR: –
FYE: December 31
Type: Public

Baxano Surgical (formerly TranS1) wants to keep your lower lumbar limber. The medical device company designs develops and sells products that treat degenerative disc disease of the spine's lower lumbar region. Its AxiaLIF products allow spine surgeons to perform procedures on discs in the lower lumbar through an incision by the tailbone; doctors perform a fusion procedure through a tube that provides direct access to the degenerative disc. Baxano Surgical added the iO-Flex system which is used in spinal decompression procedures through the acquisition of Baxano Inc. in 2013; the company changed its name from TranS1 to Baxano Surgical following the purchase.

	Annual Growth	12/09	12/10	12/11	12/12	12/13
Sales ($ mil.)	(11.1%)	29.8	26.2	19.2	14.6	18.6
Net income ($ mil.)	–	(23.2)	(19.5)	(18.3)	(29.9)	(32.0)
Market value ($ mil.)	(28.9%)	182.3	96.0	85.9	114.5	46.6
Employees	(1.4%)	148	129	86	89	140

BAXTER COUNTY REGIONAL HOSPITAL, INC.

624 HOSPITAL DR
MOUNTAIN HOME, AR 726532955
Phone: 870-508-1000
Fax: –
Web: www.baxterregional.org

CEO: –
CFO: Ivan Holleman
HR: –
FYE: December 31
Type: Private

Hark! If you trip in the Ozarks rest assured that Baxter Regional Medical Center (BRMC) will be there to help. The not-for-profit acute care hospital provides services to residents of north central Arkansas and south central Missouri and has about 270 all-private rooms. BRMC provides general and advanced medical-surgical care in more than 30 medical specialties including cardiology oncology orthopedics women's health and physical rehabilitation. BRMC also runs several primary care and specialty clinics and a home health and hospice agency. The hospital started in 1963 with about 40 beds and four doctors.

	Annual Growth	12/13	12/14	12/15	12/16	12/19
Sales ($ mil.)	9.0%	–	164.0	167.5	178.5	252.2
Net income ($ mil.)	(7.8%)	–	10.6	(1.6)	0.4	7.0
Market value ($ mil.)	–	–	–	–	–	–
Employees	–	–	–	–	–	1,358

BAXTER INTERNATIONAL INC   NYS: BAX

One Baxter Parkway
Deerfield, IL 60015
Phone: 224 948-2000
Fax: 847 948-2964
Web: www.baxter.com

CEO: Jose Almeida
CFO: James Saccaro
HR: Jeanne Mason
FYE: December 31
Type: Public

Baxter International Inc. through its subsidiaries provides a broad portfolio of essential healthcare products including acute and chronic dialysis therapies; sterile intravenous (IV) solutions; infusion systems and devices; parenteral nutrition therapies; inhaled anesthetics; generic injectable pharmaceuticals; and surgical hemostat and sealant products. Baxter's products are sold in more than 100 countries; the company generates more than 40% of sales from the Americas segment (North and South America).

	Annual Growth	12/17	12/18	12/19	12/20	12/21
Sales ($ mil.)	4.9%	10,561.0	11,127.0	11,362.0	11,673.0	12,784.0
Net income ($ mil.)	15.7%	717.0	1,624.0	1,001.0	1,102.0	1,284.0
Market value ($ mil.)	7.3%	32,424.4	33,016.3	41,945.1	40,249.6	43,058.7
Employees	6.3%	47,000	50,000	50,000	50,000	60,000

BAY BANCORP INC   NAS: BYBK

7151 Columbia Gateway Drive, Suite A
Columbia, MD 21046
Phone: 410 494-2580
Fax: –
Web: www.baybankmd.com

CEO: –
CFO: –
HR: –
FYE: December 31
Type: Public

Carrollton Bancorp can babysit your money from Babe Ruth's hometown. It is the holding company for commercial banks serving Baltimore and surrounding areas from about two dozen branches operating under the Bay Bank and Carrollton Bank banners. It offers standard retail services such as checking and savings accounts money market accounts and IRAs. Commercial real estate and residential mortgages account for about 45% and 20% respectively of its loan portfolio. Subsidiary Carrollton Financial Services sells stocks bonds mutual funds and annuities; Carrollton Mortgage Services originates and sells residential mortgages. In 2013 Carrollton Bancorp merged with Jefferson Bancorp holding company of Bay Bank.

	Annual Growth	12/12	12/13	12/14	12/15	12/16
Assets ($ mil.)	14.2%	365.2	419.1	479.9	491.2	620.3
Net income ($ mil.)	–	(0.1)	3.2	3.0	1.9	1.8
Market value ($ mil.)	4.8%	57.1	51.4	45.9	52.9	69.0
Employees	(1.1%)	137	49	166	156	131

BAY CITIES PAVING & GRADING, INC.

1450 CIVIC CT STE 400
CONCORD, CA 945207950
Phone: 925-687-6666
Fax: –
Web: www.baycities.us

CEO: Ben L Rodriguez
CFO: –
HR: –
FYE: September 30
Type: Private

Up among the tall trees or down by the bay Bay Cities Paving & Grading is on the job. The company provides highway and street construction services for private and public projects primarily in Northern California. Bay Cities Paving also performs road improvements renovations and extensions on existing roads. The company has provided work for such clients as the cities of Elk Grove Brentwood and Pleasant Hill and the school district of West Contra Costa. Bay Cities Paving & Grading is one of the largest Hispanic-owned firms in the US.

	Annual Growth	09/05	09/06	09/07	09/08	09/09
Sales ($ mil.)	17.3%	–	73.9	100.3	96.2	119.1
Net income ($ mil.)	48.2%	–	1.5	7.7	9.4	4.9
Market value ($ mil.)	–	–	–	–	–	–
Employees	–	–	–	–	–	250

BAY COUNTY HEALTH SYSTEM, LLC

615 N BONITA AVE
PANAMA CITY, FL 324013623
Phone: 850-769-1511
Fax: –
Web: www.baymedical.org

CEO: Steve Grubbs
CFO: Chris Brooks
HR: –
FYE: September 30
Type: Private

Bay Medical Center is a 320-bed regional hospital located in the Florida panhandle. the center provides general medical and surgical services. The hospital's specialized services and programs include an open-heart surgery program a cancer center women's and children's health and emergency care. It also operates centers for sleep disorder and childhood communication disorders. Bay Medical Center has a staff of more than 300 physicians. The hospital also operates outpatient facilities for primary care and diagnostics. Bay Medical Center is operated by a joint venture between Sacred Heart Health System and LHP Hospital Group.

	Annual Growth	09/06	09/07	09/08	09/09	09/10
Sales ($ mil.)	(52.3%)	–	–	966.2	231.6	219.7
Net income ($ mil.)	–	–	–	0.0	4.4	(5.9)
Market value ($ mil.)	–	–	–	–	–	–
Employees	–	–	–	–	–	1,150

BAYCARE HEALTH SYSTEM, INC.

2985 DREW ST
CLEARWATER, FL 337593012
Phone: 727-820-8200
Fax: –
Web: www.baycare.org

CEO: Steve Mason
CFO: –
HR: –
FYE: December 31
Type: Private

BayCare Health System is the leading not-for-profit health care system that connects individuals and families to a wide range of services at hundreds of locations in the Tampa Bay and West Central Florida regions. The system's member hospitals boast approximately 4000 beds; the facilities offer a variety of specialty services ranging from orthopedics to cancer care to women's services. BayCare has about 6000 physicians and medical professionals. Established in 1997 the health system operates approximately 15 not-for-profit hospitals nearly 15 outpatient imaging facilities and about 20 urgent care centers.

	Annual Growth	12/11	12/12	12/13	12/14	12/19
Sales ($ mil.)	12.0%	–	–	–	464.0	818.6
Net income ($ mil.)	6.9%	–	–	–	163.6	228.4
Market value ($ mil.)	–	–	–	–	–	–
Employees	–	–	–	–	–	20,000

BAYER CORPORATION

100 Bayer Rd.
Pittsburgh PA 15205-9741
Phone: 412-777-2000
Fax: 412-777-3883
Web: www.bayerus.com

CEO: –
CFO: –
HR: –
FYE: December 31
Type: Subsidiary

For when you can't "bayer" the pain Bayer Corporation makes your medicine. The US headquarters of pharmaceuticals and materials giant Bayer AG (or Bayer Group) the company oversees the US subsidiaries of Bayer's three global divisions: Bayer HealthCare (pharmaceuticals animal health and over-the-counter medicines) MaterialScience (plastics coatings and polyurethanes) and Bayer CropScience (herbicides fungicides and insecticides). Bayer Corp.'s internal services unit Bayer Business and Technology Services handles administrative technology human resources legal and procurement functions for the Bayer Group's US operations. Bayer Corp. has around 50 sales and manufacturing locations in the US.

BAYER HEALTHCARE PHARMACEUTICALS INC.

6 W. Belt
Wayne NJ 07470-6806
Phone: 973-694-4100
Fax: 973-487-2003
Web: pharma.bayer.com

CEO: -
CFO: -
HR: -
FYE: December 31
Type: Subsidiary

Bayer HealthCare Pharmaceuticals Inc. brings the Bayer recipe for health to the US market. The company develops and markets prescription medicines for sale in the US and is part of the global Bayer HealthCare Pharmaceuticals (formerly Bayer Schering Pharma) division which is based in Germany. In addition to being a leading provider of women's health products including birth control and hormone therapies (YAZ and Mirena) Bayer HealthCare Pharmaceuticals sells specialty therapeutics in areas including diagnostic imaging hematology neurology and cancer. It makes products that target serious chronic diseases such as multiple sclerosis (Betaseron) and general health ailments such as infections (Avelox).

BAYLAKE CORP. (WI)
NAS: BYLK

217 North Fourth Avenue
Sturgeon Bay, WI 54235
Phone: 920 743-5551
Fax: -
Web: www.baylake.com

CEO: -
CFO: -
HR: -
FYE: December 31
Type: Public

Baylake Corp. is the holding company for Baylake Bank which provides financial services from about 25 offices in northeastern Wisconsin. Serving individuals and local businesses the bank provides standard products and services such as checking and savings accounts IRAs CDs credit cards mortgages and personal and business loans. It also offers trust financial planning asset management and brokerage services. Additionally Baylake Bank owns an insurance agency and holds a 49.8% stake in United Financial Services which performs electronic banking and data processing services for Baylake and other banks. Nicolet Bankshares agreed to acquire Baylake in September 2015.

	Annual Growth	12/10	12/11	12/12	12/13	12/14
Assets ($ mil.)	(0.7%)	1,052.5	1,086.9	1,024.0	996.8	1,021.6
Net income ($ mil.)	67.4%	1.1	4.5	7.6	8.0	8.9
Market value ($ mil.)	32.1%	37.1	38.0	68.8	117.9	113.1
Employees	(5.2%)	323	310	274	267	261

BAYLOR HEALTH CARE SYSTEM

3500 Gaston Ave.
Dallas TX 75246
Phone: 214-820-0111
Fax: 214-820-4697
Web: www.bhcs.com

CEO: Joel T Allison
CFO: Fredrick Savelsberg
HR: -
FYE: June 30
Type: Private - Not-for-Pr

The Baylor Health Care System (BHCS) offers an array of health care services throughout the Dallas-Fort Worth metroplex. BHCS owns or operates about two dozen acute care and specialty hospitals including the Baylor University Medical Center complex one of the state's major teaching and referral facilities. Other facilities include about 25 surgery centers and more than 250 physician and outpatient care centers as well as senior health clinics pharmacies and research labs. The faith-based (with Baptist roots) non-for-profit system also provides home health care and specialized pediatric services. BHCS is exploring a merger with Scott & White Healthcare.

BAYLOR UNIVERSITY

700 S UNIV PKS DR STE 67
WACO, TX 767061003
Phone: 254-710-1561
Fax: -
Web: www.baylor.edu

CEO: Robert Sloan PHD
CFO: -
HR: -
FYE: May 31
Type: Private

Don't mess with Texas and don't mess around at Baylor University. The world's largest Baptist institution of higher learning requires its more than 15000 students to follow a strict code of conduct. The university has approximately 150 undergraduate degree programs as well as about 75 masters and more than 30 doctoral programs. With a student-to-faculty ratio of 15:1 the private co-educational university also offers degrees from its law school (juris doctor) and theological seminary (master of divinity and doctor of ministry) as well as extensive research programs. Founded in 1845 the college is affiliated with the Baptist General Convention of Texas.

	Annual Growth	05/17	05/18	05/19	05/20	05/21
Sales ($ mil.)	10.9%	-	674.7	710.3	791.7	920.5
Net income ($ mil.)	76.0%	-	96.2	19.8	142.4	524.1
Market value ($ mil.)	-	-	-	-	-	-
Employees		-	-	-	-	2,500

BAYLOR UNIVERSITY MEDICAL CENTER

2001 BRYAN ST STE 2200
DALLAS, TX 752013024
Phone: 214-820-3151
Fax: -
Web: www.bswhealth.com

CEO: -
CFO: -
HR: -
FYE: June 30
Type: Private

Baylor University Medical Center at Dallas is the flagship institution of the Baylor Health Care System. The medical center (known as Baylor Dallas) serves more than 300000 patients annually with more than 1000 inpatient beds and some 1200 physicians. It offers general medical and surgical services to specialty care in a wide range of fields including oncology cardiovascular disease and neuroscience. The hospital also features a Level I trauma center neonatal ICU and organ transplantation center. Founded in 1903 the Baylor Dallas campus includes the Charles A. Sammons Cancer Center and the Baylor Research Institute which conducts basic and clinical research across numerous medical specialties.

	Annual Growth	06/05	06/06	06/08	06/09	06/15
Sales ($ mil.)	4.5%	-	937.2	155.9	1,072.7	1,394.6
Net income ($ mil.)	14.3%	-	114.1	16.1	0.0	379.0
Market value ($ mil.)	-	-	-	-	-	-
Employees		-	-	-	-	5,003

BAYOU CITY EXPLORATION INC
NBB: BYCX

632 Adams Street, Suite 700
Bowling Green, KY 42101
Phone: 270 282-8544
Fax: -
Web: www.bcexploration.com

CEO: Stephen C Larkin
CFO: Stephen Larkin
HR: -
FYE: December 31
Type: Public

An affiliate of the Blue Ridge Group Bayou City Exploration is engaged in oil and gas exploration primarily in Texas and Louisiana. It conducts its activities through partnerships and the acquisition of direct stakes in oil and gas properties and in exploratory and development wells. In 2008 the company reported proved reserves of about 1.1 billion cu. ft. of natural gas equivalent. The Blue Ridge Group owns 14% of Bayou City Exploration. Shifting its exploration focus from Appalachia to the Gulf Coast in 2005 Blue Ridge Energy the exploration and production unit of Blue Ridge Group renamed itself Bayou City Exploration. To raise cash in 2010 the company sold its stakes in two wells in Texas.

	Annual Growth	12/08	12/09	12/10	12/11	12/12
Sales ($ mil.)	84.2%	0.3	1.0	1.4	1.4	3.3
Net income ($ mil.)	-	(0.2)	0.8	0.5	0.3	0.8
Market value ($ mil.)	-	0.0	0.1	0.0	0.0	0.4
Employees	0.0%	1	-	2	2	1

BAYOU CITY EXPLORATION INC.

OTC: BYCX

632 Adams St. Ste. 710
Bowling Green KY 42101
Phone: 800-798-3389
Fax: 312-220-6212
Web: www.lapizusa.com

CEO: Stephen C Larkin
CFO: Stephen Larkin
HR: –
FYE: December 31
Type: Public

An affiliate of the Blue Ridge Group Bayou City Exploration is engaged in oil and gas exploration primarily in Texas and Louisiana. It conducts its activities through partnerships and the acquisition of direct stakes in oil and gas properties and in exploratory and development wells. In 2008 the company reported proved reserves of about 1.1 billion cu. ft. of natural gas equivalent. The Blue Ridge Group owns 14% of Bayou City Exploration. Shifting its exploration focus from Appalachia to the Gulf Coast in 2005 Blue Ridge Energy the exploration and production unit of Blue Ridge Group renamed itself Bayou City Exploration. To raise cash in 2010 the company sold its stakes in two wells in Texas.

BAYSIDE FUEL OIL DEPOT CORP

1776 SHORE PKWY
BROOKLYN, NY 112146546
Phone: 718-372-9800
Fax: –
Web: www.baysidedepot.com

CEO: –
CFO: –
HR: –
FYE: December 31
Type: Private

A tree isn't the only thing that has grown in Brooklyn. So has Bayside Fuel Oil Depot which provides heating oil to customers in New York through its own four Brooklyn terminals and from two other locations the 149th Street terminal in the Bronx and the Western Nassau terminal in Nassau County. The company was founded in 1937 as a retail distributor of heating oil by Sergio Allegretti In 1965 Bayside Fuel became a wholesale oil terminal operator. It sold its retail business in 2001. Vincent Allegretti the grandson of the company's founder runs the business.

	Annual Growth	12/02	12/03	12/04	12/05	12/12
Sales ($ mil.)	7.4%	–	146.0	152.8	195.5	276.5
Net income ($ mil.)	–	–	0.7	1.1	1.2	(3.3)
Market value ($ mil.)	–	–	–	–	–	–
Employees	–	–	–	–	–	36

BAYSTATE HEALTH INC.

759 CHESTNUT ST
SPRINGFIELD, MA 011991001
Phone: 413-794-0000
Fax: –
Web: www.baystatehealth.org

CEO: Mark Alvin Keroack
CFO: Dennis W Chalke
HR: –
FYE: September 30
Type: Private

Baystate Medical Center is the flagship facility of the not-for-profit Baystate Health System. It is a tertiary care facility and Level I trauma center that provides comprehensive acute care services to residents of Springfield Massachusetts and the surrounding region. The more than 700-bed medical center is also a teaching hospital serving as a secondary campus for Tufts University School of Medicine. The Baystate Medical Center campus includes Baystate Children's Hospital a 110-bed/57-bassinette unit that boasts neonatal and pediatric ICUs. Other Baystate Medical Center operations include specialty programs in radiology cardiac care cancer and neurology.

	Annual Growth	09/14	09/15	09/16	09/17	09/18
Sales ($ mil.)	7.0%	–	1,048.4	1,095.7	1,217.9	1,284.5
Net income ($ mil.)	(6.4%)	–	76.8	108.4	107.4	63.0
Market value ($ mil.)	–	–	–	–	–	–
Employees	–	–	–	–	–	11,000

BAYSTATE HEALTH SYSTEM HEALTH SERVICES, INC.

280 CHESTNUT ST
SPRINGFIELD, MA 011991000
Phone: 413-794-9939
Fax: –

CEO: –
CFO: –
HR: –
FYE: September 30
Type: Private

Patients in need of medical care can dock at this bay. Not-for-profit Baystate Health is the largest health care services provider in western Massachusetts. The system operates five acute-care and specialty hospitals with a total of approximately 1000 beds including the flagship Baystate Medical Center which operates a Level 1 Trauma Center and a specialized children's hospital. Baystate Health also offers ancillary medical services such as cancer care respiratory care infusion therapy visiting nurse and hospice services through its regional clinics and agencies. The system controls for-profit health plan provider Health New England as well as clinical pathology firm Baystate Reference Laboratories.

	Annual Growth	09/03	09/04	09/05	09/06	09/07
Sales ($ mil.)	–	–	0.0	0.0	1,209.9	1,286.3
Net income ($ mil.)	–	–	0.0	0.0	83.7	125.0
Market value ($ mil.)	–	–	–	–	–	–
Employees	–	–	–	–	–	5,000

BAZAARVOICE INC.

NMS: BV

10901 South Stonelake Blvd.
Austin, TX 78759-5749
Phone: 512 551-6000
Fax: –
Web: www.bazaarvoice.com

CEO: Keith Nealon
CFO: –
HR: –
FYE: April 30
Type: Public

Bazaarvoice considers itself the voice of the marketplace. Its e-commerce software helps retailers and other companies collect socially-generated online consumer feedback about their brands in order to tailor their sales marketing and customer service initiatives. Clients use its flagship Bazaarvoice Conversations platform to offer features such as rate and review Q&A and syncing to Facebook profiles. The Bazaarvoice Connections platform provides a brand interaction network to share captured information. Its Media Solutions creates advertising from word-of-mouth content. Bazaarvoice also offers search engine optimization (SEO) services. Altogether it counts more than 1000 retailers as customers.

	Annual Growth	04/12	04/13	04/14	04/15	04/16
Sales ($ mil.)	17.1%	106.1	160.3	168.1	191.2	199.8
Net income ($ mil.)	–	(24.3)	(63.8)	(63.2)	(34.4)	(25.3)
Market value ($ mil.)	(35.9%)	1,625.8	595.0	551.5	441.5	274.9
Employees	(2.6%)	840	783	799	826	756

BBDO WORLDWIDE INC.

1285 Avenue of the Americas
New York NY 10019
Phone: 212-459-5000
Fax: 212-459-6645
Web: www.bbdo.com

CEO: Kirsten Flanik
CFO: James Cannon
HR: –
FYE: December 31
Type: Subsidiary

This alphabet soup of advertising begins here. As the flagship agency of media conglomerate Omnicom Group BBDO Worldwide offers creative development services for some of the world's top brands using television print and other media. BBDO Worldwide also provides campaign planning and management services as well as other brand promotion services. The firm's Atmosphere BBDO unit offers interactive marketing services in North America. BBDO's clients have included such heavy hitters as Chrysler FedEx and PepsiCo (including the famous "Pepsi Generation" campaign). It operates through some 290 offices in about 80 countries featuring outposts like Abbott Mead Vickers Barefoot Proximity and Proximity London.

BBQ HOLDINGS INC
NMS: BBQ

12701 Whitewater Drive, Suite 100
Minnetonka, MN 55343
Phone: 952 294-1300
Fax: –
Web: www.bbq-holdings.com

CEO: Jeffery Crivello
CFO: Paul M Malazita
HR: –
FYE: January 03
Type: Public

Barbecue made this Dave famous. Famous Dave's of America operates and franchises about 185 barbecue restaurants in some 35 states primarily Minnesota Illinois California and Wisconsin. The eateries serve St. Louis-style ribs Georgia chopped pork and Texas brisket. Most of the restaurants are designed to resemble 1930s-era roadhouse shacks complete with antique items and Americana touches. Other units try to recreate the feeling of a hunting lodge or a Chicago-style blues club featuring live music. The company also distributes barbecue sauce seasonings and prepared meats through grocery stores and other retail outlets. Famous Dave's owns and operates about 50 of its restaurants and franchises the rest.

	Annual Growth	01/17*	12/17	12/18	12/19*	01/21
Sales ($ mil.)	5.2%	99.2	64.6	54.9	82.3	121.4
Net income ($ mil.)	–	(2.4)	(8.1)	4.9	(0.6)	4.9
Market value ($ mil.)	(0.4%)	46.1	61.0	39.4	38.4	45.4
Employees	10.1%	1,645	722	779	1,677	2,417

*Fiscal year change

BBX CAPITAL CORP
NYS: BBX

401 East Las Olas Boulevard, Suite 800
Fort Lauderdale, FL 33301
Phone: 954 940-4000
Fax: –
Web: www.bbxcapital.com

CEO: Alan Levan
CFO: Raymond Lopez
HR: –
FYE: December 31
Type: Public

BBX Capital is a diversified holding company that invests in real estate and development projects confectioneries manufacturers and other businesses. Its BBX Asset Management subsidiary manages the commercial loan portfolio and real estate properties. Renin Holdings manufacturers building supplies and home improvement products. Florida Asset Resolution (FAR) provides asset liquidation services for tax certificates loans and real estate properties. BBX Sweet Holdings owns confectioneries including Hoffman's Chocolates Boca Bons S&F Good Fortunes Williams & Bennett Jer's Helen Grace and Anastasia. Formerly the owner of BankAtlantic BBX sold the struggling bank to BB&T in 2012.

	Annual Growth	12/10	12/11	12/12	12/13	12/14
Assets ($ mil.)	(45.7%)	4,509.4	3,678.1	470.7	431.1	392.9
Net income ($ mil.)	–	(144.2)	(29.1)	235.8	47.8	4.7
Market value ($ mil.)	94.5%	18.6	54.7	108.4	252.3	266.0
Employees	(22.1%)	1,372	1,036	34	366	506

BCB BANCORP INC
NMS: BCBP

104-110 Avenue C
Bayonne, NJ 07002
Phone: 201 823-0700
Fax: –
Web: www.bcb.bank

CEO: Thomas Coughlin
CFO: Thomas Keating
HR: –
FYE: December 31
Type: Public

BCB Bancorp be the holding company for BCB Community Bank which opened its doors in late 2000. The independent bank serves Hudson County and the surrounding area from about 15 offices in New Jersey's Bayonne Hoboken Jersey City and Monroe. The bank offers traditional deposit products and services including savings accounts money market accounts CDs and IRAs. Funds from deposits are used to originate mortgages and loans primarily commercial real estate and multi-family property loans (which together account for more than half of the bank's loan portfolio). BCB agreed to acquire IA Bancorp in a $20 million deal in 2017.

	Annual Growth	12/16	12/17	12/18	12/19	12/20
Assets ($ mil.)	13.4%	1,708.2	1,942.8	2,674.7	2,907.5	2,821.0
Net income ($ mil.)	27.1%	8.0	10.0	16.8	21.0	20.9
Market value ($ mil.)	(3.9%)	222.4	248.1	179.1	235.9	189.4
Employees	(3.8%)	353	314	365	365	302

BCT INTERNATIONAL INC.

3000 NE 30th Place 5th Fl.
Fort Lauderdale FL 33306
Phone: 954-563-1224
Fax: 954-565-0742
Web: www.bct-net.com

CEO: William Wilkerson
CFO: Andyara Mata
HR: –
FYE: February 28
Type: Private

BCT International focuses on TCB (takin' care of business). The company operates a commercial printing chain of about 70 shops in the US and Canada most of which are franchised. BCT shops specialize in thermographed (a raised printing effect) and offset printed products such as business cards and forms envelopes letterhead rubber stamps and labels. Customers include retail printers superstores mailing centers and advertising and design professionals. The company's Pelican Paper Products unit supplies paper and printing equipment to franchisees. It also operates orderprinting.com and printdesigner.com which provide stationery products to retailers and corporate clients.

BDO USA LLP

130 E. Randolph Ste. 2800 1 Prudential Plaza
Chicago IL 60601
Phone: 312-240-1236
Fax: 312-240-3311
Web: www.bdo.com

CEO: Wayne Berson
CFO: –
HR: –
FYE: June 30
Type: Private - Partnershi

BDO knows accounting. BDO USA is the US member of BDO International one of the largest accounting firms outside of the Big Four (Deloitte Touche Tohmatsu Ernst & Young KPMG and PricewaterhouseCoopers). BDO USA offers midsized companies a broad range of accounting and consulting services such as auditing tax planning litigation consulting and appraisals and valuations. The company has almost 2200 staff members and about 270 partners. It has more than 40 offices in the US. More than 400 additional offices are operated by independent US firms that are members of the BDO Seidman Alliance.

BDP INTERNATIONAL INC.

510 Walnut St.
Philadelphia PA 19106
Phone: 215-629-8900
Fax: 215-629-8940
Web: www.bdpinternational.com

CEO: –
CFO: Katherine Harper
HR: –
FYE: December 31
Type: Private

Be it by air ground or ocean BDP International is in the business of moving raw materials and finished products around the globe. The company provides logistics services such as customs brokerage freight forwarding and warehousing and distribution for customers in a variety of industries including chemicals and retail. It serves more than 4000 customers worldwide including DuPont Panasonic Revlon and Johnson & Johnson. BDP International and its subsidiaries have about 25 offices in the US; internationally it operates through subsidiaries joint ventures and agents in some 120 countries. President and CEO Richard Bolte Jr. and his family own the company which was founded by his father in 1966.

BEACON CAPITAL PARTNERS LLC

200 State St. 5th Fl.
Boston MA 02109
Phone: 617-457-0400
Fax: 617-457-0499
Web: www.beaconcapital.com

CEO: –
CFO: –
HR: –
FYE: December 31
Type: Private

Beacon earns its bacon by collecting offices. A private real estate investment trust (REIT) Beacon Capital Partners invests in renovates and operates commercial and mixed-use properties in major metropolitan markets throughout the US. Beacon also has properties in London and Paris. It buys properties that can be improved through redevelopment repositioning or through managing the capital markets after which it sells its holdings at a profit. The company manages investment funds on behalf of institutional corporate and government investors. Beacon Capital Partners was formed in 1998 after predecessor public REIT Beacon Properties merged with Equity Office Properties Trust in a $4 billion transaction.

BEACON MEDICAL GROUP, INC.

615 N MICHIGAN ST
SOUTH BEND, IN 466011033
Phone: 574-647-1000
Fax: –

CEO: Philip A Newbold
CFO: –
HR: –
FYE: December 31
Type: Private

When you're on a fishing trip in northern Indiana and feel a little green around the gills you can rely on Memorial to help you get back in the swim. The health network provides wellness services in northern Indiana and southern Michigan. The Memorial Hospital of South Bend has some 620 acute care beds; it also operates a network of outpatient care and specialty clinics. Other divisions include Memorial Medical Group (physician practice organization) Memorial MedFlight (emergency air transportation) and Memorial Home Care (visiting nurse association). Memorial is part of regional care organization Beacon Health System along with Elkhart General.

	Annual Growth	12/09	12/10	12/14	12/15	12/16
Sales ($ mil.)	(20.7%)	–	461.0	–	106.8	114.3
Net income ($ mil.)	27.5%	–	1.5	–	(1.0)	6.4
Market value ($ mil.)	–	–	–	–	–	–
Employees	–	–	–	–	–	1,900

BEACON POWER CORPORATION

NASDAQ: BCON

65 Middlesex Rd.
Tyngsboro MA 01879
Phone: 978-694-9121
Fax: 978-694-9127
Web: www.beaconpower.com

CEO: Barry R Brits
CFO: Brian Battle
HR: –
FYE: December 31
Type: Private

Beacon Power beckons companies seeking backup power. The development-stage company's flywheel energy storage systems provide uninterruptible electric power for communications networks computers industrial manufacturing and other power generation applications. Beacon Power's flywheel systems draw electrical energy from a power source such as an electric power grid or a fuel cell and then store it. The power can then be delivered as needed when a primary energy source either fails or is disrupted. The company also makes photovoltaic power conversion systems (solar inverters). Beacon Power entered Chapter 11 bankruptcy protection in late 2011 and was acquired by private equity firm Rockland Capital in 2012.

BEACON ROOFING SUPPLY INC

NMS: BECN

505 Huntmar Park Drive, Suite 300
Herndon, VA 20170
Phone: 571 323-3939
Fax: –
Web: www.becn.com

CEO: Julian Francis
CFO: Frank Lonegro
HR: Sean McDevitt
FYE: September 30
Type: Public

Beacon Roofing Supply (BRS) is the leading publicly traded distributor of roofing materials and complementary building products in North America. Along with roofing products BRS distributes complementary building materials such as siding windows and weatherproofing systems. The company operates about 445 branches in the 50 US states and six Canadian provinces. BRS carries more than 100000 stock keeping units (SKUs) available for more than 80000 customers including contractors home builders building owners and other resellers. Most of BRS's business involves new construction projects as well as the repair or remodeling of residential and non-residential properties. Majority of the company's sales is generated from the US amounting more than 95%.

	Annual Growth	09/17	09/18	09/19	09/20	09/21
Sales ($ mil.)	11.0%	4,376.7	6,418.3	7,105.2	6,943.9	6,642.0
Net income ($ mil.)	–	100.9	98.6	(10.6)	(80.9)	(45.5)
Market value ($ mil.)	(1.7%)	3,592.6	2,536.9	2,350.5	2,178.0	3,348.0
Employees	5.4%	5,406	8,356	8,147	7,582	6,676

BEAD INDUSTRIES INC.

11 Cascade Blvd.
Milford CT 06460
Phone: 203-301-0270
Fax: 203-301-0280
Web: www.beadindustries.com

CEO: Jill Bryant Mayer
CFO: Kristen Sawyer
HR: Rosa Dimicco
FYE: December 31
Type: Private

For nearly 100 years Bead Industries has had its chain yanked. The company makes the beaded chains used to flush toilets and operate ceiling fans and window blinds. The ubiquitous metal swag (branded Bead Chain) has a number of other uses including securing gas tanks attaching commercial shower curtains and leashing bank pens as well as key chains dog tags and neck chains. The company's Bead Electronics division makes various pins and connectors found in PC boards cars and telecom devices. Bead Industries also owns UK-based chain manufacturer Sturge Industries and McGuire Manufacturing a US maker of plumbing products. Founded by Waldo D. Bryant the company is still led by members of his family.

BEAL BANK S.S.B.

6000 Legacy Dr.
Plano TX 75024
Phone: 469-467-5000
Fax: 469-241-9564
Web: www.bealbank.com

CEO: Margaret Jaques
CFO: –
HR: –
FYE: December 31
Type: Private

Everything's bigger in Texas and Beal Bank is no exception. One of the largest private financial services firms based in the state Beal is a wholesale bank that buys and sells pools of loans and debt securities on the secondary market. It also engages in more traditional banking activities offering certificates of deposit money market accounts IRAs and savings accounts to businesses and consumers nationwide. However it does not originate commercial or residential loans. The company has offices in Texas New York California Florida and other states. Beal Bank was founded in 1988 by chairman primary owner and famed poker player Andy Beal.

BEALL'S, INC.

E R BALL CTR 700 13TH AVE
BRADENTON, FL 34208
Phone: 941-747-2355
Fax: –
Web: www.beallsinc.com

CEO: Robert Beall III
CFO: –
HR: –
FYE: August 01
Type: Private

Residents of the Sun Belt have been known to leave their homes with Beall's on. The retail holding company operates through subsidiaries Beall's Department Stores Beall's Outlet and Burke's Outlet Stores in a dozen states. The multi-brand retailer has more than 530 department and outlet stores (about 200 are in Florida) located throughout states in the southern and western US including Arizona California Georgia Louisiana and Texas. Products range from off-price clothing and footwear for men and women to cosmetics gifts and housewares. Each chain has its own online shopping destination. The family-owned company was founded in 1915 by the grandfather of chairman Robert Beall (pronounced "bell").

	Annual Growth	07/09	07/10	07/11	07/12*	08/15
Sales ($ mil.)	3.2%	–	–	1,166.8	1,232.2	1,321.9
Net income ($ mil.)	12.8%	–	–	15.5	14.2	25.0
Market value ($ mil.)	–	–	–	–	–	9,700
Employees	–	–	–	–	–	–

*Fiscal year change

BEAM INC

510 Lake Cook Road
Deerfield, IL 60015
Phone: 847 948-8888
Fax: –
Web: www.beamglobal.com

NYS: BEAM
CEO: Albert Baladi
CFO: Marc Andre Tousignant
HR: –
FYE: December 31
Type: Public

Beam Inc. is one spirited company! Beam is a big producer and distributor of premium-branded distilled spirits. Its lineup ranges from bourbon whiskey to Scotch and tequila rum and ready-to-drink cocktails. Beam's portfolio of best-selling brands includes Jim Beam Bourbon Sauza Tequila Canadian Club Whisky Teacher's Scotch and Courvoisier Cognac among many. The company which operates distilleries and other sites worldwide sells primarily through direct sales forces to distributors. The US is Beam's #1 market. Once a cocktail of businesses known as Fortune Brands Beam became a stand-alone company in 2011 after spinning off its home products and hardware business Fortune Brands Home & Security.

	Annual Growth	12/08	12/09	12/10	12/11	12/12
Sales ($ mil.)	(24.5%)	7,608.9	6,694.7	7,141.5	2,311.1	2,465.9
Net income ($ mil.)	5.3%	311.1	242.8	487.6	911.4	382.4
Market value ($ mil.)	10.3%	6,609.8	6,917.2	9,647.3	8,203.0	9,781.8
Employees	(40.5%)	27,100	24,248	24,600	3,200	3,400

BEAR STATE FINANCIAL INC

9900 South Shackleford Rd, Suite 401
Little Rock, AR 72211
Phone: 501 975-6033
Fax: –
Web: www.ffbh.com

NMS: BSF
CEO: –
CFO: –
HR: –
FYE: December 31
Type: Public

Bear State Financial (formerly First Federal Bancshares of Arkansas) is the holding company for Bear State Bank and Metropolitan Bank which serve businesses and individuals through a total of 55 branches mostly in Arkansas but also in southeastern Oklahoma and southwestern Missouri. Founded in 1934 the thrift offers standard retail services such as checking and savings accounts money markets and CDs. More than 50% of the bank's loan portfolio is made up of one-to-four-family residential and commercial real estate mortgages while business loans make up another 15%. The bank changed its name in mid-2014 to match its holding company's brand.

	Annual Growth	12/12	12/13	12/14	12/15	12/16
Assets ($ mil.)	40.3%	530.4	548.9	1,514.6	1,920.2	2,053.2
Net income ($ mil.)	119.3%	0.8	0.7	24.3	10.6	17.5
Market value ($ mil.)	1.0%	366.8	327.3	413.4	407.4	381.8
Employees	27.2%	192	190	423	586	502

BEARING DISTRIBUTORS, INC.

8000 HUB PKWY
CLEVELAND, OH 441255788
Phone: 216-642-9100
Fax: –
Web: www.bearingdistributors.com

CEO: –
CFO: Dan Maisonville
HR: –
FYE: December 31
Type: Private

Bearing Distributors Inc. (BDI) began as a regional Midwestern distributor of replacement parts to OEMs. Among the world's largest industrial suppliers today the company also provides maintenance and repair services as well as training and inventory management. Its offerings include bearings electrical power products material handling systems and motion control products hydraulic and pneumatic systems and fluid power components. BDI serves customers in automotive to power generation industries and from mining to food and beverage paper processing and package handling operations. Founded in 1935 the company a unit of Forge Industries has locations dotting North America Europe and Asia.

	Annual Growth	12/04	12/05	12/06	12/07	12/08
Sales ($ mil.)	–	–	–	0.0	502.7	528.9
Net income ($ mil.)	–	–	–	0.0	13.0	5.6
Market value ($ mil.)	–	–	–	–	–	–
Employees	–	–	–	–	–	896

BEASLEY BROADCAST GROUP INC

3033 Riviera Drive, Suite 200
Naples, FL 34103
Phone: 239 263-5000
Fax: 239 263-8191
Web: www.bbgi.com

NMS: BBGI
CEO: Caroline Beasley
CFO: Marie Tedesco
HR: –
FYE: December 31
Type: Public

Beasley Broadcast Group is a leading radio broadcaster with some 52 stations operating in about a dozen large and mid-sized markets in seven states primarily Florida Georgia and North Carolina. The company's stations (serving 7.7 million listeners per week) broadcast a variety of formats including news sports and talk radio as well as Top 40 Urban Oldies and other music formats. Most of its stations operate as part of a cluster within a specific market allowing the company to combine certain business functions between those stations and achieve greater operating efficiencies. Beasley Broadcast Group was founded by George Beasley in 1961.

	Annual Growth	12/16	12/17	12/18	12/19	12/20
Sales ($ mil.)	10.8%	136.7	232.2	257.5	261.6	206.1
Net income ($ mil.)	–	47.5	87.1	6.5	13.5	(17.8)
Market value ($ mil.)	(29.8%)	180.4	393.2	110.0	90.7	43.7
Employees	(5.2%)	1,406	1,484	1,488	1,438	1,135

BEAUFORT MEMORIAL HOSPITAL

955 RIBAUT RD
BEAUFORT, SC 299025454
Phone: 843-522-5200
Fax: –
Web: www.bmhsc.org

CEO: –
CFO: Jeff White
HR: –
FYE: September 30
Type: Private

Beaufort Memorial Hospital provides medical surgical and therapeutic services in southern South Carolina. As the largest hospital between Savannah Georgia and Charleston South Carolina the not-for-profit community hospital is a regional referral center providing inpatient acute care and outpatient service s. The about 200-bed facility offers specialties in areas including cancer treatment cardiology emergency medicine mental health rehabilitation and obstetrics/gynecology. Beaufort Memorial Hospital operates the Keyserling Cancer Center through its affiliation with the South Carolina Health System . It also offers outpatient care at satellite facilities. The medical center opened its doors in 1944.

	Annual Growth	09/13	09/14	09/15	09/17	09/18
Sales ($ mil.)	6.4%	–	173.3	188.1	207.1	222.3
Net income ($ mil.)	2.1%	–	7.0	(10.2)	(10.1)	7.6
Market value ($ mil.)	–	–	–	–	–	–
Employees	–	–	–	–	–	1,300

BEAUMONT HEALTH

3601 W 13 MILE RD
ROYAL OAK, MI 480736712
Phone: 248-898-5000
Fax: –
Web: www.beaumont.org

CEO: John Fox
CFO: John Keuten
HR: Michael Woolsey
FYE: December 31
Type: Private

Beaumont Health is an eight-hospital regional health system in southeastern Michigan. The health system boasts about 3400 hospital beds 150 outpatient sites and 5000 affiliated physicians. Outpatient facilities include community medical centers nursing homes a home health agency a research institute and primary and specialty care clinics as well as rehabilitation cardiology and cancer centers. Beaumont is the exclusive clinical teaching site for the Oakland University William Beaumont School of Medicine; it also has affiliations with Michigan State University College of Osteopathic Medicine and Wayne State University School of Medicine. In 2019 it agreed to acquire Ohio hospital operator Summa Health.

	Annual Growth	12/16	12/17	12/18	12/19	12/20
Sales ($ mil.)	1.1%	–	4,438.6	4,659.9	4,703.3	4,580.8
Net income ($ mil.)	(6.7%)	–	392.7	142.1	401.1	318.4
Market value ($ mil.)	–	–	–	–	–	–
Employees	–	–	–	–	–	35,000

BEAUTICONTROL INC.

2121 Midway Rd.
Carrollton TX 75006-5039
Phone: 972-458-0601
Fax: 972-341-3071
Web: www.beauticontrol.com

CEO: –
CFO: –
HR: –
FYE: December 31
Type: Subsidiary

BeautiControl is looking to be ageless in the business of aesthetics and enjoys calling the Lone Star State home alongside rival Mary Kay. A unit of household products maker Tupperware BeautiControl sells its personal care items through more than 140000 independent sales consultants who in turn sell to consumers in the US Puerto Rico and Canada. Consultants provide computer-assisted head-to-toe makeup advice through in-home demos. Its products include skin and nail care fragrances cosmetics toiletries nutritional and weight-management food supplements and in-home spa retreats. Tupperware purchased BeautiControl in 2000 in a bid to expand its direct-selling reach to beauty and personal care items.

BEAUTY SYSTEMS GROUP LLC

3001 Colorado Blvd.
Denton TX 76210
Phone: 940-898-7500
Fax: 940-383-8143
Web: www.sallybeautyholdings.com/holdings/bsg.asp

CEO: –
CFO: –
HR: –
FYE: September 30
Type: Subsidiary

Hair stylists and colorists manicurists and cosmetologists stock up at stores operated by Beauty Systems Group (BSG). The beauty supplies distributor operates about 995 company-owned CosmoProf stores open only to the beauty trade. The company also supplies more than 150 franchised Armstrong McCall shops and distributes products directly to salons through a sales force of more than 1100 professional consultants. Customers primarily include salons spas licensed beauticians and nail technicians. Its 10000 products include brands such as Paul Mitchell Wella and more. BSG which covers all 50 US states Puerto Rico and parts of Canada Mexico and Europe is a subsidiary of Sally Beauty Holdings (SBH).

BEAVER DAM COMMUNITY HOSPITALS, INC.

707 S UNIVERSITY AVE
BEAVER DAM, WI 539163027
Phone: 920-887-7181
Fax: –
Web: www.bdch.com

CEO: Kim Miller
CFO: Donna Hutchinson
HR: –
FYE: June 30
Type: Private

Beaver Dam Community Hospitals (BDCH) provides medical services for the residents of south central Wisconsin. The non-profit medical center includes the 60-bed Beaver Dam Community Hospital as well as its Hillside Manor skilled nursing facility. Other facilities include an assisted living retirement center community-based residential facilities home health care services and a wellness center. BDCH also operates FastCare clinics in two towns and a dialysis center. BDCH has invested in an electronic medical records system and upgrades to its dialysis services.

	Annual Growth	06/13	06/14	06/15	06/17	06/18
Sales ($ mil.)	(1.8%)	–	111.3	91.3	101.2	103.3
Net income ($ mil.)	(4.6%)	–	6.8	7.2	3.7	5.6
Market value ($ mil.)	–	–	–	–	–	–
Employees	–	–	–	–	–	830

BEAVER STREET FISHERIES, INC.

1741 W BEAVER ST
JACKSONVILLE, FL 322097570
Phone: 904-354-5661
Fax: –
Web: www.beaverstreetfisheries.com

CEO: –
CFO: –
HR: Andrea Favarelli
FYE: May 28
Type: Private

After more than 60 years of fishing Beaver Street Fisheries can tell a tale or two of the one that got away. It's a top supplier of fish and other seafood products to wholesalers retailers and food service operators. Sourcing its products from more than 50 countries family-owned Beaver Street Fisheries offers one of the largest selections of seafood in the US. It boasts a variety of fresh and frozen seafood — including octopus shrimp and turtle — sold under its flagship Sea Best brand as well as the HF's and Island Queen names. Beaver Street Fisheries also imports lamb from New Zealand and sells Silver Fern-brand pork and beef via its Florida-New Zealand Lamb & Meat unit.

	Annual Growth	05/07	05/08	05/09	05/10	05/11
Sales ($ mil.)	(1.9%)	–	–	468.2	442.9	450.7
Net income ($ mil.)	(11.8%)	–	–	17.2	19.6	13.4
Market value ($ mil.)	–	–	–	–	–	–
Employees	–	–	–	–	–	350

BEAZER HOMES USA, INC.

1000 Abernathy Road, Suite 260
Atlanta, GA 30328
Phone: 770 829-3700
Fax: –
Web: www.beazer.com

NYS: BZH
CEO: Allan Merrill
CFO: David Goldberg
HR: –
FYE: September 30
Type: Public

Beazer Homes USA builds for the middle-class buyer who's ready to make the move into the white-picket-fence scene. Building homes with an average price of about $385000 the company courts the entry-level move-up and active adult markets. Beazer Homes focuses on high-growth regions in over a dozen states across the East Southeast and West; it tends to close around 5500 homes each year. The company also offers homebuyers upgrades on features such as cabinetry countertops and flooring. Like most large homebuilders Beazer relies on subcontractors to build its homes.

	Annual Growth	09/17	09/18	09/19	09/20	09/21
Sales ($ mil.)	2.8%	1,916.3	2,107.1	2,087.7	2,127.1	2,140.3
Net income ($ mil.)	39.9%	31.8	(45.4)	(79.5)	52.2	122.0
Market value ($ mil.)	(2.1%)	586.5	328.6	466.3	413.1	539.8
Employees	(1.1%)	1,100	1,280	1,205	1,063	1,052

BEBE STORES INC
NAS: BEBE

400 Valley Drive
Brisbane, CA 94005
Phone: 415 715-3900
Fax: -
Web: www.bebe.com

CEO: Manny Mashouf
CFO: Walter Parks
HR: -
FYE: July 02
Type: Public

Retailer bebe stores offers apparel in two main sizes: slim and none. bebe (pronounced "beebee") designs and sells contemporary women's career evening and casual clothing and accessories under the bebe banner through more than 200 stores in the US Canada and Puerto Rico; abroad through licensees; and online. The company targets hip "body-conscious" (some say skinny) 21- to 34-year-olds. bebe also licenses its name for items such as eyewear and swimwear. The majority of bebe's products are designed in-house and produced by contract manufacturers. Chairman and former CEO Manny Mashouf who founded bebe in 1976 controls the company.

	Annual Growth	06/12*	07/13	07/14	07/15	07/16
Sales ($ mil.)	(7.2%)	530.8	484.7	425.1	428.0	393.6
Net income ($ mil.)	-	11.7	(77.4)	(73.4)	(27.7)	(27.5)
Market value ($ mil.)	(46.3%)	47.0	47.0	25.2	15.9	3.9
Employees	(5.7%)	3,294	3,107	3,254	2,924	2,601

*Fiscal year change

BECHTEL GROUP INC.

50 Beale St.
San Francisco CA 94105-1895
Phone: 415-768-1234
Fax: 415-768-9038
Web: www.bechtel.com

CEO: Brendan Bechtel
CFO: -
HR: Camille Sanchez
FYE: December 31
Type: Private

Whether the job is raising an entire city or razing a nuclear power plant you can bet the Bechtel Group will be there to bid on the business. The engineering construction and project management company serves the oil and gas energy transportation communications mining and government services sectors. It operates worldwide and has participated in such historic projects as the construction of Hoover Dam and the cleanup of the Chernobyl nuclear plant. Bechtel's Oil Gas & Chemical business unit (particularly liquefied natural gas) and its Mining & Metals group are its leading revenue producers. The group is in its fourth generation of Bechtel family leaders with chairman and CEO Riley Bechtel at the helm.

BECK SUPPLIERS, INC.

1000 N FRONT ST
FREMONT, OH 434201921
Phone: 800-232-5645
Fax: -
Web: www.becksuppliers.com

CEO: Daryl Becker
CFO: Loren Owens
HR: -
FYE: December 31
Type: Private

More than willing to be at the beck and call of its customers Beck Suppliers provides its clients in Ohio with fuel oil diesel gasoline kerosene and propane. The company annually delivers more than 170 million gallons of fuel at Sunoco Marathon and other gas stations in northwestern Ohio. Beck Suppliers also operates 20 Friendship Food Stores. The company's truck fleet delivers diesel fuel oil gasoline kerosene and propane for farm construction and industrial purposes as well as home heating oil and propane for residential use. Beck Suppliers also operates car washes and has a construction division that builds convenience stores gas stations and car washes.

	Annual Growth	12/05	12/06	12/07	12/08	12/09
Sales ($ mil.)	(7.3%)	-	-	293.3	316.6	252.3
Net income ($ mil.)	14.6%	-	-	1.0	0.8	1.4
Market value ($ mil.)	-	-	-	-	-	-
Employees	-	-	-	-	-	250

BECTON, DICKINSON & CO
NYS: BDX

1 Becton Drive
Franklin Lakes, NJ 07417-1880
Phone: 201 847-6800
Fax: -
Web: www.bd.com

CEO: Thomas Polen
CFO: Christopher DelOrefice
HR: Betty Larson
FYE: September 30
Type: Public

Becton Dickinson and Company (BD) is a global medical technology company that develops manufactures and sells a broad range of medical supplies devices laboratory equipment and diagnostic products. These products are used and offered to healthcare institutions physicians life science researchers clinical laboratories the pharmaceutical industry and the general public. The company provides innovative solutions that help advance medical research and genomics enhance the diagnosis of infectious disease and cancer improve medication management promote infection prevention equip surgical and interventional procedures and support the management of diabetes. The company's domestic operations accounts for about 55% of the total revenue.

	Annual Growth	09/17	09/18	09/19	09/20	09/21
Sales ($ mil.)	13.8%	12,093.0	15,983.0	17,290.0	17,117.0	20,248.0
Net income ($ mil.)	17.4%	1,100.0	311.0	1,233.0	874.0	2,092.0
Market value ($ mil.)	5.8%	55,743.1	74,248.2	71,961.0	66,191.9	69,929.9
Employees	15.6%	41,933	76,032	70,093	72,000	75,000

BED, BATH & BEYOND, INC.
NMS: BBBY

650 Liberty Avenue
Union, NJ 07083
Phone: 908 688-0888
Fax: 908 810-8813
Web: www.bedbathandbeyond.com

CEO: Mark Tritton
CFO: Gustavo Arnal
HR: -
FYE: February 27
Type: Public

Bed Bath & Beyond sells a wide assortment of merchandise in the Home Baby and Beauty & Wellness markets and operates under the names Bed Bath & Beyond (BBB) buybuy BABY (BABY) and Harmon Harmon Face Values. It also operates Decorist an online interior design platform that provides personalized home design services. The company also operates 1020 retail stores consisting of about 835 BBB stores in all 50 states the District of Columbia Puerto Rico and Canada more than 130 BABY stores in more than 35 states and Canada and about 55 Harmon stores in five states.

	Annual Growth	02/17*	03/18	03/19*	02/20	02/21
Sales ($ mil.)	(6.8%)	12,215.8	12,349.3	12,028.8	11,158.6	9,233.0
Net income ($ mil.)	-	685.1	424.9	(137.2)	(613.8)	(150.8)
Market value ($ mil.)	(10.1%)	4,498.8	2,393.0	1,829.6	1,185.0	2,944.4
Employees	(12.8%)	65,000	65,000	62,000	55,000	37,600

*Fiscal year change

BEEBE MEDICAL CENTER, INC.

424 SAVANNAH RD
LEWES, DE 199581462
Phone: 302-645-3300
Fax: -
Web: www.beebehealthcare.org

CEO: Rick Schaffner
CFO: -
HR: -
FYE: June 30
Type: Private

Sea shells on the sea shore can be found near Beebe Medical Center. The health care provider offers emergency inpatient long-term care women's health and other medical services to residents of Sussex County Delaware. The hospital is located in the town of Lewes near Rehoboth Beach. It has approximately 210 beds and offers specialized services including cardiology orthopedic rehabilitation and oncology treatments. Beebe Medical Center offers outpatient services including wound care diabetes management surgery radiology and sleep disorder diagnosis. It also operates senior care centers home health agencies medical laboratories and a nursing school.

	Annual Growth	06/17	06/18	06/19	06/20	06/21
Sales ($ mil.)	6.0%	-	419.7	447.8	450.8	500.4
Net income ($ mil.)	6.2%	-	54.8	21.2	(8.2)	65.7
Market value ($ mil.)	-	-	-	-	-	-
Employees	-	-	-	-	-	1,606

BEECH-NUT NUTRITION CORPORATION

100 Hero Dr.
Amsterdam NY 12010
Phone: 518-595-6600
Fax: 910-814-3899
Web: www.boonedam.us/inc/

CEO: –
CFO: –
HR: –
FYE: June 30
Type: Private

Peas and applesauce — Beech-Nut Nutrition puts them in jars for baby's lunch or baby's finger-painting. As one of the top branded baby food makers (along with Gerber and Heinz) Beech-Nut Nutrition hopes baby will open up wider for their airplane. In addition to jars of pureed fruits vegetables meats and meals the company makes instant and jarred cereals meals plus juices and water for the youngest palates. It offers more than 150 baby and toddler food products; it was the first baby food manufacturer to offer products (beginning in 2002) containing DHA an essential fatty acid found in human breast milk. Beech-Nut is owned by Swiss branded-food manufacturer Hero.

BEHLEN MFG. CO.

4025 E. 23rd St.
Columbus NE 68602-0569
Phone: 402-564-3111
Fax: 402-563-7405
Web: www.behlenmfg.com

CEO: –
CFO: Tom Burton
HR: –
FYE: April 30
Type: Private

Behlen has the metal to grain and bear it.. Behlen makes metal livestock equipment pallets grain storage bins and silos as well as metal buildings and trailers. Over the past 20 years Behlen Country the company's livestock equipment unit has acquired farm gate maker Farmaster cattle handling equipment makers Big Valley and Universal Mfg. and storage tank provider Agri-Engineering to become the industry's largest livestock equipment manufacturer. Behlen Building Systems focuses on making products for the agricultural building market while Behlen's International Ag Systems unit makes silos and other grain storage structures. BMC Transportation maker truck trailers.

BEHRMAN CAPITAL L.P.

126 E. 56th St. 27th Fl.
New York NY 10022
Phone: 212-980-6500
Fax: 212-980-7024
Web: www.behrmancap.com

CEO: –
CFO: Gary Dieber
HR: –
FYE: December 31
Type: Private

Private equity firm Behrman Capital engages in management buyouts recapitalizations acquisitions and consolidations within fragmented industries. Targeting established firms with annual revenues from $50 million to $500 million the company typically makes equity investments from $25 million to $100 million per transaction. It prefers to be the lead investor and assists its portfolio companies in formulating business and financial strategies. Behrman Capital focuses on the defense health care information technology specialty manufacturing and telecommunications sectors. It has stakes in about a dozen companies and more than $2 billion of assets under management.

BEKAERT CORPORATION

3200 W. Market St. Ste. 303
Akron OH 44333-3326
Phone: 330-867-3325
Fax: 330-867-3424
Web: www.bekaert.com

CEO: Matthew Taylor
CFO: Beatriz Garcia-Cos
HR: –
FYE: December 31
Type: Subsidiary

Bekaert Corporation goes right down to the wire on a daily basis. The company the US subsidiary of Belgium-based NV Bekaert SA manufactures a variety of wire and wire and film coatings. For automobiles Bekaert makes tire cord control cables spring wire and clips. It also produces high carbon low carbon and stainless steel wire for industrial applications. Other Bekaert products include telecom and power cables agricultural fencing material and sawing cable. North America represents approximately 20% of its parent company's revenues.

BEKINS HOLDING CORP.

330 S. Mannheim Rd.
Hillside IL 60162
Phone: 708-547-2000
Fax: 708-547-3228
Web: www.bekins.com

CEO: Michael Petersen
CFO: William Kelly
HR: –
FYE: December 31
Type: Private

Bekins would like to be a beacon of help to families and businesses on the move. Through its Bekins Van Lines subsidiary and its 300 US locations the company provides household and corporate relocation services in North America as well as tradeshow logistics services and transportation of high-value items. In addition Bekins handles international moves through a network of partners around the world; specialties include service to government and military clients. The company is owned by its agents who bought it from former parent GeoLogistics in 2002. Bekins was founded by the Bekins brothers — John and Martin — in 1891.

BEL FUSE INC

NMS: BELF B

206 Van Vorst Street
Jersey City, NJ 07302
Phone: 201 432-0463
Fax: –
Web: www.belfuse.com

CEO: Daniel Bernstein
CFO: Farouq Tuweiq
HR: Sherry Urban
FYE: December 31
Type: Public

Bel Fuse designs manufactures and markets a broad array of products that power protect and connect electronic circuits. These products are primarily used in the networking telecommunications computing military transportation and broadcasting industries. Its magnetic products include discrete components power transformers and MagJack connector modules. It also offers power conversion modules for a variety of applications. Bel Fuse's ircuit protection products include board level fuses (miniature micro and surface-mounted) and Polymeric PTC (Positive Temperature Coefficient) devices designed for the global electronic and telecommunication markets. The company also makes passive jacks plugs and cable assemblies. Top customers include Hon Hai/Foxconn Technology Group (over 10% of sales). Majority of the company's sales were generated from North America.

	Annual Growth	12/16	12/17	12/18	12/19	12/20
Sales ($ mil.)	(1.8%)	500.2	491.6	548.2	492.4	465.8
Net income ($ mil.)	–	(64.8)	(11.9)	20.7	(8.7)	12.8
Market value ($ mil.)	(16.5%)	381.7	311.0	227.6	253.2	185.7
Employees	(4.5%)	7,694	7,491	8,098	6,935	6,400

BELCAN CORPORATION

10200 ANDERSON WAY
BLUE ASH, OH 45242-4718
Phone: 513-891-0972
Fax: –
Web: www.belcan.com

CEO: Lance H Kwasneiwski
CFO: Beth Ferris
HR: –
FYE: December 31
Type: Private

Belcan provides engineering technical recruiting and staffing services to clients in the aviation consumer products and manufacturing industries among others. Its Belcan Engineering division offers design engineering engineering analysis and computer modeling to customers such as Lockheed Martin and UTC. The company also offers recruiting services — including interviewing screening and workforce management — to fill openings for highly skilled technical personnel through Belcan TechServices. BelFlex Staffing Network supplies light industrial and clerical employees to clients. Family-owned Belcan founded in 1958 by Ralph Anderson operates some 70 offices primarily in the US.

	Annual Growth	12/08	12/09	12/10	12/11	12/12
Sales ($ mil.)	15.0%	–	452.8	538.7	623.5	688.7
Net income ($ mil.)	117.6%	–	1.9	13.5	22.9	19.3
Market value ($ mil.)	–	–	–	–	–	–
Employees		–	–	–	–	10,000

BELDEN & BLAKE CORPORATION

1001 Fannin St. Ste. 800
Houston TX 77002
Phone: 713-659-3500
Fax: 310-826-6139
Web: www.cytrx.com

CEO: Mark A Houser
CFO: James M Vanderhider
HR: –
FYE: December 31
Type: Private

It may sound like a law firm but Belden & Blake is in fact an energy company that obeys the laws of supply and demand in the oil and gas market. It acquires properties explores for and develops oil and gas reserves and gathers and markets natural gas in the Appalachian and Michigan basins. In 2010 Belden & Blake reported interests in 1216 gross wells and leases on more than 1.1 million gross acres and it owned and operated 1600 miles of gas gathering lines. That year the company reported estimated proved reserves of 202.4 billion cu. ft. of gas equivalent. Belden & Blake is controlled by Capital C Energy Operations itself controlled by EnerVest Ltd.

BELDEN INC

NYS: BDC

1 North Brentwood Boulevard, 15th Floor
St. Louis, MO 63105
Phone: 314 854-8000
Fax: 314 854-8001
Web: www.belden.com

CEO: Roel Vestjens
CFO: Jeremy Parks
HR: Dean McKenna
FYE: December 31
Type: Public

Belden designs and manufactures cable connectivity and networking products for the transmission of data sound and video signals. Offerings include copper cables (shielded/unshielded twisted coaxial and stranded) and fiber optic and composite cables (multiconductor coaxial and fiber optic). It also makes fiber and copper connectors and networking products such as Ethernet switches. Products are used in industrial (robotics) enterprise broadcast and consumer electronics applications. Customers in the US account for about 55% of Belden's sales. The company's roots going back to its founding in 1902 by Joseph Belden.

	Annual Growth	12/17	12/18	12/19	12/20	12/21
Sales ($ mil.)	0.2%	2,388.6	2,585.4	2,131.3	1,862.7	2,408.1
Net income ($ mil.)	(9.0%)	93.2	160.9	(377.0)	(55.2)	63.9
Market value ($ mil.)	(3.9%)	3,470.7	1,878.6	2,473.6	1,884.5	2,956.2
Employees	(11.1%)	9,100	9,400	7,200	6,400	–

BELFOR USA GROUP INC.

185 Oakland Ave. Ste. 300
Birmingham MI 48009
Phone: 248-594-1144
Fax: 248-594-3190
Web: www.us.belfor.com

CEO: Sheldon Yellen
CFO: Joe Ciolino
HR: –
FYE: December 31
Type: Subsidiary

When bad things happen BELFOR USA steps in to clean up and repair the damage. The company provides disaster recovery and property restoration services to businesses and residences through some 80 offices across the US. Services include reconstruction drying fire storm and water damage restoration emergency power mold remediation semiconductor services and data recovery. Subsidiary DUCTZ International provides air duct cleaning and HVAC restoration services. Additionally BELFOR USA provides consulting and pre-planning services to help minimize potential problems its clients might encounter. Founded in 1995 BELFOR USA is part of global group Belfor International.

BELK INC (DE)

OTC: BLKI B

2801 West Tyvola Road
Charlotte, NC 28217-4500
Phone: 704 357-1000
Fax: –
Web: www.belk.com

CEO: Nir Patel
CFO: William Langley
HR: Angela Watson
FYE: February 01
Type: Public

Belk is busy bulking up. Already the nation's largest family owned and operated department store chain Belk operates about 300 stores in more than 15 states following its purchase of the Parisian chain from Saks. Previously Belk acquired Saks' McRae's and Proffitt's divisions. Belk stores are located primarily in the southeastern US and offer mid-priced brand-name and private-label apparel shoes jewelry cosmetics gifts and home furnishings. Its stores usually anchor malls or shopping centers in small to midsized markets and target 35-to-54-year-old middle- and upper-income women. Founded in 1888 by William Henry Belk the chain is run by chairman and CEO Thomas Belk.

	Annual Growth	01/10	01/11	01/12*	02/13	02/14
Sales ($ mil.)	4.8%	3,346.3	3,513.3	3,699.6	3,956.9	4,038.1
Net income ($ mil.)	24.0%	67.1	127.6	183.1	188.4	158.5
Market value ($ mil.)	36.1%	656.3	1,004.3	1,242.0	1,602.7	2,253.7
Employees	0.8%	23,880	24,000	23,000	23,800	24,700

*Fiscal year change

BELKIN INTERNATIONAL INC.

12045 E. Waterfront Dr.
Playa Vista CA 90094
Phone: 310-751-5100
Fax: 281-933-0044
Web: www.rose.com

CEO: Christopher Lu
CFO: Jasjit Jay Singh
HR: Megan Allen
FYE: December 31
Type: Private

Got a gadget? There's a good chance it's attached to an accessory from Belkin. The company makes a variety of products for Apple's iPod iPhone and iPad as well as eReaders laptops netbooks and TVs. A leading manufacturer of Universal Serial Bus (USB) devices such as networking hubs Belkin also provides media player accessories surge protectors and battery backups. Other products include fiber optic cables router pickers and home theater networking gear. For commercial and government customers Belkin provides security infrastructure and server-room products that include Keyboard-Video-Mouse (KVM) switches rackmount consoles and converters and adaptors. Founder and CEO Chet Pipkin owns Belkin.

BELL HELICOPTER TEXTRON INC.

600 E. Hurst Blvd.
Hurst TX 76053
Phone: 817-280-2011
Fax: 817-280-2321
Web: www.bellhelicopter.com

CEO: Mitch Snyder
CFO: Jim Tarallo
HR: –
FYE: December 31
Type: Subsidiary

Bell Helicopter a Textron company prefers a light lift and a heavy payload. It is a leading manufacturer of commercial helicopters manned and unmanned vertical lift aircraft and military tiltrotor aircraft which lift like a helicopter but fly like an airplane with twice the speed and triple the payload as a traditional helicopter. Different models are suited for transporting troops emergency medical provisioning search and rescue and warfighting. With partner Boeing Bell produces the V-22 Osprey tiltrotor aircraft for the US Department of Defense. Bell also provides training and maintenance repair and overhaul (MRO) services. It maintains operations in North America Europe and Asia.

BELL PARTNERS INC.

300 N. Greene St. Ste. 1000
Greensboro NC 27401
Phone: 336-232-1999
Fax: 336-232-1901
Web: www.bellpartnersinc.com

CEO: Lili F Dunn
CFO: John E Tomlinson
HR: –
FYE: December 31
Type: Private

If someone's ringing you up about a real estate deal it might be Bell Partners. The privately-held firm buys sells and manages multi-family residential and commercial real estate. It invests on behalf of individuals and institutional investors. Bell Partners' $5 billion portfolio includes about 200 apartment communities with nearly 60000 individual units; 30 commercial properties with more than 4 million sq. ft. of space; and more than 25 senior housing communities. Bell Partners targets markets in nearly 110 cities throughout the Northeast Southeast and Southwest. The company also offers property management services. CEO Steven D. Bell founded the company in 1976.

BELOIT COLLEGE

700 COLLEGE ST
BELOIT, WI 535115595
Phone: 608-363-2000
Fax: –
Web: www.campus.beloit.edu

CEO: –
CFO: –
HR: –
FYE: May 31
Type: Private

Beloit College home of the famed Beloit Poetry Journal is a liberal arts and sciences college with an enrollment of about 1300 students. The school offers more than 50 majors in nearly 30 departments and has some 100 full-time faculty members. Academic fields include anthropology health and society and philosophy. Beloit College also offers pre-professional programs in medicine law engineering and environmental management. The town of Beloit (population 36500) is home to a Frito-Lay cheese powder plant and incoming freshman are warned about the "cheese breeze" prevalent in winter months.

	Annual Growth	05/08	05/09	05/10	05/11	05/13
Sales ($ mil.)	3.5%	–	59.4	69.6	68.9	68.2
Net income ($ mil.)	–	–	–	1.8	0.9	(3.8)
Market value ($ mil.)	–	–	–	–	–	–
Employees	–	–	–	–	–	450

BELOIT HEALTH SYSTEM, INC.

1969 W HART RD
BELOIT, WI 535112298
Phone: 608-364-5011
Fax: –
Web: www.beloithealthsystem.org

CEO: Gregory Britton
CFO: –
HR: –
FYE: December 31
Type: Private

Beloit Wisconsin: Home of the world's largest can of chili the Beloit Snappers and... Beloit Health System. Its Beloit Memorial Hospital acute care facility provides medical care to the city's residents and surrounding areas. Specialty services include emergency medicine cardiology home care and occupational health. Its North-Pointe integrative medicine campus provides traditional and alternative medical approaches including massage Tai Chi and yoga. Beloit Health also provides primary care and specialized services through numerous outreach medical centers and operates an assisted living complex called Riverside Terrace. Beloit Health is affiliated with the University of Wisconsin Hospital and Clinics.

	Annual Growth	12/12	12/13	12/14	12/17	12/19
Sales ($ mil.)	4.8%	–	198.0	211.3	247.0	262.0
Net income ($ mil.)	6.7%	–	7.3	9.3	10.6	10.7
Market value ($ mil.)	–	–	–	–	–	–
Employees	–	–	–	–	–	1,400

BEMIS CO INC   NYS: BMS

2301 Industrial Drive
Neenah, WI 54956
Phone: 920 527-5000
Fax: –
Web: www.bemis.com

CEO: William F Austen
CFO: –
HR: Meghan L Heiman
FYE: December 31
Type: Public

Bemis makes a broad line of flexible packaging materials including polymer films barrier laminates and paper-bag packaging used by the food industry to bundle a range of edibles. In addition to the food industry which accounts for 80% of revenue the company sells to the agricultural chemical medical personal care and printing industries. Bemis has sales offices and plants in North America Latin America Europe and the Asia/Pacific region to serve its thousands of customers. US sales account for about 75% of revenue. In 2018 Bemis agreed to be acquired by Amcor for $6.8 billion (including debt).

	Annual Growth	12/13	12/14	12/15	12/16	12/17
Sales ($ mil.)	(5.3%)	5,029.8	4,343.5	4,071.4	4,004.4	4,046.2
Net income ($ mil.)	(18.5%)	212.6	191.1	239.3	236.2	94.0
Market value ($ mil.)	3.9%	3,719.2	4,105.1	4,057.9	4,342.1	4,339.3
Employees	(3.5%)	19,106	17,000	17,500	17,500	16,582

BENCHMARK ELECTRONICS, INC.   NYS: BHE

56 South Rockford Drive
Tempe, AZ 85281
Phone: 623 300-7000
Fax: –
Web: www.bench.com

CEO: Jeffrey Benck
CFO: Roop Lakkaraju
HR: –
FYE: December 31
Type: Public

Benchmark Electronics provides innovative product design engineering services technology solutions and advanced manufacturing services (both electronics manufacturing services (EMS) and precision technology services). Customers include manufacturers of computers and related products for business enterprises industrial equipment medical devices telecommunications equipment semi-cap equipment and equipment for the A&D industries. The company also offers design fulfillment solutions manufacturing engineering automation and testing services. About 65% of Benchmark's sales are from customers in the US while its 10 largest customers account for around 40% of sales. The company was founded in 1979.

	Annual Growth	12/16	12/17	12/18	12/19	12/20
Sales ($ mil.)	(2.9%)	2,310.4	2,466.8	2,566.5	2,268.1	2,053.1
Net income ($ mil.)	(31.6%)	64.0	(32.0)	22.8	23.4	14.1
Market value ($ mil.)	(3.0%)	1,107.0	1,056.2	768.7	1,247.1	980.3
Employees	3.2%	9,900	10,600	10,500	10,600	11,234

BENCO DENTAL SUPPLY CO.

295 CENTERPOINT BLVD
PITTSTON, PA 186406136
Phone: 570-602-7781
Fax: -
Web: www.benco.com

CEO: -
CFO: -
HR: -
FYE: January 04
Type: Private

Benco Dental Supply is a one-stop shop for the tooth doc. Through regional showrooms and distribution centers Benco provides dental and dentistry supplies to more than 30000 dental professionals throughout the US. Its offerings include dental hand pieces furniture and disposable supplies. Its BencoNET division develops and distributes custom computers and proprietary programming and networking systems for dentists. Other services include dental office design practice consulting financing and real estate planning wealth management and equipment repairs.

	Annual Growth	12/05	12/06	12/07	12/12*	01/14
Sales ($ mil.)	6.9%	-	-	389.2	600.8	620.4
Net income ($ mil.)	8.5%	-	-	5.0	7.4	8.9
Market value ($ mil.)	-	-	-	-	-	-
Employees						1,600

*Fiscal year change

BENDERSON DEVELOPMENT COMPANY LLC

8441 Cooper Creek Blvd.
University Park FL 34201
Phone: 941-359-8303
Fax: 941-359-1836
Web: www.benderson.com

CEO: -
CFO: -
HR: -
FYE: March 31
Type: Private

Benderson Development could probably bend your ear about its real estate portfolio. It develops manages and leases more than 250 properties including shopping centers residential communities industrial properties hotels office buildings self-storage facilities and mixed-use projects throughout the US. About a quarter of its portfolio is in Florida. The company which has more than 25 million sq. ft. of leasable space and more than 4 million sq. ft. of space under development also does business through subsidiaries Buffalo Lodging Associates and Kings Gate Homes. Its construction division designs and manages projects. CEO Nate Benderson founded the firm which he and his family control.

BENEDICTINE COLLEGE

1020 N 2ND ST
ATCHISON, KS 660021499
Phone: 913-367-5340
Fax: -
Web: www.benedictine.edu

CEO: -
CFO: -
HR: -
FYE: June 30
Type: Private

Benedictine College is a Roman Catholic liberal arts school that provides instruction to nearly 1200 students. It offers bachelor's degrees in nearly 40 major fields as well as three graduate degree programs. The school's Atchison Kansas campus overlooks the Missouri River. The college which opened its doors in 1859 is sponsored by brothers and sisters of the Benedictine monastic order.

	Annual Growth	06/12	06/13	06/14	06/16	06/17
Sales ($ mil.)	8.1%	-	57.3	67.6	74.1	78.2
Net income ($ mil.)	-	-	(0.3)	6.5	3.6	2.6
Market value ($ mil.)	-	-	-	-	-	-
Employees						184

BENEDICTINE HEALTH SYSTEM

4560 NORWAY PINES PL
HERMANTOWN, MN 558111253
Phone: 218-786-2370
Fax: -
Web: www.benedictineliving.org

CEO: Jerry Carley
CFO: Kevin Rymanowski
HR: -
FYE: June 30
Type: Private

The Benedictine Health System (BHS) is a peaceful provider of senior care services across the Midwest. The health system mostly serves rural and smaller communities in seven states. It owns or operates about 40 long-term care facilities including nursing homes assisted-living centers and independent senior housing developments. Other offerings include adult day-care transitional care and outpatient rehabilitation. Many of its facilities are integrated campuses that provide a spectrum of services. BHS was founded in 1892 and took its present form in 1985. It is sponsored by the Benedictine Sisters of St. Scholastica Monastery.

	Annual Growth	06/14	06/15	06/16	06/17	06/18
Sales ($ mil.)	2.2%	-	-	-	266.3	272.2
Net income ($ mil.)	82.4%	-	-	-	3.4	6.2
Market value ($ mil.)	-	-	-	-	-	-
Employees						8,000

BENEFICIAL LIFE INSURANCE COMPANY

36 S. State St.
Salt Lake City UT 84136
Phone: 801-933-1100
Fax: 801-521-0903
Web: www.beneficialfinancialgroup.com/

CEO: Kent Cannon
CFO: -
HR: -
FYE: December 31
Type: Subsidiary

Beneficial Life Insurance (doing business as Beneficial Financial Group) provides a variety of insurance and financial products and services primarily to customers in the western US. Its financial division Beneficial Investment Services offers brokerage and investment advisory services. Previously the company offered universal and whole life disability insurance employee benefits and annuities. However in 2009 the company quit selling new insurance and annuities and placed its existing business in run-off. Beneficial Financial was founded in 1905 and is owned by Mormon Church-affiliated Deseret Management Corporation.

BENEFICIAL MUTUAL BANCORP INC

510 Walnut Street
Philadelphia, PA 19106
Phone: 215 864-6000
Fax: 215 864-1770
Web: www.thebeneficial.com

NMS: BNCL
CEO: -
CFO: -
HR: -
FYE: December 31
Type: Public

You would expect something beneficial from the city of brotherly love. Beneficial Mutual Bancorp is the holding company for Beneficial Bank which serves the greater Philadelphia area and southern New Jersey through about 65 branches. Founded in 1853 as Beneficial Mutual Savings Bank the bank provides traditional deposit products such as checking savings and money market accounts; IRAs; and CDs. Commercial real estate business and construction loans together account for nearly half of the company's loan portfolio; consumer loans (nearly 30%) and residential mortgages (almost 25%) round out its lending activities. The bank is looking to grow its commercial loan portfolio.

	Annual Growth	12/08	12/09	12/10	12/11	12/12
Assets ($ mil.)	5.8%	4,002.1	4,673.7	4,929.8	4,596.1	5,006.4
Net income ($ mil.)	(3.8%)	16.5	17.1	(9.0)	11.0	14.2
Market value ($ mil.)	(4.1%)	892.1	780.3	700.2	662.9	753.3
Employees	(2.6%)	970	965	965	842	874

BENEFIT COSMETICS LLC

685 Market St. 7th Fl.
San Francisco CA 94105
Phone: 415-781-8153
Fax: 415-781-3930
Web: www.benefitcosmetics.com

CEO: Christie Fleischer
CFO: –
HR: –
FYE: December 31
Type: Subsidiary

BeneFit Cosmetics will make you look lovely and for a good cause. The company which donates a portion of proceeds to charity boasts products that have clever names and pin-up lasses on nearly every package. BeneFit sells its lines and offers facial services through more than 2000 counters (called "Beauty Bars") in department stores and beauty specialty shops in nearly 40 countries worldwide. It also has more than a dozen dedicated boutiques. BeneFit Cosmetics whose celebrity-endorsed Benetint product brought the fledgling company into the mainstream was founded in 1976 in San Francisco by sisters Jean Ann and Jane Ann Ford as The Face Place. Glamour leviathan LVMH holds a 70% stake.

BENEFIT SOFTWARE INC.

212 Cottage Grove Ave. Ste. A
Santa Barbara CA 93101
Phone: 805-568-0240
Fax: 805-568-0239
Web: www.bsiweb.com

CEO: –
CFO: –
HR: –
FYE: December 31
Type: Private

The benefits of Benefit Software's products are clear to human resources managers. Founded in 1978 Benefit Software provides employee benefit communications and workers' compensation case management software for businesses. The company's Fringe Facts Communicator software enables human resources departments to produce personalized employee benefits statements that summarize and explain employer-paid benefits. Its CompWatch software helps employers lower their workers' compensation costs by more efficiently managing their claims and cases. Benefit Software also offers Fringe Facts Online a hosted application for Internet-based employee benefits program communications.

BENEFITMALL INC.

4851 LBJ Fwy. Ste. 100
Dallas TX 75244
Phone: 469-791-3300
Fax: 469-791-3313
Web: www.benefitmall.com

CEO: –
CFO: –
HR: –
FYE: December 31
Type: Private

Only in insurance would you find a middle man poised to serve the middle men. Such is the business of BenefitMall an online exchange for insurance brokers who sell employee benefits to small businesses. As one of the largest general agencies in the US the company offers access to thousands of employee benefits plans from more than 125 insurance carriers. Its services are free to brokers as carriers pay to be represented. Insurance brokers use the nationwide service to get real-time quotes online and from sales and support offices in about a dozen states. Management bought the company from investors in 2006 and in 2012 privately held payroll company CompuPay Inc. merged with BenefitMall.

BENJAMIN MOORE & CO.

101 Paragon Dr.
Montvale NJ 07645
Phone: 201-573-9600
Fax: 201-573-0046
Web: www.benjaminmoore.com

CEO: Dan Calkins
CFO: –
HR: –
FYE: December 31
Type: Subsidiary

Not only can you paint the town red (or any other color) with Benjamin Moore paints you can stain and finish it as well. The company is a leading formulator manufacturer and retailer of a broad range of architectural coatings. In addition to ready-mixed colors — sold under such brands as Benjamin Moore Paints Moorcraft and Coronado Paint — the company can match almost any shade with roughly 3300 colors. Benjamin Moore (a subsidiary of Warren Buffett's Berkshire Hathaway) also makes industrial coatings and coatings for manufacturers of furniture and roof decking.

BENTLEY SYSTEMS INCORPORATED

685 Stockton Dr.
Exton PA 19341-0678
Phone: 610-458-5000
Fax: +886-3-579-2668
Web: www.winbond.com

CEO: Gregory S Bentley
CFO: David J Hollister
HR: –
FYE: May 31
Type: Private

Bentley Systems wants to be the premier ride for infrastructure engineers. The company's computer-aided design (CAD) software is used to design and build large-scale infrastructure projects such as airports transit and utilities systems manufacturing plants and buildings. Available on both a subscription basis (nearly three quarters of revenue) and as a perpetual license Bentley's software lets architects engineers builders and property owners collaborate over the Web to develop and maintain projects. The company also offers content management applications as well as consulting integration and training. It largely serves the architecture construction engineering and utilities industries.

BENTLEY UNIVERSITY

175 FOREST ST
WALTHAM, MA 024524713
Phone: 781-891-2000
Fax: –
Web: www.bentley.edu

CEO: –
CFO: Paul Clemente
HR: –
FYE: June 30
Type: Private

Bentley University is not the Rolls-Royce of universities but is fairly prestigious nevertheless. It offers undergraduate graduate and doctoral degree programs to its nearly 5670 enrolled students from 82 countries. The university also offers professional development and certificate programs for executives and corporations. The focus at Bentley is on business; the school was a pioneer in integrating information technology into the business curriculum. In the belief that businesspeople need a broad education Bentley requires a liberal arts core of classes in behavioral and social sciences English and other subjects in the humanities as well as math and natural sciences.

	Annual Growth	06/11	06/12	06/13	06/15	06/20
Sales ($ mil.)	6.9%	–	185.3	192.7	288.1	316.6
Net income ($ mil.)	–	–	(21.0)	40.5	18.7	9.4
Market value ($ mil.)	–	–	–	–	–	–
Employees	–	–	–	–	–	911

BEREA COLLEGE

101 CHESTNUT ST
BEREA, KY 404031516
Phone: 859-985-3000
Fax: –
Web: www.berea.edu

CEO: –
CFO: –
HR: –
FYE: June 30
Type: Private

Berea College is a Christian school that provides a private tuition-free liberal arts education to about 1600 students each year most of whom come from Kentucky and the Appalachian region. In lieu of tuition Berea has a work program that requires its students to work in on-campus jobs for at least 10 hours each week in their choice of some 130 different departments. Berea offers about 30 majors leading to Bachelor of Arts and Bachelor of Science degrees and each student is required to attend seven convocations (guest lectures concerts or other cultural events) each term. It also offers 15 teacher education programs.

	Annual Growth	06/17	06/18	06/19	06/20	06/21
Sales ($ mil.)	3.3%	–	126.7	140.0	151.0	139.8
Net income ($ mil.)	124.4%	–	30.8	43.4	25.6	347.7
Market value ($ mil.)	–	–	–	–	–	–
Employees	–	–	–	–	–	550

BERGELECTRIC CORP.

3182 LIONSHEAD AVE
CARLSBAD, CA 920104701
Phone: 760-638-2374
Fax: –
Web: www.bergelectric.com

CEO: William Wingrning
CFO: –
HR: –
FYE: January 31
Type: Private

One of the nation's top electrical contractors Bergelectric provides design/build and design/assist services on projects that include office buildings public-sector facilities bioscience labs entertainment complexes hotels data centers and hospitals. Its projects also consist of parking garages water treatment plants residential towers and correctional facilities. The company boasts expertise in building information modeling fire alarms and security and telecommunications and data infrastructure. Bergelectric operates mainly in the western and southeastern US from about a dozen offices.

	Annual Growth	01/13	01/14	01/15	01/16	01/17
Sales ($ mil.)	(2.7%)	–	525.2	494.1	507.6	483.1
Net income ($ mil.)	(5.0%)	–	5.0	1.2	2.2	4.7
Market value ($ mil.)	–	–	–	–	–	–
Employees	–	–	–	–	–	2,100

BERGEN COMMUNITY COLLEGE

400 PARAMUS RD STE A330-C
PARAMUS, NJ 076521508
Phone: 201-447-7100
Fax: –
Web: www.bergen.edu

CEO: –
CFO: –
HR: Patti Bonomolo
FYE: June 30
Type: Private

Bergen Community College offers academic degree programs as well as adult and continuing education. Its students work to earn Associate in Arts Associate in Science and Associate in Applied Science degrees as well as to complete certificate and continuing education programs. It has an enrollment of approximately 17000 students at its main campus in Paramus New Jersey as well as at two satellite campuses. The college offers courses in more than 100 areas of study. More than half of its students are able to transfer to four-year institutions in New Jersey and nationwide. Bergen Community College was founded in 1965.

	Annual Growth	06/04	06/05	06/08	06/16	06/17
Sales ($ mil.)	38.1%	–	1.4	1.1	69.6	68.1
Net income ($ mil.)	–	–	1.2	0.5	1.8	(1.2)
Market value ($ mil.)	–	–	–	–	–	–
Employees	–	–	–	–	–	1,054

BERGEN PINES COUNTY HOSPITAL INC

230 E RIDGEWOOD AVE
PARAMUS, NJ 076524142
Phone: 800-730-2762
Fax: –
Web: www.bergenregional.com

CEO: –
CFO: Connie Magdangal
HR: –
FYE: December 31
Type: Private

Bergen Regional Medical Center (BRMC) is not just the biggest hospital in Paramus New Jersey — it's one of the biggest in the state. BRMC provides acute care long-term care and behavioral health care services to the residents of northeastern New Jersey. The not-for-profit medical center with approximately 1190 beds also offers specialized services including orthopedics cardiology neurology emergency medicine and surgery as well as substance abuse treatment and hospice services. About half of the facility is devoted to long-term nursing care; and about 325 beds serve behavioral health patients.

	Annual Growth	12/05	12/06	12/07	12/08	12/15
Sales ($ mil.)	5.1%	–	–	–	146.2	207.5
Net income ($ mil.)	–	–	–	–	(78.9)	(8.4)
Market value ($ mil.)	–	–	–	–	–	–
Employees	–	–	–	–	–	2,700

BERKELEY FARMS LLC

25500 Clawiter Rd.
Hayward CA 94545
Phone: 510-265-8600
Fax: 510-265-8754
Web: www.berkeleyfarms.com

CEO: –
CFO: –
HR: –
FYE: December 31
Type: Subsidiary

Founded in 1910 California's oldest continuously operating milk processor Berkeley Farms "mooved" right in. The company produces milk ice cream and other dairy products that are sold in northern and central California. Berkeley Farms is one of the largest producers of bovine growth hormone (BGH)-free milk on the West Coast. Its other products include butter buttermilk eggnog cottage cheese eggs juice and sour and whipping cream. The dairy's foodservice division that along with dairy other products offers a full line of cheeses including mozzarella ricotta Parmesan Cheddar Jack Swiss and American varieties. Berkeley Farms is a subsidiary of US dairy giant Dean Foods.

BERKLEE COLLEGE OF MUSIC, INC.

1140 BOYLSTON ST
BOSTON, MA 022153693
Phone: 617-266-1400
Fax: –
Web: www.berklee.edu

CEO: –
CFO: –
HR: –
FYE: May 31
Type: Private

If you get accepted to this school you've no doubt hit a high note in your musical career. Berklee College of Music is one of the largest independent music college in the world offers bachelor's degrees in a dozen majors including film scoring jazz composition music education music production and engineering performance and songwriting. Located in Boston the school has some 6440 students and some 940 faculty members. Berklee has a student-to-faculty ratio of 12:1. Notable alumni include Branford Marsalis Quincy Jones Charlie Puth Steely Dan vocalist Donald Fagen. Pianist Lawrence Berk founded the college in 1945. The school was named after his son Lee Berk who served as Berklee president from 1979 to 2004.

	Annual Growth	05/13	05/14	05/15	05/17	05/20
Sales ($ mil.)	6.5%	–	252.9	259.6	276.0	368.6
Net income ($ mil.)	(0.1%)	–	27.3	12.6	107.9	27.1
Market value ($ mil.)	–	–	–	–	–	–
Employees	–	–	–	–	–	716

BERKLEY (WR) CORP
NYS: WRB

475 Steamboat Road
Greenwich, CT 06830
Phone: 203 629-3000
Fax: –
Web: www.wrberkley.com

CEO: W. Robert Berkley
CFO: Richard Baio
HR: –
FYE: December 31
Type: Public

Holding company W. R. Berkley offers an assortment of niche commercial property/casualty insurance across two segments ? Insurance and Reinsurance. The Insurance segment comprising more than 50 operating companies underwrites commercial insurance coverage including excess and surplus lines and admitted lines. It also develops self-insuring programs aimed at employers and employer groups. The Reinsurance segment allows insurance companies to pool their risks in order to reduce their liability. Berkley serves customers in 60 countries in the Americas Europe and the Asia/Pacific region.

	Annual Growth	12/16	12/17	12/18	12/19	12/20
Assets ($ mil.)	5.2%	23,364.8	24,299.9	24,896.0	26,643.4	28,606.9
Net income ($ mil.)	(3.1%)	601.9	549.1	640.7	681.9	530.5
Market value ($ mil.)	(0.0%)	11,827.2	12,741.2	13,143.1	12,287.7	11,811.1
Employees	(0.6%)	7,683	7,722	7,448	7,493	7,495

BERKLEY INSURANCE COMPANY

475 Steamboat Rd.
Greenwich CT 06830
Phone: 203-542-3800
Fax: 203-542-3839
Web: www.wrbc.com/index.shtml

CEO: –
CFO: –
HR: –
FYE: December 31
Type: Subsidiary

Berkley Insurance is the principal reinsurance subsidiary of property/casualty insurance firm W. R. Berkley. Its seven affiliated operating companies provide underwriting for specialty lines including professional liability workers' compensation and commercial automobile and trucking; treaty (automatic) and facultative (individual) reinsurance products; and provide specialty insurance through program administrators and managing general underwriters. Underwriting affiliates include BF Re Underwriters Berkley Risk Solutions Facultative ReSources and Signet Star Re. Chairman William Berkley founded parent firm W. R. Berkley in 1967.

BERKSHIRE BANCORP INC (DE)
NBB: BERK

160 Broadway
New York, NY 10038
Phone: 212 791-5362
Fax: –
Web: www.berkbank.com

CEO: Moses Krausz
CFO: David Lukens
HR: –
FYE: December 31
Type: Public

While the company is not looking to win a Tony Award for its work it is on Broadway. Headquartered on this famous Manhattan street Berkshire Bancorp is the holding company for The Berkshire Bank which operates about a dozen branches mostly in New York but also in New Jersey. The bank's products and services include individual and business checking and savings accounts money market accounts and CDs. Lending activities consist mostly of non-residential mortgages (about half of the company's total loan portfolio) and one- to four-family real estate loans (about 30%). Through subsidiaries the bank offers title insurance and property investment services.

	Annual Growth	12/16	12/17	12/18	12/19	12/20
Assets ($ mil.)	(0.3%)	723.5	705.5	764.0	684.9	715.7
Net income ($ mil.)	(30.5%)	5.2	4.9	5.6	6.3	1.2
Market value ($ mil.)	2.0%	133.3	181.8	188.9	145.6	144.2
Employees	–	–	–	–	–	–

BERKSHIRE HATHAWAY INC
NYS: BRK A

3555 Farnam Street
Omaha, NE 68131
Phone: 402 346-1400
Fax: –
Web: www.berkshirehathaway.com

CEO: Warren E Buffett
CFO: Marc D Hamburg
HR: –
FYE: December 31
Type: Public

Berkshire Hathaway is the holding company where Warren Buffett one of the world's richest men makes his money and spreads his risk. The company invests in a variety of industries. The most important of these are insurance businesses conducted on both a primary basis and a reinsurance basis a freight rail transportation business and a group of utility and energy generation and distribution businesses. Its core insurance subsidiaries include GEICO National Indemnity and reinsurance giant General Re. The company's other large holdings include Marmon Group McLane Company MidAmerican Energy and Shaw Industries.

	Annual Growth	12/16	12/17	12/18	12/19	12/20
Assets ($ mil.)	8.9%	620,854.0	702,095.0	707,794.0	817,729.0	873,729.0
Net income ($ mil.)	15.3%	24,074.0	44,940.0	4,021.0	81,417.0	42,521.0
Market value ($ mil.)	9.3%	376,913.1	459,482.5	472,451.8	524,313.4	537,012.4
Employees	(0.5%)	367,700	377,000	389,000	391,500	360,000

BERKSHIRE HEALTH SYSTEMS INC.

725 North St.
Pittsfield MA 01201
Phone: 413-447-2000
Fax: 413-447-2066
Web: www.berkshirehealthsystems.org

CEO: David E Phelps
CFO: Sean Fitzpatrick
HR: –
FYE: December 31
Type: Private - Not-for-Pr

Berkshire Health Systems serves the residents of Massachusetts and surrounding regions. The system operates two acute-care hospitals: Berkshire Medical Center with 300 beds and Fairview Hospital with 25 beds. Berkshire Medical Center is a teaching hospital affiliated with the University of Massachusetts' medical school. It also operates the Berkshire Visiting Nurse Association (home health care) a family health center (BMC Hillcrest) and several outpatient clinics and physician practices. In addition affiliate Berkshire Healthcare runs about 20 long-term care facilities in Massachusetts Ohio and Pennsylvania. Not-for-profit Berkshire Health Systems was founded in 1983.

BERKSHIRE HILLS BANCORP INC
NYS: BHLB

60 State Street
Boston, MA 02109
Phone: 800 773-5601
Fax: –
Web: www.berkshirebank.com

CEO: Nitin Mhatre
CFO: Subhadeep Basu
HR: –
FYE: December 31
Type: Public

Berkshire Hills Bancorp is the holding company for Berkshire Bank (the Bank) and Berkshire Insurance Group Inc. The company offers a wide range of deposit lending insurance and wealth management products to retail and commercial customers in its market areas. The Bank operates a socially responsible platform Reevx Labs to support emerging entrepreneurs artists and small non-profit organizations. The Insurance Group offers a full line of personal and commercial property and casualty insurance. It also offers employee benefits insurance and a full line of personal life health and financial services insurance products. Headquartered in Boston Berkshire has $12.8 billion in assets and operates some 120 banking offices primarily in New England and New York.

	Annual Growth	12/16	12/17	12/18	12/19	12/20
Assets ($ mil.)	8.8%	9,162.5	11,570.8	12,212.2	13,216.0	12,838.0
Net income ($ mil.)	–	58.7	55.2	105.8	97.5	(533.0)
Market value ($ mil.)	(17.4%)	1,873.2	1,860.5	1,371.0	1,671.4	870.3
Employees	(3.4%)	1,731	1,992	1,917	1,550	1,505

BERKSHIRE INCOME REALTY INC
ASE: BIR PRA

One Beacon Street
Boston, MA 02108
Phone: 617 523-7722
Fax: -
Web: www.berkshireincomerealty.com

CEO: -
CFO: David E Doherty
HR: -
FYE: December 31
Type: Public

If you enjoy attractive landscaping and swimming pools but can't stand the upkeep and maintenance Berkshire Income Realty might have just the spot for you. The real estate investment trust (REIT) invests and operates apartment communities. It owns more than 25 properties in major cities in Texas Georgia Florida California Oregon North Carolina and Pennsylvania as well as the Washington D.C. metropolitan area. The company (which is controlled by chairman Donald Krupp and his family) often acquires neglected properties and then rehabilitates them. Affiliate Berkshire Property Advisors provides day-to-day management and business operations services to the company.

	Annual Growth	12/09	12/10	12/11	12/12	12/13
Sales ($ mil.)	0.2%	79.5	81.7	84.7	79.0	80.0
Net income ($ mil.)	3.4%	5.9	5.9	6.4	7.0	6.7
Market value ($ mil.)	4.8%	30.9	35.9	36.2	37.1	37.3
Employees		-	-	-	-	-

BERKSHIRE PARTNERS LLC

200 Clarendon St. 35th Fl.
Boston MA 02116
Phone: 617-227-0050
Fax: 617-227-6105
Web: www.berkshirepartners.com

CEO: -
CFO: -
HR: -
FYE: December 31
Type: Private

No not that Berkshire — the other one. Berkshire Partners is a private equity firm that targets established North American and European companies worth $200 million to $2 billion. It targets varied industries including industrial manufacturing consumer products transportation communications business services energy and retailing. An active investor the company usually puts up between $50 million to $500 million per transaction in leveraged buyouts recapitalizations privatizations growth capital investments and special situations. Its Stockbridge affiliate invests in marketable securities to compliment Berkshire Partners' core private equity activities.

BERKSHIRE PRODUCTION SUPPLY LLC

40333 W 14 MILE RD
NOVI, MI 483771609
Phone: 586-755-2200
Fax: -
Web: www.pts-tools.com

CEO: -
CFO: -
HR: -
FYE: December 31
Type: Private

Production Tool Supply totes the tools of the trade — and it distributes them to customers worldwide. With nine showrooms in Michigan and Ohio the company (PTS) distributes brand-name discount industrial tools and machinery. It markets approximately 235000 products through a 1700-page catalog on the Internet and through independent distributors. Products include cutting tools carbide tools abrasives measuring tools clamps and vises power tools tool safety products and power machinery by blue chip OEMs such as Bosch Porter-Cable and Sandvik. D. Dan Kahn founded PTS in 1951 to serve small factories and shops in the Detroit area. The Kahn family still controls the company.

	Annual Growth	10/07	10/08	10/09	10/10*	12/13
Sales ($ mil.)	18.2%	-	-	117.2	129.1	228.5
Net income ($ mil.)	21.7%	-	-	10.7	15.0	23.5
Market value ($ mil.)	-	-	-	-	-	-
Employees		-	-	-	-	357

*Fiscal year change

BERLIN PACKAGING L.L.C.

525 W. Monroe 14th Fl.
Chicago IL 60661
Phone: 312-876-9292
Fax: 312-876-9290
Web: www.berlinpackaging.com

CEO: William Hayes
CFO: James Walters
HR: Edmar Petterson
FYE: December 31
Type: Private

Berlin is rigid and closed off but only when it comes to its plastics and lids. Chicago-based Berlin Packaging is a US distributor of rigid packaging such as glass metal and plastic stock bottles and closures dispensing systems and other components used in the personal care chemical food and beverage and pharmaceutical industries. It also offers packaging design inventory management delivery and financing services. Berlin markets and sells its more than 24000 products through its 80 or so sales offices and warehouses in the US and Puerto Rico. Equity group Investcorp owns a majority stake in the company.

BERLITZ LANGUAGES INC.

400 Alexander Park
Princeton NJ 08540-6306
Phone: 609-514-3400
Fax: 609-514-3405
Web: www.berlitz.com

CEO: Yukako Uchinaga
CFO: -
HR: -
FYE: March 31
Type: Subsidiary

Want to speak Dansk Deutsch Espa?ol or Portugues? If so Berlitz can help. Berlitz owns or franchises more than 550 language centers in 70 countries. Founded in 1878 to teach languages through a conversational approach to pleasure travelers Berlitz now serves schools military and government clientele and such corporate clients as Johnson & Johnson Procter & Gamble and ABC News. Besides small-group and one-on-one language courses Berlitz offers study-abroad and cultural-awareness training and online programs for all ages. Japanese education group Benesse Corporation owns parent Berlitz Corporation which it purchased in 2001.

BERNARD CHAUS INC.
OTC: CHBD

530 7th Ave.
New York NY 10018
Phone: 212-354-1280
Fax: 201-863-6307
Web: www.bernardchaus.com

CEO: Ariel Chaus
CFO: William Runge
HR: -
FYE: June 30
Type: Private

Bernard Chaus' clothes are made for the days when a woman "has nothing to wear." The company designs and sells upscale women's career and casual sportswear primarily under the Josephine Chaus Chaus Vince Camuto and Cynthia Steffe trademarks. Its jackets skirts pants blouses sweaters dresses and accessories are designed to coordinate by style color and fabric to make dressing for work easier. Manufactured mostly in Asia its apparel is sold in about 4000 US department and specialty stores. The company also makes private-label apparel for others. Widow of founder Bernard Chaus Josephine Chaus is chairwoman and CEO. She owned about 45% of the company before it was taken private in mid-2012.

BERNARD HODES GROUP INC.

220 E. 42nd St.
New York NY 10017-5806
Phone: 212-999-9000
Fax: 646-658-0445
Web: www.hodes.com

CEO: –
CFO: –
HR: –
FYE: December 31
Type: Subsidiary

Bernard Hodes Group helps companies send the right message to potential employees. The marketing communications company provides recruitment marketing response management consulting services and technology to streamline the hiring process. It also assists clients building minority recruitment programs and creating online recruiting strategies. Services include expertise in website design resume mining database creation and job posting strategies. Bernard Hodes has more than 90 offices in the Americas Asia Australasia and Europe. Founded in 1970 by Bernard Hodes the company is a subsidiary of media conglomerate Omnicom.

BERNATELLO"S PIZZA INC

200 CONGRESS ST W
MAPLE LAKE, MN 553583525
Phone: 320-963-6191
Fax: –
Web: www.bernatellos.com

CEO: William Ramsay
CFO: –
HR: –
FYE: June 30
Type: Private

This company feeds your frozen pizza amore. Bernatello's Pizza is a leading frozen-pizza maker in the US's Northeast Midwest and Rocky Mountain regions marketing its pies under the Bernatello's and Roma brands. Its product line (pumping out 100000 pizzas every day) offers a variety of different pizzas such as pan-style sausage and pepperoni Mexican-style four-cheese half-pounder and thin-and-crispy. The company also produces pizza-related frozen items such as garlic cheese bread mozzarella sticks and jalape?o snappers (Bernie's Bites). In addition Bernatello's provides manufacturing services for private-label customers. The family-owned company is controlled by food-industry veteran Bill Ramsay.

	Annual Growth	06/02	06/03	06/04	06/05	06/07
Sales ($ mil.)	2.7%	–	42.4	40.2	45.7	47.1
Net income ($ mil.)	–	–	–	(0.7)	0.1	(0.0)
Market value ($ mil.)	–	–	–	–	–	–
Employees	–	–	–	–	–	220

BERNER FOOD & BEVERAGE, LLC

2034 E FACTORY RD
DAKOTA, IL 610189736
Phone: 815-563-4222
Fax: –
Web: www.bernerfoodandbeverage.com

CEO: Stephen A Kneubuehl
CFO: Bill Marchido
HR: –
FYE: September 30
Type: Private

Berner Food & Beverage is burning up with dairy fever. The company is a producer of natural cheese (Swiss cheddar American) processed cheese (shelf-stable dips spreads aerosols and jars) and salsa con queso sauce well as energy coffee and specialty beverages. Berner contract-manufactures products for private-label customers including supermarkets drug stores club membership and dollar stores food distributors and foodservice companies. It also sells products under its own Berner labels. The company was founded in 1943 by the Kneubuehl family. It is still owned and operated by the family.

	Annual Growth	12/06	12/07	12/08*	09/12	09/14
Sales ($ mil.)	12.9%	–	–	65.4	74.8	135.5
Net income ($ mil.)	–	–	–	(1.3)	3.2	6.0
Market value ($ mil.)	–	–	–	–	–	–
Employees	–	–	–	–	–	300

*Fiscal year change

BERRY COMPANIES, INC.

2402 E 37TH ST N
WICHITA, KS 672193538
Phone: 316-832-0171
Fax: –
Web: www.berrycompaniesinc.com

CEO: –
CFO: Greg Joerg
HR: –
FYE: March 31
Type: Private

Savoring the fruit of its labor Berry Companies makes a living bulldozing big jobs. The employee-owned business runs eight divisions; each independently sells and rents new and used construction and material handling equipment. Berry Cos. specialize in graders tractors loaders excavators cranes rollers construction and woodworking supplies concrete equipment and small tools. The company's five distribution dealerships include White Star Machinery (Kansas); Bobcat of Dallas and Houston (Texas); K.C. Bobcat (Missouri); and Bobcat of the Rockies (Colorado). Berry Cos. also operates Berry Tractor and Equipment Berry Material Handling and Superior Broom (makes self-propelled road construction brooms).

	Annual Growth	03/05	03/06	03/07	03/08	03/09
Sales ($ mil.)	–	–	–	(1,240.6)	203.6	178.6
Net income ($ mil.)	9168.5%	–	–	0.0	2.6	0.6
Market value ($ mil.)	–	–	–	–	–	–
Employees	–	–	–	–	–	520

BERRY GLOBAL FILMS, LLC

95 CHESTNUT RIDGE RD
MONTVALE, NJ 076451801
Phone: 201-641-6600
Fax: –
Web: www.berryplastics.com

CEO: Tom Salmon
CFO: Mark W Miles
HR: Renee Porcile
FYE: October 31
Type: Private

Making plastic cling is this company's thing. AEP Industries manufactures plastic packaging films — more than 15000 types — including stretch wrap for industrial pallets packaging for foods and beverages and films for agricultural uses such as wrap for hay bales. AEP also makes dispenser-boxed plastic wraps which are sold to consumers as well as institutions ranging from schools to hospitals. Other industries courted by AEP are packaging transportation food autos chemicals textiles and electronics. The company operates in the US and in Canada. In the summer of 2016 AEP agreed to be acquired by rival Berry Plastics Group.

	Annual Growth	10/11	10/12	10/13	10/14	10/15
Sales ($ mil.)	(0.1%)	–	–	1,143.9	1,193.0	1,141.4
Net income ($ mil.)	63.8%	–	–	10.7	(5.5)	28.8
Market value ($ mil.)	–	–	–	–	–	–
Employees	–	–	–	–	–	2,600

BERRY GLOBAL GROUP INC

101 Oakley Street
Evansville, IN 47710
Phone: 812 424-2904
Fax: –
Web: www.berryplastics.com

NYS: BERY
CEO: Thomas Salmon
CFO: Mark Miles
HR: –
FYE: October 02
Type: Public

With a portfolio that includes tapes tubes and trash bags Berry Global is one of the top manufacturers of plastic products and engineered materials for customers across a broad range of industries. Some products of the company also include dispensing systems pharmaceutical devices and packaging overcaps bottles prescription vials and other products in each of its segments. Key markets include the healthcare personal care and food and beverage industries. Berry Global operates worldwide but the US together with Canada is by far its largest market.

	Annual Growth	09/17	09/18	09/19	09/20*	10/21
Sales ($ mil.)	18.2%	7,095.0	7,869.0	8,878.0	11,709.0	13,850.0
Net income ($ mil.)	21.2%	340.0	496.0	404.0	559.0	733.0
Market value ($ mil.)	2.0%	7,676.1	6,556.8	5,327.9	6,426.8	8,306.2
Employees	19.6%	23,000	24,000	48,000	47,000	47,000

*Fiscal year change

BERTUCCI'S CORPORATION

155 Otis St.
Northborough MA 01532
Phone: 508-351-2500
Fax: 508-393-8046
Web: www.bertuccis.com

CEO: David Lloyd
CFO: Brian P Connell
HR: –
FYE: December 31
Type: Private

New Englanders in need of a taste of Italy can turn to Bertucci's. The company owns and operates more than 90 casual-dining establishments operating under the Bertucci's Italian Restaurant banner. The restaurants located in about 10 states primarily in the Northeast feature a wide array of Tuscan-style dishes including pasta chicken and seafood dishes as well as appetizers and desserts. Bertucci's also offers a variety of premium brick oven pizzas available with a number of different topping combinations. Chairman Benjamin Jacobson controls the company through his Jacobson Partners holding company. The first Bertucci's opened in 1981.

BEST BRANDS CORP.

111 Cheshire Ln. Ste. 100
Minnetonka MN 55305
Phone: 952-404-7500
Fax: 952-404-7501
Web: www.bestbrandscorp.com

CEO: –
CFO: –
HR: –
FYE: December 31
Type: Subsidiary

Best Brands believes it can be the best in the baking industry. The company makes an oven full of fillings frozen doughs and batters icings and baked goods such as cakes cookies muffins croissants puff pastry and baking ingredients — more than 1000 different products. Under the Multifoods Bakery Products brand it produces muffins and baking mixes; the Telco Food Products brand offers retail-ready brownies and Bundt and loaf cakes; and its Fantasia brands makes chocolate desserts. Best Brands has customers in the retail food foodservice and wholesale food and baking industries across North America. The company was acquired by baking-ingredient giant Netherlands-based CSM in early 2010

BEST BUY INC

NYS: BBY

7601 Penn Avenue South
Richfield, MN 55423
Phone: 612 291-1000
Fax: –
Web: www.investors.bestbuy.com

CEO: Corie Barry
CFO: Matthew Bilunas
HR: –
FYE: January 30
Type: Public

The multinational retailer sells both products and services through some 1170 stores in the US Canada and Mexico under the Best Buy Best Buy Express Best Buy Mobile Best Buy Health CST Geek Squad GreatCall Lively Magnolia and Pacific Kitchen and Home Sales banners. Its stores sell a variety of electronic gadgets and wearables tablets movies music computers mobile phones and appliances. On the services side it offers installation and maintenance delivery design in-home consultations memberships protection plans repair set-up technical support and health-related services.

	Annual Growth	01/17*	02/18	02/19	02/20*	01/21
Sales ($ mil.)	4.7%	39,403.0	42,151.0	42,879.0	43,638.0	47,262.0
Net income ($ mil.)	10.0%	1,228.0	1,000.0	1,464.0	1,541.0	1,798.0
Market value ($ mil.)	25.8%	11,171.8	18,308.7	15,026.8	21,765.3	27,966.7
Employees	(5.0%)	125,000	125,000	125,000	125,000	102,000

*Fiscal year change

BEST FRIENDS PET CARE INC.

520 Main Ave.
Norwalk CT 06851
Phone: 203-846-3360
Fax: 203-849-1092
Web: www.bestfriendspetcare.com

CEO: John A Heyder
CFO: Linda Fayerweather
HR: –
FYE: December 31
Type: Private

Best Friends Pet Care takes care of man's best friend. The company provides pet boarding grooming and day care services through more than 40 locations in about 20 states including California Illinois and Florida. It offers dog and cat grooming and boarding as well as dog training through its Canine College. Doggy Day Camp (daytime dog sitting services) is available at some locations. Best Friends also sells a wide range of pet products (such as dishes carriers collars and treats) and apparel cards and accessories adorned with animal images. The company was founded as Windsor Pet Care in 1991.

BEST MEDICAL INTERNATIONAL INC.

7643 Fullerton Rd.
Springfield VA 22153
Phone: 703-451-2378
Fax: 703-451-0922
Web: www.teambest.com

CEO: –
CFO: –
HR: –
FYE: December 31
Type: Private

Best Medical International has set a high standard for the medical equipment it manufactures. The vertically-integrated company has rolled up a collection of businesses in the US and Canada that manufacture and distribute radiotherapy systems and supplies. Its product lines include brachytherapy systems (radioactive seeds implanted to zap tumors) external beam therapy systems blood irradiators and other supporting equipment used to deliver and monitor radiation therapy. Its subsidiaries include Best Cyclotron Systems Best NOMOS Best Theratronics CNMC Huestis Medical and Novoste. The company was founded by its president Krishnan Suthanthiran in 1977.

BEST WESTERN INTERNATIONAL, INC.

6201 N 24TH PKWY
PHOENIX, AZ 850162023
Phone: 602-957-4200
Fax: –
Web: www.bestwestern.com

CEO: David Kong
CFO: Mark Straszynski
HR: –
FYE: November 30
Type: Private

Founded in 1946 by M.K. Guertin Best Western is a privately held hotel brand with more than 4700 independently owned and operated hotels in over 100 countries and territories. Its WorldHotels Collection is a curated global offering of the finest independent hotels and resorts around the world. The SureStay Hotel Group offers value-oriented travelers an exceptional experience at an affordable price. Comprised of four distinct brands SureStay Hotel Group offers traditional and longer stay travelers comfort and value while away from home.

	Annual Growth	11/03	11/04	11/05	11/06	11/07
Sales ($ mil.)	5.4%	–	–	198.8	205.5	220.9
Net income ($ mil.)	–	–	–	(1.3)	2.5	(3.0)
Market value ($ mil.)	–	–	–	–	–	–
Employees	–	–	–	–	–	1,015

BEST WINGS USA INC.

101 Chestnut St.
Sharon PA 16146
Phone: 724-981-3123
Fax: 724-981-5946
Web: www.lubewings.com

CEO: –
CFO: –
HR: –
FYE: December 31
Type: Private

Get in touch with your inner chicken-lovin' grease monkey at one of this company's restaurants. Best Wings USA operates and franchises the Quaker Steak & Lube full-service dining chain with more than 35 locations found in a dozen states mostly in Ohio and Pennsylvania. The auto-themed eateries are best known for chicken wings that can be ordered in a wide range of flavors. The menu also features burgers and other sandwiches ribs and steaks as well as a selection of appetizers. In addition to dining most of the restaurants offer full bar service. Vice chairmen George Warren and Gary Meszaros opened the first Quaker Steak outlet in 1974.

BET INTERACTIVE LLC

BET Plaza 1235 W St. NE
Washington DC 20018
Phone: 202-608-2000
Fax: 202-608-2988
Web: www.bet.com

CEO: Robert L Johnson
CFO: –
HR: –
FYE: July 31
Type: Subsidiary

This company is hoping to create a cultural connection online. BET Interactive operates the BET.com portal a leading provider of Internet content and services targeted to African-Americans. Other digital assets include BET on Blast (broadband media player) BET on Demand (video on demand) and BET Mobile (a mobile content subscription service). BET.com offers information on such topics as news health music and careers to an audience of more than 3 million registered users. It generates revenue from advertisements and sponsorships. BET Interactive is a unit of Viacom subsidiary Black Entertainment Television.

BETH ISRAEL DEACONESS MEDICAL CENTER, INC.

330 BROOKLINE AVE
BOSTON, MA 022155400
Phone: 617-667-7000
Fax: –
Web: www.bidmc.org

CEO: Kevin Tabb
CFO: Steve Fischer
HR: –
FYE: September 30
Type: Private

Beth Israel Deaconess Medical Center (BIDMC) is part of Beth Israel Lahey Health a new health care system that brings together academic medical centers and teaching hospitals community and specialty hospitals with more than 4000 physicians and 35000 employees. BIDMC has about 675 beds including around 495 medical/surgical beds more than 75 critical care beds and more than 60 OB/GYN beds. It also provides a full range of emergency services including a Level 1 Trauma Center and roof-top heliport. BIDMC a patient care teaching and research affiliate of Harvard Medical School. The health system traces its roots to Deaconess Hospital founded in 1896 and Beth Israel Hospital established in 1916.

	Annual Growth	09/14	09/15	09/16	09/17	09/19
Sales ($ mil.)	12.9%	–	1,198.8	1,280.0	1,335.8	1,945.1
Net income ($ mil.)	11.1%	–	44.6	28.9	37.5	68.0
Market value ($ mil.)	–	–	–	–	–	–
Employees	–	–	–	–	–	6,500

BETH ISRAEL MEDICAL CENTER

281 1ST AVE
NEW YORK, NY 100032925
Phone: 212-420-2000
Fax: –
Web: www.bethisraelny.org

CEO: Kenneth L Davis
CFO: Donald Scanlon
HR: –
FYE: December 31
Type: Private

Residents of New York City's Lower East Side look to Mount Sinai Beth Israel (formerly Beth Israel Medical Center) to keep them healthy. A member of Mount Sinai Health System the tertiary care medical facility has about 800 inpatient beds located in Manhattan. It emphasizes its services in heart disease cancer neurology orthopedics gastrointestinal disease chemical dependency psychiatric disorders pain management and palliative care and HIV/AIDS research and treatment. It is notable for its unique approach to combining medical excellence with clinical innovation. Its wide array of services have included addiction emergency department heart (cardiology) lung and pulmonology musictherapy neurology orthopedics pediatric emergency care psychiatry radiology surgery and urology. Headquartered in New York Mount Sinai Beth Israel has played an important role in providing health care to New Yorkers since the mid-20th century.

	Annual Growth	12/05	12/06	12/07	12/08	12/09
Sales ($ mil.)	34.8%	–	–	–	932.4	1,256.6
Net income ($ mil.)	–	–	–	–	(59.7)	15.2
Market value ($ mil.)	–	–	–	–	–	–
Employees	–	–	–	–	–	8,100

BETHESDA HOSPITAL, INC.

4750 WESLEY AVE
CINCINNATI, OH 452122244
Phone: 513-569-6100
Fax: –
Web: www.trihealth.com

CEO: –
CFO: Craig Rucker
HR: –
FYE: June 30
Type: Private

From modest beginnings as a informal cottage hospital Bethesda North Hospital has grown into the fourth largest medical center in Cincinnati Ohio. Bethesda North is a full-service acute care hospital with some 360 beds for adults and 60 for children. It provides comprehensive medical and surgical care including maternity and fertility services emergency care and diagnostic imaging. The hospital joined with fellow Cincinnati health care provider Good Samaritan Hospital in 1995 to form TriHealth. Together the two hospitals offer care at some 80 locations including primary care offices fitness centers and occupational health facilities.

	Annual Growth	06/17	06/18	06/19	06/20	06/21
Sales ($ mil.)	5.2%	–	639.8	624.1	643.1	744.5
Net income ($ mil.)	8.5%	–	52.5	32.6	(37.0)	67.0
Market value ($ mil.)	–	–	–	–	–	–
Employees	–	–	–	–	–	3,000

BETHUNE-COOKMAN UNIVERSITY INC.

640 DR MARY MCLEOD BETHUN
DAYTONA BEACH, FL 321143012
Phone: 386-481-2000
Fax: –
Web: www.cookman.edu

CEO: –
CFO: –
HR: –
FYE: June 30
Type: Private

Founded by educator Dr. Mary McLeod Bethune as a school for African-American women Bethune-Cookman University (B-CU) is in the top tier of Historically Black Colleges & Universities (HBCUs) in the US. The Daytona Florida-based university has about 3600 students enrolled in undergraduate and graduate programs in some 40 majors. Approximately 54% of the school's students live in on-campus residential housing. B-CU has about 200 full-time faculty members and faculty/student ratio of 1:17. The university also offers a NCAA Division One athletic program. B-CU charges some $14410 in annual tuition and fees.

	Annual Growth	06/08	06/09	06/11	06/13	06/14
Sales ($ mil.)	9.3%	–	58.8	76.1	71.4	92.0
Net income ($ mil.)	–	–	(4.6)	11.2	2.1	(0.3)
Market value ($ mil.)	–	–	–	–	–	–
Employees	–	–	–	–	–	600

BETSEY JOHNSON LLC

498 7th Ave. 21st Fl.
New York NY 10018
Phone: 212-244-0843
Fax: 212-244-0855
Web: www.betseyjohnson.com/

CEO: –
CFO: –
HR: –
FYE: December 31
Type: Private

Betsey Johnson the person and the brand is a favorite for women with a funky fashion sense. The apparel label named after its eclectic designer is sewn into dresses and other merchandise shoes handbags and accessories (sunglasses legwear and perfume). Private equity firm Castanea Partners and Steven Madden have owned Betsey Johnson's trademark and intellectual property since the company recapitalized in 2010. Betsey Johnson filed for Chapter 11 bankruptcy liquidation in 2012. Subsequently The Levy Group which licenses Betsey Johnson outerwear and other labels picked up the license to make and sell her dresses to boutique retailers and department stores including Bloomingdale's Saks and Nordstrom.

BEXIL CORP

NBB: BXLC

11 Hanover Square
New York, NY 10005
Phone: 212 785-0900
Fax: 212 785-0400
Web: www.bexil.com

CEO: Thomas Winmill
CFO: Thomas O'malley
HR: –
FYE: December 31
Type: Public

Bexil Corporation is on a quest to seek out new business ventures. The shell corporation has left the insurance business behind and is hoping to acquire another promising business. The holding company's primary operation had been a 50% stake in York Insurance Services Group which provided independent adjustment and third-party administration services to insurance companies and self-insured groups. In 2006 however Bexil sold its stake in York to Odyssey Investment Partners and began seeking other opportunities for investment.

	Annual Growth	12/07	12/08	12/09	12/18	12/19
Assets ($ mil.)	(4.2%)	38.6	38.7	38.3	19.3	23.1
Net income ($ mil.)	26.9%	0.3	0.3	(0.6)	(1.3)	4.5
Market value ($ mil.)	(5.3%)	24.9	21.9	20.7	8.3	12.9
Employees		–	–	–	–	–

BG MEDICINE INC

NBB: BGMD

303 Wyman Street, Suite 300
Waltham, MA 02451
Phone: 781 890-1199
Fax: –
Web: www.bg-medicine.com

CEO: Paul Sohmer
CFO: Stephen Hall
HR: –
FYE: December 31
Type: Public

BG Medicine wants to fill big gaps in diagnostic medicine. The biosciences researcher specializes in developing biomarkers (substances used to detect disease at a molecular level) that enable research into the causes of disease and the effectiveness of drugs used to treat them. Products in commercialization development and discovery stages include molecular diagnostic tests for heart disease neurological disorders and immune-system ailments. BG Medicine also provides drug research and development services to global pharmaceutical makers US government agencies and other health care organizations. The company built through venture capital backing held its IPO in 2011.

	Annual Growth	12/11	12/12	12/13	12/14	12/15
Sales ($ mil.)	(1.1%)	1.6	2.8	4.1	2.8	1.6
Net income ($ mil.)	–	(17.6)	(23.8)	(15.8)	(8.1)	(5.3)
Market value ($ mil.)	(47.4%)	53.4	26.1	11.8	5.2	4.1
Employees	(40.2%)	39	30	23	7	5

BGC PARTNERS INC

NMS: BGCP

499 Park Avenue
New York, NY 10022
Phone: 212 610-2200
Fax: –
Web: www.bgcpartners.com

CEO: Howard Lutnick
CFO: Steven Bisgay
HR: –
FYE: December 31
Type: Public

A leading global brokerage and financial technology company BGC Partners wheels and deals in financial markets. Specializing in inter-dealer brokerage for financial institutions the firm's BGC Trader Capitalab and FENICS branded platforms provide voice electronic and hybrid trade brokerage services for a broad range of financial products including government and corporate bonds and other debt instruments as well as related interest rate derivatives and credit derivatives. It also provides a wide variety of services including trade execution brokerage services clearing compression post-trade information and other back-office services to a broad assortment of financial and non-financial institutions. The company provides market data and analytics services. Majority of the company's sales are generated from international markets.

	Annual Growth	12/16	12/17	12/18	12/19	12/20
Sales ($ mil.)	(5.8%)	2,612.6	3,353.4	1,937.8	2,104.2	2,056.7
Net income ($ mil.)	(16.9%)	102.5	51.5	197.5	55.7	48.9
Market value ($ mil.)	(20.9%)	3,773.9	5,574.1	1,907.2	2,191.3	1,475.6
Employees	(11.3%)	8,091	9,235	4,688	5,200	5,000

BHE ENVIRONMENTAL INC.

11733 Chesterdale Rd.
Cincinnati OH 45246
Phone: 513-326-1500
Fax: 513-326-1550
Web: www.bheenv.com

CEO: –
CFO: –
HR: –
FYE: December 31
Type: Private

Engineering and consulting firm BHE Environmental provides services related to remediation resource management and brownfield restoration to industrial commercial and government clients. The company's specialties include industrial hygiene and safety land reuse management of cultural and natural resources site assessment and wind energy support services. It uses Ultimap technology to provide an online means to collect store and communicate geospatial information and to display it on aerial photographs and maps. BHE Environmental operates from offices in Ohio Missouri Tennessee and West Virginia. The company was founded in 1988.

BI-LO HOLDING LLC

208 BI-LO Blvd.
Greenville SC 29607
Phone: 864-213-2500
Fax: 312-602-8099
Web: www.grantthornton.com

CEO: –
CFO: Brian Carney
HR: –
FYE: December 31
Type: Private

"Combine and conquer" is the motto at BI-LO Holding. The newly-formed parent company for the BI-LO and Winn-Dixie supermarket chains boasts about 690 stores across eight southeastern states. The BI-LO supermarket chain operates more than 200 BI-LO and Super BI-LO grocery stores in the Carolinas Georgia and Tennessee. Winn-Dixie operates about 480 combination food and drug stores in Alabama Florida Georgia Louisiana and Mississippi under the Winn-Dixie and Winn-Dixie Marketplace banners. BI-LO Holding was formed in 2012 when BI-LO's owner Dallas-based investment firm Lone Star Funds acquired Winn-Dixie for about $560 million and merged the two companies.

BI-RITE RESTAURANT SUPPLY CO., INC.

123 S HILL DR
BRISBANE, CA 940051203
Phone: 415-656-0187
Fax: –
Web: www.birite.com

CEO: William Barulich
CFO: Zachary Barulich
HR: –
FYE: December 31
Type: Private

Bi-Rite Restaurant Supply which does business as BiRite Foodservice Distributors is a leading food service supplier serving the San Francisco Bay area and Northern California. The company distributes a full line of food equipment and supplies including meat and dairy items seafood frozen foods dry groceries cleaning supplies china kitchen equipment and disposables. Its customers include restaurant operators hotels universities and hospitals. The company's international arm supplied food to the Middle East and Asia. A member of the UniPro Foodservice cooperative the family-owned company was founded in 1966 by cousins Victor and John Barulich.

	Annual Growth	12/14	12/15	12/16	12/17	12/18
Sales ($ mil.)	0.3%	–	321.6	305.6	314.8	324.0
Net income ($ mil.)	50.6%	–	8.5	12.2	13.3	29.2
Market value ($ mil.)	–	–	–	–	–	–
Employees	–	–	–	–	–	300

BIDZ.COM INC.

2400 Marine Ave.
Redondo Beach CA 90278
Phone: 310-280-7373
Fax: 310-280-7375
Web: www.bidz.com

NASDAQ: BIDZ
CEO: David Zinberg
CFO: Lawrence Y Kong
HR: –
FYE: December 31
Type: Private

Bidz.com combines the discounts of a dollar store the format of an auction house and the convenience of the Internet to bring sparkling deals to shoppers. The firm buys closeout merchandise and sells it using a live-auction format with $1 opening bids. It mostly sells jewelry including gold platinum and silver items set with diamonds as well as precious and semi-precious stones. Visitors can also find deals on electronics apparel and a range of collectibles (such as fine art antiques coins and sports cards). The company's Buyz.com is a fixed-price e-commerce site that offers similar items listed for auction. In a deal that took the company private Bidz.com was acquired by Glendon Group in 2012.

BIG 5 SPORTING GOODS CORP

2525 East El Segundo Boulevard
El Segundo, CA 90245
Phone: 310 536-0611
Fax: –
Web: www.big5sportinggoods.com

NMS: BGFV
CEO: Steven Miller
CFO: Barry Emerson
HR: Jeffrey Fraley
FYE: January 03
Type: Public

Big 5 Sporting Goods which started out with five army surplus shops in California in 1955 is a sporting goods retailer with approximately 430 stores in which more than half of the stores are located in California. The company sells brand-name and private-label equipment apparel and footwear for indoor and outdoor activities such as camping hunting fishing tennis golf snowboarding and accessories. Its revenue is generated pretty evenly from soft goods (non-durable items such as apparel and footwear) and hard goods (durable items such as exercise equipment). Big 5 has stuck with a neighborhood-store format (averaging approximately 11000 sq. ft.) instead of opening massive superstores.

	Annual Growth	01/17*	12/17	12/18	12/19*	01/21
Sales ($ mil.)	0.5%	1,021.2	1,009.6	987.6	996.5	1,041.2
Net income ($ mil.)	34.9%	16.9	1.1	(3.5)	8.4	55.9
Market value ($ mil.)	(12.4%)	380.5	166.7	56.1	66.2	223.9
Employees	(1.7%)	9,000	9,000	8,700	8,800	8,400

*Fiscal year change

BIG LOTS, INC.

4900 E. Dublin-Granville Road
Columbus, OH 43081
Phone: 614 278-6800
Fax: 614 278-6666
Web: www.biglots.com

NYS: BIG
CEO: Bruce Thorn
CFO: Jonathan Ramsden
HR: Michael Schlonsky
FYE: January 30
Type: Public

One of North America's largest broadline closeout retailers Big Lots operates nearly 1410 stores across the US. It sells a variety of brand-name products that include food decor consumables furniture housewares seasonal items and electronics toys and accessories among others. Furniture represents the company's largest product line accounting for about 30% of sales. Big Lots which has been shuttering physical stores in recent years also offers products via its website including some items only available online. The company was founded by Sol Shenk in 1967.

	Annual Growth	01/17*	02/18	02/19	02/20*	01/21
Sales ($ mil.)	4.5%	5,200.4	5,271.0	5,238.1	5,323.2	6,199.2
Net income ($ mil.)	42.4%	152.8	189.8	156.9	242.5	629.2
Market value ($ mil.)	5.2%	1,729.5	2,051.8	1,113.0	961.6	2,120.7
Employees	1.3%	35,100	34,800	35,600	34,000	37,000

*Fiscal year change

BIG WEST OIL, LLC

333 W CENTER ST
NORTH SALT LAKE, UT 840542805
Phone: 801-624-1000
Fax: –
Web: www.bigwestoil.com

CEO: –
CFO: –
HR: –
FYE: January 31
Type: Private

Big West Oil keeps the wagon trains rolling across the big West — at least the station wagons. The company is in the oil processing and products business centered around its 35000 barrels-a-day refinery in North Salt Lake Utah to its fleet of tanker trucks that gather crude oil from the refinery and other purchases and deliver to wholesale customers and gas station/convenience stores in seven Western states including Colorado Idaho Nevada Utah and Wyoming. The company's refinery processes crude oil produced in Utah Wyoming and Canada. Big West Oil is a subsidiary of FJ Management.

	Annual Growth	01/04	01/05	01/06	01/07	01/08
Sales ($ mil.)	60.7%	–	735.6	2,014.1	2,399.5	3,053.3
Net income ($ mil.)	55.6%	–	50.8	102.9	89.0	191.1
Market value ($ mil.)	–	–	–	–	–	–
Employees	–	–	–	–	–	460

BIG Y FOODS INC.

2145 Roosevelt Ave.
Springfield MA 01102-7840
Phone: 413-784-0600
Fax: 908-673-9920
Web: authentidate.com

CEO: William Mahoney
CFO: –
HR: Drew Golaski
FYE: December 31
Type: Private

Why call it Big Y? Big Y Foods began as a 900-sq.-ft. grocery at a Y intersection in Chicopee Massachusetts. It now operates some 60 supermarkets throughout Massachusetts and Connecticut. Most of its stores are Big Y World Class Markets offering specialty areas such as bakeries and floral shops as well as banking. The rest consist of Big Y Supermarkets and a single gourmet food and liquor store called Table & Vine in Springfield Massachusetts. Some Big Y stores provide child care dry cleaning photo processing and even propane sales and their delis and food courts offer to-go foods. Big Y is owned and run by the D'Amour family and is one of New England's largest independent supermarket chains.

BIG-D CONSTRUCTION CORP.

404 W 400 S
SALT LAKE CITY, UT 841011108
Phone: 801-415-6000
Fax: -
Web: www.big-d.com

CEO: Rob Moore
CFO: -
HR: -
FYE: December 31
Type: Private

Big-D builds big things. Founded in 1967 by Dee Livingood (who carried the nickname "Big-Dee") the family-run construction firm offers design/build services to customers in a dozen states from offices in Utah Arizona California and Wyoming. Known for its work on projects in the food and beverage sector Big-D also works on light commercial office and retail properties manufacturing health care and hospitality projects among others. Its clients have included Hampton and Marriott. Big-D's Signature Group division builds high-end luxury homes as well as condominiums spas and other special projects in resort communities. Its Self-Performed Services unit works on parking garage architectural and structural projects. Big-D ranked 2nd in Top Utah General Contractor by Utah Design & Construction Magazine (rankings are based on revenues).

	Annual Growth	12/08	12/09	12/10	12/11	12/12
Sales ($ mil.)	44.4%	-	-	259.8	554.8	541.6
Net income ($ mil.)	-	-	-	0.0	0.0	0.0
Market value ($ mil.)	-	-	-	-	-	-
Employees	-	-	-	-	-	1,384

BIGLARI HOLDINGS INC (NEW)   NYS: BH

17802 IH 10 West, Suite 400
San Antonio, TX 78257
Phone: 210 344-3400
Fax: 317 633-4105
Web: www.biglariholdings.com

CEO: Sardar Biglari
CFO: -
HR: -
FYE: December 31
Type: Public

Beef and ice cream is an unbeatable combination for this restaurant company. Biglari Holdings is a multi-concept dining operator with two chains operating under the names Steak n Shake and Western Sizzlin. Its flagship concept encompasses more than 660 company-owned and franchised family dining spots in more than 30 states mostly in the Midwest and Southeast. The diners open 24-hours a day are popular for its Steakburger sandwiches and milkshakes as well as breakfast items and other dishes. More than 370 of the units are company-owned while the rest are franchised. Western Sizzlin meanwhile oversees nearly 50 franchised steak buffet restaurants in about 15 states. The company also has operations in insurance and media.

	Annual Growth	12/16	12/17	12/18	12/19	12/20
Sales ($ mil.)	(15.5%)	850.1	839.8	809.9	668.8	433.7
Net income ($ mil.)	-	99.5	50.1	19.4	45.4	(38.0)
Market value ($ mil.)	(30.4%)	1,076.8	943.0	258.5	260.4	253.0
Employees	(34.9%)	21,519	20,732	18,684	10,906	3,862

BILL & MELINDA GATES FOUNDATION

500 5th Ave. North
Seattle WA 98102
Phone: 206-709-3100
Fax: 206-709-3180
Web: www.gatesfoundation.org

CEO: Mark Suzman
CFO: -
HR: -
FYE: December 31
Type: Private - Foundation

You don't have to be one of the world's richest men or know one to make a difference with your charitable gifts — but it helps. Established by the chairman of Microsoft Corporation and his wife the Bill & Melinda Gates Foundation works in developing countries to improve health and reduce poverty and in the US to support education and libraries nationwide and children and families in the Pacific Northwest. With an endowment of about $33.5 billion the foundation is the largest in the US distributing more than $26 billion in total grants since 1994. Investor Warren Buffett plans to give the Bill & Melinda Gates Foundation about $30 billion worth of Berkshire Hathaway stock in installments.

BILLING SERVICES GROUP LTD.   LON: BILL

7411 John Smith Drive, Suite 1500
San Antonio, TX 78229
Phone: 210 949-7000
Fax: 210 949-7101
Web: www.bsgclearing.com

CEO: Norman M Phipps
CFO: Norman Phipps
HR: -
FYE: December 31
Type: Public

The idea behind Billing Services Group (doing business as BSG Clearing Solutions) is simple: Leave the bills to someone else. The company provides outsourced bill processing and settlement to telecommunications companies around the world. Its technology platform tracks direct long-distance calls as well as operator-assisted and calling-card calls and enables authentication invoicing collection and settlement. Originally a subsidiary of U.S. Long Distance the company (then Billing Concepts) was spun off as a public company in 1996. ABRY Partners took the company private in 2003 and merged it with ACI Billing Services the next year to form parent Billing Services Group which is domiciled in Bermuda.

	Annual Growth	12/14	12/15	12/16	12/17	12/18
Sales ($ mil.)	(21.5%)	42.4	36.4	30.2	21.1	16.1
Net income ($ mil.)	-	2.1	8.7	10.9	(6.7)	(7.8)
Market value ($ mil.)	-	-	-	-	-	-
Employees	-	-	-	-	-	-

BILLINGS CLINIC

2800 10TH AVE N
BILLINGS, MT 591010703
Phone: 406-657-4000
Fax: -
Web: www.billingsclinic.com

CEO: Nicholas Wolter
CFO: Priscilla Needham
HR: -
FYE: June 30
Type: Private

Billings Clinic is an integrated health care system that serves the residents of Big Sky Country. Through a group of more than 450 doctors and other providers the clinic caters a vast region covering much of Montana northern Wyoming and the western Dakotas. It offers 50-plus specialties such as emergency and trauma cancer orthopedics birthing cardiovascular neurosciences dialysis and pediatrics. Its operations include a more than 300-bed hospital and the organization's main clinic. Additionally Billings Clinic has nearly 15 regional partnerships including management agreements with more than 10 Critical Access Hospitals and a joint venture in Community Medical Center (Missoula MT) with RegionalCare Hospital Partners. The not-for-profit health care system is owned by the community.

	Annual Growth	06/12	06/13	06/14	06/15	06/16
Sales ($ mil.)	1.6%	-	560.2	593.6	565.5	586.8
Net income ($ mil.)	-	-	14.5	38.9	30.3	(2.4)
Market value ($ mil.)	-	-	-	-	-	-
Employees	-	-	-	-	-	3,300

BIMINI CAPITAL MANAGEMENT INC   NBB: BMNM

3305 Flamingo Drive
Vero Beach, FL 32963
Phone: 772 231-1400
Fax: -
Web: www.biminicapital.com

CEO: Robert Cauley
CFO: George Haas
HR: -
FYE: December 31
Type: Public

Bimini Capital Management (formerly Opteum) invests in residential mortgage-backed securities and related securities issued by the likes of Fannie Mae Freddie Mac and Ginnie Mae. The real estate investment trust (REIT) manages a portfolio worth more than $100 million mainly consisting of mortgage-related securities backed by adjustable-rate mortgages. Bimini Capital also invests in fixed-rate mortgage-backed securities and inverse interest-only securities. The company sold its residential mortgage origination business which consisted of about 25 offices in five states to Prospect Mortgage in 2007. It also ceased conduit and wholesale lending.

	Annual Growth	12/11	12/12	12/13	12/14	12/15
Sales ($ mil.)	(26.6%)	3.1	1.2	0.5	35.6	0.9
Net income ($ mil.)	-	(2.6)	(2.0)	(2.3)	7.7	59.2
Market value ($ mil.)	21.1%	4.6	1.6	3.4	23.6	9.9
Employees	0.0%	-	-	7	6	7

BIND THERAPEUTICS INC   NMS: BIND

325 Vassar Street   CEO: –
Cambridge, MA 02139   CFO: –
Phone: 617 491-3400   HR: –
Fax: –   FYE: December 31
Web: www.bindtherapeutics.com   Type: Public

BIND Therapeutics believes it's bound on a path and to products that will lead to a breakthrough in the treatment of certain cancers. The company designs nanoparticles with a prolonged circulation in the bloodstream called Accurins that target tumors at the the tissue cellular and molecular levels. Its lead candidate BIND-1014 which seeks out prostate tumors and lung cancers is in Phase 2 clinical trials. The company also aims to produce Accurins to treat non-oncological ailments such as cardiovascular disease and autoimmune disorders and is collaborating with Amgen AstraZeneca and Pfizer to develop such products. BIND founded in 2006 went public in September 2013 raising more than $70 million.

	Annual Growth	12/10	12/11	12/12	12/13	12/14
Sales ($ mil.)	–	0.0	0.9	1.0	10.9	10.4
Net income ($ mil.)	–	0.0	(16.9)	(19.2)	(27.7)	(32.5)
Market value ($ mil.)	–	–	0.0	–	249.7	89.4
Employees	33.4%	–	–	50	59	89

BINGHAM MCCUTCHEN LLP

1 Federal St.   CEO: –
Boston MA 02110-1726   CFO: –
Phone: 617-951-8000   HR: –
Fax: 617-951-8736   FYE: December 31
Web: www.bingham.com   Type: Private - Partnershi

Big and getting bigger Bingham McCutchen has about 1000 lawyers overall. Bingham has grown over the years by absorbing other law firms — adding 10 firms since 1997. It maintains 15 offices in the US Europe and the Asia/Pacific region with concentrations in California and New England. Bingham's wide range of practice areas is divided into major groups such as corporate finance litigation and securities. Along with its law practices the firm offers consulting services through subsidiaries such as Bingham Consulting Group and Bingham Strategic Advisors. Clients have included Guantanamo Bay detainees and ESPN reporter Erin Andrews. The firm was founded in 1891.

BIO-KEY INTERNATIONAL INC   NAS: BKYI

3349 Highway 138, Building A, Suite E   CEO: Michael DePasquale
Wall, NJ 07719   CFO: Cecilia Welch
Phone: 732 359-1100   HR: –
Fax: –   FYE: December 31
    Type: Public

BIO-key International has its finger securely on the pulse of biometrics. The company develops biometric security software and technology designed to secure access to enterprise applications and mobile devices. Its products incorporate biometric technology to scan and analyze fingerprints in order to grant or deny user access to wireless and enterprise data. BIO-key licenses its technology to original equipment manufacturers systems integrators and application developers. End users of its technology include corporations government agencies and other organizations concerned about the theft or misuse of sensitive data.

	Annual Growth	12/16	12/17	12/18	12/19	12/20
Sales ($ mil.)	(1.2%)	3.0	6.3	4.0	2.3	2.8
Net income ($ mil.)	–	(4.2)	(4.3)	(6.9)	(14.6)	(9.7)
Market value ($ mil.)	7.4%	20.7	13.8	5.9	3.9	27.5
Employees	(2.6%)	40	19	15	22	36

BIO-RAD LABORATORIES INC   NYS: BIO

1000 Alfred Nobel Drive   CEO: Norman Schwartz
Hercules, CA 94547   CFO: Ilan Daskal
Phone: 510 724-7000   HR: –
Fax: –   FYE: December 31
Web: www.bio-rad.com   Type: Public

Bio-Rad Laboratories is a leading maker of products for clinical diagnostics laboratory research and medical testing. Bio-Rad's clinical diagnostics segment makes products used in blood fluid and tissue testing to detect diseases such as diabetes. Its life science unit offers instruments apparatus reagents and software used in lab settings to study life processes potential drugs and food pathogens. Bio-Rad's customers include clinical labs pharmaceutical firms hospitals government agencies and universities. Majority of BioRad's sales come from international customers.

	Annual Growth	12/17	12/18	12/19	12/20	12/21
Sales ($ mil.)	7.8%	2,160.2	2,289.4	2,311.7	2,545.6	2,922.5
Net income ($ mil.)	142.8%	122.2	365.6	1,758.7	3,806.3	4,245.9
Market value ($ mil.)	33.4%	7,144.0	6,950.9	11,075.9	17,448.8	22,616.1
Employees	(0.8%)	8,150	8,260	8,120	8,000	7,900

BIO-REFERENCE LABORATORIES, INC.   NMS: BRLI

481 Edward H. Ross Drive   CEO: –
Elmwood Park, NJ 07407   CFO: –
Phone: 201 791-2600   HR: –
Fax: 201 791-1941   FYE: October 31
Web: www.bioreference.com   Type: Public

Bio-Reference Laboratories tests positive as the lab of choice for many in the Northeast. Primarily serving the greater New York Metropolitan Area the company offers routine clinical tests including Pap smears pregnancy tests cholesterol checks and blood cell counts. Through its GenPath business unit it also performs more sophisticated esoteric testing such as cancer pathology and molecular diagnostics. It gets most of its orders (close to 8 million per year) from doctors' offices collecting specimens at draw stations scattered throughout its primary service area in the New York area. Bio-Reference Laboratories also provides services in Connecticut Delaware Maryland New Jersey and Pennsylvania.

	Annual Growth	10/10	10/11	10/12	10/13	10/14
Sales ($ mil.)	16.1%	458.0	558.6	661.7	715.4	832.3
Net income ($ mil.)	15.4%	26.4	36.4	42.2	45.8	46.8
Market value ($ mil.)	8.6%	597.8	555.7	769.7	898.7	832.9
Employees	15.7%	2,424	3,155	3,564	4,427	4,347

BIO-SOLUTIONS MANUFACTURING INC.   OTC: BSOM

4440 Arville St. Ste. 6   CEO: –
Las Vegas NV 89103-3813   CFO: –
Phone: 702-222-9532   HR: –
Fax: 702-222-9126   FYE: October 31
Web: www.todaysalternativeenergy.net   Type: Public

Clogged drains? Nothing at all! Backed up pipes? P'shaw! Diesel tank empty? No problem for the guys at Bio-Solutions Manufacturing (BSM). The company has two divisions: a Cleaning Division and a Bio Diesel Division. The Cleaning Division's products make use of microbes and enzymes that can be used to treat sites contaminated by such pollutants as hydrocarbons grease hydrogen sulfide and ammonia. In addition Bio-Solutions' micro-organisms can clean up oil spills and contaminated groundwater by literally eating the contaminants. The Bio Diesel Division turns many of the waste products the company collects into biodiesel fuel. BSM distributes its products through subsidiary Bio-Solutions Franchise.

BIO-TECHNE CORP
NMS: TECH

614 McKinley Place N.E.
Minneapolis, MN 55413
Phone: 612 379-8854
Fax: -
Web: www.bio-techne.com

CEO: Chuck Kummeth
CFO: James Hippel
HR: -
FYE: June 30
Type: Public

Bio-Techne is a biotechnology research specialist. Through subsidiaries including Research and Diagnostic Systems (R&D Systems) Boston Biochem Bionostics and Tocris the company makes and distributes life science reagents instruments and services for the research diagnostics and bioprocessing markets worldwide. Bio-Techne's product lines extend to more than 350000 products most of which the company manufactures itself in multiple locations in North America as well as the UK and China. It also makes hematology controls and calibrators for blood analysis systems and sells them to equipment makers. The US accounts the largest for about 55% of total revenue.

	Annual Growth	06/17	06/18	06/19	06/20	06/21
Sales ($ mil.)	13.4%	563.0	643.0	714.0	738.7	931.0
Net income ($ mil.)	16.6%	76.1	126.2	96.1	229.3	140.4
Market value ($ mil.)	39.9%	4,577.3	5,763.5	8,121.8	10,287.0	17,540.1
Employees	9.6%	1,800	2,000	2,250	2,300	2,600

BIOCARDIA INC
NAS: BCDA

125 Shoreway Road, Suite B
San Carlos, CA 94070
Phone: 650 226-0120
Fax: -
Web: www.biocardia.com

CEO: Peter Altman
CFO: David McClung
HR: -
FYE: December 31
Type: Public

A healthy ticker really makes BioCardia (formerly Tiger X Medical) tick. The biopharma and diagnostics firm is exploring a stem cell therapy system to treat heart failure. Its CardiAMP therapy derived from a patients' bone marrow is in phase III clinical trials for the treatment of those who have already had a heart attack. The therapy is enabled by BioCardia's Helix delivery system through which treatments are injected into the walls of the heart. The firm has other regenerative biologic therapies under development for cardiovascular disease. The biotech was established in October 2016 after private company BioCardia conducted a reverse merger with publicly traded medical device shell company Tiger X Medical.

	Annual Growth	12/16	12/17	12/18	12/19	12/20
Sales ($ mil.)	(29.2%)	0.6	0.5	0.6	0.7	0.1
Net income ($ mil.)	-	(10.3)	(12.3)	(14.0)	(14.7)	(15.0)
Market value ($ mil.)	33.8%	17.6	38.3	19.6	60.0	56.4
Employees	20.0%	14	24	27	24	29

BIOCEPT INC
NAS: BIOC

9955 Mesa Rim Road
San Diego, CA 92121
Phone: 858 320-8200
Fax: -
Web: www.biocept.com

CEO: Michael Nall
CFO: Timothy Kennedy
HR: -
FYE: December 31
Type: Public

The concept at Biocept is to make cancer tumor identification quicker and more accurate. The company's products detect circulating tumor cells (CTCs) in a standard blood sample. Only one test is in production OncoCEE-BR for breast cancer. Its pipeline contains tests for lung gastric colorectal prostate and skin cancers; it plans to launch five new tests by 2017. Biocept collaborates with doctors and researchers at The University of Texas M.D. Anderson Cancer Center and the Dana-Farber Cancer Institute. The company was formed in 1997 and went public in 2014. It raised $18.8 million that it plans to use for sales and marketing R&D and development of tests and scaling up its production capabilities.

	Annual Growth	12/16	12/17	12/18	12/19	12/20
Sales ($ mil.)	70.8%	3.2	5.1	3.3	5.5	27.5
Net income ($ mil.)	-	(18.4)	(21.6)	(24.6)	(25.1)	(17.8)
Market value ($ mil.)	54.7%	10.4	9.3	11.5	3.8	59.5
Employees	16.4%	73	96	91	95	134

BIOCLINCA

7707 GATEWAY BLVD FL 3
NEWARK, CA 945601160
Phone: 415-817-8900
Fax: -
Web: www.synarc.com

CEO: Claus Christiansen
CFO: -
HR: -
FYE: December 31
Type: Private

You put up the compounds Synarc puts up the trials. The biomedical testing and contract research organization provides medical imaging patient recruitment and biomechanical marker services for clinical trials conducted by drug development companies around the globe. Synarc operates clinical research centers in North America Europe and Asia. The company has a main focus on neurological research including Alzheimer's disease studies; other clinical areas include oncology cardiovascular disease orthopedics infectious disease arthritis and osteoporosis. Synarc also conducts studies on medical devices.

	Annual Growth	09/97	09/98	09/99	09/00*	12/07
Sales ($ mil.)	36.3%	-	-	8.6	12.2	102.2
Net income ($ mil.)	-	-	-	(1.8)	(3.0)	(3.1)
Market value ($ mil.)	-	-	-	-	-	-
Employees	-	-	-	-	-	400

*Fiscal year change

BIOCRYST PHARMACEUTICALS INC
NMS: BCRX

4505 Emperor Blvd., Suite 200
Durham, NC 27703
Phone: 919 859-1302
Fax: 919 859-1314
Web: www.biocryst.com

CEO: Jon Stonehouse
CFO: Anthony Doyle
HR: -
FYE: December 31
Type: Public

BioCryst Pharmaceuticals is tackling the bad enzymes that spread disease. The firm creates small molecule compounds that inhibit enzymes associated with viral diseases autoimmune conditions and cancer. BioCryst's peramivir is a treatment for acute influenza that was developed with funding from the Department of Health and Human Services (HHS). Peramivir is marketed in Japan by Shionogi under the commercial name Rapiacta; in Korea it is marketed by Green Cross Corporation under the name PeramiFlu. Additional development programs include Berotralstat oral plasma kallikrein inhibitors for the treatment of angioedema and viral RNA polymerase inhibitor BCX4430.

	Annual Growth	12/16	12/17	12/18	12/19	12/20
Sales ($ mil.)	(9.3%)	26.4	25.2	20.7	48.8	17.8
Net income ($ mil.)	-	(55.1)	(65.8)	(101.3)	(108.9)	(182.8)
Market value ($ mil.)	4.2%	1,119.7	868.5	1,427.4	610.2	1,317.8
Employees	39.5%	65	85	100	140	246

BIODELIVERY SCIENCES INTERNATIONAL INC
NMS: BDSI

4131 ParkLake Avenue, Suite 225
Raleigh, NC 27612
Phone: 919 582-9050
Fax: -
Web: www.bdsi.com

CEO: Jeffrey Bailey
CFO: John Golubieski
HR: -
FYE: December 31
Type: Public

BioDelivery Sciences International (BDSI) is a specialty pharmaceutical firm that takes already approved drugs to patients living with chronic pain and associated conditions. Drugs delivered via its BEMA (BioErodible MucoAdhesive) systems focus on the areas of pain management and opioid-induced constipation. Its BEMA fentanyl product ONSOLIS is a buccally delivered polymer film used for the treatment of cancer pain. Other FDA-approved product includes BUNAVAIL for the treatment of opioid dependence and BELBUCA for chronic severe pain management.

	Annual Growth	12/16	12/17	12/18	12/19	12/20
Sales ($ mil.)	78.1%	15.5	62.0	55.6	111.4	156.5
Net income ($ mil.)	-	(67.1)	5.3	(33.9)	(15.3)	25.7
Market value ($ mil.)	24.5%	177.4	299.0	375.0	640.6	425.7
Employees	15.5%	99	116	164	178	176

BIOGEN INC
NMS: BIIB

225 Binney Street
Cambridge, MA 02142
Phone: 617 679-2000
Fax: –
Web: www.biogen.com

CEO: Michel Vounatsos
CFO: Michael R McDonnell
HR: –
FYE: December 31
Type: Public

With its pipeline full of biotech drugs Biogen aims to meet the unmet needs of patients around the world. The biotech giant is focused on developing treatments in the areas of multiple sclerosis and neuroimmunology. Its product roster includes best-selling drugs Tecfidera and Avonex for the treatment of relapsing multiple sclerosis (MS); Tysabri a drug treatment for MS and Crohn's disease; and Fampyra which improves walking in adults with MS. Other products include Plegridy for RMS. Biogen which serves customers around the world gets majority of its revenue from the US.

	Annual Growth	12/17	12/18	12/19	12/20	12/21
Sales ($ mil.)	(2.7%)	12,273.9	13,452.9	14,377.9	13,444.6	10,981.7
Net income ($ mil.)	(11.5%)	2,539.1	4,430.7	5,888.5	4,000.6	1,556.1
Market value ($ mil.)	(6.8%)	46,829.8	44,235.2	43,619.3	35,994.4	35,268.2
Employees	7.1%	7,300	7,800	7,400	9,100	9,610

BIOHORIZONS INC.

2300 Riverchase Center
Birmingham AL 35244
Phone: 205-967-7880
Fax: 205-870-0304
Web: www.biohorizons.com

CEO: R Steve Boggan
CFO: David Wall
HR: –
FYE: December 31
Type: Private

BioHorizons offers its customers a beautiful set of choppers with its tools. The company manufactures and sells dental implants — or individual screw-in teeth — as an alternative to conventional dentures. It also sells soft tissue regeneration products called biologics to help patients' gums grow back around the implant. Targeted to oral surgeons BioHorizons offers tools and specialty instruments (including those by Hu-Friedy) as well as a software program under the Virtual Implant Placement (VIP) name to map treatment procedures. BioHorizons sells its products in more than 80 countries and online. The company is owned by private equity firm HealthpointCapital.

BIOJECT MEDICAL TECHNOLOGIES INC.
OTC: BJCT

20245 SW 95th Ave.
Tualatin OR 97062
Phone: 503-692-8001
Fax: 503-692-6698
Web: www.bioject.com

CEO: Tony K Chow
CFO: –
HR: –
FYE: December 31
Type: Public

Bioject Medical Technologies wants to give the medical community a shot in the arm. Its Biojector 2000 jet injection system delivers injectable medication without a needle (and thus without needle-associated risks) by using a fine high-pressure stream that goes through the skin; the injector is powered by CO2 disposable cartridges or tanks. The accompanying vial adapter device allows the Biojector system to be filled without a needle. The company also markets Vitajet a spring-powered needle-free self-injection device that has been cleared for administering injections of insulin and Merck Serono's human growth hormones. Investment firm Signet Healthcare Partners and affiliates own one-third of Bioject.

BIOLA UNIVERSITY, INC.

13800 BIOLA AVE
LA MIRADA, CA 906390001
Phone: 562-903-6000
Fax: –
Web: www.biola.edu

CEO: –
CFO: –
HR: Judith Rood
FYE: June 30
Type: Private

The bio of Biola University is that it is a faith-based institution. The university is a private evangelical Christian institution of higher learning that provides more than 150 academic programs through nine schools. The nondenominational school offers bachelors masters and doctoral degrees and has an enrollment of more than 6000 students. Biola University was founded as the Bible Institute in 1908 and its campuses rests on the border of Orange and Los Angeles counties. Biola students and faculty donate some 200000 hours of volunteer work annually participating in off-campus activities such as leading Bible studies in nearby churches and evangelizing on the streets of inner cities.

	Annual Growth	06/13	06/14	06/15	06/16	06/20
Sales ($ mil.)	4.5%	–	199.7	161.5	165.3	260.7
Net income ($ mil.)	15.9%	–	13.6	29.1	10.6	32.9
Market value ($ mil.)	–	–	–	–	–	–
Employees	–	–	–	–	–	3,914

BIOLARGO INC
NBB: BLGO

14921 Chestnut St.
Westminster, CA 92683
Phone: 888 400-2863
Fax: –
Web: www.biolargo.com

CEO: Dennis Calvert
CFO: Charles Dargan
HR: –
FYE: December 31
Type: Public

After morphing identities several times over the past few years BioLargo (formerly NuWay Medical) hopes that it has found its way. The company went from car dealership and casino ownership to being a medical device maker and application service provider (ASP). It believes it has found its future in designing sanitizing chemicals for specialty packaging (such as pads protective liners and surgical drapes) used for shipping blood biohazardous materials meat and poultry and other items requiring sanitary containment. Consultant Kenneth Code controls 56% of BioLargo.

	Annual Growth	12/16	12/17	12/18	12/19	12/20
Sales ($ mil.)	71.5%	0.3	0.5	1.4	1.9	2.4
Net income ($ mil.)	–	(7.8)	(9.1)	(10.2)	(10.7)	(8.4)
Market value ($ mil.)	(37.9%)	186.8	87.0	54.1	48.8	27.8
Employees	9.2%	19	29	25	25	27

BIOLASE INC
NAS: BIOL

27042 Towne Centre Drive, Suite 270
Lake Forest, CA 92610
Phone: 949 361-1200
Fax: –
Web: www.biolase.com

CEO: John Beaver
CFO: –
HR: –
FYE: December 31
Type: Public

BioLase is causing dentists to drop the knife and pick up the laser. The company develops manufactures and sells laser-based systems for use primarily in dental applications. BioLase's surgical cutting system Waterlase uses laser pulses to turn water droplets into high-speed particles that can cut both hard and soft tissues and bones in the mouth. Waterlase is used in procedures traditionally performed with dental drills and scalpels. The company's Diode laser systems are used to perform soft tissue and cosmetic dental procedures as well as non-dental procedures. BioLase markets its products in more than 60 countries.

	Annual Growth	12/16	12/17	12/18	12/19	12/20
Sales ($ mil.)	(18.6%)	51.8	46.9	46.2	37.8	22.8
Net income ($ mil.)	–	(15.4)	(16.9)	(21.5)	(17.9)	(16.8)
Market value ($ mil.)	(26.1%)	136.7	41.6	96.7	54.0	40.7
Employees	(12.0%)	225	195	190	157	135

BIOLIFE SOLUTIONS INC   NAS: BLFS

3303 Monte Villa Parkway, Suite 310
Bothell, WA 98021
Phone: 425 402-1400
Fax: –
Web: www.biolifesolutions.com

CEO: Michael Rice
CFO: Troy Wichterman
HR: Sarah Aebersold
FYE: December 31
Type: Public

BioLife Solutions makes sure your tissues and organs don't get freezer burn. The company has designed liquid media technologies for frozen (cryogenic) storage and cold (hypothermic) storage of biological products including cells tissues and organs. Its HypoThermosol and CryoStor products minimize the damage done to these biological products during refrigeration and freezing making them viable for transplant or experimentation for longer periods. The company sells its products directly to academic institutions companies and laboratories conducting clinical research.

	Annual Growth	12/16	12/17	12/18	12/19	12/20
Sales ($ mil.)	55.5%	8.2	11.0	19.7	27.4	48.1
Net income ($ mil.)	–	(6.9)	(2.5)	3.3	(1.7)	2.7
Market value ($ mil.)	123.1%	53.2	198.2	397.5	534.6	1,317.9
Employees	53.3%	36	40	54	158	199

BIOMED REALTY TRUST INC   NYS: BMR

17190 Bernardo Center Drive
San Diego, CA 92128
Phone: 858 485-9840
Fax: 858 485-9843
Web: www.biomedrealty.com

CEO: Alan D Gold
CFO: Greg N Lubushkin
HR: –
FYE: December 31
Type: Public

BioMed Realty knows its niche. A self-administered real estate investment trust (REIT) the firm acquires develops leases and manages laboratory and office space for biotechnology and pharmaceutical companies scientific research institutions government agencies and other life science tenants. BioMed owns more than 80 properties with around 185 buildings and more than 16 million sq. ft. of rentable space. The REIT's properties which span about a dozen states are often located near universities; its preferred markets include research and development hubs such as Boston New York San Diego San Francisco and Seattle. In 2013 BioMed acquired Wexford Science & Technology.

	Annual Growth	12/09	12/10	12/11	12/12	12/13
Sales ($ mil.)	15.3%	361.2	386.4	439.7	518.2	637.3
Net income ($ mil.)	(5.6%)	58.7	38.8	42.2	11.8	46.6
Market value ($ mil.)	3.5%	3,031.6	3,582.9	3,473.4	3,713.6	3,481.1
Employees	15.5%	132	159	166	175	235

BIOMERICA INC   NAS: BMRA

17571 Von Karman Avenue
Irvine, CA 92614
Phone: 949 645-2111
Fax: –
Web: www.biomerica.com

CEO: Zackary Irani
CFO: Steven Sloan
HR: –
FYE: May 31
Type: Public

God bless Biomerica. The firm makes diagnostic tests for use worldwide in hospitals and other clinical laboratories as well as in doctors' offices and homes. Its clinical laboratory products are immunoassay tests for conditions such as food allergies diabetes infectious diseases and hyperthyroidism. Its point-of-care product portfolio which includes products that produce rapid results provides tests for prostate cancer pregnancy cat allergies and drugs of abuse. Biomerica has manufacturing facilities in the US and in Mexico. It once owned a minority interest in Lancer Orthodontics a maker of orthodontic products such as arch wires lingual attachments and buccal tubes but it sold its stake in 2008.

	Annual Growth	05/17	05/18	05/19	05/20	05/21
Sales ($ mil.)	5.6%	5.8	5.6	5.2	6.7	7.2
Net income ($ mil.)	–	(0.9)	(1.5)	(2.4)	(2.3)	(6.5)
Market value ($ mil.)	9.9%	30.8	50.1	27.7	79.6	44.9
Employees	5.9%	39	39	39	45	49

BIOMET INC.

56 E. Bell Dr.
Warsaw IN 46582-0587
Phone: 574-267-6639
Fax: 574-267-8137
Web: www.biomet.com

CEO: –
CFO: –
HR: –
FYE: May 31
Type: Private

When the leg bone and the knee bone don't connect so well anymore Biomet may have a solution. Orthopedic specialists use the medical devices made by Biomet whose wares include reconstructive products (hips knees and shoulders) dental implants bone cement systems orthopedic support devices and operating-room supplies. Through Biomet Trauma and other units the firm also sells fixation devices (bone screws and pins) electrical bone-growth stimulators and bone grafting materials. Subsidiary Biomet Microfixation markets implants and bone substitute material for craniomaxillofacial (head and face) surgeries. Biomet is controlled by LVB Acquisition which is owned by a group of private equity firms.

BIOMIMETIC THERAPEUTICS INC.   NASDAQ: BMTI

389-A Nichol Mill Ln.
Franklin TN 37067
Phone: 615-844-1280
Fax: 615-844-1281
Web: www.biomimetics.com

CEO: –
CFO: –
HR: –
FYE: December 31
Type: Public

BioMimetic Therapeutics' GEM might not sparkle but it does attract cells that promote tissue and bone growth when applied to damaged tissue or a bone fracture. The company's products and candidates are based on the GEM (Growth-factor Enhanced Matrix) technology a combination drug and medical device platform that includes a human tissue growth factor with a synthetic bone matrix. BioMimetic Therapeutics develops the GEM technology as a treatment for various fractures where its bone matrix can be used to repair reinforce or fuse broken bones as well as repair tendons ligaments and cartilage. BioMimetic was acquired by Wright Medical Group for $380 million in 2013.

BION ENVIRONMENTAL TECHNOLOGIES, INC.   NBB: BNET

Box 566 / 1774 Summitview Way
Crestone, CO 81131
Phone: 212 758-6622
Fax: –
Web: www.biontech.com

CEO: Dominic Bassani
CFO: Mark Smith
HR: –
FYE: June 30
Type: Public

A "moo moo" here and an "oink oink" there are music to the ears of Bion Environmental Technologies. The company provides waste stream remediation for animal operations primarily for large dairy and hog farms. To reduce pollution caused by animal waste Bion Environmental uses organic nutrients bacteria and other microbes to treat the waste before disposal. The treatment creates organic soil and fertilizer products which the company markets for use on athletic fields gardens and golf courses. The company is working closely with government bodies and universities in Pennsylvania to address the major problem of animal waste run-off from farms into the Chesapeake Bay.

	Annual Growth	06/12	06/13	06/14	06/15	06/16
Sales ($ mil.)	(32.4%)	–	0.0	0.0	0.0	0.0
Net income ($ mil.)	–	(6.4)	(8.2)	(5.8)	(5.6)	(4.5)
Market value ($ mil.)	(20.0%)	49.9	42.3	25.2	26.1	20.4
Employees	(12.6%)	12	8	6	6	7

BIOPHAN TECHNOLOGIES INC. OTC: BIPH

15 Schoen Place
Pittsford NY 14534
Phone: 585-267-4800
Fax: 585-267-4819
Web: www.biophan.com

CEO: –
CFO: –
HR: –
FYE: February 28
Type: Public

Biophan Technologies appreciates high visibility and smooth circulation. The company develops blood circulation support systems and technologies to help make medical devices compatible with MRI (magnetic resonance imaging) equipment. Its majority-owned Myotech unit is developing a system to restore and sustain blood flow in patients with acute heart failure. The system is based on a device that even a general surgeon can fit directly on a patient's heart to restart its pumping. Biophan's other technologies improve the visibility of coronary stents and vena cava filters in MRIs.

BIORELIANCE CORPORATION

14920 Broschart Rd.
Rockville MD 20850-3349
Phone: 301-738-1000
Fax: 301-610-2590
Web: www.bioreliance.com

CEO: David A Dodd
CFO: David S Walker
HR: –
FYE: December 31
Type: Subsidiary

BioReliance is one lab rat whose testing and manufacturing wheels are turning. Founded in 1947 the company is a contract testing and manufacturing services provider hired by drug developers to enhance their products' safety. With laboratories and other operations in the US the UK India and Japan BioReliance conducts biologics safety testing animal diagnostics toxicology and clinical trial assay services. It also manufactures vaccines gene therapies and other biologics for use in clinical trials. Clients include biotech pharmaceutical and chemical companies medical device makers academic institutions and government agencies. Laboratory chemicals supplier Sigma-Aldrich acquired BioReliance in 2012.

BIOSPECIFICS TECHNOLOGIES CORP. NMS: BSTC

35 Wilbur Street
Lynbrook, NY 11563
Phone: 516 593-7000
Fax: –
Web: www.biospecifics.com

CEO: Blaise Coleman
CFO: Mark Bradley
HR: Helen Piazza
FYE: December 31
Type: Public

BioSpecifics Technologies specifically uses collagenase (an enzyme that breaks the bonds of collagen) to treat a variety of skin-thickening diseases and conditions. Its current product named Xiaflex (Xiapex in Europe) is an injectable collagenase that treats Dupuytren's disease and Peyronie's disease. It partners with Endo International to market Xiaflex in the US and with Swedish Orphan Biovitrum to market Xiapex in Europe and Eurasia. BioSpecifics is also testing collagenase treatments for human and canine lipoma (benign fatty tumor) frozen shoulder cellulite plantar fibromatosis and lateral hip fat.

	Annual Growth	12/14	12/15	12/16	12/17	12/18
Sales ($ mil.)	23.7%	14.1	22.8	26.3	27.4	33.0
Net income ($ mil.)	44.1%	4.6	9.6	11.4	11.3	20.1
Market value ($ mil.)	11.9%	281.0	312.6	405.3	315.3	440.9
Employees	0.0%	5	5	5	5	5

BIOSYNERGY, INC. NL:

1940 East Devon Avenue
Elk Grove Village, IL 60007
Phone: 847 956-0471
Fax: 847 956-6050
Web: www.biosynergyinc.com

CEO: Fred Suzuki
CFO: Laurence Mead
HR: –
FYE: April 30
Type: Public

Biosynergy does its part to keep the good blood good. Biosynergy makes blood monitoring devices most of which are used in blood banks to keep blood healthy and at the right temperature. Its products are disposable cholesteric (asymmetrical) liquid crystal devices that cool heat and monitor blood and other lab materials or samples. The company also distributes some third-party products. In addition Biosynergy is developing antibacterial compounds for use in food and other products. The company sells its products to hospitals laboratories product dealers and clinical end-users. Chairman president and CEO Fred Suzuki controls about 35% of the company which was founded in 1976.

	Annual Growth	04/17	04/18	04/19	04/20	04/21
Sales ($ mil.)	(2.4%)	1.3	1.2	1.3	1.2	1.2
Net income ($ mil.)	(38.0%)	0.1	0.0	0.1	0.0	0.0
Market value ($ mil.)	–	0.0	0.0	–	–	–
Employees	(4.5%)	6	6	6	6	5

BIOTELEMETRY INC NMS: BEAT

1000 Cedar Hollow Road
Malvern, PA 19355
Phone: 610 729-7000
Fax: –
Web: www.gobio.com

CEO: Joseph H Capper
CFO: Heather C Getz
HR: –
FYE: December 31
Type: Public

BioTelemetry knows how to keep a beat. The company provides real-time outpatient cardiac rhythm monitoring and telemetry services for patients throughout the US. Its core product Mobile Cardiac Outpatient Telemetry (MCOT) helps physicians diagnose and monitor heart arrhythmia in patients by providing continuous heartbeat monitoring and transmitting a complete picture of the heart's functions to physicians. The system which uses real-time two-way wireless communication accommodates patient mobility and remote physician adjustment. BioTelemetry also manufactures and sells traditional cardiac event and Holter monitors that record patient heart rhythm data but cannot transmit the data in real time.

	Annual Growth	12/15	12/16	12/17	12/18	12/19
Sales ($ mil.)	25.2%	178.5	208.3	286.8	399.5	439.1
Net income ($ mil.)	41.6%	7.4	53.4	(16.0)	42.8	29.8
Market value ($ mil.)	41.1%	397.4	760.4	1,017.3	2,031.9	1,575.3
Employees	16.0%	938	1,087	1,600	1,500	1,700

BIRDS EYE FOODS LLC

90 Linden Oaks
Rochester NY 14625
Phone: 585-383-1850
Fax: 585-385-2857
Web: www.birdseyefoods.com

CEO: –
CFO: –
HR: –
FYE: June 30
Type: Subsidiary

Whether from a bird's eye or with an eye on the bottom line the view is sure to inspire health at Birds Eye Foods. Its namesake packaged frozen vegetables (boxed and bagged) are the #1 brand in the US frozen vegetable industry a more than $2 billion market in terms of retail sales. The company is also the #2 producer of frozen complete bagged meals providing a protein starch and vegetable. Birds Eye also makes such staples as canned pie fillings and chili and bottled salad dressings. It supplies US retail food retailers as well as foodservice and industrial food customers. Birds Eye operates as a division of diversified foods producer Pinnacle Foods itself owned by investment giant The Blackstone Group.

BIRKENSTOCK USA GP LLC

6 Hamilton Landing
Novato CA 94949
Phone: 415-884-3200
Fax: 888-937-2475
Web: www.birkenstockusa.com

CEO: –
CFO: –
HR: –
FYE: September 30
Type: Private

From Woodstock to the stock market Birkenstock wants you to put your best foot forward. Birkenstock USA is the exclusive US importer and distributor of the German-made footwear that was transformed from cult status to mainstream hip as the look of the 1970s re-emerged. The company's high-comfort products include hundreds of styles of shoes sandals clogs and arch supports for men women and children. Birkenstock's footwear is designed around the concept that the shape of the shoe should follow the shape of the foot. Birkenstock sells shoes through more than 1800 retailers and more than 200 licensed specialty shops. Birkenstock employees own 100% of the company.

BIRMINGHAM-SOUTHERN COLLEGE INC

900 ARKADELPHIA RD
BIRMINGHAM, AL 352540002
Phone: 205-226-4600
Fax: –
Web: www.bsc.edu

CEO: –
CFO: –
HR: –
FYE: May 31
Type: Private

Birmingham-Southern College is a private liberal arts college affiliated with the United Methodist Church. The school offers bachelor's degrees in more than 50 fields of study including art history math physics and religion. It has an enrollment of approximately 1300 students. In addition to core curriculum in areas of arts fine arts music and science the college has study abroad independent study research honors interdisciplinary study and internship programs. Birmingham-Southern College is the result of the 1918 merger between Southern University (founded in 1856) and Birmingham College (founded in 1898).

	Annual Growth	05/10	05/11	05/13	05/15	05/16
Sales ($ mil.)	(1.3%)	–	75.5	73.9	66.6	70.5
Net income ($ mil.)	–	–	0.2	7.9	(4.1)	(4.4)
Market value ($ mil.)	–	–	–	–	–	–
Employees						299

BIRNER DENTAL MANAGEMENT SERVICES INC   NBB: BDMS

1777 S. Harrison Street, Suite 1400
Denver, CO 80210
Phone: 303 691-0680
Fax: –
Web: www.perfectteeth.com

CEO: Frederic W J Birner
CFO: Dennis N Genty
HR: Lindsay Higgins
FYE: December 31
Type: Public

Birner Dental Management Services hopes to leave its customers smiling. The company acquires develops and manages dental practice networks freeing dentists of their administrative duties by providing management services such as billing accounting and marketing. Birner Dental manages about 60 offices under the Perfect Teeth brand name; more than 40 of the practices are located in Colorado and the rest are in Arizona and New Mexico. Some locations offer special services such as orthodontics oral surgery and periodontics. Brothers and co-founders Frederic (chairman and CEO) and Mark Birner (president) together own more than one-quarter of the company.

	Annual Growth	12/12	12/13	12/14	12/15	12/16
Sales ($ mil.)	(0.2%)	62.4	64.1	65.1	63.8	61.8
Net income ($ mil.)	–	0.8	0.1	(0.9)	(0.7)	(1.4)
Market value ($ mil.)	(1.6%)	31.8	32.5	27.9	20.9	29.8
Employees	(4.5%)	588	594	526	502	489

BISCOM INC.

321 Billerica Rd.
Chelmsford MA 01824
Phone: 978-250-1800
Fax: 978-250-4449
Web: www.biscom.com

CEO: Bill Ho
CFO: –
HR: –
FYE: June 30
Type: Private

Biscom can help you get right down to seemingly mundane business details such as faxing and e-mailing. The company provides enterprise fax server and fax software products including products to make various messaging formats and data such as voicemail fax and e-mail accessible and integrated into various applications. Biscom also provides tools for securly tranferring files throughout enterprises as well as document capture and routing products. Biscom's customers come from a variety of industries such as financial services manufacturing retail and health care.

BISON BUILDING MATERIALS LTD.

1445 W. Sam Houston Pkwy. North
Houston TX 77043-3110
Phone: 713-467-6700
Fax: 713-935-1223
Web: www.bisonbuilding.com

CEO: –
CFO: –
HR: –
FYE: April 30
Type: Private

Bison Building Materials provides lumber and building materials to primarily residential contractors and remodelers through about five locations in the Houston area and Central Texas. Besides lumber and plywood Bison Building Materials specializes in engineered wood products such as flooring structural beams fiberglass insulation and millwork. Founded in 1962 by Roy Bierschwale as a small retail store and lumber shed Bison Building Materials filed for Chapter 11 bankruptcy protection in 2009 following the crash in the housing market. Rival Stock Building Supply (SBS) acquired the company in July 2010.

BISSELL HOMECARE INC.

2345 Walker St. NW
Grand Rapids MI 49544
Phone: 616-453-4451
Fax: 616-453-1383
Web: www.bissell.com

CEO: Mark J Bissell
CFO: –
HR: –
FYE: December 31
Type: Private

BISSELL's in the business of seeing spots and taking care of dust bunnies. A pioneer in the carpet-cleaning industry BISSELL Homecare makes a full line of vacuum cleaners sweepers steam cleaners deep cleaners and cleaning chemicals for home use. Its models include the Powersteamer Big Green and Spotlifter machines. The firm sells its products worldwide under the BISSELL and Woolite brand names through mass merchandisers (Best Buy Target Wal-Mart) home centers (Lowe's Home Depot) hardware stores (Ace Hardware) and through BISSELL.com. It entered the deep-cleaning rental business in 2010. Founded in 1876 by Melville and Anna Bissell the company is still owned and operated by the Bissell family.

BITCO CORPORATION

320 18th St.
Rock Island IL 61201
Phone: 309-786-5401
Fax: 309-786-3847
Web: www.bituminousinsurance.com

CEO: Greg Ator
CFO: –
HR: –
FYE: December 31
Type: Subsidiary

Bitco which operates as the Bituminous Insurance Companies provides insurance services with industry specialization in construction construction materials forest products oil and gas and structural moving. The group consists of Bituminous Casualty and Bituminous Fire and Marine Insurance and underwrites primarily commercial automobile commercial property general liability and workers' compensation insurance lines. Bitco also sells insurance through Great West Casualty Company which specializes in coverage primarily for the motor carrier industry. Its products are marketed through independent insurance agents. Bitco and the Bituminous Insurance Companies are subsidiaries of Old Republic International.

BITNILE HOLDINGS INC   ASE: NILE

11411 Southern Highlands Pkwy., Suite 240
Las Vegas, NV 89141
Phone: 949 444-5464
Fax: –
Web: www.dpwholdings.com

CEO: Amos Kohn
CFO: William B Horne
HR: –
FYE: December 31
Type: Public

Digital Power is a real switch hitter. The company makes power supplies such as AC/DC switchers and DC/DC converters for OEMs in the industrial medical military and telecommunications markets. Its products protect electronic components and circuits from power surges while converting a single input voltage into different output voltages. Most of Digital Power's products which can be easily modified to meet the specific needs of its 400 customers are made by subcontractors in China and Mexico. UK-based subsidiary Digital Power Limited doing business as Gresham Power Electronics makes AC/DC power supplies uninterruptible power supplies and power inverters; it accounts for more than half of sales.

	Annual Growth	12/16	12/17	12/18	12/19	12/20
Sales ($ mil.)	33.1%	7.6	10.2	27.2	26.5	23.9
Net income ($ mil.)	–	(1.1)	(10.6)	(32.2)	(32.9)	(32.7)
Market value ($ mil.)	60.5%	18.2	89.1	2.8	33.0	120.7
Employees	56.0%	26	77	248	210	154

BITSTREAM INC.   NASDAQ: BITS

500 Nickerson Rd.
Marlborough MA 01752
Phone: 617-497-6222
Fax: 617-868-0784
Web: www.bitstream.com

CEO: Amos Kaminski
CFO: James P Dore
HR: –
FYE: December 31
Type: Public

Bitstream counts on its fonts to keep business flowing. The company's Font Fusion and Bitstream Panorama technologies help deliver typographic capabilities to hardware software and Web applications. Font Fusion is the company's base text rendering technology designed specifically for small form factors such as mobile phones and set-top boxes. Bitstream Panorama specializes in complex language printing needs such as for Arabic Hebrew and Thai. Bitstream also offers some 62000 fonts to consumers through MyFonts.com. In 2011 Bitstream spun off its mobile browsing and data publishing businesses to facilitate the company's acquisition by Monotype Imaging in 2012.

BJ'S RESTAURANTS INC   NMS: BJRI

7755 Center Avenue, Suite 300
Huntington Beach, CA 92647
Phone: 714 500-2400
Fax: –
Web: www.bjsrestaurants.com

CEO: Gregory A Trojan
CFO: Gregory S Levin
HR: –
FYE: December 29
Type: Public

BJ's Restaurants (BJ's) owns and operates some 210 restaurants in California and almost 30 other states. BJ's more than 100 menu includes a wide variety of offerings and has something for everyone: slow-roasted entrees like prime rib; BJ's EnLIGHTened Entrees including Cherry Chipotle Glazed Salmon; signature deep dish pizza; and the world-famous Pizookie dessert. The company takes pride in serving BJ's award-winning proprietary handcrafted beers brewed on its own brewing facilities and certain third party craft brewers. It offers high-quality ingredients bold flavors moderate prices sincere service and a cool contemporary atmosphere. The first BJ's opened in California in 1978.

	Annual Growth	01/17	01/18	01/19*	12/19	12/20
Sales ($ mil.)	(7.8%)	993.1	1,031.8	1,116.9	1,161.5	778.5
Net income ($ mil.)	–	45.6	44.8	50.8	45.2	(57.9)
Market value ($ mil.)	(0.2%)	852.5	820.2	1,128.6	847.2	847.9
Employees	(8.2%)	22,000	21,500	22,215	22,500	17,000

*Fiscal year change

BJ'S WHOLESALE CLUB INC.

25 Research Dr.
Westborough MA 01581
Phone: 508-651-7400
Fax: 508-651-6114
Web: www.bjs.com

CEO: –
CFO: Robert Eddy
HR: –
FYE: January 31
Type: Private

"Exclusive membership" has never been as common as it is at BJ's Wholesale Club. The firm is the nation's #3 membership warehouse club (far behind leaders Costco and SAM'S CLUB) and #1 in New England with more than nine million members and about 195 locations in 15 states mostly along the Eastern Seaboard. Food including canned fresh and frozen items accounts for about two-thirds of sales at BJ's. The remainder comes from general merchandise including apparel housewares office equipment small appliances and gas. Unlike its major rivals BJ's targets individual retail customers rather than small businesses. BJ's was taken private in 2011.

BJT, INC.

2233 CAPITAL BLVD
RALEIGH, NC 276041421
Phone: 919-828-3842
Fax: –
Web: www.mutualdistributing.com

CEO: –
CFO: –
HR: –
FYE: December 31
Type: Private

A wholesaler of Southern comfort Mutual Distributing distributes alcoholic and nonalcoholic beverages in North Carolina. The company started in 1946 operates from seven locations across the state. Alcoholic beverage brands handled by Mutual Distributing include domestic and imported wine labels by Wyndham Estate Robert Mondavi Moet & Chandon and Folie a Deux and beers by Anchor Tecate Heineken and Sapporo. The company distributes bottled waters too such as Evian Perrier San Pellegrino and Fiji. Mutual Distributing caters to retail customers (supermarkets convenience stores and specialty package outlets restaurants and hotels) in every county in North Carolina.

	Annual Growth	12/04	12/05	12/06	12/08	12/09
Sales ($ mil.)	6.1%	–	158.3	172.7	192.0	200.4
Net income ($ mil.)	17.8%	–	3.2	4.2	7.8	6.2
Market value ($ mil.)	–	–	–	–	–	–
Employees	–	–	–	–	–	650

BK TECHNOLOGIES CORP
ASE: BKTI

7100 Technology Drive
West Melbourne, FL 32904
Phone: 321 984-1414
Fax: –
Web: www.relm.com

CEO: John M Suzuki
CFO: William P Kelly
HR: –
FYE: December 31
Type: Public

RELM Wireless spreads communications across the land. The company makes portable land mobile radio (LMR) products used for mobile handheld and vehicle communications. In addition to radios its products include base stations repeaters and related subsystems. The US government and public safety agencies account for the vast majority of RELM's sales but the company also markets to hotels construction firms schools and transportation service providers. RELM Wireless sells its radio communications systems under the BK Radio RELM and RELM/BK brands.

	Annual Growth	12/16	12/17	12/18	12/19	12/20
Sales ($ mil.)	(3.4%)	50.7	39.4	49.4	40.1	44.1
Net income ($ mil.)	(44.9%)	2.7	(3.6)	(0.2)	(2.6)	0.2
Market value ($ mil.)	(10.6%)	59.4	44.4	46.9	38.8	37.9
Employees	(2.9%)	107	119	119	111	95

BKF CAPITAL GROUP INC
NBB: BKFG

31248 Oak Crest Drive, Suite 110
Westlake Village, CA 91361
Phone: 805 416-7054
Fax: –
Web: www.bkfcapital.com

CEO: Steven N Bronson
CFO: David Burnett
HR: –
FYE: December 31
Type: Public

Wanted: business opportunity for former investment firm. Contact BKF Capital Group. BKF is evaluating strategic alternatives including a possible merger acquisition or other business combination. The company has no operations and only a small revenue stream (more like a trickle) from its days as an asset manager and broker dealer; it is no longer a registered investment advisor and has also surrendered its broker license. Its primary subsidiary is BKF Asset Management but as the company itself points out it has no operations either. BKF Capital's search for a new raison d'etre was put on hold when it was named in a class action shareholder lawsuit but the suit was dropped in 2007 and the search resumed.

	Annual Growth	12/12	12/13	12/14	12/15	12/16
Sales ($ mil.)	(63.3%)	0.1	0.0	0.0	0.0	0.0
Net income ($ mil.)	–	(0.8)	(2.3)	(1.0)	(0.6)	(0.2)
Market value ($ mil.)	68.9%	0.7	0.8	1.0	0.6	5.7
Employees	(42.3%)	3	1	1		

BLACK & VEATCH CORPORATION

11401 LAMAR AVE
OVERLAND PARK, KS 662111598
Phone: 913-458-2000
Fax: –
Web: www.bv.com

CEO: Steven Edwards
CFO: Kenneith Williams
HR: –
FYE: December 31
Type: Private

Black & Veatch (BV) is one of the world's top global engineering procurement consulting and construction firms specializing in infrastructure development for the energy oil and gas water environmental and telecommunications industries and governments. BV offers microconsulting experts on demand engineering consulting and management consulting. The employee-owned contractor has offices in more than 20 countries including coal nuclear and combustion turbine plants; drinking water and coastal water operations; and wireless and broadband installations. The company was founded by engineers E. B. Black and Tom Veatch in 1915.

	Annual Growth	12/05	12/06	12/07	12/08	12/09
Sales ($ mil.)	(4.9%)	–	–	1,287.3	1,267.3	1,163.0
Net income ($ mil.)	31.7%	–	–	33.5	16.9	58.2
Market value ($ mil.)	–	–	–	–	–	–
Employees		–	–	–	–	4,065

BLACK BOX CORP. (DE)
NMS: BBOX

1000 Park Drive
Lawrence, PA 15055
Phone: 724 746-5500
Fax: –
Web: www.blackbox.com

CEO: Sanjeev Verma
CFO: Deepak Bansal
HR: Lisa Davidson
FYE: March 31
Type: Public

Black Box packs a lot of equipment in its box of networking products. The company distributes and supports voice and data networking infrastructure offering more than 118000 products including modems routers switches and testing equipment. It also sells cabinets cables and training materials. Black Box primarily distributes and services third-party equipment some of which carries its brand but it also manufactures some products. Most of the company's sales come from its on-site services such as design installation technical support and maintenance. Black Box sells to corporations schools and government agencies primarily in North America and Europe. Key industries served include business services manufacturing banking retail and health care.

	Annual Growth	03/13	03/14	03/15	03/16	03/17
Sales ($ mil.)	(3.8%)	997.8	971.7	992.4	912.7	855.7
Net income ($ mil.)	–	28.8	(115.9)	15.3	(171.1)	(7.1)
Market value ($ mil.)	(20.0%)	326.3	364.1	313.1	201.5	133.9
Employees	(3.0%)	3,900	3,959	3,803	3,631	3,448

BLACK ENTERTAINMENT TELEVISION LLC

1 BET Plaza 1235 W St. NE
Washington DC 20018
Phone: 202-608-2000
Fax: 202-608-2589
Web: www.bet.com

CEO: Debra L Lee
CFO: Michael Pickrum
HR: –
FYE: December 31
Type: Subsidiary

You might say this network gives cable TV some street cred. Black Entertainment Television operates BET the leading cable channel targeting young African-American audiences with a mix of entertainment music and news programming. Reaching about 91 million US homes BET boasts a lineup that includes 106 & Park (music videos); BET Awards and Soul Train Awards (award shows); Harlem Heights (reality shows); The Game (scripted series) and Sunday Best (gospel music). The network is the flagship property of BET Networks which includes sister outlets BET Gospel BET Hip Hop and Centric (targeting multicultural viewers). Launched in 1980 BET is owned by media conglomerate Viacom.

BLACK HILLS CORPORATION
NYS: BKH

7001 Mount Rushmore Road
Rapid City, SD 57702
Phone: 605 721-1700
Fax: –
Web: www.blackhillscorp.com

CEO: Linden Evans
CFO: Richard Kinzley
HR: Jennifer Landis
FYE: December 31
Type: Public

The Black Hills distributes power to approximately 216000 customers in Colorado Montana South Dakota and Wyoming. Black Hills' gas utilities segment serves 1083000 natural gas customers in Arkansas Colorado Iowa Kansas Nebraska and Wyoming. Power Generation segment produces electric power from its wind natural gas and coal-fired generating plants and sells the electric capacity and energy. The company's mining segment produces coal at mine near Gillette Wyoming and sells and delivers it primarily under long-term contracts to adjacent mine-mouth electric generation facilities owned by Electric Utilities and Power Generation businesses.

	Annual Growth	12/17	12/18	12/19	12/20	12/21
Sales ($ mil.)	3.8%	1,680.3	1,754.3	1,734.9	1,696.9	1,949.1
Net income ($ mil.)	7.5%	177.0	258.4	199.3	227.6	236.7
Market value ($ mil.)	4.1%	3,891.5	4,064.3	5,084.6	3,978.2	4,568.6
Employees	1.3%	2,744	2,863	2,944	3,011	2,884

BLACK HILLS POWER INC.

7001 Mount Rushmore Road
Rapid City, SD 57702
Phone: 605 721-1700
Fax: –
Web: www.blackhillspower.com

CEO: Linden Evans
CFO: Richard Kinzley
HR: –
FYE: December 31
Type: Public

Mount Rushmore is a monument to the powerful in the Black Hills of South Dakota. Black Hills Power formed in 1941 the same year the Mount Rushmore was completed gets power to the people. It generates transmits and distributes electricity to 66000 customers. Its 9300 sq.ml. service area encompasses western South Dakota northeastern Wyoming and southeastern Montana. The utility became a subsidiary of Black Hills Corporation in 2000. Its five electric power plants are fueled by low-sulphur Wyoming coal mined by Black Hills Corp.'s unit Wyodak Resource Development Corp.

	Annual Growth	12/15	12/16	12/17	12/18	12/19
Sales ($ mil.)	1.2%	277.9	267.6	288.4	298.1	291.2
Net income ($ mil.)	0.9%	45.2	45.1	51.3	45.6	46.9
Market value ($ mil.)	–	–	–	–	–	–
Employees		–	–	–	–	217

BLACK RAVEN ENERGY INC.

1875 Lawrence St. Ste. 450
Denver CO 80202
Phone: 303-308-1330
Fax: 303-308-1590
Web: www.blackravenenergy.com

CEO: Robert Watson Jr
CFO: Douglas Wright
HR: –
FYE: December 31
Type: Private

Black Raven Energy (formerly PRB Energy) is engaged in coal-bed methane production in the Rocky Mountains. The company focuses on natural gas gathering and exploration and production. Its exploration and gathering and processing operations are primarily located in the Powder River Basin. In 2007 PRB Energy was targeting reserves of about 100 billion cu. ft. of natural gas equivalent before deteriorating finances hurt its expansion plans. The company filed for Chapter 11 bankruptcy protection in 2008. In preparation to emerge from bankruptcy it reorganized as Black Raven Energy in 2009.

BLACKBAUD, INC.

NMS: BLKB

65 Fairchild Street
Charleston, SC 29492
Phone: 843 216-6200
Fax: 843 216-6100
Web: www.blackbaud.com

CEO: Michael Gianoni
CFO: Anthony Boor
HR: –
FYE: December 31
Type: Public

Blackbaud wants to make it easy to give. The company provides financial fundraising and administrative software for not-for-profit organizations and educational institutions. Software offerings include The Raiser's Edge for fundraising management Blackbaud CRM for customer relationship management The Financial Edge for accounting and The Education Edge for managing school admissions registration and billing. Blackbaud has about 45000 customers in more than 100 countries including higher educations K-12 schools healthcare organizations faith communities and more. The company generates most of its sales in the US.

	Annual Growth	12/16	12/17	12/18	12/19	12/20
Sales ($ mil.)	5.7%	730.8	788.3	848.6	900.4	913.2
Net income ($ mil.)	(34.3%)	41.5	65.9	44.8	11.9	7.7
Market value ($ mil.)	(2.6%)	3,126.4	4,615.9	3,072.7	3,888.5	2,811.8
Employees	(0.4%)	3,156	3,182	3,353	3,611	3,100

BLACKBOARD INC.

650 Massachusetts Ave. NW 6th Fl.
Washington DC 20001-3796
Phone: 202-463-4860
Fax: 202-463-4863
Web: www.blackboard.com

CEO: William L Ballhaus
CFO: Edwin Scholte
HR: –
FYE: December 31
Type: Private

Chalk up Blackboard's success to the Internet. Blackboard develops software that lets schools create Internet-based learning programs and communities. Its applications connect teachers students parents and administrators via the Web enabling Internet-based assignments class websites and online collaboration with classmates. The software also includes a content management system for creating and managing digital course content. Other modules include transaction community and payment management tools that enable students to use their college IDs for meal plans events and tuition payments. In 2011 Blackboard was acquired by Providence Equity for about $1.64 billion.

BLACKFOOT TELEPHONE COOPERATIVE INC.

1221 N RUSSELL ST
MISSOULA, MT 598081898
Phone: 406-541-2121
Fax: –
Web: www.blackfoot.com

CEO: Bill Squires
CFO: Theodore Otis
HR: –
FYE: December 31
Type: Private

Blackfoot Telecommunications Cooperative provides phone services to rural communities along the Blackfoot River in western Montana and central Idaho. Founded in 1954 it is the first of the Blackfoot Communications Group of companies which includes competitive local-exchange carrier (CLEC) Blackfoot Communications Blackfoot.net Internet services provider and telecom software maker TeleSphere. The company's services include local and long-distance phone service dial-up and DSL Internet access and PCS wireless. It also owns a stake in video conferencing specialist Vision Net.

	Annual Growth	12/05	12/06	12/07	12/08	12/09
Sales ($ mil.)	0.6%	–	31.6	33.1	33.9	32.1
Net income ($ mil.)	15.5%	–	–	2.9	3.7	3.9
Market value ($ mil.)	–	–	–	–	–	–
Employees		–	–	–	–	214

BLACKHAWK BANCORP INC

NBB: BHWB

400 Broad Street
Beloit, WI 53511
Phone: 608 364 8911
Fax: 608 363 6186
Web: www.blackhawkbank.com

CEO: R Richard Bastian
CFO: Todd J James
HR: –
FYE: December 31
Type: Public

This Blackhawk's mission is to increase your bottom line. Blackhawk Bancorp is the holding company for Blackhawk State Bank (aka Blackhawk Bank) which has nearly 10 locations in south-central Wisconsin and north-central Illinois. Serving area consumers and businesses the bank offers standard financial services such as checking savings and money market accounts CDs credit cards and wealth management. It also caters to the Hispanic community by offering bilingual services at some of its branches. Blackhawk Bank maintains a somewhat diverse loan portfolio with residential mortgages commercial and industrial loans and commercial real estate loans accounting for the bulk of its lending activities.

	Annual Growth	12/16	12/17	12/18	12/19	12/20
Assets ($ mil.)	14.4%	665.7	720.6	817.3	963.9	1,141.6
Net income ($ mil.)	16.1%	6.0	6.2	8.1	9.6	10.8
Market value ($ mil.)	5.0%	77.6	91.2	89.7	93.9	94.4
Employees						

BLACKHAWK NETWORK HOLDINGS INC   NMS: HAWK

6220 Stoneridge Mall Road
Pleasanton, CA 94588
Phone: 925 226-9990
Fax: –
Web: www.blackhawknetwork.com

CEO: Talbott Roche
CFO: Chuck Garner
HR: –
FYE: December 31
Type: Public

With this Blackhawk think shoppers not choppers. Blackhawk Network sells gift phone sports ticket prepaid debit and prepaid wireless phone cards through a network of more than 244000 retailers around the world. The cards can be found in convenience drug grocery and specialty stores including Chevron Food Lion Kroger and Safeway (Blackhawk's founder). Blackhawk offers more than 600 brands of cards from companies such as Apple Barnes & Noble Starbucks Visa and Best Buy. The cards can be found online or at Gift Card Mall racks which display hundreds of cards that can be redeemed online or on-site at retail locations.

	Annual Growth	12/12	12/13*	01/15	01/16*	12/16
Sales ($ mil.)	18.6%	959.1	1,138.1	1,445.0	1,801.1	1,899.8
Net income ($ mil.)	(44.2%)	48.2	54.1	45.5	45.6	4.7
Market value ($ mil.)	13.7%	–	1,428.4	2,060.2	2,461.0	2,097.3
Employees	44.8%	725	1,316	1,860	2,331	3,191

*Fiscal year change

BLACKROCK INC   NYS: BLK

55 East 52nd Street
New York, NY 10055
Phone: 212 810-5300
Fax: –
Web: www.blackrock.com

CEO: Laurence Fink
CFO: Gary Shedlin
HR: –
FYE: December 31
Type: Public

With over $8 trillion in assets under management BlackRock is the world's largest public investment management firm. It specializes in equity and fixed income products as well as alternative and money market instruments which it invests in on behalf of institutional and retail investors worldwide. Clients include pension plans governments insurance companies financial institutions endowments foundations charities third party fund sponsors and retail investors. BlackRock also provides technology products and services through its Aladdin Aladdin Wealth eFront Cachematrix and FutureAdvisor systems. The firm has offices in more than 30 countries. The company's largest geographical market is the Americas with more than 65% of the total revenue.

	Annual Growth	12/16	12/17	12/18	12/19	12/20
Sales ($ mil.)	9.8%	11,155.0	12,491.0	14,198.0	14,539.0	16,205.0
Net income ($ mil.)	11.7%	3,172.0	4,970.0	4,305.0	4,476.0	4,932.0
Market value ($ mil.)	17.3%	58,044.9	78,357.7	59,918.0	76,678.3	110,058.6
Employees	6.1%	13,000	13,900	14,900	16,200	16,500

BLACKSTONE INC   NYS: BX

345 Park Avenue
New York, NY 10154
Phone: 212 583-5000
Fax: –
Web: www.blackstone.com

CEO: Stephen Schwarzman
CFO: Michael Chae
HR: –
FYE: December 31
Type: Public

The Blackstone Group is one of the world's largest real estate private equity and alternative asset managers in the world with more than $618.6 billion in assets under management. Of approximately $618.6 billion private equity make up the firm's largest asset category with more than $197.5 billion under management. Its real estate investment holdings constitute more than $187.2 billion making Blackstone one of the world's largest real estate investors. The firm manages investment vehicles including real estate private equity public debt and equity growth equity opportunistic non-investment grade credit real assets and secondary funds all on a global basis.

	Annual Growth	12/16	12/17	12/18	12/19	12/20
Sales ($ mil.)	4.5%	5,125.8	7,119.1	6,833.3	7,338.3	6,101.9
Net income ($ mil.)	0.1%	1,039.2	1,470.8	1,541.8	2,049.7	1,045.4
Market value ($ mil.)	24.4%	18,485.2	21,897.7	20,386.3	38,256.0	44,322.0
Employees	10.5%	2,120	2,360	2,615	2,905	3,165

BLACKSTONE MORTGAGE TRUST INC   NYS: BXMT

345 Park Avenue, 24th Floor
New York, NY 10154
Phone: 212 655-0220
Fax: –
Web: www.blackstonemortgagetrust.com

CEO: Katharine Keenan
CFO: Anthony Marone
HR: –
FYE: December 31
Type: Public

Capital Trust thinks investing in commercial mortgages is a capital idea. The self-managed real estate investment trust (REIT) originates underwrites and invests in commercial real estate assets on its own behalf and for other investors. Its portfolio includes first mortgage and bridge loans mezzanine loans and collateralized mortgage-backed securities. Subsidiary CT Investment Management which the company is selling manages five private equity funds and a separate account for third parties. Most Capital Trust's assets are related to US properties but the REIT does make occasional investments in international instruments.

	Annual Growth	12/17	12/18	12/19	12/20	12/21
Sales ($ mil.)	12.3%	537.9	756.1	882.7	779.6	854.7
Net income ($ mil.)	17.8%	217.6	285.1	305.6	137.7	419.2
Market value ($ mil.)	(1.2%)	5,412.0	5,358.2	6,259.7	4,630.0	5,149.7
Employees	–	–	–	–	–	–

BLAIR CORPORATION

220 Hickory St.
Warren PA 16366
Phone: 814-723-3600
Fax: 814-726-6376
Web: www.blair.com

CEO: –
CFO: –
HR: –
FYE: December 31
Type: Subsidiary

Before its customers pick up the phone to arrange a game of pinochle with their peeps Blair hopes they'll give some attention to its latest mailing. Through its catalogs letter pitches and website Blair sells men's and women's clothing (its biggest sales generators) to middle-aged and senior low- to middle-income customers. The company also sells home decor bedspreads bath accessories drapes kitchenware rugs and vacuums. Most of Blair's merchandise is made to specifications by independent suppliers. Established in 1910 it operates a retail store and a factory outlet in Pennsylvania. Apparel marketer Orchard Brands (formerly Appleseed's Topco) owns Blair.

BLANK ROME LLP

1 Logan Sq.
Philadelphia PA 19103-6998
Phone: 215-569-5500
Fax: 215-569-5555
Web: www.blankrome.com

CEO: –
CFO: –
HR: –
FYE: December 31
Type: Private - Partnershi

Blank Rome has more than 500 lawyers in about 10 offices located mostly in the eastern US with one office in Hong Kong and one in Shanghai. The firm practices in such areas as bankruptcy corporate governance employment government relations intellectual property litigation maritime real estate and tax. Through its Blank Rome Government Relations affiliate the firm provides advocacy and communications services. Blank Rome caters to a wide array of industries such as life sciences chemical private equity real estate and financial institutions. Blank Rome opened a Houston office in 2011 the firm's first Texas office.

BLARNEY CASTLE OIL CO.

12218 WEST ST
BEAR LAKE, MI 496149453
Phone: 231-864-3111
Fax: –
Web: www.blarneycastleoil.com

CEO: –
CFO: Joe Taraskavage
HR: –
FYE: March 31
Type: Private

While kissing the Blarney stone has a reputation for reliably making people loquacious Blarney Castle Oil and Propane has a reputation for reliably supplying its customers with fuels. The family-owned company transports petroleum products to customers through about 10 office locations in Michigan. Its products include agricultural and commercial fuels (diesel and gasoline) commercial and industrial lubricants and coolants home heating oil fuel oil and propane. Blarney Castle Oil and Propane also operates 90 convenience stores under the EZ Mart brand name.

	Annual Growth	03/09	03/10	03/11	03/12	03/13
Sales ($ mil.)	11.2%	–	–	415.3	501.5	513.6
Net income ($ mil.)	42.7%	–	–	3.0	4.0	6.0
Market value ($ mil.)	–	–	–	–	–	–
Employees		–	–	–	–	700

BLESSING HOSPITAL

BROADWAY AT 11TH ST
QUINCY, IL 62301
Phone: 217-223-1200
Fax: –
Web: www.blessinghealth.org

CEO: Maureen A Kahn
CFO: –
HR: –
FYE: September 30
Type: Private

Blessing Hospital is a not-for-profit acute care medical center that provides a wide range of health services to residents in areas of western Illinois northeast Missouri and southeast Iowa. Through its main campus location it provides primary and emergency care as well as specialty services including diagnostics and surgery. The hospital is home to centers of excellence in the treatment of cancer heart and cardiovascular ailments wound care and women's health issues. Blessing Hospital provides outpatient and behavioral health services at a nearby campus. It also operates family practice centers and provides home and hospice care services. It is part of the Blessing Health System.

	Annual Growth	09/07	09/08	09/12	09/15	09/16
Sales ($ mil.)	5.1%	–	238.4	289.1	316.3	355.2
Net income ($ mil.)	–	–	(2.2)	14.8	15.2	52.6
Market value ($ mil.)	–	–	–	–	–	–
Employees	–	–	–	–	–	2,500

BLISH-MIZE CO.

223 S 5TH ST
ATCHISON, KS 660022801
Phone: 913-367-1250
Fax: –
Web: www.blishmize.com

CEO: Jonathan Mize
CFO: Tom Hottovy
HR: –
FYE: December 31
Type: Private

Hardware supplier Blish-Mize distributes more than 52000 products to hardware stores home centers lumberyards and paint stores in a dozen states in the heartland of the US. Its catalog includes hand and power tools lawn equipment hardware paint heating and cooling products housewares plumbing and electrical supplies and sporting goods. The company has distribution centers in Colorado and Kansas. Aside from its wholesaling business Blish-Mize operates toolmaker Hardware House with House-Hasson. Brothers-in-law David Blish Edward Mize and Jack Silliman founded the firm in 1871 to outfit wagon trains. President and CEO John Mize Jr. represents the fourth generation of the family-owned company.

BLIZZARD ENTERTAINMENT INC.

16215 Alton Pkwy.
Irvine CA 92623
Phone: 949-955-1380
Fax: +44-20-7802-5600
Web: www.capreg.com

CEO: Mike Morhaime
CFO: –
HR: –
FYE: December 31
Type: Subsidiary

Blizzard Entertainment hopes to continue to produce a flurry of hit games. A unit of Activision Blizzard the company is the leading video game maker in the massively multiplayer online role-playing games (MMORPG) niche. It develops and publishes software titles such as the genre-dominating World of Warcraft (about 10 million subscribers) Starcraft and Diablo series available for play on PCs. Blizzard offers its Battle.net online gaming service that enables the worldwide social gaming experience for its titles. The games are sold through retailers and online download. The company has also leveraged its popular games into related products such as action figures board games graphic novels and comic books.

BLOCK (H & R), INC.

NYS: HRB

One H&R Block Way
Kansas City, MO 64105
Phone: 816 854-3000
Fax: –
Web: www.hrblock.com

CEO: Jeffrey Jones
CFO: Tony Bowen
HR: –
FYE: June 30
Type: Public

H&R Block is one of the largest tax return preparers in the US where it boasts over 9270 company-owned and franchised retail locations. The company offers customers the options of filing taxes online or in person and doing their own taxes or having them done by an H&R Block professional. Through Block Advisors and Wave the company helps small business owners thrive with innovative products like Wave Money a small business banking and bookkeeping solution and the only business bank account to manage bookkeeping automatically. H&R was founded in 1955 by brothers Henry and Richard Bloch.

	Annual Growth	04/18	04/19	04/20	04/21*	06/21
Sales ($ mil.)	(47.2%)	3,159.9	3,094.9	2,639.7	3,414.0	466.1
Net income ($ mil.)	(47.3%)	613.1	422.5	(7.5)	583.8	89.6
Market value ($ mil.)	(5.3%)	5,027.1	4,947.1	3,027.2	4,047.2	4,269.0
Employees	10.1%	2,700	3,100	3,500	3,600	–

*Fiscal year change

BLOCKBUSTER L.L.C.

9601 S. Meridian Blvd
Englewood CO 80112
Phone: 303-723-1000
Fax: 414-259-5773
Web: www.briggsandstratton.com

CEO: –
CFO: –
HR: –
FYE: December 31
Type: Subsidiary

With video stores going the way of the dinosaurs (and record stores) movie rental chain Blockbuster has seen its business take a Hollywood-sized hit. With a library of more than 125000 movie and video game titles Blockbuster has struggled to transform its store-based distribution system to a multi-channel content delivery model. The company's customers can either download movies to their home or mobile devices order them by mail or visit one of a dwindling number of Blockbuster stores. Amid rapid technological change and competition from Netflix and Redbox Blockbuster filed for Chapter 11 bankruptcy protection in 2010 and was sold to satellite TV service provider DISH Network.

	Annual Growth	12/05	12/06	12/07	12/08	12/09
Sales ($ mil.)	–	–	–	(1,647.8)	64.0	60.5
Net income ($ mil.)	12586.3%	–	–	0.0	1.8	0.7
Market value ($ mil.)	–	–	–	–	–	–
Employees	–	–	–	–	–	175

BLONDER TONGUE LABORATORIES, INC.   ASE: BDR

One Jake Brown Road
Old Bridge, NJ 08857
Phone: 732 679-4000
Fax: –
Web: www.blondertongue.com

CEO: Edward Grauch
CFO: Eric Skolnik
HR: –
FYE: December 31
Type: Public

Blonder Tongue Laboratories isn't involved in genetic modification — it makes equipment for acquiring and distributing cable TV signals. Founded by Isaac Blonder and Ben Tongue the company's offerings center on analog and digital video products for headend facilities (television signal-receiving centers) such as encoders receivers and modulators as well as hybrid fiber-coax (HFC) distribution products which deliver the signal to the viewer. Blonder Tongue mainly serves cable operators TV broadcasters the lodging and hospitality sector and institutional facilities such as schools hospitals stadiums airports and prisons.

	Annual Growth	12/16	12/17	12/18	12/19	12/20
Sales ($ mil.)	(7.6%)	22.5	23.3	21.7	19.8	16.4
Net income ($ mil.)	–	(1.2)	(0.4)	(1.3)	(0.7)	(7.5)
Market value ($ mil.)	30.0%	5.4	7.0	12.8	8.8	15.4
Employees	(8.6%)	122	117	117	93	85

BLOODWORKS

921 TERRY AVE
SEATTLE, WA 981041239
Phone: 206-292-6500
Fax: –
Web: www.bloodworksnw.org

CEO: James P Aubuchon
CFO: Bob Gleason
HR: –
FYE: June 30
Type: Private

Residents of the Emerald City can go here to give red. Bloodworks Northwest (formerly Puget Sound Blood Center) is a not-for-profit blood and tissue bank serving nearly 90 hospitals and clinics in the Pacific Northwest. The blood center collects and processes donated blood through about a dozen donation centers and several mobile units; it also registers bone marrow donors provides testing and training services to patients with hemophilia and collects cord blood for use in stem cell transplantation. Bloodworks Northwest Research Institute conducts research on improving transfusion and transplantation medicine. The organization was formed in 1944.

	Annual Growth	06/12	06/13	06/14	06/15	06/16
Sales ($ mil.)	5.9%	–	152.4	162.9	175.7	180.9
Net income ($ mil.)	–	–	(2.4)	1.4	9.5	0.1
Market value ($ mil.)	–	–	–	–	–	–
Employees	–	–	–	–	–	750

BLOOMBERG L.P.

731 Lexington Ave.
New York NY 10022
Phone: 212-318-2000
Fax: 917-369-5000
Web: www.bloomberg.com

CEO: Alexius Fenwick
CFO: Mike McCarty
HR: –
FYE: December 31
Type: Private

What do you do when you've conquered Wall Street? You become mayor of the city the famous financial district calls home. After leading his financial news and information company to success Michael Bloomberg left to run the Big Apple. His namesake company remains a leader in the market for business media. Its core Bloomberg Professional Service offering is accessed through terminals that provides real-time financial news market data and analysis. The firm also has a syndicated news service publishes magazines (including Bloomberg Businessweek) and disseminates business information via Bloomberg Television radio and the Web. Michael Bloomberg founded the company in 1981; he owns a majority of the firm.

BLOOMIN' BRANDS INC   NMS: BLMN

2202 North West Shore Boulevard, Suite 500
Tampa, FL 33607
Phone: 813 282-1225
Fax: –
Web: www.bloominbrands.com

CEO: David Deno
CFO: Christopher Meyer
HR: Lori Malcolm
FYE: December 27
Type: Public

The company owns nearly 1200 restaurants in almost 50 US states and roughly 20 countries. It also franchises around 300 restaurants. Bloomin' Brands has four founder-inspired concepts: Outback Steakhouse Carrabba's Italian Grill Bonefish Grill and Fleming's Prime Steakhouse & Wine Bar. The company's restaurant concepts range in price point and degree of formality from casual (Outback Steakhouse and Carrabba's Italian Grill) to upscale casual (Bonefish Grill) and fine dining (Fleming's Prime Steakhouse & Wine Bar). OSI Restaurant Partners LLC ("OSI") a wholly-owned subsidiary of Bloomin' Brands is its primary operating entity. Around 725 of its restaurants are Outback Steakhouses. The US accounts for about 90% of the company's revenue.

	Annual Growth	12/16	12/17	12/18	12/19	12/20
Sales ($ mil.)	(7.1%)	4,252.3	4,213.3	4,126.4	4,139.4	3,170.6
Net income ($ mil.)	–	41.7	100.2	107.1	130.6	(158.7)
Market value ($ mil.)	0.9%	1,605.1	1,874.8	1,546.3	1,904.7	1,664.9
Employees	(5.6%)	97,000	94,000	93,000	94,000	77,000

BLOUNT INTERNATIONAL, INC.

4909 SE INTERNATIONAL WAY
PORTLAND, OR 972224679
Phone: 503-653-8881
Fax: –
Web: www.oregontool.com

CEO: Paul Tonnesen
CFO: Calvin Jenness
HR: Barbara Wallis
FYE: December 31
Type: Private

Formerly Blount International Oregon Tool produces cutting chain guide bars sprockets and accessories for chainsaws concrete-cutting equipment and lawnmower blades. Blount's lineup is sold under brands Oregon Carlton and KOX to dealers and consumers in key markets. End users are professionals and consumers engaged in forestry lawn and garden farming and construction activities. Blount was founded in 1947 as Oregon Saw Chain Company by Joe Cox. In 2021 Blount International Inc. is renamed to Oregon Tool Inc. to honor the company's legacy and unite all of its brands under one name moving forward.

	Annual Growth	12/11	12/12	12/13	12/14	12/15
Sales ($ mil.)	(3.7%)	–	927.7	900.6	944.8	828.6
Net income ($ mil.)	–	–	39.6	4.8	36.6	(49.9)
Market value ($ mil.)	–	–	–	–	–	–
Employees	–	–	–	–	–	4,000

BLOUNT MEMORIAL HOSPITAL, INCORPORATED

907 LAMAR ALEXANDER PKWY
MARYVILLE, TN 378045015
Phone: 865-983-7211
Fax: –
Web: www.blountmemorial.org

CEO: Don Heinemann
CFO: –
HR: –
FYE: June 30
Type: Private

Blount Memorial Hospital provides health care services in eastern Tennessee. Founded in 1947 the hospital offers area communities cardiopulmonary care cancer care radiology women's health and laboratory services. As part of its operations Blount Memorial boasts satellite clinics devoted to family care diagnostic imaging occupational health services and outpatient rehabilitation. The hospital serves seniors through its focus on specialty services including senior care home health care hospice home life assistance occupational health and wellness care.

	Annual Growth	06/02	06/03	06/05	06/06	06/15
Sales ($ mil.)	4.3%	–	131.9	0.5	0.2	218.9
Net income ($ mil.)	(47.7%)	–	14.3	(0.0)	0.2	0.0
Market value ($ mil.)	–	–	–	–	–	–
Employees	–	–	–	–	–	2,060

BLUCORA, INC.

NMS: BCOR

3200 Olympus Blvd, Suite 100
Dallas, TX 75019
Phone: 972 870-6400
Fax: –
Web: www.blucora.com

CEO: Chris Walters
CFO: Marc Mehlman
HR: –
FYE: December 31
Type: Public

Blucora Inc. is a leading provider of tax-smart financial solutions. The company helps clients manage their finances through its Avantax Wealth Management as well as prepare and file taxes with its TaxAct tax preparation product. Nearly 4000 financial advisers throughout the US use the Avantax platform to help their clients manage their money. The company claims Avantax supports approximately $83.0 billion of total client assets. TaxAct is a digital tax prep product used by individuals small business owners and professional tax preparers. Approximately 3.2 million individuals file taxes electronically with TaxAct with another 2.1 million returns going through tax preparers. Blucora does all its business in the US.

	Annual Growth	12/16	12/17	12/18	12/19	12/20
Sales ($ mil.)	13.4%	455.9	509.6	560.5	717.9	755.0
Net income ($ mil.)	–	(65.2)	27.0	50.6	48.1	(342.8)
Market value ($ mil.)	1.9%	710.6	1,064.7	1,283.4	1,259.3	766.5
Employees	15.5%	476	487	529	690	846

BLUE BIRD CORPORATION

402 Blue Bird Blvd.
Fort Valley GA 31030
Phone: 478-825-2021
Fax: 478-822-2457
Web: www.blue-bird.com

CEO: Phil Horlock
CFO: Keith Romundo
HR: –
FYE: December 31
Type: Private

Blue Bird is from the "old school" of bus manufacturers. The largest school bus maker in the US Blue Bird also produces commercial and specialty/activity buses such as security buses shell buses and buses for export. School buses vary in size engine location and fuel used. Independent distributors sell the buses to school districts churches businesses government agencies and non-profit organizations. It also provides financing services through its Blue Bird Financial Services affiliate. The company's buses are globally exported to 60 countries throughout the Middle East Asia/Pacific Europe Africa and Latin America. Parent company Traxis Group is a subsidiary of Cerberus Capital Management L.P.

BLUE BUFFALO PET PRODUCTS, INC.

11 RIVER RD STE 103
WILTON, CT 068976011
Phone: 203-762-9751
Fax: –
Web: www.bluebuffalo.com

CEO: –
CFO: –
HR: –
FYE: December 31
Type: Private

Blue Buffalo makes natural dog and cat food using whole meats fruits and vegetables with no by-products or artificial ingredients; some products are also grain-free. The company's products undergo a robust formulation manufacturing and testing process to ensure they are safe effective and compliant with all nutrient requirements outlined by AAFCO and the Global Nutrition Committee of the World Small Animal Veterinary Association (WSAVA). BLUE's exclusive LifeSource Bits are "cold-formed" to minimize heat exposure which can degrade the potency of many vitamins minerals antioxidants and enzymes. Blue Buffalo started in 2003.

	Annual Growth	12/13	12/14	12/15	12/16	12/17
Sales ($ mil.)	11.4%	–	–	1,027.4	1,149.8	1,274.6
Net income ($ mil.)	47.1%	–	–	89.4	130.2	193.5
Market value ($ mil.)	–	–	–	–	–	–
Employees	–	–	–	–	–	1,800

BLUE CARE NETWORK OF MICHIGAN

20500 Civic Center Dr.
Southfield MI 48076
Phone: 248-799-6400
Fax: 248-799-6327
Web: www.mibcn.com

CEO: –
CFO: Susan Kluge
HR: –
FYE: December 31
Type: Subsidiary

Blue Care Network of Michigan (BCN) keeps its state residents healthy. The health maintenance organization (HMO) provides health insurance products and related services to some 700000 Michigan members. The company's health insurance plans include HMO traditional indemnity and supplemental Medicare. The network also provides wellness and disease management services to its members. Parent company Blue Cross Blue Shield of Michigan (BCBSM) formed BCN one of the largest HMOs in Michigan in 1998 to create a statewide coverage organization. Its network includes about 130 hospitals and 19000 primary and specialty physicians throughout the state.

BLUE CROSS & BLUE SHIELD ASSOCIATION

225 N MICHIGAN AVE FL 5
CHICAGO, IL 606017658
Phone: 312-297-6000
Fax: –
Web: www.bcbs.com

CEO: Kim A Keck
CFO: –
HR: –
FYE: December 31
Type: Private

The Blue Cross and Blue Shield Association is a national federation of about 35 independent community-based and locally operated Blue Cross and Blue Shield companies that collectively provide health care coverage for one in three Americans across all 50 US states the District of Columbia and Puerto Rico. The association owns and manages the Blue Cross and Blue Shield trademarks and names in more than 170 countries. In addition the BCBS Federal Employee Program insures over 5.8 million federal employees retirees and their families. The company traces its roots back to 1929.

	Annual Growth	12/03	12/04	12/05	12/06	12/17
Sales ($ mil.)	6.2%	–	270.9	275.4	320.5	592.0
Net income ($ mil.)	–	–	11.7	8.2	14.5	(1.4)
Market value ($ mil.)	–	–	–	–	–	–
Employees	–	–	–	–	–	1,880

BLUE CROSS & BLUE SHIELD OF MISSISSIPPI

3545 Lakeland Dr.
Flowood MS 39232
Phone: 601-932-3704
Fax: 601-939-7035
Web: www.bcbsms.com

CEO: Rick Hale
CFO: –
HR: Otinma Robinson
FYE: December 31
Type: Private - Mutual Com

Like the river that gives the state its name Blue Cross & Blue Shield of Mississippi (BCBSMS) is big and broad. The mutual insurance company which provides health care coverage and related services to members is the state's largest health plan provider. It is an independent licensee of the Blue Cross and Blue Shield Association with managed care offerings that include group (Network Blue) individual (Blue Care) and supplemental Medicare (Blue 65) health plans. Policies are marketed through a statewide network of agents. BCBSMS members have access to a contracted network of some 7500 family care and specialty doctors as well as about 100 hospitals across the state.

BLUE CROSS & BLUE SHIELD OF RHODE ISLAND

500 Exchange St
Providence RI 02903
Phone: 401-459-1000
Fax: 312-943-5316
Web: www.flairpromo.com

CEO: Kim Keck
CFO: –
HR: Genivieve Bassett
FYE: December 31
Type: Private - Not-for-Pr

As the state's largest health insurer Blue Cross & Blue Shield of Rhode Island (BCBSRI) has the Ocean State's citizens covered. In fact BCBSRI provides health insurance products and related services to more than 600000 members or more than half of the state's residents primarily through their employers. The company offers a variety of plan types including PPO (HealthMate Coast-to-Coast) HMO (BlueCHiP) and traditional indemnity (Classic Blue). It also sells Medicare Advantage and Medicare supplemental coverage as well as dental coverage plans. A not-for-profit licensee of the Blue Cross and Blue Shield Association

BLUE CROSS AND BLUE SHIELD OF MASSACHUSETTS INC.

Landmark Center 401 Park Dr.
Boston MA 02215-3326
Phone: 617-246-5000
Fax: 617-246-4832
Web: www.bluecrossma.com

CEO: Andrew Dreyfus
CFO: Andreana Santangelo
HR: –
FYE: December 31
Type: Private - Not-for-Pr

The dominant health insurer in the Bay State Blue Cross and Blue Shield of Massachusetts (BCBSMA) covers some 3 million members. The company an independent licensee of the Blue Cross and Blue Shield Association offers a variety of individual and employer-sponsored health care plans including HMO (HMO Blue) PPO (Blue Options) and point-of-service (Blue Choice) plans as well as various hybrid options and personal spending accounts to cover out-of-pocket costs. BCBSMA also provides Medicare options and dental vision and prescription drug coverage. Its provider network includes more than 20000 physicians and about 75 hospitals across the state. The health care firm was founded in 1937.

BLUE CROSS AND BLUE SHIELD OF ALABAMA

450 Riverchase Pkwy. East
Birmingham AL 35244
Phone: 205-220-2100
Fax: 205-220-6477
Web: www.bcbsal.com

CEO: Tim Vines
CFO: Cynthia Mizell
HR: –
FYE: December 31
Type: Private - Not-for-Pr

Folks who hang their hats in Tuscaloosa or Birmingham (or any other Alabama city) may depend on Blue Cross and Blue Shield of Alabama when they need medical coverage. The state's largest health benefits provider Blue Cross and Blue Shield of Alabama administers individual corporate and federal employer-sponsored and Medicare health plans to more than 3 million members representing about 30000 companies. Its insurance products include PPO and high-deductible health plans as well as dental policies. The company also sells long-term care insurance (dubbed Preferred LTC) and it provides disease management services and wellness programs. It is a licensee of the Blue Cross and Blue Shield Association.

BLUE CROSS AND BLUE SHIELD OF MINNESOTA

3535 Blue Cross Rd.
Eagan MN 55122-1154
Phone: 651-662-8000
Fax: 651-662-2777
Web: www.bluecrossmn.com

CEO: Dana Erickson
CFO: Pamela Sedmak
HR: –
FYE: December 31
Type: Private - Not-for-Pr

Blue Cross and Blue Shield of Minnesota is the state's oldest and largest not-for-profit health insurer serving some 2.7 million members including employees for General Mills and Northwest Airlines. The company's insurance plans include traditional indemnity coverage HMOs (Blue Plus and Preferred Gold) PPOs (Aware) and major medical plans. Blue Cross Blue Shield of Minnesota also offers Medicare Advantage PPOs and other products aimed at seniors. Dental coverage is provided through a partnership with Delta Dental. Additionally its health support programs offer disease management assistance for those with chronic conditions as well as health improvement programs such as fitness center discounts.

BLUE CROSS AND BLUE SHIELD OF ARIZONA, INC.

2444 W LAS PALMARITAS DR
PHOENIX, AZ 850214860
Phone: 602-864-4100
Fax: –
Web: www.azblue.com

CEO: Pam Kehaly
CFO: Tony M Astorga CPA
HR: –
FYE: December 31
Type: Private

Blue Cross Blue Shield of Arizona (BCBSAZ) provides health insurance products and services to more than 1.9 million Arizonans. The not-for-profit company offers a variety of managed care plans to small and large employer groups individuals and families including PPO HMO and high-deductible health plans. It also provides dental vision and prescription drug coverage as well as supplemental health plans for Medicare beneficiaries. Founded in 1933 the company is an independent licensee of the Blue Cross and Blue Shield Association.

BLUE CROSS AND BLUE SHIELD OF MONTANA

560 N. Park Ave.
Helena MT 59604
Phone: 406-444-8200
Fax: 406-447-3454
Web: www.bcbsmt.com

CEO: –
CFO: –
HR: –
FYE: December 31
Type: Private - Not-for-Pr

Nearly a quarter of a million residents of Big Sky Country depend on Blue Cross and Blue Shield of Montana for health insurance. The state's largest private health insurer the company provides a variety of coverage types including traditional indemnity policies HMOs POS plans and supplemental Medicare plans to about 240000 customers. It also administers the state-sponsored children's Medicaid and low-income health insurance plans (dubbed Healthy Montana Kids) and participates in InsureMontana a state-sponsored subsidized program designed to encourage small businesses to cover their employees. The not-for-profit company's provider network includes about 1900 physicians and all of the state's hospitals.

	Annual Growth	12/05	12/06	12/07	12/08	12/09
Assets ($ mil.)	8.6%	–	–	–	975.9	1,059.5
Net income ($ mil.)	(9.9%)	–	–	–	71.7	64.6
Market value ($ mil.)	–	–	–	–	–	–
Employees	–	–	–	–	–	1,278

BLUE CROSS AND BLUE SHIELD OF NORTH CAROLINA

5901 Chapel Hill Rd.
Durham NC 27707
Phone: 919-489-7431
Fax: 919-765-7818
Web: www.bcbsnc.com

CEO: Tunde Sotunde
CFO: Daniel E Glaser
HR: –
FYE: December 31
Type: Private - Not-for-Pr

Blue Cross and Blue Shield of North Carolina (BCBSNC) provides health care insurance products and related services to about 3.7 million members in North Carolina. Founded in 1933 the company's individual and group health plans include Blue Care (HMO) and Blue Options (PPO) as well as consumer-directed plans that couple high-deductible policies with a health savings account. BCBSNC also provides dental life disability long-term care and Medicare supplemental insurance as well as prescription drug coverage. The company's Partners National Health Plans subsidiary offers Medicare Advantage health plans. BCBSNC is a licensee of the Blue Cross and Blue Shield Association.

BLUE CROSS BLUE SHIELD OF GEORGIA INC

3350 Peachtree Rd. NE
Atlanta GA 30326
Phone: 404-842-8000
Fax: 404-842-8100
Web: www.bcbsga.com

CEO: John Watts
CFO: Randall A Edwards
HR: –
FYE: December 31
Type: Subsidiary

Blue Cross Blue Shield of Georgia (BCBSGA) is the Empire State of the South's #1 provider of health insurance and related services. With more than 3 million members the company offers a variety of insurance plans including HMO PPO indemnity and point-of-service (POS) programs to groups and individuals throughout the state. BCBSGA also provides disease management services and supplemental insurance products such as dental vision life and disability coverage as well as Medicare plans. BCBSGA an independent licensee of Blue Cross and Blue Shield Association is a subsidiary of WellPoint.

BLUE CROSS AND BLUE SHIELD OF TEXAS

901 S. Central Expwy.
Richardson TX 75080
Phone: 972-766-6900
Fax: 972-766-6234
Web: www.bcbstx.com

CEO: –
CFO: –
HR: –
FYE: December 31
Type: Subsidiary

If an apple a day could keep the doctor away Blue Cross and Blue Shield of Texas (BCBSTX) would stock up for its 4.8 million customers. Instead the not-for-profit insurer strives to keep Texans healthy by providing HMO PPO point-of-service (POS) and indemnity insurance health care plans for large to small employer groups. It also provides coverage for individuals families seniors and low-income customers. The company's provider network has about 40000 doctors and 400 hospitals throughout the state. A division of Chicago-based mutual insurance firm Health Care Service Corporation BCBSTX counts among its customers American Airlines the University of Texas System H.E. Butt Grocery and Halliburton.

BLUE CROSS BLUE SHIELD OF MICHIGAN

600 E. Lafayette Blvd.
Detroit MI 48226-2998
Phone: 313-225-9000
Fax: 312-819-1220
Web: www.hcsc.com

CEO: Daniel J Loepp
CFO: Mark Bartlett
HR: –
FYE: December 31
Type: Private - Not-for-Pr

Blue Cross Blue Shield of Michigan (BCBSM) covers Michigan residents from one great lake to another. The company is the state's leading health benefits organization serving some 4.4 million members residing in the state or employed by companies headquartered there and 1.1 million more members in other states. The not-for-profit company's insurance offerings include traditional indemnity PPO and POS plans in addition to its Blue Care Network HMO plans. It also provides consumer-directed Flexible Blue plans paired with health savings accounts (HSAs) as well as options for individual buyers and Medicare beneficiaries. The organization is an independent licensee of the Blue Cross and Blue Shield Association.

BLUE CROSS AND BLUE SHIELD OF VERMONT

445 Industrial Ln.
Berlin VT 05602-4415
Phone: 802-223-6131
Fax: 802-223-4229
Web: www.bcbsvt.com

CEO: –
CFO: Ruth K Greene
HR: –
FYE: December 31
Type: Private - Not-for-Pr

Blue Cross and Blue Shield of Vermont (BCBSVT) lauds on healthy Vermont hikers. The company a licensee of the Blue Cross and Blue Shield Association stakes its claim as the largest and oldest health insurance company in Vermont and serves about 150000 members. The company's group and individual health insurance plans include Vermont Freedom Plan (PPO) Vermont Health Partnership Plan (POS) and BlueCare (HMO) as well as high-deductable plans and state-supplemented coverage for low-income members. BCBSVT also offers supplemental Medicare life dental and vision coverage. The company founded in 1944 also provides third-party administrative (TPA) services for medical dental COBRA and other employee benefits.

BLUE CROSS OF CALIFORNIA

One WellPoint Way
Thousand Oaks CA 91362-5035
Phone: 805-557-6655
Fax: 805-557-6872
Web: www.anthem.com/ca

CEO: –
CFO: Kenneth C Zurek
HR: –
FYE: December 31
Type: Subsidiary

Blue Cross of California which does business as Anthem Blue Cross provides health insurance and related services to more than 8 million residents of the Golden State. Along with its Anthem Blue Cross Life and Health Insurance affiliate it offers HMO PPO and point-of-service health plans for individuals employer groups and public entities. It also sells Medicare supplemental and Medicare Advantage plans to seniors and manages the health care of participants in state-funded programs such as Medi-Cal (Medicaid) and Healthy Families. Blue Cross of California is a licensee of the Blue Cross and Blue Shield Association and a subsidiary of WellPoint.

BLUE CROSS OF IDAHO HEALTH SERVICE INC.

3000 E. Pine Ave.
Meridian ID 83642
Phone: 208-345-4550
Fax: 208-331-7311
Web: www.bcidaho.com
CEO: Zelda Geyer-Sylvia
CFO: –
HR: Heidi Jones
FYE: December 31
Type: Private - Not-for-Pr

Blue Cross of Idaho Health Service shine's like a diamond in the Gem State's health market. The organization is a leading provider of health insurance products and related services to about 650000 Idaho members including individuals corporate groups and government institutions. The company's health insurance products include traditional indemnity HMO PPO and supplemental Medicare plans. It also offers high-deductable plans paired with a health savings accounts. Blue Cross of Idaho a licensee of the Blue Cross and Blue Shield Association also provides dental coverage behavioral health and disease management and access to hearing vision and fitness discount programs.

BLUE DOLPHIN ENERGY CO.   NBB: BDCO

801 Travis Street, Suite 2100
Houston, TX 77002
Phone: 713 568-4725
Fax: –
Web: www.blue-dolphin-energy.com
CEO: Jonathan Carroll
CFO: –
HR: –
FYE: December 31
Type: Public

Blue Dolphin Energy is trying to stay afloat in the waters of the Gulf of Mexico. The company's primary asset is its 40-mile-long Blue Dolphin Pipeline System which includes an offshore platform for separation metering and compression; the onshore Buccaneer oil pipeline; onshore facilities including 85000 barrels of surface tankage separation and dehydration facilities; 360 acres of land; and a barge-loading terminal. Blue Dolphin Energy owns interests in three producing blocks in the High Island area in the Gulf of Mexico and has two exploratory prospects for sale. In 2010 the company reported estimated proved reserves of 155.5 cu. ft. of natural gas and 134122 barrels of oil.

	Annual Growth	12/16	12/17	12/18	12/19	12/20
Sales ($ mil.)	1.0%	167.9	258.4	340.8	309.3	174.8
Net income ($ mil.)	–	(15.8)	(22.3)	(0.5)	7.4	(14.5)
Market value ($ mil.)	(46.1%)	48.6	12.7	15.2	5.9	4.1
Employees	–	–	–	–	–	–

BLUE NILE INC   NMS: NILE

411 First Avenue South, Suite 700
Seattle, WA 98104
Phone: 206 336-6700
Fax: –
Web: www.bluenile.com
CEO: Sean Kell
CFO: Bill Koefoed
HR: –
FYE: January 04
Type: Public

Blue Nile helps tech-savvy Marc Antonys bejewel their Cleopatras. The leader in online jewelry sales through its bluenile.com the company offers luxury-grade jewelry loose diamonds settings and engagement rings as well as non-bridal jewelry made of gold platinum and silver set with diamonds pearls emeralds rubies and sapphires. While engagement rings account for about 70% of its sales the e-tailer also sells watches and provides custom jewelry design services. Blue Nile's web sites serve customers in the US Canada Europe and the Asia-Pacific region — more than 40 countries in all. Chairman Mark Vadon and Ben Elowitz formerly of Fatbrain.com founded the site in 1999.

	Annual Growth	01/11	01/12*	12/12	12/13*	01/15
Sales ($ mil.)	9.2%	332.9	348.0	400.0	450.0	473.5
Net income ($ mil.)	(8.9%)	14.1	11.4	8.4	10.9	9.7
Market value ($ mil.)	(11.5%)	676.7	484.8	447.1	566.6	415.5
Employees	11.8%	193	212	253	291	301

*Fiscal year change

BLUE RIDGE AUDUBON

225 VARICK ST FL 7
NEW YORK, NY 100144396
Phone: 212-979-3000
Fax: –
Web: www.audubon.org
CEO: David Yarnold
CFO: Mary Beth Henson
HR: –
FYE: June 30
Type: Private

Audubon has gone to the birds. The National Audubon Society is a not-for-profit organization dedicated to preserving birds and other wildlife and their habitats by conserving and restoring their natural ecosystems. The society operates programs and educational centers in every US state and in several South American and Caribbean countries to encourage grassroots conservation and promote environmental public policy reform. Projects have included saving habitats in the Everglades Arctic Wildlife Refuge Long Island Sound and Mississippi River basin. Audubon also publishes Audubon Magazine . A precursor to the society formed in 1886 but disbanded when it grew too quickly. The current society began in 1905.

	Annual Growth	06/08	06/09	06/10	06/16	06/18
Sales ($ mil.)	5.2%	–	74.0	80.1	102.6	116.7
Net income ($ mil.)	–	–	0.0	(1.8)	(19.2)	24.3
Market value ($ mil.)	–	–	–	–	–	–
Employees	–	–	–	–	–	600

BLUE RIDGE HEALTHCARE HOSPITALS, INC.

2201 S STERLING ST
MORGANTON, NC 286554044
Phone: 828-580-5000
Fax: –
Web: www.carolinashealthcareblueridge.org
CEO: Kathy C Bailey
CFO: Patricia Moll
HR: Cindy Cross
FYE: December 31
Type: Private

Perhaps it is a lack of grace that lands patients in the Grace Hospital emergency room? Whether treatment for a broken ankle or more serious cancer care is needed Grace Hospital provides general medical services for the residents of Burke County North Carolina. The 200-bed not-for-profit hospital also serves as the anchor of Blue Ridge HealthCare Systems. Specialty services include cancer and cardiac care behavioral health rehabilitation senior services and home health care. Other services include advanced imaging Level 2 neonatology and pediatrics.

	Annual Growth	12/08	12/09	12/13	12/14	12/19
Sales ($ mil.)	9.3%	–	104.5	209.2	191.0	253.1
Net income ($ mil.)	–	–	(3.2)	34.7	28.8	47.1
Market value ($ mil.)	–	–	–	–	–	–
Employees	–	–	–	–	–	1,400

BLUE RIDGE HEALTHCARE SYSTEM, INC..

2201 S STERLING ST
MORGANTON, NC 286554044
Phone: 828-580-5000
Fax: –
Web: www.carolinashealthcareblueridge.org
CEO: Kathy Bailey
CFO: Jackie Garner
HR: –
FYE: December 31
Type: Private

Blue Ridge HealthCare wants to keep you as far from the thin blue line as possible. Blue Ridge HealthCare provides health care services to Burke County North Carolina and the surrounding area via two acute-care hospitals (Grace Hospital and Valdese Hospital with nearly 350 beds between the two) and several outpatient facilities (behavioral health care rehabilitation cancer care senior care and wellness services). Blue Ridge HealthCare also provides senior living services including in-house medical care and hospice services through its Grace Ridge retirement community. The company is an affiliate of the Carolinas HealthCare System.

	Annual Growth	12/12	12/13	12/14	12/16	12/18
Sales ($ mil.)	106.0%	–	7.3	7.4	263.1	271.3
Net income ($ mil.)	–	–	(0.3)	(0.4)	16.6	(7.6)
Market value ($ mil.)	–	–	–	–	–	–
Employees	–	–	–	–	–	1,200

BLUE SKY STUDIOS INC.

One American Ln.
Greenwich CT 06831
Phone: 203-992-6000
Fax: 203-992-6001
Web: www.blueskystudios.com

CEO: –
CFO: Brian Keane
HR: –
FYE: June 30
Type: Subsidiary

Fox Filmed Entertainment hopes its animation sees nothing but blue skies. Its Blue Sky Entertainment division develops and produces animation for feature films and television shows and the studio's CGI Studio proprietary software integrates animation and live action as it did for such Fox films as Fight Club and Alien Resurrection. Blue Sky has produced full-length feature films including Ice Age: Dawn of the Dinosaurs and Horton Hears A Who!. Founded in 1987 the company originally served the advertising industry until its purchase by Fox ten years later. All total Blue Sky has produced about a dozen movies since its first release Bunny which won the Academy Award for Best Animated Short Film in 1999.

BLUEARC CORPORATION

50 Rio Robles
San Jose CA 95134
Phone: 408-576-6600
Fax: 408-576-6601
Web: www.bluearc.com

CEO: –
CFO: –
HR: –
FYE: March 31
Type: Subsidiary

BlueArc is redefining the network storage performance curve. The company provides high-end and mid-range data storage systems used in network-attached storage (NAS) and storage area network (SAN) configurations. Companies involved in drug discovery oil and gas exploration legal electronic discovery high-performance computing media and entertainment Internet services and other data-intensive industries use its scalable Titan servers. BlueArc's servers which are manufactured by Sanmina-SCI utilize programmable chips designed by Altera. Customers in North America account for nearly three-quarters of the company's sales. In 2011 BlueArc filed for an IPO and was then acquired by Hitachi Data Systems (HDS).

BLUE TEE CORP.

387 PARK AVE S FL 5
NEW YORK, NY 100161495
Phone: 212-598-0880
Fax: –
Web: www.bluetee.com

CEO: William M Kelly
CFO: David P Alldian
HR: –
FYE: December 31
Type: Private

Handling a variety of steel products and scrap materials suits Blue Tee to a tee. The holding company which operates through two primary subsidiaries distributes steel building materials and scrap metal. Blue Tee's Brown-Strauss Steel subsidiary is one of the largest distributors of wide flange beam and structural steel products (beams pipe and tubing) in North America. The metal distributor's other primary business is Azcon a leading scrap processor broker and mill services management company which handles scrap metal sales rail cars and other steel parts.

	Annual Growth	12/06	12/07	12/08	12/09	12/10
Sales ($ mil.)	(27.7%)	–	–	1,549.3	564.6	809.8
Net income ($ mil.)	(34.4%)	–	–	33.2	(10.1)	14.3
Market value ($ mil.)	–	–	–	–	–	–
Employees	–	–	–	–	–	900

BLUEBIRD BIO INC

60 Binney Street
Cambridge, MA 02142
Phone: 339 499-9300
Fax: –
Web: www.bluebirdbio.com

NMS: BLUE
CEO: Andrew Obenshain
CFO: Gina Consylman
HR: –
FYE: December 31
Type: Public

bluebird bio is ready to fly in the faces of rare genetic diseases. The company is using gene therapy to develop orphan drugs for two rare diseases. Its lead drug candidate Lenti-D is being developed to treat childhood cerebral adrenoleukodystrophy (CCALD) a rare neurological disorder that affects boys. Its second drug candidate LentiGlobin is being developed to treat the blood disorders beta-thalassemia major and sickle cell disease. Both drugs will begin studies by 2014. In addition bluebird bio partnered with Celgene to develop gene therapies for cancer. Founded in 1992 as Genetix Pharmaceuticals the company changed its name to bluebird bio in 2010 and filed an IPO in 2013.

	Annual Growth	12/16	12/17	12/18	12/19	12/20
Sales ($ mil.)	152.6%	6.2	35.4	54.6	44.7	250.7
Net income ($ mil.)	–	(263.5)	(335.6)	(555.6)	(789.6)	(618.7)
Market value ($ mil.)	(8.5%)	4,098.9	11,831.5	6,590.1	5,829.4	2,874.5
Employees	38.7%	328	479	764	1,090	1,213

BLUE VALLEY BAN CORP (KS)

11935 Riley St., PO Box 26128
Overland Park, KS 66213
Phone: 913 338-1000
Fax: 913 234-7145
Web: www.bankbv.com

NBB: BVBC
CEO: –
CFO: –
HR: –
FYE: December 31
Type: Public

Protect your green at Blue Valley Ban Corp the holding company of Bank of Blue Valley. Founded in 1989 the bank targets closely-held small to midsized businesses and their owners plus professionals and residents in Johnson County Kansas. Through about a half dozen branches located within the Kansas City metropolitan area the bank provides traditional deposit products cash management services investment brokerage and trust services. Its lending activities are focused on construction loans which account for about 30% of its portfolio as well as business and commercial real estate loans which each account for about a quarter.

	Annual Growth	12/13	12/14	12/15	12/16	12/17
Assets ($ mil.)	3.1%	609.1	638.4	638.2	674.4	687.5
Net income ($ mil.)	(13.8%)	1.0	12.8	0.7	1.6	0.6
Market value ($ mil.)	18.3%	34.1	36.9	45.4	53.9	66.7
Employees	–	173	–	–	–	–

BLUEBONNET ELECTRIC COOPERATIVE, INC.

155 ELECTRIC AVE
BASTROP, TX 78602
Phone: 800-842-7708
Fax: –
Web: www.bluebonnetelectric.coop

CEO: Matt Bentke
CFO: Elizabeth Kana
HR: Rachel Meinke
FYE: December 31
Type: Private

Bluebonnet Electric Cooperative's mission has echoes of the late Lady Bird Johnson's quest to spread bluebonnets and other wildflower seeds along Texas' highways. In this case the cooperative spreads power to homes and businesses in rural central and southeast Texas. One of the largest power distribution cooperatives in the state Bluebonnet Electric serves more than 81000 customers in 14 counties (a service area of more than 3800 square miles). The member-owned company which was formed in 1939 operates approximately 11000 miles of transmission and distribution lines and 19 substations. It purchases its wholesale power supply at 21 Lower Colorado River Authority-owned substations.

	Annual Growth	12/16	12/17	12/18	12/19	12/20
Sales ($ mil.)	2.6%	–	208.9	228.0	221.1	225.4
Net income ($ mil.)	18.1%	–	19.7	24.8	29.0	32.4
Market value ($ mil.)	–	–	–	–	–	–
Employees	–	–	–	–	–	265

BLUECHOICE HEALTHPLAN OF SOUTH CAROLINA INC.

4101 Percival Rd.
Columbia SC 29229
Phone: 803-786-8466
Fax: 803-754-6386
Web: www.bluechoicesc.com

CEO: M Edward Sellers
CFO: Robert A Leichtle
HR: –
FYE: December 31
Type: Subsidiary

BlueChoice HealthPlan of South Carolina wants Palmetto State residents to get the health care Blues. The company is a health maintenance organization (HMO) offering managed health care products to some 200000 members in South Carolina. The company's group health plans include a basic HMO plan (Primary Choice) open access HMOs (BlueChoice Advantage) and point-of-service and high-deductable options. Its CarolinaADVANTAGE offering is aimed at small businesses with fewer than 50 employees. The company also offers individual health plans for adults families and children. The company is a subsidiary of Blue Cross & Blue Shield of South Carolina.

BLUECROSS BLUESHIELD OF TENNESSEE INC.

1 Cameron Hill Cir. Sheila Clemons 1 5
Chattanooga TN 37402-9815
Phone: 423-535-5600
Fax: 423-535-6255
Web: www.bcbst.com

CEO: –
CFO: John F Giblin
HR: –
FYE: December 31
Type: Private - Not-for-Pr

BlueCross BlueShield of Tennessee (BCBST) is the oldest and largest not-for-profit managed care provider in the state of Tennessee. Serving around 3 million people through group and individual policies the company offers HMO PPO and high-deductable health plans. Founded in 1945 BCBST also provides Medicare plans to another 1 million customers and its Group Insurance Services unit brokers vision dental life accident and disability plans. Its Volunteer State Health Plan unit provides coverage for low-income members and children through state-sponsored programs. BCBST is a member of the Blue Cross and Blue Shield Association.

BLUEGREEN VACATIONS HOLDINGS CORP

NYS: BVH

4960 Conference Way North, Suite 100
Boca Raton, FL 33431
Phone: 561 912-8000
Fax: –
Web: www.bbxcapital.com

CEO: Alan B Levan
CFO: Raymond S Lopez
HR: –
FYE: December 31
Type: Public

Holding company BFC Financial controls Florida-based investment firm Woodbridge Holdings which has holdings in real estate companies Core Communities and Bluegreen Corporation and restaurant franchise Pizza Fusion. BFC also owns a minority stake in Asian-themed restaurant chain Benihana. Chairman president and CEO Alan Levan and vice chairman Jack Abdo control BFC Financial. In 2016 the company agreed to merge with BBX Capital Corporation which owns the remaining 46% of Woodbridge Holdings that BFC doesn't own. The merger will create a simplified corporate structure.

	Annual Growth	12/16	12/17	12/18	12/19	12/20
Sales ($ mil.)	(9.2%)	764.0	815.8	947.6	946.9	519.5
Net income ($ mil.)	–	28.4	82.2	35.1	17.7	(80.5)
Market value ($ mil.)	29.0%	94.3	154.0	110.7	92.1	261.4
Employees	(6.8%)	6,141	6,914	7,307	7,185	4,637

BLUEKNIGHT ENERGY PARTNERS LP

NMS: BKEP

6060 American Plaza, Suite 600
Tulsa, OK 74135
Phone: 918 237-4000
Fax: –
Web: www.bkep.com

CEO: D Andrew Woodward
CFO: Matthew Lewis
HR: –
FYE: December 31
Type: Public

Blueknight Energy Partners (formerly SemGroup Energy Partners) provides gathering transporting terminalling and storage of crude oil in Oklahoma Kansas and Texas. It operates two pipeline systems (1285 miles of pipeline) delivering crude oil to refineries and provides storage services with a capacity of about 8.1 million barrels. It also provides asphalt services. Blueknight Energy Partners has about 7.4 million barrels of asphalt and residual fuel storage in 45 terminals located in 22 states. Blueknight Energy Partners' top customer is Netherlands-based natural resources group Vitol (54% of total revenues in 2010). Vitol and investment firm Charlesbank Capital Partners indirectly own the company.

	Annual Growth	12/16	12/17	12/18	12/19	12/20
Sales ($ mil.)	(11.2%)	177.4	181.9	384.8	371.1	110.2
Net income ($ mil.)	–	(4.8)	20.0	(42.0)	18.4	(13.5)
Market value ($ mil.)	(26.6%)	290.7	216.4	48.8	48.0	84.5
Employees	(21.1%)	380	370	285	270	147

BLUELINX HOLDINGS INC

NYS: BXC

1950 Spectrum Circle, Suite 300
Marietta, GA 30067
Phone: 770 953-7000
Fax: –
Web: www.bluelinxco.com

CEO: Dwight Gibson
CFO: Kelly Janzen
HR: –
FYE: January 01
Type: Public

You won't find many building products missing at BlueLinx. Through some 65 offices and distribution centers across the US the company is a leading U.S. wholesale distributor of residential and commercial building products with over 50000 branded and private-label SKUs. Products include plywood oriented strand board rebar and remesh lumber engineered wood products moulding siding cedar metal products and insulation. BlueLinx serves national regional and local dealers specialty distributors national home centers and manufactured housing customers of building products in the US. It was established as a division of Georgia-Pacific in 1954.

	Annual Growth	12/17	12/18	12/19*	01/21	01/22
Sales ($ mil.)	18.7%	1,815.5	2,862.9	2,637.3	3,097.3	4,277.2
Net income ($ mil.)	36.3%	63.0	(48.1)	(17.7)	80.9	296.1
Market value ($ mil.)	57.9%	94.9	246.2	127.9	284.6	931.3
Employees	6.5%	1,500	2,400	2,200	2,100	2,055

*Fiscal year change

BLUEPOINT SOLUTIONS INC.

1221 Liberty Way
Vista CA 92081
Phone: 760-410-9000
Fax: 760-410-9010
Web: www.bluepointsolutions.com

CEO: –
CFO: –
HR: –
FYE: December 31
Type: Private

You have to give Bluepoint credit for its document management skills. Bluepoint Solutions develops sofware used by companies in the financial services industry credit unions in particular to process checks and digitally manage forms. The company's products help credit unions organize information into a single database (Receipt Manager) create loan applications and other electronic forms and enable customers to view an electronic image of member signatures for check verification purposes. Other products are used to import check images (Remote Deposit Capture) enable Internet-based account access (WebShare) and manage branch operations. Bluepoint was founded in 2000 by chairman and CEO Hal Tilbury.

BLUESTAR ENERGY SERVICES INC.

363 W. Erie St. Ste. 700
Chicago IL 60610
Phone: 312-327-0900
Fax: 866-996-3782
Web: www.bluestarenergy.com

CEO: –
CFO: Brian X Tierney
HR: –
FYE: December 31
Type: Subsidiary

BlueStar Energy intends to burn bright in the firmament of independent electricity providers. Serving more than 23000 customers in the deregulated markets of Delaware Maryland New Jersey Ohio Illinois Pennsylvania and Washington DC it offers variable- and fixed-rate and custom plans along with green energy to industrial commercial and residential customers. Its energy efficiency program examines customers' energy usage and offers services to decrease costs including reworking lighting fixtures monitoring power use rewiring fixtures and performing exterior maintenance. To harness the financial heft of a major company for future growth in 2012 BlueStar Energy was bought by American Electric Power.

BLUESTEM BRANDS INC.

6509 Flying Cloud
Eden Prairie MN 55344-3307
Phone: 952-656-3700
Fax: 952-830-3293
Web: www.jostens.com

CEO: Bruce Cazenave
CFO: –
HR: –
FYE: January 31
Type: Private

You might say this company lets your fingers do the shopping. Bluestem Brands (formerly Fingerhut Direct Marketing) offers an array of private-label and brand-name merchandise including apparel appliances electronics furniture health and beauty products jewelry kitchenware luggage sporting goods tools and toys through its Fingerhut catalog and e-commerce site and via the Gettington.com site. It also offers credit in partnership with MetaBank and WebBank. In addition it also owns PayCheck Direct an employee purchase plan whereby employers can offer high-ticket items to employees who pay for them interest-free via payroll deductions. The company filed an IPO in 2011 but withdrew it a year later.

BLYTH, INC.   NYS: BTH

One East Weaver Street
Greenwich, CT 06831
Phone: 203 661-1926
Fax: 203 661-1969
Web: www.blyth.com

CEO: Harry Slatkin
CFO: –
HR: –
FYE: December 31
Type: Public

Blyth lights up the party with its wicked products. As the largest candle maker in the US Blyth's PartyLite Worldwide subsidiary sells its scented and unscented candles flameless products and reed diffusers all under the PartyLite brand. Blyth's portfolio extends beyond the candle business with ViSalus nutritional supplements as well as a variety of catalog and online businesses that market household goods and gifts under the Silver Star Brands umbrella. Blyth's products are sold through home parties online and by retailers worldwide. The company also supplies institutional customers such as restaurants and hotels. Blyth which is focused on the direct to consumer market was founded in 1977.

	Annual Growth	01/10	01/11*	12/11	12/12	12/13
Sales ($ mil.)	(2.6%)	958.1	900.9	888.3	1,179.5	885.5
Net income ($ mil.)	(48.4%)	17.7	25.6	16.2	44.0	2.4
Market value ($ mil.)	(27.1%)	449.9	538.5	909.7	249.1	174.3
Employees	(9.6%)	2,300	2,300	1,800	1,700	1,700

*Fiscal year change

BMC STOCK HOLDINGS INC   NMS: BMCH

8020 Arco Corporate Drive, Suite 400
Raleigh, NC 27617
Phone: 919 431-1000
Fax: –
Web: www.buildwithbmc.com

CEO: David E Flitman
CFO: James F Major Jr
HR: Celinda Downey
FYE: December 31
Type: Public

BMC Stock Holdings has crafted itself into a leading supplier of lumber and building materials to large homebuilding companies and contractors. BMC Stock operates about 105 distribution centers in about 20 US states and Washington DC. Products include lumber plywood sheetrock tools and trusses. It also operates commercial flooring and roofing services. Founded in 1922 by B. B. Benson to sell boards and plaster base Stock Building Supply acquired Building Materials Holding Corporation in 2015 and changed its name to BMC Stock Holdings.

	Annual Growth	12/14	12/15	12/16	12/17	12/18
Sales ($ mil.)	29.8%	1,295.7	1,576.7	3,093.7	3,366.0	3,682.4
Net income ($ mil.)	84.1%	10.4	(4.8)	30.9	57.4	119.7
Market value ($ mil.)	0.3%	1,030.0	1,126.1	1,311.0	1,700.9	1,040.7
Employees	32.3%	3,104	9,600	9,000	9,100	9,500

BMO FINANCIAL CORP.

111 W. Monroe St.
Chicago IL 60603
Phone: 312-461-2121
Fax: 973-245-6714
Web: www.basf.us

CEO: James M Cracchiolo
CFO: –
HR: –
FYE: October 31
Type: Subsidiary

BMO Bankcorp (formerly Harris Bankcorp) represents the US retail banking operations of Canada's Bank of Montreal. It is the holding company for BMO Harris Bank (Harris) which offers personal and commercial banking and other financial services through about 700 bank branches in the Chicago area and the Midwest as well as Arizona Florida and a handful of other states. In addition to BMO Harris Bank the company's operations include financial planner Harris Private Bank and its Harris SBSB division and wealth manager Harris myCFO. BMO Bankcorp is growing Harris through such acquisitions as Milwaukee-based Marshall & Ilsley (M&I) in 2011 and the FDIC-assisted purchase of the failed AMCORE Bank in 2010.

BMW OF NORTH AMERICA LLC

300 Chestnut Ridge Rd.
Woodcliff Lake NJ 07677
Phone: 201-307-4000
Fax: 201-307-0880
Web: www.bmwgroupna.com

CEO: Ludwig Willisch
CFO: Dr Gunter Niedernhuber
HR: –
FYE: December 31
Type: Subsidiary

A key subsidiary of BMW BMW of North America provides marketing sales and financial services through almost 900 dealerships and motorcycle retailers. The company imports and manufactures BMW brands such as the 1 3 5 6 7 Series; the X5 X6 and M Series models; and the MINI and Rolls-Royce brands. Styles include coupes convertibles sedans roadsters sports activity and luxury vehicles. Divisions include BMW Manufacturing (South Carolina) industrial-design firm DesignworksUSA a parts distribution center a technology office a technical training center and other operations in the US. Charged to oversee the group's largest single market — the US — BMW of North America was established in 1975.

BNC BANCORP
NAS: BNCN

3980 Premier Drive, Suite 210 — CEO: -
High Point, NC 27265 — CFO: -
Phone: 336 476-9200 — HR: -
Fax: - — FYE: December 31
Web: www.bankofnc.com — Type: Public

BNC Bancorp knows the ABCs of the financial world. The firm is the holding company for Bank of North Carolina which boasts more than 55 branches mostly across North and South Carolina but also in Virginia. In addition to offering traditional loan and deposit products (including checking savings and money market accounts credit cards and certificates of deposits) for local business and retail customers BNC also offers wealth management retirement planning and brokerage services and insurance products. Nearly 40% of its loans are commercial real estate loans while residential mortgages make up another 15%. Founded in 1991 the bank now has more than $5 billion in total assets.

	Annual Growth	12/11	12/12	12/13	12/14	12/15
Assets ($ mil.)	23.3%	2,454.9	3,083.8	3,229.6	4,072.5	5,668.2
Net income ($ mil.)	59.1%	6.9	10.5	17.2	29.4	44.5
Market value ($ mil.)	36.8%	295.6	326.6	698.9	701.7	1,034.8
Employees	16.9%	455	564	620	823	850

BNCCORP INC
NBB: BNCC

322 East Main Avenue — CEO: Richard Milne
Bismarck, ND 58501 — CFO: -
Phone: 701 250-3040 — HR: Connie Froelich
Fax: 701 222-3653 — FYE: December 31
Web: www.bnccorp.com — Type: Public

BNCCORP is the holding company for BNC National Bank which has about 20 branches in Arizona North Dakota and Minnesota. Serving individuals and small and midsized businesses the bank offers deposit accounts credit cards and wealth management services. It also has residential mortgage banking operations in Iowa Kansas and Missouri. Real estate loans account for nearly half of the company's portfolio; commercial industrial construction agricultural and consumer loans make up most of the remainder. BNCCORP sold BNC Insurance Services to Hub International in 2007 for more than $37 million. It arranged to sell some of its operations in Arizona and Minnesota to Alerus Financial in 2010.

	Annual Growth	12/16	12/17	12/18	12/19	12/20
Assets ($ mil.)	4.2%	910.4	946.2	971.0	966.8	1,074.1
Net income ($ mil.)	58.0%	7.2	4.9	6.8	10.2	44.6
Market value ($ mil.)	14.8%	92.2	109.8	72.6	122.7	160.2
Employees	-	-	-	-	-	-

BNS HOLDING INC.
PINK SHEETS: BNSSA

61 E. Main St. Ste. B — CEO: -
Los Gatos CA 95031 — CFO: -
Phone: 401-848-6300 — HR: -
Fax: 314-854-4274 — FYE: October 31
Web: www.brownshoe.com — Type: Public

After trying out a variety of businesses and settling on one that serves the energy market BNS is shutting down. The company is selling North Dakota Sun Well Services a work-over rig service for oil and gas exploration companies to Steel Excel for about $85 million. BNS had acquired Sun Well Services for some $51 million in 2011 after selling its 80% stake in bus maker Collins Industries (purchased in 2006). Once BNS sells Sun Well Services its operating subsidiary it will liquidate and distribute its assets pro rata to its stockholders. Affiliates of private equity firm Steel Partners own about 85% of BNS and 40% of Steel Excel.

BNSF RAILWAY COMPANY

2650 LOU MENK DR — CEO: Kathryn Farmer
FORT WORTH, TX 761312830 — CFO: Julie A Piggott
Phone: 800-795-2673 — HR: -
Fax: - — FYE: December 31
Web: www.bnsf.com — Type: Private

BNSF Railway operates one of the largest railroad networks in North America. A wholly-owned subsidiary of Burlington Northern Santa Fe itself a unit of Berkshire Hathaway the company provides freight transportation over a network of about 32500 route miles of track across some 30 US states and three provinces in Canada. BNSF Railway owns or leases a fleet of about 8000 locomotives. It also has some 25 intermodal facilities that help to transport agricultural consumer and industrial products as well as coal. In addition to major cities and ports BNSF Railway serves smaller markets in alliance with short-line partners.

	Annual Growth	12/12	12/13	12/14	12/16	12/17
Sales ($ mil.)	(0.9%)	-	21,552.0	22,714.0	19,278.0	20,747.0
Net income ($ mil.)	29.8%	-	4,271.0	4,397.0	4,260.0	12,119.0
Market value ($ mil.)	-	-	-	-	-	-
Employees	-	-	-	-	-	41,000

BOARD OF REGENTS OF THE UNIVERSITY OF NEBRASKA

3835 HOLDREGE ST — CEO: -
LINCOLN, NE 685031435 — CFO: -
Phone: 402-472-3906 — HR: -
Fax: - — FYE: June 30
Web: www.nebraska.edu — Type: Private

The University of Nebraska has sprouted four campuses out in the fields of the Cornhusker State. Founded in 1869 the university confers bachelor's master's and doctoral degrees in more than 200 majors including agriculture business education and engineering at its campuses in Kearney Lincoln and Omaha. The university's Medical Center in Omaha trains doctors performs research and is affiliated with a nearly 720-bed teaching hospital. The school also operates research and extension services across the state. More than 51420 students attend classes in the system that has a student-teacher ratio of about 17:1. It was founded as a land-grant university just two years after the Nebraska became a state.

	Annual Growth	06/12	06/13	06/14	06/15	06/16
Sales ($ mil.)	4.3%	-	1,313.5	1,333.6	1,405.0	1,491.0
Net income ($ mil.)	(5.4%)	-	254.8	222.6	221.3	215.5
Market value ($ mil.)	-	-	-	-	-	-
Employees	-	-	-	-	-	15,200

BOARD OF TRUSTEES OF COMMUNITY COLLEGE DISTRICT 508 (INC)

226 W JACKSON BLVD # 103 — CEO: -
CHICAGO, IL 606066959 — CFO: -
Phone: 312-553-2752 — HR: -
Fax: - — FYE: June 30
Web: www.ccc.edu — Type: Private

City Colleges of Chicago (CCC) is one of the largest urban community college systems in the US. It includes seven separately accredited schools — Daley College Kennedy-King College Malcolm X College Olive-Harvey College Truman College Washington College and Wright College. CCC offers associate degrees continuing education IT certifications industry training GED and ESL classes and other programs to some 120000 students each year. Other institutions under the CCC umbrella include the French Pastry School the Washburne Culinary Institute three learning centers and the public television station WYCC-TV. City Colleges of Chicago was founded in 1911 as Crane Junior College.

	Annual Growth	06/06	06/07	06/08	06/09	06/11
Sales ($ mil.)	832.8%	-	-	-	0.6	54.5
Net income ($ mil.)	-	-	-	-	0.0	30.3
Market value ($ mil.)	-	-	-	-	-	-
Employees	-	-	-	-	-	3,500

BOARD OF TRUSTEES OF ILLINOIS STATE UNIVERSITY

302 HOVEY HALL
NORMAL, IL 617900001
Phone: 309-438-2111
Fax: -
Web: www.illinoisstate.edu

CEO: -
CFO: -
HR: -
FYE: June 30
Type: Private

Normal doesn't quite describe it. Illinois State University (ISU) in Normal-Bloomington provides advanced education courses in more than 150 academic fields including business fine arts education and science nursing and technology. The school has a student body of more than 19920 graduate and undergraduate students; about 95% are Illinois residents. ISU's facilities include a public planetarium 490-acre arboretum two primary laboratory schools and the Milner Library with more than 1.6 million volumes. The university is governed by a board of trustees selected by the Illinois governor.

	Annual Growth	06/04	06/05	06/06	06/07	06/08
Sales ($ mil.)	-	-	-	(1,265.6)	225.1	247.8
Net income ($ mil.)	-	-	-	0.0	34.1	36.0
Market value ($ mil.)	-	-	-	-	-	-
Employees	-	-	-	-	-	3,441

BOARDRIDERS, INC.

5600 ARGOSY AVE STE 100
HUNTINGTON BEACH, CA 926491063
Phone: 714-889-5404
Fax: -
Web: www.boardriders.com

CEO: Arne Arens
CFO: Thomas Chambolle
HR: -
FYE: October 31
Type: Private

Boardriders rides the wave of youth appeal. Formerly Quiksilver the company caters to the young and athletic with surfwear snowboardwear sportswear and swimwear sold under the Quiksilver Billabong Element VonZipper and Roxy names among others. It also owns the DC Shoes brand of footwear and apparel for young men and juniors. It sells its apparel footwear and accessories in specialty and department stores worldwide as well as through its own network of about 570 retail stores. It emerged from Chapter 11 bankruptcy protection in 2016 and is now owned by Oaktree Capital Management; in 2018 it bought rival Billabong.

	Annual Growth	10/10	10/11	10/12	10/13	10/14
Sales ($ mil.)	(11.7%)	-	-	2,013.2	1,810.6	1,570.4
Net income ($ mil.)	-	-	-	(9.7)	(233.5)	(320.1)
Market value ($ mil.)	-	-	-	-	-	-
Employees	-	-	-	-	-	600

BOARDWALK PIPELINE PARTNERS LP

NYS: BWP

9 Greenway Plaza, Suite 2800
Houston, TX 77046
Phone: 866 913-2122
Fax: -

CEO: Stanley Horton
CFO: Jamie Buskill
HR: Mercy Kamps
FYE: December 31
Type: Public

Boardwalk Pipeline Partners walks a fine (pipe) line. The limited partnership owns and operates three US interstate natural gas pipeline systems — totaling 14450 miles — that originate in the Gulf Coast region Arkansas and Oklahoma and extend to the Midwest. It provides transportation and storage to customers that include gas producers marketers local distribution companies and interstate and intrastate pipelines. It operates through Boardwalk Pipelines LP and its subsidiaries Gulf Crossing Pipeline Company Gulf South Pipeline Company and Texas Gas Transmission. The company's systems carry 11% of the daily US consumption of natural gas. Boardwalk Pipeline Partners is controlled by Loews Corporation.

	Annual Growth	12/12	12/13	12/14	12/15	12/16
Sales ($ mil.)	2.5%	1,185.0	1,205.6	1,233.8	1,249.2	1,307.2
Net income ($ mil.)	(0.3%)	306.0	253.7	233.6	222.0	302.2
Market value ($ mil.)	(8.6%)	6,232.4	6,387.6	4,447.8	3,248.9	4,345.2
Employees	1.6%	1,200	1,200	1,230	1,260	1,280

BOB EVANS FARMS INC

NMS: BOBE

8111 Smith's Mill Road
New Albany, OH 43054
Phone: 614 491-2225
Fax: -
Web: www.bobevans.com

CEO: Saed Mohseni
CFO: Mark E Hood
HR: -
FYE: April 29
Type: Public

This farm is focused on cooks in the kitchen rather than seeds in the ground. Bob Evans Farms is a leading full-service restaurant company with more than 650 locations operating under the names Bob Evans and Mimi's Café. Its namesake chain includes about 565 family-style restaurants in 20 states that are best known for breakfast items such as bacon eggs hotcakes and sausage products. Its Mimi's Café casual dining chain operated through subsidiary SWH Corporation serves American-style dishes at about 150 locations. In addition to its restaurants Bob Evans Farms markets its own sausage and bacon products under the Bob Evans and Owens brands at supermarkets and other grocery retailers.

	Annual Growth	04/12	04/13	04/14	04/15	04/16
Sales ($ mil.)	(5.2%)	1,654.4	1,608.9	1,328.6	1,349.2	1,338.8
Net income ($ mil.)	(24.1%)	72.9	(2.9)	33.7	16.6	24.2
Market value ($ mil.)	4.2%	764.0	840.1	924.6	894.8	899.7
Employees	(10.1%)	46,818	34,023	34,470	32,341	30,625

BOB ROSS BUICK, INC.

85 LOOP RD
DAYTON, OH 454592199
Phone: 937-433-0990
Fax: -
Web: www.bobrossauto.com

CEO: -
CFO: -
HR: -
FYE: December 31
Type: Private

The Bob Ross Group sells new and used cars made by Buick for sure as well as by GMC Alfa Romeo Fiat and Mercedes Benz in Centerville Ohio. Bob Ross also provides financing parts service and collision repair. The company's bobrossauto.com Web site allows customers to search new and used inventory as well as schedule service order parts and apply for financing. Bob Ross ranks near the top of many categories (Buick sales customer satisfaction GMC truck sales) for Buick dealerships in Ohio. The company was founded in 1979 by the late Bob Ross Sr. and his wife Norma Ross (daughter Jenell is now the owner). It was the first African-American owned Mercedes-Benz dealership in the world.

	Annual Growth	12/12	12/13	12/14	12/15	12/16
Sales ($ mil.)	4.2%	-	66.8	72.8	77.5	75.6
Net income ($ mil.)	2.0%	-	0.5	0.5	0.6	0.5
Market value ($ mil.)	-	-	-	-	-	-
Employees	-	-	-	-	-	100

BODDIE-NOELL ENTERPRISES, INC.

1021 NOELL LN
ROCKY MOUNT, NC 278041761
Phone: 252-937-2000
Fax: -
Web: www.bneinc.com

CEO: Bill Boddie
CFO: W Craig Worthy
HR: Mitzi L Aldridge
FYE: December 29
Type: Private

Boddie-Noell Enterprises (BNE) is a hearty competitor in the fast-food business. The company is one of the largest franchise operators of Hardee's a fast-food chain owned by CKE Restaurants with about 330 locations the four southeastern states of Kentucky North Carolina South Carolina and Virginia. In addition the company owns The Highway Diner restaurant concept. BNE is also involved in real estate development through BNE Land & Development. The family owned company was started in 1962 by Carleton Noell and his nephews Nick and Mayo Boddie.

	Annual Growth	12/10	12/11	12/12	12/13	12/14
Sales ($ mil.)	(1.2%)	-	395.3	395.3	369.9	381.3
Net income ($ mil.)	-	-	(9.6)	14.0	16.6	17.0
Market value ($ mil.)	-	-	-	-	-	-
Employees	-	-	-	-	-	12,000

BODY CENTRAL CORP. NBB: BODY

6225 Powers Avenue
Jacksonville, FL 32217
Phone: 904 737-0811
Fax: 904 730-0638
Web: www.bodycentral.com

CEO: -
CFO: -
HR: -
FYE: December 28
Type: Public

Body Central likely has something in store for young women who feel that image is everything. The company offers trendy apparel shoes and accessories to women in their late teens and early 20s through about 290 Body Central and Body Shop retail stores. Located primarily in malls in more than 25 states in the South Midwest and Mid-Atlantic the shops carry dresses tops jewelry and shoes sold under its Body Central and Lipstick brands. It also sells its merchandise through catalogs and its e-commerce site. A holding company Body Central operates primarily through its Body Shop of America (not affiliated with The Body Shop) and Catalogue Ventures subsidiaries. Body Central went public in 2010.

	Annual Growth	01/10	01/11*	12/11	12/12	12/13
Sales ($ mil.)	12.6%	198.8	243.4	296.5	311.0	283.6
Net income ($ mil.)	-	2.8	9.8	19.7	11.9	(42.3)
Market value ($ mil.)	(46.8%)	-	23.7	41.5	15.8	6.7
Employees	19.3%	2,300	2,410	2,869	3,305	3,901

*Fiscal year change

BOEING CAPITAL CORP

500 Naches Ave. S.W., 3rd Floor
Renton, WA 98057
Phone: 425 965-4000
Fax: -
Web: www.boeing.com

CEO: -
CFO: Kelvin E Council
HR: -
FYE: December 31
Type: Public

Need financing for that 747? Boeing Capital a major subsidiary of Boeing provides asset-backed leasing and lending services through two divisions: Aircraft Financial Services offers financing and leasing services for airlines and governmental customers interested in Boeing aircraft; Space & Defense Financial Services offers similar services for Boeing's Integrated Defense Systems customers. AirTran is Boeing Capital's biggest customer followed by American Airlines Hawaiian Airlines and Continental Airlines. Boeing Capital was founded in 1968 as McDonnell Douglas Finance and changed its name when Boeing acquired McDonnell Douglas in 1997.

	Annual Growth	12/08	12/09	12/10	12/11	12/12
Sales ($ mil.)	(11.3%)	703.0	660.0	639.0	532.0	436.0
Net income ($ mil.)	(20.5%)	120.0	57.0	92.0	83.0	48.0
Market value ($ mil.)	-	-	-	-	-	-
Employees	(2.3%)	160	161	150	146	146

BOEING CO. (THE) NYS: BA

100 North Riverside Plaza
Chicago, IL 60606-1596
Phone: 312 544-2000
Fax: -
Web: www.boeing.com

CEO: David L Calhoun
CFO: Brian J West
HR: -
FYE: December 31
Type: Public

Boeing is one of the world's largest aerospace company that designs develops and manufactures the sale service and support of commercial jetliners military aircraft satellites missile defense human space flight and launch systems and services. The company is one of the two major manufacturers of 100-plus seat airplanes. Its commercial jet aircraft models include 737 747 767 777 and 787 families of airplanes and the Boeing Business Jet range. New product development efforts include the Boeing 787-10 Dreamliner the 737 MAX and the 777X. The company generates about two-thirds of its revenue domestically.

	Annual Growth	12/17	12/18	12/19	12/20	12/21
Sales ($ mil.)	(9.6%)	93,392.0	101,127.0	76,559.0	58,158.0	62,286.0
Net income ($ mil.)	-	8,197.0	10,460.0	(636.0)	(11,873.0)	(4,202.0)
Market value ($ mil.)	(9.1%)	173,677.6	189,925.9	191,845.7	126,063.7	118,560.9
Employees	0.2%	140,800	153,000	161,100	141,000	142,000

BOEING EMPLOYEES' CREDIT UNION

12770 Gateway Dr.
Tukwila WA 98168
Phone: 206-439-5700
Fax: 206-439-5804
Web: www.becu.org

CEO: Benson Porter
CFO: -
HR: -
FYE: December 31
Type: Private - Not-for-Pr

Boeing Employees' Credit Union (BECU) was founded in 1935 to serve the employees of Boeing (naturally) which called Seattle home until 2001. Today membership in the credit union is open to all who live work go to school or belong to a church in Washington State. BECU has about 45 locations in the state's Puget Sound region many of them in Safeway supermarkets. The credit union offers standard retail financial services such as checking and savings accounts credit cards home mortgages and other loans. The credit union also participates in a shared-branch system giving its members access to financial services at more than 4000 locations worldwide. BECU boasts some 800000 members.

BOEING SATELLITE SYSTEMS INTERNATIONAL INC.

2260 E. Imperial Hwy.
El Segundo CA 90245
Phone: 310-364-4000
Fax: 604-681-8240

CEO: Craig R Cooning
CFO: -
HR: -
FYE: December 31
Type: Subsidiary

Boeing Satellite Systems International is happiest when its products are far far away. The company is a contracting unit for commercial and military spacecraft within the Boeing Space & Intelligence Systems division. It manufactures communications meteorological and research satellites. Boeing Satellite Systems International built the world's first geosynchronous communications satellite (Syncom) and estimates that it has manufactured about 40% of all the communications satellites in commercial service today (since its inception in 1961). Other satellite applications include cover radar mapping satellite television and national security. Contracts with the DoD constitute the majority of its revenues.

BOGEN COMMUNICATIONS INTERNATIONAL INC. PINK SHEETS: BOGN

50 Spring St.
Ramsey NJ 07446
Phone: 201-934-8500
Fax: 201-934-9832
Web: www.bogen.com

CEO: Jonathan Guss
CFO: Maureen Flotard
HR: -
FYE: December 31
Type: Public

Bogen Communications knows how the soothing sounds of smooth jazz can make time fly while holding on the telephone. Through subsidiaries Bogen Communications and Speech Design the company makes telecommunications peripherals and sound equipment. Bogen Communications sells telecom equipment including music-on-hold devices unified messaging systems call distributors and voice mail systems. Speech Design sells call processing and PBX products primarily in Germany. Bogen also makes audio amplifiers and speaker systems. Schools restaurants and stores use the company's line of intercom and paging systems for public address and background music. Executives and directors together own a majority of Bogen.

BOINGO WIRELESS INC

NMS: WIFI

10960 Wilshire Blvd., 23rd Floor
Los Angeles, CA 90024
Phone: 310 586-5180
Fax: –
Web: www.boingo.com

CEO: Mike Finley
CFO: Peter Hovenier
HR: –
FYE: December 31
Type: Public

Boingo keeps travelers connected as they bounce through often unfamiliar locales. The company sells access to a global Wi-Fi network of over 1.3 million hot spots to more than 340000 subscribers through wholesale agreements with wireless network and hot spot operators. Access is offered mainly in such venues as hotels convention centers airports and restaurants. Additionally Boingo offers its roaming network and software to ISPs and managed network service providers. AT&T Verizon and Sprint Corporation are among the company's corporate customers. The company was established in 2001.

	Annual Growth	12/15	12/16	12/17	12/18	12/19
Sales ($ mil.)	17.2%	139.6	159.3	204.4	250.8	263.8
Net income ($ mil.)	–	(22.3)	(27.3)	(19.4)	(1.2)	(10.3)
Market value ($ mil.)	13.4%	292.8	539.1	995.0	909.7	484.3
Employees	9.5%	286	315	334	463	411

BOISE CASCADE CO. (DE)

NYS: BCC

1111 West Jefferson Street, Suite 300
Boise, ID 83702-5389
Phone: 208 384-6161
Fax: –
Web: www.bc.com

CEO: Nate Jorgensen
CFO: Kelly Hibbs
HR: Erin Nuxoll
FYE: December 31
Type: Public

Boise Cascade has more than a trickle of building materials. The company is one of North America's largest producer of environmentally friendly engineered wood products (EWP) and plywood in North America. Boise Cascade is also a leading building materials distributors. Customers include lumberyards home improvement centers and industrial converters (makers of windows doors and other assembled products) in North America. Boise Cascade was formed in 2004.

	Annual Growth	12/16	12/17	12/18	12/19	12/20
Sales ($ mil.)	8.8%	3,911.2	4,432.0	4,995.3	4,643.4	5,474.8
Net income ($ mil.)	46.2%	38.3	83.0	20.5	80.9	175.0
Market value ($ mil.)	20.7%	882.0	1,564.1	934.9	1,432.0	1,873.8
Employees	(0.6%)	6,190	6,370	6,210	6,010	6,040

BOISE STATE UNIVERSITY

1910 UNIVERSITY DR
BOISE, ID 837250002
Phone: 208-426-1000
Fax: –

CEO: Bob Kustra
CFO: Martin Schimpf
HR: –
FYE: June 30
Type: Private

Boise State University (BSU) provides higher education in the shadows of the Rocky Mountains. BSU has an enrollment of approximately 23000 students and a faculty and staff of more than 2400. The university offers about 200 undergraduate graduate and technical fields of study through seven colleges: Arts and Sciences Business and Economics Education Engineering Health Sciences Social Sciences and Public Affairs and Graduate Studies. In addition to its main campus in Boise Idaho it operates a satellite campus in Nampa (Boise State West) which offers academic non-credit and applied technology courses. BSU also has three centers elsewhere in the state as well as online learning programs.

	Annual Growth	06/16	06/17	06/18	06/19	06/20
Sales ($ mil.)	5.5%	–	244.1	258.7	275.0	286.5
Net income ($ mil.)	49.0%	–	9.8	35.2	28.9	32.6
Market value ($ mil.)	–	–	–	–	–	–
Employees	–	–	–	–	–	1,879

BOJANGLES' RESTAURANTS INC.

9432 Southern Pines Blvd.
Charlotte NC 28273
Phone: 704-527-2675
Fax: 704-523-6803
Web: www.bojangles.com/

CEO: Randy Kibler
CFO: John Jordan
HR: Acadia Manning
FYE: December 31
Type: Private

This Bojangles doesn't dance in worn-out shoes but it will cook some chicken for you. Bojangles' Holdings operates and franchises more than 520 quick-service eateries in North Carolina and about a dozen other states. Operating under the name Bojangles' Famous Chicken & Biscuits the restaurants specialize in Cajun-style chicken and biscuits. The menu also includes sandwiches chicken wings and breakfast items. The chain includes more than 150 company-owned locations; the rest are operated by franchisees. Bojangles was founded in 1977 by former KFC president Richard Thomas and partner Jack Fulk. Private equity firm Advent International agreed to buy the chain from Falfurrias Capital Partners in 2011.

BOK FINANCIAL CORP

NMS: BOKF

Bank of Oklahoma Tower, Boston Avenue at Second Street
Tulsa, OK 74172
Phone: 918 588-6000
Fax: –
Web: www.bokf.com

CEO: Norman Bagwell
CFO: Steven Nell
HR: –
FYE: December 31
Type: Public

BOK Financial began in 1910 as a regional source of capital for the energy industry. It has seven principal banking divisions in eight midwestern and southwestern states. In addition to traditional deposit lending and trust services its banks provide investment management wealth advisory and mineral and real estate management services through a network of branches in Arizona Arkansas Colorado Kansas Missouri New Mexico Oklahoma and Texas. With nearly 120 branches in the US more than half of the bank's deposit franchise are located in Oklahoma and over 30% of its loan portfolio are in Texas.

	Annual Growth	12/16	12/17	12/18	12/19	12/20
Assets ($ mil.)	9.2%	32,772.3	32,272.2	38,020.5	42,172.0	46,671.1
Net income ($ mil.)	16.9%	232.7	334.6	445.6	500.8	435.0
Market value ($ mil.)	(4.7%)	5,782.7	6,428.9	5,106.5	6,086.3	4,768.8
Employees	0.2%	4,884	4,930	5,313	5,107	4,915

BOLLINGER SHIPYARDS INC.

8365 Hwy. 308 South
Lockport LA 70374
Phone: 985-532-2554
Fax: 985-532-7225
Web: www.bollingershipyards.com

CEO: Ben Bordelon
CFO: Andrew Fc Germain
HR: –
FYE: September 30
Type: Private

Bollinger Shipyards is a leading provider of shipbuilding and ship repair services for both the military and commercial marine industry on the US Gulf Coast. The company specializes in the construction repair and conversion of US Navy and Coast Guard patrol boats oil tankers and supply and utility vessels such as barges and tugboats. It operates from some 13 shipyards primarily in Louisiana but also in Texas and has access to the Mississippi River. Its more than 30 dry docks have the capability to accommodate ships ranging in size from 100 tons to 22000 tons. It also has a more than 460000-sq.-ft. facility for constructing vessels indoors. Bollinger Shipyards was founded in 1946 by Donald Bollinger.

BOLLORE LOGISTICS USA INC.

423 RXR PLZ
UNIONDALE, NY 115563811
Phone: 718-525-5038
Fax: –
Web: www.sdvusa.com

CEO: Thomas Duplan
CFO: –
HR: Angela Lotito
FYE: December 31
Type: Private

SDV (USA) aims to arrange the transportation of its customers' freight PDQ. The company which provides international air and ocean freight forwarding and logistics services specializes in serving customers from industries such as in aerospace high technology manufacturing and oil and gas. (As a freight forwarder SDV (USA) buys transportation capacity from carriers and resells it to customers.) The company operates from more than a dozen offices in major US trade gateways. SDV (USA) is a unit of France-based SDV International Logistics which itself is a unit of the diversified Bolloré group.

	Annual Growth	12/06	12/07	12/08	12/09	12/13
Sales ($ mil.)	11.3%	–	–	–	211.8	324.6
Net income ($ mil.)	12.6%	–	–	–	5.5	8.8
Market value ($ mil.)	–	–	–	–	–	–
Employees	–	–	–	–	–	480

BOLT TECHNOLOGY CORP.

Four Duke Place
Norwalk, CT 06854
Phone: 203 853-0700
Fax: 203 854-9601
Web: www.bolt-technology.com

NMS: BOLT
CEO: –
CFO: –
HR: –
FYE: June 30
Type: Public

Bolt Technology's action is technology the kind used to map out oil and gas discoveries. Its product suite consists of the key components needed by seismic exploration vessels to acquire seismic data: an energy source (air guns); synchronization (controllers); and communication (cables) linking the guns and the controllers. Its marine air guns help produce 3-D seismic maps for oil and gas exploration by firing high-pressure air into the water producing elastic waves that penetrate deep into the earth. These waves create a "map" of the subsurface geography. The company also operates a fleet of remotely operated vehicles (ROVs). Bolt Technology's major customers include CCG-Veritas and Schlumberger.

	Annual Growth	06/09	06/10	06/11	06/12	06/13
Sales ($ mil.)	4.3%	48.9	31.5	38.9	52.6	57.8
Net income ($ mil.)	(10.6%)	10.5	5.0	5.5	2.0	6.7
Market value ($ mil.)	11.0%	97.0	75.5	107.0	129.5	147.3
Employees	7.3%	139	123	165	176	184

BON SECOURS - RICHMOND COMMUNITY HOSPITAL, INCORPORATED

1500 N 28TH ST
RICHMOND, VA 232235332
Phone: 804-225-1700
Fax: –
Web: www.richmondobgyn.com

CEO: Mark Gordon
CFO: –
HR: –
FYE: August 31
Type: Private

Part of the Bon Secours Health System Bon Secours-Richmond Community Hospital is a 100-bed facility that provides general medical and surgical care to the residents of Richmond Virginia. Located in the city's historic Church Hill neighborhood the hospital provides inpatient care as well as emergency services diagnostic imaging services and outpatient rehabilitation. The hospital also features an inpatient psychiatric unit and provides primary health care services at a medical office building next door. Bon Secours-Richmond Community Hospital was founded in 1903 by a husband-and-wife duo of African American doctors Sarah and Miles Jones.

	Annual Growth	08/02	08/03	08/05	08/09	08/16
Sales ($ mil.)	15.1%	–	21.6	31.0	49.6	134.3
Net income ($ mil.)	–	–	(4.6)	(3.7)	(3.2)	41.3
Market value ($ mil.)	–	–	–	–	–	–
Employees	–	–	–	–	–	189

BON SECOURS MERCY HEALTH, INC.

1701 MERCY HEALTH PL
CINCINNATI, OH 452376147
Phone: 513-952-5000
Fax: –
Web: www.bsmhealth.org

CEO: John M Starcher Jr
CFO: –
HR: –
FYE: December 31
Type: Private

Bon Secours Mercy Health is one of the 20 largest health systems in the US and the fifth-largest Catholic health system in the country. The ministry's quality compassionate care is provided by more than 60000 associates serving communities in Florida Kentucky Maryland New York Ohio South Carolina Virginia and throughout Ireland.

	Annual Growth	08/08	08/09	08/10*	12/19	12/20
Sales ($ mil.)	11.9%	–	2,895.2	3,084.9	8,717.6	9,969.7
Net income ($ mil.)	–	–	(291.9)	(41.4)	2,593.2	609.1
Market value ($ mil.)	–	–	–	–	–	–
Employees	–	–	–	–	–	19,000

*Fiscal year change

BON-TON STORES INC

2801 East Market Street
York, PA 17402
Phone: 717 757-7660
Fax: –
Web: www.bonton.com

NBB: BONT Q
CEO: William Tracy
CFO: Michael Culhane
HR: –
FYE: January 28
Type: Public

Age wasn't enough to protect Bon-Ton Stores from major shifts in the department store industry. Founded in 1898 by the Grumbacher family the company filed for Chapter 11 bankruptcy in early 2018 and later that year sold its inventory and assets to liquidators. All of its stores will close. Amid a decline in mall traffic and overall harsh retail environment Bon-Ton struggled with falling revenue and debt which limited its ability to invest in all-important e-commerce operations.

	Annual Growth	02/13	02/14*	01/15	01/16	01/17
Sales ($ mil.)	(2.7%)	2,978.8	2,834.1	2,822.9	2,789.5	2,674.4
Net income ($ mil.)	–	(21.6)	(3.6)	(7.0)	(57.1)	(63.4)
Market value ($ mil.)	(44.2%)	282.8	232.1	118.3	36.7	27.4
Employees	(3.5%)	26,900	25,800	25,200	24,100	23,300

*Fiscal year change

BONITZ, INC.

645 ROSEWOOD DR
COLUMBIA, SC 292014699
Phone: 803-799-0181
Fax: –
Web: www.bonitz.us

CEO: –
CFO: Doug Dozier
HR: –
FYE: December 31
Type: Private

Bonitz is a veteran US acoustical ceiling and drywall contractor. Founded by chairman Bill Rogers in 1954 the company got a humble start in South Carolina and has grown to operate in more than a dozen US locations primarily in the Southeast including Alabama Colorado Georgia Tennessee Virginia and the Carolinas. Through its operating divisions Bonitz also offers commercial and residential flooring contracting roofing contracting and manufacturing of prefabricated light gage metal wall panels and trusses for educational institutional and commercial buildings. Its clients include architects interior designers general contractors and building owners. Bonitz is employee owned.

	Annual Growth	12/11	12/12	12/13	12/14	12/15
Sales ($ mil.)	11.6%	–	129.0	143.9	178.8	179.2
Net income ($ mil.)	26.0%	–	3.9	6.7	6.1	7.8
Market value ($ mil.)	–	–	–	–	–	–
Employees	–	–	–	–	–	850

BONNEVILLE POWER ADMINISTRATION

905 NE 11TH AVE
PORTLAND, OR 972324169
Phone: 503-230-3000
Fax: -
Web: www.bpa.gov

CEO: John Hairston
CFO: Claudia Andrews
HR: -
FYE: September 30
Type: Private

Bonneville Power Administration (BPA) keeps the lights on in the Pacific Northwest. The US Department of Energy power marketing agency operates a transmission grid (with more than 15000 miles of high-voltage lines) that delivers about 30% of the electrical power consumed in the region. The electricity that BPA wholesales is generated primarily by around 30 federal hydroelectric dams (operated by the US Army Corp of Engineers) and one nonfederal nuclear facility and several small nonfederal power plants.

	Annual Growth	09/06	09/07	09/08	09/09	09/10
Sales ($ mil.)	0.3%	-	-	3,036.6	2,870.3	3,055.1
Net income ($ mil.)	-	-	-	264.8	(101.1)	(127.6)
Market value ($ mil.)	-	-	-	-	-	-
Employees	-	-	-	-	-	3,100

BONNIER CORPORATION

460 N. Orlando Ave. Ste. 200
Winter Park FL 32789
Phone: 407-628-4802
Fax: 407-628-7061
Web: www.bonniercorp.com

CEO: David Ritchie
CFO: -
HR: -
FYE: December 31
Type: Subsidiary

Packing Salade Nicoise for a typical afternoon cruising the bay on your yacht? If so you would be a target reader of Bonnier Corporation publisher of magazine titles such as to "Saveur" (an award-winning gourmet foods magazine) Cruising World and "Boating Life". Additional titles include Popular Science Field & Stream and Outdoor Life. Its Garden Design and Florida Travel & Life titles make up the company's Lifestyle & Shelter Group with other groups devoted to Travel Luxury and Parenting. All total Bonnier Corporation publishes about 50 special-interest magazines and produces related multimedia projects and events. The company is owned by 200-year-old Swedish media firm Bonnier AB.

BOOKING HOLDINGS INC   NMS: BKNG

800 Connecticut Avenue
Norwalk, CT 06854
Phone: 203 299-8000
Fax: 203 595-0160
Web: www.bookingholdings.com

CEO: Glenn Fogel
CFO: David Goulden
HR: -
FYE: December 31
Type: Public

Booking Holdings (formerly The Priceline Group) operates six of the world's leading online travel tools. Booking.com is its namesake and top brand and offers online reservation services for nearly 2.4 million properties — including hotels motels resorts apartments and homes — across over 220-plus countries. The holding company also owns Priceline which features discount bookings for hotels cars airline tickets cruises and vacation packages; other brands include Agoda KAYAK RentalCars and OpenTable. Booking Holdings generates revenues from credit card processing rebates and customer processing fees advertising services restaurant reservations and management services and various other services such as travel-related insurance. It was founded in 1997 and generates about 90% of sales outside the US.

	Annual Growth	12/17	12/18	12/19	12/20	12/21
Sales ($ mil.)	(3.6%)	12,681.1	14,527.0	15,066.0	6,796.0	10,958.0
Net income ($ mil.)	(16.0%)	2,340.8	3,998.0	4,865.0	59.0	1,165.0
Market value ($ mil.)	8.4%	71,362.1	70,733.0	84,338.6	91,465.2	98,526.9
Employees	(3.0%)	22,900	24,500	26,400	20,300	20,300

BOOKS-A-MILLION, INC.   NMS: BAMM

402 Industrial Lane
Birmingham, AL 35211
Phone: 205 942-3737
Fax: -
Web: www.booksamillioninc.com

CEO: Terrance G Finley
CFO: R Todd Noden
HR: -
FYE: February 01
Type: Public

Books-A-Million (BAM) caters to readers who aren't millionaires. One of the nation's largest booksellers (behind Amazon and Barnes & Noble) the company operates some 260 stores in 30-plus states and Washington DC and sells books online. BAM operates superstores under the Books-A-Million Books & Co. and 2nd & Charles banners and traditional smaller stores under the Bookland title. All the stores sell discounted hardcover and paperback books magazines toys music DVDs and general merchandise. Many stores include Joe Muggs cafés and sell frozen yogurt. Other activities comprise online unit booksamillion.com gift card issuer BAM Card Services and book wholesaler American Wholesale Book.

	Annual Growth	01/10	01/11	01/12*	02/13	02/14
Sales ($ mil.)	(1.9%)	508.7	495.0	468.5	503.8	470.3
Net income ($ mil.)	-	13.8	8.9	(2.8)	2.5	(7.6)
Market value ($ mil.)	(22.4%)	97.7	85.7	38.5	38.5	35.4
Employees	(0.5%)	5,500	5,300	6,000	5,500	5,400

*Fiscal year change

BOOKSPAN

501 Franklin Ave.
Garden City NY 11530-5945
Phone: 516-490-4561
Fax: 516-490-4714
Web: www.booksonline.com

CEO: Deborah I Fine
CFO: -
HR: -
FYE: December 31
Type: Private

Spanning the globe to bring you ... books. Bookspan is a direct marketer of books operating book clubs under such familiar names as the Book-of-the-Month Club Doubleday Book Club and The Literary Guild. The company operates about 20 clubs that offer bestsellers and feature titles from specific genres including history military mystery and science fiction. Book selections are chosen by editors in various areas. The company was created through a partnership between Bertelsmann and Time Warner which sold its stake to Bertelsmann in 2007. Bertelsmann sold Bookspan Columbia House and its other direct marketing operations in the US to Phoenix-based private investment firm Najafi Cos. in 2008.

BOONE HOSPITAL CENTER

1600 E BROADWAY
COLUMBIA, MO 652015897
Phone: 573-815-8000
Fax: -
Web: www.boone.health

CEO: -
CFO: -
HR: Deanna Weiner
FYE: December 31
Type: Private

If you're torn apart by tigers you might end up here. Boone Hospital Center is a 390-bed full-service hospital that serves St. Louis and a 25-county area in central Missouri. Boone provides a range of programs and services including emergency care and emergency transportation. The hospital offers specialized care in the areas of cardiology neurology oncology surgery and obstetrics. It also operates outreach clinics and provides home health care services through Boone Hospital Home Care. Its Wellaware center focuses on behavioral and occupational medicine. Boone Hospital is part of the BJC HealthCare network.

	Annual Growth	12/14	12/15	12/16	12/17	12/18
Sales ($ mil.)	0.3%	-	284.3	299.5	288.8	286.8
Net income ($ mil.)	-	-	(1.8)	6.3	(10.9)	(16.4)
Market value ($ mil.)	-	-	-	-	-	-
Employees	-	-	-	-	-	3,150

BOOZ ALLEN HAMILTON HOLDING CORP.   NYS: BAH

8283 Greensboro Drive   CEO: Horacio Rozanski
McLean, VA 22102   CFO: Lloyd Howell
Phone: 703-902-5000   HR: –
Fax: –   FYE: March 31
Web: www.boozallen.com   Type: Public

Booz Allen Hamilton is a leading contractor for US Government defense and intelligence departments assisting in the fields of cyber security and intelligence operations. The company which acts as prime contractor in nearly every instance generates billions in sales each year from the delivery of highly technical skills to the Department of Defense the National Security Agency the IRS and nearly every cabinet-level US Government department. It increasingly works with foreign governments and commercial clients as well. Investment company The Carlyle Group owns a majority interest in the consulting company which was founded in 1914.

	Annual Growth	03/17	03/18	03/19	03/20	03/21
Sales ($ mil.)	7.9%	5,804.3	6,171.9	6,704.0	7,463.8	7,858.9
Net income ($ mil.)	24.6%	252.5	305.1	418.5	482.6	609.0
Market value ($ mil.)	22.8%	4,821.7	5,275.4	7,921.3	9,351.9	10,971.9
Employees	4.4%	23,300	24,600	26,100	27,200	27,700

BORGHESE INC.

10 E. 34th St. 3rd Fl.   CEO: –
New York NY 10016   CFO: Frank Palladino
Phone: 212-659-5300   HR: –
Fax: 212-659-5301   FYE: December 31
Web: www.borghese.com   Type: Private

You can ring up Borghese when you need to be made beautiful. Borghese makes and markets its namesake Italian cosmetics skin care fragrances and hair care products and sells its collections through high-end department stores nationwide including Bloomingdale's Lord & Taylor and Nordstrom. Its products are also marketed internationally in such countries as China Germany Ireland and Mexico. President and CEO Georgette Mosbacher (also a well-known New York City Republican) holds a substantial equity stake in the company while the rest is retained by the original group of Saudi investors who purchased it upon Revlon's divestiture of the firm in 1992.

BORGWARNER INC   NYS: BWA

3850 Hamlin Road   CEO: Frederic Lissalde
Auburn Hills, MI 48326   CFO: Kevin Nowlan
Phone: 248-754-9200   HR: –
Fax: –   FYE: December 31
Web: www.borgwarner.com   Type: Public

BorgWarner is a global product leader in clean and efficient technology solutions for combustion hybrid and electric vehicles. Products include turbochargers timing chain systems emissions and thermal systems rear-wheel-drive and all-wheel-drive transfer cases starters alternators hybrid electric motors and electric motors. Together automakers Ford and Volkswagen account for about 25% of sales. Other customers include BMW Daimler and General Motors. In addition to automotive customers BorgWarner also serves OEMs of commercial and off-highway vehicles. The company gets some 80% of its sales from outside the US. The company traces its roots back to 1880.

	Annual Growth	12/17	12/18	12/19	12/20	12/21
Sales ($ mil.)	10.9%	9,799.3	10,529.6	10,168.0	10,165.0	14,838.0
Net income ($ mil.)	5.1%	439.9	930.7	746.0	500.0	537.0
Market value ($ mil.)	(3.1%)	12,250.2	8,329.8	10,401.5	9,265.0	10,806.7
Employees	14.2%	29,000	30,000	29,000	49,700	49,300

BOSCH COMMUNICATIONS SYSTEMS

12000 Portland Ave. South   CEO: –
Burnsville MN 55337   CFO: –
Phone: 952-884-4051   HR: –
Fax: 916-928-6404   FYE: December 31
Web: www.daegis.com   Type: Business Segment

Bosch Communications Systems (formerly Telex Communications) makes sure its customers' voices are heard. The company makes audio and communications equipment for commercial professional and industrial use. Its sound systems can be heard in venues from the Metropolitan Opera to Wrigley Field. A large portion of commercial airline pilots use Telex headsets. Other brand names include Electro-Voice Dynacord Klark Teknik Midas and RTS. Telex Communications was founded in 1936 as a hearing aid manufacturer; Robert Bosch GmbH acquired the company in 2006 and renamed it Bosch Communications Systems.

BOSCH SECURITY SYSTEMS INC.

130 Perinton Pkwy.   CEO: –
Fairport NY 14450-9199   CFO: –
Phone: 585-223-4060   HR: –
Fax: 585-223-9180   FYE: December 31
Web: www.boschsecurity.com   Type: Subsidiary

Bosch Security Systems has a sixth sense for finding business. The company makes electronic detection and communications equipment for use in government banking education and gaming sectors as well as at airports and train stations. Products include cameras fire and intrusion alarm systems conference communications and access control. Some of the products send alarm signals over telephone lines or wireless networks. Its personal safety systems transmit the user's identity and location to a monitoring station when activated. The company has sales offices and distribution centers worldwide. Bosch Security Systems is a subsidiary of German manufacturing giant Robert Bosch GmbH.

BOSS HOLDINGS, INC.   NBB: BSHI

1221 Page Street   CEO: G. Louis Graziadio
Kewanee, IL 61443   CFO: Steve Witte
Phone: 309-852-2131   HR: –
Fax: –   FYE: December 31
Web: www.bossgloves.com   Type: Public

Boss Holdings would rather take orders (for its gloves boots and rainwear) than give them. Its primary subsidiary Boss Manufacturing Company (BMC) imports and markets gloves and protective wear that it sells through mass merchandisers hardware stores and other retailers in North America. The company also sells its products directly to commercial users in industries such as agriculture and automotive. The holding company's Boss Pet Products markets pet supplies to US retailers while its Galaxy Balloons subsidiary sells latex balloons. Boss Holdings was founded in 1893 as a manufacturer of work gloves. Today gloves and protective gear account for a majority of annual sales.

	Annual Growth	12/12	12/13	12/14	12/15	12/16
Sales ($ mil.)	(1.0%)	64.8	64.0	67.9	67.9	62.2
Net income ($ mil.)	2.3%	1.5	1.8	1.9	2.0	1.6
Market value ($ mil.)	12.1%	16.7	20.7	23.4	24.1	26.4
Employees		–	–	–	–	–

BOSSELMAN INC.

3123 W. Stolley Park Rd.
Grand Island NE 68801
Phone: 308-381-2800
Fax: 308-381-2801
Web: www.bosselman.com

CEO: –
CFO: –
HR: –
FYE: December 31
Type: Private

Bosselman depends on truckers needing a pit stop to pump it up and pack it in. The diversified family-owned-and-operated firm runs about 45 Pump & Pantry convenience stores across Nebraska. Other ventures include a full-service Bosselman Travel Center in Grand Island Nebraska as well as 30-plus Boss Truck Shops in 20 states that offer truck repair services. Bosselman also operates restaurants (mostly Grandma Max's) and motels under the Motel 6 Hampton Inn and Pump & Pantry brands. Other operations include Bosselman Energy (wholesale oil fuel and propane delivery) and a sport team. Founder Frederick H. Bosselman — a farmer and part-time truck driver — opened his first truck stop in 1948.

BOSTON ACOUSTICS INC.

300 Jubilee Dr.
Peabody MA 01960
Phone: 978-538-5000
Fax: 978-538-5199
Web: www.bostonacoustics.com

CEO: Yvonne Hao
CFO: –
HR: –
FYE: March 31
Type: Subsidiary

Play Dark Side of the Moon on a set of Boston Acoustics' speakers and you'll see the light. The company designs and makes moderately priced and high-end loudspeaker systems for the home and automotive markets. It also makes home entertainment systems amplifiers and ancillary speaker equipment including selectors and volume controls. Boston Acoustics mostly tunes out mass retailers selling its products through a select group of specialty dealers. Its products are manufactured by third parties in the Asia/Pacific region Europe and North America. Former chairman Andrew Kotsatos and ex-CEO Frank Reed founded the company in 1979. D&M Holdings acquired Boston Acoustics in 2005.

BOSTON BEER CO INC (THE)   NYS: SAM

One Design Center Place, Suite 850
Boston, MA 02210
Phone: 617 368-5000
Fax: 617 368-5500
Web: www.bostonbeer.com

CEO: David Burwick
CFO: Frank Smalla
HR: –
FYE: December 26
Type: Public

The Boston Beer Company Inc. is a high-end alcoholic beverage company and one of the largest craft brewers in the United States. In fiscal 2020 Boston Beer sold approximately 7.4 million barrels of its proprietary products. The company's brands include Truly Hard Seltzer Twisted Tea Samuel Adams Angry Orchard Hard Cider and Dogfish Head Craft Brewery as well as other local craft beer brands. Boston Beer produces alcohol beverages including hard seltzer malt beverages (beers) and hard cider at company-owned breweries and its cidery and under contract arrangements at other brewery locations.

	Annual Growth	12/16	12/17	12/18	12/19	12/20
Sales ($ mil.)	17.6%	906.4	863.0	995.6	1,249.8	1,736.4
Net income ($ mil.)	21.8%	87.3	99.0	92.7	110.0	192.0
Market value ($ mil.)	56.3%	2,069.2	2,328.1	2,909.5	4,614.2	12,364.6
Employees	12.6%	1,505	1,439	1,543	2,128	2,423

BOSTON MEDICAL CENTER CORPORATION

1 BOSTON MEDICAL CTR PL # 1
BOSTON, MA 021182999
Phone: 617-414-5000
Fax: –
Web: www.bmc.org

CEO: Kate Walsh
CFO: –
HR: –
FYE: September 30
Type: Private

Located in Boston's South End neighborhood Boston Medical Center (BMC) offers a full spectrum of health care services from prenatal care and obstetrics to surgery and rehabilitation. BMC is also the city's largest provider of indigent care spending millions of dollars annually on care for uninsured patients and offering free screenings and other community outreach programs. The not-for-profit hospital boasts more than nearly 500 licensed beds more than 700about 755 physicians and includes a Level 1 trauma center acute rehabilitation facilities and neonatal and pediatric intensive care units. The center is the primary teaching hospital of Boston University'sBoston University's School of Medicine.

	Annual Growth	09/10	09/11	09/12	09/15	09/17
Sales ($ mil.)	4.2%	–	–	886.3	1,004.7	1,089.4
Net income ($ mil.)	38.0%	–	–	2.6	7.6	12.8
Market value ($ mil.)	–	–	–	–	–	–
Employees	–	–	–	–	–	4,200

BOSTON MUTUAL LIFE INSURANCE COMPANY

120 Royall St.
Canton MA 02021
Phone: 781-828-7000
Fax: 781-770-0490
Web: www.bostonmutual.com

CEO: Paul Quaranto Jr
CFO: –
HR: –
FYE: December 31
Type: Private - Mutual Com

If life insurance gives you a good feeling at Boston Mutual Life Insurance the feeling is mutual. The company sells traditional group and individual life insurance as well as disability and supplemental accident and illness coverage. The company distributes its products to individuals through its in-house General Agencies division while its Group and Worksite Divisions distribute through employers. Additional products include employee assistance programs and voluntary supplemental insurance products. The company reaches customers in New York through its subsidiary The Life Insurance Company of Boston & New York. Boston Mutual has remained a mutual company since it was founded in 1891.

BOSTON PRIVATE FINANCIAL HOLDINGS, INC.   NMS: BPFH

Ten Post Office Square
Boston, MA 02109
Phone: 617 912-1900
Fax: –
Web: www.bostonprivate.com

CEO: –
CFO: –
HR: –
FYE: December 31
Type: Public

Boston Private Financial Holdings (BPFH) is a holding company for firms engaged in wealth management and private banking including Boston Private Bank & Trust which operates branches in New England New York Los Angeles and the San Francisco Bay Area. (The bank sold its branches in the Pacific Northwest in 2013.) BPFH also owns four other wealth advisory and investment management firms. The company offers private banking wealth advisory investment management deposits and lending and trust services to wealthy individuals corporations and institutional clients. All told BPFH and its affiliates have more than $30 billion in managed or advised assets.

	Annual Growth	12/15	12/16	12/17	12/18	12/19
Assets ($ mil.)	4.0%	7,542.5	7,970.5	8,311.7	8,494.6	8,830.5
Net income ($ mil.)	5.4%	64.9	71.6	40.6	80.4	80.0
Market value ($ mil.)	1.5%	944.2	1,378.0	1,286.5	880.1	1,001.7
Employees	(3.3%)	890	888	925	774	779

BOSTON PROPERTIES INC
NYS: BXP

Prudential Center, 800 Boylston Street, Suite 1900 — CEO: Owen Thomas
Boston, MA 02199-8103 — CFO: Michael LaBelle
Phone: 617 236-3300 — HR: –
Fax: – — FYE: December 31
Web: www.bostonproperties.com — Type: Public

Boston Properties knows real estate in more than just its home city. The self-administered and self- managed real estate investment trust (REIT) owns develops and manages mostly Class A office buildings in large US cities. Its core markets are Boston Los Angeles New York San Francisco and Washington DC. As one of the nation's largest office owners and developers Boston Properties owns around 175 office properties with some 51.2 million rentable square feet. Its largest tenants include the US government Salesforce.com Arnold & Porter Kaye Scholer and Biogen. The REIT also owns a handful of retail hotel and residential properties. The firm's chairman Mort Zuckerman was the co-founder of Boston Properties.

	Annual Growth	12/16	12/17	12/18	12/19	12/20
Sales ($ mil.)	2.0%	2,550.8	2,602.1	2,717.1	2,960.6	2,765.7
Net income ($ mil.)	14.2%	512.8	462.4	582.8	521.5	872.7
Market value ($ mil.)	(6.9%)	19,586.3	20,248.1	17,526.2	21,467.4	14,720.1
Employees	(1.1%)	785	740	760	760	750

BOSTON RED SOX BASEBALL CLUB LIMITED PARTNERSHIP

4 Yawkey Way — CEO: Sam Kennedy
Boston MA 02215-3496 — CFO: –
Phone: 617-267-9440 — HR: –
Fax: 617-375-0944 — FYE: December 31
Web: boston.redsox.mlb.com — Type: Private

You might say this team is now a curse on the other clubs in Major League Baseball. Boston Red Sox Baseball Club operates one of the oldest and most storied sports franchises. Founded as a charter member of the American League in 1901 the team owns seven World Series titles but at one time suffered through an 86-year championship drought popularly attributed to "The Curse of the Bambino." Boston broke The Curse in 2004 and then won its seventh championship three years later. Red Sox fans root for their home team at venerable Fenway Park the oldest pro baseball stadium in the country. Businessman John Henry leads a group that has owned the Red Sox franchise since 2002.

BOSTON RESTAURANT ASSOCIATES INC.

6 Kimball Ln. Ste. 210 — CEO: –
Lynnfield MA 01940 — CFO: Fran V Ross
Phone: 339-219-0466 — HR: Donna Devlin
Fax: 781-231-5225 — FYE: April 30
Web: www.reginapizza.com — Type: Private

Boston Restaurant Associates (BRA) is rolling in New England dough. The company operates more than 15 Pizzeria Regina pizza parlors located in shopping mall food courts and other high-traffic areas in Massachusetts and three other states. The restaurants specialize in brick-oven style thin crust Neapolitan pizzas that are available with a variety of toppings (and by the slice). In addition to its food court kiosk units BRA operates the original Regina Pizzeria (built in 1926) in Boston's North End as well as three full-service family-style Polcari's Italian Restaurant locations in the Boston area. The company is controlled by private equity firm Dolphin Asset Management.

BOSTON SCIENTIFIC CORP.
NYS: BSX

300 Boston Scientific Way — CEO: Michael Mahoney
Marlborough, MA 01752-1234 — CFO: Daniel Brennan
Phone: 508 683-4000 — HR: Wendy Carruthers
Fax: – — FYE: December 31
Web: www.bostonscientific.com — Type: Public

Boston Scientific makes medical supplies and devices used in interventional medical procedures. The firm focuses on manufacturing cardiovascular and cardiac rhythm management (CRM) products. It also makes devices used for electrophysiology endoscopy pain management (neuromodulation) urology and pelvic health. Its diagnostic and treatment products ? made in nearly a dozen factories worldwide ? include biopsy forceps catheters coronary and urethral stents defibrillators needles and pacemakers. Boston Scientific markets its products in about 120 countries but the US generates about 60% of sales.

	Annual Growth	12/17	12/18	12/19	12/20	12/21
Sales ($ mil.)	7.1%	9,048.0	9,823.0	10,735.0	9,913.0	11,888.0
Net income ($ mil.)	77.9%	104.0	1,671.0	4,700.0	(82.0)	1,041.0
Market value ($ mil.)	14.4%	35,338.6	50,377.9	64,462.0	51,247.5	60,556.1
Employees	9.0%	29,000	32,000	36,000	38,000	41,000

BOSTON SYMPHONY ORCHESTRA, INC.

301 MASSACHUSETTS AVE — CEO: Mark Volpe
BOSTON, MA 021154511 — CFO: –
Phone: 617-266-1492 — HR: –
Fax: – — FYE: August 31
Web: www.bso.org — Type: Private

If you want to venture out for some live music but are not in the mood for rock or pop then a performance by The Boston Symphony Orchestra (BSO) might strike the right chord with you. Featuring compositions by composers like Beethoven Mozart and Stravinsky the BSO performs more than 100 concerts during the regular season at Symphony Hall. The BSO also performs during the summer at the Tanglewood music center; other BSO-related performances are given by the smaller and lighter Boston Pops orchestra. One of the more prominent orchestras in the US the BSO was founded in 1881 by businessman Henry Lee Higginson. Current music director James Levine is the BSO's first America-born conductor.

	Annual Growth	08/08	08/09	08/10	08/11	08/14
Sales ($ mil.)	–	–	(1,675.6)	39.7	38.3	100.7
Net income ($ mil.)	274.8%	–	0.0	12.7	41.7	12.1
Market value ($ mil.)	–	–	–	–	–	–
Employees	–	–	–	–	–	350

BOSTONCOACH

69 Norman St. — CEO: –
Everett MA 02149 — CFO: Hilary Simons
Phone: 617-394-3900 — HR: –
Fax: 617-381-8725 — FYE: December 31
Web: www.bostoncoach.com — Type: Subsidiary

We don't know whether any Celtics coaches call on BostonCoach but the company does provide car and bus transportation for business and leisure travelers as well as shuttle and charter services for groups. Its fleet includes more than 25000 sedans along with limousines vans SUVs minibuses and buses. Through its network of affiliates the company serves more than 450 cities in some 35 countries including North America Asia and Europe. BostonCoach is a subsidiary of investment powerhouse FMR (Fidelity Investments) which founded the company in 1985 with three vehicles to serve its own employees.

BOTTOMLINE TECHNOLOGIES (DELAWARE) INC   NMS: EPAY

325 Corporate Drive
Portsmouth, NH 03801-6808
Phone: 603 436-0700
Fax: 603 436-0300
Web: www.bottomline.com

CEO: Robert Eberle
CFO: A.Bruce Bowden
HR: –
FYE: June 30
Type: Public

Bottomline Technologies provides digital transformation for business payments and corporations and banks rely on the company for domestic and international payments efficient cash management automated workflows for payment processing and bill review and fraud detection behavioral analytics and regulatory compliance solutions. Its Paymode-X product allows businesses to easily transition from legacy invoice-to-pay processes maximizing cost-savings efficiency and security. Bottomline operates payment platforms that facilitate electronic payment and transaction settlement between businesses their vendors and banks. The company's customers do business in financial services health care insurance retail communications manufacturing and government. Among Bottomline's customers are Bank of America Merrill Lynch Cleveland Clinic State Farm Insurance and Tesco Stores.

	Annual Growth	06/17	06/18	06/19	06/20	06/21
Sales ($ mil.)	7.8%	349.4	394.1	422.0	442.2	471.4
Net income ($ mil.)	–	(33.1)	9.3	9.4	(9.2)	(16.3)
Market value ($ mil.)	9.6%	1,110.8	2,154.5	1,912.8	2,195.1	1,603.2
Employees	10.0%	1,600	1,700	1,900	2,000	2,344

BOULDER BRANDS INC   NMS: BDBD

1600 Pearl Street, Suite 300
Boulder, CO 80302
Phone: 303 652-0521
Fax: –
Web: www.boulderbrands.com

CEO: –
CFO: –
HR: –
FYE: December 31
Type: Public

Walking a nutrition tightrope? Boulder Brands (formerly Smart Balance) may help; its growing portfolio of food brands target the health conscious and those with health problems such as diabetes and glutin allergies. The company makes Smart Balance buttery spreads and other alternative food products including peanut butter popcorn and cooking oils. As the company has grown its Smart Balance business has been outweighed by its Natural foods segment including the Glutino and Gluten-Free Pantry Udi's Earth Balance and the EVOL brands of shelf-stable and frozen products. Boulder Brands' products are sold by food retailers throughout North America. Founded in 2005 the company became Boulder Brands in 2013.

	Annual Growth	12/09	12/10	12/11	12/12	12/13
Sales ($ mil.)	17.8%	239.5	242.0	274.3	369.6	461.3
Net income ($ mil.)	31.7%	3.5	(128.2)	9.7	4.2	10.4
Market value ($ mil.)	27.5%	361.3	260.8	322.8	776.9	955.1
Employees	77.2%	73	69	203	613	720

BOWDOIN COLLEGE

255 MAINE ST
BRUNSWICK, ME 04011
Phone: 207-725-3000
Fax: –
Web: www.bowdoin.edu

CEO: –
CFO: –
HR: –
FYE: June 30
Type: Private

Bowdoin College churns out graduates from its campus on the coast of Maine. The private liberal arts school serves some 1800 students offering undergraduate degrees in about 40 fields of study including English psychology history mathematics and biology. It has about 200 faculty members and a student-to-teacher ratio of 9:1. Most classes are conducted on the main campus in Brunswick Maine; Bowdoin also includes a Coastal Studies Center some eight miles from campus on Orr's Island. Notable alumni include writers Nathanial Hawthorne and Henry Wadsworth Longfellow as well as former president Franklin Pierce. Established in 1794 Bowdoin is Maine's oldest college.

	Annual Growth	06/17	06/18	06/19	06/20	06/21
Sales ($ mil.)	1.4%	–	169.5	177.9	183.5	176.8
Net income ($ mil.)	75.2%	–	174.2	116.8	61.6	936.8
Market value ($ mil.)	–	–	–	–	–	–
Employees	–	–	–	–	–	949

BOWEN ENGINEERING CORPORATION

8802 N MERIDIAN ST STE X
INDIANAPOLIS, IN 462605319
Phone: 219-661-9770
Fax: –
Web: www.bowenengineering.com

CEO: A Douglas Bowen III
CFO: Scot Evans Sr
HR: –
FYE: September 30
Type: Private

Bowen Engineering understands the elements of earth wind and water. The company provides engineering and construction services for water wastewater earthwork concrete industrial power and underground utility projects. It operates through three divisions: Power and industrial; private water; and public works. The company which has offices in Indiana Tennessee and Ohio offers design/build general contracting and construction management services to public and private clients. Bowen Engineering was founded in 1967 by Robert Bowen. The Bowen family continues to lead the company.

	Annual Growth	09/05	09/06	09/07	09/08	09/09
Sales ($ mil.)	26.5%	–	–	228.2	288.9	365.2
Net income ($ mil.)	2.8%	–	–	15.3	17.5	16.2
Market value ($ mil.)	–	–	–	–	–	–
Employees	–	–	–	–	–	700

BOWL AMERICA INC.   ASE: BWL A

6446 Edsall Road
Alexandria, VA 22312
Phone: 703 941-6300
Fax: –
Web: www.bowlamericainc.com

CEO: Leslie H Goldberg
CFO: Cheryl A Dragoo
HR: –
FYE: June 28
Type: Public

This company is looking to make a strike in the recreation business. Bowl America owns and operates about 20 bowling centers in four markets including the Baltimore-Washington DC area; Jacksonville and Orlando Florida; and Richmond Virginia. The bowling centers offer a total of more than 750 lanes for both league and non-league bowling as well as Cosmic Bowling (with glow-in-the-dark balls and laser light shows) for younger patrons. The centers also feature game rooms food and beverage services and other amenities. President Leslie Goldberg and his sister Merle Fabian together own more than 50% of Bowl America.

	Annual Growth	07/16	07/17	07/18*	06/19	06/20
Sales ($ mil.)	(7.3%)	24.1	23.9	24.8	24.4	17.8
Net income ($ mil.)	(34.2%)	2.2	2.5	3.8	3.0	0.4
Market value ($ mil.)	(9.5%)	74.7	73.9	77.9	82.1	50.1
Employees	0.0%	500	500	500	500	500

*Fiscal year change

BOWLIN TRAVEL CENTERS INC.   OTC: BWTL

150 Louisiana NE
Albuquerque NM 87108
Phone: 505-266-5985
Fax: 504-539-5427
Web: www.luzianne.com

CEO: Michael Bowlin
CFO: Nina Pratz
HR: –
FYE: January 31
Type: Public

Dotting the desert with gas pumps and gifts Bowlin Travel Centers (BTC) operates about 10 full-service southwestern-themed travel centers along desolate stretches of interstates I-10 and I-40 in arid Arizona and New Mexico. Its travel centers offer snacks souvenirs provided by Native American tribes or imported from Mexico gas (Shell and ExxonMobil brands) and restaurants (Dairy Queen at five locations). It also sells gasoline wholesale. BTC traces its roots to 1912 when founder Claude Bowlin started trading goods and services with Native Americans in New Mexico. Today BTC is controlled by its chairman president and CEO Michael Bowlin and his family.

BOY SCOUTS OF AMERICA

1325 W WALNUT HILL LN
IRVING, TX 750383096
Phone: 972-580-2000
Fax: -
Web: www.scouting.org

CEO: Robert Mazzuca
CFO: -
HR: -
FYE: December 31
Type: Private

Boy Scouts of America (BSA) is one of the US's largest youth organizations with approximately 2.2 million members and 800000 volunteers. It offers educational and character-building programs emphasizing leadership. In addition to traditional scouting programs (Tiger Cub Webelos and Boy Scouts) BSA offers the Venturing program for boys and girls ages 14-20. The organization was founded in 1910. It generates revenue through membership and council fees food and magazine sales and contributions.

	Annual Growth	12/09	12/10	12/13	12/14	12/15
Sales ($ mil.)	1.6%	-	310.5	0.0	244.0	335.9
Net income ($ mil.)	-	-	90.1	(33.7)	46.3	(25.5)
Market value ($ mil.)	-	-	-	-	-	-
Employees	-	-	-	-	-	2,800

BOYD COFFEE COMPANY

19730 NE Sandy Blvd.
Portland OR 97230
Phone: 503-666-4545
Fax: 503-669-2223
Web: www.boyds.com

CEO: -
CFO: -
HR: -
FYE: October 31
Type: Private

Boy oh Boyd! Boyd Coffee Company sells coffees teas and other beverage products (such as flavoring syrups drink mixes) under the names Boyds Coffee Italia D'Oro Coffee House Roasters Coffee House Freezers and Island Mist. The company also markets brewing equipment through its Techni-Brew International division and it offers the Today Foods brand of soups and soup bases. Boyd Coffee supplies retail food outlets and restaurants hotels hospitals and other foodservice venues in about 25 states as well as US military commissaries worldwide. Products are also available to consumers via Boyd's online store. In addition the firm operates three coffee shops in the Portland Oregon area.

BOYD GAMING CORP.

NYS: BYD

6465 South Rainbow Boulevard
Las Vegas, NV 89118
Phone: 702 792-7200
Fax: -
Web: www.boydgaming.com

CEO: Keith Smith
CFO: Josh Hirsberg
HR: -
FYE: December 31
Type: Public

Boyd Gaming operates about 30 wholly owned casino properties in Nevada and nine other US states. Most of its properties are resorts or hotels that feature pools full casinos restaurants shops and on-site entertainment options for guests. The company also has a partnership with digital gaming company FanDuel Group through which it uses FanDuel's technology for its own online and mobile gambling and sports betting services. In addition to its casinos Boyd owns and operates a travel agency and a travel insurance company in Hawaii. Founded in 1975 the company generates approximately 70% of revenue from Midwest & South.

	Annual Growth	12/16	12/17	12/18	12/19	12/20
Sales ($ mil.)	(0.1%)	2,184.0	2,383.7	2,626.7	3,326.1	2,178.5
Net income ($ mil.)	-	418.0	189.2	115.0	157.6	(134.7)
Market value ($ mil.)	20.8%	2,255.6	3,919.6	2,323.8	3,348.2	4,799.8
Employees	(9.1%)	19,932	19,707	23,477	24,300	13,583

BOYS & GIRLS CLUBS OF AMERICA

1275 PEACHTREE ST NE # 100
ATLANTA, GA 303093576
Phone: 404-487-5700
Fax: -
Web: www.bgca.org

CEO: James Clark
CFO: -
HR: -
FYE: December 31
Type: Private

The Boys & Girls Clubs of America (BGCA) runs after-school programs nationwide to give children and teenagers a safe and supervised environment. Operating through local affiliates BGCA boasts nearly 4740 locations that serve approximately 4.6 million youth. Members engage in sports recreation and fitness activities as well as in programs centered on character development leadership and life skills. BGCA alumni include Bill Clinton Jackie Joyner-Kersee Martin Sheen Michael Jordan and Queen Latifah. Boys & Girls Clubs of America had its beginnings in 1860.

	Annual Growth	12/09	12/10	12/17	12/18	12/19
Sales ($ mil.)	1.5%	-	120.6	141.3	158.3	138.0
Net income ($ mil.)	-	-	0.1	(33.0)	(10.1)	(18.2)
Market value ($ mil.)	-	-	-	-	-	-
Employees	-	-	-	-	-	360

BOZZUTO'S, INC.

275 SCHOOLHOUSE RD
CHESHIRE, CT 064101257
Phone: 203-272-3511
Fax: -
Web: www.bozzutos.com

CEO: Michael A Bozzuto
CFO: -
HR: -
FYE: September 27
Type: Private

Bozzuto's is a leading wholesale grocery distribution company that supplies food and household products to retailers in New Jersey New York Pennsylvania and in New England. The company distributes a full line of grocery items including meat products produce and floral grocery dairy and frozen food bakery and deli fresh meat and seafood as well as seasonal and GM/HBC and specialty and organics. It carries goods sold under both the IGA and Hy-Top labels in addition to national brands. Bozzuto's also owns about five distribution centers in Connecticut and Pennsylvania. The company was founded in 1945.

	Annual Growth	09/04	09/05	09/06	09/07	09/08
Sales ($ mil.)	(96.4%)	-	-	955,449.3	1,180.7	1,244.0
Net income ($ mil.)	-	-	-	-	0.2	(0.4)	(5.9)
Market value ($ mil.)	-	-	-	-	-	-
Employees	-	-	-	-	-	3,100

BPZ RESOURCES, INC.

NYS: BPZ

580 Westlake Park Blvd., Suite 525
Houston, TX 77079
Phone: 281 556-6200
Fax: 281 556-6377
Web: www.bpzenergy.com

CEO: Manuel Pablo Zuniga-Pflucker
CFO: Richard S Menniti
HR: -
FYE: December 31
Type: Public

BPZ Resources is committed to exploring for oil and gas resources in South America. The company is focusing on oil and gas exploration and production in recent years. It operates through its BPZ Energy subsidiary and that unit's BPZ Energy International Holdings subsidiary. BPZ Resources owns 2.2 million acres of oil and gas properties in northwest Peru. It also holds acreage in Ecuador where it holds a 10% stake in producing block. In 2012 the company reported proved reserves of 16.4 million barrels of oil equivalent (of which 13.4 million barrels was in the Corvina field and 3 million barrels in the Albacora field both of which are located offshore of northwest Peru in the Block Z-1 field).

	Annual Growth	12/09	12/10	12/11	12/12	12/13
Sales ($ mil.)	(0.8%)	52.5	110.5	143.7	123.0	50.7
Net income ($ mil.)	-	(35.8)	(59.8)	(33.8)	(39.1)	(57.7)
Market value ($ mil.)	(33.8%)	1,116.5	559.4	333.8	370.2	213.9
Employees	(15.5%)	182	262	270	245	93

BRADFORD SOAP WORKS INC.

200 Providence St.
West Warwick RI 02893-2508
Phone: 401-821-2141
Fax: 401-821-1660
Web: www.bradfordsoap.com

CEO: Stuart Benton
CFO: –
HR: –
FYE: December 31
Type: Private

Bradford Soap Works is far from being a dud with suds. As a top manufacturer of private-label bath soaps the company makes soap and personal care formulations specifically for consumer products firms. Products which include bar soaps gels powders and mousses are manufactured under names AngelSkin Eco-Ex Organic-Choices Chakra Body Buffing Grain and Watercolors among others. Bradford Soap also makes certified organic ingredients as well as detergent lubricants and foam stabilizers for industrial use. Bradford which has operations in the US and Mexico was founded in 1876 to make soaps for the textile industry. The company grows its operations chiefly through acquisitions of smaller soap makers.

BRADFORD WHITE CORPORATION

725 Talamore Dr.
Ambler PA 19002
Phone: 215-641-9400
Fax: 215-641-1670
Web: www.bradfordwhite.com

CEO: –
CFO: –
HR: Justin Kulwicki
FYE: December 31
Type: Private

Bradford White Corporation helps folks get in (and stay in) hot water. The company manufactures water heaters for residential commercial and industrial heating applications. It makes oil-fired products gas power burners and indirect-fired units. Through subsidiaries Bradford White-Canada and LAARS Heating Systems it also manufactures products such as pool heaters oil burners and air handlers. The company wholesales its products through a network of plumbing and heating professionals. Subsidiary Niles Steel Tank produces custom steel tanks for companies in the automotive petrol-chemical pharmaceutical and refrigeration industries. Bradford White Corporation was founded in 1881.

BRADLEY UNIVERSITY

1501 W BRADLEY AVE
PEORIA, IL 616250003
Phone: 309-676-7611
Fax: –
Web: www.bradley.edu

CEO: –
CFO: –
HR: –
FYE: May 31
Type: Private

Bradley University is a private university offering a wide breadth of higher education opportunitites. The school provides 100 undergraduate programs in fields ranging from art science and education to business media and health. Bradley also confers graduate degrees in more than 30 academic fields including a Doctorate of Physical Therapy. With a student-to-teacher ratio of 12:1 the university has an enrollment of approximately 6000 students — more than 5000 of whom are undergraduates -- that receive instruction from some 350 full-time faculty members.

	Annual Growth	05/12	05/13	05/16	05/20	05/21
Sales ($ mil.)	(0.5%)	–	153.2	194.8	238.6	147.4
Net income ($ mil.)	18.3%	–	28.3	7.0	5.8	108.1
Market value ($ mil.)	–	–	–	–	–	–
Employees	–	–	–	–	–	1,000

BRADY CORP

NYS: BRC

6555 West Good Hope Road
Milwaukee, WI 53223
Phone: 414 358-6600
Fax: –
Web: www.bradycorp.com

CEO: J. Michael Nauman
CFO: Aaron Pearce
HR: Helena Nelligan
FYE: July 31
Type: Public

Brady Corporation makes a diversified array of industrial identification and workplace safety products. The company's ID products include label printing systems lockout/tagout devices wire markers and tags hospital and entertainment wristbands ID badges and safety compliance software and services. Other products include safety and compliance signs tags and labels; informational signage; compliance posters; asset tracking labels; and first aid products. Brady operates in about 40 manufacturing and distribution across the globe. . The US accounts for around 55% of the company's sales.

	Annual Growth	07/17	07/18	07/19	07/20	07/21
Sales ($ mil.)	0.7%	1,113.3	1,173.9	1,160.6	1,081.3	1,144.7
Net income ($ mil.)	7.9%	95.6	91.1	131.3	112.4	129.7
Market value ($ mil.)	13.3%	1,728.6	1,991.6	2,693.4	2,393.5	2,847.0
Employees	(2.5%)	6,300	6,200	6,100	5,400	5,700

BRAKE PARTS INC.

4400 Prime Pkwy.
McHenry IL 60050-7003
Phone: 815-363-9000
Fax: 815-363-9030
Web: www.raybestos.com

CEO: David Overbeeke
CFO: –
HR: Maria Estrada
FYE: December 31
Type: Private

Brake Parts Inc. knows how to pull out all of the stops. The company doing business under the Raybestos brand manufactures aftermarket motor vehicle brake systems and parts. Products include brake pads and shoes rotors drums calipers wheel cylinders master cylinders and hardware. Brake Parts operates as part the Affinia Under Vehicle Group which includes AIMCO (brake parts) Spicer (chassis and steering components) and Wix (air fuel and oil filters). The automotive collection is held by investment firm The Cypress Group.

BRANCH BUILDS, INC.

5732 AIRPORT RD NW
ROANOKE, VA 240121122
Phone: 540-989-5215
Fax: –
Web: www.branch-associates.com

CEO: –
CFO: –
HR: –
FYE: December 31
Type: Private

Branch & Associates is no twig in the Branch Group family tree. The employee-owned subsidiary offers general contracting design/build and construction management services for commercial and industrial construction projects in the Carolinas Tennessee Virginia and West Virginia. The company builds retail health care educational multi-unit residential government hospitality and industrial facilities. Billy Branch founded the company in 1963. It was reorganized and became Branch Associates under the Branch Group in 1985. Other Branch Group subsidiaries include Branch Highways E.V. Williams and G.J. Hopkins.

	Annual Growth	12/16	12/17	12/18	12/19	12/20
Sales ($ mil.)	23.2%	–	121.9	177.7	268.6	227.7
Net income ($ mil.)	–	–	0.0	0.0	0.0	0.0
Market value ($ mil.)	–	–	–	–	–	–
Employees	–	–	–	–	–	90

BRANDEIS UNIVERSITY

298 CRESCENT ST
WALTHAM, MA 024533803
Phone: 781-736-8318
Fax: –
Web: www.brandeis.edu

CEO: –
CFO: –
HR: –
FYE: June 30
Type: Private

Brandeis University offers about 45 undergraduate majors and 50 minors programs in the creative arts humanities sciences and social sciences. Located just west of Boston it comprises the College of Arts and Sciences the Graduate School of Arts and Sciences the International Business School the Heller School for Social Policy and Management the Lown School for Near Eastern and Judaic Studies and the Rabb School of Continuing Studies. The university has an enrollment of more than 5800 students; the student/faculty ratio is 10-to-1. A non-sectarian Jewish community-sponsored institution named after the late Justice Louis Brandeis of the US Supreme Court Brandeis University was founded in 1948.

	Annual Growth	06/08	06/09	06/10	06/15	06/16
Sales ($ mil.)	4.3%	–	248.6	323.3	508.9	333.7
Net income ($ mil.)	–	–	(174.0)	(24.1)	80.1	(64.7)
Market value ($ mil.)	–	–	–	–	–	–
Employees	–	–	–	–	–	1,200

BRANDYWINE REALTY TRUST

NYS: BDN

2929 Arch Street, Suite 1800
Philadelphia, PA 19104
Phone: 610 325-5600
Fax: –
Web: www.brandywinerealty.com

CEO: Gerard Sweeney
CFO: Thomas Wirth
HR: –
FYE: December 31
Type: Public

If the thought of making it big in real estate intoxicates you look into Brandywine. A self-managed real estate investment trust (REIT) Brandywine buys leases sells and manages commercial properties. It owns more than 200 office properties about 20 industrial properties a handful of mixed-use properties and some 500 acres of undeveloped land. Its portfolio comprises more than 25 million sq. ft. of rentable space located mainly in urban and suburban areas of the mid-Atlantic region as well as California and Texas. Jerry Sweeney who founded Brandywine in 1986 remains president and CEO of the company.

	Annual Growth	12/16	12/17	12/18	12/19	12/20
Sales ($ mil.)	0.4%	525.5	520.5	544.3	580.4	534.9
Net income ($ mil.)	66.0%	40.2	120.9	136.3	34.3	305.5
Market value ($ mil.)	(7.8%)	2,816.2	3,102.7	2,195.3	2,686.5	2,031.5
Employees	(1.6%)	363	342	329	337	341

BRANT INDUSTRIES INC.

80 Field Point Rd.
Greenwich CT 06830
Phone: 203-661-3344
Fax: 203-661-3349
Web: www.whitebirchpaper.com

CEO: Peter M Brant
CFO: –
HR: –
FYE: December 31
Type: Private

Brant Industries does its part to keep newspaper delivery boys busy. Operating through White Birch Paper and its subsidiaries the company produces about 1.3 million tons of newsprint and directory paper annually. It also manufactures uncoated specialty paper and paperboard with recycled content. Brant operates four pulp and paper mills three in Canada and one in the US; its lineup is distributed in North America and to some overseas markets. Brant has a saw mill which produces lumber and wood chips and 30000 acres of forestland. The family-run company is owned by CEO Peter Brant and COO Christopher Brant. In early 2010 White Birch filed for bankruptcy in the US and Canada and subsequently sought a buyer.

BRAVO BRIO RESTAURANT GROUP INC

NMS: BBRG

777 Goodale Boulevard, Suite 100
Columbus, OH 43212
Phone: 614 326-7944
Fax: 614 326-7943
Web: www.bbrg.com

CEO: Steven R Layt
CFO: Diane D Reed
HR: –
FYE: December 25
Type: Public

Standing ovations are welcomed but not required at these restaurants. Bravo Brio Restaurant Group owns and operates more than 100 upscale casual-dining locations in more than 30 states. The restaurants operate under the names BRAVO! Cucina Italiana and BRIO Tuscan Grille. The company's flagship BRAVO! Cucina Italiana restaurants offer pasta pizza and other affordable Italian-inspired cuisine. The group's BRIO Tuscan Grille concept meanwhile specializes in upscale Tuscan-style ambiance and entrees such as steaks chops and fresh seafood. Bravo Brio Restaurant Group went public in 2010.

	Annual Growth	12/12	12/13	12/14	12/15	12/16
Sales ($ mil.)	0.1%	409.1	411.1	408.3	424.0	410.3
Net income ($ mil.)	–	16.1	7.5	11.8	4.6	(74.7)
Market value ($ mil.)	(25.8%)	198.9	252.2	196.5	136.6	60.4
Employees	(1.1%)	9,500	9,500	11,000	9,500	9,100

BRAVO MEDIA LLC

30 Rockefeller Plaza 8th Fl. East
New York NY 10112
Phone: 212-664-4444
Fax: 845-424-8286
Web: www.outwardbound.org

CEO: –
CFO: –
HR: –
FYE: December 31
Type: Subsidiary

Fans of this TV channel give a standing ovation to reality programming. Bravo Media operates the popular cable channel Bravo which reaches 90 million homes with a heavy dose of competition shows celebrity reality series and other reality-based programming. The channel's schedule includes such hit shows as Millionaire Matchmaker The Fashion Show Top Chef and the Real Housewives franchise. Bravo also broadcasts movies and reruns as well as such specialty programming as the Inside the Actors Studio interview program. Launched in 1980 by Rainbow Media Holdings (now known as AMC Networks) Bravo is a unit of NBCUniversal one of the largest media and entertainment companies in the world.

BRAZOS ELECTRIC POWER COOPERATIVE, INC.

7616 BAGBY AVE
WACO, TX 767126924
Phone: 254-750-6500
Fax: –
Web: www.brazoselectric.com

CEO: –
CFO: Khaki Bordovsky
HR: –
FYE: December 31
Type: Private

Brazos means "arms" in Spanish and the generation and transmission arms of Brazos Electric Power Cooperative reach across 68 Texas counties. It serves 16 member/owner distribution cooperatives and one municipality in Northern and Central Texas. Brazos Electric Power annually generates (through its four power stations) and/or accesses from other power marketers some 3655 MW of electric power. The cooperative's members include Comanche Electric Cooperative Association Heart of Texas Electric Co-op (McGregor) Mid-South Synergy (Navasota) United Coop Services (Cleburne) and Wise Electric (Decatur).

	Annual Growth	12/97	12/98	12/99	12/09	12/17
Sales ($ mil.)	6.2%	–	–	307.4	963.4	905.3
Net income ($ mil.)	12.6%	–	–	6.9	56.6	58.8
Market value ($ mil.)	–	–	–	–	–	–
Employees	–	–	–	–	–	366

BRE PROPERTIES, INC.

525 Market Street, 4th Floor
San Francisco, CA 94105-2712
Phone: 415 445-6530
Fax: –
Web: www.breproperties.com

NYS: BRE
CEO: –
CFO: –
HR: –
FYE: December 31
Type: Public

The huddled masses that yearn to live and breathe California life turn to BRE Properties. The real estate investment trust (REIT) acquires develops and manages multifamily properties in the western US. It owns more than 75 apartment communities with nearly 22000 units in Northern and Southern California and Seattle. Most properties offer amenities including clubhouses exercise facilities business centers and swimming pools. The REIT also has several properties under development and owns stakes in about a dozen more. BRE Properties has shed its holdings in Colorado and Nevada to focus on markets in California where high housing costs and a stable occupancy rate make for an attractive environment.

	Annual Growth	12/08	12/09	12/10	12/11	12/12
Sales ($ mil.)	2.7%	350.9	344.6	342.0	371.4	390.1
Net income ($ mil.)	(0.7%)	140.8	62.5	53.4	77.9	137.1
Market value ($ mil.)	16.1%	2,152.4	2,544.7	3,346.3	3,883.2	3,910.1
Employees	(4.1%)	793	737	628	690	670

BREEZE-EASTERN CORP

35 Melanie Lane
Whippany, NJ 07981
Phone: 973 602-1001
Fax: –
Web: www.breeze-eastern.com

ASE: BZC
CEO: –
CFO: –
HR: –
FYE: March 31
Type: Public

Does your cargo need a lift? Breeze-Eastern makes electric and hydraulic rescue hoist systems for helicopters as well as cargo winches and tie-downs hook systems and weapons handling systems. Its external helicopter cargo hook systems range in capacity from 1500 pounds to 36000 pounds. The company's weapons-handling systems include hoists for missiles and gearboxes for specialty weapons applications. It also offers overhaul/repair and engineering sales services. Breeze-Eastern caters mainly to the US government in addition to major aerospace manufacturers and airlines.

	Annual Growth	03/10	03/11	03/12	03/13	03/14
Sales ($ mil.)	5.6%	69.0	78.2	84.9	80.0	85.9
Net income ($ mil.)	–	(6.0)	5.0	3.8	4.1	5.6
Market value ($ mil.)	9.3%	67.1	83.3	81.5	80.1	95.9
Employees	1.3%	172	164	182	187	181

BREITBURN ENERGY PARTNERS LP

707 Wilshire Boulevard, Suite 4600
Los Angeles, CA 90017
Phone: 213 225-5900
Fax: –
Web: www.breitburn.com

NBB: BBEP Q
CEO: –
CFO: –
HR: –
FYE: December 31
Type: Public

Oil and gas futures burn brightly for BreitBurn Energy Partners one of California's largest independent exploration and production companies. With assets in Antrim Shale (Michigan) the Los Angeles Basin the Wind River and Big Horn Basins (both in Wyoming) the Sunniland Trend (Florida) the New Albany Shale (Indiana and Kentucky) and the Permian Basin (West Texas) in 2011 the company reported estimated proved reserves of 151.1 million barrels of oil equivalent (65% of which was natural gas). That year 49% of its reserves were in Michigan 29% in Wyoming 14% in California 7% in Florida and 1% in Indiana and Kentucky. The company filed for Chapter 11 bankruptcy protection in 2016.

	Annual Growth	12/12	12/13	12/14	12/15	12/16
Sales ($ mil.)	2.6%	423.0	634.7	1,430.0	1,108.7	469.0
Net income ($ mil.)	–	(40.8)	(43.7)	421.3	(2,583.3)	(815.0)
Market value ($ mil.)	(65.9%)	3,948.9	4,348.7	1,496.6	143.2	53.5
Employees	10.5%	450	563	901	833	671

BRENTWOOD INDUSTRIES, INC.

500 SPRING RIDGE DR
READING, PA 196101069
Phone: 610-374-5109
Fax: –
Web: –

CEO: –
CFO: –
HR: –
FYE: September 30
Type: Private

Brentwood Industries can help you wheel it around flush it mold it and cool it among other things. The company manufactures a variety of plastic products including wheelbarrows cooling towers wastewater treatment systems and specialty plastic forming and molding services. Brentwood has expanded its product line with the additions of Polychem Systems (non-metallic chain and flight sludge collectors) NRG Products (non-metallic clarifier systems for municipal and industrial markets) and medical thermoform packaging. It is the world's largest manufacturer of plastic media supplying more than 100 million cubic feet of material for cooling tower and wastewater applications.

	Annual Growth	09/09	09/10	09/11	09/12	09/13
Sales ($ mil.)	(76.3%)	–	–	1,953.8	110.2	110.2
Net income ($ mil.)	16326.4%	–	–	0.0	6.4	4.5
Market value ($ mil.)	–	–	–	–	–	–
Employees	–	–	–	–	–	700

BRG SPORTS, INC.

1700 E HIGGINS RD STE 500
DES PLAINES, IL 600183800
Phone: 224-585-5200
Fax: –
Web: www.brgsports.com

CEO: Dan Arment
CFO: Mark A Tripp
HR: –
FYE: December 29
Type: Private

BRG Sports is a corporate holding company of leading brands that design develop and market innovative sports equipment smart helmet technology team apparel and accessories. The company's Riddell brand is a premier designer and developer of football helmets protective sports equipment head impact monitoring technologies apparel and related accessories. A recognized leader in helmet technology and innovation Riddell is the leading manufacturer of football helmets and shoulder pads and a top provider of reconditioning services (cleaning repairing repainting and recertifying existing equipment).

	Annual Growth	01/09	01/10	01/11*	12/11	12/12
Sales ($ mil.)	7.0%	–	–	772.8	834.9	827.2
Net income ($ mil.)	–	–	–	8.1	10.0	(3.4)
Market value ($ mil.)	–	–	–	–	–	–
Employees	–	–	–	–	–	2,370

*Fiscal year change

BRICKELL BIOTECH INC

5777 Central Avenue
Boulder, CO 80301
Phone: 720 505-4755
Fax: –
Web: www.ir.brickellbio.com

NAS: BBI
CEO: Robert Brown
CFO: Albert Marchio
HR: –
FYE: December 31
Type: Public

Vical counts DNA as its main ally in tackling disease. The biopharmaceutical firm researches and develops vaccines based on its DNA delivery technology which uses portions of the genetic code of a pathogen to induce an immune response. Faced with a number of failed trials Vical announced cut around half of its workforce in early 2018. Later that year it abandoned its lead program a vaccine candidate for HSV-2. It then announced plans to focus on the development of antifungal candidate VL-2397 but put those plans on hold when it had problems finding trial participants. The company is now exploring its options including possibly selling itself or its assets.

	Annual Growth	12/16	12/17	12/18	12/19	12/20
Sales ($ mil.)	(40.5%)	14.5	13.8	1.6	7.9	1.8
Net income ($ mil.)	–	(9.0)	(13.0)	(16.3)	(23.9)	(20.9)
Market value ($ mil.)	(23.7%)	123.2	98.0	63.2	80.3	41.8
Employees	(35.0%)	73	74	30	15	13

BRIDGE CAPITAL HOLDINGS   NMS: BBNK

55 Almaden Boulevard
San Jose, CA 95113
Phone: 408 423-8500
Fax: -
Web: www.bridgebank.com

CEO: -
CFO: -
HR: -
FYE: December 31
Type: Public

Bridge Capital Holdings helps its business clients get from here to there. It is the holding company of Bridge Bank which caters to small midsized and emerging businesses in California's Silicon Valley and San Francisco Bay area. The bank has regional branches in Palo Alto and San Jose; it also has Small Business Administration (SBA) loan production offices in Pleasanton and San Francisco. Additional SBA offices are located in Irvine California; Dallas; Boston; and Reston Virginia. The bank also has groups devoted to technology banking IPO services and international banking. Its Bridge Capital Finance unit provides factoring and asset-based lending services.

	Annual Growth	12/09	12/10	12/11	12/12	12/13
Assets ($ mil.)	17.4%	844.1	1,029.7	1,161.0	1,343.6	1,604.1
Net income ($ mil.)	78.9%	1.4	2.6	7.8	13.8	14.7
Market value ($ mil.)	29.7%	115.0	138.0	164.9	246.8	325.7
Employees	9.4%	164	170	193	207	235

BRIDGELINE DIGITAL INC   NAS: BLIN

100 Sylvan Road, Suite G700
Woburn, MA 01801
Phone: 781 376-5555
Fax: -
Web: www.bridgeline.com

CEO: Roger Kahn
CFO: Thomas Windhausen
HR: -
FYE: September 30
Type: Public

Bridgeline Digital believes the Web is the causeway to the customer. The company develops and sells Web application creation and management software. Its iAPPS product suite offers tools for content and relationship management e-commerce website creation and analytics. Bridgeline also offers usability engineering search engine optimization and rich media development services. Bridgeline's target markets are financial services technology health services and life sciences retailers transportation and storage foundations and associations and the US government. Its customers have included Honeywell John Hancock AARP Budget Rent A Car and the Washington Redskins. Bridgeline operates in the US and India.

	Annual Growth	09/17	09/18	09/19	09/20	09/21
Sales ($ mil.)	(5.0%)	16.3	13.6	10.0	10.9	13.3
Net income ($ mil.)	-	(1.6)	(7.2)	(9.5)	0.3	(6.7)
Market value ($ mil.)	9.4%	29.2	10.0	19.4	18.9	41.9
Employees	(2.7%)	67	55	72	39	60

BRIDGEPORT HOSPITAL & HEALTHCARE SERVICES INC

267 GRANT ST
BRIDGEPORT, CT 06610-2805
Phone: 203-384-3000
Fax: -
Web: www.bridgeporthospital.org

CEO: -
CFO: -
HR: -
FYE: September 30
Type: Private

Serving as a bridge to wellness and a port in the stormy waters of health care is the 425-bed Bridgeport Hospital. Part of the Yale New Haven Health System the facility offers acute care and specialized services to residents of Bridgeport Connecticut and surrounding counties. The hospital operates a cancer center a burn treatment center a heart center and a rehabilitation therapy center. Its medical staff includes nearly 600 physicians representing more than 60 specialties. Founded in 1878 as Fairfield County's first hospital Bridgeport Hospital has grown into a nearly $350 million regional health care organization.

	Annual Growth	09/06	09/07	09/08	09/09	09/10
Sales ($ mil.)	151445.7%	-	-	-	0.3	380.0
Net income ($ mil.)	7585.1%	-	-	-	0.2	13.9
Market value ($ mil.)	-	-	-	-	-	-
Employees						150

BRIDGESTONE RETAIL OPERATIONS LLC

333 E. Lake St.
Bloomingdale IL 60108
Phone: 630-259-9000
Fax: 630-259-9158
Web: www.bsro.com/

CEO: Larry Magee
CFO: -
HR: Mark Frankel
FYE: December 31
Type: Subsidiary

You'll find plenty of rolling stock at Bridgestone Retail Operations' (BSRO) stores. BSRO is the US retail division of Japan-based tire giant Bridgestone and it owns and operates more than 2140 service centers in about 45 states under the Firestone Complete Auto Care Expert Tire Tires Plus and Wheel Works banners. BSRO's stores offer a variety of automotive repair services including drive train engine heating and cooling steering and suspension maintenance as well as tire sales. The business serves both consumers and commercial clients. BSRO which was named BFS Retail & Commercial until 2009 also maintains its own credit card operation Credit First National Association.

BRIDGFORD FOODS CORP.   NMS: BRID

1707 South Good-Latimer Expressway
Dallas, TX 75226
Phone: 214 428-1535
Fax: -
Web: www.bridgford.com

CEO: William L Bridgford
CFO: Raymond Lancy
HR: -
FYE: October 29
Type: Public

Bridgford Foods manufactures markets and distributes a slew of frozen refrigerated and snack foods. Its lineup ranges from biscuits and bread dough to deli meats dry sausage and beef jerky. Bridgford adds to its offerings by buying for resale some snack and refrigerated foods made by other processors. The company sells to food service (restaurants and institutions) and retailers (supermarkets mass merchandise and convenience stores) in the US and Canada largely through distributors brokers and a direct store delivery network. Bridgford traces its roots back to 1932 when its founder Hugh H. Bridgford (1908-1992) opened a retail meat market in San Diego California.

	Annual Growth	11/17	11/18	11/19*	10/20	10/21
Sales ($ mil.)	9.5%	167.2	174.3	188.8	198.0	240.4
Net income ($ mil.)	-	8.8	6.5	6.5	7.3	(5.5)
Market value ($ mil.)	(2.7%)	118.9	157.0	228.7	165.6	106.5
Employees	6.5%	544	544	564	563	699

*Fiscal year change

BRIGGS & STRATTON CORP.   NYS: BGG

12301 West Wirth Street
Wauwatosa, WI 53222
Phone: 414 259-5333
Fax: 414 259-9594
Web: www.basco.com

CEO: Stephen Andrews
CFO: -
HR: -
FYE: June 30
Type: Public

Briggs & Stratton is one of the world's largest manufacturers of gasoline engines for lawn mowers. It designs makes markets and services these engines primarily for lawn and garden OEMs worldwide including Husqvarna MTD Products and Deere & Company. It is also a top North American manufacturer of portable generators and pressure washers and a leading maker of lawn mowers garden tillers and related service parts and accessories sold through retailers and independent dealers. Briggs & Stratton has offices and manufacturing facilities in North America Europe Asia and Australia.

	Annual Growth	06/15*	07/16	07/17	07/18*	06/19
Sales ($ mil.)	(0.8%)	1,894.8	1,808.8	1,786.1	1,881.3	1,836.6
Net income ($ mil.)	-	45.7	26.6	56.7	(11.3)	(54.1)
Market value ($ mil.)	(14.9%)	821.0	886.6	1,013.6	740.6	430.7
Employees	(1.3%)	5,480	5,445	5,300	5,185	5,200

*Fiscal year change

BRIGGS & STRATTON POWER PRODUCTS GROUP LLC

12301 W. Wirth St.
Wauwatosa WI 53222
Phone: 414-259-5333
Fax: 863-965-2222
Web: www.coloradoboxedbeef.com

CEO: -
CFO: -
HR: -
FYE: June 30
Type: Subsidiary

Briggs & Stratton Power Products Group (BSPPG) — the power equipment manufacturing subsidiary of Briggs & Stratton designs manufacturers and sells pressure washers pumps portable and home generators powered lawn equipment snow throwers and other related products. BSPPG sells its products through multiple distribution channels including home centers warehouse clubs independent dealers and mass merchants. Customers include Lowe's The Home Depot Sears Wal-Mart Deere & Company and Tractor Supply Company. The Power Products Group accounts for about 40% of its parent company's sales.

BRIGHAM EXPLORATION COMPANY NASDAQ: BEXP

6300 Bridge Point Pkwy. Building 2 Ste. 500
Austin TX 78730
Phone: 512-427-3300
Fax: 512-427-3400
Web: www.bexp3d.com/

CEO: Andrea Kubik
CFO: Eugene B Shepherd Jr
HR: -
FYE: December 31
Type: Subsidiary

Still a young company Brigham Exploration was one of the first small independent exploration and production firms to use 3-D seismic imaging. The company continues to rely on 3-D and other advanced technologies for onshore exploration. It traditionally explored in the Anadarko Basin the onshore Texas/Louisiana Gulf Coast and West Texas but has shifted its focus in recent years to the lucrative oil shale plays in the Rockies. In 2010 Brigham Exploration reported proved reserves of 66.8 million barrels of oil equivalent. Since its founding in 1990 Brigham Exploration has drilled more than 1070 gross wells. In 2011 the company was acquired by Norway's Statoil in a $4.4 billion deal.

BRIGHT HORIZONS FAMILY SOLUTIONS INC. NYSE: BFAM

200 Talcott Ave. South
Watertown MA 02472
Phone: 617-673-8000
Fax: 617-673-8001
Web: www.brighthorizons.com

CEO: -
CFO: -
HR: -
FYE: December 31
Type: Private

With Bright Horizons Family Solutions kids learn while parents earn. The company offers full-service child care and early education services to employer clients through more than 700 child care and early education centers with a capacity to serve more than 87000 children in the US Canada India Ireland the Netherlands and the UK. Some of its centers also provide back-up elder and dependent care services. Under multiyear contracts it provides these services to companies hospitals universities and government agencies as part of their employee benefits packages. After being taken private by Bain Capital in 2008 Bright Horizons went public in early 2013 in an IPO worth $222.2 million.

BRIGHT HOUSE NETWORKS LLC

5000 Campuswood Dr.
E. Syracuse NY 13057-1254
Phone: 315-463-7675
Fax: 760-929-8072
Web: www.socogroup.com

CEO: -
CFO: -
HR: -
FYE: December 31
Type: Private

Bright House Networks lights up living rooms — more than 2.5 million of them in fact. The company offers digital cable television video-on-demand (VOD) digital phone service and broadband Internet connections to both residential and business customers in select metropolitan markets in Florida Alabama Indiana Michigan and California. Its Florida systems offer about 300 cable channels. Bright House Networks also owns and operates two 24-hour local news TV stations: Central Florida News 13 in the Orlando area and Bay News 9 for the Tampa Bay area. Bright House Networks is owned by the Advance/Newhouse Partnership (part of Advance Publications).

BRIGHTCOVE INC NMS: BCOV

290 Congress Street
Boston, MA 02210
Phone: 888 882-1880
Fax: -
Web: www.brightcove.com

CEO: Hugh Ray
CFO: Robert Noreck
HR: -
FYE: December 31
Type: Public

Brightcove is a leading global provider of cloud-based services for video. The company sells five core video products which includes Brightcove Video Cloud and Brightcove Live that helps its customers use video to further their businesses in meaningful ways. It has some 3330 customers including media companies broadcasters publishers sports and entertainment companies fashion and hospitality brands faith-based institutions retail and e-commerce platforms and hi-tech organizations as well as governments educational institutions and non-profit organizations. Brightcove delivers an average of about 3.78 billion streams a month. Majority of the company's sales were generated in North America.

	Annual Growth	12/17	12/18	12/19	12/20	12/21
Sales ($ mil.)	7.9%	155.9	164.8	184.5	197.4	211.1
Net income ($ mil.)	-	(19.5)	(14.0)	(21.9)	(5.8)	5.4
Market value ($ mil.)	9.5%	292.9	290.4	358.5	759.0	421.6
Employees	8.4%	498	495	610	623	687

BRIGHTPOINT INC. NASDAQ: CELL

7635 Interactive Way Ste. 200
Indianapolis IN 46278
Phone: 317-707-2355
Fax: 317-707-2512
Web: www.brightpoint.com

CEO: Shailendra Gupta
CFO: Vincent Donargo
HR: -
FYE: December 31
Type: Public

Brightpoint makes money moving mobiles. The company is a top global distributor of mobile phones and other wireless products acting as a middleman between manufacturers and wireless service providers. It ships the equipment to companies that sell mobile phones and accessories including wireless carriers dealers and retailers; customers include Vodafone RadioShack and Sprint Nextel. Brightpoint also offers logistics services such as warehousing product fulfillment purchasing contract manufacturing call center outsourcing customized packaging and activation through subsidiaries the likes of Brightpoint North America. In late 2012 it was acquired by world-leading IT products distributor Ingram Micro.

BRIGHTSTAR CORP.

9725 NW 117th Ave. Ste. 300
Miami FL 33178
Phone: 305-421-6000
Fax: 630-472-7817
Web: www.bcsf.com

CEO: Rod Millar
CFO: Jack Negro
HR: –
FYE: December 31
Type: Private

Brightstar hopes to outshine its rivals with service. The company distributes wireless products such as cell phones and prepaid wireless products. It also offers value-added services including merchandising channel sales inventory management logistics packaging and assembly services as well as supply chain and reverse logistics services. It distributes cell phones made by Nokia Samsung Electronics LG Motorola Mobility and RIM among others. Brightstar was founded in 1997 by its Bolivia-born CEO Marcelo Claure who owns more than 40% of the company.

BRILLSTEIN ENTERTAINMENT PARTNERS LLC

9150 Wilshire Blvd. Ste. 350
Beverly Hills CA 90212
Phone: 310-275-6135
Fax: 310-275-6180

CEO: –
CFO: Brian Taylor
HR: –
FYE: December 31
Type: Private

Brillstein Entertainment Partners (formerly Brillstein-Grey Entertainment) has its eyes on the talent. The agency is a powerful Hollywood management firm with a roster of some 200 clients including such stars as Brad Pitt Jennifer Aniston Adam Sandler and Lorne Michaels. It also produces TV shows and films that showcase the talents of its clients. Producer Bernie Brillstein founded the agency in 1969 and later partnered with his protege Brad Grey. Following Grey's departure the company changed its name to Brillstein Entertainment Partners in 2007.

BRINKER INTERNATIONAL, INC. NYS: EAT

3000 Olympus Blvd.
Dallas, TX 75019
Phone: 972 980-9917
Fax: –
Web: www.brinker.com

CEO: Wyman Roberts
CFO: Joseph Taylor
HR: –
FYE: June 30
Type: Public

One of the world's largest casual dining companies Brinker International operates the Chili's Grill & Bar and Maggiano's Little Italy restaurant brands. Chili's a recognized leader in the bar & grill category of casual dining has built a reputation for gourmet burgers sizzling fajitas hand shaken margaritas and its popular baby back ribs. Maggiano's is a full-service national polished casual restaurant brand offering Italian-American cuisine.

	Annual Growth	06/17	06/18	06/19	06/20	06/21
Sales ($ mil.)	1.5%	3,150.8	3,135.4	3,217.9	3,078.5	3,337.8
Net income ($ mil.)	(3.4%)	150.8	125.9	154.9	24.4	131.6
Market value ($ mil.)	12.9%	1,750.2	2,276.6	1,758.4	1,080.0	2,838.9
Employees	0.7%	57,906	58,478	56,147	62,200	59,491

BRINKS CO (THE) NYS: BCO

1801 Bayberry Court
Richmond, VA 23226-8100
Phone: 804 289-9600
Fax: –
Web: www.brinks.com

CEO: Douglas Pertz
CFO: Ronald Domanico
HR: –
FYE: December 31
Type: Public

The Brink's Company generates about half of its revenue from core services including cash-in-transit (CIT) and ATM replenishment and maintenance services. Its high-value services comprise secure long-distance transportation of valuables supply chain management of cash payment services and guarding services (including airport security often used by government agencies). The Brink's Company serves customers in more than 100 countries. Its operations include approximately 1300 facilities and some 16300 vehicles. The company's largest geographic market is the US which generates about a third of total revenue.

	Annual Growth	12/16	12/17	12/18	12/19	12/20
Sales ($ mil.)	5.1%	3,020.6	3,347.0	3,488.9	3,683.2	3,690.9
Net income ($ mil.)	(17.5%)	34.5	16.7	(33.3)	29.0	16.0
Market value ($ mil.)	14.9%	2,041.9	3,895.7	3,200.2	4,488.7	3,564.0
Employees	6.0%	60,700	62,300	62,400	64,600	76,500

BRISTOL HOSPITAL INCORPORATED

41 BREWSTER RD
BRISTOL, CT 060105141
Phone: 860-585-3000
Fax: –
Web: www.bristolhealth.org

CEO: –
CFO: –
HR: –
FYE: September 30
Type: Private

Bristol Hospital bristles with health care services for central Connecticut residents. The health care facility has more than 130 beds and offers a range of services including counseling diagnostic imaging inpatient and outpatient care surgery home health and physical therapy. Specialty services include oncology obstetrics neurology pediatrics and orthopedic care. Its wellness center is dedicated to cardiac and pulmonary rehabilitation diabetes care health education health screenings nutrition fitness and pain management. Bristol Hospital also operates Ingraham Manor a skilled nursing residence for seniors.

	Annual Growth	09/14	09/15	09/18	09/19	09/20
Sales ($ mil.)	2.6%	–	133.3	143.5	150.4	151.7
Net income ($ mil.)	12.0%	–	1.3	8.7	(18.2)	2.3
Market value ($ mil.)	–	–	–	–	–	–
Employees	–	–	–	–	–	1,600

BRISTOL MYERS SQUIBB CO. NYS: BMY

430 E. 29th Street, 14th Floor
New York, NY 10016
Phone: 212 546-4200
Fax: 212 546-4020
Web: www.bms.com

CEO: Giovanni Caforio
CFO: David Elkins
HR: –
FYE: December 31
Type: Public

Bristol-Myers Squibb (BMS) offers drugs such as Eliquis for stroke prevention cancer treatment Opdivo and rheumatoid arthritis treatment Orencia. Most of the firm's sales come from products in the areas of hematology oncology cardiovascular fibrosis and immunology. BMS has global research facilities and manufacturing plants mainly in the America Europe and Asia. The US accounts for over 60% of sales. In 2020 BMS completed the acquisition of MyoKardia for approximately $13.1 billion in cash.

	Annual Growth	12/17	12/18	12/19	12/20	12/21
Sales ($ mil.)	22.2%	20,776.0	22,561.0	26,145.0	42,518.0	46,385.0
Net income ($ mil.)	62.3%	1,007.0	4,920.0	3,439.0	(9,015.0)	6,994.0
Market value ($ mil.)	–	0.0	0.0	0.0	0.0	0.0
Employees	8.0%	23,700	23,300	30,000	30,250	32,200

BRISTOW GROUP INC (DE) — NYS: VTOL

3151 Briarpark Drive, Suite 700
Houston, TX 77042
Phone: 713 267-7600
Fax: –
Web: www.erahelicopters.com

CEO: Christopher S Bradshaw
CFO: Jennifer Whalen
HR: –
FYE: March 31
Type: Public

Bristow Group (formerly known as Era Group) is a global provider of vertical flight solutions. The company primarily provides aviation services to a broad base of major integrated national and independent energy companies. It also provides commercial search and rescue services in multiple countries and public sector SAR services in the United Kingdom on behalf of the Maritime & Coastguard Agency. Additionally it offers fixed wing transportation and other aviation related solutions. Its oil and gas customers charter its helicopters primarily to transport personnel to from and between onshore bases and offshore production platforms drilling rigs and other installations.

	Annual Growth	03/19*	10/19*	12/19*	03/20	03/21
Sales ($ mil.)	(7.3%)	1,369.7	757.2	226.1	485.8	1,178.1
Net income ($ mil.)	–	(336.8)	(836.4)	(3.6)	139.2	(56.1)
Market value ($ mil.)	49.7%	342.7	287.1	302.0	158.3	768.5
Employees	111.6%	–	–	707	–	3,167

*Fiscal year change

BRITTON & KOONTZ CAPITAL CORP. — NBB: BKBK

500 Main Street
Natchez, MS 39120
Phone: 601 445-5576
Fax: –
Web: www.bkbank.com

CEO: W. Page Ogden
CFO: William Salters
HR: –
FYE: December 31
Type: Public

You'll find this bank along the banks of the Mississippi. Britton & Koontz Capital is the holding company for Britton & Koontz Bank which has about a half-dozen branches in Natchez and Vicksburg Mississippi and Baton Rouge Louisiana where the company plans to expand. Targeting individual and local business customers the bank offers such standard deposit products as checking savings and money market accounts; CDs; and trust services. A majority of the bank's loan portfolio consists of real estate loans however Britton & Koontz Capital also makes agricultural business and consumer loans. Brothers William and Audley Britton along with George Koontz established the bank in 1836.

	Annual Growth	12/08	12/09	12/10	12/11	12/12
Assets ($ mil.)	(7.3%)	413.1	393.1	375.4	366.1	305.0
Net income ($ mil.)	(55.6%)	3.5	1.6	1.9	0.4	0.1
Market value ($ mil.)	(8.9%)	25.8	24.8	24.3	16.1	17.8
Employees	(1.9%)	110	113	112	104	–

BRIXMOR PROPERTY GROUP INC — NYS: BRX

450 Lexington Avenue
New York, NY 10017
Phone: 212 869-3000
Fax: –
Web: www.brixmor.com

CEO: James Taylor
CFO: Angela Aman
HR: –
FYE: December 31
Type: Public

Brixmor Property Group hopes you swing by the grocery store more than once a week. The internally-managed real estate investment trust (REIT) owns a portfolio of about 520 strip mall-style shopping centers across 38 states. Its properties are situated in high-traffic commercial areas anchored by grocery store chains such as Ahold Kroger Publix Safeway and Wal-Mart. Besides the main grocery store tenant its shopping centers offer a mix of smaller retailers such as Dollar Tree or other big box stores such as Best Buy Kmart and TJX Cos. Altogether Brixmor Property Group owns some 87 million sq. ft. of leasable space; each shopping center averages about 166100 sq. ft. The trust went public in 2013.

	Annual Growth	12/17	12/18	12/19	12/20	12/21
Sales ($ mil.)	(2.7%)	1,283.2	1,234.3	1,168.3	1,053.3	1,152.3
Net income ($ mil.)	(2.6%)	300.3	366.3	274.8	121.2	270.2
Market value ($ mil.)	8.0%	5,545.9	4,366.0	6,422.7	4,918.8	7,552.1
Employees	1.9%	464	458	477	480	501

BROADCAST INTERNATIONAL INC — NBB: BCST

6952 S. High Tech Drive Suite C
Salt Lake City, UT 84047
Phone: 801 562-2252
Fax: –
Web: www.brin.com

CEO: –
CFO: –
HR: –
FYE: December 31
Type: Public

Broadcast International (BI) provides communication network integration services for large retailers and other geographically dispersed businesses. The company utilizes satellite Internet video streaming and Wi-Fi technologies to connect businesses with employees and customers. Clients use its networks to deliver training programs and make product announcements. BI primarily uses third-party equipment but it also supplies some proprietary technologies. BI also offers hosting of video streaming as well as audio and video production services. Its customers have included Caterpillar Safeway and Chevron.

	Annual Growth	12/08	12/09	12/10	12/11	12/12
Sales ($ mil.)	21.9%	3.4	3.6	7.3	8.4	7.5
Net income ($ mil.)	–	(12.5)	(13.4)	(18.7)	1.3	1.6
Market value ($ mil.)	(56.3%)	236.4	126.8	129.0	58.0	8.6
Employees	(10.9%)	38	49	45	51	24

BROADCAST INTERNATIONAL INC. — OTC: BCST

7050 Union Park Ave. Ste. 600
Salt Lake City UT 84047
Phone: 801-562-2252
Fax: 801-562-1773
Web: www.brin.com

CEO: –
CFO: –
HR: –
FYE: December 31
Type: Public

Broadcast International (BI) provides communication network integration services for large retailers and other geographically dispersed businesses. The company utilizes satellite Internet video streaming and Wi-Fi technologies to connect businesses with employees and customers. Clients use its networks to deliver training programs and make product announcements. BI primarily uses third-party equipment but it also supplies some proprietary technologies. BI also offers hosting of video streaming as well as audio and video production services. Its customers have included Caterpillar Safeway and Chevron.

BROADCAST MUSIC INC.

7 World Trade Center 250 Greenwich St.
New York NY 10007
Phone: 212-220-3000
Fax: 212-621-8453
Web: www.ascap.com

CEO: Michael O'Neill
CFO: Bruce Esworthy
HR: –
FYE: June 30
Type: Private - Not-for-Pr

If you are a composer or musician Broadcast Music Inc. (BMI) is here to see that your royalties are paid. The not-for-profit organization collects licensing fees from a host of outlets and venues (such as radio stations TV programs websites restaurants and nightclubs) and distributes them to the more than 550000 songwriters composers and music publishers it represents. Its catalog of compositions includes more than 7.5 million works by a diverse range of artists including Adele Elton John Eric Clapton Gotye Merle Haggard Natalie Cole Herbie Hancock Kanye West and Sting. BMI was founded in 1939.

BROADCOM CORP. NMS: BRCM

5300 California Avenue — CEO: Hock Tan
Irvine, CA 92617-3038 — CFO: Kristen Spears
Phone: 949 926-5000 — HR: –
Fax: – — FYE: December 31
Web: www.broadcom.com — Type: Public

As a semiconductor supplier for the global wired and wireless communications industry Broadcom's reach is far and wide. With locations around the globe Broadcom manufactures billions of chips annually and is one of the world's leading semiconductor companies. Its system-on-a-chip (SoC) technologies and software products deliver voice video data and multimedia in several major market segments: home and office (cable modems DSL and set-top boxes) mobile (Bluetooth and GPS) and infrastructure (controllers embedded processors and security). Broadcom's customer roster includes such elite technology names as Apple Cisco and ZTE. It generates most of its sales from Asia.

	Annual Growth	12/10	12/11	12/12	12/13	12/14
Sales ($ mil.)	5.4%	6,818.3	7,389.0	8,006.0	8,305.0	8,428.0
Net income ($ mil.)	(11.9%)	1,081.8	927.0	719.0	424.0	652.0
Market value ($ mil.)	(0.1%)	26,086.5	17,586.6	19,892.8	17,757.4	25,954.7
Employees	4.4%	8,950	9,590	11,300	12,550	10,650

BROADCOM INC (DE) NMS: AVGO

1320 Ridder Park Drive — CEO: –
San Jose, CA 95131-2313 — CFO: –
Phone: 408 433-8000 — HR: –
Fax: – — FYE: October 31
Web: www.broadcom.com — Type: Public

Broadcom Limited's products cover a broad range of semiconductors. The products include chips for wireless and wired communications as well as optoelectronics radio-frequency and microwave components power amplifiers and application-specific integrated circuits (custom chips). The company's thousands of products are used in a wide range of applications including mobile phones data networking and telecommunications equipment consumer appliances displays printers servers and storage networking gear and factory automation. Broadcom Limited was created with Avago Technologies acquired Broadcom Inc. The company took the Broadcom Limited name when the deal closed in early 2016.

	Annual Growth	10/17*	11/18	11/19	11/20*	10/21
Sales ($ mil.)	11.7%	17,636.0	20,848.0	22,597.0	23,888.0	27,450.0
Net income ($ mil.)	41.3%	1,692.0	12,259.0	2,724.0	2,960.0	6,736.0
Market value ($ mil.)	20.4%	104,447.7	91,178.0	122,491.7	144,397.2	219,579.7
Employees	9.3%	14,000	15,000	19,000	21,000	20,000

*Fiscal year change

BROADRIDGE FINANCIAL SOLUTIONS INC NYS: BR

5 Dakota Drive — CEO: Adam Amsterdam
Lake Success, NY 11042 — CFO: Edmund Reese
Phone: 516 472-5400 — HR: –
Fax: – — FYE: June 30
Web: www.broadridge.com — Type: Public

Broadridge Financial Solutions does business by proxy. The company provides global financial technology leader providing investor communications and technology-driven solutions. Clients include banks broker-dealers asset management firms/ mutual funds and institutional investors. Through its proprietary ProxyEdge system Broadridge processes and distributes proxy materials voting instructionsfor institutional investors processing over 6 billion billion investor communications per year. It also offers related services such as marketing and customer communications and virtual shareholder meetings.

	Annual Growth	06/17	06/18	06/19	06/20	06/21
Sales ($ mil.)	4.8%	4,142.6	4,329.9	4,362.2	4,529.0	4,993.7
Net income ($ mil.)	13.8%	326.8	427.9	482.1	462.5	547.5
Market value ($ mil.)	20.9%	8,772.5	13,363.1	14,823.6	14,650.7	18,753.6
Employees	8.2%	10,000	10,000	11,000	12,000	13,704

BROADSOFT INC NMS: BSFT

9737 Washingtonian Boulevard, Suite 350 — CEO: –
Gaithersburg, MD 20878 — CFO: –
Phone: 301 977-9440 — HR: –
Fax: – — FYE: December 31
Web: www.broadsoft.com — Type: Public

BroadSoft hopes to remove some of the hard work from the process of supplying voice and data services. The company develops software that more than 500 fixed-line mobile and cable telecommunications service providers use to deliver voice and data services. Its BroadWorks software enables carriers to offer their subscribers unified communications services such as video calling hosted multimedia communications business telephone systems and collaboration tools. A hosted program is sold under the BroadCloud platform. Customers include Alteva Axiom Broadconnect Telecom and Birch Telecom.

	Annual Growth	12/11	12/12	12/13	12/14	12/15
Sales ($ mil.)	19.2%	138.1	164.8	178.5	216.9	278.8
Net income ($ mil.)	(72.7%)	32.3	12.1	(8.9)	1.0	0.2
Market value ($ mil.)	4.0%	878.2	1,056.5	794.5	843.9	1,028.3
Employees	26.5%	487	611	725	867	1,247

BROADVIEW INSTITUTE INC NBB: BVII

8147 Globe Drive — CEO: Terry Myhre
Woodbury, MN 55125 — CFO: Kenneth J McCarthy
Phone: 651 332-8000 — HR: –
Fax: – — FYE: March 31
Web: www.broadviewmedia.com — Type: Public

Broadview Institute isn't narrow-minded about education. The company owns and operates C Square Educational Enterprises dba Utah Career College or UCC which offers career vocational training programs in the Salt Lake City area to about 1000 students. Its degree programs span four growing industries: business and accounting health sciences (including veterinary studies) information technology and legal science. Classes are offered at three campuses in Utah and through online and accelerated programs. Chairman Terry Myhre owns about 65% of Broadview. Additionally Myhre has controlling interest in two other post-secondary career colleges Globe University and Minnesota School of Business.

	Annual Growth	03/10	03/11	03/12	03/13	03/14
Sales ($ mil.)	(8.3%)	19.0	20.5	17.8	14.6	13.4
Net income ($ mil.)	–	2.0	(0.1)	(4.2)	(5.1)	(4.9)
Market value ($ mil.)	(66.4%)	242.2	83.5	25.1	13.4	3.1
Employees	(2.6%)	233	246	214	236	210

BROADVIEW NETWORKS HOLDINGS INC.

800 Westchester Ave. Ste. N501 — CEO: Kristi M Moody
Rye Brook NY 10573 — CFO: Corey Rinker
Phone: 914-922-7000 — HR: –
Fax: +65-67933-8156 — FYE: December 31
Web: www.parkwayholdings.com — Type: Private

Broadview Networks seeks to expand its customers' horizons along with its own. The company provides such telecommunications services as local and long-distance computer telephony broadband Internet access and Web hosting. Enterprise data services include hosted business networks and hosted computer telephony services (sold under the OfficeSuite brand). It caters primarily to small and mid-sized businesses serving 10 states in the northeastern and mid-Atlantic US. Key markets include Baltimore Boston New York Philadelphia and Washington DC. Most of Broadview's sales are made to retail customers but it also serves wholesalers and other telecom carriers. Its majority shareholder is MCG Capital.

BROADVISION INC

NAS: BVSN

460 Seaport Court, Suite 102
Redwood City, CA 94063
Phone: 650 331-1000
Fax: –
Web: www.broadvision.com

CEO: Scott Brighton
CFO: –
HR: –
FYE: December 31
Type: Public

BroadVision gives companies a peek into the world of customer self-service. The company develops software that enables businesses to offer their customers personalized self-service via the Internet. Its software suite includes tools for integrating business processes with self-service operations; managing the sales process including lead generation execution and customer service; connecting customers to personalized online views of content; and managing content from creation through distribution. BroadVision serves such industries as travel retail health care and entertainment. Clients have included Canon Oreck PETCO Vodafone and the US Air Force. Founder and CEO Pehong Chen owns 37% of BroadVision.

	Annual Growth	12/14	12/15	12/16	12/17	12/18
Sales ($ mil.)	(21.9%)	13.6	9.4	7.9	6.4	5.1
Net income ($ mil.)	–	(9.5)	(11.4)	(9.5)	(9.9)	(7.0)
Market value ($ mil.)	(33.9%)	30.4	30.3	23.5	18.2	5.8
Employees	(27.9%)	163	156	145	104	44

BROADWAY BANCSHARES INC.

1177 NE Loop 410
San Antonio TX 78209
Phone: 210-283-6500
Fax: 210-283-5623
Web: www.broadwaybank.com

CEO: –
CFO: Chris Bannwolf
HR: –
FYE: December 31
Type: Private

Broadway Bancshares is the holding company for Broadway National Bank (dba Broadway Bank) and its Eisenhower Bank division. The former is a community-oriented financial institution with about 30 branches in San Antonio and Central Texas; the latter has seven offices on military bases throughout the Lone Star State and serves military personnel worldwide. The banks offer traditional deposit products such as checking and savings accounts IRAs and CDs. Both originate various personal consumer construction and commercial loans as well as commercial and residential mortgages. The banks also provide private banking trust investment management and wealth advisory services.

BROADWAY FINANCIAL CORP. (DE)

NAS: BYFC

5055 Wilshire Boulevard, Suite 500
Los Angeles, CA 90036
Phone: 323 634-1700
Fax: –
Web: www.broadwayfederalbank.com

CEO: Brian Argrett
CFO: Brenda Battey
HR: –
FYE: December 31
Type: Public

This company won't quit 'til it's a star! Broadway Financial is the holding company for Broadway Federal Bank a savings and loan that serves the low- and moderate-income minority neighborhoods of central and south central Los Angeles and nearby Inglewood. Through about a half-dozen branches and loan offices the bank primarily originates multi-family (about 40% of its loan portfolio) and commercial real estate loans (another 40%). These loans are secured primarily by multi-family dwellings and properties used for business and religious purposes. Deposit products include CDs and savings checking money market and NOW accounts.

	Annual Growth	12/16	12/17	12/18	12/19	12/20
Assets ($ mil.)	3.0%	429.1	413.7	409.4	440.4	483.4
Net income ($ mil.)	–	3.5	1.9	0.8	(0.2)	(0.6)
Market value ($ mil.)	3.2%	45.8	66.2	29.4	43.2	51.9
Employees	(1.1%)	67	68	65	64	64

BROADWIND INC

NAS: BWEN

3240 S. Central Avenue
Cicero, IL 60804
Phone: 708 780-4800
Fax: –
Web: www.bwen.com

CEO: Eric Blashford
CFO: Jason L Bonfigt
HR: –
FYE: December 31
Type: Public

If you're a wind energy producer Broadwind Energy wants to be the wind beneath your wings. The company serves the wind power generation industry with wind turbine towers and gear systems along with engineering repair and logistics services. Its gear systems are also used by other energy and mining companies. Broadwind's logistics segment specializes in transporting the oversize and overweight components used in constructing wind power generation facilities. The company's locations are spread across North America in areas where wind energy production is heavy.

	Annual Growth	12/16	12/17	12/18	12/19	12/20
Sales ($ mil.)	2.4%	180.8	146.8	125.4	178.2	198.5
Net income ($ mil.)	–	0.3	(3.6)	(24.1)	(4.5)	(1.5)
Market value ($ mil.)	18.3%	68.5	46.1	22.0	28.1	134.3
Employees	(3.9%)	600	399	425	521	512

BROAN-NUTONE LLC

926 W. State St.
Hartford WI 53027-1066
Phone: 262-673-4340
Fax: 262-673-8638
Web: www.broan-nutone.com

CEO: –
CFO: Ryan Haines
HR: –
FYE: December 31
Type: Subsidiary

Customers are big fans of Broan-NuTone products. Henry Broan started the company in 1932 with the Motordor kitchen fan; today Broan-NuTone a subsidiary of Nortek is a leading maker of residential ventilation products. Offerings include ventilation and ceiling fans heaters indoor air quality products and trash compactors. Central vacuums intercom systems medicine cabinets speakers and doorbells are marketed under the NuTone name. Range hoods are sold under the Best and Broan brands. The company's products are available at retail stores such as Lowe's and The Home Depot and also sold by distributors. Broan-NuTone also makes private label products for GE Sears Whirlpool and others.

BROCADE COMMUNICATIONS SYSTEMS, INC.

NMS: BRCD

130 Holger Way
San Jose, CA 95134-1376
Phone: 408 333-8000
Fax: 408 333-8101
Web: www.brocade.com

CEO: Hock E Tan
CFO: Thomas H Krause Jr
HR: –
FYE: October 29
Type: Public

Brocade Communications Systems maintains silky smooth computer network operations. A leading supplier of data center networking products Brocade makes Fibre Channel switches and related software for connecting corporate storage systems and servers. Its products are used in storage area networks (SANs) which pool storage resources across enterprises for easier management and more efficient asset use. Brocade's products support internet connectivity and enterprise mobility as well as key technologies such as software defined networking (SDN) network function virtualization (NFV) and cloud computing. It generates about half of its sales in the US. Brocade agreed to sell to Broadcom for $5.9 billion in 2016.

	Annual Growth	10/12	10/13*	11/14*	10/15	10/16
Sales ($ mil.)	1.2%	2,237.8	2,222.9	2,211.3	2,263.5	2,345.6
Net income ($ mil.)	2.3%	195.2	208.6	238.0	340.4	213.8
Market value ($ mil.)	13.2%	2,129.3	3,145.7	4,310.8	4,186.2	3,491.2
Employees	7.1%	4,536	4,143	4,161	4,640	5,960

*Fiscal year change

BROCKTON HOSPITAL, INC.

680 CENTRE ST
BROCKTON, MA 023023395
Phone: 508-941-7000
Fax: –
Web: www.brocktonhospital.org

CEO: Kim Hollon
CFO: –
HR: –
FYE: September 30
Type: Private

Signature Healthcare Brockton Hospital is a not-for-profit acute medical facility that serves southeastern Massachusetts. The hospital has 245 beds including about 30 beds in its skilled nursing unit. Its emergency department sees more than 62000 patients per year. Specialized services include radiation oncology cardiac care pediatrics orthopedics and joint replacement and inpatient and outpatient psychiatry. It is a community-based teaching hospital and part of the Signature Healthcare network. Brockton Hospital also formed a clinical affiliation with Beth Israel Deaconess Medical Center in 2013.

	Annual Growth	09/11	09/12	09/13	09/14	09/15
Sales ($ mil.)	3.8%	–	222.2	211.8	236.3	248.5
Net income ($ mil.)	(12.0%)	–	19.8	19.6	(15.6)	13.5
Market value ($ mil.)	–	–	–	–	–	–
Employees	–	–	–	–	–	1,500

BRODER BROS., CO.

6 NESHAMINY INTERPLEX DR 6T
TREVOSE, PA 190536964
Phone: 215-291-0300
Fax: –
Web: www.alphabroder.com

CEO: Norman Hullinger
CFO: –
HR: –
FYE: December 26
Type: Private

Selling clothes had been in the genes of sportswear distributor Broder Bros. for years. Begun as a haberdashery in 1919 the company evolved from making hats and gloves into a leading distributor of imprintable sportswear distributing 40000-plus SKUs across more than 40 retail brands including adidas Golf Champion Russell Athletic alternative Dickies and private labels. It operates under the Broder Alpha and NES divisions. Private labels include Devon & Jones Chestnut Hill and Harriton. Customers mostly small US retailers order merchandise through seasonal catalogs or online. Private investment firm Bain Capital has held a majority interest in the company since 2000 when the Broder family sold the company.

	Annual Growth	12/05	12/06	12/07	12/08	12/09
Sales ($ mil.)	(12.9%)	–	–	929.1	926.1	705.2
Net income ($ mil.)	–	–	–	(124.1)	(68.9)	(13.2)
Market value ($ mil.)	–	–	–	–	–	–
Employees	–	–	–	–	–	1,826

BROMLEY COMMUNICATIONS

401 E. Houston St.
San Antonio TX 78205
Phone: 210-244-2000
Fax: 210-244-2442
Web: www.bromleyville.com

CEO: –
CFO: –
HR: –
FYE: December 31
Type: Subsidiary

Marketers looking to put a multicultural spin on their brand can turn to this company. Bromley Communications is the #1 advertising agency offering communications services targeting the Hispanic population in the US. The firm provides creative ad development and strategic planning services as well as media buying and allied marketing and promotional services. It also offers public relations services through a partnership with PR firm Manning Selvage & Lee. Bromley has served such clients as Burger King Procter & Gamble and Western Union. Founded as Sosa Bromley & Aguilar Associates in 1981 the agency is part of Publicis Worldwide's regional operating unit Publicis USA.

BRONSON BATTLE CREEK HOSPITAL

300 NORTH AVE
BATTLE CREEK, MI 490173396
Phone: 269-966-8000
Fax: –
Web: www.bronsonbattlecreek.com

CEO: –
CFO: –
HR: –
FYE: December 31
Type: Private

Bronson Battle Creek Hospital fights against injury and disease in residents of south central Michigan. The hospital is located on two campuses with a total of some 220 beds; it also operates a mental health facility (Fieldstone Center) a variety of outpatient clinics and a home health care and hospice network (Lifespan). The health care provider's hospital and outpatient facilities house general and specialty care clinics including a wound healing center a diagnostic imaging center a sleep center and cardiac and cancer care centers. Its Employer Health Services program features two occupational health and therapy clinics. Bronson Battle Creek is part of the Bronson Health Care Group.

	Annual Growth	12/12	12/13	12/14	12/17	12/18
Sales ($ mil.)	1.3%	–	212.4	159.1	244.9	227.0
Net income ($ mil.)	–	–	(4.5)	(3.8)	(16.4)	(26.4)
Market value ($ mil.)	–	–	–	–	–	–
Employees	–	–	–	–	–	1,882

BRONSON HEALTH CARE GROUP, INC.

301 JOHN ST
KALAMAZOO, MI 490075295
Phone: 269-341-6000
Fax: –
Web: www.bronsonhealth.com

CEO: –
CFO: Kenneth L Taft
HR: –
FYE: December 31
Type: Private

Bronson Health Care Group has a strong presence as a provider of a wide range of medical services in southern Michigan and northern Indiana. The company operates several regional hospitals and health clinics including Bronson Methodist Hospital (some 400 beds) Bronson Battle Creek (220 beds) and Bronson Lakeview Hospital (35 beds). The not-for-profit health care system's facilities provide general and specialty services including trauma stroke burn cancer and cardiac care as well as emergency medicine pediatrics obstetrics rehabilitation and home health care.

	Annual Growth	12/08	12/09	12/16	12/17	12/19
Sales ($ mil.)	11.0%	–	119.6	1,136.1	1,233.9	338.8
Net income ($ mil.)	–	–	16.5	28.7	63.5	(39.1)
Market value ($ mil.)	–	–	–	–	–	–
Employees	–	–	–	–	–	4,180

BRONSON METHODIST HOSPITAL INC

601 JOHN ST STE E-012
KALAMAZOO, MI 490075346
Phone: 269-341-7654
Fax: –
Web: www.bronsonhealth.com

CEO: –
CFO: Mary Meitz
HR: –
FYE: December 31
Type: Private

From your leg bone to your knee bone; your neck bone to your head bone Bronson Methodist Hospital has the specialists to cure what ails you. The 435-bed hospital is the flagship facility of the Bronson Healthcare Group a not-for-profit health care system. Bronson Methodist provides care in just about every specialty including orthopedics surgery and oncology. The hospital also contains specialist units for critical care (level I trauma center) neurology (primary stroke center) cardiology (Chest pain emergency center) women's health (BirthPlace) and pediatrics (children's hospital).

	Annual Growth	12/14	12/15	12/17	12/18	12/19
Sales ($ mil.)	7.0%	–	726.6	864.8	864.3	952.8
Net income ($ mil.)	(55.6%)	–	69.0	85.2	26.9	2.7
Market value ($ mil.)	–	–	–	–	–	–
Employees	–	–	–	–	–	2,861

BRONXCARE HEALTH SYSTEM

1276 FULTON AVE
BRONX, NY 104563402
Phone: 718-590-1800
Fax: –
Web: www.bronxcare.org

CEO: Miguel Fuentes
CFO: –
HR: –
FYE: December 31
Type: Private

Bronx-Lebanon Hospital Center cares for patients in the central and south Bronx no doubt while rooting for the Yankees a few blocks away. The health care provider maintains more than 970 beds across its two campuses as well as psychiatric and nursing home facilities. Hospital specialty units include chest pain orthopedic cancer and women's health centers. Bronx-Lebanon also manages a network of about 70 owned and affiliated medical practices (under the BronxCare brand). This network includes primary care doctors and specialty clinics as well as rehabilitation facilities. The hospital is also a primary teaching hospital for the Albert Einstein College of Medicine.

	Annual Growth	12/13	12/14	12/15	12/16	12/17
Sales ($ mil.)	7.9%	–	598.5	631.3	641.1	750.8
Net income ($ mil.)	–	–	(34.2)	18.9	6.5	12.1
Market value ($ mil.)	–	–	–	–	–	–
Employees	–	–	–	–	–	4,000

BROOKDALE SENIOR LIVING INC

111 Westwood Place, Suite 400
Brentwood, TN 37027
Phone: 615 221-2250
Fax: –
Web: www.brookdale.com

NYS: BKD
CEO: Lucinda Baier
CFO: Steven Swain
HR: –
FYE: December 31
Type: Public

Brookdale Senior Living operates assisted and independent living centers and retirement communities for middle- and upper-income elderly clients. The US largest senior living provider Brookdale owns leases or manages about 725 communities offering studio one-bedroom and two-bedroom units in some 45 states. It has the capacity to serve about 64000 residents. Services for its residents include health assessments meals 24-hour emergency response personal care housekeeping concierge services transportation and recreational activities. Brookdale's continuing care retirement centers include skilled nursing units; the firm also operates memory care units for Alzheimer's and dementia patients.

	Annual Growth	12/17	12/18	12/19	12/20	12/21
Sales ($ mil.)	(12.7%)	4,747.1	4,531.4	4,057.1	3,540.2	2,758.3
Net income ($ mil.)	–	(571.4)	(528.3)	(267.9)	82.0	(99.3)
Market value ($ mil.)	(14.6%)	1,813.5	1,252.6	1,359.2	828.2	964.7
Employees	(18.7%)	75,600	65,400	58,400	45,000	33,000

BROOKFIELD PROPERTY REIT INC

250 Vesey Street, 15th Floor
New York, NY 10281-1023
Phone: 212 417-7000
Fax: –
Web: www.brookfieldpropertiesretail.com

NMS: BPYU
CEO: Brian W Kingston
CFO: Bryan K Davis
HR: –
FYE: December 31
Type: Public

Brookfield Property REIT (formerly GGP) has an idea for an economic stimulus plan: Let's all hang out at the mall! Brookfield Property is one of the largest commercial real estate companies with nearly $90 billion in total assets. It owns manages leases and redevelops its malls which generates annual sales of nearly $800 per square foot. The real estate investment trust (REIT) has a portfolio that includes more than 120 primarily Class A regional shopping malls in major US markets; the malls have approximately 120 million sq. ft. of space. Top tenants include L Brands Foot Locker and LVMH. GGP was acquired for $14.8 billion by Brookfield Asset Management's property division in mid-2018; now trading as Brookfield Property REIT the company is nearly 90%-owned by institutional investors.

	Annual Growth	12/15	12/16	12/17	12/18	12/19
Sales ($ mil.)	(10.2%)	2,403.9	2,346.4	2,327.9	2,064.0	1,564.0
Net income ($ mil.)	(25.1%)	1,374.6	1,288.4	657.3	4,090.5	432.9
Market value ($ mil.)	14.6%	–	–	–	16,024.4	18,358.4
Employees	0.0%	1,700	1,800	1,700	–	–

BROOKHAVEN MEMORIAL HOSPITAL MEDICAL CENTER, INC.

101 HOSPITAL RD
EAST PATCHOGUE, NY 117724870
Phone: 631-654-7100
Fax: –
Web: www.licommunityhospital.org

CEO: Richard T Margulis
CFO: Brenda Farrell
HR: –
FYE: December 31
Type: Private

Brookhaven Memorial Hospital Medical Center is an acute-care facility with more than 300 beds that serves patients primarily in Suffolk County on Long Island New York. The not-for-profit community hospital's Emergency Trauma and Chest Pain Pavilion is one of the largest emergency rooms on Long Island. Founded in 1956 Brookhaven Memorial also offers behavioral health services including inpatient and outpatient mental health and alcohol treatment services. In addition to hospital services the medical center operates two community health clinics and a specialty center that provides hemodialysis women's imaging and home health and hospice services.

	Annual Growth	12/14	12/15	12/16	12/17	12/19
Sales ($ mil.)	1.7%	–	254.1	261.3	271.4	272.2
Net income ($ mil.)	125.2%	–	0.2	(1.2)	(6.9)	4.8
Market value ($ mil.)	–	–	–	–	–	–
Employees	–	–	–	–	–	2,100

BROOKLINE BANCORP INC (DE)

131 Clarendon Street
Boston, MA 02116
Phone: 617 425-4600
Fax: –
Web: www.brooklinebancorp.com

NMS: BRKL
CEO: Paul Perrault
CFO: Carl Carlson
HR: Sandra Jenkins
FYE: December 31
Type: Public

Boston-based Brookline Bancorp is the holding company for Brookline Bank Bank Rhode Island (BankRI) and First Ipswich Bank which together operate more than 50 full-service branches in eastern Massachusetts and Rhode Island. Commercial and multifamily mortgages backed by real estate such as apartments condominiums and office buildings account for the largest portion of the company's loan portfolio followed by indirect auto loans commercial loans and consumer loans. Established in 1997 as Brookline Savings Bank the bank went public five years later and changed its name to Brookline Bank in 2003.

	Annual Growth	12/16	12/17	12/18	12/19	12/20
Assets ($ mil.)	8.6%	6,438.1	6,780.2	7,392.8	7,856.9	8,942.4
Net income ($ mil.)	(2.3%)	52.4	50.5	83.1	87.7	47.6
Market value ($ mil.)	(7.4%)	1,289.9	1,234.8	1,087.0	1,294.6	947.0
Employees	2.3%	743	765	791	811	813

BROOKLYN HOSPITAL CENTER

121 DEKALB AVE
BROOKLYN, NY 112015493
Phone: 718-250-8000
Fax: –
Web: www.tbh.org

CEO: –
CFO: –
HR: –
FYE: December 31
Type: Private

The Brooklyn Hospital Center has been taking care of ailing Kings County residents since before Brooklyn was a borough. Established in 1845 (before Brooklyn became part of New York City) the hospital houses some 460 beds and is a member of the NewYork-Presbyterian Healthcare System. It provides general medical and surgical care as well as a wide variety of specialty medical services including dialysis pediatrics obstetrics and cardiovascular care. The Brooklyn Hospital Center is affiliated with Weill Medical College of Cornell University. The hospital also operates a network of outpatient clinics providing primary and specialty care throughout the borough.

	Annual Growth	12/14	12/15	12/16	12/17	12/19
Sales ($ mil.)	4.0%	–	345.8	349.6	347.5	404.6
Net income ($ mil.)	–	–	3.5	4.0	(10.0)	(24.5)
Market value ($ mil.)	–	–	–	–	–	–
Employees	–	–	–	–	–	3,300

BROOKLYN IMMUNOTHERAPEUTICS INC   NMS: BTX

140 58th Street, Suite 2100
Brooklyn, NY 11220
Phone: 212 582-1199
Fax: –
Web: www.buzztime.com

CEO: Allen Wolff
CFO: Sandra Gurrola
HR: Amy Biondo
FYE: December 31
Type: Public

Brooklyn ImmunoTherapeutics is a clinical stage biopharmaceutical company committed to developing IRX-2 a novel hd-IL-2 -based therapy to treat patients with cancer. IRX-2 delivers hd-IL-2 and other key cytokines to potentially restore immune function in the tumor microenvironment enabling the immune system to attack cancer cells. The company is also exploring opportunities to advance oncology and blood disorder therapies using leading edge gene editing/cell therapy technology through the newly acquired license from Factor Bioscience and Novellus. Its headquarters laboratories and manufacturing facilities are located in the historic Brooklyn Army Terminal.

	Annual Growth	12/16	12/17	12/18	12/19	12/20
Sales ($ mil.)	(28.6%)	22.3	21.3	23.3	19.8	5.8
Net income ($ mil.)	–	(2.9)	(1.1)	(0.3)	(2.0)	(4.4)
Market value ($ mil.)	(28.4%)	25.1	12.4	5.8	6.5	6.6
Employees	(51.6%)	402	446	281	39	22

BROOKLYN NAVY YARD DEVELOPMENT CORPORATION

63 FLUSHING AVE UNIT 300
BROOKLYN, NY 112051080
Phone: 718-237-6740
Fax: –

CEO: David Ehrenberg
CFO: Dan Conlon
HR: –
FYE: June 30
Type: Private

After the federal government closed the military facilities at Brooklyn Navy Yard in 1966 the property on the East River was taken over and converted into commercial real estate by The City of New York. Brooklyn Navy Yard Development Corporation is in charge of the management and development of the old Navy Yard which contains about 4 million sq. ft. of leasable office and industrial space. Located near the Brooklyn Bridge the Navy Yard is home to about 250 tenants including small businesses high-tech startups and film and television studios. Since 2006 the company has been managing a Mayor Bloomberg-sanctioned expansion of the yard including some 1.7 million sq. ft. of new industrial space.

	Annual Growth	06/12	06/13	06/14	06/15	06/16
Assets ($ mil.)	11.1%	–	403.7	422.7	453.7	553.7
Net income ($ mil.)	65.6%	–	12.9	9.6	12.3	58.6
Market value ($ mil.)	–	–	–	–	–	–
Employees	–	–	–	–	–	165

BROOKMOUNT EXPLORATIONS INC   NBB: BMXI

1 East Liberty, Suite 600
Reno, NV 89501
Phone: 775 525-6012
Fax: –
Web: www.brookmountcorp.com

CEO: Peter Flueck
CFO: –
HR: –
FYE: November 30
Type: Public

Brookmount Explorations hopes it has the Midas touch. Formed in 1999 the exploration-stage mining company is engaged in the exploration of precious metal resource properties located Peru and Canada. Its primary project is the Mercedes 100 gold/silver/lead/zinc property in Peru. The company is also on the lookout for potential acquisitions in Canada and elsewhere in South America. President Peter Flueck controls approximately 40% of Brookmount Explorations having joined the company when he sold his ownership interests in the Mercedes property to Brookmount in 2005.

	Annual Growth	11/16	11/17	11/18	11/19	11/20
Sales ($ mil.)	35.0%	–	–	6.0	7.0	11.0
Net income ($ mil.)	128.8%	0.2	(0.1)	2.0	2.8	5.7
Market value ($ mil.)	137.8%	0.3	0.1	0.2	0.1	9.6
Employees	–	–	–	–	–	–

BROOKS TROPICALS HOLDING INC.

18400 SW 256TH ST
HOMESTEAD, FL 33031-1892
Phone: 305-247-3544
Fax: –
Web: www.brookstropicals.com

CEO: Greg Smith
CFO: Janice Kolar
HR: –
FYE: December 31
Type: Private

Brooks Tropicals offers exotic tastes with every bite. The company is a producer importer and supplier of tropical fruits and vegetables. Brooks product line consists of about 25 fruits and vegetables — some familiar some virtually unknown to American palates. They include avocados boniato calabaza chayote coconut ginger key lime kumquat lime malanga mamey sapote mango papaya Scotch bonnet pepper star fruit sugar cane and yuca. Brooks' produce is grown on its more than 6000 acres located in Florida as well as growing operations in Belize. The company was founded in 1928 by J.R. Brooks and is still owned and managed by his son and company president Neal (Pal) Brooks.

	Annual Growth	12/07	12/08	12/09	12/10	12/11
Sales ($ mil.)	5.0%	–	44.8	42.1	48.3	51.8
Net income ($ mil.)	–	–	(1.7)	(2.0)	2.9	3.8
Market value ($ mil.)	–	–	–	–	–	–
Employees	–	–	–	–	–	200

BROOKSTONE INC.

1 Innovation Way
Merrimack NH 03054
Phone: 603-880-9500
Fax: 405-270-1089
Web: www.bancfirst.com

CEO: Steven Goldsmith
CFO: Valen Tong
HR: –
FYE: December 31
Type: Private

Need a putting green for the office? How about an alarm clock that responds to your spoken commands? Then Brookstone is the place for you. It sells gifts gadgets and other doodads targeted primarily at men through about 295 stores in 40-plus states and Puerto Rico. The company's products fall into categories such as technology travel time and weather outdoor living fitness and automotive. Brookstone also sells its wares online and through its eponymous catalog. Because gifts contribute to most of its sales the company operates temporary kiosks during Father's day and busy holiday seasons. Brookstone is owned by a consortium led by Osim International J.W. Childs and Temasek Holdings.

BROTHER INTERNATIONAL CORPORATION

200 CROSSING BLVD FL 1
BRIDGEWATER, NJ 088072861
Phone: 908-704-1700
Fax: –
Web: www.support.brother-usa.com

CEO: –
CFO: –
HR: –
FYE: March 31
Type: Private

Brother International is a leading supplier of innovative products for the home sewing and crafting enthusiast. A subsidiary of Japan-based Brother Industries Brother International sells a host of products ? including inkjet and laser printers fax machines scanners typewriters sewing machines gear motors and machine tools ? manufactured by its parent company. Its products are marketed to consumers and businesses in North America and across Latin America. Through its subsidiaries Brother International operates production and sales facilities in more than 30 countries worldwide and it serves customers in over 100 countries. The business was formed in 1954.

	Annual Growth	03/12	03/13	03/14	03/15	03/18
Sales ($ mil.)	(1.0%)	–	–	1,826.4	1,852.7	1,751.5
Net income ($ mil.)	6.1%	–	–	26.8	3.8	34.0
Market value ($ mil.)	–	–	–	–	–	–
Employees	–	–	–	–	–	2,000

BROWN & BROWN INC
NYS: BRO

300 North Beach Street
Daytona Beach, FL 32114
Phone: 386 252-9601
Fax: –
Web: www.bbinsurance.com

CEO: J. Powell Brown
CFO: R. Andrew Watts
HR: –
FYE: December 31
Type: Public

Insurance agency Brown & Brown is the sixth largest independent insurance brokerages in the US. The company provides property/casualty life and health insurance plus risk management services through its Retail segment mainly to commercial clients. Its National Programs division designs customized programs for such niche clients as dentists lawyers and optometrists. Brown & Brown's Wholesale Brokerage unit distributes excess and surplus commercial insurance as well as reinsurance to retail agents while the firm's Services segment provides self-insured and third-party administrator services. The company has more than 300 offices in about 45 states and in England the Cayman Islands and Bermuda.

	Annual Growth	12/17	12/18	12/19	12/20	12/21
Sales ($ mil.)	12.9%	1,881.3	2,014.2	2,392.2	2,613.4	3,051.4
Net income ($ mil.)	10.1%	399.6	344.3	398.5	480.5	587.1
Market value ($ mil.)	8.1%	14,537.2	7,785.6	11,152.9	13,393.1	19,853.8
Employees	9.1%	8,491	1,281	10,083	11,136	12,023

BROWN BROTHERS HARRIMAN & CO.

140 Broadway
New York NY 10005-1101
Phone: 212-483-1818
Fax: 916-327-0489
Web: www.calottery.com

CEO: –
CFO: –
HR: –
FYE: December 31
Type: Private

Brown Brothers Harriman (BBH) is one of the oldest largest and most prestigious private banks in the US. Founded in 1818 and known for its conservative investment approach the company specializes in asset management for wealthy families and institutional investors and corporate banking finance and mergers and acquisitions advisory for closely held middle-market companies. It has expertise in wealth planning and investment advisory banking public and private equity fixed-income strategies commodities and fiduciary services. It also manages four mutual funds. BBH has more than 15 offices in North America Europe and Asia.

BROWN JORDAN INTERNATIONAL INC.

475 W. Town Place Ste. 201
St. Augustine FL 32092
Phone: 904-495-0717
Fax: 408-325-6444
Web: www.ultratech.com

CEO: Gene J Moriarty
CFO: Jeff Leonard
HR: –
FYE: December 31
Type: Private

Brown Jordan International (BJI) prefers that its customers take a seat — inside or out. The firm designs and makes upscale indoor and outdoor furniture including chairs tables sofas and loveseats for home and commercial use. Its brands include Brown Jordan Casual Living Charter La-Z-Boy (under license) Lodging by Liberty Wabash and Winston. Residential products are sold by mass merchants (Home Depot and SAM'S CLUB); commercial lines are sold to hotels restaurants health care facilities and schools. BJI is controlled by a trio of hedge funds: TCW Group Stonehill Capital Management and Litespeed Capital.

BROWN PRINTING COMPANY

2300 Brown Ave.
Waseca MN 56093-0517
Phone: 507-835-2410
Fax: 507-835-0420
Web: www.bpc.com

CEO: –
CFO: –
HR: –
FYE: June 30
Type: Subsidiary

Brown doesn't mind getting its hands dirty — with four-color or black and white — with plenty of printer ink. Founded by Wayne "Bumps" Brown in 1949 Brown Printing Company is one of the largest publication printers in the US. The company prints magazines (more than 700 of them) catalogs and inserts for some 400 customers such as catalog retailer Hanover Direct and marketing company Valassis. Brown also provides direct-mail production and distribution through its Alliance List Services division while its Specialty Printing segment concentrates on digital print services. The company is a unit of large European magazine publisher Gruner + Jahr (G+J).

BROWN UNIVERSITY

1 PROSPECT ST
PROVIDENCE, RI 029129127
Phone: 401-369-0294
Fax: –
Web: www.it.brown.edu

CEO: Christina Paxson
CFO: –
HR: –
FYE: June 30
Type: Private

Brown is a leading research university distinct for its student-centered learning and deep sense of purpose. The University's academic programs include: undergraduate graduate and professional schools and colleges academic departments centers and institutes libraries and collections global education as well as non-degree programs. The University founded in 1764 is located in Providence Rhode Island ? Brown's home for more than two and a half centuries.

	Annual Growth	06/09	06/10	06/11	06/12	06/13
Sales ($ mil.)	4.8%	–	–	666.5	704.9	732.1
Net income ($ mil.)	(10.2%)	–	–	359.4	(69.1)	289.6
Market value ($ mil.)	–	–	–	–	–	–
Employees	–	–	–	–	–	5,100

BROWN-FORMAN CORP
NYS: BF B

850 Dixie Highway
Louisville, KY 40210
Phone: 502 585-1100
Fax: 502 774-7876
Web: www.brown-forman.com

CEO: Lawson Whiting
CFO: Leanne Cunningham
HR: –
FYE: April 30
Type: Public

Distiller Brown-Forman (B-F) spreads its spirits around the world. The company's portfolio of mid-priced to super-premium alcoholic beverages includes such well-known brands as Jack Daniel's Canadian Mist Finlandia and Woodford Reserve. Its wine labels include Sonoma-Cutrer and Korbel champagnes. Jack Daniel's is the company's signature brand and the largest-selling American whiskey in the world (by volume). Offering more than 40 brands the company sells its beverages in more than 170 countries across the globe; sales outside the US account for approximately half of revenue.

	Annual Growth	04/17	04/18	04/19	04/20	04/21
Sales ($ mil.)	3.7%	2,994.0	3,248.0	3,324.0	3,363.0	3,461.0
Net income ($ mil.)	7.8%	669.0	717.0	835.0	827.0	903.0
Market value ($ mil.)	12.7%	22,653.5	26,828.0	25,511.5	29,776.9	36,517.4
Employees	0.0%	4,700	4,800	4,700	4,800	4,700

BRYAN MEDICAL CENTER

1600 S 48TH ST
LINCOLN, NE 685061283
Phone: 402-481-1111
Fax: –
Web: www.bryanhealth.com

CEO: Kim Russel
CFO: Russell Gronewold
HR: –
FYE: December 31
Type: Private

Bryan Medical Center is the centerpiece of a not-for-profit health care system serving residents of Lincoln Nebraska and surrounding communities. The medical center which operates as part of Bryan Health features two acute-care hospitals (Bryan East and Bryan West) housing a combined 670 beds. In addition to providing general medical and surgical care it serves as a regional trauma center and provides specialty care in areas such as cancer orthopedics and cardiology. The Bryan Health organization also includes a rural hospital and several outpatient clinics and it provides medical training home health care services and wellness programs.

	Annual Growth	12/14	12/15	12/16	12/17	12/19
Sales ($ mil.)	8.9%	–	558.8	586.8	606.4	785.7
Net income ($ mil.)	31.2%	–	43.6	60.7	74.7	129.4
Market value ($ mil.)	–	–	–	–	–	–
Employees	–	–	–	–	–	3,970

BRYCE CORPORATION

4505 Old Lamar Ave.
Memphis TN 38118
Phone: 901-369-4400
Fax: 901-369-4419
Web: www.brycecorp.com

CEO: Thomas J Bryce
CFO: Ramon Marus Jr
HR: –
FYE: December 31
Type: Private

Sweet! Bryce Corporation produces plastic-film (using polypropylene polyethylene and polyester laminations) packaging for markets including candy snack pet food and other consumer products from its five production facilities in the US. Its Bryce Company business is a pro in film conversion and flexible packaging while its Cyber Graphics business provides package design; product photography; flexographic printing in up to 10 colors; a range of laminations such as solvent adhesives multilayer barrier extrusions and tandem laminations; and barrier coextrusion emulsion and wax coatings. Chairman and CEO Thomas J. Bryce preserves the family's stake in the company which was founded in 1969.

BRYN MAWR BANK CORP

NMS: BMTC

801 Lancaster Avenue
Bryn Mawr, PA 19010
Phone: 610 525-1700
Fax: –
Web: www.bmtc.com

CEO: Francis J Leto
CFO: Michael W Harrington
HR: –
FYE: December 31
Type: Public

Bryn Mawr Bank Corporation stands atop a "big hill" in Pennsylvania. Bryn Mawr (which in Welsh translates as "big hill") is the bank holding company for Bryn Mawr Trust operates some 20 offices in Pennsylvania and Delaware. The bank offers traditional services as checking and savings accounts CDs mortgages and business and consumer loans in addition to insurance products equipment leasing investment management retirement planning tax planning and preparation and trust services. Founded in 1889 Bryn Mawr boasts more than $5 billion of assets under administration and management.

	Annual Growth	12/15	12/16	12/17	12/18	12/19
Assets ($ mil.)	14.8%	3,031.0	3,421.5	4,449.7	4,652.5	5,263.3
Net income ($ mil.)	37.1%	16.8	36.0	23.0	63.8	59.2
Market value ($ mil.)	9.5%	578.0	848.3	889.6	692.3	830.0
Employees	6.6%	530	544	680	696	684

BRYN MAWR COLLEGE

101 N MERION AVE
BRYN MAWR, PA 190102899
Phone: 610-526-5000
Fax: –
Web: www.brynmawr.edu

CEO: Hannah Holborn Gray
CFO: –
HR: –
FYE: May 31
Type: Private

These Mawrters aren't sacrificing anything especially when it comes to their education. Bryn Mawr is a college for women often referred to as Mawrters who hail from 60 countries. Its undergraduate programs including biology English math political science and psychology enroll 1300 students. Bryn Mawr also offers degrees through its co-educational Graduate School of Arts and Sciences and Graduate School of Social Work and Social Research which enrolls some 425 students. The college pools resources with Haverford Swarthmore and The University of Pennsylvania. Founded in 1885 Bryn Mawr is one of the nation's oldest women's colleges and the first to offer women an education through the Ph.D. level.

	Annual Growth	05/12	05/13	05/14	05/15	05/20
Sales ($ mil.)	8.6%	–	114.4	200.5	225.0	204.1
Net income ($ mil.)	(11.7%)	–	75.9	43.7	67.3	31.7
Market value ($ mil.)	–	–	–	–	–	–
Employees	–	–	–	–	–	777

BSB BANCORP INC. (MD)

NAS: BLMT

2 Leonard Street
Belmont, MA 02478
Phone: 617 484-6700
Fax: –
Web: www.belmontsavings.com

CEO: –
CFO: –
HR: –
FYE: December 31
Type: Public

BSB Bancorp is the holding company for Belmont Savings Bank a community back with about half a dozen branches in southeastern Middlesex County in the suburbs of Boston. Serving local businesses and individuals the $2 billion-asset bank offers checking savings money market retirement accounts and a variety of lending products. Almost 50% of its loan portfolio is made up of one-to-four family residential mortgages while commercial real estate loans make up another 30%. While Belmont Savings Bank traces its roots back to 1885 BSB Bancorp was formed in 2011 to take the company public.

	Annual Growth	12/13	12/14	12/15	12/16	12/17
Assets ($ mil.)	26.2%	1,054.6	1,425.6	1,812.9	2,158.7	2,676.6
Net income ($ mil.)	64.6%	2.0	4.3	6.9	12.0	14.4
Market value ($ mil.)	18.0%	146.5	180.9	227.1	281.0	283.9
Employees	(0.2%)	127	128	132	125	126

BSD MEDICAL CORP.

NAS: BSDM

2188 West 2200 South
Salt Lake City, UT 84119
Phone: 801 972-5555
Fax: 801 972-5930
Web: www.bsdmedical.com

CEO: Clinton E Carnell Jr
CFO: William S Barth
HR: –
FYE: August 31
Type: Public

BSD Medical has developed equipment to provide hyperthermia treatment specifically for treating cancer (including melanoma breast cancer brain cancer and cervical cancer). Its systems are used in tandem with chemotherapy and radiation therapy or as a stand-alone treatment. BSD Medical was the first to develop an approvable hyperthermia system which uses focused radio frequencies and microwaves to heat cancer cells until they die. The company's devices are designed to target superficial tumors as well as tumors located deep within a patient's body. Its products are sold to clinics hospitals and other cancer-treatment institutions through its sales force and external distributors.

	Annual Growth	08/10	08/11	08/12	08/13	08/14
Sales ($ mil.)	35.5%	1.6	3.0	2.1	3.7	5.3
Net income ($ mil.)	–	(7.5)	(5.3)	(8.0)	(8.3)	(7.1)
Market value ($ mil.)	(26.4%)	87.3	116.3	68.7	60.3	25.6
Employees	13.8%	31	41	50	48	52

BSH HOME APPLIANCES CORPORATION

5551 McFadden Ave.
Huntington Beach CA 92649
Phone: 714-901-6600
Fax: 714-901-5980
Web: www.bsh-group.us/

CEO: Michael Traub
CFO: Stefan Koss
HR: –
FYE: December 31
Type: Subsidiary

BSH can help make an HSH — a home sweet home that is. The company makes and distributes a variety of high-end home appliances under the Gaggenau Bosch and Thermador brands including dishwashers ovens cooktops ranges washing machines and dryers. BSH serves the US and Canadian markets selling products directly to new homebuilders as well as through retailers such as Home Depot Lowe's and Sears. Most BSH appliances which are locally manufactured at plants in North Carolina and Tennessee are made from recyclable materials. Founded in 1997 BSH Home Appliances is a subsidiary of German manufacturer BSH Bosch und Siemens Hausgerate.

BSQUARE CORP

1415 Western Ave., Suite 700
Seattle, WA 98101
Phone: 425 519-5900
Fax: –
Web: www.bsquare.com

NAS: BSQR
CEO: Ralph Derrickson
CFO: Christopher Wheaton
HR: –
FYE: December 31
Type: Public

Bsquare hips its clients on how to integrate Microsoft applications with their own products. The company primarily resells software from Microsoft. Domestically its sales center around the Microsoft General Embedded operating system (OS) while international customers look to Bsquare for Microsoft's Windows Mobile OS. Makers of consumer electronics (cell phones) and automobiles in particular power portions of their goods with Microsoft's applications. Bsquare sells software from such other vendors as Adobe and McAfee. Additionally it provides engineering and development services to clients who require help integrating Windows products. The company also sells its own electronics testing software.

	Annual Growth	12/16	12/17	12/18	12/19	12/20
Sales ($ mil.)	(16.6%)	97.4	80.8	73.4	59.3	47.1
Net income ($ mil.)	–	(1.1)	(9.1)	(13.7)	(9.2)	(1.9)
Market value ($ mil.)	(28.6%)	77.4	61.5	20.5	18.4	20.1
Employees	(19.8%)	169	192	139	75	70

BT CONFERENCING

150 Newport Avenue Extension Ste. 400
North Quincy MA 02171
Phone: 617-801-6600
Fax: 617-845-1058
Web: www.btconferencing.com

CEO: Aaron McCormack
CFO: Bernard Barlow
HR: –
FYE: December 31
Type: Subsidiary

BT Conferencing wants to connect people wherever they may be. The company provides audio video and Web conferencing and scheduling services and it resells and integrates conferencing systems. Businesses schools and government agencies worldwide use hardware software and services supplied by BT Conferencing to enable meetings and training sessions between participants in far-flung locations. The company offers products from such vendors as Avaya Cisco Polycom and TANDBERG. It also offers consulting installation project management and support. Clients have included food products giant Nestle and clothing maker Tommy Hilfiger. BT Conferencing is a subsidiary of UK-based telecom service provider BT Group.

BTU INTERNATIONAL, INC.

23 Esquire Road
North Billerica, MA 01862-2596
Phone: 978 667-4111
Fax: 978 667-9068
Web: www.btu.com

NMS: BTUI
CEO: Michael Whang
CFO: Lisa Gibbs
HR: –
FYE: December 31
Type: Public

Things are heating up at BTU International. BTU makes sells and services thermal processing equipment and controls for the manufacture of printed circuit boards and for semiconductor packaging. The company provides its PYRAMAX branded systems for solder reflow (for printed circuit boards) as well as technical ceramic sintering electrical component brazing and the deposition of film coatings. BTU equipment is also used to make photovoltaic solar cells and solid oxide fuel cells and for sintering nuclear fuel. The company sells its products to the alternative energy and electronics assembly markets mostly manufacturers of computers printed circuit board assemblies and consumer electronics products.

	Annual Growth	12/08	12/09	12/10	12/11	12/12
Sales ($ mil.)	(5.3%)	72.3	45.1	81.6	76.1	58.1
Net income ($ mil.)	–	(1.1)	(14.6)	2.2	(2.7)	(11.0)
Market value ($ mil.)	(16.4%)	38.1	60.5	84.7	24.8	18.6
Employees	(5.6%)	381	352	383	356	302

BUBBA GUMP SHRIMP CO. RESTAURANTS INC.

209 Avenida Fabricante Ste. 200
San Clemente CA 92672-6270
Phone: 949-366-6260
Fax: 949-366-6261
Web: www.bubbagump.com

CEO: –
CFO: Dan Bylund
HR: –
FYE: December 31
Type: Subsidiary

Maybe for this company the restaurant business is like a box of chocolates. Bubba Gump Shrimp Co. Restaurants operates and franchises about 30 themed eateries. Inspired by the 1994 film Forrest Gump the casual dining restaurants offer a menu of seafood appetizers entrees and sandwiches. The chain has about 20 restaurants in 10 states along with another dozen international locations; most Bubba Gump units are found at tourist destinations such as the Mall of America and the Universal Orlando theme park. The chain started after cutting a licensing deal with Paramount Pictures in 1996 and was acquired by multi-concept dining operator Landry's Restaurants in 2010.

BUCKEYE PARTNERS LP

One Greenway Plaza, Suite 600
Houston, TX 77046
Phone: 832 615-8600
Fax: –
Web: www.buckeye.com

NYS: BPL
CEO: –
CFO: Keith St.Clair
HR: Mark Esselman
FYE: December 31
Type: Public

Buckeye Partners keeps the home fires burning and ship engines humming with its gas pipeline and marine terminals operations. The company owns and operates a diversified network of midstream assets stretching from the US upper Midwest to the East Coast. It also operates or is a JV partner in a number of global marine terminals that provide fuel to the shipping industry. It has more than 100 product terminals with capacity for nearly 55 million barrels of liquid petroleum product storage capacity A key subsidiary Buckeye Pipe Line stretches a pipeline some 1800 miles from Massachusetts to Illinois.

	Annual Growth	12/13	12/14	12/15	12/16	12/17
Sales ($ mil.)	(7.8%)	5,054.1	6,620.2	3,453.4	3,248.4	3,648.1
Net income ($ mil.)	31.5%	160.3	273.0	437.2	535.6	478.8
Market value ($ mil.)	(8.6%)	10,415.6	11,097.6	9,674.8	9,704.2	7,267.9
Employees	7.8%	1,270	1,430	1,765	1,590	–

BUCKEYE PIPE LINE COMPANY, L P

5002 BUCKEYE RD
EMMAUS, PA 180495347
Phone: 610-904-4000
Fax: –
Web: www.buckeye.com

CEO: –
CFO: –
HR: –
FYE: December 31
Type: Private

It's the octane in fuel in the pipes of Buckeye Pipe Line that gets engines to buck up. A partnership subsidiary of Buckeye Partners the company operates an interstate common carrier refined petroleum pipeline that runs some 2643 miles from Massachusetts to Illinois. The refined petroleum products carried include gasoline turbine fuel diesel fuel heating oil and kerosene. The company serves major population centers in nine states. It is also the major jet engine fuel provider to John F. Kennedy International Airport LaGuardia Airport Newark International Airport and a number of other airports within the territory served by the pipeline operator.

	Annual Growth	12/01	12/02	12/03	12/04	12/16
Sales ($ mil.)	4.6%	–	179.9	196.3	323.5	335.5
Net income ($ mil.)	8.5%	–	55.7	14.1	83.0	173.6
Market value ($ mil.)	–	–	–	–	–	–
Employees	–	–	–	–	–	504

BUCKEYE POWER, INC.

6677 BUSCH BLVD
COLUMBUS, OH 432291101
Phone: 614-781-0573
Fax: –
Web: www.buckeyepower.com

CEO: Anthony J Ahern
CFO: –
HR: –
FYE: June 30
Type: Private

It has cost a few bucks to generate power but the effort has been well worth it for Buckeye Power an electricity generation and transmission cooperative that provides electricity to 24 distribution companies in Ohio and one in Michigan. Together they serve about 400000 homes and businesses in 77 of Ohio's 88 counties. The company was established by Ohio's rural electric co-ops to produce and transmit electric power for member systems throughout the state. Buckeye Power contracts with other Ohio electric companies to use their transmission systems to transmit power to its member electric distribution cooperatives.

	Annual Growth	06/09	06/10	06/11	06/12	06/18
Sales ($ mil.)	2.9%	–	–	580.7	626.9	708.2
Net income ($ mil.)	4.9%	–	–	32.9	31.2	45.9
Market value ($ mil.)	–	–	–	–	–	–
Employees	–	–	–	–	–	300

BUCKHEAD LIFE RESTAURANT GROUP INC.

265 Pharr Rd.
Atlanta GA 30305-2241
Phone: 404-237-2060
Fax: 404-237-2160
Web: www.buckheadrestaurants.com

CEO: –
CFO: –
HR: –
FYE: December 31
Type: Private

Buckhead Life Restaurant Group is a leading multi-concept dining operator in Atlanta with about a dozen upscale and casual-dining restaurants. Its portfolio includes Pricci and Veni Vidi Vici (Italian cuisine) Kyma (Greek food) and Nava (Southwestern) along with Atlanta Fish Market Chops Lobster Bar and the Buckhead Diner. The company also operates private dining and party destination 103 West. In addition to its locations in Atlanta Buckhead Life has a small number of restaurants in Boca Raton Florida. Owner Pano Karatassos started the restaurant business in 1979.

BUCKLE, INC. (THE)

2407 West 24th Street
Kearney, NE 68845-4915
Phone: 308 236-8491
Fax: –
Web: www.buckle.com

NYS: BKE
CEO: Dennis Nelson
CFO: Thomas Heacock
HR: –
FYE: January 30
Type: Public

The Buckle has done away with the notion that Midwestern kids' fashion sense favors overalls. With nearly 450 mostly mall-based stores in 40-plus states The Buckle sells fashion-conscious 15- to 30-year-olds the clothes they've just got to have. The company retails a variety of clothing items including mid- to higher-priced casual apparel (pants tops and outerwear) shoes and accessories. Its products portfolio boasts such brands as Oakley Fox Hurley Billabong Fossil and American Fighter. The Buckle operates under the names Buckle and The Buckle; it also has an online store. Born in Nebraska in 1948 under the name Mills Clothing the chain has expanded into the South and West.

	Annual Growth	01/17*	02/18	02/19	02/20*	01/21
Sales ($ mil.)	(1.9%)	974.9	913.4	885.5	900.3	901.3
Net income ($ mil.)	7.4%	98.0	89.7	95.6	104.4	130.1
Market value ($ mil.)	17.6%	1,015.3	968.4	858.7	1,206.0	1,942.7
Employees	(4.3%)	8,600	7,400	7,400	7,000	7,200

*Fiscal year change

BUCKNELL UNIVERSITY

1 DENT DR
LEWISBURG, PA 178372029
Phone: 570-577-2000
Fax: –
Web: www.bucknell.edu

CEO: –
CFO: –
HR: –
FYE: June 30
Type: Private

Just getting into Bucknell University is an accomplishment. The highly selective private liberal arts school accepts only about 10% of applicants each year. Students who do get in some 3600 of them from around the world have the option to specialize in more than 50 majors and 60 minors. Bucknell confers both undergraduate and master's degrees in the liberal arts sciences engineering and music. It also offers programs in pre-law and pre-med. Bucknell tuition and fees total more than $58000; more than half of the student body typically receives financial aid. The school's student-to-faculty ratio is 10-to-1.

	Annual Growth	06/17	06/18	06/19	06/20	06/21
Sales ($ mil.)	1.7%	–	240.5	247.2	247.7	253.3
Net income ($ mil.)	56.7%	–	73.4	22.6	(23.3)	282.6
Market value ($ mil.)	–	–	–	–	–	–
Employees	–	–	–	–	–	1,300

BUDGET RENT A CAR SYSTEM INC.

6 Sylvan Way
Parsippany NJ 07054
Phone: 973-496-3500
Fax: 888-304-2315
Web: www.budget.com

CEO: –
CFO: David B Wyshner
HR: –
FYE: December 31
Type: Subsidiary

When your budget won't allow for the fanciest rental car on the lot Budget Rent A Car System might very well have your ride. Budget rents cars through a network of about 1800 locations some 770 of which are company-owned in the Americas and the Asia/Pacific region. The Budget car rental brand is pitched mainly to leisure travelers and the cost-conscious. Together with sister company Avis Rent A Car System the company operates a fleet of more than 400000 rental cars. Affiliate Budget Truck Rental rents some 29000 trucks from about 2550 franchised and company-owned locations in the US. Founded in 1958 Budget Rent A Car System is a unit of Avis Budget Group and accounts for about a third of its sales.

BUFFALO BILLS INC.

1 Bills Dr.
Orchard Park NY 14127
Phone: 716-648-1800
Fax: 716-649-6446
Web: www.buffalobills.com

CEO: Ralph C Wilson Jr
CFO: Jeffrey C Littman
HR: –
FYE: December 31
Type: Private

It doesn't involve horses or gunplay but these Buffalo Bills can put on a wild show for football fans. Buffalo Bills Inc. operates the Buffalo Bills professional football team one of the more storied franchises in the National Football League. A founding member of the American Football League the team made four straight trips to the Super Bowl in the early 1990s but has yet to claim an NFL title. Buffalo has fielded teams with such Hall of Fame talent as OJ Simpson and Jim Kelly. Team owner and Detroit businessman Ralph Wilson founded the franchise in 1960; the Bills joined the NFL in 1970 when the AFL and NFL merged.

BUFFALO WILD WINGS INC

5500 Wayzata Boulevard, Suite 1600
Minneapolis, MN 55416
Phone: 952 593-9943
Fax: –
Web: www.buffalowildwings.com

NMS: BWLD

CEO: Sally J Smith
CFO: Alexander H Ware
HR: –
FYE: December 27
Type: Public

Hot sauce fuels the flight of this restaurateur. Buffalo Wild Wings (BWW) operates a chain of more than 1120 Buffalo Wild Wings Grill & Bar quick-casual dining spots that specialize in serving Buffalo-style chicken wings. The eateries found throughout North America the Philippines and the UAE offer more than a dozen unique dipping sauces to go with the spicy wings as well as a complement of other items such as chicken tenders and legs. BWW's menu also features appetizers burgers tacos salads and desserts along with beer wine and other beverages. The company owns and operates about 515 of the restaurants while the rest are operated by franchisees.

	Annual Growth	12/11	12/12	12/13	12/14	12/15
Sales ($ mil.)	23.3%	784.5	1,040.5	1,266.7	1,516.2	1,812.7
Net income ($ mil.)	17.2%	50.4	57.3	71.6	94.1	95.1
Market value ($ mil.)	24.2%	1,290.9	1,360.9	2,763.5	3,463.5	3,070.0
Employees	20.7%	21,000	25,500	31,700	37,200	44,500

BUILD-A-BEAR WORKSHOP INC

415 South 18th St.
St. Louis, MO 63103
Phone: 314 423-8000
Fax: 314 423-8188
Web: www.buildabear.com

NYS: BBW

CEO: Sharon John
CFO: Vojin Todorovic
HR: –
FYE: January 30
Type: Public

The Build-A-Bear Workshop (BBW) is a multi-channel retailer offering a "make your own stuffed animal" interactive retail-entertainment experience. Located mainly in malls the company's stores allow kids to design their own teddy bears and other stuffed animals complete with clothing shoes and a barrage of accessories. Build-A-Bear founded by Maxine Clark in 1997 boasts about 355 corporately-managed locations including some 305 stores in the US and Canada nearly 50 stores in the UK Ireland and China and about 70 franchised stores operating internationally under the Build-A-Bear Workshop brand. Most of the company's revenue comes from North America.

	Annual Growth	12/17*	02/18	02/19	02/20*	01/21
Sales ($ mil.)	(8.1%)	357.9	30.2	336.6	338.5	255.3
Net income ($ mil.)	–		7.9	(0.8)	(17.9)	0.3	(23.0)
Market value ($ mil.)	(11.6%)	146.6	133.0	73.8	66.6	89.4
Employees	(3.1%)	4,200	–	–	4,300	3,700

*Fiscal year change

BUILDERS FIRSTSOURCE INC.

2001 Bryan Street, Suite 1600
Dallas, TX 75201
Phone: 214 880-3500
Fax: 214 880-3599
Web: www.bldr.com

NYS: BLDR

CEO: David Flitman
CFO: Peter Jackson
HR: –
FYE: December 31
Type: Public

Builders FirstSource supplier and manufacturer of building materials manufactured components and construction services to professional homebuilders sub-contractors remodelers and consumers. It also offers construction-related services. The company's products and services ? which manufactured products include the factory-built roof and floor trusses wall panels and stairs vinyl windows custom millwork and trim as well as engineered wood ?are offered through some 550 locations across roughly 40 US states. Homebuilders such as Pulte Homes and Lennar are among its largest customers. Builders' residential building products industry is driven by the level of activity in both the US residential new construction market and the U.S. residential repair and remodeling market. Builders FirstSource Inc. is a Delaware corporation formed in 1998 as BSL Holdings Inc. In 1999 the name changed to Builders FirstSource Inc.

	Annual Growth	12/16	12/17	12/18	12/19	12/20
Sales ($ mil.)	7.7%	6,367.3	7,034.2	7,724.8	7,280.4	8,558.9
Net income ($ mil.)	21.4%	144.3	38.8	205.2	221.8	313.5
Market value ($ mil.)	38.9%	1,281.6	2,545.7	1,274.6	2,968.6	4,767.8
Employees	16.7%	14,000	15,000	15,000	15,800	26,000

BUILDERS FIRSTSOURCE-SOUTHEAST GROUP LLC

2001 Bryan St. Ste. 1600
Dallas TX 75201
Phone: 214-880-3500
Fax: 214-880-3599
Web: www.buildersfirstsource.com

CEO: –
CFO: –
HR: –
FYE: December 31
Type: Subsidiary

Builders FirstSource-Southeast Group knows the true meaning of bricks and mortar. A subsidiary of Builders FirstSource the regional group manufactures roof and floor trusses wall panels stair parts doors and windows and it distributes these products along with lumber and other building supplies (such as concrete paint and power tools) to new home builders. The company's operations include about 50 manufacturing centers and more than 50 distribution facilities in Alabama Florida Georgia Maryland Tennessee Texas Virginia and the Carolinas. Owned by Builders FirstSource since 1998 the business was originally named Pelican Companies when it was founded in 1947.

BULLDOG SOLUTIONS INC.

7600 N. Capital of Texas Hwy. Bldg. C Ste. 250
Austin TX 78731
Phone: +65-6216-0244
Fax: +65-6223-6635
Web: www.wilmar-international.com

CEO: –
CFO: –
HR: –
FYE: December 31
Type: Private

If dog is man's best friend then Bulldog Solutions is a marketer's best friend. The company helps companies looking to generate revenue by creating custom marketing campaigns including Webinars podcasts white papers e-mail blasts and Web site ads. Bulldog tracks analyzes and breaks down benchmarking data into easy-to-read language and graphs for clients in the financial services health care insurance publishing and telecom industries. Among its major clients are Motorola Solutions Avaya and NetIQ. The firm was founded by CEO Rob Solomon and President Todd Davison.

BULOVA CORPORATION

1 Bulova Ave.
Woodside NY 11377-7874
Phone: 718-204-3300
Fax: 718-204-3546
Web: www.bulova.com

CEO: –
CFO: –
HR: –
FYE: December 31
Type: Subsidiary

Bulova is working to keep perfect time in the watch industry. It sells watches clocks and timepiece parts under brands such as Accutron and Wittnauer (luxury) Bulova and Caravelle (lower-priced) as well as licensed Harley-Davidson and Frank Lloyd Wright styles. Its watches range in price from about $150 to $4495. The firm also sells miniature collectible clocks mostly under the Bulova name and has expanded its licensing efforts to include items such as eyewear. Bulova sells its products primarily through department and jewelry stores mostly in North America (about 90% of sales). Founded in 1875 Bulova is a wholly-owned subsidiary of Japan's Citizen Holdings.

BULOVA TECHNOLOGIES GROUP, INC

NBB: BTGI

1501 Lake Avenue SE
Largo, FL 33771
Phone: 727 536-6666
Fax: –
Web: www.bulovatechgroup.com

CEO: Stephen L Gurba
CFO: Michael J Perfetti
HR: –
FYE: September 30
Type: Public

Bulova Technologies Group believes defense manufacturing and technology is a recipe for business success. Bulova operates in three primary segments: defense contract manufacturing and technologies. Its defense operations provide the DoD with explosive simulators ammunition and pyrotechnic devices as well as integration services. Bulova's contract manufacturing division assembles printed circuit boards and cable assemblies. It sold its BulovaTech Labs which developed and licensed applications for the defense energy and health care markets to Growth Technologies International in 2010. Bulova completed a reverse merger with 3Si Holdings in late 2009 in order to become a publicly traded company.

	Annual Growth	09/13	09/14	09/15	09/16	09/17
Sales ($ mil.)	40.6%	6.4	3.2	1.8	18.7	25.2
Net income ($ mil.)	(53.1%)	11.2	(3.8)	(5.3)	(8.1)	0.5
Market value ($ mil.)	100.0%	0.1	14.0	36.5	1.4	1.6
Employees	–	–	–	–	–	–

BUNGE LTD.

NYS: BG

1391 Timberlake Manor Parkway
St. Louis, MO 63017
Phone: 314 292-2000
Fax: –
Web: www.bunge.com

CEO: –
CFO: –
HR: –
FYE: December 31
Type: Public

Bunge's businesses stretch from the farm field to your local supermarket shelf. A leading integrated agribusiness and food company Bunge produces stores and sells agricultural products such as oilseeds and grains which it turns into vegetable oils and protein meals. Customers include animal feed poultry and aquaculture producers. The agribusiness markets vegetable oils used in the biodiesel industry. The company's edible oil products segment sells packaged oils like shortening and margarine under brands Bunge Pro Floriol and Olek. A sugar and bioenergy unit produces sugar and ethanol which are sold primarily in Brazil. Bunge also mixes and distributes crop fertilizers to farmers in South America.

	Annual Growth	12/16	12/17	12/18	12/19	12/20
Sales ($ mil.)	(0.8%)	42,679.0	45,794.0	45,743.0	41,140.0	41,404.0
Net income ($ mil.)	11.3%	745.0	160.0	267.0	(1,280.0)	1,145.0
Market value ($ mil.)	–	–	–	–	–	–
Employees	(7.9%)	32,000	31,000	31,000	24,000	23,000

BUNGE MILLING INC.

11720 Borman Dr.
St. Louis MO 63146-1000
Phone: 314-292-2000
Fax: 314-292-2533
Web: www.bungemilling.com

CEO: Carl L Hausmann
CFO: –
HR: –
FYE: December 31
Type: Subsidiary

Talk about America's breadbasket. Bunge Milling is definitely in the running as a contender for the title and then some. The company is the largest dry corn miller in the world. It processes wheat corn and soybeans for domestic and import sales. Bunge's products include grits corn flour corn oil bulgar wheat hominy feed soy oil soybean hull pellets and soybean meal and pellets all of which are sold as ingredients to feed manufacturers food processors and the foodservice and bakery industries. The company's five mills are located in Mexico and the US. Bunge Milling is a division of Bunge North America a subsidiary of Bunge Limited.

BURGER KING WORLDWIDE INC.

NYSE: BKW

5505 Blue Lagoon Dr.
Miami FL 33126
Phone: 305-378-3000
Fax: 503-472-1048
Web: www.evergreenaviation.com

CEO: Bernardo Hees
CFO: Daniel S Schwartz
HR: –
FYE: June 30
Type: Private

This king rules one whopper of a fast-food empire. Burger King Worldwide operates the world's #3 hamburger chain by sales (behind McDonald's and Wendy's) with more than 12500 restaurants in the US and more than 80 other countries. In addition to its popular Whopper sandwich the chain offers a selection of burgers chicken sandwiches salads and breakfast items along with beverages desserts and sides. Many of the eateries are stand-alone locations offering dine-in seating and drive-through services; the chain also includes units in high-traffic locations such as airports and shopping malls. Investment firm 3G Capital took the company in private in 2010 before taking it public again in mid-2012.

BURGETT INC.

4111 N. Freeway Blvd.
Sacramento CA 95834
Phone: 916-567-9999
Fax: 916-567-1941
Web: www.pianodisc.com

CEO: Gary Burgett
CFO: Edward Ringgold
HR: –
FYE: December 31
Type: Private

"Program it again Hal" says Burgett maker of player pianos for the 21st century. Doing business as PianoDisc the company makes electronic reproduction systems that enable acoustic pianos to automatically play music ranging from Mozart to Broadway show tunes to Billy Joel. The company's SilentDrive technology controls the piano keys precisely enough to create whisper-soft notes. Its Opus7 wireless playback device stores hours of uninterrupted piano music and can be used from any room in the house. The firm's products are sold through more than 600 distributors in 45 countries. Burgett was founded in 1979 by two brothers co-CEOs Gary and Kirk Burgett who made their first PianoDisc player in 1989.

BURKHART DENTAL SUPPLY CO.

2502 S 78TH ST
TACOMA, WA 984099053
Phone: 253-474-7761
Fax: –
Web: www.burkhartdental.com

CEO: –
CFO: –
HR: –
FYE: December 31
Type: Private

Burkhart Dental Supply is dedicated to supplying dentists with the tools they need. The family-owned company provides dental equipment and supplies to more than 5000 dentists throughout the midwestern southwestern and western US. The company also offers a variety of technical services equipment repairs office management software continuing education financing and consulting services such as office design and equipment planning. It distributes products made by some 100 manufacturers including Dentsply Sirona and Kimberly Clark. Its operating subsidiaries include ADC Group Financial Services Burkhart Consulting and Summit Dental Study Group.

	Annual Growth	12/05	12/06	12/07	12/08	12/09
Sales ($ mil.)	1.0%	–	–	140.1	157.1	142.8
Net income ($ mil.)	14.6%	–	–	1.3	2.1	1.7
Market value ($ mil.)	–	–	–	–	–	–
Employees	–	–	–	–	–	400

BURLINGTON NORTHERN SANTA FE LLC

2650 Lou Menk Dr.
Fort Worth TX 76131-2830
Phone: 817-352-1000
Fax: 817-352-7171
Web: www.bnsf.com

CEO: Kathryn M Farmer
CFO: Julie A Piggott
HR: Denise Kramer
FYE: December 31
Type: Subsidiary

Over the years the number of major US railroads has dwindled but Burlington Northern Santa Fe (BNSF) thrives as one of the survivors. Through its primary subsidiary BNSF Railway the company is one of the largest railroad operators in the US along with rival Union Pacific. BNSF makes tracks through 28 states in the West Midwest and SunBelt regions of the US and in two Canadian provinces. The company operates its trains over a system of about 32000 route miles. Along with its rail operations BNSF generates revenue from its BNSF Logistics unit a provider of transportation management services. Already owning 23% of BNSF Warren Buffett's Berkshire Hathaway bought the remaining 77% stake in February 2010.

BURLINGTON STORES INC

NYS: BURL

2006 Route 130 North
Burlington, NJ 08016
Phone: 609 387-7800
Fax: –
Web: www.burlingtoninvestors.com

CEO: Michael O'Sullivan
CFO: John Crimmins
HR: –
FYE: January 30
Type: Public

Burlington Stores (Burlington) a nationally recognized off-price retailer of high-quality branded apparel at everyday low prices. The clothing retailer which made its name selling coats operates nearly 760 no-frills retail stores offering off-price current brand-name clothing in about 45 states plus Puerto Rico. Although it is one of the nation's largest coat sellers the stores also sell a full wardrobe of products including children's apparel bath items furniture gifts jewelry linens and shoes. Sister chains include a pair of Super Baby Depot stores a higher-priced Cohoes Fashions shop and oneMJM Designer Shoe store. Burlington was founded in 1972.

	Annual Growth	01/17*	02/18	02/19	02/20*	01/21
Sales ($ mil.)	0.8%	5,591.0	6,110.0	6,668.5	7,286.4	5,764.0
Net income ($ mil.)	–	215.9	384.9	414.7	465.1	(216.5)
Market value ($ mil.)	32.4%	5,371.3	7,684.2	11,409.8	14,437.0	16,523.6
Employees	8.8%	40,000	40,000	44,000	47,000	55,959

*Fiscal year change

BURRELL COMMUNICATIONS GROUP LLC

233 N. Michigan Ave.
Chicago IL 60601
Phone: 312-297-9600
Fax: 312-297-9601
Web: www.burrell.com

CEO: McGhee Williams Osse
CFO: Louis Disilvestro
HR: –
FYE: December 31
Type: Private

Corporate America comes to Burrell to get some street cred. Burrell Communications Group specializes in developing advertising and marketing campaigns targeted to African-American consumers and the urban market. It also offers expertise in reaching consumers in the general and youth marketplaces. The advertising agency provides services such as brand consulting account planning public relations event marketing and research in addition to its creative work. Burrell's clients have included McDonald's Procter & Gamble Toyota General Mills Verizon Marriott International Nielsen Media Research and Bacardi. French ad giant Publicis Groupe owns 49% of the shop which was founded by Thomas Burrell in 1971.

BURRILL & COMPANY LLC

1 Embarcadero Center Ste. 2700
San Francisco CA 94111
Phone: 415-591-5400
Fax: 415-591-5401
Web: www.burrillandco.com

CEO: –
CFO: –
HR: –
FYE: December 31
Type: Private

Burrill & Company is banking on biotech. The merchant bank serves only life sciences companies involved in such sectors as biotechnology pharmaceuticals diagnostics drug discovery medical devices and nutraceuticals. The firm works with life sciences companies seeking strategic partners mergers acquisitions or financing. It also helps larger companies spin off divisions or technology. Burrill helps steer the industry's growth through its venture capital funds which have more than $1 billion under management. The company also makes private equity investments. Its international arm seeks investments and merchant banking business in developing economies such as China India and Russia.

BURROUGHS & CHAPIN COMPANY INC.

2411 N. Oak St.
Myrtle Beach SC 29577
Phone: 843-448-5123
Fax: 843-448-9838
Web: burroughschapin.com

CEO: James W Apple Jr
CFO: J Bratton Fennell
HR: –
FYE: December 31
Type: Private

Burroughs & Chapin believes in family values and property values. A top land developer in the Myrtle Beach South Carolina area the company owns more than 40 commercial resort recreational and hospitality developments. Its portfolio includes malls strip centers hotels both championship and miniature golf courses land and family-friendly developments such as shopping and recreation venue Broadway at the Beach and Myrtle Waves Water Park. Subsidiary Prudential Burroughs & Chapin Realty a partnership with Prudential Real Estate provides real estate brokerage sales relocation and residential development services in coastal portions of North and South Carolina.

BURSON-MARSTELLER INC.

230 Park Ave. South
New York NY 10003-1556
Phone: 212-614-4000
Fax: 212-598-5407
Web: www.bm.com

CEO: –
CFO: –
HR: –
FYE: December 31
Type: Subsidiary

Burson-Marsteller is a one-stop shop for public relations services. It offers a range of related services including advertising brand building investor and media relations crisis management and Internet strategy and Web development. Serving such clients as SmithKline Beecham American Airlines and Champion Enterprises in the past the company operates through more than 130 offices (including affiliates) in almost 100 countries. Burson-Marsteller was established in 1953 by Harold Burson and Bill Marsteller and joined the Young & Rubicam group of companies in 1979. Young & Rubicam is a subsidiary of media services conglomerate WPP Group.

BURST MEDIA CORPORATION

8 New England Executive Park
Burlington MA 01803
Phone: 781-272-5544
Fax: 434-817-1010
Web: www.crutchfield.com

CEO: –
CFO: –
HR: –
FYE: March 31
Type: Subsidiary

Burst Media helps advertisers reach nearly one in five Web surfers with interests ranging from art to real estate. It sells advertising based on its network of more than 130 million unique users. It offers advertising packages that cover the whole network and smaller packages focusing on a specific category or a few selected sites. Burst Media's AdConductor software automates a variety of services including inventory management ad performance reporting and ad delivery. The company also operates a targeted e-mail delivery service. In May 2011 Burst Media was acquired by blinkx a provider of video search engine services that searches the Web for video clips.

BURTON LUMBER & HARDWARE CO.

1170 S 4400 W
SALT LAKE CITY, UT 841044413
Phone: 801-952-3700
Fax: –
Web: www.burtonlumber.com

CEO: –
CFO: –
HR: –
FYE: December 31
Type: Private

Family-owned-and-run Burton Lumber & Hardware designs makes and installs truss and floor packages wall panels and doors (interior and exterior) from its facility in Salt Lake City. It also sells and installs Heatilator-brand fireplaces and building materials made by Trex James Hardie and other companies. Burton Lumber & Hardware operates half a dozen locations in Utah and offers delivery services throughout the state. Its customers have included contractors home builders and government agencies. The company was founded in 1911 by Willard C. Burton.

	Annual Growth	12/13	12/14	12/15	12/16	12/17
Sales ($ mil.)	13.0%	–	131.2	137.5	167.7	189.5
Net income ($ mil.)	26.3%	–	8.8	9.1	13.4	17.7
Market value ($ mil.)	–	–	–	–	–	–
Employees	–	–	–	–	–	250

BUSH INDUSTRIES INC.

1 Mason Dr.
Jamestown NY 14702-0460
Phone: 716-665-2000
Fax: 716-665-2510
Web: www.bushindustries.com

CEO: Mike Evans
CFO: Neil A Frederick
HR: Kim Tatoian
FYE: December 31
Type: Private

Bush Industries is jockeying for a permanent seat in the ready-to-assemble (RTA) furniture industry. A leading maker of furniture for homes and offices the company sells its products worldwide with the help of about 10000 retail outlets including furniture and department stores electronics and office product retailers and mass merchandisers. It boasts two operating divisions: Bush Furniture (which sells through retail and ecommerce channels) and BBF (named Bush Business Furniture until 2010). The company's European business operates under the Rohr banner. Founded by the Bush family in 1959 the furniture maker is owned by a group led by DDJ Capital Management and JPMorgan Chase Bank.

BUSHNELL INC.

9200 Cody St.
Overland Park KS 66214
Phone: 913-752-3400
Fax: 913-752-6112
Web: www.bushnell.com/

CEO: –
CFO: Stephen M Nolan
HR: –
FYE: December 31
Type: Private

Bushnell is one highly focused firm. Also known as Bushnell Outdoor Products the company makes binoculars riflescopes laser-guided rangefinders night vision items trail cameras and other high-end optical equipment. It also produces performance eyewear and has a licensing agreement with Bausch & Lomb (which sold Bushnell in the mid-'90s). The firm's brand portfolio includes Bushnell Bolle Butler Creek Cebe Hoppe's Serengeti Stoney Point Tasco and Uncle Mike's. Bushnell operates offices in the US Canada France Hong Kong and Australia and its products are distributed to more than 25 countries. Established in 1948 the company today is owned by private equity firm MidOcean Partners.

BUSKEN BAKERY INC.

650 WALNUT ST DOWNTOWN
CINCINNATI, OH 45202
Phone: 513-871-2114
Fax: –
Web: www.busken.com

CEO: D Page Busken
CFO: –
HR: –
FYE: December 26
Type: Private

Fans of schnecken can make a connection at these bakery stores. Busken Bakery operates a dozen bakery stores in the Cincinnati area known for schnecken a kind of cinnamon roll that is a regional favorite. The bakeries also make cookies coffee cakes and pies as well as donuts muffins several varieties of bread and custom-made cakes. Its products are also sold through Remke Markets a regional supermarket chain. In addition Busken Bakery offers catering services and provides baked goods for fundraising efforts. Joe Busken Sr. started the family-owned company in 1928.

	Annual Growth	12/04	12/05	12/06	12/08	12/09
Sales ($ mil.)	(82.8%)	–	–	2,057.5	10.7	10.4
Net income ($ mil.)	635.5%	–	–	0.0	0.1	0.1
Market value ($ mil.)	–	–	–	–	–	–
Employees	–	–	–	–	–	175

BUSY BEAVER BUILDING CENTERS INC.

3130 WILLIAM PITT WAY
PITTSBURGH, PA 152381360
Phone: 412-828-2323
Fax: –
Web: www.busybeaver.com

CEO: Frank Filmelk
CFO: –
HR: –
FYE: December 29
Type: Private

|They're busy as well you know what kind of animals at Busy Beaver Building Centers. The company has 15 stores in Ohio Pennsylvania and West Virginia selling ceilings flooring lumber plumbing fixtures and other building materials along with garden supplies hardware power equipment and tools. Busy Beaver serves the professional contractor as well as the do-it-yourselfer. The regional home improvement center chain was founded in 1962. A management group led by chairman and former CEO Charles Bender acquired the company in 1988 and now owns about one-quarter of Busy Beaver which is facing heavyweight competition from big-box chains such as Home Depot and Lowe's.

	Annual Growth	12/09	12/10	12/11	12/12	12/13
Sales ($ mil.)	(1.0%)	–	41.5	40.8	40.4	40.2
Net income ($ mil.)	(86.0%)	–	–	0.4	0.3	0.0
Market value ($ mil.)	–	–	–	–	–	–
Employees		–	–	–	–	350

BUTLER HEALTH SYSTEM, INC.

1 HOSPITAL WAY
BUTLER, PA 160014670
Phone: 724-283-6666
Fax: –
Web: www.butlerhealthsystem.org

CEO: Ken Defurio
CFO: Anne Krebs
HR: –
FYE: June 30
Type: Private

Butler Health System (BHS) ushers in health care services for Pennsylvania residents. The not-for-profit provider operates a network of inpatient and outpatient health care facilities. Its primary location is the 300-bed Butler Memorial Hospital which provides general surgical and medical care and specialty programs for the treatment of women's health behavioral health cancer pain management and other conditions. Other BHS locations include diagnostic family practice urgent care and specialist facilities.

	Annual Growth	06/04	06/05	06/10	06/15	06/16
Sales ($ mil.)	(3.2%)	–	366.5	0.0	240.8	255.7
Net income ($ mil.)	14.9%	–	9.6	0.0	12.9	44.3
Market value ($ mil.)	–	–	–	–	–	–
Employees	–	–	–	–	–	3,000

BUTLER MANUFACTURING COMPANY

1540 Genessee St.
Kansas City MO 64102
Phone: 816-968-3000
Fax: 816-968-3279
Web: www.butlermfg.com

CEO: –
CFO: –
HR: –
FYE: December 31
Type: Subsidiary

Need an eight-story building fast? Not a problem for Butler Manufacturing maker of pre-engineered buildings structural systems and roof and wall systems for non-residential construction. A subsidiary of Australia-based BlueScope Steel Butler produces pre-engineered and custom-designed steel structures used in a range of projects from offices to schools to shopping centers. Through its BUCON and Butler Heavy Structures units the company provides general contracting services for large-scale projects. Butler also offers real estate development services. It distributes its products throughout North America.

BUTLER NATIONAL CORP.

NBB: BUKS

19920 West 161st Street
Olathe, KS 66062
Phone: 913 780-9595
Fax: –
Web: www.butlernational.com

CEO: Clark Stewart
CFO: Tad McMahon
HR: –
FYE: April 30
Type: Public

This Butler is at the service of aircraft operators. Butler National's Avcon subsidiary (over half of sales) provides aircraft modification services including the conversion of passenger planes to freighters. The company works mainly on Learjet models; it also modifies Beechcraft Cessna and Dassault Falcon aircraft. It adds aerial photography capability to aircraft and offers stability enhancements. The company's avionics unit makes airborne electronic switching components. Other Butler National businesses provide remote water and wastewater monitoring (SCADA Systems) and architectural services (BCS Design) as well as gaming management services to Indian tribes (Butler National Service Corporation; BNSC).

	Annual Growth	04/17	04/18	04/19	04/20	04/21
Sales ($ mil.)	5.0%	50.6	48.3	58.7	65.9	61.5
Net income ($ mil.)	(1.7%)	1.5	0.3	3.9	4.2	1.4
Market value ($ mil.)	17.0%	24.1	18.8	30.1	38.4	45.2
Employees	(23.7%)	349	342	349	114	118

BUZZI UNICEM USA INC.

100 Brodhead Rd.
Bethlehem PA 18017-8989
Phone: 610-882-5000
Fax: 610-866-9430
Web: www.buzziunicemusa.com

CEO: Massimo Toso
CFO: –
HR: –
FYE: December 31
Type: Subsidiary

Buzzi Unicem USA has a concrete goal — to secure a top market spot in US cement manufacturing. The company produces portland and masonry cement and ready-mix concrete used in highway and airport paving and concrete block manufacturing. It runs more than half a dozen cement plants with an annual production capacity of about 8.5 million metric tons and about 30 terminals from which it distributes its products mainly throughout the Midwest Northeast and Southeast. Formed out of the merger of RC Cement and Dyckerhoff's Lone Star Industries Buzzi Unicem USA is a subsidiary of Italy-based BUZZI UNICEM.

BWAY HOLDING COMPANY

8607 Roberts Dr. Ste. 250
Atlanta GA 30350
Phone: 770-645-4800
Fax: 770-645-4810
Web: www.bwaycorp.com

CEO: Kenneth M Roessler
CFO: Michael Clauer
HR: –
FYE: September 30
Type: Private

Trouble containing yourself? BWAY Holding may be of some help. The company manufactures and distributes metal containers from aerosol cans to paint cans steel pails and specialty boxes. It also makes rigid plastic pails drums and other blow-molded containers. BWAY products are used to pack industrial and consumer goods including ammunition deck sealants personal care items and food. Core subsidiaries are BWAY Packaging (metal containers) ICL Industrial Containers (pails) and NAMPAC Packaging (plastic containers). In late 2012 its parent company was acquired by an affiliate of Platinum Equity for approximately $1.24 billion.

BWX TECHNOLOGIES INC
NYS: BWXT

800 Main Street, 4th Floor
Lynchburg, VA 24504
Phone: 980 365-4300
Fax: –

CEO: Rex Geveden
CFO: Robb Lemasters
HR: –
FYE: December 31
Type: Public

BWX Technologies is a specialty manufacturer of nuclear components a developer of nuclear technologies and a service provider with an operating history of more than 100 years. Its core businesses focus on the design engineering and manufacture of precision naval nuclear components reactors and nuclear fuel for the US government. It also provides precision manufactured components nuclear fuel and services to the commercial nuclear industry and provides special nuclear materials processing environmental site restoration services and a variety of products and services to customers in the critical medical radioisotopes and radiopharmaceuticals industries. US government agencies are its largest customers. Additionally the US is responsible for about 85% of the sales. The company was founded in 1867.

	Annual Growth	12/16	12/17	12/18	12/19	12/20
Sales ($ mil.)	8.2%	1,550.6	1,687.7	1,799.9	1,894.9	2,123.5
Net income ($ mil.)	11.1%	183.1	147.8	227.0	244.1	278.7
Market value ($ mil.)	11.0%	3,783.8	5,765.3	3,643.7	5,916.9	5,745.3
Employees	3.2%	5,900	6,100	6,250	6,450	6,700

BYCOR GENERAL CONTRACTORS, INC.

6490 MARINDUSTRY DR STE A
SAN DIEGO, CA 921215297
Phone: 858-587-1901
Fax: –
Web: www.bycor.com

CEO: Scott Kaats
CFO: –
HR: –
FYE: December 31
Type: Private

Bycor General Contractors provides construction services for a variety of commercial retail institutional civic and leisure facilities in the San Diego area. Its offerings include tenant improvements shell construction build-to-suit and LEED-certified services and projects range from church sanctuaries to auto dealerships. The company has served clients including Western University of Health Sciences Northrop Grumman and San Diego National Bank. President Rich Byer CEO Scott Kaats and Van Smith founded co-founded Bycor General Contractors in 1981.

	Annual Growth	12/15	12/16	12/17	12/18	12/19
Sales ($ mil.)	7.5%	–	106.1	89.1	134.4	131.8
Net income ($ mil.)	2.6%	–	4.9	2.8	5.8	5.3
Market value ($ mil.)	–	–	–	–	–	–
Employees	–	–	–	–	–	90

C & F FINANCIAL CORP.
NMS: CFFI

3600 La Grange Parkway
Toano, VA 23168
Phone: 804 843-2360
Fax: 804 843-3017
Web: www.cffc.com

CEO: Thomas Cherry
CFO: Jason Long
HR: –
FYE: December 31
Type: Public

C&F Financial Corporation is the holding company for C&F Bank (aka Citizens and Farmers Bank) which operates about 20 branches in eastern Virginia. The bank targets individuals and local businesses offering such products and services as checking and savings accounts CDs credit cards and trust services. Commercial industrial and agricultural loans account for the largest portion of the company's loan portfolio (about 40%) which also includes residential mortgages consumer auto loans and consumer and construction loans.

	Annual Growth	12/16	12/17	12/18	12/19	12/20
Assets ($ mil.)	9.5%	1,452.0	1,509.1	1,521.4	1,657.4	2,086.3
Net income ($ mil.)	13.2%	13.5	6.6	18.0	18.9	22.1
Market value ($ mil.)	(7.1%)	183.0	212.9	195.3	203.1	136.2
Employees	2.3%	636	650	634	643	697

C & K MARKET, INC.

850 OHARE PKWY STE 100
MEDFORD, OR 975047720
Phone: 541-469-3113
Fax: –
Web: www.ckmarket.com

CEO: Karl Wissmann
CFO: David D Doty
HR: –
FYE: December 31
Type: Private

Family-owned C&K Market operates more than 40 supermarkets in southern Oregon and northern California mostly under the name Ray's Food Place but also under Shop Smart and C&K banners. The Shop Smart warehouse-style stores focus on value-priced groceries and household goods. Most of C&K's stores are situated in small rural communities. C&K Market was founded in 1957 by Raymond "Ray" Nidiffer. Stung by competition from large national discounters including Wal-Mart and Costco the regional chain filed for bankruptcy in late 2013 and closed 15 supermarkets and sold 15 pharmacies. It emerged from bankruptcy in 2014.

	Annual Growth	12/05	12/06	12/07	12/09	12/10
Sales ($ mil.)	(1.6%)	–	–	479.3	467.0	457.1
Net income ($ mil.)	245.6%	–	–	0.1	5.2	3.5
Market value ($ mil.)	–	–	–	–	–	–
Employees	–	–	–	–	–	2,000

C&A INDUSTRIES INC.

C & A Plaza 13609 California St. Ste. 500
Omaha NE 68154
Phone: 402-891-0009
Fax: 402-891-9461
Web: www.ca-industries.com

CEO: Scott Thompson
CFO: Mike Morgan
HR: –
FYE: December 31
Type: Private

C&A Industries provides staffing services in areas such as finance medicine engineering and administration to clients in the Midwest and elsewhere in the US. The company is made up of Aureus Group (specialty divisions offering staffing services in health care executive recruiting finance IT and travel) AurStaff (industrial and technical staffing) and Celebrity Staffing (administrative managerial and office support staffing). In addition the company has several community outreach units aimed at serving the Nebraska area.

C&D ZODIAC INC.

5701 Bolsa Ave.
Huntington Beach CA 92647
Phone: 714-934-0000
Fax: 714-934-0088
Web: zodiac.com/

CEO: Christophe Bernardini
CFO: Jeff Henry
HR: –
FYE: December 31
Type: Subsidiary

Without companies like C&D Zodiac air passengers would tumble around in cavernous flying tubes. The company makes the storage bins that people insist on levering trunk-sized objects into the seats from which your invariably large and bathroom-visiting seatmates invade your space the overhead panels that pinlight your book and keep you cool(ish) the phone-booth-sized lavatories the oft-maligned (and now seldom-used) galleys the ceiling panels you pray to in rough weather and the sidewalls you lean your head against when weary. Thank goodness C&D also makes upgrade and retrofit security kits for cockpit doors. The company is part of the cabin interiors business of France-based Zodiac.

C&S WHOLESALE GROCERS INC.

7 Corporate Dr.
Keene NH 03431
Phone: 603-354-7000
Fax: 661-861-9870
Web: www.calcot.com

CEO: –
CFO: Kevin McNamara
HR: –
FYE: September 30
Type: Private

C&S Wholesale Grocers is at the bottom of the food chain — and likes it that way. The company is the second-largest wholesale grocery distributor in the US (after SUPERVALU) supplying goods to some 3900 independent and major supermarkets (including A&P and Safeway) mass marketers and wholesale clubs. C&S Wholesale which serves about a dozen states (from Vermont to Hawaii) distributes more than 95000 food and nonfood items. Its ES3 logistics unit provides warehousing and supply-chain management services. The grocery distributor is exiting the food retail business with the sale of its Grand Union and Southern Family Markets chains in 2012. Israel Cohen started the company with Abraham Siegel in 1918.

C.H. GUENTHER & SON INC.

129 E. Guenther St.
San Antonio TX 78204
Phone: 210-227-1401
Fax: 210-227-1409
Web: www.chguenther.com

CEO: Dale W Tremblay
CFO: Janelle M Sykes
HR: –
FYE: April 30
Type: Private

Business is a grind for C.H. Guenther & Son; the flourmill produces the Pioneer brand of pancake biscuit and gravy mixes as well as the White Wings Peter Pan and Morrison brand name fours tortilla mixes and ready-to-eat tortillas used in homes restaurants and commercial kitchens across the US. Guenther also makes frozen bakery products to supply McDonalds Burger King and other customers in the foodservice industry. In addition the family-owned company operates The Guenther House home of founder Carl Hilmar Guenther restored as a restaurant museum and gift shop located in San Antonio Texas. C.H. Guenther & Son was started in Fredericksburg Texas in 1951.

C. B. FLEET COMPANY INCORPORATED

4615 MURRAY PL
LYNCHBURG, VA 24502-2235
Phone: 434-528-4000
Fax: –
Web: www.fleetlabs.com

CEO: Jeffrey R Rowan
CFO: Robert Lemon
HR: –
FYE: December 31
Type: Private

Some of C.B. Fleet's products are tucked away in medicine cabinets worldwide for those times of need. Established as a small family-run pharmacy in 1869 by Dr. Charles Browne Fleet today the company makes about 100 personal health and beauty care products that are distributed to more than 100 countries globally. C.B. Fleet's products include feminine care laxatives oral care skin care and oral rehydration product lines sold under brand names Summer's Eve Vera by CCS Norforms Clinomyn Oliva by CCS BioralSuero and Casen-Fleet among others. It also operates several subsidiaries such as CSS (Europe) DeWitt Personal Care (the UK) and Fleet Laboratories (Asia and Latin America).

	Annual Growth	12/04	12/05	12/06	12/07	12/08
Sales ($ mil.)	2.9%	–	213.7	223.9	235.4	232.6
Net income ($ mil.)	–	–	9.9	21.3	13.6	(2.1)
Market value ($ mil.)	–	–	–	–	–	–
Employees	–	–	–	–	–	696

C.R. ENGLAND, INC.

4701 W 2100 S
SALT LAKE CITY, UT 841201223
Phone: 800-421-9004
Fax: –
Web: www.crengland.com

CEO: Chad England
CFO: Tj McGeean
HR: –
FYE: December 31
Type: Private

The world's top refrigerated trucking company and one of North America's largest transportation firms C.R. England hauls refrigerated and dry cargo throughout the US. The family-owned company also serves parts of Canada and through alliances points in Mexico. C.R. England's fleet includes more than 3500 Freightliner Peterbilt Volvo and International tractors and 8000 trailers. Besides for-hire freight hauling C.R. England offers dedicated contract carriage in which drivers and equipment are assigned to a customer long-term; logistics services including freight brokerage; and intermodal railroad service.

	Annual Growth	12/05	12/06	12/07	12/11	12/12
Sales ($ mil.)	13.7%	–	–	829.8	1,315.3	1,579.3
Net income ($ mil.)	6.2%	–	–	41.8	55.9	56.5
Market value ($ mil.)	–	–	–	–	–	–
Employees	–	–	–	–	–	6,500

C.D. SMITH CONSTRUCTION INC.

889 E JOHNSON ST
FOND DU LAC, WI 549352933
Phone: 920-924-2900
Fax: –
Web: www.cdsmith.com

CEO: –
CFO: Robert Baker
HR: –
FYE: September 30
Type: Private

One of the Midwest's top contractors C.D. Smith Construction works on commercial institutional and industrial projects. It builds manufacturing retail correctional health care and education facilities as well as water treatment plants. The company offers general contracting and design/build services and also provides specialty contracting services such as steel erection masonry and concrete work carpentry and demolition. Charles D. Smith grandfather of president Gary Smith founded the company in 1936.

	Annual Growth	09/09	09/10	09/11	09/12	09/13
Sales ($ mil.)	–	–	0.0	0.0	252.1	252.1
Net income ($ mil.)	–	–	–	0.0	0.0	0.0
Market value ($ mil.)	–	–	–	–	–	–
Employees	–	–	–	–	–	440

CA INC

NMS: CA

520 Madison Avenue
New York, NY 10022
Phone: 631 342-3550
Fax: 631 342-6800
Web: www.ca.com

CEO: Michael P Gregoire
CFO: Kieran J McGrath
HR: –
FYE: March 31
Type: Public

Once known as Computer Associates CA Technologies is becoming known as Computer Apps. One of the world's largest software companies CA provides tools for managing networks databases applications storage security and other systems. Primarily serving large enterprises its applications work across both mainframes and cloud computing environments. It current focus is on developing applications for cloud and mobile computing and DevOps (development operations). Most of its software license sales come from subscriptions. The company also offers consulting implementation and training services. It sells worldwide to businesses government agencies and schools directly and through resellers.

	Annual Growth	03/13	03/14	03/15	03/16	03/17
Sales ($ mil.)	(3.4%)	4,643.0	4,515.0	4,262.0	4,025.0	4,036.0
Net income ($ mil.)	(5.1%)	955.0	914.0	846.0	783.0	775.0
Market value ($ mil.)	5.9%	10,409.6	12,807.4	13,481.3	12,728.9	13,113.3
Employees	(3.5%)	13,600	12,700	11,600	11,000	11,800

CABELA'S INC   NYS: CAB

One Cabela Drive
Sidney, NE 69160
Phone: 308 254-5505
Fax: –
Web: www.cabelas.com

CEO: Thomas L Millner
CFO: Ralph W Castner
HR: –
FYE: December 31
Type: Public

Cabela is a major seller of outdoor sporting goods that operates more than 75 stores in 35-plus US states plus nine stores in Canada. Located mainly in the Midwest the stores are as big as 247000 sq. ft. and include such features as waterfalls mountain replicas aquariums in-store shooting galleries and banquet and meeting facilities. Cabela's sells footwear clothing and gear for fishing hunting camping and other outdoor activities. Cabela's also mails more than 132 million catalogs each year sells magazines and merchandise online and has an outdoors show on television. Cabela's was founded in 1961 by chairman Dick Cabela and his younger brother Jim. In 2016 the company agreed to be acquired by rival Bass Pro Shops for $65.50 per share or $5.5 billion.

	Annual Growth	12/12	12/13	12/14*	01/16*	12/16
Sales ($ mil.)	7.3%	3,112.7	3,599.6	3,647.7	3,997.7	4,129.4
Net income ($ mil.)	(4.1%)	173.5	224.4	201.7	189.3	146.9
Market value ($ mil.)	9.5%	2,790.8	4,496.5	3,524.4	3,201.1	4,010.8
Employees	5.9%	15,200	16,400	19,300	19,700	19,100

*Fiscal year change

CABLE MANUFACTURING AND ASSEMBLY CO. INC.

10896 Industrial Pkwy. NW
Bolivar OH 44612
Phone: 330-874-2900
Fax: 330-874-2373
Web: www.cmacable.com

CEO: Daniel Pappano
CFO: Nicholas Hoff
HR: Beth Carpenter
FYE: June 30
Type: Private

Cable Manufacturing and Assembly — the name says it all. The company designs and manufactures cable (metal polymer and carbon fiber) for industrial and commercial uses. Its products include mechanical cable assemblies in a wide range of galvanized stainless steel and its proprietary PlastiCable in diameters of 1/32 inches to 3/8 inches and miniature stainless steel mechanical cable assemblies in diameters from .006 inches to .045 inches. Cable Manufacturing and Assembly also offers a wide range of actuators custom cable controls and operators for the remote operation of latches catches mechanisms and locking gas springs. The company has facilities in the US and Mexico.

CABLE NEWS NETWORK INC.

1 CNN Center
Atlanta GA 30348
Phone: 404-827-1700
Fax: 404-827-1099
Web: www.cnn.com

CEO: Tom Johnson
CFO: Wayne H Pace
HR: –
FYE: December 31
Type: Subsidiary

Whether it's reporting on the news or just talking about it this network does both all day long. Cable News Network (CNN) operates one of the top 24-hour news channels reaching more than 100 million US homes. In addition to its flagship channel the company offers HLN (formerly CNN Headline News) and it has an international division that keeps viewers informed in nearly 200 other countries. CNN has about 45 news bureaus around the world including 15 in the US. Away from the television CNN operates the top-ranked CNN.com news website and it offers syndicated news services. Founded in 1980 by cable broadcasting pioneer Ted Turner CNN operates as part of Time Warner's Turner Broadcasting division.

CABLE ONE INC   NYS: CABO

210 E. Earll Drive
Phoenix, AZ 85012
Phone: 602 364-6000
Fax: –
Web: www.cableone.net

CEO: Julia Laulis
CFO: Steven Cochran
HR: –
FYE: December 31
Type: Public

Sparklight (formerly Cable ONE) gives small-town folk CNN and The Cartoon Network. The company provides cable television service primarily to non- metropolitan secondary and tertiary markets. Its core service areas are the Gulf Coast region and Boise Idaho. Approximately 773000 subscribers receive data services from Sparklight some 314000 subscribers to video services and around 139000 subscribers to voice services. The company also offers voice-over-Internet-protocol (VoIP) computer telephony and digital video services. Quarter-fifth of revenue comes from Residential. In 2019 the company rebrand its business as Sparklight.

	Annual Growth	12/16	12/17	12/18	12/19	12/20
Sales ($ mil.)	12.8%	819.6	960.0	1,072.3	1,168.0	1,325.2
Net income ($ mil.)	32.4%	98.9	234.0	164.8	178.6	304.4
Market value ($ mil.)	37.6%	3,747.6	4,239.6	4,943.3	8,972.1	13,428.0
Employees	9.7%	1,877	2,310	2,224	2,751	2,716

CABLEVISION SYSTEMS CORP.   NYS: CVC

1111 Stewart Avenue
Bethpage, NY 11714
Phone: 516 803-2300
Fax: –
Web: www.cablevision.com

CEO: –
CFO: –
HR: –
FYE: December 31
Type: Public

Cablevision Systems is a leading provider of digital television phone and Internet services in the New York City metropolitan area. Through its Optimum brand the company serves nearly 3 million subscribers who receive at least one of the services. It also provides voice data and managed technology services to commercial customers through Cablevision Lightpath. Other operations include newspaper publishing (NYC's Newsday and community papers) regional news and sports networks and cable television advertising. Cablevision agreed to be bought by Altice a telecommunications company based in France. The $17.7 billion deal reached in 2015 was expected to face regulatory scrutiny.

	Annual Growth	12/10	12/11	12/12	12/13	12/14
Sales ($ mil.)	(2.8%)	7,231.2	6,700.8	6,705.5	6,232.2	6,460.9
Net income ($ mil.)	(3.6%)	360.9	291.9	233.5	465.7	311.4
Market value ($ mil.)	(11.6%)	9,284.3	3,901.4	4,098.9	4,919.2	5,662.7
Employees	(5.9%)	19,065	17,815	18,889	15,369	14,968

CABLEXPRESS CORPORATION

5404 S BAY RD
SYRACUSE, NY 132123885
Phone: 315-476-3000
Fax: –
Web: www.cxtec.com

CEO: Peter E Belyea
CFO: Barbara Ashkin
HR: –
FYE: December 31
Type: Private

CABLExpress (dba CXtec) is hard wired for hardware. The company sells new and refurbished computer and communications equipment such as networking hardware phone systems and accessories storage products cables and media converters. It also provides such services as asset recovery consulting project management systems integration and technical support. CXtec distributes its products primarily in North America and serves various sectors including education financial services government and health care. The company sells products made by the likes of 3Com and Hewlett-Packard. CEO William Pomeroy founded the company from his home in 1978 as a distributor of used IBM mainframe cables and computer parts.

	Annual Growth	12/09	12/10	12/12	12/13	12/14
Sales ($ mil.)	5.1%	–	61.7	68.2	75.3	75.3
Net income ($ mil.)	–	–	–	0.0	0.0	0.0	0.0
Market value ($ mil.)	–	–	–	–	–	–
Employees	–	–	–	–	–	340

CABOT CORP.
NYS: CBT

Two Seaport Lane
Boston, MA 02210-2019
Phone: 617 345-0100
Fax: –
Web: www.cabotcorp.com

CEO: Sean Keohane
CFO: Erica Mclaughlin
HR: –
FYE: September 30
Type: Public

Cabot is a global specialty chemicals and performance materials company. The company is a leading maker of carbon black a compound that strengthens tires hoses belts and molded products. It also makes specialty carbons and metal oxides used in automotive construction infrastructure and energy applications. Cabot's activated carbon products are used to purify air and water and food and beverages. One of the few carbon black manufacturers with a worldwide presence Cabot's biggest market is China. The company goes back to 1882 when Godfrey and Samuel Cabot opened a carbon black plant in Pennsylvania.

	Annual Growth	09/17	09/18	09/19	09/20	09/21
Sales ($ mil.)	5.8%	2,717.0	3,242.0	3,337.0	2,614.0	3,409.0
Net income ($ mil.)	0.9%	241.0	(113.0)	157.0	(238.0)	250.0
Market value ($ mil.)	(2.6%)	3,165.4	3,557.9	2,570.9	2,043.9	2,843.1
Employees	0.0%	4,500	4,600	4,500	4,500	4,500

CACHE INC
NMS: CACH

256 West 38th Street
New York, NY 10018
Phone: 212 575-3200
Fax: –
Web: www.cache.com

CEO: Jay Margolis
CFO: Anthony F Dipippa
HR: –
FYE: December 28
Type: Public

Cach © sells fashions — from ball gowns to blue jeans — that bring cachet to the soir ©e. The upscale women's apparel retailer owns and operates about 280 specialty stores in shopping malls in 40-plus US states Puerto Rico and the US Virgin Islands under the Cach © and Cach © Luxe banners as well as an online shopping site. Sportswear including casual wear collections and separates accounts for more than 55% of apparel sales. The retailer courts women ages 25 to 45 with its own brand of apparel and accessories in a boutique-like atmosphere. (Stores average about 2000 square feet.) The firm buys its merchandise primarily from domestic suppliers but it has begun to source more overseas.

	Annual Growth	01/10	01/11*	12/11	12/12	12/13
Sales ($ mil.)	(0.5%)	219.8	206.5	223.9	224.2	216.7
Net income ($ mil.)	–	(8.7)	(22.4)	2.1	(12.1)	(34.4)
Market value ($ mil.)	5.8%	98.4	95.6	133.3	52.1	116.5
Employees	5.6%	2,250	2,204	3,156	2,735	2,652

*Fiscal year change

CACI INTERNATIONAL INC
NYS: CACI

12021 Sunset Hills Road
Reston, VA 20190
Phone: 703 841-7800
Fax: 703 841-7882
Web: www.caci.com

CEO: John Mengucci
CFO: Thomas Mutryn
HR: –
FYE: June 30
Type: Public

CACI International Inc (CACI) is a provider of information technology solutions and services. It provides business systems command and control communications cyber security intelligence services enterprise information technology and investigation and litigation support. CACI serves to the US Department of Defense (DoD) government and commercial markets. It also offers solutions and services for intelligence defense and federal civilian customers in support of government transformation and national security missions. The company operates through offices and subsidiaries in North America and Europe. CACI is headquartered in Arlington Virginia. Majority of the company's sales were generated in the US.

	Annual Growth	06/17	06/18	06/19	06/20	06/21
Sales ($ mil.)	8.5%	4,354.6	4,467.9	4,986.3	5,720.0	6,044.1
Net income ($ mil.)	29.3%	163.7	301.2	265.6	321.5	457.4
Market value ($ mil.)	19.5%	2,945.4	3,970.0	4,818.9	5,108.4	6,009.1
Employees	4.3%	18,600	18,800	22,100	22,900	22,000

CACTUS FEEDERS INC.

2209 W. 7th St.
Amarillo TX 79106
Phone: 806-373-2333
Fax: 806-371-4767
Web: www.cactusfeeders.com

CEO: –
CFO: Matt Forrester
HR: Andy Etheredge
FYE: October 31
Type: Private

Cactus Feeders founder and chairman Paul Engler may operate one of the world's largest cattle feedlot businesses but he was no match for Oprah Winfrey. Cactus Feeders operates 10 feedlots with a capacity of some 520000 head of cattle which it beefs up and sells to meat packers. The company's feedyards are located in Texas and Kansas. It also provides market analysis marketing services Cactus Feeders offers financing for its rancher/suppliers. Oh and about Oprah Engler and other cattle ranchers unsuccessfully sued Winfrey and a guest after a 1996 broadcast of Winfrey's TV program The Oprah Show disparaged the beef industry.

CADENCE BANK
NYS: CADE

One Mississippi Plaza, 201 South Spring Street
Tupelo, MS 38804
Phone: 662 680-2000
Fax: –
Web: www.bancorpsouth.com

CEO: –
CFO: –
HR: –
FYE: December 31
Type: Public

Like Elvis Presley BancorpSouth has grown beyond its Tupelo roots. It's the holding company for BancorpSouth Bank which operates some 290 branches in nine southern and midwestern states. Catering to consumers and small and midsized businesses the bank offers checking and savings accounts loans credit cards and commercial banking services. BancorpSouth also sells insurance and provides brokerage investment advisory and asset management services throughout most of its market area. Real estate loans including consumer and commercial mortgages and home equity construction and agricultural loans comprise approximately three-quarters of its loan portfolio. BancorpSouth has assets of $13 billion.

	Annual Growth	12/16	12/17	12/18	12/19	12/20
Assets ($ mil.)	13.1%	14,724.4	15,298.5	18,001.5	21,052.6	24,081.2
Net income ($ mil.)	14.5%	132.7	153.0	221.3	234.3	228.1
Market value ($ mil.)	(3.0%)	3,184.5	3,225.6	2,681.0	3,221.5	2,814.3
Employees	3.5%	3,998	3,947	4,445	4,693	4,596

CADENCE DESIGN SYSTEMS INC
NMS: CDNS

2655 Seely Avenue, Building 5
San Jose, CA 95134
Phone: 408 943-1234
Fax: –
Web: www.cadence.com

CEO: Lip-Bu Tan
CFO: John Wall
HR: –
FYE: January 01
Type: Public

Cadence Design Systems is a leader in electronic design building upon more than 30 years of computational software expertise. Customers use Cadence products to design integrated circuits (ICs) printed circuit boards (PCBs) smartphones laptop computers gaming systems and more. The company offer software hardware services and reusable IC design blocks which are commonly referred to as intellectual property (IP). The company also provides maintenance and support and design and methodology consulting services. International customers account for nearly 60% of the company's sales.

	Annual Growth	12/17	12/18	12/19*	01/21	01/22
Sales ($ mil.)	9.0%	1,943.0	2,138.0	2,336.3	2,682.9	2,988.2
Net income ($ mil.)	27.8%	204.1	345.8	989.0	590.6	696.0
Market value ($ mil.)	34.8%	11,575.6	11,996.3	19,456.0	37,763.3	51,580.9
Employees	5.3%	7,200	7,500	8,100	8,800	9,300

*Fiscal year change

CADENCE MCSHANE CONSTRUCTION COMPANY LLC

5057 KELLER SPRINGS RD # 5
ADDISON, TX 750016231
Phone: 972-239-2336
Fax: -
Web: www.cadencemcshane.com
CEO: James A McShane P E
CFO: -
HR: -
FYE: September 30
Type: Private

With a certain cadence Cadence McShane Construction has been right in step with the top contractors in the US. A part of development and construction group The McShane Companies it provides general construction construction management and design/build services for commercial institutional and industrial projects in Texas and the central US. The firm is known for its school and community projects throughout Texas. It also provides services to the manufacturing office multi-family residential government hospitality and retail markets. Cadence McShane was founded in 1995.

	Annual Growth	09/05	09/06	09/07	09/09	09/10
Sales ($ mil.)	(12.7%)	-	-	237.5	259.2	158.2
Net income ($ mil.)	(45.9%)	-	-	7.8	4.9	1.2
Market value ($ mil.)	-	-	-	-	-	-
Employees	-	-	-	-	-	225

CADENCE PHARMACEUTICALS INC   NMS: CADX

12481 High Bluff Drive, Suite 200
San Diego, CA 92130
Phone: 858 436-1400
Fax: 858 436-1401
Web: www.cadencepharm.com
CEO: -
CFO: -
HR: -
FYE: December 31
Type: Public

Cadence Pharmaceuticals figures that if a drug had success in one area it might do well in others. The company licenses rights to compounds and develops them for sale in untapped markets or for new indications. Cadence's sole marketed product is Ofirmev an injectable form of acetaminophen. Cadence licensed the drug from Bristol-Myers Squibb which markets it in Europe under the name Perfalgan. Cadence markets Ofirmev in the US for the treatment of acute pain and fever in children and adults in hospital settings. With one drug on the market Cadence is also on the lookout for other new drugs for its sales force to carry into hospitals.

	Annual Growth	12/08	12/09	12/10	12/11	12/12
Sales ($ mil.)	200.6%	-	-	-	16.7	50.2
Net income ($ mil.)	-	(57.1)	(45.5)	(56.6)	(93.0)	(81.0)
Market value ($ mil.)	(9.8%)	619.4	828.4	646.8	338.4	410.4
Employees	39.1%	55	90	247	220	206

CADIZ INC   NMS: CDZI

550 South Hope Street, Suite 2850
Los Angeles, CA 90071
Phone: 213 271-1600
Fax: -
Web: www.cadizinc.com
CEO: Scott Slater
CFO: Stanley Speer
HR: -
FYE: December 31
Type: Public

Cadiz hopes to strike gold with water. The land and water resource development firm owns some 45000 acres of land — and the groundwater underneath it — in eastern San Bernardino County California near the Colorado River Aqueduct and in the eastern Mojave Desert. Cadiz is betting on its groundwater storage and distribution project as water supplies become increasingly scarce in Southern California and as the state aims to increase its renewable energy production levels. Cadiz is also looking into commercial and residential development of its land. It has some agricultural assets that are leased as lemon groves and grape vineyards.

	Annual Growth	12/16	12/17	12/18	12/19	12/20
Sales ($ mil.)	7.0%	0.4	0.4	0.4	0.4	0.5
Net income ($ mil.)	-	(26.3)	(33.9)	(26.3)	(29.5)	(37.8)
Market value ($ mil.)	(3.9%)	461.3	525.9	380.1	406.7	393.0
Employees	2.7%	9	10	9	9	10

CADUS CORPORATION   OTC: KDUS

767 5th Ave. 47th Fl.
New York NY 10153
Phone: 212-702-4351
Fax: 212-750-5815
CEO: Hunter C Gary
CFO: -
HR: -
FYE: December 31
Type: Public

Cadus had hoped to make some dough from yeast but now is barely more than a hollow crust. Previously the company's drug discovery technologies used genetically engineered yeast cells but the firm sold its discovery programs to OSI Pharmaceuticals years ago and halted all research efforts. Its subsidiary Cadus Technologies still holds some assets related to its yeast cell technology and is seeking interested parties to license the intellectual properties. Its revenues consist of the payments on a sale of technology discoveries it made years ago. Investor Carl Icahn a director and former chairman of the company owns almost 40% of Cadus and effectively controls the company.

CADWALADER WICKERSHAM & TAFT LLP

1 World Financial Center
New York NY 10281
Phone: 212-504-6000
Fax: 212-504-6666
Web: www.cadwalader.com
CEO: -
CFO: -
HR: -
FYE: December 31
Type: Private - Partnershi

Founded during the presidency of George Washington Cadwalader Wickersham & Taft is one of the oldest law firms in the US. Since 1792 the firm has grown to include about 450 lawyers and to encompass offices not only in the US but also in Europe and the Asia/Pacific region. Among the areas of practice for which the firm is regularly recognized are capital markets financial restructuring and mergers and acquisitions. Banks and other financial institutions have been prominently represented on Cadwalader's client list; in addition the firm undertakes work for other large businesses and for government entities health care organizations nonprofits and individuals.

CAESARS ENTERTAINMENT CORP   NMS: CZR

One Caesars Palace Drive
Las Vegas, NV 89109
Phone: 702 407-6000
Fax: -
Web: www.caesars.com
CEO: Thomas R Reeg
CFO: Bret D Yunker
HR: -
FYE: December 31
Type: Public

The palaces owned by this Caesar are part of a vast gaming empire. One of the world's largest gambling companies Caesars Entertainment Corporation owns and operates about 50 casinos mostly in the US and the UK. Properties include some of the biggest names on the Las Vegas Strip including Caesars Palace and Planet Hollywood. Operations which comprise hotels riverboat casinos and gaming establishments boast millions of square feet of casino space and thousands of hotel rooms. The company owns the World Series of Poker brand and tournaments through Caesars Interactive. Most revenue is generated in the US. Caesars has agreed to be acquired by Eldorado Resorts in a deal worth $17.3 billion.

	Annual Growth	12/14	12/15	12/16	12/17	12/18
Sales ($ mil.)	(0.4%)	8,516.0	4,654.0	3,877.0	4,852.0	8,391.0
Net income ($ mil.)	-	(2,783.0)	5,920.0	(3,569.0)	(375.0)	303.0
Market value ($ mil.)	(18.9%)	9,790.6	4,923.4	5,304.0	7,893.6	4,237.0
Employees	(0.7%)	68,000	33,000	31,000	65,000	66,000

CAFE ENTERPRISES INC.

4324 Wade Hampton Blvd. Ste. B — CEO: -
Taylors SC 29687 — CFO: -
Phone: 864-322-1331 — HR: -
Fax: 864-322-1332 — FYE: December 31
Web: www.cafeent.com — Type: Private

You might say this company wantz to feed you lotz. Cafe Enterprises owns and operates almost 50 FATZ Eatz & Drinkz casual-dining establishments in Georgia North Carolina South Carolina Tennessee and Virginia. The restaurants known for their down-home atmosphere and large portions offer standard American fare such as burgers chicken pasta steaks and seafood. In 2012 the company launched two new concepts — Tavern 24 a casual pub-style restaurant that serves burgers sandwiches and pizza and Tablefields a farm-to-table restaurant that serves fresh locally sourced menu items with a focus on southern comfort fare. Both are in South Carolina.

CAFEPRESS INC — NMS: PRSS

11909 Shelbyville Road — CEO: Jasbir Patel
Louisville, KY 40243 — CFO: Phillip Milliner
Phone: 502 995-2229 — HR: -
Fax: - — FYE: December 31
Web: www.cafepressinc.com — Type: Public

Call it a craft fair that meets Amazon.com. CafePress operates an online service that connects millions of buyers and sellers of print-on-demand products. If you've dreamed up a catchy slogan or an arresting image the company's flagship website CafePress.com will print it for you on a T-shirt hat mug poster or other product; post it on cafepress.com for sale; and then ship it off and collect payments keeping a nominal base fee for itself. The company's growing portfolio of websites includes ezprints.com GreatBigCanvas.com CanvasOnDemand.com Imagekind.com. and InvitationBox.com and boasts more than 19 million members across all of its properties. Founded in 1999 CafePress went public in 2012.

	Annual Growth	12/12	12/13	12/14	12/15	12/16
Sales ($ mil.)	(17.2%)	217.8	245.9	153.2	104.5	102.2
Net income ($ mil.)	-	(0.1)	(13.5)	(15.9)	2.2	(26.5)
Market value ($ mil.)	(15.5%)	96.0	105.4	39.1	63.9	48.9
Employees	(19.2%)	742	775	452	357	316

CAHILL GORDON & REINDEL LLP

80 Pine St. — CEO: -
New York NY 10005-1702 — CFO: -
Phone: 212-701-3000 — HR: -
Fax: 212-269-5420 — FYE: December 31
Web: www.cahill.com — Type: Private - Partnershi

Here's a name plenty of high-profile clients have banked on: Cahill Gordon & Reindel. The firm's roster of clients has included investment banks such as Goldman Sachs J.P. Morgan Chase and Merrill Lynch as well as commercial banks and big companies from a variety of other industries. The firm maintains a broad range of practice areas; among its specialties are corporate transactions intellectual property litigation media law and tax. Cahill which has about 300 lawyers has offices in New York; Washington DC; and London. The firm was founded in 1919.

CAI INTERNATIONAL INC — NYS: CAI

Steuart Tower, 1 Market Plaza, Suite 2400 — CEO: Timothy B Page
San Francisco, CA 94105 — CFO: Timothy B Page
Phone: 415 788-0100 — HR: -
Fax: - — FYE: December 31
Web: www.capps.com — Type: Public

Is it bigger than a breadbox? CAI International (CAI) can pack it. The company leases large steel boxes to ship freight by ship truck and rail around the world. More than 95% of its container fleet is owned by CAI and the balance owned by container investors is managed by CAI. The leasing segment offers 280-plus shipping companies short-term and long-term leases with some leases giving the lessees the option to purchase the container. In operating its fleet CAI lease re-lease and dispose of its container portfolio; services also include container repair relocation and storage. The company was founded in 1989. Around 30% of company's total revenue comes from the US.

	Annual Growth	12/15	12/16	12/17	12/18	12/19
Sales ($ mil.)	13.7%	249.7	294.4	348.4	432.1	416.5
Net income ($ mil.)	3.7%	26.8	6.0	72.1	78.6	31.0
Market value ($ mil.)	30.2%	176.2	151.5	495.0	406.0	506.5
Employees	14.2%	128	212	215	261	218

CAITHNESS CORPORATION

565 5th Ave. 29th Fl. — CEO: James D Bishop Jr
New York NY 10017 — CFO: -
Phone: 212-921-9099 — HR: -
Fax: 212-921-9239 — FYE: December 31
Web: www.caithnessenergy.com — Type: Private

Scotland's windswept Caithness region might well serve as an inspiration for Caithness Corp. which develops wind and other renewable power plants in the US under the Caithness Energy brand. Although the firm has focused on the development acquisition operation and management of geothermal hydroelectric wind and solar energy power projects it also develops environmentally friendly fossil-fueled plants. Caithness is one of the largest producers of renewable energy in the US and has developed more than 350 MW of geothermal projects 160 MW of solar plants and 440 MW produced by wind turbines. On the cleaner fossil fuel plant side it has also developed more than 2000 MW of gas-turbine powered capacity.

CAJUN INDUSTRIES HOLDINGS, LLC

15635 AIRLINE HWY — CEO: Todd Grigsby
BATON ROUGE, LA 708177318 — CFO: Shane Recile
Phone: 225-753-5857 — HR: -
Fax: - — FYE: September 30
Web: www.cajunusa.com — Type: Private

Offering a mixed gumbo of services Cajun Industries builds oil refineries power plants process plants water-treatment plants and other industrial and infrastructure projects primarily in Louisiana and Texas. Subsidiary Cajun Constructors provides a full range of services from design/build to maintenance; Cajun Deep Foundations offers drilling piles installation and related services. Cajun Maritime focuses on marine coastal and oilfield services including construction repair and power distribution. Cajun Equipment Services manages a fleet of trucks and trailers that transport heavy and specialized loads. Chairman and owner Lane Grigsby founded the company as Cajun Contractors and Engineers in 1973.

	Annual Growth	09/16	09/17	09/18	09/19	09/20
Sales ($ mil.)	(11.4%)	-	616.3	515.8	478.8	429.3
Net income ($ mil.)	(36.7%)	-	56.5	19.8	5.9	14.3
Market value ($ mil.)	-	-	-	-	-	-
Employees		-	-	-	-	1,500

CAL DIVE INTERNATIONAL INC
NBB: CDVI

2500 CityWest Boulevard, Suite 2200
Houston, TX 77042
Phone: 713 361-2600
Fax: –
Web: www.caldive.com

CEO: –
CFO: –
HR: –
FYE: December 31
Type: Public

Cal Dive International may or may not be California dreaming but its waking hours are spent beneath the waters of the world's oceans. The subsea contractor operates a fleet of 18 surface and saturation diving support vessels and a handful of shallow water pipelay vessels dedicated pipebury barges combination pipelay/derrick barges and derrick barges. It installs and maintains offshore platforms pipelines and production systems on the Outer Continental Shelf of the Gulf of Mexico as well as in the Middle East Southeast Asia Europe and elsewhere. Cal Dive also provides shallow water diving services and performs salvage operations on abandoned fields.

	Annual Growth	12/09	12/10	12/11	12/12	12/13
Sales ($ mil.)	(11.1%)	829.4	536.5	479.8	464.8	517.0
Net income ($ mil.)	–	76.6	(315.8)	(66.9)	(65.0)	(36.6)
Market value ($ mil.)	(28.2%)	736.6	552.5	219.2	168.6	195.8
Employees	(6.8%)	2,050	1,900	1,700	1,200	1,550

CAL-MAINE FOODS INC
NMS: CALM

1052 Highland Colony Pkwy, Suite 200
Ridgeland, MS 39157
Phone: 601 948-6813
Fax: 601 969-0905
Web: www.calmainefoods.com

CEO: Adolphus B Baker
CFO: Max P Bowman
HR: –
FYE: May 29
Type: Public

Cal-Maine Foods is the nation's largest fresh shell egg producer and marketer with egg products processing facilities capable of producing 60 million lbs per year. It is also one of the top suppliers of specialty shell eggs such as Omega-3 enhanced and organic eggs marketed under the Egg-Land's Best Land O' Lakes and 4-Grain brand among others. Cal-Maine's operations consist of hatching chicks growing and maintaining flocks of pullets layers and breeders making feed and producing processing packaging and distributing shell eggs. Customers include national and regional grocery stores supermarkets club stores and foodservice distributors and consumers of egg products.

	Annual Growth	06/17	06/18	06/19*	05/20	05/21
Sales ($ mil.)	5.9%	1,074.5	1,502.9	1,361.2	1,351.6	1,349.0
Net income ($ mil.)	–	(74.3)	125.9	54.2	18.4	2.1
Market value ($ mil.)	(2.4%)	1,883.5	2,286.6	1,808.7	2,177.1	1,705.6
Employees	(2.1%)	3,578	3,573	3,490	3,636	3,286

*Fiscal year change

CALADRIUS BIOSCIENCES INC
NAS: CLBS

110 Allen Road, 2nd Floor
Liberty Corner, NJ 07920
Phone: 908 842-0100
Fax: –

CEO: David Mazzo
CFO: Joseph Talamo
HR: –
FYE: December 31
Type: Public

Caladrius Biosciences has a vision and it stems from life's building blocks. Operating in the US and China the clinical-stage company is working on developing cell-based therapies. Its lead candidate CLBS03 is in studies to treat recent-onset type 1 diabetes; it is targeted at adolescents. Another Caladius program aims to treat ischemia.

	Annual Growth	12/12	12/13	12/14	12/15	12/16
Sales ($ mil.)	25.3%	14.3	14.7	17.9	22.5	35.3
Net income ($ mil.)	–	(53.8)	(39.0)	(54.9)	(80.9)	(32.7)
Market value ($ mil.)	47.5%	4.9	55.9	30.9	8.9	23.2
Employees	21.2%	97	108	182	221	209

CALAMOS ASSET MANAGEMENT INC
NMS: CLMS

2020 Calamos Court
Naperville, IL 60563
Phone: 630 245-7200
Fax: –
Web: www.calamos.com

CEO: John S Koudounis
CFO: –
HR: –
FYE: December 31
Type: Public

Calamos Asset Management wants to make the most of your assets. Through its subsidiaries the company provides money management and investment advice to institutional and individual investors. The firm manages more than 30 mutual funds closed-end funds separately managed portfolios private funds exchange-traded funds and UCITS funds representing a range of investment strategies and risk levels. Calamos has nearly $25 billion of assets under management with most of it invested in US and global equities though it also employs fixed income convertible and alternative investment strategies. The firm mainly distributes its products through large broker-dealers.

	Annual Growth	12/11	12/12	12/13	12/14	12/15
Sales ($ mil.)	(10.0%)	352.3	326.7	269.1	251.0	230.9
Net income ($ mil.)	(32.3%)	15.9	18.2	18.6	13.5	3.3
Market value ($ mil.)	(6.2%)	211.6	178.8	200.3	225.3	163.8
Employees	0.5%	341	360	361	363	348

CALAMP CORP
NMS: CAMP

15635 Alton Parkway, Suite 250
Irvine, CA 92618
Phone: 949 600-5600
Fax: –
Web: www.calamp.com

CEO: Jeffery Gardner
CFO: Kurtis Binder
HR: –
FYE: February 28
Type: Public

CalAmp is a global connected intelligence company helping people and business work smarter. The company partners with transportation and logistics government industrial equipment and automotive industries to track monitor and recover vital assets with real-time visibility and insights that allow people and businesses everywhere to thrive. It provides asset tracking units mobile telematics devices fixed and mobile wireless gateways and routers for mobile resource management (MRM) and original equipment manufacturers (OEM). CalAmp keeps track of it all through cloud-based telematics and applications offered through as-a-service models. It generates about two-thirds of revenue in its home country the US. Spireon has acquired the LoJack US Stolen Vehicle Recovery (SVR) business from the company in 2021.

	Annual Growth	02/17	02/18	02/19	02/20	02/21
Sales ($ mil.)	(3.2%)	351.1	365.9	363.8	366.1	308.6
Net income ($ mil.)	–	(7.9)	16.6	18.4	(79.3)	(56.3)
Market value ($ mil.)	(8.9%)	571.1	824.4	489.7	338.9	393.5
Employees	0.3%	970	900	931	1,090	983

CALATLANTIC GROUP INC
NYS: CAA

15360 Barranca Parkway
Irvine, CA 92618-2215
Phone: 949 789-1600
Fax: –
Web: www.calatlantichomes.com

CEO: Larry T Nicholson
CFO: Jeff J McCall
HR: –
FYE: December 31
Type: Public

CalAtlantic builds homes from California to the Pacific Coast. Targeting entry level move-up and luxury market homebuyers the builder formerly known as Standard Pacific constructs homes in 40 metropolitan markets in the West Southwest Southeast and North that typically range in size from 1100 sq. ft. to more than 6000 sq. ft. with prices ranging from $165000 to more than $2 million and averaging around $480000 each. It also builds townhomes and condominiums and buys and develops tracts of high-quality land (both alone and through joint ventures). CalAtlantic offers home loans to its customers in all of its markets as well. Then-Standard Pacific acquired The Ryland Group in 2015 to form the fourth-largest builder in the US then changed its name to CalAtlantic.

	Annual Growth	12/11	12/12	12/13	12/14	12/15
Sales ($ mil.)	41.1%	893.9	1,258.3	1,939.5	2,435.3	3,540.1
Net income ($ mil.)	–	(16.4)	531.4	188.7	215.9	213.5
Market value ($ mil.)	85.8%	385.7	891.5	1,097.6	884.2	4,599.2
Employees	39.6%	750	820	1,115	1,250	2,850

CALAVO GROWERS, INC.   NMS: CVGW

1141-A Cummings Road
Santa Paula, CA 93060
Phone: 805 525-1245
Fax: 805 921-3223
Web: www.calavo.com

CEO: Brian Kocher
CFO: Mariela Matute
HR: Graciela Montgomery
FYE: October 31
Type: Public

Calavo Growers is a global leader in the avocado industry and a provider of value added fresh food. The company are experts in marketing and distributing avocados prepared avocados and other perishable foods allows the company to deliver a wide array fresh and prepared food products retail grocery foodservice club stores mass merchandisers food distributors and wholesalers on worldwide basis. Calavo procures and processes avocados papaya pineapple tomatoes and other fresh fruits grown mainly in California but the company also uses fruit from Colombia Peru and Mexico.

	Annual Growth	10/17	10/18	10/19	10/20	10/21
Sales ($ mil.)	(0.5%)	1,075.6	1,088.8	1,195.8	1,059.4	1,055.8
Net income ($ mil.)	–	37.3	32.3	36.6	(13.6)	(11.8)
Market value ($ mil.)	(14.1%)	1,303.5	1,715.5	1,533.9	1,187.3	711.0
Employees	9.9%	2,516	2,979	3,657	3,971	3,676

CALCOT, LTD.

2131 MARS CT
BAKERSFIELD, CA 933086830
Phone: 661-395-6866
Fax: –
Web: www.calcot.com

CEO: Paul Bush
CFO: Roxanne Wang
HR: –
FYE: August 31
Type: Private

With cotton-producing members in Arizona California New Mexico and Texas Calcot is one of the top cotton-marketing cooperatives in the US. Members of the co-op primarily grow premium-grade Far Western cottons including California Upland Pima and San Joaquin Acala (SJV Acala). The company operates three warehousing locations which can store 600000 bales of cotton per year. Calcot has gained and maintained a highly-regarded reputation among cotton producers textile mills and the entire cotton industry.

	Annual Growth	08/09	08/10	08/11	08/12	08/13
Sales ($ mil.)	(30.0%)	–	–	399.6	306.2	195.7
Net income ($ mil.)	61.5%	–	–	0.6	5.3	1.6
Market value ($ mil.)	–	–	–	–	–	–
Employees	–	–	–	–	–	43

CALENDAR HOLDINGS LLC

6411 Burleson Rd.
Austin TX 78744
Phone: 512-386-7220
Fax: 512-369-6192
Web: www.calendarholdings.com

CEO: Marc Winkelman
CFO: Jim Hull
HR: –
FYE: January 31
Type: Private

During the holiday season Calendar Holdings (aka Calendar Club) transforms empty retail space into shops under the banners Go! Calendar Go! Games and Go! Toys. The company's temporary stores range in size from kiosks to some 6000 sq. ft. Founded in 1993 with about 60 stores Calendar Club now operates more than 1200 locations in the US. The company also sells merchandise year-round on its websites including Calendars.com and DogBreedStore.com. Bookseller Barnes & Noble sold its majority stake in Calendar Club to CEO Marc Winkelman and the firm's management in 2009 for $7 million.

CALERES INC   NYS: CAL

8300 Maryland Avenue
St. Louis, MO 63105
Phone: 314 854-4000
Fax: –
Web: www.caleres.com

CEO: Diane Sullivan
CFO: Kenneth Hannah
HR: –
FYE: January 30
Type: Public

Caleres operates about 915 value-priced family footwear stores under the Famous Footwear banner in the US Canada and Guam plus approximately 170 Naturalizer Allen Edmonds and Sam Edelman stores in the US Canada and China. The company also sells shoes online and licenses Dr. Scholl's LifeStride Franco Sarto Ryka and Blowfish Malibu-branded footwear among others. It distributes footwear worldwide through approximately 4200 retailers including independent retailers chain (DSW) department stores (Nordstrom) catalogs and online retailers. The company was originally founded as Brown Shoe Company in 1878.

	Annual Growth	01/17*	02/18	02/19	02/20*	01/21
Sales ($ mil.)	(4.8%)	2,579.4	2,785.6	2,834.8	2,921.6	2,117.1
Net income ($ mil.)	–	65.7	87.2	(5.4)	62.8	(439.1)
Market value ($ mil.)	(15.6%)	1,129.5	1,093.0	1,124.2	666.3	573.7
Employees	(8.5%)	12,000	12,000	11,500	11,400	8,400

*Fiscal year change

CALGON CARBON CORPORATION

3000 GSK DR
MOON TOWNSHIP, PA 151081381
Phone: 412-787-6700
Fax: –
Web: www.calgoncarbon.com

CEO: Stevan R Schott
CFO: Robert Fortwangler
HR: –
FYE: December 31
Type: Private

Calgon Carbon is a global leader in activated carbons and purification systems. It offers purification and a variety of industrial and commercial manufacturing processes. Services include ballast water treatment ultraviolet light disinfection and advanced ion-exchange technologies used in the treatment of drinking water wastewater odor control pollution abatement and a variety of industrial and commercial manufacturing processes. With more than 240 patents its products find usage in more than 700 discrete market applications including air drinking water foods and pharmaceuticals purification and the removal of mercury emissions from coal-powered electrical plants.

	Annual Growth	12/13	12/14	12/15	12/16	12/17
Sales ($ mil.)	3.7%	–	555.1	535.0	514.2	619.8
Net income ($ mil.)	(24.7%)	–	49.4	43.5	13.8	21.1
Market value ($ mil.)	–	–	–	–	–	–
Employees	–	–	–	–	–	1,334

CALIBRE SYSTEMS, INC.

6361 WALKER LN STE 1100
ALEXANDRIA, VA 223103284
Phone: 703-797-8500
Fax: –
Web: www.calibresys.com

CEO: Richard Y Pineda
CFO: Craig College
HR: –
FYE: February 28
Type: Private

When it comes to information technology CALIBRE aims to please. The employee-owned company provides information technology and management services to government and commercial clients in the US. It specializes in data analytics modeling and simulation financial and cost management land management logistics and strategic planning among other areas. The company serves clients in the public and private sectors: Defense Federal / Civil National Security and Commercial. To expand its capabilities the company partners with academia large and small businesses and has entered a joint venture with VC Solutions. CALIBRE operates from a handful of US offices as well as on-site at customer facilities.

	Annual Growth	02/06	02/07	02/08	02/09	02/11
Sales ($ mil.)	16.8%	–	–	99.0	109.0	157.9
Net income ($ mil.)	25.4%	–	–	5.2	6.2	10.3
Market value ($ mil.)	–	–	–	–	–	–
Employees	–	–	–	–	–	767

CALIENT NETWORKS INC.

2665 N. 1st St. Ste. 204
San Jose CA 95134
Phone: 408-232-6400
Fax: 408-232-6422
Web: www.calient.net

CEO: Saiyed Atiq Raza
CFO: Jag Setlur
HR: –
FYE: December 31
Type: Private

All light's all right with Calient Networks. The company designs switches used to direct signals in fiber-optic communications networks. Unlike conventional switches that convert light to electrical impulses and back again Calient's DiamondWave switches use MEMS (micro-electromechanical system) technology that redirects optical transmissions using tiny movable mirrors. Its fiber cross-connect systems are used to manage and troubleshoot fiber networks. The company targets telecom service carriers and ISPs. Founded in 1999 Calient has attracted investments from venture capital firms including Enterprise Partners and TeleSoft Partners as well as networking companies such as Juniper Networks and Tellabs.

CALIFORNIA BANK & TRUST

11622 El Camino Real Ste. 200
San Diego CA 92130
Phone: 858-793-7400
Fax: 858-793-7438
Web: www.calbanktrust.com

CEO: –
CFO: –
HR: –
FYE: December 31
Type: Subsidiary

California Bank & Trust (CB&T) is the second-largest subsidiary of mulitbank holding company Zions Bancorporation (behind flagship affiliate Zions Bank). CB&T operates more than 100 branches in greater Los Angeles Orange County San Diego Northern California and the Inland Empire. It serves business and consumer clients offering standard services such as checking and savings accounts investments and wealth management residential and commercial mortgages credit cards personal loans and business loans including Small Business Administration loans. Specialized services for businesses include cash management lines of credit merchant services and international banking.

CALIFORNIA COASTAL COMMUNITIES INC.

6 Executive Circle Ste. 250
Irvine CA 92614
Phone: 949-250-7700
Fax: 949-250-7705
Web: www.californiacoastalcommunities.com

CEO: Raymond J Pacini
CFO: Sandra G Sciutto
HR: –
FYE: December 31
Type: Private

The tide is turning for California Coastal Communities. Through operating subsidiaries Hearthside Homes and Signal Landmark the company builds homes and develops residential communities in Southern California. Long wrapped up in a battle over land development rights California Coastal Communities has begun development of its Brightwater project some 215 acres (about half of which is undevelopable land) situated near important wetlands in Bolsa Chica the last undeveloped strip of coastal property in Orange County. Besides the controversial parcels the company has homebuilding operations in Los Angeles County. California Coastal Communities emerged from Chapter 11 bankruptcy in March 2011.

CALIFORNIA COMMUNITY FOUNDATION

221 S FIGUEROA ST STE 400
LOS ANGELES, CA 900123760
Phone: 213-413-4130
Fax: –
Web: www.calfund.org

CEO: Antonia Hernandez
CFO: Steve Cobb
HR: –
FYE: June 30
Type: Private

California Community Foundation supports not-for-profit organizations and public institutions in the Los Angeles area. The organization performs its function by offering funding for health and human services affordable housing early childhood education and community arts and culture. The 24th Street Theatre Antelope Valley Hospital and Community Arts Partnership are among the organizations to have received the foundation's grant funding. In times of emergency it has also pitched in to help groups in other areas. California Community Foundation was founded in 1915.

	Annual Growth	06/08	06/09	06/10	06/11	06/12
Assets ($ mil.)	(1.3%)	–	–	1,120.5	1,242.4	1,092.0
Net income ($ mil.)	(9.0%)	–	–	85.4	139.6	70.7
Market value ($ mil.)	–	–	–	–	–	–
Employees	–	–	–	–	–	60

CALIFORNIA DAIRIES INC.

2000 N. Plaza Dr.
Visalia CA 93291
Phone: 559-625-2200
Fax: 559-625-5433
Web: www.californiadairies.com

CEO: Brad Anderson
CFO: Phil Girard
HR: –
FYE: April 30
Type: Private - Cooperativ

Herding dairies together to gain "ag"-gregate strength makes California Dairies the largest dairy processing cooperative in the US. Its 470 member/farmers provide the co-op with more than 17 billion pounds of milk a year. Its plants process milk into mainly butter but also cheese and powdered milk for commercial and consumer use. The co-op's subsidiaries are Challenge Dairy Products (retail food service and ingredient products) and Los Banos Foods (cheddar cheese for food manufacturers). California Dairies also owns majority control of DairyAmerica which markets about 50% of all the milk powder produced in the US as well as other dairy products. The co-op exports to 50-plus countries worldwide.

CALIFORNIA DEPARTMENT OF WATER RESOURCES

1416 9TH ST
SACRAMENTO, CA 958145511
Phone: 916-653-9394
Fax: –
Web: www.ca.gov

CEO: –
CFO: –
HR: –
FYE: June 30
Type: Private

The California Department of Water Resources knows that water is gold. The agency is dedicated to managing the state's water resources in partnership with other agencies. Its core areas include designing the State Water Project (which supplies water to some 25 million farms businesses and residents) providing legislative guidance creating recreational opportunities educating the public and offering technical and financial support for local planning and regional water management. The department also provides flood control and dam safety services as well as plans for future water needs for the state.

	Annual Growth	06/04	06/05	06/17	06/18	06/19
Sales ($ mil.)	–	–	0.0	1,223.3	1,206.5	1,149.7
Net income ($ mil.)	–	–	0.0	0.0	0.0	(27.7)
Market value ($ mil.)	–	–	–	–	–	–
Employees	–	–	–	–	–	3,000

CALIFORNIA FIRST LEASING CORP
NBB: CFNB

5000 Birch Street, Suite 500
Newport Beach, CA 92660
Phone: 949 255-0500
Fax: 949 255-0501
Web: www.calfirstlease.com

CEO: Patrick Paddon
CFO: S. Leslie Jewett
HR: –
FYE: June 30
Type: Public

California First National Bancorp (CFNB) is a leasing company and a bank. Its California First Leasing (CalFirst Leasing) subsidiary leases equipment for a wide variety of industries including computers and software. Other leases include retail point-of-sale systems office furniture and manufacturing telecommunications and medical equipment. The bank holding company also operates California First National Bank (CalFirst Bank) a branchless FDIC-insured retail bank that conducts business mainly over the Internet but also by mail and phone. About three-quarters of its revenue comes from interest.

	Annual Growth	06/17	06/18	06/19	06/20	06/21
Assets ($ mil.)	(23.7%)	715.6	389.2	304.9	267.8	242.9
Net income ($ mil.)	34.3%	11.1	12.5	7.3	(2.4)	36.2
Market value ($ mil.)	(0.7%)	193.9	162.5	162.5	157.3	188.3
Employees	–		98	–	–	–

CALIFORNIA INDEPENDENT SYSTEM OPERATOR CORPORATION

250 OUTCROPPING WAY
FOLSOM, CA 956308773
Phone: 916-351-4400
Fax: –
Web: www.caiso.com

CEO: –
CFO: William J Regan
HR: Katherine Woodward
FYE: December 31
Type: Private

The California Independent System Operator (California ISO) manages a 25627-mile power transmission system (about 80% of California's power grid) balancing wholesale supply to meet retail demand. The enterprise directs the flow of electricity along long-distance high-voltage power lines that connect California with neighboring states as well as with Mexico and Canada. It manages the transmission lines and supervises maintenance but the transmission systems are owned and maintained by individual utilities. The not-for-profit public benefit corporation also acts as a transmission planner.

	Annual Growth	12/15	12/16	12/17	12/18	12/19
Sales ($ mil.)	1.7%	–	212.0	220.6	223.9	222.7
Net income ($ mil.)	23.8%	–	9.8	20.6	7.3	18.5
Market value ($ mil.)	–	–	–	–	–	–
Employees	–	–	–	–	–	530

CALIFORNIA INSTITUTE OF TECHNOLOGY

1200 E CALIFORNIA BLVD
PASADENA, CA 911250001
Phone: 626-395-6811
Fax: –
Web: www.caltech.edu

CEO: –
CFO: –
HR: –
FYE: September 30
Type: Private

The California Institute of Technology (Caltech) is a world-renowned science and engineering Institute that marshals some of the world's brightest mind and most innovative tools to address fundamental scientific questions and pressing societal challenges. The institute has approximately 938 undergraduate students and 1299 graduate students. Caltech has a very low student-teacher ratio of 3:1. Caltech operates the Jet Propulsion Laboratory (JPL) which supervises robotic Mars exploration programs and other interplanetary missions under contract to NASA. The school was founded in 1891.

CALIFORNIA PHYSICIANS' SERVICE

50 Beale St.
San Francisco CA 94105-1808
Phone: 415-229-5000
Fax: 415-229-5070
Web: www.blueshieldca.com

CEO: Paul Markovich
CFO: Sandra Clarke
HR: –
FYE: December 31
Type: Private - Not-for-Pr

California Physicians' Service which operates as Blue Shield of California provides health insurance products and related services to some 3.4 million members in the state of California. The not-for-profit mutual organization's health plans include HMO PPO dental and Medicaid or Medicare supplemental plans for individuals families and employer groups. Accidental death and dismemberment executive medical reimbursement life insurance vision and short-term health plans are provided by the company's Blue Shield of California Life & Health Insurance subsidiary. Blue Shield of California was established in 1939 and is an independent Blue Cross and Blue Shield Association member.

CALIFORNIA PIZZA KITCHEN INC.

6053 W. Century Blvd. 11th Fl.
Los Angeles CA 90045-6438
Phone: 310-342-5000
Fax: 310-342-4640
Web: www.cpk.com

CEO: Jim Hyatt
CFO: Susan M Collyns
HR: –
FYE: December 31
Type: Private

This company's cookeries are putting a West Coast twist on an old favorite. California Pizza Kitchen (CPK) operates a chain of about 265 casual-dining restaurants that specialize in gourmet pizzas featuring unique topping combinations including duck barbecued chicken and grilled shrimp. The chain also serves Neapolitan pizzas from Italy as well as American-style pies. CPK rounds out its menu with pastas soups salads and desserts. The restaurants are found in more than 30 states and about a dozen other countries; more than 200 of the locations are company-owned. Private equity firm Golden Gate Capital acquired CPK in 2011.

CALIFORNIA PRODUCTS CORPORATION

150 Dascomb Rd.
Andover MA 01810
Phone: 978-623-9980
Fax: 978-623-9960
Web: www.calprocorp.com

CEO: –
CFO: Sven Doerge
HR: –
FYE: November 30
Type: Private

Don't expect nominal consistency from California Products; no matter its name the company is based in New England. Through its California Paints division the company makes paints and coatings for home and office uses ceiling whites and enamels for hard wall interiors and finishes and primers. Its Plexipave Sport Surfacing Systems and DecoSystems divisions make tennis track and other sport surfaces and subsidiary Fiberlock Technologies manufactures environmental containment products. Employees are majority shareholders in the company whose name dates back to its founding as a subsidiary of a West Coast stucco manufacturer. In 2007 private equity behemoth Apollo Management took a stake in the company.

	Annual Growth	09/16	09/17	09/18	09/19	09/20
Sales ($ mil.)	5.0%	–	2,894.6	3,303.1	3,434.1	3,354.4
Net income ($ mil.)	(41.5%)	–	412.9	165.5	(11.2)	82.7
Market value ($ mil.)	–	–	–	–	–	–
Employees	–	–	–	–	–	11,643

CALMARE THERAPEUTICS INC
NBB: CTTC

1375 Kings Highway East, Suite 400
Fairfield, CT 06824
Phone: 203 368-6044
Fax: –
Web: www.calmaretherapeutics.com

CEO: Conrad Mir
CFO: Thomas Richtarich
HR: Deborah McQuade
FYE: December 31
Type: Public

It doesn't matter how great your invention is if you can't get it to market — that's where Competitive Technologies (CTT) comes in. The company helps individuals corporations government agencies and universities commercialize their inventions. Clients such as Sony and the University of Illinois have used CTT's services which include feasibility and marketability evaluations as well as application for and enforcement of patents. CTT focuses on inventions in life and physical sciences as well as digital technologies. The company established in 1971 also represents companies seeking to license technologies for commercial purposes.

	Annual Growth	12/12	12/13	12/14	12/15	12/16
Sales ($ mil.)	2.2%	1.1	0.8	1.2	1.0	1.2
Net income ($ mil.)	–	(3.0)	(2.7)	(3.4)	(3.7)	(3.8)
Market value ($ mil.)	(26.2%)	18.5	9.3	4.5	5.1	5.5
Employees	8.8%	5	5	6	7	7

CALNET INC.

12359 SUNRISE VALLEY DR # 270
RESTON, VA 20191-3462
Phone: 703-547-6800
Fax: –
Web: www.calnet.com

CEO: Kaleem Shah
CFO: –
HR: –
FYE: December 31
Type: Private

CALNET provides information technology (IT) consulting and services for businesses and public sector agencies. The company's IT services include application development and testing; e-commerce consulting; network management and security; and technical staffing. Industries served include technology telecommunications and financial services. In addition CALNET provides intelligence analysis including linguist services in a variety of languages for the US military. Customers have included the Food and Drug Administration Cisco Systems and Intel. The company has offices in Reston Virginia and San Diego. CALNET was founded in 1989 by president Kaleem Shah.

	Annual Growth	12/07	12/08	12/10	12/11	12/12
Sales ($ mil.)	(7.3%)	–	83.7	0.0	82.7	61.7
Net income ($ mil.)	–	–	(0.4)	0.0	14.4	11.7
Market value ($ mil.)	–	–	–	–	–	–
Employees	–	–	–	–	–	362

CALPINE CORP
NYS: CPN

717 Texas Avenue, Suite 1000
Houston, TX 77002
Phone: 713 830-2000
Fax: –
Web: www.calpine.com

CEO: John B Hill III
CFO: Zamir Rauf
HR: –
FYE: December 31
Type: Public

Independent power producer and marketer Calpine controls nearly 26000 MW of generating capacity and some 830 MW under construction through interests in about 80 primarily natural gas-fired power plants in 25 US states Canada and Mexico. This fleet also includes more than 10 geothermal power plants in California. Calpine the leading geothermal power producer in North America owns 760 MW of capacity at the largest geothermal facility in the US (the Geysers in northern California) which accounts for 40% of the country's geothermal energy. The company has major presence in the wholesale power markets in California the Mid-Atlantic and Texas. In 2017 the company agreed to sell itself to a consortium led by private equity firm Energy Capital Partners for $5.6 billion.

	Annual Growth	12/12	12/13	12/14	12/15	12/16
Sales ($ mil.)	5.2%	5,478.0	6,301.0	8,030.0	6,472.0	6,716.0
Net income ($ mil.)	(17.5%)	199.0	14.0	946.0	235.0	92.0
Market value ($ mil.)	(10.9%)	6,509.8	7,005.3	7,946.0	5,195.6	4,104.1
Employees	2.5%	2,151	2,157	2,052	2,209	2,372

CALPORTLAND COMPANY

2025 E. Financial Way Ste. 200
Glendora CA 91741-4692
Phone: 626-852-6200
Fax: 317-295-9434
Web: www.graindealers.com

CEO: Allen Hamblen
CFO: James A Wendoll
HR: –
FYE: March 31
Type: Subsidiary

CalPortland supplies building materials such as ready-mix concrete aggregates (sand gravel and rock products) asphalt and cement. It also offers precast building materials and performs road construction and earth moving services for clients such as CalTrans. CalPortland is active in western US and Canada; its operations include more than 60 ready-mix concrete plants in addition to about 25 aggregate yards and plants more than a dozen cement plants and transfer terminals three asphalt plants and five building materials distribution facilities in Alaska Arizona California Idaho Nevada Oregon and Washington as well as Alberta and British Columbia. CalPortland is owned by Taiheiyo Cement.

CALUMET SPECIALTY PRODUCT PARTNERS LP
NMS: CLMT

2780 Waterfront Parkway East Drive, Suite 200
Indianapolis, IN 46214
Phone: 317 328-5660
Fax: –
Web: www.calumetspecialty.com

CEO: Stephen Mawer
CFO: Louis Borgmann
HR: –
FYE: December 31
Type: Public

Crude oil refiner Calumet Specialty Products Partners turns crude oil into specialty hydrocarbon products such as lubricating oils solvents petrolatums and waxes under brands such as Royal Purple Bel-Ray and TruFuel. Additionally it refines crude into fuels such as gasoline diesel and jet fuel; it also makes asphalt. The company's operations are scattered across the US while it sells to both US and non-US customers. Calumet's products are used as a raw material component for basic industrial consumer and automotive goods.

	Annual Growth	12/16	12/17	12/18	12/19	12/20
Sales ($ mil.)	(10.9%)	3,599.4	3,763.8	3,497.5	3,452.6	2,268.2
Net income ($ mil.)	–	(328.6)	(103.8)	(55.1)	(43.6)	(149.0)
Market value ($ mil.)	(5.9%)	312.2	601.1	172.5	284.9	244.3
Employees	(8.5%)	2,000	1,600	1,700	1,500	1,400

CALVARY HOSPITAL, INC.

1740 EASTCHESTER RD
BRONX, NY 104612392
Phone: 718-518-2000
Fax: –
Web: www.calvaryhospital.org

CEO: Frank A Calamari
CFO: –
HR: –
FYE: December 31
Type: Private

Calvary Hospital rallies its doctors and nurses around advanced cancer patients hoping to keep them as comfortable as possible. The facility specializes in palliative care the practice of relieving the pain and symptoms associated with an illness (not curing the illness itself). Calvary Hospital offers both inpatient and outpatient services to adult patients in the advanced stages of cancer through two campuses; the main hospital has about 200 beds and a satellite location in Brooklyn has about 25 beds. In addition the hospital operates home health and hospice agencies and provides case management and family support services. The not-for-profit organization is sponsored by the Archdiocese of New York.

	Annual Growth	12/12	12/13	12/14	12/15	12/17
Sales ($ mil.)	3.9%	–	102.3	106.2	110.4	119.2
Net income ($ mil.)	–	–	13.1	(14.9)	(6.4)	(3.0)
Market value ($ mil.)	–	–	–	–	–	–
Employees	–	–	–	–	–	900

CALVERT COMPANY INC.

218 N V ST
VANCOUVER, WA 986617701
Phone: 360-693-0971
Fax: –
Web: www.calvert.com

CEO: –
CFO: –
HR: –
FYE: December 31
Type: Private

Strange as it may sound this company makes glulams in Washougal. Calvert manufactures and supplies glulams or pre-shaped glued-laminated lumber products for use in decorative construction work including arches beams bridges domes trusses s-curves columns and even playground equipment. It uses species such as Douglas fir Alaska yellow cedar redwood western red cedar spruce pine fir and more. The company manufactures glulams for export to Asia Canada and the Middle East and provides container loading at its plants in Vancouver and Washougal Washington. Calvert Company was founded by Ray Calvert and others in 1947.

	Annual Growth	12/04	12/05	12/06	12/07	12/08
Sales ($ mil.)	–	–	–	0.0	18.8	12.5
Net income ($ mil.)	–	–	–	0.0	0.9	0.2
Market value ($ mil.)	–	–	–	–	–	–
Employees	–	–	–	–	–	60

CALVERTHEALTH MEDICAL CENTER, INC.

100 HOSPITAL RD
PRINCE FREDERICK, MD 206784017
Phone: 410-535-4000
Fax: –
Web: www.calverthospital.com

CEO: James J Xinis
CFO: Kirk Blandford
HR: –
FYE: June 30
Type: Private

Calvert Memorial Hospital provides health care to Chesapeake Bay area residents in Southern Maryland. The medical facility along with Dunkirk Medical Center Solomons Medical Center and a handful of specialty centers and clinics comprise Calvert Health System. In addition to acute care Calvert Memorial Hospital and its affiliates offer same-day surgery outpatient behavioral health care and diagnostic imaging. They also provide such alternative therapies as acupuncture massage and hypnotherapy. For long-term and critical care Calvert Memorial Hospital partners with area facilities including Washington Hospital Center Children's National Medical Center Johns Hopkins and University of Maryland.

	Annual Growth	06/14	06/15	06/16	06/18	06/20
Sales ($ mil.)	1.9%	–	129.7	132.1	138.5	142.5
Net income ($ mil.)	(5.5%)	–	7.6	7.2	(1.3)	5.7
Market value ($ mil.)	–	–	–	–	–	–
Employees	–	–	–	–	–	1,000

CALYPSO TECHNOLOGY INC.

595 Market St. Ste. 1800
San Francisco CA 94105
Phone: 415-817-2400
Fax: 415-284-1222
Web: www.calypso.com

CEO: Didier Bouillard
CFO: –
HR: –
FYE: December 31
Type: Private

Calypso Technology moves not to the tropical rhythms of the Caribbean but to the insistent beat of Wall Street and world financial markets. The company markets an integrated software system used to trade bonds currencies derivatives stocks and other financial instruments. It also provides related services such as consulting implementation support and training. Calypso primarily targets global financial services firms; the company claims more than 125 clients including eight of the world's ten largest global banks. Other customers include local and regional banks asset managers hedge funds and stock exchanges. Founded in 1997 the employee-owned company operates from 16 locations worldwide.

CALYPTE BIOMEDICAL CORPORATION OTC: CBMC

16290 SW Upper Boones Ferry Rd.
Portland OR 97224
Phone: 503-726-2227
Fax: 503-601-6299
Web: www.calypte.com

CEO: Adel Karas
CFO: Kartlos Edilashvili
HR: –
FYE: December 31
Type: Public

Fear of needles need not stop you from getting tested for HIV infection. Calypte Biomedical's line of HIV testing products includes several tests that use saliva rather than blood. These rapid-detection tests (sold under the Aware brand name) don't require sophisticated laboratory equipment and Calypte hopes that such products will appeal to markets in developing countries where the incidence of HIV is high but health care infrastructure is lacking. The company has obtained regulatory approval for its Aware Rapid HIV tests in several foreign markets including South Africa India and Russia. The company has also developed an Aware HIV blood test and an over-the-counter version of its oral test.

CAMBER ENERGY INC ASE: CEI

1415 Louisiana, Suite 3500
Houston, TX 77002
Phone: 210 998-4035
Fax: 713 337-1510
Web: www.camber.energy

CEO: James Doris
CFO: Frank Barker
HR: –
FYE: March 31
Type: Public

Lucas Energy puts a good amount of energy into drilling. The independent crude oil and gas company owns and operates about 35 production wells and holds more than 1.5 million barrels of oil in proved reserves. Its operations are spread over some 11000 acres primarily in the Austin Chalk region of Texas. The company leases its well-producing properties from local landowners and small operators and is building up its reserve base by acquiring and re-drilling older or underperforming wells that have been overlooked by larger oil and gas companies. Most of Lucas Energy's revenue comes from sales of crude oil to customers such as Gulfmart and Texon with the remainder derived from natural gas sales.

	Annual Growth	03/16	03/17	03/18	03/19	03/20
Sales ($ mil.)	(20.0%)	1.0	5.3	6.9	2.7	0.4
Net income ($ mil.)	–	(25.4)	(89.1)	(24.8)	16.6	(3.9)
Market value ($ mil.)	(22.0%)	15.4	2.9	3.8	1.9	5.7
Employees	–	–	7	10	–	–

CAMBIUM LEARNING GROUP, INC. NAS: ABCD

17855 Dallas Parkway, Suite 400
Dallas, TX 75287
Phone: 888 399-1995
Fax: –
Web: www.cambiumlearning.com

CEO: John Campbell
CFO: Barbara Benson
HR: –
FYE: December 31
Type: Public

Cambium cells carry nutrients and form the bark and wood of a tree and Cambium Learning Group carries educational materials to schools to help students succeed. Operating through its Voyager Learning Sopris Learning Learning A-Z and Cambium Learning Technologies business units the company provides comprehensive reading and math programs as well as academic support services for pre-K through 12th grade students particularly those who are at risk or have special learning needs. Its products include instructional software print materials and interactive online tools. Cambium Learning Group offers these products and services to school districts across the US.

	Annual Growth	12/12	12/13	12/14	12/15	12/16
Sales ($ mil.)	0.6%	148.6	150.5	141.7	144.9	152.4
Net income ($ mil.)	–	(133.8)	(14.3)	(10.0)	(1.3)	10.4
Market value ($ mil.)	45.6%	51.3	76.7	76.7	224.1	230.6
Employees	4.2%	526	517	528	585	619

CAMBREX CORP
NYS: CBM

One Meadowlands Plaza
East Rutherford, NJ 07073
Phone: 201 804-3000
Fax: 201 804-9852
Web: www.cambrex.com

CEO: Steven M Klosk
CFO: Gregory P Sargen
HR: Noreen Pattermann
FYE: December 31
Type: Public

Cambrex focuses on health. Providing products services and technologies which help to accelerate the development and commercialization of small molecule therapeutics the company develops products for the human health care market that include active pharmaceutical ingredients (APIs) and intermediates for over-the-counter and prescription branded and generic pharmaceuticals. Cambrex focuses on developing drug delivery technologies and the manufacture of high-potency compounds and controlled substances.

	Annual Growth	12/13	12/14	12/15	12/16	12/17
Sales ($ mil.)	13.8%	318.2	374.6	433.3	490.6	534.5
Net income ($ mil.)	41.0%	25.9	57.3	57.2	81.7	102.5
Market value ($ mil.)	28.1%	585.7	710.1	1,546.8	1,772.1	1,576.6
Employees	7.0%	936	1,117	1,228	1,295	1,228

CAMBRIDGE BANCORP
NAS: CATC

1336 Massachusetts Avenue
Cambridge, MA 02138
Phone: 617 876-5500
Fax: –
Web: www.cambridgetrust.com

CEO: Denis Sheahan
CFO: Michael Carotenuto
HR: Pilar Pueyo
FYE: December 31
Type: Public

Cambridge Bancorp is the nearly $2 billion-asset holding company for Cambridge Trust Company a community bank serving Cambridge and the Greater Boston area through about a dozen branch locations in Massachusetts. It offers standard retail products and services including checking and savings accounts CDs IRAs and credit cards. Residential mortgages including home equity loans account for about 50% of the company's loan portfolio while commercial real estate loans make up more than 40%. The company also offers commercial industrial and consumer loans. Established in 1892 the bank also offers trust and investment management services.

	Annual Growth	12/16	12/17	12/18	12/19	12/20
Assets ($ mil.)	20.9%	1,849.0	1,949.9	2,101.4	2,855.6	3,949.3
Net income ($ mil.)	17.3%	16.9	14.8	23.9	25.3	32.0
Market value ($ mil.)	2.9%	431.5	552.8	576.7	555.2	483.1
Employees	15.7%	–	247	262	321	383

CAMBRIDGE HEART INC.
OTC: CAMH

1 Oak Park Dr.
Bedford MA 01730
Phone: 781-271-1200
Fax: 781-275-8431
Web: www.cambridgeheart.com

CEO: Ali Haghighi-Mood
CFO: Vincenzo Licausi
HR: –
FYE: December 31
Type: Public

It's not just a heart — it's a "Cambridge" heart. Cambridge Heart makes noninvasive tools for diagnosing cardiac arrest and ventricular arrhythmia. Its CH 2000 system conducts cardiac stress tests and measures extremely low levels of T-wave alternans an irregularity in an electrocardiogram indicating the risk of sudden cardiac death. Another product the Heartwave II System allows T-wave alternans screenings to be performed with any stress test system. The company's Microvolt T-Wave Alternans technology can detect the smallest heartbeat variation measuring from one-millionth of a volt. The company markets its products in the US through direct sales and representatives; it also has international distributors.

CAMBRIDGE PUBLIC HEALTH COMMISSION

1493 CAMBRIDGE ST
CAMBRIDGE, MA 021391047
Phone: 617-665-1000
Fax: –

CEO: Patrick Wardell
CFO: Jill Batty
HR: –
FYE: June 30
Type: Private

Because not everyone in the college town of Cambridge Massachusetts can walk into student health centers there is the Cambridge Public Health Commission (doing business as Cambridge Health Alliance or CHA). The health care system operates the Cambridge Public Health Department and three hospitals — Cambridge Hospital Somerville Hospital and Whidden Hospital — with a combined total of more than 490 beds. It also operates 20 primary care and specialty practices specializing in such areas as pediatrics gerontology family medicine psychiatry and dentistry. CHA is a teaching affiliate of Harvard's Medical School and School of Public Health as well as Tufts University's School of Medicine.

	Annual Growth	06/01	06/02	06/03	06/05	06/09
Sales ($ mil.)	(20.9%)	–	384.3	466.1	644.2	74.2
Net income ($ mil.)	–	–	0.3	(17.0)	6.1	0.0
Market value ($ mil.)	–	–	–	–	–	–
Employees	–	–	–	–	–	2,700

CAMBRIDGE SOUNDWORKS INC.

120 Water St.
Andover MA 01845
Phone: 978-623-4400
Fax: 978-794-2903
Web: www.cambridgesoundworks.com

CEO: –
CFO: Robert Cardin
HR: –
FYE: June 30
Type: Subsidiary

Cambridge SoundWorks wants to be speaker of the house the car and the computer. The company is a leading manufacturer of speaker systems for consumer use including floor speakers and bookshelf models. It also makes home theater speaker systems outdoor speakers and surround sound units. In addition to its own brand Cambridge SoundWorks markets audio and video items from such manufacturers as Samsung Sony and Toshiba as well as products made by its parent company Creative Technology. Steep discounting of consumer electronics contributed to its decision to shut down its 30-store chain to focus on online and catalog sales in 2008.

CAMCO FINANCIAL CORP
NMS: CAFI

814 Wheeling Avenue
Cambridge, OH 43725-9757
Phone: 740 435-2020
Fax: –
Web: www.camcofinancial.com

CEO: –
CFO: –
HR: –
FYE: December 31
Type: Public

Camco Financial tries to give customers a financial edge through its Advantage Bank subsidiary. The company operates about 20 branches loan offices and Camco Title Agency offices in Ohio northern Kentucky and western West Virginia. The bank primarily uses funds from deposits (checking savings and money market accounts; CDs; and IRAs) to originate residential mortgages which make up about 60% of its loan portfolio; the bank also issues nonresidential real estate consumer and construction loans. In 2013 Ohio-based Huntington Bancshares agreed to buy Camco Financial.

	Annual Growth	12/08	12/09	12/10	12/11	12/12
Assets ($ mil.)	(6.5%)	1,000.4	842.7	815.0	767.0	764.3
Net income ($ mil.)	–	(15.3)	(11.2)	(14.6)	0.2	4.2
Market value ($ mil.)	(10.5%)	42.1	26.2	19.3	16.5	27.0
Employees	(5.5%)	276	252	254	222	220

CAMDEN NATIONAL CORP. (ME)
NMS: CAC

2 Elm Street
Camden, ME 04843
Phone: 207 236-8821
Fax: 207 236-6256
Web: www.camdennational.com/healthprofunding

CEO: Gregory Dufour
CFO: Michael Archer
HR: –
FYE: December 31
Type: Public

Camden National Corporation is the holding company for Camden National Bank which boasts nearly 45 branches in about a dozen Maine counties and provides standard deposit products such as checking and savings accounts CDs and IRAs. Commercial mortgages and loans make up 50% of its loan portfolio while residential mortgages make up another 40% and consumer loans constitute the remainder. Subsidiary Acadia Trust provides trust fiduciary investment management and retirement plan administration services while Camden Financial Consultants offers brokerage and insurance services. The largest bank headquartered in Maine Camden National Bank was founded in 1875 and once issued its own US currency.

	Annual Growth	12/16	12/17	12/18	12/19	12/20
Assets ($ mil.)	6.1%	3,864.2	4,065.4	4,297.4	4,429.5	4,898.7
Net income ($ mil.)	10.4%	40.1	28.5	53.1	57.2	59.5
Market value ($ mil.)	(5.3%)	662.7	628.1	536.3	686.7	533.4
Employees	(0.9%)	631	636	634	639	609

CAMDEN PROPERTY TRUST
NYS: CPT

11 Greenway Plaza, Suite 2400
Houston, TX 77046
Phone: 713 354-2500
Fax: –
Web: www.camdenliving.com

CEO: Richard Campo
CFO: Alexander Jessett
HR: –
FYE: December 31
Type: Public

Camden Property Trust and all its consolidated subsidiaries are primarily engaged in the ownership management development redevelopment acquisition and construction of multifamily apartment communities. The real estate investment trust (REIT) has some 175 urban and suburban properties with some 59100 apartment units. Its portfolio is made up of both wholly owned and joint-venture holdings; most communities carry the Camden name. Around 30% of the REIT's properties are in Texas while the rest are in top markets such as Atlanta Denver Florida North Carolina Phoenix California and Washington DC.

	Annual Growth	12/17	12/18	12/19	12/20	12/21
Sales ($ mil.)	5.9%	928.7	957.3	1,061.9	1,069.6	1,169.7
Net income ($ mil.)	11.5%	196.4	156.1	219.6	123.9	303.9
Market value ($ mil.)	18.0%	10,363.9	9,912.5	11,944.5	11,248.8	20,115.4
Employees	1.5%	1,600	1,600	1,650	1,700	1,700

CAMELOT ENTERTAINMENT GROUP INC.
OTC: CMLT

8001 Irvine Center Dr. Ste. 400
Irvine CA 92618
Phone: 949-754-3030
Fax: 949-754-4309
Web: www.camelotfilms.com

CEO: Robert P Atwell
CFO: Steven Istock
HR: –
FYE: December 31
Type: Public

Camelot Entertainment Group is participating in the quest for the holy grail of movie studios: making low-budget films that sell mountains of tickets. The company plans to produce and distribute low-budget motion pictures with a business model focusing on pre-production digital photography profit participation and stock incentives for its directors and writers. Previously a development stage company Camelot has exited that phase; it got the ball rolling in 2010 with the purchase of the assets of Liberation Entertainment. Included in the deal is 750 titles from Liberation's film library.

CAMERON INTERNATIONAL CORPORATION

4646 W SAM HOUSTON PKWY N
HOUSTON, TX 770418214
Phone: 713-939-2282
Fax: –
Web: www.slb.com

CEO: Robert Scott Rowe
CFO: Charles Sledge
HR: –
FYE: December 31
Type: Private

Cameron is a leading manufacturer provider and servicer of oil and gas industry equipment. The company makes products that control pressure at oil and gas wells including blowout preventers chokes controls wellheads measurement tools and valves. The company's products are used for offshore onshore and subsea applications. Cameron is a wholly owned subsidiary of oilfield product and services giant Schlumberger (a major provider of technology for reservoir characterization drilling production and processing services to the oil and gas industry).

	Annual Growth	12/10	12/11	12/12	12/13	12/14
Sales ($ mil.)	10.5%	–	–	8,502.1	9,838.4	10,381.0
Net income ($ mil.)	6.3%	–	–	750.5	724.2	848.0
Market value ($ mil.)	–	–	–	–	–	–
Employees	–	–	–	–	–	23,000

CAMERON MITCHELL RESTAURANTS LLC

515 Park St.
Columbus OH 43215
Phone: 614-621-3663
Fax: 614-621-1020
Web: www.cameronmitchell.com

CEO: –
CFO: –
HR: Katie Laudick
FYE: December 31
Type: Private

Cameron Mitchell Restaurants lays out the white tablecloth in Columbus Ohio and beyond. The company operates about 20 upscale establishments encompassing more than half a dozen dining concepts including Cameron's American Bistro Cap City Fine Diner & Bar Marcella's Martini Modern Italia Martini Italian Bistro Molly Woo's Asian Bistro and Ocean Prime. Many of the company's restaurants are found in and around Columbus but it also has dining operations in about half a dozen other states. In addition Cameron Mitchell offers catering services. Founder chef and president Cameron Mitchell left cross-town rival Fifty-Five Restaurant Group in 1992 to open his first restaurant Cameron's American Bistro.

CAMPAGNA-TURANO BAKERY INC.

6501 ROOSEVELT RD
BERWYN, IL 604021100
Phone: 708-788-9220
Fax: –
Web: www.turano.com

CEO: –
CFO: –
HR: –
FYE: December 31
Type: Private

The Campagna - Turano Bakery which does does business as the Turano Bakery manufactures fully and partially baked European-style artisan breads. The company's more than 400 varieties include French baguettes ciabatta bread focaccia and kaiser rolls as well as sweet baked goods including cannoli biscotti cakes and cookies. Operating three commercial bakeries Turano serves restaurant in-store bakery and retail grocery customers throughout the US. Its foodservice operation supplies customers in Illinois Wisconsin and northwestern Indiana with parbaked and fully baked goods.

	Annual Growth	12/06	12/07	12/08	12/09	12/12
Sales ($ mil.)	9.8%	–	–	–	5.3	7.0
Net income ($ mil.)	–	–	–	–	(0.7)	0.3
Market value ($ mil.)	–	–	–	–	–	–
Employees	–	–	–	–	–	470

CAMPBELL MITHUN INC.

222 S. 9th St.
Minneapolis MN 55402
Phone: 612-347-1000
Fax: 612-347-1515
Web: www.campbellmithun.com

CEO: Rob Buchner
CFO: Steve Arndt
HR: -
FYE: December 31
Type: Subsidiary

This company brings a little Madison Avenue savvy to the Midwest. Campbell Mithun is one of the leading advertising agencies in the US offering creative development and campaign services for both print and broadcast marketing efforts especially for clients in such industries as food health care and consumer products. It also provides insight into youth marketing through its Boing consultancy as well as general brand marketing services. In addition its Compass Point Media unit offers media planning and buying for spot TV print and radio time. Campbell Mithun is part of global advertising and marketing services conglomerate Interpublic Group.

CAMPBELL SOUP CO

1 Campbell Place
Camden, NJ 08103-1799
Phone: 856 342-4800
Fax: 856 342-3878
Web: www.campbellsoupcompany.com

NYS: CPB
CEO: Mark Clouse
CFO: Mick Beekhuizen
HR: Diane Johnson May
FYE: August 01
Type: Public

The one of the world's top soup maker Campbell Soup Company's range of products include Campbell's condensed and ready to-serve soups Swanson broth and stocks and Pacific Foods broth. Campbell also makes many other simple foods snacks and beverages including Pace Mexican sauce V8 juices and beverages and Pepperidge Farm baked goods (including those popular tiny Goldfish crackers). The company sold its U.S. refrigerated business Garden Fresh Gourmet business and Bolthouse Farms business in 2019. The company also sold its Kelsen business Arnott's business and European chips business also in 2019. Its biggest customer Wal-Mart accounts for around a fifth of all sales.

	Annual Growth	07/17	07/18	07/19*	08/20	08/21
Sales ($ mil.)	1.8%	7,890.0	8,685.0	8,107.0	8,691.0	8,476.0
Net income ($ mil.)	3.1%	887.0	261.0	211.0	1,628.0	1,002.0
Market value ($ mil.)	(4.6%)	15,960.7	12,363.9	12,369.9	14,970.1	13,203.4
Employees	(5.9%)	18,000	23,000	19,000	14,500	14,100

*Fiscal year change

CAMPBELL-EWALD COMPANY

30400 Van Dyke Ave.
Warren MI 48093
Phone: 586-574-3400
Fax: 586-575-9925
Web: www.campbell-ewald.com

CEO: Kevin Wertz
CFO: Jarilyn Auger
HR: -
FYE: December 31
Type: Subsidiary

This agency knows it takes more than a good name to make a great brand. Campbell-Ewald is one of the Midwest's leading advertising agencies offering creative development and campaign management services for broadcast print and interactive media. In addition to traditional advertising the firm provides services for direct response marketing event marketing and business-to-business selling. Major clients have included Carrier Michelin and the United States Postal Service. Its Campbell-Ewald Publishing unit offers custom publishing services for creating branded content. The agency is part of global marketing services conglomerate Interpublic Group and has a half dozen offices in major cities in the US.

CAMPUS CREST COMMUNITIES INC

2100 Rexford Road, Suite 414
Charlotte, NC 28211
Phone: 704 496-2500
Fax: 704 496-2599
Web: www.campuscrest.com

NYS: CCG
CEO: -
CFO: -
HR: -
FYE: December 31
Type: Public

College dorms have moved beyond cinder block walls and Murphy beds thanks to Campus Crest Communities. The real estate investment trust (REIT) develops builds and manages on- and off-campus student housing apartment communities at medium-sized colleges and universities. Campus Crest owns interests in more than 25 communities which are branded as The Grove located mostly in the South. Its properties feature furnished apartments with such amenities as a pool library volleyball and basketball courts fitness center tanning beds and gated entry with keyed bedroom locks. The student-friendly rental rates include utilities.

	Annual Growth	12/10	12/11	12/12	12/13	12/14
Sales ($ mil.)	77.1%	10.9	94.8	137.4	142.3	106.7
Net income ($ mil.)	-	(1.6)	3.8	10.8	1.6	(164.0)
Market value ($ mil.)	(15.0%)	907.7	651.3	793.7	609.2	473.3
Employees	4.7%	525	527	650	522	632

CAMPUS CREST COMMUNITIES, INC.

2100 Rexford Road, Suite 414
Charlotte, NC 28211
Phone: 704 496-2500
Fax: 704 496-2599
Web: www.campuscrest.com

NYS: CCG
CEO: -
CFO: -
HR: -
FYE: December 31
Type: Public

College dorms have moved beyond cinder block walls and Murphy beds thanks to Campus Crest Communities. The company develops builds and manages on- and off-campus student housing apartment communities at medium-sized colleges and universities. Campus Crest owns interests in more than 25 communities which are branded as The Grove located mostly in the South. Its properties feature furnished apartments with such amenities as a pool library volleyball and basketball courts fitness center tanning beds and gated entry with keyed bedroom locks. The student-friendly rents include utilities. Campus Crest which went public via a 2010 IPO has converted to a real estate investment trust (REIT).

	Annual Growth	10/10*	12/10	12/11	12/12	12/13
Sales ($ mil.)	22.9%	76.6	10.9	94.8	137.4	142.3
Net income ($ mil.)	-	(20.7)	(1.6)	3.8	10.8	1.6
Market value ($ mil.)	(9.5%)	819.2	904.3	648.9	790.8	607.0
Employees	(0.2%)	-	525	527	650	522

*Fiscal year change

CAMSTAR SYSTEMS INC.

13024 Ballantyne Corporate Place Ste. 300
Charlotte NC 28277
Phone: 704-227-6600
Fax: 704-227-6783
Web: www.camstar.com

CEO: -
CFO: -
HR: -
FYE: December 31
Type: Private

Camstar wants your manufacturing operations to play a starring role. The company makes manufacturing execution systems (MES) software for such industries as semiconductors biotechnology electronics medical devices and outsourced operations. Its InSite application helps manufacturers to quickly change production lines and synchronize plant output to meet demand. Other applications include LiveConnect (integration with ERP and CRM applications) LiveSync (replication of processes in other plants) and LiveView (reporting). Customers have included Agilent Technologies Corning JDS Uniphase IBM and Kodak. The company also offers services such as consulting training and support.

CAN-CAL RESOURCES LTD.   OTC: CCRE

2500 Vista Mar Dr.
Las Vegas NV 89128
Phone: 702-243-1849
Fax: 702-243-1869
Web: www.can-cal.com

CEO: –
CFO: –
HR: –
FYE: December 31
Type: Public

Can Can-Cal strike it rich? The question hasn't been answered. Can-Cal Resources is an exploration-stage mining company that owns exploration-stage precious mineral and metal properties in the southwestern US. Its focus is currently on the Pisgah and Wikieup properties in California and Arizona respectively. It also owns the Owl Canyon in California but is holding that property in reserve for exploration at a later date.

CANAAN MANAGEMENT INC.

285 Riverside Ave. Ste. 250
Westport CT 06880
Phone: 203-855-0400
Fax: 203-854-9117
Web: www.canaan.com

CEO: –
CFO: –
HR: –
FYE: December 31
Type: Private

It's the land of milk and honey for start-up companies. Canaan Management (also known as Canaan Partners) is a venture capital firm that invests primarily in early-stage technology and health care companies in the US and abroad. It focuses on digital media mobile communications enterprise software clean technology biopharmaceuticals medical devices and diagnostics. The company typically invests $1 million to $20 million per transaction and has approximately $3 billion in capital under management. Founded in 1987 Canaan has raised eight funds (its most recent in 2008). Notable past investments include Acme Packet Amicus Therapeutics DoubleClick and Match.com.

CANACCORD GENUITY INC.

99 High St. Ste. 1200
Boston MA 02110
Phone: 617-371-3900
Fax: 801-476-9138
Web: www.ut.regence.com

CEO: –
CFO: Donald Macfayden
HR: –
FYE: March 31
Type: Subsidiary

Canaccord Genuity (formerly Canaccord Adams) provides equities research sales and trading services and investment banking services such as securities underwriting sales trading mergers and acquisitions advice and industry research. Formed in 1969 through the merger of Weston W. Adams & Company and Harkness & Hill the company specializes in the technology metals mining life sciences real estate and financial services sectors. Canaccord Genuity also acts as a market maker for small- and mid-cap stocks in the US. The company is part of Canaccord Financial.

CANANDAIGUA NATIONAL CORP.   NBB: CNND

72 South Main Street
Canandaigua, NY 14424
Phone: 585 394-4260
Fax: 585 394-4001
Web: www.cnbank.com

CEO: Frank Hamlin
CFO: Vincent Yacuzzo
HR: –
FYE: December 31
Type: Public

Canandaigua National can undoubtedly stake its claim as the holding company for Canandaigua National Bank and Trust which operates more than two dozen branches in the Finger Lakes region of upstate New York. In addition to traditional deposits and loans the bank also offers online brokerage insurance and wealth management services including corporate retirement plan management and individual financial planning. The company also owns Genesee Valley Trust Company and the recently formed Canandaigua National Trust Company of Florida. Canandaigua National's loan portfolio is composed largely of commercial mortgages other business loans and residential mortgages.

	Annual Growth	12/16	12/17	12/18	12/19	12/20
Assets ($ mil.)	10.1%	2,476.1	2,661.7	2,862.5	3,015.7	3,635.4
Net income ($ mil.)	17.1%	22.5	22.0	35.9	39.2	42.3
Market value ($ mil.)	7.6%	261.9	284.3	327.3	378.3	351.6
Employees	2.1%	533	541	556	572	580

CANDELA CORPORATION

530 Boston Post Rd.
Wayland MA 01778
Phone: 508-358-7400
Fax: 508-358-5602
Web: www.candelalaser.com

CEO: –
CFO: –
HR: –
FYE: December 31
Type: Subsidiary

Tattoo regrets? Candela's medical laser technology can remove them and other cosmetic skin issues as well. The company makes light-based (laser) systems including Alex TriVantage for birthmarks lesions sun spots and tattoos; GentleLASE for permanent hair removal facial veins and wrinkles; Vbeam for acne skin rejuvenation scars and warts. Candela sells to cosmetic and surgical markets through a direct sales force and distributors in the US and abroad. Its patent portfolio consists of roughly 25 issued US patents (with some 20 patents applications pending) and 35 international patents. Candela is a wholly-owned subsidiary of aesthetic lasermaker Syneron Medical

CANDLEWICK PRESS INC.

99 Dover St.
Somerville MA 02144
Phone: 617-661-3330
Fax: 617-661-0565
Web: www.candlewick.com

CEO: –
CFO: –
HR: –
FYE: December 31
Type: Private

Candlewick Press shines a light in the children's book world. The company has published more than 3000 children's books. Its catalog is comprised of picture books easy readers middle grade and young adult fiction nonfiction poetry collections and novelty and activity books. Candlewick titles include Can't You Sleep Little Bear? Guess How Much I Love You My Very First Mother Goose and It's Perfectly Normal. Its books are distributed in the US by Random House. The company is 100%-owned by its employees.

CANNABIS GLOBAL INC
NBB: CBGL

520 S. Grand Avenue, Suite 320
Los Angeles, CA 90071
Phone: 310 986-4929
Fax: –
Web: www.cannabisglobalinc.com

CEO: Garry McHenry
CFO: Garry McHenry
HR: –
FYE: August 31
Type: Public

MicroChannel Technologies is trying to get on your nerves. The development-stage company is studying the use of stem cells to regenerate optical and bodily nerve damage caused by injury diabetes or post-surgical complications. The research involves scraping out tiny grooves in the damaged cells and filling them with stem cells (hence the micro channel) to accelerate new growth. The company was spun off from technology incubator Octillion in 2007 and up until mid-2008 it continued to fund studies conducted by the Research Foundation at Iowa State University. However the project failed to find any commercially viable cells and MicroChannel Technologies is now trying to find another commercial opportunity.

	Annual Growth	08/17	08/18	08/19	08/20	08/21
Sales ($ mil.)	5828.9%	–	–	–	0.0	1.6
Net income ($ mil.)	–	(0.0)	(0.1)	(0.4)	(4.9)	(7.8)
Market value ($ mil.)	134.0%	0.1	1.7	3.8	10.2	3.0
Employees	–	–	–	–	–	–

CANNONDALE BICYCLE CORPORATION

16 Trowbridge Dr.
Bethel CT 06801
Phone: 203-749-7000
Fax: 203-748-4012
Web: www.cannondale.com

CEO: –
CFO: Sean Jacobs
HR: –
FYE: June 30
Type: Subsidiary

Cannondale's lightweight products are heavyweights in the high-performance bicycle market. The company is a leading maker of mountain road racing multisport recreational and specialty bicycles — most of them with aluminum frames. Cannondale also peddles bicycle-related apparel accessories and gear. The bicycle-maker offers some 80 bike models through specialty bike retailers in about 70 countries. It also co-sponsors bike-racing teams to promote its products. The company boasts major facilities in Japan and Taiwan. Cannondale is owned by juvenile products and bicycle company Dorel Industries and operates as part of its recreational/leisure business generating about one-third of total corporate sales.

CANON U.S.A. INC.

1 Canon Plaza
Lake Success NY 11042
Phone: 516-328-5000
Fax: 718-260-4375
Web: www.trackdata.com

CEO: Kazuto Ogawa
CFO: –
HR: Arlene Erbeck
FYE: December 31
Type: Subsidiary

Canon U.S.A. expanded its canon beyond cameras. The US arm of Tokyo-based printer and peripherals giant Canon sells and services office and consumer imaging equipment including copiers printers fax machines and scanners. Its focus on cameras hasn't softened though offering still and video digital cameras for both consumers and professionals in photography broadcast and motion pictures. Industrial and other products include semiconductor and LCD lithography equipment small motors and medical equipment such as eye care cameras and radiography systems. Canon U.S.A. oversees subsidiaries Canon Canada Canon Latin America and Canon Mexicana; the Americas account for more than one-fourth of Canon's global sales.

CANON VIRGINIA INC.

12000 Canon Blvd.
Newport News VA 23606-4299
Phone: 757-881-6000
Fax: 312-565-5823
Web: www.fhlbc.com

CEO: Shingo Shigeta
CFO: –
HR: –
FYE: December 31
Type: Subsidiary

Canon Virginia provides contract manufacturing and parts fabrication services. The company assembles new and remanufactured office equipment including copiers toner and toner cartridges and laser printers. Its manufacturing capabilities include plastic injection molding metal fabrication and metal stamping. In addition to assembly it offers painting and packaging services as well as reverse-logistics contracts. The unit also provides return product repair services. Canon Virginia is a subsidiary of Canon U.S.A. the US arm of Japanese imaging giant Canon. Canon Virginia was founded in 1985.

CANTALOUPE INC
NMS: CTLP

100 Deerfield Lane, Suite 300
Malvern, PA 19355
Phone: 610 989-0340
Fax: –
Web: www.cantaloupe.com

CEO: Sean Feeney
CFO: Scott Stewart
HR: –
FYE: June 30
Type: Public

Since you can't get much from a vending machine with a quarter these days USA Technologies decided to make them take plastic. Its ePort device attaches onto vending machines and its eSuds works on washing machines and clothes dryers to allow them to accept debit and credit cards. With the Business Express device hotels libraries and universities can run their business centers as self-pay operations; customers simply swipe their cards to use a PC fax machine or copier. USA Technologies also sells energy-saving devices for such "always-on" appliances as vending machines and office equipment. Information from the company's remote devices is transmitted through the company's USALive network.

	Annual Growth	06/17	06/18	06/19	06/20	06/21
Sales ($ mil.)	12.5%	104.1	132.5	143.8	163.2	166.9
Net income ($ mil.)	–	(1.9)	(11.3)	(32.0)	(40.6)	(8.7)
Market value ($ mil.)	22.9%	370.5	997.6	529.4	310.7	845.1
Employees	16.3%	101	–	126	147	185

CANTEL MEDICAL CORP
NYS: CMD

150 Clove Road
Little Falls, NJ 07424
Phone: 973 890-7220
Fax: 973 890-7270
Web: www.cantelmedical.com

CEO: George L Fotiades
CFO: Shaun Blakeman
HR: –
FYE: July 31
Type: Public

Just ask Cantel Medical — cleanliness is second to nothing when it comes to medical and scientific equipment. Through its subsidiaries the firm sells infection prevention and control products to hospitals dentists drug makers researchers and others in the US and abroad in the field of health care. Its diverse offerings include medical device reprocessing systems and disinfectants for dialyzers and endoscopes water purification equipment masks and bibs used in dental offices and therapeutic filtration systems. The US market accounts the largest for nearly 75% of total revenue.

	Annual Growth	07/16	07/17	07/18	07/19	07/20
Sales ($ mil.)	11.2%	664.8	770.2	871.9	918.2	1,016.0
Net income ($ mil.)	(30.9%)	60.0	71.4	91.0	55.0	13.7
Market value ($ mil.)	(8.3%)	2,822.8	3,128.4	3,908.9	3,890.7	1,992.2
Employees	16.4%	2,000	2,337	2,693	2,775	3,669

CANTERBURY PARK HOLDING CORP (NEW)　　　NMS: CPHC

1100 Canterbury Road　　　CEO: –
Shakopee, MN 55379　　　CFO: Randy J Dehmer
Phone: 952 445-7223　　　HR: –
Fax: –　　　FYE: December 31
Web: www.canterburypark.com　　　Type: Public

The tails of this Canterbury are connected to horses running around a track. The operator of the Canterbury Park racetrack in Shakopee Minnesota Canterbury Park Holding offers live pari-mutuel horse racing from May through September. The racetrack also offers year-round betting on simulcast races from racetracks such as Churchill Downs Hollywood Park and Belmont Park. When horses aren't dashing down the track the company stages other events (snowmobile races concerts crafts shows private parties) at Canterbury Park. It also offers gambling for card sharks at its on-site Card Club. Chairman Curtis Sampson owns more than 20% of the company.

	Annual Growth	12/16	12/17	12/18	12/19	12/20
Sales ($ mil.)	(10.8%)	52.5	57.0	59.1	59.2	33.1
Net income ($ mil.)	(29.1%)	4.2	4.1	5.7	2.7	1.1
Market value ($ mil.)	4.5%	47.7	77.2	66.0	58.9	56.8
Employees	(8.3%)	864	1,213	854	930	610

CANTOR ENTERTAINMENT TECHNOLOGY INC.

2575 S. Highland Dr.　　　CEO: Lee M Amaitis
Las Vegas NV 89109　　　CFO: Douglas R Barnard
Phone: 702-677-3800　　　HR: –
Fax: 201-528-9201　　　FYE: December 31
Web: cancergenetics.com　　　Type: Private

Cantor Entertainment Technology is willing to bet that high-rollers wouldn't mind replacing that slot machine with a tablet computer. Doing business as Cantor Gaming the company is the only provider of mobile gaming and mobile wagering systems in Nevada. (Mobile betting in casino hotel rooms was legalized in 2011.) Cantor Gaming supplies a handful of Las Vegas resorts with handheld touchscreen computers that offer race and sports books and other mobile casino games; players rent the computers from the casino. In addition it launched a sports wagering app for Android phones that can be used anywhere in Nevada and is developing apps for Apple and Windows phones. The company filed an IPO in 2011 but withdrew it in 2012.

CANTOR FITZGERALD L.P.

110 E. 59th St.　　　CEO: –
New York NY 10022　　　CFO: Jeffrey Chertoff
Phone: 212-938-5000　　　HR: –
Fax: 212-829-5280　　　FYE: December 31
Web: www.cantor.com　　　Type: Private

Neither a choir leader nor a Jazz Age novelist this Cantor Fitzgerald probably does sing the praises of strong returns. Cantor Fitzgerald provides a variety of investment services including trading and brokerage asset management investment banking and market research. One of the largest traders of US Treasury securities it also deals in global equities bonds and derivatives. Niche operations include UK spread specialist Cantor Index the Cantor FX (foreign exchange trading) and Cantor Gaming (technology services for the gaming industry). Cantor Fitzgerald serves more than 5000 institutional clients around the world. B. Gerald Cantor and John Fitzerald co-founded the company in 1945.

CAPCOM U.S.A. INC.

800 Concar Dr. Ste. 300　　　CEO: –
San Mateo CA 94402-2649　　　CFO: Koko Ishikawa
Phone: 650-350-6500　　　HR: –
Fax: +49-1805252587　　　FYE: March 31
Web: www.sony.de　　　Type: Subsidiary

Capcom USA sets its cap at the US video game market. The subsidiary of Japan's Capcom Co. Ltd. was established as the administrative arm for Capcom's US operations in 1985. It is best known for blockbuster video game franchises such as Devil May Cry Mega Man Resident Evil and Street Fighter made for Sony Nintendo and Microsoft game consoles as well as for PCs. Recent hit franchises include Dead Rising and Monster Hunter. Mobile and social games such as Smurf's Village and Shrek's Fairytale Kingdom are developed through the Beeline brand. Beeline avoids established Capcom brands to focus strictly on family-friendly games. The US accounts for about 20% of parent Capcom's overall revenues.

CAPE BANCORP, INC.　　　NMS: CBNJ

225 North Main Street　　　CEO: –
Cape May Court House, NJ 08210　　　CFO: –
Phone: 609 465-5600　　　HR: –
Fax: –　　　FYE: December 31
Web: www.capebanknj.com　　　Type: Public

Cape Bank is a permanent fixture serving the ebb and flow of New Jersey's touristy coastal and inland towns. Serving both commercial and residential customers the community bank provides traditional deposit options such as checking and savings accounts as well as loan services like home equity lines of credit and commercial mortgages (which represents more than half its loan portfolio). The company operates about 15 locations and serves customers in Atlantic and Cape May counties. It was formed in 2007 to be the holding company for Cape Bank and went public the following year; the bank's roots go back to the 1920s. OceanFirst Financial agreed to buy Cape Bancorp for $208.1 million in early 2016.

	Annual Growth	12/10	12/11	12/12	12/13	12/14
Assets ($ mil.)	0.4%	1,061.0	1,071.1	1,040.8	1,092.9	1,079.9
Net income ($ mil.)	13.8%	4.0	8.0	4.6	5.6	6.8
Market value ($ mil.)	2.6%	97.5	90.1	99.7	116.6	108.0
Employees	(1.7%)	213	202	212	203	199

CAPE COD HEALTHCARE, INC.

27 PARK ST　　　CEO: Michael K Lauf
HYANNIS, MA 026015230　　　CFO: Michael Connors
Phone: 508-862-5030　　　HR: –
Fax: –　　　FYE: September 30
Web: www.capecodhealth.org　　　Type: Private

Cape Cod Healthcare (CCHC) is a not-for-profit healthcare organization that operates two acute care hospitals (Cape Cod Hospital and Falmouth Hospital). Specializations include heart and vascular women's health bones and muscles cancer care and brain spine and nerves. CCHC also operates a home health services agency (Visiting Nurse Association of Cape Cod) more than 130-bed skilled nursing and rehabilitation facility (JML Care Center) and assisted living facility (Heritage at Falmouth). The health care system has affiliations with UMass Medical School Boston University University of New England and Cape Cod Community College. CCHC is the Cape's largest private employer with more than 5300 staff members 450 physicians and 790 volunteers.

	Annual Growth	09/16	09/17	09/18	09/19	09/20
Sales ($ mil.)	2.2%	–	872.6	921.4	978.6	931.4
Net income ($ mil.)	(28.4%)	–	74.3	80.5	29.1	27.3
Market value ($ mil.)	–	–	–	–	–	–
Employees	–	–	–	–	–	1,850

CAPE COD HOSPITAL

27 PARK ST
HYANNIS, MA 026015203
Phone: 508-771-1800
Fax: -
Web: www.capecodhealth.org

CEO: Michael K Lauf
CFO: -
HR: -
FYE: September 30
Type: Private

Get too much sun or eat too much lobster while visiting Cape Cod? Never fear Cape Cod Hospital can treat whatever ails you. Cape Cod Hospital a subsidiary of Cape Cod Healthcare is a 260-bed acute care hospital that serves the Cape Cod Massachusetts area. Its specialty services include pediatrics maternity care cancer treatment and infectious disease therapeutics. The not-for-profit Cape Cod Hospital also includes a specialty cardiovascular center a psychiatry unit a surgical pavilion and a diagnostic imaging facility as well as outpatient medical offices.

	Annual Growth	09/16	09/17	09/18	09/19	09/20
Sales ($ mil.)	2.7%	-	526.7	564.0	599.3	569.8
Net income ($ mil.)	(36.3%)	-	47.4	46.6	26.0	12.3
Market value ($ mil.)	-	-	-	-	-	-
Employees	-	-	-	-	-	1,700

CAPE ENVIRONMENTAL MANAGEMENT INC.

500 PINNACLE CT STE 100
NORCROSS, GA 300713630
Phone: 770-908-7200
Fax: -
Web: www.cape-inc.com

CEO: Fernando J Rios
CFO: Les Flynn
HR: -
FYE: December 27
Type: Private

Cape Environmental Management offers a number of engineering and environmental services including facility construction and demolition remediation and water and wastewater utility-related services. Clients include government agencies such as the US Air Force and the US Army Corps of Engineers and industrial clients in the petroleum chemical telecommunications and transportation sectors. Specialty areas include engineering scientific construction and industrial hygiene/safety. The company operates from more than a dozen offices located across the US. It also has two offices in Iraq. Cape Environmental Management was founded in 1965 and acquired by its executive team in 1991.

	Annual Growth	12/02	12/03	12/04	12/06	12/08
Sales ($ mil.)	19.2%	-	-	46.1	117.7	92.9
Net income ($ mil.)	-	-	-	0.0	20.3	4.0
Market value ($ mil.)	-	-	-	-	-	-
Employees	-	-	-	-	-	315

CAPELLA EDUCATION COMPANY   NMS: CPLA

Capella Tower, 225 South Sixth Street, 9th Floor
Minneapolis, MN 55402
Phone: 888 227-3552
Fax: -
Web: www.capellaeducation.com

CEO: J Kevin Gilligan
CFO: Steven L Polacek
HR: -
FYE: December 31
Type: Public

Capella Education is all about the digital age. The fast-growing company operates Capella University an online school that offers more than 1840 online courses about 160 undergraduate and graduate degree programs with some 160 specializations. Its 37000 students from the US and abroad are primarily composed of working adults 72% of which are pursuing master's or doctoral degrees. Capella Education's faculty members are mostly part-time employees typically teaching one to three courses per semester. The firm's programs range across a variety of subjects including business health human resources information technology and psychology. Capella Education is merging with Strayer Education in a $1.9 billion transaction.

	Annual Growth	12/12	12/13	12/14	12/15	12/16
Sales ($ mil.)	0.4%	421.9	415.6	422.0	430.3	429.4
Net income ($ mil.)	4.2%	36.5	35.2	37.9	40.2	43.0
Market value ($ mil.)	32.8%	325.9	767.0	888.5	533.6	1,013.7
Employees	0.9%	2,829	2,804	2,944	2,887	2,928

CAPGEMINI NORTH AMERICA INC.

623 5th Ave. 33rd Fl.
New York NY 10022
Phone: 212-314-8000
Fax: 212-314-8001
Web: www.us.capgemini.com

CEO: Paul Hermelin
CFO: -
HR: -
FYE: December 31
Type: Subsidiary

Vive la technologie! Capgemini North America oversees the US Canadian and Mexican operations of Paris-based consulting giant Cap Gemini. Like its parent the subsidiary offers management and IT consulting services systems integration technology development design and outsourcing services through nearly 30 offices in about a dozen US states Puerto Rico and Canada. Its consultants serve clients in a variety of industries including automotive energy and utilities financial services high-tech manufacturing and transportation. The unit was formed in 2000 after Capgemini acquired the consulting arm of accounting giant Ernst & Young. Capgemini North America represents almost 20% of its parent's annual sales.

CAPITAL BANK CORPORATION   NASDAQ: CBKN

333 Fayetteville Ste. 700
Raleigh NC 27601-2950
Phone: 919-645-6400
Fax: 919-645-6435
Web: www.capitalbank-nc.com

CEO: -
CFO: -
HR: -
FYE: December 31
Type: Public

Capital Bank Corporation owns about a quarter of Capital Bank NA which has more than 140 offices in the Carolinas Florida Tennessee and Virginia. The bank provides consumer and commercial banking services such as savings checking and health savings accounts as well as CDs IRAs and credit cards. Real estate loans including commercial and residential mortgages as well as construction land development and farmland loans make up about 85% of the bank's loan portfolio. Business and consumer loans help to round out its lending activities. The bank offers private banking trust and investment services through affiliate Naples Capital Advisors.

CAPITAL BANK FINANCIAL CORP   NMS: CBF

4725 Piedmont Row Drive Suite 110
Charlotte, NC 28210
Phone: 704 554-5901
Fax: -
Web: www.capitalbank-us.com

CEO: -
CFO: -
HR: -
FYE: December 31
Type: Public

Capital Bank Financial Corporation (formerly North American Financial Holdings) owns $7.5 billion-asset Capital Bank NA which operates more than 150 branches in North Carolina Tennessee Florida South Carolina and Virginia. The bank offers standard savings and checking accounts as well as mortgages consumer and commercial loans. More than 40% of its loan portfolio consists of business loans while consumer loans make up another one-third and commercial real estate mortgages make up an additional 20%. The bank also offers trust and investment management and mortgage banking services. Formed in 2009 Capital Bank Financial went public in 2012.

	Annual Growth	12/11	12/12	12/13	12/14	12/15
Assets ($ mil.)	3.1%	6,587.2	7,295.7	6,617.6	6,831.4	7,449.5
Net income ($ mil.)	72.3%	6.2	51.2	38.8	50.9	54.7
Market value ($ mil.)	23.3%	-	736.5	981.5	1,156.2	1,379.7
Employees	(1.6%)	1,480	1,588	1,610	1,515	1,389

CAPITAL BLUECROSS

2500 Elmerton Ave.
Harrisburg PA 17177
Phone: 717-541-7000
Fax: 717-541-6915
Web: htttps://www.capbluecross.com

CEO: Todd A Shamash
CFO: Michael Cleary
HR: –
FYE: December 31
Type: Private - Not-for-Pr

If you dwell in the Lehigh Valley Capital BlueCross could be your direct link to health care coverage. A licensee of the Blue Cross and Blue Shield Association the company provides health insurance products to individuals and employer groups with a total of about 1 million members in central and eastern Pennsylvania. It offers traditional PPO HMO and POS health care plans as well as dental and vision coverage and Medicare Advantage plans. Capital BlueCross' network includes more than 11000 health care providers and some 40 hospitals. The company also provides benefits administration services to self-funded customers through for-profit subsidiary Capital Administrative Services (dba NCAS Pennsylvania).

CAPITAL HEALTH SYSTEM INC.

750 BRUNSWICK AVE
TRENTON, NJ 086384143
Phone: 609-394-6000
Fax: –
Web: www.capitalhealth.org

CEO: Al Maghazehe
CFO: Shane Fleming
HR: –
FYE: December 31
Type: Private

Capital Health System (CHS) serves the residents of New Jersey's capital city through two hospitals. Together they have about 430 beds. The not-for-profit organization offers emergency surgical and acute health care and it serves as a hands-on teaching facility to nursing and medical students. It also operates outpatient care facilities. CHS primarily serves residents of Mercer County and parts of Bucks County in central New Jersey. Capital Health System offers centers for maternal and pediatric health neurology emergency and trauma services oncology orthopedics mental health surgery and sleep diagnostics.

	Annual Growth	12/06	12/07	12/08	12/12	12/14
Sales ($ mil.)	248.7%	–	–	0.3	538.8	585.5
Net income ($ mil.)	–	–	–	0.0	(58.1)	(18.9)
Market value ($ mil.)	–	–	–	–	–	–
Employees	–	–	–	–	–	3,000

CAPITAL CITY BANK GROUP, INC.   NMS: CCBG

217 North Monroe Street
Tallahassee, FL 32301
Phone: 850 402-7821
Fax: –
Web: www.ccbg.com

CEO: William Smith
CFO: J. Kimbrough Davis
HR: –
FYE: December 31
Type: Public

Capital City Bank Group is the holding company for Capital City Bank (CCB). The bank provides traditional deposit and credit services mortgage banking asset management trust merchant services bank cards data processing and securities brokerage services through some 60 banking offices in Florida Georgia and Alabama. Through Capital City Home Loans the company has about 30 additional offices in mortgage banking in the Southeast. In addition to CCB other assets include Capital City Trust Company and Capital City Investments. The bank was founded in 1895.

	Annual Growth	12/16	12/17	12/18	12/19	12/20
Assets ($ mil.)	7.5%	2,845.2	2,898.8	2,959.2	3,089.0	3,798.1
Net income ($ mil.)	28.0%	11.7	10.9	26.2	30.8	31.6
Market value ($ mil.)	4.7%	343.9	385.2	389.7	512.1	412.7
Employees	(2.4%)	853	825	819	815	773

CAPITAL ONE FINANCIAL CORP   NYS: COF

1680 Capital One Drive
McLean, VA 22102
Phone: 703 720-1000
Fax: –
Web: www.capitalone.com

CEO: Kevin Borgmann
CFO: Andrew Young
HR: Jory Berson
FYE: December 31
Type: Public

Capital One Financial is one of the most recognizable issuers of Visa and MasterCard credit cards in the US. It offers credit and debit card products auto loans and other consumer lending products in markets across the US The company also offer products outside of the US principally through Capital One (Europe) plc (COEP) and through a branch of COBNA in Canada. It boasts a banking network of branches and Caf ©s (mostly in over five US states) and maintains a strong online presence with ists internet and mobile banking applications.

	Annual Growth	12/16	12/17	12/18	12/19	12/20
Assets ($ mil.)	4.2%	357,033.0	365,693.0	372,538.0	390,365.0	421,602.0
Net income ($ mil.)	(7.8%)	3,751.0	1,982.0	6,015.0	5,546.0	2,714.0
Market value ($ mil.)	3.2%	40,040.7	45,704.5	34,693.7	47,232.8	45,369.4
Employees	2.4%	47,300	49,300	47,600	51,900	51,985

CAPITAL DISTRICT PHYSICIANS' HEALTH PLAN, INC.

500 PATROON CREEK BLVD
ALBANY, NY 122061057
Phone: 518-641-3700
Fax: –
Web: www.cdphp.com

CEO: –
CFO: –
HR: –
FYE: December 31
Type: Private

Capital District Physicians' Health Plan (CDPHP) is an independent not-for-profit health plan serving some 448000 members in two dozen New York counties. It offers employer-sponsored and individual managed care plans (including HMO PPO and consumer-directed plans) as well as a Medicare Advantage plan for seniors. The company's coverage include full coverage for some preventative medical services as well as options for covering prescription drugs dental work and vision services. CDPHP also provides wellness programs that help members with weight loss smoking cessation and chronic disease management.

	Annual Growth	12/01	12/02	12/03	12/09	12/13
Sales ($ mil.)	4.9%	–	–	818.3	1,037.4	1,314.7
Net income ($ mil.)	–	–	–	(1.8)	33.5	23.0
Market value ($ mil.)	–	–	–	–	–	–
Employees	–	–	–	–	–	700

CAPITAL PROPERTIES, INC.   NBB: CPTP

5 Steeple Street, Unit 303
Providence, RI 02903
Phone: 401 435-7171
Fax: 401 435-7179
Web: www.capitalproperties.com

CEO: Robert Eder
CFO: –
HR: –
FYE: December 31
Type: Public

Was it providence or clear foresight that led Capital Properties to buy land in what is now Capital Center a downtown revitalization project in Providence Rhode Island? The company owns and leases out about a dozen parcels of land totaling some 18 acres in the area making it Capital Center's largest landowner. It leases parcels for the long term (at least 99 years) and leaves development and improvement to its tenants. Subsidiaries own and operate a petroleum storage facility in East Providence used by Global Partners and lease land to Lamar Advertising for roadside billboards in Rhode Island and Massachusetts. Chairman and CEO Robert Eder and his wife Linda together own a majority of Capital Properties.

	Annual Growth	12/16	12/17	12/18	12/19	12/20
Sales ($ mil.)	(2.7%)	5.1	5.2	5.3	5.2	4.6
Net income ($ mil.)	2.1%	1.8	6.0	1.3	2.5	2.0
Market value ($ mil.)	(2.2%)	89.1	92.3	100.6	101.6	81.5
Employees	(27.7%)	11	4	3	3	3

CAPITAL SOUTHWEST CORP.   NMS: CSWC

5400 Lyndon B. Johnson Freeway, Suite 1300
Dallas, TX 75240
Phone: 214 238-5700
Fax: –
Web: www.capitalsouthwest.com

CEO: Bowen Diehl
CFO: Michael Sarner
HR: –
FYE: March 31
Type: Public

A private equity firm Capital Southwest owns significant minority stakes in around 30 companies many of them in Texas. The business development company (BDC) offers growth capital recapitalization and acquisition financing and funding for management buyouts to companies in a variety of industries. It typically invests between $5 million to $15 million per transaction in target firms which do not include troubled companies startups real estate developments or other less-than-stable ventures. The company is also focused on investments in the US especially firms located in the Southwest Southeast Midwest and Mountain regions.

	Annual Growth	03/15	03/16	03/17	03/18	03/19
Assets ($ mil.)	(8.2%)	776.9	284.5	325.8	417.5	551.8
Net income ($ mil.)	–	(2.4)	(10.7)	7.9	16.2	23.7
Market value ($ mil.)	(17.9%)	812.5	242.8	296.0	297.9	368.3
Employees	6.7%	17	15	17	19	22

CAPITALSOURCE INC.   NYSE: CSE

633 W. 5th St. 33rd Fl.
Los Angeles CA 90071
Phone: 213-443-7700
Fax: 800-543-2095
Web: www.wrighttool.com

CEO: –
CFO: –
HR: –
FYE: December 31
Type: Public

CapitalSource is a capital source of capital for small- and middle-market businesses. Its CapitalSource Bank subsidiary formed in 2008 provides commercial and multifamily mortgages operating loans equipment leases and other finance options to small and midsized companies from about 10 offices throughout the US. It also has about 20 bank branches in central and southern California that offer retail deposit products such as savings and money market accounts CDs and IRAs to help fund its lending activities. Target sectors include health care security technology consumer lending and professional practices such as dentist and physician offices.

CAPITOL FEDERAL FINANCIAL INC   NMS: CFFN

700 South Kansas Avenue
Topeka, KS 66603
Phone: 785 235-1341
Fax: –
Web: www.capfed.com

CEO: John Dicus
CFO: Kent Townsend
HR: –
FYE: September 30
Type: Public

Capital Federal Financial is a savings and loan holding company. The bank competes for commercial banking business through a wide variety commercial deposit and expanded lending products. Capital Federal Financial offers consumer lending that offers a variety of secured consumer loans including home equity loans and lines of credit home improvement loans vehicle loans and loans secured by savings deposits as well as commercial lending. The savings bank serves metropolitan areas of the Topeka Wichita Lawrence Manhattan Emporia and Salina as well as Kansas City Missouri through a network of more than 50 branches.

	Annual Growth	09/17	09/18	09/19	09/20	09/21
Assets ($ mil.)	1.2%	9,192.9	9,449.5	9,340.0	9,487.2	9,631.2
Net income ($ mil.)	(2.5%)	84.1	98.9	94.2	64.5	76.1
Market value ($ mil.)	(6.0%)	2,040.8	1,768.7	1,913.1	1,286.3	1,595.2
Employees	1.5%	708	775	773	793	750

CAPRI CAPITAL PARTNERS LLC

875 N. Michigan Ave. Ste. 3430
Chicago IL 60611
Phone: 312-573-5300
Fax: 312-573-5273
Web: www.capricapital.com

CEO: –
CFO: –
HR: –
FYE: December 31
Type: Private

Capri Capital wants its investors to experience the Mediterranean isle's legendary spirit of "la dolce vita" "the sweet life." The company provides capital in the lending and equity investments arenas to public and private real estate companies. Its Capri Capital Advisors is a real estate investment management firm specializing in multi-family (more than two-thirds of its investments) industrial retail and office projects in major US markets. Capri Capital named after founders Daryl Carter and Quintin Primo was created in 1992 and manages nearly $5 billion in loans and investments related to real estate.

CAPRICOR THERAPEUTICS INC   NAS: CAPR

8840 Wilshire Blvd., 2nd Floor
Beverly Hills, CA 90211
Phone: 310 358-3200
Fax: –
Web: www.capricor.com

CEO: Linda Marban
CFO: Anthony Bergmann
HR: –
FYE: December 31
Type: Public

While its operations are far from the Nile river Nile Therapeutics makes products aimed at getting cardiovascular systems moving like a river. A biopharmaceutical company Nile Therapeutics has a handful of candidates in development in its pipeline that are designed to treat acute heart failure. Its primary candidate CD-NP is a peptide (short specialized amino acid chain) engineered to treat acute decompensated heart failure (ADHF) or the rapid degeneration of the heart resulting from a heart attack or other medical conditions. Nile's other prominent candidate is an early-stage peptide also designed to treat similar cardiovascular conditions.

	Annual Growth	12/16	12/17	12/18	12/19	12/20
Sales ($ mil.)	(47.2%)	4.0	2.7	1.7	1.0	0.3
Net income ($ mil.)	–	(18.8)	2.4	(15.2)	(7.6)	(13.7)
Market value ($ mil.)	6.6%	54.7	32.5	8.4	26.3	70.6
Employees	(10.2%)	40	40	22	16	26

CAPRIUS INC.   PINK SHEETS: CAPI

10 Forest Ave. Ste. 220
Paramus NJ 07652
Phone: 201-342-0900
Fax: 913-647-0132
Web: www.elecsyscorp.com

CEO: Dwight Morgan
CFO: Jonathan Joels
HR: –
FYE: September 30
Type: Public

Caprius helps doctors take out the trash. The company owns a majority interest in MCM Environmental Technologies which provides systems for disposal of medical waste. Its SteriMed system can crush grind shred and mix all types of medical waste including metal sharps and needles plastic tubing and IV bags and glass items. Once this process is complete MCM's Steri-Cid chemical process disinfects the waste which can then be discarded as regular waste at as little as 10% of the original volume. MCM manufactures the SteriMed system in Israel; the company distributes parts and supplies from facilities in Israel. In 2011 the company was acquired by Vintage Capital Group LLC.

CAPROCK COMMUNICATIONS INC.

4400 S. Sam Houston Pkwy. East
Houston TX 77048
Phone: 832-668-2300
Fax: 832-668-2388
Web: www.caprock.com

CEO: –
CFO: –
HR: –
FYE: December 31
Type: Subsidiary

CapRock Communications provides satellite communications services where others fear to tread. The company's network enables the secure transmission of voice data and video primarily for customers operating in remote locations or harsh environments such as offshore drilling platforms. Clients come from the construction maritime military mining and energy exploration industries. CapRock also provides systems integration and project management services including engineering design equipment installation and testing. CapRock operates a global communications network in cooperation with other satellite fleet operators. The company was acquired by Harris Corporation in 2010 for about $525 million in cash.

CAPSONIC GROUP LLC

460 2nd St.
Elgin IL 60123-7008
Phone: 847-888-7300
Fax: 847-888-7543
Web: www.capsonic.com

CEO: Greg G Liautaud
CFO: Thomas Gillespie
HR: Maryann Scordas
FYE: December 31
Type: Private

Following the belief that specialization makes money Capsonic Group specializes in high-volume production of custom molded plastic inserts and composites. Its products include connectors for electronics and vehicles; sensors for telecommunication devices; switch bases for power tools; and brush holders for office machines and appliances. About half of its sales are from automakers and component makers such as GM Ford and Hewlett-Packard. The company operates a plant housing 50 30-ton to 300-ton presses that bind multiple plastic and metal materials to create one part. Its services include product design and prototyping. Sister company Capsonic Automotive produces solenoid switches and lighting components.

CAPSTEAD MORTGAGE CORP.   NYS: CMO

8401 North Central Expressway, Suite 800
Dallas, TX 75225-4404
Phone: 214 874-2323
Fax: –
Web: www.capstead.com

CEO: –
CFO: –
HR: –
FYE: December 31
Type: Public

Capstead Mortgage is a self-managed real estate investment trust (REIT) with holdings in mortgage-backed securities. It makes leveraged investments in single-family residential adjustable-rate mortgage securities issued and backed by government agencies such as Fannie Mae Freddie Mac and Ginnie Mae. It occasionally makes limited investments in credit-sensitive commercial mortgage assets as well. The REIT typically funds its investment activities through short-term borrowings or equity offerings. Founded in 1985 Capstead is one of the oldest publicly traded mortgage REITs in the US and manages an investment portfolio worth nearly $1.17 billion.

	Annual Growth	12/15	12/16	12/17	12/18	12/19
Assets ($ mil.)	(5.5%)	14,446.4	13,576.9	13,733.4	12,186.5	11,520.0
Net income ($ mil.)	–	108.3	82.9	79.6	50.1	(35.3)
Market value ($ mil.)	(2.4%)	826.9	964.0	818.3	631.0	749.3
Employees	0.0%	14	14	13	15	14

CAPSTONE GREEN ENERGY CORP   NAS: CGRN

16640 Stagg Street
Van Nuys, CA 91406
Phone: 818 734-5300
Fax: –
Web: www.capstoneturbine.com

CEO: Darren Jamison
CFO: Frederick Hencken
HR: –
FYE: March 31
Type: Public

Capstone Turbine's (Capstone) products are here when the lights go out. The company makes the Capstone MicroTurbine a power-generating system that produces environmentally friendly electricity and heat. The microturbines which can operate on a stand-alone basis or be connected to the utility grid run on a variety of liquid and gaseous fuels such as natural gas diesel kerosene propane and flare gases from landfills and sewage plants. In the event of a power outage customers can use microturbines to produce its own secure power for extended periods of time; microturbines can also be used as onboard battery chargers for hybrid electric vehicles. Around 45% of the company's revenue comes from the US.

	Annual Growth	03/17	03/18	03/19	03/20	03/21
Sales ($ mil.)	(3.2%)	77.2	82.8	83.4	68.9	67.6
Net income ($ mil.)	–	(23.9)	(10.0)	(16.7)	(21.9)	(18.4)
Market value ($ mil.)	86.0%	9.8	14.7	11.5	15.4	117.2
Employees	(7.5%)	168	151	154	112	123

CAPTAIN D'S LLC

1717 Elm Hill Pike Ste. A-1
Nashville TN 37210
Phone: 615-391-5461
Fax: 615-231-2309
Web: www.captainds.com

CEO: Phil Greifeld
CFO: Keith Davis
HR: –
FYE: October 31
Type: Private

This Captain sails the fast food seas. Captain D's operates Captain D's Seafood Kitchen a leading quick-service seafood chain with more than 525 company-owned and franchised locations in about 25 states. The eateries feature a menu of fried and broiled fish shrimp and chicken as well as french fries hush puppies and corn on the cob. Captain D's also serves fish and chicken sandwiches salads and menu items for kids. Most of the restaurants are located in such southern states as Georgia Tennessee and Alabama. Ray Danner started the business as Mr. D's in 1969. Private equity firm Sun Capital Partners acquired the chain in 2010.

CAPTECH VENTURES INC.

7100 FOREST AVE STE 204
RICHMOND, VA 232263742
Phone: 804-355-0511
Fax: –
Web: www.captechconsulting.com

CEO: Sandy Williamson
CFO: –
HR: Jess Navon
FYE: December 31
Type: Private

CapTech Ventures provides management and IT consulting and related services to business and public sector clients primarily in the Mid-Atlantic region. The company specializes in providing technology services and products (covering big data agile methodology mobile app development and digital strategies for top companies and government agencies). Areas of specialty include data warehousing network design systems integration software interface design training and network security. CapTech serves retailers health care providers and financial services companies among others. Clients have included Campbell Soup Company the Richmond Virginia Chamber of Commerce and the US Navy.

	Annual Growth	12/01	12/02	12/04	12/11	12/12
Sales ($ mil.)	23.0%	–	8.7	14.4	49.8	69.1
Net income ($ mil.)	66.4%	–	–	0.1	2.3	5.7
Market value ($ mil.)	–	–	–	–	–	–
Employees	–	–	–	–	–	415

CARA THERAPEUTICS INC
NMS: CARA

4 Stamford Plaza, 107 Elm Street, 9th Floor
Stamford, CT 06902
Phone: 203 406-3700
Fax: –
Web: www.caratherapeutics.com

CEO: Christopher Posner
CFO: Thomas Reilly
HR: –
FYE: December 31
Type: Public

Cara Therapeutics cares about pain therapy. The clinical-stage biopharmaceutical company focuses on developing and commercializing new chemical products designed to alleviate pain by selectively targeting kappa opioid receptors. Its proprietary class of product candidates targets the body's peripheral nervous system. In a test with patients with moderate-to-severe pain they have demonstrated efficacy without inducing many of the undesirable side effects often associated with pain therapeutics. Cara's most advanced product candidates are KORSUVA (CR845/difelikefalin) injection and Oral KORSUVA (CR845/difelikefalin). Founded in 2004 the company is based in Stamford Connecticut.

	Annual Growth	12/16	12/17	12/18	12/19	12/20
Sales ($ mil.)	529.5%	0.1	0.9	13.5	19.9	135.1
Net income ($ mil.)	–	(57.3)	(58.1)	(74.0)	(106.4)	8.4
Market value ($ mil.)	13.0%	463.3	610.4	648.3	803.4	754.6
Employees	23.9%	34	37	55	67	80

CARACO PHARMACEUTICAL LABORATORIES LTD.
NYSE AMEX: CPD

1150 Elijah McCoy Dr.
Detroit MI 48202
Phone: 313-871-8400
Fax: 313-871-8314
Web: www.caraco.com

CEO: Abhay Gandhi
CFO: Mukul Rathi
HR: –
FYE: March 31
Type: Public

Caraco Pharmaceutical Laboratories peddles cheaper versions of prescription drugs. The drug company sells generic knock-offs of a wide variety of pharmaceuticals including about 40 prescription products in various strengths and dosages. Its product lineup includes treatments for high blood pressure cancer nervous system conditions diabetes allergies and pain. Indian drugmaker Sun Pharmaceutical Industries owns a majority stake in the firm and licenses US marketing rights to Caraco for a number of generic drugs. Caraco markets its products throughout the US and Puerto Rico selling primarily to pharmaceutical wholesalers. However it has halted manufacturing operations due to regulatory concerns.

CARAHSOFT TECHNOLOGY CORP.

12369 Sunrise Valley Dr. Ste. D2
Reston VA 20191
Phone: 703-871-8500
Fax: 703-871-8505
Web: www.carahsoft.com

CEO: –
CFO: John Bukman
HR: –
FYE: December 31
Type: Private

Carahsoft loves it when the government spends money (on technology that is.) It is a B2G (business to government) contractor that distributes software products by Adobe Red Hat SAP Symantec and VMware to local state and federal agencies especially through the General Services Administration. Carahsoft's technology partners offer data storage cloud computing resources encryption and open-source software and intelligence and human resources technologies among others. Founded in 2004 the company was named after CEO Craig Abod's daughter Carah.

CARAUSTAR RECOVERED FIBER GROUP INC.

5000 Austell-Powder Springs Rd. Ste. 300
Austell GA 30106-3227
Phone: 770-948-3101
Fax: 718-292-6348
Web: www.manhattanbeer.com

CEO: –
CFO: –
HR: Linda Simmons
FYE: December 31
Type: Subsidiary

Caraustar Recovered Fiber Group (RFG) a division of Caraustar Industries provides recovered fiber for use as paperboard through its processing plants and recycling centers located across the US. Recovered paper is processed into paperboard which in turn is converted into products such as tubes cores composite containers cartons and custom packaging. Through its own facilities and through brokerage operations Caraustar RFG distributes over a million tons of paper stock annually. Caraustar Industries filed Chapter 11 in May 2009; it reorganized and emerged as a private company in August 2009 after eliminating approximately $135 million in debt. Wayzata Investment Partners is the controlling stakeholder.

CARBO CERAMICS INC.

5050 WESTWAY PARK BLVD # 150
HOUSTON, TX 770412018
Phone: 281-921-6400
Fax: –
Web: www.carboceramics.com

CEO: Don P Conkle
CFO: Ernesto Bautista III
HR: Kim Eeson
FYE: December 31
Type: Private

CARBO Ceramics is a global technology company that provides products and services to several markets including oil and gas industrial agricultural and environmental markets. To increase well production operators often pump fluids down wells at high pressure to create fractures in the hydrocarbon-bearing rock formation (hydraulic fracturing). Proppants filled fracture creates a conductive channels through which the hydrocarbons can flow more freely from the formation to the well and then to the surface. CARBO Ceramics also offers related software fracture design and consulting services. The company filed its bankruptcy case with Houston's Southern District of Texas Bankruptcy Court in early 2020 and emerged from Chapter 11 bankruptcy protection in mid-2020.

	Annual Growth	12/15	12/16	12/17	12/18	12/19
Sales ($ mil.)	16.2%	–	103.1	188.8	210.7	161.7
Net income ($ mil.)	–	–	(80.1)	(253.1)	(75.4)	(304.2)
Market value ($ mil.)	–	–	–	–	–	–
Employees	–	–	–	–	–	407

CARBONITE INC
NMS: CARB

Two Avenue de Lafayette
Boston, MA 02111
Phone: 617 587-1100
Fax: –
Web: www.carbonite.com

CEO: Steve Munford
CFO: Anthony Folger
HR: –
FYE: December 31
Type: Public

Carbonite wishes that everyone followed the No. 1 piece of advice from any IT person ever: “Backup your data.” Carbonite's cloud-based backup and protection services preserve documents emails music photos and settings for PCs (Windows or Mac) and mobile devices such as Apple's iPhone and Google OS Android phones. Most of the company's revenue comes from subscriptions many in effect over several years. Carbonite targets the small and medium business market for its services while also operating a sizable business with consumers. The Boston-based company makes most of its sales in the US.

	Annual Growth	12/13	12/14	12/15	12/16	12/17
Sales ($ mil.)	22.3%	107.2	122.6	136.6	207.0	239.5
Net income ($ mil.)	–	(10.6)	(9.4)	(21.6)	(4.1)	(4.0)
Market value ($ mil.)	20.7%	333.4	402.2	276.2	462.2	707.4
Employees	22.2%	434	589	623	840	967

CARDEAN LEARNING GROUP LLC

111 N. Canal St. Ste. 455
Chicago IL 60606-7204
Phone: 312-669-5222
Fax: 954-360-7081
Web: www.valveresearch.com

CEO: –
CFO: –
HR: –
FYE: December 31
Type: Private

A maker of Masters of the Universe? Well not quite but Cardean Learning which operates Cardean University can make you a Master of Business. The company offers more than 60 online graduate and undergraduate degrees certificates and specializations including a fully accredited MBA program. Cardean Learning created its MBA courses in collaboration with Carnegie Mellon University Columbia Business School the London School of Economics and Political Science Stanford University and the University of Chicago Graduate School of Business. The institution is accredited by the Accrediting Commission of the Distance Education Training Council (DETC).

CARDIAC SCIENCE CORPORATION

3303 Monte Villa Pkwy.
Bothell WA 98021
Phone: 425-402-2000
Fax: 909-357-2020
Web: www.maisto.com

CEO: –
CFO: –
HR: –
FYE: December 31
Type: Subsidiary

The heart can't lie to Cardiac Science. The medical device company makes cardiovascular monitoring and therapeutic equipment including automated external defibrillators (AEDs) and electrocardiograms (ECGs/EKGs) as well as systems that analyze the heart's performance under stress. Its monitoring systems are used for extended surveillance and include telemetry devices for evaluation of the heart during rehabilitation exercise. Cardiac Science sells accessories such as lead wires and electrodes and provides product repair and technical support services. The company which has direct and indirect sales channels in more than 100 countries is a subsidiary of India-based health equipment manufacturer Opto Circuits.

CARDINAL BANKSHARES CORP. NBB: CDBK

101 Jacksonville Circle, P.O. Box 215
Floyd, VA 24091
Phone: 540 745-4191
Fax: 540 745-4133
Web: www.bankoffloyd.com

CEO: –
CFO: –
HR: –
FYE: December 31
Type: Public

Cardinal Bankshares may not answer to the Pope but it does pay attention to what its shareholders have to say. It is the holding company for The Bank of Floyd which serves southwest Virginia's Floyd County and surrounding areas from about 10 locations. The bank offers standard retail products and services including checking and savings accounts CDs IRAs and credit cards. It uses funds from deposits to write loans primarily real estate mortgages and loans. Bank subsidiary FBC has interests in two Virginia title insurance firms and an investment services company.

	Annual Growth	12/10	12/11	12/12	12/13	12/14
Assets ($ mil.)	2.7%	249.1	266.2	282.1	268.8	276.8
Net income ($ mil.)	(26.3%)	1.0	1.1	(4.2)	(7.2)	0.3
Market value ($ mil.)	1.4%	12.7	20.3	20.7	17.7	13.4
Employees	(2.5%)	40	39	—	—	—

CARDINAL BANKSHARES CORPORATION OTC: CDBK

101 Jacksonville Cir.
Floyd VA 24091
Phone: 540-745-4191
Fax: 540-745-4133
Web: www.bankoffloyd.com

CEO: –
CFO: –
HR: –
FYE: December 31
Type: Public

Cardinal Bankshares may not answer to the Pope but it does pay attention to what its shareholders have to say. It is the holding company for The Bank of Floyd which serves southwest Virginia's Floyd County and surrounding areas from about 10 locations. The bank offers standard retail products and services including checking and savings accounts CDs IRAs and credit cards. It uses funds from deposits to write loans primarily real estate mortgages and loans. Bank subsidiary FBC has interests in two Virginia title insurance firms and an investment services company.

CARDINAL FINANCIAL CORP NMS: CFNL

8270 Greensboro Drive, Suite 500
McLean, VA 22102
Phone: 703 584-3400
Fax: –
Web: www.cardinalbank.com

CEO: –
CFO: –
HR: –
FYE: December 31
Type: Public

Cardinal Financial can help you keep out of the red. The holding company owns Cardinal Bank which operates some 30 branches in northern Virginia and the Washington DC metropolitan area. Serving commercial and retail customers it offers such deposit options as checking savings and money market accounts; IRAs; and CDs as well as trust services. Commercial real estate loans make up more than 40% of Cardinal Financial's loan portfolio; residential mortgages construction loans business loans and home equity and consumer loans round out the bank's lending activities. West Virginia-based United Bankshares is buying Cardinal Financial for $912 million.

	Annual Growth	12/11	12/12	12/13	12/14	12/15
Assets ($ mil.)	11.5%	2,602.7	3,039.2	2,894.2	3,399.1	4,029.9
Net income ($ mil.)	14.0%	28.0	45.3	25.5	32.7	47.3
Market value ($ mil.)	20.6%	347.7	527.7	582.4	642.0	736.5
Employees	13.7%	510	706	809	733	851

CARDINAL HEALTH PHARMACY SOLUTIONS

1330 Enclave Pkwy.
Houston TX 77077
Phone: 281-749-4000
Fax: 281-749-2068
Web: www.cardinal.com/us/en/pharmacysolutions/overv

CEO: –
CFO: –
HR: –
FYE: June 30
Type: Business Segment

Cardinal Health Pharmacy Solutions soars above the playing field as a leading pharmacy management provider for hospitals in the US. The company provides services for all aspects of its institutional clients' pharmacy operations including full-service outsourcing staffing purchasing cost control regulatory compliance consulting finance and efficiency consulting quality and safety control and information technology. Its inventory control products include the Rxe-source remote order entry software (online prescription processing by remote pharmacists) and the Rxe-view medication order management system (for prescription use tracking and metrics). The company is a division of drug distributor Cardinal Health.

CARDINAL HEALTH, INC.   NYS: CAH

7000 Cardinal Place | CEO: Michael Kaufmann
Dublin, OH 43017 | CFO: Jason Hollar
Phone: 614-757-5000 | HR: –
Fax: – | FYE: June 30
Web: www.cardinalhealth.com | Type: Public

Cardinal Health is a top distributor of pharmaceuticals and other medical supplies and equipment in the US. Its pharmaceutical division provides supply chain services including branded generic and specialty pharmaceutical and OTC drug distribution. Cardinal's medical division parcels out medical laboratory and surgical supplies. Customers include retail pharmacies hospitals health care systems surgery centers nursing homes doctor's offices clinical labs and other health care businesses. The US accounts for the majority of Cardinal's revenue.

	Annual Growth	06/17	06/18	06/19	06/20	06/21
Sales ($ mil.)	5.7%	129,976.0	136,809.0	145,534.0	152,922.0	162,467.0
Net income ($ mil.)	(17.0%)	1,288.0	256.0	1,363.0	(3,696.0)	611.0
Market value ($ mil.)	(7.5%)	22,674.7	14,209.5	13,706.1	15,187.3	16,613.2
Employees	4.0%	40,400	50,200	49,500	30,000	47,300

CARDINAL LOGISTICS MANAGEMENT CORPORATION

5333 Davidson Hwy. | CEO: –
Concord NC 28027 | CFO: Michael Roberts
Phone: 704-786-6125 | HR: Lindsay Sexton
Fax: 704-788-6618 | FYE: December 31
Web: www.cardlog.com | Type: Private

Cardinal Logistics Management sings a sweet song when it comes to freight transportation. The company is a leading North American logistics provider with one of the largest dedicated fleet operations in the US. Its services include less-than-truckload (LTL) transportation in which freight from multiple shippers is combined into a single trailer; dedicated contract carriage in which drivers and equipment are assigned to customers long term; bulk transport; supply chain consulting; and warehousing and distribution. Cardinal Logistics which is owned by New York private equity firm Centerbridge Partners merged with another Centerbridge owned company Greatwide Logistics Services in early 2013.

CARDINGTON YUTAKA TECHNOLOGIES INC.

575 W. Main St. | CEO: –
Cardington OH 43315 | CFO: –
Phone: 419-864-8777 | HR: –
Fax: 419-864-7771 | FYE: March 31
Web: www.yutakatech.com | Type: Subsidiary

Cardington Yutaka Technologies (CYT) and its parent company Honda Motor Co. possess a certain synergy; subsidiary CYT supplies its parent with automotive parts and never wishes to appear exhausted. Primary parts manufactured by the company include exhaust systems and torque and catalytic converters. It also manufactures an assortment of other parts for manufacturers of both automobiles and all-terrain vehicles. CYT operates three manufacturing plants in the US — Alabama Ohio and South Carolina. The company's main customers are the various manufacturing plants of Honda of America Mfg. Inc.

CARDIOGENESIS CORPORATION

11 Musick | CEO: –
Irvine CA 92618-1638 | CFO: William R Abbott
Phone: 949-420-1800 | HR: –
Fax: 949-420-1888 | FYE: December 31
Web: www.cardiogenesis.com | Type: Subsidiary

Cardiogenesis will leave a hole in your heart and not feel a pang of guilt. The company's laser and fiber-optic systems are used for transmyocardial revascularization (TMR) and percutaneous myocardial channeling (PMC) procedures that use a laser to cut channels through the heart muscle into the heart chamber to help circulation in cardiac patients. Its SolarGen 2100 system is FDA-approved and is marketed through Cardiogenesis' sales force in the US and through international distributors. The company's PMC system is available outside the US. It also sells catheters and other related equipment to operate its laser systems. Tissue preservation firm CryoLife bought Cardiogenesis in 2010 for about $22 million.

CARDIOVASCULAR SYSTEMS, INC   NMS: CSII

1225 Old Highway 8 Northwest | CEO: Scott Ward
St. Paul, MN 55112-6416 | CFO: Jeffrey Points
Phone: 651 259-1600 | HR: –
Fax: – | FYE: June 30
Web: www.csi360.com | Type: Public

While Cardiovascular Systems Inc. (CSI) deals with blood there's no crime scene investigation here. Its Orbital Atherectomy Systems (OAS) treat calcified and fibrotic plaque in arterial vessels throughout the leg and heart in a few minutes of treatment time and address many of the limitations associated with existing surgical catheter and pharmacological treatment alternatives. CSI's Diamondback 360° and Stealth 360° products are minimally invasive catheter systems that help restore blood flow to the legs of patients with peripheral arterial disease (PAD) a condition that occurs when plaque builds up on limb arteries; and address the effects of coronary arterial disease (CAD). Vast majority of its revenue comes from its domestic operation.

	Annual Growth	06/17	06/18	06/19	06/20	06/21
Sales ($ mil.)	6.0%	204.9	217.0	248.0	236.5	259.0
Net income ($ mil.)	–	(1.8)	1.7	(0.3)	(27.2)	(13.4)
Market value ($ mil.)	7.3%	1,296.1	1,300.6	1,726.5	1,268.8	1,715.2
Employees	7.7%	579	652	731	779	780

CARDONE INDUSTRIES INC.

5501 Whitaker Ave. | CEO: Michael Carr
Philadelphia PA 19124-1799 | CFO: Margaret Ferrer
Phone: 215-912-3000 | HR: Sal Lo Dico
Fax: 215-912-3700 | FYE: December 31
Web: www.cardone.com | Type: Private

Old car parts are the new cool thanks to Cardone Industries. The company is one of the largest remanufacturers of auto parts for the aftermarket. Cardone offers seven lines under the A1 Cardone brand: brakes (master cylinders) drivetrain parts (constant-velocity axles) electronics (ignition distributors mass air flow sensors) fuel/air systems (intake manifolds) motors (window-lift and wiper) pumps (water and vacuum) and steering (power-steering pumps). New parts are also sold under the Cardone Select name. Cardone's eco-friendly benefits include material and energy conservation and landfill reduction.

CARDTRONICS PLC
NMS: CATM

2050 West Sam Houston Parkway South, Suite 1300
Houston, TX 77042
Phone: 832 308-4000
Fax: —
Web: www.cardtronics.com

CEO: Edward H West
CFO: —
HR: —
FYE: December 31
Type: Public

Cardtronics is the largest non-bank owner and operator of automated teller machines (ATMs) and related financial services equipment in the world. It maintains more than 112600 cash machines in Europe and North America including 92000 locations in the US many of which are branded by banks such as Chase PNC and Citibank. The company also leases and sells machines to airports convenience stores supermarkets malls and drug stores including Walgreens and CVS stores. Most clients pay the company to handle some or all of the maintenance services or operational services of their ATMs. Cardtronics also operates Allpoint which is the largest surcharge-free ATM network in the US with 55000 machines.

	Annual Growth	12/15	12/16	12/17	12/18	12/19
Sales ($ mil.)	3.0%	1,200.3	1,265.4	1,507.6	1,345.2	1,349.4
Net income ($ mil.)	(7.9%)	67.1	88.0	(145.4)	3.7	48.3
Market value ($ mil.)	—	—	—	—	—	—
Employees	3.4%	1,739	1,734	2,271	2,104	1,987

CARE NEW ENGLAND HEALTH SYSTEM INC

45 WILLARD AVE
PROVIDENCE, RI 029053218
Phone: 401-453-7900
Fax: —
Web: www.carenewengland.org

CEO: James Finale
CFO: —
HR: Dean Carlson
FYE: September 30
Type: Private

Care New England Health System take pains to ease its patients' pain. The system operates four hospitals: Kent Hospital a general acute care facility with about 360 beds; the 290-bed Memorial Hospital of Rhode Island; psychiatric facility Butler Hospital; and Women & Infants Hospital of Rhode Island which specializes in obstetrics gynecology and newborn pediatrics. All told the system has more than 963 licensed beds. Care New England formed in 1996 by three member hospitals also operates a home health agency and outpatient care facilities. In late 2016 the system dropped its plans to merge with Southcoast Health. The following year it agreed to be acquired by Partners HealthCare which is expanding outside of Massachusetts.

	Annual Growth	09/15	09/16	09/17	09/19	09/20
Sales ($ mil.)	(0.7%)	—	1,154.7	1,132.6	1,146.4	1,123.8
Net income ($ mil.)	—	—	(63.2)	21.9	(30.4)	(26.0)
Market value ($ mil.)	—	—	—	—	—	—
Employees	—	—	—	—	—	6,500

CARE.COM INC
NYS: CRCM

77 Fourth Avenue, Fifth Floor
Waltham, MA 02451
Phone: 781 642-5900
Fax: —
Web: www.care.com

CEO: Timothy Allen
CFO: Emily Neff
HR: —
FYE: December 29
Type: Public

Care.com lets families shop for child care senior care special needs care pet care tutoring and housekeeping services via web and mobile platforms. The site has more than 14 million members including more than 7.5 million families and more than 6 million caregivers who use Care.com to market their services and find employment. The service which is actively used in more than 15 countries (primarily the US but also Canada the UK and other parts of Western Europe) averages about 6.5 million unique visitors each month including about 4 million visitors per month from mobile devices. Care.com also offers household payroll management (HomePay) and other services. In early 2014 Care.com went public.

	Annual Growth	12/14	12/15	12/16	12/17	12/18
Sales ($ mil.)	13.3%	116.7	138.7	161.8	174.1	192.3
Net income ($ mil.)	—	(80.3)	(35.0)	7.0	10.7	52.9
Market value ($ mil.)	24.0%	267.0	233.1	274.7	578.3	630.6
Employees	29.2%	853	799	787	891	2,376

CARECENTRIC INC.

Overlook II 2839 Paces Ferry Rd. Ste. 900
Atlanta GA 30339
Phone: 678-264-4400
Fax: 770-384-1650
Web: www.carecentric.com

CEO: John Driscoll
CFO: Lyle Newkirk
HR: —
FYE: December 31
Type: Subsidiary

CareCentric helps health care providers spend less time managing their business operations and more time paying attention to patients. Formerly Simione Central Holdings the company offers software and services to help manage billing collections back office human resource development and process improvement systems for post-acute and long-term care providers. In addition to its software offerings CareCentric also provides outsourced scheduling patient intake marketing and quality assurance services. In early 2011 Mediware acquired CareCentric.

CAREFIRST INC.

10455 Mill Run Circle
Owings Mills MD 21117-5559
Phone: 410-528-7000
Fax: 513-381-0149
Web: www.firststudentinc.com

CEO: Chuck Burrell
CFO: —
HR: Lashawna May
FYE: December 31
Type: Private - Not-for-Pr

CareFirst makes health care coverage its No.1 priority. The firm is a not-for-profit non-stock holding company with subsidiaries providing managed health care plans to about 3.4 million members in Maryland and Washington DC. The company's main subsidiaries CareFirst of Maryland and Group Hospitalization and Medical Services are licensees of the Blue Cross and Blue Shield Association. Together the subsidiaries do business as CareFirst BlueCross BlueShield and offer Blue-branded HMO and PPO plans as well as consumer-driven coverage to individuals and employers throughout their service areas. Non-Blue subsidiaries and affiliates provide third-party benefits administration and claims processing services.

CAREFUSION CORP
NYS: CFN

3750 Torrey View Court
San Diego, CA 92130
Phone: 858 617-2000
Fax: —
Web: www.carefusion.com

CEO: —
CFO: Christopher R Reidy
HR: —
FYE: June 30
Type: Public

CareFusion cares about eliminating confusion and infection in hospital settings. It sells medical equipment - infusion and respiratory ventilation systems - and accompanying disposables for infection prevention. The company's Pyxis automated medication dispensing units cut down on clinician error when dealing with patients in critical care settings. Its Alaris infusion products include software to reduce IV medication errors. The company also makes AVEA respiratory ventilation devices SensorMedics pulmonary care products and V. Mueller surgical instruments. Other products and software help prevent the spread of hospital-acquired infections. Medical equipment maker Becton Dickenson is buying CareFusion.

	Annual Growth	06/10	06/11	06/12	06/13	06/14
Sales ($ mil.)	(0.6%)	3,929.0	3,528.0	3,598.0	3,550.0	3,842.0
Net income ($ mil.)	21.1%	194.0	244.0	293.0	385.0	417.0
Market value ($ mil.)	18.2%	4,639.9	5,553.5	5,249.0	7,532.1	9,065.1
Employees	1.6%	15,000	14,000	15,000	15,000	16,000

CAREGROUP, INC.

375 LONGWOOD AVE FL 7
BOSTON, MA 022155395
Phone: 617-667-1715
Fax: –
Web: www.caregroup.org

CEO: –
CFO: –
HR: –
FYE: September 30
Type: Private

Thanks to CareGroup there's well-bein' in Beantown. CareGroup serves Massachusetts residents through its flagship facility the 672-bed Beth Israel Deaconess Medical Center (BIDMC) and five other hospital campuses. With more than 1100 beds total the system provides a comprehensive range of general acute care as well as specialty care in a number of areas including orthopedics obstetrics diabetes and cardiovascular disease. In addition to its hospitals CareGroup operates a network of outpatient clinics and physician practices in the Boston area. It is also heavily involved in biomedical research and medical education.

	Annual Growth	09/08	09/09	09/10	09/11	09/12
Sales ($ mil.)	2.9%	–	–	–	2,380.1	2,448.8
Net income ($ mil.)	179.5%	–	–	–	47.0	131.3
Market value ($ mil.)	–	–	–	–	–	–
Employees	–	–	–	–	–	12,000

CAREY INTERNATIONAL INC.

4530 Wisconsin Ave. NW
Washington DC 20016
Phone: 202-895-1200
Fax: 202-895-1269
Web: www.carey.com

CEO: Sandy Miller
CFO: Mitchell Lahr
HR: –
FYE: November 30
Type: Private

Carey International carries passengers in about 550 major cities in some 60 countries. The company provides chauffeured car services primarily to business travelers as well as ground transportation logistics management through a global network of franchisees operated by the Carey family of subsidiaries licensees and affiliates. Services include airport pick-ups and drop-offs hourly charters special events and leisure travel. The company's fleet consists of sedans limousines vans minibuses and buses. Carey links its centralized reservation system to terminals at travel agencies corporate travel departments and government offices. It also offers online reservations. Carey was founded in 1921.

CARHARTT INC.

5750 Mercury Dr.
Dearborn MI 48126
Phone: 313-271-8460
Fax: 313-271-3455
Web: www.carhartt.com

CEO: Mark Valade
CFO: Susan Telang
HR: Lacey Royalty
FYE: December 31
Type: Private

Real workers don't leave home without first donning their Carhartts. The clothing maker produces rugged overalls flame-resistant workwear outerwear sweatshirts sportswear and pants favored by farmers and other hard-working people. Its products have even appeared in such films as "The Perfect Storm" and "The Horse Whisperer". Most of Carhartt's items sold to men women and children are made in US factories; the rest are produced in Mexico and Europe. Besides its own shops Carhartt's apparel is carried by major chains including Bass Pro Shops and Cabela's and international retailers in North America Europe Japan and Australia. The family of founder Hamilton Carhartt owns the firm which was founded in 1889.

CARILION CLINIC

1906 BELLEVIEW AVE SE
ROANOKE, VA 240141838
Phone: 540-981-7900
Fax: –
Web: www.goodneighborpharmacy.com

CEO: Nancy Howell Agee
CFO: Don Lorton
HR: Jamie Ghypes
FYE: September 30
Type: Private

If the name rings a bell for Virginians it may be because Carilion Clinic provides medical care for the citizens of southwestern Virginia. The regional health system includes eight not-for-profit hospitals a network of physicians and a research partnership with Virginia Tech. Carilion Clinic (including its handful of affiliates) has some 1200 beds and 60 neonatal ICU beds available. In addition to providing a range of medical treatments Carilion Clinic provides continuing medical education through its affiliation with medical schools including Virginia Tech Carilion School of Medicine and Research Institute (VTC).

	Annual Growth	09/13	09/14	09/15*	03/16*	09/16
Sales ($ mil.)	(0.2%)	–	1,489.5	1,510.5	800.9	1,482.7
Net income ($ mil.)	–	–	(28.1)	(42.6)	19.2	(1.8)
Market value ($ mil.)	–	–	–	–	–	–
Employees	–	–	–	–	–	9,200

*Fiscal year change

CARL BUDDIG & COMPANY

950 W. 175 St.
Homewood IL 60430
Phone: 708-798-0900
Fax: 708-798-1284
Web: www.buddig.com

CEO: Thomas Buddig
CFO: –
HR: Pam Spencer
FYE: December 31
Type: Private

Less is more at the Carl Buddig & Company which manufactures and markets some of the thinnest lunch meats available. The company's most popular brand Original Buddig is a svelte 10-15 calories per slice and comes in choices such as beef chicken turkey ham pastrami and corned beef. It also offers Old Wisconsin brand smoked beef jerky sticks and snack bites along with wieners bratwurst Polish sausage summer sausage and ring bologna. Carl Buddig's meat products are available in the US Puerto Rico and Canada and are sold at retail food outlets including Kroger Albertson's Safeway Food Lion Giant Roundy's and others.

CARLE FOUNDATION HOSPITAL

611 W PARK ST
URBANA, IL 618012529
Phone: 217-326-2900
Fax: –
Web: www.carle.org

CEO: –
CFO: –
HR: –
FYE: December 31
Type: Private

Carle Foundation Hospital is a nearly 435-bed acute-care facility that serves the residents of east central Illinois. The hospital includes the region's only Level I trauma center as well as a Level III perinatal center a neonatal ICU and centers devoted to cardiac and cancer care. It also runs a handful of specialty centers in the region. Carle Foundation Hospital is the primary teaching hospital for the University of Illinois College of Medicine at Urbana-Champaign. With more than 20 primary care locations throughout the region it is controlled by the not-for-profit Carle Foundation; sister company Carle Physician Group which boasts approximately 280 physicians representing early 75 specialties is one of the nation's largest private physician groups.

	Annual Growth	12/14	12/15	12/16	12/17	12/18
Sales ($ mil.)	7.5%	–	754.5	812.7	900.8	937.8
Net income ($ mil.)	9.8%	–	163.7	185.3	247.6	216.5
Market value ($ mil.)	–	–	–	–	–	–
Employees	–	–	–	–	–	2,500

CARLE PHYSICIAN GROUP

602 W. University Ave.
Urbana IL 61801
Phone: 217-383-3311
Fax: 217-383-6818
Web: www.carle-clinic.com

CEO: –
CFO: –
HR: –
FYE: December 31
Type: Private - Not-for-Pr

Carle Physician Group takes care of patients in east central Illinois. The company formerly named Carle Clinic Association is a not-for-profit physician-owned group made up of some 300 physicians practicing in more than 50 medical specialties at about a dozen locations. The organization's facilities which are spread out over seven different towns are linked by a network of electronic medical records allowing Carle Physician Group's medical providers to access a patient's medical information at any of its locations. The company also has its own managed care company Health Alliance Medical Plans. Carle Physician Group was acquired by Carle Foundation parent of Carle Foundation Hospital in 2010.

CARLISLE COMPANIES INC.

16430 North Scottsdale Road, Suite 400
Scottsdale, AZ 85254
Phone: 480 781-5000
Fax: –
Web: www.carlisle.com

NYS: CSL
CEO: –
CFO: Kevin Zdimal
HR: Lori Snyder
FYE: December 31
Type: Public

Through its four business segments multinational commercial manufacturing group Carlisle Companies creates and distributes an array of products including construction materials automotive products brake and friction products and interconnection technologies. Its largest segments produce construction material?including rubber and plastic roofing systems rigid foam insulation and waterproofing and protective coatings?and technologies for power and data transfer (wire cable connectors and contacts for aerospace and defense electronics). Carlisle strives to be a market leader in various niche markets. The US accounts for around 80% of company's total sales.

	Annual Growth	12/17	12/18	12/19	12/20	12/21
Sales ($ mil.)	4.1%	4,089.9	4,479.5	4,811.6	4,245.2	4,810.3
Net income ($ mil.)	3.6%	365.5	611.1	472.8	320.1	421.7
Market value ($ mil.)	21.6%	5,909.8	5,227.0	8,415.7	8,121.4	12,902.2
Employees	(7.3%)	15,600	14,900	15,000	13,000	11,500

CARLETON COLLEGE

1 N COLLEGE ST
NORTHFIELD, MN 550574044
Phone: 507-222-4000
Fax: –
Web: www.carleton.edu

CEO: –
CFO: –
HR: –
FYE: June 30
Type: Private

Curiosity is key at Carleton College. In addition to providing a traditional undergraduate liberal arts education the school encourages critical thinking and creativity at its campus in southern Minnesota. It has an enrollment of some 2000 students and a student-to-teacher ratio of 9:1. The college confers Bachelor of Arts degrees in more than 35 academic majors with a focus on fields including biology chemistry physics mathematics and computer science. The school offers education and foreign language certification and pre-professional programs as well. Carleton College was founded in 1866 by the Minnesota Conference of Congregational Churches under the name of Northfield College.

	Annual Growth	06/17	06/18	06/19	06/20	06/21
Sales ($ mil.)	0.7%	–	147.8	154.1	240.3	151.0
Net income ($ mil.)	60.2%	–	79.6	29.8	40.8	327.0
Market value ($ mil.)	–	–	–	–	–	–
Employees	–	–	–	–	–	650

CARLISLE FOODSERVICE PRODUCTS INCORPORATED

4711 E. Hefner Rd.
Oklahoma City OK 73131
Phone: 405-475-5600
Fax: 405-475-5607
Web: www.carlislefsp.com

CEO: –
CFO: –
HR: –
FYE: December 31
Type: Subsidiary

Carlisle FoodService doesn't play tennis but the company does know something about serving. A subsidiary of Carlisle Companies Carlisle FoodService (CFSP) manufactures food service products that range from dinnerware and salad bar display cases to serving spoons and service carts. It also makes janitorial/sanitation products (brooms and brushes). CFSP caters to both commercial and institutional markets including restaurants schools and hospitals. It has manufacturing plants in the US China and Mexico. North America and Europe generate most of CFSP's business which represents about 10% of its parent's sales. Founded in 1955 as Continental Plastics CFSP joined the Carlisle group of companies in 1978.

CARLISLE BRAKE & FRICTION INC.

6180 Cochran Rd.
Solon OH 44139
Phone: 440-528-4000
Fax: 440-528-4098
Web: www.carlislecbf.com

CEO: –
CFO: –
HR: –
FYE: December 31
Type: Subsidiary

Whether race car or dump truck Carlisle Brake & Friction (CBF) enables smoother starts and stops. The company provides high-performance brake clutch and transmission products to the off-highway aerospace agricultural construction industrial military and motorsports markets. Geared at OEMs and the aftermarket products include parking brakes wind turbine brakes brake pads transmission discs insulators and carbon-based friction materials. It has 10 manufacturing facilities in North America Europe and Asia/Pacific with additional R&D centers in the US and Wales and satellite sales offices in India and the Netherlands. CBF was formed in 2011 as a business segment of Carlisle Companies.

CARLISLE TIRE & WHEEL COMPANY

23 Windham Blvd.
Aiken SC 29805-9320
Phone: 803-643-2900
Fax: 803-643-2919
Web: www.carlisletire.com

CEO: Jacob Thomas
CFO: Max Narancich
HR: –
FYE: December 31
Type: Subsidiary

Big biters golf gliders and turf handlers are the wheels that keep business in motion at Carlisle Tire & Wheel. The company produces bias-ply steel-belted radial trailer tires rubber tires for non-automotive use as well as roll-formed and stamped steel wheels and tire and wheel assemblies. It sells to OEMs mass retailers and replacement markets for outdoor power equipment and power sports construction agricultural and recreational vehicles and home appliances. Manufacturing facilities in the US and China serve its diverse customer base in the US and Canada and less so Europe and Asia. Carlisle Tire & Wheel operates as a subsidiary within Carlisle Companies' family of transportation products.

CARLSON COMPANIES INC.

701 Carlson Pkwy.
Minnetonka MN 55305
Phone: 763-212-5000
Fax: 763-212-2219
Web: www.carlson.com

CEO: –
CFO: –
HR: –
FYE: December 31
Type: Private

Carlson Companies began in 1938 as the Gold Bond Stamp Company but has evolved into a leisure services juggernaut. The company owns a majority (55%) of travel giant Carlson Wagonlit. Its Carlson Hotels Worldwide owns and operates approximately 1075 hotels in more than 70 countries under brands such as Radisson Country Inns & Suites By Carlson and Park Plaza. In addition its Carlson Restaurants Worldwide includes the T.G.I. Friday's and Pick Up Stix chains. Chairman Marilyn Carlson Nelson and director Barbara Carlson Gage daughters of founder Curtis Carlson each own half of Carlson Companies.

CARLSON HOTELS WORLDWIDE INC.

701 Carlson Pkwy.
Minnetonka MN 55305
Phone: 763-212-5000
Fax: 763-212-3400
Web: www.carlsonhotels.com

CEO: John Kidd
CFO: –
HR: –
FYE: December 31
Type: Subsidiary

Carlson Hotels Worldwide has a little R&R on its mind. One of the world's leading hotel franchisors Carlson operates four lodging chains with more than 1000 properties in more than 75 countries including the upscale Radisson Hotel brand. The Radisson chain offers upscale amenities at more than 420 locations in about 70 countries. Carlson also owns the Park Plaza Hotels & Resorts (mid-market) Park Inn (economy) and Radisson Blu (upscale) brands. In addition its Country Inn & Suites chain provides extended-stay service at more than 480 locations. And with a 50.1% stake Carlson is the largest shareholder in The Rezidor Hotel Group. Carlson Hotels is a division of leisure conglomerate Carlson Companies.

CARLSON RESTAURANTS WORLDWIDE INC.

4201 Marsh Ln.
Carrollton TX 75007
Phone: 972-662-5400
Fax: 972-307-2822
Web: www.fridays.com

CEO: Nicholas P Shepherd
CFO: –
HR: –
FYE: December 31
Type: Subsidiary

Carlson Restaurants Worldwide (CRW) has a lot of Friday's for which to be thankful. A leader in full-service restaurants the company operates and franchises more than 900 T.G.I. Friday's casual dining locations across the US and in about 60 other countries. The restaurant chain offers a menu featuring beef chicken and seafood entrees along with a selection of popular appetizers. About 300 T.G.I. Friday's units are company-owned while the rest are franchised. The company also operates Pick Up Stix an Asian-themed fast-casual chain with more than 90 locations in California Nevada and Arizona. CRW is a subsidiary of travel and leisure conglomerate Carlson Companies.

CARLTON FIELDS P.A.

Corporate Center 3 Intl Plaza Ste. 1000 4221 W. Boy Scout Blvd.
Tampa FL 33607
Phone: 813-223-7000
Fax: 813-229-4133
Web: www.carltonfields.com

CEO: –
CFO: –
HR: –
FYE: January 31
Type: Private - Partnershi

Fielding complex questions of law is no monumental task for the firm Carlton Fields. The full service law firm offers expertise in such practice areas as intellectual property business litigation real estate health care and taxation. The firm employs about 300 attorneys in eight offices (six in Florida) serving clients throughout the Southeastern US and Latin America. In Florida its offices are located in Miami Orlando St. Petersburg Tallahassee Tampa and West Palm Beach. The firm also has offices in Atlanta and New York City. Carlton Fields was founded in 1901 by Milton and Giddings Mabry.

CARLYLE GROUP INC (THE)

1001 Pennsylvania Avenue, N.W.
Washington, DC 20004-2505
Phone: 202 729-5626
Fax: –
Web: www.carlyle.com

NMS: CG
CEO: Kewsong Lee
CFO: Curtis Buser
HR: –
FYE: December 31
Type: Public

A global investment firm The Carlyle Group is a global alternative asset manager with more than $246 billion in assets under management. Through three business segments the company invests in real estate power infrastructure energy distressed credit energy credit opportunistic credit corporate mezzanine funds aircraft financing and servicing other closed-end credit funds vehicles and corporate buyouts across numerous industries and regions. Carlyle currently has direct investments in about 255 companies and serve more than 2650 active carry fund investors from 95 countries. Most of the company's sales were generated from the Americas accounting to more than 60% of sales.

	Annual Growth	12/17	12/18	12/19	12/20	12/21
Sales ($ mil.)	24.3%	3,676.2	2,427.2	3,377.0	2,934.6	8,782.1
Net income ($ mil.)	86.8%	244.1	116.5	380.9	348.2	2,974.7
Market value ($ mil.)	24.4%	8,137.9	5,597.0	11,400.2	11,172.8	19,509.7
Employees	3.7%	1,600	1,650	1,775	1,825	1,850

CARMA LABORATORIES INC.

9750 S FRANKLIN DR
FRANKLIN, WI 531328848
Phone: 414-421-7707
Fax: –
Web: www.mycarmex.com

CEO: Eric Woelbing
CFO: –
HR: Beth Maloney
FYE: December 31
Type: Private

Carma Laboratories wants to make it easier for you to smile and sit. The family-owned-and-operated company is most famous for its retro yellow-lidded vials of Carmex lip balm. The company also makes Am-Ren a zinc-oxide based diaper rash ointment and LANEX hemorrhoid ointment to soothe cracked and painful tissues elsewhere. Once sold mostly in the Midwest and the ski areas of the Rockies Carmex (now also in cherry and strawberry flavors) soothes lips in all 50 states Canada Australia and Europe. The company was founded by Alfred Woelbing who developed the formula for Carmex in 1937 as a treatment for his own cold sores.

	Annual Growth	12/03	12/04	12/05	12/07	12/09
Sales ($ mil.)	(38.0%)	–	–	272.7	42.7	40.2
Net income ($ mil.)	433.4%	–	–	0.0	14.9	13.3
Market value ($ mil.)	–	–	–	–	–	–
Employees	–	–	–	–	–	70

CARMAX INC.
NYS: KMX

12800 Tuckahoe Creek Parkway
Richmond, VA 23238
Phone: 804 747-0422
Fax: -
Web: www.carmax.com

CEO: William Nash
CFO: Enrique Mayor-Mora
HR: -
FYE: February 28
Type: Public

CarMax is the US's largest specialty used-car retailer buys reconditions and sells cars and light trucks through approximately 220 superstores in 100-plus television markets (markets in which CarMax has a television advertising presence). Typically selling vehicles that are approximately ten years old with more than 100000 miles CarMax sells more than 751860 used cars per year. CarMax also operates one new-car franchises and sells about 426270 vehicles in-store auctions each year at about 75 stores. Additionally it sells older cars and trucks with higher mileage and offers vehicle financing through its CarMax Auto Finance unit.

	Annual Growth	02/17	02/18	02/19	02/20	02/21
Sales ($ mil.)	4.5%	15,875.1	17,120.2	18,173.1	20,320.0	18,950.1
Net income ($ mil.)	4.5%	627.0	664.1	842.4	888.4	746.9
Market value ($ mil.)	16.7%	10,531.1	10,103.6	10,133.0	14,246.6	19,500.7
Employees	2.5%	24,344	25,110	25,946	27,050	26,889

CARMIKE CINEMAS, INC.
NMS: CKEC

1301 First Avenue
Columbus, GA 31901-2109
Phone: 706 576-3400
Fax: -
Web: www.carmike.com

CEO: Adam M Aron
CFO: Craig R Ramsey
HR: -
FYE: December 31
Type: Public

At Carmike Cinemas the show must go on. The movie exhibitor owns operates or has stakes in about 250 theaters with more than 2500 screens in 35 states across the US. The company's theaters are located mostly in small to midsized communities where the chain hosts the only theater in town. Revenues come from the sale of admission tickets and concessions. Carmike also owns two Hollywood Connection family entertainment centers (one in Georgia and one in Utah) which feature multiplex theaters along with skating rinks miniature golf and arcades.

	Annual Growth	12/10	12/11	12/12	12/13	12/14
Sales ($ mil.)	8.9%	491.3	482.2	539.3	634.8	689.9
Net income ($ mil.)	-	(12.6)	(7.7)	96.3	5.8	(8.9)
Market value ($ mil.)	35.8%	188.5	168.0	366.3	679.9	641.5
Employees	6.1%	6,165	6,276	7,119	7,800	7,800

CARNEGIE INSTITUTION OF WASHINGTON

1530 P ST NW
WASHINGTON, DC 200051910
Phone: 202-387-6400
Fax: -
Web: www.carnegiescience.edu

CEO: -
CFO: -
HR: -
FYE: June 30
Type: Private

The folks that work at the Carnegie Institution of Washington aren't exactly melon heads. The organization known to the public as the Carnegie Institution for Science supports scientific research in areas such as plant biology developmental biology Earth and planetary sciences astronomy and global ecology. It operates via six scientific departments on the East and West Coasts. The institution funded primarily by an endowment of more than $530 million was established in 1902 by steel magnate Andrew Carnegie (whose other philanthropic endeavors included the Carnegie Corporation of New York and Carnegie Mellon University).

	Annual Growth	06/14	06/15	06/16	06/17	06/18
Sales ($ mil.)	(10.4%)	-	187.0	12.8	161.4	134.5
Net income ($ mil.)	(22.6%)	-	85.3	(90.5)	63.0	39.6
Market value ($ mil.)	-	-	-	-	-	-
Employees	-	-	-	-	-	500

CARNEGIE MELLON UNIVERSITY

5000 FORBES AVE
PITTSBURGH, PA 152133890
Phone: 412-268-2000
Fax: -
Web: www.cmu.edu

CEO: -
CFO: Amir Rahnamay- Azar
HR: -
FYE: June 30
Type: Private

Carnegie Mellon University is a private global research university and one of the world's most renowned educational institutions. Drama is not all Carnegie Mellon teaches though ? the school has seven colleges and schools that offer academic programs in areas such as psychology computer science engineering biology and public policy. It has about 14190 students and more than 1470 faculty and it has a relatively small student-teacher ratio of 7:1. Carnegie Mellon was founded by philanthropist and industrialist Andrew Carnegie who established the Carnegie Technical Schools in 1900 for the sons and daughters of Pittsburgh's blue-collar workers.

	Annual Growth	06/17	06/18	06/19	06/20	06/21
Sales ($ mil.)	8.4%	-	1,313.4	1,363.1	1,850.1	1,672.7
Net income ($ mil.)	72.6%	-	296.5	207.5	411.6	1,525.8
Market value ($ mil.)	-	-	-	-	-	-
Employees	-	-	-	-	-	4,913

CARNIVAL CORP
NYS: CCL

3655 N.W. 87th Avenue
Miami, FL 33178-2428
Phone: 305 599-2600
Fax: -
Web: www.carnivalcorp.com

CEO: Michael Thamm
CFO: David Bernstein
HR: -
FYE: November 30
Type: Public

Carnival Corporation offers a boatload of fun. The company is the world's most popular cruise line boasting nine leading cruise lines and over 80 ships with a total passenger capacity of more than 230000. Carnival operates in North America primarily through its Princess Cruise Line Holland America and Seabourn luxury cruise brand as well as its flagship Carnival Cruise Lines unit. Brands such as AIDA P&O Cruises Costa Cruises and Cunard offer services to passengers in Europe and Asia. While P&O Cruises offer services to passengers in Australia. Carnival operates as a dual-listed company with UK-based Carnival plc forming a single enterprise under a unified executive team. North America accounts for about 55% of total sales.

	Annual Growth	11/17	11/18	11/19	11/20	11/21
Sales ($ mil.)	(42.5%)	17,510.0	18,881.0	20,825.0	5,595.0	1,908.0
Net income ($ mil.)	-	2,606.0	3,152.0	2,990.0	(10,236.0)	(9,501.0)
Market value ($ mil.)	(28.0%)	74,567.0	68,489.4	51,210.9	22,697.3	20,016.3
Employees	(25.8%)	99,200	88,000	92,000	58,000	30,000

CAROLINA POWER & LIGHT COMPANY

410 S. Wilmington St.
Raleigh NC 27601-1748
Phone: 919-546-6111
Fax: 919-546-2920
Web: www.progress-energy.com

CEO: Lynn J Good
CFO: Steven K Young
HR: -
FYE: December 31
Type: Subsidiary

The Palmetto state and Tarheels both have Carolina Power & Light on their minds when they need some power. The company which operates as Progress Energy Carolinas transmits and distributes electricity to some 1.5 million homes and businesses in the Carolinas. The utility generates almost 12600 MW of capacity from its fossil-fueled nuclear and hydroelectric power plants. Carolina Power & Light purchases about 5% of the power it distributes. The Duke Energy subsidiary also sells power to wholesale customers primarily other utilities and energy marketers including North Carolina Eastern Municipal Power Agency and North Carolina Electric Membership Corporation.

CAROLINA BANK HOLDINGS INC

NMS: CLBH

101 North Spring Street
Greensboro, NC 27401
Phone: 336-288-1898
Fax: –

CEO: –
CFO: –
HR: –
FYE: December 31
Type: Public

Carolina Bank Holdings owns Carolina Bank which serves individuals and small to midsized businesses through some 10 branches in northern portions of North Carolina. The community-oriented financial institution offers standard services such as checking and savings accounts money market and individual retirement accounts CDs ATM and debit cards and online banking and bill payment. Loans secured by commercial properties account for about 40% of the company's portfolio followed by residential mortgages construction and land development loans commercial and industrial loans and consumer loans.

	Annual Growth	12/11	12/12	12/13	12/14	12/15
Assets ($ mil.)	1.0%	673.3	691.9	661.8	679.3	700.8
Net income ($ mil.)	24.5%	2.4	7.5	4.0	3.3	5.8
Market value ($ mil.)	65.6%	12.3	36.9	50.8	48.5	92.6
Employees	2.5%	174	208	191	189	192

CAROLINA CARE PLAN INC.

201 Executive Center Dr.
Columbia SC 29210-8438
Phone: 803-750-7400
Fax: 803-750-7480
Web: www.carolinacareplan.com

CEO: –
CFO: –
HR: –
FYE: December 31
Type: Subsidiary

From Charleston to Greenville Carolina Care Plan has the health costs of South Carolina on its mind. The managed health care company provides coverage to about 50000 members in the state some individually and many through employer groups. Its products include a direct-access HMO that allows users to see any doctor within the network without a referral. The organization also offers a point-of-service plan that covers out-of-network costs and a high-deductible plan paired with a health savings account. Additionally Medicare beneficiaries can buy prescription drug coverage or Medicare Advantage plans. The company is a subsidiary of Medical Mutual of Ohio.

CAROLINA HANDLING, LLC

4835 SIRONA DR STE 100
CHARLOTTE, NC 282733253
Phone: 704-357-6273
Fax: –
Web: www.carolinahandling.com

CEO: –
CFO: –
HR: –
FYE: December 31
Type: Private

The company offers design implementation and support services of all material handling needs through three primary divisions. Power Solutions makes a full line of batteries chargers and battery handling systems for lift trucks and pallet jacks while Fleet Solutions offers fleet products and services which help to reduce unnecessary capital expenditures. Finally Warehouse Solutions provides warehouse services that help to utilize floor space more efficiently increase order selection productivity and improve workplace ergonomics.

	Annual Growth	12/04	12/05	12/06	12/07	12/08
Sales ($ mil.)	(66.7%)	–	–	1,045.5	107.5	116.2
Net income ($ mil.)	33722.9%	–	–	0.0	4.3	4.1
Market value ($ mil.)	–	–	–	–	–	–
Employees	–	–	–	–	–	356

CAROLINA TRUST BANCSHARES INC

NAS: CART

901 East Main Street
Lincolnton, NC 28092
Phone: 704-735-1104
Fax: –
Web: www.carolinatrust.com

CEO: –
CFO: –
HR: –
FYE: December 31
Type: Public

Carolina Trust BancShares is the holding company of Carolina Trust Bank which serves southwestern North Carolina through about 10 locations. It provides a variety of commercial and personal financial services including checking and savings accounts IRAs CDs and credit cards. The bank is mainly a real estate lender with one- to four-family residential mortgage commercial real estate construction and land development loans comprising most of its portfolio. The company acquired the single-branch Carolina Commerce Bank in 2009. Carolina Trust was founded in 2000.

	Annual Growth	12/13	12/14	12/15	12/16	12/17
Assets ($ mil.)	11.1%	266.4	293.0	334.0	374.9	406.6
Net income ($ mil.)	–	(1.4)	6.9	1.1	1.3	0.4
Market value ($ mil.)	30.4%	15.4	23.5	28.9	29.8	44.5
Employees	7.3%	61	74	83	80	81

CAROLINAS MEDICAL CENTER-LINCOLN

433 MCALISTER RD
LINCOLNTON, NC 280924147
Phone: 980-212-2000
Fax: –
Web: www.carolinashealthcare.org/locations/carolinas-healthca

CEO: –
CFO: –
HR: –
FYE: December 31
Type: Private

Honestly this Lincoln County hospital is there to care for all its citizens' health needs. Carolinas Medical Center-Lincoln (formerly Lincoln Medical Center) provides a host of medical services to Tar Heelers that range from general acute care to home health imaging surgery and heart care. The 100-bed medical center also offers pain management services rehabilitation a birthing center and comprehensive diabetes care. Carolinas Medical Center-Lincoln conducts research and clinical trials focused on a range of maladies including cardiology oncology and pediatric ailments. The hospital became part of the Carolinas HealthCare System (CHS) several years ago; it is led by CEO Michael Tarwater.

	Annual Growth	12/13	12/14	12/15	12/16	12/17
Sales ($ mil.)	5.6%	–	105.2	116.4	116.4	124.1
Net income ($ mil.)	12.5%	–	14.0	24.0	17.0	20.0
Market value ($ mil.)	–	–	–	–	–	–
Employees	–	–	–	–	–	550

CAROMONT HEALTH, INC.

2525 COURT DR
GASTONIA, NC 280542140
Phone: 704-834-2000
Fax: –
Web: www.caromonthealth.org

CEO: Douglas Luckett
CFO: David O'Connor
HR: –
FYE: June 30
Type: Private

CaroMont Health is an independent not-for-profit health care system serving residents of North Carolina's Piedmont region. Anchoring CaroMont Health is Gaston Memorial Hospital a 435-bed medical and surgical facility that features a birthing center an inpatient psychiatric ward and specialized facilities for heart disease cancer sleep disorders diabetes and wound care. Other operations include a nearly 100-bed nursing home outpatient surgery and urgent care centers and a network of primary and specialty medical practices. CaroMont Health also provides home health and hospice care services. CaroMont Health is governed by the North Carolina Medical Care Commission.

	Annual Growth	06/14	06/15	06/17	06/18	06/19
Sales ($ mil.)	91.1%	–	38.3	552.4	602.7	510.6
Net income ($ mil.)	10.5%	–	36.5	80.6	63.3	54.3
Market value ($ mil.)	–	–	–	–	–	–
Employees	–	–	–	–	–	2,400

CARPARTS.COM INC (NEW)
NMS: PRTS

2050 W. 190th Street, Suite 400 — CEO: Lev Peker
Torrance, CA 90504 — CFO: David Meniane
Phone: 424 702-1455 — HR: –
Fax: – — FYE: January 02
Web: www.carparts.com — Type: Public

CarParts.com Inc. (formerly U.S. Auto Parts Network) is a leading online provider of aftermarket auto parts and accessories. The company offers over 820 thousand SKUs with detailed product descriptions attributes and photographs through its user-friendly website and mobile-friendly platform. Its inventory includes replacement performance body and engine parts as well as accessories (such as seat covers alarms). The company generates the bulk of its revenue online; a retail store in Illinois and mail-order catalogs also bring in sales. It also distributes its own house brands (formerly referred to as private-label line of mirrors to auto parts stores nationwide

	Annual Growth	12/16	12/17	12/18	12/19*	01/21
Sales ($ mil.)	7.9%	303.6	303.4	289.5	280.7	443.9
Net income ($ mil.)	–	0.7	24.0	(4.9)	(31.5)	(1.5)
Market value ($ mil.)	28.6%	169.3	121.2	45.2	102.0	595.8
Employees	8.8%	1,080	1,069	1,054	843	1,649

*Fiscal year change

CARPENTER CONTRACTORS OF AMERICA, INC.

3900 AVE D NW — CEO: –
WINTER HAVEN, FL 33880 — CFO: –
Phone: 863-294-6449 — HR: Bob Johnston
Fax: – — FYE: February 03
Web: www.carpentercontractors.com — Type: Private

Carpenter Contractors of America has been working with wood for more than half of a century. The company manufactures roof trusses and wall panels and supplies building materials through its manufacturing facilities in Florida. The company also has offices in North Carolina and Illinois where it operates under the name R&D Thiel. The company's products and services are used in both residential and commercial construction. In 1955 brothers Robert and Donald Thiel founded the company as R&D Thiel in Belvidere Illinois. Carpenter Contractors of America filed for Chapter 11 bankruptcy in 2010.

	Annual Growth	01/0-1	01/00*	02/01	02/02	02/07
Sales ($ mil.)	12.1%	–	159.0	174.2	183.8	353.6
Net income ($ mil.)	13.6%	–	5.0	8.0	8.1	12.3
Market value ($ mil.)	–	–	–	–	–	–
Employees	–	–	–	–	–	1,000

*Fiscal year change

CARPENTER TECHNOLOGY CORP.
NYS: CRS

1735 Market Street, 15th Floor — CEO: Tony Thene
Philadelphia, PA 19103 — CFO: Timothy Lain
Phone: 610 208-2000 — HR: –
Fax: – — FYE: June 30
Web: www.cartech.com — Type: Public

This carpenter works with metal not wood. Carpenter Technology (Carpenter) is a specialty materials producer that processes basic raw materials like cobalt nickel manganese and titanium to make engineered materials for applications in a wide variety of end-user markets. Most of its sales come from special alloy products — including billet bar rod and wire ? and it is a recognized leader in high-performance specialty alloy-based materials and process solutions for critical applications. Its titanium powder technology supports additive manufacturing and soft magnetics applications. Major customers operate in the aerospace and defense industry as well as in the energy automotive medical and other industries. Carpenter's primary geographic market is the US (some 65% of sales) but the company claims customers worldwide.

	Annual Growth	06/17	06/18	06/19	06/20	06/21
Sales ($ mil.)	(4.8%)	1,797.6	2,157.7	2,380.2	2,181.1	1,475.6
Net income ($ mil.)	–	47.0	188.5	167.0	1.5	(229.6)
Market value ($ mil.)	1.8%	1,798.2	2,525.5	2,305.0	1,166.4	1,932.2
Employees	(4.0%)	4,600	4,800	5,100	4,600	3,900

CARQUEST CORPORATION

2635 E. Millbrook Rd. — CEO: –
Raleigh NC 27604 — CFO: –
Phone: 919-573-3000 — HR: –
Fax: 610-725-0570 — FYE: December 31
Web: www.dfyoung.com — Type: Business Segment

Searching for a sensor solenoid or switches? CARQUEST can steer you in the right direction. The replacement auto parts distribution group boasts more than 3400 member-owned locations in the US Canada and Mexico and it runs about 40 distribution centers. CARQUEST sells its own line of auto parts (made by Moog Automotive Dana and Gates) to independent jobbers and wholesalers for eventual resale to professional repair centers service stations dealerships and do-it-yourselfers. CARQUEST was rolled out by General Parts in 1974 as a national marketing program for independent distributors. General Parts is the largest single member-owner in CARQUEST's network with about 1400 locations.

CARR-GOTTSTEIN FOODS CO.

6401 A St. — CEO: Lawrence H Hayward
Anchorage AK 99518 — CFO: Donald J Anderson
Phone: 907-561-1944 — HR: –
Fax: 412-788-8353 — FYE: December 31
Web: www.indsci.com — Type: Subsidiary

Carr-Gottstein Foods could sell ice to the Eskimos ... and it does. Alaska's largest grocery retailer operates more than 30 stores primarily in Anchorage as well as in Fairbanks Kenai and other locations throughout the state. Banners include Carrs Quality Centers which sell food general and drugstore merchandise as well as its smaller food stores in more rural areas under the Eagle Quality Centers banner and other trade names. Carr-Gottstein also runs Oaken Keg Spirit Shops (wine and liquor stores) mostly adjacent to Carrs stores and The Great Alaska Tobacco Company stores. Carr-Gottstein is a wholly owned subsidiary of Safeway one of North America's largest food retailers.

CARRIAGE SERVICES, INC.
NYS: CSV

3040 Post Oak Boulevard, Suite 300 — CEO: Melvin Payne
Houston, TX 77056 — CFO: Carl Brink
Phone: 713 332-8400 — HR: –
Fax: – — FYE: December 31
Web: www.carriageservices.com — Type: Public

When people's lives come to an end Carriage Services' business gets rolling. The company is a large US death care company though it trails far behind Service Corporation International and smaller rival StoneMor Partners. Carriage Services runs more than 185 funeral homes (owned and leased) in about 30 states and more than 30 cemeteries (owned and leased) operating in nearly a dozen states mostly in California Florida and Texas. The company removes and prepares remains sells caskets and memorials provides transportation services performs ceremonies and burials and maintains cemeteries.

	Annual Growth	12/16	12/17	12/18	12/19	12/20
Sales ($ mil.)	7.3%	248.2	258.1	268.0	274.1	329.4
Net income ($ mil.)	(4.8%)	19.6	37.2	11.6	14.5	16.1
Market value ($ mil.)	2.3%	515.4	462.7	278.9	460.7	563.6
Employees	2.0%	2,509	2,659	2,617	2,797	2,718

CARRIZO OIL & GAS, INC.

NMS: CRZO

500 Dallas Street, Suite 2300
Houston, TX 77002
Phone: 713 328-1000
Fax: –
Web: www.carrizo.com

CEO: –
CFO: –
HR: –
FYE: December 31
Type: Public

Carrizo Oil & Gas focuses on exploration development and production of crude oil NGLs and gas in the Eagle Ford Shale in South Texas and the Delaware Basin in West Texas. It specializes in horizontal development drilling and completion in unconventional resource plays. Currently the company holds leases covering approximately 145200 net acres containing more than 560 net oil and gas wells. It boasts proved reserves of 262 MMBoe consisting of 64% crude oil 16% natural gas liquids and 20% natural gas. Its production output is around 54000 Boe/d.

	Annual Growth	12/13	12/14	12/15	12/16	12/17
Sales ($ mil.)	9.4%	520.2	710.2	429.2	443.6	745.9
Net income ($ mil.)	18.8%	43.7	226.3	(1,155.2)	(675.5)	87.1
Market value ($ mil.)	(17.0%)	3,646.7	3,388.5	2,409.4	3,042.3	1,733.4
Employees	2.1%	229	247	215	227	249

CARROLS RESTAURANT GROUP INC

NMS: TAST

968 James Street
Syracuse, NY 13203
Phone: 315 424-0513
Fax: –
Web: www.carrols.com

CEO: –
CFO: Anthony Hull
HR: Gerald DiGenova
FYE: January 03
Type: Public

Carrols Restaurant Group (also known as Carrols) is one of the leading quick-service restaurant operator and the world's largest Burger King franchisee with more than 7000 locations in the US. As a franchisee of Burger King and Popeyes the company also has contractual rights to use certain trademarks service marks and other intellectual property relating to the Burger King and Popeyes concepts. The company has no proprietary intellectual property other than the Carrols logo and trademark. In addition almost all of the company's restaurants are freestanding. It operates Burger King restaurants since 1976.

	Annual Growth	01/17*	12/17	12/18	12/19*	01/21
Sales ($ mil.)	13.2%	943.6	1,088.5	1,179.3	1,462.8	1,547.5
Net income ($ mil.)	–	45.5	7.2	10.1	(31.9)	(29.5)
Market value ($ mil.)	(19.9%)	753.2	600.1	463.3	339.3	310.2
Employees	5.4%	21,500	23,500	24,500	31,500	26,500

*Fiscal year change

CARRY TRANSIT, LLC

711 JORIE BLVD STE 101N
OAK BROOK, IL 605232285
Phone: 630-573-2555
Fax: –
Web: www.heniff.com

CEO: –
CFO: –
HR: –
FYE: December 31
Type: Private

Superior Bulk Logistics through subsidiaries Superior Carriers and Carry Transit hauls liquid and dry bulk cargo including both chemical and food-grade products. Overall the trucking units of Superior Bulk Logistics operate a fleet of some 875 tractors and 2000 trailers. The company's SuperFlo unit provides transloading services — the transfer of cargo between railcars and trucks. Superior Bulk Logistics' Sanicare Wash Systems unit cleans tank truck trailers and other bulk containers used for food products. Superior Bulk Logistics offers service between Mexico and the US and Canada through a partnership with Transpormex a division of Grupo Dexel.

	Annual Growth	12/04	12/05	12/06	12/07	12/09
Sales ($ mil.)	(5.1%)	–	–	220.5	235.0	188.2
Net income ($ mil.)	(26.0%)	–	–	5.1	7.2	2.0
Market value ($ mil.)	–	–	–	–	–	–
Employees	–	–	–	–	–	2,201

CARSON TAHOE REGIONAL HEALTHCARE

1600 MEDICAL PKWY
CARSON CITY, NV 897034625
Phone: 775-445-8000
Fax: –
Web: www.carsontahoe.com

CEO: –
CFO: Ann Beck
HR: –
FYE: December 31
Type: Private

Carson Tahoe Regional Healthcare which includes the Carson Tahoe Regional Medical Center (CTRMC) serves Nevada's Carson Valley and its surrounding areas. The not-for-profit CTRMC boasts about 220 beds and provides a wide range of services such as acute general surgical specialty and outpatient care. The medical center also includes a rehabilitation center cardiovascular center surgical unit free-standing cancer center emergency room and women and children's center. Carson Tahoe Regional Healthcare also operates smaller urgent care behavioral health physical therapy and outpatient care centers in Carson City and nearby communities.

	Annual Growth	12/15	12/16	12/17	12/18	12/19
Sales ($ mil.)	4.8%	–	270.8	284.6	298.3	312.1
Net income ($ mil.)	5.6%	–	26.8	20.2	7.9	31.5
Market value ($ mil.)	–	–	–	–	–	–
Employees	–	–	–	–	–	2,000

CARTER & ASSOCIATES ENTERPRISES INC.

171 17th St. NW Ste. 1200
Atlanta GA 30363-1032
Phone: 404-888-3000
Fax: 404-888-3006
Web: www.carterusa.com

CEO: Robert E Peterson
CFO: –
HR: –
FYE: December 31
Type: Private

Carter knows more than just peanuts about real estate. The company provides commercial real estate development project management investment and consulting services. It has more than $2.5 billion in assets under management. Carter also has developed several projects including Atlantic Station a 800000 sq. ft. mixed use property in Atlanta. Carter has offices in Atlanta; Birmingham Alabama; Raleigh North Carolina; and Tampa Florida. A member of the ONCOR International consortium the privately held company was founded in 1958. Carter sold its property management and brokerage business to commercial real estate company Cassidy Turley in 2011.

CARTER'S INC

NYS: CRI

Phipps Tower, 3438 Peachtree Road NE, Suite 1800
Atlanta, GA 30326
Phone: 678 791-1000
Fax: –
Web: www.carters.com

CEO: Michael Casey
CFO: Richard Westenberger
HR: Jill Wilson
FYE: January 02
Type: Public

Operating through William Carter Company Carter's is the largest maker in the US of branded apparel exclusively for babies and young children. Primary products include newborn layette clothing sleepwear and playwear. It markets its items under the Carter's OshKosh B'Gosh and Skip Hop brands as well as private labels Child of Mine Just One You and Simple Joys. Carter's distributes their products through multiple channel such as retail store e-commerce and wholesale sales channels. Its channels included over 1100 retail stores more than 19000 wholesale locations and it also operates in more than 850 Carter's and OshKosh stores in the US and approximately 200 stores in Canada.

	Annual Growth	12/16	12/17	12/18	12/19*	01/21
Sales ($ mil.)	(1.1%)	3,199.2	3,400.4	3,462.3	3,519.3	3,024.3
Net income ($ mil.)	(15.7%)	258.1	302.8	282.1	263.8	109.7
Market value ($ mil.)	1.7%	3,782.2	5,143.7	3,568.5	4,818.4	4,118.4
Employees	(0.3%)	18,300	20,900	21,000	20,300	18,000

*Fiscal year change

CARTESIAN INC   NBB: CRTN

7300 College Boulevard, Suite 302   CEO: Jim Serafin
Overland Park, KS 66210   CFO: –
Phone: 913 345-9315   HR: –
Fax: –   FYE: December 31
Web: www.cartesian.com   Type: Public

The Management Network Group which does business as TMNG Global helps its clients answer the call in the ever-changing communications industry. The company provides management strategic and operational consulting services to communications service providers technology companies and financial services firms. Its TMNG Marketing unit offers a full range of marketing and customer relationship management services including product development market research and customer retention programs. The company's Ascertain suite of software products allows customers to manage billing services analyze customer data and monitor trends. Founded in 1990 TMNG Global serves clients primarily in the US and the UK.

	Annual Growth	12/12	12/13*	01/15	01/16*	12/16
Sales ($ mil.)	7.9%	53.0	55.4	71.7	78.3	71.7
Net income ($ mil.)	–	(1.2)	(2.1)	(1.4)	(7.7)	(13.9)
Market value ($ mil.)	(20.6%)	20.6	25.3	38.2	19.9	8.2
Employees	0.0%	298	283	299	360	298

*Fiscal year change

CARUS PUBLISHING COMPANY

140 S. Dearborn Ste. 1450   CEO: –
Chicago IL 60603   CFO: –
Phone: 312-701-1720   HR: –
Fax: 312-701-1728   FYE: December 31
Web: www.cricketmag.com   Type: Private

Carus Publishing Company weaves a literary web aimed at capturing kids' imaginations. With a focus on high quality stories and illustrations the company's "Cricket" magazine targets young teens. Other publications include "Babybug" for the youngest tots "Ladybug" for toddlers and preschoolers "Spider" for elementary school kids and "Cicada" magazine for teens. Carus Publishing also publishes a variety of books through its Cricket Books and Open Court divisions. Carus launched in 1887. Its flagship magazine "Cricket" debuted in 1973. Marianne Carus formed the publishing company to bring quality literature to children. Today ePals Corporation operater of an educational digital platform owns Carus Publishing.

CARVEL CORPORATION

200 Glenridge Point Pkwy. Ste. 200   CEO: Steve Desutter
Atlanta GA 30342   CFO: –
Phone: 404-255-3250   HR: –
Fax: 404-255-4978   FYE: December 31
Web: www.carvel.com   Type: Subsidiary

If Fudgie the Whale and Cookie Puss conjure up childhood memories of ice cream you're probably a true fan of Carvel's. The company operates a chain of more than 500 franchised ice cream outlets known for their soft serve ice cream and other frozen treats including character-shaped frozen ice cream cakes. Typically found in high-traffic areas such as airports malls and sports arenas Carvel has locations in 25 mostly Northeastern states Puerto Rico and some Middle Eastern countries. In addition the company sells ice cream cakes through more than 8500 supermarkets. Tom Carvel a traveling salesman founded the chain in 1934. It is owned by FOCUS Brands an affiliate of Atlanta-based Roark Capital Group.

CARVER BANCORP INC.   NAS: CARV

75 West 125th Street   CEO: Michael Pugh
New York, NY 10027   CFO: Christina Maier
Phone: 718 230-2900   HR: –
Fax: –   FYE: March 31
Web: www.carverbank.com   Type: Public

Carver Bancorp one of the largest minority-led financial institutions in the US is the holding company for Carver Federal Savings Bank. The bank was founded in 1948 to provide community banking services to New York City's African-American and Caribbean-American population. From about 10 branches in mostly low- to moderate-income neighborhoods in Harlem Brooklyn and Queens the thrift offers deposit accounts insurance and investment products. Carver Federal's lending activities are focused on housing (residential mortgages and multifamily real estate loans) and non-residential real estate (churches and commercial properties.) The latter makes up about 40% of Carver's loan portfolio.

	Annual Growth	03/17	03/18	03/19	03/20	03/21
Assets ($ mil.)	(0.4%)	687.9	693.9	563.7	578.8	676.7
Net income ($ mil.)	–	(2.9)	5.4	(5.9)	(5.4)	(3.9)
Market value ($ mil.)	25.5%	12.2	9.4	12.4	6.3	30.3
Employees	(5.2%)	129	123	114	107	104

CAS MEDICAL SYSTEMS INC   NAS: CASM

44 East Industrial Road   CEO: Thomas Patton
Branford, CT 06405   CFO: Jeffery Baird
Phone: 203 488-6056   HR: Silvia Taylor
Fax: –   FYE: December 31
Web: www.casmed.com   Type: Public

It's not a doctor or a nurse but CAS Medical Systems (CASMED) is standing bedside keeping a watchful eye on patients. CASMED makes non-invasive monitoring devices used in critical care settings. Its leading products include its FORE-SIGHT oximeters which monitor oxygen levels in brain and muscle tissue. Other products include bedside monitors and neonatal vital sign supplies (electrodes skin surface probes). CASMED sells its products in North America Europe Latin America Africa and the Pacific Rim to hospitals and other health care professionals through sales representatives and specialty distributors.

	Annual Growth	12/13	12/14	12/15	12/16	12/17
Sales ($ mil.)	(3.8%)	21.9	22.9	21.6	22.2	18.8
Net income ($ mil.)	–	(10.4)	(7.6)	(6.9)	(3.2)	(2.3)
Market value ($ mil.)	(17.9%)	48.5	47.1	50.5	45.9	22.0
Employees	(5.9%)	97	97	101	96	76

CASCADE BANCORP   NAS: CACB

1100 N.W. Wall Street   CEO: –
Bend, OR 97701   CFO: –
Phone: 877 617-3400   HR: –
Fax: –   FYE: December 31
Web: www.botc.com   Type: Public

Forget the dirty dishes. Cascade Bancorp wants to provide sparkling customer service. It's the holding company for Bank of the Cascades which operates some 40 branches serving the Oregon and Boise Idaho markets. Catering to individuals and small to mid-sized businesses the banks offer traditional deposit services like checking and savings accounts CDs and IRAs as well as credit cards and trust services. Commercial real estate loans make up more than half of the company's loan portfolio; business loans comprise nearly a quarter. To a far lesser extent the bank also originates consumer loans and mortgages. Cascade Bancorp acquired Home Federal Bancorp in 2014 boosting assets to more than $2.3 billion.

	Annual Growth	12/11	12/12	12/13	12/14	12/15
Assets ($ mil.)	17.3%	1,303.5	1,301.4	1,406.2	2,341.1	2,468.0
Net income ($ mil.)	–	(47.3)	6.0	50.8	3.7	20.6
Market value ($ mil.)	8.5%	318.8	455.7	380.7	377.8	441.9
Employees	4.1%	436	432	399	513	513

CASCADE ENGINEERING, INC.

3400 INNOVATION CT SE
GRAND RAPIDS, MI 495122085
Phone: 616-975-4800
Fax: -
Web: www.cascadeng.com

CEO: Christina Keller
CFO: Janice Oshinski
HR: -
FYE: August 29
Type: Private

Ideas about plastic parts cascade down from Cascade Engineering's collection of companies ending up as practical components for many applications. The company manufactures and markets under the Cascade and other brands plastic injection molded products as well as parts for OEMs in the automotive truck material handling waste and recycling and home and office industries. Its auto lineup includes interior and exterior trim HVAC cases and ducts and acoustical parts along with heavy truck fairings fenders and grills. Catering to resource conservation markets Cascade also makes and services an eco-lineup comprising building-mountable wind turbines waste collection bins and water filtration systems.

	Annual Growth	09/11	09/12*	08/13	08/14	08/15
Sales ($ mil.)	14.7%	-	238.0	238.0	358.8	358.8
Net income ($ mil.)	-	-	0.0	0.0	0.0	0.0
Market value ($ mil.)	-	-	-	-	-	-
Employees						1,800

*Fiscal year change

CASCADE MICROTECH INC   NMS: CSCD

9100 S.W. Gemini Drive
Beaverton, OR 97008
Phone: 503 601-1000
Fax: -
Web: www.cascademicrotech.com

CEO: -
CFO: -
HR: -
FYE: December 31
Type: Public

In the foothills of the Cascade Range Cascade Microtech makes test systems for microelectronics. Semiconductor makers such as Broadcom Fujitsu Semiconductor IBM Intel Samsung and Toshiba use the company's probe cards probe stations and analytical probes to ensure the quality of their integrated circuits (ICs). Many of Cascade's customers use its tools to test their wireless broadband or other communications ICs at the wafer level before the wafers are cut into individual chips. The company has a development alliance with test equipment giant Agilent Technologies.

	Annual Growth	12/10	12/11	12/12	12/13	12/14
Sales ($ mil.)	9.2%	95.8	104.6	113.0	120.0	136.0
Net income ($ mil.)	-	(10.3)	(5.8)	6.1	13.4	9.9
Market value ($ mil.)	35.4%	71.6	56.1	92.2	153.5	240.6
Employees	2.9%	401	365	383	426	449

CASCADE NATURAL GAS CORPORATION

222 Fairview Ave. North
Seattle WA 98109-5312
Phone: 206-624-3900
Fax: 206-624-7215
Web: www.cngc.com

CEO: David W Stevens
CFO: -
HR: -
FYE: December 31
Type: Subsidiary

To approximately 100 small communities in Washington and Oregon Cascade Natural Gas is the main man. The gas utility transmits and distributes natural gas to more than 250000 residential commercial and industrial customers. It also distributes gas to approximately 200 noncore customers mostly large industrial users buying their supplies from third parties. Cascade Natural Gas' service territory covers more than 3000 sq. miles and 700 highway miles. The utility obtains its gas mainly from Canadian suppliers and producers in the Rocky Mountains. Cascade Natural Gas is a subsidiary of energy giant MDU Resources.

CASE FINANCIAL INC.   OTC: CSEF

7720 El Camino Real Ste. 2E
Carlsbad CA 92009
Phone: 760-804-1449
Fax: 760-804-1566

CEO: Michael A Schaffer
CFO: Lawrence C Schaffer
HR: -
FYE: September 30
Type: Public

Case Financial went from the courtroom to the goldmine. The former business litigation financing business shifted its focus away from loaning money to lawyers in 2005 and now wants to invest in mine exploration. Setbacks have prevented the company from operating since 2004. However in 2008 Case Financial announced that it would provide $4 million in funding to Canada-based Trio Gold Corp for a gold mine exploration project in Nevada.

CASE WESTERN RESERVE UNIVERSITY

10900 EUCLID AVE
CLEVELAND, OH 441064901
Phone: 216-368-6062
Fax: -
Web: www.case.edu

CEO: -
CFO: Hossein Sadid
HR: -
FYE: June 30
Type: Private

Case Western Reserve University (CWRU) is an independent research school with an enrollment of about 12070 students from all US states and around 90 countries more than half of whom are graduate and professional students. CWRU offers approximately 230 undergraduate graduate and professional options and almost 140 dual-degree programs from its eight colleges and schools ? management engineering law arts and sciences dentistry social work nursing and medicine ? as well as a graduate school at its campus in Cleveland. The university has more than 3655 faculty members and a student-to-teacher ratio of 11:1.

	Annual Growth	06/16	06/17	06/18	06/20	06/21
Sales ($ mil.)	1.9%	-	1,022.6	1,016.3	1,075.6	1,101.1
Net income ($ mil.)	34.4%	-	208.2	111.1	(49.2)	679.1
Market value ($ mil.)	-	-	-	-	-	-
Employees	-	-	-	-	-	6,599

CASELLA WASTE SYSTEMS, INC.   NMS: CWST

25 Greens Hill Lane
Rutland, VT 05701
Phone: 802 775-0325
Fax: -
Web: www.casella.com

CEO: John Casella
CFO: Edmond Coletta
HR: -
FYE: December 31
Type: Public

The wasteful habits of Americans are big business for Casella Waste Systems which operates regional waste-hauling businesses mainly in the northeastern US. The company serves residential commercial industrial and municipal customers. In 2019 it owned and/or operated about 45 solid waste collection operations about 60 transfer stations about 20 recycling facilities more than five Subtitle D landfills less than landfill gas-to-energy facilities and one landfill permitted to accept construction and demolition materials. With a strategy focused on increasing waste volumes at its landfills Casella Waste Systems added about 1.2 million tons in 2019. The company were founded in 1975.

	Annual Growth	12/17	12/18	12/19	12/20	12/21
Sales ($ mil.)	10.4%	599.3	660.7	743.2	774.6	889.2
Net income ($ mil.)	-	(21.8)	6.4	31.7	91.1	41.1
Market value ($ mil.)	38.8%	1,183.5	1,464.7	2,366.4	3,184.9	4,391.5
Employees	9.7%	2,000	2,300	2,500	2,500	2,900

CASEY'S GENERAL STORES, INC.

NMS: CASY

One SE Convenience Boulevard
Ankeny, IA 50021
Phone: 515 965-6100
Fax: –
Web: www.caseys.com

CEO: Darren Rebelez
CFO: Steve Bramlage
HR: –
FYE: April 30
Type: Public

Casey's provides convenience for small-town customers. One of the largest convenience store chains in the country Casey's General Stores owns nearly 2245 stores across 15-plus states primarily in the Midwest. Its stores most of which operate in areas with fewer than 5000 people offer gasoline prepared foods such as pizza and donuts and other food and nonfood items traditionally found in convenience stores. In addition to Casey's and Casey's General Store locations the company operates two tobacco stores one liquor store and one grocery store. The company derives its revenue primarily from the retail sale of fuel.

	Annual Growth	04/17	04/18	04/19	04/20	04/21
Sales ($ mil.)	3.8%	7,506.6	8,391.1	9,352.9	9,175.3	8,707.2
Net income ($ mil.)	15.2%	177.5	317.9	203.9	263.8	312.9
Market value ($ mil.)	18.7%	4,141.0	3,569.4	4,890.3	5,594.6	8,209.9
Employees	1.5%	35,014	37,205	36,841	–	37,205

CASH AMERICA INTERNATIONAL, INC.

NYS: CSH

1600 West 7th Street
Fort Worth, TX 76102
Phone: 817 335-1100
Fax: –

CEO: T Brent Stuart
CFO: Thomas A Bessant Jr
HR: –
FYE: December 31
Type: Public

If cash is king then Cash America International is king of pawns. Cash America operates more than 960 stores under the banners Cash America Pawn SuperPawn and Pawn X-Change in the US and Cash America casa de empeño in Mexico. The company is one of the largest providers of secured non-recourse loans (also known as pawn loans). As part of its business Cash America also provides cash advances in half a dozen states through shops operating under the Cashland and Cash America Payday Advance banners. The company offers check cashing money orders and money transfers through about 90 owned and franchised Mr. Payroll stores in about 15 states.

	Annual Growth	12/10	12/11	12/12	12/13	12/14
Sales ($ mil.)	(4.1%)	1,293.3	1,540.6	1,800.4	1,797.2	1,094.7
Net income ($ mil.)	(3.9%)	115.5	136.0	107.5	142.5	98.6
Market value ($ mil.)	(11.5%)	1,063.8	1,343.3	1,142.8	1,103.3	651.6
Employees	1.7%	6,017	6,619	7,035	7,637	6,426

CASH-WA DISTRIBUTING CO. OF KEARNEY, INC.

401 W 4TH ST
KEARNEY, NE 688457825
Phone: 308-237-3151
Fax: –
Web: www.cashwa.com

CEO: –
CFO: Edward Bloomfield
HR: –
FYE: November 28
Type: Private

This company keeps the Quik-E Marts in merchandise. Cash-Wa Distributing supplies food produce beverages equipment cleaning supplies and more to foodservice operators and convenience stores throughout Nebraska and in all or parts of 10 surrounding states. It operates three distribution centers and serves more than 6500 customers with an inventory of some 20000 items. The family-owned and -operated company was formed in 1934 as a candy and tobacco wholesaler and was purchased by the Henning family in 1957. Cash-Wa Distributing is a member of the UniPro distribution cooperative.

	Annual Growth	12/11	12/12*	11/13	11/14	11/15
Sales ($ mil.)	(0.3%)	–	398.8	377.6	387.2	395.3
Net income ($ mil.)	(15.9%)	–	11.9	6.6	8.4	7.1
Market value ($ mil.)	–	–	–	–	–	–
Employees	–	–	–	–	–	539

*Fiscal year change

CASI PHARMACEUTICALS, INC.

NAS: CASI

9620 Medical Center Drive, Suite 300
Rockville, MD 20850
Phone: 240 864-2600
Fax: –
Web: www.casipharmaceuticals.com

CEO: Wei-Wu He
CFO: –
HR: –
FYE: December 31
Type: Public

EntreMed wants to get in between cancer and the blood vessels that feed it. The biotech pharmaceutical company develops drugs that inhibit angiogenesis or the growth of new blood vessels. Its lead candidate ENMD-2076 inhibits aurora kinases which regulate cell division and are linked to several cancers. The company has several other product candidates in its pipeline. EntreMed receives royalties from sales of Thalomid a multiple myeloma therapy marketed by EntreMed's minority shareholder Celgene.

	Annual Growth	12/16	12/17	12/18	12/19	12/20
Sales ($ mil.)	266.5%	–	–	–	4.1	15.1
Net income ($ mil.)	–	(9.5)	(10.8)	(27.5)	(46.0)	(48.3)
Market value ($ mil.)	26.6%	142.5	402.8	498.3	383.0	365.6
Employees	52.0%	27	50	125	125	144

CASIO AMERICA INC.

570 Mt. Pleasant Ave.
Dover NJ 07801
Phone: 973-361-5400
Fax: 973-537-8926
Web: www.casio.com

CEO: Makoto Ori
CFO: –
HR: –
FYE: March 31
Type: Subsidiary

You might be (G-)shocked to learn how many products Casio America sells. As the US subsidiary of Japanese electronics giant CASIO COMPUTER the firm markets products ranging from handheld computers and calculators to electronic keyboards and its popular G-Shock and high-end Oceanus watch lines. Established in 1957 Casio also makes and markets cell phones digital cameras electronic dictionaries label printers clocks portable TVs and other items. Going beyond the consumer market Casio targets the retail hospitality and industrial markets (cash registers and industrial handheld PDAs). And to make sure that young consumers remember its name the company also sells to the education market.

CASPIAN SERVICES INC

NBB: CSSV

2319 Foothill Drive, Suite 160
Salt Lake City, UT 84109
Phone: 801 746-3700
Fax: –
Web: www.caspianservicesinc.com

CEO: Alexey Kotov
CFO: Indira Kaliyeva
HR: –
FYE: September 30
Type: Public

Caspian Services (formerly EMPS Corporation) provides geophysical and seismic data acquisition and interpretation services to the oil and gas industry operating in the Caspian Sea region. It also owns or leases a fleet of 15 shallow draft vessels that provide offshore marine services including transportation housing and supplies for production personnel. Caspian Services' ships are chartered primarily to Agip KCO a consortium of oil companies operating in the Caspian Sea and CMOC/Shell joint venture. The company owns 56% of a joint venture that operates a desalinization plant and sells purified drinking water.

	Annual Growth	09/11	09/12	09/13	09/14	09/15
Sales ($ mil.)	(23.9%)	49.1	24.9	33.1	29.9	16.4
Net income ($ mil.)	–	(9.7)	(14.0)	(11.5)	(16.6)	(28.0)
Market value ($ mil.)	(41.1%)	5.8	1.5	2.5	1.6	0.7
Employees	(14.7%)	757	516	574	509	400

CASS INFORMATION SYSTEMS INC.

NMS: CASS

12444 Powerscourt Drive, Suite 550
St. Louis, MO 63131
Phone: 314 506-5500
Fax: –
Web: www.cassinfo.com

CEO: Eric Brunngraber
CFO: Michael Normile
HR: –
FYE: December 31
Type: Public

Cass Information Systems provides freight payment and information processing services to large manufacturing distribution and retail companies across the US. Its offerings include payment and rating services as well as bill processing and payments. Its telecommunications division manages telecom expenses for large companies. Cass grew out of Cass Commercial Bank (now a subsidiary) which provides banking services to Its target markets which include privately-owned businesses and faith-based ministries in the St. Louis metropolitan area as well as other selected cities in the US. Other major customer bases include Columbus Ohio and South Carolina.

	Annual Growth	12/16	12/17	12/18	12/19	12/20
Assets ($ mil.)	10.0%	1,504.8	1,603.2	1,695.2	1,764.2	2,203.2
Net income ($ mil.)	0.8%	24.3	25.0	30.3	30.4	25.2
Market value ($ mil.)	(14.7%)	1,058.9	837.8	761.7	831.0	560.0
Employees	0.6%	1,075	1,116	1,143	1,122	1,101

CASTLE (AM) & CO

NBB: CTAM

1420 Kensington Road, Suite 220
Oak Brook, IL 60523
Phone: 847 455-7111
Fax: –
Web: www.castlemetals.com

CEO: Marec Edgar
CFO: –
HR: –
FYE: December 31
Type: Public

Providing alloys for its allies metals service company A. M. Castle distributes highly engineered metals and metal alloys to a broad range of industrial manufacturers. It sells steel (alloy carbon and stainless) nickel alloys aluminum copper brass cast iron and titanium in bar sheet plate and tube form. Its Transtar Metals unit distributes high-performance metals to the aerospace and defense markets. Through its Total Plastics unit it distributes plastics in forms (such as plate rod and tube). A. M. Castle operates 47 steel service centers throughout North America Europe and Asia. It also holds 50% of steel distributor Kreher Steel. In 2017 the company filed for Chapter 11 bankruptcy protection.

	Annual Growth	08/17*	12/17	12/18	12/19	12/20
Sales ($ mil.)	1.3%	353.9	164.9	582.0	559.6	368.3
Net income ($ mil.)	–	36.2	(13.3)	(37.1)	(38.5)	(40.7)
Market value ($ mil.)	(6.3%)	–	26.9	20.6	12.0	22.1
Employees	(9.9%)	–	930	979	873	681

*Fiscal year change

CASTLE BRANDS INC.

ASE: ROX

122 East 42nd Street, Suite 5000
New York, NY 10168
Phone: 646 356-0200
Fax: –
Web: www.castlebrandsinc.com

CEO: Richard J Lampen
CFO: Alfred J Small
HR: –
FYE: March 31
Type: Public

Castle Brands hopes to earn a king's ransom selling imported distilled spirits. Among its brands are Tierras tequila Pallini liqueur Jefferson's bourbon Brady's Irish cream liqueur Betts & Scholl wine and Knappogue Castle Whiskey. As part of its business the company also owns 60% of Celtic Crossing Irish liqueur. Castle Brands distributes its products nationwide and in a dozen international markets as well as in duty-free markets. Castle Brands boasts marketing and distribution rights for other brands such as Gosling's Rum and Travis Hasse's Original Apple Pie Liqueur. Castle Brands formed in 2003 mainly contracts with other firms to distill and bottle its products.

	Annual Growth	03/14	03/15	03/16	03/17	03/18
Sales ($ mil.)	16.9%	48.1	57.5	72.2	77.3	89.9
Net income ($ mil.)	–	(8.9)	(3.8)	(2.5)	(0.9)	(0.8)
Market value ($ mil.)	0.8%	199.6	232.9	156.4	257.8	206.3
Employees	6.1%	45	51	55	55	57

CASTLE ROCK ENTERTAINMENT INC.

335 N. Maple Dr. Ste. 135
Beverly Hills CA 90210-3879
Phone: 310-285-2300
Fax: 310-285-2345

CEO: Martin Shafer
CFO: –
HR: –
FYE: December 31
Type: Subsidiary

This castle is looking for a few good movies. Castle Rock Entertainment producer of acclaimed films such as "When Harry Met Sally" "A Few Good Men" and The Shawshank Redemption is also responsible for duds such as Miss Congeniality 2: Armed and Fabulous. The company's TV credits include the hit show "Seinfeld". Castle Rock was formed in 1987 by five media moguls including director Rob Reiner Warner Bros. president and COO Alan Horn and Castle Rock CEO Martin Shafer. The company has produced seven movies based on Stephen King novels and takes its name from the fictional Maine town that serves as the setting for many King stories. Castle Rock's films and TV shows are distributed by parent Warner Bros.

CASTLEROCK SECURITY HOLDINGS INC.

2101 S. Arlington Heights Rd. Ste. 150
Arlington Heights IL 60005
Phone: 847-768-6300
Fax: 858-334-2199
Web: www.ambitbio.com

CEO: –
CFO: –
HR: –
FYE: December 31
Type: Private

CastleRock Security Holdings wants to be the moat around your castle. Through its subsidiaries CastleRock provides security system monitoring services and maintenance to residential and light commercial customers. The company which operates in 46 states and select markets in Canada and Puerto Rico monitors a variety of systems including burglary fire environmental and medical alarm systems. CastleRock serves its own retail customer accounts but also offers wholesale monitoring services to third-party alarm system companies. Formed in 2008 CastleRock Security filed to go public in late 2010.

CATALENT PHARMA SOLUTIONS INC.

14 Schoolhouse Rd.
Somerset NJ 08873
Phone: 732-537-6200
Fax: 732-537-6480
Web: www.catalent.com

CEO: –
CFO: –
HR: Allison Mackay
FYE: June 30
Type: Private

Catalyst + talent = Catalent. At least that's the brand Catalent Pharma Solutions is using to try to ensure its customers' success. The company provides contract development and manufacturing of oral (soft and hardshell capsules) topical (ointment applicators) sterile (syringes) and inhaled (nasal sprays) drug delivery products to pharmaceutical and biotechnology companies in some 100 countries. Catalent also provides packaging services using bottles pouches and strips used to hold tablet powder and liquid medicines. Catalent operates 30 facilities worldwide. The company is owned by The Blackstone Group.

CATALINA MARKETING CORPORATION

200 Carillon Pkwy.   CEO: Wayne Powers
St. Petersburg FL 33716   CFO: –
Phone: 727-579-5000   HR: –
Fax: 727-556-2700   FYE: December 31
Web: www.catalinamarketing.com   Type: Private

To reach shoppers when they are shopping consumer packaged-goods manufacturers call on Catalina Marketing. The company's network installed at the cash registers of more than 26000 supermarkets and drugstores throughout the US prints out coupons and other marketing communications for consumers based on the products they have just purchased. A similar system installed at more than 18300 pharmacies delivers health-related information to consumers based on the prescriptions they pick up. Outside the US Catalina has installed its networks at about 8000 retail locations in Europe and Japan.

CATALINA RESTAURANT GROUP INC.

2200 Faraday Ave. Ste. 250   CEO: –
Carlsbad CA 92008   CFO: –
Phone: 760-804-5750   HR: –
Fax: 760-476-5141   FYE: December 31
Web: www.catalinarestaurantgroup.com   Type: Subsidiary

Catalina Restaurant Group is pretty casual about dining. The company operates and franchises more than 175 casual-dining restaurants under the Carrows and Coco's names. Its Carrows Restaurant chain offers family dining fare for breakfast lunch and dinner at about 65 locations. Several of the eateries are open 24 hours a day. Coco's Bakery Restaurants feature fresh-baked goods burgers sandwiches and breakfast items at more than 110 locations. Most of Catalina Restaurant Group's properties are found in California with additional locations in Arizona Colorado and Nevada. Formed in 2002 the company is a subsidiary of Tokyo-based Zensho Co.

CATALYST BIOSCIENCES INC   NAS: CBIO

611 Gateway Blvd., Suite 710   CEO: Nassim Usman
South San Francisco, CA 94080   CFO: Clinton Musil
Phone: 650 871-0761   HR: –
Fax: –   FYE: December 31
Web: www.catalystbiosciences.com   Type: Public

Catalyst Biosciences (formerly Targacept) is a clinical-stage biopharmaceutical focused on developing products in the fields of hemostasis and inflammation. Its candidates treat such ailments as hemophilia and surgical bleeding delayed graft function in kidney transplants and dry age-related macular degeneration. The company's lead candidate is a next-generation coagulation Factor VIIa variant — CB 813d — which has completed Phase 1 clinical trials in severe hemophilia patients. The company was formed in 1997 and went public in 2006. Targacept was acquired by Catalyst Biosciences in a reverse merger mid-2015 after which the firm adopted the Catalyst moniker.

	Annual Growth	12/14	12/15	12/16	12/17	12/18
Sales ($ mil.)	(61.6%)	0.3	1.8	0.4	1.0	0.0
Net income ($ mil.)	–	(32.6)	(14.8)	(16.9)	(21.6)	(30.1)
Market value ($ mil.)	31.6%	31.4	37.4	7.8	163.1	94.3
Employees	2.5%	19	19	28	13	21

CATALYST HEALTH SOLUTIONS INC.   NASDAQ: CHSI

800 King Farm Blvd.   CEO: –
Rockville MD 20850   CFO: –
Phone: 301-548-2900   HR: –
Fax: 301-548-2991   FYE: December 31
Web: www.catalysthealthsolutions.com   Type: Public

Catalyst Health Solutions cooks up efficiencies in the prescription benefits market. The company provides pharmacy benefit management (PBM) services to clients including managed care organizations (MCOs) self-insured employers third-party benefit administrators and hospices. Its Catalyst Rx business helps clients design drug benefit plans that encourage the use of preferred prescriptions bought from one of about 65000 pharmacies (including contracted mail order pharmacies) in the company's nationwide network. It also provides customized reporting and data analysis services. In 2012 Catalyst Health Solutions agreed to be acquired by PBM software firm SXC Health Solutions in a deal worth some $4.4 billion.

CATALYST PHARMACEUTICALS INC   NAS: CPRX

355 Alhambra Circle, Suite 801   CEO: Patrick McEnany
Coral Gables, FL 33134   CFO: Alicia Grande
Phone: 305 420-3200   HR: –
Fax: –   FYE: December 31
Web: www.catalystpharma.com   Type: Public

Catalyst Pharmaceutical a development-stage biopharmaceutical firm is developing treatments for rare neurological diseases such as Lambert-Eaton myasthenic syndrome (LEMS) and infantile spasms. Its amifampridine phosphate named Firdapse is under development for LEMS but also being tested for the treatment of other neuromuscular disorders; it was granted the breakthrough therapy designation by the FDA. Another candidate CPP-115 is a GABA-aminotransferase inhibitor that is in studies for infantile spasms — a rare form of epileptic seizures. It holds orphan drug designations in the US and Europe. Catalyst Pharma was previously engaged in developing drugs to treat addiction.

	Annual Growth	12/16	12/17	12/18	12/19	12/20
Sales ($ mil.)	1443.2%	–	–	0.5	102.3	119.1
Net income ($ mil.)	–	(18.1)	(18.4)	(34.0)	31.9	75.0
Market value ($ mil.)	33.5%	109.0	405.8	199.3	389.2	346.6
Employees	42.4%	18	21	51	76	74

CATAMOUNT CONSTRUCTORS, INC.

1527 COLE BLVD STE 100   CEO: Geoffrey G Wormer
LAKEWOOD, CO 804013421   CFO: –
Phone: 303-679-0087   HR: –
Fax: –   FYE: December 31
Web: www.catamountinc.com   Type: Private

A solid foundation is tantamount to Catamount's success. The company provides general contracting services for the construction of commercial industrial health care institutional and residential developments around the US. It offers services from conceptualization and design-build to construction management. Subsidiary CC Residential specializes in midrise multifamily residences including condominiums apartments and mixed-use developments. Catamount Constructors boasts a high customer return rate; it has provided services for such return clients as CarMax Walgreen and Chase Bank. CEO Geoff Wormer and other executives Kurt Kenchel Jeff Sidwell and Jeff Cochran founded the company in 1997.

	Annual Growth	12/04	12/05	12/06	12/07	12/08
Sales ($ mil.)	–	–	–	(156.4)	183.4	226.2
Net income ($ mil.)	1499.4%	–	–	0.0	7.5	4.2
Market value ($ mil.)	–	–	–	–	–	–
Employees	–	–	–	–	–	142

CATCHMARK TIMBER TRUST INC
NYS: CTT

5 Concourse Parkway, Suite 2650
Atlanta, GA 30328
Phone: 855 858-9794
Fax: -
Web: www.catchmark.com

CEO: Brian Davis
CFO: Ursula Godoy-Arbelaez
HR: -
FYE: December 31
Type: Public

Wood you be interested in investing in CatchMark Timber Trust? The real estate investment trust (REIT) which specializes in buying owning and selling commercial timberland owns interests in about 435000 acres of such property - mostly pine forest but also hardwood - across Alabama Georgia Florida Louisiana North Carolina South Carolina Tennessee and Oregon. Unlike other landowning REITs CatchMark only owns the land; it doesn't have logging operations or make wood products. Its largest customer is packaging manufacturer WestRock which contributes around 15% to the REIT's annual revenues.

	Annual Growth	12/16	12/17	12/18	12/19	12/20
Sales ($ mil.)	6.2%	81.9	91.3	97.9	106.7	104.3
Net income ($ mil.)	-	(11.1)	(13.5)	(122.0)	(93.3)	(17.5)
Market value ($ mil.)	(4.5%)	549.1	640.3	346.2	559.3	456.4
Employees	10.1%	17	19	25	26	25

CATERPILLAR FINANCIAL SERVICES CORP

2120 West End Ave.
Nashville, TN 37203-0001
Phone: 615 341-1000
Fax: -
Web: www.caterpillar.com

CEO: -
CFO: -
HR: -
FYE: December 31
Type: Public

Cat Financial is a wholly owned finance subsidiary of Caterpillar Inc. and it provides retail and wholesale financing to customers and dealers around the world for Caterpillar products as well as financing for vehicles power generation facilities and marine vessels that in most cases incorporate Caterpillar products. Retail financing is primarily comprised of installment sale contracts and other equipment-related loans working capital loans finance leases and operating leases. Wholesale financing to Caterpillar dealers consists primarily of inventory and rental fleet financing. A significant portion of Cat Financial's activity is conducted in North America with additional offices and subsidiaries in Latin America Asia/Pacific Europe Africa and the Middle East.

	Annual Growth	12/17	12/18	12/19	12/20	12/21
Sales ($ mil.)	(1.2%)	2,689.0	2,847.0	2,966.0	2,550.0	2,562.0
Net income ($ mil.)	(3.7%)	586.0	305.0	410.0	293.0	505.0
Market value ($ mil.)	-	-	-	-	-	-
Employees	3.1%	1,855	1,877	1,973	2,000	2,100

CATERPILLAR INC.
NYS: CAT

510 Lake Cook Road, Suite 100
Deerfield, IL 60015
Phone: 224 551-4000
Fax: -
Web: www.caterpillar.com

CEO: -
CFO: Andrew Bonfield
HR: -
FYE: December 31
Type: Public

Caterpillar Inc. is the world's #1 manufacturer of construction and mining equipment which includes excavators loaders and tractors as well as forestry paving and tunneling machinery. It also manufactures diesel and natural engines industrial gas turbines and diesel-electric locomotives. Subsidiary Caterpillar Financial Services offers financing products and services for dealers and customers and its Energy & Transportation segment supports customers in oil and gas power generation marine rail and industrial applications including Cat machines. The US supplies about 45% of sales.

	Annual Growth	12/17	12/18	12/19	12/20	12/21
Sales ($ mil.)	2.9%	45,462.0	54,722.0	53,800.0	41,748.0	50,971.0
Net income ($ mil.)	71.3%	754.0	6,147.0	6,093.0	2,998.0	6,489.0
Market value ($ mil.)	7.0%	84,445.2	68,095.3	79,139.9	97,542.3	110,789.5
Employees	2.3%	98,400	104,000	102,300	97,300	107,700

CATHAY GENERAL BANCORP
NMS: CATY

777 North Broadway
Los Angeles, CA 90012
Phone: 213 625-4700
Fax: -
Web: www.cathaybank.com

CEO: Chang M Liu
CFO: Heng Chen
HR: -
FYE: December 31
Type: Public

Cathay General Bancorp is the holding company for Cathay Bank which mainly serves Chinese and Vietnamese communities from some 30 branches in California and about 20 more in Illinois New Jersey New York Massachusetts Washington and Texas. It also has a branch in Hong Kong and offices in Shanghai and Taipei. Catering to small to medium-sized businesses and individual consumers the bank offers standard deposit services and loans. Commercial mortgage loans account for more than half of the bank's portfolio; business loans comprise nearly 25%. The bank's Cathay Wealth Management unit offers online stock trading mutual funds and other investment products and services through an agreement with PrimeVest.

	Annual Growth	12/16	12/17	12/18	12/19	12/20
Assets ($ mil.)	7.0%	14,520.8	15,640.2	16,784.7	18,094.1	19,043.1
Net income ($ mil.)	6.9%	175.1	176.0	271.9	279.1	228.9
Market value ($ mil.)	(4.1%)	3,023.7	3,352.9	2,665.9	3,025.3	2,559.4
Employees	1.6%	1,129	1,271	1,277	1,219	1,205

CATHOLIC HEALTH EAST

3805 WEST CHESTER PIKE # 100
NEWTOWN SQUARE, PA 19073-2329
Phone: 610-355-2000
Fax: -
Web: www.che.org

CEO: -
CFO: -
HR: -
FYE: December 31
Type: Private

Catholic Health East (CHE) marries the physical and the spiritual in its vast network of not-for-profit health care facilities. As one of the largest religious health systems in the country CHE carries out its mission of healing the sick through more than 35 acute-care hospitals (7300 beds) four long-term acute care (LTAC) hospitals and 25 freestanding and hospital-based long-term care facilities as well as assisted living behavioral health and rehabilitation centers. Operating in 11 states along the East Coast from Maine to Florida CHE is also one of the country's largest providers of home health care services. The health care organization is sponsored by 10 religious congregations and ministries.

	Annual Growth	12/05	12/06	12/07	12/09	12/10
Sales ($ mil.)	(0.7%)	-	4,175.9	4,364.5	106.6	4,057.5
Net income ($ mil.)	(8.1%)	-	199.2	199.9	(3.3)	142.3
Market value ($ mil.)	-	-	-	-	-	-
Employees	-	-	-	-	-	50,000

CATHOLIC HEALTH SERVICES OF LONG ISLAND

992 N. Village Ave.
Rockville Centre NY 11570
Phone: 516-705-3700
Fax: 516-705-3730
Web: www.chsli.org

CEO: Alan D Guerci
CFO: William Armstrong
HR: -
FYE: December 31
Type: Private - Not-for-Pr

The long and the short of it is that Catholic Health Services of Long Island (CHS) provides health care to the residents of Long Island. Founded in 1997 and sponsored by the Diocese of Rockville Centre CHS's operations consist of six hospitals and three nursing homes as well as regional home care and hospice services. Within the CHS system member organizations offer virtually any medical specialty or clinical service. The system's hospitals which include Good Samaritan Hospital Medical Center Mercy Medical Center and St. Francis Hospital house some 1725 beds more than 15000 employees and a medical staff of 3300. CHS's MaryHaven Center provides services to people of all ages with disabilities.

CATHOLIC HEALTH SYSTEM, INC.

144 GENESEE ST FL 1
BUFFALO, NY 142031560
Phone: 716-685-4870
Fax: –
Web: www.chsbuffalo.org

CEO: –
CFO: –
HR: –
FYE: December 31
Type: Private

The Catholic Health System gives residents of its home state even more reason to proclaim "I heart New York." The non-profit health care system recognized for its cardiac services serves residents of western New York through four hospitals and more than a dozen primary care centers as well as long-term care facilities diagnostic and treatment centers and other health care sites. Catholic Health is also well-known for its women's health cancer treatment and rehabilitation services and is a leading provider of elderly care in the region. Its hospitals (including Kenmore Mercy Sisters of Charity — formerly St. Joseph's Mercy Hospital of Buffalo and St. Joseph's) have a capacity of about 825 beds.

	Annual Growth	12/04	12/05	12/06	12/09	12/13
Sales ($ mil.)	(20.6%)	–	–	622.0	84.8	123.6
Net income ($ mil.)	–	–	–	20.3	(0.1)	0.0
Market value ($ mil.)	–	–	–	–	–	–
Employees	–	–	–	–	–	8,400

CATO CORP.

8100 Denmark Road
Charlotte, NC 28273-5975
Phone: 704 554-8510
Fax: –
Web: www.catofashions.com

NYS: CATO
CEO: John Cato
CFO: Chuck Knight
HR: –
FYE: January 30
Type: Public

The Cato Corp. caters to fashion-minded women on a budget. The retailer operates more than 1281 apparel stores in 31-plus states (primarily in the Southeast) under the names Cato Cato Fashions Cato Plus Versona It's Fashion and It's Fashion Metro. Its mostly private-label merchandise includes missy juniors' girls' and plus-sized casual sportswear career clothing coats shoes and accessories. Cato's stores are typically located in shopping centers anchored by a Wal-Mart store or another major discounter or supermarket. Founded in 1946 the company is led by chairman John Cato the third generation of Catos in the family business.

	Annual Growth	01/17*	02/18	02/19	02/20*	01/21
Sales ($ mil.)	(11.9%)	956.6	850.0	829.7	825.3	575.1
Net income ($ mil.)	–	47.2	8.5	30.5	35.9	(47.5)
Market value ($ mil.)	(18.6%)	585.0	257.9	332.9	362.6	257.0
Employees	(7.7%)	10,200	10,500	10,350	10,060	7,400

*Fiscal year change

CAVALIER TELEPHONE LLC

2134 W. Laburnum Ave.
Richmond VA 23227
Phone: 804-422-4100
Fax: 804-422-4392
Web: www.cavtel.com

CEO: –
CFO: –
HR: –
FYE: December 31
Type: Subsidiary

Despite its name Cavalier Telephone takes a serious approach to residential and business telecommunications. The facilities-based telephone and data services company offers local and long-distance voice broadband Internet and computer telephony services in 15 states in the eastern southeastern and midwestern US. It provides commercial communications services such as private networks and broadband Internet connections largely through its Intellifiber Networks division. Digital television programming is offered through an agreement with direct broadcast satellite provider DIRECTV. Key residential markets include Baltimore Philadelphia and Pittsburgh. The company was acquired by PAETEC Holding in late 2010.

CAVCO INDUSTRIES INC (DE)

3636 North Central Ave., Ste. 1200
Phoenix, AZ 85012
Phone: 602 256-6263
Fax: –
Web: www.cavco.com

NMS: CVCO
CEO: William Boor
CFO: –
HR: –
FYE: April 03
Type: Public

Cavco Industries designs makes and sells manufactured homes under brands that include Cavco Palm Harbor Friendship and Fleetwood. Its products include full-sized homes (about 500 sq. ft. to 3300 sq. ft.); park model homes (less than 400 sq. ft.) for use as recreational and retirement units; camping cabins; and commercial structures for use as portable classrooms showrooms and offices. Cavco sold some 14200 factory-built homes through company-owned and independent distribution channels. The company's finance arm offers mortgages and insurance.

	Annual Growth	04/17*	03/18	03/19	03/20*	04/21
Sales ($ mil.)	9.4%	773.8	871.2	962.7	1,061.8	1,108.1
Net income ($ mil.)	19.2%	38.0	61.5	68.6	75.1	76.6
Market value ($ mil.)	18.9%	1,074.9	1,604.5	1,085.3	1,371.1	2,146.2
Employees	2.2%	4,300	4,500	4,650	5,000	4,700

*Fiscal year change

CAVIUM INC

2315 N. First Street
San Jose, CA 95131
Phone: 408 943-7100
Fax: –
Web: www.caviumnetworks.com

NMS: CAVM
CEO: –
CFO: Jean Hu
HR: –
FYE: December 31
Type: Public

Cavium provides integrated circuits for use in networking equipment such as routers switches security appliances gateway devices and storage networking equipment. The company designs specialized microprocessors used in secure network transmissions based on ARM and MIPS architecture technologies. Manufacturing is contracted out to Taiwan Semiconductor Manufacturing and United Microelectronics among others. Cavium also provides related software and services. Customers outside the US account for more than two-thirds of the company's sales.

	Annual Growth	12/12	12/13	12/14	12/15	12/16
Sales ($ mil.)	26.5%	235.5	304.0	373.0	412.7	603.3
Net income ($ mil.)	–	(112.6)	(3.0)	(15.3)	(17.1)	(147.2)
Market value ($ mil.)	18.9%	2,096.7	2,318.4	4,153.2	4,414.5	4,194.8
Employees	21.8%	831	830	936	1,005	1,831

CAZENOVIA COLLEGE

22 SULLIVAN ST
CAZENOVIA, NY 130351085
Phone: 315-655-7000
Fax: –
Web: www.cazenovia.edu

CEO: –
CFO: Mark Edwards
HR: –
FYE: June 30
Type: Private

Students wanting individualized attention and a well-rounded education can apply to Cazenovia College. With a a student-faculty ratio of 15 to 1 the school, focuses on liberal arts offering bachelor's and associate degrees in more than 20 fields of study. The school, has, about 1000 students and some 140 full- and part-time faculty members., Cazenovia College opened in 1824 in what had been the Madison County (New York) Courthouse., The school, was founded as the Seminary of the Genesee Conference the second Methodist seminary to be established in the US. Among its early notable alumni is Leland Stanford who founded and endowed Stanford University.

	Annual Growth	06/07	06/08	06/09	06/10	06/11
Sales ($ mil.)	–	–	–	(115.7)	25.8	24.7
Net income ($ mil.)	1765.4%	–	–	0.0	3.6	5.7
Market value ($ mil.)	–	–	–	–	–	–
Employees	–	–	–	–	–	369

CBEYOND INC   NMS: CBEY

320 Interstate North Parkway, Suite 500
Atlanta, GA 30339
Phone: 678 424-2400
Fax: –
Web: www.cbeyond.com

CEO: –
CFO: Edward James III
HR: –
FYE: December 31
Type: Public

Cbeyond isn't looking past the millions of small businesses in the US to find customers. The company offers local long-distance and cellular telephone and broadband Internet services as well as a host of network and cloud-based services (data center Web hosting security application migration administration management) to more than 60000 small and midsized businesses with fewer than 250 employees. It targets businesses in more than a dozen large metropolitan areas divided between established (Atlanta Dallas Denver) and emerging (Boston Seattle Washington DC) markets. Typical customers include law firms physicians' offices real estate companies and accounting firms.

	Annual Growth	12/08	12/09	12/10	12/11	12/12
Sales ($ mil.)	8.7%	349.7	413.8	452.0	485.4	488.0
Net income ($ mil.)	–	3.7	(2.2)	(1.7)	(8.0)	(2.3)
Market value ($ mil.)	(13.3%)	478.2	471.3	457.2	239.7	270.5
Employees	2.8%	1,493	1,677	1,944	1,928	1,667

CBIZ INC   NYS: CBZ

6050 Oak Tree Boulevard South, Suite 500
Cleveland, OH 44131
Phone: 216 447-9000
Fax: 216 447-4809
Web: www.cbiz.com

CEO: Jerome Grisko
CFO: Ware Grove
HR: Katie Gisztl
FYE: December 31
Type: Public

CBIZ provides outsourced services such as accounting and financial services group health benefits consulting property and casualty services retirement plan services payroll services and IT services. The company serves small and midsize businesses (SMBs) government agencies individuals and not-for-profits organizations. CBIZ has more than 100 offices in more than 30 states and the District of Columbia. The company was founded in 1996 and generates almost all of its revenue in the US.

	Annual Growth	12/16	12/17	12/18	12/19	12/20
Sales ($ mil.)	4.8%	799.8	855.3	922.0	948.4	963.9
Net income ($ mil.)	18.2%	40.1	50.4	61.6	70.7	78.3
Market value ($ mil.)	18.1%	741.2	835.8	1,065.8	1,458.5	1,439.6
Employees	1.1%	4,600	4,600	4,800	4,800	4,800

CBL & ASSOCIATES PROPERTIES INC   NYS: CBL

2030 Hamilton Place Blvd., Suite 500
Chattanooga, TN 37421-6000
Phone: 423 855-0001
Fax: –
Web: www.cblproperties.com

CEO: Stephen Lebovitz
CFO: Farzana Khaleel
HR: –
FYE: December 31
Type: Public

CBL & Associates Properties is a self-managed real estate investment trust (REIT) owns develops manages and finances shopping malls and other retail properties primarily in the Southeast and Midwest US. Its largest tenants include Signet Jewelers L Brands Foot Locker Hot Topic and Luxottica Group. The REIT wholly owns or has interests in about 100 properties around 60 are regional malls and open-air shopping centers. Regional shopping malls open-air and mixed-use centers outlet centers associated centers community centers office and other properties round out its portfolio.

	Annual Growth	12/16	12/17	12/18	12/19	12/20
Sales ($ mil.)	(13.5%)	1,028.3	927.3	858.6	768.7	575.9
Net income ($ mil.)	–	172.9	120.9	(78.6)	(108.8)	(295.1)
Market value ($ mil.)	–	–	–	–	–	–
Employees	(9.2%)	697	685	650	594	474

CBOE GLOBAL MARKETS INC   BZX: CBOE

433 West Van Buren Street
Chicago, IL 60607
Phone: 312 786-5600
Fax: –
Web: www.cboe.com

CEO: Edward Tilly
CFO: Brian Schell
HR: –
FYE: December 31
Type: Public

CBOE or Chicago Board Options Exchange provides cutting-edge trading and investment solutions to market participants around the world. The company is committed to defining markets through product innovation leading edge technology and seamless trading solutions. The company offers trading across a diverse range of products in multiple asset classes and geographies including options futures US Canadian and European equities exchange-traded products (ETPs) global foreign exchange (FX) and volatility products based on the Cboe Volatility Index (VIX Index) recognized as the world's premier gauge of US equity market volatility. In addition the company operates one of the largest stock exchanges by value traded in Europe and owns EuroCCP a leading pan-European equities clearing house. Cboe Global Markets also is a leading market globally for ETP listings and trading.

	Annual Growth	12/17	12/18	12/19	12/20	12/21
Sales ($ mil.)	11.9%	2,229.1	2,768.8	2,496.1	3,427.1	3,494.8
Net income ($ mil.)	7.1%	401.7	426.5	374.9	468.2	529.0
Market value ($ mil.)	1.1%	13,287.1	10,433.2	12,797.6	9,930.9	13,906.7
Employees	7.7%	889	842	823	1,010	1,196

CBRE GROUP INC   NYS: CBRE

2100 McKinney Avenue, 12th Floor
Dallas, TX 75201
Phone: 214 979-6100
Fax: –
Web: www.cbre.com

CEO: Michael Lafitte
CFO: Leah Stearns
HR: –
FYE: December 31
Type: Public

As the largest commercial real estate services company CBRE Group provides leasing property sales occupier outsourcing and valuation businesses from about 500 offices worldwide. Subsidiary Trammell Crow provides commercial real estate development services in the US. CBRE Global Investors provides investment management services to pension funds insurance companies sovereign wealth funds foundations endowments and other institutional investors seeking to generate returns and diversification through investment in real assets such as real estate infrastructure master limited partnerships and other assets. The company garners over 55% of its revenue from the US. CBRE was founded in San Francisco in 1906.

	Annual Growth	12/16	12/17	12/18	12/19	12/20
Sales ($ mil.)	16.2%	13,071.6	14,209.6	21,340.1	23,894.1	23,826.2
Net income ($ mil.)	7.1%	572.0	691.5	1,063.2	1,282.4	752.0
Market value ($ mil.)	18.8%	10,566.8	14,533.2	13,435.9	20,566.6	21,046.4
Employees	7.5%	75,000	80,000	90,000	100,000	100,000

CBS BROADCASTING INC.

51 W. 52nd St.
New York NY 10019
Phone: 212-975-4321
Fax: 212-975-4516
Web: www.cbs.com

CEO: Leslie Moonves
CFO: –
HR: –
FYE: December 31
Type: Subsidiary

The forensic evidence shows this company is tops in the TV ratings. CBS Broadcasting owns and operates the CBS Television Network the #1 watched broadcast network in the US. Its top shows include CSI: Crime Scene Investigation and its two spinoffs as well as The Mentalist NCIS and a host of primetime comedies. It boasts more than 200 affiliate stations around the country including about 15 stations that are company-owned and -operated. In addition CBS Broadcasting oversees The CW Network a 50%-owned joint venture with Time Warner's Warner Bros. Entertainment. The company is a unit of media conglomerate CBS Corporation.

CBS RADIO INC.

40 W. 57th St. 14th Fl.
New York NY 10019
Phone: 212-649-9600
Fax: 212-315-2162
Web: www.cbsradio.com

CEO: Andre Fernandez
CFO: Jacques Tortoroli
HR: –
FYE: December 31
Type: Subsidiary

This company keeps its eye on radio listeners. CBS Radio is one of the country's leading radio broadcasters with about 130 stations serving about 30 major markets over the airwaves. Its stations offer a variety of programming from news talk and sports to a wide range of music styles; many of the stations are affiliates of the Westwood One radio network. (CBS Radio owns nearly 10% of the radio programming syndicator.) In addition to traditional broadcasting many CBS stations broadcast digital over-the-air signals along with online streaming and on-demand content. CBS Radio is a subsidiary of media giant CBS Corporation.

CC INDUSTRIES INC.

222 N. LaSalle St. Ste. 1000
Chicago IL 60601
Phone: 312-855-4000
Fax: 919-573-3551

CEO: William H Crown
CFO: –
HR: –
FYE: December 31
Type: Subsidiary

A few of the Crown family's affairs are handled by CC Industries. The private equity firm which is controlled by Chicago's Henry Crown and Company manages several investments for its parent including Great Dane which is one of the largest manufacturers of truck trailers in North America. CC Industries also oversees Provisur Technologies a manufacturer of meat processing equipment sold under the Formax Beehive and Weiler brands. CC Industries which was founded in 1986 mostly invests in manufacturing companies in North America and Latin America.

CCA INDUSTRIES, INC.

1099 Wall Street West, Suite 275
Lyndhurst,, NJ 07071
Phone: 201 935-3232
Fax: 201 935-6784
Web: www.ccaindustries.com

NBB: CAWW
CEO: Christopher Dominello
CFO: Stephen Heit
HR: –
FYE: November 30
Type: Public

Consumers count on CCA Industries for health and beauty care. The company makes and markets health and beauty aids each under its own brand name including Plus+White (oral care) Bikini Zone (shave gels) Sudden Change (skin care) Solar Sense (sun protection) and Nutra Nail and Gel Perfect (nail care) among many. It also sells dietary supplements (tea and chewing gum) under the Mega-T label. CCA items are made under contract and several such as Hair-Off Mega-T and Kids Sense are made and marketed under licensing agreements. The firm caters to food and drug retailers such as Walgreens and CVS mass merchandisers Wal-Mart and Target warehouse club Sam's and wholesale distributors mainly in the US.

	Annual Growth	11/16	11/17	11/18	11/19	11/20
Sales ($ mil.)	(7.9%)	19.6	19.8	16.6	17.1	14.1
Net income ($ mil.)	–		1.2	1.8	(3.3)	0.6	(0.1)
Market value ($ mil.)	(5.6%)	19.4	22.6	17.7	21.5	15.4
Employees	8.0%	12	12	14		

CCC GROUP INC.

5797 Dietrich Rd.
San Antonio TX 78219
Phone: 210-661-4251
Fax: 210-661-6060
Web: www.cccgroupinc.com

CEO: Joe Garza
CFO: –
HR: –
FYE: December 31
Type: Private

Construction is at the core of CCC Group. The general contractor founded in 1947 specializes in industrial construction manufacturing and specialty engineering and design services. It performs a laundry list of construction services including site development civil engineering construction management marine construction mining equipment erection and dismantling and plant expansions. CCC Group also installs specialized equipment. The company serves utilities and municipalities as well as the oil and gas and metals and chemicals industries. It operates mostly out of its home state of Texas but maintains offices throughout the South Southwestern and Southeastern US and three international offices.

CCC INFORMATION SERVICES GROUP INC.

222 Merchandise Mart Ste. 900
Chicago IL 60654-1005
Phone: 312-222-4636
Fax: 312-527-2298
Web: www.cccis.com

CEO: Githesh Ramamurthy
CFO: Andrew G Balbirer
HR: –
FYE: December 31
Type: Subsidiary

CCC Information Services Group helps smooth the dents in auto claims processing. The company's software and services help insurance agencies independent appraisers and collision repair shops process auto claims. CCC's offerings include its Pathways application for estimating collision and repair cost and its Valuescope claim settlement services application for estimating the worth of totaled vehicles. Its claims management software is linked to about 21000 auto body collision repair shops and 350 insurance companies. CCC Information Services was founded in 1980 and taken private by Investcorp for about $496 million in 2006.

CCFNB BANCORP INC.

232 East Street
Bloomsburg, PA 17815
Phone: 570 784-4400
Fax: –
Web: www.firstcolumbiabank.com

NBB: CCFN
CEO: Lance Diehl
CFO: Jeffrey Arnold
HR: –
FYE: December 31
Type: Public

CCFNB Bancorp knows the ABCs of banking. It is the holding company for First Columbia Bank & Trust a community institution serving Pennsylvania's Columbia Montour Northumberland and Luzerne counties from some 15 locations. The bank offers standard products and services as well as wealth management and trust services. It uses funds from deposits to write a variety of loans; real estate loans account for more than 80% of its loan portfolio. The bank also offers consumer and construction loans. CCFNB Bancorp owns a 50% stake in Neighborhood Group (dba Neighborhood Advisors) an insurance and financial products agency. CCFNB Bancorp merged with Columbia Financial Corporation in 2008.

	Annual Growth	12/16	12/17	12/18	12/19	12/20
Assets ($ mil.)	6.1%	673.6	709.5	726.2	742.7	855.1
Net income ($ mil.)	6.8%	7.2	7.3	8.0	8.9	9.3
Market value ($ mil.)	1.2%	87.2	102.1	103.3	101.1	91.3
Employees	0.2%	138	136	143	133	139

CCH INCORPORATED

2700 Lake Cook Rd.
Riverwoods IL 60015-3888
Phone: 847-267-7000
Fax: 773-866-3095
Web: www.cch.com

CEO: Jason Marx
CFO: Eric Bartholome
HR: –
FYE: December 31
Type: Subsidiary

Tax season must be CCH's favorite time of year. Also known as Wolters Kluwer Tax and Accounting CCH publishes more than 700 publications in print and electronic form primarily concerning the subjects of tax and business law. Publications are available in a variety of print and electronic formats that reach a target audience of accountants attorneys and compliance professionals. The company's flagship product is "The Standard Federal Tax Reporter". Its Tax and Accounting unit produces software used for tax preparation audits and office productivity. The company was founded in 1913 the same year the US federal income tax was created. CCH is a subsidiary of Dutch publisher Wolters Kluwer.

CD INTERNATIONAL ENTERPRISES INC   NBB: CDII Q

1333 S. University Drive, Suite 202
Plantation, FL 33342
Phone: 954 363-7333
Fax: –
Web: www.cdii.net

CEO: –
CFO: –
HR: –
FYE: September 30
Type: Public

China Direct Industries cuts out the middleman and goes directly to the source. The company invests in and manages Chinese companies that sell industrial metals and related products. Its portfolio includes controlling stakes in companies that produce and/or distribute magnesium synthetic chemicals steel and other commodities. The company is increasingly focused on the production and distribution of pure magnesium a high-demand commodity. China Direct provides its subsidiaries with management advisory services and strategic planning; its consulting segment specializes in providing services for US companies that primarily do business in China.

	Annual Growth	09/12	09/13	09/14	09/15	09/16
Sales ($ mil.)	(83.6%)	114.1	2.0	1.7	0.4	0.1
Net income ($ mil.)	–	(41.7)	(24.7)	16.5	(3.1)	(20.4)
Market value ($ mil.)	–	2.4	0.5	0.6	0.2	0.0
Employees	(66.2%)	610	25	10	9	8

CCOM GROUP INC   NBB: CCOM P

275 Wagaraw Road
Hawthorne, NJ 07506
Phone: 973 427-8224
Fax: –
Web: www.ccomgrp.com

CEO: Peter Gasiewicz
CFO: William Salek
HR: –
FYE: December 31
Type: Public

Colonial Commercial through subsidiaries Universal Supply Group The RAL Supply Group and S&A Supply provides HVAC products climate-control systems and plumbing fixtures to mostly builders and contractors in New York and New Jersey. It supplies control-system design custom fabrication technical support training and consultation services (but not installation) for engineers and installers. RAL Supply Group offers plumbing fixtures water systems and water-treatment products and heating and cooling equipment. More than 80% of Colonial's sales come from the replacement market while the balance is generated by new construction. Chairman Michael Goldman owns about 30% of the company.

	Annual Growth	12/16	12/17	12/18	12/19	12/20
Sales ($ mil.)	4.0%	87.3	92.3	104.7	113.7	101.9
Net income ($ mil.)	10.2%	0.7	0.5	3.1	1.3	1.1
Market value ($ mil.)	11.0%	5.4	6.0	6.1	10.5	8.2
Employees	–	–	–	–	–	–

CDC SUPPLY CHAIN

8989 N. Deerwood Dr.
Milwaukee WI 53223
Phone: 414-362-6800
Fax: 414-362-6794
Web: www.cdcsupplychain.com

CEO: Michael Eleftheriou
CFO: David H Jacobson
HR: –
FYE: December 31
Type: Subsidiary

CDC Supply Chain serves as an agent of change in supply chains. The company's supply chain execution performance and process management software helps clients manage inventory and fulfillment monitor their supply chain activities and automate a range of warehouse functions including receiving loading and storage. The company targets clients in the transportation retail consumer packaged goods and processed goods industries. CDC Supply Chain counts multinational companies such as AstraZeneca Boeing Saks and Smucker among its customers. CDC Supply Chain is a unit of CDC Software.

CCUR HOLDINGS INC   NBB: CCUR

6470 East Johns Crossing, Suite 490
Duluth, GA 30097
Phone: 770 305-6434
Fax: –
Web: www.ccurholdings.com

CEO: Wayne Barr Jr
CFO: Warren Sutherland
HR: –
FYE: June 30
Type: Public

Watch a video on multiple devices? Simulate the performance of a car or aircraft part in real time? Such processes might be courtesy of Concurrent Computer. The company's video segment is mainly geared toward broadband and content providers worldwide to allow streaming video and collecting viewer data. The company also develops real-time products that allow manufacturers such as those in the aerospace and automotive industries to run their products through advanced computer simulations. The real-time computing products combine Linux and similar operating systems and software development tools with off-the-shelf hardware for time-critical applications.

	Annual Growth	06/16	06/17	06/18	06/19	06/20
Sales ($ mil.)	(44.3%)	61.1	27.6	–	3.5	5.9
Net income ($ mil.)	–	(11.1)	28.4	16.1	0.7	12.2
Market value ($ mil.)	–	–	–	–	–	–
Employees	(60.7%)	251	110	3	7	6

CDI CONTRACTORS, LLC

3000 CANTRELL RD
LITTLE ROCK, AR 722022010
Phone: 501-666-4300
Fax: –
Web: www.cdicon.com

CEO: E Lloyd Garrison
CFO: Chris Johnson
HR: –
FYE: December 31
Type: Private

CDI Contractors means big buildings in Little Rock and beyond. The company has completed commercial industrial and institutional projects including the William J. Clinton Presidential Library. Other areas of specialty include health care facilities parking decks condos hotels and educational institutions. CDI Contractors provides a range of services including pre-construction scheduling general contracting and construction and project management. The company was founded in 1987 as a partnership between the late Bill Clark and Dillard's head Bill Dillard II. CDI has built several Dillard's department stores. Dillard's bought the remaining 50% of CDI it did not already own in 2008.

	Annual Growth	12/13	12/14	12/15	12/16	12/17
Sales ($ mil.)	(2.0%)	–	213.2	284.5	261.0	200.8
Net income ($ mil.)	6.8%	–	2.0	4.7	4.2	2.4
Market value ($ mil.)	–	–	–	–	–	–
Employees	–	–	–	–	–	300

CDTI ADVANCED MATERIALS INC
NBB: CDTI

1700 Fiske Place
Oxnard, CA 93033
Phone: 805 639-9458
Fax: –
Web: www.cdti.com

CEO: Matthew Beale
CFO: Tracy Kern
HR: –
FYE: December 31
Type: Public

Clean Diesel Technologies (which operates as CDTi) has developed a few cool technologies to counteract global warming. The company is starting to commercialize its chemical fuel additives and other products for reducing diesel engine emissions and improving fuel economy. These include its platinum fuel catalysts which are marketed in Europe and the US under the Platinum Plus brand. CDTi also manufactures and licenses nitrogen oxide reduction systems (under the brand name ARIS) and chemical fuel additives to help control diesel engine emissions. The company has a licensing deal with Mitsui to use the ARIS technology.

	Annual Growth	12/13	12/14	12/15	12/16	12/17
Sales ($ mil.)	(15.4%)	55.3	41.2	39.7	36.8	28.4
Net income ($ mil.)	–	(7.1)	(9.3)	(8.5)	(23.5)	(5.3)
Market value ($ mil.)	1.6%	4.7	5.7	3.0	6.8	5.0
Employees	(25.3%)	151	117	125	99	47

CDW CORPORATION

200 N. Milwaukee Ave.
Vernon Hills IL 60061
Phone: 847-465-6000
Fax: 336-852-2096
Web: www.tangeroutlet.com

CEO: Christine Leahy
CFO: Albert Miralles
HR: –
FYE: December 31
Type: Private

People who get IT shop for it at CDW. The company offers about 100000 information technology products including notebook and desktop computers software printers servers storage devices networking tools and accessories under more than 1000 brands. Top brands include Adobe Apple Cisco Hewlett-Packard Microsoft VMware among others. CDW operates a retail store at its corporate headquarters and manages an e-commerce site. Almost all of the company's sales come from public-sector clients and private businesses. Founded in 1984 as Computer Discount Warehouse today CDW is owned by private equity firms Madison Dearborn Partners and Providence Equity Partners.

CEB INC.

1201 WILSON BLVD STE 1800
ARLINGTON, VA 222092316
Phone: 571-303-3000
Fax: –
Web: www.cebglobal.com

CEO: Thomas L Monahan III
CFO: Richard S Lindahl
HR: –
FYE: December 31
Type: Private

Don't fear the competition; learn from it. So says CEB a provider of business research and analysis services to more than 10000 companies worldwide. Its program areas cover "best practices" in such topics as finance human resources information technology operations and sales and marketing. Unlike consulting firms which engage with one client at a time CEB operates on a membership-based business model. Members subscribe to one or more of the company's programs and participate in the research and analysis thus sharing expertise with others. Besides reports on best practices CEB offers seminars customized research briefs and decision-support tools.

	Annual Growth	12/12	12/13	12/14	12/15	12/16
Sales ($ mil.)	5.0%	–	820.1	909.0	928.4	949.8
Net income ($ mil.)	–	–	32.0	51.2	92.5	(34.7)
Market value ($ mil.)	–	–	–	–	–	–
Employees	–	–	–	–	–	4,600

CEC ENTERTAINMENT, INC.

1707 MARKET PL STE 200
IRVING, TX 750638049
Phone: 972-258-8507
Fax: –
Web: www.chuckecheese.com

CEO: David McKillips
CFO: James Howell
HR: Nancy Harris
FYE: December 29
Type: Private

Don't let the mouse mascot fool you: This amusement kingdom is founded on the power of pizza. CEC Entertainment operates the Chuck E. Cheese's chain of pizza parlors with more than 610 locations in over 45 states and approximately 15 foreign countries and territories. The restaurants cater mostly to families with children and feature a broad array of entertainment offerings including arcade-style and skill-oriented games rides live entertainment shows. Entertainment and merchandise account for some 55% of sales. The menu features pizzas wings appetizers salads and desserts. CEC Entertainment owns and operates more than 550 of the pizza and fun joints while the rest are franchised.

	Annual Growth	01/16	01/17*	12/17	12/18	12/19
Sales ($ mil.)	(0.6%)	–	923.7	886.8	896.1	912.9
Net income ($ mil.)	–	–	(3.7)	53.1	(20.5)	(28.9)
Market value ($ mil.)	–	–	–	–	–	–
Employees	–	–	–	–	–	17,200

*Fiscal year change

CECIL BANCORP, INC.
NBB: CECB

127 North Street, P.O. Box 568
Elkton, MD 21921
Phone: 410 398-1650
Fax: –
Web: www.cecilbank.com

CEO: Terrie Spiro
CFO: R. Lee Whitehead
HR: –
FYE: December 31
Type: Public

Cecil Bancorp is the holding company for Cecil Federal Bank which serves northeastern Maryland's Cecil and Harford counties through about a dozen branches. The bank offers standard deposit products such as checking and savings accounts NOW and money market accounts CDs and IRAs. The bank focuses on real estate lending; commercial mortgages make up the largest portion of the bank's loan portfolio followed by one- to four-family residential mortgages and construction loans. It offers investment and insurance services through an agreement with third-party provider Community Bankers Securities. First Mariner Bancorp acquired nearly 25% of Cecil Bancorp in 2012 through the collection of a defaulted loan.

	Annual Growth	12/08	12/09	12/10	12/11	12/12
Assets ($ mil.)	(2.8%)	492.4	509.8	487.2	463.7	439.8
Net income ($ mil.)	–	1.9	(2.5)	1.1	(4.7)	(20.3)
Market value ($ mil.)	(46.2%)	50.1	26.0	23.8	4.1	4.2
Employees	(0.5%)	92	91	93	92	90

CECO ENVIRONMENTAL CORP.
NMS: CECE

14651 North Dallas Parkway, Suite 500
Dallas, TX 75254
Phone: 214 357-6181
Fax: –
Web: www.cecoenviro.com

CEO: Todd Gleason
CFO: Matthew Eckl
HR: –
FYE: December 31
Type: Public

CECO Environmental makes industrial ventilation and pollution control systems including air filters to improve air quality. The company serves customers in the automotive chemical electronics refining pharmaceutical and aquaculture industries among others. Its brands include Peerless Emtrol-Buell Fybroc Sethco Zhongli Adwest and Busch International. CECO Environmental also provides custom metal fabrication services making components for its own ventilation systems. The company operates across the US Canada the UK and China. CECO Environmental generates approximately 35% of revenue outside US.

	Annual Growth	12/16	12/17	12/18	12/19	12/20
Sales ($ mil.)	(6.7%)	417.0	345.1	337.3	341.9	316.0
Net income ($ mil.)	–	(38.2)	(3.0)	(7.1)	17.7	8.2
Market value ($ mil.)	(16.0%)	493.4	181.4	238.7	270.9	246.2
Employees	(7.2%)	985	900	800	830	730

CEDAR FAIR LP
NYS: FUN

One Cedar Point Drive
Sandusky, OH 44870-5259
Phone: 419 626-0830
Fax: –
Web: www.cedarfair.com

CEO: Richard Zimmerman
CFO: Brian Witherow
HR: Craig Heckman
FYE: December 31
Type: Public

Cedar Fair is one of the largest regional amusement park operators in the world. The company owns and manages nearly 15 amusement parks water parks and complementary resort facilities. Properties include the flagship Cedar Point on Lake Erie in Ohio; Knott's Berry Farm in Buena Park California (outside of Los Angeles); and Michigan's Adventure near Muskegon Michigan. The company also has a contract to manage Gilroy Gardens in California. Knott's Berry Farm and Castaway Bay Indoor Waterpark Resort (also in Sandusky) operate year-round while other parks are open daily from Memorial Day through Labor Day plus additional seasonal weekends. Cedar Fair parks together draw approximately 28 million visitors each year.

	Annual Growth	12/16	12/17	12/18	12/19	12/20
Sales ($ mil.)	(38.7%)	1,288.7	1,322.0	1,348.5	1,474.9	181.6
Net income ($ mil.)	–	177.7	215.5	126.7	172.4	(590.2)
Market value ($ mil.)	(11.5%)	3,640.5	3,685.3	2,682.2	3,143.8	2,230.8
Employees	2.7%	45,600	46,900	47,300	51,200	50,700

CEDAR REALTY TRUST INC
NYS: CDR

928 Carmans Road
Massapequa, NY 11758
Phone: 516 767-6492
Fax: –
Web: www.cedarrealtytrust.com

CEO: Bruce Schanzer
CFO: Jennifer Bitterman
HR: –
FYE: December 30
Type: Public

Cedar Realty Trust (formerly Cedar Shopping Centers) has tended its portfolio from a sapling to a full-grown evergreen. The self-managed real estate investment trust (REIT) owns develops and manages retail space mainly supermarket-anchored strip centers from Washington D.C. to Boston. It owns about 55 properties totaling more than 8.3 million sq. ft. of leasable space. Its portfolio spans eight states with the heaviest concentration of shopping centers in Pennsylvania and Maryland. Major tenants include Giant Foods LA Fitness and Farm Fresh. The REIT usually redevelops or expands existing properties after it buys them.

	Annual Growth	12/16	12/17	12/18	12/19	12/20
Sales ($ mil.)	(2.7%)	151.1	146.0	152.0	144.1	135.5
Net income ($ mil.)	–	8.9	19.1	3.9	1.1	(1.1)
Market value ($ mil.)	10.9%	88.4	82.3	42.5	39.9	133.7
Employees	(2.2%)	70	76	76	75	64

CEDARBURG HAUSER PHARMACEUTICALS INC.

870 Badger Circle
Grafton WI 53024-9436
Phone: 262-376-1467
Fax: 262-376-1068
Web: www.cedarburgpharma.com

CEO: John Ratliff
CFO: –
HR: Breanna Warmka
FYE: December 31
Type: Private

Cedarburg Hauser formerly Cedarburg Pharmaceuticals makes drugs components of drugs and ingredients for drugs. The contract manufacturer does everything from project management to manufacturing to validating study results. It produces custom chemicals natural and synthetic active pharmaceutical ingredients dietary supplements and cosmetics. And because Cedarburg Hauser also holds Drug Enforcement Agency permits it makes controlled substances including pain killers and other narcotics. Other services include process development and a whole host of analytical services including quality control and stability studies.

CEDARS-SINAI MEDICAL CENTER

8700 BEVERLY BLVD
WEST HOLLYWOOD, CA 900481804
Phone: 310-423-3277
Fax: –
Web: www.cedars-sinai.org

CEO: Thomas M Priselac
CFO: Edward M Pronchunas
HR: –
FYE: June 30
Type: Private

Cedars-Sinai is a nonprofit academic healthcare organization serving the diverse Los Angeles community and beyond. Cedars-Sinai is consistently listed as a top-ranked hospital by US News & World Report in such specialties as cancer cardiology endocrinology gastrointestinal disorders gynecology heart surgery kidney disease neurology orthopedics and respiratory disorders. Cedars-Sinai is a partner institution in the UCLA Clinical and Translational Science Institute (CTSI) an academic-clinical-community partnership and is engaged in hundreds of research programs in areas such as cancer neuroscience and genetics. It also partners with some 30 leading community service organizations advocacy groups health delivery networks churches and schools.

	Annual Growth	06/17	06/18	06/19	06/20	06/21
Sales ($ mil.)	6.1%	–	3,470.2	3,649.3	3,648.0	4,142.3
Net income ($ mil.)	37.4%	–	418.0	389.0	443.9	1,083.5
Market value ($ mil.)	–	–	–	–	–	–
Employees	–	–	–	–	–	8,000

CEGEDIM RELATIONSHIP MANAGEMENT

1425 Rt. 26 S.
Bedminster NJ 07921
Phone: 908-443-2000
Fax: 908-470-9900
Web: crm.cegedim.com/pages/default.aspx

CEO: –
CFO: –
HR: –
FYE: December 31
Type: Subsidiary

Cegedim Relationship Management helps pharmaceutical companies conduct business. A subsidiary of Cegedim the company offers services and software that manage and analyze sales efforts for pharmaceutical and other life sciences companies. Its products include applications that can access product information and physician databases evaluate competitors and catalog client and prospect data. The company does business in more than 80 countries and serves small to large companies and government agencies. It routinely partners with consulting and technology companies looking to develop and cross-promote products for the life sciences market. Capgemini Informatica Microsoft TAKE and TIBCO are among its partners.

CEL-SCI CORPORATION
ASE: CVM

8229 Boone Boulevard, Suite 802
Vienna, VA 22182
Phone: 703 506-9460
Fax: 703 506-9471
Web: www.cel-sci.com

CEO: Geert Kersten
CFO: Geert R Kersten
HR: –
FYE: September 30
Type: Public

CEL-SCI hopes to make L.E.A.P.S. and bounds in preventing and treating deadly diseases. Its L.E.A.P.S. (Ligand Epitope Antigen Presentation System) technology modulates T-cells and may lead to synthetic vaccines for herpes viral encephalitis smallpox and other diseases; the National Institutes of Health is testing CEL-1000 (a compound developed using L.E.A.P.S. technology) as a potential avian flu vaccine. The firm's lead drug candidate however is Multikine which might make tumors more susceptible to radiation therapy and help a patient's body produce tumor-fighting antibodies. Multikine is undergoing clinical trials for the treatment of head and neck tumors. The company was founded in 1983.

	Annual Growth	09/16	09/17	09/18	09/19	09/20
Sales ($ mil.)	18.3%	0.3	0.1	0.5	0.5	0.6
Net income ($ mil.)	–	(11.5)	(14.4)	(31.8)	(22.1)	(30.3)
Market value ($ mil.)	154.3%	11.8	64.3	156.9	346.2	493.8
Employees						

CELADON GROUP, INC.   NYS: CGI

9503 East 33rd Street, One Celadon Drive
Indianapolis, IN 46235-4207
Phone: 317 972-7000
Fax: –
Web: www.celadontrucking.com

CEO: Paul Svindland
CFO: Vincent Donargo
HR: –
FYE: June 30
Type: Public

Celadon Group provides long-haul dry van truckload service throughout North America via subsidiaries Celadon Trucking Services Celadon Canada and Mexico-based Jaguar. The group maintains a fleet of about 3300 tractors and 8700 trailers. Celadon also offers dedicated contract carriage in which drivers and equipment are assigned to a customer long-term as well as freight brokerage and warehousing services. Its clients have included large shippers with strict time-delivery requirements such as Arconic Procter & Gamble Philip Morris and Wal-Mart. An e-commerce unit TruckersB2B serves as a purchasing cooperative for smaller trucking fleets and provides discounts on fuel tires and satellite systems.

	Annual Growth	06/12	06/13	06/14	06/15	06/16
Sales ($ mil.)	15.5%	599.0	613.6	759.3	900.8	1,065.4
Net income ($ mil.)	(0.7%)	25.5	27.3	30.7	37.2	24.8
Market value ($ mil.)	(16.0%)	462.2	514.9	601.5	583.5	230.5
Employees	16.3%	3,982	4,351	4,876	7,606	7,286

CELANESE CORP (DE)   NYS: CE

222 W. Las Colinas Blvd., Suite 900N
Irving, TX 75039-5421
Phone: 972 443-4000
Fax: –
Web: www.celanese.com

CEO: Lori Ryerkerk
CFO: Scott Richardson
HR: Allison St John
FYE: December 31
Type: Public

Celanese Corp. is a leading manufacturer of high performance engineered polymers and acetyl products serving a diverse set of end-use applications including automotive chemical additives construction consumer and industrial adhesives consumer and medical energy storage food and beverage paints paper and performance industrial and textiles among others. The company makes and supplies acetyl products including acetic acid VAM acetic anhydride and acetate esters which are used as starting materials for colorants paints adhesives coatings and pharmaceuticals. The company sells through industry-leading brands including Celcon and Hostaform (polycetals) GUR (thermoplastics) Celanex Nylfor Ecomid Frianyl (nylon). Texas-based Celanese which has manufacturing plants throughout the world gets more than 25% of sales from the US.

	Annual Growth	12/17	12/18	12/19	12/20	12/21
Sales ($ mil.)	8.6%	6,140.0	7,155.0	6,297.0	5,655.0	8,537.0
Net income ($ mil.)	22.4%	843.0	1,207.0	852.0	1,985.0	1,890.0
Market value ($ mil.)	11.9%	11,567.2	9,718.9	13,299.9	14,036.6	18,154.5
Employees	3.0%	7,592	7,684	7,714	7,658	8,529

CELEBRATE INTERACTIVE HOLDINGS INC.

11220 120th Ave. NE
Kirkland WA 98033
Phone: 425-250-1064
Fax: 425-828-6252
Web: www.celebrateexpress.com

CEO: –
CFO: –
HR: –
FYE: December 31
Type: Subsidiary

Celebrate Interactive Holdings seeks to provide everything for a birthday party except the birthday suit (although it does sell costumes). The online (and catalog) retailer operates four e-commerce sites: the online party store Celebrate Express; Birthday Express offering more than 150 themed party packages targeting families with young children; 1st Wishes (launched in 2006) specializing in those all-important first birthdays; and Costume Express an online Halloween superstore. Founded in 1994 as Celebrate Express Celebrate Interactive Holdings was formed in 2010 to provide one-stop online party planning and shopping. It is a subsidiary of video and e-commerce conglomerate Liberty Interactive Corp.

CELERA CORPORATION

1401 Harbor Bay Pkwy.
Alameda CA 94502
Phone: 510-749-4200
Fax: 650-854-1515
Web: www.baypartners.com

CEO: Kathy Ordoez
CFO: –
HR: –
FYE: December 31
Type: Subsidiary

Celera spent years mapping the human genome and has put that knowledge to use. Formerly a researcher the firm is now focused on developing diagnostics and providing clinical services. Its genotyping products are used to track genetic mutations that indicate drug resistance in HIV screen for cystic fibrosis and identify the best matches for organ transplants. The company's Berkeley HeartLab (BHL) and 4myheart businesses provide cardiology testing and disease management services respectively. Abbott Laboratories distributes the company's diagnostics. Celera is wholly owned subsidiary of Quest Diagnostics.

CELGENE CORP   NMS: CELG

86 Morris Avenue
Summit, NJ 07901
Phone: 908 673-9000
Fax: –
Web: www.celgene.com

CEO: Mark J Alles
CFO: David V Elkins
HR: –
FYE: December 31
Type: Public

Celgene lines up cells and genes to create good health. The biopharmaceutical company's lead product is Revlimid which is approved in the US Europe and other select markets as a treatment for multiple myeloma (bone marrow cancer). Revlimid also is used to treat a blood disorder called myelodysplastic syndrome (MDS). The company's second-biggest seller is Pomalyst/Imnovid which is approved in various markets for the treatment of multiple myeloma. Other products include Otezla for the treatment of psoriatic arthritis and chemotherapy agent Abraxane. The firm has other drugs in development that combat inflammatory diseases and cancer. Bristol-Myers Squibb is buying Celgene in a $74 billion deal.

	Annual Growth	12/13	12/14	12/15	12/16	12/17
Sales ($ mil.)	19.0%	6,493.9	7,670.4	9,256.0	11,229.2	13,003.0
Net income ($ mil.)	19.3%	1,449.9	1,999.9	1,602.0	1,999.2	2,940.0
Market value ($ mil.)	(11.3%)	128,297.4	84,935.3	90,933.8	87,889.0	79,240.5
Employees	10.0%	5,100	6,012	6,971	7,132	7,467

CELLCO PARTNERSHIP

1 Verizon Way
Basking Ridge NJ 07920
Phone: 908-559-5490
Fax: 919-379-3600
Web: www.xsinc.com

CEO: Hans Erik Vestberg
CFO: Andrew Davies
HR: –
FYE: December 31
Type: Joint Venture

Cellco Partnership is the #1 US wireless phone operator in terms of sales and subscribers (ahead of top rival AT&T Mobility). Serving nearly 110 million consumer business and government customers nationwide under the Verizon Wireless brand the joint venture is controlled with a 55% stake by Verizon Communications; UK-based global communications giant Vodafone owns the remainder. Offering both standard post-paid (about 95% of its customers) and prepaid subscriptions it distributes phones from manufacturers including Samsung Electronics Research in Motion LG and Apple. The company also offers mobile data services including text messaging multimedia content (V CAST) and Web access.

CELLDEX THERAPEUTICS, INC.

NAS: CLDX

Perryville III Building, 53 Frontage Road, Suite 220
Hampton, NJ 08827
Phone: 908 200-7500
Fax: -
Web: www.celldex.com

CEO: Anthony Marucci
CFO: Samuel Martin
HR: -
FYE: December 31
Type: Public

Celldex Therapeutics develops cellular therapies to treat specific forms of cancer autoimmune diseases and infections. The biopharmaceutical company's focused on the development and commercialization of immunotherapies and other targeted biologics. It has candidates in clinical development for the treatment of thyroid breast cancer and other oncology-related ailments. Its clinical stage product include CDX-1140 an agonist monoclonal antibody targeted to CD40 a key activator of immune response currently being studied as a single-agent and in combination with CDX-301 a dendritic cell growth factor and CDX-3379 a monoclonal antibody designed to block the activity of ErbB3 (HER3) in an early phase 2 study in advanced head and neck squamous cell cancer in combination with Erbitux.

	Annual Growth	12/16	12/17	12/18	12/19	12/20
Sales ($ mil.)	2.3%	6.8	12.7	9.5	3.6	7.4
Net income ($ mil.)	-	(128.5)	(93.0)	(151.2)	(50.9)	(59.8)
Market value ($ mil.)	49.2%	140.2	112.5	7.8	88.3	693.9
Employees	(12.2%)	210	197	137	130	125

CELSION CORP

NAS: CLSN

997 Lenox Drive, Suite 100
Lawrenceville, NJ 08648
Phone: 609 896-9100
Fax: -
Web: www.celsion.com

CEO: Michael Tardugno
CFO: Jeffrey Church
HR: -
FYE: December 31
Type: Public

Celsion is trying to turn up the heat on cancer. The company is developing a heat-activated cancer therapy in the form of its lead drug ThermoDox. ThermoDox combines a common oncology drug doxorubicin with a heat-activated liposome that may help deliver and release the drug more accurately. The drug is being studied as a treatment for liver cancer and breast cancer. Celsion was previously a device maker and developed the Prolieve Thermodilatation system an FDA-approved device used to treat benign prostatic hyperplasia (prostate enlargement). Celsion sold the product line to Boston Scientific in 2007.

	Annual Growth	12/16	12/17	12/18	12/19	12/20
Sales ($ mil.)	0.0%	0.5	0.5	0.5	0.5	0.5
Net income ($ mil.)	-	(22.1)	(20.4)	(11.9)	(16.9)	(21.5)
Market value ($ mil.)	23.6%	12.4	109.1	57.4	69.6	28.9
Employees	9.2%	19	21	29	29	27

CELSIUS HOLDINGS INC

NAS: CELH

2424 N. Federal Highway, Suite 208
Boca Raton, FL 33431
Phone: 561 276-2239
Fax: -
Web: www.celsius.com

CEO: John Fieldly
CFO: Edwin Negron-Carballo
HR: -
FYE: December 31
Type: Public

Celsius Holdings wants consumers to enjoy the taste of burning calories. The company develops markets and distributes nutritional drinks that claim to burn calories raise metabolism and boost energy. Its first product Celsius is a canned sparkling beverage that comes in a variety of flavors and is marketed as an alternative to soda coffee and traditional energy drinks. Although it has undergone independent clinical studies results have not been US FDA approved. Its products which also include non-carbonated Celsius green tea drinks and single-serving powder mix packets that can be added to water are manufactured by third-party co-packers. Celsius Holdings was founded in 2004 under the name Elite FX.

	Annual Growth	12/16	12/17	12/18	12/19	12/20
Sales ($ mil.)	54.8%	22.8	36.2	52.6	75.1	130.7
Net income ($ mil.)	-	(3.1)	(8.2)	(11.2)	10.0	8.5
Market value ($ mil.)	230.7%	30.4	379.4	250.8	349.0	3,635.5
Employees	41.0%	39	39	50	120	154

CEM HOLDINGS CORPORATION

3100 Smith Farm Rd.
Matthews NC 28106
Phone: 704-821-7015
Fax: 704-821-7894
Web: www.cem.com

CEO: Michael J Collins
CFO: -
HR: -
FYE: September 30
Type: Private

Scientists mad or otherwise probably love to browse CEM's product catalog. CEM — short for chemistry electronics and mechanics — makes microwave-based instruments that perform testing analysis and process control in laboratory and industrial environments. The company's MARS heating system analyzes samples by dissolving them in acid. CEM's other products include moisture/solids analysis systems and fat analyzers. CEM sells directly in the US and worldwide through subsidiaries and distributors in about 50 countries. It serves such industries as food tobacco to plastics chemicals and textiles. Established in 1978 CEM was taken private in 2000 by founder and CEO Michael J. Collins.

CENAMA INC.

1410 Commonwealth Dr. Ste. #202
Wilmington NC 28403
Phone: 910-395-5300
Fax: 910-395-6691
Web: www.vpsstores.com/

CEO: -
CFO: Jeff W Turpin
HR: -
FYE: December 31
Type: Private

Cenama which does business as VPS Convenience Store Group can help road hogs to top off their tanks and their tummies. The company operates about 420 convenience stores in the Southeast and Midwest under the Scotchman Young's Li'l Cricket Village Pantry Next Door Stores and Everyday Shop banners. VPS's stores sell name-brand fuels (including BP Exxon and Shell) in addition to its proprietary Carolina Petro brand. Many stores offer Subway Quiznos and Noble Roman's fast food as well as ready-made breakfast and lunch items. The company also runs two truck stops and provides fleet fueling services. VPS is owned by private investment firm Sun Capital Partners.

CENTAUR TECHNOLOGY INC.

7600-C N. Capital of Texas Hwy. Ste. 300
Austin TX 78731
Phone: 512-418-5700
Fax: 512-794-0717
Web: www.centtech.com/

CEO: -
CFO: -
HR: -
FYE: December 31
Type: Subsidiary

The horsepower provided by Centaur Technology's processors is a breed apart. An independent subsidiary and design house of chipset stalwart VIA Technologies Centaur makes low-cost microprocessors for use in mobile PCs and other portable electronics. The company designed VIA's C7-M processor one of the world's smallest lowest-power and most secure x86-architecture processors. Centaur was established in Austin Texas in 1995 and prides itself on its employee-friendly work environment with free breakfasts and lunches and an onsite fitness facility. VIA purchased Centaur in 1999. The company has no management hierarchy save for founder and president Glenn Henry.

CENTEGRA HEALTH SYSTEM FOUNDATION

385 MILLENNIUM DR STE A
CRYSTAL LAKE, IL 600123761
Phone: 815-788-5800
Fax: –
Web: www.centegra.org

CEO: –
CFO: –
HR: –
FYE: June 30
Type: Private

Centegra Health System seeks integrity in the health care services realm. The health network serves residents of the greater McHenry County region in northern Illinois and southern Wisconsin. The company operates two main medical centers Centegra Hospital-McHenry and Centegra Hospital-Woodstock with a total of some 325 beds. They offer emergency and trauma care as well as general medicine surgery and obstetrics services. Centegra has dedicated cancer diabetes and heart centers and also offers rehabilitation behavioral health and fitness services. In addition the community-based health system operates a network of primary care and specialty outpatient clinics.

	Annual Growth	06/09	06/10	06/11	06/12	06/17
Sales ($ mil.)	32.0%	–	80.8	0.0	428.0	564.2
Net income ($ mil.)	–	–	(12.0)	0.0	(13.1)	(45.4)
Market value ($ mil.)	–	–	–	–	–	–
Employees	–	–	–	–	–	3,700

CENTENE CORP

NYS: CNC

7700 Forsyth Boulevard
St. Louis, MO 63105
Phone: 314 725-4477
Fax: 314 725-5180
Web: www.centene.com

CEO: Rich Fisher
CFO: Andrew Asher
HR: H. Robert Sanders
FYE: December 31
Type: Public

Centene provides health insurance to more than 25 million members in all 50 US states and three international markets. Centene is a leading Medicaid managed care provider serving low-income families and disabled people through state Medicaid plans the Children's Health Insurance Program (CHIP) Long-Term Services and Supports (LTSS) and other programs. Centene also offers Medicare military and commercial insurance plans. It provides specialty services in areas such as vision and dental benefits wellness home health and pharmacy benefits management. In 2020 Centene has bought Medicaid insurer WellCare for nearly $20 billion.

	Annual Growth	12/17	12/18	12/19	12/20	12/21
Sales ($ mil.)	27.0%	48,382.0	60,116.0	74,639.0	111,115.0	125,982.0
Net income ($ mil.)	12.9%	828.0	900.0	1,321.0	1,808.0	1,347.0
Market value ($ mil.)	(4.9%)	58,760.5	67,159.8	36,620.5	34,966.2	47,996.3
Employees	21.1%	33,700	47,300	56,500	71,300	72,500

CENTER FOR CREATIVE LEADERSHIP INC

1 LEADERSHIP PL
GREENSBORO, NC 274109427
Phone: 336-288-7210
Fax: –
Web: www.ccl.org

CEO: John R Ryan
CFO: Bradley E Shumaker
HR: Sabine Van Craen
FYE: March 31
Type: Private

The Center for Creative Leadership (CCL) is a not-for-profit organization that provides coaching in management training to public private nonprofit government and education sectors worldwide. The center is headquartered in Greensboro North Carolina and offers its programs through open enrollment courses and customized training at its campuses and affiliates across North America Europe Africa and Asia. Virtual learning through webinars podcasts and eBooks also is available. CCL serves some 20000 individuals and 2000 organizations each year with clients such as Wells Fargo Time Warner Cable and the US Army.

	Annual Growth	03/09	03/10	03/11	03/14	03/20
Sales ($ mil.)	3.2%	–	86.1	92.6	113.7	117.5
Net income ($ mil.)	–	–	8.0	3.8	0.5	(11.1)
Market value ($ mil.)	–	–	–	–	–	–
Employees	–	–	–	–	–	600

CENTERBEAM INC.

30 Rio Robles Dr.
San Jose CA 95134
Phone: 408-750-0500
Fax: 408-750-0555
Web: www.centerbeam.com

CEO: –
CFO: –
HR: –
FYE: December 31
Type: Private

CenterBeam takes on the day-to-day management and support of everything IT. The company provides outsourced computing and communications infrastructure management services primarily to midsized businesses in North America. Areas of specialty include desktop management (virus protection software patches and data back-up) server and network management (performance and fault management virus protection updates asset tracking and network monitoring) and other support services. Its customers come from a range of industries including construction financial services and health care. Founded in 1999 CenterBeam has received funding from such investors as Intel Apax Partners and New Enterprise Associates.

CENTERLINE CAPITAL GROUP INC.

625 Madison Ave.
New York NY 10022
Phone: 212-317-5700
Fax: 212-751-3550
Web: www.centerline.com

CEO: –
CFO: –
HR: –
FYE: December 31
Type: Subsidiary

Centerline Capital finds its center in real estate financing and asset management for affordable and multifamily housing developments. The subsidiary of Centerline Holding Company has raised about $10 billion used to finance and develop more than 15000 affordable housing properties throughout the US and Puerto Rico. Centerline Capital provides equity and debt financing through low-income housing tax credits. It also underwrites and services mortgages on behalf of Fannie Mae and Freddie Mac. Clients include developers owners and investors. Centerline Capital currently provides asset management for 1300 affordable housing properties in the US.

CENTERPLATE INC.

201 E. Broad St.
Spartanburg SC 29306
Phone: 864-598-8600
Fax: 864-598-8693
Web: www.centerplate.com

CEO: Chris Verros
CFO: Kevin F McNamara
HR: Tina Moore
FYE: December 31
Type: Private

Wherever there's a sporting event this concessions operator likes to be front and center. Centerplate is a leading provider of catering concessions and merchandise services in the US to about 250 sports stadiums convention centers and other entertainment venues. The company's clients include professional baseball and football stadiums minor league parks and college sports stadiums. It provides catering and other services at convention centers including the Jacob K. Javits Center in Manhattan as well as at airports parks performing arts centers and ski resorts. It also handles a number of special events such as the Kentucky Derby Festival.

CENTERPOINT ENERGY HOUSTON ELECTRIC LLC

1111 Louisiana St.
Houston TX 77002
Phone: 713-207-1111
Fax: 414-383-4339
Web: www.badgermutual.com

CEO: –
CFO: –
HR: –
FYE: December 31
Type: Subsidiary

Houston we don't have a problem. CenterPoint Energy Houston Electric's glow spreads across the fourth-largest US city and surrounding areas of the Texas Gulf Coast. The utility operates the regulated power transmission and distribution systems in the Houston metropolitan area. CenterPoint Energy Houston Electric a subsidiary of utility holding company CenterPoint Energy serves more than 2 million metered customers over its more than 48230 miles of electric distribution lines and more than 230 substations; the utility's 3780 miles of transmission lines are managed by the Electric Reliability Council of Texas (ERCOT).

CENTERPOINT ENERGY, INC

1111 Louisiana
Houston, TX 77002
Phone: 713 207-1111
Fax: –
Web: www.centerpointenergy.com

NYS: CNP
CEO: David Lesar
CFO: Jason Wells
HR: –
FYE: December 31
Type: Public

CenterPoint Energy is one of the largest public utilities in the US distributes natural gas and electricity to more than 7 million customers. Through subsidiary CenterPoint Energy Resources Corp this holding company distributes natural gas to 4.6 million customers in eight states. The company's other major subsidiary Houston Electric distributes electricity that reaches about 2.6 million customers in the Texas Gulf Coast region including Houston. These customers range from large industries and utilities to municipalities health care and educational institutions. In addition to its portfolio of about 4866 transmission lines and approximately 63130 distribution lines the holding company also owns interests in Enable a publicly traded MLP.

	Annual Growth	12/17	12/18	12/19	12/20	12/21
Sales ($ mil.)	(3.5%)	9,614.0	10,589.0	12,301.0	7,418.0	8,352.0
Net income ($ mil.)	(4.6%)	1,792.0	368.0	791.0	(773.0)	1,486.0
Market value ($ mil.)	(0.4%)	17,836.3	17,754.5	17,150.7	13,609.9	17,553.3
Employees	4.2%	7,977	7,977	14,262	9,541	9,418

CENTERPOINT PROPERTIES TRUST

1808 Swift Dr.
Oak Brook IL 60523
Phone: 630-586-8000
Fax: 630-586-8010
Web: www.centerpoint-prop.com

CEO: –
CFO: Michael J Kraft
HR: –
FYE: December 31
Type: Private

CenterPoint Properties invests in develops and manages industrial and infrastructure projects in transportation hubs throughout the US primarily in Chicago and the Midwest where it is the largest industrial owner. It owns some 28 million sq. ft. of space including warehouses light manufacturing centers distribution facilities and container yards. CenterPoint also provides renovation services for ports and rail terminals and develops industrial and commercial properties for other owners. Subsidiary CenterPoint Capital helps secure project financing. Founded in 1984 the company is owned by CalEast Global Logistics a group which includes Jones Lang LaSalle and CalPERS.

CENTERS FOR DISEASE CONTROL AND PREVENTION

1600 Clifton Rd.
Atlanta GA 30333
Phone: 404-639-3311
Fax: 404-498-1177
Web: www.cdc.gov

CEO: –
CFO: –
HR: –
FYE: December 31
Type: Business Segment

The name really says it all for the Centers for Disease Control and Prevention (CDC). The lead federal agency for protecting the health and safety of US citizens the CDC investigates health problems performs research and develops public health policies as well as developing and applying disease prevention and control. It is one of the major operating components of the Department of Health and Human Services and comprises seven coordinating centers and the National Institute for Occupational Safety and Health. The CDC which has nine US locations and workers in more than 50 countries partners with public and private entities to improve the flow of information throughout the health care community.

CENTERS FOR MEDICARE & MEDICAID SERVICES

7500 Security Blvd.
Baltimore MD 21244-1850
Phone: 410-786-3000
Fax: 410-786-8060
Web: cms.gov

CEO: –
CFO: –
HR: –
FYE: September 30
Type: Government Agency

The Centers for Medicare & Medicaid Services (CMS) was created in 1977 to administer the Medicare and Medicaid programs which together provide health care coverage to millions of Americans. Medicare provides hospital medical and prescription coverage for people over age 65 and for people with certain disabilities; Medicaid provides health care for people with low incomes (as defined by the government). CMS also runs the Children's Health Insurance Program (CHIP) which in partnership with state legislations provides health care for children and pregnant women that don't qualify for Medicaid. CMS is part of the Department of Health and Human Services; its annual budget was more than $486 billion in 2011.

CENTERSPACE

3100 10th Street SW, Post Office Box 1988
Minot, ND 58702-1988
Phone: 701 837-4738
Fax: –
Web: www.centerspacehomes.com

NYS: CSR
CEO: Mark Decker
CFO: Bhairav Patel
HR: Chantelle Oveson
FYE: December 31
Type: Public

Investors Real Estate Trust (IRET) is a self-advised umbrella partnership real estate investment trust (UPREIT) that invests in develops and maintains a portfolio of office retail and multifamily residential properties. IRET owns some 70 apartment communities composing nearly 12000 individual units. More than 85% of its revenue comes from multi-family residential properties while all others properties bring in nearly 15%.

	Annual Growth	04/17	04/18*	12/18	12/19	12/20
Sales ($ mil.)	(4.7%)	205.7	169.7	121.9	185.8	178.0
Net income ($ mil.)	(53.2%)	43.3	116.8	(4.4)	78.7	4.4
Market value ($ mil.)	128.6%	77.0	69.4	639.2	944.5	920.2
Employees	(11.3%)	523	527	435	392	365

*Fiscal year change

CENTERSTATE BANK CORP
NMS: CSFL
1101 First Street South, Suite 202
Winter Haven, FL 33880
Phone: 863 293-4710
Fax: –
Web: www.centerstatebanks.com
CEO: –
CFO: –
HR: –
FYE: December 31
Type: Public

CenterState Banks is the holding company for CenterState Bank of Florida which serves the Sunshine State through about 60 branches. The bank offers standard deposit products such as checking and savings accounts money market accounts and CDs. Real estate loans primarily residential and commercial mortgages make up 85% of the company's loan portfolio while the rest is made up of business loans and consumer loans. The bank's correspondent division provides bond securities accounting and loans to small and mid-sized banks across the Southeast and Texas. It also sells mutual funds annuities and other investment products.

	Annual Growth	12/14	12/15	12/16	12/17	12/18
Assets ($ mil.)	34.4%	3,776.9	4,022.7	5,078.6	7,124.0	12,337.6
Net income ($ mil.)	86.4%	13.0	39.3	42.3	55.8	156.4
Market value ($ mil.)	15.3%	1,139.5	1,497.4	2,408.3	2,461.8	2,013.1
Employees	28.1%	785	784	952	1,200	2,113

CENTIMARK CORPORATION
12 GRANDVIEW CIR
CANONSBURG, PA 153178533
Phone: 724-514-8700
Fax: –
Web: www.centimark.com
CEO: –
CFO: John L Heisey
HR: –
FYE: April 30
Type: Private

Shout it from the rooftops Centimark is one of the commercial and industrial roofing contractors in the US Canada and Mexico. The company provides roof installation inspection repair and emergency leak service. Centimark typically works on flat roofs using EPDM rubber thermoplastic bitumen metal and coatings. Its Quest-Mark division offers commercial industrial and retail flooring do-it-yourself (DIY) products and floor maintenance and cleaning products. The company has more than 85 offices throughout US Canada and Mexico.

	Annual Growth	04/14	04/15	04/17	04/18	04/21
Sales ($ mil.)	–	–	(817.2)	625.8	670.5	783.9
Net income ($ mil.)	952.3%	–	0.0	51.2	54.0	73.3
Market value ($ mil.)	–	–	–	–	–	–
Employees	–	–	–	–	–	3,500

CENTRA HEALTH, INC.
1920 ATHERHOLT RD
LYNCHBURG, VA 245011120
Phone: 434-200-3204
Fax: –
Web: www.centrahealth.com
CEO: Andrew Mueller
CFO: –
HR: –
FYE: December 31
Type: Private

Centra Health is a regional nonprofit healthcare system based in Lynchburg Virginia. Its entity's core are two acute care facilities in Lynchburg: The Lynchburg General which is the region's main emergency center and specializes in orthopedic pediatric and cardiac care; and Virginia Baptist facility focused on surgery women's health infant care mental health and rehabilitation. With nearly 800 physicians and medical staff Centra Health provides care to over 500000 people in some 50 locations throughout central and southern Virginia. It was founded on 1987.

	Annual Growth	12/08	12/09	12/14	12/15	12/19
Sales ($ mil.)	7.3%	–	535.0	553.3	742.7	1,078.6
Net income ($ mil.)	(6.6%)	–	16.8	63.4	25.3	8.5
Market value ($ mil.)	–	–	–	–	–	–
Employees	–	–	–	–	–	6,000

CENTRA INC.
12225 Stephen Rd.
Warren MI 48089-2010
Phone: 586-939-7000
Fax: 586-755-5607
Web: www.centraltransportint.com
CEO: –
CFO: Hal Briand
HR: –
FYE: December 31
Type: Private

At the center of CenTra is Central Transport International a less-than-truckload (LTL) carrier that hauls across North America. (LTL carriers combine freight from multiple shippers into a single truckload.) Central Transport and its affiliates operate via some 200 terminals mainly in the eastern US. CenTra's interests include expedited freight transporter CTX freight forwarder Central Global Express broker/warehouser Custom Services International and supply chain manager Logistics Insight (LINC). CenTra also owns the Ambassador Bridge connecting Detroit with Windsor Ontario. CEO Manuel Moroun and his son Matthew control freight hauler Universal Truckload as well as CenTra (founded by Manuel's father).

CENTRAL DUPAGE HOSPITAL
25 North Winfield Rd.
Winfield IL 60190
Phone: 630-933-1600
Fax: 630-933-1300
Web: www.cdh.org
CEO: –
CFO: James T Spear
HR: –
FYE: June 30
Type: Private - Not-for-Pr

Central DuPage Hospital attends to the health needs of Windy City suburbanites. Located in DuPage County just west of Chicago the hospital has more than 310 beds and provides general medical and surgical care including specialty care in areas such as oncology cardiovascular disease neuroscience and orthopedics. The hospital is the focal point of a network of health services that include a physician medical group home health care services occupational care and about half a dozen urgent care centers. Central DuPage Hospital opened its doors in 1964.

CENTRAL DUPAGE HOSPITAL ASSOCIATION
25 N WINFIELD RD
WINFIELD, IL 601901295
Phone: 630-933-1600
Fax: –
Web: www.cdh.org
CEO: –
CFO: James T Spear
HR: –
FYE: June 30
Type: Private

Central DuPage Hospital attends to the health needs of Windy City suburbanites. Located in DuPage County just west of Chicago the hospital has more than 310 beds and provides general medical and surgical care including specialty care in areas such as oncology cardiovascular disease neuroscience and orthopedics. The hospital is the focal point of a network of health services that include a physician medical group home health care services occupational care and about half a dozen urgent care centers. Central DuPage Hospital opened its doors in 1964.

	Annual Growth	06/09	06/10	06/11	06/12	06/13
Sales ($ mil.)	10.2%	–	633.6	667.7	773.2	849.1
Net income ($ mil.)	166.5%	–	–	26.0	112.2	184.4
Market value ($ mil.)	–	–	–	–	–	–
Employees	–	–	–	–	–	1,600

CENTRAL FREIGHT LINES INC.

5601 W. Waco Dr.
Waco TX 76710
Phone: 254-772-2120
Fax: 254-741-5370
Web: www.centralfreight.com

CEO: -
CFO: -
HR: -
FYE: December 31
Type: Private

The Southwest the Midwest and the Northwest are all central to the business of Central Freight Lines a leading regional less-than-truckload (LTL) carrier. (LTL carriers consolidate freight from multiple shippers into a single truckload.) The company focuses on next-day and second-day services within each of its regions. It operates a fleet of more than 1950 tractors and nearly 8500 trailers from a network of about 50 terminals and provides service to 49 US states. Central Freight Lines serves the rest of the US through alliances with other carriers. Trucking magnate Jerry Moyes owns the company.

CENTRAL GARDEN & PET CO

NMS: CENT A

1340 Treat Boulevard, Suite 600
Walnut Creek, CA 94597
Phone: 925 948-4000
Fax: -
Web: www.central.com

CEO: Timothy Cofer
CFO: Nicholas Lahanas
HR: -
FYE: September 25
Type: Public

Central Garden & Pet is among the leading US producers and distributors of consumer lawn garden and pet supplies providing its products to retailers home improvement centers nurseries and mass merchandisers. Central Garden & Pet operates about 55 manufacturing plants and nearly 70 sales and distribution centers throughout the US. The company sells private label brands as well as brands from other manufacturers. It offers product lines such as AMDRO fire ant bait Four Paws animal products Kaytee bird seed Nylabone dog chews and TFH pet books. The company was founded by Bill Brown in 1980 as Central Garden Supply.

	Annual Growth	09/17	09/18	09/19	09/20	09/21
Sales ($ mil.)	12.6%	2,054.5	2,215.4	2,383.0	2,695.5	3,303.7
Net income ($ mil.)	17.8%	78.8	123.6	92.8	120.7	151.7
Market value ($ mil.)	3.2%	2,054.0	1,830.4	1,543.7	1,890.6	2,327.4
Employees	14.3%	4,100	5,400	5,800	6,300	7,000

CENTRAL GROCERS, INC.

2600 HAVEN AVE
JOLIET, IL 604338467
Phone: 815-553-8800
Fax: -
Web: www.central-grocers.com

CEO: -
CFO: -
HR: -
FYE: July 28
Type: Private

In a city of big stores Central Grocers helps keep neighborhood markets stocked. Founded in 1917 the cooperative wholesale food distributor is owned by some 225 members. It supplies 40000 food items and general merchandise to more than 400 independent grocery stores serving several states such as Illinois Indiana Iowa Michigan and Wisconsin. Central Grocers distributes products under both national brands and its own Centrella brand which is marketed exclusively to its member stores. The co-op also operates about 30 stores under a handful of banner names including Strack & Van Til Town & Country Key Market and the low-cost Ultra Foods chain. In 2017 the company filed for Chapter 11 bankruptcy protection.

	Annual Growth	07/03	07/04	07/05	07/06	07/07
Sales ($ mil.)	4.5%	-	1,047.9	1,103.2	1,108.9	1,197.2
Net income ($ mil.)	-	-	3.2	4.8	5.5	(10.3)
Market value ($ mil.)	-	-	-	-	-	-
Employees	-	-	-	-	-	2,300

CENTRAL IOWA POWER COOPERATIVE

1400 HIGHWAY 13
CEDAR RAPIDS, IA 524039060
Phone: 319-366-8011
Fax: -
Web: www.cipco.net

CEO: Dennis Murdock
CFO: -
HR: -
FYE: December 31
Type: Private

Keeping a sharp eye out for the well-being of Iowa's citizens Central Iowa Power Cooperative provides electricity transmission and generation services to 13 member distribution cooperatives (12 rural electric cooperatives and one municipal cooperative) which in turn serve about 320000 residential and 7000 industrial and commercial customers. Central Iowa Power's member distribution cooperatives deliver power to commercial businesses farmsteads industrial parks manufacturers urban residences and other customers in a service area that stretches 300 miles diagonally across the state from Shenandoah in the southwest to the Mississippi River in the east.

	Annual Growth	12/12	12/13	12/14	12/15	12/17
Sales ($ mil.)	(0.7%)	-	193.1	195.0	188.4	188.0
Net income ($ mil.)	(28.2%)	-	12.1	11.5	7.0	3.2
Market value ($ mil.)	-	-	-	-	-	-
Employees	-	-	-	-	-	117

CENTRAL MICHIGAN UNIVERSITY

1280 E CAMPUS DR
MOUNT PLEASANT, MI 488592033
Phone: 989-774-3015
Fax: -
Web: www.cmich.edu

CEO: -
CFO: -
HR: -
FYE: June 30
Type: Private

Academic advancement is central at Central Michigan University (CMU). The university offers more than 200 academic programs for undergraduate graduate and professional coursework through eight colleges including business communication and fine arts medicine and education and human services. The university enrolls more than 20000 students at the main campus in Mt. Pleasant. The institution also enrolls another 7000 students online and at 50 locations throughout North America. In addition CMU offers study abroad programs in 40 countries.

	Annual Growth	06/17	06/18	06/19	06/20	06/21
Sales ($ mil.)	(6.8%)	-	328.1	314.3	289.5	265.8
Net income ($ mil.)	68.1%	-	21.5	2.3	(6.9)	102.3
Market value ($ mil.)	-	-	-	-	-	-
Employees	-	-	-	-	-	2,388

CENTRAL MUTUAL INSURANCE COMPANY

800 S. Washington St.
Van Wert OH 45891-2357
Phone: 419-238-1010
Fax: 800-736-7026
Web: www.central-insurance.com

CEO: -
CFO: -
HR: -
FYE: December 31
Type: Private - Mutual Com

Central Mutual Insurance Company is aptly if modestly named: The company is centrally located is mutually held and by golly it does sell insurance. Along with its affiliates All America Insurance and CMI Lloyds Central Mutual operates as Central Insurance Companies. The group offers personal auto and homeowners insurance as well as commercial property/casualty policies. It also provides equipment protection workers' compensation professional liability and other specialty coverage. Central Insurance Companies sells its products through independent agents in almost 20 states. Chairman and president Francis Purmort III is the fifth generation of his family to lead the firm which was founded in 1876.

CENTRAL PACIFIC FINANCIAL CORP — NYS: CPF

220 South King Street
Honolulu, HI 96813
Phone: 808 544-0500
Fax: 808 531-2875
Web: www.centralpacificbank.com

CEO: Paul Yonamine
CFO: David Morimoto
HR: –
FYE: December 31
Type: Public

When in the Central Pacific do as the islanders do. This may include doing business with Central Pacific Financial the holding company for Central Pacific Bank which operates more than 35 branch locations and 110 ATMs across the Hawaiian Islands. Targeting individuals and local businesses the $5 billion bank provides such standard retail banking products as checking and savings accounts money market accounts and CDs. About 70% of the bank's loan portfolio is made up of commercial real estate loans residential mortgages and construction loans though it also provides business and consumer loans.

	Annual Growth	12/16	12/17	12/18	12/19	12/20
Assets ($ mil.)	5.2%	5,384.2	5,623.7	5,807.0	6,012.7	6,594.6
Net income ($ mil.)	(5.6%)	47.0	41.2	59.5	58.3	37.3
Market value ($ mil.)	(11.8%)	885.5	840.7	686.3	833.7	535.8
Employees	(0.5%)	837	838	844	854	822

CENTRAL REFRIGERATED SERVICE, LLC

5175 W 2100 S
WEST VALLEY CITY, UT 841201252
Phone: 801-924-7000
Fax: –
Web: www.driveknight.com

CEO: Jon Isaacson
CFO: Robert Baer
HR: –
FYE: December 31
Type: Private

No matter the weather conditions trucking company Central Refrigerated Service stays cool when it's on the move. The carrier provides temperature-controlled transportation and dry cargo services for major food suppliers and retailers across the US. It specializes in providing a wide array of offerings from private fleet conversion to inner city and solo driver deliveries to long haul truckload transportation services. Central Refrigerated operates a fleet of about 1800 tractors and 2700 refrigerated trailers or reefers. The company was acquired by truckload carrier Swift Transportation in mid-2013.

	Annual Growth	12/04	12/05	12/06	12/07	12/08
Sales ($ mil.)	(27.6%)	–	–	775.6	361.9	406.9
Net income ($ mil.)	17487.7%	–	–	0.0	6.7	9.6
Market value ($ mil.)	–	–	–	–	–	–
Employees	–	–	–	–	–	1,650

CENTRAL STEEL AND WIRE COMPANY

3000 W 51ST ST
CHICAGO, IL 606322198
Phone: 773-471-3800
Fax: –
Web: www.centralsteel.com

CEO: Stephen E Fuhrman
CFO: Kevin G Powers
HR: –
FYE: December 31
Type: Private

When it comes to metal service center Central Steel & Wire Company (CS&W) can shape up and ship out. CS&W distributes ferrous and nonferrous metals in a variety of shapes and forms including bars coils plates sheets structurals tubing and wire. Among the company's processing services are annealing blanking computer numerical control (CNC) laser cutting galvanizing and structural fabrication. CS&W distributes its products throughout North America from five facilities that are located primarily in the Midwestern US. The company has metallurgical engineers on its staff to support customers with metal specifications and interpretation expertise.

	Annual Growth	12/10	12/11	12/12	12/13	12/14
Sales ($ mil.)	(3.6%)	–	–	750.9	678.9	698.0
Net income ($ mil.)	–	–	–	10.6	2.2	(2.8)
Market value ($ mil.)	–	–	–	–	–	–
Employees	–	–	–	–	–	1,075

CENTRAL SUFFOLK HOSPITAL

1 HEROES WAY
RIVERHEAD, NY 119012058
Phone: 631-548-6000
Fax: –
Web: www.pbmchealth.org

CEO: –
CFO: –
HR: –
FYE: December 31
Type: Private

Central Suffolk Hospital (CSH—doing business as PBMC Health System) provides a sea of medical care services to residents of Long Island. The not-for-profit hospital covers a broad range of general and specialty care services including oncology emergency medicine general surgery neurosurgery orthopedics and women's health care. With a medical staff of more than 200 the medical center has roughly 200 beds. PBMC also operates a 60-bed skilled nursing and rehabilitation center a certified home health agency a palliative care center and a network of primary care centers. PBMC is affiliated with Stony Brook University Medical Center.

	Annual Growth	12/12	12/13	12/15	12/16	12/17
Sales ($ mil.)	3.9%	–	151.1	156.0	165.8	175.9
Net income ($ mil.)	(3.4%)	–	3.9	1.8	3.5	3.4
Market value ($ mil.)	–	–	–	–	–	–
Employees	–	–	–	–	–	1,350

CENTRAL VALLEY COMMUNITY BANCORP — NAS: CVCY

7100 N. Financial Dr., Suite 101
Fresno, CA 93720
Phone: 559 298-1775
Fax: –
Web: www.cvcb.com

CEO: James Kim
CFO: David Kinross
HR: Marcia Madsen
FYE: December 31
Type: Public

Central Valley Community Bancorp is the holding company for Central Valley Community Bank which offers individuals and businesses traditional banking services through about 25 offices in California's San Joaquin Valley. Deposit products include checking savings and money market accounts; IRAs; and CDs. The bank founded in 1979 offers credit card services and originates a variety of loans including residential and commercial mortgage Small Business Administration and agricultural loans. Through Central Valley Community Insurance Services it markets health property and casualty insurance products primarily to business customers.

	Annual Growth	12/16	12/17	12/18	12/19	12/20
Assets ($ mil.)	8.6%	1,443.3	1,661.7	1,537.8	1,596.8	2,004.1
Net income ($ mil.)	7.6%	15.2	14.0	21.3	21.4	20.3
Market value ($ mil.)	(7.1%)	249.7	252.4	236.1	271.1	186.3
Employees	0.0%	287	316	290	288	287

CENTRAL VERMONT PUBLIC SERVICE CORPORATION — NYSE: CV

77 Grove St.
Rutland VT 05701
Phone: 800-649-2877
Fax: 802-747-2199
Web: www.cvps.com

CEO: Mary Powell
CFO: Pamela J Keefe
HR: –
FYE: December 31
Type: Public

Moonlight in Vermont may be beautiful but it doesn't provide any power. Vermont's largest electric utility Central Vermont Public Service (CVPS) provides power to more than 159000 customers in 163 communities across the state. It generates approximately 110 MW of nuclear hydroelectric and fossil-fueled capacity; it purchases most of its energy supply of 516 MW. CVPS owns 59% of Vermont Yankee Nuclear Power Corporation and 47% of state transmission firm Vermont Electric Power Company (VELCO). Nonregulated businesses include investments (Catamount Resources) home maintenance contracting real estate (C.V. Realty) and energy-related services. In 2012 CVPS was acquired by Canada-based GazMetro.

CENTRASTATE HEALTHCARE SYSTEM INC

901 W MAIN ST
FREEHOLD, NJ 077282537
Phone: 732-431-2000
Fax: –
Web: www.centrastate.com

CEO: John T Gribbin
CFO: John A Dellocono
HR: –
FYE: December 31
Type: Private

CentraState Healthcare System makes healing its central mission while serving residents of central New Jersey. The health system operates CentraState Medical Center an acute-care teaching hospital with more than 280 beds that offers emergency surgical and diagnostic imaging services as well as specialty services including cardiovascular care and women's health. Other CentraState Healthcare facilities include three nursing homes wellness centers and outpatient clinics. CentraState Healthcare is an affiliate of the Robert Wood Johnson Health System and Network.

	Annual Growth	12/15	12/16	12/17	12/18	12/19
Sales ($ mil.)	4.6%	–	322.0	326.0	355.0	368.1
Net income ($ mil.)	36.3%	–	13.2	9.3	0.1	33.5
Market value ($ mil.)	–	–	–	–	–	–
Employees	–	–	–	–	–	2,527

CENTRE COLLEGE OF KENTUCKY

600 W WALNUT ST
DANVILLE, KY 404221394
Phone: 859-238-5200
Fax: –
Web: www.centre.edu

CEO: –
CFO: Robert Keasler
HR: –
FYE: June 30
Type: Private

Centre College's name reflects its location in the geographic center of Kentucky (near Lexington) as well as its founders' preponderance for British spellings. The private liberal arts school enrolls some 1200 students majoring in about 30 academic areas. Some 85% of students participate in study-abroad opportunities which cost little more than regular tuition. Centre boasts a fraternity that carries an oil portrait of alum former Supreme Court Chief Justice Fred Vinson (Dead Fred) to all home football games. Living alums seem to like the place too: The school is ranked #1 in the nation in terms of percentage of alumni making annual contributions. Centre College was founded in 1819 by Presbyterian leaders.

	Annual Growth	06/09	06/10	06/13	06/15	06/17
Sales ($ mil.)	2.6%	–	58.8	89.2	86.6	70.2
Net income ($ mil.)	–	–	(6.8)	6.8	0.0	38.2
Market value ($ mil.)	–	–	–	–	–	–
Employees	–	–	–	–	–	340

CENTRIA INC.

1005 Beaver Grade Rd.
Moon Township PA 15108
Phone: 800-759-7474
Fax: 412-299-8317
Web: www.centria.com

CEO: –
CFO: –
HR: –
FYE: December 31
Type: Private

The metal panel is central to the business of CENTRIA which manufactures architectural industrial nonresidential and institutional metal buildings. The company is the world leader in custom-engineered architectural metal enclosure systems. CENTRIA also provides extensive coil-coating capabilities for a range of industries including automotive and residential building products. Through its H. H. Robertson Floor Systems unit the company offers electrified cellular decking and related products. CENTRIA Worldwide sells factory foamed metal panel systems and profiled panel systems for both walls and roofs worldwide.

CENTRIC BRANDS INC

350 5th Avenue, 6th Floor
New York, NY 10118
Phone: 646 582-6000
Fax: –
Web: www.centricbrands.com

NAS: CTRC
CEO: Jason Rabin
CFO: Anurup S Pruthi
HR: –
FYE: December 31
Type: Public

A pair of jeans that fit just right; Joe's Jeans gets us. The company designs develops and markets premium designer denim jeans under the Joe's Hudson and Else brands. Its Joe's line also includes men's jeans and pants as well as shirts sweaters jackets and accessories for both sexes. Newly-acquired Hudson targets a more fashion forward customers looking for a great fit. Joe's Jeans sells its lineup to US retailers such as Saks Nordstrom and Macy's boutiques and through its namesake stores and website. It operates about 35 full-price retail and outlet stores in the US and now Canada. Founded in 1987 Joe's Jeans nearly doubled in size with the purchase of Hudson in 2013.

	Annual Growth	11/14	11/15*	12/16	12/17	12/18
Sales ($ mil.)	33.3%	188.8	80.2	149.3	164.1	596.6
Net income ($ mil.)	–	(27.7)	(32.3)	(17.8)	(2.5)	(123.8)
Market value ($ mil.)	54.6%	35.0	12.0	136.9	55.4	200.2
Employees	77.8%	400	588	387	421	4,000

*Fiscal year change

CENTRIC GROUP L.L.C.

1260 Andes Blvd.
St. Louis MO 63132
Phone: 314-214-2700
Fax: 314-214-2766
Web: www.centricgp.com

CEO: –
CFO: –
HR: –
FYE: December 31
Type: Private

Coffee baggage and commissary essentials are the focal points of Centric Group's business. The holding company operates three manufacturing and distribution divisions. Its Courtesy Products unit distributes coffee irons hair dryers and other guestroom supplies for the hospitality industry. The company's TRG Group manufactures luggage and other travel bags under such brands as Callaway Golf Soren and Victorinox Swiss Army. In addition Centric provides toiletries clothing electronics snacks and beverages to commissaries at correctional facilities through its Keefe Group. The company which is controlled by the Taylor family was formed in 1974 as part of Enterprise Rent-A-Car and spun off in 1999.

CENTRUS ENERGY CORP

6901 Rockledge Drive, Suite 800
Bethesda, MD 20817
Phone: 301 564-3200
Fax: –
Web: www.centrusenergy.com

ASE: LEU
CEO: Daniel Poneman
CFO: Philip Strawbridge
HR: –
FYE: December 31
Type: Public

Centrus Energy (formerly USEC) beats radioactive swords into enriched uranium plowshares. The company processes used uranium — about half of which comes from old Russian atomic warheads — into enriched uranium which it then supplies for commercial nuclear power plants. Centrus Energy is the radioactive recycler of choice for the "Megatons-to-Megawatts" program a US-Russian agreement to convert uranium from warheads into nuclear fuel. In addition Centrus Energy develops low-enriched uranium for the nuclear materials industry and also processes uranium for the US Department of Energy. The company filed for Chapter 11 bankruptcy protection in 2014 and emerged later the same year.

	Annual Growth	12/16	12/17	12/18	12/19	12/20
Sales ($ mil.)	(5.6%)	311.3	218.4	193.0	209.7	247.2
Net income ($ mil.)	–	(67.0)	12.2	(104.1)	(16.5)	54.4
Market value ($ mil.)	38.0%	77.3	48.6	20.5	83.3	280.1
Employees	(5.7%)	338	290	226	230	267

CENTURY 21 REAL ESTATE LLC

1 Campus Dr.
Parsippany NJ 07054
Phone: 877-221-2765
Fax: +44-118-923-1001
Web: www.adeptra.com

CEO: Michael Miedler
CFO: –
HR: –
FYE: December 31
Type: Subsidiary

Home is where the money is for Century 21. A subsidiary of Realogy Corporation Century 21 provides franchises for one of the world's largest residential real-estate sales networks with about 7600 independently owned offices in more than 70 countries and territories worldwide. While homes are its core focus the company also helps customers buy and sell commercial and vacation properties and provides relocation services for individuals corporations and members of the military. Century 21 Fine Homes & Estates offers services for luxury home buyers. Realogy Corporation licenses the Century 21 name among several other major real estate brands. In 2012 Realogy parent Domus filed to go public.

CENTURY ALUMINUM CO.   NMS: CENX

One South Wacker Drive, Suite 1000
Chicago, IL 60606
Phone: 312 696-3101
Fax: –
Web: www.centuryaluminum.com

CEO: Jesse Gary
CFO: Craig Conti
HR: –
FYE: December 31
Type: Public

Century Aluminum is a global producer of primary aluminum and operates aluminum reduction facilities or smelters in the US and Iceland. It operates three US aluminum smelters in Kentucky and South Carolina and one aluminum smelter in Iceland. With an annual production capacity of more than 1 million tons per year the company produced approximately 794000 tons of primary aluminum. Century Aluminum also owns a carbon anode production facility in Vlissingen Netherlands. Glencore accounts for the vast majority of Century Aluminum's sales. Century Aluminum generates about 65% of sales in the US.

	Annual Growth	12/16	12/17	12/18	12/19	12/20
Sales ($ mil.)	5.0%	1,319.1	1,589.1	1,893.2	1,836.6	1,605.1
Net income ($ mil.)	–	(252.4)	48.6	(66.2)	(80.8)	(123.3)
Market value ($ mil.)	6.5%	770.9	1,768.7	658.3	676.8	993.3
Employees	4.5%	1,741	1,864	2,069	2,079	2,078

CENTURY BANCORP, INC.   NMS: CNBK A

400 Mystic Avenue
Medford, MA 02155
Phone: 781 391-4000
Fax: –
Web: www.centurybank.com

CEO: Barry R Sloane
CFO: William P Hornby
HR: Starks Lyndsey
FYE: December 31
Type: Public

Century Bancorp is the holding company for Century Bank and Trust which serves Boston and surrounding parts of northeastern Massachusetts from more than 25 branches. Boasting some $3.6 billion in total assets the bank offers standard deposit products including checking savings and money market accounts; CDs; and IRAs. Nearly two-thirds of its loan portfolio is comprised of commercial and commercial real estate loans. while residential mortgages and home equity loans make up around 30%. The bank also writes construction and land development loans business loans and personal loans. It offers brokerage services through an agreement with third-party provider LPL Financial.

	Annual Growth	12/15	12/16	12/17	12/18	12/19
Assets ($ mil.)	8.6%	3,947.4	4,462.6	4,785.6	5,163.9	5,492.4
Net income ($ mil.)	14.6%	23.0	24.5	22.3	36.2	39.7
Market value ($ mil.)	19.9%	242.0	334.1	435.7	377.1	500.9
Employees	1.2%	438	438	447	460	460

CENTURY CASINOS INC.   NAS: CNTY

455 E. Pikes Peak Ave., Suite 210
Colorado Springs, CO 80903
Phone: 719 527-8300
Fax: –
Web: www.cnty.com

CEO: Erwin Haitzmann
CFO: Margaret Stapleton
HR: –
FYE: December 31
Type: Public

In the 19th century people rushed to Cripple Creek Colorado seeking their fortune in gold. Today thanks to Century Casinos they can do basically the same thing (but via midsized regional casinos rather than through prospecting). The company's Womacks Casino & Hotel in Cripple Creek offers some 440 slot machines and video devices as well as a handful of gaming tables. It also owns the Century Casino & Hotel in Central City Colorado and another Century Casino & Hotel in Edmonton Canada. In addition it operate four cruise ship casinos and is the casino concessionaire for cruise lines run by TUI Cruises a joint venture between German travel operator TUI and #2 cruise ship operator Royal Caribbean.

	Annual Growth	12/16	12/17	12/18	12/19	12/20
Sales ($ mil.)	21.6%	139.2	154.1	168.9	218.2	304.3
Net income ($ mil.)	–	9.2	6.3	3.4	(19.2)	(48.0)
Market value ($ mil.)	(6.1%)	243.4	270.0	218.6	234.2	189.0
Employees	5.9%	1,791	1,910	2,172	3,515	2,254

CENTURY ENERGY LTD.   PINK SHEETS: CEYFF

4605 Post Oak Place Dr. Ste. 250
Houston TX 77027
Phone: 713-658-0161
Fax: 713-222-7158
Web: www.centuryenergyltd.com

CEO: –
CFO: –
HR: –
FYE: August 31
Type: Public

What can top Topper Resources? How about Century Energy. The junior natural resources company (formerly Topper Resources) buys interests in gas and oil exploration sites in Canada and the US. It owns the petroleum and natural gas rights to 1100 acres in the Bakken oil formation in southern Saskatchewan. In conjunction with TriAxon Resources Ltd. (its joint venture partner with extensive experience in the Bakken Shale play) the company has succeeded in producing oil from its first exploratory Bakken well and plans to develop several others.

CENTURY FOODS INTERNATIONAL LLC

400 Century Ct.
Sparta WI 54656
Phone: 800-269-1901
Fax: 608-269-1910
Web: www.centuryfoods.com

CEO: –
CFO: –
HR: Elizabeth Neitzel
FYE: October 31
Type: Subsidiary

Century Foods International knows where there's swill there's a whey. The company provides dairy and vegetable proteins and nutraceuticals used for muscle-building and weight-loss powders bars and beverages. Clients include food manufacturers and heath nutritional supplement and sports companies. The company serves customers in more than 45 countries. Century Foods provides services such as development manufacturing testing and packaging from its four plants in central Wisconsin. The company is a division of Hormel Foods.

CENVEO INC
NBB: CVOV Q

200 First Stamford Place
Stamford, CT 06902
Phone: 203 595-3000
Fax: -
Web: www.cenveo.com

CEO: -
CFO: -
HR: -
FYE: December 31
Type: Public

Commercial printer Cenveo knows that when you send mail it's important to consider the envelope. The company provides direct mail and customized envelopes for advertising billing and remittance. It also sells labels and specialty packaging. In addition Cenveo has commercial printing operations devoted to the production of scientific technical and medical (STM) journals. Included in its services are design content management fulfillment and distribution solutions. Cenveo encompasses more than two dozen entities operating 100-plus facilities worldwide.

	Annual Growth	12/12	12/13	12/14*	01/16*	12/16
Sales ($ mil.)	(2.0%)	1,797.6	1,777.8	1,949.0	1,741.8	1,660.0
Net income ($ mil.)	-	(79.9)	(68.8)	(83.9)	(30.9)	67.9
Market value ($ mil.)	26.8%	23.1	30.2	18.6	7.5	59.8
Employees	(1.0%)	7,600	8,700	8,100	7,300	7,300

*Fiscal year change

CEPHALON INC.

41 Moores Rd.
Malvern PA 19355
Phone: 610-344-0200
Fax: 561-438-4001
Web: www.officedepot.com

CEO: J Kevin Buchi
CFO: Wilco Groenhuysen
HR: -
FYE: December 31
Type: Subsidiary

Cephalon has a handful of powerful specialty drugs. The company's research development manufacturing and marketing activities focus on therapies for central nervous system (CNS) disorders cancer pain and inflammatory disease. Its NUVIGIL and PROVIGIL drugs treat the sleep disorder narcolepsy. The company's other top sellers are cancer drug TREANDA cancer pain medications ACTIQ and FENTORA epilepsy treatment GABITRIL and muscle relaxant AMRIX. Its eight major products are primarily sold in the US and Europe. Cephalon was acquired by top generic drugmaker Teva Pharmaceutical Industries in 2011.

CEPHAS HOLDING CORP
NBB: CEHC

215 Dino Dr.
Ann Arbor, MI 48103
Phone: 623 738-5792
Fax: -

CEO: Peter Klamka
CFO: -
HR: -
FYE: December 31
Type: Public

Cephas Holding (formerly Legend Mobile) would like you to see its face when you pick up the phone. The company designs and markets accessories for wireless phones such as personalized faceplate covers. It also offers text-messaging services and mobile software. Several of Cephas' products feature branded themes representing such organizations as NASCAR. The company's 50%-owned Legend Credit unit markets promotional stored-value gift cards. Neither of the company's business lines has generated significant revenue however and its auditor has questioned the financial viability of the company. CEO Peter Klamka controls a majority of voting stock of Cephas which changed its name from Legend Mobile in 2009.

	Annual Growth	12/08	12/09	12/10	12/11	12/12
Sales ($ mil.)	(22.9%)	-	0.0	0.0	0.0	0.0
Net income ($ mil.)	-	(0.6)	(0.5)	(0.5)	(0.8)	(4.6)
Market value ($ mil.)	49.5%	0.3	0.3	0.5	0.1	1.5
Employees	0.0%	1	1	1	1	1

CEPHEID
NMS: CPHD

904 Caribbean Drive
Sunnyvale, CA 94089-1189
Phone: 408 541-4191
Fax: -
Web: www.cepheid.com

CEO: -
CFO: Daniel E Madden
HR: Kari N Vaatveit
FYE: December 31
Type: Public

Cepheid helps doctors and scientists see DNA faster. The molecular diagnostics firm develops and manufactures systems that automate the process of preparing and amplifying DNA in order to quickly detect diseases and harmful agents. Its two instrument platforms — GeneXpert and SmartCycler — can perform rapid molecular testing for a number of purposes including diagnosing infectious diseases and cancer as well as detecting biothreats such as anthrax. Cepheid also makes reagents (testing chemicals) and other disposable testing components for use with its systems.

	Annual Growth	12/10	12/11	12/12	12/13	12/14
Sales ($ mil.)	22.0%	212.5	277.6	331.2	401.3	470.1
Net income ($ mil.)	-	(5.9)	2.6	(20.0)	(18.0)	(50.1)
Market value ($ mil.)	24.2%	1,613.1	2,439.8	2,400.8	3,309.2	3,838.8
Employees	24.9%	576	717	945	1,200	1,400

CEQUEL COMMUNICATIONS HOLDINGS I LLC

12444 Powerscourt Dr. Ste. 450
St. Louis MO 63131
Phone: 314-315-9400
Fax: 949-486-3995
Web: www.clickerinc.com

CEO: Dexter Goei
CFO: Charles F Stewart
HR: Terry Cordova
FYE: December 31
Type: Private

Cequel Communications which operates through subsidiary Suddenlink provides cable TV high-speed Internet access and phone services to about 1.4 million business and residential customers. The company primarily serves rural markets in Arkansas Louisiana North Carolina Oklahoma Texas and West Virginia among other states. It also offers home security system installation and monitoring services. Suddenlink's services for business clients include high-capacity networking and Web hosting. The company's CoStreet division provides fiber optic networking and backhaul services to other carriers. A group of investors and company executives are acquiring Cequel for $6.6 billion including $4.1 billion in debt.

CERADYNE INC.
NASDAQ: CRDN

3169 Red Hill Ave.
Costa Mesa CA 92626
Phone: 714-549-0421
Fax: 714-549-5787
Web: www.ceradyne.com

CEO: Joel P Moskowitz
CFO: Jerrold J Pellizzon
HR: -
FYE: December 31
Type: Public

A bull in a china shop wouldn't stand a chance against Ceradyne's ceramics. The company's advanced technical ceramics products combine hardness with light weight and the ability to withstand high temperatures resist corrosion and insulate against electricity. Some uses of Ceradyne's materials include armor for military helicopters missile nose cones body armor and helmets for soldiers diesel engine components ceramic industrial products solar glass products and orthodontic brackets. The company sells to contractors and OEMs and the US government and government agencies represent more than 37% of sales. In late 2012 3M Company acquired Ceradyne.

CEREPLAST INC
NBB: CERP

2213 Killion Avenue
Seymour, IN 47274
Phone: 812 200-5400
Fax: -
Web: www.cereplast.com

CEO: -
CFO: -
HR: -
FYE: December 31
Type: Public

Cereplast aims to make plastics greener. The company develops and manufactures bio-based plastic resins that are designed to be eco-friendly alternatives to petroleum-based plastics often used in converting processes such as extrusion coating injection molding and thermoforming. Its family of products include: US- and Europe-certified compostable and biodegradable resins made from corn potato tapioca and wheat starches; hybrid resins that combine bio-based plant starches with traditional plastic; and a technology still in development to convert algae into bioplastics. Cereplast primarily markets to the automotive construction consumer goods electronics and medical packaging industries.

	Annual Growth	12/08	12/09	12/10	12/11	12/12
Sales ($ mil.)	(33.3%)	4.5	2.7	6.3	20.3	0.9
Net income ($ mil.)	-	(12.7)	(6.1)	(7.5)	(14.0)	(30.2)
Market value ($ mil.)	(33.8%)	7.3	6.1	262.7	60.9	1.4
Employees	(14.9%)	-	26	53	46	16

CERES SOLUTIONS, LLP

2112 INDIANAPOLIS RD
CRAWFORDSVILLE, IN 479333137
Phone: 765-362-6108
Fax: -
Web: www.ceres.coop

CEO: Jeff Troike
CFO: -
HR: Mary Lubbehusen
FYE: July 31
Type: Private

Ceres Solutions is a growth business. The agricultural partnership provides farmers in about a dozen Indiana counties with crop farming support services and supplies. It sells stores and distributes such goods as fertilizers and fuel (gasoline propane home-heating). The company's agronomy services include field mapping crop and pest management soil sampling and yield analysis. Ceres Solutions also offers crop-financing programs sells crop insurance and provides marketing services. Its Green Notes newsletter offers the state's farmers market and technical advice and analysis.

	Annual Growth	07/13	07/14	07/15	07/16	07/17
Sales ($ mil.)	(9.1%)	-	412.2	368.1	299.7	309.9
Net income ($ mil.)	(14.4%)	-	22.2	16.5	10.7	13.9
Market value ($ mil.)	-	-	-	-	-	-
Employees	-	-	-	-	-	125

CERNER CORP.
NMS: CERN

2800 Rock Creek Parkway
North Kansas City, MO 64117
Phone: 816 221-1024
Fax: -
Web: www.cerner.com

CEO: David Feinberg
CFO: Marc G Naughton
HR: -
FYE: December 31
Type: Public

Cerner is a leading supplier of health care information technology (HCIT) solutions and tech-enabled services. The company offers a wide range of intelligent solutions and tech-enabled services that support the clinical financial and operational needs of organizations of all sizes. Complementary services include support and maintenance implementation and training remote hosting data analytics and transaction processing among others. The company has operations in more than 35 countries although the US is by far its largest market.

	Annual Growth	12/17	12/18	12/19	12/20	12/21
Sales ($ mil.)	2.9%	5,142.3	5,366.3	5,692.6	5,505.8	5,764.8
Net income ($ mil.)	(10.5%)	867.0	630.1	529.5	780.1	555.6
Market value ($ mil.)	8.3%	19,735.1	15,231.1	21,460.0	22,982.9	27,197.0
Employees	(0.8%)	26,000	29,200	27,400	26,400	25,150

CERRITOS COMMUNITY COLLEGE DISTRICT

11110 ALONDRA BLVD
NORWALK, CA 906506203
Phone: 562-860-2451
Fax: -
Web: www.cerritosfalcons.com

CEO: -
CFO: -
HR: -
FYE: June 30
Type: Private

Cerritos College provides comprehensive learning programs to communities in southeastern Los Angeles County. The public community college offers degrees and certificates in more than 200 fields of study through its nine divisions including business education fine arts liberal arts and technology. It also conducts vocational training programs such as health-related programs for nurses dental hygienists pharmacy technicians and physical therapy assistants. Cerritos College has more than 830 full- and part-time faculty members an enrollment of more than 23650 students. Cerritos College was founded in 1955.

	Annual Growth	06/13	06/14	06/15	06/16	06/17
Sales ($ mil.)	92.3%	-	-	-	87.1	167.6
Net income ($ mil.)	(73.7%)	-	-	-	29.4	7.7
Market value ($ mil.)	-	-	-	-	-	-
Employees	-	-	-	-	-	2,005

CERTAINTEED CORPORATION

750 E. Swedesford Rd.
Valley Forge PA 19482
Phone: 610-341-7000
Fax: 610-341-7777
Web: www.certainteed.com

CEO: Mark Rayfield
CFO: Robert J Panaro
HR: -
FYE: December 31
Type: Subsidiary

There's no uncertainty about CertainTeed's business. A subsidiary of French industrial giant Compagnie de Saint-Gobain CertainTeed manufactures building products for both commercial and residential construction. CertainTeed's products include fiberglass insulation asphalt roofing shingles gypsum wallboard windows fiber cement siding foundations fencing pipes PVC trim and composite decking and railing. The company sells its products under the Bufftech CertainTeed Form-A-Drain Prestige and Wolverine brands. CertainTeed operates some 65 manufacturing plants in the US and Canada.

CERTCO, INC.

5321 VERONA RD
FITCHBURG, WI 537116050
Phone: 608-271-4500
Fax: -
Web: www.certcoinc.com

CEO: Randy Simon
CFO: Amy Niemetscheck
HR: -
FYE: April 26
Type: Private

Certco has built a business serving about 200 independent grocers in Minnesota Wisconsin Iowa and Illinois. The food distribution cooperative offers customers an inventory of more than 57000 items including bakery goods frozen foods meat products produce and general merchandise. It distributes products under the Shurfine Shurfresh and Top Care labels. Additionally Certco offers its member-operators such services as advertising accounting client data services warehousing merchandising store planning and design and other business support services. The cooperative was founded in 1930 as Central Wisconsin Cooperative Food Stores.

	Annual Growth	04/10	04/11	04/12	04/13	04/14
Sales ($ mil.)	6.0%	-	-	569.7	607.3	640.5
Net income ($ mil.)	5.6%	-	-	5.0	5.5	5.6
Market value ($ mil.)	-	-	-	-	-	-
Employees	-	-	-	-	-	325

CERUS CORP.
NMS: CERS

1220 Concord Avenue, Suite 600
Concord, CA 94520
Phone: 925 288-6000
Fax: –
Web: www.cerus.com

CEO: William Greenman
CFO: Kevin Green
HR: –
FYE: December 31
Type: Public

Cerus biomedical products company focused on developing and commercializing the INTERCEPT Blood System to enhance blood safety. The INTERCEPT Blood System which is based on its proprietary technology for controlling biological replication is designed to reduce blood-borne pathogens in donated blood components intended for transfusion. Its INTERCEPT Blood Systems for platelets and plasma are approved for sale in some European and Middle Eastern countries where they are marketed directly to customers through subsidiary Cerus Europe. Most of its revenue accounts from outside the US. The company was incorporated in California in 1991 and reincorporated in Delaware in 1996.

	Annual Growth	12/16	12/17	12/18	12/19	12/20
Sales ($ mil.)	30.6%	39.3	51.3	76.1	93.8	114.2
Net income ($ mil.)	–	(62.9)	(60.6)	(57.6)	(71.2)	(59.9)
Market value ($ mil.)	12.3%	731.5	568.4	852.6	709.7	1,163.7
Employees	7.3%	204	215	240	254	270

CESSNA AIRCRAFT COMPANY

1 Cessna Blvd.
Wichita KS 67215
Phone: 316-517-6000
Fax: 610-341-7797
Web: www.saint-gobain-corporation.com

CEO: –
CFO: –
HR: –
FYE: December 31
Type: Subsidiary

Blue-sky thinking is encouraged at Cessna Aircraft one of the most famous names in small planes. A subsidiary of Textron the company designs and manufactures light and midsize Citation business jets Caravan utility turboprops (primarily used in the US for overnight express package shipments) and single-engine piston and light lift aircraft. It has delivered more than 190000 aircraft over the course of more than eight decades in business making it the world's leading general aviation company by unit sales. In addition to aircraft sales Cessna's other principal line of business is aftermarket services including parts maintenance inspection and repair.

CEVA INC
NMS: CEVA

15245 Shady Grove Road, Suite 400
Rockville, MD 20850
Phone: 240 308-8328
Fax: –
Web: www.ceva-dsp.com

CEO: Gideon Wertheizer
CFO: Yaniv Arieli
HR: –
FYE: December 31
Type: Public

CEVA has a fever for semiconductor design. CEVA specializes in technology — both integrated circuit and software designs — used in cell phones handheld computers MP3 players watches and other wireless devices as well as mouse and thermostat. It licenses its silicon intellectual property (SIP) designs to such industry heavyweights as Lenovo Philips Samsung and Xiaomi. The company partners with semiconductor companies and OEMs worldwide to create power-efficient intelligent and connected devices for a range of end markets including mobile consumer automotive robotics industrial and IoT.

	Annual Growth	12/16	12/17	12/18	12/19	12/20
Sales ($ mil.)	8.4%	72.7	87.5	77.9	87.2	100.3
Net income ($ mil.)	–	13.1	17.0	0.6	0.0	(2.4)
Market value ($ mil.)	7.9%	746.9	1,027.3	491.7	600.2	1,012.9
Employees	9.8%	278	313	341	382	404

CF BANKSHARES INC
NAS: CFBK

7000 North High Street
Worthington, OH 43085
Phone: 614 334-7979
Fax: 614 334-7980
Web: www.cfbankonline.com

CEO: Timothy O'Dell
CFO: Kevin Beerman
HR: –
FYE: December 31
Type: Public

Central Federal Corporation is the holding company for CFBank. Traditionally a retail-focused savings and loan CFBank has added business banking commercial real estate and business lending to its foundation. It now serves not only local individuals but also businesses through five branches in eastern Ohio and the state capital Columbus. Its deposit products include checking savings NOW and money market accounts as well as CDs. Commercial commercial real estate and multifamily residential mortgages represent nearly 80% of the company's loan portfolio. Single-family mortgages make up about 13% of loans. CFBank traces its roots to 1892.

	Annual Growth	12/16	12/17	12/18	12/19	12/20
Assets ($ mil.)	35.7%	436.1	481.4	665.0	880.5	1,477.0
Net income ($ mil.)	106.5%	1.6	1.3	4.3	9.6	29.6
Market value ($ mil.)	78.3%	11.5	18.1	76.7	91.6	116.1
Employees	29.0%	64	66	95	125	177

CF INDUSTRIES HOLDINGS INC
NYS: CF

4 Parkway North, Suite 400
Deerfield, IL 60015
Phone: 847 405-2400
Fax: –
Web: www.cfindustries.com

CEO: W. Anthony Will
CFO: Christopher Bohn
HR: Susan Menzel
FYE: December 31
Type: Public

Owners of Terra Nitrogen Company agricultural firm CF Industries manufactures and distributes nitrogen products serving agricultural and industrial customers as well as distributors traders and wholesalers worldwide. It serves its customers in North America through its production storage transportation and distribution network. Its core product is anhydrous ammonia (ammonia) which contains 82% nitrogen and 18% hydrogen. Its nitrogen products that are upgraded from ammonia are granular urea urea ammonium nitrate solution (UAN) and ammonium nitrate (AN). Other nitrogen products include diesel exhaust fluid (DEF) urea liquor nitric acid and aqua ammonia. The company also has nitrogen manufacturing complexes in Canada and the UK. Almost 75% of the company's revenue comes from the US.

	Annual Growth	12/16	12/17	12/18	12/19	12/20
Sales ($ mil.)	2.9%	3,685.0	4,130.0	4,429.0	4,590.0	4,124.0
Net income ($ mil.)	–	(277.0)	358.0	290.0	493.0	317.0
Market value ($ mil.)	5.3%	6,735.3	9,101.6	9,309.2	10,214.2	8,282.2
Employees	0.0%	3,000	3,000	3,000	3,000	3,000

CFC INTERNATIONAL INC.

500 State St.
Chicago Heights IL 60411
Phone: 708-891-3456
Fax: 708-758-5989
Web: www.cfcintl.com

CEO: –
CFO: Dennis W Lakomy
HR: Susan Contri
FYE: December 31
Type: Subsidiary

At CFC International beauty by design is only skin deep. The company makes transferable chemical coatings to beautify protect and add other kinds of functionality to consumer products. It makes complex functional coatings such as simulated metal used on cosmetic containers and simulated wood grain for ready-to-assemble furniture. CFC also makes holographic authentication seals (popular on tickets and software) heat transfer labels for pharmaceuticals and magnetic strips for security and credit card uses. The company is a part multi-industry conglomerate Illinois Tool Works (ITW).

CGB ENTERPRISES, INC.

1127 HWY 190 E SERVICE RD
COVINGTON, LA 704334929
Phone: 985-867-3500
Fax: -
Web: www.cgb.com

CEO: Kevin D Adams
CFO: Richard S Pemberton
HR: -
FYE: May 31
Type: Private

CGB Enterprises is a leader in the grain and transportation industries. Located in Louisiana the agricultural company provides US farmers with a range of services including grain handling storage lending and merchandising. It offers inland grain transportation by barge rail and truck and also markets and sells seeds agricultural products and insurance. CGB's Consolidated Terminals and Logistics Co. (CTLC) subsidiary provides transportation logistics and bulk commodity services for both agricultural and non-agricultural customers. The company operates more than 125 locations across the US. Japanese trading conglomerates ITOCHU and ZEN-NOH own CGB.

	Annual Growth	05/17	05/18	05/19	05/20	05/21
Sales ($ mil.)	1.4%	-	6,802.0	6,498.0	5,955.3	7,081.2
Net income ($ mil.)	1.8%	-	110.4	67.7	50.1	116.4
Market value ($ mil.)	-	-	-	-	-	-
Employees	-	-	-	-	-	3,250

CH2M HILL COMPANIES, LTD.

9191 S JAMAICA ST
ENGLEWOOD, CO 801125946
Phone: 303-771-0900
Fax: -
Web: www.ch2m.com

CEO: -
CFO: -
HR: -
FYE: December 30
Type: Private

Engineering and construction firm CH2M HILL (named for its founders Cornell Howland Hayes and Merryfield; dba CH2M) operates five divisions that offer up consulting design build operations and maintenance services. It is active across five markets: energy and industrial; environment and nuclear transportation water and power. CH2M's top client is the US Government and public sector clients include the US Department of Energy and the Department of Defense. CH2M also works for state and local governments building water and wastewater systems airports highways and other transportation projects. Founded in 1946 the privately held company is owned by private equity firm Apollo Global Management.

	Annual Growth	12/12	12/13	12/14	12/15	12/16
Sales ($ mil.)	(3.8%)	-	5,931.8	5,468.4	5,408.3	5,287.9
Net income ($ mil.)	-	-	131.2	(318.6)	92.1	(124.3)
Market value ($ mil.)	-	-	-	-	-	-
Employees	-	-	-	-	-	22,000

CHA HOLLYWOOD MEDICAL CENTER LP

1300 N VERMONT AVE
LOS ANGELES, CA 900276098
Phone: 213-413-3000
Fax: -
Web: www.hollywoodpresbyterian.com

CEO: Jeff A Nelson
CFO: Galen Gorman
HR: -
FYE: December 31
Type: Private

As one might expect from a Hollywood hospital the staff at Hollywood Presbyterian Medical Center (HPMC) includes bellmen concierges and parking valets in addition to nurses and doctors. HPMC aims to blur the lines between acute-care hospital and hotel caring for the oft-pampered community of Hollywood California. Its health care services include a cancer treatment center; physical speech and occupational therapy; and the Institute of Maternal Fetal Health which performs fetal surgeries. Other services include community health outreach programs and The Chalet a skilled nursing facility. The 430-plus-bed hospital with 500 physicians is part of CHA Health Systems.

	Annual Growth	12/12	12/13	12/14	12/15	12/16
Sales ($ mil.)	10.9%	-	-	-	260.5	289.0
Net income ($ mil.)	83.0%	-	-	-	18.5	33.8
Market value ($ mil.)	-	-	-	-	-	-
Employees	-	-	-	-	-	1,500

CHADBOURNE & PARKE LLP

30 Rockefeller Plaza
New York NY 10112
Phone: 212-408-5100
Fax: 212-541-5369
Web: www.chadbourne.com

CEO: -
CFO: -
HR: -
FYE: December 31
Type: Private - Partnershi

International law firm Chadbourne & Parke doesn't shy away from controversy. Representing Brown & Williamson Tobacco put the firm on the frontlines in the war between state governments and big tobacco. Its clients also have included liquor producers and a nuclear bomb manufacturer. Chadbourne & Parke is a leader in mergers and acquisitions and project finance; about 420 attorneys also work in areas such as bankruptcy environmental litigation product liability and tax. The firm has about a dozen offices with international locations in Brazil China Kazakhstan Mexico Poland Russia the UK the Ukraine and the United Arab Emirates. The late Thomas Chadbourne founded the firm in 1902.

CHAMPION INDUSTRIES INC (WV)

2450-90 1st Avenue, P.O. Box 2968
Huntington, WV 25728
Phone: 304 528-2700
Fax: -

NBB: CHMP

CEO: Adam Reynolds
CFO: Justin Evans
HR: Justin Carpenter
FYE: October 31
Type: Public

This Champion hopes to win business in the printing and office supply fields. Through more than a dozen operating units Champion Industries prints books brochures business cards business forms posters and tags including complex four- to six-color products. Printing accounts for the majority of sales. The company also sells a wide range of office products and office furniture that it orders from manufacturers and provides office design services. Champion Industries operates primarily in regional markets east of the Mississippi and publishes The Herald-Dispatch the daily newspaper of its hometown in Huntington West Virginia.

	Annual Growth	10/11	10/12	10/13	10/14	10/15
Sales ($ mil.)	(16.9%)	128.5	104.4	72.3	63.5	61.3
Net income ($ mil.)	-	(4.0)	(22.9)	5.7	(1.1)	(1.2)
Market value ($ mil.)	-	0.1	0.0	0.0	0.0	0.0
Employees	(16.8%)	660	550	330	330	316

CHAMPION LABORATORIES INC.

200 S. Fourth St.
Albion IL 62806
Phone: 618-445-6011
Fax: 618-445-5489
Web: www.champlabs.com

CEO: -
CFO: -
HR: -
FYE: December 31
Type: Subsidiary

Champion Laboratories wants to keep your machine cool and clean. It manufactures oil fuel and air filters for motor vehicle OEMs and aftermarket. Other products include breather filters cabin air filters and transmission filters. It also makes engine management systems driveline components and lighting systems for the marine mining construction industrial and agricultural markets. Its primary brand names include Champ Luber-Finer and Kleener. Champion Laboratories has 10 manufacturing and distribution locations in North and South America Europe and Asia. The company is owned by UCI International (formerly United Components) which is owned by New Zealand investment firm Rank Group Limited.

CHAMPIONS ONCOLOGY INC
NAS: CSBR

One University Plaza, Suite 307
Hackensack, NJ 07601
Phone: 201 808-8400
Fax: -
Web: www.championsoncology.com

CEO: Ronnie Morris
CFO: David Miller
HR: -
FYE: April 30
Type: Public

Champions Oncology (formerly Champions Biotechnology) is hoping to win big in the field of cancer research. Its Champions Tumorgraft platform allows the company to implant human tumors of various cancer types into mice allowing scientists to study the effects of investigational drugs on human cancers. The company uses the platform in its own research and also provides tumor-specific research to doctors as well as the Tumorgraft platform to other drug developers. The company has licensed the rights to explore Irinophore a nanoparticle in preclinical development.

	Annual Growth	04/17	04/18	04/19	04/20	04/21
Sales ($ mil.)	27.7%	15.4	20.2	27.1	32.1	41.0
Net income ($ mil.)	-	(6.9)	(1.5)	0.1	(2.0)	0.4
Market value ($ mil.)	39.9%	37.6	58.2	121.8	103.6	143.9
Employees	25.2%	79	92	115	143	194

CHANCELIGHT, INC.

1321 MURFREESBORO PIKE
NASHVILLE, TN 372172626
Phone: 615-361-4000
Fax: -
Web: www.esa-education.com

CEO: Mark Claypool
CFO: -
HR: -
FYE: July 31
Type: Private

Educational Services of America (ESA) knows that public school isn't a one-size-fits-all model for every student. A provider of K-12 and post-secondary alternative and specialized education programs ESA targets and teaches students with special needs learning disabilities and emotional and behavioral difficulties through five divisions. Its Ombudsman division partners with school districts to provide off-campus education to at-risk stiudents while College Living Experience teaches independent living and social skills to those with learning disabilities. It also offers an academic program for exceptional students. Founded in 1999 ESA owns and operates more than 130 accredited schools in 17 states.

	Annual Growth	12/05	12/06	12/07*	07/08	07/09
Sales ($ mil.)	110.9%	-	8.6	74.9	85.1	80.7
Net income ($ mil.)	-	-	91.7	(8.6)	(10.6)	(12.8)
Market value ($ mil.)	-	-	-	-	-	-
Employees	-	-	-	-	-	2,600

*Fiscal year change

CHANNELADVISOR CORP
NYS: ECOM

3025 Carrington Mill Boulevard
Morrisville, NC 27560
Phone: 919 228-4700
Fax: -
Web: www.channeladvisor.com

CEO: David Spitz
CFO: Richard Cornetta
HR: Stephanie Levin
FYE: December 31
Type: Public

ChannelAdvisor's proprietary software-as-a-service or SaaS cloud platform helps brands and retailers worldwide improve their online performance by expanding sales channels connecting with consumers around the world optimizing their operations for peak performance and providing actionable analytics to improve competitiveness. The company offers software and support services for brands and retailer worldwide looking for greater product visibility and brand management in marketplaces (such as eBay Amazon and Google) comparison shopping sites (Google Shopping) search engines (Google and Bing) and their own Web stores. Founded in 2001 the company generates around three-quarters of sales domestically.

	Annual Growth	12/17	12/18	12/19	12/20	12/21
Sales ($ mil.)	8.2%	122.5	131.2	130.0	145.1	167.7
Net income ($ mil.)	-	(16.6)	(7.6)	3.5	18.8	47.2
Market value ($ mil.)	28.7%	271.7	342.6	272.9	482.4	745.1
Employees	3.5%	737	730	642	725	846

CHAPARRAL ENERGY L.L.C.

701 Cedar Lake Blvd.
Oklahoma City OK 73114
Phone: 405-478-8770
Fax: 405-478-1947
Web: www.chaparralenergy.com

CEO: -
CFO: Joseph O Evans
HR: -
FYE: December 31
Type: Private

Chaparral Energy searches the scrublands of America's Mid-Continent and Permian Basin looking for oil and natural gas. The exploration and production company also drills in North Texas the Gulf Coast the Ark-La-Tex region and the Rocky Mountains. In 2010 the company reported estimated proved reserves of some 149.3 million barrels of oil equivalent. About 30% of the its reserves are in enhanced oil recovery project areas primarily in Oklahoma and Texas where the company uses carbon dioxide (CO_2) to flood wells to release trapped oil in mature and well-worked fields. Securing CO_2 supply from third party plants is key to its enhanced oil recovery an area of expertise the company has pursued since 2000.

CHAPMAN UNIVERSITY

1 UNIVERSITY DR
ORANGE, CA 928661005
Phone: 714-997-6815
Fax: -
Web: www.chapman.edu

CEO: -
CFO: -
HR: -
FYE: May 31
Type: Private

Chapman University enrolls 7000 students at campuses throughout California as well as in Washington State. From its main campus in Orange California the university offers traditional undergraduate graduate and professional programs at seven colleges and schools. It also confers bachelor and master's degrees and teaching credentials to non-traditional students at its two-dozen satellite campuses. The university offers some 50 undergraduate majors and 40 graduate programs. It has 650 faculty members and a student-to-teacher ratio of 15:1. Chapman University includes Brandman University a distance learning program for some 10000 working adults that operates two dozen locations and offers online courses.

	Annual Growth	05/17	05/18	05/19	05/20	05/21
Sales ($ mil.)	(2.6%)	-	483.1	530.8	461.4	446.9
Net income ($ mil.)	36.5%	-	90.8	70.9	90.7	230.7
Market value ($ mil.)	-	-	-	-	-	-
Employees	-	-	-	-	-	3,300

CHARGERS FOOTBALL COMPANY LLC

4020 Murphy Canyon Rd.
San Diego CA 92123
Phone: 858-874-4500
Fax: 858-292-2760
Web: www.chargers.com

CEO: -
CFO: Jeanne Bonk
HR: -
FYE: December 31
Type: Private

This company energizes football fans in Southern California. Chargers Football owns and operates the San Diego Chargers professional football team a charter member of the American Football League (AFL) and current member of the National Football League (NFL). Barron Hilton (the son of hotelier Conrad Hilton) founded the team in 1959 as the Los Angeles Chargers; it moved to San Diego in 1961 and won the AFL championship two years later. The AFL and NFL merged in 1970. Despite its lengthy history the franchise has made just one trip to the Super Bowl (a loss to the San Francisco 49ers following the 1994 season). Alex Spanos who owns construction firm A. G. Spanos Companies has owned the Bolts since 1984.

CHARLES & COLVARD LTD
NAS: CTHR

170 Southport Drive
Morrisville, NC 27560
Phone: 919 468-0399
Fax: –
Web: www.charlesandcolvard.com

CEO: Don O'Connell
CFO: Clint Pete
HR: –
FYE: June 30
Type: Public

Charles & Colvard hopes that it isn't just some shooting star. The company makes gemstones made from moissanite a diamond substitute created in laboratories. Composed of silicon and carbon moissanite (aka silicon carbide or SiC) is typically found in meteorites. Charles & Colvard makes its gemstones from SiC crystals purchased primarily from Cree Inc. and Swedish company Norstel. Charles & Colvard markets its gemstones through two distributors (Stuller and Rio Grande) and jewelry manufacturers such as K&G Creations Reeves Park and Samuel Aaron International.

	Annual Growth	12/17*	06/18	06/19	06/20	06/21
Sales ($ mil.)	9.8%	27.0	13.2	32.2	29.2	39.2
Net income ($ mil.)	–	(0.5)	(1.3)	2.3	(6.2)	12.8
Market value ($ mil.)	21.9%	40.4	32.0	47.3	21.8	89.1
Employees	(9.5%)	76	60	63	48	51

*Fiscal year change

CHARLES C PARKS CO INC

500 N BELVEDERE DR
GALLATIN, TN 370665408
Phone: 615-452-2406
Fax: –
Web: www.charlescparks.com

CEO: –
CFO: Tom Cripps
HR: –
FYE: April 30
Type: Private

The Charles C. Parks Company is a grocery distributor that primarily supplies convenience stores in more than half a dozen Southern states. It distributes a variety of food items and dry goods as well as beverages cigarettes candy and general merchandise. The company also offers support programs for in-store delis and other quick-service food operations. Carl C. Parks Jr. started the family-run business in 1934.

	Annual Growth	04/09	04/10	04/11	04/12	04/13
Sales ($ mil.)	(2.0%)	–	292.3	264.3	268.3	275.5
Net income ($ mil.)	(32.8%)	–	1.5	0.3	(0.7)	0.4
Market value ($ mil.)	–	–	–	–	–	–
Employees	–	–	–	–	–	145

CHARLES INDUSTRIES LTD.

5600 Apollo Dr.
Rolling Meadows IL 60008-4049
Phone: 847-806-6300
Fax: 847-806-6231
Web: www.charlesindustries.com

CEO: Richard Adam Norwitt
CFO: –
HR: –
FYE: December 31
Type: Private

Charles Industries goes for cash "and" charge. Charles Industries manufactures telecommunications products industrial chargers and charger components such as transformers and capacitors. It also has a joint venture with Telmax Communications to develop high-speed digital subscriber line access systems and maintains alliances with Corning Cable Systems among other manufacturers. Although Charles Industries has sold its dockside marina products division the company still makes marine battery chargers power cables and related products. Founder president and CEO Joseph Charles owns the company.

CHARLES PANKOW BUILDERS LTD.

199 S.Los Robles Ave. Ste. 300
Pasadena CA 91101
Phone: 626-304-1190
Fax: 626-696-1782
Web: www.pankow.com

CEO: Scott Anderson
CFO: –
HR: –
FYE: December 31
Type: Private

Charles Pankow Builders has some pretty concrete ideas on how to build high-rises. The design/build general contractor specializes in quake-resistant concrete frames for structures including department stores hotels condominiums medical facilities and office buildings. The firm is primarily active in California and Hawaii. Affiliate Pankow Special Projects focuses on small-scale projects including renovations interior build-outs and seismic upgrades. Unit Mid-State Precast provides structural and architectural precast concrete components for Pankow-managed projects. Employee-owned Charles Pankow Builders was founded in 1963 by the late Charles Pankow who helped pioneer the design/build delivery system.

CHARLES REGIONAL MEDICAL CENTER FOUNDATION INC.

5 GARRETT AVE
LA PLATA, MD 206465960
Phone: 301-609-4000
Fax: –
Web: www.charlesregional.org

CEO: –
CFO: –
HR: –
FYE: June 30
Type: Private

Civista Health sees a civic vista wherever it looks. The organization brings medical care to the residents of Charles County and surrounding areas in southern Maryland. The regional not-for-profit hospital system includes acute care facility Civista Medical Center Civista Women's Health Center Civista Surgery Center (an outpatient facility) and Civista OB/GYN Associates. Civista Health's services include emergency care rehabilitation surgery and cancer treatment offered by more than 230 physicians. The system also offers a chronic pain program radiology and laboratory services. Nearly half the system's revenue comes from Medicare payments.

	Annual Growth	06/04	06/05	06/06	06/09	06/10
Sales ($ mil.)	(24.6%)	–	–	318.4	0.1	102.7
Net income ($ mil.)	626.4%	–	–	0.0	0.0	1.8
Market value ($ mil.)	–	–	–	–	–	–
Employees	–	–	–	–	–	668

CHARLES RIVER LABORATORIES INTERNATIONAL INC.
NYS: CRL

251 Ballardvale Street
Wilmington, MA 01887
Phone: 781 222-6000
Fax: –
Web: www.criver.com

CEO: James Foster
CFO: David Smith
HR: –
FYE: December 25
Type: Public

Charles River Laboratories International provides early-stage contract research organization (CRO) services to pharmaceutical firms and other manufacturers and institutions. The company provides contract drug discovery services including target identification and toxicology through its Discovery and Safety Assessment segment. Its Research Models and Services (RMS) segment is a leading global provider of research models (lab rats and mice) bred specifically for use in medical testing. The Manufacturing Support unit offers biologics testing and chicken eggs for vaccines. Charles River has operations in over 20 countries but generates around 55% of sales in the US. Charles River began operating in 1947 and went public in 2000.

	Annual Growth	12/17	12/18	12/19	12/20	12/21
Sales ($ mil.)	17.5%	1,857.6	2,266.1	2,621.2	2,923.9	3,540.2
Net income ($ mil.)	33.4%	123.4	226.4	252.0	364.3	391.0
Market value ($ mil.)	35.5%	5,525.0	5,639.6	7,669.4	12,706.3	18,637.2
Employees	14.1%	11,800	14,700	17,100	18,400	20,000

CHARLES RIVER SYSTEMS INC.

7 New England Executive Park
Burlington MA 01803-5010
Phone: 781-238-0099
Fax: 781-238-0088
Web: www.crd.com

CEO: John Plansky
CFO: -
HR: -
FYE: December 31
Type: Private

The streams of global finance come flowing together in Charles River Systems' software and services. The company (which does business as Charles River Development) provides investment software that performs front- and middle-office functions for clients in the financial services industry. Among its customers are banks hedge funds insurance firms mutual funds and wealth managers. Its offerings include software applications for portfolio management investment management decision support compliance monitoring trading and post-trade order management and performance measurement and risk. Charles River also offers professional services such as remote and hosted application management and consulting.

CHARLESTON AREA MEDICAL CENTER, INC.

501 MORRIS ST
CHARLESTON, WV 253011326
Phone: 304-348-5432
Fax: -
Web: www.camc.org

CEO: -
CFO: -
HR: -
FYE: December 31
Type: Private

CAMC Health System is a catalyst for care in Charleston. The health network includes flagship facility Charleston Area Medical Center (CAMC) which is the largest hospital in West Virginia and consists of three campuses with some 840 beds total. The system also includes the CAMC Health Education and Research Institute which coordinates education programs for medical students from West Virginia University. In addition the health system operates smaller rural hospital CAMC Teays Valley and several urgent care and family practice clinics. CAMC Health System operates an online medical information system and physician services company Integrated Health Care Providers.

	Annual Growth	12/13	12/14	12/15	12/16	12/19
Sales ($ mil.)	7.7%	-	877.1	932.6	1,044.6	1,273.4
Net income ($ mil.)	(1.0%)	-	42.9	37.0	(17.5)	40.8
Market value ($ mil.)	-	-	-	-	-	-
Employees	-	-	-	-	-	4,000

CHARLESTON HOSPITAL, INC.

333 LAIDLEY ST
CHARLESTON, WV 253011614
Phone: 304-347-6500
Fax: -
Web: www.stfrancishospital.com

CEO: -
CFO: -
HR: -
FYE: September 30
Type: Private

If you get a little overzealous doing the Charleston while you're in Charleston West Virginia head to Charleston Hospital! Doing business as Saint Francis Hospital the 155-bed facility provides a range of services that include the patching up of twisted ankles inpatient surgery nuclear medicine and skilled nursing. Founded in 1913 Saint Francis Hospital is one-half of Thomas Health System (Thomas Memorial Hospital in South Charleston comprises the other half). Since acquiring Saint Francis Hospital a couple of years ago Thomas Health System has invested about $8 million in St. Francis to provide it with updated equipment and a new pain management center.

	Annual Growth	09/12	09/13	09/14	09/15	09/16
Sales ($ mil.)	(5.2%)	-	105.0	106.3	99.7	89.4
Net income ($ mil.)	-	-	1.7	1.8	(1.3)	(0.3)
Market value ($ mil.)	-	-	-	-	-	-
Employees	-	-	-	-	-	570

CHARLIES HOLDINGS INC

NBB: CHUC

1007 Brioso Drive
Costa Mesa, CA 92627
Phone: 949 531-6855
Fax: -
Web: www.charlieschalkdust.com

CEO: Robert Van Boerum
CFO: Matt Montesano
HR: -
FYE: December 31
Type: Public

True Drinks is focused on providing all-natural healthy alternatives to sodas and other high-calorie beverages. Its flagship product is AquaBall Naturally Flavored Water which is sweetened with all-natural stevia and infused with various vitamins. Marketed directly to children it comes in a variety of fruit flavors and features Disney and Marvel characters on the bottles. True Drinks also makes and markets Bazi All Natural Energy which is designed to boost energy through a combination of 12 vitamins and eight so-called super-fruits (such as jujube goji berry and acai). The products are sold primarily through mass-market retailers across the US.

	Annual Growth	12/16	12/17	12/18	12/19	12/20
Sales ($ mil.)	59.6%	2.6	3.8	1.9	22.7	16.7
Net income ($ mil.)	-	(5.4)	(12.4)	(3.9)	(2.1)	(7.2)
Market value ($ mil.)	(61.5%)	22.8	3.0	0.5	0.3	0.5
Employees	33.9%	14	11	1	59	45

CHART INDUSTRIES INC

NYS: GTLS

3055 Torrington Drive
Ball Ground, GA 30107
Phone: 770 721-8800
Fax: -
Web: www.chartindustries.com

CEO: Jillian Evanko
CFO: Joe Brinkman
HR: -
FYE: December 31
Type: Public

Chart Industries is a leading independent global manufacturer of highly engineered equipment servicing multiple applications in the Energy and Industrial Gas markets. Its unique product portfolio is used in every phase of the liquid gas supply chain including upfront engineering service and repair. Being at the forefront of the clean energy transition Chart is a leading provider of technology equipment and services related to liquefied natural gas hydrogen biogas and CO2 Capture amongst other applications. Chart's customers are mainly large multinational producers and distributors of hydrocarbon and industrial gases. The company generates more than half its sales in the US.

	Annual Growth	12/16	12/17	12/18	12/19	12/20
Sales ($ mil.)	8.2%	859.2	988.8	1,084.3	1,299.1	1,177.1
Net income ($ mil.)	81.7%	28.2	28.2	88.0	46.4	308.1
Market value ($ mil.)	34.5%	1,303.4	1,695.7	2,353.2	2,442.2	4,262.3
Employees	1.6%	4,050	4,424	4,605	5,743	4,318

CHARTER COMMUNICATIONS INC (NEW)

NMS: CHTR

400 Washington Blvd.
Stamford, CT 06902
Phone: 203 905-7801
Fax: -
Web: www.charter.com

CEO: -
CFO: -
HR: -
FYE: December 31
Type: Public

Charter Communications navigated its way to the #2 cable company by making a bigger boat. The cable system operator leaped to the second spot behind Comcast with its acquisitions of Time Warner Cable and Bright House Networks for a total of some $70 billion in 2016. The deal expanded the reach of the company which has taken the name Charter Spectrum. Serving 17 million video subscribers and 19 million broadband customers it offers a full range of services to residential and business subscribers including cable TV high-speed Internet Voice over IP telephone and entertainment packages. Its Charter Business unit provides Internet access data networking phone and wireless backhaul services to about 500000 commercial clients.

	Annual Growth	12/17	12/18	12/19	12/20	12/21
Sales ($ mil.)	5.6%	41,581.0	43,634.0	45,764.0	48,097.0	51,682.0
Net income ($ mil.)	(17.2%)	9,895.0	1,230.0	1,668.0	3,222.0	4,654.0
Market value ($ mil.)	18.0%	58,034.1	49,226.1	83,793.3	114,277.0	112,622.1
Employees	(0.3%)	94,800	98,000	95,100	96,100	93,700

CHARTER MANUFACTURING COMPANY, INC.

12121 CORPORATE PKWY
MEQUON, WI 530923332
Phone: 262-243-4700
Fax: –
Web: www.chartermfg.com

CEO: –
CFO: Todd Endres
HR: –
FYE: December 31
Type: Private

Charter Manufacturing's magna carta calls for it to make steel products. The family-owned company manufactures such steel products as special bar quality (SBQ) bar rod wire and stainless steel rod. The company also supplies precision cold-rolled custom profiles and engineered components including driveline engine and transmission parts for the automotive industry. It operates primarily in the US but also in Europe and Asia through subsidiaries Charter Steel (general steel products) Charter Wire (precision cold-rolled custom profiles flat wire and standard shapes) Charter Dura-Bar (cast iron bar and bronze alloys) and Charter Automotive (engineered components for automotive applications).

	Annual Growth	12/06	12/07	12/08	12/09	12/10
Sales ($ mil.)	(4.8%)	–	–	996.1	517.8	903.3
Net income ($ mil.)	66.8%	–	–	26.8	2.2	74.6
Market value ($ mil.)	–	–	–	–	–	–
Employees	–	–	–	–	–	2,000

CHARTIS INC.

175 Water St.
New York NY 10038
Phone: 212-770-7000
Fax: 512-441-9222
Web: www.texasfolklife.org

CEO: –
CFO: –
HR: –
FYE: December 31
Type: Private

Chartis has mapped out a new course for its slimmed down parent AIG. The company operating as AIG Property Casualty handles all of AIG's property/casualty operations and serves more than 70 million clients in the US and abroad. The company's commercial offerings include general liability workers' compensation specialty insurance and risk management services for businesses. Consumer lines account for 40% of the company's business including home auto travel and health and accident insurance. AIG Property Casualty is comprised of the operations of many subsidiary companies and affiliates that offer industry-specific insurance coverage to international aerospace marine and energy companies.

CHASE CORP.   ASE: CCF

295 University Avenue
Westwood, MA 02090
Phone: 781 332-0700
Fax: –
Web: www.chasecorp.com

CEO: Adam Chase
CFO: Michael Bourque
HR: –
FYE: August 31
Type: Public

Duct tape is great but when the job calls for higher-tech stuff Chase has it. The company has made and sold Chase & Sons branded protective tape and coatings including conducting and insulating products for cable and wire makers for more than 50 years. Chase processes almost any flexible material produced on a roll — films to fabrics. It makes laminates sealants and coatings for pipeline construction electronics as well as printing markets. Chase pipe coating tapes Tapecoat and Royston are sold to oil companies and gas utilities. The company also offers expansion/control joint systems and asphalt additives for roads bridges and stadiums. US customers represent about 84% of revenues.

	Annual Growth	08/17	08/18	08/19	08/20	08/21
Sales ($ mil.)	3.8%	252.6	284.2	281.4	261.2	293.3
Net income ($ mil.)	1.7%	42.0	43.1	32.7	34.2	44.9
Market value ($ mil.)	5.2%	883.4	1,171.1	946.9	921.8	1,081.8
Employees	(1.2%)	695	769	726	619	661

CHASE GENERAL CORPORATION   PINK SHEETS: CSGN

1307 S. 59th St.
St. Joseph MO 64507
Phone: 816-279-1625
Fax: 816-279-1997
Web: www.cherrymash.com

CEO: –
CFO: –
HR: Joe Merklin
FYE: June 30
Type: Public

They not only chase but catch the sweet life at Chase General Corporation. Its subsidiary Dye Candy Company makes and distributes candy and confections. Combining chocolate and chopped peanuts and using crushed maraschino cherries for a smooth fondant center the company's Dye Candy division produces its flagship "Cherry Mash" candy bars. Its Seasonal Candy division makes Chase brand coconut haystacks fudge jelly candies peanut brittle and peanut clusters. Chase General's products are distributed mainly in the Midwest. Associated Wholesale Grocers accounted for 26% of the company's 2008 sales; Wal-Mart accounted for 15%.

CHATHAM LODGING TRUST   NYS: CLDT

222 Lakeview Avenue, Suite 200
West Palm Beach, FL 33401
Phone: 561 802-4477
Fax: –
Web: www.chathamlodgingtrust.com

CEO: Jeffrey Fisher
CFO: Jeremy Wegner
HR: –
FYE: December 31
Type: Public

Self-advised real estate investment trust (REIT) Chatham Lodging acquires upscale extended-stay hotels including Residence Inn by Marriott Homewood Suites by Hilton and Hyatt House locations To a lesser extent the firm will also buy select-service and full-service hotels such as Courtyard by Marriott Hampton Inn and Hilton Garden Inn. Chatham Lodging owns about 40 hotels with more than 6090 rooms across about 15 US states. Through two joint ventures it also has minority interests in more than 45 other hotels with nearly 5950 rooms/suites.

	Annual Growth	12/16	12/17	12/18	12/19	12/20
Sales ($ mil.)	(16.2%)	293.8	298.9	324.2	328.3	144.9
Net income ($ mil.)	–	31.5	29.5	30.6	18.7	(76.0)
Market value ($ mil.)	(14.9%)	965.3	1,069.1	830.5	861.5	507.3
Employees	(15.4%)	45	45	40	39	23

CHATHAM SEARCH INTERNATIONAL INC.

3 Lion Gardiner
Cromwell CT 06416
Phone: 860-635-5538
Fax: 216-929-0042
Web: www.diseco.com

CEO: –
CFO: –
HR: –
FYE: December 31
Type: Private

In need of an executive? Chatham Search International can help. The company is a generalist executive search firm recruiting senior-level and mid-level management personnel for companies in a variety of industries and across the full spectrum of functional disciplines. The firm operates a division dedicated to recruiting executives from diverse social and cultural backgrounds. Additionally Chatham provides strategic human resources coaching and consulting.

CHATHAM UNIVERSITY

WOODLAND RD
PITTSBURGH, PA 15232
Phone: 412-365-1100
Fax: –
Web: www.chatham.edu

CEO: –
CFO: –
HR: –
FYE: June 30
Type: Private

Men need not apply to Chatham University at least not for its undergraduate program. The university consists of Chatham College for Women which offers bachelor's degrees to women only; Chatham College for Graduate Studies which offers graduate degrees and teaching certificates to both men and women; and Chatham College for Continuing and Professional Studies its co-educational online school. Undergraduate students can choose from more than 30 majors in such areas as the sciences humanities arts environmental studies and pre-professional studies. Chatham has an enrollment of more than 2000 students. The private liberal arts school was founded in 1869 as Pennsylvania Female College.

	Annual Growth	06/13	06/14	06/15	06/16	06/17
Sales ($ mil.)	(8.9%)	–	80.3	59.8	52.9	60.8
Net income ($ mil.)	–	–	27.4	0.1	(6.3)	(2.5)
Market value ($ mil.)	–	–	–	–	–	–
Employees						300

CHATTANOOGA BAKERY INC.

900 Manufacturers Rd.
Chattanooga TN 37405
Phone: 423-267-3351
Fax: 423-266-2169
Web: www.moonpie.com

CEO: –
CFO: –
HR: Terry Humphrey
FYE: December 31
Type: Private

Despite the name of its best-selling product Chattanooga Bakery is no pie-in-the-sky outfit. It is the one and only maker of the MoonPie a four-inch-round sandwich cookie made of marshmallow fluff layered between graham crackers and coated with chocolate. In addition to the original iteration MoonPies are available in double-decker and mini versions — and with banana or vanilla coating. Its most recent variation is the crispy-shelled MoonPie Crunch which comes with mint or peanut butter filling. The company also makes pecan and coconut pie snacks under the LookOut! name. Chattanooga's treats are sold nationwide at food retailers mass merchandisers convenience stores and through vending machines.

CHATTEM INC.

1715 W. 38th St.
Chattanooga TN 37409
Phone: 423-821-4571
Fax: 423-821-0395
Web: www.chattem.com

CEO: Zan Guerry
CFO: Robert B Long
HR: Angela Acuff
FYE: November 30
Type: Subsidiary

If it's a well known cream oil paste pill or powder it's likely that Chattem owns that brand name. The Sanofi subsidiary markets some two-dozen over-the-counter branded personal care products and dietary supplements including skin care and pain treatments such as Aspercreme Cortizone-10 Icy Hot muscle pain reliever and Pamprin menstrual symptom reliever. The company also makes the Unisom sleep aid medicated powder Gold Bond Bullfrog sunscreen Mudd clay-based facial masks and Selsun Blue dandruff shampoo. Chattem sells its products to wholesalers and retail merchandisers.

CHCA CONROE, L.P.

504 MEDICAL CENTER BLVD
CONROE, TX 773042808
Phone: 936-539-1111
Fax: –
Web: www.hcahoustonhealthcare.com

CEO: Matt Davis
CFO: Tom Holt
HR: James Fitch
FYE: December 31
Type: Private

CHCA Conroe operates its health care business under the Conroe Regional Medical Center name. Either way the hospital is an acute care 360-bed facility serving the residents of Montgomery County Texas and surrounding areas. The medical center's Heart and Vascular Institute includes a cardiac care unit and catheterization laboratory. Conroe Regional Medical Center also provides wound cancer diabetes diagnostic sleep disorder rehabilitation trauma and women's and children's care. Hospital operator HCA owns and manages the health care facility.

	Annual Growth	12/12	12/13	12/14	12/15	12/16
Sales ($ mil.)	0.0%	–	–	224.1	233.7	224.3
Net income ($ mil.)	–	–	–	17.2	9.6	(6.6)
Market value ($ mil.)	–	–	–	–	–	–
Employees						1,200

CHECKPOINT SYSTEMS INC

NYS: CKP

101 Wolf Drive, P.O. Box 188
Thorofare, NJ 08086
Phone: 856 848-1800
Fax: –
Web: www.checkpointsystems.com

CEO: George Babich Jr
CFO: James M Lucania
HR: –
FYE: December 28
Type: Public

Checkpoint Systems wants to keep shoplifters in check. The company makes electronic article surveillance systems (EAS) radio frequency identification (RFID) tags and electronic security devices (using electromagnetic technology) such as intrusion alarms digital video recorders and electronic access control systems used by retailers that have included Barnes & Noble Sears Target and Walgreen. Its EAS units employ paper-thin disposable circuit tags attached to merchandise that are disarmed at checkout; if not disarmed the tags trigger electronic sensors when the customer tries to leave. The company operates in some 30 countries worldwide; about 60% of its sales come from outside the Western Hemisphere.

	Annual Growth	12/10	12/11	12/12	12/13	12/14
Sales ($ mil.)	(5.6%)	834.5	865.3	690.8	689.7	662.0
Net income ($ mil.)	(20.5%)	27.4	(66.6)	(145.9)	(18.9)	11.0
Market value ($ mil.)	(9.4%)	869.5	469.9	436.4	637.9	586.5
Employees	(4.2%)	5,814	6,565	5,132	4,710	4,894

CHEESECAKE FACTORY INC. (THE)

NMS: CAKE

26901 Malibu Hills Road
Calabasas Hills, CA 91301
Phone: 818 871-3000
Fax: –
Web: www.thecheesecakefactory.com

CEO: David Overton
CFO: Matthew Clark
HR: –
FYE: December 29
Type: Public

The Cheesecake Factory's restaurants offer more than 250 menu items ranging from sandwiches and salads to steaks and seafood. The highlight of the menu of course is cheesecake which comes in about 50 varieties. In addition to its flagship locations the company operates Grand Lux Cafes and a few other Asian-themed restaurants. The Cheesecake Factory also sells desserts to foodservice operators retailers and distributors.

	Annual Growth	01/17	01/18	01/19*	12/19	12/20
Sales ($ mil.)	(4.5%)	2,275.7	2,260.5	2,332.3	2,482.7	1,983.2
Net income ($ mil.)	–	139.5	157.4	99.0	127.3	(253.4)
Market value ($ mil.)	(14.6%)	2,711.1	2,249.5	1,984.9	1,772.7	1,687.0
Employees	3.1%	38,800	39,100	38,700	46,250	42,500

*Fiscal year change

CHEFS INTERNATIONAL INC.

62 Broadway
Point Pleasant Beach NJ 08742
Phone: 732-295-0350
Fax: 732-295-4514

CEO: –
CFO: Martin W Fletcher
HR: –
FYE: January 31
Type: Private

These chefs are busy boiling seafood. Chefs International operates about a dozen casual dining restaurants in New Jersey and Florida mostly doing business under the Lobster Shanty name such as Point Pleasant Lobster Shanty Toms River Lobster Shanty and its flagship Jack Baker's Lobster Shanty. Other locations include Jack Baker's Wharfside & Patio Bar and The Sunset Ballroom event and banquet hall. The restaurants serve a variety of seafood dishes in a casual setting. Jack Baker a New Jersey fisherman opened his first Jack Baker's Lobster Shanty in 1979. Chairman Robert Lombardi and his family control the company.

CHELSEA & SCOTT LTD.

75 Albrecht Dr.
Lake Bluff IL 60044
Phone: 847-615-2110
Fax: 847-615-2290
Web: www.onestepahead.com

CEO: –
CFO: –
HR: –
FYE: December 31
Type: Private

Chelsea & Scott wants children to grow up with its products. Through its One Step Ahead catalog and website the company sells apparel home furnishings feeding and safety products toys and travel accessories for newborns to children under 3. It also provides educational toys and developmental products for children ages 3 to 8 through its Leaps and Bounds catalog and website. Chelsea & Scott offers such brands as ALEX Infantino Lamaze and Manhattan Group as well as its own One Step Ahead branded lines. The company started doing business in 1989 when founders Karen and Ian Scott decided they wanted to offer an easier way for parents to find quality children's products.

CHEFS' WAREHOUSE INC (THE) NMS: CHEF

100 East Ridge Road
Ridgefield, CT 06877
Phone: 203 894-1345
Fax: –
Web: www.chefswarehouse.com

CEO: Christopher Pappas
CFO: James Leddy
HR: –
FYE: December 24
Type: Public

A distributor of specialty food products Chefs' Warehouse sells such gourmet food items as artisan charcuterie specialty cheeses hormone-free protein truffles caviar and chocolates as well as basic food ingredients like cooking oils flour butter milk and eggs. The company provides more than 55000 items sourced from 2200 suppliers to a core customer base comprising chefs from independent restaurants fine dining establishments culinary schools hotels and country clubs. Its Allen Brothers subsidiary sells prime cuts direct to consumers via mail and online. Chefs' Warehouse typically focuses on culinary hotbeds such as New York City San Francisco Los Angeles and Washington DC. Tracing its roots back to 1985 Chefs' Warehouse went public in 2011.

	Annual Growth	12/17	12/18	12/19	12/20	12/21
Sales ($ mil.)	7.6%	1,301.5	1,444.6	1,591.8	1,111.6	1,745.8
Net income ($ mil.)	–	14.4	20.4	24.2	(82.9)	(4.9)
Market value ($ mil.)	12.3%	776.7	1,187.0	1,438.6	905.1	1,234.0
Employees	8.0%	1,994	2,316	2,447	2,221	2,712

CHELSEA PROPERTY GROUP INC.

105 Eisenhower Pkwy.
Roseland NJ 07068
Phone: 973-228-6111
Fax: 973-228-3891
Web: www.premiumoutlets.com

CEO: –
CFO: –
HR: –
FYE: December 31
Type: Subsidiary

Chelsea Property Group (also known as Premium Outlets) a subsidiary of retail giant Simon Property Group owns develops leases and manages some 50 factory outlet shopping centers in the US and abroad. The properties typically are located near metropolitan areas and tourist destinations such as Disney World in Orlando Florida Branson Missouri and California's Monterey Peninsula. The shopping centers feature some 750 tenants including such high-end fashion names as Gucci Versace Coach and Michael Kors. Most of its centers operate under the Premium Outlet name. Through joint ventures Chelsea Property also operates seven outlet malls in Japan one in Korea and one in Mexico.

CHEGG INC NYS: CHGG

3990 Freedom Circle
Santa Clara, CA 95054
Phone: 408 855-5700
Fax: –
Web: www.chegg.com

CEO: Daniel Rosensweig
CFO: Andrew Brown
HR: –
FYE: December 31
Type: Public

Chegg offers products and services that help students improve their outcomes throughout their educational journey. The company operates an online library that rents out textbooks to cash-strapped students; it has e-textbook titles from major publishers such as Cengage Learning Pearson Sage Publications McGraw Hill and John Wiley & Sons Inc. In addition to approximately 8.2 million individuals who paid for its products and services the company's primary Chegg Services include Chegg Study Chegg Writing Chegg Math Solver Chegg Study Pack Thinkful and Mathway Formed in 2005 Chegg went public in 2013.

	Annual Growth	12/16	12/17	12/18	12/19	12/20
Sales ($ mil.)	26.2%	254.1	255.1	321.1	410.9	644.3
Net income ($ mil.)	–	(42.2)	(20.3)	(14.9)	(9.6)	(6.2)
Market value ($ mil.)	87.0%	954.6	2,110.9	3,675.9	4,903.4	11,683.6
Employees	26.2%	766	893	1,087	1,401	1,941

CHEMED CORP NYS: CHE

255 E. Fifth Street, Suite 2600
Cincinnati, OH 45202
Phone: 513 762-6690
Fax: –
Web: www.chemed.com

CEO: Kevin McNamara
CFO: David Williams
HR: –
FYE: December 31
Type: Public

Operating through two major subsidiaries Chemed offers hospice care to terminally ill patients through its VITAS Healthcare subsidiary which operates in about 15 US states including California Connecticut Georgia and Florida. VITAS employs doctors nurses and other professionals to provide at-home and inpatient services in care facilities. Chemed's better-known Roto-Rooter subsidiary was founded in 1935 and offers plumbing and drain-cleaning services for residential and commercial customers through company-owned contractor-operated and franchised locations. Roto-Rooter system offers services to more than 90% of the US population and approximately 40% of the Canadian population. The vast majority of its revenues are generated from business within the US.

	Annual Growth	12/16	12/17	12/18	12/19	12/20
Sales ($ mil.)	7.2%	1,576.9	1,666.7	1,782.6	1,938.6	2,079.6
Net income ($ mil.)	30.9%	108.7	98.2	205.5	219.9	319.5
Market value ($ mil.)	35.0%	2,551.7	3,865.7	4,506.2	6,987.3	8,472.3
Employees	1.6%	14,613	14,813	15,707	16,641	15,544

CHEMOCENTRYX, INC.

NMS: CCXI

835 Industrial Road
San Carlos, CA 94070
Phone: 650 210-2900
Fax: 650 210-2910
Web: www.chemocentryx.com

CEO: Thomas Schall
CFO: Susan Kanaya
HR: -
FYE: December 31
Type: Public

Biopharmaceutical ChemoCentryx is developing drugs that target inflammatory disorders autoimmune diseases and cancer. It focuses on orally administered drugs that block specific chemoattractant receptors. Its lead candidates have an initial focus on kidney disease. Avacopan is being studied for its effectiveness in treating a number of orphan diseases while CCX140 is in development for the treatment of chronic and orphan kidney diseases. ChemoCentryx also has candidates in early stage development.

	Annual Growth	12/16	12/17	12/18	12/19	12/20
Sales ($ mil.)	52.7%	11.9	82.5	42.9	36.1	64.9
Net income ($ mil.)	-	(40.0)	17.9	(38.0)	(55.5)	(55.4)
Market value ($ mil.)	70.1%	513.9	413.2	757.7	2,746.8	4,300.5
Employees	21.0%	62	66	76	82	133

CHEMTURA CORP

NYS: CHMT

1818 Market Street, Suite 3700
Philadelphia, PA 19103
Phone: 203 573-2000
Fax: -
Web: www.chemtura.com

CEO: -
CFO: -
HR: -
FYE: December 31
Type: Public

Chemtura aspires to be the future of chemicals-making. The company ranks among the top specialty chemical companies in the US along with the likes of Ecolab and Hexion and among the leading plastics additives maker globally. It makes chemical products that makes other products more durable safer cleaner and more efficient. Major industries served include transportation energy electronics and agriculture. Aside from plastic additives Chemtura holds niche-leading positions in petroleum additives flame retardants and swimming pool chemicals. Its other products include urethanes. In 2016 the company agreed to be acquired by LANXESS in a $2.5 billion deal.

	Annual Growth	12/11	12/12	12/13	12/14	12/15
Sales ($ mil.)	(12.9%)	3,025.0	2,629.0	2,231.0	2,190.0	1,745.0
Net income ($ mil.)	3.4%	119.0	101.0	(177.0)	763.0	136.0
Market value ($ mil.)	24.5%	762.0	1,428.7	1,876.2	1,661.9	1,832.5
Employees	(13.7%)	4,500	4,600	3,300	2,700	2,500

CHEMUNG FINANCIAL CORP.

NMS: CHMG

One Chemung Canal Plaza
Elmira, NY 14901
Phone: 607 737-3711
Fax: -
Web: www.chemungcanal.com

CEO: Anders Tomson
CFO: Karl Krebs
HR: -
FYE: December 31
Type: Public

Everybody Chemung Financial Tonight probably wouldn't make much of a pop record. The firm is parent to Chemung Canal Trust Company which provides bank and trust services from about 30 offices in upstate New York. The trust company offers such deposit services as savings checking and money market accounts; IRAs; and CDs. It also offers credit cards and originates a variety of loans including personal small business and residential mortgage loans. Other services include retirement and estate planning and tax services. Another Chemung Financial subsidiary CFS Group offers mutual funds discount brokerage and other financial services.

	Annual Growth	12/16	12/17	12/18	12/19	12/20
Assets ($ mil.)	8.3%	1,657.2	1,707.6	1,755.3	1,787.8	2,279.5
Net income ($ mil.)	17.7%	10.0	7.4	19.6	15.6	19.3
Market value ($ mil.)	(1.7%)	169.7	224.5	192.8	198.4	158.5
Employees	(1.9%)	368	371	374	362	341

CHENEGA CORPORATION

3000 C ST STE 301
ANCHORAGE, AK 995033975
Phone: 907-277-5706
Fax: -
Web: www.chenega.com

CEO: Charles Totemoff
CFO: -
HR: Jeff Doty
FYE: September 30
Type: Private

An Alaska Native Corporation Chenega Corporation has gone from landowner to business titan. Representing the Chenega people residing in the central Alaskan Prince William Sound region it operates mostly through its subsidiaries. Chenega Integrated Systems and Chenega Technology Services offer information technology security training manufacturing research and development network engineering and military operation support services. Chenega Corporation's clients have included the Department of Defense Department of Homeland Security and EPA.

	Annual Growth	09/16	09/17	09/18	09/19	09/20
Sales ($ mil.)	2.7%	-	875.9	829.9	871.0	948.6
Net income ($ mil.)	16.7%	-	12.2	19.3	19.6	19.4
Market value ($ mil.)	-	-	-	-	-	-
Employees	-	-	-	-	-	4,500

CHENIERE ENERGY INC.

ASE: LNG

700 Milam Street, Suite 1900
Houston, TX 77002
Phone: 713 375-5000
Fax: -
Web: www.cheniere.com

CEO: Jack Fusco
CFO: Zach Davis
HR: -
FYE: December 31
Type: Public

Cheniere Energy is a producer of liquefied natural gas (LNG) in the US exporting LNG to customers in over 30 nations around the world. The company purchases natural gas and processes it into LNG and offers customers the option to load the LNG onto their vessels at its terminals or it delivers the LNG to regasification facilities around the world. The company has two terminals on the US Gulf Coast in various stages of development: its Sabine Pass liquefaction project in southwest Louisiana and its Corpus Christi liquefaction facility in South Texas. Over 70% of revenue come from outside the US. Cheniere also has pipeline assets and operates an LNG and natural gas marketing business.

	Annual Growth	12/16	12/17	12/18	12/19	12/20
Sales ($ mil.)	64.3%	1,283.2	5,601.0	7,987.0	9,730.0	9,358.0
Net income ($ mil.)	-	(610.0)	(393.0)	471.0	648.0	(85.0)
Market value ($ mil.)	9.7%	10,452.8	13,583.8	14,933.6	15,408.0	15,145.6
Employees	13.6%	911	1,230	1,372	1,530	1,519

CHENIERE ENERGY PARTNERS L P

ASE: CQP

700 Milam Street, Suite 1900
Houston, TX 77002
Phone: 713 375-5000
Fax: -
Web: www.cheniere.com

CEO: Jack Fusco
CFO: Zach Davis
HR: -
FYE: December 31
Type: Public

Cheniere Energy Partners a subsidiary of Cheniere Energy plans to be North America's biggest gas station — natural gas that is. The Sabine Pass LNG (liquefied natural gas) receiving terminal is one of North America's largest: It boasts 4 billion cu. ft. per day of regasification capacity as well as 17 billion cu. ft. of LNG storage capacity. All of the Sabine Pass LNG receiving terminal's capacity has already been contracted to Total Gas and Power North America Chevron and Cheniere Energy's subsidiary Cheniere Marketing.

	Annual Growth	12/16	12/17	12/18	12/19	12/20
Sales ($ mil.)	53.9%	1,100.2	4,304.0	6,426.0	6,838.0	6,167.0
Net income ($ mil.)	-	(171.2)	490.0	1,274.0	1,175.0	1,183.0
Market value ($ mil.)	5.2%	14,234.2	14,639.2	17,829.8	19,662.2	17,410.0
Employees	-	-	-	-	-	-

CHENIERE ENERGY PARTNERS LP HOLDINGS LLC   ASE: CQH

700 Milam Street, Suite 1900
Houston, TX 77002
Phone: 713 375-5000
Fax: –
Web: www.cheniere.com

CEO: Jack A Fusco
CFO: Michael J Wortley
HR: –
FYE: December 31
Type: Public

Three's not a crowd for Cheniere Energy Partners LP Holdings. The LLC was formed by Cheniere Energy Partners to own a 55.9% stake in Cheniere Energy Partners which operates the Sabine Pass LNG terminal in Louisiana. (Cheniere Energy Partners is itself an offshoot of Cheniere Energy.) By creating a stock-owning holding company Cheniere Energy Partners reduces its risk to early-stage development projects and marketing activities. Shareholders of Cheniere Energy Partners LP Holdings are also entitled to quarterly cash dividends. Cheniere Energy Partners LP Holdings completed an IPO in 2013 and raised $720 million which it will use to pay down debt and make a distribution to Cheniere Energy.

	Annual Growth	12/12	12/13	12/14	12/15	12/16
Sales ($ mil.)	(47.3%)	264.5	–	20.3	20.3	20.3
Net income ($ mil.)	–	(150.1)	(0.1)	18.1	18.2	17.8
Market value ($ mil.)	6.1%	–	4,344.4	5,220.2	4,031.6	5,183.1
Employees	–	–	–	–	–	–

CHEP INTERNATIONAL INC.

8517 S. Park Cir.
Orlando FL 32819-9040
Phone: 407-370-2437
Fax: 407-363-5354
Web: www.chep.com

CEO: Graham Chipchase
CFO: Scott Spivey
HR: –
FYE: June 30
Type: Subsidiary

CHEP knows it's sink or swim in the pallet and plastic container pooling services business. The company a unit of Australia-based Brambles manages the movement of more than 300 million pallets and containers used by companies in the automotive consumer goods food and beverage home improvement petrochemical and raw materials industries. It collects cleans and refurbishes the pallets and containers which are used throughout the supply chain. The company's 500000-plus customers have included industry leaders such as General Motors Kraft and Procter & Gamble. CHEP operates from a network of more than 500 service facilities in about 45 countries worldwide.

CHERRY BEKAERT LLP

200 S 10TH ST STE 900
RICHMOND, VA 232194064
Phone: 804-673-5700
Fax: –
Web: www.artisantalent.com

CEO: Michelle Thompson
CFO: Matthew Grossman
HR: –
FYE: April 30
Type: Private

Life's a bowl of accounting and consulting services at Cherry Bekaert (formerly Cherry Bekaert & Holland). The firm provides financial and management consulting services in the southeastern US. It specializes in serving such sectors as government financial services not-for-profit higher education healthcare retail and manufacturing. In addition to tax and accounting services Cherry Bekaert provides business valuations litigation support M&A advisory and other services. It also has a wealth management arm for well-to-do families. The firm enjoys an international reach through its affiliation with Baker Tilly International.

	Annual Growth	04/05	04/06	04/07	04/10	04/11
Sales ($ mil.)	(52.2%)	–	–	2,130.8	98.4	111.2
Net income ($ mil.)	530.2%	–	–	0.0	24.0	25.8
Market value ($ mil.)	–	–	–	–	–	–
Employees	–	–	–	–	–	850

CHERRY CENTRAL COOPERATIVE, INC.

1771 N US HIGHWAY 31 S
TRAVERSE CITY, MI 496858748
Phone: 231-946-1860
Fax: –
Web: www.cherrycentral.com

CEO: Melanie Laperriere
CFO: Catherine Collins
HR: –
FYE: April 30
Type: Private

Serving as a central hub for cherry pickers' crops Cherry Central Cooperative is a fruit marketing co-operative that consists of more than a dozen member cooperatives representing hundreds of growers in Michigan New York Utah Washington Wisconsin and Ontario. It processes cherries cranberries apples and other fruit products including the Indian Summer brand of apple and cherry juices and ciders. Its Oceana Foods unit makes dried fruit sold under the Traverse Bay label while its Dunkley International subsidiary makes fruit-processing equipment. Cherry Central's products are sold to retail foodservice and ingredient customers. The cooperative was formed in 1973.

	Annual Growth	04/13	04/14	04/15	04/16	04/17
Sales ($ mil.)	(3.2%)	–	–	167.7	150.6	157.2
Net income ($ mil.)	–	–	–	0.1	(0.8)	(0.2)
Market value ($ mil.)	–	–	–	–	–	–
Employees	–	–	–	–	–	308

CHERRY HILL MORTGAGE INVESTMENT CORP   NYS: CHMI

1451 Route 34, Suite 303
Farmingdale, NJ 07727
Phone: 877 870-7005
Fax: –
Web: www.chmireit.com

CEO: Jeffrey Lown
CFO: Michael Hutchby
HR: –
FYE: December 31
Type: Public

Cherry Hill Mortgage Investment is interested in real estate assets that lie far beyond Cherry Hill New Jersey. Formed in 2012 Cherry Hill is a real estate investment trust or REIT that looks to acquire invest in and manage real estate assets across the US. It plans to build a portfolio that comprises excess mortgage servicing rights (excess MSRs are servicing fees that exceed basic MSR servicing fees) agency residential mortgage-backed securities (secured by the government agencies like Fannie Mae and Freddie Mac) and other residential mortgage assets. The REIT is externally managed by Cherry Hill Mortgage Management an affiliate of Freedom Mortgage. It went public in 2013.

	Annual Growth	12/16	12/17	12/18	12/19	12/20
Sales ($ mil.)	–	42.3	82.4	94.2	17.8	(18.4)
Net income ($ mil.)	–	24.8	47.4	37.3	(42.8)	(52.2)
Market value ($ mil.)	(15.8%)	310.6	307.2	299.5	249.2	156.1
Employees	39.2%	4	4	4	5	15

CHESAPEAKE ENERGY CORP.   NMS: CHK

6100 North Western Avenue
Oklahoma City, OK 73118
Phone: 405 848-8000
Fax: –
Web: www.chk.com

CEO: Domenic Dell'osso
CFO: Mohit Singh
HR: –
FYE: December 31
Type: Public

Chesapeake Energy is an independent exploration and production company with oil and gas assets across the US. The company owns interests in approximately 7400 oil and natural gas wells. Chesapeake has exploration and production assets in Marcellus Eagle Ford Brazos Valley Powder River Basin and Haynesville shale plays. Its customer Valero Energy Corporation constitutes nearly 20% of the company's total revenues.

	Annual Growth	12/16	12/17	12/18	12/19	12/20
Sales ($ mil.)	(9.4%)	7,872.0	9,496.0	10,231.0	8,595.0	5,296.0
Net income ($ mil.)	–	(4,401.0)	949.0	873.0	(308.0)	(9,734.0)
Market value ($ mil.)	–	–	–	–	–	–
Employees	(20.8%)	3,300	3,200	2,350	2,300	1,300

CHESAPEAKE LODGING TRUST
NYS: CHSP

4300 Wilson Boulevard, Suite 625
Arlington, VA 22203
Phone: 571 349-9450
Fax: –
Web: www.chesapeakelodgingtrust.com

CEO: –
CFO: –
HR: –
FYE: December 31
Type: Public

As a real estate investment trust (REIT) focused on the hospitality industry Chesapeake Lodging Trust targets upper-upscale hotels located in major US business centers and popular convention markets. The company owns 22 hotels with a total of nearly 6700 rooms in nine US states and Washington DC. Southern California is a major market for the company. Chesapeake Lodging's properties operate under several major brands including Hyatt Marriott and W Hotels. In evaluating properties for purchase the company considers rebranding and renovation options. Formed in mid-2009 Chesapeake Lodging Trust went public in 2010.

	Annual Growth	12/13	12/14	12/15	12/16	12/17
Sales ($ mil.)	9.2%	420.2	478.0	582.6	619.7	598.3
Net income ($ mil.)	13.9%	45.3	61.0	67.5	76.7	76.2
Market value ($ mil.)	1.7%	1,515.9	2,230.4	1,508.1	1,550.1	1,623.8
Employees	1.9%	13	13	12	15	14

CHESAPEAKE OILFIELD SERVICES INC.

6100 N. Western Ave.
Oklahoma City OK 73118
Phone: 405-848-8000
Fax: 732-393-6025
Web: www.blackstratus.com

CEO: –
CFO: –
HR: –
FYE: December 31
Type: Private

"Divide and conquer" might be the strategy behind Chesapeake Oilfield Services a company spun off from Chesapeake Energy one of the top onshore energy companies in the US. Chesapeake Energy reorganized six of its oilfield services subsidiaries into Chesapeake Oilfield Services to create a new publicly traded entity that offers drilling hydraulic fracturing and trucking services as well as renting tools and manufacturing natural gas compressor equipment. With about 110 land drilling rigs Chesapeake Oilfield Services has the fourth-largest rig fleet in the US. The company was formed in October 2011 and filed to go public in April 2012 in an initial public offering seeking up to $862.5 million.

CHESAPEAKE UTILITIES CORP.
NYS: CPK

909 Silver Lake Boulevard
Dover, DE 19904
Phone: 302 734-6799
Fax: –
Web: www.chpk.com

CEO: Jeffry Householder
CFO: Beth W Cooper
HR: –
FYE: December 31
Type: Public

Chesapeake Utilities (Chesapeake) is an energy delivery company engaged in the distribution of natural gas electricity and propane; the transmission of natural gas; the generation of electricity and steam and in providing related services to its customers. Chesapeake's regulated natural gas distribution divisions serve customers in central and southern Delaware Maryland's eastern shore and Florida. Another unit distributes electricity to nearly 32325 customers in northeast and northwest Florida. On the unregulated side the company also serves retail propane customers in Mid-Atlantic region and Florida. In addition Chesapeake has an interstate gas pipeline.

	Annual Growth	12/16	12/17	12/18	12/19	12/20
Sales ($ mil.)	(0.5%)	498.9	617.6	717.5	479.6	488.2
Net income ($ mil.)	12.5%	44.7	58.1	56.6	65.2	71.5
Market value ($ mil.)	12.8%	1,169.1	1,371.6	1,419.6	1,673.4	1,889.5
Employees	1.2%	903	945	983	955	947

CHEVIOT FINANCIAL CORP
NAS: CHEV

3723 Glenmore Avenue
Cincinnati, OH 45211
Phone: 513 661-0457
Fax: –
Web: www.cheviotsavings.com

CEO: –
CFO: –
HR: –
FYE: December 31
Type: Public

Cheviot Financial happily puts the "buck" in "Buckeye State." It is the holding company for Cheviot Savings Bank which operates about a dozen branches in and around Cincinnati. The community-oriented thrift offers traditional products such as checking and savings accounts CDs IRAs and credit cards. Its lending activities primarily consist of residential mortgages; construction consumer and commercial loans round out its loan book. Investment services are offered through through third-party Souders Financial. The bank nearly doubled in size when it acquired First Franklin Corporation in 2011. Formerly 61%-owned by Cheviot Mutual Cheviot Financial converted to a 100% publicly traded stock company in 2012.

	Annual Growth	12/10	12/11	12/12	12/13	12/14
Assets ($ mil.)	12.4%	358.1	616.3	632.0	587.1	571.2
Net income ($ mil.)	11.7%	2.0	3.4	3.4	1.4	3.1
Market value ($ mil.)	12.4%	59.8	50.0	62.5	69.2	95.5
Employees	(2.6%)	–	120	124	111	111

CHEVRON CORPORATION
NYS: CVX

6001 Bollinger Canyon Road
San Ramon, CA 94583-2324
Phone: 925 842-1000
Fax: 925 894-6017
Web: www.chevron.com

CEO: Michael Wirth
CFO: Pierre Breber
HR: –
FYE: December 31
Type: Public

Chevron has earned its stripes as the #2 integrated oil company in the US behind Exxon Mobil. Its global operations explore for and produce oil and oil equivalents refines them into various fuels and other end products and sells them through gas stations airport fuel depots and industrial channels. Chevron boasts approximately 11.4 billion barrels of proved reserves produces about 3.1 million barrels of oil per day and has refining capacity for nearly 1.7million barrels per day. The company sells refined products branded under the Chevron Texaco and Caltex names through approximately 7900 gas stations in the US and around 5100 outside the US.

	Annual Growth	12/16	12/17	12/18	12/19	12/20
Sales ($ mil.)	(4.6%)	114,472.0	141,722.0	166,339.0	146,516.0	94,692.0
Net income ($ mil.)	–	(497.0)	9,195.0	14,824.0	2,924.0	(5,543.0)
Market value ($ mil.)	(8.0%)	226,594.4	241,014.1	209,441.0	232,004.2	162,582.0
Employees	(3.6%)	55,200	51,900	48,600	48,200	47,736

CHEVRON PHILLIPS CHEMICAL COMPANY LLC

10001 SIX PINES DR
THE WOODLANDS, TX 773801498
Phone: 832-813-4100
Fax: –
Web: www.cpchem.com

CEO: Mark Lashier
CFO: Carolyn Burke
HR: –
FYE: December 31
Type: Private

Among the world's largest petrochemical firms Chevron Phillips Chemical (CPChem) produces ethylene propylene polyethylene and polypropylene — sometimes used as building blocks for the company's other products such as pipes and food containers. CPChem also produces aromatics such as benzene and styrene specialty chemicals such as acetylene black (a form of carbon black) and mining chemicals. Chevron Phillips Chemical Company LP is CPChem's wholly-owned primary US operating subsidiary. CPChem is 50% owned by Chevron U.S.A. Inc. an indirect wholly-owned subsidiary of Chevron Corporation and 50% by wholly-owned subsidiaries of Phillips 66.

	Annual Growth	12/12	12/13	12/14	12/15	12/16
Sales ($ mil.)	(21.3%)	–	–	14,148.0	9,859.0	8,769.0
Net income ($ mil.)	(28.4%)	–	–	3,288.0	2,651.0	1,687.0
Market value ($ mil.)	–	–	–	–	–	–
Employees	–	–	–	–	–	6,472

CHEVRON PIPE LINE COMPANY

1500 LOUISIANA ST
HOUSTON, TX 770027308
Phone: 877-596-2800
Fax: –
Web: www.chevron.com/operations/transportation/chevron-pipe-l

CEO: –
CFO: –
HR: –
FYE: December 31
Type: Private

Many US users of oil petrochemicals and natural gas rely on Chevron Pipe Line Company for delivery of these products. The pipeline company a subsidiary of oil giant Chevron transports crude oil refined petroleum products liquefied petroleum gas natural gas and chemicals. Through about 4100 miles of pipeline the company moves more than 1.3 million barrels of crude and other products across the US every day. Chevron Pipe Line also supplies other Chevron businesses with the supplies they need to run their operations efficiently. The company also makes use of joint ventures and third parties to move additional volumes.

	Annual Growth	12/13	12/14	12/15	12/16	12/17
Sales ($ mil.)	(29.6%)	–	–	–	122.4	86.1
Net income ($ mil.)	20.8%	–	–	–	74.9	90.5
Market value ($ mil.)	–	–	–	–	–	–
Employees		–	–	–	–	715

CHEVYS RESTAURANTS LLC

5660 Katella Ave.
Cypress CA 90630
Phone: 510-475-5236
Fax: 510-475-9828
Web: www.chevys.com

CEO: –
CFO: Terrie Robinson
HR: –
FYE: December 31
Type: Subsidiary

Fresh Mexican food is the driving force behind this chain. Chevys Restaurants operates and franchises nearly 100 full-service Mexican eateries in about 15 states under the Chevys Fresh Mex banner. The restaurants feature mesquite-grilled beef chicken and vegetarian fajitas as well as such traditional favorites as enchiladas tacos and burritos. The chain also serves a selection of margaritas and tequilas for happy hour celebrations. Nearly 70 locations are company-owned while the rest are franchised. Chevys was formed in 1986 by Warren Simmons Sr. and his son. It is owned by leading Mexican restaurant operator Real Mex Restaurants.

CHICAGO AIRPORT SYSTEM

Chicago Department of Aviation 10510 W. Zemke Rd.
Chicago IL 60666
Phone: 773-686-3700
Fax: 773-686-3573
Web: www.flychicago.com

CEO: –
CFO: –
HR: –
FYE: December 31
Type: Government-owned

Chicago Airport System manages airports in the Windy City including one of the busiest on the planet — O'Hare International. Handling more than 76 million travelers a year O'Hare serves as a hub for such airlines as United and American. The Chicago Airport System also operates Midway Airport which was the world's busiest before the introduction of large jets that needed longer runways; it still serves about 20 million passengers a year who use carriers such as Southwest Airlines. Gary-Chicago International Airport in Indiana also is managed by Chicago Airport System. The system is overseen by the City of Chicago's Department of Aviation.

CHICAGO BEARS FOOTBALL CLUB INC.

1000 Football Dr.
Lake Forest IL 60045
Phone: 847-295-6600
Fax: 847-295-8986
Web: www.chicagobears.com

CEO: –
CFO: –
HR: –
FYE: February 28
Type: Private

These Monsters of the Midway have been scaring opponents since the very beginning. Chicago Bears Football Club operates the storied Chicago Bears professional football team which lays claim to nine National Football League titles (its last in Super Bowl XX at the end of the 1985 season). More than 25 Hall of Fame players have graced the roster of "Da Bears" including Red Grange Dick Butkus Gale Sayers and Walter Payton. Loyal Chicago fans root on their team at venerable Soldier Field. The franchise originally known as the Decatur Staleys was a charter member of the NFL in 1920. Chairman Michael McCaskey (grandson of founder George "Papa Bear" Halas) and his family control the club.

CHICAGO BLACKHAWK HOCKEY TEAM INC.

1901 W. Madison St.
Chicago IL 60612
Phone: 312-455-7000
Fax: 312-455-7041
Web: www.chicagoblackhawks.com

CEO: –
CFO: –
HR: –
FYE: June 30
Type: Subsidiary

When the Windy City turns cold these Hawks start flying on the ice. One of the Original Six professional hockey franchises of the National Hockey League the Chicago Blackhawks boast a long history that includes four Stanley Cup championships and a roster that has featured such Hall of Fame players as Phil and Tony Esposito Bobby Hull and Stan Mikita. The club won its most recent NHL championship title in 2010 breaking a drought that lasted 49 years the longest in league history. Loyal fans support the team at Chicago's United Center. The Wirtz family has owned the Blackhawks franchise through their Wirtz Corporation since 1954.

CHICAGO COMMUNITY TRUST

225 N MICHIGAN AVE # 2200
CHICAGO, IL 606017672
Phone: 312-616-8000
Fax: –
Web: www.cct.org

CEO: –
CFO: –
HR: –
FYE: September 30
Type: Private

You can trust this group to do the giving thing. The Chicago Community Trust gave more than $105 million in 2008 to not-for-profit organizations such as social services agencies schools health centers museums and theaters in the Chicago area. The grant program targets groups working in arts and culture basic human needs community development education and health. Past projects have included after-school programs for impoverished children funding a senior citizens center and health services for people with AIDS. Chicago Community Trust gets its funds from corporate and private donations. It was founded in 1915.

	Annual Growth	09/13	09/14	09/15	09/16	09/19
Sales ($ mil.)	14.1%	–	291.6	363.3	389.6	564.2
Net income ($ mil.)	12.9%	–	105.9	136.2	135.4	194.0
Market value ($ mil.)	–	–	–	–	–	–
Employees		–	–	–	–	100

CHICAGO MEAT AUTHORITY INC.

1120 W. 47th Place
Chicago IL 60609
Phone: 773-254-3811
Fax: 773-254-5851
Web: www.chicagomeat.com

CEO: Jordan Dorfman
CFO: -
HR: Patricia Almanza
FYE: December 31
Type: Private

When Chicago needs meat it turns to an authority. Chicago Meat Authority (CMA) processes beef and pork into a variety of sizes and cuts and sells its products not only in Chicago but worldwide. The company's fresh and frozen meats are specially cut for a range of customers including food retailers ethnic markets further processors (such as sausage makers) healthcare providers restaurants and broadline distributors. It also offers services such as aging custom cutting and trimming marinating and precooking as well as a variety of packaging options. Headquartered in the historic Chicago Stockyards Chicago Meat Authority was founded in 1990.

CHICAGO TRANSIT AUTHORITY (INC)

567 W LAKE ST STE CTA
CHICAGO, IL 606611465
Phone: 312-664-7200
Fax: -
Web: www.transitchicago.com

CEO: -
CFO: -
HR: -
FYE: December 31
Type: Private

The Chicago Transit Authority (CTA) is the nation's second largest public transportation system in the US. On a typical weekday CTA passengers take about 1.6 million rides on the agency's buses and trains which travel in and around Chicago and about 35 suburbs. The CTA operates a fleet of some 1865 buses on almost 130 routes. Its rail system includes eight rail lines with over 1490 rail cars operating on 224 miles of track at some 145 stations. The agency created by the Illinois legislature in 1947 is part of the state's Regional Transportation Authority which also oversees Metra (commuter rail system) and Pace (suburban bus system).

	Annual Growth	12/09	12/10	12/16	12/19	12/20
Sales ($ mil.)	(6.6%)	-	548.3	625.1	654.0	278.5
Net income ($ mil.)	-	-	(323.8)	(79.5)	(115.2)	17.1
Market value ($ mil.)	-	-	-	-	-	-
Employees	-	-	-	-	-	12,000

CHICAGO NATIONAL LEAGUE BALL CLUB INC.

Wrigley Field 1060 W. Addison St.
Chicago IL 60613-4397
Phone: 773-404-2827
Fax: 773-404-4129
Web: www.cubs.com

CEO: -
CFO: -
HR: -
FYE: December 31
Type: Private

This company has thrilled and (mostly) disappointed baseball fans for a long time. Chicago National League Ball Club operates the Chicago Cubs franchise of Major League Baseball which has gone without a World Series title since 1908. The team was formed as the Chicago White Stockings in 1876 and became the Cubs in 1907. Despite the lack of championships Chicagoans still flock to the charming and famed Wrigley Field (the second-oldest ballpark in MLB after Boston's Fenway Park) to see their Cubbies play. A group led by billionaire Tom Ricketts acquired a majority of the Cubs in 2009.

CHICAGO WHITE SOX LTD.

333 W. 35th St.
Chicago IL 60616
Phone: 312-674-1000
Fax: 312-924-3296
Web: chicago.whitesox.mlb.com

CEO: -
CFO: -
HR: -
FYE: October 31
Type: Private

In the summer in Chicago you can either "root root root for the Cubbies" or you can cheer on these southsiders. The venerable Chicago White Sox franchise is one of the oldest clubs in Major League Baseball having joined the American League in 1900. The team boasts just three World Series championships two from the early 1900s and it latest in 2005. (A World Series appearance in 1919 was marred by the "Black Sox" scandal that saw eight teammates banned from baseball for throwing the championship.) Playing host at US Cellular Field the White Sox franchise is owned by real estate developer and chairman Jerry Reinsdorf who also owns the Chicago Bulls basketball team.

CHICAGO RIVET & MACHINE CO.

901 Frontenac Road
Naperville, IL 60563
Phone: 630 357-8500
Fax: -
Web: www.chicagorivet.com

ASE: CVR
CEO: Walter Morrissey
CFO: -
HR: -
FYE: December 31
Type: Public

Rosie the Riveter might have used rivets made by Chicago Rivet & Machine. The company's main business is making fasteners including rivets screw machine products and cold-formed fasteners. In addition to manufacturing assembly equipment such as automatic rivet-setting equipment and rivet-working tools it leases rivet-setting machines. Chicago Rivet sells its products through internal and independent sales representatives to US automotive and auto parts manufacturers. Major customers include Fisher & Company (accounting for about 20% of the company's sales) and TI Automotive (16% of sales).

	Annual Growth	12/16	12/17	12/18	12/19	12/20
Sales ($ mil.)	(7.1%)	37.0	35.8	37.2	32.9	27.6
Net income ($ mil.)	(61.8%)	2.4	2.1	2.0	0.5	0.1
Market value ($ mil.)	(13.9%)	40.2	30.7	30.4	24.9	22.1
Employees	(2.5%)	231	219	228	217	209

CHICKASAW HOLDING COMPANY

124 W VINITA AVE
SULPHUR, OK 730863821
Phone: 580-622-2111
Fax: -
Web: www.chickasawholding.com

CEO: RE Gauntt
CFO: -
HR: -
FYE: December 31
Type: Private

Chickasaw Holding's family of businesses keeps south central Oklahoma connected. The company's original business Chickasaw Telephone Company was founded in 1909 and offers local phone service to about 9000 business and residential customers. Its other subsidiaries provide such services as long-distance (Chickasaw Long Distance) Internet access (BrightNet Oklahoma) wireless service (Chickasaw Cellular) and wholesale fiber-optic networking for business customers and other communications carriers (Indian Nations Fiber Optics). The group also installs telecommunications equipment including private branch exchange (PBX) and voice mail systems through its Telco Supply Company subsidiary.

	Annual Growth	12/12	12/13	12/14	12/15	12/16
Sales ($ mil.)	(0.8%)	-	103.0	22.9	106.8	100.6
Net income ($ mil.)	(1.2%)	-	24.6	21.2	22.3	23.7
Market value ($ mil.)	-	-	-	-	-	-
Employees	-	-	-	-	-	600

CHICO'S FAS INC

NYS: CHS

11215 Metro Parkway
Fort Myers, FL 33966
Phone: 239 277-6200
Fax: –
Web: www.chicos.com

CEO: Molly Langenstein
CFO: Patrick Guido
HR: Kristin Gwinner
FYE: January 30
Type: Public

Chico's FAS is a Florida-based fashion company founded in 1983 on Sanibel Island Florida. Chico's owns and operates more than 1300 specialty stores nationwide and about 70 franchised locations in Mexico. Its stores are mostly located in enclosed malls and shopping centers under the banners Chico's White House Black Market (WHBM) and Soma. The company has launched a digital-only intimate apparel store called TellTale. Its casual wear includes tops pants shorts skirts and dresses as well as jewelry and accessories. WHBM offers a modern collection to support her every lifestyle moment selling stylish and versatile clothing and accessory items including everyday basics polished casual apparel relaxed workwear black and white pieces and feminine all-occasion dresses.

	Annual Growth	01/17*	02/18	02/19	02/20*	01/21
Sales ($ mil.)	(14.5%)	2,476.4	2,282.4	2,131.1	2,037.9	1,324.1
Net income ($ mil.)	–	91.2	101.0	35.6	(12.8)	(360.1)
Market value ($ mil.)	(35.4%)	1,520.6	1,121.9	686.1	465.8	264.6
Employees	(12.2%)	21,000	19,000	18,500	17,100	12,500

*Fiscal year change

CHICOPEE BANCORP INC

NMS: CBNK

70 Center Street
Chicopee, MA 01013
Phone: 413 594-6692
Fax: –

CEO: –
CFO: –
HR: –
FYE: December 31
Type: Public

Chicopee Bancorp is the holding company for Chicopee Savings Bank a community bank which serves the residents and businesses of Hampden and Hampshire counties in western Massachusetts. Through a handful of branches the bank offers deposit services such as savings and checking accounts as well as a variety of lending services. Its loan portfolio consists of one-to-four-family residential real estate loans (its largest loan segment) and commercial real estate loans. Other lending services include multi-family construction home equity commercial business and consumer loans. Chicopee Bank was founded in 1854.

	Annual Growth	12/10	12/11	12/12	12/13	12/14
Assets ($ mil.)	2.7%	573.7	616.3	600.0	587.7	639.2
Net income ($ mil.)	–	0.5	1.1	2.5	2.6	(0.6)
Market value ($ mil.)	7.3%	66.7	74.3	83.8	91.8	88.3
Employees	0.2%	129	130	138	139	130

CHIEF INDUSTRIES INC.

3942 W OLD HIGHWAY 30
GRAND ISLAND, NE 688035051
Phone: 308-389-7200
Fax: –
Web: www.agri.chiefind.com

CEO: Dj Eihusen
CFO: David Ostdiek
HR: Anastacia Glinsmann
FYE: June 30
Type: Private

When it comes serving the agriculture and transportation industries through its eclectic range of businesses Chief Industries is the head honcho. Chief makes ethanol fuel and manufactures a host of supplies for agricultural industrial correctional building transportation and wastewater treatment applications. Its agri/industrial unit makes grain-drying and storage bins crop-drying fans and aeration systems. Its transportation business makes rail car products while division Chief Custom Homes makes modular homes and RVs. Chief offers services including metal fabrication powder coating design/build general contracting electrical/lighting design and for-hire freight hauling.

	Annual Growth	06/98	06/99	06/00	06/01	06/08
Sales ($ mil.)	(30.0%)	–	256.2	325.2	294.7	10.4
Net income ($ mil.)	–	–	–	6.0	1.6	(0.1)
Market value ($ mil.)	–	–	–	–	–	–
Employees	–	–	–	–	–	1,645

CHILDFUND INTERNATIONAL, USA

2821 EMERYWOOD PKWY
RICHMOND, VA 232943726
Phone: 804-756-2700
Fax: –
Web: www.childfund.org

CEO: –
CFO: James Tuite
HR: –
FYE: June 30
Type: Private

ChildFund International (CFI) serves the little ones. The worldwide non-profit organization provides education medical care food and safe water to more than 13 million children — of all faiths — in about 30 countries in Africa Asia the Caribbean Eastern Europe Latin America and the US. It works in areas of early childhood development education family income generation nutrition and sanitation. The group also tries to get child soldiers away from the military and reintegrated into daily life. Founded in 1938 as China's Children Fund the group changed its name to Christian Children's Fund in 1951. In 2009 it again renamed itself ChildFund International.

	Annual Growth	06/10	06/11	06/14	06/19	06/20
Sales ($ mil.)	(1.6%)	–	228.2	235.9	196.0	197.6
Net income ($ mil.)	2.1%	–	12.1	6.5	3.9	14.6
Market value ($ mil.)	–	–	–	–	–	–
Employees	–	–	–	–	–	160

CHILDREN'S HEALTH SYSTEM

1600 7th Ave. S.
Birmingham AL 35233
Phone: 205-939-9100
Fax: 205-939-9064
Web: www.chsys.org

CEO: –
CFO: –
HR: April Mize
FYE: December 31
Type: Private - Not-for-Pr

Children's Health System is an integrated health network that operates Birmingham's Children's Hospital and a group of medical offices clinics and outpatient facilities located primarily in the Greater Birmingham area. Not-for-profit Children's Hospital is licensed for about 275 beds and provides treatment for pediatric cancers blood disorders sickle cell disease and many other childhood illnesses. It serves as a Level 1 trauma center and houses a regional burn center a poison control center and a pediatric dialysis facility. Founded in 1911 Children's Hospital is also a teaching hospital for the University of Alabama at Birmingham.

CHILDREN'S HEALTH SYSTEM INC.

601 Children's Ln.
Norfolk VA 23507
Phone: 757-668-7500
Fax: 757-668-7745
Web: www.chkd.org

CEO: –
CFO: –
HR: –
FYE: June 30
Type: Private - Not-for-Pr

You don't have to be royalty to be a patient at Children's Hospital of The King's Daughters (CHKD). CHKD is Virginia's only free-standing full-service pediatric facility and as such provides medical dental and therapeutic services to children and adolescents through the age of 21 years old. The 210-bed hospital has a staff of more than 500 physicians and has the state's only dedicated pediatric emergency center which gets more than 47000 patient visits each year. CHKD also operates several outpatient pediatric centers throughout the state. The not-for-profit system was formed in 1961.

CHILDREN'S HEALTHCARE OF CALIFORNIA

1201 W LA VETA AVE
ORANGE, CA 928684203
Phone: 714-997-3000
Fax: –
Web: www.choc.org

CEO: Kimberly C Cripe
CFO: Kerri Ruppert
HR: –
FYE: June 30
Type: Private

Children's Hospital of Orange County (aka CHOC) fights kid-sized ailments in southern California. The not-for-profit hospital's main campus in Orange has about 240 beds and provides a comprehensive range of care to young patients including pediatric and neonatal intensive care. Its CHOC Mission facility (located within the Mission Hospital in Mission Viejo) has nearly 50 beds for pediatric patients as well as neonatal and pediatric ICUs. CHOC also runs a handful of primary care community clinics and several mobile clinics. It also conducts research and educational programs. The hospital was founded in 1964.

	Annual Growth	06/07	06/08	06/09	06/10	06/19
Sales ($ mil.)	(16.1%)	–	879.9	8.3	6.4	127.1
Net income ($ mil.)	–	–	0.0	0.0	(1.7)	106.8
Market value ($ mil.)	–	–	–	–	–	–
Employees	–	–	–	–	–	1,800

CHILDREN'S HOSPITAL & RESEARCH CENTER AT OAKLAND

747 52ND ST
OAKLAND, CA 946091809
Phone: 510-428-3000
Fax: –
Web: www.childrenshospitaloakland.org

CEO: –
CFO: Rina Smith
HR: –
FYE: June 30
Type: Private

Children's Hospital & Research Center at Oakland (operating as Children's Hospital Oakland) does just what its name says provides medical care for children and performs research to advance the treatment of pediatric diseases. The freestanding hospital has about 190 beds and a staff of some more than 200 hospital-based physicians professionals with more than 30 medical specialties. Its services include orthopedics neurology oncology and cardiology as well as surgery trauma neonatal and intensive care. Additionally the hospital operates several satellite outpatient clinics providing general and specialized care. Children's Hospital Oakland also conducts teaching and community outreach programs.

	Annual Growth	12/04	12/05	12/13*	06/15	06/20
Sales ($ mil.)	5.1%	–	313.5	541.7	178.6	661.6
Net income ($ mil.)	–	–	15.6	44.8	34.9	(8.2)
Market value ($ mil.)	–	–	–	–	–	–
Employees	–	–	–	–	–	2,000

*Fiscal year change

CHILDREN'S HOSPITAL AND HEALTH SYSTEM, INC.

8915 W CONNELL AVE
MILWAUKEE, WI 532263067
Phone: 414-266-2000
Fax: –
Web: www.childrenswi.org

CEO: –
CFO: Tim Birkenstock
HR: –
FYE: December 31
Type: Private

The Children's Hospital and Health System serves children and their families in Milwaukee and throughout the Great Lakes region. Its dozen entities dedicated to pediatric health care include the flagship 300-bed Children's Hospital of Wisconsin which is also an affiliate of the Medical College of Wisconsin. Satellite facilities include the 42-bed Fox Valley pediatric hospital as well as a surgical center specialty care clinics in Wisconsin and Illinois and research facilities. The organization also has a network of affiliated primary care pediatricians and manages an HMO that covers Medicaid recipients (children and adults) in several Wisconsin counties.

	Annual Growth	12/96	12/97	12/00*	06/05*	12/13
Sales ($ mil.)	(10.7%)	–	744.1	246.0	401.1	121.2
Net income ($ mil.)	–	–	0.0	25.6	0.0	(4.1)
Market value ($ mil.)	–	–	–	–	–	–
Employees	–	–	–	–	–	3,000

*Fiscal year change

CHILDREN'S HOSPITAL COLORADO

13123 E 16TH AVE
AURORA, CO 800457106
Phone: 720-777-1234
Fax: –
Web: www.childrenscolorado.org

CEO: Jena Hausemann
CFO:
HR: –
FYE: December 31
Type: Private

Children's Hospital Colorado is a private nonprofit pediatric healthcare network dedicated to caring for kids at all ages and stages of growth. With more than 3000 pediatric specialists the company provides comprehensive pediatric care at its hospital on Anschutz Medical Campus and at several locations throughout the region. Children's Hospital Colorado also operates more than a dozen satellite locations in and around Denver that specialize in providing children with emergency and specialty care. Its affiliation with the University of Colorado School of Medicine means that its doctors are not only expert clinicians but also active researchers working toward better ways to care for kids.

	Annual Growth	12/15	12/16	12/17	12/18	12/19
Sales ($ mil.)	13.3%	–	911.9	960.8	1,102.8	1,327.5
Net income ($ mil.)	8.0%	–	50.6	76.8	138.8	63.6
Market value ($ mil.)	–	–	–	–	–	–
Employees	–	–	–	–	–	2,200

CHILDREN'S HOSPITAL MEDICAL CENTER

3333 BURNET AVE
CINCINNATI, OH 452293039
Phone: 513-636-4200
Fax: –
Web: www.cincinnatichildrens.org

CEO: Steve Davis
CFO: Teresa Bowling
HR: –
FYE: June 30
Type: Private

Cincinnati Children's Hospital Medical Center has a special place in its heart for kids. The pediatric health care facility offers specialty treatments for children and adolescents suffering from just about any malady including ailments of the heart and liver as well as blood diseases and cancer. Cincinnati Children's Hospital has some 600 beds and operates about a dozen outpatient care centers. Founded in 1883 the not-for-profit hospital runs the only level I pediatric trauma center in the region and serves as a teaching and research facility for the University of Cincinnati College of Medicine. It is also ranked in the top 10 for all 10 pediatric specialties by U.S. News & World Report.

	Annual Growth	06/10	06/11	06/14	06/15	06/16
Sales ($ mil.)	(1.2%)	–	1,693.4	2,116.5	1,527.9	1,597.9
Net income ($ mil.)	32.0%	–	53.4	140.7	209.6	213.5
Market value ($ mil.)	–	–	–	–	–	–
Employees	–	–	–	–	–	18,000

CHILDREN'S HOSPITAL OF PITTSBURGH OF UPMC HEALTH SYSTEM

3705 5th Ave.
Pittsburgh PA 15213
Phone: 412-692-5325
Fax: 412-692-6920
Web: www.chp.edu

CEO: –
CFO: –
HR: –
FYE: June 30
Type: Subsidiary

From polio to poison control Children's Hospital of Pittsburgh has long been at the forefront of children's health care. Jonas Salk developed the polio vaccine there in the 1950s and the ubiquitous Mr. Yuk poison label also got its start there. Founded in 1890 the hospital cares for thousands of sick kids each year — both those who stay in one of its 300 inpatient beds and those who visit its outpatient ambulatory surgery and primary care centers. The hospital's doctors handle everything from flu to organ transplantation and they engage in wide-ranging pediatric medical research as well much of it funded by grants from the National Institutes of Health.

CHILDREN'S MEDICAL CENTER OF DALLAS

1935 MEDICAL DISTRICT DR
DALLAS, TX 752357701
Phone: 214-456-7000
Fax: –
Web: www.childrens.com

CEO: –
CFO: –
HR: –
FYE: December 31
Type: Private

Children's Medical Center of Dallas one of the largest and most prestigious pediatric health care providers and the leading pediatric health system in North Texas. Through the academic affiliation with UT Southwestern and leader in life changing treatments innovative technology and groundbreaking research. Among the campus Children's Health is licensed for around 600 beds including 490 beds at the main campus in the Southwestern Medical District and over 70 beds at Children's House facility in Dallas. Around 800 patients visits annually for 50 estates around the world. It was founded in 1913 when a group of nurses led by public health nurse May Forster Smith organized the Dallas Baby Camp.

	Annual Growth	12/07	12/08	12/13	12/14	12/15
Sales ($ mil.)	(0.6%)	–	744.9	1,111.2	1,120.4	712.6
Net income ($ mil.)	–	–	(4.1)	166.7	135.4	(185.6)
Market value ($ mil.)	–	–	–	–	–	–
Employees	–	–	–	–	–	5,318

CHILDREN'S NATIONAL MEDICAL CENTER

111 MICHIGAN AVE NW
WASHINGTON, DC 200102916
Phone: 202-476-5000
Fax: –
Web: www.childrensnational.org

CEO: –
CFO: –
HR: –
FYE: June 30
Type: Private

Children's National Hospital was established in 1870 has ranked as one of the top 10 pediatric hospitals in the nation ? with the #1 ranked neonatology program ? by US News & World Report for the fifth year in a row. The hospital is a Level 1 pediatric trauma center with some 325 beds. It also has critical care transport program via ambulance helicopter and fixed-wing airplane. Additionally it operates roughly 15 specialty care centers spread throughout Maryland Virginia and Washington DC an ambulatory surgery center in Maryland and two large emergency departments located at the main campus and on the United Medical Center campus. Children's National Health Network links more than 1500 primary and specialty care physicians.

	Annual Growth	06/05	06/06	06/07	06/09	06/20
Sales ($ mil.)	(10.3%)	–	574.0	694.6	516.6	126.1
Net income ($ mil.)	–	–	86.0	76.3	16.4	0.0
Market value ($ mil.)	–	–	–	–	–	–
Employees	–	–	–	–	–	6,000

CHILDREN'S PLACE INC (THE)

500 Plaza Drive
Secaucus, NJ 07094
Phone: 201 558-2400
Fax: –
Web: www.childrensplace.com

NMS: PLCE
CEO: Jane Elfers
CFO: Robert Helm
HR: –
FYE: January 30
Type: Public

The Children's Place is the largest pure-play children's specialty apparel retail in North America. It operates around 750 Children's Place stores throughout the US Canada and Puerto Rico as well as its online stores. In addition the company's eight international partners operates approximately 230 international points of distribution in about 20 countries. It also sells apparel online. The Children's Place outfits children in its own brand of value-priced apparel shoes and accessories most of which is produced by contract manufacturers. (The company also owns the Gymboree and Crazy 8 brands.) Approximately 90% of its sales come from stores in the US.

	Annual Growth	01/17*	02/18	02/19	02/20*	01/21
Sales ($ mil.)	(3.9%)	1,785.3	1,870.3	1,938.1	1,870.7	1,522.6
Net income ($ mil.)	–	102.3	84.7	101.0	73.3	(140.4)
Market value ($ mil.)	(6.2%)	1,382.6	2,123.4	1,343.6	870.2	1,071.5
Employees	(3.8%)	15,500	15,800	18,700	15,400	13,300

*Fiscal year change

CHILDREN'S SPECIALIZED HOSPITAL INC

150 NEW PROVIDENCE RD # 1
MOUNTAINSIDE, NJ 070922590
Phone: 888-244-5373
Fax: –
Web: www.rwjbh.org

CEO: Amy Mansue
CFO: –
HR: –
FYE: December 31
Type: Private

No grown-ups allowed! Children's Specialized Hospital (CSH) is the largest pediatric rehabilitation hospital in the US. The hospital provides rehabilitation medical and developmental health care services to patients from infancy through young adulthood. CSH's areas of specialization include burn care spinal cord and brain injury and physical therapy. In addition the hospital offers developmental care such as speech therapy nutritional services and audiology and it operates a network of outpatient and care facilities throughout New Jersey. The hospital an affiliate of the Robert Wood Johnson Health Network also performs research in children's disorders. CSH founded in 1892 is led by CEO Amy Mansue.

	Annual Growth	12/15	12/16	12/17	12/18	12/19
Sales ($ mil.)	9.8%	–	119.5	141.9	146.5	158.4
Net income ($ mil.)	(35.5%)	–	6.7	9.4	6.0	1.8
Market value ($ mil.)	–	–	–	–	–	–
Employees	–	–	–	–	–	1,200

CHILDRENS HOSPITAL & MEDICAL CENTER

8200 DODGE ST
OMAHA, NE 681144113
Phone: 402-955-5400
Fax: –
Web: www.childrensomaha.org

CEO: –
CFO: –
HR: –
FYE: December 31
Type: Private

Junior Cornhuskers can have their medical needs met at Children's Hospital & Medical Center. The not-for-profit center Nebraska's only pediatric hospital (and a top US children's hospital) is a 145-bed facility offering pediatric in patient services. The Omaha hospital has neonatal and pediatric intensive care units along with units dedicated surgery child development eating disorders and conditions including asthma allergies cardiac care diabetes nephrology and respiratory care. Children's serves as the teaching hospital for the University of Nebraska and Creighton University. It also operates urgent care and outreach clinics in the area.

	Annual Growth	12/14	12/15	12/16	12/17	12/18
Sales ($ mil.)	9.2%	–	327.6	339.4	373.0	427.1
Net income ($ mil.)	(22.4%)	–	42.9	57.6	81.7	20.0
Market value ($ mil.)	–	–	–	–	–	–
Employees	–	–	–	–	–	1,400

CHILDRENS HOSPITAL MEDICAL CENTER OF AKRON

1 PERKINS SQ
AKRON, OH 443081063
Phone: 330-543-1000
Fax: –
Web: www.akronchildrens.org

CEO: William Considine
CFO: Spencer A Kowal
HR: –
FYE: December 31
Type: Private

Akron Children's Hospital is the largest pediatric health care system in northeast Ohio. The health system operates through approximately 50 urgent primary and specialty care locations scattered around the state. Among Children's specialized services are cardiology orthopedics rehabilitation and home care. It added two new pediatric primary care locations: Akron Children's Hospital Pediatrics East Liverpool and Akron Children's Health Center Wooster The main hospital's emergency department treats nearly 70000 patients each year. With about 16445 urgent care visits the health system also has more than 337245 specialty visits per year. Akron Children's Hospital started as a nursery more than 100 years ago.

	Annual Growth	12/11	12/12	12/13	12/14	12/19
Sales ($ mil.)	8.5%	–	–	623.3	701.2	1,014.5
Net income ($ mil.)	4.8%	–	–	80.9	93.6	107.0
Market value ($ mil.)	–	–	–	–	–	–
Employees	–	–	–	–	–	4,763

CHILDRESS KLEIN PROPERTIES INC.

301 S. College St. Ste. 2800
Charlotte NC 28202
Phone: 704-342-9000
Fax: 704-342-9039
Web: www.childressklein.com

CEO: J Donald Childress
CFO: Harry Clements
HR: –
FYE: December 31
Type: Private

Childress Klein develops owns leases and manages commercial real estate in the southeastern US. It owns some 20 million sq. ft. of office industrial retail and mixed-use space mostly in the Atlanta and Charlotte North Carolina metropolitan areas. (Nearly 60% of its portfolio is office buildings and business centers.) The company's projects include Atlanta Galleria and LakePointe Corporate Center as well as the Wachovia Center a two-block office residential and hospitality complex in downtown Charlotte. Childress Klein also develops retail properties ranging from strip centers to big box-anchored shopping centers.

CHILTON HOSPITAL

97 W PARKWAY
POMPTON PLAINS, NJ 074441647
Phone: 973-831-5000
Fax: –
Web: www.chiltonhealth.org

CEO: Deborah K Zastocki
CFO: –
HR: Michele Bianco
FYE: December 31
Type: Private

Chilton Medical Center (formerly Chilton Memorial Hospital) serves the residents of northern New Jersey's Morris and Passaic counties. The acute-care facility has some 260 beds and provides emergency diagnostic inpatient surgical and outpatient care. The hospital operates with a staff of about 650 physicians who practice in 60 fields of health care. Chilton Medical Center offers such specialties as a cancer center surgical weight-loss programs occupational health orthopedics stroke care pediatrics and dialysis. Chilton Medical Center merged with Atlantic Health System in 2014.

	Annual Growth	12/03	12/04	12/05	12/08	12/14
Sales ($ mil.)	3.6%	–	–	128.8	0.0	176.4
Net income ($ mil.)	46.3%	–	–	2.5	0.0	76.5
Market value ($ mil.)	–	–	–	–	–	–
Employees	–	–	–	–	–	1,188

CHIMERA INVESTMENT CORP   NYS: CIM

630 Fifth Ave, Ste 2400
New York, NY 10111
Phone: 888 895-6557
Fax: –
Web: www.chimerareit.com

CEO: Mohit Marria
CFO: Subramaniam Viswanathan
HR: –
FYE: December 31
Type: Public

This Chimera has the body of a mortgage real estate investment trust (REIT) but its head is that of its external manager FIDAC (Fixed Income Discount Advisory Company) a fixed-income investment management firm wholly-owned by Annaly Capital Management. Formed in 2007 Chimera invests in residential mortgage loans; residential mortgage-backed securities (RMBS) such as those guaranteed by government agencies Fannie Mae and Freddie Mac; real estate-related securities; and other assets including collateralized debt obligations or CDOs. The REIT went public in 2007 shortly after it was formed.

	Annual Growth	12/17	12/18	12/19	12/20	12/21
Assets ($ mil.)	(7.7%)	21,222.1	27,708.6	27,118.7	17,523.0	15,407.4
Net income ($ mil.)	6.3%	524.7	411.6	413.6	88.9	670.1
Market value ($ mil.)	(5.0%)	4,378.9	4,222.5	4,871.7	2,428.8	3,573.2
Employees	0.0%	38	38	39	41	38

CHIMERIX INC.   NMS: CMRX

2505 Meridian Parkway, Suite 100
Durham, NC 27713
Phone: 919 806-1074
Fax: –
Web: www.chimerix.com

CEO: Michael Sherman
CFO: Michael Andriole
HR: –
FYE: December 31
Type: Public

All that shimmers isn't ? enhanced by lipid conjugate technology. Chimerix is a development-stage biopharmaceutical company dedicated to accelerating the advancement of innovative for patients living with cancer and other serious diseases. Its two clinical-stage development programs include dociparstat sodium (DSTAT) and brincidofovir (BCV). DSTAT is a glycosaminoglycan derivative of heparin with known anti-inflammatory properties and BCV is an oral antiviral in development for the treatment of smallpox.

	Annual Growth	12/16	12/17	12/18	12/19	12/20
Sales ($ mil.)	(1.5%)	5.7	4.5	7.2	12.5	5.4
Net income ($ mil.)	–	(76.4)	(71.0)	(69.5)	(112.6)	(43.5)
Market value ($ mil.)	1.2%	289.0	290.8	161.4	127.5	303.4
Employees	(11.2%)	87	82	82	43	54

CHINDEX INTERNATIONAL INC   NMS: CHDX

4340 East West Highway, Suite 1100
Bethesda, MD 20814
Phone: 301 215-7777
Fax: 301 215-7719
Web: www.chindex.com

CEO: –
CFO: –
HR: –
FYE: December 31
Type: Public

Chindex International provides health care services through its United Family Healthcare (UFH) network of private hospitals and satellite medical clinics in Beijing Shanghai Tianjin and Guangzhou. The growing network's hospitals have a combined licensed bed count of about 200 and cater primarily to the expatriate community and to affluent Chinese patients. Chindex also operates a joint venture — Chindex Medical Limited (CML) — with Shanghai Fosun Pharmaceutical to distribute medical equipment and supplies including diagnostic imaging and robotic surgery systems to hospitals in China and Hong Kong. Western manufacturers including Siemens Hologic and Candela supply these medical products.

	Annual Growth	03/09	03/10*	12/10	12/11	12/12
Sales ($ mil.)	(3.8%)	171.4	171.2	136.7	114.4	152.4
Net income ($ mil.)	(6.2%)	5.0	8.2	5.8	3.2	4.1
Market value ($ mil.)	28.3%	84.8	201.6	281.4	145.4	179.2
Employees	11.1%	1,276	1,328	1,090	1,448	1,749

*Fiscal year change

CHIPOTLE MEXICAN GRILL INC   NYS: CMG

610 Newport Center Drive, Suite 1400
Newport Beach, CA 92660
Phone: 949 524-4000
Fax: –
Web: www.chipotle.com

CEO: Brian Niccol
CFO: John Hartung
HR: –
FYE: December 31
Type: Public

US restaurant chain Chipotle Mexican Grill owns and operates more than 2900 quick-casual eateries popular for burritos tacos burrito bowls and salads. It also has about 45 international restaurants and four non-Chipotle restaurants. Chipotle offers a variety of menu that includes chicken steak carnitas sofritas barbecue or free-range pork as well as beans rice guacamole and various other veggies and salsas. The company claims that with extras its menu offers thousands of choices. Chipotle restaurants also serve soft tacos crispy tacos chips and salsa beer and margaritas. Chipotle has about 25 independently owned and operated regional distribution centers. The company was founded in 1993 in Denver Colorado.

	Annual Growth	12/17	12/18	12/19	12/20	12/21
Sales ($ mil.)	13.9%	4,476.4	4,865.0	5,586.4	5,984.6	7,547.1
Net income ($ mil.)	38.7%	176.3	176.6	350.2	355.8	653.0
Market value ($ mil.)	56.8%	8,116.0	12,124.7	23,506.0	38,938.8	49,090.9
Employees	9.1%	68,890	73,000	83,000	88,000	97,660

CHIPPEWA VALLEY BEAN COMPANY INC.

N2960 730TH ST
MENOMONIE, WI 547516615
Phone: 715-664-8342
Fax: –
Web: www.cvbean.com

CEO: –
CFO: –
HR: –
FYE: November 30
Type: Private

Chippewa Valley Bean has found its niche in the world through kidney beans. The company processes and wholesales dried light and dark red kidney beans. It grows and purchases beans grown on irrigated land in Wisconsin and three adjacent states. Chippewa Valley Bean's processing facility handles 40 million pounds of kidney beans every year. It exports its products to European and developing countries. The company also deals in pinto beans and dried green peas and sells prepackaged bean soups. Chippewa Valley Bean is a family-owned and -operated business.

	Annual Growth	11/08	11/09	11/10	11/11	11/12
Sales ($ mil.)	2.4%	–	22.4	19.8	17.2	24.0
Net income ($ mil.)	(14.2%)	–	–	0.8	0.1	0.6
Market value ($ mil.)	–	–	–	–	–	–
Employees	–	–	–	–	–	15

CHIQUITA BRANDS INTERNATIONAL, INC.   NYS: CQB

550 South Caldwell Street
Charlotte, NC 28202
Phone: 980 636-5000
Fax: –
Web: www.chiquita.com

CEO: Brian Kocher
CFO: –
HR: –
FYE: December 31
Type: Public

As one of the world's top banana producers Chiquita Brands deals in big bunches. The company grows procures markets and sells bananas and other fresh fruits and vegetables under the Chiquita name and several others. Bananas account for about 65% of Chiquita's sales. Its other offerings include whole citrus fruits melons grapes apples and tomatoes as well as packaged fresh-cut items processed fruit ingredients and juices. The company's Fresh Express unit generates about a third of sales and is the leading US seller of packaged ready-to-eat salads. Chiquita's products are sold in nearly 70 countries mainly in North America and Europe. Lesser markets include the Middle East Japan and South Korea.

	Annual Growth	12/08	12/09	12/10	12/11	12/12
Sales ($ mil.)	(3.9%)	3,609.4	3,470.4	3,227.4	3,139.3	3,078.3
Net income ($ mil.)	–	(323.7)	90.5	57.4	56.8	(405.0)
Market value ($ mil.)	(13.6%)	684.6	835.6	649.4	386.3	382.1
Employees	(3.4%)	23,000	21,000	21,000	21,000	20,000

CHOICE HOTELS INTERNATIONAL, INC.   NYS: CHH

1 Choice Hotels Circle, Suite 400
Rockville, MD 20850
Phone: 301 592-5000
Fax: –
Web: www.choicehotels.com

CEO: Patrick Pacious
CFO: Dominic Dragisich
HR: –
FYE: December 31
Type: Public

This company offers a lot of hospitality choices. Choice Hotels is a leading hotel franchisor with about 7150 locations and approximately 600000 rooms throughout the US and more than 40 other countries. The company operates about a dozen brands which include upper midscale hotels (Comfort Inn and Comfort Suites) midscale brands (Quality and Clarion and Clarion Pointe) and economy that offers sensible lodging for travelers on a budget (Econo Lodge and Rodeway Inn) Ascend Hotel (boutique). It also operates extended stay hotels such as MainStay Suites and WoodSpring Suites. Choice Hotels also launched Everhome Suites a new-construction midscale extended-stay brand.

	Annual Growth	12/16	12/17	12/18	12/19	12/20
Sales ($ mil.)	(4.3%)	924.6	1,007.4	1,041.3	1,114.8	774.1
Net income ($ mil.)	(14.2%)	139.4	114.9	216.4	222.9	75.4
Market value ($ mil.)	17.5%	3,112.8	4,309.6	3,975.2	5,744.0	5,927.3
Employees	(4.3%)	1,789	1,987	1,882	1,807	1,498

CHOICEONE FINANCIAL SERVICES, INC.   NAS: COFS

109 East Division Street
Sparta, MI 49345
Phone: 616 887-7366
Fax: –
Web: www.choiceone.com

CEO: Heather Brolick
CFO: Adom J Greenland
HR: –
FYE: December 31
Type: Public

One choice for a place to park your money is ChoiceOne Financial Services. The institution is the holding company for ChoiceOne Bank which has more than a dozen offices in the western part of Michigan's Lower Peninsula. The bank serves consumers and area businesses offering checking and savings accounts CDs investment planning and other services. Real estate loans including residential and commercial mortgages constitute more than two-thirds of the company's loan portfolio. Agricultural consumer and business loans help to round out the bank's lending activities. ChoiceOne Financial Services sells life health and disability coverage through its ChoiceOne Insurance Agencies subsidiaries.

	Annual Growth	12/16	12/17	12/18	12/19	12/20
Assets ($ mil.)	33.3%	607.4	646.5	670.5	1,386.1	1,919.3
Net income ($ mil.)	26.5%	6.1	6.2	7.3	7.2	15.6
Market value ($ mil.)	6.7%	185.2	185.6	194.9	249.2	240.2
Employees	22.4%	160	173	174	339	359

CHRISTIAN HOSPITAL NORTHEAST - NORTHWEST

11133 DUNN RD
SAINT LOUIS, MO 631366163
Phone: 314-355-2300
Fax: –
Web: www.christianhospital.org

CEO: –
CFO: –
HR: –
FYE: December 31
Type: Private

Christian or heathen if you're in the St. Louis area and need medical care Christian Hospital wants to help. The not-for-profit hospital which has some 485 beds is part of BJC HealthCare. Established in 1903 it specializes in a range of treatment areas including diabetes and cancer care and cardiothoracic surgery. Its more than 430 physicians also offer services in 40 other specialties from primary care to pulmonology. Christian Hospital offers a comprehensive mental health and substance abuse program that includes an inpatient option as well as specialization in geriatric mental wellness. The hospital is headed by president Ron McMullen a long-time health care administrator.

	Annual Growth	12/14	12/15	12/16	12/17	12/18
Sales ($ mil.)	1.7%	–	249.9	253.1	253.5	262.8
Net income ($ mil.)	–	–	(12.6)	(20.0)	(45.6)	(35.1)
Market value ($ mil.)	–	–	–	–	–	–
Employees	–	–	–	–	–	2,493

CHRISTIANA CARE HEALTH SYSTEM

501 W. 14th St.
Wilmington DE 19801
Phone: 302-733-1900
Fax: 302-428-5770
Web: www.christianacare.org

CEO: –
CFO: –
HR: –
FYE: June 30
Type: Private - Not-for-Pr

Christiana Care Health System cares for the Brandywine Valley. The not-for-profit health care network serves patients in northern Delaware and surrounding areas of Pennsylvania Maryland and New Jersey. The company operates Christiana Hospital and Wilmington Hospital which together have some 1100 beds. The hospitals provide cardiac care cancer treatment women's health pediatrics rehabilitation general medicine and surgery. Other specialties include urology and gastroenterology. The system also operates area physician clinics and offers home health and adult day care services. In addition Christiana Care conducts education training and research programs.

CHRISTOPHER & BANKS CORP.

NBB: CBKC Q

2400 Xenium Lane North
Plymouth, MN 55441
Phone: 763 551-5000
Fax: –
Web: www.christopherandbanks.com

CEO: –
CFO: Richard Bundy
HR: –
FYE: February 01
Type: Public

Women's specialty apparel retailer Christopher & Banks has been slimming down. The largely mall-based chain sells moderately priced private-label women's casual fashions through more than 445 locations. Its portfolio of stores span about 45 states operating under the Christopher & Banks C.J. Banks banners and Missy Petite Women. It also operates outlet and MPW dual-concept stores which offer merchandise from both Christopher & Banks and C.J. Banks and sells items online. Christopher & Banks targets women of all sizes typically ages 50 and older with an income level from moderate to above average. In early 2021 the company filed voluntary petitions for relief under Chapter 11 of the Bankruptcy Code in the United States Bankruptcy Court for the District of New Jersey.

	Annual Growth	01/16	01/17*	02/18	02/19	02/20
Sales ($ mil.)	(2.4%)	383.8	381.6	365.9	348.9	348.9
Net income ($ mil.)	–	(49.1)	(17.8)	(22.0)	(32.8)	(16.7)
Market value ($ mil.)	(27.4%)	66.4	50.7	47.6	22.0	18.4
Employees	(3.4%)	4,355	4,100	3,900	3,700	3,800

*Fiscal year change

CHRISTOPHER RANCH, LLC

305 BLOOMFIELD AVE
GILROY, CA 950209565
Phone: 408-847-1100
Fax: –
Web: www.christopherranch.com

CEO: –
CFO: –
HR: –
FYE: December 31
Type: Private

There are probably a lot of breath mints available at Christopher Ranch the largest garlic producer in the US. Christopher Ranch sells dozens of types of fresh and jarred garlic as well as specialty onions sun-dried tomatoes broccoli dried chilies herbs and spices. Christopher Ranch nestled in California's Santa Clara Valley ships more than 60 million pounds of garlic every year to foodservice companies and grocery stores such as Kroger Safeway and Whole Foods. Its garlic is also exclusively used in Michael Angelo's frozen foods. Christopher Ranch was founded in 1953 by brothers Don and Art Christopher. Don's son Bill now runs the company.

	Annual Growth	12/05	12/06	12/07	12/08	12/09
Sales ($ mil.)	(0.1%)	–	–	108.6	111.3	108.5
Net income ($ mil.)	(3.7%)	–	–	13.9	7.0	12.9
Market value ($ mil.)	–	–	–	–	–	–
Employees	–	–	–	–	–	200

CHRISTUS HEALTH

919 HIDDEN RDG
IRVING, TX 750383813
Phone: 469-282-2000
Fax: –
Web: www.christushealth.org

CEO: Ernie Sadau
CFO: Jay Herron
HR: –
FYE: June 30
Type: Private

In CHRISTUS there is no east or west but plenty of care nonetheless. The not-for-profit Catholic health care system operates about 350 medical facilities from its more than 60 hospitals including general hospitals and long-term acute care facilities to clinics and outpatient centers. It operates mostly in Louisiana and Texas where its hospitals are but also has facilities in Arkansas Georgia Iowa Missouri and New Mexico and in six states in Mexico and one in Chile. In addition to its acute care facilities CHRISTUS runs medical groups home health and hospice agencies and senior living facilities. Specialized services include oncology pediatrics rehabilitation and women's and children's health care.

	Annual Growth	06/14	06/15	06/16	06/19	06/20
Sales ($ mil.)	(8.8%)	–	658.8	4,212.4	736.5	415.2
Net income ($ mil.)	–	–	–	(44.3)	149.7	(41.1)	30.8
Market value ($ mil.)	–	–	–	–	–	–
Employees	–	–	–	–	–	25,700

CHRISTUS HEALTH CENTRAL LOUISIANA

3330 MASONIC DR
ALEXANDRIA, LA 713013841
Phone: 318-487-1122
Fax: –
Web: www.christushealth.org

CEO: Stephen Wright
CFO: –
HR: –
FYE: June 30
Type: Private

CHRISTUS St. Frances Cabrini Hospital provides a wide range of medical services to the denizens of Alexandria Louisiana. If you're ailing down south there's not much the hospital can't do to help especially in the area of cancer. Founded in 1950 the 240-bed St. Frances Cabrini Hospital has a staff of more than 320 physicians providing services that include emergency care women's health surgery and cardiology. For the insomniacs among us the hospital provides specialized care through its sleep center. St. Francis Cabrini's parent company is one of the nation's major hospital operators — with about 50 facilities located around the country.

	Annual Growth	06/08	06/09	06/10	06/13	06/15
Sales ($ mil.)	1.4%	–	217.4	219.5	222.3	236.9
Net income ($ mil.)	50.5%	–	1.6	(0.6)	5.0	18.4
Market value ($ mil.)	–	–	–	–	–	–
Employees	–	–	–	–	–	2,000

CHRISTUS ST. CATHERINE HOSPITAL

701 S. Fry Rd.
Katy TX 77450
Phone: 281-599-5700
Fax: 281-398-2265
Web: www.christusstcatherine.org

CEO: –
CFO: –
HR: –
FYE: June 30
Type: Subsidiary

CHRISTUS St. Catherine Hospital serves the Houston-area community of Katy Texas with acute health care services. The hospital which has about 100 beds offers a variety of adult pediatric and surgical medical care services to patients in Katy and surrounding areas. Specialized services include emergency medicine cardiac and orthopedic care rehabilitation women's health home health care and medical imaging and sleep centers. It also offers cancer care through a partnership with the University of Texas MD Anderson Cancer Center. The hospital is part of the not-for-profit CHRISTUS Health system which includes more than 40 hospitals and other facilities in the US and Mexico.

CHRISTY SPORTS L.L.C.

875 PARFET ST
LAKEWOOD, CO 802155507
Phone: 303-237-6321
Fax: –
Web: www.patio.christysports.com

CEO: Matt Gold
CFO: Lindsay Goszulak
HR: –
FYE: April 30
Type: Private

Christy Sports isn't some girly group of ponytailed cheerleaders. It's the largest specialty ski and snowboard retailer in the Rocky Mountains. With more than 40 retail stores in skiing hot spots like Snowmass Crested Butte Steamboat Springs and Vail the company sells skiing snowboarding snow-shoeing mountain biking and golf equipment along with shoes shirts gloves and bags to carry it all. Stores also carry patio furniture grills hammocks and other accessories for the outdoor life and rent skiing and snowboarding gear. Christy's staff are all serious skiers and snowboarders who use the equipment they sell. The company was founded in 1958 by avid skiers Ed and Gale Crist.

	Annual Growth	04/09	04/10	04/11	04/12	04/13
Sales ($ mil.)	5.3%	–	50.4	56.5	56.0	59.0
Net income ($ mil.)	20.0%	–	–	2.4	1.5	3.5
Market value ($ mil.)	–	–	–	–	–	–
Employees	–	–	–	–	–	450

CHROMADEX CORP
NAS: CDXC

10900 Wilshire Blvd., Suite 600
Los Angeles, CA 90024
Phone: 310 388-6706
Fax: –
Web: www.chromadex.com

CEO: Robert Fried
CFO: Kevin Farr
HR: –
FYE: December 31
Type: Public

ChromaDex can talk a blue streak about the health benefits of blueberries. The company markets pterostilbene a plant-based chemical found in blueberries that is said to lower cholesterol and reduce the risk of cancer. Sold under the brand pTeroPure the phytochemical is used in about 20 different nutritional supplements including Nutraceutical's Solaray Super Resveratrol with Pterostilbene. ChromaDex also launched its own line of supplements in 2011 called BluScience that are sold at GNC and Walgreens. Biotech investor Philip Frost the chairman of Teva Pharmaceuticals owns almost 20% of ChromaDex.

	Annual Growth	12/16	12/17	12/18	12/19	12/20
Sales ($ mil.)	21.9%	26.8	21.2	31.6	46.3	59.3
Net income ($ mil.)	–	(2.9)	(11.4)	(33.3)	(32.1)	(19.9)
Market value ($ mil.)	9.7%	204.8	363.9	212.3	266.7	297.0
Employees	4.3%	93	74	100	110	110

CHRYSLER GROUP LLC

1000 Chrysler Dr.
Auburn Hills MI 48326-2766
Phone: 248-576-5741
Fax: 908-903-2027
Web: www.chubb.com

CEO: Christine Feuell
CFO: Richard Palmer
HR: –
FYE: December 31
Type: Private

Chrysler hopes its crisis remains in its rearview mirror. After engineering an automotive resurrection by choosing a back-to-basics alliance with Fiat in 2009 the carmaker continues to manufacture its Chrysler brands including its Dodge Dart Fiat 500 Jeep Grand Cherokee SRT8 Jeep Wrangler Town & Country and Ram 1500 vehicles. Chrysler's trademarked MOPAR (MOtor PARts) automobile parts and service division carries almost 300000 parts options and accessories for vehicle customization. Chrysler Group LLC emerged from a US government backed Chapter 11 bankruptcy in mid-2009. It was first founded by Walter Chrysler and organized as Chrysler Corporation in 1925.

CHS INC
NMS: CHSC L

5500 Cenex Drive
Inver Grove Heights, MN 55077
Phone: 651 355-6000
Fax: –
Web: www.chsinc.com

CEO: Jay Debertin
CFO: Olivia Nelligan
HR: Mary Kaul-Hottinger
FYE: August 31
Type: Public

CHS is the leading integrated agricultural cooperative which provides grains foods and energy resources to businesses and consumers worldwide owned by farmers and ranchers as well as their member cooperatives across the US. The company provides products and services ranging from initial agricultural inputs such as fuels farm supplies crop nutrients and protection products to agricultural outputs which include grains and oilseeds among others. CHS also operates petroleum refineries that sell Cenex-brand fuels lubricants and other energy products. The company does approximately 95% of its business in North America.

	Annual Growth	08/17	08/18	08/19	08/20	08/21
Sales ($ mil.)	4.7%	31,934.8	32,683.3	31,900.5	28,406.4	38,448.0
Net income ($ mil.)	44.3%	127.9	775.9	829.9	422.4	554.0
Market value ($ mil.)	–	0.0	0.0	0.0	0.0	0.0
Employees	(3.8%)	11,626	10,495	10,703	10,493	9,941

CHS MCPHERSON REFINERY INC.

2000 S MAIN ST
MCPHERSON, KS 674609402
Phone: 620-241-2340
Fax: –
Web: www.chsinc.com

CEO: –
CFO: Timothy Skidmore
HR: –
FYE: August 31
Type: Private

Cooperation is a refined art and refining a cooperative art for the National Cooperative Refinery Association (NCRA) which provides its member owners farm supply cooperatives CHS GROWMARK and MFA Oil with gasoline and diesel fuel through its oil refinery in McPherson Kansas. The refinery's production rate is 85000 barrels per day. Fuel from the refinery is allocated to member/owners on the basis of ownership percentages. In addition to the refinery NCRA owns Jayhawk Pipeline stakes in two other pipeline companies and an underground oil storage facility.

	Annual Growth	08/09	08/10	08/11	08/12	08/13
Sales ($ mil.)	9.5%	–	–	3,405.1	4,045.1	4,081.0
Net income ($ mil.)	34.7%	–	–	378.6	705.2	686.8
Market value ($ mil.)	–	–	–	–	–	–
Employees	–	–	–	–	–	700

CHUBB CORP.
NYS: CB

15 Mountain View Road
Warren, NJ 07059
Phone: 908 903-2000
Fax: 908 903-2003
Web: www.chubb.com

CEO: –
CFO: –
HR: –
FYE: December 31
Type: Public

Here's the skinny on Chubb: The insurer is best known for comprehensive personal homeowners insurance for the demographic that owns yachts (the company insures those too). Chubb also offers commercial property/casualty insurance including multiple peril property and marine and workers' compensation. Its specialty insurance arm offers professional liability policies for executives across a spectrum of industries and also provides construction and commercial surety bonds. Chubb distributes its products through 8500 independent agents and brokers in 120 offices across the US and in more than 25 countries. The company began in 1882 when Thomas Chubb and his son began writing marine insurance in New York City.

	Annual Growth	12/09	12/10	12/11	12/12	12/13
Assets ($ mil.)	(0.0%)	50,449.0	50,249.0	50,865.0	52,184.0	50,433.0
Net income ($ mil.)	1.8%	2,183.0	2,174.0	1,678.0	1,545.0	2,345.0
Market value ($ mil.)	18.4%	12,211.7	14,809.0	17,187.8	18,702.4	23,993.9
Employees	0.0%	10,200	10,100	10,100	10,200	10,200

CHUGACH ALASKA CORPORATION

3800 CNTRPINT DR STE 1200
ANCHORAGE, AK 99503
Phone: 907-563-8866
Fax: –
Web: www.chugach.com

CEO: Sheri Buretta
CFO: –
HR: –
FYE: December 31
Type: Private

At the heart of Chugach Alaska Corporation is a vision of indigenous people running their own businesses on their own land. Chugach Alaska was formed following the activation of the Alaska Native Claims Settlement Act (which was passed by the US Congress in 1971) to provide land management services for the 928000-acre Chugach region of Alaska. The company derives the bulk of its sales from oil and gas production mining commercial timber and tourist activities that occur in the region and from its engagement in military base construction projects at more than 30 locations in Alaska the US Pacific Northwest and the Western Pacific. Chugach Alaska's shareholders consist of Aleut Eskimo and Indian natives.

	Annual Growth	12/13	12/14	12/15	12/16	12/17
Sales ($ mil.)	387.6%	–	7.9	758.5	842.4	919.7
Net income ($ mil.)	–	–	(12.7)	22.7	35.7	20.8
Market value ($ mil.)	–	–	–	–	–	–
Employees	–	–	–	–	–	4,822

CHUGACH ELECTRIC ASSOCIATION, INC.

5601 Electron Drive
Anchorage, AK 99518
Phone: 907 563-7494
Fax: –
Web: www.chugachelectric.com

CEO: Lee Thibert
CFO: Sherri McKay-Highers
HR: –
FYE: December 31
Type: Public

Deriving its name from an old Eskimo tribal word Chugach Electric Association generates transmits distributes and sells electricity in Alaska's railbelt region. This area extends from the coastal Chugach Mountains into central Alaska and includes the state's two largest cities (Anchorage and Fairbanks). The member-owned cooperative utility has 530 MW of generating capacity from its natural gas-fired and hydroelectric power plants. Serving 80300 metered retail locations Chugach Electric the largest electric utility in Alaska also sells wholesale power to other municipal and cooperative utilities in the region. In 2016 it agreed to buy Chicago-based Rex Electric and Technologies.

	Annual Growth	12/15	12/16	12/17	12/18	12/19
Sales ($ mil.)	(0.5%)	216.4	197.7	224.7	202.3	212.5
Net income ($ mil.)	(5.8%)	6.5	5.8	6.0	5.4	5.1
Market value ($ mil.)	–	–	–	–	–	–
Employees	0.3%	291	288	291	293	295

CHURCH & DWIGHT CO INC
NYS: CHD

500 Charles Ewing Boulevard
Ewing, NJ 08628
Phone: 609 806-1200
Fax: 609 497-7269
Web: www.churchdwight.com

CEO: Matthew Farrell
CFO: Richard Dierker
HR: –
FYE: December 31
Type: Public

Church & Dwight develops manufactures and markets a broad range of consumer household and personal care products and specialty products under the ARM & HAMMER brand and about 15 other brands. The company's household products and specialty products include laundry detergent fabric softener sheets cat litter antiperspirants oral care products depilatories reproductive health products oral analgesics nasal saline moisturizers and dietary supplements. Beyond Arm & Hammer the company's top brands include XTRA and Oxiclean detergents Nair depilatories First Response pregnancy tests Orajel toothpaste L'il Critters and Vitafusion gummy vitamins SpinBrush toothbrushes FLAWLESS hair removal products and Trojan-brand condoms. More than 80% of sales comes from US.

	Annual Growth	12/17	12/18	12/19	12/20	12/21
Sales ($ mil.)	8.3%	3,776.2	4,145.9	4,357.7	4,895.8	5,190.1
Net income ($ mil.)	2.7%	743.4	568.6	615.9	785.9	827.5
Market value ($ mil.)	19.6%	12,168.5	15,949.8	17,060.7	21,157.3	24,861.0
Employees	2.1%	4,700	4,700	4,800	5,100	5,100

CHURCH PENSION GROUP SERVICES CORPORATION

445 Fifth Ave.
New York NY 10016
Phone: 212-592-1800
Fax: 801-250-6099
Web: www.cobblestones.com

CEO: T Period D Sullivan
CFO: Daniel Kasle
HR: –
FYE: March 31
Type: Private - Not-for-Pr

Broken stained glass window? Fractured clerical clavicle? Church Pension Group can help. Its Church Pension Fund Church Medical Trust and Church Life Insurance divisions provide pensions health plans life insurance disability coverage and other benefits for clergy and workers of the Protestant Episcopal Church in the US. Church Pension Group also maintains the Episcopal Church Clergy and Employees' Benefit Trust (the "Medical Trust") which was created in 1978 to provide benefits for the Church's employees and their families. The group's Church Insurance Companies division provides specialty property/casualty insurance plans tailored specifically for churches.

CHURCHILL DOWNS, INC.
NMS: CHDN

600 North Hurstbourne Parkway, Suite 400
Louisville, KY 40222
Phone: 502 636-4400
Fax: –
Web: www.churchilldownsincorporated.com

CEO: William Carstanjen
CFO: Marcia Dall
HR: –
FYE: December 31
Type: Public

Churchill Downs is most famous for owning its namesake horse racing track online wagering and gaming entertainment company anchored by its iconic flagship event ? the world-famous Kentucky Derby. The gaming segment has approximately 11000 slot machines and VLTs and some 200 table games located in about 10 states. Its horse racing operations include major race courses including Churchill Downs (Kentucky) Arlington International Race Course (Illinois) and Calder Casino and Racing. Finally the company also operates a number of simulcast networks and off-track betting (OTB) facilities as well as a TwinSpires wagering deposit service that allows bettors to place bets online.

	Annual Growth	12/16	12/17	12/18	12/19	12/20
Sales ($ mil.)	(5.3%)	1,308.6	882.6	1,009.0	1,329.7	1,054.0
Net income ($ mil.)	–	108.1	140.5	352.8	137.5	(81.9)
Market value ($ mil.)	6.7%	5,942.8	9,191.7	9,635.6	5,419.4	7,694.2
Employees	15.0%	4,000	4,300	4,100	5,500	7,000

CHUY'S HOLDINGS INC
NMS: CHUY

1623 Toomey Road
Austin, TX 78704
Phone: 512 473-2783
Fax: –
Web: www.chuys.com

CEO: Steve Hislop
CFO: Jon Howie
HR: –
FYE: December 27
Type: Public

Chuy's Holdings operates the Chuy's Tex-Mex casual dining restaurant chain which serves up a menu of enchiladas fajitas tacos burritos combination platters and daily specials complemented by a variety of appetizers soups and salads as well as a variety of homemade sauces including Chuy's signature Hatch Green Chile Boom-Boom and Creamy Jalape ±o sauces. Operates in over 15 states each of the company's more than 90 restaurants offer patrons a funky upbeat vibrant and eclectic atmosphere. Originally founded in Austin Texas in 1982 the company went public in mid-2012.

	Annual Growth	12/16	12/17	12/18	12/19	12/20
Sales ($ mil.)	(0.7%)	330.6	369.6	398.2	426.4	321.0
Net income ($ mil.)	–	17.2	29.0	5.5	6.2	(3.3)
Market value ($ mil.)	(4.1%)	649.5	552.9	354.0	509.1	550.5
Employees	(7.1%)	8,200	9,000	9,000	9,000	6,100

CHYRONHEGO CORP
NMS: CHYR

5 Hub Drive
Melville, NY 11747
Phone: 631 845-2000
Fax: –
Web: www.chyron.com

CEO: Ariel Garcia
CFO: Carl Blandino
HR: –
FYE: December 31
Type: Public

ChyronHego (formerly Chyron) wants customers to stay tuned. The company develops makes and sells software hardware and cloud-based services providing graphics creation and management for live and pre-recorded television broadcasts. Its Windows-based products are used to create logos text and other images that can be superimposed over existing images to display information such as sports scores stock tickers and weather data. The firm's clients include ABC ESPN FOX News CNN and the BBC. In addition to broadcasters ChyronHego markets to post-production facilities government agencies schools health care providers and telecom service providers. In 2013 Chyron merged with Hego AB to form ChyronHego.

	Annual Growth	12/09	12/10	12/11	12/12	12/13
Sales ($ mil.)	16.6%	25.6	27.7	31.6	30.2	47.4
Net income ($ mil.)	–	(3.1)	(2.4)	(4.2)	(22.3)	(7.8)
Market value ($ mil.)	0.5%	64.0	67.7	42.8	21.9	65.3
Employees	16.3%	104	114	126	111	190

CIANBRO CORPORATION

101 CIANBRO SQ
PITTSFIELD, ME 049676301
Phone: 207-487-3311
Fax: –
Web: www.cianbro.com

CEO: Peter A Vigue
CFO: Kyle K Holmstrom
HR: –
FYE: December 31
Type: Private

One of the largest most diverse successful open shop 100% employee-owned construction and construction services companies in the US Cianbro and its subsidiaries presently operate in more than 40 states including operational facilities in Maine Massachusetts Connecticut Maryland New Jersey South Carolina Kentucky Illinois Louisiana Texas and Washington. Working with a fleet of 3500 owned equipment units Cianbro provides construction services from concept through implementation and works start-up commissioned and turn-key operations to markets such as building industrial and manufacturing infrastructure and power and energy industries. Cianbro manages and self-performs civil structural mechanical electrical instrumentation telecommunications thermal fabrication and coating. The company headquartered in Maine was founded in 1949.

	Annual Growth	12/05	12/06	12/07	12/08	12/16
Sales ($ mil.)	–	–	0.0	0.0	429.0	385.0
Net income ($ mil.)	–	–	0.0	0.0	0.0	(6.4)
Market value ($ mil.)	–	–	–	–	–	–
Employees	–	–	–	–	–	1,639

CIB MARINE BANCSHARES INC   NBB: CIBH

19601 West Bluemound Road
Brookfield, WI 53045
Phone: 262 695-6010
Fax: 630 735-2841
Web: www.cibmarine.com

CEO: J. Brian Chaffin
CFO: Patrick Straka
HR: –
FYE: December 31
Type: Public

CIB Marine Bancshares is semper fi to its banking strategy. The company owns CIBM Bank which operates in the Indianapolis Milwaukee and Phoenix markets. Through some 20 branches the bank caters to individuals and small- and midsized-business customers offering checking and savings accounts ATM and debit cards CDs and IRAs. The company's loan portfolio mainly consists of commercial mortgages business loans and commercial real estate construction loans. CIB Marine Bancshares emerged from Chapter 11 bankruptcy protection in early 2010.

	Annual Growth	12/16	12/17	12/18	12/19	12/20
Assets ($ mil.)	3.5%	653.6	662.4	721.3	703.8	751.0
Net income ($ mil.)	19.1%	4.1	27.0	3.3	2.0	8.2
Market value ($ mil.)	94.4%	1.4	1.8	2.0	1.8	20.0
Employees	7.0%	171	183	–	–	–

CIBER, INC.   NYS: CBR

6312 South Fiddler's Green Circle, Suite 600E
Greenwood Village, CO 80111
Phone: 303 220-0100
Fax: 303 220-7100
Web: www.ciber.com

CEO: Christian Mezger
CFO: Christian Mezger
HR: –
FYE: December 31
Type: Public

CIBER (Consultants in Business Engineering and Research) is a global IT consultancy that provides enterprise systems integration through consulting practices specializing in such software systems as Lawson Microsoft Oracle SAP and Salesforce.com as well as custom software development. It serves corporate customers in such industries as communications financial services manufacturing health care and education as well as not-for-profits. Its diverse client list includes Boeing The University of Texas System Duke Energy and Disney. Founded in 1974 CIBER earns just over half of its sales overseas; international offices in Europe operate through CIBER (UK) Ltd.

	Annual Growth	12/11	12/12	12/13	12/14	12/15
Sales ($ mil.)	(5.3%)	976.9	884.4	877.3	863.6	787.0
Net income ($ mil.)	–	(67.3)	(14.6)	(14.5)	(19.6)	3.3
Market value ($ mil.)	(2.3%)	308.9	267.3	331.3	284.1	280.9
Employees	(2.0%)	6,500	6,700	6,500	6,500	6,000

CIC GROUP, INC.

1509 OCELLO DR
FENTON, MO 630262406
Phone: 314-682-2900
Fax: –
Web: www.cicgroup.com

CEO: Donald H Lange
CFO: –
HR: –
FYE: November 30
Type: Private

CIC Group can see clearly that its future (like its present) is in heavy manufacturing and construction. Its group of commercial and industrial subsidiaries specialize in the manufacture maintenance and repair of equipment for the crude oil natural gas coal and other energy industries. Its largest subsidiary is Nooter/Eriksen which supplies heat recovery steam generators for combustion gas turbines worldwide. CIC's Nooter Construction is a construction contractor serving the refining petro-chemical pulp and paper and power industries among others. The employee-owned holding company was formed in 2002.

	Annual Growth	11/06	11/07	11/08	11/10	11/11
Sales ($ mil.)	(9.2%)	–	–	1,120.6	758.0	838.9
Net income ($ mil.)	–	–	–	0.0	0.0	0.0
Market value ($ mil.)	–	–	–	–	–	–
Employees	–	–	–	–	–	1,500

CICERO INC   NBB: CICN

8000 Regency Parkway, Suite 542
Cary, NC 27518
Phone: 919 380-5000
Fax: –
Web: www.ciceroinc.com

CEO: John Broderick
CFO: John Broderick
HR: Rachel Wendel
FYE: December 31
Type: Public

Cicero takes a philosophical approach to integrating computer applications. The company provides application integration software used to link a variety of enterprise applications (including mainframe client/server and Web-based environments) primarily for financial service firms' contact centers. It also provides consulting project management and training services which account for more than a third of revenue. Customers include Affiliated Computer Services Deutsche Bank and Merrill Lynch. Cicero's roster of strategic partners includes resellers such as BluePhoenix MphasiS and Tata Consultancy. The company gets all of its sales in the US.

	Annual Growth	12/15	12/16	12/17	12/18	12/19
Sales ($ mil.)	(5.7%)	1.9	1.3	1.3	0.8	1.5
Net income ($ mil.)	–	(2.8)	(3.9)	(2.1)	(2.1)	(1.6)
Market value ($ mil.)	(20.0%)	4.4	1.3	1.7	0.9	1.8
Employees	(12.6%)	24	16	15	15	14

CIENA CORP   NYS: CIEN

7035 Ridge Road
Hanover, MD 21076
Phone: 410 694-5700
Fax: 410 694-5750
Web: www.ciena.com

CEO: Gary Smith
CFO: James Moylan
HR: –
FYE: October 30
Type: Public

Ciena's optical transport and switching equipment increases the capacity of fiber-optic networks to meet the rising demands of video data and voice traffic. Users include telecommunications providers cable TV companies large-scale web services firms submarine network operators and governments. In addition to its systems and software Ciena also offer a broad range of services that help its customers build operate and improve their networks and associated operational environments. These include network transformation consulting implementation systems integration maintenance network operations center (NOC) management and optimization services. About 60% of sales are to US customers.

	Annual Growth	10/17	10/18	10/19	10/20	10/21
Sales ($ mil.)	6.6%	2,801.7	3,094.3	3,572.1	3,532.2	3,620.7
Net income ($ mil.)	(20.7%)	1,262.0	(344.7)	253.4	361.3	500.2
Market value ($ mil.)	26.4%	3,293.9	4,840.9	5,748.4	6,099.9	8,407.3
Employees	6.0%	5,737	6,013	6,383	7,032	7,241

CIFC CORP.

250 PARK AVE STE 400
NEW YORK, NY 101770502
Phone: 212-624-1200
Fax: –
Web: www.cifc.com

CEO: –
CFO: Rahul Agarwal
HR: –
FYE: December 31
Type: Private

CIFC is searching for a new world of investments. Through subsidiaries the specialty finance company invests in and manages client assets such as asset-backed securities bank loans and government securities. It offers some 30 investment products including separately managed accounts and a private investment fund. CIFC has some $14 billion of assets under management. Nearly 90% of its portfolio was once devoted to residential mortgage-backed securities (RMBS) but CIFC broadened its investment mix in the wake of the mortgage meltdown. Alternative investment platform F.A.B. Partners is buying CIFC for $333 million.

	Annual Growth	12/11	12/12	12/13	12/14	12/15
Assets ($ mil.)	(71.4%)	–	10,504.9	11,600.2	13,148.1	244.6
Net income ($ mil.)	–	–	(240.3)	96.8	(12.3)	1.0
Market value ($ mil.)	–	–	–	–	–	–
Employees	–	–	–	–	–	82

CIGNA CORP (NEW) NYS: CI

900 Cottage Grove Road
Bloomfield, CT 06002
Phone: 860 226-6000
Fax: 860 226-6741
Web: www.cigna.com

CEO: David Cordani
CFO: Eric Palmer
HR: –
FYE: December 31
Type: Public

With a significant position in the US health insurance market CIGNA covers some 16 million Americans with its various medical plans. The firm's offerings include PPO HMO point-of-service (POS) indemnity and consumer-directed products as well as specialty coverage in the form of dental vision pharmacy and behavioral health plans. It also sells group accident life and disability insurance. Customers include employers government entities unions Medicare recipients and other groups and individuals in North America. Internationally CIGNA sells life accident and health insurance in parts of Europe and Asia and provides health coverage to expatriate employees of multinational companies.

	Annual Growth	12/16	12/17	12/18	12/19	12/20
Assets ($ mil.)	27.2%	59,360.0	61,753.0	153,226.0	155,774.0	155,451.0
Net income ($ mil.)	45.9%	1,867.0	2,237.0	2,637.0	5,104.0	8,458.0
Market value ($ mil.)	11.8%	47,322.9	72,050.4	67,378.1	72,547.1	73,856.2
Employees	15.8%	41,000	46,000	73,800	73,700	73,700

CIM COMMERCIAL TRUST CORP NMS: CMCT

17950 Preston Road, Suite 600
Dallas, TX 75252
Phone: 972 349-3200
Fax: –
Web: www.cimcommercial.com

CEO: David Thompson
CFO: Nathan DeBacker
HR: –
FYE: December 31
Type: Public

PMC Commercial Trust likes lending to little businesses. The real estate investment trust (REIT) makes small business loans primarily to limited-service hotel franchisees. The loans ranging from $100000 to $4 million are secured by first liens on real estate and written for hotel owner/operators of national franchises such as Comfort Inn and Holiday Inn Express. PMC Commercial Trust also lends to owners of convenience stores restaurants and other small businesses. About 20% of its loan portfolio is concentrated in Texas. Subsidiaries are active in Small Business Administration (SBA) lending and in investing (as small business investment companies or SBICs). The company was founded in 1993.

	Annual Growth	12/16	12/17	12/18	12/19	12/20
Assets ($ mil.)	(23.7%)	2,022.9	1,336.4	1,342.4	667.6	685.6
Net income ($ mil.)	–	34.5	379.7	1.1	345.7	(15.0)
Market value ($ mil.)	(2.0%)	229.1	283.2	225.1	215.0	211.1
Employees	(20.5%)	10	2	5	5	4

CIMAREX ENERGY CO NYS: XEC

1700 Lincoln Street, Suite 3700
Denver, CO 80203
Phone: 303 295-3995
Fax: –
Web: www.cimarex.com

CEO: Thomas E Jorden
CFO: G Mark Burford
HR: –
FYE: December 31
Type: Public

Cimarex Energy's energy is devoted to oil and natural gas exploration and production. The independent is focusing its operations developing assets in two regions — the Mid-Continent and the Permian Basin. The company has proved reserves of nearly 620 million boe (barrels of oil equivalents including gas oil and natural gas liquids). Cimarex's daily production averages about 280000 boe. The company's three biggest assets are the Watonga-Chickasha field in the Mid-Continent (nearly 30% of proved reserves) Dixieland in the Permian Basin (more than 20%) and Ford West in the Permian Basin (over 15%). Denver Colorado-based Cimarex's customers include major energy companies pipeline operators local distributors and other end users.

	Annual Growth	12/15	12/16	12/17	12/18	12/19
Sales ($ mil.)	12.9%	1,452.6	1,257.3	1,918.2	2,339.0	2,363.0
Net income ($ mil.)	–	(2,408.9)	(431.0)	494.3	791.9	(124.6)
Market value ($ mil.)	(12.5%)	9,129.7	13,881.4	12,462.7	6,297.2	5,361.6
Employees	1.6%	925	856	910	955	987

CINCINNATI BELL INC NYS: CBB

221 East Fourth Street
Cincinnati, OH 45202
Phone: 513 397-9900
Fax: –
Web: www.cincinnatibell.com

CEO: Leigh R Fox
CFO: Andrew R Kaiser
HR: –
FYE: December 31
Type: Public

Cincinnati Bell isn't hanging up on copper yet but it is moving to provide telecommunication services through fiber optic cable as well as IT services. The company which has provide telephone service to the Cincinnati area since 1870 has invested in fiber optics to bring high-speed internet and entertainment services to residential customers through its Fioptics service. It also provides communications and IT services and hardware to businesses. In the meantime it divested its wireless licenses and de-emphasized its legacy landline business. It also provides IT and telecommunications services including telephony network and infrastructure services equipment sales and staffing services.

	Annual Growth	12/15	12/16	12/17	12/18	12/19
Sales ($ mil.)	7.1%	1,167.8	1,185.8	1,288.5	1,378.2	1,536.7
Net income ($ mil.)	–	353.7	102.1	35.1	(69.8)	(66.6)
Market value ($ mil.)	30.6%	181.5	1,126.9	1,051.3	392.3	527.9
Employees	7.9%	3,250	3,400	3,500	4,300	4,400

CINCINNATI BENGALS INC.

1 Paul Brown Stadium
Cincinnati OH 45202
Phone: 513-621-3550
Fax: 513-621-3570
Web: www.bengals.com

CEO: Michael Brown
CFO: William Scanlom
HR: –
FYE: February 28
Type: Private

These Bengals prowl the jungle of the NFL. The Cincinnati Bengals professional football franchise traces an elite heritage having been formed by Hall of Fame coach Paul Brown in 1968 as part of the American Football League (AFL). Cincinnati joined the National Football League in 1970 when the AFL and NFL merged and went on to make two trips to the Super Bowl (losing both times to the San Francisco 49ers). The team plays host at Paul Brown Stadium which opened in 2000. Brown's family led by his son Mike Brown continues to control the Bengals.

CINCINNATI FINANCIAL CORP.   NMS: CINF

6200 S. Gilmore Road   CEO: Steven Johnston
Fairfield, OH 45014-5141   CFO: Michael Sewell
Phone: 513 870-2000   HR: –
Fax: –   FYE: December 31
Web: www.cinfin.com   Type: Public

Cincinnati Financial Corporation (CFC) provides property casualty insurance marketed through independent insurance agencies in around 45 states primarily in the midwestern and southeastern US. Its flagship firm Cincinnati Insurance (operating through four subsidiaries) sells commercial property and casualty liability excess and surplus auto bond and fire insurance. Personal lines include homeowners auto and other personal line products. The Cincinnati Insurance companies also sell life coverage and annuities. Other CFC subsidiaries include CFC Investment (leasing and financing services) CSU Producers Resources (excess and surplus lines brokerage) and Cincinnati Global Underwriting (global specialty insurance). The Cincinnati Insurance Company was founded in 1950 while CFC was formed in 1968.

	Annual Growth	12/16	12/17	12/18	12/19	12/20
Assets ($ mil.)	7.8%	20,386.0	21,843.0	21,935.0	25,408.0	27,542.0
Net income ($ mil.)	19.8%	591.0	1,045.0	287.0	1,997.0	1,216.0
Market value ($ mil.)	3.6%	12,188.2	12,062.7	12,456.9	16,918.6	14,057.8
Employees	2.6%	4,754	4,925	4,999	5,148	5,266

CINER RESOURCES LP   NYS: CINR

Five Concourse Parkway, Suite 2500   CEO: Oguz Erkan
Atlanta, GA 30328   CFO: Ahmet Tohma
Phone: 770 375-2300   HR: –
Fax: –   FYE: December 31
Web: www.ciner.us.com   Type: Public

They say baking soda has plenty of household uses but soda ash provides even more. Ciner Resources operates a soda ash mining and production plant in Wyoming that annually produces about 2.5 million short tons of the raw material used in flat glass container glass detergents chemicals paper and other consumer and industrial products. Ciner Resources sells most of its soda ash to export firm American Natural Soda Ash Corporation (ANSAC). Turkey's Ciner Group's acquired OCI Chemical in 2015 and renamed it Ciner Resources.

	Annual Growth	12/16	12/17	12/18	12/19	12/20
Sales ($ mil.)	(4.7%)	475.2	497.3	486.7	522.8	392.2
Net income ($ mil.)	(27.1%)	41.4	41.6	49.9	49.6	11.7
Market value ($ mil.)	(18.8%)	585.8	507.2	433.3	350.5	254.3
Employees	0.8%	473	476	488	497	489

CINEDIGM CORP   NMS: CIDM

237 West 35th Street, Suite 605   CEO: Christopher McGurk
New York, NY 10001   CFO: John Canning
Phone: 212 206-8600   HR: –
Fax: –   FYE: March 31
Web: www.cinedigm.com   Type: Public

Cinedigm Digital Cinema (formerly known as Access Integrated Technologies or AccessIT) hopes to make digital the new cinema paradigm. The company provides software and services for the managed storage and electronic delivery of digital content to movie theaters for major film studios. It also provides alternative digital content to customers such as museums and educational venues. Major customers include Warner Bros. and Universal Pictures. Cinedigm in 2011 sold its digital delivery assets to Technicolor. It kept assets in key areas related to alternative content and digital cinema operational software.

	Annual Growth	03/17	03/18	03/19	03/20	03/21
Sales ($ mil.)	(23.2%)	90.4	67.7	53.5	39.3	31.4
Net income ($ mil.)	–	(15.1)	(18.5)	(16.2)	(14.7)	(62.8)
Market value ($ mil.)	1.9%	257.1	227.7	315.8	60.7	277.6
Employees	(10.9%)	114	110	104	72	72

CINTAS CORPORATION   NMS: CTAS

6800 Cintas Boulevard, P.O. Box 625737   CEO: Scott Farmer
Cincinnati, OH 45262-5737   CFO: Jon Hansen
Phone: 513 459-1200   HR: –
Fax: 513 573-4030   FYE: May 31
Web: www.cintas.com   Type: Public

Cintas is one of the North America's leading provider of corporate identity uniforms as well as a significant provider of related business services including entrance mats restroom cleaning services and supplies first aid and safety services and fire protection products and services. It provides products and services to over one million businesses of all types through the company's nearly 475 facilities in more than 330 cities. Besides offering rental and servicing of uniforms and other garments the company also offers flame-resistant clothing mats mops and shop towels and other ancillary items. Founded by Richard T. Farmer in 1968 Cintas is now run by Scott D. Farmer.

	Annual Growth	05/17	05/18	05/19	05/20	05/21
Sales ($ mil.)	7.5%	5,323.4	6,476.6	6,892.3	7,085.1	7,116.3
Net income ($ mil.)	23.3%	480.7	842.6	885.0	876.0	1,111.0
Market value ($ mil.)	29.5%	13,099.2	18,965.2	23,083.9	25,803.1	36,789.9
Employees	(1.2%)	42,000	41,000	45,000	40,000	40,000

CINEMARK HOLDINGS INC   NYS: CNK

3900 Dallas Parkway   CEO: Sean Gamble
Plano, TX 75093   CFO: Melissa Thomas
Phone: 972 665-1000   HR: Sid Srivastava
Fax: –   FYE: December 31
Web: www.cinemark.com   Type: Public

Cinemark Holdings is one of the largest movie exhibitor in the US and one of the most geographically diverse operators in the motion picture exhibition industry with about 5960 screens in nearly 530 theaters in the US and Latin America. The company prefers to build new theaters reinvesting and acquiring existing theaters where the Cinemark theater is the only game in town. As part of the Digital Cinema Distribution Coalition joint venture with certain exhibitors and distributors Cinemark's US theaters receive films and other media via satellite. The company generates majority of its revenue domestically.

	Annual Growth	12/16	12/17	12/18	12/19	12/20
Sales ($ mil.)	(30.4%)	2,918.8	2,991.5	3,221.7	3,283.1	686.3
Net income ($ mil.)	–	255.1	264.2	213.8	191.4	(616.8)
Market value ($ mil.)	(17.9%)	4,548.6	4,128.8	4,245.0	4,013.8	2,064.4
Employees	10.4%	19,200	28,100	20,000	22,000	28,500

CIPHERLOC CORP   NBB: CLOK

6836 Bee Cave Road, Bldg.1, Suite 279   CEO: David Chasteen
Austin, TX 78746   CFO: Ryan Polk
Phone: 512 337-3728   HR: –
Fax: –   FYE: September 30
Web: www.cipherloc.net   Type: Public

National Scientific keeps an eye on kids and it doesn't mind riding the bus. The company makes location-tracking products that incorporate digital video recording (DVR) devices Global Positioning System (GPS) technology and software. Its Gotcha! radio device alerts parents when a child wanders too far away while the Travado IBUS system provides position tracking and video monitoring of school buses. The company's Travado Mini product tracks the location of government and first responder vehicles. National Scientific has yet to be profitable. The company is owned by its executives and other shareholders.

	Annual Growth	09/17	09/18	09/19	09/20	09/21
Sales ($ mil.)	(57.4%)	0.5	0.3	0.0	0.0	0.0
Net income ($ mil.)	–	(4.4)	(4.4)	(6.8)	(7.0)	(3.1)
Market value ($ mil.)	(43.1%)	150.1	170.0	45.6	37.3	15.7
Employees	(13.1%)	7	11	11	3	4

CIRCOR INTERNATIONAL INC — NYS: CIR

30 Corporate Drive, Suite 200
Burlington, MA 01803-4238
Phone: 781 270-1200
Fax: –
Web: www.circor.com

CEO: Tony Najjar
CFO: Arjun Sharma
HR: –
FYE: December 31
Type: Public

CIRCOR International designs manufactures and markets differentiated technology products and sub-systems for the industrial and aerospace and defense markets. It has a diversified flow and motion control product portfolio with recognized market-leading brands that fulfill its customers' mission critical and severe service needs. Its products are also used in the aerospace military and commercial aircraft as well as analytical equipment oil & gas refining power generation chemical processing and maritime industries. Products are sold directly and through distributors in some 100 countries around the world. Majority of the company's sales were generated in the US.

	Annual Growth	12/16	12/17	12/18	12/19	12/20
Sales ($ mil.)	7.0%	590.3	661.7	1,175.8	964.3	773.3
Net income ($ mil.)	–	10.1	11.8	(39.4)	(133.9)	(185.5)
Market value ($ mil.)	(12.3%)	1,297.7	973.7	426.0	924.9	768.9
Employees	6.9%	2,400	4,400	4,400	4,000	3,138

CIRRUS LOGIC INC — NMS: CRUS

800 W. 6th Street
Austin, TX 78701
Phone: 512 851-4000
Fax: –
Web: www.cirrus.com

CEO: John Forsyth
CFO: Thurman Case
HR: –
FYE: March 27
Type: Public

Cirrus Logic is a leader in low-power high-precision mixed-signal processing solutions that create innovative user experiences for the world's top mobile and consumer applications that are used in smartphones tablets truly wireless headsets and more. It also has an extensive portfolio of products including "codecs" - chips that integrate analog-to-digital converters (ADCs) and digital-to-analog converters (DACs) into a single integrated circuit (IC) smart codecs - codecs with digital signal processing integrated boosted amplifiers as well as standalone digital signal processors (DSPs). The company gets most of its sales from customers in China. The company was incorporated in 1984 and became public in 1989.

	Annual Growth	03/17	03/18	03/19	03/20	03/21
Sales ($ mil.)	(2.9%)	1,538.9	1,532.2	1,185.5	1,281.1	1,369.2
Net income ($ mil.)	(4.5%)	261.2	162.0	90.0	159.5	217.3
Market value ($ mil.)	8.4%	3,462.6	2,342.4	2,425.4	3,569.8	4,785.7
Employees	0.6%	1,444	1,596	1,551	1,443	1,481

CIRTRAN CORP. — NBB: CIRC

4125 South 6000 West
West Valley City, UT 84128
Phone: 801 963-5112
Fax: –
Web: www.cirtran.com

CEO: Iehab Hawatmeh
CFO: Iehab Hawatmeh
HR: –
FYE: December 31
Type: Public

CirTran provides contract electronics manufacturing services through which it makes printed circuit boards and cables for customers in consumer electronics networking equipment the automotive industry and other markets. The company has established an Asian subsidiary in Shenzhen China that undertakes manufacturing services for a wider variety of products including cooking appliances fitness equipment and hair products. CirTran's Racore Technology subsidiary makes Ethernet adapter cards for PCs. Racore's customers include the Fire Department of New York City Lear Siegler Lockheed Martin the US Air Force and Walt Disney World.

	Annual Growth	12/09	12/10	12/11	12/12	12/13
Sales ($ mil.)	(22.7%)	9.7	9.0	3.1	4.3	3.5
Net income ($ mil.)	–	(5.8)	(2.6)	(6.3)	(0.2)	0.9
Market value ($ mil.)	–	0.0	0.0	0.0	0.0	0.0
Employees	40.8%	15	88	11	3	59

CISCO SYSTEMS INC — NMS: CSCO

170 West Tasman Drive
San Jose, CA 95134
Phone: 408 526-4000
Fax: –
Web: www.cisco.com

CEO: Charles Robbins
CFO: R Scott Herren
HR: –
FYE: July 31
Type: Public

Cisco Systems (Cisco) designs and sells a broad range of technologies that power the Internet. It is integrating its platforms across networking security collaboration applications and the cloud. These platforms are designed to help its customers manage more users devices and things connecting to their networks. This will enable the company to provide customers with a highly secure intelligent platform for their digital business. Most sales come from customers in the Americas. Cisco's primary customers including businesses of all sizes public institution government telecommunications service providers including large webscale providers.

	Annual Growth	07/17	07/18	07/19	07/20	07/21
Sales ($ mil.)	0.9%	48,005.0	49,330.0	51,904.0	49,301.0	49,818.0
Net income ($ mil.)	2.5%	9,609.0	110.0	11,621.0	11,214.0	10,591.0
Market value ($ mil.)	–	0.0	0.0	0.0	0.0	0.0
Employees	2.2%	72,900	74,200	75,900	77,500	79,500

CIT GROUP INC (NEW) — NYS: CIT

11 West 42nd Street
New York, NY 10036
Phone: 212 461-5200
Fax: –
Web: www.cit.com

CEO: Ellen Alemany
CFO: John Fawcett
HR: James Duffy
FYE: December 31
Type: Public

A stalwart in the big-business landscape for over a century CIT Group is a financial holding company that offers lending leasing deposit products as well as ancillary products and services including cash management capital markets and advisory services to small- and mid-sized businesses in such industries as erospace & defense aviation communication power and energy entertainment gaming health care industrial maritime restaurants services and technology. It operates a physical branch network in southern California and spans the US with its online banking platform. Founded in 1908 CIT expanded its consumer presence with the 2015 acquisition of OneWest. Majority of the company's revenue is generated from the US.

	Annual Growth	12/15	12/16	12/17	12/18	12/19
Assets ($ mil.)	(6.8%)	67,498.8	64,170.2	49,278.7	48,537.4	50,832.8
Net income ($ mil.)	(15.8%)	1,056.6	(848.0)	468.2	447.1	529.9
Market value ($ mil.)	3.5%	3,761.3	4,043.6	4,664.2	3,625.8	4,323.1
Employees	(7.4%)	4,900	4,410	4,167	3,678	3,609

CITATION OIL & GAS CORP.

14077 CUTTEN RD
HOUSTON, TX 770692212
Phone: 281-891-1000
Fax: –
Web: www.cogc.com

CEO: –
CFO: Chris Phelps
HR: –
FYE: December 31
Type: Private

Citation Oil & Gas is writing its own ticket to prosperity in the petroleum industry. The oil and gas development and production company has interests in about 15000 wells (in more than 480 separately designated fields) and reported 210 million barrels of proved oil equivalent reserves (91% oil) in 2012. Its oil fields are in the Mid-Continent Illinois Basin Permian Basin and Rocky Mountain regions. Citation seeks out properties with high levels of crude oil declining production with long reserve life and low risk. The company uses a variety of techniques to recover oil and gas including waterflood and infill drilling. Subsidiary Citation Crude Marketing sells the company's products to refiners.

	Annual Growth	12/15	12/16	12/17	12/18	12/20
Sales ($ mil.)	3.2%	–	179.7	191.9	283.5	204.0
Net income ($ mil.)	–	–	(129.8)	74.1	125.9	(9.0)
Market value ($ mil.)	–	–	–	–	–	–
Employees	–	–	–	–	–	507

CITGO PETROLEUM CORPORATION

1293 ELDRIDGE PKWY
HOUSTON, TX 770771670
Phone: 832-486-4000
Fax: –
Web: www.citgo.com

CEO: Carlos Jorda
CFO: Curtis Rowe
HR: –
FYE: December 31
Type: Private

CITGO Petroleum is the fifth-largest independent refiner in the US. It refines and markets petroleum products including transportation fuels lubricants and petrochemicals. It markets CITGO branded gasoline through about 5300 independent retail outlets in about 30 US states mainly east of the Rockies. CITGO Petroleum owns oil refineries in Illinois Louisiana and Texas. The company has the refining capacity to process more than 749000 barrels of crude oil per day. It markets more than 600 types of lubricants and sells over 13 billion gallons of refined products annually. CITGO Petroleum is the operating subsidiary of PDV America itself a subsidiary of Venezuela's national oil company PDVSA.

	Annual Growth	12/03	12/04	12/15	12/16	12/17
Sales ($ mil.)	(2.2%)	–	32,277.1	–	19,914.2	24,100.4
Net income ($ mil.)	1.0%	–	625.0	–	234.0	715.3
Market value ($ mil.)	–	–	–	–	–	–
Employees	–	–	–	–	–	4,000

CITI TRENDS INC

104 Coleman Boulevard
Savannah, GA 31408
Phone: 912 236-1561
Fax: –
Web: www.cititrends.com

CEO: David Makuen
CFO: Pamela Edwards
HR: Ivy Council
FYE: January 30
Type: Public

NMS: CTRN

Citi Trends hopes to transport its customers to Trend City as quickly as possible. The fast-growing urban fashion apparel and accessory chain focuses primarily on the African-American market. Its brand-name includes Citi Steps Citi Trends Fashion for Less Lil Ms Hollywood Red Ape and Vintage Harlem ? which include men's women's and children's clothing; shoes; fashion accessories; and housewares ? sell for 20%?70% lower than department and specialty stores' regular prices. Citi Trends operates about 570 stores in about 35 states. The company was founded in 1946 as Allied Department Stores.

	Annual Growth	01/17*	02/18	02/19	02/20*	01/21
Sales ($ mil.)	3.0%	695.2	755.2	769.6	781.9	783.3
Net income ($ mil.)	15.8%	13.3	14.6	21.4	16.5	24.0
Market value ($ mil.)	37.8%	161.4	223.2	201.4	230.0	582.7
Employees	(1.8%)	5,600	5,600	5,500	5,700	5,200

*Fiscal year change

CITIGROUP INC

388 Greenwich Street
New York, NY 10013
Phone: 212 559-1000
Fax: –
Web: www.citigroup.com

CEO: Paco Ybarra
CFO: Mark Mason
HR: Sara Wechter
FYE: December 31
Type: Public

NYS: C

Citigroup is a global diversified financial services holding company whose businesses provide consumers corporations governments and institutions with a broad yet focused range of financial products and services including consumer banking and credit corporate and investment banking securities brokerage trade and securities services and wealth management. Citi has approximately 200 million customer accounts and does business in more than 160 countries and jurisdictions. Citi has some $2.3 trillion in assets and some $1.3 trillion in deposits. Citigroup generates almost half of its sales from North America.

	Annual Growth	12/16	12/17	12/18	12/19	12/20
Assets ($ mil.)	6.0%	1,792,077.0	1,842,465.0	1,917,383.0	1,951,158.0	2,260,090.0
Net income ($ mil.)	(7.2%)	14,912.0	(6,798.0)	18,045.0	19,401.0	11,047.0
Market value ($ mil.)	0.9%	123,738.6	154,928.3	108,393.6	166,338.1	128,381.6
Employees	(1.0%)	219,000	209,000	204,000	200,000	210,153

CITIZENS & NORTHERN CORP

90-92 Main Street
Wellsboro, PA 16901
Phone: 570 724-3411
Fax: –
Web: www.cnbankpa.com

CEO: J. Scovill
CFO: Mark Hughes
HR: Tracy Watkins
FYE: December 31
Type: Public

NAS: CZNC

Citizens & Northern Corp. is the holding company for Citizens & Northern (C&N) Bank Citizens & Northern Investment Corp. and Bucktail Life Insurance Company. Its primary business and largest subsidiary is C&N Bank a community bank that serves individuals and commercial customers in Pennsylvania and New York. The bank operates more than 25 branches and offers online and telebanking services. The firm's other subsidiaries are Citizens & Northern Investment Corp. which provides investment services and Bucktail Life Insurance a provider of credit life and property/casualty reinsurance. The bank holding company has assets of more than $1.3 billion.

	Annual Growth	12/17	12/18	12/19	12/20	12/21
Assets ($ mil.)	16.2%	1,277.0	1,290.9	1,654.1	2,239.1	2,327.6
Net income ($ mil.)	22.8%	13.4	22.0	19.5	19.2	30.6
Market value ($ mil.)	2.1%	378.2	416.5	445.2	312.7	411.6
Employees	6.5%	296	299	336	–	–

CITIZENS BANCSHARES CORP. (GA)

230 Peachtree Street, NW, Suite 2700
Atlanta, GA 30303
Phone: 678 406-4000
Fax: –
Web: www.ctbconnect.com

CEO: Cynthia N Day
CFO: Samuel J Cox
HR: –
FYE: December 31
Type: Public

NBB: CZBS

One of the largest minority-led financial institutions in the US Citizens Bancshares is the holding company for Citizens Trust Bank which serves the Atlanta and Columbus Georgia and Birmingham and Eutaw Alabama communities from about 10 branch offices. The bank provides standard services such as checking and savings accounts CDs IRAs credit cards financial planning and investments. Its lending portfolio mainly consists of loans secured by one- to four-family residences multifamily dwellings or commercial or industrial real estate. Former chairman and Atlanta-area entrepreneur and philanthropist Herman J. Russell owns about 30% of Citizens Bancshares' stock.

	Annual Growth	12/16	12/17	12/18	12/19	12/20
Assets ($ mil.)	9.6%	395.8	429.1	410.6	417.8	571.9
Net income ($ mil.)	26.6%	2.0	1.6	4.0	3.7	5.2
Market value ($ mil.)	2.8%	21.8	33.4	25.1	27.3	24.3
Employees	–	–	–	–	–	–

CITIZENS COMMUNITY BANCORP INC (MD)

2174 EastRidge Center
Eau Claire, WI 54701
Phone: 715 836-9994
Fax: –
Web: www.ccf.us

CEO: Stephen Bianchi
CFO: James Broucek
HR: –
FYE: December 31
Type: Public

NMS: CZWI

Citizens Community Bancorp is the holding company for Citizens Community Federal a community bank with about 20 branches in Wisconsin southern Minnesota and northern Michigan. Serving consumers and businesses the bank offers standard deposit services such as savings checking money market and retirement accounts as well as a variety of loan products. The bank focuses its lending activities on one- to four-family mortgages which represent more than half of its loan portfolio. The bank also offers consumer loans such as auto and personal loans; it does not routinely make commercial loans. Founded in 1938 Citizens Community was a state-chartered credit union until 2001.

	Annual Growth	09/17	09/18*	12/18	12/19	12/20
Assets ($ mil.)	20.6%	940.7	975.4	1,287.9	1,531.2	1,649.1
Net income ($ mil.)	72.0%	2.5	4.3	1.3	9.5	12.7
Market value ($ mil.)	(7.9%)	154.2	154.8	120.5	135.1	120.4
Employees	3.9%	224	282	265	288	251

*Fiscal year change

CITIZENS ENERGY GROUP

2020 N MERIDIAN ST
INDIANAPOLIS, IN 462021306
Phone: 317-924-3341
Fax: –
Web: www.citizensenergygroup.com

CEO: Jeffrey Harrison
CFO: –
HR: Robyn Nelson
FYE: September 30
Type: Private

Hoosiers are happy to have their homes provided with gas and water services by Public Utilities of the City of Indianapolis (dba Citizens Energy and CWA Authority public charitable trusts). Its Citizens Water unit provides water and wastewater services to 300000 customers in Indianapolis; Citizens Gas serves more than 266000 gas customers. Citizens Energy also provides steam heating and chilled water cooling services to about 250 customers through Citizens Thermal Energy. The regional utility also has a small oil production unit (Citizens Oil Division). Its Citizens Resources unit has joint venture stakes in some companies not regulated by the Indiana Utility Regulatory Commission such as ProLiance Energy.

	Annual Growth	09/08	09/09	09/10	09/11	09/12
Sales ($ mil.)	25.7%	–	–	440.7	463.6	696.4
Net income ($ mil.)		–	–	(1.8)	32.4	(11.8)
Market value ($ mil.)	–	–	–	–	–	–
Employees		–	–	–	–	1,100

CITIZENS EQUITY FIRST CREDIT UNION

5401 W. Dirksen Pkwy.
Peoria IL 61607
Phone: 309-633-7000
Fax: 309-633-3926
Web: www.cefcu.com

CEO: –
CFO: Charles E Walker
HR: Cindy Sarff
FYE: December 31
Type: Private - Not-for-Pr

Citizens Equity First Credit Union (CEFCU) first gained traction in 1937 as the credit union of mammoth equipment manufacturer Caterpillar. Through some 20 branches CEFCU now serves employees of more than 550 companies and people who live and work in about a dozen counties in central Illinois and portions of northern California. It boasts more than 275000 members who have access to financial services such as checking and savings accounts CDs home auto and education loans credit cards investments and life and auto insurance. The credit union offers estate retirement and tax planning services through subsidiary CEFCU Financial Services and its partnership with MEMBERS Trust Company.

CITIZENS FINANCIAL CORP.

213 3rd St.
Elkins WV 26241-1519
Phone: 304-636-4095
Fax: 304-636-6924
Web: www.cnbelkins.com

OTC: CIWV
CEO: Robert Schoonover
CFO: Nathaniel Bonnell
HR: –
FYE: December 31
Type: Public

The proletariat should not confuse Citizens Financial with Citizens Financial Corporation (in Kentucky) Citizens Financial Group (Rhode Island) or Citizens Financial Services (Pennsylvania). This Citizens Financial is the holding company of Citizens National Bank which has about a half-dozen offices in central and eastern West Virginia. Citizens National Bank offers savings and checking accounts consumer and commercial loans trust services and other financial services and products. Real estate loans — including mortgages home equity loans and construction loans — account for some 80% of the bank's lending portfolio.

CITIZENS FINANCIAL CORP. (WV)

213 Third Street
Elkins, WV 26241
Phone: 304 636-4095
Fax: 304 636-6924
Web: www.cnbelkins.com

NBB: CIWV
CEO: Robert Schoonover
CFO: Nathaniel Bonnell
HR: –
FYE: December 31
Type: Public

The proletariat should not confuse Citizens Financial with Citizens Financial Corporation (in Kentucky) Citizens Financial Group (Rhode Island) or Citizens Financial Services (Pennsylvania). This Citizens Financial is the holding company of Citizens National Bank which has about a half-dozen offices in central and eastern West Virginia. Citizens National Bank offers savings and checking accounts consumer and commercial loans trust services and other financial services and products. Real estate loans — including mortgages home equity loans and construction loans — account for some 80% of the bank's lending portfolio.

	Annual Growth	12/06	12/07	12/08	12/13	12/14
Assets ($ mil.)	(1.2%)	243.0	246.6	282.5	208.7	220.8
Net income ($ mil.)	0.1%	2.1	1.0	0.9	1.5	2.1
Market value ($ mil.)	(10.5%)	35.3	20.4	12.7	12.2	14.5
Employees	(3.9%)	91	88	84	–	–

CITIZENS FINANCIAL GROUP INC (NEW)

One Citizens Plaza
Providence, RI 02903
Phone: 203 900-6715
Fax: –
Web: www.citizensbank.com

NYS: CFG
CEO: Bruce Van Saun
CFO: John Woods
HR: –
FYE: December 31
Type: Public

Citizens Financial Group offers a broad range of retail and commercial banking products and services to more than five million individuals small businesses middle-market companies large corporations and institutions. The company's main operating subsidiary is consumer bank Citizens Bank which spans approximately 1000 branches across eleven states in the New England Mid-Atlantic and Midwest regions and boasts more than $183 billion in assets and over $147 billion in deposits. The bank's branches offer standard retail and commercial services including loans leases trade financing deposits cash management commercial cards foreign exchange and others.

	Annual Growth	12/17	12/18	12/19	12/20	12/21
Assets ($ mil.)	5.5%	152,336.0	160,518.0	165,733.0	183,349.0	188,409.0
Net income ($ mil.)	8.8%	1,652.0	1,721.0	1,791.0	1,057.0	2,319.0
Market value ($ mil.)	3.0%	17,721.3	12,550.1	17,143.0	15,095.6	19,946.0
Employees	(0.2%)	17,600	18,100	18,000	17,584	17,463

CITIZENS FINANCIAL SERVICES INC

15 South Main Street
Mansfield, PA 16933
Phone: 570 662-2121
Fax: –
Web: www.firstcitizensbank.com

NBB: CZFS
CEO: Randall Black
CFO: Stephen Guillaume
HR: Amy Wood
FYE: December 31
Type: Public

Citizens Financial Services is an upstanding resident of the financial community. The holding company for First Citizens National Bank serves north-central Pennsylvania's Tioga Potter and Bradford counties and southern New York. Through some 15 branches the bank offers checking savings time and deposit accounts as well as real estate commercial industrial residential and consumer loans. Residential mortgage loans account for more than half of the bank's total loan portfolio. The Trust and Investment division offers investment advice and employee benefits coordination as well as estate and retirement planning services. Insurance is offered through the First Citizen's Insurance Agency subsidiary.

	Annual Growth	12/16	12/17	12/18	12/19	12/20
Assets ($ mil.)	11.5%	1,223.0	1,361.9	1,430.7	1,466.3	1,891.7
Net income ($ mil.)	18.7%	12.6	13.0	18.0	19.5	25.1
Market value ($ mil.)	1.4%	209.9	249.5	220.0	243.6	221.8
Employees	3.2%	270	273	274	268	306

CITIZENS FIRST CORP.

NMS: CZFC

1065 Ashley Street
Bowling Green, KY 42103
Phone: 270 393-0700
Fax: -
Web: www.citizensfirstbank.com

CEO: -
CFO: -
HR: -
FYE: December 31
Type: Public

Citizens First puts the folks of southwestern Kentucky before all else. Founded in 1975 as a small private-investment club Citizens First is the holding company for Citizens First Bank which serves consumers and area businesses through about a dozen locations and 20 ATMs. The company's loan portfolio includes primarily commercial and residential mortgages and business loans. The company also provides title insurance services. Through alliances with other firms it offers its customers trust and investment services as well as insurance products. Fellow Kentucky bank Porter Bancorp withdrew its offer to acquire a controlling stake in Citizens First in late 2009..

	Annual Growth	12/13	12/14	12/15	12/16	12/17
Assets ($ mil.)	3.2%	410.2	412.8	432.2	455.4	465.4
Net income ($ mil.)	22.1%	1.8	3.2	3.6	4.2	4.1
Market value ($ mil.)	24.9%	24.9	30.1	34.7	45.5	60.6
Employees	(0.5%)	100	97	98	95	98

CITIZENS HOLDING CO

NMS: CIZN

521 Main Street
Philadelphia, MS 39350
Phone: 601 656-4692
Fax: -
Web: www.citizensholdingcompany.com

CEO: Greg McKee
CFO: Phillip Branch
HR: -
FYE: December 31
Type: Public

Citizens Holding Company has taken the proletariat approach to banking. The firm is the holding company for The Citizens Bank of Philadelphia Mississippi which operates some 20 locations in the eastern part of the state. Founded in 1908 the bank targets individuals and local businesses offering products such as checking and savings accounts money market accounts CDs IRAs and trust services. Lending activities consist mostly of real estate loans (about 70% of the loan portfolio) and commercial industrial and agricultural loans (more than 10%). Citizens Holding offers discount brokerage services through an agreement with First Tennessee Bank. Subsidiary Title Services offers title insurance.

	Annual Growth	12/16	12/17	12/18	12/19	12/20
Assets ($ mil.)	9.1%	1,025.2	993.1	958.6	1,195.4	1,450.7
Net income ($ mil.)	0.7%	6.7	3.7	6.7	5.9	6.9
Market value ($ mil.)	(5.1%)	144.4	129.1	117.3	122.2	117.0
Employees	2.3%	264	265	259	290	289

CITIZENS, INC. (AUSTIN, TX)

NYS: CIA

11815 Alterra Pkwy, Floor 15
Austin, TX 78758
Phone: 512 837-7100
Fax: -
Web: www.citizensinc.com

CEO: Gerald Shields
CFO: Jeffrey Conklin
HR: -
FYE: December 31
Type: Public

Citizens is an insurance holding company. Through its Life Insurance it issues life insurance in US dollars to wealthy individuals in Latin America and Taiwan. Its Home Service segment sells life insurance to middle and lower-income individuals in a Louisiana Mississippi and Arkansas through employee and independent agents in its home service distribution channel and through funeral homes. Citizens operates through CICA Life Insurance Company of America (CICA) CICA Life Ltd. Citizens National Life Insurance Company which constitute the Life Insurance segment and Security Plan Life Insurance Company (SPLIC) Security Plan Fire Insurance Company and Magnolia Guaranty Life Insurance Company which constitute the Home Service Insurance segment. The company has about $1.7 billion of assets and approximately $4.2 billion of insurance in force.

	Annual Growth	12/16	12/17	12/18	12/19	12/20
Assets ($ mil.)	3.9%	1,583.7	1,644.5	1,615.6	1,744.9	1,843.4
Net income ($ mil.)	-	2.0	(38.1)	(11.1)	(1.4)	(11.0)
Market value ($ mil.)	(12.6%)	496.1	371.3	379.9	341.0	289.5
Employees	(23.9%)	730	443	650	400	245

CITRIX SYSTEMS INC

NMS: CTXS

851 West Cypress Creek Road
Fort Lauderdale, FL 33309
Phone: 954 267-3000
Fax: 954 267-9319
Web: www.citrix.com

CEO: Robert Calderoni
CFO: Arlen Shenkman
HR: -
FYE: December 31
Type: Public

Citrix is an enterprise software company focused on helping organizations deliver a consistent and secure work experience no matter where work needs to get done ? in the office at home or in the field. The company does this by delivering a digital workspace solution that gives each employee the resources and space they need to do their best work. Its product line includes application virtualization software (Citrix Virtual Apps and Desktops) network access devices (Citrix ADC) and mobility applications (Citrix Endpoint Management). The US accounts for more than 50% of revenue.

	Annual Growth	12/17	12/18	12/19	12/20	12/21
Sales ($ mil.)	3.3%	2,824.7	2,973.9	3,010.6	3,236.7	3,217.2
Net income ($ mil.)	-	(20.7)	575.7	681.8	504.4	307.5
Market value ($ mil.)	1.8%	10,987.8	12,793.3	13,847.1	16,244.4	11,810.6
Employees	6.6%	7,500	8,200	8,400	9,000	9,700

CITY & COUNTY OF HONOLULU

530 S KING ST RM 300
HONOLULU, HI 968103019
Phone: 808-768-4141
Fax: -
Web: www.honolulu.gov

CEO: -
CFO: -
HR: -
FYE: June 30
Type: Private

With a population of almost 1 million people Honolulu County located on the island of Oahu is the largest city and county in Hawaii. The city and county are governed by a mayor and a nine-member legislative council. Honolulu's largest industry is tourism but the city is also the financial center of Hawaii.

	Annual Growth	06/16	06/17	06/18	06/19	06/20
Sales ($ mil.)	8.6%	-	1,728.6	1,849.0	2,013.9	2,211.4
Net income ($ mil.)	-	-	(89.2)	482.4	315.1	336.2
Market value ($ mil.)	-	-	-	-	-	-
Employees	-	-	-	-	-	8,000

CITY & COUNTY OF SAN FRANCISCO

1 DR CARLTON B GOODLETT P
SAN FRANCISCO, CA 941024604
Phone: 415-554-7500
Fax: -
Web: www.sf.gov

CEO: -
CFO: -
HR: -
FYE: June 30
Type: Private

The City of San Francisco is the 14th largest in the US and its dense population geographic detachment and cultural diversity have made San Francisco a favorite with both tourists and residents. San Francisco's government is a consolidated city-county bureaucracy with both entities led by an elected mayor. The government includes an executive branch led by the mayor and consisting of other elected officials and city departments and a legislative branch consisting of an 11-member Board of Supervisors. The city is also home to several federal institutions including the Federal Reserve Bank and the US Mint.

	Annual Growth	06/16	06/17	06/18	06/19	06/20
Sales ($ mil.)	6.3%	-	5,971.6	6,411.4	7,561.9	7,181.4
Net income ($ mil.)	-	-	569.3	1,172.5	563.3	(100.7)
Market value ($ mil.)	-	-	-	-	-	-
Employees	-	-	-	-	-	30,000

CITY HARVEST, INC.

6 E 32ND ST FL 5
NEW YORK, NY 100165415
Phone: 646-412-0600
Fax: –
Web: www.cityharvest.org

CEO: –
CFO: –
HR: –
FYE: June 30
Type: Private

The folks at City Harvest have found a way to harvest food straight from the asphalt of New York City streets. City Harvest is a not-for-profit organization that delivers food to soup kitchens food pantries and community food programs in New York. The organization distributes almost 110 million pounds of good food each year. Founded by Helen verDuin Palit in 1982 City Harvest works with nearly 2500 food donors such as Blue Apron Baldor PRET Vita Coco Whole Foods Market as well as financial supporters to bring food to the city streets.

	Annual Growth	06/16	06/17	06/18	06/19	06/20
Sales ($ mil.)	19.2%	–	123.6	136.7	142.4	209.4
Net income ($ mil.)	312.5%	–	0.5	0.5	0.2	36.4
Market value ($ mil.)	–	–	–	–	–	–
Employees	–	–	–	–	–	140

CITY HOLDING CO.

25 Gatewater Road
Charleston, WV 25313
Phone: 304 769-1100
Fax: –
Web: www.bankatcity.com

NMS: CHCO
CEO: Charles Hageboeck
CFO: David Bumgarner
HR: –
FYE: December 31
Type: Public

City Holding conducts its principal activities through its wholly owned subsidiary City National Bank of West Virginia. City National offers full range of commercial banking services to corporation and other business customers and provides banking services to consumers including checking savings and money market accounts as well as certificates of deposit and individual retirement accounts. It also provides mortgage banking services and offers specialized services and expertise in the areas of wealth management trust investment and custodial services for commercial and individual customers. City Nationals operates more than 90 branches along the I-64 corridor from Lexington Kentucky through Lexington Virginia and along the I-81 corridor through the Shenandoah Valley from Lexington Virginia to Martinsburg West Virginia.

	Annual Growth	12/16	12/17	12/18	12/19	12/20
Assets ($ mil.)	9.6%	3,984.4	4,132.3	4,899.0	5,018.8	5,758.6
Net income ($ mil.)	14.5%	52.1	54.3	70.0	89.4	89.6
Market value ($ mil.)	0.7%	1,065.9	1,063.8	1,065.7	1,292.1	1,096.6
Employees	2.3%	847	839	891	918	926

CITY NATIONAL CORP. (BEVERLY HILLS, CA)

City National Plaza, 555 South Flower Street
Los Angeles, CA 90071
Phone: 213 673-7700
Fax: –
Web: www.cnb.com

NYS: CYN
CEO: –
CFO: –
HR: –
FYE: December 31
Type: Public

For celebrity sightings forget the Hollywood Homes Tour and camp out at City National Bank. The flagship subsidiary of City National Corporation has been known as "Bank to the Stars" since opening in Beverly Hills in 1954. The bank has since grown to some 80 branches in Southern California the San Francisco Bay area and Nevada as well as New York City Nashville and Atlanta. It focuses on personal and business banking investment management and trust services. The bank provides customized service tailoring its offerings to meet the needs of its high-powered clientele. Its target market includes small to midsized businesses entrepreneurs professionals and affluent individuals in urban markets.

	Annual Growth	12/09	12/10	12/11	12/12	12/13
Assets ($ mil.)	9.0%	21,078.8	21,353.1	23,666.3	28,618.5	29,718.0
Net income ($ mil.)	45.5%	51.3	131.2	172.4	208.0	230.0
Market value ($ mil.)	14.8%	2,470.8	3,324.7	2,393.8	2,683.2	4,292.4
Employees	4.3%	3,017	3,178	3,256	3,472	3,566

CITY OF AKRON

166 S HIGH ST RM 502
AKRON, OH 443081622
Phone: 330-375-2720
Fax: –
Web: www.akronohio.gov

CEO: –
CFO: –
HR: –
FYE: December 31
Type: Private

Akron Ohio once known as the "Rubber Capital of the World" is the fifth-largest city in Ohio. It is located about 40 miles south of Cleveland in the north-central part of the state. Akron's largest corporation is the Goodyear Tire & Rubber Company (founded 1898); it's also home to the University of Akron. Akron was founded in 1825. Its population in 2015 was about 200000 people.

	Annual Growth	12/16	12/17	12/18	12/19	12/20
Sales ($ mil.)	9.6%	–	330.9	359.8	384.6	436.2
Net income ($ mil.)	–	–	(36.2)	(1.4)	(20.2)	13.2
Market value ($ mil.)	–	–	–	–	–	–
Employees	–	–	–	–	–	2,866

CITY OF ALBUQUERQUE

400 MARQUETTE AVE NW
ALBUQUERQUE, NM 871022117
Phone: 505-768-3000
Fax: –
Web: www.cabq.gov

CEO: –
CFO: Sanjay Bhakta
HR: –
FYE: June 30
Type: Private

Albuquerque is by far New Mexico's largest city with a 2015 estimated population of 561380 (about 970680 in the greater metropolitan area). Albuquerque is located in the central part of the state and is home to The University of New Mexico. While Pueblo Indians lived in the general area for several centuries Spanish explorers arrived in the 16th century. The city of Albuquerque was founded in 1706 and named after the Spanish town of Albuquerque (with an extra "r"). The City of Albuquerque is administered by a Mayor and a nine-person City Council.

	Annual Growth	06/16	06/17	06/18	06/19	06/20
Sales ($ mil.)	8.8%	–	709.5	722.8	825.1	913.7
Net income ($ mil.)	–	–	(5.6)	45.1	20.6	209.7
Market value ($ mil.)	–	–	–	–	–	–
Employees	–	–	–	–	–	6,500

CITY OF ALEXANDRIA

301 KING ST
ALEXANDRIA, VA 223143211
Phone: 703-746-4000
Fax: –
Web: www.alexandriava.gov

CEO: –
CFO: –
HR: –
FYE: June 30
Type: Private

Historically a wartime victim of occupying forces modern Alexandria is home to many Defense Department contractors and employees. It uses a council-manager form of government wherein the mayor is part of the six-member city council (all elected at large) which determines city policy. The city manager works to carry out the policy and run the day-to-day operations of Alexandria. In addition to the city manager the council also appoints the city attorney city clerk and members of various commissions and boards. Alexandria's more than 30 departments operate on an annual budget of about $400 million and serve about 130000 citizens. The city was founded in 1749.

	Annual Growth	06/17	06/18	06/19	06/20	06/21
Sales ($ mil.)	3.2%	–	842.3	880.9	911.0	924.6
Net income ($ mil.)	–	–	108.9	(8.3)	167.7	(76.0)
Market value ($ mil.)	–	–	–	–	–	–
Employees	–	–	–	–	–	2,375

CITY OF ANAHEIM

200 S ANAHEIM BLVD
ANAHEIM, CA 928053820
Phone: 714-765-5162
Fax: –
Web: www.anaheim.net

CEO: –
CFO: –
HR: –
FYE: June 30
Type: Private

Anaheim is a city in sunny southern Orange County California. The state's 10th largest city is home to Disneyland Resort one of Walt Disney Parks and Resorts' theme parks. The city also features a number of professional sports franchises such as the Anaheim Ducks hockey team and the Angels baseball team. Anaheim was founded in 1857.

	Annual Growth	06/16	06/17	06/18	06/19	06/20
Sales ($ mil.)	(1.6%)	–	602.9	566.2	592.7	574.9
Net income ($ mil.)	–	–	93.0	27.7	12.9	(100.4)
Market value ($ mil.)	–	–	–	–	–	–
Employees	–	–	–	–	–	3,100

CITY OF ARLINGTON

101 W ABRAM ST
ARLINGTON, TX 760107102
Phone: 817-275-3271
Fax: –
Web: www.arlingtontx.gov

CEO: –
CFO: –
HR: –
FYE: September 30
Type: Private

This City of Arlington is in Texas though it's named for the one in Virginia. Established in 1876 Arlington was named for Confederate General Robert E. Lee's Arlington House in Arlington Virginia. The city which is between Dallas and Fort Worth is the seventh-largest city in Texas and home to about 380000 people. Its most popular attraction is the Six Flags Over Texas theme park. It also plays host to the Texas Rangers Major League Baseball team and the Dallas Cowboys AT&T Stadium. The city also boasts the second largest unit of the University of Texas System UT Arlington and a General Motors assembly plant built in 1954.

	Annual Growth	09/13	09/14	09/15	09/16	09/17
Sales ($ mil.)	3.5%	–	338.0	355.1	405.9	374.8
Net income ($ mil.)	–	–	15.1	6.4	48.9	(9.4)
Market value ($ mil.)	–	–	–	–	–	–
Employees	–	–	–	–	–	2,477

CITY OF ATLANTA

55 TRINITY AVE SW # 3900
ATLANTA, GA 303033543
Phone: 404-330-6100
Fax: –
Web: www.atlantaga.gov

CEO: –
CFO: J Anthony Beard
HR: –
FYE: June 30
Type: Private

City of Atlanta leaders have a dream to improve Atlantans' quality of life. The birthplace of civil rights activist Martin Luther King Jr. Atlanta is run by a mayor and a 16-member council. With a metropolitan population of more than 5 million Atlanta is the most populous city in Georgia. It's also the state capital and home to such major companies as The Coca-Cola Company The Home Depot and UPS. In addition Atlanta has a number of professional sports franchises namely the Atlanta Braves Hawks and Falcons.

	Annual Growth	06/12	06/13	06/14	06/15	06/17
Sales ($ mil.)	5.3%	–	850.6	883.3	920.2	1,044.6
Net income ($ mil.)	79.0%	–	14.2	9.1	274.1	146.2
Market value ($ mil.)	–	–	–	–	–	–
Employees	–	–	–	–	–	8,885

CITY OF AUSTIN

301 W 2ND ST
AUSTIN, TX 787014652
Phone: 512-974-2000
Fax: –
Web: www.austintexas.gov

CEO: –
CFO: –
HR: –
FYE: September 30
Type: Private

Deep in the heart of Texas you'll find Austin the capital of the state and self-proclaimed Live Music Capital of the World. The city covering more than 300 square miles follows the council/manager model where the mayor and six city council members all elected to three-year terms enact policy and the city manager carries it out. The manager's office oversees about 30 departments/offices the municipal court system city utilities and the city's airport. Austin has a city population of more than 820000 and a greater metro population of more than 1.8 million. Stephen F. Austin brought the first Anglo settlers to the area in 1821.

	Annual Growth	09/16	09/17	09/18	09/19	09/20
Sales ($ mil.)	6.9%	–	1,186.6	1,279.2	1,352.9	1,449.5
Net income ($ mil.)	–	–	28.5	67.0	33.7	(34.9)
Market value ($ mil.)	–	–	–	–	–	–
Employees	–	–	–	–	–	10,922

CITY OF BAKERSFIELD

1600 TRUXTUN AVE FL 5TH
BAKERSFIELD, CA 933015140
Phone: 661-326-3000
Fax: –
Web: www.mechanicsbankarena.com

CEO: –
CFO: –
HR: Anthony Gonzales
FYE: June 30
Type: Private

Californians can enjoy sunny weather with fewer crowds in the City of Bakersfield. With a population of about 350000 Bakersfield is the 9th largest city in the state. Governed by the mayor and seven city council members (elected for four-year terms) the City of Bakersfield operates through 15 departments including water resources animal services and recreation and parks. Bakersfield was founded in 1858 and named after early settler Colonel Thomas Baker. The city is home to the Bakersfield Panthers California State University and the Rabobank Arena.

	Annual Growth	06/16	06/17	06/18	06/19	06/20
Sales ($ mil.)	9.6%	–	340.8	334.4	359.9	448.8
Net income ($ mil.)	–	–	(5.7)	2.1	12.7	27.1
Market value ($ mil.)	–	–	–	–	–	–
Employees	–	–	–	–	–	1,570

CITY OF BALTIMORE

100 HOLLIDAY ST STE 250
BALTIMORE, MD 212023459
Phone: 410-396-3835
Fax: –
Web: www.baltimorecity.gov

CEO: –
CFO: –
HR: Catherine B Phr
FYE: June 30
Type: Private

Although it is the birthplace of the National Anthem home to the first commercial ice cream factory in the US and among the nation's oldest cities Baltimore is more than an asterisk to history. With a population of about 620000 the city — Maryland's largest — supports a major seaport and is part of the Baltimore-Washington metropolis. The city's economy is founded on shipping transportation auto manufacturing and steel processing. It is however shifting to a diverse service base attractive to tourists. Baltimore is home to two professional sports teams the Baltimore Orioles and the Baltimore Ravens.

	Annual Growth	06/16	06/17	06/18	06/19	06/20
Sales ($ mil.)	3.3%	–	2,167.5	2,147.6	2,413.1	2,391.8
Net income ($ mil.)	–	–	63.4	126.2	133.1	(6.0)
Market value ($ mil.)	–	–	–	–	–	–
Employees	–	–	–	–	–	26,400

CITY OF BELLEVUE

450 110TH AVE NE
BELLEVUE, WA 980045514
Phone: 425-452-6800
Fax: -
Web: www.bellevuewa.gov

CEO: -
CFO: -
HR: -
FYE: December 31
Type: Private

The pretty view from the City of Bellevue Washington is of its larger neighbor across Lake Washington the City of Seattle. The bedroom community boasts a population of more than 130000 and a council-manager form of government where the post of mayor is mostly ceremonial. The seven-member council serves staggered four-year terms and chooses the mayor from its ranks. Day-to-day operations are carried out by the city manager city attorney and city clerk. Bellevue sits right next to Microsoft hometown Redmond Washington and the Lake Washington "Gold Coast" where Bill Gates and other technology millionaires make their homes. Bellevue was founded in 1869.

	Annual Growth	12/16	12/17	12/18	12/19	12/20
Sales ($ mil.)	5.1%	-	338.3	342.8	379.1	392.2
Net income ($ mil.)	53.8%	-	8.9	29.8	12.4	32.2
Market value ($ mil.)	-	-	-	-	-	-
Employees	-	-	-	-	-	1,175

CITY OF BERKELEY

2120 MILVIA ST
BERKELEY, CA 947041113
Phone: 510-981-7300
Fax: -
Web: www.cityofberkeley.info

CEO: -
CFO: -
HR: -
FYE: June 30
Type: Private

Situated on the eastern shore of San Francisco Bay the City of Berkeley has a population of more than 100000 within the confines of roughly 18 square miles. It is home to the University of California Berkeley considered the flagship institution of the California higher education system. Since 1823 the city has operated under the council-manager form of government. Eight council members (elected by separate districts) and the mayor are responsible for decisions regarding the city's economic development health and human services housing public works and transportation.

	Annual Growth	06/16	06/17	06/18	06/19	06/20
Sales ($ mil.)	6.4%	-	276.4	298.6	334.5	332.7
Net income ($ mil.)	9.4%	-	18.4	60.8	36.6	24.1
Market value ($ mil.)	-	-	-	-	-	-
Employees	-	-	-	-	-	1,520

CITY OF BOSTON

1 CITY HALL SQ STE 242
BOSTON, MA 022011020
Phone: 617-635-4545
Fax: -
Web: www.boston.gov

CEO: -
CFO: -
HR: -
FYE: June 30
Type: Private

Boston's legacy includes a famous Tea Party Paul Revere's Ride and clam chowder. With about 625000 residents Boston has been called the economic and cultural hub of New England. The Greater Boston metro area is home to about 4.6 million people making it the 10th largest city in the US. Boston also boasts world class educational institutions (Harvard Massachusetts Institute of Technology) champion sports teams (Red Sox Celtics Patriots) and a rich cultural and historical identity. Boston is also the capital of Massachusetts.

	Annual Growth	06/14	06/15	06/16	06/17	06/19
Sales ($ mil.)	4.8%	-	3,278.1	3,393.1	3,542.4	3,953.0
Net income ($ mil.)	28.1%	-	79.3	139.0	93.9	213.6
Market value ($ mil.)	-	-	-	-	-	-
Employees	-	-	-	-	-	18,760

CITY OF BROCKTON

45 SCHOOL ST
BROCKTON, MA 023014063
Phone: 508-580-7123
Fax: -
Web: www.brockton.ma.us

CEO: -
CFO: -
HR: -
FYE: June 30
Type: Private

Owing to the success of native boxers Rocky Marciano and "Marvelous" Marvin Hagler the City of Brockton has been hailed "The City of Champions." With a population of more than 90000 the city covers 22 square miles in southeastern Massachusetts. It is primarily urban in nature and is situated along the Salisbury River which once fueled the city's many shoe factories. During the American Civil War Brockton was the largest producer of shoes in the country. Incorporated in 1881 its city government today consists of the mayor (elected to a two-year term) and 11 city council members.

	Annual Growth	06/05	06/06	06/12	06/13	06/14
Sales ($ mil.)	3.2%	-	294.2	361.2	368.9	379.7
Net income ($ mil.)	-	-	(4.6)	(9.4)	(10.1)	2.4
Market value ($ mil.)	-	-	-	-	-	-
Employees	-	-	-	-	-	30,000

CITY OF BUFFALO

65 NIAGARA SQ RM 201
BUFFALO, NY 142023392
Phone: 716-851-4200
Fax: -
Web: www.buffalony.gov

CEO: -
CFO: -
HR: -
FYE: June 30
Type: Private

Buffalo New York is the second-largest city in the state (behind New York City of course). Located in the western part of the state of the state by Lake Erie Buffalo is home to more than 260000 people. The greater metropolitan area including the famed Niagara Falls is home to more 1.2 million people. It also has two professional sports franchises the Buffalo Bills football team and the Sabres hockey team.

	Annual Growth	06/17	06/18	06/19	06/20	06/21
Sales ($ mil.)	4.4%	-	516.4	525.9	504.9	587.7
Net income ($ mil.)	-	-	(25.2)	(19.3)	(18.2)	59.1
Market value ($ mil.)	-	-	-	-	-	-
Employees	-	-	-	-	-	3,426

CITY OF CAMBRIDGE

795 MASSACHUSETTS AVE
CAMBRIDGE, MA 021393219
Phone: 617-349-4260
Fax: -
Web: www.cambridgema.gov

CEO: -
CFO: -
HR: -
FYE: June 30
Type: Private

The City of Cambridge houses an abundance of prominent minds. Part of the Greater Boston area it is home to prestigious universities Harvard and the Massachusetts Institute of Technology (MIT). With a population of more than 100000 the city covers just seven square miles. Most of its commercial districts are major street intersections (which act as neighborhood centers) which have given rise to its nickname "City of Squares." They include: Central Harvard Inman Kendall Lechmere and Porter Squares. Cambridge's city government is a bit unusual. The city manager (appointed by its nine city council members) rather than the mayor (also elected by the council) serves as the chief executive of the city.

	Annual Growth	06/16	06/17	06/18	06/19	06/20
Sales ($ mil.)	5.4%	-	667.4	726.6	754.7	782.3
Net income ($ mil.)	(22.6%)	-	55.3	65.7	38.2	25.7
Market value ($ mil.)	-	-	-	-	-	-
Employees	-	-	-	-	-	2,000

CITY OF CHANDLER

175 S ARIZONA AVE
CHANDLER, AZ 852257526
Phone: 480-782-2000
Fax: –
Web: www.chandleraz.gov

CEO: –
CFO: –
HR: –
FYE: June 30
Type: Private

Chandler Arizona is just one of the many popular cities located in Maricopa County. This suburb of Phoenix has a population of more than 240000 residents but don't call it a bedroom community — Chandler is home to a number of high tech companies including an Intel plant that makes semiconductors. The city is named after Dr. Alexander Chandler a veterinarian who moved to the area in the late 19th century.

	Annual Growth	06/16	06/17	06/18	06/19	06/20
Sales ($ mil.)	8.1%	–	298.6	306.3	330.3	376.9
Net income ($ mil.)	62.6%	–	11.5	47.5	5.9	49.5
Market value ($ mil.)	–	–	–	–	–	–
Employees	–	–	–	–	–	1,498

CITY OF CHARLOTTE

600 E 4TH ST
CHARLOTTE, NC 282022816
Phone: 704-336-7600
Fax: –
Web: www.charlottenc.gov

CEO: –
CFO: –
HR: –
FYE: June 30
Type: Private

You can bank on Charlotte ... the nation's second-largest banking center (behind New York City). The City of Charlotte delivers public services and promotes safety and health among residents. Policies are set by a mayor and 11 council members elected for two-year terms. The day-to-day operations are handled by a city manager. Charlotte has a population of more than 750000 and covers about 280 square miles. It's home to a handful of Fortune 500 companies including Bank of America Family Dollar and Duke Energy as well as the Carolina Panthers and Charlotte Motor Speedway. It also boasts some 700 places of worship earning it the nickname "The City of Churches."

	Annual Growth	06/16	06/17	06/18	06/19	06/20
Sales ($ mil.)	5.2%	–	945.5	997.1	1,065.6	1,102.2
Net income ($ mil.)	–	–	(36.0)	(10.2)	148.6	(83.4)
Market value ($ mil.)	–	–	–	–	–	–
Employees	–	–	–	–	–	5,011

CITY OF CHESAPEAKE

306 CEDAR RD
CHESAPEAKE, VA 233225597
Phone: 757-382-6586
Fax: –
Web: www.cityofchesapeake.net

CEO: –
CFO: –
HR: –
FYE: June 30
Type: Private

The City of Chesapeake attracts both beachcombers and history buffs. Located about 20 miles from Virginia Beach Chesapeake was established in 1963 through the merging of the city of South Norfolk and Norfolk County which was created in 1691. The first English settlement in the area began around 1620 along the banks of the Elizabeth River. The mayor vice mayor and seven city council members (elected for four-year terms) govern the city which has a population of more than 233370. The third-largest city in Virginia Chesapeake is home to the College of William and Mary and Hampton University.

	Annual Growth	06/13	06/14	06/15	06/16	06/20
Sales ($ mil.)	–	–	0.0	595.8	621.9	703.0
Net income ($ mil.)	53.3%	–	4.2	4.6	15.0	54.1
Market value ($ mil.)	–	–	–	–	–	–
Employees	–	–	–	–	–	2,893

CITY OF CHULA VISTA

276 FOURTH AVE
CHULA VISTA, CA 919102699
Phone: 619-691-5137
Fax: –
Web: www.chulavistaca.gov

CEO: –
CFO: –
HR: –
FYE: June 30
Type: Private

Chula Vista (which means "beautiful view" in Spanish) is a suburb of city of San Diego. With a population of nearly 250000 Chula Vista is governed by a mayor and four city council members. As a bedroom community the city's largest employers are the local school districts.

	Annual Growth	06/16	06/17	06/18	06/19	06/20
Sales ($ mil.)	9.7%	–	210.8	253.6	276.7	278.1
Net income ($ mil.)	29.0%	–	4.9	99.8	31.7	10.6
Market value ($ mil.)	–	–	–	–	–	–
Employees	–	–	–	–	–	942

CITY OF CINCINNATI

801 PLUM ST RM 246
CINCINNATI, OH 452025704
Phone: 513-352-3221
Fax: –
Web: www.cincinnati-oh.gov

CEO: –
CFO: –
HR: –
FYE: June 30
Type: Private

Founded in 1788 Cincinnati is home to almost 300000 people and covers roughly 80 square miles. It is the third-largest city in Ohio trailing behind Columbus and Cleveland. The city's government consists of the mayor and nine city council members (elected at large). Council committees deal with a wide range of issues including public education health economic concerns and community development. The city is also home to two major-league sports franchises — baseball's Cincinnati Reds and football's Cincinnati Bengals.

	Annual Growth	06/15	06/16	06/17	06/18	06/19
Sales ($ mil.)	4.2%	–	–	708.6	729.0	769.2
Net income ($ mil.)	52.5%	–	–	10.9	(22.2)	25.3
Market value ($ mil.)	–	–	–	–	–	–
Employees	–	–	–	–	–	5,964

CITY OF CLEVELAND

601 LAKESIDE AVE E RM 210
CLEVELAND, OH 441141015
Phone: 216-664-2000
Fax: –
Web: www.clevelandohio.gov

CEO: –
CFO: –
HR: –
FYE: December 31
Type: Private

It's only rock and roll but Cleveland residents like it. The City of Cleveland Ohio (C-Town) is home to the Rock and Roll Hall of Fame and is the nation's 45th largest city and Ohio's second largest (behind Columbus). C-Town with more than 390000 residents is run by a mayor-council form of government. The legislative branch consists of a 21-member council and the executive branch comprises the mayor his adjunct offices advisors and the city's administrative departments. The mayor is the city's CEO and is elected to enforce its charter ordinances and state laws. The Village of Cleveland was incorporated in 1814.

	Annual Growth	12/14	12/15	12/17	12/19	12/20
Sales ($ mil.)	2.9%	–	706.9	801.3	839.5	816.9
Net income ($ mil.)	(15.8%)	–	21.0	75.9	31.0	8.9
Market value ($ mil.)	–	–	–	–	–	–
Employees	–	–	–	–	–	8,073

CITY OF COLORADO SPRINGS

107 N NEVADA AVE
COLORADO SPRINGS, CO 809031305
Phone: 719-385-5900
Fax: –
Web: www.coloradosprings.gov

CEO: –
CFO: –
HR: –
FYE: December 31
Type: Private

There may not be much gold in them thar hills anymore but Colorado Springs is still a glitzy place to live. With more than 415000 residents it's the second-largest city in Colorado behind Denver. (Colorado Springs is located about 70 miles south of Denver along Interstate 25.) The city was incorporated in 1871 chosen for its scenic location in the valley of Pikes Peak and the Rocky Mountains.

	Annual Growth	12/11	12/12	12/13	12/14	12/15
Sales ($ mil.)	5.1%	–	272.6	279.1	304.6	316.8
Net income ($ mil.)	(55.1%)	–	17.3	(2.2)	2.8	1.6
Market value ($ mil.)	–	–	–	–	–	–
Employees	–	–	–	–	–	7,000

CITY OF COLUMBUS

90 W BROAD ST RM B33
COLUMBUS, OH 432159061
Phone: 614-645-7671
Fax: –
Web: www.columbus.gov

CEO: –
CFO: –
HR: –
FYE: December 31
Type: Private

So what if European explorer Christopher Columbus didn't sail the Scioto River? Columbus the capital of Ohio is located smack dab in the middle of the state. With a population of almost 836000 people Columbus is the largest city in the Buckeye State. (Cleveland and Cincinnati however have larger populations in their greater metropolitan areas.) Columbus is home to a handful of Fortune 500 companies including Nationwide Insurance and retailer L Brands. While the area had been home to European fur trappers since the 1700s and Native Americans for centuries Columbus became a city in 1812.

	Annual Growth	12/16	12/17	12/18	12/19	12/20
Sales ($ mil.)	7.8%	–	1,442.7	1,478.7	1,630.7	1,805.7
Net income ($ mil.)	–	–	(1.4)	94.3	29.2	(73.0)
Market value ($ mil.)	–	–	–	–	–	–
Employees	–	–	–	–	–	8,385

CITY OF CORPUS CHRISTI

1201 LEOPARD ST
CORPUS CHRISTI, TX 784012120
Phone: 361-880-3000
Fax: –
Web: www.cctexas.com

CEO: –
CFO: –
HR: –
FYE: September 30
Type: Private

Corpus Christi (which means "body of Christ" in Latin) is a port city that sits on the Gulf of Mexico in south Texas. With a population of more than 305000 it's the eighth-largest city in Texas. Its Port of Corpus Christi is one of the top 10 ports in the country.

	Annual Growth	09/14	09/15	09/16	09/18	09/20
Sales ($ mil.)	2.3%	–	340.5	348.9	372.8	381.7
Net income ($ mil.)	(6.0%)	–	95.2	12.0	13.7	69.8
Market value ($ mil.)	–	–	–	–	–	–
Employees	–	–	–	–	–	3,518

CITY OF DAYTON

101 W 3RD ST
DAYTON, OH 454021859
Phone: 937-333-3333
Fax: –
Web: www.daytonohio.gov

CEO: Warren Price
CFO: –
HR: –
FYE: December 31
Type: Private

If you "heart" nerds The City of Dayton Ohio is the place for you. Dayton boasts one of the highest concentrations of engineers and patents in the US with aerospace and high tech bolstering its economy. Dayton is run by a commission comprised of the mayor and four commissioners who are elected for four-year terms. The commission passes ordinances and resolutions adopts regulations and appoints the city manager. The manager oversees the day-to-day workings of about 20 departments that provide such services as water supply and treatment police protection and street and bridge maintenance. Dayton covers nearly 60 square miles has more than 166000 residents and an annual budget of about $155 million.

	Annual Growth	12/16	12/17	12/18	12/19	12/20
Sales ($ mil.)	4.6%	–	224.2	223.6	236.3	256.5
Net income ($ mil.)	–	–	(13.0)	7.7	6.3	27.0
Market value ($ mil.)	–	–	–	–	–	–
Employees	–	–	–	–	–	2,000

CITY OF DENTON

215 E MCKINNEY ST
DENTON, TX 762014299
Phone: 940-349-8200
Fax: –
Web: www.cityofdenton.com

CEO: –
CFO: –
HR: –
FYE: September 30
Type: Private

Texans who prefer a more laid-back atmosphere than Dallas or Houston can find a home in the City of Denton. The mayor and six city council members (elected for two-year terms) govern the city which has a population of about 120000. Founded in 1857 by lawyer and preacher John Denton the city is home to the University of North Texas (third-largest in the state with 40000 students) and Texas Woman's University. Denton which operates with an annual budget of about $550 million has about 20 public schools some 30 parks and a public library with three branches.

	Annual Growth	09/16	09/17	09/18	09/19	09/20
Sales ($ mil.)	–	–	0.0	192.0	193.8	204.0
Net income ($ mil.)	–	–	0.0	40.1	(0.6)	10.0
Market value ($ mil.)	–	–	–	–	–	–
Employees	–	–	–	–	–	1,000

CITY OF EL PASO

300 N CAMPBELL ST
EL PASO, TX 799011402
Phone: 915-212-0000
Fax: –
Web: www.eppension.org

CEO: –
CFO: Robert Cortinas
HR: –
FYE: August 31
Type: Private

Out in the West Texas Town of El Paso the sprawling metropolis is administered by the City of El Paso. The sixth-largest city in Texas with a population of about 650000 (2.5 million in the region including Ciudad Ju rez Mexico) El Paso is built around the base of the Franklin Mountains across the Rio Grande from Ju rez. Its city government consists of the mayor and eight council members (elected to four-year terms) along with a hired city manager. US Army post Fort Bliss and The University of Texas at El Paso are among the city's largest employers.

	Annual Growth	08/15	08/16	08/17	08/18	08/19
Sales ($ mil.)	5.1%	–	550.5	569.9	609.9	638.8
Net income ($ mil.)	(38.2%)	–	270.8	(41.0)	(89.2)	64.0
Market value ($ mil.)	–	–	–	–	–	–
Employees	–	–	–	–	–	6,500

CITY OF FONTANA

8353 SIERRA AVE
FONTANA, CA 923353598
Phone: 909-350-7605
Fax: –
Web: www.fontana.org

CEO: –
CFO: –
HR: –
FYE: June 30
Type: Private

Historic Route 66 runs through the heart of Fontana making it a major Southern California thoroughfare. Formerly an agricultural community then a steel town the city serves as a transportation hub with heavy industrial facilities and warehousing/distribution centers serving railroad and truck operations. Fontana supports a growing population of 150000 by offering some of the most affordable housing in the area. It is governed by an elected mayor and four city council members. They appoint a city manager who runs four main departments which oversee human resources information technology public works and community development. The city's annual budget tops $200 million.

	Annual Growth	06/16	06/17	06/18	06/19	06/20
Sales ($ mil.)	5.6%	–	204.8	220.7	233.1	241.2
Net income ($ mil.)	(21.8%)	–	18.4	10.1	29.7	8.8
Market value ($ mil.)	–	–	–	–	–	–
Employees	–	–	–	–	–	1,300

CITY OF FORT WAYNE

200 E BERRY ST STE 425
FORT WAYNE, IN 468022739
Phone: 260-427-1111
Fax: –
Web: www.cityoffortwayne.org

CEO: –
CFO: –
HR: –
FYE: December 31
Type: Private

Fort Wayne Indiana is the state's second-largest city after Indianapolis. Located in the northeast part of Indiana near the borders of Michigan and Ohio and covering more than 110.7 square miles the city counts more than 258500 residents. The city has more than 1380 miles of water lines and 1302 miles of streets. As part of America's "Rust Belt" Fort Wayne has one Fortune 500 company metal maker Steel Dynamics. Other major employers include insurance company Lincoln National and branches of defense contractors BAE Systems Exelis and Raytheon.

	Annual Growth	12/16	12/17	12/18	12/19	12/20
Sales ($ mil.)	12.6%	–	260.7	274.8	298.3	371.9
Net income ($ mil.)	31.4%	–	12.8	9.1	15.9	29.1
Market value ($ mil.)	–	–	–	–	–	–
Employees	–	–	–	–	–	1,910

CITY OF FREMONT

3300 CAPITOL AVE
FREMONT, CA 945381514
Phone: 510-284-4000
Fax: –
Web: www.fremont.gov

CEO: –
CFO: –
HR: –
FYE: June 30
Type: Private

Fremont California is a city located on the southeast side of San Francisco Bay about 25 miles south of Oakland. Fremont is home to about 215000 residents. It is overseen by a mayor an appointed city manager and four elected city council members. Situated near Silicon Valley Fremont is home to a number of tech companies. Major employers include Lam Research and branches of Tesla Motors and Western Digital.

	Annual Growth	06/16	06/17	06/18	06/19	06/20
Sales ($ mil.)	8.0%	–	304.1	317.4	350.4	382.8
Net income ($ mil.)	12.2%	–	24.8	33.6	36.1	35.0
Market value ($ mil.)	–	–	–	–	–	–
Employees	–	–	–	–	–	1,000

CITY OF FRESNO

2600 FRESNO ST
FRESNO, CA 937213620
Phone: 559-621-7001
Fax: –
Web: www.fresno.gov

CEO: –
CFO: –
HR: –
FYE: June 30
Type: Private

Fresno (which means "ash" or "ash tree" in Spanish) is California's fifth-largest city. Located in the fertile San Joaquin Valley Fresno counts about 500000 residents in the city and about 940000 residents across Fresno County. The City's residents represent more than 80 different nationalities. Centrally located Fresno is the financial industrial trade and commercial capital of the Central San Joaquin Valley. The area is home to many agricultural concerns including Sun-Maid Raisins Valley Fig Growers and Zacky Farms. Fresno was founded by the Central Pacific Railroad Company in 1872.

	Annual Growth	06/16	06/17	06/18	06/19	06/20
Sales ($ mil.)	2.1%	–	435.2	397.3	436.2	462.6
Net income ($ mil.)	(13.9%)	–	36.2	(13.0)	22.3	23.1
Market value ($ mil.)	–	–	–	–	–	–
Employees	–	–	–	–	–	2,600

CITY OF GARLAND

200 N 5TH ST
GARLAND, TX 750406314
Phone: 972-205-2000
Fax: –
Web: www.garlandtx.gov

CEO: –
CFO: –
HR: –
FYE: September 30
Type: Private

Garland is a city in North Texas considered part of the Dallas/Fort Worth Metroplex. With a population of almost 230000 people the city is governed by a mayor an appointed city manager and eight city council members. Garland was incorporated in 1891 and is named after 19th century US Attorney General Augustus Hill Garland. Its top employer is military contractor Raytheon.

	Annual Growth	09/16	09/17	09/18	09/19	09/20
Sales ($ mil.)	7.3%	–	207.8	213.7	227.5	256.5
Net income ($ mil.)	6.0%	–	19.3	1.9	(6.1)	22.9
Market value ($ mil.)	–	–	–	–	–	–
Employees	–	–	–	–	–	2,000

CITY OF GLENDALE

5850 W GLENDALE AVE FL 4
GLENDALE, AZ 853012599
Phone: 623-930-2000
Fax: –
Web: www.glendaleaz.com

CEO: –
CFO: –
HR: Shannon Rodriguez
FYE: June 30
Type: Private

There are more than a dozen cities in the US named Glendale but Glendale Arizona is the largest. A suburb of Phoenix Glendale has more than 250000 residents and is one of the many cities that make up Maricopa County. The city is governed by a mayor an appointed city manager and six city council members. Glendale was settled in the late 1800s after a canal was built.

	Annual Growth	06/16	06/17	06/18	06/19	06/20
Sales ($ mil.)	7.1%	–	306.5	315.5	331.5	376.1
Net income ($ mil.)	–	–	(5.7)	34.4	(6.4)	24.0
Market value ($ mil.)	–	–	–	–	–	–
Employees	–	–	–	–	–	1,000

CITY OF GLENDALE

141 N GLENDALE AVE FL 2
GLENDALE, CA 912064975
Phone: 818-548-2085
Fax: -

CEO: -
CFO: -
HR: Matthew Doyle
FYE: June 30
Type: Private

Glendale California (not to be confused with Glendale Arizona) is a suburb of Los Angeles. The city encompasses about 30 square miles of land and with a population of more than 190000 it's the third-largest city in Los Angeles County. Mostly a bedroom community Glendale's two largest employers are hospitals Glendale Adventist and Glendale Memorial.

	Annual Growth	06/16	06/17	06/18	06/19	06/20
Sales ($ mil.)	4.1%	–	314.4	331.4	363.1	354.6
Net income ($ mil.)	(46.1%)	–	24.2	43.9	62.9	3.8
Market value ($ mil.)	–	–	–	–	–	–
Employees	–	–	–	–	–	2,000

CITY OF GREENSBORO

300 W WASHINGTON ST
GREENSBORO, NC 274012624
Phone: 336-373-2002
Fax: -
Web: www.greensboro-nc.gov

CEO: -
CFO: -
HR: -
FYE: June 30
Type: Private

Greensboro is the third-largest city in North Carolina (behind Charlotte and Raleigh) with a population of about 275000 people. The city government is organized in the style of council-manager where the city manager heads executive affairs and the mayor and eight council members make up the legislative body. Greensboro is home to two Fortune 1000 companies — apparel manufacturer V.F. Corporation and tobacco maker Lorillard.

	Annual Growth	06/16	06/17	06/18	06/19	06/20
Sales ($ mil.)	4.5%	–	300.2	315.3	327.0	342.4
Net income ($ mil.)	(26.2%)	–	15.5	16.2	77.6	6.2
Market value ($ mil.)	–	–	–	–	–	–
Employees	–	–	–	–	–	2,650

CITY OF HENDERSON

240 S WATER ST
HENDERSON, NV 890157227
Phone: 702-267-2323
Fax: -
Web: www.cityofhenderson.com

CEO: -
CFO: -
HR: -
FYE: June 30
Type: Private

Henderson Nevada may be a suburb of Las Vegas but it's a far cry from Sin City with its focus on arts gallerias recreational venues and a host of family friendly activities. With a population of more than 277400 Henderson is the state's second-largest city. It is governed by a mayor and four city council members. Situated more than a mile high the high desert city gets less than six inches of rainfall per year. Founded in 1941 Henderson quickly became a main supplier of magnesium to the US military through its Basic Magnesium Plant (which closed after WWII). The City of Henderson was founded in 1953.

	Annual Growth	06/16	06/17	06/18	06/19	06/20
Sales ($ mil.)	5.8%	–	302.9	332.2	368.0	358.8
Net income ($ mil.)	241.1%	–	1.9	14.3	42.2	75.8
Market value ($ mil.)	–	–	–	–	–	–
Employees	–	–	–	–	–	3,775

CITY OF HIALEAH

501 PALM AVE
HIALEAH, FL 330104719
Phone: 305-883-8075
Fax: -
Web: www.hialeahfl.gov

CEO: -
CFO: -
HR: -
FYE: September 30
Type: Private

Hialeah a suburb of Miami is located in Miami-Dade County and is Florida's fifth-largest city. Its population of more than 235000 residents lives in only 20 sq. mi. of land. Hialeah is governed by a mayor and seven city council members. While Native Americans lives in the area for centuries the city of Hialeah was incorporated in 1925.

	Annual Growth	09/15	09/16	09/17	09/18	09/19
Sales ($ mil.)	6.0%	–	179.6	185.3	200.2	213.9
Net income ($ mil.)	(29.6%)	–	32.7	5.7	9.7	11.4
Market value ($ mil.)	–	–	–	–	–	–
Employees	–	–	–	–	–	1,800

CITY OF HOUSTON

901 BAGBY ST
HOUSTON, TX 770022049
Phone: 832-393-1000
Fax: -
Web: www.houstontx.gov

CEO: -
CFO: Tantri Emo
HR: -
FYE: June 30
Type: Private

It is bigger in Texas when you consider the City of Houston. As the largest city in the state and one of the largest cities nationwide Houston is more than an oil town. Founded in 1836 and home to Rice University and the Astros it also has a noteworthy museum district and operates the Texas Medical Center one of the world's largest health care facilities. While a mayor oversees Houston's management 14 council members (elected for two-year terms) have the power to enact and enforce city ordinances. With a population of more than 2 million Houston operates through some 20 departments including health and human services police and parks and recreation. It has an annual budget of about $2 billion.

	Annual Growth	06/16	06/17	06/18	06/19	06/20
Sales ($ mil.)	89.3%	–	494.0	3,110.5	3,253.3	3,351.8
Net income ($ mil.)	(44.0%)	–	128.1	52.3	98.4	22.4
Market value ($ mil.)	–	–	–	–	–	–
Employees	–	–	–	–	–	23,235

CITY OF IRVING

825 W IRVING BLVD
IRVING, TX 750602860
Phone: 972-721-2600
Fax: -
Web: www.cityofirving.org

CEO: -
CFO: -
HR: -
FYE: September 30
Type: Private

This city makes up the Dallas-Plano-Irving metropolitan division which is part of the larger Dallas-Fort Worth Metroplex. With a population of more than 220000 the City of Irving covers approximately 68 square miles. It contains Las Colinas a developed area founded in 1972 by cattle ranching millionaire Ben H. Carpenter. Las Colinas is known for its landmark office towers luxury hotels private country clubs and gated residencies. Irving's city government consists of its mayor eight council members (serving three-year terms) and a city manager.

	Annual Growth	09/16	09/17	09/18	09/19	09/20
Sales ($ mil.)	2.3%	–	307.4	318.0	342.3	329.2
Net income ($ mil.)	–	–	52.2	(2.2)	(30.8)	(11.4)
Market value ($ mil.)	–	–	–	–	–	–
Employees	–	–	–	–	–	1,635

CITY OF JACKSONVILLE

117 W DUVAL ST
JACKSONVILLE, FL 322023700
Phone: 904-630-1776
Fax: –
Web: www.coj.net

CEO: –
CFO: –
HR: –
FYE: September 30
Type: Private

In Jacksonville residents and visitors can enjoy the Florida wilderness. The city which offers some 57000 acres of parks provides more land for recreation than any other city in the US. Its 19 city council members (five at-large members and 14 representing geographic districts) enact the legislation for the Jacksonville. Elected for four-year terms the mayor oversees the administration of the central government and appoints directors for its 10 departments. The 14th-largest city in the US Jacksonville has a population of more than 850000 residents.

	Annual Growth	09/14	09/15	09/16	09/17	09/18
Sales ($ mil.)	4.2%	–	1,414.1	1,493.3	1,560.4	1,599.4
Net income ($ mil.)	8.7%	–	50.3	33.7	12.8	64.7
Market value ($ mil.)	–	–	–	–	–	–
Employees	–	–	–	–	–	7,908

CITY OF LAREDO

1110 HOUSTON ST
LAREDO, TX 780408019
Phone: 956-791-7308
Fax: –
Web: www.cityoflaredo.com

CEO: –
CFO: –
HR: Monica Flores
FYE: September 30
Type: Private

Laredo is Texas' 10 th -largest city. Located right across the Rio Grande River from Nuevo Laredo Mexico the city has a population of more than 235000. Due to its location along the border Laredo is a major point of entry for trade between Mexico and the US. The area's major employers are government agencies such as those with the local school district city Webb County and US Border Patrol.

	Annual Growth	09/15	09/16	09/17	09/18	09/20
Sales ($ mil.)	2.3%	–	280.4	281.8	291.9	306.9
Net income ($ mil.)	4.6%	–	14.0	(8.6)	17.7	16.8
Market value ($ mil.)	–	–	–	–	–	–
Employees	–	–	–	–	–	2,100

CITY OF LAS VEGAS

495 S MAIN ST
LAS VEGAS, NV 891012986
Phone: 702-229-6321
Fax: –
Web: www.lasvegasnevada.gov

CEO: –
CFO: –
HR: –
FYE: June 30
Type: Private

Some 585000 people call Sin City home. Las Vegas Nevada's largest city is the gaming capital of the US. The city is overseen by a mayor an appointed city manager and six elected city council members. Its largest industry is tourism; the casino resorts attract visitors seeking business and pleasure — Las Vegas hosts almost 20000 conventions every year.

	Annual Growth	06/16	06/17	06/18	06/19	06/20
Sales ($ mil.)	13.2%	–	688.4	782.9	857.7	999.2
Net income ($ mil.)	–	–	10.8	69.4	58.9	(95.0)
Market value ($ mil.)	–	–	–	–	–	–
Employees	–	–	–	–	–	2,500

CITY OF LINCOLN

555 S 10TH ST RM B115
LINCOLN, NE 685082803
Phone: 402-441-7511
Fax: –
Web: www.lincoln.ne.gov

CEO: –
CFO: –
HR: –
FYE: August 31
Type: Private

Welcome to Cornhusker nation. Lincoln is Nebraska's second-largest city (behind Omaha) with a population of more than 255000 people. Of course the University of Nebraska is located in Lincoln. The city is also the state capital and the state of Nebraska is the city's top employer. Other government agencies such as the school system the city and the federal government are also major employers.

	Annual Growth	08/16	08/17	08/18	08/19	08/20
Sales ($ mil.)	1.3%	–	351.8	355.4	349.9	365.4
Net income ($ mil.)	(31.7%)	–	23.1	10.2	(23.6)	7.4
Market value ($ mil.)	–	–	–	–	–	–
Employees	–	–	–	–	–	2,000

CITY OF LONG BEACH

411 W OCEAN BLVD
LONG BEACH, CA 908024664
Phone: 562-570-6450
Fax: –
Web: www.longbeach.gov

CEO: –
CFO: –
HR: –
FYE: September 30
Type: Private

It's a city it's a port it's Long Beach. The City of Long Beach boasts the Port of Long Beach one of the busiest ports in the nation. With a population of more than 460000 Long Beach is part of the greater Los Angeles metropolitan area. The city uses a charter form of government with an elected mayor and city council as well as an appointed city manager. It's also known for its large oil reserves managed by the Long Beach Gas & Oil Department.

	Annual Growth	09/16	09/17	09/18	09/19	09/20
Sales ($ mil.)	7.5%	–	716.4	779.1	864.6	889.8
Net income ($ mil.)	29.0%	–	9.2	26.6	36.8	19.8
Market value ($ mil.)	–	–	–	–	–	–
Employees	–	–	–	–	–	5,028

CITY OF LOS ANGELES

200 N SPRING ST STE 303
LOS ANGELES, CA 900123239
Phone: 213-978-0600
Fax: –
Web: www.lacity.org

CEO: –
CFO: –
HR: –
FYE: June 30
Type: Private

Los Angeles may be a Mecca for the rich and famous but there is little glamour in running a city of more than 4 million people. Governing responsibilities are shared among the city's mayor and city council while various commissions departments and bureaus see to the daily operations that keep the wheels spinning. Elected every four years the mayor appoints most commission members (subject to approval by the city council) and serves as the city's executive officer. The City of Los Angeles is located in the County of Los Angeles.

	Annual Growth	12/06	12/07	12/08*	06/09	06/16
Sales ($ mil.)	217.6%	–	–	0.7	6,281.3	7,196.2
Net income ($ mil.)	–	–	–	0.0	(285.4)	231.1
Market value ($ mil.)	–	–	–	–	–	–
Employees	–	–	–	–	–	41,000

*Fiscal year change

CITY OF LUBBOCK

1314 AVENUE K
LUBBOCK, TX 794014051
Phone: 806-775-2016
Fax: –
Web: www.ci.lubbock.tx.us

CEO: –
CFO: –
HR: Scott Snider
FYE: September 30
Type: Private

Lubbock or leave it! Famous as the home to Texas Tech and rock and roll legend Buddy Holly the City of Lubbock is located in northwest Texas at the center of the area known as the South Plains. Main industries within the region include agriculture (primarily cotton) ranching oil and gas mining and manufacturing. Lubbock has a population of about 238000 and is governed by a council-manager system consisting of a seven- person city council headed by the mayor and its city manager. The City was formed in 1890 and named after a former Texas Ranger and Confederate officer.

	Annual Growth	09/16	09/17	09/18	09/19	09/20
Sales ($ mil.)	14.8%	–	197.3	228.5	254.1	298.8
Net income ($ mil.)	–	–	(6.9)	12.6	36.0	6.0
Market value ($ mil.)	–	–	–	–	–	–
Employees	–	–	–	–	–	2,700

CITY OF MADISON

210 MRTIN LTHER KING JR B
MADISON, WI 537033341
Phone: 608-266-4671
Fax: –
Web: www.cityofmadison.com

CEO: –
CFO: –
HR: –
FYE: December 31
Type: Private

Named for the forth president of the United States James Madison Madison Wisconsin is located in the southern part of the state. It is the second largest city in Wisconsin behind Milwaukee and is the state's capital. The City of Madison is governed by a mayor and city council composed of 20 alders that each represents a district. The city was incorporated in 1856.

	Annual Growth	12/16	12/17	12/18	12/19	12/20
Sales ($ mil.)	3.3%	–	360.7	383.6	408.0	398.0
Net income ($ mil.)	28.7%	–	26.7	(22.7)	(14.4)	57.0
Market value ($ mil.)	–	–	–	–	–	–
Employees	–	–	–	–	–	2,918

CITY OF MEMPHIS

125 N MAIN ST STE 628
MEMPHIS, TN 381032032
Phone: 901-676-6657
Fax: –
Web: www.memphistn.gov

CEO: –
CFO: Shirley Ford
HR: –
FYE: June 30
Type: Private

Home to Graceland and Beale Street Memphis has both feet entrenched in the world of music. With a population of more than 670000 it is located in the southwestern corner of the state and stretches over 300 square miles. Serving the largest urban population in Tennessee it is run by a mayor and 13 city council members (elected from nine districts). City government is responsible for economic development public education housing public utilities homeland security and landmark preservation. Set atop the eastern bank of the Mississippi River and named after the ancient capital of Egypt Memphis was founded in 1820.

	Annual Growth	06/12	06/13	06/14	06/15	06/16
Sales ($ mil.)	2.3%	–	845.8	840.9	863.4	906.5
Net income ($ mil.)	–	–	(25.0)	26.6	1.4	8.0
Market value ($ mil.)	–	–	–	–	–	–
Employees	–	–	–	–	–	6,000

CITY OF MESA

20 E MAIN ST
MESA, AZ 852017425
Phone: 480-644-2011
Fax: –
Web: www.mesaaz.gov

CEO: –
CFO: –
HR: –
FYE: June 30
Type: Private

This city which literally covers a "mesa" or plateau stands roughly 100 feet higher than Phoenix and spreads across 130 square miles. With a population of more than 468000 the City of Mesa is the third-largest city in Arizona behind Phoenix and Tucson. Its city government consists of the mayor six city council members (elected to four-year terms) and a city manager. Mesa is also home to the Chicago Cubs baseball team during spring training. The city was founded in 1878 by Mormon (Latter-day Saint or LDS) pioneers who gave it its name; Mesa still has a large Mormon population. It was incorporated in 1883.

	Annual Growth	06/16	06/17	06/18	06/19	06/20
Sales ($ mil.)	10.7%	–	476.3	515.6	539.1	646.2
Net income ($ mil.)	32.6%	–	38.4	47.0	50.1	89.6
Market value ($ mil.)	–	–	–	–	–	–
Employees	–	–	–	–	–	4,068

CITY OF MIAMI

3500 PAN AMERICAN DR FL 2
MIAMI, FL 331335595
Phone: 305-250-5300
Fax: –
Web: www.miamigov.com

CEO: –
CFO: –
HR: –
FYE: September 30
Type: Private

Thankfully the City of Miami is much more than Dolphins sound-machines and vice cops. With a population of more than 400000 the city has little trouble attracting tourists and residents alike to the bustling international hub of business entertainment and culture. Thanks to its status as a transportation hub and the businesses that make the city home to international operations the city is also known as the Gateway to Latin America. The city government consists of its elected mayor five commissioners a city manager and the heads of Miami's various public services departments.

	Annual Growth	09/08	09/09	09/12	09/15	09/16
Sales ($ mil.)	2.8%	–	691.3	675.2	792.7	837.6
Net income ($ mil.)	–	–	(30.2)	(18.6)	(1.7)	15.3
Market value ($ mil.)	–	–	–	–	–	–
Employees	–	–	–	–	–	3,000

CITY OF MINNEAPOLIS

350 S 5TH ST STE 325M
MINNEAPOLIS, MN 554151315
Phone: 612-673-3000
Fax: –
Web: www.minneapolismn.gov

CEO: –
CFO: –
HR: –
FYE: December 31
Type: Private

One half of Minnesota's famed Twin Cities Minneapolis is a combination of the Sioux word for water with the Greek word for city. With 20 lakes and wetlands plus the Mississippi River waterfront and many creeks and streams the City of Minneapolis is known as the City of Lakes. It is governed by a mayor and city council with 13 members representing the city's wards. The mayor appoints the chief of police but has little other power. Independent boards oversee public housing the tax office and public parks and libraries. The city's more than 80 parks serve as a model for city park systems nationwide. Formed in 1856 Minneapolis is now home to a population of almost 400000.

	Annual Growth	12/16	12/17	12/18	12/19	12/20
Sales ($ mil.)	2.2%	–	846.9	858.1	916.4	903.3
Net income ($ mil.)	–	–	36.1	84.0	85.5	(21.4)
Market value ($ mil.)	–	–	–	–	–	–
Employees	–	–	–	–	–	5,000

CITY OF NEW ORLEANS

1300 PERDIDO ST BSMT FL2
NEW ORLEANS, LA 701122128
Phone: 504-658-4900
Fax: –
Web: www.nola.gov

CEO: –
CFO: –
HR: –
FYE: December 31
Type: Private

New Orleans is a city with a story. The city was founded in 1718 and became famous for its architecture music food and parties. The city is home to a major port the New Orleans Saints the French Quarter and is the regarded as the birthplace of jazz. Devastated by Hurricane Katrina and the flooding which ensued in 2005 the city has undertaken a massive rebuilding and recovery effort utilizing state and federal assistance. The city of New Orleans is governed by a city council consisting of seven members and an elected mayor.

	Annual Growth	12/14	12/15	12/16	12/17	12/18
Sales ($ mil.)	5.2%	–	905.9	881.5	902.0	1,056.1
Net income ($ mil.)	(71.4%)	–	65.4	39.9	(74.2)	1.5
Market value ($ mil.)	–	–	–	–	–	–
Employees	–	–	–	–	–	6,658

CITY OF NEWPORT NEWS

2400 WASHINGTON AVE MAIN
NEWPORT NEWS, VA 236074300
Phone: 757-926-8411
Fax: –
Web: www.newportnewshistory.org

CEO: –
CFO: –
HR: –
FYE: June 30
Type: Private

There are nearly as many theories on where the unusual city name came from as there are citizens of Newport News Virginia. Whether it was founded on land chosen by Sir William Newce or the point where Captain Newport delivered good news to early settlers Newport News today boasts a population of some 193000. The mayor and six-member city council (representing three districts) work together to serve residents and visitors backed by an annual budget of about $750 million. The council sets up city policies and controls funding while the city manager attorney and clerk carry out the day-to-day administration of Newport News. The city which was settled around 1621 is well known as a military shipbuilding hub.

	Annual Growth	06/15	06/16	06/17	06/19	06/20
Sales ($ mil.)	2.4%	–	544.6	563.6	603.0	598.6
Net income ($ mil.)	–	–	10.2	33.3	50.4	(30.6)
Market value ($ mil.)	–	–	–	–	–	–
Employees	–	–	–	–	–	5,000

CITY OF NORFOLK

810 UNION ST STE 508
NORFOLK, VA 235108048
Phone: 757-664-7300
Fax: –
Web: www.norfolk.gov

CEO: –
CFO: –
HR: –
FYE: June 30
Type: Private

You could say that the City of Norfolk Virginia is at home on the water. The second-largest city in Virginia with a population of more than 245400 Norfolk sports miles of lake river and bay front as well as a bustling international port and the world's largest naval base. The city was founded in 1682 and offers such attractions as the battleship USS Wisconsin the National Maritime Center and Old Dominion University. Norfolk Southern Railway's corporate headquarters are also located in the city. Norfolk city government consists of its seven-member city council and mayor. The city manager serves as the city's COO and is appointed by the city council.

	Annual Growth	06/16	06/17	06/18	06/19	06/20
Sales ($ mil.)	2.2%	–	702.8	730.5	751.1	749.5
Net income ($ mil.)	–	–	22.9	73.4	162.4	(16.0)
Market value ($ mil.)	–	–	–	–	–	–
Employees	–	–	–	–	–	4,364

CITY OF OAKLAND

1 FRANK H OGAWA PLZ 2ND
OAKLAND, CA 946121904
Phone: 510-238-3280
Fax: –
Web: www.oaklandca.gov

CEO: –
CFO: –
HR: Lisette Del Pino
FYE: June 30
Type: Private

Joining San Francisco and San Jose Oakland makes up one-third of Northern California's Golden Triangle . Founded in 1852 Oakland boasts of a diverse population numbering more than 390000 residents a Mediterranean climate and thriving hip arts scene. The city is a hub for the port of San Francisco Bay as well as for the business elite and the higher educated. Environmental policies have helped propel Oakland to stand among the top green economies in the US. The city is served by a mayor and eight council members who oversee a budget of almost $1 billion. It is home to the NBA's Golden State Warriors NFL's Oakland Raiders and national landmark Lake Merritt.

	Annual Growth	06/16	06/17	06/18	06/19	06/20
Sales ($ mil.)	5.0%	–	1,071.6	1,164.5	1,211.7	1,239.9
Net income ($ mil.)	17.6%	–	100.3	184.1	28.2	163.1
Market value ($ mil.)	–	–	–	–	–	–
Employees	–	–	–	–	–	4,000

CITY OF OKLAHOMA CITY

100 N WALKER AVE
OKLAHOMA CITY, OK 731022230
Phone: 405-297-2506
Fax: –
Web: www.okc.gov

CEO: –
CFO: –
HR: –
FYE: June 30
Type: Private

Oklahoma City was born overnight as a boomtown named Oklahoma Station in 1889 during the celebrated land rush in Oklahoma Territory. It became in time the state capital and largest city (with a population approaching 600000) and is headquarters of oil and gas companies Chesapeake Energy and Devon Energy as well as electric utility OGE Energy and service station operator Love's Truck Stops. City government is headed by a mayor and council members representing eight wards. The city captured its first top-rank sports franchise when the Oklahoma City Thunder NBA team began play in 2008.

	Annual Growth	06/14	06/15	06/16	06/17	06/18
Sales ($ mil.)	2.5%	–	804.0	800.7	806.1	865.8
Net income ($ mil.)	19.5%	–	66.0	26.1	(21.6)	112.4
Market value ($ mil.)	–	–	–	–	–	–
Employees	–	–	–	–	–	4,500

CITY OF OMAHA

1819 FARNAM ST RM 300
OMAHA, NE 681831000
Phone: 402-444-5000
Fax: –
Web: www.cityofomaha.org

CEO: –
CFO: –
HR: –
FYE: December 31
Type: Private

Owing it name to one the tribes living in the area the City Omaha was once bypassed by the Lewis and Clark expedition. Founded in 1854 Omaha has become the 42nd largest city in the U.S. with a population of almost 409.000 in an area measuring little more than 130 square miles. The city is ruled by a mayor-council consisting of of an "at-large" mayor and 7 district councilmembers. The City of Omaha is home for megacompanies Berkshire Hathaway ConAgra Peter Kiewit Sons Mutual of Omaha TD Ameritrade Union Pacific West Corporation Valmont Industries and Werner Enterprises.

	Annual Growth	12/16	12/17	12/18	12/19	12/20
Sales ($ mil.)	6.3%	–	589.5	593.4	636.3	707.8
Net income ($ mil.)	(41.8%)	–	24.5	(29.1)	1.3	4.8
Market value ($ mil.)	–	–	–	–	–	–
Employees	–	–	–	–	–	2,800

CITY OF OXNARD

300 W 3RD ST
OXNARD, CA 930305729
Phone: 805-385-7803
Fax: –
Web: www.visitoxnard.com

CEO: –
CFO: –
HR: –
FYE: June 30
Type: Private

If California is truly full of fruits and nuts then Oxnard supplies much of the former. The City of Oxnard's economy is driven by agricultural (including a huge annual strawberry crop) as well as international trade defense manufacturing and tourism. It has a council-manager form of government. The city council — comprised of a mayor mayor pro tem and three council members — establishes city policies. The city manager supports the needs of the council implements council directives and manages the day-to-day operations of some 15 departments. Incorporated in 1903 Oxnard is the largest city in Ventura County. It's located some 60 miles northwest of Los Angeles and has a population of about 200000.

	Annual Growth	06/16	06/17	06/18	06/19	06/20
Sales ($ mil.)	2.0%	–	196.8	192.4	219.4	209.1
Net income ($ mil.)	(50.4%)	–	26.8	(8.8)	8.3	3.3
Market value ($ mil.)	–	–	–	–	–	–
Employees	–	–	–	–	–	1,100

CITY OF PEORIA

8401 W MONROE ST
PEORIA, AZ 853456560
Phone: 623-773-7148
Fax: –
Web: www.peoriaaz.gov

CEO: –
CFO: –
HR: –
FYE: June 30
Type: Private

Peoria Arizona was established in the 1880s based on the vision of William J. Murphy to use water from the Salt River to create fertile farm lands in Arizona. After the completion of the Arizona Canal Murphy went east to sell his vision eventually convincing four families from Peoria Illinois to make the move and establish the farming community. Now considered a suburb of Phoenix Peoria has a population of about 120000 and is growing steadily. The ninth largest city in Arizona Peoria's six-person city council and mayor set policy and serve the legislative role for the city the City Manager oversees daily operations and acts as the city's CEO.

	Annual Growth	06/16	06/17	06/18	06/19	06/20
Sales ($ mil.)	7.3%	–	210.2	222.0	231.3	259.6
Net income ($ mil.)	–	–	(8.2)	(4.1)	36.6	(16.0)
Market value ($ mil.)	–	–	–	–	–	–
Employees	–	–	–	–	–	1,600

CITY OF PHILADELPHIA

215 CITY HALL
PHILADELPHIA, PA 191073214
Phone: 215-686-2181
Fax: –
Web: www.phila.gov

CEO: –
CFO: –
HR: –
FYE: June 30
Type: Private

Known as the City of Brotherly Love Philadelphia is the fifth largest city in the nation with a population of more than 1.5 million. The city which covers 135 square miles operates through some 50 departments boards offices and other units that include emergency medical services sanitation services and street maintenance. Founded in 1682 by William Penn Philadelphia has a mayor 10 districts and 17 council members. The city which hosts millions of tourists each year is home to the Phillies the Eagles the Flyers the 76ers Bryn Mawr College the Liberty Bell and the National Constitution Center. The City of Philadelphia has an annual budget of more than $3.5 billion.

	Annual Growth	06/13	06/14	06/15	06/16	06/17
Sales ($ mil.)	3.8%	–	5,947.1	6,070.8	6,264.8	6,646.5
Net income ($ mil.)	–	–	(10.1)	(92.2)	(65.0)	20.8
Market value ($ mil.)	–	–	–	–	–	–
Employees	–	–	–	–	–	29,862

CITY OF PHOENIX

200 W WASHINGTON ST FL 11
PHOENIX, AZ 850031611
Phone: 602-262-7111
Fax: –
Web: www.phoenix.gov

CEO: –
CFO: –
HR: –
FYE: June 30
Type: Private

Phoenix the capital of Arizona has a population of about 1.4 million and is the sixth largest city in the US. Located in the south-central portion of the state Phoenix covers a sprawling 500 square miles and is geographically larger than Los Angeles. The City of Phoenix operates through some 30 departments including street transportation water services human services and public transit. Eight city council members (representing eight districts) and the mayor make up the city council which develop laws and policy for governing the city. Phoenix was incorporated in 1881.

	Annual Growth	06/16	06/17	06/18	06/19	06/20
Sales ($ mil.)	6.3%	–	2,318.3	2,522.0	2,588.3	2,786.5
Net income ($ mil.)	(48.1%)	–	198.7	(35.0)	54.4	27.8
Market value ($ mil.)	–	–	–	–	–	–
Employees	–	–	–	–	–	14,000

CITY OF PITTSBURGH

414 GRANT ST
PITTSBURGH, PA 152192409
Phone: 412-255-2640
Fax: –
Web: www.pittsburghpa.gov

CEO: –
CFO: –
HR: –
FYE: December 31
Type: Private

Take one look at the skyline and it's no wonder Pittsburgh's been nicknamed "The City of Bridges." With more than 440 bridges 150 skyscrapers and a countless number of steel behemoths Pittsburgh is Pennsylvania's second largest city (behind Philadelphia) with a population of more than 305700. The city is composed of nine districts each represented by a council member while the mayor rounds out the executive side. Its annual budget goes toward enhancements to health care and retirement as well as hiring police and fire prevention personnel; most of its revenue comes from real estate taxes. Pittsburgh was founded in 1758.

	Annual Growth	12/12	12/13	12/14	12/18	12/19
Sales ($ mil.)	3.1%	–	542.2	538.0	635.6	651.7
Net income ($ mil.)	–	–	(30.2)	22.7	2.0	48.1
Market value ($ mil.)	–	–	–	–	–	–
Employees	–	–	–	–	–	3,500

CITY OF PLANO

1520 AVE K
PLANO, TX 75074
Phone: 972-941-7121
Fax: –
Web: www.plano.gov

CEO: –
CFO: –
HR: –
FYE: September 30
Type: Private

Plano isn't located deep in the heart of Texas but it is nonetheless a proud Texas city. Part of the Dallas-Fort Worth metropolitan area Plano is located in the northeastern region of the state just north of Dallas. It is the ninth-largest city in Texas and is governed by a city council made up of a mayor and seven city council members. Incorporated in 1873 the City of Plano comprises large suburban areas and boasts safe neighborhoods and high-performing schools.

	Annual Growth	09/15	09/16	09/18	09/19	09/20
Sales ($ mil.)	4.4%	–	340.8	369.5	409.4	404.2
Net income ($ mil.)	(2.1%)	–	17.9	23.1	31.1	16.4
Market value ($ mil.)	–	–	–	–	–	–
Employees	–	–	–	–	–	2,000

CITY OF PORTLAND

1221 SW 4TH AVE RM 340
PORTLAND, OR 972041900
Phone: 503-823-4120
Fax: –
Web: www.prosperportland.us

CEO: –
CFO: –
HR: –
FYE: June 30
Type: Private

A rose by any other name would smell as sweet may be only way to tell this city from 18 other Portlands in the US. Portland has been known as the City of Roses since 1888 and has hosted an annual rose festival since 1905.

	Annual Growth	06/17	06/18	06/19	06/20	06/21
Sales ($ mil.)	6.0%	–	1,483.2	1,604.8	1,648.9	1,768.1
Net income ($ mil.)	–	–	110.9	138.7	269.4	(9.7)
Market value ($ mil.)	–	–	–	–	–	–
Employees	–	–	–	–	–	5,684

CITY OF RICHMOND

900 E BROAD ST STE 201
RICHMOND, VA 232141907
Phone: 804-646-7970
Fax: –
Web: www.rva.gov

CEO: –
CFO: –
HR: –
FYE: June 30
Type: Private

Music legends Joan Baez and Jerry Garcia both sang about seeing Richmond fall but these days Richmond is rising. The city which made its living on tobacco and slave trading early in its history now thrives on business law and the research center at the Virginia Biotechnology Research Park. Richmond is home to several major corporations including CarMax Dominion Resources Genworth Financial and MeadWestvaco. It's also home to more than 200000 people who are governed by a city council representing nine districts along with an at-large mayor. The city follows a council-manager system and the mayor is not part of the council. Richmond which was founded in 1737 has an annual budget of about $1.4 billion.

	Annual Growth	06/16	06/17	06/18	06/19	06/20
Sales ($ mil.)	1.6%	–	786.6	757.5	800.8	824.7
Net income ($ mil.)	–	–	51.9	(41.8)	72.2	(6.2)
Market value ($ mil.)	–	–	–	–	–	–
Employees	–	–	–	–	–	5,315

CITY OF RICHMOND

450 CIVIC CENTER PLAZA
RICHMOND, CA 948041661
Phone: 510-620-6727
Fax: –
Web: www.ci.richmond.ca.us

CEO: –
CFO: –
HR: Kristi Florence
FYE: June 30
Type: Private

In the shadows of San Francisco's East Bay the City of Richmond stands on the shoulders of its shipbuilding past. Richmond's shipyards home of Rosie the Riveter Museum broke records building American ships for WWII. The city government uses a council-manager system with nine at-large members and a mayor all elected to four-year terms. Major employers include Chevron USA and HMO Kaiser Permanente (originally the medical system for the shipyard workers); the Port of Richmond does a brisk business importing automobiles. With a population of nearly 104000 Richmond has a budget of about $315 million. It was incorporated in 1905 and in 2007 became the largest city in the nation with a Green Party mayor.

	Annual Growth	06/16	06/17	06/18	06/19	06/20
Sales ($ mil.)	1.8%	–	223.3	238.7	242.8	235.5
Net income ($ mil.)	(7.7%)	–	10.3	10.8	13.4	8.1
Market value ($ mil.)	–	–	–	–	–	–
Employees	–	–	–	–	–	1,158

CITY OF RIVERSIDE

3900 MAIN ST FL 7
RIVERSIDE, CA 925220002
Phone: 951-826-5311
Fax: –
Web: www.riversideca.gov

CEO: –
CFO: Paul Sundeen
HR: –
FYE: June 30
Type: Private

This city's cup will likely not runneth over. The City of Riverside California is home to the World's Largest Paper Cup (68 feet tall) set in front of a former Dixie cup plant. Riverside operates under a council-manager form of government with a seven-member council presided over by a mayor. The council passes ordinances appoints committees and hires the city manager attorney and clerk. Its city manager carries out the council's policies and ordinances and oversees city day-to-day operations. Incorporated in 1883 Riverside planted the seeds for the US navel orange-growing industry. It is located about 60 miles east of Los Angeles occupies about 80 square miles and has a population of some 300000.

	Annual Growth	06/16	06/17	06/18	06/19	06/20
Sales ($ mil.)	7.3%	–	273.6	318.4	338.6	338.1
Net income ($ mil.)	–	–	(5.1)	41.3	71.3	10.5
Market value ($ mil.)	–	–	–	–	–	–
Employees	–	–	–	–	–	2,700

CITY OF ROCHESTER

30 CHURCH ST
ROCHESTER, NY 146141206
Phone: 585-428-6755
Fax: –
Web: www.cityofrochester.gov

CEO: –
CFO: –
HR: –
FYE: June 30
Type: Private

Known as "The World's Image Center" the City of Rochester situated on the south of Lake Ontario encompasses some 37 sq. mi. The city incorporated in 1703 was one of the first "boomtowns" in the US due to a large number of flour mills. Rochester is now a center of higher education medical and technological research with University of Rochester Rochester Institute of Technology Bausch & Lomb and Kodak calling it home. Xerox still has a large presence in the city. A population of over 200000 makes the city the third largest in the state. The government is a "strong mayor" style with 4 district and 5 at-large council members. Previously known as "The Flower City" it hosts an annual lilac festival.

	Annual Growth	06/16	06/17	06/18	06/19	06/20
Sales ($ mil.)	(1.3%)	–	581.4	584.0	577.4	559.6
Net income ($ mil.)	–	–	(20.0)	17.0	(3.9)	(44.5)
Market value ($ mil.)	–	–	–	–	–	–
Employees	–	–	–	–	–	3,200

CITY OF SACRAMENTO

915 I ST FL 5
SACRAMENTO, CA 958142622
Phone: 916-808-5300
Fax: –
Web: www.cityofsacramento.org

CEO: –
CFO: –
HR: –
FYE: June 30
Type: Private

With its Mediterranean climate and location at the foot of the Sierra Nevadas living in the city of Sacramento is no sacrifice. Founded in 1849 Sacramento is the oldest incorporated city in the state and its seventh most populated comprising about 470000 residents. California's capital city uses a council-manager form of government with council members from eight districts elected to four-year terms. The council sets up city policies approves contracts and a budget of nearly $800 million as well as hears appeals of city decisions. The four council-appointed officers that carry out the city's business are the city manager attorney treasurer and clerk. A Legislative Affairs Unit supports the council.

	Annual Growth	06/15	06/16	06/17	06/18	06/19
Sales ($ mil.)	5.7%	–	709.9	694.4	723.9	838.2
Net income ($ mil.)	(1.9%)	–	91.4	46.5	2.0	86.5
Market value ($ mil.)	–	–	–	–	–	–
Employees	–	–	–	–	–	4,500

CITY OF SAINT PAUL

15 KELLOGG BLVD W STE 390
SAINT PAUL, MN 551021615
Phone: 651-266-8500
Fax: –
Web: www.stpaul.gov

CEO: –
CFO: –
HR: Mary Nash
FYE: December 31
Type: Private

In a Pig's Eye once referred to the City of Saint Paul. Founded in 1849 in the Territory of Minnesota the city of 285000 has gone through a few other name changes finally settling on its current name in 1854. Saint Paul is located on the east bank of the Mississippi River and with its twin city Minneapolis forms the 16th largest metropolis in the US. The mayor-council government consists of an "at large" mayor and seven ward councilmembers. Minnesota's capital Saint Paul is home to professional sports teams Minnesota Wild of the NHL and Minnesota Swarm of the National Lacrosse League (NLL).

	Annual Growth	12/15	12/16	12/17	12/18	12/19
Sales ($ mil.)	3.2%	–	463.5	454.7	488.4	509.1
Net income ($ mil.)	36.0%	–	14.5	(11.0)	(24.1)	36.5
Market value ($ mil.)	–	–	–	–	–	–
Employees		–	–	–	–	3,358

CITY OF SAINT PETERSBURG

175 5TH ST N
SAINT PETERSBURG, FL 337013708
Phone: 727-893-7111
Fax: –
Web: www.golfstpete.com

CEO: –
CFO: –
HR: –
FYE: September 30
Type: Private

Luckily for all those Midwesterners escaping snowy weather St. Pete is nothing like its Russian namesake. The city of St. Petersburg known almost universally as St. Pete is surrounded by warm Gulf water and boasts nearly 360 days of sunshine per year. Along with Tampa and Clearwater it makes up the Tampa Bay Area on Florida's west coast. St. Pete's mayor-council government includes eight council members each representing their home district. The first deputy mayor oversees the city's daily operations. Tourism and marine research are major industries with about a dozen oceanographic institutes in the area. St. Pete founded in 1892 spends about $500 million each year on a population of about 400000.

	Annual Growth	09/16	09/17	09/18	09/19	09/20
Sales ($ mil.)	7.6%	–	296.4	309.6	336.3	368.8
Net income ($ mil.)	(21.4%)	–	66.5	(49.9)	(16.9)	32.3
Market value ($ mil.)	–	–	–	–	–	–
Employees		–	–	–	–	2,800

CITY OF SALINAS

200 LINCOLN AVE
SALINAS, CA 939012639
Phone: 831-758-7489
Fax: –
Web: www.cityofsalinas.org

CEO: –
CFO: –
HR: –
FYE: June 30
Type: Private

It isn't known as the "Salad Bowl of America" for nothing; Salinas Valley is responsible for more than 80% of the lettuce grown in the US. With a population of more than 140000 the City of Salinas' economy is primarily based on agriculture. Many major vegetable producers are headquartered in the city and the area is well known for fruits and vegetables including broccoli carrots lettuce spinach strawberries and watermelons. The city's government consists of the mayor (two-year term) and six city council members (four-year terms). Salinas is also the hometown of famed writer and Nobel price laureate John Steinbeck.

	Annual Growth	06/16	06/17	06/18	06/19	06/20
Sales ($ mil.)	4.1%	–	152.2	161.8	171.6	171.9
Net income ($ mil.)	32.4%	–	3.3	(7.8)	59.4	7.7
Market value ($ mil.)	–	–	–	–	–	–
Employees		–	–	–	–	735

CITY OF SAN ANTONIO

100 W HOUSTON ST STE 1800
SAN ANTONIO, TX 782051404
Phone: 210-207-6000
Fax: –
Web: www.sanantonio.gov

CEO: –
CFO: –
HR: –
FYE: September 30
Type: Private

When you "Remember the Alamo" don't forget San Antonio! The second-largest Texas city (behind Houston) with a population of about 1.5 million San Antonio was the site of the Battle of the Alamo. Today it's home to major tourist attractions like the River Walk SeaWorld and Six Flags Fiesta Texas as well as the San Antonio Spurs NBA franchise and more than 50 golf courses. It has a huge military presence with three major Army and Air Force bases. San Antonio is run by a mayor and 10 district representatives who pass laws and establish policies for the city. Its city manager oversees day-to-day operations including nearly 40 departments. San Antonio has an annual budget of more than $2 billion.

	Annual Growth	09/15	09/16	09/18	09/19	09/20
Sales ($ mil.)	–	–	–	0.0	2,056.6	2,150.0	2,168.0
Net income ($ mil.)	–	–	–	0.0	284.1	192.7	(15.8)
Market value ($ mil.)	–	–	–	–	–	–
Employees		–	–	–	–	12,000

CITY OF SAN DIEGO

202 C ST
SAN DIEGO, CA 921013860
Phone: 619-236-6330
Fax: –
Web: www.sandiego.gov

CEO: –
CFO: –
HR: –
FYE: June 30
Type: Private

The City of San Diego offers more than just warm weather and beautiful beaches. The second-largest city in California (with a population of more than 1.3 million) known as Telecom Valley is also one of the centers in the US for technological manufacturing. Its council members each represent one of its nine districts. Founded in 1769 San Diego is the home to 3 universities as well as professional sports teams Padres of MLB and Chargers of the NFL. The city operates through some 50 programs and departments including environmental services homeland security parks and recreation and the commission for arts and culture. The City of San Diego has an annual budget of approximately $3 billion.

	Annual Growth	06/15	06/16	06/18	06/19	06/20
Sales ($ mil.)	3.1%	–	1,978.8	2,021.2	2,283.5	2,237.5
Net income ($ mil.)	–	–	264.0	(82.9)	62.2	(103.4)
Market value ($ mil.)	–	–	–	–	–	–
Employees		–	–	–	–	11,200

CITY OF SAN JOSE

200 E SANTA CLARA ST 13TH
SAN JOSE, CA 951131905
Phone: 408-535-3500
Fax: –
Web: www.sanjoseca.gov

CEO: –
CFO: –
HR: –
FYE: June 30
Type: Private

Do you know the way to San Jos ©? If so you're probably a high tech worker and hopefully one with a salary to match its real estate prices. The city is known for its Silicon Valley location and technology-driven economy. More than 500 tech firms are the major employers in the area which is also known for its premium home prices (median $495000). San Jos © was founded in 1777 and incorporates some 180 square miles. 950000 residents make San Jos © the third largest city in the state. The city government uses the council/manager model wherein the council made up of the mayor (elected at large) and the 10 council members (one from each district) sets policy and the council-appointed city manager carries it out.

	Annual Growth	06/16	06/17	06/18	06/19	06/20
Sales ($ mil.)	7.0%	–	1,526.1	1,629.7	1,731.6	1,868.7
Net income ($ mil.)	86.2%	–	48.0	9.0	135.0	309.9
Market value ($ mil.)	–	–	–	–	–	–
Employees		–	–	–	–	7,500

CITY OF SANTA ANA

20 CIVIC CENTER PLZ FL 8
SANTA ANA, CA 927014058
Phone: 714-647-5400
Fax: –
Web: www.santa-ana.org

CEO: –
CFO: –
HR: –
FYE: June 30
Type: Private

The area was named by a Spanish army sergeant in 1810 and the city of Santa Ana was founded in 1869 by William Spurgeon. The city encompasses 27.5 sq. mi. and coupled with a population of almost 330000 is the fourth most densely populated city in the US. Santa Ana is home for Behr Paint CoreLogic Corinthian Colleges Ingram Micro and Rickenbacker with regional headquarters for T-Mobile Ultimate Software and Xerox. A Mediterranean climate and proximity to Disneyland Knotts Berry Farm and Huntington and Newport beaches offer residents and visitors with ample recreational activities. The city is governed by a council-manager system consisting of a mayor and six councilmembers elected to 4-year terms.

	Annual Growth	06/16	06/17	06/18	06/19	06/20
Sales ($ mil.)	7.6%	–	339.4	342.9	381.1	422.7
Net income ($ mil.)	–	–	(1.1)	(12.6)	16.7	14.5
Market value ($ mil.)	–	–	–	–	–	–
Employees	–	–	–	–	–	2,044

CITY OF SEATTLE

700 5TH AVE STE 5500
SEATTLE, WA 981045016
Phone: 206-684-7999
Fax: –
Web: www.seattle.gov

CEO: –
CFO: –
HR: –
FYE: December 31
Type: Private

In the Emerald City it's not just the name that's green. The City of Seattle is known for rain-fed lush greenery but also for its environmentalism. It uses a charter form of government which features an elected mayor and city council along with a city attorney. The nine council members are elected at large annually. Among some 25 other departments Seattle has an Office of Sustainability and Environment it's restoring salmon habitat and it celebrates Earth Month rather than just Earth Day. The city serves a population of more than 600000 with an annual budget of around $4 billion. It was first settled by Europeans in 1851 and takes its name from Chief Seattle a local tribal leader.

	Annual Growth	12/15	12/16	12/17	12/18	12/19
Sales ($ mil.)	6.7%	–	2,099.4	2,210.0	2,395.8	2,549.2
Net income ($ mil.)	(2.4%)	–	124.0	120.9	44.7	115.2
Market value ($ mil.)	–	–	–	–	–	–
Employees	–	–	–	–	–	10,000

CITY OF SHREVEPORT

505 TRAVIS ST STE 600
SHREVEPORT, LA 711013028
Phone: 318-423-5611
Fax: –
Web: www.shreveportla.gov

CEO: –
CFO: –
HR: –
FYE: December 31
Type: Private

As industry goes in the Ark-La-Tex so it goes in the City of Shreveport located on the banks of the Red River. The third largest city in Louisiana and ranked 108th in the US Shreveport has a population of nearly 200000 encompassing almost 118 sq. mi. Founded in 1805 by the Shreve Town Company and later incorporated in 1893 Shreveport along with its neighbor Bossier City boast a thriving service economy. The elected mayor and seven district councilmembers run the city government.

	Annual Growth	12/16	12/17	12/18	12/19	12/20
Sales ($ mil.)	16.6%	–	268.9	265.3	260.4	425.8
Net income ($ mil.)	–	–	(36.7)	(10.9)	(8.4)	(18.3)
Market value ($ mil.)	–	–	–	–	–	–
Employees	–	–	–	–	–	3,000

CITY OF ST. LOUIS

1200 MARKET ST RM 212
SAINT LOUIS, MO 631032805
Phone: 314-622-3201
Fax: –
Web: www.stlouis-mo.gov

CEO: –
CFO: –
HR: –
FYE: June 30
Type: Private

The Gateway to the West is bordered by the Mississippi River on the east and occupies approximately 62 square miles with a population of more than 300000. The government of the City of St. Louis is comprised of the city's mayor and a Board of Aldermen (made up of 28 elected members in addition to the board president). Unlike most city governments the mayor shares executive authority with other independent citywide elected officials such as the treasurer and comptroller. During the 21st century St. Louis has transitioned from a manufacturing and industrial economy to one heavily dependent on medicine biotechnology and other sciences. It is home to MLB's St. Louis Cardinals and NFL's St. Louis Rams.

	Annual Growth	06/16	06/17	06/18	06/19	06/20
Sales ($ mil.)	2.7%	–	796.6	849.0	870.1	863.3
Net income ($ mil.)	(14.9%)	–	14.2	50.4	111.1	8.8
Market value ($ mil.)	–	–	–	–	–	–
Employees	–	–	–	–	–	4,500

CITY OF STOCKTON

425 N EL DORADO ST
STOCKTON, CA 952021997
Phone: 209-937-8212
Fax: –

CEO: –
CFO: –
HR: Pamela Summerville
FYE: June 30
Type: Private

Tuleburg Fat City and Mudville were just a few of the early names for the City of Stockton. A German immigrant and gold miner founding father Captain Charles Webber settled on Stockton in honor of Commodore Robert Stockton a leader in the capture of California in the Mexican-American War. A population of over 290000 is packed into an area of almost 65 sq. mi. Historically a farming community for asparagus cherries tomatoes walnuts and almonds Stockton is home to the University of the Pacific and Diamond Foods.

	Annual Growth	06/16	06/17	06/18	06/19	06/20
Sales ($ mil.)	8.1%	–	293.7	344.0	369.8	371.3
Net income ($ mil.)	48.2%	–	9.5	8.8	39.5	30.8
Market value ($ mil.)	–	–	–	–	–	–
Employees	–	–	–	–	–	2,200

CITY OF SYRACUSE

233 E WSHNGTN ST STE 231
SYRACUSE, NY 132021423
Phone: 315-448-8005
Fax: –
Web: www.syrgov.net

CEO: –
CFO: –
HR: –
FYE: June 30
Type: Private

Syracuse New York is located in the center of the state but it is a world apart from the "Big Apple". Named after the Sicilian city of Syracuse the city owes much of its growth and history to two things— salt and the Erie Canal. Although neither is as important as it once was to the city Syracuse is still a regional transportation hub and the city has managed to weather the economic trends supplanting a salt-centric economy with industrial manufacturing before evolving to a service industry centered economy. The city has a population of about 150000 and is governed by its mayor and a ten-person Common Council.

	Annual Growth	06/16	06/17	06/18	06/19	06/20
Sales ($ mil.)	1.7%	–	741.5	758.8	775.9	779.1
Net income ($ mil.)	51.2%	–	6.2	122.8	16.0	21.3
Market value ($ mil.)	–	–	–	–	–	–
Employees	–	–	–	–	–	6,456

CITY OF TAMPA

306 E JACKSON ST
TAMPA, FL 336025223
Phone: 813-274-8211
Fax: –
Web: www.tampa.gov

CEO: –
CFO: –
HR: Carrie Ortolano
FYE: September 30
Type: Private

Disregarded by its first owners the Spanish in 1517 and the British in 1763 Tampa is now a thriving city on the Gulf Coast of Florida. It joins Clearwater and St. Petersburg in forming the Tampa Bay Area. The city uses a mayor-council form of government with seven council members one from each of four districts and three at-large. The mayor and council members are elected to four year terms. They set policy and the chief of staff carries it out by running the day-to-day operations of the city. In addition to tourism and the port of Tampa major area industry includes agriculture construction health care and military operations. Tampa which has a population of about 350000 was incorporated in 1855.

	Annual Growth	09/16	09/17	09/18	09/19	09/20
Sales ($ mil.)	9.9%	–	491.6	558.8	610.2	652.2
Net income ($ mil.)	–	–	(9.0)	64.5	33.8	43.8
Market value ($ mil.)	–	–	–	–	–	–
Employees	–	–	–	–	–	4,500

CITY OF TOLEDO

1 GOVERNMENT CTR STE 2050
TOLEDO, OH 436042281
Phone: 419-245-1050
Fax: –
Web: www.toledo.oh.gov

CEO: Paula Hicks-Hudson
CFO: –
HR: –
FYE: December 31
Type: Private

Known as the Glass City because of its strong presence in the glass and auto manufacturing industry the City of Toledo is by no means fragile. The city incorporated in Ohio in 1837 is situated in the northwestern part of the state along the Michigan border. It is the fourth most populous city in Ohio. Toledo's heavy dependence on manufacturing has made it particularly susceptible to the country's economic lows but the city has bounced back each time through revitalization and redevelopment efforts. The City of Toledo is governed by a mayor and a 12-member city council.

	Annual Growth	12/15	12/16	12/17	12/18	12/19
Sales ($ mil.)	3.3%	–	326.6	328.3	338.9	360.5
Net income ($ mil.)	(13.4%)	–	21.3	16.9	12.1	13.8
Market value ($ mil.)	–	–	–	–	–	–
Employees	–	–	–	–	–	3,000

CITY OF TRENTON

319 E STATE ST
TRENTON, NJ 086081809
Phone: 609-989-3030
Fax: –
Web: www.trentonnj.org

CEO: –
CFO: –
HR: –
FYE: June 30
Type: Private

Trenton New Jersey is a city with a lot of history. The first settlement in the area dates to 1679 with the town adopting the name "Trent-towne" in 1719. Eventually shortened to Trenton the city became famous for the Battle of Trenton in which Washington crossed the Delaware on December 26 to defeat the Hession troops stationed there. The city was also briefly the capital of the United States. Although it is no longer the nation's capital the city is the capital of New Jersey sporting a population of about 85000. Trenton's city government consists of a seven-member city council and its elected mayor.

	Annual Growth	06/11	06/12	06/13	06/15	06/16
Sales ($ mil.)	2.0%	–	300.3	307.0	290.9	324.7
Net income ($ mil.)	8.7%	–	14.9	8.1	12.3	20.7
Market value ($ mil.)	–	–	–	–	–	–
Employees	–	–	–	–	–	13,000

CITY OF TUCSON

255 W ALAMEDA ST
TUCSON, AZ 857011362
Phone: 520-791-4561
Fax: –
Web: www.tucsonaz.gov

CEO: –
CFO: –
HR: –
FYE: June 30
Type: Private

There's no such thing as too much sun in Tucson. The City of Tucson Arizona enjoys 360 sunny days a year is divided into six wards each represented by a council member. Together with the mayor the members form the Tucson City Council which sets city policies; a city manager leads all departments in implementing these policies. Tucson has about half a million residents and a culture that blends Native American and Mexican influences. It's home to The University of Arizona Davis-Monthan Air Force Base and The National Optical Astronomy Observatories. The Arizona Diamondbacks are based in Tucson and the Chicago White Sox hold spring training here. The city has an annual budget of greater than $2 billion.

	Annual Growth	06/13	06/14	06/15	06/16	06/19
Sales ($ mil.)	4.4%	–	728.7	723.8	763.5	903.6
Net income ($ mil.)	12.8%	–	31.7	(16.3)	19.4	58.0
Market value ($ mil.)	–	–	–	–	–	–
Employees	–	–	–	–	–	5,900

CITY OF TULSA

175 E 2ND ST STE 15129
TULSA, OK 741033201
Phone: 918-596-2100
Fax: –
Web: www.cityoftulsa.org

CEO: –
CFO: –
HR: –
FYE: June 30
Type: Private

Named for the Tulsa Lochapokas indian tribe the City of Tulsa was incorporated in 1898. The finding of oil in 1901 resulted in rapid growth and still links Tulsa to the US oil industry. The city with a population of over 395000 straddles the Arkansas River and maintains a temperate climate. AAON Mazzios Nordam Group ONEOK and The Williams Companies headquarter in Tulsa. The University of Tulsa Oral Roberts University and Rogers State University form the base of the 15 institutions in the city.

	Annual Growth	06/13	06/14	06/15	06/16	06/17
Sales ($ mil.)	1.4%	–	467.2	469.0	478.4	487.5
Net income ($ mil.)	97.0%	–	21.5	45.2	15.2	164.4
Market value ($ mil.)	–	–	–	–	–	–
Employees	–	–	–	–	–	3,897

CITY OF VIRGINIA BEACH

2401 COURTHOUSE DR 13R
VIRGINIA BEACH, VA 234569120
Phone: 757-385-3111
Fax: –
Web: www.malibues.vbschools.com

CEO: –
CFO: –
HR: –
FYE: June 30
Type: Private

Whether you're looking for seaside peace and seclusion or bustling boardwalk adventure Virginia Beach is the spot. With nearly 40 miles of Chesapeake Bay and Atlantic Ocean coastline the city's economy thrives largely on travel and tourism and supports a population of more than 435000 people. Virginia Beach's city council consists of 11 elected members (including its mayor) and is responsible for legislative duties including levying taxes adopting an annual budget and appointing a city manager. The city manager carries out executive and administrative tasks in this city's Council-Manager government.

	Annual Growth	06/17	06/18	06/19	06/20	06/21
Sales ($ mil.)	2.6%	–	1,356.6	1,379.5	1,412.5	1,463.6
Net income ($ mil.)	–	–	61.1	(70.2)	156.8	(12.5)
Market value ($ mil.)	–	–	–	–	–	–
Employees	–	–	–	–	–	7,500

CITY OF YONKERS

40 S BROADWAY STE 1
YONKERS, NY 107013715
Phone: 914-377-6000
Fax: –
Web: www.yonkersny.gov

CEO: –
CFO: –
HR: –
FYE: June 30
Type: Private

The city of Jonk Herr (Dutch for young gentleman) has gone through many changes since its founding in 1670. Incorporated in 1872 the City of Yonkers now has a population of almost 200000 nestled into an area of about 20 sq. mi. overlooking the Hudson River. Home to Sarah Lawrence College Yonkers' mayor/council style of government is run by an "at large" mayor and seven district councilmembers.

	Annual Growth	06/16	06/17	06/18	06/19	06/20
Sales ($ mil.)	1.4%	–	1,171.3	1,199.8	1,263.1	1,219.7
Net income ($ mil.)	–	–	(15.2)	(6.3)	(41.1)	69.4
Market value ($ mil.)	–	–	–	–	–	–
Employees	–	–	–	–	–	2,500

CITY PUBLIC SERVICES OF SAN ANTONIO

500 MCCULLOUGH AVE
SAN ANTONIO, TX 782152104
Phone: 210-353-2222
Fax: –
Web: www.cpsenergy.com

CEO: Paula Gold-Williams
CFO: Delores Lenzy-Jones
HR: –
FYE: January 31
Type: Private

CPS Energy (formerly City Public Service of San Antonio) is owned by the City of San Antonio. It is the largest municipally-owned gas and electric utility in the US. About 15% of its gross revenues support over one-fourth of the general operating budget of San Antonio's municipal government providing financial resources for the delivery of basic services such as streets and infrastructure public safety parks and youth programs and libraries. It serves about 840750 electricity customers and some 352585 natural gas customers in the greater San Antonio Texas area.

	Annual Growth	01/08	01/09	01/10	01/11	01/12
Sales ($ mil.)	8.1%	–	–	1,930.9	2,068.7	2,258.4
Net income ($ mil.)	(55.5%)	–	–	107.6	78.8	21.3
Market value ($ mil.)	–	–	–	–	–	–
Employees	–	–	–	–	–	3,100

CITY UTILITIES OF SPRINGFIELD MO

301 E CENTRAL ST
SPRINGFIELD, MO 658023858
Phone: 417-863-9000
Fax: –
Web: www.cityutilities.net

CEO: –
CFO: –
HR: –
FYE: September 30
Type: Private

City Utilities of Springfield Missouri springs to action with multiple services and products. The multi-utility supplies electricity natural gas and water for residents and businesses in the southwestern Missouri town. It has about 1870 miles of power lines and 1260 miles of natural gas mains serves about 110000 electric customers 82000 natural gas customers and 81000 water customers. It also operates the municipal bus system which has 25 regular street buses and five demand/response buses and serves about 790 broadband contracts through SpringNet Telecommunications. City Utilities of Springfield has a service region of 320 sq. mi. and serves a base population of 229000.

	Annual Growth	09/16	09/17	09/18	09/19	09/20
Sales ($ mil.)	(0.2%)	–	432.8	459.7	457.7	429.8
Net income ($ mil.)	20.5%	–	34.9	61.0	66.9	60.9
Market value ($ mil.)	–	–	–	–	–	–
Employees	–	–	–	–	–	980

CITYSERVICEVALCON, LLC

640 W MONTANA ST
KALISPELL, MT 599013834
Phone: 406-755-4321
Fax: –
Web: www.cityservicevalcon.com

CEO: –
CFO: –
HR: –
FYE: September 30
Type: Private

You don't have to live in the city to get the services of CityServiceValcon which markets and distributes petroleum products throughout the Inland Northwest and Rocky Mountain regions of the US as well as in the adjacent Plains states. Its products include gasoline diesel aviation fuels lubricants propane and heating oil. The company has diesel gasoline and heating oils for delivery through its network of bulk plants. CityServiceValcon also operates cardlock fueling facilities under the Pacific Pride brand name. Regional independent petroleum marketers City Service and Valcon merged their operations in 2003 to form CityServiceValcon.

	Annual Growth	09/04	09/05	09/06	09/07	09/08
Sales ($ mil.)	16.6%	–	–	459.5	490.1	625.1
Net income ($ mil.)	(8.0%)	–	–	4.7	3.0	4.0
Market value ($ mil.)	–	–	–	–	–	–
Employees	–	–	–	–	–	150

CIVISTA BANCSHARES INC

NAS: CIVB

100 East Water Street
Sandusky, OH 44870
Phone: 419 625-4121
Fax: –

CEO: Dennis Shaffer
CFO: –
HR: –
FYE: December 31
Type: Public

First Citizens Banc Corp. is the holding company for The Citizens Banking Company and its Citizens Bank and Champaign Bank divisions which together operate more than 30 branches in northern Ohio. The banks offer such deposit products as checking and savings accounts and CDs in addition to trust services. They concentrate on real estate lending with residential mortgages and commercial mortgages each comprising approximately 40% of the company's loan portfolio. The Citizens Banking Company's Citizens Wealth Management division provides financial planning brokerage insurance and investments through an agreement with third-party provider UVEST (part of LPL Financial).

	Annual Growth	12/16	12/17	12/18	12/19	12/20
Assets ($ mil.)	19.0%	1,377.3	1,525.9	2,139.0	2,309.6	2,762.9
Net income ($ mil.)	16.9%	17.2	15.9	14.1	33.9	32.2
Market value ($ mil.)	(2.5%)	308.9	349.8	276.9	381.6	278.7
Employees	8.0%	337	350	432	457	459

CIVITAS RESOURCES INC

NYS: CIVI

410 17th Street, Suite 1400
Denver, CO 80202
Phone: 720 440-6100
Fax: 720 305-0804
Web: www.bonanzacrk.com

CEO: Benjamin Dell
CFO: Marianella Foschi
HR: –
FYE: December 31
Type: Public

Bonanza Creek Energy searches for a treasure of black gold. The independent oil and natural gas company has exploration and production assets in Arkansas California Colorado and Texas. Unlike many in the industry it operates nearly all of its projects and has an 89% working interest in its holdings. The company reported a 32% increase in proved reserves in 2013 to 69.8 million barrels of oil equivalent resulting primarily from the development of the Wattenberg Field in Colorado. Most of the company's proved reserves are in its Rocky Mountains (Niobara oil shale) and Arkansas (Cotton Valley sands) holdings. Bonanza Creek Energy filed for and emerged from Chapter 11 bankruptcy protection in 2017.

	Annual Growth	04/17*	12/17	12/18	12/19	12/20
Sales ($ mil.)	47.0%	68.6	123.5	276.7	313.2	218.1
Net income ($ mil.)	238.9%	2.7	(5.0)	168.2	67.1	103.5
Market value ($ mil.)	(11.2%)	–	575.0	430.7	486.4	402.8
Employees	(11.3%)	–	156	144	125	109

*Fiscal year change

CKX INC.

650 Madison Ave.
New York NY 10022
Phone: 212-838-3100
Fax: 212-872-1473
Web: ir.ckx.com

CEO: –
CFO: –
HR: –
FYE: December 31
Type: Private

CKX is ready to sing "Viva Las Vegas" but any performance will be critiqued by the judges of American Idol. The company controls 85% of Elvis Presley Enterprises which manages the King's estate and licenses his likeness songs and name and operates tours of Graceland. CKX also owns 19 Entertainment the firm responsible for TV shows such as American Idol and So You Think You Can Dance. It owns the rights to the IDOLS brand which appears in more than 100 countries around the world. Additionally CKX has an 80% stake in the name image likeness and intellectual property of Muhammad Ali. Private equity firm Apollo Global Management owns CKX.

CKX LANDS INC

2417 Shell Beach Drive
Lake Charles, LA 70601
Phone: 337 493-2399
Fax: –
Web: www.ckxlands.com

ASE: CKX
CEO: –
CFO: –
HR: –
FYE: December 31
Type: Public

Revenues come naturally to CKX Lands. The company owns or has stakes in about 14000 acres in Louisiana that contain oil and gas wells mines timber and agricultural operations. Formed in 1930 the company does not perform any of these operations and is not involved in oil and gas exploration. Instead it generates revenues through royalties from the natural resources produced on its land. Originally set up to receive mineral royalties spun off by a bank to its shareholders CKX Lands' growth strategy is built around acquiring land in southwestern Louisiana. Its largest customers Mayne and Mertz and Cox & Perkins account for nearly 40% of sales.

	Annual Growth	12/16	12/17	12/18	12/19	12/20
Sales ($ mil.)	(6.1%)	0.9	1.1	1.2	0.8	0.7
Net income ($ mil.)	18.7%	0.2	0.5	1.1	0.2	0.3
Market value ($ mil.)	(3.7%)	21.5	19.8	20.0	18.1	18.5
Employees	(24.0%)	3	3	1	1	1

CLARCOR INC.

840 CRESCENT CENTRE DR # 600
FRANKLIN, TN 370674687
Phone: 615-771-3100
Fax: –
Web: www.parker.com

CEO: –
CFO: –
HR: –
FYE: November 30
Type: Private

CLARCOR cleans up with filters. The company's industrial and environmental filtration unit makes air and antimicrobial filters for commercial industrial and residential buildings along with filters used in industrial processes. Brands include Airguard Facet ATI Transweb UAS Keddeg MKI TFSand Purolator. Companies in CLARCOR's engine and mobile filtration business make products under brands such as Baldwin Hastings Filters and Clark that filter the air oil fuel coolant and hydraulic fluids. In 2017 in order to expand its filtration portfolio Parker-Hannifin acquired CLARCOR for about $4.3 billion.

	Annual Growth	11/12	11/13	11/14	11/15	11/16
Sales ($ mil.)	7.1%	–	1,130.8	1,512.9	1,481.0	1,389.6
Net income ($ mil.)	5.6%	–	118.4	144.2	134.9	139.4
Market value ($ mil.)	–	–	–	–	–	–
Employees						5,773

CLARE ROSE, INC.

100 ROSE EXECUTIVE BLVD
EAST YAPHANK, NY 119671524
Phone: 631-475-2337
Fax: –
Web: www.clarerose.com

CEO: –
CFO: Monica Ray
HR: –
FYE: December 31
Type: Private

Clare Rose has risen to the top with help from The King of Beers. The company a top beer wholesaler in the US primarily markets Anheuser-Busch products including Budweiser Michelob Bacardi and Busch branded products. Clare Rose dominates distribution of the US beer maker's brands on New York's Long Island and Staten Island. The firm also carries other products including those of Heineken Redhook Ale and Widmer Brothers (both owned by Craft Brewers Alliance) Kona Brewing China's Harbin and Japan's Kirin. Founded in 1936 by Clare Rose the company is still owned and operated by the Rose family.

	Annual Growth	12/09	12/10	12/11	12/12	12/13
Sales ($ mil.)	0.5%	–	–	199.8	209.9	202.0
Net income ($ mil.)	(11.4%)	–	–	8.4	9.5	6.6
Market value ($ mil.)	–	–	–	–	–	–
Employees						267

CLAREMONT GRADUATE UNIVERSITY

150 E 10TH ST
CLAREMONT, CA 917115909
Phone: 909-607-8632
Fax: –
Web: www.cgu.edu

CEO: Deborah Freund
CFO: –
HR: –
FYE: June 30
Type: Private

Claremont Graduate University (CGU) offers sunshine as well as strong academics to students. About 35 miles from Los Angeles the university provides master's and doctoral degrees in 22 disciplines including education mathematics and psychology. A member of the Claremont University Consortium the university is made up of nine academic schools including arts and humanities educational studies and politics and economics. The Peter F. Drucker Graduate School of Management also is housed on the Claremont Graduate University campus. The relatively small university with an enrollment of about 2000 focuses on giving its students individualized attention. CGU was founded in 1925.

	Annual Growth	06/08	06/09	06/10	06/13	06/15
Sales ($ mil.)	7.7%	–	57.7	59.1	62.6	89.9
Net income ($ mil.)	–	–	(15.2)	(16.1)	10.6	6.6
Market value ($ mil.)	–	–	–	–	–	–
Employees						250

CLAREMONT MCKENNA COLLEGE FOUNDATION

500 E 9TH ST
CLAREMONT, CA 917115929
Phone: 909-621-8088
Fax: –
Web: www.cmc.edu

CEO: –
CFO: –
HR: –
FYE: June 30
Type: Private

Claremont McKenna College (CMC) is an coeducational undergraduate liberal arts college with an annual enrollment of some 1250 students. It offers 33 majors and 8 sequences (programs of related courses). Double dual individualized off campus majors and more than 2000 courses available for cross registration across a network of CMC and six affiliated schools. CMC is also home to nearly a dozen research centers including The Keck Center for International and Strategic Studies and The Center for Human Rights Leadership. The college is managed by the Claremont University Consortium which supports seven independent Claremont colleges and is modeled after the University of Oxford.

	Annual Growth	06/09	06/10	06/11	06/12	06/15
Sales ($ mil.)	7.2%	–	109.6	159.1	154.6	155.1
Net income ($ mil.)	25.8%	–	8.6	53.6	22.9	27.0
Market value ($ mil.)	–	–	–	–	–	–
Employees						370

CLARK CONSTRUCTION GROUP LLC

7500 Old Georgetown Rd.
Bethesda MD 20814
Phone: 301-272-8100
Fax: 301-272-1928
Web: www.clarkconstruction.com

CEO: Robert D Moser Jr
CFO: Sameer Bhargava
HR: –
FYE: December 31
Type: Subsidiary

Clark Construction Group specializes in building landmarks. The general contractor has constructed iconic structures such as the Boston Convention and Exhibition Center Dulles International Airport and FedEx Field the home of the Washington Redskins. Clark Construction serves commercial institutional and heavy construction customers around the US and is part of Clark Enterprises. It offers construction management design/build and general contracting services. Projects include convention centers sports facilities office complexes hotels airports correctional facilities manufacturing facilities water treatment plants highways and bridges and high-rise apartments.

CLARK ENTERPRISES INC.

7500 Old Georgetown Rd. 15th Fl.
Bethesda MD 20814-6195
Phone: 301-657-7100
Fax: 301-657-7263
Web: www.clarkenterprisesinc.com

CEO: –
CFO: James J Brinkman
HR: –
FYE: December 31
Type: Private

Like Clark Kent this firm holds some super powers. Clark Enterprises Inc. (CEI) is a holding company with diverse investments in real estate construction financial markets and venture capital. Its flagship subsidiary Clark Construction Group is one of the largest private general contractors in the US and provides construction management design/build and consulting services. Other CEI units develop manage and lease residential and office real estate. Private equity and venture capital arm CNF Investments is an active investor in the technology life sciences telecom and energy sectors. Chairman and CEO James Clark owns CEI which was founded in 1972.

CLARKSON UNIVERSITY

8 CLARKSON AVE
POTSDAM, NY 136761402
Phone: 315-268-6400
Fax: –
Web: www.clarkson.edu

CEO: –
CFO: James Fish
HR: –
FYE: June 30
Type: Private

Clarkson University knows that quality research never sleeps in The Empire State. The research institution confers bachelor's master's and doctoral degrees in more than 95 fields of study including engineering business science liberal arts and health sciences. It also has well-regarded programs in advanced materials biotech environment and energy entrepreneurship and global supply chain management. The university employs around 870 faculty and staff catering to more than 4300 students. Clarkson University was founded in 1896 as a memorial to Thomas Clarkson a businessman from Potsdam New York where the primary campus is located. Its Capital Region satellite is located in Schenectady.

	Annual Growth	06/16	06/17	06/18	06/19	06/20
Sales ($ mil.)	21.0%	–	139.4	132.8	135.3	247.2
Net income ($ mil.)	(29.7%)	–	26.5	(7.0)	17.4	9.2
Market value ($ mil.)	–	–	–	–	–	–
Employees	–	–	–	–	–	700

CLAROCITY CORP

3115 Melrose Drive, Suite 130
Carlsbad, CA 92010
Phone: 403 984-9246
Fax: 403 770-8780
Web: www.clarocity.com

TVX: CLY
CEO: –
CFO: –
HR: –
FYE: December 31
Type: Public

How much is your home sweet home worth? Zaio — short for Zone Appraisal and Imaging Operations — aims to provide instant access (through its Web site) to property information on almost every residential property in the 250 largest US cities. Its proprietary GeoScore property rating system uses comprehensive property data including real estate appraisals and property photos provided by contracted independent appraisers and photographers to calculate an estimated valuation. Revenues are generated by selling geographic zones to appraisers and photographers and property information to customers including mortgage companies county tax assessors investors and property owners.

	Annual Growth	12/13	12/14	12/15	12/16	12/17
Sales ($ mil.)	115.6%	–	–	2.3	4.7	10.6
Net income ($ mil.)	–	(6.4)	(4.7)	(9.4)	(7.3)	(11.6)
Market value ($ mil.)	(21.2%)	35.0	47.2	16.0	17.8	13.5
Employees	–	–	–	–	–	–

CLARUS CORP (NEW)

2084 East 3900 South
Salt Lake City, UT 84124
Phone: 801 278-5552
Fax: –

NMS: CLAR
CEO: John C Walbrecht
CFO: Aaron J Kuehne
HR: –
FYE: December 31
Type: Public

Black Diamond caters to expert skiers snowboarders rock and ice climbers and other hardy-outdoor types. The company makes and distributes climbing and mountaineering equipment (carabiners harnesses helmets) backpacks tents trekking poles headlamps and lanterns gloves and mittens skis bindings boots avalanche safety equipment mountain biking gear and more under the Black Diamond and PIEPS brands. Black Diamond sells its products across more than 5000 retail locations. The US account for almost 50% of its sales.

	Annual Growth	12/16	12/17	12/18	12/19	12/20
Sales ($ mil.)	10.9%	148.2	170.7	212.1	229.4	224.0
Net income ($ mil.)	–	(9.0)	(0.7)	7.3	19.0	5.5
Market value ($ mil.)	30.2%	167.1	245.1	316.0	423.5	480.9
Employees	10.7%	400	500	500	500	600

CLASSIFIED VENTURES LLC

175 W. Jackson Blvd. Ste. 800
Chicago IL 60604
Phone: 312-601-5000
Fax: +65-6532-6816
Web: www.hwahongcorp.com

CEO: Alex Vetter
CFO: Robert Gallagher
HR: –
FYE: December 31
Type: Joint Venture

You don't need top secret clearance to work with Classified Ventures. It operates a network of websites offering classified advertising space primarily for real estate and automobile sales. Its sites including Apartments.com (rental listings) Cars.com (new and used autos) and HomeGain.com (home sales) also distribute their content to a network of 170 Web sites owned and operated by newspapers and television stations around the country as well as top portal operators such as Yahoo! and MSN. Classified Ventures is a partnership of five leading media companies: A. H. Belo Gannett McClatchy Washington Post and Tribune Company.

CLAY ELECTRIC COOPERATIVE, INC.

225 W WALKER DR
KEYSTONE HEIGHTS, FL 326567617
Phone: 352-473-8000
Fax: –
Web: www.clayelectric.com

CEO: Richard K Davis
CFO: –
HR: –
FYE: December 31
Type: Private

Clay Electric Cooperative covers a lot of ground in Florida. The utility distributes electricity to 14 counties in the northeastern part of the state including the suburbs of Jacksonville and Gainesville. It delivers power to about 170000 residential commercial and industrial members over more than 13000 miles of distribution and transmission lines. The consumer-owned utility offers electronic funds transfer average billing and a seniors' payment plan to residential customers and backup diesel power generation and special rate plans to businesses. The consumer-owned utility has a stake in Seminole Electric Cooperative which provides generation services to Clay Electric and nine other cooperatives.

	Annual Growth	12/16	12/17	12/18	12/19	12/20
Sales ($ mil.)	1.5%	–	355.7	373.2	364.7	371.7
Net income ($ mil.)	11.2%	–	16.2	22.3	19.4	22.3
Market value ($ mil.)	–	–	–	–	–	–
Employees	–	–	–	–	–	444

CLAYCO, INC.

35 E WACKER DR STE 1300
CHICAGO, IL 606012110
Phone: 312-658-0747
Fax: –
Web: www.claycorp.com

CEO: Russ Burns
CFO: James Havel
HR: –
FYE: December 31
Type: Private

Clayco is a top US general building contractor that offers real estate architecture design engineering and construction services. The privately owned company serves a range of industries with a focus on industrial corporate government residential institutional and financial facilities. Projects include distribution and logistics centers industrial facilities and food and beverage industry warehouses and plants. Clayco also has constructed headquarters and operation centers call and data centers sports and education facilities and retail centers. Its Clayco Realty Group provides land development site selection and project financing.

	Annual Growth	12/08	12/09	12/10	12/11	12/12
Sales ($ mil.)	(6.0%)	–	–	443.2	511.3	391.3
Net income ($ mil.)	(26.2%)	–	–	4.4	2.4	2.4
Market value ($ mil.)	–	–	–	–	–	–
Employees	–	–	–	–	–	1,200

CLEAN ENERGY FUELS CORP   NMS: CLNE

4675 MacArthur Court, Suite 800
Newport Beach, CA 92660
Phone: 949 437-1000
Fax: –
Web: www.cleanenergyfuels.com

CEO: Andrew J Littlefair
CFO: Robert Vreeland
HR: –
FYE: December 31
Type: Public

Clean Energy Fuels is renewable energy company focused on the procurement and distribution of renewable natural gas (RNG) and conventional natural gas in the form of compressed natural gas (CNG) and liquefied natural gas (LNG) for the US and Canadian transportation markets. It owns and supplies approximately 560 natural gas fueling stations. These enable Clean Energy's over 1000 fleet customers to tank up their more than 48000 fleet vehicles with CNG or LNG. Clean Energy also helps customers buy natural gas vehicles and obtain government incentives. Most of the company's revenue comes from the US.

	Annual Growth	12/16	12/17	12/18	12/19	12/20
Sales ($ mil.)	(7.7%)	402.7	341.6	346.4	344.1	291.7
Net income ($ mil.)	–	(12.2)	(79.2)	(3.8)	20.4	(9.7)
Market value ($ mil.)	28.8%	567.7	402.9	341.4	464.5	1,560.1
Employees	(13.5%)	832	431	401	412	465

CLEAN HARBORS INC   NYS: CLH

42 Longwater Drive
Norwell, MA 02061-9149
Phone: 781 792-5000
Fax: –
Web: www.cleanharbors.com

CEO: Alan McKim
CFO: Michael Battles
HR: Jeff Knapp
FYE: December 31
Type: Public

Clean Harbors is one of the leading provider of environmental energy and industrial services throughout North America. The company is also the largest re-refiner and recycler of used oil in the world and the largest provider of parts cleaning and related environmental services to commercial industrial and automotive customers in North America. Its services include end-to-end hazardous waste management emergency response industrial cleaning and maintenance and recycling services. The company has an annual collection capacity of about 200 million gallons of waste oil and some 485 service locations across the US and parts of Canada Puerto Rico and Mexico. More than 85% of its revenue comes from the US.

	Annual Growth	12/16	12/17	12/18	12/19	12/20
Sales ($ mil.)	3.4%	2,755.2	2,945.0	3,300.3	3,412.2	3,144.1
Net income ($ mil.)	–	(39.9)	100.7	65.6	97.7	134.8
Market value ($ mil.)	8.1%	3,048.1	2,968.7	2,703.0	4,696.8	4,168.2
Employees	3.1%	12,400	12,700	14,200	14,400	14,000

CLEANNET U.S.A., INC.

9861 BROKEN LAND PKWY # 208
COLUMBIA, MD 210461185
Phone: 410-720-6444
Fax: –
Web: www.cleanetinc.com

CEO: –
CFO: –
HR: Kelly Wiseman
FYE: December 31
Type: Private

If Mr. Clean himself can't make a personal appearance at your office building Clean-Net USA will happily come to your rescue. The company provides commercial building cleaning services to clients nationwide through franchises in at more than 35000 locations totaling more than 160 million square feet across the US. Its clients' properties include commercial and retail buildings and facilities including banks airports entertainment venues convention centers restaurants and medical facilities as well as places of worship. Its trained personnel are uniformed and carry identification badges. CleanNet USA was founded in 1987 by president Mark Salek.

	Annual Growth	12/11	12/12	12/13	12/15	12/17
Sales ($ mil.)	(0.9%)	–	71.8	77.9	76.8	68.8
Net income ($ mil.)	(0.7%)	–	4.6	(2.1)	5.2	4.4
Market value ($ mil.)	–	–	–	–	–	–
Employees	–	–	–	–	–	150

CLEAR CHANNEL COMMUNICATIONS INC.

200 E. Basse Rd.
San Antonio TX 78209
Phone: 210-822-2828
Fax: 210-822-2299
Web: www.clearchannel.com

CEO: Robert W Pittman
CFO: Richard J Bressler
HR: –
FYE: December 31
Type: Private

This company leaves few open channels on the radio dial. Clear Channel Communications is the #1 radio company in the US with about 860 stations that reach more than 239 million people. Its Premier Radio Networks produces syndicated radio content for more than 5000 stations. Clear Channel also sells spot advertising for about 4000 radio stations and 600 TV stations through Katz Media. (Meanwhile sister company Clear Channel Outdoor Holdings is one of the world's largest outdoor advertising companies with about 840000 display locations worldwide.) Clear Channel Communications a part of CC Media Holdings which is in turn owned by Thomas H. Lee Partners and Bain Capital.

CLEAR CHANNEL OUTDOOR HOLDINGS INC (NEW) NYS: CCO

4830 North Loop 1604 West, Suite 111
San Antonio, TX 78249
Phone: 210 547-8800
Fax: –
Web: www.clearchanneloutdoor.com

CEO: Scott Wells
CFO: Brian Coleman
HR: –
FYE: December 31
Type: Public

Clear Channel Outdoor Holdings is a leading display advertising operator with over 500000 displays in more than 25 countries across Asia Europe Latin America and North America. Besides billboards Clear Channel Outdoor Holdings sells advertising on buses and trains and on street furniture such as bus stops and information kiosks in metropolitan markets. The company sells advertising space in airports and malls and on the sides of high-profile buildings and also creates displays that feature video and moving parts. About 55% of the company's revenue comes from Americas operation. In early 2020 Clear Channel sold its 50.91% stake in Clear Media a company based in China.

	Annual Growth	12/16	12/17	12/18	12/19	12/20
Sales ($ mil.)	(9.0%)	2,702.4	2,591.3	2,721.7	2,683.8	1,854.6
Net income ($ mil.)	–	141.4	(639.7)	(218.2)	(363.3)	(582.7)
Market value ($ mil.)	(24.4%)	2,360.1	2,149.8	2,425.5	1,336.6	771.1
Employees	(4.6%)	5,800	5,700	5,800	5,900	4,800

CLEARDAY INC NBB: CLRD

8800 Village Drive, Suite 106
San Antonio, TX 78217
Phone: 210 451-0839
Fax: –
Web: www.suptech.com

CEO: James Walesa
CFO: John Bergeron
HR: –
FYE: December 31
Type: Public

Superconductor Technologies Inc. (STI) can cool even the most heated conversation. The company uses high-temperature superconducting (HTS) technology in its line of communications products which combine low-noise amplifiers and filters are designed to improve the quality of radio-frequency (RF) transmissions between cellular base stations and mobile devices in wireless networks. It also makes cryogenic cooling devices used to cool HTS materials. STI relies on government contracts to fund its R&D operations; on the commercial side the company serves such top wireless network operators as AT&T Verizon Wireless Sprint Nextel and T-Mobile.

	Annual Growth	12/16	12/17	12/18	12/19	12/20
Sales ($ mil.)	8.9%	0.1	0.4	1.6	0.5	0.2
Net income ($ mil.)	–	(11.1)	(9.5)	(8.1)	(9.2)	(3.0)
Market value ($ mil.)	(9.6%)	1.8	1.6	1.9	0.3	1.2
Employees	(39.9%)	23	22	25	7	3

CLEARFIELD INC NMS: CLFD

7050 Winnetka Avenue North, Suite 100
Brooklyn Park, MN 55428
Phone: 763 476-6866
Fax: –
Web: www.clearfieldconnection.com

CEO: Cheryl Beranek
CFO: Daniel Herzog
HR: –
FYE: September 30
Type: Public

Broadband providers can get all the fiber they need from Clearfield Inc. The company designs manufactures and distributes fiber protection fiber management and fiber delivery solutions to enable rapid and cost-effective fiber-fed deployment throughout the broadband service provider space across North America. Products include a series of panels cabinets wall boxes and other enclosures that house the Clearfield components; optical components integrated for signal coupling splitting termination and multiplexing among others for a seamless integration within their fiber management platform; fiber management and fiber pathway and protection method. More than 95% of Clearfield's revenue comes from customers in the US.

	Annual Growth	09/17	09/18	09/19	09/20	09/21
Sales ($ mil.)	17.5%	73.9	77.7	85.0	93.1	140.8
Net income ($ mil.)	51.6%	3.8	4.3	4.6	7.3	20.3
Market value ($ mil.)	34.2%	186.8	184.7	162.7	277.0	606.3
Employees	2.1%	230	225	240	230	250

CLEARONE INC NAS: CLRO

5225 Wiley Post Way, Suite 500
Salt Lake City, UT 84116
Phone: 801 975-7200
Fax: –
Web: www.clearone.com

CEO: Zeynep Hakimoglu
CFO: –
HR: –
FYE: December 31
Type: Public

ClearOne Communications wants voices to carry loud and clear. The company provides audio conferencing systems to small and large enterprises educational institutions churches and government agencies largely in the US. It also sells related products including microphones and equipment carts. ClearOne's conferencing systems connect large venues such as auditoriums and board rooms as well as desktops and small conference rooms. The company markets its products worldwide selling primarily through distributors who in turn sell to systems integrators and resellers. Customers in the US account for about 60% of sales.

	Annual Growth	12/16	12/17	12/18	12/19	12/20
Sales ($ mil.)	(12.1%)	48.6	41.8	28.2	25.0	29.1
Net income ($ mil.)	(32.6%)	2.4	(14.2)	(16.7)	(8.4)	0.5
Market value ($ mil.)	(33.2%)	214.0	168.0	23.5	31.2	42.6
Employees	(4.4%)	151	–	130	127	126

CLEARPOINT NEURO INC NAS: CLPT

120 S. Sierra Ave., Suite 100
Solana Beach, CA 92075
Phone: 888 287-9109
Fax: –
Web: www.clearpointneuro.com

CEO: Joseph Burnett
CFO: Danilo D Alessandro
HR: –
FYE: December 31
Type: Public

SurgiVision designs products with surgical focus. A medical devices company SurgiVision develops imaging technologies and precision instruments (i.e. needles that deliver radiation) designed for surgeons performing minimally invasive procedures by way of MRI (magnetic resonance imaging) scanners. The company received FDA approval for its first commercial product the ClearPoint system for use in neurological procedures in 2010. It also has candidates in earlier stages of development including its ClearTrace and SafeLead products which are designed for cardiac procedures. SurgiVision was established in 1998; it filed to go public through an IPO in 2009.

	Annual Growth	12/16	12/17	12/18	12/19	12/20
Sales ($ mil.)	22.2%	5.7	7.4	7.4	11.2	12.8
Net income ($ mil.)	–	(8.1)	(7.2)	(6.2)	(5.5)	(6.8)
Market value ($ mil.)	47.0%	58.0	46.9	26.8	81.8	270.9
Employees	19.4%	33	15	38	49	67

CLEARSIGN TECHNOLOGIES CORP NAS: CLIR

12870 Interurban Avenue South
Seattle, WA 98168
Phone: 206 673-4848
Fax: –
Web: www.clearsign.com

CEO: Colin Deller
CFO: Brian G Fike
HR: –
FYE: December 31
Type: Public

Improved energy efficiency and lower emissions? Clearsign believes it has found a way to do what many said couldn't be done. The company's proprietary Electrodynamic Combustion Control (ECC) system uses a computer connected to electrodes inside a combustion system to electrostatically control the process. ECC uses existing ions to manipulate chemical combustion thereby reducing pollution and directing the heat transfer for greater efficiency. The process which can be part of new construction or a retrofit works in combustion power generation (from coal natural gas and other fuels) in petrochemical refining and in other industrial heat processes. Formed in 2008 Clearsign filed to go public in 2011.

	Annual Growth	12/14	12/15	12/16	12/17	12/18
Sales ($ mil.)	105.6%	–	0.1	0.6	0.5	0.5
Net income ($ mil.)	–	(7.3)	(7.9)	(11.2)	(9.7)	(9.5)
Market value ($ mil.)	(38.9%)	195.7	129.5	90.8	96.1	27.2
Employees	6.5%	14	19	20	18	18

CLEARWATER PAPER CORP   NYS: CLW

601 West Riverside, Suite 1100 — CEO: Arsen Kitch
Spokane, WA 99201 — CFO: Michael Murphy
Phone: 509 344-5900 — HR: Kari Moyes
Fax: - — FYE: December 31
Web: www.clearwaterpaper.com — Type: Public

Clearwater Paper is a manufacturer and premier supplier of quality consumer tissue parent roll tissue and bleached paperboard. Business is divided into two primary divisions: Its Pulp and Paperboard segment manufactures bleached paperboard for the high-end segment of the packaging industry and is a leading producer of Solid Bleached Sulfate (SBS) paperboard. A Consumer Products arm produces a private label tissue largely for grocery chains. Vast Majority of Clearwater sales are made in the US. The company traces its roots back in 1926.

	Annual Growth	12/17	12/18	12/19	12/20	12/21
Sales ($ mil.)	0.6%	1,730.4	1,724.2	1,761.5	1,868.6	1,772.6
Net income ($ mil.)	-	97.3	(143.8)	(5.6)	77.1	(28.1)
Market value ($ mil.)	(5.2%)	757.8	406.8	356.5	630.1	612.1
Employees	(2.2%)	3,280	3,130	3,290	3,340	3,000

CLEARWAY ENERGY INC   NYS: CWEN

300 Carnegie Center, Suite 300 — CEO: Christopher Sotos
Princeton, NJ 08540 — CFO: Chad Plotkin
Phone: 609 608-1525 — HR: -
Fax: - — FYE: December 31
Web: www.nrgyield.com — Type: Public

Clearway Energy is one of the largest renewable energy owners in the US with over 4200 net MW of installed wind and solar generation projects. The company also owns approximately 2500 net MW of environmentally-sound highly efficient natural gas generation facilities as well as a portfolio of district energy systems. Clearway Energy is indirectly owned by Global Infrastructure Partners III. Global Infrastructure Management LLC is an independent fund manager that invests in infrastructure assets in the energy and transport sectors and Global Infrastructure Partners III is its third equity fund. The company is sponsored by GIP through GIP's portfolio company CEG.

	Annual Growth	12/16	12/17	12/18	12/19	12/20
Sales ($ mil.)	4.1%	1,021.0	1,009.0	1,053.0	1,032.0	1,199.0
Net income ($ mil.)	(21.8%)	67.0	(8.0)	52.0	(11.0)	25.0
Market value ($ mil.)	19.2%	3,185.8	3,810.9	3,478.2	4,022.6	6,438.2
Employees	-	-	-	269	307	301

CLEARY GOTTLIEB STEEN & HAMILTON LLP

1 Liberty Plaza — CEO: -
New York NY 10006 — CFO: Renee M Lercher
Phone: 212-225-2000 — HR: -
Fax: 212-225-3999 — FYE: December 31
Web: www.cgsh.com — Type: Private - Partnershi

Cleary Gottlieb Steen & Hamilton may be a big cheese in the Big Apple but the law firm also has made a name for itself in the international arena. Cleary Gottlieb's attorneys work from nearly 15 offices scattered across the globe and are known for their work in such practice areas as corporate finance mergers and acquisitions litigation and intellectual property. The firm boasts about 1200 attorneys with almost half of those based outside the US. Representative clients have included British Airways Deutsche Telekom Nortel and other international corporations. The firm was founded in 1946 by former Root Clark Buckner partners George Cleary Leo Gottlieb Fowler Hamilton and Mel Steen.

CLEARY UNIVERSITY

3601 PLYMOUTH RD — CEO: -
ANN ARBOR, MI 481052659 — CFO: -
Phone: 734-332-4477 — HR: -
Fax: - — FYE: June 30
Web: www.cleary.edu — Type: Private

Cleary University helps students navigate the murky waters of business education. The school offers associate bachelor's and master's degrees in business administration. Cleary University focuses on adult undergraduate students first-time college students wanting to begin a business career and senior managers seeking to advance their careers through a graduate degree. It has two campuses (Howell and Ann Arbor) and three extension sites (Flint Garden City and Warren) in Michigan. The school also offers distance learning courses online through its eCleary program. Patrick Roger Cleary founded the school as The Cleary School of Penmanship in 1883.

	Annual Growth	06/10	06/11	06/12	06/13	06/14
Sales ($ mil.)	(5.4%)	-	8.8	7.8	7.6	7.5
Net income ($ mil.)	-	-	-	(0.4)	(0.4)	0.1
Market value ($ mil.)	-	-	-	-	-	-
Employees	-	-	-	-	-	200

CLECO CORP.   NYS: CNL

2030 Donahue Ferry Road — CEO: William G Fontenot
Pineville, LA 71360-5226 — CFO: Kazi Hasan
Phone: 318 484-7400 — HR: -
Fax: - — FYE: December 31
Web: www.cleco.com — Type: Public

Down in the Louisiana bayous Cleco comes alive with the click of a light switch. The holding company's utility unit Cleco Power generates transmits and distributes electricity to approximately 283000 residential and business customers in 108 communities in Louisiana. Cleco Power has a net generating capacity of about 2565 MW from its interests in nine fossil-fueled power plants. It also purchases power from other utilities and energy marketers and it sells some excess power to wholesale customers. Subsidiary Cleco Midstream Resources owns and operates two gas-fired wholesale power plants a gas interconnection link to access the natural gas supply market and offers energy management services. Macquarie is buying Cleco.

	Annual Growth	12/10	12/11	12/12	12/13	12/14
Sales ($ mil.)	2.5%	1,148.7	1,117.3	993.7	1,096.7	1,269.5
Net income ($ mil.)	(11.8%)	255.4	195.8	163.6	160.7	154.7
Market value ($ mil.)	15.4%	1,858.6	2,302.1	2,417.5	2,816.8	3,295.4
Employees	(1.4%)	1,277	1,234	1,259	1,205	1,206

CLEVELAND BROWNS FOOTBALL COMPANY LLC

76 Lou Groza Blvd. — CEO: Joe Banner
Berea OH 44017 — CFO: David A Jenkins
Phone: 440-891-5000 — HR: -
Fax: 440-891-5009 — FYE: March 31
Web: www.clevelandbrowns.com — Type: Private

The Dawg Pound is the place to be for football fans in Cleveland. The Cleveland Browns Football Company owns and operates the Cleveland Browns one of the more storied franchises in the National Football League. Started in 1944 by Arthur McBride as part of the All-American Football Conference the club joined the NFL in 1949 and boasts four championship titles its last in 1964. The present team was awarded to the late Alfred Lerner and former 49ers president Carmen Policy after Art Modell relocated the original Browns to Baltimore in 1996. (A deal struck with the NFL allowed Cleveland to retain the team name colors and history.) Lerner's family led by son Randy continues to control the team.

CLEVELAND CONSTRUCTION, INC.

8620 TYLER BLVD
MENTOR, OH 440604348
Phone: 440-255-8000
Fax: –
Web: www.clevelandconstruction.com

CEO: –
CFO: Mark T Small
HR: –
FYE: December 31
Type: Private

Cleveland Construction Inc. (CCI) has ventured beyond Cleveland to offer its services nationwide. Beyond general contractor work CCI provides design build construction management and interior trades services for commercial and institutional projects. Also a top interior contractor in the US the contractor installs finishes such as drywall acoustic wall panels and specialty ceilings. Its projects have included hospitals universities correctional facilities hotels convention centers sports complexes retail outlets (including Wal-Mart stores) and public projects such as Charlotte Douglas International Airport and Offutt Air Force Base.. Founded in 1980 the company remains family-owned.

	Annual Growth	12/05	12/06	12/07	12/08	12/09
Sales ($ mil.)	(2.4%)	–	–	228.0	186.5	217.0
Net income ($ mil.)	25.2%	–	–	16.4	24.0	25.7
Market value ($ mil.)	–	–	–	–	–	–
Employees	–	–	–	–	–	800

CLEVELAND STATE UNIVERSITY

2121 EUCLID AVE
CLEVELAND, OH 441152226
Phone: 216-687-2000
Fax: –
Web: www.csuohio.edu

CEO: Lee Fisher
CFO: –
HR: –
FYE: June 30
Type: Private

Cleveland State University offers a well-rounded education in the land of the Buckeyes. The university provides some 1000 courses in the arts and sciences business administration law engineering and other areas. The school which enrolls more than 17000 students offers undergraduate and graduate degrees in 200 fields of study through eight colleges and two academic divisions. The university has more than 570 faculty members on its staff. Tuition for undergraduate residents is about $7900. Its Maxine Goodman Levin College of Urban Affairs is nationally recognized for its public administration programs. Established in 1964 Cleveland State merged with Cleveland-Marshall College of Law in 1969.

	Annual Growth	06/16	06/17	06/18	06/19	06/20
Sales ($ mil.)	(3.2%)	–	204.5	199.4	191.9	185.4
Net income ($ mil.)	–	–	(7.1)	73.4	9.4	(10.3)
Market value ($ mil.)	–	–	–	–	–	–
Employees	–	–	–	–	–	2,600

CLEVELAND-CLIFFS INC (NEW) — NYS: CLF

200 Public Square
Cleveland, OH 44114-2315
Phone: 216 694-5700
Fax: –
Web: www.clevelandcliffs.com

CEO: Lourenco Goncalves
CFO: Celso Goncalves
HR: Maurice Harapiak
FYE: December 31
Type: Public

Cleveland is the largest flat-rolled steel and iron ore pellets producer in North America.- Its fully integrated portfolio includes custom-made pellets and HBI; flat-rolled carbon steel stainless electrical plate tinplate and long steel products; as well as carbon and stainless steel tubing hot and cold stamping and tooling. Cleveland-Cliffs' operations including Tilden Mine Northshore Minorca and United Taconite mines produce about 18.1 million tons of iron ore pellets annually. The company sells its ore primarily in North America. In 2020 Cleveland-Cliffs completed the acquisition with Ohio-based AK Steel Holding Corporation in a deal valued at about $1 billion.

	Annual Growth	12/17	12/18	12/19	12/20	12/21
Sales ($ mil.)	72.1%	2,330.2	2,332.4	1,989.9	5,354.0	20,444.0
Net income ($ mil.)	68.9%	367.0	1,128.1	292.8	(122.0)	2,988.0
Market value ($ mil.)	31.8%	3,606.1	3,846.2	4,201.3	7,282.3	10,888.5
Employees	72.5%	2,938	2,926	2,372	25,000	26,000

CLICKER, INC. — NBB: CLKZ

1111 Kane Concourse, Suite 304
Bay Harbor Islands, FL 33154
Phone: 786 309-5190
Fax: –
Web: www.clickercorporate.com

CEO: Willis Arndt Jr
CFO: Mark Noffke
HR: –
FYE: August 31
Type: Public

This company is much more interested in the mouse than the remote control. Clicker operates a network of websites focused around such topics as celebrity news classified advertising investing and sports. Its online properties include the For-Want (classified ads) Sippin' It (celebrity news and gossip) and Wall Street Network (investment community). Most of its sites include social networking functions to help foster interactivity and generate revenue through advertising and rewards programs. Chairman and CEO Albert Aimers owns nearly 45% of Clicker.

	Annual Growth	08/08	08/09	08/10	08/11	08/12
Sales ($ mil.)	(86.4%)	7.8	1.3	0.8	0.0	0.0
Net income ($ mil.)	–	(2.9)	(3.3)	(7.5)	(4.1)	(1.8)
Market value ($ mil.)	(24.0%)	0.3	0.0	0.2	0.0	0.1
Employees	(53.8%)	22	9	6	1	1

CLIENT NETWORK SERVICES, LLC

2277 RESEARCH BLVD
ROCKVILLE, MD 208503224
Phone: 301-634-4600
Fax: –
Web: www.cns-inc.com

CEO: Todd Stottlemyer
CFO: Lawrence Sinnott
HR: Gopal Lakshmynarayana
FYE: December 31
Type: Private

Client Network Services Inc. (CNSI) provides IT and business process outsourcing services to corporate and government clients in the US. Its offerings include consulting systems integration project management application development legacy migration and software architecture. The company is particularly active in the health care industry and worked as a subcontractor to support the Federal Health Exchange. It also supports the defense transportation energy and financial industries. CNSI takes an agnostic approach to technology and partners with a range of vendors including IBM Microsoft and Oracle. The company counts Best Buy Health and Human Services and the National Institutes of Health among its clients.

	Annual Growth	12/11	12/12	12/13	12/14	12/15
Sales ($ mil.)	13.7%	–	109.1	148.6	143.0	160.2
Net income ($ mil.)	29.0%	–	8.9	12.1	15.6	19.0
Market value ($ mil.)	–	–	–	–	–	–
Employees	–	–	–	–	–	1,000

CLIENT SERVICES INC.

3451 HARRY S TRUMAN BLVD
SAINT CHARLES, MO 63301-4047
Phone: 636-947-2321
Fax: –
Web: www.clientservices.com

CEO: Brad Franta
CFO: –
HR: –
FYE: October 31
Type: Private

This CSI investigates debt. Client Services Inc. (CSI) is a collections agency that provides accounts receivable management and customer care services nationwide. CSI markets its services to banks and credit card companies utilities and other government and commercial clients. It performs a range of services from pre-collection consultation to skiptracing debt purchasing and recovery consulting. Debtors can also make payments on the company's website. However call centers are the heart of its daily operations. CSI has four call centers that are staffed 24/7 and can handle 10000 calls per day. The company was founded in 1987.

	Annual Growth	10/08	10/09	10/10	10/11	10/12
Sales ($ mil.)	4.5%	–	48.5	68.2	64.3	55.3
Net income ($ mil.)	(7.8%)	–	3.5	8.3	5.7	2.7
Market value ($ mil.)	–	–	–	–	–	–
Employees	–	–	–	–	–	955

CLIFTON SAVINGS BANCORP INC   NMS: CSBK

1433 Van Houten Avenue
Clifton, NJ 07015
Phone: 973 473-2200
Fax: -
Web: www.cliftonsavings.com

CEO: -
CFO: -
HR: -
FYE: March 31
Type: Public

You don't need CliffsNotes to figure out that Clifton Savings Bancorp is the holding company of Clifton Savings Bank which operates about a dozen branches in northeastern New Jersey's Bergen and Passaic counties. Founded in 1928 the bank serves consumer and business clients offering checking and savings accounts IRAs CDs and mortgages and other loans. Its lending portfolio is dominated by real estate loans primarily one- to four-family residential mortgages; the bank also issues multifamily and commercial real estate construction and consumer loans. Bank subsidiary Botany manages investments and securities. Clifton's majority stockholder is Clifton MHC a mutual holding company.

	Annual Growth	03/09	03/10	03/11	03/12	03/13
Assets ($ mil.)	1.4%	959.8	1,067.7	1,122.6	1,101.4	1,016.1
Net income ($ mil.)	6.5%	5.1	6.3	8.8	7.9	6.6
Market value ($ mil.)	5.6%	261.7	242.6	310.6	272.9	326.0
Employees	(0.2%)	101	110	100	102	100

CLIFTONLARSONALLEN LLP

220 S 6TH ST STE 300
MINNEAPOLIS, MN 554021418
Phone: 612-376-4500
Fax: -
Web: www.blogs.claconnect.com

CEO: Jen Leary
CFO: Heidi Hillman
HR: -
FYE: December 04
Type: Private

CliftonLarsonAllen (CLA) is all about the CPAs. Boasting more than $7.5 billion in client assets under management CLA is on the list of top 10 largest accounting firm that serves privately-owned firms and the firm's principals along with not-for-profits and government agencies. Also serving as a financial advisory and business consultancy CLA is organized as a holding company with three main business segments: wealth advisory outsourcing and audit tax and consulting. It mostly serves clients in the agribusiness financial employee benefit plan healthcare manufacturing and government sectors. With more than 6200 professionals in approximately 120 US locations and a global affiliation the firm's annual revenues was about $955 million.

	Annual Growth	12/11	12/12	12/13	12/14	12/15
Sales ($ mil.)	7.5%	-	-	563.0	598.7	650.7
Net income ($ mil.)	5.1%	-	-	154.8	163.3	170.8
Market value ($ mil.)	-	-	-	-	-	-
Employees	-	-	-	-	-	4,786

CLINCH VALLEY MEDICAL CENTER, INC.

6801 GOV GC PEERY HWY
RICHLANDS, VA 246412194
Phone: 276-596-6000
Fax: -
Web: www.clinchvalleymedicalcenter.com

CEO: Peter Mulkey
CFO: -
HR: David Darden
FYE: November 30
Type: Private

Clinch Valley Medical Center oversees southwestern Virginia's acute medical needs. The regional hospital provides medical and emergency care services in about a dozen counties around Richlands Virginia. Clinch Valley Medical Center offers cancer care cardiac catheterization diagnostic imaging laboratory services women's services pediatrics physical rehabilitation services sleep studies and surgical services. The medical center has a 200-bed capacity and is part of the LifePoint Health network. The hospital's medical staff represent 33 medical specialties.

	Annual Growth	12/13	12/14*	11/15	11/16	11/17
Sales ($ mil.)	0.7%	-	84.2	85.7	82.1	86.0
Net income ($ mil.)	(14.8%)	-	4.0	3.9	0.8	2.5
Market value ($ mil.)	-	-	-	-	-	-
Employees	-	-	-	-	-	715

*Fiscal year change

CLOPAY CORPORATION

8585 Duke Blvd.
Mason OH 45040-3101
Phone: 513-770-4800
Fax: 513-770-3984
Web: www.clopay.com

CEO: -
CFO: Franklin Smith Jr
HR: -
FYE: September 30
Type: Subsidiary

Just like Aldous Huxley and Jim Morrison Clopay knows something about doors. Subsidiary Clopay Building Products makes residential and commercial garage doors for the remodel and new-build markets. Brands include Avante Canyon Ridge Reserve and Coachman and its products are distributed nationwide by independent contractors home improvement stores and wholesalers. The Home Depot and Menard are among its largest customers. Another subsidiary Clopay Plastic Products makes specialty plastic films for hygienic medical and industrial applications. (Procter & Gamble uses the film for its disposable diapers.) Clopay Corp. is owned by holding company Griffon which also owns Telephonics and Ames True Temper.

CLOROX CO (THE)   NYS: CLX

1221 Broadway
Oakland, CA 94612-1888
Phone: 510 271-7000
Fax: -
Web: www.thecloroxcompany.com

CEO: Linda Rendle
CFO: Kevin Jacobsen
HR: -
FYE: June 30
Type: Public

Although Clorox may be best known for its namesake bleach the leading consumer and professional products maker has a plethora of market-leading brands. It sells laundry and cleaning items (Formula 409 Pine-Sol) as well as dressings and sauces (Hidden Valley Soy Vay) charcoal (Kingsford Match Light) plastic wrap and containers (Glad) and cat litters (Fresh Step Scoop Away). Other items include filtration systems (Brita) dietary supplements (Rainbow Light Natural Vitality) and personal care items (Burt's Bees). Clorox makes and sells its products worldwide although the US accounts for the most revenue by far.

	Annual Growth	06/17	06/18	06/19	06/20	06/21
Sales ($ mil.)	5.3%	5,973.0	6,124.0	6,214.0	6,721.0	7,341.0
Net income ($ mil.)	0.3%	701.0	823.0	820.0	939.0	710.0
Market value ($ mil.)	7.8%	16,359.2	16,606.0	18,798.9	26,934.3	22,089.4
Employees	2.7%	8,100	8,700	8,800	8,800	9,000

CLOUD PEAK ENERGY INC   NYS: CLD

748 T-7 Road
Gillette, WY 82718
Phone: 307 687-6000
Fax: -
Web: www.cloudpeakenergy.com

CEO: Todd Myers
CFO: Heath Hill
HR: Jeanie Fox
FYE: December 31
Type: Public

Cloud Peak Energy owns and operates three surface coal mines in the Powder River Basin of Montana and Wyoming. One of the largest producers of coal in the US it sells mainly to utilities and industrial customers and accounts for about 3% of the electricity generated in the US. Formerly part of Rio Tinto it sells about 60 million tons of coal annually and controls almost 1.1 billion tons in proved and probable reserves. Cloud Peak supplies coal to more than 45 domestic and foreign electric utilities. The company was formed in 1993 as Kennecott Coal.

	Annual Growth	12/13	12/14	12/15	12/16	12/17
Sales ($ mil.)	(10.7%)	1,396.1	1,324.0	1,124.1	800.4	887.7
Net income ($ mil.)	-	52.0	79.0	(204.9)	21.8	(6.6)
Market value ($ mil.)	(29.5%)	1,353.0	690.0	156.3	421.7	334.5
Employees	(7.4%)	1,959	1,815	1,750	1,485	1,440

CLOVER TECHNOLOGIES GROUP LLC

2700 W. Higgins Rd. Ste. 100
Hoffman Estates IL 60169
Phone: 815-431-8100
Fax: 847-885-6400
Web: www.clovertech.com

CEO: George Milton
CFO: Brent Sallee
HR: –
FYE: December 31
Type: Private

Clover Technologies makes its mark inside many a printer. The company makes toner cartridges for laser and inkjet printers and copiers and sells refurbished printers. Its supplies work with devices made by such vendors as Brother Canon Dell and HP. Clover's products are sold under its own Dataproducts and Genuine Recycled Cartridge brands as well as its private label brand CTG. It also makes ink and ribbon for postage meters and magnetically charged ink and toner cartridges for check printers. It recycles printer cartridges cell phones and other small electronics through its Clover Environmental unit. Golden Gate Capital and company management bought Clover from Key Principal Partners in 2010.

CLOVIS ONCOLOGY INC

NMS: CLVS

5500 Flatiron Parkway, Suite 100
Boulder, CO 80301
Phone: 303 625-5000
Fax: –
Web: www.clovisoncology.com

CEO: Patrick J Mahaffy
CFO: Daniel W Muehl
HR: –
FYE: December 31
Type: Public

Clovis Oncology is a biopharmaceutical company that acquires develops and commercializes therapies for subsets of ovarian lung and other cancers that do not respond well to existing commercial drugs. Its first marketed product Rubraca is approved in the US for the treatment of ovarian cancer. The company has additional candidates in its pipeline including oral treatments for ovarian solid tumors as well as a drug for gastrointestinal cancer. Clovis also works with partners to develop companion diagnostics for its treatment drugs.

	Annual Growth	12/16	12/17	12/18	12/19	12/20
Sales ($ mil.)	577.7%	0.1	55.5	95.4	143.0	164.5
Net income ($ mil.)	–	(349.1)	(346.4)	(368.0)	(400.4)	(369.2)
Market value ($ mil.)	(42.7%)	4,606.3	7,051.5	1,862.4	1,081.1	497.8
Employees	11.5%	278	360	468	484	429

CLUBCORP HOLDINGS INC

NYS: MYCC

3030 LBJ Freeway, Suite 600
Dallas, TX 75234
Phone: 972 243-6191
Fax: –
Web: www.clubcorp.com

CEO: Eric L Affeldt
CFO: Andrew Lacko
HR: –
FYE: December 29
Type: Public

This company makes its green from the green — the golf green that is. ClubCorp is one of the world's largest operators of golf courses and private clubs with more than 200 facilities in some 25 states (mostly in the fair weather states of California Florida and Texas) and three in Cozumel Mexico. In addition the company operates about 135 private business sports and alumni clubs across the US as well as one in Beijing China. Its golf courses include such well known venues as Country Club of Hilton Head (Hilton Head South Carolina) Mission Hills Country Club (Palm Springs California) and Woodside Plantation Country Club (Augusta Georgia). Founded in 1957 ClubCorp went public in 2013.

	Annual Growth	12/11	12/12	12/13	12/14	12/15
Sales ($ mil.)	10.0%	720.0	754.9	815.1	884.2	1,052.9
Net income ($ mil.)	–	(36.2)	(27.3)	(40.9)	13.2	(9.5)
Market value ($ mil.)	1.6%	–	–	1,148.5	1,160.8	1,186.1
Employees	6.3%	–	14,800	13,300	16,900	17,800

CMC MATERIALS INC

NMS: CCMP

870 North Commons Drive
Aurora, IL 60504
Phone: 630 375-6631
Fax: –
Web: www.cmcmaterials.com

CEO: David Li
CFO: Jeanette Press
HR: –
FYE: September 30
Type: Public

CMC Materials Inc (formerly Cabot Microelectronics) is a leading global supplier of consumable materials to semiconductor manufacturers and pipeline companies. It operates its business within two reportable segments: Electronic Materials and Performance Materials. Pipeline and Industrial Materials ("PIM") products are sold under the brands Flowchem Sealweld and Val-Tex. Samsung and Intel are among its largest customers. Asia is its largest market accounting for about 55% of the sales. In 2020 the company changed its name from "Cabot Microelectronics Corporation" to "CMC Materials Inc.

	Annual Growth	09/17	09/18	09/19	09/20	09/21
Sales ($ mil.)	24.0%	507.2	590.1	1,037.7	1,116.3	1,199.8
Net income ($ mil.)	–	87.0	110.0	39.2	142.8	(68.6)
Market value ($ mil.)	11.4%	2,272.1	2,932.7	4,014.0	4,059.5	3,502.9
Employees	16.9%	1,179	1,219	2,047	2,082	2,200

CME GROUP INC

NMS: CME

20 South Wacker Drive
Chicago, IL 60606
Phone: 312 930-1000
Fax: –
Web: www.cmegroup.com

CEO: Terry Duffy
CFO: John Pietrowicz
HR: –
FYE: December 31
Type: Public

CME Group owns the Chicago Mercantile Exchange the Chicago Board of Trade (CBOT) the New York Mercantile Exchange (NYMEX) and the Commodity Exchange (COMEX). The exchanges provide marketplaces for agricultural commodities energy and metals as well as for interest rate sensitive instruments equity and foreign exchange futures. Products are traded on CME's Globex electronic trading system on its floors via technology-assisted open outcry and through privately negotiated deals. Easily the world's largest futures exchange CME owns more than 25% of Dow Jones' index business including the Dow Jones Industrial Average.

	Annual Growth	12/16	12/17	12/18	12/19	12/20
Sales ($ mil.)	8.0%	3,595.2	3,644.7	4,309.4	4,868.0	4,883.6
Net income ($ mil.)	8.2%	1,534.1	4,063.4	1,962.2	2,116.5	2,105.2
Market value ($ mil.)	12.1%	41,308.3	52,302.4	67,368.2	71,880.5	65,194.5
Employees	12.8%	2,700	2,830	4,590	4,360	4,370

CMS BANCORP INC

NAS: CMSB

123 Main Street
White Plains, NY 10601
Phone: 914 422-2700
Fax: –
Web: www.cmsbk.com

CEO: –
CFO: –
HR: –
FYE: September 30
Type: Public

CMS Bancorp was formed in 2007 to be the holding company for Community Mutual Savings Bank which serves the northern suburbs of New York City. Operating through five branches in Westchester County (one of the richest counties in the country) the bank collects deposits from area consumers and small businesses and uses the funds mainly to originate residential mortgages which account for more than 85% of its loan portfolio. It also issues commercial mortgages consumer loans and business loans and lines of credit. Deposit products include checking savings and money market accounts; CDs; and IRAs. Community Mutual Savings Bank was founded in 1887. Pennsylvania-based Customers Bancorp is buying CMS Bancorp.

	Annual Growth	09/10	09/11	09/12	09/13	09/14
Assets ($ mil.)	2.5%	247.4	253.8	264.7	258.3	273.3
Net income ($ mil.)	41.0%	0.2	0.2	(0.6)	0.9	0.7
Market value ($ mil.)	6.6%	18.6	15.1	14.9	16.0	24.0
Employees	(1.2%)	44	50	46	43	42

CMS ENERGY CORP
NYS: CMS

One Energy Plaza
Jackson, MI 49201
Phone: 517 788-0550
Fax: –
Web: www.cmsenergy.com

CEO: Garrick Rochow
CFO: Rejji Hayes
HR: –
FYE: December 31
Type: Public

Michigan relies on CMS Energy. The energy holding company's regulated utility subsidiary Consumers serves electricity and/or natural gas to 6.8 million of Michigan's 10 million residents It has electric generating capacity of more than 5300 MW and purchases an additional of approximately 2600 MW from third party electricity providers. Another subsidiary CMS Enterprises operates the nonutility operations and investments and is an operator of independent power production. CMS Enterprises' independent power production (coal- gas- and solar wood waste) have a capacity of more than 1800 MW and are located in Michigan North Carolina Ohio Texas and Wisconsin. EnerBank provides primarily unsecured fixed-rate installment loans throughout the US to finance home improvements.

	Annual Growth	12/17	12/18	12/19	12/20	12/21
Sales ($ mil.)	2.7%	6,583.0	6,873.0	6,845.0	6,680.0	7,329.0
Net income ($ mil.)	31.0%	460.0	657.0	680.0	755.0	1,353.0
Market value ($ mil.)	8.3%	13,705.6	14,386.5	18,208.4	17,678.1	18,848.8
Employees	3.5%	7,952	8,625	8,789	8,837	9,122

CNA FINANCIAL CORP
NYS: CNA

151 N. Franklin
Chicago, IL 60606
Phone: 312 822-5000
Fax: 312 822-6419
Web: www.cna.com

CEO: Dino Robusto
CFO: Larry Haefner
HR: –
FYE: December 31
Type: Public

CNA Financial is an umbrella organization for a wide range of insurance providers including Continental Casualty and Continental Insurance. CNA also sells specialty insurance including professional liability (real estate agents lawyers architects) and vehicle warranty service contracts. Its insurance products primarily include commercial property and casualty coverages including surety. Its services include warranty risk management information services and claims administration. Holding company Loews which owns nearly 90% of can Financial.

	Annual Growth	12/17	12/18	12/19	12/20	12/21
Assets ($ mil.)	4.2%	56,567.0	57,152.0	60,612.0	64,026.0	66,639.0
Net income ($ mil.)	7.5%	899.0	813.0	1,000.0	690.0	1,202.0
Market value ($ mil.)	(4.5%)	14,395.9	11,980.7	12,159.8	10,572.3	11,961.7
Employees	(2.9%)	6,300	6,100	5,900	5,800	5,600

CNA SURETY CORPORATION

333 S. Wabash Ave.
Chicago IL 60604
Phone: 312-822-5000
Fax: 312-822-7517
Web: www.cnasurety.com

CEO: –
CFO: John F Corcoran
HR: –
FYE: December 31
Type: Subsidiary

If the job doesn't get done CNA Surety pays the price. One of the largest surety companies in the US CNA Surety offers contract and commercial surety bonds which guarantee fulfillment of contracts. The company's Western Surety and Universal Surety of America units handle fidelity commercial and contract bonds and international surety and credit insurance; Surety Bonding another subsidiary specializes in commercial and contract bonds to small businesses. Contract surety (for construction contractors) accounts for a majority of CNA Surety's premiums. CNA Surety sells its products throughout the US via a network of independent agents and brokers. CNA Surety is a subsidiary of CNA Financial.

CNB CORP (MI)
NBB: CNBZ

303 North Main Street
Cheboygan, MI 49721
Phone: 231 627-7111
Fax: –
Web: www.cnbismybank.com

CEO: Susan Eno
CFO: Shanna Hanley
HR: –
FYE: December 31
Type: Public

CNB Corporation is the holding company for Citizens National Bank of Cheboygan which serves individuals and local businesses through more than five branches in the northern reaches of Michigan's Lower Peninsula. Serving the counties of Cheboygan Emmet and Presque Isle the bank offers standard fare such as checking savings and money market accounts CDs and IRAs. CNB Mortgage a subsidiary of the bank handles residential mortgage lending activities which account for approximately half of the company's loan portfolio; commercial mortgages make up most of the remainder. Bank affiliate CNB Financial Services provides insurance and financial planning. Citizens National Bank was founded in 1931.

	Annual Growth	12/10	12/11	12/12	12/13	12/14
Assets ($ mil.)	(0.1%)	255.1	250.1	260.9	247.7	253.9
Net income ($ mil.)	56.0%	0.3	(2.7)	1.4	2.7	1.9
Market value ($ mil.)	10.3%	11.5	7.9	12.4	13.3	17.0
Employees	1.3%	78	79	–	–	–

CNB FINANCIAL CORP. (CLEARFIELD, PA)
NMS: CCNE

1 South Second Street, P.O. Box 42
Clearfield, PA 16830
Phone: 814 765-9621
Fax: –
Web: www.cnbbank.bank

CEO: Joseph B Bower Jr
CFO: Tito Lima
HR: –
FYE: December 31
Type: Public

CNB Financial is the holding company for CNB Bank ERIEBANK and FCBank. The banks and subsidiaries provide traditional deposit and loan services as well as wealth management merchant credit card processing and life insurance through nearly 30 CNB Bank- and ERIEBANK-branded branches in Pennsylvania and nine FCBank branches in central Ohio. Commercial industrial and agricultural loans make up more than one-third of the bank's loan portfolio while commercial mortgages make up another one-third. It also makes residential mortgages consumer and credit card loans. The company's non-bank subsidiaries include CNB Securities Corporation Holiday Financial Services Corporation and CNB Insurance Agency.

	Annual Growth	12/16	12/17	12/18	12/19	12/20
Assets ($ mil.)	16.4%	2,573.8	2,768.8	3,221.5	3,763.7	4,729.4
Net income ($ mil.)	12.4%	20.5	23.9	33.7	40.1	32.7
Market value ($ mil.)	(5.5%)	450.1	441.7	386.3	550.1	358.4
Employees	6.4%	507	528	556	559	651

CNO FINANCIAL GROUP INC
NYS: CNO

11825 N. Pennsylvania Street
Carmel, IN 46032
Phone: 317 817-6100
Fax: –
Web: www.cnoinc.com

CEO: Gary Bhojwani
CFO: Paul McDonough
HR: –
FYE: December 31
Type: Public

CNO Financial Group is a holding company for a group of insurance companies operating throughout the US that develop market and administer health insurance annuity individual life insurance and other insurance products. The company serves middle-income pre-retiree and retired Americans. Prior to 2020 the company managed its business through the following operating segments: Bankers Life Washington National and Colonial Penn. In 2020 CNO announced a new operating models viewing their operations as three insurance product lines: annuity health and life and the investment and fee revenue segments. The company also offers reinsurance. CNO Financial operates nationwide.

	Annual Growth	12/16	12/17	12/18	12/19	12/20
Assets ($ mil.)	2.5%	31,975.2	33,110.3	31,439.8	33,630.9	35,339.9
Net income ($ mil.)	(4.2%)	358.2	175.6	(315.0)	409.4	301.8
Market value ($ mil.)	3.8%	2,590.6	3,340.0	2,013.0	2,452.6	3,007.3
Employees	0.0%	3,400	3,300	3,300	3,300	3,400

CNX RESOURCES CORP

NYS: CNX

CNX Center, 1000 CONSOL Energy Drive, Suite 400
Canonsburg, PA 15317-6506
Phone: 724 485-4000
Fax: –
Web: www.cnx.com

CEO: Nicholas Deluliis
CFO: Donald Rush
HR: –
FYE: December 31
Type: Public

CNX Resources formerly known as CONSOL Energy is an independent upstream oil and gas company operating mainly in Appalachian Basin. The company explores for develops produces gathers acquires and processes natural gas found in unconventional shale formations primarily the Marcellus Shale and Utica Shale covering parts of Pennsylvania West Virginia and Ohio. It also operates and develops Coal Bed Methane properties in Virginia. CNX has an average daily production of around 1.4 Mcfe and boasts approximately 9.5 Tcfe of proved reserves with about 20 years of reserve life ratio.

	Annual Growth	12/17	12/18	12/19	12/20	12/21
Sales ($ mil.)	(15.1%)	1,455.1	1,730.4	1,922.4	1,258.0	756.8
Net income ($ mil.)	–	380.7	796.5	(80.7)	(483.8)	(498.6)
Market value ($ mil.)	(1.5%)	2,977.7	2,324.3	1,801.3	2,198.1	2,798.6
Employees	(5.8%)	561	564	467	451	441

CO HOLDINGS, LLC

KEENE, NH 03431
Phone: 603-352-0001
Fax: –
Web: www.deadriver.com

CEO: –
CFO: –
HR: –
FYE: October 31
Type: Private

Cheshire Oil is confident that the smile it has put on customers' faces in Southern New Hampshire and Vermont won't suddenly disappear. The company's services (under the Cheshire Oil and T-Bird Fuel brands) to residential and commercial clients include heating oil delivery oil and propane furnace and boiler installation service and repair fleet fueling and central air-conditioning installation and repair. Cheshire Oil also operates gas stations and convenience stores under the T-Bird Mini-Marts moniker. It also offers storage rental services through Keene Mini Storage. Cheshire Oil is owned and managed by members of the founding Robertson family.

	Annual Growth	10/07	10/08	10/09	10/10	10/11
Sales ($ mil.)	15.1%	–	–	70.0	77.4	92.7
Net income ($ mil.)	(1.4%)	–	–	0.7	0.2	0.7
Market value ($ mil.)	–	–	–	–	–	–
Employees	–	–	–	–	–	175

COAST CITRUS DISTRIBUTORS

7597 BRISTOW CT
SAN DIEGO, CA 921547419
Phone: 619-661-7950
Fax: –
Web: www.coasttropical.com

CEO: James M Alvarez
CFO: –
HR: Jorge Gutierrez
FYE: December 28
Type: Private

Coast Citrus Distributors is a leading wholesale distributor of fresh fruits and vegetables in Mexico and the US. The company supplies a variety of produce including bananas lettuce limes and potatoes to retail grocers and other food customers. It distributes under the names Coast Citrus Coast Tropical Olympic Fruit and Vegetable and Importadora y Exportadora. Coast Citrus Distributors operates half a dozen distribution facilities in California Texas and Florida. It also has about five locations in Mexico. The late Roberto Alvarez founded the family-owned business in 1950.

	Annual Growth	12/15	12/16	12/17	12/18	12/19
Sales ($ mil.)	5.0%	–	290.2	293.4	306.9	335.6
Net income ($ mil.)	64.6%	–	1.7	2.0	3.7	7.7
Market value ($ mil.)	–	–	–	–	–	–
Employees	–	–	–	–	–	320

COAST DISTRIBUTION SYSTEM

ASE: CRV

350 Woodview Avenue
Morgan Hill, CA 95037
Phone: 408 782-6686
Fax: –
Web: www.coastdistribution.com

CEO: James Musbach
CFO: Sandra A Knell
HR: –
FYE: December 31
Type: Public

Be it on wheels or on the water there's no place like home with accessories from The Coast. The Coast Distribution System wholesales accessories replacement parts and supplies for recreational vehicles (RVs). Tapping outdoor recreational markets with much in common the company also distributes boating and marine accessories and parts. Its lineup includes close to 11000 products many of them Coast branded from various appliances to awnings boat covers life jackets and trailer hitches. Products are channeled from 17 distribution centers in the US and Canada to more than 15000 customers primarily RV and boat dealerships supply stores and service centers.

	Annual Growth	12/09	12/10	12/11	12/12	12/13
Sales ($ mil.)	2.5%	103.2	108.6	108.2	113.5	113.9
Net income ($ mil.)	–	0.1	0.2	(0.9)	(2.0)	(0.6)
Market value ($ mil.)	(4.3%)	19.7	19.5	11.4	10.1	16.5
Employees	0.9%	265	265	275	275	275

COAST ELECTRIC POWER ASSOCIATION

18020 HIGHWAY 603
KILN, MS 395568487
Phone: 228-363-7000
Fax: –
Web: www.coastepa.com

CEO: Robert J Occhi
CFO: John Holston
HR: –
FYE: December 31
Type: Private

There's no coasting for the Coast Electric Power Association when it comes to providing residents in three southern Mississippi counties with electricity. The utility uses a 6400-mile distribution network to serve its more than 76000 members (the great majority or which are residential customers) in Hancock Pearl River and Harrison counties. Coast offers electronic fund transfer and average monthly payment plans and rebates on energy efficient home improvements. The utility's power is generated by South Mississippi Electric Power an association of Coast and 10 other cooperatives. It partners with Touchstone Energy Cooperatives.

	Annual Growth	12/13	12/14	12/15	12/17	12/18
Sales ($ mil.)	(0.2%)	–	201.6	202.9	187.6	200.2
Net income ($ mil.)	(9.8%)	–	14.6	15.9	9.5	9.6
Market value ($ mil.)	–	–	–	–	–	–
Employees	–	–	–	–	–	238

COASTAL BANKING CO INC

NBB: CBCO

1891 South 14th Street
Fernandina Beach, FL 32034
Phone: 904 321-0400
Fax: 843 524-4510
Web: www.coastalbanking.com

CEO: –
CFO: –
HR: –
FYE: December 31
Type: Public

Hoping to provide traditional small-town banking amid rapid growth in the Southeast a group of area banking veterans formed Coastal Banking Company in 2000. The holding company owns CBC National Bank which does business as Lowcountry National Bank from around five branches in southern South Carolina and First National Bank of Nassau County which operates loan offices in Atlanta and Savannah Georgia and Jacksonville Florida in addition to one bank branch in Meigs Georgia under The Georgia Bank name. The banks offer standard products and services including business and consumer loans checking and savings accounts and CDs.

	Annual Growth	12/12	12/13	12/14	12/15	12/16
Assets ($ mil.)	4.3%	475.0	375.6	421.9	464.7	561.4
Net income ($ mil.)	38.6%	1.9	1.6	3.1	5.8	7.0
Market value ($ mil.)	31.7%	18.2	0.3	33.7	43.8	54.8
Employees	(1.8%)	362	333	349	–	–

COASTAL CAROLINA UNIVERSITY ALUMNI ASSOCIATION, INC.

642 CENTURY CIR
CONWAY, SC 295268279
Phone: 843-347-3161
Fax: -
Web: www.coastal.edu

CEO: -
CFO: -
HR: -
FYE: June 30
Type: Private

It's hard for students at Coastal Carolina University not to be cocky. The university (whose rooster mascot Chanticleer appears in Chaucer's Canterbury Tales) offers bachelor's degrees in about 60 fields of study through schools of science humanities education and business. It also offers about 10 master's degrees in fields including business administration education and coastal marine and wetland studies. Coastal Carolina University has an enrollment of more than 9000 students and about 1000 faculty members. Its student-to-teacher ratio is 17:1.

	Annual Growth	06/09	06/10	06/11	06/12	06/13
Sales ($ mil.)	10.0%	-	-	117.0	128.8	141.6
Net income ($ mil.)	(3.0%)	-	-	29.5	29.8	27.7
Market value ($ mil.)	-	-	-	-	-	-
Employees	-	-	-	-	-	900

COASTAL PACIFIC FOOD DISTRIBUTORS, INC.

1015 PERFORMANCE DR
STOCKTON, CA 952064925
Phone: 909-947-2066
Fax: -
Web: www.cpfd.com

CEO: -
CFO: -
HR: -
FYE: December 29
Type: Private

Coastal Pacific Food Distributors (CPF) fuels the military forces from facility to fork. The company is one of the top wholesale food distributors that primarily serves the US armed forces across the Western US and in the Far East. As part of its business CPF provides a full line of groceries to military bases run by the US Army Navy Air Force and Marines. It delivers a variety of products from distribution centers located in California Washington and Hawaii. CPF also offers information system programming services for its customers to track sales and shipping as well as procurement and logistics through partnerships in Iraq Kuwait and Saudi Arabia. The company was founded in 1986.

	Annual Growth	01/09	01/10	01/11*	12/11	12/12
Sales ($ mil.)	8.9%	-	-	1,113.6	1,162.7	1,213.0
Net income ($ mil.)	(14.6%)	-	-	17.7	25.2	15.1
Market value ($ mil.)	-	-	-	-	-	-
Employees	-	-	-	-	-	459

*Fiscal year change

COATES INTERNATIONAL LTD
NBB: COTE

2100 Highway 34
Wall Township, NJ 07719
Phone: 732 449-7717
Fax: -
Web: www.coatesengine.com

CEO: George J Coates
CFO: Barry C Kaye
HR: -
FYE: December 31
Type: Public

Coates International Ltd. (CIL) may be sparking the next industrial revolution. CEO George J. Coates founded CIL to develop his many patents the most noteworthy being the Coates Spherical Rotary Valve (CSRV). The CSRV is designed to replace the century-old technology of the internal combustion engine's camshaft and poppet valve system. An engine equipped with the CSRV can run on different fuels while reducing emissions and increasing efficiency; the need for maintenance is also reduced. CIL licenses its CSRV engine technology to makers of heavy-duty vehicles automobiles and industrial engines. Major customer Almont Energy (Canada) took first delivery of CSRV engines in 2010.

	Annual Growth	12/13	12/14	12/15	12/16	12/17
Sales ($ mil.)	0.0%	0.0	0.0	0.1	0.0	0.0
Net income ($ mil.)	-	(2.8)	(12.8)	(10.2)	(8.4)	(8.4)
Market value ($ mil.)	(12.6%)	1.2	0.3	0.1	0.0	0.7
Employees	(13.1%)	7	6	5	5	4

COBALT INTERNATIONAL ENERGY L.P.
NYSE: CIE

2 Post Oak Central 1980 Post Oak Blvd. Ste. 1200
Houston TX 77056
Phone: 713-579-9100
Fax: 713-579-9196
Web: www.cobaltintl.com

CEO: -
CFO: -
HR: -
FYE: December 31
Type: Public

Cobalt International Energy scours the deep blue seas in search of oil. An exploration and development company Cobalt International owns interests in offshore properties located in the Gulf of Mexico and West Africa. The company's assets include majority and minority stakes in more than 600000 net acres in almost 50 blocks in the Gulf and more than 2 million acres in more than 100 prospects located off the coast of Gabon and Angola. It focuses primarily on searching for oil pockets encased beneath salt layers which until recently was traditionally untapped geological territory in the oil industry. Cobalt International Energy contracts two drilling rigs one from Ensco and one from Diamond Offshore.

COBANK, ACB

6340 S FIDDLERS GREEN CIR
GREENWOOD VILLAGE, CO 801114951
Phone: 303-740-6527
Fax: -
Web: www.cobank.com

CEO: Robert B Engel
CFO: David P Burlage
HR: -
FYE: December 31
Type: Private

CoBank is a national cooperative bank serving vital industries across rural of America. The bank provides loans; leases export financing and other financial services to agribusiness and rural power water and communication providers in all 50 estates and a member of Farm Credit System a nationwide network of banks and retail lending associations. The bank farm credit leasing offers flexible leasing options vehicles such as equipment and facilities that can deliver significant benefits to agriculture and utility business. Its core agribusiness customers range from local and single facility grain cooperatives to national global food beverage and agribusiness companies. Formed in 1989 CoBank merged with US AgBank in early 2012.

	Annual Growth	12/14	12/15	12/16	12/17	12/18
Assets ($ mil.)	5.8%	-	117,470.6	126.1	129,210.8	139,015.7
Net income ($ mil.)	8.3%	-	936.7	945.7	1,125.3	1,190.8
Market value ($ mil.)	-	-	-	-	-	-
Employees	-	-	-	-	-	500

COBB ELECTRIC MEMBERSHIP CORPORATION

1000 EMC PKWY NE
MARIETTA, GA 300607908
Phone: 770-429-2100
Fax: -
Web: www.cobbemc.com

CEO: W T Chip Nelson III
CFO: Robert Steele
HR: -
FYE: December 31
Type: Private

Cobb Electric Membership Corporation (Cobb EMC) makes sure that Cobb County Georgia residents can cook corn on the cob (and anything else) using either electric power or natural gas. The utility distributes electricity to more than 200000 meters (more than 177000 residential commercial and industrial members) in Cobb County and four other north metro Atlanta counties. Cobb EMC operates about 10000 miles of power lines. The company's Gas South unit markets natural gas to customers who receive their service on Atlanta Gas & Light's natural gas distribution pipelines in Georgia.

	Annual Growth	04/08	04/09*	12/13*	04/18*	12/20
Sales ($ mil.)	2.1%	-	641.0	416.3	849.7	802.4
Net income ($ mil.)	26.9%	-	3.6	(8.1)	25.4	49.2
Market value ($ mil.)	-	-	-	-	-	-
Employees	-	-	-	-	-	548

*Fiscal year change

COBIZ FINANCIAL INC
NMS: COBZ

1401 Lawrence St., Ste. 1200
Denver, CO 80202
Phone: 303 312-3400
Fax: –
Web: www.cobizbank.com

CEO: Steven Bangert
CFO: Lyne B Andrich
HR: –
FYE: December 31
Type: Public

CoBiz Financial is reaching new heights in the Rockies and in the Valley of the Sun. The $3.5 billion-asset holding company for CoBiz Bank operates Colorado Business Bank and Arizona Business Bank. The former operates more than 10 branches in the Denver Boulder and Vail areas while the latter has about a half-dozen branches in and around Phoenix. CoBiz mostly originates business loans and commercial and residential real estate mortgages. The company also offers insurance through CoBiz Insurance and wealth management services through CoBiz Investment Management CoBiz Trust and Financial Designs.

	Annual Growth	12/12	12/13	12/14	12/15	12/16
Assets ($ mil.)	8.1%	2,653.6	2,800.7	3,062.2	3,351.8	3,630.3
Net income ($ mil.)	9.2%	24.6	27.6	29.0	26.1	34.9
Market value ($ mil.)	22.6%	310.4	497.0	545.6	557.7	701.9
Employees	1.0%	512	513	534	532	533

COBORN'S, INCORPORATED

1921 COBORN BLVD
SAINT CLOUD, MN 563012100
Phone: 320-252-4222
Fax: –
Web: www.cobornsinc.com

CEO: Christopher Coborn
CFO: James Shaw
HR: –
FYE: December 28
Type: Private

Coborn's operates more than 120 stores across Midwest of the US under the Coborn's Cash Wise Captain Jack's Marketplace Foods and Hornbacher's. Coborn's operates its own central bakery fuel and convenience division pharmacy division in-house grocery warehouse and distribution center and tops cleaners. Along with its grocery stores the firm owns and operates pharmacies and convenience and liquor stations. The company manages the delivery logistics of hundreds of grocery products for its entire family of stores throughout the upper Midwest. Founded in 1921 Coborn's is a fourth generation business managed by its CEO Chris Coborn.

	Annual Growth	12/09	12/10	12/11	12/12	12/13
Sales ($ mil.)	2.1%	–	–	–	1,220.5	1,246.7
Net income ($ mil.)	(5.0%)	–	–	–	32.4	30.8
Market value ($ mil.)	–	–	–	–	–	–
Employees	–	–	–	–	–	7,200

COBRA ELECTRONICS CORP.
NMS: COBR

6500 West Cortland Street
Chicago, IL 60707
Phone: 773 889-8870
Fax: –
Web: www.cobra.com

CEO: Chris Cowger
CFO: Gail Babitt
HR: Irma Fonseca
FYE: December 31
Type: Public

Cobra Electronics' citizens band radios and radar detectors are good buddies when you're on the road. Its principal Cobra division markets CB and marine radios two-way radios radar detectors power inverters jump-starters and GPS navigation systems for professional drivers under the Cobra brand. The firm's PPL unit peddles personal navigation systems and speed camera location detectors under the Snooper name. Cobra Electronics also manages the AURA database of photo-enforcement locations (including speed camera and red-light detector positions) in North America and Europe. Cobra's products are sold in the US Canada and Europe through consumer electronics stores discount retailers and truck stops.

	Annual Growth	12/08	12/09	12/10	12/11	12/12
Sales ($ mil.)	(1.2%)	124.7	105.2	110.5	123.3	118.9
Net income ($ mil.)	–	–	(18.8)	(10.3)	1.6	3.1	3.2
Market value ($ mil.)	38.1%	6.9	11.0	21.2	29.3	25.1
Employees	(2.7%)	174	150	152	150	156

COCA-COLA CO (THE)
NYS: KO

One Coca-Cola Plaza
Atlanta, GA 30313
Phone: 404 676-2121
Fax: 404 676-6792
Web: www.coca-colacompany.com

CEO: James Quincey
CFO: John Murphy
HR: –
FYE: December 31
Type: Public

The Coca-Cola company is home to numerous beverage brands including four of the top five soft drinks: Coca-Cola Diet Coke Fanta and Sprite. In addition to soft drinks it markets waters enhanced water and sports drinks; juice drinks dairy and plant-based beverages ready-to-drink teas and coffees and and energy drinks. Other top brands include Minute Maid Powerade Dasani Honest Tea and vitaminwater. With the world's largest beverage distribution system Coca-Cola reaches thirsty consumers in more than 200 countries. Nearly 70% of its sales comes from outside the US.

	Annual Growth	12/17	12/18	12/19	12/20	12/21
Sales ($ mil.)	2.2%	35,410.0	31,856.0	37,266.0	33,014.0	38,655.0
Net income ($ mil.)	67.3%	1,248.0	6,434.0	8,920.0	7,747.0	9,771.0
Market value ($ mil.)	–	0.0	0.0	0.0	0.0	0.0
Employees	6.3%	61,800	62,600	86,200	80,300	79,000

COCA-COLA CONSOLIDATED INC
NMS: COKE

4100 Coca-Cola Plaza
Charlotte, NC 28211
Phone: 704 557-4400
Fax: –
Web: www.cokeconsolidated.com

CEO: J. Frank Harrison
CFO: F. Scott Anthony
HR: James Matte
FYE: December 31
Type: Public

As the largest independent Coke bottler in the US Coca-Cola Consolidated Inc. (formerly Coca-Cola Bottling Co. Consolidated) offers thirst-quenchers to approximately 66 million consumers across some 15 states. It produces bottles and distributes a few hundred brands and flavors of beverages principally the products of The Coca-Cola Company which account for about 85% of total sales. Other beverages bottled and distributed by Coca-Cola Consolidated include Dr. Pepper and Monster Energy drinks. In addition to bottles and cans the company sells products to other bottlers and offers post-mix products that allow retailers to sell fountain drinks. Coca-Cola Company owns over 25% of CCBCC.

	Annual Growth	01/17*	12/17	12/18	12/19	12/20
Sales ($ mil.)	16.6%	3,156.4	4,323.7	4,625.4	4,826.5	5,007.4
Net income ($ mil.)	51.0%	50.1	96.5	(19.9)	11.4	172.5
Market value ($ mil.)	14.2%	1,676.5	2,017.8	1,683.0	2,752.6	2,495.9
Employees	6.2%	13,200	16,500	16,200	16,900	15,800

*Fiscal year change

COCA-COLA ENTERPRISES INC
NYS: CCE

2500 Windy Ridge Parkway
Atlanta, GA 30339
Phone: 678 260-3000
Fax: –
Web: www.cokecce.com

CEO: –
CFO: –
HR: –
FYE: December 31
Type: Public

Scientists at The Coca-Cola Company concoct the secret syrup but it's up to Coca-Cola Enterprises (CCE) to do the heavy lifting. CCE buys it combines it with other ingredients then bottles and distributes Coke products in Western Europe. One of the world's largest Coca-Cola bottlers by volume CCE bottles and distributes energy drinks sports drinks still and sparkling waters (Dr Pepper Snapple's Schweppes Abbey Well) juices and coffees and teas. The company's European reach includes distribution in Belgium France the Netherlands Norway Sweden and the UK. All told CCE operates more than 15 production and about 50 distribution facilities in Europe.

	Annual Growth	12/11	12/12	12/13	12/14	12/15
Sales ($ mil.)	(4.1%)	8,284.0	8,062.0	8,212.0	8,264.0	7,011.0
Net income ($ mil.)	(5.6%)	749.0	677.0	667.0	663.0	596.0
Market value ($ mil.)	17.6%	5,860.7	7,213.4	10,032.3	10,052.8	11,194.0
Employees	(3.5%)	13,250	13,000	11,750	11,650	11,492

CODALE ELECTRIC SUPPLY, INC.

5225 W 2400 S
SALT LAKE CITY, UT 841201264
Phone: 801-975-7300
Fax: -
Web: www.codale.com

CEO: -
CFO: -
HR: -
FYE: December 25
Type: Private

Codale Electric Supply distributes lighting fixtures electrical supplies and datacomm products to wholesale customers through 11 locations in Nevada Utah Idaho and Wyoming. It stocks products from such manufacturers as Brad Harrison Chromalox Greenlee Philips Lighting Southwire and Western Tube & Conduit. The company sells to the aerospace construction mining healthcare schools government and utility markets. Codale Electric also offers consulting and training energy and safety audits and inventory management services. The company was founded in 1975 by CEO Dale Holt who owns nearly all of Codale Electric's equity.

	Annual Growth	12/06	12/07	12/08	12/09	12/10
Sales ($ mil.)	(13.8%)	-	-	235.5	175.8	175.1
Net income ($ mil.)	(39.3%)	-	-	16.3	6.3	6.0
Market value ($ mil.)	-	-	-	-	-	-
Employees	-	-	-	-	-	290

CODEXIS INC

200 Penobscot Drive
Redwood City, CA 94063
Phone: 650 421-8100
Fax: -
Web: www.codexis.com

NMS: CDXS
CEO: John Nicols
CFO: Ross Taylor
HR: -
FYE: December 31
Type: Public

The pharmaceutical and the biodiesel industries don't seem like they have much in common but they both use the chemicals produced by Codexis. The company develops biocatalysts — chemicals used to manufacture other chemicals in a way that's easy on the environment. Its technology is used to make the active ingredients in pharmaceuticals and produce biofuel from plant material. Codexis has a research agreement with Shell to develop new ways of converting biomass to biofuel; Shell accounts for more than half of Codexis' sales. The company is also working within other markets to use its technology to manage carbon emissions from coal-fired power plants and treat wastewater.

	Annual Growth	12/16	12/17	12/18	12/19	12/20
Sales ($ mil.)	9.0%	48.8	50.0	60.6	68.5	69.1
Net income ($ mil.)	-	(8.6)	(23.0)	(10.9)	(11.9)	(24.0)
Market value ($ mil.)	47.6%	295.7	536.8	1,073.5	1,027.9	1,403.3
Employees	13.8%	108	116	132	161	181

CODORUS VALLEY BANCORP, INC.

105 Leader Heights Road, P.O. Box 2887
York, PA 17405-2287
Phone: 717 747-1519
Fax: -

NMS: CVLY
CEO: Craig Kauffman
CFO: -
HR: -
FYE: December 31
Type: Public

Codorus Valley Bancorp is a people-oriented business. The firm is the holding company for PeoplesBank which operates about 20 branches in southeastern Pennsylvania's York County and Hunt Valley and Bel Air Maryland. The bank offers the standard fare including checking and savings accounts and CDs. It uses funds from deposits to write a variety of loans primarily commercial loans and commercial real estate loans but also residential mortgages and consumer installment loans. Bank subsidiary Codorus Valley Financial Advisors offers investment products while SYC Settlement Services provides real estate settlement services.

	Annual Growth	12/16	12/17	12/18	12/19	12/20
Assets ($ mil.)	7.6%	1,611.6	1,709.2	1,807.5	1,886.5	2,162.2
Net income ($ mil.)	(10.4%)	13.1	12.0	19.5	18.6	8.4
Market value ($ mil.)	(12.2%)	280.9	270.4	208.7	226.2	166.6
Employees	3.3%	304	339	348	363	346

COE COLLEGE

1220 1ST AVE NE
CEDAR RAPIDS, IA 524025092
Phone: 319-399-8000
Fax: -
Web: www.coe.edu

CEO: -
CFO: -
HR: Kristina Bridges
FYE: June 30
Type: Private

Coe College is a private liberal arts college with a residential campus in Cedar Rapids Iowa. The school offers more than 40 academic majors and grants undergraduate degrees (Bachelor of Arts Bachelor of Music and Bachelor of Science in Nursing) as well as a Master of Arts in Teaching. Coe College's has an annual enrollment of more than 1400 students (from across more than 30 US states and more than 15 other countries) who are required to participate in an internship student research project practicum or study abroad program as they matriculate. Approximately half of the school's students go on to post-graduate studies.

	Annual Growth	06/13	06/14	06/15	06/16	06/17
Sales ($ mil.)	20.5%	-	42.2	36.0	70.6	73.9
Net income ($ mil.)	-	-	3.5	(2.1)	(0.3)	(0.3)
Market value ($ mil.)	-	-	-	-	-	-
Employees	-	-	-	-	-	272

COEUR MINING INC

104 S. Michigan Avenue, Suite 900
Chicago, IL 60603
Phone: 312 489-5800
Fax: -
Web: www.coeur.com

NYS: CDE
CEO: Mitchell Krebs
CFO: Thomas Whelan
HR: Emilie Schouten
FYE: December 31
Type: Public

Coeur Mining (formerly Coeur d'Alene Mines) is a leading primary gold and silver producer the company holds interests in silver and gold properties in the US Canada Mexico and exploration projects in North America including the wholly-owned Crown and Sterling projects in southern Nevada and the La Preciosa project in Mexico other mineral interests strategic equity investments among other items. It has proven and probable reserves of approximately 260 million ounces of silver and over 3 million ounces of gold. Its two main mines are at Kensington in Alaska and Palmarejo in Mexico. The US accounts for roughly 65% of the company's revenue.

	Annual Growth	12/17	12/18	12/19	12/20	12/21
Sales ($ mil.)	4.1%	709.6	625.9	711.5	785.5	832.8
Net income ($ mil.)	-	(1.3)	(48.4)	(341.2)	25.6	(31.3)
Market value ($ mil.)	(9.5%)	1,926.9	1,148.4	2,075.9	2,659.1	1,294.9
Employees	(1.7%)	2,257	2,075	2,155	1,959	2,105

COFFEE HOLDING CO INC

3475 Victory Boulevard
Staten Island, NY 10314
Phone: 718 832-0800
Fax: -
Web: www.coffeeholding.com

NAS: JVA
CEO: Andrew Gordon
CFO: Andrew Gordon
HR: -
FYE: October 31
Type: Public

Coffee Holding Co. brewed up the idea of selling a wide spectrum of raw and roasted Arabica coffee beans to coffee purveyors. Its products are divided into three categories: Wholesale Green Coffee Private Label Coffee and Branded Coffee. The company's private label and branded coffee products are sold throughout the US Canada and abroad to supermarkets wholesalers and individually owned and multi-unit retail customers. Established in 1972 Coffee Holding has operated under the leadership of the founding Gordon family including Andrew Gordon and David Gordon who have both worked with the company for more than 35 years.

	Annual Growth	10/17	10/18	10/19	10/20	10/21
Sales ($ mil.)	(4.6%)	77.1	90.7	86.5	74.3	63.9
Net income ($ mil.)	28.0%	0.5	1.1	(0.1)	(0.1)	1.3
Market value ($ mil.)	1.5%	23.8	24.8	21.6	21.7	25.3
Employees	0.3%	74	79	79	82	75

COGENT COMMUNICATIONS HOLDINGS, INC.   NMS: CCOI

2450 N Street N.W.
Washington, DC 20037
Phone: 202 295-4200
Fax: -
Web: www.cogentco.com
CEO: David Schaeffer
CFO: Thaddeus G Weed
HR: -
FYE: December 31
Type: Public

Cogent Communications offers fiber-optic data network that serves customers in North America Europe and Asia. It offers dedicated Internet access and data transport services to businesses through Ethernet connections that link its nearly 35 data center facilities directly to customer office buildings. Clients include financial services companies law firms ad agencies and other professional services businesses including Cloudhelix Cadwalader Chartright air group and CHF industries. Cogent also sells access to its network and provides colocation management services to ISPs hosting companies and other high-volume bandwidth users. Cogent serves almost 210 markets in more than 45 countries globally.

	Annual Growth	12/16	12/17	12/18	12/19	12/20
Sales ($ mil.)	6.2%	446.9	485.2	520.2	546.2	568.1
Net income ($ mil.)	(19.7%)	14.9	5.9	28.7	37.5	6.2
Market value ($ mil.)	9.7%	1,952.3	2,138.8	2,134.5	3,107.2	2,826.7
Employees	4.8%	897	928	978	1,051	1,083

COGENTIX MEDICAL INC   NAS: CGNT

5420 Feltl Road
Minnetonka, MN 55343
Phone: 952 426-6140
Fax: -
Web: www.cogentixmedical.com
CEO: Michael Frazzette
CFO: -
HR: -
FYE: December 31
Type: Public

Even those outside California know Cogentix Medical's products are totally tubular. The firm (formerly named Vision-Sciences) makes endoscopic tools — tubular instruments that let doctors see into the body and perform procedures without invasive surgery. It makes traditional endoscopes and the EndoSheath System which consists of a disposable sterile sheath covering the reusable endoscope. The system allows health care providers to save money by avoiding costly cleaning and repairs and reduces the risk of cross-contamination. Subsidiary Machida makes flexible borescopes endoscope-like tools used in industrial applications. In 2015 Vison-Sciences merged with Uroplasty to create Cogentix Medical.

	Annual Growth	03/13	03/14	03/15*	12/15	12/16
Sales ($ mil.)	50.2%	15.3	17.1	26.5	36.6	51.9
Net income ($ mil.)	—	(10.6)	(7.7)	(7.7)	(7.0)	(22.1)
Market value ($ mil.)	23.4%	64.7	72.5	21.2	78.0	121.5
Employees	17.9%	108	105	214	181	177

*Fiscal year change

COGNEX CORP   NMS: CGNX

One Vision Drive
Natick, MA 01760-2059
Phone: 508 650-3000
Fax: -
Web: www.cognex.com
CEO: Robert Willett
CFO: Paul Todgham
HR: -
FYE: December 31
Type: Public

Cognex is a leading worldwide provider of machine vision products that capture and analyze visual information in order to automate manufacturing and distribution tasks where vision is required. Manufacturers of consumer electronics and vehicles as well as logistics companies use the company's machine vision and industrial identification systems to position and identify products gauge sizes and locate defects. It also offers a full range of machine vision systems and sensors vision software and industrial image-based barcode readers designed to meet customer needs at different performance and price points. Sales to customers based in the US account for about 40% of sales.

	Annual Growth	12/17	12/18	12/19	12/20	12/21
Sales ($ mil.)	8.5%	748.0	806.3	725.6	811.0	1,037.1
Net income ($ mil.)	12.1%	177.2	219.3	203.9	176.2	279.9
Market value ($ mil.)	6.2%	10,732.4	6,785.9	9,834.0	14,088.5	13,645.4
Employees	6.2%	1,771	2,124	2,267	2,055	2,257

COGNIZANT TECHNOLOGY SOLUTIONS CORP.   NMS: CTSH

300 Frank W. Burr Blvd.
Teaneck, NJ 07666
Phone: 201 801-0233
Fax: 201 801-0243
Web: www.cognizant.com
CEO: Brian Humphries
CFO: Jan Siegmund
HR: -
FYE: December 31
Type: Public

Cognizant Technology Solutions is one of the world's leading professional services companies engineering modern business for the digital era. To help customers make the switch the information technology outsourcing company provides intelligent systems automation cloud technologies and cyber security tools. Cognizant also offers digital services and solutions consulting application development systems integration application testing application maintenance infrastructure services and business process services. The company targets companies in financial services health care manufacturing retail and logistics as well as communications and media. Most of Cognizant's software development centers and employees are in India. Most of the company's revenue is generated in North America.

	Annual Growth	12/17	12/18	12/19	12/20	12/21
Sales ($ mil.)	5.7%	14,810.0	16,125.0	16,783.0	16,652.0	18,507.0
Net income ($ mil.)	9.2%	1,504.0	2,101.0	1,842.0	1,392.0	2,137.0
Market value ($ mil.)	5.7%	37,285.5	33,327.0	32,560.5	43,023.8	46,578.0
Employees	6.2%	260,000	281,600	292,500	289,500	330,600

COHEN & COMPANY INC (NEW)   ASE: COHN

Cira Centre, 2929 Arch Street, Suite 1703
Philadelphia, PA 19104
Phone: 215 701-9555
Fax: -
Web: www.cohenandcompany.com
CEO: Lester Brafman
CFO: Joseph Pooler
HR: -
FYE: December 31
Type: Public

Institutional Financial Markets Inc. (IFMI) believes in the institution of the markets. Formerly a real estate investment trust named Alesco Financial (and later Cohen & Company) the company now manages and trades financial investments specializing in credit-related fixed income assets. The company serves institutional investors. IFMI's asset management arm offers funds separately managed accounts collateralized debt obligations international hybrid securities and other investment products; it manages some $10 billion in assets. The firm also has a capital markets division which sells trades and issues corporate and securitized products. IFMI has about 10 offices in the US and London.

	Annual Growth	12/16	12/17	12/18	12/19	12/20
Sales ($ mil.)	23.8%	55.3	47.5	49.4	49.7	130.1
Net income ($ mil.)	58.2%	2.3	2.1	(2.5)	(2.1)	14.2
Market value ($ mil.)	91.9%	1.6	10.6	11.2	5.2	21.7
Employees	2.4%	79	88	88	94	87

COHEN & STEERS INC   NYS: CNS

280 Park Avenue
New York, NY 10017
Phone: 212 832-3232
Fax: 212 832-3622
Web: www.cohenandsteers.com
CEO: Joseph Harvey
CFO: Matthew Stadler
HR: Michele Nolty
FYE: December 31
Type: Public

Cohen & Steers founded in 1986 is a global investment manager specializing in liquid real assets including real estate securities listed infrastructure and natural resource equities as well as preferred securities and other income solutions. The company offer strategies through a variety of investment vehicles including US and non-US registered funds and other commingled vehicles separate accounts and subadvised portfolios. Cohen & Steers has nearly $80 billion of assets under management. Majority of its sales were generated in the North America.

	Annual Growth	12/16	12/17	12/18	12/19	12/20
Sales ($ mil.)	5.1%	349.9	378.2	381.1	410.8	427.5
Net income ($ mil.)	(4.7%)	92.9	91.9	113.9	134.6	76.6
Market value ($ mil.)	21.9%	1,605.7	2,259.9	1,640.1	2,999.2	3,550.7
Employees	4.9%	287	303	328	328	347

COHERENT INC
NMS: COHR

5100 Patrick Henry Drive
Santa Clara, CA 95054
Phone: 408 764-4000
Fax: -
Web: www.coherent.com

CEO: Andreas Mattes
CFO: Kevin Palatnik
HR: -
FYE: October 02
Type: Public

Coherent is a leading maker of lasers solutions and optics for microelectronics life sciences industrial manufacturing scientific and aerospace and defense markets. The company's lasers and laser technologies are used in microelectronics manufacturing medical diagnostics therapeutic medical applications and scientific research. Its products also are used to make vehicles machine tools consumer goods and medical devices. Coherent's biggest market is the microelectronics industry. Coherent gets over 75% of its revenue from international customers. The company has been turning out laser technology since it was founded in 1966.

	Annual Growth	09/17	09/18	09/19*	10/20	10/21
Sales ($ mil.)	(3.6%)	1,723.3	1,902.6	1,430.6	1,229.0	1,487.5
Net income ($ mil.)	-	207.1	247.4	53.8	(414.1)	(106.8)
Market value ($ mil.)	1.9%	5,770.6	4,225.2	3,718.5	2,699.2	6,211.1
Employees	(0.6%)	5,218	5,418	5,184	4,875	5,085

*Fiscal year change

COHU INC
NMS: COHU

12367 Crosthwaite Circle
Poway, CA 92064-6817
Phone: 858 848-8100
Fax: -
Web: www.cohu.com

CEO: Luis Muller
CFO: Jeffrey Jones
HR: -
FYE: December 25
Type: Public

Cohu is a leading supplier of semiconductor test and inspection handlers microelectromechanical system (MEMS) test modules test contactors thermal sub-systems semiconductor automated test equipment and bare board PCB test systems used by global semiconductor and electronics manufacturers and semiconductor test subcontractor. Customers include device manufacturers fabless design houses PCB manufacturers and test subcontractors. China is the California-based company's single biggest market. Cohu was founded in 1957.

	Annual Growth	12/17	12/18	12/19	12/20	12/21
Sales ($ mil.)	25.9%	352.7	451.8	583.3	636.0	887.2
Net income ($ mil.)	50.2%	32.8	(32.2)	(69.7)	(13.8)	167.3
Market value ($ mil.)	14.7%	1,070.2	770.8	1,087.3	1,889.3	1,853.2
Employees	15.8%	1,800	3,500	3,200	3,250	3,240

COLAVITA USA L.L.C.

1 RUNYONS LN
EDISON, NJ 088172219
Phone: 732-404-8300
Fax: -
Web: www.colavita.com

CEO: Giovanni Colavita
CFO: Simon Boltuch
HR: -
FYE: December 31
Type: Private

This company helps bring Italian flavors to American palates. Colavita USA is a leading importer and distributor of Italian foods notably olive oil pastas sauces and vinegars sold under the Colavita label. It supplies products to retail grocery store chains specialty food stores and wholesale distributors as well as restaurants caterers and other foodservice operators. The company was started by John J. Profaci who struck a distribution agreement with Italy's Colavita family in 1978. Rome-based Colavita S.p.A owns 80% of the US importer.

	Annual Growth	12/08	12/09	12/10	12/11	12/12
Sales ($ mil.)	7.5%	-	-	-	85.3	91.7
Net income ($ mil.)	(1.6%)	-	-	-	1.2	1.2
Market value ($ mil.)	-	-	-	-	-	-
Employees	-	-	-	-	-	80

COLDWATER CREEK INC.
NMS: CWTR

One Coldwater Creek Drive
Sandpoint, ID 83864
Phone: 208 263-2266
Fax: 208 263-1582
Web: www.coldwatercreek.com

CEO: -
CFO: -
HR: -
FYE: February 02
Type: Public

Women quench their thirst for classic casual clothing and accessories from Coldwater Creek's stores catalog and Web site. The upscale multi-channel retailer sells mostly traditional apparel through some 360 full-line stores and about 35 retail outlets targeting middle- and upper-income women 35 years of age and older. It also sells directly to consumers via its Coldwater Creek catalog and online store and operates about 10 namesake day spas that typically span 5400 sq. ft. While it got its start as a catalog operator today the company's retail presence is felt more at the mall than the mailbox with stores accounting for more than 75% of sales. Coldwater Creek was founded in 1984 by Dennis and Ann Pence.

	Annual Growth	01/09	01/10	01/11	01/12*	02/13
Sales ($ mil.)	(7.7%)	1,024.2	1,038.6	981.1	773.0	742.5
Net income ($ mil.)	-	(26.0)	(56.1)	(44.1)	(99.7)	(81.8)
Market value ($ mil.)	7.0%	86.1	136.2	89.5	27.5	112.7
Employees	(12.4%)	11,200	9,531	9,198	6,900	6,600

*Fiscal year change

COLE HAAN

1 Cole Haan Dr.
Yarmouth ME 04096-6670
Phone: 207-846-2500
Fax: 207-846-6374
Web: www.colehaan.com

CEO: Jack Boys
CFO: Tom Linko
HR: -
FYE: May 31
Type: Subsidiary

Cole Haan caters to the well-heeled. It designs and sells upscale footwear and accessories and was once the fashion-footed subsidiary of athletic products firm NIKE. The shoe maker peddles its products through about 110 Cole Haan stores in the US as well as nearly 70 stores in Japan. It also sells its shoes belts hosiery handbags small leather goods fine outerwear and watches online and in stores run by other retailers. Cole Haan has reached into high-end accessories (encroaching on Coach) in recent years. Most of Cole Haan's products are distributed from New Hampshire; its outerwear is made in Italian factories by G-III Apparel. Cole Haan was founded in Chicago in 1928 by Trafton Cole and Eddie Haan.

COLFAX CORP
NYS: CFX

2711 Centerville Road, Suite 400
Wilmington, DE 19808
Phone: 302 252-9160
Fax: -
Web: www.colfaxcorp.com

CEO: Shyam Kambeyanda
CFO: Christopher Hix
HR: -
FYE: December 31
Type: Public

Colfax provides fabrication technology and medical technology products and services. Marketed primarily under the ESAB brand and DJO brands. Colfax offers a wide range of consumable products and equipment for use in the cutting joining and automated welding of steels aluminum and other metals and metal alloys. Colfax also makes portable welding machines and large customized and automated metal cutting and welding systems. The company's DJO division is a maker and distributor of medical devices with applications including orthopedic bracing reconstructive implants and physical therapy. More than 40% of the company's total sales is generated from the US.

	Annual Growth	12/17	12/18	12/19	12/20	12/21
Sales ($ mil.)	4.0%	3,300.2	3,666.8	3,327.5	3,070.8	3,854.3
Net income ($ mil.)	(17.0%)	151.1	140.2	(527.6)	42.6	71.7
Market value ($ mil.)	3.8%	6,190.6	3,265.6	5,684.3	5,975.0	7,182.8
Employees	3.2%	14,300	15,500	15,000	15,400	16,200

COLGATE UNIVERSITY

13 OAK DR
HAMILTON, NY 133461386
Phone: 315-228-1000
Fax: –
Web: www.colgate.edu

CEO: –
CFO: –
HR: –
FYE: June 30
Type: Private

Colgate University is located in upstate New York. The university is a liberal arts college with an enrollment of about 3000 students. Most students are undergrads though the school has a small graduate program that offers master's degrees in arts and teaching. Colgate offers some 50 major fields of study plus about 15 minor study programs. Its most popular programs include business communications finance education medicine law and technology. The university has about 300 full-time faculty members.

	Annual Growth	06/15	06/16	06/18	06/19	06/20
Sales ($ mil.)	12.9%	–	189.6	209.7	226.1	307.5
Net income ($ mil.)	–	–	(57.7)	48.1	52.7	35.7
Market value ($ mil.)	–	–	–	–	–	–
Employees	–	–	–	–	–	1,014

COLGATE-PALMOLIVE CO.

NYS: CL

300 Park Avenue
New York, NY 10022
Phone: 212 310-2000
Fax: 212 310-3284
Web: www.colgatepalmolive.com

CEO: Noel Wallace
CFO: Stanley Sutula
HR: Sally Massey
FYE: December 31
Type: Public

Colgate-Palmolive is a global leader in oral personal and home care products. The company also offers pet nutrition products through subsidiary Hill's Pet Nutrition which makes Science Diet and Prescription Diet pet foods. Many of its oral care products fall under the Colgate brand and include toothbrushes and mouthwashes. Its oral care segment also includes pharmaceutical products for dentists and other oral health professionals. Personal and home care items include Ajax brand household cleaner Palmolive bar soap and dishwashing liquid Softsoap shower gel and Sanex deodorant and soap as well as Speed Stick deodorants. Colgate-Palmolive sells its products in more than 200 countries and generates most of its sales outside the US.

	Annual Growth	12/17	12/18	12/19	12/20	12/21
Sales ($ mil.)	3.0%	15,454.0	15,544.0	15,693.0	16,471.0	17,421.0
Net income ($ mil.)	1.7%	2,024.0	2,400.0	2,367.0	2,695.0	2,166.0
Market value ($ mil.)	3.1%	63,414.2	50,025.4	57,858.7	71,869.5	71,726.6
Employees	(1.5%)	35,900	34,500	34,300	34,200	33,800

COLLABERA INC.

25 Airport Rd.
Morristown NJ 07960
Phone: 973-889-5200
Fax: 973-292-1643
Web: www.collabera.com

CEO: Karthik Krishnamurthy
CFO: Sham Patel
HR: –
FYE: December 31
Type: Private

Collabera knows the value of enabling people to work together effectively. The company provides outsourced IT management consulting and related services such as software development to companies in such industries as inancial services manufacturing media utilities and retail. It specializes in such areas as consulting enterprise resource planning software implementation and data migration. The company also offers IT staffing services. Collabera operates from about 20 US offices a London office seven offices and software development facilities in India and locations in Manila and Singapore. The company was founded in 1991 by chairman Hiten Patel CFO Sham Patel CIO Dhar Patadia and EVP Hemin Shah.

COLLECTORS UNIVERSE INC

NMS: CLCT

1610 E. Saint Andrew Place
Santa Ana, CA 92705
Phone: 949 567-1234
Fax: –
Web: www.collectorsuniverse.com

CEO: Joseph Orlando
CFO: Joseph Wallace
HR: –
FYE: June 30
Type: Public

Before you sell that silver dollar or those baseball cards you might want to check with Collectors Universe. The company provides authentication grading and information services for sellers and buyers of trading cards event tickets vintage autographs and other memorabilia. The company charges a fee — usually between $2 and $10000 per item — to determine the authenticity quality and worth of the collectible. Coins and sports cards account for most of the company's business; notable offerings include its Professional Coin Grading Service (PCGS). Collectors Universe also publishes price guides market reports rarity reports and other information in print form as well as on its website.

	Annual Growth	06/15	06/16	06/17	06/18	06/19
Sales ($ mil.)	4.1%	61.7	61.0	70.2	68.4	72.5
Net income ($ mil.)	7.8%	7.4	7.6	8.5	6.2	10.0
Market value ($ mil.)	1.7%	182.5	180.8	227.5	134.9	195.3
Employees	10.6%	290	302	369	387	434

COLLEGE ENTRANCE EXAMINATION BOARD

250 VESEY ST
NEW YORK, NY 102811052
Phone: 212-713-8000
Fax: –
Web: www.collegeboard.org

CEO: –
CFO: Tho Higgins
HR: –
FYE: June 30
Type: Private

There are three letters every high school student must learn: S A and T. The College Board is a not-for-profit association that owns and administers the Scholastic Assessment Test (SAT) College-Level Examination Program (CLEP) and the Advanced Placement Program (AP) at high schools across the US. It also offers guidance counseling financial aid student assessment standardized testing and professional development courses. The College Board was founded in 1900; its members include nearly 6000 schools colleges universities and other educational institutions.

	Annual Growth	06/10	06/11	06/12	06/13	06/14
Sales ($ mil.)	6.0%	–	705.1	746.0	779.5	840.7
Net income ($ mil.)	(1.1%)	–	102.3	26.9	93.6	98.9
Market value ($ mil.)	–	–	–	–	–	–
Employees	–	–	–	–	–	1,259

COLLEGE OF SAINT BENEDICT

37 COLLEGE AVE S
SAINT JOSEPH, MN 563742099
Phone: 320-363-5011
Fax: –
Web: www.csbsju.edu

CEO: –
CFO: –
HR: –
FYE: June 30
Type: Private

The College of Saint Benedict (CSB) is an all-female Catholic liberal arts college with an enrollment of more than 2000 students about 70% of which are Catholic (though students of all faith are welcome). Saint John's University (SJU) located six miles from from CSB in central Minnesota is the school's male counterpart. SJU and CSB share a common curriculum and students from both institutions attend classes together. The schools offer some 60 areas of study with more than 35 majors. CSB was incorporated when it separated from the Saint Benedict's Monastery in 1961.

	Annual Growth	06/14	06/15	06/16	06/17	06/18
Sales ($ mil.)	0.7%	–	69.2	70.6	69.1	70.6
Net income ($ mil.)	7.0%	–	7.2	6.2	23.4	8.8
Market value ($ mil.)	–	–	–	–	–	–
Employees	–	–	–	–	–	431

COLLEGE OF THE HOLY CROSS (INC)

1 COLLEGE ST
WORCESTER, MA 016102395
Phone: 508-793-2011
Fax: –
Web: www.holycross.edu

CEO: –
CFO: –
HR: –
FYE: June 30
Type: Private

College of The Holy Cross has some real Crusaders. The Jesuit-founded college with sports teams nicknamed the Crusaders is a liberal arts undergraduate institution in central Massachusetts with more than 2900 students. Some of the school's more popular areas of study include liberal arts' favorites such as English history and political science but also multidisciplinary concentrations and specialty programs including biochemistry Latin American studies and women's studies. The co-educational school has more than 300 full- and part-time faculty with a 10:1 student-to-faculty ratio. Holy Cross is the oldest Catholic college in New England.

	Annual Growth	06/17	06/18	06/19	06/20	06/21
Sales ($ mil.)	(2.1%)	–	189.6	200.7	193.4	177.9
Net income ($ mil.)	60.2%	–	71.0	10.5	(14.7)	292.2
Market value ($ mil.)	–	–	–	–	–	–
Employees		–	–	–	–	949

COLOMBO BANK

1229 Connecticut Ave., N.W.
Washington, DC 20036
Phone: 202 628-5500
Fax: –
Web: www.ifsb.com

NBB: IFSB
CEO: –
CFO: –
HR: –
FYE: December 31
Type: Public

Founded in 1968 to provide loans to African-Americans living in Washington DC Independence Federal Savings Bank continues that mission today. Through three branches in the US capital and nearby Maryland the bank offers standard deposit products such as checking and savings accounts money market accounts and CDs. Mortgages secured by residential or commercial real estate make up almost all of its loan portfolio; the bank ceased providing guaranteed student loans through Sallie Mae in 2008. Chairman Morton Bender owns a majority of Independence Federal. The company withdrew a plan to merge with Maryland-based Colombo Bank after regulatory approvals were delayed indefinitely in 2010.

	Annual Growth	12/12	12/13	12/14	12/15	12/16
Assets ($ mil.)	(2.0%)	217.5	198.6	200.8	202.6	200.9
Net income ($ mil.)	–	(4.5)	(3.1)	(1.6)	0.0	0.2
Market value ($ mil.)	(14.5%)	206.5	79.2	106.7	120.7	110.2
Employees		–	–	–	–	–

COLONIAL FINANCIAL SERVICES, INC.

2745 S. Delsea Drive
Vineland, NJ 08360
Phone: 856 205-0058
Fax: –
Web: www.colonialbankfsb.com

NMS: COBK
CEO: Edward J Geletka
CFO: L Joseph Stella III
HR: –
FYE: December 31
Type: Public

Community banking is a revolutionary idea for Colonial Financial Services. The holding company owns Colonial Bank a regional thrift serving southern New Jersey from about 10 locations. The bank offers products and services including checking and savings accounts bank cards loans and brokerage. It originates primarily real estate loans with one- to four-family home mortgages accounting for nearly 50% of its loan portfolio. Colonial Bank also writes construction business home equity and consumer loans. Colonial Financial Services converted from a mutual holding structure to a stock holding company in 2010.

	Annual Growth	12/09	12/10	12/11	12/12	12/13
Sales ($ mil.)	(6.8%)	27.6	27.9	25.9	23.3	20.9
Net income ($ mil.)	–	1.4	3.9	3.3	(1.7)	(1.8)
Market value ($ mil.)	16.3%	28.0	47.0	48.0	50.5	51.2
Employees	2.8%	104	106	108	116	116

COLONIAL PIPELINE COMPANY

1185 SANCTUARY PKWY # 100
ALPHARETTA, GA 300094765
Phone: 678-762-2200
Fax: –
Web: www.colpipe.com

CEO: Joseph A Blount Jr
CFO: –
HR: –
FYE: December 31
Type: Private

Colonial Pipeline delivers about 100 million gallons of gasoline diesel jet fuel home heating oil and military fuels per day to cities and businesses across the eastern and southern US. The more than 5500-mile Colonial Pipeline system transports the fuels from Houston Texas to Linden New Jersey to more than 270 marketing terminals near major urban centers in the Southeast and along the Eastern Seaboard. Colonial provides a portfolio of information and logistics management services to its customers. Colonial Pipeline is owned by a consortium of companies including Koch KKR-Keats Pipeline Investors L.P. Caisse de depot et placement du Quebec IFM (US) Colonial Pipeline 2 and Shell Midstream Operating. Colonial Pipeline was founded in 1962.

	Annual Growth	12/15	12/16	12/17	12/18	12/19
Sales ($ mil.)	4.5%	–	1,215.0	1,231.4	1,340.1	1,385.6
Net income ($ mil.)	20.2%	–	233.1	509.3	407.2	404.7
Market value ($ mil.)	–	–	–	–	–	–
Employees		–	–	–	–	700

COLONY BANKCORP, INC.

115 South Grant Street
Fitzgerald, GA 31750
Phone: 229 426-6000
Fax: –
Web: www.colonybank.com

NMS: CBAN
CEO: T. Heath Fountain
CFO: Tracie Youngblood
HR: –
FYE: December 31
Type: Public

Colony Bankcorp seems to be colonizing Georgia. The multibank holding company owns seven financial institutions doing business under variations of the Colony Bank name throughout central and southern portions of the state. The banks operate more than 25 branches in all. They offer traditional fare such as checking and savings accounts NOW and IRA accounts and CDs. Real estate loans including residential and commercial mortgages and construction and farmland loans make up the largest portion of the company's loan portfolio at more than 80%. The banks also issue business and consumer loans.

	Annual Growth	12/16	12/17	12/18	12/19	12/20
Assets ($ mil.)	9.9%	1,210.4	1,232.8	1,251.9	1,515.3	1,764.0
Net income ($ mil.)	8.0%	8.7	7.8	11.9	10.2	11.8
Market value ($ mil.)	2.6%	125.4	138.7	138.7	156.7	139.2
Employees	3.1%	333	326	330	370	376

COLONY FINANCIAL INC.

2450 Broadway, 6th Floor
Santa Monica, CA 90404
Phone: 310 282-8820
Fax: –
Web: www.colonyfinancial.com

NYS: CLNY
CEO: –
CFO: –
HR: –
FYE: December 31
Type: Public

When most real estate investors are heading for the nearest exit Colony Financial is knocking on the doors of opportunity. The real estate investment and finance company which formed in 2009 and immediately filed for an initial public offering was established to acquire originate and manage commercial mortgage loans and other commercial real estate related debts. The firm's portfolio also includes real estate equity including single- and multifamily homes. It also has an interest in about 100 hotels acquired through foreclosure. Colony Financial is externally managed by affiliate Colony Financial Manager a wholly-owned subsidiary of the global real estate firm Colony Capital.

	Annual Growth	12/09	12/10	12/11	12/12	12/13
Sales ($ mil.)	258.5%	1.1	27.4	65.5	107.2	180.2
Net income ($ mil.)	–	(0.4)	17.8	43.4	62.0	101.8
Market value ($ mil.)	(0.1%)	1,558.1	1,531.4	1,201.7	1,491.6	1,552.0
Employees		–	–	–	–	–

COLORADO COLLEGE

14 E CACHE LA POUDRE ST
COLORADO SPRINGS, CO 809033243
Phone: 719-389-6000
Fax: –
Web: www.coloradocollege.edu

CEO: –
CFO: –
HR: –
FYE: June 30
Type: Private

Colorado College does things a little differently but it shares its mission with other institutions of higher learning. The private liberal arts and sciences college in 1970 adopted the Block Plan which divides the school year into eight three-and-a-half week blocks. Students take one course per three-and-a-half week block allowing them to focus on a single subject at a time. Its class size averages about 15 students with most classes capped at 25. Colorado College's 12000 students can choose from more than 40 majors and 30-plus minors. They are required to live on campus the first three years. Established in 1874 the Colorado Springs school boasts a 10:1 student-faculty ratio.

	Annual Growth	06/17	06/18	06/19	06/20	06/21
Sales ($ mil.)	(3.2%)	–	160.7	169.5	166.4	145.9
Net income ($ mil.)	100.8%	–	23.9	40.9	48.2	193.7
Market value ($ mil.)	–	–	–	–	–	–
Employees	–	–	–	–	–	800

COLORADO INTERSTATE GAS COMPANY LLC

1001 LA ST STE 1000
HOUSTON, TX 77002
Phone: 713-369-9000
Fax: –
Web: www.kindermorgan.com

CEO: –
CFO: David P Michels
HR: –
FYE: December 31
Type: Private

Colorado Interstate Gas knows that there is no fuel like an old fuel — natural gas. The company an indirect subsidiary of Kinder Morgan ransports natural gas from fields in the Rocky Mountains and the Anadarko Basin to customers in the Rocky Mountains Midwest Southwest Pacific Northwest and California. All told Colorado Interstate Gas has some 4300 miles of pipeline that can carry more than 4.6 billion cu. ft. per day. It has 38 billion cu. ft. of storage capacity in facilities in Colorado and Kansas. It also has a 50% stake in WYCO Development LLC a joint venture with an affiliate of Xcel Energy which owns and operates an intrastate gas pipeline.

	Annual Growth	12/13	12/14	12/15	12/16	12/17
Sales ($ mil.)	(12.5%)	–	–	–	365.5	320.0
Net income ($ mil.)	(6.1%)	–	–	–	97.3	91.4
Market value ($ mil.)	–	–	–	–	–	–
Employees	–	–	–	–	–	4

COLORADO MESA UNIVERSITY

1100 NORTH AVE
GRAND JUNCTION, CO 815013122
Phone: 970-248-1020
Fax: –
Web: www.coloradomesa.edu

CEO: –
CFO: –
HR: –
FYE: June 30
Type: Private

Colorado Mesa University is a small liberal arts university with an enrollment of more than 10600 students and a student-to-faculty ratio of 22:1. The school has three campuses in Colorado: the main campus in Grand Junction; another campus in Grand Junction that houses two-year affiliate Western Colorado Community College; and a third campus located in nearby Montrose. Colorado Mesa University offers more than 70 liberal arts and sciences programs and a limited number of professional technical and graduate programs. It was founded as Grand Junction State Junior College in 1925.

	Annual Growth	06/15	06/16	06/17	06/18	06/19
Sales ($ mil.)	5.1%	–	112.1	118.5	120.0	130.2
Net income ($ mil.)	6.1%	–	16.6	5.5	(12.0)	19.8
Market value ($ mil.)	–	–	–	–	–	–
Employees	–	–	–	–	–	850

COLORADO SPRINGS UTILITIES

121 S TEJON ST STE 200
COLORADO SPRINGS, CO 809032187
Phone: 719-448-4800
Fax: –
Web: www.csu.org

CEO: Phillip H Tollefson
CFO: –
HR: –
FYE: December 31
Type: Private

Even one of the country's most scenic areas needs creature comforts and that's where utilities come in. Community-owned Colorado Springs Utilities is a multi-utility company that provides natural gas electric water and wastewater services in the Pikes Peak region. Colorado Springs Utilities' service territories include Colorado Springs Manitou Springs and several of the suburban residential areas surrounding the city. The City of Colorado Springs is the only customer of the streetlight system and is responsible for all streetlight service charges. The military installations of Fort Carson Peterson Air Force Base and the US Air Force Academy are also serviced by the multi-utility.

	Annual Growth	12/14	12/15	12/16	12/17	12/18
Sales ($ mil.)	2.3%	–	830.8	793.3	839.8	890.5
Net income ($ mil.)	(14.4%)	–	174.2	130.5	74.2	109.3
Market value ($ mil.)	–	–	–	–	–	–
Employees	–	–	–	–	–	1,800

COLORADO STATE UNIVERSITY

6003 CAMPUS DELIVERY
FORT COLLINS, CO 805236003
Phone: 970-491-1372
Fax: –
Web: www.lib.colostate.edu

CEO: –
CFO: –
HR: –
FYE: June 30
Type: Private

Colorado State University (CSU) got its start as an agricultural college in 1870 six years before Colorado was even a state. The school still has agricultural and forestry programs as well as a veterinary medicine school but it also offers degrees in liberal arts business engineering and the sciences. True to its roots as a land-grant college CSU engages the larger community in research and outreach through statewide Cooperative Extension programs and centers like the Colorado Agricultural Experiment Station. More than 30000 students are enrolled at CSU about 80% of whom are Colorado residents. It employs about 1500 faculty members and has a student-to-teacher ratio of 19:1.

	Annual Growth	06/03	06/04	06/05	06/06	06/08
Sales ($ mil.)	14.7%	–	–	–	562.9	740.3
Net income ($ mil.)	–	–	–	–	26.4	(44.5)
Market value ($ mil.)	–	–	–	–	–	–
Employees	–	–	–	–	–	6,701

COLQUITT ELECTRIC MEMBERSHIP CORPORATION

15 ROWLAND DR
MOULTRIE, GA 317684169
Phone: 229-985-3620
Fax: –
Web: www.colquittemc.com

CEO: –
CFO: –
HR: –
FYE: December 31
Type: Private

There's no quit in the electric service to Colquitt and surrounding counties in Georgia thanks to Colquitt Electric Membership Corporation (Colquitt EMC). The consumer-owned non-profit utility distributes electricity to more than 41000 members in Berrien Brooks Colquitt Cook Lowndes Tift and Worth counties. Colquitt EMC distributes electricity via more than 8020 miles of power line. In 1976 the cooperative changed its name from Colquitt County Rural Electric Company to Colquitt EMC. The utility is the largest EMC in south Georgia with some of the lowest electric rates in the state.

	Annual Growth	12/16	12/17	12/18	12/19	12/20
Sales ($ mil.)	0.3%	–	128.1	134.1	137.0	129.2
Net income ($ mil.)	171.3%	–	0.3	5.6	8.5	5.4
Market value ($ mil.)	–	–	–	–	–	–
Employees	–	–	–	–	–	164

COLSA CORPORATION

6728 ODYSSEY DR NW
HUNTSVILLE, AL 358063305
Phone: 256-964-5361
Fax: –
Web: www.colsa.com

CEO: Francisco J Collazo
CFO: –
HR: –
FYE: December 31
Type: Private

COLSA doesn't mind being called a little defensive. The company provides advanced technology systems and services to US government agencies such as the Missile Defense Agency and NASA. COLSA which specializes in radar and guidance system technology offers services including engineering and testing developing war games simulations analyzing radar technology and virtual prototyping. Its information systems services include integration maintenance and administration for large computer centers. COLSA also offers a software system for nuclear power plants and a gateway for sending simulation data to remote systems. COLSA was founded in 1980.

	Annual Growth	12/15	12/16	12/17	12/18	12/19
Sales ($ mil.)	24.0%	–	190.1	0.0	336.1	362.7
Net income ($ mil.)	15.7%	–	15.2	0.0	16.5	23.6
Market value ($ mil.)	–	–	–	–	–	–
Employees	–	–	–	–	–	1,100

COLUMBIA BANKING SYSTEM INC

NMS: COLB

1301 A Street
Tacoma, WA 98402-2156
Phone: 253 305-1900
Fax: –
Web: www.columbiabank.com

CEO: Clint Stein
CFO: Aaron Deer
HR: –
FYE: December 31
Type: Public

Columbia Banking System (CBS) is the roughly $16.6 billion-asset holding company for Columbia Bank. The regional community bank has some 145 branches in Washington from Puget Sound to the timber country in the southwestern part of the state as well as in northern Oregon and Idaho. Targeting retail and small to medium-sized business customers the bank offers standard retail services such as checking and savings accounts CDs IRAs credit cards loans and mortgages. Commercial real estate loans make up about 45% of the company's loan portfolio while business loans make up another nearly 40%. Most of its branches were generated in Washington.

	Annual Growth	12/16	12/17	12/18	12/19	12/20
Assets ($ mil.)	14.9%	9,509.6	12,716.9	13,095.1	14,079.5	16,584.8
Net income ($ mil.)	10.1%	104.9	112.8	172.9	194.5	154.2
Market value ($ mil.)	(5.3%)	3,199.0	3,110.2	2,598.3	2,913.0	2,570.4
Employees	3.5%	1,819	2,120	2,137	2,162	2,091

COLUMBIA COLLEGE CHICAGO

600 S MICHIGAN AVE FL 5
CHICAGO, IL 606051996
Phone: 312-663-1600
Fax: –
Web: www.colum.edu

CEO: –
CFO: –
HR: –
FYE: August 31
Type: Private

Columbia College Chicago revels in its creative reputation. Specializing in arts and media the private not-for-profit school offers undergraduate and graduate degrees in the visual performing media and communication arts. The college offers more than 120 academic programs including architecture and interior design photography dance television theater film music composition journalism and marketing communications. Comedian Andy Richter and Wheel of Fortune host Pat Sajak are among the school's notable alumni. Founded in 1890 as the Columbia School of Oratory the college is located in several buildings in downtown Chicago and has about 12000 students. Average teacher to student ratio is 20:1.

	Annual Growth	08/09	08/10	08/14	08/16	08/19
Sales ($ mil.)	(0.8%)	–	244.1	261.5	210.8	226.2
Net income ($ mil.)	(24.9%)	–	18.5	6.6	6.3	1.4
Market value ($ mil.)	–	–	–	–	–	–
Employees	–	–	–	–	–	1,000

COLUMBIA GAS OF OHIO, INC.

290 W NATIONWIDE BLVD # 1
COLUMBUS, OH 432151082
Phone: 614-460-6000
Fax: –
Web: www.nisource.com

CEO: –
CFO: –
HR: –
FYE: December 31
Type: Private

Columbia Gas of Ohio takes pride in the fact that it can deliver gas first class en masse without impasse to the working class the middle class and the upper class. The utility is the largest natural gas utility in the state serving 1.4 million customers (including about 1.3 million residential 112000 commercial and 2600 industrial customers in more than 1030 communities in more than 60 of Ohio's 88 counties). The NiSource subsidiary offers a customer choice program which allows customers to choose their energy suppliers while Columbia Gas of Ohio continues to deliver the gas.

	Annual Growth	12/13	12/14	12/15	12/16	12/17
Sales ($ mil.)	(3.0%)	–	993.9	872.2	854.1	908.2
Net income ($ mil.)	(1.9%)	–	102.8	113.1	114.8	96.9
Market value ($ mil.)	–	–	–	–	–	–
Employees	–	–	–	–	–	2,500

COLUMBIA GULF TRANSMISSION, LLC

700 LOUISIANA ST
HOUSTON, TX 770022700
Phone: 713-623-0124
Fax: –
Web: www.tcenergy.com

CEO: Glen Kettering
CFO: –
HR: –
FYE: December 31
Type: Private

Gas many people need it and Columbia Gulf Transmission likes to pass it. The company operates a 3400 mile pipeline that delivers natural gas to customers in Louisiana Mississippi Kentucky and Tennessee. Its transportation services unit moves gas from the Gulf of Mexico to pipelines in southern Louisiana. The company also provides electric power services for power generation plants. Through its affiliate Columbia Gas Transmission Company it provides markets in the East Mid-Atlantic Midwest and Northeast US. Columbia Gulf Transmission founded in 1954 is a subsidiary of NiSource.

	Annual Growth	12/13	12/14	12/15	12/16	12/17
Sales ($ mil.)	(7.1%)	–	–	–	171.2	159.0
Net income ($ mil.)	414.2%	–	–	–	10.6	54.3
Market value ($ mil.)	–	–	–	–	–	–
Employees	–	–	–	–	–	1,300

COLUMBIA OGDEN MEDICAL CENTER, INC.

5475 S 500 E
OGDEN, UT 844056905
Phone: 801-479-2111
Fax: –
Web: www.mountainstar.com

CEO: Mark Adams
CFO: Judd Taylor
HR: –
FYE: May 31
Type: Private

Ogden Regional Medical Center is a nearly 240-bed hospital in Ogden Utah. The regional hospital offers general medical and acute care services. It operates specialty units for the treatment of alcoholism cancer and heart ailments as well as blood collection women's health and radiology. The hospital employs more than 300 medical staff members. Ogden Regional Medical Center is part of HCA's MountainStar Healthcare Network a group of hospitals and regional health clinics in Utah and Idaho.

	Annual Growth	06/05	06/06*	12/08*	05/15	05/16
Sales ($ mil.)	10.5%	–	75.0	0.0	192.8	204.0
Net income ($ mil.)	–	–	0.0	0.0	70.8	74.0
Market value ($ mil.)	–	–	–	–	–	–
Employees	–	–	–	–	–	950

*Fiscal year change

COLUMBIA SPORTSWEAR CO.   NMS: COLM

14375 Northwest Science Park Drive
Portland, OR 97229
Phone: 503 985-4000
Fax: —
Web: www.columbia.com

CEO: Timothy Boyle
CFO: Jim Swanson
HR: —
FYE: December 31
Type: Public

Columbia Sportswear connects active people with their passions through its portfolio of well-known brands making it a global leader in upscale outdoor active and lifestyle apparel footwear accessories and equipment products. It operates around the world but generates about 65% of sales in US. Its key brands are Columbia Mountain Hard Wear Sorel and prAna. The company was founded as a hat distributor in 1938 in Oregon.

	Annual Growth	12/16	12/17	12/18	12/19	12/20
Sales ($ mil.)	1.3%	2,377.0	2,466.1	2,802.3	3,042.5	2,501.6
Net income ($ mil.)	(13.4%)	191.9	105.1	268.3	330.5	108.0
Market value ($ mil.)	10.6%	3,862.5	4,762.2	5,571.1	6,637.8	5,789.1
Employees	4.8%	6,023	6,188	6,511	8,900	7,275

COLUMBIA ST. MARY'S INC.

2025 E. Newport Ave.
Milwaukee WI 53211
Phone: 414-961-3300
Fax: 414-961-8712
Web: www.columbia-stmarys.com

CEO: —
CFO: —
HR: —
FYE: June 30
Type: Subsidiary

Columbia St. Mary's mission is to provide medical care to residents of southeastern Wisconsin. The company operates a health care network that includes two acute care hospitals — Columbia St. Mary's Milwaukee Campus and Columbia St. Mary's Ozaukee Campus — and two specialty hospital the Sacred Heart Rehabilitation Institute and the Columbia St. Mary's Women's Hospital. Altogether the medical centers have some 660 patient beds. The health system also includes about 60 community urgent care and specialist clinics as well as the Columbia College of Nursing. The company which was founded by the Catholic Sisters of Charity in Milwaukee in 1848 is sponsored by Ascension Health and Columbia Health System.

COLUMBUS MCKINNON CORP. (NY)   NMS: CMCO

205 Crosspoint Parkway
Buffalo, NY 14068
Phone: 716 689-5400
Fax: —
Web: www.columbusmckinnon.com

CEO: David Wilson
CFO: —
HR: Adrienne Williams
FYE: March 31
Type: Public

Columbus McKinnon's machinery products can be extremely uplifting — literally. The company is one of North America's largest producers of equipment for lifting positioning or securing all kinds of large materials. Columbus McKinnon's hoists cranes actuators and steel lifting and rigging tools are used in construction general manufacturing and industrial machinery forestry mining and even wind energy. Well known in the marketplace its brand names include Coffing Duff-Norton Shaw-Box and Yale (made by NACCO). In addition to OEMs the company sells to hardware distributors and merchandiser outlets. About 55% of its revenue comes from domestic customers.

	Annual Growth	03/17	03/18	03/19	03/20	03/21
Sales ($ mil.)	0.5%	637.1	839.4	876.3	809.2	649.6
Net income ($ mil.)	0.3%	9.0	22.1	42.6	59.7	9.1
Market value ($ mil.)	20.7%	595.3	859.6	823.9	599.6	1,265.4
Employees	(3.9%)	3,107	3,328	3,128	2,997	2,651

COMARCO INC.   NBB: CMRO

25541 Commercentre Drive, Suite 250
Lake Forest, CA 92630
Phone: 949 599-7400
Fax: 800 792-0250
Web: www.comarco.com

CEO: Thomas W Lanni
CFO: —
HR: —
FYE: January 31
Type: Public

Comarco develops universal power supplies that charge various portable devices. Operating solely through wholly owned subsidiary Comarco Wireless Technologies the company's flagship product is its ChargeSource line of adapters that recharge consumer electronic devices such as notebooks mobile phones and music players. Comarco sells directly to consumers through its chargesource.com retail website and to notebook OEMs such as Lenovo who brand the accessories and sell them in conjunction with their notebooks. Comarco was spun off from Genge Industries in 1971. Elkhorn Partners Limited Partnership holds a 49% stake in Comarco.

	Annual Growth	01/10	01/11	01/12	01/13	01/14
Sales ($ mil.)	(36.0%)	26.4	28.9	8.1	6.3	4.4
Net income ($ mil.)	—	(7.4)	(6.0)	(5.3)	(5.6)	(2.1)
Market value ($ mil.)	(49.2%)	38.9	5.0	2.3	2.3	2.6
Employees	(59.2%)	36	24	15	10	1

COMBE INCORPORATED

1101 Westchester Ave.
White Plains NY 10604
Phone: 914-694-5454
Fax: 914-461-4402
Web: www.combe.com

CEO: —
CFO: —
HR: —
FYE: June 30
Type: Private

Combe comes to the rescue when a touch of grey or other personal indignity appears. The company's health and beauty aids nix the itch with below-the-belt Vagisil as well as color the head turned salt and pepper (Grecian Formula and Just For Men). Combe also combats loose dentures (sold under the Sea-Bond brand) and tough beards (Lectric Shave). Combe's acquisition of J.B. Williams in 2002 added popular personal care brands Aqua Velva after-shave and Brylcreem hair styling cream among others. Founded in 1949 by Ivan Combe and his wife Mary Elizabeth Deming the family-owned company created Clearasil in 1950 the #1 acne medication (later sold) and other familiar brands. Combe's products are sold worldwide.

COMBIMATRIX CORP   NAS: CBMX

310 Goddard, Suite 150
Irvine, CA 92618
Phone: 949 753-0624
Fax: —
Web: www.combimatrix.com

CEO: Mark McDonough
CFO: Scott R Burell
HR: —
FYE: December 31
Type: Public

CombiMatrix works to untangle the complicated matrix of genetic profiles. The company develops and sells diagnostic testing supplies and provides related laboratory services. Through its CombiMatrix Molecular Diagnostics subsidiary it provides molecular diagnostic testing assays and other genetic analysis products. The tests evaluate a patient's DNA to find genetic irregularities which can then help to diagnose health conditions or predict disease susceptibility. CombiMatrix markets its products and services to physician practices hospitals and other health care centers.

	Annual Growth	12/11	12/12	12/13	12/14	12/15
Sales ($ mil.)	22.0%	4.6	5.4	6.4	8.0	10.1
Net income ($ mil.)	—	(7.6)	(9.5)	(3.9)	(8.7)	(6.6)
Market value ($ mil.)	(22.9%)	1.7	4.5	1.9	1.1	0.6
Employees	9.6%	45	41	43	56	65

COMCAST CORP   NMS: CMCS A

One Comcast Center
Philadelphia, PA 19103-2838
Phone: 215 286-1700
Fax: –
Web: www.comcastcorporation.com

CEO: Brian Roberts
CFO: Michael Cavanagh
HR: –
FYE: December 31
Type: Public

Comcast is a global media and technology company with three primary businesses: Comcast Cable NBCUniversal and Sky. On the content side the company owns NBCUniversal including the NBC TV network and movie studios Universal Pictures and DreamWorks Animation. Cable channels CNBC MSNBC and the USA Network are also under the Comcast tent. Other Comcast properties include the Universal Studios theme parks and Telemundo a leading Spanish-language TV network. Majority of sales were generated in US. The company traces its roots back in 1936 when NBC covered the Berlin Olympics as its first live radio broadcast.

	Annual Growth	12/17	12/18	12/19	12/20	12/21
Sales ($ mil.)	8.3%	84,526.0	94,507.0	108,942.0	103,564.0	116,385.0
Net income ($ mil.)	(11.1%)	22,714.0	11,731.0	13,057.0	10,534.0	14,159.0
Market value ($ mil.)	–	0.0	0.0	0.0	0.0	0.0
Employees	3.6%	164,000	184,000	190,000	168,000	189,000

COMENITY BANK

12921 S VISTA STATION BLV
DRAPER, UT 840202377
Phone: 614-729-4000
Fax: –
Web: www.comenity.com

CEO: –
CFO: –
HR: –
FYE: December 31
Type: Private

World Financial Network National Bank (WFNNB) will take credit for the credit it extends. The company is the private-label and co-branded credit card banking subsidiary of Alliance Data Systems. Along with affiliate World Financial Capital Bank the company underwrites cards on behalf of more than 85 businesses. The company's largest clients include apparel retailers L Brands and Redcats USA. WFNNB oversees about 120 million cardholder accounts and roughly $4 billion in receivables. Private equity giant Blackstone planned to acquire parent Alliance Data Systems for more than $6 billion but that deal was terminated in 2008.

	Annual Growth	12/02	12/03	12/05	12/13	12/14
Assets ($ mil.)	26.8%	–	672.1	332.6	7,453.2	9,149.2
Net income ($ mil.)	14.4%	–	88.8	10.8	350.0	389.3
Market value ($ mil.)	–	–	–	–	–	–
Employees	–	–	–	–	–	200

COMERICA, INC.   NYS: CMA

Comerica Bank Tower, 1717 Main Street, MC 6404
Dallas, TX 75201
Phone: 214 462-6831
Fax: –
Web: www.comerica.com

CEO: Curtis Farmer
CFO: James Herzog
HR: –
FYE: December 31
Type: Public

Comerica is the holding company for Comerica Bank which operates primarily in five US states (Texas California Michigan Arizona & Florida) and in Canada and Mexico. The company is organized into three main segments. The Commercial Bank division is the largest offering commercial loans deposits and capital markets products to small- and middle-market businesses multinational corporations and government clients. The Retail Bank serves consumers while the Wealth Management arm provides fiduciary services investment management and advisory and retirement services. Comerica categorizes its securities portfolio and asset and liability management under an additional Finance segment. The company boasts total assets of more than $88 billion and deposits of about $73 billion.

	Annual Growth	12/17	12/18	12/19	12/20	12/21
Assets ($ mil.)	7.2%	71,567.0	70,818.0	73,402.0	88,129.0	94,616.0
Net income ($ mil.)	12.0%	743.0	1,235.0	1,198.0	474.0	1,168.0
Market value ($ mil.)	0.1%	11,345.0	8,977.0	9,376.9	7,300.2	11,369.9
Employees	(1.8%)	8,190	8,051	7,948	7,870	7,611

COMFORT SYSTEMS USA INC   NYS: FIX

675 Bering Drive, Suite 400
Houston, TX 77057
Phone: 713 830-9600
Fax: 713 830-9696
Web: www.comfortsystemsusa.com

CEO: Brian Lane
CFO: William George
HR: –
FYE: December 31
Type: Public

Comfort Systems USA sells and services commercial HVAC (heating ventilation and air conditioning) systems in apartments health care facilities office buildings manufacturing plants retail centers and schools. Some company locations also offer fire protection and electrical services. More than 45% of its revenue was attributable to installation services in newly constructed facilities and nearly 55% was attributable to renovation expansion maintenance repair and replacement services in existing buildings. Comfort Substantially all of its revenue is generated in the US. Systems was established in 1997.

	Annual Growth	12/16	12/17	12/18	12/19	12/20
Sales ($ mil.)	15.0%	1,634.3	1,787.9	2,182.9	2,615.3	2,856.7
Net income ($ mil.)	23.3%	64.9	55.3	112.9	114.3	150.1
Market value ($ mil.)	12.1%	1,205.1	1,579.6	1,580.7	1,804.0	1,905.7
Employees	9.6%	7,700	8,700	9,900	12,000	11,100

COMMAND SECURITY CORP   ASE: MOC

512 Herndon Parkway, Suite A
Herndon, VA 20170
Phone: 703 464-4735
Fax: –
Web: www.commandsecurity.com

CEO: Larry Parrotte
CFO: N Paul Brost
HR: Victor Lewis
FYE: March 31
Type: Public

Somebody's watching me is a song but also a service thanks to Command Security. The company provides security guards for commercial governmental financial and industrial clients. About half of Command Security's business comes from its aviation services. Although passenger screening services have been taken over by the US government Command Security manages support services such as aircraft and baggage-related security duties and skycap and wheelchair escort services. In addition to general security tasks the company offers recruiting hiring training and supervisory assistance of operating personnel. Federal Express the company's most significant customer accounts for over 20% of total sales.

	Annual Growth	03/14	03/15	03/16	03/17	03/18
Sales ($ mil.)	4.7%	156.7	139.2	133.1	162.2	188.0
Net income ($ mil.)	–	1.1	1.3	(2.7)	(2.3)	(1.4)
Market value ($ mil.)	14.6%	17.9	19.5	23.4	25.7	30.9
Employees	(1.9%)	5,300	4,750	4,300	5,200	4,900

COMMERCE BANCSHARES INC   NMS: CBSH

1000 Walnut
Kansas City, MO 64106
Phone: 816 234-2000
Fax: 816 234-2369
Web: www.commercebank.com

CEO: John Kemper
CFO: Charles Kim
HR: –
FYE: December 31
Type: Public

Commerce Bancshares owns bank branch operator Commerce Bank. The financial institution boasts a network of more than 300 locations across several US states including Missouri Kansas Illinois Oklahoma and Colorado. The bank focuses on retail and commercial banking services such as deposit accounts mortgages loans and credit cards. Commerce Bank also runs a wealth management division that offers asset management trust private banking brokerage and estate planning services and also manages proprietary mutual funds. As part of its operations Commerce Bank has subsidiaries devoted to insurance leasing and private equity investments.

	Annual Growth	12/16	12/17	12/18	12/19	12/20
Assets ($ mil.)	6.4%	25,641.4	24,833.4	25,463.8	26,065.8	32,923.0
Net income ($ mil.)	6.5%	275.4	319.4	433.5	421.2	354.1
Market value ($ mil.)	3.3%	7,124.6	6,881.8	6,947.1	8,373.0	8,097.0
Employees	(1.5%)	4,877	4,857	4,869	4,835	4,588

COMMERCE GROUP CORP.　　　　　　　　　　OTC: CGCO

6001 N. 91st St.　　　　　　　　　　　　CEO: Edward Machulak
Milwaukee WI 53225-1795　　　　　　　　　　　　　CFO: –
Phone: 414-462-5310　　　　　　　　　　　　　　　HR: –
Fax: 414-462-5312　　　　　　　　　　　　FYE: March 31
Web: www.commercegroupcorp.com　　　　　　Type: Public

Commerce Group owns El Salvador's San Sebastian Gold Mine which contains some 1.5 million ounces of gold reserves. Production at the mine has been suspended since 1999 however while the company works to raise money to upgrade the facility's gold-processing equipment. Commerce Group also explores for other gold and silver mining opportunities in El Salvador. In 2009 the Commerce Group filed a motion for arbitration hearings with the government of El Salvador which revoked the company's permits to explore the San Sebastian Gold Mine in 2006. The company has postponed all business activity pending the outcome of the arbitration.

COMMERCIAL BANCSHARES, INC. (OH)　　　　　NBB: CMOH

118 S. Sandusky Avenue　　　　　　　　　　　　　CEO: –
Upper Sandusky, OH 43351　　　　　　　　　　　　CFO: –
Phone: 419 294-5781　　　　　　　　　　　　　　　HR: –
Fax: –　　　　　　　　　　　　　　　　　FYE: December 31
Web: www.csbanking.com　　　　　　　　　　Type: Public

If Commercial Bancshares were planning to produce a commercial it's quite probable the subject would be Commercial Savings Bank. The holding company owns the community bank which serves northwestern Ohio from about 10 branches. The bank offers standard retail and business services including checking and savings accounts certificates of deposit and loans. Commercial loans make up the largest portion of the bank's loan portfolio (more than two-thirds); other offerings include consumer finance loans home equity loans credit card loans and residential mortgages. Fellow Ohio firm First Defiance Financial is buying Commercial Bancshares for $63 million.

	Annual Growth	12/11	12/12	12/13	12/14	12/15
Assets ($ mil.)	4.3%	287.8	301.6	318.0	336.5	341.1
Net income ($ mil.)	5.4%	2.8	2.9	3.1	3.3	3.4
Market value ($ mil.)	13.9%	21.6	22.4	26.9	32.6	36.3
Employees	(1.5%)	104	102	103	100	98

COMMERCIAL METALS CO.　　　　　　　　　　NYS: CMC

6565 North MacArthur Blvd.　　　　　　　　CEO: Barbara Smith
Irving, TX 75039　　　　　　　　　　　　CFO: Paul Lawrence
Phone: 214 689-4300　　　　　　　　　　HR: Jennifer Durbin
Fax: 214 689-5886　　　　　　　　　　　　FYE: August 31
Web: www.cmc.com　　　　　　　　　　　　Type: Public

Commercial Metals (CMC) manufactures recycles and fabricates steel and metal products related materials and services through a network of facilities that includes seven electric arc furnace (EAF) mini mills two EAF micro mills two rerolling mill steel fabrication and processing plants construction-related product warehouses and metal recycling facilities in the US and Poland. CMC operates through two reportable segments: North America and Europe. The US accounts for nearly 80% of revenue. CMC traces its roots back to 1915 where Moses Feldman established his first scrap operations in Dallas.

	Annual Growth	08/17	08/18	08/19	08/20	08/21
Sales ($ mil.)	10.2%	4,569.7	4,643.7	5,829.0	5,476.5	6,729.8
Net income ($ mil.)	72.8%	46.3	138.5	198.1	279.5	412.9
Market value ($ mil.)	14.6%	2,277.9	2,604.7	1,889.6	2,516.6	3,933.5
Employees	6.0%	8,797	8,900	11,524	11,297	11,089

COMMERCIAL NATIONAL FINANCIAL CORP. (PA)　　NBB: CNAF

900 Ligonier Street　　　　　　　　　　　　CEO: Gregg Hunter
Latrobe, PA 15650　　　　　　　　　　　CFO: Thomas Watters
Phone: 724 539-3501　　　　　　　　　　HR: Charles Taylor
Fax: 724 539-1137　　　　　　　　　　　FYE: December 31
Web: www.cnbthebank.com　　　　　　　　Type: Public

Commercial National Financial is the holding company for Commercial Bank & Trust of PA which serves individuals and local businesses through more than five branches in western Pennsylvania's Westmoreland County. Founded in 1934 the bank offers standard deposit services like checking and savings accounts money market investments CDs and IRAs as well as trust and asset management services. Commercial Bank & Trust of PA's loan portfolio consists mostly of residential mortgages and commercial mortgages in addition to business construction consumer and municipal loans.

	Annual Growth	12/17	12/18	12/19	12/20	12/21
Assets ($ mil.)	5.2%	386.0	419.6	419.6	425.4	472.0
Net income ($ mil.)	(8.1%)	6.9	4.3	4.7	5.7	4.9
Market value ($ mil.)	(5.0%)	63.7	60.2	58.4	47.2	51.8
Employees	(6.9%)	99	98	46	80	–

COMMERCIAL VEHICLE GROUP INC　　　　　　　NMS: CVGI

7800 Walton Parkway　　　　　　　　　　　CEO: Harold Bevis
New Albany, OH 43054　　　　　　　　CFO: Christopher Bohnert
Phone: 614 289-5360　　　　　　　　　　HR: Kristin Mathers
Fax: –　　　　　　　　　　　　　　　　　FYE: December 31
Web: www.cvgrp.com　　　　　　　　　　　Type: Public

Commercial Vehicle Group (CVG) is a global provider of components and assemblies into two primary end markets ? the global vehicle market and the US technology integrator markets. Products include static and suspension seat systems interior trim (instrument panels door panels headliners) mirrors wiper systems and controls and switches. Its customers have included heavy-duty truck manufacturers such as AB Volvo and Daimler. Besides truck manufacturers CVG sells its electrical systems electrical wire harnesses electro-mechanical assemblies for warehouses electro-mechanical cable assemblies for the agricultural mining and construction equipment among others. CVG generates some three-quarters of total sales from its home country the US.

	Annual Growth	12/16	12/17	12/18	12/19	12/20
Sales ($ mil.)	2.0%	662.1	755.2	897.7	901.2	717.7
Net income ($ mil.)	–	6.8	(1.7)	44.5	15.8	(37.0)
Market value ($ mil.)	11.8%	172.8	334.1	178.1	198.4	270.3
Employees	2.5%	7,000	8,250	8,355	7,347	7,740

COMMONSPIRIT HEALTH

444 W LAKE ST STE 2500　　　　　　　　　　CEO: Lloyd Dean
CHICAGO, IL 606060097　　　　　　　　　CFO: Dan Morissette
Phone: 312-741-7000　　　　　　　　　　　　　　　HR: –
Fax: –　　　　　　　　　　　　　　　　　　　FYE: June 30
Web: www.commonspirit.org　　　　　　　　Type: Private

Formed in 2019 through the merger of Catholic hospital systems Catholic Health Initiatives and Dignity Health CommonSpirit Health is a not-for-profit organization with more than 140 hospitals in about 20 states. Its hospitals range from large urban medical centers (many with educational and research programs) to small hospitals in rural areas. The company also operates clinics long-term care assisted-living and senior residential facilities (totaling more than 1500 care sites) and provides home-based care services.

	Annual Growth	06/16	06/17	06/18	06/19	06/21
Sales ($ mil.)	20.9%	–	15,547.5	14,982.1	7,170.0	33,253.0
Net income ($ mil.)	183.6%	–	128.4	222.1	9,008.0	8,303.0
Market value ($ mil.)	–	–	–	–	–	–
Employees	–	–	–	–	–	72,500

COMMUNICATIONS SYSTEMS, INC. NMS: JCS

10900 Red Circle Drive
Minnetonka, MN 55343
Phone: 952 996-1674
Fax: –
Web: www.commsystems.com

CEO: Roger Lacey
CFO: Mark Fandrich
HR: –
FYE: December 31
Type: Public

Aptly named Communications Systems makes connectors and wiring systems for telecommunications networks. The company operates through subsidiaries. Its Suttle and Austin Taylor units make connectors adapters and other devices for voice data and video communications. Transition Networks makes converters that move data between copper wire and fiber-optic networks LAN switches and print servers. JDL Technologies provides schools and businesses with telecom network development services and software. Communications Systems sells directly and through distributors. Major customers include AT&T and Verizon.

	Annual Growth	12/16	12/17	12/18	12/19	12/20
Sales ($ mil.)	(19.1%)	99.4	82.3	65.8	50.9	42.6
Net income ($ mil.)	–	(8.1)	(11.8)	(6.8)	6.5	(0.2)
Market value ($ mil.)	(0.3%)	43.2	33.2	18.9	57.5	42.6
Employees	(21.6%)	398	291	241	203	150

COMMUNICATIONS TEST DESIGN, INC.

1373 ENTERPRISE DR
WEST CHESTER, PA 193805959
Phone: 610-436-5203
Fax: –

CEO: –
CFO: –
HR: –
FYE: December 31
Type: Private

Communications Test Design (CTDI) repairs installs tests and manufactures telecommunications equipment. The company's main business is providing repair and maintenance services to wireless and wireline carriers and cable companies as well as equipment makers such as Alcatel Lucent and Cisco. It offers warehousing and distribution services product testing and equipment installation — from laying cable to integrating customer premise equipment. CTDI also makes a line of broadband switching and access equipment and provides contract manufacturing services. The company was founded in 1975 by chairman and CEO Jerry Parsons his father Donald and brother Dick. CTDI is owned and led by the Parsons family.

	Annual Growth	12/05	12/06	12/07	12/08	12/09
Sales ($ mil.)	–	–	–	(1,551.2)	761.9	740.5
Net income ($ mil.)	27743.5%	–	–	0.0	15.5	24.0
Market value ($ mil.)	–	–	–	–	–	–
Employees	–	–	–	–	–	3,750

COMMUNICATIONS WORKERS OF AMERICA, AFL-CIO, CLC

501 3RD ST NW
WASHINGTON, DC 200012760
Phone: 202-434-1100
Fax: –
Web: www.cwa-union.org

CEO: –
CFO: –
HR: –
FYE: May 31
Type: Private

CWA knows how to get its message across. Communications Workers of America is a labor union representing more than 700000 employees in the communications and media industries. Members work in a variety of sectors including telecommunications journalism publishing manufacturing and customer service. With about 1200 locals across the US Canada and Puerto Rico CWA is one of the most geographically diverse unions. It holds more than 2000 collective bargaining agreements guaranteeing wages benefits and good working conditions for members. The group is affiliated with the AFL-CIO the Canadian Labour Congress and Union Network International.

	Annual Growth	05/09	05/10	05/11	05/13	05/16
Sales ($ mil.)	0.8%	–	156.7	155.3	146.0	164.8
Net income ($ mil.)	–	–	9.2	2.0	(4.2)	(13.5)
Market value ($ mil.)	–	–	–	–	–	–
Employees	–	–	–	–	–	510

COMMUNITY ASPHALT CORP.

9675 NW 117TH AVE STE 108
MEDLEY, FL 331781244
Phone: 305-884-9444
Fax: –
Web: www.cacorp.net

CEO: Ashok Patel
CFO: Miren Sotomayor
HR: –
FYE: December 31
Type: Private

Community Asphalt provides paving services for the road more traveled. The company's services include grading and paving pavement milling surveying excavation on- and off-road hauling drainage utilities base finishing and highway sweeping. It also provides engineering contracting and design/build services; projects include parking lots industrial and retail complexes auto race tracks and airport runways. Formed in 1980 Community Asphalt has three asphalt plants in southeastern Florida. It also operates a limestone quarry and a fleet of dump trucks. In 2006 Community Asphalt and Spain's Obrasc n Huarte Lain (OHL) made a stock purchase agreement which gave OHL a controlling interest in the company.

	Annual Growth	12/08	12/09	12/10	12/11	12/12
Sales ($ mil.)	(14.1%)	–	–	330.7	260.8	243.9
Net income ($ mil.)	(70.6%)	–	–	27.7	3.1	2.4
Market value ($ mil.)	–	–	–	–	–	–
Employees	–	–	–	–	–	640

COMMUNITY BANCORP. (DERBY, VT) NBB: CMTV

4811 U.S. Route 5
Derby, VT 05829
Phone: 802 334-7915
Fax: –
Web: www.communitybancorpvt.com

CEO: Kathryn Austin
CFO: Louise Bonvechio
HR: –
FYE: December 31
Type: Public

Winters may be cold in Vermont but Community Bancorp. hopes to warm the hearts of its customers with its hometown banking services. It is the holding company for Community National Bank which has been serving Vermont since 1851. Through nearly 20 branches the bank offers such products and services as checking and savings accounts CDs IRAs residential and commercial mortgages and business consumer and other loans. In conjunction with two other regional banks the company is part of Community Financial Services Group which offers trust and investment planning services. At the end of 2007 Community Bancorp. acquired LyndonBank which added about a half-dozen branches to its network.

	Annual Growth	12/16	12/17	12/18	12/19	12/20
Assets ($ mil.)	9.5%	637.7	667.0	720.3	738.0	918.2
Net income ($ mil.)	18.3%	5.5	6.2	8.4	8.8	10.8
Market value ($ mil.)	(1.0%)	82.4	98.4	87.7	85.1	79.0
Employees	0.2%	135	138	135	136	136

COMMUNITY BANK SHARES OF INDIANA, INC. NAS: CBIN

101 W. Spring Street
New Albany, IN 47150
Phone: 812 944-2224
Fax: –
Web: www.yourcommunitybank.com

CEO: –
CFO: –
HR: –
FYE: December 31
Type: Public

Community Bank Shares of Indiana is the holding company for Your Community Bank and Scott County State Bank. The banks serve customers from about 20 locations in southern Indiana and Louisville Kentucky. Both banks offer deposit products such as checking money market and savings accounts as well as IRAs and CDs. Their lending activities center on commercial mortgages and residential real estate loans (each around 25% of the company's loan portfolio) but also include business construction and consumer (including home equity home improvement and auto) loans and credit cards. Community Bank Shares of Indiana is focused on organic growth within existing markets.

	Annual Growth	12/09	12/10	12/11	12/12	12/13
Assets ($ mil.)	0.8%	819.2	801.5	797.4	819.5	846.7
Net income ($ mil.)	–	(22.0)	7.0	7.4	7.7	8.7
Market value ($ mil.)	31.3%	22.2	32.7	31.9	44.1	65.9
Employees	0.4%	206	205	201	202	209

COMMUNITY BANK SYSTEM INC
NYS: CBU

5790 Widewaters Parkway
DeWitt, NY 13214-1883
Phone: 315 445-2282
Fax: –
Web: www.communitybankna.com

CEO: Mark Tryniski
CFO: Joseph Sutaris
HR: –
FYE: December 31
Type: Public

Community Bank System is right up front about what it is. The holding company owns Community Bank which operates about 195 branches across upstate New York and northeastern Pennsylvania where it operates as First Liberty Bank and Trust. Focusing on small underserved towns and non-urban markets the bank offers standard products and services such as checking and savings accounts certificates of deposit and loans and mortgages to consumer business and government clients. Boasting over $11.0 billion in assets the bank's loan portfolio consists of mostly business loans residential mortgages and consumer loans. Community Bank System's subsidiaries offer employee benefit services wealth management and insurance products and services.

	Annual Growth	12/16	12/17	12/18	12/19	12/20
Assets ($ mil.)	12.6%	8,666.4	10,746.2	10,607.3	11,410.3	13,931.1
Net income ($ mil.)	12.2%	103.8	150.7	168.6	169.1	164.7
Market value ($ mil.)	0.2%	3,311.5	2,880.6	3,124.5	3,801.9	3,339.4
Employees	5.1%	2,499	2,874	2,933	3,038	3,047

COMMUNITY BANKERS TRUST CORP
NAS: ESXB

9954 Mayland Drive, Suite 2100
Richmond, VA 23233
Phone: 804 934-9999
Fax: –
Web: www.cbtrustcorp.com

CEO: Rex L Smith III
CFO: Bruce E Thomas
HR: –
FYE: December 31
Type: Public

Community Bankers Trust Corporation formerly Community Bankers Acquisition is the holding company for the Bank of Essex and TransCommunity Bank. Additional divisions of TransCommunity operate as Bank of Goochland Bank of Powhatan Bank of Louisa and Bank of Rockbridge. The company grew in 2008 when it merged with former bank holding companies TransCommunity Financial and BOE Financial Services of Virginia. The company now includes about a dozen bank branches west and north of Richmond Virginia. Subsidiaries offer securities and insurance products. Community Bankers Trust expanded into Georgia when it acquired the branches and deposits of The Community Bank which was the 20th bank to fail in 2008.

	Annual Growth	12/15	12/16	12/17	12/18	12/19
Assets ($ mil.)	4.9%	1,180.6	1,249.8	1,336.2	1,393.2	1,430.8
Net income ($ mil.)	–	(2.5)	9.9	7.2	13.7	15.7
Market value ($ mil.)	13.4%	120.4	162.6	182.7	161.9	199.1
Employees	0.7%	236	232	264	255	243

COMMUNITY CAPITAL BANCSHARES INC
NBB: ALBY

2815 Meredyth Drive, P.O. Drawer 71269
Albany, GA 31708-1269
Phone: 229 446-2265
Fax: 229 446-7030
Web: www.comcapbancshares.com

CEO: James Flatt
CFO: David Baranko
HR: –
FYE: December 31
Type: Public

Community Capital Bancshares has taken hometown to heart. The bank holding company owns Albany Bank & Trust a community bank serving southwestern Georgia through three branches. It also includes AB&T National Bank which operates two branches in Alabama. The banks offer standard deposit products and services including checking and savings accounts money market accounts CDs and IRAs. The company mainly uses these deposits to fund residential and commercial construction loans and mortgages as well as business and consumer loans. Real estate loans comprise about 80% of the company's loan book. The company plans to combine all of its banks under the AB&T National Bank name.

	Annual Growth	12/16	12/17	12/18	12/19	12/20
Assets ($ mil.)	16.9%	151.2	180.3	194.2	195.6	281.8
Net income ($ mil.)	29.3%	0.6	(1.4)	1.2	1.5	1.8
Market value ($ mil.)	63.2%	2.0	3.3	11.8	14.5	14.2
Employees	–	–	–	–	–	–

COMMUNITY CHOICE FINANCIAL INC
NL:

6785 Bobcat Way, Suite 200
Dublin, OH 43016
Phone: 888 513-9395
Fax: –
Web: www.ccfi.com

CEO: Ted Saunders
CFO: Michael Durbin
HR: –
FYE: December 31
Type: Public

Dire Straits may have gotten their money for nothing but the rest of us sometimes need to hit up payday lenders like Community Choice Financial. Formed in 2011 the company issues unsecured short-term consumer loans of up to $5000 charging fees from $8 to $15 per $100 borrowed in addition to interest rates which vary by state but typically range from 60% to 120% APR. Its stores operated under the CheckSmart and California Check Cashing Stores brands also issue title loans prepaid MasterCard debit cards and offer check cashing money transfers bill payments and money orders in 9 US states.

	Annual Growth	12/13	12/14	12/15	12/16	12/17
Sales ($ mil.)	(4.6%)	439.2	518.3	527.4	402.3	364.1
Net income ($ mil.)	–	8.2	(51.8)	(70.0)	(1.5)	(180.9)
Market value ($ mil.)	–	–	–	–	–	–
Employees	(5.3%)	3,523	3,831	3,356	2,819	2,829

COMMUNITY FINANCIAL CORP (THE)
NAS: TCFC

3035 Leonardtown Road
Waldorf, MD 20601
Phone: 301 645-5601
Fax: –
Web: www.cbtc.com

CEO: William Pasenelli
CFO: Todd Capitani
HR: –
FYE: December 31
Type: Public

Tri-County Financial is trying to create some interest in the Old Line State. The financial institution is the holding company for Community Bank of Tri-County which operates about 10 branches in Calvert Charles and St. Mary's counties in southern Maryland. The bank which was first organized as a savings and loan association in 1950 offers standard retail products and services including checking and savings accounts IRAs and CDs. It uses funds from deposits to write a variety of loans including commercial mortgages (about 40% of its loan book) residential mortgages and business loans. Home equity construction equipment and consumer loans round out its loan portfolio.

	Annual Growth	12/16	12/17	12/18	12/19	12/20
Assets ($ mil.)	11.0%	1,334.3	1,406.0	1,689.2	1,797.5	2,026.4
Net income ($ mil.)	21.8%	7.3	7.2	11.2	15.3	16.1
Market value ($ mil.)	(2.3%)	171.2	226.1	172.6	210.0	156.3
Employees	4.2%	162	165	189	194	191

COMMUNITY FIRST BANCORPORATION
OTC: CFOK

449 Hwy. 123 Bypass
Seneca SC 29678
Phone: 864-886-0206
Fax: 864-886-0912
Web: www.c1stbank.com

CEO: –
CFO: –
HR: –
FYE: December 31
Type: Public

Community First Bancorporation puts financial matters first in the northwestern corner of South Carolina. The holding company owns Community First Bank which operates more than five branches in Oconee and Anderson counties. The commercial bank offers traditional deposit products such as checking and savings accounts CDs and IRAs. Deposit funds are primarily used to originate single- to four-family mortgages and commercial mortgages. The bank also writes construction consumer and business loans. In late 2011 Community First Bancorporation bought the single-branch Bank of Westminster which was merged with Community First Bank's existing location in Westminster South Carolina.

COMMUNITY HEALTH GROUP

2420 FENTON ST 200
CHULA VISTA, CA 919143516
Phone: 619-422-0422
Fax: -
Web: www.chgsd.com

CEO: Norma A Diaz
CFO: William Rice
HR: -
FYE: December 31
Type: Private

Community Health Group is the oldest and one of the largest locally based HMOs in San Diego. Founded in 1982 the not-for-profit HMO provides health insurance products and related services to more than 100000 members. Community Health Group's product offerings include its California's Healthy Families program which provides low-cost health dental and vision coverage to children. The company also provides other managed care services to California communities such as Medi-Cal low-income coverage and Medicare Advantage Special Needs plans as well as third-party administration services.

	Annual Growth	12/02	12/03	12/05	12/09	12/12
Sales ($ mil.)	(8.0%)	-	110.2	79.3	40.0	52.2
Net income ($ mil.)	19.5%	-	-	1.2	2.2	4.3
Market value ($ mil.)	-	-	-	-	-	-
Employees	-	-	-	-	-	140

COMMUNITY HEALTH NETWORK, INC.

1500 N RITTER AVE
INDIANAPOLIS, IN 462193027
Phone: 317-355-1411
Fax: -
Web: www.ecommunity.com

CEO: -
CFO: Kyle Fisher
HR: -
FYE: December 31
Type: Private

As a non-profit health system with more than 200 sites of care and affiliates throughout Central Indiana Community's full continuum of care integrates hundreds of physicians specialty and acute care hospitals surgery centers home care services MedChecks behavioral health and employer health services. Its state-of-the-art emergency departments are open 24/7 to treat emergency medical conditions including stroke head trauma heart attack chest pain broken bones wounds and more. Community Health has partnership with Marian University's College of Osteopathic Medicine. Community Health has been deeply committed to the communities it serves since opening its first hospital Community Hospital East in 1956.

	Annual Growth	12/11	12/12	12/13	12/14	12/19
Sales ($ mil.)	(1.1%)	-	-	1,763.4	1,942.1	1,645.9
Net income ($ mil.)	15.0%	-	-	179.1	(0.9)	413.4
Market value ($ mil.)	-	-	-	-	-	-
Employees	-	-	-	-	-	5,000

COMMUNITY HEALTH SYSTEMS, INC.   NYS: CYH

4000 Meridian Boulevard
Franklin, TN 37067
Phone: 615 465-7000
Fax: -
Web: www.chs.net

CEO: -
CFO: Kevin Hammons
HR: Beverly Ray
FYE: December 31
Type: Public

Community Health Systems (CHS) owns or leases about 90 hospitals in around 15 states. Its hospitals (which house roughly 14110 beds) is comprised of over 85 general acute care hospitals and two stand-alone rehabilitation or psychiatric hospitals. Facilities supports a wide array of diagnostic medical and surgical services in an outpatient setting for the nearby hospital. CHS also operates a couple of stand-alone rehabilitation or psychiatric facilities. The CHS network also includes physician practices urgent care clinics surgery centers imaging and diagnostic centers and internal medicine clinics. The company was founded in 1986 and were incorporated in 1996.

	Annual Growth	12/17	12/18	12/19	12/20	12/21
Sales ($ mil.)	(5.3%)	15,353.0	14,155.0	13,210.0	11,789.0	12,368.0
Net income ($ mil.)	-	(2,459.0)	(788.0)	(675.0)	511.0	230.0
Market value ($ mil.)	33.0%	562.9	372.7	383.2	981.8	1,758.9
Employees	(8.7%)	95,000	87,000	80,000	70,000	66,000

COMMUNITY HOSPITAL OF ANDERSON AND MADISON COUNTY, INCORPORATED

1515 N MADISON AVE
ANDERSON, IN 460113453
Phone: 765-298-4242
Fax: -
Web: www.communityanderson.com

CEO: Beth Tharp
CFO: -
HR: -
FYE: December 31
Type: Private

The folks of Madison County Indiana needn't race south to Indianapolis to find medical care. Community Hospital Anderson is an acute care facility with some 200 beds. Departments and services include a sleep analysis lab ECG (electrocardiogram) tests for cardiopulmonary conditions and specialized treatment for cancer and diabetes among other conditions. Community Hospital Anderson operates four intermediate and supervised care facilities in the area. The hospital is part of Community Hospitals of Indiana (also known as Community Health Network) a not-for-profit health care system that serves the health care needs of patients in Indiana.

	Annual Growth	12/12	12/13	12/14	12/15	12/19
Sales ($ mil.)	5.9%	-	152.0	159.2	167.5	214.0
Net income ($ mil.)	-	-	35.4	25.7	23.8	(10.2)
Market value ($ mil.)	-	-	-	-	-	-
Employees	-	-	-	-	-	1,250

COMMUNITY HOSPITAL OF SAN BERNARDINO

1805 MEDICAL CENTER DR
SAN BERNARDINO, CA 924111217
Phone: 909-887-6333
Fax: -
Web: www.dignityhealth.org

CEO: -
CFO: Ed Sorenson
HR: Jon Webb
FYE: June 30
Type: Private

You really don't have to feel deserted in the desert: CHSB will make you realize you aren't alone when you're illin'. The Community Hospital of San Bernardino is an acute care facility with more than 320 beds. Special health care services available at the hospital include pediatric and adult behavioral health neurological care surgery laboratory testing a long-term care unit for children and home health care. Serving the city and its surrounding areas since 1908 Community Hospital of San Bernardino is a member of Catholic Healthcare West.

	Annual Growth	06/10	06/11	06/12	06/13	06/16
Sales ($ mil.)	8.2%	-	-	-	193.2	244.8
Net income ($ mil.)	-	-	-	-	(22.5)	(11.0)
Market value ($ mil.)	-	-	-	-	-	-
Employees	-	-	-	-	-	1,400

COMMUNITY HOSPITAL OF THE MONTEREY PENINSULA

23625 HOLMAN HWY
MONTEREY, CA 939405902
Phone: 831-624-5311
Fax: -
Web: www.montagehealth.org

CEO: Steven J Packer
CFO: Laura Zehm
HR: -
FYE: December 31
Type: Private

Community Hospital of the Monterey Peninsula has a sunny disposition when it comes to medical care. The not-for-profit health care facility provides general medical and surgical services to residents of Monterey California. It has about 235 acute care and skilled nursing beds and offers specialty services including cardiac and cancer care obstetrics orthopedics and rehabilitation. In addition to its main facility the hospital operates several ancillary centers including a mental health clinic an inpatient hospice medical laboratory branches and several outpatient centers offering diagnostic imaging diabetes care and other services.

	Annual Growth	12/11	12/12	12/15	12/16	12/19
Sales ($ mil.)	6.6%	-	442.9	560.7	526.9	693.6
Net income ($ mil.)	(0.7%)	-	81.4	66.7	72.0	77.6
Market value ($ mil.)	-	-	-	-	-	-
Employees	-	-	-	-	-	1,947

COMMUNITY HOSPITALS OF CENTRAL CALIFORNIA

2823 FRESNO ST
FRESNO, CA 937211324
Phone: 559-459-6000
Fax: –
Web: www.communitymedical.org

CEO: Tim A Joslin
CFO: Joseph Nowicki
HR: Ginny R Burdick
FYE: August 31
Type: Private

Community Medical Centers helps California's San Joaquin Valley stay healthy. The not-for-profit system operates four hospitals ? along with nursing homes and free-standing outpatient facilities ? in the greater Fresno area. Its Community Regional Medical Center is a roughly 685-bed academic hospital that provides advanced care in areas such as trauma cardiac care neuroscience and orthopedics. Clovis Community Medical Center (nearly 210 beds) provides general medical-surgical care with expertise in women's health and bariatric surgery. Specialty hospitals Fresno Heart & Surgical Hospital and Community Behavioral Health Center (the largest psychiatric care facility in the area) each have about 60 beds.

	Annual Growth	06/09	06/10*	08/18	08/19	08/20
Sales ($ mil.)	49.4%	–	33.5	1,667.6	1,813.2	1,857.2
Net income ($ mil.)	64.0%	–	0.7	108.5	117.7	100.4
Market value ($ mil.)	–	–	–	–	–	–
Employees	–	–	–	–	–	6,200

*Fiscal year change

COMMUNITY INVESTORS BANCORP, INC   NBB: CIBN

119 South Sandusky Avenue, P.O. Box 749
Bucyrus, OH 44820
Phone: 419 562 7055
Fax: 419 562 5516
Web: www.ffcb.com

CEO: Phillip Gerber
CFO: Thomas Kalb
HR: –
FYE: June 30
Type: Public

You won't find these investors on Wall Street or in Omaha. You'll find Community Investors Bancorp the holding company for First Federal Community Bank of Bucyrus in north central Ohio's Crawford County. The bank provides traditional deposit options like CDs checking and savings accounts money market accounts and NOW accounts. First Federal's lending activities include residential and non-residential real estate mortgages commercial loans construction loans and land loans. Its consumer loan options include automobile and home equity loans. Community Investors Bancorp plans to become private after a reverse stock split transaction.

	Annual Growth	06/02	06/03	06/04	06/16	06/17
Assets ($ mil.)	1.2%	119.8	122.7	121.9	140.3	143.4
Net income ($ mil.)	(6.3%)	1.2	1.1	0.9	0.9	0.5
Market value ($ mil.)	2.5%	8.3	10.3	11.7	10.9	12.0
Employees	14.6%	32	36	42	–	–

COMMUNITY MEDICAL CENTER, INC.

99 ROUTE 37 W
TOMS RIVER, NJ 087556423
Phone: 732-557-8000
Fax: –
Web: www.rwjbh.org

CEO: –
CFO: Mark Ostrander
HR: –
FYE: December 31
Type: Private

When Garden Staters in Ocean County get sick they look to the community for help. Community Medical Center (CMC) that is. Part of the Saint Barnabas Health Care System CMC is a full-service 590-bed acute care hospital that provides a range of health services including primary and emergency care obstetrics and maternity care pediatrics diabetes and cancer treatment surgery senior care and rehabilitative care. CMC's community wellness centers provide ambulatory health services diagnostic services and primary care as well as prevention and wellness education to the communities they serve. CMC is one of New Jersey's largest non-teaching hospitals.

	Annual Growth	12/14	12/15	12/17	12/18	12/19
Sales ($ mil.)	1.5%	–	372.7	380.7	391.7	395.2
Net income ($ mil.)	–	–	33.5	25.8	19.4	(13.4)
Market value ($ mil.)	–	–	–	–	–	–
Employees	–	–	–	–	–	2,500

COMMUNITY SHORES BANK CORP   NBB: CSHB

1030 W. Norton Avenue
Muskegon, MI 49441
Phone: 231 780-1800
Fax: –
Web: www.communityshores.com

CEO: –
CFO: –
HR: –
FYE: December 31
Type: Public

Community Shores Bank Corporation is the holding company for Community Shores Bank which has about five branches that serve western Michigan's Muskegon and Ottawa counties. The bank provides deposit services such as checking and savings accounts money market accounts health savings accounts CDs and IRAs. Commercial operating and real estate loans to area businesses make up approximately three-quarters of the company's loan portfolio which also includes residential real estate consumer and construction loans. The bank also offers investment products and services through an agreement with a third-party provider. The bank was founded in 1999.

	Annual Growth	12/14	12/15	12/16	12/17	12/18
Assets ($ mil.)	0.1%	184.7	181.0	191.4	184.7	185.1
Net income ($ mil.)	(32.4%)	4.3	(0.4)	0.2	(1.0)	0.9
Market value ($ mil.)	15.1%	6.2	9.0	9.5	12.3	10.9
Employees	(2.0%)	77	72	74	–	–

COMMUNITY TRUST BANCORP, INC.   NMS: CTBI

346 North Mayo Trail, P.O. Box 2947
Pikeville, KY 41502
Phone: 606 432-1414
Fax: –
Web: www.ctbi.com

CEO: Jean Hale
CFO: Kevin Stumbo
HR: –
FYE: December 31
Type: Public

Community Trust Bancorp is the holding company for Community Trust Bank one of the largest Kentucky-based banks. It operates 70-plus branches throughout the state as well as in northeastern Tennessee and southern West Virginia. The bank offers standard services to area businesses and individuals including checking and savings accounts credit cards and CDs. Loans secured by commercial properties and other real estate account for nearly 70% of the bank's portfolio which also includes business consumer and construction loans. Subsidiary Community Trust and Investment Company provides trust estate retirement brokerage and insurance services through a handful of offices in Kentucky and Tennessee.

	Annual Growth	12/16	12/17	12/18	12/19	12/20
Assets ($ mil.)	6.9%	3,932.2	4,136.2	4,201.6	4,366.0	5,139.1
Net income ($ mil.)	5.9%	47.3	51.5	59.2	64.5	59.5
Market value ($ mil.)	(7.0%)	883.4	838.9	705.5	830.7	659.9
Employees	0.1%	996	990	978	1,000	998

COMMUNITY WEST BANCSHARES   NMS: CWBC

445 Pine Avenue
Goleta, CA 93117
Phone: 805 692-5821
Fax: 805 692-5835
Web: www.communitywest.com

CEO: Martin Plourd
CFO: Richard Pimentel
HR: Jennifer Ofner
FYE: December 31
Type: Public

Community West Bancshares is the holding company for Community West Bank which serves individuals and small to midsized businesses through five branches along California's Central Coast. Services include checking and savings accounts and CDs as well as health savings accounts. Approximately 40% of the bank's loan portfolio is secured by manufactured housing loans; real estate mortgages account for more than 30%. A preferred Small Business Administration lender Community West also writes SBA loans through offices in about a dozen other states.

	Annual Growth	12/16	12/17	12/18	12/19	12/20
Assets ($ mil.)	8.2%	710.6	833.3	877.3	913.9	975.4
Net income ($ mil.)	12.1%	5.2	4.9	7.4	8.0	8.2
Market value ($ mil.)	(0.5%)	78.3	90.2	85.0	94.1	76.9
Employees	1.6%	120	128	139	133	128

COMMUNITYONE BANCORP   NAS: COB

1017 E. Morehead Street
Charlotte, NC 28204
Phone: 336 626-8300
Fax: –
Web: www.community1.com

CEO: –
CFO: –
HR: –
FYE: December 31
Type: Public

CommunityOne Bancorp (formerly FNB United) is the holding company for CommunityOne Bank (formerly First National Bank and Trust) which has about 50 branches in North Carolina. The bank's offerings include checking savings and money market accounts CDs IRAs credit cards and trust services. It concentrates on real estate lending: Commercial mortgages account for more than 35% of the company's loan portfolio while residential mortgages and construction loans are about 25% apiece. The bank also makes business and consumer loans. Subsidiary Dover Mortgage Company originates mortgages for sale into the secondary market through about five loan production offices in its home state.

	Annual Growth	12/10	12/11	12/12	12/13	12/14
Assets ($ mil.)	3.6%	1,921.3	2,409.1	2,151.6	1,985.0	2,215.5
Net income ($ mil.)	–	(112.9)	(137.3)	(40.0)	(1.5)	150.5
Market value ($ mil.)	143.3%	7.9	309.6	280.6	308.4	276.9
Employees	2.1%	526	609	629	581	571

COMMVAULT SYSTEMS INC   NMS: CVLT

1 Commvault Way
Tinton Falls, NJ 07724
Phone: 732 870-4000
Fax: –
Web: www.commvault.com

CEO: Sanjay Mirchandani
CFO: Brian Carolan
HR: –
FYE: March 31
Type: Public

Commvault Systems wants to have a lock on data management. The company provides software including cloud-based programs that customers use to store and manage enterprise data. Its Commvault Data Platform handles resource management backup archiving data replication disaster recovery and search. Altogether Commvault counts more than 26000 customers that come from industries such as financial services health care manufacturing and utilities as well as from the public sector. Commvault's strategic partners include systems integrators and professional services firms distributors and resellers and technology providers. Nearly 60% of its revenue comes from US customers.

	Annual Growth	03/17	03/18	03/19	03/20	03/21
Sales ($ mil.)	2.7%	650.5	699.4	711.0	670.9	723.5
Net income ($ mil.)	–	0.5	(61.9)	3.6	(5.6)	(31.0)
Market value ($ mil.)	6.2%	2,361.3	2,658.8	3,009.2	1,881.6	2,998.1
Employees	0.1%	2,656	2,839	2,559	2,533	2,671

COMP-VIEW INC.

10035 SW ARCTIC DR
BEAVERTON, OR 97005-4181
Phone: 503-641-8439
Fax: –
Web: www.compviewmedical.com

CEO: –
CFO: –
HR: –
FYE: December 31
Type: Private

CompView rents and sells audio-visual computer peripherals (primarily projectors and conferencing systems) to corporations educational organizations and government agencies; it also provides system installation and integration services. Its CompView Medical subsidiary specializes in providing audio-visual equipment for medical applications such as projectors for surgical operating rooms. CompView has facilities in California Minnesota Oregon Utah and Washington state. The company was started in 1987 by Paul White who is the majority owner.

	Annual Growth	12/98	12/99	12/00	12/01	12/11
Sales ($ mil.)	5.9%	–	28.2	38.9	36.3	56.0
Net income ($ mil.)	2.7%	–	0.6	(0.1)	0.1	0.9
Market value ($ mil.)	–	–	–	–	–	–
Employees	–	–	–	–	–	129

COMPASS DIVERSIFIED   NYS: CODI

301 Riverside Avenue, Second Floor
Westport, CT 06880
Phone: 203 221-1703
Fax: –
Web: www.compassdiversifiedholdings.com

CEO: Elias Sabo
CFO: Ryan Faulkingham
HR: –
FYE: December 31
Type: Public

Compass Diversified Holdings helps niche companies navigate their way toward profitability. The holding company owns controlling stakes in and manages promising middle-market businesses throughout North America. Its strategy is two-fold: help its portfolio firms grow and increase their profits and increase the size of its own portfolio. Compass invests in niche businesses across a variety of industries including furniture maker AFM Holdings (sold in 2015) and home and gun safes maker Liberty Safe and Security Products. Its arsenal includes helping its holdings make strategic acquisitions enter new business arenas or improve operations to increase profitability.

	Annual Growth	12/16	12/17	12/18	12/19	12/20
Sales ($ mil.)	12.4%	978.3	1,269.7	1,691.7	1,450.3	1,560.8
Net income ($ mil.)	(19.7%)	54.7	28.0	(5.7)	301.9	22.8
Market value ($ mil.)	2.1%	1,161.7	1,100.1	808.0	1,613.4	1,262.3
Employees	62.8%	655	837	2,416	3,456	4,598

COMPASS GROUP USA INC.

2400 Yorkmont Rd.
Charlotte NC 28217
Phone: 704-329-4000
Fax: 704-329-4010
Web: compass-usa.com

CEO: Gary Green
CFO: Adrian Meredith
HR: –
FYE: September 30
Type: Subsidiary

This company points the way to managed foodservices. Compass Group USA provides catering and dining services to corporate clients educational and healthcare facilities and sports and entertainment venues in Canada Mexico and the US. Its operating units include Bon Appetit Management Co. (corporate dining) Chartwells (school dining services) and Morrison Management Specialists (healthcare dining). The company's Levy Restaurants unit also operates fine dining locations as well as concessions at sports and entertainment venues. In addition the company offers vending services and on-site dining. It is a division of UK-based Compass Group.

COMPASS MINERALS INTERNATIONAL INC   NYS: CMP

9900 West 109th Street, Suite 100
Overland Park, KS 66210
Phone: 913 344-9200
Fax: –
Web: www.compassminerals.com

CEO: Kevin Crutchfield
CFO: Lorin Crenshaw
HR: –
FYE: September 30
Type: Public

Compass Minerals is one of the salt producers in North America. Its salt products include rock evaporated solar salt brine and flake magnesium chloride and are used for applications such as water softening plant nutrition road deicing dust control industrial and food preparation. Highway deicing salt ? generally sold to states provinces counties municipalities and road maintenance contractors ? and salt used in sulfate of potash (SOP) fertilizer and other plant nutrient products together account for more than a third of the company's annual sales. Compass Minerals has more than 20 production and packaging facilities and operates a number of salt mines in Canada the UK Brazil and the US. The US accounts for over half of sales.

	Annual Growth	12/17	12/18	12/19	12/20*	09/21
Sales ($ mil.)	(11.5%)	1,364.4	1,493.6	1,490.5	1,373.5	836.6
Net income ($ mil.)	–	42.7	68.8	62.5	59.5	(213.3)
Market value ($ mil.)	(2.8%)	2,460.4	1,419.7	2,075.9	2,101.8	2,193.1
Employees	(7.9%)	3,090	3,071	3,131	3,229	2,223

*Fiscal year change

COMPLETE PRODUCTION SERVICES INC. NYSE: CPX

11700 Katy Fwy. Ste. 300 — CEO: –
Houston TX 77079 — CFO: Jose A Bayardo
Phone: 281-372-2300 — HR: –
Fax: 281-372-2301 — FYE: December 31
Web: www.completeproduction.com — Type: Subsidiary

Complete Production Services tries to live up to its name as it serves customers in the Rocky Mountains Arkansas Louisiana Oklahoma Pennsylvania and Texas. It is a major provider of services and products that help oil and gas companies develop reserves enhance production and reduce costs. Focusing on basins in North America that have long-term growth potential the company offers a range of oil field services including drilling completion and production services and product sales. In 2012 the company was acquired by Superior Energy Services in a $2.7 billion deal.

COMPSYCH CORPORATION

NBC Tower 455 N. Cityfront Plaza Dr. — CEO: Richard A Chaifetz
Chicago IL 60611-5322 — CFO: –
Phone: 312-595-4000 — HR: –
Fax: 716-627-3999 — FYE: December 31
Web: goldenhire.com — Type: Private

ComPsych provides employee assistance programs such as behavioral health work-life wellness and crisis intervention services. The company's services offered under the GuidanceResources brand are designed to help clients' employees improve behavioral and physical health and address personal family and life issues. Clients employ GuidanceResources in order to retain workers and improve employee productivity and performance. ComPsych serves more than 45 million individuals at 17000 organizations across the US and about 100 other countries. Clients consist of FORTUNE 500 companies small businesses and government organizations among other firms. ComPsych was founded in 1984 by Dr. Richard Chaifetz.

COMPUCOM SYSTEMS INC.

7171 Forest Ln. — CEO: Greg Hoogerland
Dallas TX 75230 — CFO: –
Phone: 972-856-3600 — HR: –
Fax: 972-856-5395 — FYE: December 31
Web: www.compucom.com — Type: Private

CompuCom Systems urges clients to leave IT management to them. The company provides outsourced information technology infrastructure services that range from planning and purchasing to systems integration and life-cycle support. Its application services include consulting and staffing custom software development and quality assurance. CompuCom also offers third-party hardware and software management services acting as a value-added reseller of products from such providers as Cisco Hewlett-Packard IBM Microsoft and Sony. The company markets primarily to midsized and large enterprises in North America and Mexico. CompuCom is owned by private equity firm Court Square Capital Partners.

COMPUMED INC NBB: CMPD

5777 West Century Blvd., Suite 360 — CEO: David Pointer
Los Angeles, CA 90045 — CFO: Laura Carroll
Phone: 310 258-5000 — HR: –
Fax: 310 645-5880 — FYE: September 30
Web: www.compumedinc.com — Type: Public

CompuMed won't comp your meds but it might interpret your ECG. Through its CardioGram software the telemedicine company provides online analyses of ECGs (electrocardiograms) for more than 1000 hospitals clinics and other health care facilities throughout the US. The firm's ECG services are available 24 hours a day. CompuMed also rents and to a lesser extent sells ECG equipment. The company's additional product OsteoGram monitors osteoporosis by analyzing bone density; the test involves taking a hand X-ray and can be performed using standard X-ray equipment.

	Annual Growth	09/16	09/17	09/18	09/19	09/20
Sales ($ mil.)	25.8%	2.1	2.3	3.5	5.0	5.3
Net income ($ mil.)	–	(0.1)	0.1	0.2	1.0	0.3
Market value ($ mil.)	33.1%	2.1	1.6	4.8	5.8	6.6
Employees	–	–	–	–	–	–

COMPUTER PROGRAMS & SYSTEMS INC NMS: CPSI

54 St. Emanuel Street — CEO: John Boyd Douglas
Mobile, AL 36602 — CFO: Matthew Chambless
Phone: 251 639-8100 — HR: –
Fax: – — FYE: December 31
Web: www.cpsi.com — Type: Public

Computer Programs and Systems Inc. (CPSI) is a leading provider of healthcare solutions and services for community hospitals and other healthcare systems and post-acute care facilities. CPSI offers its products and services through four companies - Evident American HealthTech TruBridge and iNetXperts. These combined companies are focused on improving the health of the communities it serves connecting communities for a better patient care experience and improving the financial operations of its clients. In the US there are approximately 3900 community hospitals with fewer than 200 acute care beds with approximately 2900 of these having fewer than 100 acute care beds. Almost all of the company's sales were generated from its domestic markets. The company traces its roots back in 1979.

	Annual Growth	12/16	12/17	12/18	12/19	12/20
Sales ($ mil.)	(0.3%)	267.3	276.9	280.4	274.6	264.5
Net income ($ mil.)	38.0%	3.9	(17.4)	17.6	20.5	14.2
Market value ($ mil.)	3.3%	341.4	434.6	363.0	381.8	388.2
Employees	0.0%	2,000	2,000	2,000	2,000	2,000

COMPUTER SCIENCES CORPORATION

1775 TYSONS BLVD FL 8 — CEO: J Michael Lawrie
TYSONS, VA 221024251 — CFO: Paul N Saleh
Phone: 855-716-0853 — HR: –
Fax: – — FYE: March 31
Web: www.dxc.com — Type: Private

Computer Sciences Corporation (CSC) has been one of the world's leading providers of systems integration and other information technology services. It offers application development data center management communications and networking development IT systems management and business consulting. It also provides business process outsourcing (BPO) services in such areas as billing and payment processing customer relationship management (CRM) and human resources. CSC boasts 2500 clients in more than 70 countries. In 2017 CSC merged with the Enterprise Services segment of Hewlett-Packard Enterprise to form DXC Technology Co. This report is based on CSC's last year as an independent company.

	Annual Growth	03/13	03/14*	04/15	04/16*	03/17
Sales ($ mil.)	(16.4%)	–	12,998.0	12,173.0	7,106.0	7,607.0
Net income ($ mil.)	–	–	690.0	7.0	263.0	(100.0)
Market value ($ mil.)	–	–	–	–	–	–
Employees	–	–	–	–	–	66,000

*Fiscal year change

COMPUTER TASK GROUP, INC.   NMS: CTG

300 Corporate Parkway, Suite 214N
Amherst, NY 14226
Phone: 716 882-8000
Fax: –
Web: www.ctg.com

CEO: Filip Gyde
CFO: John Laubacker
HR: –
FYE: December 31
Type: Public

Computer Task Group (CTG) offers a range of technology staffing and consulting services to about 520 clients in North America and Europe. IT and other staffing (and to a lesser extent administrative warehouse and other employee staffing) accounts for about 65% of revenues. IT solutions account for the remaining over 35%. The company's clients are primarily technology service providers as well as manufacturing health care financial services and energy companies. CTG's largest client IBM accounts for more than 20% of revenue. The company was founded in 1966 and has approximately 20 offices across North America Western Europe and India. The US accounts for beyond 60% of revenues.

	Annual Growth	12/16	12/17	12/18	12/19	12/20
Sales ($ mil.)	3.0%	324.9	301.2	358.8	394.2	366.1
Net income ($ mil.)	–	(34.6)	0.8	(2.8)	4.1	7.6
Market value ($ mil.)	9.8%	63.9	77.4	61.9	78.6	92.9
Employees	3.5%	3,400	3,200	4,150	3,950	3,900

COMPUWARE CORP.   NMS: CPWR

One Campus Martius
Detroit, MI 48226-5099
Phone: 313 227-7300
Fax: –
Web: www.compuware.com

CEO: Chris O'Malley
CFO: Joe Aho
HR: –
FYE: March 31
Type: Public

Compuware is more than aware of the power of diversity. The company's software includes testing development and management tools for programs running on traditional mainframe computer systems distributed computer networks and newer Web-based systems. It also makes application development implementation and support software for programmers as well as file data and systems management tools. The company's Gomez platform is a Web-based software testing and monitoring tool sold on a subscription basis. Compuware's services include consulting systems integration custom programming maintenance and support. It sells directly and through distributors to such clients as the BBC the NHL Google and Facebook.

	Annual Growth	03/09	03/10	03/11	03/12	03/13
Sales ($ mil.)	(3.5%)	1,090.5	892.2	928.9	1,009.8	944.5
Net income ($ mil.)	–	139.6	140.8	107.4	88.4	(17.3)
Market value ($ mil.)	17.3%	1,405.1	1,791.0	2,462.7	1,959.5	2,663.1
Employees	(2.7%)	5,006	4,336	4,396	4,564	4,491

COMPX INTERNATIONAL, INC.   ASE: CIX

5430 LBJ Freeway, Suite 1700, Three Lincoln Centre
Dallas, TX 75240-2620
Phone: 972 448-1400
Fax: –
Web: www.compx.com

CEO: Scott James
CFO: Michael Simmons
HR: –
FYE: December 31
Type: Public

CompX International tries to keep the workday smooth theft-free and painless. Through CompX's three operating divisions — security products furniture components and marine components — the company makes ball bearing slides cabinet locks and ergonomic computer support systems. The company's primary customers are office furniture makers but its components are used in recreational marine vehicles ignition systems vending equipment mailboxes appliances and computer equipment. CompX International believes that it is a North American market leader in the manufacture and sale of cabinet locks and other locking mechanisms. The company is majority-owned by NL Industries.

	Annual Growth	12/16	12/17	12/18	12/19	12/20
Sales ($ mil.)	1.3%	108.9	112.0	118.2	124.2	114.5
Net income ($ mil.)	(0.3%)	10.5	13.2	15.3	16.0	10.3
Market value ($ mil.)	(3.0%)	200.5	165.6	169.5	181.7	177.2
Employees	(0.1%)	516	520	547	547	513

COMSCORE INC   NMS: SCOR

11950 Democracy Drive, Suite 600
Reston, VA 20190
Phone: 703 438-2000
Fax: –
Web: www.comscore.com

CEO: William Livek
CFO: Jon Carpenter
HR: –
FYE: December 31
Type: Public

comScore Inc. is a global information and analytics company that measures advertising content and the consumer audiences of each across media platforms. The company create its products using a global data platform that combines information on digital platforms (connected (Smart) televisions mobile devices tablets and computers) television ("TV") over the top devices ("OTT") direct to consumer applications and movie screens with demographics and other descriptive information. The company was established in 1999. The US accounts for more than 85% of total sales.

	Annual Growth	12/16	12/17	12/18	12/19	12/20
Sales ($ mil.)	(2.8%)	399.5	403.5	419.5	388.6	356.0
Net income ($ mil.)	–	(117.2)	(281.4)	(159.3)	(339.0)	(47.9)
Market value ($ mil.)	(47.0%)	2,303.4	2,078.7	1,052.5	360.3	181.6
Employees	(9.9%)	–	1,830	1,800	1,300	1,340

COMSTOCK HOLDING COMPANIES, INC   NAS: CHCI

1900 Reston Metro Plaza, 10th Floor
Reston, VA 20190
Phone: 703 230-1985
Fax: –
Web: www.comstockcompanies.com

CEO: Christopher Clemente
CFO: Christopher Guthrie
HR: –
FYE: December 31
Type: Public

While people take stock of their lives Comstock takes stock of its portfolio. The homebuilder develops land and builds single-family homes townhouses and mid- and high-rise condominiums in and around Washington DC. The company annually delivers some 200 homes with an average price of approximately $289000. Its customer base includes first-time homebuyers buyers looking to move up empty nesters and active retirees. The company also rents resdential properties under the Comstock Communities name. Average rent is approximately $1500 a month.

	Annual Growth	12/16	12/17	12/18	12/19	12/20
Sales ($ mil.)	(8.8%)	41.6	45.4	56.7	25.3	28.7
Net income ($ mil.)	–	(9.0)	(5.0)	(4.5)	0.9	2.1
Market value ($ mil.)	15.1%	14.6	13.8	13.6	15.8	25.6
Employees	42.2%	36	51	85	109	147

COMSTOCK RESOURCES INC   NYS: CRK

5300 Town and Country Blvd., Suite 500
Frisco, TX 75034
Phone: 972 668-8800
Fax: –
Web: www.comstockresources.com

CEO: M. Jay Allison
CFO: Roland Burns
HR: –
FYE: December 31
Type: Public

Comstock Resources' stock in trade is exploring for and producing natural gas and oil. In 2012 the midsized independent oil and gas company reported proved reserves of 711.9 trillion cu. ft. of natural gas equivalent (67% natural gas 33% oil) on its properties primarily located in three major areas — East Texas/North Louisiana South Texas and West Texas. Comstock Resources operates more than 960 of the 1640 producing wells in which it holds an interest. The company has grown through the drill bit (by exploiting existing reserves) and through complementary acquisitions.

	Annual Growth	08/18*	12/18	12/19	12/20	12/21
Sales ($ mil.)	123.1%	166.6	223.6	768.7	858.2	1,850.7
Net income ($ mil.)	–	(92.8)	64.1	96.9	(52.4)	(241.7)
Market value ($ mil.)	(2.6%)	2,040.4	1,055.1	1,917.0	1,017.9	1,884.4
Employees	22.0%	–	113	207	204	205

*Fiscal year change

COMTECH TELECOMMUNICATIONS CORP.
NMS: CMTL

68 South Service Road, Suite 230
Melville, NY 11747
Phone: 631 962-7000
Fax: 631 962-7001
Web: www.comtechtel.com

CEO: Michael Porcelain
CFO: Michael Bondi
HR: –
FYE: July 31
Type: Public

Comtech is a global provider of next-generation 911 emergency systems ("NG-911") and secure wireless communications technologies. The company's solutions fulfill its customers' needs for secure wireless communications in some of the most demanding environments including those where traditional communications are unavailable or cost-prohibitive and in mission-critical and other scenarios where performance is crucial. In recent years an increase in market demand for global voice video and data usage has contributed to its growth. It provides solutions to both commercial and governmental customers. The company generates about 75% of its revenue from its domestic operations.

	Annual Growth	07/17	07/18	07/19	07/20	07/21
Sales ($ mil.)	1.4%	550.4	570.6	671.8	616.7	581.7
Net income ($ mil.)	–	15.8	29.8	25.0	7.0	(73.5)
Market value ($ mil.)	8.5%	472.5	881.9	781.2	431.0	655.4
Employees	3.0%	1,813	1,852	2,013	2,034	2,038

COMTEX NEWS NETWORK INC.
OTC: CMTX

625 N. Washington St. Ste. 301
Alexandria VA 22314
Phone: 703-820-2000
Fax: 703-820-2005
Web: www.comtexnews.net

CEO: Chip Brian
CFO: –
HR: –
FYE: June 30
Type: Public

Comtex News Network is a leading distributor of electronic news and alerts that specializes in the business and financial markets. The company gathers news and content from more than 10000 national and international news agencies and publications including PR Newswire United Press International and The Associated Press and packages those feeds into several different product offerings. In addition to individual and institutional customers Comtex supplies news to such information distributors as MarketWatch Dow Jones' Factiva and Thomson Financial.

COMVERGE INC.
NASDAQ: COMV

5390 Trianlge Pkwy. Ste. 300
Norcross GA 30092
Phone: 888-565-5525
Fax: 770-696-7665
Web: www.comverge.com

CEO: Gregory J Dukat
CFO: –
HR: –
FYE: December 31
Type: Private

Comverge seeks a convergence of communications enabling the lights to stay on. The company provides demand management software and systems to electric utilities and other energy suppliers and sells automated meters and related equipment with communications links. The company's products are used by more than 500 utilities and energy providers including PEPCO as well as some 2100 commercial and industrial customers such as Barnes and Noble and Foot Locker. Its products include software and hardware that help control energy load read meters remotely manage billing and detect theft and outages. Comverge was acquired in 2012 by H.I.G. Capital for about $49 million.

COMVERSE INC.
NASDAQ: CNSI

200 Quannapowitt Pkwy.
Wakefield MA 01880
Phone: 781-246-9000
Fax: 781-224-8143
Web: www.comverse.com

CEO: Philippe Tartavull
CFO: Jacky Wu
HR: –
FYE: January 31
Type: Public

Comverse is conversant with communications technology. The company provides communication software and systems that handle messaging billing and accounts call management and data delivery services. It also provides related services such as consulting design implementation interoperability testing maintenance support and training. Its services are sold to more than 450 wireline wireless and cable network providers in more than 125 countries. Top customer Verizon accounts for about 15% of sales. Comverse has offices in about 40 countries and generates most of its revenues in the EMEA (Europe Middle East and Africa) region. The company was spun off by former parent Comverse Technology (CTI) in 2012.

CON-WAY FREIGHT INC.

2211 Old Earhart Rd. Ste. 100
Ann Arbor MI 48105-2751
Phone: 734-994-6600
Fax: 734-757-1153
Web: www.con-way.com/en/freight

CEO: –
CFO: –
HR: –
FYE: December 31
Type: Subsidiary

A shipper picks a day then Con-way hits the highway. Con-way Freight specializes in next-day and second-day less-than-truckload (LTL) freight transportation. (LTL carriers consolidate loads from multiple shippers into a single truckload.) The company operates throughout the US with an extended network in North America via Con-way Freight Canada and Con-way Mexico. Transborder services extend to Canada Mexico Asia Europe and the Caribbean. Overall Con-way Freight operates a fleet of about 9100 tractors and 26300 trailers from some 290 owned or leased terminals. Con-way Freight is the main subsidiary of Con-way which also owns supply chain management and truckload freight transportation businesses.

CON-WAY INC
NYS: CNW

2211 Old Earhart Road, Suite 100
Ann Arbor, MI 48105
Phone: 734 994-6600
Fax: 734 757-1153
Web: www.con-way.com

CEO: Douglas W Stotlar
CFO: Stephen L Bruffett
HR: –
FYE: December 31
Type: Public

Providing trucking and logistics services Con-way is at home on the high-way. Con-way Freight the company's less-than-truckload (LTL) unit provides regional inter-regional and transcontinental service throughout North America. (LTL carriers consolidate loads from multiple shippers into a single truckload.) Con-way Freight operates a fleet of about 9300 tractors and some 25000 trailers. Con-way offers full truckload transportation services through its Con-way Truckload subsidiary which maintains a fleet of about 2700 tractors and more than 8000 trailers. Con-way's Menlo Worldwide unit provides contract logistics freight brokerage warehousing and supply chain management services.

	Annual Growth	12/09	12/10	12/11	12/12	12/13
Sales ($ mil.)	6.4%	4,269.2	4,952.0	5,290.0	5,580.2	5,473.4
Net income ($ mil.)	–	(107.7)	4.0	88.4	104.5	99.2
Market value ($ mil.)	3.3%	1,987.2	2,081.7	1,659.9	1,583.6	2,260.4
Employees	1.9%	27,400	27,900	27,800	29,100	29,500

CONAGRA BRANDS INC   NYS: CAG

222 West Merchandise Mart Plaza, Suite 1300
Chicago, IL 60654
Phone: 312 549-5000
Fax: –
Web: www.conagrabrands.com

CEO: Sean M Connolly
CFO: David S Marberger
HR: –
FYE: May 30
Type: Public

Conagra Brands is one of North America's leading branded food companies. The company makes and markets name-brand packaged and frozen foods that are sold widely across the US including in Walmart stores. Conagra's cornucopia of America's best-known brands includes Duncan Hines Birds Eye Slim Jim Reddi-wip Vlasic Angie's BOOMCHICKAPOP Duke's Earth Balance Gardein Frontera Healthy Choice and Marie Callender's. About 40 domestic manufacturing facilities located in Arkansas California Colorado Illinois Indiana Iowa Kentucky Maryland Michigan Minnesota Missouri Nebraska Nevada Ohio Pennsylvania Tennessee Washington and Wisconsin. Conagra began as a flour-milling company in Nebraska in 1919 and over the decades transformed into a consumer goods company.

	Annual Growth	05/17	05/18	05/19	05/20	05/21
Sales ($ mil.)	9.3%	7,826.9	7,938.3	9,538.4	11,054.4	11,184.7
Net income ($ mil.)	19.4%	639.3	808.4	678.3	840.1	1,298.8
Market value ($ mil.)	(0.6%)	18,745.5	17,967.4	13,846.6	16,709.1	18,298.8
Employees	10.2%	12,600	12,400	18,000	16,500	18,600

CONCERT PHARMACEUTICALS INC   NMS: CNCE

65 Hayden Avenue, Suite 3000N
Lexington, MA 02421
Phone: 781 860-0045
Fax: –
Web: www.concertpharma.com

CEO: Roger Tung
CFO: Marc Becker
HR: –
FYE: December 31
Type: Public

Concert Pharmaceuticals wants to use deuterium chemistry to conduct a symphony of drugs. The company's process lets it substitute deuterium (also called heavy hydrogen) for hydrogen in a chemical compound thereby making the compound more stable without changing its other properties. It believes this process will lead to a shorter time from discovery to trial for certain drugs. Concert has a handful of clinical-stage candidates in various stages of the approval process including treatments for autoimmune and central nervous system (CNS) disorders. It collaborates with Avanir and Celgene on development.

	Annual Growth	12/16	12/17	12/18	12/19	12/20
Sales ($ mil.)	159.6%	0.2	143.9	10.5	1.1	7.9
Net income ($ mil.)	–	(50.7)	95.6	(56.0)	(78.2)	(74.8)
Market value ($ mil.)	5.3%	327.9	824.3	399.9	293.9	402.7
Employees	0.7%	69	64	71	70	71

CONCHO RESOURCES INC   NYS: CXO

One Concho Center, 600 West Illinois Avenue
Midland, TX 79701
Phone: 432 683-7443
Fax: 432 683-7441
Web: www.concho.com

CEO: Timothy A Leach
CFO: Brenda R Schroer
HR: –
FYE: December 31
Type: Public

Fracking company Concho Resources explores develops and extracts oil and gas assets in the Permian Basin the hottest energy resource region on US shores. It has about 640000 net acres to its name along with 270 net wells primarily underground in Southeastern New Mexico and West Texas. Its around 840 million barrels of proved reserves is split between crude oil (60%) and natural gas (40%). Concho produces roughly 260 million barrels of oil equivalent each day ranking it among the region's top producers and the only companies operating exclusively in the Permian.

	Annual Growth	12/14	12/15	12/16	12/17	12/18
Sales ($ mil.)	11.8%	2,660.1	1,803.6	1,635.0	2,586.0	4,151.0
Net income ($ mil.)	43.6%	538.2	65.9	(1,462.4)	956.0	2,286.0
Market value ($ mil.)	0.8%	19,975.7	18,595.9	26,554.1	30,082.6	20,584.4
Employees	10.1%	1,022	1,121	1,085	1,203	1,503

CONCORD HOSPITAL, INC.

250 PLEASANT ST
CONCORD, NH 033012598
Phone: 603-227-7000
Fax: –
Web: www.concordhospital.org

CEO: Robert Steigmeyer
CFO: Bruce R Burns
HR: –
FYE: September 30
Type: Private

Concord Hospital is agreeably an acute care regional hospital serving central New Hampshire. The hospital has some 300 licensed beds and provides general inpatient and outpatient medical care as well as specialist centers for cardiology orthopedics cancer care urology and women's health. Concord Hospital operates other medical facilities either on its main campus or nearby including surgery imaging diagnostic hospice and rehabilitation facilities as well as physician practice locations. With roots reaching back to 1884 Concord Hospital is part of the Capital Region Health Care system which also offers mental health and home health care services.

	Annual Growth	09/16	09/17	09/18	09/19	09/20
Sales ($ mil.)	2.3%	–	481.6	500.3	528.8	516.1
Net income ($ mil.)	(34.5%)	–	35.4	23.1	9.4	10.0
Market value ($ mil.)	–	–	–	–	–	–
Employees	–	–	–	–	–	2,000

CONCORD LITHO GROUP

92 OLD TURNPIKE RD
CONCORD, NH 033017305
Phone: 603-224-1202
Fax: –
Web: www.concordlitho.com

CEO: Peter Cook
CFO: Marlin Kaufman
HR: –
FYE: December 31
Type: Private

Concord Litho Group is all about the commercially printed word. The company specializes in producing promotional and marketing materials of all sizes for retailers publishers ad agencies and consumer products brands. It prints catalogs brochures calendars greeting cards and maps as well as point-of-purchase displays art prints and other large-format items. Concord Litho Group also offers product and program development services. Clients have included Macy's Rodale Dunkin' Donuts Publishers Clearing House Prudential Financial and TV Guide. Concord Litho Group was founded in 1958.

	Annual Growth	12/09	12/10	12/11	12/12	12/13
Sales ($ mil.)	9.9%	–	39.0	44.7	50.3	51.8
Net income ($ mil.)	(27.6%)	–	–	1.1	1.9	0.6
Market value ($ mil.)	–	–	–	–	–	–
Employees	–	–	–	–	–	200

CONCUR TECHNOLOGIES INC   NMS: CNQR

601 108th Avenue N.E., Suite 1000
Bellevue, WA 98004
Phone: 425 702-8808
Fax: –
Web: www.concur.com

CEO: –
CFO: –
HR: –
FYE: September 30
Type: Public

Concur Technologies can ensure that all of your expense reports are in perfect harmony with budgeting and accounting. The company offers expense and spend management cloud computing software that enables businesses to automate and streamline the process for submitting and approving employee expense reports. Concur's software features modules for tracking submitting and processing reports for travel and entertainment costs as well as applications to track employee requests for vendor payments. Other applications include business process management travel booking invoicing auditing and business intelligence. Concur licenses its software to clients primarily on a subscription basis.

	Annual Growth	09/09	09/10	09/11	09/12	09/13
Sales ($ mil.)	21.8%	247.6	292.9	349.5	439.8	545.8
Net income ($ mil.)	–	25.7	20.6	(10.7)	(7.0)	(24.4)
Market value ($ mil.)	29.1%	2,228.3	2,770.8	2,086.5	4,132.1	6,192.9
Employees	36.3%	1,100	1,200	1,600	2,400	3,800

CONCURRENT TECHNOLOGIES CORPORATION

100 CTC DR
JOHNSTOWN, PA 159041935
Phone: 800-282-4392
Fax: -
Web: www.ctc.com

CEO: Edward J Sheehan Jr
CFO: -
HR: -
FYE: June 30
Type: Private

Concurrent Technologies Corporation (CTC) helps customers keep pace with all the current technologies. The not-for-profit research and development organization provides IT services to public and private sectors although it primarily serves the needs of the Department of Defense and about 20 other federal departments. CTC provides training rapid prototyping studies and analysis network design project management design and development and systems integration. It serves clients in advanced materials and manufacturing IT healthcare energy environmental sustainability training and intelligence among others. CTC has about 50 locations across the US and one in Canada.

	Annual Growth	06/11	06/12	06/13	06/14	06/15
Sales ($ mil.)	(20.4%)	-	-	219.7	140.0	139.1
Net income ($ mil.)	-	-	-	1.2	(0.0)	(2.6)
Market value ($ mil.)	-	-	-	-	-	-
Employees	-	-	-	-	-	450

CONDOR HOSPITALITY TRUST INC

ASE: CDOR

P.O. Box 153 Battle Creek
NE 68715
Phone: 301 861-3305
Fax: -
Web: www.condorhospitality.com

CEO: J William Blackham
CFO: Jill Burger
HR: -
FYE: December 31
Type: Public

Condor Hospitality (formerly Supertel Hospitality) wants to help business and leisure travelers have a super overnight stay. The self-administered real estate investment trust (REIT) owns some 39 limited-service and midscale hotels operated by third parties. The hotels are located in 18 primarily midwestern and eastern states and operate under such franchised brand names as Super 8 Comfort Inn Holiday Inn Express Days Inn Hampton Inn and Sleep Inn. The hotels are leased to the REIT's taxable subsidiaries. Condor Hospitality also develops hotel properties on a limited basis.

	Annual Growth	12/17	12/18	12/19	12/20	12/21
Sales ($ mil.)	(3.6%)	55.5	65.1	61.1	35.2	47.8
Net income ($ mil.)	101.1%	2.9	5.4	(5.0)	(19.1)	47.1
Market value ($ mil.)	(26.6%)	146.5	101.4	162.5	58.0	-
Employees	(48.3%)	14	14	14	6	1

CONMED CORP

NYS: CNMD

11311 Concept Blvd.
Largo, FL 33773
Phone: 727 392-6464
Fax: 315 797-0321
Web: www.conmed.com

CEO: Curt Hartman
CFO: Todd Garner
HR: -
FYE: December 31
Type: Public

CONMED is a global manufacturer of medical equipment for minimally invasive surgical procedures. The medical technology company develops and manufactures a wide range of electronic instruments such as electrosurgical systems powered surgical instruments and endomechanical devices. Its arthroscopic (joint surgery) products include reconstruction tools scopes implants and fluid management systems. Brands include CONMED Linvatec Hall Concept and Shutt. The company sells its products in more than 100 countries; about 55% of sales come from the US market.

	Annual Growth	12/17	12/18	12/19	12/20	12/21
Sales ($ mil.)	6.1%	796.4	859.6	955.1	862.5	1,010.6
Net income ($ mil.)	3.0%	55.5	40.9	28.6	9.5	62.5
Market value ($ mil.)	29.1%	1,497.2	1,885.8	3,284.8	3,289.8	4,164.0
Employees	5.2%	3,100	3,100	3,200	3,400	3,800

CONNECTICARE INC.

175 Scott Swamp Rd.
Farmington CT 06032
Phone: 860-674-5700
Fax: 860-674-2030
Web: www.connecticare.com

CEO: -
CFO: -
HR: -
FYE: December 31
Type: Subsidiary

ConnectiCare is one of the largest HMOs in Connecticut. In 1979 a group of doctors at Hartford Hospital planted the seeds for what would become ConnectiCare; today the company's 240000 members in Connecticut and western Massachusetts choose from HMO PPO or point-of-service options. It also provides supplemental dental and Medicare plans as well as health savings accounts (HSAs) and disease management programs. ConnectiCare has a network of some 125 acute-care hospitals and about 22000 care providers. The company is a subsidiary of Health Insurance Plan of Greater New York (HIP) which is itself a unit of EmblemHealth.

CONNECTICUT CHILDREN'S MEDICAL CENTER

282 WASHINGTON ST
HARTFORD, CT 061063322
Phone: 860-545-9000
Fax: -
Web: www.connecticutchildrens.org

CEO: -
CFO: Gerald J Boisvert
HR: -
FYE: September 30
Type: Private

When their tiny tykes need some TLC Nutmeg Staters turn to Connecticut Children's Medical Center. The roughly 190-bed children's hospital is located on two campuses and provides a variety of pediatric services including surgery behavioral care and emergency medicine. The not-for-profit medical center also conducts clinical research and is the primary pediatric teaching facility for the UConn School of Medicine. In addition Connecticut Children's operates outpatient facilities throughout Connecticut and a school for children with physical and behavioral challenges.

	Annual Growth	09/09	09/10	09/13	09/14	09/19
Sales ($ mil.)	7.2%	-	210.1	264.5	256.4	393.9
Net income ($ mil.)	15.8%	-	10.1	(2.8)	(1.6)	37.9
Market value ($ mil.)	-	-	-	-	-	-
Employees	-	-	-	-	-	1,117

CONNECTICUT COLLEGE

270 MOHEGAN AVE
NEW LONDON, CT 063204150
Phone: 860-447-1911
Fax: -
Web: www.conncoll.edu

CEO: -
CFO: -
HR: Cheryl Miller
FYE: June 30
Type: Private

With its picturesque campus overlooking Long Island Sound Connecticut College (CC) strives to be the quintessential New England college. It is a private co-educational liberal arts college in New London which is close to Providence Hartford and New Haven. The college offers approximately 55 majors has an enrollment of 1900 and a reputation as one of the most selective schools in the nation. Top majors include biology English government international relations and psychology. CC is known for its interdisciplinary studies. The school has a 9-to-1 student-faculty ratio. The comprehensive fee (tuition room board and fees) for the 2009-10 academic year is just over $51000. CC was founded in 1911.

	Annual Growth	06/12	06/13	06/14	06/15	06/16
Sales ($ mil.)	(0.1%)	-	149.4	151.0	162.7	148.9
Net income ($ mil.)	(46.4%)	-	14.2	9.5	18.5	2.2
Market value ($ mil.)	-	-	-	-	-	-
Employees	-	-	-	-	-	684

CONNECTICUT LIGHT & POWER CO
NBB: CNLT P

107 Selden Street
Berlin, CT 06037-1616
Phone: 800 286-5000
Fax: –
Web: www.eversource.com

CEO: Werner Schweiger
CFO: James Judge
HR: Christine Carmody
FYE: December 31
Type: Public

Northeast utility Connecticut Light and Power Company (CL&P) keeps the folks in the Constitution State connected. CL&P provides electric utility services to 1.2 million customers in nearly 150 Connecticut communities. The electric utility a subsidiary of Eversource Energy has 225 substations and more than 288400 transformers and owns and operates regulated transmission and distribution assets in its 4400-sq.-mile service territory. It has more than 22800 miles of distribution lines and more than 1770 miles of transmission lines. CL&P's transmission assets are monitored by ISO New England.

	Annual Growth	12/17	12/18	12/19	12/20	12/21
Sales ($ mil.)	5.9%	2,887.4	3,096.2	3,232.6	3,547.5	3,637.4
Net income ($ mil.)	1.6%	376.7	377.7	410.9	457.9	401.7
Market value ($ mil.)	0.0%	283.7	279.4	285.2	294.0	283.7
Employees	2.1%	1,270	1,307	1,343	1,381	1,382

CONNECTICUT STATE UNIVERSITY SYSTEM

61 WOODLAND ST
HARTFORD, CT 061052345
Phone: 860-493-0000
Fax: –
Web: www.ct.edu

CEO: –
CFO: Pamela J Kedderis
HR: –
FYE: June 30
Type: Private

The Connecticut State University System (CSUS) is the largest public university system in Connecticut and consists of four universities — Central Connecticut State University Eastern Connecticut State University Southern Connecticut State University and Western Connecticut State University. CSUS has an enrollment of more than 36000 students and its schools offer undergraduate and graduate degrees in some 180 subjects. Programs include courses in liberal arts sciences (including meteorology) business nursing education and technology. CSUS traces its roots to 1849 when Central Connecticut State University was founded. It is part of the broader Connecticut State Colleges & Universities (ConnSCU) system.

	Annual Growth	06/10	06/11	06/17	06/19	06/20
Sales ($ mil.)	(0.2%)	–	428.0	429.2	438.5	419.3
Net income ($ mil.)	–	–	55.5	(55.2)	(38.1)	(195.6)
Market value ($ mil.)	–	–	–	–	–	–
Employees	–	–	–	–	–	2,800

CONNECTICUT WATER SERVICE INC
NMS: CTWS

93 West Main Street
Clinton, CT 06413
Phone: 860 669-8630
Fax: –
Web: www.ctwater.com

CEO: –
CFO: –
HR: –
FYE: December 31
Type: Public

Connecticut Water Service is the holding company of six wholly-owned utility subsidiaries in Maine and Connecticut primarily Connecticut Water Company Heritage Village Water Company Avon Water Company and Maine Water Company. It also owns two active unregulated companies Chester Realty and New England Water Utility Services that provide real estate transactions and sewer operations respectively. The company has around 136000 customers spread over 80 municipalities with 185 million gallons of water supplied each day. In 2018 the company entered into a merger agreement with SJW Group and Hydro Sub Inc. for $750 million. After the merger Connecticut Water Services would become a subsidiary with SJW Group and Hydro Sub Inc will become part of Connecticut Water Services.

	Annual Growth	12/13	12/14	12/15	12/16	12/17
Sales ($ mil.)	4.0%	91.5	94.0	96.0	98.7	107.1
Net income ($ mil.)	8.2%	18.3	21.3	22.8	23.4	25.1
Market value ($ mil.)	12.8%	428.4	437.8	458.6	673.8	692.7
Employees	3.2%	259	265	266	266	294

CONNECTONE BANCORP INC (NEW)
NMS: CNOB

301 Sylvan Avenue
Englewood Cliffs, NJ 07632
Phone: 201 816-8900
Fax: –
Web: www.centerbancorp.com

CEO: Frank Sorrentino
CFO: William Burns
HR: –
FYE: December 31
Type: Public

ConnectOne Bancorp (formerly Center Bancorp) is the holding company for ConnectOne Bank which operates some two dozen branches across New Jersey. Serving individuals and local businesses the bank offers such deposit products as checking savings and money market accounts; CDs; and IRAs. It also performs trust services. Commercial loans account for about 60% of the bank's loan portfolio; residential mortgages account for most of the remainder. It also has a subsidiary that sells annuities and property/casualty life and health coverage. The former Center Bancorp acquired rival community bank ConnectOne Bancorp in 2014 and took that name.

	Annual Growth	12/16	12/17	12/18	12/19	12/20
Assets ($ mil.)	14.3%	4,426.3	5,108.4	5,462.1	6,174.0	7,547.3
Net income ($ mil.)	23.1%	31.1	43.2	60.4	73.4	71.3
Market value ($ mil.)	(6.5%)	1,032.4	1,024.5	734.8	1,023.3	787.4
Employees	–	–	–	–	–	413

CONNECTRIA CORPORATION

10845 OLIVE BLVD STE 300
SAINT LOUIS, MO 631417760
Phone: 314-395-7787
Fax: –
Web: www.connectria.com

CEO: –
CFO: –
HR: –
FYE: December 31
Type: Private

Businesses around the world hook up with Connectria for their information technology needs. The company provides outsourced IT services such as onsite and offsite management of clients' applications databases and networks. It specializes in products from such vendors as IBM and Oracle among others. Connectria also provides managed data hosting disaster recovery and consulting services. The company operates primary data center facilities in St. Louis and Philadelphia with more than 20 additional data centers scattered across the US. Clients have included 3M Anheuser-Busch and Charter Communications. Connectria was founded in 1996 by Richard Waidmann.

	Annual Growth	12/06	12/07	12/08	12/09	12/10
Sales ($ mil.)	(70.3%)	–	–	273.0	21.1	24.0
Net income ($ mil.)	891.4%	–	–	0.0	1.3	1.6
Market value ($ mil.)	–	–	–	–	–	–
Employees	–	–	–	–	–	167

CONNEXUS ENERGY

14601 RAMSEY BLVD NW
RAMSEY, MN 553036775
Phone: 763-323-2600
Fax: –
Web: www.connexusenergy.com

CEO: Mike Rajala
CFO: Michael Bash
HR: –
FYE: December 31
Type: Private

Connexus Energy connects more Minnesotans to electricity than any other cooperative. The member-owned organization distributes power to more than 127000 customers in the northern suburbs of Minneapolis-St. Paul. Connexus buys its power from generation and transmission cooperative Great River Energy and distributes it through more than 8880 miles of overhead and underground power lines. It also operates 47 electrical substations. Residential customers account for the bulk of sales. The cooperative is governed by a board of directors elected by its members.

	Annual Growth	12/15	12/16	12/17	12/18	12/19
Sales ($ mil.)	(2.0%)	–	262.2	263.8	273.9	246.8
Net income ($ mil.)	–	–	15.1	13.8	21.7	0.0
Market value ($ mil.)	–	–	–	–	–	–
Employees	–	–	–	–	–	250

CONNOR CO.

2800 NE ADAMS ST
PEORIA, IL 616032806
Phone: 309-693-7229
Fax: –
Web: www.connorco.com

CEO: –
CFO: –
HR: Dawn Edwards
FYE: December 31
Type: Private

Goldilocks would like Connor Co. If it's too hot or too cold the heating and A/C company can make it just right. Through about 20 locations in Illinois and one in St. Louis the company distributes heating and air conditioning equipment along with boilers fittings furnaces pipes pumps valves wells and other industrial equipment. The company also conducts its business online. Connor Co. boasts sheet metal fabrication and valve automation facilities and peddles Kohler products within its showrooms in many locations. The company was founded as Kinsey & Mahler a brass valve manufacturer in 1850. It became Connor Co. in 1936.

	Annual Growth	12/03	12/04	12/05	12/06	12/07
Sales ($ mil.)	6.2%	–	91.5	100.6	106.0	109.5
Net income ($ mil.)	12.0%	–	4.5	4.8	6.9	6.4
Market value ($ mil.)	–	–	–	–	–	–
Employees	–	–	–	–	–	230

CONNS INC

2445 Technology Forest Blvd., Suite 800
The Woodlands, TX 77381
Phone: 936 230-5899
Fax: –
Web: www.conns.com

NMS: CONN

CEO: Chandra Holt
CFO: George Bchara
HR: Brian Daly
FYE: January 31
Type: Public

A top consumer goods retailer in the US Conn's sells consumer electronics home appliances home office furniture and mattresses through nearly 145 stores located in about 15 states including Texas (accounting for nearly half) Arizona Colorado Louisiana and North Carolina. It also trades online. Conn's markets its products under brands such as Corinthian and Serta (furniture and mattresses) Samsung and LG (home appliances and consumer electronics) and HP Apple and Microsoft (home office including computers printers and accessories). A major part of Conns' business is its financing arm which allows customers to extend payment over months or years. Originally a plumbing and heating business Conn's has been around for 130 years.

	Annual Growth	01/17	01/18	01/19	01/20	01/21
Sales ($ mil.)	(3.5%)	1,596.8	1,516.0	1,549.8	1,543.7	1,386.0
Net income ($ mil.)	–	(25.6)	6.5	73.8	56.0	(3.1)
Market value ($ mil.)	10.5%	308.3	973.2	612.0	256.0	459.7
Employees	0.4%	4,200	4,250	4,475	4,425	4,260

CONOLOG CORP.

5 Columbia Road
Somerville, NJ 08876
Phone: 908 722-8081
Fax: 908 722-5461
Web: www.conolog.com

NBB: CNLG

CEO: –
CFO: –
HR: –
FYE: July 31
Type: Public

Conolog makes small electronic and electromagnetic components that military industrial and utilities customers use for microwave radio and telephone transmission. Its products include transducers receivers electromagnetic-wave filters and signal-processing equipment. Its products for commercial customers electrical and industrial utilities in particular are carried under the INIVEN brand name taken from a company Conolog acquired in 1981. Leading customers include the US military and power utilities Bonneville Power Administration NSTAR and Tucson Electric Power.

	Annual Growth	07/08	07/09	07/10	07/11	07/12
Sales ($ mil.)	(9.2%)	1.2	1.5	1.2	1.7	0.8
Net income ($ mil.)	–	(7.0)	(2.4)	(24.9)	(4.3)	(1.8)
Market value ($ mil.)	(45.5%)	19.2	23.1	18.4	1.7	1.7
Employees	(1.7%)	15	16	15	15	14

CONOLOG CORPORATION

5 Columbia Rd.
Somerville NJ 08876
Phone: 908-722-8081
Fax: 908-722-5461
Web: www.conolog.com

PINK SHEETS: CNLG

CEO: –
CFO: –
HR: –
FYE: July 31
Type: Public

Conolog makes small electronic and electromagnetic components that military industrial and utilities customers use for microwave radio and telephone transmission. Its products include transducers receivers electromagnetic-wave filters and signal-processing equipment. Its products for commercial customers electrical and industrial utilities in particular are carried under the INIVEN brand name taken from a company Conolog acquired in 1981. Leading customers include the US military and power utilities Bonneville Power Administration NSTAR and Tucson Electric Power.

CONRAD INDUSTRIES INC

1100 Brashear Avenue, Suite 200
Morgan City, LA 70380
Phone: 985 702-0195
Fax: 985 702-1126
Web: www.conradindustries.com

NBB: CNRD

CEO: John Conrad
CFO: Carl Hebert
HR: –
FYE: December 31
Type: Public

Like the story of Noah's Ark Conrad Industries starts anew by rescuing the things its likes. Conrad Industries builds converts and repairs small to midsized vessels for commercial and government customers. More than half of the company's work is in constructing barges liftboats towboats and tugboats. Its boat-conversion projects mainly involve lengthening vessel mid-bodies or modifying vessels to perform different functions. Conrad Industries operates shipyards along the Gulf Coast in Louisiana and Texas. Conrad also offers fabrication of modular components used on offshore drilling rigs as well as storage and offloading of vessels. Established in 1948 the company is led by the founding Conrad family.

	Annual Growth	12/16	12/17	12/18	12/19	12/20
Sales ($ mil.)	(0.9%)	164.4	189.1	182.3	207.4	158.7
Net income ($ mil.)	–	(1.7)	(2.1)	0.2	0.1	(4.0)
Market value ($ mil.)	(14.4%)	107.2	83.8	66.0	56.9	57.6
Employees	(1.3%)	455	460	442	489	432

CONSERVATION INTERNATIONAL FOUNDATION

2011 CRYSTAL DR STE 600
ARLINGTON, VA 222023715
Phone: 703-341-2400
Fax: –
Web: www.conservation.org

CEO: Peter N Seligman
CFO: Barbara Dipietro
HR: –
FYE: June 30
Type: Private

Conservation International (CI) is dedicated to protecting the environment and its inhabitants. The not-for-profit has helped protect some 2.3 million square miles of land and sea across 70-plus countries. Its projects focus on areas such as climate change agriculture fresh water hotspots seascapes and wildlife poaching. CI which has offices in over 30 countries has a worldwide network of thousands of partners. It generates revenue primarily through contributions and grants and contracts and has total assets of some $322 million. The not-for-profit was formed in 1987.

	Annual Growth	06/07	06/08	06/18	06/19	06/20
Sales ($ mil.)	(3.4%)	–	240.1	149.0	140.4	159.5
Net income ($ mil.)	(18.3%)	–	104.8	(12.0)	(7.5)	9.2
Market value ($ mil.)	–	–	–	–	–	–
Employees	–	–	–	–	–	950

CONSOLIDATED COMMUNICATIONS HOLDINGS INC   NMS: CNSL

2116 South 17th Street
Mattoon, IL 61938
Phone: 217 235-3311
Fax: –
Web: www.consolidated.com

CEO: Bob Udell
CFO: Steven Childers
HR: –
FYE: December 31
Type: Public

Consolidated Communications is just what its name implies. The rural local exchange carrier operates systems in Illinois Kansas Missouri Pennsylvania Texas and California providing voice and data telecommunications to business and residential customers. It operates RLECs that offer local access and long-distance internet and TV business phone systems and related services through about 270000 local access lines 167000 voice connections and 290000 data and Internet connections. It also offers directory publishing and carrier services. Subsidiaries include Illinois Consolidated Telephone Company Consolidated Communications of Fort Bend Company and Consolidated Communications of Texas Company.

	Annual Growth	12/16	12/17	12/18	12/19	12/20
Sales ($ mil.)	15.1%	743.2	1,059.6	1,399.1	1,336.5	1,304.0
Net income ($ mil.)	25.4%	14.9	64.9	(50.8)	(20.4)	37.0
Market value ($ mil.)	(34.7%)	2,127.3	965.8	782.8	307.4	387.4
Employees	17.5%	1,676	3,930	3,600	3,400	3,200

CONSOLIDATED EDISON CO. OF NEW YORK, INC.

4 Irving Place
New York, NY 10003
Phone: 212 460-4600
Fax: –
Web: www.coned.com

CEO: Timothy Cawley
CFO: Robert Hoglund
HR: –
FYE: December 31
Type: Public

Consolidated Edison Company of New York (CECONY) distributes electricity to approximately 3.5 million customers in all of New York City and most Westchester County. It also delivers natural gas to about 1.1 million customers in Manhattan Bronx parts of Queens and most part of Westchester County. The utility also provides steam services to some 1575 customers in parts of Manhattan. CECONY owns and operates more than 135500 miles of overhead and underground power distribution lines. CECONY is a subsidiary of Consolidated Edison.

	Annual Growth	12/16	12/17	12/18	12/19	12/20
Sales ($ mil.)	1.2%	10,165.0	10,468.0	10,680.0	10,821.0	10,647.0
Net income ($ mil.)	2.9%	1,056.0	1,104.0	1,196.0	1,250.0	1,185.0
Market value ($ mil.)	–	–	–	–	–	–
Employees	(2.0%)	13,531	14,010	13,685	14,890	12,477

CONSOLIDATED EDISON INC   NYS: ED

4 Irving Place
New York, NY 10003
Phone: 212 460-4600
Fax: –
Web: www.conedison.com

CEO: Stuart Nachmias
CFO: Robert Hoglund
HR: –
FYE: December 31
Type: Public

Consolidated Edison (Con Edison) is a holding company that owns Consolidated Edison Company of New York the company's main subsidiary that distributes electricity to some 3.5 million residential and business customers in some 660-mile service territory centered on New York City. It delivers natural gas to approximately 1.1 million customers and operates the country's largest steam distribution service to deliver energy to parts of Manhattan. Subsidiary Orange and Rockland Utilities serves approximately 0.3 million electric and gas customers in New York and New Jersey. Con Edison also owns or operates renewable energy facilities and advises large clients on energy efficiency programs.

	Annual Growth	12/17	12/18	12/19	12/20	12/21
Sales ($ mil.)	3.3%	12,033.0	12,337.0	12,574.0	12,246.0	13,676.0
Net income ($ mil.)	(3.1%)	1,525.0	1,382.0	1,343.0	1,101.0	1,346.0
Market value ($ mil.)	0.1%	30,070.9	27,065.6	32,024.9	25,582.4	30,201.9
Employees	(2.9%)	15,591	15,307	14,890	14,071	13,871

CONSOLIDATED PIPE & SUPPLY COMPANY, INC.

1205 HILLTOP PKWY
BIRMINGHAM, AL 352045002
Phone: 205-323-7261
Fax: –
Web: www.consolidatedpipe.com

CEO: –
CFO: –
HR: –
FYE: December 31
Type: Private

Consolidated Pipe and Supply lives up to its name: Its nine divisions supply pipe and pipeline materials to a swath of industries from energy to water and waste treatment chemical mining nuclear oil and gas and pulp and paper. Its industrial unit specializes in carbon and stainless alloy pipe valves and fittings. Vulcan makes all types of PVC. Corrosion resistant coatings are offered by a Line Pipe and Tubular unit and liquid applied coatings by Specialty Coatings. Its Consolidated Power Supply is the largest in the business of safety related metallic materials for commercial nuclear generation. Another unit caters to utilities. Consolidated also provides engineering services and inventory systems.

	Annual Growth	12/14	12/15	12/16	12/18	12/19
Sales ($ mil.)	8.9%	–	575.7	550.7	810.7	808.7
Net income ($ mil.)	36.9%	–	7.4	17.9	44.0	26.0
Market value ($ mil.)	–	–	–	–	–	–
Employees	–	–	–	–	–	900

CONSTANT CONTACT INC   NMS: CTCT

1601 Trapelo Road, Third Floor
Waltham, MA 02451
Phone: 781 472-8100
Fax: –
Web: www.constantcontact.com

CEO: Frank Vella
CFO: Michael Pellegrino
HR: –
FYE: December 31
Type: Public

Constant Contact makes sure businesses never lose touch with their prospects and customers. The company provides small businesses with Web-based marketing software and services for managing e-mail and social media campaigns as well as offering local deals managing digital storefronts and creating online surveys. Its offerings include tools for creating implementing tracking managing and analyzing marketing materials. Customers include retailers restaurants and other businesses as well as non-profit organizations alumni associations and churches; two-thirds of its clients have fewer than 10 employees. It claims more than 555000 customers for its products.

	Annual Growth	12/09	12/10	12/11	12/12	12/13
Sales ($ mil.)	21.9%	129.1	174.2	214.4	252.2	285.4
Net income ($ mil.)	–	(1.3)	2.9	23.7	12.8	7.2
Market value ($ mil.)	18.0%	499.3	967.0	724.2	443.4	969.5
Employees	18.6%	625	734	367	1,162	1,235

CONSTELLATION BRANDS INC   NYS: STZ

207 High Point Drive, Building 100
Victor, NY 14564
Phone: 585 678-7100
Fax: –
Web: www.cbrands.com

CEO: Bill Newlands
CFO: Garth Hankinson
HR: Tom Kane
FYE: February 28
Type: Public

Constellation Brands is a leading wine beer and spirits company in North America. The company is the world's largest premium wine producer offering more than 100 brands sourced from the world's premier wine-growing regions; brands include Robert Mondavi Corona Extra and Meiomi. On the beer front Constellation holds the exclusive license to produce import and sell Mexican beer giant Grupo Modelo's Corona and Modelo brand in the US; it also owns a number of small-scale craft beer brands. Spirits the company's smallest business includes the premium spirits Casa Noble and SVEDKA vodka. Brothers Richard and Robert Sands control the company which was founded by the late Marvin Sands in 1954. The majority of the company's revenue is generated from the US.

	Annual Growth	02/17	02/18	02/19	02/20	02/21
Sales ($ mil.)	4.1%	7,331.5	7,585.0	8,116.0	8,343.5	8,614.9
Net income ($ mil.)	6.8%	1,535.1	2,318.9	3,435.9	(11.8)	1,998.0
Market value ($ mil.)	7.8%	30,810.9	41,805.5	32,818.9	33,443.6	41,545.5
Employees	1.7%	8,700	9,600	9,800	9,000	9,300

CONSTELLATION ENERGY GROUP INC.
NYSE: CEG

100 Constellation Way
Baltimore MD 21202
Phone: 410-470-2800
Fax: 563-262-1069
Web: www.bandag.com

CEO: –
CFO: –
HR: –
FYE: December 31
Type: Subsidiary

Constellation Energy Group's leading light Baltimore Gas and Electric (BGE) distributes electricity and natural gas in Maryland. Constellation Energy operates a number of independent power plants with 11750 MW of generating capacity through its Constellation Generation unit and it competes in retail energy supply through Constellation NewEnergy. Other operations include HVAC services appliance sales nuclear plant development and energy consulting services. In 2012 the company was acquired by Exelon in a $7.9 billion industry-consolidation deal. (Constellation Energy's recent losses made it a prime takeover target).

CONSUMER PORTFOLIO SERVICES, INC.
NMS: CPSS

3800 Howard Hughes Parkway, Suite 1400
Las Vegas, NV 89169
Phone: 949 753-6800
Fax: 949 753-6805
Web: www.consumerportfolio.com

CEO: Charles Bradley
CFO: Jeffrey Fritz
HR: –
FYE: December 31
Type: Public

Consumer Portfolio Services (CPS) buys sells and services auto loans made to consumers who probably don't have portfolios. The company finances vehicles for subprime borrowers who can't get traditional financing due to poor or limited credit; these loans typically carry a higher interest rate than prime loans. CPS purchases contracts from both new car and independent used car dealers in more than 45 states; the company then securitizes (bundles and sells) them on the secondary market. Its total managed portfolio comprises some $900 million in contracts. The bulk of the contracts CPS acquires finance used vehicles. The company has servicing operations in California Florida Illinois and Virginia.

	Annual Growth	12/16	12/17	12/18	12/19	12/20
Sales ($ mil.)	(10.5%)	422.3	434.4	389.8	345.8	271.2
Net income ($ mil.)	(7.3%)	29.3	3.8	14.9	5.4	21.7
Market value ($ mil.)	(4.6%)	116.4	94.4	68.4	76.6	96.4
Employees	(4.8%)	960	999	1,032	1,010	787

CONSUMER PRODUCT DISTRIBUTORS, LLC

705 MEADOW ST
CHICOPEE, MA 010134820
Phone: 413-592-4141
Fax: –
Web: www.jpolep.com

CEO: Jeff Polep
CFO: Bill Fitzsimmons
HR: –
FYE: September 29
Type: Private

Consumer Product Distributors helps convenience stores provide convenient services to their customers. The company which operates as J. Polep Distribution Services is a leading wholesale supplier serving more than 4000 convenience retailers in New York Pennsylvania and the New England states. J. Polep distributes a variety of products including cigarettes and other tobacco items candy dairy products frozen foods snack items and general merchandise as well as alcohol and other beverages. As part of its business J. Polep provides merchandising sales and marketing and technology services. The family-owned company was founded as Polep Tobacco in 1898 by Charles Polep.

	Annual Growth	10/14	10/15	10/16*	09/17	09/18
Sales ($ mil.)	8.8%	–	968.9	1,005.3	1,101.8	1,249.0
Net income ($ mil.)	(14.4%)	–	2.5	5.5	5.9	1.5
Market value ($ mil.)	–	–	–	–	–	–
Employees	–	–	–	–	–	400

*Fiscal year change

CONSUMER REPORTS, INC.

101 TRUMAN AVE
YONKERS, NY 107031044
Phone: 914-378-2000
Fax: –
Web: www.advocacy.consumerreports.org

CEO: Marta L Tellado
CFO: –
HR: –
FYE: May 31
Type: Private

Consumers Reports (CR) inspires both trust and fear. CR is an independent non-profit member organization that works side by side with consumers for truth transparency and fairness in the marketplace. Print products include subscription or newsstand sales of Consumer Reports Magazine a Health based newsletter and special interest publications. CR derives income from the sale of Consumer Reports and other services and from non-commercial contributions subscriptions newsstands and other. CR traces its roots to 1936 when consumers had very few options to gauge the value quality or authenticity of goods and services.

	Annual Growth	05/17	05/18	05/19	05/20	05/21
Sales ($ mil.)	3.2%	–	239.0	241.7	245.4	262.3
Net income ($ mil.)	114.1%	–	11.4	(0.5)	9.4	111.8
Market value ($ mil.)	–	–	–	–	–	–
Employees	–	–	–	–	–	480

CONSUMERS BANCORP, INC. (MINERVA, OH)
NBB: CBKM

614 East Lincoln Way, P.O. Box 256
Minerva, OH 44657
Phone: 330 868-7701
Fax: –
Web: www.consumers.bank

CEO: Ralph Lober
CFO: Renee Wood
HR: –
FYE: June 30
Type: Public

You don't have to be a consumer to do business with Consumers — it's happy to serve businesses as well. Consumers Bancorp is the holding company for Consumers National Bank which has about 10 branches in eastern Ohio. The bank offers standard services such as savings and checking accounts CDs and NOW accounts. Business loans make up more than half of the bank's loan portfolio; real estate consumer and construction loans round out its lending activities. CNB Investment Services a division of the bank offers insurance brokerage financial planning and wealth management services through a third-party provider UVEST. Chairman Laurie McClellan owns more than 20% of Consumers Bancorp.

	Annual Growth	06/17	06/18	06/19	06/20	06/21
Assets ($ mil.)	16.2%	457.9	502.6	553.9	740.8	833.8
Net income ($ mil.)	31.6%	3.0	3.6	5.6	5.5	9.0
Market value ($ mil.)	0.6%	57.5	72.7	56.0	43.0	59.0
Employees	8.3%	128	139	144	172	176

CONSUMERS ENERGY CO.
NYS: CMS PRB

One Energy Plaza
Jackson, MI 49201
Phone: 517 788-0550
Fax: –
Web: www.consumersenergy.com

CEO: Garrick J Rochow
CFO: Rejji P Hayes
HR: –
FYE: December 31
Type: Public

Consumers Energy Company makes life better for the people of Michigan by providing safe reliable energy delivered with hometown service.. The company's customer base consists of a mix of primarily residential commercial and diversified industrial customers in Michigan's lower peninsula. All told Consumers Energy (the principal subsidiary of CMS Energy) has a generating capacity of some 5885 MW (primarily fossil-fueled) and distributes electricity to some 1.8 million customers and natural gas to approximately 1.8 million customers. Included in the utility's arsenal of power production is electricity generated from coal natural gas wind and hydroelectric power plants.

	Annual Growth	12/17	12/18	12/19	12/20	12/21
Sales ($ mil.)	3.1%	6,222.0	6,464.0	6,376.0	6,189.0	7,021.0
Net income ($ mil.)	8.3%	632.0	705.0	743.0	816.0	868.0
Market value ($ mil.)	1.2%	8,743.0	8,536.2	9,209.0	9,171.1	9,176.2
Employees	6.3%	7,496	8,777	8,762	8,738	9,583

CONTAINER STORE GROUP, INC
NYS: TCS

500 Freeport Parkway
Coppell, TX 75019
Phone: 972 538-6000
Fax: -
Web: www.containerstore.com

CEO: Satish Malhotra
CFO: Jeffrey Miller
HR: -
FYE: April 03
Type: Public

With its packets pockets and boxes The Container Store (TCS) has the storage products niche well-contained. Its merchandise ranges from hanging storage bags to pantry organizers. The home-organization pioneer operates about 95 stores in about 35 states and the District of Columbia. It also runs an e-commerce site. The company offers free shipping on orders over $75 and same-day home delivery in select markets. Stores carry more than 11000 items; the company's Elfa brand of wire shelving (made in Sweden) accounts for over 5% of its sales.

	Annual Growth	04/17*	03/18	03/19	03/20*	04/21
Sales ($ mil.)	4.8%	819.9	857.2	895.1	916.0	990.1
Net income ($ mil.)	40.5%	15.0	19.4	21.7	14.5	58.3
Market value ($ mil.)	40.4%	206.6	265.7	429.8	155.3	801.9
Employees	0.0%	5,100	4,950	5,110	5,100	5,100

*Fiscal year change

CONTANGO OIL & GAS CO.
ASE: MCF

717 Texas Avenue, Suite 2900
Houston, TX 77002
Phone: 713 236-7400
Fax: -
Web: www.contango.com

CEO: David C Rockecharlie
CFO: -
HR: -
FYE: December 31
Type: Public

It takes two to tango but a lot more people to make independent oil and natural gas company Contango work. Contango Oil & Gas (named after a term used by oil and gas traders to describe anticipated rising prices in the futures market) explores develop exploit and acquires oil and gas properties across the US. The company has offshore production of 20.3 million cubic feet equivalent per day which consists primarily in the shallow waters of the Gulf of Mexico. Contango which like other oil and gas explorers has been hurt by lower commodity prices in recent years also has assets in onshore Texas Oklahoma Louisiana and Wyoming. The company were originally formed in 1999.

	Annual Growth	12/15	12/16	12/17	12/18	12/19
Sales ($ mil.)	(10.0%)	116.5	78.2	78.5	77.1	76.5
Net income ($ mil.)	-	(335.0)	(58.0)	(17.6)	(121.6)	(159.8)
Market value ($ mil.)	(13.0%)	826.7	1,204.7	607.5	419.2	473.3
Employees	14.2%	73	67	63	46	124

CONTI ENTERPRISES, INC.

2045 LINCOLN HWY
EDISON, NJ 088173334
Phone: 908-791-4800
Fax: -
Web: www.contienterprises.com

CEO: Gerard Maurer
CFO: Dominic Mustillo
HR: Erin Pia
FYE: December 31
Type: Private

Conti Enterprises is continuing its tour of duty as a civil and heavy construction firm. With clients such as the Army Corps of Engineers the company provides construction management general contracting and design/build services for a range of projects including commercial and industrial buildings power plants environmental remediation physical security upgrades and infrastructure such as dams roads bridges and rail systems. The contractor often participates in public-private partnerships. Active primarily in the Northeastern US clients have included Newark Airport Volvo Palmetto Navy Base and West Bank.

	Annual Growth	12/03	12/04	12/05	12/08	12/09
Sales ($ mil.)	11.4%	-	115.4	123.4	198.2	198.2
Net income ($ mil.)	-	-	0.2	0.0	0.0	0.0
Market value ($ mil.)	-	-	-	-	-	-
Employees	-	-	-	-	-	500

CONTINENTAL AIRLINES INC.

1600 Smith St. Dept. HOSEO
Houston TX 77002
Phone: 713-324-2950
Fax: 973-357-3065
Web: www.cytec.com

CEO: Jeffery Smisek
CFO: John Rainey
HR: Cris Minard
FYE: December 31
Type: Subsidiary

If it's a continent chances are it's accessible via Continental Airlines. The carrier serves about 140 US destinations and another 135 abroad from hubs in Cleveland Houston Newark and Guam (hub of Continental Micronesia). Its network includes regional flights by subsidiary lines. Continental has about 350 jets and more than 250 regional aircraft. It extends its offerings through code-sharing with fellow members of the Star Alliance led by United Continental's United Air Lines Lufthansa and Air Canada. (Code-sharing allows airlines to sell tickets on one another's flights.) In fall 2010 Continental was acquired by United parent UAL Corp. in a $3 billion stock swap to create United Continental Holdings.

CONTINENTAL BUILDING PRODUCTS INC
NYS: CBPX

12950 Worldgate Drive, Suite 700
Herndon, VA 20170
Phone: 703 480-3800
Fax: -
Web: www.continental-bp.com

CEO: James Bachmann
CFO: Dennis Schemm
HR: -
FYE: December 31
Type: Public

Continental Building Products (CBP) has got homeowners surrounded. The company is a leading manufacturer of gypsum wallboard (aka drywall) and complementary finishing products used in new residential and commercial construction and for repairs and remodels. CBP manufactures its products at plants in Florida Kentucky and New York for sale east of the Mississippi River and in eastern Canada. The company claims to be the only US producer of gypsum wallboard to use only 100% synthetic gypsum. Product lines include LiftLite a lightweight product Mold Defense which protects against mildew and Weather Defense exterior sheeting. The wallboard producer went public in 2014 in an offering valued at $185 million.

	Annual Growth	12/13	12/14	12/15	12/16	12/17
Sales ($ mil.)	34.4%	150.1	424.5	421.7	461.4	489.2
Net income ($ mil.)	130.9%	2.1	15.9	16.7	44.0	59.8
Market value ($ mil.)	16.7%	-	665.5	655.3	867.0	1,056.6
Employees	6.7%	480	538	546	617	621

CONTINENTAL MATERIALS CORP.
NL:

440 South La Salle Street, Suite 3100
Chicago, IL 60605
Phone: 312 541-7200
Fax: -
Web: www.continental-materials.com

CEO: James G Gidwitz
CFO: Paul A Ainsworth
HR: -
FYE: December 28
Type: Public

Continental Materials provides construction and heating ventilation and air conditioning (HVAC) services. Its HVAC segment which sccounts for a majority of sales makes wall furnaces console heaters and fan coils through Williams Furnace and evaporative air coolers through Phoenix Manufacturing. Customers include wholesale distributors and retail home centers in the Southwest. The construction products segment produces ready-mix concrete and aggregates through three subsidiaries and metal doors from McKinney Door and Hardware. Contractors government entities and consumers in Colorado are the segment's primary customers. CEO James Gidwitz and family own more than 60% of Continental Materials.

	Annual Growth	01/16*	12/16	12/17	12/18	12/19
Sales ($ mil.)	(6.1%)	136.8	151.6	152.8	164.0	113.3
Net income ($ mil.)	-	1.4	3.7	1.8	(5.9)	(13.9)
Market value ($ mil.)	(20.4%)	25.6	41.0	32.6	19.2	12.9
Employees	(6.5%)	563	590	590	612	460

*Fiscal year change

CONTINENTAL RESOURCES INC.
NYS: CLR

20 N. Broadway
Oklahoma City, OK 73102
Phone: 405-234-9000
Fax: -
Web: www.clr.com

CEO: William Berry
CFO: John Hart
HR: -
FYE: December 31
Type: Public

One of the top independent energy companies in the US Continental Resources primarily focuses on exploration development and production of crude oil and natural gas in the country's premier oil field the Bakken of North Dakota Red River units and Montana. Additionally the company has leading positions in two major plays near its home-base of Oklahoma?the SCOOP (South Central Oklahoma Oil Province) and STACK (Sooner Trend Anadarko Canadian Kingfisher). With around 1.6 million net acres of leased land to its name Continental Resources maintains around 1600 MMboe of proved reserves more than 45% being crude oil. It reports a production average around 365000 Boe per day from about 2800 net producing wells.

	Annual Growth	12/17	12/18	12/19	12/20	12/21
Sales ($ mil.)	16.4%	3,120.8	4,709.6	4,631.9	2,586.5	5,719.3
Net income ($ mil.)	20.4%	789.4	988.3	775.6	(596.9)	1,661.0
Market value ($ mil.)	(4.1%)	19,296.8	14,641.1	12,495.4	5,938.0	16,306.0
Employees	2.7%	1,127	1,221	1,260	1,201	1,254

CONTINENTAL RESOURCES, INC.

175 MIDDLESEX TPKE STE 1
BEDFORD, MA 017301469
Phone: 781-275-0850
Fax: -
Web: www.conres.com

CEO: Mary Nardella
CFO: James M Bunt
HR: -
FYE: December 31
Type: Private

Continental Resources is a family-owned global IT solutions provider that offers a broad range of technologies and services you'd expect from a distributor combined with the personalized touch and flexibility you'd expect from a family business. Also known as ConRes the company designs procures implements and manages IT solutions that solve business-specific problems. The company's managed services include service desk and end user support cloud and managed backup services. Professional services uses a multi-vendor solution approach coupled with extensive technical expertise that consistently develops long-term client relationships.

	Annual Growth	12/14	12/15	12/16	12/18	12/19
Sales ($ mil.)	(4.0%)	-	479.1	455.6	547.2	407.1
Net income ($ mil.)	(19.3%)	-	8.4	6.2	7.8	3.6
Market value ($ mil.)	-	-	-	-	-	-
Employees	-	-	-	-	-	300

CONTINUCARE CORPORATION

7200 Corporate Center Dr. Ste. 600
Miami FL 33126
Phone: 305-500-2000
Fax: 305-500-2080
Web: www.continucare.com

CEO: Gemma Rosello
CFO: -
HR: -
FYE: June 30
Type: Subsidiary

Continucare continues to care for South and Central Florida's Medicare recipients. The company provides primary care medical services through a network of some 20 centers in Broward Miami-Dade Hillsborough and Palm Beach counties. It also provides practice management services to independent doctors' offices affiliated with Humana and other insurers. A majority of patients who seek medical assistance at Continucare clinics and practices are members of Medicare Advantage health plans. The company has branched out and also operates a growing number of sleep diagnostic centers. Continucare has been part of neighboring Metropolitan Health Networks (MetCare) since it was acquired in 2011.

CONTRACTORS STEEL COMPANY

36555 AMRHEIN RD
LIVONIA, MI 481501182
Phone: 734-464-4000
Fax: -
Web: www.upgllc.com

CEO: -
CFO: Steve Letnich
HR: -
FYE: October 31
Type: Private

When you contract with Contractors Steel you get steel products delivered to you. Steel service center operator Contractors Steel provides products such as bars (cold-rolled and hot-rolled) pipe plate sheet structural members (angles beams and channels) and tubing. The company's fabricating and processing services include burning grinding plasma cutting sawing and shearing. Contractors Steel operates from facilities in Michigan Indiana Arizona and Ohio. Chairman president and CEO Donald Simon founded Contractors Steel in 1960.

	Annual Growth	10/08	10/09	10/10*	04/16*	10/16
Sales ($ mil.)	4.9%	-	153.1	101.2	101.2	213.9
Net income ($ mil.)	-	-	(24.1)	0.8	0.8	4.9
Market value ($ mil.)	-	-	-	-	-	-
Employees	-	-	-	-	-	439

*Fiscal year change

CONTROL4 CORP
NMS: CTRL

11734 S. Election Road
Salt Lake City, UT 84020
Phone: 801-523-3100
Fax: -
Web: www.control4.com

CEO: John Heyman
CFO: -
HR: -
FYE: December 31
Type: Public

Control4 gives homes a personal touch far beyond throw pillows and new paint. The company makes and sells home automation systems that allow users to control music video lighting temperature and security systems with the touch of a button on a wall panel or mobile device. For example homeowners may program their system to lock the doors close the blinds and turn on the alarm when they leave for work and open the garage door and adjust the thermostat to a particular temperature upon arrival. Control4 systems are only sold through authorized dealers and distributors who design a custom solution for each home (and to a smaller extent businesses).

	Annual Growth	12/13	12/14	12/15	12/16	12/17
Sales ($ mil.)	17.5%	128.5	148.8	163.2	208.8	244.7
Net income ($ mil.)	46.1%	3.5	8.2	(1.7)	13.0	16.0
Market value ($ mil.)	13.9%	457.2	397.1	187.8	263.5	768.8
Employees	13.3%	386	417	449	546	635

CONVAID PRODUCTS INC.

2830 CALIFORNIA ST
TORRANCE, CA 905033908
Phone: 310-618-0111
Fax: -
Web: www.convaid.com

CEO: Chris Braun
CFO: -
HR: -
FYE: December 31
Type: Private

Convaid makes lightweight compact-folding wheelchairs that are made for clients with orthopedic conditions and limited upper body control. The company also offers accessories such as travel bags canopies footplates incontinence liners and torso support vests. Convaid sells the wheelchairs to the pediatric adult and geriatric markets. The company was founded in 1976.

	Annual Growth	12/03	12/04	12/05	12/06	12/07
Sales ($ mil.)	-	-	-	0.0	9.4	9.2
Net income ($ mil.)	-	-	-	0.0	0.9	0.3
Market value ($ mil.)	-	-	-	-	-	-
Employees	-	-	-	-	-	89

CONVERGENT OUTSOURCING, INC.

800 SW 39TH ST
RENTON, WA 980574927
Phone: 206-322-4500
Fax: –
Web: www.convergentusa.com

CEO: –
CFO: –
HR: –
FYE: December 31
Type: Private

Companies send their ailing accounts receivable to Convergent Outsourcing. A subsidiary of Convergent Resources (CRI) one of the largest collections companies in the US Convergent Outsourcing (formerly ER Solutions) provides receivables collections services to creditors in the retail telecommunications utilities and financial services industries. Utilizing a mixture of state-of-the-art technology and old-fashioned diplomacy the company tracks down delinquent customers and encourages voluntary repayment of debt. It also provides customer service both for outbound communications (contacting customers to remind them of their debt and payment options) and inbound customer relations.

	Annual Growth	12/06	12/07	12/08	12/10	12/11
Sales ($ mil.)	5.4%	–	–	81.2	86.2	95.0
Net income ($ mil.)	6.4%	–	–	8.6	8.7	10.4
Market value ($ mil.)	–	–	–	–	–	–
Employees	–	–	–	–	–	730

CONVERGINT TECHNOLOGIES LLC

1 COMMERCE DR
SCHAUMBURG, IL 601735302
Phone: 847-620-5000
Fax: –
Web: www.convergint.com

CEO: Ken Lochiatto
CFO: –
HR: –
FYE: December 31
Type: Private

Convergint Technologies is a global service-based systems integrator whose top priority is service in every way ? service to customers colleagues and community. Its advanced solutions create innovative solutions by working strategically with its customers to help reduce risk meet a regulation or deliver a positive business?return. It also works with top artificial intelligence partners to provide customers with the latest innovations in deep learning to improve safety and security. The company designs installs as well as repairs electronic security fire alarm and life safety and building automation systems for a diverse group of commercial industrial and government customers.

	Annual Growth	12/07	12/08	12/09	12/12	12/14
Sales ($ mil.)	19.9%	–	–	164.8	96.8	408.2
Net income ($ mil.)	(17.0%)	–	–	13.6	(7.4)	5.4
Market value ($ mil.)	–	–	–	–	–	–
Employees	–	–	–	–	–	3,658

CONVERGYS CORP

201 East Fourth Street
Cincinnati, OH 45202
Phone: 513 723-7000
Fax: –
Web: www.convergys.com

NYS: CVG
CEO: Dennis J Polk
CFO: Marshall W Witt
HR: –
FYE: December 31
Type: Public

Convergys is conversant in the languages of global customer satisfaction. The company provides business services designed to maximize customer service acquisition and retention from about 130 customer contact centers in about 30 countries. Convergys' call center agents handle customer service interactions such as account service billing inquiries and technical support. The company targets customers in industries such as communications financial services technology retail healthcare and government. Convergys was formed as a division of Cincinnati Bell and spun off in 1998.

	Annual Growth	12/12	12/13	12/14	12/15	12/16
Sales ($ mil.)	9.8%	2,005.0	2,046.1	2,855.5	2,950.6	2,913.6
Net income ($ mil.)	9.2%	100.6	60.9	120.0	169.0	143.0
Market value ($ mil.)	10.6%	1,554.0	1,993.4	1,929.0	2,357.1	2,325.8
Employees	14.0%	77,000	84,000	125,000	130,000	130,000

CONVERSANT INC

30699 Russell Ranch Road, Suite 250
Westlake Village, CA 91362
Phone: 818 575-4500
Fax: 818 575-4501
Web: www.valueclick.com

NMS: CNVR
CEO: John Giuliani
CFO: John Pitstick
HR: –
FYE: December 31
Type: Public

If you think that banner ad is worth a look ValueClick will put a price on it. The company brings Web publishers together with advertisers providing the technology necessary for each side to manage online advertising. ValueClick's media services segment offers e-mail marketing search marketing and ad placement services. The company's affiliate marketing tools track and analyze online marketing programs through its Commission Junction subsidiary while its Mediaplex unit provides online ad serving and management tools. Pricerunner Shopping.net and Smarter.com allow consumers to compare and research products online.

	Annual Growth	12/08	12/09	12/10	12/11	12/12
Sales ($ mil.)	1.4%	625.8	422.7	430.8	560.2	660.9
Net income ($ mil.)	–	(214.1)	68.6	90.5	101.1	101.7
Market value ($ mil.)	29.8%	515.1	762.1	1,207.1	1,226.7	1,461.6
Employees	(1.7%)	1,189	686	1,062	1,331	1,111

CONVERSE INC.

1 High St.
North Andover MA 01845-2601
Phone: 978-983-3300
Fax: 978-983-3502
Web: www.converse.com

CEO: Scott Uzzell
CFO: Lisa Kempa
HR: –
FYE: May 31
Type: Subsidiary

With its roots as a popular basketball shoe worn by professionals Converse has morphed under NIKE into a fashionable footwear maker for those off the court too. It has sold some 750 million pairs of its classic Chuck Taylor All Star canvas basketball shoes which appeal to consumers ranging from kids to clothing designers. It also licenses its name to sports apparel makers. Converse produces products under the One Star Star Chevron and Jack Purcell names. It sells them through about 60 of its own stores and through retailers the likes of Target and even DSW. Converse operates as a separate unit from NIKE's competing sports brands reining in the kitsch value of Converse's vintage Chuck Taylor brand.

CONVIO INC.

11501 Domain Dr. Ste. 200
Austin TX 78758
Phone: 512-652-2600
Fax: 512-652-2699
Web: www.convio.com

NASDAQ: CNVO
CEO: Gene Austin
CFO: James R Offerdahl
HR: –
FYE: December 31
Type: Subsidiary

Convio takes a community approach to helping not-for-profit organizations institutions of higher education and associations raise money organize volunteer efforts manage online content and get their message out. The company's online Common Ground customer relationship management (CRM) software and services connect potential donors and volunteers to groups they may support and vice versa. Convio's more than 1600 clients include The American Red Cross Meals on Wheels Susan G. Komen and the World Wildlife Fund. Nearly all sales come from customers in North America. Founded in 1999 the company went public in 2010. It was acquired by not-for-profit software maker Blackbaud in 2012.

CONWAY REGIONAL MEDICAL CENTER, INC.

2302 COLLEGE AVE
CONWAY, AR 720346297
Phone: 501-329-3831
Fax: –
Web: www.conwayregional.org

CEO: Matt Troup
CFO: Steven Rose
HR: –
FYE: December 31
Type: Private

Ailing Arkansans have a health services provider in Conway Regional Health System. The health system is composed of not-for-profit 154-bed acute care hospital Conway Regional Medical Center as well as four health clinics a home health agency a health and fitness center and an inpatient rehabilitation hospital. Conway Regional provides specialized cardiovascular neurology oncology orthopedics physical therapy and women's services (including obstetrics and gynecology). Its facilities serve the health needs of residents of several central Arkansas counties including Cleburne Conway Faulkner Perry and Van Buren.

	Annual Growth	12/16	12/17	12/18	12/19	12/20
Sales ($ mil.)	13.8%	–	157.5	181.7	200.5	232.1
Net income ($ mil.)	34.3%	–	2.9	3.3	12.7	7.0
Market value ($ mil.)	–	–	–	–	–	–
Employees	–	–	–	–	–	1,200

COOK CHILDREN'S HEALTH CARE SYSTEM

801 7TH AVE
FORT WORTH, TX 761042733
Phone: 682-885-4000
Fax: –
Web: www.cookchildrens.org

CEO: Russell Tolman
CFO: Stephen W Kimmel
HR: –
FYE: September 30
Type: Private

Cook Children's Health Care System is one of the largest freestanding pediatric health care systems in the country with a complete network of care including a medical center pediatric surgery centers specialty clinics pediatrician offices urgent care centers and an emergency department. It encompasses the Cook Children's Medical Center Cook Children's Home Health and Cook Children's Health Plan. In addition its physician network has offices at dozens of locations in Denton Hood Johnson Parker Tarrant and Wise counties. Specialties include behavioral health/psychology/psychiatry endocrinology hematology/oncology bone marrow and stem cell transplant and pain management and trauma services. Cook's Life After Cancer Program is funded by the Livestrong Foundation and helps people manage and survive cancer.

	Annual Growth	09/04	09/05	09/07	09/09	09/15
Sales ($ mil.)	12.6%	–	42.9	500.8	75.8	140.6
Net income ($ mil.)	(5.7%)	–	3.6	59.9	(1.5)	2.0
Market value ($ mil.)	–	–	–	–	–	–
Employees	–	–	–	–	–	2,000

COOPER COMMUNITIES INC.

903 N 47TH ST
ROGERS, AR 727569622
Phone: 479-246-6500
Fax: –
Web: www.ccias.com

CEO: –
CFO: M Kent Burger
HR: –
FYE: December 31
Type: Private

Feeling cooped up in your cookie-cutter house with its bare minimum of surrounding green space? Cooper Communities develops master-planned communities and resorts in the southeastern US. Some properties feature golf courses and lakes with 20-30% of their land set aside for natural landscape. Subsidiaries include custom builder Cooper Homes Cooper Land Development and Escapes! which sells timeshare options for Cooper's resorts. Cooper Realty Investments acquires and manages commercial properties. The largest homebuilder in Arkansas Cooper Communities also has developments in eight other states. Cooper Communities was founded by John Cooper in 1954 and builds about 1300 new homes each year.

	Annual Growth	12/05	12/06	12/07	12/08	12/10
Assets ($ mil.)	10.2%	–	–	170.6	398.6	228.2
Net income ($ mil.)	–	–	–	0.0	(29.5)	(65.4)
Market value ($ mil.)	–	–	–	–	–	–
Employees	–	–	–	–	–	400

COOPER COMPANIES, INC. (THE)   NYS: COO

6101 Bollinger Canyon Road, Suite 500
San Ramon, CA 94583
Phone: 925 460-3600
Fax: 925 460-3648
Web: www.coopercos.com

CEO: Albert White
CFO: Brian Andrews
HR: –
FYE: October 31
Type: Public

The Cooper Companies specializes in eye care and to a lesser extent lady care. The global company makes specialty medical devices in two niche markets: vision care and gynecology. Its CooperVision subsidiary makes specialty contact lenses including toric lenses for astigmatism multifocal lenses for presbyopia and cosmetic lenses. The company also offers spherical lenses for more common vision problems such as nearsightedness and farsightedness. Subsidiary CooperSurgical specializes in women's health care; its wide range of products that are based on the point of health care delivery used in medical office and surgical procedures primarily by Obstetricians/Gynecologists (OB/GYN) as well as fertility products and genetic testing services used primarily in fertility clinics and laboratories. Cooper's products are sold in more than 100 countries. The company primarily earns about 45% of revenue from its domestic sales.

	Annual Growth	10/17	10/18	10/19	10/20	10/21
Sales ($ mil.)	8.1%	2,139.0	2,532.8	2,653.4	2,430.9	2,922.5
Net income ($ mil.)	67.6%	372.9	139.9	466.7	238.4	2,944.7
Market value ($ mil.)	14.8%	11,844.8	12,734.7	14,346.3	15,729.2	20,554.2
Employees	0.4%	11,800	12,000	12,000	12,000	12,000

COOPER TIRE & RUBBER CO.   NYS: CTB

701 Lima Avenue
Findlay, OH 45840
Phone: 419 423-1321
Fax: 419 424-4305
Web: www.coopertire.com

CEO: Bradley E Hughes
CFO: Gerald C Bialek
HR: –
FYE: December 31
Type: Public

Cooper Tire & Rubber Company is a real wheeler dealer. The company makes and sells replacement tires mainly for passenger cars and light trucks but also for medium truck motorcycles and race cars for North American and international markets. Cooper operates almost 10 manufacturing facilities and more than 20 distribution centers worldwide. Unlike some of its rivals Cooper does not typically sell to automotive OEMs; instead it markets its tires to customers including independent tire dealers wholesale distributors and regional and national tire chains. The company generates about 80% of its sales in the US.

	Annual Growth	12/15	12/16	12/17	12/18	12/19
Sales ($ mil.)	(1.9%)	2,972.9	2,924.9	2,854.7	2,808.1	2,752.6
Net income ($ mil.)	(18.0%)	212.8	248.4	95.4	76.6	96.4
Market value ($ mil.)	(6.6%)	1,900.2	1,950.4	1,774.7	1,623.1	1,443.3
Employees	(1.1%)	9,119	10,540	9,204	9,027	8,720

COOPER-STANDARD HOLDINGS INC   NYS: CPS

40300 Traditions Drive
Northville, MI 48168
Phone: 248 596-5900
Fax: –
Web: www.cooperstandard.com

CEO: Jeffrey S Edwards
CFO: Jonathan P Banas
HR: –
FYE: December 31
Type: Public

Cooper-Standard Holdings is a leading manufacturer of sealing fuel and brake delivery and fluid transfer systems. Its products are primarily for use in passenger vehicles and light trucks that are manufactured by global automotive original equipment manufacturers (OEMs) and replacement markets. Its sealing products protect interiors from noise dust and weather. Fluid transfer systems deliver and control fluids to fuel and brake systems and HVAC systems. The company sells to virtually every global OEM although Ford GM and Fiat Chrysler combined generate about 55% of sales. CSA also generates about half its revenue in North America.

	Annual Growth	12/17	12/18	12/19	12/20	12/21
Sales ($ mil.)	(10.4%)	3,618.1	3,629.3	3,108.4	2,375.4	2,330.2
Net income ($ mil.)	–	135.3	107.8	67.5	(267.6)	(322.8)
Market value ($ mil.)	(34.6%)	2,081.5	1,055.5	563.5	589.1	380.8
Employees	(8.3%)	32,000	32,000	28,000	25,000	22,600

COOPERATIVE ELEVATOR CO.

7211 E MICHIGAN AVE
PIGEON, MI 487555202
Phone: 989-453-4500
Fax: –
Web: www.coopelev.com

CEO: Scott Gordon
CFO: –
HR: –
FYE: January 31
Type: Private

Cooperative Elevator represents and serves northern Michigan bean and grain farmers. The agricultural cooperative is made up of approximately 900 member/owners. It operates storage facilities and processing plants offers crop marketing and agronomy services and provides farm supplies to its members including seed feed fertilizer herbicides fuel and agricultural chemicals. The co-op's bean farmers grow black red pinto and navy beans which are distributed in bulk throughout the US as well as in Africa and the Caribbean. Cooperative Elevator's grain farmers produce wheat soy corn barley and oats and the co-op provides storage and market services such as price updates for these commodities.

	Annual Growth	01/12	01/13	01/14	01/15	01/16
Sales ($ mil.)	(13.0%)	–	–	277.1	216.6	209.9
Net income ($ mil.)	(24.3%)	–	–	10.0	8.3	5.7
Market value ($ mil.)	–	–	–	–	–	–
Employees						164

COOPERATIVE FOR ASSISTANCE AND RELIEF EVERYWHERE, INC. (CARE)

151 ELLIS ST NE
ATLANTA, GA 303032420
Phone: 404-681-2552
Fax: –
Web: www.care.org

CEO: Michelle Nunn
CFO: Vickie J Barrow-Klien
HR: –
FYE: June 30
Type: Private

The Cooperative for Assistance and Relief Everywhere (CARE) strives to be the beginning of the end of poverty. The organization works to reduce poverty in about 85 countries by helping communities in areas such as health education economic development emergency relief and agriculture. CARE supports more than 1100 projects to combat poverty. It also operates a small economic activity development (SEAD) unit that supports moneymaking activities. Through SEAD CARE provides technical training and savings and loans programs to help people — particularly women — open or expand small businesses. CARE was founded in 1945 to give aid to WWII survivors.

	Annual Growth	06/15	06/16	06/18	06/19	06/20
Sales ($ mil.)	3.5%	–	530.5	604.5	621.0	609.3
Net income ($ mil.)	–	–	(21.5)	15.6	16.5	(38.0)
Market value ($ mil.)	–	–	–	–	–	–
Employees						10,000

COOPERATIVE REGIONS OF ORGANIC PRODUCER POOLS

1 ORGANIC WAY
LA FARGE, WI 546396604
Phone: 608-625-2602
Fax: –
Web: www.organicvalley.coop

CEO: Bob Kirchoff
CFO: Michael Bedessem
HR: –
FYE: December 31
Type: Private

Cooperative Regions of Organic Producers Pool (CROPP) is the largest organic farming cooperative in North America. The group's 1840-plus farmer/members produce the co-op's Organic Valley Family of Farms and Organic Prairie brands of fluid and shelf-stable milk along with cheese butter and soy milk. Beyond the dairy barn the cooperative also offers organic citrus juices produce eggs meats and poultry. Its Organic Valley products are sold by food retailers and its ingredients are marketed to other organic food processors. Wisconsin-headquartered CROPP's farmer/members are located throughout North America and Australia. The co-op was founded in 1988.

	Annual Growth	12/05	12/06	12/07	12/08	12/10
Sales ($ mil.)	12.7%	–	–	432.6	527.8	619.7
Net income ($ mil.)	24.6%	–	–	6.2	3.8	12.1
Market value ($ mil.)	–	–	–	–	–	–
Employees						764

COPART INC

NMS: CPRT

14185 Dallas Parkway, Suite 300
Dallas, TX 75254
Phone: 972 391-5000
Fax: –
Web: www.copart.com

CEO: A. Jayson Adair
CFO: John North
HR: –
FYE: July 31
Type: Public

Copart is one of the leading provider of online auctions and vehicle remarketing services. It takes those vehicles and auctions them for insurers as well as auto dealers fleet operations charities and banks. The buyers are mostly rebuilders licensed dismantlers and used-car dealers and exporters. The company has replaced live auctions with internet auctions using a platform known as Virtual Bidding Third Generation (VB3 for short). It also provides services such as towing and storage to buyers and other salvage companies. Copart serves customers throughout North America Europe the Middle East and Brazil although the US accounts for about 85% of sales.

	Annual Growth	07/17	07/18	07/19	07/20	07/21
Sales ($ mil.)	16.8%	1,448.0	1,805.7	2,042.0	2,205.6	2,692.5
Net income ($ mil.)	24.1%	394.2	417.9	591.7	699.9	936.5
Market value ($ mil.)	47.0%	7,463.6	13,602.2	18,375.7	22,101.6	34,841.1
Employees	12.7%	5,323	6,026	7,327	7,600	8,600

CORAM LLC

555 17th St. Ste. 1500
Denver CO 80202
Phone: 303-292-4973
Fax: 303-298-0043
Web: www.coramhc.com

CEO: –
CFO: –
HR: Cindy Cassel
FYE: December 31
Type: Subsidiary

Coram infuses healing for its patients. The company also known as Coram Specialty Infusion Services provides intravenous administration of drugs as well as specialty pharmaceuticals distribution through CoramRx. With more than 85 branches nationwide Coram administers infusion therapies such as parenteral nutrition antibiotics pain medications and hemophilia treatments. It serves patients in their homes and through more than 70 ambulatory infusion sites (located inside some Coram branches). The company also supplies patients with home respiratory equipment. Its CoramRx unit distributes to patients the high-cost drugs needed for serious diseases. The company is a subsidiary of Apria Healthcare.

CORCEPT THERAPEUTICS INC

NAS: CORT

149 Commonwealth Drive
Menlo Park, CA 94025
Phone: 650 327-3270
Fax: –
Web: www.corcept.com

CEO: Joseph Belanoff
CFO: Atabak Mokari
HR: –
FYE: December 31
Type: Public

Corcept Therapeutics is a commercial-stage firm exploring treatments that regulate the presence of cortisol a steroid hormone associated with some psychiatric and metabolic disorders. Its sole commercial product Korlym is a version of the compound mifepristone (commonly known as RU-486 or the "abortion pill") used to regulate release patterns of cortisol. The drug is approved in the US for use in patients with Cushing's Syndrome a metabolic disorder caused by high levels of cortisol in the blood. The company's lead compounds have other potential treatments for weight gain caused by antipsychotic medications.

	Annual Growth	12/17	12/18	12/19	12/20	12/21
Sales ($ mil.)	23.1%	159.2	251.2	306.5	353.9	366.0
Net income ($ mil.)	(3.4%)	129.1	75.4	94.2	106.0	112.5
Market value ($ mil.)	2.3%	1,913.3	1,415.4	1,281.9	2,771.4	2,097.6
Employees	15.0%	136	166	206	236	238

CORDIS CORPORATION

430 Route 22 East
Bridgewater NJ 08807
Phone: 908-541-4100
Fax: 800-997-1122
Web: www.cordis.com

CEO: Shar Matin
CFO: Christopher Scully
HR: Nancy Pounder
FYE: December 31
Type: Subsidiary

Cordis is a hearty subsidiary of Johnson & Johnson. The company develops products to treat circulatory system diseases including congestive heart failure and cerebral aneurysms. Cordis is divided into five units: Cordis Cardiology focuses on cardiovascular disease diagnosis and treatment; Cordis Endovascular develops devices for endovascular and liver diseases; Biosense Webster develops medical sensor and electrophysiology technology for cardiovascular use; Conor Medsystems provides vascular drug delivery technologies; and the Biologics Delivery Systems division makes cardiac mapping equipment used to improve the delivery of biological therapies. Cordis was founded in 1959 and bought by Johnson & Johnson in 1996.

CORE MOLDING TECHNOLOGIES INC — ASE: CMT

800 Manor Park Drive
Columbus, OH 43228-0183
Phone: 614 870-5000
Fax: –
Web: www.coremt.com

CEO: David Duvall
CFO: John Zimmer
HR: Renee Anderson
FYE: December 31
Type: Public

The core business of Core Molding Technologies is fiberglass reinforced plastic and sheet molding composite materials. Through compression molding sprayup hand layup and vacuum-assisted resin infusion molding the company makes truck components (air deflectors fenders hoods) and personal watercraft parts (decks hulls and engine hatches). It divides its operations into two segments: Products and Tooling. Navistar International accounts for one-third sales and other major customers include heavy-duty truck manufacturers Volvo and PACCAR. The company's sales are confined to North America.

	Annual Growth	12/16	12/17	12/18	12/19	12/20
Sales ($ mil.)	6.2%	174.9	161.7	269.5	284.3	222.4
Net income ($ mil.)	2.5%	7.4	5.5	(4.8)	(15.2)	8.2
Market value ($ mil.)	(4.7%)	136.5	173.2	56.7	25.9	112.4
Employees	6.7%	1,247	1,304	2,190	1,821	1,617

CORE CONSTRUCTION, INC.

3036 E GREENWAY RD
PHOENIX, AZ 850324414
Phone: 602-494-0800
Fax: –
Web: www.coreconstruction.com

CEO: –
CFO: –
HR: –
FYE: December 31
Type: Private

CORE Construction fits into the core clique of contractors in the southwestern US. The company formerly Targent General is one of the top contractors in the region; it also has offices in Florida and Illinois. CORE offers construction management general contracting and design/build services for municipal educational health care office residential retail sports institutional and industrial projects. It has worked on projects as diverse as Phoenix's Chase Field Ballpark Dodge Theatre and Lower Buckeye Jail. German immigrant Otto Baum founded the company in 1937.

CORECARD CORP — NYS: CCRD

4355 Shackleford Road
Norcross, GA 30093
Phone: 770 381-2900
Fax: –
Web: www.intelsys.com

CEO: James Strange
CFO: Matthew White
HR: –
FYE: December 31
Type: Public

Intelligent Software Solutions (ISS) is no dummy when it comes to software development and IT systems analysis. The privately-held company develops and integrates custom software for data visualization and analysis pattern detection and mission planning for the aerospace defense and maritime industries. Its products include a software tool that counters improvised explosive devices (Dfuze) and public safety management software tool (WebTAS). The company provides on-site product and development support and training. Customers include government military intelligence agencies and local law enforcement in the US and abroad.

	Annual Growth	12/15	12/16	12/17	12/18	12/19
Sales ($ mil.)	–	–	0.0	223.8	262.6	194.8
Net income ($ mil.)	–	–	0.0	0.0	3.9	5.0
Market value ($ mil.)	–	–	–	–	–	–
Employees	–	–	–	–	–	60

	Annual Growth	12/16	12/17	12/18	12/19	12/20
Sales ($ mil.)	44.7%	8.2	9.3	20.1	34.3	35.9
Net income ($ mil.)	–	(1.1)	0.5	6.2	11.0	8.2
Market value ($ mil.)	75.3%	37.7	40.5	114.8	354.9	356.4
Employees	18.8%	286	350	430	530	570

CORE MARK HOLDING CO INC — NMS: CORE

1500 Solana Boulevard, Suite 3400
Westlake, TX 76262
Phone: 940 293-8600
Fax: –
Web: www.core-mark.com

CEO: Scott E McPherson
CFO: Christopher M Miller
HR: –
FYE: December 31
Type: Public

A convenience store wholesale distributors Core-Mark Holding supplies packaged consumables (including cigarettes alternative nicotine products candy snacks and food) to over 40000 customer locations. Traditional convenience stores are the company's primary customer as well as alternative outlets selling consumer packaged goods grocery stores mass merchandisers drug stores liquor stores cigarette and tobacco shops hotel gift shops military exchanges college and corporate campuses casinos hardware stores airport concessions and other specialty and small format stores. Cigarettes and other tobacco products are Core-Mark's top sellers generating more than three-fourths of net sales. The company operates primarily in the US serving customers in all 50 US states; it also has customers in five Canadian provinces.

CORECIVIC INC — NYS: CXW

5501 Virginia Way
Brentwood, TN 37027
Phone: 615 263-3000
Fax: –
Web: www.corecivic.com

CEO: Damon Hininger
CFO: David Garfinkle
HR: Andrea Cooper
FYE: December 31
Type: Public

The company is the nation's largest owner of partnership correctional detention and residential reentry facilities and one of the largest prison operators in the US. Through its CoreCivic Safety segment it has about 50 correctional and detention facilities which it owns or manages for federal state and local government agencies. Federal clients account for about 50% of sales. The company also has a real estate ownership and leasing segment (CoreCivic Properties and operates residential reentry centers designed to address recidivism (CoreCivic Community).

	Annual Growth	12/15	12/16	12/17	12/18	12/19
Sales ($ mil.)	10.8%	11,069.4	14,529.4	15,687.6	16,395.3	16,670.5
Net income ($ mil.)	2.9%	51.5	54.2	33.5	45.5	57.7
Market value ($ mil.)	(24.1%)	3,696.6	1,943.0	1,424.7	1,048.9	1,226.6
Employees	6.5%	6,655	7,688	8,413	8,087	8,555

	Annual Growth	12/17	12/18	12/19	12/20	12/21
Sales ($ mil.)	1.3%	1,765.5	1,835.8	1,980.7	1,905.5	1,862.6
Net income ($ mil.)	–	178.0	159.2	188.9	54.2	(51.9)
Market value ($ mil.)	(18.4%)	2,706.4	2,144.7	2,090.6	787.9	1,199.2
Employees	(5.3%)	12,875	13,890	14,075	12,415	10,348

CORENERGY INFRASTRUCTURE TRUST INC
NYS: CORR

1100 Walnut, Ste. 3350
Kansas City, MO 64106
Phone: 816 875-3705
Fax: —
Web: www.corenergy.reit

CEO: David J Schulte
CFO: Robert L Waldron
HR: —
FYE: December 31
Type: Public

A closed-end investment management firm CorEnergy Infrastructure Trust (formerly Tortoise Capital Resources) invests in privately held and public micro-cap energy companies including midstream and downstream oil and gas companies and coal companies. The firm typically makes equity or debt investments in low-risk established energy companies that will generate steadily increasing returns on its investments over the long term. CorEnergy which has more than $90 million in assets under management is managed by Tortoise Capital Advisors a fund manager with five other publicly traded funds under management.

	Annual Growth	12/16	12/17	12/18	12/19	12/20
Sales ($ mil.)	(40.3%)	89.3	88.7	89.2	85.9	11.3
Net income ($ mil.)	—	29.7	32.6	43.7	4.1	(306.1)
Market value ($ mil.)	(33.4%)	476.2	521.5	451.6	610.4	93.5
Employees	(1.2%)	22	20	22	16	21

CORESITE REALTY CORP
NYS: COR

1001 17th Street, Suite 500
Denver, CO 80202
Phone: 866 777-2673
Fax: —
Web: www.coresite.com

CEO: Paul E Szurek
CFO: Jeffrey S Finnin
HR: —
FYE: December 31
Type: Public

CoreSite Realty leases data center space to those with data center needs. The real estate investment trust (REIT) owns develops and operates these specialized facilities which require enough power security and network interconnection to handle often complex IT operations. Its property portfolio includes more than 20 operating data center facilities with additional space under development. These properties comprise around 4.6 million rentable sq. ft. and are located in major US tech hubs including Silicon Valley. Tenants include enterprise organizations communications service providers media and content companies and government agencies. The REIT has grown along with demand for data center space.

	Annual Growth	12/15	12/16	12/17	12/18	12/19
Sales ($ mil.)	14.5%	333.3	400.4	481.8	544.4	572.7
Net income ($ mil.)	21.6%	34.7	58.7	74.9	77.9	75.8
Market value ($ mil.)	18.6%	2,138.4	2,992.3	4,294.1	3,288.7	4,227.0
Employees	4.4%	391	422	465	454	464

CORESOURCE INC.

400 Field Dr.
Lake Forest IL 60045
Phone: 847-604-9200
Fax: 847-615-3900
Web: www.coresource.com

CEO: —
CFO: Clare Smith
HR: —
FYE: December 31
Type: Subsidiary

CoreSource is a third-party administrator (TPA) of employee benefits programs. As a TPA it manages the health insurance benefits of self-insured employers and their workers throughout the US. Among other services the company handles claims provides access to nationwide and specialty provider networks and manages a variety of ancillary programs such pharmacy benefits flexible spending accounts and COBRA administration. It serves more than 900 clients mostly midsized and large corporations representing about 1.4 million employee members. Other clients include public retiree plans and state high-risk pools. CoreSource is a subsidiary of insurance provider Trustmark Mutual.

CORGENIX MEDICAL CORP.
NBB: CONX

11575 Main Street
Broomfield, CO 80020
Phone: 303 457-4345
Fax: —
Web: www.corgenix.com

CEO: Jim Widergren
CFO: —
HR: —
FYE: June 30
Type: Public

Corgenix Medical wants to take a peek inside you. The company makes in vitro diagnostics to detect autoimmune liver and vascular diseases. Its line of more than 50 diagnostics are used by reference labs hospitals and clinics researchers and other medical facilities around the world. It sells directly to customers in the US and the UK and through independent distributors elsewhere. To expand its product line Corgenix Medical has released an aspirin resistance diagnostic and it is developing new tests to diagnose fibromyalgia (pain disorder) and cardiovascular disease. It is also developing tests that detect potential bioterrorism agents using grant funding from the National Institutes of Health.

	Annual Growth	06/10	06/11	06/12	06/13	06/14
Sales ($ mil.)	7.5%	8.3	7.9	9.3	10.2	11.0
Net income ($ mil.)	253.0%	0.0	(0.4)	(0.6)	0.3	0.4
Market value ($ mil.)	30.7%	5.8	5.3	5.5	9.5	16.9
Employees	3.6%	40	40	48	46	46

CORINTHIAN COLLEGES, INC.
NMS: COCO

6 Hutton Centre Drive, Suite 400
Santa Ana, CA 92707
Phone: 714 427-3000
Fax: —
Web: www.cci.edu

CEO: —
CFO: —
HR: —
FYE: June 30
Type: Public

Corinthian Colleges believes more in marketable skills than in ivory towers. It was one of the largest for-profit post-secondary education companies in North America focused on career-oriented students. It had more than 80000 students enrolled in about 110 schools in some 25 US states as well as in Canada. Corinthian's institutions operate under the Everest College WyoTech (for automotive training) and Heald College brand names. Under pressure from state and federal government investigations into its practices and finances the company is winding down operations by selling off campuses. It has identified buyers for most of its schools.

	Annual Growth	06/09	06/10	06/11	06/12	06/13
Sales ($ mil.)	5.2%	1,307.8	1,763.8	1,868.8	1,605.5	1,600.2
Net income ($ mil.)	—	68.8	146.0	(111.2)	(10.2)	(1.7)
Market value ($ mil.)	(39.7%)	1,459.1	848.9	367.1	249.1	193.0
Employees	8.2%	11,100	15,900	16,600	15,200	15,200

CORMEDIX INC
NMS: CRMD

300 Connell Drive, Suite 4200
Berkeley Heights, NJ 07922
Phone: 908 517-9500
Fax: 908 429-4307
Web: www.cormedix.com

CEO: Matthew David
CFO: —
HR: —
FYE: December 31
Type: Public

CorMedix is a commercial-stage biopharmaceutical company which seeks to in-license develop and commercialize therapeutic products for the prevention and treatment of cardiac renal and infectious diseases. Its first commercial product in Europe is Neutrolin a catheter lock for the prevention of catheter related bloodstream infections and maintenance of catheter patency in tunneled cuffed central venous catheters used for vascular access in hemodialysis oncology critical care and other patients. CorMedix controlled by a group of its officers went public in early 2010.

	Annual Growth	12/16	12/17	12/18	12/19	12/20
Sales ($ mil.)	1.6%	0.2	0.3	0.4	0.3	0.2
Net income ($ mil.)	—	(24.6)	(33.0)	(26.8)	(16.4)	(22.0)
Market value ($ mil.)	48.5%	51.3	16.8	43.3	244.3	249.1
Employees	25.7%	14	14	22	30	35

CORNELL UNIVERSITY

308 DUFFIELD HALL
ITHACA, NY 148532700
Phone: 607-254-4636
Fax: –
Web: www.cornell.edu

CEO: –
CFO: –
HR: –
FYE: June 30
Type: Private

Cornell is the federal land-grant institution of New York State a private endowed university a member of the ivy League/Ancient Eight and a partner of the State University of New York. The Ivy League school's some 23620 students can select undergraduate graduate and professional courses from around 16 colleges and schools. In addition to its Ithaca New York campus the university has medical and professional programs in New York City and Doha Qatar. Cornell's faculty includes some 1695 of regular and part time employee. It was founded 1865 by Ezra Cornell and Andrew Dickson White.

	Annual Growth	06/10	06/11	06/12	06/16	06/17
Sales ($ mil.)	5.2%	–	2,955.8	2,956.8	3,809.2	4,013.9
Net income ($ mil.)	3.2%	–	814.0	(342.0)	(442.4)	985.6
Market value ($ mil.)	–	–	–	–	–	–
Employees		–	–	–	–	12,207

CORNERSTONE BANCORP

1670 E. Main St.
Easley SC 29640
Phone: 864-306-1444
Fax: 864-306-1473
Web: www.cornerstonenatlbank.com

OTC: CTOT
CEO: –
CFO: –
HR: –
FYE: December 31
Type: Public

Cornerstone Bancorp has laid the groundwork for three banking branches in northwestern South Carolina. The institution is the holding company for Cornerstone National Bank which offers traditional products and services including checking and savings accounts money market accounts CDs and credit cards. Commercial real estate loans comprise the largest portion of its lending portfolio; other offerings include residential mortgages business and industrial loans real estate construction and consumer loans. Cornerstone National Bank has three offices in Easley Greenville and Powdersville South Carolina. Cornerstone Bancorp also has an insurance agency that operates as Crescent Financial Services.

CORNERSTONE BUILDING BRANDS INC

5020 Weston Parkway, Suite 400
Cary, NC 27513
Phone: 866 419-0042
Fax: –
Web: www.cornerstonebuildingbrands.com

NYS: CNR
CEO: James Metcalf
CFO: Jeffrey Lee
HR: –
FYE: December 31
Type: Public

Cornerstone Building Brands (formerly NCI Building System) is a leading North American integrated manufacturer of external building products including vinyl windows vinyl siding stone veneer installation metal accessories metal roofing/wall systems insulated metal panels and a top-three position in engineered metal building systems for the commercial residential and repair and remodel construction industries. Its collection of leading brands include Ply Gem Simonton Atrium American Craftsman Silver Line Great Lakes Window and North Star. The company has about 65 manufacturing facilities in the US and Canada supported by a network of some 40 distribution and branch office facilities. About 95% of total sales come from the US.

	Annual Growth	10/17	10/18*	12/18	12/19	12/20
Sales ($ mil.)	37.7%	1,770.3	2,000.6	559.9	4,889.7	4,617.4
Net income ($ mil.)	–	54.7	63.1	(76.2)	(15.4)	(482.8)
Market value ($ mil.)	(15.8%)	1,950.0	1,561.2	909.2	1,067.2	1,163.7
Employees	56.3%	5,300	5,300	–	20,100	20,230

*Fiscal year change

CORNERSTONE ONDEMAND, INC.

1601 Cloverfield Blvd., Suite 620 South
Santa Monica, CA 90404
Phone: 310 752-0200
Fax: –
Web: www.cornerstoneondemand.com

NMS: CSOD
CEO: Himanshu Palsule
CFO: Chirag Shah
HR: –
FYE: December 31
Type: Public

Cornerstone OnDemand provides software to help companies get the most from their cornerstone asset their employees. Cornerstone offers cloud-based applications for recruiting and hiring training and development tracking employee performance and administration. Customers can draw data from Cornerstone applications that help them use resources more efficiently. The company's Cornerstone Growth Edition product is for small businesses; it also offers a learning program designed for salesforce.com customers. Cornerstone offers its programs in more than 40 languages and it has users in more than 190 countries. Still more than two-thirds of the company's revenue comes from customers in the US.

	Annual Growth	12/15	12/16	12/17	12/18	12/19
Sales ($ mil.)	14.1%	339.7	423.1	482.0	537.9	576.5
Net income ($ mil.)	–	(85.5)	(66.8)	(61.3)	(33.8)	(4.1)
Market value ($ mil.)	14.1%	2,107.6	2,582.5	2,156.5	3,078.1	3,573.8
Employees	5.0%	1,645	1,823	1,891	1,953	2,000

CORNING INC

One Riverfront Plaza
Corning, NY 14831
Phone: 607 974-9000
Fax: –
Web: www.corning.com

NYS: GLW
CEO: Wendell Weeks
CFO: Edward Schlesinger
HR: Robert France
FYE: December 31
Type: Public

Corning Incorporated makes a diverse range of glass and ceramic products for optical communications mobile consumer electronics display technology automotive and life sciences markets. Its products include damage-resistant cover glass for mobile devices precision glass for advanced displays optical fiber and automotive emissions control products to name a few. Corning's signature Gorilla Glass is a chemically strengthened thin glass designed specifically to function as a cover or back-enclosure glass for mobile consumer electronic devices such as mobile phones tablets laptops and smartwatches. The company operates about 120 manufacturing and processing facilities in around 15 countries but generates more than half of its sales in the Asia Pacific region. It was founded in 1936.

	Annual Growth	12/17	12/18	12/19	12/20	12/21
Sales ($ mil.)	8.6%	10,116.0	11,290.0	11,503.0	11,303.0	14,082.0
Net income ($ mil.)	–	(497.0)	1,066.0	960.0	512.0	1,906.0
Market value ($ mil.)	3.9%	26,551.7	25,074.3	24,161.3	29,880.0	30,900.9
Employees	7.3%	46,200	51,500	49,500	50,110	61,200

CORPORATE OFFICE PROPERTIES TRUST

6711 Columbia Gateway Drive, Suite 300
Columbia, MD 21046
Phone: 443 285-5400
Fax: 443 285-7650
Web: www.copt.com

NYS: OFC
CEO: Stephen Budorick
CFO: Anthony Mifsud
HR: –
FYE: December 31
Type: Public

The name says "corporate" but it's really about the government. A real estate investment trust (REIT) Corporate Office Properties Trust owns and manages some 170 properties totaling some 19.2 million sq. ft. of leasable space. The REIT focuses on large suburban business parks near federal government hubs and military installations. More than 50% of its office space is located in in the Fort Meade/ BW Corridor regions; other major markets include Northern Virginia Lackland Air Force Base and Redstone Arsenal. Subsidiaries provide property management construction and development and HVAC services. Founded in 1998 the REIT's largest tenants are the US Government and defense information technology concerns.

	Annual Growth	12/16	12/17	12/18	12/19	12/20
Sales ($ mil.)	1.5%	574.3	612.8	578.1	641.2	609.4
Net income ($ mil.)	70.8%	11.4	70.1	74.7	191.7	97.4
Market value ($ mil.)	(4.4%)	3,502.3	3,275.7	2,359.2	3,295.9	2,925.7
Employees	1.9%	376	375	378	394	406

CORPORATE TRAVEL CONSULTANTS INC

1717 N NAPER BLVD STE 300
NAPERVILLE, IL 605638839
Phone: 630-691-9100
Fax: –
Web: www.frosch.com

CEO: –
CFO: Gerry Lazar
HR: –
FYE: December 31
Type: Private

Corporate Travel Consultants (CorpTrav) brings order to the chaos of globetrotting go-getters and far-flung meetings on foreign soil. The company offers Internet-based booking reporting compliance and management tools through CorpTrav On-line as well as meeting and incentive travel arrangements. Its online tools allow customers to check health advisories travel alerts and strike updates for planned destinations. CorpTrav has offices in Chicago Dallas New York and San Francisco. The agency partners with GlobalStar to provide global support and service to travelers. CEO Bonnie Lorefice founded CorpTrav in 1976.

	Annual Growth	12/09	12/10	12/12	12/14	12/16
Sales ($ mil.)	8.3%	–	135.8	209.4	222.4	219.6
Net income ($ mil.)	13.9%	–	0.5	1.9	1.6	1.1
Market value ($ mil.)	–	–	–	–	–	–
Employees	–	–	–	–	–	120

CORPORATION FOR PUBLIC BROADCASTING

401 9TH ST NW STE 200
WASHINGTON, DC 200042129
Phone: 202-879-9600
Fax: –
Web: www.cpb.org

CEO: –
CFO: William Tayman
HR: Deborah Carr
FYE: September 30
Type: Private

This organization is made possible by a grant from the federal government and by support from viewers like you. The Corporation for Public Broadcasting (CPB) is a private not-for-profit corporation created by the federal government that receives appropriations from Congress to help fund programming for more than 1000 locally-owned public TV and radio stations. CPB-funded programs are distributed by the Public Broadcasting Service (PBS) National Public Radio (NPR) and Public Radio International (PRI). Funds are also used for research on media and education. CPB was created by Congress in 1967.

	Annual Growth	09/14	09/15	09/16	09/18	09/19
Sales ($ mil.)	1.9%	–	461.4	510.5	493.6	498.3
Net income ($ mil.)	–	–	(11.1)	31.0	(55.6)	17.2
Market value ($ mil.)	–	–	–	–	–	–
Employees	–	–	–	–	–	99

CORSAIR COMPONENTS INC.

46221 Landing Pkwy.
Fremont CA 94538
Phone: 510-657-8747
Fax: 510-657-8748
Web: www.corsair.com

CEO: –
CFO: –
HR: –
FYE: December 31
Type: Private

Hardcore gaming requires hardcore hardware and that's where Corsair Components comes into play. Through subsidiaries Corsair Components is a designer and supplier of high-performance components and peripherals for the PC gaming market. Its two product segments which each generate about half of sales include high-performance memory components (DRAM modules USB flash drives) and gaming components and peripherals (power supply units computer cooling units gaming keyboards and mice headsets and cases). Corsair distributes its products in about 60 countries across the globe under its own name as well as under the Dominator and XMS brands among others. It generates more than half its sales from Europe.

CORTLAND BANCORP (OH)

194 West Main Street
Cortland, OH 44410
Phone: 330 637-8040
Fax: –
Web: www.cortland-banks.com

NAS: CLDB
CEO: –
CFO: –
HR: –
FYE: December 31
Type: Public

Cortland Bancorp is the place to keep your bucks in the Buckeye State. Cortland Bancorp is the holding company for Cortland Savings and Banking Company (aka Cortland Banks) a community-oriented institution serving northeastern Ohio from about 15 banking locations. Cortland Banks offers standard banking services including checking and savings accounts debit cards and business and consumer loans. More than half of Cortland's loan portfolio is composed of commercial mortgages. Other offerings include discount brokerage and trust services.

	Annual Growth	12/15	12/16	12/17	12/18	12/19
Assets ($ mil.)	4.7%	612.4	655.2	711.1	714.7	737.2
Net income ($ mil.)	13.6%	4.4	4.9	4.4	8.8	7.3
Market value ($ mil.)	8.2%	68.7	75.7	88.6	88.6	94.3
Employees	0.2%	163	161	159	166	164

CORVEL CORP

5128 Apache Plume Road, Suite 400
Fort Worth, TX 76109
Phone: 817 390-1416
Fax: –
Web: www.corvel.com

NMS: CRVL
CEO: Michael Combs
CFO: Brandon O'Brien
HR: –
FYE: March 31
Type: Public

CorVel has carved out a niche providing medical cost containment for US workers' compensation programs auto and liability insurers and group health plans. CorVel helps insurers third-party administrators government agencies and self-insured employers keep down costs associated with workers' compensation and other medical claims and to get employees back on the job as soon as is practicable. Among other things CorVel reviews medical bills to make sure they are in line with state fee schedules. It also maintains a health provider network and provides case management and vocational rehabilitation services. Clients access CorVel's range of services through its CareMC web portal.

	Annual Growth	03/17	03/18	03/19	03/20	03/21
Sales ($ mil.)	1.6%	518.7	558.4	595.7	592.2	552.6
Net income ($ mil.)	12.0%	29.5	35.7	46.7	47.4	46.4
Market value ($ mil.)	23.9%	777.6	903.6	1,166.2	974.4	1,833.9
Employees	0.4%	3,629	3,788	3,904	3,824	3,681

COSCO FIRE PROTECTION, INC.

29222 RANCHO VIEJO RD # 205
SAN JUAN CAPISTRANO, CA 926751045
Phone: 714-974-8770
Fax: –
Web: www.coscofire.com

CEO: Keith R Fielding
CFO: –
HR: –
FYE: December 31
Type: Private

COSCO Fire Protection designs installs and inspects automatic fire sprinkler systems as well as fire alarm and detection systems. The company also designs and installs fire suppression systems. Its target customers include owners of office buildings and manufacturing facilities; hospitals and extended-care facilities; schools and universities; retail shopping malls; and government complexes and military facilities. COSCO operates in the western US (from offices in Alaska California Nevada Oregon and Washington). The company was founded in 1959 and is owned by Consolidated Fire Protection which is itself a subsidiary of German fire protection firm Minimax.

	Annual Growth	12/13	12/14	12/15	12/16	12/17
Sales ($ mil.)	12.8%	–	121.6	155.6	170.5	174.3
Net income ($ mil.)	33.7%	–	6.1	10.4	12.1	14.5
Market value ($ mil.)	–	–	–	–	–	–
Employees	–	–	–	–	–	601

COSI INC
NBB: COSI Q

294 Washington Street, Suite 510
Boston, MA 02108
Phone: 857 415-5000
Fax: –
Web: www.getcosi.com

CEO: Andrew Berger
CFO: James O'Connor
HR: –
FYE: December 28
Type: Public

Cosi's recipe calls for one part coffee house one part sandwich shop and one part cocktail bar. The company operates and franchises about 75 eclectic Cosìcafés offering coffee and made-to-order sandwiches. Its menu also features breakfast items (including its bagel-inspired Squagels) salads soups and desserts. Most of the company's restaurants also offer dinner and drinks after 5 p.m. while its Così Downtown units (primarily located in non-residential business districts) close in the evening. Cosi also offers delivery and catering services. About 45 of the locations are company-owned while the rest are franchised. In 2016 Cosi filed for Chapter 11 bankruptcy protection.

	Annual Growth	01/12*	12/12	12/13	12/14	12/15
Sales ($ mil.)	(4.2%)	102.1	98.0	86.3	77.8	89.9
Net income ($ mil.)	–	(6.5)	(4.4)	(11.4)	(16.6)	(15.7)
Market value ($ mil.)	(14.5%)	33.8	37.3	82.4	74.7	21.1
Employees	(4.1%)	1,953	1,820	1,674	1,725	1,725

*Fiscal year change

COSKATA INC.

4575 Weaver Pkwy. Ste. 100
Warrenville IL 60555
Phone: 630-657-5800
Fax: 630-657-5801
Web: www.coskata.com

CEO: William Roe
CFO: David Blair
HR: –
FYE: December 31
Type: Private

Coskata is looking to turn biowaste into biotreasure. Through a proprietary process Coskata produces cellulosic ethanol from plant-derived biomass agricultural residues municipal wastes and other feedstock. The company which is currently developing and refining its production technology operates a semi-commercial facility in Pennsylvania and intends to begin producing fuel-grade ethanol on a fully commercial scale at a future plant in Alabama. In an effort to secure funding for its new plant Coskata filed a $100 million IPO in late 2011. It has also received financing from the USDA for the construction of the facility.

COSTAR GROUP, INC.
NMS: CSGP

1331 L Street, N.W.
Washington, DC 20005
Phone: 202 346-6500
Fax: 877 739-0486
Web: www.costargroup.com

CEO: Andrew Florance
CFO: Scott Wheeler
HR: –
FYE: December 31
Type: Public

CoStar is the leading provider of information analytics and online marketplace services through its comprehensive proprietary database of commercial real estate information in the US Canada the UK France Spain and Germany. Its hundreds of data points include location ownership and tenant names. Clients include government agencies real estate brokerages real estate investment trusts (REITs) and property owners and managers who stand to benefit from insight on property values market conditions and current availabilities. Most of CoStar's sales come from subscription fees. The company was founded in 1987. Majority of the company's sales were generated from the North America.

	Annual Growth	12/16	12/17	12/18	12/19	12/20
Sales ($ mil.)	18.6%	837.6	965.2	1,191.8	1,399.7	1,659.0
Net income ($ mil.)	27.8%	85.1	122.7	238.3	315.0	227.1
Market value ($ mil.)	48.8%	74,291.4	117,039.9	132,959.2	235,814.0	364,295.7
Employees	11.6%	3,064	3,711	3,705	4,337	4,753

COSTCO WHOLESALE CORP
NMS: COST

999 Lake Drive
Issaquah, WA 98027
Phone: 425 313-8100
Fax: –
Web: www.costco.com

CEO: W. Craig Jelinek
CFO: Richard Galanti
HR: –
FYE: August 29
Type: Public

Operating approximately 815 membership warehouse stores Costco is the nation's largest wholesale club operator. Primarily under the Costco Wholesale banner it serves more than 111 million cardholders in some 45 US states Washington DC and Puerto Rico and about 10 other countries. The company carries an average of approximately 4000 active stock keeping units (SKUs) per warehouse in its core warehouse business significantly less than other broadline retailers (many in bulk packaging) ranging from alcoholic beverages and appliances to fresh food pharmaceuticals and tires. Certain club memberships also offer products and services such as car and home insurance real estate services and travel packages. Costco generates most of its sales in the US.

	Annual Growth	09/17	09/18	09/19*	08/20	08/21
Sales ($ mil.)	11.0%	129,025.0	141,576.0	152,703.0	166,761.0	195,929.0
Net income ($ mil.)	16.9%	2,679.0	3,134.0	3,659.0	4,002.0	5,007.0
Market value ($ mil.)	29.9%	69,914.4	103,002.7	130,232.3	153,918.6	198,971.5
Employees	5.7%	231,000	245,000	254,000	273,000	288,000

*Fiscal year change

COTERRA ENERGY INC
NYS: CTRA

Three Memorial City Plaza, 840 Gessner Road, Suite 1400
Houston, TX 77024
Phone: 281 589-4600
Fax: 281 589-4653
Web: www.cabotog.com

CEO: Thomas Jorden
CFO: Scott Schroeder
HR: –
FYE: December 31
Type: Public

Cabot Oil & Gas Corporation is an independent oil and gas development exploitation exploration and production company. It sells gas to industrial customers local utilities power generation facilities and gas marketers in the US and has proved reserves of some 12.9 Tcfe (trillion cubic feet of natural gas equivalent). The company focuses its natural gas development efforts on the Marcellus Shale in Northeast Pennsylvania (Susquehanna County) which accounts for substantially all of its production. Cabot Oil & Gas has approximately 173000 net acres in the dry gas window of the Marcellus Shale. The company has drilled approximately 950 net horizontal wells in its 10 years of drilling in the basin. Cabot Oil & Gas began its horizontal drilling program in 2008.

	Annual Growth	12/16	12/17	12/18	12/19	12/20
Sales ($ mil.)	6.1%	1,155.7	1,764.2	2,188.1	2,066.3	1,466.6
Net income ($ mil.)	–	(417.1)	100.4	557.0	681.1	200.5
Market value ($ mil.)	(8.6%)	9,317.6	11,407.7	8,914.8	6,944.4	6,493.6
Employees	(3.3%)	576	468	303	274	503

COTTON INCORPORATED

6399 WESTON PKWY
CARY, NC 275132314
Phone: 919-677-9228
Fax: –
Web: www.cottoninc.com

CEO: J Berrye Worsham III
CFO: David N Byrd
HR: –
FYE: December 31
Type: Private

Cotton Incorporated battles both boll weevils and synthetic fibers. The organization bolsters the demand and profitability of the US cotton industry through its research and marketing efforts. To the public Cotton Incorporated is known for its white-on-brown "Seal of Cotton" logo and its advertising slogan "The fabric of our lives." Founded in 1970 Cotton Incorporated is funded by US growers of upland cotton cotton importers and cotton-product makers. Its board consists of representatives from each cotton-growing state — all of whom are cotton producers — and is overseen by the US Department of Agriculture.

	Annual Growth	12/04	12/05	12/13	12/14	12/15
Sales ($ mil.)	0.6%	–	72.6	81.1	77.0	77.3
Net income ($ mil.)	(3.6%)	–	0.5	5.5	(3.9)	0.3
Market value ($ mil.)	–	–	–	–	–	–
Employees	–	–	–	–	–	157

COTY, INC.
NYS: COTY

350 Fifth Avenue
New York, NY 10118
Phone: 212 389-7300
Fax: –
Web: www.coty.com

CEO: Sue Nabi
CFO: Laurent Mercier
HR: –
FYE: June 30
Type: Public

Coty is one of the leading makers of fragrances and beauty products for men and women across the globe. Its lineup ranges from moderately priced scents and cosmetics sold by mass retailers to prestige fragrances and premium skincare products found in hypermarkets department stores drugstores and pharmacies. The company's nearly 40 owned or licensed brands include some of the world's most well-known including COVERGIRL Max Factor philosophy Escada Calvin Klein and Stetson. It generates most of its revenue outside the Americas. With a history that dates to 1904 Coty operates in approximately 130 countries and territories.

	Annual Growth	06/17	06/18	06/19	06/20	06/21
Sales ($ mil.)	(11.8%)	7,650.3	9,398.0	8,648.5	4,717.8	4,629.9
Net income ($ mil.)	–	(422.2)	(168.8)	(3,784.2)	(1,006.7)	(201.3)
Market value ($ mil.)	(16.0%)	14,370.2	10,800.6	10,264.4	3,424.0	7,154.4
Employees	(15.1%)	22,000	20,000	19,000	18,260	11,430

COUNCIL OF BETTER BUSINESS BUREAUS INC.

3033 WILSON BLVD STE 600
ARLINGTON, VA 222013863
Phone: 703-276-0100
Fax: –

CEO: Stephen A Cox
CFO: Joseph E Dillon
HR: –
FYE: December 31
Type: Private

The Council of Better Business Bureaus (BBB) helps North American consumers and businesses know who's on the up-and-up. The non-profit organization comprises independent BBBs and branches in about 125 locations throughout North America as well as some 240 national companies that have shown a commitment to business ethics. More than 300000 companies that have demonstrated a similar commitment belong to local BBBs. The companies can promote their adherence to BBB standards; in return they are subject to "reliability reports" that consist of any complaints clients or partners have had about them. BBBs work to resolve disputes between consumers and businesses and review companies' advertising.

	Annual Growth	12/06	12/07	12/08	12/09	12/11
Sales ($ mil.)	(70.3%)	–	2,010.8	17.8	18.5	15.7
Net income ($ mil.)	–	–	–	(0.6)	(0.1)	(1.0)
Market value ($ mil.)	–	–	–	–	–	–
Employees	–	–	–	–	–	119

COUNCIL ON FOREIGN RELATIONS, INC.

58 E 68TH ST
NEW YORK, NY 100655953
Phone: 212-434-9400
Fax: –
Web: www.cfr.org

CEO: Carla Hills
CFO: –
HR: –
FYE: June 30
Type: Private

The Council on Foreign Relations (CFR) was established in 1921 with support from the Rockefeller family to provide a forum for government officials corporate executives journalists students and other interested parties to study and discuss world issues and the related impact on American foreign policy. The independent nonpartisan council publishes Foreign Affairs a magazine that comes out six times a year along with books and studies by its own scholars. It also sponsors task forces and hosts meetings attended by world leaders government officials and diplomats. Prospective members must be US citizens (native-born or naturalized) and are nominated by an existing member. CFR currently has about 4700 members.

	Annual Growth	06/14	06/15	06/16	06/18	06/19
Sales ($ mil.)	16.0%	–	77.5	82.9	94.2	140.1
Net income ($ mil.)	49.6%	–	12.7	4.4	20.5	63.7
Market value ($ mil.)	–	–	–	–	–	–
Employees	–	–	–	–	–	200

COUNTERPART INTERNATIONAL INC

2345 CRYSTAL DR STE 301
ARLINGTON, VA 222024810
Phone: 571-447-5700
Fax: –
Web: www.counterpart.org

CEO: Jeffrey T Lariche
CFO: Kathleen Rowan
HR: –
FYE: September 30
Type: Private

Counterpart International finds perfect partners to work together in improving the quality of life for communities worldwide. The not-for-profit humanitarian relief organization provides food medical supplies disaster relief technical and economic assistance and training to countries in the former Soviet Union Central Asian republics Southeast Asia Eastern Europe and Africa. It helps to form coalitions of companies governments and grass roots organizations to build schools and hospitals foster micro-businesses and develop tourism in war-torn or disaster-affected areas. Counterpart was founded in 1965 as the Foundation for the Peoples of the South Pacific.

	Annual Growth	09/07	09/08	09/09	09/15	09/16
Sales ($ mil.)	(6.6%)	–	107.6	87.2	64.6	62.3
Net income ($ mil.)	–	–	(0.2)	(0.6)	(0.0)	(0.3)
Market value ($ mil.)	–	–	–	–	–	–
Employees	–	–	–	–	–	45

COUNTRY PRIDE COOPERATIVE, INC.

648 W 2ND ST
WINNER, SD 575801230
Phone: 605-842-2711
Fax: –
Web: www.countrypridecoop.com

CEO: –
CFO: –
HR: –
FYE: June 30
Type: Private

The Country Pride Cooperative has provided assistance to farmers in south central South Dakota since 1935. Country Pride offers it members an agronomy center seed sales grain storage and merchandising a feed mill and an equipment-rental center as well as finance programs and farm supply stores an auto-service center and bulk refined fuel delivery. It also operates five convenience stores under the Cenex name. The co-op was created through the 2000 merger of two area cooperatives Freeman Oil Cooperative (formed in 1935) and Dakota Pride Cooperative.

	Annual Growth	06/08	06/09	06/10	06/11	06/12
Sales ($ mil.)	25.0%	–	–	109.4	139.6	170.8
Net income ($ mil.)	64.1%	–	–	1.3	2.3	3.4
Market value ($ mil.)	–	–	–	–	–	–
Employees	–	–	–	–	–	200

COUNTY BANK CORP.(LAPEER, MI)
NBB: CBNC

83 West Nepessing St.
Lapeer, MI 48446
Phone: 810 664-2977
Fax: –
Web: www.lakestonebank.com

CEO: –
CFO: –
HR: –
FYE: December 31
Type: Public

County Bank Corp is the holding company for Lapeer County Bank & Trust (LCBT) which operates about 10 branches in southeastern Michigan's Lapeer County north of Detroit. Founded in 1902 the bank offers traditional services such as checking and savings accounts CDs IRAs and and trust services. LCBT focuses on real estate lending: Commercial and single-family residential mortgages together make up approximately three-quarters of its loan portfolio. The bank also originates business construction municipal land and consumer loans. Its CBC Financial Services subsidiary offers insurance investment and financial planning services.

	Annual Growth	12/12	12/13	12/14	12/15	12/16
Assets ($ mil.)	17.9%	301.8	311.9	321.5	324.2	583.8
Net income ($ mil.)	11.7%	1.9	3.5	3.6	3.5	2.9
Market value ($ mil.)	22.9%	27.0	32.8	38.9	49.2	61.6
Employees	–	–	–	–	–	–

COUNTY OF ALAMEDA

1221 OAK ST STE 555
OAKLAND, CA 946124224
Phone: 510-272-6691
Fax: –
Web: www.acgov.org

CEO: –
CFO: –
HR: Sharen Stanek
FYE: June 30
Type: Private

Just east of San Francisco Bay lies Alameda County. Governed by a five-member board of supervisors it includes 14 cities among them Hayward Oakland and San Leandro. Nearly 60 departments handle services like behavioral health care emergency medical and human resources along with law enforcement property tax assessment and collection and community development for a population of more than 1.5 million. The county also serves as the keeper of birth death and marriage certificates and other public records. Its budget is more than $2.7 billion; most of it goes to public assistance public protection and health care. Alameda was incorporated in 1853 from parts of neighboring Contra Costa and Santa Clara counties.

	Annual Growth	06/11	06/12	06/13	06/14	06/15
Sales ($ mil.)	4.1%	–	2,403.0	2,622.5	2,579.8	2,714.7
Net income ($ mil.)	–	–	(155.8)	65.7	203.0	(26.6)
Market value ($ mil.)	–	–	–	–	–	–
Employees	–	–	–	–	–	8,000

COUNTY OF LOS ANGELES

500 W TEMPLE ST STE 437
LOS ANGELES, CA 900122724
Phone: 213-974-1101
Fax: –
Web: www.lacounty.gov

CEO: Fesia Davenport
CFO: –
HR: –
FYE: June 30
Type: Private

The County of Los Angeles could easily be its own country; all it really needs is just an "r." It encompasses more than 4000 square miles 88 cities two islands and has a population of more than 10 million. The regional level of state government provides such services as law enforcement property assessment tax collection public health protection and other social services within its boundaries (sometimes sharing and often providing municipal services for unincorporated cities). The county's elected Board of Supervisors provide political direction filling executive legislative and judicial roles while the various departments manage daily operations. LA County has an annual budget of nearly $30 billion.

	Annual Growth	06/16	06/17	06/18	06/19	06/20
Sales ($ mil.)	7.9%	–	20,065.0	21,191.2	23,510.6	25,198.2
Net income ($ mil.)	(6.3%)	–	393.5	403.5	915.5	324.0
Market value ($ mil.)	–	–	–	–	–	–
Employees	–	–	–	–	–	100,000

COURIER CORP.
NMS: CRRC

15 Wellman Avenue
North Chelmsford, MA 01863
Phone: 978 251-6000
Fax: –
Web: www.courier.com

CEO: –
CFO: –
HR: –
FYE: September 27
Type: Public

Courier dispatches books for playing praying and puzzling over. One of the largest book printers in the US Courier manufactures a variety of books for educational religious and specialty trade publishers and organizations. Most of its business comes from book printing operations which produce more than 175 million books per year and serve more than 500 customers; clients include Bible distributor The Gideons International and publishing giant Pearson. A book publisher itself Courier offers books for niche markets through subsidiaries Creative Homeowner (home and garden topics) Dover Publications (fiction and non-fiction) and Research & Education Association (education materials).

	Annual Growth	09/10	09/11	09/12	09/13	09/14
Sales ($ mil.)	2.5%	257.1	259.4	261.3	274.9	283.3
Net income ($ mil.)	2.3%	7.1	0.1	9.2	11.2	7.8
Market value ($ mil.)	(3.2%)	167.6	79.7	139.6	181.0	147.3
Employees	(1.3%)	1,662	1,568	1,501	1,560	1,576

COUSINS PROPERTIES INC
NYS: CUZ

3344 Peachtree Road NE, Suite 1800
Atlanta, GA 30326-4802
Phone: 404 407-1000
Fax: –
Web: www.cousins.com

CEO: M Colin Connolly
CFO: Gregg Adzema
HR: –
FYE: December 31
Type: Public

Cousins Properties a real estate investment trust (REIT) which buys develops and manages Class-A office properties mainly in high-growth markets in the Sunbelt region of the US. Its portfolio includes 19.7 million sq. ft. of office space and 310000 square feet of mixed-use space in Atlanta Austin Dallas and Charlotte. The company conducts its operations through Cousins Properties LP ("CPLP"). Its other subsidiary Cousins TRS Services LLC ("CTRS") also manages its own real estate portfolio and also provides real estate related services for other parties.

	Annual Growth	12/17	12/18	12/19	12/20	12/21
Sales ($ mil.)	12.8%	466.2	475.2	657.5	740.3	755.1
Net income ($ mil.)	6.5%	216.3	79.2	150.4	237.3	278.6
Market value ($ mil.)	44.5%	1,375.4	1,174.6	6,125.9	4,981.0	5,989.2
Employees	3.0%	261	257	331	316	294

COVANCE INC.
NYS: CVD

210 Carnegie Center
Princeton, NJ 08540
Phone: 609 452-4440
Fax: 609 452-9375
Web: www.covance.com

CEO: Joseph L Herring
CFO: Alison A Cornell
HR: –
FYE: December 31
Type: Public

Behind every great big drug company stands a great big contract research organization (CRO) and Covance is one of the biggest. Covance helps pharmaceutical and biotech companies worldwide develop new drugs by providing the fullest range of testing services from preclinical investigations all the way through designing and carrying out human clinical trials and conducting post-marketing studies to determine if drugs are safe and/or effective. Services include toxicology studies and biostatistical analysis. Among the company's customers are pharmaceutical biotech and medical device companies. Covance also offers laboratory testing services to companies in the chemical agrochemical and food industries.

	Annual Growth	12/08	12/09	12/10	12/11	12/12
Sales ($ mil.)	6.7%	1,827.1	1,962.6	2,038.5	2,236.4	2,365.8
Net income ($ mil.)	(16.7%)	196.8	175.9	68.3	132.2	94.7
Market value ($ mil.)	5.8%	2,531.0	3,000.6	2,826.8	2,513.9	3,176.5
Employees	7.0%	9,000	10,320	10,528	11,292	11,790

COVANTA HOLDING CORP
NYS: CVA

445 South Street
Morristown, NJ 07960
Phone: 862 345-5000
Fax: –
Web: www.covanta.com

CEO: Azeez Mohammed
CFO: Bradford J Helgeson
HR: –
FYE: December 31
Type: Public

Covanta Holding Corporation provides sustainable waste services to municipalities across the US. It treats and recycles municipal solid waste?some 21 million tons annually?into electricity through some 75 energy-from-waste (EfW) mass-burn facilities. Though the company makes most of its revenue from waste management services Covanta also sells electricity (around 10 million megawatt hours in a year) and recycles ferrous and non-ferrous metals as part of its waste treatment process. Beyond the US the company manages some EfW projects in Ireland Italy and UK and China which were currently under development and construction. Its largest market is in US.

	Annual Growth	12/15	12/16	12/17	12/18	12/19
Sales ($ mil.)	3.3%	1,645.0	1,699.0	1,752.0	1,868.0	1,870.0
Net income ($ mil.)	(38.1%)	68.0	(4.0)	57.0	152.0	10.0
Market value ($ mil.)	(1.1%)	2,029.2	2,043.6	2,213.9	1,758.0	1,944.0
Employees	1.3%	3,800	3,600	3,700	4,000	4,000

COVENANT HEALTH

100 FORT SANDERS W BLVD
KNOXVILLE, TN 379223353
Phone: 865-531-5555
Fax: –
Web: www.covenanthealth.com

CEO: Jim Vandersteeg
CFO: John Geppi
HR: –
FYE: December 31
Type: Private

Covenant Health has made a pact to provide good health to the good people of Tennessee. The not-for-profit health care system established in 1996 provides a variety of medical services through seven acute care hospitals a psychiatric hospital and a number of specialty outpatient centers offering geriatrics pediatric care cancer services weight management and diagnostics. Covenant Health also operates home health and hospice agencies and a physician practice management company. Covenant Health provides staffing and medical management services to its affiliated facilities and to make itself a really well-rounded health care provider it operates the Covenant Health Federal Credit Union.

	Annual Growth	12/16	12/17	12/18	12/19	12/20
Sales ($ mil.)	5.0%	–	1,268.2	1,296.5	1,407.0	1,470.1
Net income ($ mil.)	3.1%	–	144.5	(49.1)	183.9	158.6
Market value ($ mil.)	–	–	–	–	–	–
Employees	–	–	–	–	–	2,469

COVENANT HEALTH SYSTEM

3615 19TH ST
LUBBOCK, TX 794101209
Phone: 806-725-1011
Fax: –
Web: www.covenanthealth.org

CEO: Richard Parks
CFO: Denise Saenz
HR: –
FYE: June 30
Type: Private

Covenant Health System ties West Texas and Eastern New Mexico together with quality health care. The health services provider offers some 1100 beds in its five primary acute-care and specialty hospitals; it also manages about a dozen affiliated community hospitals. Covenant Health System part of Providence St. Joseph Health also maintains a network of family health care and medical clinics. Covenant Health System's major facilities are Covenant Medical Center Covenant Specialty Hospital and Covenant Women's and Children's Hospital. The health system also includes some 20 clinics and 50 physician practices and its extensive outreach programs target isolated rural communities with mobile services.

	Annual Growth	06/07	06/08	06/09	06/13	06/15
Sales ($ mil.)	(8.3%)	–	–	1,185.2	552.9	703.0
Net income ($ mil.)	–	–	–	(38.3)	35.7	76.3
Market value ($ mil.)	–	–	–	–	–	–
Employees	–	–	–	–	–	5,000

COVENANT LOGISTICS GROUP INC   NMS: CVLG

400 Birmingham Hwy.
Chattanooga, TN 37419
Phone: 423 821-1212
Fax: 423 821-5442
Web: www.covenanttransport.com

CEO: David Parker
CFO: –
HR: –
FYE: December 31
Type: Public

Truckload freight carrier Covenant Transportation Group (CTG) promises its customers speedy service on long-haul cross-border and regional routes. The company operates a fleet of about 2550 tractors and about 7100 trailers including both dry vans and temperature-controlled units (through its Southern Refrigerated Transport subsidiary). In addition to for-hire transportation Covenant offers dedicated contract carriage (where drivers and equipment are assigned long-term to a customer or route) and freight brokerage services. The company gets business from manufacturers retailers and other transportation companies; among its top customers are Walmart and UPS. Covenant operates primarily in North America.

	Annual Growth	12/16	12/17	12/18	12/19	12/20
Sales ($ mil.)	5.7%	670.7	705.0	885.5	894.5	838.6
Net income ($ mil.)	–	16.8	55.4	42.5	8.5	(42.7)
Market value ($ mil.)	(6.5%)	331.4	492.3	329.0	221.5	253.8
Employees	2.5%	4,619	4,540	5,819	5,850	5,100

COVENANT MEDICAL CENTER, INC.

1447 N HARRISON ST
SAGINAW, MI 486024727
Phone: 989-583-0000
Fax: –
Web: www.covenanthealthcare.com

CEO: Edward Bruff
CFO: Mark Gronda
HR: –
FYE: June 30
Type: Private

Covenant Medical Center (operating as Covenant HealthCare) has made a pact with Wolverine Staters to try to keep them in good health. The not-for-profit health care provider operates more than 20 inpatient and outpatient care facilities including its two main Covenant Medical Center campuses. It serves residents in a 20-county area of east-central Michigan with additional facilities in Bay City Frankenmuth and Midland. Specialized care services include cardiovascular health cancer treatment and obstetrics. The regional health care system has more about 650 beds.

	Annual Growth	06/09	06/10	06/14	06/15	06/16
Sales ($ mil.)	2.2%	–	508.5	566.6	536.0	579.6
Net income ($ mil.)	6.2%	–	28.1	34.3	31.3	40.3
Market value ($ mil.)	–	–	–	–	–	–
Employees	–	–	–	–	–	4,000

COVER-ALL TECHNOLOGIES, INC.   ASE: COVR

412 Mt. Kemble Avenue, Suite 110C
Morristown, NJ 07960
Phone: 973 461-5200
Fax: –
Web: www.cover-all.com

CEO: –
CFO: –
HR: –
FYE: December 31
Type: Public

Cover-All Technologies keeps insurers covered. The company offers software and services for carriers agents and brokers in the property/casualty insurance industry. Cover-All's software which the company licenses and offers as a hosted application automates insurance rating and policy issuance. Its My Insurance Center site an Internet-based portal for insurance professionals helps agents with policy quoting rating issuance and billing; provides quick access to policy information; and offers applications for managing insurance agencies. The company also provides product customization data integration and other support services that keep the software up-to-date on industry information and regulations.

	Annual Growth	12/09	12/10	12/11	12/12	12/13
Sales ($ mil.)	9.0%	14.5	17.5	17.6	16.2	20.5
Net income ($ mil.)	–	3.9	3.0	1.2	(5.0)	(2.9)
Market value ($ mil.)	5.7%	29.6	42.8	47.5	32.9	37.0
Employees	5.7%	48	82	71	76	60

COVERALL NORTH AMERICA, INC.

350 SW 12TH AVE
DEERFIELD BEACH, FL 334423106
Phone: 561-922-2500
Fax: –
Web: www.coverall.com

CEO: –
CFO: Marilyn Felos
HR: –
FYE: December 31
Type: Private

Coverall North America operating as Coverall Health-Based Cleaning System has commercial cleaning covered. The company is a franchisor of commercial cleaning businesses. Through more than 35 support centers and over 8000 franchisees worldwide the company offers franchises that provides janitorial services to fitness facilities retail locations office buildings health care facilities manufacturing and industrial plants and educational facilities. The company's local Support Centers provide training support commercial cleaning and other programs to its Coverall Franchised Businesses. Headquartered in Deerfield Beach Florida the company was founded in 1985.

	Annual Growth	12/03	12/04	12/05	12/06	12/07
Assets ($ mil.)	6.0%	–	–	50.1	53.4	56.3
Net income ($ mil.)	201.3%	–	–	1.5	6.7	13.2
Market value ($ mil.)	–	–	–	–	–	–
Employees	–	–	–	–	–	476

COVISINT CORPORATION

26533 EVERGREEN RD # 500　　　　　　CEO: Mark J Barrenechea
SOUTHFIELD, MI 480764234　　　　　　CFO: John Doolittle
Phone: 248-483-2000　　　　　　　　　HR: –
Fax: –　　　　　　　　　　　　　　　　FYE: March 31
Web: www.covisint.com　　　　　　　　Type: Private

Covisint keeps things copacetic between buyers and suppliers partners and customers with its enterprise and supply chain software. The company provides cloud-based systems for integrating business information and processes between links in the supply chain. The Compuware subsidiary offers industry-tailored products and services to customers in the automotive energy financial services and health care sectors. Customers which include a number of major car manufacturers use its products to share applications with registered users automate partner lifecycle administration and management and create partner portals for information exchange and data messaging. Covisint agreed to sell to Open Text in 2017.

	Annual Growth	03/13	03/14	03/15	03/16	03/17
Sales ($ mil.)	(10.9%)	–	–	88.5	76.0	70.2
Net income ($ mil.)	–	–	–	(38.6)	(14.9)	(12.7)
Market value ($ mil.)	–	–	–	–	–	–
Employees	–	–	–	–	–	382

COWAN SYSTEMS, LLC

4555 HOLLINS FERRY RD　　　　　　　CEO: Dennis Morgan
BALTIMORE, MD 212274610　　　　　　CFO: –
Phone: 410-247-0800　　　　　　　　　HR: –
Fax: –　　　　　　　　　　　　　　　　FYE: December 31
Web: www.cowansystems.com　　　　　Type: Private

Cowan Systems is a leader in the transportation industry. Cowan has more than 2000 tractors a fleet of approximately 2000 power units and over 6000 trailers. The company arranges the transportation of freight through its logistics unit. Working with a full scope of customers including many Fortune 500 companies and small businesses Cowan specializes in dedicated truckload intermodal warehousing brokerage and driver staffing. Its warehousing division is a premier 3PL with warehousing facilities located throughout the Mid-Atlantic area. It offers 100% supply chain solutions including local and long haul trucking in and out of Cowan facilities. Headquartered in Baltimore Maryland the company delivers to nearly 40 states.

	Annual Growth	12/12	12/13	12/14	12/15	12/16
Sales ($ mil.)	–	–	0.0	421.0	435.0	434.0
Net income ($ mil.)	–	–	0.0	0.0	0.0	21.0
Market value ($ mil.)	–	–	–	–	–	–
Employees	–	–	–	–	–	2,250

COWEN INC　　　　　　　　　　　　　NMS: COWN

599 Lexington Avenue　　　　　　　　CEO: Jeffrey Solomon
New York, NY 10022　　　　　　　　　CFO: Stephen Lasota
Phone: 646 562-1010　　　　　　　　　HR: –
Fax: –　　　　　　　　　　　　　　　　FYE: December 31
Web: www.cowen.com　　　　　　　　 Type: Public

Cowen along with its subsidiaries offers investment banking research sales and trading prime brokerage global clearing and commission management services and investment management through its business segments the operating company and the asset company. It provides services primarily to companies and institutional investor clients as well as media and telecommunications consumer and industrials sectors in the US and Europe. Some of its subsidiaries includes UK broker-dealer Cowen International Limited Cowen Execution Services Limited and Cowen and Company (Asia) Limited.

	Annual Growth	12/16	12/17	12/18	12/19	12/20
Sales ($ mil.)	36.2%	471.6	658.8	966.9	1,049.4	1,623.3
Net income ($ mil.)	–	(19.3)	(60.9)	42.8	24.6	216.4
Market value ($ mil.)	13.8%	416.1	366.4	358.1	422.8	697.7
Employees	12.8%	843	1,124	1,212	1,325	1,364

COX COMMUNICATIONS INC.

1400 Lake Hearn Dr.　　　　　　　　　CEO: Patrick J Esser
Atlanta GA 30319　　　　　　　　　　CFO: Mark F Bowser
Phone: 404-843-5000　　　　　　　　　HR: –
Fax: 949-595-7913　　　　　　　　　　FYE: December 31
Web: www.charismabrands.com　　　　Type: Subsidiary

Cox Communications carries the full complement of cable capacity. The company provides basic cable service to more than 6 million customers including about 3 million digital cable subscribers and 3.5 million Internet access subscribers in 15 states making it the third-largest US cable company behind Comcast and Time Warner Cable. Cox also provides telephone service as a competitive local-exchange carrier (CLEC). In addition Cox offers voice and data communications services to businesses and has investments in television programming and broadband technology companies. Cox Communications is a subsidiary of media conglomerate Cox Enterprises.

CPA2BIZ INC.

100 Broadway 6th Fl.　　　　　　　　 CEO: –
New York NY 10005　　　　　　　　　CFO: –
Phone: 646-233-5000　　　　　　　　　HR: –
Fax: 646-233-5090　　　　　　　　　　FYE: July 31
Web: www.cpa2biz.com　　　　　　　　Type: Subsidiary

CPA2Biz wants to help certified public accountants make their practices perfect. As the for-profit marketing arm of the American Institute of Certified Public Accountants (AICPA) the company offers resources to accounting professionals that include continuing professional education career resources online literature and other products and services. CPA2Biz markets its offerings nationwide through catalogs direct mail conferences specialty brochures e-newsletters e-mail Webcasts and industry tradeshows. It also offers member clients special programs such as small business banking through JPMorgan Chase payroll through Paychex and bill pay services through Bill.com.

CPI AEROSTRUCTURES, INC.　　　　　ASE: CVU

91 Heartland Blvd.　　　　　　　　　 CEO: Douglas McCrosson
Edgewood, NY 11717　　　　　　　　　CFO: Andrew Davis
Phone: 631 586-5200　　　　　　　　　HR: –
Fax: –　　　　　　　　　　　　　　　　FYE: December 31
Web: www.cpiaero.com　　　　　　　　Type: Public

To build an aircraft some assembly is required and CPI Aerostructures is ready. CPI Aero delivers contract production of structural aircraft subassemblies chiefly for the US Air Force and other US military customers. Military products include skin panels flight control surfaces leading edges wing tips engine components cowl doors and nacelle and inlet assemblies. The lineup is used on military aircraft such as the C-5A Galaxy and C-130 Hercules cargo jets E-3 Sentry AWACs jet and T-38 Talon jet trainer. As a subcontractor to OEMs CPI Aero also makes aprons and engine mounts for commercial aircraft such as business jets. Government prime and subcontracts represent a majority of CPI Aero's sales

	Annual Growth	12/16	12/17	12/18	12/19	12/20
Sales ($ mil.)	1.9%	81.3	81.3	83.9	87.5	87.6
Net income ($ mil.)	–	(3.6)	5.8	2.2	(4.5)	(1.3)
Market value ($ mil.)	(19.8%)	110.5	107.0	76.1	80.4	45.8
Employees	0.8%	259	230	281	258	267

CPI INTERNATIONAL INC.

5580 Skylane Blvd.
Santa Rosa CA 95403
Phone: 707-525-5788
Fax: 707-545-7901
Web: www.cpii.com

CEO: Robert A Fickett
CFO: Robert J Kemp
HR: –
FYE: September 30
Type: Private

CPI International makes broadcast and wireless components such as satellite communications transmitters amplifiers sensors X-ray equipment power supplies transmitters and microwave components. Its radio-frequency (RF) and microwave components go into a great deal of military hardware including Aegis-class cruisers and destroyers Patriot missile systems and fighter aircraft. The company serves clients in about 90 countries from sales and service offices across the US Europe Canada and Japan. In 2011 investment firm Veritas Capital took the company private in a transaction valued at around $525 million.

CPS TECHNOLOGIES CORP

NAS: CPSH

111 South Worcester Street
Norton, MA 02766-2102
Phone: 508 222-0614
Fax: –
Web: www.alsic.com

CEO: Michael McCormack
CFO: Charles Griffith
HR: –
FYE: December 26
Type: Public

CPS Technologies makes thermal management components for electronics using aluminum silicon carbide (ALSiC) metal matrix composites. Products include substrates baseplates and heat spreaders that are used by customers in motor controller and wireless communications component applications. CPS is working with the US Army on using its composite technology in armor for military vehicles. The company also licenses its technology to other manufacturers; revenue from licenses and royalties however has dwindled away to virtually nothing. CPS Technologies makes more than two-thirds of its sales to locations outside the US although the majority of its customers are actually based in the US.

	Annual Growth	12/16	12/17	12/18	12/19	12/20
Sales ($ mil.)	8.0%	15.4	14.6	21.6	21.5	20.9
Net income ($ mil.)	–	(0.5)	(1.7)	(3.7)	(0.6)	0.9
Market value ($ mil.)	5.2%	24.9	22.1	14.0	14.0	30.5
Employees	0.0%	104	143	156	152	104

CRA INTERNATIONAL INC

NMS: CRAI

200 Clarendon Street
Boston, MA 02116-5092
Phone: 617 425-3000
Fax: 617 425-3132
Web: www.crai.com

CEO: Paul Maleh
CFO: Daniel Mahoney
HR: –
FYE: January 02
Type: Public

CRA International doing business as Charles River Associates employs nearly 780 consultants offering economic financial and management counsel to corporate clients attorneys government agencies and other clients. Practices are organized into two areas. Litigation Regulatory and Financial Consulting advises on topics such as antitrust and competition damages valuation financial accounting and insurance economics. Management Consulting focus areas include auctions and competitive bidding business strategy and enterprise risk management. Charles River Associates has about 20 offices mainly in North America but also in Europe. Most business is conducted in the US. The firm was founded in 1965.

	Annual Growth	12/16	12/17	12/18	12/19*	01/21
Sales ($ mil.)	9.4%	324.8	370.1	417.6	451.4	508.4
Net income ($ mil.)	13.7%	12.9	7.6	22.5	20.7	24.5
Market value ($ mil.)	6.8%	281.6	345.8	314.8	412.1	391.8
Employees	9.0%	540	631	687	779	831

*Fiscal year change

CRACKER BARREL OLD COUNTRY STORE INC

NMS: CBRL

305 Hartmann Drive
Lebanon, TN 37087-4779
Phone: 615 444-5533
Fax: –
Web: www.cbrlgroup.com

CEO: Sandra Cochran
CFO: Craig Pommells
HR: Donna Roberts
FYE: July 30
Type: Public

Cracker Barrel Old Country Store owns and operates about 700 of its flagship restaurants known for their rustic old country-store design offering a full-service restaurant menu that features home-style country food and a wide variety of decorative and functional items such as rocking chairs holiday and seasonal gifts toys apparel cookware and foods. The eateries located mostly along interstate highways in about 45 states offer mostly standard American fare such as chicken ham and roast beef dishes but they are most popular as breakfast spots. It also operates a small number of Holler & Dash Biscuit House locations and holds a non-controlling stake in entertainment venue chain Punch Bowl Social.

	Annual Growth	07/17*	08/18	08/19*	07/20	07/21
Sales ($ mil.)	(0.9%)	2,926.3	3,030.4	3,072.0	2,522.8	2,821.4
Net income ($ mil.)	6.0%	201.9	247.6	223.4	(32.5)	254.5
Market value ($ mil.)	(3.3%)	3,653.1	3,420.7	4,047.4	2,595.7	3,199.8
Employees	(1.0%)	73,000	73,000	73,000	55,000	70,000

*Fiscal year change

CRAFT BREW ALLIANCE INC

NMS: BREW

929 North Russell Street
Portland, OR 97227-1733
Phone: 503 331-7270
Fax: –
Web: www.craftbrew.com

CEO: Andrew J Thomas
CFO: Christine Perich
HR: –
FYE: December 31
Type: Public

Competing with the big boys is more effective in an alliance. The Craft Brew Alliance brings together Redhook Ale Brewery (Seattle) Widmer Brothers Brewing (Portland) and Kona Brewing (Kona Hawaii) to brew market and sell their beers throughout the US and in international markets. The Alliance divides its business between beer comprising brewing and selling craft beers and pubs and other operations including five pubs four of which neighbor its breweries. Its lineup offers year-round and flagship brands (Pilsner Hefeweizen Longboard Lager). The Alliance competes against big beer makers and works with them. Its beers are distributed through an agreement with Anheuser-Busch which owns about 32% of the Alliance.

	Annual Growth	12/14	12/15	12/16	12/17	12/18
Sales ($ mil.)	0.8%	200.0	204.2	202.5	207.5	206.2
Net income ($ mil.)	7.7%	3.1	2.2	(0.3)	9.5	4.1
Market value ($ mil.)	1.8%	258.6	162.2	327.6	372.1	277.4
Employees	(4.1%)	785	820	800	665	665

CRAFTMADE INTERNATIONAL INC.

PINK SHEETS: CRFT

650 S. Royal Ln. Ste. 100
Coppell TX 75019-3810
Phone: 972-393-3800
Fax: 972-304-3754
Web: www.craftmade.com

CEO: Jean Liu
CFO: –
HR: Jack Grandel
FYE: June 30
Type: Public

Craftmade International is no celebrity but it is accustomed to fans and bright lights. The company designs manufactures and distributes Craftmade brand ceiling fans as well as lights for home use. Through its subsidiaries — Woodard Prime/Home Impressions and Trade Source International — it sells more than 80 fan models separate light kits doorbells and accessories. It also offers bathstrip and outdoor lighting lamps and Woodard brand outdoor furniture. Asian manufacturers produce most Craftmade lines sold to specialty retailers and mass merchandisers including Lowe's (31% of revenues) and Costco (7%). Craftmade also owns a 50% stake in Design Trends a Chinese distributor of lamps and shades.

CRANE CO.   NYS: CR

100 First Stamford Place
Stamford, CT 06902
Phone: 203 363-7300
Fax: –
Web: www.craneco.com

CEO: Max Mitchell
CFO: Richard Maue
HR: –
FYE: December 31
Type: Public

Crane Co. is a diversified manufacturer of highly engineered industrial products. Founded in 1855 Crane Co. provides products and solutions to customers in the chemicals oil & gas power automated payment solutions banknote design and production and aerospace & defense markets along with a wide range of general industrial and consumer related end markets. The company has four business segments: Fluid Handling Payment & Merchandising Technologies Aerospace & Electronics and Engineered Materials. Crane which operates in more than two dozen countries generates around 65% of total sales in US.

	Annual Growth	12/16	12/17	12/18	12/19	12/20
Sales ($ mil.)	1.7%	2,748.0	2,786.0	3,345.5	3,283.1	2,936.9
Net income ($ mil.)	10.2%	122.8	171.8	335.6	133.3	181.0
Market value ($ mil.)	1.9%	4,192.2	5,186.2	4,195.7	5,021.1	4,514.2
Employees	0.0%	11,000	10,600	12,000	13,000	11,000

CRAWFORD & CO.   NYS: CRD A

5335 Triangle Parkway
Peachtree Corners, GA 30092
Phone: 404 300-1000
Fax: –
Web: www.crawfordandcompany.com

CEO: Rohit Verma
CFO: William Swain
HR: –
FYE: December 31
Type: Public

Crawford & Company is the world's largest publicly listed independent provider of claims management and outsourcing services for risk management and insurance companies as well as self-insured entities. It operates through a global network of service providers in more than 70 countries. Clients turn to Crawford for field investigation and the evaluation and resolution of claims related to property damage from natural disasters and other incidents. It has another unit devoted to disability insurance and workers comp medical management and liability insurance. It also has a business line that handles large and complex claims. Crawford & Company was founded in 1941 by Jim Crawford.

	Annual Growth	12/16	12/17	12/18	12/19	12/20
Sales ($ mil.)	(3.6%)	1,177.6	1,163.7	1,123.0	1,047.6	1,016.2
Net income ($ mil.)	(5.8%)	36.0	27.7	26.0	12.5	28.3
Market value ($ mil.)	(6.0%)	505.3	453.5	474.9	612.0	394.3
Employees	(0.6%)	9,190	8,800	9,000	9,000	8,985

CRAWFORD UNITED CORP   NBB: CRAW A

10514 Dupont Avenue
Cleveland, OH 44108
Phone: 216 243-2614
Fax: –
Web: www.crawfordunited.com

CEO: Brian Powers
CFO: Jay Daly
HR: Karen Walker
FYE: December 31
Type: Public

Like "Wild Bill" of Wild West lore Hickok is quite comfortable shooting it out with competitors on its own measured road to success. The company manufactures testing equipment used by automotive technicians to repair cars. Hickok also makes instruments indicators and gauges for manufacturers of aircraft and locomotives. While Ford and General Motors traditionally were the company's largest customers its biggest customer now is Environmental Systems Products (ESP) at 53% of sales. Hickok sells products primarily in the US. In 2019 Hickok bought Data Genomix which develops social media marketing applications for political legal and recruiting campaigns. The companies are based in Cleveland Ohio.

	Annual Growth	09/17*	12/17	12/18	12/19	12/20
Sales ($ mil.)	52.9%	23.8	11.8	66.4	89.7	85.1
Net income ($ mil.)	60.7%	1.4	0.5	3.6	7.0	5.8
Market value ($ mil.)	25.9%	31.3	34.9	34.9	65.7	62.4
Employees	13.0%	180	200	275	271	260

*Fiscal year change

CRAY INC   NMS: CRAY

901 Fifth Avenue, Suite 1000
Seattle, WA 98164
Phone: 206 701-2000
Fax: –
Web: www.cray.com

CEO: Peter J Ungaro
CFO: Brian C Henry
HR: –
FYE: December 31
Type: Public

Cray makes computers that aren't just good — they're super. Its massively parallel and vector supercomputers provide the firepower behind research ranging from weather forecasting and scientific research to design engineering and classified government projects. The company also sells its own and third-party high-performance data storage products and provides maintenance and support services. Cray's largest customer is the US government which accounts for more than half of sales. Cray also targets academic institutions and industrial companies. Around two-thirds of sales come from customers in the US.

	Annual Growth	12/13	12/14	12/15	12/16	12/17
Sales ($ mil.)	(7.0%)	525.7	561.6	724.7	629.8	392.5
Net income ($ mil.)	–	–	32.2	62.3	27.5	10.6
Market value ($ mil.)	(3.1%)	1,111.2	1,395.2	1,313.1	837.6	979.3
Employees	5.1%	1,042	1,138	1,282	1,312	1,273

Note: Net income 12/17 = (133.8)

CREATIVE GROUP INC.

619 N LYNNDALE DR
APPLETON, WI 54914-3087
Phone: 920-739-8850
Fax: –
Web: www.creativegroupinc.com

CEO: Ronald Officer
CFO: Martin Van Stippen
HR: –
FYE: September 30
Type: Private

Creative Group Inc. has devoted its energy towards business improvement. The company provides a variety of marketing services specializing in building and managing incentive programs and planning corporate meetings and events. The company's incentive programs target sales reseller and employees offering travel merchandise and gift certificates as rewards for good performance. Creative Group also offers personal travel services including travel planning and emergency services that benefit from the company's large corporate travel business.

	Annual Growth	09/08	09/09	09/10	09/11	09/12
Sales ($ mil.)	0.0%	–	80.0	80.0	80.0	80.0
Net income ($ mil.)	–	–	0.0	0.0	0.0	0.0
Market value ($ mil.)	–	–	–	–	–	–
Employees	–	–	–	–	–	173

CREATIVE REALITIES INC   NAS: CREX

13100 Magisterial Drive, Suite 100
Louisville, KY 40223
Phone: 502 791-8800
Fax: –
Web: www.cri.com

CEO: Richard Mills
CFO: Will Logan
HR: –
FYE: December 31
Type: Public

Wireless Ronin Technologies makes the signs of the time. The company's Ronin-Cast electronic display products combine digital media players video monitors and wireless networking systems to enable the remote distribution of video marketing materials. Its digital signage is used for corporate logos and branding promotional displays interactive touchscreens movie theater schedules and restaurant menus. Wireless Ronin serves the automotive financial services gaming restaurant and retail industries among others. Customers include Chrysler Canada Carnival Ford KFC Thomson Reuters and Travelocity.

	Annual Growth	12/16	12/17	12/18	12/19	12/20
Sales ($ mil.)	6.3%	13.7	17.7	22.5	31.6	17.5
Net income ($ mil.)	–	(5.9)	(7.0)	(10.6)	1.0	(16.8)
Market value ($ mil.)	42.7%	3.4	3.5	24.9	16.7	14.1
Employees	1.7%	70	100	120	100	75

CREDIT ACCEPTANCE CORP (MI)   NMS: CACC

25505 West Twelve Mile Road
Southfield, MI 48034-8339
Phone: 248 353-2700
Fax: –

CEO: Kenneth Booth
CFO: –
HR: –
FYE: December 31
Type: Public

Credit Acceptance Corporation (CAC) offers financing programs that enable automobile dealers to sell vehicles to consumers. CAC makes the effort a reality. Working with approximately 60000 independent and franchised automobile dealers in the US CAC provides financing programs through a nationwide network of automobile dealers who benefit from sales of vehicles to consumers who otherwise could not obtain financing; from repeat and referral sales generated by these same customers; and from sales to customers responding to advertisements for the company's financing programs. CAC which concentrates its operations in a handful of US states typically funds about 3.6 million auto loans per year.

	Annual Growth	12/17	12/18	12/19	12/20	12/21
Sales ($ mil.)	13.7%	1,110.0	1,285.8	1,489.0	1,669.3	1,856.0
Net income ($ mil.)	19.5%	470.2	574.0	656.1	421.0	958.3
Market value ($ mil.)	20.7%	4,575.9	5,400.3	6,257.2	4,896.5	9,727.8
Employees	3.4%	1,817	2,040	2,016	2,033	2,073

CREDIT SUISSE (USA) INC

Eleven Madison Avenue
New York, NY 10010
Phone: 212 325-2000
Fax: –

CEO: Brady W Dougan
CFO: David C Fisher
HR: –
FYE: December 31
Type: Public

Credit Suisse (USA) is one of the top US investment banks offering advisory services on mergers and acquisitions raising capital securities underwriting and trading research and analytics and risk management products. Clients include corporations governments institutional investors such as hedge funds and private individuals. The company provides asset management services through Credit Suisse Private Equity; while Credit Suisse Private Banking USA offers wealth services to the rich throughout the country. Credit Suisse (USA) is a wholly owned subsidiary of Swiss banking powerhouse Credit Suisse Group and part of Credit Suisse Americas which includes North and South America and the Caribbean.

	Annual Growth	12/03	12/04	12/05	12/11	12/12
Sales ($ mil.)	8.3%	4,993.0	6,341.0	7,025.0	6,738.0	10,232.0
Net income ($ mil.)	5.0%	1,329.0	787.0	127.0	(272.0)	2,063.0
Market value ($ mil.)	0.0%	0.1	0.1	0.1	–	–
Employees	11.9%	8,706	9,344	10,899	–	–

CREDITRISKMONITOR.COM, INC.   NBB: CRMZ

704 Executive Boulevard, Suite A
Valley Cottage, NY 10989
Phone: 845 230-3000
Fax: –
Web: www.creditriskmonitor.com

CEO: Jerome Flum
CFO: Steven Gargano
HR: –
FYE: December 31
Type: Public

Need to monitor credit risk? CreditRiskMonitor.com (also called CRMZ) provides online financial information and news about some 40000 public companies worldwide marketing the service to corporate credit managers who use the data to make credit decisions. Subscribers get access to such information as company background financial statements trend reports and comparative analysis in addition to proprietary credit scores. The firm also provides access to information on more than 6 million public and private US companies through affiliations with third-party providers. CreditRiskMonitor.com was formed in 1999 after buying Market Guide's credit information database.

	Annual Growth	12/16	12/17	12/18	12/19	12/20
Sales ($ mil.)	5.3%	12.8	13.4	13.9	14.5	15.7
Net income ($ mil.)	–	0.1	0.0	(0.2)	0.2	(0.0)
Market value ($ mil.)	(6.7%)	33.2	18.8	20.4	16.8	25.2
Employees	0.5%	98	102	96	101	100

CREDO PETROLEUM CORPORATION   NASDAQ: CRED

1801 Broadway Ste. 900
Denver CO 80202-3837
Phone: 303-297-2200
Fax: 303-297-2204
Web: www.credopetroleum.com

CEO: Michael D Davis
CFO: Chris Nines
HR: –
FYE: October 31
Type: Public

CREDO Petroleum believes strongly in fossil fuels: It explores for produces and markets natural gas and crude oil in the US Gulf Coast Midcontinent and Rocky Mountain regions. The company has traditionally concentrated on shallow and medium-depth properties (7000-9000 ft.) but in recent years it has launched projects in Kansas and South Texas (where it is drilling to well depths ranging from 10000 to 17000 ft.). Subsidiary United Oil operates the company's properties in Oklahoma and CREDO Petroleum's other subsidiary SECO Energy owns royalty interests in the Rocky Mountains. In 2012 the company was acquired by the Forestar Group for about $146 million.

CRESCENT FINANCIAL BANCSHARES INC.   NASDAQ: CRFN

3600 Glenwood Ave. Ste. 300
Raleigh NC 27612
Phone: 919-659-9000
Fax: 919-460-2512
Web: www.crescentstatebank.com

CEO: –
CFO: –
HR: –
FYE: December 31
Type: Public

This Crescent helps your financial health take shape. Crescent Financial Bancshares is the holding company for Crescent State Bank which operates some 15 branches in central North Carolina. The bank focuses on serving businesses business owners and professionals. It offers standard products and services including checking and savings accounts CDs and credit cards. Commercial mortgages make up more than half of the company's loan portfolio; the bank also writes construction loans commercial and industrial loans home equity loans and residential mortgages. Through Crescent Investment Services it offers financial planning products and services.

CREST OPERATIONS, LLC

4725 HIGHWAY 28 E
PINEVILLE, LA 713604730
Phone: 318-448-0274
Fax: –
Web: www.crestoperations.com

CEO: –
CFO: –
HR: –
FYE: December 31
Type: Private

Crest Operations part of Crest Industries distributes and installs electrical substations and transmission products for electric power generation and utility customers worldwide through its DIS-TRAN and Beta Engineering subsidiaries. Other subsidiaries grow pine and hardwood trees in Louisiana and Texas (Crest Natural Resources) and make wooden utility poles and cross arms. Crest's Mid-State Supply Company subsidiary is a Louisiana-based distributor of electrical products that has showrooms for appliances and lighting. Crest Operations was founded in 1958.

	Annual Growth	12/15	12/16	12/17	12/18	12/19
Sales ($ mil.)	9.3%	–	254.7	278.8	273.9	332.9
Net income ($ mil.)	21.4%	–	5.6	(5.5)	(4.9)	10.1
Market value ($ mil.)	–	–	–	–	–	–
Employees	–	–	–	–	–	300

CRESTED BUTTE LLC

12 Snowmass Rd.
Mt. Crested Butte CO 81225
Phone: 970-349-2333
Fax: 970-349-2250
Web: www.skicb.com

CEO: –
CFO: –
HR: –
FYE: April 30
Type: Private

Whether it's cross country or downhill this butte is made for skiing. Crested Butte is a leading Colorado ski operator that owns the Crested Butte Mountain Resort within the Gunnison National Forest and the Elk Mountain Range. The ski resort offers more than 1100 acres of skiable terrain 16 lifts and a full range of accommodations and amenities. Crested Butte has hosted such events as Colorado's first X Games the US Extreme Freeskiing Championships and the Elk Mountain Grand Traverse. CNL Lifestyle Properties a real estate investment trust affiliated with CNL Financial Group owns the resort property and leases it to Triple Peaks a ski operator controlled by husband and wife team Tim and Diane Mueller.

CRESTWOOD MIDSTREAM PARTNERS LP

700 LOUISIANA ST STE 2550
HOUSTON, TX 770022756
Phone: 832-519-2200
Fax: –

CEO: Robert Phillips
CFO: Robert Halpin
HR: –
FYE: December 31
Type: Private

The middle of the oil and gas stream is best for Crestwood Midstream Partners (formerly Quicksilver Gas Services). The company gathers and processes natural gas and natural gas liquids from the Barnett Shale formation near Fort Worth Texas. Crestwood Midstream Partners' assets include a pipeline and a processing plant with 200 million cu. ft. a day capacity a processing unit at the existing plant extensions to the existing pipeline and pipelines in other drilling areas in Texas. In 2013 it merged with Inergy Midstream to become an $8 billion midstream entity.

	Annual Growth	12/12	12/13	12/14	12/15	12/16
Sales ($ mil.)	56.4%	–	658.6	2,565.5	2,632.8	2,520.5
Net income ($ mil.)	–	–	(15.1)	(21.9)	(1,410.6)	(197.5)
Market value ($ mil.)	–	–	–	–	–	–
Employees	–	–	–	–	–	1,300

CRETE CARRIER CORPORATION

400 NW 56TH ST
LINCOLN, NE 685288843
Phone: 800-998-4095
Fax: –
Web: www.cretecarrier.com

CEO: Tonn Ostergard
CFO: –
HR: –
FYE: September 30
Type: Private

Holding company Crete Carrier Corporation's flagship business Crete Carrier provides dry van truckload freight transportation services in the 48 contiguous states. It operates from some two dozen terminals mainly in the mid-western and southeastern US. The company's Shaffer Trucking unit transports temperature-controlled cargo and Hunt Transportation (no relation to J.B. Hunt Transport Services) hauls heavy equipment and other cargo on flatbed trailers. Overall the companies operate more than 5400 tractors and 13000 trailers. Family-owned Crete Carrier was founded in 1966 by chairman Duane Acklie; president and CEO Tonn Ostergard is his son-in-law.

	Annual Growth	09/13	09/14	09/15	09/16	09/18
Sales ($ mil.)	2.7%	–	1,034.1	0.0	984.1	1,150.6
Net income ($ mil.)	2.3%	–	127.1	0.0	95.8	139.2
Market value ($ mil.)	–	–	–	–	–	–
Employees	–	–	–	–	–	6,000

CREXENDO INC

NAS: CXDO

1615 South 52nd Street
Tempe, AZ 85281
Phone: 602 714-8500
Fax: –
Web: www.crexendo.com

CEO: Steven Mihaylo
CFO: Ronald Vincent
HR: –
FYE: December 31
Type: Public

Crexendo (formerly iMergent) would like to help increase the volume on your e-commerce business. Catering to home-based small and medium-sized businesses the company's cloud-based software helps merchants create manage and promote their e-commerce website and process orders. Premium services include site and logo design supplier integration and search engine optimization. The company has primarily used training seminars around the country to sell its products to aspiring e-commerce mavens but hopes to open more sales channels. More than 90% of sales come from customers in North America (US and Canada). Chairman and CEO Steven Mihaylo founder and former CEO of Inter-Tel owns more than a third of Crexendo.

	Annual Growth	12/16	12/17	12/18	12/19	12/20
Sales ($ mil.)	15.8%	9.1	10.4	11.9	14.4	16.4
Net income ($ mil.)	–	(2.8)	(1.0)	(0.2)	1.1	7.9
Market value ($ mil.)	47.8%	26.1	37.8	36.0	76.4	124.6
Employees	2.3%	53	54	56	56	58

CRISTA MINISTRIES

19303 FREMONT AVE N
SHORELINE, WA 981333800
Phone: 206-546-7200
Fax: –
Web: www.crista.org

CEO: Robert Lonac
CFO: Brian Kirkpatrick
HR: –
FYE: June 30
Type: Private

World Concern is concerned with the poorest of the poor around the world. The Christian not-for-profit helps about 4 million people a year in more than 30 nations. The group uses its own index of nine factors like economy health issues conflict and food availability along with prayer to determine which nations most need assistance. World Concern provides emergency relief and community development including small business loans agriculture starter kits prenatal education Christian literature village sanitation kits and donated goods (clothing plant seeds bedding). Founded in 1973 the group uses about 1300 volunteers throughout the world working from offices in the US Bolivia Kenya and Thailand.

	Annual Growth	06/12	06/13	06/14	06/15	06/16
Sales ($ mil.)	3.9%	–	102.8	101.7	105.5	115.2
Net income ($ mil.)	56.6%	–	1.5	6.0	4.6	5.7
Market value ($ mil.)	–	–	–	–	–	–
Employees	–	–	–	–	–	1,200

CROCS INC

NMS: CROX

13601 Via Varra
Broomfield, CO 80020
Phone: 303 848-7000
Fax: –
Web: www.crocs.com

CEO: Andrew Rees
CFO: Anne Mehlman
HR: –
FYE: December 31
Type: Public

Crocs is one of the world's largest footwear companies. Its shoe collection has grown by leaps and bounds from its ubiquitous classic slip-on clog to a range of trainers sandals and boots. Branded as Crocs its shoes are made of proprietary closed-cell resin and designed for men women and children. Jibbitz are the company's decorative add-on charms. It reaches customers via nearly 350 owned stores first- and third-party e-commerce sites and third-party retailers. Sold approximately 69.1 million pairs of shoes worldwide the company has customers in more than 80 countries and earns most of its sales outside the US. Every pair of Crocs is manufactured by other companies mostly in Vietnam and China.

	Annual Growth	12/17	12/18	12/19	12/20	12/21
Sales ($ mil.)	22.6%	1,023.5	1,088.2	1,230.6	1,386.0	2,313.4
Net income ($ mil.)	190.2%	10.2	50.4	119.5	312.9	725.7
Market value ($ mil.)	78.5%	736.9	1,514.6	2,442.2	3,653.1	7,475.2
Employees	7.1%	4,382	3,901	3,803	4,600	5,770

CROGHAN BANCSHARES, INC.   NBB: CHBH

323 Croghan Street   CEO: Rick Robertson
Fremont, OH 43420   CFO: Kendall Rieman
Phone: 419 332-7301   HR: –
Fax: –   FYE: December 31
Web: www.croghan.com   Type: Public

Croghan Bancshares is helping to share the wealth in the Buckeye state. The firm is the holding company for Croghan Colonial Bank which has about 10 branches in northern Ohio. Founded in 1888 the bank provides standard products and services including checking and savings accounts money market accounts certificates of deposit and credit cards Its lending activities primarily consist of residential and commercial mortgages and to a lesser extent agricultural business construction and consumer loans. In addition the bank offers wealth management investments estate planning private banking and trust services.

	Annual Growth	12/16	12/17	12/18	12/19	12/20
Assets ($ mil.)	5.8%	819.6	843.0	847.6	876.8	1,028.5
Net income ($ mil.)	10.8%	9.1	10.2	12.0	12.5	13.7
Market value ($ mil.)	3.1%	102.5	112.2	111.0	119.3	116.0
Employees	(1.1%)	208	205	203	207	199

CROPKING INCORPORATED

134 West Dr.   CEO: Paul Brentlinger
Lodi OH 44254   CFO: –
Phone: 330-302-4203   HR: –
Fax: 330-302-4204   FYE: July 31
Web: www.cropking.com   Type: Private

Marketing controlled environment agriculture for fun and profit CropKing makes and sells greenhouses equipment and supplies for growing hydroponic crops (that is growing crops without soil in a controlled environment). CropKing's hydroponic greenhouse systems protect crops from environmental elements allowing year-round production of such plants as tomatoes lettuce and herbs. The company sells to hobbyists as well as to commercial customers. It offers grower workshops videos and literature through its Web site. Other products include aquaculture (fish farming) systems and mushroom production units. CropKing sells to customers throughout the US Canada Mexico Europe and the Caribbean.

CROSS BORDER RESOURCES INC.   NBB: XBOR

2515 McKinney Avenue, Suite 900   CEO: –
Dallas, TX 75201   CFO: –
Phone: 210 226-6700   HR: –
Fax: –   FYE: December 31
Web: www.xbres.com   Type: Public

Cross Border Resources is focusing its oil and gas exploration and development efforts on New Mexico and Texas. The company owns some 300000 net acres primarily in New Mexico with more than 30000 of those acres located in the prolific Permian Basin in West Texas. Its properties consist of working mineral and royalty interests in various oil and gas wells and lease acreage located in the counties of Chaves Eddy Lea and Roosevelt in New Mexico and the counties of Borden and Dawson in Texas. They produce more than 200 barrels of oil equivalent per day. Cross Border Resources formed in early 2011 following the business combination of Doral Energy and Pure Energy.

	Annual Growth	07/10*	12/11	12/12	12/13	12/14
Sales ($ mil.)	65.1%	1.7	7.3	14.8	13.1	12.4
Net income ($ mil.)	–	(13.8)	(1.2)	(2.4)	3.4	(2.5)
Market value ($ mil.)	128.0%	0.5	28.8	15.6	6.4	13.5
Employees	–	–	2	5	–	–

*Fiscal year change

CROSS COUNTRY HEALTHCARE INC   NMS: CCRN

6551 Park of Commerce Boulevard, N.W.   CEO: Kevin Clark
Boca Raton, FL 33487   CFO: William Burns
Phone: 561 998-2232   HR: Colin McDonald
Fax: –   FYE: December 31
Web: www.crosscountryhealthcare.com   Type: Public

Cross Country Healthcare (Cross Country) is one of the largest health care staffing firms in the US. Under several brands the company places traveling nurses and other health care professionals through approximately 5300 active contracts with acute care hospitals pharmaceutical companies nursing homes schools and other related facilities across the nation. The firm coordinates travel and housing arrangements for its nurses whose assignments usually last about three months at a time. Cross Country also provides consulting services health care personnel technical assistance on policies implementation and training related to children and youth with special needs in school settings. Subsidiaries and brands include Cross Country Nurses Cross Country Allied Cross Country Medical Staffing Network Cross Country Workforce Solutions Cross Country Education and Cejka Search.

	Annual Growth	12/16	12/17	12/18	12/19	12/20
Sales ($ mil.)	0.1%	833.5	865.0	816.5	822.2	836.4
Net income ($ mil.)	–	8.0	37.5	(17.0)	(57.7)	(13.0)
Market value ($ mil.)	(13.2%)	564.7	461.6	265.2	420.4	320.9
Employees	(4.4%)	1,737	1,800	1,750	1,700	1,450

CROSS TIMBERS ROYALTY TRUST   NYS: CRT

c/o The Corporate Trustee, Simmons Bank, 2911 Turtle Creek Blvd., Suite 850   CEO: –
Dallas, TX 75219   CFO: –
Phone: 855 588-7839   HR: –
Fax: –   FYE: December 31
Web: www.crt-crosstimbers.com   Type: Public

Cross Timbers Royalty Trust distributes royalties from more than 2900 oil and natural gas producing properties in Texas Oklahoma and New Mexico. The trust which was formed in 1991 does not operate or control any of its properties. Instead it owns stakes in wells located primarily in gas properties in the San Juan Basin of northwestern New Mexico. The trust's estimated proved reserves are 856000 barrels of oil and 25.6 billion cu. ft. of gas. XTO Energy which markets the trust's oil and gas owns the underlying propeties and distributed all of its trust units as a dividend to its stockholders in 2003.

	Annual Growth	12/16	12/17	12/18	12/19	12/20
Sales ($ mil.)	(8.5%)	7.6	6.6	9.2	6.0	5.3
Net income ($ mil.)	(7.4%)	6.4	6.1	8.6	5.3	4.7
Market value ($ mil.)	(17.7%)	107.8	88.1	65.5	52.4	49.4
Employees		–	–	–	–	–

CROSSAMERICA PARTNERS LP   NYS: CAPL

600 Hamilton Street, Suite 500   CEO: Charles Nifong
Allentown, PA 18101   CFO: Maura Topper
Phone: 610 625-8000   HR: –
Fax: –   FYE: December 31
Web: www.crossamericapartners.com   Type: Public

CrossAmerica Partners (formerly Lehigh Gas Partners) won't leave motorists running on empty as they drive across America. The company distributes gasoline and diesel fuel to 1174 gas stations in 16 US states mostly along the East Coast. CrossAmerica owns or leases about 660 gas stations franchised under various brands including BP ExxonMobil Shell and Valero; it also distributes branded motor fuel to Gulf and Sunoco gas stations. About 95% of the more than 906.2 million gallons of motor fuels distributed yearly by CrossAmerica is branded (including the Chevron Sunoco Valero Gulf and CITGO brands).

	Annual Growth	12/16	12/17	12/18	12/19	12/20
Sales ($ mil.)	0.8%	1,869.8	2,094.8	2,445.9	2,149.4	1,932.3
Net income ($ mil.)	78.0%	10.7	23.2	5.3	18.1	107.5
Market value ($ mil.)	(9.1%)	953.9	899.4	536.2	683.5	650.2
Employees	(27.7%)	744	604	548	–	203

CROSSLAND CONSTRUCTION COMPANY, INC.

833 S EAST AVE
COLUMBUS, KS 667252307
Phone: 620-429-1414
Fax: –
Web: www.crossland.com

CEO: Ivan E Crossland Jr
CFO: –
HR: –
FYE: July 31
Type: Private

Crossland Construction has crossed the prairie transitioning from a local player in Columbus Kansas to a firm with a strong regional presence. The company designs builds and manages construction of government education healthcare retail and other buildings from a handful of offices in Kansas Missouri Arkansas Oklahoma Colorado and Texas. Customers have included Harley-Davidson SAM'S CLUB McCune Brooks Hospital Embassy Suites and a variety of school districts and municipalities. Crossland builds everything from office buildings and warehouses to veteran's memorials and airports. The company which often works in partnership with PBA Architects was founded by Ivan Crossland Sr. in 1978.

	Annual Growth	07/02	07/03	07/04	07/07	07/08
Sales ($ mil.)	25.3%	–	–	176.3	336.1	434.2
Net income ($ mil.)	44.5%	–	–	2.3	11.4	10.2
Market value ($ mil.)	–	–	–	–	–	–
Employees	–	–	–	–	–	715

CROSSROADS SYSTEMS INC (NEW)

NBB: CRSS

4514 Cole Avenue, Suite 1600
Dallas, TX 75205
Phone: 214 999-0149
Fax: –
Web: www.crossroads.com

CEO: Eric Donnelly
CFO: Jennifer Ray Crane
HR: –
FYE: October 31
Type: Public

Crossroads Systems sets up shop where business and information intersect. The company provides storage networking equipment and data archiving systems used to manage and protect critical data. Its products include StrongBox (network attached storage appliance that uses linear tape file system technology) RVA (monitoring tape media and the condition of disk drives) and SPHiNX (protecting data by working as a network attached storage device or virtual tape library). Crossroads Systems sells directly to manufacturers such as HP (45% of sales) and EMC and through distributors. The company was founded in 1996.

	Annual Growth	10/17	10/18	10/19	10/20	10/21
Sales ($ mil.)	970.0%	0.1	28.4	37.7	36.6	930.6
Net income ($ mil.)	–	(1.7)	23.8	1.8	3.0	194.8
Market value ($ mil.)	54.1%	19.7	41.2	50.8	53.7	111.1
Employees	25.9%	–	–	–	27	34

CROSSTEX ENERGY INC

NMS: XTXI

2501 Cedar Springs
Dallas, TX 75201
Phone: 214 953-9500
Fax: –

CEO: Barry E Davis
CFO: Pablo Mercado
HR: –
FYE: December 31
Type: Public

Crosstex Energy Inc. owns and controls the general partner of and has a 17% limited partnership stake in major operating unit Crosstex Energy L.P. Crosstex Energy's energy sources (the Barnett and Haynesville shale plays) and markets are found in East Texas North Texas and the Louisiana Gulf Coast. It is engaged in natural gas gathering processing transmission and marketing. The company buys natural gas from independent producers. Crosstex Energy's assets include 3500 miles of natural gas gathering and transmission pipeline 10 processing plants and four fractionators. It also operates barge and rail terminals product storage facilities brine disposal wells and an major fleet of trucks.

	Annual Growth	12/08	12/09	12/10	12/11	12/12
Sales ($ mil.)	(23.8%)	4,907.0	1,459.1	1,792.7	2,013.9	1,655.9
Net income ($ mil.)	–	24.2	15.6	(11.7)	(6.0)	(12.5)
Market value ($ mil.)	38.5%	184.9	286.9	420.1	599.3	679.9
Employees	(1.4%)	780	456	469	494	736

CROWDER CONSTRUCTION COMPANY INC

6425 BROOKSHIRE BLVD
CHARLOTTE, NC 282160301
Phone: 800-849-2966
Fax: –
Web: www.crowdercc.com

CEO: –
CFO: –
HR: –
FYE: March 31
Type: Private

Seeking to stand out from the crowd of US-based construction companies Crowder Construction specializes in bridge and highway civil environmental and industrial construction serving a range of customers primarily in the Southeast US. The specialty construction company's projects include parking decks highway and bridge water and sewer treatment plant construction. Projects that have been completed by its Crowder Electrical unit range from power substations to light rail facilities. The now employee-owned company was founded in Charlotte North Carolina in 1947 by Bill and O. P. Crowder; it continues to be led by the Crowder family.

	Annual Growth	03/11	03/12	03/13	03/14	03/15
Sales ($ mil.)	(6.9%)	–	222.0	233.0	233.0	179.4
Net income ($ mil.)	–	–	0.0	0.0	0.0	0.4
Market value ($ mil.)	–	–	–	–	–	–
Employees	–	–	–	–	–	900

CROWLEY MARITIME CORPORATION

9487 REGENCY SQUARE BLVD # 101
JACKSONVILLE, FL 322257800
Phone: 904-727-2200
Fax: –
Web: www.crowley.com

CEO: Thomas Crowley Jr
CFO: Dan Warner
HR: –
FYE: December 31
Type: Private

Crowley founded in 1892 is a privately-held US-owned and operated logistics government marine and energy solutions company headquartered in Jacksonville Florida. Crowley owns operates and/or manages a fleet of more than 200 vessels consisting of RO/RO (roll-on-roll-off) vessels LO/LO (lift-on-lift-off) vessels articulated tug-barges (ATBs) LNG-powered container/roll-on roll-off ships (ConRos) and multipurpose tugboats and barges. Land-based facilities and equipment include port terminals warehouses tank farms gas stations office buildings trucks trailers containers chassis cranes and other specialized vehicles.

	Annual Growth	12/04	12/05	12/06	12/07	12/08
Sales ($ mil.)	18.0%	–	1,190.8	1,467.7	1,622.3	1,955.8
Net income ($ mil.)	30.3%	–	38.9	38.4	122.3	86.0
Market value ($ mil.)	–	–	–	–	–	–
Employees	–	–	–	–	–	4,329

CROWN BATTERY MANUFACTURING COMPANY

1445 MAJESTIC DR
FREMONT, OH 434209190
Phone: 419-334-7181
Fax: –
Web: www.crownbattery.com

CEO: –
CFO: Tim Hack
HR: –
FYE: September 30
Type: Private

Crown Battery Manufacturing doesn't let its power go to its head. The company manufactures and sells industrial batteries and chargers automotive batteries and commercial battery products to clients across North America. Products serve clients in the marine railroad mining and automotive industries; the company also offers products with deep-cycle and other heavy-duty applications. Other products include battery chargers and battery cleaners for industrial applications. The company was founded in 1926 by German immigrant William J. Koenig.

	Annual Growth	09/10	09/11	09/12	09/13	09/14
Sales ($ mil.)	5.9%	–	–	191.1	196.2	214.2
Net income ($ mil.)	40.1%	–	–	6.1	10.8	12.0
Market value ($ mil.)	–	–	–	–	–	–
Employees	–	–	–	–	–	615

CROWN CRAFTS, INC.

NAS: CRWS

916 South Burnside Avenue
Gonzales, LA 70737
Phone: 225 647-9100
Fax: –
Web: www.crowncrafts.com

CEO: E. Randall Chestnut
CFO: Craig Demarest
HR: –
FYE: March 28
Type: Public

Prospects for new business opportunities keep Crown Crafts drooling. Operating through its subsidiaries Hamco and Crown Crafts Infant Products the company designs and sells textile products for infants and juveniles. Crown Crafts designs makes and markets baby bibs burp cloths bathing accessories and bedding. The childcare products firm founded in 1957 has worked to regain profitability by selling or shuttering its US manufacturing operations and relying on foreign contractors mainly in China to make its goods. Crown Crafts' products are sold in department and specialty stores mass retailers catalog houses and outlet stores.

	Annual Growth	04/17	04/18*	03/19	03/20	03/21
Sales ($ mil.)	4.7%	66.0	70.3	76.4	73.4	79.2
Net income ($ mil.)	2.2%	5.6	3.0	5.0	6.6	6.1
Market value ($ mil.)	(1.7%)	82.2	59.0	51.6	47.5	76.8
Employees	2.4%	119	179	163	138	131

*Fiscal year change

CROWN GOLD CORPORATION

TSX VENTURE: CWM

970 Caughlin Crossing Ste 100
Reno NV 89509
Phone: 775-284-7200
Fax: 775-284-7202
Web: www.goldsummitcorp.com

CEO: –
CFO: –
HR: –
FYE: April 30
Type: Public

The top of the gold heap is where Crown Gold (formerly Gold Summit) aims to be. The company explores for and develops gold and silver prospect properties in the eastern and western US. Crown Gold focuses on explorations at several properties across Nevada including Monte Cristo Gold Basin and Blue Sphinx. The company with partner Astral Mining is also developing properties in North and South Carolina (Saluda and Bear Creek) where miners have not explored underground since the mid-1800s. It also plans to buy Pasofino Gold Corp. which holds assets in Colombia. The former Gold Summit merged with Crown Minerals in 2010 to form Crown Gold.

CROWN HOLDING COMPANY

Pasquerilla Plaza
Johnstown PA 15901
Phone: 814-536-4441
Fax: 814-535-9388
Web: www.crownamericanhotels.com

CEO: –
CFO: –
HR: –
FYE: January 31
Type: Private

Crown Holding's jewels are in the form of a couple of midscale hotels a restaurant and convention center. Formed as a masonry company in 1950 Crown Holding now focuses on managing a handful of properties in its hometown. Through privately held Crown American Hotels the company owns and manages four hotel restaurant and convention center properties in downtown Johnstown Pennsylvania. Its Holiday Inn and Holiday Inn Express there are both franchised through InterContinental Hotels. The company also owns Harrigan's Cafe and Wine Deck (attached to the Holiday Inn) and the Pasquerilla Conference Center named after company cofounder Frank Pasquerilla.

CROWN HOLDINGS INC

NYS: CCK

770 Township Line Road
Yardley, PA 19067-4232
Phone: 215 698-5100
Fax: –
Web: www.crowncork.com

CEO: Timothy J Donahue
CFO: Thomas A Kelly
HR: –
FYE: December 31
Type: Public

Crown Holdings is a leading global supplier of rigid packaging products to consumer marketing companies as well as transit and protective packaging products equipment and services to a broad range of end markets. Its portfolio includes beverage food and aerosol cans and ends glass bottles specialty packaging metal vacuum closures steel crowns and aluminum caps under brands Liftoff SuperEnd and Easylift. Crown also supplies can-making equipment and parts. Its roster of customers has included Anheuser-Busch InBev Coca-Cola SC Johnson Unilever FrieslandCampina and Procter & Gamble. Crown traces its historical roots all the way back to 1892. Most of its net sales is generated outside the US.

	Annual Growth	12/16	12/17	12/18	12/19	12/20
Sales ($ mil.)	8.7%	8,284.0	8,698.0	11,151.0	11,665.0	11,575.0
Net income ($ mil.)	3.9%	496.0	323.0	439.0	510.0	579.0
Market value ($ mil.)	17.5%	7,086.5	7,582.6	5,603.7	9,778.5	13,507.1
Employees	8.3%	24,000	24,000	33,000	33,000	33,000

CROWN MEDIA HOLDINGS INC

NMS: CRWN

12700 Ventura Boulevard, Suite 200
Studio City, CA 91604
Phone: 818 755-2400
Fax: –
Web: www.hallmarkchannel.com

CEO: William J Abbott
CFO: Andrew Rooke
HR: –
FYE: December 31
Type: Public

All for the Family would be the name of a TV series about family-friendly Crown Media Holdings. It owns and operates the Hallmark Channel a cable network that specializes in family-oriented TV fare. It features mostly third-party programming including such TV series as Golden Girls Little House on the Prairie and Matlock as well as made-for-TV movies feature films and miniseries which includes original programming. The channel reaches about 87 million US homes through cable providers such as Comcast and Cox. Crown Media also operates the Hallmark Movies & Mysteries channel a 24-hour channel that primarily offers feature films miniseries and lighter mysteries; it reaches nearly 30 million homes. Hallmark Cards controls more than 90% of the company.

	Annual Growth	12/10	12/11	12/12	12/13	12/14
Sales ($ mil.)	9.7%	287.3	323.4	349.9	377.8	415.6
Net income ($ mil.)	40.7%	24.1	319.0	107.4	67.7	94.5
Market value ($ mil.)	7.8%	942.4	435.2	665.4	1,269.7	1,273.3
Employees	5.2%	170	173	175	187	208

CROZER-KEYSTONE HEALTH SYSTEM

100 W SPROUL RD
SPRINGFIELD, PA 190642033
Phone: 610-338-8200
Fax: –

CEO: Peter Adamo
CFO: Philip J Ryan
HR: –
FYE: June 30
Type: Private

Crozer-Keystone Health System provides a full range of health care in the Philadelphia metropolitan area. The health system's facilities include five acute care hospitals four outpatient care centers and a sports science and technology center. Combined its not-for-profit member hospitals have about 840 beds. The hospitals' specialty units include trauma cardiac cancer orthopedic wound healing obesity sleep disorder and women's and children's health centers. The system also operates family occupational and diagnostic health clinics as well as home health and hospice agencies. In early the company agreed to be acquired by for-profit hospital operator Prospect Medical Holdings.

	Annual Growth	06/07	06/08	06/09	06/10	06/13
Sales ($ mil.)	–	–	–	(170.9)	49.0	50.8	807.5
Net income ($ mil.)	–	–	–	(1.1)	0.8	102.4
Market value ($ mil.)	–	–	–	–	–	–
Employees	–	–	–	–	–	7,100

CRST INTERNATIONAL, INC.

201 1ST ST SE STE 400
CEDAR RAPIDS, IA 524011423
Phone: 319-396-4400
Fax: –
Web: www.crst.com

CEO: Hugh Ekberg
CFO: Wesley Brackey
HR: –
FYE: December 31
Type: Private

CRST International promises f-a-s-t freight transportation through its operating units. CRST Expedited provides standard dry van truckload transportation primarily on long-haul routes along with dedicated and expedited transportation services. CRST Malone hauls steel and other freight requiring flatbed trailers or trailers with removable sides and CRST Logistics arranges freight transportation and provides other third-party logistics services. The family-owned business' other operations include CRST Dedicated Services and Specialized Transportation. Overall the companies operate a fleet of about 4500 tractors and 7300 van trailers.

	Annual Growth	12/08	12/09	12/10	12/11	12/12
Sales ($ mil.)	10.1%	–	–	–	1,143.1	1,258.0
Net income ($ mil.)	(7.8%)	–	–	–	81.6	75.3
Market value ($ mil.)	–	–	–	–	–	–
Employees	–	–	–	–	–	5,960

CRUM & FORSTER HOLDINGS CORP.

305 Madison Ave.
Morristown NJ 07962
Phone: 973-490-6600
Fax: 973-490-6940
Web: www.cfins.com

CEO: Douglas M Libby
CFO: –
HR: –
FYE: December 31
Type: Subsidiary

Crum & Forster looks out for the best interests of employers. Through its subsidiaries the company offers an array of property/casualty insurance products to businesses including general liability automobile property and workers' compensation coverage. Crum & Forster also offers The Defender a broad commercial umbrella policy. The company's specialty policies include management protection crime insurance; it also offers personal auto and homeowners policies. In addition Crum & Forster provides risk management services. The company's products are sold through some 1500 independent brokers across the US. Crum & Forster is a subsidiary of Fairfax Financial Holdings.

CRYO-CELL INTERNATIONAL INC

700 Brooker Creek Boulevard
Oldsmar, FL 34677
Phone: 813 749-2100
Fax: 813 723-0444
Web: www.cryo-cell.com

NAS: CCEL
CEO: Mark Portnoy
CFO: Jill Taymans
HR: –
FYE: November 30
Type: Public

Cryo-Cell International freezes the ties that bind. The company collects and cryogenically stores umbilical cord blood stem cells giving expectant parents some insurance in case disease (such as diabetes heart disease or stroke) should strike in the future. Specimens collected in the US are processed and stored at Cryo-Cell's facility in Oldsmar Florida. The company also offers services through subsidiaries in certain countries in Asia Europe Latin America and the Middle East. Cryo-Cell markets its services directly to consumers online through its website and by providing information and education to obstetricians pediatricians childbirth educators and other health care providers.

	Annual Growth	11/17	11/18	11/19	11/20	11/21
Sales ($ mil.)	3.3%	25.4	29.2	31.8	31.1	28.9
Net income ($ mil.)	(2.6%)	2.3	(0.9)	2.3	3.6	2.1
Market value ($ mil.)	57.8%	17.1	17.1	17.1	17.1	105.9
Employees	3.5%	81	101	97	98	93

CRYSTAL FLASH, INC.

1754 ALPINE AVE NW
GRAND RAPIDS, MI 495042810
Phone: 616-363-4851
Fax: –
Web: www.crystalflash.com

CEO: –
CFO: –
HR: Krinn Vandersloot
FYE: December 31
Type: Private

Energy in a flash while keeping those streams and rivers crystal clear. Why not? Environmentally friendly Crystal Flash Limited Partnership (dba Crystal Flash Energy) one of Michigan's largest energy-related products suppliers delivers heating oil propane and other energy options. The company's fleet of approximately 150 trucks deliver propane and heating oil to thousands of homes and gasoline and diesel fuel to trucking companies construction firms and farms. The company was founded in 1932 by John E. Fehsenfeld.

	Annual Growth	12/07	12/08	12/09	12/10	12/11
Sales ($ mil.)	26.4%	–	–	112.9	123.8	180.5
Net income ($ mil.)	123.8%	–	–	1.1	2.3	5.5
Market value ($ mil.)	–	–	–	–	–	–
Employees	–	–	–	–	–	240

CRYSTAL ROCK HOLDINGS INC

1050 Buckingham Street
Watertown, CT 06795
Phone: 860 945-0661
Fax: –
Web: www.crystalrock.com

ASE: CRVP
CEO: –
CFO: –
HR: –
FYE: October 31
Type: Public

When co-workers gather around the water cooler or the coffeepot to discuss the Celtics the Patriots or the Red Sox (or even the Yankees) Crystal Rock wants to be there. The company delivers water and coffee to offices and homes throughout New England and in New York and New Jersey. Non-sparkling water which the company bottles at facilities in Connecticut Vermont and New York is offered under the Vermont Pure Hidden Springs and Crystal Rock brands and private labels. Vermont Pure Holdings' coffee brands include Baronet Coffee and Green Mountain Coffee Roasters. Company president Peter Baker and his family own a majority of Crystal Rock.

	Annual Growth	10/13	10/14	10/15	10/16	10/17
Sales ($ mil.)	(4.5%)	71.0	75.2	73.9	65.3	59.1
Net income ($ mil.)	(0.5%)	0.6	0.2	(0.6)	1.2	0.6
Market value ($ mil.)	(4.3%)	18.6	16.7	10.9	17.9	15.6
Employees	(6.8%)	390	374	333	311	294

CSG SYSTEMS INTERNATIONAL INC.

6175 S. Willow Drive, 10th Floor
Greenwood Village, CO 80111
Phone: 303 200-2000
Fax: –
Web: www.csgi.com

NMS: CSGS
CEO: Brian Shepherd
CFO: Hai Tran
HR: –
FYE: December 31
Type: Public

CSG Systems International is one of the world's leading providers of revenue management customer experience and payment solutions that enable a growing list of companies around the world to monetize relationships with their customers in an era of rapid change and digital transformation. The company offers an award-winning solutions taht are built on proven public and private cloud platforms available out-of-the-box custom or through end-to-end managed services. The company serves primarily North American cable TV direct broadcast satellite online services and telecom companies such as AT&T America Movil and Comcast. Majority of the company's sales were generated in the Americas.

	Annual Growth	12/17	12/18	12/19	12/20	12/21
Sales ($ mil.)	7.3%	789.6	875.1	996.8	990.5	1,046.5
Net income ($ mil.)	4.2%	61.4	66.1	82.8	58.7	72.3
Market value ($ mil.)	7.1%	1,423.9	1,032.4	1,682.6	1,464.5	1,872.4
Employees	11.4%	3,373	3,965	4,339	4,807	5,200

CSI COMPRESSCO LP
NMS: CCLP

24955 Interstate 45 North
The Woodlands, TX 77380
Phone: 281 364-2244
Fax: –
Web: www.compressco.com

CEO: John Jackson
CFO: Jonathan Byers
HR: –
FYE: December 31
Type: Public

Compressco Partners puts the pressure on before the natural gas and oil wells run dry. The company specializes in providing services to more than 400 natural gas and oil companies across 14 states to increase production and total recoverable reserves. The company offers compression liquids separation and gas metering services as well as the GasJack units that perform these operations. It applies its services primarily to mature wells but also on newer wells which have declined in production. Compressco Partners which was spun-off from TETRA Technologies in 2011 also provides well evaluations and well testing and monitoring services in Mexico.

	Annual Growth	12/16	12/17	12/18	12/19	12/20
Sales ($ mil.)	(0.8%)	311.4	295.6	438.7	476.6	301.6
Net income ($ mil.)	–	(138.1)	(40.5)	(37.0)	(21.0)	(73.8)
Market value ($ mil.)	(42.5%)	460.7	259.0	109.9	128.5	50.2
Employees	5.0%	600	635	750	791	730

CSI LEASING, INC.

9990 OLD OLIVE STREET RD
SAINT LOUIS, MO 631415965
Phone: 314-997-4934
Fax: –
Web: www.csileasing.com

CEO: Bill Gillula
CFO: Phil Cagney
HR: –
FYE: June 30
Type: Private

CSI Leasing is an industry leader that provides lease financing in 50 countries. The company sees leasing as a way to gain the benefits of using equipment without many of the hassles costs and limitations associated with ownership. It provides off-lease services through its EPC subsidiary which helps hundreds of organizations around the world dispose of end-of-life IT and maximize their return in secondary markets. CSI serves clients in such industries as technology healthcare government and education. It is a wholly-owned subsidiary of Tokyo Century Corporation. The company was founded in 1972.

	Annual Growth	06/00	06/01	06/02	06/03	06/09
Sales ($ mil.)	(5.6%)	–	576.5	502.4	531.3	362.1
Net income ($ mil.)	5.2%	–	11.0	13.7	14.4	16.4
Market value ($ mil.)	–	–	–	–	–	–
Employees	–	–	–	–	–	540

CSL BEHRING LLC

1020 1st Ave.
King of Prussia PA 19406-0901
Phone: 610-878-4000
Fax: 610-878-4009
Web: www.cslbehring.com

CEO: –
CFO: –
HR: –
FYE: June 30
Type: Subsidiary

Take away the red and white blood cells from blood and you get plasma a protein-rich fluid. CSL Behring is among the world's largest fully integrated plasma collection companies. Through subsidiary CSL Plasma (formerly ZLB Plasma) the company collects plasma through dozens of facilities in the US and Germany. CSL Behring then develops plasma-based protein biotherapeutics to treat a range of health ailments including bleeding disorders (such as hemophilia) immune system deficiencies and respiratory disease (including emphysema). Biotherapeutics are also used in critical care settings for surgical and wound healing applications. CSL Behring is a subsidiary of Australian biopharmaceutical firm CSL Limited.

CSP INC
NMS: CSPI

175 Cabot Street, Suite 210
Lowell, MA 01854
Phone: 978 954-5038
Fax: –
Web: www.cspi.com

CEO: Victor Dellovo
CFO: Gary Levine
HR: –
FYE: September 30
Type: Public

CSP knows IT. The company provides information technology services including the resale and integration of computer hardware and software through its Modcomp subsidiary. Modcomp serves clients in the UK and the US. Its MultiComputer product line includes systems used for radar sonar and surveillance. The company generates most of its revenue in the Americas. CSP Inc. was incorporated in 1968 and is based in Lowell Massachusetts.

	Annual Growth	09/17	09/18	09/19	09/20	09/21
Sales ($ mil.)	(18.5%)	111.5	72.9	79.1	61.8	49.2
Net income ($ mil.)	(27.3%)	2.5	14.4	(0.4)	(1.4)	0.7
Market value ($ mil.)	(5.2%)	48.6	57.6	59.0	37.9	39.2
Employees	(13.5%)	200	124	114	112	112

CSS INDUSTRIES, INC.
NYS: CSS

450 Plymouth Road, Suite 300
Plymouth Meeting, PA 19462
Phone: 610 729-3959
Fax: –
Web: www.cssindustries.com

CEO: Christopher J Munyan
CFO: Keith W Pfeil
HR: –
FYE: March 31
Type: Public

Every day is cause for celebration at CSS Industries a designer maker and distributor of seasonal and everyday decorative products such as ribbons and bows gifts and gift tags boxes and wrap tissue paper and boxed Christmas cards. The company also makes dye for Easter eggs (Dudley's) and valentines for classroom exchange. Customers include mass-merchandise retailers warehouse clubs and retail drug and food stores primarily in the US and Canada. Wal-Mart and Target are CSS's largest customers. Originally founded as a furniture and department store retailer in 1923 the company operates through subsidiaries The Paper Magic Group Berwick Offray and C.R. Gibson.

	Annual Growth	03/15	03/16	03/17	03/18	03/19
Sales ($ mil.)	5.1%	313.0	317.0	322.4	361.9	382.3
Net income ($ mil.)	–	17.0	17.2	28.5	(36.5)	(53.5)
Market value ($ mil.)	(33.2%)	266.4	246.8	229.1	154.7	52.9
Employees	13.4%	1,450	1,530	1,830	2,075	2,400

CSSI INC.

400 VRGNIA AVE SW STE 710
WASHINGTON, DC 20024
Phone: 202-863-2175
Fax: –
Web: www.cssiinc.com

CEO: –
CFO: Christopher Giusti
HR: Poniesa Johnson
FYE: December 31
Type: Private

CSSI turns an eye toward R&D. A technology and engineering services company the company specializes in air traffic management. Areas of expertise include decision support systems safety management and cost-benefit analysis. Its services include information management and custom software development operational analysis and implementation investment strategy and analysis and systems engineering. CSSI's clients have included NASA the US Department of Defense the Federal Aviation Administration and the airline industry. The company has satellite offices in Charleston South Carolina; Landover Maryland; and Northfield New Jersey.

	Annual Growth	12/04	12/05	12/06	12/08	12/12
Sales ($ mil.)	16.6%	–	22.4	21.4	31.2	65.5
Net income ($ mil.)	(25.9%)	–	–	20.1	1.9	3.3
Market value ($ mil.)	–	–	–	–	–	–
Employees	–	–	–	–	–	265

CST BRANDS INC
NYS: CST

19500 Bulverde Road, Suite 100
San Antonio, TX 78259
Phone: 210 692-5000
Fax: –
Web: www.cstbrands.com

CEO: Kimberly S Bowers
CFO: Clayton Killinger
HR: –
FYE: December 31
Type: Public

CST Brands is hoping to corner the market on convenience stores. The holding company spun off from energy giant Valero in 2013 operates around 1050 gas stations/convenience stores in the US under the Corner Store moniker. Its gasoline is sold under the Valero and Diamond Shamrock brands while its stores are located in 10 US states and sell the usual — snacks drinks tobacco products health and beauty products automotive products and other convenience items. CST Brands has another 860 Dépanneur du Coin stores in eastern Canada (mostly in Quebec); however the bulk of its Canadian stores are operated by independent dealers. In 2016 the company agreed to be acquired by Alimentation Couche-Tard.

	Annual Growth	12/11	12/12	12/13	12/14	12/15
Sales ($ mil.)	(2.9%)	12,863.0	13,135.0	12,777.0	12,758.0	11,444.0
Net income ($ mil.)	(8.7%)	214.0	210.0	139.0	200.0	149.0
Market value ($ mil.)	3.2%	–	–	2,776.6	3,297.6	2,959.6
Employees	(2.1%)	–	11,640	12,321	13,496	10,923

CSU FULLERTON AUXILIARY SERVICES CORPORATION

2600 NUTWOOD AVE STE 275
FULLERTON, CA 928313137
Phone: 657-278-4140
Fax: –
Web: www.csufasc.org

CEO: –
CFO: –
HR: –
FYE: June 30
Type: Private

CSU Fullerton Auxiliary Services (formerly California State University Fullerton Foundation) keeps an eye on auxiliary operations at Cal State. The organization administers research and education grants and oversees commercial operations such as the Titan Shops (which stock textbooks computers gifts and clothing) and franchise foodservices. It is also involved in real estate providing affordable housing for sale and lease to the university's faculty and staff. A 25-member board governs CSU Fullerton Auxiliary Services Corporation which was established in 1959.

	Annual Growth	06/07	06/08	06/09	06/10	06/12
Sales ($ mil.)	(50.4%)	–	1,035.7	54.0	55.2	62.9
Net income ($ mil.)	–	–	–	(0.5)	2.3	(2.8)
Market value ($ mil.)	–	–	–	–	–	–
Employees	–	–	–	–	–	1,400

CSX CORP
NMS: CSX

500 Water Street, 15th Floor
Jacksonville, FL 32202
Phone: 904 359-3200
Fax: –
Web: www.csx.com

CEO: James Foote
CFO: Sean Pelkey
HR: –
FYE: December 31
Type: Public

Through its main subsidiary CSX Transportation (CSXT) CSX Corporation operates a major rail system of around 19000 route miles in the eastern US. The freight carrier links some 25 states 70 ports 230 short-line railroads the District of Columbia and two Canadian provinces (Ontario and Quebec). Freight hauled by the company includes a wide variety of merchandise (food and agricultural products chemicals and consumer goods among others) coal and automotive products. CSX also transports via intermodal containers and trailers.

	Annual Growth	12/17	12/18	12/19	12/20	12/21
Sales ($ mil.)	2.4%	11,408.0	12,250.0	11,937.0	10,583.0	12,522.0
Net income ($ mil.)	(8.8%)	5,471.0	3,309.0	3,331.0	2,765.0	3,781.0
Market value ($ mil.)	–	0.0	0.0	0.0	0.0	0.0
Employees	(3.4%)	24,000	22,500	21,000	19,300	20,900

CTI BIOPHARMA CORP
NAS: CTIC

3101 Western Avenue, Suite 800
Seattle, WA 98121
Phone: 206 282-7100
Fax: –
Web: www.celltherapeutics.com

CEO: Adam Craig
CFO: David Kirske
HR: –
FYE: December 31
Type: Public

CTI Biopharma is a toxic avenger. The firm creates more effective and less toxic treatments for various forms of cancer. CTI is developing a number of cancer-fighting compounds including Pixuvri (pixantrone) a treatment for non-Hodgkin's lymphoma and other tumorous cancers; Pixuvri has conditional approval in Europe. Another candidate pacritinib is being studied for myelofibrosis. The company's Systems Medicine subsidiary is working on a potential sarcoma-fighter called brostallicin. Other subsidiaries include Aequus Biopharma and CTI Life Sciences.

	Annual Growth	12/15	12/16	12/17	12/18	12/19
Sales ($ mil.)	(32.5%)	16.1	57.4	25.1	26.3	3.3
Net income ($ mil.)	–	(119.4)	(52.0)	(40.7)	(29.3)	(40.0)
Market value ($ mil.)	6.5%	71.3	23.6	155.4	42.5	91.6
Employees	(36.0%)	149	104	57	46	25

CTI GROUP HOLDINGS INC.
NBB: CTIG

333 North Alabama Street, Suite 240
Indianapolis, IN 46204
Phone: 317 262-4666
Fax: –

CEO: Manfred Hanuschek
CFO: Nathan Habegger
HR: –
FYE: December 31
Type: Public

CTI Group (Holdings) helps companies act on their transactions. The company provides software and services for billing customer care and telemanagement. Targeting service providers in the telecom information technology financial cable and health care industries CTI offers software that analyzes billing data (SmartBill) automates telecommunications spending manages electronic invoicing and handles call accounting. The company also offers professional services and outsourced call center management output processing training support and marketing services.

	Annual Growth	12/09	12/10	12/11	12/12	12/13
Sales ($ mil.)	(0.4%)	15.7	15.2	17.0	16.8	15.5
Net income ($ mil.)	–	(1.3)	(3.3)	(0.6)	0.6	(1.1)
Market value ($ mil.)	55.4%	1.8	3.1	2.8	6.7	10.5
Employees	(4.5%)	137	124	111	113	114

CTO REALTY GROWTH INC (NEW)
NYS: CTO

1140 N. Williamson Blvd., Suite 140
Daytona Beach, FL 32114
Phone: 386 274-2202
Fax: 386 274-1223
Web: www.ctoreit.com

CEO: –
CFO: –
HR: –
FYE: December 31
Type: Public

From retail centers to hay farms land developer CTO Realty Growth (formerly Consolidated-Tomoka) owns and manages sometimes utilizing third-party property management companies about 35 commercial real estate properties in more than 10 states in the United States. Its portfolio includes single- and multi-tenant retail properties (tenants include Wells Fargo Big Lots and Lowe's). Through its subsidiaries it also holds subsurface oil gas and mineral interests on land throughout Florida. The company traces its roots to 1910 and change its name to CTO Realty Growth Inc. from Consolidated-Tomoka Land Co. in mid-2020.

	Annual Growth	12/16	12/17	12/18	12/19	12/20
Sales ($ mil.)	(5.6%)	71.1	91.4	86.7	44.9	56.4
Net income ($ mil.)	48.3%	16.3	41.7	37.2	115.0	78.5
Market value ($ mil.)	(5.7%)	316.0	375.7	310.6	356.8	249.4
Employees	5.0%	14	14	14	15	17

CTPARTNERS EXECUTIVE SEARCH INC
NBB: CTPR

1166 Avenue of the Americas, 3rd Fl.
New York, NY 10036
Phone: 212 588-3500
Fax: -
Web: www.ctnet.com

CEO: David Nocifora
CFO: William Keneally
HR: -
FYE: December 31
Type: Public

CTPartners finds the hidden treasures of senior management. The company performs CEO board member and senior-level executive management searches for both large and emerging companies worldwide. Operating through more than 20 global offices it has special expertise in filling top-level technology positions but also operates a number of other industry practices including financial services human resources life sciences media and telecommunications. The company delivers talent within an average of about 100 days; it has placed executives with such companies as Sony American Express and RELX Group. CTPartners was founded in 1980.

	Annual Growth	12/10	12/11	12/12	12/13	12/14
Sales ($ mil.)	108.3%	9.4	126.1	132.9	134.3	176.8
Net income ($ mil.)	-	(5.8)	(3.2)	(3.6)	(1.6)	3.3
Market value ($ mil.)	(0.9%)	114.5	38.6	33.2	40.7	110.4
Employees	17.1%	336	369	453	460	631

CTPARTNERS EXECUTIVE SEARCH LLC
ASE: CTP

1166 Avenue of the Americas, 3rd Fl.
New York, NY 10036
Phone: 212 588-3500
Fax: -
Web: www.ctnet.com

CEO: David Nocifora
CFO: William Keneally
HR: -
FYE: December 31
Type: Public

CTPartners finds the hidden treasures of senior management. The company performs CEO board member and senior-level executive management searches for both large and emerging companies worldwide. Operating through more than 20 global offices it has special expertise in filling top-level technology positions but also operates a number of other industry practices including financial services human resources life sciences media and telecommunications. The company delivers talent within an average of about 100 days; it has placed executives with such companies as Sony American Express and Reed Elsevier Group. CTPartners was founded in 1980.

	Annual Growth	11/10*	12/10	12/11	12/12	12/13
Sales ($ mil.)	7.4%	108.3	9.4	126.1	132.9	134.3
Net income ($ mil.)	-	7.6	(5.8)	(3.2)	(3.6)	(1.6)
Market value ($ mil.)	(29.2%)	-	112.0	37.8	32.4	39.8
Employees	11.0%	-	336	369	453	460

*Fiscal year change

CTS CORP
NYS: CTS

4925 Indiana Avenue
Lisle, IL 60532
Phone: 630 577-8800
Fax: -
Web: www.ctscorp.com

CEO: Kieran O'Sullivan
CFO: Ashish Agrawal
HR: -
FYE: December 31
Type: Public

CTS designs manufactures and sells a broad line of sensors connectivity components and actuators primarily to original equipment manufacturers. CTS-made products are used in the aerospace and defense industrial telecommunications information technology medical equipment and transportation markets. Customers have included industry leaders such as Cummins Honda and Toyota. The US account for over 55% of the company's total sales. It was founded in 1896.

	Annual Growth	12/16	12/17	12/18	12/19	12/20
Sales ($ mil.)	1.7%	396.7	423.0	470.5	469.0	424.1
Net income ($ mil.)	0.2%	34.4	14.4	46.5	36.1	34.7
Market value ($ mil.)	11.3%	723.0	831.1	835.6	968.6	1,108.1
Employees	7.9%	2,796	3,222	3,230	3,570	3,786

CTS VALPEY CORPORATION
NASDAQ: VPF

75 South St.
Hopkinton MA 01748-2204
Phone: 508-435-6831
Fax: 508-497-6377
Web: www.valpeyfisher.com

CEO: -
CFO: Michael J Kroll
HR: -
FYE: December 31
Type: Subsidiary

CTS Valpey (formerly Valpey-Fisher) is all about time and control. The company makes quartz crystals and crystal-based products such as oscillators used for timing and frequency control in telecom computer and aerospace equipment. It also makes ultrasonic transducers which are used in non-destructive testing research and medical applications. Customers include contract electronics manufacturers Celestica and Flextronics. Valpey-Fisher has divested other operations including its AcoustoSizer optical components and piezoelectric product lines. More than two-thirds of sales are to customers in the US. In 2012 the company was acquired by electronic component manufacturer CTS Corporation for about $18 million.

CTSC LLC

10505 FURNACE RD STE 205
LORTON, VA 220792636
Phone: 703-493-9880
Fax: -
Web: www.chenega.jobs

CEO: Ken Ogden
CFO: -
HR: -
FYE: September 30
Type: Private

CTSC (Chenega Technology Services Corporation) is a certified Alaska Native Corporation (ANC) that provides support services to federal agencies. Its core competencies include base operations and facilities management engineering information technology intelligence support logistics and training. Partnering with prime government contractors and sub-contractors CTSC offers information systems development system integration support to military operations network engineering and technical analysis. As an ANC the company enjoys no-bid contracts with the government. CTSC is a subsidiary of Chenega Corporation.

	Annual Growth	09/05	09/06	09/07	09/08	09/09
Sales ($ mil.)	-	-	-	0.0	582.7	181.3
Net income ($ mil.)	-	-	-	0.0	14.0	15.9
Market value ($ mil.)	-	-	-	-	-	-
Employees	-	-	-	-	-	620

CUBESMART
NYS: CUBE

5 Old Lancaster Road
Malvern, PA 19355
Phone: 610 535-5000
Fax: -
Web: www.cubesmart.com

CEO: Christopher P Marr
CFO: Timothy M Martin
HR: -
FYE: December 31
Type: Public

CubeSmart is a real estate investment trust (REIT) that owns about 545 self-storage facilities with about 38.5 million sq. ft. of rentable space in about 25 states and in the District of Columbia. The company also manages some 725 self-storage facilities for third parties. Its self-storage properties are designed to offer affordable and easily-accessible storage space for our residential and commercial customers. CubeSmart's customers rent storage cubes for their exclusive use typically on a month-to-month basis. Additionally some of its stores offer outside storage areas for vehicles and boats. Its stores are designed to accommodate both residential and commercial customers with features such as wide aisles and load-bearing capabilities for large truck access.

	Annual Growth	12/16	12/17	12/18	12/19	12/20
Sales ($ mil.)	7.4%	510.0	558.9	597.9	643.9	679.2
Net income ($ mil.)	17.2%	87.9	134.3	163.9	169.1	165.6
Market value ($ mil.)	5.9%	5,284.6	5,709.0	5,663.6	6,214.3	6,634.8
Employees	9.9%	2,136	2,508	2,815	3,011	3,111

CUBIC CORP
NYS: CUB

9333 Balboa Avenue
San Diego, CA 92123
Phone: 858 277-6780
Fax: –
Web: www.cubic.com

CEO: Stevan Slijepcevic
CFO: Anshooman AGA
HR: –
FYE: September 30
Type: Public

Cubic's products and services fit squarely within the global defense and transportation industries. With its business divided into three main segments Cubic Corporation provides mission support services including actual combat rehearsal exercises to national military organizations and US security forces and their allies. It manufactures air and ground combat instrumentation systems for live and virtual training as well as communications global asset tracking and cyber security equipment for the defense market. It also provides automated fare collection (AFC) management systems and services for mass transit (including bus light rail ferry and parking) worldwide. The US accounts for about 60% of the company's revenue.

	Annual Growth	09/16	09/17	09/18	09/19	09/20
Sales ($ mil.)	0.2%	1,461.7	1,485.9	1,202.9	1,496.5	1,476.2
Net income ($ mil.)	–	1.7	(11.2)	12.3	49.7	(3.2)
Market value ($ mil.)	5.6%	1,466.5	1,597.8	2,288.6	2,206.5	1,822.4
Employees	(8.0%)	8,500	8,700	5,600	6,200	6,100

CUBIC SIMULATION SYSTEMS INC.

2001 W. Oak Ridge Rd.
Orlando FL 32809-3803
Phone: 407-859-7410
Fax: 407-855-4840
Web: cubic.com/ecc

CEO: Robert L Collins
CFO: Melissa A Van Valkenburgh
HR: –
FYE: September 30
Type: Subsidiary

Ready aim simulate fire and repair! Cubic Simulation Systems Division (SSD) provides a full range of virtual training devices to military and commercial customers worldwide. It develops simulation-based training systems for armor missile small arms and aircraft applications so that military personnel can gain weapons and maintenance experience in a realistic but safe environment before the bits hit the fan. Major products include the Close Combat Tactical Trainer which trains tank crews; the Engagement Skills Trainer 2000 a small arms trainer; Javelin trainers which teach personnel how to use the Javelin missile; and F-16 and F/A-18 Maintenance Trainers which provide aircraft maintenance training.

CUBIST PHARMACEUTICALS INC.
NMS: CBST

65 Hayden Avenue
Lexington, MA 02421
Phone: 781 860-8660
Fax: 781 240-0256
Web: www.cubist.com

CEO: Michael W Bonney
CFO: Michael J Tomsicek
HR: –
FYE: December 31
Type: Public

Fighting infection is a modern art at Cubist Pharmaceuticals. The company develops antimicrobial agents to treat drug-resistant bacterial strains including methicillin-resistant Staphylococcus aureus (MRSA) typically found in hospitals and other health care institutions. Its flagship product Cubicin (daptomycin for injection) is an FDA-approved intravenous antibiotic to fight MRSA infections of the skin and blood. Cubist also markets Entereg a drug to speed patient recovery following bowel resection surgery in the US. Cubist's pipeline includes candidates in various stages of clinical and pre-clinical development.

	Annual Growth	12/08	12/09	12/10	12/11	12/12
Sales ($ mil.)	20.9%	433.6	562.1	636.5	754.0	926.4
Net income ($ mil.)	(2.4%)	169.8	79.6	94.3	33.0	154.1
Market value ($ mil.)	14.9%	1,563.5	1,227.6	1,384.9	2,564.0	2,721.2
Employees	8.3%	554	600	638	669	762

CUIVRE RIVER ELECTRIC COOPERATIVE, INC.

1112 E CHERRY ST
TROY, MO 633791518
Phone: 636-528-8261
Fax: –
Web: www.cuivre.com

CEO: Doug Tracy
CFO: –
HR: Debbie Bicker
FYE: December 31
Type: Private

Show me the power. Cuivre River Electric Cooperative provides power to four eastern counties in the "Show Me" state: Lincoln Pike St. Charles and Warren. The membership utility which is one of Missouri's largest cooperatives with more than 58000 residential commercial and industrial customers gets its wholesale power supply from the Associated Electric Cooperative and the Central Electric Power Cooperative. Cuivre River Propane jointly owned and operated by Cuivre River Electric Cooperative and MFA Oil Company supplies propane to co-op members from four locations Bowling Green Elsberry Troy and Wright City.

	Annual Growth	12/08	12/09	12/11	12/14	12/15
Sales ($ mil.)	1.4%	–	101.5	102.6	110.8	110.7
Net income ($ mil.)	(13.4%)	–	8.5	10.0	4.4	3.6
Market value ($ mil.)	–	–	–	–	–	–
Employees	–	–	–	–	–	138

CULLEN/FROST BANKERS, INC.
NYS: CFR

111 W. Houston Street
San Antonio, TX 78205
Phone: 210 220-4011
Fax: 210 220-5578
Web: www.frostbank.com

CEO: Philip Green
CFO: Jerry Salinas
HR: Annette Alonzo
FYE: December 31
Type: Public

Cullen/Frost Bankers owns Frost Bank is one of the largest independent bank holding companies in Texas. The community-oriented bank serves individuals and local businesses. It offers commercial and consumer deposit products and loans trust and investment management services mutual funds insurance brokerage and leasing. Subsidiaries include Frost Insurance Agency Frost Brokerage Services Frost Investment Advisors and investment banking arm Frost Securities. Cullen/Frost has total assets of $42.4 billion.

	Annual Growth	12/17	12/18	12/19	12/20	12/21
Assets ($ mil.)	12.5%	31,747.9	32,293.0	34,027.4	42,391.3	50,878.5
Net income ($ mil.)	5.0%	364.1	454.9	443.6	331.2	443.1
Market value ($ mil.)	7.4%	6,056.3	5,626.9	6,256.6	5,581.5	8,066.7
Employees	1.6%	4,270	4,370	4,659	4,685	4,553

CULP INC
NYS: CULP

1823 Eastchester Drive
High Point, NC 27265-1402
Phone: 336 889-5161
Fax: –
Web: www.culp.com

CEO: Robert Culp
CFO: Kenneth Bowling
HR: Angela Cranfill
FYE: May 02
Type: Public

Culp just wants to keep on ticking. The company is a maker of furniture upholstery fabrics and mattress fabrics (known as ticking). Culp delivers fashion-conscious stylish fabrics with broad appeal to some of the largest home furnishing retailers and manufacturers. Its upholstery fabrics include wovens (jacquards and dobbies) knits screen-prints and velvets (woven and tufted). Its fabrics are used in upholstering residential and commercial furniture such as recliners sofas chairs sectionals sofa-beds love seats and office seating. Culp's mattress fabrics and sewn covers is used for covering mattresses foundations other bedding products and upholstery fabrics. About a third-quarter of the company's revenue comes from the US.

	Annual Growth	04/17	04/18	04/19*	05/20	05/21
Sales ($ mil.)	(0.8%)	309.5	323.7	296.7	256.2	299.7
Net income ($ mil.)	(38.4%)	22.3	20.9	5.7	(24.0)	3.2
Market value ($ mil.)	(18.5%)	395.2	370.6	255.4	85.1	174.2
Employees	1.9%	1,325	1,392	1,440	1,399	1,430

*Fiscal year change

CULVER FRANCHISING SYSTEM, INC.

1240 WATER ST
PRAIRIE DU SAC, WI 535781091
Phone: 608-643-7980
Fax: –
Web: www.culvers.com

CEO: Enrique Silva
CFO: –
HR: –
FYE: December 31
Type: Private

If you think ButterBurgers are better burgers then you're probably a fan of Culver's. Culver Franchising System operates a chain of about 500 Culver's quick-service restaurants popular for their signature ButterBurgers (hamburgers served on a grilled buttered bun) and frozen custard. The chain's menu also includes chicken fish and pork sandwiches; salads; and dinner items such as shrimp and Norwegian cod. Nearly all of the restaurants are operated by franchisees. Chairman and CEO Craig Culver started the restaurant as a family business back in 1984.

	Annual Growth	12/06	12/07	12/08	12/11	12/12
Assets ($ mil.)	–	–	–	0.0	57.6	54.8
Net income ($ mil.)	470.4%	–	–	0.0	14.5	17.3
Market value ($ mil.)	–	–	–	–	–	–
Employees	–	–	–	–	–	290

CUMBERLAND COUNTY HOSPITAL SYSTEM, INC.

1638 OWEN DR
FAYETTEVILLE, NC 283043424
Phone: 910-609-4000
Fax: –
Web: www.capefearvalley.com

CEO: Michael Nagowski
CFO: Sandra Williams
HR: –
FYE: September 30
Type: Private

Don't fear for a lack of medical services at Cumberland County Hospital System (doing business as Cape Fear Valley Health System). The medical provider comprises five acute-care and specialty hospitals with about 915 total beds serving a six-county region of Southeastern North Carolina and more than 935000 patients annually. The hospital system serves residents of coastal North Carolina providing general and specialized medical services such as cancer treatment open-heart surgery psychiatric care and rehabilitation. It also operates the HealthPlex fitness and wellness facility that has over 140 pieces of next-generation cardiovascular and strength-building equipment and provides home health and hospice services. Among its medical facilities include Cape Fear Valley Medical Center Highsmith-Rainey Specialty Hospital Cape Fear Valley Rehabilitation Center Bladen County Hospital and Hoke Hospital.

	Annual Growth	09/03	09/04	09/05	09/06	09/07
Sales ($ mil.)	6.4%	–	–	446.0	492.7	504.6
Net income ($ mil.)	16.7%	–	–	17.0	29.7	23.1
Market value ($ mil.)	–	–	–	–	–	–
Employees	–	–	–	–	–	5,000

CUMBERLAND FARMS INC.

100 Crossing Blvd.
Framingham MA 01702
Phone: 508-270-1400
Fax: 206-722-2569
Web: www.darigold.com

CEO: –
CFO: –
HR: –
FYE: September 30
Type: Private

Once a one-cow dairy Cumberland Farms now operates a network of 900-plus convenience stores and gas stations in about a dozen eastern seaboard states from Maine to Florida. The company operates its own grocery distribution and bakery operations to supply its stores as well. Cumberland owns a two-thirds limited partnership in petroleum wholesaler Gulf Oil LP giving it the right to use and license Gulf trademarks in Delaware New Jersey New York most of Ohio Pennsylvania and the New England states. The first convenience-store operator in New England Cumberland Farms was founded in 1939 by Vasilios and Aphrodite Haseotes. Their descendants including chairman Lily Haseotes Bentas own the company.

CUMBERLAND PHARMACEUTICALS INC

NMS: CPIX

2525 West End Avenue, Suite 950
Nashville, TN 37203
Phone: 615 255-0068
Fax: –
Web: www.cumberlandpharma.com

CEO: A. Kazimi
CFO: John Hamm
HR: –
FYE: December 31
Type: Public

Cumberland Pharmaceuticals wants to make your search for the right drugs less cumbersome. The specialty pharmaceutical company focuses on acquiring developing and commercializing branded prescription drugs. Targeting the hospital acute care and gastroenterology segments Cumberland's FDA-approved drugs include Acetadote for the treatment of acetaminophen poisoning; Kristalose a prescription strength laxative; Vaprisol for low sodium levels; and Caldolor (ne © Amelior) the first injectable dosage form of ibuprofen. The company also has several projects in development. Acetadote and Kristalose are marketed through Cumberland's own hospital and gastroenterology sales forces. The company went public in a mid-2009 IPO.

	Annual Growth	12/16	12/17	12/18	12/19	12/20
Sales ($ mil.)	3.2%	33.0	41.2	40.7	47.5	37.4
Net income ($ mil.)	–	(0.9)	(8.0)	(7.0)	(3.5)	(3.3)
Market value ($ mil.)	(14.4%)	82.4	110.3	90.4	77.2	44.2
Employees	2.4%	82	84	80	94	90

CUMMINS, INC.

NYS: CMI

500 Jackson Street, P.O. Box 3005
Columbus, IN 47202-3005
Phone: 812 377-5000
Fax: 812 377-4937
Web: www.cummins.com

CEO: Tom Linebarger
CFO: Mark Smith
HR: Mark Osowick
FYE: December 31
Type: Public

Cummins is a global power leader that makes diesel- and natural gas-powered engines for the heavy- and mid-duty truck RV automotive and industrial markets as well as for the marine rail mining and construction industries. In addition to its flagship Engine segment other business segments include Distribution (product distributors and servicing) Components (filtration products and fuel systems) Power Systems (vehicle and residential generators) and New Power (electric and hybrid powertrain systems). Cummins' major customers include OEMs Chrysler Daimler Ford Komatsu PACCAR Navistar and Volvo. About 55% of the company's total sales come from the US. The company traces its historical roots back to 1919 when it was founded by Clessie Cummins.

	Annual Growth	12/17	12/18	12/19	12/20	12/21
Sales ($ mil.)	4.1%	20,428.0	23,771.0	23,571.0	19,811.0	24,021.0
Net income ($ mil.)	20.9%	999.0	2,141.0	2,260.0	1,789.0	2,131.0
Market value ($ mil.)	5.4%	25,171.2	19,043.7	25,501.8	32,361.8	31,085.0
Employees	0.6%	58,600	62,610	61,615	57,825	59,900

CUMULUS MEDIA INC

NMS: CMLS

3280 Peachtree Road N.W., Suite 2200
Atlanta, GA 30305
Phone: 404 949-0700
Fax: –
Web: www.cumulusmedia.com

CEO: –
CFO: –
HR: –
FYE: December 31
Type: Public

Cumulus Media reigns over an empire of radio stations. The company is a radio station ownership group in the US (behind Clear Channel) with about 430 owned or operated stations in more than 85 markets throughout the country. In many of its markets Cumulus provides advertisers with personal connections local impact and national reach through on-air and on-demand digital mobile social and voice-activated platforms as well as integrated digital marketing services powerful influencers full-service audio solutions industry-leading research and insights and live event experiences. The company delivers nationally-syndicated sports news talk and entertainment programming from iconic brands including the NFL the NCAA the Masters the Olympics the Academy of Country Music Awards and many other world-class partners through Westwood One an audio network in America.

	Annual Growth	12/17*	06/18*	12/18	12/19	12/20
Sales ($ mil.)	(10.4%)	1,135.7	453.9	686.4	1,113.4	816.2
Net income ($ mil.)	–	(206.6)	696.2	61.4	61.3	(59.7)
Market value ($ mil.)	(10.1%)	–	–	220.1	358.0	177.7
Employees	(10.1%)	5,213	–	5,135	4,732	3,787

*Fiscal year change

CUPERTINO ELECTRIC INC.

1132 N. 7th St.
San Jose CA 95112
Phone: 408-808-8000
Fax: 408-275-8575
Web: www.cei.com

CEO: Tom Schott
CFO: Bill Slakey
HR: –
FYE: December 31
Type: Private

Cupertino Electric Inc. (CEI) likes to get its customers wired. The electrical contractor builds and maintains electrical power and data infrastructure systems for commercial industrial and institutional facilities including semiconductor plants biotech installations data centers network systems and schools. It provides generation facilities for companies that are not on a grid or need additional power. CEI works mostly for companies and schools in the western US. The company's energy alternatives division also offers design and installation of photovoltaics (solar cells) as well as fuel cells. Customers include Apple Google Hyatt Microsoft Oracle and Safeway.

CURAEGIS TECHNOLOGIES INC   NBB: CRGS

350 Linden Oaks
Rochester, NY 14625
Phone: 585 254-1100
Fax: –
Web: www.curaegis.com

CEO: James Donnelly
CFO: Jason Burke
HR: –
FYE: December 31
Type: Public

A development-stage company Torvec hopes to bring its Torvec FTV (full-terrain vehicle) to the markets of developing nations. The FTV has the body of a truck but has tracks similar to those of a tank. The tracks enable the FTV to venture where a mere wheeled vehicle would fear to tread. Several technologies developed by the late Vernon Gleasman and members of his family including an infinitely variable transmission and a steering drive and suspension system for tracked vehicles are being incorporated into the FTV. The company is working with Ford Motor to develop a version of the FTV to be manufactured and distributed in the US initially and then marketed globally.

	Annual Growth	12/15	12/16	12/17	12/18	12/19
Sales ($ mil.)	(16.8%)	0.0	0.0	0.0	0.0	0.0
Net income ($ mil.)	–	(2.7)	(4.2)	(5.4)	(6.3)	(4.3)
Market value ($ mil.)	(30.6%)	16.8	34.7	15.3	9.7	3.9
Employees	(14.3%)	13	24	24	15	7

CURIS INC   NMS: CRIS

128 Spring Street, Building C, Suite 500
Lexington, MA 02421
Phone: 617 503-6500
Fax: –
Web: www.curis.com

CEO: James Dentzer
CFO: William Steinkrauss
HR: –
FYE: December 31
Type: Public

Curis' cancer patients and Sega's gamers might one day have an unlikely hero in common: Sonic the Hedgehog. Drug development firm Curis is studying hedgehog signaling pathways (including the sonic hedgehog pathway named after the Sega mascot) to find treatments for oncology ailments and other conditions. Its commercialize product Erivedge is an orally bioavailable small molecule which is designed to selectively inhibit the Hedgehog signaling pathway by targeting a protein called Smoothened. Erivedge is FDA approved for treatment of adults with metastatic basal cell carcinoma. Its collaborating partner Genentech (a member of the Roche Group) and Roche are responsible for the clinical development and global commercialization of Erivedge. The company also has internal development programs for cancer treatments using other signaling pathways.

	Annual Growth	12/16	12/17	12/18	12/19	12/20
Sales ($ mil.)	9.5%	7.5	9.9	10.4	10.0	10.8
Net income ($ mil.)	–	(60.4)	(53.3)	(32.6)	(32.1)	(29.9)
Market value ($ mil.)	27.7%	281.8	64.1	63.1	155.6	749.4
Employees	(16.6%)	58	55	31	28	28

CURTISS-WRIGHT CORP.   NYS: CW

130 Harbour Place Drive, Suite 300
Davidson, NC 28036
Phone: 704 869-4600
Fax: –
Web: www.curtisswright.com

CEO: Lynn Bamford
CFO: Glenn E Tynan
HR: –
FYE: December 31
Type: Public

Curtiss-Wright makes a variety of flow control metal treatment and motion control products. It provides commercial and industrial customers with products and services that support critical applications across the aerospace automotive and general industrial markets. The company manufactures and services main coolant pumps power-dense compact motors generators and secondary propulsion systems. Curtiss-Wright also provides embedded computing board level modules integrated subsystems flight testing systems turret aiming and weapons handling systems to defense customers. The company's manufacturing footprint spans about 155 facilities worldwide while it generates the majority of sales in the US.

	Annual Growth	12/16	12/17	12/18	12/19	12/20
Sales ($ mil.)	3.2%	2,108.9	2,271.0	2,411.8	2,488.0	2,391.3
Net income ($ mil.)	1.8%	187.3	214.9	275.7	307.6	201.4
Market value ($ mil.)	4.3%	4,024.5	4,985.7	4,178.4	5,764.7	4,760.6
Employees	0.6%	8,000	8,600	9,000	9,100	8,200

CUSO FINANCIAL SERVICES, L.P.

10150 MEANLEY DR FL 1
SAN DIEGO, CA 921313008
Phone: 800-686-4724
Fax: –
Web: www.cusonet.com

CEO: Valorie Seyfert
CFO: Daniel J Kilroy
HR: –
FYE: December 31
Type: Private

For credit unions looking to expand their investment offerings CUSO can do so. CUSO Financial Services (CFS) provides credit unions with online securities trading retirement planning wealth management insurance and other investment services from more than 300 providers that the credit unions can in turn offer to their members. Founded in 1996 by Valorie Seyfert and Amy Beattie (company president and COO respectively) CFS serves about 100 credit unions throughout the US; more than 40 of them are limited partners that hold ownership stakes in the company.

	Annual Growth	12/04	12/05	12/06	12/07	12/08
Assets ($ mil.)	0.8%	–	22.3	24.7	28.0	22.8
Net income ($ mil.)	(11.0%)	–	4.8	6.0	6.0	3.4
Market value ($ mil.)	–	–	–	–	–	–
Employees	–	–	–	–	–	95

CUSTOMERS BANCORP INC   NYS: CUBI

701 Reading Avenue
West Reading, PA 19611
Phone: 610 933-2000
Fax: –
Web: www.customersbank.com

CEO: Jay Sidhu
CFO: Carla Leibold
HR: –
FYE: December 31
Type: Public

Customers Bancorp makes it pretty clear who they want to serve. Boasting some $8.5 billion in assets the bank holding company operates about 15 branches mostly in southeastern Pennsylvania but also in New York and New Jersey. It offers personal and business checking savings and money market accounts as well as loans certificates of deposit credit cards and concierge or appointment banking (they come to you seven days a week). Around 95% of the bank's loan portfolio is made up of commercial loans while the rest consists of consumer loans. It was formed in 2010 as a holding company for Customers Bank which was created in 1994 as New Century Bank.

	Annual Growth	12/16	12/17	12/18	12/19	12/20
Assets ($ mil.)	18.4%	9,382.7	9,839.6	9,833.4	11,520.7	18,439.2
Net income ($ mil.)	13.9%	78.7	78.8	71.7	79.3	132.6
Market value ($ mil.)	(15.6%)	1,135.7	824.0	577.0	754.9	576.4
Employees	2.9%	739	765	827	867	830

CUSTOMINK LLC

2910 DISTRICT AVE STE 100
FAIRFAX, VA 220312283
Phone: 703-891-2273
Fax: –
Web: www.customink.com

CEO: –
CFO: –
HR: –
FYE: December 31
Type: Private

CustomInk knows a T-shirt is not just a T-shirt. (It can also be an advertisement a form of self-expression or a fashion statement.) The firm provides screen printing and embroidery services for customers across the US through its online storefront. Customers pick the clothing type (short and long sleeve Ts tank tops sweats) and color and then add text and graphics (picking from available graphics or designing their own). CustomInk team members — or Inkers as they call themselves — then print and ship orders. The firm also offers anout 200 other customized products (pens hats drinkware). CustomInk was founded in 1999 by president Marc Katz and former classmates Mike Driscoll and Dave Christensen.

	Annual Growth	12/03	12/04	12/05	12/06	12/08
Sales ($ mil.)	44.5%	–	13.7	0.0	34.0	59.6
Net income ($ mil.)	–	–	–	0.0	3.8	4.6
Market value ($ mil.)	–	–	–	–	–	–
Employees	–	–	–	–	–	500

CUTERA INC

NMS: CUTR

3240 Bayshore Blvd.
Brisbane, CA 94005
Phone: 415 657-5500
Fax: –
Web: www.cutera.com

CEO: David Mowry
CFO: Rohan Seth
HR: –
FYE: December 31
Type: Public

Cutera was founded in 1998 and is a global provider of Face + Body laser light and other energy-based aesthetic systems. The company designs develops manufactures and markets its platforms for use by physicians and other qualified practitioners enabling them to provide safe and effective aesthetic treatments to their customers. excel V excel HR xeo enlighten truSculpt and Genesis Plus are the main product platforms sold globally for a wide-range of aesthetic indications. The company sells both single and multi-application platforms and all feature upgradability and customization to match customer need. Cutera distributes its products globally through distributors in over 65 countries but generates 40% of its revenue in US.

	Annual Growth	12/16	12/17	12/18	12/19	12/20
Sales ($ mil.)	5.8%	118.1	151.5	162.7	181.7	147.5
Net income ($ mil.)	–	2.6	30.0	(30.8)	(12.3)	(23.9)
Market value ($ mil.)	8.6%	306.7	801.8	300.9	633.1	426.2
Employees	2.1%	297	367	402	447	323

CUTTER & BUCK INC.

701 N. 34th St. Ste. 400
Seattle WA 98103
Phone: 206-830-6812
Fax: 206-448-0589
Web: www.cutterbuck.com

CEO: Joel Freet
CFO: –
HR: Chris Nguyen
FYE: April 30
Type: Private

Relatively unknown less than a decade ago Cutter & Buck has climbed onto the leader board of the nation's top makers of golf apparel. Cutter & Buck sells men's and women's golf apparel and other sportswear through golf pro shops resorts and specialty stores throughout North America as well as to corporate accounts. It sells its products in other countries through distributors. Most of its sales come from men's apparel. Cutter & Buck divides its apparel into two lines: the ephemeral fashion line with brighter colors and the seasonless and less-expensive classics line. Its corporate marketing division puts company logos on products for corporate golf events and programs. New Wave Group AB owns the company.

CVB FINANCIAL CORP

NMS: CVBF

701 North Haven Ave., Suite 350
Ontario, CA 91764
Phone: 909 980-4030
Fax: –
Web: www.cbbank.com

CEO: David Brager
CFO: E. Allen Nicholson
HR: –
FYE: December 31
Type: Public

CVB Financial is into the California Vibe Baby. The holding company's Citizens Business Bank offers community banking services to primarily small and midsized businesses but also to consumers through nearly 50 branch and office locations across central and southern California. Boasting more than $7 billion in assets the bank offers checking money market CDs and savings accounts trust and investment services and a variety of loans. Commercial real estate loans account for about two-thirds of the bank's loan portfolio which is rounded out by business consumer and construction loans; residential mortgages; dairy and livestock loans; and municipal lease financing.

	Annual Growth	12/16	12/17	12/18	12/19	12/20
Assets ($ mil.)	15.6%	8,073.7	8,270.6	11,529.2	11,282.5	14,419.3
Net income ($ mil.)	15.0%	101.4	104.4	152.0	207.8	177.2
Market value ($ mil.)	(4.0%)	3,109.3	3,194.7	2,743.2	2,926.3	2,644.2
Employees	–	–	–	–	–	1,052

CVD EQUIPMENT CORP.

NAS: CVV

355 South Technology Drive
Central Islip, NY 11722
Phone: 631 981-7081
Fax: –
Web: www.cvdequipment.com

CEO: Emmanuel Lakios
CFO: Thomas McNeill
HR: –
FYE: December 31
Type: Public

CVD Equipment has expanded well beyond the chemical vapor deposition (CVD) equipment that gave it its name. (During CVD precise layers of chemicals are deposited onto semiconductor wafers during chip manufacturing.) The company's specialized equipment is also used in the development of nanotechnology — namely solar cells smart glass carbon nanotubes nanowires LEDs and microelectromechanical systems (MEMS). CVD Equipment still makes custom-designed products for major semiconductor companies but its newer technologies are used by universities research labs and startup companies. Its largest shareholder is Chairman and CEO Leonard A. Rosenbaum who founded the company in 1982 and owns 29%.

	Annual Growth	12/16	12/17	12/18	12/19	12/20
Sales ($ mil.)	(5.2%)	21.0	41.1	24.3	19.6	16.9
Net income ($ mil.)	–	(0.1)	5.3	(5.2)	(6.3)	(6.1)
Market value ($ mil.)	(19.6%)	58.0	77.6	23.7	21.5	24.2
Employees	(6.9%)	173	231	197	172	130

CVENT, INC

NYS: CVT

1765 Greensboro Station Place, 7th Floor
Tysons Corner, VA 22102
Phone: 703 226-3500
Fax: –
Web: www.cvent.com

CEO: Rajeev K Aggarwal
CFO: Cynthia Russo
HR: –
FYE: December 31
Type: Public

Cvent does everything for event planners except set up the chairs. The company's software automates the event planning process for conferences trade shows and industry events. Its database of more than 200000 hotels and convention centers in more than 175 countries helps event planners in selecting a venue. Its software manages the budget registrations marketing (including social media and event-specific apps) logistics such as travel and lodging and post-event surveys. Customers include more than 6000 event marketing firms (such as Aimia and Maritz) and almost 5000 hotel groups (such as Marriott and Starwood). Founded in 1999 Cvent went public in 2013 raising $117.6 million in its IPO.

	Annual Growth	12/10	12/11	12/12	12/13	12/14
Sales ($ mil.)	–	0.0	60.9	83.5	111.1	142.2
Net income ($ mil.)	–	0.0	(0.2)	4.3	(3.2)	1.8
Market value ($ mil.)	–	0.0	–	–	1,498.0	1,146.0
Employees	15.7%	–	–	1,300	1,450	1,740

CVR ENERGY INC
NYS: CVI

2277 Plaza Drive, Suite 500
Sugar Land, TX 77479
Phone: 281 207-3200
Fax: –
Web: www.cvrenergy.com

CEO: David Lamp
CFO: Dane Neumann
HR: –
FYE: December 31
Type: Public

CVR Energy refines and markets high value transportation fuels to retailers railroads and farm cooperatives and other refiners/marketers in Kansas Oklahoma and Iowa. Located approximately 100 miles of Cushing Oklahoma (a major crude oil trading and storage hub) the company's two oil refineries?in Coffeyville Kansas and Wynnewood Oklahoma?represent close to a quarter of the region's refining capacity. Through a limited partnership the company also produces and distributes ammonia and ammonium nitrate to farmers in Illinois Iowa Kansas Nebraska and Texas. The company is founded in 2006.

	Annual Growth	12/16	12/17	12/18	12/19	12/20
Sales ($ mil.)	(4.8%)	4,782.4	5,988.4	7,124.0	6,364.0	3,930.0
Net income ($ mil.)	–	24.7	234.4	289.0	380.0	(256.0)
Market value ($ mil.)	(12.5%)	2,552.5	3,743.8	3,466.3	4,064.5	1,497.9
Employees	(1.1%)	1,487	1,440	1,450	1,486	1,423

CVR PARTNERS LP
NYS: UAN

2277 Plaza Drive, Suite 500
Sugar Land, TX 77479
Phone: 281 207-3200
Fax: –
Web: www.cvrpartners.com

CEO: Mark Pytosh
CFO: Dane Neumann
HR: –
FYE: December 31
Type: Public

Farmers dreaming of fertile fields can turn to CVR Partners. The company makes nitrogen fertilizers. From its fertilizer manufacturing facility in Kansas CVR Partners produces ammonia and urea ammonia nitrate (UAN). The company sells ammonia to agricultural and industrial customers such as Brandt Consolidated Interchem and National Cooperative Refinery Association and provides UAN products to retailers and distributors. To lower production costs CVR Partners uses petroleum coke instead of the more expensive natural gas. It obtains the majority of its petroleum coke from parent company CVR Energy which founded CVR Partners in 2007. CVR Partners went public in April 2011 raising $307 million.

	Annual Growth	12/16	12/17	12/18	12/19	12/20
Sales ($ mil.)	(0.4%)	356.3	330.8	351.1	404.2	350.0
Net income ($ mil.)	–	(26.9)	(72.8)	(50.0)	(35.0)	(98.2)
Market value ($ mil.)	27.8%	64.3	35.1	36.4	33.2	171.5
Employees	(1.0%)	299	304	290	286	287

CVR REFINING LP
NYS: CVRR

2277 Plaza Drive, Suite 500
Sugar Land, TX 77479
Phone: 281 207-3200
Fax: –
Web: www.cvrrefining.com

CEO: David L Lamp
CFO: –
HR: –
FYE: December 31
Type: Public

Oil refinery Coffeyville Resources may be located in Coffeyville Kansas but new parent CVR Refining is thinking "We're not just in Kansas anymore." CVR Refining was formed by CVR Energy in September 2012 as an indirect wholly owned subsidiary to take over its downstream operations. CVR Refining is taking ownership of the 115000 barrels-per-day Coffeyville refinery and a 70000 barrels-per-day refinery in Wynnewood Oklahoma both of which are not too far from a crude oil hub at Cushing Oklahoma. In addition CVR Refining will control 350 miles of pipeline 125 oil tanker trucks tank farms and 6 million barrels of storage capacity. CVR Refining went public in 2013 with an offering worth $600 million.

	Annual Growth	12/12	12/13	12/14	12/15	12/16
Sales ($ mil.)	(14.5%)	8,281.7	8,683.5	8,829.7	5,161.9	4,431.5
Net income ($ mil.)	(60.0%)	595.3	590.4	358.7	291.2	15.3
Market value ($ mil.)	(22.8%)	–	3,338.7	2,479.7	2,794.1	1,535.0
Employees	3.9%	832	891	982	968	968

CVS HEALTH CORPORATION
NYS: CVS

One CVS Drive
Woonsocket, RI 02895
Phone: 401 765-1500
Fax: 401 762-2137
Web: www.cvshealth.com

CEO: Karen Lynch
CFO: Shawn Guertin
HR: –
FYE: December 31
Type: Public

CVS Health Corp. is a leading pharmacy benefits manager with approximately 110 million plan members as well as the nation's largest drugstore chain. It runs approximately 9900 retail and specialty drugstores. In addition to its standalone pharmacy operations the company operates CVS locations inside Target stores and runs a panel of healthcare professionals Caremark National Pharmacy and Therapeutics Committee. The company also offers walk-in health services through its retail network of MinuteClinics that are located in around 1200 CVS stores. CVS also serves an estimated 35 million people through traditional voluntary and consumer-directed health insurance products and related services.

	Annual Growth	12/17	12/18	12/19	12/20	12/21
Sales ($ mil.)	12.1%	184,765.0	194,579.0	256,776.0	268,706.0	292,111.0
Net income ($ mil.)	4.5%	6,622.0	(594.0)	6,634.0	7,179.0	7,910.0
Market value ($ mil.)	9.2%	95,845.0	86,617.4	98,211.4	90,292.6	136,377.5
Employees	5.1%	246,000	295,000	290,000	300,000	300,000

CYALUME TECHNOLOGIES HOLDINGS, INC
NBB: CYLU

910 S.E. 17th Street, Suite 300
Fort Lauderdale, FL 33316
Phone: 954 315-4939
Fax: –
Web: www.cyalume.com

CEO: Zivi Nedivi
CFO: Andrea Settembrino
HR: –
FYE: December 31
Type: Public

Cyalume Technologies Holdings believes in walking softly and carrying a big chemstick. Through two main subsidiaries the company provides an array of tactical gear and training services to militaries and law enforcement agencies. Subsidiary Cyalume Technologies Inc. makes chemical light sticks and other reflective items as well as explosion simulation products. It also offers combat training. Customers include NATO and US militaries and Canadian and German defense procurement agencies. Subsidiary Cyalume Specialty Products makes specialty chemical products for military pharmaceutical and other markets. Cyalume which has manufacturing plants in the US and France filed a $5.8 million IPO in April 2012.

	Annual Growth	12/11	12/12	12/13	12/14	12/15
Sales ($ mil.)	2.2%	34.7	38.6	31.8	33.3	37.8
Net income ($ mil.)	77.9%	0.3	(50.2)	(15.7)	(7.7)	3.3
Market value ($ mil.)	(57.6%)	80.3	44.9	14.8	1.0	2.6
Employees	(5.3%)	236	271	190	179	190

CYANOTECH CORP.
NAS: CYAN

73-4460 Queen Kaahumanu Highway, Suite 102
Kailua-Kona, HI 96740
Phone: 808 326-1353
Fax: –
Web: www.cyanotech.com

CEO: Gerald Cysewski
CFO: Felicia Ladin
HR: Amy Nordin
FYE: March 31
Type: Public

Cyanotech transforms the scum of the earth into health products. The majority of the company's sales come from Spirulina Pacifica a nutritional supplement made from tiny blue-green vegetable algae and sold as powder flakes and tablets. The firm also produces BioAstin an astaxanthin-based dietary supplement full of antioxidants. Cyanotech produces the microalgae used in its product lines at a 90-acre production facility on the Kona Coast of Hawaii. It sells them primarily to health food and dietary supplement makers. In order to focus on its nutritional supplement business the company has discontinued some other product lines including NatuRose an algae-based pigmentation used to color farm-raised fish.

	Annual Growth	03/17	03/18	03/19	03/20	03/21
Sales ($ mil.)	0.2%	32.0	34.1	30.2	31.9	32.3
Net income ($ mil.)	–	(1.2)	1.0	(3.6)	0.4	0.9
Market value ($ mil.)	(3.7%)	23.5	31.2	19.8	12.6	20.2
Employees	(6.2%)	124	118	109	95	96

CYBERDEFENDER CORPORATION
NASDAQ: CYDE

617 W. 7th St. 10th Fl.
Los Angeles CA 90017
Phone: 213-689-8631
Fax: 213-689-8639
Web: www.cyberdefendercorp.com

CEO: Kevin Harris
CFO: Kevin Harris
HR: –
FYE: December 31
Type: Public

If the best defense is a good offense then CyberDefender's got your lineup. Its CyberDefender line of Internet security software protects Windows-based PCs against identity theft viruses malware and spyware. The company boasts about 600000 active subscribers who renew its products on a monthly or yearly basis. CyberDefender markets its applications to consumers and small businesses through e-mails banners and search ads; it also runs a direct marketing campaign with Guthy-Renker. In addition CyberDefender operates a tech-support call center called LiveTech where its 500 help desk agents handle about 160000 calls a month. Co-founder and CEO Gary Guseinov owns almost a quarter of the company's stock.

CYBERNET SOFTWARE SYSTEMS INC.

3031 Tisch Way Ste. 1002
San Jose CA 95128
Phone: 408-615-5700
Fax: 408-615-5707
Web: www.csscorp.com

CEO: Suranjan Pramanik
CFO: Sivaramakrishnan Sundaram
HR: –
FYE: March 31
Type: Private

Cybernet Software Systems (which does business as CSS) helps large corporations consumers and technology vendors worldwide improve software quality and the operations of their IT systems. Among the services the company offers are software testing and development remote infrastructure management application lifecycle management cloud enablement and enterprise and consumer technical support. It serves customers in a wide range of industries including technology (NETGEAR) financial services (Deutsche Bank) and healthcare (Purdue Pharma). The company partners with such tech firms as Blackberry Microsoft and VMware. Privately held CSS has received investments from Goldman Sachs SAIF and Sierra Ventures.

CYBERONICS, INC.
NMS: CYBX

100 Cyberonics Boulevard
Houston, TX 77058
Phone: 281 228-7200
Fax: –
Web: www.cyberonics.com

CEO: Daniel J Moore
CFO: Gregory H Browne
HR: Jonathan Brown
FYE: April 25
Type: Public

It may sound futuristic but Cyberonics is all about treating an age-old neurological disorder. The company is the maker of the first medical device to gain clearance by the FDA for treating epilepsy. Its Vagus Nerve Stimulation Therapy system (VNS Therapy) is a pacemaker-like device that is implanted under the collarbone with a lead that connects it to the vagus nerve in the neck. The device delivers intermittent signals to the brain to control epileptic seizures. Physicians can program the signals by computer and patients can start or stop signals with hand-held magnets. VNS Therapy is also used for treating depression that has been treatment-resistant. Cyberonics sells its systems worldwide.

	Annual Growth	04/10	04/11	04/12	04/13	04/14
Sales ($ mil.)	13.9%	167.8	190.5	218.5	254.3	282.0
Net income ($ mil.)	(8.5%)	78.4	46.7	36.1	46.4	54.9
Market value ($ mil.)	32.4%	522.3	951.9	1,031.8	1,149.8	1,605.3
Employees	8.3%	465	484	536	581	639

CYBEROPTICS CORP.
NMS: CYBE

5900 Golden Hills Drive
Minneapolis, MN 55416
Phone: 763 542-5000
Fax: –
Web: www.cyberoptics.com

CEO: Subodh Kulkarni
CFO: Jeffrey Bertelsen
HR: –
FYE: December 31
Type: Public

CyberOptics keeps a close eye on the printed circuit board market. The company makes non-contact sensors and integrated systems used during and after the assembly of printed circuit boards and solar cells. Incorporating proprietary laser and optics three-dimensional sensing technology most of the company's products are used in surface mount technology (SMT) assembly and solar cell manufacturing as components used by assembly system manufacturers and as stand-alone products sold directly to end users. It also offers products used for yield improvement in semiconductor fabrication.

	Annual Growth	12/16	12/17	12/18	12/19	12/20
Sales ($ mil.)	1.4%	66.2	53.3	64.7	59.3	70.1
Net income ($ mil.)	(16.1%)	11.6	1.3	2.8	0.8	5.7
Market value ($ mil.)	(3.4%)	190.4	109.4	128.6	134.1	165.5
Employees	2.8%	164	177	178	173	183

CYCLACEL PHARMACEUTICALS INC
NAS: CYCC

200 Connell Drive, Suite 1500
Berkeley Heights, NJ 07922
Phone: 908 517-7330
Fax: 866 271-3466
Web: www.cyclacel.com

CEO: Spiro Rombotis
CFO: Paul McBarron
HR: –
FYE: December 31
Type: Public

Cyclacel Pharmaceuticals wants to stop the cycle of disease. The company's main focus is on cancer but it is also working on treatments for inflammation type II diabetes and HIV/AIDS. Its cancer programs which seek to halt cell cycles related to disease progression target such ailments as leukemia and non-small cell lung cancer. Cyclacel's R&D operations are supported by commercial products sold through subsidiary ALIGN Pharmaceuticals including Xclair cream for radiation-induced skin conditions and Numoisyn lozenge and liquid formulas for xerostomia (dry mouth often related to chemotherapy).

	Annual Growth	12/12	12/13	12/14	12/15	12/16
Sales ($ mil.)	87.0%	0.1	1.1	1.7	1.9	0.8
Net income ($ mil.)	–	(13.2)	(10.2)	(19.4)	(14.3)	(11.8)
Market value ($ mil.)	(3.4%)	25.8	17.1	3.0	2.1	22.5
Employees	(6.5%)	17	18	18	16	13

CYCLE COUNTRY ACCESSORIES CORP.
NYSE AMEX: ATC

1701 38th Ave. West
Spencer IA 51301
Phone: 712-262-4191
Fax: 712-262-0248
Web: www.cyclecountry.com

CEO: –
CFO: –
HR: –
FYE: September 30
Type: Public

Cycle Country Accessories turns ATVs into beasts of burden. The company makes all-terrain vehicle (ATV) accessories such as snowplow blades lawnmowers spreaders sprayers tillage equipment winch mounts utility boxes and wheel covers for Honda Yamaha Kawasaki Suzuki Polaris Arctic Cat and other ATV models. Cycle Country also makes hubcaps for golf carts riding lawnmowers and light-duty trailers. Its products are sold through 20 distributors in the US and more than 30 other countries. The company also makes pull-behind implements and other accessories for riding mowers under the Weekend Warrior brand and offers contract manufacturing services. Cycle Country makes most of its sales in the US.

CYIOS CORPORATION
OTC: CYIO

1300 Pennsylvania Ave. NW Ste. 700
Washington DC 20004
Phone: 202-204-3006
Fax: 202-315-3458
Web: www.cyios.com

CEO: –
CFO: –
HR: –
FYE: December 31
Type: Public

CYIOS is a holding company for two operating subsidiaries. The first which has the same name as the parent company and is referred to as CYIOS DC is a provider of information technology (IT) systems integration services for agencies within the Department of Defense. The second subsidiary CKO offers an online office management software product called XO Office software. The company had previously provided telecommunications services as WorldTeq but has ceased those operations. CEO Tim Carnahan owns 67% of the company.

CYOPTICS INC.
CEO: Ed J Coringrato Jr

9999 Hamilton Blvd.
Breinigsville PA 18031
Phone: 484-397-2000
Fax: 484-397-2014
Web: www.cyoptics.com

CFO: Warren Barratt
HR: –
FYE: December 31
Type: Private

CyOptics sees its way clear to optical networks. The company makes optical components based on indium phosphide (InP) a compound semiconductor that runs faster than silicon the material in most microchips. Its chips lasers and receivers are integrated telecommunications network equipment. CyOptics also offers contract design and manufacturing services from facilities in Mexico and the US. Customers include telecom equipment makers module suppliers and defense contractors. Founded in 1999 CyOptics has received funding from equity investors Jerusalem Venture Partners (which owns 54% of the company) Sprout Group Birchmere Ventures and Eurofund. The company filed an IPO in 2011 but withdrew it in 2012.

CYNERGISTEK INC
ASE: CTEK

11940 Jollyville Road, Suite 300-N
Austin, TX 78759
Phone: 949 614-0700
Fax: –
Web: www.cynergistek.com

CEO: Michael McMillan
CFO: Paul T Anthony
HR: –
FYE: December 31
Type: Public

Hospitals count on AUXILIO to streamline their printing processes; you can print copy scan and fax that. The company is a managed print services provider meaning it does not sell printing equipment and related supplies. Rather it is vendor neutral and procures different makes and models of equipment depending on the needs of its US health care industry clients which include California Pacific Medical Center Saddleback Memorial Medical Center and St. Joseph Health System. Often working with IT departments AUXILIO's consultants assess clients' print environments and assist them with plans to minimize costs on supplies that will maximize their productivity and also reduce unnecessary paper waste.

	Annual Growth	12/16	12/17	12/18	12/19	12/20
Sales ($ mil.)	(25.2%)	60.2	71.6	71.1	21.4	18.9
Net income ($ mil.)	–	5.0	(0.4)	1.9	14.9	(18.5)
Market value ($ mil.)	16.0%	9.6	48.7	57.0	39.7	17.4
Employees	(21.6%)	283	303	297	142	107

CYPRESS ENVIRONMENTAL PARTNERS LP
NYS: CELP

5727 South Lewis Avenue, Suite 300
Tulsa, OK 74105
Phone: 918 748-3900
Fax: –
Web: www.cypressenergy.com

CEO: Peter Boylan
CFO: Jeffrey Herbers
HR: –
FYE: December 31
Type: Public

It's a dirty job but someone's got to do it. After oil and gas companies drill wells Cypress Energy Partners comes in and cleans up the mess. The company provides saltwater disposal and other water and environmental services to oil and natural gas companies that perform hydraulic fracturing a process that pumps sand water and chemicals into shale reservoirs to release oil and gas. It owns and operates nine fluid management disposal facilities in North Dakota and Texas. It also provides independent pipeline inspection and integrity services to producers and pipeline companies through subsidiary Tulsa Inspection Resources. Cypress Energy Partners went public in early 2014.

	Annual Growth	12/16	12/17	12/18	12/19	12/20
Sales ($ mil.)	(8.8%)	298.0	286.3	315.0	401.6	206.0
Net income ($ mil.)	–	(4.7)	(0.8)	11.4	16.0	(1.4)
Market value ($ mil.)	(31.7%)	128.8	73.3	68.6	112.4	28.1
Employees	–	–	–	–	–	–

CYNOSURE INC
NMS: CYNO

5 Carlisle Road
Westford, MA 01886
Phone: 978 256-4200
Fax: –
Web: www.cynosure.com

CEO: Todd Tillemans
CFO: –
HR: –
FYE: December 31
Type: Public

HologicIf beauty is only skin deep then Cynosure can surely enhance it. The company develops makes and markets aesthetic laser and pulsed light systems used by dermatologists and doctors to remove hair reduce pigmentation rejuvenate the skin and treat vascular lesions. For patients who want to go deeper its Smartlipo workstation allows cosmetic surgeons to perform a less-invasive procedure than conventional liposuction to target and reduce fat. Cynosure's laser systems consist of a control console and one or more hand pieces. The company's direct sales force and international distributors market and sell its products worldwide under such names as Accolade Affirm Cynergy Elite and PicoSure. Hologic is buying Cynosure for $1.7 billion.

	Annual Growth	12/11	12/12	12/13	12/14	12/15
Sales ($ mil.)	32.4%	110.6	153.5	226.0	292.4	339.5
Net income ($ mil.)	–	(2.9)	11.0	(1.6)	31.3	15.8
Market value ($ mil.)	39.6%	266.9	547.3	604.7	622.4	1,014.0
Employees	25.5%	346	378	576	755	857

CYPRESS SEMICONDUCTOR CORP.
NMS: CY

198 Champion Court
San Jose, CA 95134
Phone: 408 943-2600
Fax: –
Web: www.cypress.com

CEO: Robert LeFort
CFO: Jack Artman
HR: –
FYE: December 30
Type: Public

Cypress Semiconductor makes an array of embedded and memory processors for automotive industrial and consumer machines and devices. Its microcontroller devices which generate most of the company's revenue are embedded in products that range from Audi and Subaru autos to Samsung and Under Armour wearable fitness devices as well as smart TVs and smartphones. Cypress memory products are used in automated driver assist systems networking modems medical instruments and other devices. The company makes significant sales through distributors such as Fujitsu Electronics and Arrow Electronics. In 2019 Cypress agreed to be bought by Germany-based Infineon Technologies for $10.1 billion (?9 billion).

	Annual Growth	12/14*	01/16	01/17*	12/17	12/18
Sales ($ mil.)	36.0%	725.5	1,607.9	1,923.1	2,327.8	2,483.8
Net income ($ mil.)	110.9%	17.9	(378.9)	(686.3)	(80.9)	354.6
Market value ($ mil.)	(3.5%)	5,277.2	3,545.8	4,135.0	5,508.5	4,572.4
Employees	14.9%	3,350	6,279	6,546	6,099	5,846

*Fiscal year change

CYS INVESTMENTS, INC.

NYS: CYS

500 Totten Pond Road, 6th Floor
Waltham, MA 02451
Phone: 617 639-0440
Fax: –
Web: www.cysinv.com

CEO: Kevin E Grant
CFO: Jack Decicco
HR: –
FYE: December 31
Type: Public

CYS Investments (formerly Cypress Sharpridge Investments) is a real estate investment trust (REIT) that invests in residential mortgage-backed securities (RMBS) primarily collateralized by adjustable-rate mortgage loans and guaranteed by government agencies Fannie Mae Freddie Mac and Ginnie Mae. (As a REIT CYS is exempt from paying federal income tax so long as it distributes dividends back to shareholders.) More than three-quarters of its portfolio is backed by hybrid adjustable-rate mortgages (ARMs) and 15-year fixed-rate single-family mortgages. The REIT's investment activities are usually financed through major commercial and investment banks.

	Annual Growth	12/12	12/13	12/14	12/15	12/16
Sales ($ mil.)	(28.5%)	437.4	(402.0)	573.1	62.2	114.3
Net income ($ mil.)	(54.2%)	372.8	(475.8)	425.6	(4.8)	16.4
Market value ($ mil.)	(10.1%)	1,788.4	1,122.1	1,320.5	1,079.7	1,170.6
Employees	1.5%	16	16	16	15	17

CYSTIC FIBROSIS FOUNDATION

4550 MONTGOMERY AVE 1150N
BETHESDA, MD 208145200
Phone: 301-951-4422
Fax: –
Web: www.cff.org

CEO: Michael Boyle
CFO: –
HR: –
FYE: December 31
Type: Private

The Cystic Fibrosis Foundation funds cystic fibrosis (CF) research and medical programs. Founded in 1955 the organization funds research and drug development through matching funds and offers CF-related information and educational materials. Its Cystic Fibrosis Foundation Therapeutics (CFFT) subsidiary studies and address manifestations of CF including infection inflammation and mucus clearance. The foundation provides funding training and accreditation for more than 130 treatment centers in the US. It has about 70 chapters and branch offices nationwide.

	Annual Growth	12/07	12/08	12/12	12/13	12/15
Sales ($ mil.)	3.2%	–	138.5	297.7	405.5	173.1
Net income ($ mil.)	–	–	(2.1)	175.2	247.1	(134.9)
Market value ($ mil.)	–	–	–	–	–	–
Employees	–	–	–	–	–	550

CYTEC INDUSTRIES, INC.

NYS: CYT

Five Garret Mountain Plaza
Woodland Park, NJ 07424
Phone: 973 357-3100
Fax: –
Web: www.cytec.com

CEO: Shane D Fleming
CFO: Daniel G Darazsdi
HR: –
FYE: December 31
Type: Public

Cytec Industries makes products that help companies do everything from lifting off driving fast and mining ores. Its Aerospace Materials segment makes advanced composites carbon fiber and structural film adhesives for aerospace markets. The Industrial Materials segment makes structural composite materials (for automotive motorsports and recreation markets) and process materials (for aerospace wind energy and other process materials markets). The In Process Separation segment makes mining chemicals and phosphines primarily used in applications to separate targeted minerals from host ores. The Additive Technologies segment makes polymer additives specialty additives and formulated resins.

	Annual Growth	12/09	12/10	12/11	12/12	12/13
Sales ($ mil.)	(8.7%)	2,789.5	2,748.3	3,073.1	1,708.1	1,935.0
Net income ($ mil.)	–	(2.5)	172.3	207.8	188.0	173.5
Market value ($ mil.)	26.5%	2,586.1	3,767.7	3,170.5	4,887.5	6,615.2
Employees	(6.7%)	5,800	6,000	5,500	6,600	4,400

CYTOKINETICS INC

NMS: CYTK

280 East Grand Avenue
South San Francisco, CA 94080
Phone: 650 624-3000
Fax: –
Web: www.cytokinetics.com

CEO: Robert Blum
CFO: Ching Jaw
HR: David Cragg
FYE: December 31
Type: Public

Cytokinetics is a late-stage biopharmaceutical company focused on discovering developing and commercializing first-in-class muscle activators and best-in-class muscle inhibitors as potential treatments for people with debilitating diseases in which muscle performance is compromised and/or declining. Its clinical-stage drug candidates are omecamtiv mecarbil a novel cardiac myosin activator CK-136 (formerly known as AMG 594) a novel cardiac troponin activator reldesemtiv a novel fast skeletal muscle troponin activator (FSTA) CK-3773274 (CK-274) a novel cardiac myosin inhibitor and CK-3772271 (CK-271) its second novel cardiac myosin inhibitor. Cytokinetics was founded in 1998 by pioneers in the field of muscle biology.

	Annual Growth	12/16	12/17	12/18	12/19	12/20
Sales ($ mil.)	(14.9%)	106.4	13.4	31.5	26.9	55.8
Net income ($ mil.)	–	16.5	(127.8)	(106.3)	(121.7)	(127.3)
Market value ($ mil.)	14.4%	862.8	578.8	448.8	753.5	1,475.7
Employees	9.7%	127	137	130	156	184

CYTOSORBENTS CORPORATION

OTC: CTSO

7 Deer Park Dr. Ste. K
Monmouth Junction NJ 08852
Phone: 732-329-8885
Fax: 732-329-8650
Web: www.cytosorbents.com

CEO: –
CFO: –
HR: –
FYE: December 31
Type: Public

CytoSorbents (formerly Medasorb Technologies) gets the gunk out of blood. The medical device firm is developing blood purification systems for treating patients with infections and kidney disease. Its top priority is its clinical-stage CytoSorb device which draws a patient's blood pumps it through a cartridge with cleansing polymers and returns it to the patient in a closed loop; the company is developing the device as a treatment for sepsis (or blood infection) in collaboration with UPMC. CytoSorbents is also working on BetaSorb a similar system for treating chronic kidney failure in combination with dialysis; Fresenius Medical Care has agreed to help market the device if approved.

CYTRX CORP

NBB: CYTR

11726 San Vicente Blvd, Suite 650
Los Angeles, CA 90049
Phone: 310 826-5648
Fax: 310 826-6139
Web: www.cytrx.com

CEO: Stephen Snowdy
CFO: John Caloz
HR: –
FYE: December 31
Type: Public

CytRx is fighting cancer at the scene of the crime. The clinical-stage biopharmaceutical is researching and developing drug candidates to treat conditions such as chronic and acute forms of leukemia pancreatic cancer stomach cancer and soft-tissue sarcomas (malignant tumors). Its lead candidate is aldoxorubicin a conjugate of the chemotherapic agent doxorubicin. In mid-2017 CytRx out-licensed Aldoxorubicin to NantCell which is testing for its efficacy in treating advanced soft-tissue sarcomas. CytRx subsidiary Centurion BioPharma is focused on specialized treatments that are delivered directly to solid tumors.

	Annual Growth	12/14	12/15	12/16	12/17	12/18
Sales ($ mil.)	25.7%	0.1	0.1	0.2	0.1	0.3
Net income ($ mil.)	–	(30.1)	(58.6)	(50.8)	(35.0)	(12.7)
Market value ($ mil.)	(36.4%)	92.2	89.1	12.5	56.8	15.1
Employees	(30.7%)	26	31	27	20	6

D W W CO., INC.

1400 N TUSTIN ST
ORANGE, CA 928673902
Phone: 714-516-3111
Fax: –
Web: www.toyota.com

CEO: –
CFO: –
HR: Michelle Chauvin
FYE: December 31
Type: Private

First Orange County then the world — or at least as far as Arizona and Mexico. Megadealer David Wilson Automotive Group has its roots in Orange County California with 16 branches that stretch to east to Scottsdale and now south to Puerto Vallarta Mexico. David Wilson's Automotive locations sell new and used Acura Ford Honda and Mazda cars as well as Toyota and Lexus brand vehicles. The group's dealerships also operate parts and service departments; some offer fleet services. Dealership Web sites allow customers to search inventory schedule service appointments and request quotes. David Wilson owns the company that bears his name

	Annual Growth	12/04	12/05	12/06	12/07	12/08
Sales ($ mil.)	(8.8%)	–	214.6	229.9	199.9	162.8
Net income ($ mil.)	(9.2%)	–	10.0	12.0	7.6	7.5
Market value ($ mil.)	–	–	–	–	–	–
Employees	–	–	–	–	–	135

D'AGOSTINO SUPERMARKETS INC.

1385 Boston Post Rd.
Larchmont NY 10538-3904
Phone: 914-833-4000
Fax: 914-833-4060
Web: www.dagnyc.com

CEO: –
CFO: –
HR: –
FYE: July 31
Type: Private

D'Agostino Supermarkets sells food for the body and soul to New York City residents. The company operates more than a dozen grocery stores mostly in Manhattan but also in Westchester County New York that feature deli and floral departments seafood and meat counters and an ample supply of fresh and organic produce. In addition to name-brand items the grocer sells everything from ice cream to chips and chickens under its D'Agostino label; it also has developed the Earth Goods product line for environment- and health-conscious shoppers. Founded in 1932 by Nicola and Pasquale D'Agostino the regional supermarket chain in still owned and operated by the D'Agostino family.

D. C. TAYLOR CO.

312 29TH ST NE
CEDAR RAPIDS, IA 524024816
Phone: 319-363-2073
Fax: –
Web: www.dctaylorco.com

CEO: William W Taylor
CFO: –
HR: –
FYE: December 31
Type: Private

D. C. Taylor is one of the largest commercial and industrial roofing contractors in the US providing roof installation repair and maintenance services. It has some 60 service and roofing crews that operate from offices in Arizona California Georgia Illinois and Iowa. Dudley C. Taylor started Taylor Tuckpointing a tuckpointing (cosmetic brick finishing commonly found on Federation houses and Californian bungalows) and masonry repair company in Chicago in 1949; the company's name was changed to D. C. Taylor in 1954 and the firm was formally incorporated in 1960. Chairman and CEO Bill Taylor is the company's majority shareholder.

	Annual Growth	12/06	12/07	12/08	12/09	12/10
Sales ($ mil.)	–	–	–	(1,140.6)	8.4	40.4
Net income ($ mil.)	18944.5%	–	–	0.0	1.2	1.9
Market value ($ mil.)	–	–	–	–	–	–
Employees	–	–	–	–	–	350

D/L COOPERATIVE INC.

5001 BRITTONFIELD PKWY
EAST SYRACUSE, NY 130579201
Phone: 315-233-1000
Fax: –
Web: www.dairylea.com

CEO: –
CFO: –
HR: –
FYE: March 31
Type: Private

Yes the farmer takes a wife then hi-ho the dairy-o the farmer takes membership in milk-marketing organizations such as Dairylea Cooperative. Owned by some 2000 dairy farmers in the northeastern US Dairylea processes and markets 6.3 billion pounds of milk for its farmers annually to dairy-product customers including food manufacturers. Its Agri-Services holding company provides members with a full range of financial and farm-management services as well as insurance. Its Empire Livestock Marketing unit operates regional livestock auction locations. Dairylea which was established in 1907 by New York dairy farmers merged with the US's largest milk marketing coop Dairy Farmers of America in 2014.

	Annual Growth	03/07	03/08	03/09	03/10	03/11
Sales ($ mil.)	25.1%	–	–	–	1,066.4	1,333.9
Net income ($ mil.)	7.6%	–	–	–	1.5	1.7
Market value ($ mil.)	–	–	–	–	–	–
Employees	–	–	–	–	–	107

DAEGIS INC

NAS: DAEG

600 E. Las Colinas Blvd., Suite 1500
Irving, TX 75039
Phone: 214 584-6400
Fax: –
Web: www.daegis.com

CEO: Timothy P Bacci
CFO: Susan K Conner
HR: –
FYE: April 30
Type: Public

Daegis formerly Unify Corporation has a firm business plan. The company targets corporate law departments and law firms with products and services for the legal discovery process including search analysis review and production. Legal clients also use Daegis's archiving software to manage electronically stored information. The company additionally serves software value-added resellers systems integrators and independent software vendors among others with products that aid in the development and management of business applications and data. Services provided by Daegis include project management maintenance and consulting.

	Annual Growth	04/10	04/11	04/12	04/13	04/14
Sales ($ mil.)	2.0%	28.6	47.0	43.5	40.2	31.0
Net income ($ mil.)	–	(1.8)	(16.7)	(16.7)	0.5	(1.6)
Market value ($ mil.)	(22.8%)	59.0	47.5	22.9	18.7	21.0
Employees	(0.8%)	127	204	213	160	123

DAILY EXPRESS, INC.

1072 HARRISBURG PIKE
CARLISLE, PA 170131615
Phone: 717-243-5757
Fax: –
Web: www.dailyexp.com

CEO: Todd Long
CFO: –
HR: –
FYE: December 31
Type: Private

Daily Express moves freight not seen every day. The trucking company carries mostly oversized loads (construction machinery industrial equipment even gigantic telescope mirrors) on various-sized trailers. Delivery of wind turbine components is a Daily Express specialty as the demand for alternative energy production surges globally. The company's fleet consists of more than 700 trailers. It operates throughout the US from a network of about 10 terminals primarily east of the Mississippi. An affiliate Plant Site Logistics provides transportation management services.

	Annual Growth	12/11	12/12	12/13	12/14	12/15
Sales ($ mil.)	0.0%	–	92.8	–	92.8	92.8
Net income ($ mil.)	0.0%	–	8.4	–	8.4	8.4
Market value ($ mil.)	–	–	–	–	–	–
Employees	–	–	–	–	–	200

DAILY JOURNAL CORPORATION
NAS: DJCO

915 East First Street
Los Angeles, CA 90012-4050
Phone: 213 229-5300
Fax: 213 229-5481
Web: www.dailyjournal.com

CEO: Gerald Salzman
CFO: Gerald L Salzman
HR: –
FYE: September 30
Type: Public

Legal matters dominate in these papers. Daily Journal Corporation offers legal software and services to US courts and other justice agencies including browser-based case processing systems (eCourt eProsecutor eDefender and eProbation) and electronic filing and payment tools (eFile ePayIt). The company is also a newspaper publisher with about a dozen papers serving markets primarily in California and Arizona. Its flagship papers include the Los Angeles Daily Journal and the San Francisco Daily Journal which offer in-depth coverage of legal cases and court matters in addition to general interest news. Board members Charles Munger (who also serves as vice chairman of Berkshire Hathaway) and J.P. Guerin together control Daily Journal Corporation.

	Annual Growth	09/17	09/18	09/19	09/20	09/21
Sales ($ mil.)	4.5%	41.4	40.7	48.7	49.9	49.4
Net income ($ mil.)	–	(0.9)	8.2	(25.2)	4.0	112.9
Market value ($ mil.)	10.0%	301.8	332.8	341.8	334.1	442.3
Employees	(5.1%)	370	375	385	320	300

DAIRY FARMERS OF AMERICA, INC.

1405 N 98TH ST
KANSAS CITY, KS 661111865
Phone: 816-801-6455
Fax: –
Web: www.dfamilk.com

CEO: Rick Smith
CFO: Kevin Strathman
HR: –
FYE: December 31
Type: Private

Dairy Farmers of America (DFA) is one of the world's largest dairy cooperatives with more than 12500 member farmers across the US. Along with fresh and shelf-stable fluid milk the co-op produces cheese butter powders and sweetened condensed milk for industrial wholesale and retail customers. It also offers contract manufacturing services. The company's brands include Borden and Cache Valley for consumer cheese; Keller's Creamery Plugra Breakstone's Falfurrias and Oakhurst Dairy; and other dairy products under Sport Shake (sports beverage) La Vaquita (queso) Kemps Guida's and Cass Clay. The company owns around 85 production plants nationwide.

	Annual Growth	12/12	12/13	12/14	12/15	12/16
Sales ($ mil.)	(13.0%)	–	–	17,856.1	13,803.1	13,528.3
Net income ($ mil.)	67.6%	–	–	48.6	98.3	136.6
Market value ($ mil.)	–	–	–	–	–	–
Employees	–	–	–	–	–	21,000

DAIRYLAND POWER COOPERATIVE

3200 EAST AVE S
LA CROSSE, WI 546017291
Phone: 608-788-4000
Fax: –
Web: www.dairylandpower.com

CEO: Brent Ridge
CFO: Phillip Moilien
HR: –
FYE: December 31
Type: Private

Dairyland Power Cooperative provides its customers with lots of juice in the land of lactose. The firm provides electricity generation (1366 MW of generating capacity) and transmission services for 25 member distribution cooperatives and 16 municipal utilities in five states (including Wisconsin). The member cooperatives and municipal utilities in turn distribute electricity to almost 254460 consumers. Dairyland Power generates 1030 MW of capacity from its coal-fired power plants; it also operates more than 3180 miles of transmission lines and 228 substations. The power cooperative also markets electricity and offers energy management services.

	Annual Growth	12/16	12/17	12/18	12/19	12/20
Sales ($ mil.)	0.1%	–	441.4	472.8	470.6	442.4
Net income ($ mil.)	(18.3%)	–	27.0	16.5	18.3	14.7
Market value ($ mil.)	–	–	–	–	–	–
Employees	–	–	–	–	–	500

DAIS CORP
NBB: DLYT

11552 Prosperous Drive
Odessa, FL 33556
Phone: 727 375-8484
Fax: –
Web: www.daisanalytic.com

CEO: Timothy Tangredi
CFO: –
HR: –
FYE: December 31
Type: Public

Dais Corporation develops nano polymers it hopes can be used to solve tough global problems like cleaning air and water and reducing harmful emissions. Its only current product is ConsERV an energy recovery ventilator that uses nano technology to improve the efficiency of existing heating and cooling systems. Other Dais products in the development stage including NanoAir NanoClear and NanoCap use the same technology to cleaning air and water and storing energy more efficiently. Formed in 1993 as fuel cell developer Dais the company bought fellow fuel cell firm Analytic in 1999 and changed its name. In 2002 it shifted focus to nano polymers.

	Annual Growth	12/16	12/17	12/18	12/19	12/20
Sales ($ mil.)	(17.9%)	2.2	0.4	1.4	0.9	1.0
Net income ($ mil.)	–	(0.3)	(3.4)	(3.0)	(4.0)	(2.8)
Market value ($ mil.)	–	0.0	0.0	0.0	0.1	0.1
Employees	(5.9%)	14	13	12	11	11

DAKOTA ELECTRIC ASSOCIATION

4300 220TH ST W
FARMINGTON, MN 550249583
Phone: 651-463-6212
Fax: –
Web: www.dakotaelectric.com

CEO: Greg Miller
CFO: –
HR: –
FYE: December 31
Type: Private

The Dakota Electric Association delivers electricity to residents of southeastern Minnesota the Gopher State so they don't have to burrow underground to outlast those long cold winters. The member-owned utility serves more than 103000 customers in portions of Dakota Goodhue Rice and Scott counties south of Minneapolis-St. Paul. The co-op gets its power wholesale from transmission cooperative Great River Energy and distributes it more than 4010 miles of power lines nearly two-thirds of which are buried. Dakota Electric is pushing energy efficiency programs and products to help save its customers money.

	Annual Growth	12/15	12/16	12/17	12/18	12/19
Sales ($ mil.)	0.8%	–	202.7	202.3	210.5	207.9
Net income ($ mil.)	(30.1%)	–	13.5	11.1	5.1	4.6
Market value ($ mil.)	–	–	–	–	–	–
Employees	–	–	–	–	–	200

DAKOTA GASIFICATION COMPANY INC

420 COUNTY RD 26
BEULAH, ND 58523
Phone: 701-873-2100
Fax: –
Web: www.dakotagas.com

CEO: Paul M Sukut
CFO: Steve Johnson
HR: Scott Fritz
FYE: December 31
Type: Private

A miracle on the prairie? A subsidiary of Basin Electric Power Cooperative Dakota Gasification does not turn water into wine but it does something pretty neat anyway: It turns coal into natural gas. The Great Plains Synfuels Plant harnesses the abundant coal resources underlying the North Dakota prairie. The gasification process transforms more than 6 million tons of coal into more than 57 billion cu. ft. of natural gas annually which is then used to supply the eastern US. In addition to natural gas the company's Synfuels plant produces carbon dioxide fertilizers solvents phenol and other chemicals.

	Annual Growth	12/16	12/17	12/18	12/19	12/20
Sales ($ mil.)	(6.0%)	–	337.2	381.4	345.6	279.7
Net income ($ mil.)	–	–	(87.2)	(397.8)	(70.5)	(94.9)
Market value ($ mil.)	–	–	–	–	–	–
Employees	–	–	–	–	–	725

DAKOTA SUPPLY GROUP, INC.

2601 3RD AVE N
FARGO, ND 581024016
Phone: 701-237-9440
Fax: –
Web: www.dsgsupply.com

CEO: Paul Kennedy
CFO: Ross Westby
HR: –
FYE: December 31
Type: Private

Dakota Supply Group (DSG) distributes electrical communications and mechanical equipment to customers through more than a dozen branch locations in Minnesota North Dakota and South Dakota. The company stocks approximately 25000 products. DSG carries products from 3Com 3M A. O. Smith Buckingham Manufacturing Corning Emerson Electric Ferraz Shawmut General Electric Honeywell Hubbell Moen Schneider Electric and Zurn Industries among other manufacturers. The company was founded in 1898. An employee stock ownership plan holds nearly all of Dakota Supply.

	Annual Growth	12/13	12/14	12/15	12/16	12/17
Sales ($ mil.)	(1.4%)	–	380.4	401.2	359.5	364.9
Net income ($ mil.)	(24.8%)	–	15.1	11.0	5.9	6.4
Market value ($ mil.)	–	–	–	–	–	–
Employees	–	–	–	–	–	888

DAKTRONICS INC.

NMS: DAKT

201 Daktronics Drive
Brookings, SD 57006
Phone: 605 692-0200
Fax: –
Web: www.daktronics.com

CEO: Reece Kurtenbach
CFO: Sheila Anderson
HR: Carla Gatzke
FYE: May 01
Type: Public

Daktronics always knows the score. The company is a leading manufacturer of electronic displays audio systems and timing products. Its products include scoreboards game timers shot clocks and animation displays for sports facilities; billboards and price displays for businesses; and displays used by transportation agencies. Other applications include patented mounting system self-adjusting brightness and outdoor advertising. Daktronics products are used in major sports arenas including venues such as the Olympic Games. While most sales come from the US Daktronics has about 15 offices worldwide.

	Annual Growth	04/17	04/18	04/19*	05/20	05/21
Sales ($ mil.)	(4.8%)	586.5	610.5	569.7	608.9	482.0
Net income ($ mil.)	1.4%	10.3	5.6	(1.0)	0.5	10.9
Market value ($ mil.)	(10.1%)	425.4	405.2	328.3	200.1	277.4
Employees	(6.0%)	2,709	2,713	2,722	2,671	2,117

*Fiscal year change

DALE CARNEGIE & ASSOCIATES INC.

290 Motor Pkwy.
Hauppauge NY 11788-5102
Phone: 800-231-5800
Fax: 212-644-5532
Web: www.dale-carnegie.com

CEO: Peter Handal
CFO: Chris Noonan
HR: –
FYE: August 31
Type: Private

Be a good listener remember names and network and you might find success the Dale Carnegie way. Dale Carnegie & Associates started by the author of the 1936 bestseller "How to Win Friends and Influence People" teaches sales teamwork and public-speaking skills. The company founded in 1912 runs courses and franchisees operate offices in more than 85 countries. Dale Carnegie's enduring self-improvement and job skills message has reached some 8 million people who have completed training courses and seminars over the years. The company which boasts a training staff of more than 2700 offers multilingual courses for individuals and custom-made programs for corporations such as AT&T Coca-Cola and BASF.

DALE JARRETT RACING ADVENTURE INC

NBB: DJRT

116 3rd Street N.W., Suite 302
Hickory, NC 28601
Phone: 888 467-2231
Fax: –
Web: www.racingadventure.com

CEO: Timothy B Shannon
CFO: Timothy B Shannon
HR: –
FYE: December 31
Type: Public

Gentlemen start your engines! Dale Jarrett Racing Adventure brings the thrills (but hopefully not the spills) of NASCAR racing to doctors lawyers Indian chiefs — and even average joes assuming they have enough "fuel" to foot the bill. The company gives racing fans the opportunity to race on a major track. Packages range from riding three laps in the passenger seat with a professional driver to 60 laps of actual driving at speeds of up to 165 mph (after instruction). Events are held at racetracks around the country (including Talladega Superspeedway and Atlanta Motor Speedway). The Dale Jarrett Racing Adventure was founded in 1998 when CEO Tim Shannon approached NASCAR driver Dale Jarrett with the concept.

	Annual Growth	12/10	12/11	12/12	12/13	12/14
Sales ($ mil.)	(6.2%)	3.1	2.9	3.5	2.7	2.4
Net income ($ mil.)	–	0.1	(0.3)	(0.2)	(0.2)	(0.4)
Market value ($ mil.)	(12.0%)	1.5	0.8	2.1	0.5	0.9
Employees	40.1%	7	3	3	2	27

DALLAS COUNTY HOSPITAL DISTRICT

5200 HARRY HINES BLVD
DALLAS, TX 752357709
Phone: 214-590-8000
Fax: –
Web: www.parklandhospital.com

CEO: Frederick Cerise
CFO: John Moore
HR: –
FYE: September 30
Type: Private

Parkland Health & Hospital System (PHHS) is one of the largest public hospital systems and a level I Trauma Center and second largest civilian burn center in the U.S. and Level III Neonatal Intensive Care Unit. Parkland Memorial sits at the heart of the health system and is Dallas' only public hospital. PHHS also manages a network of about 20 community clinics as well as Parkland Community Health Plan a regional HMO for Medicaid and CHIP (Children's Health Insurance Program) members. Additionally the system offers Parkland Financial Assistance a program to help residents of Dallas County pay for health care services. Founded in 1894.

	Annual Growth	09/16	09/17	09/18	09/19	09/20
Sales ($ mil.)	2.2%	–	1,734.3	1,456.5	1,600.9	1,850.7
Net income ($ mil.)	–	–	(17.9)	17.3	208.3	297.5
Market value ($ mil.)	–	–	–	–	–	–
Employees	–	–	–	–	–	11,000

DALLAS COWBOYS FOOTBALL CLUB LTD.

1 Cowboys Pkwy.
Irving TX 75063
Phone: 972-556-9900
Fax: 972-556-9304
Web: www.dallascowboys.com

CEO: –
CFO: –
HR: –
FYE: February 28
Type: Private

Proclaiming itself "America's Team" this football franchise certainly has the loyalty of many Texans. Dallas Cowboys Football Club operates the famed Dallas Cowboys professional football franchise one of the most popular teams in the National Football League and the winner of five Super Bowl titles (a mark it shares with the San Francisco 49ers). Dallas has been home to such Hall of Fame players as Troy Aikman Michael Irvin and Roger Staubach as well as famed head coach Tom Landry. The team was founded in 1960 by Clint Murchison Jr. and Bedford Wynne. Oilman Jerry Jones has owned the team since 1989.

DALLAS-FORT WORTH INTERNATIONAL AIRPORT FACILITY IMPROVEMENT CORPORATION

2400 AVIATION DR
DFW AIRPORT, TX 75261
Phone: 972-973-5400
Fax: -
Web: www.dfwairport.com

CEO: Jeff P Fegan
CFO: -
HR: -
FYE: September 30
Type: Private

Many things are bigger in Texas and Dallas/Fort Worth International Airport (DFW) is no exception. Covering some 30 square miles DFW is one of the world's largest airports by land mass. The facility includes seven runways two active control towers five terminals and 165 gates. Some 65 million passengers pass through DFW annually to destinations domestic and international. Aside from airport fare DFW provides private warehouse and distribution centers to tenants and features Grand Hyatt and Hyatt Regency hotels. Opened in 1974 DFW is owned by the cities of Dallas and Fort Worth; it is situated halfway between them and within about a four-hour flight time of most US destinations.

	Annual Growth	09/05	09/06	09/07	09/16	09/18
Sales ($ mil.)	7.5%	-	389.0	567.6	745.6	929.4
Net income ($ mil.)	(7.6%)	-	140.9	28.5	(88.7)	54.7
Market value ($ mil.)	-	-	-	-	-	-
Employees	-	-	-	-	-	1,700

DALLASNEWS CORP
NAS: DALN

P.O. Box 224866
Dallas, TX 75222-4866
Phone: 214 977-7342
Fax: -
Web: www.ahbelo.com

CEO: Robert W Decherd
CFO: Mary Kathryn Murray
HR: -
FYE: December 31
Type: Public

This company gives the Big D a helping of news with breakfast. A. H. Belo is a leading newspaper publisher with a portfolio of three daily newspapers anchored by The Dallas Morning News one of the country's top papers with a circulation of about 260000. It also owns The Press-Enterprise (Riverside California). In addition to its flagship papers A. H. Belo publishes the Denton Record-Chronicle (Texas) and several niche papers such as the Spanish-language paper Al Dia (Dallas) along with websites serving most of its publications. The company was spun off from TV station operator Belo Corp. in 2008.

	Annual Growth	12/16	12/17	12/18	12/19	12/20
Sales ($ mil.)	(12.2%)	260.0	248.6	202.3	183.6	154.3
Net income ($ mil.)	-	(19.3)	10.2	(5.4)	9.3	(6.9)
Market value ($ mil.)	(30.1%)	34.0	25.7	18.0	15.1	8.1
Employees	(11.5%)	1,211	1,090	982	830	743

DANA INC
NYS: DAN

3939 Technology Drive
Maumee, OH 43537
Phone: 419 887-3000
Fax: 419 887-5200
Web: www.dana.com

CEO: James Kamsickas
CFO: Timothy Kraus
HR: -
FYE: December 31
Type: Public

Dana is a global leader in providing power-conveyance and energy-management solutions for vehicles and machinery. In addition to its core offerings the company also offers driveline products (rear and front axles driveshafts transmissions) it provides power technologies (sealing and thermal-management products) and service parts. It makes products for vehicles in the light medium/heavy (commercial) and off-highway markets that carry brand names such as Spicer Victor Reinz and Long. Dana operates in about 140 facilities across the globe. It traces its historical roots back to 1904 when it introduced the automotive universal joint. More than 50% of its sales comes from North America.

	Annual Growth	12/16	12/17	12/18	12/19	12/20
Sales ($ mil.)	5.1%	5,826.0	7,209.0	8,143.0	8,620.0	7,106.0
Net income ($ mil.)	-	640.0	111.0	427.0	226.0	(31.0)
Market value ($ mil.)	0.7%	2,742.9	4,625.9	1,969.7	2,630.2	2,820.9
Employees	11.3%	24,900	30,100	20,900	36,300	38,200

DANA-FARBER CANCER INSTITUTE, INC.

450 BROOKLINE AVE
BOSTON, MA 022155450
Phone: 617-632-3000
Fax: -
Web: www.dana-farber.org

CEO: Edward J Benz Jr
CFO: -
HR: -
FYE: September 30
Type: Private

The Dana-Farber Cancer Institute fights cancer on two fronts: It provides treatment to cancer patients young and old and researches new cancer diagnostics treatments and preventions. The organization's scientists also research AIDS treatments and cures for a host of other deadly diseases. Patients receive treatment from Dana-Farber through its cancer centers operated in conjunction with Brigham and Women's Hospital Boston Children's Hospital and Massachusetts General Hospital. The institute is also a principal teaching affiliate of Harvard Medical School. Dana-Farber is funded by the National Cancer Institute the National Institute of Allergy and Infectious Diseases and private contributions.

	Annual Growth	09/09	09/10	09/13	09/14	09/19
Sales ($ mil.)	9.3%	-	894.2	635.5	672.4	1,985.5
Net income ($ mil.)	22.2%	-	16.8	56.2	34.6	102.2
Market value ($ mil.)	-	-	-	-	-	-
Employees	-	-	-	-	-	3,000

DANAHER CORP
NYS: DHR

2200 Pennsylvania Avenue, N.W., Suite 800W
Washington, DC 20037-1701
Phone: 202 828-0850
Fax: 202 828-0860
Web: www.danaher.com

CEO: Rainer Blair
CFO: Matthew McGrew
HR: Angela Lalor
FYE: December 31
Type: Public

Danaher is a diversified industrial and medical conglomerate whose products test analyze and diagnose. Its subsidiaries design manufacture and market products and offer services geared to worldwide professional medical and dental industrial and commercial markets. Danaher operates through three segments: Life Sciences Diagnostics (research and clinical tools) Environmental & Applied Solutions (turbine pumps and air/water analysis and treatment equipment). It has facilities in more than 60 countries and generates about 40% of sales from customers in the US.

	Annual Growth	12/17	12/18	12/19	12/20	12/21
Sales ($ mil.)	12.6%	18,329.7	19,893.0	17,911.1	22,284.0	29,453.0
Net income ($ mil.)	26.8%	2,492.1	2,650.9	3,008.2	3,646.0	6,433.0
Market value ($ mil.)	37.2%	66,366.3	73,730.8	109,738.2	158,830.1	235,242.2
Employees	4.5%	67,000	71,000	60,000	69,000	80,000

DANCKER, SELLEW & DOUGLAS, INC.

291 EVANS WAY
BRANCHBURG, NJ 088763766
Phone: 908-429-1200
Fax: -
Web: www.dancker.com

CEO: Steven Lang
CFO: Bill Hendry
HR: -
FYE: March 31
Type: Private

Dancker Sellew & Douglas (DS&D) is a furniture dealership serving the New York City metropolitan area upstate New York and New Jersey. It specializes in providing furniture to businesses with clients including AT&T and Coldwell Banker. DS&D offers chairs desks lighting and storage from a variety of manufacturers including Peter Pepper Products Steelcase and Teknion. The company also offers furniture rental and warehousing along with design consulting inventory management and refurbishment services. DS&D also caters to hospitals and universities and provides lab furniture and equipment to pharmaceutical companies. The firm was founded in 1829 as the T.G. Seller Company making roll-top desks.

	Annual Growth	03/02	03/03	03/04	03/06	03/07
Sales ($ mil.)	(10.2%)	-	111.8	97.9	135.8	72.8
Net income ($ mil.)	-	-	(1.7)	(0.8)	0.5	(0.4)
Market value ($ mil.)	-	-	-	-	-	-
Employees	-	-	-	-	-	150

DANFOSS POWER SOLUTIONS INC.

2800 E 13TH ST
AMES, IA 500108600
Phone: 515-239-6000
Fax: –
Web: www.danfoss.com

CEO: Eric Alstrom
CFO: Jesper V Christensen
HR: –
FYE: December 31
Type: Private

Danfoss Power Solutions (formerly Sauer-Danfoss) is one of the largest companies in the mobile hydraulics industry which designs manufactures and sells a complete range of engineered hydraulic electronic and electric components and solutions. The mobile equipment manufacturers rely on its expertise for the most innovative propel control work function and steering solutions around the world. Its solutions have included motors pumps valves and software among others. Danfoss Power Solutions is a wholly-owned subsidiary of Denmark-based industrial company Danfoss A/S. The company traces its roots back in 1946.

	Annual Growth	12/07	12/08	12/09	12/10	12/11
Sales ($ mil.)	33.2%	–	–	1,159.0	1,640.6	2,057.5
Net income ($ mil.)	–	–	–	(332.3)	246.3	259.8
Market value ($ mil.)	–	–	–	–	–	–
Employees	–	–	–	–	–	6,400

DANIS BUILDING CONSTRUCTION COMPANY

3233 NEWMARK DR
MIAMISBURG, OH 453425422
Phone: 937-228-1225
Fax: –
Web: www.danis.com

CEO: John Danis
CFO: Tim Carlson
HR: –
FYE: December 31
Type: Private

Danis Building Construction can reach from the Buckeye state to the Sunshine state. The company provides commercial and industrial construction services in Ohio Indiana Kentucky Tennessee North Carolina Georgia and Florida. The third-generation family-owned company offers construction management design/build general construction and build-to-suit lease-back services. It specializes in public and private building and industrial projects such as offices health care facilities retail complexes hotels cultural facilities schools and industrial plants. Its projects have included the Cincinnati Children's Hospital and a federal courthouse in Kentucky. B.G. Danis established the company in 1916.

	Annual Growth	12/03	12/04	12/06	12/07	12/08
Sales ($ mil.)	–	–	0.0	0.0	208.6	217.4
Net income ($ mil.)	–	–	0.0	0.0	0.0	0.0
Market value ($ mil.)	–	–	–	–	–	–
Employees	–	–	–	–	–	475

DANONE US, INC.

12002 AIRPORT WAY
BROOMFIELD, CO 800212546
Phone: 303-635-4000
Fax: –
Web: www.danonenorthamerica.com

CEO: Gregg L Engles
CFO: –
HR: –
FYE: December 31
Type: Private

WhiteWave Foods rides a wave of dietary changes as consumers seek alternatives to conventional foods. The company is best known for its refrigerated Silk soymilk in the US and Alpro brand soy products in Europe. WhiteWave also produces organic dairy products under the Horizon Organic label and dairy related foods including International Delight coffee creamers and LAND O'LAKES-branded creamers and dairy dessert toppings (licensed from dairy co-op Land O'Lakes). WhiteWave products are sold through natural food and grocery stores as well as mass merchandisers and restaurants and food service businesses in the US and Canada and parts of Europe. WhiteWave has been part of French dairy giant Danone since 2017.

	Annual Growth	12/11	12/12	12/13	12/14	12/15
Sales ($ mil.)	23.3%	–	–	2,542.1	3,436.6	3,866.3
Net income ($ mil.)	30.4%	–	–	99.0	140.2	168.4
Market value ($ mil.)	–	–	–	–	–	–
Employees	–	–	–	–	–	500

DANVILLE REGIONAL MEDICAL CENTER, LLC

142 S MAIN ST
DANVILLE, VA 245412987
Phone: 434-799-2100
Fax: –
Web: www.sovahhealth.com

CEO: Alan Larson
CFO:
HR: –
FYE: June 30
Type: Private

If your name is Dan you should feel right at home at Danville Regional Medical Center (DRMC) serving residents of the Dan River Region in Danville Virginia. Founded in 1884 as the Ladies Benevolent Society Home for the Sick the hospital provides a variety of health care services such as home care cancer treatment psychiatry and rehabilitation. Outpatient options include endoscopy (for gastrointestinal care) imaging neurosurgical treatments and pain management. DRMC administers a range of senior care services such as skilled nursing and coordination of assisted and independent living options. The health system is owned by LifePoint Health.

	Annual Growth	02/04	02/05*	06/09	06/15	06/16
Sales ($ mil.)	83.6%	–	0.2	153.4	172.2	172.2
Net income ($ mil.)	–	–	0.0	(12.0)	(2.9)	(3.6)
Market value ($ mil.)	–	–	–	–	–	–
Employees	–	–	–	–	–	1,400

*Fiscal year change

DARA BIOSCIENCES, INC.

NAS: DARA

8601 Six Forks Road, Suite 160
Raleigh, NC 27615
Phone: 919 872-5578
Fax: –
Web: www.darabiosciences.com

CEO: Peter Melnyk
CFO: Ernest De Paolantonio
HR: –
FYE: December 31
Type: Public

Metabolism out of whack? DARA BioSciences is working on it. The drug development company is testing drugs for metabolic diseases such as diabetes. However it was not always thus for the company. Formerly called Point Therapeutics the firm failed in its previous efforts to advance lead cancer drug talabostat and was forced to regroup and consider its options. The company turned to its preclinical pipeline which included a potential diabetes drug and then in 2008 executed a reverse merger with privately held DARA BioSciences which brought along a complementary set of metabolic compounds as well as programs focused on neuropathic pain and psoriasis.

	Annual Growth	12/09	12/10	12/11	12/12	12/13
Sales ($ mil.)	681.9%	–	–	–	0.1	0.4
Net income ($ mil.)	–	(3.3)	(5.7)	(6.2)	(7.3)	(10.0)
Market value ($ mil.)	5.1%	2.7	20.4	7.7	4.8	3.3
Employees	29.4%	5	6	9	18	14

DARDEN RESTAURANTS, INC.

NYS: DRI

1000 Darden Center Drive
Orlando, FL 32837
Phone: 407 245-4000
Fax: –
Web: www.darden.com

CEO: Eugene Lee
CFO: Rajesh Vennam
HR: –
FYE: May 30
Type: Public

Darden Restaurants is a full-service restaurant company that has been fueled by its Olive Garden chain of more than 905 Italian-themed restaurants. But Darden is more than garden operating about 1835 restaurants in the US and Canada (fully-owned and franchises). Other concepts include LongHorn Steakhouse The Capital Grille (upscale steakhouse) Bahama Breeze (Caribbean food and drinks) Eddie V's (seafood) Yard House (American food) Seasons 52 (casual grill and wine bar) and Cheddar's Scratch Kitchen (meals from scratch). Overall Darden restaurants serve over 320 million diners in fiscal 2021.

	Annual Growth	05/17	05/18	05/19	05/20	05/21
Sales ($ mil.)	0.1%	7,170.2	8,080.1	8,510.4	7,806.9	7,196.1
Net income ($ mil.)	7.1%	479.1	596.0	713.4	(52.4)	629.3
Market value ($ mil.)	13.0%	11,500.6	11,491.4	15,708.5	10,050.4	18,729.1
Employees	(3.2%)	178,729	180,656	184,514	177,895	156,883

DARLING INGREDIENTS INC NYS: DAR

5601 N. MacArthur Blvd.
Irving, TX 75038
Phone: 972 717-0300
Fax: -
Web: www.darlingii.com

CEO: Randall Stuewe
CFO: Brad Phillips
HR: -
FYE: January 02
Type: Public

Darling Ingredients is the largest publicly traded rendering operation in the US. The company collects and recycles animal by-products into specialty ingredients such as collagen edible fats animal proteins plasma fertilizers fuel feedstocks and natural casings. Darling also recovers and converts used cooking grease and bakery waste and offers grease-trap cleaning services. It primarily collects animal by-products from slaughterhouses butcher shops grocery stores and food service establishments. Darling also produces yellow grease tallow and meat bone and blood meal. The company sells its products nationwide and overseas to makers of soap rubber oils animal feed and chemicals. North America accounts for some 55% its total sales.

	Annual Growth	12/16	12/17	12/18	12/19*	01/21
Sales ($ mil.)	1.0%	3,398.1	3,662.3	3,387.7	3,363.9	3,571.9
Net income ($ mil.)	23.7%	102.3	128.5	101.5	312.6	296.8
Market value ($ mil.)	34.9%	2,094.0	2,940.7	3,088.3	4,541.6	9,355.7
Employees	0.0%	10,000	9,800	9,800	10,100	10,000

*Fiscal year change

DARTMOUTH-HITCHCOCK CLINIC

1 MEDICAL CENTER DR
LEBANON, NH 037560001
Phone: 603-650-5000
Fax: -
Web: www.dartmouth-hitchcock.org

CEO: James N Weinstein
CFO: Robin Mackey
HR: -
FYE: June 30
Type: Private

The New England Alliance for Health (NEAH) brings together health care facilities and professionals looking to improve health in the New England region. Members of the alliance include about 20 community hospitals home health care agencies and mental health centers in New Hampshire Vermont and Massachusetts. While the members collaborate on wellness quality and communication initiatives each member of the alliance is an independently owned and operated not-for-profit organization with its own board of directors. Collaborative services provided by NEAH include procurement staff training information technology quality control and finance as well as the coordination of facility policies and planning.

	Annual Growth	06/12	06/13	06/14	06/15	06/19
Sales ($ mil.)	313.1%	-	-	-	6.5	1,888.0
Net income ($ mil.)	-	-	-	-	0.0	22.0
Market value ($ mil.)	-	-	-	-	-	-
Employees	-	-	-	-	-	7,999

DATA I/O CORP. NAS: DAIO

6645 185th Avenue NE, Suite 100
Redmond, WA 98052
Phone: 425 881-6444
Fax: -
Web: www.dataio.com

CEO: Anthony Ambrose
CFO: Joel S Hatlen
HR: -
FYE: December 31
Type: Public

Data I/O knows the chip-programming business inside and out. The company makes programming systems used by electronics manufacturers to tailor their integrated circuits (ICs) to suit a broad range of products. Data I/O manufactures both manual and automated programming systems used to manufacture semiconductor components for wireless consumer electronics automotive electronics and flash memory cards. Data I/O sells its devices to manufacturers such as LG Delphi and Foxconn. The company does most of its business outside the US; in fact Singapore-based Flextronics is its largest customer. Data I/O has locations in Brazil Canada China Germany Guam and Hong Kong.

	Annual Growth	12/16	12/17	12/18	12/19	12/20
Sales ($ mil.)	(3.5%)	23.4	34.1	29.2	21.6	20.3
Net income ($ mil.)	-	1.7	5.4	1.6	(1.2)	(4.0)
Market value ($ mil.)	(0.4%)	35.2	101.3	42.1	35.7	34.7
Employees	1.3%	91	103	102	96	96

DATACOLOR INC.

5 Princess Rd.
Lawrence NJ 08648
Phone: 609-924-2189
Fax: 609-895-7414
Web: www.datacolor.com

CEO: Albert Busch
CFO: -
HR: -
FYE: September 30
Type: Business Segment

Datacolor takes its cue from hue. The company makes instruments and software that control color measuring matching and quality control for use in textile paint automotive printing photography and home theater applications. Its Spyder brand targets the consumer market. Datacolor also offers a variety of services including calibration of spectrophotometers on-site consulting product training and education in color theory. The company sells directly to consumers online and through resellers. It also integrates its products with those of partners such as Lectra Fongs and Lawer. Established in 1970 Datacolor is a subsidiary of Datacolor AG (formerly Eichhof Holdings) a Swiss firm.

DATALINK CORP NMS: DTLK

10050 Crosstown Circle, Suite 500
Eden Prairie, MN 55344
Phone: 952 944-3462
Fax: -
Web: www.datalink.com

CEO: -
CFO: -
HR: -
FYE: December 31
Type: Public

Datalink builds and implements high-end custom-designed data storage systems for large corporations. Its storage systems include disk- and tape-based storage devices storage networking components and data management software. The company employs an open-system standard building networks from products made by leading manufacturers such as Brocade EMC and Hitachi Data Systems. Datalink also provides ongoing support and maintenance services. The company markets its products directly to customers in the US. It has designed systems for clients including AT&T Harris Corporation NAVTEQ and St. Jude Medical. It has about 35 locations across the US.

	Annual Growth	12/10	12/11	12/12	12/13	12/14
Sales ($ mil.)	21.0%	293.7	380.0	491.2	594.2	630.2
Net income ($ mil.)	48.1%	2.3	9.8	10.5	10.0	11.1
Market value ($ mil.)	28.9%	106.8	189.0	195.6	249.4	295.1
Employees	22.5%	299	389	459	510	674

DATASITE GLOBAL CORPORATION

733 MARQUETTE AVE STE 600
MINNEAPOLIS, MN 554022357
Phone: 651-632-4000
Fax: -
Web: www.datasite.com

CEO: Rusty Wiley
CFO: Tom Donnelly
HR: -
FYE: January 31
Type: Private

Datasite formerly known as Merrill Corporation is a leading SaaS provider for the M&A industry empowering dealmakers around the world with the tools they need to succeed across the entire deal lifecycle. As the premiere virtual data room for M&A due diligence globally Datasite is consistently recognized for breakthrough technologies like its AI/ML-enabled capabilities and automated redaction tools. Beyond due diligence Datasite provides transaction and document management solutions for investment banks corporate development private equity and law firms across industries. In late 2020 Datasite agreed to be acquire by funds managed by CapVest Partners LLP an international private equity firm.

	Annual Growth	01/13	01/14	01/15	01/16	01/17
Sales ($ mil.)	(6.1%)	-	-	691.5	579.4	609.1
Net income ($ mil.)	(8.5%)	-	-	64.5	78.1	54.0
Market value ($ mil.)	-	-	-	-	-	-
Employees	-	-	-	-	-	6,010

DATATRAK INTERNATIONAL INC.   NBB: DTRK

5900 Landerbrook Dr., Suite 170
Mayfield Heights, OH 44124
Phone: 440 443-0082
Fax: 440 442-3482
Web: www.datatrak.com

CEO: James Bob Ward
CFO: Julia Henderson
HR: Laura Stuebbe
FYE: December 31
Type: Public

Researchers rely on DATATRAK to keep tabs on their clinical data. The company develops online hosted electronic data capture (EDC) software for the biotechnology medical device contract research and pharmaceutical industries. Its software speeds up the process of gathering data during clinical trials by collecting and electronically transmitting trial data from remote research sites to sponsors. DATATRAK also offers project management site assessment training and hosting services. Its products have been used to support hundreds of clinical trials involving patients in more than 50 countries.

	Annual Growth	12/16	12/17	12/18	12/19	12/20
Sales ($ mil.)	(5.5%)	9.0	7.5	7.4	7.7	7.2
Net income ($ mil.)	—	1.0	0.2	0.2	0.4	(0.1)
Market value ($ mil.)	(11.9%)	23.4	14.9	7.2	15.6	14.1
Employees	—	—	—	—	—	—

DATAWATCH CORP.   NAS: DWCH

4 Crosby Drive
Bedford, MA 01730
Phone: 978 441-2200
Fax: –
Web: www.datawatch.com

CEO: Michael A Morrison
CFO: James Eliason
HR: Brigid Macdonald
FYE: September 30
Type: Public

Datawatch want its customers do more than watch data. It wants to help them see the information available in data through visualizations. The company makes enterprise information management software that includes data mining business intelligence and help desk management. Its products include Datawatch Modeler for extracting and manipulating data from ASCII PDF or HTML files; Datawatch Automator a data replication and migration tool used to populate and refresh data marts and data warehouses; Datawatch RMS Web-based report mining and analysis; and Datawatch Report Mining Server. The company serves more than 40000 customers across a broad range of industries worldwide although it generates most of its sales in the US.

	Annual Growth	09/13	09/14	09/15	09/16	09/17
Sales ($ mil.)	4.6%	30.3	35.1	30.2	30.5	36.3
Net income ($ mil.)	—	(4.2)	(22.4)	(49.8)	(14.6)	(4.0)
Market value ($ mil.)	(19.8%)	342.0	125.6	72.1	90.8	141.6
Employees	(6.5%)	192	199	164	153	147

DATS TRUCKING, INC.

321 N OLD HIGHWAY 91
HURRICANE, UT 847373194
Phone: 435-673-1886
Fax: –
Web: www.datstrucking.com

CEO: –
CFO: –
HR: –
FYE: December 31
Type: Private

DATS Trucking specializes in less-than-truckload (LTL) freight transportation in the western US but that's not all there is to the company's operations. In addition to its LTL operations in which freight from multiple shippers is combined into a single trailer DATS Trucking provides truckload transportation. The company's tanker division Overland Petroleum transports gasoline diesel fuel and other petroleum products. Overall DATS Trucking operates a fleet of about 500 tractors and 2500 trailers. It offers LTL service outside its home territory via The Reliance Network a group of regional carriers that covers the US and Canada. President and CEO Don Ipson founded DATS Trucking in 1988.

	Annual Growth	12/03	12/04	12/05	12/06	12/07
Sales ($ mil.)	22.3%	—	391.7	600.1	658.9	717.3
Net income ($ mil.)	4.6%	—	1.6	1.2	7.8	1.8
Market value ($ mil.)	—	—	—	—	—	—
Employees	—	—	—	—	—	475

DAVE & BUSTERS ENTERTAINMENT INC   NMS: PLAY

2481 Manana Drive
Dallas, TX 75220
Phone: 214 357-9588
Fax: –
Web: www.daveandbusters.com

CEO: Kevin Sheehan
CFO: Michael Quartieri
HR: Robert Edmund
FYE: January 31
Type: Public

Dave & Buster's Entertainment owns and operates about 140 stores that offer casual dining full bar service and a cavernous game room. The company's Midway features virtual reality platform and some games that are activated by game play credits on cards or other RFID devices (Power Cards). For dining Dave & Buster's offers a menu that features traditional American fare such as burgers and steak. Dave & Buster's was founded in 1982.

	Annual Growth	01/17*	02/18	02/19	02/20*	01/21
Sales ($ mil.)	(18.8%)	1,005.2	1,139.8	1,265.3	1,354.7	436.5
Net income ($ mil.)	—	90.8	120.9	117.2	100.3	(207.0)
Market value ($ mil.)	(11.2%)	2,611.0	2,272.7	2,446.2	2,104.1	1,620.9
Employees	(11.6%)	13,983	14,840	16,098	15,908	8,547

*Fiscal year change

DAVENPORT UNIVERSITY

6191 KRAFT AVE SE
GRAND RAPIDS, MI 495129396
Phone: 616-698-7111
Fax: –
Web: www.davenport.edu

CEO: –
CFO: –
HR: –
FYE: June 30
Type: Private

Couch potatoes need not apply to Davenport. A private not-for-profit school Davenport University offers its 9000 students — many of whom are working adults — associate's bachelor's and master's degrees as well as certification and diploma programs. Founded in 1866 Davenport offers more than 50 undergraduate majors in fields including business health and technology plus an MBA and several other master's programs. With campuses across Michigan online offerings and a study abroad program Davenport is a top independent university system in Michigan. Davenport University was founded by Union Army veteran Conrad Swensburg in 1866. It was originally named Grand Rapids Business College.

	Annual Growth	06/09	06/10	06/11	06/13	06/20
Sales ($ mil.)	(0.7%)	—	132.7	137.2	126.8	124.3
Net income ($ mil.)	—	—	12.7	9.4	(7.5)	(1.7)
Market value ($ mil.)	—	—	—	—	—	—
Employees	—	—	—	—	—	927

DAVEY TREE EXPERT CO. (THE)   NBB: DVTX

1500 North Mantua Street, P.O. Box 5193
Kent, OH 44240
Phone: 330 673-9511
Fax: –
Web: www.davey.com

CEO: Patrick Covey
CFO: Joseph Paul
HR: –
FYE: December 31
Type: Public

The company's roots extend back to 1880 when John Davey founded the arboricultural horticultural services environmental and consulting firm which branched into residential commercial utility and other natural resource management services. With offices in the US and Canada Davey's services include treatment preservation maintenance and removal of trees shrubs and other plants; landscaping; grounds maintenance; tree surgery; tree feeding and tree spraying; the application of fertilizers herbicides and insecticides. It also natural resource management and consulting forestry research and development and environmental planning. Davey has been employee-owned since 1979. The US generates some 95% of Davey's total revenue.

	Annual Growth	12/16	12/17	12/18	12/19	12/20
Sales ($ mil.)	11.1%	845.7	916.0	1,024.8	1,143.7	1,287.6
Net income ($ mil.)	28.6%	22.3	22.1	28.0	40.8	60.9
Market value ($ mil.)	—	—	—	—	—	—
Employees	4.7%	8,000	8,200	8,900	9,700	9,600

DAVID'S BRIDAL INC.

1001 Washington St.
Conshohocken PA 19428
Phone: 610-943-5000
Fax: 610-943-5048
Web: www.davidsbridal.com

CEO: James Marcum
CFO: Curt Kroll
HR: Elaine Nicoloudakis
FYE: January 31
Type: Private

From prom night to the big day itself David's Bridal begs to make an entrance. The largest retail chain specializing in bridal gowns numbers more than 300 stores in 45 US states Canada and Puerto Rico. All gowns are available off the rack and priced from $300 to $1500 to meet most consumers' budgets. David's Bridal also sells invitations and gifts veils and other bridal accessories and apparel for formal occasions such as church communions and Quincea?eras. Besides its brick-and-mortar locations David's Bridal operates an online catalog and spotlights the latest trends through Style Council blogs and podcasts. In 2012 the retailer agreed to be acquired by private equity firm Clayton Dubilier & Rice.

DAVIDSON COMPANIES

Davidson Bldg. 8 3rd St. North
Great Falls MT 59401
Phone: 406-727-4200
Fax: 406-791-7238
Web: www.davidsoncompanies.com

CEO: William Johnstone
CFO: Scott Witeby
HR: -
FYE: September 30
Type: Private

Employee-owned Davidson Companies offers investment banking asset management brokerage and trust services through its operating subsidiaries. The company's flagship firm D.A. Davidson & Co. was founded in 1935 and offers investment banking services such as mergers and acquisitions advisory capital raising institutional sales and trading and fundamental research. The group provides brokerage trust wealth management and financial planning services for private clients through Davidson Trust Co. and Davidson Investment Advisors. Altogether Davidson has some $30 billion of assets under management. Davidson has more than 60 offices in some 15 states though it is mainly active in the Northwest.

DAVIESS COUNTY HOSPITAL

1314 E WALNUT ST
WASHINGTON, IN 475012132
Phone: 812-254-2760
Fax: -
Web: www.dchosp.org

CEO: David Dixler
CFO: Brad Hardcastle
HR: -
FYE: December 31
Type: Private

Daviess Community Hospital serves Daviess County in southwestern Indiana. The acute care facility has about 120 beds and offers behavioral health cardiac rehabilitation hospice obstetric physical therapy and pediatric services. In addition the hospital also has centers dedicated to women's health and diabetes management. Daviess Community Hospital opened its doors in 1915.

	Annual Growth	12/15	12/16	12/17	12/18	12/19
Sales ($ mil.)	23.5%	-	158.9	248.5	291.8	299.2
Net income ($ mil.)	-	-	(0.4)	6.9	9.5	8.2
Market value ($ mil.)	-	-	-	-	-	-
Employees	-	-	-	-	-	550

DAVITA INC

2000 16th Street
Denver, CO 80202
Phone: 720 631-2100
Fax: -
Web: www.davita.com

NYS: DVA

CEO: Javier Rodriguez
CFO: Joel Ackerman
HR: -
FYE: December 31
Type: Public

DaVita performs dialysis treatments for patients suffering from end-stage renal disease (ESRD or chronic kidney failure). The firm is one of the US' largest providers of dialysis — its administrative services reach some 204200 patients through about 2815 outpatient centers across the US. The company also offers home-based dialysis services as well as inpatient dialysis in some 900 hospitals. It operates one separately licensed and highly automated clinical laboratory that specializes in routine testing of dialysis patients and serve the company's network of clinics.

	Annual Growth	12/17	12/18	12/19	12/20	12/21
Sales ($ mil.)	1.7%	10,876.6	11,404.9	11,388.5	11,550.6	11,618.8
Net income ($ mil.)	10.2%	663.6	159.4	811.0	773.6	978.5
Market value ($ mil.)	12.0%	7,029.1	5,006.5	7,299.6	11,421.7	11,067.6
Employees	(1.9%)	74,500	77,700	65,000	67,000	69,000

DAWSON GEOPHYSICAL CO (NEW)

508 West Wall, Suite 800
Midland, TX 79701
Phone: 432 684-3000
Fax: -

NMS: DWSN

CEO: Stephen Jumper
CFO: James Brata
HR: -
FYE: December 31
Type: Public

3-D technology has made Dawson Geophysical (formerly TGC Industries) one of the movers and shakers in the North American oil patch as it conducts seismic surveys for oil exploration companies. The company principally employs land surveys using Geospace Technologies and ARAM ARIES seismic systems which obtain 3-D seismic data related to subsurface geological features. Employing radio-frequency telemetry and multi-channel recorders the system enables the exploration of rivers swamps and inaccessible terrain. It also sells gravity information from its data bank to oil and gas exploration companies. In 2014 it was acquired by Dawson Operating then known as Dawson Geophysical.

	Annual Growth	12/16	12/17	12/18	12/19	12/20
Sales ($ mil.)	(10.4%)	133.3	157.1	154.2	145.8	86.1
Net income ($ mil.)	-	(39.8)	(31.3)	(24.4)	(15.2)	(13.2)
Market value ($ mil.)	(28.3%)	188.8	116.7	79.4	56.3	49.8
Employees	(28.0%)	814	851	582	455	219

DAWSON GEOPHYSICAL CO.

508 West Wall, Suite 800
Midland, TX 79701
Phone: 432 684-3000
Fax: -
Web: www.dawson3d.com

NMS: DWSN

CEO: -
CFO: -
HR: -
FYE: September 30
Type: Public

The oil industry can be shaky at times but Dawson Geophysical always looks for good vibrations. The company provides data acquisition and data processing services including the analysis of 2-D and 3-D seismic data to assess potential underground oil and gas deposits. Dawson Geophysical's customers both major and independent oil and gas operators use the data in exploration and development activities. The company's 3-D seismic data acquisition crews work in the lower 48 states; data processing is performed by geophysicists at the firm's computer center in Midland Texas.

	Annual Growth	09/09	09/10	09/11	09/12	09/13
Sales ($ mil.)	5.8%	244.0	205.3	333.3	319.3	305.3
Net income ($ mil.)	0.6%	10.2	(9.4)	(3.2)	11.1	10.5
Market value ($ mil.)	4.4%	220.6	214.7	190.0	203.5	261.6
Employees	7.4%	942	1,170	1,507	1,452	1,252

DAWSON METAL COMPANY INC.

825 ALLEN ST
JAMESTOWN, NY 147013998
Phone: 716-664-3811
Fax: –
Web: www.dawsondoors.com

CEO: –
CFO: Guy F Lombardo
HR: –
FYE: December 31
Type: Private

Don't knock Dawson Metal's open-door policy. Dawson Metal (which does business as Dawson Doors) manufactures custom-made stainless steel aluminum and bronze doors for businesses and storefronts. The company also manufactures balanced doors which open in an elliptical arch. It mainly serves US corporations and the construction industry and makes doors for private residences as well. Dawson Metal was established in Jamestown New York in 1946 as an industrial and architectural metal fabrication business by Axel Dawson and his son George. The Dawson family continues to own the company.

	Annual Growth	12/09	12/10	12/11	12/12	12/13
Sales ($ mil.)	(0.6%)	–	15.0	14.6	12.9	14.8
Net income ($ mil.)	(22.1%)	–	–	0.5	0.2	0.3
Market value ($ mil.)	–	–	–	–	–	–
Employees	–	–	–	–	–	110

DAXOR CORPORATION
NYSE AMEX: DXR

350 5th Ave. Ste. 7120
New York NY 10118
Phone: 212-330-8500
Fax: 212-244-0806
Web: www.daxor.com

CEO: Michael Feldschuh
CFO: Robert Michel
HR: Diane Fox
FYE: December 31
Type: Public

They might not give you a toaster with that new account but Daxor's blood and sperm banks are open to attract new uh deposits. The company offers blood banking through subsidiary Scientific Medical Systems and operates sperm banks through its Idant division. Its main business however has been the development and commercialization of a blood volume analyzer the BVA-100 which hospitals and other health care providers use to diagnose and treat heart and kidney failure anemia and other conditions as well as to manage blood transfusions. The BVA-100 measures a patient's blood volume within 90 minutes.

DAY KIMBALL HEALTHCARE, INC.

320 POMFRET ST
PUTNAM, CT 062601836
Phone: 860-928-6541
Fax: –
Web: www.daykimball.org

CEO: Robert Smanik
CFO: –
HR: –
FYE: September 30
Type: Private

With more than 100 beds Day Kimball Hospital is a non-profit acute-care facility that caters primarily to Connecticut with an extended reach into parts of Massachusetts and Rhode Island. The health care provider founded in 1894 offers general medical and surgical care along with the option of home care services. Logging an average of nearly 29000 emergency department visits and 550 births Day Kimball offers specialized services such as pediatrics gynecology emergency medicine and psychiatric health care. It also provides hospice and palliative care for terminally ill patients. Outpatient surgery and other medical services are provided through the facility's Ambulatory Care Unit.

	Annual Growth	09/16	09/17	09/18	09/19	09/20
Sales ($ mil.)	8.6%	–	99.0	138.1	136.5	126.6
Net income ($ mil.)	–	–	1.7	8.1	(15.6)	(20.5)
Market value ($ mil.)	–	–	–	–	–	–
Employees	–	–	–	–	–	900

DAYLIGHT DONUT FLOUR COMPANY LLC

11707 E 11TH ST
TULSA, OK 741284401
Phone: 918-438-0800
Fax: –
Web: www.daylightdonuts.com

CEO: John Bond
CFO: Jimmy Keeter
HR: –
FYE: December 31
Type: Private

|Daylight Donut wants to tempt you whether it's day or night. The company sells a variety of sweet and savory pastries from nearly 1000 Daylight Donuts locations in all 50 states plus single shops in Australia China Mexico and Romania. It offers licenses instead of franchises allowing owners to avoid franchise fees by agreeing to use company products in exchange for the use of the name and trademark. The products licensees agree to use include company-made dry mixes for the stores' signature donuts bear claws cinnamon rolls sausage wraps and other pastries as well as private-label coffee for use in-store and for resale. Formed in 1954 Daylight Donut is owned by John and Sheila Bond husband and wife.

	Annual Growth	12/09	12/10	12/11	12/12	12/13
Sales ($ mil.)	2.9%	–	14.2	15.6	15.2	15.4
Net income ($ mil.)	11.9%	–	–	1.7	1.8	2.1
Market value ($ mil.)	–	–	–	–	–	–
Employees	–	–	–	–	–	30

DAYSTAR TECHNOLOGIES INC.
NASDAQ: DSTI

2972 Stender Way
Santa Clara CA 95054
Phone: 408-907-4600
Fax: 408-907-4637
Web: www.daystartech.com

CEO: L Mark Roseborough
CFO: –
HR: –
FYE: December 31
Type: Public

Old Sol otherwise known as the sun is the "day star" providing energy through the solar cells of this company. DayStar Technologies makes energy-generating and storing devices out of copper indium gallium and selenium dubbed CIGS solar cells. The company is developing manufacturing processes for its thin-film photovoltaic foil CIGS solar cells that will be cheaper to produce than conventional polycrystalline silicon solar cells which currently dominate the market. DayStar got out of the business of installing and maintaining solar panels for residences. Running out of cash in 2009 the company warned that it may have to seek Chapter 11 protection from creditors if it is unable to raise capital.

DCB FINANCIAL CORP
OTC: DCBF

110 Riverbend Avenue
Lewis Center, OH 43035
Phone: 740 657-7000
Fax: –
Web: www.dcbfinancialcorp.com

CEO: –
CFO: –
HR: –
FYE: December 31
Type: Public

DCB Financial is the holding company for The Delaware County Bank and Trust which serves individual and commercial customers through some 15 branches in central Ohio. The bank offers traditional products and services such as checking and savings accounts CDs IRAs credit and debit cards and safe deposit facilities. Its loan portfolio primarily consists of commercial mortgages residential mortgages and home equity loans. The bank also writes construction land development industrial and consumer loans. The Delaware County Bank and Trust provides insurance investments wealth management and trust services as well. First Commonwealth Financial is buying DBC Financial for some $106 million.

	Annual Growth	12/11	12/12	12/13	12/14	12/15
Assets ($ mil.)	0.9%	522.9	506.5	502.4	515.4	541.3
Net income ($ mil.)	–	–	(2.7)	0.6	(2.9)	0.4	11.7
Market value ($ mil.)	27.8%	20.4	33.5	44.8	51.0	54.5
Employees	(0.3%)	166	181	171	162	164

DCP MIDSTREAM LP

NYS: DCP

370 17th Street, Suite 2500
Denver, CO 80202
Phone: 303 595-3331
Fax: –
Web: www.dcpmidstream.com

CEO: wouter van Kempen
CFO: Sean O'Brien
HR: –
FYE: December 31
Type: Public

DCP Midstream is one of the natural gas gatherers in North America and a producer and marketer of natural gas liquids (NGLs). It also engages in natural gas compressing treating processing transporting and selling. DCP Midstream also transports and sells NGLs and distributes propane wholesale. The company operates natural gas gathering and transmission systems (51000 miles of pipe) in more than 15 states.

	Annual Growth	12/16	12/17	12/18	12/19	12/20
Sales ($ mil.)	43.2%	1,497.0	8,462.0	9,822.0	7,625.0	6,302.0
Net income ($ mil.)	–	312.0	229.0	298.0	17.0	(306.0)
Market value ($ mil.)	(16.7%)	7,996.5	7,569.4	5,519.2	5,102.5	3,858.7
Employees	–	–	–	–	–	–

DCT INDUSTRIAL TRUST INC

NYS: DCT

555 17th Street, Suite 3700
Denver, CO 80202
Phone: 303 597-2400
Fax: –
Web: www.dctindustrial.com

CEO: –
CFO: –
HR: –
FYE: December 31
Type: Public

In industry DCT trusts. DCT Industrial Trust is a real estate investment trust (REIT) that owns develops and manages bulk distribution warehouses light industrial properties and service centers located in high-density high-volume markets in the US. It owns interests in or manages some 400 buildings spanning more than 73 million sq. ft. of leasable space in about 15 US states and Mexico. Bulk distribution warehouses account for a majority of the company's rentable space. Companies in the manufacturing wholesale and retail trade and transportation and warehousing sectors make up most of DCT's clients. Major tenants include Clorox Kellogg and DHL.

	Annual Growth	12/12	12/13	12/14	12/15	12/16
Sales ($ mil.)	10.8%	260.8	289.0	336.5	354.7	392.8
Net income ($ mil.)	–	(15.1)	15.9	49.2	94.0	93.1
Market value ($ mil.)	64.8%	593.9	652.5	3,263.5	3,420.0	4,381.8
Employees	2.7%	131	136	145	143	146

DDI CORP.

NASDAQ: DDIC

1220 N. Simon Circle
Anaheim CA 92806
Phone: 714-688-7200
Fax: 714-688-7400
Web: www.ddiglobal.com

CEO: –
CFO: –
HR: –
FYE: December 31
Type: Public

DDi takes a dynamic approach to manufacturing. DDi provides time-critical customized printed circuit board (PCB) design fabrication and assembly services for makers of communications and networking gear computers medical instruments and military equipment. The company produces PCBs backpanels and wire harnesses. Its more than 1000 customers include electronics manufacturers and contract manufacturers worldwide. DDi gets the majority of its business from customers in North America. In 2012 the company was acquired by rival Viasystems in a transaction valued at about $283 million including debt.

DE PAUL UNIVERSITY

1 E JACKSON BLVD
CHICAGO, IL 606042287
Phone: 312-362-6714
Fax: –
Web: www.depaul.edu

CEO: –
CFO: Bonnie Frankel
HR: –
FYE: June 30
Type: Private

In the land of da Bulls and da Bears there's DePaul. One of the largest private not-for-profit universities in the US DePaul has more than 21920 students attending classes at its Chicago-area campuses and its increasing offerings of online learning courses. The university offers more than 300 undergraduate and graduate programs through 10 colleges and schools including the Driehaus College of Business and the College of Communication. It has a student teacher ratio of 16 to 1. One of the country's largest Catholic institutions of higher learning DePaul was founded in 1898 by the Vincentian religious community and is named after 17th century French priest St. Vincent de Paul.

	Annual Growth	06/17	06/18	06/19	06/20	06/21
Sales ($ mil.)	(0.4%)	–	575.0	580.7	595.2	569.0
Net income ($ mil.)	56.0%	–	67.0	45.9	67.3	254.6
Market value ($ mil.)	–	–	–	–	–	–
Employees	–	–	–	–	–	3,895

DEACON INDUSTRIAL SUPPLY CO. INC.

1510 GEHMAN RD
HARLEYSVILLE, PA 19438-2929
Phone: 215-256-1715
Fax: –
Web: www.deaconind.com

CEO: –
CFO: Bill Hardie
HR: –
FYE: March 31
Type: Private

In the cold dark night who will be a beacon when the pipes burst? Deacon Industrial Supply will. Through four locations in Delaware New Jersey and Pennsylvania the company distributes pipes valves fittings and other products for plumbing HVAC and waterworks projects. It stocks more than 35000 items from manufacturers such as Cornerstone Valves NIBCO Sure Seal and Victaulic. The company also offers pipe fabrication specialized gasket cutting and emergency services. Deacon serves commercial contractors and professionals in a range of industries including automotive food processing petrochemical steel and pharmaceutical. It was founded in 1963 by Ben Deacon and Les Vail.

	Annual Growth	03/05	03/06	03/07	03/08	03/09
Sales ($ mil.)	11.2%	–	46.4	47.8	55.8	63.9
Net income ($ mil.)	40.1%	–	1.6	1.5	2.3	4.4
Market value ($ mil.)	–	–	–	–	–	–
Employees	–	–	–	–	–	80

DEACONESS HEALTH SYSTEM, INC.

600 MARY ST
EVANSVILLE, IN 477101658
Phone: 812-450-5000
Fax: –
Web: www.deaconess.com

CEO: Shawn McCoy
CFO: Cheryl Wathen
HR: –
FYE: September 30
Type: Private

While it primarily presides over numerous health care facilities in the southwestern corner of Indiana Deaconess Health System also serves residents in parts of southeastern Illinois and western Kentucky. The system consists of two general acute-care hospitals as well as specialty hospitals for women's health mental health and medical rehabilitation. Its flagship Deaconess Hospital boasts 365 beds and serves as a regional referral center. Deaconess Health also operates a standalone cancer treatment center medical group practice Deaconess Clinic and about 20 outpatient and urgent care clinics. Its Deaconess Health Plans unit is a PPO network that contracts with various health insurers.

	Annual Growth	09/14	09/15	09/16	09/17	09/18
Sales ($ mil.)	628.6%	–	2.7	2.8	930.9	1,058.4
Net income ($ mil.)	–	–	(24.8)	(27.4)	127.3	170.6
Market value ($ mil.)	–	–	–	–	–	–
Employees	–	–	–	–	–	6,086

DEACONESS HOSPITAL INC

600 MARY ST
EVANSVILLE, IN 477101674
Phone: 812-450-5000
Fax: –
Web: www.deaconess.com

CEO: Linda E White
CFO: Richard Stivers
HR: –
FYE: September 30
Type: Private

Deaconess Hospital provides benevolent medical assistance to residents of southern Indiana western Kentucky and southeastern Illinois. The not-for-profit hospital is a 365-bed acute care medical facility that is the flagship hospital of the Deaconess Health System. Specialized services include cardiovascular surgery cancer treatment orthopedics neurological and trauma care. The hospital also offers home health care hospice services and medical equipment rental and it operates outpatient family practice surgery wellness and community outreach centers. Founded in 1892 Deaconess Hospital is a teaching and research facility affiliated with the Indiana University School of Medicine.

	Annual Growth	09/15	09/16	09/17	09/18	09/19
Sales ($ mil.)	14.5%	–	698.7	725.7	823.4	1,047.6
Net income ($ mil.)	13.6%	–	108.6	94.1	153.1	159.3
Market value ($ mil.)	–	–	–	–	–	–
Employees	–	–	–	–	–	5,300

DEALERS SUPPLY COMPANY INC.

82 KENNEDY DR
FOREST PARK, GA 302972536
Phone: 404-361-6800
Fax: –
Web: www.dealerssupply.net

CEO: Richard E Laurens
CFO: Earl C Hunter
HR: –
FYE: December 31
Type: Private

Dealers Supply Company (DSC) strives to keep cool during those long Southern summers. Through about 15 locations in Georgia and North Carolina the company distributes air conditioning and heating products to residential customers contractors and small businesses. Products include air conditioners heaters motors insulation lifts sealants and other items from such brands as Airgas, Honeywell RUUD Trion, and WeatherKing. DSC sells the tools needed to install and maintain all the heating and cooling equipment it sells and it offers classes and reference guides. The company's Web site includes an online catalog and searchable database of licensed conditioned air contractors.

	Annual Growth	03/09	03/10	03/11	03/12*	12/12
Sales ($ mil.)	(9.4%)	–	38.5	41.0	40.8	31.6
Net income ($ mil.)	(7.4%)	–	–	0.7	0.5	0.6
Market value ($ mil.)	–	–	–	–	–	–
Employees	–	–	–	–	–	126

*Fiscal year change

DEALERTRACK TECHNOLOGIES, INC.   NMS: TRAK

1111 Marcus Avenue, Suite M04
Lake Success, NY 11042
Phone: 516 734-3600
Fax: –
Web: www.dealertrack.com

CEO: Mark F O'Neil
CFO: Eric D Jacobs
HR: –
FYE: December 31
Type: Public

DealerTrack keeps auto dealers lenders OEMs and car buyers on track with its Web-based software and services. Using a Software-as-a-Service (SaaS) model the company offers a suite of dealer management system (DMS) vehicle inventory management and merchandising sales and financing compliance and processing (including e-registration and titling application) tools that provide real-time on-demand data for auto dealers to operate more efficiently and cost effectively. Dealer-Track also operates the largest online credit application network in the US and Canada.

	Annual Growth	12/09	12/10	12/11	12/12	12/13
Sales ($ mil.)	20.9%	225.6	243.8	353.3	388.9	481.5
Net income ($ mil.)	–	(4.3)	(27.8)	65.1	20.5	5.9
Market value ($ mil.)	26.5%	826.7	883.0	1,199.3	1,263.6	2,115.3
Employees	20.1%	1,200	1,200	1,900	2,000	2,500

DEAN & DELUCA INCORPORATED

2402 E. 37th St. North
Wichita KS 67219-3538
Phone: 316-821-3200
Fax: 800-781-4050
Web: www.deandeluca.com

CEO: Mark Daley
CFO: –
HR: –
FYE: January 31
Type: Private

You could go to Manhattan's tony SoHo neighborhood for a taste of Dean & DeLuca but increasingly you don't have to. The purveyor of pricey gourmet foods fine wines cheeses baked goods coffees and teas and high-end kitchenware operates about 15 specialty markets and cafes in select US cities and is growing rapidly in Japan. The company opened its first cafe in the Middle East located in Dubai in 2008 and now has a store in Kuwait. Dean & DeLuca also offers its goods through consumer and corporate gift catalogs as well as online. It has operated in Japan since 2003 through a distribution agreement with ITOCHU there. Joel Dean and Giorgio DeLuca opened their first market in SoHo in 1977.

DEAN FOODS CO.   NBB: DFOD Q

2711 North Haskell Avenue, Suite 3400
Dallas, TX 75204
Phone: 214 303-3400
Fax: –
Web: www.deanfoods.com

CEO: Eric Beringause
CFO: Gary W Rahlfs
HR: –
FYE: December 31
Type: Public

Dean Foods is one of the nation's largest milk bottler and purveyor of dairy products. The company markets fluid milk ice cream and cultured dairy products as well as beverages (juices teas and bottled water). It operates under more than 50 local regional and private label brands including DairyPure Mayfield Pet Country Fresh Meadow Gold and TruMoo a leading national flavored milk brand. Dean Foods owns and operates a number of smaller regional dairy companies including Friendly's Berkeley Farms and Garelick Farms. The company distributes dairy products across the US from regional manufacturing facilities. In late 2019 Dean Foods filed for Chapter 11 bankruptcy with the intention of selling itself.

	Annual Growth	12/15	12/16	12/17	12/18	12/19
Sales ($ mil.)	(2.5%)	8,121.7	7,710.2	7,795.0	7,755.3	7,328.7
Net income ($ mil.)	–	(8.5)	119.9	61.6	(326.9)	(499.9)
Market value ($ mil.)	(75.7%)	1,576.8	2,002.5	1,062.8	350.3	5.5
Employees	(3.8%)	16,960	17,000	16,000	15,000	14,500

DEBT RESOLVE INC   NBB: DRSV

1133 Westchester Ave., Suite S-223
White Plains, NY 10604
Phone: 914 949-5500
Fax: –
Web: www.debtresolve.com

CEO: –
CFO: –
HR: –
FYE: December 31
Type: Public

Debt Resolve isn't intimidated by mountains of debt. The company provides a hosted software service that allows credit card companies and collection agencies to collect money from consumers who are past due on their credit card bills. The online service branded as DebtResolve uses an Internet-based bidding system that allows debtors and creditors to agree on acceptable repayment schedules. Customers include banks and other credit originators credit card issuers and third-party collection agencies as well as assignees and buyers of consumer debt.

	Annual Growth	12/12	12/13	12/14	12/15	12/16
Sales ($ mil.)	124.0%	0.2	0.1	0.2	5.7	4.4
Net income ($ mil.)	–	(1.6)	(0.5)	(0.8)	(0.8)	(1.8)
Market value ($ mil.)	(22.5%)	3.6	2.5	0.8	1.1	1.3
Employees	(6.9%)	4	4	4	4	3

DECISION DIAGNOSTICS CORP NBB: DECN

2660 Townsgate Road, Suite 300
Westlake Village, CA 91361
Phone: 805 446-1973
Fax: 805 446-1983
Web: www.decisiondiagnostics.com

CEO: -
CFO: Keith Berman
HR: -
FYE: December 31
Type: Public

Decision Diagnostics Corp. (DDC) hopes IT plus pharmaceuticals will equal success. Previously focused on wireless systems for the health care and lodging markets in 2005 the company added a pharmaceuticals distribution unit through its purchases of CareGeneration and the Pharmaceutical Solutions unit of Kelly Company. DDC drives customers to its pharmaceuticals business by providing wireless computing devices to doctors in clinics for the poor and uninsured; in return doctors direct their patients to the company's discount mail-order prescription service. The company continues to sell its wireless PDA devices for the health care and lodging industries. Clearing company Cede & Co. owns 40% of DDC.

	Annual Growth	12/16	12/17	12/18	12/19	12/20
Sales ($ mil.)	16.0%	1.1	1.9	2.2	2.4	2.0
Net income ($ mil.)	-	(3.2)	(3.0)	(2.2)	(3.1)	(29.7)
Market value ($ mil.)	(35.2%)	36.4	26.6	7.1	5.1	6.4
Employees	-	-	-	9	-	-

DECKERS OUTDOOR CORP. NYS: DECK

250 Coromar Drive
Goleta, CA 93117
Phone: 805 967-7611
Fax: -
Web: www.deckers.com

CEO: David Powers
CFO: Steven Fasching
HR: -
FYE: March 31
Type: Public

Deckers Outdoor is a global leader in designing marketing and distributing innovative footwear apparel and accessories developed for both everyday casual lifestyle use and high-performance activities. It designs and markets the iconic UGG brand of luxury sheepskin footwear in addition to Teva sports sandals ? a cross between a hiking boot and a flip-flop used for walking hiking and rafting among other pursuits. Other product lines include Sanuk HOKA One One and Koolaburra. Deckers Outdoor which generates most of its revenue in the US sells its footwear through approximately 140 retail stores worldwide independent distributors and e-commerce sites such as Amazon.com Zappos.com and Zalando.com.

	Annual Growth	03/17	03/18	03/19	03/20	03/21
Sales ($ mil.)	9.2%	1,790.1	1,903.3	2,020.4	2,132.7	2,545.6
Net income ($ mil.)	186.1%	5.7	114.4	264.3	276.1	382.6
Market value ($ mil.)	53.4%	1,667.1	2,512.7	4,102.5	3,739.9	9,222.0
Employees	0.7%	3,300	3,500	3,500	3,600	3,400

DECO, INC.

11156 ZEALAND AVE N
CHAMPLIN, MN 553163594
Phone: 763-576-9572
Fax: -
Web: www.deco-inc.com

CEO: Chris Bauer
CFO: Constance O'Brien
HR: -
FYE: December 31
Type: Private

This DECO has nothing to do with art and everything to do with security. The private Native American-owned firm provides professional security services including anti-terrorism training armed and unarmed guards escorts and patrols security system monitoring security consulting and administrative staffing support to federal corporate and tribal clients. Security services account for about 90% of the firm's revenue. The remainder comes from its contracting division which offers construction services for large-scale remodeling projects and electrical and security system installations. DECO counts the US Department of Homeland Security FAA and US Environmental Protection Agency among its clients.

	Annual Growth	12/08	12/09	12/10	12/11	12/12
Sales ($ mil.)	9.8%	-	-	82.9	94.9	100.0
Net income ($ mil.)	(59.5%)	-	-	0.6	1.2	0.1
Market value ($ mil.)	-	-	-	-	-	-
Employees	-	-	-	-	-	1,600

DEEP DOWN INC NBB: DPDW

18511 Beaumont Highway
Houston, TX 77049
Phone: 281 517-5000
Fax: 281 517-5001
Web: www.deepdowninc.com

CEO: Charles Njuguna
CFO: Charles K Njuguna
HR: -
FYE: December 31
Type: Public

Deep down Deep Down understands itself to be in the subsea sector. The company (formerly medical equipment provider Mediquip Holdings) acquired Deep Down in a reverse merger taking on that company's subsea service business as well as its name. An umbilical and flexible pipe installation engineering and installation management company Deep Down also fabricates component parts for subsea distribution systems and assemblies that specialize in the development of offshore subsea fields. The company's product include umbilicals flowlines distribution systems pipeline terminations controls winches and launch and retrieval systems. It serves clients in the Gulf of Mexico and internationally.

	Annual Growth	12/16	12/17	12/18	12/19	12/20
Sales ($ mil.)	(15.4%)	25.4	19.5	16.2	18.9	13.0
Net income ($ mil.)	-	0.2	(0.1)	(4.7)	(2.8)	(6.1)
Market value ($ mil.)	(25.6%)	17.6	11.7	10.6	8.4	5.4
Employees	(11.4%)	73	59	58	48	45

DEERE & CO. NYS: DE

One John Deere Place
Moline, IL 61265
Phone: 309 765-8000
Fax: 309 765-9929
Web: www.johndeere.com

CEO: John May
CFO: Ryan Campbell
HR: -
FYE: October 31
Type: Public

Deere & Co. is one of the world's largest makers of farm equipment and a major producer of construction forestry and commercial and residential lawn care equipment. Deere offers a portfolio of more than 25 brands to provide a full line of innovative solutions for its customers in a variety of production systems throughout the lifecycle of their machines. Some of its brands include Wirtgen Hagie Mazzotti Monosem Blue River Technology and Harvest Profit among others. Deere famous for its "Nothing Runs Like a Deere" slogan sells John Deere and other brands through dealer networks and also sells lawn and garden products through home improvement retailers like The Home Depot and Lowes. Most of the company's revenue is generated in the US.

	Annual Growth	10/17	10/18*	11/19	11/20*	10/21
Sales ($ mil.)	10.3%	29,737.7	37,357.7	39,258.0	35,540.0	44,024.0
Net income ($ mil.)	28.9%	2,159.1	2,368.4	3,253.0	2,751.0	5,963.0
Market value ($ mil.)	26.6%	41,049.7	40,972.7	54,253.3	69,595.0	105,453.8
Employees	5.7%	60,476	74,413	73,489	69,634	75,550

*Fiscal year change

DEFFENBAUGH INDUSTRIES INC.

2601 Midwest Dr.
Kansas City KS 66111
Phone: 913-631-3300
Fax: 954-447-7979
Web: www.spiritair.com

CEO: -
CFO: Ron Anderson
HR: -
FYE: April 30
Type: Private

Deffenbaugh Industries doesn't turn a deaf ear to its customers' waste management needs in the Plains and the Midwest. The company collects transports and disposes of commercial and residential waste in Kansas Iowa Missouri and Nebraska. It also provides industrial waste services quarrying services the disposal of construction waste and commercial and residential recycling. Deffenbaugh Industries' more than 700-acre Johnson County Landfill is the largest disposal facility in Kansas. The company's Johnny on the Spot division rents portable toilets.

DEFOE CORP.

800 S COLUMBUS AVE
MOUNT VERNON, NY 105505019
Phone: 914-699-7440
Fax: –
Web: www.defoecorp.com

CEO: –
CFO: Dennis Brands
HR: –
FYE: December 31
Type: Private

DeFoe makes sure you can safely cross those proverbial bridges when you get to them. The heavy construction firm specializes in the design and construction of bridges highways airport terminals railroads and other transit projects throughout the New York Metropolitan and Tri-State area. Other areas of expertise include rehabilitation and reconstruction foundations and architectural concrete work. DeFoe which was founded in 1946 often works for the New York State Department of Transportation as well as the The Port Authority of New York and New Jersey. President John Amicucci Sr. who is the son-in-law of former president Dario Cioti owns the company.

	Annual Growth	12/10	12/11	12/12	12/13	12/17
Sales ($ mil.)	9.2%	–	59.4	54.6	45.7	100.7
Net income ($ mil.)	29.2%	–	1.3	(1.4)	(7.3)	6.1
Market value ($ mil.)	–	–	–	–	–	–
Employees	–	–	–	–	–	150

DEKALB MEDICAL CENTER, INC.

2701 N DECATUR RD
DECATUR, GA 300335918
Phone: 404-501-1000
Fax: –
Web: www.dekalbmedical.org

CEO: –
CFO: –
HR: –
FYE: June 30
Type: Private

As far as DeKalb is concerned da healthier da better! Beginning as a rural hospital DeKalb Regional Health System now serves all of the Atlanta metropolitan area. The health system operating as DeKalb Medical is home to two acute care hospitals -- DeKalb Medical at North Decatur and DeKalb Medical at Hillandale (with a combined total of about 550 beds). It also operates a 75-bed long-term rehabilitation hospital — DeKalb Medical at Downtown Decatur. Specialty hospital services include oncology cardiology orthopedics and diabetes care. The health system which was founded in 1961 also operates primary specialty and mobile health care clinics partly through the DeKalb Medical Physicians Group. DeKalb is merging with Emory Healthcare.

	Annual Growth	06/09	06/10	06/11	06/14	06/15
Sales ($ mil.)	(5.3%)	–	397.1	422.9	524.8	303.0
Net income ($ mil.)	–	–	(15.0)	0.9	1.6	5.0
Market value ($ mil.)	–	–	–	–	–	–
Employees	–	–	–	–	–	2,700

DEL FRISCO'S RESTAURANT GROUP INC

NMS: DFRG

2900 Ranch Trail
Irving, TX 75063
Phone: 469 913-1845
Fax: –
Web: www.dfrg.com

CEO: Norman Abdallah
CFO: Neil Thomson
HR: –
FYE: December 26
Type: Public

Del Frisco's Restaurant Group operates two upscale steakhouse chains Del Frisco's Double Eagle Steak House and Sullivan's with about 30 locations in more than 15 states. The group also runs two more casual Del Frisco's Grille restaurants. Del Frisco's Double Eagle Steak House has about 10 locations and offer upscale dining in a contemporary surrounding. The somewhat less pricey version of the 20-unit Sullivan's chain features an atmosphere reminiscent of a Chicago-style steakhouse. Both concepts serve premium cuts of beef along with seafood lamb and pork dishes and both offer an extensive wine list. The company controlled by Dallas-based private equity firm Lone Star Funds went public in 2012.

	Annual Growth	12/13	12/14	12/15	12/16	12/17
Sales ($ mil.)	7.4%	271.8	301.8	331.6	351.7	361.4
Net income ($ mil.)	–	12.2	16.6	16.0	17.8	(11.5)
Market value ($ mil.)	(10.0%)	478.7	476.3	328.8	354.4	313.8
Employees	3.7%	4,222	4,745	4,921	4,809	4,890

DEL MONACO SPECIALTY FOODS INC.

18675 MADRONE PKWY # 150
MORGAN HILL, CA 950372868
Phone: 408-500-4100
Fax: –
Web: www.delmonacofoods.com

CEO: –
CFO: –
HR: –
FYE: December 31
Type: Private

Del Monaco Specialty Foods makes products that any Tuscan Roman or Venetian mama would give her blessing to. The company cooks up and freezes Italian-style food items for the foodservice industry. Del Monaco's certified-organic food products include pastas sauces ravioli tortellini gnocchi polenta pestos and desserts. It offers American-style foods as well including barbecue sauce pot pies and New England clam chowder. It makes its own Del Monaco products and also offers services such as recipe creation duplication and enhancement plus the manufacture of custom products. The company was founded in 1964 by its namesakes the late Mike Del Monaco and his wife Ernestine.

	Annual Growth	12/08	12/09	12/10	12/11	12/12
Sales ($ mil.)	22.2%	–	–	–	21.1	25.8
Net income ($ mil.)	52.4%	–	–	–	2.2	3.3
Market value ($ mil.)	–	–	–	–	–	–
Employees	–	–	–	–	–	88

DEL MONTE CORPORATION

1 Maritime Plaza
San Francisco CA 94111
Phone: 415-247-3000
Fax: 415-247-3565
Web: www.delmonte.com

CEO: Richard K Smucker
CFO: Mark R Belgya
HR: –
FYE: April 30
Type: Private

How does Del Monte's garden grow? Quite well. The company is one of the largest makers of branded canned fruit vegetables and broths in the US. Del Monte Foods manufactures tomato-based items such as ketchup and tomato sauce under brands College Inn Del Monte and Contadina. It owns no farms but instead purchases fruits and vegetables from growers. The company helps pets grow too with a stable of popular brands: 9Lives Gravy Train Milk-Bone and Meow Mix. Del Monte Foods makes private-label products as well as ingredients for other food makers and supplies products to foodservice operators. A trio of private equity firms led by Kohlberg Kravis Roberts (KKR) took Del Monte Foods private in 2011.

DELAWARE NORTH COMPANIES INC.

40 Fountain Plaza
Buffalo NY 14202
Phone: 716-858-5000
Fax: 716-858-5479
Web: www.delawarenorth.com

CEO: Charlie Jacobs
CFO: Christopher Feeney
HR: David Bolz
FYE: December 31
Type: Private

This company makes few concessions when it comes to selling hot dogs and sodas at the ball game. Delaware North is a leading provider of food services and hospitality at airports sports stadiums and tourist destinations throughout the US and in a handful of other countries. The company oversees concessions at more than 50 major and minor league sporting arenas and it owns Boston's TD Garden arena. Delaware North also manages concessions and retail operations at more than 25 airports provides hospitality services at several tourist destinations and runs racing and gaming operations in half a dozen states. In all family-owned Delaware North operates at 200 locations and serves 500 million guests a year.

DELAWARE RIVER PORT AUTHORITY

2 RIVERSIDE DR STE 603
CAMDEN, NJ 081031019
Phone: 856-968-2000
Fax: –
Web: www.drpa.org

CEO: –
CFO: James M White
HR: –
FYE: December 31
Type: Private

The famous painting of George Washington crossing the Delaware would have lacked a good deal of its drama if the Delaware River Port Authority of Pennsylvania and New Jersey (DRPA) had been around in 1776. DRPA keeps commuters (and leaders of revolutionary armies) out of small boats by operating the Benjamin Franklin Betsy Ross Commodore Barry and Walt Whitman toll bridges over the Delaware River which divides Pennsylvania from New Jersey. Bridge operations account for 90% of the agency's revenue. Through its Port Authority Transit Corp. (PATCO) subsidiary DRPA operates PATCO a rail service that links Philadelphia with communities on the New Jersey side of the Delaware.

	Annual Growth	12/14	12/15	12/16	12/18	12/20
Sales ($ mil.)	(3.4%)	–	341.3	354.7	371.8	287.2
Net income ($ mil.)	(11.0%)	–	102.3	66.9	124.0	57.0
Market value ($ mil.)	–	–	–	–	–	–
Employees	–	–	–	–	–	900

DELAWARE STATE UNIVERSITY

1200 N DUPONT HWY
DOVER, DE 199012202
Phone: 302-857-6060
Fax: –
Web: www.desu.edu

CEO: –
CFO: –
HR: –
FYE: June 30
Type: Private

One of the top historically black colleges and universities in the US Delaware State University (DSU) offers more than 50 bachelor's degree programs 25 graduate degree programs and five doctoral degree programs through more than 20 academic departments and five colleges. In addition to its main 400-acre campus in Dover the university has satellite locations in Georgetown and Wilmington. The school began as a land-grant educational institution founded in 1891 as the State College for Colored Students. It became known as Delaware State College in 1947 and gained university status in 1993. The university has a student-teacher ratio of 14:1 and enrolls more than 3800 students each year.

	Annual Growth	06/10	06/11	06/13	06/14	06/15
Sales ($ mil.)	(1.6%)	–	75.2	82.4	146.6	70.5
Net income ($ mil.)	–	–	9.8	2.1	(2.0)	(4.4)
Market value ($ mil.)	–	–	–	–	–	–
Employees	–	–	–	–	–	600

DELAWARE VALLEY UNIVERSITY

700 E BUTLER AVE
DOYLESTOWN, PA 189012607
Phone: 215-345-1500
Fax: –
Web: www.delval.edu

CEO: –
CFO: –
HR: –
FYE: June 30
Type: Private

Delaware Valley College (DelVal) serves about 2000 undergraduate and graduate students and boasts a student/faculty ratio of 15:1. The school offers associate's bachelor's and master's degrees in fields such as agriculture biology business administration chemistry environmental science media and secondary education; overall it offers about two dozen undergraduate majors. DelVal's campus is located on 570 acres 30 miles north of Philadelphia. The college was founded in 1896 by activist rabbi Joseph Krauskopf.

	Annual Growth	06/14	06/15	06/16	06/17	06/18
Sales ($ mil.)	2.3%	–	–	55.6	56.9	58.2
Net income ($ mil.)	–	–	–	(3.8)	2.3	(0.0)
Market value ($ mil.)	–	–	–	–	–	–
Employees	–	–	–	–	–	405

DELCATH SYSTEMS INC

NAS: DCTH

1633 Broadway, Suite 22C
New York, NY 10019
Phone: 212 489-2100
Fax: –
Web: www.delcath.com

CEO: Gerard Michel
CFO: –
HR: –
FYE: December 31
Type: Public

A cancer-stricken liver might be a lonely little organ thanks to Delcath Systems. The company's technology allows blood infused with chemotherapy drugs to be pumped directly to the liver and then filtered before being returned into the circulation system. By isolating the liver Delcath's proprietary Hepatic CHEMOSAT® Delivery System is designed to protect other parts of the body from side effects and allow stronger doses of drugs to be used to treat liver cancer and malignant melanoma that has spread to the liver. The system approved and available in Europe is undergoing clinical trials to gain FDA approval. Delcath is also developing the system for use in treating other cancers and viral hepatitis.

	Annual Growth	12/16	12/17	12/18	12/19	12/20
Sales ($ mil.)	(4.7%)	2.0	2.7	3.4	1.6	1.6
Net income ($ mil.)	–	(18.0)	(45.1)	(19.2)	(8.9)	(24.2)
Market value ($ mil.)	110.3%	5.5	0.6	1.7	127.4	107.5
Employees	(4.3%)	43	46	43	33	36

DELEK LOGISTICS PARTNERS LP

NYS: DKL

7102 Commerce Way
Brentwood, TN 37027
Phone: 615 771-6701
Fax: –
Web: www.deleklogistics.com

CEO: Ezra Yemin
CFO: Reuven Spiegel
HR: –
FYE: December 31
Type: Public

Oil is on the move at Delek Logistics Partners. An oil transportation and storage company Delek Logistics owns and operates crude oil pipelines storage and distribution facilities and other assets in West Texas and the southeastern US. Core assets include 400 miles of crude oil transportation pipelines and a 600-mile crude oil gathering system. The company also offers wholesale marketing of refined petroleum products. The majority of Delek Logistics' operations serve oil company Delek US Holdings and the holding company's Texas and Arkansas-based refineries. The company was formed in 2012 when Delek US Holdings spun off its pipeline assets; Delek Logistics Partners subsequently went public.

	Annual Growth	12/16	12/17	12/18	12/19	12/20
Sales ($ mil.)	5.9%	448.1	538.1	656.7	584.0	563.4
Net income ($ mil.)	26.2%	62.8	69.4	90.2	96.7	159.3
Market value ($ mil.)	2.9%	1,240.3	1,377.2	1,270.7	1,388.4	1,390.2
Employees	–	–	–	–	–	–

DELEK US HOLDINGS INC (NEW)

NYS: DK

7102 Commerce Way
Brentwood, TN 37027
Phone: 615 771-6701
Fax: –
Web: www.delekus.com

CEO: Ezra Uzi Yemin
CFO: Kevin L Kremke
HR: –
FYE: December 31
Type: Public

Delek US Holdings' US petroleum business is a delectable mix of crude oil refining and marketing. The company a subsidiary of Israeli-based conglomerate Delek Group sources crude oil from producers in Texas and Arkansas for refining into transportation fuels such as gasoline distillate and jet fuel. Some of its production also consists of residual products such as paving asphalt and roofing flux. Delek US' Tyler Texas and El Dorado Arkansas refineries have total production capacity of 155000 barrels per day. Delek US Holdings' marketing segment sells refined products on a wholesale basis in west Texas through company owned and third-party operated terminals. It sold off its gas station retail business in 2016.

	Annual Growth	12/16	12/17	12/18	12/19	12/20
Sales ($ mil.)	14.8%	4,197.9	7,267.1	10,233.1	9,298.2	7,301.8
Net income ($ mil.)	–	(153.7)	288.8	340.1	310.6	(608.0)
Market value ($ mil.)	(9.6%)	1,775.9	2,577.9	2,398.6	2,473.9	1,185.7
Employees	27.8%	1,326	3,941	3,717	3,814	3,532

DELHAIZE AMERICA LLC

2110 Executive Dr.
Salisbury NC 28145-1330
Phone: 704-633-8250
Fax: 704-645-4499
Web: www.delhaizegroup.com

CEO: Frans W H Muller
CFO: –
HR: –
FYE: December 31
Type: Subsidiary

Belgian food retailer Delhaize "Le Lion" has one big cub — Delhaize America. With some 1625 supermarkets and discount grocery stores in 17 states from Maine to Florida the holding company is the third-largest supermarket operator on the East Coast. Banners include: Food Lion (some 1075 stores located mainly in the Carolinas and Virginia but also in eight other eastern seaboard states); the Hannaford Bros. supermarket chain (about 180 stores in New England and New York); and 70 Harveys supermarkets. The grocery operator's Sweetbay chain does business along the west coast of Florida. Delhaize America provides shared services for all of its banners. Delhaize Group established its US subsidiary in 1999.

DELI MANAGEMENT, INC.

350 PINE ST STE 1775
BEAUMONT, TX 777012458
Phone: 409-838-1976
Fax: –
Web: www.jasonsdeli.com

CEO: –
CFO: Troy Cormier
HR: –
FYE: December 31
Type: Private

This company knows a good sandwich when serves one. Deli Management operates Jason's Deli a chain of sandwich shops with more than 240 company-owned and franchised locations. The quick casual eateries specialize in deli-style sandwiches including such signature varieties as Bird to the Wise The New York Yankee and Rueben THE Great. The chain also serves panini and po'boy sandwiches pasta dishes soups and salads. Many Jason's outposts provide delivery and catering services as well as online ordering. President Joe Tortorice and partner Rusty Coco started the company in 1976.

	Annual Growth	12/03	12/04	12/05	12/06	12/08
Sales ($ mil.)	11.7%	–	–	247.0	344.2	344.2
Net income ($ mil.)	(22.5%)	–	–	12.4	5.8	5.8
Market value ($ mil.)	–	–	–	–	–	–
Employees	–	–	–	–	–	6,000

DELMARVA POWER & LIGHT CO.

500 North Wakefield Drive
Newark, DE 19702
Phone: 202 872-2000
Fax: –
Web: www.delmarva.com

CEO: David Velazquez
CFO: Phillip Barnett
HR: –
FYE: December 31
Type: Public

Delmarva Power & Light (DPL) has a delmarvellous proposition — connecting people to an extensive energy supply network. The company is engaged in the transmission and distribution of electricity in Delaware and a portion of Maryland (the Eastern Shore); it delivers electricity to about 501000 customers. DPL also provides natural gas (in northern Delaware) to more than 124000 customers. DPL is an indirect subsidiary of Pepco Holdings which owns two other utilities (Potomac Electric Power and Atlantic City Electric) as well as competitive energy generation marketing and supply businesses. As part of the 2016 acquisition of Pepco Holdings Delmarva P&L joined the Exelon family of utilities.

	Annual Growth	12/16	12/17	12/18	12/19	12/20
Sales ($ mil.)	(0.1%)	1,277.0	1,300.0	1,332.0	1,306.0	1,271.0
Net income ($ mil.)	–	(9.0)	121.0	120.0	147.0	125.0
Market value ($ mil.)	–	–	–	–	–	–
Employees	1.8%	871	944	940	936	936

DELOITTE & TOUCHE LLP

Paramount Bldg. 1633 Broadway
New York NY 10019-6754
Phone: 212-489-1600
Fax: 212-489-1687
Web: www.deloitte.com/view/en_us/us/services/audit-

CEO: Joseph Ucuzoglu
CFO: –
HR: –
FYE: May 31
Type: Subsidiary

Deloitte & Touche LLP touches on all aspects of accounting in the US. The firm is the accounting arm of Deloitte LLP the US affiliate of international Big Four accounting firm Deloitte Touche Tohmatsu. Deloitte & Touche LLP offers audit and enterprise risk services. As part of its business the firm provides clients with audits and financial statement reviews. Other services include financial reporting regulatory updates employee benefit audits and venture capital services. Deloitte & Touche LLP has operations in about 90 US cities. Deloitte LLP also manages other US subsidiaries that offer tax consulting and financial advisory services.

DELOITTE CONSULTING LLP

1633 Broadway
New York NY 10019-6754
Phone: 212-489-1600
Fax: 212-489-1687
Web: www.deloitte.com/view/en_us/us/services/consul

CEO: Dan Helfrich
CFO: –
HR: –
FYE: May 31
Type: Subsidiary

One of the world's largest consulting firms Deloitte Consulting serves customers in industries such as aviation consumer products and services energy financial services health care manufacturing and technology as well as government agencies. The firm's areas of expertise include human resources information technology services outsourcing and strategy and operations. Along with accounting firm Deloitte & Touche Deloitte Consulting is a unit of Deloitte LLP which in turn is an affiliate of global accounting powerhouse Deloitte Touche Tohmatsu. Other Deloitte LLP units offer financial advisory and tax services.

DELOITTE LLP

Paramount Bldg. 1633 Broadway
New York NY 10019-6754
Phone: 212-489-1600
Fax: 212-489-1687
Web: www.deloitte.com/view/en_us/us/index.htm

CEO: Joseph Ucuzoglu
CFO: Frank Friedman
HR: –
FYE: May 31
Type: Private

Deloitte LLP is a US-based member firm of Deloitte Touche Tohmatsu one of the big four global accounting firms. Deloitte LLP does not provide services to clients itself. Rather it does so through its operating subsidiaries primarily Deloitte & Touche LLP Deloitte Consulting LLP Deloitte Financial Advisory Services LLP and Deloitte Tax LLP. Those companies offer audit and enterprise risk consulting financial advisory and tax preparation services. Industry specializations include automotive banking consumer products life sciences oil and gas technology and government. Deloitte LLP and its subsidiaries operate from more than 100 offices across the US employing some 9300 accountants.

DELOITTE TOUCHE TOHMATSU SERVICES INC.

1633 Broadway
New York NY 10019-6754
Phone: 212-489-1600
Fax: 212-489-1687
Web: www.deloitte.com

CEO: James Copeland Jr
CFO: -
HR: -
FYE: May 31
Type: Private

This company is "deloitted" to make your acquaintance particularly if you're a big business in need of accounting services. Deloitte Touche Tohmatsu (or Deloitte) is one of accounting's Big Four along with Ernst & Young KPMG and PricewaterhouseCoopers. Deloitte operates through more than 50 independent firms in some 150 locations around the world including US-based Deloitte LLP and its accounting arm Deloitte & Touche LLP. Each member firm works in a specific geographic area offering audit tax consulting risk management and financial advisory services in addition to human resources and technology services. Deloitte coordinates its member firms but does not provide services directly to clients.

DELPHI FINANCIAL GROUP INC.   NYSE: DFG

1105 N. Market St. Ste. 1230
Wilmington DE 19899
Phone: 302-478-5142
Fax: 302-427-7663
Web: www.delphifin.com

CEO: Robert Rosenkranz
CFO: -
HR: -
FYE: December 31
Type: Public

One doesn't need an oracle to see that Delphi Financial Group knows a thing or two about employee benefits and insurance. Through Reliance Standard Life and Safety National Casualty Delphi sells disability excess workers' compensation group life and personal accident insurance to small and midsized businesses. Its Matrix Absence Management subsidiary provides disability and absence management services to larger employers. The company also offers asset accumulation products mainly annuities to individuals and groups. Delphi Financial's products are sold through independent brokers and agents in the US. In 2012 the insurance group was acquired by leading Japanese insurer Tokio Marine Holdings.

DELTA AIR LINES INC (DE)   NYS: DAL

Post Office Box 20706
Atlanta, GA 30320-6001
Phone: 404 715-2600
Fax: -
Web: www.delta.com

CEO: Ed Bastian
CFO: Dan Janki
HR: -
FYE: December 31
Type: Public

Delta Air Lines is one of the world's largest airlines by traffic and revenues. Through its regional carriers the company serves over 800 destinations in about 130 countries and it operates a mainline fleet of 1200 aircraft as well as maintenance repair and overhaul (MRO) and cargo operations. The company serves more than 200 million customers each year and offer more than 5000 departures daily. Delta is a founding member of the SkyTeam marketing and code-sharing alliance (airlines extend their networks by selling tickets on flights) which includes carriers Aeroméxico Air France-KLM China Eastern Korean Air and Virgin Atlantic. Customers from the US account for approximately 80% of sales.

	Annual Growth	12/17	12/18	12/19	12/20	12/21
Sales ($ mil.)	(7.7%)	41,244.0	44,438.0	47,007.0	17,095.0	29,899.0
Net income ($ mil.)	(47.1%)	3,577.0	3,935.0	4,767.0	(12,385.0)	280.0
Market value ($ mil.)	(8.6%)	35,838.2	31,934.4	37,425.3	25,733.1	25,009.9
Employees	(1.2%)	87,000	89,000	91,224	74,000	83,000

DELTA APPAREL INC.   ASE: DLA

2750 Premiere Parkway, Suite 100
Duluth, GA 30097
Phone: 864 232-5200
Fax: -
Web: www.deltaapparelinc.com

CEO: Robert Humphreys
CFO: Simone Walsh
HR: -
FYE: October 02
Type: Public

Delta Apparel's wares are a wardrobe basic: the t-shirt. The company manufactures knitted cotton and polyester/cotton t-shirts tank tops sweatshirts and caps for screen printers. Through subsidiary M.J. Soffe Delta Apparel also designs makes and sells branded and private-label activewear apparel to mainly to US distributors sporting goods and specialty stores mass merchants traditional and upscale department stores the US military college bookstores and online. The company's garments are finished at plants in North Carolina and abroad in Mexico El Salvador and Honduras. Delta entered the business of custom apparel design by acquiring Art Gun Technologies and hats by taking over Gekko Brands.

	Annual Growth	09/17	09/18	09/19*	10/20	10/21
Sales ($ mil.)	3.2%	385.1	395.5	431.7	381.0	436.8
Net income ($ mil.)	17.9%	10.5	1.3	8.2	(10.6)	20.3
Market value ($ mil.)	6.3%	150.0	124.1	160.8	102.4	191.5
Employees	2.4%	7,700	7,700	8,500	7,860	8,469

*Fiscal year change

DELTA COMMUNITY CREDIT UNION

1025 Virginia Ave.
Atlanta GA 30354
Phone: 404-715-4725
Fax: 404-677-4773
Web: www.deltacommunitycu.com

CEO: Hank Halter
CFO: Jay Gratwick
HR: -
FYE: December 31
Type: Private - Not-for-Pr

Delta Community Credit Union serves employees of Delta Air Lines and its affiliates and group members as well as residents of the Atlanta metro region. It offers traditional banking products such as deposit accounts credit cards home mortgages and consumer loans. The credit union also provides financial planning services and insurance. Delta Community has about a dozen offices in and around Atlanta (where Delta Air Lines is headquartered) and locations near Delta's hub airports including Cincinnati Dallas/Fort Worth and Salt Lake City. Established in 1940 Delta Community is a member-owned and operated institution; it has more than 250000 members and exceeds $4 billion in assets.

DELTA DENTAL OF CALIFORNIA

100 1st St.
San Francisco CA 94105
Phone: 415-972-8300
Fax: 415-972-8466
Web: www.deltadentalins.com

CEO: Mike Castro
CFO: Alicia Weber
HR: -
FYE: December 31
Type: Private - Not-for-Pr

Delta Dental of California doesn't just help keep the mouths of movie stars clean. The not-for-profit company is a member of the Delta Dental Plans Association (DDPA) and has affiliates nationwide. Delta Dental of California provides dental coverage for individuals and groups through HMOs preferred provider plans (PPOs) and such government programs as the TRICARE Retiree Dental Program and California's Denti-Cal (Medicaid) program. The company serves more than 18 million enrollees in California; its programs cover more than one-third of California residents. It also provides dental benefits administration support to employers

DELTA HEALTH SYSTEM

1400 E UNION ST
GREENVILLE, MS 387033246
Phone: 662-378-3783
Fax: –
Web: www.deltahealthsystem.org

CEO: Scott Christensen
CFO: –
HR: –
FYE: September 30
Type: Private

If you're feeling bad down in the Lower Delta Delta Regional Medical Center (DRMC) can help perk you up. The only full service hospital and Level III trauma center in northwest Mississippi DRMC also serves as the tri-state Delta's safety-net hospital. The four medical centers provide heart and vascular care a full service emergency room diagnostics center outpatient rehab a sleep center a wound healing center maternal child center and inpatient psychiatric care. Delta Medical Group includes about 15 clinics specializing in everything from gastroenterology to women's health. Founded as the Washington County General Hospital in 1953 the 358-bed DRMC serves more than 35000 patients each year.

	Annual Growth	09/13	09/14	09/15	09/16	09/17
Sales ($ mil.)	(6.3%)	–	146.1	123.4	123.1	120.0
Net income ($ mil.)	(18.0%)	–	2.2	5.4	4.2	1.2
Market value ($ mil.)	–	–	–	–	–	–
Employees	–	–	–	–	–	800

DELTA MUTUAL INC.

OTC: DLTM

14301 N. 87th St. Ste.310
Scottsdale AZ 85260
Phone: 480-221-1989
Fax: 480-584-6138
Web: www.deltamutual.com

CEO: Scott Stoegbauer
CFO: Matthew McCormack
HR: –
FYE: December 31
Type: Public

Delta Mutual tried to clean up during the Internet boom by providing online mortgage services. Today it really does clean up. Literally. This development stage company has shifted its direction to being an environmental services provider. Delta Mutual offers waste processing and reclamation technology and equipment as well as energy-efficient construction technologies to low-cost housing development projects. Its operations are concentrated in the US the Asia/Pacific region the Middle East and Puerto Rico. In 2008 the company acquired American Hedge Fund LLC a limited liability company that intends to make investments in South America.

DELTA NATURAL GAS CO INC

NMS: DGAS

3617 Lexington Road
Winchester, KY 40391
Phone: 859 744-6171
Fax: –
Web: www.deltagas.com

CEO: Glenn R Jennings
CFO: –
HR: –
FYE: June 30
Type: Public

Delta digs blue grass and natural gas. Delta Natural Gas provides gas to some 36000 retail customers in central and southeastern Kentucky and has 2500 miles of gathering transmission and distribution lines. It also provides transportation services to wholesale customers and operates an underground gas storage field. The regulated utility buys almost all of its gas supply from interstate gas marketers. Delta Natural Gas's production subsidiary Enpro has interests in 35 producing gas wells and it has proved developed reserves of 3 billion cu. ft. of natural gas. Other subsidiaries include Delta Resources and Delgasco. In 2017 Delta Natural Gas agreed to be acquired by Peoples Gas.

	Annual Growth	06/12	06/13	06/14	06/15	06/16
Sales ($ mil.)	(3.5%)	74.1	80.7	95.8	86.2	64.1
Net income ($ mil.)	(1.1%)	5.8	7.2	8.3	6.5	5.5
Market value ($ mil.)	5.5%	154.0	150.6	155.6	142.5	190.9
Employees	(0.5%)	151	150	150	142	148

DELTA TUCKER HOLDINGS, INC.

1700 OLD MEADOW RD
MC LEAN, VA 221024302
Phone: 571-722-0210
Fax: –
Web: www.dyn-intl.com

CEO: George C Krivo
CFO: William T Kansky
HR: –
FYE: December 31
Type: Private

Through operating company DynCorp International (DI) Delta Tucker Holdings works behind the scenes to support military and diplomatic efforts on front lines. A US national security contractor the company supports the US Departments of State and Defense by providing linguist services and international police force training especially in Afghanistan and Iraq. It provides turnkey solutions for post-conflict countries to rebuild infrastructure install utilities and telecommunications provide security transport equipment and remove and dismantle weapons. About 40% the holding company's sales come from the US.

	Annual Growth	12/14	12/15	12/16	12/17	12/18
Sales ($ mil.)	3.8%	–	1,923.2	1,836.2	2,004.4	2,148.3
Net income ($ mil.)	–	–	(132.6)	0.0	30.6	85.6
Market value ($ mil.)	–	–	–	–	–	–
Employees	–	–	–	–	–	13,200

DELTATHREE INC

NBB: DDDC

1 Bridge Plaza, Fort Lee
West New York, NJ 07024
Phone: 212 500-4850
Fax: –

CEO: –
CFO: –
HR: –
FYE: December 31
Type: Public

Deltathree supplies the pipes that make phone calls via the Internet possible. The company manages an international voice over Internet Protocol (VoIP) network that offers distribution through both service provider and reseller channels. Deltathree sells consumer phone service over the Web under the iConnectHere (or ICH) and joip brands. Using the company's software and network connection customers can place calls from their computers to traditional telephones. Deltathree also provides operational management services such as account provisioning billing and payment processing. The company's network connects points in New Jersey and Georgia plus Frankfurt Germany. It makes more than half of its sales overseas.

	Annual Growth	12/09	12/10	12/11	12/12	12/13
Sales ($ mil.)	(4.1%)	19.0	14.2	10.5	13.7	16.1
Net income ($ mil.)	–	(3.2)	(2.5)	(3.1)	(1.6)	(1.8)
Market value ($ mil.)	(44.7%)	26.7	12.3	2.2	1.4	2.5
Employees	(9.4%)	43	48	32	30	29

DELTEK INC.

NASDAQ: PROJ

2291 Wood Oak Dr.
Herndon VA 20171
Phone: 703-734-8606
Fax: 703-734-1146
Web: www.deltek.com

CEO: Michael Corkery
CFO: Michael Krone
HR: –
FYE: December 31
Type: Private

Deltek provides project management software designed to meet the needs of professional services firms and project-based businesses. Its applications handle expense reporting HR administration materials management customer management and sales force automation. Deltek integrates tools from partners such as Microsoft with its own software and provides consulting and other services. Deltek targets the aerospace construction engineering and information technology sectors. It also serves government agencies and contractors an area of strength for Deltek where it holds a large market share. The company which operates primarily in the US is owned by Thoma Bravo.

DELTIC TIMBER CORP. NYS: DEL

210 East Elm Street, P.O. Box 7200
El Dorado, AR 71731-7200
Phone: 870 881-9400
Fax: –
Web: www.deltic.com

CEO: –
CFO: –
HR: –
FYE: December 31
Type: Public

Money doesn't grow on trees? Deltic Timber might beg to differ. The company annually grows and harvests some 605000 tons of timber from the more than 450000 acres of timberland that it owns primarily in Arkansas and northern Louisiana. The company's two sawmills convert the timber (mainly Southern Pine) into softwood lumber products; this is then sold to wholesale distributors lumber treaters and truss manufacturers for use in residential construction to make roof trusses laminated beams and decking. In addition to its timber and lumber businesses Deltic Timber develops real estate in central Arkansas and manufactures medium density fiberboard (MDF) through Del-Tin Fiber.

	Annual Growth	12/11	12/12	12/13	12/14	12/15
Sales ($ mil.)	12.3%	121.8	140.9	199.7	227.4	193.9
Net income ($ mil.)	(0.0%)	2.7	9.2	26.2	19.7	2.7
Market value ($ mil.)	(0.6%)	747.8	874.5	841.5	847.0	729.0
Employees	5.2%	438	438	537	541	536

DELUXE CORP NYS: DLX

801 S. Marquette Ave. Minneapolis
Shoreview, MN 55126-2966
Phone: 651 483-7111
Fax: 651 483-7337
Web: www.deluxe.com

CEO: Barry Mccarthy
CFO: Scott Bomar
HR: Jane Elliott
FYE: December 31
Type: Public

Deluxe is a Trusted Business Technology company for enterprises small businesses and financial institutions offering solutions to help customers manage and grow their businesses. Deluxe offers industry-leading programs in marketing services and data analytics treasury management solutions website development and hosting promotional products and fraud solutions as well as forms. The company is also a leading provider of checks and accessories sold directly to consumers. Most of its sales come from the US but it also sells its products and services in Canada Australia and portions of Europe and South America.

	Annual Growth	12/16	12/17	12/18	12/19	12/20
Sales ($ mil.)	(0.8%)	1,849.1	1,965.6	1,998.0	2,008.7	1,790.8
Net income ($ mil.)	(55.7%)	229.4	230.2	149.6	(199.9)	8.8
Market value ($ mil.)	(20.1%)	3,005.7	3,225.2	1,613.4	2,095.3	1,225.6
Employees	3.3%	5,433	5,886	5,934	6,352	6,185

DELUXE ENTERTAINMENT SERVICES GROUP INC.

5433 Fernwood Ave.
Hollywood CA 90027
Phone: 323-960-3600
Fax: 323-960-7016
Web: www.bydeluxe.com

CEO: –
CFO: –
HR: –
FYE: June 30
Type: Subsidiary

There's nothing standard about this company's movie production and distribution services. Deluxe Entertainment Services Group provides a plethora of services to the motion picture industry including film processing and distribution and post-production and visual effects work. It has offices throughout Australia Canada Europe India and the US. Clients include all major Hollywood studios. Since 1943 Deluxe has received 10 Academy Awards for technical achievement. The firm can trace its history back to 1919 when Fox Film Corporation built Deluxe Laboratory on its lot for film processing and printing. Deluxe is part of MacAndrews & Forbes Holdings (the holding company of billionaire Ronald Perelman).

DEMANDWARE INC NYS: DWRE

5 Wall Street
Burlington, MA 01803
Phone: 888 553-9216
Fax: –
Web: www.demandware.com

CEO: Thomas D Ebling
CFO: Timothy M Adams
HR: –
FYE: December 31
Type: Public

Consumers make a lot of demands on retailers and Demandware is there to provide demand satisfaction. The company's Demandware Commerce is an on-demand software-as-a-service (SaaS) platform that connects users to up-to-date tools for designing and maintaining websites mobile apps and other digital shopping avenues. It uses data centers to monitor customers' websites worldwide. Major customers include retailers Barneys New York Crocs Jones Group and Columbia Sportswear. Demandware receives a share of the revenue its customers generate using the SaaS; it also collects subscription fees for platform use.

	Annual Growth	12/10	12/11	12/12	12/13	12/14
Sales ($ mil.)	44.6%	36.7	56.5	79.5	103.7	160.6
Net income ($ mil.)	–	0.3	(1.4)	(8.1)	(20.9)	(27.1)
Market value ($ mil.)	45.1%	–	–	963.8	2,262.1	2,030.0
Employees	40.0%	–	215	298	383	590

DEMOULAS SUPER MARKETS INC.

875 East St.
Tewksbury MA 01876
Phone: 978-851-8000
Fax: 978-640-8390
Web: www.mydemoulas.net

CEO: Felicia Thornton
CFO: –
HR: –
FYE: December 31
Type: Private

The Demoulas supermarket chain is ripe with family history all rolled up into numerous Market Baskets. Demoulas Super Markets runs 60-plus grocery stores under the Market Basket banner in Massachusetts and New Hampshire. One store still operates under the DeMoulas banner. The grocery retailer also manages real estate interests. Market Basket supermarkets are typically located in shopping centers with other retail outlets including properties owned by the company through its real estate arm Retail Management and Development (RMD) Inc. Begun as a mom-and-pop grocery store the chain has since transformed into a traditional yet modern concept. The business is run by CEO Arthur Demoulas.

DENBURY INC (NEW) NYS: DEN

5851 Legacy Circle
Plano, TX 75024
Phone: 972 673-2000
Fax: –
Web: www.denbury.com

CEO: Christian Kendall
CFO: Mark Allen
HR: Jenny Cochran
FYE: December 31
Type: Public

Denbury Resources is a combined oil and natural gas producer in Mississippi Texas Louisiana North Dakota Wyoming and Montana. In 2019 it reported estimated proved reserves of 230.2 million barrels of oil equivalent of which almost was oil. It owns the largest reserves of carbon dioxide (CO_2) used in enhanced (also called tertiary) oil recovery east of the Mississippi River and it holds operating acreage in its two core regions Gulf Coast and Rocky Mountains. Using CO_2 in enhanced oil recovery is one of the most efficient tertiary recovery methods for producing crude oil. Denbury Resources generates substantially all of its revenue from sales of oil natural gas and related products.

	Annual Growth	12/17	12/18	12/19*	09/20*	12/20
Sales ($ mil.)	(42.0%)	1,129.8	1,473.6	1,274.9	530.1	220.6
Net income ($ mil.)	–	163.2	322.7	217.0	(1,432.6)	(50.7)
Market value ($ mil.)	126.5%	110.5	85.5	70.5	1.5	1,284.5
Employees	(9.2%)	879	847	806	–	657

*Fiscal year change

DENDREON CORP
NMS: DNDN

1301 2nd Avenue
Seattle, WA 98101
Phone: 206 256-4545
Fax: –
Web: www.dendreon.com

CEO: –
CFO: –
HR: –
FYE: December 31
Type: Public

Dendreon wants to boost your immunity from the start. It is developing therapeutic vaccines that help the body's immune system fight cancer by targeting dendritic cells which initiate an immune response to disease-causing antigens. Its sole commercial product Provenge is a therapeutic vaccine that targets prostate cancer. In 2010 Provenge gained the status of being the first therapeutic cancer vaccine to receive FDA approval. Dendreon is working to expand use of Provenge; it is also working on therapeutic vaccines to treat other types of cancer and it has research programs investigating other cancer-fighting biotech and small molecule drugs. In late 2014 Dendreon filed for Chapter 11 bankruptcy protection.

	Annual Growth	12/09	12/10	12/11	12/12	12/13
Sales ($ mil.)	628.0%	0.1	48.1	341.6	325.5	283.7
Net income ($ mil.)	–	(220.2)	(439.5)	(337.8)	(393.6)	(296.8)
Market value ($ mil.)	(41.9%)	4,133.2	5,492.0	1,195.3	832.0	470.3
Employees	11.8%	484	1,497	1,475	1,050	755

DENISON UNIVERSITY

100 W COLLEGE ST
GRANVILLE, OH 430231100
Phone: 740-587-0810
Fax: –
Web: www.denison.edu

CEO: –
CFO: David English
HR: –
FYE: June 30
Type: Private

Denizens of Denison University have a desire to dedicate themselves to higher learning. The small-town college is a private undergraduate school with an enrollment of about 2200. It has some 220 faculty members and a low student-to-teacher ratio of about 10:1. Denison University offers some 60 majors concentrations and pre-professional programs. Its degrees range across a number of liberal arts and science fields including a pre-medical program and an athletic training program as well as social science and humanities programs.

	Annual Growth	06/16	06/17	06/19	06/20	06/21
Sales ($ mil.)	4.0%	–	127.1	138.1	145.7	148.6
Net income ($ mil.)	35.2%	–	93.5	50.1	20.0	312.6
Market value ($ mil.)	–	–	–	–	–	–
Employees	–	–	–	–	–	757

DENMARK BANCSHARES INC
NBB: DMKB A

103 East Main Street, P.O. Box 130
Denmark, WI 54208
Phone: 920 863-2161
Fax: 920 863-6159
Web: www.denmarkstate.com

CEO: John Olsen
CFO: Dennis Heim
HR: Evonne Kreft
FYE: December 31
Type: Public

Hold the Shakespeare jokes: Denmark Bancshares is the holding company for Denmark State Bank which serves the Green Bay Wisconsin area through more than five branches. The bank offers a variety of deposit products such as checking and savings accounts CDs individual retirement accounts and health savings accounts in addition to credit cards. Real estate loans including residential and commercial mortgages and agricultural and construction loans comprise the bulk of the bank's lending activities; it also originates consumer and business loans.

	Annual Growth	12/16	12/17	12/18	12/19	12/20
Assets ($ mil.)	8.9%	459.6	474.5	506.2	552.6	646.4
Net income ($ mil.)	(0.2%)	3.9	2.8	4.1	5.0	3.9
Market value ($ mil.)	(8.4%)	–	–	–	79.9	73.2
Employees	–	–	–	–	–	–

DENNY'S CORP
NAS: DENN

203 East Main Street
Spartanburg, SC 29319-0001
Phone: 864 597-8000
Fax: 864 597-8135
Web: www.dennys.com

CEO: John Miller
CFO: Robert Verostek
HR: –
FYE: December 30
Type: Public

Denny's is one of America's largest franchised full-service restaurant chains based on the number of restaurants. Denny's is known as America's Diner or in the case of international locations "the local diner". Open 24/7 in most locations the company provides guests with quality foods In addition to breakfast-all-day items Denny's offers a wide selection of lunch and dinner items including burgers sandwiches salads and skillet entr©es along with an assortment of beverages appetizers and desserts. The company consists of approximately 1650 franchised licensed and company restaurants around the world including nearly 1505 restaurants in the US and about 145 international restaurant locations.

	Annual Growth	12/16	12/17	12/18	12/19	12/20
Sales ($ mil.)	(13.1%)	506.9	529.2	630.2	541.4	288.6
Net income ($ mil.)	–	19.4	39.6	43.7	117.4	(5.1)
Market value ($ mil.)	2.3%	823.2	857.1	1,040.0	1,295.2	902.5
Employees	(22.7%)	8,700	8,900	9,000	4,000	3,100

DENSO INTERNATIONAL AMERICA INC.

24777 Denso Dr.
Southfield MI 48033-5244
Phone: 248-350-7500
Fax: 248-213-2337
Web: www.densocorp-na.com

CEO: Kenichiro Ito
CFO: –
HR: –
FYE: March 31
Type: Subsidiary

No spherical measurement DIAM (DENSO International America) does encompass the North American operations of Japanese auto parts maker DENSO. The company oversees more than 30 joint ventures and affiliate businesses — mostly in the US but also in Mexico and Canada. In addition to manufacturing everything from automotive radiators and fuel injectors to alternators and air conditioners DIAM manages research and development of electronic components that improve vehicle fuel efficiency emissions reduction safety and comfort. The company's customers include Toyota General Motors Ford Motor Honda of America Cummins Deere & Company Volvo Trucks Mercedes-Benz U.S. International and Harley-Davidson.

DENTON COUNTY ELECTRIC COOPERATIVE, INC.

7701 S STEMMONS FWY
CORINTH, TX 76210
Phone: 940-321-7800
Fax: –
Web: www.coserv.com

CEO: Michael A Dreyspring
CFO: Donnie Clary
HR: Denise Smithers
FYE: December 31
Type: Private

Denton County Electric Cooperative makes a dent in the heat of a North Texas summer. Operating under the CoServ Electric name the member-owned cooperative distributes power to more than 156000 rural homes and businesses in North Texas. The second-largest member-owned co-op in Texas behind Pedernales Electric it receives its wholesale electricity from Brazos Electric Power Cooperative. CoServ Electric also distributes natural gas to more than 70000 customers through its CoServ Gas subsidiary. Through its affiliates the cooperative also provides infrastructure project management and construction services.

	Annual Growth	06/00	06/01	06/02*	12/09	12/13
Sales ($ mil.)	–	–	–	0.0	395.8	430.7
Net income ($ mil.)	–	–	–	0.0	22.9	(1.8)
Market value ($ mil.)	–	–	–	–	–	–
Employees	–	–	–	–	–	900

*Fiscal year change

DENTSPLY SIRONA INC

NMS: XRAY

13320 Ballantyne Corporate Place
Charlotte, NC 28277-3607
Phone: 844 848-0137
Fax: -
Web: www.dentsplysirona.com

CEO: Donald Casey
CFO: Jorge Gomez
HR: -
FYE: December 31
Type: Public

Dentsply Sirona makes a range of dental tools and supplies from artificial teeth precious metal dental alloys dental ceramics and crown and bridge materials. The company also manufactures dental equipment and supplies including root canal instruments ultrasonic polishers imaging systems CAD/CAM machines and dentist chairs. It sells through distributors and directly to dentists dental assistants dental labs and dental schools in more than 120 countries. In addition Dentsply Sirona offers medical equipment to urologists continence care nurses general practitioners and direct-to-patients.. About 35% of the company's annual sales come from customers in the US.

	Annual Growth	12/16	12/17	12/18	12/19	12/20
Sales ($ mil.)	(2.8%)	3,745.3	3,993.4	3,986.3	4,029.2	3,342.0
Net income ($ mil.)	-	-	429.9	(1,550.0)	(1,011.0)	262.9	(83.0)
Market value ($ mil.)	(2.4%)	12,625.6	14,397.0	8,137.8	12,376.2	11,451.1
Employees	(1.1%)	15,700	16,100	16,400	15,200	15,000

DENVER BOARD OF WATER COMMISSIONERS

1600 W 12TH AVE
DENVER, CO 802043412
Phone: 303-893-2444
Fax: -
Web: www.denverwater.org

CEO: James Loughhead
CFO: Angela Bircmont
HR: -
FYE: December 31
Type: Private

Denver Water keeps the Broncos' troughs full. The Board of Water Commissioners City and County of Denver Colorado which operates as Denver Water distributes water to more than 1.5 million people in the Denver metropolitan area. The company serves about 319230 customers for treated water almost 168675 is from inside city and county of Denver. The utility gets its water primarily from the Blue River Fraser River watersheds the South Platte River and Williams Fork River. Denver Water is an independently operated division of the City and County of Denver. The utility was founded in 1918.

	Annual Growth	12/16	12/17	12/18	12/19	12/20
Sales ($ mil.)	6.2%	-	298.5	320.6	317.2	357.2
Net income ($ mil.)	12.7%	-	83.1	113.9	68.1	119.1
Market value ($ mil.)	-	-	-	-	-	-
Employees	-	-	-	-	-	1,100

DENVER HEALTH AND HOSPITALS AUTHORITY INC

777 BANNOCK ST
DENVER, CO 802044597
Phone: 720-956-2580
Fax: -
Web: www.denverhealth.org

CEO: Arthur Gonzalez
CFO: Lorraine Montoya
HR: -
FYE: December 31
Type: Private

When you live a mile high you sometimes need a safety net; that's where Denver Health and Hospital Authority comes in. Though it serves all the people of Colorado's capital annually attending to a fourth of the city's population and a third of its children Denver Health is also the "safety net" care provider for the city's indigent uninsured mentally ill and other high-risk patients. The medical system's primary facility is the Denver Health Medical Center a 525-bed hospital offering care in more than 50 medical specialties that also houses a regional trauma center. It also includes a network of family health and dental clinics; a poison and drug center; and a 911 response system for Denver County.

	Annual Growth	12/15	12/16	12/17	12/18	12/19
Sales ($ mil.)	30.0%	-	505.6	1,056.9	1,119.5	1,111.9
Net income ($ mil.)	-	-	(6.5)	14.1	62.6	127.2
Market value ($ mil.)	-	-	-	-	-	-
Employees	-	-	-	-	-	3,541

DEPAUW UNIVERSITY

313 S LOCUST ST
GREENCASTLE, IN 461351736
Phone: 765-658-4800
Fax: -
Web: www.depauw.edu

CEO: David Greising
CFO: -
HR: -
FYE: June 30
Type: Private

DePauw University is a private co-educational liberal arts university with an approximate enrollment of 2300 students. Its campus boasts some 36 major buildings across nearly 700 acres including a 520-acre nature preserve located 45 miles west of Indianapolis. The university offers undergraduate degrees from more than 30 academic departments and programs as well as fellowships in media management and science. Prominent alumni include former US Vice President Dan Quayle former US Rep. Lee Hamilton and best-selling author Barbara Kingsolver. DePauw was founded in 1837 by the Methodist Church. The university's School of Music founded in 1884 is one of the oldest in the US.

	Annual Growth	06/16	06/17	06/18	06/19	06/20
Sales ($ mil.)	(7.9%)	-	-	136.5	128.2	115.8
Net income ($ mil.)	-	-	-	54.1	(13.4)	(51.9)
Market value ($ mil.)	-	-	-	-	-	-
Employees	-	-	-	-	-	652

DERMA SCIENCES INC

NAS: DSCI

214 Carnegie Center, Suite 300
Princeton, NJ 08540
Phone: 609 514-4744
Fax: -
Web: www.dermasciences.com

CEO: Stephen T Wills
CFO: John E Yetter
HR: -
FYE: December 31
Type: Public

Time may eventually heal all wounds but in the meantime there's Derma Sciences. The company operates in three segments: advanced wound care traditional wound care and pharmaceutical wound care products. Advanced wound care products include dressings bandages and ointments designed to promote wound healing and/or prevent infection. Traditional wound care products consist of commodity related dressings ointments gauze bandages adhesive bandages wound closer strips catheter fasteners and skin care products. Integra Lifesciences a manufacturer of specialty medical devices reached an agreement to acquire Derma Sciences in early 2017.

	Annual Growth	12/11	12/12	12/13	12/14	12/15
Sales ($ mil.)	7.8%	62.6	72.6	79.7	83.7	84.5
Net income ($ mil.)	-	(4.3)	(12.1)	(24.0)	(39.8)	(38.1)
Market value ($ mil.)	(11.9%)	196.1	287.5	280.0	240.9	118.3
Employees	5.3%	214	244	262	303	263

DESALES UNIVERSITY

2755 STATION AVE
CENTER VALLEY, PA 180349568
Phone: 610-282-1100
Fax: -
Web: www.desales.edu

CEO: -
CFO: Robert Snyder
HR: -
FYE: June 30
Type: Private

Named after scholar writer and Doctor of the Church St. Francis de Sales DeSales University prides itself on providing its students an education based on the philosophy of Christian humanism. The private four-year Catholic university offers bachelor of arts (BA) and bachelor of science (BS) degrees in about 30 major fields of studies. It also administers graduate degrees in education business nursing criminal justice information systems physical therapy and physician assistant studies. Total enrollment is about 3300 students taught by more than 100 faculty members. DeSales University was founded in 1964.

	Annual Growth	06/10	06/11	06/12	06/13	06/15
Sales ($ mil.)	4.5%	-	83.1	87.7	97.5	98.9
Net income ($ mil.)	(8.2%)	-	8.0	7.9	13.3	5.6
Market value ($ mil.)	-	-	-	-	-	-
Employees	-	-	-	-	-	580

DESERET GENERATION AND TRANSMISSION CO-OPERATIVE

10714 S JORDAN GTWY # 30
SOUTH JORDAN, UT 840953922
Phone: 435-781-5737
Fax: –
Web: www.deseretgt.com

CEO: Kimball Rasmussen
CFO: Greg Humphreys
HR: Susan M Cornia
FYE: December 31
Type: Private

Its service area may be dry but it is not a power desert thanks to Deseret Generation and Transmission Cooperative (aka Deseret Power) which supplies wholesale electricity to its members (six retail distribution cooperatives) and other bulk energy customers in Arizona Colorado Nevada Utah and Wyoming. The member-owned utility operates 223 miles of transmission lines and it has interests in two power generation facilities in Utah that give it 550 MW of capacity. Deseret Power also operates its own coal mine which fuels its main power plant through subsidiary Blue Mountain Energy; other operations include the transportation of coal by railroad and the development of a limestone extraction facility.

	Annual Growth	12/04	12/05	12/06	12/07	12/16
Sales ($ mil.)	(17.1%)	–	1,732.6	218.8	242.7	221.5
Net income ($ mil.)	–	–	0.0	10.8	(9.7)	(3.5)
Market value ($ mil.)	–	–	–	–	–	–
Employees	–	–	–	–	–	250

DESERT SCHOOLS FEDERAL CREDIT UNION

148 N. 48th St.
Phoenix AZ 85034
Phone: 602-433-7000
Fax: 604-608-6717
Web: www.amica.ca

CEO: –
CFO: –
HR: –
FYE: December 31
Type: Private - Not-for-Pr

Arizona's largest not-for-profit credit union with $3 billion in assets Desert Schools Federal Credit Union operates more than 50 locations in the Phoenix area and serves some 370000 members. Established by a group of 15 teachers in 1939 the credit union offers traditional banking products and services including checking savings and money market accounts certificates of deposit and credit cards. Its lending activities include home mortgage vehicle personal and student loans as well as business loans and lines of credit. Subsidiary Desert Schools Financial Services provides investment advisory retirement insurance and tax planning services.

DESIGNER BRANDS INC   NYS: DBI

810 DSW Drive
Columbus, OH 43219
Phone: 614 237-7100
Fax: –
Web: www.designerbrands.com

CEO: Roger Rawlins
CFO: Jared Poff
HR: –
FYE: January 30
Type: Public

Designer Brands (formerly DSW) is one of North America's largest designers producers and retailers of footwear and accessories. The company offers its products to men women and kids through around 665 stores and on e-commerce platforms. Its DSW banner stores average of approximately 20300 square feet and offer a wide assortment of brand name of dress casual and athletic shoes as well as a complementary array of handbags hosiery jewelry and accessories. The company also operates nearly 290 Stein Mart stores in the US. Designer Brands designs and produces footwear and accessories through Camuto Group. Designer Brands was founded in 1969.

	Annual Growth	01/17*	02/18	02/19	02/20*	01/21
Sales ($ mil.)	(4.7%)	2,711.4	2,799.8	3,183.7	3,492.5	2,234.7
Net income ($ mil.)	–	124.5	67.3	(20.5)	94.5	(488.7)
Market value ($ mil.)	(11.9%)	1,472.6	1,419.0	1,938.1	1,031.0	886.9
Employees	(2.5%)	12,600	12,000	16,100	15,800	11,400

*Fiscal year change

DESTINATION MATERNITY CORP   NBB: DEST Q

232 Strawbridge Drive
Moorestown, NJ 08057
Phone: 856 291-9700
Fax: –
Web: www.destinationmaternitycorp.com

CEO: Marla Ryan
CFO: David Helkey
HR: –
FYE: February 02
Type: Public

The destination for moms-to-be may be a store operated by Destination Maternity a designer and seller of mid-priced to high-end maternity apparel. Its three chains (A Pea in the Pod Destination Maternity and Motherhood Maternity) occupy more than 2000 retail locations including more than 650 company-owned sites and about 1400 leased spaces in department and specialty stores (Boscov's Macys) in the US Canada and Puerto Rico. The company is also the exclusive supplier of maternity apparel to more than 1100 Kohl's stores nationwide. Most of its merchandise is designed by the company and made by third-party contractors. The company was founded in 1982 as Mothers Work. The company filed for bankruptcy protection in 2019 citing a challenging retail environment. Destination Maternity agreed to be acquired by Marquee Brands in December 2019.

	Annual Growth	01/15	01/16	01/17*	02/18	02/19
Sales ($ mil.)	23.4%	165.6	498.8	433.7	406.2	383.8
Net income ($ mil.)	–	(17.4)	(4.5)	(32.8)	(21.6)	(14.3)
Market value ($ mil.)	(33.8%)	220.7	96.4	81.3	34.5	42.5
Employees	(6.8%)	–	4,200	4,000	3,700	3,400

*Fiscal year change

DESTINATION XL GROUP INC   NMS: DXLG

555 Turnpike Street
Canton, MA 02021
Phone: 781 828-9300
Fax: –
Web: www.dxl.com

CEO: Harvey Kanter
CFO: Peter Stratton
HR: –
FYE: January 30
Type: Public

Destination XL Group (formerly Casual Male Retail Group) is the largest specialty retailer of big and tall men's clothing and shoes with retail locations in the US and Toronto Canada. It sells moderately-priced private-label and name-brand casual wear dresswear and suits for big-and-tall men at about 310 DXL and Casual Male XL retail and outlet stores in more than 45 US states and two retail outlets in Canada as well as online and through catalogs. Founded in 1976 as Designs Inc. the company has changed its name twice most recently to Destination XL Group.

	Annual Growth	01/17*	02/18	02/19	02/20*	01/21
Sales ($ mil.)	(8.3%)	450.3	468.0	473.8	474.0	318.9
Net income ($ mil.)	–	(2.3)	(18.8)	(13.5)	(7.8)	(64.5)
Market value ($ mil.)	(49.7%)	171.3	133.6	130.8	57.6	11.0
Employees	(15.9%)	2,625	2,634	2,543	2,353	1,316

*Fiscal year change

DETERMINE INC   NBB: DTRM

615 West Carmel Drive, Suite 100
Carmel, IN 46032
Phone: 650 532-1500
Fax: –
Web: www.determine.com

CEO: Patrick Stakenas
CFO: John Nolan
HR: –
FYE: March 31
Type: Public

Selectica's offerings are choice. Clients use Selectica's applications to sell complex goods and services over intranets extranets and the Internet. Selectica's software helps clients develop and deploy online sales channels that guide their customers through the selection configuration pricing and fulfillment process for consumer goods loans and insurance. The cloud-based software also suggests optimum product configurations (based on sales objectives marketing information and product constraints). Selectica primarily serves clients from the manufacturing retail and consumer goods sectors.

	Annual Growth	03/14	03/15	03/16	03/17	03/18
Sales ($ mil.)	15.5%	15.8	20.9	26.8	27.5	28.1
Net income ($ mil.)	–	(8.2)	(13.7)	(14.0)	(9.5)	(9.9)
Market value ($ mil.)	(32.0%)	99.3	96.9	27.6	50.7	21.2
Employees	19.5%	75	117	140	224	153

DETREX CORP.

24901 Northwestern Highway, Suite 410
Southfield, MI 48075
Phone: 248 358-5800
Fax: 248 799-7192
Web: www.detrex.com

NBB: DTRX
CEO: Thomas E Mark
CFO: –
HR: –
FYE: December 31
Type: Public

Detrex Corporation has one word for you: plastics. OK three words: plastics and specialty chemicals. Detrex's subsidiary Harvel Plastics which accounts for more than two-thirds of Detrex's sales makes PVC and CPVC pipe and custom extrusions. Detrex's other division The Elco Corporation makes lubricant additives (such as hydraulic fluid additives) fine chemicals and semiconductor-grade hydrochloric acid. The company has operations throughout the US and customers in 50 countries though a clear majority of Detrex's sales are in the US. Those customers include manufacturers of appliances automobiles and farm implements. Summit Capital Partners owns 37% of Detrex.

	Annual Growth	12/11	12/12	12/13	12/14	12/15
Sales ($ mil.)	(5.6%)	48.9	43.4	41.0	40.8	38.9
Net income ($ mil.)	(14.3%)	4.3	7.7	2.6	1.0	2.3
Market value ($ mil.)	15.6%	23.5	28.5	54.0	53.6	41.9
Employees	(26.2%)	219	65	68	66	65

DETROIT PISTONS BASKETBALL COMPANY

6 Championship Dr.
Auburn Hills MI 48326
Phone: 248-377-0100
Fax: 248-377-3260
Web: www.nba.com/pistons

CEO: –
CFO: –
HR: Justen Johnson
FYE: June 30
Type: Private

Basketball fans get revved up thanks to these Pistons. Detroit Pistons Basketball Company owns and operates the Detroit Pistons professional basketball team which boasts three National Basketball Association championships its last coming in 2004. The team was formed in 1941 as the Fort Wayne (Indiana) Zollner Pistons by auto piston maker Fred Zollner who moved the team to Detroit in 1957. The Pistons roster has included such stars as Joe Dumars Bill Laimbeer and Isiah Thomas. Karen Davidson widow of the late William Davidson controls the team. The family also owns Palace Sports & Entertainment a holding company that owns Detroit's Palace of Auburn Hills arena.

DETROIT TIGERS INC.

Comerica Park 2100 Woodward Ave.
Detroit MI 48201-3470
Phone: 313-471-2000
Fax: 206-346-4100
Web: seattle.mariners.mlb.com

CEO: –
CFO: Steve Quinn
HR: Kelsey Shuck
FYE: December 31
Type: Subsidiary

These Tigers prowl in the jungle of Major League Baseball. The Detroit Tigers franchise was a charter member of the American League in 1901 and has won 10 league pennants and four World Series championships (the last in 1984). For all its past success however the team struggled to finish with a winning record for more than a decade until the 2006 season when the club won its first AL pennant since 1984. (Detroit lost the World Series though to the St. Louis Cardinals.) The baseball franchise is part of Ilitch Holdings owned by Mike and Marian Ilitch. The Ilitches who bought the Tigers in 1992 also own the Detroit Red Wings hockey team part of MotorCity Casino and Little Caesar Enterprises.

DEUTSCHE BANK SECURITIES INC.

60 Wall St.
New York NY 10005-2858
Phone: 212-250-2500
Fax: 212-797-4664
Web: www.db.com/us

CEO: –
CFO: Doug Barnard
HR: –
FYE: December 31
Type: Subsidiary

Deutsche Bank Securities is the US arm of German banking colossus Deutsche Bank. Its Deutsche Bank USA is the only investment bank physically located on Wall Street; it offers securities brokerage and investment advisory services to both domestic and international private clients and institutions and correspondent clearing services to broker-dealers. Deutsche Bank Securities also provides investment products brokerage and financial advice to wealthy individual investors through its Deutsche Bank Alex. Brown division. Deutsche Bank opened its first branch in New York in 1979 and now has offices in some 90 cities in nearly 30 US states.

DEVCON CONSTRUCTION INCORPORATED

690 GIBRALTAR DR
MILPITAS, CA 950356317
Phone: 408-942-8200
Fax: –
Web: www.devcon-const.com

CEO: Gary Filizetti
CFO: Brett Sisney
HR: –
FYE: December 31
Type: Private

Devcon Construction has built a sturdy business from building in the Bay Area. One of the area's top general building contractors Devcon has constructed more than 30 million sq. ft. of office industrial and commercial space. Its focus is on Northern California mainly in the San Francisco Bay Area and Silicon Valley. The company provides engineering design/build and interior design services. It specializes in high-tech projects including data centers and industrial research and development facilities. In addition to building company facilities and offices Devcon works on such projects as hotels restaurants parking structures retail stores sports facilities and schools.

	Annual Growth	12/10	12/11	12/12	12/13	12/14
Sales ($ mil.)	23.1%	–	–	779.0	1,012.4	1,181.4
Net income ($ mil.)	138.8%	–	–	3.5	12.5	20.2
Market value ($ mil.)	–	–	–	–	–	–
Employees	–	–	–	–	–	550

DEVEREUX FOUNDATION

2012 RENAISSANCE BLVD # 200
KING OF PRUSSIA, PA 194062786
Phone: 610-542-3057
Fax: –
Web: www.devereux.org

CEO: Carl E Clark II
CFO: –
HR: –
FYE: June 30
Type: Private

Devereux Foundation endeavors to make a difference in the lives of people with behavioral psychological intellectual or neurological problems. A not-for-profit organization Devereux serves children adolescents and adults and their families through about 15 centers in about a dozen states. Its offerings include hospitalization group homes respite care family counseling and vocational training. Devereux also conducts behavioral health research and provides consulting services for other organizations with similar concerns. The group's work began in 1912 when Philadelphia educator Helena Devereux began working with three special education students in her parents' home.

	Annual Growth	06/06	06/07	06/08	06/11	06/12
Sales ($ mil.)	0.7%	–	–	384.9	395.2	395.7
Net income ($ mil.)	–	–	–	5.3	17.9	(5.4)
Market value ($ mil.)	–	–	–	–	–	–
Employees	–	–	–	–	–	6,000

DEVON ENERGY CORP.
NYS: DVN

333 West Sheridan Avenue
Oklahoma City, OK 73102-5015
Phone: 405 235-3611
Fax: -
Web: www.devonenergy.com

CEO: Richard Muncrief
CFO: Jeffrey Ritenour
HR: Tana Cashion
FYE: December 31
Type: Public

An independent energy company Devon Energy explores for develops and produces oil natural gas and NGLs (natural gas liquids) assets onshore in the US. Its primary productive assets are in the Eagle Ford Powder River Basin Anadarko Basin Williston Basin and Delaware Basin. In total Devon boasts proved developed and undeveloped reserves of nearly 180 million barrels of oil equivalent with more than 2300 net producing wells. In 2021 Devon and WPX completed an all-stock merger of equals.

	Annual Growth	12/17	12/18	12/19	12/20	12/21
Sales ($ mil.)	(3.3%)	13,949.0	10,734.0	6,220.0	4,828.0	12,206.0
Net income ($ mil.)	33.0%	898.0	3,064.0	(355.0)	(2,680.0)	2,813.0
Market value ($ mil.)	1.6%	27,448.2	14,944.0	17,218.1	10,482.0	29,205.2
Employees	(24.4%)	4,900	2,900	1,800	1,400	1,600

DEWEY & LEBOEUF LLP

1301 Avenue of the Americas
New York NY 10019-6092
Phone: 212-259-8000
Fax: 212-259-6333
Web: www.deweyleboeuf.com

CEO: -
CFO: -
HR: -
FYE: September 30
Type: Private - Partnershi

International law firm Dewey & LeBoeuf has 1100 lawyers in about 25 offices worldwide in 15 countries. Dewey & LeBoeuf's areas of expertise include antitrust bankruptcy government investigations real estate tax and trade law as well as mergers and acquisitions. The firm is the result of the October 2007 merger between law firms Dewey Ballantine and LeBoeuf Lamb Greene & MacRae. Dewey Ballantine was initially founded in 1909; the Dewey in the name refers to former partner Thomas Dewey a three-term New York governor and two-time Republican presidential nominee in the 1940s. LeBoeuf Lamb was established in 1929. Dewey & LeBoeuf filed for Chapter 11 bankruptcy protection in 2012.

DEWEY ELECTRONICS CORP.
NBB: DEWY

27 Muller Road
Oakland, NJ 07436
Phone: 201 337-4700
Fax: -
Web: www.deweyelectronics.com

CEO: John Dewey
CFO: -
HR: -
FYE: June 30
Type: Public

The Dewey Electronics Corporation powers the military and powders the slopes. The company's electronics segment which accounts for nearly all of Dewey's sales provides the US Army with diesel-operated tactical generator sets and produces underwater speed and distance measuring instrumentation for the US Navy. The US Department of Defense and its various agencies provide around 72% of sales. Dewey's HEDCO division designs manufactures and services the Snow Cub brand of snowmaking equipment which it has sold to more than 300 ski resorts around the world. The family of late CEO Gordon Dewey owns about 37% of the company.

	Annual Growth	06/13	06/14	06/15	06/16	06/17
Sales ($ mil.)	(20.3%)	8.3	6.5	6.6	5.8	3.3
Net income ($ mil.)	-	0.1	(0.1)	(0.1)	0.1	(1.0)
Market value ($ mil.)	0.0%	2.1	3.0	2.9	2.7	2.1
Employees	(7.2%)	30	29	31	24	-

DEXCOM INC
NMS: DXCM

6340 Sequence Drive
San Diego, CA 92121
Phone: 858 200-0200
Fax: -
Web: www.dexcom.com

CEO: Kevin Sayer
CFO: Jereme Sylvain
HR: -
FYE: December 31
Type: Public

DexCom is a medical device company that develops and markets continuous glucose monitoring or CGM systems for the management of diabetes by patients caregivers and clinicians around the world. It develops and manufactures continuous glucose monitoring systems such as its G7 features are 60% reduction in size of the on-body wearable fully disposable and reduced packaging. DexCom launched its latest generation system the Dexcom G6 integrated Continuous Glucose Monitoring System or G6 in 2018. DexCom's products are marketed to physicians endocrinologists and diabetes educators in the US and selected international markets. The company's largest geographic market is the US.

	Annual Growth	12/17	12/18	12/19	12/20	12/21
Sales ($ mil.)	35.9%	718.5	1,031.6	1,476.0	1,926.7	2,448.5
Net income ($ mil.)	-	(50.2)	(127.1)	101.1	493.6	154.7
Market value ($ mil.)	74.9%	5,566.8	11,620.6	21,217.8	35,862.8	52,084.2
Employees	23.7%	2,990	3,900	5,200	6,400	7,000

DEXTERA SURGICAL INC
NBB: DXTR

900 Saginaw Drive
Redwood City, CA 94063
Phone: 650 364-9975
Fax: -
Web: www.dexterasurgical.com

CEO: -
CFO: -
HR: -
FYE: June 30
Type: Public

Dextera Surgical (formerly Cardica) wants to help surgeons treat patients with coronary heart disease. The company makes products including the C-Port and PAS-Port systems that are used in coronary artery bypass surgery. The automated systems connect blood vessels that restore blood flow beyond the closed sections of coronary arteries. Its products offer a less time-consuming and simpler alternative to hand-sewn suturing. Dextera markets its C-Port and PAS-Port systems in the US via direct sales and in the EU through distributors. Century Medical is the exclusive distributor of PAS-Port systems in Japan. The company has a co-development agreement with Cook for a vascular access closure device.Dextera Surgical filed for Chapter 11 bankruptcy protection in December 2017. It plans to sell its assets to Aesculap an affiliate of B. Braun Group.

	Annual Growth	06/13	06/14	06/15	06/16	06/17
Sales ($ mil.)	(0.5%)	3.5	3.6	3.0	4.1	3.4
Net income ($ mil.)	-	(16.1)	(17.0)	(19.2)	(16.0)	(17.2)
Market value ($ mil.)	(27.9%)	44.8	46.0	20.1	72.7	12.1
Employees	(5.6%)	63	69	44	50	50

DFB PHARMACEUTICALS, LLC

3909 HULEN ST
FORT WORTH, TX 761077224
Phone: 817-900-4050
Fax: -
Web: www.dfb.com

CEO: H Paul Dorman
CFO: -
HR: -
FYE: December 31
Type: Private

DFB Pharmaceuticals contributes to drug development and manufacturing processes by providing essential ingredients. The company produces various pharmaceutical ingredients for its own use and for other drug makers through its Phyton Biotech operating subsidiary. Phyton Biotech uses its plant cell culture technology to make APIs (active pharmaceutical ingredients). Phyton Biotech is a global provider of chemotherapeutic agents including paclitaxel and docetaxel APIs and taxane intermediates. Affiliate Phyton LTD. operates Phyton Biotech LLC and Phyton Biotech GmbH.

	Annual Growth	12/05	12/06	12/07	12/08	12/10
Sales ($ mil.)	(44.8%)	-	-	1,916.0	318.7	322.4
Net income ($ mil.)	-	-	-	0.0	0.0	0.0
Market value ($ mil.)	-	-	-	-	-	-
Employees	-	-	-	-	-	700

DFC GLOBAL CORP.

NMS: DLLR

1436 Lancaster Avenue
Berwyn, PA 19312
Phone: 610 296-3400
Fax: –
Web: www.dfcglobalcorp.com

CEO: Jeffrey A Weiss
CFO: Randy Underwood
HR: –
FYE: June 30
Type: Public

If your wallet is flat and payday is far away DFC Global can tide you over. The company owns some 1350 check-cashing and payday loan stores (and franchises about 50 additional locations) in North America and Europe. The stores operate under such names as Money Mart Money Shop Insta-Cheques Sefina Suttons and Robertsons and The Check Cashing Store. In addition to check cashing and short-term loans the stores offer money transfer services money orders tax filing services gold purchasing foreign exchange and reloadable Visa and MasterCard debit cards to customers who choose not to use or don't have access to traditional banks or financial institutions.

	Annual Growth	06/09	06/10	06/11	06/12	06/13
Sales ($ mil.)	20.8%	527.9	610.9	788.4	1,061.7	1,122.3
Net income ($ mil.)	–	1.8	(4.9)	65.8	52.4	(0.7)
Market value ($ mil.)	0.0%	553.1	793.8	868.4	739.3	554.0
Employees	9.9%	4,522	4,966	5,375	6,528	6,600

DGT HOLDINGS CORP

NBB: DGTC

c/o Steel Partners Holdings L.P., 590 Madison Avenue, 32nd floor
New York, NY 10022
Phone: 212 520-2300
Fax: –
Web: www.dgtholdings.com

CEO: John J Quicke
CFO: Terry Gibson
HR: –
FYE: July 28
Type: Public

Del Global Technologies can see the beauty of the inner you. And your pet. The firm's Medical Systems group makes medical and dental X-ray systems used by hospitals and doctors dentists and veterinarians. It sells its products through distributors worldwide under the Villa brand name; it also provides some of its products to OEMs under private-label agreements. Through its RFI subsidiary Del Global Technologies' Power Conversion Group makes precision electronic components and sub-assemblies for makers of everything from weapons systems to satellites to MRI machines; brands include RFI Filtron Sprague and Stanley. The company was formed in 1954.

	Annual Growth	08/08	08/09*	07/10	07/11	07/12
Sales ($ mil.)	(43.0%)	108.3	80.4	56.2	67.9	11.4
Net income ($ mil.)	14.5%	3.0	(4.1)	(0.8)	1.1	5.1
Market value ($ mil.)	62.2%	5.8	2.3	3.1	34.6	40.1
Employees	(25.8%)	310	263	217	212	94

*Fiscal year change

DHI GROUP INC

NYS: DHX

6465 South Greenwood Plaza, Suite 400
Centennial, CO 80111
Phone: 212 448-6605
Fax: –
Web: www.dhigroupinc.com

CEO: Arthur Zeile
CFO: Kevin Bostick
HR: –
FYE: December 31
Type: Public

DHI is a leading provider of software products online tools and services to deliver career marketplaces to candidates and employers globally. The company's three brands (Dice ClearanceJobs and eFinancialCareers) enable recruiters and hiring managers to efficiently search match and connect with highly skilled technologists in specialized fields particularly technology those with active government security clearances and in financial services. Most of DHI's revenue comes from the sale of recruitment packages which allow customers to post jobs on its websites and source candidates through its resume databases. Recruitment packages are typically provided through contractual arrangements with annual quarterly or monthly terms.

	Annual Growth	12/17	12/18	12/19	12/20	12/21
Sales ($ mil.)	(12.9%)	208.0	161.6	149.4	136.9	119.7
Net income ($ mil.)	–	16.0	7.2	12.6	(30.0)	(29.7)
Market value ($ mil.)	34.6%	92.6	74.1	146.8	108.2	304.2
Employees	(6.5%)	615	484	559	524	470

DIAGNOSTIC LABORATORY SERVICES, INC.

99-859 IWAIWA ST
AIEA, HI 967013267
Phone: 808-589-5100
Fax: –
Web: www.dlslab.com

CEO: –
CFO: Rebecca S Roberts
HR: –
FYE: June 30
Type: Private

Diagnostic Laboratory Services (DLS) provides clinical laboratory and employee drug screening services in Hawaii and other Pacific islands. The company's toxicology department provides drug testing services for private companies federal and state agencies and health care providers. DLS' microbiology department provides infectious disease testing services. The company also provides provides diagnostic pathology lab services including biopsy and pap smear analysis through affiliate Hawaii Pathology Laboratory. DLS operates satellite locations throughout the Hawaiian Islands Guam and Saipan and has hospital-based laboratories including one at the affiliated Queen's Medical Center in Honolulu.

	Annual Growth	06/03	06/04	06/05	06/06	06/07
Sales ($ mil.)	7.7%	–	55.9	60.2	65.0	69.8
Net income ($ mil.)	13.5%	–	4.0	6.7	7.3	5.9
Market value ($ mil.)	–	–	–	–	–	–
Employees	–	–	–	–	–	55

DIAKON

1 S HOME AVE
TOPTON, PA 195621317
Phone: 610-682-1262
Fax: –
Web: www.diakon.org

CEO: Mark T Pile
CFO: Richard Barger
HR: Jennifer Rautzhan
FYE: December 31
Type: Private

Taking its name from the Greek word for service Diakon Lutheran Social Ministries offers a range of health and community services including more than a dozen retirement communities home health care pregnancy and adoption services hospice care and counseling. The not-for-profit organization's Housing and Development subsidiary works to provide community planning affordable housing and property management. Diakon Lutheran also offers clinical pastoral education for seminary students. Its services cover tens of thousands of residents throughout Pennsylvania Maryland and Delaware. Diakon was established in 2000 through a merger of Lutheran Services Northeast and Tressler Lutheran Services.

	Annual Growth	12/16	12/17	12/18	12/19	12/20
Sales ($ mil.)	1.0%	–	256.9	259.6	269.9	265.1
Net income ($ mil.)	(23.3%)	–	25.7	(16.4)	(5.8)	11.6
Market value ($ mil.)	–	–	–	–	–	–
Employees	–	–	–	–	–	4,600

DIALOGIC INC

NBB: DLGC

1504 McCarthy Boulevard
Milpitas, CA 95035-7405
Phone: 408 750-9400
Fax: 408 750-9450
Web: www.dialogic.com

CEO: –
CFO: –
HR: –
FYE: December 31
Type: Public

Dialogic serves as a gateway to Internet protocol (IP)-based communications. The company provides hardware and software systems used to build and integrate computer telephony networks over IP connections. Its products include software (PowerMedia) computer signaling boards that handle multimedia and message processing and media gateways (I-Gate) for delivering voice calls over digital lines with a level of quality comparable to analog landline phone systems. Dialogic sells its products worldwide to enterprises and service providers through resellers distributors and systems integrators including Advantech and Syntellect. The company merged with Veraz Networks in 2010.

	Annual Growth	12/08	12/09	12/10	12/11	12/12
Sales ($ mil.)	–	0.0	176.3	178.8	198.1	160.0
Net income ($ mil.)	–	0.0	(37.6)	(46.7)	(54.8)	(37.8)
Market value ($ mil.)	–	0.0	–	56.9	17.3	19.7
Employees	(14.5%)	–	–	935	808	684

DIALYSIS CLINIC, INC.

1633 CHURCH ST STE 500
NASHVILLE, TN 372032948
Phone: 615-327-3061
Fax: –
Web: www.dciinc.org

CEO: –
CFO: –
HR: –
FYE: September 30
Type: Private

Dialysis Clinic Inc. or DCI is dedicated to caring for patients with end-stage renal disease (ESRD). The not-for-profit company which operates a network of more than 210 dialysis centers serving more than 14000 patients in 27 states also provides kidney transplant assistance services. Affiliate DCI Donor Services is an organ and tissue procurement agency. DCI also funds kidney-related research and educational programs and is affiliated with various universities and teaching hospitals throughout the US including Tufts University the University of Arizona and Tulane University.

	Annual Growth	09/15	09/16	09/17	09/18	09/19
Sales ($ mil.)	0.9%	–	719.7	736.2	760.1	739.1
Net income ($ mil.)	(30.0%)	–	22.7	24.0	5.5	7.8
Market value ($ mil.)	–	–	–	–	–	–
Employees	–	–	–	–	–	5,000

DIAMOND DISCOVERIES INTERNATIONAL CORP.

PINK SHEETS: DMDD

45 Rockefeller Plaza Ste. 2000
New York NY 10111
Phone: 212-332-8016
Fax: 212-332-3401
Web: www.diamonddiscoveries.com

CEO: –
CFO: –
HR: –
FYE: December 31
Type: Public

Diamond Discoveries International: The name says it all. The company is a minerals exploration company that leases property in the Torngat fields in northern Quebec. The company is firmly in the exploration and development phase of the project which will last at least through 2008. Former chairman and CEO Teodosia Pangia holds nearly 25% of Diamond Discoveries.

DIAMOND FOODS INC

NMS: DMND

600 Montgomery Street, 13th Floor
San Francisco, CA 94111-2702
Phone: 415 445-7444
Fax: –
Web: www.diamondfoods.com

CEO: Gary Ford
CFO: Ray Silcock
HR: –
FYE: July 31
Type: Public

Diamond Foods has come out of its shell. While the company still sells plenty of walnuts peanuts almonds and other varieties of nuts primarily under the Diamond and Emerald brands snacks are a growing part of its business. Diamond Foods sells microwave popcorn under the Pop Secret brand and Kettle brand potato chips. The snack food maker sells its products to food retailers; Wal-Mart and Costco combined account for about 25% of sales. Non-retail customers include food processors restaurants bakeries and food service operators. Snack maker Synder's-Lance the maker of Cape Cod chips Lance crackers and Synder's of Hanover pretzels agreed to buy Diamond Foods for nearly $1.3 billion in late 2015.

	Annual Growth	07/11	07/12	07/13	07/14	07/15
Sales ($ mil.)	(2.7%)	965.9	981.4	864.0	865.2	864.2
Net income ($ mil.)	(9.9%)	50.2	(86.3)	(163.2)	(164.7)	33.0
Market value ($ mil.)	(18.0%)	2,254.4	512.4	642.1	845.8	1,017.5
Employees	(1.4%)	1,797	1,407	1,266	1,731	1,696

DIAMOND HILL INVESTMENT GROUP INC.

NMS: DHIL

325 John H. McConnell Blvd., Suite 200
Columbus, OH 43215
Phone: 614 255-3333
Fax: –
Web: www.diamond-hill.com

CEO: Heather Brilliant
CFO: Tom Line
HR: –
FYE: December 31
Type: Public

Diamond Hill Investment Group takes a shine to investment management. Operating through flagship subsidiary Diamond Hill Capital Management the firm oversees some $11.5 billion in assets most of it invested in mutual funds. Serving institutional and individual clients the company administers several mutual funds and sells them mainly through independent investment advisers broker-dealers financial planners investment consultants and third-party marketing firms. The firm hews to a value-based investment philosophy and takes a long-term perspective to investing. Formed in 1990 Diamond Hill Investment Group also manages separate accounts and hedge funds.

	Annual Growth	12/16	12/17	12/18	12/19	12/20
Sales ($ mil.)	(1.8%)	136.1	145.2	145.6	136.6	126.4
Net income ($ mil.)	(4.3%)	46.1	50.0	47.4	55.0	38.7
Market value ($ mil.)	(8.2%)	666.7	654.9	473.6	445.1	473.0
Employees	3.0%	112	118	125	129	126

DIAMOND OFFSHORE DRILLING, INC.

NBB: DOFS Q

15415 Katy Freeway
Houston, TX 77094
Phone: 281 492-5300
Fax: 281 492-5316
Web: www.diamondoffshore.com

CEO: Bernie Wolford
CFO: Dominic Savarino
HR: Bettina Ortiz
FYE: December 31
Type: Public

This Diamond is an oiler's best friend. Diamond Offshore Drilling is a contract offshore oil and gas driller capable of descending in the deep blue to depths of 10000 feet and deeper. Diamond Offshore has some 15 offshore drilling rigs including about five drillships and over 10 semisubmersible rigs including less than five rigs that are currently cold stacked. This fleet enables the company to offer services in the floater market on a worldwide basis. A floater rig is a type of mobile offshore drilling rig that floats and does not rest on the seafloor. The US generates about 55% of the company's total sales.

	Annual Growth	12/15	12/16	12/17	12/18	12/19
Sales ($ mil.)	(20.2%)	2,419.4	1,600.3	1,485.7	1,083.2	980.6
Net income ($ mil.)	–	(274.3)	(372.5)	18.3	(180.3)	(357.2)
Market value ($ mil.)	(23.6%)	2,905.6	2,437.4	2,559.9	1,299.9	990.1
Employees	(7.4%)	3,400	2,800	2,400	2,300	2,500

DIAMOND RESORTS HOLDINGS LLC

3745 Las Vegas Blvd South
Las Vegas NV 89109
Phone: 702-261-1010
Fax: 602-852-6686
Web: www.drivetime.com

CEO: Stephen J Cloobeck
CFO: –
HR: –
FYE: December 31
Type: Private

Diamond Resorts Holdings formerly Sunterra Corporation can help you shine on in all your crazy vacation adventures. The time-share vacation company doing business as Diamond Resorts International owns or manages more than 220 resorts across the globe including 70 managed resorts and some 130 affiliated resorts. About 495000 owners and members vacation at the resorts through the purchase of either vacation intervals (generally a one-week stay) or vacation points (redeemable for varying lengths of stay). The company's holdings also include four cruise ships. Stephen Cloobeck a real estate developer and time share industry executive owns Diamond Resorts.

DIAMONDBACK ENERGY INC.

NASDAQ: FANG

500 West Texas Ste. 1225
Midland TX 79701
Phone: 432-617-0511
Fax: 432-689-5299
Web: www.legacylp.com

CEO: Raty Straehla
CFO: –
HR: –
FYE: December 31
Type: Private

Diamondback Energy is not selling snake oil. It is selling crude oil. The company is engaged in the exploration and production of unconventional oil and natural gas reserves in the Permian Basin in West Texas. In particular it is focusing on the oil-rich Wolfberry play which has a long production history long-lived reserves and proven drilling success rates. In 2011 Diamondback Energy reported estimated proved oil and natural gas reserves of 24.8 billion barrels of oil equivalent and more than 28140 net acres of leasehold properties. It operates more than 140 wells. The company raised $218 million in an initial public offering (IPO) in 2012.

DIAMONDBACK ENERGY, INC.

NMS: FANG

500 West Texas, Suite 1200
Midland, TX 79701
Phone: 432 221-7400
Fax: –
Web: www.diamondbackenergy.com

CEO: Travis Stice
CFO: Kaes Van't Hof
HR: –
FYE: December 31
Type: Public

Upstream oil and gas company Diamondback Energy engages in the exploration and production of unconventional oil and natural gas reserves in the Permian Basin in West Texas. In particular it is focusing on the oil-rich Wolfcamp play which has a long production history long-lived reserves and proven drilling success rates. It is also active in the Spraberry Clearfork Bone Spring and Cline formations. Diamondback has three main customers: Shell Trading Company Koch Supply & Trading and Occidental Energy Marketing. Its proved oil and natural gas reserves total nearly 1 million MBOE and has interests in some 7300 productive wells. Diamondback first entered the Permian in 2007 and went public in 2012.

	Annual Growth	12/16	12/17	12/18	12/19	12/20
Sales ($ mil.)	52.0%	527.1	1,205.1	2,176.3	3,964.0	2,813.0
Net income ($ mil.)	–	(165.0)	482.3	845.7	240.0	(4,517.0)
Market value ($ mil.)	(16.8%)	15,976.4	19,958.6	14,654.8	14,680.1	7,651.5
Employees	46.7%	158	251	711	712	732

DIAMONDROCK HOSPITALITY CO.

NYS: DRH

2 Bethesda Metro Center, Suite 1400
Bethesda, MD 20814
Phone: 240 744-1150
Fax: –
Web: www.drhc.com

CEO: Mark Brugger
CFO: Jeffrey Donnelly
HR: Kathy Johnson
FYE: December 31
Type: Public

Operating as an umbrella partnership real estate investment trust (UPREIT) DiamondRock Hospitality owns about 30 upper-upscale hotels with over 10100 rooms in the North America and the US Virgin Islands with an emphasis on major urban markets such as Chicago and Boston. Its hotels are operated under the banners of Hilton Worldwide Marriott International Starwood Hotels & Resorts Worldwide and Westin. DiamondRock mostly operates through its taxable REIT subsidiary Bloodstone TRS.

	Annual Growth	12/16	12/17	12/18	12/19	12/20
Sales ($ mil.)	(24.0%)	896.6	870.0	863.7	938.1	299.5
Net income ($ mil.)	–	114.8	91.9	87.8	183.5	(394.7)
Market value ($ mil.)	(8.0%)	2,422.1	2,371.7	1,907.5	2,327.6	1,733.1
Employees	2.8%	26	29	31	31	29

DICERNA PHARMACEUTICALS INC

NMS: DRNA

33 Hayden Avenue
Lexington, MA 02421
Phone: 617 621-8097
Fax: –
Web: www.dicerna.com

CEO: –
CFO: John B Green
HR: –
FYE: December 31
Type: Public

Dicerna Pharmaceuticals is trying to discern a viable treatment for rare diseases. The company is developing four drug candidates that aim to treat rare inherited liver diseases and cancer. Its treatments are based on RNA interference (RNAi) a biological process where ribonucleic acid (RNA) molecules inhibit gene expression. Two of the drug candidates are being developed with Japanese pharmaceutical firm Kyowa Hakko Kirin (KHK). Formerly funded by Oxford Biosciences the company went public in early 2014 and raised $90 million in its IPO. It plans to use the proceeds to fund preclinical and clinical trials of its drug candidates.

	Annual Growth	12/15	12/16	12/17	12/18	12/19
Sales ($ mil.)	237.6%	0.2	0.3	2.3	6.2	23.9
Net income ($ mil.)	–	(62.8)	(59.5)	(60.0)	(88.9)	(120.5)
Market value ($ mil.)	16.7%	849.6	206.1	646.3	765.1	1,576.8
Employees	40.5%	48	47	44	78	187

DICK CLARK PRODUCTIONS INC.

9200 Sunset Blvd. 10th Fl.
Los Angeles CA 90069
Phone: 310-786-8900
Fax: 310-777-2187
Web: www.dickclarkproductions.com

CEO: Allen Shapiro
CFO: –
HR: –
FYE: June 30
Type: Private

From the Bandstand to the red carpet this company is anywhere there is celebrity entertainment. dick clark productions is best-known for producing televised awards shows ceremonies such as The American Music Awards and the Golden Globes. In addition to awards shows dick clark productions produces ABC's Bloopers and current FOX hit So You Think You Can Dance. It also owns the rights to the iconic music and dance program American Bandstand licensing TV clips as well as the Bandstand brand for use by restaurants and theatres. The company was founded by legend Dick Clark in 1957. A consortium of private equity firms including Guggenheim Partners and Mandalay Entertainment acquired the company in 2012.

DICK'S SPORTING GOODS, INC

NYS: DKS

345 Court Street
Coraopolis, PA 15108
Phone: 724 273-3400
Fax: –
Web: www.dicks.com

CEO: Lauren Hobart
CFO: Lee Belitsky
HR: –
FYE: January 30
Type: Public

Dick's Sporting Goods is a leading omni-channel sporting goods retailer offering an extensive assortment of authentic high-quality sports equipment apparel footwear and accessories. Aside from the company's nearly 730 stores across the US its products are also sold through an eCommerce platform that is integrated with our store network In addition to well-known brand names Dick's carries exclusive brands such as Walter Hagen Alpine Design and Top-Flite. The company also operates about 100 Golf Galaxy and more than 20 Field & Stream stores.

	Annual Growth	01/17*	02/18	02/19	02/20*	01/21
Sales ($ mil.)	4.9%	7,922.0	8,590.5	8,436.6	8,750.7	9,584.0
Net income ($ mil.)	16.5%	287.4	323.4	319.9	297.5	530.3
Market value ($ mil.)	6.9%	4,357.8	2,674.5	2,993.8	3,756.5	5,691.2
Employees	5.5%	40,500	45,200	40,700	41,600	50,100

*Fiscal year change

DICKINSON COLLEGE

28 N COLLEGE ST
CARLISLE, PA 170132311
Phone: 717-245-1943
Fax: -
Web: www.dickinson.edu

CEO: -
CFO: -
HR: -
FYE: June 30
Type: Private

Located in Carlisle Pennsylvania Dickinson College is a private liberal arts college with a penchant for international study. The small but selective college has an annual enrollment of some 2400 students half of which study abroad in programs that span 24 countries on six continents. The college offers more than 40 programs in arts and humanities (including a significant foreign language program) social sciences and natural sciences. It also offers minors in fields including astronomy creative writing and film studies. Dickinson College traces its roots back to 1773; it is named for John Dickinson who signed the US Constitution and was known as "The Penman of the [American] Revolution."

	Annual Growth	06/17	06/18	06/19	06/20	06/21
Sales ($ mil.)	16.4%	-	162.5	147.9	113.3	256.3
Net income ($ mil.)	77.8%	-	26.4	17.9	(11.2)	148.2
Market value ($ mil.)	-	-	-	-	-	-
Employees	-	-	-	-	-	632

DIEBOLD NIXDORF INC

NYS: DBD

5995 Mayfair Road, P.O. Box 3077
North Canton, OH 44720-8077
Phone: 330 490-4000
Fax: -
Web: www.dieboldnixdorf.com

CEO: Gerrard B Schmid
CFO: Jeffrey Rutherford
HR: -
FYE: December 31
Type: Public

Diebold Nixdorf is the leading global producer of automated teller machines (ATMs) with about a million in operation around the world. In addition it offers remote teller systems cash dispensers and intelligent deposit terminals. The company's software encompasses front-end applications for consumer connection points as well as back-end platforms which manage channel transactions operations and channel integration. These hardware-agnostic software applications facilitate millions of transactions via ATMs kiosks and other self-service devices as well as via online and mobile digital channels. Diebold Nixdorf gets about three-quarters of its sales outside the US. The company has a presence in more than 100 countries with approximately 22000 employees worldwide.

	Annual Growth	12/16	12/17	12/18	12/19	12/20
Sales ($ mil.)	4.2%	3,316.3	4,609.3	4,578.6	4,408.7	3,902.3
Net income ($ mil.)	-	(33.0)	(233.1)	(568.7)	(341.3)	(269.1)
Market value ($ mil.)	(19.3%)	1,953.6	1,270.1	193.4	820.3	828.1
Employees	(3.1%)	25,000	23,000	23,000	22,000	22,000

DIEDRICH COFFEE INC.

28 Executive Park Ste. 200
Irvine CA 92614
Phone: 949-260-1600
Fax: 949-260-1610
Web: www.diedrich.com

CEO: Carl Diedrich
CFO: Sean M McCarthy
HR: -
FYE: June 30
Type: Subsidiary

This company keeps caffeine lovers buzzing. Diedrich Coffee is a leading coffee producer and wholesale supplier that distributes coffee products to retailers and food-service customers. The company produces a variety of specialty coffee blends and flavors under the brands Coffee People Diedrich Coffee and Gloria Jean's. Its primary product is K-Cup single-serving portion packs produced under license for Keurig's single-service coffee machines. Diedrich Coffee produces and distributes fresh roasted coffee from its facility in California. In 2010 the company was acquired by Green Mountain Coffee Roasters.

DIGERATI TECHNOLOGIES INC

NBB: DTGI

825 W. Bitters, Suite 104
San Antonio, TX 78216
Phone: 210 775-0888
Fax: -
Web: www.digerati-inc.com

CEO: Arthur Smith
CFO: Antonio Estrada
HR: -
FYE: July 31
Type: Public

Digerati Technologies (formerly ATSI Communications) has its head in the clouds and its feet in the oil wells. Digerati is a diversified holding company with operating subsidiaries that specialize in cloud-based technology services most notably Shift8 Technologies. Shift8 provides telecommunications solutions to commercial consumers. Digerati is also actively pursuing possible investments in the fossil fuels sector.

	Annual Growth	07/17	07/18	07/19	07/20	07/21
Sales ($ mil.)	183.2%	0.2	2.0	6.0	6.3	12.4
Net income ($ mil.)	-	0.4	(3.2)	(4.5)	(3.4)	(16.7)
Market value ($ mil.)	(27.4%)	73.4	73.7	20.8	4.0	20.4
Employees	60.1%	7	26	23	22	46

DIGI INTERNATIONAL INC

NMS: DGII

9350 Excelsior Blvd., Suite 700
Hopkins, MN 55343
Phone: 952 912-3444
Fax: -
Web: www.digi.com

CEO: Ronald Konezny
CFO: James Loch
HR: -
FYE: September 30
Type: Public

Digi International is a global provider of business and mission-critical Internet of Things (IoT) connectivity products services and solutions. The IoT Products & Services segment provides its customers with a device management platform and other professional services to enable customers to capture and manage data from devices they connect to networks. Digi serves over 81000 customer including industries such as food service retail healthcare (primarily pharmacies) and supply chain. The company sells directly and through resellers and distributors. About 75% of company's total revenue comes from North America.

	Annual Growth	09/17	09/18	09/19	09/20	09/21
Sales ($ mil.)	14.2%	181.6	228.4	254.2	279.3	308.6
Net income ($ mil.)	2.6%	9.4	1.3	10.0	8.4	10.4
Market value ($ mil.)	18.7%	363.2	460.8	466.7	535.5	720.2
Employees	6.4%	514	516	543	656	659

DIGIMARC CORP

NMS: DMRC

9405 SW Gemini Drive
Beaverton, OR 97008
Phone: 503 469-4800
Fax: -
Web: www.digimarc.com

CEO: Riley McCormack
CFO: Charles Beck
HR: -
FYE: December 31
Type: Public

Digimarc provides digital watermarking software that embeds code in printed and digital content including photographs music plastic fabric e-book labels as well as currency documents and packages. Customers — which include movie studios record labels broadcasters creative professionals and government agencies — use Digimarc's software to control copyrights deter piracy license online content and manage digital assets. The company generates revenue from software development consulting services and technology licensing and subscription fees. Its licensees include AlpVision SA Intellectual Ventures Kantar SAS and NexGuard Labs B.V.

	Annual Growth	12/16	12/17	12/18	12/19	12/20
Sales ($ mil.)	2.4%	21.8	25.2	21.2	23.0	24.0
Net income ($ mil.)	-	(21.7)	(25.8)	(32.5)	(32.8)	(32.5)
Market value ($ mil.)	12.0%	502.1	605.0	242.7	561.6	790.6
Employees	3.1%	180	207	213	216	203

DIGITAL ALLY INC
NAS: DGLY

15612 College Blvd.
Lenexa, KS 66219
Phone: 913 814-7774
Fax: –
Web: www.digitalally.com

CEO: Stanton Ross
CFO: Thomas Heckman
HR: –
FYE: December 31
Type: Public

Digital video systems manufacturer Digital Ally is an ally to police and other law enforcement that want more than a paper record of their traffic stops. Targeted to city state and commercial law enforcement agencies the company designs and manufactures specialized digital video cameras including a rear-view mirror with a built-in digital video camera (used to capture video from inside police vehicles) as well as a portable digital video flashlight which can be used to record routine traffic stops sobriety tests and other law enforcement/civilian interactions. The company also offers a version of their video camera that can be worn on law enforcement officers' uniforms. Digital Ally was formed in 2004.

	Annual Growth	12/16	12/17	12/18	12/19	12/20
Sales ($ mil.)	(10.8%)	16.6	14.6	11.3	10.4	10.5
Net income ($ mil.)	–	(12.7)	(12.3)	(15.5)	(10.0)	(2.6)
Market value ($ mil.)	(13.6%)	112.4	70.9	71.7	27.3	62.6
Employees	(13.6%)	154	128	95	119	86

DIGITAL ANGEL CORPORATION
OTC: DIGA

490 Villaume Ave.
South St. Paul MN 55075
Phone: 651-455-1621
Fax: 651-455-0413
Web: www.digitalangel.com

CEO: Kenneth Shapiro
CFO: –
HR: –
FYE: December 31
Type: Public

Digital Angel puts a British accent on two-way communication equipment. The company develops emergency identification products for use in global positioning systems and other applications and distributes them in the UK. Digital Angel's conventional radio systems provide such services as site monitoring for construction companies and manufacturers while its trunked radio systems serve the security needs of large customers such as local governments and public utilities. In mid-2012 the company announced a strategic shift toward the development of games and applications for mobile devices. It has several titles in progress.

DIGITAL CINEMA DESTINATIONS CORP.

250 East Broad St.
Westfield NJ 07090
Phone: 908-396-1360
Fax: 908-396-1361
Web: www.digiplexdest.com

CEO: Bud Mayo
CFO: –
HR: –
FYE: June 30
Type: Private

It's out with the celluloid and in with the megapixels at Digital Cinema Destinations (DCDC). Operating under the Digiplex Destinations brand DCDC owns a small but growing chain of movie theaters that show first-run movies in an entirely digital format. Its theaters located in New Jersey and Connecticut also show non-movie recorded and broadcasted events such as concerts operas and ballets and live sporting events. DCDC's theaters offer an interactive element as well allowing patrons to text comments and questions sing along and host tailgate parties. Founded in 2010 the company filed to go public in late 2011.

DIGITAL FEDERAL CREDIT UNION

220 Donald Lynch Blvd.
Marlborough MA 01752
Phone: 508-263-6700
Fax: 508-263-6430
Web: www.dcu.org

CEO: James Regan
CFO: –
HR: –
FYE: December 31
Type: Private - Not-for-Pr

Digital Federal Credit Union (DCU) provides old-fashioned financial services with modern technology. Its more than 370000 members can conduct business online at about 20 branch locations in Massachusetts and New Hampshire or at some 6400 credit unions that accept transactions on behalf of DCU. The credit union offers a range of commercial and retail products and services including savings and checking accounts; Visa credit cards; residential and commercial mortgages; and auto business construction and home equity loans. Founded in 1979 the credit union also operates DCU Insurance residential real estate brokerage DCU Realty DCU Financial which offers investments and financial planning services.

DIGITAL REALTY TRUST INC
NYS: DLR

5707 Southwest Parkway, Building 1, Suite 275
Austin, TX 78735
Phone: 737 281-0101
Fax: 415 738-6501
Web: www.digitalrealty.com

CEO: A William Stein
CFO: Andrew Power
HR: –
FYE: December 31
Type: Public

One of the largest publicly traded Real estate investment trust (REIT) Digital Realty Trust owns or leases some 290 data center and technology properties with around 43.6 million sq. ft. of rentable space. Active in around 50 metropolitan areas across some two dozen countries on six continents the company provides data center colocation and interconnection services for tenants in fields such as financial services cloud and IT tech manufacturing energy healthcare and consumer products. It also holds some 45 properties with approximately 4.75 million rentable square feet as investments. The company operates through Digital Realty Trust LP. The US operation generates some two-thirds of company's total sales.

	Annual Growth	12/16	12/17	12/18	12/19	12/20
Sales ($ mil.)	16.2%	2,142.2	2,457.9	3,046.5	3,209.2	3,903.6
Net income ($ mil.)	(4.4%)	426.2	248.3	331.2	579.8	356.4
Market value ($ mil.)	9.2%	27,541.3	31,925.0	29,864.9	33,561.9	39,103.2
Employees	20.9%	1,345	1,436	1,530	1,550	2,878

DIGITAL RIVER, INC.
NMS: DRIV

10380 Bren Road West
Minnetonka, MN 55343
Phone: 952 253-1234
Fax: –
Web: www.digitalriver.com

CEO: Adam Coyle
CFO: CJ Bernander
HR: –
FYE: December 31
Type: Public

Digital River helps keep the e-commerce flowing. The company provides technology and services that enable its clients to sell their products on the Web without building an e-commerce platform from the ground up. Using its own proprietary server technology Digital River offers Web development and hosting transaction processing fulfillment and fraud screening services to tens of thousands of customers operating online retail and distribution businesses. It also provides its customers with Web traffic data that allows them to better market their online presence. Digital River was established in 1994 and began offering online stores for its clients in 1996.

	Annual Growth	12/08	12/09	12/10	12/11	12/12
Sales ($ mil.)	(0.5%)	394.2	403.8	363.2	398.1	386.2
Net income ($ mil.)	–	63.6	49.8	15.7	17.2	(195.9)
Market value ($ mil.)	(12.7%)	876.9	954.4	1,217.1	531.1	508.5
Employees	2.5%	1,335	1,239	1,280	1,419	1,473

DIGITAL TURBINE INC
NAS: APPS

110 San Antonio Street, Suite 160
Austin, TX 78701
Phone: 512 387-7717
Fax: –
Web: www.digitalturbine.com

CEO: William Stone
CFO: Barrett Garrison
HR: April Collazo
FYE: March 31
Type: Public

When it comes to mobile digital content Digital Turbine (formerly Mandalay Digital) doesn't play games (but it does make them). Through its Twistbox and AMV subsidiaries the company develops content for 3G mobile phones including games images chat services and other products. Its content is targeted to users aged 18 to 40 and covers a variety of themes including mature entertainment. The company distributes its products in 40 European North American Latin American and Asian countries through agreements with major mobile phone operators including Verizon Virgin Mobile T-Mobile and Vodafone.

	Annual Growth	03/17	03/18	03/19	03/20	03/21
Sales ($ mil.)	36.0%	91.6	74.8	103.6	138.7	313.6
Net income ($ mil.)	–	(24.3)	(52.9)	(6.0)	13.9	54.9
Market value ($ mil.)	204.0%	84.6	180.8	314.8	387.7	7,228.4
Employees	17.7%	146	161	161	207	280

DIGITALGLOBE INC
NYS: DGI

1300 West 120th Avenue
Westminster, CO 80234
Phone: 303 684-4000
Fax: –
Web: www.digitalglobe.com

CEO: –
CFO: –
HR: –
FYE: December 31
Type: Public

Look up and smile. DigitalGlobe might be capturing an image of you — and the rest of the planet. From its array of satellites the company captures imagery used for a variety of applications including mapping urban planning oil exploration land management disaster assessment and humanitarian relief. DigitalGlobe's products include standard images panchromatic images multispectral images and color infrared images as well as mosaics and digital elevation models. About 60% of its revenues come from the US government; commercial customers include oil and gas exploration companies and GPS navigation system makers. DigitalGlobe's images and services are incorporated into popular mapping applications such as Google Maps and Microsoft Virtual Earth as well as into GPS systems from DeLorme and Garmin.

	Annual Growth	12/11	12/12	12/13	12/14	12/15
Sales ($ mil.)	19.9%	339.5	421.4	612.7	654.6	702.4
Net income ($ mil.)	–	(28.1)	39.0	(68.3)	18.5	23.3
Market value ($ mil.)	(2.2%)	1,153.2	1,647.3	2,773.5	2,087.4	1,055.5
Employees	13.8%	708	749	1,235	1,339	1,189

DIGITAS INC.

33 Arch St.
Boston MA 02110
Phone: 617-867-1000
Fax: 617-867-1111
Web: www.digitasinc.com

CEO: –
CFO: Joseph Tomasulu
HR: –
FYE: December 31
Type: Subsidiary

This company knows the important bits (and bytes) about interactive marketing. Digitas provides digital communications and direct marketing services through several operating agencies: Digitas Health Prodigious Solutions Digitas and Publicis Modem (formerly Modem Media). Operating from about 30 offices spanning 16 countries the agency offers website design e-mail management and demand generation services which enable clients to build marketing campaigns across a plethora of media channels. It has worked with such big clients as American Express Kraft General Motors and MillerCoors. Digitas is a part of VivaKi an advertising and marketing communications division of Publicis.

DIGNITY HEALTH

185 BERRY ST STE 200
SAN FRANCISCO, CA 941071777
Phone: 415-438-5500
Fax: –
Web: www.dignityhealth.org

CEO: Lloyd Dean
CFO: Michael Blaszyk
HR: –
FYE: June 30
Type: Private

Dignity Health is the largest hospital provider in California and the fifth largest health system in the US. The not-for-profit health care provider operates a network of more than 400 care centers including nearly 40 hospitals urgent and occupational care imaging and surgery centers home health and primary care clinics in more than 20 states. Dignity Health is the official health care provider of the San Francisco Giants. With more than 60000 caregivers and staff who deliver excellent care to diverse communities the company has more than 10000 active physicians.

	Annual Growth	06/06	06/07	06/08	06/09	06/19
Sales ($ mil.)	1.0%	–	–	–	8,957.9	9,916.6
Net income ($ mil.)	–	–	–	–	(799.1)	119.3
Market value ($ mil.)	–	–	–	–	–	–
Employees	–	–	–	–	–	55,494

DILLARD'S INC.
NYS: DDS

1600 Cantrell Road
Little Rock, AR 72201
Phone: 501 376-5200
Fax: –
Web: www.dillards.com

CEO: William Dillard
CFO: Chris B Johnson
HR: –
FYE: January 30
Type: Public

Dillard's Inc. is one of the nation's largest fashion apparel cosmetics and home furnishing retailers that operates more than 280 locations in about 30 US states. It also operates about 30 clearance centers and an Internet store that offers a wide selection of merchandise including fashion apparel for women men and children accessories cosmetics home furnishings and other consumer goods. Dillard's exclusive brand merchandise includes Antonio Melani Gianni Bini GB Roundtree & Yorke and Daniel Cremieux. The company also operates a general contracting construction company CDI Contractors a portion of whose business includes constructing and remodeling stores for the company. Founded in 1938 by William Dillard family members through the W. D. Company control the company.

	Annual Growth	01/17*	02/18	02/19	02/20*	01/21
Sales ($ mil.)	(8.8%)	6,418.0	6,422.7	6,503.3	6,343.2	4,433.2
Net income ($ mil.)	–	169.2	221.3	170.3	111.1	(71.7)
Market value ($ mil.)	12.6%	1,203.1	1,401.9	1,444.4	1,336.8	1,933.2
Employees	(7.7%)	40,000	40,000	39,000	38,000	29,000

*Fiscal year change

DILLON COMPANIES INC.

2700 E. 4th Ave.
Hutchinson KS 67504-1608
Phone: 620-665-5511
Fax: 620-669-3160
Web: www.dillons.com

CEO: –
CFO: –
HR: Frank J Remar
FYE: January 31
Type: Subsidiary

Dillon Companies which began as J.S. Dillon and Sons Stores has been selling bread to America's breadbasket bread since 1921. The regional supermarket operator has more than 200 combination food and drug stores under several banners; Dillons and Dillons Marketplace stores in Kansas; Baker's Supermarkets and Food-4-Less in Nebraska; Gerbes in Missouri; and City Market and King Soopers in Colorado. In addition to traditional supermarket fare Dillon's supermarkets have in-store pharmacies and many sell gas in the parking lot. Dillon Companies is losing market share to discounters including Wal-Mart Supercenters which has surpassed Dillon's parent company Kroger to become the #1 seller of groceries in the US.

DIME COMMUNITY BANCSHARES INC (NEW) — NMS: DCOM

898 Veterans Memorial Highway, Suite 560
Hauppauge, NY 11788
Phone: 631 537-1000
Fax: -
Web: www.bridgenb.com

CEO: Kevin O'connor
CFO: Avinash Reddy
HR: -
FYE: December 31
Type: Public

The Bridgehampton National Bank which operates 40 branches on primary market areas of Suffolk and Nassau Counties on Long Island and the New York City boroughs. Founded in 1910 the bank offers traditional deposit services to area individuals small businesses and municipalities including savings money market accounts and CDs. Deposits are invested primarily in mortgages which account for some 80% of the bank's loan portfolio. Title insurance services are available through bank subsidiary Bridge Abstract. In addition it offers merchant credit and debit card ATMs cash management services and individual retirement accounts through Bridge Financial Services LLC. Bridge Bancorp bought Hamptons State Bank in 2011 to fortify its presence on Long Island.

	Annual Growth	12/16	12/17	12/18	12/19	12/20
Assets ($ mil.)	12.2%	4,054.6	4,430.0	4,700.7	4,921.5	6,434.3
Net income ($ mil.)	4.3%	35.5	20.5	39.2	51.7	42.0
Market value ($ mil.)	(10.6%)	748.3	691.0	503.3	662.0	477.4
Employees	1.3%	477	480	473	496	502

DIME COMMUNITY BANCSHARES, INC — NMS: DCOM

300 Cadman Plaza West, 8th Floor
Brooklyn, NY 11201
Phone: 718 782-6200
Fax: -
Web: www.dime.com

CEO: -
CFO: -
HR: -
FYE: December 31
Type: Public

Dime Community Bancshares is in a New York state of mind. It is the holding company for Dime Community Bank (formerly The Dime Savings Bank of Williamsburgh) which boasts $4.5 billion in assets and operates more than 25 branches in Brooklyn Queens and the Bronx as well as Nassau County on Long Island. Founded in 1864 the bank provides standard products and services including checking savings retirement money market and club accounts accounts. Multifamily residential and commercial real estate loans comprise the vast majority of the bank's loan portfolio. Subsidiary Dime Insurance Agency (formerly Havemeyer Investments) offers life policies fixed annuities and wealth management services.

	Annual Growth	12/14	12/15	12/16	12/17	12/18
Assets ($ mil.)	8.9%	4,497.1	5,032.9	6,005.4	6,403.5	6,320.6
Net income ($ mil.)	3.8%	44.2	44.8	72.5	51.9	51.3
Market value ($ mil.)	1.1%	587.4	631.1	725.2	755.9	612.7
Employees	2.0%	409	388	386	421	443

DIMENSIONS HEALTH CORPORATION

901 HARRY S TRUMAN DR N
LARGO, MD 207745477
Phone: 301-618-2000
Fax: -
Web: www.umms.org

CEO: Nathaniel Richardson Jr
CFO: -
HR: -
FYE: June 30
Type: Private

Dimensions Healthcare System takes care of the many many facets of a human's dimensions. Dimensions Healthcare System operates a handful of medical facilities serving the residents in Prince George's County Maryland and the surrounding area. Acute care centers include Prince George's Hospital Center and Laurel Regional Hospital. Specialty services include rehabilitation behavioral health cardiology emergency medicine senior care pediatrics and a sleep disorders center. The not-for-profit health care system was established in 1982.

	Annual Growth	06/03	06/04	06/05	06/06	06/21
Sales ($ mil.)	32.7%	-	3.1	338.3	367.0	386.9
Net income ($ mil.)	-	-	0.0	3.9	17.7	(29.0)
Market value ($ mil.)	-	-	-	-	-	-
Employees	-	-	-	-	-	2,800

DIMEO CONSTRUCTION COMPANY

75 CHAPMAN ST
PROVIDENCE, RI 029055496
Phone: 401-781-9800
Fax: -
Web: www.dimeo.com

CEO: -
CFO: Steven B Avery
HR: -
FYE: June 30
Type: Private

Dimeo Construction has built a reputation in New England. The company provides general contracting design/build and construction management services ranging from pre-planning to post-construction commissioning. It focuses on projects in the corporate academic health care life sciences/R&D public commercial and residential markets working on schools hospitals corporate headquarters research and development facilities and shopping centers for clients including University of Rhode Island National Elevator Industry Educational Program and Washington Village. It also has worked on renovation projects such as Hasbro Children's Hospital Underway and Yale University ? Swartwout & Street Halls. Founded in 1930 the employee-owned firm is still run by the Dimeo family.

	Annual Growth	06/07	06/08	06/09	06/10	06/11
Sales ($ mil.)	(27.2%)	-	-	567.8	356.1	300.9
Net income ($ mil.)	5.5%	-	-	8.4	9.6	9.3
Market value ($ mil.)	-	-	-	-	-	-
Employees	-	-	-	-	-	300

DINE BRANDS GLOBAL INC — NYS: DIN

450 North Brand Boulevard
Glendale, CA 91203-1903
Phone: 818 240-6055
Fax: -
Web: www.dinebrands.com

CEO: John Peyton
CFO: Vance Chang
HR: -
FYE: December 31
Type: Public

Dine Brands Global is one of the leading chain restaurant companies in the US with two flagship concepts IHOP (the International House of Pancakes) and Applebee's Neighborhood Grill + Bar. IHOP has about 1770 mostly franchised restaurants that are open 24 hours a day. The chain is best known for its breakfast menu but it also offers standard family fare for lunch and dinner. One of the world's largest casual dining brands Applebee's has more than 1640 locations in the US and more than 10 other countries offering a wide variety of appetizers and entrees.

	Annual Growth	12/16	12/17	12/18	12/19	12/20
Sales ($ mil.)	2.1%	634.0	604.8	780.9	910.2	689.3
Net income ($ mil.)	-	98.0	(330.5)	80.4	104.3	(104.0)
Market value ($ mil.)	(6.8%)	1,266.8	834.6	1,107.9	1,374.1	954.2
Employees	37.7%	960	520	3,300	3,560	3,447

DIODES, INC. — NMS: DIOD

4949 Hedgcoxe Road, Suite 200
Plano, TX 75024
Phone: 972 987-3900
Fax: -
Web: www.diodes.com

CEO: Keh-Shew Lu
CFO: Brett Whitmire
HR: -
FYE: December 31
Type: Public

Diodes Incorporated (also known as Diodes) knows how important it is to be discrete in business. The company makes discrete semiconductors — fixed-function devices that are much less complex than integrated circuits. Diodes' products include diodes transistors amplifiers comparators and rectifiers; they are used by computer and consumer electronics manufacturers in products such as notebooks LCD monitors smartphones and game consoles. Other applications include power supplies climate control systems GPS devices and networking gear. The company's products are sold throughout Asia (accounts for some 80% of sales; the largest among its geographic regions) Europe and the Americas.

	Annual Growth	12/17	12/18	12/19	12/20	12/21
Sales ($ mil.)	14.4%	1,054.2	1,214.0	1,249.1	1,229.2	1,805.2
Net income ($ mil.)	-	(1.8)	104.0	153.3	98.1	228.8
Market value ($ mil.)	39.9%	1,290.7	1,452.3	2,537.7	3,173.8	4,943.4
Employees	1.0%	8,586	7,710	7,271	8,939	8,921

DIONEX CORPORATION

1228 Titan Way
Sunnyvale CA 94085-3603
Phone: 408-737-0700
Fax: 408-730-9403
Web: www.dionex.com

CEO: Mark Casper
CFO: Craig A McCollam
HR: –
FYE: June 30
Type: Subsidiary

Dionex's instruments keep the contaminants away while scientists play. The company makes instruments used for substance analysis including identifying contaminants in everything from drinking water to industrial chemicals. Dionex is a leading maker of ion chromatography instruments devices used by chemists to isolate and quantify charged molecules in complex chemical mixtures. It also makes high-performance liquid chromatography (used to separate and identify biological molecules such as amino acids carbohydrates and proteins) sample extraction and sample handling equipment. It gets about 70% of its sales outside the US. In 2011 rival Thermo Fisher bought Dionex for $2.1 billion.

DIRECT RELIEF

6100 WALLACE BECKNELL RD
SANTA BARBARA, CA 931173265
Phone: 805-964-4767
Fax: –
Web: www.directrelief.org

CEO: Thomas Tighe
CFO: Bhupi Singh
HR: –
FYE: June 30
Type: Private

Direct Relief International wants to relieve the health problems of people around the world. The not-for-profit organization is dedicated to providing health care support and emergency relief to people in developing countries as well as victims of disasters and war. Active in 50 US states and 70 countries it gives medicine supplies and equipment through partnerships with local groups that make specific requests and coordinates distribution. The group also has partnered with nonprofit clinics and community health centers to provide medical care and medicine for homeless and low-income people in California. Direct Relief was founded in 1948 by Estonian immigrant William Zimdin.

	Annual Growth	06/08	06/09	06/11	06/12	06/17
Sales ($ mil.)	–	–	(1,554.6)	405.0	299.7	1,114.3
Net income ($ mil.)	200.1%	–	0.0	95.6	(17.9)	105.3
Market value ($ mil.)	–	–	–	–	–	–
Employees	–	–	–	–	–	2

DIRECTV   NMS: DTV

2260 East Imperial Highway
El Segundo, CA 90245
Phone: 310 964-5000
Fax: –
Web: www.directv.com

CEO: Michael White
CFO: Patrick Doyle
HR: –
FYE: December 31
Type: Public

DIRECTV takes television straight to the masses. The company operates the largest direct-to-home (DTH) digital TV service in the US ahead of #3 DISH Network and in direct competition with cable providers Comcast (#1 overall in the pay-TV market) and Time Warner. In addition to its roughly 20 million US customers the company counts about another 18 million subscribers in Latin America under the DIRECTV and SKY brands. Services include HD 3D and video-on-demand (VOD) programming. Phone companies such as Verizon and AT&T bundle the company's video services with their own traditional voice digital telephone and Internet packages. In 2014 DIRECTV and AT&T agreed to take their relationship a big step further. A deal for AT&T to buy DIRECTV is awaiting regulatory approval.

	Annual Growth	12/09	12/10	12/11	12/12	12/13
Sales ($ mil.)	10.2%	21,565.0	24,102.0	27,226.0	29,740.0	31,754.0
Net income ($ mil.)	32.0%	942.0	2,198.0	2,609.0	2,949.0	2,859.0
Market value ($ mil.)	20.0%	17,318.9	20,735.9	22,205.5	26,048.4	35,863.3
Employees	8.0%	23,300	25,100	26,800	29,700	31,700

DISABLED AMERICAN VETERANS

860 DOLWICK DR
ERLANGER, KY 410182774
Phone: 859-441-7300
Fax: –
Web: www.dav.org

CEO: J Marc Burgess
CFO: –
HR: –
FYE: December 31
Type: Private

Disabled American Veterans (DAV) helps ex-military men and women fight personal battles. The nonprofit group strives to improve the quality of life for some 200000 wounded veterans and their families by helping them navigate the US Department of Veterans Affairs system to obtain benefits. DAV also represents the political interests of veterans and provides various outreach and volunteer programs. The group which generates most of its revenue from tax-exempt contributions has about 1.2 million members and boasts some 110 offices in the US and Puerto Rico. DAV was formed in 1920 and chartered by Congress in 1932. The organization has partnered with large corporations to help veterans get assistance.

	Annual Growth	12/13	12/14	12/16	12/17	12/19
Sales ($ mil.)	(5.9%)	–	196.9	134.9	137.1	145.4
Net income ($ mil.)	–	–	–	(2.0)	(11.8)	(6.8)	1.4
Market value ($ mil.)	–	–	–	–	–	–
Employees	–	–	–	–	–	630

DISCOVER FINANCIAL SERVICES   NYS: DFS

2500 Lake Cook Road
Riverwoods, IL 60015
Phone: 224 405-0900
Fax: –
Web: www.discover.com

CEO: Roger Hochschild
CFO: John Greene
HR: –
FYE: December 31
Type: Public

Discover Financial Services is best known for issuing Discover-brand credit cards. The company provides digital banking products and services and payment services through their subsidiaries. It offers credit card loans private student loans personal loans home equity loans and deposit products. Discover also licenses Diners Club which processes transactions for Discover-branded credit and debit cards provides payment transaction processing and settlement services. The company also runs the PULSE Network ATM system an electronic funds transfer network providing financial institutions issuing debit cards on the PULSE network with access to ATMs domestically and internationally as well as merchant acceptance throughout the United States for debit card transactions. It was incorporated in Delaware in 1960.

	Annual Growth	12/16	12/17	12/18	12/19	12/20
Assets ($ mil.)	5.2%	92,308.0	100,087.0	109,553.0	113,996.0	112,889.0
Net income ($ mil.)	(16.9%)	2,393.0	2,099.0	2,742.0	2,957.0	1,141.0
Market value ($ mil.)	5.9%	22,102.6	23,583.5	18,083.1	26,005.6	27,756.3
Employees	3.1%	15,549	16,500	16,600	17,200	17,600

DISCOVERY INC   NMS: DISC A

230 Park Avenue South
New York, NY 10003
Phone: 212 548-5555
Fax: –
Web: www.discoverycommunications.com

CEO: Jean-Briac Perrette
CFO: –
HR: –
FYE: December 31
Type: Public

Discovery is a global media company that provides content across multiple distribution platforms including linear platforms such as pay-television (pay-TV) free-to-air (FTA) and broadcast television authenticated GO applications digital distribution arrangements content licensing arrangements and direct-to-consumer (DTC) subscription products. The company is one of the world's largest pay-TV programmers that provides original and purchased content and live events to almost 4 billion subscribers and viewers worldwide through networks that it wholly or partially owns. Properties include the Discovery Channel HGTV Food Network TLC Animal Planet Investigation Discovery Travel Channel Science Channel MotorTrend (previously known as Velocity domestically and currently known as Turbo in most international countries) and OWN. Discovery also operates stream mobile devices video on demand ("VOD") and broadband channels..

	Annual Growth	12/16	12/17	12/18	12/19	12/20
Sales ($ mil.)	13.2%	6,497.0	6,873.0	10,553.0	11,144.0	10,671.0
Net income ($ mil.)	0.5%	1,194.0	(337.0)	594.0	2,069.0	1,219.0
Market value ($ mil.)	2.4%	13,348.7	10,899.1	12,048.4	15,944.4	14,653.8
Employees	8.8%	7,000	7,000	9,000	9,200	9,800

DISH NETWORK CORP
NMS: DISH

9601 South Meridian Boulevard
Englewood, CO 80112
Phone: 303 723-1000
Fax: 303 723-1499
Web: www.dishnetwork.com

CEO: W. Erik Carlson
CFO: Paul Orban
HR: –
FYE: December 31
Type: Public

The company is one of the biggest pay-TV providers in the US serving about 11 million household subscribers as well as hotels motels and other commercial accounts. Programming includes premium movies on-demand video service regional and specialty sports local and international channels and pay-per-view in addition to basic video programming. Its relatively Sling TV offering provides streaming video over the internet. DISH generates almost all sales in the US. As of December 31 2020 DISH had 9.055 million retail wireless subscribers.

	Annual Growth	12/16	12/17	12/18	12/19	12/20
Sales ($ mil.)	0.7%	15,094.6	14,391.4	13,621.3	12,807.7	15,493.4
Net income ($ mil.)	5.0%	1,449.9	2,098.7	1,575.1	1,399.5	1,762.7
Market value ($ mil.)	(13.6%)	30,480.2	25,124.0	13,138.1	18,662.8	17,015.9
Employees	(4.2%)	16,000	17,000	16,000	16,000	13,500

DISNEY (WALT) CO. (THE)
NYS: DIS

500 South Buena Vista Street
Burbank, CA 91521
Phone: 818 560-1000
Fax: –
Web: www.disney.com

CEO: –
CFO: –
HR: –
FYE: October 02
Type: Public

The monarch of this magic kingdom is no man but a mouse: Mickey Mouse. The Walt Disney Company is the world's largest media conglomerate with assets encompassing movies television publishing and theme parks. Its Disney/ABC Television Group includes the ABC television network and almost ten television stations as well as a portfolio of cable networks including ABC Family Disney Channel and ESPN (80%-owned). Walt Disney Studios produces films through imprints Walt Disney Pictures Disney Animation and Pixar. It also owns Marvel Entertainment and Lucasfilm two extremely successful film producers. In addition Walt Disney Parks and Resorts runs its popular theme parks including Walt Disney World and Disneyland.

	Annual Growth	09/17	09/18	09/19*	10/20	10/21
Sales ($ mil.)	5.2%	55,137.0	59,434.0	69,570.0	65,388.0	67,418.0
Net income ($ mil.)	(31.3%)	8,980.0	12,598.0	11,054.0	(2,864.0)	1,995.0
Market value ($ mil.)	15.6%	175,553.2	208,270.1	231,458.8	218,261.6	313,473.8
Employees	(1.2%)	199,000	201,000	223,000	203,000	190,000

*Fiscal year change

DITECH HOLDING CORPORATION

500 OFFICE CENTER DR # 400
FORT WASHINGTON, PA 190343219
Phone: 844-714-8603
Fax: –
Web: www.ditechholding.com

CEO: Thomas F Marano
CFO: Gerald A Lombardo
HR: –
FYE: December 31
Type: Private

Walter Investment Management does its best to collect from the credit-challenged. The firm owns and services residential mortgages (particularly those of the subprime and nonconforming variety) for itself as well as for government sponsored entities government agencies third-party securitization trusts and other credit owners. Operating through subsidiaries Walter Mortgage Company; Hanover Capital; Marix Servicing; Ditech; and third-party credit servicer Green Tree Walter Investment Management services 2 million residential loan accounts with unpaid balances of $256 billion making it one of the 10 largest mortgage servicers in the US. The firm also originates residential loans including reverse loans. The firm filed for Chapter 11 bankruptcy in 2017 and is expected to emerged from it less $800 million in debt overhang in early 2018.

	Annual Growth	12/14	12/15	12/16	12/17	12/18
Sales ($ mil.)	(19.7%)	–	1,274.3	995.7	831.3	658.9
Net income ($ mil.)	–	–	(263.2)	(529.2)	(426.9)	(205.1)
Market value ($ mil.)	–	–	–	–	–	–
Employees	–	–	–	–	–	3,800

DIVERSIFIED CHEMICAL TECHNOLOGIES, INC.

15477 WOODROW WILSON ST
DETROIT, MI 482381586
Phone: 313-867-5444
Fax: –

CEO: –
CFO: –
HR: –
FYE: January 28
Type: Private

True to its name Diversified Chemical Technologies manufactures a diverse range of specialty chemical products for a diverse range of customers. It serves a number of industries but is best known for its process and maintenance chemicals for metalworking and cleaning and sanitation chemicals for the food and beverage markets. Working through subsidiaries it produces various adhesives (hot melt pressure sensitive and water-based adhesives) polymeric materials (including PVC seals epoxies acrylics polyesters and polyurethanes) custom-formulated specialty products and recycled polymeric materials to make polyurethane foam for autos. It also offers office supplies through Detroit-based Paperworks.

	Annual Growth	01/07	01/08	01/09	01/10	01/11
Sales ($ mil.)	–	–	–	(373.9)	59.8	70.3
Net income ($ mil.)	33223.2%	–	–	0.0	1.0	7.1
Market value ($ mil.)	–	–	–	–	–	–
Employees	–	–	–	–	–	225

DIVERSIFIED HEALTHCARE TRUST
NMS: DHC

Two Newton Place, 255 Washington Street, Suite 300
Newton, MA 02458-1634
Phone: 617 796-8350
Fax: 617 796-8349
Web: www.dhcreit.com

CEO: –
CFO: Richard Siedel
HR: –
FYE: December 31
Type: Public

Diversified Healthcare Trust (formerly Senior Housing Properties Trust) offers those in their golden years a place to rest their weary bones. The real estate investment trust (REIT) owns some 425 health care-related properties in about 40 states and Washington DC. Its portfolio includes senior apartments independent and assisted living facilities nursing homes medical office buildings and gymnasiums. Tenants sign triple-net leases which require them not only to pay rent but to also pay operating expenses remove hazardous waste and carry insurance on their properties.

	Annual Growth	12/16	12/17	12/18	12/19	12/20
Sales ($ mil.)	11.4%	1,058.0	1,074.8	1,117.2	1,040.2	1,632.0
Net income ($ mil.)	–	141.3	147.6	286.9	(88.2)	(139.5)
Market value ($ mil.)	(31.7%)	4,510.4	4,562.8	2,792.5	2,011.0	981.7
Employees	–	–	–	–	–	–

DIVERSIFIED RESTAURANT HOLDINGS INC.
NAS: SAUC

5750 New King Drive, Suite 320
Troy, MI 48098-2634
Phone: 833 374-7282
Fax: 248 223-9165
Web: www.diversifiedrestaurantholdings.com

CEO: –
CFO: Toni Werner
HR: Krystal White
FYE: December 30
Type: Public

Diversified Restaurant Holdings owns and operates about 25 Buffalo Wild Wings Grill & Bar locations in Florida Illinois Indiana and Michigan. Franchised from Buffalo Wild Wings (BWW) the quick-casual eateries are popular for their Buffalo-style chicken wings served with a variety of dipping sauces. The restaurants also serve burgers sandwiches and tacos along with beer and other beverages. Many of the eateries are located near large suburban shopping and entertainment areas. Diversified Restaurant Holdings also operates its own dining concept Bagger Dave's Legendary Burgers and Fries an upscale hamburger joint with two locations in Michigan.

	Annual Growth	12/14	12/15	12/16	12/17	12/18
Sales ($ mil.)	4.5%	128.4	172.5	166.5	165.5	153.1
Net income ($ mil.)	–	(1.3)	(16.2)	(6.0)	(20.5)	(5.0)
Market value ($ mil.)	(33.2%)	165.7	86.7	46.8	53.1	32.9
Employees	–	–	–	–	–	–

DIXIE GAS AND OIL CORPORATION

229 LEE HWY
VERONA, VA 244822500
Phone: 540-438-9811
Fax: –
Web: www.dixiegas.com

CEO: –
CFO: –
HR: –
FYE: June 30
Type: Private

Far from looking away local petroleum retailers look to Dixie Gas & Oil a distributor of propane heating oil industrial lubricants and other petroleum products to customers in Virginia and West Virginia. The company also operates gas stations and convenience stores and provides fleeting fueling services. In addition to propane and petroleum Dixie Gas & Oil supplies CITGO- and Castrol-branded commercial and food grade lubricants; it also supplies some retailers with BP and Pure petroleum products. The company was founded as Dixie Bottled Gas Company in 1946. Dixie Gas & Oil's five gas stations/convenience stores offer BP fuels Subway sandwiches and salads as well as convenience food items.

	Annual Growth	06/10	06/11	06/12	06/13	06/14
Sales ($ mil.)	7.6%	–	56.0	62.1	70.6	69.8
Net income ($ mil.)	16.5%	–	–	0.3	0.5	0.4
Market value ($ mil.)	–	–	–	–	–	–
Employees	–	–	–	–	–	115

DIXIE GROUP INC.
NMS: DXYN

475 Reed Road
Dalton, GA 30720
Phone: 706 876-5800
Fax: –
Web: www.theDixieGroup.com

CEO: Daniel Frierson
CFO: Allen Danzey
HR: W. Derek Davis
FYE: December 26
Type: Public

The Dixie Group takes its business to the rug. Once a textile concern the company has evolved into a maker of tufted broadloom carpets and custom rugs and proprietary yarns used in manufacturing the soft floorcoverings. Its brands Dixie Home Masland Carpets Fabrica International and Candlewick Yarn are differentiated by product price and styling. Dixie markets and sells carpets to high-end residential customers including interior decorators retailers home builders and motorhome and yacht OEMs. Less so it supplies carpet for the specified (contract) market such as architectural and commercial customers as well as consumers through specialty floorcovering retailers.

	Annual Growth	12/16	12/17	12/18	12/19	12/20
Sales ($ mil.)	(5.6%)	397.5	412.5	405.0	374.6	315.9
Net income ($ mil.)	–	(5.3)	(9.6)	(21.4)	15.3	(9.2)
Market value ($ mil.)	(7.7%)	55.6	59.4	10.8	17.8	40.3
Employees	(4.7%)	1,746	1,930	1,646	1,526	1,441

DIXON TICONDEROGA COMPANY

615 CRESCENT EXECUTIVE CT # 500
LAKE MARY, FL 327465036
Phone: 407-829-9000
Fax: –
Web: www.dixonusa.com

CEO: James Schmitz
CFO: –
HR: Lillian Gonzalez
FYE: December 31
Type: Private

Dixon Ticonderoga is number one in No. 2 pencils. A top US maker of wood-cased graphite pencils (it developed the ubiquitous No. 2 pencil in 1913) the company also makes pencil grips Dixon markers Prang art materials a line of school supplies featuring Looney Tunes and Scooby Doo characters and general office supplies under the Ticonderoga Prang Dixon Oriole Das Maimeri and Lyra brands. In addition Dixon Ticonderoga offers advertising specialty pencils crayons markers and pens. Customers include major discounters like Wal-Mart office products superstores (Office Depot and Staples) and supermarkets (Publix). Dixon Ticonderoga is owned by FILA S.p.A. of Milan Italy.

	Annual Growth	12/06	12/07	12/08	12/09	12/12
Sales ($ mil.)	13.2%	–	–	–	52.1	75.7
Net income ($ mil.)	(8.0%)	–	–	–	9.9	7.7
Market value ($ mil.)	–	–	–	–	–	–
Employees	–	–	–	–	–	100

DLH HOLDINGS CORP
NAS: DLHC

3565 Piedmont Road, Building 3, Suite 700
Atlanta, GA 30305
Phone: 770 554-3545
Fax: –
Web: www.dlhcorp.com

CEO: Zachary Parker
CFO: Kathryn JohnBull
HR: G. Maliek Ferebee
FYE: September 30
Type: Public

Dlh Holdings provides temporary and permanent medical office administration and technical staffing services to US government facilities nationwide. Its services on behalf of government agencies include case management healthcare IT systems and tools physical and behavioral health examinations; health and nutritional support for children and adults biological research disaster and emergency response staffing among others. The company has contracts with the Department of Defense Health and Human Services and Veterans Affairs. It traces its roots back to 1969.

	Annual Growth	09/17	09/18	09/19	09/20	09/21
Sales ($ mil.)	20.8%	115.7	133.2	160.4	209.2	246.1
Net income ($ mil.)	32.5%	3.3	1.8	5.3	7.1	10.1
Market value ($ mil.)	17.4%	82.4	73.2	56.7	92.2	156.4
Employees	13.2%	1,400	1,500	1,900	2,200	2,300

DLT SOLUTIONS LLC

13861 SUNRISE VALLEY DR # 400
HERNDON, VA 20171-6124
Phone: 703-709-7172
Fax: –
Web: www.dlt.com

CEO: Art Richer
CFO: Joe Donohue
HR: –
FYE: December 31
Type: Private

DLT Solutions is a middleman for G-men. The company resells IT products and services primarily to local state and federal government clients in the US. The company sells and integrates hardware and software from such vendors as Autodesk Oracle NetApp Red Hat and Symantec. DLT's contracts are primarily with the US Department of Defense's Enterprise Software Initiative (ESI) and the US Navy. It also has more than a dozen other contracts with state and city governments. To a smaller extent it offers consulting network design application development training and other professional services. The company's areas of expertise include cloud computing data center consolidation cybersecurity and computer-aided design.

	Annual Growth	12/07	12/08	12/09	12/10	12/11
Sales ($ mil.)	9.3%	–	271.7	–	447.7	354.5
Net income ($ mil.)	18.8%	–	8.7	–	13.0	14.5
Market value ($ mil.)	–	–	–	–	–	–
Employees	–	–	–	–	–	253

DMC GLOBAL INC
NMS: BOOM

11800 Ridge Parkway, Suite 300
Broomfield, CO 80021
Phone: 303 665-5700
Fax: –
Web: www.dmcglobal.com

CEO: Kevin Longe
CFO: Michael Kuta
HR: –
FYE: December 31
Type: Public

Dynamic Materials Corporation (DMC) has an explosive personality when it comes to working with metal. Formerly Explosive Fabricators the company uses explosives to metallurgically bond or "clad" metal plates; the process usually joins a corrosion-resistant alloy with carbon steel — metals that do not bond easily. Its clad metal plates are central to making heavy-duty pressure vessels and heat exchangers used in such industries as alternative energy and shipbuilding. Its Oilfield Products segment (operating as DYNAenergetics) makes explosive devices used to knock open oil and gas wells. Its AMK Welding unit machines and welds parts for commercial and military aircraft engines and power-generation turbines.

	Annual Growth	12/16	12/17	12/18	12/19	12/20
Sales ($ mil.)	9.6%	158.6	192.8	326.4	397.6	229.2
Net income ($ mil.)	–	(6.5)	(18.9)	30.5	34.0	(1.4)
Market value ($ mil.)	28.5%	243.9	385.5	540.5	691.6	665.6
Employees	5.5%	428	536	665	741	531

DNB FINANCIAL CORP.

NAS: DNBF

4 Brandywine Avenue
Downingtown, PA 19335
Phone: 610 269-1040
Fax: –
Web: www.dnbfirst.com

CEO: –
CFO: –
HR: –
FYE: December 31
Type: Public

DNB Financial Corporation is the holding company for DNB First a bank with about 15 branches in Chester and Delaware counties in southeastern Pennsylvania. Founded in 1861 the bank serves area consumers but mainly lends to small and midsized businesses with mortgages secured by commercial property (approximately 35% of its loan portfolio) commercial operating loans (more than 25%) and equipment leases representing most of its financing activity. The bank also writes residential mortgages and consumer loans. Deposit products include checking savings and money market accounts.

	Annual Growth	12/13	12/14	12/15	12/16	12/17
Assets ($ mil.)	13.1%	661.5	723.3	748.8	1,070.7	1,081.9
Net income ($ mil.)	19.3%	3.9	4.8	5.1	5.0	7.9
Market value ($ mil.)	12.9%	88.9	92.6	126.4	121.7	144.4
Employees	7.1%	139	133	129	166	183

DO IT BEST CORP.

6502 NELSON RD
FORT WAYNE, IN 468031947
Phone: 260-748-5300
Fax: –
Web: www.doitbestonline.com

CEO: Dan Starr
CFO: –
HR: –
FYE: June 25
Type: Private

Founded in 1945 Do it Best Corp. is a member-owned wholesaler of hardware lumber builder supplies and related products operating as a wholesaler cooperative. Besides the usual tools and building materials merchandise includes automotive items bicycles camping gear housewares office supplies and small appliances. Customers also can have products specially shipped to their local stores through Do it Best's e-commerce site. The co-op's buying power enables members to offer items at competitive prices.

	Annual Growth	06/08	06/09	06/10	06/11	06/16
Sales ($ mil.)	4.1%	–	–	2,296.1	2,328.6	2,925.9
Net income ($ mil.)	(5.7%)	–	–	1.0	0.5	0.7
Market value ($ mil.)	–	–	–	–	–	–
Employees	–	–	–	–	–	1,519

DOALL COMPANY

1480 S. Wolf Rd.
Wheeling IL 60090
Phone: 847-495-6800
Fax: 203-595-3070
Web: www.cenveo.com

CEO: –
CFO: –
HR: –
FYE: May 31
Type: Private

DoALL wants to be the end-all and be-all of metal cutting. For more than eight decades it has engineered and manufactured saw machinery and accessories and distributed industrial products. Its four businesses include DoALL Sawing which makes saw blades sawing machines and cutting oils; Greenlee Diamond Tool makes diamond and superabrasive products; Continental Hydraulics makes hydraulic pumps valves and power units; and DGI Supply distributes 1500 industrial brands through a national network of more than 40 supply centers. DoALL is owned by the Wilkie family who founded it in 1927.

DOC'S DRUGS, LTD.

455 E REED ST
BRAIDWOOD, IL 604082090
Phone: 815-458-6104
Fax: –
Web: www.docsdrugs.com

CEO: –
CFO: –
HR: –
FYE: October 31
Type: Private

After visiting the doc customers in northeastern Illinois can fill their prescriptions at Doc's Drugs. The regional drugstore chain operates more than 15 pharmacies under the Doc's Discount Drugs banner. In addition to dispensing prescription medications Doc's Drugs sells medical equipment collectibles electronics and toys as well as offering in-store photo processing. Doc's Drugs also sells more than 100 products online. The company is remodeling many of its stores to focus on its pharmacy operation which accounts for 80% of sales. To that end it is eliminating hardware liquor and groceries from its shelves. Doc's Drugs was founded by Dave Sartoris who runs the company with his son Tony.

	Annual Growth	10/11	10/12	10/13	10/14	10/15
Sales ($ mil.)	6.9%	–	60.1	60.8	65.7	73.4
Net income ($ mil.)	17.3%	–	0.3	0.8	0.8	0.6
Market value ($ mil.)	–	–	–	–	–	–
Employees	–	–	–	–	–	210

DOCTOR'S ASSOCIATES INC.

325 SUB WAY
MILFORD, CT 064613081
Phone: 203-877-4281
Fax: –
Web: www.subway.com

CEO: –
CFO: –
HR: –
FYE: December 31
Type: Private

Doctor's Associates owns the Subway chain of sandwich shops the world's largest quick-service restaurant chain by number of locations surpassing burger giant McDonald's. The company boasts more than 44000 restaurants in greater than 110 countries. Virtually all Subway restaurants are franchised and offer such fare as hot and cold sub sandwiches turkey wraps and salads. The widely recognized eateries are in freestanding buildings as well as in airports convenience stores sports facilities and other locations.

	Annual Growth	12/05	12/06	12/07	12/08	12/10
Sales ($ mil.)	10.4%	–	–	780.5	926.6	1,049.5
Net income ($ mil.)	9.8%	–	–	5.6	6.3	7.5
Market value ($ mil.)	–	–	–	–	–	–
Employees	–	–	–	–	–	650

DOCTORS HOSPITAL OF AUGUSTA, LLC

3651 WHEELER RD
AUGUSTA, GA 309096426
Phone: 706-651-3232
Fax: –
Web: www.doctors-hospital.net

CEO: Doug Welch
CFO: –
HR: Frances Lester
FYE: March 31
Type: Private

Doctors Hospital of Augusta serves up physician care in eastern Georgia and western South Carolina. The general and acute health care facility has more than 350 beds and is part of hospital giant HCA. Its specialty units include the Joseph M. Still Advanced Wound and Burn Clinic and the Healthy Living Center. In addition the hospital offers centers for cardiopulmonary health digestive diseases occupational medicine orthopedics cancer care sleep disorders stroke care surgery and women's health. Doctors Hospital of Augusta also operates freestanding surgical centers diagnostic imaging centers and Human Motion Institute rehabilitation clinics.

	Annual Growth	12/00	12/01	12/02*	03/09	03/17
Sales ($ mil.)	–	–	(1,254.6)	162.8	271.6	392.9
Net income ($ mil.)	66.8%	–	0.0	28.1	89.6	121.9
Market value ($ mil.)	–	–	–	–	–	–
Employees	–	–	–	–	–	1,300

*Fiscal year change

DOCTORS' HOSPITAL, INC.

8118 GOOD LUCK RD
LANHAM, MD 207063574
Phone: 301-552-8118
Fax: –
Web: www.dchweb.org

CEO: Philip B Down
CFO: –
HR: –
FYE: June 30
Type: Private

Doctors Community Hospital is an acute care and surgical hospital serving the Washington DC area. The not-for-profit medical center admits 12000 patients each year and has some 220 beds and offers standard and specialty services such as diagnostics emergency and cardiac care diagnostics rehabilitation wound care and neurology. The hospital which has some 600 doctors on staff also includes a women's health center a sleep therapy division and the Joslin Diabetes Center. Established in 1975 Doctors Community Hospital provides community health services such as educational programs and support groups for specific medical conditions.

	Annual Growth	06/12	06/13	06/14	06/15	06/19
Sales ($ mil.)	5.5%	–	181.6	188.2	197.2	250.1
Net income ($ mil.)	37.5%	–	1.3	2.2	7.7	8.7
Market value ($ mil.)	–	–	–	–	–	–
Employees	–	–	–	–	–	1,509

DOCUMENT CAPTURE TECHNOLOGIES INC   NBB: DCMT

4255 Burton Drive
San Jose, CA 95054
Phone: 408 436-9888
Fax: –
Web: www.docucap.com

CEO: –
CFO: –
HR: –
FYE: December 31
Type: Public

Like The Lorax Document Capture Technologies speaks for the trees. The company makes digital scanners used to upload paper documents into electronic data. Its line of USB-powered portable image scanners sold under the TravelScan and DocketPORT brand names are used in bank note and check verification devices ID card and passport scanners barcode scanners and business card readers. A handful of customers including Brother Industries NCR and Newell Rubbermaid account for more than half of sales. Subsidiary Syscan Inc. develops contact image sensor (CIS) modules used in fax machines and scanners. Investor Richard Dietl owns more than 35% of the company; Hong Kong-based Syscan Imaging Ltd. holds around 15%.

	Annual Growth	12/08	12/09	12/10	12/11	12/12
Sales ($ mil.)	10.5%	11.6	11.5	14.8	17.7	17.3
Net income ($ mil.)	–	(0.1)	(0.3)	0.3	(0.4)	(0.7)
Market value ($ mil.)	(22.3%)	10.4	7.1	11.9	8.6	3.8
Employees	16.9%	15	22	25	30	28

DOLAN COMPANY (THE)   NBB: DOLN

222 South Ninth Street, Suite 2300
Minneapolis, MN 55402
Phone: 612 317-9420
Fax: –
Web: www.thedolancompany.com

CEO: Mark McEachen
CFO: Vicki J Duncomb
HR: –
FYE: December 31
Type: Public

Helping law firms is a big part of the process for this publisher. Formerly Dolan Media Company The Dolan Company is a diversified professional services provider with a significant interest in local business news publishing. Through subsidiary National Default Exchange (NDeX) the company offers mortgage default processing services to lenders loan servicers and law firms around the country. Dolan's Counsel Press and DiscoverReady units provide services for law firms including outsourced document management to support litigation discovery. The company changed its name in 2010 to reflect its focus on providing diversified professional services.

	Annual Growth	12/08	12/09	12/10	12/11	12/12
Sales ($ mil.)	7.6%	189.9	262.9	311.3	285.6	254.3
Net income ($ mil.)	–	14.3	30.8	32.4	19.5	(101.8)
Market value ($ mil.)	(12.4%)	204.0	316.1	430.9	263.7	120.4
Employees	(1.5%)	1,812	1,903	2,034	2,006	1,708

DOLBY LABORATORIES INC   NYS: DLB

1275 Market Street
San Francisco, CA 94103-1410
Phone: 415 558-0200
Fax: –
Web: www.dolby.com

CEO: Kevin Yeaman
CFO: Robert Park
HR: –
FYE: September 24
Type: Public

Dolby Laboratories (Dolby) is the market leader in developing sound processing and noise reduction systems for use in professional and consumer audio and video equipment. Though it does make some of its own products Dolby mostly licenses its technology to other manufacturers. The company has approximately 15500 issued patents and approximately 1400 trademarks worldwide. In film the Dolby Digital format has become the de facto audio standard. Its systems equip movie screens around the globe. American engineer and physicist Ray Dolby and his family own the more than 55-year-old company. The company generates most of its sales internationally.

	Annual Growth	09/17	09/18	09/19	09/20	09/21
Sales ($ mil.)	4.3%	1,081.5	1,171.9	1,241.6	1,161.8	1,281.3
Net income ($ mil.)	11.3%	201.8	122.2	255.2	231.4	310.2
Market value ($ mil.)	12.6%	5,813.7	7,072.1	6,447.5	6,568.7	9,346.2
Employees	2.8%	2,122	2,151	2,193	2,289	2,368

DOLLAR BANK FSB

3 Gateway Center
Pittsburgh PA 15222
Phone: 412-261-4900
Fax: 412-261-7567
Web: www.dollarbank.com

CEO: Robert Oeler
CFO: Jerry Ritzert
HR: –
FYE: December 31
Type: Private

Founded in 1855 Dollar Bank serves business and retail customers from more than 60 branches and loan offices in the Pittsburgh and Cleveland metropolitan areas. Serving consumers and small business clients the bank offers standard products such as checking and savings accounts CDs mortgages and loans. Dollar Bank also performs private banking corporate banking and correspondent banking services. In addition it offers payment protection insurance and mortgage life/disability coverage; subsidiary Dollar Bank Insurance Agency sells term life insurance.

DOLLAR GENERAL CORP   NYS: DG

100 Mission Ridge
Goodlettsville, TN 37072
Phone: 615 855-4000
Fax: 615 855-5527
Web: www.dollargeneral.com

CEO: Todd Vasos
CFO: John Garratt
HR: Alyssa Brogdon
FYE: January 29
Type: Public

Dollar General is one of the largest discount retailers in the United States by number of stores with more than 17260 stores located in some 45 states with the greatest concentration of stores in the southern southwestern midwestern and eastern US. It generates most of its sales from consumables (including paper and cleaning products; health and beauty aids; and refrigerated shelf-stable and perishable foods). The stores also offer seasonal items cookware and small appliances and apparel. The no-frills stores typically measure around 7400 sq. ft. and approximately 75% of its stores are located in towns of 20000 or fewer people.

	Annual Growth	02/17	02/18	02/19*	01/20	01/21
Sales ($ mil.)	11.3%	21,986.6	23,471.0	25,625.0	27,754.0	33,746.8
Net income ($ mil.)	20.7%	1,251.1	1,539.0	1,589.5	1,712.6	2,655.1
Market value ($ mil.)	27.7%	17,611.0	23,943.7	27,699.9	36,938.8	46,859.2
Employees	6.9%	121,000	129,000	135,000	143,000	158,000

*Fiscal year change

DOLLAR THRIFTY AUTOMOTIVE GROUP INC.   NYSE: DTG

5330 E. 31st St.
Tulsa OK 74135
Phone: 918-660-7700
Fax: 918-669-2934
Web: www.dtag.com

CEO: –
CFO: –
HR: –
FYE: December 31
Type: Public

Thrifty drivers looking to get the most for a buck might try Dollar Thrifty Automotive Group (DTG) which rents cars under the Dollar Rent A Car and Thrifty Car Rental brands. Combined Dollar and Thrifty rent cars from some 280 company-owned locations in the US and Canada as well as about 1300 franchise locations in 80-plus countries. Both brands target the airport market; Thrifty also has off-airport locations. The combined DTG fleet of over 100000 vehicles comprises mainly Chrysler Ford and GM cars. Although the brands retain their separate identities key operations and administrative functions have been consolidated under the company umbrella. DTG is owned by Hertz Global Holdings.

DOLLAR TREE INC   NMS: DLTR

500 Volvo Parkway
Chesapeake, VA 23320
Phone: 757 321-5000
Fax: –
Web: www.dollartree.com

CEO: Michael Witynski
CFO: Kevin Wampler
HR: –
FYE: January 30
Type: Public

Dollar Tree is a leading operator of discount variety stores. The fast-growing company operates approximately 15685 Dollar Tree and Family Dollar discount stores across the US and in about five provinces in Canada. The stores carry a mix of durable housewares toys seasonal items food health and beauty aids. At Dollar Tree shops most goods are priced at $1 or less while Family Dollar merchandise is usually less than $10. The stores are generally located in high-traffic strip centers and malls often in mid-sized cities and small towns.

	Annual Growth	01/17*	02/18	02/19	02/20*	01/21
Sales ($ mil.)	5.3%	20,719.2	22,245.5	22,823.3	23,610.8	25,509.3
Net income ($ mil.)	10.6%	896.2	1,714.3	(1,590.8)	827.0	1,341.9
Market value ($ mil.)	8.2%	17,282.0	25,399.1	22,565.8	20,320.7	23,725.7
Employees	3.0%	176,800	176,100	182,100	193,100	199,327

*Fiscal year change

DOMINION ENERGY INC (NEW)   NYS: D

120 Tredegar Street
Richmond, VA 23219
Phone: 804 819-2000
Fax: 804 775-5819
Web: www.dom.com

CEO: Robert Blue
CFO: James Chapman
HR: –
FYE: December 31
Type: Public

Dominion Energy dominates the American energy market as one of its top distributors of electricity and natural gas. The company serves some 7 million retail energy customers across eight US states with a special concentration in Virginia the Carolinas and Ohio. The company boasts an impressive energy portfolio with about 30200 MW of generating capacity 10500 miles of electric transmission lines 85600 miles of electric distribution lines and 94200 miles of gas distribution mains and related service facilities which are supported by 6200 miles of gas transmission gathering and storage pipeline. Operating subsidiaries include Virginia Power.

	Annual Growth	12/16	12/17	12/18	12/19	12/20
Sales ($ mil.)	4.8%	11,737.0	12,586.0	13,366.0	16,572.0	14,172.0
Net income ($ mil.)	–	2,123.0	2,999.0	2,447.0	1,358.0	(401.0)
Market value ($ mil.)	(0.5%)	61,731.5	65,334.4	57,596.8	66,752.9	60,611.2
Employees	1.7%	16,200	16,200	21,300	19,100	17,300

DOMINION RESOURCES BLACK WARRIOR TRUST   NBB: DOMR

Royalty Trust Management, Southwest Bank, 2911 Turtle Creek Boulevard, Suite 850
Dallas, TX 75219
Phone: 855 588-7839
Fax: –
Web: www.dom-dominionblackwarriortrust.com

CEO: –
CFO: –
HR: –
FYE: December 31
Type: Public

Dominion Resources Black Warrior Trust knows that when the wells get old financial warriors (aka shareholders) don't give up on the economic possibilities. The trust holds royalty interests in 532 natural gas producing wells and is set to terminate when these wells no longer produce enough gas to be profitable. The trust receives then distributes to shareholders 65% of the gross proceeds that Dominion Resources (via its subsidiary Dominion Black Warrior Basin) earns by selling the natural gas from its wells in the Black Warrior Basin of Alabama. In 2008 the trust had proved reserves of 22.6 billion cu. ft. of natural gas equivalent.

	Annual Growth	12/10	12/11	12/12	12/13	12/14
Sales ($ mil.)	(8.8%)	10.2	8.4	5.3	6.4	7.1
Net income ($ mil.)	(10.7%)	9.2	7.4	4.2	5.4	5.8
Market value ($ mil.)	(22.1%)	121.3	62.7	23.2	43.7	44.7
Employees	–	–	–	–	–	–

DOMINOS PIZZA INC.   NYS: DPZ

30 Frank Lloyd Wright Drive
Ann Arbor, MI 48105
Phone: 734 930-3030
Fax: –
Web: www.dominos.com

CEO: Richard Allison
CFO: –
HR: –
FYE: January 03
Type: Public

Domino's Pizza is a pizza company with more than 17600 delivery and take-out locations in over 90 countries. (The chain includes more than 5990 stores throughout the US.) Besides a wide range of pizza styles and toppings Domino's menu also includes oven-baked sandwiches pasta boneless chicken and chicken wings bread side items desserts and soft drink products. Its stores are principally delivery locations and generally do not have any dine-in seating. Less than 365 locations are directly owned and operated by Domino's; the vast majority are franchised.

	Annual Growth	01/17*	12/17	12/18	12/19*	01/21
Sales ($ mil.)	13.6%	2,472.6	2,788.0	3,432.9	3,618.8	4,117.4
Net income ($ mil.)	23.0%	214.7	277.9	362.0	400.7	491.3
Market value ($ mil.)	24.6%	6,189.4	7,344.6	9,715.1	11,361.6	14,904.5
Employees	0.5%	14,100	14,100	14,500	13,100	14,400

*Fiscal year change

DONALDSON CO. INC.   NYS: DCI

1400 West 94th Street
Minneapolis, MN 55431
Phone: 952 887-3131
Fax: –
Web: www.donaldson.com

CEO: Tod E Carpenter
CFO: Scott J Robinson
HR: Sheila G Kramer
FYE: July 31
Type: Public

Donaldson is one of the top companies making filtration systems designed to remove contaminants from air and liquids. The company makes products for engine that include air intake and exhaust systems liquid-filtration systems and replacement parts. Its products are sold to manufacturers of construction mining and transportation equipment as well as parts distributors and fleet operators around the world. The company also makes dust fume and mist collectors and air filtration systems used in industrial gas turbines computer disk drives and other items. The US and Canada account for about 40% of revenue.

	Annual Growth	07/17	07/18	07/19	07/20	07/21
Sales ($ mil.)	4.7%	2,371.9	2,734.2	2,844.9	2,581.8	2,853.9
Net income ($ mil.)	5.4%	232.8	180.3	267.2	257.0	286.9
Market value ($ mil.)	8.7%	5,937.3	5,963.6	6,244.9	6,043.6	8,275.2
Employees	(0.2%)	13,200	14,000	14,100	12,400	13,100

DONEGAL GROUP INC.

NMS: DGIC A

1195 River Road, P.O. Box 302
Marietta, PA 17547
Phone: 717 426-1931
Fax: –
Web: www.donegalgroup.com

CEO: Kevin Burke
CFO: Jeffrey Miller
HR: –
FYE: December 31
Type: Public

Risk is Donegal Group's middle name. Through its subsidiaries including Atlantic States Insurance and Southern Insurance Company of Virginia Donegal Group provides personal farm and commercial property/casualty insurance products. It is active in about 20 states in the mid-Atlantic Midwest New England and South. The group's personal insurance offerings range from private passenger automobile and homeowners coverage; its commercial insurance products include business owners multi-peril and workers' compensation. Donegal Mutual Insurance controls more than 70% of the company's voting stock.

	Annual Growth	12/16	12/17	12/18	12/19	12/20
Assets ($ mil.)	7.4%	1,623.1	1,737.9	1,832.1	1,923.2	2,160.5
Net income ($ mil.)	14.4%	30.8	7.1	(32.8)	47.2	52.8
Market value ($ mil.)	(5.3%)	528.3	522.9	412.4	447.9	425.3
Employees	–	–	–	–	–	879

DONNELLEY (RR) & SONS COMPANY

NYS: RRD

35 West Wacker Drive
Chicago, IL 60601
Phone: 312 326-8000
Fax: –
Web: www.rrd.com

CEO: Daniel Knotts
CFO: Terry Peterson
HR: –
FYE: December 31
Type: Public

If you can read it RR Donnelley & Sons (RRD) can print it (and digitize distribute and market it too). The company is evolving from a provider of printing services to a full-on communications services firm. Its primary offerings fall under the Business Services category and include commercial print packaging labels and forms as well as supply chain management and business process outsourcing. For about 155 years in the business the company has operations in more than 250 locations and in nearly 30 countries but most revenue comes from the US.

	Annual Growth	12/15	12/16	12/17	12/18	12/19
Sales ($ mil.)	(13.6%)	11,256.8	6,895.7	6,939.6	6,800.2	6,276.2
Net income ($ mil.)	–	151.1	(495.9)	(34.4)	(11.0)	(93.2)
Market value ($ mil.)	(28.0%)	1,043.6	1,157.1	659.4	280.8	280.1
Employees	(14.6%)	68,400	44,360	42,700	39,500	36,400

DONNELLEY FINANCIAL SOLUTIONS INC

NYS: DFIN

35 West Wacker Drive
Chicago, IL 60601
Phone: 800 823-5304
Fax: –
Web: www.dfinsolutions.com

CEO: Daniel Leib
CFO: David Gardella
HR: –
FYE: December 31
Type: Public

Donnelley Financial Solutions is a leading global risk and compliance solutions company. The company provides regulatory filing and deal solutions via its software technology-enabled services and print distribution to public and private companies mutual funds and other regulated investment firms to serve its clients' regulatory compliance needs. The company offers filing agent service digital document creation online content management tools regulatory reporting virtual data rooms and more. Investment market customers include alternative investment and insurance investment companies while language service customers include legal partnerships life sciences firms and corporations. Printing company R.R. Donnelley spin-off Donnelley Financial Solutions in 2016. Most of Donnelley Financial Solutions' revenue comes from the US.

	Annual Growth	12/16	12/17	12/18	12/19	12/20
Sales ($ mil.)	(2.3%)	983.5	1,004.9	963.0	874.7	894.5
Net income ($ mil.)	–	59.1	9.7	73.6	37.6	(25.9)
Market value ($ mil.)	(7.3%)	765.2	649.0	467.2	348.7	565.1
Employees	(10.1%)	3,600	3,400	3,100	2,900	2,350

DORCHESTER MINERALS LP

NMS: DMLP

3838 Oak Lawn Avenue, Suite 300
Dallas, TX 75219
Phone: 214 559-0300
Fax: –
Web: www.dmlp.net

CEO: William McManemin
CFO: Leslie Moriyama
HR: –
FYE: December 31
Type: Public

The stakeholders of Dorchester Minerals are enjoying the benefits of three natural resource exploitation enterprises which came together as one. The oil and gas exploration company was formed by the 2003 merger of oil trust Dorchester Hugoton with Republic Royalty and Spinnaker Royalty. Dorchester Minerals' holdings include about 141600 net acres in Texas and 62850 net acres in Montana. The company holds assets (producing and nonproducing mineral royalty overriding royalty net profits and leasehold interests) in properties in 574 counties in 25 states. In 2009 Dorchester Minerals reported proved reserves of 60.3 billion cu. ft. of natural gas and 3.3 million barrels of oil and condensate.

	Annual Growth	12/16	12/17	12/18	12/19	12/20
Sales ($ mil.)	5.7%	37.6	57.3	73.3	78.8	46.9
Net income ($ mil.)	1.1%	21.0	38.4	53.9	52.8	21.9
Market value ($ mil.)	(11.2%)	608.6	527.1	507.7	676.6	378.4
Employees	0.0%	24	30	31	34	24

DORMAN PRODUCTS INC

NMS: DORM

3400 East Walnut Street
Colmar, PA 18915
Phone: 215 997-1800
Fax: –
Web: www.dormanproducts.com

CEO: Kevin Olsen
CFO: David Hession
HR: –
FYE: December 25
Type: Public

Markets approximately 81000 unique parts Dorman Products is a leading supplier of automotive replacement parts (including brake parts) fasteners and service line products to the automotive aftermarket. Approximately 75% of the company's products are sold under brands that the company owns. Dorman sells to auto aftermarket retailers and warehouse distributors (such as Advance AutoZone and O'Reilly) as well as to parts manufacturers for resale under private labels. The company services over 3600 active accounts. Dorman distributes its products primarily into Canada and Mexico Europe the Middle East and Australia. About 95% of the company's total sales is generated from the US.

	Annual Growth	12/17	12/18	12/19	12/20	12/21
Sales ($ mil.)	10.5%	903.2	973.7	991.3	1,092.7	1,345.2
Net income ($ mil.)	5.4%	106.6	133.6	83.8	106.9	131.5
Market value ($ mil.)	14.9%	1,932.5	2,792.5	2,374.0	2,830.8	3,363.7
Employees	13.0%	2,061	2,370	2,742	2,681	3,360

DORSEY & WHITNEY LLP

50 S. 6th St. Ste. 1500
Minneapolis MN 55402-1498
Phone: 612-340-2600
Fax: 612-340-2868
Web: www.dorsey.com

CEO: –
CFO: Roderick N Dolan
HR: –
FYE: December 31
Type: Private - Partnershi

Dorsey & Whitney is more than a big fish in the land of 1000 lakes. Founded in 1912 the law firm has grown into a truly global practice with more than 600 lawyers operating in about 20 offices across the US Canada Europe and Asia. Traditionally strong in matters of mergers and acquisitions corporate finance and litigation the firm is focused on intellectual property patent and trademark issues in the international arena. It has expertise in Canadian cross-border transactions and has conducted US securities work in India China and Hong Kong.

DOT FOODS INC.

1 Dot Way
Mt. Sterling IL 62353
Phone: 217-773-4411
Fax: 217-773-3321
Web: www.dotfoods.com

CEO: Joe Tracy
CFO: Anita Montgomery
HR: Jennifer Evans
FYE: December 31
Type: Private

You don't have to buy a lot to work with Dot. A leading foodservice redistributor Dot Foods hauls more than 60000 dry frozen and refrigerated products from roughly 700 food industry manufacturers to customers who buy in less-than-truckload quantities. The company also offers foodservice equipment and supplies. Dot's customer base consists of more than 3300 distributors nationwide (including convenience store retail food and vending wholesalers as well as foodservice suppliers). The company also sells food ingredients to dairies bakeries confectioners and meat processors.

DOT HILL SYSTEMS CORP. NMS: HILL

1351 S. Sunset Street
Longmont, CO 80501
Phone: 303 845-3200
Fax: –
Web: www.dothill.com

CEO: –
CFO: –
HR: –
FYE: December 31
Type: Public

Dot Hill Systems designs and markets RAID (redundant array of independent disks) storage devices that are used in corporate data centers and other network environments by enterprises in data-intensive industries such as financial services and telecommunications. It also makes entry-level and and mid-range storage area network (SANs) and fibre channel systems and it provides storage system and data management software. Dot Hill's products are sold under the Assured brand. Most of the company's sales are made to manufacturing partners namely including Hewlett-Packard which accounts for nearly three-quarters of sales. Dot Hill has international offices in Germany Israel Japan and the UK.

	Annual Growth	12/09	12/10	12/11	12/12	12/13
Sales ($ mil.)	(3.1%)	234.4	252.5	197.5	194.5	206.5
Net income ($ mil.)	–	(13.6)	(13.3)	(22.0)	(15.0)	5.1
Market value ($ mil.)	15.4%	112.4	103.5	78.7	55.4	199.3
Employees	3.4%	285	293	322	324	326

DOUGHERTY'S PHARMACY INC NBB: MYDP

5924 Royal Lane, Suite 250
Dallas, TX 75230
Phone: 972 250-0945
Fax: –
Web: www.ascendantsolutions.com

CEO: Stewart Edington
CFO: –
HR: Leigh Dillard
FYE: December 31
Type: Public

Ascendant Solutions holds stakes in companies involved in health care retailing real estate and other sectors. It seeks out opportunities among corporate divestitures distressed or bankrupt firms and entrepreneurs looking to sell their companies. Its investments include Dallas-based specialty pharmacy Dougherty's and CRESA Partners which provides tenant representation and lease management services. Ascendant Solutions also owns stakes in Ampco Safety Tools and Dallas-area mixed-use real estate development firm Frisco Square. In 2008 Ascendant Solutions sold its stake in the Medicine Man chain of pharmacies to a subsidiary of Medicine Shoppe.

	Annual Growth	12/14	12/15	12/16	12/17	12/18
Sales ($ mil.)	6.1%	28.5	41.0	42.8	40.2	36.1
Net income ($ mil.)	–	0.5	(0.4)	(4.9)	(2.1)	(3.5)
Market value ($ mil.)	(49.2%)	6.0	5.2	4.7	3.2	0.4
Employees	(5.7%)	–	–	–	105	99

DOUGLAS DYNAMICS, INC. NYS: PLOW

7777 North 73rd Street
Milwaukee, WI 53223
Phone: 414 354-2310
Fax: –
Web: www.douglasdynamics.com

CEO: Robert Mccormick
CFO: Sarah Lauber
HR: Linda Evans
FYE: December 31
Type: Public

Douglas Dynamics makes snowplows and sand-and-salt spreading equipment for light trucks. One of the biggest manufacturers in its industry the company sells its lineup under brand names Western Fisher Snowex Henderson Turfex Sweepex and Blizzard via equipment distributors. It also supplies related parts and accessories. End customers are mainly snowplowers in the business of removing snow and ice for municipalities and commercial and private owners in the Midwest East and Northeast US as well as throughout Canada. Douglas traces its roots back to the 1970s.

	Annual Growth	12/16	12/17	12/18	12/19	12/20
Sales ($ mil.)	3.6%	416.3	474.9	524.1	571.7	480.2
Net income ($ mil.)	–	39.0	55.3	43.9	49.2	(86.6)
Market value ($ mil.)	6.2%	769.2	864.0	820.4	1,257.2	977.6
Employees	2.0%	1,633	1,664	1,663	1,677	1,767

DOUGLAS EMMETT INC NYS: DEI

1299 Ocean Avenue, Suite 1000
Santa Monica, CA 90401
Phone: 310 255-7700
Fax: –
Web: www.douglasemmett.com

CEO: Jordan Kaplan
CFO: Peter Seymour
HR: –
FYE: December 31
Type: Public

Office Space is more than the name of a cult movie to Douglas Emmett. The self-administered and self-managed real estate investment trust (REIT) invests in commercial real estate in Southern California and Hawaii. It owns about 70 Class A office properties (totaling 17.8 million sq. ft.) mostly in the heart of Hollywood and surrounding areas. Its office holdings account for more than 85% of its total revenues. The REIT also owns nearly 4160 apartment units in tony neighborhoods of West Los Angeles and Honolulu. Douglas Emmett's portfolio includes some of the most notable addresses on the West Coast including the famed Sherman Oaks Galleria Burbank's Studio Plaza and Beverly Hills. California accounts for the highest revenue by location which accounts for nearly 90%.

	Annual Growth	12/17	12/18	12/19	12/20	12/21
Sales ($ mil.)	3.1%	812.1	881.3	936.7	891.5	918.4
Net income ($ mil.)	(8.8%)	94.4	116.1	363.7	50.4	65.3
Market value ($ mil.)	(5.0%)	7,207.2	5,990.8	7,705.7	5,121.9	5,880.2
Employees	3.9%	600	670	713	700	700

DOVER CORP NYS: DOV

3005 Highland Parkway
Downers Grove, IL 60515
Phone: 630 541-1540
Fax: –
Web: www.dovercorporation.com

CEO: Richard Tobin
CFO: Brad Cerepak
HR: Kimberly Bors
FYE: December 31
Type: Public

Dover is a diversified global manufacturer and solutions provider delivering innovative equipment and components consumable supplies aftermarket parts software and digital solutions and support services through five operating segments: Engineered Products Clean & Energy Fueling Pumps & Process solutions Imaging & Identification and Refrigeration and Climate & Sustainability Technologies. Dover serves industries such as chemical hygienic oil & gas food and beverages heating & cooling and other end markets. It generates around 55% of revenue in the US. Dover traces its historical roots back to 1947.

	Annual Growth	12/17	12/18	12/19	12/20	12/21
Sales ($ mil.)	0.2%	7,830.4	6,992.1	7,136.4	6,683.8	7,907.1
Net income ($ mil.)	8.5%	811.7	570.3	677.9	683.5	1,123.8
Market value ($ mil.)	15.8%	14,547.2	10,220.0	16,602.7	18,185.8	26,158.7
Employees	(3.6%)	29,000	24,000	24,000	23,000	25,000

DOVER MOTORSPORTS, INC.   NYS: DVD

1131 North DuPont Highway
Dover, DE 19901
Phone: 302 883-6500
Fax: 302 672-0100
Web: www.dovermotorsports.com

CEO: Denis McGlynn
CFO: Timothy R Horne
HR: Janie Libby
FYE: December 31
Type: Public

This company makes its money when rubber meets the pavement at its racetrack. Dover Motorsports host more several auto racing events each year at its flagship Dover International Speedway in Delaware. The track hold events sponsored by all the major US racing leagues including NASCAR the Indy Racing League and the National Hot Rod Association though stock car racing accounts for 80% of sales. Dover Motorsports and Dover Downs Gaming & Entertainment were operating as one company before being separated in a spin-off in 2002. In 2014 the company sold off its Nashville area racetrack.

	Annual Growth	12/15	12/16	12/17	12/18	12/19
Sales ($ mil.)	(0.3%)	46.5	45.9	46.7	47.0	46.0
Net income ($ mil.)	1.0%	5.3	3.8	8.4	6.9	5.5
Market value ($ mil.)	(5.5%)	84.7	83.6	70.9	68.3	67.6
Employees	1.3%	57	57	60	54	60

DOVER SADDLERY INC   NAS: DOVR

525 Great Road
Littleton, MA 01460
Phone: 978 952-8062
Fax: –
Web: www.doversaddlery.com

CEO: Brad Wolansky
CFO: David R Pearce
HR: –
FYE: December 31
Type: Public

Dover Saddlery is an upscale specialty retailer and direct marketer of equestrian products. The company's specialty is English-style riding gear and its selection features riding apparel tack and stable supplies as well as horse health care products. Its brand-name products include names such as Ariat Grand Prix Mountain Horse Passier and Prestige. Dover operates more than 20 retail stores mostly on the East Coast and in Texas under the Dover Saddlery and Smith Brothers banners (Western-style gear) and it also markets products on its website and in catalogs. The company was founded in 1975 by US Equestrian Team members including company directors Jim and Dave Powers.

	Annual Growth	12/09	12/10	12/11	12/12	12/13
Sales ($ mil.)	5.3%	76.2	78.2	80.8	86.0	93.8
Net income ($ mil.)	15.2%	0.9	2.0	1.7	1.6	1.6
Market value ($ mil.)	24.2%	12.0	13.9	21.4	17.7	28.6
Employees	8.8%	520	497	565	614	729

DOW CHEMICAL CO.   NYS: DOW

2030 Dow Center
Midland, MI 48674
Phone: 989 636-1000
Fax: 989 638 1740
Web: www.dow.com

CEO: James R Fitterling
CFO: Howard Ungerleider
HR: –
FYE: December 31
Type: Public

The Tao of Dow Chemical is its integrated production of plastics chemicals hydrocarbons and agrochemicals. The largest chemical company in the US and #2 worldwide behind BASF Dow also makes performance plastics (engineering plastics polyurethanes and materials) for Dow Automotive. It uses chlorine-based and hydrocarbon-based raw materials to make more than 6000 finished chemical products at 179 sites in 35 countries. The maker of Styrofoam insulation also is the world's #1 producer of chlorine and caustic soda and a top maker of ethylene dichloride and vinyl chloride monomer. Dow also owns silicone products maker Dow Corning. In late 2015 Dow agreed to merge with rival Dupont.

	Annual Growth	12/12	12/13	12/14	12/15	12/16
Sales ($ mil.)	(4.0%)	56,786.0	57,080.0	58,167.0	48,778.0	48,158.0
Net income ($ mil.)	38.3%	1,182.0	4,787.0	3,772.0	7,685.0	4,318.0
Market value ($ mil.)	15.3%	39,155.2	53,774.3	55,239.8	62,349.1	69,301.0
Employees	0.9%	54,000	53,000	53,000	49,500	56,000

DOWLING COLLEGE

150 IDLE HOUR BLVD
OAKDALE, NY 11769-1999
Phone: 631-244-3000
Fax: –
Web: www.dowling.edu

CEO: –
CFO: –
HR:
FYE: June 30
Type: Private

Dowling College is private but not exclusive. The college offers undergraduate and graduate educational opportunities from campuses in Oakdale Shirley and Melville New York. Dowling enrolls about 6500 students who can earn bachelors masters and doctoral degrees from four schools: Arts and Sciences the Townsend School of Business Education and Aviation. Popular degrees include business administration psychology elementary education and special education. Dowling's Aviation program includes a fleet of aircraft and offers flight simulation and air traffic control courses. Dowling College has a student/faculty ratio of 17:1.

	Annual Growth	06/07	06/08	06/09	06/09	06/10
Sales ($ mil.)	–	–	–	(1,491.7)	73.6	78.5
Net income ($ mil.)	6824.8%	–	–	0.0	(3.6)	1.1
Market value ($ mil.)	–	–	–	–	–	–
Employees	–	–	–	–	–	1,030

DOYLESTOWN HOSPITAL HEALTH AND WELLNESS CENTER, INC.

595 W STATE ST
DOYLESTOWN, PA 189012597
Phone: 215-345-2200
Fax: –
Web: www.doylestownhealth.org

CEO: –
CFO: Dan Upton
HR: –
FYE: June 30
Type: Private

It takes a village to own a hospital and Doylestown Hospital is owned by the local women's civic organization Village Improvement Association (VIA). Founded in 1923 the hospital serves southeastern Pennsylvania and neighboring areas of New Jersey. With some 240 beds and a medical staff of more than 435 physicians in over 50 specialties Doylestown Hospital provides a variety of acute and tertiary medical services. Specialties include cardiac surgery cancer care (as part of the University of Pennsylvania Cancer Network) and orthopedics. Affiliated with the hospital are two Pine Run nursing and assisted-living centers. Doylestown Hospital the flagship facility of the Doylestown Health system.

	Annual Growth	06/17	06/18	06/19	06/20	06/21
Sales ($ mil.)	5.2%	–	310.0	313.3	310.6	361.3
Net income ($ mil.)	50.6%	–	10.2	11.3	(18.3)	34.9
Market value ($ mil.)	–	–	–	–	–	–
Employees	–	–	–	–	–	2,853

DPL INC.   NYSE: DPL

1065 Woodman Dr.
Dayton OH 45432
Phone: 937-224-6000
Fax: 937-259-7147
Web: www.dplinc.com

CEO: Phil Herrington
CFO: Caroline Muhlenkamp
HR: –
FYE: December 31
Type: Public

When it's dark in Dayton DPL turns on the lights. The holding company's main subsidiary regulated utility Dayton Power and Light (DP&L) which was established in 1911 brightens the night for more than 500000 electricity customers in 24 counties in west central Ohio. Nonregulated subsidiary DPL Energy operates DPL's 10 power plants which produce more than 3800 MW of primarily coal-fired generating capacity. It also sells power to energy marketing affiliate DPL Energy Resources to meet the electric requirements of its retail customers. Other activities include street lighting and financial support services. In 2011 DPL was acquired by AES in a $4.7 billion transaction.

DPR CONSTRUCTION, INC.

1450 VETERANS BLVD
REDWOOD CITY, CA 940632617
Phone: 650-474-1450
Fax: –
Web: www.dpr.com

CEO: –
CFO: Michele Leiva
HR: –
FYE: December 31
Type: Private

From bio labs to wafer fabs DPR Construction runs the gamut for its high-tech and health care clients. The employee-owned firm provides general contracting and construction management services for the advanced technology/mission-critical life sciences health care higher education and corporate office markets. The construction firm specializes in developing retail stores hospitals data centers clean rooms laboratories manufacturing facilities and green buildings. Altogether DPR Construction boasts more than 25 regional offices nationwide. Company head Doug Woods former CEO Peter Nosler and secretary/treasurer Ron Davidowski (the D P and R in DPR Construction) founded the firm in 1990.

	Annual Growth	12/0-3	12/0-2	12/0-1	12/00	12/08
Sales ($ mil.)	(0.8%)	–	–	–	1,958.1	1,836.1
Net income ($ mil.)	13.0%	–	–	–	25.7	68.5
Market value ($ mil.)	–	–	–	–	–	–
Employees	–	–	–	–	–	8,002

DRAKE UNIVERSITY

2507 UNIVERSITY AVE
DES MOINES, IA 503114505
Phone: 515-271-2011
Fax: –
Web: www.drake.edu

CEO: –
CFO: –
HR: –
FYE: June 30
Type: Private

You won't find duck duck goose as part of the curriculum at Drake University. The Des Moines Iowa school provides undergraduate and graduate education programs for some 5500 students through its six colleges and schools: arts and sciences business and public administration education journalism and mass communications law and pharmacy and health sciences. It has a 15:1 student-to-faculty ratio. A private school Drake University was founded in 1881 with seed money from General Francis Marion Drake a Civil War general and former Iowa governor banker railroad builder and attorney. Drake University also hosts the Drake Relays one of the largest track and field events in the US.

	Annual Growth	06/16	06/17	06/18	06/19	06/20
Sales ($ mil.)	16.5%	–	140.5	144.5	150.1	222.3
Net income ($ mil.)	(64.5%)	–	27.6	9.2	13.8	1.2
Market value ($ mil.)	–	–	–	–	–	–
Employees	–	–	–	–	–	830

DREAMS INC.

NYSE AMEX: DRJ

2 S. University Dr. Ste. 325
Plantation FL 33324
Phone: 954-377-0002
Fax: 954-475-8785
Web: www.fanaticsinc.com/

CEO: –
CFO: –
HR: –
FYE: December 31
Type: Private

Talk about a dream team: Troy Aikman Emmitt Smith Randy Moss and Jerry Rice; these sports heroes mean money to Dreams. It owns and operates about 15 US stores under the Field of Dreams and FansEdge banners as well as about five franchised stores. The stores network sells signed balls jerseys photos plaques and other collectibles which it licenses from the NFL MLB NHL NBA NCAA and NASCAR. It also reaches shoppers via the FansEdge catalog and online at FansEdge.com and ProSportsMemorabilia.com. The company's Mounted Memories makes and distributes sports memorabilia; its Greene Organization handles special appearances endorsements and other off-field activities for athletes. It's owned by Fanatics.

DREAMWORKS ANIMATION SKG INC

NMS: DWA

1000 Flower Street
Glendale, CA 91201
Phone: 818 695-5000
Fax: –
Web: www.dreamworksanimation.com

CEO: Jeffrey Katzenberg
CFO: Fazal Merchant
HR: –
FYE: December 31
Type: Public

While live action isn't a nightmare for DreamWorks Animation SKG this company definitely prefers CGI. DreamWorks Animation has produced more than 30 computer-animated family-friendly features — including high-earning hits such as Shrek the Third Shrek 2 and Madagascar. (Its Shrek 2 is one of the highest grossing films of all time at the domestic box office.) The studio's movies are distributed and marketed by Twentieth Century Fox. DreamWorks Animation earns most of its revenues from distributing its films in theaters and ancillary markets such as home entertainment and cable and broadcast TV. In 2004 former parent DreamWorks spun off DreamWorks Animation as a separate company.

	Annual Growth	12/10	12/11	12/12	12/13	12/14
Sales ($ mil.)	(3.4%)	784.8	706.0	749.8	706.9	684.6
Net income ($ mil.)	–	170.6	86.8	(36.4)	55.1	(309.6)
Market value ($ mil.)	(6.7%)	2,524.8	1,421.7	1,419.6	3,041.4	1,913.1
Employees	6.5%	2,100	2,100	2,400	2,200	2,700

DRESSER-RAND GROUP INC.

NYSE: DRC

10205 Westheimer Rd. West8 Tower Ste. 1000
Houston TX 77042
Phone: 713-354-6100
Fax: 713-354-6110
Web: www.dresser-rand.com

CEO: Paulo Ruiz Sternadt
CFO: Heribert Stumpf
HR: –
FYE: December 31
Type: Public

Dresser-Rand is going in circles but that's a good thing. The company is a leading maker of industrial rotating equipment that includes steam and gas turbines centrifugal and reciprocating compressors hot gas expanders and control systems. It makes new and replacement units and offers aftermarket repair and upgrades for its own and third-party products. Dresser-Rand serves customers in the oil and gas power and chemical and petrochemical markets through 12 manufacturing and nearly 40 service facilities in about 30 countries. More than 80% of its sales come from energy infrastructure and oilfield projects. Chevron BP Royal Dutch Shell Exxon Mobil and Dow Chemical are among its blue-chip customers.

DREW UNIVERSITY

36 MADISON AVE
MADISON, NJ 079401434
Phone: 973-408-3000
Fax: –
Web: www.drewrangers.com

CEO: –
CFO: –
HR: –
FYE: June 30
Type: Private

Drew University draws interest with its seminary. The school is a liberal arts college that offers both graduate school and as many as 30 undergraduate degrees including master's and Ph.D. studies in religion from the Drew Theological School. It's the home of the Caspersen School of Graduate Studies. The educational institution's campus is located in Madison New Jersey on 186 wooded acres in the foothills of northern New Jersey. The school boasts an enrollment of about 2370 students and has NCAA Division III teams playing as the Drew Rangers. With more than 150 faculty members of which 98% hold terminal degrees Drew University boasts a student/faculty ratio of 10:1 and an average class size of 17.

	Annual Growth	06/08	06/09	06/14	06/15	06/16
Sales ($ mil.)	3.8%	–	55.5	120.1	128.2	72.2
Net income ($ mil.)	–	–	0.0	(0.8)	5.9	(28.5)
Market value ($ mil.)	–	–	–	–	–	–
Employees	–	–	–	–	–	550

DREXEL UNIVERSITY

3141 CHESTNUT ST
PHILADELPHIA, PA 191042875
Phone: 215-895-2000
Fax: –
Web: www.drexel.edu

CEO: –
CFO: Thomas J Elzey
HR: –
FYE: June 30
Type: Private

Drexel doesn't want to train its dragons but to educate them in a wide range of disciplines. Drexel University (home of the Drexel Dragons) is a private coeducational institution of higher learning with an enrollment of more than 24200 undergraduate and graduate students and a student-teacher ratio of about 9:1. It operates more than a dozen schools and colleges in the US; the Drexel University College of Medicine is the one of the country's largest private medical schools. Drexel runs a mandatory co-operative education program that helps students gain real-world experience while supplying local employers with trained workers. Philadelphia financier and philanthropist Anthony Drexel founded the university in 1891.

	Annual Growth	12/07	12/08*	06/11	06/12	06/17
Sales ($ mil.)	–	–	0.0	897.0	910.8	985.3
Net income ($ mil.)	–	–	0.0	166.4	34.4	34.8
Market value ($ mil.)	–	–	–	–	–	–
Employees	–	–	–	–	–	2,868

*Fiscal year change

DRI CORPORATION

13760 Noel Rd. Ste. 830
Dallas TX 75240
Phone: 214-378-8992
Fax: 214-378-8437
Web: www.digrec.com

NASDAQ: TBUS
CEO: David L Turney
CFO: –
HR: –
FYE: December 31
Type: Public

DRI drives transportation technology. The company designs automatic voice announcement systems and electronic destination signs for mass transit operators as well as vehicle location systems. Its Talking Bus announcement systems broadcast stops and transfer information for buses subways trains and other private and commercial vehicles. DRI also makes electronic destination signs that display transit information for buses. The company counts vehicle makers transit operators and state and local governments among its customers. It operates through subsidiaries in the US (Digital Recorders TwinVision) and abroad (Mobitec). DRI filed for chapter 11 bankruptcy in 2012 and is looking for a buyer for its assets.

DRIL-QUIP INC

6401 N. Eldridge Parkway
Houston, TX 77041
Phone: 713 939-7711
Fax: –
Web: www.dril-quip.com

NYS: DRQ
CEO: Blake T Deberry
CFO: Kyle McClure
HR: –
FYE: December 31
Type: Public

Dril-Quip designs manufactures sells and services the global deepwater oil and gas industry. The company specializes in deepwater harsh-environment and/or severe-condition equipment. Its products include drilling and production riser systems subsea and surface wellheads and production trees subsea control systems and manifolds mudline hanger systems (which support the weight of each casing string at the mudline) and specialty connectors and pipe. Dril-Quip's offshore rig equipment includes drilling riser systems wellhead connectors diverters safety valves and cement manifolds. The company also provides reconditioning and technical advisory services. The Western Hemisphere accounts the majority of sales with about 60% of sales.

	Annual Growth	12/16	12/17	12/18	12/19	12/20
Sales ($ mil.)	(9.3%)	538.7	455.5	384.6	414.8	365.0
Net income ($ mil.)	–	93.2	(100.6)	(95.7)	1.7	(30.8)
Market value ($ mil.)	(16.2%)	2,126.8	1,689.4	1,063.6	1,661.4	1,049.1
Employees	(11.8%)	2,355	2,019	1,926	1,814	1,424

DRIVE SHACK INC

10670 N. Central Expressway, Suite 700
Dallas, TX 75231
Phone: 646 585-5591
Fax: –
Web: www.driveshack.com

NYS: DS
CEO: Hana Khouri
CFO: Michael Nichols
HR: –
FYE: December 31
Type: Public

Drive Shack (formerly Newcastle Investment) owns and operates golf- and leisure-related assets. Its portfolio includes some 80 public private and managed golf properties in 13 states. The company is also developing a line of entertainment facilities that combine technology-enhanced golf and dining. Drive Shack is managed by Fortress Investment Group which also owns a minority stake in the company. Newcastle transformed from a real estate investment trust (REIT) to a C-Corporation in 2017; now named Drive Shack it still holds a portfolio of real estate securities primarily Fannie Mae- or Freddie Mac-backed assets. .

	Annual Growth	12/16	12/17	12/18	12/19	12/20
Sales ($ mil.)	(7.4%)	298.9	292.6	314.4	272.1	220.0
Net income ($ mil.)	–	77.1	(42.2)	(38.7)	(54.9)	(56.4)
Market value ($ mil.)	(10.8%)	253.1	372.3	263.9	246.4	160.2
Employees	(10.1%)	4,700	4,400	3,923	4,658	3,072

DRIVETIME AUTOMOTIVE GROUP, INC.

1720 W RIO SALADO PKWY
TEMPE, AZ 852816590
Phone: 602-852-6600
Fax: –
Web: www.drivetime.com

CEO: –
CFO: Kurt Wood
HR: –
FYE: December 31
Type: Private

In this story the ugly duckling changes into DriveTime Automotive Group. Formerly known as Ugly Duckling the company is a used-car dealership chain that primarily targets low-income customers and those with less-than-stellar credit. To cater to subprime clients it's a "buy here-pay here" dealer meaning it finances and services car loans rather than using outside lenders. DriveTime operates more than 125 dealerships in 50 US metropolitan areas in 24 mostly southern and western states. The company provides customers with a comprehensive end-to-end solution for their automotive needs including the sale financing and maintenance of their vehicle.

	Annual Growth	12/12	12/13	12/14	12/15	12/17
Sales ($ mil.)	23.6%	–	1,400.9	–	2,372.2	3,267.1
Net income ($ mil.)	–	–	29.8	–	32.2	(16.7)
Market value ($ mil.)	–	–	–	–	–	–
Employees	–	–	–	–	–	991

DROPCAR INC

1412 Broadway, Suite 2105
New York, NY 10018
Phone: 646 342-1595
Fax: –
Web: www.wpcs.com

NAS: DCAR
CEO: Thomas Wittenschlaeger
CFO: David Hollingsworth
HR: –
FYE: December 31
Type: Public

WPCS International provides the engineering behind communications networks. Through subsidiaries the company designs and installs broadband wireless video security systems and specialty communications systems. Services include product integration fiber-optic cabling project management and technical support. The company also provides engineering services to support wireless networks. Its specialty communication systems division offers support for telematics and telemetry systems as well as networks designed for asset tracking. WPCS serves the enterprise government and education sectors. Clients have included Amtrak the Jacksonville Jaguars and Wake Forest University Baptist Medical Center.

	Annual Growth	04/14	04/15	04/16	04/17*	12/18
Sales ($ mil.)	(26.9%)	21.3	24.4	14.6	16.7	6.1
Net income ($ mil.)	–	(11.1)	(8.8)	(2.8)	(1.2)	(18.7)
Market value ($ mil.)	(35.2%)	1.7	4.7	2.2	2.2	0.3
Employees	(21.1%)	240	68	72	77	93

*Fiscal year change

DRUGSTORE.COM INC.

411 108th Ave. NE Ste. 1400
Bellevue WA 98004
Phone: 425-372-3200
Fax: 425-372-3800
Web: www.drugstore.com

CEO: –
CFO: Eleuth RE Du Pont
HR: –
FYE: August 31
Type: Subsidiary

drugstore.com hopes it has the right Rx for e-commerce success. The e-tailer sells some 60000 name-brand and private-label health and beauty items personal care products household goods and over-the-counter (OTC) drugs through its website and by telephone. A partnership with GNC Corporation allows drugstore.com to offer the retailer's vitamins and wellness products online. It also sells high-end cosmetics and skin care items through its Beauty.com unit. The company markets contact lenses through its Vision Direct subsidiary and customized nutritional supplement programs through its Custom Nutrition Services subsidiary. In 2011 behemoth retailer Walgreen bought drugstore.com in a deal valued at $410 million.

DSC LOGISTICS INC.

1750 S. Wolf Rd.
Des Plaines IL 60018
Phone: 800-372-1960
Fax: 847-390-7276
Web: www.dsclogistics.com

CEO: –
CFO: David Copeland
HR: Jain Hayes
FYE: December 31
Type: Private

DSC Logistics knows the ABCs of supply chain management. The third-party logistics company manages services such as warehousing transportation and packaging for its customers; it also offers logistics consulting services. DSC maintains a network of logistics centers spread throughout the US. Customers have included Georgia-Pacific Heinz Kimberly-Clark and Wal-Mart. DSC founder Jim McIlrath the father of CEO Ann Drake started the company as Dry Storage Corporation in 1960 after a former boss refused to offer dry storage along with refrigerated storage services.

DSP GROUP, INC.
NMS: DSPG

2055 Gateway Place, Suite 480
San Jose, CA 95110
Phone: 408 986-4300
Fax: –

CEO: Michael Hurlston
CFO: Dean Butler
HR: –
FYE: December 31
Type: Public

DSP Group loves the sound of its own voice ... chips. The company's name derives from the digital signal processors (DSPs) and related speech compression software it develops that convert speech and other audio data into digital values for cordless telephones wireless phones answering devices PCs and other consumer electronics. Top customers include landline makers VTech Panasonic and Cisco. 85% of the company's sales are to customers in Asia. The company was founded in 1987.

	Annual Growth	12/15	12/16	12/17	12/18	12/19
Sales ($ mil.)	(5.0%)	144.3	137.9	124.8	117.4	117.6
Net income ($ mil.)	–	–	1.6	4.8	(3.0)	(2.0)	(1.2)
Market value ($ mil.)	13.6%	218.2	301.6	288.9	258.8	363.8
Employees	2.0%	314	333	328	320	340

DSS INC
ASE: DSS

6 Framark Drive
Victor, NY 14564
Phone: 585 325-3610
Fax: –
Web: www.dsssecure.com

CEO: Frank Heuszel
CFO: Todd Macko
HR: –
FYE: December 31
Type: Public

Document Security Systems (DSS) caters to those who are insecure about their security particularly on paper. The company develops anti-counterfeiting products. Its offerings include technology that prevents documents from being accurately scanned or copied and authentication coding that can be used in conjunction with a handheld reader to verify that a document is genuine. DSS also sells paper that displays words such as "void" or "unauthorized copy" if it goes through a copier fax machine or scanner. Customers include corporations governments and financial institutions. DSS is slated to merge with Lexington Technology Group (LTG) in 2013.

	Annual Growth	12/16	12/17	12/18	12/19	12/20
Sales ($ mil.)	(2.4%)	19.2	18.7	18.5	19.4	17.4
Net income ($ mil.)	–	(1.0)	(0.6)	1.5	(2.9)	1.9
Market value ($ mil.)	74.8%	3.9	10.5	4.3	1.8	36.4
Employees	(2.8%)	104	98	106	100	93

DST SYSTEMS, INC.

333 W 11TH ST FL 5
KANSAS CITY, MO 641051628
Phone: 816-654-6067
Fax: –
Web: www.ssctech.com

CEO: William C Stone
CFO: Patrick J Pedonti
HR: –
FYE: December 31
Type: Private

Financial firms and health institutions focus on making clients wealthy and healthy respectively. So they might be wise to turn to DST Systems to handle their information processing tasks. The company provides information processing software and services to the mutual fund insurance retirement and healthcare industries. The company's financial services segment offers software and systems used to handle a wide range of tasks including shareowner recordkeeping investment management and business process management. Among the healthcare offerings are claims adjudication and benefit and care management. DST makes most of its sales to customers in the US. The company was acquired by SS&C Technologies Holdings in 2018.

	Annual Growth	12/13	12/14	12/15	12/16	12/17
Sales ($ mil.)	(6.9%)	–	2,749.3	2,825.1	1,556.7	2,218.2
Net income ($ mil.)	(8.7%)	–	593.3	358.1	426.4	452.1
Market value ($ mil.)	–	–	–	–	–	–
Employees	–	–	–	–	–	15,700

DTE ELECTRIC COMPANY

One Energy Plaza
Detroit, MI 48226-1279
Phone: 313 235-4000
Fax: –
Web: www.dteenergy.com

CEO: –
CFO: Peter B Oleksiak
HR: –
FYE: December 31
Type: Public

Ford Motors is not the only powerhouse operating in Detroit — DTE Electric is another. The utility (formerly known as Detroit Edison) generates and distributes electricity to 2.2 million customers in Michigan mainly around Detroit with expansion north to Lake Huron and east to Ann Arbor. The company a unit of regional power player DTE Energy has more than 11000 MW of generating capacity from its interests in primarily fossil-fueled nuclear and hydroelectric power plants. It operates more than 46000 circuit miles of distribution lines and owns and operates more than 670 distribution substations.

	Annual Growth	12/17	12/18	12/19	12/20	12/21
Sales ($ mil.)	3.3%	5,102.0	5,298.0	5,224.0	5,506.0	5,809.0
Net income ($ mil.)	9.6%	601.0	664.0	716.0	778.0	866.0
Market value ($ mil.)	–	–	–	–	–	–
Employees	0.0%	4,700	4,900	4,900	10,600	4,700

DTE ENERGY CO
NYS: DTE

One Energy Plaza
Detroit, MI 48226-1279
Phone: 313 235-4000
Fax: –
Web: www.dteenergy.com

CEO: Gerardo Norcia
CFO: David Ruud
HR: –
FYE: December 31
Type: Public

DTE Energy is a diversified energy company involved in the development and management of energy-related businesses and services nationwide. DTE Electric distributes electricity to some 2.2 million customers in southeastern Michigan. The utility's power plants have a generating capacity of more than 11700 MW. The company's DTE Gas unit distributes natural gas to 1.3 million customers throughout Michigan. DTE Energy runs non-regulated businesses in gas storage & pipelines power & industrial operations and energy trading.

	Annual Growth	12/17	12/18	12/19	12/20	12/21
Sales ($ mil.)	4.4%	12,607.0	14,212.0	12,669.0	12,177.0	14,964.0
Net income ($ mil.)	(5.4%)	1,134.0	1,120.0	1,169.0	1,368.0	907.0
Market value ($ mil.)	2.2%	21,207.6	21,370.4	25,162.0	23,522.9	23,160.6
Employees	0.2%	10,200	10,600	10,700	10,600	10,300

DTS INC
NMS: DTSI

5220 Las Virgenes Road
Calabasas, CA 91302
Phone: 818 436-1000
Fax: –
Web: www.dts.com

CEO: Jon E Kirchner
CFO: Melvin L Flanigan
HR: Kathleen Gelineau
FYE: December 31
Type: Public

DTS (formerly Digital Theater Systems) surrounds movie lovers with sound. The company's multi-channel audio systems are used in consumer electronic devices such as audio/video receivers DVD and Blu-ray HD players PCs car audio products video game consoles and home theater systems. DTS has licensing agreements with major consumer electronics manufacturers (Sony Samsung and Philips). It also provides DTS-encoded soundtracks in movies TV shows and music content. The firm was founded in 1990 as Digital Theater Systems by scientist Terry Beard. It received initial funding from Universal Pictures in 1993 and used that relationship to debut its audio system in the soundtrack to Universal's Jurassic Park.

	Annual Growth	12/10	12/11	12/12	12/13	12/14
Sales ($ mil.)	13.4%	87.1	96.9	100.6	125.1	143.9
Net income ($ mil.)	14.1%	16.0	18.3	(15.9)	15.8	27.1
Market value ($ mil.)	(11.0%)	852.1	473.2	290.1	415.4	534.2
Employees	13.0%	228	258	369	373	372

DUCKS UNLIMITED, INC.

1 WATERFOWL WAY
MEMPHIS, TN 381202351
Phone: 901-758-3825
Fax: –
Web: www.ducks.org

CEO: Dale Hall
CFO: Randy L Graves
HR: –
FYE: June 30
Type: Private

If it walks like a duck and talks like a duck ... Ducks Unlimited wants to protect its habitat. The not-for-profit group works to conserve manage and restore wetlands and other waterfowl habitat through projects across North America and in more than 10 South American countries. With some 13 million acres under its care DU's efforts are aimed at ducks but also benefit more than 900 other wildlife species. Most of the organization's members and volunteers are sport hunters and DU puts out a magazine cable TV show and daily radio show for them. It also offers training in hunter ethics firearm safety and conservation and programs for children. DU was founded in 1937 and has more than 691000 members.

	Annual Growth	06/12	06/13	06/14	06/15	06/20
Sales ($ mil.)	0.6%	–	–	178.4	209.6	185.7
Net income ($ mil.)	–	–	–	5.7	23.3	(24.3)
Market value ($ mil.)	–	–	–	–	–	–
Employees	–	–	–	–	–	500

DUCOMMUN INC.
NYS: DCO

200 Sandpointe Avenue, Suite 700
Santa Ana, CA 92707-5759
Phone: 657 335-3665
Fax: –
Web: www.ducommun.com

CEO: Stephen Oswald
CFO: Christopher Wampler
HR: –
FYE: December 31
Type: Public

Ducommun is a leading global provider of engineering and manufacturing services for high-performance products and high-cost-of failure applications used primarily in the aerospace and defense (A&D) industrial medical and other industries (collectively Industrial). Structural Systems engineers and manufactures structures and assemblies such as aircraft wing spoilers and large fuselage skins rotor blades on rotary-wing aircraft and components. Electronic Systems makes electromechanical components such as switch assemblies actuators keyboard panels and avionics racks. Products for military and space applications account for over 65% of its sales each year.

	Annual Growth	12/16	12/17	12/18	12/19	12/20
Sales ($ mil.)	3.4%	550.6	558.2	629.3	721.1	628.9
Net income ($ mil.)	3.7%	25.3	20.1	9.0	32.5	29.2
Market value ($ mil.)	20.4%	299.8	333.7	426.0	592.6	629.8
Employees	(2.4%)	2,700	2,600	2,600	2,800	2,450

DUCOMMUN LABARGE TECHNOLOGIES

9900 Clayton Rd.
St. Louis MO 63124
Phone: 314-997-0800
Fax: 314-812-9438
Web: www.ducommun.com/dti

CEO: –
CFO: Joseph Bellino
HR: –
FYE: December 31
Type: Subsidiary

Contract manufacturer Ducommun LaBarge Technologies (formerly LaBarge Inc.) designs and produces complex electronics and interconnect systems able to withstand the physical extremes of combat space sea and inner earth. Its printed circuit boards cables electronic assemblies and other products are used for such applications as military communication systems commercial aircraft satellites medical equipment airport security glass container fabrication systems and oil drilling equipment. Customers have included Owens-Illinois and Raytheon. Ducommun acquired LaBarge for $340 million in 2011 to expand its manufacturing capabilities. LaBarge was combined with Ducommun's technologies subsidiary and renamed.

DUKE ENERGY CORP
NYS: DUK

550 South Tryon Street
Charlotte, NC 28202-1803
Phone: 704 382-3853
Fax: –
Web: www.duke-energy.com

CEO: Lynn J Good
CFO: Steven K Young
HR: –
FYE: December 31
Type: Public

Duke Energy is one of the top electric power holding companies in the US serving about 7.9 million retail customers in six US states covering more than 90000s quare miles of service area in the Southeast and Midwest. Its electric utilities and infrastructure owns approximately 50800 MW of generation capacity. The company also serves about 1.6 million natural gas customers through more than 60000 miles of pipelines and service lines. Duke Energy's rate-regulated utilities serve customers in the Carolinas Florida Ohio Indiana and Kentucky. The company also owns some renewable energy assets like wind and solar farms.

	Annual Growth	12/16	12/17	12/18	12/19	12/20
Sales ($ mil.)	1.2%	22,743.0	23,565.0	24,521.0	25,079.0	23,868.0
Net income ($ mil.)	(10.6%)	2,152.0	3,059.0	2,666.0	3,748.0	1,377.0
Market value ($ mil.)	4.2%	59,689.8	64,680.6	66,364.7	70,140.5	70,409.6
Employees	(1.1%)	28,798	29,060	30,083	28,793	27,535

DUKE ENERGY FLORIDA LLC

NL: –

299 First Avenue North
St. Petersburg, FL 33701
Phone: 704 382-3853
Fax: –

CEO: Vincent Dolan
CFO: Mark Mulhern
HR: –
FYE: December 31
Type: Public

Sometimes the sunshine state just isn't bright enough and that's when Florida Power (doing business as Progress Energy Florida) really shines. The utility transmits and distributes electricity to 1.6 million customers and oversees 10025 MW of generating capacity from interests in 14 nuclear and coal- oil- and gas-fired power plants. Additionally Florida Power purchases about 20% of the energy it provides. Florida Power operates 5100 miles of transmission lines and 52000 miles of overhead and 18700 miles of underground distribution cable. It also has 500 electric substations. A subsidiary of holding company Duke Energy the company also sells wholesale power to other utilities and marketers.

	Annual Growth	12/16	12/17	12/18	12/19	12/20
Sales ($ mil.)	3.2%	4,568.0	4,646.0	5,021.0	5,231.0	5,188.0
Net income ($ mil.)	8.8%	551.0	712.0	554.0	692.0	771.0
Market value ($ mil.)	–	–	–	–	–	–
Employees	–	–	–	–	–	–

DUKE ENERGY INDIANA, INC.

1000 East Main Street
Plainfield, IN 46168
Phone: 704 382-3853
Fax: –
Web: www.duke-energy.com

CEO: Lynn J Good
CFO: Steven Young
HR: –
FYE: December 31
Type: Public

Duke Energy Indiana helps to light up the Hoosier state. Indiana's largest utility Duke Energy subsidiary Duke Energy Indiana transmits and distributes electricity to 69 of the state's 92 counties (approximately 790000 customers). The utility also owns power plants (about 7000 MW of primarily fossil-fueled capacity) which are operated by its parent's merchant energy division. Duke Energy Indiana's service area covers about 22000 sq. miles with an estimated population of 2.4 million. The company operates about 31000 miles of distribution lines and a 5400-mile transmission system.

	Annual Growth	12/16	12/17	12/18	12/19	12/20
Sales ($ mil.)	(1.4%)	2,958.0	3,047.0	3,059.0	3,004.0	2,795.0
Net income ($ mil.)	1.7%	381.0	354.0	393.0	436.0	408.0
Market value ($ mil.)	–	–	–	–	–	–
Employees	–	–	–	–	–	–

DUKE REALTY CORP

NYS: DRE

8711 River Crossing Boulevard
Indianapolis, IN 46240
Phone: 317 808-6000
Fax: –
Web: www.dukerealty.com

CEO: James Connor
CFO: Mark Denien
HR: –
FYE: December 31
Type: Public

Duke Realty is a self-managed and self-administered real estate investment trust (REIT). It owns and develops industrial properties primarily in major cities that are key logistics markets. In addition to about 535 properties totaling more than 159.6 million sq. ft. of rentable space the company owns some 1000 acres of land and control an additional 800 acres through purchase options. The REIT leases its properties to a variety of tenants including e-commerce manufacturing retail wholesale and distribution firms. Duke's service operations include construction and development asset and property management and leasing. The company was founded in 1972.

	Annual Growth	12/17	12/18	12/19	12/20	12/21
Sales ($ mil.)	9.1%	780.9	947.9	973.8	993.2	1,105.9
Net income ($ mil.)	(15.0%)	1,634.4	383.7	429.0	299.9	852.9
Market value ($ mil.)	24.6%	10,408.2	9,907.1	13,261.7	15,289.0	25,108.2
Employees	(4.0%)	400	400	400	350	340

DUKE UNIVERSITY

CEO: –

2200 W MAIN ST STE 710
DURHAM, NC 277054677
Phone: 919-684-8111
Fax: –
Web: www.duke.edu

CFO: Kenneth Morris
HR: –
FYE: June 30
Type: Private

Duke University has 15 551 undergraduate and graduate students. Duke School and Colleges includes Trinity College of Art and Sciences the Fuqua School of Business and the Pratt School of Engineering and more. The private institution which boasts some 3956 faculty members also operates the Duke University Health System (DUHS). Duke was founded in 1924 but traces its roots to 1838.

	Annual Growth	06/02	06/03	06/04	06/05	06/12
Sales ($ mil.)	6.4%	–	–	2,806.8	1,832.9	4,611.9
Net income ($ mil.)	–	–	–	679.7	246.9	(508.0)
Market value ($ mil.)	–	–	–	–	–	–
Employees	–	–	–	–	–	8,852

DUKE UNIVERSITY HEALTH SYSTEM, INC.

2301 ERWIN RD
DURHAM, NC 277054699
Phone: 919-684-8111
Fax: –
Web: www.dukehealth.org

CEO: –
CFO: –
HR: –
FYE: June 30
Type: Private

Duke University Health System is a world-class hospital and health care network supported by outstanding and renowned clinical faculty nurses and care teams. In addition to its hospitals Duke Health has an extensive geographically dispersed network of outpatient facilities that include primary care offices urgent care centers multi-specialty clinics and outpatient surgery centers. Its Duke Health & Well-Being includes a medically-based weight loss program medically-based fitness wellness and rehabilitation programs at the Duke Health & Fitness Center and Duke Integrative Medicine which combines evidence-based treatment with proven complementary therapies.

	Annual Growth	06/17	06/18	06/19	06/20	06/21
Sales ($ mil.)	5.9%	–	3,597.9	3,836.8	3,951.5	4,269.5
Net income ($ mil.)	47.2%	–	688.1	160.5	(296.6)	2,195.0
Market value ($ mil.)	–	–	–	–	–	–
Employees	–	–	–	–	–	2,400

DUN & BRADSTREET CORP (DE)

NYS: DNB

103 JFK Parkway
Short Hills, NJ 07078
Phone: 973 921-5500
Fax: –
Web: www.dnb.com

CEO: Anthony Jabbour
CFO: Bryan Hipsher
HR: –
FYE: December 31
Type: Public

The Dun & Bradstreet Corporation is one of the world's leading suppliers of business information and research. Its global database contains commercial data on more than 265 million companies and it holds the world's largest volume of business-credit information. The company mines its data to create software products web-based applications and marketing information and purchasing-support services for its customers. Its data and content can be integrated into clients' systems workflows and apps. The company's operations are split into two main segments: risk management and sales and marketing solutions. Dun & Bradstreet is the publisher of this profile.

	Annual Growth	12/12	12/13	12/14	12/15	12/16
Sales ($ mil.)	0.6%	1,663.0	1,655.2	1,681.8	1,637.1	1,703.7
Net income ($ mil.)	(24.2%)	295.5	258.5	294.4	168.8	97.4
Market value ($ mil.)	11.4%	2,894.3	4,517.2	4,451.3	3,824.6	4,464.6
Employees	1.1%	4,600	4,600	4,900	5,000	4,800

DUN & BRADSTREET HOLDINGS INC
NYS: DNB

101 John F. Kennedy Parkway
Short Hills, NJ 07078
Phone: 973 921-5500
Fax: –
Web: www.dnb.com

CEO: Anthony M Jabbour
CFO: Bryan T Hipsher
HR: –
FYE: December 31
Type: Public

Dun & Bradstreet Holdings is primarily engaged in providing mercantile and consumer credit reporting services. Through its operating company The Dun & Bradstreet Corporation the company helps companies around the world improve their business performance by transforming data into valuable business insights which are the foundation of its global solutions that clients rely on to make mission critical business decisions. In mid-2020 the company went public again with an initial public offering price of approximately $22.00 per share resulting in gross proceeds of approximately $2381047464.

	Annual Growth	12/17	12/18*	02/19*	12/19	12/20
Sales ($ mil.)	(0.1%)	1,742.5	1,716.4	178.7	1,413.9	1,738.1
Net income ($ mil.)	–	141.7	288.1	(75.6)	(674.0)	(175.6)
Market value ($ mil.)	–	–	–	–	–	10,531.5
Employees	0.0%	–	–	–	4,037	4,039

*Fiscal year change

DUNCAN ENERGY PARTNERS L.P.

1100 Louisiana St. 10th Fl.
Houston TX 77002
Phone: 713-381-6500
Fax: 713-381-6668
Web: www.deplp.com

CEO: W Randall Fowler
CFO: Bryan F Bulawa
HR: –
FYE: December 31
Type: Subsidiary

Duncan Energy Partners (DEP) went deep and wide to make its money. The midstream operator a former spinoff from Enterprise Products Partners found stored and transported natural gas and other petrochemicals. Its operations included Mont Belvieu Caverns (with a 100-million-barrel capacity) the 1000-mile-long Acadian Gas pipeline in Louisiana propylene pipelines between Texas and Louisiana and a 297-mile-long intrastate natural gas liquids (NGLs) pipeline. It owned stakes in 9430 miles of natural gas pipelines and more than 1480 miles of NGL pipelines. Reconsolidating to boost its market share in 2011 Enterprise Products Partners bought the 40% of DEP it did not own for $2.4 billion.

DUNCAN EQUIPMENT COMPANY

3450 S MACARTHUR BLVD
OKLAHOMA CITY, OK 73179-7638
Phone: 405-688-2300
Fax: –
Web: www.blackhawkid.com

CEO: –
CFO: –
HR: –
FYE: December 31
Type: Private

Industrial companies run on Dunkin' — Duncan Equipment that is. Doing business as Duncan Industrial Solutions the company supplies its industrial customers with a slew of maintenance repair and overhaul (MRO) tools. Duncan distributes name brand process equipment pumps electronic and cutting tools power transmission supplies safety supplies and material handling supplies. It also offers bar coding supply chain and inventory management services as well as safety compliance and product training. Duncan has offices in Oklahoma Texas and through Atlantic Tool Systems (ATS) New Jersey. Founded in 1948 the company is owned by BlackHawk Industrial Distribution and Brazos Private Equity.

	Annual Growth	12/03	12/04	12/05	12/06	12/07
Sales ($ mil.)	–	–	–	(895.4)	74.6	77.8
Net income ($ mil.)	23676.1%	–	–	0.0	13.9	2.4
Market value ($ mil.)	–	–	–	–	–	–
Employees	–	–	–	–	–	170

DUNE ENERGY, INC.
NBB: DUNR

811 Louisiana Street,, Suite 2300
Houston, TX 77002
Phone: 713 229-6300
Fax: –
Web: www.duneenergy.com

CEO: –
CFO: –
HR: –
FYE: December 31
Type: Public

Like sand piling up in a windblown sand dune Dune Energy is looking to pile up profits from its Texas and Louisiana oil and gas properties. The oil and gas exploration and production independent has leases on 100000 gross acres across 23 producing oil and natural gas fields along the Texas and Louisiana Gulf Coast. In 2008 Dune Energy reported proved reserves of 8.2 million barrels of oil and 83.8 billion cu. ft. of natural gas. It has a more than two-year current drilling inventory for its properties along the Gulf Coast. Swiss bank UBS owns 35% of the company; Russian gas company ITERA's Tierra Holdings BV unit 33%.

	Annual Growth	12/09	12/10	12/11	12/12	12/13
Sales ($ mil.)	(3.8%)	64.9	64.2	62.9	52.1	55.5
Net income ($ mil.)	–	(59.1)	(75.5)	(60.4)	(7.9)	(47.0)
Market value ($ mil.)	55.0%	16.3	29.0	2.0	112.4	94.2
Employees	(8.3%)	48	38	34	32	34

DUNKIN' BRANDS GROUP INC
NMS: DNKN

130 Royall Street
Canton, MA 02021
Phone: 781 737-3000
Fax: –
Web: www.dunkinbrands.com

CEO: David Hoffmann
CFO: Kate Jaspon
HR: –
FYE: December 29
Type: Public

Dunkin' Brands Group is a leading quick service restaurant franchisor operating both the Dunkin' and Baskin-Robbins chains with more than 20900 locations in about 60 countries. Dunkin' is the world's leading donut chain boasting nearly 13000 units in about 45 countries (including approximately 3500 in the US). Baskin-Robbins is a top ice cream and frozen snacks outlet with more than 8000 locations in about 55 countries (some 2600 in the US). Having divested all its company-operated restaurants Dunkin' Brands counts royalty income and franchise fees as a key revenue source. The company ropped the "Donuts" from its name in 2019. It was founded in 1950.

	Annual Growth	12/14	12/15	12/16	12/17	12/18
Sales ($ mil.)	15.3%	748.7	810.9	828.9	860.5	1,321.6
Net income ($ mil.)	6.9%	176.4	105.2	195.6	350.9	229.9
Market value ($ mil.)	10.6%	3,498.1	3,497.3	4,329.5	5,322.7	5,236.0
Employees	(0.6%)	1,134	1,145	1,163	1,148	1,107

DUNKIN' BRANDS GROUP INC.
NASDAQ: DNKN

130 Royall St.
Canton MA 02021
Phone: 781-737-3000
Fax: 781-737-4000
Web: www.dunkinbrands.com

CEO: Nigel Travis
CFO: Cornelius F Moses
HR: –
FYE: December 31
Type: Public

Doughnuts and ice cream make sweet bedfellows at Dunkin' Brands Group. The company is a leading multi-concept quick-service restaurant franchisor that operates both the Dunkin' Donuts and Baskin-Robbins chains. It has more than 16800 franchise locations operating in about 60 countries. With some 10000 units in about 30 countries (including approximately 7000 in the US) Dunkin' Donuts is the world's leading doughnut chain. Baskin-Robbins is a top ice cream and frozen snacks outlet with more than 6700 locations in 45 countries (2450 in the US). The company went public in mid-2011.

DUPONT DE NEMOURS INC
NYS: DD

974 Centre Road, Building 730　　　　　　　　　CEO: Edward Breen
Wilmington, DE 19805　　　　　　　　　　　　　　CFO: Lori Koch
Phone: 302-774-3034　　　　　　　　　　　　　　HR: –
Fax: –　　　　　　　　　　　　　　　　　　　　　FYE: December 31
Web: www.investors.dupont.com　　　　　　　　Type: Public

DuPont is a global innovation leader with technology-based materials and solutions that help transform industries and everyday life by applying diverse science and expertise to help customers advance their best ideas and deliver essential innovations in key markets including electronics transportation building and construction healthcare and worker safety. The company has subsidiaries in about 60 countries worldwide and manufacturing operations in about 40 countries. In conjunction with the closing of the N&B Transaction in early 2020 DuPont realigned its segments to Electronics & Industrial Mobility & Materials and Water & Protection effective in February 2021. About 30% of the company's revenue comes from US.

	Annual Growth	12/17	12/18	12/19	12/20	12/21
Sales ($ mil.)	9.3%	11,672.0	22,594.0	21,512.0	20,397.0	16,653.0
Net income ($ mil.)	53.7%	1,159.0	3,845.0	498.0	(2,951.0)	6,467.0
Market value ($ mil.)	3.2%	36,449.9	27,370.7	32,857.1	36,393.6	41,342.6
Employees	(10.6%)	–	–	35,000	34,000	28,000

DUPONT FABROS TECHNOLOGY INC
NYS: DFT

401 9th Street NW, Suite 600　　　　　　　　　CEO: Christopher P Eldredge
Washington, DC 20004　　　　　　　　　　　　　CFO: Jeffrey H Foster
Phone: 202-728-0044　　　　　　　　　　　　　　HR: –
Fax: –　　　　　　　　　　　　　　　　　　　　　FYE: December 31
Web: www.dft.com　　　　　　　　　　　　　　　Type: Public

DuPont Fabros Technology's server farms corral a lot of data. The company owns develops operates and manages 12 wholesale data centers — the facilities that house power and cool computer servers for such technology companies as Facebook Rackspace Microsoft and Yahoo! Other tenants come from the media communications health care and financial services industries. Organized as a real estate investment trust (REIT) DuPont Fabros is exempt from paying federal income tax as long as it makes quarterly distributions to shareholders.

	Annual Growth	12/11	12/12	12/13	12/14	12/15
Sales ($ mil.)	12.0%	287.4	332.4	375.1	417.6	452.4
Net income ($ mil.)	(58.6%)	65.0	53.0	48.4	105.9	1.9
Market value ($ mil.)	7.0%	1,601.1	1,597.1	1,633.5	2,197.4	2,101.5
Employees	5.6%	91	93	92	97	113

DUQUESNE LIGHT COMPANY

411 7TH AVE 6-1　　　　　　　　　　　　　　　　CEO: Kevin Walker
PITTSBURGH, PA 152191942　　　　　　　　　　CFO: Mark E Kaplan
Phone: 412-393-6000　　　　　　　　　　　　　　HR: –
Fax: –　　　　　　　　　　　　　　　　　　　　　FYE: December 31
Web: www.duquesnelight.com　　　　　　　　　Type: Private

Duquesne Light is the first and last resort for light for many residential customers in the Keystone State. The utility company provides electricity to more than 588000 customers (90% of which are residential) in southwestern Pennsylvania via an extensive transmission and distribution system. The utility a subsidiary of Duquesne Light Holdings (formerly DQE) acts as a generation Provider of Last Resort (POLR) for customers who do not choose an alternative supplier. A consortium led by Macquarie Infrastructure Partners controls the company's parent.

	Annual Growth	12/15	12/16	12/17	12/18	12/19
Sales ($ mil.)	2.2%	–	903.3	911.1	937.5	963.1
Net income ($ mil.)	15.9%	–	118.6	130.5	152.1	184.4
Market value ($ mil.)	–	–	–	–	–	–
Employees	–	–	–	–	–	1,000

DUQUESNE UNIVERSITY OF THE HOLY SPIRIT

600 FORBES AVE　　　　　　　　　　　　　　　　CEO: –
PITTSBURGH, PA 152193016　　　　　　　　　　CFO: –
Phone: 412-396-6000　　　　　　　　　　　　　　HR: –
Fax: –　　　　　　　　　　　　　　　　　　　　　FYE: June 30
Web: www.duq.edu　　　　　　　　　　　　　　　Type: Private

Duquesne University of The Holy Spirit keeps a keen eye on the spiritual as well as the academic. The Catholic university offers 80 undergraduate degree programs and 90 master's doctoral and professional programs at nine schools including ones devoted to business education law liberal arts health sciences and music. Duquesne also offers more than 20 online programs. The college has an annual enrollment of more than 9300 undergraduate graduate and professional students and a student-faculty ratio of 14:1. Duquesne was founded in 1878 as the Pittsburgh Catholic College.

	Annual Growth	06/11	06/12	06/15	06/20	06/21
Sales ($ mil.)	1.3%	–	262.7	400.4	434.2	296.0
Net income ($ mil.)	40.7%	–	7.3	25.6	12.1	158.7
Market value ($ mil.)	–	–	–	–	–	–
Employees	–	–	–	–	–	3,601

DURA AUTOMOTIVE SYSTEMS LLC

1780 Pond Run　　　　　　　　　　　　　　　　　CEO: –
Auburn Hills MI 48326　　　　　　　　　　　　　 CFO: –
Phone: 248-299-7500　　　　　　　　　　　　　　HR: –
Fax: 248-475-4378　　　　　　　　　　　　　　　FYE: December 31
Web: www.duraauto.com　　　　　　　　　　　　Type: Private

You wouldn't be able to keep the pedal to the metal without DURA Automotive Systems' driver control systems. The company is a leading supplier of pedal systems parking brake mechanisms manual and automatic transmission gear shifter systems and auto cables. DURA also designs and makes engineered assemblies such as tailgate latches and seating adjustment controls as well as structural door modules and exterior trim. The company sells to auto OEMs and many suppliers in North America Europe and Asia. Customers include Ford Volkswagen GM Chrysler and BMW. DURA has about 30 facilities in 17 countries. In late 2009 private equity Patriarch Partners bought a majority interest in DURA for about $125 million.

DURA COAT PRODUCTS INC.

5361 VIA RICARDO　　　　　　　　　　　　　　　CEO: Myung K Hong
RIVERSIDE, CA 925092414　　　　　　　　　　　CFO: –
Phone: 951-341-6500　　　　　　　　　　　　　　HR: Raul Muytoy
Fax: –　　　　　　　　　　　　　　　　　　　　　FYE: December 31
Web: www.duracoatproducts.com　　　　　　　Type: Private

Durability is fundamental to Dura Coat Products. The company specializes in high-performance coatings for metal surfaces. Dura Coat develops and makes coil-applied coatings to protect metal building exteriors and roofing trim and sidewall rain ware and HVAC components. Coatings are also used on garage doors appliances hardware and vehicles. Spray coatings protect aluminum extrusions such as window frames and storefronts. For galvanized tubing its high-solids exterior and water-based interior coatings are made to meet mechanical and electrical tubing markets. Dura Coat operates manufacturing plants in Huntsville Alabama and Riverside California.

	Annual Growth	12/09	12/10	12/11	12/12	12/13
Sales ($ mil.)	–	–	–	0.0	0.0	100.0	100.0
Net income ($ mil.)	–	–	–	–	0.0	0.0	0.0
Market value ($ mil.)	–	–	–	–	–	–
Employees	–	–	–	–	–	120

DURATA THERAPEUTICS INC.   NASDAQ: DRTX

89 Headquarters Plaza North 14th Fl.
Morristown NJ 07960
Phone: 973-993-4865
Fax: 610-930-2042
Web: www.globusmedical.com
CEO: –
CFO: –
HR: –
FYE: December 31
Type: Private

You don't even want to think about the infections Durata Therapeutics is hoping to treat. Its lead candidate dalbavancin is designed for people with acute bacterial skin and skin structure infections (abSSSI) usually caused by Strep and Staph bacteria. Dalbavancin is given once a week by IV as opposed to the current treatment which must be given several times a day. The development stage company is conducting clinical trials in the US and Western Europe and hopes to begin selling dalbavancin to hospitals through its own sales force in late 2013. Durata's other drug candidates include pleuromutalins and lincosamide also high level antibacterials. The company formed in 2009 went public in 2012.

DURECT CORP   NAS: DRRX

10260 Bubb Road
Cupertino, CA 95014
Phone: 408 777-1417
Fax: –
Web: www.durect.com
CEO: James E Brown
CFO: Matthew J Hogan
HR: –
FYE: December 31
Type: Public

Biopharmaceutical DURECT is developing drug delivery systems to provide long-term therapy for such conditions as chronic pain and cancer. Its drug delivery technologies include ORADUR a sustained release oral gel-cap; SABER an injectable delivery system. In the field of epigenetics or treatments that don't involve DNA alteration the company seeks to discover and develop new therapeutic molecules. Its lead candidate is DUR-928 which may help treat organ injuries liver diseases and inflammatory skin conditions. The firm also sells absorbable polymers (LACTEL) and osmotic pumps (ALZET) to pharmaceutical and medical research firms. Its US accounts for the majority of sales of the company.

	Annual Growth	12/16	12/17	12/18	12/19	12/20
Sales ($ mil.)	21.0%	14.0	49.2	18.6	29.6	30.1
Net income ($ mil.)	–	(34.5)	(3.7)	(25.3)	(20.6)	(0.6)
Market value ($ mil.)	11.5%	272.7	187.6	98.3	773.4	421.3
Employees	(4.7%)	98	93	–	90	81

DUSA PHARMACEUTICALS INC.   NASDAQ: DUSA

25 Upton Dr.
Wilmington MA 01887
Phone: 978-657-7500
Fax: 978-657-9193
Web: www.dusapharma.com
CEO: Robert F Doman
CFO: Richard Christopher
HR: –
FYE: December 31
Type: Public

DUSA Pharmaceuticals has seen the light. The company develops photodynamic therapy (PDT) devices and drugs for treating and diagnosing dermatological conditions using a combination of drugs and light. DUSA markets its Levulan Kerastick topical solution and applicator which are used in combination with the BLU-U light to treat actinic keratoses or pre-cancerous skin lesions caused by sun exposure. When used together Levulan Kerastick and BLU-U are known as the Levulan PDT process; on its own BLU-U is also FDA approved to treat moderate acne. While DUSA packages Levulan into its Kerastick applicator products third parties manufacture its drugs and light systems. DUSA is being acquired by Sun Pharmaceutical.

DXP ENTERPRISES, INC.   NMS: DXPE

5301 Hollister
Houston, TX 77040
Phone: 713 996-4700
Fax: –
Web: www.dxpe.com
CEO: David Little
CFO: Kent Yee
HR: –
FYE: December 31
Type: Public

DXP Enterprises (DXP) is a distributor of industrial maintenance repair and operations (MRO) products and services through its three main segments?Service Centers Innovative Pumping Solutions and Supply Chain Services. The company's Service Centers segment offers more than one million items in the bearing rotating equipment fluid power power transmission and safety product categories. It also provides technical design and logistics services. DXP serves the oil and gas agriculture chemical construction food and beverage mining and transportation markets. It operates from about 170 locations throughout the US and Canada as well as in Mexico and Dubai. The US accounts for more than 90% of total revenue.

	Annual Growth	12/16	12/17	12/18	12/19	12/20
Sales ($ mil.)	1.1%	962.1	1,006.8	1,216.2	1,267.2	1,005.3
Net income ($ mil.)	–	7.7	16.9	35.6	36.0	(28.7)
Market value ($ mil.)	(10.6%)	667.3	568.0	534.8	764.7	427.0
Employees	1.0%	2,453	2,511	1,576	1,586	2,550

DYADIC INTERNATIONAL INC   NAS: DYAI

140 Intracoastal Pointe Drive, Suite 404
Jupiter, FL 33477
Phone: 561 743-8333
Fax: 561 743-8343
Web: www.dyadic.com
CEO: Mark Emalfarb
CFO: Ping Rawson
HR: –
FYE: December 31
Type: Public

Dyadic International hopes to unlock biotechnology dynasties using its C1 technology. The company uses its C1 Expression System to develop biological and chemical substances for a variety of life sciences and industrial applications. The firm's enzyme business makes enzymes and other products for commercial and industrial uses employing C1 know-how. Industries served include textiles agriculture and paper mills. Dyadic's biopharma division uses the expression system to make therapeutic proteins for drugmakers. The company is also developing its enzymes for bioenergy applications including biofuels.

	Annual Growth	12/16	12/17	12/18	12/19	12/20
Sales ($ mil.)	28.2%	0.6	0.8	1.3	1.7	1.6
Net income ($ mil.)	–	(3.6)	(2.1)	(5.7)	(8.3)	(9.3)
Market value ($ mil.)	34.2%	45.6	38.2	52.0	142.4	147.9
Employees	(3.8%)	7	7	8	9	6

DYAX CORP   NMS: DYAX

55 Network Drive
Burlington, MA 01803
Phone: 617 225-2500
Fax: –
Web: www.dyax.com
CEO: –
CFO: –
HR: –
FYE: December 31
Type: Public

Dyax has two ways to make a difference — by developing its own drugs or by licensing its proprietary discovery technology to help others discover and develop drugs. The biopharmaceutical company's phage display technology rapidly identifies proteins peptides and antibodies useful in treating disease. Dyax's first commercial drug Kalbitor (ecallantide) is approved in the US to treat hereditary angioedema (HAE a condition causing tissue swelling) and enjoys orphan drug designation. The company is also investigating the drug for use in treating other types of angioedema and working to obtain regulatory approval for the drug in overseas markets.

	Annual Growth	12/09	12/10	12/11	12/12	12/13
Sales ($ mil.)	25.6%	21.6	51.4	48.7	54.7	53.9
Net income ($ mil.)	–	(62.4)	(24.5)	(34.6)	(29.3)	(27.8)
Market value ($ mil.)	22.1%	412.6	262.9	165.5	423.5	917.0
Employees	(0.2%)	121	137	120	125	120

DYCOM INDUSTRIES, INC.

NYS: DY

11780 US Highway 1, Suite 600
Palm Beach Gardens, FL 33408
Phone: 561 627-7171
Fax: 561 627-7709
Web: www.dycomind.com

CEO: Steven Nielsen
CFO: H. Andrew DeFerrari
HR: Kimberly Dickens
FYE: January 30
Type: Public

Dycom Industries is a leading provider of specialty contracting services throughout the United States. Operating through a nationwide network of some 45 subsidiaries Dycom designs builds and maintains coaxial copper and fiber-optic cable systems as well as wireless infrastructure for phone companies and cable television operators. Dycom also supplies telecommunications providers with a comprehensive portfolio of specialty services such as program management planning and engineering and design among others. Most of the company's revenue comes from major telecommunications companies. The company traces its roots back in 1969.

	Annual Growth	07/17*	01/18	01/19	01/20	01/21
Sales ($ mil.)	1.1%	3,066.9	1,411.3	3,127.7	3,339.7	3,199.2
Net income ($ mil.)	(31.6%)	157.2	68.8	62.9	57.2	34.3
Market value ($ mil.)	(2.6%)	2,764.5	3,652.4	1,811.8	1,362.7	2,484.1
Employees	0.1%	14,225	14,365	14,920	15,230	14,276

*Fiscal year change

DYNACQ HEALTHCARE INC

NBB: DYII

4301 Vista Road
Pasadena, TX 77504
Phone: 713 378-2000
Fax: -
Web: www.dynacq.com

CEO: Eric K Chan
CFO: Hemant Khemka
HR: -
FYE: August 31
Type: Public

Dynacq Healthcare is a holding company that owns and operates acute-care specialty hospitals providing electively scheduled surgeries such as bariatric (weight loss) and orthopedic surgeries and pain management procedures. Dynacq operates Vista Hospital in Garland Texas and Surgery Specialty Hospitals of America in Pasadena Texas (suburbs of Dallas and Houston respectively). Most of the Dynacq's revenues come from workers' compensation insurance and commercial insurers on an out-of-network basis. Chairman and CEO Chiu Moon Chan owns more than half of Dynacq.

	Annual Growth	08/11	08/12	08/13	08/14	08/15
Sales ($ mil.)	-	(2.0)	5.5	6.1	10.2	7.0
Net income ($ mil.)	-	(19.2)	(12.2)	(3.3)	(3.8)	(3.8)
Market value ($ mil.)	(31.3%)	24.3	7.6	0.4	0.1	5.4
Employees	(2.1%)	137	111	127	131	126

DYNAMEX INC.

5429 LBJ Fwy. Ste. 1000
Dallas TX 75240
Phone: 214-560-9000
Fax: 214-560-9349
Web: www.dynamex.com

CEO: -
CFO: -
HR: -
FYE: July 31
Type: Subsidiary

Dynamex knows the dynamics of same-day delivery. The company provides both scheduled and on-demand delivery of time-sensitive items such as medical supplies and financial documents. It operates from more than 60 company-owned (but locally managed) facilities in the US and Canada. A network of ground couriers focuses on intracity deliveries while hird-party air and ground carriers fulfill same-day intercity services. Dynamex also supports clients in outsourcing certain logistics functions including management of dedicated vehicle fleets and facilities such as mailrooms and inventory-tracking call centers. The company has been owned by Canada's TransForce since 2011.

DYNAMIC OFFSHORE RESOURCES LLC

1301 McKinney Ste. 900
Houston TX 77010
Phone: 713-728-7840
Fax: 713-728-7860
Web: www.dynamicosr.com

CEO: George McCarroll
CFO: Howard Tate
HR: -
FYE: December 31
Type: Private

Dynamic Offshore Resources isn't giving up on the Gulf of Mexico. While other companies are pulling out of the gulf it has amassed offshore oil and natural gas properties stretching from Texas to Alabama. The company has interests in about 200 producing wells mostly located in water depths of less than 300 feet and 200 offshore leases covering 315000 net acres. It also owns a 49% interest in the deep-water Bullwinkle field and platform located at 1350 feet. (Superior Energy owns the other 51%). Dynamic Offshore Resources reported proved reserves of 62.5 million barrels of oil equivalent at the end of 2011. In 2012 the debt-laden company was acquired by SandRidge Energy for about $1.2 billion.

DYNAMIX GROUP, INC

1905 WOODSTOCK RD # 4150
ROSWELL, GA 300755625
Phone: 770-643-8877
Fax: -
Web: www.dynamixgroup.com

CEO: -
CFO: David A Delong
HR: -
FYE: December 31
Type: Private

Dynamix Group provides information technology (IT) products and services including the implementation and configuration of software and hardware as well as network systems maintenance and technical support from its offices throughout the southeastern US. The company offers a full range of products and services including top-of-the-line hardware software and maintenance. With decades of combined experience and deep knowledge of IBM and Cisco products the company has excellent client and technology partner relationships. Additional data network services include disaster recovery and storage management. The company targets the healthcare retail manufacturing as well as a variety of other industries. Dynamix was founded in 1995.

	Annual Growth	12/15	12/16	12/17	12/18	12/19
Sales ($ mil.)	(9.8%)	-	175.1	155.1	164.3	128.5
Net income ($ mil.)	(6.2%)	-	11.1	9.6	8.8	9.2
Market value ($ mil.)	-	-	-	-	-	-
Employees	-	-	-	-	-	97

DYNASIL CORP OF AMERICA

NBB: DYSL

313 Washington Street, Suite 403
Newton, MA 02458
Phone: 617 668-6855
Fax: -
Web: www.dynasil.com

CEO: Peter Sulick
CFO: Holly Hicks
HR: -
FYE: September 30
Type: Public

Dynasil Corporation of America likes playing with the dynamics of silica. The company manufactures custom synthetic-fused silica and quartz products primarily used in industrial optical materials. Its products include filters lenses prisms reflectors windows and mirrors. Customers use the company's fabricated optical products in lasers aircraft optical equipment analytical instruments semiconductors and electronics. Manufacturers Corning Schott Glass Technologies and General Electric supply the company with some fused silica fused quartz and optical materials. Dynasil sells its products in the US and overseas.

	Annual Growth	09/15	09/16	09/17	09/18	09/19
Sales ($ mil.)	1.9%	40.5	43.4	37.3	40.7	43.7
Net income ($ mil.)	-	(0.2)	0.7	2.2	1.8	(0.4)
Market value ($ mil.)	(16.7%)	28.7	14.7	18.5	19.1	13.8
Employees	(1.3%)	230	226	204	214	218

DYNATRONICS CORP. NAS: DYNT

1200 Trapp Road
Eagan, MN 55121
Phone: 801 568-7000
Fax: 801 568-7711
Web: www.dynatronics.com

CEO: John Krier
CFO: Norman Roegner
HR: Karen Morgan
FYE: June 30
Type: Public

Dynatronics makes medical equipment to keep active people on the go. Its physical medicine products include electrotherapy ultrasound and infrared light therapy equipment; medical supplies such as wraps braces bandages walking aids and training equipment; and rehabilitation therapy tables. Dynatronics also sells aesthetic products under the Synergie brand including the Synergie Aesthetic Massage System (AMS) for cosmetic weight loss and the Synergie Elite microdermabrasion device that reduces wrinkles. The company's products are sold directly through its own distributors and catalogs as well as through independent dealers. Customers include physicians surgeons and physical therapists.

	Annual Growth	06/17	06/18	06/19	06/20	06/21
Sales ($ mil.)	7.5%	35.8	64.4	62.6	53.4	47.8
Net income ($ mil.)	–	(1.9)	(1.6)	(0.9)	(3.4)	2.0
Market value ($ mil.)	(19.1%)	48.6	49.9	28.7	15.3	20.8
Employees	(6.9%)	233	336	284	195	175

DYNAVAX TECHNOLOGIES CORP NAS: DVAX

2100 Powell Street, Suite 900
Emeryville, CA 94608
Phone: 510 848-5100
Fax: –
Web: www.dynavax.com

CEO: Ryan Spencer
CFO: Kelly Macdonald
HR: –
FYE: December 31
Type: Public

Dynavax Technologies is trying to reprogram the way the body reacts to disease. The firm is a biopharmaceutical company focused on developing and commercializing novel vaccines. Its first commercial product HEPLISAV-B is approved by FDA for prevention of infection caused by all known subtypes of hepatitis B virus in adults age 18 years and above. Its other products and development programs target a number of areas including vaccine adjuvants cancer immunotherapy and autoimmune and inflammatory diseases. To share the expense and risk of development Dynavax has partnered with drugmakers including Merck and GlaxoSmithKline.

	Annual Growth	12/16	12/17	12/18	12/19	12/20
Sales ($ mil.)	43.3%	11.0	0.3	8.2	35.2	46.6
Net income ($ mil.)	–	(112.4)	(95.2)	(158.9)	(152.6)	(75.2)
Market value ($ mil.)	3.0%	435.2	2,060.6	1,008.2	630.3	490.3
Employees	(0.5%)	250	170	249	231	245

DYNAVOX INC. NASDAQ: DVOX

2100 Wharton St. Ste. 400
Pittsburgh PA 15203
Phone: 412-381-4883
Fax: 412-381-5241
Web: www.dynavoxtech.com

CEO: –
CFO: –
HR: –
FYE: June 30
Type: Public

DynaVox gives its customers a voice — literally. The company provides speech generation communication and environment control devices used by persons with speech learning and physical disabilities. Its products which come in various keyboard- and touchscreen-based form factors are used by individuals diagnosed with amyotrophic lateral sclerosis (ALS or Lou Gehrig's disease) autism cerebral palsy stroke traumatic brain injury and similar conditions. Besides the proprietary technology that drives its devices DynaVox also develops and sells the Boardmaker special education and text-to-speech software. The company generates most of its sales from the US.

DYNCORP INTERNATIONAL INC.

3190 Fairview Park Dr. Ste. 700
Falls Church VA 22042
Phone: 571-722-0210
Fax: 571-722-0252
Web: www.dyn-intl.com

CEO: George Krivo
CFO: William Kansky
HR: –
FYE: December 31
Type: Private

DynCorp International works behind the scenes to support military and diplomatic efforts on front lines. A US national security contractor DynCorp (DI) supports the US departments of State and Defense by providing linguist services and international police force training especially in Afghanistan and Iraq. It provides turnkey solutions for post-conflict countries to rebuild infrastructure install utilities/telecommunications provide security transport equipment and remove/dismantle weapons. It also constructs barracks hangars and provides aircraft repairs and service.

DYNEGY INC (NEW) (DE) NYS: DYN

601 Travis, Suite 1400
Houston, TX 77002
Phone: 713 507-6400
Fax: –
Web: www.dynegy.com

CEO: –
CFO: –
HR: –
FYE: December 31
Type: Public

Power company Dynegy (a mashup of "dynamic energy") has lost some of its dynamism in recent years but is looking to get some of that energy back as a reorganized company. Dynegy provides wholesale power capacity and other services to a broad range of customers (utilities cooperatives municipalities and other energy operations) in about a dozen states in the Midwest the Northeast Texas and on the West Coast. The company's power generation portfolio consists of about 50 power plants totaling about 27000 MW of generating capacity. More than 60% of its power generation is from natural gas. In 2017 Dynegy agreed to be bought by Vistra Energy for $1.74 billion in an all-stock deal.

	Annual Growth	12/12	12/13	12/14	12/15	12/16
Sales ($ mil.)	92.9%	312.0	1,466.0	2,497.0	3,870.0	4,318.0
Net income ($ mil.)	–	(107.0)	(356.0)	(273.0)	50.0	(1,240.0)
Market value ($ mil.)	(18.5%)	2,244.0	2,524.3	3,560.1	1,571.8	992.4
Employees	19.4%	1,210	1,710	1,679	2,591	2,457

DYNEX CAPITAL INC NYS: DX

4991 Lake Brook Drive, Suite 100
Glen Allen, VA 23060-9245
Phone: 804 217-5800
Fax: –
Web: www.dynexcapital.com

CEO: Byron Boston
CFO: Stephen Benedetti
HR: –
FYE: December 31
Type: Public

Dynex Capital is a real estate investment trust (REIT) that invests in loans and fixed-income securities backed by single-family residential and commercial mortgage loans. Its Investments consist primarily of Agency MBS including residential MBS (RMBS) commercial MBS (CMBS) and CMBS interest-only (IO) securities and non-Agency MBS which consist mainly of CMBS IO. Agency MBS have an implicit guaranty of principal payment by an agency of the US government or a US government-sponsored entity (GSE) such as Fannie Mae and Freddie Mac. Non-Agency MBS are issued by non-governmental enterprises and do not have a guaranty of principal payment.

	Annual Growth	12/16	12/17	12/18	12/19	12/20
Sales ($ mil.)	1.2%	91.9	94.5	110.1	170.2	96.5
Net income ($ mil.)	42.5%	43.1	33.9	7.0	(152.7)	177.5
Market value ($ mil.)	27.1%	161.6	166.1	135.6	401.4	421.8
Employees	1.4%	18	17	19	20	19

DYNTEK INC.

PINK SHEETS: DYNE

4440 Von Karman Ste. 200
Newport Beach CA 92660
Phone: 949-271-6700
Fax: 949-271-6794
Web: www.dyntek.com

CEO: Ron Ben-Yishay
CFO: Karen Rosenberger
HR: –
FYE: June 30
Type: Public

DynTek sees a bright future in technology services. The company previously a provider of medication and services to diabetes patients now provides a variety of information technology services to local and state governments schools and commercial enterprises. Its services include technology procurement systems integration business process outsourcing network engineering and technical support. While its marketing emphasis focuses on its IT services business the bulk of its sales are derived from the resale of hardware and software from partners such as Cisco IBM Microsoft and Novell.

DZS INC

NAS: DZSI

5700 Tennyson Parkway, Suite 400
Plano, TX 75024
Phone: 469 327-1531
Fax: –
Web: www.zhone.com

CEO: Charles Vogt
CFO: Misty Kawecki
HR: –
FYE: December 31
Type: Public

Zhone Technologies helps network service providers get into the SLMS zone. The company's all-IP Single Line Multi-Service (SLMS) platform uses existing local-loop infrastructures to deliver broadband services. Telecommunications service providers and wireless and cable operators use SLMS to offer their business and residential subscribers bundled broadband Internet access local and long-distance voice and broadcast video services. Its products are assembled at its plant in Florida using components manufactured in Asia. The company serves some 1000 customers worldwide; about 70% of sales come from outside the US.

	Annual Growth	12/16	12/17	12/18	12/19	12/20
Sales ($ mil.)	18.9%	150.3	247.1	282.3	306.9	300.6
Net income ($ mil.)	–	(15.3)	1.1	2.8	(13.5)	(23.1)
Market value ($ mil.)	99.1%	21.6	203.3	305.4	194.5	339.7
Employees	7.5%	622	629	670	789	830

E Z LOADER BOAT TRAILERS INC.

717 N HAMILTON ST
SPOKANE, WA 992022044
Phone: 574-266-0092
Fax: –
Web: www.estore.ezloader.com

CEO: –
CFO: –
HR: Sheila Harris
FYE: December 31
Type: Private

Nine years after manufacturing its first boat trailer in 1953 EZ Loader invented the all-roller trailer and made loading boats easier for everyone. Its patented design has rubber rollers in key locations along the top of the trailer to allow boats to avoid damage and slide easily into place. The company's website includes an e-store that sells trailer kits for home assembly and replacement and spare parts. EZ Loader also sells its trailers through independent distributors located in the US Japan the Middle East Asia Australia and Africa. The company has grown to include 10 divisions across the country. It is owned by Dave Thielman and president Randy Johnson.

	Annual Growth	12/02	12/03	12/04	12/06	12/08
Sales ($ mil.)	(2.6%)	–	–	56.3	66.3	50.6
Net income ($ mil.)	–	–	–	0.0	0.5	(0.1)
Market value ($ mil.)	–	–	–	–	–	–
Employees	–	–	–	–	–	275

E*TRADE FINANCIAL CORP

NMS: ETFC

11 Times Square, 32nd Floor
New York, NY 10036
Phone: 646 521-4300
Fax: –
Web: www.etrade.com

CEO: Michael A Pizzi
CFO: –
HR: –
FYE: December 31
Type: Public

Known for its brokerage services E*TRADE Financial provides products tools services and advice to individual investors and stock plan participants wanting to manage their own investments. For corporate clients it offers market making trade clearing and employee stock option plan administration services. Subsidiary E*TRADE Bank provides deposits savings and credit cards online and from some 30 financial centers in major US cities. Its other units include E*TRADE Financial Corporate Services — an equity compensation plan management software and services company for corporate customers — and E*TRADE Securities — a broker-dealer that offers mutual funds options fixed income products exchange-traded funds and portfolio management services.

	Annual Growth	12/14	12/15	12/16	12/17	12/18
Assets ($ mil.)	9.3%	45,530.0	45,427.0	48,999.0	63,365.0	65,003.0
Net income ($ mil.)	37.7%	293.0	268.0	552.0	614.0	1,052.0
Market value ($ mil.)	16.0%	5,978.7	7,306.1	8,541.1	12,218.8	10,816.2
Employees	5.7%	3,200	3,400	3,600	3,600	4,000

E. C. BARTON & COMPANY

2929 BROWNS LN
JONESBORO, AR 724017208
Phone: 870-932-6673
Fax: –
Web: www.bartons-lumber.com

CEO: Niel Crowson
CFO: –
HR: Allen Devereux
FYE: October 26
Type: Private

E. C. Barton & Company sells a variety of homebuilding tools and goods under a handful of banner names. A member of industry cooperative Do It Best the company sells lumber and building materials through more than 100 locations throughout Texas as well as 15 other states in the US Southeast and the Northeast. It operates several divisions including Barton's Builders Material Company E.C.B. Brokerage and Surplus Purchasing Surplus Warehouse and Grossman's Bargain Outlet. E. C. Barton also manages an e-commerce site. Professional builders and remodelers generate most of the company's revenue. The company is employee-owned.

	Annual Growth	10/13	10/14	10/15	10/16	10/17
Sales ($ mil.)	6.2%	–	247.3	253.2	269.9	296.2
Net income ($ mil.)	145.1%	–	0.9	5.2	10.6	13.8
Market value ($ mil.)	–	–	–	–	–	–
Employees	–	–	–	–	–	600

E.DIGITAL CORP.

NBB: EDIG

16870 West Bernardo Drive, Suite 120
San Diego, CA 92127
Phone: 858 304-3016
Fax: –
Web: www.edigital.com

CEO: –
CFO: –
HR: –
FYE: March 31
Type: Public

e.Digital believes that the future is digital. The company provides engineering services product reference designs and technology platforms to customers focusing on the digital video and audio markets. e.Digital however plans to focus future growth on selling its eVU mobile entertainment device which features a 7-inch LCD screen dual stereo headphone jacks embedded credit card reader and touch screen capabilities. The eVu is geared towards customers in the airline health care military and travel and leisure industries.

	Annual Growth	03/12	03/13	03/14	03/15	03/16
Sales ($ mil.)	(37.8%)	4.7	0.4	2.3	2.2	0.7
Net income ($ mil.)	–	1.2	(1.5)	0.1	(0.2)	(1.3)
Market value ($ mil.)	(1.1%)	11.8	49.5	20.3	31.2	11.3
Employees	(24.0%)	9	7	7	5	3

E.N.M.R. TELEPHONE COOPERATIVE

7111 N PRINCE ST
CLOVIS, NM 881019730
Phone: 575-389-5100
Fax: –
Web: www.plateautel.com

CEO: Tom Phelps
CFO: David Robinson
HR: –
FYE: December 31
Type: Private

ENMR-Plateau Telecommunications is a telephone cooperative providing wireless and wired communications services in about two dozen communities in eastern New Mexico and western Texas. Mobile services are offered through its Plateau Wireless unit while Plateau Internet provides Internet access and other services including Web hosting. ENMR-Plateau has about 42000 wireless accounts 10000 landline customers and more than 13000 internet subscribers. Area farmers ranchers and other residents founded the company in 1949 as Eastern New Mexico Rural Telephone Cooperative. It operates from offices in Roswell and Carlsbad New Mexico as well as in Levelland and Plainview Texas among other cities.

	Annual Growth	12/08	12/09	12/10	12/11	12/12
Sales ($ mil.)	(5.9%)	–	–	110.8	106.5	98.0
Net income ($ mil.)	55.7%	–	–	16.9	30.6	40.9
Market value ($ mil.)	–	–	–	–	–	–
Employees	–	–	–	–	–	270

EA ENGINEERING, SCIENCE, AND TECHNOLOGY, INC., PBC

225 SCHILLING CIR STE 400
HUNT VALLEY, MD 210311124
Phone: 410-584-7000
Fax: –
Web: www.eaest.com

CEO: –
CFO: Peter Ney
HR: –
FYE: December 31
Type: Private

EA Engineering Science and Technology wants to stop pollution before it starts by offering environmental consulting services. The company's specialties include brownfields and urban redevelopment environmental compliance management and natural resources management. Its more than 450 professionals have completed more than 100000 environmental projects worldwide (more than $1 billion of services). Customers include government agencies and industrial manufacturers. EA Engineering operates from more than 25 offices — 23 in the US (including facilities in Alaska and Hawaii) and one in Guam.

	Annual Growth	06/11	06/12	06/13*	12/15	12/16
Sales ($ mil.)	22.4%	–	59.5	105.0	68.9	133.4
Net income ($ mil.)	(0.6%)	–	3.6	2.8	6.2	3.5
Market value ($ mil.)	–	–	–	–	–	–
Employees	–	–	–	–	–	440

*Fiscal year change

EACO CORP

5065 East Hunter Avenue
Anaheim, CA 92807
Phone: 714 876-2490
Fax: –
Web: www.eacocorp.com

NBB: EACO
CEO: Glen Ceiley
CFO: –
HR: –
FYE: August 31
Type: Public

EACO Corporation lost its appetite for the buffet business. For a half-dozen years after selling its restaurant operations to pursue a new line of business the company generated revenues from a handful of rental properties including restaurant and industrial properties. (Tenant NES Rentals accounts for about half of its rental revenues.) In 2010 the company acquired Bisco Industries which distributes electronics components in the US and Canada. EACO was once the sole franchisee of Ryan's Restaurant Group restaurants in Florida; it also owned a chain of 16 Whistle Junction and Florida Buffet locations. CEO Glen Ceiley owns 98.9% of EACO.

	Annual Growth	08/16	08/17	08/18	08/19	08/20
Sales ($ mil.)	11.0%	148.5	157.0	193.3	221.2	225.2
Net income ($ mil.)	17.5%	4.1	4.1	6.9	9.4	7.8
Market value ($ mil.)	30.7%	29.0	30.7	68.1	95.0	84.5
Employees	6.1%	414	407	464	489	525

EAGLE BANCORP INC (MD)

7830 Old Georgetown Road, Third Floor
Bethesda, MD 20814
Phone: 301 986-1800
Fax: –
Web: www.eaglebankcorp.com

NAS: EGBN
CEO: Susan Riel
CFO: Charles Levingston
HR: –
FYE: December 31
Type: Public

For those nest eggs that need a little help hatching holding company Eagle Bancorp would recommend its community-oriented EagleBank subsidiary. The bank serves businesses and individuals through more than 20 branches in Maryland Virginia and Washington DC and its suburbs. Deposit products include checking savings and money market accounts; certificates of deposit; and IRAs. Commercial real estate loans represent more than 70% of its loan portfolio while construction loans make up another more than 20%. The bank which has significant expertise as a Small Business Administration lender also writes business consumer and home equity loans. EagleBank offers insurance products through an agreement with The Meltzer Group.

	Annual Growth	12/16	12/17	12/18	12/19	12/20
Assets ($ mil.)	12.7%	6,890.1	7,479.0	8,389.1	8,988.7	11,117.8
Net income ($ mil.)	7.9%	97.7	100.2	152.3	142.9	132.2
Market value ($ mil.)	(9.3%)	1,937.0	1,840.0	1,548.0	1,545.4	1,312.5
Employees	2.4%	469	466	470	492	515

EAGLE BANCORP MONTANA, INC.

1400 Prospect Avenue
Helena, MT 59601
Phone: 406 442-3080
Fax: –
Web: www.opportunitybank.com

NMS: EBMT
CEO: Peter Johnson
CFO: Laura Clark
HR: –
FYE: December 31
Type: Public

Eagle Bancorp Montana hopes to swoop down on every potential account holder in its home state. The holding company owns American Federal Savings Bank a thrift that serves businesses and residents of southwestern Montana through six branches and seven ATMs. American Federal primarily writes mortgages on one- to four-family residences (these comprise almost half of its loan book); the rest of its portfolio consists of commercial mortgages (25%) home equity (about 20%) and consumer business and construction loans. The bank's deposit products include checking money market and savings accounts; CDs; IRAs; and Visa debit cards. Eagle Bancorp Montana is buying seven branches from Sterling Financial.

	Annual Growth	12/16	12/17	12/18	12/19	12/20
Assets ($ mil.)	16.9%	673.9	716.8	853.9	1,054.3	1,257.6
Net income ($ mil.)	42.6%	5.1	4.1	5.0	10.9	21.2
Market value ($ mil.)	0.1%	143.0	141.9	111.8	144.9	143.8
Employees	15.3%	200	207	249	298	354

EAGLE BULK SHIPPING INC

300 First Stamford Place, 5th Floor
Stamford, CT 06902
Phone: 203 276-8100
Fax: –
Web: www.eagleships.com

NMS: EGLE
CEO: Gary Vogel
CFO: Frank De Costanzo
HR: –
FYE: December 31
Type: Public

Some eagles soar through the skies but Eagle Bulk Shipping rides the waves. The company owns a fleet of 45 Handymax dry bulk carriers that it charters to customers typically on one- to three-year contracts. Most of its vessels are classified as Supramaxes and range in capacity from 50000 to 60000 deadweight tons (DWT). Overall the company's fleet has a carrying capacity of more than 1.1 million DWT. Cargo carried by charterers of Eagle Bulk Shipping's vessels includes cement coal fertilizer grain and iron ore. In mid-2014 Eagle Bulk Shipping filed for Chapter 11 bankruptcy protection and emerged in October of the same year.

	Annual Growth	12/16	12/17	12/18	12/19	12/20
Sales ($ mil.)	21.9%	124.5	236.8	310.1	292.4	275.1
Net income ($ mil.)	–	(223.5)	(43.8)	12.6	(21.7)	(35.1)
Market value ($ mil.)	–	–	–	–	–	–
Employees	2.4%	820	941	912	974	900

EAGLE MATERIALS INC   NYS: EXP

5960 Berkshire Lane, Suite 900
Dallas, TX 75225
Phone: 214 432-2000
Fax: 214 432-2100
Web: www.eaglematerials.com

CEO: Michael Haack
CFO: Dale Craig Kesler
HR: –
FYE: March 31
Type: Public

Eagle Materials company manufactures and distributes cement and gypsum wallboard. Eagle Materials also produces ready-mix concrete aggregates and recycled paperboard. Its products are sold to residential commercial and industrial construction customers throughout the US. The company operates about 30 cement storage and distribution facilities. It also produce and market other cementitious products including slag cement and fly ash. Slag is used in concrete mix designs to improve the durability of concrete and reduce future maintenance costs. Fly ash is a by-product of a coal-fired power plant and acts as an extender of cement in concrete. Founded in 1963 Eagle Materials was spun off by homebuilder Centex Corporation in 2004.

	Annual Growth	03/17	03/18	03/19	03/20	03/21
Sales ($ mil.)	7.6%	1,211.2	1,386.5	1,393.2	1,450.8	1,622.6
Net income ($ mil.)	14.4%	198.2	256.6	68.9	70.9	339.4
Market value ($ mil.)	8.5%	4,115.9	4,366.3	3,571.9	2,475.3	5,695.1
Employees	0.0%	2,200	2,200	2,300	2,400	2,200

EAGLE PHARMACEUTICALS, INC.   NMS: EGRX

50 Tice Boulevard, Suite 315
Woodcliff Lake, NJ 07677
Phone: 201 326-5300
Fax: –
Web: www.eagleus.com

CEO: Scott Tarriff
CFO: Brian Cahill
HR: –
FYE: December 31
Type: Public

Like the talons of its namesake Eagle Pharmaceuticals specializes in sharps. The firm develops and commercializes injectable treatments primarily to address unmet needs in oncology and critical care. The company has five FDA-approved products — blood thinner Argatroban malignant hyperthermia treatment Ryanodex anti-inflammatory drug diclofenac-misoprostol cancer drug Non-Alcohol Docetaxel Injection and leukemia and non-Hodgkin lymphoma treatment Bendeka. Eagle Pharmaceuticals also has a handful of candidates under development. Commercial and development partners include Cephalon Albany Molecular Research Sandoz and The Medicines Company.

	Annual Growth	12/16	12/17	12/18	12/19	12/20
Sales ($ mil.)	(0.2%)	189.5	236.7	213.3	195.9	187.8
Net income ($ mil.)	(38.1%)	81.5	51.9	31.9	14.3	12.0
Market value ($ mil.)	(12.5%)	1,035.9	697.5	526.1	784.5	608.1
Employees	8.3%	77	108	96	108	106

EAGLE ROCK ENERGY PARTNERS LP   NMS: EROC

1415 Louisiana Street, Suite 2700
Houston, TX 77002
Phone: 281 408-1200
Fax: –
Web: www.eaglerockenergy.com

CEO: –
CFO: Richard A Robert
HR: –
FYE: December 31
Type: Public

The Eagles are into soft rock whereas Eagle Rock Energy Partners is into developing and producing hydrocarbons. The company has oil and gas properties that include more than 560 gross operated productive wells and 1200 gross non-operated wells. The company's upstream operations have exploration and production assets in Alabama Louisiana Mississippi and Texas and has proved reserves of 252.5 billion cu. ft. of natural gas of equivalent. Eagle Rock's former midstream business which included 8100 miles of gathering pipeline and over 800 million cu. ft. of processing plants was sold to Regency Energy Partners in mid-2014.

	Annual Growth	12/09	12/10	12/11	12/12	12/13
Sales ($ mil.)	18.3%	610.5	758.4	1,059.9	984.0	1,195.3
Net income ($ mil.)	–	(171.3)	(5.3)	73.1	(150.6)	(278.0)
Market value ($ mil.)	0.7%	907.0	1,381.6	1,824.9	1,354.9	932.0
Employees	13.5%	353	367	462	510	586

EARL L. HENDERSON TRUCKING COMPANY

8118 BUNKUM RD
CASEYVILLE, IL 622322104
Phone: 618-548-4667
Fax: –
Web: www.hendersontrucking.com

CEO: –
CFO: –
HR: –
FYE: December 31
Type: Private

This Earl aspires to hold a royal rank in the world of refrigerated transportation. Earl L. Henderson Trucking hauls food and other perishable products throughout the US. The company operates a fleet of some 400 tractors and 600 trailers including about 500 refrigerated trailers. It offers long-haul service in the US and parts of Canada and regional service in the eastern half of the US. In addition to perishable products Henderson Trucking transports time-sensitive printed matter. Company president John Kaburick owns Henderson Trucking which was founded by Earl Henderson in 1978.

	Annual Growth	12/04	12/05	12/06	12/07	12/08
Sales ($ mil.)	12.1%	–	–	79.5	94.9	100.0
Net income ($ mil.)	(45.8%)	–	–	1.8	93.0	0.5
Market value ($ mil.)	–	–	–	–	–	–
Employees	–	–	–	–	–	600

EARLHAM COLLEGE

801 NATIONAL RD W
RICHMOND, IN 473744095
Phone: 765-983-1200
Fax: –
Web: www.earlham.edu

CEO: –
CFO: –
HR: –
FYE: June 30
Type: Private

Earlham College is a private liberal arts college located in Richmond Indiana. The venerable school originally founded by Quakers enrolls about 1100 undergraduate students a year and offers 40 courses of study in the fine arts humanities natural sciences and social sciences. Earlham also offers a three-year pre-professional course of study as well as master's degree programs in teaching and education. The college's annual tuition is approximately $34000. The affiliated Earlham School of Religion established in 1960 offers graduate degrees in religion and ministry.

	Annual Growth	06/08	06/09	06/10	06/15	06/17
Sales ($ mil.)	2.2%	–	53.2	76.4	84.6	63.1
Net income ($ mil.)	–	–	(91.0)	6.6	(0.3)	37.5
Market value ($ mil.)	–	–	–	–	–	–
Employees	–	–	–	–	–	365

EARTHSTONE ENERGY INC   NYS: ESTE

1400 Woodloch Forest Drive, Suite 300
The Woodlands, TX 77380
Phone: 281 298-4246
Fax: –
Web: www.earthstoneenergy.com

CEO: Robert Anderson
CFO: Mark Lumpkin
HR: –
FYE: December 31
Type: Public

Earthstone Energy (also known as Earthstone) taps into some of Planet Earth's basic energy sources — oil and gas. It is involved in acquisition and development activities of oil and gas assets in Midland Basin of west Texas and the Eagle Ford Trend of south Texas. The company drills about 45 net wells a year and has proved reserves of over 94335 barrels of oil and nearly 110 million cu. ft. of gas. Most of Earthstone's productive wells are in west and south Texas

	Annual Growth	12/16	12/17	12/18	12/19	12/20
Sales ($ mil.)	36.0%	42.3	108.1	165.4	191.3	144.5
Net income ($ mil.)	–	(54.5)	(12.5)	42.3	0.7	(13.5)
Market value ($ mil.)	(21.1%)	897.9	694.7	295.4	413.7	348.3
Employees	5.2%	49	58	65	69	60

EAST ALABAMA HEALTH CARE AUTHORITY

2000 PEPPERELL PKWY
OPELIKA, AL 368015452
Phone: 334-749-3411
Fax: -
Web: www.eamc.org

CEO: Terry Andrus
CFO: -
HR: -
FYE: September 30
Type: Private

From babies to seniors The East Alabama Health Care Authority cares for all of Alabama's denizens. The authority's flagship facility is East Alabama Medical Center (EAMC) a general acute-care hospital include services such as cancer center surgery maternity care orthopaedic care women's health as well as hearth and vascular care. Other services have included eye care HIV care and counseling infectious disease and more. The system also operates EAMC-Lanier which offers a variety of services including a Nasal & Sinus Institute a nursing home a 24-hour emergency room imaging services in-patient and out-patient rehabilitation services an urgent care clinic and others. Headquartered in Alabama the company traces its roots back in 1945.

	Annual Growth	09/14	09/15	09/16	09/17	09/18
Sales ($ mil.)	3.4%	-	289.0	6.1	298.6	319.4
Net income ($ mil.)	25.3%	-	9.0	0.6	9.7	17.7
Market value ($ mil.)	-	-	-	-	-	-
Employees	-	-	-	-	-	2,250

EAST ORANGE GENERAL HOSPITAL (INC)

300 CENTRAL AVE
EAST ORANGE, NJ 070182897
Phone: 973-672-8400
Fax: -
Web: www.evh.org

CEO: -
CFO: Al Aboud
HR: -
FYE: December 31
Type: Private

East Orange General Hospital pairs medical services with community action. Established in 1903 the not-for-profit hospital is the home of the first Candy Striper program in 1944 and continues with a number of community outreach programs. The 210-bed facility provides inpatient acute care in a wide range of specialties including critical care oncology behavioral health surgery and intensive care. East Orange General Hospital also offers cardiology physical rehabilitation dialysis respiratory care diagnostic testing and wound care among other services. The hospital's Family Health Center provides primary and specialty care as well as outpatient surgery. East Orange General Hospital is part of Essex Valley Healthcare.

	Annual Growth	12/07	12/08	12/09	12/10	12/11
Sales ($ mil.)	-	-	-	(141.6)	112.5	118.2
Net income ($ mil.)	8297.4%	-	-	0.0	0.4	1.3
Market value ($ mil.)	-	-	-	-	-	-
Employees	-	-	-	-	-	801

EAST TENNESSEE CHILDREN'S HOSPITAL ASSOCIATION, INC.

2018 CLINCH AVE
KNOXVILLE, TN 379162301
Phone: 865-541-8000
Fax: -
Web: www.etch.com

CEO: Matt Schaefer
CFO: -
HR: -
FYE: June 30
Type: Private

ETCH has made a permanent mark on the lives of countless children over the years. Knoxville-based East Tennessee Children's Hospital (ETCH) with more than 150 beds provides a full range of health care services to children from eastern Tennessee and portions of surrounding states. Among its 30 specialized services are cardiology neonatal care orthopedics and psychiatry as well as cystic fibrosis and hearing impairment services. The hospital also offers support such as for families of children stricken by cancer. The hospital's roots are in the foundation of Knox County Crippled Children's Hospital in 1937 with less than 50 beds.

	Annual Growth	06/14	06/15	06/16	06/19	06/20
Sales ($ mil.)	0.9%	-	210.7	219.5	210.6	220.4
Net income ($ mil.)	44.7%	-	3.6	23.9	11.4	22.7
Market value ($ mil.)	-	-	-	-	-	-
Employees	-	-	-	-	-	1,500

EAST TENNESSEE STATE UNIVERSITY FOUNDATION

1276 GILBREATH DR
JOHNSON CITY, TN 376146503
Phone: 423-439-1000
Fax: -
Web: www.etsu.edu

CEO: -
CFO: -
HR: -
FYE: June 30
Type: Private

East Tennessee State University (ETSU) is a public coeducational member of the Tennessee Board of Regents' network of 45 postsecondary educational institutions. The university has 11 colleges and schools representing arts and sciences business and technology clinical and rehabilitative health sciences education medicine nursing pharmacy public health honors as well as continuing and graduate studies. It offers approximately 125 undergraduate programs 95 master's programs and a dozen doctoral programs as well as graduate certificates teacher licensure and specialist programs. Founded as East Tennessee State Normal School in 1911 ETSU has an enrollment of more than 15000 students.

	Annual Growth	06/04	06/05	06/06	06/08	06/13
Sales ($ mil.)	40.9%	-	-	16.3	14.7	179.7
Net income ($ mil.)	(4.3%)	-	-	8.8	7.6	6.4
Market value ($ mil.)	-	-	-	-	-	-
Employees	-	-	-	-	-	2,400

EAST TEXAS MEDICAL CENTER REGIONAL HEALTHCARE SYSTEM

1000 S BECKHAM AVE
TYLER, TX 757011908
Phone: 903-596-3267
Fax: -
Web: www.uthealtheasttexas.com

CEO: Elmer G Ellis
CFO: -
HR: -
FYE: October 31
Type: Private

East Texas Medical Center (ETMC) Regional Healthcare System works to meet the health care needs of residents of the Piney Woods. The not-for-profit health system operates more than a dozen hospitals across eastern Texas along with behavioral rehabilitation and home health care businesses. Its flagship 450-bed Tyler location serves as the hub and referral center for satellite medical centers located in more rural locations. The system also runs numerous primary care and outpatient clinics throughout the region. Serving more than 300000 patients each year ETMC operates an emergency ambulance service subsidiary and a clinical laboratory which provide services to the ETMC Regional Healthcare System.

	Annual Growth	10/04	10/05	10/06	10/07	10/08
Sales ($ mil.)	1.5%	-	837.5	837.5	827.9	877.0
Net income ($ mil.)	20.4%	-	17.2	0.0	40.0	30.1
Market value ($ mil.)	-	-	-	-	-	-
Employees	-	-	-	-	-	7,600

EAST WEST BANCORP, INC

135 North Los Robles Ave., 7th Floor
Pasadena, CA 91101
Phone: 626 768-6000
Fax: -
Web: www.eastwestbank.com

NMS: EWBC

CEO: Dominic Ng
CFO: Irene Oh
HR: Gary Teo
FYE: December 31
Type: Public

East Wes Bancorp is the holding company for East West Bank which provides standard banking services and loans operating in more than 120 locations in the US and China. Boasting $52 billion in assets East West Bank focuses on making commercial and industrial real estate loans which account for the majority of the company's loan portfolio. Catering to the Asian-American community it also provides international banking and trade financing to importers/exporters doing business in the Asia/Pacific region.

	Annual Growth	12/16	12/17	12/18	12/19	12/20
Assets ($ mil.)	10.7%	34,788.8	37,150.2	41,042.4	44,196.1	52,156.9
Net income ($ mil.)	7.1%	431.7	505.6	703.7	674.0	567.8
Market value ($ mil.)	(0.1%)	7,195.8	8,611.4	6,162.3	6,894.2	7,178.8
Employees	2.7%	2,873	3,000	3,200	3,300	3,200

EASTER SEALS, INC.

233 S WACKER DR STE 2400
CHICAGO, IL 606066410
Phone: 312-726-6200
Fax: -

CEO: Angela F Williams
CFO: -
HR: -
FYE: December 31
Type: Private

A year round effort that has nothing to do with Easter seals or flowers the National Easter Seal Society annually helps more than one million children and adults with disabilities through over 550 service centers in the US Puerto Rico Canada and Australia. The organization offers medical rehabilitation job training child care and adult day services. It began in 1907 as the National Society for Crippled Children and launched its first "seal" campaign around Easter in 1934. Supporters placed stickers or seals depicting the lily a symbol of renewal on letters and envelopes. The campaign was so successful and the symbol so associated with the organization that it changed its name in 1967.

	Annual Growth	12/07	12/08	12/09	12/13	12/14
Sales ($ mil.)	(10.0%)	-	-	123.7	82.2	73.0
Net income ($ mil.)	(8.6%)	-	-	1.1	0.8	0.7
Market value ($ mil.)	-	-	-	-	-	-
Employees						120

EASTERN AMERICAN NATURAL GAS TRUST

919 Congress Ave. Ste. 500
Austin TX 78701
Phone: 800-852-1422
Fax: 512-479-2553

NYSE: NGT
CEO: -
CFO: -
HR: -
FYE: December 31
Type: Public

Shareholders of Eastern American Natural Gas Trust know all about the clean-burning royalty-producing attributes of natural gas. The trust receives royalty interests from 650 producing natural gas wells in West Virginia and Pennsylvania and operated by Eastern American Energy. The trust distributes the royalties to its shareholders quarterly. As a grantor trust Eastern American Natural Gas Trust does not pay federal income taxes and the production on some of its wells qualifies for tax credits because the wells are located on hard-to-drill formations. The trust which in 2008 reported proved reserves of 12.9 billion cu. ft. of natural gas equivalent on its properties will be liquidated no later than 2013.

EASTERN BAG AND PAPER COMPANY, INCORPORATED

200 RESEARCH DR
MILFORD, CT 064602880
Phone: 203-878-1814
Fax: -
Web: www.ebpsupply.com

CEO: Meredith Reuben
CFO: William J O Donnell
HR: -
FYE: December 31
Type: Private

Eastern Bag and Paper Co. (dba EBP Supply) is a leading distributor of paper products in the northeastern US. In addition to disposable tableware and packaging the company offers foodservice products (including china and glassware) restaurant equipment (can openers refrigerators) personal care items (bath mats roll towels) and cleansers and maintenance supplies (air fresheners vacuums). Its name-brand products are used by the industrial healthcare foodservice and janitorial industries. Founded in 1918 by Samuel Baum the company is owned and run by CEO Meredith Baum Reuben.

	Annual Growth	12/16	12/17	12/18	12/19	12/20
Sales ($ mil.)	1.3%	-	198.8	204.8	212.7	207.0
Net income ($ mil.)	10.7%	-	2.4	2.3	1.8	3.3
Market value ($ mil.)	-	-	-	-	-	-
Employees						285

EASTERN BANK CORPORATION

265 Franklin St.
Boston MA 02110-3113
Phone: 617-897-1008
Fax: 617-897-1105
Web: www.easternbank.com

CEO: -
CFO: Charles M Johnston
HR: -
FYE: December 31
Type: Private - Mutual Com

Eastern Bank wants to help you count your clams. The holding company owns Eastern Bank which operates approximately 100 branch locations in Massachusetts. Eastern Bank offers retail and commercial products including deposit accounts investments and credit cards. Its lending activities are focused on commercial loans and leases residential mortgages and consumer loans. Eastern Bank also provides wealth management services through a third-party provider. Insurance subsidiary Eastern Insurance offers personal and commercial coverage group health and life insurance employee benefit plans and 401(k) administration through some 25 locations. Eastern Bank Corporation is mutually owned.

EASTERN CO.

112 Bridge Street
Naugatuck, CT 06770
Phone: 203 729-2255
Fax: -
Web: www.easterncompany.com

NMS: EML
CEO: August Vlak
CFO: John Sullivan
HR: -
FYE: January 02
Type: Public

The Eastern Company has latched on to the security industry. The company's security products group makes coin acceptors used in laundry facilities smart card payment systems and keyless locks sold under such brands as Big Tag Duo Warlock Searchalert Sesamee Prestolock and Huski. It also manufactures industrial hardware including latches locks and hinges used by the transportation industry. Eastern owns a foundry that makes metal anchoring devices to support underground mine roofs clamps for construction and railroad brake system components. The company sells mainly to manufacturers distributors and locksmiths through its operations in North America China Mexico and Taiwan.

	Annual Growth	12/16	12/17	12/18	12/19*	01/21
Sales ($ mil.)	11.8%	137.6	204.2	234.3	251.7	240.4
Net income ($ mil.)	(7.0%)	7.8	5.0	14.5	13.3	5.4
Market value ($ mil.)	2.9%	130.6	163.4	152.0	187.2	150.6
Employees	8.9%	862	1,189	1,327	1,399	1,323

*Fiscal year change

EASTERN KENTUCKY UNIVERSITY

521 LANCASTER AVE
RICHMOND, KY 404753102
Phone: 859-622-1791
Fax: -
Web: www.eku.edu

CEO: -
CFO: -
HR: -
FYE: June 30
Type: Private

Deep in the heart of bluegrass country Eastern Kentucky University offers more than 100 degree programs including some 30 masters degree programs through its five colleges (Arts & Sciences Business & Technology Education Health Sciences and Justice & Safety). The school has an annual enrollment of some 16000 students on eight campuses. It also offers online courses and degree programs. Eastern Kentucky University was founded in 1906 with a faculty of just seven; in 1909 the school's first graduating class consisted of 11 students. Originally Eastern Kentucky State Normal School it gained university status in 1966 and began offering graduate degrees in fields other than education.

	Annual Growth	06/16	06/17	06/18	06/19	06/20
Sales ($ mil.)	(4.2%)	-	183.9	180.3	172.4	161.6
Net income ($ mil.)	-	-	(21.4)	(27.0)	43.3	66.3
Market value ($ mil.)	-	-	-	-	-	-
Employees						2,100

EASTERN MAINE HEALTHCARE SYSTEMS

43 WHITING HILL RD # 500
BREWER, ME 044121005
Phone: 207-973-7000
Fax: –
Web: www.northernlighthealth.org

CEO: –
CFO: –
HR: Diane Simpson
FYE: September 30
Type: Private

Eastern Maine Healthcare Systems (EMHS) keeps the folks in the Pine Tree State feeling fine. With more than a dozen member hospitals and multiple medical practices and clinics the organization offers patients emergency primary mental-health laboratory and other specialty services. It primarily serves eastern central and northern portions of rural Maine. Some hospitals include Eastern Maine Medical Center (410 beds) Acadia Hospital (100 beds) Aroostook Medical Center (75 beds) and Inland Hospital (50 beds). The system also operates long-term care hospice and home health facilities as well as emergency transportation and administrative services businesses.

	Annual Growth	09/16	09/17	09/18	09/19	09/20
Sales ($ mil.)	2.0%	–	1,654.2	1,672.1	1,744.5	1,753.2
Net income ($ mil.)	–	–	43.5	8.9	16.2	(77.4)
Market value ($ mil.)	–	–	–	–	–	–
Employees	–	–	–	–	–	8,175

EASTERN MICHIGAN UNIVERSITY

202 WELCH HALL
YPSILANTI, MI 481972214
Phone: 734-487-2031
Fax: –
Web: www.emich.edu

CEO: –
CFO: –
HR: –
FYE: June 30
Type: Private

Eastern Michigan University (known affectionately as just plain Eastern) has long been an affordable place to study your way into a better career. The university began as a teachers' college in 1849 and it still graduates one out of every four teachers in Michigan. Eastern has an enrollment of more than 23000 students (90% are Michigan residents) who participate in undergraduate and graduate degree programs on its campus in the southeastern part of the state. Its 200 majors minors and concentrations are offered through colleges of arts and sciences business education technology and health and human services.

	Annual Growth	06/14	06/15	06/16	06/17	06/18
Sales ($ mil.)	(1.5%)	–	–	–	244.3	240.7
Net income ($ mil.)	(29.2%)	–	–	–	9.7	6.9
Market value ($ mil.)	–	–	–	–	–	–
Employees	–	–	–	–	–	2,000

EASTERN MOUNTAIN SPORTS INC.

1 Vose Farm Rd.
Peterborough NH 03458
Phone: 603-924-9571
Fax: 603-924-9138
Web: www.emsonline.com

CEO: –
CFO: –
HR: –
FYE: January 31
Type: Private

Eastern Mountain Sports (EMS) can prepare you for a life of climb. EMS sells a wide range of outdoor gear apparel footwear and accessories from more than 65 stores in a dozen East Coast states from Maine to Virginia and through its website. Outdoor enthusiasts can purchase or rent tents sleeping bags and other equipment — choosing from brands such as Patagonia Columbia The North Face REEF and Teva. The retailer's own EMS-branded products account for about a third of sales. Founded in 1967 by two New England rock climbers EMS offers outdoor skills clinics provides guides for hire arranges day and overnight trips and operates climbing and kayaking schools.

EASTERN VIRGINIA BANKSHARES, INC

10900 Nuckols Road, Suite 325
Glen Allen, VA 23060
Phone: 804 443-8400
Fax: –
Web: www.evb.org

NMS: EVBS
CEO: –
CFO: –
HR: –
FYE: December 31
Type: Public

Founded in 1997 Eastern Virginia Bankshares is the holding company for EVB a community bank that operates more than two dozen branches in — believe it or not — eastern Virginia. Targeting individuals and local business customers the bank offers such standard retail services as checking and savings accounts money market accounts CDs IRAs and credit cards. Residential mortgages make up nearly half of the the company's loan portfolio which also includes commercial real estate construction business and consumer loans. Subsidiary EVB Financial Services owns interests in companies that offer investments and insurance.

	Annual Growth	12/11	12/12	12/13	12/14	12/15
Assets ($ mil.)	4.6%	1,063.0	1,075.6	1,027.1	1,182.0	1,270.4
Net income ($ mil.)	42.3%	1.8	3.5	(2.6)	5.7	7.3
Market value ($ mil.)	37.5%	26.2	70.4	91.2	84.3	93.6
Employees	0.3%	307	306	315	353	311

EASTERN VIRGINIA MEDICAL SCHOOL

735 FAIRFAX AVE STE 909C
NORFOLK, VA 235072007
Phone: 757-446-6052
Fax: –
Web: www.evms.edu

CEO: –
CFO: –
HR: –
FYE: June 30
Type: Private

Eastern Virginia Medical School (EVMS) sends graduated physicians down the Hampton Roads. The school offers medical and doctoral degrees residencies and specialty programs such as reproductive medicine. The community-oriented school does not have a teaching hospital but rather partners with about a dozen regional hospitals. Its main campus is part of the Eastern Virginia Medical Center which is also home to Sentara Norfolk General Hospital and Children's Hospital of The King's Daughters located in the Hampton Roads region of southeastern Virginia. The south campus hosts pediatric and diabetes research programs. EVMS also has research programs devoted to cancer infectious diseases and heart disease.

	Annual Growth	06/17	06/18	06/19	06/20	06/21
Sales ($ mil.)	4.3%	–	255.8	336.5	294.5	289.9
Net income ($ mil.)	52.8%	–	26.0	71.8	54.8	92.8
Market value ($ mil.)	–	–	–	–	–	–
Employees	–	–	–	–	–	1,500

EASTERN WASHINGTON UNIVERSITY INC

307 SHOWALTER HALL
CHENEY, WA 990042445
Phone: 509-359-6200
Fax: –
Web: www.ewu.edu

CEO: –
CFO: Toni Havegger
HR: –
FYE: June 30
Type: Private

Eagles — the mascot kind at any rate — soar around Eastern Washington University (EWU). The university serves about 13000 undergraduate and graduate students in the area around metropolitan Spokane Washington. Most students study at EWU's Cheney campus but the school includes other learning centers around the state. EWU has 23:1 student-to-faculty ratio. About 140 fields of study are offered through four colleges: Arts Letters and Education; Business and Public Administration; Science Health and Engineering; and Social and Behavioral Sciences and Social Work. The school was founded in 1882 as the Benjamin P. Cheney Academy.

	Annual Growth	06/16	06/17	06/18	06/19	06/20
Sales ($ mil.)	1.0%	–	148.0	148.7	154.0	152.6
Net income ($ mil.)	58.2%	–	9.6	(6.6)	13.2	38.1
Market value ($ mil.)	–	–	–	–	–	–
Employees	–	–	–	–	–	1,550

EASTGROUP PROPERTIES INC   NYS: EGP

400 W Parkway Place, Suite 100
Ridgeland, MS 39157
Phone: 601 354-3555
Fax: –
Web: www.eastgroup.net
CEO: Marshall A Loeb
CFO: Brent W Wood
HR: –
FYE: December 31
Type: Public

EastGroup Properties points its compass all across the Sunbelt. The self-administered real estate investment trust (REIT) invests in develops and manages industrial properties with a particular emphasis on Florida Texas Arizona and California. EastGroup's distribution space properties are typically multitenant buidings. Its distribution space for location sensitive customers ranges from about 15000 to 70000 sq. ft. in size located near major transportation hubs. Its portfolio includes some 360 industrial properties and an office building totaling more than 40 million sq. ft. of leasable space.

	Annual Growth	12/17	12/18	12/19	12/20	12/21
Sales ($ mil.)	10.6%	274.2	300.4	331.4	363.0	409.5
Net income ($ mil.)	17.3%	83.2	88.5	121.7	108.4	157.6
Market value ($ mil.)	26.7%	3,647.3	3,785.6	5,475.1	5,697.6	9,403.1
Employees	3.7%	71	75	77	80	82

EASTMAN CHEMICAL CO   NYS: EMN

200 South Wilcox Drive
Kingsport, TN 37662
Phone: 423 229-2000
Fax: –
Web: www.eastman.com
CEO: Mark Costa
CFO: William Mclain
HR: Perry Stuckey
FYE: December 31
Type: Public

Eastman Chemical Company is a chemical manufacturer with a focus on additives chemical intermediates advanced materials and fibers. The company has more than 45 manufacturing facilities and has equity interests in three manufacturing joint ventures in about 15 countries that supply products to customers worldwide. Eastman's products wind up in scores of consumer and industrial products including building materials automotive paints tires personal and home care products packaging animal nutrition and crop protection products water treatment and health and wellness products. The company was once part of film giant Eastman Kodak. US and Canada generate the largest sales at more than 40%.

	Annual Growth	12/16	12/17	12/18	12/19	12/20
Sales ($ mil.)	(1.5%)	9,008.0	9,549.0	10,151.0	9,273.0	8,473.0
Net income ($ mil.)	(13.5%)	854.0	1,384.0	1,080.0	759.0	478.0
Market value ($ mil.)	7.5%	10,214.3	12,581.5	9,929.1	10,764.4	13,619.1
Employees	0.9%	14,000	14,000	14,500	14,500	14,500

EASTMAN KODAK CO.   NYS: KODK

343 State Street
Rochester, NY 14650
Phone: 585 724-4000
Fax: –
Web: www.kodak.com
CEO: James Continenza
CFO: David Bullwinkle
HR: –
FYE: December 31
Type: Public

Eastman Kodak the inventor of the Brownie camera has put consumer photography in albums on a shelf to focus on imaging for businesses. The company generates nearly 60% of sales from print systems and services for the book publishing newspaper and magazine publishing commercial printing and packaging industries among others. It makes presses and imprinting systems as well as technology to print documents publications and product packaging. Kodak's other operations include hardware software consumables and services related to printing and imaging for consumers and customers in a host of industries. The company which generates most of its sales outside the US was founded in 1880 by George Eastman.

	Annual Growth	12/16	12/17	12/18	12/19	12/20
Sales ($ mil.)	(9.6%)	1,543.0	1,531.0	1,325.0	1,242.0	1,029.0
Net income ($ mil.)	–	15.0	94.0	(16.0)	116.0	(541.0)
Market value ($ mil.)	(14.9%)	1,196.6	239.3	196.9	359.0	628.4
Employees	(7.3%)	6,100	5,800	5,400	4,922	4,500

EASYLINK SERVICES INTERNATIONAL CORPORATION   NASDAQ: ESIC

6025 The Corners Pkwy. Ste. 100
Norcross GA 30092
Phone: 678-533-8000
Fax: 203-755-5105
Web: www.diasys.com
CEO: Mark J Barrenechea
CFO: Paul McFeeters
HR: –
FYE: July 31
Type: Public

EasyLink Services International made sure that clients got the message. The company provided electronic data interchange (EDI) and telex software and services through its supply chain messaging division. Its data translation systems allowed trading partners with incompatible information systems to exchange invoices purchase orders shipping notices and other documents. EasyLink's on-demand messaging segment provided a document delivery system that handles fax e-mail and messaging communications. The company offered services ranging from consulting and training to outsourced document processing. EasyLink was acquired by Open Text in 2012 for $232 million.

EATON VANCE CORP   NYS: EV

Two International Place
Boston, MA 02110
Phone: 617 482-8260
Fax: 617 482-2396
Web: www.eatonvance.com
CEO: James P Gorman
CFO: –
HR: –
FYE: October 31
Type: Public

Formed in 1924 Eaton Vance now manages $515.7 billion in assets on behalf of retail high-net-worth and institutional clients. Its investment specialties include tax-managed equity funds municipal bond funds floating-rate bank-loan funds income and value equity funds global and high-yield bonds closed-end funds and alternative investments such as private equity funds commodity-based investments and absolute return strategies. Its Eaton Vance Distributors unit markets and sells Calvert Eaton Vance and Parametric-branded funds and separately managed accounts offered through financial intermediaries. In late 2020 Eaton Vance agreed to acquire by Morgan Stanley for about $7 billion. More than 95% of total sales comes from US customers.

	Annual Growth	10/16	10/17	10/18	10/19	10/20
Sales ($ mil.)	6.5%	1,342.9	1,529.0	1,702.2	1,683.3	1,730.4
Net income ($ mil.)	(13.0%)	241.3	282.1	381.9	400.0	138.5
Market value ($ mil.)	14.3%	4,020.0	5,787.0	5,165.5	5,228.6	6,855.6
Employees	7.0%	1,510	1,638	1,764	1,871	1,983

EAU TECHNOLOGIES INC   NBB: EAUI

1890 Cobb International Blvd., Suite A
Kennesaw, GA 30152
Phone: 678 388-9492
Fax: –
Web: www.eau-x.com
CEO: Doug Kindred
CFO: Brian Heinhold
HR: –
FYE: December 31
Type: Public

Of all the vowels O is EAU's bread and butter (as in H2O). Using water electrolysis technology EAU Technologies (formerly Electric Aquagenics Unlimited) makes equipment and process systems that clean and disinfect surfaces and foods. Its Empowered Water generators are sold and leased to companies in search of improved cleaning and sanitizing. The firm's water-based non-toxic products reduce bacteria viruses spores and molds in food processing living surfaces and other environments. Director Peter Ullrich individually and through his Water Science firm is EAU Technologies largest shareholder. Water Science is also EAU's biggest customer and it licenses EAU technology in Latin America.

	Annual Growth	12/10	12/11	12/12	12/13	12/14
Sales ($ mil.)	9.2%	0.7	1.9	0.5	2.0	1.0
Net income ($ mil.)	–	2.4	(3.0)	(2.0)	(2.0)	(1.9)
Market value ($ mil.)	(40.8%)	4.9	5.7	0.6	1.1	0.6
Employees	(10.7%)	11	11	11	9	7

EBAY INC.

NMS: EBAY

2025 Hamilton Avenue
San Jose, CA 95125
Phone: 408 376-7008
Fax: –
Web: www.ebay.com

CEO: –
CFO: –
HR: –
FYE: December 31
Type: Public

eBay is a global commerce leader through its Marketplace platforms which connect millions of buyers and sellers in more than 190 markets around the world and boasts around 185 million users and over 1.7 billion listings globally. The platforms include its online marketplace located at www.ebay.com and its localized counterparts including off-platform businesses in South Korea Japan and Turkey as well as eBay's suite of mobile apps. It generates revenue through final value fees feature fees including fees to promote listing and listing fees from sellers in its Marketplace. eBay is available across digital platforms including mobile. Some 60% of its sales are outside the US. In 2020 eBay completed the sale of StubHub to viagogo for a purchase price $4.1 billion in cash and enters an agreement to transfer its Classifieds business to Adevinta for $2.5 billion in cash.

	Annual Growth	12/16	12/17	12/18	12/19	12/20
Sales ($ mil.)	3.4%	8,979.0	9,567.0	10,746.0	10,800.0	10,271.0
Net income ($ mil.)	(6.0%)	7,266.0	(1,016.0)	2,530.0	1,786.0	5,667.0
Market value ($ mil.)	14.1%	20,308.0	25,814.2	19,199.9	24,699.2	34,371.0
Employees	0.2%	12,600	14,100	14,000	13,300	12,700

EBIX INC

NMS: EBIX

1 Ebix Way
Johns Creek, GA 30097
Phone: 678 281-2020
Fax: –
Web: www.ebix.com

CEO: Robin Raina
CFO: Steven Hamil
HR: –
FYE: December 31
Type: Public

Ebix Inc. supplies on-demand software designed to streamline the way insurance professionals manage distribution marketing sales customer service and accounting activities. Its EbixCash Exchange (EbixCash) is primarily derived from the sales of prepaid gift cards and consideration paid by customers for financial transaction services including services like transferring or exchanging money. It also offers several other services including payment services and ticketing and travel services for which revenue is impacted by varying factors. Ebix also Software-as-a-Service (SaaS) enterprise solutions in the area of customer relationship management (CRM) front-end & back-end systems outsourced administrative and risk compliance. Ebix generated majority of its sales in India.

	Annual Growth	12/16	12/17	12/18	12/19	12/20
Sales ($ mil.)	20.3%	298.3	364.0	497.8	580.6	625.6
Net income ($ mil.)	(0.4%)	93.8	100.6	93.1	96.7	92.4
Market value ($ mil.)	(9.7%)	1,740.9	2,418.3	1,298.7	1,019.5	1,158.7
Employees	34.6%	2,988	4,515	9,263	7,975	9,802

EBSCO INDUSTRIES INC.

5724 Hwy. 280 East
Birmingham AL 35242
Phone: 205-991-6600
Fax: 256-430-4030
Web: www.avocent.com

CEO: David Walker
CFO: –
HR: –
FYE: June 30
Type: Private

Few portfolios are more diverse than that of EBSCO Industries (short for Elton B. Stephens Company). Among the conglomerate's more than 50 information services manufacturing and sales subsidiaries are magazine subscription and fulfillment firms a fishing lure manufacturer (the world's largest) a rifle manufacturer a specialty office and computer furniture retailer and real estate holdings. Its main businesses revolve around the publishing industry: EBSCO operates a subscription management agency and is one of the largest publishers of digital information. It offers about 375000 articles from more than 95000 publishers worldwide. The family of founder Elton B. Stephens Sr. owns the company.

EBY CORPORATION

610 N MAIN ST STE 500
WICHITA, KS 672033619
Phone: 316-268-3500
Fax: –
Web: www.ebycorp.com

CEO: James R Greir III
CFO: –
HR: Karman Diehl
FYE: December 31
Type: Private

General contractor Eby Corporation operating primarily through its Martin K. Eby Construction subsidiary provides design-build construction management general contracting and related services on projects such as office buildings medical facilities athletic facilities and historical renovations. Eby serves major corporations universities hospitals and state and local governments. Clients have included Disney The University of Texas Wichita State University and The Salvation Army. Martin K. Eby Construction named after the group's founder and the father of chairman Martin K. Eby Jr. was founded in 1937.

	Annual Growth	12/05	12/06	12/08	12/09	12/13
Sales ($ mil.)	–	–	(1,566.5)	43.5	33.8	93.3
Net income ($ mil.)	30.0%	–	–	0.5	(2.3)	1.7
Market value ($ mil.)	–	–	–	–	–	–
Employees	–	–	–	–	–	135

EBY-BROWN COMPANY LLC

280 SHUMAN BLVD STE 280
NAPERVILLE, IL 60563-8106
Phone: 630-778-2800
Fax: –
Web: www.eby-brown.com

CEO: –
CFO: –
HR: –
FYE: October 01
Type: Private

Eby-Brown makes its money on such vices as munchies and nicotine. The company is a leading convenience store supplier that distributes more than 11000 products to some 13500 retail locations in 30 states mostly east of the Mississippi. Eby-Brown operates about half a dozen distribution centers (with total capacity of about 2 million sq. ft.) that supply such items as beverages candy and snack foods frozen and refrigerated foods tobacco products and general merchandise. The convenience store supplier also offers advertising and promotion services for its customers. Eby-Brown which is still family-owned was founded in 1887 by the Wake family.

	Annual Growth	09/06	09/07	09/08*	10/10	10/11
Sales ($ mil.)	–	–	0.0	0.0	4,730.4	4,730.4
Net income ($ mil.)	–	–	0.0	0.0	0.0	0.0
Market value ($ mil.)	–	–	–	–	–	–
Employees	–	–	–	–	–	2,500

*Fiscal year change

ECC CAPITAL CORP

NBB: ECRO

2600 East Coast Highway, Suite 250
Corona Del Mar, CA 92625
Phone: 949 955-8700
Fax: –
Web: www.ecccapital.com

CEO: Steven Holder
CFO: Roque Santi
HR: –
FYE: December 31
Type: Public

ECC Capital refused to conform — to credit scoring criteria. The real estate investment trust (REIT) was formed to invest in non-conforming residential real estate loans. In the height of the subprime mortgage crisis the REIT's revenues plummeted and ECC Capital was forced to close offices reduce its workforce and sell assets. In 2007 it sold wholesale mortgage banking arm Encore Credit to Bear Stearns; it also sold its portfolio of direct-to-consumer loans to ResCap. The REIT is seeking a buyer for the rest of its securitized assets. Subsidiary Performance Credit was formerly engaged in the origination of wholesale loans but now provides financing to ECC Capital's clients.

	Annual Growth	12/05	12/06	12/18	12/19	12/20
Sales ($ mil.)	(17.7%)	95.7	30.7	1.7	(1.4)	5.1
Net income ($ mil.)	–	(64.1)	(134.6)	(2.7)	(4.8)	1.1
Market value ($ mil.)	(21.1%)	240.7	126.8	1.5	0.8	6.9
Employees	(57.1%)	1,667	715	–	–	–

ECHELON CORP.

NMS: ELON

2901 Patrick Henry Drive
Santa Clara, CA 95054
Phone: 408 938-5200
Fax: –
Web: www.echelon.com

CEO: Ronald Sege
CFO: –
HR: –
FYE: December 31
Type: Public

Echelon Corp. has made the infrastructure that connected industrial devices into networks that morphed into the Internet of Things. The company's combination of computer chips routers and controllers network interfaces and software have enabled connections for about 100 million devices for lighting heating and cooling security manufacturing lighting and building automation around the world. Echelon is moving to develop networking resources for the Industrial Internet of Things (IIoT) providing the capability for things such as sensors inside jet engines to communicate their operating status. The company also develops and sells an array of lighting control systems another portion of the Internet of Things.

	Annual Growth	12/12	12/13	12/14	12/15	12/16
Sales ($ mil.)	(29.9%)	134.0	86.2	38.7	38.8	32.4
Net income ($ mil.)	–	(12.8)	(17.6)	(24.3)	(13.2)	(4.1)
Market value ($ mil.)	17.5%	10.9	9.5	7.5	25.0	20.8
Employees	(22.4%)	223	192	106	87	81

ECHO GLOBAL LOGISTICS INC

NMS: ECHO

600 West Chicago Avenue, Suite 725
Chicago, IL 60654
Phone: 800 354-7993
Fax: –
Web: www.echo.com

CEO: Douglas R Waggoner
CFO: Peter M Rogers
HR: –
FYE: December 31
Type: Public

Echo Global Logistics' main business is arranging transportation by truckload (TL) and less than truckload (LTL) carriers for customers in a wide range of industries. It manages more than three million shipments annually. Echo Global provides its transportation and supply chain management services using advanced proprietary technology platforms for truckload quoting and transit times. It also offers intermodal services (a combination of truck and rail delivery) and some air and ocean delivery services. Its logistics solutions encompass services such as rate negotiation shipment tracking and freight management and reporting. The company was founded in 2005.

	Annual Growth	12/15	12/16	12/17	12/18	12/19
Sales ($ mil.)	9.6%	1,512.3	1,716.2	1,943.1	2,439.7	2,185.0
Net income ($ mil.)	17.3%	7.8	1.6	12.6	28.7	14.8
Market value ($ mil.)	0.4%	534.8	657.1	734.4	533.3	543.0
Employees	2.1%	2,335	2,350	2,453	2,595	2,539

ECHO THERAPEUTICS INC

NAS: ECTE

99 Wood Avenue South, Suite 302
Iselin, NJ 08830
Phone: 732 549-0128
Fax: –
Web: www.echotx.com

CEO: Alan W Schoenbart
CFO: Alan W Schoenbart
HR: –
FYE: December 31
Type: Public

Echo Therapeutics tries not to scratch the surface. The company develops instruments for transdermal (through the skin) drug delivery and diagnostics. Its devices use gentle abrasion and ultrasound technologies to painlessly extract analytes or introduce drugs without breaking the skin. The firm's proprietary Prelude Skin-Prep technology platform is being developed for use in glucose monitoring under the name Symphony. Echo is also developing a system to provide needle-free drug administration of lidocaine and other pharmaceuticals. Echo is also developing Azone a transdermal technology used for reformulated drugs already on the market.

	Annual Growth	12/10	12/11	12/12	12/13	12/14
Sales ($ mil.)	(39.5%)	0.4	0.4	0.0	0.0	0.1
Net income ($ mil.)	–	(4.1)	(10.0)	(12.3)	(19.1)	(15.0)
Market value ($ mil.)	(4.1%)	20.2	28.5	13.1	39.7	17.1
Employees	13.1%	11	29	44	28	18

ECHOSTAR CORP

NMS: SATS

100 Inverness Terrace East
Englewood, CO 80112-5308
Phone: 303 706-4000
Fax: –
Web: www.echostar.com

CEO: Michael Dugan
CFO: David Rayner
HR: –
FYE: December 31
Type: Public

EchoStar Corporation a global provider of broadband satellite technologies broadband internet services for consumer customers which include home and small to medium-sized businesses and satellite services. The company owns or leases around 10 satellites. The company's Hughes unit has approximately 1.6 million consumer and business broadband subscribers. The EchoStar Satellite Services unit provides satellite service operations and video delivery to DISH Network and other customers. The North America region accounts for most of EchoStar's revenue.

	Annual Growth	12/16	12/17	12/18	12/19	12/20
Sales ($ mil.)	(11.3%)	3,056.7	1,885.5	2,091.4	1,886.1	1,887.9
Net income ($ mil.)	–	179.9	392.6	(40.5)	(62.9)	(40.2)
Market value ($ mil.)	(19.9%)	4,961.7	5,783.4	3,545.3	4,181.6	2,045.9
Employees	(12.0%)	4,000	2,100	2,200	2,300	2,400

ECKERD YOUTH ALTERNATIVES, INC.

100 N STARCREST DR
CLEARWATER, FL 337653224
Phone: 727-461-2990
Fax: –
Web: www.eckerd.org

CEO: –
CFO: –
HR: –
FYE: June 30
Type: Private

Eckerd Youth Alternatives (EYA) provides early intervention and prevention wilderness education residential and day treatment and re-entry and aftercare programs for at-risk youths. The not-for-profit organization has worked to help more than 80000 kids through its operations in about 10 states located primarily in the eastern US. Many of EYA's some 40 programs are offered under contract with state juvenile justice agencies. EYA was established in 1968 by Jack Eckerd the founder of the Eckerd drugstore chain and his wife Ruth Eckerd. During the past few years the company has been focused on expanding its community-based support programs.

	Annual Growth	06/14	06/15	06/16	06/19	06/20
Sales ($ mil.)	10.6%	–	172.1	193.2	236.5	284.7
Net income ($ mil.)	(0.1%)	–	2.1	4.6	3.2	2.1
Market value ($ mil.)	–	–	–	–	–	–
Employees	–	–	–	–	–	1,400

ECLINICALWORKS LLC

2 TECHNOLOGY DR
WESTBOROUGH, MA 01581-1727
Phone: 508-475-0450
Fax: –

CEO: Girish Navani
CFO: –
HR: –
FYE: December 31
Type: Private

eClinicalWorks helps physicians focus on their patients by offering a hand in organizing their administrative records. The company provides medical software that manages medical documents also known as electronic health records. It serves both small and mid-sized health care practitioners and large practice groups such as Houston's Memorial Hermann Healthcare System and Chicago's Rush Health. The eClinicalWorks client roster includes some 85000 physicians and more than 470000 medical professionals operating businesses throughout the US. Owned by its executives and employees the company provides software for primary care practices and most medical specialties.

	Annual Growth	12/05	12/06	12/07	12/08	12/10
Sales ($ mil.)	–	–	–	0.0	64.7	140.4
Net income ($ mil.)	–	–	–	0.0	1.9	34.7
Market value ($ mil.)	–	–	–	–	–	–
Employees	–	–	–	–	–	2,800

ECOLAB INC — NYS: ECL

1 Ecolab Place
St. Paul, MN 55102
Phone: 800 232-6522
Fax: –
Web: www.ecolab.com

CEO: Christophe Beck
CFO: Scott D Kirkland
HR: –
FYE: December 31
Type: Public

Ecolab Inc. offers cleaning sanitation pest-elimination and maintenance products and services to the energy healthcare hospitality and industrial sectors among others. Its cleaning and sanitizing operations serve hotels schools commercial and institutional laundries and quick-service restaurants. Other units focus on products for textile care water care healthcare food and beverage processing and pest control. It also makes chemicals used in water treatment for industrial processes including in the paper and energy industries. The US is Ecolab's largest market accounting for about 55% of revenue.

	Annual Growth	12/16	12/17	12/18	12/19	12/20
Sales ($ mil.)	(2.7%)	13,152.8	13,838.3	14,668.2	14,906.3	11,790.2
Net income ($ mil.)	–	1,229.6	1,508.4	1,429.1	1,558.9	(1,205.1)
Market value ($ mil.)	16.6%	33,495.9	38,342.3	42,105.6	55,147.4	61,825.4
Employees	(1.9%)	47,565	48,400	49,000	50,200	44,000

ECOLOGY AND ENVIRONMENT, INC. — NMS: EEI

368 Pleasant View Drive
Lancaster, NY 14086
Phone: 716 684-8060
Fax: 716 684-0844
Web: www.ene.com

CEO: –
CFO: Peter F Sorci
HR: –
FYE: July 31
Type: Public

Every day is Earth Day at environmental consulting and testing company Ecology and Environment (E & E). The company which has completed more than 50000 projects in some 120 countries provides engineering permitting and environmental support for all types of energy development including offshore energy power plants pipelines and renewables. Services include environmental impact assessments air pollution control wastewater analyses and site-planning. It also consults on natural resource restoration programs green initiatives emergency planning and hazardous waste projects. E & E which generates most of its sales in the US targets government industrial and engineering clients.

	Annual Growth	07/13	07/14	07/15	07/16	07/17
Sales ($ mil.)	(6.2%)	134.9	128.4	126.7	105.8	104.5
Net income ($ mil.)	–	(2.1)	(1.4)	3.4	0.9	3.0
Market value ($ mil.)	3.8%	45.8	44.6	48.7	43.7	53.2
Employees	(6.2%)	1,130	1,013	952	893	876

ECOTALITY INC — NBB: ECTY Q

Post Montgomery Center, One Montgomery Street, Suite 2525
San Francisco, CA 94104
Phone: 415 992-3000
Fax: –
Web: www.ecotality.com

CEO: –
CFO: –
HR: –
FYE: December 31
Type: Public

ECOtality is all juiced up for the electric car revolution. The company develops power storage technologies including battery chargers and charging stations for electric vehicles. Its Minit-Charger system takes about 15 minutes to charge the batteries for electric forklifts golf carts airport trucks and other off-road electric vehicles; the company has sold about 6000 chargers since 2008. Now that the all-electric Nissan Leaf and the hybrid-electric Chevrolet Volt are in production ECOtality is marketing car charging stations called Blink in select cities. ECOtality is also involved in developing solar modules and distributing fuel cell systems. CEO Jonathan Read owns 10% of the company's stock.

	Annual Growth	12/08	12/09	12/10	12/11	12/12
Sales ($ mil.)	48.7%	11.2	8.6	13.5	28.4	54.7
Net income ($ mil.)	–	(8.1)	(29.5)	(16.4)	(22.5)	(9.6)
Market value ($ mil.)	96.3%	0.7	131.6	76.5	25.7	10.4
Employees	38.2%	45	67	116	179	164

ECOVA INC.

1313 N. Atlantic Ste. 5000
Spokane WA 99201
Phone: 509-329-7600
Fax: 509-329-7287
Web: www.ecova.com

CEO: Mathias Lelievre
CFO: Vincent Manier
HR: –
FYE: December 31
Type: Subsidiary

Ecova (formerly Advantage IQ) maintains that intelligence plays a key role in business success. The company helps multi-site commercial customers in the US manage their facilities utilities and telecommunications costs by providing outsourced services for such tasks as estimating and managing facility-related expenses handling billing and managing invoices and vendor contracts. It serves clients in industries including communications retail financial services and health care. The company was founded in 1995 as an affiliate of parent Avista Corporation a provider of utilities services in the northwestern US. Ecova has satellite offices in Colorado Minnesota Ohio and Oregon.

ECS FEDERAL, LLC

2750 PROSPERITY AVE # 600
FAIRFAX, VA 220314312
Phone: 703-270-1540
Fax: –
Web: www.ecs-federal.com

CEO: –
CFO: Thomas Weston
HR: –
FYE: December 31
Type: Private

Electronic Consulting Services (ECS) provides computer and telecommunications network consulting services primarily in the Eastern US. The company specializes in such areas as systems engineering enterprise communications project management and program support. It also offers information assurance help desk operations and Web development services. ECS primarily serves government agencies and defense contractors. Customers have included Lockheed Martin Titan the US Department of Housing and Urban Development and Advanced Technology Systems. The company has satellite offices in Florida Missouri North Carolina Pennsylvania and Washington D.C. Electronic Consulting Services was founded in 1993.

	Annual Growth	12/08	12/09	12/10	12/11	12/12
Sales ($ mil.)	36.0%	–	–	112.4	138.8	208.1
Net income ($ mil.)	21.4%	–	–	11.1	8.0	16.4
Market value ($ mil.)	–	–	–	–	–	–
Employees	–	–	–	–	–	1,184

EDELBROCK LLC

2700 California St.
Torrance CA 90503
Phone: 310-781-2222
Fax: 310-3201187-
Web: www.edelbrock.com

CEO: Don Barry
CFO: Steve Zitkus
HR: Talisa Kohan
FYE: June 30
Type: Private

Speed enthusiast Edelbrock makes performance-enhancing parts for race cars and motorcycles recreational and passenger vehicles light trucks and watercraft. The short list includes carburetors intake manifolds cylinder heads water pumps air cleaners camshafts exhaust systems an array of other aftermarket parts and even some branded sportswear. Specifically for Harley-Davidson motorcycles Edelbrock tailors a line of aftermarket engine parts. The company markets its products mainly through automotive chain stores online dealers mail-order houses and warehouse distributors. The Edelbrock family — led by company chairman president and CEO Vic Edelbrock Jr. — runs the 70-plus year old company.

EDGEWELL PERSONAL CARE CO
NYS: EPC

6 Research Drive
Shelton, CT 06484
Phone: 203 944-5500
Fax: –
Web: www.edgewell.com

CEO: Rod Little
CFO: Daniel Sullivan
HR: –
FYE: September 30
Type: Public

Edgewell Personal Care Company is one of the world's largest manufacturers and marketers of portfolio of personal care products includes razors sunscreen moist wipes infant and pet care products and feminine care products sold under brands such as Schick Edge Banana Boat Hawaiian Tropic Stayfree Wet Ones and Diaper Genie. The company distributes its products to consumers through numerous retail locations worldwide including mass merchandisers and warehouse clubs food drug and convenience stores and military stores. It operates in more than 20 countries and has a global footprint in more than 50 countries. The US accounts for more than 55% of its total revenue.

	Annual Growth	09/17	09/18	09/19	09/20	09/21
Sales ($ mil.)	(2.4%)	2,298.4	2,234.4	2,141.0	1,949.7	2,087.3
Net income ($ mil.)	112.9%	5.7	103.3	(372.2)	67.6	117.0
Market value ($ mil.)	(16.0%)	3,956.5	2,513.5	1,766.5	1,515.8	1,973.6
Employees	3.6%	6,000	5,900	6,000	5,800	6,900

EDISON INTERNATIONAL
NYS: EIX

2244 Walnut Grove Avenue, P.O. Box 976
Rosemead, CA 91770
Phone: 626 302-2222
Fax: –
Web: www.edisoninvestor.com

CEO: Pedro Pizarro
CFO: Maria Rigatti
HR: Jacqueline Trapp
FYE: December 31
Type: Public

Edison International is a major power provider in California through its Southern California Edison (SCE) subsidiary which distributes electricity to 15 million people in a 50000 square-mile area of central coastal and southern California. The distribution system which takes power from substations to customers includes over 53000 line-miles of overhead lines 38000 line-miles of underground lines and approximately 800 substations all of which are located in California. SCE also has about 7000 MW of generating capacity and energy storage facilities primarily located in California. Through its Edison Energy subsidiary Edison International owns and operates additional solar and wind power projects.

	Annual Growth	12/16	12/17	12/18	12/19	12/20
Sales ($ mil.)	3.4%	11,869.0	12,320.0	12,657.0	12,347.0	13,578.0
Net income ($ mil.)	(13.4%)	1,311.0	565.0	(423.0)	1,284.0	739.0
Market value ($ mil.)	(3.3%)	27,277.5	23,962.1	21,510.6	28,573.4	23,802.9
Employees	1.9%	12,390	12,521	12,574	12,937	13,351

EDISON MISSION ENERGY

3 MacArthur Place, Suite 100
Santa Ana, CA 92707
Phone: 714 513-8000
Fax: –
Web: www.edisonmissionenergy.com

CEO: –
CFO: –
HR: –
FYE: December 31
Type: Public

At one time the mission of Edison Mission Energy (EME) was to conquer the non-regulated energy sector around the world but it has since settled for focusing on a big slice of the US market. An indirect subsidiary of Edison International it has interests in more than 40 coal-fired natural gas-fired and wind power plants in the US and one in Turkey (Doga project) that give it a net physical generating capacity of more than 8900 MW. EME sells power wholesale through contracts with large utilities regional distributors and other energy companies; it also trades and hedges energy on the open power markets through Edison Mission Marketing & Trading.

	Annual Growth	12/08	12/09	12/10	12/11	12/12
Sales ($ mil.)	(17.7%)	2,811.0	2,377.0	2,423.0	2,180.0	1,287.0
Net income ($ mil.)	–	–	501.0	197.0	164.0	(1,078.0)	(925.0)
Market value ($ mil.)	–	–	–	–	–	–
Employees	(9.2%)	1,889	1,843	1,828	1,783	1,283

EDP RENEWABLES NORTH AMERICA LLC

808 Travis St. Ste. 700
Houston TX 77002
Phone: 713-265-0350
Fax: 713-265-0365
Web: www.edpr.com

CEO: Miguel Prado
CFO: –
HR: –
FYE: December 31
Type: Subsidiary

EDP Renewables North America (formerly Horizon Wind Energy) is the US subsidiary of Spain-based EDP Renovaveis. The US company owns and operates more than 20 onshore wind farms across nine states that have a generating capacity of 2800 MW. It has another 20000 MW of wind projects in various stages of development around the country. EDP Renewables North America sells its electricity wholesale as Power Purchase Agreements (PPAs) to utility companies such as AmerenUE Direct Energy Great River and the TVA. It has also developed and sold seven farms to Entergy Florida Power & Light and Puget Energy.

EDUCATION MANAGEMENT CORP
NBB: EDMC

210 Sixth Avenue, 33rd Floor
Pittsburgh, PA 15222
Phone: 412 562-0900
Fax: 412 562-0598
Web: www.edmc.edu

CEO: –
CFO: –
HR: –
FYE: June 30
Type: Public

Worried that traditional higher education could leave you enlightened but unemployed? Education Management may have the solution. The company operates five main branches with about 110 locations in more than 30 states and in Canada. The Art Institutes Argosy University South University and Brown Mackie College offer degree programs from associate to postgraduate and Western State University College of Law offers juris doctoral degrees. The company also offers online courses through three of its divisions. Education Management institutions boast a combined enrollment of more than 125500 students and some 21000 faculty and staff. Education Management voluntarily delisted from the NASDAQ in 2014.

	Annual Growth	06/10	06/11	06/12	06/13	06/14
Sales ($ mil.)	(2.4%)	2,508.5	2,887.6	2,761.0	2,498.6	2,272.7
Net income ($ mil.)	–	168.5	229.5	(1,515.7)	(268.0)	(663.9)
Market value ($ mil.)	(42.3%)	1,922.2	3,017.5	876.0	708.4	213.0
Employees	(1.7%)	22,300	16,900	24,700	23,400	20,800

EDUCATION REALTY TRUST INC
NYS: EDR

999 South Shady Grove Road, Suite 600
Memphis, TN 38120
Phone: 901 259-2500
Fax: –
Web: www.edrtrust.com

CEO: –
CFO: –
HR: –
FYE: December 31
Type: Public

This company can give your college student a home away from home. Education Realty Trust a self-administered real estate investment trust (REIT) develops buys owns and operates residential communities for university students. It owns roughly 50 communities in more than 20 US states consisting of almost 28000 beds in nearly 10500 units. Through its Allen & O'Hara Education Services subsidiary the REIT manages another 20-plus student housing properties owned by others. Education Realty Trust communities offer private rooms as well as amenities such as Internet access fitness centers game rooms dining facilities swimming pools — and even study rooms.

	Annual Growth	12/12	12/13	12/14	12/15	12/16
Sales ($ mil.)	18.8%	145.0	184.4	225.8	255.2	289.0
Net income ($ mil.)	52.0%	8.4	4.3	47.1	19.9	44.9
Market value ($ mil.)	41.2%	777.5	644.5	2,673.8	2,768.1	3,091.1
Employees	1.2%	1,222	1,288	1,283	1,237	1,280

EDUCATIONAL & INSTITUTIONAL COOPERATIVE SERVICE INC.

2 JERICHO PLZ STE 309
JERICHO, NY 117531681
Phone: 631-273-7900
Fax: –
Web: www.eandi.org

CEO: Tom Fitzgerald
CFO: John D Orlando
HR: –
FYE: December 31
Type: Private

Educational & Institutional Cooperative Service (E&I) is a not-for-profit buying cooperative that provides goods and services to its members at discounted prices. E&I seeks and enters contracts with athletic equipment furniture computer and electronics maintenance food service office products and transportation and delivery service suppliers. Established in 1934 the cooperative is owned by more than 1600 tax-exempt organizations including colleges universities private schools health care institutions and hospitals.

	Annual Growth	12/03	12/04	12/05	12/06	12/07
Sales ($ mil.)	0.7%	–	10.9	12.5	13.8	11.1
Net income ($ mil.)	–	–	–	1.4	1.9	(0.6)
Market value ($ mil.)	–	–	–	–	–	–
Employees	–	–	–	–	–	55

EDUCATIONAL DEVELOPMENT CORP.   NMS: EDUC

5402 South 122nd East Avenue
Tulsa, OK 74146
Phone: 918 622-4522
Fax: –
Web: www.edcpub.com

CEO: Craig White
CFO: Dan O'Keefe
HR: –
FYE: February 28
Type: Public

Educational Development Corporation (EDC) likes being in a bind as long as the cover appeals to youngsters. The company is the exclusive US distributor of a line of about 1500 children's books published by the UK's Usborne Publishing Limited. EDC's Home Business Division markets the books to individuals using independent sales reps who sell through personal websites home parties direct sales and book fairs; this division also distributes books to public and school libraries. EDC's Publishing Division distributes the Usborne line to a network of book toy and other retail stores. EDC bought multi-cultural children's book publisher Kane/Miller in 2008 to complement its product offerings.

	Annual Growth	02/17	02/18	02/19	02/20	02/21
Sales ($ mil.)	17.7%	106.6	112.0	118.8	113.0	204.6
Net income ($ mil.)	44.9%	2.9	5.2	6.7	5.6	12.6
Market value ($ mil.)	13.1%	79.7	161.5	67.2	43.1	130.3
Employees	1.5%	202	193	178	201	214

EDUCATIONAL FUNDING OF THE SOUTH, INC.

12700 KINGSTON PIKE
FARRAGUT, TN 379340917
Phone: 865-342-0684
Fax: –
Web: www.corp.elfi.com

CEO: Ron Gambill
CFO: –
HR: –
FYE: September 30
Type: Private

Reading is fundamental but funding is crucial to higher education. That's where Educational Funding of the South comes in. Known as Edsouth the not-for-profit public benefit corporation provides student loan funding by purchasing loans from originators. Nearly 500 lending institutions participate in one or more of Edsouth's educational loan programs. Edsouth is one of the nation's largest holders of student loans. The organization was founded in 1988. Formerly known as Volunteer State Student Funding Corporation it changed its name to Educational Funding of the South in 1996.

	Annual Growth	12/03	12/04	12/05	12/06*	09/12
Assets ($ mil.)	(3.5%)	–	3,881.5	4,484.5	4,223.0	2,924.2
Net income ($ mil.)	–	–	30.6	26.1	252.2	(20.1)
Market value ($ mil.)	–	–	–	–	–	–
Employees	–	–	–	–	–	3

*Fiscal year change

EDUCATIONAL TESTING SERVICE

660 ROSEDALE RD
PRINCETON, NJ 085402218
Phone: 609-921-9000
Fax: –
Web: www.ets.org

CEO: –
CFO: Jack Hayon
HR: –
FYE: September 30
Type: Private

Please completely fill in each circle on the answer sheet as prepared by Educational Testing Service (ETS). ETS develops and administers the Graduate Record Examinations (GRE) and Test of English as a Foreign Language (TOEFL). The nonprofit group develops and administers more than 50 million achievement admissions academic and professional tests a year at more than 9000 locations in more than 180 countries. It also develops assessment programs for corporations professional associations and state entities. ETS' research unit conducts advancing educational measurement and policy studies; test-development firm Prometric is a for-profit subsidiary.

	Annual Growth	09/16	09/17	09/18	09/19	09/20
Sales ($ mil.)	(9.1%)	–	1,398.1	1,392.9	1,358.0	1,050.3
Net income ($ mil.)	–	–	53.2	686.5	(22.1)	(85.4)
Market value ($ mil.)	–	–	–	–	–	–
Employees	–	–	–	–	–	2,756

EDWARDS LIFESCIENCES CORP   NYS: EW

One Edwards Way
Irvine, CA 92614
Phone: 949 250-2500
Fax: –
Web: www.edwards.com

CEO: Michael Mussallem
CFO: Scott Ullem
HR: –
FYE: December 31
Type: Public

Edwards Lifesciences Corporation is the global leader in patient-focused medical innovations for structural heart disease and critical care monitoring. Offerings include transcatheter heart valves for minimally invasive procedures surgical heart valves and annuloplasty rings that repair damaged valves. The company also makes monitoring systems that measure heart function during surgery and fluid status in surgical and intensive care settings. Edwards Lifesciences markets its products worldwide; more than 55% of sales come from the US.

	Annual Growth	12/17	12/18	12/19	12/20	12/21
Sales ($ mil.)	11.1%	3,435.3	3,722.8	4,348.0	4,386.3	5,232.5
Net income ($ mil.)	26.7%	583.6	722.2	1,046.9	823.4	1,503.1
Market value ($ mil.)	3.5%	70,342.3	95,593.4	145,596.3	56,936.6	80,852.2
Employees	6.5%	12,200	12,800	13,900	14,900	15,700

EEI HOLDING CORPORATION

700 N MACARTHUR BLVD
SPRINGFIELD, IL 627022304
Phone: 217-523-0108
Fax: –
Web: www.eeiholding.com

CEO: Robert Egizii
CFO: John Hinkle
HR: –
FYE: December 31
Type: Private

Electricity comes easy for EEI Holding. The company owns Egizii Electric and other firms that provide electrical and general construction and contracting services throughout the US. It has expertise in utilities medical facilities infrastructure telecommunications data systems and traffic control. The company also assists clients with site selection budget development and property lease-back transactions. EEI Holding began operations in the late 1940s. Chairman and CEO Robert Egizii is the firm's majority shareholder. The company has offices in Illinois and Florida.

	Annual Growth	12/98	12/99	12/00	12/01	12/09
Sales ($ mil.)	(12.0%)	–	71.3	98.4	117.4	19.8
Net income ($ mil.)	–	–	–	(2.4)	1.0	0.2
Market value ($ mil.)	–	–	–	–	–	–
Employees	–	–	–	–	–	500

EGAIN CORP
NAS: EGAN

1252 Borregas Avenue
Sunnyvale, CA 94089
Phone: 408 636-4500
Fax: -
Web: www.egain.com

CEO: Ashutosh Roy
CFO: Eric Smit
HR: -
FYE: June 30
Type: Public

eGain Corporation automates customer engagement with an innovative software as a service (SaaS) platform powered by deep digital artificial intelligence (AI) and knowledge capabilities. It sells mostly to large enterprises across financial services telecommunications retail government healthcare and utilities. More than 180 leading brands use eGain's cloud software to improve customer satisfaction empower agents reduce service cost and boost sales. North America generates nearly 70% of its revenue.

	Annual Growth	06/17	06/18	06/19	06/20	06/21
Sales ($ mil.)	7.7%	58.2	61.3	67.2	72.7	78.3
Net income ($ mil.)	-	(6.0)	(2.0)	4.2	7.2	7.0
Market value ($ mil.)	62.4%	51.5	471.6	254.2	347.0	358.5
Employees	4.4%	479	464	475	522	570

EGPI FIRECREEK INC
NBB: EFIR

6564 Smoke Tree Lane
Scottsdale, AZ 85253
Phone: 480 948-6581
Fax: -
Web: www.egpifirecreek.com

CEO: Dennis Alexander
CFO: Dennis R Alexander
HR: -
FYE: December 31
Type: Public

The fire in EGPI Firecreek's belly is for oil and gas exploration and production and traffic systems. Once dependent on the sale of private leisure and commercial vessels EGPI Firecreek has refocused on US oil and gas activities. The company produces and sells oil and natural gas from wells in Sweetwater County Wyoming and Knox County Texas. In 2009 in a diversification move EGPI Firecreek subsidiary Asian Ventures Corp. acquired M3 Lighting as the company expanded into light and traffic fixture manufacturing. It picked up communications technology firm Terra Telecom in 2010. That year it moved to expand its assets by agreeing to acquire Caddo International and by buying Arctic Solar Engineering in 2011

	Annual Growth	12/08	12/09	12/10	12/11	12/12
Sales ($ mil.)	(53.2%)	-	1.2	0.0	0.3	0.1
Net income ($ mil.)	-	3.3	(3.4)	(4.5)	(5.0)	(6.1)
Market value ($ mil.)	-	0.0	0.0	0.0	0.0	0.0
Employees	-	-	-	-	-	-

EGPI FIRECREEK INC.
OTC: EFCR

6564 Smoke Tree Ln.
Scottsdale AZ 85253
Phone: 480-948-6581
Fax: 480-443-1403
Web: www.egpifirecreek.com

CEO: Dennis Alexander
CFO: Dennis R Alexander
HR: -
FYE: December 31
Type: Public

The fire in EGPI Firecreek's belly is for oil and gas exploration and production and traffic systems. Once dependent on the sale of private leisure and commercial vessels EGPI Firecreek has refocused on US oil and gas activities. The company produces and sells oil and natural gas from wells in Sweetwater County Wyoming and Knox County Texas. In 2009 in a diversification move EGPI Firecreek subsidiary Asian Ventures Corp. acquired M3 Lighting as the company expanded into light and traffic fixture manufacturing. It picked up communications technology firm Terra Telecom in 2010. That year it moved to expand its assets by agreeing to acquire Caddo International and by buying Arctic Solar Engineering in 2011

EHEALTH INC
NMS: EHTH

2625 Augustine Drive, Second Floor
Santa Clara, CA 95054
Phone: 650 584-2700
Fax: -
Web: www.ehealth.com

CEO: Francis Soistman
CFO: Christine Janofsky
HR: -
FYE: December 31
Type: Public

eHealth is a leading health insurance marketplace with a technology and service platform that provides consumer engagement education and health insurance enrollment solutions. The company created a marketplace that offers consumers a broad choice of insurance products that includes thousands of Medicare Advantage Medicare Supplement Medicare Part D prescription drug individual and family small business and other ancillary health insurance products. Licensed to sell insurance policies throughout the US the company has partnerships with more than 200 health insurance carriers for which it processes and delivers potential members' applications in return for commission on policy sales. It lets consumers compare products online ? including health dental and vision insurance products from the likes of Aetna Humana and UnitedHealth.

	Annual Growth	12/16	12/17	12/18	12/19	12/20
Sales ($ mil.)	32.9%	187.0	172.4	251.4	506.2	582.8
Net income ($ mil.)	-	(4.9)	(25.4)	0.2	66.9	45.5
Market value ($ mil.)	60.5%	276.1	450.3	996.0	2,490.8	1,830.5
Employees	20.0%	944	1,079	1,079	1,500	1,960

EIDE BAILLY LLP

4310 17TH AVE S
FARGO, ND 581033339
Phone: 701-239-8500
Fax: -
Web: www.eidebailly.com

CEO: -
CFO: -
HR: -
FYE: April 30
Type: Private

Eide Bailly is how the West was audited. The company which was founded in 1917 provides clients with audit accounting tax and consulting services from more than 20 offices in nearly a dozen western and central US states. Eide Bailly's target industries include construction agricultural processing oil and gas real estate renewable energy government financial services manufacturing health care and not-for-profit organizations. Additional services are provided by subsidiaries and affiliates including Eide Bailly Technology Consulting. International services are provided through Eide Bailly's affiliation with HLB International. The accounting firm serves some 44000 clients annually.

	Annual Growth	04/15	04/16	04/17	04/18	04/19
Sales ($ mil.)	9.4%	-	259.4	269.4	296.6	339.7
Net income ($ mil.)	5.8%	-	93.9	98.5	100.9	111.1
Market value ($ mil.)	-	-	-	-	-	-
Employees	-	-	-	-	-	2,500

EILEEN FISHER, INC.

2 BRIDGE ST STE 230
IRVINGTON, NY 105331595
Phone: 914-591-5700
Fax: -
Web: www.eileenfisher.com

CEO: -
CFO: Vincent Phelan
HR: -
FYE: December 31
Type: Private

EILEEN FISHER designs women's clothing that embraces simplicity sustainability and timeless design. The company is committed to responsible business practices that create positive change ? giving to causes that support women and girls building a more sustainable fashion industry and creating a more responsible supply chain. The company makes and sells upscale women's business and casual clothing (tops jackets pants skirts and dresses) made mostly from organic and natural fabrics. EILEEN FISHER operates more than 65 stores in the US Canada and the UK. It also offers personal shopping services for US customers. After working in the fields of graphic arts and interior design Eileen Fisher founded the company in 1984.

	Annual Growth	12/04	12/05	12/06	12/07	12/08
Sales ($ mil.)	(55.2%)	-	-	1,361.8	253.8	272.9
Net income ($ mil.)	5435.0%	-	-	0.0	7.4	2.7
Market value ($ mil.)	-	-	-	-	-	-
Employees	-	-	-	-	-	1,000

EINSTEIN NOAH RESTAURANT GROUP INC NMS: BAGL

555 Zang Street, Suite 300
Lakewood, CO 80228
Phone: 303 568-8000
Fax: -
Web: www.einsteinnoah.com
CEO: Frank G Paci
CFO: John A Coletta
HR: -
FYE: January 01
Type: Public

Bagels and coffee are key ingredients for this company. Einstein Noah Restaurant Group is the largest bagel shop operator in the US with more than 815 company-owned and franchised locations. Its flagship chain Einstein Bros. Bagels offers more than a dozen varieties of fresh-made bagels and spreads along with coffee pastries and a menu of sandwiches and salads at its 685 outlets. In addition to Einstein Bros. the company operates the Noah's New York Bagels and Manhattan Bagel chains. Some 460 of the bagel shops are company-owned while the rest are operated by franchisees or licensees. Investment firm Greenlight Capital controls about 65% of Einstein Noah.

	Annual Growth	12/08	12/09	12/10*	01/12	01/13
Sales ($ mil.)	0.6%	413.5	408.6	411.7	423.6	427.0
Net income ($ mil.)	(9.6%)	21.1	72.0	10.6	13.2	12.7
Market value ($ mil.)	18.0%	91.2	166.7	234.8	257.9	208.5
Employees	(2.1%)	7,698	7,054	6,796	6,506	6,912

*Fiscal year change

EISAI INC.

100 Tice Blvd.
Woodcliff Lake NJ 07677
Phone: 201-692-1100
Fax: 201-692-1804
Web: us.eisai.com
CEO: -
CFO: -
HR: -
FYE: March 31
Type: Subsidiary

Eisai Inc. develops and markets pharmaceuticals to treat a variety of ills. As the US production arm of Eisai Co. its roster includes Alzheimer's treatment Aricept Aciphex for acid reflux anti-seizure medication Banzel anticoagulant Fragmin lymphoma drug Ontak and anti-convulsant Zonegran. In addition to neurology oncology and vascular ailments the firm has drug research development marketing and manufacturing programs in areas including infectious disease inflammation and critical care. The company supplies its products to health care professionals pharmacies and hospitals through wholesale distributors.

EISENHOWER MEDICAL CENTER

39000 BOB HOPE DR
RANCHO MIRAGE, CA 922703221
Phone: 760-340-3911
Fax: -
Web: www.emc.org
CEO: G Aubrey Serfling
CFO: Kimberly Osborne
HR: -
FYE: June 30
Type: Private

The Eisenhower Medical Center is perhaps better known for the name of a first lady than the 34th US president: The not-for-profit medical campus is the home of the Betty Ford Center. In addition to the renowned alcohol and drug rehabilitation center Eisenhower Medical Center comprises the more than 540-bed Eisenhower Memorial Hospital the Barbara Sinatra Children's Center and the Annenberg Center for Health Sciences. In addition to medical surgical and emergency services the hospital offers cancer care neurology orthopedics cardiology and rehabilitation. An accredited teaching hospital it also conducts training and research programs and operates outpatient clinics in surrounding areas.

	Annual Growth	06/08	06/09	06/10	06/13	06/15
Sales ($ mil.)	6.8%	-	-	411.2	501.4	571.8
Net income ($ mil.)	19.3%	-	-	6.9	(27.3)	16.6
Market value ($ mil.)	-	-	-	-	-	-
Employees	-	-	-	-	-	3,000

EISNERAMPER LLP

733 3RD AVE FL 9
NEW YORK, NY 100173242
Phone: 212-949-8700
Fax: -
Web: www.eisneramper.com
CEO: -
CFO: -
HR: -
FYE: January 31
Type: Private

EisnerAmper is one of the largest accounting tax and business advisory firms in the US serving more than 200 US public companies as well as with family offices and high net worth individuals. Most EisnerAmper clients are based in the US or comprised of US business interests of foreign entities. To serve domestically-based clients with interests in financial services opportunities overseas it offers the resources of offices in the UK Israel India and EisnerAmper Global with offices in the Cayman Islands Singapore and Ireland; as well as the services of?Allinial Global.

	Annual Growth	01/10	01/11	01/12	01/13	01/14
Sales ($ mil.)	35.8%	-	-	230.7	247.6	425.6
Net income ($ mil.)	(1.0%)	-	-	59.7	55.7	58.5
Market value ($ mil.)	-	-	-	-	-	-
Employees	-	-	-	-	-	1,920

EKIMAS CORP NBB: ASNB

229 Andover Street
Wilmington, MA 01887
Phone: 424 256-8560
Fax: 978 657-0074
Web: www.advbiomaterials.com
CEO: -
CFO: -
HR: -
FYE: March 31
Type: Public

If artificial blood becomes a reality the manufacturers can hook up with AdvanSource Biomaterials maker of synthetic blood vessels. The company's products replace or bypass damaged and diseased arteries and provide access for dialysis needles in kidney disease patients undergoing hemodialysis. These man-made blood vessels also called vascular grafts are made of ChronoFlex the company's polyurethane-based biomaterial. Its CardioPass product candidate is a synthetic coronary artery bypass graft. AdvanSource's HydroThane polymer-based biomaterial mimics living tissue and is marketed for use by other medical device makers.

	Annual Growth	03/15	03/16	03/17	03/18	03/19
Sales ($ mil.)	6.8%	2.6	3.2	2.3	2.9	3.3
Net income ($ mil.)	-	(0.3)	0.0	(0.5)	(0.2)	0.3
Market value ($ mil.)	24.1%	0.8	3.9	0.9	0.9	1.9
Employees	0.0%	11	12	12	11	11

EL DORADO FURNITURE CORP

4200 NW 167TH ST
MIAMI GARDENS, FL 330546112
Phone: 305-624-9700
Fax: -
Web: www.eldoradofurniture.com
CEO: Luis E Capo
CFO: -
HR: -
FYE: December 31
Type: Private

The road to El Dorado Furniture is covered in sand. The company sells home furnishings in South Florida through about a dozen retail showrooms and a pair of outlets located in Broward Miami-Dade Palm Beach and Lee counties. El Dorado Furniture stores offer wood upholstered and leather furniture for every room in the house as well as mattresses bedding and decorative accessories. Its stores are designed to look like small towns with building fa §ades situated along a boulevard; some locations also feature caf ©s. Founded in 1967 and run by the Cap family El Dorado Furniture has become the nation's largest Hispanic-owned retail enterprises.

	Annual Growth	12/15	12/16	12/17	12/18	12/20
Sales ($ mil.)	(2.7%)	-	218.7	219.7	233.8	196.3
Net income ($ mil.)	(1.7%)	-	39.8	38.7	36.8	37.2
Market value ($ mil.)	-	-	-	-	-	-
Employees	-	-	-	-	-	705

EL PASO CORPORATION

NYSE: EP

El Paso Bldg. 1001 Louisiana St.
Houston TX 77002
Phone: 713-420-2600
Fax: 713-420-4417
Web: www.elpaso.com

CEO: Richard D Kinder
CFO: John R Sult
HR: -
FYE: December 31
Type: Public

Out in the West Texas town of El Paso this company fell in love with the natural gas industry. Founded in 1928 in its namesake city El Paso Corporation is primarily engaged in gas transportation and storage (including liquefied natural gas LNG) oil and gas exploration and production and gas gathering and processing. The operator of the largest gas transportation system in the US El Paso has interests in 44000 miles of interstate pipeline. In 2011 subsidiary El Paso Exploration and Production had estimated proved reserves of about 3.9 trillion cu. ft. of natural gas equivalent in Brazil Egypt and the US. In a major move in 2012 El Paso Corp. was acquired by Kinder Morgan for about $38 billion.

EL PASO COUNTY HOSPITAL DISTRICT

4815 ALAMEDA AVE
EL PASO, TX 799052705
Phone: 915-544-1200
Fax: -
Web: www.umcelpaso.org

CEO: James N Valenti
CFO: Michael Nunez
HR: -
FYE: September 30
Type: Private

University Medical Center is a community not-for-profit health care system serving West Texas and southern New Mexico. The network includes the 330-bed University Medical Center of El Paso (formerly also known as Thomason General Hospital) several neighborhood primary care clinics and the El Paso First Health Plans HMO. The hospital is an acute-care teaching hospital affiliated with Texas Tech. It specializes in emergency/trauma care obstetrics pediatric medicine and orthopedics. The hospital district through its affiliates provides a range of outpatient services including physical rehabilitation speech therapy family planning dental care cancer treatment diagnostics and pharmacy services.

	Annual Growth	09/15	09/16	09/18	09/19	09/20
Sales ($ mil.)	7.4%	-	578.3	599.1	679.6	769.5
Net income ($ mil.)	187.2%	-	0.5	(31.3)	(10.9)	30.9
Market value ($ mil.)	-	-	-	-	-	-
Employees	-	-	-	-	-	1,898

EL PASO ELECTRIC COMPANY

NYS: EE

Stanton Tower, 100 North Stanton Street
El Paso, TX 79901
Phone: 915 543-5711
Fax: -
Web: www.epelectric.com

CEO: Kelly Tomblin
CFO: Richard Ostberg
HR: -
FYE: December 31
Type: Public

El Paso Electric (EPE) creates currents along the Rio Grande River. The utility transmits and distributes electricity to some 404500 customers in West Texas and southern New Mexico. More than half of the company's sales come from its namesake city and nearby Las Cruces New Mexico. The firm has 2055 MW of nuclear fossil-fuel and wind-based generating capacity. EPE also purchases power from other utilities and marketers and sells wholesale power in Texas and New Mexico as well as in Mexico. Its largest customers include military installations such as Fort Bliss in Texas and White Sands Missile Range and Holloman Air Force Base in New Mexico.

	Annual Growth	12/14	12/15	12/16	12/17	12/18
Sales ($ mil.)	(0.4%)	917.5	849.9	886.9	916.8	903.6
Net income ($ mil.)	(2.0%)	91.4	81.9	96.8	98.3	84.3
Market value ($ mil.)	5.8%	1,629.7	1,566.2	1,891.7	2,251.7	2,039.3
Employees	2.4%	1,000	1,100	1,100	1,100	1,100

EL PASO PIPELINE PARTNERS LP

NYS: EPB

500 Dallas Street, Suite 1000
Houston, TX 77002
Phone: 713 369-9000
Fax: -
Web: www.eppipelinepartners.com

CEO: -
CFO: -
HR: -
FYE: December 31
Type: Public

El Paso Pipeline Partners is a natural gas pipeline and storage company with interests that extend far beyond its West Texas roots. The firm which consists primarily of Wyoming Interstate Company (WIC) Cheyenne Plains Gas (CPG) Colorado Interstate Gas Company (CIG) Elba Express and Southern Natural Gas Company (SNG) has 12900 miles of pipeline and storage facilities totaling 97 billion cu. ft. El Paso Pipeline Partners' customers include local distribution companies industrial users electricity generators and natural gas marketing and trading companies. Kinder Morgan controls the company.

	Annual Growth	12/08	12/09	12/10	12/11	12/12
Sales ($ mil.)	81.0%	141.1	537.6	1,344.1	1,425.0	1,515.0
Net income ($ mil.)	50.0%	114.5	213.5	378.5	472.0	579.0
Market value ($ mil.)	24.1%	3,435.0	5,716.2	7,365.5	7,623.1	8,140.5
Employees	-	-	-	-	-	-

ELAH HOLDINGS INC

NBB: ELLH

4514 Cole Avenue, Suite 1600
Dallas, TX 75205
Phone: 805 435-1255
Fax: -
Web: www.elahholdings.com

CEO: Michael Hobey
CFO: -
HR: -
FYE: December 31
Type: Public

Elah Holdings Inc. formerly known as Real Industry Inc. is a holding company that is continuing to execute its longstanding business strategy of seeking to acquire profitable businesses in the commercial industrial financial and other markets. Elah seeks transaction partners with established businesses or assets to generate sustainable profitability and cash flows to unlock the value of its considerable tax assets. Its acquisition approach uses win-win deal structures to meet the particular exit or growth needs of business owners position the acquired businesses for continued success reduce risk and ultimately create long-term value for its shareholders. Further Elah Holdings is committed to supporting the performance of such acquisitions post-closing seeking new opportunities and managing its legacy assets.

	Annual Growth	12/16	12/17	12/18	12/19	12/20
Sales ($ mil.)	(89.1%)	1,249.7	1,346.4	0.1	0.1	0.2
Net income ($ mil.)	-	(102.9)	(121.7)	73.6	(0.2)	(1.7)
Market value ($ mil.)	17.0%	-	-	44.3	45.3	60.6
Employees	2.8%	1,800	1,850	-	-	-

ELDORADO ARTESIAN SPRINGS INC

NBB: ELDO

1783 Dogwood Street
Louisville, CO 80027
Phone: 303 499-1316
Fax: -

CEO: -
CFO: Cathleen M Shoenfeld
HR: -
FYE: March 31
Type: Public

If Cortez had sought a wealth of water instead of streets of gold he might have headed for Eldorado Artesian Springs. The company bottles water from springs it owns in the foothills of the Rocky Mountains. About 70% of its sales come from home and office delivery of three and five gallon bottles of its natural spring water (and water cooler rentals); it also supplies smaller bottles to wholesalers and distributors for retail sale. Eldorado's water is distributed primarily in Colorado but also in regions of bordering states. In addition to its bottled water business the company owns and operates a resort on its property.

	Annual Growth	03/11	03/12	03/13	03/14	03/15
Sales ($ mil.)	9.4%	8.9	9.2	9.9	11.4	12.7
Net income ($ mil.)	-	(0.5)	0.1	0.5	0.5	0.6
Market value ($ mil.)	36.1%	2.1	1.1	3.1	11.4	7.2
Employees	6.3%	76	78	82	89	97

ELECSYS CORP.
NAS: ESYS

846 N. Mart-Way Court
Olathe, KS 66061
Phone: 913 647-0158
Fax: 913 647-0132
Web: www.elecsyscorp.com

CEO: Karl B Gemperli
CFO: Todd A Daniels
HR: Monica Stowers
FYE: April 30
Type: Public

Many companies elect Elecsys to make their electronics. Elecsys is a contract manufacturer of electronic assemblies and displays. The company makes custom electronic assemblies — including printed circuit boards electronic modules LCDs light-emitting diodes (LEDs) and wireless communication interface modules — for OEMs in the aerospace industrial communications safety transportation military and other industries. Elecsys also makes ruggedized handheld computers and printers as well as remote monitoring equipment for customers in the oil and gas exploration and production industries. About 85% of the company's sales come from customers located in the US.

	Annual Growth	04/09	04/10	04/11	04/12	04/13
Sales ($ mil.)	3.8%	21.9	17.0	23.6	23.1	25.4
Net income ($ mil.)	25.6%	0.7	(0.7)	0.9	1.2	1.7
Market value ($ mil.)	10.5%	14.1	15.6	19.8	20.9	21.0
Employees	(1.4%)	132	120	129	127	125

ELECTRIC POWER BOARD OF CHATTANOOGA

10 W MRTIN LTHER KING BLV
CHATTANOOGA, TN 374021832
Phone: 423-756-2706
Fax: –
Web: www.epb.com

CEO: Harold De Priest
CFO: Greg Eaves
HR: –
FYE: June 30
Type: Private

Pardon me .... is that the Electric Power Board (EPB) of Chattanooga? EPB keeps on choo-chooin' along by providing electricity to more than 167410 residents and businesses. The utility (a non-profit agency of the City of Chattanooga) distributes energy in a 600 sq.-ml. area that includes greater Chattanooga as well as parts of surrounding counties in Georgia and Tennessee. It gets its wholesale power supply from the Tennessee Valley Authority. EPB also provides telecommunications (telephone and Internet) services to area homes and businesses through its EPB Fiber Optics unit.

	Annual Growth	06/15	06/16	06/17	06/18	06/19
Sales ($ mil.)	2.7%	–	683.9	716.7	729.7	741.7
Net income ($ mil.)	4.8%	–	32.1	35.3	43.8	36.9
Market value ($ mil.)	–	–	–	–	–	–
Employees	–	–	–	–	–	400

ELECTRIC POWER BOARD OF THE METROPOLITAN GOVERNMENT OF NASHVILLE & DAVIDSON COUNTY

1214 CHURCH ST
NASHVILLE, TN 372460001
Phone: 615-747-3831
Fax: –
Web: www.nespower.com

CEO: –
CFO: Teresa Broyles Aplin
HR: Cheryl Cole
FYE: June 30
Type: Private

The Electric Power Board of the Metropolitan Government of Nashville and Davidson County is a mouthful. Its operating name Nashville Electric Service (NES) sounds much better. And talking of sound the legendary "Nashville Sound" would be hard to hear without the resources of this power distributor which serves more than 360000 customers in central Tennessee. NES is one of the largest government-owned utilities in the US. The company is required to purchase all its power from another government-owned operator the Tennessee Valley Authority (TVA).

	Annual Growth	06/14	06/15	06/16	06/18	06/19
Sales ($ mil.)	1.9%	–	1,246.6	1,203.5	380.7	1,342.2
Net income ($ mil.)	12.7%	–	55.8	28.6	94.2	90.0
Market value ($ mil.)	–	–	–	–	–	–
Employees	–	–	–	–	–	950

ELECTRIC POWER RESEARCH INSTITUTE, INC.

3420 HILLVIEW AVE
PALO ALTO, CA 943041382
Phone: 650-855-2000
Fax: –
Web: www.epri.com

CEO: Michael Howard
CFO: –
HR: –
FYE: December 31
Type: Private

The Electric Power Research Institute (EPRI) conducts research development and demonstration projects for the benefit of the public in the US and internationally. From its headquarters in Palo Alto California the institute works to bring benefits for the US and other countries. EPRI is a nonprofit organization for public interest energy and environmental research that focuses on electricity generation delivery and use including questions related to environmental protection. EPRI was founded in 1972.

	Annual Growth	12/16	12/17	12/18	12/19	12/20
Sales ($ mil.)	0.9%	–	408.7	416.6	396.6	420.2
Net income ($ mil.)	37.7%	–	6.8	1.2	(0.6)	17.7
Market value ($ mil.)	–	–	–	–	–	–
Employees	–	–	–	–	–	891

ELECTRIC RELIABILITY COUNCIL OF TEXAS, INC.

7620 METRO CENTER DR
AUSTIN, TX 787441613
Phone: 512-225-7000
Fax: –
Web: www.ercot.com

CEO: Bill Magness
CFO: –
HR: –
FYE: December 31
Type: Private

ERCOT works to ensure that Texas power grid errors are caught before triggering a massive blackout. The Electric Reliability Council of Texas (ERCOT) is responsible for the reliable operation of 550 generation units (74000 MW capacity) and a 40500-mile power transmission system carrying about 85% of the state's electric load and serving 23 million customers. A member of the North American Electric Reliability Council ERCOT functions as the independent system operator for the region. It also administers financial settlement for the competitive wholesale bulk-power market and oversees customer switching for 6.7 million Texans who live in areas where they have a competitive choice of power supplier.

	Annual Growth	12/08	12/09	12/10	12/11	12/15
Sales ($ mil.)	(2.2%)	–	206.9	272.5	279.8	181.4
Net income ($ mil.)	–	–	28.7	19.1	(2.0)	(2.1)
Market value ($ mil.)	–	–	–	–	–	–
Employees	–	–	–	–	–	625

ELECTRO RENT CORP.
NMS: ELRC

6060 Sepulveda Boulevard
Van Nuys, CA 91411-2501
Phone: 818 787-2100
Fax: –
Web: www.electrorent.com

CEO: Michael Clark
CFO: Allen Sciarillo
HR: –
FYE: May 31
Type: Public

Electro Rent rents leases and resells electronic test and measurement equipment computers servers and related equipment. The company's test instruments come from suppliers that include Agilent Technologies and Tektronix while its computers and workstations are primarily sourced from from such manufacturers as Apple Dell Hewlett-Packard and Toshiba. Electro Rent provides new and used equipment to government agencies and companies in the aerospace and defense electronics semiconductor and telecommunications industries.

	Annual Growth	05/11	05/12	05/13	05/14	05/15
Sales ($ mil.)	1.0%	228.7	248.6	248.7	241.1	238.3
Net income ($ mil.)	(10.2%)	23.8	25.8	22.8	20.4	15.4
Market value ($ mil.)	(9.5%)	369.8	333.7	410.1	389.3	247.6
Employees	2.5%	371	393	417	420	410

ELECTRO SCIENTIFIC INDUSTRIES INC   NMS: ESIO

13900 N.W. Science Park Drive
Portland, OR 97229
Phone: 503 641-4141
Fax: –
Web: www.esi.com
CEO: Michael Burger
CFO: Allen Muhich
HR: –
FYE: April 01
Type: Public

Electro Scientific Industries (ESI) has a laser focus locked on lasers. Lasers that help its customers make and test micron- and submicron-sized electronics that go into bigger electronics. The company's laser-based fabrication equipment is used for ultra-fine work in semiconductors interconnect devices and other microtechnology components as well as thin films and glass for touch screens. Its products provide yield improvement optical inspection wafer scribing high-capacity test and inspection and more. ESI's customers include Apple which accounts for about 15% of sales. Most sales come from customers in Asia.

	Annual Growth	03/13	03/14	03/15*	04/16	04/17
Sales ($ mil.)	(7.1%)	216.6	181.2	159.1	184.4	161.0
Net income ($ mil.)	–	(54.7)	(38.3)	(43.8)	(12.3)	(37.4)
Market value ($ mil.)	(10.9%)	367.5	328.9	204.9	240.5	231.8
Employees	4.7%	599	658	739	698	720

*Fiscal year change

ELECTRO-MATIC VENTURES, INC.

23409 INDUSTRIAL PARK CT
FARMINGTON HILLS, MI 483352849
Phone: 248-478-1182
Fax: –
Web: www.electro-matic.com
CEO: James C Baker Jr
CFO: –
HR: –
FYE: September 30
Type: Private

Electro-Matic Products are not "as seen on TV." The company distributes industrial automation equipment and electrical supplies to customers in the industrial chemical pharmaceutical utility and automotive industries. Products include cables connectors sensors fuses and control devices along with automation tools indoor and outdoor LED displays and industrial computer hardware. Electro-Matic stocks products from Littelfuse Molex Rittal Corporation Siemens and Woodhead Industries among other vendors. Founded in 1969 the company sells worldwide through sales engineering and support offices in Michigan and Ohio. Electro-Matic established an employee stock ownership plan in 2007.

	Annual Growth	09/06	09/07	09/08	09/10	09/11
Sales ($ mil.)	–	–	–	(729.4)	53.9	81.9
Net income ($ mil.)	2838.3%	–	–	0.0	0.3	2.8
Market value ($ mil.)	–	–	–	–	–	–
Employees	–	–	–	–	–	111

ELECTRO-SENSORS, INC.   NAS: ELSE

6111 Blue Circle Drive
Minnetonka, MN 55343-9108
Phone: 952 930-0100
Fax: –
Web: www.electro-sensors.com
CEO: David Klenk
CFO: David L Klenk
HR: –
FYE: December 31
Type: Public

Electro-Sensors supports the manufacturing process with sensitive loving care. The company's Product Monitoring Division which accounts for the bulk of sales makes computerized systems that monitor and regulate the production speed of industrial machinery. Products are sold worldwide. Electro-Sensors also has an AutoData Systems unit which makes software that reads hand-printed characters check marks and bar code information from scanned or faxed forms. The unit has an exclusive license to use a neural network algorithm developed by PPT Vision. Its software sells mostly in North America and Western Europe. Electro-Sensors director and secretary Peter Peterson and his family own 38% of the company.

	Annual Growth	12/16	12/17	12/18	12/19	12/20
Sales ($ mil.)	1.8%	7.1	7.8	7.5	8.3	7.6
Net income ($ mil.)	–	0.2	0.3	(0.0)	0.2	(0.1)
Market value ($ mil.)	8.6%	11.7	13.8	11.5	12.3	16.3
Employees	2.1%	34	36	33	40	37

ELECTROMED, INC.   ASE: ELMD

500 Sixth Avenue NW
New Prague, MN 56071
Phone: 952 758-9299
Fax: –
Web: www.electromed.com
CEO: Kathleen Skarvan
CFO: Michael MacCourt
HR: –
FYE: June 30
Type: Public

Electromed aims to clear the way for patients suffering from respiratory ailments. A medical device maker the company manufactures respiratory products designed to treat patients with cystic fibrosis chronic obstructive pulmonary disease (COPD) and other ailments that affect respiratory systems. Its FDA-approved SmartVest System is a vest worn by patients that helps loosen lung congestion. A self-administered therapy the vest works by administering high frequency pulsations that compress and release the patient's chest area. Electromed sells its SmartVest and related products primarily in the US to patients home health care professionals and hospitals. Founded in 1992 the company went public in 2010.

	Annual Growth	06/17	06/18	06/19	06/20	06/21
Sales ($ mil.)	8.4%	25.9	28.7	31.3	32.5	35.8
Net income ($ mil.)	1.5%	2.2	1.9	2.0	4.2	2.4
Market value ($ mil.)	19.5%	47.2	46.3	46.5	131.3	96.3
Employees	3.5%	115	132	119	120	132

ELECTRONIC ARTS, INC.   NMS: EA

209 Redwood Shores Parkway
Redwood City, CA 94065
Phone: 650 628-1500
Fax: –
Web: www.ea.com
CEO: Andrew Wilson
CFO: Blake Jorgensen
HR: –
FYE: March 31
Type: Public

Electronic Arts (EA) is a global leader in digital interactive entertainment which develops markets publishes and delivers games content and services that can be played and watched on game consoles PCs mobile phones and tablets. Its leading titles are Madden NFL FIFA and Star Wars all of which it licenses from other companies and its own Battlefield and The Sims. While EA generates increasing sales for games on mobile devices it still makes most of its revenue from games played on consoles from Sony and Microsoft and on personal computers. EA gets majority of revenue from international customers. The company was founded in 1982.

	Annual Growth	03/17	03/18	03/19	03/20	03/21
Sales ($ mil.)	3.8%	4,845.0	5,150.0	4,950.0	5,537.0	5,629.0
Net income ($ mil.)	(3.5%)	967.0	1,043.0	1,019.0	3,039.0	837.0
Market value ($ mil.)	10.9%	25,644.3	34,731.0	29,113.4	28,695.2	38,778.8
Employees	5.7%	8,800	9,300	9,700	9,800	11,000

ELECTRONIC CONTROL SECURITY INC.   NBB: EKCS

790 Bloomfield Avenue
Clifton, NJ 07012
Phone: 973 574-8555
Fax: 973 574-8562
Web: www.ecsiinternationalgov.com
CEO: Arthur Barchenko
CFO: Daryl Holcomb
HR: –
FYE: June 30
Type: Public

Electronic Control Security (ECSI) is a leading provider of integrated security systems for government and commercial facilities worldwide. Its products include command and control intrusion detection and sensing and surveillance systems used at airports military bases ports and other sensitive facilities such as embassies and power plants. ECSI also provides risk assessment and other security consulting services. Its customers include a number of government agencies such as the US Department of Energy and the Department of Defense. In addition to offices in the US the company has operations in the Middle East and Latin America.

	Annual Growth	06/17	06/18	06/19	06/20	06/21
Sales ($ mil.)	(9.9%)	1.3	1.0	1.8	0.6	0.8
Net income ($ mil.)	–	(0.3)	(0.1)	0.2	(0.3)	0.2
Market value ($ mil.)	131.1%	0.4	1.9	1.1	1.9	11.4
Employees	–	–	–	–	–	–

ELECTRONIC SYSTEMS TECHNOLOGY, INC. NBB: ELST

415 North Roosevelt St. Ste. B1
Kennewick, WA 99336
Phone: 509 735-9092
Fax: –
Web: www.esteem.com

CEO: Michael Eller
CFO: Michael W Eller
HR: –
FYE: December 31
Type: Public

Electronic Systems Technology (EST) makes wireless modems that it markets under the ESTeem brand. EST targets the modems for applications in industrial automation the military and public safety. The ESTeem line includes Ethernet radios that can be used for handling video and voice over Internet protocol (VoIP) transmissions. EST buys parts from Hitachi Intersil Integrated Microelectronics Mitsubishi Murata Manufacturing Rakon and Toko America for its products. Assembly of EST's products is farmed out to Manufacturing Services.

	Annual Growth	12/16	12/17	12/18	12/19	12/20
Sales ($ mil.)	(4.8%)	1.5	1.4	1.4	1.4	1.2
Net income ($ mil.)	–	(0.1)	(0.4)	(0.1)	(0.2)	(0.2)
Market value ($ mil.)	(7.4%)	1.9	2.6	1.9	2.0	1.4
Employees	(7.7%)	11	10	9	9	8

ELECTRONICS FOR IMAGING, INC. NMS: EFII

6750 Dumbarton Circle
Fremont, CA 94555
Phone: 650 357-3500
Fax: –
Web: www.efi.com

CEO: Jeff Jacobson
CFO: Grant Fitz
HR: –
FYE: December 31
Type: Public

Electronics For Imaging (EFI) wants to take control of your color. The company makes hardware and software systems for commercial and enterprise digital printing and print management. EFI's Fiery line includes print servers as well as print controllers that copier and printer vendors such as Ricoh Xerox Canon Epson and Konica Minolta integrate into their equipment. EFI's Print MIS (management information systems) software provides supply chain and customer relationship management from job submission to fulfillment. Its Inkjet segment products include super-wide format (VUTEk) and industrial printers (Jetrion). It's also the world's largest manufacturer of digital UV ink.

	Annual Growth	12/13	12/14	12/15	12/16	12/17
Sales ($ mil.)	8.1%	727.7	790.4	882.5	992.1	993.3
Net income ($ mil.)	–	109.1	33.7	33.5	45.5	(15.3)
Market value ($ mil.)	(6.6%)	1,749.8	1,935.0	2,111.7	1,981.6	1,334.1
Employees	7.5%	2,523	2,672	3,136	3,235	3,366

ELEMENT SOLUTIONS INC NYS: ESI

500 East Broward Boulevard, Suite 1860
Fort Lauderdale, FL 33394
Phone: 561 207-9600
Fax: –
Web: www.elemetsolutionsinc.com

CEO: Benjamin Gliklich
CFO: Carey Dorman
HR: –
FYE: December 31
Type: Public

Element Solutions (formerly Platform Specialty Products) is a leading global specialty chemicals company whose businesses supply a broad range of solutions that enhance the performance of products people use every day. Its offerings include electronic assembly materials and hydraulic control fluids for the electronics automotive oil and gas and consumer packaged goods among others. Its businesses provide products that are consumed by customers as part of their production process providing customers with reliable and recurring revenue streams as the products are replenished in order to continue production. The company was incorporates in 2014. About three-fourths of sales were generated outside US.

	Annual Growth	12/16	12/17	12/18	12/19	12/20
Sales ($ mil.)	(15.2%)	3,585.9	3,775.9	1,961.0	1,835.9	1,853.7
Net income ($ mil.)	–	–	(73.7)	(296.2)	(324.4)	92.2	75.7
Market value ($ mil.)	15.9%	2,424.1	2,451.2	2,552.6	2,886.1	4,381.1
Employees	(13.2%)	7,750	7,850	4,450	4,400	4,400

ELEVANCE RENEWABLE SCIENCES INC.

2501 W. Davey Rd.
Woodridge IL 60440
Phone: 866-625-7103
Fax: 630-633-7295
Web: www.elevance.com

CEO: K'Lynne Johnson
CFO: David H Kelsey
HR: –
FYE: December 31
Type: Private

If cars can run on vegetable oil why can't palm oil clean clothes? Elevance Renewable Sciences figured it out. The chemical company is developing new applications to use plant-based oils as an eco-friendly alternative to petrochemicals. It plans to make chemicals from palm soy and rapeseed oil to use in household and personal care products as well as lubricants coatings and plastics. The company is building a biorefinery with Wilmar International in Indonesia to manufacture specialty chemicals oleochemicals and olefins. Currently it only makes vegetable wax candles sold under the NatureWax brand through a partnership with Cargill. In mid-2012 Elevance withdrew an initial public offering that was originally filed in 2011.

ELITE PHARMACEUTICALS INC NBB: ELTP

165 Ludlow Avenue
Northvale, NJ 07647
Phone: 201 750-2646
Fax: –
Web: www.elitepharma.com

CEO: Nasrat Hakim
CFO: Marc Bregman
HR: –
FYE: March 31
Type: Public

Elite Pharmaceuticals isn't above peddling generics. Subsidiary Elite Laboratories develops generic versions of existing controlled-release drugs whose patents are about to expire. Its commercial products include allergy therapeutics Lodrane 24 and Lodrane 24D which are marketed by ECR Pharmaceuticals. Products in various stages of testing and preclinical development include oxycodone pain medications anti-infectives and treatments for gastrointestinal disorders. Elite Laboratories also provides contract research and development services for other drugmakers.

	Annual Growth	03/17	03/18	03/19	03/20	03/21
Sales ($ mil.)	27.4%	9.6	7.5	7.6	18.0	25.4
Net income ($ mil.)	7.5%	3.8	(3.7)	(9.3)	(2.2)	5.1
Market value ($ mil.)	(19.9%)	149.3	100.9	99.9	72.7	61.6
Employees	(1.7%)	46	43	35	43	43

ELIXIR INDUSTRIES

24800 CHRISANTA DR # 210
MISSION VIEJO, CA 926914833
Phone: 949-860-5000
Fax: –

CEO: –
CFO: –
HR: –
FYE: December 31
Type: Private

Elixir Industries is a diversified manufacturer of aluminum extrusions aluminum fabrication and custom metal fabrication products. Its portfolio of offerings includes doors siding and roofing window guards recreational vehicle products cargo trailers and aluminum painted coil. It also makes a variety of coatings sealants and tapes. The company operates from about a dozen locations in half a dozen states serving clients across the US as well as in selected international markets. Roland Sahm founded what is now Elixir Industries in 1948.

	Annual Growth	12/02	12/03	12/04	12/05	12/11
Sales ($ mil.)	(6.7%)	–	–	–	221.0	146.0
Net income ($ mil.)	–	–	–	–	0.0	14.4
Market value ($ mil.)	–	–	–	–	–	–
Employees	–	–	–	–	–	64

ELIZABETH ARDEN INC.
NMS: RDEN

2400 S.W. 145 Avenue
Miramar, FL 33027
Phone: 954 364-6900
Fax: –
Web: www.elizabetharden.com

CEO: E Scott Beattie
CFO: Rod R Little
HR: –
FYE: June 30
Type: Public

Sweet scents and more are behind Elizabeth Arden's auspicious red door. The firm owns and licenses prestige and mass market celebrity lifestyle and designer fragrances and distributes about 280 prestige fragrance brands. Fragrance generated some 77% of 2014 sales. Established labels include Red Door Elizabeth Arden 5th Avenue and Elizabeth Taylor's White Diamonds. Scents aimed at younger wearers include the Justin Bieber and Nicki Minaj licensed brands. Its fragrances cosmetics and skin care lines (Ceramide PREVAGE Visible Difference) are sold to US department stores and mass retailers as well as international retailers.

	Annual Growth	06/11	06/12	06/13	06/14	06/15
Sales ($ mil.)	(4.7%)	1,175.5	1,238.3	1,344.5	1,164.3	971.1
Net income ($ mil.)	–	41.0	57.4	40.7	(145.7)	(224.0)
Market value ($ mil.)	(16.3%)	865.4	1,157.0	1,342.7	638.6	425.1
Employees	(1.1%)	2,665	2,789	2,990	2,790	2,550

ELKHART GENERAL HOSPITAL, INC.

600 EAST BLVD
ELKHART, IN 465142499
Phone: 574-294-2621
Fax: –
Web: www.beaconhealthsystem.org

CEO: Gregory W Lintjer
CFO: Kevin Higdon
HR: Amanda Flick
FYE: June 30
Type: Private

From Nappanee to Edwardsburg Elkhart General serves residents of northern Indiana and southwestern Michigan. The community-owned Elkhart General Hospital has about 325 beds. The system also operates about ten general practice clinics throughout its region and provides home care rehabilitation and occupational health services. The system's Michiana Linen unit provides linen and laundry services to other hospitals clinics and physician offices in the region. Its hospital staff includes about 300 physicians representing about 30 medical specialties. Elkhart General is affiliated with Memorial Hospital of South Bend through the Beacon Health System organization.

	Annual Growth	12/14	12/15	12/16	12/17*	06/18
Sales ($ mil.)	(20.7%)	–	274.1	281.6	274.7	136.9
Net income ($ mil.)	13.0%	–	10.9	20.9	17.8	15.8
Market value ($ mil.)	–	–	–	–	–	–
Employees	–	–	–	–	–	1,900

*Fiscal year change

ELKINS CONSTRUCTORS, INC.

701 W ADAMS ST STE 1
JACKSONVILLE, FL 322041600
Phone: 904-353-6500
Fax: –

CEO: Barry L Allred
CFO: –
HR: –
FYE: December 31
Type: Private

Elkins Constructors builds it all. The company one of Florida's largest privately held construction companies works on commercial industrial multi-family residential institutional and retail projects mainly in the Southeast. It offers general contracting design/build and construction management services and its retail market clients have included Lowe's British Airways and Castleton Beverage. Other projects include the America Online call center and headquarters for PGA Tour Productions. Elkins also has been named one of the top green contractors in the US by Engineering News-Record. Founded in 1955 by Martin Elkins the company was acquired in 1984 by CEO Barry Allred and a team of investors.

	Annual Growth	12/04	12/05	12/06	12/07	12/08
Sales ($ mil.)	117.0%	–	–	60.8	231.7	286.0
Net income ($ mil.)	2391.3%	–	–	0.0	8.1	10.2
Market value ($ mil.)	–	–	–	–	–	–
Employees	–	–	–	–	–	55

ELLIE MAE INC
NYS: ELLI

4420 Rosewood Drive, Suite 500
Pleasanton, CA 94588
Phone: 925 227-7000
Fax: 925 227-9030
Web: www.elliemae.com

CEO: Jonathan Corr
CFO: Dan Madden
HR: –
FYE: December 31
Type: Public

Ellie Mae might sound like Fannie Mae's cousin but they're just in related industries not bloodlines. The company provides automation software and operates the Ellie Mae Network that facilitates the residential mortgage origination and funding process. Its Encompass software suite combines loan origination with CRM (customer relationship management) to gather review and verify data from a single database. Other programs handle regulatory compliance appraisal and title services underwriting tax transcripts and document preparation and management. More than 136000 mortgage professionals use its software and network to process more than 3 million new mortgages an estimated 20% of its addressable market.

	Annual Growth	12/13	12/14	12/15	12/16	12/17
Sales ($ mil.)	34.2%	128.5	161.5	253.9	360.3	417.0
Net income ($ mil.)	43.2%	12.6	14.8	22.3	37.8	52.9
Market value ($ mil.)	35.1%	919.7	1,380.1	2,061.5	2,864.2	3,060.0
Employees	38.1%	407	640	857	1,069	1,480

ELLINGTON FINANCIAL INC
NYS: EFC

53 Forest Avenue
Old Greenwich, CT 06870
Phone: 203 698-1200
Fax: –
Web: www.ellingtonfinancial.com

CEO: Laurence Penn
CFO: J. R. Herlihy
HR: –
FYE: December 31
Type: Public

Mortgage-related assets are music to Ellington Financial's ears. The specialty finance company manages a portfolio of primarily non-agency residential mortgage-backed securities valued at more than $366 million. It also seeks to acquire other target assets such as residential whole mortgage loans commercial mortgage-backed securities commercial real estate debt and asset-backed securities. Riskier residential whole mortgage loans which are generally not guaranteed by the US government include subprime non-performing and sub-performing mortgage loans. Founded in 2007 Ellington Financial went public in 2010 in hopes of taking advantage of the current credit environment.

	Annual Growth	12/16	12/17	12/18	12/19	12/20
Sales ($ mil.)	(2.6%)	80.2	94.0	135.0	45.4	72.1
Net income ($ mil.)	(8.6%)	35.8	35.2	43.1	57.9	25.0
Market value ($ mil.)	(1.1%)	679.5	635.3	671.2	802.5	649.7
Employees	(1.6%)	160	160	150	150	150

ELLINGTON RESIDENTIAL MORTGAGING REAL ESTATE INVESTMENT TRUST
NYS: EARN

53 Forest Avenue
Old Greenwich, CT 06870
Phone: 203 698-1200
Fax: –
Web: www.earnreit.com

CEO: Laurence Penn
CFO: Christopher Smernoff
HR: –
FYE: December 31
Type: Public

Ellington Financial LLC is ready to double its money. The investment firm formed Ellington Residential Mortgage REIT a real estate residential trust (REIT) to invest in agency residential mortgage-backed securities (Agency RMBS) or those guaranteed by federally sponsored entities Fannie Mae Freddie Mac and Ginnie Mae. (Agency RMBS carry less risk than privately issued mortgage securities.) The trust's portfolio is balanced out with about 10% non-Agency RMBS such as residential whole mortgage loans mortgage servicing rights (MSRs) and residential real properties. (Non-Agency RMBS carry more risk but might offer better returns.) The trust went public in 2013.

	Annual Growth	12/16	12/17	12/18	12/19	12/20
Assets ($ mil.)	(4.4%)	1,429.1	1,887.1	1,675.6	1,489.1	1,194.8
Net income ($ mil.)	14.0%	11.9	10.8	(11.3)	22.3	20.1
Market value ($ mil.)	0.1%	160.6	148.6	126.3	133.9	161.0
Employees	(1.6%)	160	160	150	–	150

ELLIOT HOSPITAL OF THE CITY OF MANCHESTER

1 ELLIOT WAY
MANCHESTER, NH 031033502
Phone: 603-669-5300
Fax: –
Web: www.elliothospital.org

CEO: Douglas Dean
CFO: Richard Elwell
HR: –
FYE: June 30
Type: Private

Elliot Health System provides medical care to southern New Hampshire. The health care organization operates Elliot Hospital an acute care hospital with nearly 300 beds that is home to a regional cancer center a designated regional trauma center and a level III neonatal intensive care unit (NICU). In addition to general and surgical care the hospital offers rehabilitation behavioral health obstetrics cardiology and lab services. The system also operates the Elliot Physician Network which operates primary care centers specialty clinics and surgery centers in various regional communities. Elliot Hospital was founded in 1890.

	Annual Growth	06/15	06/16	06/19	06/20	06/21
Sales ($ mil.)	9.5%	–	394.7	560.2	549.4	621.6
Net income ($ mil.)	23.1%	–	49.5	(4.7)	(27.7)	139.9
Market value ($ mil.)	–	–	–	–	–	–
Employees	–	–	–	–	–	2,000

ELLIS (PERRY) INTERNATIONAL INC

3000 N.W. 107th Avenue
Miami, FL 33172
Phone: 305 592-2830
Fax: –
Web: www.pery.com

NMS: PERY
CEO: Oscar Feldenkreis
CFO: Jorge Narino
HR: –
FYE: January 28
Type: Public

You'll find Perry Ellis International (PEI) apparel worn about town during the workweek and on the links most weekends. It designs distributes and licenses men's and women's sportswear under 30-plus company-owned or licensed brands including Jantzen Laundry Manhattan Munsingwear Original Penguin and namesake Perry Ellis among others. PEI also distributes PGA and Champions Tour golf apparel and NIKE swimwear under licenses. PEI's customers include some of the nation's largest retailers (Wal-Mart Kohl's and Macy's) and it distributes its products to 20000 stores. The apparel maker also operates more than 40 Perry Ellis stores in the US Puerto Rico and the UK and several Original Penguin US shops.

	Annual Growth	02/13	02/14*	01/15	01/16	01/17
Sales ($ mil.)	(2.9%)	969.6	912.2	890.0	899.5	861.1
Net income ($ mil.)	(0.5%)	14.8	(22.8)	(37.2)	(7.3)	14.5
Market value ($ mil.)	5.0%	300.7	243.4	371.3	295.2	365.0
Employees	(1.0%)	2,600	2,700	2,600	2,700	2,500

*Fiscal year change

ELLIS HOSPITAL

1101 NOTT ST
SCHENECTADY, NY 123082489
Phone: 518-243-4000
Fax: –
Web: www.ellismedicine.org

CEO: James W Connolly
CFO: –
HR: –
FYE: December 31
Type: Private

Schenectady-based Ellis Hospital (dba Ellis Medicine) serves the residents of New York's capital area as part of Ellis Medicine a 438-bed community and teaching health care system. The hospital provides emergency inpatient medical/surgical and psychiatric care including diagnostic primary and rehabilitative care. The hospital is also home to centers of excellence in the treatment of and care for heart and cardiovascular ailments cancer women's health issues stroke-related problems and behavioral health concerns. It also operates the Ellis Center the Bellvue Woman's Center the satellite outpatient clinic Ellis Health Center and recently-constructed Medical Center of Clifton Park.

	Annual Growth	12/15	12/16	12/17	12/18	12/19
Sales ($ mil.)	5.5%	–	400.3	401.8	401.4	469.8
Net income ($ mil.)	21.1%	–	3.4	1.5	11.0	6.0
Market value ($ mil.)	–	–	–	–	–	–
Employees	–	–	–	–	–	3,000

ELLSWORTH COOPERATIVE CREAMERY

232 WALLACE ST
ELLSWORTH, WI 540113500
Phone: 715-273-4311
Fax: –
Web: www.ellsworthcheese.com

CEO: Paul Bauer
CFO: –
HR: –
FYE: December 31
Type: Private

Ellsworth Cooperative Creamery processes and markets the cream of its members' crops which in this instance are dairy cows. The creamery manufactures and distributes butter cheese whey powder cheese curds and other dairy foods. Founded in 1908 (as the Milton Dairy Company and taking its current name in 1910) the cooperative processes 1.5 million pounds of milk daily. The co-op has more than 500 farmer/members whose dairy operations are located in Minnesota and Wisconsin. It is known for its cheddar cheese curds; the company was officially nicked-named the "Cheese Curd Capital of the World" by (former) Wisconsin's governor Anthony Earl.

	Annual Growth	12/03	12/04	12/05	12/06	12/07
Sales ($ mil.)	21.8%	–	–	98.2	92.2	145.7
Net income ($ mil.)	21.7%	–	–	2.3	2.8	3.5
Market value ($ mil.)	–	–	–	–	–	–
Employees	–	–	–	–	–	60

ELMA ELECTRONIC INC.

44350 S GRIMMER BLVD
FREMONT, CA 945386385
Phone: 510-656-3400
Fax: –

CEO: Fred Ruegg
CFO: –
HR: –
FYE: December 31
Type: Private

Elma Electronic thinks your electronics equipment should be contained not your enthusiasm. The US subsidiary of Elma Electronic AG manufactures and distributes an array of electronic enclosures backplanes and server racks. It also makes passive electronic components from rotary switches to knobs and light-emitting diodes. Elma Electronic's slate of services includes component customization design engineering manufacture systems integration and verification. Subsidiary Elma Bustronic offers custom backplane applications and Optima EPS makes electronic enclosures. The company courts industries worldwide in telecommunications medical electronics industrial control defense and aerospace.

	Annual Growth	12/13	12/14	12/15	12/16	12/17
Sales ($ mil.)	1.2%	–	70.5	66.7	66.0	73.2
Net income ($ mil.)	0.4%	–	2.3	2.8	2.5	2.3
Market value ($ mil.)	–	–	–	–	–	–
Employees	–	–	–	–	–	280

ELMHURST MEMORIAL HOSPITAL INC

155 E BRUSH HILL RD
ELMHURST, IL 601265658
Phone: 331-221-9003
Fax: –
Web: www.emhc.org

CEO: Pamela Davis
CFO: James Doyle
HR: –
FYE: June 30
Type: Private

Elmhurst Memorial Healthcare operates Elmhurst Memorial Hospital an acute care facility located in DuPage County Illinois in the western suburbs of Chicago. Founded in 1926 the hospital provides a comprehensive range of medical services — from emergency care to specialty cancer and orthopedics care to behavioral health services. In addition to the 310-bed main hospital Elmhurst Memorial Healthcare operates several facilities such as doctors' offices outpatient centers occupational health programs and other ancillary health care operations. Elmhurst Memorial Healthcare is part of Edward-Elmhurst Healthcare after it merged with Edward Hospital & Health Services and Linden Oaks.

	Annual Growth	06/06	06/07	06/08	06/09	06/15
Sales ($ mil.)	1.3%	–	341.8	345.8	305.7	379.8
Net income ($ mil.)	–	–	43.3	(22.1)	20.1	(9.9)
Market value ($ mil.)	–	–	–	–	–	–
Employees	–	–	–	–	–	2,444

ELMIRA SAVINGS BANK (NY)   NAS: ESBK

333 East Water Street
Elmira, NY 14901
Phone: 607 735-8660
Fax: –
Web: www.elmirasavingsbank.com

CEO: Thomas Carr
CFO: Jason Sanford
HR: –
FYE: December 31
Type: Public

The Elmira Savings Bank is a community bank that serves individuals and small to midsized businesses through about a dozen branch offices in upstate New York's Cayuga Chemung Steuben and Tompkins counties. The bank offers traditional deposit products such as checking and savings accounts CDs and IRAs. With these funds it mainly originates residential and commercial mortgages business loans and auto and other consumer loans. The bank offers investments and financial planning through its ESB Advisory Services subsidiary. Elmira Savings Bank was organized in 1869.

	Annual Growth	12/16	12/17	12/18	12/19	12/20
Assets ($ mil.)	3.0%	573.5	554.6	590.0	606.8	644.6
Net income ($ mil.)	(1.0%)	4.3	4.9	4.2	3.5	4.2
Market value ($ mil.)	(13.4%)	72.0	72.0	61.5	53.2	40.5
Employees	(3.6%)	132	132	127	125	114

ELOQUA LIMITED   NASDAQ: ELOQ

1921 Gallows Rd. Ste. 250
Vienna VA 22182-3900
Phone: 703-584-2750
Fax: 956-381-5706
Web: www.fronteraproduce.com

CEO: Joseph P Payne
CFO: Donald E Clarke
HR: –
FYE: December 31
Type: Private

Eloqua wants its clients to be fluent in customer data and lead generation. The company makes demand generation software that helps corporate marketing and sales personnel pull data from website tracking and customer relationship management (CRM) applications. Its software captures search terms used by website visitors and translates those into relevant data to improve revenue performance management. Customers have included Ellie Mae Nokia Sybase and Pitney Bowes. The company has sales partnerships with Omniture Microsoft Dynamics and Oracle. Founded in 1999 Eloqua received funding from JMI Equity Fund prior to going public on the NASDAQ exchange in 2012. It is being acquired by Oracle.

ELVIS PRESLEY ENTERPRISES INC.

3734 Elvis Presley Blvd.
Memphis TN 38116-0508
Phone: 901-332-3322
Fax: 901-345-8511
Web: www.elvis.com

CEO: Jack Soden
CFO: –
HR: –
FYE: September 30
Type: Subsidiary

Elvis may have permanently left the building but his legacy is still taking care of business. Elvis Presley Enterprises (EPE) manages the late singer's estate and licenses his name likeness and songs for a variety of commercial purposes. Revenue mostly comes from operating Presley's Graceland mansion in Memphis. The company runs tours at Graceland and also operates the associated museum visitor's center and the Heartbreak Hotel. EPE was created in 1981 (four years after Presley's death) and was owned by The Elvis Presley Trust. EPE and The Elvis Presley Trust were wholly owned by Elvis' daughter Lisa Marie Presley until 2005 when she sold an 85% stake to entertainment investor Robert Sillerman's CKX.

ELWYN OF PENNSYLVANIA AND DELAWARE

111 ELWYN RD
MEDIA, PA 190634622
Phone: 610-891-2000
Fax: –
Web: www.elwyn.org

CEO: Charles McLister
CFO: Cindy Bertrando
HR: –
FYE: June 30
Type: Private

Elwyn isn't a character out of Harry Potter or Lord of the Rings. It's a not-for-profit organization that serves more than 13000 disabled and disadvantaged people of all ages at multiple sites through education rehabilitation and vocational counseling. The organization also operates residential communities including more than 80 group homes and apartments and provides a variety of health care services for persons with developmental physical and emotional disabilities. The group also publishes training materials and hosts conferences and seminars for human services professionals. Founded in 1852 as a school for children with mental retardation Elwyn is one of the oldest organizations of its kind in the US.

	Annual Growth	06/10	06/11	06/14	06/15	06/17
Sales ($ mil.)	3.0%	–	264.0	268.4	218.2	314.6
Net income ($ mil.)	4.9%	–	14.6	13.1	2.5	19.5
Market value ($ mil.)	–	–	–	–	–	–
Employees	–	–	–	–	–	2,500

ELXSI CORP   NBB: ELXS

3600 Rio Vista Avenue, Suite A
Orlando, FL 32805
Phone: 407 849-1090
Fax: –

CEO: –
CFO: –
HR: –
FYE: December 31
Type: Public

This restaurant operator comes with a side of technology. ELXSI Corporation's hospitality division operates about 15 family-style restaurants in New England while its CUES division manufactures sewer inspection equipment. The eateries operate under the Bickford's Grille brand and offer casual dining with an emphasis on breakfast items served throughout the day. Its equipment manufacturing operation makes remote-control video cameras and robotic cutting devices used by municipalities and contractors. ELXSI is controlled by chairman and CEO Alexander Milley.

	Annual Growth	12/12	12/13	12/14	12/15	12/16
Sales ($ mil.)	8.5%	63.9	64.4	76.5	83.4	88.7
Net income ($ mil.)	22.0%	4.6	4.5	7.1	26.1	10.2
Market value ($ mil.)	26.3%	39.0	31.3	48.9	59.9	99.3
Employees	–	–	–	–	–	–

EMAGIN CORP   ASE: EMAN

700 South Drive, Suite 201
Hopewell Junction, NY 12533
Phone: 845 838-7900
Fax: –
Web: www.emagin.com

CEO: Andrew Sculley
CFO: Mark Koch
HR: –
FYE: December 31
Type: Public

eMagin is imagining eye-opening technology. The company develops virtual imaging and organic light-emitting diodes (OLEDs) that can be used in applications ranging from wearable PCs and virtual imaging devices to more mundane products such as DVD headset systems video games and high-definition televisions. The technology also extends to military uses. eMagin's products use microcircuits and displays to magnify images of text or video. Subsidiary Virtual Vision develops near-eye and virtual image display products including headset viewer systems. eMagin markets to OEMs and directly to customers in the government industrial and medical sectors.

	Annual Growth	12/16	12/17	12/18	12/19	12/20
Sales ($ mil.)	8.3%	21.4	22.0	26.2	26.7	29.4
Net income ($ mil.)	–	(8.0)	(7.8)	(9.5)	(4.3)	(11.4)
Market value ($ mil.)	(6.4%)	147.8	113.4	70.8	23.6	113.4
Employees	2.0%	96	100	105	96	104

EMANATE HEALTH MEDICAL GROUP

210 W SAN BERNARDINO RD
COVINA, CA 917231515
Phone: 626-331-7331
Fax: –
Web: www.emanatehealth.org

CEO: Robert Curry
CFO: Lois Conyers
HR: –
FYE: December 31
Type: Private

Citrus Valley Health Partners is a 660-bed hospital system that serves the residents of California's San Gabriel Valley region located between Los Angeles and San Bernardino. It operates through four health care facilities: Citrus Valley Medical Center (CVMC) Queen of the Valley Campus CVMC Inter-Community Campus Foothill Presbyterian Hospital and Citrus Valley Hospice. Citrus Valley Health Partners also operates a home health care provider that offers nursing and rehabilitation care. The hospital system boasts several areas of specialty including diabetes care cancer treatment palliative care wound care and cardiac therapy.

	Annual Growth	12/14	12/15	12/16	12/17	12/18
Sales ($ mil.)	118.5%	–	58.2	61.1	64.4	606.3
Net income ($ mil.)	–	–	(2.1)	0.9	2.5	21.1
Market value ($ mil.)	–	–	–	–	–	–
Employees	–	–	–	–	–	2,800

EMBARCADERO TECHNOLOGIES INC.

100 California St. 12th Fl.
San Francisco CA 94111
Phone: 415-834-3131
Fax: 415-434-1721
Web: www.embarcadero.com

CEO: Wayne Williams
CFO: Robert Levin
HR: –
FYE: December 31
Type: Private

Thinking of setting out on a database development adventure? Embarcadero wants to be along for the ride. The company makes data lifecycle management software used to build test optimize and manage application infrastructure and databases for large corporations and government agencies. Its applications are used in the food services health care IT financial services education travel utilities industries among others. Embarcadero's software is used for modeling change management performance optimization and administration of database platforms made by Oracle IBM and Microsoft. It has offices in nearly 30 countries. Founded in 1993 the company is owned by private equity group Thoma Cressey Bravo.

EMBLEMHEALTH INC.

55 Water St.
New York NY 10041
Phone: 646-447-5000
Fax: 646-447-3011
Web: www.emblemhealth.com

CEO: Anthony L Watson
CFO: Heather Tamborino
HR: –
FYE: December 31
Type: Private

EmblemHealth is set on being the mark of good health in the Northeast. The not-for-profit company provides health insurance through subsidiaries Group Health Incorporated (GHI) and the Health Insurance Plan of Greater New York (HIP). Collectively the two health insurers cover some 2.8 million New Yorkers primarily state government and New York City employees. The two companies cover upwards of 90% of Big Apple city workers and retirees. Both provide a variety of managed health plans to their members including prescription drug and dental coverage and Medicare plans. GHI and HIP joined together under the EmblemHealth banner in 2006.

EMBREE CONSTRUCTION GROUP, INC.

4747 WILLIAMS DR
GEORGETOWN, TX 786333799
Phone: 512-819-4700
Fax: –
Web: www.embreegroup.com

CEO: Jim Embree
CFO:
HR: –
FYE: December 31
Type: Private

The Embree Construction Group develops designs and builds free-standing buildings for business chains across the US. The group serves as a general contractor or construction manager primarily for major national companies. It is active throughout the US. Ground-up and remodeling projects include retail properties restaurants gas stations convenience stores automotive service centers and correctional facilities. Operating companies include Embree Healthcare Group which develops assisted-living and specialty medical projects and Embree Asset Group which develops build-to-suit single-tenant buildings and leases them back to clients. Owner and chairman Jim Embree founded the firm in 1979 in Kansas City.

	Annual Growth	12/13	12/14	12/15	12/16	12/17
Sales ($ mil.)	16.2%	–	140.9	190.4	177.0	220.9
Net income ($ mil.)	57.3%	–	2.8	8.9	9.8	11.0
Market value ($ mil.)	–	–	–	–	–	–
Employees	–	–	–	–	–	175

EMBRY-RIDDLE AERONAUTICAL UNIVERSITY INC.

600 S CLYDE MORRIS BLVD
DAYTONA BEACH, FL 321143966
Phone: 386-226-6000
Fax: –
Web: www.erau.edu

CEO:
CFO: –
HR: –
FYE: June 30
Type: Private

Embry-Riddle Aeronautical University (ERAU) helps students solve the mysteries of space and flying. The not-for-profit corporation teaches aviation aerospace and engineering to about 30000 students a year (and a student-teacher ratio of about 13:1). ERAU which offers hands-on training through a fleet of 90 instructional aircraft has residential campuses in Daytona Beach Florida and Prescott Arizona. Its Embry-Riddle Worldwide program provides learning through more than 150 teaching centers and online training in the US Canada Europe and Middle East. It offers bachelor's master's and doctoral degrees in 35 areas.

	Annual Growth	06/10	06/11	06/12	06/13	06/14
Sales ($ mil.)	(1.7%)	–	359.4	318.0	384.6	340.9
Net income ($ mil.)	19.2%	–	–	24.3	26.7	34.5
Market value ($ mil.)	–	–	–	–	–	–
Employees	–	–	–	–	–	4,719

EMC CORP. (MA)

176 South Street
Hopkinton, MA 01748
Phone: 508 435-1000
Fax: 508 435-5222
Web: www.emc.com

NYS: EMC
CEO:
CFO:
HR: –
FYE: December 31
Type: Public

EMC has its head in the cloud ... and rightly so for a company that's helping businesses build Web-based computing systems with its data storage products and services. Its hardware and software platforms enable enterprises to store manage protect and analyze massive volumes of data. EMC also offers data security products through its RSA Security business and virtualization software through majority-owned VMware. The company serves both large FORTUNE 500 organizations and smaller businesses across many industries. Banks government agencies ISPs and manufacturers are among its customers. EMC serves a global client base from facilities and partners worldwide; it generates nearly half its sales outside the US. In October 2015 EMC agreed to be bought by Dell Inc. for $67 billion.

	Annual Growth	12/10	12/11	12/12	12/13	12/14
Sales ($ mil.)	9.5%	17,015.1	20,007.6	21,713.9	23,222.0	24,440.0
Net income ($ mil.)	9.3%	1,900.0	2,461.3	2,732.6	2,889.0	2,714.0
Market value ($ mil.)	6.8%	45,456.5	42,756.9	50,220.5	49,922.8	59,033.9
Employees	9.6%	48,500	53,600	60,000	63,900	70,000

EMC INSURANCE GROUP INC.
NMS: EMCI

717 Mulberry Street
Des Moines, IA 50309
Phone: 515 345-2902
Fax: –
Web: www.emcins.com

CEO: Bruce G Kelley
CFO: Mark E Reese
HR: –
FYE: December 31
Type: Public

Holding company EMC Insurance Group may be publicly traded but in its heart it's a mutual insurance company. Subsidiaries EMCASCO Insurance Illinois EMCASCO and Dakota Fire Insurance sell commercial and personal property/casualty insurance including automobile property liability and workers' compensation. Its commercial customers are primarily small and medium-sized businesses. Other group companies include EMC Underwriters which offers excess and surplus lines of insurance and EMC Reinsurance which provides reinsurance for the group and other unaffiliated insurers. Employers Mutual Casualty a multiple-line property/casualty insurance company owns about 55% of EMC Insurance Group; it plans to acquire the rest and take the firm private.

	Annual Growth	12/13	12/14	12/15	12/16	12/17
Assets ($ mil.)	5.1%	1,378.9	1,497.8	1,536.0	1,588.8	1,681.9
Net income ($ mil.)	(2.6%)	43.5	30.0	50.2	46.2	39.2
Market value ($ mil.)	(1.6%)	657.0	760.8	542.8	643.9	615.6
Employees	–	–	–	–	–	–

EMCLAIRE FINANCIAL CORP.
NAS: EMCF

612 Main Street
Emlenton, PA 16373
Phone: 844 767-2311
Fax: –
Web: www.emclairefinancial.com

CEO: William Marsh
CFO: Amanda Engles
HR: –
FYE: December 31
Type: Public

Emclaire Financial is the holding company for the Farmers National Bank of Emlenton which operates about a dozen branches in northwestern Pennsylvania. Serving area consumers and businesses the bank offers standard deposit products and services including checking and savings accounts money market accounts and CDs. The bank is mainly a real estate lender with commercial mortgages residential first mortgages and home equity loans and lines of credit making up most of its loan portfolio. Emclaire Financial also owns title insurance and real estate settlement services provider Emclaire Settlement Services.

	Annual Growth	12/16	12/17	12/18	12/19	12/20
Assets ($ mil.)	10.5%	692.1	750.1	898.9	915.3	1,032.3
Net income ($ mil.)	14.1%	4.0	4.3	4.2	8.0	6.7
Market value ($ mil.)	1.1%	79.6	82.6	82.6	88.5	83.3
Employees	5.1%	131	137	164	162	160

EMCOR GROUP, INC.
NYS: EME

301 Merritt Seven
Norwalk, CT 06851-1092
Phone: 203 849-7800
Fax: –
Web: www.emcorgroup.com

CEO: Anthony Guzzi
CFO: Mark Pompa
HR: –
FYE: December 31
Type: Public

EMCOR Group is an electrical and mechanical construction specialist and facilities services firms. Its electrical and mechanical construction services primarily involve the design integration installation start-up operation and maintenance and provision of services relating to electrical power transmission and distribution systems lighting water and wastewater treatment voice and data communications fire protection plumbing and heating ventilation and air-conditioning (HVAC). EMCOR also provides facilities services including management and maintenance support. Through some 85 subsidiaries the company serves a range of commercial industrial institutional and utility customers. EMCOR's domestic operations account for most of its revenue.

	Annual Growth	12/16	12/17	12/18	12/19	12/20
Sales ($ mil.)	3.9%	7,551.5	7,687.0	8,130.6	9,174.6	8,797.1
Net income ($ mil.)	(7.5%)	181.9	227.2	283.5	325.1	132.9
Market value ($ mil.)	6.6%	3,874.5	4,476.3	3,268.4	4,725.4	5,008.0
Employees	1.6%	31,000	32,000	33,000	36,000	33,000

EMCORE CORP.
NMS: EMKR

2015 W. Chestnut Street
Alhambra, CA 91803
Phone: 626 293-3400
Fax: –
Web: www.emcore.com

CEO: Jeffrey Rittichier
CFO: Thomas Minichiello
HR: –
FYE: September 30
Type: Public

EMCORE Corporation (also known as EMCORE) is a provider of sensors for navigation in the aerospace and defense market as well as a manufacturer of lasers and optical subsystems for use in the Cable TV (CATV) industry. The company pioneered the linear fiber optic transmission technology that enabled the world's first delivery of CATV directly on fiber. Its best-in-class components and systems support a broad array of applications including navigation and inertial sensing defense optoelectronics broadband communications optical sensing and specialty chips for telecom and data center applications. The company makes almost 90% of its revenue from companies based in the US.

	Annual Growth	09/17	09/18	09/19	09/20	09/21
Sales ($ mil.)	6.6%	122.9	85.6	87.3	110.1	158.4
Net income ($ mil.)	32.8%	8.2	(17.5)	(36.0)	(7.0)	25.6
Market value ($ mil.)	(2.3%)	303.3	175.7	113.5	120.2	276.6
Employees	0.1%	364	391	420	387	365

EMDEON INC.
NYSE: EM

3055 Lebanon Pike
Nashville TN 37214
Phone: 615-932-3000
Fax: 615-231-7972
Web: www.emdeon.com

CEO: Neil De Crescenzo
CFO: Randy Giles
HR: –
FYE: December 31
Type: Private

Emdeon wants to make the servicing of medical accounts a little easier. The company's offerings are designed to simplify and streamline health care billing for insurance companies health care systems and doctors. Emdeon offers discounted office supplies online automated billing and document mailing services and insurance card printing and has products specifically for dental and pharmaceutical offices. It processes more than 5 billion health care-related transactions each year. It also owns Chamberlin Edmonds & Associates a provider of revenue recovery assistance to healthcare clients. Emdeon was acquired by The Blackstone Group in 2011.

EMERALD DAIRY INC.
OTC: EMDY

11990 Market St. Ste. 205
Reston VA 20190
Phone: 703-867-9247
Fax: +61-3-5563-2156
Web: www.wcbf.com.au

CEO: Yang Yong Shan
CFO: Shu Kaneko
HR: –
FYE: December 31
Type: Public

Emerald Dairy's formula for success is turning milk into milk powder. The company produces milk powder (infant formula and enriched milk powders for children and adults) as well as rice and soybean powders. Its product line includes two brands: Xing An Ling which is marketed to low-end customers and Yi Bai which is marketed to middle and high-end customers. Producing more than 9000 tons of milk powder annually the dairy distributes its products to more than 5800 retail stores located in 20 of China's 30 provinces. Emerald Dairy gets its milk supply through contracting with local dairy farmers. Chairman and CEO Yong Shan Yang owns 47% of Emerald John Winfield owns 10% and Farallon Partners owns 9%.

EMERALD OIL, INC
ASE: EOX

200 Columbine Street, Suite 500
Denver, CO 80206
Phone: 303 595-5600
Fax: -
Web: www.voyageroil.com

CEO: McAndrew Rudisill
CFO: Ryan Smith
HR: -
FYE: December 31
Type: Public

Emerald Oil (formerly Voyager Oil & Gas) is involved in energy exploration and production in the northern US. It has oil and gas rights in properties Colorado Montana and North Dakota primarily in the Bakken and Three Forks formations in the Williston Basin. Growing its assets in the Rockies in 2012 Voyager Oil & Gas acquired fellow oil and gas exploration and production company Emerald Oil and assumed that company's name. That year the company reported proved reserves of approximately 5.35 million barrels of oil equivalent all of which were located in the Williston Basin.

	Annual Growth	12/10	12/11	12/12	12/13	12/14
Sales ($ mil.)	230.6%	0.9	8.4	27.9	51.3	112.6
Net income ($ mil.)	-	(4.3)	(1.3)	(62.3)	(10.9)	(52.1)
Market value ($ mil.)	(31.3%)	420.3	200.0	407.8	596.2	93.4
Employees	93.4%	3	5	15	30	42

EMERGE ENERGY SERVICES LP
NYS: EMES

5600 Clearfork Main Street, Suite 400
Fort Worth, TX 76109
Phone: 817 618-4020
Fax: -
Web: www.emergelp.com

CEO: -
CFO: Deborah Deibert
HR: Kara Dahm
FYE: December 31
Type: Public

Emerge Energy Services is ready to come into being. The company formed in April 2012 by an investment firm Insight Equity to take over three of its portfolio investments — Allied Energy Company LLC; Direct Fuels Partners L.P.; and Superior Silica Sands LLC. Allied Energy and Direct Fuels distribute petroleum products including ethanol and biodiesel while Superior Silica Sands owns three processing plants that supply sand to natural gas production companies. (Sand is one of the key components in hydraulic fracturing the process in producing natural gas.) When Emerge Energy Services went public in March 2013 it took ownership of the three companies.

	Annual Growth	12/13	12/14	12/15	12/16	12/17
Sales ($ mil.)	(19.6%)	873.3	1,111.3	711.6	128.4	364.3
Net income ($ mil.)	-	35.2	89.1	(9.4)	(72.8)	(6.8)
Market value ($ mil.)	(36.5%)	1,337.7	1,629.4	139.7	371.5	217.0
Employees	-	-	-	-	-	-

EMERGENT BIOSOLUTIONS INC
NYS: EBS

400 Professional Drive Suite 400
Gaithersburg, MD 20879
Phone: 240 631-3200
Fax: -
Web: www.emergentbiosolutions.com

CEO: Robert Kramer
CFO: Richard Lindahl
HR: Katherine Strei
FYE: December 31
Type: Public

Emergent BioSolutions a global life sciences company focused on providing innovative preparedness and response solutions addressing accidental deliberate and naturally occurring public health threats (PHTs). Primary product BioThrax is the only FDA-approved anthrax vaccine. Most BioThrax revenue comes from direct sales to US federal agencies including the Department of Defense (DOD) and the Department of Health and Human Services (HHS). Other offerings include vaccines ACAM2000 (smallpox) Vivotif (typhoid fever) and Vaxchora (cholera); opioid overdose drug Narcan; and inhaled anthrax treatment raxibacumab. Emergent also has contract manufacturing and research operations.

	Annual Growth	12/16	12/17	12/18	12/19	12/20
Sales ($ mil.)	33.6%	488.8	560.9	782.4	1,106.0	1,555.4
Net income ($ mil.)	55.8%	51.8	82.6	62.7	54.5	305.1
Market value ($ mil.)	28.5%	1,743.8	2,467.6	3,147.8	2,864.7	4,757.8
Employees	(10.6%)	1,098	1,256	1,705	1,834	700

EMERGENT CAPITAL INC
NBB: EMGC

5355 Town Center RoadSuite 701
Boca Raton, FL 33486
Phone: 561 995-4200
Fax: -
Web: www.imperial.com

CEO: -
CFO: -
HR: -
FYE: December 31
Type: Public

Specialty finance company Emergent Capital (formerly Imperial Holdings) offers loans allowing policyholders to postpone or consolidate insurance premium payments using the policy as collateral. Emergent Capital has issued loans mostly to senior citizens secured by about $4 billion in insurance policies. The average loan is for $216000 on policies with an average death payout of $4 million. In addition to premium financing the company also purchases structured settlements allowing customers to exchange a long-term settlement plan for an immediate lump sum of lesser value. Formed in 2006 Emergent Capital went public in 2011.

	Annual Growth	12/11	12/12	12/13	12/14	12/15
Assets ($ mil.)	23.0%	222.6	160.3	348.1	459.9	509.9
Net income ($ mil.)	-	(39.2)	(44.6)	65.3	(5.5)	(31.0)
Market value ($ mil.)	18.4%	52.9	125.2	184.0	183.4	103.8
Employees	(29.6%)	130	119	107	39	32

EMERGENT GROUP INC.
NYSE AMEX: LZR

10939 Pendleton St.
Sun Valley CA 91352
Phone: 818-394-2800
Fax: 818-394-2850
Web: www.emergentgroupinc.com

CEO: Bruce J Haber
CFO: William M McKay
HR: -
FYE: December 31
Type: Public

Mobile medical equipment for rent? Emergent Group's got it. Through wholly-owned operating subsidiary PRI Medical Technologies the company rents mobile medical laser and surgical equipment in more than 15 states on a per-procedure basis to hospitals surgical care centers and doctors' offices. The equipment comes with operation and maintenance services from technical support personnel. The company serves both small health care providers that cannot afford to purchase expensive medical equipment for their facilities and larger hospitals that cannot justify buying certain equipment due to infrequent usage. Universal Hospital Services (UHS) acquired Emergent Group in 2011 in a transaction worth about $70 million.

EMERGING VISION INC.
OTC: ISEE

520 8th Ave. 23rd Fl.
New York City NY 10018
Phone: 646-737-1500
Fax: 724-720-1530
Web: www.tollgrade.com

CEO: -
CFO: Brian P Alessi
HR: -
FYE: December 31
Type: Public

Emerging Vision doesn't have to strain to keep its business in focus. The firm owns and franchises about 130 optical outlets under the Sterling Optical Site For Sore Eyes Kindy Optical and Singer Specs names in more than a dozen states the District of Columbia and the US Virgin Islands. It also runs an optical purchasing group offering vendor discounts to independent eyewear retailers in the US under the Combine Optical name and in Canada under The Optical Group name. In addition the company operates VisionCare of California a specialized HMO whose dues-paying members may receive eye care services at Emerging Vision's optical outlets throughout the state.

EMERITUS CORP.   NYS: ESC

3131 Elliott Avenue, Suite 500 — CEO: –
Seattle, WA 98121 — CFO: Robert C Bateman
Phone: 206 298-2909 — HR: –
Fax: 206 378-4205 — FYE: December 31
Web: www.emeritus.com — Type: Public

The Emeritus Corporation honors the retirement set. The company operates assisted living communities for senior citizens who need help with daily activities such as feeding bathing housekeeping and managing their medications as well as for those patients suffering from dementia. Emeritus' communities also organize social and recreational activities for residents and most of them provide special services (called Join Their Journey programs) to support residents with Alzheimer's disease or other forms of dementia. Throughout the US Emeritus owns leases or manages about 480 communities. It also manages communties through joint ventures and for third parties.

	Annual Growth	12/08	12/09	12/10	12/11	12/12
Sales ($ mil.)	19.5%	769.4	898.7	1,007.1	1,254.8	1,568.1
Net income ($ mil.)	–	(104.8)	(53.9)	(57.0)	(71.9)	(84.8)
Market value ($ mil.)	25.3%	459.5	859.0	903.0	802.2	1,132.5
Employees	12.8%	18,671	12,577	29,300	28,100	30,236

EMERSON COLLEGE

120 BOYLSTON ST STE 414 — CEO: –
BOSTON, MA 021164624 — CFO: –
Phone: 617-824-8500 — HR: –
Fax: – — FYE: June 30
Web: www.emerson.edu — Type: Private

Emerson College specializes in teaching subjects in the fields of communication and the arts in a liberal arts context. Areas of study include journalism; marketing; organizational and political communication; performing arts; visual and media arts; and writing literature and publishing. Its also has an acclaimed communication sciences and disorders program. The college enrolls about 3200 full-time undergraduates and 1000 full and part-time graduate students on its Boston-based campus. Among its alumni are producer Norman Lear talk show host Jay Leno and journalist Morton Dean. The college has additional facilities in Los Angeles and in the Netherlands. Emerson was founded in 1880 as a school of oratory.

	Annual Growth	06/09	06/10	06/15	06/17	06/20
Sales ($ mil.)	6.2%	–	154.3	216.2	189.8	281.1
Net income ($ mil.)	(4.7%)	–	17.8	8.2	20.7	11.0
Market value ($ mil.)	–	–	–	–	–	–
Employees	–	–	–	–	–	425

EMERSON ELECTRIC CO.   NYS: EMR

8000 W. Florissant Avenue, P.O. Box 4100 — CEO: Surendralal Karsanbhai
St. Louis, MO 63136 — CFO: Frank Dellaquila
Phone: 314 553-2000 — HR: –
Fax: – — FYE: September 30
Web: www.emerson.com — Type: Public

Emerson Electric is a global leader that designs and manufactures products and delivers services that bring technology and engineering together to provide innovative solutions for customers in a wide range of industrial commercial and consumer markets around the world. The company operates globally in the Americas Europe Asia and the Middle East & Africa. The company offers its products through its segments such as automation solutions that manufacture products and integrated solutions which include measurement and analytical instrumentation. Its Tools & Home Products segment includes brands such as Emerson Emerson Professional Tools Badger Greenlee Grind2Energy InSinkErator Klauke ProTeam and RIDGID. About 55% of total sales were from the Americas region.

	Annual Growth	09/17	09/18	09/19	09/20	09/21
Sales ($ mil.)	4.5%	15,264.0	17,408.0	18,372.0	16,785.0	18,236.0
Net income ($ mil.)	11.0%	1,518.0	2,203.0	2,306.0	1,965.0	2,303.0
Market value ($ mil.)	10.7%	37,440.1	45,626.4	39,835.2	39,066.6	56,124.4
Employees	3.2%	76,500	87,500	88,000	83,500	86,700

EMERSON HOSPITAL

133 OLD RD TO 9 ACRE COR — CEO: –
CONCORD, MA 017424169 — CFO: –
Phone: 978-369-1400 — HR: –
Fax: – — FYE: September 30
Web: www.emersonhospital.org — Type: Private

Ralph Waldo Emerson said "the first wealth is health" and Emerson Hospital would agree. The not-for-profit hospital tends to the well-being of patients in and around historic Concord Massachusetts. The 179-bed community hospital is staffed by more than 300 doctors and specialists. Emerson is well known for its outstanding nursing care and patient-centered facilities including the Mass General Cancer Center at Emerson Hospital ? Bethke and the Clough Birthing Center which has the area's only Special Care Level 2 Nursery for moderately ill newborns. Emerson Hospital provides medical services to people in some 25 communities in Massachusetts including Concord Groton Sudbury and Westford. All told Emerson provides advanced medical services to more than 300000 people.

	Annual Growth	09/15	09/16	09/17	09/18	09/19
Sales ($ mil.)	8.4%	–	213.6	225.5	242.6	272.1
Net income ($ mil.)	–	–	(3.6)	8.1	12.4	3.7
Market value ($ mil.)	–	–	–	–	–	–
Employees	–	–	–	–	–	1,450

EMERSON NETWORK POWER-EMBEDDED COMPUTING INC.

2900 S. Diablo Way Ste. 190 — CEO: Steven Dow
Tempe AZ 85282 — CFO: –
Phone: 602-438-5720 — HR: –
Fax: 602-438-5825 — FYE: September 30
Web: www.emerson.com/sites/network_power/en-us/page — Type: Subsidiary

Emerson Network Power-Embedded Computing Inc. (dba Emerson Network Power) makes some powerful products for a broad range of applications. The company makes standard and custom power supplies including switches rectifiers breaker interface panels AC/DC and DC/DC power supplies and related accessories. Its products are used in computing medical networking and telecommunications process control and test instrumentation applications. One of the largest manufacturers of power supplies in the world Emerson Network Power also a company brand is a subsidiary of Emerson Electric. It has manufacturing and direct sales force operations in Asia Europe and North America. The US represents about 40% of sales.

EMERSON RADIO CORP.   ASE: MSN

35 Waterview Blvd., Suite 140 — CEO: Wing On Ho
Parsippany, NJ 07054 — CFO: Richard Li
Phone: 973 428-2000 — HR: –
Fax: – — FYE: March 31
Web: www.emersonradio.com — Type: Public

Emerson Radio is tuned to the crowd that thinks a new television or microwave oven shouldn't cost an arm and a leg. The company designs imports sells and licenses housewares and audio and video products under the Emerson H.H. Scott and Olevia brand names. Its products are sold primarily by mass merchants in the US. (Wal-Mart and Target account for more than 85% of the company's sales.) Emerson's products include microwave ovens compact refrigerators wine openers and coolers clock radios televisions and other audio and video products. Its products are sourced from foreign suppliers primarily in China. Emerson Radio was founded in 1948.

	Annual Growth	03/17	03/18	03/19	03/20	03/21
Sales ($ mil.)	(23.1%)	21.3	15.0	9.0	6.3	7.4
Net income ($ mil.)	–	(0.2)	(6.9)	(2.4)	(4.3)	(4.0)
Market value ($ mil.)	(1.5%)	28.6	30.7	27.4	14.7	26.9
Employees	(6.9%)	32	27	23	22	24

EMISPHERE TECHNOLOGIES, INC. NBB: EMIS

4 Becker Farm Road, Suite 103 — CEO: Alan L Rubino
Roseland, NJ 07068 — CFO: Alan Gallantar
Phone: 973 532-8000 — HR: –
Fax: – — FYE: December 31
Web: www.emisphere.com — Type: Public

Needle prick be gone. Development-stage Emisphere Technologies is offering an alternative to traditional injection of certain drugs with an oral drug delivery technology called eligen which is designed to improve the way certain therapeutic molecules (such as proteins carbohydrates and peptides) are administered to and absorbed by the body. With collaborative partners including Novartis Roche and Genta Emisphere is developing oral formulations that incorporate eligen to deliver drugs that treat such health problems as osteoporosis diabetes growth disorders and cardiovascular disease. Emisphere was formed in 1986.

	Annual Growth	12/12	12/13	12/14	12/15	12/16
Sales ($ mil.)	190.8%	–	–	–	0.4	1.2
Net income ($ mil.)	–	(1.9)	(20.9)	(25.4)	(40.4)	(10.0)
Market value ($ mil.)	38.7%	9.9	10.7	17.1	41.2	36.6
Employees	(15.9%)	12	11	10	10	6

EMJ CORPORATION

2034 HAMILTON PLACE BLVD # 400 — CEO: James Jolley
CHATTANOOGA, TN 374216102 — CFO: Chuck McGlothlen
Phone: 423-855-1550 — HR: –
Fax: – — FYE: March 07
Web: www.emjcorp.com — Type: Private

EMJ does it all for the mall. Founded in 1968 by namesake Edgar M. Jolley the company specializes in building and renovating retail outlets and shopping centers throughout the US. It is also known for other building projects such as offices warehouses churches hotels multifamily residences hospitals and wind farms. Working from five offices nationwide EMJ provides general construction and construction management. The company's pre-construction services include creating detailed budgets and construction schedules and coordinating permitting utility companies and municipal requirements. To track a project's progress and monitor costs EMJ offers quality control and safety and warranty management.

	Annual Growth	12/06	12/07	12/08	12/11*	03/17
Sales ($ mil.)	0.0%	–	959.2	821.8	437.5	960.3
Net income ($ mil.)	(7.1%)	–	10.2	7.9	0.4	4.9
Market value ($ mil.)	–	–	–	–	–	–
Employees	–	–	–	–	–	210

*Fiscal year change

EMKAY INC.

805 W. Thorndale Ave. — CEO: –
Itasca IL 60143 — CFO: –
Phone: 630-250-7400 — HR: –
Fax: 630-250-7077 — FYE: February 28
Web: www.emkay.com — Type: Private

Emkay is an ehiclevay easerlay. Or for the Pig Latin challenged: Emkay is a vehicle leaser. One of the oldest and largest fleet leasing and management companies in the nation it leases and manages some 75000 cars trucks and electric vehicles to more than 500 corporate clients. The employee-owned company offers open- and closed-end leasing programs as well as assistance with fleet purchase and disposal. Other services include maintenance and fuel management It also operates Emkay Motors a retail used vehicle outlet in Illinois. Founded in 1946 Emkay has 10 US offices and is active in Canada Mexico and the Caribbean. It operates Unico Car-Lease in Europe.

EMMIS COMMUNICATIONS CORP NBB: EMMS

One Emmis Plaza, 40 Monument Circle, Suite 700 — CEO: Jeffrey Smulyan
Indianapolis, IN 46204 — CFO: Ryan Hornaday
Phone: 317 266-0100 — HR: –
Fax: – — FYE: February 29
Web: www.emmis.com — Type: Public

Emmis Communications is into communicating — whether it's through the radio or magazines. The company operates two radio stations in New York through a local marketing agreement with ESPN Radio (WLIB 1190 AM and WEPN 98.7 FM). It also owns four radio stations in Indianapolis. In addition Emmis has a controlling interest in Digonex a dynamic pricing company and Indianapolis Monthly a city regional magazine. Significantly smaller than it once was Emmis has been busy as of late selling off radio and publishing properties in order to pay off debt.

	Annual Growth	02/16	02/17	02/18	02/19	02/20
Sales ($ mil.)	(35.6%)	231.4	214.6	148.5	114.1	39.7
Net income ($ mil.)	121.1%	2.1	13.1	82.1	23.4	50.5
Market value ($ mil.)	61.4%	7.1	37.0	55.7	51.3	48.2
Employees	(21.5%)	1,085	830	620	560	412

EMPIRE RESORTS INC NMS: NYNY

c/o Monticello Casino and Raceway, 204 State Route 17B, P.O. Box 5013 — CEO: Ryan Eller
Monticello, NY 12701 — CFO: Laurette J Pitts
Phone: 845 807-0001 — HR: Eileen Cavanaugh
Fax: – — FYE: December 31
Web: www.empireresorts.com — Type: Public

Empire Resorts has taken up permanent residence in New York's playground. The company operates Catskills-area harness horseracing track Monticello Gaming and Raceway which features pari-mutuel wagering and more than 1100 video gaming machines (VGMs). The property located 90 miles northwest of New York City also includes a clubhouse entertainment lounge bar and food court. Its VGMs are owned by the State of New York and are overseen by the state's Division of the Lottery which distributes a percentage of VGM revenue to Empire Resorts. Other company revenues primarily come from wagering fees admission fees program and racing form sales and food and beverages sales.

	Annual Growth	12/13	12/14	12/15	12/16	12/17
Sales ($ mil.)	(1.9%)	71.0	65.2	68.2	67.5	65.9
Net income ($ mil.)	–	(21.5)	(23.9)	(36.6)	(24.2)	(46.3)
Market value ($ mil.)	53.7%	157.6	252.7	586.1	740.7	879.1
Employees	57.0%	288	290	277	–	1,750

EMPIRE RESOURCES, INC.

2115 LINWOOD AVE STE 200 — CEO: Johnny Hsieh
FORT LEE, NJ 070245022 — CFO: –
Phone: 201-944-2200 — HR: –
Fax: – — FYE: December 31
Web: www.empireresources.com — Type: Private

When it comes to aluminum Empire Resources is especially resourceful. The company distributes semi-finished aluminum products including sheet foil wire plate and coil. Products are sold primarily to manufacturers of appliances automobiles packaging and housing materials. Empire Resources provides a variety of related services including sourcing of aluminum products storage and delivery and handling foreign exchange transactions. Company president and CEO Nathan Kahn and CFO Sandra Kahn who are husband and wife own some 40% of Empire Resources.

	Annual Growth	12/12	12/13	12/14	12/15	12/16
Sales ($ mil.)	(1.7%)	–	482.7	582.3	521.7	458.9
Net income ($ mil.)	11.3%	–	2.4	3.7	2.8	3.3
Market value ($ mil.)	–	–	–	–	–	–
Employees	–	–	–	–	–	60

EMPIRE SOUTHWEST, LLC

1725 S COUNTRY CLUB DR
MESA, AZ 852106099
Phone: 480-633-4000
Fax: –
Web: www.caterpillar.com

CEO: Jeffrey S Whiteman
CFO: –
HR: –
FYE: October 31
Type: Private

Empire Southwest is a third-generation family-owned Cat Dealer that sells rents and services heavy equipment tractors and power generation equipment to clients throughout Arizona and Southeastern California. One of the largest Caterpillar dealerships in the US Empire Southwest operates through four divisions: hydraulic service fluid labs precision machining and rebuilds. The company's equipment includes backhoe loaders compactors dozers electric rope shovels track loaders pipelayers telehandlers and tractors. It also handles equipment used for mining and forestry projects. The company was founded by Jack Whiteman in 1950 as Empire Machinery an Eastern Oregon Caterpillar dealer.

	Annual Growth	10/07	10/08	10/09	10/10	10/11
Sales ($ mil.)	23.5%	–	–	448.2	528.5	683.9
Net income ($ mil.)	127.0%	–	–	7.4	22.5	38.0
Market value ($ mil.)	–	–	–	–	–	–
Employees		–	–	–	–	1,450

EMPIRE STATE REALTY TRUST INC

NYS: ESRT

111 West 33rd Street, 12th Floor
New York, NY 10120
Phone: 212 850-2600
Fax: –
Web: www.empirestaterealtytrust.com

CEO: Anthony Malkin
CFO: Christina Chiu
HR: –
FYE: December 31
Type: Public

If King Kong were around he'd be an executive at Empire State Realty Trust. The self-administered and self-managed real estate investment trust (REIT) formed in mid-2011 to take over a portfolio of high-profile Manhattan properties from its previous owners the Malkin family. Its flagship property is of course the 102-story Empire State Building but the trust also owns more than a dozen other buildings in the greater New York area totaling almost 7.7 million sq. ft. of office and retail space. In addition it plans to build a 340000-sq.-ft. building at the train station in Stamford Connecticut. Empire State Realty Trust went public in 2013 raising $929 million.

	Annual Growth	12/16	12/17	12/18	12/19	12/20
Sales ($ mil.)	(2.6%)	678.0	712.5	731.5	731.3	609.2
Net income ($ mil.)	–	52.4	63.6	66.5	51.2	(12.5)
Market value ($ mil.)	(17.6%)	3,463.9	3,522.2	2,441.4	2,395.1	1,599.0
Employees	(2.0%)	819	831	813	831	755

EMPIRIX INC.

600 TECHNOLOGY PARK DR # 1
BILLERICA, MA 01821-4154
Phone: 978-313-7000
Fax: –
Web: www.empirix.com

CEO: John Danna
CFO: Ray Dezenzo
HR: –
FYE: December 31
Type: Private

Empirix elucidates about communications service quality. The company provides testing and monitoring applications that manage and enhance IP communications networks and systems for service providers equipment manufacturers and corporate contact centers. Its systems rely on the Hammer Test Engine a technology that duplicates user behavior to test and validate the performance of voice data video and mobile communications networks under real-world conditions. Empirix's global customer base includes Amtrak Cisco China Mobile Sonus Networks Time Warner Cable and lastminute.com.

	Annual Growth	12/03	12/04	12/05	12/06	12/07
Sales ($ mil.)	7.2%	–	58.8	70.6	73.0	72.4
Net income ($ mil.)	–	–	(3.6)	(2.3)	(3.7)	(7.6)
Market value ($ mil.)	–	–	–	–	–	–
Employees		–	–	–	–	380

EMPLOYERS HOLDINGS INC

NYS: EIG

10375 Professional Circle
Reno, NV 89521
Phone: 888 682-6671
Fax: –
Web: www.employers.com

CEO: Katherine Antonello
CFO: Michael Paquette
HR: John Mutschink
FYE: December 31
Type: Public

Because workers' compensation is nothing to gamble with small business owners can turn to Employers Holdings. The Reno-based holding company provides workers' compensation services including claims management and services focused on select small businesses in low and medium hazard industries. The company provides workers' compensation through its Employer Insurance Company of Nevada (EICN) and Employers Compensation Insurance Company. Employers Holdings also operates Employers Assurance and Employers Preferred Insurance Company both of which also offer workers' compensation.

	Annual Growth	12/16	12/17	12/18	12/19	12/20
Assets ($ mil.)	1.0%	3,773.4	3,840.1	3,919.2	4,004.1	3,922.6
Net income ($ mil.)	2.9%	106.7	101.2	141.3	157.1	119.8
Market value ($ mil.)	(5.0%)	1,131.2	1,268.3	1,198.9	1,192.6	919.5
Employees	(0.1%)	693	672	704	704	691

EMPORIA STATE UNIVERSITY

1200 COMMERCIAL ST CA
EMPORIA, KS 668015087
Phone: 620-341-1200
Fax: –
Web: www.emporia.edu

CEO: –
CFO: –
HR: –
FYE: June 30
Type: Private

Emporia State University (ESU) offers more than 35 undergraduate and roughly two dozen graduate degrees and programs as well as certification programs specialist degrees and doctoral degrees. It has four schools and colleges: the School of Business School of Library and Information Management College of Liberal Arts and Sciences and The Teachers College. Some 6500 students are enrolled at the school which employs about 260 full-time faculty members. ESU is said to be the first and only university to offer a four-year degree in Engraving Arts. The school offers an additional 35 programs online. ESU was founded as Kansas State Normal School in 1863. It adopted its current name in 1977.

	Annual Growth	06/05	06/06	06/08	06/13	06/14
Sales ($ mil.)	3.3%	–	37.3	10.4	42.3	48.4
Net income ($ mil.)	(15.5%)	–	–	6.1	(0.7)	2.2
Market value ($ mil.)	–	–	–	–	–	–
Employees		–	–	–	–	1,700

EMRISE CORP

NBB: EMRI

2530 Meridian Parkway
Durham, NC 27713
Phone: 408 200-3040
Fax: –
Web: www.emrise.com

CEO: –
CFO: –
HR: –
FYE: December 31
Type: Public

The sun doesn't set on EMRISE. Through its worldwide subsidiaries the company makes electronic components and communications equipment for customers in the aerospace military and telecommunications industries. Its CXR Larus units produce network transmission and access equipment and a range of testing gear. EMRISE's EEC Corporation subsidiary manufactures power converters digital and rotary switches and subsystem assemblies. The company counts BAE SYSTEMS EMS Technologies Harris ITT Raytheon Rockwell Collins and Thales Air Defence among its top clients. EMRISE gets more than 80% of sales outside the US principally in the UK.

	Annual Growth	12/09	12/10	12/11	12/12	12/13
Sales ($ mil.)	(12.2%)	53.8	30.6	33.5	34.0	31.9
Net income ($ mil.)	–	–	1.0	(3.4)	(1.6)	0.1	(0.4)
Market value ($ mil.)	2.7%	8.1	9.2	4.6	5.2	9.0
Employees	(11.8%)	335	213	213	213	203

EMS TECHNOLOGIES INC.

660 Engineering Dr.
Norcross GA 30092
Phone: 770-263-9200
Fax: 770-263-9207
Web: www.ems-t.com

CEO: Darius Adamczyk
CFO: John J Tus
HR: –
FYE: December 31
Type: Subsidiary

EMS Technologies' wireless systems can help you communicate whether you're walking the warehouse floor or floating in space. The company's LXE unit provides rugged mobile computers and wireless networks for logistics and other applications. EMS also makes engineered hardware for civilian and military applications through its Defense & Space (D&S) unit. Its Aviation unit makes data communications equipment that provides Internet video conferencing and other capabilities on aircraft. Global Tracking provides tracking and mapping products and services for transport and emergency operations. Customers in the US account for more than two-thirds of sales. In 2011 Honeywell bought EMS for about $491 million.

EMTEC INC.

NBB: ETEC

11 Diamond Road
Springfield, NJ 07081
Phone: 973 376-4242
Fax: –
Web: www.emtecinc.com

CEO: Sunil Misra
CFO: Gregory P Chandler
HR: –
FYE: August 31
Type: Public

Emtec provides information technology services including product procurement and infrastructure design and implementation. The company primarily resells and supports computer hardware and software from leading providers such as Cisco Dell Hewlett-Packard and Oracle but it is building its newer IT consulting and application services business which also includes training technical staffing and network management services. Federal government agencies including the US Department of Defense Department of Justice and Department of Homeland Security account for nearly half of sales; other customers include state governments corporations and educational organizations.

	Annual Growth	08/08	08/09	08/10	08/11	08/12
Sales ($ mil.)	1.6%	211.2	223.8	224.6	212.1	224.6
Net income ($ mil.)	–	1.3	1.7	(0.5)	(4.3)	(12.4)
Market value ($ mil.)	3.9%	17.4	15.9	20.1	14.1	20.3
Employees	6.3%	574	572	649	761	733

EMULEX CORPORATION

NYS: ELX

3333 Susan Street
Costa Mesa, CA 92626
Phone: 714 662-5600
Fax: –
Web: www.emulex.com

CEO: –
CFO: –
HR: –
FYE: June 29
Type: Public

Emulex sets an example in the data storage market. The company is a leading maker of host server products (HSP) and embedded storage products (ESP). Its LightPulse fibre channel host bus adapters (HBA) are used to connect storage devices in direct-attached storage configurations as well as storage area network (SAN) and network-attached storage (NAS) systems. Emulex also develops HBAs based on the fibre channel over Ethernet protocol. The company primarily sells directly to equipment makers who incorporate Emulex components into their own storage platforms; its top customers are IBM (29% of sales) and Hewlett-Packard (16%).

	Annual Growth	06/10*	07/11	07/12*	06/13	06/14
Sales ($ mil.)	2.9%	399.2	452.5	501.8	478.6	447.3
Net income ($ mil.)	–	23.6	(83.6)	(11.1)	(5.2)	(29.5)
Market value ($ mil.)	(13.5%)	687.3	617.1	510.7	462.5	385.2
Employees	9.1%	791	972	1,011	1,264	1,122

*Fiscal year change

ENABLE MIDSTREAM PARTNERS L.P.

NYS: ENBL

499 West Sheridan Avenue, Suite 1500
Oklahoma City, OK 73102
Phone: 405 525-7788
Fax: –
Web: www.enablemidstream.com

CEO: Marshall S McCrea III
CFO: –
HR: –
FYE: December 31
Type: Public

Enable Midstream Partners is an American limited partnership energy company between CenterPoint Energy OGE Energy and ArcLight. It gathers processes transports and stores crude oil and natural gas to its customers. With 13900 miles of pipelines 15 major processing plants and some 10 natural gas storage facilities and an additional 10000 miles of combined interstate and intra-state pipelines Enable's operations serve Oklahoma Texas Arkansas Louisiana Alabama and Illinois.

	Annual Growth	12/15	12/16	12/17	12/18	12/19
Sales ($ mil.)	5.2%	2,418.0	2,272.0	2,803.0	3,431.0	2,960.0
Net income ($ mil.)	–	(752.0)	312.0	436.0	521.0	396.0
Market value ($ mil.)	2.2%	4,003.9	6,845.7	6,188.6	5,888.3	4,365.1
Employees	1.4%	1,640	1,600	1,630	1,705	1,735

ENANTA PHARMACEUTICALS INC

NMS: ENTA

500 Arsenal Street
Watertown, MA 02472
Phone: 617 607-0800
Fax: –
Web: www.enanta.com

CEO: Jay Luly
CFO: Paul Mellett
HR: –
FYE: September 30
Type: Public

Enanta Pharmaceuticals is getting hip to Hep C. The biotech firm is developing treatments for viral infections including hepatitis C (HCV) a virus that can lead to chronic liver diseases such as cirrhosis organ failure and cancer. The company's first licensed product which is licensed to AbbVie is paritaprevir is a protease inhibitor for use against HCV. Enanta also has five small molecule drugs under development: glecaprevir another protease inhibitor for the treatment for HCV; EDP-938 (treatment to respiratory syncytial virus); EDP-297 (an FXR agonist candidate for NASH); EDP-514 (treatment of chronic infection with hepatitis B virus or HBV); and EDP-305 which is being studied for the treatment of non-alcoholic steatohepatitis (NASH) and primary biliary cholangitis (PBC).

	Annual Growth	09/17	09/18	09/19	09/20	09/21
Sales ($ mil.)	(1.4%)	102.8	206.6	205.2	122.5	97.1
Net income ($ mil.)	–	17.7	72.0	46.4	(36.2)	(79.0)
Market value ($ mil.)	5.0%	947.1	1,729.5	1,215.9	926.5	1,149.7
Employees	14.9%	89	113	132	141	155

ENBRIDGE ENERGY MANAGEMENT LLC

NYS: EEQ

1100 Louisiana Street, Suite 3300
Houston, TX 77002
Phone: 713 821-2000
Fax: 713 821-2230
Web: www.enbridgemanagement.com

CEO: –
CFO: –
HR: –
FYE: December 31
Type: Public

Enbridge Energy Management bridging the gap over a complex structure of pipeline partnerships manages and controls the business of Enbridge Energy Partners (formerly Lakehead Pipe Line Partners). The company's only asset is its 10% limited partner interest and 2% general partner interest in Enbridge Energy Partners which owns the US part of North America's longest liquid petroleum pipeline (Lakehead System) and also has interests in natural gas gathering treating processing and transmission operations in East Texas. Enbridge Energy Company a wholly owned subsidiary of Enbridge Inc. holds a 17% stake in the company and serves as the general partner of Enbridge Energy Partners.

	Annual Growth	12/12	12/13	12/14	12/15	12/16
Sales ($ mil.)	–	50.5	(26.3)	43.7	(379.7)	(121.9)
Net income ($ mil.)	–	31.8	(18.1)	27.1	(512.4)	(120.1)
Market value ($ mil.)	(2.7%)	2,364.9	2,347.7	3,175.2	1,827.9	2,120.1
Employees	–	–	–	–	–	–

ENBRIDGE ENERGY PARTNERS, L.P.   NYS: EEP

1100 Louisiana Street, Suite 3300
Houston, TX 77002
Phone: 713 821-2000
Fax: –
Web: www.enbridgepartners.com

CEO: Mark A Maki
CFO: –
HR: –
FYE: December 31
Type: Public

Head of the class in transporting petroleum around the Great Lakes is Enbridge Energy Partners which owns the 2211-mile US portion (Lakehead System) of the world's longest liquid petroleum pipeline. When combined with the Canadian segment (owned and operated by Enbridge Inc.) the pipeline system spans some 5100 miles across North America. Other midstream assets include 5300 miles of crude oil gathering and transportation lines and 34 million barrels of crude oil storage and terminaling capacity and 11100 miles of natural gas gathering and transportation pipelines. Enbridge's US unit Enbridge Energy Management owns a 23% stake in the company.

	Annual Growth	12/12	12/13	12/14	12/15	12/16
Sales ($ mil.)	(9.6%)	6,706.1	7,117.1	7,964.7	5,146.1	4,481.9
Net income ($ mil.)	–	493.1	72.1	476.7	233.2	(67.7)
Market value ($ mil.)	(2.2%)	12,167.4	13,026.5	17,400.7	10,061.0	11,112.0
Employees	–	–	–	–	–	–

ENCISION INC.   NBB: ECIA

6797 Winchester Circle
Boulder, CO 80301
Phone: 303 444-2600
Fax: –
Web: www.encision.com

CEO: Gregory Trudel
CFO: –
HR: –
FYE: March 31
Type: Public

Encision enables doctors to make the cut during surgery. The company makes instruments for use in laparoscopic surgical procedures including electrodes graspers monitors and scissor inserts. Encision's products sold under the brand name AEM Surgical Instruments work like conventional electrosurgical instruments but incorporate proprietary technology that reduces the risk of accidental damage to surrounding tissues caused by stray electrosurgical energy. The company has been working to expand its marketing and distribution network using independent distributors and sales representatives as well as agreements with group purchasing organizations such as Novation and Premier.

	Annual Growth	03/17	03/18	03/19	03/20	03/21
Sales ($ mil.)	(4.0%)	8.9	8.8	8.8	7.7	7.5
Net income ($ mil.)	–	(0.7)	0.3	(0.2)	(0.2)	0.6
Market value ($ mil.)	17.1%	4.2	4.5	3.9	6.0	7.9
Employees	0.0%	35	38	38	31	35

ENCOMPASS HEALTH CORP   NYS: EHC

9001 Liberty Parkway
Birmingham, AL 35242
Phone: 205 967-7116
Fax: –
Web: www.encompasshealth.com

CEO: Mark Tarr
CFO: Douglas Coltharp
HR: –
FYE: December 31
Type: Public

Encompass Health (formerly HealthSouth) is there when the body's functioning abilities go south. One of the US' providers of post-acute healthcare services the company boasts a variety of facilities including inpatient rehabilitation hospitals hospice agencies and home health agencies. These agencies provide nursing and therapy to patients who are recovering from brain and spinal cord injuries complex orthopedic conditions amputations cardiac and pulmonary conditions or neurological disorders (such as strokes or aneurysms). Encompass Health operates some 460 inpatient outpatient home health and hospice centers in some 40 states and in Puerto Rico.

	Annual Growth	12/16	12/17	12/18	12/19	12/20
Sales ($ mil.)	6.2%	3,646.0	3,919.0	4,277.3	4,605.0	4,644.4
Net income ($ mil.)	3.5%	247.6	256.3	292.3	358.7	284.2
Market value ($ mil.)	19.0%	4,099.6	4,911.7	6,133.4	6,886.0	8,220.0
Employees	11.5%	27,968	29,370	30,060	31,570	43,178

ENCORE BANCSHARES INC.   NASDAQ: EBTX

9 Greenway Plaza Ste. 1000
Houston TX 77046
Phone: 713-787-3100
Fax: 585-321-1707
Web: www.harperhewes.com

CEO: –
CFO: –
HR: –
FYE: December 31
Type: Public

Encore! Encore! Encore Bancshares is taking its bows as the holding company for Encore Bank. Encore operates a dozen branches in Houston offering traditional retail banking products such as deposits mortgages and loans as well as wealth management and insurance through subsidiaries Town & Country Insurance Agency Encore Trust Company and Linscomb & Williams. The bank mostly caters to wealthy clients investment firms investors and privately owned business. Its staff of private bankers and relationship managers even makes house calls. Bank holding company Cadence Bancorp is buying Encore Bancshares for some $250 million; the acquiring firm was formed in 2010 to invest in community banks in the Southeast.

ENCORE CAPITAL GROUP INC   NMS: ECPG

350 Camino De La Reina, Suite 100
San Diego, CA 92108
Phone: 877 445-4581
Fax: –
Web: www.encorecapital.com

CEO: Craig Buick
CFO: Jonathan Clark
HR: –
FYE: December 31
Type: Public

Encore Capital Group is an international specialty finance company that provides debt recovery solutions and other related services across a broad range of financial assets. Encore Capital purchase portfolios of defaulted consumer receivables at deep discounts to face value and manage them by working with individuals as they repay their obligations and work toward financial recovery. Defaulted receivables are consumers' unpaid financial commitments to credit originators including banks credit unions consumer finance companies and commercial retailers. Defaulted receivables may also include receivables subject to bankruptcy proceedings. The company also provide debt servicing and other portfolio management services to credit originators for non-performing loans. Around 65% of total revenue comes from domestic operation.

	Annual Growth	12/16	12/17	12/18	12/19	12/20
Sales ($ mil.)	9.9%	1,029.3	1,187.0	1,362.0	1,397.7	1,501.4
Net income ($ mil.)	29.0%	76.6	83.2	115.9	167.9	211.8
Market value ($ mil.)	8.0%	898.0	1,319.6	736.6	1,108.4	1,220.9
Employees	3.6%	6,700	8,200	7,900	7,300	7,725

ENCORE ENERGY PARTNERS LP   NYSE: ENP

777 Main St. Ste. 1400
Fort Worth TX 76102
Phone: 817-877-9955
Fax: +86-790-666-9000
Web: www.ldksolar.com

CEO: –
CFO: –
HR: –
FYE: December 31
Type: Subsidiary

Encore Energy Partners is banking on a second trip to the well. The partnership acquires exploits and develops existing oil and natural gas properties. Encore Energy's primary assets consist of oil and natural gas properties in the Big Horn Basin of Wyoming and Montana the Permian Basin of West Texas and the Williston Basin of North Dakota. In 2009 the company reported proved reserves of 28.9 million barrels of oil and 84.7 billion cu. ft. of natural gas. In a move to expand its property base Denbury Resources acquired Encore Energy's former parent Encore Acquisition in early 2010 for $4.5 billion. Vanguard Natural Resourcesthen acquired Denbury Resources' 46% stake in Encore Energy for $380 million.

ENCORE NATIONWIDE INC.

18150 S FIGUEROA ST STE B
GARDENA, CA 902484215
Phone: 866-438-7823
Fax: –
Web: www.encorenationwide.com

CEO: Larry Hess
CFO: Tom Gowrie
HR: Lisa Vasquez
FYE: December 31
Type: Private

Encore Nationwide provides event staffing services for marketing and promotional campaigns. With a talent database of more than 12000 people across the US Encore can match the right person with appropriate event to create successful promotional events. The company can supply everything from promotional models and product demonstrators to emcees tour managers and all manner of casual laborers. Events include trade shows bar and nightclub promotions fashion shows and guerilla marketing campaigns.

	Annual Growth	12/09	12/10	12/11	12/12	12/13
Sales ($ mil.)	(0.6%)	–	–	–	11.8	11.7
Net income ($ mil.)	1118.5%	–	–	–	0.0	0.2
Market value ($ mil.)	–	–	–	–	–	–
Employees	–	–	–	–	–	25

ENCORE WIRE CORP.

NMS: WIRE

1329 Millwood Road
McKinney, TX 75069
Phone: 972 562-9473
Fax: 972 562-4744
Web: www.encorewire.com

CEO: Daniel Jones
CFO: Bret Eckert
HR: –
FYE: December 31
Type: Public

A low-cost manufacturer of copper electrical building wire and cable Encore Wire produces NM-B cable a sheathed cable used to wire homes apartments and manufactured housing and UF-B cable an underground feeder cable for outside lighting and remote residential building connections. Its inventory of stock-keeping units include THWN-2 cable an insulated feeder circuit and branch wiring for commercial and industrial buildings and other wires like armored cable. The company's principal customers are wholesale electrical distributors that sells its products to electrical contractors. The company was founded in 1989.

	Annual Growth	12/17	12/18	12/19	12/20	12/21
Sales ($ mil.)	22.2%	1,164.2	1,288.7	1,275.0	1,276.9	2,592.7
Net income ($ mil.)	68.6%	67.0	78.2	58.1	76.1	541.4
Market value ($ mil.)	31.0%	979.8	1,010.6	1,156.0	1,219.8	2,881.9
Employees	3.9%	1,235	1,278	1,380	1,289	1,440

ENDEAVOUR INTERNATIONAL CORP

NBB: ENDR Q

811 Main Street, Suite 2100
Houston, TX 77002
Phone: 713 307-8700
Fax: –
Web: www.endeavourcorp.com

CEO: Catherine L Stubbs
CFO: Catherine L Stubbs
HR: –
FYE: December 31
Type: Public

Like famous British explorer Captain James Cook and his vessel the Endeavour Endeavour International is looking to make new discoveries of great economic benefit. The exploration and production company has traditionally sought developed new oil assets by buying stakes in mature North Sea fields that the oil majors are moving away from. Endeavour International is also developing a second core area the US and has bought stakes in oil and gas properties particularly shale plays in Louisiana New Mexico and Texas and elsewhere. In 2012 Endeavour International reported proved reserves of 25.7 million barrels of oil equivalent (90% of which is in the North Sea).

	Annual Growth	12/09	12/10	12/11	12/12	12/13
Sales ($ mil.)	52.6%	62.3	71.7	60.1	219.1	337.7
Net income ($ mil.)	–	(41.0)	56.5	(131.0)	(126.2)	(95.5)
Market value ($ mil.)	48.5%	50.7	648.3	408.3	243.4	246.7
Employees	(1.2%)	43	58	102	87	41

ENDO HEALTH SOLUTIONS INC

NMS: ENDP

1400 Atwater Drive
Malvern, PA 19355
Phone: 484 216-0000
Fax: –
Web: www.endo.com

CEO: Rajiv De Silva
CFO: Suketu P Upadhyay
HR: –
FYE: December 31
Type: Public

Endo Health Solutions formerly known as Endo Pharmaceuticals wants the pain to end preferably through the drugs it acquires and markets. The company has a portfolio of both branded and generic prescription products for pain management and other health conditions. Its best-selling drug is Lidoderm a lidocaine patch that treats nerve pain caused by shingles. Endo also sells pain medications Percocet and Opana migraine therapy Frova cancer drug Valstar and urology treatment Sanctura. Its generics include morphine and oxycodone tablets. In addition the firm makes and sells urology and prostate devices and provides related medical services.

	Annual Growth	12/08	12/09	12/10	12/11	12/12
Sales ($ mil.)	24.5%	1,260.5	1,460.8	1,716.2	2,730.1	3,027.4
Net income ($ mil.)	–	261.7	266.3	259.0	187.6	(740.3)
Market value ($ mil.)	0.3%	2,867.3	2,273.5	3,956.4	3,825.7	2,906.1
Employees	39.7%	1,216	1,487	2,947	4,566	4,629

ENDOCYTE INC

NMS: ECYT

3000 Kent Avenue, Suite A1-100
West Lafayette, IN 47906
Phone: 765 463-7175
Fax: –
Web: www.endocyte.com

CEO: Michael A Sherman
CFO: Michael T Andriole
HR: –
FYE: December 31
Type: Public

Endocyte develops receptor-targeted therapeutics (or "smart drugs") that aim to take out bad cells without causing collateral damage. Receptor-targeted therapeutics are a precision alternative to non-targeted cancer drugs that can destroy healthy cells. Founded in 1996 Endocyte uses its drug guidance system to deliver drugs including small molecule cancer drugs and RNA-based therapies directly to cancerous cells while leaving other cells unaffected. The firm has a pipeline of small molecule drug conjugates (SMDCs) in various stages of development. Its lead candidate Vynfinit (vintafolide) is designed to treat ovarian cancer.

	Annual Growth	12/12	12/13	12/14	12/15	12/16
Sales ($ mil.)	(78.8%)	34.7	64.9	70.4	0.1	0.1
Net income ($ mil.)	–	(17.3)	(18.0)	5.5	(41.3)	(43.9)
Market value ($ mil.)	(27.0%)	380.6	452.6	266.6	169.9	108.1
Employees	1.7%	71	91	81	78	76

ENDOLOGIX INC

NMS: ELGX

2 Musick
Irvine, CA 92618
Phone: 949 595-7200
Fax: –

CEO: John Onopchenko
CFO: Cindy Pinto
HR: –
FYE: December 31
Type: Public

Medical device maker Endologix strengthens weak arteries. The company makes endovascular systems that use stents graft material and catheter delivery devices to treat abdominal aortic aneurysm (AAA or weakening of the aortic wall). Its endovascular aneurysm repair (EVAR) products include the Endologix AFX Endovascular AAA System (AFX) the VELA Proximal Endograft and the Ovation Abdominal Stent Graft System. Its endovascular aneurysm sealing (EVAS) products (available outside of the US) include the Nellix EVAS System; aortic and limb extensions; and accessories such as compatible guidewires and inflation devices. Most of the company's revenue comes from the US.

	Annual Growth	12/14	12/15	12/16	12/17	12/18
Sales ($ mil.)	1.5%	147.6	153.6	192.9	181.2	156.5
Net income ($ mil.)	–	(32.4)	(50.4)	(154.7)	(66.4)	(79.7)
Market value ($ mil.)	(53.5%)	158.2	102.4	59.2	55.3	7.4
Employees	(2.7%)	590	619	782	675	528

ENDURANCE INTERNATIONAL GROUP HOLDINGS INC
NMS: EIGI

10 Corporate Drive, Suite 300
Burlington, MA 01803
Phone: 781 852-3200
Fax: –
Web: www.endurance.com

CEO: –
CFO: –
HR: –
FYE: December 31
Type: Public

Endurance International helps small businesses thrive on the Internet. The company owns a portfolio of brands that offer website design and hosting domain name registry and web security as well as e-commerce tools online marketing and search engine optimization. Bluehost targets small businesses (fewer than five employees) with technical know-how while HostGator helps those who need to offer more customer support. Altogether the company offers a comprehensive suite of some 150 products and services under the brands A Small Orange Domain.com Dotster FatCow Homestead HostMonster JustHost iPage and iPower. Endurance International counts more than 3 million subscribers. The company went public in 2013.

	Annual Growth	12/15	12/16	12/17	12/18	12/19
Sales ($ mil.)	10.7%	741.3	1,111.1	1,176.9	1,145.3	1,113.3
Net income ($ mil.)	–	(25.8)	(72.8)	(107.3)	4.5	(12.3)
Market value ($ mil.)	(19.0%)	1,598.6	1,360.2	1,228.6	972.6	687.4
Employees	9.7%	2,593	4,005	3,664	3,901	3,762

ENEL GREEN POWER NORTH AMERICA INC.

1 Tech Dr. Ste. 220
Andover MA 01810
Phone: 978-681-1900
Fax: 978-681-7727
Web: www.enelgreenpower.com/en-gb/ena/

CEO: –
CFO: Marco Fossataro
HR: –
FYE: December 31
Type: Subsidiary

You can't spell renewable without Enel. The North American arm of Italy's Enel Green Power S.p.A. owns and operates more than 70 renewable energy plants in 20 states and two Canadian provinces. Enel Green Power North America's plants have a capacity to generate 800 MW of power through wind hydropower biomass and geothermal energy. Its wind farms use Vestas and GE Energy turbines; its largest project the Smoky Hills Wind Farm in Kansas has 155 wind turbines that alone generate 250 MW of power (enough to power 85000 homes for a year). Enel North America's only biomass plant is located in Quebec where it offsets 1 million tons of carbon dioxide by burning wood waste each year.

ENERGEN CORP.
NYS: EGN

605 Richard Arrington Jr. Boulevard North
Birmingham, AL 35203-2707
Phone: 205 326-2700
Fax: –
Web: www.energen.com

CEO: James T McManus II
CFO: Charles W Porter Jr
HR: –
FYE: December 31
Type: Public

Energen develops acquires explores for and produces oil natural gas and natural gas liquids across the continental US. The oil and gas exploration and production company operates principally through Energen Resources Corporation which in 2015 had proved reserves of 355 million barrels of oil equivalent mainly located in the Permian Basin (West Texas). Oil accounted for 49% of the company's proved reserves; natural gas 31%; and natural gas liquids 20%. In 2014 Energen exited the gas utility business selling Alabama Gas Corporation (Alagasco) to Spire Inc. for $1.6 billion.

	Annual Growth	12/12	12/13	12/14	12/15	12/16
Sales ($ mil.)	(24.2%)	1,617.2	1,738.7	1,679.2	878.6	532.9
Net income ($ mil.)	–	253.6	204.6	568.0	(945.7)	(167.5)
Market value ($ mil.)	6.3%	4,374.3	6,863.7	6,185.6	3,976.6	5,594.7
Employees	(29.5%)	1,575	1,434	550	470	390

ENERGY & ENVIRONMENTAL SERVICES INC
NBB: EESE

2601 N.W. Expressway, Suite 605W
Oklahoma, OK 73112
Phone: 405 843-8996
Fax: 405 843-0819
Web: www.eesokc.com

CEO: –
CFO: –
HR: –
FYE: December 31
Type: Public

Turning subterranean natural gas into a useful energy is the goal of exploration and development independent Energas Resources. Operating through its A.T. Gas Gathering Systems and TGC subsidiaries the company is primarily focused on exploring and producing in the Arkoma Basin in Oklahoma and the Powder River Basin in Wyoming. Energas Resources has proved reserves of 22143 barrels of oil and 1.9 billion cu. ft. of natural gas. In 2007 the company sold most of its assets in the shallow Devonian Shale natural gas strata in the Appalachian Basin of Kentucky. President George Shaw owns about 24% of the company.

	Annual Growth	12/16	12/17	12/18	12/19	12/20
Sales ($ mil.)	44.3%	2.0	3.8	7.2	8.6	8.5
Net income ($ mil.)	–	(2.1)	(2.4)	0.1	(0.3)	(1.7)
Market value ($ mil.)	(47.2%)	32.1	31.6	10.2	4.8	2.5
Employees	31.4%	–	–	22	64	38

ENERGY & EXPLORATION PARTNERS INC.

Two City Place Ste. 1700 100 Throckmorton
Fort Worth TX 76102
Phone: 817-789-6712
Fax: 510-995-9092
Web: www.singulex.com

CEO: –
CFO: –
HR: –
FYE: December 31
Type: Private

After exploring for energy Energy & Exploration Partners Inc. (ENEXP) might need a little R&R. The independent exploration and production company formed in July 2012 to begin buying rights to three different oil and natural gas plays across the US. ENEXP has almost 45000 net acres in three areas: the Eagle Ford Shale and Woodbine Sandstone formations in East Texas; the Wolfcamp play in the Permian Basin in West Texas; and the Niobrara Shale in the Denver-Julesburg Basin in Colorado and Wyoming. The company has not yet commenced operations but it did file a $275 million initial public offering in September 2012.

ENERGY CONVERSION DEVICES INC.
NASDAQ: ENER

2956 Waterview Dr.
Rochester Hills MI 48309
Phone: 248-293-0440
Fax: 248-844-1214
Web: www.energyconversiondevices.com

CEO: –
CFO: –
HR: –
FYE: June 30
Type: Public

Energy Conversion Devices (ECD) gets a charge out of its technology. ECD makes storage products that generate and store power or store information electronically. Subsidiary United Solar Ovonic which accounts for more than 90% of sales makes flexible solar panels mainly for roofs but also for telecom lighting and other uses. The Ovonic Materials Division produces materials for use in NiMH and other batteries. ECD's largest customers are Enel Green Power EDF En Developpement Solardis-Soprasolar and Centrosolar AG. Around 85% of sales come from outside the US; customers in France Italy Germany and Spain account for more than two-thirds of sales. In 2012 ECD filed for Chapter 11 bankruptcy.

ENERGY FOCUS INC
NAS: EFOI

32000 Aurora Road, Suite B
Solon, OH 44139
Phone: 440 715-1300
Fax: –
Web: www.energyfocusinc.com

CEO: James Tu
CFO: Tod Nestor
HR: –
FYE: December 31
Type: Public

The Illuminator may be coming to a theater near you but it isn't a movie— its what Energy Focus does. The company makes products such as energy-efficient fiber-optic light-emitting diode ceramic metal halide and high-intensity discharge lighting systems. Serving the commercial/industrial and pool lighting markets Energy Focus' systems illuminate cinemas shopping malls parking garages performing arts centers restaurants pools/spas and homes. Its lighting products include acrylic accent fixtures downlight fixtures spotlights and display-case lighting. The company's Stones River Companies (SRC) unit concentrates on turnkey lighting projects and solar retrofit jobs.

	Annual Growth	12/16	12/17	12/18	12/19	12/20
Sales ($ mil.)	(14.2%)	31.0	19.8	18.1	12.7	16.8
Net income ($ mil.)	–	(16.9)	(11.3)	(9.1)	(7.4)	(6.0)
Market value ($ mil.)	(1.4%)	15.0	8.6	2.2	1.7	14.2
Employees	(18.1%)	131	74	66	46	59

ENERGY FUTURE HOLDINGS CORP
NYS: TXU 19

1601 Bryan Street
Dallas, TX 75201-3411
Phone: 214 812-4600
Fax: –
Web: www.energyfutureholdings.com

CEO: Paul M Keglevic
CFO: Anthony R Horton
HR: –
FYE: December 31
Type: Public

Energy Future Holdings has seen the future and it works — with electricity. It operates the largest nonregulated retail electric provider in Texas (TXU Energy) with more than 1.7 million customers and its Luminant unit has a generating capacity of more than 13700 MW in the state. Energy Future Holdings has regulated power transmission and distribution operations through 80%-owned Oncor Electric Delivery which operates the largest regulated distribution and transmission system in Texas providing power to more than 3.2 million electric delivery points over 120000 miles of transmission and distribution lines. The company filed for bankruptcy protection in 2014 and expected to exit bankruptcy in 2016.

	Annual Growth	12/11	12/12	12/13	12/14	12/15
Sales ($ mil.)	(6.5%)	7,040.0	5,636.0	5,899.0	5,978.0	5,370.0
Net income ($ mil.)	–	(1,913.0)	(3,360.0)	(2,218.0)	(6,406.0)	(5,342.0)
Market value ($ mil.)	–	–	–	–	–	–
Employees	(1.2%)	9,300	9,100	9,000	8,920	8,860

ENERGY RECOVERY INC
NMS: ERII

1717 Doolittle Drive
San Leandro, CA 94577
Phone: 510 483-7370
Fax: –
Web: www.energyrecovery.com

CEO: yu Lang Mao
CFO: Joshua Ballard
HR: –
FYE: December 31
Type: Public

Desalination makes seawater potable; Energy Recovery (ERI) makes desalination practical. The company designs develops and manufactures energy recovery devices used in sea water reverse osmosis (SWRO) desalination plants. The SWRO process is energy intensive using high pressure to drive salt water through membranes to produce fresh water. The company's main product the PX Pressure Exchanger helps recapture and recycle up to 98% of the energy available in the high-pressure reject stream a by-product of the SWRO process. The PX can reduce the energy consumption of a desalination plant by up to 60% compared with a plant lacking an energy recovery device. Subsidiary Pump Engineering also makes high pressure pumps.

	Annual Growth	12/16	12/17	12/18	12/19	12/20
Sales ($ mil.)	21.4%	54.7	63.2	74.5	86.9	119.0
Net income ($ mil.)	124.8%	1.0	12.4	22.1	10.9	26.4
Market value ($ mil.)	7.1%	583.1	493.0	379.2	551.6	768.5
Employees	15.8%	120	133	143	188	216

ENERGY RESEARCH AND DEVELOPMENT AUTHORITY, NEW YORK STATE

17 COLUMBIA CIR
ALBANY, NY 122035156
Phone: 518-862-1090
Fax: –
Web: www.energyplan.ny.gov

CEO: John B Rhodes
CFO: –
HR: –
FYE: March 31
Type: Private

The New York State Energy Research and Development Authority (NYSERDA) uses technological innovation to solve the state's energy and environmental problems. The public benefit corporation funds energy supply and conservation research and energy-related environmental issues. It also conducts research projects that help state and city groups solve their energy problems. Its Energy Efficiency Services group works helps more than 450 schools businesses and municipalities find ways to reduce their energy costs. Investor-owned electric and gas utilities grants and contributions from the New York Power Authority and the Long Island Power Authority fund NYSERDA which was created in 1975.

	Annual Growth	03/14	03/15	03/16	03/17	03/19
Sales ($ mil.)	7215.0%	–	–	–	0.2	1,091.6
Net income ($ mil.)	–	–	–	–	(0.6)	51.2
Market value ($ mil.)	–	–	–	–	–	–
Employees	–	–	–	–	–	345

ENERGY SERVICES OF AMERICA CORP.
NBB: ESOA

75 West 3rd Ave.
Huntington, WV 25701
Phone: 304 522-3868
Fax: –
Web: www.energyservicesofamerica.com

CEO: Douglas Reynolds
CFO: Charles Crimmel
HR: –
FYE: September 30
Type: Public

When energy companies don't want to get their hands dirty they can call on Energy Services of America (ESA). The service company provides installation repair and maintenance work primarily for natural gas and electricity providers. It also installs water and sewer lines for government agencies. ESA operates mostly in the Mid Atlantic region; its customers include Spectra Energy Hitachi Columbia Gas Transmission Toyota MarkWest Energy and American Electric Power. Typically the pipes steel plates wire and fittings used by the company are supplied by their customer keeping costs low. The company operates through subsidiaries ST Pipeline and C.J. Hughes Construction which it purchased in 2008.

	Annual Growth	09/17	09/18	09/19	09/20	09/21
Sales ($ mil.)	(3.4%)	140.5	135.5	174.5	119.2	122.5
Net income ($ mil.)	–	(0.7)	2.5	2.0	2.4	9.1
Market value ($ mil.)	12.1%	14.3	15.6	10.2	11.2	22.6
Employees	2.1%	648	842	484	553	703

ENERGY SERVICES PROVIDERS, INC.

3700 LAKESIDE DR 6
MIRAMAR, FL 330273264
Phone: 305-947-7880
Fax: –

CEO: Douglas W Marcille
CFO: –
HR: –
FYE: December 31
Type: Private

Energy Services Providers Inc. (ESPI) is an electricity and natural gas supplier dedicated to providing more efficient energy services in New York's deregulated power market. ESPI is one of about 20 energy service company (ESCOs) offered to customers of public utility Niagara Mohawk. ESPI also offers cost-saving services such as energy audits energy-efficient lighting HVAC compressors and controls. The company promises to save its customers some 7% of their electric bills through its energy-efficient offerings. ESPI was founded in 2002 by CEO Franklin Lewis. In 2009 the company was acquired by US Gas & Electric a portfolio company of investment firm MVC Capital.

	Annual Growth	12/07	12/08	12/09	12/10	12/11
Sales ($ mil.)	30.5%	–	–	–	73.9	96.5
Net income ($ mil.)	81.3%	–	–	–	4.1	7.4
Market value ($ mil.)	–	–	–	–	–	–
Employees	–	–	–	–	–	41

ENERGY TRANSFER LP — NYS: ET

8111 Westchester Drive, Suite 600
Dallas, TX 75225
Phone: 214 981-0700
Fax: –
Web: www.energytransfer.com

CEO: Thomas Long
CFO: Bradford Whitehurst
HR: –
FYE: December 31
Type: Public

Energy Transfer LP transfers natural gas and other energy resources through its massive network of US-based pipelines. The primary activities in which the company is engaged which are in the US and Canada and the operating subsidiaries through which it conduct those activities are natural gas midstream and intrastate transportation and storage oil NGL and refined products transportation terminaling services and acquisition and marketing activities as well as NGL storage and fractionation services. In addition Energy Transfer own investments in other businesses including Sunoco LP and USAC. Energy Transfer was formed in 1996 and became a publicly traded partnership in 2004.

	Annual Growth	12/16	12/17	12/18	12/19	12/20
Sales ($ mil.)	1.0%	37,504.0	40,523.0	54,087.0	54,213.0	38,954.0
Net income ($ mil.)	–	995.0	954.0	1,694.0	3,592.0	(648.0)
Market value ($ mil.)	–	0.0	0.0	0.0	0.0	0.0
Employees	(22.1%)	30,992	29,486	11,768	12,812	11,421

ENERGY TRANSFER OPERATING LP — NYS: ETP PRE

8111 Westchester Drive, Suite 600
Dallas, TX 75225
Phone: 214 981-0700
Fax: –
Web: www.energytransfer.com

CEO: –
CFO: –
HR: –
FYE: December 31
Type: Public

Energy Transfer Operating (ETO) is the main operating subsidiary of diversified energy asset firm Energy Transfer LP. ETO's crude oil segment (about 30% of sales) operates more than 9500 miles of pipelines that provide crude transportation services to oil markets in the Southwest Midwest and Northeast US. The NGL and Refined Products segment (20% of sales) operates about 4700 miles of natural gas liquids (NGL) pipelines and fractionation facilities. The company's midstream activities (nearly 15% of sales) include the gathering compression and treating of natural gas. Other operations include more than 28000 miles of interstate and intrastate natural gas pipelines and an LNG import terminal and regasification facility in Louisiana. The company derives about 30% of revenue through a 35% stake in Sunoco LP.

	Annual Growth	12/15	12/16	12/17	12/18	12/19
Sales ($ mil.)	50.7%	10,486.0	9,151.0	29,054.0	54,087.0	54,032.0
Net income ($ mil.)	79.5%	393.0	705.0	2,081.0	3,020.0	4,084.0
Market value ($ mil.)	–	–	–	–	0.0	0.0
Employees	49.6%	2,500	2,575	506,829	11,768	12,517

ENERGYUNITED ELECTRIC MEMBERSHIP CORPORATION

567 MOCKSVILLE HWY
STATESVILLE, NC 286258269
Phone: 704-873-5241
Fax: –
Web: www.energyunited.com

CEO: H Wayne Wilkins
CFO: –
HR: Lynn Bear
FYE: December 31
Type: Private

Electrical energy and propane energy come together under the auspices of EnergyUnited Electric Membership. One of North Carolina's largest power utilities EnergyUnited distributes electricity to more than 120000 residential and business customers in 19 counties. The member-owned not-for-profit cooperative also provides propane to 23000 customers in 74 counties in North and South Carolina and it also offers home security bill management and facility monitoring services. The third largest supplier of residential electricity in the state its service territory includes three of the largest cities in North Carolina - Charlotte Greensboro and Winston-Salem.

	Annual Growth	12/13	12/14	12/15	12/16	12/17
Sales ($ mil.)	0.9%	–	274.8	281.3	291.3	282.6
Net income ($ mil.)	(12.5%)	–	9.6	9.8	9.2	6.5
Market value ($ mil.)	–	–	–	–	–	–
Employees	–	–	–	–	–	185

ENERNOC INC — NMS: ENOC

One Marina Park Drive, Suite 400
Boston, MA 02210
Phone: 617 224-9900
Fax: –
Web: www.enernoc.com

CEO: Mike Storch
CFO: –
HR: –
FYE: December 31
Type: Public

EnerNOC knocks on the door of large energy customers and kindly asks them to dim the lights. Not literally of course but the company has added its technology to utility companies' traditional demand response model. Rather than manually calling up their largest end users EnerNOC's Network Operations Center (NOC) through its DemandSMART program remotely monitors their customers' energy assets and has the capability to adjust their electrical use. It caters to commercial industrial and technological educational and other institutional organizations as well as electric power grid operators and utilities. EnerNOC has operations around the world.

	Annual Growth	12/11	12/12	12/13	12/14	12/15
Sales ($ mil.)	8.7%	286.6	278.0	383.5	471.9	399.6
Net income ($ mil.)	–	(13.4)	(22.3)	22.1	12.1	(185.1)
Market value ($ mil.)	(22.9%)	334.8	361.9	530.0	475.8	118.6
Employees	22.9%	599	685	716	1,125	1,366

ENERPAC TOOL GROUP CORP — NYS: EPAC

N86 W12500 Westbrook Crossing
Menomonee Falls, WI 53051
Phone: 262 293-1500
Fax: –
Web: www.enerpactoolgroup.com

CEO: Paul Sternlieb
CFO: Ricky Dillon
HR: –
FYE: August 31
Type: Public

Founded in 1910 Enerpac Tool Group Corp. (formerly Actuant) is a premier industrial tools and services company serving a broad and diverse set of customers in more than 100 countries. It provides engineering and manufacturing of high pressure hydraulic tools controlled force products and solutions for precise positioning of heavy loads that help customers safely and reliably tackle some of the most challenging jobs around the world. It generates over 30% of its revenue from the US.

	Annual Growth	08/17	08/18	08/19	08/20	08/21
Sales ($ mil.)	(16.7%)	1,095.8	1,182.6	654.8	493.3	528.7
Net income ($ mil.)	–	(66.2)	(21.6)	(249.1)	0.7	38.1
Market value ($ mil.)	1.1%	1,448.3	1,773.6	1,337.5	1,252.6	1,515.2
Employees	(21.0%)	5,400	5,300	4,900	2,300	2,100

ENERSYS — NYS: ENS

2366 Bernville Road
Reading, PA 19605
Phone: 610 208-1991
Fax: –
Web: www.enersys.com

CEO: David Shaffer
CFO: Michael J Schmidtlein
HR: –
FYE: March 31
Type: Public

EnerSys is a world leader in stored energy solutions for industrial applications. The company manufactures markets and distributes industrial batteries and related products such as chargers outdoor cabinet enclosures power equipment and battery accessories and provides related after-market and customer-support services for its products. The battery manufacturer sells directly and through distributors to more than 10000 customers in more than 100 countries. It serves distributors warehouse operators retailers airports and mine operators as well as customers in the telecom electric utilities emergency lighting security systems and space satellites markets.

	Annual Growth	03/17	03/18	03/19	03/20	03/21
Sales ($ mil.)	5.9%	2,367.1	2,581.9	2,808.0	3,087.9	2,977.9
Net income ($ mil.)	(2.7%)	160.2	119.6	160.2	137.1	143.4
Market value ($ mil.)	3.6%	3,374.9	2,965.8	2,785.8	2,117.1	3,882.0
Employees	4.2%	9,400	9,600	11,000	11,400	11,100

ENERVEST LTD.

1001 Fannin St. Ste. 800
Houston TX 77002-6707
Phone: 713-659-3500
Fax: +974-4429-3750
Web: www.industriesqatar.com.qa

CEO: John B Walker
CFO: James M Vanderhider
HR: –
FYE: December 31
Type: Private

Want to invest in energy? Call up EnerVest. The investment group manages oil and gas properties on behalf of institutional investors such as pension plans university endowments and family foundations. Investors pool their money into a fund for EnerVest to buy and operate oil and gas wells; the company acts as a general partner and distributes dividends from the proceeds. Its 12th fund closed in December 2010 raising $1.5 billion from about 115 investors. EnerVest owns 19000 onshore wells spanning 4 million acres in a dozen states. It also owns 71% of EV Energy Partners a publicly traded master limited partnership through general partner is EV Energy GP.

ENGLEFIELD OIL COMPANY

447 James Pkwy.
Heath OH 43056
Phone: 740-928-8215
Fax: 740-928-1531
Web: www.englefieldoil.com

CEO: –
CFO: –
HR: –
FYE: June 30
Type: Private

Englefield Oil Company supplies fuel and lubricants and operates about 100 convenience stores under the Duke and Duchess Shoppe banner in Ohio and West Virginia. Many of the company's convenience stores sell BP brand gasoline. In addition Englefield Oil operates several truck stops a pair of Super 8 motels several Taco Bell Express restaurants and other various businesses in Ohio and West Virginia. Englefield also operates more than a dozen Pacific Pride automated commercial fueling sites. Chairman F. W. "Bill" Englefield III founded the company in 1961 with three service stations and an office operating out of his basement.

ENGELBERTH CONSTRUCTION, INC.

463 MOUNTAIN VIEW DR # 201
COLCHESTER, VT 054465952
Phone: 802-655-0100
Fax: –
Web: www.engelberth.com

CEO: –
CFO: Thomas J Clavelle
HR: Gina Catanzarita
FYE: December 31
Type: Private

Engelberth Construction has spent more than thirty years building its business but it doesn't take nearly as long in the business of building. Specializing in commercial construction the company offers construction management design/build general contracting and additional services for educational commericial multi-family residential and industrial clients. Engelberth Construction works primarily in the New England region (Vermont and New Hampshire) of the US. Otto Engelberth founded Engelberth Construction as a small two-person home-based construction business in 1972.

	Annual Growth	12/11	12/12	12/13	12/14	12/15
Sales ($ mil.)	–	–	0.0	94.4	94.4	94.4
Net income ($ mil.)	–	–	0.0	1.1	1.1	1.1
Market value ($ mil.)	–	–	–	–	–	–
Employees	–	–	–	–	–	150

ENGLOBAL CORP.   NAS: ENG

11740 Katy Fwy - Energy Tower III, 11th floor
Houston, TX 77079
Phone: 281 878-1000
Fax: –
Web: www.englobal.com

CEO: Mark Hess
CFO: Darren Spriggs
HR: –
FYE: December 26
Type: Public

ENGlobal is engineering its way into the hearts of energy companies. A leading provider of engineering and automation services the company provides engineering and systems services procurement construction management inspection and control system automation design fabrication and implementation to the pipeline and process divisions of major oil and gas companies primarily in the US. Following a downturn in its business and heavy losses ENGlobal has repositioned itself as a leaner operation by selling or discontinuing certain lines of business including its Field Solutions and Electrical Services divisions closing offices and shedding about 75% of its workforce. ENGlobal was founded in 1994.

	Annual Growth	12/16	12/17	12/18	12/19	12/20
Sales ($ mil.)	2.1%	59.2	55.8	54.0	56.4	64.4
Net income ($ mil.)	–	(2.3)	(16.3)	(5.7)	(1.5)	(0.6)
Market value ($ mil.)	5.4%	65.9	24.0	18.7	27.3	81.3
Employees	(3.6%)	279	252	238	251	241

ENGILITY HOLDINGS INC (NEW)   NYS: EGL

4803 Stonecroft Blvd.
Chantilly, VA 20151
Phone: 703 633-8300
Fax: –
Web: www.engilitycorp.com

CEO: –
CFO: –
HR: –
FYE: December 31
Type: Public

When Uncle Sam says "I want you for the US Army" Engility Holdings strives to answer the call and then some. A government services provider Engility offers government agencies a myriad of support services including systems engineering and software development program management defense-related education training and staffing field management and logistics and language translation services. Its customers have included the US Department of Defense and foreign governments as well as US civilian agencies and commercial entities. Engility was formed in 2012 when L-3 Communications spun off five of its government services businesses which were in turn organized under the Engility Holdings banner.

	Annual Growth	12/12	12/13	12/14	12/15	12/16
Sales ($ mil.)	5.8%	1,655.3	1,407.4	1,367.1	2,085.6	2,076.4
Net income ($ mil.)	–	(350.4)	49.5	35.4	(235.4)	(10.8)
Market value ($ mil.)	15.0%	708.3	1,228.3	1,574.0	1,194.5	1,239.4
Employees	3.9%	7,800	6,600	6,600	9,800	9,100

ENLINK MIDSTREAM LLC   NYS: ENLC

1722 Routh St., Suite 1300
Dallas, TX 75201
Phone: 214 953-9500
Fax: –
Web: www.enlink.com

CEO: Barry Davis
CFO: Pablo Mercado
HR: –
FYE: December 31
Type: Public

EnLink Midstream LLC is a US midstream energy company that transports stores and sells natural gas NGLs crude oil and condensates to industrial end-users utilities marketers and other pipelines. Its asset network includes approximately 11900 miles of pipelines more than 20 natural gas processing plants seven fractionators barge and rail terminals storage and crude oil trucking services. EnLink Midstream primarily focuses in gathering compressing treating processing fractioning transporting and stabilizing gasses. Generates all of its sales from the US the company also offers purchasing and marketing capabilities brine disposal wells and equity investments in certain joint ventures.

	Annual Growth	12/16	12/17	12/18	12/19	12/20
Sales ($ mil.)	(2.2%)	4,252.4	5,739.6	7,699.0	6,052.9	3,893.8
Net income ($ mil.)	–	(460.0)	212.8	(13.2)	(1,119.3)	(421.5)
Market value ($ mil.)	(33.6%)	9,322.7	8,613.1	4,644.2	2,999.9	1,815.6
Employees	(7.7%)	1,472	1,494	1,449	1,355	1,069

ENLINK MIDSTREAM PARTNERS LP   NYS: ENLK

1722 ROUTH ST., SUITE 1300
Dallas, TX 75201
Phone: 214 953-9500
Fax: –
Web: www.crosstexenergy.com

CEO: Barry E Davis
CFO: Pablo Mercado
HR: –
FYE: December 31
Type: Public

Across the Gulf of Mexico region in Louisiana and in East and North Texas EnLink Midstream Partners (formerly Crosstex Energy LP) is hard at work pushing natural gas. The company gathers transports processes and fractionates natural gas and natural gas liquids through its infrastructure of about 3500 miles of natural pipeline 12 processing plants and six fractionators. EnLink Midstream Partners provides services for 3.3 billion cu. ft. of natural gas per day (6% of US daily production). In 2014 Crosstex Energy combined its assets with Devon Energy's US midstream assets and became EnLink Midstream Partners.

	Annual Growth	12/12	12/13	12/14	12/15	12/16
Sales ($ mil.)	26.6%	1,655.9	1,943.2	3,500.4	4,452.1	4,252.4
Net income ($ mil.)	–	(40.1)	(113.1)	181.1	(1,377.8)	(565.2)
Market value ($ mil.)	6.1%	4,988.5	9,462.8	9,946.3	5,684.6	6,315.4
Employees	18.9%	736	817	1,148	1,432	1,472

ENNIS INC   NYS: EBF

2441 Presidential Pkwy.
Midlothian, TX 76065
Phone: 972 775-9801
Fax: 972 775-9820
Web: www.ennis.com

CEO: Keith Walters
CFO: Vera Burnett
HR: Sheila McGuire
FYE: February 28
Type: Public

Ennis is the largest provider of business forms pressure-seal forms labels tags envelopes and presentation folders to independent distributors in the US. Its print units include Northstar Computer Forms Witt Printing and Adams McClure. Customers include fulfillment companies payroll and accounts payable software companies and advertising agencies among others. About 95% of the business products it manufactures are custom and semi-custom products constructed in a wide variety of sizes colors number of parts and quantities on an individual job basis depending upon the customers' specifications. Founded in 1909 the company operates more than 55 manufacturing plants in the US.

	Annual Growth	02/17	02/18	02/19	02/20	02/21
Sales ($ mil.)	0.1%	356.9	370.2	400.8	438.4	358.0
Net income ($ mil.)	91.8%	1.8	32.9	37.4	38.3	24.1
Market value ($ mil.)	4.9%	424.3	506.0	550.1	521.6	514.3
Employees	(2.8%)	2,348	2,183	2,470	2,505	2,096

ENOVA SYSTEMS INC   NBB: ENVS

2945 Columbia Street
Torrance, CA 90503
Phone: 650 346-4770
Fax: –
Web: www.enovasystems.com

CEO: –
CFO: –
HR: –
FYE: December 31
Type: Public

Enova Systems makes commercial digital power management systems for controlling and monitoring electric power in automobiles and stationary power generators. Products include hybrid-electric drive systems electric drive motors electric motor controllers hybrid drive systems battery care units safety disconnect units generator units fuel cell management units and fuel cell power conditioning units. The company counts EDO First Auto Works of China Ford Motor Hyundai Motor Navistar International and Volvo/Mack among its customers. Enova gets more than half of its sales outside the US primarily in China.

	Annual Growth	12/09	12/10	12/11	12/12	12/13
Sales ($ mil.)	(47.5%)	5.6	8.6	6.6	1.1	0.4
Net income ($ mil.)	–	(7.0)	(7.4)	(7.0)	(8.2)	(2.9)
Market value ($ mil.)	(73.6%)	82.4	57.1	7.4	0.7	0.4
Employees	(51.5%)	36	59	30	3	2

ENPHASE ENERGY INC.   NMS: ENPH

47281 Bayside Parkway
Fremont, CA 94538
Phone: 877 774-7000
Fax: –
Web: www.enphase.com

CEO: Badrinarayanan Kothandaraman
CFO: Eric Branderiz
HR: –
FYE: December 31
Type: Public

Enphase Energy is ready to usher in a new phase of solar power. The company makes all-in-one solar panel systems for residential and commercial use in the US and Canada. Unlike typical small-scale photovoltaic systems Enphase's solar modules are connected on a microinverter system where each panel has its own inverter that converts the sun's rays into electricity. The company claims its microinverter technology is more energy efficient than having all the panels hooked up to one big inverter. Enphase Energy sells its solar power systems to a network of thousands of distributors.

	Annual Growth	12/17	12/18	12/19	12/20	12/21
Sales ($ mil.)	48.2%	286.2	316.2	624.3	774.4	1,382.0
Net income ($ mil.)	–	(45.2)	(11.6)	161.1	134.0	145.4
Market value ($ mil.)	195.2%	322.7	633.3	3,498.7	23,494.4	24,494.6
Employees	61.0%	336	427	577	850	2,260

ENPRO INDUSTRIES INC   NYS: NPO

5605 Carnegie Boulevard, Suite 500
Charlotte, NC 28209
Phone: 704 731-1500
Fax: –
Web: www.enproindustries.com

CEO: Eric Vaillancourt
CFO: J. Milton Childress
HR: –
FYE: December 31
Type: Public

EnPro is a US manufacturer of sealing systems engineered products and heavy-duty engines. The company has three principal business lines: Sealing Products (gaskets dynamic seals joints compression packing brake pads milometers); Engineered Materials (engineered plastics and bearings and rings and valve assemblies for engines and compressors); and Advanced Surface Technologies segment (cleaning coating testing refurbishment and verification services for critical components and assemblies). These serve the automotive aerospace chemical and petrochemical and food processing power generation and semiconductor industries. More than 50% of sales are generated in the US.

	Annual Growth	12/16	12/17	12/18	12/19	12/20
Sales ($ mil.)	(2.5%)	1,187.7	1,309.6	1,532.0	1,205.7	1,074.0
Net income ($ mil.)	–	(40.1)	539.8	24.6	38.3	184.4
Market value ($ mil.)	2.9%	1,383.3	1,920.3	1,234.2	1,373.5	1,550.9
Employees	(3.1%)	5,000	6,000	5,900	5,300	4,400

ENSERVCO CORP   ASE: ENSV

14133 County Road 9 1/2
Longmont, CO 80504
Phone: 303 333-3678
Fax: 702 974-3417
Web: www.enservco.com

CEO: Richard Murphy
CFO: Marjorie Hargrave
HR: –
FYE: December 31
Type: Public

Aspen Exploration (which does business as ENSERVCO) is a leading provider of fluid-related services to the oil and gas production industry in the US. In 2008 Aspen Exploration announced that because of high expenses and rising debt it was pursuing strategic alternatives and subsequently sold its exploration and production oil and gas assets. In 2010 the shell company merged with oilfield services provider Dillco Fluid Service and reorganized under the ENSERVCO brand name. Its two operating subsidiaries (Dillco Fluid Services and Heat Wave Hot Oil) operate a fleet of 200 vehicles. Services include acidizing water hauling and disposal and well-site construction.

	Annual Growth	12/16	12/17	12/18	12/19	12/20
Sales ($ mil.)	(10.7%)	24.6	40.8	46.9	43.0	15.7
Net income ($ mil.)	–	(8.6)	(6.9)	(5.9)	(7.7)	(2.5)
Market value ($ mil.)	35.5%	3.5	4.1	2.3	1.2	11.8
Employees	(19.0%)	204	249	231	186	88

ENSIGN GROUP INC

NMS: ENSG

29222 Rancho Viejo Road, Suite 127
San Juan Capistrano, CA 92675
Phone: 949 487-9500
Fax: –
Web: www.ensigngroup.net

CEO: Barry Port
CFO: Suzanne Snapper
HR: –
FYE: December 31
Type: Public

The Ensign Group offers skilled nursing senior living and rehabilitative care services through nearly 230 senior living facilities as well as other ancillary businesses (including mobile diagnostics and medical transportation) in about a dozen of states. In addition it acquire lease and own healthcare real estate in addition to servicing the post-acute care continuum through accretive acquisition and investment opportunities in healthcare properties. Its transitional and skilled services companies provided skilled nursing care at nearly 220 operations with more than 23170 operational beds. It provides short and long-term nursing care services for patients with chronic conditions prolonged illness and the elderly.

	Annual Growth	12/17	12/18	12/19	12/20	12/21
Sales ($ mil.)	9.2%	1,849.3	2,040.7	2,036.5	2,402.6	2,627.5
Net income ($ mil.)	48.1%	40.5	92.4	110.5	170.5	194.7
Market value ($ mil.)	39.5%	1,225.2	2,140.8	2,504.0	4,024.5	4,633.8
Employees	5.0%	21,301	23,463	24,500	24,400	25,900

ENSYNC INC

NBB: ESNC

N88 W13901 Main Street, Suite 200
Menomonee Falls, WI 53051
Phone: 262 253-9800
Fax: –
Web: www.ensync.com

CEO: Sandeep Gupta
CFO: William Dallapiazza
HR: –
FYE: June 30
Type: Public

ZBB Energy makes and sells energy storage systems designed to store surplus energy for use at times when energy demand is higher than the utility company (or other generator) can provide. Its products — based on the company's zinc-bromine battery technology — also provide a source of power protection from voltage current or frequency deviations that can cause brownouts or power outages. While ZBB Energy markets its products primarily to utility companies and renewable energy generators in Australia China Europe and North America it has had only one customer to date the California Energy Commission. ZBB Energy operates one manufacturing facility in Menomonee Falls Wisconsin.

	Annual Growth	06/14	06/15	06/16	06/17	06/18
Sales ($ mil.)	11.0%	7.9	1.8	2.1	12.5	11.9
Net income ($ mil.)	–	(8.9)	(12.9)	(17.9)	(4.1)	(13.0)
Market value ($ mil.)	(31.1%)	91.7	49.8	20.9	20.9	20.7
Employees	2.5%	58	59	78	66	64

ENT FEDERAL CREDIT UNION

7250 Campus Dr.
Colorado Springs CO 80920
Phone: 719-574-1100
Fax: 719-388-0104
Web: www.entfederal.com

CEO: Chad Graves
CFO: Mj Coon
HR: –
FYE: December 31
Type: Private - Not-for-Pr

Ent Federal Credit Union (Ent FCU) is named for Uzal Girard Ent a WWII Air Force commander for which Ent Air Force Base in Colorado Springs is also named. Founded in 1957 the credit union provides personal business and corporate financial services including checking and savings accounts credit cards home mortgages business and personal loans and insurance as well as wealth management private banking and trust services. FCU serves more than 200000 members in the Front Range area of Colorado including Denver through about two dozen locations

ENTECH SALES AND SERVICE, LLC

3404 GARDEN BROOK DR
DALLAS, TX 752342496
Phone: 469-522-6000
Fax: –
Web: www.entechsales.com

CEO: Gale P Rucker
CFO: –
HR: –
FYE: December 31
Type: Private

Entech keeps Texans cool and safe. The company which was founded in 1981 has business units that provide air-conditioning heating and refrigeration equipment and services in about a half-dozen cities across the Lone Star State. Entech also offers integrated-system building automation that syncs HVAC controls access controls security closed-circuit television alarms and other automated systems. The company keeps its systems running by offering design installation maintenance and repair of HVAC and refrigeration. Other products and services include rebuilt cooling towers and HVAC and power equipment rentals.

	Annual Growth	12/04	12/05	12/06	12/07	12/17
Sales ($ mil.)	(19.1%)	–	1,342.6	52.4	56.8	105.5
Net income ($ mil.)	122.1%	–	0.0	5.1	6.8	5.9
Market value ($ mil.)	–	–	–	–	–	–
Employees	–	–	–	–	–	387

ENTECH SOLAR INC.

OTC: ENSL

13301 Park Vista Blvd. Ste. 100
Fort Worth TX 76177
Phone: 817-224-3600
Fax: 817-224-3601
Web: www.entechsolar.com

CEO: David Gelbaum
CFO: Shelley Hollingsworth
HR: –
FYE: December 31
Type: Public

Entech Solar aims to shine brightly in the solar energy market. The company designs makes and markets solar energy systems that provide electricity and thermal energy for commercial industrial and utility applications. Its products include ThermoVolt System (a proprietary concentrating photovoltaic and thermal technology that produces both electricity and thermal energy) and Solar Volt System (which uses a concentrating photovoltaic technology that produces cost-competitive electricity). Entech Solar also makes energy-efficient skylights and provides engineering services. Venture capital firm Quercus Trust owns 54% of Entech Solar.

ENTEGEE, INC.

85 RANGEWAY RD STE 1
NORTH BILLERICA, MA 018622105
Phone: 800-368-3433
Fax: –
Web: www.entegee.com

CEO: Robert P Crouch
CFO: J Todd King
HR: –
FYE: December 31
Type: Private

When businesses need help with engineering and technical projects Entegee is ready. The company's staffing division places engineering and technical professionals — including assemblers designers drafters programmers and technical writers — with clients such as defense contractors government agencies and manufacturing and engineering companies. In addition Entegee offers consulting and project-based services and outsourced engineering and drafting. It operates throughout the US from a network of about 20 offices. Entegee was a unit of MPS Group which was acquired by global staffing rival Adecco in 2010.

	Annual Growth	12/04	12/05	12/06	12/07	12/08
Sales ($ mil.)	9.0%	–	245.7	277.2	306.8	318.1
Net income ($ mil.)	–	–	0.0	65.2	0.0	41.2
Market value ($ mil.)	–	–	–	–	–	–
Employees	–	–	–	–	–	2,629

ENTEGRIS INC
NMS: ENTG
129 Concord Road
Billerica, MA 01821
Phone: 978 436-6500
Fax: –
Web: www.entegris.com
CEO: Bertrand Loy
CFO: Gregory Graves
HR: Susan Rice
FYE: December 31
Type: Public

Entegris makes products integral to the manufacture of semiconductors and computer disk drives. The company makes some 21000 standard and custom products used to transport and protect semiconductor and disk drive materials during processing. Its products include filtration wafer carriers storage boxes and chip trays as well as chemical delivery systems such as pipes fittings and valves. Its disk drive offerings include shippers stamper cases and transport trays. Semiconductor manufacturers including Taiwan Semiconductor Manufacturing Co. are among the company's customers. Massachusetts-based Entegris gets about 80% of revenue from international customers.

	Annual Growth	12/17	12/18	12/19	12/20	12/21
Sales ($ mil.)	14.4%	1,342.5	1,550.5	1,591.1	1,859.3	2,298.9
Net income ($ mil.)	48.1%	85.1	240.8	254.9	295.0	409.1
Market value ($ mil.)	46.1%	4,126.5	3,780.2	6,788.0	13,023.2	18,779.9
Employees	15.1%	3,900	4,900	5,300	5,800	6,850

ENTERGY ARKANSAS LLC
425 West Capitol Avenue
Little Rock, AR 72201
Phone: 501 377-4000
Fax: –
Web: www.entergy.com
CEO: Laura R Landreaux
CFO: Andrew S Marsh
HR: –
FYE: December 31
Type: Public

Entergy Arkansas is the largest power provider in the Natural State. The utility serves approximately 700000 residential commercial industrial and government customers in 63 eastern and central Arkansas counties. Residential customers account for about 84% of total clients. The Entergy subsidiary also has interests in fossil-fueled nuclear and hydroelectric power generation facilities with 5200 MW of capacity and it offers energy conservation and management programs.

	Annual Growth	12/16	12/17	12/18	12/19	12/20
Sales ($ mil.)	(0.0%)	2,086.6	2,139.9	2,060.6	2,259.6	2,084.5
Net income ($ mil.)	10.0%	167.2	139.8	252.7	263.0	245.2
Market value ($ mil.)	–	–	–	–	–	–
Employees	0.0%	1,242	1,278	1,258	1,251	1,244

ENTERGY CORP
NYS: ETR
639 Loyola Avenue
New Orleans, LA 70113
Phone: 504 576-4000
Fax: –
Web: www.entergy.com
CEO: Leo Denault
CFO: Andrew Marsh
HR: –
FYE: December 31
Type: Public

Entergy is an integrated energy company engaged in electric power production transmission and retail distribution operations. Entergy delivers electricity to 3 million utility customers in Arkansas Louisiana Mississippi and Texas. Entergy owns power plants that have a combined generating capacity of about 30000 MW including approximately 8000 MW of nuclear power. Entergy also provides ownership operation and decommissioning of nuclear power plants in the northern US and the sale of the electric power produced by its operating plants to wholesale customers. The company's regulated utilities have little retail competition as they are deemed by state regulators as the sole providers of electricity in their service areas.

	Annual Growth	12/16	12/17	12/18	12/19	12/20
Sales ($ mil.)	(1.7%)	10,845.6	11,074.5	11,009.5	10,878.7	10,113.6
Net income ($ mil.)	–	(564.3)	425.4	862.6	1,258.2	1,406.7
Market value ($ mil.)	8.0%	14,712.0	16,297.9	17,235.1	23,989.3	19,992.4
Employees	(0.2%)	13,513	13,504	13,688	13,635	13,400

ENTERGY GULF STATES LOUISIANA LLC
OTC: EYGF N
446 North Boulevard
Baton Rouge, LA 70802
Phone: 800 368-3749
Fax: –
Web: www.entergy.com
CEO: Phillip R May Jr
CFO: –
HR: –
FYE: December 31
Type: Public

Entergy Gulf States Louisiana keeps energy flowing in the Bayou State. The utility a subsidiary of Entergy and an affiliate of Entergy Louisiana provides electrical service to about 383900 customers in the state of Louisiana; its customer base is comprised of residential commercial industrial and governmental entities. The company owns or leases about 6660 MW of generating capacity including the River Bend Steam Electric Generation Station a Louisiana-based 978 MW nuclear facility. Together Entergy Louisiana and Entergy Gulf States Louisiana serve about 1 million electric customers in 58 parishes. Entergy Gulf States Louisiana also provides natural gas service to about 92000 customers in Baton Rouge.

	Annual Growth	12/09	12/10	12/11	12/12	12/13
Sales ($ mil.)	1.3%	1,844.4	2,097.0	2,134.4	1,654.9	1,941.1
Net income ($ mil.)	1.4%	153.0	190.7	203.0	159.0	161.7
Market value ($ mil.)	–	–	–	–	–	–
Employees	(2.4%)	840	816	805	798	763

ENTERGY LOUISIANA LLC (NEW)
4809 Jefferson Highway
Jefferson, LA 70121
Phone: 504 576-4000
Fax: –
Web: www.entergy.com
CEO: Phillip May
CFO: Andrew S Marsh
HR: –
FYE: December 31
Type: Public

Entergy Louisiana energizes everything from fishing shacks and suburban enclaves to petroleum refineries and city infrastructure for the storm-weary citizens of the Bayou State. The utility serves electric customers in 58 parishes of northeast and south Louisiana. The company holds non-exclusive franchises to provide electric service in 116 incorporated Louisiana municipalities. It also supplies electric service in 45 Louisiana parishes in which it holds non-exclusive franchises. Of the Entergy subsidiary's almost 5670 MW of generating capacity about 4900 MW comes from gas- and oil-fired power plants and almost 1160 MW from nuclear power plants.

	Annual Growth	12/16	12/17	12/18	12/19	12/20
Sales ($ mil.)	(0.6%)	4,177.0	4,300.6	4,296.3	4,285.2	4,069.9
Net income ($ mil.)	14.9%	622.0	316.3	675.6	691.5	1,082.4
Market value ($ mil.)	–	–	–	–	–	–
Employees	(0.6%)	1,696	1,713	1,656	1,670	1,654

ENTERGY MISSISSIPPI LLC
308 East Pearl Street
Jackson, MS 39201
Phone: 601 368-5000
Fax: –
Web: www.entergy.com
CEO: Haley R Fisackerly
CFO: –
HR: –
FYE: December 31
Type: Public

Entergy Mississippi keeps electricity flowing across the Magnolia state. With a physical presence in 45 of the state's 82 counties the utility provides electricity to about 440000 residential business and institutional customers (roughly 16% of electric customers in Mississippi) throughout the western half of its namesake state. Residential customers account for more than 90% of the company's client base. Entergy Mississippi is a subsidiary of the Louisiana-based utility holding company Entergy.

	Annual Growth	12/16	12/17	12/18	12/19	12/20
Sales ($ mil.)	3.3%	1,094.6	1,198.2	1,335.1	1,323.0	1,247.9
Net income ($ mil.)	6.5%	109.2	110.0	126.1	119.9	140.6
Market value ($ mil.)	–	–	–	–	–	–
Employees	1.4%	709	737	713	745	750

ENTERGY NEW ORLEANS LLC

1600 Perdido Street
New Orleans, LA 70112
Phone: 504 670-3700
Fax: –

CEO: –
CFO: –
HR: –
FYE: December 31
Type: Public

Entergy New Orleans lights up the path for the unsteady libation-influenced patrons of Bourbon Street and others in the Crescent City. The regulated utility a subsidiary of Entergy distributes electricity to 200000 residential commercial and industrial customers and natural gas to some 100000 customers in Orleans Parish Louisiana. It deactivated the Michoud power plant in 2016 and is considering building new power generating facilities on the same site.

	Annual Growth	12/16	12/17	12/18	12/19	12/20
Sales ($ mil.)	(1.2%)	665.5	716.1	717.4	686.2	633.8
Net income ($ mil.)	0.2%	48.8	44.6	53.2	52.6	49.3
Market value ($ mil.)	–	–	–	–	–	–
Employees	3.0%	269	274	278	308	303

ENTERPRISE BANCORP, INC. (MA)
NMS: EBTC

222 Merrimack Street
Lowell, MA 01852
Phone: 978 459-9000
Fax: –
Web: www.enterprisebanking.com

CEO: John Clancy
CFO: Joseph Lussier
HR: Jamie Gabriel
FYE: December 31
Type: Public

Enterprise Bancorp caters to more customers than just entrepreneurs. The holding company owns Enterprise Bank and Trust which operates more than 20 branches in north-central Massachusetts and southern New Hampshire. The $2 billion-asset bank offers traditional deposit and loan products specializing in lending to businesses professionals high-net-worth individuals and not-for-profits. About half of its loan portfolio is tied to commercial real estate while another one-third is tied to commercial and industrial and commercial construction loans. Subsidiaries Enterprise Investment Services and Enterprise Insurance Services provide investments and insurance geared to the bank's target business customers.

	Annual Growth	12/16	12/17	12/18	12/19	12/20
Assets ($ mil.)	12.3%	2,526.3	2,817.6	2,964.4	3,235.0	4,014.3
Net income ($ mil.)	13.8%	18.8	19.4	28.9	34.2	31.5
Market value ($ mil.)	(9.2%)	448.4	406.5	383.9	404.3	305.0
Employees	3.0%	468	482	508	538	527

ENTERPRISE DIVERSIFIED INC
NBB: SYTE

1518 Willow Lawn Drive
Richmond, VA 23230
Phone: 434 336-7737
Fax: –
Web: www.enterprisediversified.com

CEO: G Michael Bridge
CFO: Alea Kleinhammer
HR: –
FYE: December 31
Type: Public

Sitestar wants to sparkle in the Internet firmament. The Internet service provider (ISP) primarily serves markets in the mid-Atlantic and Northwest states offering dial-up and DSL Internet access as well as Web hosting and design within its regional service area. Sitestar's retail division sells and makes computer systems and recharges toner and ink cartridges. The company sold its programming and consulting division and has acquired the dial-up customer base of IDACOMM a subsidiary of IDACORP.

	Annual Growth	12/16	12/17	12/18	12/19	12/20
Sales ($ mil.)	1.3%	5.0	9.1	4.4	3.6	5.2
Net income ($ mil.)	–	(0.1)	2.1	(3.8)	(5.4)	3.3
Market value ($ mil.)	190.8%	0.2	0.3	22.6	9.9	14.3
Employees	3.9%	6	36	20	7	7

ENTERPRISE ELECTRIC, LLC

1300 FORT NEGLEY BLVD
NASHVILLE, TN 372034854
Phone: 615-350-7270
Fax: –
Web: www.enterprisellc.com

CEO: James C Seabury III
CFO: Lera Pendergrass
HR: –
FYE: December 31
Type: Private

Enterprise Electric welcomes the power hungry. The full service electrical firms specializes in construction and design of electrical systems for institutional commercial industrial and services projects from planning through construction. The company completes projects large and small and has completed design and installation of wiring and electrical systems for health care correctional commercial and industrial clients. Services include temporary power installations voice data and fiber optic cabling systems emergency generator and substation installations maintenance services. Headquartered in Nashville Tennessee the company serves clients throughout the US.

	Annual Growth	12/09	12/10	12/11	12/12	12/13
Sales ($ mil.)	54.2%	–	–	–	59.1	91.2
Net income ($ mil.)	–	–	–	–	(2.9)	2.2
Market value ($ mil.)	–	–	–	–	–	–
Employees	–	–	–	–	–	400

ENTERPRISE FINANCIAL SERVICES CORP
NMS: EFSC

150 North Meramec
Clayton, MO 63105
Phone: 314 725-5500
Fax: –
Web: www.enterprisebank.com

CEO: James Lally
CFO: Keene Turner
HR: –
FYE: December 31
Type: Public

Enterprise Financial Services wants you to boldly bank where many have banked before. It's the holding company for Enterprise Bank & Trust which mostly targets closely-held businesses and their owners but also serves individuals in the St. Louis Kansas City and Phoenix metropolitan areas. Boasting $3.8 billion in assets and 16 branches Enterprise offers standard products such as checking savings and money market accounts and CDs. Commercial and industrial loans make up over half of the company's lending activities while real estate loans make up another 45%. The bank also writes consumer and residential mortgage loans. Bank subsidiary Enterprise Trust offers wealth management services.

	Annual Growth	12/16	12/17	12/18	12/19	12/20
Assets ($ mil.)	24.3%	4,081.3	5,289.2	5,645.7	7,333.8	9,751.6
Net income ($ mil.)	11.1%	48.8	48.2	89.2	92.7	74.4
Market value ($ mil.)	(5.0%)	1,342.0	1,409.1	1,174.4	1,504.6	1,090.8
Employees	18.9%	479	635	650	805	–

ENTERPRISE PRODUCTS PARTNERS L.P.
NYS: EPD

1100 Louisiana Street, 10th Floor
Houston, TX 77002
Phone: 713 381-6500
Fax: –
Web: www.enterpriseproducts.com

CEO: A. James Teague
CFO: W. Fowler
HR: –
FYE: December 31
Type: Public

Doing business through wholly owned subsidiary Enterprise Products Operating LLC (EPO) Enterprise Products Partners is one of the leading players in the North American midstream market. EPO connects producers of natural gas natural gas liquids (NGL) crude oil in major North American supply basins with domestic and international consumers. Operations include natural gas processing NGL fractionation propylene production petrochemical services crude oil transportation and marine transportation. The company derives nearly all its sales from the US.

	Annual Growth	12/16	12/17	12/18	12/19	12/20
Sales ($ mil.)	4.3%	23,022.3	29,241.5	36,534.2	32,789.2	27,199.7
Net income ($ mil.)	10.7%	2,513.1	2,799.3	4,172.4	4,591.3	3,775.6
Market value ($ mil.)	–	0.0	0.0	0.0	0.0	0.0
Employees	–	–	–	–	–	–

ENTRAVISION COMMUNICATIONS CORP.　　NYS: EVC

2425 Olympic Boulevard, Suite 6000 West　　CEO: Walter Ulloa
Santa Monica, CA 90404　　CFO: Christopher Young
Phone: 310 447-3870　　HR: –
Fax: –　　FYE: December 31
Web: www.entravision.com　　Type: Public

This company helps advertisers trying to reach the US Hispanic market. Entravision Communications (Entravision) has about 55 television stations and 50 radio stations located in the top 50 Hispanic markets in the US. It is the largest affiliate of Univision's two Spanish-language television networks Univision and UniMas; Entravision's TV portfolio also includes a small number of stations affiliated with The CW Network FOX and MyNetworkTV. On the radio the company offers a variety of programming formats including music news sports advertising traffic weather promotions and community events.

	Annual Growth	12/16	12/17	12/18	12/19	12/20
Sales ($ mil.)	7.4%	258.5	536.0	297.8	273.6	344.0
Net income ($ mil.)	–	20.4	176.3	12.2	(19.7)	(3.9)
Market value ($ mil.)	(20.8%)	595.3	608.0	247.5	222.8	233.9
Employees	(2.6%)	1,111	1,259	1,156	1,104	1,001

ENTROPIC COMMUNICATIONS, INC.　　NMS: ENTR

6250 Sequence Drive　　CEO: –
San Diego, CA 92121　　CFO: –
Phone: 858 768-3600　　HR: –
Fax: –　　FYE: December 31
Web: www.entropic.com　　Type: Public

Entropic Communications is far from sluggish when it comes to broadband. The fabless semiconductor company designs specialized chipsets for video and broadband multimedia applications. Through the Multimedia over Coax Alliance (MoCA) networking standard Entropic is targeting digital home entertainment networks linked by coaxial cable connections a market being promoted by cable TV services providers and others. The company's c.LINK technology enables broadband networking between an access node and cable outlets. Leading customers include Actiontec Electronics Samsung Motorola Mobility (16% of sales) and Wistron NeWeb (18%). The Asia/Pacific region accounts for most sales.

	Annual Growth	12/09	12/10	12/11	12/12	12/13
Sales ($ mil.)	22.2%	116.3	210.2	240.6	321.7	259.4
Net income ($ mil.)	–	(13.2)	64.7	26.6	4.5	(66.2)
Market value ($ mil.)	11.2%	278.7	1,096.6	463.9	480.2	426.6
Employees	25.0%	262	300	344	693	639

ENTRUST INC.

One Lincoln Centre 5400 LBJ Freeway Ste. 1340　　CEO: –
Dallas TX 75240　　CFO: –
Phone: 972-728-0447　　HR: –
Fax: 972-728-0440　　FYE: December 31
Web: www.entrust.com　　Type: Private

Entrust is like a bodyguard for your e-Identity. The company's software and services ensure the privacy of electronic communications and transactions across corporate networks and the Internet. Its applications are used to authenticate users via smart cards passwords and biometric devices to control access to e-mail databases websites and business applications. Services include consulting deployment and security systems management. Entrust serves some 5000 enterprise government and financial customers worldwide from offices in about 10 countries. The company is controlled by private equity firm Thoma Bravo which acquired it in 2009.

ENTRX CORPORATION　　PINK SHEETS: ENTX

800 Nicollet Mall Ste. 2690　　CEO: Peter L Hauser
Minneapolis MN 55402　　CFO: Brian D Niebur
Phone: 612-333-0614　　HR: –
Fax: 612-338-7332　　FYE: December 31
Web: metalclad.com　　Type: Public

The raison d'etre of Entrx as of late has been to insulate and abate. The company provides insulation and asbestos abatement services through subsidiary Metalclad Insulation. Operating primarily in California it installs insulation on pipes ducts furnaces boilers and other industrial equipment. It also maintains and removes insulation and sells specialty insulation products to public utilities oil petrochemical and heavy construction companies. Metalclad's customers have included Jacobs Engineering Group and Southern California Edison .

ENVELA CORP　　ASE: ELA

1901 Gateway Drive, Ste 100　　CEO: John Loftus
Irving, TX 75038　　CFO: Bret Pedersen
Phone: 972 587-4049　　HR: –
Fax: 972 674-2596　　FYE: December 31
Web: www.envela.com　　Type: Public

Attracted to things gold and shiny? If so DGSE is for you. The company buys and sells jewelry bullion rare coins fine watches and collectibles to retail and wholesale customers across the US through its various websites and 30-plus retail stores in California Texas and South Carolina. The company's eight e-commerce sites let customers buy and sell jewelry and bullion interactively and obtain current precious-metal prices. In all more than 7500 items are available for sale on DGSE websites including $2 million in diamonds. DGSE also owns Fairchild Watches a leading vintage watch wholesaler and the rare coin dealer Superior Galleries. The company sold its pair of pawn shops in Dallas in 2009.

	Annual Growth	12/16	12/17	12/18	12/19	12/20
Sales ($ mil.)	23.9%	48.3	62.0	54.1	82.0	113.9
Net income ($ mil.)	–	(4.0)	1.8	0.7	2.8	6.4
Market value ($ mil.)	43.1%	33.4	25.1	12.4	36.3	140.0
Employees	18.5%	77	54	52	135	152

ENVESTNET INC　　NYS: ENV

35 East Wacker Drive, Suite 2400　　CEO: William Crager
Chicago, IL 60601　　CFO: Peter D'Arrigo
Phone: 312 827-2800　　HR: –
Fax: 312 827-2801　　FYE: December 31
Web: www.envestnet.com　　Type: Public

Envestnet is a leading leader in helping transform wealth management working and its goal of building a holistics financial wellness ecosystem to improve the financial lives of millions of consumers. The company provides a financial network connecting technology solutions and data delivering better intelligence and enabling its customers to drive better outcomes. Subsidiary Portfolio Management Consultants (Envestnet | PMC) provides consulting services to financial advisors and affords them access to managed accounts multi manager-manager portfolios fund strategist portfolios as well over 900 proprietary such as quantitative portfolios and fund strategist portfolios. In additions PMC offers portfolio overlay and tax optimization services. Founded in 1999.

	Annual Growth	12/16	12/17	12/18	12/19	12/20
Sales ($ mil.)	14.6%	578.2	683.7	812.4	900.1	998.2
Net income ($ mil.)	–	(55.6)	(3.3)	5.8	(16.8)	(3.1)
Market value ($ mil.)	23.6%	1,906.8	2,696.6	2,660.9	3,766.5	4,451.4
Employees	7.4%	3,197	3,516	3,920	4,190	4,250

ENVIRO TECHNOLOGIES US INC
NBB: EVTN

821 N.W. 57th Place
Fort Lauderdale, FL 33309
Phone: 954 958-9968
Fax: –
Web: www.evtn.com

CEO: John A Dibella
CFO: John A Dibella
HR: –
FYE: December 31
Type: Public

Enviro Voraxial Technology has a voracious appetite for developing equipment to separate solids and liquids with different specific gravities. The company's Voraxial Separator can be used for wastewater treatment grit and sand separation oil and water separation marine-oil-spill cleanup bilge and ballast treatment stormwater treatment and food-processing-waste treatment. The separator is capable of processing volumes as low as 3 gallons per minute as well as volumes of more than 10000 gallons per minute with only one moving part. Chairman and CEO Alberto DiBella officers and directors control almost 35% of the company.

	Annual Growth	12/16	12/17	12/18	12/19	12/20
Sales ($ mil.)	(38.6%)	0.6	0.3	1.3	2.8	0.1
Net income ($ mil.)	–	(0.5)	2.1	(0.5)	0.6	(1.0)
Market value ($ mil.)	49.5%	0.1	0.2	0.2	0.2	0.5
Employees	0.0%	5	7	7	6	5

ENVIRONMENTAL DEFENSE FUND, INCORPORATED

257 PARK AVE S FL 17
NEW YORK, NY 100107386
Phone: 212-505-2100
Fax: –
Web: www.edfaction.org

CEO: –
CFO: –
HR: –
FYE: September 30
Type: Private

Environmental Defense fights for those without a voice. The not-for-profit group works to protect the environment through programs in areas such as ecosystem restoration environmental health ocean protection and global and regional air and energy. The organization which has tripled in size since it was founded in 1967 boasts more than 500000 members and employs some 300 scientists attorneys economists and other professionals. In addition to its New York City headquarters Environmental Defense maintains 10 regional offices nationwide and in Beijing. Environmental Defense initially funded its efforts from a battle won against the DDT pesticide which had been harming wildlife.

	Annual Growth	09/12	09/13	09/14	09/15	09/16
Sales ($ mil.)	18.3%	–	–	–	145.7	172.2
Net income ($ mil.)	–	–	–	–	0.0	7.2
Market value ($ mil.)	–	–	–	–	–	–
Employees	–	–	–	–	–	525

ENVIRONMENTAL TECTONICS CORP.
NBB: ETCC

County Line Industrial Park, 125 James Way
Southampton, PA 18966
Phone: 215 355-9100
Fax: –
Web: www.etcusa.com

CEO: Robert Laurent
CFO: Mark Prudenti
HR: –
FYE: February 26
Type: Public

Environmental Tectonics Corporation (ETC) believes virtual environments can teach us a lot about real life. Through its Aerospace Solutions segment (formerly Training Services Group) the company makes software-driven aircrew training systems and disaster simulators. Through its Commercial/Industrial Systems segment (formerly Control Systems Group) it designs manufactures and sells industrial steam and gas sterilizers for the pharmaceutical medical device and animal research industries hyperbaric chambers for the medical industry and environmental testing products for the automotive and HVAC industries.

	Annual Growth	02/17	02/18	02/19	02/20	02/21
Sales ($ mil.)	(20.1%)	39.8	48.1	48.4	40.6	16.3
Net income ($ mil.)	–	(0.9)	2.4	3.1	(4.0)	(7.5)
Market value ($ mil.)	(22.8%)	9.3	8.9	8.0	5.6	3.3
Employees	(50.2%)	277	280	270	234	17

ENVISION HEALTHCARE HOLDINGS INC
NYS: EVHC

6200 S. Syracuse Way, Suite 200
Greenwood Village, CO 80111
Phone: 303 495-1200
Fax: –
Web: www.evhc.net

CEO: –
CFO: –
HR: –
FYE: December 31
Type: Public

Municipalities and hospitals can't call 911 when they have an emergency — but they can call Envision Healthcare. The holding company (formerly Emergency Medical Services Corporation) is the parent of EmCare Holdings a leading medical management firm that specializes in staffing emergency rooms and AMR Inc. the largest private ambulance service in the US. EmCare holds about 800 staffing and service contracts with hospitals and physician groups in more than 40 states and the District of Columbia. AMR has more than 3800 contracts with clients (cities government agencies health care providers and insurance firms) in some 40 states for emergency and non-emergency transport services. The company went public in 2013.

	Annual Growth	05/11*	12/11	12/12	12/13	12/14
Sales ($ mil.)	53.3%	1,221.8	1,885.8	3,300.1	3,728.3	4,397.6
Net income ($ mil.)	82.4%	20.7	13.0	41.2	6.0	125.5
Market value ($ mil.)	(2.3%)	–	–	–	6,524.3	6,371.8
Employees	12.4%	–	–	26,700	30,339	33,748

*Fiscal year change

ENZO BIOCHEM, INC.
NYS: ENZ

527 Madison Ave.
New York, NY 10022
Phone: 212 583-0100
Fax: –
Web: www.enzo.com

CEO: Hamid Erfanian
CFO: David Bench
HR: Debbie Sohmer
FYE: July 31
Type: Public

For Enzo Biochem genomic research is the key to both diagnostic and therapeutic care. The biotech company is focused on the development and sale of gene-based tests and pharmaceuticals through its three operating divisions. The Enzo Clinical Labs unit provides diagnostic testing services in the New York City area while Enzo Life Sciences makes reagents used in research by pharmaceutical firms biotech companies academic institutions. The third division Enzo Therapeutics is a development-stage firm working to treat ophthalmic conditions gastrointestinal ailments and other diseases.

	Annual Growth	07/17	07/18	07/19	07/20	07/21
Sales ($ mil.)	2.2%	107.8	104.7	81.2	76.0	117.7
Net income ($ mil.)	–	(2.5)	(10.3)	2.5	(28.5)	7.9
Market value ($ mil.)	(26.0%)	525.9	214.2	189.5	115.4	158.0
Employees	2.2%	472	503	500	448	514

ENZON PHARMACEUTICALS INC
NBB: ENZN

20 Commerce Drive (Suite 135)
Cranford, NJ 07016
Phone: 732 980-4500
Fax: 908 575-9457
Web: www.enzon.com

CEO: Richard Feinstein
CFO: Richard L Feinstein
HR: –
FYE: December 31
Type: Public

Enzon Pharmaceuticals has PEGged its future on researching ways to fight cancer. The company has developed compounds using its PEGylation and Locked Nucleic Acid (LNA) technology platforms to improve the performance and deliverability of existing cancer drugs. PEGylation involves attaching polyethylene glycol (PEG) to a drug compound to make it more effective and less toxic for patients. However in 2012 Enzon suspended clinical efforts and began reviewing strategic options; in 2013 it refocused on minimizing expenses and maximizing royalty revenue returns.

	Annual Growth	12/16	12/17	12/18	12/19	12/20
Sales ($ mil.)	(71.9%)	8.4	8.4	6.9	0.2	0.1
Net income ($ mil.)	–	(1.1)	5.4	5.8	(1.0)	(1.3)
Market value ($ mil.)	(9.2%)	27.1	20.0	18.7	15.3	18.4
Employees	–	–	1	–	–	–

EOG RESOURCES, INC.
NYS: EOG

1111 Bagby, Sky Lobby 2
Houston, TX 77002
Phone: 713 651-7000
Fax: –
Web: www.eogresources.com

CEO: William Thomas
CFO: Timothy Driggers
HR: Keri White
FYE: December 31
Type: Public

Large-scale shale is the Holy Grail for oil prospector EOG Resources. It engages in exploration development production and marketing of natural gas and crude oil originating in the Eagle Ford Shale and Barnett Shale in Texas and the Bakken formation in North Dakota. Of its approximately 3.3 million BOE reserves EOG holds nearly 1.7 million barrels in crude oil and condensates with an approximately 5.3 billion cubic feet of natural gas. The US is the company's largest market.

	Annual Growth	12/16	12/17	12/18	12/19	12/20
Sales ($ mil.)	9.6%	7,650.6	11,208.3	17,275.4	17,380.0	11,032.0
Net income ($ mil.)	–	(1,096.7)	2,582.6	3,419.0	2,734.9	(604.6)
Market value ($ mil.)	(16.2%)	58,999.0	62,973.1	50,893.2	48,879.9	29,102.7
Employees	2.3%	2,650	2,664	2,800	2,900	2,900

EP ENERGY CORP.
NL:

1001 Louisiana Street
Houston, TX 77002
Phone: 713 997-1000
Fax: –
Web: www.epenergy.com

CEO: Russell E Parker
CFO: Kyle A McCuen
HR: James Cleary
FYE: December 31
Type: Public

EP Energy is into the (E)xploration and (P)roduction of oil and gas. The company's primary operations are at the Eagle Ford Shale in South Texas Northeastern Utah (NEU) in the Uinta basin and the Permian basin in West Texas. It owns proved reserves of around 190 million barrels of oil equivalent about 75% of which is oil and NGLs (natural gas liquids). In early 2020 EP Energy emerged from Chapter 11 bankruptcy protection. EP Energy was formed in 2012 when the former El Paso Corporation sold its exploration and production assets to an investment group for $7.2 billion.

	Annual Growth	12/15	12/16	12/17	12/18	12/19
Sales ($ mil.)	(19.0%)	1,908.0	767.0	1,066.0	1,324.0	820.0
Net income ($ mil.)	–	(3,748.0)	(27.0)	(194.0)	(1,003.0)	(943.0)
Market value ($ mil.)	(83.2%)	1,118.2	1,672.2	602.5	178.7	0.9
Employees	(13.6%)	665	502	436	372	370

EP ENERGY CORPORATION

601 TRAVIS ST STE 1400
HOUSTON, TX 770023253
Phone: 713-997-1000
Fax: –
Web: www.epenergy.com

CEO: Russell E Parker
CFO: Kyle A McCuen
HR: James Cleary
FYE: December 31
Type: Private

EP Energy is into the (E)xploration and (P)roduction of oil and gas. The company's primary operations are at the Eagle Ford Shale in South Texas Northeastern Utah (NEU) in the Uinta basin and the Permian basin in West Texas. It owns proved reserves of around 190 million barrels of oil equivalent about 75% of which is oil and NGLs (natural gas liquids). In early 2020 EP Energy emerged from Chapter 11 bankruptcy protection. EP Energy was formed in 2012 when the former El Paso Corporation sold its exploration and production assets to an investment group for $7.2 billion.

	Annual Growth	12/15	12/16	12/17	12/18	12/19
Sales ($ mil.)	2.3%	–	767.0	1,066.0	1,324.0	820.0
Net income ($ mil.)	–	–	(27.0)	(194.0)	(1,003.0)	(943.0)
Market value ($ mil.)	–	–	–	–	–	–
Employees	–	–	–	–	–	372

EPAM SYSTEMS, INC.
NYS: EPAM

41 University Drive, Suite 202
Newtown, PA 18940
Phone: 267 759-9000
Fax: –
Web: www.epam.com

CEO: Arkadiy Dobkin
CFO: Jason Peterson
HR: –
FYE: December 31
Type: Public

EPAM is the world's leading provider of digital platform engineering software development and other IT services to customers primarily in North America Europe Asia and Australia. The company provides software development product engineering services and other business processes. Its key service offerings and solutions include five practice areas such as engineering operations optimization consulting and design. The company has development centers in Russia Belarus Ukraine Hungary Poland India and China that employ more than 36735 professionals. Around 60% of sales come from North America. EPAM was founded in 1993.

	Annual Growth	12/16	12/17	12/18	12/19	12/20
Sales ($ mil.)	23.0%	1,160.1	1,450.4	1,842.9	2,293.8	2,659.5
Net income ($ mil.)	34.7%	99.3	72.8	240.3	261.1	327.2
Market value ($ mil.)	53.6%	3,608.3	6,027.7	6,509.1	11,903.9	20,106.3
Employees	16.5%	22,383	25,962	30,156	36,739	41,168

EPICORE BIONETWORKS INC.
PINK SHEETS: EPCBF

4 Lina Ln.
Eastampton NJ 08060
Phone: 609-267-9118
Fax: 609-267-9336
Web: www.epicorebionetworks.com

CEO: –
CFO: –
HR: –
FYE: June 30
Type: Public

Epicore BioNetworks puts the earth at the core of its scientific creations. The company manufactures environmentally sensitive biotechnology products for commercial industrial and consumer applications and specialty animal feeds. It mixes natural bacteria enzymes microbes and other biodegradable non-toxic ingredients to create products for diverse industries like agriculture cleaning and sanitation food processing and nutrition and environmental remediation. Those products include water treatment chemicals agrochemicals and sanitizers and deodorizers. Epicore is a major supplier of products to the aquaculture industry especially to the shrimp industries in Asia and in Latin America.

EPIQ SYSTEMS INC
NMS: EPIQ

501 Kansas Avenue
Kansas City, KS 66105-1300
Phone: 913 621-9500
Fax: –
Web: www.epiqsystems.com

CEO: John Davenport Jr
CFO: –
HR: –
FYE: December 31
Type: Public

Epiq Systems wants to make legal discovery and bankruptcy proceedings as quick and painless as possible (for attorneys that is). The company provides case and document management software for bankruptcy class action mass tort and other legal proceedings. Its software automates tasks including electronic discovery legal notice claims management and government reporting. Epiq's software line includes products for Chapter 7 liquidations as well as Chapter 13 and 11 reorganizations. The company which caters to law firms and bankruptcy trustees also offers consulting and case management services and software for class action mass tort and bankruptcy case administration. Epiq operates primarily in the US.

	Annual Growth	12/10	12/11	12/12	12/13	12/14
Sales ($ mil.)	17.7%	247.2	283.3	373.1	482.1	474.5
Net income ($ mil.)	–	–	13.9	12.1	22.4	11.1	(1.3)
Market value ($ mil.)	5.6%	503.6	440.9	467.7	593.1	626.5
Employees	18.9%	550	1,000	1,000	1,000	1,100

EPITEC, INC.

24800 DENSO DR STE 150
SOUTHFIELD, MI 480337464
Phone: 248-353-6800
Fax: –
Web: www.epitecinc.com

CEO: Jerome Sheppard
CFO: Mark J Ruma
HR: –
FYE: December 31
Type: Private

Epitec supports the idea that surrounding oneself with smart people is the key to a successful business. The company provides information technology staffing services to businesses across the US although its primary market is the Detroit area. It offers contract contract-to-hire and direct hire placement of developers analysts architects engineers and other technical staff to companies in a wide range of industries. Epitec also provides on-site management services and related custom software development. It was founded by CEO Jerry Sheppard in 1978.

	Annual Growth	12/05	12/06	12/07	12/08	12/15
Sales ($ mil.)	13.0%	–	–	–	28.5	67.0
Net income ($ mil.)	12.4%	–	–	–	0.8	1.8
Market value ($ mil.)	–	–	–	–	–	–
Employees	–	–	–	–	–	1,800

EPIZYME INC.
NMS: EPZM

400 Technology Square, 4th Floor
Cambridge, MA 02139
Phone: 617 229-5872
Fax: –
Web: www.epizyme.com

CEO: Grant Bogle
CFO: Paolo Tombesi
HR: –
FYE: December 31
Type: Public

Epizyme is a commercial-stage biopharmaceutical company that is committed to rewriting treatment for people with cancer and other serious diseases through discovery the discovery development and commercialization of novel epigenetic medicines. The company's customers are hospital pharmacies community practice pharmacies specialty pharmacies and specialty distributors. Epizyme has made the most progress with treatments for leukemia and for non-Hodgkin lymphoma. It is also working with an affiliate of GlaxoSmithKline on the development of three other enzyme inhibitors. Founded in 2007 the company went public in 2013.

	Annual Growth	12/16	12/17	12/18	12/19	12/20
Sales ($ mil.)	18.5%	8.0	10.0	21.7	23.8	15.8
Net income ($ mil.)	–	(110.2)	(134.3)	(123.6)	(170.3)	(231.7)
Market value ($ mil.)	(2.7%)	1,229.4	1,275.4	626.0	2,500.0	1,103.7
Employees	28.4%	112	131	124	203	304

EPL OIL & GAS INC
NYS: EPL

919 Milam Street, Suite 1600
Houston, TX 77002
Phone: 713 228-0711
Fax: –
Web: www.eplweb.com

CEO: –
CFO: –
HR: –
FYE: December 31
Type: Public

It pays for EPL Oil & Gas (formerly Energy Partners) to have friends in the oil and gas business. The independent explorer and producer focuses on the waters of the Gulf of Mexico off the Gulf Coast. It partners with big oil companies to explore for reserves on properties the majors have left behind; EPL Oil & Gas earns an interest in the new reserves and production. The company has grown through a combination of exploration exploitation and development drilling as well as strategic acquisitions of oil and natural gas fields. It changed its corporate name in 2012 to reflect its oil and gas focus.

	Annual Growth	09/09*	12/09	12/10	12/11	12/12
Sales ($ mil.)	46.4%	134.9	56.8	239.9	348.3	423.6
Net income ($ mil.)	–	(36.1)	(21.0)	(8.5)	26.6	58.8
Market value ($ mil.)	44.6%	291.7	334.3	581.1	570.9	881.8
Employees	19.6%	–	101	100	108	173

*Fiscal year change

EPLUS INC
NMS: PLUS

13595 Dulles Technology Drive
Herndon, VA 20171-3413
Phone: 703 984-8400
Fax: –
Web: www.eplus.com

CEO: Mark Marron
CFO: Elaine Marion
HR: –
FYE: March 31
Type: Public

ePlus is a leading solutions provider and operates through two business segments that deal in technology sales and financing. Offerings include security storage and networking products as well as consulting and systems integration services. It also offers supply chain management software and services; its proprietary applications include procurement and asset management. The company's Leasing and Financial Services arm offers lease financing and leases IT and medical equipment. In addition ePlus is an authorized reseller of more than 1000 vendors but primarily of approximately 100 vendors including Arista Networks Check Point Cisco Systems Dell EMC F5 Networks Hewlett Packard Enterprise and HP Inc. among others. Virtually about 95% of ePlus' revenue comes from the US.

	Annual Growth	03/17	03/18	03/19	03/20	03/21
Sales ($ mil.)	4.2%	1,329.4	1,411.0	1,372.7	1,588.4	1,568.3
Net income ($ mil.)	10.1%	50.6	55.1	63.2	69.1	74.4
Market value ($ mil.)	(7.3%)	3,647.2	2,098.4	2,391.1	1,691.1	2,690.9
Employees	7.4%	1,173	1,260	1,537	1,579	1,560

EPR PROPERTIES
NYS: EPR

909 Walnut Street, Suite 200
Kansas City, MO 64106
Phone: 816 472-1700
Fax: 816 472-5794
Web: www.eprkc.com

CEO: Gregory Silvers
CFO: Mark Peterson
HR: Liz Grace
FYE: December 31
Type: Public

EPR Properties (formerly Entertainment Properties Trust) invests in places to play and learn. The self-administered real estate investment trust (REIT) owns around 180 movie megaplex theaters and theater-anchored entertainment retail centers around the US and Canada. Many of its theaters are leased to AMC Entertainment. EPR also owns ski resorts golf resorts (for operator TopGolf) waterparks (including Schlitterbahn parks) public charter schools early education centers and private schools.

	Annual Growth	12/16	12/17	12/18	12/19	12/20
Sales ($ mil.)	(4.2%)	493.2	576.0	700.7	652.0	414.7
Net income ($ mil.)	–	225.0	263.0	267.0	202.2	(131.5)
Market value ($ mil.)	(18.0%)	5,354.2	4,883.5	4,776.8	5,269.9	2,424.6
Employees	(1.8%)	57	63	64	62	53

EPSILON SYSTEMS SOLUTIONS, INC.

9242 LIGHTWAVE AVE # 100
SAN DIEGO, CA 921236402
Phone: 619-702-1700
Fax: –
Web: www.epsilonsystems.com

CEO: Bryan Min
CFO: Joe Quinn
HR: Meriel Gonzalez
FYE: December 31
Type: Private

Epsilon Systems Solutions is not afraid of its alpha beta gamma and delta rivals. The diversified engineering services company offers consultation field services and IT support to the applied technology energy environmental industrial and marine markets. It also maintains and repairs ships for the US Navy and Coast Guard. Epsilon Systems caters to federal agencies including the Department of Energy the Department of Defense and the Department of Homeland Security as well as to major contractors such as Boeing Lockheed Martin SPAWAR NAVAIR Lakehurst and Raytheon.

	Annual Growth	12/04	12/05	12/06	12/07	12/08
Sales ($ mil.)	18.8%	–	–	66.4	94.1	93.8
Net income ($ mil.)	12.4%	–	–	1.3	1.7	1.7
Market value ($ mil.)	–	–	–	–	–	–
Employees	–	–	–	–	–	887

EQT CORP

NYS: EQT

625 Liberty Avenue, Suite 1700
Pittsburgh, PA 15222
Phone: 412 553-5700
Fax: –
Web: www.eqt.com

CEO: Toby Rice
CFO: David Khani
HR: –
FYE: December 31
Type: Public

EQT Corporation (EQT) is a major US producer of natural gas boasting proved reserves of about 19.8 trillion cubic feet equivalent of natural gas natural gas liquids and crude oil. Its assets are mainly in the Marcellus and Utica shale basin in Appalachia. The company's customers include Appalachian-area utilities and industrial customers as well as natural gas marketers. In addition the company also caters to markets that are accessible through the company's transportation portfolio particularly in the gulf Coast Midwest and Northeast US and Canada.

	Annual Growth	12/17	12/18	12/19	12/20	12/21
Sales ($ mil.)	(2.4%)	3,378.0	4,557.9	4,416.5	3,058.8	3,064.7
Net income ($ mil.)	–	1,508.5	(2,244.6)	(1,221.7)	(967.2)	(1,155.8)
Market value ($ mil.)	(21.3%)	21,424.6	7,110.2	4,102.7	4,784.0	8,209.3
Employees	(23.9%)	2,067	863	647	624	693

EQUIFAX INC

NYS: EFX

1550 Peachtree Street, N.W.
Atlanta, GA 30309
Phone: 404 885-8000
Fax: –
Web: www.equifax.com

CEO: Mark Begor
CFO: John Gamble
HR: –
FYE: December 31
Type: Public

A global data analytics and technology company Equifax provides information solutions for businesses governments and consumers and we provide human resources business process outsourcing services for employers. Through its Workforce Solutions unit Equifax provides services enabling customers to verify income and employment (Verification Services) of people in the US. Clients include financial institutions corporations government agencies and individuals. Equifax operates around the world but does most of its business in the US.

	Annual Growth	12/16	12/17	12/18	12/19	12/20
Sales ($ mil.)	7.0%	3,144.9	3,362.2	3,412.1	3,507.6	4,127.5
Net income ($ mil.)	1.6%	488.8	587.3	299.8	(398.8)	520.1
Market value ($ mil.)	13.0%	14,400.4	14,362.7	11,343.2	17,066.6	23,487.9
Employees	4.7%	9,500	10,300	10,900	11,200	11,400

EQUILAR INC.

1100 Marshall St.
Redwood City CA 94063
Phone: 650-286-4512
Fax: 650-701-0993
Web: www.equilar.com

CEO: David Chun
CFO: –
HR: –
FYE: December 31
Type: Private

Equilar earns its bread and butter by finding out how much everyone else gets paid. The executive compensation research company manages a database compiled with the salary information of more than 20000 executives of public companies registered with the US Securities and Exchange Commission. Equilar reports and analyses are available through a subscription; customers can also buy printed copies of its reports. Fortune 500 corporations use the information to determine executive and board member pay; consulting firms such as Deloitte and media firms such as Bloomberg and the Wall Street Journal also use Equilar's data. The company was founded in 2001 by CEO David Chun.

EQUINIX INC

NMS: EQIX

One Lagoon Drive
Redwood City, CA 94065
Phone: 650 598-6000
Fax: –
Web: www.equinix.com

CEO: Charles Meyers
CFO: Keith Taylor
HR: Brandi Morandi
FYE: December 31
Type: Public

Equinix is a global digital infrastructure company. Platform Equinix combines a global footprint of International Business Exchange (IBX) data centers in the Americas Asia-Pacific and Europe the Middle East and Africa regions interconnection solutions edge services unique business and digital ecosystems and expert consulting and support. Its customers include telecommunications carriers mobile and other network services providers cloud and IT services providers digital media and content providers financial services companies and global enterprise ecosystems in various industries. Altogether Equinix operates more than 225 data centers around the world and gets some 55% of revenue outside the Americas region.

	Annual Growth	12/17	12/18	12/19	12/20	12/21
Sales ($ mil.)	11.0%	4,368.4	5,071.7	5,562.1	5,998.5	6,635.5
Net income ($ mil.)	21.0%	233.0	365.4	507.5	369.8	500.2
Market value ($ mil.)	16.9%	41,048.8	31,931.9	52,866.5	64,684.3	76,608.9
Employees	10.8%	7,273	7,903	8,378	10,013	10,944

EQUINOR MARKETING & TRADING (US) INC.

120 LONG RIDGE RD 3E01
STAMFORD, CT 069021839
Phone: 203-978-6900
Fax: –
Web: www.equinor.com

CEO: –
CFO: –
HR: –
FYE: December 31
Type: Private

Check the stats. Oil. Hundreds of thousands of barrels of oil gasoline and more. Statoil Marketing & Trading is a wholesaler of oil and petroleum products. The company is the US trading arm of Statoil the leading Scandinavian oil and gas enterprise. Statoil Marketing & Trading delivers about 600000 barrels a day in the form of crude oil gasoline liquefied petroleum gas (LPG) propane and butane to the North American market. In addition to supplying Norwegian crude the company trades crude oil from Africa South America and North America. Statoil Marketing & Trading sells it oil products primarily to customers in Northeastern Canada the US East Coast and Gulf Coast.

	Annual Growth	12/16	12/17	12/18	12/19	12/20
Sales ($ mil.)	0.3%	–	9,874.2	14,852.2	13,594.6	9,959.5
Net income ($ mil.)	–	–	(28.8)	140.0	88.8	209.6
Market value ($ mil.)	–	–	–	–	–	–
Employees	–	–	–	–	–	5

EQUINOX PAYMENTS LLC

8901 E. Raintree Dr. Ste. 400
Scottsdale AZ 85260
Phone: 480-551-7800
Fax: 512-491-8026
Web: www.lso.com

CEO: Philippe Tartavull
CFO: –
HR: Diane Handley
FYE: December 31
Type: Private

Equinox Payments formerly Hypercom USA provides electronic payment terminals and associated software and services to customers across the US. Businesses use its products to swipe credit debit and smart cards. Its product line also includes printers keypads and networking gear. The company's software encompasses point-of-sale management systems terminal operations and systems monitoring. In addition Equinox provides asset management systems implementation and transaction services. It sells to distributors financial institutions payment processors and retailers. The company is owned by private equity firm The Gores Group.

EQUITY COMMONWEALTH
NYS: EQC

Two North Riverside Plaza, Suite 2100
Chicago, IL 60606
Phone: 312 646-2800
Fax: 617 332-2261
Web: www.eqcre.com

CEO: David Helfand
CFO: William Griffiths
HR: –
FYE: December 31
Type: Public

Equity CommonWealth (formerly CommonWealth REIT) invests in office and industrial properties primarily in the US mainly located in suburbs of major metropolitan markets. Its portfolio includes about 40 properties the majority of which are offices comprising some 17 million sq. ft. of leasable space. Equity CommonWealth was one of the largest industrial private land owners in Oahu until it spun off those assets in 2012; other markets include Boston Philadelphia Southern California and the District of Columbia. GlaxoSmithKline and Office Depot are among the REIT's largest tenants. The REIT has been selling off certain holdings; it has unloaded more than 1 billion sq. ft. since early 2016.

	Annual Growth	12/17	12/18	12/19	12/20	12/21
Sales ($ mil.)	(35.8%)	340.6	197.0	127.9	66.3	58.0
Net income ($ mil.)	–	29.7	272.8	492.7	451.3	(16.4)
Market value ($ mil.)	(4.0%)	3,514.9	3,457.3	3,782.2	3,142.8	2,983.8
Employees	(17.5%)	54	41	28	28	25

EQUITY LIFESTYLE PROPERTIES INC
NYS: ELS

Two North Riverside Plaza, Suite 800
Chicago, IL 60606
Phone: 312 279-1400
Fax: –
Web: www.equitylifestyleproperties.com

CEO: Marguerite Nader
CFO: Paul Seavey
HR: –
FYE: December 31
Type: Public

Snow birds and empty nesters flock to communities developed and owned by Equity LifeStyle Properties. The real estate investment trust (REIT) owns and operates lifestyle-oriented residential properties aimed at retirees vacationers and second home owners. Other properties provide affordable housing for families. Equity LifeStyle Properties leases lots for factory-built homes cottages cabins and recreational vehicles. Available homes range in size and style. The REIT's portfolio includes more than 380 properties containing some 141000 lots in about 30 states and Canada. Properties are similar to site-built residential subdivisions with centralized entrances utilities gutters curbs and paved streets.

	Annual Growth	12/16	12/17	12/18	12/19	12/20
Sales ($ mil.)	5.8%	870.4	925.3	986.7	1,037.3	1,091.4
Net income ($ mil.)	7.1%	173.3	197.6	212.6	279.1	228.3
Market value ($ mil.)	(3.2%)	13,138.8	16,222.2	17,700.1	12,827.2	11,546.1
Employees	(0.6%)	4,100	4,100	4,100	4,200	4,000

EQUITY ONE, INC.

1 INDEPENDENT DR STE 114
JACKSONVILLE, FL 322025005
Phone: 212-796-1760
Fax: –

CEO: –
CFO: –
HR: –
FYE: December 31
Type: Private

Equity One wants to be #1: the number one shopping center owner that is. A real estate investment trust (REIT) Equity One acquires develops and manages shopping centers in urban areas across the US targeting markets in California the northeastern US South Florida Atlanta and Washington DC. Its portfolio consists primarily of more than 120 properties including shopping centers anchored by supermarkets drug stores and other specialty retail chains totaling about 14 million sq. ft. The REIT's top five tenants include Albertsons Publix LA Fitness Food Emporium and TJX Companies. Chairman Chaim Katzman controls the REIT through his Israeli real estate firm Gazit-Globe.

	Annual Growth	12/11	12/12	12/13	12/14	12/16
Assets ($ mil.)	(0.1%)	–	3,502.7	3,354.7	3,262.2	3,494.6
Net income ($ mil.)	78.2%	–	7.2	88.7	61.1	72.8
Market value ($ mil.)	–	–	–	–	–	–
Employees	–	–	–	–	–	155

EQUITY RESIDENTIAL
NYS: EQR

Two North Riverside Plaza
Chicago, IL 60606
Phone: 312 474-1300
Fax: –
Web: www.equityapartments.com

CEO: Mark Parrell
CFO: Robert Garechana
HR: –
FYE: December 31
Type: Public

Equity Residential is one of the largest apartment owners in the US actively investing in rental properties in the urban core of cities and in high density suburban areas near transit entertainment and cultural amenities. The company acquires develops and manages multifamily residential units in the form of garden-style high-rise and mid-rise properties. A real estate investment trust (REIT) Equity Residential owns more than 300 multifamily communities composed of nearly 80000 rentable units in large metropolitan areas such as San Francisco Seattle and New York.

	Annual Growth	12/17	12/18	12/19	12/20	12/21
Sales ($ mil.)	(0.1%)	2,471.4	2,578.4	2,701.1	2,571.7	2,464.0
Net income ($ mil.)	21.9%	603.5	657.5	970.4	913.6	1,332.9
Market value ($ mil.)	9.1%	23,947.4	24,788.6	30,387.7	22,261.3	33,985.2
Employees	(2.9%)	2,700	2,700	2,700	2,600	2,400

ERBA DIAGNOSTICS
ASE: ERB

14100 NW 57th Court
Miami Lakes, FL 33014
Phone: 305 324-2300
Fax: 305 324-2385
Web: www.erbadiagnostics.com

CEO: Hayden Jeffreys
CFO: –
HR: –
FYE: December 31
Type: Public

Using blood sweat or tears ERBA Diagnostics (formerly IVAX Diagnostics) can tell if something is wrong. The company develops manufactures and distributes in vitro diagnostic products to identify autoimmune and infectious diseases based upon samples of bodily fluids. It operates through three subsidiaries. Delta Biologicals develops and manufactures the MAGO and Aptus instrument systems and distributes products to hospitals and medical laboratories in Italy. Diamedix makes and markets diagnostic test kits in the US. ImmunoVision develops makes and markets autoimmune reagents for use by clinical and research labs and other diagnostic manufacturers. ERBA Diagnostics Mannheim holds 72% of the company.

	Annual Growth	12/10	12/11	12/12	12/13	12/14
Sales ($ mil.)	11.6%	17.0	16.8	19.3	28.3	26.4
Net income ($ mil.)	–	(4.2)	(3.3)	(1.6)	0.7	0.4
Market value ($ mil.)	53.6%	25.1	19.4	39.2	120.4	139.8
Employees	6.0%	106	87	99	135	134

ERESEARCHTECHNOLOGY INC.
NASDAQ: ERT

1818 Market St. Suite 1000
Philadelphia PA 19103
Phone: 215-972-0420
Fax: 215-972-0414
Web: www.ert.com

CEO: James Corrigan
CFO: Waqar Nasim
HR: –
FYE: December 31
Type: Private

eResearchTechnology (ERT) e-cares about your e-clinical e-trial by offering support services software and hardware to help streamline the clinical trials process that drugs and medical devices must pass to earn regulatory approval. Its products automate all aspects of the process from setup and data gathering to analysis and FDA application preparation. ERT also provides site support including ECG equipment rentals and sales. Customers include contract research organizations (CROs) drugmakers and medical device firms. Flagship product EXPERT ensures cardiac safety by collecting processing and interpreting electrocardiogram (ECG) data. ERT was taken private by affiliates of Genstar Capital LLC in 2012.

ERHC ENERGY INC.

OTC: ERHE

5444 Westheimer Rd. Ste. 1570
Houston TX 77056
Phone: 713-626-4700
Fax: 713-626-4704
Web: www.erhc.com/

CEO: Peter Ntephe
CFO: -
HR: -
FYE: September 30
Type: Public

Oil out of Africa is the hope of ERHC Energy (formerly Environmental Remediation Holding Corporation) an independent oil and gas company whose sole assets are two West African oil and gas exploration concessions: in the Joint Development Zone between the Sao Tome and Nigeria; and in the Exclusive Economic Zone in Sao Tome. ERHC is teaming up with larger oil and gas companies (such as Noble Energy and Pioneer Natural Resources) to help it develop its holdings. The company is also hoping to acquire interests in high-potential non-producing international prospects in known oil producing areas. Former chairman and CEO Emeka Offor the owner of Chrome Oil Services and Chrome Energy controls about 40% of ERHC.

ERICKSON INC

NBB: EACI Q

5550 S.W. Macadam Avenue, Suite 200
Portland, OR 97239
Phone: 503 505-5800
Fax: -
Web: www.ericksonaircrane.com

CEO: Doug Kitani
CFO: Stephen Wideman
HR: -
FYE: December 31
Type: Public

No light-weight Erickson operates and manufactures S-64 Aircrane helicopters able to lift up to 25000 pounds! Its fleet of 90 rotary-wing and fixed wing aircraft includes 20 S-64s which provide aerial services for such jobs as firefighting and utility logging construction and relief work. Some S-64s are equipped with incident response kits: hose nozzle and holding tank for firefighting rescue basket and aero-medical pod. The company also offers maintenance repair and overhaul services. Customers are fire and forestry agencies construction companies utilities and governments. Founded in 1971 by Jack Erickson the company redeveloped the Sikorsky S-64 and has since expanded internationally.

	Annual Growth	12/11	12/12	12/13	12/14	12/15
Sales ($ mil.)	18.1%	152.8	180.8	318.2	346.6	297.5
Net income ($ mil.)	-	15.9	15.2	9.7	(10.3)	(86.7)
Market value ($ mil.)	(37.6%)	-	117.1	288.9	115.9	28.5
Employees	4.0%	700	700	1,200	1,000	819

ERIE INDEMNITY CO.

NMS: ERIE

100 Erie Insurance Place
Erie, PA 16530
Phone: 814 870-2000
Fax: -
Web: www.erieinsurance.com

CEO: Timothy Necastro
CFO: Gregory Gutting
HR: -
FYE: December 31
Type: Public

Founded in 1925 as an auto insurer Erie Indemnity now provides management services that relate to the sales underwriting and issuance of policies of one customer: Erie Insurance Exchange. The Exchange is a reciprocal insurance exchange that pools the underwriting of several property/casualty insurance firms. The principal personal lines products are private passenger automobile and homeowners. The principal commercial lines products are commercial multi-peril commercial automobile and workers compensation. Historically due to policy renewal and sales patterns the Exchange's direct and affiliated assumed written premiums are greater in the second and third quarters than in the first and fourth quarters of the calendar year. Erie Indemnity charges a management fee of 25% of all premiums written or assumed by the Exchange.

	Annual Growth	12/16	12/17	12/18	12/19	12/20
Assets ($ mil.)	8.1%	1,549.0	1,665.9	1,778.3	2,016.2	2,117.1
Net income ($ mil.)	8.7%	210.4	197.0	288.2	316.8	293.3
Market value ($ mil.)	21.6%	5,194.2	5,628.0	6,157.8	7,667.8	11,344.7
Employees	4.3%	5,000	5,300	5,500	5,700	5,914

EROOM SYSTEM TECHNOLOGIES INC

NBB: ERMS D

150 Airport Road, Suite 1200
Lakewood, NJ 08701
Phone: 732 730-0116
Fax: 732 810-0380
Web: www.eroomsystem.com

CEO: -
CFO: David A Gestetner
HR: -
FYE: December 31
Type: Public

eRoomSystem Technologies is keeping tabs for hotels. The company provides computer-based refreshment centers for the hospitality industry. Its eRoomSystem products track beverage and other refreshment purchases and automatically charge lodgers' accounts. The eRoomSystem generates reports on sales statistics inventory control and restocking requirements. The company's other products include room safes that feature reprogrammable electronic combinations. Through revenue-sharing agreements the company installs its systems and takes a cut of the sales they generate.

	Annual Growth	12/11	12/12	12/13	12/14	12/15
Sales ($ mil.)	3.0%	0.8	0.7	0.6	0.8	0.9
Net income ($ mil.)	-	(0.1)	(0.3)	(0.3)	0.1	0.1
Market value ($ mil.)	-	0.1	0.1	0.0	0.0	0.0
Employees	0.0%	15	17	19	15	15

EROS STX GLOBAL CORP

NYS: ESGC

3900 West Alameda Avenue, 32nd Floor
Burbank, CA 91505
Phone: 818 524-7000
Fax: -
Web: www.erosplc.com

CEO: -
CFO: -
HR: -
FYE: March 31
Type: Public

Entertainment distributor Eros International is there for moviegoers who reside outside of India yet yearn for a taste of Bollywood. The company operates under the goal of creating a global platform for Indian cinema. Its library of content includes more than 2000 Indian films. Eros International also distributes Indian TV DVDs music and digital content. It does so through its network of more than 500 distribution partners across some 50 countries. Eros has offices in India the UK the US Dubai Australia Fiji Isle of Man and Singapore. Founded in 1977 the company was listed on the London Stock Exchange in 2006.

	Annual Growth	03/16	03/17	03/18	03/19	03/20
Sales ($ mil.)	(13.2%)	274.4	253.0	261.3	270.1	155.5
Net income ($ mil.)	-	3.8	3.8	(22.6)	(423.9)	(419.0)
Market value ($ mil.)	-	-	-	-	-	-
Employees	(11.1%)	544	448	423	396	340

ESCALADE, INC.

NMS: ESCA

817 Maxwell Ave.
Evansville, IN 47711
Phone: 812 467-1358
Fax: -
Web: www.escaladeinc.com

CEO: Walter Glazer
CFO: Stephen Wawrin
HR: -
FYE: December 25
Type: Public

Escalade is the world's largest producer of tables for table tennis residential in-ground basketball goals and archery bows. Its other sporting goods include hockey and soccer tables play systems archery darts and fitness equipment. Products are sold under the STIGA Ping-Pong Goalrilla Silverback USWeight and Woodplay names as well as private labels. The company manufactures imports and distributes widely recognized products through major sporting goods retailers specialty dealers key on-line retailers traditional department stores and mass merchants. Escalade operates through more than five manufacturing and distribution facilities across North America. Almost all of Escalade's revenue comes from the North America.

	Annual Growth	12/17	12/18	12/19	12/20	12/21
Sales ($ mil.)	15.3%	177.3	175.8	180.5	273.6	313.6
Net income ($ mil.)	14.8%	14.1	20.4	7.3	25.9	24.4
Market value ($ mil.)	6.3%	166.0	154.4	132.1	292.7	211.7
Employees	7.8%	501	531	468	704	676

ESCALERA RESOURCES CO
NBB: ESCS Q

1675 Broadway, Suite 2200
Denver, CO 80202
Phone: 303 794-8445
Fax: 303 794-8451
Web: www.escaleraresources.com

CEO: -
CFO: -
HR: -
FYE: December 31
Type: Public

It's double or nothing for Double Eagle Petroleum (formerly Double Eagle Petroleum and Mining) which gambles on hitting pay dirt as it explores for and produces oil and gas in the Rocky Mountains of Utah and Wyoming. Double Eagle owns interests in about 900 producing wells; natural gas accounts for more than 95% of the oil and gas independent's production and reserves. The company has proved reserves of more than 413000 barrels of oil and 71.3 billion cu. ft. of natural gas and leases acreage in seven states. Double Eagle sells its oil and gas on the spot market.

	Annual Growth	12/10	12/11	12/12	12/13	12/14
Sales ($ mil.)	(5.4%)	55.0	64.7	38.2	35.3	44.1
Net income ($ mil.)	–	5.5	11.7	(10.3)	(13.1)	(7.6)
Market value ($ mil.)	(16.4%)	370.2	369.8	360.2	329.7	180.8
Employees	3.0%	24	24	24	22	27

ESCALON MEDICAL CORP
NBB: ESMC

435 Devon Park Drive, Suite 824
Wayne, PA 19087
Phone: 610 688-6830
Fax: 610 688-3641
Web: www.escalonmed.com

CEO: Richard DePiano
CFO: Mark Wallace
HR: -
FYE: June 30
Type: Public

Escalon Medical has an eye for ophthalmic instruments. The company develops manufactures markets and distributes diagnostic and surgical devices for use in ophthalmology specifically ultrasound digital photography and image management systems. Its subsidiary companies are branded and operate under the Sonomed Escalon name. Products include the PacScan Plus and Master-Vu ultrasound systems and AXIS image management system. Escalon Medical was founded in 1987. It divested its Escalon Clinical Diagnostics (ECD) business in 2012 to put more focus into growing its ophthalmic business.

	Annual Growth	06/17	06/18	06/19	06/20	06/21
Sales ($ mil.)	(1.7%)	11.2	11.4	9.6	9.4	10.5
Net income ($ mil.)	–	(0.7)	0.6	(0.3)	(0.7)	(0.1)
Market value ($ mil.)	0.0%	1.6	1.7	0.9	0.9	1.6
Employees	(2.8%)	46	43	38	38	41

ESCO CORPORATION

2141 NW 25th Ave.
Portland OR 97210-2578
Phone: 503-228-2141
Fax: 503-226-8071
Web: www.escocorp.com

CEO: Calvin W Collins
CFO: Eric Blackburn
HR: -
FYE: December 31
Type: Private

ESCO is well ensconced as a global manufacturer of metal parts castings and components for industrial machinery. It operates through two segments: engineered products and turbine technologies. Mining customers account for the majority of sales for ESCO's engineered products which include crusher wear-parts and bi-metallic buttons as well as screens blocks tooth systems and other heavy parts that hit the dirt and wear out. Turbine technologies makes cast parts such as blades and vanes used in the aerospace and power generation industries. ESCO was founded in 1913 as Electric Steel Foundry which primarily made trolley car replacement parts. The company filed to go public in 2011.

ESCO TECHNOLOGIES, INC.
NYS: ESE

9900A Clayton Road
St. Louis, MO 63124-1186
Phone: 314 213-7200
Fax: -
Web: www.escotechnologies.com

CEO: Victor Richey
CFO: Christopher Tucker
HR: -
FYE: September 30
Type: Public

ESCO Technologies manufactures highly-engineered filtration and fluid control products for the aviation navy space and process markets worldwide as well as composite-based products and solutions for navy defense and industrial customers; is the industry leader in RF shielding and EMC test products; and provides diagnostic instruments software and services for the benefit of industrial power users and the electric utility and renewable energy industries. Subsidiaries include PTI Doble VACCO and ETS-Lindgren. About 70% of sales are to customers in the US.

	Annual Growth	09/17	09/18	09/19	09/20	09/21
Sales ($ mil.)	1.1%	685.7	771.6	813.0	732.9	715.4
Net income ($ mil.)	4.3%	53.7	92.1	81.0	102.0	63.5
Market value ($ mil.)	6.5%	1,562.4	1,773.5	2,073.4	2,099.5	2,006.7
Employees	(3.5%)	3,254	3,117	3,239	2,844	2,822

ESCREEN INC.

7500 W. 110th St. Ste. 500
Overland Park KS 66210
Phone: 913-327-5915
Fax: 913-327-8606
Web: www.escreen.com

CEO: -
CFO: Mark Brockelman
HR: -
FYE: December 31
Type: Private

eScreen tests for a full range of drugs and e-delivers the results. The company provides drug testing products and services to occupational health facilities throughout the US. eScreen's products are primarily used for pre-employment drug testing. Sample collection takes place at its nationwide network of about 2600 contracted clinics that are equipped with eScreen's products and technology. Samples are collected in an eCup screening device optically scanned on site by the eReader and negative results are electronically reported directly to employers within minutes. Positive results are sent on for further testing before being reported. eScreen was acquired by diagnostics firm Alere in 2012.

ESL FEDERAL CREDIT UNION

225 Chestnut St.
Rochester NY 14604
Phone: 585-336-1000
Fax: +44-20-7691-7745
Web: www.africaneagle.co.uk

CEO: -
CFO: Walter F Rufnak
HR: -
FYE: June 30
Type: Private - Not-for-Pr

Founded in 1920 by George Eastman (also the founder of Eastman Kodak) ESL Federal Credit Union was known as Eastman Savings and Loan until 1996 when it changed its charter from a thrift to a credit union. The company has about 20 branches in upstate New York that offer deposit accounts credit cards insurance and investment products. It originates consumer loans and mortgages including automobile boat and home improvement loans. The credit union has some 310000 members; membership is available to employees and retirees of Eastman Kodak and its subsidiaries as well as a handful of other employer groups and residents of Rochester New York.

ESPERION THERAPEUTICS INC (NEW)   NMS: ESPR

3891 Ranchero Drive, Suite 150
Ann Arbor, MI 48108
Phone: 734 887-3903
Fax: –
Web: www.esperion.com

CEO: Sheldon Koenig
CFO: Richard Bartram
HR: –
FYE: December 31
Type: Public

'Bad' cholesterol is public enemy #1 at Esperion Therapeutics. A biopharmaceutical company with expertise in lipid management Esperion researches and develops therapies that reduce elevated LDL-C levels in patients' blood. The firm owns the global rights to bempedoic acid a novel cholesterol-lowering agent. Its primary product candidate a pill combining bempedoic acid and ezetimibe has been shown to reduce LDL-C levels in clinical studies.

	Annual Growth	12/17	12/18	12/19	12/20	12/21
Sales ($ mil.)	(27.3%)	–	–	148.4	227.5	78.4
Net income ($ mil.)	–	(167.0)	(201.8)	(97.2)	(143.6)	(269.1)
Market value ($ mil.)	(47.5%)	4,008.3	2,800.5	3,630.2	1,582.9	304.4
Employees	39.8%	57	76	193	479	218

ESPEY MANUFACTURING & ELECTRONICS CORP.   ASE: ESP

233 Ballston Avenue
Saratoga Springs, NY 12866
Phone: 518 245-4400
Fax: –
Web: www.espey.com

CEO: David O'Neil
CFO: Katrina Sparano
HR: Peggy Murphy
FYE: June 30
Type: Public

Espey is on a power trip. Espey Mfg. & Electronics makes electronic equipment for high-voltage applications including specialized electronic power supplies transformers and electronic system components. Its transformers and electronic systems include high-power radar transmitters antennas and iron-core products such as magnetic amplifiers and audio filters. The company's products are used by industrial and military customers in radar missile guidance and control communications aircraft navigation and nuclear submarine control. Customers include General Electric Lockheed Martin Raytheon and the US government. Exports account for more than 20% of Espey's sales.

	Annual Growth	06/17	06/18	06/19	06/20	06/21
Sales ($ mil.)	5.3%	22.5	32.5	36.5	31.5	27.7
Net income ($ mil.)	–	1.1	3.1	2.3	1.2	(0.2)
Market value ($ mil.)	(9.8%)	60.6	72.5	66.9	46.8	40.1
Employees	2.1%	138	164	160	151	150

ESPN INC.

ESPN Plaza 935 Middle St.
Bristol CT 06010
Phone: 860-766-2000
Fax: +60-3-2273-0608
Web: www.aet-tankers.com

CEO: Pittsburgh Penguins
CFO: –
HR: –
FYE: September 30
Type: Joint Venture

ESPN is a superstar of the sports broadcasting world. The company is the leading cable sports broadcaster reaching about 100 million US viewers per month with its stable of channels including ESPN ESPN2 and ESPN Classic. The 24-hour networks carry a variety of live sporting events as well as programs devoted to news and analysis. ESPN also creates original programming for TV and radio and lends content for ESPN.com one of the most popular sports sites on the Internet. Its international operations extend the ESPN brand to another 200 countries. ESPN is 80% owned by Walt Disney (through ABC); media conglomerate Hearst has a 20% stake.

ESSA BANCORP INC   NMS: ESSA

200 Palmer Street
Stroudsburg, PA 18360
Phone: 570 421-0531
Fax: –
Web: www.essabank.com

CEO: Gary Olson
CFO: Allan Muto
HR: Thomas Grayuski
FYE: September 30
Type: Public

ESSA Bancorp is the holding company for ESSA Bank & Trust. Founded in 1916 the bank offers deposit and lending services to consumers and businesses through more than 25 branches located in eastern Pennsylvania's Lehigh Monroe and Northampton counties. One- to four-family residential mortgages dominate the bank's lending activities representing more than 80% of its loan portfolio. Commercial real estate loans account for 10% while home equity loans and lines of credit make up ESSA's other significant loan segments. The bank also offers financial and investment services through a third-party firm. ESSA Bancorp acquired First Star Bancorp in 2012 adding nine branches in Lehigh County.

	Annual Growth	09/17	09/18	09/19	09/20	09/21
Assets ($ mil.)	1.1%	1,785.2	1,833.8	1,799.4	1,893.5	1,861.4
Net income ($ mil.)	22.3%	7.3	6.5	12.6	14.4	16.4
Market value ($ mil.)	1.2%	164.2	170.1	171.8	129.0	172.5
Employees	(6.1%)	323	277	262	252	251

ESSENDANT INC   NMS: ESND

One Parkway North Boulevard, Suite 100
Deerfield, IL 60015-2559
Phone: 847 627-7000
Fax: 847 627-7001
Web: www.unitedstationers.com

CEO: –
CFO: Janet Zelenka
HR: –
FYE: December 31
Type: Public

Essendant strives to make the workplace work. The company is a leading distributor of supplies and equipment for offices and other workplaces. Its more than 190000 products include janitorial and breakroom supplies; digital cameras printers data storage and other technology products; and traditional office supplies as well as paper products automotive products and office furniture. Essendant distributes products from major suppliers such as Hewlett-Packard Rubbermaid and Clorox and offers items under its own brand names which include Boardwalk Innovera Universal and Windsoft. It serves some 29000 customers mostly independent resellers. The company generates most of its sales in the US.

	Annual Growth	12/12	12/13	12/14	12/15	12/16
Sales ($ mil.)	1.4%	5,080.1	5,085.3	5,327.2	5,363.0	5,369.0
Net income ($ mil.)	(13.1%)	111.8	123.2	119.2	(44.3)	63.9
Market value ($ mil.)	(9.4%)	1,161.6	1,720.1	1,580.3	1,218.6	783.4
Employees	2.0%	6,100	6,100	6,500	6,400	6,600

ESSENTIAL UTILITIES INC   NYS: WTRG

762 W Lancaster Avenue
Bryn Mawr, PA 19010-3489
Phone: 610 527-8000
Fax: –
Web: www.essential.co

CEO: Christopher Franklin
CFO: Daniel Schuller
HR: –
FYE: December 31
Type: Public

Essential Utilities (Essential) formerly Aqua America provides water or wastewater services to some 3 million customers in Pennsylvania Ohio Texas Illinois North Carolina New Jersey Indiana and Virginia. It is the holding company for several regulated utilities the largest being Aqua Pennsylvania. Additionally the company provides non-utility water supply services for the natural gas drilling industry manages a water system operating and maintenance contracts as well as sewer line protection solutions and repair service to households. The company was formed in 1968. Some 55% of Essential's total sales comes from Pennsylvania.

	Annual Growth	12/16	12/17	12/18	12/19	12/20
Sales ($ mil.)	15.6%	819.9	809.5	838.1	889.7	1,462.7
Net income ($ mil.)	5.0%	234.2	239.7	192.0	224.5	284.8
Market value ($ mil.)	12.0%	7,371.5	9,626.7	8,389.9	11,518.6	11,604.5
Employees	19.7%	1,551	1,530	1,570	1,583	3,180

ESSEX PROPERTY TRUST INC
NYS: ESS

1100 Park Place, Suite 200
San Mateo, CA 94403
Phone: 650 655-7800
Fax: –
Web: www.essex.com

CEO: Michael Schall
CFO: Barbara Pak
HR: –
FYE: December 31
Type: Public

Essex Property Trust acquires develops redevelops and manages apartment communities located along the West Coast of the US. The self-managed and self-administered real estate investment trust (REIT) owns about 245 apartment communities aggregating some 60270 apartment homes excluding the company's ownership in preferred equity co-investments loan investments one operating commercial building and a development pipeline comprised of three consolidated projects and three unconsolidated joint venture projects aggregating more than 1850 apartment homes.

	Annual Growth	12/16	12/17	12/18	12/19	12/20
Sales ($ mil.)	3.7%	1,294.0	1,363.9	1,400.1	1,460.2	1,495.7
Net income ($ mil.)	8.2%	415.0	433.1	390.2	439.3	568.9
Market value ($ mil.)	0.5%	15,112.3	15,688.8	15,938.4	19,555.6	15,432.1
Employees	0.0%	1,799	1,835	1,826	1,822	1,799

ESSEX RENTAL CORP
NBB: ESSX

1110 Lake Cook Road, Suite 220
Buffalo Grove, IL 60089
Phone: 847 215-6500
Fax: –
Web: www.essexrentalcorp.com

CEO: Nicholas J Matthews
CFO: Kory M Glen
HR: –
FYE: December 31
Type: Public

Unless you employ construction workers who moonlight as super heroes you may need to rent one of Essex Rental's cranes to hoist those steel beams and concrete pipes. Specializing in lattice-boom crawler cranes (large heavy-duty cranes with dynamic lifting capabilities) Essex Rental rents a fleet of some 350 Manitowoc and Liebherr brand cranes and attachments to North American construction and industrial companies and municipalities. Its cranes are typically used in the construction of power plants petrochemical plants water treatment and purification facilities as well as in commercial and infrastructure construction. Essex also sells used equipment and offers crane transportation and repair services.

	Annual Growth	12/10	12/11	12/12	12/13	12/14
Sales ($ mil.)	25.6%	41.5	89.6	98.3	95.5	103.4
Net income ($ mil.)	–	(9.6)	(17.1)	(12.7)	(9.6)	(11.2)
Market value ($ mil.)	(30.0%)	136.5	73.2	84.9	81.2	32.8
Employees	(1.5%)	276	273	250	236	260

ESTEE LAUDER INTERNATIONAL INC.

767 5th Ave.
New York NY 10153-0023
Phone: 212-572-4200
Fax: 212-572-3941
Web: www.esteelauder.com

CEO: –
CFO: –
HR: –
FYE: June 30
Type: Subsidiary

While its parent company is well-established in the US Estee Lauder International enjoys the same prestige worldwide. The company is a subsidiary of Estee Lauder Companies and is the arm of the company that extends outside the US and Canada. The company sells cosmetics fragrances and skin care products under the Flirt! Tom Ford Beauty Bobbi Brown Clinique Prescriptives and Donna Karan Cosmetics names among others. Founded in 1946 the Estee Lauder company is known for its upscale beauty items and dedication to research and product testing. The company develops and markets men's fragrances (such as Sean John Fragrances and Aramis) as well as men's Lab Series Skin Care for Men.

ESTERLINE TECHNOLOGIES CORP
NYS: ESL

500 108th Avenue North East
Bellevue, WA 98004
Phone: 425 453-9400
Fax: –
Web: www.esterline.com

CEO: Curtis C Reusser
CFO: Stephen M Nolan
HR: –
FYE: September 28
Type: Public

You couldn't build an entire jet just from Esterline Technologies products but it would hard to fly one without them. The aerospace company's offerings extend from the cockpit to electrical subsystems to materials inside and outside aircraft. It makes avionics that control and communicate sensors and power switching devices that monitor conditions and materials necessary for commercial and military aircraft. Esterline sells mostly to the US government particularly the Department of Defense and aircraft manufacturers. About a fifth of sales come from high-end non-aerospace products. There can be as much as $1 million worth of Esterline products in jet fighters and airliners.

	Annual Growth	10/14	10/15*	09/16	09/17	09/18
Sales ($ mil.)	(0.2%)	2,051.2	1,774.4	1,992.6	2,002.2	2,034.8
Net income ($ mil.)	(9.3%)	102.4	59.6	101.7	117.4	69.5
Market value ($ mil.)	(6.1%)	3,449.3	2,109.4	2,239.6	2,655.2	2,678.8
Employees	(0.5%)	12,874	13,290	13,572	13,255	12,609

*Fiscal year change

ESTES EXPRESS LINES

3901 W BROAD ST
RICHMOND, VA 232303962
Phone: 804-353-1900
Fax: –
Web: www.estes-express.com

CEO: Robey W Estes Jr
CFO: –
HR: –
FYE: December 31
Type: Private

Estes Express is the largest privately-owned freight shipping company in North America. Its fleet of over 7000 tractors and some 30000 trailers operates via a network of more than 260 terminals dotting the US. The company provides reliable Less Than Truckload (LTL) freight solutions to and from all 50 states Canada Mexico and the Caribbean as well as asset-based and brokered Volume LTL and Truckload shipping to regional national international and offshore destinations. The company was founded in 1931 when W.W. Estes bought a used Chevrolet truck to haul livestock to market for his neighbors in rural Virginia.

	Annual Growth	12/16	12/17	12/18	12/19	12/20
Sales ($ mil.)	9.2%	–	2,731.5	3,159.8	3,259.1	3,559.2
Net income ($ mil.)	28.9%	–	231.2	252.1	251.6	495.0
Market value ($ mil.)	–	–	–	–	–	–
Employees	–	–	–	–	–	14,000

ETHAN ALLEN INTERIORS, INC.
NYS: ETD

25 Lake Avenue Ext.
Danbury, CT 06811-5286
Phone: 203 743-8000
Fax: –
Web: www.ethanallen.com

CEO: Farooq Kathwari
CFO: Matthew McNulty
HR: –
FYE: June 30
Type: Public

Ethan Allen Interiors is a leading interior design company manufacturer and retailer in the home furnishings marketplace. Named after the American patriot the vertically integrated firm boasts nine furniture factories including one saw mill and one lumberyard. The company's products include case goods (wood furniture such as beds dressers and tables) upholstery items (sofas recliners) and accessories (wall decor lighting). These products are sold through more than 300 Ethan Allen stores located primarily in the US. More than half of its stores are operated by independent dealers who are required to deal exclusively in Ethan Allen products and follow company guidelines.

	Annual Growth	06/17	06/18	06/19	06/20	06/21
Sales ($ mil.)	(2.7%)	763.4	766.8	746.7	589.8	685.2
Net income ($ mil.)	13.5%	36.2	36.4	25.7	8.9	60.0
Market value ($ mil.)	(3.9%)	815.2	618.3	531.5	298.6	696.5
Employees	(5.3%)	5,200	5,200	4,900	3,369	4,188

ETNA DISTRIBUTORS, LLC

4901 CLAY AVE SW
GRAND RAPIDS, MI 495483074
Phone: 616-245-4373
Fax: –
Web: www.etnasupply.com

CEO: David L Potgeter
CFO: –
HR: Julie Pardoe
FYE: December 31
Type: Private

Etna Supply distributes equipment and supplies for residential and commercial plumbing pipe water meters fire hydrants and the related support services.. It operates through about 20 locations in Michigan Wisconsin Indiana and Ohio. The company also offers related services such as custom pipe flaring and threading and welding services. Customers include residential and commercial industries. Etna Supply was founded in 1965.

	Annual Growth	12/08	12/09	12/10	12/11	12/12
Sales ($ mil.)	4.4%	–	–	130.2	132.8	141.8
Net income ($ mil.)	(51.8%)	–	–	2.9	0.8	0.7
Market value ($ mil.)	–	–	–	–	–	–
Employees	–	–	–	–	–	285

ETS-LINDGREN LP

1301 Arrow Point Dr.
Cedar Park TX 78613
Phone: 512-531-6400
Fax: 512-531-6500
Web: www.ets-lindgren.com

CEO: –
CFO: –
HR: –
FYE: September 30
Type: Subsidiary

ETS-Lindgren (ETS) makes working with energy emissions A-OK. The company offers products that detect measure and manage electromagnetic magnetic and acoustic energy. Its products are used in the acoustics automotive electronics health and safety medical military and wireless communications markets. ETS also provides supporting services such as consultation custom designs and site surveying. Customers include Apple Cisco GE Healthcare GM IBM Siemens Healthcare Sony Electronics Sun Microsystems and Xerox. Founded in 1951 by Erik Lindgren the company became a subsidiary of ESCO Technologies in 2000. ETS-Lindgren has offices in China Finland France Japan Singapore Taiwan the UK and the US.

EUGENE WATER & ELECTRIC BOARD

500 E 4TH AVE
EUGENE, OR 974012465
Phone: 541-685-7000
Fax: –
Web: www.eweb.org

CEO: –
CFO: –
HR: –
FYE: December 31
Type: Private

Power (and water) to the people is the the belief and practice of Eugene Water & Electric Board (EWEB) the source of power and water for residents and businesses in Eugene Oregon. The utility is one of Oregon's largest municipal utilities. It has more than 89000 electric customers and about 52000 water customers. EWEB generates 110 MW of capacity at its hydroelectric and fossil-fueled power plants; it gets the rest of its power supply from other generators including the Bonneville Power Administration. The utility gets its water supply from the McKenzie River.

	Annual Growth	12/14	12/15	12/16	12/17	12/18
Sales ($ mil.)	1.4%	–	276.5	284.2	294.2	288.4
Net income ($ mil.)	–	–	39.7	29.7	31.6	(0.6)
Market value ($ mil.)	–	–	–	–	–	–
Employees	–	–	–	–	–	460

EUREKA FINANCIAL CORP (MD)

NBB: EKFC

3455 Forbes Avenue
Pittsburgh, PA 15213
Phone: 412 681-8400
Fax: 412 681-6625
Web: www.eurekabancorp.com

CEO: Edward Seserko
CFO: Gary B Pepper
HR: –
FYE: September 30
Type: Public

Eureka will help you eke the most out of your income. Eureka Financial is the holding company of the single-branch Eureka Bank a thrift serving Pittsburgh's Oakland neighborhood near the University of Pittsburgh. Originally chartered in 1886 the bank offers standard personal and business deposit products including checking and savings accounts CDs and IRAs. Eureka Bank is focused on real estate lending: Real estate loans — mostly single-family mortgages — account for three-quarters of its total loan portfolio. It also offers commercial and consumer loans. Eureka Bancorp MHC owns a majority of Eureka Financial.

	Annual Growth	09/10	09/11	09/12	09/13	09/14
Sales ($ mil.)	3.7%	6.0	6.8	7.0	6.9	6.9
Net income ($ mil.)	20.8%	0.7	1.3	1.5	1.4	1.5
Market value ($ mil.)	15.2%	–	14.7	19.1	21.0	22.5
Employees	(3.0%)	–	23	22	21	21

EUROFINS LANCASTER LABORATORIES, INC.

2425 NEW HOLLAND PIKE
LANCASTER, PA 176015946
Phone: 717-656-2300
Fax: –
Web: www.eurofinsus.com

CEO: Timothy S Oostdyk
CFO: –
HR: –
FYE: December 31
Type: Private

Don't buy those Bunsen burners. Let Lancaster Laboratories handle it. One of the largest contract laboratories in the country it provides chemical and microbiological analytical research and testing services in the pharmaceutical and environmental sciences to commercial customers in several industries. Customers can access their analytical data around the clock on the Web through the company's LabAccess service. It also offers staffing services to clients involved in long-term projects through its Professional Scientific Staffing division. Founded in 1961 Lancaster Laboratories serves many global FORTUNE 500 companies. Thermo Fisher Scientific sold the company to Eurofins Scientific in 2011.

	Annual Growth	12/11	12/12	12/13	12/14	12/15
Sales ($ mil.)	(7.7%)	–	–	146.9	153.7	125.1
Net income ($ mil.)	4.8%	–	–	11.4	16.1	12.6
Market value ($ mil.)	–	–	–	–	–	–
Employees	–	–	–	–	–	1,500

EUROMARKET DESIGNS INC.

1250 Techny Rd.
Northbrook IL 60062
Phone: 847-272-2888
Fax: 847-272-5366
Web: www.crateandbarrel.com

CEO: Janet Hayes
CFO: –
HR: –
FYE: February 28
Type: Private

Think you've never bought anything from Euromarket Designs? Think again. The retailer which does business under the Crate & Barrel name pioneered the fashionable-yet-homey look for contemporary interiors offering furniture housewares and linens in au courant colors and styles. It operates some 160 Crate & Barrel locations (including a dozen outlet stores) in 30 states and also peddles products through its catalogs and website. Euromarket Designs' other retailing ventures include CB2 (modern home furnishings) and The Land of Nod (furniture and toys for kids). Founded by Carole and Gordon Segal in 1962 the company is majority-owned by Germany-based Otto one of the world's leading mail-order merchants.

EURONET WORLDWIDE INC.
NMS: EEFT

11400 Tomahawk Creek Parkway, Suite 300
Leawood, KS 66211
Phone: 913 327-4200
Fax: 913 327-1921
Web: www.euronetworldwide.com

CEO: Michael Brown
CFO: Rick Weller
HR: Ashwin Gawane
FYE: December 31
Type: Public

Euronet Worldwide might soon have the whole world in its net — thanks to the growing electronic payments industry. The company offers ATM and POS services prepaid mobile top-up and gift card solutions as well as cash-based and online global money remittance and payment services. It operates three primary businesses: epay (which sells prepaid mobile airtime and related products and services) EFT (electronic financial transaction processing software and ATM/POS management services); and consumer-to-consumer money transfer. Founded in 1994 Euronet operates in approximately 175 countries and its top markets are the US and Germany.

	Annual Growth	12/16	12/17	12/18	12/19	12/20
Sales ($ mil.)	6.1%	1,958.6	2,252.4	2,536.6	2,750.1	2,482.7
Net income ($ mil.)	—	174.4	156.8	232.9	346.7	(3.4)
Market value ($ mil.)	18.9%	3,819.5	4,443.9	5,398.9	8,308.8	7,642.2
Employees	6.9%	6,200	6,600	7,100	7,700	8,100

EVANGELICAL COMMUNITY HOSPITAL

1 HOSPITAL DR
LEWISBURG, PA 178379350
Phone: 570-522-2000
Fax: —
Web: www.evanhospital.com

CEO: —
CFO: Christine Martin
HR: —
FYE: June 30
Type: Private

Evangelical Community Hospital brings the good news of community health to residents in central Pennsylvania. The hospital provides a wide range of medical services to communities in the Susquehanna Valley. Among its specialized services are home health care and hospice maternity oncology rehabilitation and pediatrics. The hospital delivers more than 1000 babies annually and treats more than 30000 patients in its emergency department each year. Its outreach network includes family practice offices and other medical services. Despite its name the hospital has no affiliation with any religious organization.

	Annual Growth	06/17	06/18	06/19	06/20	06/21
Sales ($ mil.)	14.9%	—	—	211.0	205.3	278.6
Net income ($ mil.)	—	—	—	14.9	13.5	(0.4)
Market value ($ mil.)	—	—	—	—	—	—
Employees	—	—	—	—	—	1,360

EVANS & SUTHERLAND COMPUTER CORP.
NBB: ESCC

770 Komas Drive
Salt Lake City, UT 84108
Phone: 801 588-1000
Fax: —

CEO: Jonathan A Shaw
CFO: Paul L Dailey
HR: —
FYE: December 31
Type: Public

Evans & Sutherland Computer (E&S) makes products that can impartially be described as stellar. The company provides hardware and software used in digital planetariums and other theaters. Its products include laser projectors domed projection screens and complete planetarium packages. The company also produces planetarium content. E&S sells its visual systems to theaters and schools; its domes are additionally marketed to casinos theme parks and military contractors. The company counts Disney Griffith Observatory IMAX Texas A&M University and Universal Studios among its customers. E&S gets more than half of its sales in the US.

	Annual Growth	12/14	12/15	12/16	12/17	12/18
Sales ($ mil.)	8.9%	26.5	35.3	32.9	30.5	37.2
Net income ($ mil.)	—	(1.3)	(1.3)	1.7	1.5	3.7
Market value ($ mil.)	16.9%	4.5	10.2	14.8	11.2	8.4
Employees	(0.8%)	99	96	91	96	96

EVANS BANCORP, INC.
ASE: EVBN

6460 Main St
Williamsville, NY 14221
Phone: 716 926-2000
Fax: —
Web: www.evansbancorp.com

CEO: David Nasca
CFO: John Connerton
HR: —
FYE: December 31
Type: Public

Evans National Bank wants to take care of Buffalo's bills. The subsidiary of Evans Bancorp operates about a dozen branches in western New York (including Buffalo). The bank primarily uses funds gathered from deposits to originate commercial and residential real estate loans (more than 70% of its loan portfolio) and to invest in securities. Subsidiaries include ENB Insurance Agency which sells property/casualty insurance; ENB Associates offering mutual funds and annuities to bank customers; and Evans National Leasing which provides financing for business equipment throughout the US. In 2009 Evans Bancorp acquired the assets and single branch of the failed Waterford Village Bank in Clarence New York.

	Annual Growth	12/16	12/17	12/18	12/19	12/20
Assets ($ mil.)	16.7%	1,100.7	1,295.6	1,388.2	1,460.2	2,044.1
Net income ($ mil.)	8.0%	8.3	10.5	16.4	17.0	11.2
Market value ($ mil.)	(3.3%)	170.7	226.7	175.9	217.0	149.0
Employees	5.0%	254	271	237	250	309

EVENT NETWORK, INC.

9606 AERO DR STE 1000
SAN DIEGO, CA 921231869
Phone: 858-222-6100
Fax: —
Web: www.eventnetwork.com

CEO: Larry Gilbert
CFO: Larry Eyler
HR: —
FYE: September 27
Type: Private

Event Network would like you to exit through the gift shop. The company (doing business as e|n) manages the retail gift shops on behalf of museums zoos aquariums gardens and other public cultural attractions. It designs and supplies stores with distinctive merchandise such as apparel toys and games coffee mugs key chains jewelry books and art. e|n's partner network includes more than 70 cultural attractions including the American Museum of Natural History in New York City the Gettysburg National Battlefield Museum the Philadelphia Zoo and the Shedd Aquarium in Chicago. It also operates the e-commerce websites of more than 55 attractions. e|n was founded in 1998 by Larry Gilbert and Helen Sherman.

	Annual Growth	09/05	09/06	09/07	09/08	09/09
Sales ($ mil.)	20.5%	—	—	73.5	92.5	106.7
Net income ($ mil.)	83.5%	—	—	1.7	2.8	5.6
Market value ($ mil.)	—	—	—	—	—	—
Employees	—	—	—	—	—	900

EVERBANK FINANCIAL CORP
NYS: EVER

501 Riverside Ave.
Jacksonville, FL 32202
Phone: 904 281-6000
Fax: —
Web: www.everbank.com

CEO: —
CFO: Virginia M Wilson
HR: —
FYE: December 31
Type: Public

EverBank Financial and its subsidiaries provide a range of financial services including banking investment services lending commercial financing and mortgage servicing. Its EverBank subsidiary offers community banking from more than a dozen branches in Florida. The bank's wholesale lending division provides loan products to mortgage brokers nationwide while its Everhome Mortgage subsidiary services a nearly $60 billion home loan portfolio. EverBank Direct provides online banking and brokerage. EverBank Financial also has units devoted to wealth management and commercial finance. TIAA is buying EverBank for some $2.5 billion.

	Annual Growth	12/11	12/12	12/13	12/14	12/15
Assets ($ mil.)	19.5%	13,041.7	18,242.9	17,641.0	21,617.8	26,601.0
Net income ($ mil.)	25.4%	52.7	74.0	136.7	148.1	130.5
Market value ($ mil.)	2.3%	—	1,864.1	2,292.9	2,382.9	1,997.8
Employees	5.7%	2,400	3,700	4,000	3,100	3,000

EVERCORE INC

NYS: EVR

55 East 52nd Street
New York, NY 10055
Phone: 212 857-3100
Fax: 212 857-3101
Web: www.evercore.com

CEO: Ralph Schlosstein
CFO: Celeste Mellet Brown
HR: –
FYE: December 31
Type: Public

Evercore is the leading independent investment banking advisory firm in the world based on the dollar volume of announced worldwide merger and acquisition (M&A) transactions. The company provides advisory services on mergers and mergers and acquisitions strategic shareholder advisory restructurings and capital structure to corporate clients. Boasting some $10.2 billion in assets under management the company's investment management business principally manages and invests capital for clients including institutional investors and private equity businesses. Evercore also makes private equity investments. Beyond the US the company operates globally through subsidiaries such as Evercore Partners in the UK. About 75% of the company's revenue comes from its domestic operations. Evercore was founded in 1995.

	Annual Growth	12/16	12/17	12/18	12/19	12/20
Sales ($ mil.)	12.0%	1,440.1	1,704.3	2,064.7	2,008.7	2,263.9
Net income ($ mil.)	34.4%	107.5	125.5	377.2	297.4	350.6
Market value ($ mil.)	12.4%	2,799.5	3,667.5	2,916.1	3,046.5	4,467.9
Employees	5.1%	1,475	1,600	1,700	1,900	1,800

EVERGREEN FS INC

402 N HERSHEY RD
BLOOMINGTON, IL 61704-3546
Phone: 309-663-2392
Fax: –
Web: www.home.evergreen-fs.com

CEO: –
CFO: –
HR: –
FYE: August 31
Type: Private

Evergreen FS is an agricultural cooperative serving the needs of northern Illinois farmers. The co-op provides a full range of farm supplies and services including agronomy feed seed fertilizer fuel financing and marketing advice and products. It also operates six grain elevators. The co-op's 13000 member/owners operate farmland in the counties of McLean Woodford and Livingston. Evergreen FS is a member of the GROWMARK system.

	Annual Growth	08/06	08/07	08/09	08/10	08/11
Sales ($ mil.)	10.7%	–	204.9	0.0	246.7	307.9
Net income ($ mil.)	28.4%	–	3.8	0.0	7.8	10.4
Market value ($ mil.)	–	–	–	–	–	–
Employees	–	–	–	–	–	240

EVERGREEN STATE COLLEGE

2700 EVERGREEN PKWY NW
OLYMPIA, WA 985050005
Phone: 360-867-6000
Fax: –
Web: www.evergreen.edu

CEO: –
CFO: –
HR: –
FYE: June 30
Type: Private

Puget Sounders can earn their sheepskins at The Evergreen State College. The public liberal arts and sciences college the largest of its type in Washington state offers a variety of undergraduate degrees as well as graduate-level programs in environmental studies public administration and education. Evergreen is known for its unusual approach to learning; students enroll in comprehensive programs rather than a series of separate classes and courses are taught by teams of two to four professors. Students then receive "narrative" evaluations rather than traditional letter grades. Tuition per year is $5133 (residents) and $16440 (non-residents).

	Annual Growth	06/04	06/05	06/06	06/07	06/08
Sales ($ mil.)	–	–	–	0.0	56.5	56.7
Net income ($ mil.)	–	–	–	0.0	6.6	20.8
Market value ($ mil.)	–	–	–	–	–	–
Employees	–	–	–	–	–	580

EVERI HOLDINGS INC

NYS: EVRI

7250 S. Tenaya Way, Suite 100
Las Vegas, NV 89113
Phone: 800 833-7110
Fax: –
Web: www.everi.com

CEO: Michael Rumbolz
CFO: Mark Labay
HR: –
FYE: December 31
Type: Public

If you're losing your shirt at the casino tables Global Cash Access can get you more money on the spot. The company provides such services as ATM cash withdrawals credit- and debit-card advances and check guarantee to the gaming industry in the US Canada Europe Central America the Caribbean and Asia. The company provides services to some 1000 casinos such as Foxwoods Resort Casino. Global Cash Access also has developed cashless gaming systems including special ticket vouchers and systems that allow players to access funds without leaving their gaming machines. Other services include casino marketing and patron credit information through its QuikReports and CentralCredit database.

	Annual Growth	12/16	12/17	12/18	12/19	12/20
Sales ($ mil.)	(18.3%)	859.5	974.9	469.5	533.2	383.7
Net income ($ mil.)	–	(249.5)	(51.9)	12.4	16.5	(81.7)
Market value ($ mil.)	58.8%	188.1	653.6	446.4	1,164.1	1,197.1
Employees	9.6%	900	1,100	1,250	1,400	1,300

EVERSOURCE ENERGY

NYS: ES

300 Cadwell Drive
Springfield, MA 01104
Phone: 800 286-5000
Fax: –
Web: www.eversource.com

CEO: Joseph Nolan
CFO: Philip Lembo
HR: –
FYE: December 31
Type: Public

The largest energy delivery company in New England Eversource Energy serves roughly four million electric and gas customers via its six distinct utility companies in Connecticut Massachusetts and New Hampshire. Eversource delivers its energy through about 628000 overhead and underground lines and covers over 3200 square miles of natural gas distribution. Its electricity-focused utility companies include Public Service Company of New Hampshire (PSNH) The Connecticut Light and Power Company and NSTAR Electric Company. Eversource's gas utilities are NSTAR Gas and Yankee Gas which supply natural gas to about 300000 customers in central and eastern Massachusetts and about 241000 customers in Connecticut respectively. The company also operates a water utilities subsidiary Eversource Aquarion Holdings in Connecticut Massachusetts and New Hampshire.

	Annual Growth	12/17	12/18	12/19	12/20	12/21
Sales ($ mil.)	6.2%	7,752.0	8,448.2	8,526.5	8,904.4	9,863.1
Net income ($ mil.)	5.4%	988.0	1,033.0	909.1	1,205.2	1,220.5
Market value ($ mil.)	9.5%	21,759.4	22,400.0	29,298.4	29,794.3	31,333.8
Employees	3.4%	8,084	7,998	8,234	9,299	9,227

EVERSOURCE ENERGY SERVICE COMPANY

56 PROSPECT ST
HARTFORD, CT 061032818
Phone: 800-286-5000
Fax: –
Web: www.eversource.com

CEO: James Judge
CFO: Philip Lembo
HR: –
FYE: December 31
Type: Private

Northeast Utilities Service Company (NUSCO) provides support and reports for its cohorts. The company was created in 1966 to centralize corporate activities for Northeast Utilities (renamed Eversource Energy). NUSCO acts as an agent and offers centralized administrative services not only for its parent company Northeast Utilities but all of its subsidiaries (Connecticut Light and Power Public Service Company of New Hampshire Western Massachusetts Electric and Yankee Gas Services Company) as well. NUSCO duties include accounting financial legal operational information technology engineering planning and purchasing services.

	Annual Growth	12/04	12/05	12/07	12/08	12/16
Sales ($ mil.)	–	–	0.0	5,822.2	5,800.1	831.2
Net income ($ mil.)	–	–	0.0	246.5	260.8	11.6
Market value ($ mil.)	–	–	–	–	–	–
Employees	–	–	–	–	–	4,550

EVI INDUSTRIES INC   ASE: EVI

4500 Biscayne Blvd., Suite 340 — CEO: Henry Nahmad
Miami, FL 33137 — CFO: Robert Lazar
Phone: 305 402-9300 — HR: –
Fax: – — FYE: June 30
Web: www.evi-ind.com — Type: Public

EnviroStar (formerly DRYCLEAN USA) is anything but hard pressed. The firm franchises and licenses more than 400 retail dry cleaners in three US states the Caribbean and Latin America through its DRYCLEAN USA unit. However most of its sales are generated by subsidiary Steiner-Atlantic which sells coin-operated laundry machines steam boilers and other laundry equipment; most are sold under the Aero-Tech Green-Jet and Multi-Jet names to some 750 customers and include independent dry cleaners hotels cruise lines and hospitals. The company was founded in 1963 under the name Metro-Tel Corp. It changed its name to DRYCLEAN USA in 1999.

	Annual Growth	06/17	06/18	06/19	06/20	06/21
Sales ($ mil.)	26.7%	94.0	150.0	228.3	235.8	242.0
Net income ($ mil.)	27.6%	3.2	4.0	3.7	0.8	8.4
Market value ($ mil.)	1.2%	332.1	494.8	469.9	266.6	348.7
Employees	39.7%	138	264	475	493	526

EVOLUTION PETROLEUM CORP   ASE: EPM

1155 Dairy Ashford Road, Suite 425 — CEO: Jason Brown
Houston, TX 77079 — CFO: Ryan Stash
Phone: 713 935-0122 — HR: –
Fax: 713 935-0199 — FYE: June 30
Web: www.evolutionpetroleum.com — Type: Public

Just as petroleum and natural gas evolves from old living forms Evolution Petroleum has evolved by producing these ancient hydrocarbons. The company operates oil and gas producing fields in Louisiana. One method it uses is gas flooding which uses carbon dioxide to free up trapped oil deposits. Assets include a CO2 enhanced oil recovery -project in Louisiana's Delhi Field to extend the life and ultimate recoveries of wells with oil or associated water production. It reported more than 10 million barrels of oil equivalent proved reserves in fiscal 2019. The company was formed in 2003.

	Annual Growth	06/17	06/18	06/19	06/20	06/21
Sales ($ mil.)	(1.3%)	34.5	41.3	43.2	29.6	32.7
Net income ($ mil.)	–	8.0	19.6	15.4	5.9	(16.4)
Market value ($ mil.)	(11.5%)	271.5	330.1	239.6	93.8	166.2
Employees	0.0%	5	4	4	4	5

EVOLVE TRANSITION INFRASTRUCTURE LP   ASE: SNMP

1360 Post Oak Blvd., Suite 2400 — CEO: Randall Gibbs
Houston, TX 77056 — CFO: Charles Ward
Phone: 713 783-8000 — HR: –
Fax: – — FYE: December 31
Web: www.evolvetransition.com — Type: Public

Constellation Energy Partners' domain is decidedly more terrestrial than stellar. A spin off from Constellation Energy the company is a coalbed methane exploration and production company that operates in Alabama's Black Warrior Basin (one of the oldest and most lucrative coalbed methane basins in the US) the Cherokee Basin in Kansas and Oklahoma and the Woodford Shale in the Arkoma Basin in Oklahoma. In 2010 Constellation Energy Partners reported proved reserves of 221 billion cu. ft. of natural gas equivalent. That year the company operated 87% of the more than 2780 wells in which it held an interest.

	Annual Growth	12/16	12/17	12/18	12/19	12/20
Sales ($ mil.)	(5.2%)	70.7	88.1	83.6	76.6	57.0
Net income ($ mil.)	–	19.2	(3.0)	15.7	(51.1)	(118.8)
Market value ($ mil.)	(52.2%)	235.5	221.5	34.3	6.0	12.3
Employees	(20.8%)	33	8	6	9	13

EVOLVING SYSTEMS, INC.   NAS: EVOL

9800 Pyramid Court, Suite 400 — CEO: Matthew Stecker
Englewood, CO 80112 — CFO:
Phone: 303 802-1000 — HR: –
Fax: – — FYE: December 31
Web: www.evolving.com — Type: Public

Evolving Systems offers software for the ever-evolving telecommunications industry. The company provides applications used by telecom companies to automate and manage parts of their network operations including tools applications that allow users to route calls and messages to various devices. The company also provides local number portability software that allows telephone customers to keep the same phone number when changing to a new carrier. Evolving Systems has expanded its international operations in Africa Asia and Central America and added products for managing SIM cards. The company agreed to sell its number management and monitoring assets to NeuStar in 2011 for $39 million.

	Annual Growth	12/16	12/17	12/18	12/19	12/20
Sales ($ mil.)	1.6%	24.8	28.8	30.6	25.8	26.4
Net income ($ mil.)	(34.2%)	3.4	2.5	(14.8)	(9.7)	0.6
Market value ($ mil.)	(16.8%)	50.0	57.3	14.5	10.9	24.0
Employees	8.9%	197	314	280	261	277

EVONIK CORPORATION

299 Jefferson Rd. — CEO: –
Parsippany NJ 07054 — CFO: Burkhard Zoller
Phone: 973-541-8000 — HR: –
Fax: 973-541-8013 — FYE: December 31
Web: north-america.evonik.com — Type: Subsidiary

Evonik Corporation (formerly Evonik Degussa Corp.) is the North American arm of German chemical giant Evonik Degussa GmbH. Like its parent it operates through six divisions the biggest of which are Industrial Chemicals (chlorides and peroxides) and Inorganic Materials (silicon products and carbon black). The other units are Consumer Specialties Health and Nutrition Coatings and Additives and Performance Polymers. Products range from amino acids and building protection coatings to another of its specialties specialty acrylic products including its best known brand Plexiglas. In addition to the automotive industry Evonik serves makers of coatings pharmaceuticals and plastics.

EWING IRRIGATION PRODUCTS, INC.

3441 E HARBOUR DR — CEO: –
PHOENIX, AZ 850340908 — CFO: –
Phone: 602-437-9546 — HR: –
Fax: – — FYE: June 25
Web: www.store.ewingirrigation.com — Type: Private

You can thank Ewing Irrigation Products for that lush verdant golf course you occasionally call home. The company wholesales irrigation products for water drainage and erosion control for commercial and residential yards golf courses landscaping hardscape and turf maintenance. The family-owned company also supplies water features landscape lighting and pumps.

	Annual Growth	06/06	06/07	06/08	06/09	06/10
Sales ($ mil.)	(7.8%)	–	–	306.7	278.9	260.8
Net income ($ mil.)	–	–	–	11.2	11.2	0.0
Market value ($ mil.)	–	–	–	–	–	–
Employees	–	–	–	–	–	850

EXA CORP
NMS: EXA

55 Network Drive
Burlington, MA 01803
Phone: 781 564-0200
Fax: –
Web: www.exa.com

CEO: Stephen A Remondi
CFO: Richard F Gilbody
HR: –
FYE: January 31
Type: Public

Exa Corporation strives to be irresistible to its customers. A developer of engineering software for vehicle manufacturers Exa makes digital simulation software used by engineers to enhance the performance of automobiles trucks trains and off-road equipment. Its core product PowerFLOW can simulate structural and heating/cooling system fluid flow problems in vehicles namely aerodynamics thermal management and aeroacoustics. (Aeroacoustics is the generation and transfer of sound by fluid flow.) The company sells PowerFLOW and related products in Japan the US and Europe through its direct sales force; it also sells in China and India through distributors. Exa went public in a 2012 IPO.

	Annual Growth	01/12	01/13	01/14	01/15	01/16
Sales ($ mil.)	9.3%	45.9	48.9	54.5	61.4	65.4
Net income ($ mil.)	–	14.5	0.8	(0.7)	(19.2)	(4.8)
Market value ($ mil.)	2.5%	–	146.5	206.0	148.5	157.6
Employees	12.2%	203	239	257	296	322

EXACT SCIENCES CORP.
NMS: EXAS

5505 Endeavor Lane
Madison, WI 53719
Phone: 608 535-8815
Fax: –
Web: www.exactsciences.com

CEO: Kevin Conroy
CFO: Jeffrey Elliott
HR: –
FYE: December 31
Type: Public

Exact Science develops non-invasive tests for the early detection of colorectal cancer and precancerous lesions. Its Cologuard test isolates DNA in stool samples then identifies genetic mutations associated with cancer. Colorectal cancer is a common (and one of the deadliest) cancers and Exact believes its method is superior to existing diagnostic methods because it may be able to discern colorectal cancer in its early stages when it is most treatable. Almost all of its revenues came from the US.

	Annual Growth	12/17	12/18	12/19	12/20	12/21
Sales ($ mil.)	60.5%	266.0	454.5	876.3	1,491.4	1,767.1
Net income ($ mil.)	–	(114.4)	(175.1)	(84.0)	(848.5)	(595.6)
Market value ($ mil.)	–	0.0	0.0	0.0	0.0	0.0
Employees	58.0%	1,268	1,977	4,110	5,000	–

EXACTECH, INC.
NMS: EXAC

2320 NW 66th Court
Gainesville, FL 32653
Phone: 352 377-1140
Fax: 352 378-2617
Web: www.exac.com

CEO: Darin Johnson
CFO: Joel C Phillips
HR: –
FYE: December 31
Type: Public

Exactech has joint replacement technologies down to an exact science. Health professionals worldwide use the company's orthopedic devices to replace joints weakened by injury or disease. Its Optetrak knee implants Equinoxe shoulder systems and Novation hip implants either partially or totally replace patients' damaged joints. It also markets Opteform and Optefil bone allograft materials used to correct bone defects and damage. Exactech markets its products through direct sales representatives and independent dealers in the US as well as through affiliated and independent distributors in about 35 other countries. Customers include hospitals clinics surgeons and physicians.

	Annual Growth	12/11	12/12	12/13	12/14	12/15
Sales ($ mil.)	4.2%	205.4	224.3	237.1	248.4	241.8
Net income ($ mil.)	13.7%	8.8	12.7	15.4	16.5	14.8
Market value ($ mil.)	2.5%	233.1	239.9	336.3	333.6	256.9
Employees	4.1%	574	590	608	642	674

EXAMWORKS GROUP INC
NYS: EXAM

3280 Peachtree Road, N.E., Suite 2625
Atlanta, GA 30305
Phone: 404 952-2400
Fax: –
Web: www.examworks.com

CEO: James K Price
CFO: J Miguel Fernandez De Castro
HR: –
FYE: December 31
Type: Public

ExamWorks Group examines whether people should qualify for certain types of insurance. Through subsidiary ExamWorks Inc. the holding company is a leading North American provider of independent medical examinations (IMEs). IMEs are physical exams conducted by independently contracted physicians to verify illness and injury claims for individuals seeking workers' compensation automotive and personal injury liability and disability insurance coverage. Its network consists of thousands of doctors and medical providers. ExamWorks also offers medical record and medical bill reviews. Clients include insurance companies and law firms in the US and abroad.

	Annual Growth	12/10	12/11	12/12	12/13	12/14
Sales ($ mil.)	47.6%	163.5	397.9	521.2	616.0	775.6
Net income ($ mil.)	–	(6.0)	(8.3)	(14.9)	(10.2)	10.5
Market value ($ mil.)	22.5%	746.1	382.7	564.8	1,205.9	1,679.0
Employees	17.2%	1,485	1,880	2,100	2,400	2,800

EXAR CORP.
NYS: EXAR

48720 Kato Road
Fremont, CA 94538
Phone: 510 668-7000
Fax: –
Web: www.exar.com

CEO: Ryan A Benton
CFO: Keith Tainsky
HR: –
FYE: March 27
Type: Public

Exar seeks excellence in the exacting world of integrated circuits. The fabless semiconductor company's digital analog and mixed-signal integrated circuits (ICs) are used in networking equipment — especially telecom infrastructure gear — as well as in video and imaging devices such as handheld electronics set-top boxes and DVRs. It also makes ICs and subsystems for the power management and datacom and storage markets including storage optimization and network security processors. Customers include Alcatel Lucent EMC Huawei Teradata and ZTE. The company gets about 85% of its sales outside the US.

	Annual Growth	04/12*	03/13	03/14	03/15	03/16
Sales ($ mil.)	3.4%	130.6	122.0	125.3	162.1	149.4
Net income ($ mil.)	–	(28.8)	2.9	5.8	(45.0)	(16.0)
Market value ($ mil.)	(11.0%)	407.8	509.7	568.5	500.0	255.3
Employees	(3.0%)	304	291	312	327	269

*Fiscal year change

EXCEL TRUST INC.
NYS: EXL

Excel Centre, 17140 Bernardo Center Drive, Suite 300
San Diego, CA 92128
Phone: 858 613-1800
Fax: –
Web: www.exceltrust.com

CEO: –
CFO: –
HR: –
FYE: December 31
Type: Public

Excel Trust likes to buy retail space off the clearance rack. Based in San Diego the self-managed self-administered real estate investment trust (REIT) has a penchant for acquiring high-value retail properties at a reduced cost — including value-oriented community and "power" shopping centers grocery anchored neighborhood centers and freestanding retail properties — located in California Arizona Texas and about a dozen other states. Excel owns about 35 retail and office properties totaling more than 5.8 million sq. ft. of leasable space. Tenants include chain stores Bed Bath & Beyond and PetSmart among many others and health care systems operator Kaiser Permanente.

	Annual Growth	04/10*	12/10	12/11	12/12	12/13
Sales ($ mil.)	315.6%	1.6	15.9	55.2	87.1	112.5
Net income ($ mil.)	–	(0.1)	(3.7)	0.4	1.9	19.5
Market value ($ mil.)	(4.3%)	629.0	585.4	580.6	613.0	551.1
Employees	29.3%	–	31	38	45	67

*Fiscal year change

EXCHANGE BANK (SANTA ROSA, CA) NBB: EXSR

545 Fourth Street
Santa Rosa, CA 95401
Phone: 707 524-3000
Fax: –
Web: www.exchangebank.com

CEO: Troy Sanderson
CFO: Shari Demaris
HR: –
FYE: December 31
Type: Public

Exchange Bank serves personal and business customers from some 20 branch offices throughout Sonoma County California. It also has a branch in nearby Placer County. The bank provides standard products including checking and savings accounts Visa credit cards online banking and a variety of real estate business and consumer loans. It also offers investment services such as wealth management personal trust administration employee benefits plans and individual retirement accounts. Effective early 2014 Exchange Bank is on its eighth president since its inception in 1890. The Doyle Trust which was established by co-founder Frank Doyle owns a majority of the bank.

	Annual Growth	12/16	12/17	12/18	12/19	12/20
Assets ($ mil.)	9.6%	2,179.4	2,584.1	2,654.0	2,673.1	3,139.1
Net income ($ mil.)	11.9%	21.5	19.5	38.5	36.5	33.7
Market value ($ mil.)	4.3%	214.3	260.6	282.9	306.9	253.7
Employees	–	–	–	–	–	–

EXCO RESOURCES INC NBB: EXCE

12377 Merit Drive, Suite 1700
Dallas, TX 75251
Phone: 214 368-2084
Fax: –
Web: www.excoresources.com

CEO: Harold L Hickey
CFO: Tyler Farquharson
HR: –
FYE: December 31
Type: Public

Exco Resources is engaged in onshore oil and gas exploration and production in the US. Its operations are primarily in Texas Louisiana and the Appalachia region. The company has proved reserves of 1 trillion cu. ft. of natural gas equivalent and annual production at 90 billion cubic feet. It focuses on the exploitation and development of shale resources targeting shale plays like Eagle Ford Haynesville and Marcellus as well as leasing and acquisition opportunities. In 2019 the company successfully restructured and emerged from Chapter 11 bankruptcy protection.

	Annual Growth	12/14	12/15	12/16	12/17	12/18
Sales ($ mil.)	(12.1%)	660.3	328.3	271.0	283.6	394.0
Net income ($ mil.)	–	120.7	(1,192.4)	(225.3)	24.4	(182.7)
Market value ($ mil.)	(69.6%)	46.8	26.8	18.9	4.5	0.4
Employees	(27.6%)	558	315	183	168	153

EXEL INC.

570 Polaris Pkwy.
Westerville OH 43082
Phone: 614-865-8500
Fax: 614-865-8875
Web: www.exel.com

CEO: Scott Sureddin
CFO: Scot Hofacker
HR: –
FYE: December 31
Type: Subsidiary

For Exel the goal is to excel at supply chain management. The company arranges for its customers' freight to be hauled in truckload and less-than-truckload (LTL) quantities; in addition it oversees intermodal freight transportation involving the use of both trucks and trains. Exel provides services such as international freight forwarding warehousing supply chain analysis and management in-plant services assembly and packaging and transportation management. It is part of the Supply Chain business unit of DHL the global express delivery and logistics giant. DHL itself is a subsidiary of Germany's Deutsche Post. Exel has about 440 sites in the US and Canada totaling 86 million sq. ft. of warehousing.

EXELIS INC. NYS: XLS

1650 Tysons Boulevard, Suite 1700
McLean, VA 22102
Phone: 703 790-6300
Fax: –
Web: www.exelisinc.com

CEO: –
CFO: –
HR: –
FYE: December 31
Type: Public

Exelis excels when it comes to high-tech modern weaponry. The company manufactures products for integrated electronic warfare sensing and surveillance air traffic management information and cyber security and networked communications. It also focuses on composite aerostructures logistics and technical services. Exelis generates most of its business from the US government particularly the Department of Defense (about 60% of sales) the FAA and NASA. The company also serves commercial clients with international customers comprising about 10% of sales. Formerly the defense and information solutions unit of ITT Corp. Exelis was spun off in 2011 as a publicly-traded company.

	Annual Growth	12/09	12/10	12/11	12/12	12/13
Sales ($ mil.)	(5.6%)	6,061.0	5,891.0	5,839.0	5,522.0	4,816.0
Net income ($ mil.)	(12.0%)	469.0	587.0	326.0	330.0	281.0
Market value ($ mil.)	45.1%	–	–	1,714.1	2,134.5	3,610.0
Employees	(5.5%)	–	20,400	20,500	19,900	17,200

EXELIXIS INC NMS: EXEL

1851 Harbor Bay Parkway
Alameda, CA 94502
Phone: 650 837-7000
Fax: –
Web: www.exelixis.com

CEO: Michael Morrissey
CFO: Christopher Senner
HR: –
FYE: December 31
Type: Public

Exelixis is an oncology-focused biotechnology company that strives to accelerate the discovery development and commercialization of new medicines for difficult-to-treat cancers. Its flagship molecule cabozantinib is the origin of two commercial products Cabometyx a tablets approved for advanced renal cell carcinoma and Cometriq capsules approved for progressive metastatic medullary thyroid cancer. It also include Cotellic (cobimetinib) a treatment for advanced melanoma and marketed under a collaboration with Genentech. It also has other drug development candidates against multiple target classes for oncology inflammation and metabolic diseases. The US accounts for about 80% of total revenue.

	Annual Growth	12/17	12/18*	01/20	01/21*	12/21
Sales ($ mil.)	33.4%	452.5	853.8	967.8	987.5	1,435.0
Net income ($ mil.)	10.6%	154.2	690.1	321.0	111.8	231.1
Market value ($ mil.)	(11.9%)	9,692.8	6,198.3	5,423.5	6,399.2	5,828.4
Employees	26.5%	372	484	617	773	954

*Fiscal year change

EXELON CORP NMS: EXC

10 South Dearborn Street, P.O. Box 805379
Chicago, IL 60680-5379
Phone: 800 483-3220
Fax: –
Web: www.exeloncorp.com

CEO: Michael Innocenzo
CFO: Joseph Nigro
HR: –
FYE: December 31
Type: Public

Exelon is lighting up the utility industry with high-powered energy generation and extensive electricity delivery. The utility holding company does enough of both to be designated one of the largest in the US. Its Exelon Generation subsidiary holds power-generating assets of almost 35200 MW (some 18800 MW is produced at about 25 nuclear plants). Exelon distributes electricity and gas to more than 2 million customers in Illinois Maryland the District of Columbia Delaware New Jersey and Pennsylvania through its regulated utility companies. Its Constellation subsidiary sells electricity and natural gas including renewable energy in competitive energy markets to both wholesale and retail customers.

	Annual Growth	12/16	12/17	12/18	12/19	12/20
Sales ($ mil.)	1.3%	31,360.0	33,531.0	35,985.0	34,438.0	33,039.0
Net income ($ mil.)	14.7%	1,134.0	3,770.0	2,010.0	2,936.0	1,963.0
Market value ($ mil.)	4.4%	34,638.2	38,464.2	44,017.6	44,495.8	41,206.7
Employees	(1.5%)	34,396	34,621	33,383	32,713	32,340

EXELON GENERATION CO LLC

300 Exelon Way
Kennett Square, PA 19348-2473
Phone: 610 765-5959
Fax: –
Web: www.exeloncorp.com

CEO: Kenneth Cornew
CFO: Bryan Wright
HR: –
FYE: December 31
Type: Public

Exelon Generation Company has built an excellent reputation by generating electricity. The company a subsidiary of Exelon Corporation is one of the largest electric wholesale and retail power generation companies in the US. In 2013 Exelon Generation had a generation capacity of more than 44560 MW (primarily nuclear but also fossil-fired and hydroelectric and other renewable energy-based plants). Subsidiary Exelon Nuclear operates the largest fleet of nuclear power plants in the US. Exelon Generation's Exelon Power unit oversees a fleet of more than 100 fossil- and renewable-fueled plants (more than 15875 MW of capacity) in Illinois Maryland Massachusetts Pennsylvania and Texas.

	Annual Growth	12/16	12/17	12/18	12/19	12/20
Sales ($ mil.)	(0.2%)	17,751.0	18,466.0	20,437.0	18,924.0	17,603.0
Net income ($ mil.)	4.4%	496.0	2,694.0	370.0	1,125.0	589.0
Market value ($ mil.)	–	–	–	–	–	–
Employees	(4.0%)	14,717	15,011	14,110	13,082	12,482

EXIDE TECHNOLOGIES

13000 Deerfield Parkway, Building 200
Milton, GA 30004
Phone: 678 566-9000
Fax: 678 566-9188
Web: www.exide.com

NBB: XIDE Q
CEO: Timothy D Vargo
CFO: Lou Martinez
HR: –
FYE: March 31
Type: Public

Exide Technologies hopes you'll get a charge out of its products. The company makes and recycles automotive and industrial batteries for retailers and transportation manufacturers. It also makes batteries for boats farm equipment golf carts hybrid vehicles and wheelchairs. Industrial applications include computer locomotive power plant and telecommunications systems. Centra DETA Exide NASCAR Select Absolyte and Sonnenschein make up some of the company's brand names. Operations outside the US account for about 60% of sales. In mid-2013 Exide voluntarily filed for Chapter 11 bankruptcy protection and emerged in mid-2015 as a private company.

	Annual Growth	03/10	03/11	03/12	03/13	03/14
Sales ($ mil.)	1.5%	2,685.8	2,887.5	3,084.7	2,971.7	2,855.4
Net income ($ mil.)	–	(11.8)	26.4	56.7	(223.4)	(217.8)
Market value ($ mil.)	(55.3%)	455.5	883.4	247.5	213.5	18.2
Employees	(3.5%)	10,349	10,027	9,988	9,628	8,986

EXLSERVICE HOLDINGS INC

320 Park Avenue, 29th Floor
New York, NY 10022
Phone: 212 277-7100
Fax: –
Web: www.exlservice.com

NMS: EXLS
CEO: Rohit Kapoor
CFO: Maurizio Nicolelli
HR: –
FYE: December 31
Type: Public

ExlService Holdings known as EXL offers business process management (BPM) research and analytics and consulting services through its operating segments. EXL's BPM offerings which generate most of its sales include claims processing clinical operations and finance and accounting services. Customers come mainly from the banking financial services and insurance industries as well as from the utilities and telecommunications sectors. EXL operates around the world but generates nearly 85% of revenue from the US. The company was established in 1999.

	Annual Growth	12/16	12/17	12/18	12/19	12/20
Sales ($ mil.)	8.7%	686.0	762.3	883.1	991.3	958.4
Net income ($ mil.)	9.7%	61.7	48.9	56.7	67.7	89.5
Market value ($ mil.)	14.0%	1,692.6	2,025.5	1,765.9	2,331.0	2,856.9
Employees	5.2%	26,000	27,800	29,100	31,700	31,900

EXONE CO. (THE)

127 Industry Boulevard
North Huntingdon, PA 15642
Phone: 724 863-9663
Fax: –
Web: www.exone.com

NMS: XONE
CEO: –
CFO: –
HR: –
FYE: December 31
Type: Public

ExOne wants to be THE one when it comes to non-traditional manufacturing. The company "prints" three-dimensional (3D) parts and materials — literally creating a prototype or part quickly from a computer model by laying down successive layers of material to form the part. It prints in silica sand ceramic stainless steel bronze and glass. ExOne also sells 3D printing machines and makes casting molds from silica sand and ceramics from production centers in the US Germany and Japan. The company's key customers Ford BMW Boeing Caterpillar and the KSB Group operate primarily in the aerospace automotive heavy equipment and oil and gas industries. ExOne formed in 2005 and went public in 2013.

	Annual Growth	12/15	12/16	12/17	12/18	12/19
Sales ($ mil.)	7.2%	40.4	47.8	57.7	64.6	53.3
Net income ($ mil.)	–	(25.9)	(14.6)	(20.0)	(12.7)	(15.1)
Market value ($ mil.)	(7.2%)	164.1	152.7	137.3	108.2	121.9
Employees	0.2%	311	309	302	296	313

EXPEDIA GROUP INC

1111 Expedia Group Way W
Seattle, WA 98119
Phone: 206 481-7200
Fax: –
Web: www.expediainc.com

NMS: EXPE
CEO: Peter Kern
CFO: Eric Hart
HR: –
FYE: December 31
Type: Public

Expedia an online travel company leverages on its supply portfolio platform and technology capabilities across an extensive portfolio of consumer brands and provide solutions to its business partners to empower travelers to efficiently research plan book and experience travel. It offers tools that allow users to book over 2.9 million lodging properties including over 2 million online bookable alternative accommodations listings in 200 countries and territories over 500 airlines packages rental cars cruises insurance as well as activities and experiences. They include flagship Expedia.com online travel bookers Travelocity and Orbitz accommodations manager Hotels.com travel discounter Hotwire hotel meta-searcher Trivago luxury package provider Classic Vacations and several sites focused on international destinations. Nearly 70% of sales come from customers in the US.

	Annual Growth	12/17	12/18	12/19	12/20	12/21
Sales ($ mil.)	(3.8%)	10,059.8	11,223.0	12,067.0	5,199.0	8,598.0
Net income ($ mil.)	(57.8%)	378.0	406.0	565.0	(2,612.0)	12.0
Market value ($ mil.)	10.8%	18,642.0	17,533.7	16,831.8	20,607.8	28,128.7
Employees	(10.1%)	22,615	24,500	25,400	19,100	14,800

EXPEDITORS INTERNATIONAL OF WASHINGTON, INC.

1015 Third Avenue
Seattle, WA 98104
Phone: 206 674-3400
Fax: 206 674-3459
Web: www.expeditors.com

NMS: EXPD
CEO: Jeffrey Musser
CFO: Bradley Powell
HR: –
FYE: December 31
Type: Public

As a freight forwarder Expeditors International of Washington keeps cargo moving. The company purchases air and ocean cargo space on a volume basis and resells that space to its customers at lower rates than they could obtain directly. The company also acts as a customs broker for air and ocean freight shipped by its customers and offers supply chain management services. Customers include global businesses engaged in retailing and wholesaling electronics high technology industrial and manufacturing. The company's estimated average airfreight consolidation weighs approximately 3500 pounds and that a typical consolidation includes merchandise from several shippers. US accounts for more than 25% of company's revenue.

	Annual Growth	12/16	12/17	12/18	12/19	12/20
Sales ($ mil.)	13.5%	6,098.0	6,920.9	8,138.4	8,175.4	10,116.5
Net income ($ mil.)	12.7%	430.8	489.3	618.2	590.4	696.1
Market value ($ mil.)	15.8%	8,965.8	10,951.6	11,527.2	13,208.3	16,101.6
Employees	2.2%	16,000	16,500	17,400	18,000	17,480

EXPERIAN INFORMATION SOLUTIONS INC.

475 Anton Blvd.
Costa Mesa CA 92626
Phone: 714-830-7000
Fax: 714-830-2449
Web: www.experian.com

CEO: Chris Callero
CFO: –
HR: –
FYE: March 31
Type: Subsidiary

Experian Information Solutions also known as Experian Americas is the US-based arm of global credit reporting agency Experian plc. The unit provides credit reporting and lead generation services by tapping its database of more than 220 million US consumers and some 25 million US businesses. Clients include retailers financial services firms utilities not-for-profits and small businesses among others. The company also provides addresses for more than 20 billion pieces of promotional mail every year. Services include skip tracing and collections direct marketing sales prospecting demographic information and more. Experian Americas boasts about a dozen offices nationwide.

EXPERIENCE WORKS, INC.

4401 WILSON BLVD STE 210
ARLINGTON, VA 222034195
Phone: 703-522-7272
Fax: –
Web: www.experienceworks.org

CEO: Sally A Boofer
CFO: –
HR: –
FYE: June 30
Type: Private

Experience Works makes experience pay. The not-for-profit organization helps low-income individuals 55 years of age and older find jobs. It provides training as well as community service and employment opportunities for more than 125000 mature workers in 30 states and Puerto Rico. The group offers annual local state and national awards computer and technology skills services targeted to local markets and Senior Community Service Employment Program funded by the Older Americans Act to help low-income seniors. Experience Works was created in 1965. The company was called Green Thumb before it was renamed in 2002.

	Annual Growth	06/10	06/11	06/13	06/14	06/15
Sales ($ mil.)	(12.8%)	–	181.0	106.4	100.5	104.4
Net income ($ mil.)		–	0.4	(0.3)	(0.3)	(2.4)
Market value ($ mil.)	–	–	–	–	–	–
Employees	–	–	–	–	–	400

EXPONENT INC.   NMS: EXPO

149 Commonwealth Drive
Menlo Park, CA 94025
Phone: 650 326-9400
Fax: –
Web: www.exponent.com

CEO: Catherine Corrigan
CFO: Richard Schlenker
HR: –
FYE: January 01
Type: Public

Exponent is a science and engineering consulting firm that specializes in analyzing and solving complex problems and preventing disasters and product failures. The company's cadre of scientists physicians engineers and business consultants assess environmental risks regulatory issues and workplace hazards for government agencies and clients from such industries as transportation construction and manufacturing. The company divides its more than 15 practices in two units: Engineering and Other Scientific (Biomechanics Civil Engineering Human Factors and Mechanical Engineering); and Environment and Health (Health Science and Chemical Regulation & Food Safety). Established in 1967 Exponent is active in Canada Asia Pacific Europe and the Middle East and generates majority of sales in the US.

	Annual Growth	12/16	12/17	12/18*	01/20	01/21
Sales ($ mil.)	4.9%	315.1	347.8	379.5	417.2	399.9
Net income ($ mil.)	11.7%	47.5	41.3	72.3	82.5	82.6
Market value ($ mil.)	8.3%	3,123.8	3,683.3	2,586.1	3,650.1	4,663.9
Employees	2.7%	1,023	1,075	1,122	1,201	1,168

*Fiscal year change

EXPONENTIAL INTERACTIVE INC.

2200 Powell St. Ste. 600
Emeryville CA 94608
Phone: 510-250-5500
Fax: 510-250-5700
Web: www.exponential.com

CEO: Dilip Dasilva
CFO: –
HR: –
FYE: December 31
Type: Private

Exponential Interactive envisions a world where all Internet advertisements will be specifically tailored to individual users. The company's proprietary eX Advertising Intelligence Platform is used by advertising agencies to process massive amounts (2 billion user events per day) of non-personal consumer data (what you click not who you are). Agencies use the data to create custom ad campaigns for relevant demographics. The company has partnered with almost 2000 advertisers such as Coca-Cola and McDonald's to develop ad campaigns for display video and mobile platforms. It also owns a handful of digital advertising services companies including Tribal Fusion. Exponential filed a $75 million IPO in March 2012.

EXPORT-IMPORT BANK OF THE UNITED STATES

811 Vermont Ave. NW
Washington DC 20571
Phone: 202-565-3946
Fax: 202-565-3210
Web: www.exim.gov

CEO: –
CFO: –
HR: –
FYE: September 30
Type: Government Agency

Sure the US is running a huge trade deficit but don't blame the Export-Import Bank of the United States for not trying to stem the tide. The government agency (Ex-Im Bank for short) provides financing for the export of American goods and services mainly to developing countries and regions. Ex-Im Bank which assumes credit and country risks that private-sector lenders cannot or will not stomach furnishes US businesses (most of them with fewer than 100 employees) with operating credit and export credit insurance and provides loans and loan guarantees to foreign buyers of US goods. President Franklin D. Roosevelt established Ex-Im Bank as part of the New Deal in 1934.

EXPRESS INC   NYS: EXPR

1 Express Drive
Columbus, OH 43230
Phone: 614 474-4001
Fax: –
Web: www.express.com

CEO: Timothy Baxter
CFO: Periclis Pericleous
HR: –
FYE: January 30
Type: Public

Express operates about 600 stores throughout the US and Puerto Rico that sell modern versatile dual gender apparel and accessories brand that helps people get dressed for every day and any occasion trendy. The chain's fashions ? which include everything from button-downs and dresses to jeans and pants to shoes belts and handbags ? are styled to have an international influence and modern appeal. Its stores are located primarily in malls and Express also sells merchandise online and via mobile apps. Customers in Latin America can shop in more than 10 franchised locations as well as online. Express was founded in 1980.

	Annual Growth	01/17*	02/18	02/19	02/20*	01/21
Sales ($ mil.)	(13.8%)	2,192.5	2,138.0	2,116.3	2,019.2	1,208.4
Net income ($ mil.)		–	57.4	19.4	9.6	(164.4)	(405.4)
Market value ($ mil.)	(12.3%)	658.8	432.1	343.0	260.5	389.8
Employees	(12.4%)	17,000	16,000	15,700	14,000	10,000

*Fiscal year change

EXPRESS SCRIPTS HOLDING CO   NMS: ESRX

One Express Way
St. Louis, MO 63121
Phone: 314 996-0900
Fax: –
Web: www.express-scripts.com

CEO: Timothy Wentworth
CFO: James Havel
HR: –
FYE: December 31
Type: Public

Express Scripts Holding knows that its customers like their medicine delivered quickly. The company administers more than 1.4 billion prescription drug benefits of 85 million health plan members in the US and Canada. Members have access to a network of more than 69000 retail pharmacies as well as the company's own mail-order pharmacies. On behalf of its insurer clients Express Scripts processes claims for prescriptions designs drug benefit plans and offers such services as specialty drug delivery disease management programs and consumer drug data analysis.

	Annual Growth	12/12	12/13	12/14	12/15	12/16
Sales ($ mil.)	1.7%	93,858.1	104,098.8	100,887.1	101,751.8	100,287.5
Net income ($ mil.)	26.9%	1,312.9	1,844.6	2,007.6	2,476.4	3,404.4
Market value ($ mil.)	6.2%	32,697.0	42,530.3	51,267.7	52,926.8	41,652.3
Employees	(4.1%)	30,215	29,975	29,500	25,900	25,600

EXPRESS SERVICES INC

9701 BOARDWALK BLVD
OKLAHOMA CITY, OK 731626029
Phone: 405-840-5000
Fax: –
Web: www.expresspros.com

CEO: Robert A Funk
CFO: W Anthony Bostwick
HR: –
FYE: December 31
Type: Private

When you need a worker fast Express Services delivers. Operating as Express Employment Professionals the staffing company provides work for some 566000 employees each year. It operates on a franchise business model from a network of more than 800 employment agency offices across the US Canada and South Africa. It helps fill full-time temporary and part-time positions in a range of sectors that span Professional Light Industrial and Office Services. Professional employment includes accounting engineering IT sales and marketing HR and legal sector positions while Light Industrial covers assignments such as assembly maintenance and warehousing. Bob Funk and Bill Stoller founded the firm in 1983.

	Annual Growth	12/12	12/13	12/14	12/15	12/16
Sales ($ mil.)	–	–	0.0	0.0	2,648.7	2,722.5
Net income ($ mil.)	14.8%	–	58.9	55.9	99.2	89.2
Market value ($ mil.)	–	–	–	–	–	–
Employees	–	–	–	–	–	373,869

EXPRO GROUP HOLDINGS NV   NYS: XPRO

1311 Broadfield Boulevard, Suite 400
Houston, Texas 77084
Phone: 713 463-9776
Fax: –
Web: www.expro.com

CEO: Michael Jardon
CFO: Quinn Fanning
HR: –
FYE: December 31
Type: Public

If you're building an oil well drilling platform or offshore rig you probably know Frank. Frank's International supplies tools equipment and specialty services to oil exploration and production companies worldwide. Its products include pipes tools connectors casings and specialty hammers. Frank's also offers engineering design installation testing and custom fabrication services. With five affiliated companies including Antelope Oil Tools and Pilot Drilling Control operating in 11 US cities and about 40 countries on every continent it goes where the oil is. Frank's was formed in 1938 by Frank Mosing as Frank's Casing and Tool Rental. The company went public in 2013.

	Annual Growth	12/16	12/17	12/18	12/19	12/20
Sales ($ mil.)	(5.4%)	487.5	454.8	522.5	579.9	390.4
Net income ($ mil.)	–	(135.3)	(159.5)	(90.7)	(235.3)	(156.2)
Market value ($ mil.)	–	–	–	–	–	–
Employees	(5.4%)	3,000	2,900	3,100	3,100	2,400

EXTRA SPACE STORAGE INC   NYS: EXR

2795 East Cottonwood Parkway, Suite 300
Salt Lake City, UT 84121
Phone: 801 365-4600
Fax: –
Web: www.extraspace.com

CEO: Joseph Margolis
CFO: Peter Stubbs
HR: –
FYE: December 31
Type: Public

Extra Space Storage is a self-administered and self-managed real estate investment trust (REIT) that owns some 1700 self-storage properties which comprise approximately 1.4 million units and approximately 153.4 million square feet of rentable storage space offering customers conveniently located and secure storage units across the country including boat storage RV storage and business storage. Extra Space is the second largest owner and/or operator of self-storage properties in the United States and is the largest self-storage management company in the US. Founded in 1977 Extra Space Storage went public in 2004.

	Annual Growth	12/16	12/17	12/18	12/19	12/20
Sales ($ mil.)	8.1%	991.9	1,105.0	1,196.6	1,308.5	1,356.2
Net income ($ mil.)	7.1%	366.1	479.0	415.3	420.0	481.8
Market value ($ mil.)	10.7%	10,146.1	11,487.3	11,885.3	13,874.0	15,219.1
Employees	5.1%	3,287	3,380	3,624	4,048	4,013

EXTREME NETWORKS INC   NMS: EXTR

2121 RDU Center Drive, Suite 300
Morrisville, NC 27560
Phone: 408 579-2800
Fax: –
Web: www.extremenetworks.com

CEO: Edward Meyercord
CFO: Rémi Thomas
HR: –
FYE: June 30
Type: Public

Extreme Networks is a leading provider of end-to-end cloud-driven networking solutions and top-rated services and support. Providing a set of comprehensive solutions from the Internet of Things (IoT) edge to the cloud and Extreme designs develops and manufactures wired and wireless network infrastructure equipment as well a leading cloud networking platform and application portfolio using cloud management machine learning and artificial intelligence to deliver network policy analytics security and access controls. Extreme cloud-driven technologies provide flexibility and scalability in deployment management and licensing of networks globally and the global cloud footprint provides service to over 50000 customers and over 10 million daily users. Extreme founded in 1996 generates nearly half of revenue from the US.

	Annual Growth	06/17	06/18	06/19	06/20	06/21
Sales ($ mil.)	14.0%	598.1	983.1	995.8	948.0	1,009.4
Net income ($ mil.)	–	(8.5)	(46.8)	(25.9)	(126.8)	1.9
Market value ($ mil.)	4.9%	1,168.0	1,008.4	819.6	549.8	1,413.8
Employees	10.7%	1,628	2,713	2,713	2,584	2,441

EXXON MOBIL CORP   NYS: XOM

5959 Las Colinas Boulevard
Irving, TX 75039-2298
Phone: 972 940-6000
Fax: 972 444-1505
Web: www.exxonmobil.com

CEO: Darren Woods
CFO: Kathryn Mikells
HR: –
FYE: December 31
Type: Public

Exxon Mobil Corporation is the world's #1 publicly traded oil company rivaled only by giants like Shell BP and Total. Its vast portfolio holds more than 22 billion barrels of oil equivalent of proved reserves spread across some 15 countries on six continents. The company has a huge daily average output: about 1.7 million barrels of crude oil 269000 barrels of NGLs and 9.4 billion cubic feet of natural gas. Its biggest business is selling refined products through approximately 19000 gas stations around the world. Exxon Mobil is also a provider in the chemicals industry manufacturing olefins polyolefins and aromatics that form the base for many plastic products. The company's brands?ExxonMobil Exxon Esso Mobil and XTO? enjoy global recognition.

	Annual Growth	12/17	12/18	12/19	12/20	12/21
Sales ($ mil.)	4.0%	244,363.0	290,212.0	264,938.0	181,502.0	285,640.0
Net income ($ mil.)	4.0%	19,710.0	20,840.0	14,340.0	(22,440.0)	23,040.0
Market value ($ mil.)	–	–	–	–	–	–
Employees	(2.5%)	69,600	71,000	74,900	72,000	63,000

EXXONMOBIL PIPELINE COMPANY

22777 SPRNGWOODS VLG PKWY
SPRING, TX 773891425
Phone: 713-656-3636
Fax: –
Web: www.exxonmobilpipeline.com

CEO: –
CFO: –
HR: –
FYE: December 31
Type: Private

This company makes its mark by sending its business down the tubes. Each day ExxonMobil Pipeline the oil and gas transportation arm of Exxon Mobil transports about 2.7 million barrels of crude oil refined petroleum products liquefied petroleum gases natural gas liquids and chemicals through 8000 miles of pipeline that runs through 23 US states Canada and the Gulf of Mexico. The company also provides engineering and inspection services. Its joint interest pipelines include Mustang Pipeline Plantation Pipe Line and Wolverine Pipe Line. ExxonMobil Pipeline also owns a minority stake in The Trans-Alaska Pipeline System Alaska's major vehicle for moving crude from Prudhoe Bay to the port of Valdez.

	Annual Growth	12/03	12/04	12/05	12/16	12/17
Sales ($ mil.)	–	–	–	0.0	338.9	214.3
Net income ($ mil.)	–	–	–	0.0	701.5	114.4
Market value ($ mil.)	–	–	–	–	–	–
Employees	–	–	–	–	–	600

EZCORP, INC.

NMS: EZPW

2500 Bee Cave Road, Bldg One, Suite 200
Rollingwood, TX 78746
Phone: 512 314-3400
Fax: 512 314-3404
Web: www.ezcorp.com

CEO: Lachlan P Given
CFO: Timothy K Jugmans
HR: –
FYE: September 30
Type: Public

EZCORP is a leading provider of pawn shops and associated loans in the US and Latin America. The company operates more than 515 EZPAWN and Value Pawn locations in the US and about 500 stores in Mexico under the Empe ±o F cil and Cash Apoyo Efectivo brand. In addition to its core pawn business in the US and Latin America EZCORP owns about 37% in Cash Converters which has operations in Australia and UK and 13% in Rich Data a Singapore-based software-as-a-service company that utilizes global financial services expertise. Most of the company's revenue comes from its US operations.

	Annual Growth	09/17	09/18	09/19	09/20	09/21
Sales ($ mil.)	(0.6%)	748.0	813.5	847.2	822.8	729.6
Net income ($ mil.)	(27.9%)	31.9	39.1	2.5	(68.5)	8.6
Market value ($ mil.)	(5.5%)	532.5	599.8	361.8	282.0	424.3
Employees	–	–	–	–	–	6,500

F & M BANK CORP.

NBB: FMBM

P.O. Box 1111
Timberville, VA 22853
Phone: 540 896-8941
Fax: –
Web: www.fmbankva.com

CEO: Mark Hanna
CFO: Carrie Comer
HR: –
FYE: December 31
Type: Public

F & M Bank has deep roots in Virginia's Shenandoah Valley. Founded in 1908 the holding company operates about 10 Farmers & Merchants Bank branches in the northern Virginia counties of Rockingham and Shenandoah. Farmers & Merchants caters to individuals and businesses. It provides typical deposit products including checking and savings accounts CDs and IRAs. Some 40% of its loans are mortgages; it also writes agricultural business construction and consumer loans. The company offers insurance brokerage and financial services through TEB Life Insurance and Farmers & Merchants Financial Services.

	Annual Growth	12/16	12/17	12/18	12/19	12/20
Assets ($ mil.)	6.7%	744.9	753.3	780.3	814.0	966.9
Net income ($ mil.)	(2.1%)	9.6	9.0	9.1	4.5	8.8
Market value ($ mil.)	(3.0%)	83.4	106.0	96.1	92.9	73.7
Employees	(3.3%)	173	178	172	173	151

F&B MANUFACTURING COMPANY

4316 N. 39th Ave.
Phoenix AZ 85019
Phone: 602-272-3900
Fax: 602-272-4117
Web: www.fbmfg.com

CEO: –
CFO: –
HR: –
FYE: June 30
Type: Private

Don't confuse it with food and beverage production. F&B Manufacturing makes parts and assemblies for the aerospace industry among others. The company's capabilities include hydroforming machining mechanical and hydraulic stamping and spot and laser welding as well as heat treating processes. Hydroforming a company specialty involves the use of pressurized hydraulic fluid to form metal into shapes that would be difficult to achieve by other methods. F&B Manufacturing also is able to design and make the tools necessary to produce the parts requested by its customers. The family-owned company was founded in 1923.

F&S PRODUCE COMPANY, INC.

500 W ELMER RD
VINELAND, NJ 083086314
Phone: 856-453-0316
Fax: –
Web: www.freshcutproduce.com

CEO: –
CFO: –
HR: Melissa Garwood
FYE: December 31
Type: Private

F&S Produce is into slicing and dicing. The company is a supplier of processed fresh produce including chunked diced and sliced fruits and vegetables and prepared fruit and vegetable salads and trays; it also makes brined and pickled products. Customers include food processors food service distributors and chain account representatives. F&S processes more than 75 million pounds of produce annually. Affiliate Pipco Transportation distributes the company's products through a fleet of approximately 30 trucks and 50 refrigerated trailers. The company is owned by president Sam Pipitone who founded F&S in 1981.

	Annual Growth	12/16	12/17	12/18	12/19	12/20
Sales ($ mil.)	3.8%	–	111.4	107.6	114.4	124.7
Net income ($ mil.)	59.0%	–	4.1	(1.3)	4.6	16.6
Market value ($ mil.)	–	–	–	–	–	–
Employees	–	–	–	–	–	600

F5 INC

NMS: FFIV

801 5th Avenue
Seattle, WA 98104
Phone: 206 272-5555
Fax: –
Web: www.f5.com

CEO: Francois Locoh-Donou
CFO: Francis Pelzer
HR: –
FYE: September 30
Type: Public

F5 is a multi-cloud application security and delivery company. F5's portfolio of automation security performance and insight capabilities empowers its customers to create secure and operate adaptive applications that reduce costs improve operations and better protect users. Its enterprise-grade solutions are available in a range of consumption models from on-premises to managed services optimized for multi-cloud environments. The company also offers such services as consulting training installation maintenance and other technical support services. F5 customers include large enterprise businesses public sector institutions governments and service providers. More than half of its sales come from the US.

	Annual Growth	09/17	09/18	09/19	09/20	09/21
Sales ($ mil.)	5.6%	2,090.0	2,161.4	2,242.4	2,350.8	2,603.4
Net income ($ mil.)	(5.8%)	420.8	453.7	427.7	307.4	331.2
Market value ($ mil.)	13.3%	7,312.2	12,095.2	8,516.8	7,446.2	12,056.4
Employees	10.3%	4,366	4,409	5,325	6,109	6,461

FAB UNIVERSAL CORP
NBB: FABU

5001 Baum Boulevard, Suite 770
Pittsburgh, PA 15213
Phone: 412 621-0902
Fax: 412 621-2625
Web: www.fabuniversal.com

CEO: Christopher J Spencer
CFO: John Busshaus
HR: –
FYE: December 31
Type: Public

Wizzard Software has a lot to say. The company provides podcast hosting services and develops computer software products that focus on speech recognition and text-to-speech technology. The company's technology products serve as the basis for computer telephones other devices to to listen to spoken commands and respond with synthetic speech. Wizzard's Voice Tools suite enables programmers to integrate the company's speech technologies in their applications. The company also offers podcast hosting and operates a speech technology consulting services division that offers custom programming training and support services.

	Annual Growth	12/09	12/10	12/11	12/12	12/13
Sales ($ mil.)	115.0%	5.2	5.5	6.5	27.5	110.9
Net income ($ mil.)	–	(6.5)	(4.1)	(10.0)	(4.0)	20.7
Market value ($ mil.)	73.2%	7.1	5.2	2.7	67.0	63.9
Employees	15.1%	110	110	150	215	193

FACTSET RESEARCH SYSTEMS INC.
NYS: FDS

45 Glover Avenue
Norwalk, CT 06850
Phone: 203 810-1000
Fax: 203 810-1001
Web: www.factset.com

CEO: Philip Snow
CFO: Linda Huber
HR: –
FYE: August 31
Type: Public

FactSet Research Systems is a global provider of integrated financial information analytical applications and industry-leading services for the investment and corporate communities. The company offers global financial and economic information for investment analysis. It works with asset managers and owners bankers wealth managers corporate firms including private equity and venture capital firms and others. Revenues are primarily derived from subscriptions to products and services such as workstations portfolio analytics market data and research management. About 85% of revenue comes from investment management clients. Majority of its sales were generated in the US.

	Annual Growth	08/17	08/18	08/19	08/20	08/21
Sales ($ mil.)	6.8%	1,221.2	1,350.1	1,435.4	1,494.1	1,591.4
Net income ($ mil.)	11.5%	258.3	267.1	352.8	372.9	399.6
Market value ($ mil.)	24.7%	5,912.4	8,628.6	10,234.8	13,180.4	14,302.1
Employees	4.7%	9,074	9,571	9,681	10,484	10,892

FAIR ISAAC CORP
NYS: FICO

5 West Mendenhall, Suite 105
Bozema, MT 59715
Phone: 406 982-7276
Fax: –
Web: www.fico.com

CEO: William J Lansing
CFO: Michael I McLaughlin
HR: –
FYE: September 30
Type: Public

Fair Isaac also known as FICO is a company that provides credit scores and risk management tools for businesses worldwide including banks credit card issuers mortgage and auto lenders retailers insurance firms and health care providers. It also serve consumers through online services that enable people to access and understand their FICO Scores the standard measure in the US of consumer credit risk empowering them to manage their financial health. While the US accounts for more than 70% of its revenue the company operates globally in more than 120 countries.

	Annual Growth	09/17	09/18	09/19	09/20	09/21
Sales ($ mil.)	9.0%	932.2	1,032.5	1,160.1	1,294.6	1,316.5
Net income ($ mil.)	32.2%	128.3	142.4	192.1	236.4	392.1
Market value ($ mil.)	29.7%	3,873.3	6,300.7	8,367.4	11,726.9	10,970.1
Employees	2.6%	3,299	3,668	4,009	4,003	3,662

FAIRCHILD SEMICONDUCTOR INTERNATIONAL, INC.
NMS: FCS

3030 Orchard Parkway
San Jose, CA 95134
Phone: 408 822-2000
Fax: –
Web: www.fairchildsemi.com

CEO: Keith D Jackson
CFO: Bernard Gutmann
HR: Tobin Cookman
FYE: December 28
Type: Public

One of the world's oldest chip makers Fairchild Semiconductor makes semiconductors for tens of thousands of customers in the automotive computer consumer electronics industrial mobile and communications markets. Its diversified product line includes logic chips discrete power and signal components optoelectronics and many types of analog and mixed-signal chips. The company subcontracts a small amount of its fabrication assembly and test operations to companies that include TSMC Amkor and ASE among others. In late 2015 Fairchild agreed to be bought on On Semiconductor for $2.4 billion. The deal is expected to close in 2Q 2016.

	Annual Growth	12/10	12/11	12/12	12/13	12/14
Sales ($ mil.)	(2.7%)	1,599.7	1,588.8	1,405.9	1,405.4	1,433.4
Net income ($ mil.)	–	153.2	145.5	24.6	5.0	(35.2)
Market value ($ mil.)	3.4%	1,793.4	1,435.7	1,655.7	1,551.0	2,047.6
Employees	(2.0%)	8,977	8,817	9,077	8,659	8,272

FAIRFIELD UNIVERSITY

1073 N BENSON RD
FAIRFIELD, CT 068245195
Phone: 203-254-4000
Fax: –
Web: www.fairfield.edu

CEO: –
CFO: –
HR: –
FYE: June 30
Type: Private

Fairfield University is a private Jesuit school with an enrollment of more than 5000 undergraduate and graduate students. It offers about 45 undergraduate majors and nearly 15 interdisciplinary minors as well as around 40 graduate degree programs through five schools and colleges: College of Arts and Sciences; Egan School of Nursing & Health Studies; School of Engineering; Charles F. Dolan School of Business; and the Graduate School of Education and Allied Professions. With a 12:1 student to faculty ratio Fairfield University has one campus in Fairfield Connecticut and offers more than 80 study abroad programs in some 100 cities across approximately 40 countries.

	Annual Growth	06/17	06/18	06/19	06/20	06/21
Sales ($ mil.)	4.1%	–	214.9	238.4	227.7	242.7
Net income ($ mil.)	7.3%	–	94.9	24.6	5.3	117.2
Market value ($ mil.)	–	–	–	–	–	–
Employees	–	–	–	–	–	883

FAIRLEIGH DICKINSON UNIVERSITY

1000 RIVER RD STE 1
TEANECK, NJ 076661939
Phone: 800-338-8803
Fax: –
Web: www.fdu.edu

CEO: –
CFO: –
HR: –
FYE: June 30
Type: Private

It's fair to say that Fairleigh Dickinson University (FDU) is the largest private university in New Jersey. It has an enrollment of approximately 12000 students and 260 full-time faculty members. It has a student-teacher ratio of 14:1 and offers more than 100 undergraduate and graduate degree programs as well as doctoral programs in clinical psychology and school psychology. In addition to its main Metropolitan Campus in Teaneck New Jersey; the university also offers degree programs at the College at Florham in Madison New Jersey; at FDU-Vancouver in Canada; and at Wroxton College in Oxfordshire England. Fairleigh Dickinson was founded in 1942.

	Annual Growth	06/17	06/18	06/19	06/20	06/21
Sales ($ mil.)	(7.1%)	–	233.6	222.1	210.2	187.6
Net income ($ mil.)	(11.6%)	–	37.5	17.4	(0.9)	25.9
Market value ($ mil.)	–	–	–	–	–	–
Employees	–	–	–	–	–	1,505

FAIRPOINT COMMUNICATIONS INC
NAS: FRP

521 East Morehead Street, Suite 500
Charlotte, NC 28202
Phone: 704 344-8150
Fax: -
Web: www.fairpoint.com

CEO: -
CFO: -
HR: -
FYE: December 31
Type: Public

FairPoint Communications provides local and long-distance phone services as well as broadband Internet access and cable TV to residential and business customers. It counts a total of more than 735000 subscribers to its voice broadband and Ethernet services. It operates more than 30 local-exchange carriers in 17 US states. FairPoint concentrates on rural and small urban markets mainly in northern New England but it also serves spots in the Midwest South and Northwest. In December 2016 FairPoint agreed to be bought by Consolidated Communications for $1.5 billion.

	Annual Growth	12/11	12/12	12/13	12/14	12/15
Sales ($ mil.)	(2.8%)	963.1	973.6	939.4	901.4	859.5
Net income ($ mil.)	-	(414.9)	(153.3)	(93.5)	(136.3)	90.4
Market value ($ mil.)	38.8%	116.6	213.9	304.5	382.5	432.6
Employees	(6.6%)	3,541	3,369	3,171	3,052	2,700

FAIRVIEW HEALTH SERVICES

1700 UNIVERSITY AVE W
SAINT PAUL, MN 551043727
Phone: 612-672-6300
Fax: -
Web: www.fairview.org

CEO: Rulon F Stacey
CFO: James M Fox
HR: -
FYE: December 31
Type: Private

It's fair to say that when it comes to health care Fairview Health Services takes the long view. The not-for-profit system serves Minnesota's Twin Cities and nearby communities. Fairview Health is affiliated with the medical school of the University of Minnesota and counts among its 10 hospitals the University of Minnesota Medical Center. The hospitals house more than 2500 beds and provide comprehensive medical and surgical services. The system also operates primary and specialty care clinics that provide preventive and wellness care. Additionally it operates retail pharmacies and nursing homes and provides home health care and rehabilitation. Merger talks with University of Minnesota Physicians have stalled.

	Annual Growth	12/16	12/17	12/18	12/19	12/20
Sales ($ mil.)	5.1%	-	5,275.0	5,709.2	6,049.8	6,123.8
Net income ($ mil.)	-	-	511.5	5.7	13.4	(18.4)
Market value ($ mil.)	-	-	-	-	-	-
Employees	-	-	-	-	-	18,000

FAIRWAY GROUP HOLDINGS CORP
NBB: FWMH Q

2284 12th Avenue
New York, NY 10027
Phone: 646 616-8000
Fax: -
Web: www.fairwaymarket.com

CEO: Abel Porter
CFO: Erik Frederick
HR: -
FYE: March 29
Type: Public

Fairway Group Holdings Corp. keeps a well-stocked grocery cart for discerning Manhattan shoppers. The parent company of Fairway Market operates a growing chain of more than a dozen upscale grocery stores in the greater New York City metropolitan area. Three of those stores (in Connecticut New Jersey and New York) have adjacent liquor stores under the Fairway Wines & Spirits name. Fairway Markets feature fresh produce meat and seafood as well as organic products prepared foods and hard-to-find specialty and gourmet products. Some Fairway Markets have on-site cafes that serve coffee salads and sandwiches while other locations offer delivery. Fairway Group filed for Chapter 11 bankruptcy protection in June 2016 and left it a month later.

	Annual Growth	04/11	04/12*	03/13	03/14	03/15
Sales ($ mil.)	13.2%	485.7	554.9	661.2	776.0	797.6
Net income ($ mil.)	-	(18.6)	(11.9)	(62.9)	(80.3)	(46.5)
Market value ($ mil.)	(22.1%)	-	-	-	333.9	260.2
Employees	0.5%	-	4,230	4,800	4,200	4,300

*Fiscal year change

FAITH TECHNOLOGIES, INC.

225 MAIN ST
MENASHA, WI 549523186
Phone: 920-738-1500
Fax: -
Web: www.faithtechnologies.com

CEO: -
CFO: -
HR: -
FYE: December 31
Type: Private

Keeping the faith in technology is a basic commitment of Faith Technologies one of the largest privately held electrical and specialty systems contractors in the US. The company's specialties include electrical contracting and service automated controls lighting security technology and preconstruction. It primarily serves clients in the commercial government industrial institutional health care manufacturing power residential retail transportation and data center sectors. The company has worked on a range of projects such as airports bridges correctional facilities government agencies hospitals restaurants and shopping centers.

	Annual Growth	12/09	12/10	12/11	12/12	12/15
Sales ($ mil.)	13.3%	-	228.3	248.6	260.2	425.9
Net income ($ mil.)	69.0%	-	2.3	4.6	10.0	31.8
Market value ($ mil.)	-	-	-	-	-	-
Employees	-	-	-	-	-	2,581

FALCONSTOR SOFTWARE INC
NBB: FALC

701 Brazos Street, Suite 400
Austin, TX 78701
Phone: 631 777-5188
Fax: -
Web: www.falconstor.com

CEO: Todd Brooks
CFO: Brad Wolfe
HR: -
FYE: December 31
Type: Public

FalconStor Software watches data like a hawk. The company provides hardware and software used in data storage protection and virtualization applications. Its IPStor software is used to manage storage provisioning and virtualization data availability replication and disaster recovery functions in disk-based systems. Ranging from small and midsized businesses to large enterprises the company's customers come from such fields as health care insurance financial services education telecommunications and information technology. FalconStor sells predominantly through distributors manufacturers and resellers.

	Annual Growth	12/16	12/17	12/18	12/19	12/20
Sales ($ mil.)	(16.4%)	30.3	25.2	17.8	16.5	14.8
Net income ($ mil.)	-	(11.0)	1.1	(0.9)	(1.8)	1.1
Market value ($ mil.)	96.4%	2.7	0.9	0.2	17.0	40.2
Employees	(28.2%)	166	81	86	71	44

FAMC SUBSIDIARY COMPANY

6100 TOWER CIR STE 600
FRANKLIN, TN 370671505
Phone: 615-778-1000
Fax: -
Web: www.franklinamerican.com

CEO: -
CFO: Scott J Tansil
HR: -
FYE: December 31
Type: Private

Franklin American Mortgage Company (FAMC) is flying as high as a kite. The private mortgage bank is one of the country's largest and fastest-growing mortgage brokers. Franklin American Mortgage operates through three loan production channels. The correspondent lending division services lenders nationwide while the wholesale division funds and underwrites loans for mortgage brokers. The firm's retail division offers mortgages directly to individuals from about 20 offices (mostly located in the East and South). Founded in 1994 Franklin American Mortgage CEO Dan Crockett owns the company.

	Annual Growth	12/03	12/04	12/05	12/07	12/08
Assets ($ mil.)	7.7%	-	-	238.3	206.8	298.1
Net income ($ mil.)	65.9%	-	-	5.6	5.5	25.7
Market value ($ mil.)	-	-	-	-	-	-
Employees	-	-	-	-	-	700

FAMILY DOLLAR STORES, INC.   NYS: FDO

10401 Monroe Road   CEO: Gary Philbin
Matthews, NC 28105   CFO: Mary Winston
Phone: 704 847-6961   HR: –
Fax: –   FYE: August 30
Web: www.familydollar.com   Type: Public

Penny-pinching single moms are drawn to Family Dollar. The nation's #2 dollar store (behind Dollar General) targets forty-something women shopping for a family earning less than $40000 a year. It operates about 8000 stores across some 45 states and Washington DC. Consumables (food health and beauty aids and household items) account for more than 70% of sales; stores also sell apparel shoes and linens. Family Dollar runs small neighborhood stores near its fixed- low- and middle-income customers in rural and urban areas. Most merchandise costs less than $10. Family Dollar was founded in 1959 by the father of CEO Howard Levine. Family Dollar has agreed to be acquired by rival Dollar Tree.

	Annual Growth	08/10	08/11	08/12	08/13	08/14
Sales ($ mil.)	7.5%	7,867.0	8,547.8	9,331.0	10,391.5	10,489.3
Net income ($ mil.)	(5.6%)	358.1	388.4	422.2	443.6	284.5
Market value ($ mil.)	16.5%	4,940.2	5,420.0	7,107.0	8,114.7	9,099.5
Employees	4.7%	50,000	52,000	55,000	58,000	60,000

FAMILY EXPRESS CORPORATION

213 S STATE ROAD 49   CEO: –
VALPARAISO, IN 463837976   CFO: Thomas Denise
Phone: 219-531-6490   HR: –
Fax: –   FYE: December 31
Web: www.familyexpress.com   Type: Private

Convenience is all in the family at this Indiana chain. Family Express operates about 50 convenience store/gasoline stations in north central and northwestern Indiana (split almost evenly between city and rural locations). The chain's Cravin's Market in-house foodservice features fresh sandwiches fruits vegetables salads and a selection of floral items. Family Express also has launched its own proprietary brands including Java Wave gourmet coffees Squeeze Freeze carbonated beverages natural spring water and bread and milk products. In addition Family Express operates a small fleet of delivery trucks that say "moo." The company was founded in 1975.

	Annual Growth	12/05	12/06	12/07	12/09	12/10
Sales ($ mil.)	0.2%	–	–	275.6	244.8	277.4
Net income ($ mil.)	(38.0%)	–	–	18.5	2.8	4.4
Market value ($ mil.)	–	–	–	–	–	–
Employees	–	–	–	–	–	500

FAMILY HEALTH INTERNATIONAL INC

359 BLACKWELL ST STE 200   CEO: Patrick C Fine
DURHAM, NC 277012477   CFO: Hubert C Graves
Phone: 919-544-7040   HR: –
Fax: –   FYE: September 30
Web: www.fhi360.org   Type: Private

Known as FHI 360 Family Health International believes that health is wealth. From a handful of offices located in the US Asia-Pacific and South Africa FHI 360 funds and manages public health programs research education and other resources in more than 60 countries. Founded in 1971 as the International Fertility Research Program of the University of North Carolina at Chapel Hill FHI 360 primarily focuses on and supports HIV/AIDS prevention research reproductive health services and maternal and neonatal health programs. The organization works with governments private agencies and non-governmental organizations to develop the most appropriate programs for different areas.

	Annual Growth	09/08	09/09	09/13	09/14	09/19
Sales ($ mil.)	9.1%	–	327.6	664.1	653.7	781.6
Net income ($ mil.)	(10.2%)	–	2.9	10.2	(3.4)	1.0
Market value ($ mil.)	–	–	–	–	–	–
Employees	–	–	–	–	–	4,000

FANNIE MAE   NBB: FNMA

1100 15th Street, NW   CEO: Hugh Frater
Washington, DC 20005   CFO: Chryssa Halley
Phone: 800 232-6643   HR: –
Fax: –   FYE: December 31
Web: www.fanniemae.com   Type: Public

The Federal National Mortgage Association better known as Fannie Mae is a government-sponsored enterprise (GSE) that provides liquidity and stability to the residential mortgage market and to promote access to mortgage credit. It is primarily driven by guaranty fees that the company receives for assuming the credit risk on loans underlying the mortgage-backed securities it issues. It does not originate loans or lend money directly to borrowers. Rather it primarily works with lenders who originate loans to borrowers. Through its single-family and multifamily business segments Fannie Mae provided over $1.4 trillion in liquidity to the mortgage market in 2020 which enabled the financing of approximately 6 million home purchases refinancing or rental units.

	Annual Growth	12/17	12/18	12/19	12/20	12/21
Assets ($ mil.)	6.0%	3,345,529.0	3,418,318.0	3,503,319.0	3,985,749.0	4,229,166.0
Net income ($ mil.)	73.2%	2,463.0	15,959.0	14,160.0	11,805.0	22,176.0
Market value ($ mil.)	(25.4%)	3,068.9	1,227.6	3,613.2	2,767.8	949.7
Employees	0.7%	7,200	7,400	7,500	7,700	7,400

FAR EAST ENERGY CORP   NBB: FEEC

333 N. Sam Houston Parkway East, Suite 230   CEO: –
Houston, TX 77060   CFO: –
Phone: 832 598-0470   HR: –
Fax: –   FYE: December 31
Web: www.fareastenergy.com   Type: Public

Far East Energy is engaged in coalbed methane gas exploration and production in China and in the development of related technologies. The company works with ConocoPhillips and China United Coalbed Methane Company to acquire and explore assets across China. Far East Energy's Shanxi coalbed methane project when fully developed could sustain more than 3000 horizontal gas wells making it one of the world's largest coalbed methane projects. The company has drilled five coalbed methane gas exploration wells in Shanxi and six in its other major project area in Yunnan Province. It holds more than 1.3 million acres of leasehold properties.

	Annual Growth	12/09	12/10	12/11	12/12	12/13
Sales ($ mil.)	36.0%	–	–	0.9	1.6	1.6
Net income ($ mil.)	–	(13.8)	(16.2)	(21.2)	(27.2)	(34.0)
Market value ($ mil.)	(26.3%)	159.2	242.3	72.7	19.0	46.9
Employees	1.7%	29	28	25	26	31

FARM CREDIT BANK OF TEXAS

4801 PLZ ON THE LK # 1200   CEO: Amie Pala
AUSTIN, TX 787461081   CFO: Brandon Blaut
Phone: 512-465-0400   HR: –
Fax: –   FYE: December 31
Web: www.farmcreditbank.com   Type: Private

The largest member of the federal Farm Credit System the Farm Credit Bank of Texas provides loans and financial services to about 20 lending cooperatives and financial institutions in Alabama Louisiana Mississippi New Mexico and Texas. These include agricultural credit associations which provide agricultural production loans agribusiness financing and rural mortgage financing; and federal land credit associations which offer real estate loans on farms ranches and other rural property. Farm Credit Bank of Texas is owned by the lending cooperatives it serves.

	Annual Growth	12/06	12/07	12/12	12/13	12/16
Assets ($ mil.)	5.1%	–	13,520.8	–	16,212.7	21,222.4
Net income ($ mil.)	11.2%	–	74.0	–	179.8	192.4
Market value ($ mil.)	–	–	–	–	–	–
Employees	–	–	–	–	–	200

FARM CREDIT SERVICES OF MID-AMERICA ACA

1601 UPS Dr.
Louisville KY 40223
Phone: 502-420-3700
Fax: 804-225-1725
Web: www.bonsecours.com/hospitals/richmond/index.as

CEO: Bill Johnson
CFO: Paul Bruce
HR: –
FYE: December 31
Type: Private - Cooperativ

If Old McDonald's farm is in Indiana Kentucky Ohio or Tennessee he might have a loan-loan-here and a loan-loan-there from Farm Credit Services of Mid-America. The cooperative association one of the largest in the National Farm Credit System provides lending and other financial services to these states' farmers and rural homeowners. Borrowers use Farm Credit's products to purchase real estate homes livestock and farming equipment to fund capital improvements and to cover operating and living expenses. It has a loan volume of about $12 billion and serves some 85000 customers through nearly 100 offices located throughout its service area.

FARM SERVICE COOPERATIVE

2308 PINE ST
HARLAN, IA 515371884
Phone: 712-755-2207
Fax: –
Web: www.fscoop.com

CEO: –
CFO: –
HR: Sharon Kroger
FYE: August 31
Type: Private

Farm Service Cooperative (FSC) offers a big bushel basket full of products and services to farmers in west central Iowa. The agricultural co-op offers its members such farm-management supplies and services as grain elevator operations grain marketing equipment rental tires livestock feed and fertilizer sales soil sampling on-staff crop advisors farm credit and financing agronomy and Cenex energy products (diesel home-heating oil propane ethanol gasoline) from its 10 locations.

	Annual Growth	08/03	08/04	08/05	08/06	08/07
Sales ($ mil.)	(82.5%)	–	–	2,122.1	53.2	65.4
Net income ($ mil.)	34677.7%	–	–	0.0	15.0	14.4
Market value ($ mil.)	–	–	–	–	–	–
Employees	–	–	–	–	–	110

FARMER BROS. CO.   NMS: FARM

1912 Farmer Brothers Drive
Northlake, TX 76262
Phone: 682 549-6600
Fax: –
Web: www.farmerbros.com

CEO: D. Deverl Maserang
CFO: Scott Drake
HR: –
FYE: June 30
Type: Public

Farmer Bros. is a national coffee roaster wholesaler and distributor of coffee tea and culinary products. The company roasts and packages coffee and sells it mainly to institutional foodservice operators such as restaurants gourmet coffee houses hotels and hospitals. It also distributes related coffee products such as filters sugar and creamers as well as assorted teas and culinary products (spices soup gelatins and mixes). In addition Farmer Bros. provides private brand coffee programs nationwide to retail customers such as convenience and grocery stores. Founded in 1912 the company distributes products from about 95 branch warehouses across the US.

	Annual Growth	06/17	06/18	06/19	06/20	06/21
Sales ($ mil.)	(7.4%)	541.5	606.5	595.9	501.3	397.9
Net income ($ mil.)	–	24.4	(18.3)	(73.6)	(37.1)	(41.7)
Market value ($ mil.)	(19.5%)	540.0	545.4	292.3	131.0	226.6
Employees	(9.8%)	1,610	1,600	1,521	1,210	1,064

FARMERS CAPITAL BANK CORP.   NMS: FFKT

202 West Main St.
Frankfort, KY 40601
Phone: 502 227-1668
Fax: –
Web: www.farmerscapital.com

CEO: –
CFO: –
HR: –
FYE: December 31
Type: Public

Farmers Capital has found some green in the Bluegrass State. Its four bank subsidiaries — Citizens Bank of Northern Kentucky Farmers Bank & Capital Trust First Citizens Bank and United Bank & Trust Company — operate more than 35 branches in northern and central Kentucky. Serving individuals and local businesses they offer standard retail services such as checking and savings accounts and CDs as well as trust activities. Real estate loans including (primarily) residential mortgages and commercial real estate loans account for around 90% of the company's loan portfolio. Nonbank subsidiaries of Farmers Capital provide insurance and data processing services.

	Annual Growth	12/12	12/13	12/14	12/15	12/16
Assets ($ mil.)	(1.9%)	1,807.2	1,809.6	1,782.6	1,776.0	1,671.0
Net income ($ mil.)	8.1%	12.1	13.4	16.5	15.0	16.6
Market value ($ mil.)	36.1%	92.0	163.3	174.9	203.6	315.8
Employees	(2.3%)	518	519	510	501	472

FARMERS CO-OPERATIVE SOCIETY, SIOUX CENTER, IOWA

317 3RD ST NW
SIOUX CENTER, IA 512501856
Phone: 712-722-2671
Fax: –
Web: www.farmerscoopsociety.com

CEO: –
CFO: –
HR: Kelly Neuharth
FYE: July 31
Type: Private

When farmers cooperate society benefits. Through its seven centers in northwest Iowa Farmers Cooperative Society offers its member/farmers a full range of agricultural growing and marketing products and services including crop-storage facilities and business consulting. Its feedlot with room for some 5500 head of cattle helps members buy and care for feeder cattle and provides discounts on grain for members. The co-op also operates a member-only How-To Building Store in Sioux Center Iowa that sells hardware lawn-care products lumber and paint as well as brand-name home appliances. Farmers Cooperative Society has roots dating back to 1907.

	Annual Growth	07/12	07/13	07/14	07/15	07/16
Sales ($ mil.)	(8.2%)	–	496.5	418.5	405.3	384.2
Net income ($ mil.)	21.7%	–	5.0	3.9	7.6	8.9
Market value ($ mil.)	–	–	–	–	–	–
Employees	–	–	–	–	–	160

FARMERS COOPERATIVE COMPANY

105 GARFIELD AVE
FARNHAMVILLE, IA 505386712
Phone: 515-817-2100
Fax: –
Web: www.landuscooperative.com

CEO: James Chism
CFO: –
HR: –
FYE: August 31
Type: Private

The importance of cooperation — it's one of life's most important lessons. Dating back to the early 1900s the Farmers Cooperative Company (FCC) learned that lesson early on. The 5500-member-plus co-op offers agronomy and grain marketing services to its members who oversee some 3 million acres of farmland in central and north central Iowa. The largest of its kind in Iowa FCC operates 40 grain elevators and provides soil testing and mapping services. It sells supplies including seed feed and fertilizer to its members. The coop merged with another Iowa coop West Central Cooperative in 2016 to form Landus Cooperative.

	Annual Growth	08/06	08/07	08/08	08/09	08/10
Sales ($ mil.)	(12.8%)	–	–	–	894.5	779.6
Net income ($ mil.)	(19.9%)	–	–	–	13.0	10.4
Market value ($ mil.)	–	–	–	–	–	–
Employees	–	–	–	–	–	450

FARMERS NATIONAL BANC CORP. (CANFIELD, OH)
NAS: FMNB

20 South Broad Street
Canfield, OH 44406
Phone: 330 533-3341
Fax: –
Web: www.farmersbankgroup.com

CEO: Kevin Helmick
CFO: Troy Adair
HR: Mark Nicastro
FYE: December 31
Type: Public

Farmers National Banc is willing to help even nonfarmers grow their seed income into thriving bounties of wealth. The bank provides commercial and personal banking from nearly 20 branches in Ohio. Founded in 1887 Farmers National Banc offers checking and savings accounts credit cards and loans and mortgages. Farmers' lending portfolio is composed of real estate mortgages consumer loans and commercial loans. The company also includes Farmers National Insurance and Farmers Trust Company a non-depository trust bank that offers wealth management and trust services.

	Annual Growth	12/16	12/17	12/18	12/19	12/20
Assets ($ mil.)	11.8%	1,966.1	2,159.1	2,328.9	2,449.2	3,071.1
Net income ($ mil.)	19.5%	20.6	22.7	32.6	35.8	41.9
Market value ($ mil.)	(1.7%)	400.3	415.8	359.1	460.1	374.1
Employees	0.2%	441	445	453	450	444

FARMERS TELEPHONE COOPERATIVE, INC.

1101 E MAIN ST
KINGSTREE, SC 295564105
Phone: 843-382-2333
Fax: –
Web: www.ftc.net

CEO: Bradley Erwin
CFO: Jeffrey Lawrimore
HR: Leslye C Holladay
FYE: June 30
Type: Private

Farmers Telephone Cooperative (FTC) is the incumbent local-exchange carrier (ILEC) in Williamsburg Lee Sumter Clarendon and Florence counties in eastern South Carolina. Serving more than 60000 customers in a 3000 mile area the company provides traditional phone services including local-exchange access and long-distance as well as dial-up and DSL Internet access. The company also offers wireless phone service through a partnership with AT&T Mobility as well as security services and enterprise communications services. In operation since 1951 FTC claims to be the second-largest co-op in the US and should not be confused with the Farmers Telephone Cooperative serving the Rainsville Alabama area.

	Annual Growth	06/05	06/06	06/07	06/08	06/10
Sales ($ mil.)	–	–	–	0.0	83.7	131.2
Net income ($ mil.)	–	–	–	0.0	2.3	8.6
Market value ($ mil.)	–	–	–	–	–	–
Employees	–	–	–	–	–	418

FARMINGTON FOODS INC.

7419 FRANKLIN ST
FOREST PARK, IL 601301016
Phone: 708-771-3600
Fax: –
Web: www.farmingtonfoods.com

CEO: –
CFO: –
HR: –
FYE: December 29
Type: Private

Farmington Foods takes food from the farm adds value and sells the results. The company processes markets and distributes Value-added pork products including pork loin chops and ribs. Its Lean N' Juicy product line consists of case-ready enhanced pork such as bone-in or boneless loin chops baby backribs spareribs pork shoulder and tenderloin. Farmington also offers a variety of marinated pork products in flavors like Teriyaki lemon pepper and Italian. In addition to pork products the company also sells pre-packaged kabobs made with beef chicken and pork. Formerly known as the Farmington Meat Company the family-owned company was established in 1972.

	Annual Growth	12/00	12/01	12/02	12/03	12/07
Sales ($ mil.)	(4.6%)	–	90.1	67.5	73.8	68.0
Net income ($ mil.)	–	–	–	0.0	0.0	0.0
Market value ($ mil.)	–	–	–	–	–	–
Employees	–	–	–	–	–	155

FARO TECHNOLOGIES INC.
NMS: FARO

250 Technology Park
Lake Mary, FL 32746
Phone: 407 333-9911
Fax: –
Web: www.faro.com

CEO: Michael Burger
CFO: Allen Muhich
HR: –
FYE: December 31
Type: Public

FARO Technologies is a global technology company that designs develops manufactures markets and supports software driven three-dimensional (3D) measurement imaging and realization solutions for the 3D metrology architecture engineering and construction (AEC) and public safety analytics markets. With the touch of its mechanical arm FARO's measuring systems can facilitate reverse engineering of an undocumented part or a competitor's product. The portable FaroArm FARO Laser Tracker and FARO Gage are jointed devices that simulate the human arm's movement. Along with the FARO Laser Scanning Portfolio and Laser Tracker inspections and measurements are integrated with 3-D software. Aerospace automotive and metal and machine fabrication markets. Customers located outside the Americas account for around 60% of sales.

	Annual Growth	12/17	12/18	12/19	12/20	12/21
Sales ($ mil.)	(1.6%)	360.9	403.6	381.8	303.8	337.8
Net income ($ mil.)	–	(14.5)	4.9	(62.1)	0.6	(40.0)
Market value ($ mil.)	10.5%	855.7	739.9	916.7	1,285.9	1,274.8
Employees	(3.8%)	1,669	1,862	1,818	1,364	1,432

FARSTAD OIL INC.

100 27TH ST NE
MINOT, ND 58703-5164
Phone: 701-852-1194
Fax: –
Web: www.farstadoil.com

CEO: –
CFO: Bruce Hest
HR: Kelly Beck
FYE: December 31
Type: Private

When you are freezing in Fargo fuel is more than a luxury it's a necessity. Farstad Oil makes sure that gas stations lube shops and propane dealers are well stocked for those living through the cold winters in the Upper Midwest and West. Farstad Oil is a regional wholesale petroleum products distributor serving customers in North Dakota Montana Minnesota and Wyoming. The company a subsidiary of holding company SPF Energy wholesales about 250 million gallons of gas and fuel 20 million gallons of propane and 2.5 million gallons of lubricants each year. Its Minot operation is the largest lubricant plant in the region.

	Annual Growth	12/08	12/09	12/10	12/11	12/12
Sales ($ mil.)	28.5%	–	476.6	686.7	1,034.6	1,010.1
Net income ($ mil.)	47.8%	–	1.2	2.1	3.8	4.0
Market value ($ mil.)	–	–	–	–	–	–
Employees	–	–	–	–	–	125

FASHION INSTITUTE OF TECHNOLOGY

227 W 27TH ST
NEW YORK, NY 100015992
Phone: 212-217-7999
Fax: –
Web: www.fitnyc.edu

CEO: –
CFO: –
HR: –
FYE: June 30
Type: Private

Fashionistas pay homage to the Fashion Institute of Technology (FIT). The school offers degrees and classes in a variety of disciplines (about 45) within the fashion and design industry as well as in business technology and communications. More than 10000 students are enrolled at FIT; it has a student-teacher ratio of 17:1. The school also hosts The Museum at the Fashion Institute of Technology which houses collections of costumes and textiles with a focus on 20th-century fashion. Virginia Pope fashion editor of The New York Times was one of FIT's founders. FIT began in 1944 and was tuition-free until 1953; it is part of the State University of New York (SUNY) system.

	Annual Growth	06/05	06/06	06/07	06/08	06/11
Sales ($ mil.)	–	–	–	0.0	95.9	97.1
Net income ($ mil.)	–	–	–	0.0	4.5	8.4
Market value ($ mil.)	–	–	–	–	–	–
Employees	–	–	–	–	–	1,212

FASTENAL CO.
NMS: FAST

2001 Theurer Boulevard
Winona, MN 55987-1500
Phone: 507 454-5374
Fax: 507 453-8049
Web: www.fastenal.com

CEO: Daniel Florness
CFO: Holden Lewis
HR: Reyne Wisecup
FYE: December 31
Type: Public

Fastenal makes for a snug fit. The industrial and fastener distributor sells products in more than nine major product lines including threaded fasteners (such as screws nuts and bolts) which represent about 35% of overall sales. Other sales come from fluid-transfer parts for hydraulic and pneumatic power; janitorial electrical and welding supplies; material handling items; metal-cutting tool blades; and safety supplies. Founded in 1967 as a fastener shop Fastenal now operates more than 3200 branches and on-site locations in all 50 US states and in Canada Mexico Asia Africa and Europe. Its customers include construction manufacturing and other industrial professionals Fastenal generates the majority of its revenue in US.

	Annual Growth	12/17	12/18	12/19	12/20	12/21
Sales ($ mil.)	8.2%	4,390.5	4,965.1	5,333.7	5,647.3	6,010.9
Net income ($ mil.)	12.4%	578.6	751.9	790.9	859.1	925.0
Market value ($ mil.)	4.0%	31,472.2	30,091.0	21,263.4	28,099.9	36,864.3
Employees	(0.1%)	20,565	21,644	21,948	20,365	20,507

FATBURGER CORPORATION

301 Arizona Ave. Ste. 200
Santa Monica CA 90401-1364
Phone: 310-319-1850
Fax: 310-319-1863
Web: www.fatburger.com

CEO: Andrew Wiederhorn
CFO: Harold Fox
HR: –
FYE: June 30
Type: Private

It's a little more expensive than 99 cents but you don't need to be a real fat cat to enjoy one of these burgers. Fatburger operates and franchises more than 90 hamburger stands known for their 1/3 pound signature sandwich. Located primarily in Southern California the 1950s-style restaurants also offer a 1/2 pound Kingburger and 1/8 pound Baby Fat burger as well as a variety of side orders and other sandwiches. Franchisees operate more than 60 of the chain's locations. Lovie Yancey opened the first Fatburger in 1952 when "fat" was used to describe the size not the content of the burger. Fog Cutter Capital Group owns more than 80% of the company.

FATE THERAPEUTICS INC
NMS: FATE

12278 Scripps Summit Frive
San Diego, CA 92131
Phone: 858 875-1800
Fax: –
Web: www.fatetherapeutics.com

CEO: John Wolchko
CFO: Edward Dulac
HR: –
FYE: December 31
Type: Public

Fate Therapeutics believes it's destined to treat orphan diseases. The biopharmaceutical company is developing stem cell-based treatments for hematologic malignancies such as leukemia and lymphoma non-malignant orphan diseases such as lysosomal storage disorders hemoglobinopathies such as sickle cell disease and beta-thalassemia as well as anemia and other immune deficiencies. Its lead drug candidate ProHema uses umbilical cord blood to treat hematologic malignancies. The company was founded in 2007 by seven scientists who are not involved in its day-to-day operations. In 2013 it went public raising $40 million in its IPO which it will use toward R&D as well as clinical and preclinical drug development.

	Annual Growth	12/16	12/17	12/18	12/19	12/20
Sales ($ mil.)	63.5%	4.4	4.1	4.7	10.7	31.4
Net income ($ mil.)	–	(33.5)	(43.0)	(66.6)	(98.1)	(173.4)
Market value ($ mil.)	145.3%	220.2	536.0	1,125.5	1,716.7	7,976.6
Employees	43.4%	66	80	104	178	279

FATWIRE CORPORATION

330 Old Country Rd. Ste. 303
Mineola NY 11501-4143
Phone: 516-328-9473
Fax: 516-739-5069
Web: www.fatwire.com

CEO: Dorian Daley
CFO: –
HR: –
FYE: May 31
Type: Subsidiary

FatWire's Web content and experience management software helped organizations build and run online corporate portals with complex features. Its software enabled businesses to create and manage content access it through a variety of channels and deliver and reuse it across multiple applications and websites. FatWire sold to companies in the financial services manufacturing retail media and entertainment telecom health care and travel markets. The company also offered tools for managing social media and user-generated content (UGC) including Community Server and Gadget Server (Web page personalization tools). Key clients included Wal-Mart Best Buy Pfizer and Ford. FatWire was acquired by Oracle in 2011.

FAUQUIER BANKSHARES, INC.
NAS: FBSS

10 Courthouse Square
Warrenton, VA 20186
Phone: 540 347-2700
Fax: –
Web: www.tfb.bank.com

CEO: –
CFO: –
HR: –
FYE: December 31
Type: Public

Fauquier Bankshares is the holding company for The Fauquier Bank which operates about 10 branches in Fauquier and Prince William counties in northern Virginia southwest of Washington DC. The bank targets individuals and regional business customers offering standard deposit products such as checking savings and money market accounts CDs and IRAs. Its lending activities consist mostly of residential and commercial mortgages. The bank's wealth management division provides investment management trust estate retirement insurance and brokerage services. Through subsidiary Fauquier Bank Services it has equity ownership stakes in Bankers Insurance Infinex Investments and Bankers Title Shenandoah.

	Annual Growth	12/15	12/16	12/17	12/18	12/19
Assets ($ mil.)	4.7%	601.4	624.4	644.6	730.8	722.2
Net income ($ mil.)	–	(0.6)	3.7	2.5	6.1	6.8
Market value ($ mil.)	8.6%	57.7	63.0	82.9	72.6	80.4
Employees	(1.2%)	148	154	150	142	141

FAYETTE COMMUNITY HOSPITAL, INC.

1255 HIGHWAY 54 W
FAYETTEVILLE, GA 302144526
Phone: 770-719-7000
Fax: –
Web: www.piedmont.org

CEO: James Michael Burnette
CFO: John Miles
HR: –
FYE: June 30
Type: Private

If you do too much boogying at the Fayetteville Bluegrass Blast or slip in the sleet at the Christmas in Fayetteville festival Piedmont Fayette Hospital (PFH) is there to help. The acute care hospital is home to centers in cardiovascular medicine diabetes treatment sleep disorder therapy women's health fitness and rehabilitative care. With more than 500 physicians on staff the former Fayette Community Hospital has the ability to treat just about whatever comes through its doors — from ear nose throat problems to pediatric dentistry. The about 155-bed hospital opened in 1997 and is part of the not-for-profit Piedmont Healthcare network.

	Annual Growth	06/08	06/09	06/13	06/14	06/16
Sales ($ mil.)	11.3%	–	165.2	283.1	306.2	349.7
Net income ($ mil.)	5.1%	–	18.2	23.9	29.0	25.7
Market value ($ mil.)	–	–	–	–	–	–
Employees	–	–	–	–	–	1,045

FAYETTEVILLE PUBLIC WORKS COMMISSION

955 OLD WILMINGTON RD
FAYETTEVILLE, NC 283016357
Phone: 910-723-1243
Fax: –
Web: www.faypwc.com

CEO: David Trego
CFO: J Dwight Miller
HR: –
FYE: June 30
Type: Private

The taps the toilets and the plugs in Fayetteville are all the province of The Public Works Commission of the City of Fayetteville North Carolina (PWC) which is responsible for operating maintaining and upgrading the municipal electric water and wastewater utility systems. PWC distributes electricity to about 79000 residential commercial and industrial customers. The electric utility has 1312 miles of distribution lines 24770 distribution line transformers and more than 46880 poles. The water utility serves more than 83150 customers and has 1340 miles of mains; the wastewater unit serves about 79180 customers and has about 1340 miles of sewer line.

	Annual Growth	06/17	06/18	06/19	06/20	06/21
Sales ($ mil.)	0.3%	–	334.1	346.7	342.5	337.1
Net income ($ mil.)	8.5%	–	43.0	50.0	44.9	55.0
Market value ($ mil.)	–	–	–	–	–	–
Employees	–	–	–	–	–	467

FBL FINANCIAL GROUP INC

5400 University Avenue
West Des Moines, IA 50266-5997
Phone: 515 225-5400
Fax: –
Web: www.fblfinancial.com

NYS: FFG
CEO: Daniel D Pitcher
CFO: Donald J Seibel
HR: –
FYE: December 31
Type: Public

Insurance holding company FBL Financial Group (FBL) is the parent of Farm Bureau Life Insurance Company. Through its subsidiary the firm sells life insurance annuities and investment products to farmers ranchers and agricultural businesses. Farm Bureau Life sells insurance and annuities through an exclusive network of about 1860 agents across some 15 states in the Midwest and West. (In Colorado it operates as Greenfields Life Insurance.) The company markets its products through an affiliation with the American Farm Bureau Federation. FBL also manages for a fee two Farm Bureau-affiliated property/casualty insurance companies. The Iowa Farm Bureau Federation owns majority of the company.

	Annual Growth	12/15	12/16	12/17	12/18	12/19
Assets ($ mil.)	3.5%	9,132.0	9,566.1	10,066.6	9,833.6	10,480.2
Net income ($ mil.)	2.7%	113.5	107.2	194.3	93.8	126.2
Market value ($ mil.)	(1.9%)	1,569.6	1,927.5	1,717.9	1,619.2	1,453.5
Employees	1.7%	1,637	1,644	1,692	1,647	1,751

FBR & CO

1300 North Seventeenth Street
Arlington, VA 22209
Phone: 703 312-9500
Fax: –
Web: www.fbr.com

NMS: FBRC
CEO: Richard J Hendrix
CFO: Bradley J Wright
HR: –
FYE: December 31
Type: Public

Don't confuse FDR and FBR: One was a beloved US president while the other loves dead presidents. FBR & Co. provides investment banking and institutional brokerage services for institutional and corporate clients and wealthy individuals. It also conducts equities research manages mutual funds and invests its own capital in merchant banking transactions alongside its clients. The company focuses on the consumer industrials energy financial services health care real estate media telecommunications and technology markets Crestview Partners. Its principal operating subsidiaries are FBR Capital Markets & Co. and FBR Fund Advisers.

	Annual Growth	12/11	12/12	12/13	12/14	12/15
Sales ($ mil.)	(4.9%)	147.2	151.5	259.8	182.1	120.4
Net income ($ mil.)	–	(49.6)	29.7	92.9	17.0	(7.5)
Market value ($ mil.)	76.6%	13.9	26.3	179.3	167.1	135.2
Employees	0.7%	295	256	302	300	303

FCI CONSTRUCTORS INC.

3070 I-70 BUSINESS LOOP
GRAND JUNCTION, CO 81504-4468
Phone: 970-434-9093
Fax: –
Web: www.fciol.com

CEO: Shane Haas
CFO: Clayton Marshall
HR: –
FYE: March 31
Type: Private

FCI Constructors focuses on commercial building and renovation projects in the Rocky Mountain and southwestern US. Its projects range from hospitals assisted living facilities municipal projects and recreation centers to office buildings banks churches and educational manufacturing warehouse correctional and postal facilities. The company has offices in Arizona Colorado and Wyoming. Projects include the Mesa County Justice Center in Phoenix Crossroads Urgent Psychiatric Care Hospital in Durango Colorado and the Denver Public Schools Bus Terminal. The company which was founded in 1978 by M. L. Francis is owned by CEO Ed Forsman EVP Ron Choate and its employees.

	Annual Growth	03/07	03/08	03/09	03/10	03/12
Sales ($ mil.)	(13.1%)	–	–	379.1	315.0	248.8
Net income ($ mil.)	(30.1%)	–	–	3.3	1.7	1.1
Market value ($ mil.)	–	–	–	–	–	–
Employees	–	–	–	–	–	275

FEDERAL AGRICULTURAL MORTGAGE CORP

1999 K Street, N.W., 4th Floor
Washington, DC 20006
Phone: 202 872-7700
Fax: –

NYS: AGM
CEO: Bradford Nordholm
CFO: Aparna Ramesh
HR: –
FYE: December 31
Type: Public

Farmer Mac (Federal Agricultural Mortgage Corporation) is stockholder-owned federally chartered corporation that combines private capital and public sponsorship to serve a public purpose. The company provides a secondary market for a variety of loans made to borrowers in rural America. The company's market activities include purchasing eligible loans directly from lenders and more. Farmer Mac is an institution of the Farm Credit System (FCS) which is composed of the banks associations and related entities including Farmer Mac and its subsidiaries. Farmer Mac was chartered by Congress in 1987 and established under federal legislation first enacted in 1988.

	Annual Growth	12/16	12/17	12/18	12/19	12/20
Assets ($ mil.)	11.8%	15,606.0	17,792.3	18,694.3	21,709.4	24,355.5
Net income ($ mil.)	8.9%	77.3	84.5	108.1	109.5	108.6
Market value ($ mil.)	6.7%	614.9	840.1	648.9	896.5	797.2
Employees	10.6%	81	88	103	103	121

FEDERAL AVIATION ADMINISTRATION

800 Independence Ave. SW
Washington DC 20591
Phone: 866-835-5322
Fax: 617-568-5079
Web: www.massport.com

CEO: –
CFO: –
HR: William Clear
FYE: September 30
Type: Government Agency

Nobody goes up up and away until the folks at the FAA say it's OK. The Federal Aviation Administration (FAA) is the government agency responsible for overseeing air transportation in the US. An arm of the US Department of Transportation the FAA focuses on air transportation safety including the enforcement of safety standards for aircraft manufacturing operation and maintenance. It also manages air traffic in the US through a network of towers overseeing an average of 50000 flights per day. It maintains radar systems communication equipment and air traffic security systems. The FAA's annual budget is typically around $15 billion.

FEDERAL HOME LOAN BANK BOSTON

800 Boylston Street
Boston, MA 02199
Phone: 617 292-9600
Fax: –
Web: www.fhlbboston.com

CEO: Edward A Hjerpe III
CFO: Frank Nitkiewicz
HR: –
FYE: December 31
Type: Public

Federal Home Loan Bank of Boston (FHLB Boston) is banking on the continued support of other banks. The government-supported enterprise provides funds for residential mortgages and community development loans to its members which consist of more than 440 financial institutions across New England including banks thrifts credit unions and insurance companies. The bank also lends to non-member institutions the likes of state housing finance agencies primarily to promote the funding of low to moderate income housing in the region. FHLB Boston is one of 12 regional wholesale banks in the Federal Home Loan Bank System. Its region includes Connecticut Maine Massachusetts New Hampshire Rhode Island and Vermont.

	Annual Growth	12/16	12/17	12/18	12/19	12/20
Sales ($ mil.)	1.9%	737.5	959.8	1,447.4	1,487.3	794.7
Net income ($ mil.)	(8.7%)	173.2	190.2	216.8	190.7	120.3
Market value ($ mil.)	–	–	–	–	–	–
Employees	(0.8%)	202	203	200	194	196

FEDERAL HOME LOAN BANK NEW YORK

101 Park Avenue
New York, NY 10178
Phone: 212 681-6000
Fax: –
Web: www.fhlbny.com

CEO: Jose Gonzalez
CFO: Kevin Neylan
HR: –
FYE: December 31
Type: Public

Federal Home Loan Bank of New York (FHLBNY) provides funds for residential mortgages and community development to more than 330 member banks savings and loans credit unions and life insurance companies in New York New Jersey Puerto Rico and the US Virgin Islands. One of a dozen Federal Home Loan Banks in the US it is cooperatively owned by its member institutions and supervised by the Federal Housing Finance Agency. FHLBNY like others in the system is privately capitalized; it receives no taxpayer funding. The bank instead raises funds mainly by issuing debt instruments in the capital markets.

	Annual Growth	12/16	12/17	12/18	12/19	12/20
Assets ($ mil.)	(1.2%)	143,606.3	158,918.4	144,381.4	162,062.0	136,996.4
Net income ($ mil.)	2.5%	401.2	479.5	560.5	472.6	442.4
Market value ($ mil.)	–	–	–	–	–	–
Employees	6.0%	280	308	314	342	354

FEDERAL HOME LOAN BANK OF ATLANTA

1475 PEACHTREE ST NE # 400
ATLANTA, GA 303093037
Phone: 404-888-8000
Fax: –
Web: www.fhlbanks.com

CEO: Kirk Malmberg
CFO: Haig Kazazian
HR: –
FYE: December 31
Type: Private

Where do banks in the southeastern US bank? Federal Home Loan Bank of Atlanta. Known as FHLBank Atlanta for short the bank provides mortgage funding deposit community investment and cash management services to some 1100 commercial banks credit unions insurance companies and thrifts. Its territory includes Alabama Florida Georgia Maryland North Carolina South Carolina Virginia and Washington DC. The bank primarily provides funding to members to originate residential mortgages and community development loans. It also purchases mortgages on the secondary market to provide liquidity.

	Annual Growth	12/12	12/13	12/14	12/15	12/16
Assets ($ mil.)	4.3%	–	122,316.0	138,344.0	142,253.0	138,671.0
Net income ($ mil.)	(6.3%)	–	338.0	271.0	301.0	278.0
Market value ($ mil.)	–	–	–	–	–	–
Employees	–	–	–	–	–	339

FEDERAL HOME LOAN BANK OF CHICAGO

200 E RANDOLPH ST # 1700
CHICAGO, IL 606016428
Phone: 312-565-5700
Fax: –
Web: www.fhlbc.com

CEO: Michael Ericson
CFO: Roger Lundstrom
HR: –
FYE: December 31
Type: Private

Federal Home Loan Bank of Chicago (FHLB Chicago) is a government-sponsored enterprises that provides secured loans and other support services to about 760 members including commercial banks credit unions insurance companies thrifts and community development financial institutions throughout Illinois and Wisconsin. It is cooperatively owned by its member institutions who use advances from the bank to originate residential mortgages invest in government or mortgage-related securities and promote affordable housing and community development in their respective communities. FHLB Chicago is one of a dozen federal banks that comprise the Federal Home Loan Bank System that was established by Congress in 1932.

	Annual Growth	12/11	12/12	12/14	12/15	12/16
Assets ($ mil.)	3.1%	–	69,584.0	71,841.0	70,676.0	78,692.0
Net income ($ mil.)	(3.4%)	–	375.0	392.0	349.0	327.0
Market value ($ mil.)	–	–	–	–	–	–
Employees	–	–	–	–	–	405

FEDERAL HOME LOAN BANK OF PITTSBURGH

601 Grant Street
Pittsburgh, PA 15219
Phone: 412 288-3400
Fax: –
Web: www.fhlb-pgh.com

CEO: Winthrop Watson
CFO: David G Paulson
HR: –
FYE: December 31
Type: Public

The Federal Home Loan Bank of Pittsburgh helps revitalize neighborhoods and fund low-income housing in the City of Champions and beyond. One of a dozen banks in the Federal Home Loan Bank System the government-sponsored entity (FHLB Pittsburgh for short) uses private capital and public sponsorships to provide low-cost funding for residential mortgages and community and economic development loans in Delaware Pennsylvania and West Virginia. It is cooperatively owned by about 300 member banks thrifts credit unions and insurance companies in its three-state district. The bank also offers member banks correspondent banking services such as depository funds transfer settlement and safekeeping services.

	Annual Growth	12/16	12/17	12/18	12/19	12/20
Sales ($ mil.)	1.5%	1,010.6	1,485.9	2,272.4	2,690.0	1,074.6
Net income ($ mil.)	(5.2%)	260.0	339.6	347.2	316.9	210.4
Market value ($ mil.)	–	–	–	–	–	–
Employees	2.3%	214	215	224	228	234

FEDERAL HOME LOAN BANK OF SAN FRANCISCO

333 Bush Street, Suite 2700
San Francisco, CA 94104
Phone: 415 616-1000
Fax: –
Web: www.fhlbsf.com

CEO: Teresa Bazemore
CFO: Kenneth C Miller
HR: –
FYE: December 31
Type: Public

The city by the bay is the home to the Federal Home Loan Bank of San Francisco one of a dozen regional banks in the Federal Home Loan Bank System chartered by Congress in 1932 to provide credit to residential mortgage lenders. The government-sponsored enterprise is privately owned by its members which include some 400 commercial banks credit unions industrial loan companies savings and loans insurance companies and housing associates headquartered in Arizona California and Nevada. The bank links members to worldwide capital markets which provide them with low-cost funding. Members then pass these advances along to their customers in the form of affordable home mortgage and economic development loans.

	Annual Growth	12/16	12/17	12/18	12/19	12/20
Assets ($ mil.)	(7.0%)	91,941.0	123,385.0	109,326.0	106,842.0	68,634.0
Net income ($ mil.)	(17.2%)	712.0	376.0	360.0	327.0	335.0
Market value ($ mil.)	–	–	–	–	–	–
Employees	2.7%	274	287	282	282	305

FEDERAL HOME LOAN BANK TOPEKA

500 S.W. Wanamaker Road
Topeka, KS 66606
Phone: 785 233-0507
Fax: –
Web: www.fhlbtopeka.com

CEO: Mark Yardley
CFO: William Osborn
HR: –
FYE: December 31
Type: Public

Don't worry Toto Federal Home Loan Bank of Topeka is in Kansas. The institution created by Congress provides funds for residential mortgages and community-development loans to almost 900 member banks thrifts credit unions and insurance companies in Arizona Colorado Kansas Nebraska New Mexico Oklahoma and Wyoming. FHLBank Topeka also provides members with other financial services such as safekeeping shelf funding and wire transfer services. One of a dozen Federal Home Loan Banks in the US FHLBank Topeka is cooperatively owned by its member institutions.

	Annual Growth	12/16	12/17	12/18	12/19	12/20
Sales ($ mil.)	6.3%	580.4	832.0	1,257.0	1,488.8	741.1
Net income ($ mil.)	(7.6%)	161.8	197.2	170.3	185.2	118.1
Market value ($ mil.)	–	–	–	–	–	–
Employees	0.1%	238	233	234	233	239

FEDERAL PRISON INDUSTRIES INC.

320 1st St. NW Bldg. 400
Washington DC 20534
Phone: 202-305-3500
Fax: 202-305-7340
Web: www.unicor.gov

CEO: Steve V Schwalb
CFO: –
HR: –
FYE: September 30
Type: Government Agency

Some businesses benefit from captive audiences; this company benefits from captive employees. Federal Prison Industries (FPI) known by its trade name UNICOR uses prisoners to make products and provide services mainly for US government agencies. Nearly 16000 inmates (about 9% of the total eligible inmate population) are employed in 94 FPI factories in prisons across the US. UNICOR which is part of the Justice Department's Bureau of Prisons manufactures products such as office furniture clothing beds and linens and electronics equipment. It also offers services including data entry bulk mailing laundry services recycling and refurbishing of vehicle components.

FEDERAL REALTY INVESTMENT TRUST (NEW)   NYS: FRT

909 Rose Avenue, Suite 200
North Bethesda, MD 20852
Phone: 301 998-8100
Fax: –
Web: www.federalrealty.com

CEO: Donald Wood
CFO: Daniel Guglielmone
HR: Dina Barlas
FYE: December 31
Type: Public

Federal Realty Investment Trust is a real estate investment trust (REIT) which owns or has a majority interest in about 100 retail properties with approximately 23.4 million sq. ft. of leasable space including community and neighborhood shopping centers and mixed-use complexes. Its key markets are densely populated affluent areas in the Northeast Mid-Atlantic South Florida and California. It also has properties in Florida Illinois and Michigan. The REIT's real estate projects were more than 90% leased properties and around 90% are occupied. Principal tenants include Giant Food Barnes & Noble Bed Bath & Beyond and Home Depot. One of the oldest publicly traded REITs in the US Federal Realty was founded in 1962.

	Annual Growth	12/17	12/18	12/19	12/20	12/21
Sales ($ mil.)	2.6%	857.3	915.4	935.8	835.5	951.2
Net income ($ mil.)	(2.5%)	289.9	241.9	353.9	131.7	261.5
Market value ($ mil.)	0.7%	10,439.3	9,278.3	10,118.6	6,690.7	10,715.2
Employees	(0.9%)	326	303	313	311	315

FEDERAL RESERVE BANK OF ATLANTA, DIST. NO. 6

1000 Peachtree Street, N.E.
Atlanta, GA 30309-4470
Phone: 404 498-8500
Fax: –
Web: www.frbatlanta.org

CEO: Dennis P Lockhart
CFO: –
HR: –
FYE: December 31
Type: Public

One of 12 regional banks in the Federal Reserve System the Federal Reserve Bank of Atlanta oversees Fed member banks and thrifts and their holding companies throughout the Southeast including Alabama Florida Georgia and parts of Louisiana Mississippi and Tennessee. It has branches in Birmingham Jacksonville Miami Nashville and New Orleans. It conducts examinations and investigations of member institutions distributes cash issues savings bonds and Treasury securities and assists the Fed in setting monetary policy such as interest rates. The bank also processes checks and acts as a clearinghouse for payments between banks. Fed Reserve Banks are independent arms within the government and return earnings (gleaned mostly from investments in government bonds) to the US Treasury.

	Annual Growth	12/16	12/17	12/18	12/19	12/20
Sales ($ mil.)	4.2%	6,502.0	6,971.0	6,948.0	7,042.0	7,677.0
Net income ($ mil.)	–	66.0	48.0	(138.0)	(26.0)	(4.0)
Market value ($ mil.)	–	–	–	–	–	–
Employees	–	–	–	–	–	–

FEDERAL RESERVE BANK OF BOSTON, DIST. NO. 1

600 Atlantic Avenue
Boston, MA 02210
Phone: 617 973-3000
Fax: –
Web: www.bostonfed.org

CEO: Eric S Rosengren
CFO: –
HR: –
FYE: December 31
Type: Public

One of 12 regional banks in the Federal Reserve System the Federal Reserve Bank of Boston oversees more than 100 banks and bank holding companies in six New England states including Connecticut (except Fairfield County) Massachusetts Maine New Hampshire Rhode Island and Vermont. It conducts examinations and investigations of member institutions distributes money issues savings bonds and Treasury securities and assists the Fed in setting monetary policy. The bank also processes checks and acts as a clearinghouse for payments between banks. Federal Reserve Banks are not-for-profit and return most of their earnings (primarily from investments in government bonds) to the US Treasury.

	Annual Growth	12/16	12/17	12/18	12/19	12/20
Sales ($ mil.)	(2.8%)	2,829.0	2,544.0	2,213.0	2,119.0	2,529.0
Net income ($ mil.)	–	29.0	31.0	(93.0)	54.0	(1.0)
Market value ($ mil.)	–	–	–	–	–	–
Employees	–	–	–	–	–	–

FEDERAL RESERVE BANK OF CHICAGO, DIST. NO. 7

230 South La Salle Street
Chicago, IL 60604-1413
Phone: 312 322-5322
Fax: –
Web: www.chicagofed.org

CEO: Charles L Evans
CFO: –
HR: –
FYE: December 31
Type: Public

The Federal Reserve Bank of Chicago regulates banks and bank holding companies in Iowa and portions of Mochigan Illinois Indiana and Wisconsin. It supervises bank holding companies and state member banks distributes money issues savings bonds and Treasury securities and assists the Fed in setting monetary policy. The Chicago Fed also processes checks and acts as a clearinghouse for payments between banks. Like the 11 other regional banks in the Federal Reserve System it returns its profits (earned largely from investments in government and federal agency securities) to the US Treasury.

	Annual Growth	12/16	12/17	12/18	12/19	12/20
Sales ($ mil.)	6.6%	4,458.0	4,902.0	5,752.0	5,520.0	5,751.0
Net income ($ mil.)	(31.6%)	183.0	41.0	(101.0)	19.0	40.0
Market value ($ mil.)	–	–	–	–	–	–
Employees	–	–	–	–	–	–

FEDERAL RESERVE BANK OF CLEVELAND, DIST. NO. 4

P.O. Box 6387
Cleveland, OH 44101-1387
Phone: 216 579-2000
Fax: –
Web: www.clevelandfed.org
CEO: Sandra Pianalto
CFO: –
HR: –
FYE: December 31
Type: Public

One of 12 regional banks in the Federal Reserve System the Federal Reserve Bank of Cleveland has branches banks at Cincinnati Ohio and Pittsburgh Pennsylvania and covers the state of Ohio; over 55 counties in eastern Kentucky; almost 20 counties in western Pennsylvania; and 6 counties in northern West Virginia. It provides short-term loans to depository institutions distributes money issues savings bonds and Treasury securities and participates in setting monetary policy. The bank also processes checks and acts as a clearinghouse for payments between banks in its region. Federal Reserve Banks are not-for-profit and return earnings (mostly from investments in government bonds) to the US Treasury.

	Annual Growth	12/15	12/16	12/17	12/18	12/19
Sales ($ mil.)	3.8%	2,595.0	3,172.0	3,525.0	3,224.0	3,015.0
Net income ($ mil.)	–	(1,349.0)	108.0	62.0	(192.0)	88.0
Market value ($ mil.)	–	–	–	–	–	–
Employees	–	–	–	–	–	–

FEDERAL RESERVE BANK OF DALLAS, DIST. NO. 11

2200 North Pearl Street
Dallas, TX 75201-2272
Phone: 214 922-6000
Fax: –
Web: www.dallasfed.org
CEO: Richard W Fisher
CFO: –
HR: –
FYE: December 31
Type: Public

One of 12 regional banks in the Federal Reserve System the Federal Reserve Bank of Dallas covers the state of Texas; more than 25 parishes in northern Louisiana; and nearly 20 counties in southern New Mexico. It conducts examinations and investigations of member institutions distributes money issues savings bonds and Treasury securities and assists the Federal Reserve in setting monetary policy. The bank also processes checks and acts as a clearinghouse for payments between banks. Its head office is in Dallas and has branches in El Paso Houston and San Antonio.

	Annual Growth	12/16	12/17	12/18	12/19	12/20
Sales ($ mil.)	5.5%	3,876.0	4,455.0	4,626.0	4,427.0	4,796.0
Net income ($ mil.)	84.2%	6.0	24.0	(23.0)	(3.0)	69.0
Market value ($ mil.)	–	–	–	–	–	–
Employees	–	–	–	–	–	–

FEDERAL RESERVE BANK OF KANSAS CITY, DIST. NO. 10

1 Memorial Drive
Kansas City, MO 64198
Phone: 816 881-2000
Fax: –
Web: www.kansascityfed.org
CEO: –
CFO: –
HR: –
FYE: December 31
Type: Public

One of 12 regional banks in the Federal Reserve System the Federal Reserve Bank of Kansas City oversees system member banks and bank holding companies in Colorado Kansas Nebraska Wyoming Oklahoma portions of Missouri and New Mexico. The bank also has branch offices in Denver Oklahoma and Omaha. Considered the 10th District it provides providing short-term loans to depository institutions distributes money issues savings bonds and Treasury securities and assists the Fed in setting monetary policy. The bank established in 1914 also processes checks and acts as a clearinghouse for payments between banks.

	Annual Growth	12/15	12/16	12/17	12/18	12/19
Sales ($ mil.)	1.6%	1,550.0	1,614.0	1,733.0	1,847.0	1,653.0
Net income ($ mil.)	–	(189.0)	12.0	19.0	(23.0)	30.0
Market value ($ mil.)	–	–	–	–	–	–
Employees	–	–	–	–	–	–

FEDERAL RESERVE BANK OF MINNEAPOLIS, DIST. NO. 9

90 Hennepin Avenue, P.O. Box 291
Minneapolis, MN 55408-0291
Phone: 612 204-5000
Fax: –
Web: www.minneapolisfed.org
CEO: Narayana Kocherlakota
CFO: –
HR: –
FYE: December 31
Type: Public

The Federal Reserve Bank of Minneapolis one of the 12 regional banks in the Federal Reserve System regulates banks and bank holding companies in the Ninth District in Minnesota Montana North Dakota South Dakota northern Wisconsin and the Upper Peninsula of Michigan. It conducts investigations of member institutions distributes money issues savings bonds and Treasury securities and assists the Fed in setting monetary policy. The bank also processes checks and acts as a clearinghouse for payments between banks. The Federal Reserve Bank of Minneapolis like its 11 counterparts returns its profits (earned largely from investments in government and federal agency securities) to the US Treasury.

	Annual Growth	12/16	12/17	12/18	12/19	12/20
Sales ($ mil.)	3.6%	863.0	932.0	970.0	920.0	994.0
Net income ($ mil.)	20.0%	–	11.0	(12.0)	17.0	19.0
Market value ($ mil.)	–	–	–	–	–	–
Employees	–	–	–	–	–	–

FEDERAL RESERVE BANK OF NEW YORK, DIST. NO. 2

33 Liberty Street
New York, NY 10045-0001
Phone: 212 720-5000
Fax: –
Web: www.newyorkfed.org
CEO: –
CFO: –
HR: –
FYE: December 31
Type: Public

The Federal Reserve Bank of New York is one of the twelve regional Reserve Banks which together with the Board of Governors in Washington DC make up the Federal Reserve System. It issues currency clears check drawn and lends to banks in its district. In addition to the duties it shares with twelve other regional Federal Reserve Banks the New York Fed trades US government securities to regulate the money supply intervenes on foreign exchange markets and stores monetary gold for foreign central banks and governments. The New York Fed's district is relatively small but the bank is the largest in the Federal Reserve System in assets and volume of activity.

	Annual Growth	12/16	12/17	12/18	12/19	12/20
Sales ($ mil.)	(4.1%)	64,509.0	65,090.0	62,509.0	56,535.0	54,640.0
Net income ($ mil.)	41.6%	328.0	(503.0)	(652.0)	226.0	1,317.0
Market value ($ mil.)	–	–	–	–	–	–
Employees	–	–	–	–	–	–

FEDERAL RESERVE BANK OF PHILADELPHIA, DIST. NO. 3

10 Independence Mall
Philadelphia, PA 19106-1574
Phone: 215 574-6000
Fax: 215 574-6030
Web: www.philadelphiafed.org
CEO: –
CFO: Michael J Angelakis
HR: Brad Bralow
FYE: December 31
Type: Public

One of 12 regional banks in the Federal Reserve System the Federal Reserve Bank of Philadelphia oversees system member banks and bank holding companies in eastern and central Pennsylvania southern New Jersey and Delaware. It provides short-term loans to depository institutions distributes money issues savings bonds and Treasury securities and assists the Fed in setting monetary policy. The Bank also processes checks and acts as a clearinghouse for payments between banks in its region. Federal Reserve Banks are not-for-profit and return most of their income (primarily earned from investments in US government and federal agency securities) to the US Treasury.

	Annual Growth	12/16	12/17	12/18	12/19	12/20
Sales ($ mil.)	(4.7%)	2,968.0	3,103.0	2,843.0	2,518.0	2,447.0
Net income ($ mil.)	4.1%	23.0	70.0	(119.0)	(123.0)	27.0
Market value ($ mil.)	–	–	–	–	–	–
Employees	–	–	–	–	–	–

FEDERAL RESERVE BANK OF RICHMOND, DIST. NO. 5

Post Office Box 27622 CEO: -
Richmond, VA 23261 CFO: -
Phone: 804 697-8000 HR: -
Fax: - FYE: December 31
Web: www.richmondfed.org Type: Public

One of 12 regional banks in the Federal Reserve System the Federal Reserve Bank of Richmond covers the states of Maryland Virginia North Carolina and South Carolina; nearly 50 counties constituting most of West Virginia; and the District of Columbia. It conducts examinations and investigations of member institutions distributes money issues savings bonds and Treasury securities and assists the Federal Reserve System in setting monetary policy. The bank also processes checks and acts as a clearinghouse for payments between banks. It also conducts research which supports policymaking and thought leadership on issues important to the Federal Reserve and the Fifth District. Federal Reserve Banks return earnings (mostly from investments in government bonds) to the US Treasury.

	Annual Growth	12/16	12/17	12/18	12/19	12/20
Sales ($ mil.)	0.7%	6,604.0	7,217.0	6,602.0	6,232.0	6,792.0
Net income ($ mil.)	(12.1%)	67.0	165.0	(508.0)	135.0	40.0
Market value ($ mil.)	-	-	-	-	-	-
Employees	-	-	-	-	-	-

FEDERAL RESERVE BANK OF SAN FRANCISCO, DIST. NO. 12

101 Market Street CEO: John C Williams
San Francisco, CA 94105 CFO: -
Phone: 415 974-2000 HR: -
Fax: - FYE: December 31
Web: www.frbsf.org Type: Public

One of 12 regional banks in the Federal Reserve System the Federal Reserve Bank of San Francisco through four branch offices oversees the states of Alaska Arizona California Hawaii Idaho Nevada Oregon Utah and Washington and serves American Samoa Guam and the Commonwealth of the Northern Mariana Islands. It provides short-term loans to depository institutions distributes money issues savings bonds and Treasury securities and assists the Federal Reserve in setting monetary policy. The bank also processes checks and acts as a clearinghouse for payments between banks. Federal Reserve Banks are not-for-profit and return earnings (mostly from investments in government bonds) to the US Treasury.

	Annual Growth	12/16	12/17	12/18	12/19	12/20
Sales ($ mil.)	(1.4%)	13,437.0	14,660.0	13,978.0	12,188.0	12,679.0
Net income ($ mil.)	7.8%	51.0	116.0	(330.0)	133.0	69.0
Market value ($ mil.)	-	-	-	-	-	-
Employees	-	-	-	-	-	-

FEDERAL RESERVE BANK OF ST. LOUIS, DIST. NO. 8

One Federal Reserve Bank Plaza, Broadway and Locust Street CEO: James B Bullard
St. Louis, MO 63102 CFO: -
Phone: 314 444-8444 HR: -
Fax: - FYE: December 31
Web: www.stlouisfed.org Type: Public

One of 12 regional banks in the Federal Reserve System the Federal Reserve Bank of St. Louis regulates banks and bank holding companies in its region. Its territory encompasses eastern Missouri southern Illinois all of Arkansas and portions of Indiana Kentucky Mississippi and Tennessee. The bank operating from four offices conducts examinations and investigations of member institutions distributes money processes checks and payments between banks issues savings bonds and Treasury securities and assists the Fed in setting monetary policy. Federal Reserve Banks are not-for-profit and return almost all of their earnings (gleaned mostly from investments in government bonds) to the US Treasury.

	Annual Growth	12/16	12/17	12/18	12/19	12/20
Sales ($ mil.)	4.4%	1,541.0	1,759.0	1,741.0	1,702.0	1,831.0
Net income ($ mil.)	16.6%	20.0	47.0	(26.0)	15.0	37.0
Market value ($ mil.)	-	-	-	-	-	-
Employees	-	-	-	-	-	-

FEDERAL RESERVE SYSTEM

20th Street and Constitution Avenue N.W. CEO: -
Washington, DC 20551 CFO: -
Phone: 202 452-3245 HR: -
Fax: 202 728-5886 FYE: December 31
Web: www.federalreserve.gov Type: Public

The Federal Reserve was created by an act of Congress in 1913 to provide the nation with a safer more flexible and more stable monetary and financial system. In establishing the Federal Reserve System the United States was divided geographically into 12 Districts each with a separately incorporated Reserve Bank. The Fed is the central bank of the United States. It conducts the nation's monetary policy to promote maximum employment stable prices and moderate long-term interest rates in the US economy and promotes the stability of the financial system and seeks to minimize and contain systemic risks through active monitoring and engagement in the US and abroad.

	Annual Growth	12/16	12/17	12/18	12/19	12/20
Sales ($ mil.)	(1.7%)	112,207.0	116,764.0	113,120.0	103,846.0	104,976.0
Net income ($ mil.)	16.8%	894.0	133.0	(2,218.0)	565.0	1,662.0
Market value ($ mil.)	-	-	-	-	-	-
Employees	-	-	-	-	-	-

FEDERAL SCREW WORKS NBB: FSCR

34846 Goddard Road CEO: Thomas ZurSchmiede
Romulus, MI 48174-3406 CFO: W. ZurSchmiede
Phone: 734 941-4211 HR: -
Fax: - FYE: June 30
Web: www.federalscrewworks.com Type: Public

Federal Screw Works (FSW) doesn't mind if you think of your car as a bucket of bolts. The Detroit native makes fasteners and related items primarily for the automotive industry. The company produces high-volume lots to the specifications of manufacturers. Nonautomotive sales are mainly to makers of durable goods. FSW's products include locknuts bolts piston pins studs bushings shafts and other machined cold-formed hardened and ground-metal parts. It maintains five manufacturing facilities all of which are located in Michigan.

	Annual Growth	06/17	06/18	06/19	06/20	06/21
Sales ($ mil.)	(2.6%)	77.3	75.4	73.4	60.0	69.6
Net income ($ mil.)	22.9%	3.1	3.8	4.2	(2.0)	7.0
Market value ($ mil.)	(8.5%)	12.4	11.4	10.1	6.9	8.7
Employees	(0.1%)	219	221	221	184	218

FEDERAL SIGNAL CORP. NYS: FSS

1415 West 22nd Street CEO: Jennifer Sherman
Oak Brook, IL 60523 CFO: Ian Hudson
Phone: 630 954-2000 HR: -
Fax: 630 954-2030 FYE: December 31
Web: www.federalsignal.com Type: Public

Federal Signal designs manufactures and supplies a suite of products and integrated solutions for municipal governmental industrial and commercial customers. Offerings include street sweepers vacuum- and hydro-excavation trucks and water blasters for general alarm/public address systems; industrial communications and public warning systems for public safety. In addition the company engages in the sale of parts service and repair equipment rentals and training as part of a comprehensive aftermarket offering to its customers. Federal Signal generates majority of sales from the US market.

	Annual Growth	12/16	12/17	12/18	12/19	12/20
Sales ($ mil.)	12.4%	707.9	898.5	1,089.5	1,221.3	1,130.8
Net income ($ mil.)	21.7%	43.8	61.6	94.0	108.5	96.2
Market value ($ mil.)	20.7%	944.4	1,215.4	1,204.0	1,951.1	2,006.8
Employees	12.3%	2,200	3,100	3,300	3,600	3,500

FEDERAL-MOGUL HOLDINGS CORP NMS: FDML

27300 West 11 Mile Road CEO: –
Southfield, MI 48034 CFO: –
Phone: 248 354-7700 HR: –
Fax: – FYE: December 31
Web: www.federalmogul.com Type: Public

For Federal-Mogul the sum of the parts is greater than the whole. The company makes components used in cars trucks and commercial vehicles as well as in energy industrial and other transportation equipment. Its products include pistons spark plugs ignition coils bearings gaskets seals and brake pads sold under brand names such as Champion Federal-Mogul Fel-Pro Glyco and Moog. Federal-Mogul has manufacturing and distribution facilities in 34 countries worldwide; customers include global automakers BMW Ford General Motors and Volkswagen. Federal-Mogul also distributes its own and other company's auto parts to aftermarket customers. About 60% of sales come from outside the US.

	Annual Growth	12/10	12/11	12/12	12/13	12/14
Sales ($ mil.)	4.1%	6,219.0	6,910.0	6,664.0	6,786.0	7,317.0
Net income ($ mil.)	–	161.0	(90.0)	(117.0)	41.0	(168.0)
Market value ($ mil.)	(6.0%)	3,098.1	2,212.9	1,203.2	2,952.6	2,414.0
Employees	3.3%	42,700	45,000	45,000	44,275	48,600

FEDERATED HERMES INC NYS: FHI

1001 Liberty Avenue CEO: Thomas Donahue
Pittsburgh, PA 15222-3779 CFO: Thomas R Donahue
Phone: 412 288-1900 HR: Dolores Dudiak
Fax: – FYE: December 31
Web: www.federatedhermes.com Type: Public

One of the country's largest investment managers Federated Investors provides investment advisory and administrative distribution and other services to the Federated Hermes funds and separate accounts in both domestic and international markets. Federated Investors offers fixed-income and equity mutual funds separate accounts closed-end funds variable annuity funds and alternative investments though money market funds make up most of the company's approximately $376 billion in assets under management. Its products are sold through banks brokerages government entities investment advisors corporations insurance companies foundations and endowmnent. . In 2020 the company has incorporated the Hermes Investment Management brand into a new corporate name Federated Hermes The Company founded in 1955 Chairman John Donahue.

	Annual Growth	12/16	12/17	12/18	12/19	12/20
Sales ($ mil.)	6.1%	1,143.4	1,102.9	1,135.7	1,326.9	1,448.3
Net income ($ mil.)	11.8%	208.9	291.3	220.3	272.3	326.4
Market value ($ mil.)	0.5%	2,809.3	3,584.2	2,637.5	3,237.5	2,869.9
Employees	7.9%	1,463	1,441	1,878	1,826	1,986

FEDERATED INSURANCE COMPANIES

121 E. Park Sq. CEO: Jeffrey Fetters
Owatonna MN 55060 CFO: –
Phone: 507-455-5200 HR: –
Fax: 507-455-5452 FYE: December 31
Web: www.federatedinsurance.com Type: Private - Mutual Com

Federated Insurance is a mutual firm with a clear focus. The company provides multiple lines of business insurance coverage and risk management to niche businesses including automotive repair and sales building contractors printers funeral homes and jewelers among others. Its products and services include property liability and auto coverage as well as workers' compensation risk management group life and health and retirement planning. Federated Insurance markets its products across the US. Since its founding in 1904 the company has worked closely with trade associations to develop and endorse its insurance programs.

FEDEX CORP NYS: FDX

942 South Shady Grove Road CEO: Frederick Smith
Memphis, TN 38120 CFO: Michael C Lenz
Phone: 901 818-7500 HR: –
Fax: – FYE: May 31
Web: www.fedex.com Type: Public

Holding company FedEx Corporation operates through subsidiaries FedEx Express FedEx Ground and FedEx Freight among others. Its FedEx Express unit is the world's largest express transportation provider to more than 220 countries and territories from about 2200 FedEx Office shops. It maintains a fleet of about 680 aircraft and over 183000 r vehicles. To complement the express delivery business FedEx Ground provides small-package ground delivery in North America and less-than-truckload (LTL) carrier FedEx Freight hauls larger shipments. FedEx Office stores offer a variety of document-related and other business services and serve as retail hubs for other FedEx units. In addition its TNT Express subsidiary is an international express transportation and small-package ground delivery company. About 70% of revenue is generated in the US.

	Annual Growth	05/17	05/18	05/19	05/20	05/21
Sales ($ mil.)	8.6%	60,319.0	65,450.0	69,693.0	69,217.0	83,959.0
Net income ($ mil.)	14.9%	2,997.0	4,572.0	540.0	1,286.0	5,231.0
Market value ($ mil.)	12.9%	51,822.8	66,601.8	41,246.5	34,905.0	84,163.9
Employees	14.4%	169,000	227,000	239,000	245,000	289,000

FEDEX CUSTOM CRITICAL INC.

1475 Boettler Rd. CEO: Ramona Hood
Uniontown OH 44685 CFO: –
Phone: 234-310-4090 HR: Micheal Abood
Fax: 234-310-4111 FYE: May 31
Web: customcritical.fedex.com Type: Subsidiary

FedEx Custom Critical a subsidiary of FedEx specializes in surface-expedited freight delivery services when time is of the essence. It operates throughout North America. Transportation is provided door-to-door with no intermediate handling by a fleet of about 1400 vehicles owned and operated by independent contractors. FedEx Custom Critical's Air Expedite unit arranges air transportation of customers' goods while Surface Expedite offers exclusive network-based transport for critical shipments and expedited less-than-truckload deliveries. Its White Glove Services division transports sensitive cargo such as electronics medical equipment and trade show exhibits as well as temperature-controlled freight.

FEDEX GROUND PACKAGE SYSTEM INC.

1000 FedEx Dr. CEO: Henry J Maier
Coraopolis PA 15108 CFO: –
Phone: 412-269-1000 HR: –
Fax: 412-747-4290 FYE: May 31
Web: www.fedex.com/us/ground/main Type: Subsidiary

When it doesn't absolutely positively have to be there overnight there's FedEx Ground Package System. An operating company of air-express giant FedEx FedEx Ground provides ground delivery of small packages throughout the US and Canada. Deliveries are generally made within one to five business days depending on distance. The company offers both business-to-business and home delivery services via a fleet of more than 30000 motorized vehicles most of which are operated by independent contractors. FedEx Ground handles an average of more than 3.5 million shipments per day from a network of more than 30 hubs.

FEDEX OFFICE AND PRINT SERVICES INC.

3 Galleria Tower 13155 Noel Rd. Ste. 1600
Dallas TX 75240
Phone: 214-550-7000
Fax: 214-550-7001
Web: www.fedex.com/us/officeprint/main/index.html

CEO: –
CFO: –
HR: –
FYE: May 31
Type: Subsidiary

FedEx Office and Print Services has duplicated its business formula many times. The company operates 1840 stores ("business service centers") in the US and five other countries. Stores provide printing and duplication presentation support and related business assistance and serve as drop-off points for deliveries to be made by sister companies FedEx Express and FedEx Ground. Stores also sell office supplies and rent computers and videoconferencing rooms. FedEx Office has traditionally targeted small business and home offices and individual consumers. Formerly known as Kinko's FedEx Office operates as part of the Services unit of delivery giant FedEx which purchased the business for $2.4 billion in 2004.

FEDFIRST FINANCIAL CORPORATION — NASDAQ: FFCO

Donner at 6th St.
Monessen PA 15062
Phone: 724-684-6800
Fax: 724-684-4851
Web: www.firstfederal-savings.com

CEO: –
CFO: –
HR: –
FYE: December 31
Type: Public

FedFirst Financial wants to be first in the hearts of its customers. It is the holding company for First Federal Savings Bank a community-oriented thrift serving southwestern Pennsylvania. From about 10 branches the bank offers traditional products and services including checking and savings accounts money markets accounts and IRAs. Residential mortgages secured by homes in the Pittsburgh metropolitan area make up more than three-fourths of a lending portfolio that also includes multi-family and commercial mortgages and construction business and consumer loans. FedFirst Financial converted from the mutual holding company structure to a stock holding company in 2010.

FEDNAT HOLDING CO — NMS: FNHC

14050 N.W. 14th Street, Suite 180
Sunrise, FL 33323
Phone: 800 293-2532
Fax: –
Web: www.fednat.com

CEO: Michael Braun
CFO: Ronald Jordan
HR: –
FYE: December 31
Type: Public

Trashed trailer crashed car damaged dwelling? Federated National Holding Company has a policy to cover that. Through Federated National Insurance Company and other subsidiaries it underwrites a variety of personal property/casualty insurance lines in Florida Louisiana Texas South Carolina Alabama Georgia and Mississippi.. Products include homeowners federal flood liability and other lines of insurance in Florida and other states.. Recently formed property insurance unit Monarch National (established in 2015) offers a complete homeowners policy multi-peril insurance product for Florida homeowners. The firm distributes its products through independent agents and its Insure-Link agency.

	Annual Growth	12/16	12/17	12/18	12/19	12/20
Assets ($ mil.)	15.1%	813.1	904.9	925.4	1,179.0	1,428.5
Net income ($ mil.)	–	(0.2)	8.0	14.9	1.0	(78.2)
Market value ($ mil.)	(25.0%)	256.4	227.3	273.3	228.1	81.2
Employees	(0.3%)	381	419	318	357	377

FEED THE CHILDREN INC.

333 N MERIDIAN AVE
OKLAHOMA CITY, OK 731076507
Phone: 405-942-0228
Fax: –
Web: www.feedthechildren.org

CEO: Travis Arnold
CFO: –
HR: –
FYE: June 30
Type: Private

Tuppence a bag might feed some birds but it takes more to feed growing children. Feed The Children (FTC) is a not-for-profit Christian charity that distributes food medicine clothing and other necessities. In the US FTC accepts bulk contributions of surplus food from businesses packages it in various ways at six main facilities nationwide and distributes it to food banks homeless shelters churches and other organizations that help feed the hungry. In more than 120 countries overseas FTC works with organizations such as schools orphanages and churches to provide food medical supplies clothing and educational support to the needy. Larry and Frances Jones founded FTC in 1979.

	Annual Growth	06/08	06/09	06/10	06/11	06/13
Sales ($ mil.)	(21.4%)	–	1,189.2	520.1	436.5	453.9
Net income ($ mil.)	–	–	–	(368.0)	10.6	42.3
Market value ($ mil.)	–	–	–	–	–	–
Employees	–	–	–	–	–	160

FEI CO. — NMS: FEIC

5350 NE Dawson Creek Drive
Hillsboro, OR 97124-5793
Phone: 503 726-7500
Fax: –
Web: www.fei.com

CEO: Don R Kania
CFO: Anthony L Trunzo
HR: –
FYE: December 31
Type: Public

FEI makes instruments to find very small defects. The company makes structural process management systems that use ion beams to analyze and diagnose submicron structures in integrated circuits (ICs) data storage components and biological and industrial compounds. FEI makes focused ion beam and dual beam electron microscopes that analyze ICs. It also makes scanning and transmission electron microscopes that detect defects in ICs and analyze biological specimens and materials. FEI targets applications in nanotechnology R&D but still gets significant sales from the semiconductor and data storage markets.

	Annual Growth	12/10	12/11	12/12	12/13	12/14
Sales ($ mil.)	10.8%	634.2	826.4	891.7	927.5	956.3
Net income ($ mil.)	18.4%	53.5	103.6	114.9	126.7	105.1
Market value ($ mil.)	36.0%	1,103.9	1,704.5	2,318.5	3,735.0	3,776.4
Employees	10.1%	1,813	2,074	2,518	2,611	2,660

FELCOR LODGING TRUST INC — NYS: FCH

545 E. John Carpenter Freeway, Suite 1300
Irving, TX 75062
Phone: 972 444-4900
Fax: –
Web: www.felcor.com

CEO: Ross Bierkan
CFO: –
HR: –
FYE: December 31
Type: Public

FelCor Lodging welcomes weary North American travelers looking for a little luxury. One of the top hotel real estate investment trusts in the US FelCor owns interests in 60 properties with almost 18000 rooms in more than 20 US states and one in Toronto Canada. Most are upscale hotels operating under the Embassy Suites Holiday Inn Doubletree Sheraton Westin Renaissance and Hilton brands. The properties are managed by Hilton Worldwide InterContinental Hotels Marriott International Starwood Hotels & Resorts and Fairmont. It also has several independent hotels in New York. FelCor's portfolio is concentrated in major metropolitan and resort areas of Florida California and Texas.

	Annual Growth	12/11	12/12	12/13	12/14	12/15
Sales ($ mil.)	(1.6%)	946.0	909.5	893.4	921.6	886.3
Net income ($ mil.)	–	(129.9)	(128.0)	(61.5)	92.1	(8.9)
Market value ($ mil.)	24.4%	432.5	662.2	1,157.2	1,534.4	1,035.2
Employees	(1.2%)	66	63	62	61	63

FELD ENTERTAINMENT INC.

8607 Westwood Center Dr.
Vienna VA 22182
Phone: 703-448-4000
Fax: 703-448-4100
Web: www.feldentertainment.com

CEO: –
CFO: Michael Ruch
HR: –
FYE: January 31
Type: Private

A lot of clowning around has helped Feld Entertainment become one of the largest live entertainment producers in the world. The company entertains people through its centerpiece Ringling Bros. and Barnum & Bailey Circus which visits about 90 cities in North America each year. Through a partnership with Walt Disney Feld also produces touring Disney On Ice shows such as Treasure Trove. In addition its Disney Live! produces live Disney-themed touring stage productions. Chairman and CEO Kenneth Feld whose father Irvin began managing the circus in 1956 owns the company and personally oversees most of its productions. Ringling Bros. and Barnum & Bailey Circus made its first performance in 1871.

FENDER MUSICAL INSTRUMENTS CORPORATION

17600 N. Perimeter Dr. Ste. 100
Scottsdale AZ 85250
Phone: 480-596-9690
Fax: 480-596-1384
Web: www.fender.com

CEO: Andrew P Mooney
CFO: James Broenen
HR: Jami Allred
FYE: December 31
Type: Private

Jimi Hendrix's electrified version of "The Star-Spangled Banner" showed what at least one Fender guitar could do. Fender Musical Instruments Corporation (FMIC) is the world's #1 maker of stringed instruments and the nation's #1 manufacturer of solid-body electric guitars including the Stratocaster and Telecaster lines that have made it a favorite of strummers. FMIC makes other instruments and PA equipment such as acoustic guitars electric basses mandolins banjos and violins as well as amplifiers. The company's other notable brands include Guild Tacoma Gretsch Jackson Charvel EVH SWR Groove Tubes and Squier. Fender pulled the plug on its 2012 initial public offering (IPO).

FENTURA FINANCIAL INC

NBB: FETM

P.O. Box 725
Fenton, MI 48430-0725
Phone: 810 629-2263
Fax: –
Web: www.fentura.com

CEO: Ronald Justice
CFO: James Distelrath
HR: –
FYE: December 31
Type: Public

It just makes cents to say that Fentura Financial has its hands full. Fentura Financial is the holding company for Michigan community banks The State Bank Davison State Bank West Michigan Community Bank and Community Bancorp. From about 20 branch locations the banks provide commercial and consumer banking services and products including checking and savings accounts and loans. Commercial loans account for some two-thirds of the bank's combined loan portfolio. The State Bank Fentura's first subsidiary traces its origins to 1898. Fentura acquired St. Charles-based Community Bancorp in late 2016.

	Annual Growth	12/16	12/17	12/18	12/19	12/20
Assets ($ mil.)	15.5%	703.4	781.4	926.5	1,034.8	1,251.4
Net income ($ mil.)	36.6%	4.4	8.7	10.1	11.6	15.5
Market value ($ mil.)	8.3%	75.1	88.6	98.6	118.4	103.3
Employees	–	–	–	–	–	–

FERGUSON ENTERPRISES INC.

12500 Jefferson Ave.
Newport News VA 23602
Phone: 757-874-7795
Fax: 757-989-2501
Web: www.ferguson.com

CEO: Kevin Murphy
CFO: Bill Brundage
HR: –
FYE: July 31
Type: Subsidiary

Ferguson Enterprises is part of the pipeline for pipes. It is one of North America's largest wholesale distributors of plumbing supplies pipes valves and fittings. It also is a major distributor of heating and cooling equipment waterworks (water hydrants and meters) kitchen and bath lighting safety equipment fireplaces and appliances and tools and safety equipment. Ferguson has some than 1300 branches and 11 distribution centers in the US Puerto Rico Mexico and the Caribbean. Its customers include plumbing contractors home owners air conditioning dealers the government and irrigation and fire suppression equipment installers. Ferguson which was formed in 1953 is a subsidiary of Wolseley.

FERRELLGAS PARTNERS LP

NBB: FGPR

7500 College Boulevard, Suite 1000
Overland Park, KS 66210
Phone: 913 661-1500
Fax: –
Web: www.ferrellgas.com

CEO: James Ferrell
CFO: Brian Herrmann
HR: –
FYE: July 31
Type: Public

Ferrellgas Partners (FP) is a retail marketer of propane in the US. It serves residential commercial portable tank exchange agricultural wholesale and other customers in all 50 states the District of Columbia and Puerto Rico with propane delivery Blue Rhino portable tank exchanges and the sale of propane appliances and related parts and fittings as well as other retail propane related services and consumer products under the Blue Rhino brand. Also as Bridger Logistics the company provides crude oil transportation and logistics and water treatment services to major energy companies.

	Annual Growth	07/17	07/18	07/19	07/20	07/21
Sales ($ mil.)	(2.4%)	1,930.3	2,073.1	1,684.4	1,497.8	1,754.3
Net income ($ mil.)	–	(54.2)	(254.6)	(64.2)	(82.5)	(68.4)
Market value ($ mil.)	47.6%	27.7	19.5	5.2	2.5	131.6
Employees	–	–	–	–	–	–

FERRIS STATE UNIVERSITY (INC)

1201 S STATE ST
BIG RAPIDS, MI 493072714
Phone: 231-591-2000
Fax: –
Web: www.ferris.edu

CEO: –
CFO: –
HR: –
FYE: June 30
Type: Private

Going to college is no carnival but Ferris State University still hopes the experience is enjoyable. The career-oriented public university offers more than 180 degree programs including associate's bachelor's master's and doctoral degrees through the colleges of Allied Health Sciences Arts and Sciences Business Education and Human Services Optometry Pharmacy Technology and Kendall College of Art and Design. The school has some 14500 students on 21 campuses located across Michigan. Ferris State was founded in 1884 by Michigan educator and statesman Woodbridge N. Ferris.

	Annual Growth	06/14	06/15	06/16	06/17	06/19
Sales ($ mil.)	(2.0%)	–	–	–	166.3	159.6
Net income ($ mil.)	(11.5%)	–	–	–	14.4	11.2
Market value ($ mil.)	–	–	–	–	–	–
Employees	–	–	–	–	–	1,200

FERRO CORP
NYS: FOE

6060 Parkland Boulevard, Suite 250
Mayfield Heights, OH 44124
Phone: 216 875-5600
Fax: 216 875-5627
Web: www.ferro.com

CEO: Peter Thomas
CFO: Benjamin Schlater
HR: Barbara Getting
FYE: December 31
Type: Public

Ferro is a global leader in producing glass porcelain enamels and ceramic glaze coatings with nearly 50 manufacturing plants worldwide. The specialty materials and chemicals producer make various colorants including ceramic glazes pigments and porcelain enamels. It also produces electronics and color (such as conductive metals and pastes used in solar cells) and polymer and ceramic engineered materials. Its products are used in construction and by makers of appliances autos building and renovation electronics sanitary packaging consumer products and household furnishings. The Ohio-based company gets about 85% of its revenue from international customers. Its functional coatings segment accounts for nearly 65% of its revenue. In the second quarter of 2021 Prince International Corporation announced that it is acquiring Ferro Corporation in a transaction valued at approximately $2.1 billion.

	Annual Growth	12/16	12/17	12/18	12/19	12/20
Sales ($ mil.)	(4.3%)	1,145.3	1,396.7	1,612.4	1,018.4	959.0
Net income ($ mil.)	–	(20.8)	57.1	80.1	6.0	42.8
Market value ($ mil.)	0.5%	1,180.8	1,943.8	1,292.0	1,222.0	1,205.5
Employees	2.3%	5,125	5,682	6,059	5,922	5,615

FFD FINANCIAL CORP
NBB: FFDF

321 North Wooster Avenue
Dover, OH 44622
Phone: 330 364-7777
Fax: –
Web: www.firstfed.com

CEO: Trent Troyer
CFO: Robert Gerber
HR: –
FYE: June 30
Type: Public

FFD Financial is the holding company for First Federal Community Bank which serves Tuscarawas County and contiguous portions of eastern Ohio through about five branches. Founded in 1898 the bank offers a full range of retail products including checking and savings accounts CDs IRAs and credit cards. The bank mainly uses these funds to originate one- to four-family residential mortgages non-residential real estate loans and land loans. First Federal Community Bank also originates business consumer and multifamily residential real estate loans. In 2012 First Federal Community Bank converted its charter from a savings bank to a national commercial bank.

	Annual Growth	06/17	06/18	06/19	06/20	06/21
Assets ($ mil.)	14.7%	341.5	382.2	414.0	522.3	591.5
Net income ($ mil.)	20.6%	4.2	4.9	6.3	7.0	8.8
Market value ($ mil.)	16.7%	115.5	138.8	155.4	183.0	214.1
Employees	–	–	–	72	–	–

FFW CORP.
NBB: FFWC

1205 North Cass Street
Wabash, IN 46992-1027
Phone: 260 563-3185
Fax: –
Web: www.crossroadsbanking.com

CEO: Roger Cromer
CFO: Timothy Sheppard
HR: –
FYE: June 30
Type: Public

You can find this company at the intersection of Savings and Loans. FFW Corporation is the holding company for Crossroads Bank (formerly First Federal Savings Bank of Wabash) founded in 1920 as Home Loan Savings Association. Today the bank has five branches in Columbia City North Manchester South Whitley Syracuse and Wabash Indiana. Its deposit products include CDs and checking savings and NOW accounts. Lending activities consist mostly of residential mortgages (almost half of the company's loan portfolio) commercial mortgages home equity and improvement loans and auto loans; the bank also offers business construction manufactured home and consumer loans.

	Annual Growth	06/13	06/14	06/15	06/16	06/17
Assets ($ mil.)	2.1%	337.8	335.5	334.1	341.0	366.9
Net income ($ mil.)	14.9%	2.3	3.6	2.8	3.6	3.9
Market value ($ mil.)	23.4%	18.0	23.5	27.4	29.6	41.8
Employees	–	–	–	–	–	–

FHI SERVICES

500 HOSPITAL DR
WARRENTON, VA 201863027
Phone: 540-347-2550
Fax: –

CEO: –
CFO: –
HR: –
FYE: September 30
Type: Private

Fauquier Hospital takes care of the populace of rural northern Virginia. The multi-location system provides medical surgical outpatient and home health care services to a four county area. With more than 85 beds the facility is the only hospital in Fauquier and also serves Culpeper Prince William and Rappahannock Counties. Specialized services include emergency medicine oncology rehabilitation and cardiac and pulmonary care. The hospital's emergency room has more than 30 private rooms and services about 30000 patients each year. Fauquier Hospital partners with Prince William Hospital to operate the Cancer Center at Lake Manassas. Fauquier Hospital was founded in 1925.

	Annual Growth	09/03	09/04	09/05*	06/06*	09/09
Sales ($ mil.)	–	–	–	(1,451.4)	95.3	132.6
Net income ($ mil.)	1183.8%	–	–	0.0	1.9	10.3
Market value ($ mil.)	–	–	–	–	–	–
Employees	–	–	–	–	–	700

*Fiscal year change

FIBERLINK COMMUNICATIONS CORPORATION

1787 SENTRY PKWY W # 200
BLUE BELL, PA 19422-2213
Phone: 215-664-1600
Fax: –
Web: www.maas360.com

CEO: James Sheward
CFO: Mark Parin
HR: –
FYE: December 31
Type: Private

Fiberlink combines mobility with stability. The company's cloud-based offering MaaS360 provides mobile device and mobile application management for employees using mobile devices in the workplace as well as those working remotely and needing access to corporate networks data and applications. Its platform allows employees to securely and stably connect to enterprise networks while guarding against hackers viruses and data theft. The company also provides managed virtual private network (VPN) services to connect companies with branch offices. It manages some 1 million devices for more than 700 large and small clients in the financial services healthcare and government industries among others.

	Annual Growth	12/03	12/04	12/05	12/06	12/07
Sales ($ mil.)	–	–	–	(281.5)	68.9	57.4
Net income ($ mil.)	–	–	–	0.0	2.2	(1.4)
Market value ($ mil.)	–	–	–	–	–	–
Employees	–	–	–	–	–	238

FIBERTOWER CORPORATION
NASDAQ: FTWR

185 Berry St. Ste. 4800
San Francisco CA 94107
Phone: 415-659-3500
Fax: 415-659-0007
Web: www.fibertower.com

CEO: –
CFO: –
HR: –
FYE: December 31
Type: Public

FiberTower rises to the occasion with wireless backhaul (commercial wholesale bandwidth) and access services. An alternative provider of facilities-based backhaul it offers spectrum leasing mobile phone traffic and broadband connectivity and extensions to fiber-optic networks. Customers include mobile fiber and other high-speed telecommunications carriers large-volume enterprise users and government agencies. Its largest customer AT&T Mobility accounts for nearly half of revenues. FiberTower serves more than a dozen markets across the country and it owns high-frequency band wireless spectrum licenses that cover essentially all of the US. The company filed for Chapter 11 bankruptcy in 2012.

FIBROCELL SCIENCE INC
NAS: FCSC

405 Eagleview Boulevard
Exton, PA 19341
Phone: 484 713-6000
Fax: 484 713-6001
Web: www.fibrocellscience.com

CEO: John M Maslowski
CFO: Sean D Buckley
HR: –
FYE: December 31
Type: Public

No cow collagen here — Fibrocell Science (formerly Isolagen) lets you be your beautiful self using your beautiful cells. The company's autologous cellular therapy process used in its primary LAVIV product offering extracts fibroblasts (collagen-producing cells) from a small tissue sample taken from behind a patient's ear. The cells reproduce over six to eight weeks and are then injected back into the patient giving him or her a "natural" boost. The company gained FDA approval for LAVIV for use on wrinkle correction in 2011. It also hopes to gain approval for indications such as burn and acne scar treatment and to regenerate tissue lost from periodontal disease.

	Annual Growth	12/12	12/13	12/14	12/15	12/16
Sales ($ mil.)	23.4%	0.2	0.2	0.2	0.5	0.4
Net income ($ mil.)	–	(23.2)	(30.6)	(25.7)	(34.5)	(15.3)
Market value ($ mil.)	43.4%	2.2	59.6	38.0	66.8	9.3
Employees	(24.6%)	71	64	56	52	23

FIDELITONE INC.

1260 Karl Ct.
Wauconda IL 60084
Phone: 847-487-3300
Fax: 847-469-6581
Web: www.fidelitone.com

CEO: Josh Johnson
CFO: –
HR: Brittany White
FYE: December 31
Type: Private

Fidelitone has an ear for the supply chain. The company which does business as Fidelitone Logistics offers a range of key third-party logistics (3PL) services including warehousing inventory management packaging shipping freight forwarding customs brokerage and returns handling. Managing 1 million shipments per month it serves markets such as consumer goods electronics health care medical devices retail and publishing. With more than 30 locations in some 15 states the company which was started as a manufacturer/distributor of phonograph record needles in 1929 by Arthur Olsen is now run by Olsen's in-laws — the Hudson family.

FIDELITY & GUARANTY LIFE
NYS: FGL

Two Ruan Center, 601 Locust Street, 14th Floor
Des Moines, IA 50309
Phone: 800 445-6758
Fax: –
Web: www.fglife.com

CEO: –
CFO: –
HR: –
FYE: September 30
Type: Public

Fidelity & Guaranty Life is faithfully toiling away selling you life insurance and a whole range of annuity products. Through Fidelity & Guaranty Life Insurance Company (FGL Insurance) the company sells life insurance in 49 states and Washington DC; it also operates in the Empire State through Fidelity & Guaranty Life Insurance Company of New York (FGL NY Insurance). The group's products include everything from universal life insurance and fixed deferred indexed annuities to single premium immediate annuities. Fidelity & Guaranty Life which is controlled by investment firm HRG Group went public in 2013. In mid-2016 China-based insurer Anbang Insurance Group withdrew its bid to buy the company for $1.57 billion.

	Annual Growth	09/12	09/13	09/14	09/15	09/16
Assets ($ mil.)	6.5%	20,990.3	22,429.2	24,152.7	24,925.0	27,035.0
Net income ($ mil.)	(27.1%)	344.2	347.7	162.7	118.0	97.0
Market value ($ mil.)	4.2%	–	–	1,247.2	1,433.6	1,354.7
Employees	15.1%	–	175	200	220	267

FIDELITY & GUARANTY LIFE INSURANCE COMPANY

1001 Fleet St.
Baltimore MD 21202-1137
Phone: 410-895-0100
Fax: 410-895-0132
Web: https://home.fglife.com/default.aspx

CEO: Christopher Blunt
CFO: John Fleurant
HR: –
FYE: December 31
Type: Subsidiary

Fidelity & Guaranty Life Insurance (FGL Insurance) is faithfully toiling away selling you life insurance and a whole range of annuity products. FGL Insurance sells life insurance in 49 states and Washington DC; it also operates in the Empire State through sister company Fidelity & Guaranty Life Insurance Company of New York (FGL NY Insurance). FGL Insurance's products include everything from universal life insurance and fixed deferred indexed annuities to single premium immediate annuities. The company is a subsidiary of Fidelity & Guaranty Life Holdings (FGL) which is owned by investment firm Harbinger Group.

FIDELITY D&D BANCORP INC
NMS: FDBC

Blakely & Drinker Streets
Dunmore, PA 18512
Phone: 570 342-8281
Fax: –
Web: www.bankatfidelity.com

CEO: Daniel Santaniello
CFO: Salvatore DeFrancesco
HR: –
FYE: December 31
Type: Public

Fidelity D & D Bancorp has loyal banking customers. The institution is the holding company for The Fidelity Deposit and Discount Bank serving Lackawanna and Luzerne counties in northeastern Pennsylvania through about a dozen locations and about the same number of ATM locations. The bank attracts local individuals and business customers by offering such products and services as checking and savings accounts certificates of deposit investments and trust services. Commercial real estate loans account for the bulk of the company's loan portfolio followed by consumer loans business and industrial loans and residential mortgages. The bank also writes construction loans and direct financing leases.

	Annual Growth	12/16	12/17	12/18	12/19	12/20
Assets ($ mil.)	21.0%	792.9	863.6	981.1	1,009.9	1,699.5
Net income ($ mil.)	14.1%	7.7	8.7	11.0	11.6	13.0
Market value ($ mil.)	15.6%	179.7	205.6	319.5	309.7	320.4
Employees	12.2%	167	175	181	189	265

FIDELITY NATIONAL FINANCIAL INC
NYS: FNF

601 Riverside Avenue
Jacksonville, FL 32204
Phone: 904 854-8100
Fax: –
Web: www.fnf.com

CEO: Raymond R Quirk
CFO: Anthony J Park
HR: –
FYE: December 31
Type: Public

To make sure that buying a dream home does not become a nightmare Fidelity National Financial (also known as FNF) provides title insurance escrow home warranties and other services related to real estate transactions. It is now the top dog in the residential and commercial title insurance sectors (the second-largest is First American) and issues more title insurance policies than any other title company in the US. The company operates through underwriters including Fidelity National Title Insurance Commonwealth Land Title Alamo Title and National Title of New York. It sells its products both directly and through independent agents.

	Annual Growth	12/16	12/17	12/18	12/19	12/20
Assets ($ mil.)	36.7%	14,463.0	9,151.0	9,301.0	10,677.0	50,455.0
Net income ($ mil.)	21.7%	650.0	771.0	628.0	1,062.0	1,427.0
Market value ($ mil.)	3.6%	10,127.0	11,701.5	9,375.5	13,523.5	11,656.8
Employees	(16.3%)	55,219	24,367	23,436	25,063	27,058

FIDELITY NATIONAL INFORMATION SERVICES INC   NYS: FIS

601 Riverside Avenue
Jacksonville, FL 32204
Phone: 904 438-6000
Fax: –
Web: www.fisglobal.com

CEO: Gary Norcross
CFO: James Woodall
HR: –
FYE: December 31
Type: Public

Fidelity National Information Services (FIS) is a leading provider of technology solutions for merchants banks and capital markets firms globally. The company's broad portfolio of solutions includes a wide range of flexible service arrangements from managed processing arrangements either at the client site or hosted at an FIS location including data centers or its private cloud to traditional license and maintenance approaches. It also offers outsourcing and consulting for the financial services industry. For banks and other financing entities the company's offerings address financial functions such as core processing decision and risk management and retail payment solutions. North America accounts for over 75% of company's total revenue.

	Annual Growth	12/17	12/18	12/19	12/20	12/21
Sales ($ mil.)	11.1%	9,123.0	8,423.0	10,333.0	12,552.0	13,877.0
Net income ($ mil.)	(25.0%)	1,319.0	846.0	298.0	158.0	417.0
Market value ($ mil.)	3.8%	57,300.8	62,453.0	84,705.8	86,149.1	66,472.4
Employees	5.2%	53,000	47,000	55,000	62,000	65,000

FIDELITY SOUTHERN CORP   NMS: LION

3490 Piedmont Road, Suite 1550
Atlanta, GA 30305
Phone: 404 639-6500
Fax: –
Web: www.fidelitysouthern.com

CEO: –
CFO: –
HR: –
FYE: December 31
Type: Public

Fidelity Southern Corp. is the holding company for Fidelity Bank which boasts over $3 billion in assets and some 45 branches in the Atlanta metro and in northern Florida markets. The bank offers traditional deposit services such as checking and savings accounts CDs and IRAs. Consumer loans primarily indirect auto loans which the company purchases from auto franchises and independent dealers throughout the Southeast make up more than 50% of its loan portfolio. Real estate construction commercial real estate business residential mortgage and other consumer loans round out Fidelity Southern's lending activities. Subsidiary LionMark Insurance Company offers consumer credit-related insurance products.

	Annual Growth	12/13	12/14	12/15	12/16	12/17
Assets ($ mil.)	15.6%	2,564.2	3,085.2	3,849.1	4,389.7	4,576.9
Net income ($ mil.)	9.5%	27.6	30.0	39.1	38.8	39.8
Market value ($ mil.)	7.0%	448.8	435.3	602.8	639.5	589.0
Employees	11.9%	890	1,038	1,242	1,284	1,394

FIDUS INVESTMENT CORPORATION   NASDAQ: FDUS

1603 Orrington Ave. Ste. 820
Evanston IL 60201
Phone: 847-859-3940
Fax: 847-859-3953
Web: www.fdus.com

CEO: Edward Ross
CFO: Shelby Sherard
HR: –
FYE: December 31
Type: Public

Fidus Investment Corporation is faithful to earning ROI. The externally managed closed-end business development company (BDC) formed in 2011 to begin investing in low- to mid-market companies that earn between $10 million and $150 million per year. (BDCs are exempt from paying federal income tax as long as they distribute 90% of profits back to shareholders.) Fidus has provided mezzanine debt and equity financing to 25 companies representing a range of industries typically investing between $5 million and $15 million for each transaction. It has financed recapitalizations acquisitions expansions and changes in ownership. Fidus Investment is externally managed by Fidus Investment Advisors LLC.

FIELD MUSEUM OF NATURAL HISTORY

1400 S LAKE SHORE DR
CHICAGO, IL 606052429
Phone: 312-922-9410
Fax: –
Web: www.fieldmuseum.org

CEO: –
CFO: –
HR: –
FYE: December 31
Type: Private

The Field Museum is one of the world's leading natural history museums. Founded as the Columbian Museum of Chicago in 1893 the institution adopted the Field name in 1905 in honor of major benefactor (and department store mogul) Marshall Field. The museum houses enormous biological and anthropological collections — more than 24 million specimens in all — along with a quarter-million-volume natural history library. It is also home to Sue the largest most complete and best preserved Tyrannosaurus rex fossil discovered to date. The Field Museum conducts basic research in anthropology and biology as well as an extensive program of public education.

	Annual Growth	12/02	12/03	12/09	12/14	12/17
Sales ($ mil.)	0.4%	–	66.5	47.0	95.3	70.7
Net income ($ mil.)	2.3%	–	38.9	(25.2)	23.8	53.8
Market value ($ mil.)	–	–	–	–	–	–
Employees	–	–	–	–	–	600

FIELDPOINT PETROLEUM CORP   NBB: FPPP

609 Castle Ridge Road, Suite 335
Austin, TX 78746
Phone: 512 579-3560
Fax: –
Web: www.fppcorp.com

CEO: –
CFO: –
HR: –
FYE: December 31
Type: Public

Got oil and gas? FieldPoint Petroleum can point to its oil and gas fields and its interests in 480 productive oil and gas wells (96 net) in Louisiana New Mexico Oklahoma Texas and Wyoming. The independent oil and gas exploration company operates some 19 of these wells. About two-thirds of its gross productive oil wells are located in Oklahoma. FieldPoint Petroleum has proved reserves of more than 1.1 million barrels of oil and 1.9 billion cu. ft. of natural gas. Its business strategy is to expand its reserve base as well as its production and cash flow through the acquisition of producing oil and gas properties. However low oil prices have forced the company to hold back on further acquisitions.

	Annual Growth	12/14	12/15	12/16	12/17	12/18
Sales ($ mil.)	(30.4%)	9.2	4.0	2.8	3.0	2.2
Net income ($ mil.)	–	(1.9)	(11.0)	(2.5)	2.7	(3.3)
Market value ($ mil.)	(56.2%)	19.1	6.6	7.7	1.8	0.7
Employees	(6.9%)	4	3	3	3	3

FIESTA MART INC.

5235 KATY FWY
HOUSTON, TX 77007-2210
Phone: 713-869-5060
Fax: –
Web: www.fiestamart.com

CEO: Carlos Smith
CFO: Vicki J Baum
HR: –
FYE: January 03
Type: Private

Fiesta Mart celebrates food every day of the year. The company runs some 60 stores in Texas that sell ethnic and conventional groceries including items popular with its target customers: Mexican- and Asian-Americans. Its stores are located mainly in the Houston area but Fiesta also has been adding stores in the Dallas/Fort Worth area and in Austin. Fiesta purchased three supermarkets from Winn-Dixie Stores when the grocer left Texas. At its supermarkets Fiesta leases kiosks to vendors who offer such items as jewelry and cell phones. The company also runs some 15 Beverage Mart liquor stores. Fiesta Mart founded in 1972 by Donald Bonham and O. C. Mendenhall is owned by grocery wholesaler Grocers Supply Co.

	Annual Growth	12/03	12/04	12/05	12/06*	01/10
Sales ($ mil.)	6.9%	–	–	–	1,137.7	1,483.9
Net income ($ mil.)	9.3%	–	–	–	21.1	30.1
Market value ($ mil.)	–	–	–	–	–	–
Employees	–	–	–	–	–	8,200

*Fiscal year change

FIESTA RESTAURANT GROUP, INC
NMS: FRGI

14800 Landmark Boulevard, Suite 500
Dallas, TX 75254
Phone: 972 702-9300
Fax: –
Web: www.frgi.com

CEO: Richard Stockinger
CFO: Dirk Montgomery
HR: –
FYE: January 03
Type: Public

Fiesta Restaurant Group owns operates and franchises the Taco Cabana and Pollo Tropical brands. The Group owns or franchises a total of about 280 restaurants; most of the restaurants are company leased. Taco Cabana locations found mostly in Texas feature traditional Mexican food in a quick service atmosphere. Pollo Tropical found mostly in Florida is designed to create an inviting festive and tropical atmosphere. In addition both brands offer distinct and unique flavors with broad appeal at a compelling value which differentiates them in the competitive fast-casual and quick-service restaurant segments. Almost all of the group's restaurants offer the convenience of drive-thru windows.

	Annual Growth	01/17*	12/17	12/18	12/19*	01/21
Sales ($ mil.)	(6.0%)	711.8	669.1	688.6	660.9	554.8
Net income ($ mil.)	–	16.7	(36.2)	7.8	(84.4)	(10.2)
Market value ($ mil.)	(21.4%)	755.0	480.6	385.5	239.8	288.3
Employees	(9.7%)	12,080	10,290	10,220	10,480	8,020

*Fiscal year change

FIFTH THIRD BANCORP (CINCINNATI, OH)
NMS: FITB

38 Fountain Square Plaza
Cincinnati, OH 45263
Phone: 800 972-3030
Fax: –
Web: www.53.com

CEO: Gregory Carmichael
CFO: James Leonard
HR: –
FYE: December 31
Type: Public

Fifth Third Bancorp is the holding company of Fifth Third Bank which boasts assets of some $205 billion and operates about 1135 full-service Banking Centers and over 2395 Fifth Third branded ATMs in about 10 states in the Midwest and Southeast. Fifth Third offers branch banking (deposit accounts and loans for consumers and small businesses) commercial banking (lending leasing and syndicated and trade finance for corporations) consumer lending (residential mortgages home equity loans and credit cards) and wealth and asset management (private banking brokerage and asset management). The company started in 1975.

	Annual Growth	12/16	12/17	12/18	12/19	12/20
Assets ($ mil.)	9.5%	142,177.0	142,193.0	146,069.0	169,369.0	204,680.0
Net income ($ mil.)	(2.3%)	1,564.0	2,194.0	2,193.0	2,512.0	1,427.0
Market value ($ mil.)	0.6%	19,223.1	21,625.1	16,771.3	21,910.3	19,650.8
Employees	2.7%	17,844	18,125	17,437	19,869	19,872

FILEMAKER INC.

5201 Patrick Henry Dr.
Santa Clara CA 95054-1171
Phone: 408-987-7000
Fax: 408-987-7105
Web: www.filemaker.com

CEO: –
CFO: Bill Epling
HR: –
FYE: September 30
Type: Subsidiary

FileMaker believes data's place is in the database. A subsidiary of Apple FileMaker provides its eponymous database software that is compatible with Mac OS and Microsoft's Windows operating systems. The application makes it possible for multiple users to access and exchange information instantaneously over corporate intranets or the Internet. It also offers an advanced version of FileMaker that includes development tools. The company markets to customers ranging from individual users and small businesses to universities and large corporations. Licensees include AT&T Bank of America Coca-Cola Hitachi Nokia the Smithsonian Institution Time Warner and Wal-Mart Stores.

FINANCIAL ENGINES INC
NMS: FNGN

1050 Enterprise Way, 3rd Floor
Sunnyvale, CA 94089
Phone: 408 498-6000
Fax: 408 498-6010
Web: www.financialengines.com

CEO: Lawrence M Raffone
CFO:
HR: –
FYE: December 31
Type: Public

Like the little engine that could Financial Engines provides financial advice portfolio management and retirement assessment services. The company serves US retirement-plan participants sponsors and service providers across a wide range of industries that includes more than 100 FORTUNE 500 companies and several of the largest retirement plan operators. It delivers its services online as well as by telephone. Financial Engines boasts more than $88 billion in assets under management and serves some 9 million individual retirement-plan participants. The company went public in 2010 with an offering worth $127.2 million.

	Annual Growth	12/12	12/13	12/14	12/15	12/16
Sales ($ mil.)	22.9%	185.8	239.0	281.9	310.7	423.9
Net income ($ mil.)	11.4%	18.6	30.0	37.0	31.6	28.6
Market value ($ mil.)	7.3%	1,725.4	4,321.6	2,273.4	2,094.2	2,285.8
Employees	24.1%	380	442	493	527	900

FINANCIAL EXECUTIVES INTERNATIONAL

1250 Headquarters Plaza West Tower 7th Fl.
Morristown NJ 07960
Phone: 973-765-1000
Fax: 973-765-1018
Web: www.financialexecutives.org

CEO: Jim Abel
CFO: –
HR: –
FYE: June 30
Type: Private - Associatio

Financial Executives International (FEI) knows where the dough is. Or at least its members do. The group is a professional association for CFOs VPs of finance treasurers controllers tax executives and others in finance. It has 15000 members throughout the US and Canada in about 85 branches. The association advocates the views of its members notifies members of current issues and promotes ethical conduct for financial executives. FEI also hosts conferences and networking opportunities for its members and publishes Financial Executive Magazine. The group was founded at the Controllers Institute of America in 1931.

FINANCIAL INDUSTRY REGULATORY AUTHORITY, INC.

1735 K ST NW
WASHINGTON, DC 200061506
Phone: 301-590-6500
Fax: –
Web: www.finra.org

CEO: Robert Cook
CFO: Todd Diganci
HR: –
FYE: December 31
Type: Private

FINRA is dedicated to protecting investors and safeguarding market integrity in a manner that facilitates vibrant capital markets. It is a not-for-profit organization that ? working under the supervision of the SEC ? actively engages with and provides essential tools for investors member firms and policymakers. In addition it is authorized by the congress to protect America's investors by making sure the broker-dealer industry operates fairly and honestly. FINRA oversee more than 624000 brokers across the country and analyze billion dollars of market events. FINRA was formed in 2007 from the consolidation of the National Association of Securities Dealers and certain regulatory and enforcement elements of the NYSE.

	Annual Growth	12/10	12/11	12/12	12/19	12/20
Sales ($ mil.)	3.1%	–	880.1	878.6	938.5	1,162.6
Net income ($ mil.)	–	–	(84.0)	10.5	(45.9)	19.8
Market value ($ mil.)	–	–	–	–	–	–
Employees	–	–	–	–	–	3,400

FINANCIAL INSTITUTIONS INC.
NMS: FISI

220 Liberty Street
Warsaw, NY 14569
Phone: 585 786-1100
Fax: -
Web: www.fiiwarsaw.com

CEO: Martin Birmingham
CFO: W. Jack Plants
HR: -
FYE: December 31
Type: Public

Financial Institutions may not have a luxurious name but they specialize in five star service. The holding company owns Five Star Bank which provides standard deposit products such as checking and savings accounts CDs and IRAs to retail and business customers through some 50 branches across western and central New York. Indirect consumer loans originated through agreements with area franchised car dealers account for the largest percentage of the company's loan portfolio (35%) followed by commercial mortgages. The company also sells insurance while its Five Star Investment Services subsidiary offers brokerage and financial planning services.

	Annual Growth	12/16	12/17	12/18	12/19	12/20
Assets ($ mil.)	7.3%	3,710.3	4,105.2	4,311.7	4,384.2	4,912.3
Net income ($ mil.)	4.7%	31.9	33.5	39.5	48.9	38.3
Market value ($ mil.)	(9.9%)	548.6	498.9	412.3	514.9	360.9
Employees	(1.6%)	654	656	725	722	613

FINDEX.COM INC.
OTC: FIND

11204 Davenport St. Ste. 100
Omaha NE 68154
Phone: 402-333-1900
Fax: 402-778-5763
Web: www.quickverse.com/shopfiles/default.asp

CEO: Steven Malone
CFO: Steven Malone
HR: -
FYE: December 31
Type: Public

For churches needing more than divine inspiration FindEx.com answers prayers. The company develops publishes and distributes software for churches ministries and other Christian organizations. Its primary product - making up almost 90% of sales - is QuickVerse which is designed to facilitate biblical research. Other offerings include publishing software for Christian-themed printed materials a program to assist pastors in developing sermons children's Christian entertainment software and language tutorials for Greek and Hebrew. In 2008 the company bought FormTool.com which offers 800 form templates - its first non-Christian product. Director Gordon Landies controls more than 20% of FindEx.com.

FINISAR CORP
NMS: FNSR

1389 Moffett Park Drive
Sunnyvale, CA 94089
Phone: 408 548-1000
Fax: -
Web: www.finisar.com

CEO: -
CFO: Mary Jane Raymond
HR: -
FYE: April 29
Type: Public

Finisar helps put the "work" in network with optical components and subsystems that enable high-speed data communications over LANs or metro-area and storage-area networks (MANs/SANs). The company's subsystems include transmitters receivers transceivers transponders optical cables and wavelength selective switches. Its components consist primarily of packaged lasers photodetectors and passive devices. The company sells products to manufacturers of storage systems networking equipment and telecom equipment. Customers have included such tech giants as Alcatel-Lucent Brocade Cisco Systems and EMC Ericcson HP Huawei Technologies and IBM. In 2018 Finisar agreed to be bought by II-VI Inc. for about $3.2 billion.

	Annual Growth	04/14*	05/15	05/16*	04/17	04/18
Sales ($ mil.)	3.3%	1,156.8	1,250.9	1,263.2	1,449.3	1,316.5
Net income ($ mil.)	-	-	111.8	11.9	35.2	249.3	(48.3)
Market value ($ mil.)	(13.1%)	3,165.4	2,404.2	1,889.8	2,622.3	1,807.2
Employees	0.0%	13,000	13,400	13,400	14,000	13,000

*Fiscal year change

FINJAN HOLDINGS INC
NAS: FNJN

2000 University Avenue, Suite 600
East Palo Alto, CA 94303
Phone: 650 282-3228
Fax: -
Web: www.finjan.com

CEO: Philip Hartstein
CFO: Jevan Anderson
HR: -
FYE: December 31
Type: Public

Converted Organics is not a group of new and fervent farmers but a company that is religiously developing a process to turn food into fertilizer. The company uses organic food waste as raw material to make all-natural fertilizers that combine both disease suppression and nutritional characteristics. Its manufacturing process uses heat and bacteria to transform food waste into a high-value natural fertilizer. It sells its environmentally friendly products in the agribusiness turf management and retail markets. The company which acquired vertical farming operation TerraSphere Systems in 2010 also has an industrial wastewater treatment unit. Converted Organics is restructuring to streamline operations.

	Annual Growth	12/14	12/15	12/16	12/17	12/18
Sales ($ mil.)	101.4%	5.0	4.7	18.4	50.5	82.3
Net income ($ mil.)	-	(10.5)	(12.6)	0.4	22.8	20.7
Market value ($ mil.)	(1.8%)	74.4	31.7	31.2	59.5	69.2
Employees	(8.1%)	14	14	12	10	10

FINWARD BANCORP
NAS: FNWD

9204 Columbia Avenue
Munster, IN 46321
Phone: 219 836-4400
Fax: -
Web: www.ibankpeoples.com

CEO: Benjamin Bochnowski
CFO: Peymon Torabi
HR: -
FYE: December 31
Type: Public

NorthWest Indiana Bancorp is the holding company for Peoples Bank which serves individuals and businesses customers through about 10 branches in northwest Indiana's Lake County. The savings bank offers traditional deposit services such as checking and savings accounts money market accounts and CDs. It primarily uses the funds collected to originate loans secured by single-family residences and commercial real estate; it also makes construction consumer and business loans. The bank's Wealth Management Group provides retirement and estate planning investment accounts land trusts and profit-sharing and 401(k) plans.

	Annual Growth	12/16	12/17	12/18	12/19	12/20
Assets ($ mil.)	13.1%	913.6	927.3	1,096.2	1,328.7	1,497.5
Net income ($ mil.)	16.1%	9.1	9.0	9.3	12.1	16.6
Market value ($ mil.)	(1.8%)	134.5	154.1	148.9	158.9	125.0
Employees	5.0%	216	217	276	290	263

FIRELANDS REGIONAL HEALTH SYSTEM

1111 HAYES AVE
SANDUSKY, OH 448703323
Phone: 419-557-7485
Fax: -
Web: www.firelands.com

CEO: Martin E Tursky
CFO: Daniel Moncher
HR: -
FYE: December 31
Type: Private

Firelands Regional Health System primarily operates through its Firelands Regional Medical Center (FRMC). The center serves eight counties in northern Ohio. It operates two hospital campuses with a total of 400 beds a medical office building and outpatient clinics throughout the region. FRMC's medical staff of 225 represents more than 35 specialties. The center's broad range of services include cardiovascular care home health care mental health services palliative care dialysis oncology care and chemical dependency programs. It also has hospital network and teaching affiliations with several area hospitals medical schools and community colleges. The medical center is supported by a non-profit foundation.

	Annual Growth	12/15	12/16	12/17	12/18	12/19
Sales ($ mil.)	2556.9%	-	0.0	285.5	280.8	291.3
Net income ($ mil.)	210.9%	-	0.7	27.3	(24.3)	20.5
Market value ($ mil.)	-	-	-	-	-	-
Employees	-	-	-	-	-	1,635

FIRST ACCEPTANCE CORP
NBB: FACO

3813 Green Hills Village Drive
Nashville, TN 37215
Phone: 615 844-2800
Fax: –
Web: www.acceptance.com

CEO: Larry Willeford
CFO: Brent Gay
HR: –
FYE: December 31
Type: Public

First Acceptance sells car insurance to customers wanting to stay on the right side of the law. The personal auto insurer operates its business in a dozen states specializing in providing non-standard auto insurance (insurance for drivers who have trouble getting coverage because of poor driving records or payment histories). As part of its business First Acceptance sells its policies under the brand names Acceptance Insurance (in the Chicago area) Yale Insurance and Insurance Plus brand. Altogether the company operates about 350 retail offices staffed by employee agents and through independent agents at more than a dozen retail locations.

	Annual Growth	12/16	12/17	12/18	12/19	12/20
Assets ($ mil.)	(3.9%)	400.1	395.9	389.1	356.4	341.0
Net income ($ mil.)	–	(29.3)	(8.6)	17.7	15.4	10.4
Market value ($ mil.)	8.5%	39.7	45.4	39.7	30.3	55.1
Employees	(2.5%)	1,400	1,300	1,331		

FIRST ADVANTAGE BANCORP
NBB: FABK

1430 Madison Street
Clarksville, TN 37040
Phone: 931 552-6176
Fax: –
Web: www.firstadvantagebanking.com

CEO: –
CFO: –
HR: –
FYE: December 31
Type: Public

First Advantage Bancorp is the holding company for First Federal Savings Bank which serves northern Tennessee from about a half-dozen branch offices. Founded in 1953 the thrift offers standard retail products and services including deposit accounts and loans. One- to four-family residential and commercial mortgages account for about half of First Federal's loan portfolio; the company also writes construction and land loans and to a lesser extent consumer and business loans. First Advantage was established when the bank converted to a holding company structure in 2007.

	Annual Growth	12/14	12/15	12/16	12/17	12/18
Assets ($ mil.)	10.7%	442.5	487.4	528.4	571.5	664.3
Net income ($ mil.)	22.7%	3.3	3.4	2.9	4.3	7.4
Market value ($ mil.)	15.1%	54.5	64.1	70.3	91.8	95.7
Employees	–	–	–	–	–	–

FIRST AMERICAN FINANCIAL CORP
NYS: FAF

1 First American Way
Santa Ana, CA 92707-5913
Phone: 714 250-3000
Fax: 714 250-3151
Web: www.firstam.com

CEO: Dennis Gilmore
CFO: Mark Seaton
HR: –
FYE: December 31
Type: Public

First American Financial knows that when you're buying real estate you'll probably want some insurance to go along with it. In addition to title insurance closing and escrow services from its First American Title Insurance subsidiary the company's specialty insurance arm provides residential property and casualty insurance and home warranties. Its First American Trust unit offers banking and trust services to the escrow and real estate industries. Other offerings include settlement valuation and real estate data.

	Annual Growth	12/17	12/18	12/19	12/20	12/21
Assets ($ mil.)	14.5%	9,573.2	10,630.6	11,519.2	12,796.0	16,451.0
Net income ($ mil.)	30.9%	423.0	474.5	707.4	696.4	1,241.0
Market value ($ mil.)	8.7%	6,147.6	4,897.0	6,397.7	5,663.8	8,581.8
Employees	4.4%	18,705	18,251	18,412	19,597	22,233

FIRST AVIATION SERVICES, INC.
NBB: FAVS

15 Riverside Avenue
Westport, CT 06880-4214
Phone: 203 291-3300
Fax: 203 291-3330
Web: www.firstaviation.com

CEO: Aaron P Hollander
CFO: Janelle Miller
HR: –
FYE: December 31
Type: Public

The superstore of aerospace First Aviation Services (FAvS) pushes parts and components that keep aircraft flying high. FAvS sells about 200000 new and reconditioned parts from more than 150 manufacturers and OEMs such as General Electric Goodrich and Parker Hannifin. Cornerstone unit Aerospace Products International (API) and subsidiaries worldwide tap 6000-plus manufacturers maintenance providers and operators of commercial corporate and general aviation aircraft. In addition to offering maintenance overhaul and repair (MRO) services for brakes and starters/generators and builds hose assemblies API provides third-party logistics and inventory management services.

	Annual Growth	01/09*	12/09	12/10	12/11	12/12
Sales ($ mil.)	(42.6%)	114.2	100.3	128.5	113.1	21.6
Net income ($ mil.)	–	(2.5)	(0.5)	(1.2)	0.8	(13.0)
Market value ($ mil.)	124.6%	0.6	0.7	0.6	5.3	6.8
Employees						110

*Fiscal year change

FIRST BANCORP (NC)
NMS: FBNC

300 S.W. Broad St.
Southern Pines, NC 28387
Phone: 910 246-2500
Fax: –
Web: www.localfirstbank.com

CEO: Richard Moore
CFO: Elizabeth Bostian
HR: –
FYE: December 31
Type: Public

Don't confuse this First Bancorp with Virginia's First Bancorp or First BanCorp in Puerto Rico. This one is the holding company for First Bank which operates about 100 branch locations in east-central North Carolina east South Carolina and western Virginia (where it operates under the name First Bank of Virginia). In addition to offering standard commercial banking services such as deposit accounts and lending the bank offers investment products and discount brokerage services. Another subsidiary First Bank Insurance Services offers property/casualty products. First Bank focuses its lending on mortgages which account for more than half of its loan portfolio.

	Annual Growth	12/16	12/17	12/18	12/19	12/20
Assets ($ mil.)	19.2%	3,614.9	5,547.0	5,864.1	6,143.6	7,289.8
Net income ($ mil.)	31.2%	27.5	46.0	89.3	92.0	81.5
Market value ($ mil.)	5.7%	775.6	1,009.1	933.4	1,140.6	966.8
Employees	6.7%	861	1,166	1,098	1,111	1,118

FIRST BANCORP INC (ME)
NMS: FNLC

223 Main Street
Damariscotta, ME 04543
Phone: 207 563-3195
Fax: –
Web: www.thefirstbancorp.com

CEO: Tony McKim
CFO: Richard Elder
HR: –
FYE: December 31
Type: Public

It may not actually be the first bank but The First Bancorp (formerly First National Lincoln) was founded over 150 years ago. It is the holding company for The First a regional bank serving coastal Maine from more than 15 branches. The bank offers traditional retail products and services including checking and savings accounts CDs IRAs and loans. Residential mortgages make up about 40% of the company's loan portfolio; business loans account for another 40%; and home equity and consumer loans comprise the rest. Bank subsidiary First Advisors offers private banking and investment management services. Founded in 1864 the bank now boasts more than $1.4 billion in assets.

	Annual Growth	12/16	12/17	12/18	12/19	12/20
Assets ($ mil.)	8.4%	1,712.9	1,842.9	1,944.6	2,068.8	2,361.2
Net income ($ mil.)	10.8%	18.0	19.6	23.5	25.5	27.1
Market value ($ mil.)	(6.4%)	362.5	298.2	288.0	331.0	278.1
Employees	2.1%	235	235	239	245	255

FIRST BANCORP OF INDIANA INC
NBB: FBPI

5001 Davis Lant Drive
Evansville, IN 47715
Phone: 812 492-8104
Fax: –
Web: www.firstfedevansville.com

CEO: Michael Head
CFO: George J Smith
HR: –
FYE: June 30
Type: Public

First Bancorp of Indiana wants to be second to none. It's the holding company for First Federal Savings Bank which serves individuals and local businesses through nine branches in the Evansville Indiana area. The bank offers standard retail products and services like checking savings and money market accounts; certificates of deposit; and retirement savings plans. Its lending activities primarily consist of mortgage and consumer loans (approximately 50% and 40% of the company's loan portfolio respectively). The bank also offers savings account loans and business loans.

	Annual Growth	06/16	06/17	06/19	06/20	06/21
Assets ($ mil.)	3.9%	397.8	422.2	431.1	473.4	480.9
Net income ($ mil.)	14.4%	1.9	0.9	2.1	1.8	3.8
Market value ($ mil.)	13.1%	20.6	20.6	35.4	30.4	38.2
Employees	–	–	–	–	–	–

FIRST BANCSHARES INC (MS)
NMS: FBMS

6480 U.S. Highway 98 West, Suite A
Hattiesburg, MS 39402
Phone: 601 268-8998
Fax: –
Web: www.thefirstbank.com

CEO: M. Ray Cole
CFO: Donna Lowery
HR: –
FYE: December 31
Type: Public

Hoping to be first in the hearts of its customers The First Bancshares is the holding company for The First a community bank with some two dozen branch locations in southern Mississippi's Hattiesburg Alabama and Louisiana. The company provides such standard deposit products as checking and savings accounts NOW and money market accounts and IRAs. Real estate loans account for about 80% of the bank's lending portfolio including about equal portions of residential mortgages commercial mortgages and construction loans. The bank also writes business loans and consumer loans. The bank which has expanded beyond Mississippi through several acquisitions has approximately $970 million in assets.

	Annual Growth	12/16	12/17	12/18	12/19	12/20
Assets ($ mil.)	41.7%	1,277.4	1,813.2	3,004.0	3,941.9	5,152.8
Net income ($ mil.)	50.9%	10.1	10.6	21.2	43.7	52.5
Market value ($ mil.)	2.9%	580.7	722.1	638.7	750.0	652.0
Employees	24.0%	315	487	641	697	744

FIRST BANCSHARES INC. (MO)
NBB: FBSI

142 East First Street, P.O. Box 777
Mountain Grove, MO 65711
Phone: 719 955-2800
Fax: 719 442-4330
Web: www.thestockmensbank.com

CEO: Robert Alexander
CFO: Brady J Nachtrieb
HR: –
FYE: December 31
Type: Public

First Bancshares is the holding company for First Home Savings Bank which has about a dozen locations serving south-central Missouri. First Home Savings offers a range of retail banking services including checking and savings as well as NOW accounts and CDs. Residential mortgages account for more than half of First Home Savings' lending portfolio; commercial real estate loans represent another quarter. First Home Savings Bank was founded in 1911 as Mountain Grove Building and Loan Association

	Annual Growth	12/16	12/17	12/18	12/19	12/20
Assets ($ mil.)	16.6%	219.5	356.0	345.0	352.6	406.3
Net income ($ mil.)	35.6%	1.2	(0.6)	3.0	3.6	3.9
Market value ($ mil.)	3.1%	30.1	29.8	36.0	40.5	34.0
Employees	–	–	–	–	–	–

FIRST BANCTRUST CORP
NBB: FIRT

101 South Central Avenue
Paris, IL 61944
Phone: 217 465-6381
Fax: 217 465-0201
Web: www.firstbanktrust.com

CEO: –
CFO: –
HR: –
FYE: December 31
Type: Public

You can spend your money along the banks of the Seine in Paris but you can save your money at First BancTrust Corporation in Paris (Illinois that is). It's the holding company for First Bank & Trust which has offices in the rural eastern Illinois towns of Marshall Martinsville Paris Rantoul and Savoy. Founded in 1887 the bank attracts deposits by offering such services as checking and savings accounts CDs and IRAs. Its lending activities primarily consist of residential mortgages commercial mortgages farmland loans commercial and industrial loans and consumer loans. First Bank also offers trust investment and financial planning services.

	Annual Growth	12/12	12/13	12/14	12/15	12/16
Assets ($ mil.)	3.9%	389.6	407.3	433.8	450.3	453.5
Net income ($ mil.)	0.7%	3.4	3.1	3.2	3.2	3.5
Market value ($ mil.)	17.0%	23.2	29.4	32.7	33.8	43.5
Employees	–	–	–	–	–	–

FIRST BANKS, INC. (MO)

135 North Meramec
Clayton, MO 63105
Phone: 314 854-4600
Fax: –
Web: www.firstbanks.com

CEO: Shelley Seifert
CFO: –
HR: Elaine Mintschenko
FYE: December 31
Type: Public

First Banks keeps it in the family. The holding company for First Bank it is owned by chairman James Dierberg and his family; many of the bank's branches and ATMs are located in Dierbergs Markets a Missouri-based grocery chain owned by relatives of the chairman. First Bank has about 130 branches in California Florida Illinois and Missouri with a concentration in metropolitan markets such as Los Angeles San Diego San Francisco Sacramento and St. Louis. The bank offers standard services like deposits mortgages and business and consumer loans. Additional services include brokerage insurance trust and private banking as well as commercial treasury management and international trade services.

	Annual Growth	12/10	12/11	12/12	12/13	12/14
Assets ($ mil.)	(5.3%)	7,378.1	6,608.9	6,509.1	5,919.0	5,935.5
Net income ($ mil.)	–	(191.7)	(41.2)	26.3	241.7	21.7
Market value ($ mil.)	–	–	–	–	–	–
Employees	(4.1%)	1,380	1,171	1,177	1,147	1,167

FIRST BUSEY CORP
NMS: BUSE

100 W. University Avenue
Champaign, IL 61820
Phone: 217 365-4544
Fax: –

CEO: Robin Elliott
CFO: Jeffrey Jones
HR: –
FYE: December 31
Type: Public

First Busey conducts banking related banking services asset management brokerage and fiduciary services through its wholly-owned bank subsidiary Busey Bank which boasts approximately $10.2 billion in assets and about 70 branches across Illinois Florida Missouri and Indiana. The bank offers a range of diversified financial products and services for consumers and businesses including online and mobile banking capabilities. Its primary sources of income are interest and fees on loans and investments wealth management fees and service fees. Subsidiary FirsTech provides retail payment processing services. Most of Busey Bank's branches are located in downstate Illinois.

	Annual Growth	12/16	12/17	12/18	12/19	12/20
Assets ($ mil.)	18.1%	5,425.2	7,860.6	7,702.4	9,695.7	10,544.0
Net income ($ mil.)	19.2%	49.7	62.7	98.9	103.0	100.3
Market value ($ mil.)	(8.5%)	1,674.6	1,628.9	1,335.1	1,496.1	1,172.4
Employees	1.0%	1,295	1,347	1,270	1,531	1,346

FIRST BUSINESS FINANCIAL SERVICES, INC. NMS: FBIZ

401 Charmany Drive
Madison, WI 53719
Phone: 608 238-8008
Fax: –
Web: www.firstbusiness.com

CEO: Mark Meloy
CFO: Edward Sloane
HR: –
FYE: December 31
Type: Public

Business comes first at First Business Financial Services which serves small and midsized companies entrepreneurs professionals and high-net-worth individuals through First Business Bank and First Business Bank - Milwaukee. The banks offer deposits loans cash management and trust services from a handful of offices in Wisconsin and Kansas. Over 60% of the company's loan portfolio is made up of commercial real estate loans. Subsidiary First Business Capital specializes in asset-based lending while First Business Equipment Finance provides commercial equipment financing. First Business Trust & Investments offers investment management and retirement services.

	Annual Growth	12/16	12/17	12/18	12/19	12/20
Assets ($ mil.)	9.6%	1,780.7	1,794.1	1,966.5	2,096.8	2,567.8
Net income ($ mil.)	3.3%	14.9	11.9	16.3	23.3	17.0
Market value ($ mil.)	(6.1%)	203.2	189.5	167.1	225.6	157.7
Employees	2.6%	272	264	289	301	301

FIRST CAPITAL BANCORP INC (VA) NAS: FCVA

4222 Cox Road
Glen Allen, VA 23060
Phone: 804 273-1160
Fax: –
Web: www.1capitalbank.com

CEO: –
CFO: –
HR: –
FYE: December 31
Type: Public

Moolah scratch bread chedda bucks dough ducats or skrilla — it all means business for First Capital Bank and its holding company First Capital Bancorp. Founded in 1998 the bank provides general commercial banking services through seven branches in the Richmond Virginia area. First Capital Bank offers the usual array of personal and business banking services including credit cards IRAs consumer and commercial loans Internet banking services and deposit accounts. The company terminated its agreement to merge with Eastern Virginia Bankshares in 2009 after regulatory approval for the deal stalled.

	Annual Growth	12/09	12/10	12/11	12/12	12/13
Assets ($ mil.)	0.8%	530.4	536.0	541.7	542.9	547.9
Net income ($ mil.)	88.4%	0.3	(2.2)	(3.1)	(6.0)	3.9
Market value ($ mil.)	(0.8%)	60.2	45.3	30.5	35.6	58.2
Employees	7.2%	78	82	91	101	103

FIRST CAPITAL INC. NAS: FCAP

220 Federal Drive NW
Corydon, IN 47112
Phone: 812 738-2198
Fax: –
Web: www.firstharrison.com

CEO: William Harrod
CFO: Michael Frederick
HR: Jill Keinsley
FYE: December 31
Type: Public

First Capital is the holding company for First Harrison Bank which operates about a dozen branches in Clark Floyd Harrison and Washington counties in southern Indiana. Targeting area consumers and small to midsized businesses the bank offers standard deposit products such as checking and savings accounts certificates of deposit and individual retirement accounts. Residential mortgages make up nearly half of the company's loan portfolio; consumer loans and commercial mortgages are around 20% apiece. First Harrison Bank also offers access to investments such as stocks bonds and mutual funds.

	Annual Growth	12/16	12/17	12/18	12/19	12/20
Assets ($ mil.)	8.2%	743.7	759.0	794.2	827.5	1,017.6
Net income ($ mil.)	10.2%	6.9	7.4	9.3	10.3	10.1
Market value ($ mil.)	16.9%	109.4	124.0	143.4	246.4	204.4
Employees	1.2%	204	206	210	214	214

FIRST CENTURY BANKSHARES, INC. OTC: FCBS

500 Federal Street
Bluefield, WV 24701
Phone: 304 325-8181
Fax: 304 325-3727
Web: www.firstcentury.com

CEO: –
CFO: –
HR: –
FYE: December 31
Type: Public

First Century Bankshares is the holding company for First Century Bank which serves southern West Virginia and southwestern Virginia from about a dozen branch locations. The bank provides traditional deposit services such as checking accounts statement savings money market accounts CDs and IRAs. It uses funds from deposits to write commercial and consumer loans primarily real estate mortgages which account for some 70% of the company's loan book. First Century Bank also offers real estate construction and development loans agricultural loans and check cards. Bank subsidiary First Century Financial Services provides trust investment and financial planning services. Virginia-based Summit Financial Group agreed to buy First Century for $42.8 million in June 2016.

	Annual Growth	12/11	12/12	12/13	12/14	12/15
Assets ($ mil.)	(0.7%)	417.8	410.8	412.5	401.2	406.1
Net income ($ mil.)	1.2%	2.2	2.9	3.1	3.2	2.3
Market value ($ mil.)	13.4%	23.3	28.4	32.6	33.5	38.5
Employees	–	–	153	–	–	–

FIRST CITIZENS BANCSHARES INC (DE) NMS: FCNC A

4300 Six Forks Road
Raleigh, NC 27609
Phone: 919 716-7000
Fax: –
Web: www.firstcitizens.com

CEO: Frank Holding
CFO: Craig Nix
HR: –
FYE: December 31
Type: Public

First Citizens BancShares owns First-Citizens Bank which operates more than 540 branches in nearly 20 states mainly in the southeastern and western US and urban areas scattered nationwide. The $50 billion-asset bank provides standard services such as deposits loans mortgages and trust services in addition to processing and operational support to other banks. FCB's wholly owned subsidiaries First Citizens Investor Services (FCIS) and First Citizens Asset Management (FCAM) provides various investment products and services. As a registered broker/dealer FCIS provides a full range of investment products including annuities discount brokerage services and third-party mutual funds. As registered investment advisors FCIS and FCAM provide investment management services and advice.

	Annual Growth	12/16	12/17	12/18	12/19	12/20
Assets ($ mil.)	10.9%	32,990.8	34,527.5	35,408.6	39,824.5	49,957.7
Net income ($ mil.)	21.5%	225.5	323.8	400.3	457.4	491.7
Market value ($ mil.)	12.8%	3,484.8	3,956.0	3,701.3	5,224.4	5,637.3
Employees	1.7%	6,296	6,799	6,683	7,176	6,722

FIRST CLOVER LEAF FINANCIAL CORP NAS: FCLF

6814 Goshen Road
Edwardsville, IL 62025
Phone: 618 656-6122
Fax: –

CEO: –
CFO: –
HR: –
FYE: December 31
Type: Public

First Clover Leaf Financial counts itself lucky to be in the banking business in the greater St. Louis area. The company (formerly First Federal Financial Services) is the holding company for three-branch First Clover Leaf Bank. Under its former name the company in 2006 acquired Clover Leaf Financial and merged the acquisition's Clover Leaf Bank with First Federal Savings & Loan Association of Edwardsville to form First Clover Leaf Bank. The bank serves individuals and businesses in and around Edwardsville and Glen Carbon offering such standard services as deposit accounts credit cards and loans including real estate (about 85% of its total portfolio) business and consumer loans.

	Annual Growth	12/10	12/11	12/12	12/13	12/14
Assets ($ mil.)	1.4%	575.0	562.7	600.8	622.0	607.6
Net income ($ mil.)	0.1%	3.8	1.9	4.1	3.4	3.8
Market value ($ mil.)	6.6%	47.5	42.7	43.7	68.7	61.4
Employees	4.6%	87	93	103	103	104

FIRST COMMONWEALTH FINANCIAL CORP (INDIANA, PA)   NYS: FCF

601 Philadelphia Street   CEO: Thomas Price
Indiana, PA 15701   CFO: James Reske
Phone: 724 349-7220   HR: Carrie Riggle
Fax: –   FYE: December 31
Web: www.fcbanking.com   Type: Public

First Commonwealth Financial is the holding company for First Commonwealth Bank which provides consumer and commercial banking services about 120 bank offices throughout central and western Pennsylvania counties as well as in Columbus Ohio. The bank's loan portfolio mostly consists of commercial and industrial loans including real estate operating agricultural and construction loans. It also issues consumer loans such as automobile and home equity loans and offers wealth management insurance financial planning retail brokerage and trust services. The company has total assets of some $9.1 billion with deposits of roughly $7.4 billion.

	Annual Growth	12/16	12/17	12/18	12/19	12/20
Assets ($ mil.)	7.9%	6,684.0	7,308.5	7,828.3	8,308.8	9,068.1
Net income ($ mil.)	5.4%	59.6	55.2	107.5	105.3	73.4
Market value ($ mil.)	(6.3%)	1,363.1	1,376.6	1,161.3	1,394.9	1,051.7
Employees	0.3%	1,376	1,476	1,512	1,571	1,393

FIRST COMMUNITY BANKSHARES INC (VA)   NMS: FCBC

P.O. Box 989   CEO: William Stafford
Bluefield, VA 24605-0989   CFO: David Brown
Phone: 276 326-9000   HR: –
Fax: –   FYE: December 31
Web: www.firstcommunitybank.com   Type: Public

First Community Bancshares doesn't play second fiddle to other area banks. The firm is the holding company for First Community Bank which provides traditional services like checking and savings accounts CDs and credit cards and serves communities through some 55 branches across Virginia West Virginia North Carolina and Tennessee. Commercial real estate loans make up 45% of its loan portfolio while commercial business loans make up another 5%. First Community Bancshares offers insurance through subsidiary Greenpoint Insurance and wealth management and investment advisory services through Trust Services and First Community Wealth Management.

	Annual Growth	12/16	12/17	12/18	12/19	12/20
Assets ($ mil.)	6.0%	2,386.4	2,388.5	2,244.4	2,798.8	3,011.1
Net income ($ mil.)	9.4%	25.1	21.5	36.3	38.8	35.9
Market value ($ mil.)	(8.0%)	534.2	509.2	557.9	549.8	382.5
Employees	2.3%	580	562	519	527	635

FIRST COMMUNITY CORP (SC)   NAS: FCCO

5455 Sunset Boulevard   CEO: Michael Crapps
Lexington, SC 29072   CFO: Donald Jordan
Phone: 803 951-2265   HR: –
Fax: –   FYE: December 31
Web: www.firstcommunitysc.com   Type: Public

Putting first things first First Community is the holding company for First Community Bank which serves individuals and smaller businesses in central South Carolina. Through about a dozen offices the bank which was founded in 1995 offers such products and services as checking and savings accounts money market accounts CDs IRAs credit cards insurance and investment services. Commercial mortgages make up about 60% of First Community Bank's loan portfolio which also includes residential mortgages and business consumer and construction loans. The company's First Community Financial Consultants division offers asset management and estate planning. First Community is merging with Cornerstone Bancorp expanding its presence in upstate SC.

	Annual Growth	12/16	12/17	12/18	12/19	12/20
Assets ($ mil.)	11.1%	914.8	1,050.7	1,091.6	1,170.3	1,395.4
Net income ($ mil.)	10.9%	6.7	5.8	11.2	11.0	10.1
Market value ($ mil.)	(1.5%)	135.4	169.5	145.7	162.1	127.4
Employees	4.8%	202	224	226	242	244

FIRST CONNECTICUT BANCORP INC. (MD)   NMS: FBNK

One Farm Glen Boulevard   CEO: –
Farmington, CT 06032   CFO: –
Phone: 860 676-4600   HR: –
Fax: –   FYE: December 31
Web: www.farmingtonbankct.com   Type: Public

One of the oldest states in the union also has some of the oldest banks in the union. First Connecticut Bancorp (FCB) is the holding company for Farmington Bank a Connecticut-based community bank tracing its roots back to the mid-1800s. The bank offers traditional deposit accounts and loan products to consumers businesses and government clients through about 25 branches in the suburban communities in central Connecticut and western Massachusetts. Its lending activity consists primarily of commercial and residential real estate loans. The bank also offers wealth management services.

	Annual Growth	12/12	12/13	12/14	12/15	12/16
Assets ($ mil.)	11.7%	1,822.9	2,110.0	2,485.4	2,708.5	2,837.6
Net income ($ mil.)	40.3%	3.9	3.7	9.3	12.6	15.2
Market value ($ mil.)	13.3%	218.6	256.3	259.5	276.8	360.1
Employees	1.0%	326	337	328	343	339

FIRST ELECTRIC CO-OPERATIVE CORPORATION

1000 S JP WRIGHT LOOP RD   CEO: Don Crabbe
JACKSONVILLE, AR 720765264   CFO: Bruce Andrews
Phone: 501-982-4545   HR: –
Fax: –   FYE: December 31
Web: www.firstelectric.coop   Type: Private

First Electric Cooperative wasn't the first electric cooperative ever formed but it was the first such entity created in its home state. The member-owned utility distributes power to more than 85000 customers in 17 central and southeastern Arkansas counties. It also offers its members a range of energy products and value-added services including energy efficient Marathon water heaters surge and lightning protection equipment and compact fluorescent light bulbs. Some 72% of the cooperative's revenues come from residential customers; commercial and industrial customers account for another 20% and the rest comes from such sources as irrigation and street lighting.

	Annual Growth	12/12	12/13	12/14	12/15	12/18
Sales ($ mil.)	1.9%	–	184.1	183.9	179.3	202.3
Net income ($ mil.)	–	–	0.0	0.0	0.0	0.0
Market value ($ mil.)	–	–	–	–	–	–
Employees	–	–	–	–	–	237

FIRST FEDERAL OF NORTHERN MICHIGAN BANCORP INC   NBB: FFNM

100 S. Second Avenue   CEO: –
Alpena, MI 49707   CFO: –
Phone: 989 356-9041   HR: –
Fax: –   FYE: December 31
Web: www.first-federal.com   Type: Public

First Federal of Northern Michigan Bancorp is the holding company for First Federal of Northern Michigan a savings bank serving area residents and businesses from nearly 10 locations in the northern part of the state's Lower Peninsula. Deposit services include checking savings and money market accounts CDs and IRAs. The bank's lending activities mainly consist of residential mortgages (nearly half of its loan portfolio) commercial mortgages business loans and home equity loans. It also offers construction loans consumer loans and credit cards. In 2009 First Federal sold InsuranCenter of Alpena (ICA) which provided life property/casualty and health insurance and investment products.

	Annual Growth	12/12	12/13	12/14	12/15	12/16
Assets ($ mil.)	12.7%	213.8	209.7	325.9	336.0	344.9
Net income ($ mil.)	–	(0.2)	0.1	2.2	3.4	1.3
Market value ($ mil.)	13.5%	18.6	21.8	22.2	24.3	30.9
Employees	3.2%	92	92	101	101	–

FIRST FINANCIAL BANCORP (OH)   NMS: FFBC

255 East Fifth Street, Suite 800 — CEO: Archie Brown
Cincinnati, OH 45202 — CFO: James Anderson
Phone: 877 322-9530 — HR: –
Fax: – — FYE: December 31
Web: www.bankatfirst.com — Type: Public

The holding company's flagship subsidiary First Financial Bank operates more than 140 banking centers in Ohio Indiana Kentucky and Illinois. Founded in 1863 the bank offers checking and savings accounts money market accounts CDs credit cards private banking and wealth management services through its First Financial Wealth Management subsidiary. Commercial loans including real estate and construction loans make up more than 50% of First Financial's total loan portfolio; the bank also offers residential mortgage and consumer loans. First Financial Bancorp boasts nearly $16 billion in assets including nearly $10 billion in loans.

	Annual Growth	12/17	12/18	12/19	12/20	12/21
Assets ($ mil.)	16.4%	8,896.9	13,986.7	14,511.6	15,973.1	16,329.1
Net income ($ mil.)	20.7%	96.8	172.6	198.1	155.8	205.2
Market value ($ mil.)	(1.9%)	2,480.8	2,233.2	2,395.2	1,650.4	2,295.4
Employees	10.1%	1,366	2,131	2,123	2,107	2,010

FIRST FINANCIAL BANKSHARES, INC.   NMS: FFIN

400 Pine Street — CEO: F. Scott Dueser
Abilene, TX 79601 — CFO: James Gordon
Phone: 325 627-7155 — HR: –
Fax: – — FYE: December 31
Web: www.ffin.com — Type: Public

Texas hold 'em? Well sort of. First Financial Bankshares is the holding company for eleven banks consolidated under the First Financial brand all of which are located in small and midsized markets in Texas. Together they have about 50 locations. The company maintains a decentralized management structure with each of the subsidiary banks having their own local leadership and decision-making authority. Its First Financial Trust & Asset Management subsidiary administers retirement and employee benefit plans in addition to providing trust services. First Financial Bankshares also owns an insurance agency.

	Annual Growth	12/17	12/18	12/19	12/20	12/21
Assets ($ mil.)	15.9%	7,254.7	7,731.9	8,262.2	10,904.5	13,102.5
Net income ($ mil.)	17.3%	120.4	150.6	164.8	202.0	227.6
Market value ($ mil.)	3.1%	6,378.9	8,168.6	4,970.0	5,122.2	7,198.7
Employees	3.6%	1,300	1,350	1,345	1,500	1,500

FIRST FINANCIAL CORP. (IN)   NMS: THFF

One First Financial Plaza — CEO: Norman Lowery
Terre Haute, IN 47807 — CFO: Rodger McHargue
Phone: 812 238-6000 — HR: –
Fax: – — FYE: December 31
Web: www.first-online.com — Type: Public

Which came first the First Financial in Indiana Ohio South Carolina or Texas? Regardless this particular First Financial Corporation is the holding company for First Financial Bank which offers traditional banking deposit accounts and loans as well as trust private banking wealth management and investment services through more than 70 branches in west-central Indiana and east-central Illinois. About 60% of its loan portfolio is tied to commercial loans while the rest is split between residential and consumer loans. Subsidiary Forrest Sherer sells personal and commercial insurance while subsidiary Morris Plan originates indirect auto loans through dealerships in the bank's market area.

	Annual Growth	12/16	12/17	12/18	12/19	12/20
Assets ($ mil.)	11.1%	2,988.5	3,000.7	3,008.7	4,023.6	4,557.5
Net income ($ mil.)	8.8%	38.4	29.1	46.6	48.9	53.8
Market value ($ mil.)	(7.4%)	715.9	614.9	544.4	619.9	526.7
Employees	2.0%	846	847	816	957	917

FIRST FINANCIAL NORTHWEST INC   NMS: FFNW

201 Wells Avenue South — CEO: Joseph Kiley
Renton, WA 98057 — CFO: Richard Jacobson
Phone: 425 255-4400 — HR: –
Fax: – — FYE: December 31
Web: – — Type: Public

Searching for green in The Evergreen State First Financial Northwest is the holding company for First Financial Northwest Bank (formerly First Savings Bank Northwest). The small community bank offers deposit services like checking and savings accounts and a variety of lending services to customers in western Washington. Almost 40% of First Savings Bank's loan portfolio consists of one- to four-family residential loans while commercial real estate loans made up another 35%. Because the bank focuses almost exclusively on real estate loans it writes very few unsecured consumer and commercial loans.

	Annual Growth	12/16	12/17	12/18	12/19	12/20
Assets ($ mil.)	7.5%	1,037.6	1,210.2	1,252.4	1,341.9	1,387.7
Net income ($ mil.)	(1.0%)	8.9	8.5	14.9	10.4	8.6
Market value ($ mil.)	(12.8%)	192.2	151.0	150.6	145.5	111.0
Employees	5.7%	121	145	156	158	151

FIRST FINANCIAL SERVICE CORP   NMS: FFKY

2323 Ring Road — CEO: –
Elizabethtown, KY 42701 — CFO: –
Phone: 270 765-2131 — HR: –
Fax: 270 769-5811 — FYE: December 31
Web: www.ffsbky.com — Type: Public

First Financial Service Corporation is the holding company for First Federal Savings Bank of Elizabethtown which has 18 branches in six central Kentucky counties. Founded in 1923 the bank offers CDs IRAs and savings NOW and money market accounts primarily using deposit funds to originate commercial real estate loans (about 60% of its loan portfolio) and residential mortgages (about 20%). Other loans include home equity consumer and business loans. First Service Corporation of Elizabethtown a subsidiary of the bank sells investment products to the bank's customers.

	Annual Growth	12/08	12/09	12/10	12/11	12/12
Assets ($ mil.)	(0.2%)	1,017.0	1,209.5	1,320.5	1,228.8	1,007.1
Net income ($ mil.)	–	4.8	(6.7)	(8.3)	(23.2)	(8.4)
Market value ($ mil.)	(36.1%)	56.4	43.3	19.4	7.3	9.4
Employees	(3.3%)	321	333	335	325	281

FIRST HARTFORD CORP   NBB: FHRT

149 Colonial Road — CEO: –
Manchester, CT 06042 — CFO: –
Phone: 860 646-6555 — HR: –
Fax: 860 646-8572 — FYE: April 30
Web: www.firsthartford.com — Type: Public

First Hartford puts real estate first. The company operating through subsidiary First Hartford Realty invests in and develops commercial and other real estate. Its portfolio is located primarily in the Northeast and includes shopping centers a restaurant and a business and technology school campus. First Hartford has also built single-family homes public housing units government facilities and several industrial properties. It is a preferred developer for CVS Health in areas of Lousiana New Jersey New York and Texas. The company's largest tenants include Stop & Shop Big Y Foods and Kmart. Subsidiary Lead Tech provides lead and asbestos inspection and remediation services.

	Annual Growth	04/17	04/18	04/19	04/20	04/21
Sales ($ mil.)	4.6%	75.7	83.0	80.7	67.8	90.7
Net income ($ mil.)	15.2%	3.0	1.6	2.6	(4.6)	5.3
Market value ($ mil.)	14.1%	6.6	5.5	5.1	10.4	11.2
Employees	42.9%	140	200	–	–	–

FIRST HAWAIIAN BANK

999 Bishop St. 29th Fl.
Honolulu HI 96813
Phone: 808-525-7000
Fax: 808-525-5798
Web: www.fhb.com

CEO: Robert Harrison
CFO: Ravi Mallela
HR: Iris Matsumoto
FYE: December 31
Type: Subsidiary

First Hawaiian Bank is the oldest and largest bank on the archipelago. It is a subsidiary of BancWest which in turn is owned by French bank BNP Paribas. Founded in 1858 to serve the whaling industry First Hawaiian Bank has about 60 branches in Hawaii plus locations in Guam and Saipan. The bank also has operations in the British West Indies and Japan. It offers standard deposit products such as checking and savings accounts CDs and IRAs as well as private banking and wealth management services. The bank mainly originates real estate-related loans such as residential and commercial mortgages and construction and land development loans. It also writes business and consumer loans.

FIRST HORIZON CORP

NYS: FHN

165 Madison Avenue
Memphis, TN 38103
Phone: 901 523-4444
Fax: –
Web: www.firsthorizon.com

CEO: David Jordan
CFO: Anthony Restel
HR: Tanya Hart
FYE: December 31
Type: Public

The bank holding company provide diversified financial services primarily through their principal subsidiary. Boasting more than $80 billion in total assets it offers traditional banking services like loans deposit accounts and credit cards as well as trust asset management financial advisory and investment services. In 2020 the company shortened its company name from First Horizon National Corporation to First Horizon Bank.

	Annual Growth	12/16	12/17	12/18	12/19	12/20
Assets ($ mil.)	31.0%	28,555.2	41,423.4	40,832.3	43,310.9	84,209.0
Net income ($ mil.)	38.9%	227.0	165.5	545.0	440.9	845.0
Market value ($ mil.)	(10.6%)	11,106.2	11,095.1	7,304.2	9,191.3	7,082.2
Employees	12.2%	4,288	5,984	5,577	5,017	6,802

FIRST INDEPENDENCE CORPORATION

OTC: FFSL

Myrtle and 6th
Independence KS 67301
Phone: 620-331-1660
Fax: 620-331-1600
Web: www.firstfederalsl.com

CEO: –
CFO: –
HR: –
FYE: September 30
Type: Public

First Independence is the holding company for First Federal Savings and Loan Association of Independence. Founded in 1905 First Federal has branches in Coffeyville Independence Neodesha and Pittsburg Kansas and a loan production office in Lawrence Kansas. Deposit products include checking savings health savings and retirement accounts as well as certificates of deposit. First Federal mainly originates one- to four-family residential mortgages and construction and land loans. Commercial real estate multifamily residential and consumer loans round out the bank's portfolio.

FIRST INDUSTRIAL REALTY TRUST INC

NYS: FR

1 N. Wacker Drive, Suite 4200
Chicago, IL 60606
Phone: 312 344-4300
Fax: 312 922-6320
Web: www.firstindustrial.com

CEO: Peter Baccile
CFO: Scott Musil
HR: –
FYE: December 31
Type: Public

First Industrial Realty Trust is a self-administered real estate investment trust (REIT) which owns manages and develops industrial real estate. Its portfolio consists of some 420 properties spanning about 62.4 million sq. ft. of leasable space in about 20 states. Most of the REIT's portfolio consists of light industrial properties but also includes bulk and regional warehouses research and development buildings and manufacturing facilities. Tenants include manufacturing retail wholesale trade distribution and professional services firms. Founded in 1994 First Industrial also develops customized spaces.

	Annual Growth	12/17	12/18	12/19	12/20	12/21
Sales ($ mil.)	4.7%	396.4	404.0	426.0	448.0	476.3
Net income ($ mil.)	7.7%	201.5	163.2	238.8	196.0	271.0
Market value ($ mil.)	20.4%	4,146.1	3,802.2	5,468.8	5,550.5	8,721.7
Employees	0.3%	160	145	155	153	162

FIRST INTERNET BANCORP

NMS: INBK

11201 USA Parkway
Fishers, IN 46037
Phone: 317 532-7900
Fax: –
Web: www.firstinternetbancorp.com

CEO: David Becker
CFO: Kenneth Lovik
HR: –
FYE: December 31
Type: Public

First Internet Bancorp was formed in 2006 to be the holding company for First Internet Bank of Indiana (First IB). Launched in 1999 the bank was the first state-chartered FDIC-insured institution to operate solely via the Internet. It now operates two locations in Indianapolis after adding one via its 2007 purchase of Landmark Financial (the parent of Landmark Savings Bank) a deal that also brought aboard residential mortgage brokerage Landmark Mortgage. First IB offers traditional checking and savings accounts in addition to CDs IRAs credit and check cards consumer installment and residential mortgage loans and lines of credit. It serves customers in all 50 states.

	Annual Growth	12/16	12/17	12/18	12/19	12/20
Assets ($ mil.)	23.0%	1,854.3	2,767.7	3,541.7	4,100.1	4,246.2
Net income ($ mil.)	25.0%	12.1	15.2	21.9	25.2	29.5
Market value ($ mil.)	(2.6%)	313.6	373.9	200.3	232.4	281.7
Employees	7.6%	192	206	201	231	257

FIRST INTERSTATE BANCSYSTEM INC

NMS: FIBK

401 North 31st Street
Billings, MT 59116-0918
Phone: 406 255-5390
Fax: –
Web: www.fibk.com

CEO: Kevin Riley
CFO: Marcy Mutch
HR: –
FYE: December 31
Type: Public

First Interstate BancSystem (FIB) is a financial and bank holding company focused on community banking that operates 150 banking offices including detached drive-up facilities in communities across six states?Idaho Montana Oregon South Dakota Washington and Wyoming. Through the company's bank subsidiary First Interstate Bank they deliver a comprehensive range of banking products and services?including online and mobile banking?to individuals businesses municipalities and others throughout their market areas. The company's principal business activity is lending to accepting deposits from and conducting financial transactions with and for individuals businesses municipalities and other entities.

	Annual Growth	12/16	12/17	12/18	12/19	12/20
Assets ($ mil.)	18.1%	9,063.9	12,213.3	13,300.2	14,644.2	17,648.7
Net income ($ mil.)	13.9%	95.6	106.5	160.2	181.0	161.2
Market value ($ mil.)	(1.1%)	2,642.2	2,486.9	2,270.2	2,603.1	2,531.6
Employees	9.4%	1,721	2,207	2,330	2,473	2,462

FIRST KEYSTONE CORP
NBB: FKYS

111 West Front Street
Berwick, PA 18603
Phone: 570 752-3671
Fax: –
Web: www.firstkeystonecorporation.com

CEO: Elaine Woodland
CFO: Diane C A Rosler
HR: –
FYE: December 31
Type: Public

First Keystone Corporation is the holding company for First Keystone Community Bank which serves individuals and businesses from more 18 bank locations in northeastern and central Pennsylvania. The bank provides traditional deposit products including checking and savings accounts debit cards and CDs; it also offers trust and investment advisory services. It also operates 20 ATMs and offers online banking services. Commercial mortgages constitute more than half of the bank's loan portfolio; residential mortgages business loans and consumer installment loans make up the remainder. The bank was founded in 1864.

	Annual Growth	12/16	12/17	12/18	12/19	12/20
Assets ($ mil.)	4.6%	984.3	990.1	1,012.0	1,007.2	1,179.0
Net income ($ mil.)	5.7%	9.5	8.6	9.2	10.2	11.8
Market value ($ mil.)	(4.4%)	144.7	166.2	123.3	145.6	121.1
Employees	1.3%	192	204	206	206	202

FIRST MARBLEHEAD CORP
NYS: FMD

One Cabot Road, Suite 200
Medford, MA 02155
Phone: 800 895-4283
Fax: –
Web: www.firstmarblehead.com

CEO: Daniel Meyers
CFO: Alan Breitman
HR: –
FYE: June 30
Type: Public

With a Harvard education costing six figures that government student loan just isn't going to cut it anymore. Enter First Marblehead. The firm provides underwriting and risk management services for lenders and schools who offer private student loans for undergraduate graduate and professional education and to a lesser extent continuing education and study abroad programs. First Marblehead also provides marketing and processing services. In response to deteriorating economic conditions and upheaval in the private student loan industry First Marblehead has adapted its business model to focus on providing outsourced fee-based services such as tuition planning portfolio management and asset servicing.

	Annual Growth	06/11	06/12	06/13	06/14	06/15
Sales ($ mil.)	(39.6%)	345.9	40.7	46.0	44.2	46.2
Net income ($ mil.)	–	(221.6)	1,102.2	(50.2)	(37.6)	(47.8)
Market value ($ mil.)	34.3%	20.4	13.5	13.6	60.6	66.4
Employees	(6.2%)	339	306	302	294	262

FIRST MARINER BANCORP.
OTC: FMAR Q

1501 South Clinton Street
Baltimore, MD 21224
Phone: 410 342-2600
Fax: 410 563-1594
Web: www.1stmarinerbank.com

CEO: –
CFO: –
HR: –
FYE: December 31
Type: Public

First Mariner Bancorp helps customers navigate banking seas (and fees). It's the holding company for First Mariner Bank which operates more than 20 branches along the Baltimore/Washington DC corridor. Serving retail and business clients the bank offers standard deposit products such as checking savings and money market accounts. Lending activities consist of commercial mortgages as well as consumer residential construction and mortgage and business loans. More than 95% of First Mariner's loans are secured by real estate. Subsidiary First Mariner Mortgage which has more than a dozen offices in Delaware North Carolina Maryland and Virginia originates mortgages for sale into the secondary market.

	Annual Growth	12/08	12/09	12/10	12/11	12/12
Assets ($ mil.)	1.3%	1,307.5	1,384.6	1,309.6	1,179.0	1,377.5
Net income ($ mil.)	–	–	(15.1)	(22.3)	(46.6)	(30.2)	16.1
Market value ($ mil.)	8.0%	13.6	17.9	8.3	3.0	18.5
Employees	(14.4%)	1,100	1,100	700	503	590

FIRST MERCHANTS CORP
NMS: FRME

200 East Jackson Street
Muncie, IN 47305-2814
Phone: 765 747-1500
Fax: –
Web: www.firstmerchants.com

CEO: Mark Hardwick
CFO: Michele Kawiecki
HR: Steven Harris
FYE: December 31
Type: Public

First Merchants is the holding company that owns First Merchants Bank which operates some 120 branches in Indiana Illinois and western Ohio. Through its Lafayette Bank & Trust and First Merchants Private Wealth Advisors divisions the bank provides standard consumer and commercial banking services including checking and savings accounts CDs check cards and consumer commercial agricultural and real estate mortgage loans. First Merchants also provides trust and asset management services. Founded in 1982 First Merchants has nearly $9.4 billion worth of consolidated assets.

	Annual Growth	12/16	12/17	12/18	12/19	12/20
Assets ($ mil.)	18.2%	7,211.6	9,367.5	9,884.7	12,457.3	14,067.2
Net income ($ mil.)	16.4%	81.1	96.1	159.1	164.5	148.6
Market value ($ mil.)	(0.2%)	2,030.2	2,268.0	1,847.9	2,242.6	2,017.2
Employees	7.1%	1,449	1,684	1,702	1,891	1,907

FIRST MID BANCSHARES INC
NMS: FMBH

1421 Charleston Avenue
Mattoon, IL 61938
Phone: 217 234-7454
Fax: 217 258-0485
Web: www.firstmid.com

CEO: Joseph Dively
CFO: Matthew Smith
HR: Rhonda Gatons
FYE: December 31
Type: Public

Money doesn't grow on trees so when farmers in Illinois need a little cash they turn to First Mid-Illinois Bank & Trust. The primary subsidiary of First Mid-Illinois Bancshares is a major supplier of farm credit (including real estate machinery and production loans; inventory financing; and lines of credit) in its market area. In addition to agricultural loans the bank offers commercial consumer and real estate lending. It also provides deposit products such as savings and checking accounts plus trust and investment services through a partnership with Raymond James. First Mid-Illinois Bank & Trust has about 40 branches.Other subsidiaries provide data processing services and insurance products and services.

	Annual Growth	12/16	12/17	12/18	12/19	12/20
Assets ($ mil.)	13.1%	2,884.5	2,841.5	3,839.7	3,839.4	4,726.3
Net income ($ mil.)	20.0%	21.8	26.7	36.6	47.9	45.3
Market value ($ mil.)	(0.3%)	569.2	645.2	534.4	590.1	563.5
Employees	8.3%	598	592	818	827	824

FIRST MIDWEST BANCORP, INC. (NAPERVILLE, IL)
NMS: FMBI

8750 West Bryn Mawr Avenue, Suite 1300
Chicago, IL 60631-3655
Phone: 708 831-7483
Fax: –
Web: www.firstmidwest.com

CEO: Michael L Scudder
CFO: Patrick Barrett
HR: –
FYE: December 31
Type: Public

There's a lot of cabbage in corn country. Just ask First Midwest Bancorp the holding company for First Midwest Bank. Through nearly 110 branches the bank mainly serves suburban Chicago though its market extends into central and western Illinois and neighboring portions of Iowa and Indiana. Focusing on area small to midsized businesses it offers deposit products loans trust services wealth management insurance and retirement plan services; it has $7.2 billion of client trust and investment assets under management. Commercial real estate loans account for more than half of the company's portfolio.

	Annual Growth	12/15	12/16	12/17	12/18	12/19
Assets ($ mil.)	16.4%	9,732.7	11,422.6	14,077.1	15,505.6	17,850.4
Net income ($ mil.)	24.9%	82.1	92.3	98.4	157.9	199.7
Market value ($ mil.)	5.8%	2,026.8	2,774.6	2,640.4	2,178.5	2,536.0
Employees	4.3%	1,790	1,882	2,152	2,046	2,122

FIRST NATIONAL BANK ALASKA
NBB: FBAK

101 West 36th Avenue, P.O. Box 100720
Anchorage, AK 99510-0720
Phone: 907 777-4362
Fax: 907 265-3528
Web: www.fnbalaska.com

CEO: Betsy Lawer
CFO: Michele Schuh
HR: –
FYE: December 31
Type: Public

First National Bank Alaska is a financial anchor in Anchorage. Founded in 1922 the bank is one of the state's oldest and largest financial institutions. With about 30 branches throughout The Last Frontier (and about 20 ATMs in rural communities) the bank offers traditional deposit products such as checking and savings accounts CDs and IRAs as well as loans and mortgages credit and debit cards and trust and investment management services. The family of longtime president Daniel Cuddy owns a majority of First National Bank Alaska; he took the helm of the bank in 1951.

	Annual Growth	12/16	12/17	12/18	12/19	12/20
Assets ($ mil.)	6.8%	3,609.8	3,653.1	3,753.5	3,808.3	4,695.3
Net income ($ mil.)	8.6%	41.4	36.4	54.1	55.6	57.5
Market value ($ mil.)	(42.9%)	5,542.0	6,539.6	798.1	769.6	588.7
Employees	–	–	–	–	–	–

FIRST NATIONAL CORP. (STRASBURG, VA)
NAS: FXNC

112 West King Street
Strasburg, VA 22657
Phone: 540 465-9121
Fax: –
Web: www.fbvirginia.com

CEO: Scott Harvard
CFO: Michael Bell
HR: –
FYE: December 31
Type: Public

First National Corporation knows that being number one is always good. The financial institution is the holding company for First Bank which has about a dozen branches in northern Virginia's Shenandoah Valley. The bank provides community-oriented deposit products and services including checking and savings accounts IRAs money market accounts CDs and NOW accounts. Mortgages account for about 60% of the company's loan portfolio; it also provides business construction and consumer loans. Additionally First Bank provides trust and asset management services.

	Annual Growth	12/16	12/17	12/18	12/19	12/20
Assets ($ mil.)	7.4%	716.0	739.1	753.0	800.0	950.9
Net income ($ mil.)	10.7%	5.9	6.4	10.1	9.6	8.9
Market value ($ mil.)	7.1%	62.5	87.5	94.3	104.0	82.1
Employees	(0.5%)	153	160	160	154	150

FIRST NATIONAL OF NEBRASKA, INC.
NBB: FINN

1620 Dodge Street
Omaha, NE 68197
Phone: 402 341-0500
Fax: –
Web: www.fnni.com

CEO: –
CFO: Michael A Summers
HR: –
FYE: December 31
Type: Public

First National of Nebraska is a multi-state holding company headquartered in the heart of downtown Omaha. The First National Bank of Omaha a subsidiary of First National of Nebraska has set the standard for outstanding customer service coupled with some of the most innovative financial products in the industry. Altogether the company has around 95 banking locations in seven states. It has some $23 billion in assets and nearly 5000 employee associates and was founded in 1857.

	Annual Growth	12/15	12/16	12/18	12/19	12/20
Assets ($ mil.)	6.2%	18,346.7	19,046.2	–	22,623.7	24,817.4
Net income ($ mil.)	8.1%	200.8	217.5	280.1	292.9	296.1
Market value ($ mil.)	10.8%	1,875.1	1,934.1	2,320.4	3,004.4	3,135.9
Employees	2.0%	4,757	4,851	–	–	–

FIRST NBC BANK HOLDING CO.
NMS: FNBC

210 Baronne Street
New Orleans, LA 70112
Phone: 504 566-8000
Fax: –

CEO: Carl J Chaney
CFO: Albert J Richard III
HR: –
FYE: December 31
Type: Public

First NBC Holding Company is a relatively new kid in the Old South. The bank holding company was created in 2006 to help revive New Orleans after Hurricane Katrina. First NBC Holding Company operates through subsidiary First NBC Bank which has about 40 branches in New Orleans the Mississippi Gulf Coast and the Florida panhandle. Beyond deposit accounts for individuals and businesses the bank offers low-risk SBA and US Dept. of Agriculture loans to borrowers who may not otherwise qualify for lending services. Commercial and consumer real estate mortgages make up 50% of its loan portfolio while commercial loans make up another 35%. First NBC also offers construction loans and consumer mortgages. It went public in 2013.

	Annual Growth	12/11	12/12	12/13	12/14	12/15
Assets ($ mil.)	20.7%	2,216.5	2,670.9	3,286.6	3,750.6	4,705.8
Net income ($ mil.)	–	19.4	28.9	40.9	55.6	(25.2)
Market value ($ mil.)	7.6%	–	–	616.2	671.5	713.3
Employees	9.3%	–	433	494	486	565

FIRST NIAGARA FINANCIAL GROUP, INC.
NMS: FNFG

726 Exchange Street, Suite 618
Buffalo, NY 14210
Phone: 716 819-5500
Fax: –
Web: www.firstniagara.com

CEO: –
CFO: –
HR: –
FYE: December 31
Type: Public

A lot of water and a few barrels have gone over Niagara Falls since First Niagara Bank was founded. Tracing its roots to 1870 the flagship subsidiary of acquisitive First Niagara Financial operates nearly 400 branches in upstate New York Connecticut Massachusetts and Pennsylvania. Boasting $39 billion in assets the bank offers financial services like deposits loans insurance investments and wealth management. Commercial real estate loans business loans and residential mortgages account for most of the bank's loan portfolio. Subsidiary First Niagara Risk Management offers insurance risk management and claims investigations. KeyCorp agreed to acquire the bank in 2015.

	Annual Growth	12/11	12/12	12/13	12/14	12/15
Assets ($ mil.)	5.0%	32,810.6	36,806.2	37,628.0	38,551.0	39,918.0
Net income ($ mil.)	6.5%	173.9	168.4	295.0	(715.0)	224.0
Market value ($ mil.)	5.9%	3,061.6	2,813.3	3,767.6	2,990.6	3,849.2
Employees	3.0%	4,827	5,927	5,807	5,572	5,428

FIRST NILES FINANCIAL INC.
NBB: FNFP A

55 North Main Street
Niles, OH 44446
Phone: 330 652-2539
Fax: 330 652-0911

CEO: William Stephens
CFO: –
HR: –
FYE: December 31
Type: Public

First Niles ain't a river in Egypt. It is the holding company for Home Federal Savings and Loan Association of Niles a one-branch thrift serving its namesake town in northeastern Ohio. Founded in 1897 the association offers a variety of deposit products including checking savings money market and NOW accounts and CDs. With these funds Home Federal primarily originates residential mortgages which account for approximately 70% of its loan portfolio. The thrift also originates commercial mortgages construction and development loans and consumer loans.

	Annual Growth	12/14	12/15	12/18	12/19	12/20
Assets ($ mil.)	2.2%	96.4	98.5	99.1	100.1	109.7
Net income ($ mil.)	5.0%	0.2	0.2	0.2	0.4	0.3
Market value ($ mil.)	1.5%	10.5	10.0	7.8	9.5	11.5
Employees	–	–	–	–	–	–

FIRST NORTHERN COMMUNITY BANCORP
NBB: FNRN

195 N. First Street
Dixon, CA 95620
Phone: 707 678-3041
Fax: –
Web: www.thatsmybank.com

CEO: Louise Walker
CFO: Kevin Spink
HR: –
FYE: December 31
Type: Public

First Northern Community Bancorp is the holding company for First Northern Bank which operates about 10 branches in the northern California counties of El Dorado Placer Sacramento Solano and Yolo. Founded in 1910 the bank offers community-oriented services such as checking savings and money market accounts and certificates of deposit. It also offers electronic check depositing. Its loan products include real estate mortgages (which account for about half of the bank's portfolio) commercial and construction loans and agricultural and installment loans. Investment products and services are available to customers via a pact with Raymond James Financial.

	Annual Growth	12/16	12/17	12/18	12/19	12/20
Assets ($ mil.)	9.1%	1,166.8	1,217.7	1,249.8	1,292.6	1,655.4
Net income ($ mil.)	10.9%	8.1	8.7	12.6	14.7	12.2
Market value ($ mil.)	1.3%	130.9	181.3	151.9	156.8	137.7
Employees	3.7%	185	191	201	214	214

FIRST OF LONG ISLAND CORP
NAS: FLIC

10 Glen Head Road
Glen Head, NY 11545
Phone: 516 671-4900
Fax: –
Web: www.fnbli.com

CEO: Christopher Becker
CFO: Jay Mcconie
HR: –
FYE: December 31
Type: Public

When it comes to banking The First of Long Island wants to be the first thing on Long Islanders' minds. The company owns The First National Bank of Long Island which offers a variety of lending investment and deposit services through around 45 commercial and retail branches on New York's Long Island and the boroughs of Manhattan and Queens. Residential and Commercial Mortgages (particularly tied to multifamily properties) make up more than 90% of the bank's loan portfolio though the bank also writes revolving home equity business and consumer loans. Its two bank subsidiaries include insurance agency The First of Long Island Agency and investment firm FNY Service.

	Annual Growth	12/16	12/17	12/18	12/19	12/20
Assets ($ mil.)	3.8%	3,510.3	3,894.7	4,241.1	4,097.8	4,069.1
Net income ($ mil.)	7.5%	30.9	35.1	41.6	41.6	41.2
Market value ($ mil.)	(11.1%)	679.2	678.0	474.6	596.7	424.7
Employees	2.8%	314	333	344	341	350

FIRST PHYSICIANS CAPITAL GROUP INC
NBB: FPCG D

433 North Camden Drive #810
Beverly Hills, CA 90210
Phone: 310 860-2501
Fax: –
Web: www.firstphysicianscapitalgroup.com

CEO: Sean Kirrane
CFO: Adrian Reeder
HR: –
FYE: September 30
Type: Public

First Physicians Capital Group (formerly Tri-Isthmus Group or TIGroup) is an investment and financing firm with an eye toward the health care industry. The group invests in and manages health care facilities primarily rural critical access hospitals and ambulatory surgical centers. It owns or holds stakes in about a half-dozen medical facilities in Southern California and Oklahoma. In 2009 First Physicians Capital signed a letter of intent to acquire the assets of a hospital in southeastern Texas and to develop a new community hospital in the region. Oklahoma-based investor Carol Schuster owns more than 40% of the company's common stock. Director David Hirschhorn holds about 20%.

	Annual Growth	09/09	09/10	09/11	09/12	09/13
Sales ($ mil.)	(16.1%)	39.1	39.5	6.7	16.2	19.4
Net income ($ mil.)	–	(10.1)	(9.5)	(0.5)	5.6	5.8
Market value ($ mil.)	–	0.0	0.0	0.0	0.0	0.0
Employees	(19.6%)	424	4	174	174	177

FIRST POTOMAC REALTY TRUST
NYS: FPO

7600 Wisconsin Avenue, 11th Floor
Bethesda, MD 20814
Phone: 301 986-9200
Fax: –
Web: www.first-potomac.com

CEO: –
CFO: –
HR: –
FYE: December 31
Type: Public

First Potomac Realty Trust is a self-managed real estate investment trust (REIT) whose largest tenants are the US government and government contracts. The company that acquires owns and manages a $1.6 billion portfolio of more than 130 single- and multi-tenant office and business park properties spanning some 8 million square feet of rentable space across the mid-Atlantic region in Washington DC Maryland and Virginia. More than 60% of the REIT's rental income comes from its office properties while the rest comes from its business park and industrial properties.

	Annual Growth	12/11	12/12	12/13	12/14	12/15
Sales ($ mil.)	0.1%	172.3	193.3	156.6	161.7	172.8
Net income ($ mil.)	–	(8.1)	(7.4)	11.1	16.8	(33.0)
Market value ($ mil.)	(3.3%)	753.2	713.4	671.3	713.4	658.0
Employees	(4.7%)	176	184	189	170	145

FIRST REPUBLIC BANK (SAN FRANCISCO, CA)
NYS: FRC

111 Pine Street, 2nd Floor
San Francisco, CA 94111
Phone: 415 392-1400
Fax: –
Web: www.firstrepublic.com

CEO: Michael Roffler
CFO: Olga Tsokova
HR: –
FYE: December 31
Type: Public

Founded in 1985 First Republic Bank offers private banking real estate lending wealth management trust and custody services for businesses and high-net-worth clients through more than 90 offices. Its main geographic focus is on urban markets such as San Francisco Los Angeles New York Portland and San Diego among others. The company generates most of its revenue from commercial banking operations. It also offers investment advice and brokerage and trust services through its wealth management division. First Republic Bank has around $142 billion of assets under management.

	Annual Growth	12/16	12/17	12/18	12/19	12/20
Assets ($ mil.)	18.1%	73,277.8	87,780.5	99,205.2	116,263.6	142,502.1
Net income ($ mil.)	12.1%	673.4	757.7	853.8	930.3	1,064.2
Market value ($ mil.)	12.4%	16,043.8	15,086.1	15,131.4	20,450.8	25,584.0
Employees	11.4%	3,566	4,025	4,480	4,812	5,483

FIRST ROBINSON FINANCIAL CORP.
NBB: FRFC

501 East Main Street
Robinson, IL 62454
Phone: 618 544-8621
Fax: 618 544-7506
Web: www.frsb.net

CEO: Richard Catt
CFO: Jamie McReynolds
HR: –
FYE: March 31
Type: Public

If heaven holds a place for those who pay hey hey hey then here's to you First Robinson! First Robinson Financial is the holding company for First Robinson Savings Bank which provides traditional banking services to individuals and businesses through four locations in eastern Illinois' Crawford County. In 2008 the bank opened a division in Vincennes Indiana called First Vincennes Savings Bank. The banks' services include savings checking and NOW accounts; IRAs; and CDs. They use funds from deposits primarily to originate one- to four-family real estate loans (accounting for about half of the company's loan portfolio) and to a lesser extent consumer business agricultural and municipal loans.

	Annual Growth	03/17	03/18	03/19	03/20	03/21
Assets ($ mil.)	8.4%	307.5	319.2	336.8	344.8	425.1
Net income ($ mil.)	6.7%	2.0	1.9	2.3	3.3	2.6
Market value ($ mil.)	4.9%	23.0	24.4	37.1	30.5	27.8
Employees	(0.3%)	76	81	81	80	75

FIRST SAVINGS FINANCIAL GROUP INC   NAS: FSFG

702 North Shore Drive, Suite 300
Jeffersonville, IN 47130
Phone: 812 283-0724
Fax: –
Web: www.fsbbank.net

CEO: Larry Myers
CFO: Anthony Schoen
HR: –
FYE: September 30
Type: Public

First Savings Financial Group was formed in 2008 to be the holding company for First Savings Bank a community bank serving consumers and small businesses in southern Indiana. Through more than a dozen branches the bank offers standard deposit services like savings checking and retirement accounts as well as a variety of lending services. One- to four- family residential loans make up about 60% of First Savings Bank's loan portfolio; other loans in the bank's portfolio include commercial real estate construction consumer and commercial business. In 2012 First Savings Financial expanded its footprint by acquiring the four Indiana branches of First Financial Service Corporation.

	Annual Growth	09/17	09/18	09/19	09/20	09/21
Assets ($ mil.)	17.9%	891.1	1,034.4	1,222.6	1,764.6	1,720.5
Net income ($ mil.)	33.5%	9.3	10.9	16.2	33.4	29.6
Market value ($ mil.)	(14.9%)	380.5	486.6	450.5	387.2	199.2
Employees	30.9%	201	364	473	696	590

FIRST SECURITY GROUP INC   NAS: FSGI

531 Broad Street
Chattanooga, TN 37402
Phone: 423 266-2000
Fax: –
Web: www.fsgbank.com

CEO: –
CFO: –
HR: –
FYE: December 31
Type: Public

Pardon me boy as Glenn Miller would say but if you've got your fare and a trifle to spare you might want to turn to First Security Group. The holding company for FSGBank operates about 40 branches in eastern and middle Tennessee (including Chattanooga) and northern Georgia; in addition to the FSGBank brand the company also operates certain locations under the Dalton Whitfield Bank Jackson Bank & Trust and Primer Banco Seguro names. The bank offers standard deposit and lending services including checking and savings accounts and CDs. Real estate loans and mortgages make up about three-quarters of First Security's loan portfolio which also includes business agricultural and consumer loans.

	Annual Growth	12/09	12/10	12/11	12/12	12/13
Assets ($ mil.)	(7.8%)	1,353.8	1,168.5	1,114.9	1,063.6	977.6
Net income ($ mil.)	–	(33.0)	(44.3)	(23.1)	(37.6)	(13.4)
Market value ($ mil.)	(0.8%)	158.5	59.9	156.5	148.5	153.2
Employees	(5.1%)	356	316	306	333	289

FIRST SOLAR INC   NMS: FSLR

350 West Washington Street, Suite 600
Tempe, AZ 85281
Phone: 602 414-9300
Fax: 602 414-9400
Web: www.firstsolar.com

CEO: Mark Widmar
CFO: Alexander Bradley
HR: –
FYE: December 31
Type: Public

First Solar one of the top solar energy companies in the world designs manufactures and sells photovoltaic (PV) solar modules with an advanced thin film semiconductor technology. Additionally the company provides operations and maintenance ("O&M") services to system owners. The company is currently focusing on markets including those listed below in which its cadmium (CdTe) solar modules provide certain advantages over conventional crystalline silicon solar modules including high insolation climates in which its modules provide a superior temperature coefficient humid environments in which its modules provide a superior spectral response and markets that favor the superior sustainability profile of its PV solar technology. The company generates about 70% of sales in the US.

	Annual Growth	12/16	12/17	12/18	12/19	12/20
Sales ($ mil.)	(2.1%)	2,951.3	2,941.3	2,244.0	3,063.1	2,711.3
Net income ($ mil.)	–	(358.0)	(165.6)	144.3	(114.9)	398.4
Market value ($ mil.)	32.5%	3,400.9	7,155.8	4,499.4	5,930.7	10,483.6
Employees	(1.4%)	5,400	4,100	6,400	6,600	5,100

FIRST SOUTH BANCORP INC (VA)   NMS: FSBK

1311 Carolina Avenue
Washington, NC 27889
Phone: 252 946-4178
Fax: –
Web: www.firstsouthnc.com

CEO: Bruce W Elder
CFO: Scott C McLean
HR: –
FYE: December 31
Type: Public

First South Bancorp (not to be confused with the South Carolina company of the same name) is the holding company for First South Bank. Founded in 1902 the bank has about 30 offices throughout the eastern half of North Carolina. Its deposit products include checking savings and money market accounts; CDs; and IRAs; funds generated are mainly used to fund a variety of loans. Commercial mortgages comprise more than half of the bank's loan portfolio which is rounded out by construction loans residential mortgages home equity loans and business and consumer loans. Retail investment services are offered through an alliance with UVEST; bank subsidiary First South Leasing provides equipment lease financing.

	Annual Growth	12/11	12/12	12/13	12/14	12/15
Assets ($ mil.)	6.1%	746.9	707.7	674.7	885.9	946.3
Net income ($ mil.)	31.8%	1.6	(11.0)	6.0	3.9	4.7
Market value ($ mil.)	27.8%	30.4	45.4	74.0	75.5	81.1
Employees	4.1%	267	255	261	328	313

FIRST TECH FEDERAL CREDIT UNION

3408 Hillview Ave.
Palo Alto CA 94304
Phone: 855-855-8805
Fax: 503-672-3801
Web: www.firsttechfed.com

CEO: –
CFO: –
HR: –
FYE: December 31
Type: Private - Not-for-Pr

First Tech Federal Credit Union provides deposit lending and investment services to some 350000 members through about 40 branches; most are in California Colorado Oregon and Washington with single branches in Georgia Idaho Massachusetts Texas and Puerto Rico. Its products include checking and savings accounts CDs IRAs and credit cards as well as home vehicle and personal loans. The credit union also offers insurance investment accounts and brokerage services. Membership in First Tech is open to employees of hundreds of sponsor companies most of them tech firms as well as those who work for the state of Oregon or live or work in Lane County Oregon.

FIRST UNITED CORPORATION (MD)   NMS: FUNC

19 South Second Street
Oakland, MD 21550-0009
Phone: 800 470-4356
Fax: 301 334-8351
Web: www.mybank.com

CEO: Carissa Rodeheaver
CFO: Tonya Sturm
HR: –
FYE: December 31
Type: Public

First United is the holding company for First United Bank & Trust and other financial services subsidiaries. Founded in 1900 the bank operates about 25 branches in the panhandles of western Maryland and eastern West Virginia as well as the Morgantown West Virginia area. The bank provides standard services such as checking and savings accounts money market accounts and CDs as well as retirement and trust services. Commercial loans make up the largest portion of the company's loan portfolio (more than 45%) followed by real estate mortgages (more than 35%) consumer installment loans and construction loans.

	Annual Growth	12/16	12/17	12/18	12/19	12/20
Assets ($ mil.)	7.1%	1,318.2	1,340.8	1,384.5	1,442.0	1,733.4
Net income ($ mil.)	17.4%	7.3	5.3	10.7	13.1	13.8
Market value ($ mil.)	(0.7%)	111.5	121.7	111.3	168.5	108.4
Employees	(2.7%)	356	363	356	319	319

FIRST US BANCSHARES INC
NAS: FUSB

3291 U.S. Highway 280
Birmingham, AL 35243
Phone: 205 582-1200
Fax: –
Web: www.firstusbank.com

CEO: James House
CFO: Thomas Elley
HR: –
FYE: December 31
Type: Public

First US Bancshares (formerly United Security Bancshares) is the holding company for First US Bank (formerly First United Security Bank) which has about 20 locations in central and western Alabama and eastern Mississippi. It serves area consumers and businesses offering such standard retail services as savings checking and money market accounts as well as CDs and credit and check cards. Real estate mortgages make up more than 70% of the bank's loan portfolio which also includes business and consumer loans. Bank subsidiary Acceptance Loan Company primarily makes consumer loans through about two dozen offices in Alabama and Mississippi.

	Annual Growth	12/16	12/17	12/18	12/19	12/20
Assets ($ mil.)	10.1%	606.9	625.6	791.9	788.7	890.5
Net income ($ mil.)	21.9%	1.2	(0.4)	2.5	4.6	2.7
Market value ($ mil.)	(5.1%)	68.6	79.1	49.1	71.7	55.7
Employees	(7.6%)	259	249	270	280	189

FIRST WEST VIRGINIA BANCORP INC
NBB: FWVB

1701 Warwood Avenue
Wheeling, WV 26003
Phone: 304 277-1100
Fax: 304 218-2458
Web: www.progbank.com

CEO: –
CFO: –
HR: –
FYE: December 31
Type: Public

First West Virginia and then the world! First West Virginia Bancorp is the holding company for Progressive Bank which operates about ten branches in the upper Ohio River Valley of the Mountaineer State and neighboring parts of eastern Ohio. Targeting individuals and local businesses the bank offers standard retail products like checking and savings accounts certificates of deposit and individual retirement accounts. Lending activities consist primarily of commercial and residential real estate mortgages (which together account for approximately two-thirds of the company's loan portfolio) but Progressive Bank also originates business consumer and municipal loans.

	Annual Growth	12/12	12/13	12/14	12/15	12/16
Assets ($ mil.)	2.3%	306.5	342.1	332.4	345.4	335.3
Net income ($ mil.)	(10.7%)	2.5	2.2	1.9	2.4	1.6
Market value ($ mil.)	7.2%	25.4	29.1	34.9	30.1	33.5
Employees	0.5%	95	91	96	–	–

FIRSTBANK CORP. (MI)
NMS: FBMI

311 Woodworth Avenue
Alma, MI 48801
Phone: 989 463-3131
Fax: 989 466-2042
Web: www.firstbankmi.com

CEO: –
CFO: –
HR: –
FYE: December 31
Type: Public

Firstbank Corporation is the holding company for six separately chartered subsidiary banks offering services under the Firstbank banner; it also owns Keystone Community Bank which it acquired in 2005. Through more than 50 branches in Michigan's Lower Peninsula the banks attract deposits from area residents and businesses by providing standard services such as checking and savings accounts and CDs. The company also owns subsidiaries that provide real estate appraisal services armored car services and title insurance. Firstbank bought another Michigan-based bank holding company ICNB Financial parent of Ionia County Community Bank (now Firstbank - West Michigan) in 2007.

	Annual Growth	12/08	12/09	12/10	12/11	12/12
Assets ($ mil.)	1.3%	1,425.3	1,482.4	1,458.3	1,485.3	1,498.8
Net income ($ mil.)	95.6%	0.7	2.7	3.8	5.6	10.5
Market value ($ mil.)	7.3%	64.5	67.4	46.9	41.0	85.5
Employees	(2.6%)	483	466	435	435	435

FIRSTCASH HOLDINGS INC
NMS: FCFS

1600 West 7th Street
Fort Worth, TX 76102
Phone: 817 335-1100
Fax: –
Web: www.firstcash.com

CEO: Rick Wessel
CFO: R. Douglas Orr
HR: –
FYE: December 31
Type: Public

Formed in 1988 FirstCash operates almost 2750 pawnshops and cash advance stores in the US Colombia Mexico El Salvador and Guatemala. The company lends money secured by such personal property as jewelry electronics tools sporting goods and musical equipment. The company also melts certain quantities of non-retailable scrap jewelry and sells the gold silver and diamonds in the commodity markets. Pawn stores provide a quick and convenient source of small secured consumer loans also known as pawn loans to unbanked under-banked and credit-challenged customers. Pawn loans are safe and affordable non-recourse loans for which the customer has no legal obligation to repay. The US operations generate about 65% of total revenue.

	Annual Growth	12/16	12/17	12/18	12/19	12/20
Sales ($ mil.)	10.6%	1,088.4	1,779.8	1,780.9	1,864.4	1,631.3
Net income ($ mil.)	15.4%	60.1	143.9	153.2	164.6	106.6
Market value ($ mil.)	10.5%	1,928.8	2,768.0	2,969.1	3,308.9	2,874.3
Employees	1.2%	16,200	17,000	19,000	21,000	17,000

FIRSTENERGY CORP
NYS: FE

76 South Main Street
Akron, OH 44308
Phone: 800 736-3402
Fax: –
Web: www.firstenergycorp.com

CEO: Steven Strah
CFO: K. Jon Taylor
HR: –
FYE: December 31
Type: Public

FirstEnergy's first goal is to generate and deliver power but its second goal is to stay profitable in a market undergoing deregulation. Its ten utilities provide electricity to 6 million customers in the Midwest and the Mid-Atlantic. FirstEnergy controls approximately 3790 megawatts from regulated scrubbed coal and hydro facilities in West Virginia New Jersey and Virginia. Stretching from the Ohio-Indiana border to the New Jersey shore the companies operate a vast infrastructure of more than 269000 miles of distribution lines and are dedicated to providing customers with safe reliable and responsive service.

	Annual Growth	12/17	12/18	12/19	12/20	12/21
Sales ($ mil.)	(5.6%)	14,017.0	11,261.0	11,035.0	10,790.0	11,132.0
Net income ($ mil.)	–	(1,724.0)	1,348.0	912.0	1,079.0	1,283.0
Market value ($ mil.)	8.0%	17,461.4	21,413.3	27,714.7	17,455.7	23,717.2
Employees	(5.6%)	15,617	12,494	12,316	12,153	12,395

FIRSTFLEET, INC.

202 HERITAGE PARK DR
MURFREESBORO, TN 371291556
Phone: 615-890-9229
Fax: –
Web: www.firstfleetinc.com

CEO: –
CFO: –
HR: –
FYE: March 31
Type: Private

FirstFleet helps its customers move their freight — not just by the truckload but by providing fleets of trucks. The company offers dedicated contract carriage in which it supplies its customers with tractors and trailers and the drivers to operate them. In addition FirstFleet provides related fleet management logistics and maintenance services. The company operates a fleet of about 1450 trucks and tractors from facilities in some 30 states in the US and it provides transportation services throughout the 48 contiguous states and in Canada and Mexico. FirstFleet began operations in 1986.

	Annual Growth	03/07	03/08	03/09	03/10	03/12
Sales ($ mil.)	0.1%	–	288.1	274.6	259.4	288.7
Net income ($ mil.)	20.3%	–	1.3	0.1	0.5	2.8
Market value ($ mil.)	–	–	–	–	–	–
Employees	–	–	–	–	–	2,000

FIRSTHEALTH OF THE CAROLINAS, INC.

155 MEMORIAL DR
PINEHURST, NC 283748710
Phone: 910-715-1000
Fax: −
Web: www.firsthealth.org

CEO: Mickey Foster
CFO: Lynn De Jaco
HR: −
FYE: September 30
Type: Private

FirstHealth of the Carolinas maintains a health care network that extends to 15 counties across the mid-Carolinas. The health network includes four hospitals — Moore Regional Richmond Memorial Moore Regional - Hoke and Montgomery Memorial — that provide emergency surgical acute care and diagnostic services and have a combined capacity of more than 580 beds. Moore Regional its largest hospital includes an inpatient rehabilitation center and a heart hospital. FirstHealth of the Carolinas also operates satellite facilities including family practice clinics fitness centers and dental practices. The system's FirstCarolinaCare provides home health and hospice services emergency care medical transportation and health insurance.

	Annual Growth	09/16	09/17	09/18	09/19	09/20
Sales ($ mil.)	1.1%	−	744.2	747.2	793.3	768.7
Net income ($ mil.)	6.3%	−	82.0	43.9	35.9	98.6
Market value ($ mil.)	−	−	−	−	−	−
Employees	−	−	−	−	−	3,897

FIRSTMERIT CORP
NMS: FMER

111 Cascade Plaza, 7th Floor
Akron, OH 44308
Phone: 330 996-6000
Fax: −
Web: www.firstmerit.com

CEO: −
CFO: −
HR: −
FYE: December 31
Type: Public

FirstMerit Corporation is the holding company for FirstMerit Bank which provides retail and commercial banking services through more than 360 branches in five US states primarily in the Midwest. Serving local consumers and small to midsized businesses the bank provides standard services such as deposit accounts credit and debit cards and loans as well as wealth management and trust services. Subsidiaries offer investment and brokerage services financial planning commercial lease financing life and title insurance annuities and mortgage servicing. Huntington Bancshares agreed to buy FirstMerit for $3.4 billion in January 2016.

	Annual Growth	12/10	12/11	12/12	12/13	12/14
Assets ($ mil.)	15.2%	14,136.9	14,441.7	14,913.0	23,909.0	24,902.3
Net income ($ mil.)	23.3%	102.9	119.6	134.1	183.7	238.0
Market value ($ mil.)	(1.2%)	3,273.1	2,502.4	2,346.9	3,676.6	3,124.2
Employees	9.6%	3,058	3,177	2,836	4,570	4,419

FISERV INC
NMS: FISV

255 Fiserv Drive
Brookfield, WI 53045
Phone: 262 879-5000
Fax: 262 879-5013
Web: www.fiserv.com

CEO: Frank Bisignano
CFO: Robert Hau
HR: −
FYE: December 31
Type: Public

Fiserv Inc. is a leading global provider of payments and financial services technology solutions. The company provides account processing and digital banking solutions; card issuer processing and network services; payments; e-commerce; merchant acquiring and processing; and the Clover cloud-based point-of-sale (POS) solution. Through its Fiserv Clearing Network the company provides check clearing and image exchange services. Fiserv serves customers of all sizes including banks credit unions other financial institutions and merchants across US and Canada; Europe Middle East and Africa; Latin America; and Asia Pacific.

	Annual Growth	12/16	12/17	12/18	12/19	12/20
Sales ($ mil.)	28.2%	5,505.0	5,696.0	5,823.0	10,187.0	14,852.0
Net income ($ mil.)	0.7%	930.0	1,246.0	1,187.0	893.0	958.0
Market value ($ mil.)	1.7%	71,111.9	87,739.1	49,172.2	77,368.0	76,183.7
Employees	17.6%	23,000	24,000	24,000	44,000	44,000

FISKARS BRANDS INC.

2537 Daniels St.
Madison WI 53718
Phone: 608-259-1649
Fax: 608-294-4790
Web: www2.fiskars.com

CEO: Kari Kauniskangas
CFO: −
HR: Sutton Holcomb
FYE: December 31
Type: Subsidiary

Fiskars Brands is fairly frisky in its old age. The company is the North American manufacturing and marketing subsidiary of Finland's Fiskars Corporation — the second-oldest incorporated business in the world having celebrated some 360 anniversaries. Orange-handled scissors are a signature item for consumers but Fiskars Brands' namesake line also includes garden tools (such as pruners reel mowers and axes) craft tools (hand drills punches) school and office supplies (child-sized scissors rulers and trimmers). It also makes ergonomic cutting tools for the garden as part of its PowerGear line scissors and shears for sewing and quilting under the Gingher name and outdoor cutting tools by Gerber.

FIVE BELOW INC
NMS: FIVE

701 Market Street, Suite 300
Philadelphia, PA 19106
Phone: 215 546-7909
Fax: −
Web: www.fivebelow.com

CEO: Joel Anderson
CFO: Kenneth Bull
HR: −
FYE: January 30
Type: Public

Five Below may be growing as quickly as its youthful clientele. Operating a fast-growing chain of specialty retail stores it sells a broad range of trend-right products all priced under $5. The company which targets teen and pre-teen girls and boys operates approximately 900 stores in shopping centers in some three dozen US states; it also operates an e-commerce site. Core merchandise includes fun but inexpensive items meant to entice teens such as jewelry and accessories novelty T-shirts novelty socks sports gear decor and crafts and mobile phone accessories. Five Below was founded in 2002.

	Annual Growth	01/17*	02/18	02/19	02/20*	01/21
Sales ($ mil.)	18.3%	1,000.4	1,278.2	1,559.6	1,846.7	1,962.1
Net income ($ mil.)	14.5%	71.8	102.5	149.6	175.1	123.4
Market value ($ mil.)	47.0%	2,103.2	3,520.6	6,976.8	6,333.0	9,829.5
Employees	18.9%	9,500	12,100	13,900	16,600	19,000

*Fiscal year change

FIVE PRIME THERAPEUTICS, INC
NMS: FPRX

111 Oyster Point Boulevard
South San Francisco, CA 94080
Phone: 415 365-5600
Fax: −
Web: www.fiveprime.com

CEO: Thomas Civik
CFO: David V Smith
HR: −
FYE: December 31
Type: Public

Five Prime Therapeutics is counting down the ways to fight cancer. The clinical-stage biotech which has an emphasis on immuno-oncology is developing drugs that use protein therapy to block the disease process in cancer. It has a handful of candidates in development or pre-development including the collaboration with China's Zai Lab to develop and commercialize bemarituzumab for the treatment of stomach and bladder cancer. The company also has clinical trial candidate FPA150 an antibody that targets to treat patients with cancers and also FPT155 a soluble CD80 fusion protein that enhances co-stimulation of T cells through CD28 currently in a clinical trial in multiple cancers.

	Annual Growth	12/15	12/16	12/17	12/18	12/19
Sales ($ mil.)	(55.5%)	379.8	30.7	39.5	49.9	14.9
Net income ($ mil.)	−	249.6	(65.7)	(150.2)	(140.4)	(137.2)
Market value ($ mil.)	(42.3%)	1,461.6	1,764.9	772.0	327.5	161.7
Employees	(13.7%)	157	195	216	210	87

FIVE STAR COOPERATIVE

1949 N LINN AVE
NEW HAMPTON, IA 506599406
Phone: 641-394-3052
Fax: –
Web: www.fivestar.coop

CEO: –
CFO: Laura Schwickerath
HR: –
FYE: June 30
Type: Private

If Old MacDonald actually had a farm he'd want to be a member of the Five Star Cooperative. Operating in north-central and northeast Iowa Five Star has operations in more than 15 small to midsized towns in the Hawkeye State. The cooperative is divided into five divisions according to the products and services offered — agronomy petroleum (diesel fuel and home heating oil) feed (for beef cattle and swine) grain and hardware — it operates a True Value hardware store in New Hampton that offers all the usual hardware products and services. Established in 1916 Five Star Cooperative provides a full complement for its member/farmers.

	Annual Growth	06/10	06/11	06/12	06/13	06/14
Sales ($ mil.)	(1.1%)	–	376.2	479.1	427.1	364.1
Net income ($ mil.)	(14.6%)	–	–	9.8	8.1	7.1
Market value ($ mil.)	–	–	–	–	–	–
Employees	–	–	–	–	–	140

FLAGSTAFF MEDICAL CENTER, INC.

1200 N BEAVER ST
FLAGSTAFF, AZ 860013118
Phone: 928-779-3366
Fax: –
Web: www.nahealth.com

CEO: –
CFO: –
HR: –
FYE: June 30
Type: Private

Flagstaff Medical Center serves northern Arizona's residents and those who are just passing through. Founded in 1936 the not-for-profit hospital is part of the Northern Arizona Healthcare family. It has some 270 beds and its medical staff includes about 210 physicians. The hospital offers cancer heart sports medicine joint surgery and women and infants' centers. Other medical services include behavioral health audiology diabetes care home health hospice and ambulance and air flight transportation. In addition Flagstaff Medical Center provides training courses for health care professionals. The hospital's emergency department treats about 40000 patients each year.

	Annual Growth	06/07	06/08	06/09	06/15	06/16
Sales ($ mil.)	2.2%	–	–	358.2	389.9	415.9
Net income ($ mil.)	–	–	–	0.0	53.7	55.3
Market value ($ mil.)	–	–	–	–	–	–
Employees	–	–	–	–	–	2,000

FLAGSTAR BANCORP, INC.

5151 Corporate Drive
Troy, MI 48098-2639
Phone: 248 312-2000
Fax: –
Web: www.flagstar.com

NYS: FBC
CEO: Alessandro DiNello
CFO: James Ciroli
HR: –
FYE: December 31
Type: Public

Flagstar Bancorp is the holding company for Flagstar Bank which operates around 160 branches mostly in Michigan. Beyond offering traditional deposit and loan products Flagstar's mortgages originations specializes in originating purchasing and servicing one-to-four family residential mortgage loans across roughly 30 states through a network of brokers and correspondents. Around 80% of the Flagstar's revenue is linked to mortgage origination and servicing while another some 10% comes from its community banking business. Boasting $31.0 billion in assets Flagstar is 6th largest bank mortgage originator in the nation and the 6th largest sub-servicer of mortgage loans nationwide.

	Annual Growth	12/16	12/17	12/18	12/19	12/20
Assets ($ mil.)	21.9%	14,053.0	16,912.0	18,531.0	23,266.0	31,038.0
Net income ($ mil.)	33.2%	171.0	63.0	187.0	218.0	538.0
Market value ($ mil.)	10.9%	1,418.6	1,970.4	1,390.1	2,014.1	2,146.3
Employees	15.9%	2,886	3,525	3,938	4,453	5,214

FLANDERS CORPORATION

531 FLANDERS FILTER RD
WASHINGTON, NC 278897805
Phone: 252-946-8081
Fax: –
Web: www.aafintl.com

CEO: Peter Jones
CFO: Scott Brown
HR: –
FYE: December 31
Type: Private

This Flanders handles flecks fleas flies fluff and other airborne flotsam. The company makes air filters under such brand names as Air Seal Eco-Air and Precisionaire. Its products include high-efficiency particulate air (HEPA) filters used in industrial cleanrooms as well as standard residential and commercial heating ventilation and air-conditioning filters. Flanders makes most of its sales from aftermarket replacement filters that it sells directly to wholesalers distributors and retail outlets. Customers include the likes of Home Depot Texas Instruments and Wal-Mart. Japan-based air conditioner maker Daikin Industries agreed to buy Flanders for $434 million in February 2016.

	Annual Growth	12/05	12/06	12/07	12/08	12/09
Sales ($ mil.)	(48.4%)	–	–	836.2	217.3	222.4
Net income ($ mil.)	19624.4%	–	–	0.0	(4.1)	7.0
Market value ($ mil.)	–	–	–	–	–	–
Employees	–	–	–	–	–	2,911

FLANIGAN'S ENTERPRISES, INC.

5059 N.E. 18th Avenue
Fort Lauderdale, FL 33334
Phone: 954 377-1961
Fax: –

ASE: BDL
CEO: James Flanigan
CFO: Jeffrey Kastner
HR: –
FYE: October 02
Type: Public

Seafood and sauce are the catch of the day at Flanigan's Enterprises. The company operates and manages about 20 restaurants that do business as Flanigan's Seafood Bar and Grill along with a chain of eight package liquor stores called Big Daddy's Liquors. (Four properties have combination liquor store/restaurant operations.) Six of its restaurants are franchised and owned primarily by family members of company executives. All the company's lounges and liquor stores are located in Florida. In addition Flanigan's owns the Mardi Gras adult entertainment club in Atlanta which is operated by a third party. The family of former chairman and CEO Joseph "Big Daddy" Flanigan owns more than 50% of the company.

	Annual Growth	09/17	09/18	09/19*	10/20	10/21
Sales ($ mil.)	6.5%	106.8	113.5	116.2	113.0	137.3
Net income ($ mil.)	40.5%	3.0	3.7	3.6	1.1	11.8
Market value ($ mil.)	1.5%	45.1	52.0	39.5	33.2	47.9
Employees	(2.3%)	1,707	1,740	1,870	1,804	1,555

*Fiscal year change

FLATBUSH FEDERAL BANCORP INC.

2146 Nostrand Ave.
Brooklyn NY 11210
Phone: 718-859-6800
Fax: 718-421-3210
Web: www.flatbush.com

OTC: FLTB
CEO: Jesus R Adia
CFO: John S Lotardo
HR: –
FYE: December 31
Type: Public

Flatbush Federal Bancorp is the holding company for Flatbush Federal Savings and Loan which has been serving the Flatbush neighborhood of Brooklyn New York since 1883. Through three branches the bank offers checking and savings accounts CDs IRAs credit cards and a variety of loans. One- to four-family real estate mortgages account for about three-quarters of the company's loan portfolio. The bank also writes commercial mortgages construction loans consumer loans and Small Business Administration loans. Mutual holding company Flatbush Federal Bancorp MHC owns a majority of Flatbush Federal Bancorp which was acquired by Northfield Bancorp in late 2012.

FLEETCOR TECHNOLOGIES INC
NYS: FLT

3280 Peachtree Road, Suite 2400
Atlanta, GA 30305
Phone: 770 449-0479
Fax: –
Web: www.fleetcor.com

CEO: Ronald Clarke
CFO: Charles Freund
HR: Crystal Williams
FYE: December 31
Type: Public

FLEETCOR is a leading global provider of digital payment solutions that enables businesses to control purchases and make payments more effectively and efficiently. FLEETCOR offers corporate payments solutions which simplify and automate payments and expense management solutions which help control and monitor employee spending. The company serves more than 800000 accounts and has millions of cards active in the US the UK and Brazil as well as more than 100 other countries around the world. Major customers include oil giants BP Casey's and Speedway. FLEETCOR generates about 60% of its revenue through domestic operations.

	Annual Growth	12/16	12/17	12/18	12/19	12/20
Sales ($ mil.)	6.9%	1,831.5	2,249.5	2,433.5	2,648.8	2,388.9
Net income ($ mil.)	11.7%	452.4	740.2	811.5	895.1	704.2
Market value ($ mil.)	17.8%	11,840.4	16,099.9	15,538.5	24,072.4	22,826.6
Employees	4.3%	7,100	7,890	7,580	8,700	8,400

FLEMING GANNETT INC

207 SENATE AVE
CAMP HILL, PA 170112316
Phone: 717-763-7211
Fax: –
Web: www.gannettfleming.com

CEO: Robert Scaer
CFO: Jon Kessler
HR: –
FYE: December 31
Type: Private

Engineering firm Gannett Fleming has waded through water waste and sludge for nearly a century. Gannett Fleming operates through more than a dozen subsidiaries that offer a variety of services that range from design/build construction management ground testing and soil strengthening site remediation structural rehabilitation electrical and mechanical installation geophysical mapping and surveying and 3D visualization. Founded in 1915 Gannett Fleming serves the transportation water and wastewater facilities energy and environmental industries working on projects around the world from more than 60 offices across North America and Middle East.

	Annual Growth	12/08	12/09	12/10	12/11	12/13
Sales ($ mil.)	3.9%	–	–	–	286.5	309.5
Net income ($ mil.)	27.2%	–	–	–	4.5	7.2
Market value ($ mil.)	–	–	–	–	–	–
Employees	–	–	–	–	–	1,743

FLETCHER MUSIC CENTERS INC.

3966 AIRWAY CIR
CLEARWATER, FL 337624206
Phone: 727-571-1088
Fax: –
Web: www.fletchermusic.com

CEO: John K Riley
CFO: Ken Doyle
HR: –
FYE: December 31
Type: Private

Yearning to learn to play — and maybe own — a home organ? Fletcher Music Centers would be a company to call. The firm sells a variety of Lowrey-brand organs and teaches aspiring organists to play. The company is one of the world's largest retailers of organs for home use. It boasts about 20 stores located in Arizona and Florida. Most of its locations offer lessons and the company plans special occasions such as student concerts parties and potlucks. Fletcher Music Centers operates OrganFest a three-day event featuring discussions seminars and professional concerts. Founded by Robert Fletcher in 1975 the company is still owned by the Fletcher family.

	Annual Growth	12/06	12/07	12/08	12/09	12/10
Sales ($ mil.)	(5.9%)	–	18.4	19.6	14.4	15.3
Net income ($ mil.)	(49.7%)	–	–	0.8	(0.0)	0.2
Market value ($ mil.)	–	–	–	–	–	–
Employees	–	–	–	–	–	90

FLEXERA SOFTWARE LLC

300 PARK BLVD STE 500
ITASCA, IL 601432635
Phone: 847-466-4000
Fax: –
Web: www.flexera.com

CEO: Jim Ryan
CFO: David Zwick
HR: –
FYE: December 31
Type: Private

Flexera helps companies that sell software through subscriptions manage their accounts. The company assists organizations inform their IT with total visibility into their complex hybrid ecosystems providing the IT insights that fuel better informed decisions. In addition Flexera helps to transform their IT by rightsizing across all platforms reallocating spend reducing risk and charting the most effective path on the cloud. The company's products include the Flexera Software Monetization platform. In 2020 Flexera agreed to sell its majority interest in the company to Thoma Bravo a private equity firm focused on the software and technology-enabled services sectors. Flexera's original software product InstallShield has been called the industry standard Windows installer software. The company is owned by Teachers' Private Capital and TA Associates.

	Annual Growth	12/10	12/11	12/12	12/13	12/14
Sales ($ mil.)	5.8%	–	–	–	215.3	227.7
Net income ($ mil.)	–	–	–	–	0.0	(31.4)
Market value ($ mil.)	–	–	–	–	–	–
Employees	–	–	–	–	–	1,300

FLEXION THERAPEUTICS, INC.
NMS: FLXN

10 Mall Road, Suite 301
Burlington, MA 01803
Phone: 781 305-7777
Fax: –
Web: www.flexiontherapeutics.com

CEO: Michael D Clayman
CFO: Frederick W Driscoll
HR: –
FYE: December 31
Type: Public

Flexion wants to help its customers be more flexible. The biopharmaceutical company develops anti-inflammatory and analgesic treatments for patients with osteoarthritis and other musculoskeletal conditions. Its first product Zilretta was approved in the US in 2017; it combines an existing steroid with a polymer in a formula that gets injected at the joint to relieve pain and swelling. The polymer is the company's proprietary sustained-release ingredient that allows medication to stay where it's needed. Flexion's pipeline candidates are also for post-operative pain. The company owns the worldwide rights to commercialize its Zilretta and its product candidates. All of the company's sales were generated in the US.

	Annual Growth	12/15	12/16	12/17	12/18	12/19
Sales ($ mil.)	1333.6%	–	–	0.4	22.5	73.0
Net income ($ mil.)	–	(46.3)	(71.9)	(137.5)	(169.7)	(149.8)
Market value ($ mil.)	1.8%	739.2	729.6	960.6	434.3	794.1
Employees	56.5%	48	95	251	272	288

FLEXSTEEL INDUSTRIES, INC.
NMS: FLXS

385 Bell Street
Dubuque, IA 52001-0877
Phone: 563 556-7730
Fax: –
Web: www.flexsteel.com

CEO: Jerald Dittmer
CFO: Derek Schmidt
HR: Stacy Kammes
FYE: June 30
Type: Public

Flexsteel Industries is one of the largest manufacturers importers and online marketers of residential furniture and products in the US. It offers a wide variety of furniture such as loveseats chairs swivel rockers sofa beds convertible bedding units occasional tables desks dining tables and chairs and bedroom furniture. A featured component in most of the upholstered furniture is a unique steel drop-in seat spring from which the name "Flexsteel" is derived. The company distributes its products throughout the US through its e-commerce channel and dealer network. Most of its upholstered products ? including recliners rockers and sofas ? incorporate a patented spring technology Blue Steel Spring. Flexsteel was incorporated in 1929.

	Annual Growth	06/17	06/18	06/19	06/20	06/21
Sales ($ mil.)	0.5%	468.8	489.2	443.6	366.9	478.9
Net income ($ mil.)	(0.8%)	23.8	17.7	(32.6)	(26.8)	23.0
Market value ($ mil.)	(7.0%)	370.5	273.2	116.8	86.5	276.6
Employees	(17.8%)	1,460	1,530	1,295	636	665

FLINT ELECTRIC MEMBERSHIP CORPORATION

3 S MACON ST
REYNOLDS, GA 310763104
Phone: 478-847-3415
Fax: –
Web: www.flintenergies.com

CEO: Bob Ray
CFO: Anissa Derieux
HR: –
FYE: December 31
Type: Private

The Native American inhabitants of Georgia may have used flint to spark the fires that brought light to their dwellings. Central Georgians today rely on the Flint Electric Membership Corporation which does business as Flint Energies to light their homes. Flint Energies serves 250000 residential commercial and industrial customers (through 82500 meters) in 17 counties Fort Benning and the city of Warner Robins. The customer-owned cooperative operates more than 6250 miles of distribution line and about 50 substations. Flint Energies first flicked the switch in 1937.

	Annual Growth	12/15	12/16	12/17	12/18	12/20
Sales ($ mil.)	1.6%	–	204.6	210.1	220.1	218.0
Net income ($ mil.)	4.3%	–	7.0	6.9	6.9	8.3
Market value ($ mil.)	–	–	–	–	–	–
Employees	–	–	–	–	–	227

FLINT TELECOM GROUP INC   NBB: FLTT

7500 College Blvd, Suite 500
Overland Park, KS 66210
Phone: 913 815-1570
Fax: –
Web: www.flinttelecomgroup.com

CEO: Vincent Browne
CFO: Vincent Browne
HR: –
FYE: June 30
Type: Public

Flint Telecom Group fans the flame of advanced communications. Through eight subsidiaries the holding company provides a host of products and technologies to US and international communications service providers including cable companies ISPs and telcos. It distributes advanced broadband hosted digital phone voice and data and wireless products as well as prepaid cellular and calling card products. The company's Digital Phone Solutions subsidiary offers VoIP services to independent cable companies a niche that is showing strong market growth particularly in the US.

	Annual Growth	03/08*	06/09	06/10	06/11	06/12
Sales ($ mil.)	82.6%	1.0	34.3	34.1	15.8	10.7
Net income ($ mil.)	–	(2.1)	(14.6)	(28.9)	(9.3)	0.4
Market value ($ mil.)	(80.1%)	192.4	423.3	2.9	2.7	0.3
Employees	(38.5%)	14	21	7	–	2

*Fiscal year change

FLIR SYSTEMS, INC.   NMS: FLIR

27700 S.W. Parkway Avenue
Wilsonville, OR 97070
Phone: 503 498-3547
Fax: 503 498-3911
Web: www.flir.com

CEO: Edwin Roks
CFO: Todd Booth
HR: –
FYE: December 31
Type: Public

FLIR Systems doesn't sweat it when the heat is on. It finds it. The company manufactures advanced sensors and integrated sensor systems that enable the gathering measurement and analysis of critical information through a wide variety of applications in industrial government and commercial markets worldwide. FLIR offer broad range of infrared also known as thermal imaging solutions in the world with products that range from professional-use thermal camera smartphone accessories to highly advanced aircraft-mounted imaging systems for military and search and rescue applications with products in between serving a multitude of markets customers and applications. More than half of FLIR's sales are generated in the US.

	Annual Growth	12/15	12/16	12/17	12/18	12/19
Sales ($ mil.)	4.9%	1,557.1	1,662.2	1,800.4	1,775.7	1,887.0
Net income ($ mil.)	(8.2%)	241.7	166.6	107.2	282.4	171.6
Market value ($ mil.)	16.7%	3,772.4	4,863.7	6,265.4	5,851.5	6,997.9
Employees	9.2%	3,003	3,436	3,542	3,649	4,265

FLORIDA ATLANTIC UNIVERSITY

777 GLADES RD
BOCA RATON, FL 334316496
Phone: 561-297-3000
Fax: –
Web: www.fau.edu

CEO: John W Kelly
CFO: –
HR: –
FYE: June 30
Type: Private

Who gives a hoot about tertiary education in Southeast Florida? About 30000 "owls" enrolled at Florida Atlantic University (FAU) do. The Southeast Florida university's colleges offer more than 170 undergraduate and graduate degree programs in a range of academic fields including architecture liberal arts education nursing science and engineering. The university has about a half-dozen locations in Boca Raton Ft. Lauderdale Port St. Lucie Dania Beach Jupiter Fort Pierce and Davie. FAU has a student to faculty ratio of 30:1

	Annual Growth	06/10	06/11	06/17	06/19	06/20
Sales ($ mil.)	2.8%	–	234.0	282.4	288.9	301.2
Net income ($ mil.)	(10.3%)	–	65.6	(1.7)	20.2	24.8
Market value ($ mil.)	–	–	–	–	–	–
Employees	–	–	–	–	–	3,053

FLORIDA DEPARTMENT OF LOTTERY

250 MARRIOTT DR
TALLAHASSEE, FL 323012983
Phone: 850-487-7777
Fax: –
Web: www.flalottery.com

CEO: –
CFO: –
HR: –
FYE: June 30
Type: Private

The State of Florida Department of the Lottery runs instant-play scratch tickets and lotto games including Florida Lotto Mega Money Fantasy 5 and Cash 3. In addition to its own games Florida is part of the Multi-State Lottery Association which operates the popular Powerball drawing. Proceeds from the games are contributed to Florida's Educational Enhancement Trust Fund which provides funding for a variety of education programs from pre-kindergarten up to the state university level. The lottery has returned more than $19 billion to the state since starting in 1988.

	Annual Growth	06/01	06/02	06/03	06/19	06/20
Sales ($ mil.)	56.6%	–	2.3	2,873.0	7,157.9	7,511.6
Net income ($ mil.)	28.3%	–	0.0	117.9	36.3	4.1
Market value ($ mil.)	–	–	–	–	–	–
Employees	–	–	–	–	–	400

FLORIDA GAMING CORP.   NBB: FGMG Q

3500 N.W. 37th Avenue
Miami, FL 33142
Phone: 305 633-6400
Fax: –
Web: www.fla-gaming.com

CEO: –
CFO: –
HR: –
FYE: December 31
Type: Public

Jai-alai is the high life for this company. Florida Gaming Corporation owns and operates two jai-alai frontons in Miami and Ft. Pierce Florida that feature live jai-alai competition with wagering. The gaming centers offer wagering on simulcast jai-alai from other locations as well as simulcast horse racing and dog racing. In addition its Miami location features a card room for poker. Florida Gaming also owns Tara Club Estates a real estate development project near Atlanta. Chairman W. Bennett Collett owns more than 45% of the company partially through his holding company Freedom Financial.

	Annual Growth	12/08	12/09	12/10	12/11	12/12
Sales ($ mil.)	34.2%	14.0	14.0	9.3	8.1	45.5
Net income ($ mil.)	–	(0.1)	(4.9)	(4.8)	(21.8)	(22.7)
Market value ($ mil.)	(53.1%)	8.3	18.2	8.7	12.1	0.4
Employees	5.2%	426	402	310	279	521

FLORIDA GAMING CORPORATION   OTC: FGMG

3500 NW 37th Ave.
Miami FL 33142
Phone: 305-633-6400
Fax: 305-638-1330
Web: www.fla-gaming.com

CEO: -
CFO: -
HR: -
FYE: December 31
Type: Public

Jai-alai is the high life for this company. Florida Gaming Corporation owns and operates two jai-alai frontons in Miami and Ft. Pierce Florida that feature live jai-alai competition with wagering. The gaming centers offer wagering on simulcast jai-alai from other locations as well as simulcast horse racing and dog racing. In addition its Miami location features a card room for poker. Florida Gaming also owns Tara Club Estates a real estate development project near Atlanta. Chairman W. Bennett Collett owns more than 45% of the company partially through his holding company Freedom Financial.

FLORIDA HOSPITAL WATERMAN, INC.

1000 WATERMAN WAY
TAVARES, FL 327785266
Phone: 352-253-3333
Fax: -
Web: www.adventhealth.com

CEO: David Ottati
CFO: -
HR: -
FYE: December 31
Type: Private

Florida Hospital Waterman is a 270-bed community hospital serving the residents of Lake County Florida just north of Orlando. The hospital provides a full range of acute care services including cardiac and cancer care emergency services obstetrics pediatrics and rehabilitation. It also offers outpatient surgery diagnostic imaging laboratory and home health services. As part of its portfolio of services Florida Hospital Waterman operates a primary care clinic. Established in 1938 and named after the philanthropic leader of the Waterman Fountain Pen Company Florida Hospital Waterman has been part of the Adventist Health System since 1992.

	Annual Growth	12/13	12/14	12/15	12/16	12/17
Sales ($ mil.)	5.1%	-	225.2	231.0	232.9	261.6
Net income ($ mil.)	7.4%	-	31.4	12.1	27.5	38.9
Market value ($ mil.)	-	-	-	-	-	-
Employees						1,200

FLORIDA GAS TRANSMISSION COMPANY, LLC

1300 MAIN ST
HOUSTON, TX 770026803
Phone: 713-989-7000
Fax: -

CEO: Marshall S McCrea III
CFO: Martin Salinas Jr
HR: -
FYE: December 31
Type: Private

Florida Gas Transmission gasses up the Gulf Coast. The company transports natural gas to cogeneration facilities electric utilities independent power producers municipal generators and local distribution companies through a 5400-mile natural gas pipeline extending from south Texas to south Florida. It delivers 3.1 billion cu. ft. of natural gas a day to more than 250 delivery points consisting of more than 50 natural gas-fired electric generation facilities. Florida Gas Transmission is operated by Citrus Corp. which is a joint venture of Energy Transfer Partners and Kinder Morgan.

	Annual Growth	12/14	12/15	12/16	12/17	12/18
Sales ($ mil.)	0.6%	-	-	829.5	839.3	838.9
Net income ($ mil.)	16.1%	-	-	238.3	247.6	321.0
Market value ($ mil.)	-	-	-	-	-	-
Employees						450

FLORIDA HOUSING FINANCE CORP

227 N BRONOUGH ST # 5000
TALLAHASSEE, FL 323011367
Phone: 850-488-4197
Fax: -
Web: www.floridahousing.org

CEO: -
CFO: -
HR: Jessica Cherry
FYE: December 31
Type: Private

Owning a home in Florida is just a bit easier thanks to Florida Housing Finance Corporation. Established in 1997 by the Florida Legislature as a public corporation Florida Housing's mission is to help Floridians obtain safe decent housing that might otherwise be unavailable to them. Florida Housing pursues its mission through a number of programs that provide financial assistance for first time homebuyers and for developers of multifamily dwellings that serve elderly and low income Floridians. Florida Housing partners with various local state and federal agencies as well as developers and not-for-profit organizations to achieve its goals.

	Annual Growth	12/16	12/17	12/18	12/19	12/20
Assets ($ mil.)	6.2%	-	4,764.9	4,974.5	5,373.5	5,701.3
Net income ($ mil.)	17.1%	-	206.9	125.0	224.9	332.6
Market value ($ mil.)	-	-	-	-	-	-
Employees						130

FLORIDA HEALTH SCIENCES CENTER, INC.

1 TAMPA GENERAL CIR
TAMPA, FL 336063571
Phone: 813-844-7000
Fax: -
Web: www.tgh.org

CEO: John Couris
CFO: Steve Short
HR: -
FYE: September 30
Type: Private

Florida Health Sciences Center which does business as Tampa General Hospital (TGH) provides health care services in west-central Florida serving a dozen counties. The medical center offers general medical and surgical care as well as tertiary offerings including a Level 1 trauma center a burn unit a pediatric ward women's and cardiovascular centers and an organ transplant unit. The not-for-profit hospital has more than 1005 acute-care beds as well as nearly 60 beds in its rehabilitation unit which specializes in helping patients recover from stroke head or spine trauma and other neuromuscular conditions. TGH is the primary teaching hospital for USF Health Morsani College of Medicine.

	Annual Growth	09/16	09/17	09/18	09/19	09/20
Sales ($ mil.)	8.2%	-	1,257.5	1,325.4	1,447.2	1,590.8
Net income ($ mil.)	14.2%	-	98.4	79.1	57.7	146.5
Market value ($ mil.)	-	-	-	-	-	-
Employees						8,000

FLORIDA INTERNATIONAL UNIVERSITY

11200 SW 8TH ST
MIAMI, FL 331992516
Phone: 305-348-2494
Fax: -
Web: www.fiu.edu

CEO: -
CFO: Kenneth Jessell
HR: Ana Pineda
FYE: June 30
Type: Private

Florida International University (FIU) boasts a student population representing more than 140 countries. With total enrollment of approximately 58000 students it has one of the largest student populations of all US universities. FIU offers about 300 bachelor's master's and doctoral degree options including top-ranked online programs. Its academic community is composed of nearly 10 schools and colleges ? including its prestigious Honors College. In addition FIU's exploration research and community engagement is supported by more than 40 centers and institutes. FIU is a member of the State University System of Florida. It held its first classes in 1972.

	Annual Growth	06/05	06/06	06/07	06/19	06/20
Sales ($ mil.)	5.9%	-	238.2	307.5	549.0	532.5
Net income ($ mil.)	-	-	50.7	89.9	8.4	(51.5)
Market value ($ mil.)	-	-	-	-	-	-
Employees						4,000

FLORIDA MUNICIPAL POWER AGENCY

8553 COMMODITY CIR
ORLANDO, FL 328199002
Phone: 407-355-7767
Fax: –
Web: www.fmpa.com

CEO: Jacob Williams
CFO: –
HR: –
FYE: September 30
Type: Private

Unlike some politicians Florida Municipal Power Agency (FMPA) doesn't believe in holding on to power. The non-profit public agency generates and supplies electric power to 31 county or municipally owned distribution utilities which in turn serve 2 million Florida residents and businesses. Each of the distribution utilities appoints one representative to FMPA's board of directors which governs the Agency's activities. The Agency is authorized to undertake joint power supply projects for its members and to issue tax-exempt bonds to finance the costs of such projects. It is also empowered to implement a pooled financing program for utility-related projects.

	Annual Growth	09/16	09/17	09/18	09/19	09/20
Sales ($ mil.)	(1.8%)	–	–	604.3	620.5	582.8
Net income ($ mil.)	–	–	–	32.1	0.4	(0.3)
Market value ($ mil.)	–	–	–	–	–	–
Employees	–	–	–	–	–	67

FLORIDA POWER & LIGHT CO.

700 Universe Boulevard
Juno Beach, FL 33408
Phone: 561 694-4000
Fax: –
Web: www.nexteraenergy.com

CEO: Eric Silagy
CFO: Moray Dewhurst
HR: Deborah Caplan
FYE: December 31
Type: Public

Florida Power & Light (FPL) sheds extra light onto the Sunshine State. The company a subsidiary of utility holding company NextEra Energy serves more than 5 million electricity customers in eastern and southern Florida. FPL's typical 1000-kWh residential customer bill is approximately 30% lower than the latest national average and among the lowest in the U.S. FPL's service reliability is better than 99.98%. .. FPL's has one of the cleanest power plant fleets across the US.

	Annual Growth	12/16	12/17	12/18	12/19	12/20
Sales ($ mil.)	1.7%	10,895.0	11,972.0	11,862.0	12,192.0	11,662.0
Net income ($ mil.)	11.3%	1,727.0	1,880.0	2,171.0	2,334.0	2,650.0
Market value ($ mil.)	–	–	–	–	–	–
Employees	0.6%	8,900	8,700	9,100	8,900	9,100

FLORIDA STATE UNIVERSITY

600 W COLLEGE AVE
TALLAHASSEE, FL 323061096
Phone: 850-644-5482
Fax: –
Web: www.fsu.edu

CEO: –
CFO: –
HR: –
FYE: June 30
Type: Private

Home to the Florida State Seminoles Florida State University offers more than 300 undergraduate graduate and professional programs including M.D. (medicine) and J.D. (law) programs. The educational institution has 16 colleges dedicated to academic fields ranging from liberal arts music visual arts and education to criminology engineering social work and information. A major research institution the university is home to the National High Magnetic Field Laboratory or "Mag Lab" the only national lab in Florida and the only such high-magnetic facility in the US. Florida State was founded in 1851 and is part of the 11-school State University System of Florida.

	Annual Growth	06/08	06/09	06/10	06/11	06/12
Sales ($ mil.)	7.4%	–	–	567.1	607.3	654.7
Net income ($ mil.)	(42.4%)	–	–	121.3	188.3	40.2
Market value ($ mil.)	–	–	–	–	–	–
Employees	–	–	–	–	–	13,497

FLORIDA'S NATURAL GROWERS

20205 US Hwy. 27 North
Lake Wales FL 33853
Phone: 863-676-1411
Fax: 817-837-8004
Web: www.americanhealthchoice.com

CEO: Stephen M Caruso
CFO: William Hendry
HR: –
FYE: August 31
Type: Private - Cooperativ

Florida's Natural Growers is known for squeezing out pulpy profits. The cooperative is one of the largest citrus juice sellers in the US ranking right up there with the country's two giant brand names: PepsiCo's Tropicana and Coca-Cola's Minute Maid. Some 1000 farmer/members harvest more than 50000 acres of citrus groves for the co-op's products — frozen concentrated and not-from-concentrate juices (orange grapefruit lemonade apple and fruit blends). The co-op provides juice to customers in the foodservice retail food and vending industries. Its brands include Florida's Natural Growers Pride Bluebird and Donald Duck among others.

FLORSTAR SALES, INC.

1075 TAYLOR RD
ROMEOVILLE, IL 604464265
Phone: 815-836-2800
Fax: –
Web: www.florstar.com

CEO: F Wade Cassidy
CFO: Greg Stirrett
HR: –
FYE: September 30
Type: Private

At FlorStar Sales the floor is the star. The company distributes floor coverings to retailers throughout the Midwest from four locations in Illinois Iowa Michigan and Minnesota. Florstar's product offerings include hardwoods laminates ceramic porcelain vinyl rugs and carpets from Armstrong Interceramic Milliken Wilsonart and Weyerhaeuser. From its four locations the company serves nearly 5000 customers in six additional Midwest states. In addition it offers floor installation training and certification. FlorStar was part of Carson Pirie Scott & Co. until 1988 when management purchased the flooring division and created a separate company.

	Annual Growth	09/96	09/97	09/98	09/99	09/08
Sales ($ mil.)	1.1%	–	95.2	120.3	130.9	107.9
Net income ($ mil.)	(0.2%)	–	0.7	0.8	2.6	0.7
Market value ($ mil.)	–	–	–	–	–	–
Employees	–	–	–	–	–	190

FLOTEK INDUSTRIES INC

NYS: FTK

8846 N. Sam Houston Parkway W.
Houston, TX 77064
Phone: 713 849-9911
Fax: –
Web: www.flotekind.com

CEO: John Gibson
CFO: Michael Borton
HR: –
FYE: December 31
Type: Public

Flotek Industries Inc. is a technology-driven specialty chemistry and data company that serves customers across industrial commercial and consumer markets. Flotek's Chemistry Technologies segment develops manufactures packages distributes delivers and markets high-quality sanitizers and disinfectants for commercial governmental and personal consumer use. Additionally Flotek empowers the energy industry to maximize the value of their hydrocarbon streams and improve return on invested capital through its real-time data platforms and chemistry technologies. Flotek serves downstream midstream and upstream customers both domestic and international.

	Annual Growth	12/16	12/17	12/18	12/19	12/20
Sales ($ mil.)	(32.9%)	262.8	317.1	177.8	119.4	53.1
Net income ($ mil.)	–	(49.1)	(27.4)	(70.3)	(32.3)	(136.5)
Market value ($ mil.)	(31.2%)	686.3	340.6	79.7	146.2	154.2
Employees	(27.0%)	517	334	273	174	147

FLOWERS FOODS, INC.

NYS: FLO

1919 Flowers Circle
Thomasville, GA 31757
Phone: 229 226-9110
Fax: –
Web: www.flowersfoods.com

CEO: A. Ryals Mcmullian
CFO: R. Steve Kinsey
HR: –
FYE: January 02
Type: Public

One of the largest wholesale bakeries in the US Flowers Foods makes a range of flour-based products. It bakes markets and distributes fresh breads buns rolls snack cakes and flour tortillas to retail food and foodservice customers across the US. Fresh baked foods' customers include mass merchandisers supermarkets and other retailers restaurants quick-serve chains food wholesalers institutions dollar stores and vending companies. Flowers Foods has 15 major brands including widely distributed brands such as Nature's Own Wonder Tastykake and Dave's Killer Bread and regional names such as Butternut and Sunbeam. The company traces its roots to 1919.

	Annual Growth	12/16	12/17	12/18	12/19*	01/21
Sales ($ mil.)	2.2%	3,926.9	3,920.7	3,951.9	4,124.0	4,388.0
Net income ($ mil.)	(1.4%)	163.8	150.1	157.2	164.5	152.3
Market value ($ mil.)	2.5%	4,225.7	4,086.1	3,870.2	4,600.3	4,788.6
Employees	(3.2%)	10,800	9,800	9,200	9,700	9,200

*Fiscal year change

FLOWSERVE CORP

NYS: FLS

5215 N. O'Connor Blvd., Suite 700
Irving, TX 75039
Phone: 972 443-6500
Fax: 972 443-6800
Web: www.flowserve.com

CEO: R. Scott Rowe
CFO: Amy Schwetz
HR: Elizabeth Burger
FYE: December 31
Type: Public

Flowserve is about pumps valves and other flow control equipment. The company makes highly-engineered custom and pre-configured pumps mechanical seals valves and actuators that control the flow of liquids and gases. Flowserve also provides services that include installation diagnostics repair and retrofitting. Flowserve's customers are in the chemical oil and gas power generation and water management industries as well as some others. The company operates in more than 50 countries and manufactures more than 40 different active types of pumps and approximately 185 different models of mechanical seals and sealing systems. Nearly 40% of its sales are generated from the US.

	Annual Growth	12/16	12/17	12/18	12/19	12/20
Sales ($ mil.)	(1.7%)	3,991.5	3,660.8	3,832.7	3,944.9	3,728.1
Net income ($ mil.)	(5.4%)	145.1	2.7	119.7	253.7	116.3
Market value ($ mil.)	(6.4%)	6,247.7	5,478.0	4,943.6	6,471.3	4,791.4
Employees	(2.9%)	18,000	17,000	17,000	17,000	16,000

FLOYD HEALTHCARE MANAGEMENT, INC.

304 TURNER MCCALL BLVD SW
ROME, GA 301655621
Phone: 706-509-5000
Fax: –
Web: www.floyd.org

CEO: Kurt Stuenkel
CFO: Clarice Cable
HR: –
FYE: June 30
Type: Private

If you need heart help in the Heart of Dixie Floyd Healthcare Management is there for you. Its main hospital Floyd Medical Center has more than 300 beds and serves northwestern Georgia and northeastern Alabama with more than 40 medical specialties. In addition to medical surgical and emergency care (including a Level II trauma center and Level III neonatal intensive care unit) the hospital offers rehabilitation programs hospice and home health care. It also operates a 25-bed community hospital (Polk Medical Center) and the 53-bed Floyd Behavioral Health Center. Floyd Healthcare also operates outpatient centers including primary care surgery and urgent care locations. The organization was founded in 1942.

	Annual Growth	06/10	06/11	06/15	06/16	06/20
Sales ($ mil.)	3.2%	–	332.8	316.4	326.1	442.2
Net income ($ mil.)	(7.3%)	–	11.5	33.0	13.4	5.8
Market value ($ mil.)	–	–	–	–	–	–
Employees	–	–	–	–	–	2,400

FLUIDIGM CORP (DE)

NMS: FLDM

2 Tower Place, Ste 2000
South San Francisco, CA 94080
Phone: 650 266-6000
Fax: –
Web: www.fluidigm.com

CEO: Chris Linthwaite
CFO: Vikram Jog
HR: –
FYE: December 31
Type: Public

Fluidigm creates manufactures and markets a range of products and services including instruments consumables reagents and software that are used by researchers and clinical labs worldwide. It also develops integrated fluidic circuits (IFCs) and strings them together as systems to automate certain tasks in life sciences research. Fluidigm's BioMark HD and EP1 systems enable genetic analyses including genotyping and high-throughput gene expression. Its Access Array system enables automated sample preparation for DNA sequencing. Customers include academic and government laboratories as well as pharmaceutical biotechnology plant and animal research organizations and clinical laboratories. Most of Fluidigm's revenue comes from the America (about 55%).

	Annual Growth	12/16	12/17	12/18	12/19	12/20
Sales ($ mil.)	7.2%	104.4	101.9	113.0	117.2	138.1
Net income ($ mil.)	–	(76.0)	(60.5)	(59.0)	(64.8)	(53.0)
Market value ($ mil.)	(4.7%)	542.7	439.1	642.6	259.4	447.3
Employees	1.6%	589	505	535	566	627

FLUOR CORP.

NYS: FLR

6700 Las Colinas Boulevard
Irving, TX 75039
Phone: 469 398-7000
Fax: –
Web: www.fluor.com

CEO: David Constable
CFO: Joseph Brennan
HR: –
FYE: December 31
Type: Public

Fluor is one of the world's largest international design engineering and contracting firms. Through subsidiaries it provides engineering procurement construction (EPC) fabrication and modularization operations maintenance and asset integrity as well as project management services for a variety of industrial sectors around the world. The company provides these services to its clients in a diverse set of industries worldwide including oil and gas chemicals and petrochemicals mining and metals infrastructure life sciences advanced manufacturing and advanced technologies. Fluor is also a service provider to the US federal government and governments abroad. The company generates most of its revenue in North America.

	Annual Growth	12/16	12/17	12/18	12/19	12/20
Sales ($ mil.)	(4.8%)	19,036.5	19,521.0	19,166.6	14,348.0	15,668.5
Net income ($ mil.)	–	281.4	191.4	224.8	(1,522.2)	(435.0)
Market value ($ mil.)	(25.7%)	7,390.4	7,267.9	4,531.0	2,656.7	2,247.2
Employees	(8.2%)	61,551	56,706	53,349	50,182	43,717

FLUSHING FINANCIAL CORP.

NMS: FFIC

220 RXR Plaza
Uniondale, NY 11556
Phone: 718 961-5400
Fax: –
Web: www.flushingbank.com

CEO: John Buran
CFO: Susan Cullen
HR: Ruth Filiberto
FYE: December 31
Type: Public

Flushing Financial Corp. (FFC) is the holding company for Flushing Bank which operates more than 15 branches in the New York City metropolitan area. The bank offers services catering to the sizable populations of Asians and other ethnic groups in Queens where it has the most full-service offices. Deposit products include CDs and checking savings money market and negotiable order of withdrawal (NOW) accounts. Mortgages secured by multifamily residential commercial and mixed-use real estate account for most of the company's $5.2 billion loan portfolio.

	Annual Growth	12/16	12/17	12/18	12/19	12/20
Assets ($ mil.)	7.1%	6,058.5	6,299.3	6,834.2	7,017.8	7,976.4
Net income ($ mil.)	(14.5%)	64.9	41.1	55.1	41.3	34.7
Market value ($ mil.)	(13.3%)	904.5	846.3	662.6	664.9	512.1
Employees	3.0%	470	467	480	474	530

FLYING FOOD GROUP LLC

212 N. Sangamon St. Ste. 1-A
Chicago IL 60607
Phone: 312-243-2122
Fax: 847-808-5599
Web: www.ipa-iba.com

CEO: David Cotton
CFO: Mark Noffke
HR: Gayle Hare
FYE: December 31
Type: Private

The food is really flying in this company's kitchens. Flying Food Group is a leading US provider of in-flight catering services to the airline industry. It supplies prepared meals to some 70 airline customers (primarily long-haul carriers) from more than 15 kitchen facilities located throughout the US. (The company also has one flight kitchen location in Shanghai.) In addition to in-flight meals its Fresh Food Solutions unit supplies prepared snacks salads sandwiches desserts and meals to other food service companies and specialty food retailers. With six US fresh food operations it serves customers such as HMS Host Aramark and Starbucks. Flying Food Group was founded in 1983 by CEO Sue Ling Gin.

FMC CORP.

2929 Walnut Street
Philadelphia, PA 19104
Phone: 215 299-6000
Fax: 215 299-5998
Web: www.fmc.com

NYS: FMC
CEO: Mark Douglas
CFO: Andrew Sandifer
HR: -
FYE: December 31
Type: Public

FMC Corporation is a leading agricultural sciences company FMC makes and markets insecticides herbicides and fungicides for crops including soybean corn fruits and vegetables cotton rice and cereals as well as pest control for home and garden. The company's products include herbicides (Authority Command Gamit) insecticides (Talstar Hero) and active ingredients used in insect control (Rynaxpyr and Cyazypr). FMC also makes biologicals such Quartzo and Presence bionematicides. The company generates about 55% of sales from the America. FMC dates back to 1883 when John Bean invented a piston pump for insecticides.

	Annual Growth	12/16	12/17	12/18	12/19	12/20
Sales ($ mil.)	9.1%	3,282.4	2,878.6	4,727.8	4,609.8	4,642.1
Net income ($ mil.)	27.4%	209.1	535.8	502.1	477.4	551.5
Market value ($ mil.)	19.4%	7,316.2	12,244.6	9,567.0	12,912.1	14,866.6
Employees	2.1%	5,900	7,000	7,300	6,400	6,400

FMC TECHNOLOGIES, INC.

5875 N. Sam Houston Parkway West
Houston, TX 77086
Phone: 281 591-4000
Fax: -
Web: www.fmctechnologies.com

NYS: FTI
CEO: Douglas Pferdehirt
CFO: Maryann T Mannen
HR: Jasmine Chua
FYE: December 31
Type: Public

FMC Technologies' name is a vestige of its early years as a food machinery maker but today this company's bread and butter is oil and gas equipment. FMC Technologies offers subsea drilling and production systems for the exploration and production of oil and gas. It also offers similar equipment and services for onshore oil production. In addition the company's energy infrastructure segment makes fluid control measurement marine loading separation material handling blending systems and other equipment. Its offerings are divided into three chief segments: subsea technologies surface technologies and energy infrastructure.

	Annual Growth	12/10	12/11	12/12	12/13	12/14
Sales ($ mil.)	17.8%	4,125.6	5,099.0	6,151.4	7,126.2	7,942.6
Net income ($ mil.)	16.8%	375.5	399.8	430.0	501.4	699.9
Market value ($ mil.)	(14.8%)	20,584.9	12,092.6	9,916.2	12,087.9	10,844.6
Employees	15.3%	11,500	14,200	18,400	19,300	20,300

FNB BANCORP (CA)

975 El Camino Real
South San Francisco, CA 94080
Phone: 650 588-6800
Fax: -
Web: www.fnbnorcal.com

NMS: FNBG
CEO: -
CFO: -
HR: -
FYE: December 31
Type: Public

To be or not to FNB? If that's your question you might want to look into FNB Bancorp. It's the holding company for First National Bank of Northern California which serves consumers and small to midsized businesses in San Mateo and San Francisco counties. Through about a dozen branches the bank offers traditional products such as checking and savings accounts IRAs CDs and credit cards. Real estate loans including commercial and residential mortgages account for approximately 70% of the company's loan portfolio. The bank also originates business consumer and construction loans. FNB Bancorp has agreed to acquire Oceanic Bank which has two offices in San Francisco and one branch in Guam.

	Annual Growth	12/12	12/13	12/14	12/15	12/16
Assets ($ mil.)	8.6%	875.3	891.9	917.2	1,124.3	1,219.4
Net income ($ mil.)	4.5%	8.8	7.4	9.4	8.2	10.5
Market value ($ mil.)	15.1%	135.0	203.8	202.0	219.9	237.0
Employees	(4.8%)	214	184	184	183	176

FNB CORP

One North Shore Center, 12 Federal Street
Pittsburgh, PA 15212
Phone: 800 555-5455
Fax: -
Web: www.fnb-online.com

NYS: FNB
CEO: Vincent J Delie Jr
CFO: Vincent Calabrese
HR: -
FYE: December 31
Type: Public

F.N.B. Corporation is a bank holding company and a financial holding company. Through the company's largest subsidiary it provides a full range of financial services principally to consumers corporations governments and small- to medium-sized businesses in its market areas through its subsidiary network. The company has nearly 360 banking offices throughout Pennsylvania Ohio Maryland West Virginia North Carolina and South Carolina. In addition to community banking and consumer finance FNB also has segments devoted to insurance and wealth management. It also offers leasing and merchant banking services.

	Annual Growth	12/16	12/17	12/18	12/19	12/20
Assets ($ mil.)	14.4%	21,844.8	31,417.6	33,102.0	34,615.0	37,354.0
Net income ($ mil.)	13.7%	170.9	199.2	373.0	387.0	286.0
Market value ($ mil.)	(12.3%)	5,155.7	4,444.9	3,164.8	4,084.7	3,055.5
Employees	2.4%	3,821	4,748	4,420	4,223	4,197

FNBH BANCORP INC

101 East Grand River, P.O. Box 800
Howell, MI 48844-0800
Phone: 517 546-3150
Fax: -
Web: www.fnbh.com

NBB: FNHM
CEO: Ronald L Long
CFO: Mark Huber
HR: -
FYE: December 31
Type: Public

If Thurston III and Lovey ever did get off that island they might've stashed their fortune here. FNBH Bancorp is the holding company for First National Bank of Howell which serves individuals and local businesses through nearly ten branches in Livingston County Michigan west of Detroit. The bank offers traditional deposit products such as checking and savings accounts in addition to trust investment and wealth management services. Commercial loans including loans for land development new home construction and business leasing comprise about 85% of the company's loan portfolio. Founded in 1934 the bank has traditionally served rural communities but has seen its market become increasingly suburban.

	Annual Growth	12/15	12/16	12/17	12/18	12/19
Assets ($ mil.)	5.7%	348.2	399.3	400.6	412.4	435.2
Net income ($ mil.)	14.4%	3.4	11.9	0.3	3.2	5.8
Market value ($ mil.)	15.5%	37.5	50.0	55.5	50.5	66.7
Employees						

FNCB BANCORP INC
NAS: FNCB

102 E. Drinker St.
Dunmore, PA 18512
Phone: 570 346-7667
Fax: –
Web: www.fncb.com

CEO: Gerard Champi
CFO: James Bone
HR: Dawn Gronski
FYE: December 31
Type: Public

First National Community Bancorp is the holding company for First National Community Bank which has about 20 offices in Lackawanna Luzerne Wayne and Monroe counties in northeastern Pennsylvania. The bank provides standard retail services such as checking and savings accounts certificates of deposit credit cards mortgages and other loans. It also offers wealth management services. The bank is mainly a business lender with commercial mortgages accounting for more than 40% of its loan portfolio and operating loans comprising about another quarter. Chairman Louis DeNaples and his brother Dominick who is vice chairman each own around 10% of First National Community Bancorp.

	Annual Growth	12/16	12/17	12/18	12/19	12/20
Assets ($ mil.)	5.2%	1,195.4	1,162.3	1,237.7	1,203.5	1,465.7
Net income ($ mil.)	24.9%	6.3	0.1	13.3	11.1	15.3
Market value ($ mil.)	1.4%	122.5	147.8	170.9	171.1	129.6
Employees	(4.1%)	253	242	239	224	214

FOGO DE CHAO, INC.

5908 HDQTR DR STE K200
PLANO, TX 75024
Phone: 972-960-9533
Fax: –
Web: www.fogodechao.com

CEO: George McGowan
CFO: Anthony Laday
HR: Terri Chatham
FYE: January 01
Type: Private

Fogo de Ch o operates a chain of more than 20 restaurants across the US and in Brazil and Mexico specializing in Brazilian-style churrasco a traditional way of slow-roasting meat. Customers at Fogo de Ch o (pronounced fo-go-day-shou) can help themselves from unlimited servings of meat from the ga cho chefs who keep bringing food until guests turn over their serving card from green to red. Brothers Arri and Jair Coser opened their first Fogo de Ch o in Brazil in 1979 and exported the concept to the US in 1997. The company went public in 2015.

	Annual Growth	01/13	01/14	01/15	01/16	01/17
Sales ($ mil.)	6.1%	–	–	–	271.6	288.3
Net income ($ mil.)	(13.3%)	–	–	–	28.0	24.3
Market value ($ mil.)	–	–	–	–	–	–
Employees	–	–	–	–	–	3,154

FOLEY & LARDNER LLP

777 E. Wisconsin Ave.
Milwaukee WI 53202-5306
Phone: 414-271-2400
Fax: 414-297-4900
Web: www.foley.com

CEO: Jay Rothman
CFO: Tom L Budde
HR: –
FYE: January 31
Type: Private - Partnershi

Though most famous for its cheese Wisconsin has another thing going for it: lawyers. Foley & Lardner the largest and oldest law firm in Wisconsin has nearly 1000 lawyers and has expanded far beyond its Milwaukee base with offices in more than 15 other US cities (including four in Florida and six in California). In addition Foley & Lardner has international offices in Brussels Shanghai and Tokyo. The firm founded in 1842 has one of the nation's leading health law practices and an increased focus on its intellectual property practice; other areas of expertise include business law litigation regulatory issues and tax planning.

FONAR CORP
NAS: FONR

110 Marcus Drive
Melville, NY 11747
Phone: 631 694-2929
Fax: –
Web: www.fonar.com

CEO: Timothy Damadian
CFO: Raymond Damadian
HR: –
FYE: June 30
Type: Public

SONAR finds objects hidden under the water using sound waves; FONAR uses magnetic resonance imaging (MRI) to find disease or injury hidden inside the body. The company was the first to market a commercial MRI scanner in 1980 and it is trying to stay at the forefront of the field. Its primary products include the Upright MRI which scans patients in sitting standing or bending positions and the FONAR 360 a room-sized MRI. Both systems do away with the claustrophobia-producing enclosed tubes of traditional machines. Additionally FONAR's Health Management Corporation of America (HMCA) subsidiary provides management services to more than 20 diagnostic imaging centers primarily in Florida and New York.

	Annual Growth	06/17	06/18	06/19	06/20	06/21
Sales ($ mil.)	3.6%	78.0	81.5	87.2	85.7	89.9
Net income ($ mil.)	(15.1%)	19.6	21.2	15.3	8.2	10.2
Market value ($ mil.)	(10.7%)	192.5	184.2	149.2	148.2	122.6
Employees	(0.3%)	500	525	500	424	495

FOOD FOR THE POOR, INC.

6401 LYONS RD
COCONUT CREEK, FL 330733602
Phone: 954-427-2222
Fax: –
Web: www.foodforthepoor.org

CEO: Ed Raine
CFO: Dennis North
HR: –
FYE: December 31
Type: Private

Food For The Poor feeds spiritual and physical hunger. The Christian charity provides health social economic and religious services for impoverished people in 17 countries in Latin America and the Caribbean. Food For The Poor believes its organization serves God by helping those most in need distributing requested goods through local churches and charities. The group works through Caritas the American-Nicaraguan Foundation and others to provide vocational training clinic and school construction educational materials feeding programs and medical supplies. Food For The Poor has distributed more than $3 billion in goods since its 1982 inception; the group uses 96% of its funds on programs.

	Annual Growth	12/15	12/16	12/17	12/18	12/19
Sales ($ mil.)	(2.8%)	–	994.9	948.7	942.6	914.5
Net income ($ mil.)	(1.7%)	–	14.6	(1.7)	(10.5)	13.9
Market value ($ mil.)	–	–	–	–	–	–
Employees	–	–	–	–	–	418

FOOD TECHNOLOGY SERVICE INC.
NAS: VIFL

502 Prairie Mine Road
Mulberry, FL 33860
Phone: 863 425-0039
Fax: –

CEO: –
CFO: –
HR: –
FYE: December 31
Type: Public

Food Technology Service operates a facility in Mulberry Florida that irradiates foods using gamma irradiation to kill insects and pathogens and to extend the shelf-life of foods by retarding spoilage. The company provides contract sterilization services to the food medical-device and consumer-goods industries and also irradiates packaging cosmetic ingredients and horticultural items. Given that only three customers account for 67% of its sales Food Technology has sought to diversify its customer base mainly by emphasizing its medical sterilization services which now account for 80% of its sales. Canada-based MDS Inc. a life-science services company owns about 31% of Food Technology Service.

	Annual Growth	12/08	12/09	12/10	12/11	12/12
Sales ($ mil.)	12.1%	2.5	2.5	3.0	3.7	4.0
Net income ($ mil.)	(2.6%)	1.0	0.7	1.1	0.9	0.9
Market value ($ mil.)	51.4%	2.7	4.9	10.9	14.7	14.2
Employees	3.6%	13	13	13	15	15

FOOT LOCKER, INC.
NYS: FL

330 West 34th Street
New York, NY 10001
Phone: 212 720-3700
Fax: –
Web: www.footlocker-inc.com

CEO: Richard Johnson
CFO: Andrew Page
HR: –
FYE: January 30
Type: Public

Foot Locker leads the celebration of sneaker and youth culture around the globe through a portfolio of brands including Foot Locker Lady Foot Locker Kids Foot Locker Champs Sports Eastbay Footaction and Sidestep. The company operates almost 300 primarily mall-based stores as well as stores in high-traffic urban retail areas and high streets in more than 25 countries across the US Canada Europe Australia New Zealand and Asia. It also curates special product assortments and marketing content that supports its premium position from leading global brands such as Nike Jordan Adidas and Puma as well as new and emerging brands in the athletic and lifestyle space. Foot Locker also sells via ecommerce sites mobile devices and catalogs. The US market accounts for nearly 75% of total revenue.

	Annual Growth	01/17*	02/18	02/19	02/20*	01/21
Sales ($ mil.)	(0.7%)	7,766.0	7,782.0	7,939.0	8,005.0	7,548.0
Net income ($ mil.)	(16.5%)	664.0	284.0	541.0	491.0	323.0
Market value ($ mil.)	(10.4%)	7,047.1	5,013.1	5,705.3	3,934.4	4,540.6
Employees	0.5%	50,168	49,209	49,331	50,999	51,252

*Fiscal year change

FOOTBALL NORTHWEST LLC

12 Seahawks Way
Renton WA 98056-1572
Phone: 425-203-8000
Fax: 703-726-7086
Web: www.redskins.com

CEO: –
CFO: –
HR: –
FYE: January 31
Type: Private

The Northwest is a prime nesting spot for this football team. Football Northwest owns and operates the Seattle Seahawks professional football franchise. The team joined the National Football League during the league expansion of 1976 (the same year as the Tampa Bay Buccaneers) but suffered through mostly disappointing seasons until a resurgence beginning in the late 1990s. Fans were finally treated to a Super Bowl appearance following the 2005 season; however Seattle fell to the Pittsburgh Steelers in that game. Founded by department store magnate Lloyd Nordstrom the Seahawks franchise has been owned by Microsoft co-founder Paul Allen since 1997.

FORBES ENERGY SERVICES LTD
NBB: FLSS

3000 South Business Highway 281
Alice, TX 78332
Phone: 361 664-0549
Fax: –
Web: www.forbesenergyservices.com

CEO: John E Crisp
CFO: L Melvin Cooper
HR: Katherine Clifton
FYE: December 31
Type: Public

Forbes Energy Services (FES) an independent oilfield services company offers well servicing and fluid management to onshore oil and gas drilling and production companies in Texas Mississippi and Pennsylvania. Its Fluid Logistics segment handles pumping transport and storage of fracking liquid salt water and other fluids used in drilling and extraction. FES's well-servicing segment provides well maintenance repairs cleanup and plugging; the unit also offers pressure testing. Major customers have included Apache Chesapeake Energy ConocoPhillips and EOG Resources.

	Annual Growth	12/16*	04/17*	12/17	12/18	12/19
Sales ($ mil.)	17.5%	116.2	30.8	96.5	180.9	188.4
Net income ($ mil.)	–	(109.1)	27.2	(26.0)	(32.6)	(68.4)
Market value ($ mil.)	(84.0%)	–	–	54.7	16.6	1.4
Employees	(1.6%)	825	–	843	1,178	786

*Fiscal year change

FORCE PROTECTION INC.
NASDAQ: FRPT

1520 Old Trolley Rd.
Summerville SC 29485
Phone: 843-574-7000
Fax: 843-329-0380
Web: www.forceprotectioninc.com

CEO: Michael Moody
CFO: Charles A Mathis
HR: –
FYE: December 31
Type: Subsidiary

Force Protection's vehicles protect military forces from deadly blasts. The company makes armored land vehicles designed to protect troops from landmines roadside bombs and hostile fire. It is a key provider of the US military's Mine Resistant Ambush Protected (MRAP) vehicle program. It also provides its large Buffalo and medium-sized Cougar mine-protected vehicles to foreign customers such as the UK Ministry of Defence. The Cougar family includes such variants as the Mastiff Ridgback and Wolfhound. Its other main products include the lighter-weight Cheetah Ocelot and JAMMA (joint all-terrain modular mobility asset) vehicles. In late 2011 Force Protection was bought by General Dynamics for $360 million.

FORD MOTOR CO. (DE)
NYS: F

One American Road
Dearborn, MI 48126
Phone: 313 322-3000
Fax: –
Web: www.corporate.ford.com

CEO: James Farley
CFO: John Lawler
HR: –
FYE: December 31
Type: Public

Ford Motor is a Michigan-based company that designs manufactures markets and services a full line of electrified passenger and commercial vehicles. The company's portfolio includes cars trucks and utility vehicles under the Ford and Lincoln brands. In addition the company also offers sales through Ford Motor Credit. Ford is making significant investments in a strategic shift to pursue a market position in electrification connected vehicle services and mobility solutions. Further the company is also pursuing the market of self-driving technology. Nearly 65% of total sales come from the US. The company was founded in 1903 by Henry Ford.

	Annual Growth	12/17	12/18	12/19	12/20	12/21
Sales ($ mil.)	(3.4%)	156,776.0	160,338.0	155,900.0	127,144.0	136,341.0
Net income ($ mil.)	23.9%	7,602.0	3,677.0	47.0	(1,279.0)	17,937.0
Market value ($ mil.)	–	0.0	0.0	0.0	0.0	0.0
Employees	(2.4%)	202,000	199,000	190,000	186,000	183,000

FORD MOTOR CREDIT COMPANY LLC

One American Road
Dearborn, MI 48126
Phone: 313 322-3000
Fax: –
Web: www.fordcredit.com

CEO: Bernard Silverstone
CFO: Brian E Schaaf
HR: –
FYE: December 31
Type: Public

Seems its trucks aren't the only things built Ford tough. The automaker's subsidiary Ford Motor Credit is proving to be pretty resilient too. One of the world's largest auto financing companies it funds autos for and through Ford and Lincoln dealerships in some 70 countries. It finances new used and leased vehicles and provides wholesale financing mortgages and capital loans for dealers. The company also offers business fleet financing and insurance. Founded in 1959 Ford Motor Credit generates more than half of its revenue from operating leases and more than 70% of revenue from the US.

	Annual Growth	12/17	12/18	12/19	12/20	12/21
Sales ($ mil.)	9.4%	4,067.0	4,585.0	4,599.0	4,825.0	5,834.0
Net income ($ mil.)	10.7%	3,007.0	2,224.0	2,228.0	1,924.0	4,521.0
Market value ($ mil.)	–	–	–	–	–	–
Employees	(7.4%)	7,600	7,600	6,800	6,400	5,600

FORDHAM UNIVERSITY

441 E FORDHAM RD
BRONX, NY 104589993
Phone: 718-817-1000
Fax: –
Web: www.fordham.edu

CEO: –
CFO: –
HR: –
FYE: June 30
Type: Private

A private Catholic university Fordham offers its nearly 16365 students numerous degree programs through nine graduate and undergraduate schools. Called the Jesuit University of New York Fordham has multiple locations including the original Rose Hill campus in the Bronx (often the scene of location shooting for movies TV shows and commercials) the Westchester campus and the Lincoln Center campus in Manhattan. It also operates a biological field station in Armonk New York and an international center in the UK. With about 755 full-time instructors the university has a 13:1 undergraduate student-to-faculty ratio. Fordham was founded in 1841.

	Annual Growth	06/15	06/16	06/18	06/19	06/20
Sales ($ mil.)	3.1%	–	588.4	631.6	933.5	665.6
Net income ($ mil.)	–	–	(52.4)	41.7	59.9	(20.6)
Market value ($ mil.)	–	–	–	–	–	–
Employees	–	–	–	–	–	4,070

FOREMOST GROUPS, INC.

906 MURRAY RD STE 2
EAST HANOVER, NJ 079362202
Phone: 973-428-0400
Fax: –
Web: www.foremostgroups.com

CEO: –
CFO: –
HR: –
FYE: December 31
Type: Private

Foremost Groups is a home furnishings manufacturer that markets and sells its products worldwide. The company produces a range of pieces for every room in the house including home offices (computer desks storage units) living rooms (ottomans entertainment centers) and bathrooms (cabinets vanities shower enclosures toilets). It also makes patio sets and food service equipment. Its furniture is manufactured under the Foremost Foremost Casual Contrac Craft + Main Veranda Classics and CORE PRO COOKING brands as well as private-label names for major retailers. The company was founded in 1987.

	Annual Growth	06/11	06/12	06/13	06/14*	12/15
Sales ($ mil.)	79.5%	–	–	–	100.1	179.6
Net income ($ mil.)	–	–	–	–	1.6	(0.5)
Market value ($ mil.)	–	–	–	–	–	–
Employees	–	–	–	–	–	150

*Fiscal year change

FOREST CITY ENTERPRISES, INC.

Terminal Tower, Suite 1100, 50 Public Square
Cleveland, OH 44113
Phone: 216 621-6060
Fax: –
Web: www.forestcity.net

NYS: FCE A
CEO: –
CFO: –
HR: –
FYE: December 31
Type: Public

Forest City Enterprises has grown from treeline to skyline. Founded in 1920 as a lumber dealer the company now focuses on commercial and residential real estate development in metropolitan areas across the US. Forest City which has more than $10.7 billion in assets owns and develops commercial properties including 44 retail centers and shopping malls 47 office buildings two hotels and Brooklyn's Barclays Center in 15 states. The company's residential group owns and manages 115 upscale and middle-market apartments condominiums and senior housing properties as well as more than 14000 military housing units in two dozen states. Forest City also owns about 290 acres of undeveloped land.

	Annual Growth	01/10	01/11	01/12	01/13*	12/13
Sales ($ mil.)	(6.7%)	1,257.2	1,177.7	1,090.0	1,134.7	1,020.1
Net income ($ mil.)	–	(30.7)	58.7	(86.5)	36.4	(5.3)
Market value ($ mil.)	19.1%	2,236.3	3,343.6	2,596.2	3,343.6	3,776.7
Employees	(2.2%)	3,019	2,917	2,870	2,914	2,822

*Fiscal year change

FOREST LABORATORIES, INC.

909 Third Avenue
New York, NY 10022-4731
Phone: 212 421-7850
Fax: 212 750-9152
Web: www.frx.com

NYS: FRX
CEO: –
CFO: –
HR: –
FYE: March 31
Type: Public

Forest Laboratories doesn't just blend in with the trees. The company develops and manufactures prescription drugs to address a wide field of ailments. Its central nervous system (CNS) drugs include Namenda which treats Alzheimer's disease; Savella for fibromyalgia; and antidepressants Celexa Lexapro and Viibryd. Other products include treatments for hypertension (Bystolic) thyroid disease respiratory ailments gastrointestinal conditions and pain. In addition to its branded prescription drugs Forest has limited operations in generic and over-the-counter (OTC) drug manufacturing. Forest Laboratories largely serves customers in the US.

	Annual Growth	03/09	03/10	03/11	03/12	03/13
Sales ($ mil.)	(5.5%)	3,922.8	4,192.9	4,419.7	4,586.0	3,126.1
Net income ($ mil.)	–	767.7	682.4	1,046.8	979.1	(32.1)
Market value ($ mil.)	14.7%	5,852.3	8,357.4	8,607.9	9,244.9	10,137.6
Employees	2.6%	5,225	5,200	5,600	5,700	5,800

FORESTAR GROUP INC (NEW)

2221 E. Lamar Blvd., Suite 790
Arlington, TX 76006
Phone: 817 769-1860
Fax: –
Web: www.forestargroup.com

NYS: FOR
CEO: Daniel Bartok
CFO: James Allen
HR: –
FYE: September 30
Type: Public

A majority-owned subsidiary of D.R. Horton?which is one of the largest homebuilders in the US?residential lot development company Forestar Group owns or controls over 38300 residential lots. Most of those are under contract are either under contract to sell to D.R. Horton or are assigned to D.R. Horton for right of first offer. The company owns approximately 4400 developed lots. Forestar operates in about 50 markets across about 20 states and while it sometimes develops land for commercial properties?including apartments retail centers and offices?Forestar primarily sells lots to homebuilders and developers for single-family homes.

	Annual Growth	12/17*	09/18	09/19	09/20	09/21
Sales ($ mil.)	84.5%	114.3	78.3	428.3	931.8	1,325.8
Net income ($ mil.)	21.7%	50.3	68.8	33.0	60.8	110.2
Market value ($ mil.)	(4.1%)	1,090.8	1,051.1	906.3	877.6	923.7
Employees	64.7%	34	41	78	143	250

*Fiscal year change

FOREVER 21 INC.

2001 S. Alameda St.
Los Angeles CA 90058
Phone: 213-741-5100
Fax: 213-741-5161
Web: www.forever21.com

CEO: Winnie Park
CFO: Ann Cadier Kim
HR: –
FYE: February 28
Type: Private

You don't have to be 21 or older to shop at Forever 21 stores — you just need your wallet. The fast-growing retailer operates about 500 stores under the Forever 21 XXI Forever Love 21 and Heritage 1981 banners throughout North America Asia the Middle East and the UK as well as an e-commerce site. The chain which helped to pioneer fast fashion offers cheap and chic apparel and accessories for women men teens and kids. It also carries women's footwear lingerie plus sizes and cosmetics — all at bargain basement prices. Most of Forever 21's trendy wares are private label. About 60% of its apparel is manufactured in China. CEO Don Chang and his wife founded the company as Fashion 21 in 1984.

FOREVERGREEN WORLDWIDE CORP NBB: FVRG

632 North 2000 West, Suite 101
Lindon, UT 84042
Phone: 801 655-5500
Fax: –
Web: www.forevergreen.org

CEO: Allen K Davis
CFO: John W Haight
HR: –
FYE: December 31
Type: Public

ForeverGreen Worldwide wants to give customers a piece of its mind naturally. The holding company through its ForeverGreen International subsidiary offers a menu of whole foods nutritional supplements personal care products and essential oils al sold via a network of independent distributors in the US and abroad. Company brands include LegaSea O3World Smart Food and TRUessence Oils. Its products which include energy bars drinks and snacks body oils creams lotions cleansers and shampoos claim to boost energy and mental acuity shed pounds ward off disease and help forestall biological aging with ingredients such as marine phytoplankton and organic chocolate.

	Annual Growth	12/13	12/14	12/15	12/16	12/17
Sales ($ mil.)	1.0%	17.8	58.3	67.1	40.3	18.5
Net income ($ mil.)	–	0.1	1.0	(2.6)	(5.9)	(2.2)
Market value ($ mil.)	(45.5%)	21.6	20.3	11.3	6.1	1.9
Employees	(13.3%)	69	97	103	65	39

FORGE INDUSTRIES, INC.

4450 MARKET ST
YOUNGSTOWN, OH 445121512
Phone: 330-782-8301
Fax: –

CEO: –
CFO: Dan Maisonville
HR: –
FYE: December 31
Type: Private

Forge Industries connects a diverse group of businesses. Operating via several subsidiaries the family-owned private holding company distributes thousands of products from industrial gears and bearings to asphalt and concrete construction equipment. Businesses include construction/landscape equipment maker Miller Spreader and sister companies Akron Gear & Engineering and Bearing Distributors (BDI) Forge's global product and service distributor. Forge's lineup includes curb builders and hand tools as well as rebuild and repair gearboxes redesign customer equipment customize gear reducers and machining services. Customers work in the automotive package handling food processing and landscape industries.

	Annual Growth	12/04	12/05	12/06	12/07	12/08
Sales ($ mil.)	9.9%	–	404.6	0.0	605.8	537.6
Net income ($ mil.)	(56.0%)	–	73.1	0.0	0.0	6.2
Market value ($ mil.)	–	–	–	–	–	–
Employees	–	–	–	–	–	2,000

FORMFACTOR INC NMS: FORM

7005 Southfront Road
Livermore, CA 94551
Phone: 925 290-4000
Fax: –
Web: www.formfactor.com

CEO: Michael Slessor
CFO: Shai Shahar
HR: –
FYE: December 25
Type: Public

FormFactor is a leading provider of test and measurement technologies. It provides a broad range of high-performance probe cards analytical probes probe stations metrology systems thermal systems and cryogenic systems to both semiconductor companies and scientific institutions. FormFactor designs probe cards to provide for a precise match with the thermal expansion characteristics of the wafer under test across the range of test operating temperatures. Its customers can use the same probe card for both low and high temperature testing. The majority of sales are to customers in China its largest single market. FormFactor began life in 1993 when former IBM researcher Igor Khandros began developing products for the semiconductor industry in a tiny New York lab.

	Annual Growth	12/17	12/18	12/19	12/20	12/21
Sales ($ mil.)	8.8%	548.4	529.7	589.5	693.6	769.7
Net income ($ mil.)	19.7%	40.9	104.0	39.3	78.5	83.9
Market value ($ mil.)	29.9%	1,224.5	1,096.1	2,037.4	3,331.5	3,482.5
Employees	8.0%	1,685	1,676	1,836	2,166	2,293

FORMS & SUPPLY, INC.

6410 ORR RD
CHARLOTTE, NC 282136332
Phone: 704-598-8971
Fax: –
Web: www.fsiofficefurniture.com

CEO: Jimmy D Godwin Sr
CFO: –
HR: –
FYE: December 31
Type: Private

Whether your boss needs a new mini-fridge for the office or you are just running low on staples Forms & Supply can help out. The company which does business as FSIoffice carries more than 8500 products including office supplies IT products and furniture. It operates about 10 distribution centers in five states and maintains a fleet of some 75 trucks. FSIoffice is a GSA-certified vendor and offers national account services through its partnership with American Office Products Distributors. Customers can place their orders through the company's e-commerce site. FSIoffice was founded in 1962 by Jimmy Godwin.

	Annual Growth	05/12	05/13*	12/13	12/14	12/16
Sales ($ mil.)	4.7%	–	74.5	–	78.9	85.6
Net income ($ mil.)	49.4%	–	0.7	–	1.0	2.2
Market value ($ mil.)	–	–	–	–	–	–
Employees	–	–	–	–	–	300

*Fiscal year change

FORRESTER RESEARCH INC. NMS: FORR

60 Acorn Park Drive
Cambridge, MA 02140
Phone: 617 613-6000
Fax: –
Web: www.forrester.com

CEO: George Colony
CFO: Chris Finn
HR: –
FYE: December 31
Type: Public

Forrester is one of the leading research and advisory firms in the world. The firm works closely with business and technology leaders to develop strategies for driving growth. Forrester gains powerful insights through its annual surveys of more than 675000 consumers and business leaders worldwide. The firm's reports and briefs provide insight into market forces industry trends and consumer behavior. Through proprietary research data and analytics custom consulting exclusive executive peer groups certification and events Forrester is revolutionizing how businesses grow in an era of powerful customers. The US is its largest market generating some 80% of total sales.

	Annual Growth	12/16	12/17	12/18	12/19	12/20
Sales ($ mil.)	8.3%	326.1	337.7	357.6	461.7	449.0
Net income ($ mil.)	(13.3%)	17.7	15.1	15.4	(9.6)	10.0
Market value ($ mil.)	(0.6%)	816.8	840.6	850.1	793.0	796.8
Employees	6.9%	1,378	1,392	1,432	1,795	1,798

FORSYTHE TECHNOLOGY INC.

7770 Frontage Rd.
Skokie IL 60077
Phone: 847-213-7000
Fax: 847-213-7922
Web: www.forsythe.com

CEO: –
CFO: –
HR: –
FYE: December 31
Type: Private

Forsythe Technology has the foresight to provide its clients with valuable business and information technology consulting services. The company helps businesses and government agencies manage their IT infrastructure providing services ranging from strategic planning to implementation and support. It also provides leasing and other financial services. Serving clients primarily located in the US and Canada the company works with IT product vendors such as Cisco and Oracle. Customers have included Alegent and Ricoh Canada. Chairman Richard Forsythe founded the company in 1971 as Forsythe McArthur Associates. Today the employee-owned company operates from offices in North America Singapore and the UK.

FORTEGRA FINANCIAL CORP
NYS: FRF

10151 Deerwood Park Boulevard, Building 100, Suite 330
Jacksonville, FL 32256
Phone: 866 961-9529
Fax: -
Web: www.fortegra.com

CEO: Richard S Kahlbaugh
CFO: Walter P Mascherin
HR: -
FYE: December 31
Type: Public

Fortegra Financial foresees a fortuitous future in specialty insurance. The company's payment protection division offers credit insurance debt protection and warranties under the Life of the South brand to consumer finance firms banks retailers and other lenders; it also operates several car club membership groups. Fortegra Financial's brokerage units (including Bliss & Glennon eReinsure and South Bay Acceptance) provide wholesale placement of insurance and reinsurance policies while its business process outsourcing (BPO) subsidiaries provide billing collections underwriting and call center management services for insurers.

	Annual Growth	12/08	12/09	12/10	12/11	12/12
Sales ($ mil.)	14.9%	167.1	186.1	204.3	225.3	291.6
Net income ($ mil.)	17.2%	8.0	11.6	16.2	14.5	15.2
Market value ($ mil.)	(10.3%)	-	-	217.5	131.5	175.0
Employees	16.1%	-	447	460	545	700

FORTINET INC
NMS: FTNT

899 Kifer Road
Sunnyvale, CA 94086
Phone: 408 235-7700
Fax: 408 235-7737
Web: www.fortinet.com

CEO: Ken Xie
CFO: Keith Jensen
HR: -
FYE: December 31
Type: Public

Fortinet is a global leader in cybersecurity solutions provided to a wide variety of organizations including enterprises communication service providers government organizations and small businesses. The company makes network security appliances (sold under its FortiGate line) and software that integrate antivirus firewall content filtering intrusion prevention systems (IPS) and anti-spam functions to protect against computer viruses worms and inappropriate web content. The company also offers complementary products that include its FortiManager security management and FortiAnalyzer event analysis systems. To support its broadly dispersed global channel and end-customer base it has sales professionals in over 80 countries around the world. Over 40% of the revenue comes from the Americas.

	Annual Growth	12/16	12/17	12/18	12/19	12/20
Sales ($ mil.)	19.4%	1,275.4	1,494.9	1,801.2	2,156.2	2,594.4
Net income ($ mil.)	97.4%	32.2	31.4	332.2	326.5	488.5
Market value ($ mil.)	49.0%	4,894.5	7,099.6	11,444.9	17,348.5	24,136.1
Employees	15.3%	4,665	5,066	5,845	7,082	8,238

FORTIS CONSTRUCTION, INC.

1705 SW TAYLOR ST STE 200
PORTLAND, OR 972051922
Phone: 503-459-4477
Fax: -
Web: www.fortisconstruction.com

CEO: -
CFO: -
HR: -
FYE: December 31
Type: Private

Fortis Construction isn't afraid to get its hands dirty. The fast-growing US construction company offers general contracting preconstruction construction management and environmentally-friendly green building services to customers primarily in Portland Oregon and others in the Pacific Northwest. It specializes in remodeling and upgrading corporate offices health care facilities retail complexes and schools; it also conducts seismic and structural upgrades. Customers have included Oregon State University Portland State University PPG Industries and StanCorp.

	Annual Growth	12/12	12/13	12/14	12/15	12/16
Sales ($ mil.)	66.6%	-	-	282.1	469.0	782.8
Net income ($ mil.)	48.0%	-	-	14.0	18.1	30.7
Market value ($ mil.)	-	-	-	-	-	-
Employees	-	-	-	-	-	175

FORTRESS INVESTMENT GROUP LLC
NYS: FIG

1345 Avenue of the Americas
New York, NY 10105
Phone: 212 798-6100
Fax: -

CEO: Peter Briger Jr
CFO: -
HR: -
FYE: December 31
Type: Public

Fortress Investment Group protects its investors' money. The global investment firm manages private equity and hedge funds for institutional investors wealthy individuals and on its own behalf. Its private equity arm buys long-term controlling stakes in undervalued or distressed companies and credit assets; it also manages real estate investors Newcastle Investment and Eurocastle Investment. The hedge fund arm invests in liquid markets. Fortress offers traditional asset management through Logan Circle Partners. Fortress earns fees performance-based incentive revenues and investment income on its own investments. The firm has more than $67 billion in assets under management.

	Annual Growth	12/11	12/12	12/13	12/14	12/15
Sales ($ mil.)	9.0%	858.6	969.9	1,265.0	1,811.8	1,213.9
Net income ($ mil.)	-	(431.5)	78.3	200.4	100.0	78.5
Market value ($ mil.)	10.8%	1,305.7	1,695.9	3,306.8	3,098.2	1,966.3
Employees	32.7%	979	1,996	2,324	2,860	3,040

FORTUNE BRANDS HOME & SECURITY, INC.
NYS: FBHS

520 Lake Cook Road
Deerfield, IL 60015-5611
Phone: 847 484-4400
Fax: -
Web: www.fbhs.com

CEO: Nicholas Fink
CFO: Patrick Hallinan
HR: -
FYE: December 31
Type: Public

With over 55 manufacturing facilities worldwide Fortune Brands Home & Security (FBHS) is a leading home and security products company that competes in attractive long-term growth markets in its product categories. It manufactures assembles and sells kitchen sinks and waste disposals faucets entry doors and security products. Its well-known brands include Moen faucets Sentry Safe security cabinets and Therma-Tru entry doors along with Master Lock and American Lock padlocks and other security products. Most of the company's products are the top sellers in their respective markets and are distributed via kitchen and bath dealers wholesalers oriented toward builders or professional remodelers industrial and locksmith distributors "do-it-yourself" remodeling-oriented home centers e-commerce and other retail outlets. FBHS generates about 85% of sales in the US.

	Annual Growth	12/16	12/17	12/18	12/19	12/20
Sales ($ mil.)	5.1%	4,984.9	5,283.3	5,485.1	5,764.6	6,090.3
Net income ($ mil.)	7.6%	413.2	472.6	389.6	431.9	553.1
Market value ($ mil.)	12.5%	7,412.8	9,489.9	5,267.7	9,060.1	11,885.9
Employees	4.9%	22,700	23,800	25,300	24,700	27,500

FORUM ENERGY TECHNOLOGIES INC
NYS: FET

10344 Sam Houston Park Drive, Suite 300
Houston, TX 77064
Phone: 281 949-2500
Fax: 281 949-2554
Web: www.f-e-t.com

CEO: Neal Lux
CFO: D. Lyle Williams
HR: -
FYE: December 31
Type: Public

Forum Energy Technologies (Forum) designs manufactures and sells equipment for companies in the oil and gas industry. Its products used to build and update processing centers refineries and infrastructure include drilling equipment (tubular handling equipment and drilling data-management systems) and consumable products (expendable fluid end-components for mud and centrifugal pumps valves and pressure control equipment). It also makes remote operating vehicles (ROVs) for subsea work. Complementing its product offerings Forum provides drilling contracting and oilfield services as well as equipment rental and assembly. The company was formed in 2005. Most of the company's sales were generated from the US accounting to some 70% of sales.

	Annual Growth	12/16	12/17	12/18	12/19	12/20
Sales ($ mil.)	(3.4%)	587.6	818.6	1,064.2	956.5	512.5
Net income ($ mil.)	-	(82.0)	(59.4)	(374.1)	(567.1)	(96.9)
Market value ($ mil.)	(14.2%)	122.8	86.8	23.1	9.4	66.4
Employees	(9.1%)	2,050	2,600	2,500	2,300	1,400

FORWARD AIR CORP
NMS: FWRD

1915 Snapps Ferry Road Building N
Greeneville, TN 37745
Phone: 423 636-7000
Fax: –
Web: www.forwardair.com

CEO: Thomas Schmitt
CFO: Rebecca Garbrick
HR: –
FYE: December 31
Type: Public

Forward Air is a leading asset-light freight and logistics company. Forward Air provide less-than-truckload (LTL) final mile truckload and intermodal drayage services across the United States and in Canada. It also offers premium services that typically require precision execution such as expedited transit delivery during tight time windows and special handling. The company has nearly 6010 trailers and over 230 owned and over 565 leased tractors and straight trucks in its fleet. It also provides services such as warehousing customs brokerage and other handling.

	Annual Growth	12/16	12/17	12/18	12/19	12/20
Sales ($ mil.)	6.6%	982.5	1,100.8	1,320.9	1,410.4	1,269.6
Net income ($ mil.)	(3.8%)	27.7	87.3	92.1	87.1	23.7
Market value ($ mil.)	12.8%	1,294.3	1,569.1	1,498.3	1,910.8	2,099.0
Employees	(3.9%)	4,868	4,898	5,369	5,480	4,144

FORWARD INDUSTRIES, INC.
NAS: FORD

700 Veterans Memorial Highway, Suite 100
Hauppauge, NY 11788
Phone: 631 547-3041
Fax: –
Web: www.forwardindustries.com

CEO: Tom Kramer
CFO: Anthony Camarda
HR: –
FYE: September 30
Type: Public

Forward Industries knows how to make a good case. The company designs and markets carrying cases bags clips hand straps and related items for medical monitoring kits bar code scanners and a range of consumer products (such as cell phones MP3 players cameras and firearms). Contractors in China manufacture most of the company's products which are made of leather nylon vinyl plastic PVC and other synthetic fibers. The products are primarily sold to original equipment manufacturers (OEMs). Forward's top three customers are makers of diabetic testing kits and generate more than 70% of revenues.

	Annual Growth	09/17	09/18	09/19	09/20	09/21
Sales ($ mil.)	12.0%	24.8	34.5	37.4	34.5	39.0
Net income ($ mil.)	(2.5%)	0.6	1.4	(3.6)	(1.8)	0.5
Market value ($ mil.)	17.9%	12.4	15.4	9.8	14.0	24.0
Employees	73.2%	10	73	73	85	90

FOSSIL GROUP INC
NMS: FOSL

901 S. Central Expressway
Richardson, TX 75080
Phone: 972 234-2525
Fax: –
Web: www.fossilgroup.com

CEO: Kosta Kartsotis
CFO: Sunil M Doshi
HR: Darren Hart
FYE: January 02
Type: Public

Fossil's bedrock is the watch business. It also distributes fashion accessories such as leather goods handbags sunglasses and jewelry. A leading seller of mid-priced fashion watches in the US its brands include company-owned Fossil and Relic watches and licensed names like Armani Michael Kors Chaps By Ralph Lauren DKNY and Kate Spade New York to name a few. It also offers private-label watches for Nordstrom Target and Walmart. The company peddles its products through department stores mass merchandisers and specialty shops in some 150 countries as well as online and at around 450 company-owned stores in the US and abroad. Its products are also sold on cruise ships and in airports. About 35% of the company's revenue is generated in the US.

	Annual Growth	12/16	12/17	12/18	12/19*	01/21
Sales ($ mil.)	(11.9%)	3,042.4	2,788.2	2,541.5	2,217.7	1,613.3
Net income ($ mil.)		78.9	(478.2)	(3.5)	(52.4)	(96.1)
Market value ($ mil.)	(19.6%)	1,331.1	400.0	835.4	398.4	446.3
Employees	(12.4%)	14,500	12,300	10,800	10,200	7,500

*Fiscal year change

FOSTER (L.B.) CO
NMS: FSTR

415 Holiday Drive, Suite 100
Pittsburgh, PA 15220
Phone: 412 928-3400
Fax: –
Web: www.lbfoster.com

CEO: John Kasel
CFO: William Thalman
HR: Brian Kelly
FYE: December 31
Type: Public

L. B. Foster provides products and services for the rail industry and solutions to support critical infrastructure projects. The company manufactures new and relay rail and trackwork used in railroad and mass transit systems as well as in industrial markets such as mining. L. B. Foster also supplies pipe coatings for oil and natural gas pipelines and utilities precision measurement systems for the oil and gas market and produces threaded pipe products for industrial water well and irrigation markets as well as the oil and gas markets. The US is its largest market accounting for some 80%. The company was established in 1902.

	Annual Growth	12/16	12/17	12/18	12/19	12/20
Sales ($ mil.)	0.7%	483.5	536.4	627.0	655.1	497.4
Net income ($ mil.)		(141.7)	4.1	(31.2)	42.6	7.6
Market value ($ mil.)	2.6%	143.7	286.8	168.0	204.7	159.0
Employees	(2.3%)	1,241	1,475	1,480	1,330	1,130

FOUNDATION HEALTHCARE, INC
NBB: FDNH

13900 N. Portland Avenue, Suite 200
Oklahoma City, OK 73134
Phone: 405 608-1700
Fax: –
Web: www.fdnh.com

CEO: –
CFO: –
HR: –
FYE: December 31
Type: Public

Graymark Healthcare wants its businesses to help remedy the ills of small-town Americans. Through its operating subsidiaries Graymark Healthcare acquires and operates independent pharmacies and sleep diagnostic centers many of which are located in smaller US markets. Its ApothecaryRx subsidiary manages pharmacies doing business in a handful of central US states and the company's Sleep Disorder Centers (SDC) subsidiary manages sleep diagnostics businesses in the South and Midwest. Formerly Graymark Productions (a film production firm) Graymark changed its name in 2008 following the acquisitions of ApothecaryRx and SDC. The company sold sell its ApothecaryRx stores to Walgreen in late 2010.

	Annual Growth	12/11	12/12	12/13	12/14	12/15
Sales ($ mil.)	64.3%	17.5	17.0	93.1	104.8	127.5
Net income ($ mil.)	–	(5.9)	(22.4)	(19.4)	(1.3)	5.9
Market value ($ mil.)	73.6%	8.0	3.9	5.9	5.5	72.7
Employees	54.4%	217	155	1,012	971	1,232

FOUNDATION MEDICINE INC
NMS: FMI

150 Second Street
Cambridge, MA 02141
Phone: 617 418-2200
Fax: –
Web: www.foundationmedicine.com

CEO: Brian Alexander
CFO: Jason Ryan
HR: –
FYE: December 31
Type: Public

The right course of cancer treatment starts with a good foundation — at the molecular level. Foundation Medicine's personalized medicine test kit named FoundationOne analyzes a patient's genetic profile to determine a treatment strategy. The company processes the tests for solid tumor cancers and provides doctors and oncologists with a written report that matches detected molecular alterations with relevant treatment options and clinical trials. Foundation Medicine which has received investment funding from Bill Gates went public in 2013. In 2015 Roche acquired a controlling interest in the company for just over $1 billion.

	Annual Growth	12/12	12/13	12/14	12/15	12/16
Sales ($ mil.)	82.0%	10.6	29.0	61.1	93.2	116.9
Net income ($ mil.)		(22.4)	(42.9)	(52.2)	(89.6)	(113.2)
Market value ($ mil.)	(9.4%)	–	840.4	783.9	743.0	624.5
Employees	39.3%	142	186	293	417	535

FOUR OAKS FINCORP, INC.

NBB: FOFN

6114 U.S. 301 South
Four Oaks, NC 27524
Phone: 919 963-2177
Fax: –
Web: www.fouroaksbank.com

CEO: –
CFO: –
HR: –
FYE: December 31
Type: Public

There's no need to knock on wood when trusting your money to Four Oaks Fincorp. It's the holding company for Four Oaks Bank & Trust which (with the 2008 acquisition of LongLeaf Community Bank) operates about 20 branches in central and eastern North Carolina. The bank offers standard retail products and services including checking and savings accounts CDs IRAs and money market accounts. It originates mostly real estate loans which account for nearly 90% of loans. It also writes business consumer and farm loans. Four Oaks Bank also offers insurance and investment services. The company in 2009 acquired Nuestro Banco a single-branch bank serving Hispanic customers in Raleigh.

	Annual Growth	12/11	12/12	12/13	12/14	12/15
Assets ($ mil.)	(6.8%)	916.6	865.5	821.5	820.8	691.4
Net income ($ mil.)	–	(9.1)	(7.0)	(0.4)	(4.2)	20.0
Market value ($ mil.)	16.5%	31.9	30.2	53.8	51.1	58.8
Employees	(1.2%)	194	192	177	183	185

FOX BROADCASTING COMPANY

10201 W. Pico Blvd.
Los Angeles CA 90035
Phone: 310-369-1000
Fax: 310-969-0468
Web: www.foxmovies.com

CEO: David F Devoe Jr
CFO: –
HR: –
FYE: June 30
Type: Subsidiary

TV viewers worshiping the Idol have helped make FOX a ratings superstar. FOX Broadcasting operates the #2 broadcast television network in the US (behind CBS). It has more than 200 affiliate stations including 17 company-owned TV outlets that reach 99% of all US television households. The network offers such hit primetime shows as New Girl Raising Hope Bones Glee Fringe So You Think You Can Dance and House as well as its Sunday night lineup of comedy animation programs The Simpsons Family Guy The Cleveland Show and American Dad. Launched with only six stations in 1986 FOX is a major subsidiary of Rupert Murdoch's News Corporation.

FOX CHASE BANCORP, INC.

NMS: FXCB

4390 Davisville Road
Hatboro, PA 19040
Phone: 215 283-2900
Fax: –
Web: www.foxchasebank.com

CEO: –
CFO: –
HR: –
FYE: December 31
Type: Public

Fox Chase Bancorp is the holding company for Fox Chase Bank which has served individuals and businesses in the Philadelphia area since 1867. The bank operates about a dozen offices in southeastern Pennsylvania and southern New Jersey; it offers standard products and services including checking and savings accounts CDs and money market accounts. Multifamily and commercial real estate loans make up the largest part of Fox Chase Bank's loan portfolio; commercial and industrial loans are the second-largest loan type. Other offerings include consumer residential and construction loans. Local-peer Univest Corporation of Pennsylvania agreed to buy Fox Chase for $244 million in late 2015.

	Annual Growth	12/10	12/11	12/12	12/13	12/14
Assets ($ mil.)	(0.0%)	1,095.5	1,015.9	1,088.3	1,116.6	1,094.6
Net income ($ mil.)	31.5%	2.7	4.8	5.1	5.5	8.2
Market value ($ mil.)	8.9%	139.9	149.1	196.5	203.9	196.8
Employees	0.2%	148	146	152	153	149

FOX FACTORY HOLDING CORP

NMS: FOXF

2055 Sugarloaf Circle, Suite 300
Duluth, GA 30097
Phone: 831 274-6500
Fax: –
Web: www.ridefox.com

CEO: Michael Dennison
CFO: Scott Humphrey
HR: Dale Silvia
FYE: January 01
Type: Public

Fox Factory Holding Corp. designs engineers manufactures and markets performance-defining products and systems for customers worldwide. The company's premium brand performance-defining products and systems are used primarily on bicycles side-by-side vehicles on-road vehicles with and without off-road capabilities off-road vehicles and trucks all-terrain vehicles (ATVs) snowmobiles specialty vehicles and applications motorcycles and commercial trucks. Fox generates most of its sales from North America region.

	Annual Growth	12/16	12/17	12/18*	01/20	01/21
Sales ($ mil.)	17.2%	403.1	475.6	619.2	751.0	890.6
Net income ($ mil.)	20.5%	35.7	43.1	84.0	93.0	90.7
Market value ($ mil.)	30.7%	1,160.0	1,624.0	2,505.2	2,916.9	4,418.9
Employees	12.0%	1,700	1,800	2,240	2,600	3,000

*Fiscal year change

FOX HEAD, INC.

16752 ARMSTRONG AVE
IRVINE, CA 926064912
Phone: 408-776-8800
Fax: –
Web: www.foxracing.com

CEO: Jeffrey McGuane
CFO: Tanya Fischesser
HR: –
FYE: December 31
Type: Private

Got a need for speed and big jumps? Fox Racing makes and distributes motocross and other extreme sport apparel accessories and protective gear such as racewear pants jerseys gloves boots and helmets emblazoned with its fox head graphic logo. The company also offers bicycle motocross (BMX) and mountain bike apparel T-shirts hats jeans hoodies and pullovers and jackets. Line extensions include eyewear footwear and surf and wakeboard wear. Fox Racing sells its apparel through retail sporting goods and cycle and surf shops nationwide. International offices are located in Canada and the UK. Founded in 1974 by Geoff Fox the company is family-owned and run by its second generation.

	Annual Growth	12/05	12/06	12/07	12/08	12/09
Sales ($ mil.)	1.1%	–	–	211.7	244.0	216.3
Net income ($ mil.)	4.5%	–	–	18.7	24.4	20.4
Market value ($ mil.)	–	–	–	–	–	–
Employees	–	–	–	–	–	518

FOX NEWS NETWORK LLC

1211 Avenue of the Americas
New York NY 10036
Phone: 212-301-3000
Fax: 212-301-8588
Web: www.foxnews.com

CEO: Suzanne Scott
CFO: Jack Abernethy
HR: –
FYE: June 30
Type: Subsidiary

This news channel reports and people have decided to watch ... a lot of people. FOX News Network operates the FOX News Channel the leading 24-hour cable news station reaching more than 90 million US homes. It provides round-the-clock news coverage and commentary including programs such as The O'Reilly Factor featuring commentator Bill O'Reilly and Hannity with Sean Hannity. FOX News also produces content distributed to TV affiliates of the FOX network and publishes news online; its FOX News Radio Network syndicates news to radio stations around the country. Launched by Rupert Murdoch's News Corp. in 1996 the channel's less than tacit support of conservative politics has stirred both passion and criticism.

FOX SEARCHLIGHT PICTURES INC.

10201 W. Pico Blvd. Bldg. 769 — CEO: –
Los Angeles CA 90035 — CFO: –
Phone: 310-369-4402 — HR: –
Fax: 310-369-1491 — FYE: June 30
Web: www.foxsearchlight.com — Type: Subsidiary

The light shines brightly on this specialty film division of Fox Filmed Entertainment. Rather than produce big-budget blockbusters Fox Searchlight Pictures produces smaller specialized films in genres such as drama comedy horror and science fiction. Notable titles in the Fox Searchlight canon include successful indie films such as Little Miss Sunshine Napoleon Dynamite and "Boys Don't Cry". More recent movies include Cyrus and Crazy Heart. Fox Searchlight was founded in 1994 by Fox Filmed Entertainment Co-Chairman Tom Rothman as the independent arm of Twentieth Century Fox. It has its own marketing and distribution operations. International distribution is handled by Twentieth Century Fox.

FOXWORTH-GALBRAITH LUMBER COMPANY

4965 PRESTON PARK BLVD # 400 — CEO: Walter L Foxworth
PLANO, TX 750935141 — CFO: Rich Perkins
Phone: 972-665-2400 — HR: Phr A Andrews
Fax: – — FYE: December 31
Web: www.foxgal.com — Type: Private

Foxworth-Galbraith Lumber Company is helping to build out the Southwest. The company sells hardware lumber paint plumbing equipment tools and other building supplies through more than 20 locations across Texas New Mexico Arizona and Colorado (versus about 70 stores in 2006). Foxworth-Galbraith's main customers are residential and commercial builders; other clients include do-it-yourselfers specialty contractors and federal and state agencies. Foxworth-Galbraith is still owned and operated by the families of W.L. Foxworth and H.W. Galbraith who founded the company in Dalhart Texas in 1901 to take advantage of railroad construction.

	Annual Growth	12/08	12/09	12/10	12/11	12/12
Sales ($ mil.)	13.0%	–	–	154.7	164.4	197.6
Net income ($ mil.)	–	–	–	(10.2)	(3.9)	0.8
Market value ($ mil.)	–	–	–	–	–	–
Employees	–	–	–	–	–	2,500

FPB BANCORP INC.
NASDAQ: FPBI

1301 SE Port St. Lucie Blvd. — CEO: David W Skiles
Port St. Lucie FL 34952 — CFO: –
Phone: 772-398-1388 — HR: –
Fax: 772-398-1399 — FYE: December 31
Web: www.1stpeoplesbank.com — Type: Public

FPB Bancorp is for the birds. Snow birds that is. It's the holding company for First Peoples Bank which targets retired winter visitors as well as year-round residents and small to midsized businesses in southeastern Florida. The six-branch bank operates in Fort Pierce Palm City Port St. Lucie Stuart and Vero Beach offering such standard deposit products as CDs and checking savings and money market accounts. Commercial real estate and business loans together account for about 85% of its loan portfolio; consumer loans make up most of the rest. The bank sells into the secondary market all of the fixed-rate residential mortgages that it writes. First Peoples Bank opened two new branches in 2008.

FPIC INSURANCE GROUP INC.
NASDAQ: FPIC

1000 Riverside Ave. Ste. 800 — CEO: John R Byers
Jacksonville FL 32204 — CFO: Charles Divita III
Phone: 904-354-2482 — HR: –
Fax: 904-475-1159 — FYE: December 31
Web: www.fpic.com — Type: Public

Pulled the wrong tooth or read an X-ray backwards? FPIC Insurance Group knows that these things happen. Through its First Professionals Insurance subsidiary the company sells medical professional liability insurance (including medical error and malpractice) to more than 18000 physicians and dentists. Its Anesthesiologists Professional Assurance subsidiary serves that specialty market. Although FPIC operates in more than a dozen states Florida accounts for more than 70% of its premiums written. Its subsidiaries sell policies through independent agents and First Professionals Insurance is an endorsed carrier for several regional medical associations. FPIC was acquired by The Doctors Company in 2011.

FRANCHISE GROUP INC
NMS: FRG

109 Innovation Court, Suite J — CEO: Brian Kahn
Delaware, OH 43015 — CFO: Eric Seeton
Phone: 740 363-2222 — HR: –
Fax: – — FYE: December 26
Web: www.franchisegrp.com — Type: Public

Franchise Group Inc. formerly known as Liberty Tax is an owner and operator of franchised and franchisable businesses that continually looks to grow its portfolio of brands while utilizing its operating and capital allocation philosophies to generate strong cash flows. Its business lines include American Freight The Vitamin Shoppe Liberty Tax Service Buddy's Home Furnishings and Pet Supplies Plus which was acquired in 2021 for $700 million. Franchise Group operates more than 4000 locations predominantly located in the US and Canada consisting of some 2750 franchised locations and 1280 company run locations.

	Annual Growth	04/17	04/18	04/19*	12/19	12/20
Sales ($ mil.)	131.3%	174.0	174.9	132.5	149.5	2,152.5
Net income ($ mil.)	24.4%	13.0	0.1	(2.2)	(68.4)	25.1
Market value ($ mil.)	26.8%	563.3	413.0	360.8	967.4	1,148.2
Employees	75.4%	1,498	1,514	795	8,038	8,083

*Fiscal year change

FRANCIS SAINT MEDICAL CENTER

211 SAINT FRANCIS DR — CEO: Mary Ann Reese
CAPE GIRARDEAU, MO 637035049 — CFO: David Prather
Phone: 573-331-3000 — HR: –
Fax: – — FYE: June 30
Web: www.sfmc.net — Type: Private

It may be guided by Catholic principles but you don't have to be a saint to get medical care at Saint Francis Medical Center. The hospital serves a five-state region from Missouri (its home base) to Arkansas with about 285 beds. Services include emergency medicine orthopedics cancer rehabilitation and women's health care. It also offers heart and neurosciences institutes as well as diabetes education and wound healing centers. The health care provider which was established in 1875 partners with Poplar Bluff Medical Partners to provide outpatient care at Poplar Bluff Medical Complex. Services include family practice OB-GYN and pain management.

	Annual Growth	06/10	06/11	06/14	06/15	06/16
Sales ($ mil.)	1.2%	–	423.1	433.9	424.2	449.8
Net income ($ mil.)	(8.4%)	–	48.2	37.7	41.0	31.1
Market value ($ mil.)	–	–	–	–	–	–
Employees	–	–	–	–	–	1,500

FRANCISCAN ALLIANCE, INC.

1515 W DRAGOON TRL
MISHAWAKA, IN 465444710
Phone: 574-273-3867
Fax: –
Web: www.franciscanhealth.org

CEO: Kevin D Leahy
CFO: –
HR: –
FYE: December 31
Type: Private

Franciscan Alliance is a not-for-profit organization operating more than a dozen hospitals in Indiana and south suburban Chicago. The hospitals include specialist centers for cancer care heart and vascular care weight loss pediatrics and women's health. In addition to inpatient acute care services they operate numerous outpatient facilities and medical practices within their local service areas. Other subsidiaries and affiliates perform clinical laboratory tests offer home health services and provide support services to the system. Franciscan Alliance was founded and is sponsored by the Sisters of St. Francis of Perpetual Adoration.

	Annual Growth	12/13	12/14	12/15	12/18	12/19
Sales ($ mil.)	4.4%	–	2,661.2	2,731.1	3,144.5	3,302.7
Net income ($ mil.)	8.3%	–	274.1	250.7	14.2	409.0
Market value ($ mil.)	–	–	–	–	–	–
Employees	–	–	–	–	–	19,000

FRANCISCAN HEALTH SYSTEM

1717 S J ST
TACOMA, WA 984054933
Phone: 253-426-4101
Fax: –
Web: www.chifranciscan.org

CEO: Joseph W Wilczek
CFO: Mike Fitzgerald
HR: –
FYE: June 30
Type: Private

St. Francis himself may have hailed from Italy but his followers look after the health of the residents of the South Puget Sound area through the Franciscan Health System. The not-for-profit system includes five full-service hospitals. The oldest and largest hospital is St. Joseph Medical Center in Tacoma Washington a 320-bed facility. Its facilities include community hospitals St. Clare Hospital (in Lakewood) and St. Francis Hospital (in Federal Way) as well as a hospice program and numerous primary and specialty care clinics. Its St. Anthony Hospital is an 80-bed full service pharmacy and home medical equipment retail location at Gig Harbor.

	Annual Growth	06/09	06/10	06/14	06/15	06/16
Sales ($ mil.)	(8.6%)	–	1,094.0	1,190.7	610.2	637.6
Net income ($ mil.)	(5.4%)	–	71.4	(106.7)	56.1	51.3
Market value ($ mil.)	–	–	–	–	–	–
Employees	–	–	–	–	–	3,183

FRANCISCAN UNIVERSITY OF STEUBENVILLE

1235 UNIVERSITY BLVD
STEUBENVILLE, OH 439521792
Phone: 740-283-3771
Fax: –
Web: www.franciscan.edu

CEO: –
CFO: –
HR: –
FYE: May 31
Type: Private

Franciscan University of Steubenville is a Roman Catholic school that provides instruction to more than 2300 students. It offers more than 30 undergraduate majors as well as master's degrees in six separate fields. The college was established in 1946 when Steubenville Ohio's first bishop John King Mussio invited Franciscan friars to establish a college to serve the needs of local students especially veterans of WWII.

	Annual Growth	05/09	05/10	05/13	05/15	05/17
Sales ($ mil.)	2.5%	–	63.5	73.7	83.5	75.5
Net income ($ mil.)	17.2%	–	1.9	7.6	8.3	5.8
Market value ($ mil.)	–	–	–	–	–	–
Employees	–	–	–	–	–	375

FRANK'S INTERNATIONAL INC.

10260 Westheimer Rd.
Houston TX 77042
Phone: 281-966-7300
Fax: 281-966-0948
Web: www.franksinternational.com

CEO: Donald Keith Mosing
CFO: Mark Margavio
HR: –
FYE: December 31
Type: Private

If you are building an oil well drilling platform or offshore rig you probably know Frank. Frank's International supplies tools equipment and specialty services to oil exploration and production companies worldwide. Its products include pipes tools connectors casings and specialty hammers. Frank's also offers engineering design installation testing and custom fabrication services. With five affiliated companies including Antelope Oil Tools and Pilot Drilling Control operating in 11 US cities and about 40 countries on every continent it goes where the oil is. Frank's was formed in 1938 by Frank Mosing as Frank's Casing and Tool Rental. The Mosing family continues to own and run the company.

FRANKLIN AND MARSHALL COLLEGE

415 HARRISBURG AVE
LANCASTER, PA 176032827
Phone: 717-291-3911
Fax: –
Web: www.fandm.edu

CEO: –
CFO: Eileen Austin
HR: –
FYE: June 30
Type: Private

Franklin & Marshall College named after Benjamin Franklin and John Marshall is a private liberal arts institution serving about 2400 students. It offers academic and research programs in about 60 fields including biology chemistry English history mathematics political science art sociology and environmental studies. It offers programs in 11 languages including Arabic and Greek. Franklin & Marshall College was created in 1853 through the merger of Franklin College (founded in 1787 with a contribution from Ben Franklin) and Marshall College (opened in 1836 and named after Chief Justice John Marshall).

	Annual Growth	06/12	06/13	06/15	06/17	06/20
Sales ($ mil.)	1.0%	–	165.0	208.1	151.3	176.4
Net income ($ mil.)	–	–	9.2	37.1	28.5	(17.6)
Market value ($ mil.)	–	–	–	–	–	–
Employees	–	–	–	–	–	800

FRANKLIN COMMUNITY HEALTH NETWORK

111 FRANKLIN HEALTH CMNS
FARMINGTON, ME 049386144
Phone: 207-779-2265
Fax: –
Web: www.fchn.org

CEO: Rebecca Ryder
CFO: –
HR: Judith M West
FYE: June 30
Type: Private

When it comes to providing health care Franklin Community Health Network would rather rough it. The not-for-profit health care system serves mountainous rural areas in western Maine. Franklin Community Health Network consists of a 70-bed acute care hospital a behavioral health facility and several physician management groups. Its Franklin Memorial Hospital offers specialized services such as cardiology orthopedics emergency medicine and occupational health care. The health network's unique Contract for Care program allows former patients to volunteer at the hospital if they do not have the means to pay all of their bill.

	Annual Growth	06/10	06/11	06/12	06/13	06/14
Sales ($ mil.)	172.3%	–	3.7	1.0	0.7	75.6
Net income ($ mil.)	(2.0%)	–	0.2	0.1	(1.2)	0.2
Market value ($ mil.)	–	–	–	–	–	–
Employees	–	–	–	–	–	900

FRANKLIN COVEY CO
NYS: FC

2200 West Parkway Boulevard
Salt Lake City, UT 84119-2099
Phone: 801 817-1776
Fax: –
Web: www.franklincovey.com

CEO: Paul Walker
CFO: Stephen Young
HR: –
FYE: August 31
Type: Public

Franklin Covey publisher of the popular book The 7 Habits of Highly Effective People knows a thing or two about performance improvement. Targeted at individuals teams and organizations the company is a global provider of training programs consulting services books and planning products designed around six practice areas: execution sales performance productivity customer royalty and educational improvement. Franklin Covey's clients include the FORTUNE 100 the FORTUNE 500 and thousands of small and midsized businesses. In addition to companies it serves government entities and educational institutions mostly in the US. Majority of the company's sales are from the Americas region.

	Annual Growth	08/17	08/18	08/19	08/20	08/21
Sales ($ mil.)	4.9%	185.3	209.8	225.4	198.5	224.2
Net income ($ mil.)	–	(7.2)	(5.9)	(1.0)	(9.4)	13.6
Market value ($ mil.)	23.3%	266.3	362.7	521.2	279.7	615.8
Employees	4.1%	850	890	940	940	1,000

FRANKLIN CREDIT HOLDING CORPORATION
PINK SHEETS: FCMC

101 Hudson St.
Jersey City NJ 07302
Phone: 201-604-1800
Fax: 201-604-4400
Web: www.franklincredit.com

CEO: –
CFO: Paul D Colasono
HR: –
FYE: December 31
Type: Public

Franklin Credit Holding is the holding company of mortgage servicer Franklin Credit Management. In 2009 the company entered into a restructuring agreement with The Huntington National Bank in which a large number (about 83%) of Franklin's subprime mortgages were transferred to the bank's real estate investment trust (REIT); in exchange Franklin received a capital infusion of more than $13 million and services the mortgages transferred to the bank's books in order to generate fee income. Chairman and president Thomas Axon owns some 45% of Franklin Credit Holdings. Director Frank Evans more than 10%.

FRANKLIN ELECTRIC CO., INC.
NMS: FELE

9255 Coverdale Road
Fort Wayne, IN 46809
Phone: 260 824-2900
Fax: –
Web: www.franklin-electric.com

CEO: Gregg C Sengstack
CFO: Jeffery L Taylor
HR: –
FYE: December 31
Type: Public

Franklin Electric manufactures and distributes pumps and motors including submersible and specialty electric motors electronic drives and controls and related items. Its fueling systems products include electronic tank monitoring equipment fittings flexible piping nozzles and vapor recovery systems. Franklin Electric's products are used by OEMs for underground petroleum pumping systems sewage pumps vacuum pumping systems and freshwater pumping systems. Some customers such as independent distributors and repair shops buy the company's products as replacement motors. Franklin Electric serves customers worldwide but generates more than 55% of sales from the US. The company was founded in 1944.

	Annual Growth	12/16	12/17	12/18	12/19	12/20
Sales ($ mil.)	7.0%	949.9	1,124.9	1,298.1	1,314.6	1,247.3
Net income ($ mil.)	6.3%	78.7	78.2	105.9	95.5	100.5
Market value ($ mil.)	15.5%	1,798.0	2,121.6	1,982.0	2,649.4	3,199.0
Employees	0.9%	5,200	5,600	5,600	5,400	5,400

FRANKLIN FINANCIAL SERVICES CORP
NAS: FRAF

20 South Main Street
Chambersburg, PA 17201-0819
Phone: 717 264-6116
Fax: 717 264-7129
Web: www.franklinfin.com

CEO: Timothy Henry
CFO: Mark Hollar
HR: Karen Carmack
FYE: December 31
Type: Public

Ben Franklin said "A penny saved is a penny earned" but Franklin Financial might be able to convert those pennies into dollars. It's the holding company for Farmers and Merchants Trust Company (F&M Trust) a community bank serving south-central Pennsylvania from more than 20 locations. Established in 1906 F&M Trust offers standard deposit products including checking and savings accounts IRAs and CDs. It also provides discount brokerage insurance retirement planning and other investment services. More than half of the company's lending portfolio is devoted to commercial industrial and agricultural loans; the bank also makes consumer construction and residential mortgage loans.

	Annual Growth	12/16	12/17	12/18	12/19	12/20
Assets ($ mil.)	8.0%	1,127.4	1,179.8	1,209.6	1,269.2	1,535.0
Net income ($ mil.)	12.2%	8.1	2.2	6.1	16.1	12.8
Market value ($ mil.)	(1.4%)	125.5	164.0	138.3	169.8	118.6
Employees	3.4%	247	255	255	283	282

FRANKLIN HOSPITAL

900 FRANKLIN AVE
VALLEY STREAM, NY 115802190
Phone: 516-256-6000
Fax: –

CEO: –
CFO: –
HR: –
FYE: December 31
Type: Private

Franklin Hospital is part of the North Shore-Long Island Jewish Health System. The medical center has more than 300 beds and provides emergency and specialty care services. Franklin Hospital includes the 120-bed Orzac Center a long-term care rehabilitation unit as well as a 21-bed psychiatric unit and an adult day care center. Franklin Hospital also provides outpatient care — including pediatrics and women's health — and home health services. Established in 1963 as a small community hospital Franklin offers services and programs to the residents of Nassau and southeastern Queens Counties.

	Annual Growth	12/07	12/08	12/12	12/13	12/14
Sales ($ mil.)	0.2%	–	169.5	175.3	192.0	171.1
Net income ($ mil.)	–	–	(3.8)	5.6	0.7	(0.7)
Market value ($ mil.)	–	–	–	–	–	–
Employees	–	–	–	–	–	1,300

FRANKLIN RESOURCES INC
NYS: BEN

One Franklin Parkway
San Mateo, CA 94403
Phone: 650 312-2000
Fax: 650 312-3655
Web: www.franklinresources.com

CEO: Jennifer Johnson
CFO: Matthew Nicholls
HR: –
FYE: September 30
Type: Public

Operating as Franklin Templeton Investments Franklin Resources manages mutual funds that invest in international and domestic stocks taxable and tax-exempt money market instruments and corporate municipal and US government bonds. Franklin Resources also offers separately managed accounts closed-end funds insurance product funds and retirement and college savings plans. The products are housed under the company's Franklin Templeton Legg Mason Franklin Mutual Series Franklin Bissett Fiduciary Trust International K2 LibertyShares and Martin Currie brands. Franklin Resources and its subsidiaries boast roughly $1.5 billion in assets under management. The US is the company's largest market accounting for about 70% of total revenue.

	Annual Growth	09/17	09/18	09/19	09/20	09/21
Sales ($ mil.)	7.1%	6,392.2	6,319.1	5,774.5	5,566.5	8,425.5
Net income ($ mil.)	1.9%	1,696.7	764.4	1,195.7	798.9	1,831.2
Market value ($ mil.)	(9.6%)	22,335.5	15,260.0	14,482.2	10,211.8	14,913.7
Employees	2.3%	9,400	9,700	9,600	11,800	10,300

FRANKLIN SQUARE HOSPITAL CENTER, INC.

9000 FRANKLIN SQUARE DR
BALTIMORE, MD 212373901
Phone: 410-933-2777
Fax: –
Web: www.medstarfranklinsquare.org

CEO: –
CFO: Robert P Lally Jr
HR: –
FYE: June 30
Type: Private

Franklin Square Hospital Center has made a declaration to care for the residents of eastern Baltimore County Maryland. The facility offers a wide range of specialties through some 700 doctors and about 380 beds. Since 1998 the hospital has been part of MedStar Health the region's largest integrated health system. As a teaching hospital Franklin Square offers a number of residency programs including internal and family medicine OB-GYN and surgery. The not-for-profit hospital offers its medical services through half a dozen primary service lines: Medicine Surgery Women's and Children's Care Oncology Behavioral Health and Community Health and Wellness.

	Annual Growth	06/10	06/11	06/15	06/16	06/20
Sales ($ mil.)	3.3%	–	452.9	492.9	506.2	605.8
Net income ($ mil.)	13.4%	–	18.1	17.3	10.8	56.0
Market value ($ mil.)	–	–	–	–	–	–
Employees	–	–	–	–	–	3,019

FRANKLIN STREET PROPERTIES CORP

ASE: FSP

401 Edgewater Place, Suite 200
Wakefield, MA 01880
Phone: 781 557-1300
Fax: –
Web: www.fspreit.com

CEO: George Carter
CFO: John Demeritt
HR: –
FYE: December 31
Type: Public

Franklin Street Properties acquires finances leases and manages office properties in about a dozen states across the US. The real estate investment trust (REIT) owns more than 30 properties located mainly in suburban areas and manages about 5 others. Its top markets include Atlanta Dallas Denver Houston and Minneapolis. The company's FSP Investment unit is an investment bank and brokerage that organizes REITs that invest in single properties and raises equity for them through private placements. Another subsidiary FSP Property Management manages properties for Franklin Street as well as for some of the REITs sponsored by FSP Investments.

	Annual Growth	12/17	12/18	12/19	12/20	12/21
Sales ($ mil.)	(6.4%)	272.6	268.9	269.1	245.8	209.4
Net income ($ mil.)	–	(15.9)	13.1	6.5	32.6	92.7
Market value ($ mil.)	(13.7%)	1,116.9	647.9	890.2	454.5	618.8
Employees	(3.4%)	39	38	37	37	34

FRANKLIN WIRELESS CORP

NAS: FKWL

9707 Waples Street, Suite 150
San Diego, CA 92121
Phone: 858 623-0000
Fax: 858 623-0050
Web: www.franklinwireless.com

CEO: –
CFO: David Brown
HR: –
FYE: June 30
Type: Public

Franklin Wireless hopes lightning strikes with its wireless data products. The company makes high speed connectivity products for wireless devices. Its products include USB embedded and standalone modems as well as modules PC cards and Wi-Fi hotspot routers. Customers use its products to connect their mobile computers to wireless broadband networks. Franklin Wireless primarily sells directly to wireless operators but also through partners and distributors. The US is its largest market but the Caribbean and South America have collectively grown to nearly 25% of sales. The company uses contract manufacturers such as South Korea-based shareholder (about 13%) C-Motech and Samsung Electro-Mechanics.

	Annual Growth	06/17	06/18	06/19	06/20	06/21
Sales ($ mil.)	39.5%	48.6	30.1	36.5	75.1	184.1
Net income ($ mil.)	112.1%	0.9	(2.1)	(1.3)	5.6	17.7
Market value ($ mil.)	42.1%	26.1	21.4	28.4	64.0	106.3
Employees	(0.7%)	76	67	71	71	74

FRASER/WHITE INC.

1631 PONTIUS AVE
LOS ANGELES, CA 900253307
Phone: 310-319-3737
Fax: –
Web: www.frasercommunications.com

CEO: Renee Fraser
CFO: –
HR: –
FYE: December 31
Type: Private

Fraser/White speaks the languages of advertising and marketing. The agency — which does business as Fraser Communications — offers market research media planning and buying interactive (Web design) and public relations services. The company takes an approach it calls 360 Communications — surrounding consumers with a client's message. Clients which tend to come from such industries as automotive consumer goods financial services and health care have included Cedars-Sinai Frederick's of Hollywood and Toyota. President and CEO Renee Fraser founded Fraser Communications in 1992.

	Annual Growth	11/03	11/04	11/05*	12/06	12/08
Sales ($ mil.)	–	–	–	(1,239.4)	32.7	42.0
Net income ($ mil.)	1631.7%	–	–	0.0	3.6	0.1
Market value ($ mil.)	–	–	–	–	–	–
Employees	–	–	–	–	–	35

*Fiscal year change

FRAZIER INDUSTRIAL COMPANY

91 FAIRVIEW AVE
LONG VALLEY, NJ 078533381
Phone: 908-876-3001
Fax: –
Web: www.frazier.com

CEO: William L Mascharka
CFO: Peter Acerra
HR: –
FYE: December 31
Type: Private

This company's racket is structural steel storage systems. Frazier Industrial Co. is a leading manufacturer of structural as opposed to roll-formed steel storage racks at nearly a dozen production centers located across the US Canada and Mexico. These facilities can adapt production to demand and receive just-in-time delivery of raw materials. Customers use Frazier Industrial's storage racks in warehouses factories farms and other industrial and commercial facilities. Among the company's storage products is the Glide 'N Pick pallet cart that automatically rolls out for greater ease in retrieving items. Frazier Industrial is owned by CEO William Mascharka.

	Annual Growth	12/16	12/17	12/18	12/19	12/20
Sales ($ mil.)	0.1%	–	288.1	281.2	336.8	288.6
Net income ($ mil.)	17.8%	–	11.7	21.6	25.6	19.2
Market value ($ mil.)	–	–	–	–	–	–
Employees	–	–	–	–	–	750

FRED MEYER STORES INC.

3800 SE 22nd Ave.
Portland OR 97202
Phone: 503-232-8844
Fax: 503-797-5609
Web: www.fredmeyer.com

CEO: –
CFO: David Deatherage
HR: –
FYE: January 31
Type: Subsidiary

Fred Meyer Stores went out for groceries and wound up in Kroger's cart. Freddy's — as the chain is known — is a supercenter pioneer providing food and general merchandise to cost-conscious consumers in the Pacific Northwest and Alaska. One of the largest supercenter operators in the US (along with Wal-Mart and Costco Wholesale) Fred Meyer's 130 multidepartment stores (averaging more than 165000 sq. ft.) offer everything from apparel and home goods to groceries consumer electronics fuel and jewelry. Its Web store delivers to the Alaska Bush. Kroger has leveraged Fred Meyer's general merchandising expertise as defense against Wal-Mart which has overtaken Kroger as the #1 seller of groceries in the US.

FRED'S INC.
NBB: FRED Q

4300 New Getwell Road
Memphis, TN 38118
Phone: 901 365-8880
Fax: –
Web: www.fredsinc.com

CEO: –
CFO: –
HR: –
FYE: February 02
Type: Public

Generally serving customers with modest or fixed incomes Fred's operates more than 620 discount stores and 360 pharmacies in some 15 states primarily in small- to medium-sized towns in the Southeast. The stores carry more than 12000 brand-name off-brand and private-label products including pharmaceuticals household goods clothing and linens food and tobacco items health and beauty aids and paper and cleaning supplies. The company also provides goods and services to some 15 franchised Fred's stores. Fred's traces its historical roots back to 1947.

	Annual Growth	01/15	01/16	01/17*	02/18	02/19
Sales ($ mil.)	(10.4%)	1,970.0	2,150.7	2,125.4	1,805.4	1,271.7
Net income ($ mil.)	–	(28.9)	(7.4)	(66.5)	(150.2)	(13.0)
Market value ($ mil.)	(35.5%)	580.8	577.3	493.7	107.8	100.8
Employees	(7.9%)	9,148	9,336	9,816	9,106	6,572

*Fiscal year change

FREDDIE MAC
NBB: FMCC

8200 Jones Branch Drive
McLean, VA 22102-3110
Phone: 703 903-2000
Fax: –
Web: www.freddiemac.com

CEO: Michael DeVito
CFO: Christian Lown
HR: –
FYE: December 31
Type: Public

These siblings know there's no place like home. Government-sponsored enterprises (GSEs) Freddie Mac (officially Federal Home Loan Mortgage Corporation) and Fannie Mae were established to provide liquidity stability and affordability to the US housing market. They do so by purchasing mortgages from lenders and packaging them for resale thereby mitigating risk and allowing lenders to provide mortgages to those who may not otherwise qualify. The agency also provides assistance for rental housing. Freddie Mac generates the vast majority of its revenue from mortgage loans. Due to losses related to the subprime mortgage crisis the government seized Fannie and Freddie in 2008.

	Annual Growth	12/17	12/18	12/19	12/20	12/21
Assets ($ mil.)	10.2%	2,049,776.0	2,063,060.0	2,203,623.0	2,627,415.0	3,025,586.0
Net income ($ mil.)	21.1%	5,625.0	9,235.0	7,214.0	7,326.0	12,109.0
Market value ($ mil.)	(24.2%)	1,638.2	689.1	1,952.5	1,514.6	539.5
Employees	4.3%	6,185	6,642	6,912	6,939	7,318

FREDERICK MEMORIAL HOSPITAL, INC.

400 W 7TH ST
FREDERICK, MD 217014593
Phone: 240-566-3300
Fax: –
Web: www.fmh.org

CEO: Thomas A Kleinhanzl
CFO: Michelle Nahan
HR: –
FYE: June 30
Type: Private

Frederick Memorial Healthcare System cares for the sick and unhealthy across The Old Line State. The system operates Frederick Memorial Hospital an acute care facility with some 240 beds and 20 satellite facilities in and around Frederick Maryland. Specialty services include cardiology oncology pediatrics and psychiatry. Other facilities in the system include FMH Immediate Care at Oak Street FMH Crestwood FMH Medical Fitness FMH Rose Hill FMH Wellness FMH Urbana Mt. Airy Health Services and the FMH Regional Cancer Therapy Center. The hospital traces its historical roots all the way back to 1902.

	Annual Growth	06/12	06/13	06/14	06/15	06/16
Sales ($ mil.)	(0.3%)	–	344.8	327.2	327.3	341.9
Net income ($ mil.)	61.3%	–	4.5	7.5	11.1	18.7
Market value ($ mil.)	–	–	–	–	–	–
Employees	–	–	–	–	–	2,600

FREDERICK'S OF HOLLYWOOD GROUP INC
NBB: FOHL

6255 Sunset Boulevard
Hollywood, CA 90028
Phone: 323 466-5151
Fax: 212 684-3400
Web: www.fredericks.com; www.fohgroup.com

CEO: Thomas Lynch
CFO: Thomas Rende
HR: –
FYE: July 27
Type: Public

Frederick's of Hollywood Group makes big money out of little somethings. Initially formed by the merger of Frederick's of Hollywood and Movie Star it sells intimates wigs hosiery and dresses through its catalog division (which mails more than 13 million) website and about 120 namesake stores in the US. It's also developing a presence in the Middle East. The manufacturer now soley focuses on its retail business. Years after acquiring Movie Star the group shed the wholesaler which made intimate apparel sleepwear leisurewear and loungewear. Additionally Frederick's of Hollywood Group in late 2010 sold off its wholesale unit to Dolce Vita Intimates amid declining revenues.

	Annual Growth	07/09	07/10	07/11	07/12	07/13
Sales ($ mil.)	(16.3%)	176.3	133.9	119.6	111.4	86.5
Net income ($ mil.)	–	(34.0)	(21.2)	(12.1)	(6.4)	(22.5)
Market value ($ mil.)	(32.3%)	33.3	36.0	26.2	15.3	7.0
Employees	(15.6%)	1,779	1,179	1,044	926	902

FREDERICK'S OF HOLLYWOOD INC.

6255 W. Sunset Blvd. Suite 600
Hollywood CA 90028
Phone: 323-466-5151
Fax: 323-464-5149
Web: www.fredericks.com

CEO: William Soncini
CFO: Thomas Rende
HR: –
FYE: July 31
Type: Subsidiary

Even in a town not known for modesty Frederick's of Hollywood is an eye-opener. Operating about 120 women's intimate apparel shops in the US (primarily in malls) it sells lingerie bras panties foundations dresses wigs and hosiery under the Frederick's of Hollywood brand name. The firm pioneered the push-up bra and other dainties designed from a man's point of view but has extended its reach by adding ready-to-wear items jewelry and perfume. It operates a mail-order catalog unit in the US and Canada which produces some 13 million catalogs and an online store. When Frederick's of Hollywood merged with Movie Star the combined entity and new parent became known as Frederick's of Hollywood Group.

FREEDOM FROM HUNGER

1644 Da Vinci Ct.
Davis CA 95618
Phone: 530-758-6200
Fax: 530-758-6241
Web: www.freefromhunger.org

CEO: –
CFO: –
HR: –
FYE: June 30
Type: Private - Not-for-Pr

Freedom from Hunger wants to give everybody just that. The not-for-profit organization strives to solve the problem of chronic hunger and poverty in 16 countries worldwide. The group provides self-help programs and training for more than 650000 poor women to learn to better feed and tend the health of their families and turn a small enterprise into a sustaining business. Its main program Credit With Education is a microcredit program that provides loans to small groups of women who attend classes on nutrition health family planning and sound business practices. Freedom From Hunger was founded in 1946 as Meals for Millions.

FREEDOM RESOURCES ENTERPRISES INC. OTC: FRDR

901 E. 7800 South
Midvale UT 84047
Phone: 801-566-5931
Fax: 904-280-7794
Web: www.syfobeverages.com

CEO: –
CFO: –
HR: –
FYE: December 31
Type: Public

Freedom Resources Enterprises is a development stage company. It developed a series of eight self-help self-improvement workshops. Each self-taught workshop consisted of an audio tape and a workbook which Freedom Resources marketed over the Internet. The company's workshops did not generated expected revenue and Freedom Resources has announced plans to pursue other business opportunities.

FREEDOMROADS LLC

250 Parkway Dr. Ste. 270
Lincolnshire IL 60069
Phone: 847-808-3000
Fax: 713-621-9545
Web: www.copanoenergy.com

CEO: Marcus A Lemonis
CFO: –
HR: –
FYE: December 31
Type: Private

"Home home on the road where the semis and the SUVs play..." That's how FreedomRoads would sing it. The nation's largest RV retailer FreedomRoads (dba Camping World RV Sales) sells and rents new and used recreational vehicles and accessory products through more than 75 locations in 30-plus states. Its locations feature Camping World stores which offer RV-specific items not usually carried by general merchandise retailers including bedding furniture replacement hardware and sanitation systems. Camping World RV Sales dealers provide maintenance and repair services as well as financing. Chairman and CEO Marcus Lemonis founded the company in 2003.

FREEMAN HEALTH SYSTEM

1102 W 32ND ST
JOPLIN, MO 648043503
Phone: 417-347-1111
Fax: –
Web: www.freemanhealth.com

CEO: Paula Baker
CFO: Steven Graddy
HR: –
FYE: March 31
Type: Private

Freeman Health System (FHS) offers comprehensive health and behavioral health services to the residents of Arkansas Kansas Missouri and Oklahoma through three hospitals with a total of more than 500 beds. Specialty facilities include a full-service cardiothoracic and vascular program at the Freeman Heart Institute and behavioral health services through its Ozark Health Center. Community-owned not-for-profit FHS also operates two urgent care centers a separate sleep center several doctors' office buildings and serves as a teaching hospital with three residency programs (ear nose and throat; emergency medicine; and internal medicine). FHS employs more than 300 physicians in 60 specialties.

	Annual Growth	03/17	03/18	03/19	03/20	03/21
Sales ($ mil.)	4.8%	–	588.3	624.4	562.1	676.5
Net income ($ mil.)	47.6%	–	51.2	57.3	16.9	164.7
Market value ($ mil.)	–	–	–	–	–	–
Employees	–	–	–	–	–	4,500

FREEPORT REGIONAL HEALTH CARE FOUNDATION

1045 W STEPHENSON ST
FREEPORT, IL 610324864
Phone: 815-599-6000
Fax: –
Web: www.fhn.org

CEO: –
CFO: –
HR: –
FYE: December 31
Type: Private

FHN is a regional health care system serving residents in northwestern Illinois and southern Wisconsin. At its heart is the nearly 200-bed FHN Memorial Hospital which provides general medical and surgical care emergency services and specialty care in areas such as sleep disorders orthopedics obstetrics and cardiology. The health system also features a cancer center home health care and hospice operations and a network of satellite facilities providing primary medical and dental care as well as occupational health chiropractic and counseling services. Its Northern Illinois Health Plan subsidiary supplies PPO health plans and third-party administrative services to the region's employers.

	Annual Growth	12/05	12/06	12/07	12/08	12/09
Sales ($ mil.)	(29.7%)	–	158.5	164.5	169.5	55.0
Net income ($ mil.)	–	–	–	7.6	(13.2)	(16.1)
Market value ($ mil.)	–	–	–	–	–	–
Employees	–	–	–	–	–	1,500

FREEPORT-MCMORAN INC NYS: FCX

333 North Central Avenue
Phoenix, AZ 85004-2189
Phone: 602 366-8100
Fax: –
Web: www.fcx.com

CEO: Richard Adkerson
CFO: Kathleen Quirk
HR: –
FYE: December 31
Type: Public

Freeport McMoran (FCX) is one of the world's major mining companies with holdings in copper molybdenum and gold. It is a leading copper producer with proven or probable reserves of 113.2 billion pounds; the company also has about 28.9 million ounces of gold reserves and about 3.71 billion pounds of molybdenum reserves. FCX's mines are in the Americas and Indonesia. The company consumes much of its raw output itself manufacturing copper rods and other intermediate goods. With customers across the Americas Europe and Asia the US is FCX's biggest market at around 35% of company revenue.

	Annual Growth	12/17	12/18	12/19	12/20	12/21
Sales ($ mil.)	8.6%	16,403.0	18,628.0	14,402.0	14,198.0	22,845.0
Net income ($ mil.)	24.1%	1,817.0	2,602.0	(239.0)	599.0	4,306.0
Market value ($ mil.)	21.8%	27,624.7	15,021.7	19,115.8	37,911.1	60,800.6
Employees	(3.1%)	53,200	50,200	68,100	58,300	46,900

FREESE AND NICHOLS, INC.

801 CHERRY ST STE 2800
FORT WORTH, TX 761026804
Phone: 817-735-7300
Fax: –
Web: www.freese.com

CEO: Brian Coltharp
CFO: Cynthia Milrany
HR: –
FYE: December 31
Type: Private

Freese and Nichols (FNI) keeps water in the Lone Star State flowing in the right direction. The consulting firm specializes in water management engineering but also offers architecture environmental science and construction management to clients in the Southwest primarily Texas and the Southeast. The company has designed more than 150 dams and reservoirs and also works on such projects as municipal waterworks water treatment facilities and highways. Freese and Nichols serves the private and public sectors; its clients include all levels of government. The company has offices in about 15 Texas cities and in North Carolina. It traces its roots to a Fort Worth firm founded in 1894 by John B. Hawley.

	Annual Growth	12/14	12/15	12/16	12/17	12/20
Sales ($ mil.)	14.2%	–	117.6	129.7	150.7	228.1
Net income ($ mil.)	41.3%	–	1.4	1.9	2.9	7.9
Market value ($ mil.)	–	–	–	–	–	–
Employees	–	–	–	–	–	968

FREMONT BANCORPORATION

39150 Fremont Blvd.
Fremont CA 94538
Phone: 510-505-5226
Fax: 510-795-5758
Web: www.fremontbank.com

CEO: –
CFO: –
HR: Jackie McCormick
FYE: December 31
Type: Private

Fremont Bancorporation lets freedom ka-ching! It's the holding company for Fremont Bank which operates more than 20 branches in the San Francisco Bay area. Serving area consumers and businesses the bank provides traditional banking services such as savings checking and money market accounts; check cards; IRAs; and CDs. It uses funds from deposits mainly to originate home mortgages and commercial real estate loans as well as commercial industrial construction and land development loans. The bank which was founded in 1964 provides investments wealth management retirement planning and insurance products through an agreement with UVEST (a division of LPL Financial).

FREMONT CONTRACT CARRIERS, INC.

865 BUD BLVD
FREMONT, NE 680256270
Phone: 402-721-3020
Fax: –
Web: www.fcc-inc.com

CEO: Michael F Herre
CFO: –
HR: –
FYE: December 31
Type: Private

Truckload carrier Fremont Contract Carriers (FCC) hauls general and non-hazardous freight throughout the US and Canada. Its fleet consists of some 315 trucks 700 high-cubed dry van trailers and 100 flatbed curtain-side and step-deck trailers. The company's FCC Transportation Services unit provides freight brokerage and logistics services in which customers' freight is matched with carriers' capacity. In addition to offering traditional trucking services the company provides online load tracking and reporting on its Web site. The company transports food products consumer products retail products construction and manufactured products as well as packaging and grocery goods. FCC was founded in 1966.

	Annual Growth	12/12	12/13	12/14	12/15	12/17
Sales ($ mil.)	3.0%	–	73.1	75.0	70.7	82.4
Net income ($ mil.)	–	–	(0.4)	1.0	2.3	2.8
Market value ($ mil.)	–	–	–	–	–	–
Employees	–	–	–	–	–	91

FREMONT HEALTH

450 E 23RD ST
FREMONT, NE 680252387
Phone: 402-727-3795
Fax: –
Web: www.fremonthealth.com

CEO: Patrick Booth
CFO: –
HR: –
FYE: June 30
Type: Private

Fremont Area Medical Center's area of expertise is serving patients in Nebraska's Dodge County and surrounding areas. The non-profit healthcare facility has more than 200 beds with about 112 beds dedicated to long-term care patients. Specialized services include cancer care emergency medicine rehabilitation home health and hospice and surgery. Fremont Area Medical Center is owned by Dodge County and its operations are funded by taxpayers. The institution is licensed by the Nebraska State Board of Health and maintains accreditation through the Joint Commission.

	Annual Growth	06/02	06/03	06/04	06/05	06/07
Sales ($ mil.)	8.4%	–	–	72.1	77.7	91.8
Net income ($ mil.)	34.0%	–	–	5.4	6.7	12.9
Market value ($ mil.)	–	–	–	–	–	–
Employees	–	–	–	–	–	900

FREQUENCY ELECTRONICS INC

NMS: FEIM

55 Charles Lindbergh Blvd.
Mitchel Field, NY 11553
Phone: 516 794-4500
Fax: 516 794-4340
Web: www.frequencyelectronics.com

CEO: Stanton Sloane
CFO: Steven Bernstein
HR: –
FYE: April 30
Type: Public

Frequency Electronics Inc. (FEI) lets the good times roll. The company makes quartz- rubidium- and cesium-based time and frequency control products such as oscillators and amplifiers used to synchronize voice data and video transmissions in satellite and wireless communications. The US military uses its products for navigation communications surveillance and timing systems in aircraft satellites radar and missiles. Though FEI has diversified into commercial markets nearly half of its sales still come from the US government. Other top clients include AT&T Lockheed Martin Northrop Grumman and Thales Alenia Space. The company was formed in 1961 as a time and frequency control R&D firm.

	Annual Growth	04/17	04/18	04/19	04/20	04/21
Sales ($ mil.)	1.9%	50.4	39.4	49.5	41.5	54.3
Net income ($ mil.)	–	(4.8)	(23.8)	(2.5)	(10.0)	0.7
Market value ($ mil.)	0.6%	96.9	81.3	111.2	92.6	99.1
Employees	(7.3%)	325	300	280	220	240

FRESH MARK, INC.

1888 SOUTHWAY ST SW
MASSILLON, OH 446469429
Phone: 330-832-7491
Fax: –
Web: www.freshmark.com

CEO: Neil Genshaft
CFO: David Cochenour
HR: –
FYE: January 01
Type: Private

Fresh Mark is a leading producer of smoked and processed pork products for the domestic and international retail and foodservice industries. From its four plants in Ohio the company makes and markets such products as bacon (raw par-cooked and cooked) dry sausage ham (natural and smoked) hot dogs and lunch meats under the Sugardale and Superior's brands. Sugardale label is available in all 50 states and over 20 countries. The company also produces private-label processed meat products for others and supplies the foodservice industry through its Sugardale Food Service business. Founded in 1920 Ohio-based Fresh Mark is owned and operated by the Genshaft family.

	Annual Growth	12/04	12/05	12/06	12/07*	01/11
Sales ($ mil.)	8.7%	–	481.7	481.5	534.6	795.7
Net income ($ mil.)	16.7%	–	23.5	21.7	31.0	59.5
Market value ($ mil.)	–	–	–	–	–	–
Employees	–	–	–	–	–	2,300

*Fiscal year change

FRESHPOINT INC.

1390 Enclave Pkwy.
Houston TX 77077-2025
Phone: 281-584-1390
Fax: 281-584-1188
Web: www.freshpoint.com

CEO: –
CFO: –
HR: –
FYE: June 30
Type: Subsidiary

Fresh produce is the ingredient for success at FreshPoint. The company is one of the largest foodservice distributors of fresh fruits and vegetables in North America. Its operations span more than 30 distribution centers in the US and Canada. In addition to produce the company offers some fresh dairy items as well as value-added and fancy foods. It targets regional and national foodservice customers in such markets as catering healthcare hospitality restaurants and schools. FreshPoint also supplies certain retail grocery stores and other wholesale suppliers. The company is a subsidiary of foodservice titan SYSCO. Although increasing in importance fresh produce generates less than 10% of SYSCO's sales.

FRIED FRANK HARRIS SHRIVER & JACOBSON LLP

1 New York Plaza
New York NY 10004-1980
Phone: 212-859-8000
Fax: 212-859-4000
Web: www.friedfrank.com

CEO: -
CFO: -
HR: -
FYE: February 28
Type: Private - Partnershi

Known for its mergers and acquisitions practice law firm Fried Frank Harris Shriver & Jacobson also offers expertise in such fields as bankruptcy intellectual property litigation real estate and securities regulations. The firm serves as counsel to many of the world's largest companies financial institutions and investment firms. Clients have included such big names as Bank of America Deutsche Bank Dow Jones Thomson Reuters Goldman Sachs and Credit Suisse. Fried Frank has more than 500 lawyers. The modern Fried Frank was formed in 1971 but the firm traces its roots to law practices that began early in the 1900s.

FRIEDMAN INDUSTRIES, INC.   ASE: FRD

1121 Judson Road, Suite 124
Longview, TX 75601
Phone: 903 758-3431
Fax: -

CEO: Michael Taylor
CFO: Alex Larue
HR: -
FYE: March 31
Type: Public

Steel processor Friedman Industries operates in two business segments: coil products and tubular products. The company's Texas Tubular Products unit the larger of Friedman Industries' segments buys pipe and coil material and processes it for use in pipelines oil and gas drilling and piling and structural applications. Friedman Industries' coil products unit purchases hot-rolled steel coils and processes them into sheet and plate products. The company's XSCP unit sells surplus prime secondary and transition steel coils. Friedman Industries' processing facilities are located near mills operated by U.S. Steel and Nucor Corp. and work closely with both facilities.

	Annual Growth	03/17	03/18	03/19	03/20	03/21
Sales ($ mil.)	12.8%	77.8	121.2	187.2	142.1	126.1
Net income ($ mil.)	-	(2.7)	2.8	5.1	(5.2)	11.4
Market value ($ mil.)	5.8%	44.5	40.5	52.9	30.4	55.8
Employees	3.5%	82	91	104	103	94

FRIENDFINDER NETWORKS INC   NBB: FFNT Q

6800 Broken Sound Parkway, Suite 200
Boca Raton, FL 33487
Phone: 561 912-7000
Fax: -
Web: www.ffn.com

CEO: -
CFO: -
HR: -
FYE: December 31
Type: Public

If you're looking for friendship try knocking on some doors below the penthouse. FriendFinder Networks (publisher of the venerable adult magazine Penthouse and producer of adult video content and images) now owns and operates some 38000 social networking websites including AdultFriendFinder.com Amigos.com AsiaFriendFinder.com Cams.com FriendFinder.com BigChurch.com and SeniorFriendFinder.com. In total its sites are offered to about 528 million members in more than 200 countries. FriendFinder also distributes original pictorial and video content and engages in brand licensing. It emerged from Chapter 11 bankruptcy protection in late 2013 returning control to company founder Andrew Conru.

	Annual Growth	12/09	12/10	12/11	12/12	12/13
Sales ($ mil.)	(4.6%)	327.7	346.0	331.3	314.4	271.4
Net income ($ mil.)	-	(41.2)	(43.2)	(31.1)	(49.4)	175.2
Market value ($ mil.)	(20.0%)	-	-	0.5	0.4	-
Employees	(8.3%)	-	407	692	342	-

FRISBIE MEMORIAL HOSPITAL

11 WHITEHALL RD
ROCHESTER, NH 038673297
Phone: 603-332-5211
Fax: -
Web: www.frisbiehospital.com

CEO: John Marzinzik
CFO: -
HR: -
FYE: September 30
Type: Private

Frisbie Memorial Hospital hopes to maintain a high-flying reputation as it serves southeastern New Hampshire and southern Maine. The acute-care facility has nearly 90 beds and about 250 physicians on staff. The not-for-profit community hospital offers patients a variety of services including emergency radiology cardiology neurology and respiratory and surgical care. Frisbie Memorial also operates outpatient and primary medical care facilities and it provides oncology services through a partnership with the Dartmouth-Hitchcock Medical Center in Lebanon New Hampshire.

	Annual Growth	09/14	09/15	09/16	09/17	09/18
Sales ($ mil.)	1.0%	-	132.4	135.8	122.2	136.6
Net income ($ mil.)	-	-	(4.7)	3.2	(21.2)	(11.0)
Market value ($ mil.)	-	-	-	-	-	-
Employees	-	-	-	-	-	900

FRISCH'S RESTAURANTS, INC.   ASE: FRS

2800 Gilbert Avenue
Cincinnati, OH 45206
Phone: 513 961-2660
Fax: -
Web: www.frischs.com

CEO: Aziz Hashim
CFO: -
HR: Ebonie Weems
FYE: June 03
Type: Public

Buddie Boy Big Boy Super Big Boy Brawny Lad — Frisch's burger menu reads like an arm-wrestling contest marquee. Frisch's Restaurants operates and licenses about 95 Frisch's Big Boy family-style restaurants in Indiana Kentucky and Ohio (25 locations are operated by licensees) targeting the family-dining segment. Famous for its double-decker hamburgers the Big Boy chain also offers chicken roast beef pasta and seafood dinners as well as a breakfast bar that converts to a soup and salad bar at lunch. President and CEO Craig Maier owns about 25% of the company.

	Annual Growth	06/10*	05/11	05/12	05/13*	06/14
Sales ($ mil.)	(8.1%)	292.9	303.5	205.1	203.7	209.2
Net income ($ mil.)	(1.4%)	10.0	9.5	2.1	6.8	9.4
Market value ($ mil.)	3.1%	106.4	110.8	140.7	87.4	120.1
Employees	(7.7%)	8,400	8,400	6,050	5,860	6,100

*Fiscal year change

FRITO-LAY NORTH AMERICA INC.

7701 Legacy Dr.
Plano TX 75024
Phone: 972-334-7000
Fax: 972-334-2019
Web: www.fritolay.com

CEO: Albert P Carey
CFO: Hugh F Johnston
HR: -
FYE: December 31
Type: Subsidiary

Frito-Lay is the undisputed chip champ of North America. The company makes some of the best-known and top-selling savory snacks around including Cheetos Doritos Lay's Ruffles SunChips and Tostitos. On the sweet side Frito-Lay also makes Grandma's cookies Funyuns onion-flavored rings Cracker Jack candy-coated popcorn and Smartfood popcorn. It also makes a line of chips made with the fat substitute Olestra under the Light brand name. Owned by PepsiCo Frito-Lay North America's operations span the US and Canada and account for about a quarter of the soda maker's sales. Frito-Lay's Mexican sales are reported within PepsiCo's Latin America Foods segment.

FROEDTERT MEMORIAL LUTHERAN HOSPITAL, INC.

9200 W WISCONSIN AVE
MILWAUKEE, WI 532263522
Phone: 414-805-3000
Fax: –
Web: www.froedtert.com

CEO: William Petasnick
CFO: –
HR: –
FYE: June 30
Type: Private

Patients in southeastern Wisconsin count on Froedtert Memorial Lutheran Hospital for a full range of health services including trauma transplant sports medicine and senior care. The 500-bed hospital also known as Froedtert & The Medical College of Wisconsin is part of the Froedtert (pronounced "fray-dert") Health system. Specialty units include cancer dermatology neuroscience birthing fertility urology and vein clinics. The hospital also serves as a teaching facility for the Medical College of Wisconsin and it partners with the Children's Hospital of Wisconsin to provide pediatric services. Froedtert Hospital which was founded in 1980 operates the only adult Level I trauma center in the region.

	Annual Growth	06/09	06/10	06/11	06/14	06/20
Sales ($ mil.)	8.2%	–	894.4	980.4	1,164.8	1,958.7
Net income ($ mil.)	9.2%	–	59.7	79.1	92.4	143.6
Market value ($ mil.)	–	–	–	–	–	–
Employees	–	–	–	–	–	3,400

FRONTIER COMMUNICATIONS PARENT INC

NMS: FYBR

401 Merritt 7
Norwalk, CT 06851
Phone: 203 614-5600
Fax: –
Web: www.frontier.com

CEO: Nick Jeffery
CFO: Scott Beasley
HR: –
FYE: December 31
Type: Public

Frontier Communications provides data and internet video voice services access services and advanced hardware and network solutions for its consumer and commercial customers in some 25 US states. The company has about 3.6 million customer some 3.1 million broadband subscribers. Frontier is active mostly in small to mid-sized markets as well as larger enterprise customer where it is the incumbent local-exchange carrier (ILEC). In 2020 the sale of Frontier Communications' Northwest operations completed with Ziply Fiber taking over nearly 500000 residential and business internet phone and TV subscribers. The $1.35 billion deal covers customers across Washington Oregon Idaho and Montana. The new owner also committed $500 million in improvements to the network. The company also filed Chapter 11 bankruptcy was filed as part of its restructuring support agreement to cut its debt by more than $10 billion.

	Annual Growth	12/16	12/17	12/18	12/19	12/20
Sales ($ mil.)	(5.3%)	8,896.0	9,128.0	8,611.0	8,107.0	7,155.0
Net income ($ mil.)	–	(373.0)	(1,804.0)	(643.0)	(5,911.0)	(402.0)
Market value ($ mil.)	(59.6%)	354.2	708.4	249.4	93.2	9.4
Employees	(13.0%)	28,300	22,700	21,200	18,300	16,200

FRONTIER OILFIELD SERVICES INC.

PINK SHEETS: TBXC

3030 LBJ Freeway Ste. 1320
Dallas TX 75234
Phone: 972-243-2613
Fax: 972-243-2066
Web: www.tbxresources.com

CEO: Donald Ray Lawhorne
CFO: Channing Chen
HR: –
FYE: November 30
Type: Public

Frontier Oilfield Services (formerly TBX Resources) has switched from exploring for and producing natural gas to providing oilfield services to other companies that do. Frontier Oilfield Services now focuses on saltwater and drilling fluid disposal services for oil and gas producers and operators in East Texas. The company is targeting the Haynesville share area where it believes as many as 35000 additional wells will be drilled by 2023. Frontier currently manages the operations of Trinity Disposal and Trucking which owns saltwater disposal wells and a fleet of trucks and trailers and is seeking to buy the service. In 2012 it bought salt water disposal firm Chico Coffman Tank Trucks for $17 million.

FRONTRANGE SOLUTIONS INC.

5675 Gibraltar Dr.
Pleasanton CA 94588
Phone: 925-398-1800
Fax: 719-536-0620
Web: www.frontrange.com

CEO: –
CFO: –
HR: –
FYE: June 30
Type: Private

FrontRange Solutions has a GoldMine for customer relationship management. Customers use its GoldMine software to maintain customer contacts and automate sales marketing scheduling and project management functions. Its HEAT software offers help desk ticket processing reporting and analysis. FrontRange also provides a VoIP telephone system that integrates with its software. Other offerings include hosted versions of its help desk service management and asset management software and a Web-based services catalog that functions like a shopping cart. FrontRange primarily targets small and midsized businesses. It has customers in some 45 countries. Private equity firm Francisco Partners bought FrontRange in 2005.

FROST BROWN TODD LLC

3300 Great American Tower 301 E. 4th St.
Cincinnati OH 45202
Phone: 513-651-6800
Fax: 513-651-6981
Web: www.frostbrowntodd.com

CEO: –
CFO: Frank C Szabo
HR: –
FYE: December 31
Type: Private - Partnershi

Middle America deserves a top law firm. Frost Brown Todd's more than 450 attorneys practice business law across nine offices in Ohio Kentucky Indiana Tennessee and West Virginia. Areas of specialty include corporate mergers tax law subprime lending environmental law financial restructuring intellectual property technology issues arbitration and antitrust litigation. It has conducted legal work for such high-profile clients as Ford Motor Company Toyota Motor Manufacturing General Electric and E.W. Scripps Co. The firm was created by the 2000 merger of Kentucky law firm Brown Todd & Heyburn with Ohio's Frost & Jacobs. It traces the roots of its legacy firms back to 1917.

FROZEN SPECIALTIES INC.

8600 S WILKINSON WAY G
PERRYSBURG, OH 43551-2598
Phone: 419-445-9015
Fax: –
Web: www.frozenspecialties.com

CEO: Terry O'Brien
CFO: –
HR: –
FYE: June 26
Type: Private

Frozen Specialties' specialty arena lies in frozen pizza pies. The company makes private-label frozen pizzas (in value-priced lean and microwaveable variations) and a frozen pizza-flavored snack called Pizza Bites for the North American convenience and grocery store markets. Its pizzas are primarily sold under store-brand names at major grocery chains. Frozen Specialties Inc. (also known as FSI) is a top player in the frozen pizza industry and produces more than 100 million pizzas every year. Investment firm Swander Pace Capital is the majority owner of Frozen Specialties.

	Annual Growth	06/01	06/02	06/03	06/04	06/11
Sales ($ mil.)	(2.5%)	–	–	–	67.0	56.2
Net income ($ mil.)	–	–	–	–	0.0	(1.1)
Market value ($ mil.)	–	–	–	–	–	–
Employees	–	–	–	–	–	140

FRP HOLDINGS INC

NMS: FRPH

200 West Forsyth Street, 7th Floor
Jacksonville, FL 32202
Phone: 904 396-5733
Fax: –
Web: www.frpholdings.com

CEO: –
CFO: –
HR: –
FYE: December 31
Type: Public

Patriot Transportation Holding has plenty of tanks but hasn't fired a shot. The company's Transportation segment comprising Florida Rock & Tank Lines subsidiary transports liquid and dry bulk commodities mainly petroleum (including ethanol) and chemicals in tank trucks. Patriot Transportation's combined fleet of about 435 trucks and 530 trailers operates primarily in the southeastern and mid-Atlantic US. The company's Real Estate unit comprising Florida Rock Properties and FRP Development owns office and warehouse properties as well as sand and gravel deposits on the East Coast that are leased to Vulcan Materials Company.

	Annual Growth	12/16	12/17	12/18	12/19	12/20
Sales ($ mil.)	25.5%	9.5	43.2	22.0	23.8	23.6
Net income ($ mil.)	65.8%	1.7	41.8	124.5	16.2	12.7
Market value ($ mil.)	4.8%	353.0	414.3	430.8	466.4	426.5
Employees	(11.9%)	–	19	10	12	13

FRUIT GROWERS SUPPLY COMPANY INC

27770 N ENTRMT DR FL 3 FLR 3
VALENCIA, CA 91355
Phone: 888-997-4855
Fax: –
Web: www.fruitgrowerssupply.com

CEO: Jim Phillips
CFO: Charles Boyce
HR: –
FYE: December 31
Type: Private

Shipping cartons are the real fruit of labor for Fruit Growers Supply (FSG). The non-profit cooperative association supplies affiliate Sunkist Growers and other agricultural businesses with packing materials fertilizer and related implements. Offerings include a range of equipment used to grow pick package and transport many commodity cash crops. FSG also provides packing services and custom design and installation of irrigation systems. It owns and operates some 335000 acres of timberland along the West coast (a source of box material and income) a carton manufacturing and supply plant and seven retail operations centers. FGS is owned by 6000-plus citrus growers and shippers in the US.

	Annual Growth	12/14	12/15	12/16	12/17	12/18
Sales ($ mil.)	0.6%	–	218.8	214.5	220.7	222.6
Net income ($ mil.)	13.1%	–	5.1	0.9	(9.5)	7.4
Market value ($ mil.)	–	–	–	–	–	–
Employees	–	–	–	–	–	300

FRUTH, INC.

4016 OHIO RIVER RD
POINT PLEASANT, WV 255503257
Phone: 304-675-1612
Fax: –
Web: www.fruthpharmacy.com

CEO: –
CFO: Bob Messick
HR: –
FYE: June 30
Type: Private

Fruth Pharmacy operates about 25 drugstores in southern Ohio and West Virginia. While prescriptions account for the majority of sales Fruth pharmacies also sell gift items and computer supplies and have floral departments and digital printing. The regional drugstore chain competes by constantly trying new things such as participating in the Face2Face diabetes program and testing in-store dollar departments. It is countering Wal-Mart Stores's $4 generic offering with a discount generic drug program created by Cardinal Health. Founded in 1952 by its namesake — the late Jack Fruth — the company is family-owned and -operated.

	Annual Growth	06/05	06/06	06/07	06/08	06/09
Sales ($ mil.)	1.3%	–	128.7	136.0	135.7	133.7
Net income ($ mil.)	–	–	4.7	0.3	0.9	(0.5)
Market value ($ mil.)	–	–	–	–	–	–
Employees	–	–	–	–	–	545

FRY'S FOOD AND DRUG STORES

500 S. 99th Ave.
Tolleson AZ 85353
Phone: 623-936-2100
Fax: 623-907-1910
Web: www.frysfood.com

CEO: Dennis R Hood
CFO: Ron Schuster
HR: –
FYE: January 31
Type: Subsidiary

Fry's Food Stores operates about 100 supermarkets under the Fry's Food Stores and Fry's Mercado banners mostly in Phoenix but also in Tucson and Prescott Arizona. The grocery store chain also also operates about two dozen Fry's Marketplace stores large (up to 120000 sq. ft.) multi-department stores that offer full-service grocery and pharmacy departments as well as expanded general merchandise electronics home goods and toy sections. In addition to traditional supermarket fare many Fry's stores have in-store pharmacies and offer full-service banking through Kroger Personal Finance. Fry's is owned by The Kroger Co. the #1 pure grocery chain in the US.

FS BANCORP INC (WASHINGTON)

NAS: FSBW

6920 220th Street SW
Mountlake Terrace, WA 98043
Phone: 425 771-5299
Fax: –
Web: www.fsbwa.com

CEO: Joseph Adams
CFO: Matthew Mullet
HR: Vickie Jarman
FYE: December 31
Type: Public

FS Bancorp is the holding company for 1st Security Bank of Washington which operates six branches in the Puget Sound region. The bank provides standard deposit products such as checking and savings accounts CDs and IRAs to area businesses and consumers. Its lending activities are focused on consumer loans (more than half of its portfolio) including home improvement boat and automobile loans. The bank also writes business and construction loans and commercial and residential mortgages. FS Bancorp went public via in initial public offering in 2012.

	Annual Growth	12/16	12/17	12/18	12/19	12/20
Assets ($ mil.)	26.4%	827.9	981.8	1,621.6	1,713.1	2,113.2
Net income ($ mil.)	39.1%	10.5	14.1	24.3	22.7	39.3
Market value ($ mil.)	11.1%	304.7	462.5	363.4	540.7	464.5
Employees	13.4%	306	326	424	452	506

FTD COMPANIES, INC.

3113 WOODCREEK DR
DOWNERS GROVE, IL 605155420
Phone: 630-719-7800
Fax: –
Web: www.ftdcompanies.com

CEO: –
CFO: –
HR: –
FYE: December 31
Type: Private

Mercury the Roman god of speed and commerce with winged feet comes bearing flowers. FTD is a leader in the floral industry for over a century supported by the iconic Mercury Man logo displayed in more than 30000 floral shops in over 125 countries. The company works with local florists to hand-craft floral arrangements available for same-day delivery on FTD.com and ProFlowers.com. In addition the company provides technology marketing and digital services to members of its florist network. The company was founded by John A. Valentine in 1910.

	Annual Growth	12/14	12/15	12/16	12/17	12/18
Sales ($ mil.)	(6.0%)	–	1,219.8	1,122.0	1,084.0	1,014.2
Net income ($ mil.)	–	–	(78.8)	(83.2)	(234.0)	(224.7)
Market value ($ mil.)	–	–	–	–	–	–
Employees	–	–	–	–	–	1,501

FTI CONSULTING INC.
NYS: FCN

555 12th Street NW
Washington, DC 20004
Phone: 202 312-9100
Fax: –
Web: www.fticonsulting.com

CEO: Steven Gunby
CFO: Ajay Sabherwal
HR: –
FYE: December 31
Type: Public

FTI Consulting Inc. is a global business advisory firm dedicated to helping organisations manage change mitigate risk and resolve disputes: financial legal operational political & regulatory reputational and transactional. With more than 6300 employees located in roughly 30 countries FTI Consulting professionals work closely with clients to anticipate illuminate and overcome complex business challenges and make the most of opportunities. FTI was founded in 1982. FTI Consulting generates most of its revenue in the US with the UK accounting for the next largest share of business.

	Annual Growth	12/16	12/17	12/18	12/19	12/20
Sales ($ mil.)	8.0%	1,810.4	1,807.7	2,027.9	2,352.7	2,461.3
Net income ($ mil.)	25.3%	85.5	108.0	150.6	216.7	210.7
Market value ($ mil.)	25.5%	1,554.4	1,481.3	2,297.8	3,815.7	3,852.2
Employees	7.6%	4,718	4,609	4,768	5,567	6,321

FTS INTERNATIONAL INC.

777 Main St. Ste. 3000
Fort Worth TX 76102
Phone: 817-862-2000
Fax: 817-339-3640
Web: www.fractech.net

CEO: –
CFO: –
HR: –
FYE: December 31
Type: Private

FTS International (formerly Frac Tech Services) has found a way to mix oil and water. The company helps US oil and gas firms make the most of their older assets by releasing tough-to-recover petroleum through hydraulic fracturing a process which pumps a proprietary solution of sand and water into shale reservoirs to release oil and gas. FTS International runs 33 fracturing units (1.4 million horsepower) in the shale basins of Louisiana Texas Pennsylvania West Virginia and New Mexico. It also owns sand mining and processing operations that supply most of its primary raw material. In 2011 the company was acquired by a Temasek Holdings-led consortium and reorganized as FTS International.

FUEL SYSTEMS SOLUTIONS INC
NMS: FSYS

780 Third Avenue, 25th Floor
New York, NY 10017
Phone: 646 502-7170
Fax: –
Web: www.fuelsystemssolutions.com

CEO: –
CFO: –
HR: –
FYE: December 31
Type: Public

Fuel Systems Solutions was going green before green was the way to go. Founded in 1957 the holding company operates through two subsidiaries BRC and IMPCO Technologies as a designer and manufacturer of alternative fuel components that allow engines in vehicles and industrial equipment to operate on cleaner burning gaseous fuels such as propane and compressed natural gas (CNG). BRC's customers include some of the world's largest automotive OEMs and IMPCO's customers include some of the leading engine OEMs. Products include fuel injectors electronic controls compressors and auxiliary power systems. The group also offers services ranging from system integration to environmental certification.

	Annual Growth	12/10	12/11	12/12	12/13	12/14
Sales ($ mil.)	(5.8%)	430.6	418.1	393.9	399.8	339.1
Net income ($ mil.)	–	39.7	5.2	(15.6)	(0.5)	(53.4)
Market value ($ mil.)	(21.9%)	580.8	326.0	290.8	274.2	216.3
Employees	(1.6%)	1,600	1,700	1,700	1,700	1,500

FUEL TECH INC
NAS: FTEK

27601 Bella Vista Parkway
Warrenville, IL 60555-1617
Phone: 630 845-4500
Fax: –
Web: www.ftek.com

CEO: Vincent Arnone
CFO: James M Pach
HR: –
FYE: December 31
Type: Public

Fuel Tech develops technologies and products so industrial plants and utilities around the world can run cleanly and efficiently. The company's air pollution control systems segment offers nitrogen oxide reduction products (such as NOxOUT and Over-Fire Air Systems) which reduce nitrogen oxide emissions from boilers incinerators furnaces and other combustion sources. Fuel Tech's technologies are used on more than 700 combustion units including utility industrial and municipal solid waste applications. The company's FUEL CHEM segment develops chemical products used to reduce slag formation and corrosion. Each segment accounts for about half of the company's sales.

	Annual Growth	12/16	12/17	12/18	12/19	12/20
Sales ($ mil.)	(20.0%)	55.2	45.2	56.5	30.5	22.6
Net income ($ mil.)	–	(17.4)	(11.0)	(0.0)	(7.9)	(4.3)
Market value ($ mil.)	35.5%	29.0	28.3	30.0	24.0	97.9
Employees	(15.9%)	146	122	113	82	73

FUELCELL ENERGY INC
NMS: FCEL

3 Great Pasture Road
Danbury, CT 06810
Phone: 203 825-6000
Fax: –
Web: www.fuelcellenergy.com

CEO: Jason Few
CFO: Michael Bishop
HR: –
FYE: October 31
Type: Public

FuelCell is a leading global manufacturer of proprietary fuel cell technology platforms. Founded in 1969 the company is a manufacturer of fuel cell clean power platforms delivering power and thermal energy and capable of delivering hydrogen long-duration hydrogen energy storage and carbon capture applications. The company's commercial products include SureSource which provides high efficiency with fuel conversion fuel flexibility and emits no pollution. Its SureSource power plants produce power for various industries such as commercial industrial and government. FuelCell Energy generates majority of sales domestically.

	Annual Growth	10/17	10/18	10/19	10/20	10/21
Sales ($ mil.)	(7.6%)	95.7	89.4	60.8	70.9	69.6
Net income ($ mil.)	–	(53.9)	(47.3)	(77.6)	(89.1)	(101.1)
Market value ($ mil.)	38.2%	802.9	309.9	87.4	733.2	2,929.3
Employees	(4.4%)	458	489	301	316	382

FUELSTREAM, INC.
NBB: FLST

11650 South State Street, Suite 240
Draper, UT 84020
Phone: 801 816-2510
Fax: –
Web: www.thefuelstream.com

CEO: –
CFO: Chene C Gardner
HR: –
FYE: December 31
Type: Public

Nutty about sports? SportsNuts is a sports management and marketing company that helps sports planners organize amateur sporting events and tournaments. The firm offers online event registration merchandising sponsorship and promotion services. The SportsNuts Web site is a resource for events coordinators coaches athletes and fans to post or obtain relevant information such as schedules statistics and pictures. The company spun off its Web hosting and design subsidiary Synerteck and did the same with Secure Networks which sold computer hardware.

	Annual Growth	12/10	12/11	12/12	12/13	12/14
Sales ($ mil.)	(19.2%)	–	–	1.1	0.0	0.7
Net income ($ mil.)	–	(5.6)	(2.5)	(19.7)	(4.1)	(3.2)
Market value ($ mil.)	–	0.0	0.5	2.8	0.0	0.0
Employees	56.5%	1	2	6	6	6

FULCRUM BIOENERGY INC.

4900 Hopyard Rd. Ste. 220 — CEO: Eric N Pryor
Pleasanton CA 94588 — CFO: Greg Heinlein
Phone: 925-730-0150 — HR: -
Fax: 925-730-0157 — FYE: December 31
Web: www.fulcrum-bioenergy.com — Type: Private

Fulcrum BioEnergy doesn't let anything go to waste. The development-stage company has a plan to make biofuel out of garbage (garbage!) using a proprietary process to convert solid waste into ethanol thus keeping it out of landfills. (The majority of ethanol produced in the US comes from corn which still takes time and resources to grow and is subject to commodity prices). Fulcrum BioEnergy intends to build a plant that can produce 10 million gallons of ethanol per year using solid waste purchased from Waste Management and Waste Connections. Energy marketer Tenaska has already agreed to sell its ethanol. Fulcrum BioEnergy filed a $115 million IPO in 2011 but withdrew it a year later.

FULL CIRCLE CAPITAL CORP — NMS: FULL

102 Greenwich Avenue, 2nd Floor — CEO: -
Greenwich, CT 06830 — CFO: -
Phone: 203 900-2100 — HR: -
Fax: - — FYE: June 30
Web: www.fccapital.com — Type: Public

Full Circle Capital isn't so much about circles as it is about jagged lines that trend upwards. An investment firm Full Circle Capital invests primarily in senior secured loans for small and lower middle-market companies. The firm typically targets companies in the communications business services and media sectors for investment contributing between $3 million and $10 million per transaction. Its investments help fuel growth and fund capital appreciation among its 20 portfolio companies. Full Circle leaders often sit on portfolio companies' boards and advise on business strategy and other matters. Formed in 2010 Full Circle is externally-managed by investment adviser Full Circle Advisors.

	Annual Growth	06/11	06/12	06/13	06/14	06/15
Sales ($ mil.)	22.2%	8.0	9.8	12.0	13.8	17.7
Net income ($ mil.)	18.7%	4.3	4.8	5.4	6.0	8.6
Market value ($ mil.)	(18.0%)	183.6	177.8	183.6	181.5	83.0
Employees	-	-	-	-	-	-

FULL COMPASS SYSTEMS LTD.

9770 Silicon Prairie Pkwy — CEO: Jonathan B Lipp
Madison WI 53593 — CFO: -
Phone: 608-831-7330 — HR: -
Fax: 608-831-6330 — FYE: December 31
Web: www.fullcompass.com — Type: Private

Church got a brand new big sanctuary that you want to fill with sound? Full Compass Systems can point you in the right direction for a righteous sound system. The company sells more than 700 lines of audio video and lighting equipment for audio/video recording special effects lighting and sound reinforcement via its catalogs. It also offers musical instruments (percussion keyboards and drum machines) along with furniture software and computers needed to complete a theatrical show. Retail rental and warehouse inventory is housed in the company's 140000 square foot facility in Madison Wisconsin. Customers include churches theaters hotels schools and sound studios. Full Compass was founded in 1977.

FULL HOUSE RESORTS, INC. — NAS: FLL

One Summerlin, 1980 Festival Plaza Drive, Suite 680 — CEO: Daniel Lee
Las Vegas, NV 89135 — CFO: Lewis Fanger
Phone: 702 221-7800 — HR: Elaine Guidroz
Fax: - — FYE: December 31
Web: www.fullhouseresorts.com — Type: Public

When it comes to gaming outside Sin City nothing beats a Full House. Full House Resorts owns Stockman's Casino in Fallon Nevada featuring 260 slot and gaming machines four table games and keno. In addition its Rising Star Casino Resort in Rising Son Indiana includes a riverboat casino with 40000 square feet of gaming space a 200-room hotel a theater and several restaurants. The company also operates the Grand Lodge Casino at the Hyatt Regency Lake Tahoe Resort Spa and Casino in Incline Village Nevada through a five-year lease agreement with Hyat Hotels Corporationt.

	Annual Growth	12/16	12/17	12/18	12/19	12/20
Sales ($ mil.)	(3.7%)	146.0	161.3	163.9	165.4	125.6
Net income ($ mil.)	-	(5.1)	(5.0)	(4.4)	(5.8)	0.1
Market value ($ mil.)	13.1%	65.1	105.5	54.8	90.9	106.6
Employees	(9.2%)	1,692	1,679	1,612	1,585	1,151

FULLER (HB) COMPANY — NYS: FUL

1200 Willow Lake Boulevard — CEO: James J Owens
St. Paul, MN 55110-5101 — CFO: John J Corkrean
Phone: 651 236-5900 — HR: Nathanial D Weaver
Fax: 651 236-5161 — FYE: November 27
Web: www.hbfuller.com — Type: Public

H.B. Fuller is one of the world's top adhesive sealant and specialty chemical manufacturers with sales in about 35 countries across the world. The company's core product industrial adhesives is used in the manufacturing process of a wide range of consumer and industrial goods like food and beverage containers doors and windows electronic appliances textiles marine products and automobiles among others. With some 20 independently operating regional sales offices and manufacturing plants outside of the US H.B. Fuller enjoys a wide market reach matched by only a few other global firms. The company's brands include Advantra Clarity Rakoll Silaprene and Eternabond among others. H.B. Fuller generates about 45% of sales from US.

	Annual Growth	12/17	12/18*	11/19	11/20	11/21
Sales ($ mil.)	9.2%	2,306.0	3,041.0	2,897.0	2,790.3	3,278.0
Net income ($ mil.)	29.0%	58.2	171.2	130.8	123.7	161.4
Market value ($ mil.)	7.3%	2,937.1	2,546.0	2,632.6	2,835.7	3,900.3
Employees	2.0%	6,000	6,500	6,400	6,428	6,500

*Fiscal year change

FULLER THEOLOGICAL SEMINARY

135 N OAKLAND AVE — CEO: -
PASADENA, CA 911820002 — CFO: -
Phone: 626-584-5200 — HR: -
Fax: - — FYE: June 30
Web: www.fuller.edu — Type: Private

Looking for a fuller life experience? Fuller Theological Seminary one of the world's largest multidenominational seminaries offers just that through its schools of theology psychology and intercultural studies. It offers about 20 master's and doctoral degree programs and about 10 certificate programs to more than 4000 students from more than 80 countries. In addition to its main campus in Pasadena California the seminary operates eight campuses as well as online classes. It also offers degree programs in Spanish and Korean. Fuller Theological Seminary was founded in 1947 by radio evangelist Charles E. Fuller and pastor Harold John Ockenga.

	Annual Growth	06/09	06/10	06/11	06/13	06/15
Sales ($ mil.)	2.3%	-	60.8	70.2	59.9	68.1
Net income ($ mil.)	-	-	4.6	10.9	6.2	(4.9)
Market value ($ mil.)	-	-	-	-	-	-
Employees	-	-	-	-	-	550

FULLNET COMMUNICATIONS INC
NBB: FULO

201 Robert S. Kerr Avenue, Suite 210
Oklahoma City, OK 73102
Phone: 405 236-8200
Fax: -
Web: www.fullnet.net; www.fulltel.com; www.callmultiplier.com

CEO: Roger Baresel
CFO: Roger P Baresel
HR: -
FYE: December 31
Type: Public

FullNet Communications is trying to net as many Oklahoma Internet users as possible. Established in 1995 the company provides dial-up Internet access to the state's consumers and small to midsized businesses. It sells connectivity on a retail or wholesale basis allowing other Internet service providers to resell the service under their own brand names. FullNet's wholly-owned FullTel subsidiary is a competitive local-exchange carrier (CLEC) that provides the company with the local phone numbers necessary to offer dial-up service.

	Annual Growth	12/16	12/17	12/18	12/19	12/20
Sales ($ mil.)	15.8%	1.9	1.9	2.1	2.4	3.5
Net income ($ mil.)	-	(0.0)	(0.0)	0.3	0.3	1.1
Market value ($ mil.)	41.4%	0.4	0.7	0.6	0.5	1.6
Employees	1.7%	14	15	14	15	15

FULTON FINANCIAL CORP. (PA)
NMS: FULT

One Penn Square
Lancaster, PA 17602
Phone: 717 291-2411
Fax: -
Web: www.fult.com

CEO: E. Philip Wenger
CFO: Mark McCollom
HR: -
FYE: December 31
Type: Public

Founded in 1882 Fulton Financial is a financial holding company with $25 billion in assets that owns four community banks in semi-rural and suburban areas of Pennsylvania Maryland Delaware New Jersey and Virginia. Through some 220 branches the banks offer standard products such as checking savings and credit accounts CDs retirement accounts mortgages and loans. Commercial loans — including for real estate and industrial financial and agricultural loans — account for most of the company's loan portfolio. The company owns several non-banking units including Fulton Insurance an agency selling life insurance and related products.

	Annual Growth	12/16	12/17	12/18	12/19	12/20
Assets ($ mil.)	8.1%	18,944.2	20,036.9	20,682.2	21,886.0	25,906.7
Net income ($ mil.)	2.4%	161.6	171.8	208.4	226.3	178.0
Market value ($ mil.)	(9.3%)	3,052.2	2,906.1	2,513.2	2,829.8	2,065.1
Employees	(1.5%)	3,500	3,700	3,500	3,500	3,300

FURIEX PHARMACEUTICALS INC
NMS: FURX

3900 Paramount Parkway, Suite 150
Morrisville, NC 27560
Phone: 919 456-7800
Fax: -
Web: www.furiex.com

CEO: -
CFO: -
HR: -
FYE: December 31
Type: Public

Furiex Pharmaceuticals knows two heads are better than one. The drug development company partners with pharmaceutical and biotechnology businesses in the early stages of developing new medications to combine R&D know-how. A company can reduce time and cost by teaming up with Furiex to handle safety and efficacy tests for new compounds. (It takes on average more than 10 years and almost $1 billion to bring a new drug to market.) In return Furiex receives a share of the rewards after a drug continues into the late stages of clinical development. The company began in 1998 as a division of PPD; it was named Furiex and spun off into a separate publicly traded company in mid-2010.

	Annual Growth	12/08	12/09	12/10	12/11	12/12
Sales ($ mil.)	21.8%	18.4	6.3	9.0	4.5	40.5
Net income ($ mil.)	-	-	5.8	(8.9)	(54.7)	(49.0)	(42.9)
Market value ($ mil.)	15.5%	-	-	144.7	167.4	192.9
Employees	(18.9%)	-	45	25	24	24

FURIEX PHARMACEUTICALS INC.
NASDAQ: FURX

3900 Paramount Pkwy. Ste. 150
Morrisville NC 27560
Phone: 919-456-7800
Fax: 919-456-7850
Web: furiex.com

CEO: -
CFO: -
HR: -
FYE: December 31
Type: Public

Furiex Pharmaceuticals knows two heads are better than one. The drug development company partners with pharmaceutical and biotechnology businesses in the early stages of developing new medications to combine R&D know-how. A company can reduce time and cost by teaming up with Furiex to handle safety and efficacy tests for new compounds. (It takes on average more than 10 years and almost $1 billion to bring a new drug to market.) In return Furiex receives a share of the rewards after a drug continues into the late stages of clinical development. The company began in 1998 as a division of PPD; it was named Furiex and spun off into a separate publicly traded company in mid-2010.

FURMAN FOODS, INC.

770 CANNERY RD
NORTHUMBERLAND, PA 178578615
Phone: 570-473-3516
Fax: -
Web: www.furmanosfs.com

CEO: David N Geise
CFO: Ted R Hancock
HR: -
FYE: March 28
Type: Private

Furman Foods has firm ideas about tomatoes and other food products. The Pennsylvania company has built a business producing a complete line of canned tomatoes and tomato products. It also offers canned beans; spaghetti pasta and pizza sauces; bean salads; vegetables; and ketchup and other condiments. The company's brand names include Furmano's Conte and Bella Vista. Furman Foods boasts customers in the foodservice (restaurants schools and hospitals) retail (supermarkets and grocery stores) export branded manufacturing and private-label sectors along the US's East Coast. Furman Foods is a family-owned business founded in 1921 by J. W. Furman.

	Annual Growth	04/05	04/06*	03/07	03/08	03/09
Sales ($ mil.)	9.2%	-	73.9	77.2	83.4	96.3
Net income ($ mil.)	-	-	(0.7)	13.8	1.2	1.7
Market value ($ mil.)	-	-	-	-	-	-
Employees	-	-	-	-	-	250

*Fiscal year change

FURMAN UNIVERSITY

3300 POINSETT HWY
GREENVILLE, SC 29613-1000
Phone: 864-294-2000
Fax: -
Web: www.its.furman.edu

CEO: -
CFO: -
HR: -
FYE: June 30
Type: Private

This school's slogan could be "Go Further than Furman." More than 70% of Furman University's graduates go on to law medical or other forms of graduate school. The private school offers an undergraduate liberal arts curriculum and a graduate program focused on teaching and education. Some 3000 graduate and undergraduate students from 46 states and 31 foreign countries attend Furman. Its campus — with features including lake bell tower amphitheater and rose and Japanese gardens is regarded as one of the most beautiful college campuses in the US. Furman was founded in 1826.

	Annual Growth	06/07	06/08	06/10	06/11	06/12
Sales ($ mil.)	(0.0%)	-	142.8	158.8	132.8	142.8
Net income ($ mil.)	-	-	34.0	(3.4)	83.3	(5.6)
Market value ($ mil.)	-	-	-	-	-	-
Employees	-	-	-	-	-	759

FURMAN UNIVERSITY FOUNDATION INC.

3300 POINSETT HWY
GREENVILLE, SC 296130002
Phone: 864-294-2000
Fax: –
Web: www.furman.edu

CEO: –
CFO: –
HR: –
FYE: June 30
Type: Private

The school's slogan could be "Go Further than Furman." More than 70% of Furman University's graduates go on to law medical or other graduate schools. The private school offers an undergraduate liberal arts curriculum and a graduate program focused on teaching and education. Furman offers more than 40 majors through more than 25 departments to some 2700 undergraduate and graduate students from US 46 states and 53 foreign countries. It also offers internship and study away programs. The university has 240 faculty members. The student-faculty ratio is 11:1. Its 750-acre campus features a lake bell tower amphitheater and rose and Japanese gardens and is regarded as one of the most beautiful in the US.

	Annual Growth	06/09	06/10	06/11	06/12	06/13
Sales ($ mil.)	(3.0%)	–	158.8	132.8	142.8	145.1
Net income ($ mil.)	(17.5%)	–	–	83.3	(5.6)	56.7
Market value ($ mil.)	–	–	–	–	–	–
Employees	–	–	–	–	–	759

FURMANITE CORP
NYS: FRM

10370 Richmond Avenue, Suite 600
Houston, TX 77042
Phone: 713 634-7777
Fax: –
Web: www.furmanite.com

CEO: Jeffery G Davis
CFO: Robert S Muff
HR: –
FYE: December 31
Type: Public

Furmanite thrives under pressure. The specialty contractor provides a variety of technical services for petroleum refineries chemical plants nuclear power stations and other clients in the power generation manufacturing and processing industries. Furmanite specializes in sealing leaks in valves pipes and other flow-process systems often under emergency conditions involving exposure to high temperatures and pressures potential contact with dangerous materials explosion hazards and environmental contamination. It also provides onsite machining and custom engineering services as well as consulting and support services. Company rival Team Inc agreed to buy Furmanite in late 2015 for $335 million.

	Annual Growth	12/10	12/11	12/12	12/13	12/14
Sales ($ mil.)	16.6%	286.0	316.2	326.5	427.3	529.2
Net income ($ mil.)	4.6%	9.5	24.0	0.8	14.0	11.4
Market value ($ mil.)	3.1%	260.8	238.1	202.7	400.8	295.1
Employees	18.7%	1,521	1,529	1,833	3,110	3,017

FUSION CONNECT INC
NAS: FSNN

420 Lexington Avenue, Suite 1718
New York, NY 10170
Phone: 212 201-2400
Fax: –
Web: www.fusionconnect.com

CEO: Matthew D Rosen
CFO: Keith Soldan
HR: –
FYE: December 31
Type: Public

Fusion Telecommunications International understands that modern communications is a blend of old and familiar processes with new technologies including cloud computing. The company provides VoIP (Voice over Internet Protocol) telephone and other Internet-based communications services primarily to larger US carriers. Its other clients include businesses with a need to outsource the hosting and management of their computer-based corporate telephony systems. Fusion has joined the march to the cloud offering communications infrastructure computing and managed applications from the cloud to small medium and large businesses. The company in 2017 agreed to buy Birch Communications for $280 million.

	Annual Growth	12/13	12/14	12/15	12/16	12/17
Sales ($ mil.)	25.1%	61.5	92.1	101.7	122.0	150.5
Net income ($ mil.)	–	(5.1)	(2.6)	(8.2)	(12.7)	(14.0)
Market value ($ mil.)	133.2%	1.9	47.2	48.8	22.5	56.2
Employees	8.9%	193	228	260	306	271

FUSION-IO INC.
NYS: FIO

2855 E. Cottonwood Parkway, Suite 100
Salt Lake City, UT 84121
Phone: 801 424-5500
Fax: –
Web: www.fusionio.com

CEO: Shane Robison
CFO: Ted Hull
HR: –
FYE: June 30
Type: Public

Fusion-io wants to help businesses access data in a flash. The company's ioMemory hardware modules offer storage and processing using an array of flash memory delivered through its proprietary data-path controller and virtual storage layer (VSL) software. VSL allows ioMemory to function as data storage within a server allowing data access without traditional storage devices. Fusion-io's products are used in sectors such as education energy entertainment financial services government and life sciences among others. The company's three biggest clients are Facebook (30% of sales) Apple (25%) and HP (17%). Fusion-io was formed in 2005 and went public in 2011.

	Annual Growth	06/09	06/10	06/11	06/12	06/13
Sales ($ mil.)	155.5%	10.2	36.2	197.2	359.3	432.4
Net income ($ mil.)	–	(25.6)	(31.7)	4.6	(5.6)	(38.2)
Market value ($ mil.)	(31.2%)	–	–	2,964.6	2,058.1	1,403.0
Employees	33.4%	–	395	441	669	938

FUSIONSTORM

2 Bryant St. Ste. 150
San Francisco CA 94105
Phone: 415-623-2626
Fax: 415-623-2630
Web: www.fusionstorm.com

CEO: Mike Norris
CFO: –
HR: –
FYE: December 31
Type: Private

FusionStorm whips up a combination of IT services. The company provides a variety of information technology and remote support services to businesss in a variety of industries. FusionStorm develops configures implements and hosts data networks; provides IT consultancy and training services; sources hardware and software; and performs security and vulnerability assessments. The company supplies and supports products from key IT vendors such as IBM Oracle Cisco and Hewlett-Packard. Founded in 1995 FusionStorm has offices throughout the US although more than half of its offices are in its home state of California. The firm's officers hold a majority ownership in the company.

FUSIONSTORM GLOBAL INC.

8 Cedar St. Ste. 54A
Woburn MA 01801
Phone: 781-782-1900
Fax: +48-17-888-55-50
Web: www.asseco.pl

CEO: –
CFO: –
HR: –
FYE: December 31
Type: Private

FusionStorm Global has a plan for global domination of the IT services market. The company formed in 2009 with the idea to acquire three companies — FusionStorm Red River Computer and Global Technology Resources Inc. (GTRI) that provide IT consulting and services. FusionStorm works with small businesses and large corporations while Red River sells computer products to government agencies and GTRI is focused on services for corporations and the public sector. FusionStorm Global filed a $175 million IPO in August 2011. If the company successfully goes public it will use the proceeds to buy FusionStorm for $100 million Red River for $26 million and GTRI for $12.5 million and pay off their debt.

FUTURE TECH ENTERPRISE, INC.

500 E BROWARD BLVD # 240
FORT LAUDERDALE, FL 333943000
Phone: 631-472-5500
Fax: –
Web: www.ftei.com

CEO: Robert Venero
CFO: Robert Johnson
HR: –
FYE: December 31
Type: Private

Future Tech Enterprise can help you realize the potential of all sorts of futuristic technologies. The company provides a variety of IT services including network integration services project management systems integration procurement and call center support. Future Tech also resells computer systems software and peripherals. Its customers range from small businesses to enterprise organizations with complex technology needs; clients include Hofstra University Honeywell JetBlue the New York Islanders and Northrop Grumman. The company has configuration centers and product warehouses across the US. In 1996 Future Tech got its start in the basement of president and CEO Bob Venero.

	Annual Growth	12/15	12/16	12/18	12/19	12/20
Sales ($ mil.)	8.4%	–	185.2	227.1	271.3	256.0
Net income ($ mil.)	(0.5%)	–	10.7	11.6	12.9	10.5
Market value ($ mil.)	–	–	–	–	–	–
Employees	–	–	–	–	–	92

FUTUREFUEL CORP
NYS: FF

8235 Forsyth Blvd., Suite 400
St. Louis, MO 63105
Phone: 314 854-8352
Fax: –
Web: www.futurefuelcorporation.com

CEO: Paul A Novelly
CFO: Rose M Sparks
HR: –
FYE: December 31
Type: Public

FutureFuel manufactures chemical products biofuels and bio-based specialty products for specific customers. Its annual biofuel production capacity is almost 60 million gallons. Specialty products include laundry detergent additive biocide and herbicide intermediates chlorinated polyolefin adhesion promoters and antioxidant precursors. The company serves the cosmetics and personal care specialty polymers and the fuel industries. FutureFuel generates vast majority of its sale in the US.

	Annual Growth	12/16	12/17	12/18	12/19	12/20
Sales ($ mil.)	(5.2%)	253.2	275.0	291.0	205.2	204.5
Net income ($ mil.)	(4.7%)	56.3	23.5	53.2	88.2	46.6
Market value ($ mil.)	(2.2%)	608.0	616.3	693.8	542.0	555.5
Employees	(1.5%)	500	500	548	500	470

FX ALLIANCE INC.
NYSE: FX

909 Third Ave. 10th Fl.
New York NY 10022
Phone: 646-268-9900
Fax: 646-268-9996
Web: www.fxall.com

CEO: –
CFO: –
HR: –
FYE: December 31
Type: Public

It just makes cents to use FX Alliance for foreign exchange trading online. The company operates an electronic platform for foreign exchange (FX) trading whereby market participants buy one currency and sell in another primarily on the over-the-counter (OTC) market. FX Alliance counts more than 1150 institutional clients such as asset managers banks broker-dealers corporate treasurers hedge funds and prime brokers. More than half of its trading volume comes from customers outside the US. FX Alliance has international offices in Australia India Japan Singapore and the UK. Thomson Reuters is buying FX Alliance for $616 million.

FX ENERGY INC.
NMS: FXEN

3006 Highland Drive, Suite 206
Salt Lake City, UT 84106
Phone: 801 486-5555
Fax: 801 486-5575
Web: www.fxenergy.com

CEO: David N Pierce
CFO: –
HR: –
FYE: December 31
Type: Public

FX Energy is not exactly fixated on energy in Poland but it is in western Poland's Permian Basin where it is hoping to make its big breakthrough. In 2012 the independent exploration and production company reported proved reserves of 44.1 billion cu. ft. of natural gas equivalent in Poland and 0.6 million barrels of oil equivalent in the US (from properties in Montana and Nevada). Partners include state-owned Polish Oil and Gas and CalEnergy Gas which have served as operators for exploration wells in Poland. FX Energy holds about 2.7 million gross acres (2 million net) in western Poland.

	Annual Growth	12/09	12/10	12/11	12/12	12/13
Sales ($ mil.)	23.9%	14.7	25.0	35.4	36.6	34.5
Net income ($ mil.)	–	(0.5)	(0.8)	(28.5)	4.1	(11.8)
Market value ($ mil.)	6.5%	153.1	330.5	257.9	220.8	196.7
Employees	3.4%	49	49	48	50	56

G&K SERVICES INC
NMS: GK

5995 Opus Parkway
Minnetonka, MN 55343
Phone: 952 912-5500
Fax: –
Web: www.gkservices.com

CEO: Scott D Farmer
CFO: J Michael Hansen
HR: –
FYE: July 02
Type: Public

G&K Services finds money in uniforms. The company is the third-largest uniform rental agency (behind #1 Cintas and #2 ARAMARK). G&K makes and supplies uniforms for about 170000 customers in the automotive manufacturing hospitality and technology industries among others from about 165 locations in the US Canada Ireland and the Dominican Republic. Along with rentals and sales the company provides cleaning repair and replacement services for all of its uniforms. G&K also carries clean room garments used by the semiconductor industry. In addition the company offers facility services providing restroom supplies and renting items such as dust mops floor mats and towels. G&K was founded in 1902. In 2016 Cintas agreed to acquire the company for $2.2 billion including debt.

	Annual Growth	06/12	06/13	06/14	06/15*	07/16
Sales ($ mil.)	3.0%	869.9	907.7	900.9	937.6	978.0
Net income ($ mil.)	31.6%	24.1	46.7	47.7	59.9	72.4
Market value ($ mil.)	25.2%	613.2	935.9	1,017.3	1,383.3	1,508.2
Employees	0.6%	7,800	7,800	7,800	8,000	8,000

*Fiscal year change

G&P TRUCKING COMPANY, INC.

126 ACCESS RD
GASTON, SC 290539501
Phone: 803-791-5500
Fax: –
Web: www.gptruck.com

CEO: –
CFO: Billy Lynch
HR: Martha Landreth
FYE: December 31
Type: Private

G&P Trucking provides truckload freight hauling and related logistics services mainly in the southeastern US. The company which specializes in next-day and same-day service operates a fleet of about 520 tractors and 1500 trailers from about a dozen terminals in the Carolinas Georgia Virginia Tennessee and Texas. Some of its business comes from handling cargo coming into and out of ports such as Charlotte North Carolina; Norfolk Virginia; and Savannah Georgia; it also arranges transportation to and from Mexico.

	Annual Growth	12/03	12/04	12/05	12/06	12/07
Sales ($ mil.)	8.8%	–	76.9	84.7	93.4	99.2
Net income ($ mil.)	–	–	3.9	1.9	1.1	(5.1)
Market value ($ mil.)	–	–	–	–	–	–
Employees	–	–	–	–	–	700

G-I HOLDINGS INC.

1361 Alps Rd.
Wayne NJ 07470
Phone: 973-628-3000
Fax: 303-744-4443
Web: www.gates.com

CEO: Robert B Tafaro
CFO: Susan Yoss
HR: –
FYE: December 31
Type: Private

G-I Holdings isn't your average Joe in the roofing materials business. The company and its subsidiary Building Materials Corporation of America (which do business as GAF) manufacture flashing vents and complete roofing systems. It is one of North America's leading roofing manufacturers with residential shingles and related products as well as built-up roofing single-ply roofing and modified bitumen products for commercial use. GAF markets its products under such brands as Metalastic Timberline EverGuard GAFGLAS and Ruberoid. Other products include natural stone ornamental ironwork fiber-cement siding and ducting.

G-III APPAREL GROUP LTD.

512 Seventh Avenue
New York, NY 10018
Phone: 212 403-0500
Fax: –
Web: www.g-iii.com

NMS: GIII

CEO: Morris Goldfarb
CFO: Neal Nackman
HR: –
FYE: January 31
Type: Public

G-III Apparel Group sources and markets a wide range of men's and women's apparel under 30-plus licensed and proprietary brands including global brands DKNY Donna Karan Calvin Klein Tommy Hilfiger and Karl Lagerfeld Paris. The company's offerings include outerwear dresses and sports and performance wear as well as handbags shoes leather goods and luggage. It also has a team sports business with licenses from the NFL NBA MLB and more than 150 colleges. The company also distributes its products through its retail stores and through Wilsons Leather G.H. Bass Vilebrequin and Andrew Marc websites and the websites of its retail partners such as Macy's Nordstrom Amazon and Fanatics. The US accounts for approximately 85% of sales.

	Annual Growth	01/17	01/18	01/19	01/20	01/21
Sales ($ mil.)	(3.7%)	2,386.4	2,806.9	3,076.2	3,160.5	2,055.1
Net income ($ mil.)	(17.9%)	51.9	62.1	138.1	143.8	23.5
Market value ($ mil.)	0.7%	1,270.4	1,806.9	1,686.9	1,316.3	1,308.1
Employees	(21.6%)	8,734	9,071	7,400	6,400	3,300

G.S.E. CONSTRUCTION COMPANY INC.

6950 PRESTON AVE
LIVERMORE, CA 945519545
Phone: 925-447-0292
Fax: –
Web: www.gseconstruction.com

CEO: Dennis Gutierrez
CFO: –
HR: –
FYE: December 31
Type: Private

GSE Construction Company provides heavy construction for government agencies public utilities and the private sector. The general engineering contractor specializes in building water and wastewater infrastructure. GSE provides services such as new construction renovation work and upgrades and construction labor. Projects range from retrofitting old systems and expanding capacity to constructing storage tanks treatment facilities and pump stations. The company also often teams with fellow engineering firm Applied Technologies to complete waste-to-energy conversion projects. GSE performs most of its work in California and Nevada. President and CEO Orlando Gutierrez founded GSE Construction in 1980.

	Annual Growth	12/06	12/07	12/08	12/09	12/10
Sales ($ mil.)	–	–	–	(1,344.3)	69.8	63.3
Net income ($ mil.)	12635.9%	–	–	0.0	2.1	0.3
Market value ($ mil.)	–	–	–	–	–	–
Employees	–	–	–	–	–	140

GABRIEL BROTHERS INC.

55 Scott Ave.
Morgantown WV 26508
Phone: 304-292-6965
Fax: 304-292-3874
Web: www.gabrielbrothers.com

CEO: –
CFO: –
HR: –
FYE: January 31
Type: Private

Gabriel blow your horn — your magical mystical discount horn that is. Gabriel Brothers sells discounted brand-name clothing through more than 100 stores under the Gabriel Brothers (commonly called "Gabes") and Rugged Wearhouse banners. Its stores are located in about a dozen East Coast and Mid-Atlantic states. The company's offerings include men's women's and children's apparel and footwear as well as housewares. Gabriel Brothers carries such brands as Anne Klein Kenneth Cole and Liz Claiborne and features markdowns as high as 70% off of their original retail prices. The family-run company was established in 1961 by James and Arthur Gabriel.

GADSDEN PROPERTIES INC

15150 North Hayden Road, Suite 235
Scottsdale, AZ 85260
Phone: 480 750-8700
Fax: –
Web: www.photomedex.com

NBB: FCRE

CEO: B. J. Parrish
CFO: Scott Crist
HR: –
FYE: December 31
Type: Public

For PhotoMedex beauty is skin deep. The company manufactures and markets dermatological treatments for skin disorders such as acne psoriasis and vitiligo (loss of skin pigmentation). Other products include gels and creams intended to promote skin rejuvenation and hair growth. PhotoMedex also develops lasers and fiber-optic equipment for dermatological and surgical applications. Its FDA-approved XTRAC Excimer laser system is used for the treatment of psoriasis and eczema and its VTRAC lamp system is sold outside the US to treat the same ailments. Customers in the US and overseas include consumers dermatologists cosmetic surgeons and spas. PhotoMedex plans to sell its operations to Florida-based DS Healthcare.

	Annual Growth	12/14	12/15	12/16	12/17	12/18
Sales ($ mil.)	(87.8%)	163.5	75.9	38.4	0.0	0.0
Net income ($ mil.)	–	(121.5)	(34.6)	(13.3)	(18.8)	(2.0)
Market value ($ mil.)	(52.9%)	40.8	12.0	58.6	24.2	2.0
Employees	(67.5%)	179	76	6	6	2

GADSDEN REGIONAL MEDICAL CENTER, LLC

1007 GOODYEAR AVE
GADSDEN, AL 359031195
Phone: 256-494-4000
Fax: –
Web: www.gadsdenregional.com

CEO: Justin Bryant
CFO: Michael Cotton
HR: –
FYE: September 30
Type: Private

Located in northeastern Alabama Gadsden Regional Medical Center is a general acute care hospital with about 350 beds and a medical staff of some 230 physicians. The hospital provides inpatient medical surgical and behavioral health care as well as trauma care ambulatory surgery diagnostic imaging and other outpatient services. Specialties include cardiology oncology neurology orthopedics and women's and children's care. Additionally Gadsden Regional offers home health care and hospice services and runs a retail home medical equipment store. The health system is part of the Triad Hospitals group which was acquired by Community Health Systems in 2007.

	Annual Growth	09/13	09/14	09/15	09/16	09/17
Sales ($ mil.)	(9.5%)	–	243.8	240.9	190.6	180.6
Net income ($ mil.)	–	–	2.6	7.9	8.5	(4.8)
Market value ($ mil.)	–	–	–	–	–	–
Employees	–	–	–	–	–	1,300

GAIA INC (NEW)
NMS: GAIA

833 West South Boulder Road
Louisville, CO 80027
Phone: 303 222-3600
Fax: –
Web: www.gaia.com

CEO: Jirka Rysavy
CFO: Paul Tarell
HR: –
FYE: December 31
Type: Public

If you're into living a healthy sustainable lifestyle Gaiam is your kind of company. The name Gaiam (pronounced "guy-um") is a combination of Gaia (the Earth goddess) and "I am." Most of the company's sales come from proprietary products and media for consumers interested in yoga fitness and wellness. Other merchandise includes organic cotton apparel bedding and personal care and home care products. Gaiam boasts a library of more than 7000 DVD titles and a TV channel (which the company plans to spin off). It also owns a stake in Real Goods Solar which designs and installs solar energy systems. Gaiam's offerings are sold through catalogs its e-commerce site and major retailers (including Target and Whole Foods).

	Annual Growth	12/16	12/17	12/18	12/19	12/20
Sales ($ mil.)	40.3%	17.2	28.3	43.8	54.0	66.8
Net income ($ mil.)	(72.2%)	87.1	(23.3)	(33.8)	(18.2)	0.5
Market value ($ mil.)	3.4%	165.9	237.9	198.7	153.3	189.5
Employees	1.9%	114	130	150	135	123

GAIN CAPITAL HOLDINGS INC
NYS: GCAP

Bedminster One, 135 Route 202/206
Bedminster, NJ 07921
Phone: 908 731-0700
Fax: –
Web: www.gaincapital.com

CEO: Glenn H Stevens
CFO: Nigel Rose
HR: –
FYE: December 31
Type: Public

There is plenty to lose in the foreign currency exchange market but this company would like you to focus on the potential gains. GAIN Capital Holdings provides over-the-counter foreign exchange (forex) services to retail traders (responsible for about 97% of the company's trading volume) and institutional investors and through financial intermediaries such as broker-dealers banks and futures commission merchants. The company's FOREXTrader platform provides online trading tools and educational resources to help individual investors deal in forex trading online. It has 133000 funded retail accounts.

	Annual Growth	12/14	12/15	12/16	12/17	12/18
Sales ($ mil.)	(0.8%)	369.5	435.3	411.8	308.6	358.0
Net income ($ mil.)	30.9%	31.6	10.3	35.3	(11.2)	92.9
Market value ($ mil.)	(9.1%)	341.2	306.7	248.9	378.2	233.0
Employees	7.4%	479	772	741	708	638

GAINESVILLE REGIONAL UTILITIES

301 SE 4TH AVE
GAINESVILLE, FL 326016857
Phone: 352-334-3400
Fax: –
Web: www.gru.com

CEO: –
CFO: Jennifer L Hunt
HR: –
FYE: September 30
Type: Private

Multi-service utility Gainesville Regional Utilities (GRU) started out small more than a century ago but has been gaining ground ever since. The company (now the fifth largest municipal electric utility in Florida) is the sole utilities provider in Gainesville and surrounding areas in Alachua County. The municipal utility distributes electric water wastewater natural gas and telecommunications services to approximately 93000 retail and wholesale customers. GRU has interests in power generation facilities that give it more than 600 MW of capacity. It also offers internet and other communications services. GRU gets the bulk of its revenues from its electric utility operations.

	Annual Growth	09/05	09/06	09/07	09/08	09/09
Sales ($ mil.)	12.0%	–	–	294.8	350.0	369.9
Net income ($ mil.)	32.6%	–	–	19.1	18.3	33.6
Market value ($ mil.)	–	–	–	–	–	–
Employees	–	–	–	–	–	850

GALECTIN THERAPEUTICS INC.
OTC: GALT

7 Wells Ave. Ste. 34
Newton MA 02459
Phone: 617-559-0033
Fax: 617-928-3450
Web: www.galectintherapeutics.com

CEO: Joel Lewis
CFO: Jack Callicutt
HR: –
FYE: December 31
Type: Public

Galectin Therapeutics (formerly known as Pro-Pharmaceuticals) has a knack for inhibiting galectin proteins. The drug developer is targeting galectin proteins as they play a key role in the development of a variety of diseases. It is developing such inhibitors to treat liver fibrosis which is currently untreatable. Its GM-CT-01 drug candidate is being investigated for use targeting certain melanomas and in combination with another drug to improve its effectiveness in treating colorectal cancer.

GALENA BIOPHARMA INC
NAS: GALE

2000 Crow Canyon Place, Suite 380
San Ramon, CA 94583
Phone: 855 855-4253
Fax: –
Web: –

CEO: Angelos Stergiou
CFO: Gene Mack
HR: –
FYE: December 31
Type: Public

While there's no vaccine for breast cancer Galena Biopharma has big plans for NeuVax its drug candidate. NeuVax which is in Phase III clinical trials is being tested for its efficacy in reducing the recurrence of breast cancer in patients who can't take Genentech's Herceptin. Galena Biopharma acquired the rights to NeuVax when it bought the drug's developer Arizona-based Apthera Inc. for about $7 million in April 2011. Galena itself was spun off from RXi Pharmaceuticals in a one-for-one stock split in March 2012. Galena having more potential for success with NeuVax became the public company while RXi Pharmaceuticals became a private company focused on developing RNA interference (RNAi) therapies.

	Annual Growth	12/10	12/11	12/12	12/13	12/14
Sales ($ mil.)	274.7%	–	–	–	2.5	9.3
Net income ($ mil.)	–	(12.0)	(11.5)	(35.0)	(76.7)	(36.6)
Market value ($ mil.)	(12.5%)	334.0	60.7	198.1	642.2	195.5
Employees	15.5%	32	29	12	60	57

GALENCARE, INC.

6000 49TH ST N
SAINT PETERSBURG, FL 337092114
Phone: 727-521-4411
Fax: –
Web: www.hcahealthcare.com

CEO: Valerie Stafford
CFO: Gary Searls
HR: –
FYE: September 30
Type: Private

Hurting hearts aren't the only thing Northside Hospital can treat. The acute care facility which houses the Tampa Bay Heart Institute has some 290 beds and provides a gamut of medical services to the residents of Pinellas County Florida. The Heart Institute offers surgical diagnostic and rehabilitation services for cardiac patients. In addition to its cardiovascular expertise Northside Hospital offers specialized treatment for patients with spine disorders and chronic pain conditions as well as diagnostic imaging orthopedics rehabilitation urology outpatient surgery. Northside Hospital is part of the HCA family.

	Annual Growth	09/03	09/04	09/05	09/13	09/14
Sales ($ mil.)	–	–	–	0.0	120.3	140.7
Net income ($ mil.)	–	–	–	0.0	(2.0)	10.8
Market value ($ mil.)	–	–	–	–	–	–
Employees	–	–	–	–	–	340

GALLAGHER (ARTHUR J.) & CO.   NYS: AJG

2850 Golf Road
Rolling Meadows, IL 60008-4050
Phone: 630 773-3800
Fax: –
Web: www.ajg.com

CEO: J. Patrick Gallagher
CFO: Douglas K Howell
HR: –
FYE: December 31
Type: Public

One of the world's largest insurance brokers Arthur J. Gallagher (Gallagher) provides commercial insurance brokerage consulting and third-party property/casualty claims settlement and administration services to businesses and organizations around the world through a network of subsidiaries and agencies. It places (arranges directly with underwriters) traditional and niche/practice groups in addition to offering retirement solutions and managing employee benefits programs. Risk management services include claims management insurance property appraisal services and loss control consulting. It also has investments in companies that own clean coal production facilities in the US. Most of Gallagher's revenue comes from the US.

	Annual Growth	12/17	12/18	12/19	12/20	12/21
Sales ($ mil.)	7.4%	6,159.6	6,934.0	7,195.0	7,003.6	8,209.4
Net income ($ mil.)	18.3%	463.1	633.5	668.8	818.8	906.8
Market value ($ mil.)	28.0%	13,193.9	15,366.5	19,855.5	25,793.5	35,376.2
Employees	9.8%	26,800	30,362	33,300	32,401	39,000

GALLAUDET UNIVERSITY

800 FLORIDA AVE NE
WASHINGTON, DC 200023600
Phone: 202-651-5000
Fax: –
Web: www.gallaudet.edu

CEO: –
CFO: –
HR: –
FYE: September 30
Type: Private

Gallaudet University (GU) gives deaf and hard-of-hearing students the chance to be in the majority. Designed to accommodate hearing-impaired students GU offers undergraduate and graduate degrees in more than 40 majors to about 2000 students annually. The bilingual university which uses both American Sign Language (ASL) and English admits a small number of hearing ASL-proficient students to each incoming freshman class. Through its Laurent Clerc National Deaf Education Center GU provides training and support for teachers and parents of hearing impaired children and operates demonstration schools. Founded in 1864 GU was named for Thomas Hopkins Gallaudet a pioneer in education for the deaf.

	Annual Growth	09/14	09/15	09/16	09/17	09/18
Sales ($ mil.)	0.6%	–	184.2	196.9	183.6	187.8
Net income ($ mil.)	(2.2%)	–	5.9	11.0	9.5	5.6
Market value ($ mil.)	–	–	–	–	–	–
Employees	–	–	–	–	–	1,200

GALLERY MODEL HOMES, INC.

6006 NORTH FWY
HOUSTON, TX 770764029
Phone: 713-694-5570
Fax: –
Web: www.galleryfurniture.com

CEO: –
CFO: –
HR: –
FYE: December 31
Type: Private

Gallery Furniture and its founder Jim "Mattress Mac" McIngvale have become something of a Houston institution. McIngvale's animated TV ads promise they "really will save you money." With two locations the firm has evolved into a leading regional furniture retailer accounting for about 20% of Houston's market share. Gallery Furniture also ranks as one of the nation's top sellers in terms of sales per square foot. In addition to mattresses (Simmons Beautyrest and Tempur Sealy brands) it sells bedroom dining room home office and living room furniture. The firm was founded in 1981. A fire in May 2009 destroyed its 100000-sq.-ft. warehouse and damaged its North Freeway showroom.

	Annual Growth	12/03	12/04	12/05	12/06	12/07
Sales ($ mil.)	(1.1%)	–	115.3	130.4	129.5	111.4
Net income ($ mil.)	–	–	(0.0)	0.5	1.0	3.6
Market value ($ mil.)	–	–	–	–	–	–
Employees	–	–	–	–	–	400

GALLERY OF HISTORY INC.

3601 W. Sahara Ave. Promenade Ste.
Las Vegas NV 89102-5379
Phone: 702-364-1000
Fax: 702-364-1285
Web: www.galleryofhistory.com

CEO: Todd M Axelrod
CFO: Rod R Lynam
HR: –
FYE: September 30
Type: Private

Those who don't know the Gallery of History are doomed to buy their memorabilia from another auction house. The company auctions autographs memorabilia and manuscripts from artists authors athletes entertainers politicians and scientists among other notable figures. Its inventory of about 190000 items have included baseballs autographed by Hank Aaron letters written by Albert Einstein and signed photos from Cecil B. De Mille. Although the Internet is its primary sales channel the company also offers autographs and manuscripts through a retail gallery located at its headquarters. The Gallery of History was incorporated in 1981. Founder chairman and CEO Todd Axelrod owns about 90% of the company.

GALLUP, INC.

901 F ST NW STE 400
WASHINGTON, DC 200041419
Phone: 202-715-3030
Fax: –
Web: www.gallup.com

CEO: –
CFO: James R Krieger
HR: –
FYE: December 31
Type: Private

Gallup is a global analytics and advice firm that helps leaders and organizations solve their most pressing problems. Other specialties include branding marketing and recruiting. The company delivers its services on the web and combines analytics and advice to help leaders and organizations identify opportunities and create meaningful change through some 30 global offices. It draws customers from a variety of industries including automotive business services health care hospitality manufacturing and retail. Despite its diversified business offerings the company is still most famous for its Gallup Poll surveys. George Gallup founded the company in 1935 as American Institute of Public Opinion.

	Annual Growth	12/07	12/08	12/09	12/11	12/12
Sales ($ mil.)	1.4%	–	–	264.1	303.2	275.4
Net income ($ mil.)	48.8%	–	–	7.0	34.0	23.0
Market value ($ mil.)	–	–	–	–	–	–
Employees	–	–	–	–	–	2,000

GAMCO INVESTORS INC   NYS: GBL

191 Mason Street
Greenwich, CT 06830
Phone: 203 629-2726
Fax: –
Web: www.gabelli.com

CEO: Mario Gabelli
CFO: Kieran Caterina
HR: –
FYE: December 31
Type: Public

Investing is anything but a game for "Super Mario" Gabelli the self-made billionaire investor and founder and CEO of GAMCO Investors. It provides advisory services to some 25 open-end funds and about 15 closed-end funds under the Gabelli GAMCO and Comstock brands. GAMCO has about 1700 institutional and private wealth management investors principally in the US. GAMCO has approximately $36.5 billion in assets under management. Its broker-dealer subsidiary G.distributors acts and underwriter and distributor of its open-end funds.

	Annual Growth	12/16	12/17	12/18	12/19	12/20
Sales ($ mil.)	(7.4%)	353.0	360.5	341.5	312.4	259.7
Net income ($ mil.)	(15.9%)	117.1	77.8	117.2	81.9	58.7
Market value ($ mil.)	(12.9%)	849.6	815.5	464.5	536.0	487.9
Employees	3.4%	156	159	172	189	178

GAMEFLY INC.

5340 Alla Rd. Ste. 110
Los Angeles CA 90006
Phone: 310-664-6400
Fax: +41-44-248-50-61
Web: www.tamedia.ch

CEO: Jeff Walker
CFO: –
HR: –
FYE: March 31
Type: Private

GameFly is to gamers what Netflix is to movie lovers. The video game provider offers more than 8000 titles for rent — both newer releases and classics — for entertainment systems such as Microsoft Xbox Nintendo Wii and Sony PlayStation as well as handheld consoles. Some 334000 members pay a monthly subscription fee to rent games with no due dates or late charges. To support this effort GameFly maintains shipping centers in Austin Los Angeles Pittsburgh Seattle and Tampa. Through its Direct2Drive website gamers can buy video games among 3000 choices to download to PCs or Macs. Founded in 2002 GameFly counts among its backers venture firms Sequoia Capital and Tenaya Capital.

GAMESTOP CORP   NYS: GME

625 Westport Parkway
Grapevine, TX 76051
Phone: 817 424-2000
Fax: –
Web: www.gamestop.com

CEO: Matt Furlong
CFO: Mike Recupero
HR: –
FYE: January 30
Type: Public

Established in 1996 GameStop is a retailer of new and pre-owned games and entertainment products through its e-commerce properties and thousands of stores. It boasts more than 4800 stores in the US Australia Canada and Europe. GameStop's stores and e-commerce sites operate primarily under the names GameStop EB Games and Micromania. GameStop has a buy-sell-trade program where gamers can trade-in video game consoles games and accessories as well as consumer electronics for cash or in-store credit. About two-thirds of the company's revenue comes from US operations.

	Annual Growth	01/17*	02/18	02/19	02/20*	01/21
Sales ($ mil.)	(12.3%)	8,607.9	9,224.6	8,285.3	6,466.0	5,089.8
Net income ($ mil.)	–	353.2	34.7	(673.0)	(470.9)	(215.3)
Market value ($ mil.)	91.2%	1,587.4	1,059.8	734.0	250.8	21,222.5
Employees	(6.5%)	68,000	67,000	61,000	56,000	52,000

*Fiscal year change

GAMING PARTNERS INTERNATIONAL CORP   NMS: GPIC

3945 West Cheyenne Avenue
North Las Vegas, NV 89032
Phone: 702 384-2425
Fax: –
Web: www.gpigaming.com

CEO: –
CFO: Alain M Thieffry
HR: Richelle Holmes
FYE: December 31
Type: Public

This company doesn't care if gamblers win or crap out as long as they do it using its products. Gaming Partners International is a leading manufacturer of casino gaming products including dealing shoes dice gaming chips playing cards and roulette wheels. It also supplies table furniture and layouts for blackjack poker baccarat craps and other casino games. With manufacturing facilities in the US Mexico and France the company markets its products under the brands Bourgogne et Grasset Bud Jones and Paulson to casino operators around the world. French holding company Holding Wilson owns almost 50% of Gaming Partners International.

	Annual Growth	12/13	12/14	12/15	12/16	12/17
Sales ($ mil.)	9.4%	56.2	61.0	78.2	82.1	80.6
Net income ($ mil.)	32.8%	1.2	2.7	6.9	5.2	3.6
Market value ($ mil.)	8.3%	64.8	68.3	71.1	93.8	89.2
Employees	(0.7%)	730	726	704	730	709

GAN LTD   NAS: GAN

400 Spectrum Center Drive, Suite 1900
Irvine, CA 92618
Phone: 702 964-5777
Fax: –
Web: www.gan.com

CEO: Dermot Smurfit
CFO: Karen Flores
HR: –
FYE: December 31
Type: Public

GAN lets you play cards in the cloud. The company provides its in-house GameSTACK Internet Gaming System software to online and land-based casino gaming operators. It offers simulated gaming for its customers in the US alongside real money gaming in the rest of the world (as well as New Jersey) where online gaming with cash is legal. GAN also produces and brings to market online versions of classic games for desktop tablet and mobile devices. The UK-based company's key market is the US where online gaming is slowly opening up. New Jersey was the first (and so far only) state to allow regulated real money internet-based casino gaming while much of GAN's new business comes from land-based casinos. The company was founded in 2001 by David McDowell and Kevin O'Neal.

	Annual Growth	12/16	12/17	12/18	12/19	12/20
Sales ($ mil.)	–	0.0	0.0	14.0	30.0	35.2
Net income ($ mil.)	–	0.0	0.0	(7.7)	2.0	(20.2)
Market value ($ mil.)	–	0.0	0.0	–	–	–
Employees	111.8%	–	–	–	136	288

GANDER MOUNTAIN COMPANY

180 E. 5th St. Ste. 1300
St. Paul MN 55101
Phone: 651-325-4300
Fax: 651-325-2003
Web: www.gandermountain.com

CEO: –
CFO: –
HR: –
FYE: January 31
Type: Private

Gander Mountain has got the gear to get you out of the office and up the mountain. The company operates nearly 120 outdoor sporting goods stores focused on a variety of outdoor activities such as hunting camping and fishing in some two dozen states. In addition to outdoor equipment and related accessories the stores also sell apparel and footwear. While Gander Mountain has sold fishing and pontoon boats since 2007 through an arrangement with Tracker Marine Group a unit of Bass Pro Shops the retailer exited its all terrain vehicle (ATV) and boat categories by 2010. Founded in 1960 as an outdoor catalog operation Gander Mountain went private in early 2010.

GANNETT CO INC (NEW)   NYS: GCI

7950 Jones Branch Drive
McLean, VA 22107-0910
Phone: 703 854-6000
Fax: –
Web: www.gannett.com

CEO: Michael Reed
CFO: Doug Horne
HR: Donna Marshall
FYE: December 31
Type: Public

Gannett Co. Inc. (formerly known as "New Media Investment Group Inc.") is a subscription-led and digitally focused media and marketing solutions company committed to empowering communities to thrive. The company aim to be the premiere source for clarity connections and solutions within its communities. The company's current portfolio of media assets includes USA TODAY local media organizations in around 45 states in the US and Newsquest a wholly owned subsidiary operating in the United Kingdom ("UK") with more than 120 local news media brands.

	Annual Growth	12/16	12/17	12/18	12/19	12/20
Sales ($ mil.)	28.3%	1,255.4	1,342.0	1,526.0	1,867.9	3,405.7
Net income ($ mil.)	–	31.6	(0.9)	18.2	(119.8)	(670.5)
Market value ($ mil.)	(32.3%)	2,204.1	2,317.4	1,584.0	881.1	464.0
Employees	15.8%	10,092	10,516	10,638	24,455	18,141

GARDEN FRESH RESTAURANT CORP.

15822 Bernardo Ctr. Dr. Ste. A
San Diego CA 92127
Phone: 800-874-1600
Fax: 858-675-1617
Web: www.souplantation.com

CEO: –
CFO: –
HR: –
FYE: September 30
Type: Private

Soup or salad is the question to ponder at these eateries. Garden Fresh Restaurant owns and operates more than 100 buffet-style restaurants under the names Souplantation and Sweet Tomatoes. Found mostly in California and more than a dozen other states the diners feature salad bars that include all the usual fixings as well as specialty and prepared salads. The restaurants also feature self-serve bars for pasta soups breads and fresh fruit. The company's Souplantation banner is used mostly in Southern California markets while Sweet Tomatoes is the brand outside that region. Founded in 1983 by CEO Michael Mack and partner Anthony Brooke the company is owned by private equity firm Sun Capital Partners.

GARDEN RIDGE CORPORATION

19411 Atrium Place Ste. 170
Houston TX 77084
Phone: 832-391-7201
Fax: 914-694-2286
Web: www.orthometrix.net

CEO: –
CFO: –
HR: –
FYE: January 31
Type: Private

Megastore retailer Garden Ridge offers decorating items for more than just the garden. The company owns and operates nearly 50 stores each covering some 3 acres and mostly located off major highways in about 20 states from Florida to Michigan. Its headquarters state of Texas is home to some 15 stores. Considered the "home decor depot" Garden Ridge stores sell about 500000 decorating items such as seasonal decor framed art baskets silk and dried flowers furniture home textiles and pottery as well as crafts and party supplies. Garden Ridge which began as a single store outside of San Antonio in 1979 is owned by an investment group led by the New York-based private equity firm Three Cities Research.

GARTNER INC

P.O. Box 10212, 56 Top Gallant Road
Stamford, CT 06902-7700
Phone: 203 316-1111
Fax: –
Web: www.gartner.com

NYS: IT
CEO: Eugene Hall
CFO: Craig Safian
HR: Robin Kranich
FYE: December 31
Type: Public

Gartner helps clients understand the information technology (IT) industry and make informed decisions about IT products. It provides over 15000 client organizations with competitive analysis reports industry overviews market trend data and product evaluation reports. The company offers its products and services in more than 100 countries across all major functions in every industry and enterprise size. Gartner also offers technology and management consulting services and produces conferences seminars and other events aimed at the technology sector. The US and Canada account for nearly two-thirds of the company's sales. About 80% of its revenue is garnered from its research services and products.

	Annual Growth	12/17	12/18	12/19	12/20	12/21
Sales ($ mil.)	9.3%	3,311.5	3,975.5	4,245.3	4,099.4	4,734.0
Net income ($ mil.)	294.4%	3.3	122.5	233.3	266.7	793.6
Market value ($ mil.)	28.4%	10,147.1	10,533.6	12,697.3	13,199.1	27,546.8
Employees	2.3%	15,131	15,173	16,724	15,600	16,600

GARY RABINE & SONS INC.

900 National Pkwy. Ste 260
Schaumburg IL 60173
Phone: 815-675-0555
Fax: +358-207-888-333
Web: www.rovio.com

CEO: –
CFO: –
HR: –
FYE: December 31
Type: Private

Gary Rabine & Sons known as The Rabine Group provides the Chicago region with what any US metropolitan area at its latitude needs: paving roofing and snow removal. It specializes in paving roads parking lots driveways and sidewalks. Rabine and its group of about a dozen companies also provide commercial and industrial roofing including solar panel and gardentop installation. When winter arrives it offers snow plowing blowing and rooftop shoveling. In addition the company owns a fuel distribution business hot mix asphalt plants and an operation enabling televised views inside pipelines for maintenance crews. Rabine got its start in 1981 and was founded by Gary Rabine.

GAS DEPOT OIL COMPANY

8700 N. Waukegan Rd. Ste. 200
Morton Grove IL 60053
Phone: 847-581-0303
Fax: 847-581-0309
Web: www.gasdepot.com

CEO: –
CFO: Nick Tanglis
HR: –
FYE: December 31
Type: Private

Gas Depot sits on a pot of oil but doesn't plan to hold on to it. The petroleum marketing company retails and wholesales gas and propane in the Midwest under the Gas Depot Valero CITGO Marathon Shell and Clark names. Gas Depot's nearly 20 retail locations are confined to the Chicago area while the company's wholesale business (about 160 customers) covers Illinois Indiana and Missouri. In addition to gas stations and convenience stores Gas Depot also offers store design real estate construction and financing services. The company began selling gasoline and propane to wholesale accounts in 2000. It bought into retail as many larger oil and gas firms dumped their retail holdings to focus on refining.

GAS TRANSMISSION NORTHWEST LLC

717 TEXAS ST STE 2400
HOUSTON, TX 770022834
Phone: 832-320-5000
Fax: –
Web: www.tcplus.com

CEO: Harold N Kvisle
CFO: Russell K Girling
HR: –
FYE: December 31
Type: Private

Gas Transmission Northwest (formerly PG&E Gas Transmission Northwest) takes the phrase "pipe down" literally. The company pumps nearly 3 billion cu. ft. of gas a day through more than 610 miles of pipeline running from western Canada to the Pacific Northwest California and Nevada. Gas Transmission Northwest a unit of TransCanada provides firm and interruptible transportation services to more than 100 customers including gas producers marketers and electric and gas utilities. Through Gas Transmission Northwest's pipeline customers can also store borrow or sell their excess capacity.

	Annual Growth	12/13	12/14	12/15	12/16	12/17
Sales ($ mil.)	2.8%	–	–	–	212.1	218.0
Net income ($ mil.)	(85.0%)	–	–	–	71.5	10.7
Market value ($ mil.)	–	–	–	–	–	–
Employees	–	–	–	–	–	6

GASCO ENERGY INC.
NBB: GSXN

7979 E. Tufts Avenue, Suite 1150
Denver, CO 80237
Phone: 303 483-0044
Fax: 303 483-0011
Web: www.gascoenergy.com

CEO: –
CFO: –
HR: –
FYE: December 31
Type: Public

Gasco Energy is not your local gas company or energy provider. The exploration and production independent develops and explores for natural gas and crude petroleum primarily in the Rocky Mountains. The company's exploration activities are focused on Utah's Uinta Basin and Wyoming's Green River Basin. At the end of 2008 Gasco Energy's proved reserves stood at 53.1 billion cu. ft. of natural gas equivalent. It had working interests in 330923 gross acres (214483 net acres) located in California Nevada Utah and Wyoming. That year it had stakes in 126 gross producing wells (77 net).

	Annual Growth	12/08	12/09	12/10	12/11	12/12
Sales ($ mil.)	(32.1%)	41.9	21.1	20.3	18.3	8.9
Net income ($ mil.)	–	14.5	(50.2)	10.1	(7.3)	(22.2)
Market value ($ mil.)	(34.9%)	66.2	90.0	59.4	38.2	11.9
Employees	(9.3%)	37	28	25	25	25

GATEWAY ENERGY CORPORATION
OTC: GNRG

500 Dallas St. Ste. 2615
Houston TX 77002
Phone: 713-336-0844
Fax: 713-336-0855
Web: www.gatewayenergy.com

CEO: Frederick Pevow
CFO: –
HR: Skip Paterson
FYE: December 31
Type: Public

The door swings both ways for Gateway Energy which serves as a go-between for natural gas producers and customers. It owns natural gas gathering transportation and distribution systems (totaling 280 miles of pipeline) in Texas and in the Gulf of Mexico. Gateway Offshore Pipeline Company owns pipelines and a related operating platform. Onshore Gateway Energy owns two active onshore pipeline system in Texas. The company gathers gas at the wellhead and transports it to distribution companies or its own processing facilities. It also operates a natural gas processing unit and and a gas marketing company.

GATEWAY HEALTH PLAN INC.

US Steel Tower 600 Grant St. Fl. 41
Pittsburgh PA 15219-2704
Phone: 412-255-4640
Fax: 973-633-0879
Web: www.castrolusa.com

CEO: Patricia J Darnley
CFO: –
HR: –
FYE: December 31
Type: Private

For many residents Gateway Health Plan is the keystone to health care coverage in Pennsylvania. The company provides managed health care services (as an HMO) to residents in 28 counties. Its Medicaid HMO serves some 220000 eligible recipients. In addition the company serves about 25000 members who qualify for both Medicare and Medicaid assistance through its Medicare Assured HMO special needs program (Medicare Assured?HMO SNP). Gateway's services include primary care dental prescriptions disease management and mental health services. Gateway an affiliate of Highmark was founded in 1992 as an alternative to the Department of Public Welfare's Medical Assistance Program in Pennsylvania.

GATX CORP
NYS: GATX

233 South Wacker Drive
Chicago, IL 60606-7147
Phone: 312 621-6200
Fax: –
Web: www.gatx.com

CEO: Brian Kenney
CFO: Thomas Ellman
HR: –
FYE: December 31
Type: Public

GATX Corporation founded in 1898 is the leading global railcar lessor. Its wholly owned fleet of approximately 149000 railcars is one of the largest railcar lease fleets in the world. It currently lease tank cars freight cars and locomotives in North America tank cars and freight cars in Europe and Russia and freight cars in India. In addition jointly with Rolls-Royce plc it owns one of the largest aircraft spare engine lease portfolios in the world. About 70% of company's total revenue comes from US operations. In mid-2020 GATX completed the sale of its ASC business to Rand Logistics Inc.

	Annual Growth	12/17	12/18	12/19	12/20	12/21
Sales ($ mil.)	(2.2%)	1,376.9	1,360.9	1,393.8	1,209.2	1,257.4
Net income ($ mil.)	(26.9%)	502.0	211.3	211.2	151.3	143.1
Market value ($ mil.)	13.8%	2,201.8	2,508.2	2,934.7	2,946.4	3,690.6
Employees	(4.8%)	2,267	2,225	2,165	1,904	1,863

GCT SEMICONDUCTOR INC.

2121 Ringwood Ave.
San Jose CA 95131
Phone: 408-434-6040
Fax: 408-434-6050
Web: www.gctsemi.com

CEO: John Schlaefer
CFO: Gene Kulzer
HR: –
FYE: June 30
Type: Private

While not a household name GCT Semiconductor enables activities most people are familiar with. The fabless semiconductor company's wireless communications chips include LTE-based radio-frequency (RF) transceivers for cell phones WiMAX networking chips and RF transceivers for WLAN equipment. Its single-chip LTE product for smartphones is used in mobile devices made by LG and sold by AT&T and Verizon among others. Unlike many chip developers GCT has its semiconductors fabricated with a CMOS silicon process. The company was co-founded in 1998 by CEO Kyeongho Lee. Chairman Paul Kim owns 31% GCT of GCT through Parakletos Ventures. The company filed for an IPO in 2011.

GEE GROUP INC
ASE: JOB

7751 Belfort Parkway, Suite 150
Jacksonville, FL 32256
Phone: 630 954-0400
Fax: 630 954-0447
Web: www.geegroup.com

CEO: Derek Dewan
CFO: Kim Thorpe
HR: –
FYE: September 30
Type: Public

The GEE Group Inc. is a provider of permanent and temporary professional industrial and physician staffing and placement services near several major US cities. The company specializes in the placement of professionals in the information technology engineering medical and accounting field for either direct hire or contract staffing. It also offers temporary staffing services for its commercial clients. The company is able to provide these services through its subsidiaries namely Access Data Consulting Corporation Agile Resources Inc. BMCH Inc. Paladin Consulting Inc. Scribe Solutions Inc. SNI Companies Inc. Triad Logistics Inc. and Triad Personnel Services Inc. The company operates in about 30 branches across eleven states.

	Annual Growth	09/17	09/18	09/19	09/20	09/21
Sales ($ mil.)	2.5%	135.0	165.3	151.7	129.8	148.9
Net income ($ mil.)	–	(2.4)	(7.6)	(17.8)	(14.3)	0.0
Market value ($ mil.)	(37.0%)	336.6	285.3	85.0	114.1	53.0
Employees	(13.1%)	475	389	344	258	271

GEEKNET INC
NMS: GKNT

11216 Waples Mill Rd., Suite 100
Fairfax, VA 22030
Phone: 877 433-5638
Fax: –
Web: www.geek.net

CEO: Kathryn K McCarthy
CFO: Julie A Pangelinan
HR: –
FYE: December 31
Type: Public

Geeknet is tuned in to what hipster techies crave. The company operates through its wholly-owned subsidiary ThinkGeek an online retailer of goodies for the global geek community. The company (formerly SourceForge) exited the business of producing websites for software developers to focus entirely on its ThinkGeek website which offers a broad range of apparel edibles electronics gadgets and other geek-themed merchandise for fans of movies and TV programs such as Star Wars Star Trek Dr. Who and Game of Thrones. Founded by former chairman Larry Augustin in 1993 Geeknet sold its Media business including the SourceForge Slashdot and Freecode websites in 2012 to focus on online retail.

	Annual Growth	12/09	12/10	12/11	12/12	12/13
Sales ($ mil.)	20.5%	65.6	94.6	119.5	118.9	138.3
Net income ($ mil.)	–	(14.0)	(4.4)	(1.2)	13.9	(0.2)
Market value ($ mil.)	97.5%	7.9	166.2	113.2	106.9	120.1
Employees	(8.0%)	127	122	143	76	91

GEHAN HOMES, LTD.

15725 DALLAS PKWY STE 300
ADDISON, TX 750013850
Phone: 972-383-4300
Fax: –
Web: www.gehanhomes.com

CEO: John Winniford
CFO: Scott Onderdonk
HR: Lisa Clements
FYE: December 31
Type: Private

They say everything is bigger in Texas and for Gehan Homes that hopefully applies to the number of homes sold. Gehan Homes builds single-family houses in about 60 communities in and around Austin Dallas Fort Worth Houston and San Antonio. Its houses range in price from the low $100000s to the low $300000s. Gehan Homes owns the land it builds on and provides mortgage brokerage through majority-owned Suburban Mortgage. Through cutting costs and slowing down production the homebuilder is working to stay afloat in a market that has caused several competitors to file for bankruptcy or shut down operations. John Gehan founded the family-owned company in the 1960s.

	Annual Growth	11/0-1	11/00	11/01	11/02*	12/07
Sales ($ mil.)	7.4%	–	–	–	150.5	214.6
Net income ($ mil.)	(21.8%)	–	–	–	13.8	4.0
Market value ($ mil.)	–	–	–	–	–	–
Employees	–	–	–	–	–	200

*Fiscal year change

GEICO CORPORATION

5260 Western Ave.
Chevy Chase MD 20076
Phone: 301-986-3000
Fax: 281-879-3626
Web: www.iongeo.com

CEO: Todd Combs
CFO: Mike Campbell
HR: –
FYE: December 31
Type: Subsidiary

GEICO (an acronym for Government Employees Insurance Company) has found that driving down costs brings drivers by the droves into its fold. GEICO has traditionally provided auto and other insurance to preferred low-risk demographic groups (such as government and military employees) but has also begun to sell to nonstandard (high-risk) drivers. In addition to auto coverage the company's offerings include motorcycle and RV insurance and emergency road service. GEICO eschews agents in favor of direct marketing through such vehicles as direct mail TV radio and the Internet. Its gecko mascot is one of the most recognized marketing icons. The company is a subsidiary of Warren Buffett's Berkshire Hathaway.

GEISINGER HEALTH

100 N ACADEMY AVE
DANVILLE, PA 178229800
Phone: 800-275-6401
Fax: –
Web: www.geisinger.org

CEO: Jaewon Ryu
CFO: –
HR: –
FYE: June 30
Type: Private

Geisinger Health System serves more than 1 million residents. Founded more than 100 years ago by Abigail Geisinger the system includes ten hospital campuses a health plan with more than half a million members a research institute and the Geisinger Commonwealth School of Medicine. With nearly 24000 employees and more than 1600 employed physicians Geisinger offers women's health sleep services surgery senior health dental medicine and addiction treatment among others. Its Geisinger Health Plan is an integrated health system that provides its member and patients with exceptional healthcare.

	Annual Growth	06/16	06/17	06/18	06/19	06/20
Sales ($ mil.)	4.0%	–	6,337.4	6,536.6	7,145.6	7,121.7
Net income ($ mil.)	–	–	553.0	359.4	174.1	(190.3)
Market value ($ mil.)	–	–	–	–	–	–
Employees	–	–	–	–	–	13,030

GELBER GROUP, LLC

350 N ORLEANS ST
CHICAGO, IL 606541975
Phone: 312-253-0005
Fax: –
Web: www.gelbergroup.com

CEO: –
CFO: Franklin A Gelber
HR: –
FYE: December 31
Type: Private

Gelber Group develops proprietary technology-based trading models for dealing in equities cash currencies commodities sovereign debt futures and related options markets. The company no longer has outside clients or investors; all of its trading activity is undertaken for its own account. Gelber Group which previously provided electronic trading services to individual professional traders was co-founded in 1982 by Brian Gelber (company chairman and president) and Frank Gelber (CFO). In addition to its Chicago Apparel Center headquarters the company also boasts offices in Connecticut New Jersey and New York as well as the UK.

	Annual Growth	12/01	12/02	12/03	12/04	12/07
Assets ($ mil.)	65.9%	–	–	44.8	106.8	338.9
Net income ($ mil.)	33.3%	–	–	35.8	70.2	112.9
Market value ($ mil.)	–	–	–	–	–	–
Employees	–	–	–	–	–	300

GEN-PROBE INCORPORATED
NASDAQ: GPRO

10210 Genetic Center Dr.
San Diego CA 92121-4362
Phone: 858-410-8000
Fax: 858-410-8625
Web: www.gen-probe.com

CEO: –
CFO: –
HR: –
FYE: December 31
Type: Private

Gen-Probe knows the answer is flowing through your veins. The company is a leading provider of molecular diagnostic tests and instruments to detect a host of infectious disease-causing viruses and bacteria including those behind HIV Chlamydia tuberculosis strep throat and influenza. Gen-Probe's diagnostic tests provide results within hours while traditional cultured tests can take days. In addition the firm has screening products to help identify compatible transplant matches and it also makes instruments and testing assays to screen donated blood for diseases. Customers include clinical and research laboratories and blood banks. Gen-Probe was acquired by medical equipment maker Hologic in 2012.

GENASYS INC
NAS: GNSS

16262 West Bernardo Drive
San Diego, CA 92127
Phone: 858 676-1112
Fax: –
Web: www.lradx.com

CEO: Richard Danforth
CFO: Dennis Klahn
HR: Norma Berry
FYE: September 30
Type: Public

High-tech sound may drive development for LRAD (formerly American Technology Corporation) but the firm is also banking on it to drive its bottom line. LRAD whose past sales largely came from its portable radios discontinued its portable consumer electronics division to make products that transmit sound over short and long distances. The company's Long Range Acoustic Devices generate the majority of revenues nowadays and they have been deployed by the US military and used by public safety agencies worldwide. To strengthen its identity as a global provider of long-range acoustic technology systems the company changed its name to LRAD in 2010.

	Annual Growth	09/17	09/18	09/19	09/20	09/21
Sales ($ mil.)	23.3%	20.3	26.3	37.0	43.0	47.0
Net income ($ mil.)	–	(0.9)	(3.7)	2.8	11.9	0.7
Market value ($ mil.)	24.9%	77.5	111.4	122.0	223.9	188.6
Employees	31.2%	50	75	83	105	148

GENCO DISTRIBUTION SYSTEM INC.

100 Papercraft Park
Pittsburgh PA 15238
Phone: 412-820-3700
Fax: 412-820-3689
Web: www.genco.com

CEO: Arthur F Smuck III
CFO: –
HR: –
FYE: December 31
Type: Private

Generations of businesses in need of third-party logistics have deferred to GENCO Distribution System. Founded in 1898 the company also doing business as GENCO ATC offers warehousing and distribution services reverse logistics (processing of returned goods) product liquidation supply chain analysis transportation management including parcels and damage research (analyzing the cause of customers' damaged products). Customers include manufacturers retailers and government agencies. The company manages 130 locations in North America providing a combined 38 million square feet of warehouse space. CEO Herb Shear owns the company which was started by his grandfather Hyman Shear.

GENCO SHIPPING & TRADING LTD
NYS: GNK

299 Park Avenue, 12th Floor
New York, NY 10171
Phone: 646 443-8550
Fax: –
Web: www.gencoshipping.com

CEO: John Wobensmith
CFO: Apostolos Zafolias
HR: –
FYE: December 31
Type: Public

Marine transportation company Genco Shipping & Trading transports dry cargo in a wet environment. The company maintains a fleet of about 50 oceangoing dry bulk carriers which it charters mainly on long-term contracts to shippers of bulk commodities and marine transportation companies. Its fleet has an overall capacity of almost 4 million deadweight tons (DWT). Genco Shipping's vessels transport cargo such as coal grain iron ore and steel products. More than half of its vessels are on time-charter contracts. Customers have included BHP Billiton Lauritzen Bulkers and NYK; clients Cargill and Pacific Basin Shipping make up about 10% of the company's revenues. Genco Shipping & Trading was founded in 2004.

	Annual Growth	12/16	12/17	12/18	12/19	12/20
Sales ($ mil.)	27.3%	135.6	209.7	367.5	389.5	355.6
Net income ($ mil.)	–	(217.8)	(58.7)	(32.9)	(56.0)	(225.6)
Market value ($ mil.)	–					
Employees	(9.5%)	1,432	1,385	1,346	1,255	960

GENCOR INDUSTRIES INC
NMS: GENC

5201 North Orange Blossom Trail
Orlando, FL 32810
Phone: 407 290-6000
Fax: –
Web: www.gencor.com

CEO: John E Elliott
CFO: Eric Mellen
HR: –
FYE: September 30
Type: Public

Gencor Industries is a US manufacturer of heavy machinery used in the production of highway construction materials and environmental control equipment. Subsidiary Bituma designs and manufactures hot-mix asphalt batch plants used in the production of asphalt paving materials. Subsidiary General Combustion engineers combustion systems namely large burners that can transform almost any fuel into energy or burn multiple fuels simultaneously and fluid heat transfer systems under the Hy-Way brand. Other companies include H&B (Hetherington & Berner) Thermotech Systems and Blaw-Knox. Gencor maintains two national warehouse locations (Iowa and Florida) comprising more than 50000 parts.

	Annual Growth	09/17	09/18	09/19	09/20	09/21
Sales ($ mil.)	1.4%	80.6	98.6	81.3	77.4	85.3
Net income ($ mil.)	(8.9%)	8.4	12.6	10.2	5.5	5.8
Market value ($ mil.)	(11.0%)	258.7	176.6	170.2	161.7	162.6
Employees	3.2%	335	372	334	316	380

GENELINK INC
NBB: GNLK

8250 Exchange Drive, Suite 120
Orlando, FL 32809
Phone: 407 680-1150
Fax: –
Web: www.genelink.info

CEO: Bernard Kasten
CFO: Michael Smith
HR: –
FYE: December 31
Type: Public

GeneLink has taken the science of molecular genetics and turned it into a way to sell face cream and vitamins. Although the promise of immortality is out of its reach the biosciences company aims to improve one's health beauty and wellness with customized nutritional supplements and anti-aging skin care products based upon proprietary DNA assessments obtained from a cheek swab. Other consumer genomic products in development include products to predict how an individual's skin will age or if an individual has a significant risk of developing cardiovascular disease Alzheimer's ADHD or loss of bone density.

	Annual Growth	12/08	12/09	12/10	12/11	12/12
Sales ($ mil.)	(23.9%)	6.4	8.6	7.8	4.7	2.1
Net income ($ mil.)	–	(2.6)	(2.7)	(2.4)	(3.8)	(3.1)
Market value ($ mil.)	(48.0%)	35.5	30.4	10.4	15.5	2.6
Employees	–					

GENELINK INC.
OTC: GNLK

317 Wekiva Springs Rd. Ste 200
Longwood FL 32779
Phone: 407-772-7160
Fax: 407-772-7193
Web: www.genelinkbio.com

CEO: Bernard Kasten
CFO: Michael Smith
HR: –
FYE: December 31
Type: Public

GeneLink has taken the science of molecular genetics and turned it into a way to sell face cream and vitamins. Although the promise of immortality is out of its reach the biosciences company aims to improve one's health beauty and wellness with customized nutritional supplements and anti-aging skin care products based upon proprietary DNA assessments obtained from a cheek swab. Other consumer genomic products in development include products to predict how an individual's skin will age or if an individual has a significant risk of developing cardiovascular disease Alzheimer's ADHD or loss of bone density.

GENERAC HOLDINGS INC
NYS: GNRC

S45 W29290 Hwy 59
Waukesha, WI 53189
Phone: 262 544-4811
Fax: –
Web: www.generac.com

CEO: Aaron Jagdfeld
CFO: York Ragen
HR: –
FYE: December 31
Type: Public

Generac Holdings is a leading global designer and manufacturer of a wide range of energy technology solutions. The company provides power generation equipment energy storage systems grid service solutions and other power products serving the residential light commercial and industrial markets. Generac's residential generator products provide emergency standby power for homes. The company's commercial and industrial backup generators provide standby power for everything from restaurants and gas stations to hospitals and manufacturing facilities. Other products include light towers mobile generators and heaters used in construction mining energy and other industries. Generac sells its products through retailers and wholesale distributors. The US accounts for about 85% of the company's sales.

	Annual Growth	12/17	12/18	12/19	12/20	12/21
Sales ($ mil.)	22.3%	1,672.4	2,023.5	2,204.3	2,485.2	3,737.2
Net income ($ mil.)	36.3%	159.4	238.3	252.0	350.6	550.5
Market value ($ mil.)	63.3%	3,155.4	3,166.8	6,409.5	14,490.3	22,424.0
Employees	20.3%	4,556	5,664	5,689	6,797	9,540

GENERAL BEARING CORPORATION
PINK SHEETS: GNRL

44 High St.
West Nyack NY 10994 2702
Phone: 845-358-6000
Fax: 845-358-6277
Web: www.generalbearing.com

CEO: David L Gussack
CFO: Rocky Cambrea
HR: Fran Laino
FYE: December 31
Type: Public

General Bearing has been on a roll for more than half a century. Founded in 1958 the company sources assembles and distributes roller bearings primarily under the Hyatt brand name. Products include ball bearings tapered roller bearings precision roller bearings spherical roller bearings and other related components. The lineup is sold primarily to OEMs of trains trucks trailers office equipment and appliances as well as to industrial aftermarket distributors. Based in the US General Bearing operates an array of plants and an engineering and technology center through four facilities in China. In mid-2012 General Bearing was acquired by rival bearings manufacturer SKF for about $125 million.

GENERAL CABLE CORP (DE)
NYS: BGC

4 Tesseneer Drive
Highland Heights, KY 41076-9753
Phone: 859 572-8000
Fax: 859 572-8458
Web: www.generalcable.com

CEO: Michael T McDonnell
CFO: Matti M Masanovich
HR: –
FYE: December 31
Type: Public

General Cable designs manufactures and distributes copper aluminum and fiber optic wire and cable products that are used in electrical transmission and distribution power generation and voice and data communications. Major brands include BICC (energy cables) Carol (temporary power cables) and NextGen (data communication cables). General Cable's products are sold to commercial industrial electric utility telecom military and government retail and OEM distributor customers worldwide. The company also makes copper and aluminum rod for other wire and cable manufacturers and it integrates and installs high voltage systems on land and under water.

	Annual Growth	12/12	12/13	12/14	12/15	12/16
Sales ($ mil.)	(10.5%)	6,014.3	6,421.2	5,979.8	4,225.1	3,858.4
Net income ($ mil.)	–	4.0	(17.8)	(627.6)	(121.9)	(93.8)
Market value ($ mil.)	(11.0%)	1,502.0	1,452.6	735.9	663.3	940.9
Employees	(8.1%)	14,000	15,000	13,000	12,000	10,000

GENERAL COMMUNICATION INC
NMS: GNCM A

2550 Denali Street, Suite 1000
Anchorage, AK 99503
Phone: 907 868-5600
Fax: –
Web: www.gci.com

CEO: Gregory B Maffei
CFO: –
HR: –
FYE: December 31
Type: Public

A land of long distances needs good long distance service. Through its operating subsidiaries General Communication Inc. (GCI) provides facilities-based phone services to more than 144000 local callers and 97000 long-distance customers in the five largest population areas of Alaska: Anchorage Fairbanks Juneau the Matanuska-Susitna Valley and the Kenai Peninsula. The competitive local-exchange carrier is also one of Alaska's leading cable TV providers with more than 147000 basic cable subscribers; it provides wireless services to 138000-plus customers through a partnership with AT&T Mobility. More than 116000 subscribers receive cable modem service.

	Annual Growth	12/12	12/13	12/14	12/15	12/16
Sales ($ mil.)	7.1%	710.2	811.6	910.2	978.5	933.8
Net income ($ mil.)	–	9.7	9.4	7.6	(26.0)	(3.7)
Market value ($ mil.)	19.3%	343.3	399.1	492.2	708.0	696.2
Employees	7.4%	1,734	1,924	2,255	2,370	2,310

GENERAL DYNAMICS CORP
NYS: GD

11011 Sunset Hills Road
Reston, VA 20190
Phone: 703 876-3000
Fax: –
Web: www.gd.com

CEO: Phebe Novakovic
CFO: Jason Aiken
HR: –
FYE: December 31
Type: Public

General Dynamics is a global aerospace and defense company that specializes in high-end design engineering and manufacturing of products and services in business aviation ship construction and repair land combat vehicles weapons systems and munitions. The company operates through four operating segments: Technologies Marine Systems Aerospace and Combat Systems. Working with a network of more than 90 global partners General Dynamics offers a comprehensive support for more than 2900 Gulfstream aircraft in service worldwide. The company operates in more than 70 countries worldwide. Approximately 85% of the company's total sales comes from North America.

	Annual Growth	12/17	12/18	12/19	12/20	12/21
Sales ($ mil.)	5.6%	30,973.0	36,193.0	39,350.0	37,925.0	38,469.0
Net income ($ mil.)	2.8%	2,912.0	3,345.0	3,484.0	3,167.0	3,257.0
Market value ($ mil.)	0.6%	56,482.0	43,644.8	48,958.5	41,315.5	57,875.6
Employees	1.1%	98,600	105,600	102,900	100,700	103,100

GENERAL ELECTRIC CAPITAL CORPORATION

901 Main Ave.
Norwalk CT 06851-1168
Phone: 203-840-6300
Fax: +81-3-5606-1502
Web: www.fujikura.co.jp

CEO: –
CFO: –
HR: –
FYE: December 31
Type: Subsidiary

General Electric Capital (GE Capital) encompasses the financing operations of sprawling conglomerate General Electric. The group's five segments provide commercial loans and leases consumer loans and credit cards and real estate financing services around the world. GE Capital's largest segments are commercial lending and leasing and consumer lending which together account for about 80% of revenues. Its GE Commercial Aviation Services specialist segment leases commercial aircraft while its energy financial services segment provides project funding for customers in the energy and water sectors. GE Capital is active in more than 50 countries but does most of its business in the US and Europe.

GENERAL ELECTRIC CO NYS: GE

5 Necco Street
Boston, MA 02210
Phone: 617 443-3000
Fax: –
Web: www.ge.com

CEO: Russell Stokes
CFO: Carolina Dybeck Happe
HR: –
FYE: December 31
Type: Public

Founded in 1889 by Thomas A. Edison General Electric (GE) is an American multinational company. The company produces aircraft engines locomotives and other transportation equipment generators and turbines lighting and oil and gas exploration and production equipment. GE also has a healthcare products business which it plans to separate into a standalone company and a financial services division the size of which it is reducing (especially its energy and industrial finance business). About 45% of GE's revenue comes from its US operations.

	Annual Growth	12/17	12/18	12/19	12/20	12/21
Sales ($ mil.)	(11.7%)	122,092.0	121,615.0	95,214.0	79,619.0	74,196.0
Net income ($ mil.)	–	(5,786.0)	(22,355.0)	(4,979.0)	5,704.0	(6,520.0)
Market value ($ mil.)	52.5%	19,178.0	8,319.6	12,265.1	11,869.5	103,825.1
Employees	(14.4%)	313,000	283,000	205,000	174,000	168,000

GENERAL FINANCE CORP NMS: GFN

39 East Union Street
Pasadena, CA 91103
Phone: 626 584-9722
Fax: –
Web: www.generalfinance.com

CEO: Jody E Miller
CFO: Charles E Barrantes
HR: –
FYE: June 30
Type: Public

General Finance Corporation wants to help you get your hands on some equipment. The investment holding company is building up a portfolio of specialty financing and equipment leasing companies in North America Europe and the Asia-Pacific. It made its first acquisition of RWA Holdings and its subsidiaries (collectively known as Royal Wolf) in 2007. Royal Wolf leases and sells portable storage containers portable buildings and freight containers to customers in the defense mining moving and storage and road and rail markets in Australia. General Finance acquired Pac-Van a provider of modular buildings and mobile offices in 2008. CEO Ronald Valenta owns 20% of the company.

	Annual Growth	06/16	06/17	06/18	06/19	06/20
Sales ($ mil.)	5.7%	285.9	276.9	347.3	378.2	356.5
Net income ($ mil.)	–	(5.4)	(3.0)	(8.3)	(7.5)	8.0
Market value ($ mil.)	12.1%	127.4	154.3	406.1	250.8	201.1
Employees	4.8%	773	771	875	969	934

GENERAL HEALTH SYSTEM

8585 PICARDY AVE
BATON ROUGE, LA 708093748
Phone: 225-387-7000
Fax: –
Web: www.brgeneral.org

CEO: Mark F Slyter
CFO: Kendall Johnson
HR: –
FYE: September 30
Type: Private

Injured? We're sending you to the General. General Health System provides a comprehensive range of health services to residents of southern Louisiana. The system's flagship facility is the not-for-profit community-owned Baton Rouge General Medical Center aka "the General". The medical center founded in 1927 houses some 550 beds split between two campuses in Louisiana's capital. It provides general medical and surgical care emergency services and specialty care in a number of areas including burn cancer and heart disease. General Health System is affiliated with Advanced Medical Concepts (a supplier of medical equipment) and First Care Physicians (a network of primary care physicians).

	Annual Growth	03/03	03/04*	09/05	09/09	09/15
Sales ($ mil.)	(3.2%)	–	125.0	42.9	56.0	86.9
Net income ($ mil.)	9.6%	–	1.4	0.6	(29.9)	3.9
Market value ($ mil.)	–	–	–	–	–	–
Employees	–	–	–	–	–	3,400

*Fiscal year change

GENERAL MAGNAPLATE CORPORATION

1331 Rte. 1 and 9 North
Linden NJ 07036
Phone: 908-862-6200
Fax: 908-862-6110
Web: www.magnaplate.com

CEO: Candida C Aversenti
CFO: –
HR: –
FYE: June 30
Type: Private

General Magnaplate is one slick out-of-this-world company. Magnaplate makes coatings that increase the performance of metals. Every NASA vehicle sent into space has had parts coated by Magnaplate. The company's products include HI-T-LUBE (a Guinness record holder as the most slippery solid in the world) TUFRAM coating (used to machine aluminum) and other basic metal coatings used by the food processing packaging electronics aerospace and other industries. These coatings significantly increase the durability and lubricity of both ferrous and nonferrous metals. General Magnaplate is controlled by the family of its founder the late Charles Covino including his daughter CEO Candida Aversenti.

GENERAL MARITIME CORPORATION NYSE: GMR

299 Park Ave.
New York NY 10171
Phone: 212-763-5600
Fax: 212-763-5602
Web: www.generalmaritimecorp.com

CEO: –
CFO: –
HR: –
FYE: December 31
Type: Public

Black gold on the deep blue brings in the green for General Maritime. A leading operator of midsized tankers the company transports crude oil and refined petroleum products mainly in the Atlantic Basin but also in the Black Sea. Its fleet of nearly 30 double-hull tankers includes Aframax and Suezmax vessels and Panamax Handymax and Very Large Crude Carriers (VLCCs) with an overall capacity of 5 million deadweight tons (DWT). General Maritime deploys its vessels on the spot market (short term/single voyage) and under long-term charter. Customers have included major oil companies Chevron ConocoPhillips and Exxon Mobil. In 2012 the company completed financial restructuring and emerged from Chapter 11.

GENERAL MICROWAVE CORPORATION

425 Smith St.
Farmingdale NY 11735
Phone: 631-630-2000
Fax: 631-630-2066
Web: www.herley.com/index.cfm?act=companies_farming

CEO: Deanna Lund
CFO: –
HR: –
FYE: July 31
Type: Subsidiary

General Microwave Corporation operating as Herley New York makes microwave components and electronic systems. The company's products include attenuators phase shifters couplers power and radiation meters modulators switch filters and oscillators that are used in military and commercial equipment. The company has a novel place in the wireless industry; it provides telecom companies with radiation hazard meters used to indicate dangerously high levels of microwave radio frequencies. A subsidiary of Herley Industries General Microwave Corp. was founded in 1960 and acquired by Herley in 1999.

GENESEE & WYOMING INC.
NYS: GWR

20 West Avenue
Darien, CT 06820
Phone: 203 202-8900
Fax: -
Web: www.gwrr.com

CEO: John C Hellmann
CFO: Timothy J Gallagher
HR: -
FYE: December 31
Type: Public

Genesee & Wyoming (GWI) owns stakes in more than 120 freight railroads. Its network includes 115 short-line and regional freight railroads that operate over a total of more than 22000 miles of track. Among this total about 15900 miles of track are owned and leased by the company and another 3300 miles additional miles are under contractual track access arrangements to more than 40 ports in North America Europe and Australia. Freight transported by GWI railroads includes coal forest products agricultural products automobiles and auto parts chemicals and plastics metallic ores petroleum products and pulp and paper.

	Annual Growth	12/13	12/14	12/15	12/16	12/17
Sales ($ mil.)	8.9%	1,569.0	1,639.0	2,000.4	2,001.5	2,208.0
Net income ($ mil.)	19.3%	271.3	260.8	225.0	141.1	549.1
Market value ($ mil.)	(4.8%)	6,017.3	5,633.2	3,363.5	4,348.3	4,932.2
Employees	13.6%	4,800	5,200	7,500	7,300	8,000

GENESEE VALLEY GROUP HEALTH ASSOCIATION

1425 PORTLAND AVE BLDG 1
ROCHESTER, NY 146213011
Phone: 585-338-1400
Fax: -

CEO: -
CFO: -
HR: -
FYE: December 31
Type: Private

Primary care is the primary concern of Lifetime Health Medical Group. The organization a subsidiary of The Lifetime Healthcare Companies offers up family practitioners as well as internists pediatricians OB/GYNs and specialists to about 100000 patients in Upstate New York. Lifetime Medical operates about 10 family health centers in Buffalo and Rochester that offer diagnostic therapeutic and pharmacy services; the group also includes several affiliated physicians offices a family medicine center for deaf patients and a primary care practice staffed exclusively by female physicians. Lifetime Health Medical Group has been active in the Buffalo and Rochester communities since the 1970s.

	Annual Growth	12/03	12/04*	06/06*	12/09	12/12
Sales ($ mil.)	0.2%	-	106.6	106.6	120.0	107.9
Net income ($ mil.)	(0.4%)	-	3.9	3.9	(2.1)	3.8
Market value ($ mil.)	-	-	-	-	-	-
Employees	-	-	-	-	-	576

*Fiscal year change

GENESIS CORP.

950 3RD AVE FL 26
NEW YORK, NY 100222705
Phone: 212-688-5522
Fax: -

CEO: Harley Lippman
CFO: Glenn Klein
HR: -
FYE: December 31
Type: Private

Genesis Corp.'s raison d'etre is business and technology consulting. Focused on helping organizations streamline processes manage employees and minimize costs the company (doing business as Genesis10) provides services in areas such as project management application development enterprise systems integration staffing and management support. The company's managed service program assists businesses in managing its workforce as well as outsourced work. Genesis10 founded in 1999 also helps organizations with their hiring compliance and change management issues.

	Annual Growth	12/08	12/09	12/10	12/13	12/20
Sales ($ mil.)	(0.8%)	-	-	173.6	175.1	159.7
Net income ($ mil.)	(8.1%)	-	-	10.6	2.0	4.5
Market value ($ mil.)	-	-	-	-	-	-
Employees	-	-	-	-	-	2,105

GENESIS ENERGY L.P.
NYS: GEL

919 Milam, Suite 2100
Houston, TX 77002
Phone: 713 860-2500
Fax: -
Web: www.genesisenergy.com

CEO: Grant Sims
CFO: Robert Deere
HR: -
FYE: December 31
Type: Public

Genesis Energy is a top lease-holder of oil and gas infrastructure in the US Gulf Coast serving some of the biggest oil and gas producers and refiners in the world. The company provides an integrated suite of services to refineries oil producers and industrial and commercial enterprises. Business activities are primarily focused on providing services around and within refinery complexes. The company is also one of the leading producers of natural soda ash (Na_2CO_3). Additionally Genesis is one of the largest producers of sodium hydrosulfide (NaHS) a byproduct of its sulfur-removal services from sour gas streams. Shell is one of the company's biggest customers.

	Annual Growth	12/16	12/17	12/18	12/19	12/20
Sales ($ mil.)	1.6%	1,712.5	2,028.4	2,912.8	2,480.8	1,824.7
Net income ($ mil.)	-	113.2	82.6	(6.1)	96.0	(416.7)
Market value ($ mil.)	(35.6%)	4,415.3	2,739.6	2,264.0	2,510.4	761.2
Employees	12.4%	1,200	2,142	2,100	2,200	1,914

GENESIS HEALTH INC.

3599 UNIVERSITY BLVD S # 1
JACKSONVILLE, FL 322164252
Phone: 904-858-7600
Fax: -
Web: www.brookshealth.org

CEO: Douglas M Baer
CFO: -
HR: Briana Nabors
FYE: December 31
Type: Private

Genesis Health helps people get back on their feet — literally. The company (doing business as Brooks Rehabilitation) operates a 160-bed facility dedicated to helping patients recover from injury and illness. Rehab services include physical occupational speech aquatic and recreational therapy. The hospital also helps patients coping with chronic pain cognitive disorders and other long-term disabilities. Brooks Rehabilitation provides outpatient care through a network of more than two dozen clinics a nursing home and a home health care agency in northern Florida and southeastern Georgia.

	Annual Growth	12/08	12/09	12/10	12/11	12/13
Sales ($ mil.)	9.3%	-	98.4	120.0	123.5	140.3
Net income ($ mil.)	(9.3%)	-	-	27.7	(19.6)	20.6
Market value ($ mil.)	-	-	-	-	-	-
Employees	-	-	-	-	-	1,400

GENESIS HEALTH SYSTEM

1227 E RUSHOLME ST
DAVENPORT, IA 528032459
Phone: 563-421-1000
Fax: -
Web: www.genesishealth.com

CEO: Doug Cropper
CFO: Mark Rogers
HR: -
FYE: June 30
Type: Private

Genesis Health System operates three acute care hospitals in Iowa and Illinois that have more than 660 beds total and employ some 700 doctors. Genesis Medical Center in Davenport Iowa with more than 500 beds is the system's flagship facility; the hospital offers a range of general surgical and specialist health services. The system's Illini Campus in Silvis Illinois features an assisted-living center. The Genesis Medical Center Dewitt Campus serves that Iowa town and the surrounding area with its 13-bed hospital nursing home and related care facilities. Genesis Health System also operates physician practices outpatient centers and a home health agency.

	Annual Growth	06/17	06/18	06/19	06/20	06/21
Sales ($ mil.)	11.4%	-	511.6	646.6	648.8	706.7
Net income ($ mil.)	52.3%	-	21.0	13.8	4.9	74.0
Market value ($ mil.)	-	-	-	-	-	-
Employees	-	-	-	-	-	5,000

GENERAL MILLS INC
NYS: GIS

Number One General Mills Boulevard
Minneapolis, MN 55426
Phone: 763 764-7600
Fax: 763 764-8330
Web: www.generalmills.com

CEO: Jeffrey Harmening
CFO: Kofi Bruce
HR: –
FYE: May 30
Type: Public

General Mills is one of the leading global manufacturer and marketer of branded consumer foods sold through retail stores. Some of its #1 and #2 market-leading brands include Betty Crocker dessert mixes Gold Medal flour Pillsbury cookie dough and Yoplait yogurt. It competes with Kellogg to be the top cereal maker with a brand arsenal that includes Kix Chex Cheerios Lucky Charms and Wheaties. While most of the company's sales come from the US General Mills is working to extend the reach and position of its brands globally and has facilities across five major continents. General Mills also owns the Haagen-Dazs ice cream brand in the US.

	Annual Growth	05/17	05/18	05/19	05/20	05/21
Sales ($ mil.)	3.8%	15,619.8	15,740.4	16,865.2	17,626.6	18,127.0
Net income ($ mil.)	9.0%	1,657.5	2,131.0	1,752.7	2,181.2	2,339.8
Market value ($ mil.)	2.3%	34,833.4	25,912.3	32,092.6	38,309.4	38,200.0
Employees	(2.0%)	38,000	40,000	40,000	35,000	35,000

GENERAL MOLY INC.
NYSE AMEX: GMO

1726 Cole Blvd. Ste 115
Lakewood CO 80401
Phone: 303-928-8599
Fax: 303-928-8598
Web: www.generalmoly.com

CEO: –
CFO: –
HR: –
FYE: December 31
Type: Public

General Moly reporting for molybdenum duty. The mineral development exploration and mining company (formerly Idaho General Mines) finds and exploits molybdenum oxide (moly) a mineral used primarily as an alloy in steel production. Steel makers create moly-enhanced pipes valued by the construction aircraft manufacturing and desalinization industries for their strength and resistance to heat and corrosion. Refiners use the pipes and employ the mineral to remove sulfur from diesel fuel and crude oil. General Moly owns two properties in Nevada one in an 80/20 joint venture with Korean steel company POSCO and one outright. The company's move from development to production was pending in early 2011.

GENERAL MOTORS CO
NYS: GM

300 Renaissance Center
Detroit, MI 48265-3000
Phone: 313 667-1500
Fax: –
Web: www.gm.com

CEO: Mary Barra
CFO: Paul Jacobson
HR: –
FYE: December 31
Type: Public

General Motors (GM) one of the world's largest auto manufacturers makes and sells cars and trucks worldwide under well-known brands such as Buick Cadillac Chevrolet and GMC. Business divisions GM North America and GM International handle the automotive end of the business while General Motors Financial Co. provides financing services. Looking toward the future of transportation the company is investing in developing electric vehicles and autonomous vehicles. GM's biggest single market is the US which accounts for about 85% of sales.

	Annual Growth	12/17	12/18	12/19	12/20	12/21
Sales ($ mil.)	(3.4%)	145,588.0	147,049.0	137,237.0	122,485.0	127,004.0
Net income ($ mil.)	–	(3,864.0)	8,014.0	6,732.0	6,427.0	10,019.0
Market value ($ mil.)	9.4%	59,559.3	48,603.6	53,180.6	60,503.8	85,190.6
Employees	(3.4%)	180,000	173,000	164,000	155,000	157,000

GENERAL MOTORS FINANCIAL COMPANY INC.

801 Cherry St. Ste. 3500
Fort Worth TX 76102
Phone: 817-302-7000
Fax: 817-302-7897
Web: www.gmfinancial.com

CEO: Daniel Berce
CFO: Susan Sheffield
HR: –
FYE: June 30
Type: Subsidiary

General Motors Financial Company brings motors to the general public. Formerly AmeriCredit and now operating as GM Financial the company is the in-house auto financing arm of General Motors. It works with GM dealers around the US and in Canada to offer new- and used-vehicle financing services. Founded in 1992 the former AmeriCredit traditionally provided credit to customers with less-than-ideal credit histories. Today GM Financial owns a portfolio of some $12 billion in finance receivables and leased vehicles. The company operates about 20 credit and customer service centers ithroughout the US. General Motors acquired AmeriCredit for some $3.5 billion in 2010 in an effort to boost auto sales.

GENEREX BIOTECHNOLOGY CORP (DE)
NBB: GNBT

10102 USA Today Way
Miramar, FL 33025
Phone: 416 364-2551
Fax: –
Web: www.generex.com

CEO: Joseph Moscato
CFO: Mark Corrao
HR: –
FYE: July 31
Type: Public

Generex Biotechnology knows that needles can be a real pain for diabetics so it has developed Oral-lyn an oral insulin spray that allows the drug to be absorbed through the inside lining of the cheeks. Though the product has been approved for use in some developing countries Oral-lyn is still undergoing clinical trials in the US. Generex also sells a line of over-the-counter energy and diet supplement glucose sprays available at retail stores and pharmacies in North America. The sprays are administered via Generex's handheld aerosol applicator RapidMist. Through its Antigen Express subsidiary the company is developing vaccines for disease such as cancer flu and HIV.

	Annual Growth	07/16	07/17	07/18	07/19	07/20
Sales ($ mil.)	94.5%	–	–	0.7	6.2	2.7
Net income ($ mil.)	–	(3.2)	(70.0)	36.3	(9.3)	(33.3)
Market value ($ mil.)	189.1%	0.6	415.4	168.6	230.3	41.9
Employees	–	–	–	4	4	–

GENESCO INC.
NYS: GCO

Genesco Park, 1415 Murfreesboro Pike
Nashville, TN 37217-2895
Phone: 615 367-7000
Fax: –
Web: www.genesco.com

CEO: Mimi Vaughn
CFO: Thomas George
HR: –
FYE: January 30
Type: Public

Genesco sells footwear apparel and accessories through some 1460 shoe and accessory stores in the US Canada Puerto Rico the UK and the Republic of Ireland. Genesco's shoe operations include Journeys upscale Johnston & Murphy Schuh as well as sales of licensed brands (Levi's G.H. Bass and Dockers footwear). It also sells wholesale footwear through various brands. Through the use of youth-oriented decor and multi-channel media Journeys retail footwear stores target customers in the 13 to 22 year age group. Founded in 1934 as a shoe retailer Genesco expanded overseas with the purchase of Scotland's Schuh.

	Annual Growth	01/17*	02/18	02/19	02/20*	01/21
Sales ($ mil.)	(11.2%)	2,868.3	2,907.0	2,188.6	2,197.1	1,786.5
Net income ($ mil.)	–	97.4	(111.8)	(51.9)	61.4	(56.4)
Market value ($ mil.)	(10.1%)	886.5	495.6	674.7	587.8	580.2
Employees	(8.6%)	27,200	30,500	21,000	22,050	19,000

*Fiscal year change

GENESIS HEALTHCARE INC NBB: GENN

101 East State Street
Kennett Square, PA 19348
Phone: 610 444-6350
Fax: –
Web: www.genesishcc.com
CEO: Harry Wilson
CFO: Thomas Divittorio
HR: –
FYE: December 31
Type: Public

Genesis Healthcare helps seniors begin to thrive again after suffering a medical setback. Through over 340 skilled nursing facilities and assisted/living centers. Its facilities is located in about25 states across the US house about 40200 beds. Genesis also provides third-party rehabilitation services including respiratory therapy speech-language pathology physical therapy and occupational therapy. These units serve approximately 1 400 healthcare locations in about 40 states the District of Columbia and China.

	Annual Growth	12/16	12/17	12/18	12/19	12/20
Sales ($ mil.)	(9.1%)	5,732.4	5,373.7	4,976.7	4,565.8	3,906.2
Net income ($ mil.)	–	(64.0)	(579.0)	(235.2)	14.6	(59.0)
Market value ($ mil.)	(41.9%)	708.9	127.2	196.8	273.5	80.8
Employees	(14.4%)	82,000	68,700	61,300	55,000	44,000

GENESIS HEALTHCARE LLC

101 E. State St.
Kennett Square PA 19348
Phone: 610-444-6350
Fax: 610-925-4000
Web: www.genesishcc.com
CEO: George V Hager Jr
CFO: James V McKeon
HR: –
FYE: September 30
Type: Private

Genesis HealthCare is in the business of caring for the US senior population and those in need of assistance with daily living tasks. The company is one of the largest skilled nursing care providers in the country offering both short-term transitional care and long-term hospice care through more than 400 skilled nursing centers and assisted living residences in 29 states. It also provides rehabilitation therapy to more than 1500 health care providers across the US. Some of its rehabilitation specialties include cardiac management dialysis care orthopedic care and ventilator care. In Maryland Genesis SelectCare is a licensed private duty home care agency that assists people in their own homes.

GENETHERA INC. OTC: GTHA

3930 Youngfield St.
Wheat Ridge CO 80033-3865
Phone: 303-463-6371
Fax: 303-463-6377
Web: www.genethera.net
CEO: Antonio Milici
CFO: Tannya Irizarry
HR: –
FYE: December 31
Type: Public

GeneThera does its part to protect the world's fauna. GeneThera formerly called Hand Brand Distribution develops genetic diagnostic assays for the agriculture and veterinary industries. The biotech company has developed assays that detect Chronic Wasting Disease in elk and deer and Mad Cow Disease in cattle. The company is working on cancer detection tests for animals as well as similar tests for humans through its partnership with Xpention a biotechnology company focused on oncology diagnostics. GeneThera is also developing vaccines for animal diseases such as E. coli.

GENICA CORPORATION

43195 BUSINESS PARK DR
TEMECULA, CA 925903629
Phone: 855-433-5747
Fax: –
Web: www.genica.com
CEO: –
CFO: –
HR: –
FYE: December 31
Type: Private

Think of Genica as computerdom's bargain basement. The company sells computer components peripherals and accessories — mainly overstocks and closeouts — over the Internet. It operates through two business units: Computer Geeks (which targets consumers through its geeks.com website) and Evertek Computer (which markets to small businesses and FORTUNE 500 firms via evertek.com). The company which offers more than 3000 brand-name products was formed by the merger of online seller Computer Geeks with computer importer/distributor Evertek Computer and its Hong Kong-based sister firm Evertek Trading. Chairman and CEO Frank Segler owns a majority stake in Genica.

	Annual Growth	12/05	12/06	12/07	12/08	12/09
Sales ($ mil.)	(49.4%)	–	–	672.7	164.7	172.5
Net income ($ mil.)	53932.2%	–	–	0.0	3.6	5.5
Market value ($ mil.)	–	–	–	–	–	–
Employees	–	–	–	–	–	334

GENIE ENERGY LTD NYS: GNE

520 Broad Street
Newark, NJ 07102
Phone: 973 438-3500
Fax: –
Web: www.genie.com
CEO: Michael Stein
CFO: Avraham Goldin
HR: –
FYE: December 31
Type: Public

Genie Energy is a global provider of residential and commercial energy services. The company operates through three subsidiaries ? Genie Retail Energy (GRE) Genie Solar Energy and Genie Retail Energy International (GREI). GRE resells electricity and natural gas bought from the wholesale commodities markets reselling those commodities to residential and small to large commercial customers throughout the US. Genie Solar Energy offers a variety of products and configurations to meet efficiency and ROI goals while GREI holds interests in a portfolio of innovative growing companies that supply energy to retail customers in deregulated markets outside of the US. Headquartered in Newark New Jersey Genie Energy is controlled by CEO Michael Stein.

	Annual Growth	12/16	12/17	12/18	12/19	12/20
Sales ($ mil.)	15.6%	212.1	264.2	280.3	315.3	379.3
Net income ($ mil.)	–	(24.5)	(7.0)	22.8	4.2	13.2
Market value ($ mil.)	5.8%	150.8	114.3	158.1	202.7	189.0
Employees	(8.7%)	180	178	183	163	125

GENOCEA BIOSCIENCES INC NMS: GNCA

100 Acorn Park Drive
Cambridge, MA 02140
Phone: 617 876-8191
Fax: –
Web: www.genocea.com
CEO: William Clark
CFO: Diantha Duvall
HR: –
FYE: December 31
Type: Public

Genocea Biosciences seeks a panacea for human infection. It does this using its proprietary ATLAS technology that acts through T cells to target infectious diseases. The company's lead candidate is GEN-009 an adjuvanted peptide vaccine which will begin phase 1 clinical trials targeting a range of tumor types. Genocea believes its T-cell methodology allows it to develop vaccines more quickly than the traditional method which uses B cells or antibodies. It also thinks certain infections respond better to T cell treatments which operate at the cellular level. Genocea is seeking to partner with others to develop general cancer vaccines as well as a vaccine that will target cancers caused by the Epstein-Barr Virus.

	Annual Growth	12/12	12/13	12/14	12/15	12/16
Sales ($ mil.)	(41.3%)	2.0	0.7	0.3	0.7	0.2
Net income ($ mil.)	–	(13.4)	(20.8)	(35.3)	(42.5)	(49.6)
Market value ($ mil.)	(23.3%)	–	–	199.1	149.9	117.2
Employees	25.9%	39	44	57	87	98

GENOMIC HEALTH INC
NMS: GHDX

301 Penobscot Drive
Redwood City, CA 94063
Phone: 650 556-9300
Fax: –
Web: www.genomichealth.com

CEO: –
CFO: Jeffrey T Elliott
HR: –
FYE: December 31
Type: Public

Genomic Health believes the genome is key to good health and individualized treatments. The company conducts genomic research to develop molecular diagnostics and assays that can predict the likelihood of disease recurrence as well as response to therapy and treatments. Genomic Health's Oncotype DX breast cancer test predicts the likelihood of chemotherapy effectiveness and cancer recurrence in women with newly diagnosed early-stage invasive breast cancer. Genomic Health's research efforts are targeted at providing a wider base of cancer-related tests. The company generates around 85% of its sales in the US.

	Annual Growth	12/13	12/14	12/15	12/16	12/17
Sales ($ mil.)	6.8%	261.6	275.7	287.5	327.9	340.8
Net income ($ mil.)	–	(12.8)	(24.6)	(33.3)	(13.9)	(3.9)
Market value ($ mil.)	4.0%	1,025.9	1,120.5	1,233.7	1,030.1	1,198.7
Employees	6.0%	684	752	802	846	863

GENTEX CORP.
NMS: GNTX

600 N. Centennial
Zeeland, MI 49464
Phone: 616 772-1800
Fax: 616 772-7348
Web: www.gentex.com

CEO: Steven Downing
CFO: Kevin Nash
HR: –
FYE: December 31
Type: Public

Gentex focuses on designing and manufacturing interior and exterior auto-dimming rearview mirrors and camera-based driver-assist systems for the automotive market. The company sells its products to OEM customers' sales through to Tier 1 suppliers such as Volkswagen Toyota and General Motors. To a lesser degree Gentex also makes dimmable aircraft windows found on commercial aircraft (mainly for Boeing) and fire protection products (smoke detectors fire alarms and signaling devices) primarily for commercial buildings. In 2020 Gentex acquired Aero Parts Australia Ltd. (APA) leading distributor for commercial air military and life support equipment within Australia and New Zealand. In addition on same year Gentex acquired Vaporsens a Utah-based technology company specializing in nanofiber chemical sensing research and development. Gentex serves customers worldwide but more than a third of its sales are generated in the US.

	Annual Growth	12/16	12/17	12/18	12/19	12/20
Sales ($ mil.)	0.1%	1,678.9	1,794.9	1,834.1	1,858.9	1,688.2
Net income ($ mil.)	(0.0%)	347.6	406.8	437.9	424.7	347.6
Market value ($ mil.)	14.6%	4,798.3	5,105.4	4,925.0	7,062.2	8,268.5
Employees	(0.1%)	5,315	5,481	5,707	5,874	5,303

GENTHERM INC
NMS: THRM

21680 Haggerty Road
Northville, MI 48167
Phone: 248 504-0500
Fax: –
Web: www.gentherm.com

CEO: Phillip Eyler
CFO: Matteo Anversa
HR: –
FYE: December 31
Type: Public

Don't worry TED can keep your car seat warm ... or cool. Gentherm develops thermoelectric device (TED) technology for its climate-control seats (CCS) for vehicles. CCS products can be found on the vehicles of nearly every automotive manufacturer in North America Europe and Asia. Other Gentherm products include heated and cooled cup holders steering wheel heaters and heated door and armrests. The company's industrial segment also makes battery thermal management products food temperature control products and hospital patient temperature management systems. The company sells its products worldwide but the US represents its largest market that generates around 45% of the company's total sales. In 2019 the company completed the divestiture of its environmental test equipment business Cincinnati Sub Zero industrial chamber business and also completed the divestiture of their remote power generation systemsTechnologies.

	Annual Growth	12/17	12/18	12/19	12/20	12/21
Sales ($ mil.)	1.5%	985.7	1,038.3	971.9	913.1	1,046.2
Net income ($ mil.)	27.6%	35.2	41.9	37.5	59.7	93.4
Market value ($ mil.)	28.6%	1,048.0	1,319.7	1,465.2	2,152.8	2,868.4
Employees	(5.4%)	13,069	13,755	11,726	11,519	10,474

GENTIVA HEALTH SERVICES INC
NMS: GTIV

3350 Riverwood Parkway, Suite 1400
Atlanta, GA 30339-3314
Phone: 770 951-6450
Fax: –
Web: www.gentiva.com

CEO: David Causby
CFO: Tom Dolan
HR: –
FYE: December 31
Type: Public

Gentiva Health Services is a gentle giant. As one of the nation's largest home health care and hospice services firms the company provides home nursing care through a network of about 270 agency locations in some 40 states. Gentiva's home care nurses provide services ranging from acute-care treatment to housekeeping for the elderly or disabled. Its hospice services are offered through 150 locations in 30 states. Gentiva also offers consulting services to the home care industry to help with regulatory and reimbursement issues. Gentiva also provides hospice operations through subsidiary Odyssey HealthCare.

	Annual Growth	12/08*	01/10*	12/10	12/11	12/12
Sales ($ mil.)	7.1%	1,300.4	1,152.5	1,447.0	1,798.8	1,712.8
Net income ($ mil.)	(35.4%)	153.5	59.2	52.2	(450.5)	26.8
Market value ($ mil.)	(21.9%)	829.0	830.5	817.9	207.6	309.0
Employees	(1.4%)	15,450	5,200	9,600	14,800	14,600

*Fiscal year change

GENUINE PARTS CO.
NYS: GPC

2999 Wildwood Parkway
Atlanta, GA 30339
Phone: 678 934-5000
Fax: –
Web: www.genpt.com

CEO: Paul Donahue
CFO: Carol Yancey
HR: James Neill
FYE: December 31
Type: Public

Genuine Parts Company (GPC) is a global service organization engaged in the distribution of automotive and industrial replacement parts. The company is the sole member and majority owner of National Automotive Parts Association (NAPA) a voluntary trade association that distributes auto parts nationwide. GPC operates more than 5900 NAPA Auto Parts stores in the US. It also distributes parts through chains in Canada Mexico Australasia and across Europe. Other subsidiaries include industrial parts supplier Motion Industries and UAP. Majority of the company's sales were generated in the US. GPC was founded by Carlyle Fraser in 1928 with the purchase of Motor Parts Depot in Atlanta Georgia.

	Annual Growth	12/17	12/18	12/19	12/20	12/21
Sales ($ mil.)	3.7%	16,308.8	18,735.1	19,392.3	16,537.4	18,870.5
Net income ($ mil.)	9.9%	616.8	810.5	621.1	(29.1)	898.8
Market value ($ mil.)	10.2%	13,508.6	13,652.2	15,103.9	14,279.2	19,933.7
Employees	2.0%	48,000	50,000	55,000	50,000	52,000

GENVEC INC (DE)
NAS: GNVC

910 Clopper Road, Suite 220N
Gaithersburg, MD 20878
Phone: 240 632-0740
Fax: –
Web: www.genvec.com

CEO: –
CFO: –
HR: –
FYE: December 31
Type: Public

GenVec is all over the medical map. The clinical-stage biopharmaceutical firm develops gene-based drugs and vaccines for everything from cancer to HIV. GenVec has multiple vaccine candidates for contagious diseases such as HIV malaria and foot-and-mouth through grants and partnerships with several federal agencies including the US departments of Health and Human Services Homeland Security and Agriculture. The company's other drug research and development programs target cancers and hearing and balance disorders mostly through collaborations with other drugmakers. Biotech research firm Intrexon is buying GenVec to expand its gene delivery platform; the price of the purchase was not disclosed.

	Annual Growth	12/11	12/12	12/13	12/14	12/15
Sales ($ mil.)	(52.7%)	17.7	9.4	3.7	6.0	0.9
Net income ($ mil.)	–	(7.4)	(14.1)	(10.0)	(2.5)	(6.5)
Market value ($ mil.)	–					
Employees	(33.8%)	78	45	11	11	15

GENWORTH FINANCIAL, INC. (HOLDING CO)   NYS: GNW
6620 West Broad Street
Richmond, VA 23230
Phone: 804 281-6000
Fax: –
Web: www.genworth.com
CEO: Thomas McInerney
CFO: Daniel Sheehan
HR: –
FYE: December 31
Type: Public

Insurance and investment specialist Genworth Financial has been focused on helping its customers navigate caregiving options protect and grow their retirement income and prepare for the financial challenges that come as people age. Traditionally Genworth has focused its retirement investment products including fixed annuities However facing declines in its core lines of business the company has suspended most sales of its long-term care life insurance and fixed annuity products. Chinese conglomerate China Oceanwide Holdings is buying Genworth for $2.7 billion. Majority of its sales were generated from the US.

	Annual Growth	12/16	12/17	12/18	12/19	12/20
Assets ($ mil.)	0.3%	104,658.0	105,297.0	100,923.0	101,342.0	105,747.0
Net income ($ mil.)	–	(277.0)	817.0	119.0	343.0	178.0
Market value ($ mil.)	(0.2%)	1,927.9	1,573.7	2,358.0	2,226.4	1,912.7
Employees	(3.1%)	3,400	3,500	3,500	3,100	3,000

GENZYME CORPORATION
500 Kendall St.
Cambridge MA 02142
Phone: 617-252-7500
Fax: 617-252-7600
Web: www.genzyme.com
CEO: Christopher A Viehbacher
CFO: –
HR: –
FYE: December 31
Type: Subsidiary

Genzyme makes big money off uncommon diseases. The company's product portfolio focuses on treatments for rare genetic disorders as well as kidney disease and cancer. One of its main products Cerezyme is a leading (and pricey) treatment for Gaucher disease a rare enzyme-deficiency condition. Founded in 1981 Genzyme has treatments for other enzyme disorders including Fabry disease and Pompe disease. In addition the company develops gene-based cancer treatment products renal care and immunological therapies organ transplant drugs and orthopedic biosurgery products. The company was acquired by Sanofi for some $20.1 billion in 2011.

GEO GROUP INC (THE) (NEW)   NYS: GEO
4955 Technology Way
Boca Raton, FL 33431
Phone: 561 893-0101
Fax: –
Web: www.geogroup.com
CEO: Jose Gordo
CFO: Brian Evans
HR: –
FYE: December 31
Type: Public

Its worldwide operations include some 130 maximum- medium- and minimum-security correctional detention (including immigrant detention) with roughly 95000 beds. It also conducts community supervision of more than 210000 offenders and pretrial defendants. Furthermore GEO runs educational rehabilitative and vocational training programs at its facilities. Its GEO Care unit residential treatment services for parolees probationers and pretrial defendants. About 90% of GEO's revenue derives from the US.

	Annual Growth	12/16	12/17	12/18	12/19	12/20
Sales ($ mil.)	1.9%	2,179.5	2,263.4	2,331.4	2,477.9	2,350.1
Net income ($ mil.)	(6.6%)	148.7	146.2	145.1	166.6	113.0
Market value ($ mil.)	(29.5%)	4,359.0	2,863.1	2,390.0	2,015.1	1,074.9
Employees	0.8%	19,370	18,512	22,000	22,000	20,000

GEOBIO ENERGY INC.   OTC: GBOE
601 Union St. Ste. 4500
Seattle WA 98121
Phone: 206-838-9715
Fax: 760-597-4900
Web: www.aqualung.com
CEO: –
CFO: Clayton Shelver
HR: –
FYE: September 30
Type: Public

GeoBio Energy used to think biodiesel was the way of the future but lately it's decided that the oil and gas industry isn't going anywhere anytime soon. Though it acquired GeoAlgae Technologies which develops low-cost renewable feedstock used for the production of biodiesel in 2008 GeoBio Energy has since switched directions. In 2009 it agreed to buy H&M Precision Products which makes chemicals used in the drilling of oil and gas wells. In 2010 it also agreed to acquire a Colorado-based oil field site preparation and maintenance company.

GEOKINETICS INC.
1500 CITYWEST BLVD # 800
HOUSTON, TX 770422300
Phone: 713-850-7600
Fax: –
Web: www.geokineticsinc.com
CEO: David J Crowley
CFO: Michael Muse
HR: Lina Colon
FYE: December 31
Type: Private

Using kinetic energy to assess the Earth's hydrocarbon sources Geokinetics is a global provider of geophysical services to the oil and gas industry. It acquires seismic data in North America and internationally and processes and interprets that data at processing centers in the US and the UK. The company's seismic crews work in a range of terrains including land marsh swamp shallow water and difficult transition zones (between land and water). Not dependent on any one customer its client base consists of international and national oil companies as well as smaller independent oil and gas exploration and production companies.

	Annual Growth	12/07	12/08	12/09	12/10	12/11
Sales ($ mil.)	22.3%	–	–	511.0	558.1	763.7
Net income ($ mil.)	–	–	–	(5.0)	(138.7)	(222.1)
Market value ($ mil.)	–	–	–	–	–	–
Employees	–	–	–	–	–	5,695

GEOMET INC (DE)   NBB: GMET
1221 McKinney Street, Suite 3840
Houston, TX 77010
Phone: 713 659-3855
Fax: –
Web: www.geometinc.com
CEO: Michael Y McGovern
CFO: Tony Oviedo
HR: –
FYE: December 31
Type: Public

Hoping for the day when high gas prices will result in geometric financial growth GeoMet is explores for develops and produces natural gas from coalbed methane properties in Alabama Virginia West Virginia and British Columbia. The company is developing the Gurnee field in the Cahaba Basin and the Garden City Chattanooga Shale prospect (in Alabama) as well as the Pond Creek and Lasher fields in the Central Appalachian Basin. It also has holdings in the Peace River field in British Columbia. GeoMet controls a total of 160000 net acres of coalbed methane assets. In 2010 the company had proved reserves of 215.9 billion cu. ft. of coalbed methane. Yorktown Energy Partners IV controls about 40% of GeoMet.

	Annual Growth	12/09	12/10	12/11	12/12	12/13
Sales ($ mil.)	5.4%	31.0	33.4	35.6	39.4	38.2
Net income ($ mil.)	–	(167.1)	5.8	2.8	(150.0)	35.3
Market value ($ mil.)	(49.4%)	59.4	46.8	37.8	5.7	3.9
Employees	(12.4%)	73	–	68	64	43

GEOPETRO RESOURCES CO

NBB: GEOR

150 California Street, Suite 600
San Francisco, CA 94111
Phone: 415 398-8186
Fax: –
Web: www.geopetro.com

CEO: Stuart J Doshi
CFO: –
HR: –
FYE: December 31
Type: Public

You have to drill down deep to figure out exactly what GeoPetro Resources does. It's an oil and natural gas exploration and production company with projects in Canada Indonesia and the US. These sites cover about 1 million gross acres consisting of mineral leases production-sharing contracts and exploration permits. GeoPetro operates one cash-generating property in the Madisonville Project in Texas; almost all of the revenue from this project has been derived from natural gas sales to two clients: Luminant Energy and ETC Katy Pipeline. GeoPetro Resources also has a geographically diverse portfolio of oil and natural gas prospects. In 2013 the company agreed to be bought by fuel distributor MCW Energy Group.

	Annual Growth	12/08	12/09	12/10	12/11	12/12
Sales ($ mil.)	(51.1%)	6.2	4.1	3.1	1.0	0.4
Net income ($ mil.)	–	(0.2)	(25.8)	(4.9)	(1.5)	(3.9)
Market value ($ mil.)	(44.2%)	34.0	34.0	20.5	10.7	3.3
Employees	(26.0%)	20	20	14	14	6

GEORGE E. WARREN CORPORATION

3001 OCEAN DR STE 203
VERO BEACH, FL 329631992
Phone: 772-778-7100
Fax: –
Web: www.gewarren.com

CEO: –
CFO: Michael George
HR: –
FYE: December 31
Type: Private

By barge by pipeline by tank truck by George; George E. Warren is a major private wholesale distributor of refined petroleum products. The company which has business activities in about 30 US states distributes product mostly by barge and pipeline though it uses some tank trucks as well. It distributes by pipeline via the Buckeye Colonial Magellan Nustar and Explorer pipelines and by barges and vessels from facilities on the Gulf Coast and in the New York Harbor area. It distributes a range of petroleum products including ethylene and heating oil to various industries.

	Annual Growth	12/13	12/14	12/15	12/16	12/17
Sales ($ mil.)	(4.6%)	–	103.8	124.5	121.7	90.1
Net income ($ mil.)	(6.7%)	–	34.6	43.0	42.0	28.1
Market value ($ mil.)	–	–	–	–	–	–
Employees	–	–	–	–	–	35

GEORGE FOREMAN ENTERPRISES INC.

100 N. Wilkes-Barre Blvd. 4th Fl.
Wilkes-Barre PA 18702
Phone: 570-822-6277
Fax: 330-848-4287
Web: www.juice4u.com

CEO: Chuck Gartenhaus
CFO: Jeremy Anderson
HR: –
FYE: December 31
Type: Private

George Foreman Enterprises doesn't sell the boxer's namesake grills (Salton does); however the company actively looks to make acquisitions and licensing deals to keep George Foreman's name in the ring. Through its InStride Ventures George Foreman Enterprises makes and markets therapeutic footwear under the George Foreman name to ShopKo. The company also has partnered with G-Nutritional and Vitaquest International (which later formed Vita Ventures) to market and sell vitamins and nutritional supplements using the Foreman trade name. The company signed on legendary boxing champ George Foreman to a licensing and pitchman deal in 2005 in exchange for 35% of the company and his name on the marquee.

GEORGETOWN MEMORIAL HOSPITAL

606 BLACK RIVER RD
GEORGETOWN, SC 294403368
Phone: 843-626-9040
Fax: –

CEO: Bruce Bailey
CFO: –
HR: –
FYE: September 30
Type: Private

Georgetown Hospital System may be set amidst the Antebellum grace of the South but its health care services are far from antiquated. The system on the southeast coast of South Carolina operates Georgetown Memorial Hospital an acute-care facility with more than 130 beds and Waccamaw Community Hospital which operates with about 170 beds. Georgetown Memorial Hospital features ICU cardiac and surgical services labor and delivery and a pediatric wing. Waccamaw Community Hospital covering the northern part of the system's service area provides 24-hour emergency services rehabilitation obstetrics and inpatient and outpatient surgery.

	Annual Growth	09/15	09/16	09/17	09/18	09/19
Sales ($ mil.)	11.5%	–	131.2	141.7	141.7	182.0
Net income ($ mil.)	14.7%	–	12.3	2.3	14.7	18.6
Market value ($ mil.)	–	–	–	–	–	–
Employees	–	–	–	–	–	1,300

GEORGIA FARM BUREAU MUTUAL INSURANCE COMPANY

1620 BASS RD
MACON, GA 312106500
Phone: 478-474-0679
Fax: –
Web: www.gfbinsurance.com

CEO: Vincent M Duvall
CFO: –
HR: –
FYE: December 31
Type: Private

You don't have to be a farmer to get insurance coverage here but it helps. Georgia Farm Bureau Mutual Insurance Company (GFNMIC) and its subsidiaries offer a variety of commercial and individual property/casualty products to members of the Georgia Farm Bureau. Its products include farmowners automobile homeowners marine business owners and personal liability insurance. The company specializes in writing lower-cost preferred risk policies (policies for customers that are less likely to file claims). A network of nearly 500 agents and representatives market GFNMIC's products. The company which was founded in 1959 is a part of the Georgia Farm Bureau. It is owned by its policyholders.

	Annual Growth	12/16	12/17	12/18	12/19	12/20
Sales ($ mil.)	0.1%	–	–	402.4	394.3	402.9
Net income ($ mil.)	25.7%	–	–	21.5	37.5	33.9
Market value ($ mil.)	–	–	–	–	–	–
Employees	–	–	–	–	–	1,210

GEORGIA LOTTERY CORPORATION

250 Williams St. Ste. 3000
Atlanta GA 30303
Phone: 404-215-5000
Fax: 404-215-8983
Web: www.galottery.com

CEO: Debbie Dlugolenski Alford
CFO: –
HR: Jacqueline Odejimi
FYE: June 30
Type: Government-owned

You might say these games of chance are just peachy. The Georgia Lottery Corporation (GLC) operates a number of instant-win ticket and lotto-style games including Cash 4 Fantasy 5 and Win for Life. It also takes part in the multi-state Mega Millions drawing game. Tickets are sold through more than 8200 retailers throughout the state. The GLC was established in 1992 to enhance the state's education funding. Since its founding the lottery has contributed more than $13 billion in proceeds to state education programs including the HOPE Scholarship Program and the Georgia Prekindergarten Program. The GLC has eight district offices in Atlanta Augusta Columbus Dalton Duluth Macon Savannah and Tifton.

GEORGIA POWER CO   NL:

241 Ralph McGill Boulevard, N.E.
Atlanta, GA 30308
Phone: 404 506-6526
Fax: –
Web: www.georgiapower.com
CEO: Chris Womack
CFO: Daniel Tucker
HR: Sloane Drake
FYE: December 31
Type: Public

Georgia Power is the largest subsidiary of US utility holding company Southern Company. The regulated utility provides electricity to about 2.6 million residential commercial and industrial customers throughout most of Georgia. It has interests in about 10 gas/oil nearly 15 solar one nuclear and over 15 hydroelectric power plants that give it about 14400 MW of generating capacity. Georgia Power sells wholesale electricity to several cooperatives and municipalities in the region. The utility also offers energy efficiency.

	Annual Growth	12/17	12/18	12/19	12/20	12/21
Sales ($ mil.)	2.7%	8,310.0	8,420.0	8,408.0	8,309.0	9,260.0
Net income ($ mil.)	(20.0%)	1,428.0	793.0	1,720.0	1,575.0	584.0
Market value ($ mil.)	–	–	–	–	–	–
Employees	(1.8%)	6,986	6,967	6,938	6,700	6,500

GEORGIA SOUTHERN UNIVERSITY

1582 SOUTHERN DR
STATESBORO, GA 30458
Phone: 912-681-5224
Fax: –
Web: www.georgiasouthern.edu
CEO: –
CFO: –
HR: –
FYE: June 30
Type: Private

Georgia Southern University shows students that higher education can be just peachy. Georgia Southern offers its student body more than 140 bachelor master and doctoral programs from eight colleges; academic fields include business education science and public health. One of 26 colleges and universities in the University System of Georgia it enrolls roughly 27000 students most of which hail from Georgia. The average class size of lower division courses is about 43 upper division 23 and graduate level 11. The student to faculty ratio is 22:1.

	Annual Growth	06/16	06/17	06/18	06/19	06/20
Sales ($ mil.)	0.2%	–	232.5	277.2	257.9	233.9
Net income ($ mil.)	–	–	3.5	(13.2)	27.8	(24.9)
Market value ($ mil.)	–	–	–	–	–	–
Employees	–	–	–	–	–	1,700

GEORGIA TRANSMISSION CORPORATION

2100 E EXCHANGE PL
TUCKER, GA 300845342
Phone: 770-270-7400
Fax: –
Web: www.gatrans.com
CEO: Jerry Donovan
CFO: Barbara Hampton
HR: Sharon N Williamson
FYE: December 31
Type: Private

With Georgia on its mind Georgia Transmission provides electric transmission services to power producers and distribution utilities. The company primarily transports power for its 39 member distribution cooperatives (out of Georgia's total of 42 coops) and their electricity supplier Oglethorpe Power. Georgia Transmission owns 3060 miles of transmission lines asn more that 640 substations. It jointly owns and plans the state's entire 17500 miles of transmission lines through the Integrated Transmission System in collaboration with Georgia Power MEAG Power and Dalton Utilities.

	Annual Growth	12/16	12/17	12/18	12/19	12/20
Sales ($ mil.)	5.7%	–	292.8	305.7	330.5	345.5
Net income ($ mil.)	4.7%	–	14.4	15.2	16.4	16.5
Market value ($ mil.)	–	–	–	–	–	–
Employees	–	–	–	–	–	285

GEORGIA-CAROLINA BANCSHARES, INC.   NBB: GECR

3527 Wheeler Road
Augusta, GA 30909
Phone: 706 731-6600
Fax: –
CEO: –
CFO: –
HR: –
FYE: December 31
Type: Public

Georgia-Carolina Bancshares is holding the line on banking in and around Augusta Georgia. The holding company owns First Bank of Georgia which has about a half-dozen branches along the eastern edge of the Peach State. The company also owns First Bank Mortgage which originates residential loans and other mortgage products through offices in Georgia and Florida. The bank focuses on real estate lending in addition to providing standard deposit products such as checking and savings accounts. Other lending activities include business and consumer loans. The bank's FB Financial Services division offers financial planning and investment services through an agreement with LPL Financial.

	Annual Growth	12/08	12/09	12/10	12/11	12/12
Assets ($ mil.)	2.4%	460.8	484.0	495.3	493.3	506.2
Net income ($ mil.)	24.0%	2.8	3.8	1.5	4.1	6.6
Market value ($ mil.)	5.8%	35.3	25.4	27.2	24.7	44.3
Employees	(1.2%)	167	172	166	147	159

GEOSPACE TECHNOLOGIES CORP   NMS: GEOS

7007 Pinemont
Houston, TX 77040
Phone: 713 986-4444
Fax: –
Web: www.geospace.com
CEO: Walter Wheeler
CFO: Robert Curda
HR: –
FYE: September 30
Type: Public

Geospace Technologies designs and manufactures seismic instruments and equipment. These seismic products are marketed to the oil and gas industry and used to locate characterize and monitor hydrocarbon producing reservoirs. It also market its seismic products to other industries for vibration monitoring border and perimeter security and various geotechnical applications. The company designs and manufactures other products of a non-seismic nature including water meter products imaging equipment offshore cables remote shutoff water valves and Internet of Things (IoT) platform and provide contract manufacturing services. Majority of the company's sales were generated from the US.

	Annual Growth	09/17	09/18	09/19	09/20	09/21
Sales ($ mil.)	6.5%	73.7	75.7	95.8	87.8	94.9
Net income ($ mil.)	–	(56.8)	(19.2)	(0.1)	(19.2)	(14.1)
Market value ($ mil.)	(14.4%)	231.1	177.7	199.3	80.2	123.9
Employees	(2.1%)	707	726	786	651	649

GEOSYNTEC CONSULTANTS, INC.

900 BROKEN SOUND PKWY NW
BOCA RATON, FL 334873513
Phone: 561-995-0900
Fax: –
Web: www.geosyntec.com
CEO: Peter Zeeb
CFO: Jon Dickinson
HR: –
FYE: December 31
Type: Private

An environmental engineering and consulting firm GeoSyntec Consultants provides services such as environmental management geotechnical engineering groundwater assessment and remediation pollution prevention and surface water management. The company operates from more than 75 offices primarily in the US but also in Canada Malaysia and the UK. Its clients include Aerojet-General AstraZeneca Chevron Delta Air Lines FMC Corp. Georgia Power Kimberly-Clark Lockheed Martin Pharmacia & Upjohn and Shell Oil. The company has more than 1000 engineers scientists and other specialists worldwide.

	Annual Growth	12/14	12/15	12/16	12/18	12/19
Sales ($ mil.)	11.6%	–	202.4	204.8	225.7	314.3
Net income ($ mil.)	(5.0%)	–	9.4	5.2	11.7	7.7
Market value ($ mil.)	–	–	–	–	–	–
Employees	–	–	–	–	–	1,600

GERBER CHILDRENSWEAR LLC

7005 PELHAM RD STE D
GREENVILLE, SC 296155782
Phone: 864-987-5200
Fax: –
Web: www.gerberchildrenswear.com

CEO: –
CFO: –
HR: –
FYE: January 29
Type: Private

Gerber Childrenswear may be one of the first companies to make kids brand-conscious. The company makes infant and toddler clothing sold under the licensed Gerber and Curity labels as well as its own Onesies brand. Products include sleepwear underwear playwear cloth diapers footwear and bibs. Through a licensing deal with Jockey International Gerber Childrenswear also offers Jockey-branded underwear sleepwear and thermal items for children. The company sells its products primarily through national retailers (such as Wal-Mart Kmart and Toys "R" Us) department stores and specialty shops. Gerber Childrenswear is a unit of Childrenswear LLC a portfolio company of investment firm Sun Capital Partners.

	Annual Growth	01/06	01/07	01/08	01/09	01/11
Sales ($ mil.)	(9.1%)	–	–	–	193.8	160.1
Net income ($ mil.)	(12.0%)	–	–	–	6.6	5.1
Market value ($ mil.)	–	–	–	–	–	–
Employees	–	–	–	–	–	140

GERBER SCIENTIFIC INC.

24 Industrial Park Rd. West
Tolland CT 06084
Phone: 860-644-1551
Fax: 516-478-5476
Web: www.gettyrealty.com

CEO: Michael Elia
CFO: John Capasso
HR: –
FYE: April 30
Type: Private

When it comes to its manufacturing systems Gerber Scientific is no baby. The company - not affiliated with baby food maker Gerber Products Co. — is a giant in the automated manufacturing systems industry. Its systems which include equipment and software are used by graphics apparel industrial and flexible materials companies to manufacture goods. Gerber's signage subsidiary Gerber Scientific Products makes digital imaging systems materials cutting systems and related software. Its Gerber Technology subsidiary provides CAD/CAM pattern-making and cutting systems for apparel furniture aerospace and textile companies. In 2011 Gerber Scientific was acquired by investment firm Vector Capital.

GERMAN AMERICAN BANCORP INC

NMS: GABC

711 Main Street
Jasper, IN 47546
Phone: 812 482-1314
Fax: –
Web: www.germanamerican.com

CEO: D. Dauby
CFO: Bradley Rust
HR: Marilyn Francis
FYE: December 31
Type: Public

German American Bancorp is the holding company for German American Bank which operates some 65 branches in southern Indiana and Kentucky. Founded in 1910 the bank offers such standard retail products as checking and savings accounts certificates of deposit and IRAs. It also provides trust services while sister company German American Investment Services provides trust investment advisory and brokerage services. German American Bancorp also owns German American Insurance which offers corporate and personal insurance products. The group's core banking operations provide more than 90% of its total sales.

	Annual Growth	12/16	12/17	12/18	12/19	12/20
Assets ($ mil.)	13.9%	2,956.0	3,144.4	3,929.1	4,397.7	4,977.6
Net income ($ mil.)	15.3%	35.2	40.7	46.5	59.2	62.2
Market value ($ mil.)	(10.9%)	1,394.3	936.3	736.0	944.0	877.0
Employees	6.6%	597	614	738	817	770

GERON CORP.

NMS: GERN

919 East Hillsdale Boulevard, Suite 250
Foster City, CA 94404
Phone: 650 473-7700
Fax: –
Web: www.geron.com

CEO: John Scarlett
CFO: Olivia Bloom
HR: –
FYE: December 31
Type: Public

Geron is a clinical-stage biopharmaceutical is working to developing compounds able to treat various hematologic myeloid malignancies such as myelofibrosis and myelodysplastic syndromes and acute myelogenous leukemia. The company is developing pharmaceuticals based on protein inhibitor technologies that aim to demolish enzymes that feed cancer cells. The company's lead candidate imetelstat is an enzyme inhibitor being studied for its effectiveness in treating myelofibrosis and myelodysplastic syndromes.

	Annual Growth	12/16	12/17	12/18	12/19	12/20
Sales ($ mil.)	(55.0%)	6.2	1.1	1.1	0.5	0.3
Net income ($ mil.)	–	(29.5)	(27.9)	(27.0)	(68.5)	(75.6)
Market value ($ mil.)	(6.4%)	642.9	559.9	310.6	422.4	493.8
Employees	32.2%	18	18	18	46	55

GERRITY'S SUPER MARKET, INC.

950 N SOUTH RD STE 5
SCRANTON, PA 185041430
Phone: 570-342-4144
Fax: –
Web: www.gerritys.com

CEO: –
CFO: Anna Corcoran
HR: Mari Frietto
FYE: December 31
Type: Private

Gerrity's Super Market is not yet part of a matriarchal society but does boast that it's where Mom is "always in charge!" The regional grocery chain operates about 10 supermarkets under the Gerrity's Supermarket banner in Lackawanna and Luzerne counties in northeastern Pennsylvania. The regional chain also operates an online grocery order and home delivery service. Founded in 1895 by William Gerrity the family-owned company is run by mother and son team Joyce ("Mom") and Joseph Fasula. Gerrity's Supermarkets is a member of the Shursave Supermarkets Co-op.

	Annual Growth	01/15	01/16	01/17*	12/17	12/18
Sales ($ mil.)	0.8%	–	168.8	167.8	169.8	171.5
Net income ($ mil.)	(28.9%)	–	3.6	2.7	2.3	1.8
Market value ($ mil.)	–	–	–	–	–	–
Employees	–	–	–	–	–	1,100

*Fiscal year change

GETTY REALTY CORP.

NYS: GTY

292 Madison Avenue, 9th Floor
New York, NY 10017-6318
Phone: 646 349-6000
Fax: –
Web: www.gettyrealty.com

CEO: Christopher Constant
CFO: Brian Dickman
HR: Eileen Marlow
FYE: December 31
Type: Public

Getty Realty a self-administered real estate investment trust (REIT) owns or leases about 945 gas service stations adjacent convenience stores and petroleum distribution terminals in more than 30 US states and Washington DC. Most of its properties are company-owned and located in the Northeast (about a third in New York). Major gas brands distributed at Getty properties include BP Citgo Conoco Exxon Getty Shell and Valero. The company's three most significant tenants by revenue — which together occupy about 45% of its properties — are petroleum distributors and gas station operators Global Partners Apro and Chestnut Petroleum.

	Annual Growth	12/16	12/17	12/18	12/19	12/20
Sales ($ mil.)	6.3%	115.3	120.2	136.1	140.7	147.3
Net income ($ mil.)	15.9%	38.4	47.2	47.7	49.7	69.4
Market value ($ mil.)	2.0%	1,111.5	1,184.3	1,282.4	1,433.3	1,200.9
Employees	0.0%	31	30	29	31	31

GETTYSBURG COLLEGE

300 N WASHINGTON ST
GETTYSBURG, PA 173251483
Phone: 717-337-6000
Fax: –
Web: www.gettysburgmajestic.org

CEO: –
CFO: –
HR: –
FYE: May 31
Type: Private

Four score and many years ago Gettysburg College opened its doors. The private four-year liberal arts and sciences college offers about 65 academic programs and about 40 majors to 2600 students who come from more than 40 states and 35 countries. Gettysburg's student-faculty ratio is 10:1. The campus is adjacent to the Gettysburg National Military Park in Pennsylvania. The college was founded in 1832; its first building Pennsylvania Hall served during and after the Battle of Gettysburg as a hospital for the wounded. In 1863 students and faculty of Gettysburg College walked from Pennsylvania Hall to the national cemetery in Gettysburg to hear President Lincoln deliver his legendary Gettysburg Address.

	Annual Growth	05/14	05/15	05/16	05/17	05/18
Sales ($ mil.)	2.4%	–	128.8	133.3	196.8	138.2
Net income ($ mil.)	56.7%	–	7.0	(3.8)	19.3	26.8
Market value ($ mil.)	–	–	–	–	–	–
Employees	–	–	–	–	–	108

GEVO INC

345 Inverness Drive South, Building C, Suite 310
Englewood, CO 80112
Phone: 303 858-8358
Fax: –
Web: www.gevo.com

NAS: GEVO
CEO: Patrick Gruber
CFO: L. Lynn Smull
HR: Kimberly Bowron
FYE: December 31
Type: Public

Putting sugar in a gas tank is generally not a good idea but Gevo has figured out a way to make it beneficial. A renewable chemical and biofuels company Gevo produces isobutanol a multi-purpose chemical derived from glucose and other cellulosic biomass extracted from plant matter. Its isobutanol can be used as a blendstock (additive used during the refining process) for gasoline and jet fuel production and as a chemical used in the production of plastics fibers and rubber. Gevo does not yet produce isobutanol on a commercial scale but it is in the process of building its customer and partnership base in preparation of commencing production. In 2016 the company was seeking strategic alternatives.

	Annual Growth	12/16	12/17	12/18	12/19	12/20
Sales ($ mil.)	(32.8%)	27.2	27.5	32.9	24.5	5.5
Net income ($ mil.)	–	(37.2)	(24.6)	(28.0)	(28.7)	(40.2)
Market value ($ mil.)	122.6%	22.2	75.6	251.2	296.0	544.6
Employees	(19.5%)	74	51	52	57	31

GFI GROUP INC

55 Water Street
New York, NY 10041
Phone: 212 968-4100
Fax: –
Web: www.gfigroup.com

NYS: GFIG
CEO: Colin Heffron
CFO: –
HR: Cynthia Joo
FYE: December 31
Type: Public

A financial matchmaker GFI Group is an inter-dealer hybrid brokerage that acts as an intermediary for more than 2600 institutional clients such as banks large corporations insurance companies and hedge funds. The firm deals primarily in over-the-counter (OTC) derivatives which tend to be less liquid and thus harder to trade than other assets. It also offers market data and analysis on credit equity commodity and currency derivatives and other financial instruments. Other products include foreign exchange options freight and energy derivatives including electric power coal and carbon emissions options. GFI operates in North and South America Europe Africa the Middle East and Australasia.

	Annual Growth	12/09	12/10	12/11	12/12	12/13
Sales ($ mil.)	2.4%	818.7	862.1	1,015.5	924.6	901.5
Net income ($ mil.)	–	16.3	25.6	(3.2)	(10.0)	(20.0)
Market value ($ mil.)	(3.7%)	561.0	578.2	507.9	399.4	482.1
Employees	4.2%	1,768	1,990	2,176	2,062	2,087

GGNSC HOLDINGS LLC

1000 Fianna Way
Fort Smith AR 72919
Phone: 479-201-2000
Fax: 605-721-2599
Web: www.blackhillscorp.com

CEO: Ronald Silva
CFO: Ruth Ann Harmon
HR: –
FYE: December 31
Type: Private

GGNSC Holdings puts the "Golden" in "Golden Years." The holding company does business as Golden Living and operates more than 300 skilled nursing homes (LivingCenters) and some 16 assisted living facilities nationwide. Golden Living's subsidiaries operate under a range of names including Aegis Therapies for rehabilitation therapy AseraCare hospice and home health care 360 Healthcare Staffing and Ceres a buying cooperative for health care products such as disposable gloves sanitary products and wheelchairs. The company sees patients covered by a range of payors including Medicare and Medicaid the US Department of Veterans Affairs and private insurance.

GIANT EAGLE INC.

101 Kappa Dr.
Pittsburgh PA 15238
Phone: 412-963-6200
Fax: 412-968-1617
Web: www.gianteagle.com

CEO: Laura Karet
CFO: –
HR: –
FYE: June 30
Type: Private

Giant Eagle has its talons firmly wrapped around parts of Pennsylvania and Ohio. The grocery chain a market leader in Pittsburgh and eastern Ohio operates about 175 company-owned stores and 50-plus franchised supermarkets as well as about 160 GetGo convenience stores (which feature fresh foods and sell gas at discounted prices through the fuelperks! program). The regional chain also has stores in Maryland and West Virginia. Many Giant Eagle stores feature video rental banking photo processing dry cleaning services and ready-to-eat meals. Executive chairman David Shapira is the grandson of one of the men who founded the company in 1931. The founders' families own Giant Eagle.

GIBBS DIE CASTING CORPORATION

369 COMMUNITY DR
HENDERSON, KY 424204397
Phone: 270-827-1801
Fax: –
Web: www.gibbsdc.com

CEO: –
CFO: Angela Phaup
HR: Dan Carr
FYE: December 31
Type: Private

There's plenty to die for at Gibbs Die Casting. The company manufactures aluminum and magnesium die-castings such as air conditioning compressor commercial refrigeration and engine and viscous clutch parts. Its Comac Machining Division provides precision machining and assembly work. The Audubon Tool Division uses fused deposition modeling prototyping equipment and CNC electrical discharge machines to build die-casting tools. Gibbs Engineering offers on-site product design prototype models and production tooling services. Gibbs Die Casting serves industries such as automobile and appliance manufacturing and alternative energy. The comopany is owned by Koch Enterprises.

	Annual Growth	12/13	12/14	12/15	12/16	12/17
Sales ($ mil.)	–	–	0.0	0.0	234.4	232.8
Net income ($ mil.)	–	–	0.0	0.0	0.0	0.0
Market value ($ mil.)	–	–	–	–	–	–
Employees	–	–	–	–	–	1,323

GIBRALTAR INDUSTRIES INC   NMS: ROCK

3556 Lake Shore Road, P.O. Box 2028
Buffalo, NY 14219-0228
Phone: 716 826-6500
Fax: –
Web: www.gibraltar1.com
CEO: William Bosway
CFO: Timothy Murphy
HR: Betsy Jensen
FYE: December 31
Type: Public

What rocks Gibraltar's world? A good strong structure. The company makes and distributes products for renewable energy conservation residential and commercial construction including metal roofing vents rain gutters steel framing and mailboxes. Gibraltar is a leading producer of metal roofing and accessories rain dispersion products including exterior retractable awnings products as well as metal structural connectors including foundation anchors anchor bolts and foundation straps. Its building products are sold through a number of sales channel including major retail home centers and building material wholesalers. More than 95% of its total sales came from its domestic customers.

	Annual Growth	12/16	12/17	12/18	12/19	12/20
Sales ($ mil.)	0.6%	1,008.0	986.9	1,002.4	1,047.4	1,032.6
Net income ($ mil.)	17.7%	33.7	62.6	63.8	65.1	64.6
Market value ($ mil.)	14.6%	1,355.3	1,073.8	1,158.1	1,641.3	2,340.9
Employees	0.3%	2,311	2,022	1,939	1,932	2,337

GIBRALTAR PACKAGING GROUP INC.

2000 Summit Ave.
Hastings NE 68901
Phone: 402-463-1366
Fax: 402-463-2467
Web: www.gibpack.com
CEO: Walter E Rose
CFO: –
HR: –
FYE: June 30
Type: Private

Gibraltar Packaging displays rock-solid commitment to the idea that good things come in small packages ... like the ones it makes! The company's folding carton unit makes product packaging and point-of-purchase retail displays for a variety of consumer goods. Customers supply artwork; Gibraltar Packaging prints die cuts folds and glues the cartons. Flexible poly-film packaging specialty laminated cartons and corrugated containers are also made. Gibraltar Packaging's plants in Nebraska and North Carolina market to US customers large and small in industries from textiles to pharmaceuticals office supplies auto parts and food and tobacco goods. The company was acquired by Rosmar Litho in 2008.

GIBSON DUNN & CRUTCHER LLP

333 S. Grand Ave.
Los Angeles CA 90071-3197
Phone: 213-229-7000
Fax: 213-229-7520
Web: www.gibsondunn.com
CEO: –
CFO: –
HR: –
FYE: October 31
Type: Private - Partnershi

One of the top US corporate-transactions law firms Gibson Dunn & Crutcher also practices in such areas as labor and employment crisis management litigation public policy real estate tax and white-collar defense and investigations. The firm has about 1000 lawyers working from more than 15 offices in California Colorado Texas and various financial capitals worldwide. The firm also has a significant presence in Washington DC. Along with multinational companies Gibson Dunn clients include commercial and investment banks government entities individuals and startups. The firm was founded in 1890.

GIGA-TRONICS INC   NL:

5990 Gleason Drive
Dublin, CA 94568
Phone: 925 328-4650
Fax: –
Web: www.gigatronics.com
CEO: John Regazzi
CFO: Lutz Henckels
HR: –
FYE: March 27
Type: Public

Giga-tronics has a cool gig in electronics. Its three units — Giga-tronics Instruments Microsource and ASCOR — make test measurement and control equipment for both commercial and military customers. The units make synthesizers and power measurement instruments used in electronic warfare radar satellite and telecommunications devices; switching systems for aircraft and automated test equipment; and oscillators and filters used in microwave instruments. Top customers include the US Department of Defense and its prime contractors. The majority of the company's business is done the US.

	Annual Growth	03/17	03/18	03/19	03/20	03/21
Sales ($ mil.)	(5.4%)	16.3	9.8	11.1	11.8	13.1
Net income ($ mil.)	–	(1.5)	(3.1)	(1.0)	(0.7)	(0.4)
Market value ($ mil.)	49.9%	2.2	0.9	0.9	6.5	11.1
Employees	(7.4%)	57	43	39	42	42

GIGAMON INC   NYS: GIMO

3300 Olcott Street
Santa Clara, CA 95054
Phone: 408 831-4000
Fax: –
Web: www.gigamon.com
CEO: Paul Hooper
CFO: –
HR: –
FYE: December 26
Type: Public

An invisibility cloak won't fly at Gigamon. A Unified Visibility Fabric on the other hand will definitely fly. The company's visibility fabric is a layer of technology that steers information on networks to the appropriate destination. Gigamon's products such as the GigaVUE platform can handle video voice and data. Gigamon's products which include cloud-based software help IT managers of enterprises data centers and service providers see what's happening with their networks manage risks and maintain network performance. Gigamon has customers in finance health care higher education government technology and telecom as well as other businesses. The company went public in 2013.

	Annual Growth	12/11	12/12	12/13	12/14	12/15
Sales ($ mil.)	34.4%	68.1	96.7	140.3	157.1	222.0
Net income ($ mil.)	(22.3%)	16.9	7.5	(9.5)	(40.8)	6.2
Market value ($ mil.)	(2.6%)	–	–	971.0	599.6	920.5
Employees	18.7%	–	288	352	371	482

GIGPEAK INC   ASE: GIG

130 Baytech Drive
San Jose, CA 95134
Phone: 408 522-3100
Fax: –
Web: www.gigoptix.com
CEO: Gregory L Waters
CFO: Brian C White
HR: –
FYE: December 31
Type: Public

GigPeak (formerly GigOptix) hopes its light shines bright in an optical universe. The company develops polymer materials and products for use in wireless and optical communications networks. Products include optical and radio-frequency (RF) amplifiers compact panel wireless antennas and electro-optic modulators and optical interconnects for use in telecommunications. Its products are used in fiber-optic communications networks and for connecting to other types of electronic equipment. GigPeak also develops custom electro-optic devices for the US government particularly the Department of Defense which accounts most of sales. In early 2016 it acquired Magnum Semiconductor and took its present name.

	Annual Growth	12/11	12/12	12/13	12/14	12/15
Sales ($ mil.)	5.8%	32.3	36.7	28.9	32.9	40.4
Net income ($ mil.)	–	(14.1)	(7.0)	(1.9)	(5.8)	1.2
Market value ($ mil.)	14.0%	81.4	86.8	69.2	54.3	137.5
Employees	3.6%	80	84	76	77	92

GILBANE BUILDING COMPANY

7 JACKSON WALKWAY STE 2
PROVIDENCE, RI 029033694
Phone: 401-456-5800
Fax: –
Web: www.gilbaneco.com

CEO: Michael McKelvy
CFO: John Ruggieri
HR: –
FYE: December 31
Type: Private

Gilbane Building Company has built a big business constructing for equally large customers. The firm provides construction services consulting subcontracting and facilities management to commercial institutional and governmental markets. Operating as the construction arm of Gilbane the company builds schools hospitals laboratories and prisons serving both the public and private sectors. Its completed projects include the Stroh Center at Bowling Green State University and the National WWII Memorial in Washington DC. Founded in 1870 as a carpentry and general contracting shop the family-owned Gilbane Building Company operates from more than 45 offices around the world.

	Annual Growth	12/11	12/12	12/13	12/14	12/17
Sales ($ mil.)	4.5%	–	–	4,100.7	3,840.7	4,899.2
Net income ($ mil.)	–	–	–	0.0	0.0	63.5
Market value ($ mil.)	–	–	–	–	–	–
Employees	–	–	–	–	–	2,500

GILBANE INC.

7 Jackson Walkway
Providence RI 02903
Phone: 401-456-5800
Fax: 401-456-5936
Web: www.gilbaneco.com

CEO: Thomas F Gilbane Jr
CFO: John Ruggieri
HR: –
FYE: December 31
Type: Private

Family-owned Gilbane Inc. has served the construction and real estate industry for five generations. Founded by William Gilbane in 1873 the company operates through chief subsidiaries: Gilbane Building and Gilbane Development Company. Its building arm provides construction management contracting and design and build services to construct office buildings manufacturing plants schools and prisons. Signature projects include the National WWII Memorial and Capitol Visitors Center in Washington DC. Gilbane Development offers real estate development property management financing and asset repositioning services to its clients in Maryland Ohio Pennsylvania Rhode Island Vermont.

GILBERT MAY, INC.

1125 LONGPOINT AVE
DALLAS, TX 752476809
Phone: 214-631-3331
Fax: –
Web: www.phillipsmay.com

CEO: –
CFO: –
HR: –
FYE: December 31
Type: Private

Gilbert May which does business as the Phillips/May Corporation provides general contracting services in the Dallas area. The company's projects include schools libraries and other institutional buildings and government projects including work at the DFW International Airport. The firm which was founded by president Gilbert May ranks among the fastest-growing private companies in the Dallas area.

	Annual Growth	12/13	12/14	12/15	12/16	12/17
Sales ($ mil.)	(0.4%)	–	63.1	79.4	74.9	62.4
Net income ($ mil.)	16.8%	–	0.7	0.7	0.8	1.2
Market value ($ mil.)	–	–	–	–	–	–
Employees	–	–	–	–	–	124

GILEAD SCIENCES INC

NMS: GILD

333 Lakeside Drive
Foster City, CA 94404
Phone: 650 574-3000
Fax: –
Web: www.gilead.com

CEO: Daniel O'Day
CFO: Andrew Dickinson
HR: –
FYE: December 31
Type: Public

Gilead Sciences has biotech balms for infectious diseases including hepatitis HIV and infections related to AIDS. The company's drug franchise includes Truvada an oral formulation indicated in combination with other antiretroviral agents for the treatment of HIV-1 infection in certain patients. The company co-promotes another HIV treatment called Atripla in the US and Europe with Bristol-Myers Squibb (BMS). Other products on the market include AmBisome a proprietary liposomal formulation of amphotericin B an antifungal agent for the treatment of serious invasive fungal infections caused by various fungal species in adults.. Beyond HIV/AIDS Gilead also markets Hematology and Oncology medicines and the Yescarta CAR-T cell therapy for cancer. About three-quarters of its sales are in the US.

	Annual Growth	12/17	12/18	12/19	12/20	12/21
Sales ($ mil.)	1.1%	26,107.0	22,127.0	22,449.0	24,689.0	27,305.0
Net income ($ mil.)	7.7%	4,628.0	5,455.0	5,386.0	123.0	6,225.0
Market value ($ mil.)	0.3%	89,836.6	78,437.7	81,484.9	73,058.0	91,052.9
Employees	9.5%	10,000	11,000	11,800	13,600	14,400

GILLETTE CHILDREN'S SPECIALTY HEALTHCARE

200 UNIVERSITY AVE E
SAINT PAUL, MN 551012507
Phone: 651-291-2848
Fax: –
Web: www.gillettechildrens.org

CEO: –
CFO: –
HR: –
FYE: December 31
Type: Private

Caring for the Twin Cities' tiniest tykes and most truculent teens Gillette Children's Specialty Healthcare provides diagnostic therapeutic and support services to children adolescents and young adults. Gillette Children's consists of a main campus in St. Paul Minnesota and eight clinics in the immediate and outlying areas of the city. The health system also provides adult services at its St. Paul-Phalen clinic. The main campus hospital (with about 345 beds) operates Centers of Excellence for cerebral palsy craniofacial services and pediatric neurosciences among others. The not-for-profit hospital also provides outreach services through its mobile health care unit.

	Annual Growth	12/12	12/13	12/14	12/16	12/17
Sales ($ mil.)	4.1%	–	208.1	218.1	244.2	244.7
Net income ($ mil.)	(17.8%)	–	17.4	22.1	16.7	8.0
Market value ($ mil.)	–	–	–	–	–	–
Employees	–	–	–	–	–	1,400

GINKGO RESIDENTIAL TRUST INC.

301 S. College St. Ste. 3850
Charlotte NC 28202
Phone: 704-944-0100
Fax: +82-31-387-9321
Web: www.knoc.co.kr

CEO: –
CFO: –
HR: –
FYE: December 31
Type: Private

Ginkgo Residential Trust hopes its tenants make lasting memories at its apartment properties. A self-managed self-administered real estate investment trust (REIT) Ginkgo Residential acquires owns and manages multifamily residential properties in the southern US. Its properties located predominantly in North Carolina South Carolina and Virginia comprise 24 middle-market apartment complexes that together house more than 5760 units. Ginkgo Residential was formed in early 2012 to acquire the portfolio of 24 properties from predecessor company BNP Residential Properties. Shortly after its formation the REIT filed to go public.

GIRL SCOUTS OF THE UNITED STATES OF AMERICA

420 FFTH AVE 37TH ST FL G
NEW YORK, NY 10018
Phone: 212-852-8000
Fax: –
Web: www.girlscouts.org

CEO: Judith Batty
CFO: Angela Olden
HR: –
FYE: September 30
Type: Private

For the Girl Scouts of the United States of America the calendar includes one month of cookie sales and 12 months of character-building. One of the largest groups devoted to girls it has more than 2.5 million girl members plus some 800000 adult volunteers. Girl Scouts of the USA founded in 1912 is open to girls between ages 5 and 17. It strives to develop character and leadership skills through projects using technology sports the environment literacy and the arts and sciences. Girl Scouts of the USA operates through 112 chartered regional councils. The US organization is part of the World Association of Girl Guides and Girl Scouts which numbers some 10 million girls and adults in about 145 countries.

	Annual Growth	09/10	09/11	09/15	09/16	09/19
Sales ($ mil.)	(0.8%)	–	129.8	94.7	92.4	122.1
Net income ($ mil.)	–	–	(2.6)	1.4	(5.8)	(8.0)
Market value ($ mil.)	–	–	–	–	–	–
Employees	–	–	–	–	–	500

GLACIER BANCORP, INC.   NYS: GBCI

49 Commons Loop
Kalispell, MT 59901
Phone: 406 756-4200
Fax: –
Web: www.glacierbank.com

CEO: Randall Chesler
CFO: Ronald Copher
HR: –
FYE: December 31
Type: Public

Glacier Bancorp provide a full range of banking services to both individuals and businesses to about 200 locations in Montana Idaho Utah Washington Arizona Colorado and Wyoming. The bank offers retail banking business banking real estate commercial agriculture and consumer loans as well as mortgage originating and loan servicing.

	Annual Growth	12/16	12/17	12/18	12/19	12/20
Assets ($ mil.)	18.3%	9,450.6	9,706.3	12,115.5	13,684.0	18,504.2
Net income ($ mil.)	21.8%	121.1	116.4	181.9	210.5	266.4
Market value ($ mil.)	6.2%	3,457.3	3,758.8	3,780.8	4,388.7	4,390.6
Employees	7.3%	2,291	2,354	2,723	3,046	3,032

GLACIER WATER SERVICES INC.   PINK SHEETS: GWSV

1385 Park Center Dr.
Vista CA 92081
Phone: 760-560-1111
Fax: 760-560-3333
Web: www.glacierwater.com

CEO: –
CFO: –
HR: –
FYE: December 31
Type: Public

Glacier Water Services serves those who shun the tap. The company operates more than 18000 self-service vending machines that dispense filtered drinking water making it a leading brand in vended water. Its machines which are located in more than 40 US states and Canada are connected to municipal water sources and are designed to reduce impurities in the water through processes such as micron filtration reverse osmosis carbon absorption and ultraviolet disinfection. Glacier Water's machines are placed outside supermarkets and other stores. The company conducts business in Canada through subsidiary Gestion Bi-Eau Pure. Glacier Water plans to buy the Aqua Fill water vending business.

GLADSTONE CAPITAL CORPORATION   NASDAQ: GLAD

1521 Westbranch Dr. Ste. 200
McLean VA 22102
Phone: 703-287-5800
Fax: 703-287-5801
Web: www.gladstonecapital.com

CEO: David Gladstone
CFO: Nicole Schaltenbrand
HR: –
FYE: September 30
Type: Public

If your fledgling company shows promise Gladstone Capital might be glad to provide some capital. The business development company (BDC) provides loans generally between $5 million and $20 million to small and midsized family-owned US companies or firms backed by leveraged buyout funds or venture capital outfits. Gladstone Capital particularly targets firms undergoing ownership transitions. The firm then shepherds its portfolio companies towards merger or acquisition transactions or initial public offerings. Company affiliate Gladstone Management Corporation provides management services to the firm's portfolio companies. Subsidiary Gladstone Business Loan holds the loan investment portfolio.

GLADSTONE COMMERCIAL CORP   NMS: GOOD

1521 Westbranch Drive, Suite 100
McLean, VA 22102
Phone: 703 287-5800
Fax: 703 287-5801
Web: www.gladstonecommercial.com

CEO: David Gladstone
CFO: Gary Gerson
HR: –
FYE: December 31
Type: Public

Gladstone Commercial a real estate investment trust (REIT) invests in and owns office and industrial real estate properties. The company owns more than 120 properties in more than 25 states with assets that include office buildings medical office buildings warehouses retail stores and manufacturing facilities. Gladstone generally provides net leases with terms between seven and 15 years for small to very large private and public companies. The business is managed by its external adviser Gladstone Management which is also headed by chairman and CEO David Gladstone. The company's largest revenue generating states are Texas and Florida.

	Annual Growth	12/17	12/18	12/19	12/20	12/21
Sales ($ mil.)	9.8%	94.8	106.8	114.4	133.2	137.7
Net income ($ mil.)	13.3%	5.9	12.3	9.6	14.9	9.8
Market value ($ mil.)	5.2%	801.8	682.3	832.3	685.3	981.2
Employees	–	–	–	–	–	–

GLADSTONE INVESTMENT CORP   NMS: GAIN

1521 Westbranch Drive, Suite 200
McLean, VA 22102
Phone: 703 287-5800
Fax: –
Web: www.gladstoneinvestment.com

CEO: David Gladstone
CFO: Rachael Easton
HR: –
FYE: March 31
Type: Public

Gladstone Investment is happy to invest if a business shows potential for growth. The company makes debt and equity investments typically in subordinated loans mezzanine debt and preferred stock to buy out or recapitalize small and medium-sized private US businesses. It generally does so in conjunction with a company's management team or with other buyout funds. Investments usually range from $3 million to $40 million. Gladstone invests in a variety of businesses ranging from industrial product manufacturers to media companies in TV radio and publishing. Sister companies Gladstone Capital and Gladstone Commercial provide business development loans and finance commercial and industrial real estate.

	Annual Growth	03/09	03/10	03/11	03/12	03/13
Assets ($ mil.)	3.8%	326.8	297.2	241.1	325.3	379.8
Net income ($ mil.)	5.3%	13.4	10.6	16.2	13.7	16.5
Market value ($ mil.)	17.6%	101.1	158.3	205.5	200.4	193.5
Employees	–	–	–	–	–	–

GLADSTONE LAND CORP
NMS: LAND

1521 Westbranch Drive, Suite 100
McLean, VA 22102
Phone: 703 287-5800
Fax: –
Web: www.gladstonefarms.com

CEO: David Gladstone
CFO: Lewis Parrish
HR: –
FYE: December 31
Type: Public

Gladstone Land buys farm properties in the US and rents them to corporate farming operations and medium-sized independent farmers through triple net leases arrangements in which the tenant is responsible for maintaining the property. Gladstone Land is an externally managed real estate company that owns about a dozen row crop properties in California and Florida which total more than 1600 acres. It leases most of its properties to Dole Fresh Vegetables a subsidiary of Dole Foods which uses the farmland to grow annual fruit and vegetable crops like berries melons and lettuce among others. Gladstone Land went public in early 2013 with an offering worth $50 million.

	Annual Growth	12/17	12/18	12/19	12/20	12/21
Sales ($ mil.)	31.6%	25.1	36.7	40.7	57.0	75.3
Net income ($ mil.)	–	(0.0)	2.6	1.7	4.9	3.5
Market value ($ mil.)	25.9%	459.4	392.7	443.7	500.8	1,154.9
Employees	–	–	–	–	–	–

GLASSBRIDGE ENTERPRISES INC
NBB: GLAE

411 East 57th Street, Suite 1-A
New York, NY 10022
Phone: 212 220-3300
Fax: –
Web: www.imation.com

CEO: Daniel Strauss
CFO: Francis Ruchalski
HR: –
FYE: December 31
Type: Public

GlassBridge (formerly Imation) is off to a fresh start. The company owns and operates an asset management business and a sports investment platform through majority owned Adara Enterprises Corp. (Adara) and Sport-BLX Inc. (SportBLX) among other subsidiaries. It also operates its diversified private asset management business through a number of subsidiaries (GlassBridge Investment Management LLC Adara Asset Management LLC and GlassBridge Capital LLC) that sponsor the company's fund offerings. GlassBridge acquired its sports investment platform in 2019 by purchasing a controlling interest in SportBLX. The company also sold all of its international subsidiaries (Imation Subsidiaries) to IMN Capital Holdings Inc. in 2019.

	Annual Growth	12/16	12/17	12/18	12/19	12/20
Sales ($ mil.)	(67.4%)	44.1	36.5	–	0.1	0.5
Net income ($ mil.)	–	(125.2)	(8.4)	4.1	20.2	(62.3)
Market value ($ mil.)	–	0.0	0.0	0.0	6.3	1.3
Employees	(53.3%)	167	120	5	17	–

GLASSHOUSE TECHNOLOGIES INC.

200 Crossing Blvd.
Framingham MA 01702
Phone: 508-879-5729
Fax: 508-879-7319
Web: www.glasshouse.com

CEO: –
CFO: –
HR: –
FYE: December 31
Type: Private

GlassHouse wants businesses to put down their stones and pick up its data center IT services. The company provides a range of managed services to improve the way businesses store retrieve and maintain data. Offering consulting cloud services data center management and technology integration the company specializes in such areas as virtualization data center migration and operational support services. It also resells third-party hardware and software. GlassHouse serves customers — about half of the Fortune 100 among them — in the public sector and the energy entertainment and travel industries among others and have included such companies as Biogen Idec and JPMorgan Chase.

GLATFELTER CORP
NYS: GLT

4350 Congress Street, Suite 600
Charlotte, NC 28209
Phone: 704 885-2555
Fax: 717 846-7208
Web: www.glatfelter.com

CEO: Dante Parrini
CFO: Samuel Hillard
HR: Eileen Beck
FYE: December 31
Type: Public

Glatfelter Corporation (formerly P. H. Glatfelter) is a leading supplier engineered products. Its Germany-based Composite Fibers unit makes products like coffee and tea filter paper and metallized products used in labels and packaging while the Airlaid Materials business focuses on nonwoven fabric-like materials used in feminine hygiene products and other hygiene products and wipes. Over 80% of the company's total sales are generated outside the US. The company trace its roots back in 1864. In 2020 the company changed its name to Glatfelter Corporation.

	Annual Growth	12/16	12/17	12/18	12/19	12/20
Sales ($ mil.)	(13.2%)	1,610.9	1,596.4	866.3	927.7	916.5
Net income ($ mil.)	(0.3%)	21.6	7.9	(177.6)	(21.5)	21.3
Market value ($ mil.)	(9.0%)	1,059.9	951.2	433.0	811.9	726.7
Employees	(13.7%)	4,346	4,175	2,600	2,557	2,415

GLEACHER & CO, INC. (DE)
NMS: GLCH

1290 Avenue of the Americas
New York, NY 10104
Phone: 212 273-7100
Fax: –
Web: www.gleacher.com

CEO: –
CFO: –
HR: –
FYE: December 31
Type: Public

Gleacher & Co. provides advisory services capital raising research and securities and brokerage services to institutional clients in the US and Europe. The firm's MBS/ABS & Rates arm sells and trades asset and mortgage-backed securities. Gleacher's Corporate Credit unit offers sales and trading on a range of debt securities. Its FA Technology Ventures subsidiary provides growth capital to technology firms. Gleacher is restructuring after exiting its primary business investment banking and selling its ClearPoint Funding subsidiary in 2013. The firm's namesake founder and former chairman Eric Gleacher has resigned.

	Annual Growth	12/08	12/09	12/10	12/11	12/12
Assets ($ mil.)	15.4%	694.3	1,216.2	1,657.9	3,303.6	1,229.6
Net income ($ mil.)	–	(17.4)	54.9	(20.6)	(82.1)	(77.7)
Market value ($ mil.)	(29.0%)	18.5	27.8	14.7	10.5	4.7
Employees	(3.6%)	255	342	368	453	220

GLEN BURNIE BANCORP
NAS: GLBZ

101 Crain Highway, S.E.
Glen Burnie, MD 21061
Phone: 410 766-3300
Fax: –
Web: www.thebankofglenburnie.com

CEO: John Long
CFO: Jeffrey Harris
HR: Michelle Stambaugh
FYE: December 31
Type: Public

Glen Burnie Bancorp has an interest in the Old Line State. The institution is the holding company for Bank of Glen Burnie which has about 10 branches in central Maryland's Anne Arundel County south of Baltimore. The bank offers such services as checking and savings accounts money market and individual retirement accounts CDs and remote banking services. It focuses on real estate lending with residential and commercial mortgages accounting for the largest portions of its loan portfolio. The bank also writes indirect automobile loans which are originated through a network of about 50 area car dealers. Bank of Glen Burnie was founded in 1949.

	Annual Growth	12/16	12/17	12/18	12/19	12/20
Assets ($ mil.)	1.9%	388.4	389.5	413.0	384.9	419.5
Net income ($ mil.)	11.0%	1.1	0.9	1.6	1.6	1.7
Market value ($ mil.)	(1.1%)	32.7	31.4	29.6	32.7	31.3
Employees	(0.5%)	92	99	98	102	90

GLENDALE ADVENTIST MEDICAL CENTER INC

1509 WILSON TER
GLENDALE, CA 912064007
Phone: 818-409-8000
Fax: –
Web: www.glendaleadventist.com

CEO: Kevin A Roberts
CFO: –
HR: Susan Crabtree
FYE: December 31
Type: Private

Treating ladies from Pasadena and other patients throughout the suburbs of sunny Southern California Glendale Adventist Medical Center (GAMC) is a stalwart community member. The hospital is part of Adventist Health a not-for-profit group of about 20 hospitals and health care organizations in four western states. GAMC provides a range of specialty services including cancer treatment cardiology emergency medicine neuroscience home care psychiatry rehabilitation and women's healthcare. It also provides medical training and residency programs. The 515-bed hospital was founded in 1905 by the Seventh-Day Adventist Church.

	Annual Growth	06/04	06/05*	12/07	12/09	12/12
Sales ($ mil.)	(12.5%)	–	985.2	273.7	307.8	387.1
Net income ($ mil.)	95.1%	–	–	0.2	12.7	5.5
Market value ($ mil.)	–	–	–	–	–	–
Employees	–	–	–	–	–	2,600

*Fiscal year change

GLENN O. HAWBAKER INC.

1952 WADDLE RD STE 203
STATE COLLEGE, PA 16803-1649
Phone: 814-237-1444
Fax: –
Web: www.goh-inc.com

CEO: –
CFO: –
HR: –
FYE: December 31
Type: Private

For Glenn O. Hawbaker (GOH) it's all about making the grade. Founded as an excavating and grading company GOH provides heavy construction concrete construction utility work asphalt production and heavy equipment rentals and sales. From its home base in Pennsylvania the company serves customers in the north-central portion of the state. As part of its business GOH operates two dozen quarries and eight asphalt production facilities in Pennsylvania New York and eastern Ohio (since 2012). Its Hawbaker Engineering subsidiary provides civil engineering services and site designs. The family-owned company was founded in 1952 by Glenn and Thelma Hawbaker the parents of president and CEO Daniel Hawbaker.

	Annual Growth	12/08	12/09	12/10	12/11	12/12
Sales ($ mil.)	4.4%	–	220.5	337.6	326.1	251.0
Net income ($ mil.)	(50.3%)	–	7.8	25.3	20.8	1.0
Market value ($ mil.)	–	–	–	–	–	–
Employees	–	–	–	–	–	1,300

GLIMCHER REALTY TRUST

180 East Broad Street
Columbus, OH 43215
Phone: 614 621-9000
Fax: 614 621-9311
Web: www.glimcher.com

NYS: GRT
CEO: –
CFO: –
HR: –
FYE: December 31
Type: Public

In Glimcher's ideal world we'd all be shopaholics. A self-administered and self-managed real estate investment trust (REIT) Glimcher acquires develops and manages retail real estate. Its portfolio includes about 25 enclosed and open-air shopping malls (a handful are owned through joint ventures) and three strip shopping centers. Its properties which have more than 21 million sq. ft. of space are scattered across 15 states; Ohio is home to the greatest number of its properties. The company's occupancy rate is around 95%. Major tenants include L Brands The Gap and Foot Locker.

	Annual Growth	12/08	12/09	12/10	12/11	12/12
Sales ($ mil.)	0.5%	319.1	308.4	274.8	267.9	326.0
Net income ($ mil.)	–	16.8	4.6	5.9	19.6	(2.1)
Market value ($ mil.)	40.9%	402.1	386.3	1,202.0	1,316.4	1,586.9
Employees	0.9%	1,054	1,038	1,428	1,088	1,094

GLOBAL AXCESS CORP.

7800 Belfort Parkway, Suite 165
Jacksonville, FL 32256
Phone: 904 280-3950
Fax: –
Web: www.globalaxcess.biz

NBB: GAXC Q
CEO: Kevin L Reager
CFO: Michael J Loiacono
HR: –
FYE: December 31
Type: Public

Global Axcess has no ax to grind just a bunch of kiosks to manage. Through subsidiary Nationwide Money Services the company operates a network of some 4700 ATMs around the US. More than half of the ATMs it manages are owned by merchants but Global Axcess does own around 2000 of the machines. The company provides maintenance cash management and network processing services; it processes some 1.5 million financial transactions per month. Its machine network is concentrated in the South and East. In 2009 Global Axcess formed subsidiary Nationwide Ntertainment to operate self-serve DVD rental kiosks under the InstaFlix brand. It operates more than 500 of the mini video rental stores.

	Annual Growth	12/08	12/09	12/10	12/11	12/12
Sales ($ mil.)	8.9%	22.2	21.5	22.7	31.9	31.2
Net income ($ mil.)	–	1.2	2.8	(0.9)	(1.9)	(12.1)
Market value ($ mil.)	(8.5%)	3.0	20.2	12.7	13.6	2.1
Employees	0.0%	45	48	61	54	45

GLOBAL BRASS & COPPER HOLDINGS INC

475 N. Martingale Road, Suite 1200
Schaumburg, IL 60173
Phone: 847 240-4700
Fax: –
Web: www.gbcholdings.com

NYS: BRSS
CEO: John J Wasz
CFO: Christopher J Kodosky
HR: –
FYE: December 31
Type: Public

Global Brass and Copper Holdings (GBC) is okay knowing that not all that glitters is gold. Through its subsidiaries GBC is a leading North American manufacturer and distributor of fabricated copper and copper-alloy products. The company's operations are divided into three segments: Olin Brass (fabricator of copper and brass sheet strip foil and tubing) Chase Brass (manufacturer of brass rods used by OEMs to make valves fittings and other machining products) and A.J. Oster (distributor of copper-alloy products). GBC serves customers from a variety of sectors including construction automotive coinage electronics and industrial manufacturing. Formed in 2007 the company went public in 2013.

	Annual Growth	12/13	12/14	12/15	12/16	12/17
Sales ($ mil.)	(2.9%)	1,758.5	1,711.4	1,506.2	1,338.5	1,560.8
Net income ($ mil.)	48.7%	10.4	31.7	35.6	32.2	50.9
Market value ($ mil.)	18.9%	362.6	288.3	466.6	751.4	725.1
Employees	(1.7%)	2,062	1,896	1,900	1,857	1,926

GLOBAL BRASS AND COPPER HOLDINGS INC.

1901 N. Roselle Rd. Ste. 800
Schaumburg IL 60195
Phone: 847-517-6340
Fax: 610-687-9565
Web: www.jlyonsmarketing.com

CEO: John J Wasz
CFO: –
HR: –
FYE: December 31
Type: Private

Global Brass and Copper Holdings (GBC) is okay knowing that not all that glitters is gold. Through its subsidiaries GBC is a leading North American manufacturer and distributor of fabricated copper and copper-alloy products. The company's operations are divided into three segments: Olin Brass (fabricator of copper and brass sheet strip foil and tubing) Chase Brass (manufacturer of brass rods used by OEMs to make valves fittings and other machining products) and A.J. Oster (distributor of copper-alloy products). GBC serves customers from a variety of sectors including construction automotive coinage electronics and industrial manufacturing. Formed in 2007 the company filed to go public in 2011.

GLOBAL BROKERAGE INC   NBB: GLBR

55 Water Street, Floor 50   CEO: Kenneth Grossman
New York, NY 10041   CFO: Robert Lande
Phone: 212 897-7660   HR: Amy Napolitano
Fax: –   FYE: December 31
Web: www.fxcm.com   Type: Public

Money talks in more than a dozen different languages at FXCM. The online brokerage specializes in over-the-counter (OTC) foreign exchange (forex) trading for individual investors or transactions that are bought in one currency and sold in another. FXCM operates through FXCM Holdings which processes more than 300000 trades per day for its 163000 account holders. The firm's institutional trading segment FXCM Pro used by banks hedge funds and other financial service companies accounts for less than 10% of revenue. More than three-quarters of the company's trading volume comes from outside the US. FXCM was founded in 1999 and went public in a 2010 initial public offering (IPO).

	Annual Growth	12/12	12/13	12/14	12/15	12/16
Sales ($ mil.)	(9.2%)	417.3	489.6	463.8	402.3	284.1
Net income ($ mil.)	67.6%	9.0	14.8	17.2	(553.9)	70.6
Market value ($ mil.)	(8.5%)	61.9	109.6	101.8	102.8	43.3
Employees	(2.3%)	864	934	908	871	787

GLOBAL COMMUNICATION SEMICONDUCTORS INC.

23155 Kashiwa Ct.   CEO: Bau-Hsing Ann
Torrance CA 90505-4026   CFO: –
Phone: 310-530-7274   HR: –
Fax: 310-530-7279   FYE: June 30
Web: www.gcsincorp.com   Type: Private

Global Communication Semiconductors (GCS) aspires to be a global force in communications chips. GCS offers contract manufacturing or foundry services to makers of chips used in RF communications devices such as wireless phones and base stations as well as telecommunications and high-speed networking. GCS uses compound semiconductor materials that offer various performance benefits — such as faster operation or lower power consumption — in comparison with standard silicon. Global Communication Semiconductors was founded by former CEO Owen Wu in 1997. The company is owned by several individuals and institutional investors including RF Micro Devices (12% ownership).

GLOBAL CUSTOM COMMERCE L.P.

10555 Richmond Ave. Ste. 200   CEO: –
Houston TX 77042   CFO: –
Phone: 800-505-1905   HR: –
Fax: 800-810-5919   FYE: December 31
Web: www.blinds.com   Type: Private

NoBrainerBlinds.com makes and markets custom window shades shutters and blinds. The company offers popular brand names including Hunter Douglas Bali Levolor and Graber among others. The company sells its window coverings through its Web site which also offers decorating advice on topics ranging from installation and maintenance to child- and pet-proofing customers' homes. Company president and CEO Jay Steinfeld founded NoBrainerBlinds in 1996.

GLOBAL DIVERSIFIED INDUSTRIES INC.   OTC: GDIV

1200 Airport Dr.   CEO: –
Chowchilla CA 93610   CFO: –
Phone: 559-665-5800   HR: –
Fax: 559-665-5700   FYE: April 30
Web: www.gdvi.net   Type: Public

Global Diversified Industries is the new mod squad. Through its Global Modular subsidiary the company makes pre-fabricated portable modular buildings mainly for use as classrooms. It also constructs permanent one- and two-story structures. Clients include public and private schools universities child-care facilities and municipalities. The company is active throughout California. Global Diversified divested its MBS Construction subsidiary which provided construction site management services in 2006. Company president Phil Hamilton has voting control of more than 20% of Global Diversified's stock.

GLOBAL EARTH ENERGY INC.   OTC: GLER

534 Delaware Ave. Ste. 412   CEO: –
Buffalo NY 14202   CFO: –
Phone: 716-332-7150   HR: –
Fax: 716-332-7170   FYE: August 31
Web: www.globalearthenergy.com   Type: Public

Global Earth Energy (formerly Global Wataire) believes strongly that the global earth energy to exploit is biodiesel. The company plans to build on the growing momentum for using biodiesel as way to decrease US dependency on foreign crude oil and limit carbon emissions by establishing a 1 million-gallon-per-year biodiesel production plant in North Carolina. It is also planning to move into the even greener energy sources of solar and wind power generation. The company acquired Kentucky-based Samuel Coal for $7.5 million in 2011. Formerly operating as water purification firm Global Wataire the company changed its name and industry focus in 2008. Chairman Betty-Ann Harland owns 25% of Global Earth Energy.

GLOBAL GEOPHYSICAL SERVICES INC   NYS: GGS

13927 South Gessner Road   CEO: –
Missouri City, TX 77489   CFO: –
Phone: 713 972-9200   HR: –
Fax: –   FYE: December 31
   Type: Public

Global Geophysical builds its business from the ground down. It provides seismic data acquisition services to the oil and gas industry for locating potential reservoirs and studying known reserves. Global Geophysical transmits sound waves below the earth's surface to create images of the existing subsurface geology. Its integrated suite of seismic data solutions includes high-resolution RG-3D Reservoir Grade seismic data acquisition microseismic monitoring seismic data processing and interpretation services and Multi Client data products. The firm's seismic crews work in a wide variety of terrains including deserts jungles mountains and swamps and have completed projects in more than 100 countries.

	Annual Growth	12/08	12/09	12/10	12/11	12/12
Sales ($ mil.)	(2.6%)	376.3	312.8	254.7	385.4	339.0
Net income ($ mil.)	–	(8.0)	0.4	(39.7)	5.7	(13.3)
Market value ($ mil.)	(39.1%)	–	–	390.3	252.7	144.8
Employees	13.6%	–	818	1,667	1,300	1,200

GLOBAL INDUSTRIAL COMPANY
NYS: GIC

11 Harbor Park Drive
Port Washington, NY 11050
Phone: 516 608-7000
Fax: –
Web: www.systemax.com

CEO: Barry Litwin
CFO: Thomas Clark
HR: –
FYE: December 31
Type: Public

Systemax is a direct marketer of brand name and private label industrial and business equipment and supplies in North America. Systemax also sells a wide array of material-handling equipment shelving storage items furniture and office janitorial and maintenance and other industrial products. Its customers include businesses government agencies and schools as well as individual consumers. In addition the company currently operates multiple e-commerce sites including www.globalindustrial.com www.globalindustrial.com and www.industrialsupplies.com. Systemax was founded in 1949 as Global Equipment Company. Majority of the company's revenue comes from the US.

	Annual Growth	12/16	12/17	12/18	12/19	12/20
Sales ($ mil.)	(11.5%)	1,680.1	1,265.4	896.9	946.9	1,029.0
Net income ($ mil.)	–	(32.6)	40.4	224.7	48.5	65.4
Market value ($ mil.)	42.2%	329.3	1,249.4	897.1	944.8	1,347.7
Employees	(14.7%)	2,800	1,900	1,550	1,430	1,480

GLOBAL PACIFIC PRODUCE INC.

11500 S EASTRN AVE 120
HENDERSON, NV 89052
Phone: 702-898-8051
Fax: –
Web: www.globalpacificproduce.com

CEO: –
CFO: –
HR: –
FYE: December 31
Type: Private

Global Pacific Produce is a leading exporter of fresh produce serving international retailers. It sources such goods as apples citrus grapes pears and stone fruit mostly from California and Mexico. The company supplies grocery store chains and other retailers in South America and Europe. Chris Kilvington originally from London started the business in 2000.

	Annual Growth	12/08	12/09*	01/11*	12/11	12/12
Sales ($ mil.)	26.0%	–	157.7	192.8	263.0	315.4
Net income ($ mil.)	60.6%	–	2.4	4.5	5.8	9.8
Market value ($ mil.)	–	–	–	–	–	–
Employees	–	–	–	–	–	250

*Fiscal year change

GLOBAL PARTNERS LP
NYS: GLP

P.O. Box 9161, 800 South Street
Waltham, MA 02454-9161
Phone: 781 894-8800
Fax: –
Web: www.globalp.com

CEO: Eric Slifka
CFO: Daphne H Foster
HR: –
FYE: December 31
Type: Public

Global Partners imports petroleum products from global sources but its marketing is largely regional. The company wholesales heating oil residual fuel oil diesel oil kerosene distillates and gasoline to commercial retail and wholesale customers in New England and New York. A major player in the regional home heating oil market Global Partners operates storage facilities at 25 bulk terminals each with a storage capacity of more than 50000 barrels and with a collective storage capacity of 10.8 million barrels. It also owns and supplies a network of gasoline stations. Wholesale revenues accounts for the bulk of the company's sales.

	Annual Growth	12/16	12/17	12/18	12/19	12/20
Sales ($ mil.)	0.2%	8,239.6	8,920.6	12,672.6	13,081.7	8,321.6
Net income ($ mil.)	–	(199.4)	58.8	103.9	35.9	102.2
Market value ($ mil.)	(3.9%)	665.1	571.1	557.4	689.4	568.3
Employees	18.9%	1,770	2,000	2,500	3,860	3,540

GLOBAL PAYMENTS INC
NYS: GPN

3550 Lenox Road
Atlanta, GA 30326
Phone: 770 829-8000
Fax: –
Web: www.globalpaymentsinc.com

CEO: Jeffrey Sloan
CFO: Paul Todd
HR: –
FYE: December 31
Type: Public

Global Payments provides credit and debit card processing and other electronic payment processing services for approximately 3.5 million merchant and business locations worldwide including retailers and financial institutions. The company also provides authorization services settlement and funding services customer support and help-desk functions fraud solution services prepaid debit and payroll cards demand deposit accounts and other financial service solutions to the underbanked. It also provides a variety of value-added services including specialty point-of-sale solutions analytic and customer engagement tools and payroll and human capital management services. Generates about 85% of sales from the Americas the company operates in more than 100 countries throughout North America Europe Asia-Pacific and Latin America.

	Annual Growth	12/17	12/18	12/19	12/20	12/21
Sales ($ mil.)	21.0%	3,975.2	3,366.4	4,911.9	7,423.6	8,523.8
Net income ($ mil.)	19.8%	468.4	452.1	430.6	584.5	965.5
Market value ($ mil.)	7.8%	28,543.4	29,366.3	51,984.0	61,340.9	38,492.6
Employees	25.7%	10,000	11,000	24,000	24,000	25,000

GLOBAL TELECOM & TECHNOLOGY INC.
OTC: GTLT

8484 Westpark Dr. Ste. 720
McLean VA 22102
Phone: 703-442-5500
Fax: 703-442-5501
Web: www.gt-t.net

CEO: Ernie Ortega
CFO: Donna Granato
HR: –
FYE: December 31
Type: Public

Global Telecom & Technology (GTT) gets carried away providing network integration for wide area network (WAN) dedicated Internet access and managed data services to system integrators telecom carriers and government agencies. GTT combines multiple networks and technologies such as traditional OC-x MPLS and Ethernet and has distribution partnerships with more than 800 technology suppliers including iPass for wireless services. Past customers include Avaya Lockheed Martin and Telefonica. GTT counts customers in about 80 countries; it earns almost half of its revenues outside the US. Chairman H. Brian Thompson owns nearly 31% of the company's stock.

GLOBAL TRAFFIC NETWORK INC.

880 3rd Ave. 6th Fl.
New York NY 10022
Phone: 212-896-1255
Fax: 312-669-9800
Web: www.emergenow.com

CEO: –
CFO: –
HR: –
FYE: June 30
Type: Subsidiary

Great just what we need: more traffic. Global Traffic Network (GTN) provides customized traffic reports to some 70 radio stations in nearly 20 markets in Australia. In exchange for its content GTN receives commercial airtime from the stations which the company sells to advertisers. In addition the firm produces radio and TV news reports in Australia. GTN additionally provides radio traffic reporting services to more than 10 stations in the UK and does business in the US through a deal with Metro Networks. It provides traffic reports in Canada through an agreement with Corus Entertainment and provides news weather sports and business reports in Canada through subsidiary Wise Broadcasting Network.

GLOBALOPTIONS GROUP INC.
NASDAQ: GLOI

75 Rockefeller Plaza 27th Fl.
New York NY 10019
Phone: 212-445-6262
Fax: 212-445-0053
Web: www.globaloptionsgroup.com

CEO: –
CFO: –
HR: –
FYE: December 31
Type: Public

GlobalOptions likes to think of itself as the secure choice. The firm provides security consulting and investigation services including risk mitigation decision support emergency management litigation support anti-fraud solutions business intelligence and related security services. The company provides services to government entities corporations and high net-worth and high-profile individuals. The company divested its Fraud and Special Investigative Unit (SIU) as well as its Preparedness Services and Forensic DNA Solutions and Products units in 2010. GlobalOptions was founded in 1999.

GLOBALSCAPE INC
ASE: GSB

4500 Lockhill-Selma, Suite 150
San Antonio, TX 78249
Phone: 210 308-8267
Fax: –
Web: www.globalscape.com

CEO: Robert H Alpert
CFO: Karen J Young
HR: –
FYE: December 31
Type: Public

GlobalSCAPE is pretty cute for a software company. With packages like CuteFTP and Enhanced File Transfer (EFT) Server GlobalSCAPE provides managed file transfer software for businesses and individuals. The company also offers software used to collaborate share and backup data in real-time across multiple sites. Its software which is also offered in hosted and managed versions is sold primarily to small and midsized businesses and enterprise customers worldwide. GlobalSCAPE has counted Aon Thomas Cook Lone Star Bank and the US Army among its clients. More than two-thirds of sales come from customers in the US.

	Annual Growth	12/14	12/15	12/16	12/17	12/18
Sales ($ mil.)	6.5%	26.8	30.8	33.3	33.9	34.4
Net income ($ mil.)	4.8%	3.0	4.6	4.0	1.4	3.7
Market value ($ mil.)	19.2%	38.0	68.7	69.7	60.8	76.7
Employees	(3.3%)	105	126	133	137	92

GLOBALSTAR INC
ASE: GSAT

1351 Holiday Square Blvd.
Covington, LA 70433
Phone: 985 335-1500
Fax: –
Web: www.globalstar.com

CEO: David Kagan
CFO: Rebecca Clary
HR: Colleen McDonald
FYE: December 31
Type: Public

Globalstar provides satellite voice and data service to remote areas where landlines and cell towers are few if anywhere. Its network of satellites and ground stations provides service to approximately 750000 subscribers worldwide. Customers include the US government as well as companies in the energy maritime agriculture forestry and mining industries. Half of its ground stations are operated by independent companies that buy Globalstar's services on a wholesale basis. It also sells a handheld GPS navigation system called SPOT for adventure travelers or anyone needing a GPS device.

	Annual Growth	12/16	12/17	12/18	12/19	12/20
Sales ($ mil.)	7.3%	96.9	112.7	130.1	131.7	128.5
Net income ($ mil.)	–	(132.6)	(89.1)	(6.5)	15.3	(109.6)
Market value ($ mil.)	(32.0%)	2,646.0	2,193.8	1,071.3	868.7	567.0
Employees	0.1%	344	333	353	336	346

GLOBE LIFE INC
NYS: GL

3700 South Stonebridge Drive
McKinney, TX 75070
Phone: 972 569-4000
Fax: –
Web: www.torchmarkcorp.com

CEO: Gary Coleman
CFO: Frank Svoboda
HR: –
FYE: December 31
Type: Public

Globe Life (formerly Torchmark) specializes in providing individual life insurance and supplemental health insurance to middle-income families. Globe Life's subsidiaries including American Income Life and Globe Life and Accident offer whole and term life insurance policies and supplemental health insurance coverage including illness accident and Medicare Supplement policies. Globe Life sells its products through direct marketing efforts and a network of exclusive and independent agents. Substantially all of Globe Life's business is conducted in the US.

	Annual Growth	12/16	12/17	12/18	12/19	12/20
Assets ($ mil.)	7.9%	21,436.1	23,475.0	23,095.7	25,977.5	29,046.7
Net income ($ mil.)	7.4%	549.8	1,454.5	701.5	760.8	731.8
Market value ($ mil.)	6.5%	7,656.1	9,415.5	7,736.0	10,924.7	9,856.6
Employees	1.0%	3,128	3,102	3,102	3,196	3,261

GLOBE SPECIALTY METALS INC
NMS: GSM

600 Brickell Ave, Suite 1500
Miami, FL 33131
Phone: 786 509-6900
Fax: 212 798-8185
Web: www.glbsm.com

CEO: –
CFO: Joseph Ragan
HR: –
FYE: June 30
Type: Public

Globe Specialty Metals is an apt name for a company that peddles its metals around the world. The specialty metals manufacturer sells silicon metal and silicon-based alloys to customers in the Americas Asia and Europe from facilities in the US Argentina China and Poland. Its silicon metal and alloys are used to make a variety of industrial products from aluminum and automotive parts to steel and semiconductors. It holds about one-fifth of the Western market share for magnesium ferrosilicon. Globe also recycles by-products such as silica fume (a dustlike material known as microsilica that is collected in air filtration systems) which it sells for use as a concrete additive.

	Annual Growth	06/10	06/11	06/12	06/13	06/14
Sales ($ mil.)	12.3%	472.7	641.9	705.5	757.6	752.8
Net income ($ mil.)	(19.4%)	34.1	52.8	54.6	(21.0)	14.4
Market value ($ mil.)	19.1%	761.8	1,653.5	990.5	801.7	1,532.5
Employees	8.4%	1,136	1,213	1,493	1,353	1,569

GLOBEIMMUNE, INC
NBB: GBIM

1450 Infinite Drive
Louisville, CO 80027
Phone: 303 625-2700
Fax: –
Web: www.globeimmune.com

CEO: Timothy Rodell
CFO: –
HR: –
FYE: December 31
Type: Public

GlobeImmune would like to stop disease around the world. For now it works on its proprietary Tarmogen method of stimulating cell-level immunity to cancer and other diseases. It has five cancer candidates targeting pancreatic lung colorectal and thyroid cancers while the fifth addresses the metastasis mechanism in multiple tumors. GlobeImmune's current infectious disease candidates seek to permanently cure hepatitis B and C. The company which produces its own products works with Celgene and Gilead Sciences to develop and commercialize the cancer and infectious disease drugs respectively. The company was formed in 1995 as Ceres Pharmaceutical and changed its name in 2001. It went public in 2014.

	Annual Growth	12/11	12/12	12/13	12/14	12/15
Sales ($ mil.)	–	0.0	14.6	22.5	6.0	6.5
Net income ($ mil.)	–	0.0	(2.0)	9.5	(16.3)	(2.8)
Market value ($ mil.)	–	0.0	–	–	43.7	22.3
Employees	(90.9%)	–	–	–	22	2

GLOBUS MEDICAL INC
NYS: GMED

2560 General Armistead Avenue
Audubon, PA 19403
Phone: 610 930-1800
Fax: 302 636-5454
Web: www.globusmedical.com

CEO: David Demski
CFO: Keith Pfeil
HR: –
FYE: December 31
Type: Public

Globus Medical makes procedural and therapeutic medical devices used during spinal surgery. Offerings range from screws and plates to disc replacement systems and bone void fillers. The company has two product segments: Musculoskeletal Solutions (implantable devices biologics surgical instruments and accessories) and Enabling Technologies (imaging navigation and robotic-assisted surgery systems). Globus Medical has more than 220 spinal devices on the market in the US where it earns most of its revenue; its products are also sold in more than 50 countries worldwide.

	Annual Growth	12/17	12/18	12/19	12/20	12/21
Sales ($ mil.)	10.8%	636.0	713.0	785.4	789.0	958.1
Net income ($ mil.)	8.6%	107.3	156.5	155.2	102.3	149.2
Market value ($ mil.)	15.1%	4,173.5	4,394.8	5,978.9	6,622.7	7,331.5
Employees	12.5%	1,500	1,800	2,000	2,200	2,400

GLORI ENERGY INC.

4315 South Dr.
Houston TX 77053
Phone: 713-237-8880
Fax: 860-676-8655
Web: www.horizontechnologyfinancecorp.com

CEO: Kevin Guilbeau
CFO: Victor Perez
HR: Lynn Thompson
FYE: December 31
Type: Private

"Like oil and water" may no longer be a cliche if Glori Energy has its way. The company's novel AERO System for oil recovery uses naturally occurring microbes to break down the barrier between oil and water allowing more oil to flow from underground formations. It uses a three-step approach to create custom nutrient formulas for microbes at each well site and estimates that its technology which uses existing pumps and pipelines can increase oil recovery by up to 100%. While it sounds like something from a sci-fi movie Shell Husky Merit Energy and Citation Oil are all customers; it has about 10 projects in various stages. Glori Energy filed to go public in 2011 but withdrew the IPO a year later.

GLYCOMIMETICS INC
NMS: GLYC

9708 Medical Center Drive
Rockville, MD 20850
Phone: 240 243-1201
Fax: –
Web: www.glycomimetics.com

CEO: Harout Semerjian
CFO: Brian Hahn
HR: –
FYE: December 31
Type: Public

Carbs are a good thing to GlycoMimetics. The biotechnology company uses carbohydrate chemistry to develop drug candidates for rare diseases. Its lead drug candidate is designed to treat vaso-occlusive crisis (VOC) a painful condition that affects people with sickle cell disease. If approved it would be the first drug to treat the cause of VOC and potentially reduce dependence on narcotics for pain management. Pfizer bought the rights to develop and commercialize the VOC drug. In addition the company is developing a drug to assist people with acute myeloid leukemia (AML) during chemotherapy. GlycoMimetics went public in 2014. It raised $56 million and plans to use the proceeds to further fund clinical trials.

	Annual Growth	12/12	12/13	12/14	12/15	12/16
Sales ($ mil.)	(81.3%)	15.3	4.0	15.0	20.1	0.0
Net income ($ mil.)	–	3.7	(10.6)	(11.1)	(12.8)	(31.8)
Market value ($ mil.)	(8.0%)	–	–	167.4	133.0	141.8
Employees	10.7%	28	27	34	38	42

GNC HOLDINGS INC
NYS: GNC

300 Sixth Avenue
Pittsburgh, PA 15222
Phone: 412 288-4600
Fax: –
Web: www.gnc.com

CEO: –
CFO: –
HR: –
FYE: December 31
Type: Public

Vitamins and supplements are part of the daily regimen at GNC Holdings. GNC Holdings operates the world's leading nutritional-supplements retail chain devoted to items such as vitamins supplements minerals and dietary products. The firm manufactures private-label products for Rite Aid Sam's Club and PetSmart. Altogether GNC boasts more than 8000 stores including some 3200 company-owned stores in the US Canada and Puerto Rico; 1000 franchised stores in the US; nearly 2000 franchised stores internationally in about 50 countries; and more than 2000 store-within-a-store sites in Rite Aid locations. The vast majority of its sales comes from US.

	Annual Growth	12/14	12/15	12/16	12/17	12/18
Sales ($ mil.)	(2.6%)	2,613.2	2,639.2	2,540.0	2,453.0	2,353.5
Net income ($ mil.)	(27.7%)	255.9	219.3	(286.3)	(148.9)	69.8
Market value ($ mil.)	(52.6%)	3,939.3	2,602.1	926.1	309.5	198.8
Employees	(1.6%)	16,500	16,900	16,800	16,600	15,500

GODFATHER'S PIZZA INC.

2808 N. 108th St.
Omaha NE 68114
Phone: 402-391-1452
Fax: 402-255-2687
Web: www.godfathers.com

CEO: –
CFO: Richard W Ramm
HR: –
FYE: May 31
Type: Private

Maybe the head of this family is named Don Pizzeria. Godfather's Pizza operates a leading quick-service restaurant chain with more than 600 family-oriented pizza joints in more than 40 states mostly in the Upper Midwest. The parlors offer a crew of pizzas and a mob of topping choices as well as appetizers salads and sandwiches. The company's locations typically offer dine-in delivery and carry-out service. More than 100 restaurants are company-owned while the rest are franchised. Founded by Nebraska native Willy Theisen in 1973 the business is owned by a group led by CEO Ron Gartlan.

GOLD RESERVE INC
TVX: GRZ

999 West Riverside Avenue, Suite 401
Spokane, WA 99201
Phone: 509 623-1500
Fax: 509 623-1634
Web: www.goldreserveinc.com

CEO: Rockne Timm
CFO: Robert A McGuinness
HR: –
FYE: December 31
Type: Public

Gold Reserve's primary asset was the Brisas project in Venezuela which contains estimated reserves of about 10 million ounces of gold and 1.4 billion pounds of copper. Gold Reserve had been developing Brisas since 1992. However all activity on the mine ceased in late 2009 when the Venezuelan government canceled Gold Reserve's permits and seized the assets of the Brisas project. The company is pursuing an arbitration claim through the World Bank against the Venezuelan government in an effort to recoup its investment in the Brisas project. The company is restructuring its debt while it continues it $2.1 arbitration claim.

	Annual Growth	12/16	12/17	12/18	12/19	12/20
Sales ($ mil.)	–	(0.5)	170.7	51.6	1.6	0.3
Net income ($ mil.)	–	(21.5)	89.5	41.9	(13.1)	(11.5)
Market value ($ mil.)	(21.3%)	414.6	327.0	204.8	149.8	159.0
Employees						

GOLD RESOURCE CORP
ASE: GORO

2000 South Colorado Blvd., Tower 1, Suite 10200
Denver, CO 80222
Phone: 303-320-7708
Fax: –
Web: www.goldresourcecorp.com

CEO: Allen Palmiere
CFO: Kimberly Perry
HR: –
FYE: December 31
Type: Public

Mining company Gold Resource aims to produce gold and other minerals from projects where operating costs are low. The company focuses on its El Aguila project in the southern Mexican state of Oaxaca. The El Aguila project which began in 2010 at a shallow open-pit mine now includes an underground mine La Arista. The deposit being mined at El Aguila includes not only gold and silver but also copper lead and zinc. In addition to its primary operations the company has interests in exploration properties in Oaxaca. Gold Resource was formed in 1998.

	Annual Growth	12/16	12/17	12/18	12/19	12/20
Sales ($ mil.)	2.2%	83.2	110.2	115.3	135.4	90.7
Net income ($ mil.)	(0.2%)	4.4	4.2	9.3	5.8	4.4
Market value ($ mil.)	(9.6%)	323.5	327.3	297.5	412.0	216.4
Employees	9.9%	398	506	47	630	581

GOLD'S GYM INTERNATIONAL INC.

125 E. John Carpenter Fwy Ste. 1300
Irving TX 75062
Phone: 214-574-4653
Fax: 214-296-5000
Web: www.goldsgym.com

CEO: –
CFO: –
HR: –
FYE: February 28
Type: Private

The site of America's most famous muscle beach is the birth place of one of the world's best-known muscle makers. Gold's Gym which first opened in Venice Beach California in 1965 has more than 600 gyms in some 30 countries with franchises accounting for most of its locations. The chain boasts more than 3 million members. In addition to opening franchises the firm buys smaller regional health clubs and converts them to Gold's Gyms. The company also licenses the Gold's Gym name for products such as fitness equipment and accessories luggage t-shirts and men's and women's sportswear. Gold's Gym is owned by TRT Holdings the umbrella company for Dallas-based investor Robert Rowling's holdings.

GOLD-EAGLE COOPERATIVE

415 LOCUST ST
GOLDFIELD, IA 505425092
Phone: 515-825-3161
Fax: –
Web: www.goldeaglecoop.com

CEO: –
CFO: –
HR: –
FYE: September 30
Type: Private

For Gold-Eagle Cooperative service to its member/farmers is the golden rule. The firm is a member-owned agricultural co-op located in north central Iowa. It offers its members grain drying custom crop spraying feed seed fertilizer and other bulk and packaged farm chemicals storage and warehousing as well as feed milling and marketing. The co-op runs a transportation fleet of grain-hoppers feed-bottle trucks and specialty trailers that take members' crops to and from its facilities. Gold-Eagle operates nine grain elevator/service center locations.

	Annual Growth	09/08	09/09	09/16	09/17	09/18
Sales ($ mil.)	(0.6%)	–	302.7	309.7	284.1	285.5
Net income ($ mil.)	(4.3%)	–	10.0	10.0	8.7	6.8
Market value ($ mil.)	–	–	–	–	–	–
Employees	–	–	–	–	–	215

GOLDEN ENTERPRISES, INC.

1 GOLDEN FLAKE DR
BIRMINGHAM, AL 352053312
Phone: 205-458-7316
Fax: –
Web: www.utzsnacks.com

CEO: Dylan Lissette
CFO: Todd Staub
HR: –
FYE: May 29
Type: Private

Snackers who crave a taste for the South seek Golden Enterprises. Operating through subsidiary Golden Flake Snack Foods the company makes and distributes a barbecue and other Southern flavored-varieties of potato chips fried pork skins corn chips onion rings and baked and fried cheese curls among others. It also markets peanut butter canned dips dried meat snacks pretzels and nuts packed by other manufacturers under the Golden Flake brand. The Golden Flake lineup is sold through the company's sales force to commercial enterprises that sell food products across the Southeastern US as well as through independent distributors. The company was founded in 1946 as Magic City Food Products. In 2016 snack food company Utz acquired the company for $135 million.

	Annual Growth	05/11	05/12	05/13	05/14	05/15
Sales ($ mil.)	(2.1%)	–	–	137.3	135.9	131.7
Net income ($ mil.)	25.1%	–	–	1.1	0.9	1.8
Market value ($ mil.)	–	–	–	–	–	–
Employees	–	–	–	–	–	749

GOLDEN ENTERTAINMENT INC
NMS: GDEN

6595 S Jones Boulevard
Las Vegas, NV 89118
Phone: 702-893-7777
Fax: –
Web: www.goldenent.com

CEO: Blake Sartini
CFO: Charles Protell
HR: –
FYE: December 31
Type: Public

Golden Entertainment is a gaming company. The company operates more than 12000 slot machines and video lottery terminals as well as approximately 30 table games in Nevada Montana and Maryland across four casino properties and more than 50 taverns. Its Golden Casino Group manages the Pahrump Nugget Hotel & Casino; Gold Town Casino and Lakeside Casino and RV Park and in Flintstone Maryland; and the Rocky Gap Resort. All of the properties feature gaming dining and entertainment.

	Annual Growth	12/16	12/17	12/18	12/19	12/20
Sales ($ mil.)	14.5%	403.2	509.8	851.8	973.4	694.2
Net income ($ mil.)	–	16.3	2.2	(20.9)	(39.5)	(136.6)
Market value ($ mil.)	13.2%	341.0	919.4	451.1	541.2	560.1
Employees	24.4%	2,802	6,910	6,940	8,000	6,700

GOLDEN GATE NATIONAL PARKS CONSERVANCY

FORT MASON BLDG 201
SAN FRANCISCO, CA 94123
Phone: 415-561-3000
Fax: –
Web: www.parksconservancy.org

CEO: Greg Moore
CFO: –
HR: Elena Torres
FYE: September 30
Type: Private

San Francisco open your Golden Gate — National Parks that is. The Golden Gate National Parks Conservancy is dedicated to preserving and enhancing the national parks in the San Francisco Bay area. The not-for-profit organization is a cooperating association authorized by the US Congress to assist and support the National Park Service in operating almost 40 national park sites in and around the City by the Bay. The Golden Gate National Recreation Area includes such sites as Alcatraz Island Fort Point Muir Woods in nearby Marin County and the Presidio of San Francisco (a former US Army base that was decommissioned in 1994). The conservancy was established in 1981.

	Annual Growth	09/10	09/11	09/15	09/16	09/17
Sales ($ mil.)	10.8%	–	33.2	52.3	55.2	61.5
Net income ($ mil.)	–	–	(1.1)	2.3	(3.9)	6.5
Market value ($ mil.)	–	–	–	–	–	–
Employees	–	–	–	–	–	514

GOLDEN GRAIN ENERGY, LLC

1822 43RD ST SW
MASON CITY, IA 504017071
Phone: 641-423-8525
Fax: –
Web: www.ggecorn.com

CEO: Chad Kuhlers
CFO: Brooke Peters
HR: –
FYE: October 31
Type: Private

The fruited plains with their golden grains have yielded Golden Grain Energy an ethanol production company with a plant in Iowa that converts corn into ethanol which is most commonly used as an additive to unleaded gasoline. Other uses include high octane fuel enhancer and a non-petroleum fuel substitute. Golden Grain Energy's plant has a production capacity of 110 million gallons of ethanol and 120000 tons of distillers grains per year. The distillers grains are used to produce animal feed. In 2009 with raw material costs rising and selling prices falling the company cut back production at the plant.

	Annual Growth	10/12	10/13	10/14	10/15	10/16
Sales ($ mil.)	(17.0%)	–	350.7	289.2	221.1	200.7
Net income ($ mil.)	12.9%	–	–	14.2	79.3	31.9	20.4
Market value ($ mil.)	–	–	–	–	–	–
Employees	–	–	–	–	–	47

GOLDEN MINERALS CO

350 Indiana Street, Suite 650
Golden, CO 80401
Phone: 303 839-5060
Fax: –
Web: www.goldenminerals.com

ASE: AUMN
CEO: Warren Rehn
CFO: Robert P Vogels
HR: –
FYE: December 31
Type: Public

Golden Minerals owns and operates a precious metals mine in Mexico an exploration property in Argentina and a portfolio of mining and exploration sites in parts of Mexico and South America. The company has been expanding its production at the Velarde ±a and Chicago mines in Mexico and is in the advanced evaluation stage at its El Quevar silver project in northwest Argentina. It sold most of its exploration properties in Peru in 2013. The company's strategy is focused on establishing itself as a mid-tier producer and expanding its precious metal operations in Mexico and Argentina. The company also has a joint venture with Golden Tag Resources in the San Diego silver project in Mexico.

	Annual Growth	12/16	12/17	12/18	12/19	12/20
Sales ($ mil.)	(3.1%)	6.4	6.7	7.2	7.7	5.6
Net income ($ mil.)	–	(10.7)	(3.9)	(1.9)	(5.4)	(9.1)
Market value ($ mil.)	7.0%	91.4	68.0	34.5	48.8	119.7
Employees	4.7%	160	160	178	170	192

GOLDEN STAR ENTERPRISES LTD

6490 West Desert Inn Road
Las Vegas, NV 89146
Phone: 888 488-6882
Fax: –
Web: www.goldenstarent.com

NBB: GSPT
CEO: Jaclyn Cruz
CFO: Matt Kelly
HR: –
FYE: December 31
Type: Public

Terralene Fuels (formerly Golden Spirit Enterprises) has had many lives — and many names. Founded in 1993 as Power Direct an oil-and-gas exploration company this development-stage firm has undergone several different incarnations. It took a gamble on online poker through its goldenspiritpoker.com site. After Congress passed the Unlawful Internet Gambling Enforcement Act of 2006 Golden Spirit again switched gears seeking to develop waste-recycled products. In 2010 the company launched its Terralene Fuel product an alternative to ethanol-blended gasoline. It changed its name to Terralene Fuels in 2011 to reflect its core business.

	Annual Growth	12/14	12/15	12/16	12/17	12/18
Sales ($ mil.)	(33.4%)	0.0	0.1	0.0	0.0	0.0
Net income ($ mil.)	–	(0.2)	(0.3)	(1.4)	(0.7)	(0.3)
Market value ($ mil.)	12.5%	1.5	0.0	0.1	2.2	2.4
Employees	–	–	–	–	–	–

GOLDMAN SACHS GROUP INC

200 West Street
New York, NY 10282
Phone: 212 902-1000
Fax: 212 902-3000
Web: www.gs.com

NYS: GS
CEO: David Solomon
CFO: Denis Coleman
HR: –
FYE: December 31
Type: Public

Goldman Sachs is a leading global financial institution that delivers a broad range of financial services across investment banking securities investment management and consumer banking to a large and diversified client base that includes corporations financial institutions governments and individuals. It is a world leader in merger and acquisitions advice and equities and debt underwriting. Through its Global Markets division Goldman Sachs is a major market maker offering fixed income equities currency and commodity products. The bank boasts some 2.1 trillion in assets under supervision covering all major asset classes. Goldman Sachs was founded in 1869. Vast majority of its revenue comes from its domestic operation.

	Annual Growth	12/16	12/17	12/18	12/19	12/20
Assets ($ mil.)	7.8%	860,165.0	916,776.0	931,796.0	992,968.0	1,163,028.0
Net income ($ mil.)	6.3%	7,398.0	4,286.0	10,459.0	8,466.0	9,459.0
Market value ($ mil.)	2.4%	82,392.0	87,660.0	57,480.0	79,116.3	90,739.6
Employees	4.2%	34,400	36,600	36,600	38,300	40,500

GOLDRICH MINING CO

2607 Southeast Blvd., Suite B211
Spokane, WA 99223-4942
Phone: 509 535-7367
Fax: 509 624-2787
Web: www.goldrichmining.com

NBB: GRMC
CEO: William Schara
CFO: Theodore Sharp
HR: –
FYE: December 31
Type: Public

Goldrich Mining Company is looking in a remote area of northern Alaska to get rich off gold. The development-stage company is exploring a mining site in Chandalar where gold was first discovered at the turn of the 20th century. Goldrich has mineral rights to 17000 acres on land owned by the state of Alaska. The Chandalar property does not have any proved reserves but the site did produce about 1500 ounces of fine gold and 250 ounces of fine silver in 2010. However its arctic climate creates a limited mining season; the company can only conduct business there for a few months every summer. Goldrich was incorporated in 1959 and has been public since 1970 buying its first mining claims in Chandalar in 1972.

	Annual Growth	12/13	12/14	12/15	12/16	12/17
Sales ($ mil.)	223.7%	–	–	–	0.1	0.2
Net income ($ mil.)	–	(1.9)	(2.0)	0.1	(0.7)	(1.0)
Market value ($ mil.)	(9.8%)	7.7	5.4	2.8	4.0	5.1
Employees	6.5%	49	13	69	50	63

GOLF GALAXY LLC

300 Industry Dr. RIDC Park West
Pittsburgh PA 15275
Phone: 724-273-3400
Fax: 724-227-1904
Web: www.golfgalaxy.com

CEO: –
CFO: –
HR: –
FYE: January 31
Type: Subsidiary

Let Golf Galaxy help with your galactic battle to break par. It operates about 80 golf superstores in 30 states. Stores offer "Everything for the Game" including equipment apparel and shoes gifts accessories books and videos. Golf Galaxy also sells pre-owned clubs and boasts a trade-in program. In-store amenities include computer video swing analysis onsite certified club technicians indoor driving bays full-sized putting greens and advice on equipment from a staff that includes PGA and LPGA professionals. Golf Galaxy also operates a namesake website and catalog. Founded in 1997 by former executives Randy Zanatta and Greg Maanum it is owned by Dick's Sporting Goods.

GOLFSMITH INTERNATIONAL HOLDINGS INC.   NASDAQ: GOLF

11000 N. IH-35
Austin TX 78753-3195
Phone: 512-837-8810
Fax: 512-837-1245
Web: www.golfsmith.com

CEO: Martin E Hanaka
CFO: Dave Bushland
HR: Shawna Willis
FYE: December 31
Type: Public

Golfsmith International caters to sports clubs on both sides of the US-Canada border. Formed by the combination of Texas-based Golfsmith and Canada's Golf Town newly-formed Golfsmith International operates about 95 golf stores in the US and another 55 (under the Golf Town banner) in Canada and Boston. It also sells golf and tennis equipment apparel and accessories online. Brands include TaylorMade-adidas Callaway Mizuno and Nike. Golfsmith also teaches golfers to assemble their own clubs and offers custom fitting and repair services for clubs and racquets. Founded in 1967 as a mail-order seller of custom-made golf clubs Golfsmith in 2012 was acquired by Canada's Golf Town.

GOLUB CAPITAL BDC INC.   NASDAQ: GBDC

150 S. Wacker Dr. Ste. 800
Chicago IL 60606
Phone: 312-205-5050
Fax: 607-786-8663
Web: www.mmcweb.com

CEO: David Golub
CFO: Christopher Ericson
HR: –
FYE: September 30
Type: Public

The Golub brothers are at it again. Lawrence and David Golub the investors behind Golub Capital Partners founded Golub Capital BDC to assist small businesses amid the tight credit market. Organized as a business development company (BDC) Golub Capital BDC makes debt and minority investments (between $5 million to $25 million) to smaller companies that earn between $5 million to $40 million a year. Its investment portfolio primarily consists of senior secured loans as well as some unitranche mezzanine and second lien loans. It has investments in more than 90 companies owned by private equity firms. Lawrence (Chairman) and David (CEO) control more than half its stock through various entities.

GONZAGA UNIVERSITY

502 E BOONE AVE
SPOKANE, WA 992580001
Phone: 509-328-4220
Fax: –
Web: www.gonzaga.edu

CEO: –
CFO: –
HR: –
FYE: May 31
Type: Private

Gonzaga University is a private liberal arts institution providing instruction to more than 7800 undergraduate graduate doctoral and law students. The school offers about 75 undergraduate majors two dozen master's degree programs and two leadership study doc at its six colleges and schools. The university offers a juris doctorate degree at its School of Law. The Roman Catholic university is run by the Society of Jesus — the Jesuits — and is named after a sixteenth-century Italian Jesuit Aloysius Gonzaga the patron saint of youth. The university was founded in 1887 as a men's college.

	Annual Growth	05/16	05/17	05/18	05/20	05/21
Sales ($ mil.)	1.2%	–	218.3	232.0	242.0	228.6
Net income ($ mil.)	28.1%	–	47.4	30.3	12.9	127.6
Market value ($ mil.)	–	–	–	–	–	–
Employees	–	–	–	–	–	1,200

GOOD SAM ENTERPRISES LLC

2575 Vista Del Mar
Ventura CA 93001
Phone: 805-667-4100
Fax: 805-667-4419
Web: www.affinitygroup.com

CEO: Marcus A Lemonis
CFO: Thomas F Wolfe
HR: –
FYE: December 31
Type: Private

Members needn't be good to join the Good Sam Club (formerly Affinity Group). One of several membership clubs operated by Good Sam Enterprises (GSE) the Good Sam Club and President's Club cater to the RV community offering goods and services to some 1.3 million members. GSE is also a direct marketer specialty retailer and publisher for RVers and outdoor enthusiasts. Its retail business Camping World operates 80-plus stores (plus a catalog and website) in more than 30 states that sell aftermarket RV parts and accessories and offer repair and maintenance services. GSE also publishes magazines and travel guides. Founded in 1966 members originally promised to help fellow travelers on the road.

GOOD SAMARITAN HOSPITAL

520 S 7TH ST
VINCENNES, IN 475911038
Phone: 812-882-5220
Fax: –
Web: www.gshvin.org

CEO: –
CFO: –
HR: Dean Wagoner
FYE: December 31
Type: Private

Good Samaritan Hospital provides a full slate of healthcare services to both southwest Indiana and southeast Illinois. Its services include cardiology emergency care orthopedics women's health and pediatrics among others. The 230-bed hospital is located a few blocks from the Wabash River which forms the border between the Hoosier and Prairies states. Good Samaritan operates specialty units as well including same-day surgery breast care behavioral health radiology sleep cancer care and rehabilitation centers. It also provides home health and hospice services. Established in 1908 with 25 beds Good Samaritan was Indiana's first county hospital.

	Annual Growth	12/15	12/16	12/17	12/18	12/20
Sales ($ mil.)	0.7%	–	315.6	322.4	323.3	324.7
Net income ($ mil.)	170.0%	–	0.2	(5.1)	(12.0)	10.6
Market value ($ mil.)	–	–	–	–	–	–
Employees	–	–	–	–	–	1,900

GOOD SAMARITAN HOSPITAL

2222 PHILADELPHIA DR
DAYTON, OH 454061891
Phone: 937-278-2612
Fax: –
Web: www.montortho.net

CEO: –
CFO: –
HR: –
FYE: December 31
Type: Private

Good Samaritan Hospital offers a caring hand to the residents of Dayton Ohio and the surrounding areas. The hospital has some 560 beds and offers a mix of services including primary and emergency care pediatric specialties and a family birthing center. Good Samaritan also runs the Samaritan North Health Center an outpatient health center that offers outpatient surgery rehab and sports medicine diagnostic imaging and cancer care among other services. Other operations include the Maria-Joseph Living Care Center a long-term care facility with some 400 beds and Samaritan Family Care a primary care physicians' network. Good Samaritan Hospital is part of Premier Health Partners.

	Annual Growth	12/02	12/03	12/05	12/06	12/15
Sales ($ mil.)	1.1%	–	282.8	274.3	307.2	321.6
Net income ($ mil.)	(8.5%)	–	20.5	(5.2)	12.0	7.1
Market value ($ mil.)	–	–	–	–	–	–
Employees	–	–	–	–	–	2,000

GOOD SAMARITAN HOSPITAL MEDICAL CENTER

1000 MONTAUK HWY
WEST ISLIP, NY 117954927
Phone: 631-376-3000
Fax: –
Web: www.goodsamaritan.chsli.org

CEO: –
CFO: –
HR: –
FYE: December 31
Type: Private

The folks at Good Samaritan Hospital Medical Center have plenty of reasons to feel good about their efforts. The hospital is part of Catholic Health Services of Long Island (CHS) and serves the south shore community of West Islip New York. The full-service medical center boasts 900 physicians and 440 acute care beds offering a complete range of health care counseling and rehabilitation services. Good Samaritan provides emergency medicine and trauma care in addition to oncology cardiology pediatric woman's health diagnostic and surgical care. It also operates the Good Samaritan Nursing Home a 100-bed skilled nursing facility as well as satellite clinics and a home health care agency.

	Annual Growth	12/12	12/13	12/14	12/15	12/19
Sales ($ mil.)	5.2%	–	534.1	488.1	505.1	725.2
Net income ($ mil.)	–	–	(28.5)	36.7	28.8	20.1
Market value ($ mil.)	–	–	–	–	–	–
Employees	–	–	–	–	–	3,774

GOOD SAMARITAN HOSPITAL, L.P.

2425 SAMARITAN DR
SAN JOSE, CA 951243985
Phone: 408-559-2011
Fax: –
Web: www.goodsamsanjose.com

CEO: –
CFO: Darrel Neuenschwander
HR: Stacey Lawson
FYE: January 31
Type: Private

Good Samaritan Hospital lends a hand to help Silicon Valley's techies and their neighbors stay healthy. The facility part of the HCA family of for-profit hospitals administers care through campuses in San Jose (the main campus) and Los Gatos California. Good Samaritan Hospital provides general acute care as well as a host of tertiary services that include cardiology and cardiovascular surgery; oncology; obstetrics and gynecology; and psychiatry (both inpatient and outpatient care). The main campus hospital has some 408 patient beds and 600 physicians and the Los Gatos outpatient and short-stay facility houses approximately 100 beds.

	Annual Growth	12/02	12/03*	05/05*	01/09	01/17
Sales ($ mil.)	–	–	0.0	170.0	413.9	618.5
Net income ($ mil.)	–	–	0.0	0.0	30.3	141.2
Market value ($ mil.)	–	–	–	–	–	–
Employees	–	–	–	–	–	1,800

*Fiscal year change

GOOD TIMES RESTAURANTS INC.

NAS: GTIM

651 Corporate Circle
Golden, CO 80401
Phone: 303 384-1400
Fax: –
Web: www.goodtimesburgers.com

CEO: Ryan Zink
CFO: James K Zielke
HR: –
FYE: September 28
Type: Public

Good Times Restaurants operates and franchises more than 50 Good Times Drive Thru fast-food eateries located primarily in the Denver area. The hamburger chain is made up mostly of double drive-through and walk-up eateries that feature a menu of burgers fries and frozen custard. A limited number of Good Times outlets also offer dine-in seating. More than 20 of the locations are operated by franchisees while the rest are co-owned and co-operated under joint venture agreements. The family of director Geoffrey Bailey owns almost 30% of the company.

	Annual Growth	09/17	09/18	09/19	09/20	09/21
Sales ($ mil.)	11.9%	79.1	99.2	110.8	109.9	124.0
Net income ($ mil.)	–	(2.3)	(1.0)	(5.1)	(13.9)	16.8
Market value ($ mil.)	15.9%	34.6	59.2	20.4	17.2	62.5
Employees	3.1%	1,970	2,368	2,535	2,318	2,230

GOOD360

675 N WASHINGTON ST # 330
ALEXANDRIA, VA 223141934
Phone: 703-836-2121
Fax: –
Web: www.good360.org

CEO: Cindy Hallberlin
CFO: Gerald Borenstein
HR: –
FYE: December 31
Type: Private

Good360 (formerly Gifts in Kind International) helps companies find ways to be kind. The not-for-profit organization accepts gifts of products and services from corporate clients and distributes these donations to more than 150000 community charities in the US and globally that directly help communities and people in need. About half of the FORTUNE 100 makes contributions through Good360 which has certified more than 200000 charities as potential recipients. Good360 began operating in 1983 when 3M donated $12 million in new office equipment. The organization is known for its cost-efficiency as more than 99% of its donations go directly to communities.

	Annual Growth	12/12	12/13	12/14	12/15	12/19
Sales ($ mil.)	0.8%	–	310.0	314.5	382.9	325.0
Net income ($ mil.)	–	–	(12.7)	2.6	4.1	(13.5)
Market value ($ mil.)	–	–	–	–	–	–
Employees	–	–	–	–	–	36

GOODFELLOW BROS. INC.

1407 WALLA WALLA AVE
WENATCHEE, WA 988011530
Phone: 509-667-9095
Fax: –
Web: www.goodfellowbros.com

CEO: Chad Goodfellow
CFO: –
HR: –
FYE: December 31
Type: Private

The good men at Goodfellow Bros. build everything from golf courses to runways to dams and residences. The family-owned company specializes in heavy construction infrastructure transportation systems and housing and recreation facilities in the western continental US and Hawaii. Goodfellow Bros. also offers earth moving and paving services. Its Blasting Technologies subsidiary blasts drills and demolishes rock and other structures. The company was founded in 1921 by brothers Jack Bert and Jim Sr. Their early business included the first excavation work on the Grand Coulee Dam in 1933. Now the company has a number of planned communities public facilities and other projects under its belt.

	Annual Growth	12/06	12/07	12/08	12/09	12/13
Sales ($ mil.)	(14.5%)	–	519.9	0.0	240.2	203.1
Net income ($ mil.)	–	–	–	0.0	19.8	7.3
Market value ($ mil.)	–	–	–	–	–	–
Employees	–	–	–	–	–	1,050

GOODMAN NETWORKS INCORPORATED

2801 NETWORK BLVD STE 300
FRISCO, TX 750341881
Phone: 972-406-9692
Fax: –
Web: www.goodmansolutions.com

CEO: John Goodman
CFO: John Debus
HR: –
FYE: December 31
Type: Private

Goodman Solutions builds the infrastructure for good end-to-end telecom networks. The family- and minority-owned company provides a variety of telecommunications services to the wireless industry with services such as network design engineering deployment integration and maintenance. The company also offers staffing services as well as supply chain management services such as materials management and logistics. Goodman Solutions specializes in providing equipment lifecycle services for telecom carriers and equipment manufacturers in the public and private sector.

	Annual Growth	07/04	07/05	07/06*	12/07	12/08
Sales ($ mil.)	–	–	–	(1,103.4)	102.6	220.3
Net income ($ mil.)	–	–	–	0.0	(0.9)	11.6
Market value ($ mil.)	–	–	–	–	–	–
Employees	–	–	–	–	–	3,925

*Fiscal year change

GOODRICH CORPORATION
NYSE: GR

Four Coliseum Centre 2730 W. Tyvola Rd. CEO: –
Charlotte NC 28217-4578 CFO: Scott E Kuechle
Phone: 704-423-7000 HR: –
Fax: 704-423-7002 FYE: December 31
Web: www.goodrich.com Type: Public

Goodrich is a tireless leader in aerospace systems. The company serves regional/business aircraft original equipment and aftermarket helicopters military and space markets through its three aerospace divisions. Goodrich's largest segment actuation and landing systems makes fuel systems aircraft wheels brakes landing gear and flight control systems. Nacelles and interior systems offers maintenance/repair services and makes aerostructures (cowlings and thrust reversers) as well as aircraft seats and cargo and lighting systems. Its electronic systems division makes fuel controls flight management systems and reconnaissance systems. In 2012 Goodrich was acquired by United Technologies (UTC).

GOODRICH PETROLEUM CORP
ASE: GDP

801 Louisiana, Suite 700 CEO: Walter G Goodrich
Houston, TX 77002 CFO: Kristen M McWatters
Phone: 713 780-9494 HR: –
Fax: – FYE: December 31
Web: www.goodrichpetroleum.com Type: Public

From deep in the good rich hydrocarbon-impregnated rocks of ancient Mother Earth Goodrich Petroleum brings forth oil and gas. The independent exploration and production company delves into formations in the Hayneville Shale play in Texas and Louisiana. The company also operates in the Eagle Ford Shale Trend in South Texas the Tuscaloosa Marine Shale in Louisiana and the Cotton Valley trend (in Texas and Louisiana). In the wake of a slump in oil prices Goodrich Petroleum filed for Chapter 11 bankruptcy protection in 2016 in an attempt to shed some $400 million in debt.

	Annual Growth	10/16*	12/16	12/17	12/18	12/19
Sales ($ mil.)	78.9%	20.7	6.6	46.2	88.0	118.4
Net income ($ mil.)	(67.0%)	369.9	(4.3)	(8.0)	1.8	13.3
Market value ($ mil.)	(6.8%)	–	155.4	136.7	169.2	125.8
Employees	5.9%	–	–	43	48	51	51

*Fiscal year change

GOODWILL INDUSTRIES INTERNATIONAL, INC.

15810 INDIANOLA DR CEO: Steven C Preston
ROCKVILLE, MD 208552674 CFO: –
Phone: 301-530-6500 HR: –
Fax: – FYE: December 31
  Type: Private

Goodwill Industries International supports the operations of about 165 independent Goodwill chapters in the US and Canada. While it's most well known for its more than 3000 thrift stores the group focuses on providing rehabilitation job training placement and employment services for people with disabilities and others. Goodwill is one of the world's largest providers of such services as well as one of the largest employers in the world of the physically mentally and emotionally disabled. Support for its programs is generated primarily from the sale of donated goods both at the retail stores and through an online auction site as well as from contract work and government grants.

	Annual Growth	12/08	12/09	12/13	12/14	12/15
Sales ($ mil.)	13.2%	–	37.6	46.1	42.8	79.4
Net income ($ mil.)	–	–	0.8	3.0	(3.2)	(1.0)
Market value ($ mil.)	–	–	–	–	–	–
Employees	–	–	–	–	–	100

GOODWILL INDUSTRIES OF CENTRAL TEXAS

1015 NORWOOD PARK BLVD CEO: –
AUSTIN, TX 787536608 CFO: –
Phone: 512-637-7100 HR: –
Fax: – FYE: December 31
Web: www.austingoodwill.org Type: Private

Deep in the heart of Texas there're some good folks doin' good things. Goodwill Industries of Central Texas is the Austin-area operating company for Goodwill Industries International. The organization serves people with barriers like developmental medical psychiatric and emotional problems to employment. It also works with homeless people at-risk youth dislocated workers and those over 50 seeking jobs. It operates about 20 retail outlets and two refurbished computer outlets. In 2008 the group partnered with area employers not-for-profits and community groups to help 10000 needy individuals find jobs. It teamed with Dell and the City of Austin to form a computer-recycling program and computer museum.

	Annual Growth	12/06	12/07	12/08	12/14	12/15
Sales ($ mil.)	6.7%	–	39.6	41.7	61.8	66.5
Net income ($ mil.)	–	–	0.3	(0.5)	0.7	(0.5)
Market value ($ mil.)	–	–	–	–	–	–
Employees	–	–	–	–	–	1,200

GOODWIN PROCTER LLP

Exchange Place 53 State St. CEO: –
Boston MA 02109 CFO: Michael Barton
Phone: 617-570-1000 HR: Heidi Goldstein Shepherd
Fax: 617-523-1231 FYE: September 30
Web: www.goodwinprocter.com Type: Private - Partnershi

One of the largest law firms in Beantown Goodwin Procter has branched beyond its Boston roots to establish offices on the East and West Coasts of the US. The firm has about 850 lawyers practicing in a variety of areas including corporate real estate environmental litigation tax and estate planning. It helps emerging multinational companies to achieve growth and advises on everything from critical regulatory and compliance matters to deals transactions and critical litigation issues. Goodwin Procter has offices in Boston Hong Kong London Los Angeles New York City San Diego San Francisco Silicon Valley and Washington DC. Robert Goodwin and Joseph Procter founded the firm in 1912.

GOODYEAR TIRE & RUBBER CO.
NMS: GT

200 Innovation Way CEO: Richard Kramer
Akron, OH 44316-0001 CFO: Darren Wells
Phone: 330 796-2121 HR: –
Fax: 330 796-4099 FYE: December 31
Web: www.goodyear.com Type: Public

Goodyear Tire & Rubber sells tires under the Goodyear Dunlop Kelly Fulda Debica and Sava brand names. The company manufactures and sells its tires across the Americas Europe Middle East & Africa (EMEA) and the Asia Pacific region. Goodyear also makes and markets rubber-related chemicals for various applications. It operates approximately 1000 tire and auto service centers where it offers its products for retail sale and provides automotive repair and other services. Goodyear has marketing operations in almost every country in the world although the US generates about half of its revenue.

	Annual Growth	12/17	12/18	12/19	12/20	12/21
Sales ($ mil.)	3.3%	15,377.0	15,475.0	14,745.0	12,321.0	17,478.0
Net income ($ mil.)	21.9%	346.0	693.0	(311.0)	(1,254.0)	764.0
Market value ($ mil.)	(9.9%)	9,104.7	5,751.4	4,383.3	3,074.4	6,007.8
Employees	3.0%	64,000	64,000	63,000	62,000	72,000

GORDMANS STORES INC

NMS: GMAN

1926 South 67 Street
Omaha, NE 68106
Phone: 402 691-4000
Fax: 402 691-4269
Web: www.gordmans.com

CEO: –
CFO: –
HR: –
FYE: January 30
Type: Public

Midwestern shoppers head to Gordmans Stores for deeply-discounted fashionable apparel and home décor. The department store chain operates 90-plus stores in regional shopping centers in about 20 mostly Midwestern states. The stores specialize in selling women's men's and junior's apparel accessories footwear and home décor items at up to 60% off regular department and specialty store prices (known as off-price). Gordmans competes in the off-price market of the retail industry and also separates itself from discount stores by offering brand-name fashions and a more upscale shopping environment. The discount department store chain is run by CEO Jeff Gordman grandson of founder Dan Gordman.

	Annual Growth	01/12*	02/13	02/14*	01/15	01/16
Sales ($ mil.)	4.2%	558.1	615.1	627.4	643.2	657.9
Net income ($ mil.)	–	25.2	23.5	8.0	(3.5)	(4.3)
Market value ($ mil.)	(35.6%)	287.0	240.3	142.1	72.8	49.4
Employees	3.4%	4,900	5,200	5,500	5,500	5,610

*Fiscal year change

GORDON COLLEGE

255 GRAPEVINE RD
WENHAM, MA 019841899
Phone: 978-927-2300
Fax: –
Web: www.gordon.edu

CEO: –
CFO: –
HR: –
FYE: June 30
Type: Private

Gordon College a New England non-denominational Christian liberal arts college offers nearly 40 majors and has about 1800 students. A demonstrated Christian commitment is required for admission. Undergraduate tuition is approximately $20000. In 1985 Gordon merged with Barrington College with the combined school retaining Gordon College's name. Gordon College was founded in 1889 by Reverend Dr. A.J. Gordon as a missionary training institute.

	Annual Growth	06/15	06/16	06/17	06/18	06/19
Sales ($ mil.)	–	–	0.0	65.0	62.4	116.7
Net income ($ mil.)	–	–	0.0	29.3	1.8	49.1
Market value ($ mil.)	–	–	–	–	–	–
Employees	–	–	–	–	–	496

GORDON FOOD SERVICE, INC.

1300 GEZON PKWY SW
WYOMING, MI 495099302
Phone: 888-437-3663
Fax: –
Web: www.gfs.com

CEO: James Gordon
CFO: Jeff Maddox
HR: –
FYE: October 31
Type: Private

Gordon Food Service (GFS) is North America's largest family-owned broadline food service supplier. The company boasts more than 20 distribution centers across the US and Canada. GFS's primary focus is distributing a variety of food items ingredients and beverages to restaurant operators schools health care facilities and institutional food service operators in parts of 15 states and across Canada. In addition to its distribution operation GFS operates more than 170 wholesale stores under the GFS Marketplace banner; these are open to the public. Isaac Van Westenbrugge started the family-owned business in 1897 to deliver eggs and butter.

	Annual Growth	10/10	10/11	10/12	10/13	10/15
Sales ($ mil.)	17.1%	–	–	–	64.9	89.0
Net income ($ mil.)	–	–	–	–	(1.2)	(0.2)
Market value ($ mil.)	–	–	–	–	–	–
Employees	–	–	–	–	–	10,600

GORMAN-RUPP COMPANY (THE)

NYS: GRC

600 South Airport Road
Mansfield, OH 44903
Phone: 419 755-1011
Fax: –
Web: www.gormanrupp.com

CEO: Scott King
CFO: James Kerr
HR: –
FYE: December 31
Type: Public

Gorman-Rupp was founded in 1933 by engineers J. C. Gorman and H. E. Rupp. It designs manufactures and globally sells pumps and pump systems for use in water wastewater construction dewatering industrial petroleum original equipment agriculture fire protection heating ventilating and air conditioning (HVAC) military and other liquid-handling applications. Gorman-Rupp's pumps range in size from 1/4-inch (one gallon per minute) to nearly 15 feet and ranging in rated capacity from less than one gallon per minute to nearly one million gallons per minute. Smaller pumps are used for food processing chemical processing photo processing and medical applications while large pumps include the ground refueling aircraft fluid control in HVAC applications and various agricultural purposes. The company generates most of its sales in its home country the US.

	Annual Growth	12/16	12/17	12/18	12/19	12/20
Sales ($ mil.)	(2.2%)	382.1	379.4	414.3	398.2	349.0
Net income ($ mil.)	0.3%	24.9	26.6	40.0	35.8	25.2
Market value ($ mil.)	1.2%	807.9	814.6	846.0	978.8	847.0
Employees	(0.6%)	1,180	1,165	1,200	1,200	1,150

GOTTLIEB MEMORIAL HOSPITAL

701 W NORTH AVE
MELROSE PARK, IL 601601699
Phone: 708-681-3200
Fax: –
Web: www.loyolamedicine.org

CEO: –
CFO: –
HR: –
FYE: June 30
Type: Private

Got health? Out in the western suburbs of Chicago the staff at Gottlieb Memorial Hospital can help you find it. The not-for-profit community general hospital — also known as Loyola Gottlieb — boasts more than 250 beds a staff of more than 300 physicians and dentists 200 volunteers a Level II trauma center with a heliport heart and cancer care clinics and a health and fitness center on site. The healthcare facility also offers rehabilitation services a pharmacy and a kidney dialysis center. Other Gottlieb Memorial Hospital services include outpatient clinics hospice and home health care. Gottlieb is part of Loyola University Health System.

	Annual Growth	06/12	06/13	06/14	06/15	06/20
Sales ($ mil.)	(0.5%)	–	142.2	156.2	129.6	137.3
Net income ($ mil.)	(1.3%)	–	5.6	19.6	(2.8)	5.1
Market value ($ mil.)	–	–	–	–	–	–
Employees	–	–	–	–	–	84

GOVERNMENT OF DISTRICT OF COLUMBIA

441 4TH ST NW
WASHINGTON, DC 200012714
Phone: 202-727-0252
Fax: –
Web: www.dc.gov

CEO: –
CFO: Natawar Gandhi
HR: –
FYE: September 30
Type: Private

Government of the District of Columbia manages ticket and tax payments housing and property issues children and youth services and motor vehicles registration among other duties for Washington DC. More than 689000 people live in Washington DC and many more commute to the city every day to work for the federal government. Washington DC is overseen by a mayor and a 13-member city council. It acquires contracts with more than 30 local government agencies. The Government of the District of Columbia was created in 1790 with donated land from Maryland and Virginia as part of the Residence Act.

	Annual Growth	09/04	09/05	09/11	09/15	09/16
Sales ($ mil.)	–	–	0.0	9,822.1	11,637.7	12,095.7
Net income ($ mil.)	–	–	0.0	102.5	583.9	(78.4)
Market value ($ mil.)	–	–	–	–	–	–
Employees	–	–	–	–	–	34,600

GOYA FOODS INC.

100 Seaview Dr.
Secaucus NJ 07096
Phone: 201-348-4900
Fax: 201-348-6609
Web: www.goya.com

CEO: –
CFO: –
HR: –
FYE: December 31
Type: Private

Whether you call 'em frijoles or habichuelas beans are beans and Goya's got 'em. Goya Foods produces more than 1600 Hispanic and Caribbean grocery items including canned and dried beans canned meats beverages cooking oils and olives. Its products portfolio also offers rice seasonings and sauces plantain and yucca chips ready meals and frozen treats and entrees. Goya sells many rice styles and nearly 40 types of beans and peas under the Goya and Canilla brand names. The company sells such beverages as tropical fruit nectars juices tropical sodas and coffee. Goya is owned and operated by one of the richest Hispanic "familias" in the US — the Unanues — who founded the company in 1936.

GPM INVESTMENTS, LLC

8565 MAGELLAN PKWY # 400
RICHMOND, VA 232271167
Phone: 276-328-3669
Fax: –
Web: www.gpminvestments.com

CEO: –
CFO: –
HR: –
FYE: December 31
Type: Private

Convenience is key for GPM Investments which operates or supplies fuel to more than 1100 convenience stores in about 20 US states. The stores sell BP Exxon Marathon and Valero brand gas among others as well as the usual beer smokes and snacks. Some locations also offer fresh made-to-order salads sandwiches and other items or offer branded food from Subway Taco Bell and others. The company which primarily serves the Midwest and eastern US operates or supplies stores under a host of names including Fas Mart Shore Stop Jiffi Stop Young's and Roadrunner Markets.

	Annual Growth	12/04	12/05	12/06	12/07	12/08
Sales ($ mil.)	40.2%	–	–	–	891.8	1,249.9
Net income ($ mil.)	–	–	–	–	3.2	(1.3)
Market value ($ mil.)	–	–	–	–	–	–
Employees	–	–	–	–	–	2,150

GRACE (WR) & CO

7500 Grace Drive
Columbia, MD 21044-4098
Phone: 410 531-4000
Fax: –
Web: www.grace.com

NYS: GRA
CEO: Hudson La Force
CFO: William C Dockman
HR: –
FYE: December 31
Type: Public

W. R. Grace & Co. (Grace) makes things happen. The company is a maker of catalysts used in fluid catalytic cracking (FCC) the process of refining crude oil by "cracking" its hydrocarbon chains into smaller chunks to make gasoline or diesel fuels. Grace also produces specialty catalysts used in the production of thermoplastic resins and additives used to reduce sulfur in gasoline. Additionally the company synthesizes made-to-order compounds and manufactures a range of silica products including silica gel colloidal silica zeolitic adsorbents precipitated silica and silica-aluminas. Its materials technologies business makes materials for consumer/pharma packaging coatings and chemical process. Majority of the company's sales were generated from Europe Middle East and Africa.

	Annual Growth	12/15	12/16	12/17	12/18	12/19
Sales ($ mil.)	(10.5%)	3,051.5	1,598.6	1,716.5	1,932.1	1,958.1
Net income ($ mil.)	(3.3%)	144.2	94.1	11.2	167.6	126.3
Market value ($ mil.)	(8.5%)	6,646.2	4,514.0	4,680.2	4,331.8	4,661.5
Employees	(12.1%)	6,700	3,700	3,700	3,900	4,000

GRACELAND FRUIT INC.

1123 MAIN ST
FRANKFORT, MI 496359341
Phone: 231-352-7181
Fax: –
Web: www.gracelandfruit.com

CEO: Jeff Seeley
CFO: Troy Terwilliger
HR: –
FYE: September 30
Type: Private

It's possible that Elvis would have liked Graceland Fruit's products. The company makes dried refrigerated and frozen fruit and vegetable ingredients for the food-manufacturing industry. Its product lines include infused dried fruit infused dried vegetables Soft-N-Frozen fruit and Fridg-N-Fresh vegetables. Graceland Fruit has also expanded into the fruit juice concentrate industry through a partnership with Milne Fruit Products. The company was founded in 1973 by president and CEO Donald Nugent.

	Annual Growth	09/01	09/02	09/03	09/04	09/07
Sales ($ mil.)	–	–	–	(1,021.2)	33.5	56.1
Net income ($ mil.)	847.6%	–	–	0.0	0.1	0.9
Market value ($ mil.)	–	–	–	–	–	–
Employees	–	–	–	–	–	180

GRACO INC

88 - 11th Avenue N.E.
Minneapolis, MN 55413
Phone: 612 623-6000
Fax: 612 623-6777
Web: www.graco.com

NYS: GGG
CEO: Patrick J McHale
CFO: Mark W Sheahan
HR: –
FYE: December 31
Type: Public

Graco which was founded in 1926 as Gray Company manufactures fluid-handling equipment designed to move measure control dispense and apply fluid materials. Products include pumps applicators spray guns pressure washers filters valves and accessories; these goods are used in industrial and commercial applications to handle paints adhesives sealants and lubricants. In addition to painting contractors Graco's customers include automotive construction equipment and pharmaceutical oil and natural gas and fleet service centers. Graco sells its products through independent distributors worldwide. The US accounts for almost 55% of the total revenue.

	Annual Growth	12/17	12/18	12/19	12/20	12/21
Sales ($ mil.)	7.7%	1,474.7	1,653.3	1,646.0	1,650.1	1,987.6
Net income ($ mil.)	14.9%	252.4	341.1	343.9	330.5	439.9
Market value ($ mil.)	15.6%	7,701.3	7,003.0	8,886.6	12,405.2	13,730.2
Employees	2.1%	3,500	3,700	3,700	3,700	3,800

GRADALL INDUSTRIES INC.

406 Mill Ave. SW
New Philadelphia OH 44663
Phone: 330-339-2211
Fax: 330-339-8468
Web: www.gradall.com

CEO: –
CFO: –
HR: –
FYE: July 31
Type: Subsidiary

Gradall Industries is diggin' it up and movin' it out — far out. A subsidiary of Alamo Group Gradall makes non-traditional telescopic boom material handlers traditional conventional knuckle booms rough-terrain wheeled and industrial maintenance machines and mine scalers as well as spare parts for its products. Contractors use Gradall's material handlers for lumber and other materials; its industrial machines tackle tough mining railroad construction and hazardous waste removal jobs. In 2006 parent JLG Industries sold Gradall to maintenance and agricultural equipment maker Alamo Group. Gradall supports Alamo's Vacall subsidiary which makes sewer cleaning equipment hydro-excavators and vacuum loaders.

GRAEBEL COMPANIES, INC.

16346 AIRPORT CIR
AURORA, CO 800111558
Phone: 303-214-6683
Fax: –
Web: www.graebel.com

CEO: William Graebel
CFO: Bradley Siler
HR: –
FYE: December 31
Type: Private

Graebel can move your table ... and just about anything else you need relocated. Offering both domestic and international household and commercial relocation services most of the company's business comes from firms transferring employees but it also provides individual household moving services and storage as well as freight forwarding. Graebel operates from service centers throughout the US and from international forwarding offices at major ports. It provides transportation services in Asia Europe the Middle East and Africa through hubs in Prague and Singapore and elsewhere in the world via a network of partners. Dave Graebel founded the family-run company in 1950.

	Annual Growth	12/13	12/14	12/15	12/16	12/17
Sales ($ mil.)	4.3%	–	85.3	94.0	90.9	96.9
Net income ($ mil.)	–	–	(2.9)	5.5	3.3	1.2
Market value ($ mil.)	–	–	–	–	–	–
Employees	–	–	–	–	–	753

GRAFTECH INTERNATIONAL LTD   NYS: EAF

982 Keynote Circle
Brooklyn Heights, OH 44131
Phone: 216 676-2000
Fax: –
Web: www.graftech.com

CEO: David Rintoul
CFO: Timothy Flanagan
HR: –
FYE: December 31
Type: Public

GrafTech International is a leading maker in the US of graphite electrodes which are essential to the production of electric arc furnaces steel and various other ferrous and nonferrous metals. GrafTech has the most competitive portfolio of low-cost ultra-high power (UHP) graphite electrode manufacturing facilities in the industry including three of the highest capacity facilities in the world. It is the only large scale graphite electrode producer that is substantially vertically integrated into petroleum needle coke a key raw material for graphite electrode manufacturing. Customers have included major steel producers and other ferrous and non-ferrous metal producers which sell their products into the automotive construction appliance machinery equipment and transportation industries. Majority of its sales were generated outside US. The company traces its roots back in 1886.

	Annual Growth	12/16	12/17	12/18	12/19	12/20
Sales ($ mil.)	29.3%	438.0	550.8	1,895.9	1,790.8	1,224.4
Net income ($ mil.)	–	(235.8)	8.0	854.2	744.6	434.4
Market value ($ mil.)	(3.5%)	–	–	3,056.6	3,104.7	2,848.2
Employees	0.8%	1,244	1,310	1,387	1,346	1,285

GRAHAM CORP.   NYS: GHM

20 Florence Avenue
Batavia, NY 14020
Phone: 585 343-2216
Fax: –
Web: www.graham-mfg.com

CEO: Daniel Thoren
CFO: Jeffrey Glajch
HR: –
FYE: March 31
Type: Public

Graham Corporation manufactures and sells critical equipment for the energy marine power generation and chemical/petrochemical industries. Graham provides equipment used in nuclear propulsion power systems for the US Navy and for the chemical and petrochemical industries and it offers equipment for fertilizer food processing synthetic fiber production and other chemical facilities. Its products include custom-engineered ejectors surface condensers and vacuum systems that are used in diverse applications such as metal refining pulp and paper processing and pharmaceutical. Graham Corporation sells its products worldwide with more than two-thirds of sales generated in the US.

	Annual Growth	03/17	03/18	03/19	03/20	03/21
Sales ($ mil.)	1.5%	91.8	77.5	91.8	90.6	97.5
Net income ($ mil.)	(17.1%)	5.0	(9.8)	(0.3)	1.9	2.4
Market value ($ mil.)	(11.3%)	229.1	213.3	195.5	128.5	141.8
Employees	(0.4%)	336	304	337	337	331

GRAHAM HOLDINGS CO.   NYS: GHC

1300 North 17th Street
Arlington, VA 22209
Phone: 703 345-6300
Fax: –
Web: www.ghco.com

CEO: Andrew Rosen
CFO: Wallace Cooney
HR: Sandra Stonesifer
FYE: December 31
Type: Public

Graham Holdings is a media and education company but has its hands in other arenas too. Its primary operations are in education services television broadcasting and television print and online news. The group's largest division is education conducted via Kaplan which includes tutoring and test preparation services in the US and internationally. Other operations include a portfolio of seven TV stations and online and print publications such as Slate and Foreign Policy magazine. The diverse Graham's assets also include social media advertising manufacturing and home health and hospice care businesses. The company generates about a quarter of sales outside the US.

	Annual Growth	12/16	12/17	12/18	12/19	12/20
Sales ($ mil.)	3.9%	2,481.9	2,591.8	2,696.0	2,932.1	2,889.1
Net income ($ mil.)	15.5%	168.6	302.0	271.2	327.9	300.4
Market value ($ mil.)	1.0%	2,551.0	2,782.2	3,191.9	3,184.0	2,657.7
Employees	10.2%	11,300	11,900	11,100	12,053	16,661

GRAHAM PACKAGING COMPANY L.P.

2401 Pleasant Valley Rd.
York PA 17402
Phone: 717-849-8500
Fax: +45-44-85-95-95
Web: www.dako.com

CEO: Mark Burgess
CFO: –
HR: –
FYE: December 31
Type: Subsidiary

People can't keep their hands off Graham Packaging. Graham designs manufactures and sells blow-molded plastic containers for a slew of consumer goods including food and beverages automotive lubricants and household and personal care items. Graham's 90-plus manufacturing plants dot the Americas Europe and Asia to supply such multi-national customers as Clorox Danone and PepsiCo. About one-third of plant operations are set onsite at customers' production facilities; its top 20 customers represent nearly 70% of sales each year. Reynolds Group Holdings an affiliate of New Zealand's Rank Group Limited acquired the packager in 2011 for about $4.5 billion.

GRAINGER (W.W.) INC.   NYS: GWW

100 Grainger Parkway
Lake Forest, IL 60045-5201
Phone: 847 535-1000
Fax: 847 535-0878
Web: www.grainger.com

CEO: Donald Macpherson
CFO: Deidra Merriwether
HR: –
FYE: December 31
Type: Public

W.W. Grainger distributes about 1.5 million industrial products from supplies to equipment and tools. The company offers material-handling equipment safety and security supplies lighting and electrical products power and hand tools pumps and plumbing supplies cleaning and maintenance supplies and metalworking tools. Its approximately 5 million customers are government manufacturing transportation commercial and contractors. Grainger sells through a network of branches distribution centers catalogs sales and service representatives and websites. More than three quarters of its revenue are generated from customers in the US.

	Annual Growth	12/17	12/18	12/19	12/20	12/21
Sales ($ mil.)	5.7%	10,424.9	11,221.0	11,486.0	11,797.0	13,022.0
Net income ($ mil.)	15.5%	585.7	782.0	849.0	695.0	1,043.0
Market value ($ mil.)	21.7%	12,100.8	14,462.5	17,339.1	20,915.3	26,544.4
Employees	(1.5%)	25,700	24,600	25,300	23,100	24,200

GRAMERCY PROPERTY TRUST INC
NYS: GPT

521 5th Avenue, 30th Floor
New York, NY 10175
Phone: 212 297-1000
Fax: –
Web: www.gptreit.com

CEO: –
CFO: –
HR: –
FYE: December 31
Type: Public

Gramercy Property Trust (formerly Gramercy Capital) a self-managed real estate investment trust (REIT) invests in commercial properties and real estate loan products secured throughout the US. Its Gramercy Finance arm originates and acquires mezzanine financing bridge loans interests in whole loans preferred equity private equity investments and mortgage-backed securities. Gramercy Real Estate primarily manages commercial properties mostly leased to financial institutions. Its management portfolio is made up of more than 25 million sq. ft of space in some 40 states.

	Annual Growth	12/09	12/10	12/11	12/12	12/13
Sales ($ mil.)	(45.4%)	636.1	607.1	211.2	36.8	56.7
Net income ($ mil.)	–	(519.6)	(973.7)	337.5	(171.5)	384.8
Market value ($ mil.)	22.1%	184.7	164.7	178.3	209.7	410.1
Employees	(10.8%)	131	135	121	93	83

GRAND CANYON EDUCATION INC
NMS: LOPE

2600 W. Camelback Road
Phoenix, AZ 85017
Phone: 602 247-4400
Fax: –
Web: www.gcu.edu

CEO: Brian Mueller
CFO: Daniel Bachus
HR: –
FYE: December 31
Type: Public

Grand Canyon Education (dba Grand Canyon University) spans a broad educational horizon. The regionally accredited Christian educator offers graduate and undergraduate degrees online at its campus in Phoenix and onsite at corporate facilities. Grand Canyon University offers career-oriented degree programs focused on the core disciplines of business education health care and liberal arts. Grand Canyon University has more than 103100 students enrolled in GCU's programs emphases and certificates. Most classes have a student-teacher ratio of about 20:1. The company was formed in 1949 as a not-for-profit college.

	Annual Growth	12/17	12/18	12/19	12/20	12/21
Sales ($ mil.)	(2.1%)	974.1	845.5	778.6	844.1	896.6
Net income ($ mil.)	6.4%	203.3	229.0	259.2	257.2	260.3
Market value ($ mil.)	(1.1%)	4,769.9	5,122.1	5,103.4	4,960.6	4,566.4
Employees	(16.1%)	10,000	3,500	3,400	4,625	4,955

GRAND PIANO & FURNITURE CO.

4235 ELECTRIC RD STE 100
ROANOKE, VA 240188445
Phone: 540-776-7000
Fax: –
Web: www.grandhomefurnishings.com

CEO: George B Cartledge Jr
CFO: –
HR: –
FYE: December 31
Type: Private

Grand Home Furnishings formerly Grand Piano & Furniture got its start as a piano and musical instrument store in Roanoke Virginia. Several decades later the company sells mattresses and home furnishings through more than 15 stores in Virginia West Virginia and Tennessee. The company stocks furniture from such manufacturers as Hooker La-Z-Boy Klaussner Vaughan-Bassett Meadowcraft and Thomasville and the mattresses come from Tempur Sealy to name a few. Grand Home Furnishings was founded in 1910 and acquired in 1945 by the current owners the Cartledge family. George Cartledge Jr. is the company's CEO.

	Annual Growth	10/11	10/12	10/13	10/14*	12/15
Sales ($ mil.)	0.0%	–	–	123.0	123.0	123.0
Net income ($ mil.)	–	–	–	0.0	0.0	0.0
Market value ($ mil.)	–	–	–	–	–	–
Employees	–	–	–	–	–	650

*Fiscal year change

GRAND RIVER DAM AUTHORITY

8142 HWY 412B
CHOUTEAU, OK 743376027
Phone: 918-256-5545
Fax: –
Web: www.grda.com

CEO: Dan Sullivan
CFO: Lorie Gudde
HR: –
FYE: December 31
Type: Private

It took the dam authority of the State of Oklahoma to create the body that would dam the Grand River. The resulting power provider the Grand River Dam Authority is responsible for supplying wholesale electricity to municipal and cooperative utilities and industrial customers in its service territory which encompasses 24 counties in northeastern Oklahoma. It also sells excess power to customers across a four-state region. The state-owned utility has 1480 MW of generating capacity from hydroelectric and fossil-fueled power plants and operates a 2090-mile transmission system. Grand River Dam Authority also manages two lakes and a total of 70000 surface acres of water in Northeast Oklahoma.

	Annual Growth	12/16	12/17	12/18	12/19	12/20
Sales ($ mil.)	(3.1%)	–	436.0	437.6	425.0	397.2
Net income ($ mil.)	67.7%	–	7.1	30.1	53.9	33.6
Market value ($ mil.)	–	–	–	–	–	–
Employees	–	–	–	–	–	468

GRAND STRAND REGIONAL MEDICAL CENTER, LLC

809 82ND PKWY
MYRTLE BEACH, SC 295724607
Phone: 843-692-1000
Fax: –
Web: www.mygrandstrandhealth.com

CEO: Mark Sims
CFO: –
HR: –
FYE: April 30
Type: Private

Grand Strand Regional Medical Center (GSRMC) is an acute care hospital serving Myrtle Beach South Carolina and surrounding Georgetown and Horry counties. The 220-bed hospital a designated trauma center is home to the only cardiac surgery program in those counties. GSRMC has a staff of more than 250 physicians representing a range of specializations including oncology wound treatment and emergency care women's health pediatrics rehabilitation behavioral health and treatment for sleeping disorders. Grand Strand Regional Medical Center includes the medical center and other satellite diagnostic ambulatory care and senior care facilities throughout the area.

	Annual Growth	04/07	04/08	04/09	04/13	04/15
Sales ($ mil.)	294.8%	–	–	0.1	265.2	331.6
Net income ($ mil.)	284.3%	–	–	0.0	65.3	107.1
Market value ($ mil.)	–	–	–	–	–	–
Employees	–	–	–	–	–	1,000

GRAND VALLEY STATE UNIVERSITY

1 CAMPUS DR
ALLENDALE, MI 494019403
Phone: 616-331-5000
Fax: –
Web: www.gvsu.edu

CEO: –
CFO: –
HR: –
FYE: June 30
Type: Private

Even the most average student can get a grand education at Grand Valley State University. The school operates five campuses in western Michigan. The main one is in Allendale; it has additional facilities in Grand Rapids Holland Muskegon and Traverse City. Classes at the latter two locations are offered in conjunction with local community colleges. A public university with a liberal arts emphasis Grand Valley State offers more than 200 fields of study including about 80 undergraduate majors and more than 30 graduate programs. It has an enrollment of roughly 25000 students and approximately 835 regular faculty members. Its student-teacher ratio is about 27:1.

	Annual Growth	06/15	06/16	06/17	06/18	06/19
Sales ($ mil.)	2.3%	–	355.7	370.9	375.1	381.1
Net income ($ mil.)	29.9%	–	26.8	54.2	46.3	58.7
Market value ($ mil.)	–	–	–	–	–	–
Employees	–	–	–	–	–	3,630

GRAND VIEW HOSPITAL

700 LAWN AVE
SELLERSVILLE, PA 189601548
Phone: 215-453-4000
Fax: –
Web: www.gvh.org

CEO: Jean Keeler
CFO: –
HR: –
FYE: June 30
Type: Private

Grand View Health (GVH) formerly Grand View Hospital hopes to give patients a glimpse of great health care. The hospital provide emergency inpatient surgery and specialty services including cardiology orthopedics sleep diagnostic rehabilitation women's and children's care and other medical services to the Bucks County region of Pennsylvania. GVH's oncology program is affiliated with the Fox Chase Cancer Center in Philadelphia. The medical center also operates primary care and outpatient clinics in the region and it provides home health hospice fitness and community outreach programs. The hospital has about 200 beds.

	Annual Growth	06/13	06/14	06/15	06/16	06/20
Sales ($ mil.)	0.4%	–	203.5	189.1	189.4	208.8
Net income ($ mil.)	–	–	24.0	17.3	10.1	(0.4)
Market value ($ mil.)	–	–	–	–	–	–
Employees	–	–	–	–	–	1,600

GRANITE CITY FOOD & BREWERY LTD   NBB: GCFB

3600 American Boulevard West, Suite 400
Bloomington, MN 55431
Phone: 952 215-0660
Fax: 952 215-0661
Web: www.gcfb.com

CEO: Richard Lynch
CFO: James Gilbertson
HR: –
FYE: December 25
Type: Public

Drinking and dining form the bedrock of this small restaurant chain. Granite City Food & Brewery owns and operates more than 25 casual dining brewpubs in about a dozen Midwestern states mostly in Minnesota Kansas Illinois Indiana and Iowa. The restaurants offer a variety of handcrafted beers that are brewed on-site including such varieties as Broad Axe Stout Duke of Wellington (English ale) and Northern Light Lager. Granite City's broad food menu features chicken steak and seafood entrees along with appetizers burgers sandwiches and salads. The company also owns and operates five Cadillac Ranch All American Bar & Grill restaurants.

	Annual Growth	12/14	12/15	12/16	12/17	12/18
Sales ($ mil.)	(0.4%)	136.2	150.6	150.3	141.2	133.8
Net income ($ mil.)	–	(3.1)	(0.3)	(4.7)	(9.1)	(7.4)
Market value ($ mil.)	(29.2%)	22.3	30.3	15.8	3.2	5.6
Employees	–	–	3,418	–	–	–

GRANITE CONSTRUCTION INC   NYS: GVA

585 West Beach Street
Watsonville, CA 95076
Phone: 831 724-1011
Fax: –
Web: www.graniteconstruction.com

CEO: Kyle Larkin
CFO: Elizabeth Curtis
HR: –
FYE: December 31
Type: Public

Holding company Granite Construction has a rock-hard grip on infrastructure projects. The company's main subsidiary Granite Construction Company is a transportation and heavy construction contractor that works on public infrastructure projects such as airports bridges highways mass transit dams water-related facilities utilities and tunnels. Granite's private sector projects involve residential and commercial site preparation. In addition to construction services the company operate mines and processes aggregates and has plants that produce construction materials such as asphalt concrete. The firm was incorporated in 1922.

	Annual Growth	12/16	12/17	12/18	12/19	12/20
Sales ($ mil.)	9.1%	2,514.6	2,989.7	3,318.4	3,445.6	3,562.5
Net income ($ mil.)	–	57.1	69.1	42.4	(60.2)	(145.1)
Market value ($ mil.)	(16.5%)	2,511.8	2,896.8	1,839.5	1,263.6	1,219.8
Employees	12.3%	3,400	3,600	5,700	5,600	5,400

GRANITE TELECOMMUNICATIONS LLC

100 NEWPORT AVENUE EXT # 1
QUINCY, MA 021712126
Phone: 617-933-5500
Fax: –
Web: www.granitenet.com

CEO: –
CFO: Richard Wurman
HR: –
FYE: December 31
Type: Private

Granite Telecommunications carves out an increasing block of telecommunications services to commercial clients in the US and Canada. The company is a wholesaler of local and long distance telephone service as well as broadband internet connections with more than 1.3 million lines provided by network operators. It serves corporate clients many of whom run offices in multiple states offering them no account transfer charges and no term or volume contracts on telephone service. Granite also designs and installs network cabling and security systems and provides loss prevention and risk management services.

	Annual Growth	12/08	12/09	12/10	12/11	12/12
Sales ($ mil.)	19.3%	–	–	517.2	609.0	736.2
Net income ($ mil.)	31.0%	–	–	109.4	143.0	187.8
Market value ($ mil.)	–	–	–	–	–	–
Employees	–	–	–	–	–	2,116

GRAPHIC PACKAGING HOLDING CO   NYS: GPK

1500 Riveredge Parkway, Suite 100
Atlanta, GA 30328
Phone: 770 240-7200
Fax: –
Web: www.graphicpkg.com

CEO: Michael Doss
CFO: Stephen Scherger
HR: Stacey Panayiotou
FYE: December 31
Type: Public

Graphic Packaging Holding Company (GPHC) is a leading provider of sustainable paper-based packaging solutions for a wide variety of products to food beverage foodservice and other consumer products companies. The company operates on a global basis is one of the largest producers of folding cartons in the US and holds leading market positions in coated-recycled paperboard (CRB) coated unbleached kraft paperboard (CUK) and solid bleached sulfate paperboard (SBS). The company operates eight paperboard mills across North America. It generates about 80% of its sales through US operations. Customers have included such big names as Kraft Foods MillerCoors Anheuser-Busch General Mills and various Coca-Cola and Pepsi bottlers.

	Annual Growth	12/17	12/18	12/19	12/20	12/21
Sales ($ mil.)	12.9%	4,403.7	6,023.0	6,160.1	6,559.9	7,156.0
Net income ($ mil.)	(9.2%)	300.2	221.1	206.8	167.3	204.0
Market value ($ mil.)	6.0%	4,744.7	3,267.6	5,113.3	5,202.3	5,988.5
Employees	17.8%	13,000	18,000	18,000	18,775	25,000

GRAY TELEVISION INC   NYS: GTN

4370 Peachtree Road N.E.
Atlanta, GA 30319
Phone: 404 504-9828
Fax: –
Web: www.gray.tv

CEO: Donald Laplatney
CFO: James Ryan
HR: –
FYE: December 31
Type: Public

Gray Television is one of the largest independent operators of TV stations in the US. It owns and operates local TV stations in nearly 95 markets including some 150 affiliates of ABC NBC CBS and FOX. Its station portfolio reaches about 25% of total US TV households. The company also owns video production marketing and digital businesses including Raycom Sports Tupelo-Raycom and RTM Studios. Revenue comes primarily from broadcast and internet ads and from retransmission consent fees. Gray Television's roots begin in January 1891 with the creation of the Albany Herald in Albany Georgia.

	Annual Growth	12/16	12/17	12/18	12/19	12/20
Sales ($ mil.)	30.8%	812.5	882.7	1,084.1	2,122.0	2,381.0
Net income ($ mil.)	60.2%	62.3	262.0	210.8	179.0	410.0
Market value ($ mil.)	13.3%	1,032.8	1,594.4	1,403.1	2,040.8	1,702.9
Employees	16.1%	3,996	3,938	8,523	8,018	7,262

GRAYBAR ELECTRIC CO., INC.   NBB: GRBE

34 North Meramec Avenue
St. Louis, MO 63105
Phone: 314 573-9200
Fax: –
Web: www.graybar.com

CEO: –
CFO: –
HR: –
FYE: December 31
Type: Public

Graybar Electric a Fortune 500 company specializes in supply chain management services and is a leading North American distributor of high-quality components equipment and materials. Graybar products and services support new construction infrastructure updates building renovation facility maintenance repair and operations and original equipment manufacturing. The employee-owned company operates a network of more than 300 distribution facilities across the US Canada and Puerto Rico. Graybar Electric serve customers in the construction industrial & utility vertical markets and commercial institutional and government (CIG) primarily in the US.

	Annual Growth	12/16	12/17	12/18	12/19	12/20
Sales ($ mil.)	3.3%	6,385.0	6,631.2	7,202.5	7,523.9	7,265.7
Net income ($ mil.)	7.0%	93.1	71.6	143.3	144.5	121.8
Market value ($ mil.)	–	–	–	–	–	–
Employees	(0.9%)	8,500	8,500	8,700	9,100	8,200

GRAYCOR INC.

2 Mid America Plaza Ste. 400
Oakbrook Terrace IL 60181
Phone: 630-684-7110
Fax: 630-684-7111
Web: www.graycor.com

CEO: –
CFO: Steven Gray
HR: –
FYE: September 30
Type: Private

Graycor translates blueprints into buildings. The company provides contracting construction design/build and facilities management services across the US through four main units. Graycor Industrial has expertise in the steel and energy industries and performs trade services such as concrete and carpentry work. Graycor Blasting offers industrial cleaning blast furnace delining and salamander (heat source) removal services. Graycor Construction has built edifices ranging from retail centers and hotels to manufacturing plants to corporate education health care and distribution facilities. Graycor International is active in Canada and Mexico. Chairman and CEO Melvin Gray and his family control Graycor.

GREAT AMERICAN BANCORP INC   NBB: GTPS

1311 S. Neil Street
Champaign, IL 61820
Phone: 217 356-2265
Fax: 217 356-2502
Web: www.greatamericanbancorp.com

CEO: George Rouse
CFO: Jane Adams
HR: –
FYE: December 31
Type: Public

Great American Bancorp is the holding company for First Federal Savings Bank of Champaign-Urbana which operates two branches in Champaign and one in Urbana Illinois. Targeting individuals and local businesses First Federal provides retail banking products such as checking savings and money market accounts credit cards and CDs. Lending activities consist primarily of residential mortgages as well as commercial real estate construction business and consumer loans. The bank was founded in 1908. Through a partnership with UMB Financial Corporation subsidiary UMB Financial Services First Federal Savings Bank also offers investment services.

	Annual Growth	12/16	12/17	12/18	12/19	12/20
Assets ($ mil.)	3.0%	180.6	173.7	167.4	172.7	203.7
Net income ($ mil.)	16.5%	0.7	0.5	1.0	1.5	1.2
Market value ($ mil.)	2.6%	11.3	12.5	11.9	13.7	12.5
Employees	–	–	–	–	–	–

GREAT ELM GROUP INC   NMS: GEG

800 South Street, Suite 230
Waltham, MA 02453
Phone: 617 375-3006
Fax: –
Web: www.greatelmcap.com

CEO: Peter A Reed
CFO: Brent J Pearson
HR: –
FYE: June 30
Type: Public

Unwired Planet comes from a universe where phones work without wires and companies don't need products to make money. The company (formerly Openwave Systems) developed technology behind the wireless application protocol (WAP) standard which allows mobile devices to connect to the Internet. Unwired Planet holds some 2300 US and foreign patents relating to mobile communications smart devices cloud technologies and unified messaging. The company began exploiting its intellectual property portfolio in 2012 when it sold its mediation and messaging product businesses to Marlin Equity Partners.

	Annual Growth	06/17	06/18	06/19	06/20	06/21
Sales ($ mil.)	87.5%	4.9	5.9	51.2	64.1	60.9
Net income ($ mil.)	–	(15.2)	(11.1)	(2.9)	(13.0)	(8.1)
Market value ($ mil.)	(9.8%)	88.2	93.4	111.6	60.5	58.4
Employees	123.0%	16	12	328	349	396

GREAT LAKES AVIATION LTD.   NBB: GLUX

1022 Airport Parkway
Cheyenne, WY 82001
Phone: 307 432-7000
Fax: –
Web: www.flygreatlakes.com

CEO: Douglas Voss
CFO: Michael Matthews
HR: –
FYE: December 31
Type: Public

Great Lakes Aviation goes to great lengths to get people where they need to be even if it's far from the big city. Flying as Great Lakes Airlines the regional carrier transports passengers to more than 60 destinations in the western and midwestern US mainly from Denver but also from markets such as Phoenix Kansas City and Ontario California. It maintains code-sharing agreements with Frontier Airlines and United Airlines. (Code-sharing enables carriers to sell tickets on one another's flights and thus extend their networks.) Great Lakes operates a fleet of about 40 turboprop aircraft consisting mostly of 19-passenger Beechcraft 1900Ds but also including 30-passenger Embraer Brasilia 120s.

	Annual Growth	12/10	12/11	12/12	12/13	12/14
Sales ($ mil.)	(17.1%)	125.4	124.4	137.8	117.2	59.2
Net income ($ mil.)	–	5.1	10.7	2.9	(0.4)	(7.4)
Market value ($ mil.)	(29.9%)	15.3	6.7	18.0	10.9	3.7
Employees	(16.4%)	1,122	1,068	1,164	657	548

GREAT LAKES CHEESE COMPANY INC.

17825 Great Lakes Pkwy.
Hiram OH 44234-1806
Phone: 440-834-2500
Fax: 440-834-1002
Web: www.greatlakescheese.com

CEO: Gary Vanic
CFO: –
HR: –
FYE: December 31
Type: Private

Great Lakes Cheese understands the power of provolone the charm of cheddar and the goodness of gruyere. The Ohio-based firm manufactures about 165 million pounds of cheese annually. The cheesemaker distributes natural and processed cheeses and cheese spreads including varieties such as cheddar Colby Swiss mozzarella and provolone. It also makes the premium Adams Reserve New York Cheddar. Great Lakes packages shredded chunked and sliced cheese for deli bulk and foodservice sale under the Great Lakes Adams Reserve and private-label brands. Chairman Hans Epprecht a Swiss immigrant founded the firm in 1958 as a Cleveland bulk-cheese distributor. Epprecht and Great Lakes employees own the company.

GREAT LAKES DREDGE & DOCK CORP
NMS: GLDD

9811 Katy Freeway, Suite 1200
Houston, TX 77024
Phone: 346 359-1010
Fax: –
Web: www.gldd.com

CEO: Lasse Petterson
CFO: Scott Kornblau
HR: –
FYE: December 31
Type: Public

Founded in 1890 Great Lakes Dredge & Dock is a stalwart of dredging services in the US mainly in the East West and Gulf Coast region. It also provides dredging abroad. Dredging involves enhancing or preserving waterways for navigability or protecting shorelines by removing or replenishing soil sand or rock. Great Lakes is involved in four major types of dredging work: capital (primarily port expansion projects) coastal protection (movement of sand from ocean floor to shoreline to alleviate erosion) rivers & lakes and maintenance (removal of silt and sediment from existing waterways and harbors).

	Annual Growth	12/16	12/17	12/18	12/19	12/20
Sales ($ mil.)	(1.1%)	767.6	702.5	620.8	711.5	733.6
Net income ($ mil.)	–	(8.2)	(31.3)	(6.3)	49.3	66.1
Market value ($ mil.)	33.1%	273.1	351.1	430.5	736.7	856.4
Employees	(24.8%)	1,364	1,426	1,192	1,047	437

GREAT NORTHERN IRON ORE PROPERTIES
NYS: GNI

W-1290 First National Bank Building, 332 Minnesota Street
Saint Paul, MN 55101-1361
Phone: 651 224-2385
Fax: 651 224-2387
Web: www.gniop.com

CEO: Joseph S Micallef
CFO: Thomas A Janochoski
HR: –
FYE: December 31
Type: Public

Great Northern Iron Ore Properties is the landlord of one big iron formation. The trust gets income from royalties on iron ore minerals (principally taconite) taken from its more than 67000 acres on the Mesabi Iron Formation in Minnesota. The trust was formed in 1906 to own the properties of an affiliate of Burlington Northern Santa Fe (BNSF formerly Great Northern Railway). The trust's beneficiaries were the heirs of railroad founder James Hill; however the last survivor his grandson Louis Hill died in 1995. In 2015 (20 years after Louis Hill's death) the land will be transferred to a unit of ConocoPhillips which acquired the BNSF assets in 2005.

	Annual Growth	12/09	12/10	12/11	12/12	12/13
Sales ($ mil.)	6.3%	14.8	20.9	26.7	24.2	19.0
Net income ($ mil.)	6.6%	11.4	17.5	23.0	20.1	14.8
Market value ($ mil.)	(7.7%)	141.0	214.5	165.4	100.8	102.2
Employees	0.0%	10	10	10	10	10

GREAT PLAINS ENERGY INC
NYS: GXP

1200 Main Street
Kansas City, MO 64105
Phone: 816 556-2200
Fax: –
Web: www.greatplainsenergy.com

CEO: –
CFO: –
HR: –
FYE: December 31
Type: Public

Great Plains Energy is sweeping the plains with electric power. The company serves about 850000 electricity customers in the breadbasket of America through regulated utility Kansas City Power & Light (KCP&L) and the KCP&L Greater Missouri Operations Company. The utility generates most of its own electricity which it supplements as needed with power purchase agreements. In 2017 the company agreed to a merger-of-equals transaction with its neighboring utility Westar Energy and expects the union to complete in the first half of 2018.

	Annual Growth	12/12	12/13	12/14	12/15	12/16
Sales ($ mil.)	3.7%	2,309.9	2,446.3	2,568.2	2,502.2	2,676.0
Net income ($ mil.)	9.7%	199.9	250.2	242.8	213.0	290.0
Market value ($ mil.)	7.7%	4,373.8	5,220.1	6,118.1	5,881.2	5,889.9
Employees	(1.9%)	3,090	2,964	2,935	2,899	2,865

GREAT PLAINS MANUFACTURING INCORPORATED

1525 E. North St.
Salina KS 67401
Phone: 785-823-3276
Fax: 785-822-5600
Web: www.greatplainsmfg.com

CEO: –
CFO: –
HR: –
FYE: June 30
Type: Private

Great Plains Manufacturing goes to great pains to help farmers across the fruited plain to sow grow and harvest the fruits of their labor. Through its Great Plains division the company designs manufactures and sells agricultural planting spraying and cultivating equipment. Its Land Pride unit sells landscaping products such as mowers and aerators. Great Plains Acceptance Corporation (GPAC) provides equipment financing and Great Plains Trucking provides related trucking services in the US and Canada. Great Plains Manufacturing distributes its products through a network of about 1000 Great Plains dealers and some 1600 Land Pride dealers. The company also sells equipment to more than 50 countries.

GREAT RIVER ENERGY

12300 ELM CREEK BLVD N
MAPLE GROVE, MN 553694718
Phone: 763-445-5000
Fax: –
Web: www.greatriverenergy.com

CEO: David Saggau
CFO: Larry Schmid
HR: –
FYE: December 31
Type: Private

Great River Energy is the second largest electric power supplier in Minnesota and one of the largest generation and transmission cooperatives in the country. The utility provides wholesale electricity to 1.7 million through nearly 30 distribution cooperatives. It operates some 4800 miles of transmission lines and has more than 3500 MW of generation capacity that consists of a diverse mix of baseload and peaking power plants including coal and natural gas as well as wind and solar generation facilities. The company also owns or partially owns more than 100 transmission substations. Approximately one-third of the people in Minnesota receive their electricity from a cooperative. Just like their counterparts in agriculture or housing cooperative utilities are owned by the members they serve.

	Annual Growth	12/14	12/15	12/16	12/17	12/18
Sales ($ mil.)	9.6%	–	983.0	1,022.1	1,270.2	1,295.9
Net income ($ mil.)	(17.8%)	–	15.2	21.5	18.2	8.5
Market value ($ mil.)	–	–	–	–	–	–
Employees	–	–	–	–	–	850

GREAT SOUTHERN BANCORP, INC.
NMS: GSBC

1451 E. Battlefield
Springfield, MO 65804
Phone: 417 887-4400
Fax: –
Web: www.greatsouthernbank.com

CEO: Joseph Turner
CFO: Rex Copeland
HR: –
FYE: December 31
Type: Public

Despite its name Great Southern Bancorp is firmly entrenched in the heartland. It is the holding company for nearly 200-year-old Great Southern Bank which offers loans deposit accounts CDs IRAs and credit cards through more than 75 branches in Missouri plus more than two dozen locations in Iowa Kansas Nebraska Minnesota and Arkansas. The firm's Great Southern Travel division is one of the largest travel agencies in Missouri. It serves both leisure and corporate travelers through about a dozen offices. Great Southern Insurance offers property/casualty and life insurance while Great Southern Financial provides investment products and services through an agreement with Ameriprise.

	Annual Growth	12/16	12/17	12/18	12/19	12/20
Assets ($ mil.)	5.0%	4,550.7	4,414.5	4,676.2	5,015.1	5,526.4
Net income ($ mil.)	6.9%	45.3	51.6	67.1	73.6	59.3
Market value ($ mil.)	(2.7%)	751.6	710.3	633.0	870.8	672.5
Employees	(2.2%)	1,263	1,225	1,182	1,191	1,156

GREAT WEST LIFE & ANNUITY INSURANCE CO - INSURANCE PRODUCTS

8515 East Orchard Road
Greenwood Village, CO 80111
Phone: 303 737-3000
Fax: -
Web: www.greatwest.com

CEO: Edmund F Murphy III
CFO: -
HR: -
FYE: December 31
Type: Public

Great-West Life & Annuity Insurance a subsidiary of Canada's Great-West Lifeco and a member of the Power Financial family represents the Great-West group's primary US operations. Through its Empower Retirement and Great-West Investments divisions GWL&A provides retirement and investment management services. Parent Great-West Lifeco sold substantially all of GWL&A's individual life insurance and annuity operations to Protective Life Insurance for $1.2 billion in 2019. The divested business operated under the Great-West Financial brand.

	Annual Growth	12/13	12/14	12/15	12/16	12/17
Assets ($ mil.)	3.1%	55,323.5	58,348.2	57,899.8	60,308.8	62,461.3
Net income ($ mil.)	30.1%	128.7	317.4	190.5	231.1	369.1
Market value ($ mil.)	-	-	-	-	-	-
Employees	15.1%	3,300	4,500	5,400	5,800	5,800

GREAT WOLF RESORTS INC.

525 Junction Rd. Ste. 6000 S.
Madison WI 53717
Phone: 608-662-4700
Fax: +44-141-332-2012
Web: www.carnyx.com

NASDAQ: WOLF
CEO: Kimberly K Schaefer
CFO: -
HR: -
FYE: December 31
Type: Private

Great Wolf Resorts has its customers muttering "Great Scott!" as they pull up to the company's drive-to family resorts. Great Wolf owns and operates about a dozen resorts. Nearly all of its properties operate under the Great Wolf Lodge name many of which are located in Midwestern US states. The company's properties are open year-round and include lodging indoor water parks themed restaurants and other diversions such as arcades spas and organized children's activities. Great Wolf targets families with children aged 2 to 14 years old who live within a convenient driving distance of its resorts. Private equity firm Apollo Global Management owns the company.

GREATER BALTIMORE MEDICAL CENTER, INC.

6701 N CHARLES ST
BALTIMORE, MD 212046808
Phone: 410-849-2000
Fax: -
Web: www.gbmc.org

CEO: John Chessare
CFO: Eric Melchior
HR: -
FYE: September 30
Type: Private

Greater Baltimore Medical Center also known as GBMC operates an integrated health system for residents of Baltimore and surrounding counties. The 255-bed medical center provides surgery women's health oncology cardiology and other specialty and general medical services. In addition to inpatient and outpatient services the medical center provides teaching services through an affiliation with Johns Hopkins University. GBMC also includes area clinics and physician practice locations. The GBMC Foundation coordinates fundraising for the health network.

	Annual Growth	06/14	06/15	06/19	06/20*	09/20
Sales ($ mil.)	(18.5%)	-	376.6	518.5	510.3	135.6
Net income ($ mil.)	(13.2%)	-	22.3	11.3	1.9	11.0
Market value ($ mil.)	-	-	-	-	-	-
Employees	-	-	-	-	-	308

*Fiscal year change

GREATER LAFAYETTE HEALTH SERVICES INC.

1501 HARTFORD ST
LAFAYETTE, IN 479042134
Phone: 765-423-6011
Fax: -
Web: www.franciscanalliance.org

CEO: Terry Wilson
CFO: Keith Lauter
HR: -
FYE: December 31
Type: Private

Part of Franciscan Alliance St. Elizabeth Regional Health (operating as Franciscan Saint Elizabeth Health) operates three acute care hospitals that provide health services to residents of northwestern Indiana's Tippecanoe County. The facilities are full-service acute care hospitals providing primary rehabilitative and surgery care. Specialty units include centers for diabetes cancer wound pulmonary cardiac and women's and children's care. The Franciscan St. Elizabeth Health-Lafayette East campus is home to a school of nursing. St. Elizabeth Regional Health also provides home health and hospice services and operates area poison control centers.

	Annual Growth	12/0-1	12/00	12/01	12/02	12/08
Sales ($ mil.)	(4.6%)	-	211.1	211.1	231.9	144.7
Net income ($ mil.)	-	-	-	21.3	16.5	(3.9)
Market value ($ mil.)	-	-	-	-	-	-
Employees	-	-	-	-	-	2,660

GREATER ORLANDO AVIATION AUTHORITY

1 JEFF FUQUA BLVD
ORLANDO, FL 328274392
Phone: 407-825-2001
Fax: -
Web: www.goaa.org

CEO: -
CFO: -
HR: -
FYE: December 31
Type: Private

If your destination is Disney World and you're flying into Orlando you might very well use one of the airports overseen by the Greater Orlando Aviation Authority (GOAA). The agency operates Orlando International Airport which is one of Florida's largest and Orlando Executive Airport a general aviation facility. (Orlando Sanford International Airport is overseen by the Sanford Airport Authority a separate agency.) GOAA is governed by a seven-member board that includes the mayor of Orlando a member of the Orange County Commission and five people appointed by the governor of Florida.

	Annual Growth	09/12	09/13	09/14	09/15*	12/15
Sales ($ mil.)	6.4%	-	380.6	399.2	430.7	430.7
Net income ($ mil.)	8.2%	-	87.0	90.5	101.7	101.7
Market value ($ mil.)	-	-	-	-	-	-
Employees	-	-	-	-	-	670

*Fiscal year change

GREATER WASHINGTON EDUCATIONAL TELECOMMUNICATIONS ASSOCIATION, INC.

3939 CAMPBELL AVE
ARLINGTON, VA 222063440
Phone: 703-998-2600
Fax: -
Web: www.weta.org

CEO: Sharon Percy Rockefeller
CFO: James Bond
HR: -
FYE: June 30
Type: Private

The Greater Washington Educational Telecommunications Association is a leading public broadcaster serving the Washington DC area with a television station and a radio station operating under the call letters WETA. It is also a leading producer of content for the Public Broadcasting Service including PBS NewsHour (created in partnership with MacNeil/Lehrer Productions) and Washington Week . WETA has also co-produced several documentaries by Ken Burns including The Civil War and Baseball . The not-for-profit organization was formed in 1953 and received a TV broadcast license in 1961.

	Annual Growth	06/10	06/11	06/12	06/15	06/19
Sales ($ mil.)	6.3%	-	72.1	69.9	109.6	117.9
Net income ($ mil.)	2.8%	-	16.8	12.9	15.0	20.9
Market value ($ mil.)	-	-	-	-	-	-
Employees	-	-	-	-	-	236

GREATWIDE LOGISTICS SERVICES LLC

12404 Park Central Dr. Ste. 300S
Dallas TX 75251-1803
Phone: 972-228-7300
Fax: 972-228-7328
Web: www.greatwide.com

CEO: Leo Suggs
CFO: –
HR: –
FYE: December 31
Type: Private

Greatwide Logistics Services brings together a world of freight transportation and logistics companies. The third-party logistics provider offers dedicated transportation in which drivers and equipment are assigned to a customer long-term; distribution logistics; truckload freight brokerage; and truckload freight transportation largely via a network of more than 20000 independent owner-operators. Greatwide calls upon a fleet of some 5000 trucks and has 3 million sq. ft. of warehouse space in the US. Clients have included such heavy hitters as Target Wal-Mart and IBM. Greatwide emerged from Chapter 11 bankruptcy protection in 2009 after being acquired by an investor group.

GREEN BRICK PARTNERS INC   NYS: GRBK

2805 Dallas Parkway, Suite 400
Plano, TX 75093
Phone: 469 573-6755
Fax: –
Web: www.greenbrickpartners.com

CEO: James Brickman
CFO: Richard Costello
HR: Heidi Haas
FYE: December 31
Type: Public

Green Brick Partners acquires and develops land and provides land and construction financing to its wholly owned and controlled builders. Also known as Green Brick it is engaged in all aspects of the homebuilding process including land acquisition and development entitlements design construction title and mortgage services marketing and sales and the creation of brand images at its residential neighborhoods and master planned communities. Based in Dallas the company owns or controls over 12000 prime home sites in high-growth sub-markets throughout the Dallas and Atlanta metropolitan areas and the Vero Beach Florida market.

	Annual Growth	12/16	12/17	12/18	12/19	12/20
Sales ($ mil.)	26.6%	380.3	454.4	623.6	791.7	976.0
Net income ($ mil.)	47.9%	23.8	15.0	51.6	58.7	113.7
Market value ($ mil.)	22.9%	509.2	572.5	366.8	581.6	1,163.2
Employees	18.9%	220	260	390	460	440

GREEN DOT CORP   NYS: GDOT

3465 E. Foothill Blvd.
Pasadena, CA 91107
Phone: 626 765-2000
Fax: –
Web: www.greendot.com

CEO: Daniel Henry
CFO: George Gresham
HR: –
FYE: December 31
Type: Public

Bank holding company Green Dot offers prepaid debit cards through more than 90000 retail locations in the US under brand names including Green Dot GoBank MoneyPak and TPG. Through its retail and direct bank Green Dot offers a broad set of financial products to consumers and businesses including debit prepaid checking credit and payroll cards as well as robust money processing services tax refunds cash deposits and disbursements. Founded in 1999 Green Dot has served more than 33 million customers directly.

	Annual Growth	12/16	12/17	12/18	12/19	12/20
Sales ($ mil.)	14.9%	718.8	890.2	1,041.8	1,108.6	1,253.8
Net income ($ mil.)	(13.6%)	41.6	85.9	118.7	99.9	23.1
Market value ($ mil.)	24.1%	1,272.5	3,256.1	4,296.8	1,259.0	3,015.1
Employees	5.4%	974	1,152	1,100	1,200	1,200

GREEN ENERGY GROUP (NEW)   NBB: ECEC

1150 S US Highway 1, Suite 302
Jupiter, FL 33477-7236
Phone: 561 249-1354
Fax: –
Web: www.ecec.us

CEO: Barney A Richmond
CFO: Richard C Turner
HR: –
FYE: May 31
Type: Public

eCom eCom.com has lightened its load. The company also known simply as eCom developed a diverse lineup of businesses that were spun off as separate entities. The subsidiaries were involved in a variety of diverse operations ranging from file compression software development to paintball gun sales. The company was involved in involuntary Chapter 11 bankruptcy proceedings that resulted in creditor American Capital Holdings taking control and distributing shares in eCom to American Capital Holdings shareholders. eCom has no active businesses nor revenues.

	Annual Growth	05/08	05/09	05/10	05/11	05/12
Sales ($ mil.)	–	0.0	0.0	0.0	0.0	0.0
Net income ($ mil.)	–	(0.0)	(0.1)	(0.0)	(0.0)	(0.0)
Market value ($ mil.)	(9.6%)	1.8	0.6	0.2	1.7	1.2
Employees						

GREEN MOUNTAIN POWER CORPORATION

163 ACORN LN
COLCHESTER, VT 054466611
Phone: 888-835-4672
Fax: –
Web: www.greenmountainpower.com

CEO: Mary G Powell
CFO: Dawn D Bugbee
HR: Ethan Zorzi
FYE: December 31
Type: Private

Public utility Green Mountain Power (GMP) lights up the hills of Vermont supplying electricity to more than 250000 customers in the state. The utility also markets wholesale electricity in New England. The company operates several thousand miles of transmission and distribution lines and owns a minority stake in high-voltage transmission operator Vermont Electric Power (VELCO). About half of the generation capacity GMP taps is from hydroelectric and other renewable energy sources. GMP is an indirect subsidiary of Canada's GazMetro. The company absorbed Central Vermont Public Service's assets in 2012.

	Annual Growth	12/14	12/15	12/16	12/18	12/19
Sales ($ mil.)	2.3%	–	–	652.9	713.2	698.1
Net income ($ mil.)	3.8%	–	–	69.5	80.5	77.8
Market value ($ mil.)	–	–	–	–	–	–
Employees	–	–	–	–	–	190

GREEN PLAINS INC.   NMS: GPRE

1811 Aksarben Drive
Omaha, NE 68106
Phone: 402 884-8700
Fax: –
Web: www.gpreinc.com

CEO: Todd Becker
CFO: George Simpkins
HR: Mark Hudak
FYE: December 31
Type: Public

Green Plains is one of the leading corn processors in the world which turns corn into ethanol at facilities in Illinois Indiana Iowa Nebraska Minnesota and Tennessee. The company has annual ethanol production capacity of approximately 1.0 billion gallons primarily used as an auto fuel. It also sells ethanol produced by different types of grains. Co-products of the ethanol production process are also a valuable revenue source for the company. It produces approximately 2.5 million tons of animal feed known as distiller grains the primary co-product of ethanol production as well as about 275 million pounds of corn oil sold to biodiesel manufacturers and feed lot markets.

	Annual Growth	12/17	12/18	12/19	12/20	12/21
Sales ($ mil.)	(5.8%)	3,596.2	3,843.4	2,417.2	1,923.7	2,827.2
Net income ($ mil.)	–	61.1	15.9	(166.9)	(108.8)	(66.0)
Market value ($ mil.)	19.8%	903.1	702.6	827.0	705.9	1,863.0
Employees	(11.9%)	1,427	1,194	820	839	859

GREENBERG TRAURIG P.A.

333 Avenue of the Americas (333 SE 2nd Ave.) Ste. 4400
Miami FL 33131
Phone: 305-579-0500
Fax: 305-579-0717
Web: www.gtlaw.com

CEO: Richard A Rosenbaum
CFO: –
HR: –
FYE: December 31
Type: Private - Partnershi

Greenberg Traurig is known for its entertainment practice but show business isn't the firm's only legal business. Its 1800-plus lawyers maintain a wide range of practices including corporate and securities intellectual property labor and employment litigation and real estate. The firm has about 30 offices mainly in the US but also in Latin America Europe and Asia. It extends its network in Europe and Asia via strategic alliances. In the U.K. the firm operates as Greenberg Traurig Maher LLP. Greenberg Traurig was founded in 1967 by Mel Greenberg.

GREENBRIER COMPANIES INC (THE)   NYS: GBX

One Centerpointe Drive, Suite 200
Lake Oswego, OR 97035
Phone: 503 684-7000
Fax: 503 684-7553
Web: www.gbrx.com

CEO: William Furman
CFO: Adrian Downes
HR: –
FYE: August 31
Type: Public

The Greenbrier Companies designs manufactures and markets railroad freight car equipment in North America Europe South America and other geographies. It also manufactures and markets marine barges in North America. The company manufactures primarily freight cars and marine barges. Through its primary Manufacturing segment Greenbrier produces hopper cars; intermodal and conventional railcars; center-partition flat and tank cars; and large ocean-going marine vessels. Its Wheels Repair & Parts segment provides wheel and axle services and offers railcar repair refurbishment and parts for its railcars. Its Leasing & Services unit manages a fleet of about 8800 railcars. The US market generates most of its revenue.

	Annual Growth	08/17	08/18	08/19	08/20	08/21
Sales ($ mil.)	(5.3%)	2,169.2	2,519.5	3,033.6	2,792.2	1,748.0
Net income ($ mil.)	(27.3%)	116.1	151.8	71.1	49.0	32.5
Market value ($ mil.)	0.7%	1,389.8	1,879.0	754.5	880.9	1,428.7
Employees	(3.6%)	11,917	13,400	17,100	10,600	10,300

GREENE COUNTY BANCORP INC   NAS: GCBC

302 Main Street
Catskill, NY 12414
Phone: 518 943-2600
Fax: –
Web: www.tbogc.com

CEO: Donald Gibson
CFO: Michelle Plummer
HR: –
FYE: June 30
Type: Public

This company helps put the "green" in upstate New York. Greene County Bancorp is the holding company for The Bank of Greene County serving New York's Catskill Mountains region from about a dozen branches. Founded in 1889 as a building and loan association the bank offers traditional retail products such as savings NOW checking and money market accounts; IRAs; and CDs. Real estate loans make up about 85% of the bank's lending activities; it also writes business and consumer loans. Through affiliations with Fenimore Asset Management and Essex Corp. Greene County Bancorp offers investment products. Subsidiary Greene County Commercial Bank is a state-chartered limited purpose commercial bank.

	Annual Growth	06/17	06/18	06/19	06/20	06/21
Assets ($ mil.)	22.3%	982.3	1,151.5	1,269.5	1,676.8	2,200.3
Net income ($ mil.)	21.0%	11.2	14.4	17.5	18.7	23.9
Market value ($ mil.)	0.8%	231.6	288.6	250.5	189.8	239.4
Employees	7.2%	146	164	172	186	193

GREENHILL & CO INC   NYS: GHL

1271 Avenue of Americas
New York, NY 10020
Phone: 212 389-1500
Fax: –
Web: www.greenhill.com

CEO: Scott Bok
CFO: Harold Rodriguez
HR: –
FYE: December 31
Type: Public

Greenhill is a leading independent investment bank that provides financial and strategic advice on significant domestic and cross-border mergers and acquisitions divestitures restructurings financings capital raising and other transactions to a diverse client base including corporations partnerships institutions and governments globally. It serves as a trusted advisor to its clients throughout the world on a collaborative globally integrated basis from its offices in the US Australia Canada France Germany Hong Kong Japan Singapore Spain Sweden and the UK. Its top clients include Alcoa American Axle Emerson Experian GlaxoSmithKline Teva Tesco Visa and Wells Fargo among others. About 50% of total revenue generated from clients outside US. Greenhill was established in 1996 by Robert F. Greenhill.

	Annual Growth	12/16	12/17	12/18	12/19	12/20
Sales ($ mil.)	(1.8%)	335.5	239.2	352.0	301.0	311.7
Net income ($ mil.)	(15.3%)	60.8	(26.7)	39.2	11.0	31.3
Market value ($ mil.)	(18.6%)	526.3	370.5	463.6	324.5	230.7
Employees	0.1%	356	346	365	405	358

GREENHUNTER RESOURCES, INC   ASE: GRH

1048 Texan Trail
Grapevine, TX 76051
Phone: 972 410-1044
Fax: 972 410-1066
Web: www.greenhunterenergy.com

CEO: –
CFO: –
HR: –
FYE: December 31
Type: Public

Searching for its share of the green GreenHunter Energy has renewable energy in its sights. Focusing on wind biomass (plant material and animal waste) and biofuels the company owns generation projects and refineries in California Wyoming and Texas. Its biofuels group the only segment producing revenue refines processes and stores biofuels at the company's Houston plant. It uses purchased methanol to create biodiesel up to 105 million gallons per year. GreenHunter's other operations include a biomass plant in California (currently being refurbished) and three development-stage wind energy projects in Wyoming and Texas. The company began operations in 2007 when it purchased the biofuels plant.

	Annual Growth	12/10	12/11	12/12	12/13	12/14
Sales ($ mil.)	190.6%	–	1.1	17.1	25.7	27.1
Net income ($ mil.)	–	20.6	(4.8)	(17.6)	(9.9)	(6.8)
Market value ($ mil.)	(2.9%)	29.0	31.2	58.1	41.6	25.8
Employees	94.3%	8	–	164	134	114

GREENLINK INTERNATIONAL INC   NBB: WSHE

711 Court A, Suite # 204
Tacoma, WA 98402
Phone: 833 587-4669
Fax: –
Web: www.greenlinkholdings.com

CEO: –
CFO: –
HR: –
FYE: December 31
Type: Public

Westsphere Asset Corporation is a holding company that focuses on privately owned banking services in Canada. Saddled with debt and mounting losses the company restructured in 2009 and combined most of its businesses under its Westsphere Systems subsidiary. Westsphere Systems absorbed Vencash Capital that year and took over its management of more than 800 mostly privately owned so-called "white label" automated teller machines (ATMs) and point of sale (POS) payment processing machines. Another subsidiary E-Debit International which provided pre-paid debit cards was also consolidated under Westsphere Systems. Its Kan-Can Resorts time-share resort subsidiary was dissolved.

	Annual Growth	12/11	12/12	12/18	12/19	12/20
Sales ($ mil.)	(18.2%)	3.3	2.3	0.3	0.4	0.5
Net income ($ mil.)	–	(1.1)	(0.8)	(2.9)	(0.3)	(0.5)
Market value ($ mil.)	22.7%	5.0	4.5	21.2	10.5	31.5
Employees	(18.2%)	22	18	–	–	–

GREENSHIFT CORP
NBB: GERS

1800 NE 135th Street
Oklahoma, OK 73131
Phone: 888 510-2392
Fax: –
Web: www.greenshift.com

CEO: Kevin Kreisler
CFO: Kevin Kreisler
HR: –
FYE: December 31
Type: Public

In a case of modern alchemy GreenShift (formerly GS CleanTech) is working overtime to turn organic material into biodiesel. The company's proprietary technologies are used to produce biomass-derived end products and at reduced cost and risk by extracting and refining raw materials that other producers cannot access or process. GreenShift owns and operates four proprietary corn oil extraction facilities one biodiesel production facility and one vegetable oilseed crushing plant. GreenShift claims that its technologies have the capability of extracting more than 6.5 million gallons of crude corn oil for every 100 million gallons of corn ethanol produced. The company also produces culinary oil.

	Annual Growth	12/16	12/17	12/18	12/19	12/20
Sales ($ mil.)	(51.9%)	4.7	6.9	3.8	1.5	0.3
Net income ($ mil.)	–	5.9	(2.2)	0.4	0.4	(0.5)
Market value ($ mil.)	–	0.0	4.8	0.9	1.0	1.6
Employees	–	–	–	–	–	–

GREENSTONE FARM CREDIT SERVICES ACA

3515 WEST RD
EAST LANSING, MI 488237312
Phone: 517-324-0213
Fax: –
Web: www.greenstonefcs.com

CEO: David B Armstrong
CFO: –
HR: –
FYE: December 31
Type: Private

One of the largest associations in the Farm Credit System GreenStone offers FARM CREDIT SERVICES (FCS) provides short intermediate and long-term loans; equipment and building leases; appraisal services; and life and crop insurance to farmers in Michigan and Wisconsin. It serves about 15000 members and has nearly 40 locations. Through an alliance with AgriSolutions a farm software and consulting company Greenstone provides income tax planning and preparation services farm business consulting and educational seminars. FCS Mortgage provides residential loans for rural properties as well as loans for home improvement construction and refinancing.

	Annual Growth	12/04	12/05	12/06	12/07	12/20
Assets ($ mil.)	8.1%	–	–	3,691.3	4,317.3	10,967.2
Net income ($ mil.)	10.8%	–	–	63.9	69.6	270.2
Market value ($ mil.)	–	–	–	–	–	–
Employees	–	–	–	–	–	380

GREENVILLE UTILITIES COMMISSION

401 S GREENE ST
GREENVILLE, NC 278341977
Phone: 252-551-3315
Fax: –
Web: www.guc.com

CEO: –
CFO: –
HR: –
FYE: June 30
Type: Private

For Greenville citizens the alternative to "YUK!" (no power natural gas supply potable water or sanitation) is GUC. Greenville Utilities Commission (GUC) distributes electricity natural gas water and wastewater services to residents and businesses in the city of Greenville and 75% of Pitt County in North Carolina for a combined total of more than 143000 customer connections. The utility receives wholesale power through its membership in the North Carolina Eastern Municipal Power Agency. One of 32 municipal members of the North Carolina Eastern Municipal Power Agency GUC joined the Power Agency in 1982.

	Annual Growth	06/06	06/07	06/08	06/15	06/16
Sales ($ mil.)	1.0%	–	225.5	0.0	272.0	247.2
Net income ($ mil.)	8.7%	–	11.8	12.8	13.2	24.9
Market value ($ mil.)	–	–	–	–	–	–
Employees	–	–	–	–	–	435

GREENWAY MEDICAL TECHNOLOGIES INC.
NYSE: GWAY

121 Greenway Blvd.
Carrollton GA 30117
Phone: 770-836-3100
Fax: 770-836-3200
Web: www.greenwaymedical.com

CEO: Wyche T Green III
CFO: James A Cochran
HR: –
FYE: June 30
Type: Public

Greenway Medical Technologies sees a lot of green in the health care market. The company provides doctor-centered software and services designed to integrate the clinical and business sides of physician practices. Its Web-based PrimeSUITE software is used to automate practice management electronic health records (EHR) and managed care functions as well as to link patient chart records to billing processes. Customers include some 33000 health care providers. Greenway was involved in creating definitions and certification standards related to EHR in the health IT portion of the federal stimulus bill the American Recovery and Reinvestment Act of 2009. It filed an IPO seeking $100 million in 2011.

GREIF INC
NYS: GEF

425 Winter Road
Delaware, OH 43015
Phone: 740 549-6000
Fax: –
Web: www.greif.com

CEO: Ole Rosgaard
CFO: Lawrence Hilsheimer
HR: –
FYE: October 31
Type: Public

Greif produces rigid industrial packaging products including steel plastic and fibre drums and related closure systems. It sells corrugated products and containerboard for packaging home appliances small machinery and grocery and building products. Greif also makes flexible intermediate containers (based on polypropylene woven fabric) used to ship an array of bulk industrial and consumer goods. Additionally the company owns approximately 175000 acres of timber property used to provide the raw material for some of its products. Greif caters to a diverse group of industries such as chemicals food and beverage petroleum agricultural pharmaceuticals and minerals. The company operates worldwide however it generates some 60% of revenue from US operations. It traces its history back to 1877.

	Annual Growth	10/17	10/18	10/19	10/20	10/21
Sales ($ mil.)	11.2%	3,638.2	3,873.8	4,595.0	4,515.0	5,556.1
Net income ($ mil.)	34.7%	118.6	209.4	171.0	108.8	390.7
Market value ($ mil.)	3.9%	2,696.5	2,296.8	1,902.0	1,971.0	3,140.8
Employees	5.3%	13,000	13,000	17,000	16,000	16,000

GREYSTONE POWER CORPORATION, AN ELECTRIC MEMBERSHIP CORPORATION

3400 HRAM DUGLASVILLE HWY
HIRAM, GA 301414924
Phone: 770-942-6576
Fax: –
Web: www.greystonepower.com

CEO: Gary Miller
CFO: –
HR: –
FYE: August 31
Type: Private

GreyStone's power helps to lift the grey and the darkness. GreyStone Power is an electric membership cooperative that provides transmission and distribution services to almost 116000 residential commercial and industrial customers in eight counties west of Atlanta (Bartow Carroll Cobb Coweta Douglas Fayette Fulton and Paulding). The utility operates about 3500 miles of overhead power lines. GreyStone Power also offers natural gas services through a partnership with Gas South and offers banking residential and commercial security and surge protection operations.

	Annual Growth	08/14	08/15	08/16*	12/18*	08/20
Sales ($ mil.)	1.4%	–	–	270.0	305.1	285.6
Net income ($ mil.)	(5.8%)	–	–	23.3	0.0	18.4
Market value ($ mil.)	–	–	–	–	–	–
Employees	–	–	–	–	–	260

*Fiscal year change

GRIFFITH LABORATORIES INC.

1 Griffith Center
Alsip IL 60803
Phone: 708-371-0900
Fax: 708-389-4055
Web: www.griffithlaboratories.com

CEO: –
CFO: Joseph R Maslick
HR: –
FYE: September 30
Type: Private

A little pinch here a little pinch there pretty soon you have a business. Founded in 1919 Griffith Laboratories is a food-ingredient manufacturer with operations and customers worldwide. The company's clients include food manufacturers; foodservice operators such as restaurants hotels and cruise lines; and food retailers and wholesalers. Its products include seasonings sauce and soup mixes condiments texturizers and bakery blends. Griffith's subsidiaries include Custom Culinary (food bases and mixes) and Innova (meat and savory flavors). The company also offers customized ingredient services.

GRIFFON CORP.   NYS: GFF

712 Fifth Avenue, 18th Floor
New York, NY 10019
Phone: 212 957-5000
Fax: –
Web: www.griffon.com

CEO: Ronald Kramer
CFO: Brian Harris
HR: –
FYE: September 30
Type: Public

Griffon Corporation is a diversified management and holding company that conducts business through wholly-owned subsidiaries. The company operates in two segments ? consumer and professional products and home and building products. AMES and ClosetMaid Griffon's consumer and professional products subsidiaries make wood and wire closet organizations yard tools cleaning and storage products. The home and building segment operates through Clopay which has become the largest manufacturer and marketer of garage doors and rolling steel doors in North America. The US accounts for about 75% of Griffon's total revenue.

	Annual Growth	09/17	09/18	09/19	09/20	09/21
Sales ($ mil.)	10.5%	1,525.0	1,977.9	2,209.3	2,407.5	2,270.6
Net income ($ mil.)	51.8%	14.9	125.7	37.3	53.4	79.2
Market value ($ mil.)	2.6%	1,256.8	914.3	1,187.2	1,106.2	1,392.7
Employees	9.3%	4,700	7,200	7,300	7,400	6,700

GRILL CONCEPTS INC.   PINK SHEETS: GLLC

6300 Canoga Ave. Ste. 600
Woodland Hills CA 91367
Phone: 818-251-7000
Fax: 818-999-4745
Web: www.dailygrill.com

CEO: Bob Spivak
CFO: Wayne Lipschitz
HR: –
FYE: December 31
Type: Public

You might say this company is cooking up some classics on a daily basis. Grill Concepts operates a chain of more than 20 Daily Grill restaurants offering upscale casual dining in a setting reminiscent of a classic American grill during the 1930s and 1940s. Located primarily in California the restaurants serve such fare as chicken pot pie meatloaf and cobbler as well as steak seafood and pasta. In addition to its company-owned locations Grill Concepts has a small number of licensed and managed units operating in shopping areas and hotels. The Daily Grill concept is based on the company's half dozen Grill on the Alley fine dining restaurants. CEO Robert Spivak co-founded the Daily Grill chain in 1984.

GROEN BROTHERS AVIATION INC   NBB: GNBA

2640 West California Avenue
Salt Lake City, UT 84104-4593
Phone: 801 973-0177
Fax: –

CEO: David L Groen
CFO: David L Groen
HR: –
FYE: June 30
Type: Public

A centaur is part man part horse; a griffin is part eagle part lion; and a gyroplane is part helicopter part airplane. Through its subsidiaries Groen Brothers Aviation (GBA) develops and manufactures gyroplane and gyrodyne rotor-wing aircraft. Its Hawk series gyroplane is designed to be safer in low and slow flight than either an airplane or a helicopter. Gyroplanes get lift from rotary blades and thrust from a propeller. Potential applications for the Hawk series include commercial surveying fire patrol law enforcement and military surveillance. In 2012 GBA reached an agreement with its creditors to enter a period of financial restructuring and eliminate its debt of more than $170 million.

	Annual Growth	06/08	06/09	06/10	06/11	06/12
Sales ($ mil.)	(78.8%)	5.9	1.1	0.1	0.0	0.0
Net income ($ mil.)	–	(19.8)	(16.1)	(19.4)	(23.3)	(25.8)
Market value ($ mil.)	(15.9%)	8.6	2.7	1.7	2.9	4.3
Employees	16.7%	7	9	11	12	13

GROEN BROTHERS AVIATION INC.   PINK SHEETS: GNBA

2640 W. California Ave.
Salt Lake City UT 84104-4593
Phone: 801-973-0177
Fax: 801-973-4027
Web: www.groenbros.com

CEO: David L Groen
CFO: David L Groen
HR: –
FYE: June 30
Type: Public

A centaur is part man part horse; a griffin is part eagle part lion; and a gyroplane is part helicopter part airplane. Through its subsidiaries Groen Brothers Aviation (GBA) develops and manufactures gyroplane and gyrodyne rotor-wing aircraft. Its Hawk series gyroplane is designed to be safer in low and slow flight than either an airplane or a helicopter. Gyroplanes get lift from rotary blades and thrust from a propeller. Potential applications for the Hawk series include commercial surveying fire patrol law enforcement and military surveillance. In 2012 GBA reached an agreement with its creditors to enter a period of financial restructuring and eliminate its debt of more than $170 million.

GROOVE BOTANICALS INC   NBB: GRVE

310 Fourth Avenue South, Suite 7000
Minneapolis, MN 55415
Phone: 952 746-9652
Fax: –
Web: www.avalonoilinc.com

CEO: Kent Rodriguez
CFO: Kent Rodriguez
HR: –
FYE: March 31
Type: Public

Avalon Oil & Gas is looking for that legendary prize — making consistent profits in the oil business. The company focuses on acquiring mature oil and gas wells in Kansas Louisiana Oklahoma and Texas and in 2009 it reported proved reserves of about 45650 barrels of oil equivalent. In addition to its oil and gas assets Avalon Oil & Gas' technology segment (through majority-owned Oiltek) provides explorers with oil production enhancing technologies. To develop this segment the company has a strategic partnership with UK technology group Innovaro. In 2011 the company agreed to buy Oklahoma properties from Fossiltek. CEO Kent Rodriguez owns 46% of Avalon Oil & Gas.

	Annual Growth	03/13	03/14	03/15	03/16	03/17
Sales ($ mil.)	(23.2%)	0.2	0.2	0.1	0.1	0.1
Net income ($ mil.)	–	(0.7)	(0.8)	0.1	(2.5)	(0.2)
Market value ($ mil.)	(39.1%)	2.9	1.5	0.8	0.3	0.4
Employees	(20.5%)	5	5	5	2	2

GROSSMONT HOSPITAL CORPORATION

5555 GROSSMONT CENTER DR
LA MESA, CA 919423077
Phone: 619-740-6000
Fax: –
Web: www.gemg.net

CEO: Dan Gross
CFO: –
HR: –
FYE: September 30
Type: Private

Residents of the eastern San Diego community of La Mesa California depend on Grossmont for medical care. Grossmont Hospital is a 540-bed not-for-profit health care facility. The hospital which opened in 1955 has a staff of about 700 physicians. The full-service acute care facility provides specialty services in the areas of cardiology oncology mental health orthopedics pediatrics physical therapy sleep therapy hospice and women's health care. The Grossmont Hospital Corporation is a subsidiary of Sharp HealthCare; it operates the Grossmont Hospital through a lease agreement with state-owned Grossmont Hospital District.

	Annual Growth	09/08	09/09	09/13	09/14	09/15
Sales ($ mil.)	6.1%	–	500.5	621.6	596.8	712.7
Net income ($ mil.)	3.6%	–	41.5	69.1	45.3	51.4
Market value ($ mil.)	–	–	–	–	–	–
Employees	–	–	–	–	–	2,697

GROUP 1 AUTOMOTIVE, INC.

800 Gessner, Suite 500
Houston, TX 77024
Phone: 713 647-5700
Fax: 713 647-5858
Web: www.group1auto.com

NYS: GPI

CEO: Earl Hesterberg
CFO: Daniel McHenry
HR: Frank Grese
FYE: December 31
Type: Public

Group 1 Automotive is a new and used car retailer with more than 185 dealerships nearly 240 franchises across the US UK and Brazil. The US is the biggest market and the company is present in approximately 15 US states. Group 1's largest concentration of dealerships is in its home state of Texas. Of its new and used car and light truck brands Group 1 offers Toyota/Lexus vehicles are its biggest sellers followed by BMW/MINI and Volkswagen/Audi/Porsche/SEAT/SKODA. The company also offers financing provides maintenance and repair services and sells replacement parts. It went public in 1997.

	Annual Growth	12/16	12/17	12/18	12/19	12/20
Sales ($ mil.)	(0.1%)	10,887.6	11,123.7	11,601.4	12,043.8	10,851.8
Net income ($ mil.)	18.1%	147.1	213.4	157.8	174.0	286.5
Market value ($ mil.)	13.9%	1,410.0	1,283.9	953.7	1,809.1	2,372.4
Employees	(2.2%)	13,500	14,108	14,570	15,296	12,337

GROUP HEALTH COOPERATIVE

320 Westlake Ave. North Ste. 100
Seattle WA 98109-5233
Phone: 206-448-5600
Fax: 206-448-4010
Web: www.ghc.org

CEO: –
CFO: Linda Breard
HR: –
FYE: December 31
Type: Private - Cooperativ

Group Health Cooperative gives new meaning to the term "consumer-driven health care." The organization is a not-for-profit managed health care group serving more than 600000 residents of Washington and Northern Idaho. Founded in 1947 and governed by a member-elected board the co-op offers health insurance through its Group Health Options and KPS Health Plans subsidiaries. It also operates a research institute and offers health care clinical services primarily through its affiliated Group Health Physicians organization. It also maintains partnerships with other health facility operators.

GROUP O, INC.

4905 77TH AVE E
MILAN, IL 612643250
Phone: 309-736-8100
Fax: –
Web: www.groupo.com

CEO: Gregg Ontiveros
CFO: Robert Marriott
HR: –
FYE: December 31
Type: Private

The "O" in Group O stands for optimization. It also stands for Ontiveros the family that leads this company. Founded by chairman Robert Ontiveros Group O is one of the largest Hispanic-owned companies in the US. It helps big businesses improve their operations through three divisions: marketing packaging and supply chain. It offers everything from direct mail creation to shrink wrap procurement to warehousing and distribution and business intelligence. It has served clients from various industries including food and beverage (Kerry) consumer goods (P&G) manufacturing (Johnson Controls) pharmaceutical (Bristol-Myers Squibb) and telecommunications (AT&T).

	Annual Growth	12/02	12/03	12/04	12/05	12/13
Sales ($ mil.)	11.4%	–	–	–	240.4	569.5
Net income ($ mil.)	0.9%	–	–	–	5.3	5.6
Market value ($ mil.)	–	–	–	–	–	–
Employees	–	–	–	–	–	1,066

GROUPON INC

600 W. Chicago Avenue, Suite 400
Chicago, IL 60654
Phone: 312 334-1579
Fax: –
Web: www.groupon.com

NMS: GRPN

CEO: Kedar Deshpande
CFO: Damien Schmitz
HR: –
FYE: December 31
Type: Public

Groupon taps into the power of collective buying. The company earns service revenue from transactions in which it earns commissions by selling goods or services on behalf of third-party merchants. Groupon also sells merchandise such as electronics toys apparel and household items directly to customers. Customers access the company's platform through mobile apps and websites. Groupon has some 30 million active customers. North America is Groupon's largest market accounting for nearly 60% of total sales. Groupon was founded in 2008.

	Annual Growth	12/16	12/17	12/18	12/19	12/20
Sales ($ mil.)	(18.1%)	3,143.4	2,843.9	2,636.7	2,218.9	1,416.9
Net income ($ mil.)	–	(194.6)	14.0	(11.1)	(22.4)	(287.9)
Market value ($ mil.)	83.9%	95.8	147.1	92.3	68.9	1,096.1
Employees	(15.9%)	8,323	6,672	6,576	2,358	4,159

GROWMARK, INC.

1701 TOWANDA AVE
BLOOMINGTON, IL 617012057
Phone: 309-557-6000
Fax: –
Web: www.growmark.com

CEO: Jim Spradlin
CFO: Wade Mittelstadt
HR: –
FYE: August 31
Type: Private

GROWMARK is an agricultural cooperative serving about 400000 customers across North America. It provides agronomy energy facility engineering and construction products and services as well as grain marketing and risk management services. It owns the FS trademark which is used by member cooperatives. Handles more than 3.2 million tons annually the company also operates a full-line seed company SEEDWAY and provides grain facility planning and grain marketing services. In addition to secure warehousing in facilities GROWMARK also provides truck barge and rail transport unloading and inventory control. The company has an extensive network of fertilizer terminals throughout the Midwest and Ontario.

	Annual Growth	08/16	08/17	08/18	08/19	08/20
Sales ($ mil.)	1.1%	–	7,291.2	8,522.4	8,745.2	7,541.4
Net income ($ mil.)	(16.0%)	–	115.4	65.8	75.7	68.4
Market value ($ mil.)	–	–	–	–	–	–
Employees	–	–	–	–	–	8,641

GRUMA CORPORATION

5601 EXECUTIVE DR STE 800
IRVING, TX 750382508
Phone: 972-232-5000
Fax: –
Web: www.missionfoods.com

CEO: –
CFO: –
HR: –
FYE: December 31
Type: Private

Gruma is the American subsidiary of giant Mexican food company Gruma S.A.B. de C.V. and the leading tortilla and corn flower producer in the US. The company manufactures and distributes corn flour corn tortillas and related products such as wraps and corn chips through roughly 20 production plants. The company runs the world's largest tortilla plant in Los Angeles; that facility has a production capacity of 25 million tortillas per day. Its highly recognizable brand names include Mission Calidad and Guerrero tortillas and Maseca corn flour. Gruma is its parent company's largest revenue producer.

	Annual Growth	12/13	12/14	12/15	12/16	12/19
Sales ($ mil.)	1.4%	–	–	2,086.8	2,023.7	2,202.3
Net income ($ mil.)	10.2%	–	–	152.6	179.1	224.9
Market value ($ mil.)	–	–	–	–	–	–
Employees	–	–	–	–	–	7,000

GRUNLEY CONSTRUCTION CO., INC.

15020 SHADY GROVE RD # 500
ROCKVILLE, MD 208503390
Phone: 240-399-2000
Fax: –
Web: www.grunley.com

CEO: Kenneth M Grunley
CFO: –
HR: –
FYE: December 31
Type: Private

Grunley gets it done from the monumental to the mundane. Founded in 1955 Grunley Construction Company provides general contracting engineering architectural and construction management services and specializes in the renovation restoration and modernization of historic buildings in the Washington DC area. Its projects range from prestigious undertakings — the Smithsonian Institutionthe Washington Monument and the US Treasury building — to more pedestrian endeavors such as office buildings apartment buildings schools and power plants. The company also has lent its services to the construction of embassies airports and military facilities.

	Annual Growth	12/09	12/10	12/11	12/15	12/16
Sales ($ mil.)	5.6%	–	–	324.0	403.8	425.7
Net income ($ mil.)	–	–	–	0.0	0.0	6.3
Market value ($ mil.)	–	–	–	–	–	–
Employees	–	–	–	–	–	310

GSE HOLDING INC.

19103 Gundle Rd.
Houston TX 77073
Phone: 281-443-8564
Fax: 281-230-8650
Web: www.gseworld.com

CEO: Robert Preston
CFO: Daniel C Storey
HR: –
FYE: December 31
Type: Public

NYSE: GSE

GSE has a hold on containment. The plastics company makes and sells a variety of geosynthetic materials used for lining landfills water treatment ponds canals tanks and in other infrastructure applications. It produces smooth and textured geomembranes drainage products (geonets and geocomposites) synthetic clay liners and nonwoven textiles. Specialty products include curtain walls concrete embedment strips and aquaculture tank and tunnel liners. GSE's seven manufacturing plants in Thailand Germany the US Chile and Egypt support nearly 20 sales offices in a dozen countries. A subsidiary of containment specialist Gundle/SLT Environmental formed in 2004 GSE went public in early 2012.

GSE SYSTEMS INC

6940 Columbia Gateway Dr., Suite 470
Columbia, MD 21046
Phone: 410 970-7800
Fax: –
Web: www.gses.com

CEO: Kyle Loudermilk
CFO: Emmett Pepe
HR: –
FYE: December 31
Type: Public

NAS: GVP

GSE Systems is into the appearance of power and control. The company provides simulation software to train power plant operators engineers and managers. Its systems used primarily for the nuclear power fossil energy and chemical industries can also be used to test new plant systems before they are installed. GSE Systems also offers training services through a partnership with General Physics. Customers include Slovenske electrarne American Electric Power Emerson Process Management Statoil ASA and Westinghouse Electric. With international offices in China India Sweden and the UK GSE Systems generates about 70% of sales from customers located outside the US.

	Annual Growth	12/16	12/17	12/18	12/19	12/20
Sales ($ mil.)	2.1%	53.1	70.9	92.2	83.0	57.6
Net income ($ mil.)	–	1.4	5.4	(0.4)	(12.1)	(10.5)
Market value ($ mil.)	(21.6%)	72.1	66.9	43.2	34.0	27.2
Employees	5.1%	272	430	402	363	332

GSI COMMERCE INC.

935 1st Ave.
King of Prussia PA 19406
Phone: 610-491-7000
Fax: 617-787-9355
Web: www.newbalance.com

CEO: Pierre Winand
CFO: Gary Crowe
HR: –
FYE: December 31
Type: Subsidiary

If you're not feeling generally secure in your e-commerce initiatives GSI Commerce aims to help. The company provides e-commerce services such as website development and maintenance order fulfillment payment processing and customer service. Its digital advertising offerings include brand development and e-mail marketing services. The company serves hundreds of companies and brands in markets such as retail consumer goods manufacturing and media. In 2011 GSI was acquired by auction powerhouse eBay. Under the terms of the deal eBay divested GSI's RueLaLa unit (online private sales business) and 70% of its ShopRunner operations (provides members-only online shopping and shipping services).

GSI TECHNOLOGY INC

1213 Elko Drive
Sunnyvale, CA 94089
Phone: 408 331-8800
Fax: –
Web: www.gsitechnology.com

CEO: Lee-Lean Shu
CFO: Douglas Schirle
HR: –
FYE: March 31
Type: Public

NMS: GSIT

GSI Technology makes very fast chips. The company's specialized SRAM (static random-access memory) integrated circuits are used in high-speed networking equipment. Marketed under the Very Fast brand its chips allow routers switches and other gear from the likes of Alcatel-Lucent and Cisco Systems to retrieve data at the speeds needed for broadband transmission. The fabless semiconductor company does most of its business through contract manufacturers such as Jabil Circuit (20% of sales) and Flextronics (9%) and through distributors such as Avnet (20%) and Nexcomm (11%). Other top customers include SMART Modular Technologies (11%) which buys memory chips for products it makes on behalf of Cisco.

	Annual Growth	03/17	03/18	03/19	03/20	03/21
Sales ($ mil.)	(12.9%)	48.2	42.6	51.5	43.3	27.7
Net income ($ mil.)	–	(0.1)	(4.5)	0.2	(10.3)	(21.5)
Market value ($ mil.)	(6.4%)	209.0	178.0	186.6	167.2	160.7
Employees	3.4%	156	157	166	166	178

GT ADVANCED TECHNOLOGIES INC.

NBB: GTAT Q

20 Trafalgar Square
Nashua, NH 03063
Phone: 603 883-5200
Fax: –
Web: www.gtsolar.com

CEO: Gregory C Knight
CFO: Michele P Rayos
HR: –
FYE: December 31
Type: Public

GT Advanced Technologies (formerly GT Solar International) is a beacon on the path of the solar power supply chain. The company manufactures the equipment used by other companies to produce silicon wafers and solar cells. Key products include chemical vapor deposition (CVD) reactors used to produce polysilicon the raw material in solar cells; and directional solidification systems (DSS) the furnaces used to transform polysilicon into ingots which are sliced into silicon wafers to become solar cells. GT Advanced Technologies does most of its business in Asia primarily in Malaysia. In 2014 the company filed for Chapter 11 bankruptcy protection.

	Annual Growth	04/10	04/11*	03/12*	12/12	12/13
Sales ($ mil.)	(18.1%)	544.2	899.0	955.7	379.6	299.0
Net income ($ mil.)	–	87.3	174.8	183.4	(142.3)	(82.8)
Market value ($ mil.)	18.7%	700.6	1,399.8	1,112.0	407.4	1,171.8
Employees	12.1%	384	622	663	531	541

*Fiscal year change

GTSI CORP.

NASDAQ: GTSI

2553 Dulles View Dr. Ste. 100
Herndon VA 20171
Phone: 703-502-2000
Fax: 703-463-5101
Web: www.gtsi.com

CEO: –
CFO: –
HR: –
FYE: December 31
Type: Private

When the government goes shopping GTSI supplies the goods. The company resells computers software and networking products to US federal state and local governments. It offers products from vendors including Cisco Hewlett-Packard NetApp and Microsoft. Founded in 1983 GTSI also provides asset management consulting design integration maintenance procurement and support services. It offers financing through affiliate GTSI Financial and logistics services via another unit. Business with the federal government generates close to three-quarters of sales. GTSI also sells to prime government contractors. In 2012 the company was acquired for some $76.7 million by UNICOM Systems part of the UNICOM group.

GTT COMMUNICATIONS, INC

NBB: GTTN Q

7900 Tysons One Place, Suite 1450
McLean, VA 22102
Phone: 703 442-5500
Fax: –
Web: www.gtt.net

CEO: Ernest Ortega
CFO: Donna Granato
HR: –
FYE: December 31
Type: Public

GTT Communications (formerly Global Telecom & Technology) provides network integration for wide area network (WAN) dedicated Internet access dedicated ethernet and video transport infrastructure unified communication managed data services and advanced solutions to enterprise carriers and government agencies. GTT combines multiple networks and technologies such as traditional OC-x MPLS and Ethernet and has distribution partnerships with more than 800 technology suppliers including iPass for wireless services. Past customers include Avaya Lockheed Martin and Telefónica. GTT counts customers in more than 140 countries; it earns more than half of its revenues outside the US. Founder and Chairman Brian Thompson owns about 30% of the company's stock.

	Annual Growth	12/15	12/16	12/17	12/18	12/19
Sales ($ mil.)	47.1%	369.3	521.7	827.9	1,490.8	1,727.8
Net income ($ mil.)	–	19.3	5.3	(71.5)	(243.4)	(105.9)
Market value ($ mil.)	(9.7%)	967.1	1,629.7	2,661.4	1,341.2	643.4
Employees	52.6%	572	662	1,257	3,200	3,100

GUADALUPE VALLEY TELEPHONE COOPERATIVE, INC.

36101 FM 3159
NEW BRAUNFELS, TX 781325900
Phone: 830-885-4411
Fax: –

CEO: Ritchie Sorrells
CFO: Mark J Gitter
HR: –
FYE: December 31
Type: Private

Guadalupe Valley Telephone Cooperative (GVTC) offers telecommunications services to residential and business customers in the Hill Country area of south Texas. The cooperative local exchange carrier provides traditional local and long-distance telephone services Internet access digital cable television high speed Fiber-To-The-Business (FTTB) service and high-speed Fiber-To-The-Home (FTTH) converged service packages. GVTC also installs and monitors residential and commercial security systems and provides additional enterprise services such as its ID Vault information security service. Founded in 1951 GVTC also offers Web hosting technical support domain registration and Web scam alert services.

	Annual Growth	12/13	12/14	12/15	12/16	12/17
Sales ($ mil.)	2.9%	–	63.4	65.6	63.8	69.2
Net income ($ mil.)	9.8%	–	25.1	20.9	15.9	33.3
Market value ($ mil.)	–	–	–	–	–	–
Employees	–	–	–	–	–	229

GUARANTEE ELECTRICAL COMPANY

3405 BENT AVE
SAINT LOUIS, MO 631162601
Phone: 314-772-5400
Fax: –
Web: www.geco.com

CEO: Rick Oertli
CFO: Josh Voegtli
HR: –
FYE: September 30
Type: Private

Guarantee Electrical has been a power in St. Louis since delivered on its "guarantee" to light up the 1904 World's Fair. Now a major US electrical contractor the company offers commercial institutional and industrial services including pre-construction and construction design/build communications/data systems services and maintenance. Guarantee Electrical operates throughout the country and has worked on such varied projects as the MGM Grand in Las Vegas and several post office and prison facilities. Its GECO Systems division installs and services intercom closed-circuit television and other audio-visual systems. The employee-owned firm generated $148 million in revenue during FY2015.

	Annual Growth	09/16	09/17	09/18	09/19	09/20
Sales ($ mil.)	8.0%	–	152.6	152.2	205.0	192.4
Net income ($ mil.)	–	–	0.0	0.0	0.0	0.0
Market value ($ mil.)	–	–	–	–	–	–
Employees	–	–	–	–	–	700

GUARANTY BANCORP (DE)

NMS: GBNK

1331 Seventeenth St., Suite 200
Denver, CO 80202
Phone: 303 675-1194
Fax: –
Web: www.gbnk.com

CEO: –
CFO: –
HR: –
FYE: December 31
Type: Public

Guaranty Bancorp holds Colorado's Guaranty Bank and Trust which operates 25-plus branches mostly in the metropolitan Denver and Front Range areas. Boasting $3.3 billion in assets the bank offers traditional retail and commercial banking including deposit accounts loans and trust services. Subsidiaries Private Capital Management and Cherry Hills Investment Advisors provide private banking investment management trust services and other wealth management services. The bank mostly targets small to medium-sized businesses. Over 30% of the bank's loan portfolio is made up of commercial and residential real estate property loans while another 15% consists of retail and industrial property loans.

	Annual Growth	12/12	12/13	12/14	12/15	12/16
Assets ($ mil.)	15.6%	1,886.9	1,911.0	2,124.8	2,368.5	3,366.4
Net income ($ mil.)	13.2%	15.1	14.0	13.5	22.5	24.7
Market value ($ mil.)	87.7%	55.3	398.1	409.1	468.6	685.7
Employees	8.4%	378	374	389	376	521

GUARANTY BANCSHARES INC
NMS: GNTY

16475 Dallas Parkway, Suite 600
Addison, TX 75001
Phone: 888 572-9881
Fax: –
Web: www.gnty.com

CEO: Tyson Abston
CFO: Clifton Payne
HR: –
FYE: December 31
Type: Public

Guaranty Bancshares is the holding company for Guaranty Bond Bank which operates about a dozen branches in northeast Texas and another in West Texas. Guaranty Bond Bank's deposit products and services include CDs and savings checking NOW and money market accounts. Its lending activities include one- to four-family residential mortgages (more than a third of the company's loan portfolio) in addition to commercial mortgage construction business agriculture and personal loans. The company's GB Financial division provides wealth management retirement planning and trust services.

	Annual Growth	12/16	12/17	12/18	12/19	12/20
Assets ($ mil.)	10.7%	1,828.3	1,962.6	2,267.0	2,318.4	2,740.8
Net income ($ mil.)	22.6%	12.1	14.4	20.6	26.3	27.4
Market value ($ mil.)	3.1%	289.8	335.2	326.1	359.6	327.5
Employees	4.1%	397	407	454	467	467

GUARDIAN LIFE INSURANCE CO. OF AMERICA (NYC)

7 Hanover Square, H-26-E
New York, NY 10004-2616
Phone: 212 598-8000
Fax: –
Web: www.guardianlife.com

CEO: Andrew McMahon
CFO: Kevin Molloy
HR: –
FYE: December 31
Type: Public

Guardian Life Insurance Company of America keeps a sharp eye on the investments of its policyholders. Guardian and its subsidiaries offer life insurance disability income insurance and retirement programs to individuals business owners and their employees. Its employee health indemnity plans provide HMO PPO and dental and vision plans as well as disability plans. Its Guardian Insurance & Annuity subsidiary offers retirement options that include mutual funds and annuity products which its Guardian Investor Services manages. Guardian also offers estate planning and education savings programs. The firm is a mutual company owned by its policyholders.

	Annual Growth	12/02	12/03	12/04	12/11	12/12
Assets ($ mil.)	1.0%	34,074.0	21,671.0	23,336.0	35,127.0	37,529.0
Net income ($ mil.)	–	(283.0)	218.0	286.0	196.0	253.0
Market value ($ mil.)	–	–	–	–	–	–
Employees	–	–	–	–	–	–

GUARDSMARK LLC

10 Rockefeller Plaza
New York NY 10020-1903
Phone: 212-765-8226
Fax: 212-603-3854
Web: www.guardsmark.com

CEO: Steven S Jones
CFO: –
HR: –
FYE: June 30
Type: Private

When FBI agents leave Quantico the agency's training academy they go to Guardsmark. The company provides security services to companies in the financial health care transportation utility and other industries. It is also a leading employer of former FBI agents as well as former agents of the Secret Service the DEA state and local police forces and the military. Guardsmark offers security guards private investigation and drug testing services. In addition the company conducts background checks (employment education and criminal history) and consults with architects and builders to design security programs. Chairman and president Ira Lipman owns the company which he founded in 1963.

GUESS ?, INC.
NYS: GES

1444 South Alameda Street
Los Angeles, CA 90021
Phone: 213 765-3100
Fax: –
Web: www.guess.com

CEO: Carlos Alberini
CFO: Kathryn Anderson
HR: –
FYE: January 30
Type: Public

Guess? designs markets distributes and licenses one of the world's leading lifestyle collections of contemporary apparel and accessories for men women and children under brands GUESS GUESS Kids YES Baby GUESS and GUESS by MARCIANO among others. Guess operates approximately 1570 stores and about 375 concessions in the US Canada Europe the Middle East and Asia. To capitalize on the power of its brand Guess licenses its name for apparel eyewear handbags footwear fragrance jewelry and watches. The company was founded in 1981. Approximately 75% of sales were generated outside US.

	Annual Growth	01/17*	02/18	02/19	02/20*	01/21
Sales ($ mil.)	(4.0%)	2,209.4	2,363.8	2,609.7	2,678.1	1,876.5
Net income ($ mil.)	–	22.8	(7.9)	14.1	96.0	(81.2)
Market value ($ mil.)	17.2%	790.0	938.4	1,222.3	1,367.5	1,491.4
Employees	(6.3%)	14,300	14,700	15,700	15,800	11,000

*Fiscal year change

GUEST SERVICES, INC.

3055 PROSPERITY AVE
FAIRFAX, VA 220312290
Phone: 703-849-9300
Fax: –
Web: www.guestservices.com

CEO: Gerard T Gabrys
CFO: Daniel Stoltzfus
HR: –
FYE: December 31
Type: Private

Guest Services supplies hospitality management services across a wide variety of client sites including government and business dining facilities museums hotels resorts conference centers luxury condominiums senior living centers health care systems state and national parks school and university dining facilities specialty retail stores and full-service restaurants. For leisure and resort facilities Guest Services offers water recreation activities golf spa and health club and range among other. Guest Services was founded in 1917 as a private company to serve governmental agencies.

	Annual Growth	12/15	12/16	12/17	12/18	12/20
Sales ($ mil.)	(27.0%)	–	442.6	459.6	463.7	125.7
Net income ($ mil.)	16.9%	–	1.8	(2.8)	(3.0)	3.3
Market value ($ mil.)	–	–	–	–	–	–
Employees	–	–	–	–	–	2,500

GUIDANCE SOFTWARE INC
NMS: GUID

1055 E. Colorado Blvd.
Pasadena, CA 91106
Phone: 626 229-9191
Fax: –
Web: www.guidancesoftware.com

CEO: Patrick Dennis
CFO: Barry Plaga
HR: Ruth Blanco
FYE: December 31
Type: Public

Guidance Software could be the digital version of TV's CSI only in real life. The company provides software that government authorities police agencies and corporate investigators use for digital forensic investigations information auditing e-discovery and incident response. The company's EnCase software is a forensics platform that helps organizations respond to threats and analyze information including court-validated forensics tools to conduct investigations. Guidance serves some two-thirds of FORTUNE 100 companies such as Apple Boeing Coca-Cola Facebook Whole Foods Yahoo! government agencies such as the CIA and NASA and international organizations such as NATO.

	Annual Growth	12/11	12/12	12/13	12/14	12/15
Sales ($ mil.)	0.6%	104.6	129.5	110.5	108.7	107.0
Net income ($ mil.)	–	(1.6)	(2.0)	(21.5)	(14.7)	(14.4)
Market value ($ mil.)	(1.8%)	197.8	362.3	308.3	221.3	183.8
Employees	2.7%	378	475	495	400	420

GUIDED THERAPEUTICS INC   NBB: GTHP

5835 Peachtree Corners East, Suite D
Norcross, GA 30092
Phone: 770 242-8723
Fax: –
Web: www.guidedinc.com
CEO: Gene Cartwright
CFO: Gene S Cartwright
HR: –
FYE: December 31
Type: Public

Guided Therapeutics (formerly SpectRx) can shed some light on your condition. The firm is developing diagnostic products including a cervical cancer detection device using its proprietary biophotonic technology known as LightTouch. The technology uses optics and spectroscopy to provide doctors with non-invasive diagnostic methods for finding cancer. In order to zero in on its diagnostic business the company in 2007 sold its SimpleChoice line of insulin pumps which diabetics use to control blood glucose levels to ICU Medical; it changed its name to Guided Therapeutics the following year to reflect its new focus.

	Annual Growth	12/16	12/17	12/18	12/19	12/20
Sales ($ mil.)	(35.9%)	0.6	0.2	0.1	0.0	0.1
Net income ($ mil.)	–	(4.0)	(10.7)	1.0	(1.9)	(0.3)
Market value ($ mil.)	(13.9%)	7.1	0.3	0.0	1.7	3.9
Employees	(11.4%)	13	10	10	8	8

GUIDEWIRE SOFTWARE INC   NYS: GWRE

2850 S. Delaware St., Suite 400
San Mateo, CA 94403
Phone: 650 357-9100
Fax: 650 357-9101
Web: www.guidewire.com
CEO: Michael Rosenbaum
CFO: Jeff Cooper
HR: –
FYE: July 31
Type: Public

Guidewire Software delivers a leading platform that Property and Casualty (P&C) insurers trust to engage innovate and grow efficiently. The company's InsuranceSuite via Guidewire Cloud offers applications to property and casualty insurers for underwriting policy administration (PolicyCenter) claims management (ClaimsCenter) and billing (BillingCenter). Its software is designed to support multiple releases a year to ensure that cloud customers remain on the latest version and gain rapid access to its innovation efforts. Guidewire counts more than 350 customers in around 35 countries. The company generates most of its sales from the US.

	Annual Growth	07/17	07/18	07/19	07/20	07/21
Sales ($ mil.)	9.6%	514.3	661.1	719.5	742.3	743.3
Net income ($ mil.)	–	21.2	(19.7)	20.7	(27.2)	(66.5)
Market value ($ mil.)	12.4%	6,003.3	7,171.3	8,492.5	9,788.6	9,584.0
Employees	11.7%	1,893	2,292	2,355	2,690	2,942

GUILFORD MILLS INC.

1001 Military Cutoff Rd. Ste. 300
Wilmington NC 28405
Phone: 910-794-5800
Fax: 816-854-8500
Web: www.hrblock.com
CEO: –
CFO: –
HR: –
FYE: September 30
Type: Private

Guilford Mills makes fabrics to cover your ride and your hide. The textile maker produces fabrics for car and heavy truck cab interiors from bodycloth to headliners. Its specialty products group makes consumer and industrial fabrics including loop closure fabrics (used in medical braces) window coverings technical stretch pieces for athletic wear and even shoe linings and casket liners. Customers include Johnson Controls. Founded in 1946 Guilford Mills (aka Guilford Performance Textiles) has sales and manufacturing locations in the US Asia and Europe. Lear bought Guilford Mills from private equity firm Cerberus Capital Management its owner since 2005 for about $257 million in 2012.

GUITAR CENTER INC.

5795 Lindero Canyon Rd.
Westlake Village CA 91362
Phone: 818-735-8800
Fax: 818-735-8822
Web: www.guitarcenter.com
CEO: Ron Japinga
CFO: Tim Martin
HR: Thomas Gerner
FYE: December 31
Type: Private

What AutoZone is to the garage Guitar Center is to the garage band. The #1 US retailer of guitars amps keyboards percussion and pro-audio equipment operates about 225 stores in more than 40 states. Major brands include Fender Gibson and Martin as well as Ampeg Crate and Vox. Stores also offer used and vintage instruments computer hardware and software and musician services (such as CD duplication and digital distribution). In addition to Guitar Center the firm runs about 100 Music & Arts Center stores that sell and rent band and orchestral instruments. Its Musician's Friend and Music 123 units sell merchandise online and by catalog. Guitar Center is owned by the private equity firm Bain Capital.

GULF COAST PROJECT SERVICES, INC.

5800 LAKEWOOD RNCH BLVD N
LAKEWOOD RANCH, FL 342408479
Phone: 941-921-6087
Fax: –
Web: www.dooleymack.com
CEO: –
CFO: –
HR: –
FYE: December 31
Type: Private

DooleyMack Constructors does the heavy lifting on big construction projects. The company provides design and planning construction management and general contracting services for commercial industrial multifamily residential and institutional projects. DooleyMack has built and renovated everything public schools condos and performance arts centers to waste disposal facilities and laboratories. The company mainly operates in the central and southeastern regions of the US and has several offices in Florida as well as locations in Georgia Texas North Carolina and South Carolina. The privately-owned company was founded in 1977 by executives Bill Dooley and Ken Smith. CFO Wendy Mack later joined the firm.

	Annual Growth	12/04	12/05	12/06	12/07	12/08
Sales ($ mil.)	14.8%	–	72.5	83.5	91.0	109.5
Net income ($ mil.)	81.3%	–	0.1	0.5	1.2	0.8
Market value ($ mil.)	–	–	–	–	–	–
Employees	–	–	–	–	–	93

GULF ISLAND FABRICATION, INC.   NMS: GIFI

16225 Park Ten Place, Suite 300
Houston, TX 77084
Phone: 713 714-6100
Fax: 985 876-5414
Web: www.gulfisland.com
CEO: Richard Heo
CFO: Westley Stockton
HR: –
FYE: December 31
Type: Public

Together with its subsidiaries holding company Gulf Island Fabrication (Gulf Island) is a fabricator of steel structures modules and marine vessels and a provider of project management hookup commissioning repair maintenance and civil construction services. Its subsidiaries which operate under Gulf Island and Gulf Marine monikers make offshore drilling and production platforms. Products include jackets and deck sections of fixed production platforms hull and deck sections of floating production platforms piles subsea templates wellhead protectors and various production compressor and utility modules. Gulf Island also produces and repairs pressure vessels and refurbishes existing platforms. In 2019 some 55% of the total revenue was accounted for by four customers. Gulf Island was founded in 1985.

	Annual Growth	12/16	12/17	12/18	12/19	12/20
Sales ($ mil.)	(3.2%)	286.3	171.0	221.2	303.3	251.0
Net income ($ mil.)	–	3.5	(44.8)	(20.4)	(49.4)	(27.4)
Market value ($ mil.)	(28.8%)	182.8	206.2	110.9	77.9	47.0
Employees	(7.2%)	1,178	977	875	944	875

GULF OIL LIMITED PARTNERSHIP

100 Crossing Blvd.
Framingham MA 01702
Phone: 508-270-8300
Fax: 626-440-2630
Web: www.parsons.com

CEO: Eric Johnson
CFO: Mike Campbell
HR: Lea Oneil
FYE: September 30
Type: Private - Partnershi

Gulf Oil bridges the gap between petroleum producers and retail sales outlets. The petroleum wholesaler distributes gasoline and diesel fuel to more than 2500 Gulf-brand stations in 23 northeastern and southeastern states. Gulf Oil owns 12 storage terminals and operates a network of more than 50 other terminals. It also distributes motor oils lubricants and heating oil to commercial industrial and utility customers. The company has alliances with terminal operators in areas where it does not have a proprietary terminal. Gulf Oil boasts one of the oldest and most recognizable brands in the oil business. Regional convenience store chain and gas retailer Cumberland Farms controls the company.

GULF POWER CO

One Energy Place
Pensacola, FL 32520
Phone: 850 444-6111
Fax: –
Web: www.gulfpower.com

NL:
CEO: –
CFO: –
HR: –
FYE: December 31
Type: Public

Pensacola power users patronize Gulf Power. A subsidiary of Southern Company Gulf Power is the largest energy provider in Northwest Florida serving around half a million customers. The vertically-integrated company is engaged in the generation transmission distribution and purchase of electricity as well as selling electric service to some 70 towns including Pensacola Panama City and Fort Walton Beach. In addition the company has wholesale customers in Southeast Florida. NextEra Energy Inc. announced the purchase of Gulf Power in May 2018 (purchase expected to close in 2019).

	Annual Growth	12/13	12/14	12/15	12/16	12/17
Sales ($ mil.)	1.3%	1,440.3	1,590.5	1,483.0	1,485.0	1,516.0
Net income ($ mil.)	1.3%	132.1	149.2	157.0	140.0	139.0
Market value ($ mil.)	6.5%	611.7	702.3	744.8	739.3	–
Employees	(2.2%)	1,410	1,384	1,391	1,352	1,288

GULF STATES TOYOTA INC.

1375 Enclave Pkwy.
Houston TX 77077
Phone: 713-580-3300
Fax: 713-580-3332
Web: www.gstcareers.com

CEO: Dan Friedkin
CFO: Edward E Dickinson
HR: –
FYE: December 31
Type: Private

Even good ol' boys buy foreign cars from Gulf States Toyota (GST). One of only two US Toyota distributors not owned by Toyota Motor Sales (the other is JM Family Enterprises' Southeast Toyota Distributors) GST distributes Toyota Lexus and Scion brand cars trucks and sport utility vehicles in Arkansas Louisiana Mississippi Oklahoma and Texas. GST has expanded its vehicle processing center in Houston to handle Toyota Tundra pickup trucks built in nearby San Antonio. Founded in 1969 by its Chairman and owner Thomas Friedkin GST distributes new Toyotas parts and accessories to more than 150 dealers in Texas and other states in the region. GST accounts for 13% of Toyota sales in the US.

GULF UNITED ENERGY INC.

1222 Barkdull St.
Houston TX 77006
Phone: 713-942-6575
Fax: 604-420-8711
Web: www.tenpeakscoffee.ca

OTC: GLFE
CEO: –
CFO: –
HR: –
FYE: August 31
Type: Public

The Gulf of Mexico unites this company's headquarters with its operations. Houston-based oil and gas company Gulf United Energy holds oil and gas leases on one project in Colombia and three in Peru. The exploration and development stage company doesn't have any producing wells (or revenue) but it is working with Upland Oil and Gas and SK Energy to look for resources on nearly 44 million acres. Gulf United owns between two and 40 percent working interests on the four projects. The company which was formed in 2003 exited the pipeline and liquefied natural gas business in 2010. John B. Connally III grandson of former Texas governor John B. Connally owns about 16% of Gulf United.

GULFMARK OFFSHORE INC

842 West Sam Houston Parkway North, Suite 400
Houston, TX 77024
Phone: 713 963-9522
Fax: 281 664-5057
Web: www.gulfmark.com

ASE: GLF
CEO: –
CFO: –
HR: –
FYE: December 31
Type: Public

GulfMark Offshore makes its mark on the high seas. The company offers support services for the construction positioning and operation of offshore oil and natural gas rigs and platforms. Marine services include anchor handling; cargo supply and crew transportation; towing; and emergency services. Some of its ships conduct seismic data gathering and provide diving support. It owns manages or almost 73 vessels in the North Sea offshore Southeast Asia offshore West Africa offshore the Middle East offshore Brazil and the US Gulf of Mexico offshore India offshore Australia offshore Trinidad the Persian Gulf the Mediterranean Sea offshore Russia and offshore East Africa. The company filed for Chapter 11 bankruptcy protection in 2017.

	Annual Growth	12/12	12/13	12/14	12/15	12/16
Sales ($ mil.)	(24.9%)	389.2	454.6	495.8	274.8	123.7
Net income ($ mil.)	–	19.3	70.6	62.4	(215.2)	(203.0)
Market value ($ mil.)	–	–	–	–	–	–
Employees	(16.5%)	1,850	2,000	1,800	1,100	900

GULFPORT ENERGY CORP.

3001 Quail Springs Parkway
Oklahoma City, OK 73134
Phone: 405 252-4600
Fax: –
Web: www.gulfportenergy.com

NYS: GPOR
CEO: Timothy J Cutt
CFO: William J Buese
HR: –
FYE: December 31
Type: Public

Gulfport Energy is an independent natural gas-weighted exploration and production company. The oil and gas exploration and production company's main producing properties are located in the United States with primary focus in the Appalachia and Mid-Continent basins in the Niobrara Shale Formation in western Colorado in the South Central Oklahoma Oil Province (SCOOP) in Oklahoma and in the Utica Shale in eastern Ohio. Additionally Gulfport Energy holds a sizeable acreage position in its interest in Grizzly Oil Sands ULC. The company reported proved reserves of 13 million barrels of oil and 2.2 trillion cubic feet of natural gas.

	Annual Growth	12/16	12/17	12/18	12/19	12/20
Sales ($ mil.)	22.4%	385.9	1,320.3	1,355.0	1,346.0	866.5
Net income ($ mil.)	–	(979.7)	435.2	430.6	(2,002.4)	(1,625.1)
Market value ($ mil.)	–	–	–	–	–	–
Employees	1.5%	241	331	350	298	256

GULFSTREAM NATURAL GAS SYSTEM, L.L.C.

2701 N ROCKY POINT DR # 1050
TAMPA, FL 336075554
Phone: 813-282-6600
Fax: –
Web: www.gulfstreamgas.com

CEO: –
CFO: –
HR: –
FYE: December 31
Type: Private

In the case of Gulfstream Natural Gas the name says it all. The natural gas transportation and storage company delivers approximately 1.25 billion cu. ft. of natural gas per day from source areas on the Gulf Coast (in eastern Louisiana and Mississippi) to customers in Central and South Florida. Its system consists of some 745 miles of pipeline (including 294 miles of pipeline in Florida and 419 miles offshore). The company boasts the largest pipeline in the Gulf of Mexico. Gulfstream Natural Gas is a joint venture between The Williams Companies (through Williams Partners) and Spectra Energy and its Spectra Energy Partners unit.

	Annual Growth	12/14	12/15	12/16	12/18	12/19
Sales ($ mil.)	0.4%	–	–	276.7	281.7	280.3
Net income ($ mil.)	9.3%	–	–	87.7	104.2	114.5
Market value ($ mil.)	–	–	–	–	–	–
Employees	–	–	–	–	–	50

GUNDERSEN LUTHERAN MEDICAL CENTER, INC.

1900 SOUTH AVE
LA CROSSE, WI 546015467
Phone: 608-782-7300
Fax: –
Web: www.gundersenhealth.org

CEO: Jeffery Thompson
CFO: –
HR: –
FYE: December 31
Type: Private

At the heart of the Gundersen Lutheran health system Gundersen Lutheran Medical Center serves residents of nearly 20 counties that stretch across the upper Midwest. The clinical campus for the University of Wisconsin's medical and nursing schools operates a 325-bed teaching hospital with a Level II Trauma and Emergency Center. Focused on caring for patients in western Wisconsin the hospital boasts several specialty services such as bariatrics behavioral health cancer care orthopedics palliative care pediatrics rehabilitation and women's health. The physician-led not-for-profit medical center is affiliated with a group of regional clinics and specialty centers.

	Annual Growth	12/14	12/15	12/17	12/18	12/19
Sales ($ mil.)	6.8%	–	980.7	1,071.2	1,073.8	1,275.9
Net income ($ mil.)	37.9%	–	60.0	112.1	117.0	216.9
Market value ($ mil.)	–	–	–	–	–	–
Employees	–	–	–	–	–	4,500

GUTHRIE HEALTHCARE SYSTEM

GUTHRIE SQ
SAYRE, PA 18840
Phone: 570-888-6666
Fax: –
Web: www.guthrie.org

CEO: –
CFO: –
HR: –
FYE: June 30
Type: Private

Guthrie Healthcare System is a community health care organization serving residents of the Twin Tiers region of northern Pennsylvania and southern New York through a network of hospitals community clinics physicians' practices and specialty care facilities. The flagship facility is Robert Packer Hospital in Sayre Pennsylvania a 238-bed tertiary care teaching hospital (affiliated with Pennsylvania's Mansfield University) that provides a comprehensive range of health services including emergency/trauma care pediatric care orthopedics and rehabilitative care. The system also includes two additional hospitals nursing homes a senior care community a hospice care program and a home health agency.

	Annual Growth	06/06	06/07	06/08	06/10	06/11
Sales ($ mil.)	(1.3%)	–	–	52.7	56.7	50.7
Net income ($ mil.)	(6.1%)	–	–	17.7	24.6	14.7
Market value ($ mil.)	–	–	–	–	–	–
Employees	–	–	–	–	–	2,575

GYRODYNE CO. OF AMERICA, INC.

NAS: GYRO

1 Flowerfield, Suite 24
St. James, NY 11780
Phone: 631 584-5400
Fax: 631 584-7075
Web: www.gyrodyne.com

CEO: –
CFO: –
HR: –
FYE: December 31
Type: Public

This Gyro has the wrap on real estate. Gyrodyne is a self-managed and self-administered real estate investment trust (REIT) that buys owns and manages a variety of property types. Its portfolio includes medical office parks and industrial properties as well as undeveloped land. Gyrodyne began as a helicopter maker working from its 68-acre Flowerfield site on Long Island New York but switched to real estate development as its helicopter business declined in the 1970s. Since then it has been converting its Flowerfield property for commercial industrial and residential use. The REIT has also acquired medical properties in New York and Virginia and owns a minority stake in a planned development in Florida.

	Annual Growth	12/09	12/10	12/11	12/12	12/13
Sales ($ mil.)	1.0%	4.8	5.6	5.5	5.0	5.0
Net income ($ mil.)	134.5%	1.5	(1.1)	(1.1)	99.0	46.1
Market value ($ mil.)	(25.8%)	62.1	119.1	151.2	106.8	18.8
Employees	(12.6%)	12	12	12	11	7

H&E EQUIPMENT SERVICES INC

NMS: HEES

7500 Pecue Lane
Baton Rouge, LA 70809
Phone: 225 298-5200
Fax: –
Web: www.he-equipment.com

CEO: Bradley Barber
CFO: Leslie Magee
HR: –
FYE: December 31
Type: Public

H&E Equipment Services sells and rents new and used equipment for construction earthmoving and materials handling with equipment made by lift crane and truck manufacturers such as JLG Genie Industries (Terex) and Komatsu. H&E also offers a full slate of services including multiple points of customer contact cross-selling opportunities among its rental new and used equipment sales parts sales and services operations an effective method to manage its rental fleet through efficient maintenance and profitable distribution of used equipment and a mix of business activities that enables the company to operate effectively throughout economic cycles. The company serves some 45400 customers across some two dozen US states and close to 100 service centers.

	Annual Growth	12/16	12/17	12/18	12/19	12/20
Sales ($ mil.)	4.6%	978.1	1,030.0	1,239.0	1,348.4	1,169.1
Net income ($ mil.)	–	37.2	109.7	76.6	87.2	(32.7)
Market value ($ mil.)	6.4%	839.2	1,467.2	737.0	1,206.6	1,075.9
Employees	3.1%	1,996	2,093	2,369	2,432	2,254

H. E. BUTT GROCERY COMPANY

646 S. Main Ave.
San Antonio TX 78204
Phone: 210-938-8000
Fax: 210-938-8169
Web: www.heb.com

CEO: Charles Butt
CFO: –
HR: –
FYE: October 31
Type: Private

The Muzak bounces between Tejano and country and the warm tortillas and marinated fajita meat are big sellers at H. E. Butt Grocery (H-E-B). Texas' largest private company and the #1 food retailer in South and Central Texas H-E-B owns more than 335 supermarkets including a growing number of large (70000 sq. ft.) gourmet Central Market stores in major metropolitan areas and 80-plus smaller (24000-30000 sq. ft.) H-E-B-Pantry stores often in more rural areas. H-E-B also has about 40 upscale and discount stores in Northern Mexico. H-E-B processes some of its own bread dairy products meat and tortillas. The 100-year-old company is owned by the Butt family which founded H-E-B in Kerrville Texas in 1905.

H. J. RUSSELL & COMPANY

171 17TH ST NW STE 1600
ATLANTA, GA 303631235
Phone: 404-330-1000
Fax: –
Web: www.hjrussell.com

CEO: Michael B Russell
CFO: Ed Bradford
HR: –
FYE: December 31
Type: Private

H.J. Russell & Company one of the nation's largest minority-owned enterprises helps shape southeastern cities. It's a general contractor construction manager property manager and developer that specializes in affordable multifamily housing and mixed-use communities. It also has expertise in building airports hospitals office towers retail stores and schools. Its development arm Russell New Urban Development offers such services as feasibility analysis land development and asset management. H.J. Russell also manages more than 6000 apartment and public housing units. The family-owned company was founded by chairman Herman J. Russell in 1952.

	Annual Growth	12/05	12/06	12/07	12/08	12/09
Sales ($ mil.)	(14.4%)	–	–	233.3	222.2	170.9
Net income ($ mil.)	(41.2%)	–	–	6.0	3.9	2.1
Market value ($ mil.)	–	–	–	–	–	–
Employees	–	–	–	–	–	733

H. LEE MOFFITT CANCER CENTER AND RESEARCH INSTITUTE HOSPITAL, INC.

12902 USF MAGNOLIA DR
TAMPA, FL 336129416
Phone: 813-745-4673
Fax: –
Web: www.moffitt.org

CEO: –
CFO: Yvette Tremonti
HR: –
FYE: June 30
Type: Private

The H. Lee Moffitt Cancer Center and Research Institute founded in 1986 is a National Cancer Institute-designated Comprehensive Cancer Center located on the Tampa campus of the University of South Florida. The institute carries it out its stated mission of "contributing to the prevention and cure of cancer" through patient care research and education. It operates a 210-bed medical and surgical facility as well as outpatient treatment programs and a blood and marrow transplant program. Its research programs include study in the areas of molecular oncology immunology risk assessment health outcomes and experimental therapeutics.

	Annual Growth	06/13	06/14	06/18	06/20	06/21
Sales ($ mil.)	8.5%	–	855.2	1,020.9	1,353.5	1,516.0
Net income ($ mil.)	28.9%	–	50.2	167.2	288.0	296.0
Market value ($ mil.)	–	–	–	–	–	–
Employees	–	–	–	–	–	4,200

H.C. SCHMIEDING PRODUCE COMPANY, LLC

2330 N THOMPSON ST
SPRINGDALE, AR 727641709
Phone: 479-751-4517
Fax: –
Web: www.schmieding.com

CEO: –
CFO: Chris Gryskiewicz
HR: –
FYE: December 31
Type: Private

H. C. Schmieding Produce is a leading wholesale distributor of fresh fruits and vegetables. The company supplies primarily grocery store chains and independent retailers from two distribution centers in Arkansas and Florida. President Laurence Schmieding started the family-owned company in 1961 and heads a charitable organization called The Schmieding Foundation. Through their holding company Schmieding Enterprises the family also has interests in real estate.

	Annual Growth	12/15	12/16	12/17	12/18	12/19
Sales ($ mil.)	13.9%	–	98.0	116.1	121.4	144.7
Net income ($ mil.)	(20.6%)	–	3.2	2.7	(1.3)	1.6
Market value ($ mil.)	–	–	–	–	–	–
Employees	–	–	–	–	–	35

HABASIT AMERICA

805 Satellite Blvd.
Suwanee GA 30024
Phone: 678-288-3600
Fax: 678-288-3651
Web: www.habasitamerica.com

CEO: Tim Waldner
CFO: Sathish Venugopalan
HR: Samuel Johnson
FYE: August 31
Type: Private

Need a belt? Not for your trousers but for your conveyor systems and other industrial machinery? Turn to Habasit America. The company makes power transmission belts and conveyor belts along with related gears and motors for material handling equipment in a variety of industries. Habasit America's products move automotive parts beverages electronic components food packaging paper and tissue pharmaceuticals textiles tires tobacco wood and other commodities. Its conveyor belts also are used in airport baggage handling systems and supermarket check-out stands. Habasit America's Swiss parent company Habasit Group Reinach operates globally.

HABITAT FOR HUMANITY INTERNATIONAL, INC.

285 PEACHTREE CENTER AVE
ATLANTA, GA 303031220
Phone: 800-422-4828
Fax: –
Web: www.habitat.org

CEO: Jonathan Reckford
CFO: –
HR: –
FYE: June 30
Type: Private

Thanks to Habitat for Humanity more than 5 million people worldwide know there's no place like home. The mission of the not-for-profit ecumenical Christian organization is to provide adequate and affordable shelter. It has built or remodeled more than 800000 houses at cost for families who demonstrate a need and are willing to invest "sweat equity" during construction. Homeowners make payments on no-interest mortgages; Habitat for Humanity funnels the funds back into the construction of homes for others. The group operates in all 50 states the District of Columbia Guam and Puerto Rico in addition to affiliates in nearly 80 countries. It was founded in 1976 by Linda Fuller and her late husband Millard.

	Annual Growth	06/13	06/14	06/16	06/19	06/20
Sales ($ mil.)	0.3%	–	268.2	276.1	288.1	272.8
Net income ($ mil.)	(18.2%)	–	11.8	28.5	13.2	3.5
Market value ($ mil.)	–	–	–	–	–	–
Employees	–	–	–	–	–	1,500

HACKETT GROUP INC

1001 Brickell Bay Drive, Suite 3000
Miami, FL 33131
Phone: 305 375-8005
Fax: –
Web: www.thehackettgroup.com

NMS: HCKT
CEO: Ted Fernandez
CFO: Robert Ramirez
HR: –
FYE: January 01
Type: Public

The Hackett Group a business and technology consultancy provides corporations with advisory programs benchmarking business transformation services and working capital management. It specializes in IT human resources corporate services and customer service. The Hackett Group also offers services related to best practice research with a focus on sales general and administrative functions and supply chain services. The group also provides dedicated expertise in business strategy operations finance human capital management strategic sourcing procurement and information technology including its award-winning Oracle and SAP practices. The Hackett Group generates about 90% of sales from North America.

	Annual Growth	12/16	12/17	12/18	12/19*	01/21
Sales ($ mil.)	(3.7%)	288.6	285.9	285.9	282.5	239.5
Net income ($ mil.)	(24.0%)	21.5	27.4	23.9	2.7	5.5
Market value ($ mil.)	(4.0%)	529.6	471.1	477.4	476.8	431.6
Employees	(0.6%)	1,079	1,123	1,165	1,143	1,047

*Fiscal year change

HACKLEY HOSPITAL

1700 CLINTON ST
MUSKEGON, MI 494425591
Phone: 231-728-4950
Fax: –
Web: www.hackley-health.org

CEO: –
CFO: –
HR: –
FYE: June 30
Type: Private

Medical professionals at Hackley Hospital aim to heal. Operating as as Mercy Health Partners Hackley Campus the hospital is a 210-bed acute care facility that serves patients living in Muskegon opposite the thumb on Michigan's shoreline. The teaching hospital offers such services as behavioral health care a sleep analysis lab a bariatric treatment center a cancer center stroke care emergency medicine and rehabilitation therapies. Mercy Health Partners Hackley Campus is part Mercy Health Partners Muskegon.

	Annual Growth	06/07	06/08	06/09	06/10	06/13
Sales ($ mil.)	(36.1%)	–	1,673.5	144.4	151.0	177.8
Net income ($ mil.)	559.3%	–	0.0	(6.8)	(42.2)	5.6
Market value ($ mil.)	–	–	–	–	–	–
Employees	–	–	–	–	–	1,500

HAEMONETICS CORP.

NYS: HAE

125 Summer Street
Boston, MA 02110
Phone: 781 848-7100
Fax: –
Web: www.haemonetics.com

CEO: Christopher Simon
CFO: William Burke
HR: –
FYE: April 03
Type: Public

Haemonetics company develops and produces automated blood collection systems that collect and process whole blood taking only the components (such as plasma or red blood cells) needed and returning the remainder to the donors. Typically these systems sold under the Cell Saver and TEG are bought and used by plasma centers and blood banks. Haemonetics' Hospital business has four product lines which include Hemostasis Management Cell Salvage Transfusion Management and Vascular Closure. In 1971 Jack Latham founds Haemonetics in Natick Massachusetts. About 60% of total revenue was derived from US.

	Annual Growth	04/17*	03/18	03/19	03/20*	04/21
Sales ($ mil.)	(0.4%)	886.1	903.9	967.6	988.5	870.5
Net income ($ mil.)	–	(26.3)	45.6	55.0	76.5	79.5
Market value ($ mil.)	28.9%	2,063.7	3,721.6	4,450.0	5,135.2	5,699.3
Employees	(3.4%)	3,107	3,136	3,216	3,004	2,708

*Fiscal year change

HAGGAR CLOTHING CO.

11511 Luna Rd.
Dallas TX 75234
Phone: 214-352-8481
Fax: 214-654-5500
Web: www.iphase.com

CEO: Michael B Stitt
CFO: Rob Adamek
HR: –
FYE: September 30
Type: Private

Haggar is hooked on classics. A leading maker and marketer of men's casual and dress apparel the company's products include pants sport coats suits shirts and shorts. Haggar's clothes (including its "wrinkle-free" shirts and tab-waist expandable pants) are sold through about 10000 stores in the US Canada Mexico and the UK. Its Haggar brand is sold in department stores such as Belk J. C. Penney Kohl's Macys and Sears and at more than 70 Haggar outlet stores. The men's apparel maker invented the word "slacks" and has sold plenty of them in its 80-plus years in business.

HAGGEN, INC.

2211 RIMLAND DR STE 300
BELLINGHAM, WA 982265699
Phone: 360-733-8720
Fax: –
Web: www.haggen.com

CEO: –
CFO: Ron Stevens
HR: Derek Anderson
FYE: December 31
Type: Private

Haggen showers shoppers in the Pacific Northwest with salmon coffee and other essentials. Formerly one of the area's largest independent grocers Haggen operated some 130 supermarkets in Washington and Oregon as well as California Nevada and Arizona. Most of the stores were acquired from Albertsons in late 2014. In late 2015 Haggen filed for Chapter 11 bankruptcy protection to allow it to reorganize around a reduced number of locations and in 2016 the company agreed to sell its remaining core stores to Albertsons. The chain was founded in 1933 in Bellingham Washington.

	Annual Growth	12/03	12/04	12/05	12/06	12/07
Sales ($ mil.)	–	–	–	(164.8)	758.7	787.8
Net income ($ mil.)	20237.1%	–	–	0.0	6.5	8.6
Market value ($ mil.)	–	–	–	–	–	–
Employees	–	–	–	–	–	3,900

HAHN AUTOMOTIVE WAREHOUSE INC.

415 W. Main St.
Rochester NY 14608
Phone: 585-235-1595
Fax: 585-235-8615
Web: www.hahnauto.com

CEO: –
CFO: –
HR: –
FYE: September 30
Type: Private

You rely on your mechanic and your mechanic relies on Hahn Automotive Warehouse. The company distributes aftermarket auto parts to independent jobbers (middlemen who buy from distributors and sell to retailers) and about 80 company-owned Genuine Parts Advantage Auto and Nu-Way Auto stores as well as professional installers. It operates about 30 distribution centers in the Midwest and along the East Coast. The company carries some 200 name-brand and 50 private-label parts. Eli Futerman and his son-in-law Daniel Chessin own and lead the company. Hahn Automotive Warehouse (formerly Hahn Tire and Battery) was purchased in 1958 by Futerman's father Mike and a partner.

HAIN CELESTIAL GROUP INC

NMS: HAIN

1111 Marcus Avenue
Lake Success, NY 11042
Phone: 516 587-5000
Fax: –
Web: www.hain.com

CEO: Mark Schiller
CFO: Javier Idrovo
HR: –
FYE: June 30
Type: Public

The Hain Celestial Group is a leading manufacturer and distributor of natural and organic food snacks beverages tea and personal care and grocery products worldwide. Its vast pantry of "better-for-you" brands includes Celestial Seasonings (specialty teas) Terra and Garden of Eatin' (snacks) and Earth's Best (organic baby food). Hain's products are mainstays in natural foods stores and are increasingly available in mainstream supermarkets; club mass-market and drug stores; and grocery wholesalers. Hain is also a supplier of Avalon Organics Alba Botanica Live Clean Queen Helene and JASON grooming products. The US generates about half of the group's revenue.

	Annual Growth	06/17	06/18	06/19	06/20	06/21
Sales ($ mil.)	(8.8%)	2,853.1	2,457.8	2,302.5	2,053.9	1,970.3
Net income ($ mil.)	3.5%	67.4	9.7	(183.3)	(80.4)	77.4
Market value ($ mil.)	0.8%	3,845.9	2,952.3	2,169.6	3,121.7	3,974.6
Employees	(20.7%)	7,825	7,685	5,441	4,287	3,087

HALLADOR ENERGY CO
NAS: HNRG

1183 East Canvasback Drive
Terre Haute, IN 47802
Phone: 812 299-2800
Fax: –
Web: www.halladorenergy.com

CEO: Brent Bilsland
CFO: Lawrence Martin
HR: –
FYE: December 31
Type: Public

Hallador Energy puts most of its energy into selling coal from its Carlisle Mine in Indiana to three utilities in the Midwest and one in Florida. Hallador has recoverable coal reserves of 43.5 million tons (34.2 million tons proven and 9.3 million tons probable). In addition to the Carlisle Mine it get coals from a mine in Clay County Indiana and has two inactive mines in Illinois. The company is exploring the possibility of other contracts with a number of coal purchasers. Additionally Hallador has a 45% stake in Savoy Energy L.P. an oil and gas company with operations in Michigan and a 50% interest in Sunrise Energy LLC a private oil and gas exploration and production company with assets in Indiana.

	Annual Growth	12/16	12/17	12/18	12/19	12/20
Sales ($ mil.)	(3.4%)	281.5	271.6	293.6	323.5	245.3
Net income ($ mil.)	–	12.5	33.1	7.6	(59.9)	(6.2)
Market value ($ mil.)	(36.6%)	278.2	186.4	155.2	90.9	45.0
Employees	(2.0%)	748	742	848	915	690

HALLIBURTON COMPANY
NYS: HAL

3000 North Sam Houston Parkway East
Houston, TX 77032
Phone: 281 871-2699
Fax: –
Web: www.halliburton.com

CEO: Jeffrey Miller
CFO: Lance Loeffler
HR: –
FYE: December 31
Type: Public

Founded in 1919 Halliburton is one of the world's largest providers of products and services to the energy industry. It manufactures drill bits and other downhole and completion tools provides pressure pumping services locates hydrocarbons and manages geological data drills new wells and optimizes production once the well is operational. The company serves major national and independent oil and natural gas companies throughout the world. Halliburton operates in more than 70 countries around the world. North America accounts for approximately 40% of company sales.

	Annual Growth	12/17	12/18	12/19	12/20	12/21
Sales ($ mil.)	(7.2%)	20,620.0	23,995.0	22,408.0	14,445.0	15,295.0
Net income ($ mil.)	–	(463.0)	1,656.0	(1,131.0)	(2,945.0)	1,457.0
Market value ($ mil.)	(17.3%)	43,787.5	23,815.7	21,925.1	16,934.4	20,491.5
Employees	(7.7%)	55,000	60,000	55,000	40,000	40,000

HALLMARK FINANCIAL SERVICES INC.
NMS: HALL

5420 Lyndon B., Johnson Freeway, Suite 1100
Dallas, TX 75240
Phone: 817 348-1600
Fax: –
Web: www.hallmarkgrp.com

CEO: Mark Schwarz
CFO: Christopher Kenney
HR: –
FYE: December 31
Type: Public

Personal or commercial on the ground or in the air Hallmark Financial Services sells insurance to cover risks both general and exceptional. Its specialty commercial unit markets and underwrites general commercial property/casualty insurance while its excess and surplus unit writes specialty property/casualty coverage to businesses that don't fit into standard coverage. Other Hallmark Financial units provide personal non-standard auto insurance and standard commercial auto and renters insurance products and services.

	Annual Growth	12/16	12/17	12/18	12/19	12/20
Assets ($ mil.)	6.3%	1,162.5	1,231.1	1,264.9	1,495.3	1,485.5
Net income ($ mil.)	–	6.5	(11.6)	10.3	(0.6)	(91.7)
Market value ($ mil.)	(25.6%)	211.0	189.2	193.9	318.8	64.6
Employees	0.2%	420	418	439	486	424

HALLWOOD GROUP INC.
ASE: HWG

3710 Rawlins, Suite 1500
Dallas, TX 75219
Phone: 214 528-5588
Fax: –
Web: www.hallwood.com

CEO: Anthony J Gumbiner
CFO: Richard Kelley
HR: –
FYE: December 31
Type: Public

The Hallwood Group spawns fabric for everyday life. The group is a holding company of Brookwood Companies a producer of high-tech fabric for the outdoor and sportswear industries and one of the largest suppliers of coated nylon fabric in the US. Brookwood dyes finishes coats and prints woven synthetics used in products such as consumer apparel luggage and sailcloth. A laminating arm processes fabrics for military uniforms and camouflage equipment industrial applications and waterproof gear. Roughly two-thirds of sales are made to makers of military goods such as Tennier Industries and ORC Industries. Hallwood's former interest in Hallwood Energy ended in 2009 following the latter's reorganization.

	Annual Growth	12/08	12/09	12/10	12/11	12/12
Sales ($ mil.)	(5.3%)	162.2	179.6	168.4	139.5	130.5
Net income ($ mil.)	–	1.4	17.1	9.9	(6.3)	(17.9)
Market value ($ mil.)	(27.9%)	50.3	59.2	40.3	13.8	13.6
Employees	(1.0%)	460	478	470	458	441

HALOZYME THERAPEUTICS INC
NMS: HALO

11388 Sorrento Valley Road
San Diego, CA 92121
Phone: 858 794-8889
Fax: –
Web: www.halozyme.com

CEO: Helen Torley
CFO: Nicole LaBrosse
HR: Aamara De Los Reyes
FYE: December 31
Type: Public

Halozyme Therapeutics is a biopharma technology platform company. Its Hylenex recombinant is used as an adjuvant for drug and fluid infusions. Most of Halozyme's products and candidates (including Hylenex) are based on rHuPH20 its patented recombinant human hyaluronidase enzyme while its lead cancer program is PEGPH20 which targets solid tumors. Halozyme partners with such pharmaceuticals as Roche Pfizer Janssen Baxalta and AbbVie for its ENHANZE drug delivery platform which enables biologics and small molecule compounds to be delivered subcutaneously. US generates the majority of revenue which accounts for about 40%.

	Annual Growth	12/16	12/17	12/18	12/19	12/20
Sales ($ mil.)	16.2%	146.7	316.6	151.9	196.0	267.6
Net income ($ mil.)	–	(103.0)	63.0	(80.3)	(72.2)	129.1
Market value ($ mil.)	44.2%	1,334.1	2,735.7	1,975.5	2,394.1	5,767.1
Employees	(14.9%)	259	255	281	132	136

HAMILTON CHATTANOOGA COUNTY HOSPITAL AUTHORITY

975 E 3RD ST
CHATTANOOGA, TN 374032173
Phone: 423-778-7000
Fax: –
Web: www.erlanger.org

CEO: –
CFO: Lynn Dejaco
HR: –
FYE: June 30
Type: Private

The Chattanooga-Hamilton County Hospital Authority (dba Erlanger Health System) offers a broad range of health service operations including the T.C. Thompson Children's Hospital a cancer treatment facility and centers devoted to heart treatment trauma and eye care. The system comprises five hospital campuses in Tennessee with some 810 acute care beds as well as 50 long-term care beds. A teaching center for the University of Tennessee College of Medicine Erlanger provides tertiary care for a region that includes southeastern Tennessee northern Georgia northern Alabama and western North Carolina.

	Annual Growth	06/16	06/17	06/18	06/20	06/21
Sales ($ mil.)	4.1%	–	888.1	973.7	1,021.7	1,044.2
Net income ($ mil.)	28.4%	–	13.9	26.9	29.2	37.8
Market value ($ mil.)	–	–	–	–	–	–
Employees	–	–	–	–	–	4,700

HAMILTON COLLEGE

198 COLLEGE HILL RD
CLINTON, NY 133231295
Phone: 315-859-4727
Fax: –
Web: www.hamilton.edu

CEO: –
CFO: –
HR: –
FYE: June 30
Type: Private

Hamilton College is a private liberal arts school that serves some 1800 students and employs about 180 faculty members. The school offers undergraduate programs in a variety of subjects including economics government psychology computer science education and English. Hamilton College which has a 10-to-1 student/faculty ratio is supported by a more than $500 million endowment. Located in the foothills of the Adirondack Mountains the school is one of the oldest colleges in New York State. Hamilton College was founded in 1793 by Samuel Kirkland missionary to the Oneida Indians; it was named for Alexander Hamilton the first secretary of the US Treasury.

	Annual Growth	06/09	06/10	06/11	06/12	06/13
Sales ($ mil.)	3.0%	–	–	112.7	116.8	119.6
Net income ($ mil.)	(22.2%)	–	–	142.9	(38.8)	86.4
Market value ($ mil.)	–	–	–	–	–	–
Employees	–	–	–	–	–	650

HAMPDEN BANCORP INC

19 Harrison Ave.
Springfield, MA 01102
Phone: 413 736-1812
Fax: –
Web: www.hampdenbank.com

NMS: HBNK
CEO: –
CFO: –
HR: –
FYE: June 30
Type: Public

Despite its name Hampden Bancorp's (the holding company for Hampden Bank) services extend beyond Massachusetts's Hampden County. Serving a handful of cities and towns in western Massachusetts Hampden Bank offers savings and checking deposit services as well as a variety of lending services to its consumer and business customers. The bank's primary loan products include one-to-four-family residential loans and commercial real estate loans each of which make up about a third of the bank's total loan portfolio. Loans for construction businesses and consumers make up the rest. Hampden Bancorp operates through more than a half-dozen branches.

	Annual Growth	06/10	06/11	06/12	06/13	06/14
Assets ($ mil.)	4.7%	584.0	573.3	616.0	653.0	701.5
Net income ($ mil.)	–	(0.4)	1.3	3.0	3.0	4.5
Market value ($ mil.)	15.4%	53.7	75.0	73.1	84.3	95.3
Employees	3.2%	113	115	120	118	128

HAMPSHIRE GROUP, LTD.

114 W. 41st Street
New York, NY 10036
Phone: 212 840-5666
Fax: –
Web: www.hamp.com

NBB: HAMP
CEO: Paul M Buxbaum
CFO: William Drozdowski
HR: –
FYE: December 31
Type: Public

Hampshire Group has cooled on the women's sweater business. After years of declining sales and mounting losses the company in 2011 sold its women's lines to focus exclusively on men's sweaters and woven and knit tops. The firm is licensed to manufacture men's knitwear under the Geoffrey Beene Dockers and Joseph Abboud labels. Hampshire Group's own brands include Spring+Mercer and scott james. The company's apparel is sold by major department store chains and specialty retailers throughout the US. JC Penney Kohl's and Macy's are Hampshire Group's largest customers accounting for more than 50% of total annual sales.

	Annual Growth	12/10	12/11	12/12	12/13	12/14
Sales ($ mil.)	(9.2%)	134.5	86.1	117.6	105.1	91.5
Net income ($ mil.)	–	(9.7)	(10.0)	(11.7)	(16.0)	(28.8)
Market value ($ mil.)	(17.9%)	31.9	20.4	25.7	28.9	14.5
Employees	45.2%	162	1,215	1,073	831	720

HAMPTON UNIVERSITY

100 E QUEEN ST
HAMPTON, VA 236680108
Phone: 757-727-5000
Fax: –
Web: www.hamptonu.edu

CEO: –
CFO: –
HR: –
FYE: June 30
Type: Private

Hampton University is composed of six undergraduate schools as well as a graduate college and a college of continuing education. It offers some 70 bachelor's degree programs more than 25 master's degree programs and several doctoral or professional degrees in nursing physics atmospheric and planetary science physical therapy and pharmacy. It also includes the Scripps Howard School of Journalism and Communications. The school has an enrollment of about 5000 students. Hampton University has more than 300 full-time faculty members and a student-to-teacher ratio of 16:1.

	Annual Growth	06/07	06/08	06/09	06/10	06/11
Sales ($ mil.)	–	–	–	0.0	140.2	140.2
Net income ($ mil.)	–	–	–	0.0	(1.6)	(1.6)
Market value ($ mil.)	–	–	–	–	–	–
Employees	–	–	–	–	–	1,050

HANCOCK FABRICS, INC.

One Fashion Way
Baldwyn, MS 38824
Phone: 662 365-6000
Fax: –
Web: www.hancockfabrics.com

NBB: HKFI Q
CEO: –
CFO: –
HR: –
FYE: January 31
Type: Public

Through careful piecing and pinning Hancock Fabrics has become a leading nationwide fabric chain (far behind Jo-Ann Stores). The company caters to customers who sew by offering fabrics crafts sewing machines and accessories through some 260 stores (down from more than 400 five years ago) in more than 35 states. It also sells merchandise online. To compensate for the waning popularity of sewing clothes the company has expanded its selection of craft and home decorating products including drapery and upholstery fabrics and home accent pieces. Founded in 1957 Hancock Fabrics has struggled to grow its sales in recent years and filed for Chapter 11 bankruptcy protection in 2016 to reorganize its business.

	Annual Growth	01/11	01/12	01/13	01/14	01/15
Sales ($ mil.)	0.7%	275.5	272.0	278.0	276.0	283.1
Net income ($ mil.)	–	(10.5)	(11.3)	(8.5)	(1.9)	(3.2)
Market value ($ mil.)	(17.5%)	30.8	20.7	11.0	22.0	14.3
Employees	(7.9%)	4,300	3,700	3,200	3,300	3,100

HANCOCK WHITNEY CORP

Hancock Whitney Plaza, 2510 14th Street
Gulfport, MS 39501
Phone: 228 868-4000
Fax: –
Web: www.hancockbank.com

NMS: HWC
CEO: John Hairston
CFO: Michael Achary
HR: –
FYE: December 31
Type: Public

Hancock Whitney is the holding company of Hancock Whitney Bank which has nearly 210 branches and about 275 ATMs throughout the Gulf South from Florida to Texas. The community-oriented bank offers traditional and online products and services such as deposit accounts treasury management and investment brokerage services and loans to commercial small business and retail customers. The company also provides trust and investment management services to retirement plans corporations and individuals as well as discount investment brokerage services annuity and life insurance products and consumer financing services. Formerly Hancock Holding Company Hancock Whitney consolidated its two brands (Whitney Bank and Hancock Bank) in 2018 and changed its name.

	Annual Growth	12/16	12/17	12/18	12/19	12/20
Assets ($ mil.)	8.8%	23,975.3	27,336.1	28,235.9	30,600.8	33,638.6
Net income ($ mil.)	–	149.3	215.6	323.8	327.4	(45.2)
Market value ($ mil.)	(5.7%)	3,738.0	4,293.0	3,005.1	3,805.6	2,950.5
Employees	1.7%	3,724	3,887	3,933	4,136	3,986

HANDY & HARMAN LTD   NAS: HNH

1133 Westchester Avenue, Suite N222 — CEO: Jack L Howard
White Plains, NY 10604 — CFO: Douglas B Woodworth
Phone: 914 461-1300 — HR: –
Fax: – — FYE: December 31
Web: www.handyharman.com — Type: Public

Handy & Harman (HNH) is certainly handy when it comes to producing precious metals tubing and engineered materials in the US and Canada. The company makes 40% of its sales from its Building Materials segment which makes fasteners and systems for building roofs. Other units make and supply brazing alloys steel tubing and meat-room products used in construction electronics telecommunications medical and aviation transportation appliance semiconductor signage and food industries. HNH operates through 30 locations in North America China and Europe.

	Annual Growth	12/11	12/12	12/13	12/14	12/15
Sales ($ mil.)	(0.6%)	664.0	629.4	655.2	600.5	649.5
Net income ($ mil.)	(6.4%)	138.8	26.5	42.0	25.2	106.4
Market value ($ mil.)	20.0%	120.9	184.0	295.6	561.9	250.4
Employees	7.0%	1,621	1,648	1,836	1,925	2,125

HANESBRANDS INC   NYS: HBI

1000 East Hanes Mill Road — CEO: Stephen Bratspies
Winston-Salem, NC 27105 — CFO: Michael Dastugue
Phone: 336 519-8080 — HR: –
Fax: – — FYE: January 01
Web: www.hanes.com — Type: Public

Hanesbrands Inc. is a leading marketer of basic apparel. It designs manufactures and sells bras hosiery men's and women's underwear socks and other intimate apparel under brand names such as Hanes Champion Bali Just My Size Bras N Things Playtex and Wonderbra. Hanesbrands also makes basic outerwear such as T-shirts and licensed logo apparel for college bookstores under the Champion and Gear for Sports labels and has license agreements with Polo Ralph Lauren. The lineup is sold to wholesalers major retail chains (Walmart and Target) and through Hanesbrands' own outlet stores and Internet sites. Operations in the US account for almost 75% of the company's total sales.

	Annual Growth	12/17	12/18	12/19*	01/21	01/22
Sales ($ mil.)	1.0%	6,471.4	6,804.0	6,966.9	6,664.4	6,801.2
Net income ($ mil.)	4.5%	61.9	553.1	600.7	(75.6)	77.2
Market value ($ mil.)	(4.4%)	7,316.5	4,265.3	5,189.1	5,101.6	5,850.4
Employees	(2.6%)	67,200	68,000	63,000	61,000	59,000

*Fiscal year change

HANGER INC   NYS: HNGR

10910 Domain Drive, Suite 300 — CEO: Vinit Asar
Austin, TX 78758 — CFO: Thomas Kiraly
Phone: 512 777-3800 — HR: –
Fax: – — FYE: December 31
Web: www.hanger.com — Type: Public

Hanger ranks one of the leading US operators of orthotic and prosthetic (O&P) patient care centers with about 815 facilities nationwide. The company's Southern Prosthetic Supply procures and distributes standard and customized braces and prosthetic devices to affiliated and independent O&P centers. Its therapeutic solutions units Accelerated Care Plus (ACP) and Southern Prosthetic Supply Inc. (SPS) respectively provide rehabilitation supplies to care centers and distribute O&P components to independent O&P clinics.

	Annual Growth	12/16	12/17	12/18	12/19	12/20
Sales ($ mil.)	(1.0%)	1,042.1	1,040.8	1,048.8	1,098.0	1,001.2
Net income ($ mil.)		(106.5)	(104.7)	(0.9)	27.5	38.2
Market value ($ mil.)	14.3%	491.7	491.7	723.5	1,054.1	839.6
Employees	(0.5%)	4,800	4,600	4,600	4,800	4,700

HANMI FINANCIAL CORP.   NMS: HAFC

900 Wilshire Boulevard, Suite 1250 — CEO: Bonita Lee
Los Angeles, CA 90017 — CFO: Romolo Santarosa
Phone: 213 382-2200 — HR: –
Fax: – — FYE: December 31
Web: www.hanmi.com — Type: Public

Hanmi Financial owns Hanmi Bank which serves Korean-American and other ethnic communities in California Colorado Georgia Illinois New Jersey New York Texas Virginia and Washington. The company which holds $5.5 billion in assets offers traditional banking services to small and midsized businesses from about 40 branches and eight loan offices. Real estate loans — including for retail hospitality mixed-use apartment office industrial gas station faith-based facility and warehouse properties — account for about 80% of its loan portfolio; commercial and industrial loans and leases receivable make up most of the rest.

	Annual Growth	12/16	12/17	12/18	12/19	12/20
Assets ($ mil.)	7.2%	4,701.3	5,210.5	5,502.2	5,538.2	6,201.9
Net income ($ mil.)	(7.0%)	56.5	54.7	57.9	32.8	42.2
Market value ($ mil.)	(24.5%)	1,072.1	932.3	605.1	614.2	348.3
Employees	(1.4%)	638	642	635	633	602

HANNON ARMSTRONG SUSTAINABLE INFRASTRUCTURE CAPITAL INC   NYS: HASI

1906 Towne Centre Blvd., Suite 370 — CEO: Jeffrey Eckel
Annapolis, MD 21401 — CFO: Jeffrey Lipson
Phone: 410 571-9860 — HR: –
Fax: – — FYE: December 31
Web: www.hannonarmstrong.com — Type: Public

Hannon Armstrong Sustainable Infrastructure Capital has its hands in both kinds of green. The REIT provides securitized funding for environmentally friendly infrastructure projects. It is a key provider of financing for the US government's energy efficiency projects. Hannon Armstrong focuses on energy efficiency renewable energy and other sustainable projects including water and communications that improve energy consumption and the use of natural resources. The company manages approximately $6.2 billion in assets and operates mostly in the US.

	Annual Growth	12/16	12/17	12/18	12/19	12/20
Sales ($ mil.)	23.2%	81.2	105.6	137.8	141.6	186.9
Net income ($ mil.)	54.0%	14.7	30.9	41.6	81.6	82.4
Market value ($ mil.)	35.2%	1,451.9	1,839.6	1,456.5	2,460.4	4,849.7
Employees	16.2%	40	47	49	60	73

HANOVER COLLEGE

484 BALL DR — CEO: –
HANOVER, IN 472439669 — CFO: –
Phone: 812-866-7000 — HR: –
Fax: – — FYE: June 30
Web: www.hanover.edu — Type: Private

Hanover College is a private coeducational liberal arts college affiliated with the Presbyterian Church. The school offers bachelor's degrees in about 30 areas of study. Students who are required to take four classes each fall and winter term as well as one class during the spring term can design their own majors as well. The school also offers pre-professional programs in areas of study such as medicine law and dentistry. Hanover College has an enrollment of approximately 1000. The oldest private college in Indiana it was founded in 1827 by the Rev. John Finley Crowe.

	Annual Growth	06/03	06/04	06/05	06/08	06/12
Sales ($ mil.)	4.4%	–	–	38.9	47.6	52.7
Net income ($ mil.)	–	–	–	(2.1)	3.7	0.2
Market value ($ mil.)	–	–	–	–	–	–
Employees	–	–	–	–	–	300

HANOVER FOODS CORPORATION

1486 York St.
Hanover PA 17331
Phone: 717-632-6000
Fax: 717-637-2890
Web: hanoverfoods.com

CEO: John Warehime
CFO: Gary Knisely
HR: Sally Kern
FYE: May 31
Type: Private

Hanover Foods manufactures its foods hand over fist. The company makes more than 40 million cases of prepared food each year and boasts a vast portfolio of products. It makes and markets canned and frozen vegetables canned and fresh soups frozen entrees fresh produce soft pretzels potato chips desserts and fresh deli foods such as pasta and potato salad. Hanover Foods sells its products under the Aunt Kitty's Bickel's Myers Hanover Spring Glen Fresh Foods and Sunsprout brand names. The company caters to several customer types throughout the US including those in the retail food service fresh home meal replacement private label military club store and industrial markets.

HANOVER INSURANCE GROUP INC   NYS: THG

440 Lincoln Street
Worcester, MA 01653
Phone: 508 855-1000
Fax: 508 855-6332
Web: www.hanover.com

CEO: John Roche
CFO: Jeffrey Farber
HR: –
FYE: December 31
Type: Public

Founded in 1852 The Hanover Insurance Group is one of the oldest property/casualty insurance holding companies around. Through Hanover Insurance Company the company provides personal and commercial automobile homeowners and workers' compensation coverage as well as commercial multi-peril insurance and professional liability coverage. The company sells its products through a network of independent agents throughout the US. Hanover's Opus Investment Management subsidiary provides institutional investment management services.

	Annual Growth	12/16	12/17	12/18	12/19	12/20
Assets ($ mil.)	(1.4%)	14,220.4	15,469.6	12,399.7	12,490.5	13,443.7
Net income ($ mil.)	23.3%	155.1	186.2	391.0	425.1	358.7
Market value ($ mil.)	6.5%	3,312.8	3,934.1	4,250.4	4,974.8	4,255.9
Employees	(3.2%)	4,900	4,600	4,200	4,300	4,300

HANSEN MEDICAL INC   NMS: HNSN

800 East Middlefield Road
Mountain View, CA 94043
Phone: 650 404-5800
Fax: –
Web: www.hansenmedical.com

CEO: Cary Vance
CFO: Christopher P Lowe
HR: –
FYE: December 31
Type: Public

Hansen Medical helps doctors maneuver through matters of the heart. The company develops medical devices designed to diagnose and treat common types of cardiac arrhythmia (irregular heartbeats) such as atrial fibrillation. Its core portable Sensei system (used along with its Artisan and Lynx catheters) incorporates robotics to assist in guiding the movement of flexible catheters in such places as the atria and ventricles. Sensei has received FDA and European regulatory approval for certain uses including manipulation and control of catheters during diagnostic electrophysiology procedures which detect irregular heartbeats by mapping the electrical impulses of the heart.

	Annual Growth	12/10	12/11	12/12	12/13	12/14
Sales ($ mil.)	4.0%	16.6	22.1	17.6	17.0	19.5
Net income ($ mil.)	–	(37.9)	(16.7)	(22.1)	(55.7)	(54.2)
Market value ($ mil.)	(21.9%)	19.9	34.4	27.7	23.1	7.4
Employees	(0.3%)	171	174	160	171	169

HARBOR BIOSCIENCES INC.   OTC: HRBR

4435 Eastgate Mall Ste. 400
San Diego CA 92121
Phone: 858-587-9333
Fax: 858-558-6470
Web: www.harborbiosciences.com

CEO: Christine R Deister
CFO: –
HR: –
FYE: December 31
Type: Public

Adrenal steroids do the heavy lifting in the body's natural defense and metabolic systems and Harbor Biosciences (formerly Hollis-Eden Pharmaceuticals) hopes to harness their power. The company focuses on developing adrenal steroid hormones and hormone analogs which may reduce inflammation regulate immunity and stimulate cell growth. Natural levels of adrenal steroid hormones can decline as a result of aging or stress leaving the body less able to fend off illnesses. Harbor Biosciences' TRIOLEX candidate is being tested as a possible treatment for type 2 diabetes rheumatoid arthritis and ulcerative colitis. Its APOPTONE candidate is being investigated as a therapy for prostate and breast cancer.

HARDEE'S FOOD SYSTEMS INC.

100 N. Broadway Ste. 1200
St. Louis MO 63102-2706
Phone: 314-259-6200
Fax: 314-621-1778
Web: www.hardees.com

CEO: Andrew F Puzder
CFO: Charl Jimley
HR: –
FYE: January 31
Type: Subsidiary

This might be the right place if you have a hearty appetite for burgers. Hardee's Food Systems is a leading fast food chain operator with more than 1900 locations in some 30 states primarily in the Midwest and Southeast. The chain offers a variety of premium-priced Angus beef hamburgers under such names as Thickburger Six Dollar Burger and the Monster Thickburger. Hardee's also serves up chicken sandwiches salads fries and beverages as well as dessert items. About 475 of the restaurants are operated by the company while the rest are franchised. Hardee's is a subsidiary of fast food giant CKE Restaurants.

HARDINGE INC   NMS: HDNG

One Hardinge Drive
Elmira, NY 14903
Phone: 607 734-2281
Fax: –
Web: www.hardinge.com

CEO: Ryan Levenson
CFO: Tina Mashiko
HR: –
FYE: December 31
Type: Public

Hardinge keeps on turning. The company manufactures precision turning milling and grinding machine tools that shape metals composites and plastics. It makes industrial machine tools for small and midsized shops that create machined parts for the aerospace automotive construction medical equipment and farm equipment industries. Its computer-controlled machines cut horizontally or vertically and can be connected to automatic material feeders for unattended machining. Hardinge also offers a line of work- and tool-holding devices. It gets about 70% of its sales outside of North America predominantly in China and Western Europe.

	Annual Growth	12/12	12/13	12/14	12/15	12/16
Sales ($ mil.)	(3.3%)	334.4	329.5	311.6	315.2	292.0
Net income ($ mil.)	(48.8%)	17.9	9.9	(2.1)	2.6	1.2
Market value ($ mil.)	2.8%	128.2	186.6	153.7	120.2	142.9
Employees	0.6%	1,417	1,445	1,478	1,496	1,451

HARGROVE, LLC

1 HARGROVE DR
LANHAM, MD 207061804
Phone: 301-306-9000
Fax: –
Web: www.hargroveinc.com

CEO: Timothy McGill
CFO: –
HR: –
FYE: December 31
Type: Private

Hargrove has been in the background of every Presidential inauguration for more than 50 years. A trade show and special events company Hargrove has a tradition of organizing the inaugural festivities as well as decorating the National Christmas Tree. The firm also organizes more than 1200 trade shows and events annually in the US providing design production installation and management services. Hargrove also exercises its design and production capabilities by crafting parade floats that have appeared in Mardi Gras Thanksgiving and bowl game parades. The family-owned company was founded in 1949 by Earl Hargrove Jr. when he set the stage for Harry S Truman's presidential inaugural.

	Annual Growth	12/11	12/12	12/13	12/14	12/15
Sales ($ mil.)	(8.8%)	–	100.8	67.6	75.3	76.5
Net income ($ mil.)	(11.7%)	–	3.4	1.8	2.6	2.3
Market value ($ mil.)	–	–	–	–	–	–
Employees	–	–	–	–	–	200

HARLAND CLARKE CORP.

10931 Laureate Dr.
San Antonio TX 78249
Phone: 210-697-8888
Fax: 210-696-1676
Web: www.harlandclarke.com

CEO: –
CFO: –
HR: –
FYE: December 31
Type: Subsidiary

Is your check in the mail? Ask Harland Clarke. The company produces billions of checks and deposit slips annually. In addition to checks and check-related products (such as business cards and stationary) Harland Clarke offers direct marketing services delivery and anti-fraud products and contact center services to financial institutions such as banks credit unions and securities firms. Harland Clarke maintains about 20 manufacturing and administrative facilities throughout the US and Puerto Rico. The company became Harland Clarke in 2007 after holding company M & F Worldwide the owner of Clarke American Checks bought rival printer John H. Harland and combined the two companies' check-related operations.

HARLAND M. BRAUN & CO., INC.

4010 WHITESIDE ST
LOS ANGELES, CA 900631617
Phone: 323-263-9275
Fax: –
Web: www.braunexp.com

CEO: –
CFO: –
HR: –
FYE: October 31
Type: Private

Hide (the raw material) and seek (find a buyer) are all in a day's work for Harland M. Braun & Co. Operating through its subsidiary Braun Export the company supplies raw hide goods primarily cattle hides and skins and to a lesser extent pigskin and kipskins to tanners. A slate of services is provided for leather (wet blue and crust) hide and skin manufacturing as well as brokering exporting and importing. Dotting the US Braun & Co.'s processing facilities tie in with several suppliers of Holstein steer hides. Its partners include such meat packers as JBS Packerland Group Central Valley Meat Manning Beef Nebraska Beef and American Beef Packers. The company was founded in 1957.

	Annual Growth	10/14	10/15	10/16	10/17	10/18
Sales ($ mil.)	(31.4%)	–	304.4	205.2	173.1	98.4
Net income ($ mil.)	83.3%	–	0.1	0.0	0.1	0.5
Market value ($ mil.)	–	–	–	–	–	–
Employees	–	–	–	–	–	30

HARLEY-DAVIDSON INC

NYS: HOG

3700 West Juneau Avenue
Milwaukee, WI 53208
Phone: 414 342-4680
Fax: –
Web: www.harley-davidson.com

CEO: Jochen Zeitz
CFO: Gina Goetter
HR: –
FYE: December 31
Type: Public

Harley-Davidson is a major US motorcycle manufacturer that sells its bikes worldwide through a network of about 1380 dealers. The company offers cruiser and touring models standard sportbikes and dual models that can be used on- and off-road. Its trademarks of motorcycles include Softail H-D Street Sportster and Livewire. Harley-Davidson also sells attitude with its brand-name products which include a line of riding gear and apparel (MotorClothes). Harley-Davidson Financial Services (HDFS) offers financing to dealers and consumers in the US and Canada. The US generates almost 70% of Harley's revenue.

	Annual Growth	12/16	12/17	12/18	12/19	12/20
Sales ($ mil.)	(9.3%)	5,996.5	5,647.2	5,716.9	5,361.8	4,054.4
Net income ($ mil.)	(79.2%)	692.2	521.8	531.5	423.6	1.3
Market value ($ mil.)	(10.9%)	8,922.0	7,781.1	5,218.0	5,687.5	5,612.6
Employees	(3.5%)	6,000	5,800	5,300	5,600	5,200

HARLEYSVILLE FINANCIAL CORP

NBB: HARL

271 Main Street
Harleysville, PA 19438
Phone: 215 256-8828
Fax: –
Web: www.harleysvillesavings.com

CEO: Brendan McGill
CFO: M. Michalak
HR: –
FYE: September 30
Type: Public

Get your moola runnin'! Harleysville Savings Financial is the holding company of Harleysville Savings Bank which operates about a half-dozen branches in southeastern Pennsylvania's Montgomery County. The bank offers standard deposit products such as checking and savings accounts CDs and IRAs. Its lending activities consist primarily of single-family residential mortgages which account for more than two-thirds of the company's loan portfolio; home equity loans account for nearly 15%. To a lesser extent Harleysville Savings Bank also originates commercial mortgages residential construction loans and consumer lines of credit.

	Annual Growth	09/16	09/17	09/18	09/19	09/20
Assets ($ mil.)	3.4%	747.2	762.9	768.9	779.3	854.9
Net income ($ mil.)	6.7%	5.5	5.7	7.1	8.1	7.1
Market value ($ mil.)	4.5%	68.9	85.4	89.1	85.6	82.2
Employees	–	–	–	–	–	–

HARLEYSVILLE GROUP INC.

NASDAQ: HGIC

355 Maple Ave.
Harleysville PA 19438-2297
Phone: 215-256-5000
Fax: 215-256-5799
Web: www.harleysvillegroup.com

CEO: Michael L Browne
CFO: Arthur E Chandler
HR: –
FYE: December 31
Type: Subsidiary

The reckless the accident-prone or the just plain apprehensive take heed: Harleysville Group hopes to extend a safety net to all of you. An insurance holding company Harleysville Group (also known as Harleysville Insurance) sells a broad line of commercial property/casualty insurance policies including auto commercial multi-peril and workers' compensation policies. It also sells personal auto and homeowners coverage. The company which maintains regional offices in about a dozen states markets its products in more than 30 eastern and midwestern states through some 1300 independent agencies. Harleysville Group was acquired by Nationwide Mutual Insurance in 2012.

HARMAN INTERNATIONAL INDUSTRIES INC — NYS: HAR

400 Atlantic Street, Suite 1500　　CEO: Michael Mauser
Stamford, CT 06901　　CFO: Yoonho Choi
Phone: 203 328-3500　　HR: Eileen Bergmann
Fax: –　　FYE: June 30
Web: www.harman.com　　Type: Public

Harman International makes itself heard loud and clear. It makes high-end stereo and audio equipment for consumer and professional markets. The company makes loudspeakers CD and DVD players CD recorders and amplifiers under such brands as Mark Levinson JBL Harman/Kardon Revel AKG Infinity Logic 7 and others. Harman's auto unit sells branded audio systems through several carmakers including Toyota Lexus and BMW. About 30 million vehicles are equipped with Harman technology. Its professional unit makes audio equipment such as monitors amplifiers microphones and mixing consoles for recording studios cinemas touring performers and others. Harman agreed in November 2016 to be bought by Samsung for $8 billion.

	Annual Growth	06/12	06/13	06/14	06/15	06/16
Sales ($ mil.)	12.2%	4,364.1	4,297.8	5,348.5	6,155.3	6,911.7
Net income ($ mil.)	2.4%	329.5	142.4	234.7	342.7	361.7
Market value ($ mil.)	16.0%	2,773.8	3,796.4	7,524.9	8,331.2	5,030.6
Employees	23.0%	11,366	12,221	14,202	24,197	26,000

HARMONIC, INC. — NMS: HLIT

2590 Orchard Parkway　　CEO: Patrick Harshman
San Jose, CA 95131　　CFO: Sanjay Kalra
Phone: 408 542-2500　　HR: –
Fax: –　　FYE: December 31
Web: www.harmonicinc.com　　Type: Public

Harmonic Inc. is a leading global provider of versatile and high performance video delivery software products system solutions and services that enable its customers to efficiently create prepare store playout and deliver a full range of high-quality broadcast and streaming video services to consumer devices including televisions personal computers laptops tablets and smart phones and cable access solutions that enable cable operators to more efficiently and effectively deploy high-speed internet for data voice and video services to consumers' homes. Harmonic company sells directly and through distributors and systems integrators. US customers account for nearly 50% of the Harmonic's revenue.

	Annual Growth	12/16	12/17	12/18	12/19	12/20
Sales ($ mil.)	(1.7%)	405.9	358.2	403.6	402.9	378.8
Net income ($ mil.)	–	(72.3)	(83.0)	(21.0)	(5.9)	(29.3)
Market value ($ mil.)	10.3%	491.0	412.5	463.5	766.0	725.7
Employees	(4.0%)	1,376	1,244	1,162	1,172	1,169

HARRINGTON MEMORIAL HOSPITAL, INC.

100 SOUTH ST STE 1　　CEO: Edward Moore
SOUTHBRIDGE, MA 015504047　　CFO: –
Phone: 508-765-9771　　HR: –
Fax: –　　FYE: September 30
Web: www.harringtonhospital.org　　Type: Private

Harrington Memorial Hospital works to ensure that its patients feel less harried about health care. The health care facility founded in 1931 serves south-central Massachusetts and northeastern Connecticut. Harrington Memorial boasts nearly 115 beds and some 180 physicians who provide general and emergency medical care. It offers such specialized services as obstetrics physical therapy pediatrics diagnostic imaging and substance abuse treatment. The hospital also provides patients with home health care services and operates health clinics. Harrington Memorial invests in nearby Hubbard Regional Hospital through a management agreement in an effort to shore up the finances of both facilities.

	Annual Growth	09/15	09/16	09/17	09/18	09/19
Sales ($ mil.)	5.1%	–	126.4	130.0	135.6	146.6
Net income ($ mil.)	3.5%	–	12.4	9.3	12.1	13.8
Market value ($ mil.)	–	–	–	–	–	–
Employees	–	–	–	–	–	1,100

HARRIS TEETER INC.

701 Crestdale Rd.　　CEO: –
Matthews NC 28105　　CFO: –
Phone: 704-844-3100　　HR: Arnor Alston
Fax: 704-844-3138　　FYE: September 30
Web: www.harristeeter.com　　Type: Subsidiary

Neither teetering nor tottering Harris Teeter operates more than 200 supermarkets in North Carolina and seven other southeastern states and the District of Columbia. Most of the regional chain's grocery stores feature niceties such as sushi bars gourmet delis cafes and wine departments; many also house pharmacies. Harris Teeter which also has a handful of distribution centers is accelerating its growth in Maryland northern Virginia and the competitive Washington D.C. market and nearby suburbs. Formed by the combination of Harris Super Markets and Teeter's Food Marts in 1960 Harris Teeter is owned by holding company Harris Teeter Supermarkets.

HARRY & DAVID HOLDINGS INC.

2500 S. Pacific Hwy.　　CEO: Craig Johnson
Medford OR 97501　　CFO: Edward Dunlap
Phone: 541-864-2362　　HR: –
Fax: 800-648-6640　　FYE: June 30
Web: www.hndcorp.com　　Type: Private

Harry & David Holdings (HDH) wants customers to enjoy the fruits — and flowers — of its labors. Its Harry and David Direct Marketing catalogs and e-commerce unit offers gift baskets filled with gourmet foods most notably its Royal Riviera pears Moose Munch popcorn snacks and Tower of Treats gifts. It also runs the Fruit-of-the-Month Club. Harry and David Stores sell fruits flowers gourmet specialties and wine through about 70 locations in more than 35 states. The company's products are sold under its namesake Harry & David Wolferman's and Cushman brands. HDH emerged from six months in Chapter 11 bankruptcy protection in September 2011 after the court approved its reorganization plan in August.

HARRY WINSTON INC.

1330 Avenue of the Americas　　CEO: Nayla Hayek
New York NY 10019　　CFO: Robert Scott
Phone: 212-315-7900　　HR: –
Fax: 212-581-2612　　FYE: January 31
Web: www.harrywinston.com　　Type: Subsidiary

Diamonds are Harry Winston's best friend. The diamond jeweler and luxury timepiece retailer is one of the prized assets held by Canadian diamond titan Harry Winston Diamond. Harry Winston buys designs and sells fine diamonds and gems and watches through 20 salons in Beijing Beverly Hills London New York and Paris and other prime locations. Timepieces are also sold in some 190 locations worldwide as well as online. The company draws an affluent clientele including sultans starlets and business moguls who demand the highest quality. The House of Harry Winston was established in 1932 by Harry Winston the son of a New York jeweler. Harry Winston generates more than half of its parent company's sales.

HARSCO CORP.
NYS: HSC

350 Poplar Church Road
Camp Hill, PA 17011
Phone: 717 763-7064
Fax: –
Web: www.harsco.com

CEO: F. Nicholas Grasberger
CFO: Anshooman Aga
HR: –
FYE: December 31
Type: Public

Harsco is a market-leading global provider of environmental solutions for industrial and specialty waste streams and innovative equipment and technology for the rail sector. The company works with energy steel and construction companies to find new uses for their waste or to dispose of it. It takes for example power-plant coal slag and turns it into industrial abrasives. Other reprocessed materials are fertilizer asphalt and roofing granules. Harsco's railway business makes track maintenance equipment collision avoidance and warning systems and other equipment as well as provides rail maintenance services. In recent years Harsco has reshaped itself through acquisitions and divestitures. More than 40% of the Pennsylvania-based company's revenue comes from US.

	Annual Growth	12/16	12/17	12/18	12/19	12/20
Sales ($ mil.)	6.5%	1,451.2	1,607.1	1,722.4	1,503.7	1,863.9
Net income ($ mil.)	–	(85.7)	7.8	137.1	503.9	(26.3)
Market value ($ mil.)	7.2%	1,073.4	1,471.9	1,567.4	1,816.0	1,419.1
Employees	6.3%	9,400	9,400	9,900	10,500	12,000

HARTE HANKS INC
NMS: HHS

2800 Wells Branch Parkway
Austin, TX 78728
Phone: 512 434-1100
Fax: –
Web: www.hartehanks.com

CEO: Brian Linscott
CFO: Laurilee Kearnes
HR: –
FYE: December 31
Type: Public

Harte-Hanks gives thanks to direct marketing services. One of the largest producers of shoppers (advertising circulars sent by mail) in the country the company provides integrated direct-marketing services in the US and internationally including market research and analytics. It designs contact databases tracks leads and provides telephone e-mail and printing and mailing services to connect customers with their potential clients. Customers include major retailers and companies from the financial services and health care. Its biggest market is US. The company is founded in the year 1923.

	Annual Growth	12/16	12/17	12/18	12/19	12/20
Sales ($ mil.)	(18.7%)	404.4	383.9	284.6	217.6	176.9
Net income ($ mil.)	–	(130.9)	(41.9)	17.6	(26.3)	(1.7)
Market value ($ mil.)	16.0%	10.0	6.3	16.0	23.6	18.1
Employees	(19.0%)	5,652	5,635	2,983	2,430	2,434

HARTFORD FINANCIAL SERVICES GROUP INC.
NYS: HIG

One Hartford Plaza
Hartford, CT 06155
Phone: 860 547-5000
Fax: –
Web: www.thehartford.com

CEO: Christopher Swift
CFO: Beth Costello
HR: –
FYE: December 31
Type: Public

The Hartford Financial Services Group is a major US provider of commercial and personal property/casualty insurance. Its commercial operations include workers' compensation auto and liability coverage as well as specialty insurance policies. The Hartford also offers consumer homeowners and auto coverage. The group has been the direct auto and home insurance writer for AARP's members. In addition the company provides group life accident and disability benefits. Through its mutual fund division the firm offers wealth management products and services. The Hartford has been in business since 1810.

	Annual Growth	12/17	12/18	12/19	12/20	12/21
Assets ($ mil.)	(23.6%)	225,260.0	62,307.0	70,817.0	74,111.0	76,578.0
Net income ($ mil.)	–	(3,131.0)	1,807.0	2,085.0	1,737.0	2,365.0
Market value ($ mil.)	5.2%	18,849.6	14,887.5	20,353.5	16,404.7	23,123.3
Employees	2.5%	16,400	18,500	19,500	18,500	18,100

HARTFORD HEALTHCARE CORPORATION

1 STATE ST FL 19
HARTFORD, CT 061033102
Phone: 860-263-4100
Fax: –
Web: www.hartfordhealthcare.org

CEO: Jeffrey A Flaks
CFO: Charles L Johnson III
HR: –
FYE: September 30
Type: Private

Hartford Health Care provides a variety of health services to the descendants of our founding fathers. Founded in 1854 the health care system operates a network of hospitals behavioral health centers nursing and rehabilitation facilities medical labs and numerous community programs for residents in northern Connecticut. Medical specialties range from orthopedics and women's health to cancer and heart care. Hartford Health Care's flagship facility is the Hartford Hospital an 870-bed teaching hospital affiliated with the University of Connecticut Medical School. Its network also includes MidState Medical Center (some 155 beds) Windham Hospital (145 beds) and The Hospital of Central Connecticut (415 beds).

	Annual Growth	09/14	09/15	09/18	09/19	09/20
Sales ($ mil.)	70.4%	–	298.0	3,072.3	3,541.9	4,280.9
Net income ($ mil.)	–	–	(37.1)	410.2	(101.3)	108.8
Market value ($ mil.)	–	–	–	–	–	–
Employees	–	–	–	–	–	12,500

HARVARD BIOSCIENCE INC.
NMS: HBIO

84 October Hill Road
Holliston, MA 01746
Phone: 508 893-8999
Fax: –
Web: www.harvardbioscience.com

CEO: James Green
CFO: Michael Rossi
HR: –
FYE: December 31
Type: Public

Toss an 850-page Harvard Bioscience catalog toward a bioscience researcher and it will keep him or her busy for hours. The company develops manufactures and markets the scientific gizmos and instruments used in pharmaceutical biotechnology academic and government labs worldwide. Its 11000-item product line focuses on molecular biology and ADMET (absorption distribution metabolism elimination and toxicology) testing. ADMET tests are used to screen drug candidates. Other products include spectrophotometers multi-well plate readers and protein calculators. Customers can shop directly online from its printed Harvard Apparatus catalog or through distributors.

	Annual Growth	12/16	12/17	12/18	12/19	12/20
Sales ($ mil.)	(0.6%)	104.5	101.9	120.8	116.2	102.1
Net income ($ mil.)	–	(4.3)	(0.9)	(2.9)	(4.7)	(7.8)
Market value ($ mil.)	8.9%	120.2	130.0	125.3	120.2	169.1
Employees	1.4%	435	434	547	505	459

HARVARD PILGRIM HEALTH CARE INC.

93 Worcester St.
Wellesley MA 02481
Phone: 617-509-1000
Fax: 617-495-0754
Web: www.harvard.edu

CEO: Thomas A Croswell
CFO: –
HR: –
FYE: December 31
Type: Private - Not-for-Pr

Harvard Pilgrim Health Care takes care of New Englanders. A leading provider of health benefits in Massachusetts the not-for-profit organization also offers plans to residents of New Hampshire and Maine. It has more than 1 million members enrolled in its HMO PPO point-of-service and government plans. Those members have access to regional and national networks of hospitals and doctors. Harvard Pilgrim also targets multi-state employers with its Choice Plus and Options PPO plans offered through a partnership with UnitedHealthcare. Harvard Pilgrim has a network of more than 135 hospitals and 28000 doctors and clinicians.

HARVEST NATURAL RESOURCES INC.   NYSE: HNR

1177 Enclave Pkwy. Ste. 300
Houston TX 77077
Phone: 281-899-5700
Fax: 281-899-5702
Web: www.harvestnr.com

CEO: James A Edmiston
CFO: Stephen C Haynes
HR: –
FYE: December 31
Type: Public

Harvest Natural Resources is keen to harvest the natural resources of oil and gas. The independent's main exploration and production work takes place in Venezuela where operations hit a snag in 2005 due to Venezuela's difficult political climate which has restricted the company's contracts and production activities. Harvest currently operates in Venezuela through a 40% interest in exploration firm Petrodelta. In 2008 it acquired a 50% stake in the Dussafu Marin exploration- and production-sharing contract located offshore Gabon from South African synthetic fuels firm Sasol. It has also begun exploring in the western states and the Gulf Coast in the US as well as in Indonesia the Middle East and China.

HARVEST OIL & GAS CORP   NBB: HRST

1001 Fannin, Suite 750
Houston, TX 77002
Phone: 713 651-1144
Fax: –
Web: www.hvstog.com

CEO: Michael E Mercer
CFO: Nicholas P Bobrowski
HR: –
FYE: December 31
Type: Public

Harvest Oil & Gas Corp (formerly EV Energy Partners) is a natural gas and oil exploration and production company which operates in the Appalachian Basin primarily in West Virginia and Ohio as well as in Kansas Louisiana Michigan New Mexico Oklahoma and Texas. In 2018 Harvest Oil & Gas reported estimated proved reserves of 545 billion cu. ft. equivalent of oil and natural gas. EV Energy Partners filed Chapter 11 in April 2018 and emerged two months later under a new name — Harvest Oil & Gas Corp. In 2018 Harvest Oil & Gas sold all its interests in the Barnett Shale divested certain Mid-Continent assets and announced it was exploring strategic alternatives for the company.

	Annual Growth	12/17*	05/18*	12/18	12/19	12/20
Sales ($ mil.)	(51.2%)	225.7	111.0	138.6	113.8	26.3
Net income ($ mil.)	–	(134.2)	(610.5)	24.0	(138.3)	(8.9)
Market value ($ mil.)	7.0%	–	–	18.5	6.6	21.2
Employees	(93.5%)	1,185	–	5	5	–

*Fiscal year change

HARVEY MUDD COLLEGE

301 PLATT BLVD
CLAREMONT, CA 917115901
Phone: 909-621-8000
Fax: –
Web: www.hmc.edu

CEO: –
CFO: Andrew Dorantes
HR: –
FYE: June 30
Type: Private

Mudders get down and dirty with math and science. About 800 undergraduate students (called "Mudders") attend Harvey Mudd College (HMC) a private non-profit liberal arts school that specializes in engineering mathematics and the sciences. HMC is a member of The Claremont Colleges a confederation of five independent undergraduate colleges and two graduate schools that is managed by the Claremont University Consortium. The group shares resources and offers dual degree programs. HMC alums include Jonathan Gay creator of Flash software and Unison founder Rick Sontag.

	Annual Growth	06/09	06/10	06/11	06/13	06/15
Sales ($ mil.)	3.6%	–	56.3	65.5	79.8	67.1
Net income ($ mil.)	–	–	(5.0)	1.6	41.0	(10.5)
Market value ($ mil.)	–	–	–	–	–	–
Employees	–	–	–	–	–	250

HASBRO, INC.   NMS: HAS

1027 Newport Avenue
Pawtucket, RI 02861
Phone: 401 431-8697
Fax: –
Web: www.hasbro.com

CEO: Darren Throop
CFO: Deborah Thomas
HR: –
FYE: December 26
Type: Public

It's all fun and games at Hasbro one of the largest toy maker worldwide and the producer of such childhood favorites as Nerf Magic: The Gathering My Little Pony Transformers Play-Doh Monopoly Baby Alive Power Rangers Peppa Pig And Pj Masks. Hasbro has a significant relationship with Disney producing merchandise for the entertainment giant's megabrands including Star Wars Marvel (including Spider-Man Thor and Captain America) and Frozen and other Dreamworks features. Besides toys Hasbro makes board games such as Scrabble Monopoly and Trivial Pursuit as well as trading cards including Magic: The Gathering (through its Wizards of the Coast unit) and Dungeons & Dragons. About 60% of company's total revenue comes from US operations.

	Annual Growth	12/17	12/18	12/19	12/20	12/21
Sales ($ mil.)	5.4%	5,209.8	4,579.6	4,720.2	5,465.4	6,420.4
Net income ($ mil.)	2.0%	396.6	220.4	520.5	222.5	428.7
Market value ($ mil.)	1.9%	12,562.9	11,213.8	14,618.2	12,875.2	13,534.6
Employees	5.3%	5,400	5,800	5,600	6,822	6,640

HASTINGS ENTERTAINMENT, INC.   NAS: HAST

3601 Plains Boulevard
Amarillo, TX 79102
Phone: 806 351-2300
Fax: 806 351-2424
Web: www.gohastings.com

CEO: –
CFO: –
HR: –
FYE: January 31
Type: Public

Hastings Entertainment has it all for a smaller-town Saturday night. The company operates about 135 superstores in nearly 20 Midwestern and western US states. Hastings' stores and website sell new and used CDs movies books magazines and video games in addition to related electronics such as video game consoles and DVD players. Hastings also rents DVDs and video games. Its store locations average 24000 sq. ft. and offer such amenities as music listening stations reading chairs coffee bars and children's play areas. Hastings' other store concepts include Sun Adventure Sports which offers bicycles skateboards and other sporting goods and Tradesmart a seller of mostly used entertainment products.

	Annual Growth	01/09	01/10	01/11	01/12	01/13
Sales ($ mil.)	(3.7%)	538.7	531.3	521.1	496.4	462.5
Net income ($ mil.)	–	4.1	6.9	1.7	(17.6)	(9.3)
Market value ($ mil.)	(3.7%)	20.6	34.5	45.1	13.2	17.7
Employees	(2.4%)	5,774	5,704	5,848	5,153	5,233

HAT WORLD CORPORATION

7555 Woodland Dr.
Indianapolis IN 46278
Phone: 317-334-9428
Fax: 317-337-1428
Web: www.hatworld.com

CEO: –
CFO: Richard E Cramer
HR: –
FYE: January 31
Type: Subsidiary

Hat World thanks you for putting a lid on it. The mostly mall-based retailer specializes in caps featuring licensed logos of pro sports teams (MLB NBA NFL and NHL) and collegiate athletics. It operates 985 stores under the banners Hat World Lids Head Quarters and several others in the US Puerto Rico and Canada. Its websites which run under about 15 names stock caps with popular regional team logos. The company also holds a licensing agreement with Mainland Headwear. Hat World opened its first store in 1995; six years later it bought out bankrupt rival Lids and tripled in size. Acquired in 2004 by Genesco Hat World is part of the parent's Lids Sports Group which generates about 30% of total sales.

HATTERAS FINANCIAL CORP
NYS: HTS

751 W. Fourth Street, Suite 400
Winston Salem, NC 27101
Phone: 336 760-9347
Fax: –
Web: www.hatfin.com

CEO: –
CFO: –
HR: –
FYE: December 31
Type: Public

Hatteras Financial hopes for smooth sailing on the sometimes tumultuous seas of mortgage investing. The company is a real estate investment trust (REIT) that invests in adjustable-rate and hybrid adjustable-rate single-family residential mortgages guaranteed by a US government agency or a government-backed company such as Ginnie Mae Fannie Mae or Freddie Mac. Hatteras Financial's investment portfolio valued at some $7 billion consists mostly of hybrid adjustable-rate loans with terms of three to five years. Hatteras Financial is externally managed by Atlantic Capital Advisors.

	Annual Growth	12/10	12/11	12/12	12/13	12/14
Sales ($ mil.)	7.6%	265.0	426.1	506.3	452.3	355.8
Net income ($ mil.)	(24.1%)	169.5	284.4	349.2	(134.1)	56.4
Market value ($ mil.)	(11.7%)	2,929.3	2,551.9	2,400.9	1,581.2	1,783.5
Employees		–	–	–	–	13

HAUPPAUGE DIGITAL, INC.
NBB: HAUP

91 Cabot Court
Hauppauge, NY 11788
Phone: 631 434-1600
Fax: –
Web: www.hauppauge.com

CEO: Kenneth Plotkin
CFO: Gerald Tucciarone
HR: –
FYE: September 30
Type: Public

Wanna watch TV at work? Hauppauge Digital's WinTV analog and digital video boards let viewers videoconference watch TV and view input from VCRs and camcorders in a resizable window on a PC monitor. Hauppauge (pronounced "HAW-pog") also offers boards that accommodate radio and Internet broadcasts and makes a line of PC video editing boards. The company outsources its manufacturing to companies in Europe and Asia. The company sells its products to contract electronics manufacturers including ASUSTeK Computer and Hon Hai Precision Industry (Foxconn) and partners with companies such as Intel and Microsoft. Customers outside the US make up more than half of sales.

	Annual Growth	09/09	09/10	09/11	09/12	09/13
Sales ($ mil.)	(13.0%)	59.3	56.9	42.3	44.6	34.0
Net income ($ mil.)	–	(7.1)	(1.8)	(5.8)	(2.5)	(4.0)
Market value ($ mil.)	(24.0%)	11.7	26.0	8.7	10.9	3.9
Employees	(12.5%)	169	167	146	132	99

HAWAI I PACIFIC HEALTH

55 MERCHANT ST STE 2500
HONOLULU, HI 968134306
Phone: 808-949-9355
Fax: –
Web: www.hawaiipacifichealth.org

CEO: Raymond Vara
CFO: David Okabe
HR: –
FYE: June 30
Type: Private

Hawaii may be paradise but even in paradise's some residents get sick. That's when Hawai'i Pacific Health (HPH) surfs in to save the day. HPH is a not-for-profit health care system consisting of four hospitals (Kapi'olani Medical Center for Women & Children Pali Momi Medical Center Straub Clinic & Hospital and Wilcox Memorial Hospital) across the islands with a combined capacity of 550 beds. The system offers a full array of tertiary specialty and acute care services through its hospitals which also serve as teaching and research centers as well as about 50 outpatient centers. Specialized services offered by HPH include cardiac care maternity services oncology orthopedics and pediatric care.

	Annual Growth	06/14	06/15	06/17	06/18	06/20
Sales ($ mil.)	53.8%	–	159.3	1,290.0	1,351.8	1,369.4
Net income ($ mil.)		–	0.5	153.2	130.8	(48.5)
Market value ($ mil.)		–	–	–	–	–
Employees		–	–	–	–	5,400

HAWAII DEPARTMENT OF TRANSPORTATION

869 PUNCHBOWL ST RM 509
HONOLULU, HI 968135003
Phone: 808-587-1830
Fax: –
Web: www.hidot.hawaii.gov

CEO: –
CFO: –
HR: –
FYE: June 30
Type: Private

The State of Hawaii Department of Transportation (Hawaii DOT) makes sure the state's consumers get their consumables. Hawaii imports some 80% of what it utilizes. About 99% of this enters The 50th State through the commercial harbor system; a system that's planned constructed operated and maintained by the Hawaii DOT. In addition to the state's 10 harbors the agency operates a Highways Division which manages about 2400 lane miles of highway on six islands and an Airports Division responsible for 15 airports serving commercial airlines and general aviation flights and handling more than 30 million passengers annually. The Hawaii DOT generates its own monies through independent special funds.

	Annual Growth	06/08	06/09	06/10	06/16	06/19
Sales ($ mil.)	–	–	0.0	73.3	475.0	440.8
Net income ($ mil.)	–	–	(28.7)	18.8	64.8	172.2
Market value ($ mil.)	–	–	–	–	–	–
Employees	–	–	–	–	–	2,215

HAWAII PACIFIC UNIVERSITY

1164 BISHOP ST STE 800
HONOLULU, HI 968132817
Phone: 808-544-0200
Fax: –
Web: www.hpu.edu

CEO: –
CFO: Bruce Edwards
HR: –
FYE: June 30
Type: Private

Hawai'i Pacific University infuses a little aloha spirit into the liberal arts. The state's largest private institution of higher education offers some 50 undergraduate degrees and about a dozen graduate programs to more than 7000 students with majors ranging from journalism to business administration. The university's main campus is located in downtown Honolulu while two others also on the island of Oahu focus on environmental science marine biology oceanography and nursing. Students come from more than 80 countries making it one of the most diverse campuses in the world. Founded in 1965 the not-for-profit university's student/faculty ratio is 15:1.

	Annual Growth	06/13	06/14	06/15	06/17	06/18
Sales ($ mil.)	(10.2%)	–	107.5	105.9	79.4	70.0
Net income ($ mil.)	–	–	(7.9)	(1.3)	8.8	(3.5)
Market value ($ mil.)	–	–	–	–	–	–
Employees	–	–	–	–	–	1,300

HAWAIIAN ELECTRIC INDUSTRIES INC
NYS: HE

1001 Bishop Street, Suite 2900
Honolulu, HI 96813
Phone: 808 543-5662
Fax: 808 543-7966
Web: www.hei.com

CEO: Shelee Kimura
CFO: Gregory Hazelton
HR: –
FYE: December 31
Type: Public

Aloha! Hawaiian Electric Industries (HEI) interests itself with powering the Hawaiian Islands while running a profitable banking electric utility and infrastructure investment businesses subsidiary. An unusual combination HEI operates two regulated utility companies that provide electricity for approximately 95% of Hawaii residents mainly in Oahu Hawaii Maui Lanai and Molokai. It also runs one of the state's largest financial institutions. The utilities serve more than 460000 customers across all islands except Kauai and generate the bulk of HEI's revenue and Banking serves both consumer and commercial customers and operates about 40 branches on the islands of Oahu Maui Hawaii Kauai and Molokai.

	Annual Growth	12/16	12/17	12/18	12/19	12/20
Sales ($ mil.)	2.0%	2,380.7	2,555.6	2,860.8	2,874.6	2,579.8
Net income ($ mil.)	(5.5%)	250.1	167.2	203.7	219.8	199.7
Market value ($ mil.)	1.7%	3,610.6	3,946.9	3,998.2	5,116.2	3,863.9
Employees	(0.6%)	3,796	3,880	3,898	3,841	3,702

HAWAIIAN HOLDINGS INC   NMS: HA

3375 Koapaka Street, Suite G-350   CEO: Peter Ingram
Honolulu, HI 96819   CFO: Shannon Okinaka
Phone: 808 835-3700   HR: –
Fax: –   FYE: December 31
Web: www.hawaiianairlines.com   Type: Public

Hawaiian Holdings' main subsidiary is the Hawaiian Airlines. It is engaged in the scheduled air transportation of passengers and cargo amongst the Hawaiian Islands (the Neighbor Island routes) between the Hawaiian Islands and certain cities in the United States (the North America routes and together with the Neighbor Island routes the Domestic routes) and between the Hawaiian Islands and the South Pacific Australia New Zealand and Asia (the International routes). It operates a fleet of about 20 Boeing 717-200 aircraft for the Neighbor Island routes and nearly 25 Airbus A330-200 aircraft and roughly 20 Airbus A321-200 for the North America and International routes (inclusive of charter flights). In addition to its scheduled passenger and cargo operations Hawaiian Airlines provides charter services. Domestic operations account for roughly 75% of total revenue.

	Annual Growth	12/17	12/18	12/19	12/20	12/21
Sales ($ mil.)	(12.3%)	2,695.6	2,837.4	2,832.0	844.8	1,596.6
Net income ($ mil.)	–	364.0	233.2	224.0	(510.9)	(144.8)
Market value ($ mil.)	(17.6%)	2,041.6	1,353.1	1,500.6	906.8	941.2
Employees	0.1%	6,660	7,244	7,437	5,278	6,674

HAWAIIAN MACADAMIA NUT ORCHARDS LP   NBB: NNUT U

688 Kinoole Street, Suite 121   CEO: –
Hilo, HI 96720   CFO: Bradford C Nelson
Phone: 808 747-8471   HR: –
Fax: –   FYE: December 31
Web: www.rholp.com   Type: Public

Business is nuts (and that's a good thing) at ML Macadamia Orchards. As the world's largest macadamia nut grower the company owns or leases some 4200 acres of macadamia orchards located on the southeastern portion of the island of Hawaii where it produces a yearly average of 21 million pounds of nuts. ML Macadamia is strictly a nut grower; it sells its crop to Hawaiian nut processors including the Mauna Loa Macadamia Nut Corporation MacFarms of Hawaii and others under various contract agreements. The company decided to become vertically integrated in 2008 and is looking to acquire processing operations in order to insulate itself from low commodity prices.

	Annual Growth	12/13	12/14	12/15	12/16	12/17
Sales ($ mil.)	23.5%	13.9	16.0	18.5	26.7	32.2
Net income ($ mil.)	–	(3.7)	(6.2)	(2.2)	(2.0)	1.2
Market value ($ mil.)	–	0.0	0.0	0.0	0.0	0.0
Employees	1.6%	279	269	265	244	297

HAWAIIAN TELCOM HOLDCO INC   NMS: HCOM

1177 Bishop Street   CEO: –
Honolulu, HI 96813   CFO: –
Phone: 808 546-4511   HR: Sunshine Topping
Fax: –   FYE: December 31
Web: www.hawaiiantel.com   Type: Public

Hawaiian Telcom through its operating subsidiaries provides modern telecommunications services to residential and business customers in the island state. The company has almost 320000 local access lines (aka landlines) in service. It also provides long-distance phone service to about 171000 customers and broadband Internet access to about 100000 customers. Hawaiian Telcom resells wireless communications services through an agreement with Sprint Nextel. Local voice services about for about 80% of revenue. The company has been in operation since 1883.

	Annual Growth	12/12	12/13	12/14	12/15	12/16
Sales ($ mil.)	0.5%	385.5	391.2	390.7	393.4	393.0
Net income ($ mil.)	(68.3%)	110.0	10.5	8.1	1.1	1.1
Market value ($ mil.)	6.2%	224.5	338.1	317.4	286.2	285.3
Employees	(1.8%)	1,400	1,400	1,400	1,300	1,300

HAWKINS CONSTRUCTION COMPANY

2516 DEER PARK BLVD   CEO: Fred Hawkins Jr
OMAHA, NE 681053771   CFO:
Phone: 402-342-4455   HR: –
Fax: –   FYE: December 31
Web: www.hawkins1.com   Type: Private

Hawkins Construction provides both commercial building and heavy/highway contracting services. The diversified contractor has a project portfolio that includes regional banks warehouses schools churches and prisons. It also works on highways bridges site developments and parking structures and is one of the Midwest's largest road builders. Clients include the University of Nebraska Mutual of Omaha and Hewlett-Packard. The family-owned company began with a successful contract bid in 1922 by Kenneth Hawkins and his brother Earl for what is now Lincoln Nebraska's Memorial Stadium; the firm was incorporated in 1960 by Kenneth and his son Fred.

	Annual Growth	12/07	12/08	12/12	12/13	12/14
Sales ($ mil.)	(4.0%)	–	239.0	0.0	160.6	187.0
Net income ($ mil.)	(3.8%)	–	16.0	0.0	9.0	12.7
Market value ($ mil.)	–	–	–	–	–	–
Employees	–	–	–	–	–	400

HAWKINS INC   NMS: HWKN

2381 Rosegate   CEO: Patrick Hawkins
Roseville, MN 55113   CFO: Jeffrey Oldenkamp
Phone: 612 331-6910   HR: –
Fax: –   FYE: March 28
Web: www.hawkinsinc.com   Type: Public

Hawkins distributes blends and manufactures chemicals and specialty ingredients for its customers in a wide variety of industries. The company processes and distributes bulk specialty chemicals. Its Industrial Group segment stores and distributes caustic soda phosphoric acid and aqua ammonia among others. The segment also makes bleach (sodium hypochlorite) repackages liquid chlorine and custom blends other chemicals. Hawkins' Water Treatment Group distributes products and equipment used to treat drinking water municipal and industrial wastewater and swimming pools. It also distributes laboratory-grade chemicals for the pharmaceutical industry. The company operates about 35 facilities and has a fleet of trucks and tankers to serve customers throughout the Midwest US. Hawkins Inc. was founded in 1938.

	Annual Growth	04/17	04/18*	03/19	03/20	03/21
Sales ($ mil.)	5.4%	483.6	504.2	556.3	540.2	596.9
Net income ($ mil.)	16.1%	22.6	(9.2)	24.4	28.4	41.0
Market value ($ mil.)	(9.1%)	1,027.5	737.1	772.3	697.9	701.9
Employees	3.0%	659	653	657	656	742

*Fiscal year change

HAWORTH INC.

1 Haworth Center   CEO: Franco Bianchi
Holland MI 49423-9576   CFO: –
Phone: 616-393-3000   HR: –
Fax: 616-393-1570   FYE: December 31
Web: www.haworth.com   Type: Private

Designers at Haworth sit at their cubicles and think about ... more cubicles. The company is one of the top office furniture manufacturers in the US competing with top rivals Steelcase and HNI. Known for innovative design it offers a full range of furniture including partitions desks chairs tables and storage products. Brands include Monaco Patterns PLACES and X99. The company operates 80-plus showrooms worldwide and sells its products through more than 600 dealers. Haworth is the company behind the prewired partitions that make today's cubicled workplace possible. Haworth is owned by the family of Gerrard W. Haworth who founded the company in 1948.

HAWTHORNE MACHINERY CO.

16945 CAMINO SAN BERNARDO	CEO: Tee K Ness
SAN DIEGO, CA 921272499	CFO: –
Phone: 858-674-7000	HR: –
Fax: –	FYE: December 31
Web: www.hawthornecat.com	Type: Private

Leader of the track Hawthorne Machinery a Caterpillar dealership sells and rents more than 300 CAT equipment models including tractors trucks loaders compactors harvesters graders excavators and power systems. It also provides more than 73000 parts and repair services for industrial and construction contractors and other public and private customers around San Diego County. Hawthorne Machinery offers new and used equipment and rentals of brand-name equipment by such blue chip OEMs as Kubota Spartan and Sullair. The company was founded in 1956 by Tom Hawthorne.

	Annual Growth	12/01	12/02	12/03	12/06	12/07
Sales ($ mil.)	13.9%	–	176.2	170.8	377.2	338.1
Net income ($ mil.)	–	–	0.0	44.8	7.6	0.4
Market value ($ mil.)	–	–	–	–	–	–
Employees	–	–	–	–	–	1,000

HAY HOUSE INC.

2776 LOKER AVE W	CEO: –
CARLSBAD, CA 920106611	CFO: –
Phone: 760-431-7695	HR: –
Fax: –	FYE: December 31
Web: www.hayhouse.com	Type: Private

Self-help publisher Hay House publishes books and sells audio and video content covering topics such as self-help sociology philosophy psychology alternative health and environmental issues. It has more than 300 print books and 350 audio programs from some 130 authors including TV psychic John Edward talk show host Montel Williams and radio personality Tavis Smiley. In addition to its eponymous imprint the company publishes under the New Beginnings Press Princess Books and Smiley Books labels; the firm has international divisions in Australia the UK India and South Africa. Hay House was founded in 1984 by Louise Hay to self-publish her first two books Heal Your Body and You Can Heal Your Life.

	Annual Growth	12/03	12/04	12/05	12/06	12/08
Sales ($ mil.)	–	–	–	0.0	57.0	60.5
Net income ($ mil.)	–	–	–	0.0	1.5	0.9
Market value ($ mil.)	–	–	–	–	–	–
Employees	–	–	–	–	–	92

HAYES LEMMERZ INTERNATIONAL INC.

15300 Centennial Dr.	CEO: Pieter Klinkers
Northville MI 48168	CFO: Oscar Becker
Phone: 734-737-5000	HR: Christine Rogers
Fax: 716-887-7464	FYE: January 31
Web: www.ctg.com	Type: Private

Steel Wheels is more than a Stones' album — it's a living for Hayes Lemmerz. The company rolls along as the world's #1 manufacturer of fabricated steel and cast aluminum wheels for passenger cars and light trucks and steel wheels primarily for commercial trucks and sport utility vehicles. The company operates through two segments: automotive wheels and other products. It has however eliminated most of its components and intercompany activities comprising automotive brakes suspensions and powertrain parts. Customers are major car and truck OEMs in North America Europe and Japan including GM Ford Honda Nissan and Toyota. Hayes Lemmerz was acquired by Brazil's Iochpe-Maxion in 2012.

HAYNES INTERNATIONAL, INC.   NMS: HAYN

1020 West Park Avenue	CEO: Michael Shor
Kokomo, IN 46904-9013	CFO: Daniel Maudlin
Phone: 765 456-6000	HR: –
Fax: –	FYE: September 30
Web: www.haynesintl.com	Type: Public

Haynes International is one of the world's largest producer of alloys in flat product form such as sheet coil and plate. The company develops and manufactures nickel- and cobalt-based alloys?high-temperature alloys (HTAs) able to withstand extreme temperatures and corrosion-resistant alloys (CRAs) that stand up to corrosive substances and processes. HTAs are used in jet engines gas turbines used for power generation and waste incinerators while CRAs have applications in chemical processing power plant emissions control and hazardous waste treatment. Haynes does the majority of its business in the US.

	Annual Growth	09/17	09/18	09/19	09/20	09/21
Sales ($ mil.)	(3.9%)	395.2	435.3	490.2	380.5	337.7
Net income ($ mil.)	–	(10.2)	(21.8)	9.7	(6.5)	(8.7)
Market value ($ mil.)	0.9%	451.1	446.6	450.2	214.7	467.9
Employees	(0.3%)	1,124	1,157	1,179	1,054	1,110

HAYS MEDICAL CENTER, INC.

2220 CANTERBURY DR	CEO: John H Jeter
HAYS, KS 676012370	CFO: William Overbey
Phone: 785-623-5000	HR: –
Fax: –	FYE: June 30
Web: www.haysmed.com	Type: Private

Hays Medical Center brings big city health care to rural Kansas. The not-for-profit hospital which has about 210 beds provides both acute and tertiary medical care to the Midwestern plains serving more than 13000 emergency patients each year. In addition to medical surgical and pediatric care Hays Medical Center offers home care hospice skilled nursing rehabilitation and behavioral health services. It operates centers for cardiac care (the DeBakey Heart Institute) fitness and rehabilitation (Center for Health Improvement) orthopedics (Hays Orthopedic Institute) and cancer treatment (the Dreiling/Schmidt Cancer Center). The organization also operates specialty and rural health clinics.

	Annual Growth	06/12	06/13	06/14	06/15	06/16
Sales ($ mil.)	(0.0%)	–	199.6	198.7	201.6	199.5
Net income ($ mil.)	(46.3%)	–	17.0	21.0	8.6	2.6
Market value ($ mil.)	–	–	–	–	–	–
Employees	–	–	–	–	–	1,178

HAYWOOD HEALTH AUTHORITY

262 LEROY GEORGE DR	CEO: Steve Heatherly
CLYDE, NC 287217430	CFO: Gene Winters
Phone: 828-456-7311	HR: –
Fax: –	FYE: July 31
Web: www.myhaywoodregional.com	Type: Private

Got a bad case of hay fever? Head to Haywood! Haywood Regional Medical Center (HRMC) provides a wide range of health care services to the residents of western North Carolina. Specialty services include emergency medicine home and hospice care occupational health immediate and prolonged physical rehabilitation and surgery. Founded in 1927 the medical center offers imaging services diabetes education and health and fitness centers. HRMC also houses a state-funded adult psychiatric inpatient program managed by Smoky Mountain Center a local provider of behavioral health care services. The HRMC Foundation provides charitable giving and administration services.

	Annual Growth	09/12	09/13*	07/14	07/15	07/16
Sales ($ mil.)	5.5%	–	101.3	–	110.5	118.8
Net income ($ mil.)	–	–	(2.6)	–	(1.8)	(4.2)
Market value ($ mil.)	–	–	–	–	–	–
Employees	–	–	–	–	–	1,000

*Fiscal year change

HAZEN AND SAWYER, D.P.C.

498 7TH AVE FL 11
NEW YORK, NY 100186710
Phone: 212-539-7000
Fax: –
Web: www.hazenandsawyer.com

CEO: –
CFO: –
HR: –
FYE: December 31
Type: Private

There is nothing hazy about Hazen and Sawyer's focus on water wastewater and solid waste infrastructure. The environmental engineering firm specializes in planning designing and constructing clean drinking water systems for public and private clients worldwide. Hazen and Sawyer's specific areas of expertise include architectural design aquatic sciences biosolids management buried infrastructure odor control resource economics risk management utility management services and wastewater and stormwater collection. The employee-owned firm operates from about 40 offices throughout the eastern US and several international branch offices in South America.

	Annual Growth	12/04	12/05	12/07	12/08	12/18
Sales ($ mil.)	–	–	0.0	131.4	147.6	269.6
Net income ($ mil.)	–	–	0.0	62.8	0.0	(4.8)
Market value ($ mil.)	–	–	–	–	–	–
Employees	–	–	–	–	–	950

HCA HEALTHCARE INC

One Park Plaza
Nashville, TN 37203
Phone: 615 344-9551
Fax: –
Web: www.hcahealthcare.com

NYS: HCA
CEO: Samuel Hazen
CFO: William Rutherford
HR: –
FYE: December 31
Type: Public

HCA Healthcare is one of the leading health care services companies in the US it operates about 185 hospitals — mostly acute care centers as well as five psychiatric facilities and two rehabilitation hospital — located in the US and UK. It also runs about 120 ambulatory surgery centers — as well as urgent care rehab and other outpatient centers — that form health care networks in many of the communities it serves. In total its hospitals are home to some 49000 beds. HCA's facilities are located in about 20 states; About 45 of its hospitals are in Florida and Texas. The HCA International unit operates the company's hospitals and clinics in the UK.

	Annual Growth	12/17	12/18	12/19	12/20	12/21
Sales ($ mil.)	7.7%	43,614.0	46,677.0	51,336.0	51,533.0	58,752.0
Net income ($ mil.)	33.1%	2,216.0	3,787.0	3,505.0	3,754.0	6,956.0
Market value ($ mil.)	30.8%	26,833.1	38,016.6	45,152.5	50,238.7	78,483.1
Employees	2.9%	253,000	262,000	280,000	355,000	284,000

HCC INSURANCE HOLDINGS, INC.

13403 Northwest Freeway
Houston, TX 77040-6094
Phone: 713 690-7300
Fax: –
Web: www.hcc.com

NYS: HCC
CEO: Christopher J B Williams
CFO: Brad T Irick
HR: –
FYE: December 31
Type: Public

From corporate office to offshore rig HCC Insurance Holdings sells specialized property/casualty insurance for commercial and individual customers. Through Houston Casualty Corporation and other subsidiaries the company provides insurance and reinsurance coverage in specialty markets such as directors' and officers' liability errors and omissions and surety and credit policies. It also provides medical stop-loss coverage and policies for aviation marine and energy industries. HCC's underwriting agency division provides brokerage services for affiliated and unaffiliated insurance firms. The company which underwrites more than 100 classes of specialty insurance does business in some 180 countries.

	Annual Growth	12/09	12/10	12/11	12/12	12/13
Assets ($ mil.)	4.0%	8,834.4	9,064.1	9,625.3	10,267.8	10,344.5
Net income ($ mil.)	3.6%	353.9	345.1	255.2	391.2	407.2
Market value ($ mil.)	13.3%	2,806.4	2,903.7	2,759.2	3,733.5	4,629.5
Employees	0.5%	1,864	1,883	1,874	1,870	1,900

HCI GROUP INC

3802 Coconut Palm Drive
Tampa, FL 33619
Phone: 813 849-9500
Fax: –
Web: www.hcigroup.com

NYS: HCI
CEO: Paresh Patel
CFO: Mark Harmsworth
HR: –
FYE: December 31
Type: Public

Floridian homeowners are picking HCI Group for their insurance needs — by default. The company's Homeowners Choice Property and Casualty Insurance (HCPCI) subsidiary provides homeowners' insurance and other property/casualty coverage in the state. HCI sells policies through its two subsidiaries. Other HCI Group subsidiaries provide real estate reinsurance and information technology products and services. The firm changed its name from Homeowners Choice Inc. to HCI Group in to reflect its diversified businesses.

	Annual Growth	12/16	12/17	12/18	12/19	12/20
Assets ($ mil.)	8.9%	670.1	842.3	832.9	802.6	941.3
Net income ($ mil.)	(1.3%)	29.0	(6.9)	17.7	26.6	27.6
Market value ($ mil.)	7.3%	307.4	232.8	395.6	355.4	407.2
Employees	3.1%	399	410	465	491	451

HCR MANORCARE INC.

333 N. Summit St.
Toledo OH 43604-2617
Phone: 419-252-5500
Fax: 419-252-5554
Web: www.hcr-manorcare.com

CEO: Paul A Ormond
CFO: Steven M Cavanaugh
HR: –
FYE: December 31
Type: Private

HCR Manor Care is a lord of the manor in the nursing home kingdom. The company operates about 500 nursing homes assisted living centers and rehabilitation facilities in more than 30 states. Its facilities which operate under the names Heartland ManorCare Health Services and Arden Courts provide not only long-term nursing care but also rehabilitation services and short-term post-acute care for patients recovering from serious illness or injury. Many of its facilities house special units for Alzheimer's patients. In addition to its nursing and assisted-living facilities HCR Manor Care offers hospice and home health care through offices across the US. It is owned by private equity firm The Carlyle Group.

HCSB FINANCIAL CORP

5201 Broad Street
Loris, SC 29569
Phone: 843 756-6333
Fax: –
Web: www.hcsbaccess.com

NBB: HCFB
CEO: –
CFO: –
HR: –
FYE: December 31
Type: Public

HCSB Financial has erased the state lines in the Carolinas. The institution is the holding company for Horry County State Bank which operates more than a dozen branches that serve Horry and Marion counties in South Carolina and Columbus and Brunswick counties in North Carolina. Horry County State Bank offers traditional deposit products such as checking and savings accounts CDs money market accounts and IRAs. The bank originates primarily real estate loans (more than half of its loan portfolio) followed by business loans construction and development loans consumer loans and agricultural loans. The bank also offers investment services.

	Annual Growth	12/11	12/12	12/13	12/14	12/15
Assets ($ mil.)	(9.4%)	535.7	469.0	434.6	421.6	361.5
Net income ($ mil.)	–	(29.0)	(9.5)	1.8	(0.3)	(0.2)
Market value ($ mil.)	(26.0%)	2.0	0.3	0.7	0.6	0.6
Employees	(7.3%)	122	106	106	102	90

HDR, INC.

1917 S 67TH ST
OMAHA, NE 681062973
Phone: 402-399-1000
Fax: –
Web: www.hdrinc.com

CEO: Eric Keen
CFO: Galen Meysenburg
HR: Susan V Sandt
FYE: December 29
Type: Private

With projects ranging from restoring the Pentagon and the Everglades to working on the Hoover Dam Bypass project HDR has left its mark on the US. HDR is an architecture engineering and consulting firm that specializes in such projects as bridges water- and wastewater-treatment plants and hospitals. The company also provides mechanical and plumbing services construction and project management and utilities planning. It has operation in nearly 15 countries and has offices in more than 200 global locations. The employee-owned company was founded as Henningson Engineering in 1917 to build municipal plants in the rural Midwest.

	Annual Growth	12/14	12/15	12/16	12/17	12/18
Sales ($ mil.)	(6.1%)	–	2,132.2	2,230.5	2,362.1	1,762.8
Net income ($ mil.)	15.9%	–	74.1	90.3	82.7	115.3
Market value ($ mil.)	–	–	–	–	–	–
Employees	–	–	–	–	–	10,000

HEADWATERS INC

10701 South River Front Parkway, Suite 300
South Jordan, UT 84095
Phone: 801 984-9400
Fax: –
Web: www.headwaters.com

NYS: HW
CEO: Mike Kane
CFO: –
HR: –
FYE: September 30
Type: Public

Headwaters is a modern-day alchemist turning stone and coal into money. Through subsidiaries it provides building materials such as coal combustion products (CCP) and synthetic gypsum and reclaims waste coal in North America. Headwaters' light building products segment — its largest — makes stone products and siding accessories under the Eldorado Stone brand. The heavy construction materials segment sells residuals from the coal combustion process (such as fly ash) which can be used as a substitute for Portland cement in building materials. Headwaters' energy technology segment licenses coal conversion and heavy oil upgrading technology. In late 2016 Headwaters agreed to be purchased by Australia-based Boral Limited.

	Annual Growth	09/12	09/13	09/14	09/15	09/16
Sales ($ mil.)	11.4%	632.8	702.6	791.4	895.3	974.8
Net income ($ mil.)	–	(62.2)	7.1	15.3	130.8	48.1
Market value ($ mil.)	26.6%	487.2	665.7	928.6	1,392.1	1,252.9
Employees	10.6%	2,465	2,355	2,665	2,831	3,687

HEALTH FIRST SHARED SERVICES, INC.

6450 US HIGHWAY 1
ROCKLEDGE, FL 329555747
Phone: 321-434-4300
Fax: –
Web: www.hf.org

CEO: Steve Johnson
CFO: Robert C Galloway
HR: –
FYE: September 30
Type: Private

Health First works to keep Florida's Space Coast denizens in tip-top shape. The not-for-profit health system operates four hospitals in Brevard County. Health First's biggest hospital is Holmes Regional Medical Center in Melbourne with more than 500 beds. Its Cape Canaveral Hospital and Palm Bay Community Hospital have 150 and 60 beds respectively. Its Viera Hospital is a 100-bed acute-care hospital. The system also runs outpatient clinics a home health service and a physicians group. Its for-profit subsidiary Health First Health Plans is the county's largest insurer with about 60000 commercial members and 23000 Medicare members.

	Annual Growth	09/10	09/11	09/13	09/14	09/15
Sales ($ mil.)	76.5%	–	129.4	1,059.4	1,137.0	1,255.3
Net income ($ mil.)	–	–	(0.4)	51.1	90.2	19.9
Market value ($ mil.)	–	–	–	–	–	–
Employees	–	–	–	–	–	6,900

HEALTH NET, INC.

21650 Oxnard Street
Woodland Hills, CA 91367
Phone: 818 676-6000
Fax: –
Web: www.healthnet.com

NYS: HNT
CEO: –
CFO: –
HR: –
FYE: December 31
Type: Public

Health Net has woven together a web of health plan services. The company provides managed health care medical coverage to about 6 million members. The company's health plan services unit offers HMO PPO Medicare and Medicaid plans as well as vision dental care and pharmacy benefit programs to customers in Arizona California Oregon and Washington. Health Net's Managed Health Network subsidiary provides behavioral health substance abuse and employee assistance to employer groups and traditional health plan customers. The company also provides administration services for self-funded medical plans. Medicaid insurer Centene plans to buy Health Net for $6.3 billion.

	Annual Growth	12/10	12/11	12/12	12/13	12/14
Sales ($ mil.)	0.7%	13,619.9	11,901.0	11,289.1	11,053.7	14,008.6
Net income ($ mil.)	(8.1%)	204.2	72.1	122.1	170.1	145.6
Market value ($ mil.)	18.3%	2,130.6	2,375.0	1,897.2	2,316.4	4,179.2
Employees	(0.5%)	8,169	7,471	7,378	7,659	8,014

HEALTH PARTNERS PLANS, INC.

901 MARKET ST STE 500
PHILADELPHIA, PA 191074496
Phone: 215-849-9606
Fax: –
Web: www.healthpartnersplans.com

CEO: –
CFO: Martin J Brill
HR: –
FYE: December 31
Type: Private

Health Partners wants to partner up with Pennsylvanians in need of health care. It is one of a few hospital-owned health maintenance organizations in the nation providing free and low-cost high-quality health insurance through its Medicaid Medicare and CHIP plans. The company is a not-for-profit health plan that provides health benefits to over 280000 members in the Philadelphia area. Its Health Partners Medicare plans offer three Medicare Advantage plans in the twelve-county area all of which provide more benefits than Original Medicare with no or low monthly plan premiums. Its KidzPartners program is provided in partnership with the state of Pennsylvania's Children's Health Insurance Program (CHIP). Its provider network includes over 6400 primary and specialty care doctors and more than 40 hospitals in the region. Health Partners was founded in 1984 by a group of hospitals in the Philadelphia area.

	Annual Growth	12/10	12/11	12/12	12/13	12/14
Sales ($ mil.)	(6.2%)	–	–	1,034.9	1,000.3	910.2
Net income ($ mil.)	–	–	–	(1.6)	(0.2)	(8.5)
Market value ($ mil.)	–	–	–	–	–	–
Employees	–	–	–	–	–	620

HEALTH RESEARCH, INC.

150 BROADWAY STE 280
MENANDS, NY 122042732
Phone: 518-431-1200
Fax: –
Web: www.healthresearch.org

CEO: –
CFO: –
HR: –
FYE: March 31
Type: Private

Health Research Inc. (HRI) knows where the money is. The group is a not-for-profit organization that helps the New York State Department of Health and its affiliated Roswell Park Cancer Institute solicit evaluate and administer financial support. Sources of that support come from federal and state government sources other non-profits and businesses. HRI's Technology Transfer office also assists the Department of Health in sharing its research findings with other public and private institutions and finding ways to create biomedical technologies through private sector development. HRI was founded in 1953 and has administered $7 billion over its lifetime.

	Annual Growth	03/12	03/13	03/14	03/15	03/20
Sales ($ mil.)	10.3%	–	665.9	703.4	677.9	1,326.5
Net income ($ mil.)	52.8%	–	26.0	13.5	22.6	506.2
Market value ($ mil.)	–	–	–	–	–	–
Employees	–	–	–	–	–	1,400

HEALTHCARE DISTRIBUTION MANAGEMENT ASSOCIATION

901 N GLEBE RD STE 1000
ARLINGTON, VA 222031854
Phone: 703-787-0000
Fax: –
Web: www.hdma.net

CEO: John M Gray
CFO: –
HR: –
FYE: December 31
Type: Private

The Healthcare Distribution Management Association (HDMA) helps the medicine get where it's needed. HDMA is a trade association representing healthcare and pharmaceutical products distributors. Its members include hundreds of manufacturers and some 70 distributors as well as numerous service providers that deliver to pharmacies hospitals nursing homes and health clinics. The organization provides opportunities for members to share industry best practices represents member concerns before Congress and regulatory agencies and publishes newsletters and state by state information sheets for members. HDMA was founded in the late 1800s.

	Annual Growth	12/05	12/06	12/08	12/09	12/13
Sales ($ mil.)	4.9%	–	9.2	11.3	9.6	12.9
Net income ($ mil.)	–	–	–	0.0	(2.3)	0.1
Market value ($ mil.)	–	–	–	–	–	–
Employees	–	–	–	–	–	40

HEALTHCARE PARTNERS LLC

19191 Vermont Ave. Ste. 200
Torrance CA 90502
Phone: 310-354-4200
Fax: 310-538-3385
Web: www.healthcarepartners.com

CEO: Robert J Margolis
CFO: –
HR: –
FYE: December 31
Type: Private

A health care management services and accountable care organization HealthCare Partners owns and operates groups of medical practices in California Florida New Mexico and Nevada. The company provides administrative services to subsidiary HealthCare Partners Medical Group which operates more than 65 medical practices in Los Angeles and surrounding areas. Its JSA Healthcare unit provides primary care and pharmacy services at some 40 facilities in central Florida while its HealthCare Partners of Nevada unit operates 45 facilities around Las Vegas. The company also conducts clinical research at its Health Care Partners Institute. HealthCare Partners was acquired by renal care giant DaVita in 2012.

HEALTHCARE REALTY TRUST, INC.
NYS: HR

3310 West End Avenue, Suite 700
Nashville, TN 37203
Phone: 615 269-8175
Fax: –
Web: www.healthcarerealty.com

CEO: Todd Meredith
CFO: J. Christopher Douglas
HR: –
FYE: December 31
Type: Public

Healthcare Realty Trust is a self-managed and self-administered real estate investment trust (REIT) that owns leases manages acquires finances develops and redevelops income-producing real estate properties associated primarily with the delivery of outpatient healthcare services throughout the US. The REIT owned some 230 real estate properties in about 25 states totaling 16.5 million square feet and was valued at approximately $5.9 billion. The company provided leasing and property management services to 13.1 million square feet nationwide. Healthcare Realty Trust went public in 1993.

	Annual Growth	12/17	12/18	12/19	12/20	12/21
Sales ($ mil.)	5.9%	424.5	450.4	470.3	499.6	534.8
Net income ($ mil.)	30.3%	23.1	69.8	39.2	72.2	66.7
Market value ($ mil.)	(0.4%)	4,832.7	4,279.0	5,020.8	4,453.5	4,760.5
Employees	5.5%	273	277	297	308	338

HEALTHCARE SERVICES GROUP, INC.
NMS: HCSG

3220 Tillman Drive, Suite 300
Bensalem, PA 19020
Phone: 215 639-4274
Fax: –
Web: www.hcsgcorp.com

CEO: Theodore Wahl
CFO: John C Shea
HR: Deanna May-Gospodarek
FYE: December 31
Type: Public

Healthcare Services Group provides food housekeeping laundry and linen and maintenance services to hospitals nursing homes rehabilitation centers and retirement facilities throughout the US. The company's dietary services purchases food and prepares meals for residents and monitors nutritional needs in more than 1500 facilities. Healthcare Services Group also tidies up more than 3000 facilities mostly primarily providers of long-term care many of which rely on Medicare Medicaid and third-party payors' reimbursement funds. Healthcare Services Group was established in 1976.

	Annual Growth	12/17	12/18	12/19	12/20	12/21
Sales ($ mil.)	(3.1%)	1,866.1	2,008.8	1,840.8	1,760.3	1,642.0
Net income ($ mil.)	(15.1%)	88.2	83.5	64.6	98.7	45.9
Market value ($ mil.)	(23.8%)	3,889.1	2,964.0	1,794.1	2,072.9	1,312.4
Employees	(8.1%)	55,000	55,000	51,000	44,200	39,200

HEALTHEAST ST JOHN'S HOSPITAL

1575 BEAM AVE
SAINT PAUL, MN 55109-1126
Phone: 651-232-7000
Fax: –
Web: www.stjohnshospital-mn.org

CEO: –
CFO: –
HR: –
FYE: August 31
Type: Private

St. John's Hospital provides health care to folks residing the suburbs of the Twin Cities. The hospital has about 185 beds and is an acute-care facility with emergency inpatient and outpatient medicine departments. Its facilities include specialty centers for breast care cancer care heart health maternity services and orthopedics among other offerings. St. John's started in 1910 with a private home that was converted into a 25-bed hospital. St. John's Hospital is part of the HealthEast Care System which includes other hospitals and health centers in the Minneapolis/St. Paul metropolitan area.

	Annual Growth	08/01	08/02	08/05	08/06	08/09
Sales ($ mil.)	6.0%	–	168.1	190.2	204.0	252.1
Net income ($ mil.)	(1.8%)	–	21.1	11.6	14.6	18.6
Market value ($ mil.)	–	–	–	–	–	–
Employees	–	–	–	–	–	713

HEALTHMARKETS INC.

9151 Boulevard 26
North Richland Hills TX 76180
Phone: 817-255-5200
Fax: 817-255-5390
Web: www.healthmarkets.com

CEO: Kenneth J Fasola
CFO: R Scott Donovan
HR: –
FYE: December 31
Type: Private

HealthMarkets lets the self-employed shop for better insurance. The company offers health insurance through its MEGA Life and Health Insurance Mid-West National Life Insurance Company of Tennessee Chesapeake Life Insurance Company and HealthMarkets Insurance to mostly self-employed individuals in the US. Health care options include PPOs high-deductable plans and health spending accounts (HSAs). HealthMarkets also provides supplemental dental vision accident illness and hospital indemnity insurance. The company manages a network of insurance brokers through its Insphere Insurance Solutions division. A consortium led by the Blackstone Group owns HealthMarkets.

HEALTHPEAK PROPERTIES INC NYS: PEAK

5050 South Syracuse Street, Suite 800
Denver, CO 80237
Phone: 720 428-5050
Fax: 562 733-5200
Web: www.healthpeak.com
CEO: Thomas Herzog
CFO: Peter Scott
HR: –
FYE: December 31
Type: Public

Healthpeak Properties (formerly HCP Inc.) is a self-administered real estate investment trust (REIT) that invests in develops and manages healthcare real estate across the US. Its real estate portfolio consists of senior housing lab and office space for biopharma and medical device companies and medical office buildings. Healthpeak consolidated portfolio of investment consisted of interest in about 455 properties. The company was founded in 1985.

	Annual Growth	12/17	12/18	12/19	12/20	12/21
Sales ($ mil.)	0.6%	1,848.4	1,846.7	1,997.4	1,644.9	1,896.2
Net income ($ mil.)	5.1%	414.2	1,061.1	45.5	413.6	505.5
Market value ($ mil.)	8.5%	14,059.6	15,057.0	18,582.7	16,296.9	19,456.0
Employees	0.8%	190	201	204	217	196

HEALTHSPAN INTEGRATED CARE

1701 MERCY HEALTH PL
CINCINNATI, OH 452376147
Phone: 216-621-5600
Fax: –
Web: www.payhealthspan.com
CEO: Kenneth Page
CFO: Thomas Revis
HR: –
FYE: December 31
Type: Private

Kaiser Foundation Health Plan of Ohio is a subsidiary of the Kaiser Foundation Health Plan and provides health care services to nearly 150000 people at 10 medical facilities in the Akron and Cleveland metropolitan areas. It offers specialized services at The Cleveland Clinic Lake Hospital System and Summa Health System. More than 3000 businesses offer their employees access to the company's health plans and care from more than 3000 physicians in the network. Kaiser Foundation Health Plans have an integrated care model offering both hospital and physician care through a network of hospitals and physician practices operating under the Kaiser name in 9 states and the District of Columbia.

	Annual Growth	12/10	12/11	12/12	12/13	12/14
Assets ($ mil.)	(40.6%)	–	–	–	271.1	161.1
Net income ($ mil.)	–	–	–	–	(84.4)	(42.2)
Market value ($ mil.)	–	–	–	–	–	–
Employees	–	–	–	–	–	1,240

HEALTHSPRING INC. NYSE: HS

9009 Carothers Pkwy. Ste. 501
Franklin TN 37067
Phone: 615-291-7000
Fax: 615-401-4566
Web: www.healthspring.com
CEO: Herbert A Fritch
CFO: Karey L Witty
HR: –
FYE: December 31
Type: Subsidiary

Looking to keep a spring in Grandma's step HealthSpring provides Medicare Advantage plans and Medicare Part D prescription drug benefits to members in 11 states and the District of Columbia across some 65000 pharmacies. Its Medicare Advantage plans offer the support of Medicare with additional benefits such as the Medicare Part D prescription benefits vision and hearing benefits and transportation programs. In addition HealthSpring runs a nationwide prescription drug plan (otherwise known as PDPs) and offers management services to independent physician associations in Alabama Tennessee and Texas. HealthSpring was acquired by insurance giant CIGNA in 2012.

HEALTHSTREAM INC NMS: HSTM

500 11th Avenue North, Suite 1000
Nashville, TN 37203
Phone: 615 301-3100
Fax: –
Web: www.healthstream.com
CEO: Robert Frist
CFO: Scott Roberts
HR: –
FYE: December 31
Type: Public

HealthStream supplies internet-based learning and research content to help US health care organizations meet their ongoing clinical development talent management training education assessment competency management compliance scheduling provider credentialing & privileging management and provider enrollment needs. HealthStream's core learning product is HealthStream Learning Center (HLC) which offers educational and training courseware to about 4.22 million subscribers via a software-as-a-service (SaaS) model. HealthStream's products services and operations were organized and managed under two business segments?Workforce Solutions and Provider Solutions. The company was incorporated in 1999.

	Annual Growth	12/16	12/17	12/18	12/19	12/20
Sales ($ mil.)	2.0%	226.0	247.7	231.6	254.1	244.8
Net income ($ mil.)	39.2%	3.8	10.0	32.2	15.8	14.1
Market value ($ mil.)	(3.4%)	788.9	729.4	760.6	856.6	687.8
Employees	(1.2%)	1,120	1,027	790	876	1,069

HEALTHWAREHOUSE.COM, INC. NBB: HEWA

7107 Industrial Road
Florence, KY 41042
Phone: 800 748-7001
Fax: –
Web: www.healthwarehouse.com
CEO: Joseph Peters
CFO: –
HR: –
FYE: December 31
Type: Public

HealthWarehouse.com sells over-the-counter in more than one way. The online pharmacy sells prescription and over-the-counter drugs to more than 160000 customers. It sources its products from suppliers including Masters Pharmaceutical and The Harvard Drug Group. HealthWarehouse went public through a reverse merger with OTC-traded Clacendix in 2009. Clacendix provided products that protected enterprise data and networks from security threats. Faced with declining sales and mounting losses Clacendix sold its assets to API Cryptek for $3.2 million in 2008. Clacendix later merged with HealthWarehouse and changed its name in 2009. HealthWarehouse purchased the online assets of Hocks Pharmacy in 2011.

	Annual Growth	12/16	12/17	12/18	12/19	12/20
Sales ($ mil.)	13.4%	10.4	14.8	15.7	15.8	17.2
Net income ($ mil.)	–	(1.4)	0.4	(0.8)	(0.1)	0.6
Market value ($ mil.)	(15.2%)	14.9	23.2	14.1	9.5	7.7
Employees	10.4%	74	–	–	–	110

HEARTLAND CO-OP

2829 WESTOWN PKWY STE 350
WEST DES MOINES, IA 502661340
Phone: 515-225-1334
Fax: –
Web: www.heartlandcoop.com
CEO: –
CFO: –
HR: –
FYE: June 30
Type: Private

Heartland Co-op has no need to go against the grain. The cooperative offers agricultural products and services for its central Iowa member/farmers. Heartland operates more than 50 grain elevators and service centers. It offers agronomy products and services such as seed treatments and alfalfa fertilization; grain drying storage and merchandising; petroleum products for farm vehicles and home heating; livestock and pet feed; and personal and crop credit and financing. Headquartered in West Des Moines Heartland was formed in 1987 when cooperatives in Dallas Center Minburn and Panora merged. Heartland which has grown to more than 5400-members merged with Farm Service Company of Council Bluffs in 2013.

	Annual Growth	06/15	06/16	06/17	06/18	06/19
Sales ($ mil.)	0.5%	–	854.4	932.4	901.7	867.6
Net income ($ mil.)	3.5%	–	16.0	17.9	20.1	17.7
Market value ($ mil.)	–	–	–	–	–	–
Employees	–	–	–	–	–	678

HEARTLAND EXPRESS, INC.   NMS: HTLD

901 Heartland Way | CEO: Michael Gerdin
North Liberty, IA 52317 | CFO: Christopher Strain
Phone: 319 626-3600 | HR: Jo Borden
Fax: – | FYE: December 31
Web: www.heartlandexpress.com | Type: Public

Heartland Express stays close to home as a short- to medium-haul truckload carrier — its average trip is just over 500 miles. It primarily provides nationwide asset-based dry van truckload service for major shippers from Washington to Florida and New England to California. Heartland also operates from more than 25 regional distribution hubs which are strategically located to concentrate on regional freight movements generally within a 500-mile radius of the terminals. Heartland transports general commodities including appliances auto parts consumer products food and paper products. Almost all of its operating revenue is derived from shipments within the US.

	Annual Growth	12/16	12/17	12/18	12/19	12/20
Sales ($ mil.)	1.3%	612.9	607.3	610.8	596.8	645.3
Net income ($ mil.)	5.9%	56.4	75.2	72.7	73.0	70.8
Market value ($ mil.)	(2.9%)	1,642.1	1,882.4	1,475.9	1,697.7	1,459.8
Employees	1.2%	3,600	3,800	3,450	4,050	3,780

HEARTLAND FINANCIAL USA, INC. (DUBUQUE, IA)   NMS: HTLF

1398 Central Avenue | CEO: Bruce Lee
Dubuque, IA 52001 | CFO: Janet Quick
Phone: 563 589-2100 | HR: –
Fax: 563 589-2011 | FYE: December 31
Web: www.htlf.com | Type: Public

Founded in 1981 Heartland Financial USA is an $18 billion multi-bank holding company that owns flagship subsidiary Dubuque Bank and Trust (Iowa) and ten other banks that together operate more than 125 branches in about a dozen states primarily in the West and Midwest. In addition to standard deposit loan and mortgage services the banks also offer retirement wealth management trust insurance and investment services. Heartland also owns consumer lender Citizens Finance which has about a dozen offices in Illinois Iowa and Wisconsin.

	Annual Growth	12/16	12/17	12/18	12/19	12/20
Assets ($ mil.)	21.4%	8,247.1	9,810.7	11,408.0	13,209.6	17,908.3
Net income ($ mil.)	14.5%	80.3	75.3	117.0	149.1	137.9
Market value ($ mil.)	(4.2%)	2,020.5	2,258.3	1,850.4	2,093.7	1,699.3
Employees	1.9%	1,864	2,008	2,045	1,908	2,013

HEARTLAND PAYMENT SYSTEMS, LLC

10 GLENLAKE PKWY STE 324 | CEO: Robert O Carr
ATLANTA, GA 303283495 | CFO: Samir Zabaneh
Phone: 609-683-3831 | HR: –
Fax: – | FYE: December 31
Web: www.heartlandpaymentsystems.com | Type: Private

Heartland Payment Systems (HPS) a wholly owned subsidiary of Global Payments Inc. makes sure plastic-card transactions don't get lost along their way. The company performs credit debit and prepaid card processing services at some 300000 locations nationwide. Its client list includes restaurants retailers convenience stores and professional service providers. The Heartland Payroll Solutions segment provides payroll processing such as check printing and direct deposit for more than 10000 customers. Other markets for the firm include K-12 school nutrition programs and payment processing for colleges and universities. Global Payments bought Heartland for $4.3 billion in 2016.

	Annual Growth	12/11	12/12	12/13	12/14	12/15
Sales ($ mil.)	10.0%	–	2,013.4	2,135.4	2,311.4	2,682.4
Net income ($ mil.)	8.4%	–	66.5	78.1	31.9	84.7
Market value ($ mil.)						
Employees		–	–	–	–	3,734

HEARTLAND REGIONAL MEDICAL CENTER

5325 FARAON ST | CEO: Mark Laney
SAINT JOSEPH, MO 645063488 | CFO: –
Phone: 816-271-6000 | HR: –
Fax: – | FYE: June 30
Web: www.mymlc.com | Type: Private

Heartland Regional Medical Center strives for healthy hearts minds and bodies in the US heartland. The acute care hospital a subsidiary of Heartland Health provides medical services to residents of St. Joseph Missouri and some 20 surrounding counties in northwest Missouri southeast Nebraska and northeast Kansas. Heartland Regional Medical Center encompasses specialty centers for trauma and long-term care acute rehabilitation cancer heart disease and birthing. As part of the services provided by the medical center Heartland Regional Medical Center offers services such as arthritis pain and wound treatments as well as home health and hospice care.

	Annual Growth	06/17	06/18	06/19	06/20	06/21
Sales ($ mil.)	1.7%	–	639.1	645.9	714.3	672.9
Net income ($ mil.)	(9.6%)	–	64.4	38.3	84.3	47.6
Market value ($ mil.)	–	–	–	–	–	–
Employees	–	–	–	–	–	4,000

HEARTWARE INTERNATIONAL INC   NMS: HTWR

500 Old Connecticut Path | CEO: Douglas Godshall
Framingham, MA 01701 | CFO: Peter F McAree
Phone: 508 739-0950 | HR: –
Fax: – | FYE: December 31
Web: www.heartware.com | Type: Public

HeartWare International makes hardware for your heart. The company's proprietary heart pump is an implantable device designed for patients suffering from advanced-stage heart failure. The pump branded as HVAD (for HeartWare Ventricular Assist System) is used for people who can't undergo a heart transplant or who are on a waiting list for a heart to become available. The HVAD is small fits above the diaphragm (not the abdomen like other VADs which makes it less invasive) and can generate up to 10 liters of blood flow per minute. HeartWare International is a development-stage company; the HVAD is approved for sale in Europe and Australia.

	Annual Growth	12/10	12/11	12/12	12/13	12/14
Sales ($ mil.)	49.9%	55.2	82.8	110.9	207.9	278.4
Net income ($ mil.)	–	(29.4)	(55.1)	(87.7)	(59.3)	(19.4)
Market value ($ mil.)	(4.3%)	1,502.4	1,183.8	1,440.2	1,611.0	1,259.8
Employees	29.8%	206	330	396	569	585

HEAVEN HILL DISTILLERIES INC.

1064 Loretto Rd. | CEO: –
Bardstown KY 40004 | CFO: –
Phone: 502-348-3921 | HR: –
Fax: 502-348-0162 | FYE: April 30
Web: www.heaven-hill.com/ | Type: Private

Angels don't help the Christian Brothers bottle their brandy port and sherry; Heaven Hill does. One of Kentucky's oldest and largest distilling operations Heaven Hill Distilleries makes Evan Williams Bourbon as well as super-premium bourbons under the brand names Elijah Craig and Henry McKenna. The company also owns the Christian Brothers and Old Fitzgerald brand names. Heaven Hill distributes a variety of other spirits including the aperitif Dubonnet Ansac cognac Burnett's gin and Blackheart Premium Spiced Rum among others. Founded in 1934 by five brothers from the Shapira family Heaven Hill is still family owned.

HECLA MINING CO
NYS: HL

6500 Mineral Drive, Suite 200
Coeur d'Alene, ID 83815-9408
Phone: 208 769-4100
Fax: –
Web: www.hecla-mining.com

CEO: Phillips S Baker Jr
CFO: –
HR: –
FYE: December 31
Type: Public

Not all that glisters at Hecla Mining is gold ? in fact a large proportion of the precious ores that it mines is made of silver. Hecla explores for and mines gold silver lead and zinc. In 2019 the mining and natural resource exploration company produced approximately 2.5 million ounces of silver more than 10000 ounces of gold nearly 11630 tons of zinc and about 4940 tons of lead. Hecla operates mines in the Alaska and the Lucky Friday Mine in Idaho and has interests in mines in Colorado Nevada and in Mexico.

	Annual Growth	12/16	12/17	12/18	12/19	12/20
Sales ($ mil.)	1.7%	646.0	577.8	567.1	673.3	691.9
Net income ($ mil.)	–	69.5	(23.5)	(26.6)	(99.6)	(16.8)
Market value ($ mil.)	5.5%	2,785.9	2,110.7	1,254.7	1,802.3	3,445.2
Employees	3.5%	1,396	1,431	1,714	1,622	1,600

HEERY INTERNATIONAL INC.

999 Peachtree St. NE
Atlanta GA 30309-3953
Phone: 404-881-9880
Fax: 404-946-2398
Web: www.heery.com

CEO: Glenn Jardine
CFO: Sabrina Crawley
HR: –
FYE: December 31
Type: Subsidiary

Engineering and architectural group Heery International is known as much for its program management as for the schools and stadiums it designs. Architect George Heery who helped found the firm in 1952 was an early practitioner of program management which involves consulting and client representation for complex projects at each phase of construction. Heery with its 35 offices also offers facilities and construction management and interior design services. Most of its billings come from government projects; its markets include educational medical correctional and judicial facilities. A subsidiary of UK engineering giant Balfour Beatty Heery operates as the buildings division for Parsons Brinckerhoff.

HEICO CORP
NYS: HEI

3000 Taft Street
Hollywood, FL 33021
Phone: 954 987-4000
Fax: –
Web: www.heico.com

CEO: Laurans Mendelson
CFO: Carlos Macau
HR: –
FYE: October 31
Type: Public

As one of the world's largest providers of aircraft replacement parts HEICO Corporation helps jets get airborne. Its Flight Support Group makes FAA-approved replacement parts for jet engines that can be substituted for original parts including airfoils bearings and fuel pump gears. Flight Support also repairs overhauls and distributes jet engine parts as well as avionics and instruments for commercial air carriers. HEICO's second segment Electronic Technologies Group makes a variety of electronic equipment for the aerospace/defense electronic medical and telecommunications industries. The company generates about 65% of revenue in the US.

	Annual Growth	10/17	10/18	10/19	10/20	10/21
Sales ($ mil.)	5.2%	1,524.8	1,777.7	2,055.6	1,787.0	1,865.7
Net income ($ mil.)	13.1%	186.0	259.2	327.9	314.0	304.2
Market value ($ mil.)	11.3%	12,286.1	11,358.0	16,711.1	14,233.0	18,885.7
Employees	2.4%	5,100	5,400	5,900	5,200	5,600

HEIDRICK & STRUGGLES INTERNATIONAL, INC.
NMS: HSII

233 South Wacker Drive-Suite 4900
Chicago, IL 60606-6303
Phone: 312 496-1200
Fax: –
Web: www.heidrick.com

CEO: Krishnan Rajagopalan
CFO: Mark Harris
HR: –
FYE: December 31
Type: Public

Heidrick & Struggles International is one of the largest global recruiting firms. The company has about 50 offices in nearly 30 countries filling CEO CFO director and other high-level positions for companies that range from middle market and emerging growth companies major US and non-US companies governmental higher education and not-for-profit organizations Fortune 1000 companies and other leading private and public entities. It's divided into search groups that specialize by industry such as financial services and industrial which together account for approximately 45% of sales. The company's fees are generally equal to one-third of a hired executive's first-year compensation.

	Annual Growth	12/16	12/17	12/18	12/19	12/20
Sales ($ mil.)	1.2%	600.9	640.1	735.7	725.6	629.4
Net income ($ mil.)	–	15.4	(48.6)	49.3	46.9	(37.7)
Market value ($ mil.)	5.0%	467.5	475.3	603.8	629.2	568.8
Employees	(2.3%)	1,716	1,635	1,611	1,780	1,563

HEIDTMAN STEEL PRODUCTS INC.

2401 FRONT ST
TOLEDO, OH 43605-1199
Phone: 419-691-4646
Fax: –
Web: www.heidtman.avatarsyn.com

CEO: John C Bates
CFO: Mark Ridenour
HR: –
FYE: March 31
Type: Private

Steel life is an art at Heidtman Steel Products a provider of steel processing services such as blanking leveling and pickling. One of the largest privately held flat-rolled steel service networks in the US the company processes more than five million tons of steel annually. Services include hot-rolling cold-rolling and steel coating a full-range of slitting capabilities and galvanizing. Heidtman Steel operates plants in five mainly Midwestern states that serve automotive bus and truck manufacturers as well as furniture and appliance makers. The company is an approved steel supplier to Caterpillar and Ford.

	Annual Growth	03/03	03/04	03/05	03/06	03/07
Sales ($ mil.)	12.8%	–	443.6	679.5	599.2	637.1
Net income ($ mil.)	114.4%	–	1.4	5.2	(0.3)	14.3
Market value ($ mil.)	–	–	–	–	–	–
Employees	–	–	–	–	–	1,000

HEIFER PROJECT INTERNATIONAL INC

1 WORLD AVE
LITTLE ROCK, AR 722023825
Phone: 501-907-2600
Fax: –
Web: www.heifer.org

CEO: Pierre Ferrari
CFO: Robert Bob Bloom
HR: –
FYE: June 30
Type: Private

It's not just a handout; it's a new way of life. Heifer Project International (known as Heifer International) runs more than 925 projects that help millions of impoverished families become self-sufficient. Current recipients are located in more than 50 countries around the world including about 28 US states. The non-profit organization provides more than 25 different kinds of breeding livestock and other animals (bees rabbits ducks) that can be used for food income or plowing power in addition to training in sustainable agriculture techniques. In exchange the family agrees to pass on not only the animals' first female offspring to another needy family but their knowledge too.

	Annual Growth	06/14	06/15	06/16	06/18	06/19
Sales ($ mil.)	2.6%	–	125.3	114.3	131.3	138.9
Net income ($ mil.)	–	–	(0.3)	(9.0)	10.0	6.0
Market value ($ mil.)	–	–	–	–	–	–
Employees	–	–	–	–	–	304

HELEN KELLER INTERNATIONAL

1 DAG HAMMARSKJOLD PLZ # 2
NEW YORK, NY 100172208
Phone: 212-532-0544
Fax: –
Web: www.hki.org

CEO: Kathy Spahn
CFO: Elspeth Taylor
HR: –
FYE: June 30
Type: Private

Helen Keller International (HKI) has vision. The organization fights blindness by working with doctors government agencies partner groups and individuals in 22 countries citing that 80% of all blindness is avoidable. Its core areas of focus are eye health overall health and nutrition and poverty reduction. HKI distributes antibiotics performs cataract surgery and provides eye screenings glasses and education. The group works to combat malnutrition by promoting prenatal care supplying Vitamin A and helping others set up sustainable gardens and nutrition programs. It aims to reduce poverty through projects for literacy pre-school and clean water and offers entrepreneurial support for women.

	Annual Growth	06/11	06/12	06/14	06/15	06/16
Sales ($ mil.)	(25.1%)	–	220.2	58.5	72.1	69.2
Net income ($ mil.)	–	–	2.2	(0.1)	9.8	(0.3)
Market value ($ mil.)	–	–	–	–	–	–
Employees	–	–	–	–	–	1,022

HELICOS BIOSCIENCES CORPORATION   PINK SHEETS: HLCS

1 Kendall Sq. Bldg. 700
Cambridge MA 02139
Phone: 617-264-1800
Fax: 617-252-6924
Web: www.sirtrispharma.com

CEO: –
CFO: –
HR: –
FYE: December 31
Type: Public

Helicos BioSciences is in the business of developing genetic analysis technologies. Its True Single Molecule Sequencing (tSMS) platform allows for the direct analysis of DNA and RNA samples without amplification cloning or other time-consuming preparation techniques. The company serves the research clinical diagnostic and drug discovery markets and aims to provide customers with the ability to compare thousands of samples. Its HeliScope genetic analysis system can be integrated into existing laboratories and consists of a computer-controlled instrument and related supplies and reagents.

HELIOS & MATHESON ANALYTICS INC   NBB: HMNY

Empire State Building, 350 Fifth Avenue
New York, NY 10118
Phone: 212 979-8228
Fax: –
Web: www.hmny.com

CEO: –
CFO: –
HR: –
FYE: December 31
Type: Public

Helios & Matheson Analytics Inc. (formerly Helios & Matheson Information Technology Inc.) is a source (or outsource) of IT services. The company provides database management project management network design and implementation application development and Web enablement and related e-business services. The company also markets and distributes third-party software products. HMNA primarily serves global corporations and larger organizations in the financial services banking insurance and pharmaceutical industries. The company is controlled by India-based Helios & Matheson Information Technology Ltd.

	Annual Growth	12/13	12/14	12/15	12/16	12/17
Sales ($ mil.)	(5.9%)	13.3	10.6	9.7	6.8	10.4
Net income ($ mil.)	–	0.4	(0.2)	(2.1)	(7.4)	(146.0)
Market value ($ mil.)	2.3%	137.9	48.0	33.3	79.1	151.3
Employees	12.7%	44	32	20	34	71

HELIOS TECHNOLOGIES INC   NYS: HLIO

7456 16th St. E.
Sarasota, FL 34243
Phone: 941 362-1200
Fax: –
Web: www.sunhydraulics.com

CEO: Josef Matosevic
CFO: Tricia Fulton
HR: –
FYE: January 02
Type: Public

Helios Technologies Inc. (formerly known as Sun Hydraulics) develops and manufactures solutions for both the hydraulics and electronics markets. The Hydraulics segment includes products sold under the Sun Hydraulics Faster and Custom Fluidpower brands. The Electronics segment includes products sold under the Enovation Controls Balboa and Murphy brands. Products are sold through value-add distributors and directly to OEMs. The Americas represents almost 45% of its sales. It was originally founded in 1970 as Sun Hydraulics Corporation which designed and manufactured cartridge valves for hydraulics systems.

	Annual Growth	12/16	12/17	12/18	12/19*	01/21
Sales ($ mil.)	21.6%	196.9	342.8	508.0	554.7	523.0
Net income ($ mil.)	(9.4%)	23.3	31.6	46.7	60.3	14.2
Market value ($ mil.)	5.9%	1,283.9	2,077.9	1,071.6	1,461.5	1,711.7
Employees	12.7%	1,100	1,150	2,065	1,960	2,000

*Fiscal year change

HELIX BIOMEDIX INC.   OTC: HXBM

22122 20th Ave. SE Ste. 204
Bothell WA 98021-4433
Phone: 425-402-8400
Fax: 425-806-2999
Web: www.helixbiomedix.com

CEO: R Beatty
CFO: –
HR: –
FYE: December 31
Type: Public

Helix BioMedix wants to remove wrinkles and acne without leaving red itchy skin. The company has a library of bioactive peptides with antimicrobial properties it hopes to exploit as it works to formulate wrinkle- and acne-fighting creams along with topical treatments for skin and wound infections. The firm also hopes to use its peptides to develop a treatment that will speed the healing of wounds with minimal scarring as well as to prevent drug resistant staph infections. Helix is looking to partner with large better-funded drugmakers to develop some of its product candidates. The company also licenses its peptides to consumer products makers.

HELIX ENERGY SOLUTIONS GROUP INC   NYS: HLX

3505 West Sam Houston Parkway North, Suite 400
Houston, TX 77043
Phone: 281 618-0400
Fax: 281 618-0500
Web: www.helixesg.com

CEO: Owen Kratz
CFO: Erik Staffeldt
HR: –
FYE: December 31
Type: Public

Helix Energy Solutions (Helix) is in the energy services mix as a top marine deepwater contractor. Its well intervention unit primarily works in water depths ranging from 200 to 10000 feet using dynamically positioned and remotely operated vehicles (ROVs) that offer a range of engineering repair maintenance and pipe and cable burial services in global offshore markets. Former subsidiary Energy Resource Technology (ERT) bought and operated mature fields primarily in the Gulf of Mexico but in 2013 Helix Energy Solutions sold this business in order to focus on its offshore contracting operations. About 40% of the company's total sales comes the US. Helix was incorporated in 1979 and re-incorporated in 1983.

	Annual Growth	12/16	12/17	12/18	12/19	12/20
Sales ($ mil.)	10.8%	487.6	581.4	739.8	751.9	733.6
Net income ($ mil.)	–	(81.4)	30.1	28.6	57.9	22.2
Market value ($ mil.)	(16.9%)	1,326.0	1,133.6	813.3	1,447.8	631.4
Employees	1.0%	1,474	1,600	1,546	1,650	1,536

HELLA CORPORATE CENTER USA INC.

43811 Plymouth Oaks Blvd.
Plymouth MI 48170-2539
Phone: 734-414-0900
Fax: 734-414-5098
Web: www.hella.com/produktion/hellausa/website/chan

CEO: –
CFO: –
HR: –
FYE: May 31
Type: Subsidiary

As the North American headquarters for Germany-based Hella KGaA Hueck & Co. Hella Corporate Center USA (formerly known as Hella North America) offers a helluva selection when it comes to aftermarket and OEM automotive lighting products. Through its subdivision Product Development Center for Lighting Hella Corporate Center manufactures aftermarket lighting products that include auxiliary lighting such as fog lamps replacement headlamps work lamps LED lighting warning lights and bulbs. Additionally it makes OEM automotive electronics and vehicle modules through its manufacturing facilities in the US and Mexico.

HELMERICH & PAYNE, INC.

1437 South Boulder Avenue, Suite 1400
Tulsa, OK 74119
Phone: 918 742-5531
Fax: 918 742-0237
Web: www.hpinc.com

NYS: HP
CEO: John Lindsay
CFO: Mark Smith
HR: –
FYE: September 30
Type: Public

Contract driller Helmerich & Payne (H&P) deploys its fleet of about 410 rigs mostly on the US mainland but also internationally and at sea. It operates around 360 land rigs in the US and about 35 on land outside the US in addition to a dozen of offshore platform rigs operating in the Gulf of Mexico. One of H&P's key competitive strengths is its FlexRigs its proprietary drilling platforms which have evolved and taken on new technology over the years. Besides drilling H&P has ancillary real estate operations including a shopping center and office buildings in Tulsa.

	Annual Growth	09/17	09/18	09/19	09/20	09/21
Sales ($ mil.)	(9.4%)	1,804.7	2,487.3	2,798.5	1,773.9	1,218.6
Net income ($ mil.)	–	(128.2)	482.7	(33.7)	(494.5)	(326.2)
Market value ($ mil.)	(14.8%)	5,622.6	7,420.2	4,323.5	1,580.7	2,957.5
Employees	(7.6%)	8,123	8,780	8,510	4,138	5,932

HELMSMAN MANAGEMENT SERVICES LLC

175 BERKELEY ST
BOSTON, MA 021165066
Phone: 857-224-1970
Fax: –
Web: www.helmsmantpa.com

CEO: –
CFO: –
HR: –
FYE: December 31
Type: Private

Helmsman Management Services helps businesses steer clear of risk. The third-party administrator provides risk management programs in the alternative risk marketplace for more than 300 clients across the US. The company's services which are provided on a state regional or national basis include claims management litigation management loss prevention managed care and occupational health services medical bill review and utilization review. Helmsman Management Services is part of the Boston-based Liberty Mutual Insurance group. It utilizes Liberty Mutual's national network of claims and loss prevention specialists.

	Annual Growth	12/00	12/01	12/02	12/03	12/10
Assets ($ mil.)	7.0%	–	–	–	74.6	119.9
Net income ($ mil.)	7.5%	–	–	–	3.8	6.3
Market value ($ mil.)	–	–	–	–	–	–
Employees	–	–	–	–	–	400

HEMACARE CORP.

15350 Sherman Way, Suite 350
Van Nuys, CA 91406
Phone: 818 226-1968
Fax: 818 251-5300
Web: www.hemacare.com

NBB: HEMA
CEO: James C Foster
CFO: Rochelle Martel
HR: –
FYE: December 31
Type: Public

HemaCare is not a vampire but it does need your blood to survive. A supplier of blood products and services to hospitals and researchers the company collects whole blood from donors at donor centers and mobile donor vehicles and processes it into plasma and platelets used for blood transfusions. HemaCare has blood collection centers in California and Maine. The company is focused on broadening its global bioresearch products and services operations which is its fastest growing and most profitable segment. It has sold off certain assets to help invest in that segment's growth.

	Annual Growth	12/12	12/13	12/15	12/16	12/17
Sales ($ mil.)	2.4%	17.9	1.7	9.7	13.9	20.2
Net income ($ mil.)	30.7%	1.2	(0.1)	3.2	0.8	4.4
Market value ($ mil.)	72.2%	2.4	3.0	5.3	9.6	36.3
Employees	–	–	–	–	–	–

HEMAGEN DIAGNOSTICS INC

9033 Red Branch Road
Columbia, MD 21045
Phone: 443 367-5500
Fax: –
Web: www.hemagen.com

NBB: HMGN
CEO: William Hales
CFO: M. Robert Campbell
HR: –
FYE: September 30
Type: Public

Hemagen Diagnostics lets no disease go undetected. The company makes diagnostic kits and related components. Its Virgo product line is used to identify infectious and autoimmune diseases such as rheumatoid arthritis lupus measles and syphilis. Physicians and veterinarians use its Analyst reagent system and related components to test blood for substances like cholesterol glucose and triglycerides. Hemagen sells products internationally primarily through distributors; its Brazilian subsidiary markets its products in South America.

	Annual Growth	09/08	09/09	09/10	09/11	09/12
Sales ($ mil.)	(10.8%)	6.4	5.4	5.2	5.1	4.0
Net income ($ mil.)	–	0.4	(0.8)	(0.2)	(0.9)	(0.9)
Market value ($ mil.)	(28.4%)	1.9	1.2	0.9	0.5	0.5
Employees	(14.7%)	34	25	29	31	18

HEMAGEN DIAGNOSTICS INC.

9033 Red Branch Rd.
Columbia MD 21045
Phone: 443-367-5500
Fax: 443-367-5527
Web: www.hemagen.com

OTC: HMGN
CEO: William Hales
CFO: M. Robert Campbell
HR: –
FYE: September 30
Type: Public

Hemagen Diagnostics lets no disease go undetected. The company makes diagnostic kits and related components. Its Virgo product line is used to identify infectious and autoimmune diseases such as rheumatoid arthritis lupus measles and syphilis. Physicians and veterinarians use its Analyst reagent system and related components to test blood for substances like cholesterol glucose and triglycerides. Hemagen sells products internationally primarily through distributors; its Brazilian subsidiary markets its products in South America.

HEMMINGS MOTOR NEWS

222 W. Main St.
Bennington VT 05201-2103
Phone: 802-442-3101
Fax: 802-447-1561
Web: www.hemmings.com

CEO: –
CFO: –
HR: –
FYE: July 31
Type: Subsidiary

Hemmings Motor News knows how to get a car enthusiast's motor running. The company publishes the monthly "Hemmings Motor News" (at more than 600 pages a month it is considered the bible for car collectors) "Hemmings Classic Car" Hemmings Muscle Machines and "Hemmings Sports and Exotic Car". Hemmings Motor News also publishes collector's guides and almanacs. The company's Web site provides classified listings hosts forums publishes auto blogs and posts notices of upcoming automobile shows and events. The company operates as part of American City Business Journals itself a unit of media giant Advance Publications. The company was founded in 1954 by Ernest Hemmings.

HENRICKSEN & COMPANY, INC.

1101 W THORNDALE AVE
ITASCA, IL 601431366
Phone: 630-250-9090
Fax: –
Web: www.henricksen.com

CEO: –
CFO: Tim Osborn
HR: –
FYE: April 30
Type: Private

Henricksen & Company wants your company to be comfortable. The firm is an office furniture distributor that specializes in selling mid- and high-end office furnishings. Its portfolio consists of desks chairs filing systems and partitions from manufacturers including Allsteel Gunlocke and HON. Henricksen also offers its customers furniture warehousing installation maintenance inventory and project management. Customers have included Centro Cision Gogo Enova and Beckhoff Automation. The company was founded by the Henricksen family in the 1960s.

	Annual Growth	04/09	04/10	04/11	04/12	04/13
Sales ($ mil.)	8.6%	–	–	129.6	147.4	153.0
Net income ($ mil.)	(37.4%)	–	–	0.3	0.1	0.1
Market value ($ mil.)	–	–	–	–	–	–
Employees	–	–	–	–	–	210

HENRY COUNTY MEMORIAL HOSPITAL

1000 N 16TH ST
NEW CASTLE, IN 473624395
Phone: 765-521-0890
Fax: –
Web: www.henrycountyhospitalmedicalgroup.org

CEO: Paul F Janssen
CFO: –
HR: –
FYE: December 31
Type: Private

Henry County east of Indianapolis is a perfect slice of the Midwest: farms small towns and its own county hospital system. Henry County Memorial Hospital actually serves parts of three counties with a 110-bed general hospital medical offices specialty centers a long-term care unit and an assisted living center. The hospital offers patients emergency care general medical obstetric pediatric hospice and surgical services. The Henry County Hospital Foundation funds a program to train nurses through the local schools and college. The hospital opened its doors in 1930.

	Annual Growth	12/13	12/14	12/15	12/16	12/17
Sales ($ mil.)	5.6%	–	70.3	77.4	75.1	82.8
Net income ($ mil.)	–	–	6.5	6.1	(4.8)	(4.5)
Market value ($ mil.)	–	–	–	–	–	–
Employees	–	–	–	–	–	787

HENRY FORD HEALTH SYSTEM

1 FORD PL
DETROIT, MI 482023450
Phone: 313-916-2600
Fax: –
Web: www.henryford.com

CEO: Wright Lassiter III
CFO: James M Connelly
HR: Kathy Oswald
FYE: December 31
Type: Private

Founded in 1915 by auto pioneer Henry Ford Henry Ford Health System is one of the leading healthcare provider and not-for-profit corporation and is comprised of hospitals medical centers and the Henry Ford Medical Group which includes more than 1200 physicians practicing in over 40 specialties. The system's five hospitals — including the flagship Henry Ford Hospital (877-bed) the Henry Ford Wyandotte Hospital (360-bed) and Henry Ford Allegiance Health (420-bed). Health Alliance Plan (HAP) a Henry Ford subsidiary is a Michigan-based nonprofit health plan that provides health coverage to individuals and companies of all sizes.

	Annual Growth	12/12	12/13	12/14	12/17	12/18
Sales ($ mil.)	5.3%	–	4,517.0	1,513.7	5,977.0	5,853.8
Net income ($ mil.)	(8.0%)	–	135.3	(13.8)	203.0	89.3
Market value ($ mil.)	–	–	–	–	–	–
Employees	–	–	–	–	–	23,000

HENRY MAYO NEWHALL MEMORIAL HOSPITAL

23845 MCBEAN PKWY
VALENCIA, CA 913552001
Phone: 661-253-8000
Fax: –
Web: www.henrymayo.com

CEO: Roger E Seaver
CFO: –
HR: –
FYE: September 30
Type: Private

Had a bit too much mayo? Arteries feeling a bit clogged? Henry Mayo Newhall Memorial Hospital exists for just this reason (among others). The hospital serves the healthcare needs of the Santa Clarita Valley in northern Los Angeles County. The not-for-profit community hospital houses more than 220 beds and provides general medical and surgical care as well as trauma services (it is a Level II trauma center) outpatient services psychiatric care and emergency services among other specialties. In operation since 1975 the hospital was built to serve the needs of the at-the-time unincorporated City of Santa Clara on land donated by The Newhall Land and Farming Company.

	Annual Growth	09/14	09/15	09/16	09/17	09/19
Sales ($ mil.)	7.6%	–	307.4	321.6	320.0	411.3
Net income ($ mil.)	7.3%	–	23.0	29.1	11.6	30.5
Market value ($ mil.)	–	–	–	–	–	–
Employees	–	–	–	–	–	1,600

HENRY MODELL & COMPANY, INC.

498 7TH AVE FL 20
NEW YORK, NY 100186738
Phone: 212-822-1000
Fax: –
Web: www.modells.com

CEO: –
CFO: –
HR: –
FYE: February 02
Type: Private

Operating as Modell's Sporting Goods retailer Henry Modell & Company sells sporting goods fitness equipment apparel and brand-name athletic footwear. It is America's oldest family-owned and -operated sporting goods retailer. Its top brands are Asics Champion Adidas and Smith's to name a few. It also offers fan gear such as jerseys for football. It also boasts an online presence at Modells.com.

	Annual Growth	01/09	01/10	01/11	01/12*	02/13
Sales ($ mil.)	4.3%	–	–	558.8	570.3	608.0
Net income ($ mil.)	–	–	–	(7.5)	(3.3)	0.6
Market value ($ mil.)	–	–	–	–	–	–
Employees	–	–	–	–	–	5,430

*Fiscal year change

HENSEL PHELPS CONSTRUCTION CO.

420 6TH AVE
GREELEY, CO 806312332
Phone: 970-352-6565
Fax: –
Web: www.henselphelps.com

CEO: Michael Choutka
CFO: Jenny Scholz
HR: –
FYE: December 31
Type: Private

Hensel Phelps Construction builds it all from the courthouse to the big house. The employee-owned general contractor provides a full range of development pre-construction construction and renovation services for commercial institutional and government projects throughout the US. Its project portfolio includes prisons airports arenas laboratories government complexes offices and more. Major public and private clients have included the US Intercontinental San Diego Masonic Temple Hotel NASA Samsung US Air Force and Cin ©polis Luxury Cinema. Hensel Phelps founded the eponymous company as a homebuilder in 1937.

	Annual Growth	12/15	12/16	12/17	12/18	12/19
Sales ($ mil.)	17.0%	–	3,540.4	3,360.4	4,604.3	5,676.7
Net income ($ mil.)	32.4%	–	76.2	80.9	131.5	177.1
Market value ($ mil.)	–	–	–	–	–	–
Employees	–	–	–	–	–	2,000

HERBERT MINES ASSOCIATES INC.

600 Lexington Ave. 2nd Fl.
New York NY 10022
Phone: 212-355-0909
Fax: 212-223-2186
Web: www.herbertmines.com

CEO: Hal Reiter
CFO: –
HR: –
FYE: December 31
Type: Private

Herbert Mines Associates mines the workforce to find high-performers for jobs in high fashion. The executive search firm recruits senior-level personnel in the retail food service apparel hospitality e-commerce and consumer products sectors. It has conducted work for such clients as Neiman Marcus Kimberly-Clark and Starbucks. Headquartered in New York the company strengthens its international presence through an affiliation with Globe Search Group an assortment of independently-owned executive search firms. Herbert Mines a former personnel executive with Revlon Neiman Marcus and Macy's founded the firm in 1981.

HERC HOLDINGS INC

27500 Riverview Center Blvd.
Bonita Springs, FL 34134
Phone: 239 301-1000
Fax: –
Web: www.hertz.com

NYS: HRI
CEO: Lawrence Silber
CFO: Mark Irion
HR: –
FYE: December 31
Type: Public

Herc Holdings is a heavy equipment rental company with more than 275 locations primarily in North America. Its portfolio of equipment includes aerial earthmoving material handling and specialty equipment such as air compressors compaction equipment construction-related trucks electrical equipment power generators contractor tools pumps and lighting studio and production equipment. Its equipment rental business is supported by ProSolutions its industry-specific solutions-based services which includes power generation climate control remediation and restoration and studio and production equipment and its ProContractor professional grade tools. The US accounts for about 90% of revenue.

	Annual Growth	12/17	12/18	12/19	12/20	12/21
Sales ($ mil.)	4.3%	1,754.5	1,976.7	1,999.0	1,781.3	2,073.1
Net income ($ mil.)	8.7%	160.3	69.1	47.5	73.7	224.1
Market value ($ mil.)	25.7%	1,859.5	771.9	1,453.5	1,972.4	4,649.5
Employees	3.4%	4,900	4,900	5,100	4,800	5,600

HERCULES OFFSHORE INC

9 Greenway Plaza, Suite 2200
Houston, TX 77046
Phone: 713 350-5100
Fax: 713 979-9301
Web: www.herculesoffshore.com

NMS: HERO
CEO: John T Rynd
CFO: Troy L Carson
HR: Ernest Ogbe
FYE: December 31
Type: Public

As a provider of shallow-water drilling and liftboat services Hercules Offshore supplies the muscle to major integrated energy companies and independent oil and natural gas exploration and production companies. It owns and operates a fleet of 27 jackup rigs two submersible rigs and one platform rig as well as 24 self-propelled self-elevating liftboats. About 78% of its jack up rigs are operating in the Gulf of Mexico although it works in other oil patches around the world. The company also operates a fleet of four conventional and 10 posted barge rigs that operate inland in marshes rivers lakes and shallow bay or coastal waterways along the US Gulf Coast. Hercules Offshore declared bankruptcy in 2015.

	Annual Growth	12/10	12/11	12/12	12/13	12/14
Sales ($ mil.)	8.2%	657.5	655.4	709.8	858.3	900.3
Net income ($ mil.)	–	(134.6)	(76.1)	(127.0)	(68.1)	(216.1)
Market value ($ mil.)	–	–	–	–	–	–
Employees	(4.9%)	2,200	2,300	2,600	2,200	1,800

HERCULES TECHNOLOGY GROWTH CAPITAL INC.

400 Hamilton Ave. Ste. 310
Palo Alto CA 94301
Phone: 650-289-3060
Fax: 650-473-9194
Web: www.herculestech.com

NASDAQ: HTGC
CEO: Scott Bluestein
CFO: Seth H Meyer
HR: –
FYE: December 31
Type: Public

Hercules Technology Growth Capital (HTGC) performs its feats of strength with money. The closed-end investment firm offers financing vehicles to companies in the technology and life sciences sectors. A business development company (BDC) HTGC provides primarily US-based private firms with such products as mezzanine loans senior secured loans and select private-equity investments. Loans typically range from $1 million to $25 million. HTGC's portfolio includes around 125 companies; about half of its portfolio comprises drug discovery and development Internet consumer and business services and clean tech firms. Holdings include stakes in data network provider IKANO Communications and software firm Daegis.

HERITAGE BANKSHARES, INC. (NORFOLK, VA)

150 Granby Street
Norfolk, VA 23510
Phone: 757 648-1700
Fax: 757 626-3933
Web: www.heritagebankva.com

NBB: HBKS
CEO: –
CFO: –
HR: –
FYE: December 31
Type: Public

Heritage Bankshares comes from a long line of money. Heritage Bankshares is the holding company for Heritage Bank & Trust a community-based institution in Virginia with about half a dozen branches in Chesapeake Norfolk and Virginia Beach. The bank which opened in the mid-1970s offers standard banking products and services including checking and savings accounts debit cards CDs and IRAs. Real estate loans primarily mortgages account for the largest portion of its loan portfolio; the bank also originates loans for businesses individuals and municipalities. The bank offers insurance and investment services through its subsidiary Sentinel Financial.

	Annual Growth	12/09	12/10	12/11	12/12	12/13
Assets ($ mil.)	3.0%	274.6	267.1	294.6	336.6	309.0
Net income ($ mil.)	24.4%	1.1	2.1	2.4	2.3	2.5
Market value ($ mil.)	8.1%	21.6	28.4	25.3	26.7	29.5
Employees	(6.0%)	59	58	54	49	–

HERITAGE COMMERCE CORP
NMS: HTBK

224 Airport Parkway
San Jose, CA 95110
Phone: 408 947-6900
Fax: –
Web: www.heritagecommercecorp.com

CEO: Walter Kaczmarek
CFO: Lawrence D McGovern
HR: –
FYE: December 31
Type: Public

Heritage Commerce is the holding company for Heritage Bank of Commerce which operates about 15 branches in the southern and eastern regions of the San Francisco Bay area. Serving consumers and small to midsized businesses and their owners and managers the bank offers savings and checking accounts money market accounts and CDs as well as cash management services and loans. Commercial and commercial real estate loans make up most of the company's loan portfolio which is rounded out by land construction and home equity loans.

	Annual Growth	12/16	12/17	12/18	12/19	12/20
Assets ($ mil.)	15.9%	2,570.9	2,843.5	3,096.6	4,109.5	4,634.1
Net income ($ mil.)	6.6%	27.4	23.8	35.3	40.5	35.3
Market value ($ mil.)	(11.5%)	864.6	917.9	679.5	768.7	531.5
Employees	6.2%	263	278	302	357	335

HERITAGE FINANCIAL CORP (WA)
NMS: HFWA

201 Fifth Avenue SW
Olympia, WA 98501
Phone: 360 943-1500
Fax: –
Web: www.hf-wa.com

CEO: Jeffrey Deuel
CFO: Donald Hinson
HR: –
FYE: December 31
Type: Public

Heritage Financial is ready to answer the call of Pacific Northwesterners seeking to preserve their heritage. Heritage Financial is the holding company for Heritage Bank which operates more than 65 branches throughout Washington and Oregon. Boasting nearly $4 billion in assets the bank offers a range of deposit products to consumers and businesses such as CDs IRAs and checking savings NOW and money market accounts. Commercial and industrial loans account for over 50% of Heritage Financial's loan portfolio while mortgages secured by multi-family real estate comprise about 5%. The bank also originates single-family mortgages land development construction loans and consumer loans.

	Annual Growth	12/16	12/17	12/18	12/19	12/20
Assets ($ mil.)	14.3%	3,879.0	4,113.3	5,316.9	5,553.0	6,615.3
Net income ($ mil.)	4.6%	38.9	41.8	53.1	67.6	46.6
Market value ($ mil.)	(2.4%)	924.7	1,106.1	1,067.3	1,016.3	840.0
Employees	3.0%	760	735	859	884	856

HERITAGE FINANCIAL GROUP INC.
NMS: HBOS

721 N. Westover Blvd.
Albany, GA 31707
Phone: 229 420-0000
Fax: –
Web: www.eheritagebank.com

CEO: –
CFO: –
HR: –
FYE: December 31
Type: Public

Established in the 1950s as a credit union to serve its hometown Marine base HeritageBank of the South (HBOS) has remained always faithful to its local customers. The flagship subsidiary of Heritage Financial Group operates more than 25 branches that provide traditional deposit and loan products and services to individuals and small to midsized businesses in southwestern Georgia Florida and Alabama. Nonresidential commercial real estate loans make up nearly a third of the bank's loan portfolio. HBOS also operates 15 mortgage offices and five investment offices. In late 2014 Heritage Financial Group was acquired by Renasant in a merger agreement totaling $258 million.

	Annual Growth	12/09	12/10	12/11	12/12	12/13
Sales ($ mil.)	28.1%	31.2	40.9	56.9	68.4	84.1
Net income ($ mil.)	–	(1.7)	1.4	3.8	6.8	11.3
Market value ($ mil.)	15.7%	–	97.3	92.4	108.0	150.8
Employees	21.7%	194	217	327	321	426

HERITAGE GLOBAL INC
NAS: HGBL

12625 High Bluff Drive, Suite 305
San Diego, CA 92130
Phone: 858 847-0656
Fax: –
Web: www.heritageglobalinc.com

CEO: –
CFO: –
HR: –
FYE: December 31
Type: Public

Change seems to be the only constant for Counsel RB Capital (which was known as C2 Global Technologies prior to 2011). The asset liquidation and patent licensing company sold its original business — the operation of a communications network — in 2003 and began providing phone and Internet service to residential and business customers. It sold the telecom unit which provided long-distance and business communications services to North Central Equity in 2005 to focus on the licensing of patents including two Voice-over-IP (VoIP) technologies. Counsel RB Capital is also involved in the acquisition and disposition of distressed and surplus assets in North America. Counsel Corporation owns 93% of the company.

	Annual Growth	12/16	12/17	12/18	12/19	12/20
Sales ($ mil.)	2.4%	23.8	20.1	23.7	26.2	26.2
Net income ($ mil.)	412.5%	0.0	(0.2)	3.8	3.9	9.7
Market value ($ mil.)	54.2%	16.6	13.1	16.0	34.5	93.8
Employees	0.0%	46	48	50	46	46

HERITAGE OAKS BANCORP
NAS: HEOP

1222 Vine Street
Paso Robles, CA 93446
Phone: 805 369-5200
Fax: –
Web: www.heritageoaksbancorp.com

CEO: –
CFO: –
HR: –
FYE: December 31
Type: Public

Stash your acorns at Heritage Oaks Bancorp. It's the holding company for Heritage Oaks Bank which serves retail customers farmers and small to midsized businesses in Central California's San Luis Obispo Santa Barbara and Ventura counties. Through about a dozen offices the bank offers standard products such as checking savings and money market accounts CDs IRAs and credit cards. It also has loan production offices in Goleta and Oxnard. In 2014 it took over Mission Community Bancorp and consolidated its five branches into existing locations of Heritage Oaks. Commercial real estate loans account for almost 80% of its loan portfolio; business loans make up the other 20%.

	Annual Growth	12/11	12/12	12/13	12/14	12/15
Assets ($ mil.)	17.8%	987.1	1,097.5	1,203.7	1,710.1	1,899.7
Net income ($ mil.)	18.7%	7.7	13.0	10.8	9.0	15.3
Market value ($ mil.)	22.7%	121.6	199.2	257.6	288.2	275.2
Employees	2.5%	256	251	234	294	283

HERITAGE SOUTHEAST BANCORPORATION INC
NBB: HSBI

101 North Main Street
Jonesboro, GA 30237
Phone: 770 478-8881
Fax: 770 478-8929
Web: www.heritagebank.com

CEO: David Turner
CFO: Mary Rogers
HR: Melissa Malcom
FYE: December 31
Type: Public

CCF Holding Company sees green in the Peach State. The institution is the parent of Heritage Bank which operates about a half-dozen branches in Clayton Fayette and Henry counties in greater metropolitan Atlanta. Centered in the fast-growing Hartsfield International Airport region the bank targets individuals and local businesses offering such standard services as checking and savings accounts money market accounts CDs IRAs and credit cards. Real estate loans including construction and land development loan commercial and residential mortgages and farmland loans account for about 95% of the bank's lending portfolio. Heritage Bank also writes consumer and business loans.

	Annual Growth	12/16	12/17	12/18	12/19	12/20
Assets ($ mil.)	38.5%	427.3	474.2	512.0	1,336.1	1,571.2
Net income ($ mil.)	(10.4%)	6.9	0.9	4.4	0.9	4.4
Market value ($ mil.)	70.4%	11.2	14.4	154.5	144.7	94.5
Employees						

HERITAGE VALLEY HEALTH SYSTEM, INC.

1000 DUTCH RIDGE RD
BEAVER, PA 150099727
Phone: 724-728-7000
Fax: –
Web: www.heritagevalley.org

CEO: Norman F Mitry
CFO: –
HR: –
FYE: June 30
Type: Private

Heritage Valley Health System has a legacy of serving the health care needs of residents of southwestern Pennsylvania eastern Ohio and the West Virginia Panhandle. The two-hospital system includes the flagship Heritage Valley Beaver hospital in Beaver Pennsylvania with more than 330 beds and a smaller facility in nearby Sewickley with roughly 185 beds. In addition to its acute-care facilities the system operates several satellite facilities and provides primary care through a network of three affiliated physician groups. Heritage Valley Health System was formed in 1996 when the two hospitals merged but it has roots going back to 1894.

	Annual Growth	06/10	06/11	06/13	06/14	06/18
Sales ($ mil.)	0.0%	–	449.5	4.8	5.2	450.7
Net income ($ mil.)	(3.9%)	–	40.6	3.6	4.5	30.8
Market value ($ mil.)	–	–	–	–	–	–
Employees	–	–	–	–	–	4,291

HERITAGE-CRYSTAL CLEAN INC

NMS: HCCI

2175 Point Boulevard, Suite 375
Elgin, IL 60123
Phone: 847 836-5670
Fax: –
Web: www.crystal-clean.com

CEO: Brian Recatto
CFO: Mark Devita
HR: –
FYE: January 02
Type: Public

Heritage-Crystal Clean Inc. (HCCI) operating through its wholly-owned subsidiary Heritage-Crystal Clean LLC (HCC) provides full-service parts cleaning containerized waste management used oil collection vacuum truck services antifreeze recycling field services and owns and operates a used oil re-refinery. The company provides full-service parts cleaning hazardous and non-hazardous waste services and used oil collection services to small and mid-sized customers in both the industrial and vehicle maintenance sectors in North America. It is the second largest used oil re-refiner by capacity in North America and the second largest producer of remanufactured antifreeze in the US.

	Annual Growth	12/16	12/17	12/18	12/19*	01/21
Sales ($ mil.)	3.2%	347.6	366.0	410.2	444.4	406.0
Net income ($ mil.)	15.4%	5.8	28.1	14.7	8.4	11.9
Market value ($ mil.)	6.1%	366.4	507.7	521.9	736.6	491.8
Employees	1.3%	1,195	1,274	1,338	1,392	1,275

*Fiscal year change

HERON THERAPEUTICS INC

NAS: HRTX

4242 Campus Point Court, Suite 200
San Diego, CA 92121
Phone: 858 251-4400
Fax: –
Web: www.herontx.com

CEO: Barry Quart
CFO: –
HR: Sean Ristine
FYE: December 31
Type: Public

Heron Therapeutics develops novel patient-focused solutions that apply in innovative science and technologies to already-approved pharmacological agents for patients suffering from pain or cancer. Its Biochronomer technology delivers medication directly to the site where the drug is needed. Heron's leading drug candidate SUSTOL could ease chemotherapy-induced nausea and vomiting (CINV) and CINVANTI for CINV a US approved as a 30-minute intravenous (IV) infusion and a 2-minute IV injection. The company's development programs include HTX-034 for the management of post-operative pain and HTX-019 for postoperative nausea and vomiting.

	Annual Growth	12/16	12/17	12/18	12/19	12/20
Sales ($ mil.)	188.5%	1.3	30.8	77.5	146.0	88.6
Net income ($ mil.)	–	(173.1)	(197.5)	(178.8)	(204.7)	(227.3)
Market value ($ mil.)	12.7%	1,196.2	1,652.7	2,368.6	2,145.8	1,932.6
Employees	12.5%	139	145	198	231	223

HERSCHEND FAMILY ENTERTAINMENT CORPORATION

5445 Triangle Pkwy. Ste. 200
Norcross GA 30029
Phone: 770-441-1940
Fax: 630-655-3377
Web: www.silvon.com

CEO: Andrew Wexler
CFO: –
HR: –
FYE: April 30
Type: Private

Herschend Family Entertainment (HFE) makes more than a few silver dollars. The company owns and operates (or co-owns) more than 25 amusement parks in about 10 states. Properties include Silver Dollar City in Branson Missouri and Tennessee's Dollywood in partnership with country legend Dolly Parton. HFE also owns aquariums near Philadelphia and Cincinnati and the Ride the Ducks amphibious tours in a handful of cities including Atlanta and Philadelphia. The firm touts that it offers family entertainment "with Christian values and ethics". The family-owned company was founded in 1950 by Hugo and Mary Herschend to manage the Marvel Cave in the Ozarks a tourist attraction that opened in 1894.

HERSHA HOSPITALITY TRUST

NYS: HT

44 Hersha Drive
Harrisburg, PA 17102
Phone: 717 236-4400
Fax: 717 774-7383
Web: www.hersha.com

CEO: Jay Shah
CFO: Ashish Parikh
HR: –
FYE: December 31
Type: Public

Hersha Hospitality Trust's fortune is in hotels not chocolate. The self-advised real estate investment trust (REIT) invests in hotel properties primarily midscale upscale and extended stay properties in metropolitan markets across the US. It owns or co-owns about 50 hotels containing nearly 7645 rooms most of them in Boston New York and Washington DC as well as in Miami and Los Angeles. The properties are operated under such brand names as Marriott International Hilton Hotels Intercontinental Pan Pacific and Hyatt. Hersha Hospitality Trust owns a minority stake in Hersha Hospitality Management which manages the REIT's properties.

	Annual Growth	12/16	12/17	12/18	12/19	12/20
Sales ($ mil.)	(21.6%)	466.6	498.2	495.1	530.0	176.7
Net income ($ mil.)	–	117.0	99.9	10.0	(3.7)	(166.3)
Market value ($ mil.)	(22.2%)	835.1	675.9	681.3	565.2	306.5
Employees	(10.1%)	49	51	54	49	32

HERSHEY COMPANY (THE)

NYS: HSY

19 East Chocolate Avenue
Hershey, PA 17033
Phone: 717 534 4200
Fax: 717 531-6161
Web: www.hersheys.com

CEO: Michele Buck
CFO: Steven E Voskuil
HR: Christopher Scalia
FYE: December 31
Type: Public

With a portfolio of more than 100 global brands the largest chocolate producer in North America has built a big business making such well-known chocolate and candy brands as Hershey's Kisses Reese's peanut butter cups Twizzlers Cadbury and Almond Joy candy bars York peppermint patties and Kit Kat wafer bars. Hershey also makes grocery goods ? including baking products toppings sundae syrup cocoa mix snack bites breath mints and bubble gum ? and has expanded into popcorn and other savory snacks. Products are sold to wholesale distributors and retailers throughout North America and exported overseas; the US accounts for most of sales.

	Annual Growth	12/17	12/18	12/19	12/20	12/21
Sales ($ mil.)	4.5%	7,515.4	7,791.1	7,986.3	8,149.7	8,971.3
Net income ($ mil.)	17.2%	783.0	1,177.6	1,149.7	1,278.7	1,477.5
Market value ($ mil.)	14.3%	23,395.4	22,090.8	30,293.9	31,396.6	39,875.9
Employees	2.9%	16,910	16,420	16,140	16,880	18,990

HERSHEY ENTERTAINMENT & RESORTS COMPANY

27 W CHOCOLATE AVE # 100
HERSHEY, PA 170331672
Phone: 717-534-3131
Fax: –
Web: www.thehotelhershey.com

CEO: –
CFO: –
HR: –
FYE: December 31
Type: Private

Life is sweet for Hershey Entertainment & Resorts. The company owns the many chocolate-related entertainment destinations in Hershey Pennsylvania. Its holdings include Hersheypark one of the nation's top amusement parks with more than 65 rides and attractions; ZooAmerica wildlife park; the Hotel Hershey; and the Hershey Lodge. Hershey Entertainment also owns four golf courses and the Giant Center arena in Hershey. Hershey Entertainment & Resorts is fully owned by the Hershey Trust Company which controls a majority stake in candymaker The Hershey Company. The Hershey Trust Co. also acts as trustee for the Milton Hershey School.

	Annual Growth	12/05	12/06	12/07	12/08	12/09
Sales ($ mil.)	(0.4%)	–	–	272.9	274.0	271.0
Net income ($ mil.)	(38.4%)	–	–	18.3	13.9	6.9
Market value ($ mil.)	–	–	–	–	–	–
Employees	–	–	–	–	–	7,300

HERTZ GLOBAL HOLDINGS INC (NEW)　　　　NMS: HTZ

8501 Williams Road
Estero, FL 33928
Phone: 239 301-7000
Fax: –
Web: www.hertz.com

CEO: Paul Stone
CFO: Kenny Cheung
HR: –
FYE: December 31
Type: Public

Hertz Global Holdings is one of the largest worldwide vehicle rental companies. Hertz operates about 12000 rental locations in about 160 countries under the Hertz Dollar and Thrifty brands. About 45% of its US revenue comes from off airport locations. Its fleet includes a peak rental fleet in its US and International Rental Car segments of approximately 515700 vehicles and 131500 vehicles respectively. In addition to its signature car rental services its Donlen subsidiary offers fleet leasing and management services. Majority of its sales were generated in the US.

	Annual Growth	12/16	12/17	12/18	12/19	12/20
Sales ($ mil.)	(12.1%)	8,803.0	8,803.0	9,504.0	9,779.0	5,258.0
Net income ($ mil.)	–	(491.0)	327.0	(225.0)	(58.0)	(1,714.0)
Market value ($ mil.)	(50.6%)	3,367.8	3,452.2	2,132.2	2,460.3	199.9
Employees	(9.6%)	36,000	37,000	38,000	38,000	24,000

HESKA CORP.　　　　NAS: HSKA

3760 Rocky Mountain Avenue
Loveland, CO 80538
Phone: 970 493-7272
Fax: –
Web: www.heska.com

CEO: Kevin Wilson
CFO: Catherine Grassman
HR: –
FYE: December 31
Type: Public

Heska sells veterinary and animal health diagnostic and specialty products. Its offerings include Point of Care diagnostic laboratory instruments and consumables; Point of Care digital imaging diagnostic products; digital cytology services; vaccines; local and cloud-based data services; allergy testing and immunotherapy; and single-use offerings such as in-clinic diagnostic tests and heartworm preventive products. Its core focus is on supporting veterinarians in the canine and feline healthcare space. Products are sold worldwide through direct sales representatives and independent distributors. About 60% of its revenue came from the US making it as the highest market location of the company.

	Annual Growth	12/16	12/17	12/18	12/19	12/20
Sales ($ mil.)	11.0%	130.1	129.3	127.4	122.7	197.3
Net income ($ mil.)	–	10.5	10.0	5.9	(1.5)	(14.4)
Market value ($ mil.)	19.4%	678.5	760.1	815.9	909.1	1,380.2
Employees	16.5%	327	345	347	386	602

HESS CORP　　　　NYS: HES

1185 Avenue of the Americas
New York, NY 10036
Phone: 212 997-8500
Fax: –
Web: www.hess.com

CEO: John B Hess
CFO: John P Rielly
HR: –
FYE: December 31
Type: Public

Hess Corporation is a global exploration and production company engaged in exploration development production transportation purchase and sale of crude oil natural gas liquids and natural gas. It can profess to owning about 1.2 billion barrels of oil equivalent worldwide. Its primary operations are in the US but it also has producing interests in Denmark Malaysia and Thailand. It also offers midstream services including gathering compressing and processing natural gas and fractionating and transporting crude oil and NGL as well as propane storage. Prospecting for oil since the 1920s Hess generates more than 75% of sales from the US.

	Annual Growth	12/16	12/17	12/18	12/19	12/20
Sales ($ mil.)	(0.2%)	4,844.0	5,405.0	6,466.0	6,510.0	4,804.0
Net income ($ mil.)	–	(6,132.0)	(4,074.0)	(282.0)	(408.0)	(3,093.0)
Market value ($ mil.)	(4.1%)	19,121.8	14,572.3	12,432.7	20,509.3	16,205.5
Employees	(8.4%)	2,304	2,075	1,708	1,775	1,621

HEWLETT PACKARD ENTERPRISE CO　　　　NYS: HPE

11445 Compaq Center West Drive
Houston, TX 77070
Phone: 650 687-5817
Fax: –
Web: www.hpe.com

CEO: Antonio Neri
CFO: Tarek Robbiati
HR: –
FYE: October 31
Type: Public

Hewlett Packard Enterprise (HPE) once part of the storied Hewlett-Packard Corp. designs and sells servers storage and networking equipment and provides technology services to help its large enterprise customers put together and deploy IT systems. HPE has software-defined IT offerings for private public and hybrid cloud environments as well as technologies for industrial Internet of Things (IoT) applications. HPE is a global company and around two-thirds of its revenue comes from outside the US. It maintains a cache of around 13000 worldwide patents. HPE traces its roots back to a partnership founded in 1939 by William R. Hewlett and David Packard.

	Annual Growth	10/17	10/18	10/19	10/20	10/21
Sales ($ mil.)	(1.0%)	28,871.0	30,852.0	29,135.0	26,982.0	27,784.0
Net income ($ mil.)	77.7%	344.0	1,908.0	1,049.0	(322.0)	3,427.0
Market value ($ mil.)	1.3%	18,021.3	19,743.2	21,244.9	11,185.6	18,966.4
Employees	(2.2%)	66,000	60,000	61,600	59,400	60,400

HEWLETT, WILLIAM AND FLORA FOUNDATION (INC)

2121 SAND HILL RD
MENLO PARK, CA 940256909
Phone: 650-234-4500
Fax: –
Web: www.hewlett.org

CEO: –
CFO: –
HR: –
FYE: December 31
Type: Private

The Hewlett Foundation is dedicated to helping solve the world's social and environmental problems. One of the nation's largest charitable institutions it has some $8.6 billion in assets and it disbursed approximately $240 million in grants and gifts in 2013. It provides grants in a diverse areas including education reform environmental protection in the West and population growth. The private foundation also promotes the performing arts in the San Francisco Bay Area and has funded conflict resolution and international relations programs in the past. The late Bill Hewlett co-founder of Hewlett-Packard founded the Hewlett Foundation with his wife and eldest son in 1967.

	Annual Growth	12/01	12/02	12/05	12/14	12/16
Sales ($ mil.)	9.1%	–	94.2	0.0	624.6	317.5
Net income ($ mil.)	–	–	426.8	0.0	205.0	(164.8)
Market value ($ mil.)	–	–	–	–	–	–
Employees	–	–	–	–	–	60

HEXCEL CORP.
NYS: HXL

Two Stamford Plaza, 281 Tresser Boulevard
Stamford, CT 06901
Phone: 203 969-0666
Fax: –
Web: www.hexcel.com

CEO: Nick Stanage
CFO: Patrick Winterlich
HR: Robert Hennemuth
FYE: December 31
Type: Public

Hexcel is a leading maker of composite materials. The company makes advanced structural materials used in everything from aircraft components to wind turbine blades. Its composite materials include structural adhesives honeycomb molding compounds tooling materials polyurethane systems and laminates that are incorporated into many applications including military and commercial aircraft wind turbine blades recreational products transportation. Aerospace is the largest market for honeycomb products. It designs and builds its products in about 25 manufacturing plants located in the US and Europe as well as in China and Morocco. US generates about 55% of sales.

	Annual Growth	12/17	12/18	12/19	12/20	12/21
Sales ($ mil.)	(9.5%)	1,973.3	2,189.1	2,355.7	1,502.4	1,324.7
Net income ($ mil.)	(51.2%)	284.0	276.6	306.6	31.7	16.1
Market value ($ mil.)	(4.3%)	5,195.4	4,816.6	6,158.0	4,073.2	4,351.2
Employees	(6.1%)	6,259	6,626	6,977	4,647	4,863

HEXION INC
NL: –

180 East Broad St.
Columbus, OH 43215
Phone: 614 225-4000
Fax: –
Web: www.hexion.com

CEO: Craig Rogerson
CFO: George Knight
HR: John Auletto
FYE: December 31
Type: Public

Hexion is the world's largest maker of thermosetting resins (or thermosets). Thermosets add a desired quality (heat resistance gloss adhesion durability and strength) to customer's and their customers' final products. They include an array of resins: phenolic epoxy polyester and urethane. The company also is a leading producer of adhesive and structural resins and coatings. Among the markets it serves are paints packaging consumer products composites and automotive coatings. About 45% of total revenue comes from US operations.

	Annual Growth	12/17	12/18*	07/19*	12/19	12/20
Sales ($ mil.)	(11.3%)	3,591.0	3,797.0	1,778.0	1,596.0	2,510.0
Net income ($ mil.)	–	(234.0)	(162.0)	2,894.0	(89.0)	(230.0)
Market value ($ mil.)	–	–	–	–	–	–
Employees	(15.4%)	4,300	4,000	–	4,000	2,600

*Fiscal year change

HF FINANCIAL CORP.
NMS: HFFC

225 South Main Avenue
Sioux Falls, SD 57104
Phone: 605 333-7556
Fax: –
Web: www.homefederal.com

CEO: –
CFO: –
HR: –
FYE: June 30
Type: Public

Those in South Dakota who want their finances to go north might turn to HF Financial. It's the holding company for Home Federal Bank which serves consumers and businesses through more than 30 branches in eastern and central South Dakota and a single branch in southwestern Minnesota. Deposit products include checking and savings accounts and CDs. Commercial mortgages and loans account for about 40% of HF Financial's loan portfolio. Residential multifamily and agricultural real estate loans account for another 30% of loans. Bank subsidiary Hometown Insurors sells insurance and annuities; Mid America Capital provides equipment financing. Home Federal Bank was founded in 1929. Great Western Bancorp agreed to buy HF Financial for $139.5 million in late 2015.

	Annual Growth	06/11	06/12	06/13	06/14	06/15
Assets ($ mil.)	(0.1%)	1,191.3	1,192.6	1,217.5	1,274.7	1,185.4
Net income ($ mil.)	52.0%	0.7	5.2	5.9	6.6	3.6
Market value ($ mil.)	8.5%	77.2	85.6	91.8	98.0	107.0
Employees	(4.5%)	359	311	334	285	299

HFB FINANCIAL CORP.
NBB: HFBA

1602 Cumberland Avenue
Middlesboro, KY 40965
Phone: 606 242-1071
Fax: 606 242-3432
Web: www.homefederalbank.com

CEO: David Cook
CFO: Stanley Alexander
HR: –
FYE: December 31
Type: Public

HFB Financial Corporation is the holding company for Home Federal Bank which provides community banking services to individuals and small to midsized businesses through three offices in southeastern Kentucky and two more in eastern Tennessee. Standard retail services include savings checking and money market accounts as well as certificates of deposit individual retirement accounts and Keogh plans. Home Federal focuses on residential lending but also originates commercial real estate construction business and consumer loans. Home Federal Bank was founded as People's Building and Loan Association in 1920.

	Annual Growth	12/09	12/10	12/11	12/12	12/13
Assets ($ mil.)	(0.6%)	342.4	348.0	347.1	344.3	334.8
Net income ($ mil.)	(10.9%)	3.1	1.9	1.4	2.0	2.0
Market value ($ mil.)	2.5%	20.3	23.3	21.1	21.5	22.4
Employees	–	–	90	–	–	–

HFF INC
NYS: HF

One Victory Park, 2323 Victory Avenue, Suite 1200
Dallas, TX 75219
Phone: 214 265-0880
Fax: –
Web: www.hfflp.com

CEO: Mark D Gibson
CFO: Gregory R Conley
HR: Stephanie F Messock
FYE: December 31
Type: Public

Don't huff and puff — HFF will help you finance that high-rise. The company's Holliday Fenoglio Fowler subsidiary is a large commercial real estate capital intermediary. The firm provides capital markets services including structured financing commercial loan servicing investment sales loan sales and debt placement. Real estate investment banking subsidiary HFF Securities provides advisory services seeks private and joint venture equity capital places private listings and provides institutional marketing for property investments. Unlike most commercial property brokerage firms HFF does not provide leasing or property management services. The company operates about 20 offices throughout the US.

	Annual Growth	12/13	12/14	12/15	12/16	12/17
Sales ($ mil.)	14.4%	355.6	425.9	502.0	517.4	609.5
Net income ($ mil.)	16.6%	51.4	61.3	84.0	77.2	95.0
Market value ($ mil.)	16.0%	1,035.9	1,385.8	1,198.7	1,167.0	1,876.5
Employees	11.4%	637	721	810	891	982

HG HOLDINGS INC
NBB: STLY

2115 E. 7th Street, Suite 101
Charlotte, NC 28204
Phone: 252 355-4610
Fax: –
Web: www.stanleyfurniture.com

CEO: Steven Hale
CFO: –
HR: Patrick Holbrook
FYE: December 31
Type: Public

Stanley Furniture needs lots of rooms to spread out. The company established in 1924 primarily makes wood furniture that retails in the upper-medium price range. Its products include furniture for adult bedrooms dining rooms youth bedrooms home offices and living rooms as well as for home entertainment centers. Youth furniture is made under the Young America brand. Stanley Furniture makes and markets furniture styles such as European and American traditional lines as well as contemporary/transitional and country/casual. With a manufacturing facility in North Carolina the company sells its products through furniture and department stores. International customers account for about 10% of sales.

	Annual Growth	12/13	12/14	12/15	12/16	12/17
Sales ($ mil.)	(17.4%)	96.9	60.6	57.4	44.6	45.2
Net income ($ mil.)	–	(12.6)	(29.9)	5.3	(5.3)	(7.7)
Market value ($ mil.)	(31.0%)	57.3	40.9	41.6	13.4	13.0
Employees	(33.1%)	544	135	71	70	109

HHGREGG INC   NBB: HGGG Q

4151 East 96th Street
Indianapolis, IN 46240
Phone: 317 848-8710
Fax: –
Web: www.hhgregg.com

CEO: –
CFO: –
HR: –
FYE: March 31
Type: Public

Retailer hhgregg sells a range of electronics and appliances in nearly 220 stores in 20 US states and online. It offers TV and video products (LED TVs Blu-ray disc players) home and car audio gear (CD players home theater systems) appliances (refrigerators washers and dryers) computers gaming consoles digital cameras GPS navigators and mattresses. The company also offers installation and tech services. Founded in 1955 Indianapolis-based hhgregg had expanded from southern states to the Midwest and mid-Atlantic regions. In early 2017 the company filed for Chapter 11 bankruptcy protection and was forced to liquidate its assets after failing to secure a buyer.It ceased operations in May 2017.

	Annual Growth	03/12	03/13	03/14	03/15	03/16
Sales ($ mil.)	(5.8%)	2,493.4	2,474.8	2,338.6	2,129.4	1,960.0
Net income ($ mil.)	–	81.4	25.4	0.2	(132.7)	(54.9)
Market value ($ mil.)	(34.4%)	315.3	306.2	266.3	169.8	58.5
Employees	(6.6%)	6,700	6,300	6,100	5,400	5,100

HI-SHEAR TECHNOLOGY CORPORATION

24225 Garnier St.
Torrance CA 90505
Phone: 310-784-2100
Fax: 310-325-5354
Web: www.hstc.com

CEO: –
CFO: Jan L Hauhe
HR: –
FYE: May 31
Type: Subsidiary

Hi-Shear Technology cuts loose with a slew of electronic pyrotechnic and mechanical devices used by the defense and aerospace industry. Hi-Shear's power cartridges and separation devices provide command-release for structures designed to hold together under rigorous conditions. The devices are used in rockets and satellites such as the Space Shuttle and the Patriot missile and in airplane ejector seats. Major customers include the US Government Boeing and Lockheed Martin. Hi-Shear also makes pyrotechnic-powered LifeShear cutters that slice through steel and other materials to free trapped victims. In late 2009 British defense contractor Chemring Group acquired the company for about $132 million.

HI-TECH PHARMACAL CO., INC.   NMS: HITK

369 Bayview Avenue
Amityville, NY 11701
Phone: 631 789-8228
Fax: –
Web: www.hitechpharm.com

CEO: –
CFO: William Peters
HR: –
FYE: April 30
Type: Public

Hi-Tech Pharmacal combines imitation with innovation making and distributing dozens of liquid and semi-solid prescription over-the-counter (OTC) and vitamin products. The company primarily produces generic forms of prescription drugs including versions of allergy medicine Flonase (from GlaxoSmithKline). Hi-Tech's ECR Pharmaceuticals business makes branded over-the-counter products including Bupap analgesic tablets and Zolpimist insomnia spray. Its Health Care Products division markets OTC products including nutritional products and devices for people with diabetes and the Zostrix line of pain and arthritis medications. Hi-Tech Pharmacal is being acquired by drugmaker Akorn.

	Annual Growth	04/09	04/10	04/11	04/12	04/13
Sales ($ mil.)	20.9%	108.7	163.7	190.8	230.0	232.4
Net income ($ mil.)	13.4%	9.8	31.1	41.5	48.4	16.3
Market value ($ mil.)	44.7%	102.5	330.3	375.5	442.4	448.8
Employees	4.5%	375	391	408	428	448

HIBBETT INC   NMS: HIBB

2700 Milan Court
Birmingham, AL 35211
Phone: 205 942-4292
Fax: –
Web: www.hibbett.com

CEO: Michael Longo
CFO: Robert Volke
HR: –
FYE: January 30
Type: Public

Small-town sports fans are the bread and butter for Hibbett Sports. The company sells brand-name sports equipment athletic apparel and footwear in small to mid-sized markets in about 35 states mainly in the South and Midwest. Its flagship Hibbett Sports chain boasts more than 1080 locations; stores are primarily found in malls and strip centers anchored by a Wal-Mart. Hibbett also operates nearly 150 of City Gear stores which stock urban streewear and about 20 mall-based Sports Additions shoe shops most of which are situated near Hibbett Sports stores. The company also trades online. The company was founded in 1945.

	Annual Growth	01/17*	02/18	02/19	02/20*	01/21
Sales ($ mil.)	9.9%	973.0	968.2	1,008.7	1,184.2	1,419.7
Net income ($ mil.)	5.0%	61.1	35.0	28.4	27.3	74.3
Market value ($ mil.)	14.6%	538.9	365.0	268.8	408.3	930.2
Employees	3.6%	9,300	9,200	10,600	10,200	10,700

*Fiscal year change

HICKMAN, WILLIAMS & COMPANY

250 E 5TH ST STE 300
CINCINNATI, OH 452024198
Phone: 513-621-1946
Fax: –
Web: www.hicwilco.com

CEO: –
CFO: Sander James
HR: –
FYE: March 31
Type: Private

Hickman Williams makes carbon products (anthracite coal metallurgical coke and reactive char coke) and metals and alloys (chromium manganese and silicon) used by metals producers. The company also manufactures service injection systems and cored wire feeding units for metal production facilities. Hickman Williams operates about 50 warehouse facilities throughout the nation. Founded by Richard Hickman and Harry Williams in 1891 the company is now owned by its employees.

	Annual Growth	03/12	03/13	03/14	03/15	03/16
Sales ($ mil.)	(10.6%)	–	–	245.2	247.2	195.9
Net income ($ mil.)	–	–	–	0.0	4.6	2.8
Market value ($ mil.)	–	–	–	–	–	–
Employees	–	–	–	–	–	92

HICKORY FARMS INC.

1505 Holland Rd.
Maumee OH 43537
Phone: 419-893-7611
Fax: 419-893-0164
Web: www.hickoryfarms.com

CEO: Diane Pearse
CFO: Dennis Doheny
HR: –
FYE: January 31
Type: Private

Before your relationship goes to hell in a "gift" basket try delighting your honey with a ham from Hickory Farms. The gift-food company sells high-end beef and cheese chocolates desserts fresh fruits and nuts seafood and other delectables in eco-friendly gift boxes. Prices range from about $10 to more than $200. Gift-givers may order through catalogs and the company's website. In addition Hickory Farms sells direct through about 700 shopping-mall kiosks during the holiday season and it retails at discount merchandisers and grocers (such as Target and Safeway). Founded in 1951 Hickory Farms is owned by private investment firm Sun Capital Partners.

HICKORY TECH CORP.

NMS: HTCO

221 East Hickory Street
Mankato, MN 56002-3248
Phone: 800 326-5789
Fax: –
Web: www.hickorytech.com

CEO: –
CFO: –
HR: –
FYE: December 31
Type: Public

Its name may sound like a Division II college but Hickory Tech's field of play is telecommunications. The company operates two business segments: Telecom and Enventis (Internet protocol-based voice and data services). Through its subsidiaries the company provides 55000 residential and business customers with access lines in Iowa and Minnesota. It also offers long-distance services to 36000 customers broadband Internet access services to 19000 customers and digital television service to about 10000 customers. Its National Independent Billing unit which is part of the Telecom segment provides data processing services to other telecommunications companies.

	Annual Growth	12/08	12/09	12/10	12/11	12/12
Sales ($ mil.)	4.6%	153.2	139.1	162.2	163.5	183.2
Net income ($ mil.)	0.8%	8.0	11.3	12.1	9.2	8.3
Market value ($ mil.)	15.7%	73.5	119.4	129.2	149.8	131.5
Employees	4.1%	433	448	463	500	508

HIGH CONCRETE GROUP LLC

125 DENVER RD
DENVER, PA 175179315
Phone: 717-336-9300
Fax: –
Web: www.highconcrete.com

CEO: Michael F Shirk
CFO: Karen A Biondolillo
HR: –
FYE: December 31
Type: Private

High Concrete Group offers concrete solutions for your building needs. The company produces precast concrete structures including walls architectural facades and floor slabs to create everything from office buildings to sports arenas. It is one of the leading makers of precast parking structures in the US. Its StructureCare service provides preventive maintenance to extend the life of those structures. A subsidiary of High Industries High Concrete Group counts architects contractors and building owners among its customers. It primarily serves the Mid-Atlantic Midwest and New England regions of the country with projects that include the Baltimore Ravens' stadium and a Harrah's casino parking garage.

	Annual Growth	12/05	12/06	12/07	12/08	12/09
Sales ($ mil.)	–	–	–	0.0	255.3	104.5
Net income ($ mil.)	–	–	–	0.0	22.4	0.0
Market value ($ mil.)	–	–	–	–	–	–
Employees	–	–	–	–	–	900

HIGH COUNTRY BANCORP, INC.

NBB: HCBC

7360 West US Highway 50
Salida, CO 81201
Phone: 719 539-2516
Fax: 719 539-6216

CEO: Larry Smith
CFO: –
HR: –
FYE: June 30
Type: Public

High Country Bancorp is in rarefied air. It is the holding company for High Country Bank which was founded in 1886 as the first savings and loan association chartered in Colorado. Serving the state's tourist-oriented "Fourteener" region (for the number of mountain peaks exceeding 14000 feet) the bank operates four branches in Salida Buena Vista and Canon City. It offers traditional services such as personal and business checking accounts CDs and IRAs as well as financial planning and investment services. The bank's lending activities include residential and commercial mortgages construction and land loans and home equity and personal loans. High Country Bank focuses on real estate lending with mortgages secured by one- to four-family residences comprising about 40% of the loan portfolio and commercial mortgages adding almost another quarter. The bank also makes business consumer construction and land loans.

	Annual Growth	06/17	06/18	06/19	06/20	06/21
Assets ($ mil.)	13.1%	247.5	265.4	275.4	331.8	404.3
Net income ($ mil.)	13.1%	3.0	2.7	4.0	4.3	4.9
Market value ($ mil.)	1.1%	44.5	42.8	46.3	36.2	46.5
Employees	–	–	–	–	–	–

HIGH INDUSTRIES INC.

1853 WILLIAM PENN WAY
LANCASTER, PA 176016713
Phone: 717-293-4444
Fax: –
Web: www.high.net

CEO: Michael F Shirk
CFO: Karen A Biondolillo
HR: –
FYE: December 31
Type: Private

High Industries has ascended to the top of the steel and construction business. Doing business as High Companies its subsidiaries are active in heavy construction and materials mostly along the East Coast. Its High Steel Structures is one of North America's largest steel bridge fabricators. Other group companies include High Steel Service Center (metal processing) High Concrete Group (precast concrete) High Transit (specialty hauler) and High Structural Erectors (field erection services). Affiliates of High Companies such as High Hotels are active in real estate. Tracing its roots to a welding shop founded by Sanford H. High in 1931 the family-owned company is controlled by the High Family Council.

	Annual Growth	12/05	12/06	12/07	12/08	12/09
Sales ($ mil.)	(6.5%)	–	390.2	429.5	452.9	319.2
Net income ($ mil.)	–	–	25.9	23.1	31.9	0.0
Market value ($ mil.)	–	–	–	–	–	–
Employees	–	–	–	–	–	2,107

HIGH PERFORMANCE TECHNOLOGIES INC.

11955 Freedom Dr. Ste. 1100
Reston VA 20190
Phone: 703-707-2700
Fax: 703-707-0103
Web: www.hpti.com

CEO: James P Regan
CFO: David Keleher
HR: –
FYE: December 31
Type: Subsidiary

High Performance Technologies (HPTi) hopes to take your technological efforts to the max. The company provides information technology services to the US military and other parts of the federal government. Offerings include systems development network security design financial management systems modeling and simulation and information sharing and analysis. HPTi's services are primarily used in advanced and battlefield systems computational technologies and homeland security operations. The US Army and Air Force and the departments of Justice Homeland Security and Energy are among its chief clients. Dynamics Research Corporation (DRC) agreed to buy the company in 2011 for $143 million.

HIGH POINT REGIONAL HEALTH

601 N ELM ST
HIGH POINT, NC 272624331
Phone: 336-878-6000
Fax: –
Web: www.wakehealth.edu

CEO: Ernie Bovio
CFO: Kimberly Crews
HR: –
FYE: June 30
Type: Private

Hospital stays are usually not the high point of one's life but High Point Regional Health System aims to make patients comfortable. Its main facility is High Point Regional Hospital a medical/surgical facility with about 380 beds serving the Piedmont Triad region of North Carolina. The private not-for-profit health care system also operates the Carolina Regional Heart Center Neuroscience Center Piedmont Joint Replacement Center Emergency Center Culp Women's Center and Hayworth Cancer Center. Other operations include primary care physician practices mental health wound care and home health care services. The hospital was founded in 1904. Parent company UNC Health Care System is selling High Point to Wake Forest Baptist Medical Center.

	Annual Growth	06/17	06/18	06/19	06/20	06/21
Sales ($ mil.)	3652.3%	–	–	0.3	337.1	384.9
Net income ($ mil.)	1316.6%	–	–	0.3	27.2	56.5
Market value ($ mil.)	–	–	–	–	–	–
Employees	–	–	–	–	–	2,338

HIGH POINT SOLUTIONS INC.

5 GAIL CT
SPARTA, NJ 078713438
Phone: 973-940-0040
Fax: –
Web: www.highpoint.com

CEO: –
CFO: Sandra Curran
HR: –
FYE: December 31
Type: Private

High Point Solutions can solve your networking needs. The company supplies network hardware — routers switches and access servers — to telecommunications companies and other large enterprises. High Point's procurement specialists provide equipment from leading manufactures such as Cisco Systems and Nortel Networks. The company also provides services in repair network design and installation. Owners Mike and Tom Mendiburu maintain a lean-and-mean corporate philosophy: a small staff dedicated to procurement and focused on speed and service for a short list of large clients. The brothers founded High Point in 1996.

	Annual Growth	12/14	12/15	12/16	12/17	12/18
Sales ($ mil.)	(5.6%)	–	145.9	111.5	104.5	122.7
Net income ($ mil.)	–	–	0.0	0.0	0.0	3.0
Market value ($ mil.)	–	–	–	–	–	–
Employees	–	–	–	–	–	50

HIGH STEEL STRUCTURES LLC

1915 OLD PHILADELPHIA PIKE
LANCASTER, PA 176023410
Phone: 717-299-5211
Fax: –
Web: www.highsteel.com

CEO: Michael F Shirk
CFO: Karen A Biondolillo
HR: –
FYE: December 31
Type: Private

Steel fabricator High Steel Structures helps to build bridges — literally. The company manufactures structural steel beams and girders used to build bridges and elevated roads in the US. High Steel also makes steel structures for buildings such as manufacturing plants power plants and sports arenas and offers erection services and emergency repair services. Working with contractors such as Balfour Beatty Skanska and Middlesex High Steel has fabricated steel for thousands of bridges mainly along the East Coast. The company has four fabrication plants in Pennsylvania and is a part of High Industries. High Steel traces its roots back to 1931 when it was founded as High Welding Company.

	Annual Growth	12/05	12/06	12/07	12/08	12/09
Sales ($ mil.)	15.4%	–	–	136.0	131.5	181.0
Net income ($ mil.)	–	–	–	5.9	7.1	0.0
Market value ($ mil.)	–	–	–	–	–	–
Employees	–	–	–	–	–	600

HIGHER ONE HOLDINGS INC.   NYS: ONE

115 Munson Street
New Haven, CT 06511
Phone: 203 776-7776
Fax: –
Web: www.higherone.com

CEO: Marc Sheinbaum
CFO: Christopher Wolf
HR: Donna Verdisco
FYE: December 31
Type: Public

The higher ambition at Higher One Holdings is to facilitate higher education payments. The company provides payment processing and disbursement services to nearly 2000 colleges and universities and over 13 million enrolled students across the US. To make financial transactions more efficient the firm offers Refund Management disbursement service which schools use to electronically distribute financial aid and other funds to students; CASHNet Payment Solutions which offers online and mobile billing and tuition payment options to students and parents; OneAccount banking deposit and card services for students; and Campus Labs data and analytics tools designed to help schools retain students and develop curriculum.

	Annual Growth	12/10	12/11	12/12	12/13	12/14
Sales ($ mil.)	11.0%	145.0	176.3	197.7	211.1	220.1
Net income ($ mil.)	(12.1%)	25.1	31.9	36.9	14.1	15.0
Market value ($ mil.)	(32.5%)	964.1	878.8	502.3	465.1	200.6
Employees	30.4%	450	700	880	1,000	1,300

HIGHLANDS BANKSHARES INC (VA)   NBB: HLND

P.O. Box 1128
Abingdon, VA 24212-1128
Phone: 276 628-9181
Fax: –
Web: www.hubank.com

CEO: –
CFO: –
HR: –
FYE: December 31
Type: Public

Highlands Bankshares is the holding company for Highlands Union Bank which operates about a dozen branches in Virginia North Carolina and Tennessee. Unrelated to Highlands Bankshares in West Virginia the company offers checking and savings accounts IRAs and CDs. Residential mortgages and commercial construction and land development loans make up most of its loan portfolio. The bank has two subsidiaries: Highlands Union Insurance Services is part of a consortium of more than 40 other financial institutions that owns Bankers' Insurance which in turn owns nearly 10 insurance agencies in Virginia; Highlands Union Financial Services provides trust investment and retirement services. West Virginia-based rival Summit Financial Group agreed to buy Highland in March 2016.

	Annual Growth	12/13	12/14	12/15	12/16	12/17
Assets ($ mil.)	(0.2%)	598.3	605.1	617.0	612.7	594.1
Net income ($ mil.)	–	1.5	2.5	1.3	0.0	(0.4)
Market value ($ mil.)	17.3%	31.6	28.7	39.8	48.8	59.9
Employees	(7.9%)	213	211	211	211	153

HIGHLANDS BANKSHARES INC.   NBB: HBSI

3 North Main Street, P.O. Box 929
Petersburg, WV 26847
Phone: 304 257-4111
Fax: –
Web: www.grantcountybank.com

CEO: John Van Meter
CFO: Jeffrey Reedy
HR: Marcie L Yokum
FYE: December 31
Type: Public

No matter if you take the high road or the low road Highlands Bankshares will take of your money afore ye. The company (not to be confused with Highlands Bankshares headquartered in Virginia) is the holding company for The Grant County Bank and Capon Valley Bank which together operate about a dozen branches in Virginia and West Virginia. The banks offer standard retail products and services including demand and time deposit accounts and business and consumer loans. Real estate loans account for about 80% of the company's loan book. Highlands Bankshares also offers credit life accident and health insurance through HBI Life.

	Annual Growth	12/16	12/17	12/18	12/19	12/20
Assets ($ mil.)	4.3%	402.4	404.7	413.2	418.9	475.5
Net income ($ mil.)	(2.7%)	3.7	2.5	3.9	3.5	3.3
Market value ($ mil.)	(1.0%)	47.8	55.1	61.5	52.3	45.9
Employees	–	–	–	–	–	–

HIGHMARK BCBSD INC.

800 Delaware Ave.
Wilmington DE 19801
Phone: 302-421-3000
Fax: 302-421-8864
Web: www.highmarkbcbsde.com

CEO: Timothy J Constantine
CFO: –
HR: –
FYE: December 31
Type: Private

Blue Cross Blue Shield of Delaware (BCBSD) is the first choice for health insurance for First State residents. As one of Delaware's largest health coverage providers the company administers traditional indemnity insurance and managed care plans for some 400000 members. Its coverage options include Blue Choice PPO Blue Care IPA (an HMO plan) Blue Select point-of-service (POS) plan and BlueAdvantage consumer-directed plans. The firm also provides dental vision and supplemental Medicare coverage as well as disease management programs for members with chronic and serious illnesses. Founded in 1935 BCBSD is a licensee of the Blue Cross Blue Shield Association and an affiliate of Highmark.

HIGHWOODS PROPERTIES, INC. NYS: HIW

3100 Smoketree Court, Suite 600
Raleigh, NC 27604
Phone: 919 872-4924
Fax: 919 431-1439
Web: www.highwoods.com

CEO: Theodore Klinck
CFO: Brendan Maiorana
HR: –
FYE: December 31
Type: Public

Highwoods Properties Inc. is a fully integrated office real estate investment trust (REIT) that owns develops acquires leases and managed properties primarily in the best business districts (BBDs) of Atlanta Charlotte Nashville Orlando Pittsburgh Raleigh Richmond and Tampa. The company owns a total of about 25.9 million sq. ft. of leasable space. Its largest tenants include the federal government Bank of America and Bridgestone Americas.

	Annual Growth	12/17	12/18	12/19	12/20	12/21
Sales ($ mil.)	2.2%	702.7	720.0	736.0	736.9	768.0
Net income ($ mil.)	14.0%	185.4	171.8	136.9	347.4	313.3
Market value ($ mil.)	(3.3%)	5,340.1	4,058.3	5,130.3	4,156.9	4,677.2
Employees	(5.7%)	441	442	431	359	348

HILAND DAIRY FOODS COMPANY., LLC

1133 E KEARNEY ST
SPRINGFIELD, MO 658033435
Phone: 417-862-9311
Fax: –
Web: www.hilanddairy.com

CEO: –
CFO: –
HR: Randy Hyde
FYE: September 30
Type: Private

Hiland Dairy Foods is a farmer-owned dairy foods company that offers dairy products including ice cream milk butter cheese and eggnog. It has expanded beyond dairy and has a wide variety of other beverages such as Red Diamond Tea lemonade and fresh juices. Hiland runs more than 15 processing plants and has over 50 distribution centers across the region. It partners with a larger dairy co-operative Prairie Farms Dairy to market and sell products. Beyond dairy Hiland supplies juices bottled milk and coffee as well as tea water and other to-go drinks. It features limited-run specialty items such as peanut butter banana ice cream. Hiland was founded in 1938.

	Annual Growth	09/07	09/08	09/09	09/10	09/11
Sales ($ mil.)	30.8%	–	–	559.9	588.6	958.2
Net income ($ mil.)	(53.0%)	–	–	39.3	24.6	8.7
Market value ($ mil.)	–	–	–	–	–	–
Employees	–	–	–	–	–	1,350

HILITE INTERNATIONAL, INC.

2001 PEACH ST
WHITEHALL, MI 494611844
Phone: 972-242-2116
Fax: –
Web: www.hilite.com

CEO: Karl Hammer
CFO: Stefan Eck
HR: –
FYE: December 31
Type: Private

The highlight of Hilite International's day is to manufacture high-volume high-tech auto components and systems. Its lineup is used in many powertrain (engine and transmission) applications. Hilite's hydraulic and electromagnetic products (on/off valves and variable pressure solenoids) enhance fuel efficiency emissions control and torque. Hilite sells to global auto OEMs such as GM BMW and Honda and brake systems suppliers such as BorgWarner. The company established in 1999 operates through eight locations spanning Asia Europe and North America.

	Annual Growth	12/07	12/08	12/09	12/10	12/11
Sales ($ mil.)	–	–	–	(736.1)	399.4	522.1
Net income ($ mil.)	–	–	–	0.0	7.9	(1.7)
Market value ($ mil.)	–	–	–	–	–	–
Employees	–	–	–	–	–	1,000

HILL COUNTRY MEMORIAL HOSPITAL

1020 S STATE HIGHWAY 16
FREDERICKSBURG, TX 786244471
Phone: 830-997-4353
Fax: –
Web: www.hillcountrymemorial.org

CEO: –
CFO: Mark Jones
HR: –
FYE: December 31
Type: Private

Hill Country Memorial takes care of the peaks and valleys in the wellness of area residents. The health system provides medical services to eight counties near Fredericksburg in Central Texas. Its hospital Hill Country Memorial Hospital has about 85 beds and a staff of close to 100 physicians. Specialties include cardiology obstetrics oncology orthopedics and emergency medicine. The health system also operates a wellness center that offers locals yoga stress management weight loss and massage. Other community services include hospice and home care and the administration of state-funded services for low income women infants children (WIC).

	Annual Growth	12/09	12/10	12/11	12/12	12/16
Sales ($ mil.)	3.7%	–	–	63.7	70.6	76.5
Net income ($ mil.)	–	–	–	(9.7)	3.0	25.2
Market value ($ mil.)	–	–	–	–	–	–
Employees	–	–	–	–	–	626

HILL INTERNATIONAL INC NYS: HIL

One Commerce Square, 2005 Market Street, 17th Floor
Philadelphia, PA 19103
Phone: 215 309-7700
Fax: –
Web: www.hillintl.com

CEO: Raouf Ghali
CFO: Todd Weintraub
HR: –
FYE: December 31
Type: Public

Hill International offers project and construction management consulting services worldwide. It manages all aspects of the construction process from concept to completion including estimating and cost management facilities management labor consulting and even troubled project turnaround. The company's customers include US federal state regional and local governments; foreign governments; and private sector clients. Hill International operates about 70 offices throughout the world with the Americas representing about 50% of total revenue.

	Annual Growth	12/16	12/17	12/18	12/19	12/20
Sales ($ mil.)	(8.3%)	520.8	483.7	428.7	376.4	368.5
Net income ($ mil.)	–	(18.8)	27.4	(31.5)	14.1	(8.2)
Market value ($ mil.)	(18.5%)	244.1	305.8	172.8	177.3	107.7
Employees	(5.1%)	3,330	2,856	2,664	2,718	2,703

HILL PHYSICIANS MEDICAL GROUP, INC.

2409 CAMINO RAMON
SAN RAMON, CA 945834285
Phone: 800-445-5747
Fax: –
Web: www.hillphysicians.com

CEO: David Joyner
CFO: –
HR: –
FYE: December 31
Type: Private

Hill Physicians Medical Group is the doctors' answer to HMOs. The company is an independent practice association (IPA) serving some 300000 health plan members in northern California. The company contracts with managed care organizations throughout the region — including HMOs belonging to Aetna CIGNA and Health Net— to provide care to health plan members through its provider affiliates. Its network includes about 3800 primary care and specialty physicians 38 hospitals and 24 urgent care centers. The company also provides administrative services for doctors and patients. PriMed a management services organization created Hill Physicians Medical Group in 1984 and still runs the company.

	Annual Growth	12/04	12/05	12/06	12/10	12/15
Sales ($ mil.)	2.0%	–	414.4	427.5	427.5	504.8
Net income ($ mil.)	(1.3%)	–	7.8	5.3	5.3	6.8
Market value ($ mil.)	–	–	–	–	–	–
Employees	–	–	–	–	–	600

HILL-ROM HOLDINGS, INC.   NYS: HRC

130 E. Randolph St., Suite 1000   CEO: Jose E Almeida
Chicago, IL 60601   CFO: –
Phone: 312 819-7200   HR: –
Fax: 812 934-8189   FYE: September 30
Web: www.hillrom.com   Type: Public

Hill-Rom Holdings holds Hill-Rom Company which in turn holds hospital patients safe and secure. Hill-Rom makes sells and rents hospital beds and other patient-room furniture and equipment along with stretchers surgical tables and accessories and other equipment for lifting and transporting patients. As most of its beds are designed to connect to patient monitoring equipment Hill-Rom also provides information technology products for use in health care settings. Additionally the company sells diagnostic and testing equipment through subsidiary Welch Allyn. Hill-Rom's primary customers include acute long-term and primary care facilities worldwide.

	Annual Growth	09/16	09/17	09/18	09/19	09/20
Sales ($ mil.)	2.1%	2,655.2	2,743.7	2,848.0	2,907.3	2,881.0
Net income ($ mil.)	15.8%	124.1	133.6	252.4	152.2	223.0
Market value ($ mil.)	7.7%	4,130.4	4,931.4	6,290.9	7,012.6	5,565.2
Employees	0.0%	10,000	10,000	10,000	10,000	10,000

HILLENBRAND INC   NYS: HI

One Batesville Boulevard   CEO: Kimberly Ryan-Dennis
Batesville, IN 47006   CFO: Kristina Cerniglia
Phone: 812 934-7500   HR: –
Fax: –   FYE: September 30
Web: www.hillenbrand.com   Type: Public

Hillenbrand is a global diversified industrial company with multiple leading brands that serve a wide variety of industries worldwide. It has three very distinct businesses: Advanced Process Solutions designs develops manufactures and services highly engineered industrial equipment throughout the world; Molding Technology Solutions a global leader in highly engineered and customized systems and service in plastic technology and processing; and Batesville a recognized leader in the death care industry in North America. Founded by John A. Hillenbrand in 1906 Hillenbrand generates just more than 50% of its sales in the US.

	Annual Growth	09/17	09/18	09/19	09/20	09/21
Sales ($ mil.)	15.9%	1,590.2	1,770.1	1,807.3	2,517.0	2,864.8
Net income ($ mil.)	18.6%	126.2	76.6	121.4	(60.1)	249.9
Market value ($ mil.)	2.4%	2,824.4	3,802.2	2,245.0	2,061.8	3,100.7
Employees	15.0%	6,000	6,500	6,500	11,000	10,500

HILLS BANCORPORATION   NBB: HBIA

131 Main Street   CEO: Dwight Seegmiller
Hills, IA 52235   CFO: Joseph Schueller
Phone: 319 679-2291   HR: –
Fax: –   FYE: December 31
Web: www.hillsbank.com   Type: Public

There's gold in them thar hills! Hills Bancorporation is the holding company for Hills Bank and Trust which has about a dozen branches located in the eastern Iowa counties of Johnson Linn and Washington. The bank provides standard commercial services to area individuals businesses government entities and institutional customers. Offerings include deposit accounts loans and debit and credit cards. Hills Bank and Trust also administers estates personal trusts and pension plans and provides farm management and investment advisory and custodial services. The bank traces its roots to 1904.

	Annual Growth	12/16	12/17	12/18	12/19	12/20
Assets ($ mil.)	9.2%	2,655.8	2,963.4	3,042.5	3,300.9	3,780.6
Net income ($ mil.)	5.2%	31.6	28.1	36.8	45.3	38.6
Market value ($ mil.)	6.5%	448.9	503.9	566.9	611.2	576.5
Employees	1.3%	503	499	481	484	529

HILLSBOROUGH COUNTY AVIATION AUTHORITY

4160 GEORGE J. BEAN PKWY   CEO: –
TAMPA, FL 33607   CFO: –
Phone: 813-870-8700   HR: –
Fax: –   FYE: September 30
Web: www.tampaairport.com   Type: Private

If you've ever flown to the Tampa area to catch the NFL's Buccaneers or Major League Baseball's Rays then you've probably been through an airport managed by the Hillsborough County Aviation Authority. The agency operates Tampa International Airport which handles more than 8.4 million passengers annually plus three general aviation airports. Three of the agency's five board members are residents of Hillsborough County who are appointed by the governor of Florida; other board members include the mayor of the City of Tampa and a member of the Hillsborough County Board of Commissioners. The Hillsborough County Aviation Authority was established by the Florida Legislature in 1945.

	Annual Growth	09/16	09/17	09/18	09/19	09/20
Sales ($ mil.)	(4.8%)	–	212.2	234.7	253.5	183.1
Net income ($ mil.)	(28.2%)	–	142.9	44.1	13.7	53.0
Market value ($ mil.)		–	–	–	–	–
Employees		–	–	–	–	600

HILLSHIRE BRANDS CO   NYS: HSH

400 South Jefferson Street   CEO: Sean M Connolly
Chicago, IL 60607   CFO: Maria Henry
Phone: 312 614-6000   HR: Ryan Egan
Fax: 312 558-4913   FYE: June 29
Web: www.hillshirebrands.com   Type: Public

Got meat? Hillshire Brands Company (formerly Sara Lee Corp.) certainly does. Hillshire Brands is the new home of the Hillshire Farm Ball Park Jimmy Dean and State Fair brands of deli meats and other packaged-meat products including hot dogs and sausages as well as the artisanal brands Aidells and Gallo. For dessert the company serves up Sara Lee's line of frozen desserts including cheesecake. Taking its name from its predecessor's most-recognized meat brand Hillshire Brands was formed in 2012 when Sara Lee split to form two publicly-traded companies the other being its European coffee-and-tea business D.E. Master Blenders 1753. The split followed years of divestitures and strategic acquisitions.

	Annual Growth	06/09*	07/10	07/11*	06/12	06/13
Sales ($ mil.)	(25.7%)	12,881.0	10,793.0	8,681.0	4,094.0	3,920.0
Net income ($ mil.)	(8.8%)	364.0	506.0	1,287.0	845.0	252.0
Market value ($ mil.)	36.3%	1,180.7	1,724.2	2,381.1	3,573.0	4,077.0
Employees	(31.4%)	41,000	33,000	21,000	9,500	9,100

*Fiscal year change

HILLTOP HOLDINGS, INC.   NYS: HTH

6565 Hillcrest Avenue   CEO: Jeremy Ford
Dallas, TX 75205   CFO: William Furr
Phone: 214 855-2177   HR: –
Fax: –   FYE: December 31
Web: www.hilltop-holdings.com   Type: Public

With about $16.9 billion in assets diversified financial holding company Hilltop Holdings' provides banking mortgage origination insurance and financial advisory services through its PlainsCapital Bank PrimeLending and Momentum Independent Network subsidiaries. PlainsCapital offers community commercial and private banking through about 60 branches throughout Texas and holds more than $11.4 billion in deposits. PrimeLending generates mortgages in all 50 states and District of Columbia through approximately 1250 loan officers. Momentum Independent Network is an investment bank and is among the US top financial advisors to municipalities based on transaction volume.

	Annual Growth	12/17	12/18	12/19	12/20	12/21
Assets ($ mil.)	8.7%	13,365.8	13,683.6	15,172.4	16,944.3	18,689.1
Net income ($ mil.)	29.6%	132.5	121.4	225.3	447.8	374.5
Market value ($ mil.)	8.5%	2,000.2	1,407.3	1,968.6	2,172.3	2,774.8
Employees	(2.6%)	5,500	5,200	4,950	4,950	4,950

HILTON WORLDWIDE HOLDINGS INC NYS: HLT

7930 Jones Branch Drive, Suite 1100
McLean, VA 22102
Phone: 703 883-1000
Fax: –
Web: www.hiltonworldwide.com
CEO: Christopher Nassetta
CFO: Kevin Jacobs
HR: Alexandra Donofrio
FYE: December 31
Type: Public

If you need a bed for the night Hilton has a few hundred thousand of them. Hilton Worldwide is one of the world's largest hoteliers with a lodging empire that includes over 6400 properties comprising about 1 million rooms in about 120 countries operating under such names as Doubletree Embassy Suites and Hampton Inn as well as its flagship Hilton brand. Many of its hotels serve the mid-market segment though its Hilton and Conrad hotels offer full-service upscale lodging. In addition its Homewood Suites and Home2 Suites chains offers extended-stay services. About 85% of total revenue comes from US.

	Annual Growth	12/17	12/18	12/19	12/20	12/21
Sales ($ mil.)	(10.8%)	9,140.0	8,906.0	9,452.0	4,307.0	5,788.0
Net income ($ mil.)	(24.5%)	1,259.0	764.0	881.0	(715.0)	410.0
Market value ($ mil.)	18.2%	22,288.2	20,038.7	30,954.0	31,051.7	43,535.4
Employees	(3.4%)	163,000	169,000	173,000	141,000	142,000

HINES INTERESTS LIMITED PARTNERSHIP

2800 POST OAK BLVD FL 48
HOUSTON, TX 770566123
Phone: 713-621-8000
Fax: –
Web: www.hines.com
CEO: Jeffrey C Hines
CFO: –
HR: –
FYE: December 31
Type: Private

Hines is a real estate firm that invests in develops renovates manages and finances commercial real estate including high-rise office buildings industrial parks medical facilities mixed-use developments and master-planned residential communities. Its portfolio boasts around 1425 properties completed under development managed or invested totaling over 472 million sq. ft. The firm's property and asset management portfolio includes about 575 properties representing over 246 million sq. ft. and it span in 225 cities in 25 countries. Hines has collaborated with such world-renowned architects as I. M. Pei Philip Johnson and Frank Gehry. Management services include marketing tenant relations and contract negotiations. Gerald Hines founded the family controlled firm in 1957.

	Annual Growth	12/06	12/07	12/08	12/09	12/10
Sales ($ mil.)	–	–	–	0.0	200.0	234.1
Net income ($ mil.)	–	–	–	0.0	0.0	0.0
Market value ($ mil.)	–	–	–	–	–	–
Employees	–	–	–	–	–	3,200

HINGHAM INSTITUTION FOR SAVINGS NMS: HIFS

55 Main Street
Hingham, MA 02043
Phone: 781 749-2200
Fax: 781 740-4889
Web: www.hinghamsavings.com
CEO: Robert Gaughen
CFO: Cristian Melej
HR: Brenda McGillicuddy
FYE: December 31
Type: Public

The Hingham Institution for Savings serves businesses and retail customers in Boston's south shore communities operating more than 10 branches in Massachusetts in Boston Cohasset Hingham Hull Norwell Scituate South Hingham and South Weymouth. Founded in 1834 the bank offers traditional deposit products such as checking and savings accounts IRAs and certificates of deposit. More than 90% of its loan portfolio is split between commercial mortgages and residential mortgages (including home equity loans) though the bank also originates construction business and consumer loans. More than 95% of the company's revenue comes from loan interest.

	Annual Growth	12/16	12/17	12/18	12/19	12/20
Assets ($ mil.)	9.1%	2,014.6	2,284.5	2,408.6	2,590.3	2,857.1
Net income ($ mil.)	21.3%	23.4	25.8	30.4	38.9	50.8
Market value ($ mil.)	2.4%	420.7	442.5	422.7	449.4	461.8
Employees	(4.1%)	103	101	96	90	87

HINSHAW & CULBERTSON LLP

151 N FRANKLIN ST # 2500
CHICAGO, IL 606061915
Phone: 312-704-3000
Fax: –
Web: www.hinshawlaw.com
CEO: –
CFO: –
HR: –
FYE: December 31
Type: Private

Hinshaw & Culbertson's more than 400 lawyers offer a wide range of legal services though the firm specializes in commercial and defense litigation and corporate environmental employment and construction law. It represents professionals dealing with corporate health care taxation malpractice white collar crime insurance coverage immigration intellectual property securities and real estate liability and risk management issues. The firm also offers legal advisement services to architects engineers and people residing in the financial services sector. Hinshaw has more than 20 offices in the US and one office in the UK. The firm was founded in 1934.

	Annual Growth	12/00	12/01	12/02	12/03	12/10
Sales ($ mil.)	7.2%	–	108.5	116.2	124.6	202.8
Net income ($ mil.)	9.4%	–	44.0	50.2	53.7	98.4
Market value ($ mil.)	–	–	–	–	–	–
Employees	–	–	–	–	–	1,010

HIREQUEST INC NAS: HQI

111 Springhall Drive
Goose Creek, SC 29445
Phone: 843 723-7400
Fax: –
Web: www.hirequest.com
CEO: Richard Hermanns
CFO: David Burnett
HR: –
FYE: December 31
Type: Public

Command Center wouldn't mind being regarded as the George Patton of the temporary staffing market. The company operates about 50 temporary staffing stores across 20 US states. It specializes in the placement of workers in the event services hospitality construction manufacturing janitorial telemarketing administrative clerical and accounting fields. Command Center was formed in 2005 when Temporary Financial Services acquired Command Staffing and Harborview Software then changed its name. Command Center's top executives own about 34% of the company.

	Annual Growth	12/16	12/17	12/18	12/19	12/20
Sales ($ mil.)	(38.0%)	93.3	98.1	97.4	15.9	13.8
Net income ($ mil.)	63.0%	0.8	1.7	1.0	(0.3)	5.4
Market value ($ mil.)	130.7%	4.9	80.2	51.3	96.4	138.9
Employees	13.6%	34,219	33,220	32,230	67,050	57,040

HISTOGEN INC NAS: HSTO

10655 Sorrento Valley Road, Suite 200
San Diego, CA 92121
Phone: 858 526-3100
Fax: –
Web: www.histogen.com
CEO: Steven Mento
CFO: Susan Knudson
HR: –
FYE: December 31
Type: Public

Conatus Pharmaceuticals is ready to deliver a sliver of hope to people suffering from liver disease. The biotechnology company is developing a drug named emricasan to treat patients with chronic liver failure or liver fibrosis (scarring) from Hepatitis C. Emricasan is designed to reduce the enzymes that cause inflammation and cell death in order to interrupt the progression of liver disease; currently there's no other drug like it. Pfizer initially developed the drug; Conatus bought the rights to emricasan in 2010. It is beginning Phase III trials in Europe and Phase II trials in the US in 2014. Conatus went public in mid-2013 raising $66 million in its IPO. It will use the proceeds to further fund the drug's development.

	Annual Growth	12/16	12/17	12/18	12/19	12/20
Sales ($ mil.)	26.7%	0.8	35.4	33.6	21.7	2.1
Net income ($ mil.)	–	(29.7)	(17.4)	(18.0)	(11.4)	(18.8)
Market value ($ mil.)	(38.4%)	79.2	69.4	26.0	6.0	11.4
Employees	(8.4%)	27	35	31	6	19

HITCHINER MANUFACTURING CO., INC.

594 ELM ST
MILFORD, NH 030554306
Phone: 603-673-1100
Fax: –
Web: www.hitchiner.com

CEO: –
CFO: –
HR: –
FYE: December 31
Type: Private

There's no hitch in Hitchiner Manufacturing's business plan. The family-owned supplier of thin-wall investment castings and subassemblies and components operates 4 businesses: Ferrous-USA produces countergravity castings for the auto defense and pump and valve industries; Gas Turbine specializes in hot-section parts utilizing vacuum-melted alloys for the jet engine component market; Hitchiner Manufacturing Company de Mexico makes component parts for auto OEMs; and Hitchiner S.A. de C.V. front-end casting services. Hitchiner is primarily a tier-two supplier (its parts go to another company that contracts directly with the OEM) for majors such as BorgWarner Goodrich General Motors and General Electric.

	Annual Growth	12/14	12/15	12/18	12/19	12/20
Sales ($ mil.)	(2.3%)	–	226.8	253.1	267.6	202.3
Net income ($ mil.)	(7.4%)	–	16.6	26.8	29.1	11.3
Market value ($ mil.)	–	–	–	–	–	–
Employees	–	–	–	–	–	1,843

HITT CONTRACTING, INC.

2900 FAIRVIEW PARK DR # 300
FALLS CHURCH, VA 220424513
Phone: 703-846-9000
Fax: –
Web: www.hitt-gc.com

CEO: Kimberly Roy
CFO: –
HR: –
FYE: December 31
Type: Private

HITT Contracting hits the nail on the general contracting head. The group provides turnkey construction services for corporate base building and interiors healthcare aviation legal hospitality technology research medical and institutional and governmental facilities. Projects have included construction and design for the Federal Reserve DirecTV and Greenpeace. In addition to general contracting HITT offers design interior paint preconstruction and construction management services. It handles eco-friendly projects historic renovations and infrastructure refits. Founded in 1937 the family-owned firm has operations across the US.

	Annual Growth	12/11	12/12	12/13	12/14	12/15
Sales ($ mil.)	9.4%	–	827.4	921.3	958.3	1,084.6
Net income ($ mil.)	15.8%	–	18.6	19.3	29.3	28.9
Market value ($ mil.)	–	–	–	–	–	–
Employees	–	–	–	–	–	775

HITTITE MICROWAVE CORP

NMS: HITT

2 Elizabeth Drive
Chelmsford, MA 01824
Phone: 978 250-3343
Fax: –
Web: www.hittite.com

CEO: Rick D Hess
CFO: William W Boecke
HR: Susan J Dicecco
FYE: December 31
Type: Public

And lo the Hittites did rise up out of their land (the Commonwealth of Massachusetts) and they did conquer Babylon...well semiconductors in any case. Hittite Microwave designs and develops microwave millimeter-wave and radio-frequency integrated circuits (RFICs) for aerospace broadband cellular and military applications. In addition to standard amplifiers frequency multipliers mixers modulators switches and other components the company provides custom RFICs. It gets more than half of its sales from customers in international locations. Boeing (more than 15% of sales) is Hittite Microwave's top customer.

	Annual Growth	12/08	12/09	12/10	12/11	12/12
Sales ($ mil.)	10.1%	180.3	163.0	244.3	264.1	264.4
Net income ($ mil.)	6.2%	53.8	46.2	77.0	84.7	68.6
Market value ($ mil.)	20.5%	929.8	1,286.8	1,926.6	1,558.6	1,958.8
Employees	10.0%	332	349	402	469	486

HKN INC

NBB: HKNI

180 State Street, Suite 200
Southlake, TX 76092
Phone: 817 424-2424
Fax: –
Web: www.hkninc.com

CEO: Mikel D Faulkner
CFO: Kristina M Humphries
HR: –
FYE: December 31
Type: Public

HKN (formerly Harken Energy) harkens back to the days when a certain President George W. Bush was an oil man. HKN which bought Bush's small oil company more than a decade ago explores for and produces oil and gas primarily in the US where it has interests in oil and gas wells in the Gulf Coast region of Texas and Louisiana and holds coalbed methane assets in the Midwest. Internationally it has stakes in exploration and production assets in South America (Global Energy Development 34%) and in Canada (Spitfire Energy 27%). In 2008 HKN reported proved reserves (all in the US) of 4.2 billion cu. ft. of gas and 1.5 million barrels of oil. Lyford Investments Enterprises owns 36% of the voting stock of HKN.

	Annual Growth	12/12	12/13	12/14	12/15	12/16
Sales ($ mil.)	(0.6%)	0.4	1.1	1.0	0.5	0.4
Net income ($ mil.)	–	(3.2)	(1.5)	(24.0)	(6.7)	(5.6)
Market value ($ mil.)	(41.1%)	29.1	30.1	21.9	11.7	3.5
Employees	13.4%	14	16	18	–	–

HKS, INC.

350 N SAINT PAUL ST # 100
DALLAS, TX 752014200
Phone: 214-969-5599
Fax: –
Web: www.hksinc.com

CEO: Dan Noble
CFO: Samuel Mudro
HR: –
FYE: December 31
Type: Private

HKS is a good sport when it comes to building design. As one of the world's largest architectural firms HKS has designed sports and entertainment healthcare hospitality industrial and corporate buildings in the US and overseas. The company offers structural engineering architecture project management and interior and graphic design services. It provides planning and development programming branding research and advisory services. Some of the firm's work includes the Benefield Building Lopesan Costa Bavaro Resort and Village Cambodia's First Speedway - Laumes International Motor Racing Circuit and Biolab Research Facilities in Singapore.

	Annual Growth	12/13	12/14	12/15	12/18	12/20
Sales ($ mil.)	2.7%	–	–	368.2	387.6	420.3
Net income ($ mil.)	(7.4%)	–	–	19.1	2.2	13.0
Market value ($ mil.)	–	–	–	–	–	–
Employees	–	–	–	–	–	1,400

HMG/COURTLAND PROPERTIES, INC.

ASE: HMG

1870 S. Bayshore Drive
Coconut Grove, FL 33133
Phone: 305 854-6803
Fax: –
Web: www.hmgcourtland.com

CEO: Maurice Wiener
CFO: –
HR: –
FYE: December 31
Type: Public

Sun sea and sand are key parts of the business mix for HMG/Courtland Properties a real estate investment trust (REIT) that owns and manages commercial properties in the Miami area. The company owns the posh Grove Isle — a Coconut Grove-area luxury resort which includes a hotel restaurant spa and marina. The property managed by Grand Heritage Hotel Group accounts for about 70% of HMG/Courtland's rental income. The REIT also holds a 50% interest in a 16000 sq. ft. seafood restaurant at the marina in addition to a 5000 sq. ft. corporate office building. HMG/Courtland has two properties held for development in Rhode Island and Vermont and has equity interests in other commercial real estate operations.

	Annual Growth	12/16	12/17	12/18	12/19	12/20
Sales ($ mil.)	4.4%	0.1	0.1	0.1	0.1	0.1
Net income ($ mil.)	–	(0.4)	(0.3)	4.1	0.3	(1.1)
Market value ($ mil.)	0.0%	10.6	14.6	13.9	12.9	10.6
Employees	–	–	–	–	–	–

HMH HOSPITALS CORPORATION

343 THORNALL ST
EDISON, NJ 088372206
Phone: 201-996-2000
Fax: –
Web: www.hackensackumc.org

CEO: Robert Charles Garrett
CFO: Robert Glenning
HR: –
FYE: December 31
Type: Private

Hackensack University Medical Center (HUMC) is an acute care teaching and research hospital that serves northern New Jersey and parts of New York. The hospital has about 775 beds and staffs more than 2200 medical professionals. HUMC administers general medical surgical emergency and diagnostic care. The center also includes specialized treatment centers including a children's hospital a women's hospital a cancer center and a heart and vascular hospital. HUMC is part of the Hackensack University Health Network which also includes a physician practice group and a joint venture that operates two community hospitals. In 2016 the network merged with Meridian Health to create Hackensack Meridian Health.

	Annual Growth	12/13	12/14	12/15	12/16	12/18
Sales ($ mil.)	32.2%	–	1,309.1	1,357.1	1,707.9	3,999.7
Net income ($ mil.)	19.9%	–	106.6	83.1	41.2	220.3
Market value ($ mil.)	–	–	–	–	–	–
Employees	–	–	–	–	–	1,100

HMI INDUSTRIES INC.

13325 Darice Pkwy. Unit A
Strongsville OH 44149
Phone: 440-846-7800
Fax: 440-846-7899
Web: www.filterqueen.com

CEO: Daniel Duggan
CFO: –
HR: –
FYE: September 30
Type: Private

Looking for a product that will really clear the air? HMI Industries is up to the job. Under the Filterqueen brand name the company (aka Health-Mor) sells portable vacuum cleaners and air filtration systems. Using high-efficiency filters and cartridges HMI's systems are designed to rid homes of surface and airborne particles and allergens (dust smoke pollen mold spores pet dander) better than standard vacuum cleaners. Its products are sold through distributors in more than 40 countries. Chairman Kirk Foley acquired HMI for about $3 million in 2006 through 1670255 Ontario Inc. (dba Ace Distribution Ltd.) an entity he controls.

HMN FINANCIAL INC.

NMS: HMNF

1016 Civic Center Drive Northwest
Rochester, MN 55901
Phone: 507 535-1200
Fax: –
Web: www.hmnf.com

CEO: Bradley Krehbiel
CFO: Jon Eberle
HR: –
FYE: December 31
Type: Public

HMN Financial is the holding company for Home Federal Savings Bank which operates about a dozen branches in southern Minnesota and central Iowa. Serving individuals and local businesses the bank offers such deposit products as checking and savings accounts CDs and IRAs. Its lending activities include commercial mortgages (more than 30% of the company's loan portfolio) business loans (about 25%) residential mortgages and construction development and consumer loans. The bank provides financial planning investment management and investment products through its Osterud Insurance Agency subsidiary and Home Federal Investment Management.

	Annual Growth	12/16	12/17	12/18	12/19	12/20
Assets ($ mil.)	7.5%	682.0	722.7	712.3	777.6	909.6
Net income ($ mil.)	12.9%	6.4	4.4	8.2	7.8	10.3
Market value ($ mil.)	(0.5%)	83.5	91.1	93.6	100.2	82.0
Employees	(3.7%)	209	196	194	190	180

HNI CORP

NYS: HNI

600 East Second Street, P.O. Box 1109
Muscatine, IA 52761-0071
Phone: 563 272-7400
Fax: 563 272-7114
Web: www.hnicorp.com

CEO: Jeffrey Lorenger
CFO: Marshall Bridges
HR: –
FYE: January 02
Type: Public

HNI Corporation is a manufacturer of workplace furnishings and residential building products. Workplace furnishing products include seating storage tables and architectural products and are marketed under brands such as HON Allsteel and Maxon. The company sells to furniture dealers wholesalers and wholesale distributors as well as retailers. HNI's Hearth & Home Technologies participates in the hearth products industry manufactures and markets products under various brand names. The unit operates under the Fireside Hearth & Home banner. Residential Building products are sold through independent dealers and distributors as well as company-owned distribution centers installing distributors and retail outlets. Founded in 1944 HNI is North America's largest manufacturer and marketer of prefabricated fireplaces hearth stoves and related products.

	Annual Growth	12/16	12/17	12/18	12/19*	01/21
Sales ($ mil.)	(2.4%)	2,203.5	2,175.9	2,257.9	2,246.9	1,955.4
Net income ($ mil.)	(13.3%)	85.6	89.8	93.4	110.5	41.9
Market value ($ mil.)	(9.2%)	2,400.0	1,655.4	1,510.7	1,603.9	1,479.0
Employees	(3.9%)	9,400	9,600	8,900	8,500	7,700

*Fiscal year change

HNTB CORPORATION

715 Kirk Dr.
Kansas City MO 64105
Phone: 816-472-1201
Fax: 816-472-4060
Web: www.hntb.com

CEO: Robert Slimp
CFO: –
HR: –
FYE: December 31
Type: Private

HNTB knows the ABCs of A/E. The company is a pure design firm which derives most of its revenues from architecture engineering or environmental design operations. HNTB specializes in transportation infrastructure projects and government contracts. The firm is best-known for its highway and transit system design (its portfolio includes the New Jersey Turnpike) as well as airports (Chicago's Midway) and sports arenas (Invesco Field in Denver). The company operates some 60 locations across the US. The employee-owned HNTB (its name once stood for Howard Needles Tammen & Berendoff) traces its roots to 1914.

HO-CHUNK, INC.

818 ST AUGUSTINES DR
WINNEBAGO, NE 680715167
Phone: 402-878-4135
Fax: –
Web: www.hochunkinc.com

CEO: Lance Morgan
CFO: Dennis Johnson
HR: –
FYE: December 31
Type: Private

Ho-Chunk Inc. (HCI) the economic development corporation run by the Winnebago Tribe of Nebraska manages about 18 subsidiaries in the fields of communications construction distribution gasoline and convenience store retail (under the Heritage Express banner in Iowa and Nebraska) government contracting lodging (The WinnaVegas Inn) marketing used-vehicle sales and more. The profits from these businesses are in turn managed by the Ho-Chunk Community Development Corporation a not-for-profit organization that directs commercial growth and community infrastructure development for the tribe. "Ho-Chunk" is a modernized form of Hochungra the Winnebago tribe's traditional name.

	Annual Growth	12/04	12/05	12/06	12/07	12/09
Sales ($ mil.)	24.8%	–	63.6	113.0	121.4	154.3
Net income ($ mil.)	(27.7%)	–	16.4	0.7	1.1	4.5
Market value ($ mil.)	–	–	–	–	–	–
Employees	–	–	–	–	–	310

HOAG HOSPITAL FOUNDATION

500 Superior Ave. Ste. 350 — CEO: Karen Linden
Newport Beach CA 92663-4162 — CFO: –
Phone: 949-764-7217 — HR: –
Fax: 212-423-0758 — FYE: September 30
Web: www.mcny.org — Type: Private - Foundation

Hoag Hospital Foundation supports the Hoag Memorial Hospital Presbyterian by raising money for the hospital's operations medical research education and community outreach activities through more than 1400 volunteers. Its volunteers are organized into groups such as the 552 Club and Circle 1000. The groups host events like the Christmas Carol Ball and the Toshiba Senior Classic and encourage donors to make annual gifts raising about $20 million annually. The Hoag Hospital Foundation was formed in 1948.

HOAG MEMORIAL HOSPITAL PRESBYTERIAN

1 HOAG DR — CEO: Robert Braithwaite
NEWPORT BEACH, CA 926634162 — CFO: –
Phone: 949-764-4624 — HR: –
Fax: – — FYE: June 30
Web: www.hoag.org — Type: Private

Serving California's Orange County population Hoag Memorial Hospital Presbyterian boasts several hospitals and even more clinics to cater to area residents. The not-for-profit health care system is home to two acute care hospitals nine health centers nearly 15 urgent care centers and a network of more than 1700 physicians. Its hospitals include Hoag Hospital Irvine Hoag Orthopedic Institute and Hoag Hospital Newport Beach in Southern California. Combined these hospitals have some 600 beds and provide a comprehensive range of medical and surgical services with specialized expertise in a number of areas such as cancer heart and vascular neurosciences women's health and orthopedics.

	Annual Growth	09/12	09/13*	06/14	06/15	06/16
Sales ($ mil.)	4.4%	–	784.6	–	822.5	894.0
Net income ($ mil.)	(13.7%)	–	155.7	–	107.3	100.1
Market value ($ mil.)	–	–	–	–	–	–
Employees	–	–	–	–	–	3,800

*Fiscal year change

HOBBY LOBBY STORES, INC.

7707 SW 44TH ST — CEO: David Green
OKLAHOMA CITY, OK 731794899 — CFO: Jon Cargill
Phone: 405-745-1100 — HR: Sue Cleveland
Fax: – — FYE: December 31
Web: www.hobbylobby.com — Type: Private

Hobby Lobby is the largest privately owned arts-and-crafts retailer in the world. The craft-and-fabric retailer operates more than 900 stores in the US in more than 45 states selling arts and crafts supplies baskets beads candles frames home-decorating accessories and silk flowers. Hobby Lobby Hobby Lobby also maintains offices in Hong Kong Shenzhen and Yiwu China. In addition the company operates Mardel Christian and Education Supply which sells Christian educational and homeschooling products. CEO David Green who owns the company founded Hobby Lobby in 1972 and operates it according to biblical principles including closing shop on Sunday.

	Annual Growth	12/02	12/03	12/04	12/06	12/17
Sales ($ mil.)	27.5%	–	150.9	1,363.4	196.6	4,544.2
Net income ($ mil.)	13.7%	–	58.8	88.5	58.0	352.7
Market value ($ mil.)	–	–	–	–	–	–
Employees	–	–	–	–	–	23,000

HOFSTRA UNIVERSITY

100 HOFSTRA UNIVERSITY — CEO: –
HEMPSTEAD, NY 115494001 — CFO: Joshua Robinson
Phone: 516-463-6600 — HR: –
Fax: – — FYE: August 31
Web: www.hofstra.edu — Type: Private

Hofstra University is busy. Sponsoring some 500 cultural events each year the private nonsectarian four-year university has an annual enrollment of some 11000 full- and part-time students. To encourage the success of its students Hofstra maintains a low student-faculty ratio of 14 to 1. It offers more than 140 undergraduate program options and about 150 graduate program options in liberal arts and sciences; education health and human services; business; communications; and honors studies. It has a School of Law School of Engineering and Applied Science and Hofstra North Shore-LIJ School of Medicine. Hofstra University was founded in 1935 by trustees of the estate of William and Kate Hofstra.

	Annual Growth	08/08	08/09	08/10	08/11	08/12
Sales ($ mil.)	1.5%	–	–	370.4	390.0	381.7
Net income ($ mil.)	(16.4%)	–	–	35.6	50.0	24.9
Market value ($ mil.)	–	–	–	–	–	–
Employees	–	–	–	–	–	2,000

HOLIDAY BUILDERS, INC.

2293 W EAU GALLIE BLVD — CEO: Bruce Assam
MELBOURNE, FL 329353184 — CFO: Richard Fadil
Phone: 321-610-5156 — HR: –
Fax: – — FYE: December 31
Web: www.holidaybuilders.com — Type: Private

Holiday Builders is out to make buying a new home a vacation-like experience. The company a 100% employee-owned enterprise since 1999 builds single-family detached homes throughout Florida and in Alabama South Carolina and Texas. Since its inception the company has built more than 30000 homes sold primarily to first-time and value-conscious buyers. The company offers full homebuying services to its clients through HBI Title Company Holiday Builders Real Estate HB Designs and a partnership with Shelter Mortgage. Holiday Builders was founded in 1983.

	Annual Growth	12/03	12/04	12/05	12/06	12/07
Sales ($ mil.)	(41.8%)	–	–	691.8	699.2	234.1
Net income ($ mil.)	–	–	–	42.4	40.5	(26.2)
Market value ($ mil.)	–	–	–	–	–	–
Employees	–	–	–	–	–	101

HOLIDAY WHOLESALE, INC.

225 PIONEER DR — CEO: –
WISCONSIN DELLS, WI 539658397 — CFO: –
Phone: 608-254-8321 — HR: –
Fax: – — FYE: February 28
Web: www.holidaywholesale.com — Type: Private

Holiday Wholesale services most of south and central Wisconsin with confections tobacco products paper goods and food products. The company's customers are primarily convenience stores and other small businesses. Holiday Wholesale also offers consultation services including a demographic study of the customer's location estimate of foot traffic and evaluation of proposed floor plans. In addition to its wholesale business the company also sells a number of its products (at wholesale prices) to the general public through its Showroom Store location. The company was founded in 1951 when it began operating out of a one-car garage.

	Annual Growth	02/05	02/06	02/07	02/08	02/09
Sales ($ mil.)	4.3%	–	111.4	113.3	120.2	126.5
Net income ($ mil.)	(6.3%)	–	0.8	0.8	0.8	0.6
Market value ($ mil.)	–	–	–	–	–	–
Employees	–	–	–	–	–	250

HOLLAND COMMUNITY HOSPITAL AUXILIARY, INC.

602 MICHIGAN AVE
HOLLAND, MI 494234918
Phone: 616-748-9346
Fax: –
Web: www.hollandhospital.org

CEO: Dale Sowders
CFO: –
HR: –
FYE: March 31
Type: Private

Holland Hospital (formerly Holland Community Hospital) provides a comprehensive range of health services to residents of western Michigan's Lakeshore region. The 190-bed not-for-profit hospital provides a variety of medical care and health services including primary emergency diagnostic surgical rehabilitative and inpatient behavioral health care. Holland Hospital is home to centers of excellence in the treatment of sleep disorders cancer women's health issues and cardiovascular ailments. The hospital provides community health and wellness education programs and operates a regional community health clinic. Founded in 1917 Holland Hospital employs some 330 physicians across 14 medical specialties.

	Annual Growth	03/17	03/18	03/19	03/20	03/21
Sales ($ mil.)	1.5%	–	255.6	258.6	258.3	267.6
Net income ($ mil.)	38.4%	–	23.0	6.4	(22.8)	61.0
Market value ($ mil.)	–	–	–	–	–	–
Employees	–	–	–	–	–	1,500

HOLLINGSWORTH OIL COMPANY, INC.

1503 MEMORIAL BLVD STE B
SPRINGFIELD, TN 371723269
Phone: 615-242-8466
Fax: –
Web: www.suddenservice.business.site

CEO: –
CFO: –
HR: –
FYE: December 31
Type: Private

The Hollingsworth Companies meets companies' industrial-strength needs. The company develops and builds industrial parks and facilities in the southeastern US. It provides build-to-suit and finish-to-suit structures primarily on its SouthPoint Business Park pad-ready sites located in Alabama North Carolina Tennessee and Virginia. Developments typically range from 50000 sq. ft. to 500000 sq. ft. Hollingsworth also provides facility expansion and funding services. All of the company's SouthPoint properties are located in areas convenient to interstate highways and airport services. CEO and owner Joe Hollingsworth Jr. founded The Hollingsworth Companies in 1986.

	Annual Growth	12/13	12/14	12/16	12/17	12/18
Sales ($ mil.)	(4.1%)	–	547.4	380.9	408.2	463.5
Net income ($ mil.)	9.4%	–	0.9	1.3	2.5	1.3
Market value ($ mil.)	–	–	–	–	–	–
Employees	–	–	–	–	–	300

HOLLY ENERGY PARTNERS LP
NYS: HEP

2828 N. Harwood, Suite 1300
Dallas, TX 75201
Phone: 214 871-3555
Fax: –
Web: www.hollyenergy.com

CEO: Michael Jennings
CFO: John Harrison
HR: –
FYE: December 31
Type: Public

Holly Energy Partners pipes petroleum products and crude oil from refineries. It operates petroleum product and crude gathering pipelines (in New Mexico Oklahoma Texas and Utah) distribution terminals (in Arizona Idaho New Mexico Oklahoma Texas Utah and Washington) and refinery tankage in New Mexico and Utah. It operates 1330 miles of refined petroleum pipelines (340 miles leased) 960 miles of crude oil trunk lines 10 refined product terminals one jet fuel terminal and two truck-loading facilities. It also has three 65-mile pipelines that ship feedstocks and crude oil. HollyFrontier holds a 41% stake in Holly Energy Partners.

	Annual Growth	12/16	12/17	12/18	12/19	12/20
Sales ($ mil.)	5.5%	402.0	454.4	506.2	532.8	497.8
Net income ($ mil.)	3.7%	147.6	195.0	178.8	224.9	170.5
Market value ($ mil.)	(18.4%)	3,380.4	3,425.8	3,011.4	2,335.5	1,497.3
Employees	8.5%	249	269	283	299	345

HOLLYFRONTIER CORP
NYS: HFC

2828 N. Harwood, Suite 1300
Dallas, TX 75201
Phone: 214 871-3555
Fax: –
Web: www.hollyfrontier.com

CEO: Michael Jennings
CFO: Richard Voliva
HR: –
FYE: December 31
Type: Public

HollyFrontier refines crude oil to produce gasoline diesel and jet fuel as well as lubricants and asphalt selling its products to customers in the Southwest US the Rocky Mountains (extending into the Pacific Northwest) and Plains states. The company operates refineries and other production facilities in Kansas Oklahoma New Mexico Utah and Wyoming as well as Texas Arizona and Ontario Canada. HollyFrontier has 57% stake in Holly Energy Partners (HEP) which operates crude oil and petroleum product pipelines. The company sells lubricants and other specialty products through its Petro-Canada Lubricants and Red Giant Oil subsidiaries.

	Annual Growth	12/16	12/17	12/18	12/19	12/20
Sales ($ mil.)	1.5%	10,535.7	14,251.3	17,714.7	17,486.6	11,183.6
Net income ($ mil.)	–	(260.5)	805.4	1,098.0	772.4	(601.4)
Market value ($ mil.)	(5.8%)	5,320.7	8,318.8	8,302.6	8,236.0	4,198.4
Employees	9.8%	2,676	3,522	3,622	4,074	3,891

HOLLYWOOD MEDIA CORP
NMS: HOLL

301 East Yamato Road, Suite 2199
Boca Raton, FL 33431
Phone: 561 998-8000
Fax: –
Web: www.hollywoodmedia.com

CEO: Mitchell Rubenstein
CFO: Tammy G Hedge
HR: –
FYE: December 31
Type: Public

This company helps get people to the local multiplex. Hollywood Media Corp. owns more than a quarter of movie ticket seller MovieTickets.com. In addition it owns ad sales firm CinemasOnline which maintains websites for theaters in exchange for the right to sell ads on the sites; it also sells ads on plasma TVs in cinemas hotels car dealerships and other venues in the UK and Ireland. Its growing intellectual property division owns the rights to concepts by authors such as Tom Clancy and Isaac Asimov developing them into books (through 51%-owned Tekno Books) movies and TV shows software and other merchandise. In late 2010 it sold its theater ticketing division which accounted for most of its business.

	Annual Growth	12/08	12/09	12/10	12/11	12/12
Sales ($ mil.)	(73.1%)	117.1	103.4	4.0	3.8	0.6
Net income ($ mil.)	–	(16.9)	(5.6)	4.9	(6.9)	10.4
Market value ($ mil.)	7.8%	23.2	32.4	38.0	29.4	31.3
Employees	(41.7%)	130	122	36	24	15

HOLLYWOOD MEDIA CORP.
NASDAQ: HOLL

2255 Glades Rd. Ste. 221 A.
Boca Raton FL 33431
Phone: 561-998-8000
Fax: 561-998-2974
Web: www.hollywoodmedia.com

CEO: Mitchell Rubenstein
CFO: Tammy G Hedge
HR: –
FYE: December 31
Type: Public

This company knows advertising drives the movie biz. Hollywood Media Corp. owns ad sales firm UK Theatres Online which maintains plasma TVs in cinemas hotels theaters and other venues in the UK and Ireland in exchange for the right to sell ads on the screens. In addition the company's growing intellectual property division operates through 51%-owned Tekno Books and 50%-owned NetCo Partners. The business owns the rights to concepts by authors such as Tom Clancy and Isaac Asimov developing them into movies TV shows software and other merchandise. Hollywood Media also owns more than a quarter of MovieTickets.com. In 2010 it sold its theater ticketing division which accounted for most of its business.

HOLMES LUMBER & BUILDING CENTER INC.

6139 STATE ROUTE 39
MILLERSBURG, OH 446548830
Phone: 330-674-9060
Fax: –
Web: www.holmeslumber.com

CEO: –
CFO: –
HR: –
FYE: December 31
Type: Private

Try building a home — or any, other structure — without the products that Holmes Lumber supplies. The building, materials retailer, sells, lumber blocks bricks cabinets doors paneling ceiling tiles hardware and other building materials to professional contractors and consumers at three Holmes Lumber and Building Centers, in Hartville Millersburg and Sugarcreek, Ohio. Founded in 1952 as Holmes Door & Lumber Co. the business was acquired by, family-owned Carter Lumber of Kent Ohio, in 2004 adding Holmes' operations to its 200-plus stores in 10 states.

	Annual Growth	12/04	12/05	12/06	12/07	12/08
Sales ($ mil.)	5.1%	–	–	–	47.1	49.5
Net income ($ mil.)	–	–	–	–	0.4	(0.5)
Market value ($ mil.)	–	–	–	–	–	–
Employees	–	–	–	–	–	150

HOLMES REGIONAL MEDICAL CENTER, INC.

1350 HICKORY ST
MELBOURNE, FL 329013224
Phone: 321-434-7000
Fax: –
Web: www.hf.org

CEO: Steve Johnson
CFO: Robert C Galloway
HR: –
FYE: September 30
Type: Private

If you're a Great Space Coaster you might depend on Holmes Regional Medical Center in times of medical need. The general acute-care hospital which houses about 515 beds and provides comprehensive medical and surgical care serves residents of Brevard County on Florida's Space Coast. A member of not-for-profit health care system Health First Holmes Regional Medical Center offers specialty care in a number of areas including trauma oncology cardiology orthopedics pediatrics and women's health. It also operates an air ambulance service a stroke care center a full-service endoscopy unit and an outpatient diagnostic facility as well as advanced robotic surgery and joint replacement centers.

	Annual Growth	09/05	09/06	09/12	09/13	09/14
Sales ($ mil.)	132.9%	–	0.5	411.6	391.8	412.5
Net income ($ mil.)	288.3%	–	0.0	63.1	0.6	72.2
Market value ($ mil.)	–	–	–	–	–	–
Employees	–	–	–	–	–	2,778

HOLOGIC INC

250 Campus Drive
Marlborough, MA 01752
Phone: 508 263-2900
Fax: 781 280-0669
Web: www.hologic.com

NMS: HOLX
CEO: Stephen Macmillan
CFO: Karleen Oberton
HR: Elisabeth Hellmann
FYE: September 25
Type: Public

Hologic develops manufactures and supplies a variety of women's health products focused on five areas: breast health diagnostics medical aesthetics gynecological surgical health and skeletal health. Its offerings include the Aptima line of diagnostic tests the Dimensions 3D mammography platform the ThinPrep Pap test for cervical cancer screening the NovaSure System to treat excessive bleeding and the Fluoroscan Mini C-arm Imaging system used to guide doctors during orthopedic surgery. Hologic sells its products to hospitals and clinical labs worldwide. Overall the company generates the majority of its revenue in the US.

	Annual Growth	09/17	09/18	09/19	09/20	09/21
Sales ($ mil.)	16.5%	3,058.8	3,217.9	3,367.3	3,776.4	5,632.3
Net income ($ mil.)	25.5%	755.5	(111.3)	(203.6)	1,115.2	1,871.5
Market value ($ mil.)	20.2%	9,306.5	10,394.7	12,583.7	16,322.6	19,399.4
Employees	1.8%	6,233	6,252	6,478	5,814	6,705

HOLOPHANE

Granville Business Park Bldg. A 3825 Columbus Rd. SW
Granville OH 43023
Phone: 740-345-9631
Fax: 866-637-7069
Web: www.holophane.com

CEO: Vernon J Nagel
CFO: –
HR: –
FYE: August 31
Type: Business Segment

Holophane lights things up all around the world. A company and brand of Acuity Brands Holophane makes lighting fixtures and systems for industrial commercial and outdoor markets. Its largest product line industrial fixtures features lighting for vast indoor spaces (retail spaces convention centers factories warehouses etc.). Holophane also makes lighting products for large outdoor areas such as highway interchanges and it offers commercial and institutional lighting for schools and offices. Its ISD SuperGlass prismatic lighting technology allows reflectors to cast more light. Holophane was founded in 1895 in London and its founder helped start the Illuminating Engineering Society of North America.

HOLY CROSS HOSPITAL, INC.

4725 N FEDERAL HWY
FORT LAUDERDALE, FL 333084668
Phone: 954-771-8000
Fax: –
Web: www.holy-cross.com

CEO: Patrick Taylor
CFO: Linda Wilford
HR: –
FYE: June 30
Type: Private

Holy Cross Hospital's patients have more than just doctors on their side. Holy Cross is a Catholic community hospital serving the Ft. Lauderdale Florida area. The hospital has about 560 beds and offers inpatient and outpatient medical services along with a cancer treatment center heart and vascular center women's health center orthopedic unit and home health division as well as outpatient imaging centers. It also operates family health and specialist clinics in the region. Sponsored by the Sisters of Mercy Holy Cross Hospital is a part of Trinity Health.

	Annual Growth	06/13	06/14	06/15	06/18	06/20
Sales ($ mil.)	71.2%	–	20.9	24.5	470.4	526.0
Net income ($ mil.)	–	–	(0.9)	1.0	8.9	(19.7)
Market value ($ mil.)	–	–	–	–	–	–
Employees	–	–	–	–	–	2,300

HOLY SPIRIT HOSPITAL OF THE SISTERS OF CHRISTIAN CHARITY

503 N 21ST ST
CAMP HILL, PA 170112204
Phone: 717-763-2100
Fax: –
Web: www.pennstatehealth.org

CEO: Steve Massini
CFO: –
HR: –
FYE: June 30
Type: Private

Holy Spirit Health tends to the health of the incarnate. The Holy Spirit Health System (HSHS) provides cardiology women's health care pediatric care and other acute and emergency medical services to the residents of greater Harrisburg in south-central Pennsylvania. The flagship Holy Spirit Hospital has some 310 beds as well as a level III neonatal intensive care unit. The hospital also operates an adjoining cardiac treatment facility and it has a network of affiliated family practice urgent care surgical and specialty health clinics. HSHS was established in 1963 and is an affiliate of Geisinger Health System.

	Annual Growth	06/07	06/08	06/09	06/10	06/20
Sales ($ mil.)	(12.6%)	–	1,650.1	5.6	271.7	326.2
Net income ($ mil.)	–	–	0.0	0.0	11.4	30.1
Market value ($ mil.)	–	–	–	–	–	–
Employees	–	–	–	–	–	2,698

HOMASOTE CO.
NBB: HMTC

932 Lower Ferry Road, P.O. Box 7240
West Trenton, NJ 08628-0240
Phone: 609 883-3300
Fax: 609 530-1584
Web: www.homasote.com

CEO: Warren L Flicker
CFO: Ronald Fasano
HR: Paul Volkoff
FYE: December 31
Type: Public

Homasote Company sees green when it comes to building materials. It manufactures environmentally friendly fiberboard for use in residential and commercial construction. The fiberboard is made from recycled paper and contains no asbestos or formaldehyde. Applications include roof decking concrete forming paneling insulating sound proofing and industrial packaging purposes. Its Pak-Line division creates packaging materials for electronics. Homasote processes up to 250 tons of post-consumer paper daily helping to conserve 1.4 million trees and eliminate 65 million pounds of waste per year. Formed in 1909 Homasote is the oldest manufacturer of post-consumer recycled paper building and packaging products.

	Annual Growth	12/16	12/17	12/18	12/19	12/20
Sales ($ mil.)	(3.1%)	20.9	20.6	20.6	19.8	18.4
Net income ($ mil.)	22.9%	0.5	1.4	1.0	0.4	1.2
Market value ($ mil.)	27.8%	1.2	2.9	3.7	3.3	3.2
Employees						

HOME BANCORP INC
NMS: HBCP

503 Kaliste Saloom Road
Lafayette, LA 70508
Phone: 337 237-1960
Fax: 337 264-9280
Web: www.home24bank.com

CEO: John Bordelon
CFO: David Kirkley
HR: –
FYE: December 31
Type: Public

Making its home in Cajun Country Home Bancorp is the holding company for Home Bank a community bank which offers deposit and loan services to consumers and small to midsized businesses in southern Louisiana. Through about two dozen branches the bank offers standard savings and checking accounts as well as lending services such as mortgages consumer loans and credit cards. Its loan portfolio includes commercial real estate commercial and industrial loans as well as construction and land loans. Home Bancorp also operates about half a dozen bank branches in west Mississippi which were formerly part of Britton & Koontz Bank.

	Annual Growth	12/16	12/17	12/18	12/19	12/20
Assets ($ mil.)	13.6%	1,556.7	2,228.1	2,153.7	2,200.5	2,591.9
Net income ($ mil.)	11.5%	16.0	16.8	31.6	27.9	24.8
Market value ($ mil.)	(7.7%)	337.5	377.7	309.4	342.5	244.6
Employees	–	–	–	–	–	–

HOME BANCSHARES INC
NYS: HOMB

719 Harkrider, Suite 100
Conway, AR 72032
Phone: 501 339-2929
Fax: –
Web: www.homebancshares.com

CEO: John Allison
CFO: Brian Davis
HR: –
FYE: December 31
Type: Public

Home BancShares is the holding company for Centennial Bank which operates some 160 branches in Arkansas Florida and Alabama with an additional branch in each of New York City and Los Angeles (through which the company is building out a national lending platform). With $14.9 billion in assets the bank offers traditional services such as checking savings and money market accounts and CDs. About 60% of its lending portfolio is focused on commercial real estate loans — including non-farm and non-residential and construction and land development. The bank also writes residential mortgages and business and consumer loans. Through a subsidiary Home BancShares offers insurance services.

	Annual Growth	12/16	12/17	12/18	12/19	12/20
Assets ($ mil.)	13.7%	9,808.5	14,449.8	15,302.4	15,032.0	16,398.8
Net income ($ mil.)	4.9%	177.1	135.1	300.4	289.5	214.4
Market value ($ mil.)	(8.5%)	4,584.7	3,838.5	2,697.7	3,245.8	3,216.1
Employees	7.6%	1,503	1,744	1,815	1,920	2,018

HOME CITY FINANCIAL CORP
NBB: HCFL

2454 North Limestone Street
Springfield, OH 45503
Phone: 937 390-0470
Fax: –
Web: www.homecityfederal.com

CEO: –
CFO: –
HR: –
FYE: December 31
Type: Public

Home City Financial is where the heartland is. Home City is the holding company for Home City Federal Savings Bank of Springfield a two-branch thrift serving Clark County in southwestern Ohio. The bank offers standard deposit products including checking and savings accounts NOW accounts individual retirement accounts and certificates of deposit. Residential mortgages (nearly half of the company's loan portfolio) and commercial real estate loans (almost a quarter) are its primary lending focus; the bank also makes business consumer land construction and multifamily real estate loans. The company plans to go private through a reverse stock split.

	Annual Growth	12/12	12/13	12/14	12/15	12/16
Assets ($ mil.)	2.2%	142.9	143.6	151.6	153.2	156.0
Net income ($ mil.)	12.1%	1.0	1.1	1.3	1.3	1.6
Market value ($ mil.)	20.0%	8.1	12.8	13.0	14.4	16.8
Employees						

HOME DEPOT INC
NYS: HD

2455 Paces Ferry Road
Atlanta, GA 30339
Phone: 770 433-8211
Fax: 770 431-2707
Web: www.homedepot.com

CEO: Craig Menear
CFO: Richard Mcphail
HR: Timothy Hourigan
FYE: January 31
Type: Public

As the world's largest home improvement chain and one of the largest retailers in the US the company operates nearly 2300 stores in North America. It targets the do-it-yourself (DIY) and professional markets with its selection of up to 40000 items including lumber flooring plumbing supplies garden products tools paint and appliances. Home Depot also offers installation services for carpeting cabinetry and other products for its do-it-for-me (DIFM) customers. It conducts e-commerce operations through its websites (including thecompanystore.com) and mobile apps. More than 90% of its total revenue generates within the US.

	Annual Growth	01/17	01/18*	02/19	02/20*	01/21
Sales ($ mil.)	8.7%	94,595.0	100,904.0	108,203.0	110,225.0	132,110.0
Net income ($ mil.)	12.8%	7,957.0	8,630.0	11,121.0	11,242.0	12,866.0
Market value ($ mil.)	18.3%	148,981.4	223,186.7	198,566.5	245,663.7	291,673.1
Employees	5.6%	406,000	413,000	413,000	415,700	504,800

*Fiscal year change

HOME FEDERAL BANCORP INC.
NASDAQ: HOME

500 12th Ave. South
Nampa ID 83651
Phone: 208-468-5189
Fax: 208-468-5001
Web: www.myhomefed.com

CEO: –
CFO: –
HR: –
FYE: September 30
Type: Public

Home Federal Bancorp's location provides it with a treasure trove of opportunity. Its subsidiary Home Federal Bank (formerly Home Federal Savings and Loan Association of Nampa) serves the Treasure Valley region of southwestern Idaho which includes Ada Canyon Elmore and Gem counties (where nearly 40% of the state's population resides). Home Federal has 15 branches (three in Wal-Mart stores) and a loan center in Idaho as well as seven branches in central Oregon. It also offers banking through an ATM network and on the Internet. Its primary business is attracting deposits and using them to originate loans. In 2007 Home Federal converted from a mutual holding company to a stock ownership company.

HOME FINANCIAL BANCORP
NBB: HWEN

279 E. Morgan Street
Spencer, IN 47460
Phone: 317 383-4000
Fax: 317 383-4200
Web: www.owencom.com

CEO: –
CFO: Jeff Joyce
HR: –
FYE: June 30
Type: Public

When folks southwest of Indianapolis are ownin' they turn to Owen to help pay their bills. Home Financial Bancorp is the holding company for Owen Community Bank which operates two branches in Cloverdale and Spencer Indiana. Formed in 1911 the bank attracts deposits from Owen and Putnam counties by offering CDs IRAs and checking savings money market and NOW accounts. More than half of Owen Community's loan portfolio is comprised of one- to four-family residential mortgages; the bank also makes mobile home and land loans (nearly 30%) nonresidential mortgages (14%) and industrial commercial and consumer loans.

	Annual Growth	06/15	06/16	06/17	06/18	06/19
Assets ($ mil.)	2.6%	64.9	64.5	69.7	73.3	72.0
Net income ($ mil.)	15.4%	0.2	0.2	0.3	0.2	0.3
Market value ($ mil.)	3.9%	6.6	7.9	8.1	8.9	7.7
Employees						

HOME LOAN FINANCIAL CORP
NBB: HLFN

413 Main Street
Coshocton, OH 43812
Phone: 740 622-0444
Fax: 740 622-5389
Web: www.homeloanfinancialcorp.com

CEO: Robert Hamilton
CFO: Preston Bair
HR: –
FYE: June 30
Type: Public

Home Loan Financial is the holding company for Home Loan Savings which has about five branches in eastern Ohio's Coshocton and Knox counties. True to its name the bank primarily originates one- to four-family residential mortgages which account for more than two-thirds of its loan portfolio. It also issues commercial loans and mortgages construction loans and consumer loans. Founded in 1882 as The Home Building Savings and Loan the bank offers standard deposit products including checking and savings accounts CDs and money market accounts. Home Loan Financial completed a reverse stock split transaction in August 2005 allowing it to deregister from the Nasdaq.

	Annual Growth	06/17	06/18	06/19	06/20	06/21
Assets ($ mil.)	4.9%	208.6	205.4	214.7	244.7	252.6
Net income ($ mil.)	6.0%	3.0	3.2	3.7	3.6	3.8
Market value ($ mil.)	24.4%	19.0	19.0	49.0	41.6	45.5
Employees	–	–	–	–	–	–

HOME PROPERTIES INC
NYS: HME

850 Clinton Square
Rochester, NY 14604
Phone: 585 546-4900
Fax: –
Web: www.homeproperties.com

CEO: Edward Pettinella
CFO: David Gardner
HR: –
FYE: December 31
Type: Public

It's balconies and pools for the middle-income set. Home Properties invests in develops renovates and operates multifamily residential properties primarily in growth markets in the Northeast and Mid-Atlantic. The self-administered real estate investment trust (REIT) owns and manages a portfolio of about 125 properties with around 42000 individual units. Home Properties typically invests in communities for which it can provide a little TLC (such as improved landscaping interior upgrades and amenities such as swimming pools) allowing it to benefit from increased property values post-rehabilitation. The REIT also develops new properties usually on raw land adjacent to existing properties in its portfolio.

	Annual Growth	12/09	12/10	12/11	12/12	12/13
Sales ($ mil.)	7.1%	503.6	516.6	580.0	644.3	663.6
Net income ($ mil.)	42.0%	47.1	26.3	47.7	163.6	191.6
Market value ($ mil.)	3.0%	2,717.6	3,160.8	3,279.3	3,492.3	3,054.3
Employees	2.2%	1,100	1,100	1,200	1,200	1,200

HOMEAWAY, INC.
NMS: AWAY

1011 W. Fifth Street, Suite 300
Austin, TX 78703
Phone: 512 684-1100
Fax: –
Web: www.homeaway.com

CEO: Brian H Sharples
CFO: Lynn Atchison
HR: –
FYE: December 31
Type: Public

There's no place like a home away from home for fun or functionality. HomeAway boasts nearly 1 million paid listings for vacation rental properties across 190 countries worldwide and helps property owners rent out their shack condo or chateau. Its HomeAway.com website is free to travelers who are typically affluent and is searchable by destination. Its listings include information on weekly rates availability and amenities as well as photographs descriptions and contact information. HomeAway also maintains 30 other travel-related websites. Founded in 2005 as WVR Group the company changed its name in 2006 to HomeAway launched its flagship website that year and went public in mid-2011.

	Annual Growth	12/09	12/10	12/11	12/12	12/13
Sales ($ mil.)	30.3%	120.2	167.9	230.2	280.4	346.5
Net income ($ mil.)	23.2%	7.7	16.9	6.2	15.0	17.7
Market value ($ mil.)	32.6%	–	–	2,147.4	2,031.9	3,775.7
Employees	22.3%	–	842	935	1,228	1,542

HOMEFED CORP.
NBB: HOFD

1903 Wright Place, Suite 220
Carlsbad, CA 92008
Phone: 760 918-8200
Fax: –
Web: www.homefedcorporation.com

CEO: –
CFO: –
HR: –
FYE: December 31
Type: Public

HomeFed won't provide you with room and board but it can help you get a home. The company earns its keep by investing in and developing residential real estate. Through subsidiaries HomeFed is developing a master-planned community in San Diego County called San Elijo Hills which contains approximately 3500 residences as well as commercial space and a town center. In 2014 Leucadia Financial increased its ownership in HomeFed from 31% to 65%. It also enhanced HomeFed's geographic presence by adding land and commercial real estate assets in New York Florida Maine and South Carolina.

	Annual Growth	12/13	12/14	12/15	12/16	12/17
Sales ($ mil.)	8.6%	56.6	59.5	69.5	81.0	78.6
Net income ($ mil.)	1.3%	11.3	3.9	5.8	36.7	11.9
Market value ($ mil.)	9.3%	566.3	696.3	526.9	696.3	808.5
Employees	21.6%	16	27	31	33	35

HOMESTREET INC
NMS: HMST

601 Union Street, Suite 2000
Seattle, WA 98101
Phone: 206 623-3050
Fax: –
Web: www.homestreet.com

CEO: Mark Mason
CFO: John Michel
HR: –
FYE: December 31
Type: Public

HomeStreet aims to offer home and business mortgages to all in the West Coast and Hawaii. HomeStreet principally engaged in commercial banking consumer banking and real estate lending including commercial real estate and single family mortgage lending. In addition to the banking and lending operations of its wholly owned subsidiaries HomeStreet also sells insurance products and services for consumer clients under the name HomeStreet Insurance. Founded in 1921 HomeStreet has about $6.8 billion assets.

	Annual Growth	12/16	12/17	12/18	12/19	12/20
Assets ($ mil.)	3.8%	6,243.7	6,742.0	7,042.2	6,812.4	7,237.1
Net income ($ mil.)	8.3%	58.2	68.9	40.0	17.5	80.0
Market value ($ mil.)	1.7%	688.8	631.0	462.7	741.9	735.6
Employees	(20.3%)	2,552	2,419	2,036	1,071	1,030

HONDA NORTH AMERICA INC.

700 Van Ness Ave.
Torrance CA 90501-1486
Phone: 310-783-2000
Fax: 212-818-8282
Web: www.itochu.com

CEO: –
CFO: –
HR: –
FYE: March 31
Type: Subsidiary

Its cars might not be as American as apple pie but Honda North America keeps the US appetite for Hondas sated. The subsidiary of Honda Motor coordinates the operations in North America that manufacture market and distribute Accord Civic and Acura cars as well as Gold Wing Shadow and Valkyrie motorcycles. Of the 15 models made Honda North America's best-selling cars include the Odyssey minivan and the CR-V SUV. Honda North America also markets hybrid versions of several of its sedans. New launches have included the Crosstour and Acura ZDX. Honda also makes jet and marine engines and power equipment. North America is Honda Motor's largest market representing 45% of the carmaker's sales.

HONEYWELL INTERNATIONAL INC   NMS: HON

855 South Mint Street
Charlotte, NC 28202
Phone: 704 627-6200
Fax: 973 455-4807
Web: www.honeywell.com

CEO: Que Thanh Dallara
CFO: Gregory Lewis
HR: –
FYE: December 31
Type: Public

More than a century old the company is a diverse industrial conglomerate its four segments making and selling products from aircraft engines flight safety and landing systems to smart controls for commercial buildings to personal safety products such as gas masks and footwear. The major products and services including Honeywell Forge solutions supported by Honeywell Connected Enterprise. The company does business worldwide and generates more than half its sales in the US. The company was founded in 1885 by the inventor Albert Butz.

	Annual Growth	12/17	12/18	12/19	12/20	12/21
Sales ($ mil.)	(4.0%)	40,534.0	41,802.0	36,709.0	32,637.0	34,392.0
Net income ($ mil.)	35.3%	1,655.0	6,765.0	6,143.0	4,779.0	5,542.0
Market value ($ mil.)	8.0%	105,020.9	90,475.8	121,209.6	145,657.0	142,787.6
Employees	(6.8%)	131,000	114,000	113,000	103,000	99,000

HOOKER FURNISHINGS CORP   NMS: HOFT

440 East Commonwealth Boulevard
Martinsville, VA 24112
Phone: 276 632-2133
Fax: –
Web: www.hookerfurniture.com

CEO: Jeremy Hoff
CFO: Paul Huckfeldt
HR: –
FYE: January 31
Type: Public

Hooker Furniture offers hardwood and metal furniture including wall units home office items home theater cabinets living and dining room tables bedroom furniture and accent pieces. It sells furniture under the Samuel Lawrence Furniture by Home Meridian label. Hooker Furniture's popular Bradington-Young line includes residential upholstered upscale motion and stationary leather furniture. The furniture manufacturer's Sam Moore unit makes high-end chairs. Hooker Furniture also offers home furnishings centered around an eclectic mix of unique pieces and materials that offer a fresh take on home fashion focused on e-commerce customers through Accentrics Home. Hooker Furniture was founded in 1924.

	Annual Growth	01/17	01/18*	02/19	02/20*	01/21
Sales ($ mil.)	(1.6%)	577.2	620.6	683.5	610.8	540.1
Net income ($ mil.)	–	25.3	28.3	39.9	17.1	(10.4)
Market value ($ mil.)	(2.9%)	403.6	470.2	347.1	292.9	358.2
Employees	4.8%	952	1,216	1,263	1,251	1,148

*Fiscal year change

HOOPER HOLMES INC   NBB: HPHW Q

560 N. Rogers Road
Olathe, KS 66062
Phone: 913 764-1045
Fax: –
Web: www.hooperholmes.com

CEO: –
CFO: Mark Clermont
HR: –
FYE: December 31
Type: Public

Hooper Holmes helps companies manage risk. Not financial risk but threats to employees' health. The company's Health and Wellness segment provides on-site health and wellness exams risk assessment and management and wellness coaching for companies that manage healthcare for corporate and government clients. Its Heritage Labs performs lab tests on samples collected by its own and third-party exam providers. The Hooper Holmes Services segment performs phone interviews to collect medical histories retrieves medical records and underwriting services on behalf of insurance companies. In 2017 Hooper Holmes acquired Provant Health Solutions which provides workplace well-being services.

	Annual Growth	12/13	12/14	12/15	12/16	12/17
Sales ($ mil.)	3.4%	49.2	28.5	32.1	34.3	56.2
Net income ($ mil.)	–	(11.3)	(8.5)	(10.9)	(10.3)	(16.0)
Market value ($ mil.)	(5.8%)	14.2	13.8	1.6	22.1	11.2
Employees	2.8%	300	145	200	200	335

HOOSIER ENERGY RURAL ELECTRIC COOPERATIVE INC

2501 S COOPERATIVE WAY
BLOOMINGTON, IN 474035175
Phone: 812-876-2021
Fax: –
Web: www.hoosierenergy.com

CEO: J Steven Smith
CFO: –
HR: –
FYE: December 31
Type: Private

Who's yer daddy? In terms of providing electricity for many Indianans (and some residents of Illinois) that would be Hoosier Energy Rural Electric Cooperative which provides wholesale electric power to 18 member distribution cooperatives in 59 central and southern Indiana counties and 11 counties in southeastern Illinois. These electric cooperatives serve 300000 consumers (650000 residents businesses industries and farms) in a 18000 sq. ml. service area. Hoosier Energy operates six power plants and a 1720-mile transmission system and maintains the Tuttle Creek Reservoir in Southwest Indiana. Hoosier Energy is part of the Touchstone Energy network of electric cooperatives.

	Annual Growth	12/07	12/08	12/09	12/11	12/12
Sales ($ mil.)	4.1%	–	–	575.0	649.6	647.9
Net income ($ mil.)	18.9%	–	–	16.6	30.3	27.9
Market value ($ mil.)	–	–	–	–	–	–
Employees	–	–	–	–	–	475

HOOVER'S INC.

5800 Airport Blvd.
Austin TX 78752-3812
Phone: 512-374-4500
Fax: 512-374-4501
Web: www.hoovers.com

CEO: –
CFO: –
HR: –
FYE: December 31
Type: Subsidiary

If you're reading this sentence you know where to go for company data. Hoover's the publisher of this profile offers proprietary business information through the Internet (Hoover's Online) and through integration with clients' existing enterprise infrastructure (Hoover's API). Its database of information includes about 85 million corporations and other entities and 100 million people and its First Research product covers some 900 industries. Most revenues come from selling subscriptions to a target audience of marketing sales and business development professionals. Hoover's also offers mobile apps (Hoover's Connect+) and publishes a business blog (Bizmology). It is a subsidiary of Dun & Bradstreet (D&B).

HOPFED BANCORP, INC.   NMS: HFBC

4155 Lafayette Road
Hopkinsville, KY 42240
Phone: 270 885-1171
Fax: –
Web: www.bankwithheritage.com

CEO: –
CFO: –
HR: –
FYE: December 31
Type: Public

HopFed Bancorp is the holding company for Heritage Bank which started operations in 1879 as a building and loan association. The bank has about a dozen branches in southwestern Kentucky with its market area extending into northwestern Tennessee. It offers standard products like checking savings money market and NOW accounts as well as CDs IRAs property/casualty insurance and annuities. One- to four-family residential mortgages account for about 40% of its loan portfolio. To a lesser extent Heritage Bank also writes multifamily residential construction commercial and consumer loans. In January 2019 HopFed agreed to be acquired by Indiana-based holding company First Financial.

	Annual Growth	12/13	12/14	12/15	12/16	12/17
Assets ($ mil.)	(1.5%)	973.6	935.8	903.2	891.5	917.5
Net income ($ mil.)	(3.2%)	3.8	2.2	2.4	2.9	3.3
Market value ($ mil.)	5.5%	75.6	84.4	79.7	89.3	93.6
Employees	(2.7%)	256	262	243	236	229

HOPTO INC   NBB: HPTO

189 North Main Street, Suite 102
Concord, NH 03301
Phone: 408 688-2674
Fax: –
Web: www.hopto.com

CEO: –
CFO: –
HR: –
FYE: December 31
Type: Public

GraphOn keeps its thin clients on a diet. The company provides business connectivity software that delivers applications to PCs and workstations from a host computer. The company's products enable clients to relocate desktop software to centralized servers and deploy and manage applications when needed thus conserving computing resources. GraphOn's software can be used to provide access to applications through Linux UNIX and Windows platforms. The company serves clients in a variety of industries including telecommunications software development manufacturing financial services and electronics.

	Annual Growth	12/16	12/17	12/18	12/19	12/20
Sales ($ mil.)	(2.3%)	4.0	3.9	3.2	3.5	3.6
Net income ($ mil.)	–	(1.9)	0.6	(0.0)	0.6	0.7
Market value ($ mil.)	88.8%	0.7	2.6	4.3	7.5	8.9
Employees	(6.0%)	16	14	14	12	12

HORACE MANN EDUCATORS CORP.   NYS: HMN

1 Horace Mann Plaza
Springfield, IL 62715-0001
Phone: 217 789-2500
Fax: –
Web: www.horacemann.com

CEO: Marita Zuraitis
CFO: Bret Conklin
HR: –
FYE: December 31
Type: Public

Horace Mann Educators is an insurance holding company that primarily serves K-12 school teachers administrators and other public-school employees throughout the US. Through its operating subsidiaries the company offers Property and Casualty (majority of revenue) Supplemental Retirement and Life insurance. Horace Mann employs some 1000 agents many of whom are former teachers themselves. Writing business in all 50 states and the US Virgin Islands and the District of Columbia the company derives about 35% of its direct premiums and contract deposits from top five states ? California Texas North Carolina Minnesota and Pennsylvania.

	Annual Growth	12/16	12/17	12/18	12/19	12/20
Assets ($ mil.)	6.2%	10,576.8	11,198.3	11,031.9	12,478.7	13,471.8
Net income ($ mil.)	12.3%	83.8	169.5	18.3	184.4	133.3
Market value ($ mil.)	(0.4%)	1,772.5	1,826.4	1,551.0	1,808.1	1,741.1
Employees	(7.8%)	2,061	1,496	1,495	1,538	1,490

HORIZON BANCORP INC   NMS: HBNC

515 Franklin Street
Michigan City, IN 46360
Phone: 219 879-0211
Fax: –
Web: www.horizonbank.com

CEO: Craig Dwight
CFO: Mark Secor
HR: –
FYE: December 31
Type: Public

For those in Indiana and Michigan Horizon Bancorp stretches as far as the eye can see. The company is the holding company for Horizon Bank (and its Heartland Community Bank division) which provides checking and savings accounts IRAs CDs and credit cards to customers through more than 50 branches in north and central Indiana and southwest and central Michigan. Commercial financial and agricultural loans make up the largest segment of its loan portfolio which also includes mortgage warehouse loans (loans earmarked for sale into the secondary market) consumer loans and residential mortgages. Through subsidiaries the bank offers trust and investment management services; life health and property/casualty insurance; and annuities.

	Annual Growth	12/16	12/17	12/18	12/19	12/20
Assets ($ mil.)	17.0%	3,141.2	3,964.3	4,246.7	5,246.8	5,886.6
Net income ($ mil.)	30.1%	23.9	33.1	53.1	66.5	68.5
Market value ($ mil.)	(13.2%)	1,228.7	1,219.9	692.4	833.7	695.9
Employees	5.2%	665	701	716	839	815

HORIZON HEALTH CORPORATION

2941 S. Lake Vista Dr.
Lewisville TX 75067-6011
Phone: 972-420-8200
Fax: 972-420-8252
Web: www.horizonhealth.com

CEO: –
CFO: Jack E Polson
HR: –
FYE: August 31
Type: Subsidiary

Horizon Health sees hope on the horizon for those in need of psychiatric care and physical rehabilitation. The firm provides contract psychiatric and rehabilitation management services to hospitals across the country running its clients' inpatient and outpatient mental health programs and rehab departments. Horizon also offers contract management to handle licensing and accreditation for its client hospitals' clinical programs; it also develops community awareness programs and hires most non-nursing staff. The group offers some specialty psychiatric services including geropsychiatry for people aged 65-years and older and adolescent psychiatric care. Horizon Health is owned by Universal Health Services (UHS).

HORIZON LINES INC   NBB: HRZL

4064 Colony Road, Suite 200
Charlotte, NC 28211
Phone: 704 973-7000
Fax: –
Web: www.horizonlines.com

CEO: Steven L Rubin
CFO: Michael T Avara
HR: –
FYE: December 22
Type: Public

Horizon Lines rides the waves to connect the mainland US with its far-flung states and territories. The container shipping company transports cargo such as building materials consumer goods and foodstuffs to and from the continental US and Alaska Hawaii and Puerto Rico. Horizon Lines maintains a fleet of about 15 containerships and 30000 cargo containers; it also operates five port terminals. The majority of its revenue comes from operations subject to the Jones Act which restricts marine shipping between US ports to companies with vessels that are US built/owned/crewed.

	Annual Growth	12/09	12/10	12/11	12/12	12/13
Sales ($ mil.)	(2.8%)	1,158.5	1,162.5	1,026.2	1,073.7	1,033.3
Net income ($ mil.)	–	(31.3)	(58.0)	(229.4)	(94.7)	(31.9)
Market value ($ mil.)	(34.5%)	210.8	171.9	182.8	60.3	38.9
Employees	(3.8%)	1,895	1,890	1,635	1,599	1,621

HORIZON PHARMA INC
NMS: HZNP

520 Lake Cook Road, Suite 520
Deerfield, IL 60015
Phone: 224 383-3000
Fax: –
Web: www.horizonpharma.com

CEO: Timothy P Walbert
CFO: Paul W Hoelscher
HR: Ginger Setzer
FYE: December 31
Type: Public

Horizon Pharma sees commercial drug success in its future. The biopharmaceutical company develops medicines for arthritis pain and inflammatory diseases through its two operating subsidiaries Horizon Pharma USA and Horizon Pharma AG. Its DUEXIS pill combines two existing drugs to treat mild to moderate pain from rheumatoid arthritis. Its LODOTRA is a low form of prednisone formulated to reduce morning stiffness associated with rheumatoid arthritis. DUEXIS has received approval for sale in the US while LODOTRA is approved for sale and marketed in Europe. Horizon Pharma also has a pipeline of earlier stage candidates to treat pain-related diseases and chronic inflammation. The company went public in 2011.

	Annual Growth	12/08	12/09	12/10	12/11	12/12
Sales ($ mil.)	187.4%	–	–	2.4	6.9	19.6
Net income ($ mil.)	–	(27.9)	(20.5)	(27.1)	(113.3)	(87.8)
Market value ($ mil.)	(41.8%)	–	–	–	246.9	143.8
Employees	151.7%	–	–	39	164	247

HORMEL FOODS CORP.
NYS: HRL

1 Hormel Place
Austin, MN 55912
Phone: 507 437-5611
Fax: 507 437-5489
Web: www.hormel.com

CEO: James P Snee
CFO: James N Sheehan
HR: –
FYE: October 31
Type: Public

Hormel Foods is a global branded food company bringing some of the most trusted and iconic brands to tables across the globe. It produces a slew of refrigerated processed meats and deli items ethnic entrees and frozen foods sold under the flagship Hormel brand as well as Don Miguel and MegaMex and Lloyd's (barbeque). Food service offerings include Do ±a Maria Cafe´ H Austin Blues Fast 'N Easy and Bread Ready pre-sliced meats. Hormel is also a major US turkey and pork processor churning out Jennie-O turkey Cure 81 hams and Always Tender pork. Vast majority of its total sales were from domestic operations.

	Annual Growth	10/17	10/18	10/19	10/20	10/21
Sales ($ mil.)	5.6%	9,167.5	9,545.7	9,497.3	9,608.5	11,386.2
Net income ($ mil.)	1.8%	846.7	1,012.1	978.8	908.1	908.8
Market value ($ mil.)	8.6%	16,478.5	22,331.1	22,005.7	26,909.1	22,954.9
Employees	(0.2%)	20,200	20,100	18,800	19,100	20,000

HORNBECK OFFSHORE SERVICES INC
NBB: HOSS

103 Northpark Boulevard, Suite 300
Covington, LA 70433
Phone: 985 727-2000
Fax: –
Web: www.hornbeckoffshore.com

CEO: Todd M Hornbeck
CFO: James O Harp Jr
HR: –
FYE: December 31
Type: Public

At the beck and call of oil companies Hornbeck Offshore Services provides marine transportation of oil field equipment and supplies and petroleum products. The company operates offshore supply vessels (OSVs) that support offshore oil and gas drilling and production in the deepwater regions of the Gulf of Mexico. Its fleet of about 63 OSVs and five multi-purpose support vessels (MPSVs) transports cargo such as pipe and drilling mud as well as rig crew members. In addition Hornbeck has seven additional ultra high-spec upstream vessels under construction for delivery in 2016.

	Annual Growth	12/14	12/15	12/16	12/17	12/18
Sales ($ mil.)	(23.9%)	634.8	476.1	224.3	191.4	212.4
Net income ($ mil.)	–	88.5	66.8	(63.8)	27.4	(119.1)
Market value ($ mil.)	(51.0%)	941.4	374.7	272.2	117.3	54.3
Employees	(11.4%)	1,641	1,233	797	831	1,009

HORNBLOWER YACHTS, LLC

ON THE EMBARCADERO PIER 3 ST PIER
SAN FRANCISCO, CA 94111
Phone: 415-788-8866
Fax: –
Web: www.hornblower.com

CEO: Terry Macrae
CFO: –
HR: Lisa Medulun
FYE: December 31
Type: Private

Hornblower Cruises and Events provides sightseeing dining and wedding cruises. The company has ayachts sailing from about 20 California ports including Berkeley San Diego Newport Beach Marina del Rey and San Francisco. Regularly scheduled tours include brunch dinner date night and corporate events. Hornblower also provides cruises for private events including corporate functions. Subsidiaries Alcatraz Cruises and Statue Cruises run a ferry service to Alcatraz in California and the Statue of Liberty National Monument and Ellis Island in New York through a deal with the National Park Service. CEO Terry MacRae founded Hornblower in 1980 with two yachts.

	Annual Growth	12/02	12/03	12/04	12/06	12/09
Sales ($ mil.)	29.5%	–	–	32.2	35.2	117.6
Net income ($ mil.)	9.9%	–	–	7.5	2.0	11.9
Market value ($ mil.)	–	–	–	–	–	–
Employees	–	–	–	–	–	2,404

HORNE INTERNATIONAL INC
NBB: HNIN

3975 University Drive, Suite 100
Fairfax, VA 22030
Phone: 703 641-1100
Fax: –
Web: www.horne.com

CEO: Dallas Evans
CFO: John E Donahue
HR: –
FYE: December 31
Type: Public

At the nexus where government agencies national security and environmental sustainability meet you'll find Horne International. Through its primary operating subsidiary Horne Engineering Services the company offers military base and homeland security missile defense ecosystems management and restoration and business process engineering services. It also offers public outreach services including the organization of public meetings and drafting Congressional testimony. Not surprisingly the US government's departments of Homeland Security Defense and Transportation are Horne's primary customers. Horne which has struggled in the recession owes nearly 85% of sales to its three largest customers.

	Annual Growth	12/08	12/09	12/10	12/11	12/12
Sales ($ mil.)	(4.0%)	4.9	4.7	3.4	5.7	4.1
Net income ($ mil.)	–	(6.1)	(0.3)	(1.0)	(0.1)	(1.6)
Market value ($ mil.)	(8.1%)	1.4	4.3	7.1	6.2	1.0
Employees	–	–	–	–	–	–

HORNE INTERNATIONAL INC.
OTC: HNIN

3975 University Dr. Ste. 100
Fairfax VA 22030
Phone: 703-641-1100
Fax: 703-641-0440
Web: www.horne.com

CEO: Dallas Evans
CFO: John E Donahue
HR: –
FYE: December 31
Type: Public

At the nexus where government agencies national security and environmental sustainability meet you'll find Horne International. Through its primary operating subsidiary Horne Engineering Services the company offers military base and homeland security missile defense ecosystems management and restoration and business process engineering services. It also offers public outreach services including the organization of public meetings and drafting Congressional testimony. Not surprisingly the US government's departments of Homeland Security Defense and Transportation are Horne's primary customers. Horne which has struggled in the recession owes nearly 85% of sales to its three largest customers.

HORRY TELEPHONE COOPERATIVE, INC.

3480 HIGHWAY 701 N
CONWAY, SC 295265702
Phone: 843-365-2151
Fax: –
Web: www.htcinc.net

CEO: Mike Hagg
CFO: Duane Carlton Lewis Jr
HR: –
FYE: December 31
Type: Private

Horry Telephone Cooperative (HTC) is the incumbent local exchange carrier (ILEC) serving rural Horry County in South Carolina (population: about 270000). HTC offers local and long-distance voice service Internet access cable TV home security service and mobile phone service (through AT&T Mobility). It also offers business services such as remote recovery LAN and WAN design and firewall and network security and provides bundled telecommunications services to residential and business customers via its Bluewave fiber-to-the-home business. Membership in the cooperative is open to any customer who receives at least one of HTC's primary services.

	Annual Growth	12/05	12/06	12/07	12/08	12/09
Sales ($ mil.)	–	–	–	(1,361.9)	162.9	172.8
Net income ($ mil.)	10020.7%	–	–	0.0	3.7	4.3
Market value ($ mil.)	–	–	–	–	–	–
Employees	–	–	–	–	–	690

HORSEHEAD HOLDING CORP

4955 Steubenville Pike, Suite 405
Pittsburgh, PA 15205
Phone: 724 774-1020
Fax: –
Web: www.horsehead.net

NBB: ZINC Q

CEO: Michael Griffin
CFO: Andrew Repine
HR: –
FYE: December 31
Type: Public

Bearing out the adage that one person's trash is another's treasure through Horsehead Corporation Horsehead Zinc Powders INMETCO and Zochem Horsehead Holdings turns zinc-containing dust and discarded batteries into value-added zinc and nickel-based products. Key raw materials for the company include dust from the electric-arc furnaces (EAF) used at steel minimills and residue from the galvanizing of metals. Besides zinc metal (used in galvanizing and alloying) Horsehead's products include zinc oxide (used in the agricultural chemical and pharmaceutical industries) zinc dust (used in corrosion-resistant coatings) and nickel-based metals (used as a feedstock to produce stainless and specialty steels).

	Annual Growth	12/10	12/11	12/12	12/13	12/14
Sales ($ mil.)	4.4%	382.4	451.2	435.7	441.9	453.9
Net income ($ mil.)	–	24.8	21.5	(30.4)	(14.0)	(15.5)
Market value ($ mil.)	5.0%	661.4	457.0	517.8	822.2	802.9
Employees	(9.0%)	1,089	1,064	1,062	1,074	747

HORTON (DR) INC

1341 Horton Circle
Arlington, TX 76011
Phone: 817 390-8200
Fax: –
Web: www.drhorton.com

NYS: DHI

CEO: David Auld
CFO: Bill Wheat
HR: –
FYE: September 30
Type: Public

The largest US homebuilder by volume D.R. Horton constructs single-family homes that range in size from 1000 sq. ft. to more than 4000 sq. ft. and sell for an average price range of about $150000 to more than $1000000 under the D.R. Horton America's Builder Emerald Homes Express Homes and Freedom Homes. D.R. Horton is active in roughly 100 markets in about 30 states. Through its mortgage title and insurance subsidiaries D.R. Horton provides mortgage financing title services and insurance services for its homebuyers. The company also constructs and sells both single-family and multi-family rental properties and is the majority owner of Forestar Group a national residential lot development company.

	Annual Growth	09/17	09/18	09/19	09/20	09/21
Sales ($ mil.)	18.5%	14,091.0	16,068.0	17,592.9	20,311.1	27,774.2
Net income ($ mil.)	41.6%	1,038.4	1,460.3	1,618.5	2,373.7	4,175.8
Market value ($ mil.)	20.4%	14,215.7	15,016.7	18,765.6	26,925.5	29,894.7
Employees	11.1%	7,735	8,437	8,916	9,716	11,788

HOSPICE OF MICHIGAN INC.

400 MACK AVE
DETROIT, MI 482012136
Phone: 313-578-5000
Fax: –
Web: www.hom.org

CEO: Dottie Deremo
CFO: Robert Cahill
HR: –
FYE: December 31
Type: Private

When it comes to hospice care experience counts. As the largest hospice provider in Michigan Hospice of Michigan (HOM) has plenty of it. HOM provides specialized health care to patients with terminal illnesses. The organization's nurses home health aids and volunteers help patients manage pain and other symptoms provide spiritual and emotional support and offer grief counseling to family members. The organization works with about 1000 patients on any given day at some 20 locations throughout Michigan's lower peninsula. Its services are offered in patient homes as well as in hospitals and nursing homes. Hospice of Michigan was created in 1994 when several smaller hospice programs joined forces.

	Annual Growth	12/03	12/04	12/05	12/06	12/13
Sales ($ mil.)	(28.7%)	–	1,393.6	0.0	59.0	66.0
Net income ($ mil.)	–	–	–	0.0	2.5	2.3
Market value ($ mil.)	–	–	–	–	–	–
Employees	–	–	–	–	–	500

HOSPIRA INC

275 North Field Drive
Lake Forest, IL 60045
Phone: 224 212-2000
Fax: –
Web: www.hospira.com

NYS: HSP

CEO: F Michael Ball
CFO: Thomas E Werner
HR: –
FYE: December 31
Type: Public

Hospira helps hospitals heal the hurting. The firm makes specialty injectable pharmaceuticals (primarily generics) including cardiovascular anesthesia oncology and anti-infective therapies as well as the related drug delivery systems such as prefilled syringes. Its more complicated medication delivery systems include electronic drug pumps infusion therapy devices and related medication management software. In addition Hospira makes IV nutritional solutions and provides contract manufacturing services. Key customers include hospitals alternate site facilities (such as nursing and outpatient surgical care facilities) wholesalers and other drug manufacturers. Pfizer plans to buy Hospira for some $17 billion.

	Annual Growth	12/10	12/11	12/12	12/13	12/14
Sales ($ mil.)	3.3%	3,917.2	4,057.1	4,092.1	4,002.8	4,463.7
Net income ($ mil.)	(1.7%)	357.2	(9.4)	44.2	(8.3)	333.2
Market value ($ mil.)	2.4%	9,489.6	5,175.0	5,323.3	7,034.1	10,437.0
Employees	7.9%	14,000	15,000	16,000	17,000	19,000

HOSPITAL AUTHORITY OF VALDOSTA AND LOWNDES COUNTY, GEORGIA

2501 N PATTERSON ST
VALDOSTA, GA 316021735
Phone: 229-333-1000
Fax: –
Web: www.sgmc.org

CEO: Ronald E Dean
CFO: –
HR: –
FYE: September 30
Type: Private

Hospital Authority of Valdosta and Lowndes County Georgia oversees South Georgia Medical Center (SGMC) a 335-bed regional hospital serving southern Georgia and northern Florida. The hospital offers a range of services focusing on such specialties as diabetes management pulmonary care pediatrics and women's health. SGMC's Pearlman Cancer Center is devoted to a holistic approach to cancer care. The medical center also operates a specialized wound healing center and orthopedic and spine centers. The public hospital was founded as Pineview General Hospital in 1955. Its governing board is appointed by the local city council and county commissioners.

	Annual Growth	09/14	09/15	09/16	09/17	09/18
Sales ($ mil.)	1.6%	–	310.4	305.5	314.7	325.8
Net income ($ mil.)	–	–	(2.0)	28.5	11.8	(18.4)
Market value ($ mil.)	–	–	–	–	–	–
Employees	–	–	–	–	–	3,000

HOSPITAL OF CENTRAL CONNECTICUT

100 GRAND ST
NEW BRITAIN, CT 060522016
Phone: 860-224-5011
Fax: -
Web: www.thocc.org

CEO: Clarence J Silvia
CFO: Ralph Becker
HR: -
FYE: September 30
Type: Private

The Hospital of Central Connecticut an acute care facility serves the communities of central Connecticut from two campuses. With approximately 415 beds and more than 400 physicians the hospital offers a full range of diagnostic and treatment services as well as education and prevention programs. Its diabetes treatment program is an affiliate of the Boston-based Joslin Diabetes Center; the hospital is also affiliated with the University of Connecticut School of Medicine and other universities. Central Connecticut Health Alliance (CCHA) is the parent company of The Hospital of Central Connecticut and is part of the Hartford Health Care network.

	Annual Growth	09/13	09/14	09/15	09/17	09/20
Sales ($ mil.)	4.5%	-	360.4	338.2	366.3	470.2
Net income ($ mil.)	5.2%	-	24.3	(4.2)	23.2	33.1
Market value ($ mil.)	-	-	-	-	-	-
Employees	-	-	-	-	-	2,500

HOSPITAL SERVICE DISTRICT 1 INC

1101 MEDICAL CENTER BLVD
MARRERO, LA 700723147
Phone: 504-347-5511
Fax: -

CEO: Nancy R Cassagne
CFO: -
HR: -
FYE: December 31
Type: Private

West Jefferson Medical Center keeps the suburbs of New Orleans in tune. A full-service community hospital located in Marrero Louisiana the not-for-profit hospital has about 430 beds and provides general medical-surgical care as well as specialty care in a number of areas including cardiovascular disease neurosciences orthopedics women's health and oncology. The medical center also operates several primary care clinics throughout its service area and provides behavioral health and occupational health services. The hospital is also part of The Louisiana Organ Procurement Agency.

	Annual Growth	12/05	12/06*	09/13*	12/14	12/16
Sales ($ mil.)	(0.4%)	-	234.9	59.5	200.9	226.3
Net income ($ mil.)	-	-	(9.1)	2.3	(16.9)	(2.8)
Market value ($ mil.)	-	-	-	-	-	-
Employees	-	-	-	-	-	2,000

*Fiscal year change

HOSPITAL SERVICE DISTRICT 1 OF EAST BATON ROUGE PARISH

6300 MAIN ST
ZACHARY, LA 707914037
Phone: 225-658-4000
Fax: -
Web: www.lanermc.org

CEO: Randalt Olson
CFO: Claude Hacker
HR: -
FYE: June 30
Type: Private

Lane Regional Medical Center (formerly Lane Memorial Hospital) has 137 beds and provides a full range of medical services including emergency care surgery occupational therapy pediatrics psychiatry imaging wound care and sleep studies. The hospital also operates a 30-bed medical rehabilitation center a 38-bed nursing home a 12-bed skilled nursing unit a family practice clinic and a home health agency. Founded in 1960 the hospital has a staff of more than 100 physicians.

	Annual Growth	06/02	06/03	06/04	06/15	06/16
Sales ($ mil.)	5.5%	-	38.1	40.4	72.6	76.8
Net income ($ mil.)	-	-	(1.3)	0.4	(0.2)	(0.4)
Market value ($ mil.)	-	-	-	-	-	-
Employees	-	-	-	-	-	605

HOSPITAL SERVICE DISTRICT NO. 1

8166 MAIN ST
HOUMA, LA 703603404
Phone: 985-873-4141
Fax: -
Web: www.tghealthsystem.com

CEO: Phyllis Peoples
CFO: -
HR: -
FYE: March 31
Type: Private

If you find yourself feeling puny in the parish Terrebonne General Medical Center in southeastern Louisiana is there to help (TGMC). The not-for-profit health care system is anchored by a 320-bed hospital with a staff of more than 150 physicians. The hospital provides a range of health care services including cardiac care women's health care rehabilitation and emergency medicine. TGMC also administers care through an outpatient surgery center imaging and breast centers and a psychiatric care program. The Mary Bird Perkins Cancer Center at TGMC offers a continuum of cancer care from prevention and early detection to diagnosis and treatment. Programs include surgery chemotherapy and radiation therapy.

	Annual Growth	03/12	03/13	03/17	03/18	03/21
Sales ($ mil.)	9.2%	-	170.7	185.4	271.1	345.6
Net income ($ mil.)	13.2%	-	6.0	(3.1)	(6.2)	16.1
Market value ($ mil.)	-	-	-	-	-	-
Employees	-	-	-	-	-	1,400

HOSPITAL SISTERS HEALTH SYSTEM

4936 LAVERNA RD
SPRINGFIELD, IL 627079797
Phone: 217-523-4747
Fax: -
Web: www.hshs.org

CEO: Mary Starmann-Perharrison
CFO: -
HR: -
FYE: June 30
Type: Private

These sisters want their big family to benefit everyone in the community. Hospital Sisters Health System (HSHS) a Catholic ministry of the Hospital Sisters of the Third Order of St. Francis operates more than a dozen hospitals located throughout Wisconsin and Illinois. Its facilities have a total of more than 2500 beds and range from large-scale acute care facilities such as St. John's Hospital (Springfield Illinois) St. Elizabeth's Hospital (Bellevue Illinois) and St. Vincent Hospital (Green Bay Wisconsin) to small community hospitals; it also operates regional outpatient clinics. While the organization was incorporated in 1978 the health care ministry of the HSHS goes back to 1875.

	Annual Growth	06/09	06/10	06/13	06/14	06/20
Sales ($ mil.)	11.9%	-	92.9	145.3	166.7	285.8
Net income ($ mil.)	13.2%	-	10.5	4.4	4.1	36.3
Market value ($ mil.)	-	-	-	-	-	-
Employees	-	-	-	-	-	14,676

HOSS'S STEAK & SEA HOUSE, INC.

170 PATCHWAY RD
DUNCANSVILLE, PA 166358431
Phone: 814-695-7600
Fax: -
Web: www.hosspeople.com

CEO: Willard E Campbell
CFO: Carl Raup
HR: -
FYE: December 30
Type: Private

Don't expect to find any Cartwright memorabilia here just plenty of hearty food. Hoss's Steak and Sea House operates about 40 of its signature family-style restaurants in Pennsylvania. The diners offer standard American fare and seafood for lunch and dinner along with an all-you-can-eat soup and salad bar. Each restaurant sports local memorabilia as part of its décor. The company also operates Hoss's Fresh Xpress its own warehouse and distribution system used to supply the restaurants. CEO Bill Campbell a former WesterN SizzliN franchisee opened the first Hoss's in 1983.

	Annual Growth	12/03	12/04	12/05	12/06	12/07
Sales ($ mil.)	(0.9%)	-	78.0	77.6	81.7	75.9
Net income ($ mil.)	-	-	1.3	0.7	0.7	(0.8)
Market value ($ mil.)	-	-	-	-	-	-
Employees	-	-	-	-	-	3,000

HOST HOTELS & RESORTS INC — NMS: HST

4747 Bethesda Avenue, Suite 1300
Bethesda, MD 20814
Phone: 240 744-1000
Fax: –
Web: www.hosthotels.com

CEO: James Risoleo
CFO: Sourav Ghosh
HR: Joanne Hamilton
FYE: December 31
Type: Public

Host Hotels & Resorts is the largest hospitality real estate investment trust (REIT) in the US and one of the top owners of luxury and upscale hotels. It owns around 80 luxury and "upper upscale" hotels mostly in the US (but also in Canada and Brazil) totaling some 46300 rooms. Properties are managed by third parties; most operate under the Marriott brand and are managed by sister firm Marriott International. Other brands include Hyatt Ritz-Carlton AccorHotels and Hilton. To maintain its status as a REIT which carries tax advantages Host operates through third-party managers to operate its hotels. Host generate the vast majority of its sales in the US.

	Annual Growth	12/16	12/17	12/18	12/19	12/20
Sales ($ mil.)	(26.1%)	5,430.0	5,387.0	5,524.0	5,469.0	1,620.0
Net income ($ mil.)	–	762.0	564.0	1,087.0	920.0	(732.0)
Market value ($ mil.)	(6.1%)	13,289.7	14,002.2	11,759.0	13,085.2	10,320.0
Employees	(7.2%)	220	205	184	175	163

HOUCHENS INDUSTRIES, INC.

700 CHURCH ST
BOWLING GREEN, KY 421011816
Phone: 270-843-3252
Fax: –
Web: www.houchensindustries.com

CEO: Dion Houchins
CFO: James Gordon Minter
HR: –
FYE: September 29
Type: Private

Houchens Industries is listed by Forbes as one of the largest 100% employee-owned companies in the world. The diversified company runs some 400 retail grocery convenience and neighborhood markets across around 15 US states. That includes conventional supermarkets under the Houchens Food Giant IGA Tampico and Pan-Oston banners. In addition Houchens is an extremely diversified company with businesses in more than eleven industries. Houchens Industries was originally founded in Glasgow Kentucky by Ervin G. Houchens in 1917 as Houchens Foods.

	Annual Growth	10/13	10/14	10/15	10/16*	09/18
Sales ($ mil.)	(6.7%)	–	–	3,213.0	2,987.2	2,613.6
Net income ($ mil.)	(33.4%)	–	–	99.9	104.1	29.5
Market value ($ mil.)	–	–	–	–	–	–
Employees	–	–	–	–	–	16,000

*Fiscal year change

HOUGHTON MIFFLIN HARCOURT CO. — NMS: HMHC

125 High Street
Boston, MA 02110
Phone: 617 351-5000
Fax: –
Web: www.hmhco.com

CEO: John Lynch
CFO: Joseph Abbott
HR: –
FYE: December 31
Type: Public

Houghton Mifflin Harcourt Company (HMH) is a publisher of educational material covering areas from pre-K through grade 12 as well as adult learners. HMH publishes textbooks and printed materials and provides digital content online to more than 50 million students and over 130000 school districts in some 150 countries. It also publishes fiction (including J.R.R. Tolkien's The Lord of the Rings series and the popular line of Curious George books) as well as nonfiction titles and reference materials and offers professional resources and educational services to teachers. HMH primarily sells to customers in the US.

	Annual Growth	12/16	12/17	12/18	12/19	12/20
Sales ($ mil.)	(6.9%)	1,372.7	1,407.5	1,322.4	1,390.7	1,031.3
Net income ($ mil.)	–	(284.6)	(103.2)	(94.2)	(213.8)	(479.8)
Market value ($ mil.)	(25.6%)	1,365.8	1,170.7	1,115.3	786.8	419.2
Employees	(12.8%)	4,500	3,800	3,600	3,400	2,600

HOUGHTON MIFFLIN HARCOURT PUBLISHING COMPANY

222 Berkeley St.
Boston MA 02116-3748
Phone: 617-351-5000
Fax: 703-876-3125
Web: www.gendyn.com

CEO: –
CFO: Joseph Abbott
HR: –
FYE: December 31
Type: Private

Houghton Mifflin Harcourt Publishing Company would like to thank all the professional students out there. The firm is a publisher of educational material covering areas from pre-K through grade 12 as well as adult learners. Houghton Mifflin publishes textbooks and printed materials and provides digital content online and via CD-ROM. It additionally publishes fiction (including J.R.R. Tolkien's The Lord of the Rings series) as well as nonfiction titles and reference materials and offers professional resources and educational services to teachers. Houghton Mifflin has origins dating back to 1832 and is owned by private-equity concerns including hedge fund Paulson & Co. It filed for bankruptcy in 2012.

HOUSTON AMERICAN ENERGY CORP. — ASE: HUSA

801 Travis Street, Suite 1425
Houston, TX 77002
Phone: 713 222-6966
Fax: –
Web: www.houstonamerican.com

CEO: John Terwilliger
CFO: –
HR: –
FYE: December 31
Type: Public

Houston-based with North and South American properties and energy focused Houston American Energy explores for and produces oil and natural gas primarily in Colombia but also along the US Gulf Coast (Louisiana and Texas although the oil and gas independent also holds some acreage in Oklahoma). In 2011 the company reported proved reserves of 115627 barrels of oil equivalent. President and CEO John Terwilliger owns 27.5% of Houston American Energy; director Orrie Tawes 10%. In 2012 the debt-plagued company was pursuing strategic alternatives.

	Annual Growth	12/16	12/17	12/18	12/19	12/20
Sales ($ mil.)	35.1%	0.2	0.6	2.4	1.0	0.6
Net income ($ mil.)	–	(2.6)	(2.0)	(0.3)	(2.5)	(4.0)
Market value ($ mil.)	78.6%	1.2	2.3	1.3	1.0	12.2
Employees	(9.6%)	3	3	2	2	2

HOUSTON COMMUNITY COLLEGE, INC.

3100 MAIN ST STE MC1148
HOUSTON, TX 770029331
Phone: 713-718-5001
Fax: –
Web: www.hccs.edu

CEO: –
CFO: Carloyn Dedly
HR: –
FYE: September 30
Type: Private

The Houston Community College System (HCC) has an open admission policy and offers associate degrees ongoing education workforce training and prerequisite coursework for students enrolled at universities. In addition to traditional classes the system offers online classes and other distance education courses via video and broadcast TV. HCC is the fourth largest community college in the US. It has six area colleges (Central Coleman Northeast Northwest Southeast and Southwest) throughout Houston and more than 60000 students are enrolled each year. HCC was founded in 1971.

	Annual Growth	12/04	12/05*	08/08	08/14*	09/14
Sales ($ mil.)	–	–	0.0	2.8	293.9	99.9
Net income ($ mil.)	–	–	0.0	2.1	12.2	33.5
Market value ($ mil.)	–	–	–	–	–	–
Employees	–	–	–	–	–	5,000

*Fiscal year change

HOUSTON COUNTY HEALTHCARE AUTHORITY

1108 ROSS CLARK CIR
DOTHAN, AL 363013022
Phone: 334-793-8111
Fax: –
Web: www.southeasthealth.org

CEO: Rick Sutton
CFO: Derek Miller
HR: –
FYE: September 30
Type: Private

The Houston County Health Authority is the governing body for Southeast Alabama Medical Center (SAMC) a not-for-profit acute-care hospital that serves Southeastern Alabama and adjacent parts of Georgia and Florida. In addition to providing comprehensive medical surgical and emergency care the 420-bed SAMC provides specialty services including heart cancer and women's health care. The health system also operates primary care physician offices and clinics specializing in neurology pain management and cardiovascular care as well as a home health agency. SAMC offers residency programs for medical students most of whom attend the Alabama College of Osteopathic Medicine.

	Annual Growth	09/15	09/16	09/17	09/18	09/19
Sales ($ mil.)	5.5%	–	364.0	381.6	386.0	427.4
Net income ($ mil.)	34.5%	–	9.0	16.2	11.6	21.9
Market value ($ mil.)	–	–	–	–	–	–
Employees	–	–	–	–	–	2,500

HOUSTON WIRE & CABLE CO   NMS: HWCC

10201 North Loop East
Houston, TX 77029
Phone: 713 609-2100
Fax: 713 609-2101
Web: www.houwire.com

CEO: James L Pokluda III
CFO: Eric W Davis
HR: –
FYE: December 31
Type: Public

Houston Wire & Cable (HWC) may have a Texas name but it can keep customers wired from Seattle to Tampa. The company is a conduit between cable manufacturers and electrical distributors and their customers. It distributes specialty (electrical and electronic) wire and cable products such as cable terminators fiber-optic cables and bare copper and building wire as well as voice data and premise wire. It also owns the brand LifeGuard a low-smoke zero-halogen cable. HWC operates a network of multiple distribution centers across the US and sells primarily to electrical distributors.

	Annual Growth	12/15	12/16	12/17	12/18	12/19
Sales ($ mil.)	2.4%	308.1	261.6	317.7	356.9	338.3
Net income ($ mil.)	5.7%	2.0	(6.0)	(0.2)	8.6	2.6
Market value ($ mil.)	(4.4%)	87.4	107.6	119.2	83.8	73.0
Employees	5.3%	352	403	422	427	432

HOVNANIAN ENTERPRISES, INC.   NYS: HOV

90 Matawan Road, Fifth Floor
Matawan, NJ 07747
Phone: 732 747-7800
Fax: –
Web: www.khov.com

CEO: ARA K Hovnanian
CFO: J Larry Sorsby
HR: –
FYE: October 31
Type: Public

Hovnanian Enterprises designs constructs markets and sells single-family detached homes attached townhomes and condominiums urban infill and active lifestyle homes in planned residential developments and is one of the nation's largest builders of residential homes. It designs communities that offer homes with a diversity of architecture textures and colors frequently with recreational amenities such as swimming pools tennis courts and clubhouses. Hovnanian offers a variety of home styles at base prices ranging from $173000 to $1273000 with an average sales price including options of $431000 in some 125 communities in more than two dozen markets in about 15 states throughout the US.

	Annual Growth	10/17	10/18	10/19	10/20	10/21
Sales ($ mil.)	3.2%	2,451.7	1,991.2	2,016.9	2,343.9	2,782.9
Net income ($ mil.)	–	(332.2)	4.5	(42.1)	50.9	607.8
Market value ($ mil.)	143.1%	15.1	9.1	156.9	198.7	527.0
Employees	(1.6%)	1,905	1,851	1,868	1,697	1,784

HOWARD BUILDING CORPORATION

707 WILSHIRE BLVD # 3750
LOS ANGELES, CA 900173535
Phone: 213-683-1850
Fax: –
Web: www.howardbuilding.com

CEO: Paul McGunnigle
CFO: Tony Gaudino
HR: –
FYE: December 31
Type: Private

General contracting firm Howard Building provides preconstruction design/build engineering construction and management services primarily for commercial projects throughout California. The company's portfolio includes projects ranging from corporate legal and financial buildings to entertainment showroom and high-tech facilities. Clients include BAE Systems Trammell Crow Deutsche Bank The Endeavor Agency Fox Television and Pacific Investment Management Company. Howard Building founded in 1983 maintains offices in greater Los Angeles and Orange County California.

	Annual Growth	12/14	12/15	12/16	12/17	12/18
Sales ($ mil.)	–	–	–	0.0	300.2	364.3
Net income ($ mil.)	–	–	–	0.0	3.0	5.1
Market value ($ mil.)	–	–	–	–	–	–
Employees	–	–	–	–	–	152

HOWARD HUGHES CORP   NYS: HHC

9950 Woodloch Forest Drive, Suite 1100
The Woodlands, TX 77380
Phone: 281 719-6100
Fax: –
Web: www.howardhughes.com

CEO: David O'Reilly
CFO: Carlos Olea
HR: –
FYE: December 31
Type: Public

The Howard Hughes Corporation (THHC) is involved in neither planes movies or medical research but one of the 20th century entrepreneur's later interests real estate. The company arose from the bankruptcy restructuring of shopping mall developer General Growth Properties (GGP) to oversee much of GGP's non-retail assets. THHC owns GGP's former portfolio of four master planned communities outside Columbia Maryland; Houston Texas; and Summerlin Nevada; as well as about two dozen other as-yet undeveloped sites and commercial properties in 16 states from New York to Hawaii including GGP's own headquarters building in downtown Chicago. Unlike GGP THHC does not operate as a REIT.

	Annual Growth	12/16	12/17	12/18	12/19	12/20
Sales ($ mil.)	(9.3%)	1,035.0	1,100.1	1,064.5	1,300.5	699.5
Net income ($ mil.)	–	202.3	168.4	57.0	74.0	(26.2)
Market value ($ mil.)	(8.8%)	6,272.3	7,216.2	5,366.4	6,970.5	4,339.0
Employees	(14.1%)	1,100	1,100	1,400	1,500	600

HOWMET AEROSPACE INC   NYS: HWM

201 Isabella Street, Suite 200
Pittsburgh, PA 15212-5872
Phone: 412 553-1940
Fax: –
Web: www.howmet.com

CEO: John C Plant
CFO: Kenneth J Giacobbe
HR: –
FYE: December 31
Type: Public

Formerly known as Arconic Inc the company is now renamed as Howmet Aerospace Inc. a global leader in lightweight metals engineering and manufacturing ? primarily made multi-material products which include aluminum titanium and nickel ? can help you fly drive build and generate power. Created in 2016 when it was spun off from the aluminum giant Alcoa Howmet has retained the parts businesses of its predecessor ? engineered products and forging businesses like engine products fastening systems engineered structures and forged wheels. With operations in some 20 countries Howmet is a top provider of specialty materials to the aerospace commercial transportation automotive defense building and construction and oil and gas industries. It generates about 55% of its revenue in the US.

	Annual Growth	12/17	12/18	12/19	12/20	12/21
Sales ($ mil.)	(21.3%)	12,960.0	14,014.0	14,192.0	5,259.0	4,972.0
Net income ($ mil.)	–	(74.0)	642.0	470.0	261.0	258.0
Market value ($ mil.)	4.0%	11,491.1	7,109.7	12,975.5	12,035.1	13,422.5
Employees	(16.8%)	41,500	43,000	41,700	19,700	19,900

HP HOOD LLC

6 Kimball Ln.
Lynnfield MA 01940
Phone: 617-887-3000
Fax: 617-887-8484
Web: www.hood.com

CEO: –
CFO: –
HR: –
FYE: December 31
Type: Private

HP Hood tries to cream the competition — with ice cream sour cream and whipping cream. The leading US dairy producer also makes fluid milk cottage cheese and juices. Its home turf is New England where it is one of the few remaining dairies to offer home milk delivery serving some 15000 customers. However Hood's products are distributed throughout the US to chain and independent food retailers and convenience stores and to foodservice purveyors. In addition to its own and subsidiary brands the Massachusetts company makes private-label and licensed dairy products and owns regional dairy producer Crowley Foods. Hood operates about 15 manufacturing plants throughout the US.

HP INC

1501 Page Mill Road
Palo Alto, CA 94304
Phone: 650 857-1501
Fax: –
Web: www.hp.com

NYS: HPQ
CEO: Enrique Lores
CFO: Marie Myers
HR: –
FYE: October 31
Type: Public

HP Inc. is one of two companies created from the breakup of Hewlett-Packard Co. in 2015. HP makes a full line of computing devices from desktops and laptops for commercial and consumer use to tablets and point-of-sale systems. Its printers include large format commercial printers and inkjet and laser printers as well as 3D printers. It sells to individual consumers small- and medium-sized businesses (SMBs) and large enterprises including customers in the government health and education sectors. The company generates about 35% of its revenue in the US.

	Annual Growth	10/17	10/18	10/19	10/20	10/21
Sales ($ mil.)	5.1%	52,056.0	58,472.0	58,756.0	56,639.0	63,487.0
Net income ($ mil.)	26.7%	2,526.0	5,327.0	3,152.0	2,844.0	6,503.0
Market value ($ mil.)	8.9%	23,537.0	26,365.8	18,971.6	19,616.0	33,126.6
Employees	1.0%	49,000	55,000	56,000	53,000	51,000

HSBC USA, INC.

452 Fifth Avenue
New York, NY 10018
Phone: 212 525-5000
Fax: –
Web: www.us.hsbc.com

NL:
CEO: Michael Roberts
CFO: Eric K Ferren
HR: –
FYE: December 31
Type: Public

HSBC USA a subsidiary of British banking behemoth HSBC Holdings operates HSBC Bank USA one of the largest foreign-owned banks in the country. Boasting $200 billion in assets and 230-plus branches across 10 US states (including 145 in New York making it one of the state's largest banks by branches) the bank offers personal commercial and mortgage banking services as well as wealth management investment banking private banking brokerage and trust services. Its largest markets are in New York California New Jersey and Florida. Roughly 75% of HSBC USA's loan portfolio is made up of commercial loans and around 70% of its total revenue comes from interest income.

	Annual Growth	12/16	12/17	12/18	12/19	12/20
Assets ($ mil.)	(0.6%)	201,301.0	187,235.0	172,448.0	175,375.0	196,434.0
Net income ($ mil.)	–	–	129.0	(179.0)	320.0	113.0	(940.0)
Market value ($ mil.)	–	–	–	–	–	–
Employees	(9.1%)	6,114	5,107	4,933	4,828	4,179

HSN INC (DE)

1 HSN Drive
St. Petersburg, FL 33729
Phone: 727 872-1000
Fax: –
Web: www.hsni.com

NMS: HSNI
CEO: Leslie Ferraro
CFO: William Hunter
HR: –
FYE: December 31
Type: Public

No need to worry about normal business hours when shopping with this retailer. Known to night owls and from-the-couch shoppers as Home Shopping Network HSN Inc. (HSNi) sells more than 50000 types of apparel and accessories jewelry electronics housewares health beauty and fitness products through its home shopping television network with 95 million US viewers and through fast-growing HSN.com. Its Cornerstone Brands business is a catalog and Internet retailer whose brands include Garnet Hill Ballard Designs and TravelSmith. Overall about 50% of HSNi's total sales come from home-related product sales while nearly 30% comes from beauty and health product sales. In 2015 50% of HSNi's total sales came from its e-commerce channels.

	Annual Growth	12/11	12/12	12/13	12/14	12/15
Sales ($ mil.)	3.8%	3,177.2	3,266.7	3,404.0	3,588.0	3,690.6
Net income ($ mil.)	8.3%	123.1	130.7	178.4	173.0	169.2
Market value ($ mil.)	8.7%	1,899.2	2,885.0	3,263.1	3,980.7	2,654.0
Employees	0.8%	6,400	6,700	6,800	6,900	6,600

HUB GROUP, INC.

2000 Clearwater Drive
Oak Brook, IL 60523
Phone: 630 271-3600
Fax: –
Web: www.hubgroup.com

NMS: HUBG
CEO: David Yeager
CFO: Geoffrey Demartino
HR: Michele McDermott
FYE: December 31
Type: Public

Hub Group is leading supply chain solutions provider that offers comprehensive transportation and logistics management services focused on reliability visibility and value for its customers. It offers multi-modal supply chain management solutions that serves to strengthen and deepen its relationships with its customers and allows the company to provide a more cost effective and higher service solution. Operating throughout North America the company provides services including comprehensive intermodal truck brokerage dedicated trucking managed transportation freight consolidation warehousing last mile delivery international transportation and other logistics services. The company also offers complementary services such as temperature protected transportation. Hub Group operates in every major city in the US Canada and Mexico.

	Annual Growth	12/16	12/17	12/18	12/19	12/20
Sales ($ mil.)	(0.5%)	3,572.8	4,034.9	3,683.6	3,668.1	3,495.6
Net income ($ mil.)	(0.4%)	74.8	135.2	201.7	107.2	73.6
Market value ($ mil.)	6.8%	1,496.8	1,638.8	1,268.2	1,754.7	1,950.1
Employees	16.1%	2,755	4,377	5,400	5,000	5,000

HUB INTERNATIONAL LIMITED

55 E. Jackson Blvd. Fl. 14A
Chicago IL 60604
Phone: 877-402-6601
Fax: 877-402-6606
Web: www.hubinternational.com

CEO: Martin Hughes
CFO: Joseph Hyde
HR: –
FYE: December 31
Type: Private

Hub International is an insurance broker that operates more than 250 offices in a decentralized regional hub-and-satellite-office structure. It provides property/casualty employee benefits risk management life and health reinsurance and investment products and services to clients in North America (the US and Canada) Latin America and the Caribbean. Hub is licensed in every state and all Canadian provinces. The acquisitive firm focuses on midsized commercial clients and affluent individuals. The US accounts for the bulk of its revenues. Hub is also able to facilitate cross-border business between the US and Mexico and operates in Brazil.

HUBBELL INC.   NYS: HUBB

40 Waterview Drive
Shelton, CT 06484
Phone: 475 882-4000
Fax: –
Web: www.hubbell.com

CEO: Gerben Bakker
CFO: William Sperry
HR: Stephen Mais
FYE: December 31
Type: Public

Hubbell is a manufacturer of electrical products for commercial industrial telecommunications and utility applications. Its electrical segment which accounts for about 60% of sales includes wiring connector and grounding products lighting fixtures and controls for indoor and outdoor applications. The Utility Solutions segment includes distribution transmission substation and telecommunications products used by electrical and gas utilities. Hubbell generates most of its sales in the US. However the company's products are sourced from Canada Puerto Rico Mexico China the UK Brazil among others. Founder Harvey Hubbell developed tooling and equipment to serve the growing demand for new assembly and manufacturing machinery during the industrial revolution in the late 1800s.

	Annual Growth	12/17	12/18	12/19	12/20	12/21
Sales ($ mil.)	3.4%	3,668.8	4,481.7	4,591.0	4,186.0	4,194.1
Net income ($ mil.)	13.2%	243.1	360.2	400.9	351.2	399.5
Market value ($ mil.)	11.4%	7,378.5	5,415.8	8,058.9	8,547.9	11,354.5
Employees	0.8%	17,700	19,700	18,800	19,100	18,300

HUDSON CITY BANCORP INC   NMS: HCBK

West 80 Century Road
Paramus, NJ 07652
Phone: 201 967-1900
Fax: 201 967-0559
Web: www.hcbk.com

CEO: –
CFO: –
HR: –
FYE: December 31
Type: Public

Hudson City Bancorp is the holding company for Hudson City Savings Bank one of the largest thrifts in the US. Founded in 1868 the bank has more than 130 branches in the New York City metropolitan area including northern New Jersey; Long Island; and Fairfield County Connecticut; as well as central New Jersey and that state's Philadelphia suburbs. Serving middle- to high-income consumers it issues and purchases high-quality first residential mortgages which account for about 99% of its loan portfolio. It originates loans at its branches through mortgage bankers and brokers and (to a lesser extent) on a wholesale basis nationwide. Acquisitive M&T Bank is buying Hudson City Bancorp for some $3.7 billion.

	Annual Growth	12/09	12/10	12/11	12/12	12/13
Assets ($ mil.)	(10.5%)	60,267.8	61,166.0	45,355.9	40,596.3	38,607.4
Net income ($ mil.)	(23.0%)	527.2	537.2	(736.0)	249.1	185.2
Market value ($ mil.)	(9.0%)	7,255.2	6,732.1	3,302.6	4,296.0	4,983.0
Employees	0.5%	1,552	1,626	1,645	1,792	1,581

HUDSON GLOBAL INC   NMS: HSON

53 Forest Avenue, Suite 102
Old Greenwich, CT 06870
Phone: 203 409-5628
Fax: –
Web: www.hudson.com

CEO: Jeffrey Eberwein
CFO: Matthew Diamond
HR: –
FYE: December 31
Type: Public

Hudson Global is a leading total talent solutions provider operating under the brand name Hudson RPO. The company delivers RPO recruitment and Contracting solutions tailored to the individual needs of primarily mid-to-large-cap multinational companies. The company's RPO delivery teams utilize state-of-the-art recruitment process methodologies and project management expertise in their flexible turnkey solutions to meet clients' ongoing business needs. Its RPO services include complete recruitment outsourcing project-based outsourcing contingent workforce solutions and recruitment consulting. Among the company's clients are mid to large multinational businesses and government agencies. About 75% of company's total revenue comes from Asia Pacific.

	Annual Growth	12/16	12/17	12/18	12/19	12/20
Sales ($ mil.)	(30.0%)	422.7	456.7	66.9	93.8	101.4
Net income ($ mil.)	–	(8.8)	(2.9)	7.9	(1.0)	(1.2)
Market value ($ mil.)	66.2%	3.7	6.0	3.6	32.1	28.2
Employees	(30.2%)	1,600	1,500	350	390	380

HUDSON PACIFIC PROPERTIES INC   NYS: HPP

11601 Wilshire Blvd., Ninth Floor
Los Angeles, CA 90025
Phone: 310 445-5700
Fax: –
Web: –

CEO: Victor Coleman
CFO: Harout Diramerian
HR: –
FYE: December 31
Type: Public

Hudson Pacific Properties wants to be the landlord to the stars. One of Hollywood's biggest landlords the real estate investment trust (REIT) buys and manages primarily office buildings but also and media and entertainment properties in California and the Pacific Northwest in cities such as Los Angeles Orange County San Diego San Francisco and Seattle. It owns about 55 properties totaling some 15 million sq. ft. including three production studios on Hollywood's Sunset Boulevard. Its largest tenants range from tech giants such as Google Netflix Uber Qualcomm and Nutanix.

	Annual Growth	12/17	12/18	12/19	12/20	12/21
Sales ($ mil.)	5.3%	728.1	728.4	818.2	805.0	896.8
Net income ($ mil.)	(38.1%)	68.6	98.8	43.4	1.4	10.0
Market value ($ mil.)	(7.8%)	5,176.0	4,391.7	5,689.8	3,630.0	3,734.3
Employees	17.6%	293	311	347	375	560

HUDSON TECHNOLOGIES INC   NAS: HDSN

1 Blue Hill Plaza, P.O. Box 1541
Pearl River, NY 10965
Phone: 845 735-6000
Fax: –
Web: www.hudsontech.com

CEO: Brian Coleman
CFO: Nat Krishnamurti
HR: –
FYE: December 31
Type: Public

Hudson Technologies defends the ozone. Using proprietary reclamation technology to remove moisture and impurities from refrigeration systems it recovers and reclaims chlorofluorocarbons (CFCs) used in commercial air-conditioning and refrigeration systems. The company sells both reclaimed and new refrigerants and also buys used refrigerants for reclamation and sale. In addition Hudson Technologies offers on-site decontamination services as well as services designed to improve the efficiency of customers' refrigeration systems. Customers include commercial and industrial enterprises and government entities along with refrigerant contractors distributors and wholesalers and makers of refrigeration equipment.

	Annual Growth	12/16	12/17	12/18	12/19	12/20
Sales ($ mil.)	8.8%	105.5	140.4	166.5	162.1	147.6
Net income ($ mil.)	–	10.6	11.2	(55.7)	(25.9)	(5.2)
Market value ($ mil.)	(39.3%)	347.2	263.1	38.6	42.4	47.2
Employees	12.7%	137	262	243	234	221

HUDSON VALLEY FEDERAL CREDIT UNION

159 Barnegat Rd.
Poughkeepsie NY 12601-5454
Phone: 845-463-3011
Fax: 845-463-3229
Web: www.hvfcu.org

CEO: Mary D Madden
CFO: –
HR: –
FYE: December 31
Type: Private - Not-for-Pr

Hudson Valley Federal Credit Union (HVFCU) provides financial services to more than 260000 members from about 20 branches in eastern New York's Hudson Valley region. Membership is available to all who reside work volunteer worship or attend school in Dutchess Orange Putnam or Ulster counties. In addition to savings accounts credit cards mortgages and business and personal loans the credit union offers insurance and financial planning services to its individual and small business members. It provides access to investments and asset management services through an agreement with third-party provider LPL Financial. HVFCU was founded in 1963 as the IBM Poughkeepsie Employees Federal Credit Union.

HUDSON VALLEY HOLDING CORP.   NYS: HVB

21 Scarsdale Road
Yonkers, NY 10707
Phone: 914 961-6100
Fax: –
Web: www.hudsonvalleybank.com

CEO: –
CFO: –
HR: –
FYE: December 31
Type: Public

Hudson Valley Holding is the parent company of Hudson Valley Bank which serves individuals businesses municipalities and not-for-profit organizations from more than 35 locations throughout metropolitan New York and lower Connecticut. The bank focuses on real estate lending which accounts for more than 80% of the company's loan portfolio. Hudson Valley Holding offers other standard banking products such savings checking and money market accounts commercial and industrial loans consumer loans credit cards CDs and IRAs. Bank subsidiary A.R. Schmeidler & Co. offers investment management services.

	Annual Growth	12/09	12/10	12/11	12/12	12/13
Assets ($ mil.)	3.0%	2,665.6	2,669.0	2,797.7	2,891.2	2,999.2
Net income ($ mil.)	(50.6%)	19.0	5.1	(2.1)	29.2	1.1
Market value ($ mil.)	(4.7%)	491.6	493.6	423.0	310.4	405.7
Employees	(4.2%)	498	478	489	460	419

HUGHES COMMUNICATIONS INC.

11717 Exploration Ln.
Germantown MD 20876
Phone: 301-428-5500
Fax: 301-428-1868
Web: www.hughes.com

CEO: Pradman P Kaul
CFO: Grant A Barber
HR: –
FYE: December 31
Type: Subsidiary

Hughes Communications aims even higher than visionary company namesake Howard Hughes did. Through operating subsidiary Hughes Network Systems the company provides broadband satellite equipment and services based largely on very small aperture terminal (VSAT) technology. Over a network of owned and leased satellites it provides consumers businesses and government agencies worldwide with broadband Internet access via the HughesNet service. The network also enables voice calling video transmission and data services such as credit authorization. Hughes also sells network hardware systems used by fixed and mobile communication systems operators. EchoStar bought the company for almost $2 billion in 2011.

HUGHES TELEMATICS INC.   OTC: HUTC

2002 Summit Blvd. Ste. 1800
Atlanta GA 30319
Phone: 404-573-5800
Fax: 404-573-5827
Web: www.hughestelematics.com

CEO: –
CFO: –
HR: –
FYE: December 31
Type: Public

HUGHES Telematics Inc. (HTI) wants to keep drivers and fleet managers oriented. The company provides vehicle telematics products and services such as GPS navigation emergency support and vehicle diagnostic systems. Through its Networkfleet subsidiary (more than half of sales) HTI offers fleet tracking and reporting services to companies who want to track the location of company vehicles monitor vehicle maintenance needs or track mileage. It also designs systems that allow drivers to access content on the Web and in mobile devices such as phones and digital music players as well as features such as vehicle locating and locking or unlocking the vehicle from a smartphone. It was bought in 2012 by Verizon.

HUGOTON ROYALTY TRUST (TX)   NBB: HGTX U

c/o The Corporate Trustee:, Simmons Bank 2911 Turtle Creek Blvd, Suite 850
Dallas, TX 75219
Phone: 855 588-7839
Fax: –
Web: www.hgt-hugoton.com

CEO: –
CFO: –
HR: –
FYE: December 31
Type: Public

Hugoton Royalty Trust was formed by Cross Timbers Oil Company (now XTO Energy) to pay royalties to shareholders based on the proceeds of sales from its oil and gas holdings. Payouts depend on oil and gas prices the volume of gas and oil produced and production and other costs. The trust receives 80% of the net proceeds from XTO Energy's properties located in the Hugoton fields of Kansas Oklahoma and Texas; the Anadarko Basin of Oklahoma; and the Green River Basin of Wyoming. In 2008 the trust reported proved reserves of 3.3 million barrels of oil and 366.3 billion cu. ft. of natural gas. XTO Energy controls the trust which is administered through Bank of America and has no officers.

	Annual Growth	12/16	12/17	12/18	12/19	12/20
Sales ($ mil.)	(81.9%)	2.7	5.3	1.6	0.4	0.0
Net income ($ mil.)	(55.3%)	1.9	4.5	0.4	–	–
Market value ($ mil.)	(54.8%)	86.0	56.0	21.6	6.8	3.6
Employees	–	–	–	–	–	–

HULU LLC

12312 W. Olympic Blvd.
Los Angeles CA 90064
Phone: 310-571-4700
Fax: 310-571-4701
Web: www.hulu.com

CEO: Randy Freer
CFO: –
HR: –
FYE: December 31
Type: Joint Venture

Hulu is a go-to service for online TV. The company operates an ad-supported website Hulu.com that allows viewers to watch online video content — TV shows clips and movies — for free. Its premium service Hulu Plus allows streaming of full current and past season content on everything from TV sets and PCs to mobile phones and tablets for a monthly subscription fee. Hulu's programming is provided by more than 400 content companies including network TV providers ABC FOX and NBC as well as film studios MGM Paramount and Sony. Those that have advertised on Hulu since its launch in 2008 include McDonald's Microsoft Target and Toyota.

HUMAN GENOME SCIENCES INC.   NASDAQ: HGSI

14200 Shady Grove Rd.
Rockville MD 20850-7464
Phone: 301-309-8504
Fax: 301-309-8512
Web: www.hgsi.com

CEO: H Thomas Watkins
CFO: David P Southwell
HR: –
FYE: December 31
Type: Public

Human Genome Sciences (HGS) starts at the molecular level for good health. Using its expertise in human genetics the biopharmaceutical discovery and development firm is working on therapies for infectious and autoimmune diseases cardiovascular disease and cancer. In 2011 lead candidate Benlysta gained FDA approval to treat systemic lupus and has since been extended into international markets. The company's only other commercial product is raxibacumab an antibody treatment for inhaled anthrax. In addition the company provides contract research and manufacturing services to other biotechs. Benlysta was developed through a partnership with GlaxoSmithKline (GSK). In 2012 HGS was acquired by GSK.

HUMAN PHEROMONE SCIENCES INC.
OTC: EROX

84 W. Santa Clara St. Ste. 720
San Jose CA 95113
Phone: 408-938-3030
Fax: 408-938-3025
Web: www.naturalattraction.com

CEO: William Horgan
CFO: Gregory Fredrick
HR: –
FYE: December 31
Type: Public

Human Pheromone Sciences (HPS) hopes its animal magnetism makes consumers hot under the collar. It makes fragrances that contain a patented synthetic version of a pheromone produced by the human body to stimulate the senses. It also licenses its technology to partners in the personal care products industry. The company's products are sold through its website and through direct marketing under the Natural Attraction name. It has granted non-exclusive rights to the Natural Attraction brand in the US Europe and Japan. HPS also partners with makers of consumer products to license its patented technology; CrowdGather is launching a unisex scent EroxA in 2011 with HPS. Renovatio Global Funds owns 16% of the firm.

HUMAN RIGHTS WATCH, INC.

350 5TH AVE FL 34
NEW YORK, NY 101183499
Phone: 212-290-4700
Fax: –
Web: www.hrw.org

CEO: –
CFO: –
HR: –
FYE: June 30
Type: Private

Human Rights Watch (HRW) is watching out for everyone. The organization's mission is to prevent discrimination uphold political freedom protect people during wartime and bring offenders to justice. HRW researches human rights violations around the world and publishes its findings to help generate publicity about the atrocities it uncovers. The nongovernmental organization (NGO) also meets with national and international governing officials to help steer policy change. Along with partner organizations HRW won the 1997 Nobel Peace Prize for its International Campaign to Ban Landmines. HRW is an independent organization; all funds come from private contributors. The group was founded in 1978.

	Annual Growth	06/11	06/12	06/13	06/14	06/15
Sales ($ mil.)	(2.6%)	–	70.5	59.3	74.2	65.2
Net income ($ mil.)	–	–	11.8	(3.7)	7.6	(8.3)
Market value ($ mil.)	–	–	–	–	–	–
Employees	–	–	–	–	–	348

HUMANA INC.
NYS: HUM

500 West Main Street
Louisville, KY 40202
Phone: 502 580-1000
Fax: –
Web: www.humana.com

CEO: Bruce Broussard
CFO: Susan Diamond
HR: –
FYE: December 31
Type: Public

Humana is a leading health and well-being company serving 17 million members in its medical benefit plans as well as approximately 5 million members in its specialty products. It also administers managed care plans for other government programs including Medicaid plans in Florida and Texas and TRICARE (for military personnel) in the South. Additionally Humana offers commercial health plans and specialty (life dental and vision) coverage; it also provides its members with access through their networks of health care providers such outpatient surgery centers primary care providers specialist physicians dentists and providers of ancillary health care services.

	Annual Growth	12/17	12/18	12/19	12/20	12/21
Assets ($ mil.)	13.0%	27,178.0	25,413.0	29,074.0	34,969.0	44,358.0
Net income ($ mil.)	4.6%	2,448.0	1,683.0	2,707.0	3,367.0	2,933.0
Market value ($ mil.)	16.9%	31,966.5	36,916.1	47,230.1	52,867.7	59,773.4
Employees	19.3%	47,900	43,600	47,200	49,600	96,900

HUMANGOOD NORCAL

6120 STNRDGE MALL RD STE
PLEASANTON, CA 94588
Phone: 925-924-7100
Fax: –
Web: www.humangood.org

CEO: David B Ferguson
CFO: –
HR: –
FYE: December 31
Type: Private

American Baptist Homes of the West (ABHOW) preaches the gospel of the active senior lifestyle operating more than 40 senior living facilities in four western states. Nearly three-fourths of ABHOW's communities are government-subsidized apartments for low-income seniors. About a dozen of its residences however are continuing care retirement communities which offer a continuum of care — residential living assisted living or skilled nursing — depending on residents' needs. The communities also schedule social activities and offer wellness programs and transportation services. Parent company Cornerstone Affiliates acquires and develops communities with ABHOW.

	Annual Growth	12/15	12/16	12/17	12/18	12/19
Assets ($ mil.)	(22.2%)	–	–	852.2	479.3	515.7
Net income ($ mil.)	1030.4%	–	–	0.1	(1.8)	11.2
Market value ($ mil.)	–	–	–	–	–	–
Employees	–	–	–	–	–	2,500

HUMAX USA, INC.

15621 RED HILL AVE # 120
TUSTIN, CA 927807322
Phone: 714-389-1924
Fax: –
Web: www.americas.humaxdigital.com

CEO: Keehyuk Sung
CFO: –
HR: Sally Kim
FYE: December 31
Type: Private

Humax USA prefers to connect with its customers through its products. The company develops and manufactures flat-panel TV sets and digital set-top boxes for satellite cable and terrestrial connections. Humax USA is the US-based subsidiary of Korean consumer electronics manufacturing firm Humax Co. which was founded in 1989. The brand has become one of the most popular worldwide among set-top boxes. Humax's products are available in more than 90 countries as well as in the US. The company primarily serves customers in Asia and Europe.

	Annual Growth	12/13	12/14	12/15	12/16	12/17
Sales ($ mil.)	2.5%	–	448.9	373.2	360.5	482.8
Net income ($ mil.)	–	–	0.5	0.5	(0.1)	(4.6)
Market value ($ mil.)	–	–	–	–	–	–
Employees	–	–	–	–	–	29

HUNT (J.B.) TRANSPORT SERVICES, INC.
NMS: JBHT

615 J.B. Hunt Corporate Drive
Lowell, AR 72745
Phone: 479 820-0000
Fax: –
Web: www.jbhunt.com

CEO: John Roberts
CFO: John Kuhlow
HR: Shelley Simpson
FYE: December 31
Type: Public

J.B. Hunt Transport Services is one of the largest transportation delivery and logistics companies in North America. Through its divisions the company transports freight including general merchandise automotive parts building materials chemicals electronics food and beverages and forest and paper products. Its Intermodal unit the company's largest maintains about 5165 tractors some 6745 drivers and a chassis fleet consisting of about 83260 units. The company also offers dedicated contract services truckload freight transportation and transportation management and logistics services. The company traces its roots back to 1961 and have been a publicly held company since its initial public offering in 1983.

	Annual Growth	12/16	12/17	12/18	12/19	12/20
Sales ($ mil.)	10.1%	6,555.5	7,189.6	8,614.9	9,165.3	9,636.6
Net income ($ mil.)	4.0%	432.1	686.3	489.6	516.3	506.0
Market value ($ mil.)	8.9%	10,255.8	12,148.1	9,830.0	12,338.2	14,437.6
Employees	8.1%	22,190	24,681	27,621	29,056	30,309

HUNT MEMORIAL HOSPITAL DISTRICT

4215 JOE RAMSEY BLVD E
GREENVILLE, TX 754017852
Phone: 903-408-5000
Fax: –
Web: www.huntregional.org

CEO: Richard Carter
CFO: Jerii Rich
HR: Stacey Lane
FYE: September 30
Type: Private

Hunt Memorial Hospital District doesn't want Hunt County residents to have to search high and low for a health care provider. The district also known as Hunt Regional Healthcare operates two Northeast Texas hospitals the Hunt Regional Medical Center (HRMC) at Greenville and the Hunt Regional Community Hospital at Commerce. The hospitals offer specialized services including cardiac care rehabilitation cancer treatment diabetes management diagnostic imaging surgery and sleep disorder diagnosis. In addition the district operates divisions that provide home health and EMS services as well as family medicine occupational health and specialty outpatient medical clinics.

	Annual Growth	09/16	09/17	09/18	09/19	09/20
Sales ($ mil.)	7.0%	–	129.7	137.0	149.5	158.6
Net income ($ mil.)	–	–	(3.3)	(1.6)	(0.3)	9.2
Market value ($ mil.)	–	–	–	–	–	–
Employees	–	–	–	–	–	900

HUNTER DOUGLAS INC.

1 Blue Hill Plaza
Pearl River NY 10965
Phone: 845-664-7000
Fax: 914-381-6601
Web: www.castleoil.com

CEO: Ron Kass
CFO: Leen Reijtenbagh
HR: –
FYE: December 31
Type: Subsidiary

Don't move Hunter Douglas has got you covered — well at least it has your "windows" covered. Hunter Douglas the North American subsidiary of Netherlands-based Hunter Douglas N.V. makes a variety of blinds shades and shutters. The company markets its window coverings under such brand names as Country Woods and Chalet Woods (wood blinds) Silhouette (shades) Palm Beach (custom shutters) Vignette (Roman shades) Luminette (privacy sheers) and Duette (honeycomb shades). In addition to its own sales outlets and specialty blind and home decor stores Hunter Douglas sells its window products through independent dealers in the US and Canada.

HUNTINGTON BANCSHARES INC   NMS: HBAN

41 South High Street
Columbus, OH 43287
Phone: 614 480-2265
Fax: –
Web: www.huntington.com

CEO: Stephen Steinour
CFO: Zachary Wasserman
HR: –
FYE: December 31
Type: Public

Huntington Bancshares is the holding company for The Huntington National Bank which operates about 830 branches mostly in Ohio and Michigan. In addition to traditional retail and commercial banking services the bank offers mortgage banking capital market services equipment leasing brokerage services investment management recreational vehicle and marine financing and trust and estate services. The company's automobile finance business provides car loans to consumers and real estate and inventory finance to car dealerships throughout the Midwest. Founded in 1866 the company boasts total assets of over $142 billion.

	Annual Growth	12/17	12/18	12/19	12/20	12/21
Assets ($ mil.)	13.7%	104,185.0	108,781.0	109,002.0	123,038.0	174,064.0
Net income ($ mil.)	2.2%	1,186.0	1,393.0	1,411.0	817.0	1,295.0
Market value ($ mil.)	1.4%	20,933.5	17,137.9	21,681.2	18,158.7	22,170.0
Employees	4.0%	15,770	15,693	15,664	15,578	18,442

HUNTINGTON HOSPITAL DOLAN FAMILY HEALTH CENTER, INC.

270 PARK AVE
HUNTINGTON, NY 117432787
Phone: 631-351-2000
Fax: –
Web: www.huntington.northwell.edu

CEO: Michael J Dowling
CFO: Kevin Lawlor
HR: –
FYE: December 31
Type: Private

When residents of the Gold Coast feel poorly Huntington Hospital is there to help. Part of the North Shore-Long Island Jewish Health System Huntington Hospital is a 410-bed not-for-profit tertiary care center providing a comprehensive range of medical services to residents of Huntington New York and surrounding communities. Along with general surgical services the hospital provides specialty cardiac cancer maternity pediatric and psychiatric care. Huntington also operates a number of outpatient diagnostic and community clinics where patients can turn for primary care physical rehabilitation or specialized care for other ailments.

	Annual Growth	12/14	12/15	12/16	12/17	12/18
Sales ($ mil.)	5.1%	–	302.9	339.9	336.9	351.9
Net income ($ mil.)	–	–	2.8	25.4	19.3	(0.5)
Market value ($ mil.)	–	–	–	–	–	–
Employees	–	–	–	–	–	2,000

HUNTINGTON INGALLS INDUSTRIES, INC.   NYS: HII

4101 Washington Avenue
Newport News, VA 23607
Phone: 757 380-2000
Fax: –
Web: www.huntingtoningalls.com

CEO: Christopher Kastner
CFO: Thomas Stiehle
HR: –
FYE: December 31
Type: Public

Huntington Ingalls Industries (HII) is the sole designer builder and refueler of the US Navy's nuclear aircraft carriers. Rivaling nuclear submarine builder General Dynamics HII is the largest naval shipbuilder in America; it also maintains and repairs nuclear submarines and aircraft carriers. In addition HII builds expeditionary warfare ships surface combatants submarines and Coast Guard surface ships and provides aftermarket fleet support. Almost all its offerings are sold to the US government.

	Annual Growth	12/17	12/18	12/19	12/20	12/21
Sales ($ mil.)	6.4%	7,441.0	8,176.0	8,899.0	9,361.0	9,524.0
Net income ($ mil.)	3.2%	479.0	836.0	549.0	696.0	544.0
Market value ($ mil.)	(5.7%)	9,428.0	7,612.4	10,035.2	6,819.2	7,469.6
Employees	3.7%	38,000	40,000	42,000	42,000	44,000

HUNTON & WILLIAMS LLP

Riverfront Plaza East Tower 951 E. Byrd St.
Richmond VA 23219-4074
Phone: 804-788-8200
Fax: 804-788-8218
Web: www.hunton.com

CEO: –
CFO: –
HR: –
FYE: March 31
Type: Private - Partnershi

With about 20 offices that span not only the US but also the Asia/Pacific region and Europe law firm Hunton & Williams has expanded well beyond its Virginia home. Overall the firm has more than 800 attorneys. Hunton & Williams focuses primarily on representing clients from industries such as energy financial services and life sciences but the firm has 100 separate practice specialties such as bankruptcy corporate transactions commercial litigation intellectual property and regulatory law. Major clients have included Altria MasterCard Smithfield Foods and Wells Fargo. Henry Anderson Eppa Hunton Beverley Munford and E. Randolph Williams founded Hunton & Williams in 1901.

HUNTSMAN CORP
NYS: HUN

10003 Woodloch Forest Drive
The Woodlands, TX 77380
Phone: 281 719-6000
Fax: –
Web: www.huntsman.com

CEO: Peter Huntsman
CFO: Phil Lister
HR: R. Wade Rogers
FYE: December 31
Type: Public

Huntsman Corporation manufactures differentiated organic chemical products. It offers chemicals and formulations which it markets globally to a diversified group of consumer and industrial customers. Products are used in various applications including those in the adhesives aerospace automotive construction products durable and non-durable consumer products electronics insulation medical packaging coatings and construction power generation refining synthetic fiber textile chemicals and dyes industries. Key product lines also include MDI amines maleic anhydride epoxy-based polymer formulations textile chemicals and dyes. The US and Canada are Huntsman's biggest market accounting for about 35% of sales. The company started in 1970 as a maker of small polystyrene plastics packaging.

	Annual Growth	12/17	12/18	12/19	12/20	12/21
Sales ($ mil.)	0.3%	8,358.0	9,379.0	6,797.0	6,018.0	8,453.0
Net income ($ mil.)	13.2%	636.0	337.0	562.0	1,034.0	1,045.0
Market value ($ mil.)	1.2%	7,129.7	4,131.3	5,174.4	5,384.2	7,470.3
Employees	(2.6%)	10,000	10,000	10,000	9,000	9,000

HURCO COMPANIES INC
NMS: HURC

One Technology Way
Indianapolis, IN 46268
Phone: 317 293-5309
Fax: 317 328-2811
Web: www.hurco.com

CEO: Gregory Volovic
CFO: Sonja Mcclelland
HR: Jeff McIntyre
FYE: October 31
Type: Public

Hurco is an international industrial technology company that designs and makes computerized metal cutting and forming machine tools such as vertical machining (mills) and turning (lathes) centers as well as the software that automates the machinery. Its machines are manufactured and assembled by Taiwan subsidiary Hurco Manufacturing using components produced by neighboring contract suppliers. Hurco markets its five-axis machines through its TM/TMM TMX and VMX series and other specialty product lines. It sells to customers in the aerospace/military automotive computers/electronics energy medical equipment and transportation industries. About 35% of total revenue comes from US operations.

	Annual Growth	10/17	10/18	10/19	10/20	10/21
Sales ($ mil.)	(0.9%)	243.7	300.7	263.4	170.6	235.2
Net income ($ mil.)	(18.2%)	15.1	21.5	17.5	(6.2)	6.8
Market value ($ mil.)	(7.7%)	296.1	269.6	230.2	197.5	214.7
Employees	(1.5%)	749	800	785	710	706

HURLEY MEDICAL CENTER

1 HURLEY PLZ
FLINT, MI 485035902
Phone: 810-262-9000
Fax: –
Web: www.hurleymc.com

CEO: Melanie Devalac
CFO: Kevin Murphy
HR: –
FYE: June 30
Type: Private

A community hospital owned by the City of Flint Hurley Medical Center is a teaching hospital serving Genesee Lapeer and Shiawassee counties in eastern Michigan. The 440-bed acute care facility is affiliated with the medical schools of Michigan State University and The University of Michigan. It provides care in areas such as cancer mental health rehabilitation surgery and women's health and it is a regional center for pediatrics. Hurley Medical Center also offers advanced specialty care such as trauma care neonatal intensive care kidney transplantation burn medicine and bariatric (weight loss) surgery. The center was founded in 1908 and is owned by the state of Michigan.

	Annual Growth	03/07	03/08*	06/08	06/15	06/16
Sales ($ mil.)	6.8%	–	250.1	350.2	378.5	422.1
Net income ($ mil.)	97.7%	–	0.2	3.8	24.3	44.8
Market value ($ mil.)	–	–	–	–	–	–
Employees	–	–	–	–	–	2,884

*Fiscal year change

HURON CONSULTING GROUP INC
NMS: HURN

550 West Van Buren Street
Chicago, IL 60607
Phone: 312 583-8700
Fax: –
Web: www.huronconsultinggroup.com

CEO: James H Roth
CFO: John Kelly
HR: –
FYE: December 31
Type: Public

Huron Consulting Group provides a variety of consulting services designed to assist clients in achieving growth and profitability improving quality of service and managing corporate transitions among other initiatives. Its Healthcare segment services clients such as hospitals health systems and medical groups while its Business Advisory segment serves life sciences financial services healthcare education energy and utilities industrials and manufacturing and the public sector. Its Education segment provides research enterprise and student lifecycle; digital technology and analytic solutions; and organizational transformation. The company has locations in states throughout the US as well as in Canada India Singapore Switzerland and the UK.

	Annual Growth	12/16	12/17	12/18	12/19	12/20
Sales ($ mil.)	2.2%	798.0	807.7	878.0	965.5	871.0
Net income ($ mil.)	–	37.6	(170.1)	13.6	41.7	(23.8)
Market value ($ mil.)	3.9%	1,152.9	920.8	1,168.0	1,564.3	1,341.9
Employees	7.8%	2,818	3,083	3,269	3,750	3,807

HUSSON UNIVERSITY

1 COLLEGE CIR
BANGOR, ME 044012929
Phone: 207-941-7000
Fax: –
Web: www.husson.edu

CEO: Robert A Clark
CFO: –
HR: –
FYE: June 30
Type: Private

If the hustle and bustle of college life attracts you Husson University is probably not the place for you. The university tucked away on 175 acres of fields and forests primarily caters to rural and small town residents in its home state of Maine. Enrollment is about 2500 students about 20% of whom are seeking graduate degrees. The school has about 70 faculty members and a 19-to-1 student teacher ratio. Husson offers both undergraduate and graduate degreee programs in such academic disciplines as business communications education health language studies and science and humanities. The school was founded in 1898.

	Annual Growth	06/07	06/08	06/09	06/10	06/13
Sales ($ mil.)	–	–	0.0	35.6	40.5	53.2
Net income ($ mil.)	–	–	–	0.0	2.4	4.1
Market value ($ mil.)	–	–	–	–	–	–
Employees	–	–	–	–	–	520

HUTCHESON MEDICAL CENTER INC.

100 GROSS CRESCENT CIR
FORT OGLETHORPE, GA 30742-3669
Phone: 706-858-2000
Fax: –
Web: www.hutcheson.org

CEO: –
CFO: –
HR: –
FYE: September 30
Type: Private

Hutcheson Medical Center is a community hospital that serves the residents of Catoosa Dade and Walker counties in northwestern Georgia. Founded in 1953 the nearly 200-bed hospital provides specialty services such as emergency medicine orthopedics cancer treatment physical therapy and women's and children's care as well as home health and hospice services. The hospital has more than 200 physicians on its medical staff. Hutcheson Medical Center also operates the 110-bed Parkside Nursing Home an outpatient surgery center and family practice medical clinics.

	Annual Growth	09/05	09/06	09/07	09/08	09/09
Sales ($ mil.)	(4.1%)	–	111.9	115.5	123.2	98.6
Net income ($ mil.)	–	–	(1.0)	0.3	(0.5)	(6.6)
Market value ($ mil.)	–	–	–	–	–	–
Employees	–	–	–	–	–	530

HUTCHINSON TECHNOLOGY INC.
NMS: HTCH

40 West Highland Park Drive N.E.
Hutchinson, MN 55350
Phone: 320 587-3797
Fax: –
Web: www.htch.com

CEO: Richard J Penn
CFO: David P Radloff
HR: –
FYE: September 27
Type: Public

Suspensions at Hutchinson Technology have nothing to do with getting kicked out of school. The company is a top global maker of disk drive suspension assemblies. These support the read-write head above the spinning magnetic disk in hard drives typically at a height of about a millionth of an inch — 3000 times thinner than a piece of paper. The company's products include conventional assemblies trace suspension assemblies and accessories such as base plates and flexures. Hutchinson serves OEMs primarily in Asia which accounts for most of its revenue. The company generates minimal sales from biomeasurment devices for the healthcare market.

	Annual Growth	09/11	09/12	09/13	09/14	09/15
Sales ($ mil.)	(2.4%)	278.1	248.6	249.6	261.1	252.8
Net income ($ mil.)	–	(55.6)	(48.6)	(35.1)	(40.4)	(39.1)
Market value ($ mil.)	(8.4%)	67.1	58.7	118.7	120.7	47.3
Employees	1.0%	2,317	2,060	2,436	2,489	2,412

HUTTIG BUILDING PRODUCTS, INC.
NAS: HBP

555 Maryville University Drive, Suite 400
St. Louis, MO 63141
Phone: 314 216-2600
Fax: –
Web: www.huttig.com

CEO: Jon Vrabely
CFO: Philip Keipp
HR: –
FYE: December 31
Type: Public

Huttig Building Products is one of the US's largest distributors of millwork building materials and wood products for new housing construction and remodeling and repair. Huttig sells doors windows moldings trusses wall panels lumber and other supplies through more than 25 distribution centers in more than 40 states covering a substantial portion of the US housing market. The centers primarily sell to building materials dealers (such as Lumbermen's Merchandising Corp) buying groups home centers and industrial users. Huttig's products typically end up in the hands of professional builders and contractors.

	Annual Growth	12/16	12/17	12/18	12/19	12/20
Sales ($ mil.)	2.6%	713.9	753.2	839.6	812.0	792.3
Net income ($ mil.)	–	–	16.3	(7.1)	(6.4)	(21.3)	(0.9)
Market value ($ mil.)	(13.7%)	177.7	178.8	48.4	41.4	98.7
Employees	0.0%	1,200	1,300	1,360	1,364	1,200

HY-VEE, INC.

5820 WESTOWN PKWY
WEST DES MOINES, IA 502668223
Phone: 515-267-2800
Fax: –
Web: www.hy-vee.com

CEO: Randy Edeker
CFO: Mike Skokan
HR: –
FYE: September 30
Type: Private

Hy-Vee is one of the largest privately-owned US supermarket chains despite serving some modestly sized towns in the Midwest. The company runs more than 280 stores in eight Midwestern states. It distributes products to its stores through several subsidiaries including Amber Pharmacy D & D Foods Florist Distributing Hy-Vee Construction Midwest Heritage Perishable Distributors of Iowa and Vivid Clear RX. Hy-Vee is synonymous with quality variety convenience healthy lifestyles culinary expertise and superior customer service. Charles Hyde and David Vredenburg founded the employee-owned company in 1930. It takes its name from a combination of its founders' names.

	Annual Growth	12/15	12/16*	09/18	09/19	09/20
Sales ($ mil.)	3.9%	–	9,842.3	10,290.6	10,672.5	11,449.2
Net income ($ mil.)	–	–	0.0	0.0	0.0	0.0
Market value ($ mil.)	–	–	–	–	–	–
Employees	–	–	–	–	–	83,000

*Fiscal year change

HYATT HOTELS CORP
NYS: H

150 North Riverside Plaza, 8th Floor
Chicago, IL 60606
Phone: 312 750-1234
Fax: –
Web: www.hyatt.com

CEO: Mark Hoplamazian
CFO: Joan Bottarini
HR: Malaika Myers
FYE: December 31
Type: Public

Hyatt Hotels is one of the world's top operators of luxury hotels and resorts. The company has about 925 managed franchised and owned properties (around 226000 rooms) in about 65 countries. Its core Hyatt Regency brand offers hospitality services targeted primarily to business travelers and leisure guests. The firm's hotel chains include the upscale full service Hyatt Grand Hyatt and Andaz brands as well as Park Hyatt (luxury) and Hyatt Place (select service). Hyatt also operates resorts under the names Hyatt Zilara and Hyatt Ziva. Domestic markets account for nearly 85% of total revenue.

	Annual Growth	12/17	12/18	12/19	12/20	12/21
Sales ($ mil.)	(10.3%)	4,685.0	4,454.0	5,020.0	2,066.0	3,028.0
Net income ($ mil.)	–	249.0	769.0	766.0	(703.0)	(222.0)
Market value ($ mil.)	6.9%	8,087.6	7,434.3	9,865.9	8,165.7	10,546.6
Employees	(0.6%)	45,000	54,000	55,000	37,000	44,000

HYCROFT MINING CORP
NBB: ANVG Q

9790 Gateway Drive, Suite 200
Reno, NV 89521
Phone: 775 358-4455
Fax: 775 358-4458
Web: www.alliednevada.com

CEO: –
CFO: –
HR: –
FYE: December 31
Type: Public

All that glitters is not gold; some of it's silver. That's the story at Allied Nevada Gold a mining company that produces gold primarily and silver as a by-product from its property in Nevada. Its wholly owned Hycroft Mine sitting on 96 sq. mi. has proven and probable mineral reserves of about 3 million ounces of gold and nearly 50 million ounces of silver. The company is conducting feasibility studies for a mill on the property that would process sulfide and other high oxide ores. Allied Nevada Gold also explores for gold silver and other minerals on more than 100 properties in the state. The company was spun off from Vista Gold in 2007 when it acquired its former parent's Nevada mining operations.

	Annual Growth	12/10	12/11	12/12	12/13	12/14
Sales ($ mil.)	24.1%	130.9	152.0	214.6	267.9	310.4
Net income ($ mil.)	–	34.1	36.7	47.7	1.4	(518.9)
Market value ($ mil.)	(57.4%)	3,320.1	3,821.1	3,802.2	448.0	109.8
Employees	18.7%	231	291	742	428	459

HYDROMER, INC.
NBB: HYDI

4715 Corporate Drive NW, Suite 200
Concord, NC 28027
Phone: 800 287-5208
Fax: –
Web: www.hydromer.com

CEO: Peter von Dyck
CFO: Robert Lee
HR: John Konar
FYE: June 30
Type: Public

Hydromer would say its products become lubricious when wet. Bon Jovi preferred the term "slippery" but it amounts to the same thing. The company makes lubricating and water-resistant coatings for use in medical pharmaceutical cosmetic industrial and veterinary markets. Its products include lubricated medical devices hydro-gels for drugs anti-fog coatings marine hull protective coatings barrier dips for dairy cows and intermediaries for hair and skin care products. Services include research and development medical device manufacturing (through subsidiary Biosearch Medical Products) and contract coating. Chairman and CEO Manfred Dyck owns a third of Hydromer.

	Annual Growth	06/17	06/18	06/19	06/20	06/21
Sales ($ mil.)	(9.3%)	5.4	5.6	5.2	6.2	3.7
Net income ($ mil.)	–	–	(1.3)	0.1	4.5	(3.0)	(2.7)
Market value ($ mil.)	5.2%	–	3.1	2.0	5.7	7.3	3.8
Employees	–	–	–	34	–	–

HYDRON TECHNOLOGIES INC.   OTC: HTEC

4400 34th St. North Ste. F   CEO: Helen Canetano
St. Petersburg FL 33714   CFO: William Lauby
Phone: 727-342-5050   HR: –
Fax: 727-344-3920   FYE: September 30
Web: www.hydron.com   Type: Public

The magic is in the moisture at Hydron Technologies. The company focuses on developing skin care products that contain microbubbles of pure oxygen used in treating the epidermis and underlying tissues. Hydron Technologies also manufactures personal and oral care products that contain its moisture-attracting ingredient the Hydron polymer. The company distributes about 40 skin hair and sun care products as well as bath and body items through its Web site. It also produces private-label skin care items and ships them to contract manufacturers.

HYPERDYNAMICS CORPORATION   NYSE AMEX: HDY

1 Sugar Creek Center Blvd. Ste. 125   CEO: –
Sugar Land TX 77478-3560   CFO: –
Phone: 713-353-9400   HR: –
Fax: 713-353-9421   FYE: June 30
Web: www.hypd.com   Type: Public

Not as hyper as it was but still dynamic Hyperdynamics has shifted its business focus from IT consulting services to oil and gas exploration primarily in Africa. Its SCS Corporation subsidiary concentrates on developing an oil and gas concession located offshore in the Republic of Guinea in West Africa. Hyperdynamics' HYD Resources subsidiary and gas exploration and production company focuses on low-risk shallow exploration projects in Louisiana where in 2008 it held proved reserves of 150435 barrels of oil. Chairman Kent Watts who stepped down as CEO in 2009 owns 17% of Hyperdynamics.

HYPERTENSION DIAGNOSTICS, INC.   NBB: HDII

550 Highway 7 East, Unit 316   CEO: Kenneth Brimmer
MN L4B 3Z4   CFO: Kenneth W Brimmer
Phone: 404 449-6151   HR: –
Fax: –   FYE: December 31
Web: www.hypertensiondiagnostics.com   Type: Public

Hypertension Diagnostics can tell if your cardiovascular system is about to go snap crackle and pop. The company's noninvasive instruments measure the elasticity of arteries helping physicians assess patients' risk for cardiovascular disease. Its CR-2000 Research System is marketed for research purposes to government agencies pharmaceutical companies academic research centers and cardiovascular research centers worldwide; drug heavyweights AstraZeneca and Pfizer are among the system's users. The CVProfilor DO-2020 and the CVProfilor MD-3000 are intended for general physicians cardiologists and other health care practitioners in the US and abroad.

	Annual Growth	06/10	06/11	06/12*	12/17	12/18
Sales ($ mil.)	13.4%	1.4	1.4	3.2	3.7	3.8
Net income ($ mil.)	–	(1.0)	0.4	(1.3)	(0.4)	(0.1)
Market value ($ mil.)	(42.5%)	8.4	3.1	1.3	0.1	0.1
Employees	(10.6%)	5	5	4	–	–

*Fiscal year change

HYSTER-YALE MATERIALS HANDLING INC   NYS: HY

5875 Landerbrook Drive, Suite 300   CEO: Rajiv Prasad
Cleveland, OH 44124-4069   CFO: Kenneth Schilling
Phone: 440 449-9600   HR: –
Fax: –   FYE: December 31
Web: www.hyster-yale.com   Type: Public

Hyster-Yale Materials Handling is a lift truck manufacturer the company designs manufactures and sells a variety of forklifts and other lift truck products through its Hyster-Yale Group subsidiary. In addition the company has a broad array of solutions aimed at meeting the specific materials handling needs of its customers including attachments and hydrogen fuel cell power products telematics automation and fleet management services as well as a variety of other power options for its lift trucks. Its trucks primarily are sold under the Hyster and Yale brands. The company which operates facilities in the Americas Europe and Asia gets about 60% of revenue from the US markets. The company offers a line of aftermarket parts for Hyster and Yale lift trucks as well as for competing brands.

	Annual Growth	12/16	12/17	12/18	12/19	12/20
Sales ($ mil.)	2.3%	2,569.7	2,885.2	3,174.4	3,291.8	2,812.1
Net income ($ mil.)	(3.5%)	42.8	48.6	34.7	35.8	37.1
Market value ($ mil.)	(1.7%)	1,071.7	1,431.2	1,041.3	990.8	1,000.8
Employees	4.0%	6,500	6,800	7,800	7,900	7,600

I/OMAGIC CORPORATION   OTC: IOMG

4 Marconi   CEO: Tony Shahbaz
Irvine CA 92618   CFO: –
Phone: 949-707-4800   HR: –
Fax: 949-855-3550   FYE: December 31
Web: www.iomagic.com   Type: Public

I/OMagic has some input regarding computer peripheral output. It designs and markets optical storage products such as CD-ROM and DVD-ROM playback and read-write devices. Other products include audio cards digital photo frames external hard drives headphones and Web cameras. The company also markets LCD-based HDTVs and home theater speakers through its Digital Research Technologies (DRT) division. I/OMagic sells to retailers such as Staples (nearly half of sales) OfficeMax and Costco in the US and Canada. Other significant customers include distributors Tech Data (29% of sales) and D&H Distributing. The company subcontracts the manufacturing of most of its products.

IA GLOBAL INC.   OTC: IAGI

101 California St. Ste. 2450   CEO: –
San Francisco CA 94111   CFO: –
Phone: 415-946-8828   HR: –
Fax: 415-946-8801   FYE: March 31
Web: www.iaglobalinc.com   Type: Public

IA Global has made the call to the Pacific Rim region. The holding company is focused on growing its existing businesses and making strategic acquisitions in Asia. Its primary holdings revolve around Global Hotline a Japanese business process outsourcing (BPO) company that owns two call centers and offers telemarketing services medical insurance and other products to customers in Japan. IA Global also owns call center operations in the Philippines along with parts of Japanese firms GPlus Media (online media) Slate Consulting (executive search) Taicom Securities (financial services) and Australian Secured Financial Limited (private loans and real estate investment). IA Global was formed in 1998.

IAP WORLDWIDE SERVICES, INC.

7315 N ATLANTIC AVE
CAPE CANAVERAL, FL 329203721
Phone: 973-633-5115
Fax: –

CEO: Terry Derosa
CFO: Charles Cosgrove
HR: –
FYE: December 31
Type: Private

Wherever US troops are marching IAP Worldwide Services is there to support them. The company provides a variety of logistics and facility support services chiefly for the US Department of Defense and other government customers including US states and other countries; it also undertakes work for commercial enterprises. Services include base camp facilities support logistics planning and temporary staffing. The company operates through three distinct segments: global operations and logistics; facilities management and base operations support; and professional and technical services. Investment firm Cerberus Capital Management owns a controlling interest in IAP.

	Annual Growth	12/11	12/12	12/13	12/14	12/15
Sales ($ mil.)	227.4%	–	15.6	12.0	551.2	546.7
Net income ($ mil.)	–	–	(0.4)	(1.0)	263.1	2.5
Market value ($ mil.)	–	–	–	–	–	–
Employees	–	–	–	–	–	1,647

IASIS HEALTHCARE CORPORATION

117 Seaboard Ln. Bldg. E
Franklin TN 37067
Phone: 615-844-2747
Fax: 615-846-3006
Web: www.iasishealthcare.com

CEO: Ralph De La Torre
CFO: –
HR: Clarissa Lopez
FYE: September 30
Type: Private

If you're sick in the city or have a stomach ache in the suburbs IASIS Healthcare provides a medical oasis. The company owns and operates 18 acute care hospitals and one behavioral health facility (with some 4300 beds total) in Arizona Colorado Florida Louisiana Nevada Texas and Utah. IASIS also operates several outpatient facilities and other centers providing ancillary services such as radiation therapy diagnostic imaging and ambulatory surgery. Its Health Choice subsidiary is a Medicaid and Medicare managed health plan that serves about 200000 individuals in Arizona and Utah. An investor group led by TPG Capital owns the lion's share of the company.

IASO PHARMA INC.

12707 High Bluff Dr. Ste. 200
San Diego CA 92130
Phone: 858-350-4312
Fax: +86-10-5123-8866
Web: www.mienergy.com.cn

CEO: –
CFO: –
HR: –
FYE: December 31
Type: Private

IASO Pharma aims to cure what ails ya. The development-stage drug company focuses on in-licensing potential treatments for bacterial and fungal infections. Its lead candidate is an antibiotic for the treatment of respiratory tract infections. Other potential products include an antifungal used to treat yeast and sinus infections and a process to improve the treatment of nail infections. IASO's candidates are in-licensed from Dong Wha Pharmaceutical UCB Celltech and Santee Biosciences. The company plans to exclusively license pre-tested candidates; it doesn't conduct any of its own discovery research. It was formed in 2006 as Pacific Beach Biosciences; it changed its name and filed to go public in 2010.

IBERDROLA USA INC.

52 Farm View Dr.
New Gloucester ME 04260-5116
Phone: 207-688-6300
Fax: 207-688-4354
Web: www.iberdrolausa.com

CEO: James Torgerson
CFO: Douglas K Stuver
HR: –
FYE: December 31
Type: Subsidiary

Iberdrola USA (formerly Energy East) is a major regional player and the leading US operating subsidiary of IBERDROLA. The utility holding company (98% of its assets are in regulated utilities) distributes electricity and natural gas in the US northeast through Central Maine Power New York State Electric & Gas and Rochester Gas and Electric. Iberdrola USA serves about 2.7 million electricity and natural gas customers. Other operations include power generation gas transportation and processing telecommunications and energy infrastructure and management services.

IBERIABANK CORP

NMS: IBKC

200 West Congress Street
Lafayette, LA 70501
Phone: 337 521-4003
Fax: –
Web: www.iberiabank.com

CEO: –
CFO: –
HR: –
FYE: December 31
Type: Public

Holding company IBERIABANK Corporation through its flagship bank subsidiary IBERIABANK operates some 230 branches in Louisiana and about 10 other states. It also has about 30 title insurance offices in Louisiana Arkansas and Tennessee in addition to some 90 mortgage loan offices in a dozen states and about 20 wealth management offices in four states. Offering deposit products such as checking and savings accounts CDs and IRAs the bank uses funds gathered mainly to make loans. Commercial loans and leases make up around two-thirds of the company's $22.3 billion loan portfolio which also includes consumer loans and residential mortgages. IBERIABANK Corp. has $30.1 billion in assets.

	Annual Growth	12/14	12/15	12/16	12/17	12/18
Assets ($ mil.)	18.3%	15,758.6	19,504.1	21,659.2	27,904.1	30,833.0
Net income ($ mil.)	36.9%	105.5	142.8	186.8	142.4	370.2
Market value ($ mil.)	(0.2%)	3,553.5	3,017.6	4,589.2	4,246.7	3,522.3
Employees	5.1%	2,825	3,216	3,155	3,604	3,441

IC COMPLIANCE LLC

1065 E. Hillsdale Blvd. Ste. 300
Foster City CA 94404
Phone: 650-378-4150
Fax: 650-378-4157
Web: www.gotoicon.com

CEO: Teresa Creech
CFO: Jim Hanrahan
HR: –
FYE: December 31
Type: Private

IC Compliance (doing business as ICon Professional Services) keeps the IRS off the backs of companies with contingent workforces. The consulting firm ensures that its clients are in compliance with tax rules for independent contractors providing advice on employee classification guidelines IRS audit support tax reporting and invoice submission and other services. Additionally ICon offers outsourced payroll and benefits administration for certain classes of employees including non-independent contractors non-sourced workers and former employees. The firm was established in 1997.

ICAD INC
NAS: ICAD

98 Spit Brook Road, Suite 100
Nashua, NH 03062
Phone: 603 882-5200
Fax: –
Web: www.icadmed.com

CEO: Stacey Stevens
CFO: Charles Carter
HR: –
FYE: December 31
Type: Public

Early detection is the best prevention in iCAD's eyes. The company targets the breast cancer detection market with its core SecondLook computer-aided detection (CAD) systems. The systems include workstations and analytical software that help radiologists better identify potential cancers in mammography images. iCAD sells models that can be used with film-based and digital mammography systems. In addition the company also makes similar CAD systems that are used with magnetic resonance imaging (MRI) systems to detect breast and prostate cancers. iCAD markets its products directly and through sales partnerships with the likes of GE Healthcare Siemens Medical Solutions Fuji Medical and Agfa.

	Annual Growth	12/16	12/17	12/18	12/19	12/20
Sales ($ mil.)	3.0%	26.3	28.1	25.6	31.3	29.7
Net income ($ mil.)	–	(10.1)	(14.3)	(9.0)	(13.6)	(17.6)
Market value ($ mil.)	42.1%	76.1	80.9	87.0	182.7	310.3
Employees	(0.9%)	118	119	97	138	114

ICAGEN INC.

4222 Emperor Blvd. Ste. 350
Durham NC 27703
Phone: 919-941-5206
Fax: 919-941-0813
Web: www.icagen.com

CEO: P Kay Wagoner PHD
CFO: Richard D Katz
HR: –
FYE: December 31
Type: Private

Icagen wants to set the market for ion channel modulators on fire. The development-stage biotech focuses on treatments for epilepsy asthma pain and inflammation by regulating the inflow into cells of such ions as calcium potassium and sodium. Icagen's lead candidate senicapoc for sickle cell disease died in 2007 following lackluster Phase III clinical trial results. The drug was being developed in a partnership with Johnson & Johnson subsidiary McNeil Consumer & Specialty Pharmaceuticals. Shortly thereafter Icagen announced a deal collaborating with Pfizer on the development of epilepsy and pain treatments. Then in 2011 the company decided to just go ahead and be acquired by Pfizer.

ICAHN ENTERPRISES LP
NMS: IEP

16690 Collins Avenue, PH-1
Sunny Isles Beach, FL 33160
Phone: 305 422-4100
Fax: –
Web: www.ielp.com

CEO: David Willetts
CFO: Michael Nevin
HR: –
FYE: December 31
Type: Public

Icahn Enterprises has investments in companies active across eight industry segments: investment energy automotive food packaging metals real estate home fashion and pharma. Subsidiaries include CVR Energy Viskase and WestPoint Home among others. Icahn has investments in major brands such as Herbalife Caesars Entertainment and Hertz. Most of Icahn's business is in the US which accounts for some 95% of revenue. Billionaire corporate raider Carl Icahn and his affiliates control his namesake firm.

	Annual Growth	12/16	12/17	12/18	12/19	12/20
Sales ($ mil.)	(21.8%)	16,348.0	21,744.0	11,777.0	8,992.0	6,123.0
Net income ($ mil.)	–	(1,128.0)	2,430.0	1,507.0	(1,098.0)	(1,653.0)
Market value ($ mil.)	(4.1%)	14,461.0	12,791.0	13,775.6	14,842.3	12,228.6
Employees	(28.5%)	90,960	89,034	29,034	28,033	23,800

ICE DATA SERVICES, INC.

32 CROSBY DR STE 100
BEDFORD, MA 017301448
Phone: 781-687-8500
Fax: –
Web: www.theice.com

CEO: –
CFO: –
HR: –
FYE: December 31
Type: Private

Interactive Data Corporation has something vital to the information superhighway — the information. Its subscription services provide financial market data analytics and related services to financial institutions active traders and individual investors. Interactive Data conducts business through two segments: Institutional Services and Active Trader Services. Products include Interactive Data Fixed Income Analytics (fixed-income portfolio analytics for institutions) Interactive Data Pricing and Reference Data (securities information for institutions) and Interactive Data Desktop Solutions (real-time market data for individuals). Private-equity firms Silver Lake and Warburg Pincus agreed to sell IDC to Intercontinental Exchange in 2015.

	Annual Growth	12/09	12/10	12/11	12/12	12/13
Assets ($ mil.)	(1.5%)	–	–	4,093.7	3,962.3	3,968.4
Net income ($ mil.)	–	–	–	(29.3)	1.0	33.5
Market value ($ mil.)	–	–	–	–	–	–
Employees	–	–	–	–	–	2,600

ICF INTERNATIONAL INC
NMS: ICFI

9300 Lee Highway
Fairfax, VA 22031
Phone: 703 934-3000
Fax: –
Web: www.icf.com

CEO: John Wasson
CFO: Bettina Welsh
HR: –
FYE: December 31
Type: Public

ICF International consults government entities and commercial clients on policy management and technology issues related to energy the environment and infrastructure; health education and social programs; safety and security; and consumer and financial. The company offers advisory services program implementation analytics services digital services and engagement services. ICF International has more than 75 offices in the US and over 15 outside the US in countries such as the UK Belgium China India and Canada. About two-thirds of revenue comes from government clients including US federal state and local agencies as well as governments outside the US.

	Annual Growth	12/16	12/17	12/18	12/19	12/20
Sales ($ mil.)	6.2%	1,185.1	1,229.2	1,338.0	1,478.5	1,506.9
Net income ($ mil.)	4.2%	46.6	62.9	61.4	68.9	55.0
Market value ($ mil.)	7.7%	1,043.8	992.8	1,225.0	1,732.5	1,405.6
Employees	10.7%	5,000	5,500	6,000	7,000	7,500

ICIMS.COM INC

90 MATAWAN RD FL 500
MATAWAN, NJ 077472624
Phone: 732-847-1941
Fax: –
Web: www.icims.com

CEO: Steve Lucas
CFO: Valerie Rainey
HR: –
FYE: December 31
Type: Private

|Who says good help is hard to find? iCIMS provides Web-based applicant tracking and recruiting management software for corporate human resources professionals and third-party recruiters. The company's iCIMS Talent Platform which is designed to help businesses make their hiring processes more efficient includes software for screening and storing applicant information enabling online job applications tracking candidates monitoring performance after recruitment and managing post-employment processes. It sells its applications on a Software-as-a-Service basis. iCIMS targets recruiters midsized companies and large corporations. The company was founded in 1999 by Colin Day and George Lieu.

	Annual Growth	12/09	12/10	12/11	12/12	12/13
Sales ($ mil.)	22.7%	–	25.7	30.7	37.3	47.4
Net income ($ mil.)	16.8%	–	–	3.7	(3.4)	5.0
Market value ($ mil.)	–	–	–	–	–	–
Employees	–	–	–	–	–	240

ICOA INC

NBB: ICOA

1530 Atwood Avenue, #19652
Johnston, RI 02919
Phone: 401 648-0690
Fax: -
Web: www.icoacorp.com

CEO: George Strouthopoulos
CFO: Erwin Vahlsing Jr
HR: -
FYE: December 31
Type: Public

ICOA installs and operates Wi-Fi hotspots in public areas such as airports apartment buildings and retail businesses across the US. Retail users have included such restaurants as Panera Bread and Panda Express. Airport clients have included facilities in Fresno California and Boise Idaho. The company's iDockUSA subsidiary focuses on marinas while LinkSpot targets RV parks and outdoor recreation areas. All told ICOA claims about 1500 installations in 45 states. It also provides software called Tollbooth which is used to manage wireless network user authentication billing and customer service functions.

	Annual Growth	12/16	12/17	12/18	12/19	12/20
Sales ($ mil.)	(4.8%)	0.0	0.0	0.0	0.0	0.0
Net income ($ mil.)	-	0.1	0.4	0.6	(0.1)	(0.1)
Market value ($ mil.)	-	0.0	0.0	0.0	0.0	0.0
Employees	-	-	-	-	-	-

ICON HEALTH & FITNESS INC.

1500 S. 1000 West
Logan UT 84321
Phone: 435-750-5000
Fax: 435-750-3917
Web: www.iconfitness.com

CEO: Scott Watterson
CFO: S Fred Beck
HR: -
FYE: May 31
Type: Private

ICON Health & Fitness has brawn as one of the leading US makers of home fitness equipment. Its products primarily include treadmills elliptical trainers and weight benches. Brands include NordicTrack HealthRider ProForm Image iFit Weslo and Weider. ICON also offers commercial equipment through its FreeMotion Fitness unit. It makes most of its products in Utah but it also has operations in Asia Australia Brazil Europe and Mexico. Products are sold through retailers (such as Sears Wal-Mart and Sports Authority) infomercials and the Web. The company was founded as a housewares importer in 1977. Bain Capital Credit Suisse and founders Scott Watterson and Gary Stevenson collectively own ICON.

ICON IDENTITY SOLUTIONS, INC.

1701 GOLF RD STE 1-900
ROLLING MEADOWS, IL 600084246
Phone: 847-364-2250
Fax: -
Web: www.stratusunlimited.com

CEO: Tim Eippert
CFO: John Callan
HR: -
FYE: December 31
Type: Private

Icon Identity Solutions helps its customers avoid identity crises. The firm provides a variety of services related to the building of a company's brand through the use of signs and exterior graphics. Icon can help clients manage multiple sign projects on a global scale if needed. Its services include sign design permitting and manufacturing. Icon Identity Solutions is one arm of Icon Companies which also operates subsidiaries East Coast Sign Advertising and ImageCare Maintenance Services (IMS). IMS provides sign repair and maintenance. Past clients have included BMW's Mini unit and Citigroup.

	Annual Growth	12/14	12/15	12/16	12/17	12/18
Sales ($ mil.)	16.1%	-	107.7	119.1	110.2	168.7
Net income ($ mil.)	(42.1%)	-	4.1	5.0	2.9	0.8
Market value ($ mil.)	-	-	-	-	-	-
Employees	-	-	-	-	-	450

ICONIX BRAND GROUP INC

NMS: ICON

1450 Broadway
New York, NY 10018
Phone: 212 730-0030
Fax: 212 391-2057
Web: www.iconixbrand.com

CEO: Robert C Galvin
CFO: John T McClain
HR: -
FYE: December 31
Type: Public

Once a shoemaker Iconix Brand Group (Iconix) licenses some 30 women's men's and home to retailers and manufacturers through more than 430 worldwide licenses. Consumer brands in the Iconix stable include Candie's Danskin Ocean Pacific Mossimo London Fog Mudd and Rocawear. Among the company's home brands are Cannon Fieldcrest and Waverly. Along with licensing the brands Iconix markets and promotes it through its in-house advertising and public relations services. The company maximize its brands primarily through strategic licenses and joint venture partnerships globally as well as to grow the portfolio of brands through strategic acquisitions. It generates most of its revenue in the US.

	Annual Growth	12/15	12/16	12/17	12/18	12/19
Sales ($ mil.)	(20.8%)	379.2	368.5	225.8	187.7	149.0
Net income ($ mil.)	-	(189.3)	(252.1)	(489.3)	(89.7)	(111.5)
Market value ($ mil.)	(33.3%)	80.0	109.4	15.1	1.0	15.8
Employees	(3.7%)	137	145	152	122	118

ICONMA L.L.C.

850 STEPHENSON HWY
TROY, MI 480831152
Phone: 248-583-1930
Fax: -
Web: www.iconma.com

CEO: Claudine S George
CFO: -
HR: -
FYE: December 31
Type: Private

ICONMA offers companies a number of consulting and staffing services with a focus on information technology. Its staffing services include contract contract-to-hire and direct hire IT placement as well as staffing in the areas of engineering accounting/finance and professional. The firm also provides offshore software development services and other IT consulting and has a health care services division dedicated to the technology needs of insurance providers hospitals and other medical companies. Clients include Deutsche Bank Toyota and Anthem. Established in 2000 ICONMA has offices across the US and one in India.

	Annual Growth	12/05	12/06	12/07	12/08	12/09
Sales ($ mil.)	(47.8%)	-	-	195.5	40.5	53.2
Net income ($ mil.)	906.5%	-	-	0.0	1.2	1.7
Market value ($ mil.)	-	-	-	-	-	-
Employees	-	-	-	-	-	1,556

ICU MEDICAL INC

NMS: ICUI

951 Calle Amanecer
San Clemente, CA 92673
Phone: 949 366-2183
Fax: -
Web: www.icumed.com

CEO: Vivek Jain
CFO: Brian Bonnell
HR: -
FYE: December 31
Type: Public

ICU is one of the world's leading pure-play infusion therapy companies with global operations and a wide-ranging product portfolio that includes IV solutions IV smart pumps with pain management and safety software technology dedicated and non-dedicated IV sets and needle-free connectors designed to help meet clinical safety and workflow goals. In addition ICU manufactures automated pharmacy IV compounding systems with workflow technology closed system transfer devices for preparing and administering hazardous IV drugs and cardiac monitoring systems for critically ill patients. ICU Medical which sells its products to other equipment makers and distributors gets most of its revenue from US customers.

	Annual Growth	12/16	12/17	12/18	12/19	12/20
Sales ($ mil.)	35.3%	379.4	1,292.6	1,400.0	1,266.2	1,271.0
Net income ($ mil.)	8.3%	63.1	68.6	28.8	101.0	86.9
Market value ($ mil.)	9.8%	3,102.9	4,548.5	4,835.5	3,940.4	4,516.7
Employees	29.6%	2,803	6,802	8,100	8,000	7,900

IDACORP INC
NYS: IDA

1221 W. Idaho Street
Boise, ID 83702-5627
Phone: 208 388-2200
Fax: –
Web: www.idacorpinc.com

CEO: Lisa A Grow
CFO: Steven R Keen
HR: –
FYE: December 31
Type: Public

IDACORP operating through subsidiary Idaho Power Company is an electric utility engaged in the generation transmission distribution sale and purchase of electric energy and capacity. Idaho Power provides electric utility service to approximately 587000 retail customers in southern Idaho and eastern Oregon. Approximately 491000 of these customers are residential. Other IDACORP subsidiaries include IDACORP Financial Services Inc. (IFS) an investor in affordable housing and other real estate investments; and Ida-West Energy Company an operator of small hydropower generation projects that satisfy the requirements of the Public Utility Regulatory Policies Act of 1978 (PURPA).

	Annual Growth	12/17	12/18	12/19	12/20	12/21
Sales ($ mil.)	2.0%	1,349.5	1,370.8	1,346.4	1,350.7	1,458.1
Net income ($ mil.)	3.7%	212.4	226.8	232.9	237.4	245.6
Market value ($ mil.)	5.5%	4,615.2	4,701.1	5,395.2	4,851.1	5,724.0
Employees	0.2%	1,983	1,990	1,993	1,950	1,999

IDAHO POWER CO
NL:

1221 W. Idaho Street
Boise, ID 83702-5627
Phone: 208 388-2200
Fax: 208 388-6903
Web: www.idahopower.com

CEO: Lisa A Grow
CFO: Steven R Keen
HR: –
FYE: December 31
Type: Public

Idaho Power provides electric utility service to retail customers in southern Idaho and eastern Oregon. The utility a subsidiary of holding company IDACORP provides electricity to approximately 572000 residential commercial and industrial customers over some 4830 miles of transmission and about 27970 miles distribution lines. Idaho Power holds franchises in over 70 cities in Idaho and seven in Oregon. It also owns power plant interests that give it a generating capacity of over 3540 MW. In addition through its Idaho Energy Resources unit the company has a two-third interest in the Bridger Coal Company which supplies fuel to the Jim Bridger generating plant in Wyoming.

	Annual Growth	12/17	12/18	12/19	12/20	12/21
Sales ($ mil.)	2.0%	1,344.9	1,366.6	1,342.9	1,347.3	1,455.4
Net income ($ mil.)	4.2%	206.3	222.3	224.4	233.2	243.2
Market value ($ mil.)	–	–	–	–	–	–
Employees	0.2%	1,973	1,979	1,982	1,937	1,988

IDAHO STRATEGIC RESOURCES INC
NBB: NJMC

201 N. Third Street
Coeur d'Alene, ID 83814
Phone: 208 625-9001
Fax: –
Web: www.newjerseymining.com

CEO: John Swallow
CFO: Grant A Brackebusch
HR: –
FYE: December 31
Type: Public

No product of the Garden State New Jersey Mining seeks out gold silver and base metals in the Coeur d'Alene mining district of northern Idaho and western Montana. The development and exploration company maintains two Idaho-based joint ventures one with Marathon Gold at the Golden Chest gold mine and another with United Mining Group involved in ore processing. The company also holds rights to several mineral properties including the Niagara copper-silver deposit Toboggan gold exploration project (formerly a JV with Newmont Mining) and Silver Strand mine. President Fred Brackebusch controls about a quarter of New Jersey Mining.

	Annual Growth	12/16	12/17	12/18	12/19	12/20
Sales ($ mil.)	79.7%	0.5	4.3	3.6	6.1	5.7
Net income ($ mil.)	–	(1.4)	0.0	0.8	(0.6)	(0.6)
Market value ($ mil.)	21.3%	1.2	1.5	1.6	1.3	2.6
Employees	18.0%	16	16	24	24	31

IDEALAB

130 W. Union St.
Pasadena CA 91103
Phone: 626-585-6900
Fax: 626-535-2701
Web: www.idealab.com

CEO: Bill Gross
CFO: Craig Chrisney
HR: –
FYE: January 31
Type: Private

When entrepreneur Bill Gross wanted to coddle his Internet-related brainchildren he created Idealab. The company which once teetered on the brink of bankruptcy amid the flame-outs of its erstwhile dot-com progeny nurtures business ideas (several generated by Gross) with the hopes of growing them into full-fledged companies by providing money office space strategic advice and other resources. Idealab is increasingly involved in emerging technologies such as renewable energy (eSolar Energy Innovations) automation (Evolution Robotics) and electric and hybrid vehicle development (Aptera Motors) in addition to its traditional focus on Internet companies.

IDEMIA IDENTITY & SECURITY USA LLC

11951 FREEDOM DR STE 1800
RESTON, VA 201905642
Phone: 703-775-7800
Fax: –
Web: www.idemia.com

CEO: Donald Scott
CFO: Laurent Lacroix
HR: Karen Gregory
FYE: December 31
Type: Private

Idemia Identity & Security USA (formerly MorphoTrust USA) has operated in the US for nearly half a century developing technologies and products that enhance national security while simplifying lives of Americans. It is a global leader in Augmented Identity for an increasingly digital world. It is administered managed and operated by US staff on US soil for all services provided to US government customers at the federal state local and tribal levels.

	Annual Growth	12/12	12/13	12/14	12/15	12/16
Sales ($ mil.)	17.1%	–	–	–	605.0	708.5
Net income ($ mil.)	–	–	–	–	0.0	(7.3)
Market value ($ mil.)	–	–	–	–	–	–
Employees	–	–	–	–	–	1,600

IDENIX PHARMACEUTICALS INC
NMS: IDIX

320 Bent Street
Cambridge, MA 02141
Phone: 617 995-9800
Fax: –
Web: www.idenix.com

CEO: Ronald C Renaud Jr
CFO: –
HR: –
FYE: December 31
Type: Public

Idenix Pharmaceuticals seeks to identify treatments for viral diseases. The firm is busily developing orally administered drugs to combat hepatitis C (HCV). It has one marketed drug for hepatitis B (HBV) Telbivudine sold under the brand names Tyzeka in the US and Sebivo internationally. Idenix's other candidates are in various stages of clinical testing — from preclinical to late stage trials. Most are intended to be taken in combination with other therapeutic agents to improve efficacy and convenience. Idenix's lead HCV drug candidates include IDX184 a nucleotide inhibitor in Phase II clinical testing and IDX719 an NS5A inhibitor to which the FDA granted fast-track status in 2012.

	Annual Growth	12/08	12/09	12/10	12/11	12/12
Sales ($ mil.)	62.3%	10.0	12.6	10.2	7.0	69.7
Net income ($ mil.)	–	(70.2)	(53.2)	(61.6)	(52.0)	(32.4)
Market value ($ mil.)	(4.3%)	775.6	288.0	675.1	997.3	649.7
Employees	(11.3%)	173	144	109	105	107

IDENIX PHARMACEUTICALS INC. NASDAQ: IDIX

60 Hampshire St.
Cambridge MA 02139
Phone: 617-995-9800
Fax: 617-995-9801
Web: www.idenix.com

CEO: Ronald C Renaud Jr
CFO: –
HR: –
FYE: December 31
Type: Public

Idenix Pharmaceuticals seeks to identify treatments for viral diseases. The firm is busily developing orally administered drugs to combat hepatitis C (HCV). It has one marketed drug for hepatitis B (HBV) Telbivudine sold under the brand names Tyzeka in the US and Sebivo internationally. Idenix's other candidates are in various stages of clinical testing — from preclinical to late stage trials. Most are intended to be taken in combination with other therapeutic agents to improve efficacy and convenience. Idenix's lead HCV drug candidates include IDX184 a nucleotide inhibitor in Phase II clinical testing and IDX719 an NS5A inhibitor to which the FDA granted fast-track status in 2012.

IDENTIV INC NAS: INVE

2201 Walnut Avenue, Suite 100
Fremont, CA 94538
Phone: 949 250-8888
Fax: –
Web: www.identiv.com

CEO: Steven Humphreys
CFO: Justin Scarpulla
HR: –
FYE: December 31
Type: Public

Identive Group grants secure access to the digital world. The company makes hardware and software for securely accessing digital content and services. Its products include smart card readers for electronic IDs and driver's licenses as well as health care computer network and facility access cards. Among other purposes Identive's digital media readers are used in digital photo kiosks to transfer data to and from flash media. The company sells to computer makers government contractors systems integrators financial institutions and photo processing equipment makers. Identive has international facilities in Australia Canada Germany Hong Kong India Japan the Netherlands Singapore and Switzerland.

	Annual Growth	12/16	12/17	12/18	12/19	12/20
Sales ($ mil.)	11.5%	56.2	60.2	78.1	83.8	86.9
Net income ($ mil.)	–	(13.7)	(8.1)	(4.7)	(1.2)	(5.1)
Market value ($ mil.)	27.9%	57.4	60.3	65.0	101.8	153.5
Employees	10.1%	222	223	273	289	326

IDEO LLC

100 Forest Ave.
Palo Alto CA 94301
Phone: 650-289-3400
Fax: 650-289-3707
Web: www.ideo.com

CEO: Sandy Speicher
CFO: –
HR: –
FYE: February 28
Type: Subsidiary

Ideas are IDEO's stock-in-trade. The company provides product development and branding services for a wide range of clients. It offers packaging design product research and strategic consulting services. Its work has included contributions to TiVo's digital video recorder and the Palm V for Palm. In addition IDEO (pronounced EYE-dee-oh) provides executive training and education services to help enterprises become more innovative. It operates from a network of several offices in the US Europe and the Asia/Pacific region. IDEO is a subsidiary of office furniture manufacturer Steelcase. Chairman David Kelley whose design credits include the first mouse for Apple and Bill Moggridge formed IDEO in 1991.

IDERA PHARMACEUTICALS INC NAS: IDRA

505 Eagleview Blvd., Suite 212
Exton, PA 19341
Phone: 484 348-1600
Fax: –
Web: www.iderapharma.com

CEO: Vincent Milano
CFO: John Kirby
HR: –
FYE: December 31
Type: Public

Idera Pharmaceuticals a clinical-stage biotech firm is developing DNA and RNA therapies that manipulate the immune system's response to disease. It is focused on Toll-Like Receptors (TLRs) — immune cell receptors that recognize and respond to viral and bacterial invaders. Some of Idera's drugs (such as treatments for infectious disease and cancer) mimic those invaders to stimulate an immune response; others (including treatments for autoimmune and inflammatory diseases) target TLRs to suppress the immune response. The firm's lead candidate is IMO-8400. Idera conducts some of its R&D efforts through partnerships.

	Annual Growth	12/15	12/16	12/17	12/18	12/19
Sales ($ mil.)	55.3%	0.2	16.2	0.9	0.7	1.4
Net income ($ mil.)	–	(48.6)	(38.4)	(66.0)	(59.9)	(56.5)
Market value ($ mil.)	(12.4%)	91.7	44.5	62.6	82.2	54.0
Employees	(12.7%)	62	62	62	36	36

IDEX CORPORATION NYS: IEX

3100 Sanders Road, Suite 301
Northbrook, IL 60062
Phone: 847 498-7070
Fax: –
Web: www.idexcorp.com

CEO: Eric Ashleman
CFO: William Grogan
HR: –
FYE: December 31
Type: Public

IDEX is a diversified manufacturer of pumps and other engineered products geared at different niche markets around the world. Its largest segment Fluid & Metering Technologies makes pumps flow meters and injectors used to handle or monitor water chemicals and fuels. Health & Science Technologies produces fluidics and pumps used in medical devices analytical instrumentation and photonics. The Fire & Safety/Diversified Products segment manufactures firefighting pumps and rescue tools including the branded Hurst Jaws of Life. The US accounts for around half of IDEX's sales.

	Annual Growth	12/16	12/17	12/18	12/19	12/20
Sales ($ mil.)	2.7%	2,113.0	2,287.3	2,483.7	2,494.6	2,351.6
Net income ($ mil.)	8.6%	271.1	337.3	410.6	425.5	377.8
Market value ($ mil.)	22.0%	6,841.0	10,024.5	9,590.8	13,065.2	15,131.3
Employees	(0.3%)	7,158	7,167	7,352	7,439	7,075

IDEXX LABORATORIES, INC. NMS: IDXX

One IDEXX Drive
Westbrook, ME 04092
Phone: 207 556-0300
Fax: 207 856-0346
Web: www.idexx.com

CEO: Jonathan J Mazelsky
CFO: Brian P McKeon
HR: –
FYE: December 31
Type: Public

A leading animal health care company IDEXX develops manufactures and distributes products for pets livestock dairy and poultry markets. Veterinarians use the company's VetTest analyzers for blood and urine chemistry and its SNAP in-office test kits to detect heartworms feline leukemia and other diseases. The company also provides lab testing services and practice management software. In addition IDEXX makes products to test for contaminants in water. The company sells its products worldwide but the Americas account for nearly 70% of its total revenue.

	Annual Growth	12/17	12/18	12/19	12/20	12/21
Sales ($ mil.)	13.0%	1,969.1	2,213.2	2,406.9	2,706.7	3,215.4
Net income ($ mil.)	29.7%	263.1	377.0	427.7	581.8	744.8
Market value ($ mil.)	43.2%	13,223.8	15,730.2	22,081.7	42,270.0	55,680.7
Employees	8.0%	7,600	8,377	9,200	9,300	10,350

IDT CORP

NYS: IDT

520 Broad Street
Newark, NJ 07102
Phone: 973 438-1000
Fax: –
Web: www.idt.net

CEO: Shmuel Jonas
CFO: Marcelo Fischer
HR: Nadine Shea
FYE: July 31
Type: Public

IDT is a global provider of financial technology or fintech cloud communications and traditional communications services. The communications holding company operates primarily through subsidiary IDT Telecom which provides prepaid and rechargeable international calling cards and other payment services to customers across the world through the Boss Revolution brand. Its consumer businesses make it easier for families to connect support and share across international borders. It also enables businesses to transact and communicate with their customers with enhanced intelligence and insight. The company was founded by its Chairman Howard Jonas in 1990. Majority of its sales were generated in the US.

	Annual Growth	07/17	07/18	07/19	07/20	07/21
Sales ($ mil.)	(0.9%)	1,501.7	1,547.5	1,409.2	1,345.8	1,447.0
Net income ($ mil.)	85.3%	8.2	4.2	0.1	21.4	96.5
Market value ($ mil.)	35.4%	381.5	135.2	261.7	167.7	1,282.9
Employees	7.8%	1,224	1,075	1,285	1,256	1,650

IDW MEDIA HOLDINGS INC

ASE: IDW

520 Broad Street
Newark, NJ 07102
Phone: 973 438-3385
Fax: –
Web: www.idwmh.com

CEO: Howard Jonas
CFO: Brooke Feinstein
HR: –
FYE: October 31
Type: Public

CTM Media Holdings is not embarrassed by tourists. The company distributes travel-related print and online advertising and information. Offerings include visitor maps brochures and other destination guides. Its publications are found in strategically located display stands primarily located in hotels attractions restaurants and rest stops along high-traffic throughways and interstates. In addition CTM Media publishes books and comics through its IDW Publishing subsidiary. The company was founded in 1983 as Creative Theatre Marketing. Previously known as IDT Capital the company was spun off from telecommunications firm IDT Corporation in 2009.

	Annual Growth	10/17	10/18	10/19	10/20	10/21
Sales ($ mil.)	(14.4%)	60.4	58.7	62.6	38.2	32.4
Net income ($ mil.)	–	(0.8)	(35.5)	(26.4)	(13.8)	(5.4)
Market value ($ mil.)	(48.4%)	602.8	336.9	153.9	42.1	42.8
Employees	–	–	–	–	–	81

IEC ELECTRONICS CORP.

NMS: IEC

105 Norton Street
Newark, NY 14513
Phone: 315 331-7742
Fax: –
Web: www.iec-electronics.com

CEO: Jeffrey T Schlarbaum
CFO: Thomas L Barbato
HR: Brittany Kuhn
FYE: September 30
Type: Public

IEC makes products you may never see. The company is a contract electronics manufacturer of printed circuit boards system-level assemblies extreme-condition cable and wire assemblies and precision sheet metal components. Customers come from the aerospace communications medical and military sectors. Like many contract electronics manufacturers IEC also offers a variety of auxiliary services including systems integration design and prototyping materials procurement and management engineering and testing.

	Annual Growth	09/16	09/17	09/18	09/19	09/20
Sales ($ mil.)	9.5%	127.0	96.5	116.9	157.0	182.7
Net income ($ mil.)	9.0%	4.8	0.1	10.4	4.7	6.8
Market value ($ mil.)	16.0%	50.1	51.8	55.3	72.6	90.8
Employees	7.9%	634	565	689	840	860

IES HOLDINGS INC

NMS: IESC

5433 Westheimer Road, Suite 500
Houston, TX 77056
Phone: 713 860-1500
Fax: –
Web: www.ies-corporate.com

CEO: Jeffrey Gendell
CFO: Tracy McLauchlin
HR: –
FYE: September 30
Type: Public

IES installs and maintains electrical and communications systems for residential commercial and industrial customers. Work on commercial buildings and homes includes custom design construction and maintenance on electrical and mechanical systems such as intrusion and fire alarms audio/video and data network systems. IES performs electrical and mechanical systems construction and installation for industrial properties including office buildings manufacturing facilities data centers chemical plants municipal infrastructure and health care facilities. Banking investor Jeffrey Gendell through Tontine Capital Partners owns 56% of IES.

	Annual Growth	09/17	09/18	09/19	09/20	09/21
Sales ($ mil.)	17.3%	810.7	876.8	1,077.0	1,190.9	1,536.5
Net income ($ mil.)	49.3%	13.4	(14.2)	33.2	41.6	66.7
Market value ($ mil.)	27.5%	358.7	404.3	426.9	658.7	947.3
Employees	18.0%	3,532	4,564	5,389	5,243	6,845

IGATE CORP

NMS: IGTE

100 Somerset Corporate Blvd
Bridgewater, NJ 08807
Phone: 908 219-8050
Fax: –
Web: www.igate.com

CEO: Ashok Vemuri
CFO: Sujit Sircar
HR: –
FYE: December 31
Type: Public

iGate is open to all things IT. The company provides business process outsourcing (BPO) and offshore development services including software development and maintenance outsourcing. In addition to IT-related services iGate handles such tasks as mortgage and claims processing and call center operations. The company targets midsized and large corporations in the banking financial services and insurance industries. Its more than 300 active customers include General Electric IBM Royal Bank of Canada and TEKsystems. The majority of iGate's operations are in India but the company earns most of its sales from customers in North America.

	Annual Growth	12/09	12/10	12/11	12/12	12/13
Sales ($ mil.)	56.2%	193.1	280.6	779.6	1,073.9	1,150.9
Net income ($ mil.)	46.0%	28.6	51.8	51.5	95.8	129.8
Market value ($ mil.)	41.6%	584.4	1,151.8	919.2	921.6	2,346.9
Employees	44.0%	6,910	8,338	26,889	27,616	29,733

IGNITE RESTAURANT GROUP INC

NMS: IRG

10555 Richmond Avenue
Houston, TX 77042
Phone: 713 366-7500
Fax: –
Web: www.igniterestaurants.com

CEO: Jonathan Tibus
CFO: Brad Leist
HR: –
FYE: December 28
Type: Public

Foodies with a burning passion for seafood and fun turn to this company. Ignite Restaurant Group operates Joe's Crab Shack a casual dining chain with more than 135 locations. The eateries feature a wide variety of grilled fried and stuffed seafood along with sandwiches and sides. The seafood chain is known for its quirky surf-inspired atmosphere where the servers are often part of the entertainment. In addition to its flagship restaurant brand Ignite Restaurant Group operates a small number of Brick House Tavern + Tap locations. Private equity group J. H. Whitney Capital Partners owns the company.

	Annual Growth	01/12*	12/12	12/13	12/14	12/15
Sales ($ mil.)	6.7%	405.2	465.1	760.8	837.4	492.0
Net income ($ mil.)	–	11.3	8.7	(6.6)	(53.5)	(46.4)
Market value ($ mil.)	(33.5%)	–	340.3	333.8	206.6	100.0
Employees	(6.9%)	10,900	9,700	19,800	18,600	8,800

*Fiscal year change

IGO INC

17800 N. Perimeter Dr., Suite 200
Scottsdale, AZ 85255
Phone: 480 596-0061
Fax: –
Web: www.igo.com

CEO: Terry R Gibson
CFO: Terry R Gibson
HR: –
FYE: December 31
Type: Public

NBB: IGOI

iGo has the power to keep electronics running. The company designs power products and chargers for portable consumer electronics such as notebook computers mobile phones digital music players handheld computers and gaming systems. Its product line includes AC DC combination AC/DC and battery-based universal power adapters. iGo tries to differentiate its products by incorporating interchangeable tips which let users charge and power a wide range of electronic products using the same power supply. It sells to computer makers including Dell and Lenovo as well as distributors (D&H Distributing Ingram Micro) and retailers (Wal-Mart RadioShack).

	Annual Growth	12/09	12/10	12/11	12/12	12/13
Sales ($ mil.)	(25.7%)	55.4	43.4	38.4	29.6	16.9
Net income ($ mil.)	–	(0.5)	0.8	(11.5)	(12.0)	(12.6)
Market value ($ mil.)	20.9%	3.6	11.3	2.3	0.8	7.7
Employees	(33.8%)	52	62	64	38	10

IHEARTMEDIA INC

20880 Stone Oak Parkway
San Antonio, TX 78258
Phone: 210 822-2828
Fax: –
Web: www.iheartmedia.com

CEO: Robert Pittman
CFO: Michael Mcguinness
HR: –
FYE: December 31
Type: Public

NMS: IHRT

iHeartMedia is one of the world's leading radio companies. The firm owns and operates nearly 860 radio stations in about 160 markets. Its iHeartRadio digital service available across more than 250 platforms and 2000 devices including smart speakers smartphones TVs and gaming consoles; through its influencers; social; branded iconic live music events; and podcasts as the No. 1 commercial podcast publisher. iHeartMedia also leads the audio industry in analytics targeting and attribution for its marketing partners with its SmartAudio product using data from its massive consumer base.

	Annual Growth	12/17	12/18*	05/19*	12/19	12/20
Sales ($ mil.)	(21.8%)	6,171.0	6,325.8	1,073.5	2,610.1	2,948.2
Net income ($ mil.)	–	(393.9)	(201.9)	11,184.1	112.5	(1,914.7)
Market value ($ mil.)	(23.2%)	–	–	–	1,210.3	929.5
Employees	(17.1%)	17,900	18,300	–	11,400	10,200

*Fiscal year change

IHS INC

15 Inverness Way East
Englewood, CO 80112
Phone: 303 790-0600
Fax: –
Web: www.ihs.com

CEO: Jerre L Stead
CFO: Todd Hyatt
HR: –
FYE: November 30
Type: Public

NYS: IHS

IHS (Information Handling Services) does more than handle information. Its experts process information from a variety of sources to provide analysis business and market intelligence and technical documents which it distributes in electronic formats. Products such as collections of technical specifications and standards regulations parts data and design guides are sold through its four areas of information: Energy Product Lifecycle Security and Environment. The company also offers economic-focused information and analysis through its IHS Global Insight subsidiary. IHS primarily earns revenue through subscription sales.

	Annual Growth	11/11	11/12	11/13	11/14	11/15
Sales ($ mil.)	13.3%	1,325.6	1,529.9	1,840.6	2,230.8	2,184.3
Net income ($ mil.)	15.4%	135.4	158.2	131.7	194.5	240.2
Market value ($ mil.)	8.7%	5,967.8	6,221.7	7,726.8	8,269.0	8,326.4
Employees	11.8%	5,500	6,000	8,000	8,800	8,600

II-VI INC

375 Saxonburg Boulevard
Saxonburg, PA 16056
Phone: 724 352-4455
Fax: –
Web: www.ii-vi.com

CEO: Vincent Mattera
CFO: Mary Raymond
HR: –
FYE: June 30
Type: Public

NMS: IIVI

II-VI develops manufactures and markets engineered materials optoelectronic components and devices for use in optical communications industrial aerospace and defense consumer electronics semiconductor capital equipment life sciences and automotive applications and markets. The company products are deployed in a variety of applications including optical data and wireless communications products; laser cutting welding and marking operations; 3D sensing consumer applications; aerospace and defense applications including intelligence surveillance and reconnaissance; semiconductor processing tools; and thermoelectric cooling and power-generation solutions. The company has manufacturing operations throughout the US as well as in Asia and Germany. Customers have included Coherent Inc. Nikon Corporation Aurubis AG and Apple Inc. among others. The US is its largest single market accounting for some 65% of sales.

	Annual Growth	06/17	06/18	06/19	06/20	06/21
Sales ($ mil.)	33.7%	972.0	1,158.8	1,362.5	2,380.1	3,105.9
Net income ($ mil.)	32.9%	95.3	88.0	107.5	(67.0)	297.6
Market value ($ mil.)	20.6%	3,618.2	4,583.4	3,856.6	4,981.1	7,657.2
Employees	22.1%	10,349	11,443	12,487	22,969	23,000

IKANO COMMUNICATIONS INC.

420 E SOUTH TEMPLE # 550
SALT LAKE CITY, UT 841111319
Phone: 801-924-0900
Fax: –
Web: www.ikano.com

CEO: Jim Murphy
CFO: –
HR: –
FYE: June 30
Type: Private

IKANO Communications says "I can" to businesses looking for access to the Web. The company resells wholesale Internet service in North America through agreements with network operators such as Covad enabling customers to resell Internet service under their own private brands. Clients include ISP's as well as customers in such industries as health care marketing and higher education. IKANO serves broadband customers in California through subsidiary DSL Extreme. Other brands include Dialup USA and DNAMail. The company operates from satellite offices in Los Angeles Seattle Toronto and Washington DC. Founded in 1999 IKANO has received funding from investors including Insight Venture Partners.

	Annual Growth	06/01	06/02	06/04	06/05	06/08
Sales ($ mil.)	10.4%	–	28.0	–	26.0	50.8
Net income ($ mil.)	–	–	–	–	(1.9)	13.5
Market value ($ mil.)	–	–	–	–	–	–
Employees	–	–	–	–	–	184

IKANOS COMMUNICATIONS INC

47669 Fremont Boulevard
Fremont, CA 94538
Phone: 510 979-0400
Fax: –
Web: www.ikanos.com

CEO: –
CFO: Sanjay Mehta
HR: –
FYE: December 29
Type: Public

NAS: IKAN

Ikanos Communications hopes to become an icon in the field of broadband semiconductors. The fabless semiconductor company designs DSL chipsets for use in modems and other customer premises equipment and communications processors used in gateways (multi-protocol routers). Its products allow networks to achieve fiber-like broadband speeds (up to 100 megabits per second) over copper wires enabling high-speed data features. Besides DSL its products also support wireless broadband passive optical network and Ethernet. Service providers such as AT&T and Orange are Ikanos' end users but its direct customers are manufacturers such as Alcatel-Lucent Sumitomo Electric Industries and ZTE.

	Annual Growth	01/10	01/11	01/12*	12/12	12/13
Sales ($ mil.)	(15.2%)	130.7	191.7	136.6	125.9	79.7
Net income ($ mil.)	–	(37.1)	(49.8)	(7.5)	(17.6)	(30.4)
Market value ($ mil.)	(13.9%)	18.5	13.2	8.0	16.5	11.8
Employees	(23.5%)	588	386	337	263	263

*Fiscal year change

ILG INC

NMS: ILG

6262 Sunset Drive
Miami, FL 33143
Phone: 305 666-1861
Fax: –
Web: www.iilg.com

CEO: Craig M Nash
CFO: William L Harvey
HR: –
FYE: December 31
Type: Public

Your vacation time is worth something to Interval Leisure Group. The timeshare exchange broker offers services to some 2 million member-property owners. Its primary Interval Network is an exchange program that lets owners trade their timeshare intervals for accommodations at more than 2900 resorts in approximately 80 countries. In addition the company provides exchange services to owners at timeshare properties managed by vacation services subsidiary Trading Places International (TPI) while its Preferred Residences is a luxury branded membership program with Preferred Hotel Group . The company also provides resort management services.

	Annual Growth	12/12	12/13	12/14	12/15	12/16
Sales ($ mil.)	30.1%	473.3	501.2	614.4	697.4	1,356.0
Net income ($ mil.)	59.7%	40.7	81.2	78.9	73.3	265.0
Market value ($ mil.)	(1.6%)	2,417.3	3,853.2	2,604.3	1,946.1	2,265.2
Employees	28.9%	3,800	5,000	6,100	5,600	10,500

ILLINOIS HOUSING DEVELOPMENT AUTHORITY (INC)

111 E WACKER DR STE 1000
CHICAGO, IL 606014306
Phone: 312-836-5200
Fax: –
Web: www.ihda.org

CEO: –
CFO: Robert Kugel
HR: –
FYE: June 30
Type: Private

The Illinois Housing Development Authority (IHDA) wants every Illinoisan to have a safe comfortable place to lay their head. The authority finances the construction and preservation of affordable housing for low- and moderate-income families throughout the state. Since its inception in 1967 the IHDA has allocated more than $6 billion and financed roughly 150000 units of affordable housing. An independent and self-supporting authority the IHDA raises private capital from bond markets and administers and manages a number of federal and state funding programs including the Illinois Affordable Housing Trust Fund and the Illinois Affordable Housing Tax Credit Fund.

	Annual Growth	06/15	06/16	06/17	06/18	06/19
Sales ($ mil.)	19.0%	–	113.5	227.1	57.6	191.1
Net income ($ mil.)	–	–	(3.5)	102.9	(122.6)	64.6
Market value ($ mil.)	–	–	–	–	–	–
Employees	–	–	–	–	–	200

ILLINOIS INSTITUTE OF TECHNOLOGY

10 W 35TH ST
CHICAGO, IL 606163717
Phone: 312-567-3000
Fax: –
Web: www.iit.edu

CEO: –
CFO: –
HR: –
FYE: May 31
Type: Private

Chicago has some cool architecture due in part to the Illinois Institute of Technology (IIT). The school offers more than 100 undergraduate and graduate degree programs in engineering science psychology architecture business law humanities and design. In addition to three campuses in Chicago IIT also has locations in Summit-Argo (Moffet campus) and Wheaton (Daniel F. and Ada L. Rice campus). The institute has an enrollment of some 8000 undergraduate graduate business school and law school students with a student-to-faculty ratio of 8:1.

	Annual Growth	05/15	05/16	05/18	05/19	05/21
Sales ($ mil.)	(1.3%)	–	276.8	260.8	265.0	259.2
Net income ($ mil.)	–	–	(10.4)	62.7	(10.1)	48.0
Market value ($ mil.)	–	–	–	–	–	–
Employees	–	–	–	–	–	1,662

ILLINOIS STATE OF TOLL HIGHWAY AUTHORITY

2700 OGDEN AVE
DOWNERS GROVE, IL 605151703
Phone: 630-241-6800
Fax: –
Web: www.illinoistollway.com

CEO: –
CFO: Mike Colsch
HR: –
FYE: December 31
Type: Private

The Illinois State Toll Highway Authority (ISTHA) is trying to give Illinois drivers a little relief from congestion making their morning and afternoon commutes easier to swallow. The department maintains and operates about 275 miles of interstate tollways in 12 Northern Illinois counties. ISTHA is mid-way through its 10-year $6.3 billion Congestion-Relief Program which is conducting major improvements including rebuilding widening and extending tollway segments; converting toll plazas to provide non-stop toll collection for I-PASS users; opening additional tollway oases; and adding electronic over-the-road signs to improve communication with tollway users.

	Annual Growth	12/16	12/17	12/18	12/19	12/20
Sales ($ mil.)	(3.4%)	–	1,398.5	1,436.4	1,484.5	1,261.0
Net income ($ mil.)	(29.6%)	–	356.0	353.8	374.6	124.2
Market value ($ mil.)	–	–	–	–	–	–
Employees	–	–	–	–	–	1,750

ILLINOIS TOOL WORKS, INC.

NYS: ITW

155 Harlem Avenue
Glenview, IL 60025
Phone: 847 724-7500
Fax: –
Web: www.itw.com

CEO: Ernest Santi
CFO: Michael Larsen
HR: –
FYE: December 31
Type: Public

Illinois Tool Works (ITW) manufactures and services equipment for the automotive construction electronics food beverage decorative surfaces and medical components industries. The company makes metal and plastic fasteners components and assemblies used in light vehicles automobiles and industrial applications. It also manufactures cooking equipment such as ovens ranges and broilers equipment and software for testing and measuring materials structures gases and fluids. The company's brands include Shakeproof Instron and Rain-X. ITW has operations in more than 50 countries but the customers in the US supply about 45% of the company's revenue. It was founded in 1912.

	Annual Growth	12/17	12/18	12/19	12/20	12/21
Sales ($ mil.)	0.2%	14,314.0	14,768.0	14,109.0	12,574.0	14,455.0
Net income ($ mil.)	12.4%	1,687.0	2,563.0	2,521.0	2,109.0	2,694.0
Market value ($ mil.)	10.3%	52,207.4	39,641.3	56,206.2	63,794.1	77,223.7
Employees	(2.6%)	50,000	48,000	45,000	43,000	45,000

ILLUMINA INC

NMS: ILMN

5200 Illumina Way
San Diego, CA 92122
Phone: 858 202-4500
Fax: –
Web: www.illumina.com

CEO: Francis deSouza
CFO: Sam Samad
HR: –
FYE: January 02
Type: Public

illumina is the top-ranking maker of next-generation sequencing tools used by life sciences and drug researchers to isolate and analyze genes. Its systems include the machinery and the software used to sequence pieces of DNA and RNA as well as the means to put them through large-scale testing of genetic variation and biological function. Its proprietary BeadArray technology uses microscopic glass beads that can carry samples through the genotyping process. The tests allow medical researchers to determine what genetic combinations are associated with various diseases enabling faster diagnosis better drugs and individualized treatment. Customers include pharma and biotech companies research centers and academic institutions. More than half of Illumina's revenue comes from US.

	Annual Growth	12/17	12/18	12/19*	01/21	01/22
Sales ($ mil.)	10.5%	2,752.0	3,333.0	3,543.0	3,239.0	4,526.0
Net income ($ mil.)	1.0%	726.0	826.0	1,002.0	656.0	762.0
Market value ($ mil.)	11.7%	34,302.9	46,822.1	52,169.5	58,090.0	59,729.1
Employees	11.6%	6,200	7,300	7,700	9,350	10,750

*Fiscal year change

IMAGE PROTECT INC
NBB: IMTL

1141 N. El Camino Real, Suite 203
San Clemente, CA 92672
Phone: 949 361-3959
Fax: –
Web: www.imageprotect.com

CEO: –
CFO: –
HR: –
FYE: December 31
Type: Public

Image Technology Laboratories provides medical image and information management software for radiologists and physicians. The company's WarpSpeed software includes a picture archiving and communication system which stores and distributes medical images such as CAT scans MRI images and ultrasounds and a radiology information system which manages patient insurance billing and scheduling information.

	Annual Growth	12/16	12/17	12/18	12/19	12/20
Sales ($ mil.)	(59.3%)	0.3	0.6	0.7	0.1	0.0
Net income ($ mil.)	–	(0.7)	(0.3)	(0.1)	(1.9)	(0.3)
Market value ($ mil.)	–	0.0	0.0	0.0	0.0	0.0
Employees	–	–	–	–	–	–

IMAGETREND INC.

20855 KENSINGTON BLVD
LAKEVILLE, MN 550447486
Phone: 952-469-1589
Fax: –
Web: www.imagetrend.com

CEO: Michael J McBrady
CFO: –
HR: –
FYE: December 31
Type: Private

ImageTrend hopes that the trend in your enterprise is towards increased efficiency. The company provides software development services and Web-based software used to address tasks such as content and document management e-commerce development database design and back-office integration. ImageTrend founded in 1998 also provides services including consulting support and training. The company's clients come from fields such as manufacturing health care financial services and education and have included Russell Athletic Goodyear Tire HealthEast Care System the University of Minnesota Cargill and FirstComp Insurance.

	Annual Growth	12/06	12/07	12/08	12/10	12/12
Sales ($ mil.)	10.1%	–	7.9	11.0	11.0	12.7
Net income ($ mil.)	–	–	–	2.4	0.5	(0.9)
Market value ($ mil.)	–	–	–	–	–	–
Employees	–	–	–	–	–	145

IMAGEWARE SYSTEMS INC
NBB: IWSY

11440 West Bernardo Court, Suite 300
San Diego, CA 92127
Phone: 858 673-8600
Fax: –
Web: www.iwsinc.com

CEO: Kristin Taylor
CFO: –
HR: –
FYE: December 31
Type: Public

Even if your face won't launch a thousand ships ImageWare Systems will remember it. The company's identification products are used to manage and issue secure credentials including national IDs passports driver's licenses smart cards and access-control credentials. Its software creates secure digital images and enables the enrollment and management of unlimited population sizes while its digital booking products provide law enforcement agencies with integrated mug shot fingerprint and investigative capabilities. The company markets its products worldwide to governments public safety agencies and commercial enterprises such as Unisys. The US government accounts for about 15% of revenue.

	Annual Growth	12/16	12/17	12/18	12/19	12/20
Sales ($ mil.)	5.8%	3.8	4.3	4.4	3.5	4.8
Net income ($ mil.)	–	(9.5)	(10.1)	(12.6)	(11.6)	(7.3)
Market value ($ mil.)	(50.7%)	239.5	286.3	160.3	60.3	14.1
Employees	(10.6%)	69	64	73	75	44

IMAGINE ENTERTAINMENT

9465 Wilshire Blvd. 7th Fl.
Beverly Hills CA 90212
Phone: 310-858-2000
Fax: 310-858-2020
Web: www.imagine-entertainment.com

CEO: –
CFO: –
HR: –
FYE: September 30
Type: Private

Imagine Entertainment has dreamt up a lot of success producing films and TV programs. Hollywood heavy-hitters Brian Grazer (movie producer) and Ron Howard (former child actor turned director) co-chair the studio which has a roster of critically acclaimed and commercially successful movies and TV shows. Among the company's notable films include numerous Howard-directed projects such as "Apollo 13" "A Beautiful Mind" (winner of Best Picture and Best Director Oscars) and The Da Vinci Code as well as films by others such as Eddie Murphy's The Nutty Professor. Imagine Entertainment's TV credits include the series "24" Arrested Development "Felicity" and Sports Night. Its films are distributed by Universal Pictures.

IMAGING DIAGNOSTIC SYSTEMS INC
NL:

618 E South St, Suite 500
Orlando, FL 32801
Phone: 954 581-9800
Fax: –
Web: www.imds.com

CEO: Linda B Grable
CFO: Allan L Schwartz
HR: –
FYE: June 30
Type: Public

Imaging Diagnostic Systems is a medical technology company involved in the research and development of breast-imaging devices used for detecting cancer. Using laser-based technology the company has created a more comfortable radiation-free breast examination that does not require breast compression. Its CTLM (Computed Tomography Laser Mammography) system used in conjuction with X-ray mammography may help improve early diagnosis of cancer. The company is also researching other breast screening systems using fluorescence imaging. It had been developing laser imaging products for research with lab animals but it has licensed the technology to Bioscan in order to focus on the women's health market.

	Annual Growth	06/11	06/12	06/18	06/19	06/20
Sales ($ mil.)	(16.5%)	0.1	0.2	0.1	0.2	0.0
Net income ($ mil.)	–	(5.9)	(3.2)	(1.7)	(1.7)	(1.0)
Market value ($ mil.)	–	1.8	0.0	–	–	–
Employees	(15.4%)	18	10	–	4	4

IMEDIA BRANDS INC
NMS: IMBI

6740 Shady Oak Road
Eden Prairie, MN 55344-3433
Phone: 952 943-6000
Fax: –
Web: www.imediabrands.com

CEO: Timothy Peterman
CFO: Montgomery Wageman
HR: –
FYE: January 30
Type: Public

Media Brands Inc. (formerly EVINE Live Inc.) is a leading interactive media company managing a growing portfolio of niche television networks niche national advertisers and media services. Its ShopHQ unit which trails industry leaders QVC and HSN sells jewelry and watches (more than 85% of sales) home goods and electronics beauty and fitness products and apparel and accessories. The shopping network reaches more than 80 million homes nationwide via cable and satellite TV. Programming is also streamed live across the Internet and on various mobile devices as well as through social networking sites. Typical viewers are women between the ages of approximately 45 and 70. E-commerce arm ShopHQ accounts for a growing portion of the company's sales.

	Annual Growth	01/17*	02/18	02/19	02/20*	01/21
Sales ($ mil.)	(9.1%)	666.2	648.2	596.6	501.8	454.2
Net income ($ mil.)	–	(8.7)	0.1	(22.2)	(56.3)	(13.2)
Market value ($ mil.)	41.9%	18.5	15.6	7.3	47.5	75.0
Employees	(12.0%)	1,300	1,200	1,130	990	780

*Fiscal year change

IMMERSION CORP
NMS: IMMR

330 Townsend Street, Suite 234
San Francisco, CA 94107
Phone: 408 467-1900
Fax: –
Web: www.immersion.com

CEO: Francis Jose
CFO: Aaron Akerman
HR: Lori Hioki
FYE: December 31
Type: Public

Immersion is a premier licensing company focused on the creation design development and licensing of innovative haptic technologies that allow people to use their sense of touch to engage with products and experience the digital world around them. It is one of the leading experts in haptics and its focus on innovation allows them to deliver world-class intellectual property (IP) and technology that enables the creation of products that delight end users. Immersion licenses its patents directly to Microsoft Sony and Nintendo for use in their console gaming products. Additionally we have licensed our patents to third party gaming peripheral manufacturers and distributors for use in spinning mass and force feedback devices such as controllers steering wheels and joysticks to be used with PC platforms running on Microsoft Windows and other operating systems as well as in connection with video game consoles made by Microsoft Sony Nin

	Annual Growth	12/16	12/17	12/18	12/19	12/20
Sales ($ mil.)	(14.5%)	57.1	35.0	111.0	36.0	30.5
Net income ($ mil.)	–	(39.4)	(45.3)	54.3	(20.0)	5.4
Market value ($ mil.)	1.5%	287.2	190.7	242.1	200.7	305.0
Employees	(20.0%)	132	81	64	56	54

IMMIXGROUP, INC.

8444 WESTPARK DR STE 200
MC LEAN, VA 221025112
Phone: 703-752-0610
Fax: –
Web: www.immixgroup.com

CEO: Art Richer
CFO: Noel N Samuel
HR: –
FYE: May 31
Type: Private

immixGroup offers a blend of information technology (IT) business development and consulting services to help tech firms do business with federal state and local government agencies. Through its technology sales division the company is a hardware and software reseller for such manufacturers as IBM Oracle and Hewlett-Packard. It also offers customized public sector channel development programs outsourced government contract management and IT consulting and execution. Other services include market intelligence sales training and recruiting. immixGroup serves more than 250 tech manufacturers and its government partner network includes more than 600 resellers systems integrators and other providers. Arrow Electronics acquired immixGroup in 2015.

	Annual Growth	05/09	05/10	05/11	05/12	05/13
Sales ($ mil.)	(3.5%)	–	563.6	43.6	502.1	505.9
Net income ($ mil.)	0.8%	–	11.8	16.5	13.3	12.1
Market value ($ mil.)	–	–	–	–	–	–
Employees	–	–	–	–	–	201

IMMUCELL CORP.
NAS: ICCC

56 Evergreen Drive
Portland, ME 04103
Phone: 207 878-2770
Fax: –
Web: www.immucell.com

CEO: Michael Brigham
CFO: –
HR: –
FYE: December 31
Type: Public

Many biotech companies focus on human health but ImmuCell has udder pursuits. The company develops products to help livestock farmers maintain the health of their herds. Its animal-health products include First Defense which prevents diarrhea in calves; MASTiK which diagnoses bovine mammary gland inflammation; and Wipe Out Dairy Wipes moist towelettes used to disinfect the teat area of cows prior to milking. ImmuCell makes a product for preventing disease in humans — Isolate (formerly called Crypto-Scan) a test for cryptosporidium in water. When present in municipal drinking water supplies c ryptosporidium can cause diarrheal disease in humans.

	Annual Growth	12/16	12/17	12/18	12/19	12/20
Sales ($ mil.)	12.6%	9.5	10.4	11.0	13.7	15.3
Net income ($ mil.)	–	0.5	(0.2)	(2.3)	(1.3)	(1.0)
Market value ($ mil.)	0.0%	43.0	63.5	50.9	37.2	43.0
Employees	7.9%	45	47	51	54	61

IMMUCOR INC.

3130 Gateway Dr.
Norcross GA 30091-5625
Phone: 770-441-2051
Fax: 770-441-3807
Web: www.immucor.com

CEO: AVI Pelossof
CFO: Dominique Petitgenet
HR: –
FYE: May 31
Type: Private

Immucor makes sure you can feel safe about getting a blood transfusion. The company develops makes and sells manual and automated analysis equipment used by blood banks hospitals and clinical laboratories to test blood prior to transfusions. Its traditional reagents are used to manually test samples for blood type group matching and foreign substance detection while its Galileo Galileo Echo and Galileo NEO automated instrumentation systems use traditional and proprietary Capture reagents to perform multiple blood tests at one time. The company sells its products primarily in North America Western Europe and Japan. Founded in 1982 Immucor is owned by TPG Capital.

IMMUNE PHARMACEUTICALS INC
NAS: IMNP

430 East 29th Street, Suite 940
New York, NY 10016
Phone: 646 440-9310
Fax: –
Web: www.epicept.com

CEO: –
CFO: –
HR: –
FYE: December 31
Type: Public

EpiCept's drug development mission is to help patients avoid pain leukemia remission and other conditions. The company's research pipeline includes AmiKet a topical analgesics for neuropathic pain conditions. Cancer drug candidate Ceplene is a remission maintenance therapy for acute myeloid leukemia (AML) patients; the drug is sold in the EU by Meda and EpiCept is developing Ceplene for additional markets. In 2012 EpiCept agreed to merge with Israeli drug development firm Immune Pharmaceuticals; the transaction will add additional inflammatory disease and cancer candidates to the combined pipeline.

	Annual Growth	12/10	12/11	12/12	12/13	12/14
Sales ($ mil.)	(78.8%)	1.0	0.9	7.8	0.0	0.0
Net income ($ mil.)	–	(15.5)	(15.7)	(2.6)	(5.8)	(23.6)
Market value ($ mil.)	21.3%	20.9	8.4	1.4	55.1	45.3
Employees	(5.9%)	14	11	4	8	11

IMMUNOCELLULAR THERAPEUTICS LTD.
NYSE: IMUC

21900 Burbank Blvd. 3rd Fl.
Woodland Hills CA 91367
Phone: 818-992-2907
Fax: 818-992-2908
Web: www.imuc.com

CEO: Anthony Gringeri
CFO: David Fractor
HR: –
FYE: December 31
Type: Public

ImmunoCellular Therapeutics primarily targets glioblastoma multiforme (GBM) which can hurt the brain just by trying to say or spell it. However GBM is also regarded as the most aggressive brain cancer affecting humans. The development-stage company is also going after other cancers such as those that attack the ovaries pancreas colon bones and lungs. Its immunotherapy aims not only at normal tumor cells but also the stem cells where cancers grow and recur. ImmunoCellular has a partnership and licensing agreement with Los Angeles' Cedars-Sinai Medical Center to use the latter's technology in its research. The company was founded in 1987 took its current name in 2006 and went public in 2010.

IMMUNOGEN, INC.   NMS: IMGN

830 Winter Street | CEO: Mark Enyedy
Waltham, MA 02451 | CFO: Susan Altschuller
Phone: 781 895-0600 | HR: –
Fax: – | FYE: December 31
Web: www.immunogen.com | Type: Public

ImmunoGen is a clinical-stage biotechnology company focused on developing the next generation of antibody-drug conjugates (ADC) technology targets tumors delivering an ImmunoGen cell-killing agent specifically to cancer cells. The company uses its antibodies along with its ADC platform to create product candidates; it also out-licenses the ADC technology to other companies. (Breast cancer drug Kadcyla produced by Roche is the first marketed product using ADC.) ImmunoGen's lead compounds target conditions including lung cancer acute myeloid leukemia and non-Hodgkin's lymphoma. In addition to its proprietary candidates the company has some compounds that are being developed through partnerships and licensing agreements with companies such as Genentech and Viridian.

	Annual Growth	12/16	12/17	12/18	12/19	12/20
Sales ($ mil.)	57.5%	21.5	115.4	53.4	82.3	132.3
Net income ($ mil.)	–	(78.9)	(96.0)	(168.8)	(104.1)	(44.4)
Market value ($ mil.)	33.3%	397.8	1,249.9	936.0	995.5	1,257.7
Employees	(28.8%)	308	293	296	75	79

IMMUNOMEDICS, INC.   NMS: IMMU

300 The American Road | CEO: –
Morris Plains, NJ 07950 | CFO: –
Phone: 973 605-8200 | HR: –
Fax: 973 605-8282 | FYE: June 30
Web: www.immunomedics.com | Type: Public

Immunomedics develops monoclonal antibody (MAb) medicines to treat cancer autoimmune conditions and other diseases. Its lead product epratuzumab is in development for the treatment of lupus; biopharmaceutical firm UCB has licensed the drug for further applications in autoimmune diseases but is exiting that partnership. Immunomedics is also conducting clinical trials for epratuzumab as an oncology treatment for non-Hodgkin's lymphoma. Other drugs in clinical trials aim to treat various cancers including pancreatic cancer and multiple myeloma. It also makes diagnostic imaging products; its majority-owned IBC Pharmaceuticals develops radiotherapeutics for applications in oncology treatments.

	Annual Growth	06/14	06/15	06/16	06/17	06/18
Sales ($ mil.)	(30.1%)	9.0	5.7	3.2	3.1	2.2
Net income ($ mil.)	–	(35.4)	(48.0)	(59.0)	(153.2)	(273.8)
Market value ($ mil.)	59.6%	681.7	758.3	433.3	1,649.1	4,420.8
Employees	11.4%	120	123	131	138	185

IMPAC MORTGAGE HOLDINGS, INC.   ASE: IMH

19500 Jamboree Road | CEO: George Mangiaracina
Irvine, CA 92612 | CFO: –
Phone: 949 475-3600 | HR: –
Fax: – | FYE: December 31
Web: www.impaccompanies.com | Type: Public

Impac Mortgage Holdings wants to make a positive impact on home ownership rates. The lender originates sells and services residential mortgage loans that are eligible to be sold to US government-sponsored enterprises such as Fannie Mae Freddie Mac. It does the same for government-insured mortgage loans eligible for securitization that are issued through Ginnie Mae. Beyond lending its Integrated Real Estate Services (IRES) subsidiary provides loan modifications real estate brokerage and monitoring and surveillance services. Other subsidiaries include Impac Mortgage Corp. IMH Assets Corp. and Impac Funding Corp. Founded in 1995 Impac originated and sold about $4.5 billion in loans.

	Annual Growth	12/16	12/17	12/18	12/19	12/20
Sales ($ mil.)	–	297.8	138.7	105.0	90.6	(8.1)
Net income ($ mil.)	–	46.7	(31.5)	(145.4)	(8.0)	(88.2)
Market value ($ mil.)	(31.8%)	297.8	215.8	80.3	111.7	64.6
Employees	(17.8%)	714	588	417	530	326

IMPERIAL INDUSTRIES INC.   OTC: IPII

3790 Park Central Blvd. North | CEO: Howard L Ehler Jr
Pompano Beach FL 33064 | CFO: Steven M Healy
Phone: 954-917-4114 | HR: –
Fax: 954-970-6565 | FYE: December 31
Web: www.imperialindustries.com | Type: Public

Imperial Industries manufactures roof tile mortar stucco and plaster adhesive and pool finish products through its Premix-Marbletite Manufacturing subsidiary. Founded in 1968 its primary market is the southeastern US. Its Just-Rite Supply subsidiary which distributed the company's products and such products as gypsum roofing insulation and masonry materials made by other companies ceased operation in mid-2009 and is selling its assets to satisfy creditors. (Just-Rite accounted for about two-thirds of Imperial Industries' sales.) Hardwood flooring company Q.E.P. is buying Imperial Industries.

IMPERIAL IRRIGATION DISTRICT

333 E BARIONI BLVD | CEO: Keven Kelly
IMPERIAL, CA 922511773 | CFO: –
Phone: 800-303-7756 | HR: –
Fax: – | FYE: December 31
Web: www.iid.com | Type: Private

Imperial Irrigation District (IID) keeps the lights on and the water flowing. A public agency IID is the six largest public power utility in the state of California providing generation transmission and distribution services to more than 145000 residential commercial and industrial customers. It is also the largest irrigation district in the US with more than 3000 miles of canals and drains delivering water to active farmland and providing wholesale water to local municipalities primarily in the Southern California desert corridors of Imperial Valley and Coachella Valley. The district is governed by a five-member board of directors elected by district residents.

	Annual Growth	12/16	12/17	12/18	12/19	12/20
Sales ($ mil.)	3.6%	–	634.6	615.3	642.2	705.5
Net income ($ mil.)	228.3%	–	3.3	48.6	51.5	115.4
Market value ($ mil.)	–	–	–	–	–	–
Employees	–	–	–	–	–	1,300

IMPERIAL PETROLEUM RECOVERY CORPORATION   PINK SHEETS: IREC

61 S. Concord Forest Cir. | CEO: Alan Springer
The Woodlands TX 77381 | CFO: –
Phone: 281-362-1042 | HR: –
Fax: 281-362-1051 | FYE: October 31
Web: www.iprc.com | Type: Public

Though it sticks to the sludge business Imperial Petroleum Recovery isn't bogged down. The company makes and markets oil sludge remediation equipment for oil producers and refiners pipelines and tankers. Its Microwave Separation Technology system breaks down sludge with heat and recovers hydrocarbon compounds salable oil treatable water and disposable solids. The trailer-mounted system consists of a microwave generator a series of waveguides and tuners and a sludge applicator. Imperial Petroleum Recovery has yet to post a profit and the company's auditors have questioned whether it will be able to stay in business.

IMPERIAL SUGAR COMPANY
NASDAQ: IPSU

1 Imperial Sq. 8016 Hwy. 90A
Sugar Land TX 77478
Phone: 281-491-9181
Fax: 281-490-9530
Web: www.imperialsugarcompany.com

CEO: John C Sheptor
CFO: H P Mechler
HR: –
FYE: December 31
Type: Public

I'm not going to sugar coat this for you: Imperial Sugar is one of the biggest processors and marketers of refined sugar in the US. Its white brown and powdered sugars are sold under name brands — Dixie Crystals Holly and Imperial — and under private labels to retailers. Most refined sugar which generates approximately 85% of the company's sales is sold domestically in bulk and liquid form to industrial markets (mainly food manufacturers of baked goods desserts and beverages) and food service and industrial distributors who sell the sugar to manufacturers restaurants and institutional food service customers. Imperial Sugar was acquired by a subsidiary of Louis Dreyfus Commodities (LDC) in 2012.

IMPERVA INC
NMS: IMPV

3400 Bridge Parkway
Redwood Shores, CA 94065
Phone: 650 345-9000
Fax: 650 345-9004
Web: www.imperva.com

CEO: Pam Murphy
CFO: –
HR: –
FYE: December 31
Type: Public

Imperva aims to create an impervious barrier around corporate data centers. The company's data security platform called SecureSphere protects databases files and Web applications against threats from hackers and insiders and helps its corporate customers maintain regulatory compliance. Subsidiary Incapsula provides cloud-based Web application security services for small and midsized companies. Imperva's security products cater to the energy financial services government health care higher education insurance and retail and e-commerce industries. It was established in 2002.

	Annual Growth	12/12	12/13	12/14	12/15	12/16
Sales ($ mil.)	26.2%	104.2	137.8	164.0	234.3	264.5
Net income ($ mil.)	–	(7.4)	(25.2)	(59.0)	(48.9)	(70.3)
Market value ($ mil.)	5.1%	1,043.3	1,592.6	1,635.6	2,094.9	1,270.6
Employees	20.3%	474	580	723	923	993

IMPINJ INC.

701 N. 34th St. Ste. 300
Seattle WA 98103
Phone: 206-517-5300
Fax: 206-517-5262
Web: www.impinj.com

CEO: Chris Diorio
CFO: Cary Baker
HR: –
FYE: December 31
Type: Private

Impinj designs semiconductors to adapt to their surroundings. The company's "self-adaptive silicon" technology allows analog circuits — which translate light sound and radio waves into data usable by electronic systems — to be made smaller and more efficient and allow for chip adjustment. The company focuses on designing communications chips particularly UHF Gen 2 radio-frequency identification (RFID) devices for supply chain management/automation (from pharmaceuticals to apparel) and other applications such as food safety and event timing. Impinj was founded in 2000 by chip design legend (and Caltech professor emeritus) Carver Mead and his former student Chris Diorio. The company withdrew its IPO in 2012.

IMPLANT SCIENCES CORP
NBB: IMSC Q

500 Research Drive, Unit 3
Wilmington, MA 01887
Phone: 978 752-1700
Fax: 978 752-1711
Web: www.implantsciences.com

CEO: William J McGann
CFO: Christopher Roberts
HR: –
FYE: June 30
Type: Public

Implant Sciences is giving the security industry new technologies to detect explosives. Using its ion implantation know-how the company has developed handheld and tabletop bomb detectors for use in airports and other public places. The firm is developing a walk-through portal through a contract with the Transportation Security Administration. Originally the company applied ion implantation technology into use in medical technology and semiconductor production but has since refocused its operations entirely into security sensors. It is building a customer base in China and the US.

	Annual Growth	06/12	06/13	06/14	06/15	06/16
Sales ($ mil.)	98.7%	3.4	12.0	8.6	13.0	53.1
Net income ($ mil.)	–	(14.6)	(27.4)	(21.0)	(21.5)	(10.7)
Market value ($ mil.)	(23.3%)	111.1	92.1	82.6	63.5	38.5
Employees	19.5%	47	65	74	75	96

IMPRESO INC.
NBB: ZCOM

652 Southwestern Boulevard
Coppell, TX 75019
Phone: 972 462-0100
Fax: 972 462-7764
Web: www.impreso.com

CEO: Marshall Sorokwasz
CFO: Susan Atkins
HR: –
FYE: August 31
Type: Public

Money is just paper to holding company Impreso. Impreso a Spanish word meaning "printed matter" was founded in 1976. Through its primary subsidiary TST/Impreso the company makes and distributes specialty paper and film imaging products. Its paper products include thermal fax copier wide-format continuous-feed and special surface papers such as film transparencies. Impreso operates a number of manufacturing plants and distributes in North America through its warehouses to dealers and other resellers. Impreso owns two other subsidiaries: Hotsheet.com (provides links to popular websites) and Alexa Springs (a custom-label water bottling business). Impreso suspended its SEC reporting obligations in 2006.

	Annual Growth	08/13	08/14	08/15	08/16	08/17
Sales ($ mil.)	4.2%	73.7	83.4	87.7	89.0	87.0
Net income ($ mil.)	(27.4%)	0.3	(0.1)	0.3	0.1	0.1
Market value ($ mil.)	(2.9%)	3.6	3.6	3.8	2.8	3.2
Employees	–	–	–	–	–	–

INC.JET HOLDING INC
NBB: SORT

One Winnenden Road
Norwich, CT 06360
Phone: 860 823-1427
Fax: 860 886-0135

CEO: Marc Perkins
CFO: John Carpenter
HR: –
FYE: December 31
Type: Public

When customers want help with their document processing Gunther tells them to stuff it. Gunther International makes electronic publishing mailing and billing systems that automate the assembly of printed documents. Its equipment is used to staple bind match and insert documents into envelopes for distribution. Gunther targets insurance companies such as Allstate and Metropolitan Life as well as businesses in the government retail and service bureau sectors. Subsidiary inc.jet offers industrial inkjet printers that OEMs incorporate into other devices. Gunther International was established in 1977.

	Annual Growth	03/17	03/18*	12/18	12/19	12/20
Sales ($ mil.)	(17.8%)	27.0	11.8	10.7	14.3	15.0
Net income ($ mil.)	178.5%	0.1	(1.9)	0.5	1.3	1.8
Market value ($ mil.)	–	–	–	–	–	–
Employees	–	–	–	–	–	–

*Fiscal year change

INCOME OPPORTUNITY REALTY INVESTORS INC.
NYSE AMEX: IOT

1755 Wittington Place Ste. 340 — CEO: Bradley Muth
Dallas TX 75234 — CFO: Erik Johnson
Phone: 972-407-8400 — HR: –
Fax: 972-407-8436 — FYE: December 31
Web: www.incomeopp-realty.com — Type: Public

When opportunity knocks Income Opportunity Realty Investors (IORI) is there to answer. The real estate investment firm owns commercial retail and industrial real estate and land parcels in Texas as well as an apartment complex in Indiana. Transcontinental Realty Investors (TRI) owns about 80% of IORI after buying out the majority stake of Syntek West which had overseen IORI's daily activities. American Realty Investors shares executive officers and board members with both IORI and TRI; affiliates of Prime Income Asset Management manage IORI's properties as well as those of TRI. In 2008 IORI sold six apartment properties in Texas (about half of its assets).

INCONTACT, INC.
NAS: SAAS

7730 S. Union Park Avenue, Suite 500 — CEO: Paul Jarman
Salt Lake City, UT 84047 — CFO: –
Phone: 801 320-3200 — HR: –
Fax: – — FYE: December 31
Web: www.incontact.com — Type: Public

inContact keeps customer service agents in touch with customers. The company provides call center software and an enterprise-class telecom network for a complete customer service operation. Small and midsized departments use inContact for handling inbound and outbound customer service calls as well as connectivity services and workforce optimization. Its inCloud Apps allow customers to specify and deploy services that are pre-integrated into the inContact platform. Its products are offered on a pay-as-you-go basis without the costs of premise-based systems. Customers include financial services firms retailers health care organizations utilities and government agencies.

	Annual Growth	12/10	12/11	12/12	12/13	12/14
Sales ($ mil.)	20.3%	82.2	89.0	110.3	130.0	171.8
Net income ($ mil.)	–	–	(1.1)	(9.4)	(5.4)	(9.0)	(10.6)
Market value ($ mil.)	27.9%	200.1	270.2	316.0	476.4	536.2
Employees	29.5%	330	412	424	547	928

INCYTE CORPORATION
NMS: INCY

1801 Augustine Cut-Off — CEO: Herve Hoppenot
Wilmington, DE 19803 — CFO: Christiana Stamoulis
Phone: 302 498-6700 — HR: Paula Swain
Fax: – — FYE: December 31
Web: www.incyte.com — Type: Public

Incyte is a biopharmaceutical company focused on the discovery development and commercialization of proprietary therapeutics. It is focused on developing and selling drugs that inhibit specific enzymes associated with cancer and other diseases. The company's lead program is its JAK (Janus associated kinase) inhibitor program. Its first commercial product Jakafi is approved for treatment of polycythemia vera and myelofibrosis (two rare blood cancers) and graft-versus-host-disease in the US; partner Novartis markets the drug internationally. Another inhibitor drug Iclusig is marketed for certain forms of leukemia in Europe. Incyte has a number of product candidates in research and clinical development stages partially through partnerships with other drugmakers for various cancers inflammatory ailments and other conditions.

	Annual Growth	12/17	12/18	12/19	12/20	12/21
Sales ($ mil.)	18.1%	1,536.2	1,881.9	2,158.8	2,666.7	2,986.3
Net income ($ mil.)	–	(313.1)	109.5	446.9	(295.7)	948.6
Market value ($ mil.)	(6.2%)	20,938.9	14,058.8	19,305.1	19,229.9	16,227.6
Employees	14.7%	1,208	1,367	1,456	1,773	2,094

INDEPENDENCE HOLDING COMPANY
NYS: IHC

96 Cummings Point Road — CEO: Roy Thung
Stamford, CT 06902 — CFO: Colleen P Maggi
Phone: 203 358-8000 — HR: –
Fax: 203 348-3103 — FYE: December 31
Web: www.ihcgroup.com — Type: Public

Independence Holding Company (IHC) specializes in health and life insurance in the US. Through its wholly owned subsidiaries Madison National Life Insurance and Standard Security Life Insurance Company of New York it sells and reinsures health and life insurance to groups and individuals. Though it does offer some major medical plans the company prefers to offer niche coverage such as medical stop-loss insurance (which allows employers to limit their exposure to high health insurance claims) short-term medical coverage critical illness small-group major medical and pet insurance. Subsidiary American Independence also writes medical stop-loss insurance.

	Annual Growth	12/15	12/16	12/17	12/18	12/19
Assets ($ mil.)	(3.1%)	1,198.0	1,134.5	1,040.6	1,037.5	1,054.3
Net income ($ mil.)	(19.8%)	29.9	123.3	42.0	28.5	12.4
Market value ($ mil.)	32.0%	205.9	290.6	408.0	523.2	625.5
Employees	0.3%	450	270	350	500	455

INDEPENDENT BANK CORP (MA)
NMS: INDB

2036 Washington Street — CEO: Christopher Oddleifson
Hanover, MA 02339 — CFO: Mark Ruggiero
Phone: 781 878-6100 — HR: Maria Harris
Fax: – — FYE: December 31
Web: www.rocklandtrust.com — Type: Public

Independent Bank is a state chartered federally registered bank holding company. The company is the sole stockholder of Rockland Trust Company ("Rockland Trust" or the "Bank"). Its banking subsidiary Rockland Trust operates almost 95 retail branches as well two limited service branches located in Barnstable Bristol Dukes and more in Eastern Massachusetts. Serving area consumers and small to midsized businesses the bank offers standard services such as checking and savings accounts CDs and credit cards in addition to insurance products financial planning trust services. Commercial loans including industrial construction and small business loans. Incorporated in 1985 the bank boasts total assets of some $13.2 billion.

	Annual Growth	12/16	12/17	12/18	12/19	12/20
Assets ($ mil.)	14.4%	7,709.4	8,082.0	8,851.6	11,395.2	13,204.3
Net income ($ mil.)	12.1%	76.6	87.2	121.6	165.2	121.2
Market value ($ mil.)	0.9%	2,322.4	2,302.7	2,317.8	2,744.4	2,407.8
Employees	5.7%	1,103	1,108	1,188	1,348	1,375

INDEPENDENT BANK CORPORATION (IONIA, MI)
NMS: IBCP

4200 East Beltline — CEO: William Kessel
Grand Rapids, MI 49525 — CFO: Gavin Mohr
Phone: 616 527-5820 — HR: Angela Champagne
Fax: – — FYE: December 31
Web: www.independentbank.com — Type: Public

Independent Bank Corporation is the holding company for Independent Bank which serves rural and suburban communities of Michigan's Lower Peninsula from more than 100 branches. The bank offers traditional deposit products including checking and savings accounts and CDs. Loans to businesses account for about 40% of the bank's portfolio; real estate mortgages are more than a third. Independent Bank also offers additional products and services like title insurance through subsidiary Independent Title Services and investments through agreement with third-party provider PrimeVest.

	Annual Growth	12/16	12/17	12/18	12/19	12/20
Assets ($ mil.)	13.3%	2,549.0	2,789.4	3,353.3	3,564.7	4,204.0
Net income ($ mil.)	25.3%	22.8	20.5	39.8	46.4	56.2
Market value ($ mil.)	(4.0%)	474.2	488.4	459.4	495.0	403.6
Employees	2.7%	885	911	976	994	983

INDEPENDENT BANK GROUP INC. NMS: IBTX

7777 Henneman Way
McKinney, TX 75070-1711
Phone: 972 562-9004
Fax: –
Web: www.ibtx.com

CEO: David Brooks
CFO: Michelle Hickox
HR: –
FYE: December 31
Type: Public

The bank holding company Independent Bank Group does business through subsidiary Independent Bank which operates more than 90 full-services branches which more than 70 of these branches are company-owned. The company operates in the Dallas/North Texas area Austin/Central Texas Area and the Houston Texas metropolitan area. The banks offer standard personal and business accounts and services including some focused on small business owners. IBG has total assets of more than $17 billion and loans of about $13 billion. The company traces its roots back 100 years but took its current shape in 2002.

	Annual Growth	12/16	12/17	12/18	12/19	12/20
Assets ($ mil.)	32.0%	5,852.8	8,684.5	9,850.0	14,958.2	17,753.5
Net income ($ mil.)	39.2%	53.5	76.5	128.3	192.7	201.2
Market value ($ mil.)	0.0%	2,691.8	2,916.1	1,974.4	2,391.5	2,696.9
Employees	27.3%	577	924	1,087	1,469	1,513

INDEX FRESH, INC.

1250 CORONA POINTE CT # 40
CORONA, CA 928792099
Phone: 909-877-0999
Fax: –
Web: www.indexfresh.com

CEO: –
CFO: Merrill Causey
HR: –
FYE: October 31
Type: Private

These growers are found in the index under "fresh." Index Fresh is a worldwide marketer of avocados sourcing from all major growing regions around the globe The produce it sells is grown in California or imported from Mexico Peru and Chile. Aside from Index's facilities in California it also has distribution centers and pre-conditioning facilities in Texas Pennsylvania Iowa Ohio Illinois and Colorado. It serves the retail and food service industries. The company used to organized and pack and market lemons and oranges until the 1950s when it absorbed sister cooperative United Growers Association. It became a corporation in 1999.

	Annual Growth	10/03	10/04	10/06	10/07	10/17
Sales ($ mil.)	24.6%	–	11.5	24.7	32.2	199.9
Net income ($ mil.)	(9.2%)	–	9.6	0.6	0.3	2.8
Market value ($ mil.)	–	–	–	–	–	–
Employees	–	–	–	–	–	57

INDIA GLOBALIZATION CAPITAL INC ASE: IGC

10224 Falls Road
Potomac, MD 20854
Phone: 301 983-0998
Fax: –
Web: www.igcinc.us

CEO: Ram Mukunda
CFO: –
HR: –
FYE: March 31
Type: Public

India Globalization Capital (IGC) sounds like a finance firm but its business is much more concrete. It operates mines and quarries that produce cement concrete and other highway and heavy construction materials; builds roads tunnels and other infrastructure projects exports iron ore and provides related logistics. The US-based company serves the infrastructure industry in fast-growing India and China from four offices in India. It operates through three wholly owned subsidiaries all bearing the IGC name and one 77% owned subsidiary Techni Bharathi Ltd that has built highways and tunnels for the National Highway Authority of India and the Indian Railroad.

	Annual Growth	03/17	03/18	03/19	03/20	03/21
Sales ($ mil.)	11.5%	0.6	2.2	5.1	4.1	0.9
Net income ($ mil.)	–	(1.9)	(1.8)	(4.1)	(7.3)	(8.8)
Market value ($ mil.)	39.7%	22.5	26.8	99.5	23.4	85.6
Employees	12.7%	31	26	20	50	50

INDIANA BOTANIC GARDENS INC

3401 W 37TH AVE
HOBART, IN 463421751
Phone: 219-947-4040
Fax: –
Web: www.botanicchoice.com

CEO: –
CFO: –
HR: –
FYE: December 31
Type: Private

|Indiana Botanic Gardens makes markets and sells herbal supplements cosmetics and other natural products.Its Botanic Choice and Botanic Spa lines feature such exotic ingredients as hoodia (an African desert plant) Indian Water Hyssop and emu oil. In all it sells about 1700 items to customers throughout the US and abroad. The company does most of its business through its mail-order catalogue and online retail site; it also operates a retail store and offers wholesale sales for other retailers. Joseph E. Meyer author of the classic reference book The Herbalist founded Indiana Botanic Gardens in 1910. His great-grandson Tim Cleland is the company's president.

	Annual Growth	12/07	12/08	12/11	12/12	12/13
Sales ($ mil.)	(2.7%)	–	23.9	21.6	21.3	20.8
Net income ($ mil.)	35.7%	–	–	0.5	(0.1)	1.0
Market value ($ mil.)	–	–	–	–	–	–
Employees	–	–	–	–	–	157

INDIANA HARBOR BELT RAILROAD CO

2721 161ST ST
HAMMOND, IN 463231099
Phone: 219-989-4703
Fax: –
Web: www.ihbrr.com

CEO: Jim Roots
CFO: Derek Smith
HR: –
FYE: December 31
Type: Private

Indiana Harbor Belt Railroad provides switching services on its network of more than 50 miles of mainline track in Indiana and Illinois. The company serves the Chicago area which is North America's primary railroad hub. Indiana Harbor Belt handles traffic from industrial customers such as chemical and metal producers and interchanges traffic with about 15 other rail lines. Steel companies account for the largest share of the company's freight traffic. Conrail which is controlled by Norfolk Southern and CSX owns 51% of Indiana Harbor Belt; Canadian Pacific Railway owns 49%. Indiana Harbor Belt Railroad was formed in 1907.

	Annual Growth	12/07	12/08	12/09	12/10	12/11
Sales ($ mil.)	14.3%	–	–	85.1	107.3	111.1
Net income ($ mil.)	28.2%	–	–	3.8	9.7	6.3
Market value ($ mil.)	–	–	–	–	–	–
Employees	–	–	–	–	–	750

INDIANA MUNICIPAL POWER AGENCY

11610 N COLLEGE AVE
CARMEL, IN 460325602
Phone: 317-573-9955
Fax: –
Web: www.properties.zoomprospector.com

CEO: Raj RAO
CFO: Chris Rettig
HR: –
FYE: December 31
Type: Private

Indiana Municipal Power Agency (IMPA) supplies bulk electricity to 53 community-owned distribution utilities throughout Indiana. IMPA members deliver electric service to households businesses and industries across Indiana. The company has interests in fossil-fueled power plants that give it nearly 820 MW of generating capacity; it also buys electricity through supply contracts and through purchases on the wholesale market. IMPA also owns power tranmission assets and it provides utility engineering and consulting services through its ISC subsidiary. The state's 72 public power systems provide about 6% of the state's power capacity.

	Annual Growth	12/16	12/17	12/18	12/19	12/20
Sales ($ mil.)	3.0%	–	423.4	461.1	459.7	463.2
Net income ($ mil.)	(3.2%)	–	23.2	37.6	33.9	21.0
Market value ($ mil.)	–	–	–	–	–	–
Employees	–	–	–	–	–	84

INDIANA UNIVERSITY FOUNDATION, INC.

1500 N STATE ROAD 46 BYP
BLOOMINGTON, IN 47408
Phone: 812-855-8311
Fax: –
Web: www.iufoundation.iu.edu

CEO: J Thomas Forbes
CFO: James Perin
HR: –
FYE: June 30
Type: Private

Hoosier favorite fund-raiser? If you're a fan of Indiana University then it might well be the Indiana University Foundation (IUF). The not-for-profit foundation raises more than $100 million annually in donations from individuals corporations and institutional organizations; alumni gifts account for about half of IUF's funds. It manages an endowment of about $1 billion and provides administrative services for gift accounts and scholarship and fellowship accounts. The organization has offices in Bloomington and Indianapolis. IUF was established in 1936.

	Annual Growth	06/16	06/17	06/18	06/19	06/20
Sales ($ mil.)	(26.2%)	–	–	–	309.5	228.5
Net income ($ mil.)	–	–	–	–	69.8	(9.8)
Market value ($ mil.)	–	–	–	–	–	–
Employees	–	–	–	–	–	240

INDIANA UNIVERSITY HEALTH BLOOMINGTON, INC.

601 W 2ND ST
BLOOMINGTON, IN 474032317
Phone: 812-353-5252
Fax: –

CEO: Matthew Bailey
CFO: Jim Myers
HR: –
FYE: December 31
Type: Private

Indiana University Health Bloomington wants to put a bloom back in patients' cheeks. The facility operating as IU Health Bloomington provides care in a ten-county region in south central Indiana. The not-for-profit hospital — which includes a 350-bed main campus in Bloomington and a 25-bed rural hospital in Paoli — provides care in a number of medical specialties including cardiovascular disease cancer orthopedics and neuroscience. It also runs home health and hospice urgent care lab and specialty care facilities as well as physician practices under the name Southern Indiana Physicians. IU Health Bloomington is part of the Indiana University Health (IU Health) system.

	Annual Growth	12/10	12/11	12/12	12/14	12/15
Sales ($ mil.)	(2.1%)	–	391.6	355.7	382.3	359.9
Net income ($ mil.)	33.8%	–	22.4	64.3	92.2	71.7
Market value ($ mil.)	–	–	–	–	–	–
Employees	–	–	–	–	–	3,200

INDIANA UNIVERSITY HEALTH, INC.

340 W 10TH ST
INDIANAPOLIS, IN 462023082
Phone: 317-962-2000
Fax: –
Web: www.iuhealth.org

CEO: Daniel F Evans Jr
CFO: –
HR: –
FYE: December 31
Type: Private

Indiana University Health (IU Health) is one of the largest health systems in Indiana. Not-for-profit IU Health owns or is affiliated with more than 20 hospitals throughout the state including three major facilities ? Methodist Hospital Indiana University Hospital and Riley Hospital for Children ? in downtown Indianapolis. The hospitals serve as teaching facilities for Indiana University's medical school. The largest Methodist Hospital features the Methodist Research Institute which conducts research and clinical trials. The 2700-bed IU Health system also includes primary and specialty care clinics surgery and urgent care centers a health insurance provider and a home health agency.

	Annual Growth	12/03	12/04	12/05	12/06	12/08
Sales ($ mil.)	(6.1%)	–	–	2,282.0	2,478.3	1,889.6
Net income ($ mil.)	–	–	–	69.0	159.1	(24.0)
Market value ($ mil.)	–	–	–	–	–	–
Employees	–	–	–	–	–	17,242

INDIANA UNIVERSITY OF PENNSYLVANIA

1090 SOUTH DR
INDIANA, PA 157051038
Phone: 724-357-2200
Fax: –
Web: www.iup.edu

CEO: –
CFO: –
HR: –
FYE: June 30
Type: Private

Indiana University of Pennsylvania (IUP) isn't geographically confused. It's named for the town of Indiana which is located in Western Pennsylvania east of Pittsburgh. The school serves more than 14000 students on three campuses (Indiana Northpointe and Punxsutawney); it also has a center in Monroeville that offers classes on evenings and Saturdays for professionals pursuing master's or doctoral degrees. All told the university offers some 140 undergraduate degree programs about 40 master's programs and nine doctoral programs. IUP was founded in 1875 as Indiana Normal School and was granted university status in 1965. It is part of the Pennsylvania State System of Higher Education.

	Annual Growth	06/11	06/12	06/13	06/16	06/18
Sales ($ mil.)	(1.4%)	–	188.5	176.0	173.8	172.9
Net income ($ mil.)	14.5%	–	7.8	12.9	(8.5)	17.5
Market value ($ mil.)	–	–	–	–	–	–
Employees	–	–	–	–	–	1,846

INDIANAPOLIS COLTS INC.

7001 W. 56th St.
Indianapolis IN 46254
Phone: 317-297-2658
Fax: 317-297-8971
Web: www.colts.com

CEO: –
CFO: –
HR: –
FYE: January 31
Type: Private

Fans of this team are can saddle up for football glory. The Indianapolis Colts trace a long and storied history as a franchise in the National Football League boasting five championships since joining the league in 1953. Most of those glory days though took place when the team was the Baltimore Colts and boasted the likes of Johnny Unitas on its roster. The team relocated to Indianapolis in 1984 but fans there had to wait until the 2006 season for the team to make a successful Super Bowl run with the help of such talent as Peyton Manning and Marvin Harrison. Started by Carroll Rosenbloom the team has been owned by CEO James Irsay and his family since 1972.

INDUS CORPORATION

1951 KIDWELL DR FL 8
VIENNA, VA 221823930
Phone: 703-506-6776
Fax: –
Web: www.induscorp.us.com

CEO: Shivram Krishnan
CFO: –
HR: –
FYE: December 31
Type: Private

INDUS hopes to capitalize on technology by providing a variety of information technology (IT) services to the federal government and commercial clients. The company's services include software design consulting application integration systems engineering and enterprise support services. Its areas of expertise include database management data warehousing and data mining; Web development; geographic information systems (GIS); telecommunications; and data security. The company has nine satellite offices in the US. Clients have included NASA the Department of Defense and Homeland Security agencies. INDUS CEO and majority owner Shiv Krishnan founded the company in 1993.

	Annual Growth	12/01	12/02	12/03	12/04	12/14
Sales ($ mil.)	–	–	(153.6)	61.0	75.3	51.4
Net income ($ mil.)	2.2%	–	–	2.6	3.8	3.3
Market value ($ mil.)	–	–	–	–	–	–
Employees	–	–	–	–	–	450

INDUS REALTY TRUST INC — NMS: INDT

641 Lexington Avenue
New York, NY 10022
Phone: 212 218-7910
Fax: –
Web: www.indusrt.com

CEO: Michael Gamzon
CFO: Anthony Galici
HR: –
FYE: November 30
Type: Public

Griffin Industrial Realty (formerly Griffin Land & Nurseries) has forsaken plants in favor of the dirt underneath. Following the sale of its Imperial Nurseries subsidiary which grew and distributed container-based plants to garden center operators and the garden departments of retail chain stores the company's sole business is real estate. The property holdings include about 30 buildings comprising approximately 2.5 million sq. ft. The company also owns a small stake in Centaur Media a business information publisher in the UK. Griffin was founded in 1970 and is controlled by the Cullman and Ernst families. It is one of the largest private landowners in Connecticut.

	Annual Growth	11/16	11/17	11/18	11/19	11/20
Sales ($ mil.)	4.9%	30.9	43.9	33.8	44.0	37.4
Net income ($ mil.)	–	0.6	4.6	(1.7)	3.7	(12.7)
Market value ($ mil.)	22.7%	178.1	206.7	200.8	218.9	403.5
Employees	0.0%	33	32	34	32	33

INDUSTRIAL SCIENTIFIC CORPORATION

1001 OAKDALE RD
OAKDALE, PA 150711500
Phone: 412-788-4353
Fax: –
Web: www.indsci.com

CEO: –
CFO: –
HR: –
FYE: December 31
Type: Private

Detection is a gas for Industrial Scientific. The company makes sells rents and services gas monitoring instruments systems software and related products to detect oxygen and combustible and toxic gases. Its Instrument Network (iNet) tracks the performance of customers' gas monitors and provides status reports as well as instant notification if a problem is detected. Its portable and fixed monitors ("sniffers") calibration stations transmitters controllers and accessories are designed to work alone or together through iNet. The products are used worldwide in work environments such as underground mines and oil refineries as well as by hazardous response units.

	Annual Growth	01/03	01/04	01/05	01/06*	12/07
Sales ($ mil.)	33.6%	–	59.1	63.2	72.7	140.8
Net income ($ mil.)	31.7%	–	–	7.2	8.8	12.5
Market value ($ mil.)	–	–	–	–	–	–
Employees	–	–	–	–	–	700

*Fiscal year change

INDUSTRIAL SERVICES OF AMERICA INC (FL) — NAS: IDSA

7100 Grade Lane
Louisville, KY 40213
Phone: 502 366-3452
Fax: 502 368-1440
Web: www.isa-inc.com

CEO: –
CFO: –
HR: –
FYE: December 31
Type: Public

Industrial Services of America manages solid waste and scrap metals so its customers don't have to. Its Computerized Waste Systems (CWS) unit doesn't pick up trash but instead arranges waste disposal services for its commercial and industrial customers at 2300 locations. CWS negotiates contracts with service providers and offers centralized billing and dispatching and invoice auditing services. Industrial Services of America's ISA Recycling unit handles ferrous and nonferrous metals and fiber products and the company's Waste Equipment Sales & Service unit sells leases and services waste handling and recycling equipment.

	Annual Growth	12/13	12/14	12/15	12/16	12/17
Sales ($ mil.)	(20.4%)	136.8	117.4	46.2	36.5	54.9
Net income ($ mil.)	–	(13.8)	(7.3)	(1.8)	(3.2)	(1.1)
Market value ($ mil.)	(15.1%)	25.6	48.3	10.6	14.5	13.3
Employees	(8.4%)	108	96	74	75	76

INDUSTRIAL TURNAROUND CORPORATION

13141 N ENON CHURCH RD
CHESTER, VA 238363120
Phone: 804-414-1100
Fax: –
Web: www.itacfps.com

CEO: Sidney Harrison
CFO: –
HR: –
FYE: December 31
Type: Private

Facility builder Industrial TurnAround Corporation (ITAC) makes sure that wheels turn and conveyors churn at industrial plants around the world. ITAC provides architectural and design expertise construction management and electrical and mechanical engineering to clients whose facilities are based on heavy production such as biofuels chemical metal pharmaceutical power pulp and paper and tobacco. It also offers on-site staffing (for clients who need temporary project managers draftsmen CAD operators and other support staff) as well as hazard and fall prevention assessment equipment and training. Clients include Amtrak Honeywell International and NASA.

	Annual Growth	12/11	12/12	12/13	12/14	12/17
Sales ($ mil.)	13.6%	–	42.5	50.7	64.5	80.4
Net income ($ mil.)	(26.7%)	–	3.0	4.0	6.1	0.6
Market value ($ mil.)	–	–	–	–	–	–
Employees	–	–	–	–	–	350

INDYNE, INC.

46561 EXPEDITION DR 100
LEXINGTON PARK, MD 206532118
Phone: 703-903-6900
Fax: –
Web: www.indyneinc.com

CEO: –
CFO: –
HR: Margaret James
FYE: December 31
Type: Private

InDyne offers out-of-this-world technology expertise. The company provides information technology science and engineering and technical and administrative services primarily to US government agencies including NASA. It develops custom software designs Web sites and builds computer networks. InDyne's science and engineering division designs aerospace systems provides space mission support and crew training and offers structural and fluid analysis. Its technical and administrative services unit handles imagery operations data management media services and operations support. InDyne's projects have included the development of custom database software for the CDC and the Department of Transportation.

	Annual Growth	12/06	12/07	12/08	12/09	12/10
Sales ($ mil.)	(5.0%)	–	–	288.5	256.0	260.4
Net income ($ mil.)	(12.1%)	–	–	8.9	7.7	6.9
Market value ($ mil.)	–	–	–	–	–	–
Employees	–	–	–	–	–	1,700

INFINERA CORP — NMS: INFN

6373 San Ignacio Avenue
San Jose, CA 95119
Phone: 408 572-5200
Fax: –
Web: www.infinera.com

CEO: David Heard
CFO: Nancy Erba
HR: –
FYE: December 26
Type: Public

Infinera is a global supplier of networking solutions comprised of networking equipment software and services. Its portfolio of solutions includes optical transport platforms converged packet-optical transport platforms compact modular platforms optical line systems disaggregated router platforms a suite of networking and automation software offerings and support and professional services. Infinera also optimizes the manufacturing process by using indium phosphide to build its PICs which enables the integration of hundreds of optical functions onto a set of semiconductor chips. Customers include telecommunication service providers internet content providers (ICPs) cable providers wholesale carriers research and education institutions governments and large enterprises. Over 45% of the company's sales derived from the US.

	Annual Growth	12/16	12/17	12/18	12/19	12/20
Sales ($ mil.)	11.7%	870.1	740.7	943.4	1,298.9	1,355.6
Net income ($ mil.)	–	(23.9)	(194.5)	(214.3)	(386.6)	(206.7)
Market value ($ mil.)	6.6%	1,709.9	1,274.8	789.5	1,566.9	2,209.3
Employees	8.0%	2,240	2,145	3,876	3,261	3,050

INFINITE ENERGY, LLC

7001 SW 24TH AVE
GAINESVILLE, FL 326073704
Phone: 352-331-1654
Fax: –
Web: www.gassouth.com

CEO: Darin Cook
CFO: –
HR: –
FYE: December 31
Type: Private

Infinite wisdom? No. Infinite energy? Yes. Infinite Energy does not provide its customers with the natural high of endorphins or with the latest health diet but with the more prosaic commodity of natural gas. The company supplies natural gas to clients in Florida Georgia and New York. Wholesale customers include municipalities institutions and utilities; Infinite Energy also sells to large and small commercial establishments (including restaurants) and to residential customers.

	Annual Growth	12/02	12/03	12/04	12/05	12/09
Sales ($ mil.)	6.0%	–	335.8	474.0	583.9	477.6
Net income ($ mil.)	26.7%	–	3.1	8.7	4.5	13.0
Market value ($ mil.)	–	–	–	–	–	–
Employees	–	–	–	–	–	418

INFINITE GROUP, INC. NBB: IMCI

175 Sully's Trail, Suite 202
Pittsford, NY 14534
Phone: 585 385-0610
Fax: –
Web: www.igius.com

CEO: James Villa
CFO: –
HR: –
FYE: December 31
Type: Public

As far as Infinite Group Inc. (IGI) is concerned it's capacity to handle its clients' IT outsourcing is unlimited — particularly for government clients. The company provides infrastructure management information security systems engineering server and desktop virtualization enterprise architecture and software development. US government contracts account for the majority of IGI's sales and some its government clients are the Department of Homeland Security and the US Navy. The company has offices in New York Colorado and Virginia (which serves its DC customers).

	Annual Growth	12/16	12/17	12/18	12/19	12/20
Sales ($ mil.)	(0.7%)	7.4	6.4	6.4	7.1	7.2
Net income ($ mil.)	–	(0.3)	(0.1)	0.0	0.0	0.7
Market value ($ mil.)	17.8%	1.3	0.6	0.3	1.5	2.5
Employees	(0.8%)	62	58	57	59	60

INFINITY ENERGY RESOURCES INC. PINK SHEETS: IFNY

11900 College Blvd. Ste. 204
Overland Park KS 66210
Phone: 913-948-9512
Fax: 913-338-4458
Web: www.infinity-res.com

CEO: Stanton Ross
CFO: Daniel Hutchins
HR: –
FYE: December 31
Type: Public

Maybe nothing lasts forever but Infinity Energy Resources hopes that US demand for fossil fuels won't go away for a long long time. The company focuses its oil exploration and production operations in the Fort Worth Basin of Texas in the Rocky Mountain region in the Greater Green River Basin in Wyoming and the Sand Wash and Piceance Basins in Colorado. It is also pursuing an opportunity in offshore Nicaragua. The company has proved reserves of 7.8 billion cu. ft. of natural gas equivalent. Infinity Energy Resources has exited the oil services business.

INFINITY PHARMACEUTICALS INC NMS: INFI

1100 Massachusetts Avenue, Floor 4
Cambridge, MA 02138
Phone: 617 453-1000
Fax: –
Web: www.infi.com

CEO: Adelene Perkins
CFO: –
HR: –
FYE: December 31
Type: Public

Infinity Pharmaceuticals acts on the endless possibilities for new cancer treatments. The firm works to discover and develop targeted therapies for different types of cancer including non-small cell lung cancer. Such targeted therapies aim at inhibiting specific disease signaling pathways for potential applications in oncology. It focused on advancing IPI-549 an orally administered clinical-stage immuno-oncology product candidate that selectively inhibits the enzyme phosphoinositide-3-kinase-gamma or PI3K-gamma. The company has ongoing programs in preclinical and clinical trial stages; it also investigates candidates through partnerships with other drugmakers.

	Annual Growth	12/16	12/17	12/18	12/19	12/20
Sales ($ mil.)	(45.0%)	18.7	6.0	22.1	3.0	1.7
Net income ($ mil.)	–	(30.1)	(41.8)	(11.3)	(47.1)	(40.5)
Market value ($ mil.)	12.0%	86.8	130.6	75.9	61.7	136.4
Employees	0.0%	23	22	25	25	23

INFINITY PROPERTY & CASUALTY CORP NMS: IPCC

2201 4th Avenue North
Birmingham, AL 35203
Phone: 205 870-4000
Fax: –
Web: www.infinityauto.com

CEO: James R Gober
CFO: Robert H Bateman
HR: –
FYE: December 31
Type: Public

Infinity Property and Casualty specializes in providing insurance coverage to high-risk drivers. The insurer primarily provides personal non-standard auto policies and is a leading writer of policies for high-risk drivers in the US. The company also offers standard and preferred personal auto commercial small fleet and classic collector auto insurance. Licensed in all 50 states the company currently focuses its business on targeted urban areas of a handful of states. Personal non-standard auto insurance accounts for more than 90% of its premiums; California accounts for about half of that business. Infinity distributes its products through more than 11800 independent agents. Kemper Corporation is buying Infinity for $1.4 billion.

	Annual Growth	12/12	12/13	12/14	12/15	12/16
Assets ($ mil.)	1.1%	2,303.6	2,317.3	2,384.8	2,386.8	2,402.6
Net income ($ mil.)	15.4%	24.3	32.6	57.2	51.5	43.1
Market value ($ mil.)	10.8%	643.2	792.4	853.2	908.1	970.7
Employees	1.1%	2,200	2,400	2,200	2,300	2,300

INFOBLOX INC.

2390 MISSION COLLEGE BLVD # 501
SANTA CLARA, CA 950541554
Phone: 408-986-4000
Fax: –
Web: www.infoblox.com

CEO: Jesper Andersen
CFO: Hoke Horne
HR: –
FYE: July 31
Type: Private

Infoblox products maintain the info flow across networks. Customers from various sectors use the company's hardware and software to automate consolidate and more securely operate corporate networks. Infoblox's Trinzic DDI network identity appliances manage functions such as internet domain name server (DNS) resolution IP address management and network access control. Its NetMRI product line automates network change and configuration management processes. Infoblox works more than 8000 customers including 350 of the Fortune 500. The company was acquired by Vista Equity Partners in 2016.

	Annual Growth	07/11	07/12	07/13	07/14	07/15
Sales ($ mil.)	16.6%	–	–	225.0	250.3	306.1
Net income ($ mil.)	–	–	–	(4.4)	(23.9)	(27.1)
Market value ($ mil.)	–	–	–	–	–	–
Employees	–	–	–	–	–	25

INFOGAIN CORPORATION

485 ALBERTO WAY STE 100
LOS GATOS, CA 950325476
Phone: 408-355-6000
Fax: –
Web: www.infogain.com

CEO: Sunil Bhatia
CFO: Kulesh Bansal
HR: –
FYE: March 31
Type: Private

Infogain helps clients get more from their enterprise data. The company's core services are Software Engineering and Software Quality Engineering. These services provide consulting quality assurance solutions modernization maintenance engagements DevOps automation and agile planning. Other areas of expertise include integrating and optimizing Oracle and Microsoft products as well as Azure Cloud App Engineering services. The company also provides Cloud Infrastructure Google Cloud App Engineering and IoT Services. It has expertise in the travel retail insurance and high technology industries. Infogain Corporation was founded in 1990 by Kapil Nanda. In late 2019 the company acquired Silicus Technologies and Revel Consulting.

	Annual Growth	06/07	06/08	06/09	06/11*	03/18
Sales ($ mil.)	15.6%	–	–	34.5	44.4	127.3
Net income ($ mil.)	(4.2%)	–	–	1.1	1.4	0.8
Market value ($ mil.)	–	–	–	–	–	–
Employees	–	–	–	–	–	597

*Fiscal year change

INFOR GLOBAL SOLUTIONS INC.

641 Avenue of the Americas 4th Fl.
New York NY 10011
Phone: 678-319-8000
Fax: 678-319-8682
Web: www.infor.com

CEO: Kevin Samuelson
CFO: Jay Hopkins
HR: –
FYE: May 31
Type: Private

Before manufacturers and distributors get products to the shelf Infor Global Solutions gets software to their computers. The company develops enterprise applications used for a wide range of business purposes that automate and link disparate functions across an organization. Uses for its products include managing inventories tracking shipments and managing customer interactions. Infor targets such industries as automotive chemicals consumer packaged goods food processing and pharmaceuticals. Clients have included Bristol-Myers Squibb Cargill Grohe Heinz and TRW. The company has customers in about 200 countries. Infor is controlled by a group of investors led by Golden Gate Capital and Summit Partners.

INFORELIANCE CORPORATION

4050 Legato Rd. Ste. 700
Fairfax VA 22033
Phone: 703-246-9360
Fax: 703-246-9331
Web: www.inforeliance.com

CEO: Andrew J Butler
CFO: –
HR: –
FYE: December 31
Type: Private

If you need to rely on information technology services InfoReliance could be the contractor you want. Founded in 2000 the company provides commercial and government customers with custom Web-based software development and IT services such as systems integration portal and network design project management consulting and training. Clients have included the US departments of Agriculture and Commerce; the US Army; the Centers for Disease Control and Prevention; and the Drug Enforcement Administration. Its commercial customers come from industries including financial services health care and manufacturing and have included Epson Microsoft and Diversified Lending Group.

INFORMATICA CORP.

NMS: INFA

2100 Seaport Boulevard
Redwood City, CA 94063
Phone: 650 385-5000
Fax: –
Web: www.informatica.com

CEO: Amit Walia
CFO: Eric Brown
HR: –
FYE: December 31
Type: Public

Big data is a big opportunity for Informatica. The company provides enterprise data integration software that enables companies to access integrate and consolidate their data across a variety of systems and users. Its PowerCenter platform consolidates codes and moves large data warehouses and its PowerExchange software enables access to bulk or changed data. Other products include Master Data Management (MDM) and the Informatica B2B Data Exchange as well as Fast Clone (data replication) Data Explorer (data quality) and a range of software-as-a-service (SaaS) offerings which integrate data from other business applications into a single hosted platform.

	Annual Growth	12/09	12/10	12/11	12/12	12/13
Sales ($ mil.)	17.3%	500.7	650.1	783.8	811.6	948.2
Net income ($ mil.)	7.7%	64.2	86.3	117.5	93.2	86.4
Market value ($ mil.)	12.5%	2,811.7	4,783.6	4,012.2	3,294.1	4,508.7
Employees	16.5%	1,755	2,126	2,554	2,814	3,234

INFORMATION SERVICES GROUP INC

NMS: III

2187 Atlantic Street
Stamford, CT 06902
Phone: 203 517-3100
Fax: –
Web: www.isg-one.com

CEO: Michael Connors
CFO: Humberto Alfonso
HR: –
FYE: December 31
Type: Public

True to its name Information Services Group's (ISG) service is information. ISG provides technology insights market intelligence and advisory services to companies seeking to outsource their business operations. The company specializes in marketing advertising human resources legal supply chain management and other business services. It targets North American European and Asia/Pacific markets and has operations in some 20 countries. It serves such industries as telecom financial services health care pharmaceutical and utilities. ISG operates through subsidiaries TPI Advisory Services (data and advisory) Compass (benchmarking and analysis) and STA Consulting (public sector IT services).

	Annual Growth	12/16	12/17	12/18	12/19	12/20
Sales ($ mil.)	3.6%	216.5	269.6	275.8	265.8	249.1
Net income ($ mil.)	–	(6.5)	(2.1)	5.7	3.3	2.8
Market value ($ mil.)	(2.6%)	175.4	200.9	204.3	121.9	158.1
Employees	(0.2%)	1,267	1,248	1,310	1,287	1,258

INFOVISION INC.

800 E CAMPBELL RD STE 388
RICHARDSON, TX 75081-1841
Phone: 972-234-0058
Fax: –
Web: www.infovision.net

CEO: –
CFO: –
HR: –
FYE: December 31
Type: Private

Infovision's insight is all about computer systems. The company designs and integrates large and small software systems for clients in the telecom manufacturing banking financial services retail pharmaceuticals and energy industries. With expertise in a wide range of technologies — including multi-tier architectures database administration statistical analysis graphical user interfaces and enterprise resource planning — Infovision offers contract services outsourcing engineering services vendor management and offshore software development. The company was co-founded in 1995 by chairman Sean Yalamanchi and director Raman Kovelamudi.

	Annual Growth	12/02	12/03	12/04	12/05	12/11
Sales ($ mil.)	–	–	0.0	29.0	38.2	50.7
Net income ($ mil.)	86.1%	–	0.0	13.3	4.9	2.4
Market value ($ mil.)	–	–	–	–	–	–
Employees	–	–	–	–	–	600

ING BANK FSB

1 S. Orange St.
Wilmington DE 19801
Phone: 302-658-2200
Fax: +44-1753-552-662
Web: www.adler.co.uk

CEO: Ralph Hamers
CFO: Pg Flynn
HR: –
FYE: December 31
Type: Subsidiary

Orange you glad you can count on ING Bank? The company better known as ING Direct offers the Orange Savings Account which boasts higher-than-average interest rates and one of the highest yields in the industry. Doing business in the US via the Internet over the phone by ATM and by mail ING Direct also offers certificates of deposit individual retirement accounts home mortgages and paperless checking accounts. For businesses ING Direct offers savings accounts CDs and 401(k) plans. The bank offers online brokerage services through ING Direct Investing (formerly ShareBuilder) which it acquired in 2007. Capital One bought ING Direct from Amsterdam-based ING Groep for some $9 billion in 2012.

INGLES MARKETS INC   NMS: IMKT A

P.O. Box 6676
Asheville, NC 28816
Phone: 828 669-2941
Fax: –
Web: www.ingles-markets.com

CEO: James Lanning
CFO: Ronald Freeman
HR: –
FYE: September 25
Type: Public

Ingles Markets is a leading supermarket chain in the southeast US that operates about 200 supermarkets primarily in suburbs small towns and rural areas of six southeastern states. The stores largely operate under the Ingles name although nine do business as Sav-Mor. In addition to brand-name goods Ingles Markets stocks its shelves with its Laura Lynn and Harvest Farms private label products. The company also owns milk processing and packaging plant that sells approximately 75% of its products to Ingles stores and the rest to other retailers and distributors. Ingles Markets is also in the real estate business: it owns about 165 of its supermarkets nearly all of which contain an Ingles store.

	Annual Growth	09/17	09/18	09/19	09/20	09/21
Sales ($ mil.)	5.7%	4,002.7	4,092.8	4,202.0	4,610.6	4,987.9
Net income ($ mil.)	46.7%	53.9	97.4	81.6	178.6	249.7
Market value ($ mil.)	26.3%	488.2	650.6	737.6	693.1	1,243.9
Employees	1.0%	25,000	26,000	27,000	27,000	26,000

ING U.S. INC.

230 Park Ave.
New York NY 10169
Phone: 212-309-8200
Fax: 303-532-1642
Web: www.heatwurx.com

CEO: Heather Lavallee
CFO: Michael Smith
HR: Kevin Silva
FYE: December 31
Type: Private

ING U.S. is the American arm of Dutch financial services firm ING Groep. It offers retirement investment and insurance (mostly life) services to 13 million individual and corporate customers. Retirement products include IRAs brokerage accounts and annuities; it has about $107 billion in assets under management (AUM) for this segment. ING U.S.'s investment management services with $166 billion AUM include international and domestic equity fixed-income and multi-asset products. Insurance covers individual term and universal life as well as employee benefits (stop loss group life disability) which it sells to midsized and large companies. Formed in 1999 the company filed to go public in 2012.

INGRAM MICRO INC.   NYS: IM

3351 Michelson Drive, Suite 100
Irvine, CA 92612-0697
Phone: 714 566-1000
Fax: 714 566-7604
Web: www.ingrammicro.com

CEO: Paul Bay
CFO: Mike Ziliz
HR: Debbie Bartz
FYE: December 31
Type: Public

The only things micro about Ingram are some of the smaller electronic components it sells. The world's largest wholesale distributor of information technology products Ingram Micro provides thousands of products — desktop and notebook PCs servers storage devices monitors printers and software — to more than 200000 customers in some 160 countries worldwide. Its sells products from more than 1700 suppliers including many of the world's top manufacturers; Hewlett-Packard is the company's largest supplier. Ingram Micro also offers a wide range of services to its resellers and suppliers including supply chain management business intelligence financing logistics cloud computing and network support services. The company rings up 61% of sales outside North America.

	Annual Growth	01/11*	12/11	12/12	12/13	12/14
Sales ($ mil.)	10.4%	34,589.0	36,328.7	37,827.3	42,553.9	46,487.4
Net income ($ mil.)	(5.7%)	318.1	244.2	305.9	310.6	266.7
Market value ($ mil.)	13.1%	2,982.1	2,841.5	2,583.8	3,652.3	4,317.8
Employees	11.5%	15,650	15,500	20,800	21,800	21,700

*Fiscal year change

INGERSOLL MACHINE TOOLS, INC.

707 FULTON AVE
ROCKFORD, IL 611034069
Phone: 815-987-6000
Fax: –
Web: www.camozzimachinetools.com

CEO: –
CFO: Lawrence Mocadlo
HR: –
FYE: December 31
Type: Private

At Ingersoll Machine Tools folks want to talk shop. The company leads the conversation in global production churning out advanced machine tools for other industries' goods. Products include general purpose equipment (vertical turning lathes scalpers and horizontal boring centers) to one-of-a-kind machines that produce aluminum and hard metal components and structures from composite materials. Ingersoll's contract manufacturing services offer prototype machining and short production runs of windmill hubs to small engine parts. Customers include most of the world's aerospace transportation energy and heavy industry OEMs from Caterpillar to Lockheed Martin. Ingersoll is a company of Italy's Camozzi Group.

	Annual Growth	12/08	12/09	12/15	12/16	12/17
Sales ($ mil.)	1.4%	–	56.4	0.0	55.5	63.0
Net income ($ mil.)	34.9%	–	0.3	0.0	2.6	3.5
Market value ($ mil.)	–	–	–	–	–	–
Employees	–	–	–	–	–	331

INGREDION INC   NYS: INGR

5 Westbrook Corporate Center
Westchester, IL 60154
Phone: 708 551-2600
Fax: 708 551-2700
Web: www.ingredion.com

CEO: James Zallie
CFO: James Gray
HR: –
FYE: December 31
Type: Public

Sweet sodas and diet desserts alike get their taste and feel from Ingredion's ingredients. The company is a leading global ingredients solutions provider that turns corn tapioca potatoes plant-based stevia grains fruits and vegetables into value-added ingredients and biomaterials for the food beverage brewing and other industries. Operating in more than 120 countries ilt serves markets including food beverage brewing and other industries. Ingredion's largest product line is starches used in food for stabilization feel and texture and in paper packaging and other materials for quality strength and a host of other attributes. Its other product lines include sweeteners (high-fructose corn syrup dextrose) specialty ingredients (products focused on health affordability and sustainability) and co-products (refined corn oil corn gluten feed and meal). Ingredion operates worldwide but generates most of its sales in North America.

	Annual Growth	12/17	12/18	12/19	12/20	12/21
Sales ($ mil.)	4.3%	5,832.0	5,841.0	6,209.0	5,987.0	6,894.0
Net income ($ mil.)	(31.1%)	519.0	443.0	413.0	348.0	117.0
Market value ($ mil.)	(8.8%)	9,318.6	6,092.4	6,195.7	5,243.9	6,441.7
Employees	2.2%	11,000	11,000	11,000	12,000	12,000

INKSURE TECHNOLOGIES INC.

OTC: INKS

1770 NW 64th St. Ste. 350
Fort Lauderdale FL 33309
Phone: 954-772-8507
Fax: 954-772-8509
Web: www.inksure.com

CEO: Israel Alfassi
CFO: Chanan Morris
HR: –
FYE: December 31
Type: Public

Don't think it ink it; InkSure Technologies makes the mark genuine and permanent. The company markets custom security inks that are designed to prevent counterfeiting. The company also sells readers that use the company's proprietary software to identify and analyze marks printed with its inks which can be used on a variety of paper and plastic materials and have a unique chemical code. Applications for InkSure Technologies systems include financial and government documents pharmaceutical and tobacco product packaging retail gift certificates and travel tickets. Aviation security company ICTS International holds roughly a 30% stake in InkSure Technologies.

INNOPHOS HOLDINGS INC

NMS: IPHS

259 Prospect Plains Road
Cranbury, NJ 08512
Phone: 609 495-2495
Fax: –
Web: www.innophos.com

CEO: Richard Hooper
CFO: Dennis Loughran
HR: –
FYE: December 31
Type: Public

Innophos Holdings adds a dash of its phosphate products to food beverages toothpaste detergents and asphalt. Innophos manufactures specialty phosphates used in consumer products pharmaceuticals and industrial applications. Customers use the company's phosphates to improve the quality and performance of a broad range of products from electronics and textiles to pharmaceuticals water and detergents. Innophos divides its business into three segments: specialty salts and specialty acids; purified phosphoric acid; and granular triple super phosphates (GSTP) a fertilizer.

	Annual Growth	12/13	12/14	12/15	12/16	12/17
Sales ($ mil.)	(3.8%)	844.1	839.2	789.1	725.3	722.0
Net income ($ mil.)	(17.9%)	49.5	64.5	26.3	48.0	22.4
Market value ($ mil.)	(1.0%)	949.5	1,142.0	566.2	1,021.0	913.0
Employees	(1.0%)	1,427	1,445	1,387	1,319	1,373

INNERWORKINGS INC

NMS: INWK

203 North LaSalle Street, Suite 1800
Chicago, IL 60601
Phone: 312 642-3700
Fax: –
Web: www.inwk.com

CEO: Mike Perez
CFO: –
HR: –
FYE: December 31
Type: Public

InnerWorkings has inserted itself into the nuts and bolts of the corporate printing world. The company procures manages and delivers printed products (brochures catalogs and other promotional materials) to companies in the advertising consumer products publishing and retail industries. InnerWorkings' proprietary software application and database matches customers' jobs with printing companies' equipment and capacity. The InnerWorkings system submits a job to multiple printers who then bid for the business. Approximately 10000 suppliers participate in the company's network which includes finishing and engraving firms graphic designers paper mills and merchants digital imaging companies and binders.

	Annual Growth	12/14	12/15	12/16	12/17	12/18
Sales ($ mil.)	2.9%	1,000.1	1,029.4	1,090.7	1,136.3	1,121.6
Net income ($ mil.)	–	–	44.5	(32.3)	4.4	19.0	(76.2)
Market value ($ mil.)	(16.8%)	403.6	388.6	510.3	519.6	193.8
Employees	7.0%	1,600	1,600	1,800	2,000	2,100

INNOSPEC INC

NMS: IOSP

8310 South Valley Highway, Suite 350
Englewood, CO 80112
Phone: 303 792-5554
Fax: –
Web: www.innospecinc.com

CEO: Patrick Williams
CFO: Ian Cleminson
HR: Catherine Hessner
FYE: December 31
Type: Public

Innospec develops manufactures blends markets and supplies specialty chemicals for use as fuel additives ingredients. Innospec's Fuel Specialties segment makes chemical additives that enhance fuel efficiency and engine performance and its Performance Chemicals unit makes several products used in the personal care home care agrochemical and mining. Meanwhile the Oilfield Services provide drilling and production chemical. The company's Octane Additives business which ceased trading in mid-2020 manufactures a fuel additive for use in automotive gasoline. The company generates about 45% of sales from the US and North America.

	Annual Growth	12/17	12/18	12/19	12/20	12/21
Sales ($ mil.)	3.2%	1,306.8	1,476.9	1,513.3	1,193.1	1,483.4
Net income ($ mil.)	10.8%	61.8	85.0	112.2	28.7	93.1
Market value ($ mil.)	6.4%	1,749.0	1,530.0	2,562.6	2,247.7	2,238.1
Employees	0.0%	1,900	2,000	2,000	1,900	1,900

INNODATA INC

NMS: INOD

55 Challenger Road
Ridgefield Park, NJ 07660
Phone: 201 371-8000
Fax: –
Web: www.innodata.com

CEO: Jack Abuhoff
CFO: Mark Spelker
HR: –
FYE: December 31
Type: Public

Innodata handles information inundation. The company provides content management and process outsourcing services to businesses and government agencies mainly in the US and Europe. It oversees abstracting and indexing data capture and entry research and analysis and technical writing among other tasks. Innodata manages such tasks as digitizing paper documents into a more manageable electronic form. The company also provides IT services such as consulting systems integration and software and systems engineering. It primarily serves the media publishing and information services industries. Innodata's top clients are Apple Wolters Kluwer Bloomberg and Reed Elsevier.

	Annual Growth	12/16	12/17	12/18	12/19	12/20
Sales ($ mil.)	(2.0%)	63.1	60.9	57.4	55.9	58.2
Net income ($ mil.)	–	(5.5)	(5.1)	0.0	(1.6)	0.6
Market value ($ mil.)	21.3%	63.2	35.1	38.7	29.4	136.7
Employees	(5.6%)	4,750	3,944	3,147	3,640	3,769

INNOVARO INC.

NBB: INNI

2109 Palm Avenue
Tampa, FL 33605
Phone: 813 754-4330
Fax: –
Web: www.innovaro.com

CEO: Asa Lanum
CFO: Carole Wright
HR: –
FYE: December 31
Type: Public

Innovaro's mission in life is to turn innovations into profitable ventures. The company (formerly UTEK) provides consultation services to help clients to locate new markets identify game-changing strategies and develop new platforms; it also facilitates the sale of licensing deals for potential commercial use. Areas of expertise include biotechnology energy geology manufacturing and electronics. Founded in 1997 Innovaro has worked with hundreds of big-name clients such as Disney Johnson & Johnson and Nokia. The former UTEK changed its name to Innovaro in mid-2010 after a UK consulting firm it had acquired in 2008.

	Annual Growth	09/09*	12/09	12/10	12/11	12/12
Sales ($ mil.)	(59.1%)	7.8	3.0	13.1	14.9	0.5
Net income ($ mil.)	–	(9.3)	(0.6)	(19.1)	(4.6)	(10.0)
Market value ($ mil.)	(62.5%)	75.6	68.6	23.1	15.5	4.0
Employees	(51.4%)	–	61	39	31	7

*Fiscal year change

INNOVATE CORP
NYS: VATE

295 Madison Avenue, 12th Floor
New York, NY 10017
Phone: 212 235-2690
Fax: –
Web: www.hc2.com

CEO: Wayne Barr
CFO: Michael Sena
HR: –
FYE: December 31
Type: Public

HC2 Holdings is a diversified holding company which seeks opportunities to acquire and grow businesses that can generate long-term sustainable free cash flow and attractive returns in order to maximize value for all stakeholders. HC2 has a diverse array of operating subsidiaries across multiple reportable segments including Construction Life Sciences Spectrum Insurance and Other. HC2's largest operating subsidiary is DBM Global Inc. a family of companies providing fully integrated structural and steel construction services. The company was founded in 1994.

	Annual Growth	12/16	12/17	12/18	12/19	12/20
Sales ($ mil.)	(10.4%)	1,558.1	1,634.1	1,976.7	1,984.1	1,005.8
Net income ($ mil.)	–	(94.5)	(46.9)	162.0	(31.5)	(92.0)
Market value ($ mil.)	(13.9%)	455.0	456.5	202.6	166.5	250.1
Employees	0.5%	2,744	3,358	4,119	64	2,803

INNOVATION VENTURES LLC

38955 Hills Tech Dr.
Farmington Hills MI 48331
Phone: 248-960-1700
Fax: +81-3-5201-6292
Web: www.kamipa.co.jp

CEO: Manoj Bhargava
CFO: –
HR: –
FYE: December 31
Type: Private

Just because you're tired doesn't mean you're thirsty. Innovation Ventures is a holding company that owns Living Essentials LLC which markets the two-ounce energy drink 5-hour Energy. Unlike other carbonated energy drinks 5-hour Energy doesn't contain any sugar and only has four calories thanks to its small size that packs quite a punch. Five-hour Energy is a blend of vitamins amino acids and caffeine and comes in flavors (berry grape lemon-lime) as well as a decaf and extra-strength formula. Five-hour Energy drinks are strategically placed at the checkout counter not the beverage aisle at most major grocery drug and convenience stores in the US and Canada.

INNOVATIVE SOLUTIONS AND SUPPORT INC
NMS: ISSC

720 Pennsylvania Drive
Exton, PA 19341
Phone: 610 646-9800
Fax: –
Web: www.innovative-ss.com

CEO: Shahram Askarpour
CFO: Relland Winand
HR: –
FYE: September 30
Type: Public

Pilots use products by Innovative Solutions and Support (IS&S) to gauge their success. The company makes flight information computers electronic displays and monitoring systems that measure flight information such as airspeed altitude and engine and fuel data. IS&S's reduced vertical separation minimum (RVSM) system enables planes to fly closer together; engine and fuel displays help pilots track fuel and oil levels and other engine functions. IS&S offers flat-panel displays which take up less cockpit space than conventional displays. Customers are the US DoD and other government agencies defense contractors and commercial/corporate air carriers.

	Annual Growth	09/17	09/18	09/19	09/20	09/21
Sales ($ mil.)	8.2%	16.8	13.9	17.6	21.6	23.0
Net income ($ mil.)	2.6%	4.6	(3.7)	1.9	3.3	5.1
Market value ($ mil.)	17.8%	62.8	43.8	81.1	118.0	121.1
Employees	(2.2%)	93	55	71	86	85

INNOVIVA INC
NMS: INVA

1350 Old Bayshore Highway Suite 400
Burlingame, CA 94010
Phone: 650 238-9600
Fax: –
Web: www.inva.com

CEO: Pavel Raifeld
CFO: –
HR: –
FYE: December 31
Type: Public

Innoviva (formerly Theravance) is a company with a portfolio of royalties that include respiratory assets partnered with Glaxo Group Limited (GSK). The company collaborates with GSK to develop and commercialize once-daily products for the treatment of chronic obstructive pulmonary disease (COPD) and asthma. The collaboration has developed three combination products Relvar once-daily combination medicine consisting of a LABA vilanterol and an inhaled corticosteroid fluticasone furoate; Anoro Ellipta once-daily medicine combining a long-acting muscarinic antagonist; and Trelegy Ellipta once-daily combination medicine consisting of an inhaled corticosteroid long-acting muscarinic antagonist and LABA. Founded in 1996.

	Annual Growth	12/16	12/17	12/18	12/19	12/20
Sales ($ mil.)	26.0%	133.6	217.2	261.0	261.0	336.8
Net income ($ mil.)	39.3%	59.5	134.1	395.1	157.3	224.4
Market value ($ mil.)	3.7%	1,084.9	1,438.8	1,769.3	1,435.7	1,256.2
Employees	(22.7%)	14	12	6	6	5

INNSUITES HOSPITALITY TRUST
ASE: IHT

InnSuites Hotels Centre, 1730 E. Northern Avenue, Suite 122
Phoenix, AZ 85020
Phone: 602 944-1500
Fax: –
Web: www.innsuitestrust.com

CEO: James Wirth
CFO: Sylvin Lange
HR: –
FYE: January 31
Type: Public

This company trusts you'll have a night full of sweet dreams while staying at one of its hotels. InnSuites Hospitality Trust wholly-owns and operates five studio and two-room suite hotels in Arizona New Mexico and southern California four of which are co-branded as Best Westerns. The company also provides management services for nine hotels and trademark license services for 11 hotels. InnSuites Hospitality Trust primarily operates through the InnSuites Hotels & Suites and InnSuites Boutique Hotel Collection brands. InnSuites Hospitality Trust operates through its majority-owned affiliate RRF Limited Partnership which in turn operates through subsidiary InnSuites Hotels.

	Annual Growth	01/17	01/18	01/19	01/20	01/21
Sales ($ mil.)	(24.9%)	13.2	10.8	6.2	6.6	4.2
Net income ($ mil.)	–	(2.2)	1.4	1.4	(1.7)	(1.6)
Market value ($ mil.)	6.8%	19.6	15.7	15.2	14.2	25.5
Employees	(8.5%)	200	200	120	140	140

INOGEN, INC
NMS: INGN

301 Coromar Drive
Goleta, CA 93117
Phone: 805 562-0500
Fax: –
Web: www.inogen.com

CEO: Nabil Shabshab
CFO: Mike Sergesketter
HR: –
FYE: December 31
Type: Public

Inogen is a medical technology company that primarily develops manufactures and markets innovative portable oxygen concentrators that provide supplemental oxygen by people with chronic respiratory conditions. The company's proprietary Inogen One systems concentrate the air around the patient to offer a single source of supplemental oxygen anytime anywhere with a single battery and can be plugged into an outlet when at home in a car or in a public place with outlets available. Unlike most suppliers in the market Inogen sells and rents directly to patients. The US accounts for approximately 80% of revenue. Inogen was formed in 2001 and went public in early 2014.

	Annual Growth	12/16	12/17	12/18	12/19	12/20
Sales ($ mil.)	11.1%	202.8	249.4	358.1	361.9	308.5
Net income ($ mil.)	–	20.5	21.0	51.8	21.0	(5.8)
Market value ($ mil.)	(9.7%)	1,486.6	2,635.4	2,748.1	1,512.2	988.8
Employees	11.7%	602	770	285	1,020	938

INOTIV INC
NAS: NOTV

2701 Kent Avenue
West Lafayette, IN 47906
Phone: 765 463-4527
Fax: –
Web: www.inotivco.com

CEO: Robert Leasure
CFO: Beth Taylor
HR: –
FYE: September 30
Type: Public

Bioanalytical Systems Inc. (BASi) now operating under the trade name "Inotiv" provides contract research and development services for the pharmaceutical chemical and medical device industries. The company also sells analytical instruments to these customers which include pharmaceutical biotechnology biomedical device academic and government organizations. Some of its services include analytical method development and validation stability testing archiving services among others. Vast majority of its total revenue accounted in the US. The company has been providing services involving the research of products and treatment of diseases through products since 1974.

	Annual Growth	09/17	09/18	09/19	09/20	09/21
Sales ($ mil.)	38.7%	24.2	26.3	43.6	60.5	89.6
Net income ($ mil.)	87.4%	0.9	(0.2)	(0.8)	(4.7)	10.9
Market value ($ mil.)	102.0%	28.0	25.6	57.2	76.2	465.8
Employees	38.3%	155	235	322	421	567

INOVA HEALTH SYSTEM FOUNDATION

8110 GATEHOUSE RD 200E
FALLS CHURCH, VA 220421217
Phone: 703-289-2069
Fax: –
Web: www.foundation.inova.org

CEO: John Knox Singleton
CFO: Alice H Pope
HR: –
FYE: December 31
Type: Private

Inova Health Foundation provides financial support and assistance to the Inova Health System which operates a network of not-for-profit community hospitals in northern Virginia. It also supports home health services heart care programs clinical research and trials emergency and urgent care centers outpatient services and destination institutes. To raise funds for the hospital system the foundation organizes fundraising monthly giving Inova visionaries gifts of stocks and corporate giving. Donors can also make contributions through the Inova website.

	Annual Growth	12/13	12/14	12/15	12/17	12/19
Sales ($ mil.)	(27.5%)	–	–	2,972.1	765.9	821.6
Net income ($ mil.)	34.3%	–	–	234.8	717.2	763.0
Market value ($ mil.)	–	–	–	–	–	–
Employees	–	–	–	–	–	16,000

INOVA TECHNOLOGY INC
NBB: INVA

2300 W. Sahara Ave., Suite 800
Las Vegas, NV 89102
Phone: 800 507-2810
Fax: –
Web: www.inovatechnology.com

CEO: –
CFO: –
HR: –
FYE: April 30
Type: Public

Inova Technology has innovative ways of keeping track of things. The company provides radio frequency identification (RFID) scanners and tags through its RighTag subsidiary. Its Trakkers subsidiary offers a tracking solution that allows trade show exhibitors to scan badges of attendees to capture contact information then store the data in a specially designated Web site for access from any location. Inova Technology also offers IT consulting and computer network services through its Desert Communications subsidiary. Chairman and CEO Adam Radly controls more than half of the company.

	Annual Growth	04/09	04/10	04/11	04/12	04/13
Sales ($ mil.)	(4.6%)	22.6	21.0	22.1	21.2	18.7
Net income ($ mil.)	–	(2.0)	(7.1)	(3.4)	(1.2)	(6.6)
Market value ($ mil.)	–	–	2.4	1.9	0.1	0.0	0.0
Employees	–	–	–	–	–	75

INOVIO PHARMACEUTICALS INC.
NMS: INO

660 W. Germantown Pike, Suite 110
Plymouth Meeting, PA 19462
Phone: 267 440-4200
Fax: –
Web: www.inovio.com

CEO: Joseph Kim
CFO: Peter Kies
HR: –
FYE: December 31
Type: Public

Inovio Pharmaceuticals is electrifying its vaccine delivery process. The firm's needle-free electroporation infusion therapy uses electrical pulses to open up cell membranes thus optimizing the delivery of its DNA vaccines that can protect from cancers as well as chronic infectious diseases including HIV and hepatitis C. Its SynCon process identifies shared characteristics among different strains of similar viruses to help develop a universal flu vaccine that will be effective on most influenza strains unlike traditional flu vaccines that are strain-specific. It also has a couple of anti-inflammatory drugs in its pipeline and some DNA-based animal growth hormones for livestock. Inovio was incorporated in Delaware in 2001.

	Annual Growth	12/16	12/17	12/18	12/19	12/20
Sales ($ mil.)	(32.3%)	35.4	42.2	30.5	4.1	7.4
Net income ($ mil.)	–	(73.7)	(88.2)	(97.0)	(119.4)	(166.4)
Market value ($ mil.)	6.3%	1,296.7	771.7	747.4	616.6	1,653.6
Employees	0.9%	253	280	288	194	262

INRAD OPTICS INC
NBB: INRD

181 Legrand Avenue
Northvale, NJ 07647
Phone: 201 767-1910
Fax: –
Web: www.inradoptics.com

CEO: Amy Eskilson
CFO: Theresa Balog
HR: –
FYE: December 31
Type: Public

Inrad Optics (formerly Photonic Products Group) manufactures products for use in photonics including custom optics crystals and components and provides thin-film coating services on a contract basis. Its products find applications in laser systems military gear semiconductor production equipment and telecommunications networks. The company's INRAD unit grows and finishes crystals used in commercial laser systems. Its custom optics segment includes waveplates beam displacers rotators and phase-shift plates. Inrad Optics gets about 10% of its sales from overseas customers.

	Annual Growth	12/16	12/17	12/18	12/19	12/20
Sales ($ mil.)	(2.0%)	9.8	9.9	11.5	10.0	9.0
Net income ($ mil.)	–	(0.6)	(0.7)	0.7	(0.8)	(0.9)
Market value ($ mil.)	0.3%	7.5	17.8	12.9	17.4	7.6
Employees	(5.1%)	63	62	58	58	51

INSEEGO CORP
NMS: INSG

12600 Deerfield Parkway, Suite 100
Alpharetta, GA 30004
Phone: 858 812-3400
Fax: –
Web: www.inseego.com

CEO: Dan Mondor
CFO: Michael Newman
HR: –
FYE: December 31
Type: Public

Novatel Wireless proves you can take it with you. The company designs wireless modems that let users access the Internet from anywhere. Its MiFi brand of mobile hotspot devices provides wireless connectivity for up to five users at the same time. Novatel also offers a series of wireless PC card modems (Merlin) embedded wireless modules for OEMs (Expedite) and desktop wireless gateway consoles (Ovation). Its MobiLink software bundled with modems and embedded modules connects mobile devices with wireless LANs. Novatel also offers activation provisioning and integration services. The company gets most sales from North America.

	Annual Growth	12/16	12/17	12/18	12/19	12/20
Sales ($ mil.)	6.5%	243.6	219.3	202.5	219.5	313.8
Net income ($ mil.)	–	(60.6)	(45.7)	(8.1)	(40.1)	(111.2)
Market value ($ mil.)	58.7%	242.5	160.0	412.5	728.6	1,537.7
Employees	(3.6%)	1,173	927	819	938	1,015

INSIGHT ENTERPRISES INC.

NMS: NSIT

6820 South Harl Avenue
Tempe, AZ 85283
Phone: 480 333-3000
Fax: –
Web: www.insight.com

CEO: Joyce Mullen
CFO: Helen Johnson
HR: –
FYE: December 31
Type: Public

Insight Enterprises distributes computer hardware and software and provides IT services for public sectors schools and government agencies and departments. The company offers thousands of products from hundreds of manufacturers (including Microsoft HP Inc. IBM and Cisco) as well as cloud services. Geographically Insight gets about 75% of sales from customers in the US and in terms of customers its large business clients provide about 70% of sales. Insight began operations in Arizona in 1988 incorporated in Delaware in 1991 and completed its initial public offering in 1995.

	Annual Growth	12/17	12/18	12/19	12/20	12/21
Sales ($ mil.)	8.9%	6,703.6	7,080.1	7,731.2	8,340.6	9,436.1
Net income ($ mil.)	24.7%	90.7	163.7	159.4	172.6	219.3
Market value ($ mil.)	29.2%	1,336.2	1,422.1	2,452.9	2,655.3	3,720.0
Employees	14.8%	6,697	7,420	11,261	11,006	11,624

INSIGHT HEALTH SERVICES HOLDINGS CORP.

26250 Enterprise Ct. Ste. 100
Lake Forest CA 92630
Phone: 949-282-6000
Fax: 303-254-8343
Web: www.qualmark.com

CEO: Louis E Hallman III
CFO: Keith S Kelson
HR: –
FYE: June 30
Type: Private

InSight Health Services (dba Insight Imaging) knows what lies within the hearts brains and pancreases of men. The company offers diagnostic imaging services to wholesale and retail customers in some 30 states. It mainly provides MRI (magnetic resonance imaging) services but also offers CT (computed tomography) and PET (positron emission tomography) scanning as well as conventional X-ray mammogram and ultrasound services. Customers include hospitals and physicians as well as insurance payers and Medicare or Medicaid programs. InSight restructured and emerged from bankruptcy protection in 2011. It is controlled by investment firm Black Diamond Capital Management.

INSIGNIA SYSTEMS, INC.

NAS: ISIG

212 Third Ave N, Ste 356
Minneapolis, MN 55401
Phone: 763 392-6200
Fax: –
Web: www.insigniasystems.com

CEO: Kristine Glancy
CFO: –
HR: –
FYE: December 31
Type: Public

Insignia Systems believes all signs point to greater sales. The company's point of purchase (POP) software and services help retailers and consumer goods manufacturers create promotional signage and in-store advertising that's displayed close to products on store shelving. As part of its POPSign program Insignia Systems creates customized signs based on information from retailers and manufacturers; it generates the majority of its revenue from its POPSign program. Its Stylus software suite is used to create signs labels and posters. Insignia Systems also sells specialized cardstock and other printing supplies for its systems. The company was founded in 1990.

	Annual Growth	12/16	12/17	12/18	12/19	12/20
Sales ($ mil.)	(8.2%)	24.9	26.4	33.2	22.0	17.7
Net income ($ mil.)	–	(1.3)	(0.6)	1.4	(5.0)	(4.3)
Market value ($ mil.)	(23.1%)	4.3	2.1	2.6	1.3	1.5
Employees	(10.0%)	61	62	57	54	40

INSITE VISION INC.

NBB: INSV

965 Atlantic Avenue
Alameda, CA 94501
Phone: 510 865-8800
Fax: 510 865-5700
Web: www.insitevision.com

CEO: Timothy Ruane
CFO: Louis Drapeau
HR: –
FYE: December 31
Type: Public

InSite Vision provides insight into the murky realm of eye disease. The company develops ophthalmic products using its DuraSite eyedrop-based drug delivery system. Its topical anti-infective product AzaSite is marketed in the US by licensing partner Inspire Pharmaceuticals as a treatment for conjunctivitis (pink eye). Various other AzaSite products are in development to treat eyelid inflammation and other infections. InSite Vision has licensed rights to use azithromycin (the active ingredient in AzaSite) from Pfizer. Inspire markets AzaSite in the US and Canada while international units are supplied by Catalent Pharma Solutions.

	Annual Growth	12/09	12/10	12/11	12/12	12/13
Sales ($ mil.)	33.2%	9.8	11.9	15.9	21.6	30.8
Net income ($ mil.)	–	(14.2)	(9.6)	(6.9)	(8.3)	5.8
Market value ($ mil.)	(6.0%)	50.7	44.2	58.2	40.5	39.6
Employees	34.8%	10	12	25	30	33

INSITUFORM TECHNOLOGIES INC.

17988 Edison Ave.
Chesterfield MO 63005
Phone: 636-530-8000
Fax: 636-519-8010
Web: www.insituform.com

CEO: Charles R Gordon
CFO: David A Martin
HR: Laura Villa
FYE: December 31
Type: Subsidiary

Under many a city lurks a decaying infrastructure and that's what Insituform Technologies takes care of "in situ". Serving industrial and municipal clients the company and its subsidiaries manufacture and install products for rehabilitating and protecting sewers water lines oil pipelines mining pipelines and other types of pipe systems. The heart of its business is its cured-in-place pipe process which allows for pipe rehabilitation without digging or disruption. Insituform which has operations in North America as well as in Asia Europe Australia the Middle East and South America has been expanding both geographically and by product offering. The company is part of infrastructure firm Aegion.

INSMED INC

NMS: INSM

700 US Highway 202/206
Bridgewater, NJ 08807
Phone: 908 977-9900
Fax: –
Web: www.insmed.com

CEO: William Lewis
CFO: Sara Bonstein
HR: –
FYE: December 31
Type: Public

Insmed Incorporated is a global biopharmaceutical company on a mission to transform the lives of patients with serious and rare diseases. Its first commercial products inhaled Arikayce is for the treatment of lung disease in patients who haven't responded to conventional treatment. Insmed clinical-stage pipeline includes brensocatib and TPIP. Brensocatib is a small molecule oral reversible inhibitor of dipeptidyl peptidase 1 (DPP1) which the company is developing for the treatment of patients with bronchiectasis and other neutrophil-mediated diseases. TPIP is an inhaled formulation of the treprostinil prodrug treprostinil palmitil which may offer a differentiated product profile for pulmonary arterial hypertension (PAH) and other rare pulmonary disorders.

	Annual Growth	12/17	12/18	12/19	12/20	12/21
Sales ($ mil.)	167.6%	–	9.8	136.5	164.4	188.5
Net income ($ mil.)	–	(192.6)	(324.3)	(254.3)	(294.1)	(434.7)
Market value ($ mil.)	(3.3%)	3,702.3	1,557.8	2,835.5	3,952.8	3,234.4
Employees	30.1%	214	373	435	521	613

INSPERITY INC
NYS: NSP

19001 Crescent Springs Drive
Kingwood, TX 77339
Phone: 281 358-8986
Fax: –
Web: www.insperity.com

CEO: Paul Sarvadi
CFO: Douglas Sharp
HR: –
FYE: December 31
Type: Public

Insperity handles the payroll so you don't have to. The company provides an array of human resources services to small and midsize companies in the US. As a professional employer organization (PEO) Insperity offers payroll and benefits administration workers' compensation programs and personnel records management through its flagship Workforce Optimization product. The firm also offers recruiting performance management and training and development services. Most of Insperity's clients come from industries such as information technology finance and insurance and consulting.

	Annual Growth	12/17	12/18	12/19	12/20	12/21
Sales ($ mil.)	10.8%	3,300.2	3,828.5	4,314.8	4,287.0	4,973.1
Net income ($ mil.)	10.1%	84.4	135.4	151.1	138.2	124.1
Market value ($ mil.)	19.8%	2,198.2	3,578.5	3,297.9	3,120.8	4,527.2
Employees	5.6%	2,900	3,200	3,500	3,600	3,600

INSPIRE PHARMACEUTICALS INC.

8081 Arco Corporate Dr. Ste. 400
Raleigh NC 27617
Phone: 919-941-9777
Fax: 919-941-9797
Web: www.inspirepharm.com

CEO: –
CFO: –
HR: –
FYE: December 31
Type: Subsidiary

Inspire Pharmaceuticals doesn't want to leave a dry eye in the house. The company targets treatments for various ocular diseases. Inspire Pharmaceuticals markets two North American eye products AzaSite (licensed from InSite Vision) which treats bacterial conjunctivitis (eye infections) and Elestat for allergic conjunctivitis (developed and marketed in collaboration with Allergan). The company is also working to find additional applications for AzaSite. The company also sells treatments for dry eye in Japan and the US through licensing agreements. Inspire Pharmaceuticals was acquired by Merck in 2011.

INSTALLED BUILDING PRODUCTS INC
NYS: IBP

495 South High Street, Suite 50
Columbus, OH 43215
Phone: 614 221-3399
Fax: –
Web: www.installedbuildingproducts.com

CEO: Jeffrey Edwards
CFO: Michael Miller
HR: –
FYE: December 31
Type: Public

Installed Building Products (IBP) is a leading new residential insulation installer with more than 190 branches in almost all 50 continental US states and the District of Columbia. IBP manages all aspects of the installation process for its customers including direct purchases of materials from national manufacturers delivery and installation. In addition to insulation IBP waterproofs and fireproofs homes and installs garage doors rain gutters shower doors shelving and mirrors. Founded in 1977 as Edwards Insulation.

	Annual Growth	12/16	12/17	12/18	12/19	12/20
Sales ($ mil.)	17.6%	863.0	1,132.9	1,336.4	1,511.6	1,653.2
Net income ($ mil.)	26.1%	38.4	41.1	54.7	68.2	97.2
Market value ($ mil.)	25.3%	1,223.4	2,249.9	998.0	2,040.2	3,019.5
Employees	14.0%	5,292	6,900	7,700	8,500	8,950

INSTANT WEB INC.

7951 Powers Blvd.
Chanhassen MN 55317-9502
Phone: 952-474-0961
Fax: 952-474-6467
Web: www.iwco.com

CEO: Jim Andersen
CFO: Jake Hertel
HR: Beverly Lohs
FYE: April 30
Type: Private

You might say this company gets promotional items directly into mailboxes everywhere. Doing business as IWCO Direct Instant Web provides a range of direct-mail marketing services including printing assembling and mailing. The company also makes promotional plastic and printed paper products phone cards and envelopes and it offers customized products with pull tabs peel-apart adhesive messages fragrance patches and photographic-quality images. Other services include database management automated sorting and mailing and bindery services. IWCO Direct was founded in 1969 as Instant Services Inc. Private equity firm Avista Capital Partners acquired the firm in 2007.

INSTEEL INDUSTRIES, INC.
NYS: IIIN

1373 Boggs Drive
Mount Airy, NC 27030
Phone: 336 786-2141
Fax: –
Web: www.insteel.com

CEO: H. Woltz
CFO: Mark Carano
HR: –
FYE: October 02
Type: Public

Insteel Industries manufactures steel welded wire reinforcement (WWR) which is used primarily in concrete construction materials; pre-stressed concrete strand (PC strand); engineered structural mesh (ESM); concrete pipe reinforcement (CPR); and standard welded wire reinforcement (SWWR). Its PC strand products are the spine for concrete structures from bridges to parking garages. Insteel's customers include manufacturers of concrete products distributors and rebar fabricators and contractors. A majority of its sales come from manufacturers of non-residential concrete construction products. The US is responsible for almost all of its total sales. The company was founded in 1953 by Howard O. Woltz Jr.

	Annual Growth	09/17	09/18	09/19*	10/20	10/21
Sales ($ mil.)	11.0%	388.9	453.2	455.7	472.6	590.6
Net income ($ mil.)	31.1%	22.5	36.3	5.6	19.0	66.6
Market value ($ mil.)	10.6%	506.7	696.4	401.9	367.8	756.9
Employees	3.3%	803	810	834	881	913

*Fiscal year change

INSTITUTE FOR DEFENSE ANALYSES INC

730 E GLEBE RD
ALEXANDRIA, VA 22305
Phone: 703-845-2000
Fax: –
Web: www.ida.org

CEO: Norton Schwartz
CFO: –
HR: –
FYE: September 25
Type: Private

The Institute for Defense Analyses provides technical analyses of weapons. The institute is a federally funded organization that works for the US government's defense agencies as well as for other government entities. The Institute for Defense Analyses' Science and Technology Policy Institute analyzes global science and tech trends to help the US government formula policy.

	Annual Growth	09/16	09/17	09/18	09/19	09/20
Sales ($ mil.)	1.8%	–	235.0	247.4	260.3	248.2
Net income ($ mil.)	(33.5%)	–	27.3	17.4	6.1	8.0
Market value ($ mil.)	–	–	–	–	–	–
Employees	–	–	–	–	–	1,500

INSTITUTE OF GAS TECHNOLOGY

1700 S MOUNT PROSPECT RD
DES PLAINES, IL 600181800
Phone: 847-768-0500
Fax: –
Web: www.gastechnology.org

CEO: David C Carroll
CFO: James Ingold
HR: –
FYE: December 31
Type: Private

Natural gas burns more cleanly and efficiently thanks to the Institute of Gas Technology (dba Gas Technology Institute or GTI) which provides engineering research development and training services for energy and environmental companies consumers and government clients. GTI's research focuses on expanded energy supply reduced energy delivery costs efficient energy use and clean energy systems primarily in the natural gas sector. Natural gas companies as well as large energy consumers and private industry firms comprise the majority of GTI's client base. The not-for-profit company's contract services range from market and technology analysis to product development testing and commercialization.

	Annual Growth	12/07	12/08	12/13	12/14	12/15
Sales ($ mil.)	2.0%	–	62.6	68.9	56.8	71.8
Net income ($ mil.)	–	–	(32.3)	7.4	(1.4)	8.2
Market value ($ mil.)	–	–	–	–	–	–
Employees	–	–	–	–	–	281

INSULET CORP
NMS: PODD

100 Nagog Park
Acton, MA 01720
Phone: 978 600-7000
Fax: –
Web: www.insulet.com

CEO: Shacey Petrovic
CFO: Wayde McMillan
HR: –
FYE: December 31
Type: Public

Insulet wants to isolate an insolent disease. The medical device company manufactures an insulin pump for people with insulin-dependent diabetes. Its disposable waterproof product called the OmniPod Insulin Management System a small lightweight and adheres directly to the patient's skin making it more discrete than most insulin infusion systems that typically clip to a belt or fit in a pocket. It also includes a handheld device to wirelessly program the OmniPod with insulin delivery instructions. The company have partnered with pharmaceutical and biotechnology companies to tailor the Omnipod System technology platform and sells it to customers both directly and through its distribution partners. The US is the company's largest market which accounts for about 65% of total revenue.

	Annual Growth	12/16	12/17	12/18	12/19	12/20
Sales ($ mil.)	25.3%	367.0	463.8	563.8	738.2	904.4
Net income ($ mil.)	–	(28.9)	(26.8)	3.3	11.6	6.8
Market value ($ mil.)	61.4%	2,487.5	4,555.2	5,236.5	11,302.1	16,875.9
Employees	31.3%	640	857	1,169	1,350	1,900

INSYS THERAPEUTICS INC
NBB: INSY Q

1333 S. Spectrum Blvd., Suite 100
Chandler, AZ 85286
Phone: 480 500-3127
Fax: –
Web: www.insysrx.com

CEO: –
CFO: –
HR: –
FYE: December 31
Type: Public

Insys Therapeutics a developer of pain management and nausea medicines is operating under bankruptcy protection and plans to sell substantially all of its assets. Main product Subsys which brings in virtually all of its revenue is a fast-acting oral spray version of cancer pain drug Fentanyl. Newer drug Syndros (dronabinol) is a generic liquid formulation of Marinol (a synthetic version of the active chemical in marijuana) for treatment of chemotherapy-induced nausea and vomiting. Facing scrutiny over its opioid drug marketing practices Insys filed for Chapter 11 bankruptcy protection in 2019.

	Annual Growth	12/14	12/15	12/16	12/17	12/18
Sales ($ mil.)	(22.0%)	222.1	330.8	242.3	140.7	82.1
Net income ($ mil.)	–	38.0	58.5	7.6	(228.0)	(124.5)
Market value ($ mil.)	(46.3%)	3,135.9	2,129.5	684.3	715.5	260.3
Employees	(12.3%)	382	510	423	343	226

INSYS THERAPEUTICS INC.

10220 S. 51st St. Ste. 2
Phoenix AZ 85044-5231
Phone: 602-910-2617
Fax: 602-910-2627
Web: www.insysrx.com

CEO: –
CFO: –
HR: –
FYE: December 31
Type: Private

Insys Therapeutics aims to take the rough edges off of chemo and cancer pain. The drug development company is focused on treating side effects of chemotherapy as well as therapies for pain management. Its lead candidate is a fast-acting oral spray version of cancer pain drug Fentanyl. Its Dronabinol candidate is a generic capsule form of Marinol (a synthetic version of the active chemical in marijuana) for treatment of chemotherapy-induced nausea and vomiting. Both drugs are in late stage development awaiting FDA approval. All of the company's drug candidates are reformulations of already-approved therapeutic ingredients. Insys filed to go public in 2011.

INTCOMEX INC.

3505 NW 107th Ave. Ste. A
Miami FL 33178
Phone: 305-477-6230
Fax: 305-477-5694
Web: www.intcomex.com

CEO: Michael Shalom
CFO: Humberto Lopez
HR: –
FYE: December 31
Type: Private

Intcomex is IT in Latin America and the Caribbean. The wholesaler distributes computer systems and components peripherals software accessories networking products mobile devices and digital consumer electronics to more than 42000 customers in 40 countries. Clients are primarily third-party IT distributors resellers and retailers. Intcomex offers more than 13000 products from more than 140 manufacturers including Apple Dell HP Intel Microsoft and Western Digital. Founded in 1988 the company began as a small retail store that sold computer software in South Florida. Today Intcomex operates sales offices in about a dozen countries. The company filed to go public in 2007 but has yet to do so.

INTEGER HOLDINGS CORP
NYS: ITGR

5830 Granite Parkway, Suite 1150
Plano, TX 75024
Phone: 214 618-5243
Fax: –
Web: www.integer.net

CEO: Joseph Dziedzic
CFO: Jason Garland
HR: –
FYE: December 31
Type: Public

Integer Holdings is one of the world's largest medical device outsource (MDO) manufacturing companies and serves the cardiac neuromodulation orthopedics vascular and advanced surgical and portable medical markets. The company provides innovative high quality medical technologies that enhance the lives of patients worldwide and develop batteries for high-end niche applications in energy military and environmental markets. Integer brands include Greatbatch Medical Lake Region Medical and Electrochem. The company's primary customers include large multinational original equipment manufacturers ("OEMs") and their affiliated subsidiaries. About 60% of company products are sold in the US. Its medical customers include large multi-national medical device OEMs such as Abbott Laboratories Biotronik Boehringer Ingelheim and Boston Scientific.

	Annual Growth	12/17	12/18	12/19	12/20	12/21
Sales ($ mil.)	(4.4%)	1,461.9	1,215.0	1,258.1	1,073.4	1,221.1
Net income ($ mil.)	9.8%	66.7	168.0	96.3	77.3	96.8
Market value ($ mil.)	17.2%	1,497.8	2,513.8	2,659.3	2,684.4	2,829.9
Employees	(1.9%)	9,700	8,250	8,250	7,500	9,000

INTEGRA LIFESCIENCES HOLDINGS CORP   NMS: IART

1100 Campus Road
Princeton, NJ 08540
Phone: 609 275-0500
Fax: –
Web: www.integralife.com

CEO: Jan De Witte
CFO: Carrie Anderson
HR: Lisa Evoli
FYE: December 31
Type: Public

Integra LifeSciences makes surgical equipment and instruments for neurological orthopedic and other medical procedures. The company develops medical equipment used in cranial procedures small bone and joint reconstruction and the repair and reconstruction of soft tissue nerves and tendons. Integra's products include tissue ablation equipment drainage catheters bone fixation devices regenerative technologies and basic surgical instruments. Its offerings are marketed worldwide through direct sales and distributors. The US market accounts for a majority of sales. Integra was founded in 1989 by Richard Caruso and the company acquired collagen technology.

	Annual Growth	12/16	12/17	12/18	12/19	12/20
Sales ($ mil.)	8.4%	992.1	1,188.2	1,472.4	1,517.6	1,371.9
Net income ($ mil.)	15.8%	74.6	64.7	60.8	50.2	133.9
Market value ($ mil.)	(6.7%)	7,235.3	4,036.4	3,803.6	4,915.2	5,475.2
Employees	0.0%	3,700	4,400	4,500	4,000	3,700

INTEGRA TELECOM INC.

1201 NE Lloyd Blvd. Ste. 500
Portland OR 97232
Phone: 503-453-8000
Fax: 503-453-8221
Web: www.integratelecom.com

CEO: –
CFO: –
HR: –
FYE: December 31
Type: Private

Integra Telecom wants to be a key component of the US communications network. The facilities-based telecommunications carrier provides local and long-distance telephony and broadband Internet largely to small to midsized businesses as well as some residential customers in 35 metropolitan areas in 11 mostly western states. Its enterprise data services include managed network services data and server colocation and hosted cloud computing services. Integra also sells its products to other carriers on a wholesale basis through its Electric Lightwave division. The company serves the energy food broadcasting and real estate industries among others. Clients have included SolarWorld and the Red Cross.

INTEGRAL SYSTEMS INC.

6721 Columbia Gateway Dr.
Columbia MD 21046
Phone: 443-539-5008
Fax: 410-312-2705
Web: www.integ.com

CEO: Paul G Casner Jr
CFO: Christopher Roberts
HR: –
FYE: September 30
Type: Subsidiary

Integral Systems provides high-flying customers with a sense of control. The company designs satellite command and control data processing flight simulation integration and test and signals analysis systems. Military agencies communication service providers and scientific researchers use the company's EPOCH Integrated Product Suite (IPS) to monitor and control their ground systems and satellites and to analyze the data that they gather. Integral Systems counts the US Air Force the US Navy the US NOAA and China's National Space Program Office among its largely US-based customer roster. The company was acquired in 2011 by Kratos Defense & Security in a stock swap transaction.

INTEGRAL TECHNOLOGIES INC.   NBB: ITKG

412 Mulberry
Marietta, OH 45750
Phone: 812 550-1770
Fax: –
Web: www.itkg.net

CEO: Doug Bathauer
CFO: Eli Dusenbury
HR: –
FYE: June 30
Type: Public

Integral Technologies hopes to discover that technology truly is integral to everyday life. The company has developed what it calls its "ElectriPlast" product an electrically conductive resin-based polymer that can be molded into any shape. The company's "PlasTenna" technology uses ElectriPlast for antenna design and other manufacturing processes. It can become part of the cell phone casing itself. Integral Technologies outsources its manufacturing and is marketing its products to cell phone and other wireless device manufacturers. The development stage company has yet to recognize any appreciable revenues from its products.

	Annual Growth	06/13	06/14	06/15	06/16	06/17
Sales ($ mil.)	–	0.0	0.0	0.2	0.1	0.1
Net income ($ mil.)	–	(3.7)	(4.5)	(4.4)	(4.6)	(5.7)
Market value ($ mil.)	(51.1%)	113.4	60.7	128.4	32.4	6.5
Employees	–	–	–	–	–	–

INTEGRAL VISION INC.   OTC: INVI

49113 Wixom Tech Dr.
Wixom MI 48393
Phone: 248-668-9230
Fax: 248-668-9384
Web: www.iv-usa.com

CEO: –
CFO: –
HR: –
FYE: December 31
Type: Public

Integral Vision wants manufacturers to take a closer look. The company makes machine vision systems that monitor and control manufacturing processes in the small flat-panel display industry. Its systems inspect for both cosmetic and functional defects in display components used in camcorders cell phones digital still cameras computer monitors and handheld video games. Integral Vision also offers software for developing machine vision inspection applications. Customers have included Liquavista QUALCOMM Samsung Electronics and Texas Instruments.

INTEGRAMED AMERICA INC.   NASDAQ: INMD

2 Manhattanville Rd.
Purchase NY 10577-2113
Phone: 914-253-8000
Fax: 914-253-8008
Web: www.integramed.com

CEO: Chris Throckmorton
CFO: John W Hlywak
HR: –
FYE: December 31
Type: Public

IntegraMed America's specialty is identifying and entering niche medical markets throughout the US. The company operates through two segments: its Attain Fertility Clinics and Vein Clinics. The company's fertility services include in vitro fertilization (IVF) artificial insemination and other reproductive assistance through more than 130 clinics in metropolitan markets. Its Fertility Services division supplies administrative and management support to its clinics and helps guide potential parents through the IVF process. The second division Vein Clinics operates 45 vein treatment centers throughout the US. IntegraMed America was acquired by investment firm Sagard Capital Partners in 2012.

INTEGRATED BIOPHARMA INC   NBB: INBP

225 Long Ave.   CEO: Riva Sheppard
Hillside, NJ 07205   CFO: Dina Masi
Phone: 888 319-6962   HR: –
Fax: –   FYE: June 30
Web: www.integratedbiopharma.com   Type: Public

Integrated BioPharma has taken a bounty of businesses and coalesced them into the cohesive nutraceuticals manufacturer it is today. Through numerous subsidiaries Integrated BioPharma manufactures and distributes vitamins nutritional supplements herbal products and natural chemicals. Subsidiaries include AgroLabs (nutritional drinks vitamins supplements) Chem International (vitamins) IHT Health Products (natural chemicals) Manhattan Drug Company (vitamins and nutritional supplements sold to distributors multi-level marketers and specialized health care providers) and Vitamin Factory (sells private-label Manhattan Drug products online and via mail order catalogue).

	Annual Growth	06/17	06/18	06/19	06/20	06/21
Sales ($ mil.)	7.9%	47.0	43.7	50.0	52.8	63.6
Net income ($ mil.)	35.9%	2.3	0.7	1.7	4.1	8.0
Market value ($ mil.)	54.9%	5.7	4.6	6.9	13.4	32.8
Employees	6.3%	115	128	137	143	147

INTEGRATED DEVICE TECHNOLOGY INC   NMS: IDTI

6024 Silver Creek Valley Road   CEO: Sailesh Chittipeddi
San Jose, CA 95138   CFO: Aris Bolisay
Phone: 408 284-8200   HR: Elisabeth Dumont
Fax: –   FYE: April 01
Web: www.idt.com   Type: Public

Integrated Device Technology (IDT) knows not only about integrating devices but about connecting and charging them. The company offers hundreds of high-performance semiconductors and modules available in thousands of configurations primarily for computers computer peripherals and consumer electronics as well as for the networking and communications markets. Much of IDT's sales come from its communications and high-performance logic products which include processors specialized memories logic and clock management products and chipsets and controllers for networking gear. Wireless charging products are a growing business for the company. About 75% of its sales are from the Asia/Pacific region. IDT agreed to a $6.7 billion acquisition offer from Renesas in 2018.

	Annual Growth	03/14	03/15*	04/16	04/17	04/18
Sales ($ mil.)	14.8%	484.8	572.9	697.4	728.2	842.8
Net income ($ mil.)	–	88.4	93.9	194.7	110.5	(12.1)
Market value ($ mil.)	26.5%	1,546.6	2,562.8	2,687.8	3,066.0	3,958.5
Employees	5.2%	1,484	1,447	1,767	1,623	1,821

*Fiscal year change

INTEGRATED SILICON SOLUTION, INC.   NMS: ISSI

1623 Buckeye Drive   CEO: Jimmy Lee
Milpitas, CA 95035   CFO: –
Phone: 408 969-6600   HR: Amy Guiriba
Fax: –   FYE: September 30
Web: www.issi.com   Type: Public

Fabless semiconductor company Integrated Silicon Solution Inc. (ISSI) has the right acronyms for the manufacturing process. ISSI primarily makes SRAMs (static random-access memory) chips and DRAMs (dynamic RAM) chips that are used in cars computers consumer electronics cell phones and networking devices. ISSI sells its chips to dozens of electronics manufacturers from the automotive communications consumer industrial medical and military markets either directly or through distributors and contract manufacturers. Customers include Bosch Cisco GE and Samsung. Most of its sales come from Asia.

	Annual Growth	09/10	09/11	09/12	09/13	09/14
Sales ($ mil.)	6.8%	252.5	270.5	266.0	307.6	329.0
Net income ($ mil.)	(13.8%)	42.2	56.0	(2.7)	17.5	23.3
Market value ($ mil.)	12.4%	265.5	240.8	285.5	335.8	423.6
Employees	6.9%	452	469	552	590	590

INTEGRIS BAPTIST MEDICAL CENTER, INC.

3300 NW EXPRESSWAY   CEO: –
OKLAHOMA CITY, OK 731124418   CFO: Wentz J Miller
Phone: 405-949-3011   HR: –
Fax: –   FYE: June 30
Web: www.integrisok.com   Type: Private

INTEGRIS Baptist Medical Center seeks integrity by caring for citizens from across the state of Oklahoma. The Oklahoma City-based medical center is the flagship hospital of the not-for-profit INTEGRIS Health system. With about 510 beds INTEGRIS Baptist is home to specialty care facilities for burns women's and children's health infertility stroke treatment cardiac care organ transplantation cancer treatment and more. The company also has centers for wellness hearing sleep disorders senior health and weight loss and it provides medical training and residency programs. INTEGRIS Baptist Medical Center opened its doors in 1959 with 200 beds.

	Annual Growth	06/15	06/16	06/18	06/20	06/21
Sales ($ mil.)	8.4%	–	701.4	814.1	950.5	1,051.5
Net income ($ mil.)	94.6%	–	6.9	67.7	(14.4)	192.0
Market value ($ mil.)	–	–	–	–	–	–
Employees	–	–	–	–	–	2,700

INTEGRIS HEALTH, INC.

3300 NW EXPWY   CEO: Bruce Lawrence
OKLAHOMA CITY, OK 731124418   CFO: David Hadley
Phone: 405-949-6066   HR: –
Fax: –   FYE: June 30
Web: www.integrisok.com   Type: Private

INTEGRIS Health is the state's largest Oklahoma-owned health system and one of the largest private employees and with hospitals rehabilitation centers physician clinics mental health facilities fitness centers and more. The company one of Oklahoma's largest not-for-profit health care organization operates around 15 hospitals in Oklahoma City. The hospitals provide services including primary care breast health cancer care gynecology surgery lung care transplant and rehabilitation & physical care and more. INTEGRIS also operates specialty facilities for the treatment of pain management rheumatology and neurology and for rehabilitation & physical therapy. The company operates with more than 100 primary care and specialty clinics statewide and provide medical care for all ages with high-qualified physicians.

	Annual Growth	06/17	06/18	06/19	06/20	06/21
Sales ($ mil.)	10.4%	–	1,673.5	1,950.1	2,078.0	2,250.5
Net income ($ mil.)	77.6%	–	53.6	11.6	(172.0)	300.2
Market value ($ mil.)	–	–	–	–	–	–
Employees	–	–	–	–	–	9,500

INTEGRYS ENERGY GROUP INC   NYS: TEG

200 East Randolph Street   CEO: –
Chicago, IL 60601-6207   CFO: –
Phone: 312 228-5400   HR: –
Fax: –   FYE: December 31
Web: www.integrysgroup.com   Type: Public

Integrys Energy integrates energy activities in the Windy City and surrounding areas. The energy holding company owns six regulated utilities: Michigan Gas Utilities Corp. (169000 gas customers) Minnesota Energy Resources Corp. (216000 gas customers) North Shore Gas Company (159000 customers in northern Chicago) Peoples Gas Light and Coke Company (831000 natural gas customers in Chicago) Wisconsin Public Service (445000 electric customers and 323000 natural gas customers in Wisconsin and Michigan) and Upper Peninsula Power (52000 electricity customers). The company's nonregulated subsidiary Integrys Energy Services (sold to Constellation in 2014) provided retail energy supply and services.

	Annual Growth	12/09	12/10	12/11	12/12	12/13
Sales ($ mil.)	(6.9%)	7,499.8	5,203.2	4,708.7	4,212.4	5,634.6
Net income ($ mil.)	–	(68.8)	223.7	230.5	284.3	354.8
Market value ($ mil.)	6.7%	3,335.9	3,853.9	4,304.4	4,148.6	4,322.6
Employees	(0.7%)	5,025	4,612	4,619	4,717	4,888

INTEL CORP
NMS: INTC

2200 Mission College Boulevard
Santa Clara, CA 95054-1549
Phone: 408 765-8080
Fax: 408 765-2633
Web: www.intc.com

CEO: Patrick P Gelsinger
CFO: David Zinsner
HR: –
FYE: December 25
Type: Public

Intel offers platform products that incorporate various components and technologies including a microprocessor and chipset a stand-alone SoC or a multichip package. The company makes use of technology such as Artificial Intelligence pervasive connectivity cloud to edge and ubiquitous computing to its operations and interact with its products. The company's latest data center solutions target a wide range of use cases within cloud computing network infrastructure and intelligent edge applications and support high-growth workloads including AI and 5G. More than 80% of its revenue comes from international customers. Intel was founded in 1968.

	Annual Growth	12/17	12/18	12/19	12/20	12/21
Sales ($ mil.)	5.9%	62,761.0	70,848.0	71,965.0	77,867.0	79,024.0
Net income ($ mil.)	19.9%	9,601.0	21,053.0	21,048.0	20,899.0	19,868.0
Market value ($ mil.)	–	0.0	0.0	0.0	0.0	0.0
Employees	4.2%	102,700	107,400	110,800	110,600	121,100

INTELIQUENT INC
NMS: IQNT

550 West Adams Street, Suite 900
Chicago, IL 60661
Phone: 312 384-8000
Fax: –
Web: www.inteliquent.com

CEO: Ed O'Hara
CFO: Michael Donahue
HR: –
FYE: December 31
Type: Public

Inteliquent tries to keep customers in step with smart networking choices. The company provides wholesale interconnectivity services for voice IP transit Ethernet and cloud computing via its multiprotocol label switching (MPLS)/IP network. That network exclusively uses Sonus Networks equipment and has more than 120 points of presence across North America Europe and Asia. Inteliquent's customers are competitive local exchange carriers ISPs large businesses and other telecom content and service providers. Its services are used in more than 80 countries.

	Annual Growth	12/10	12/11	12/12	12/13	12/14
Sales ($ mil.)	2.5%	199.8	268.3	275.5	211.7	220.5
Net income ($ mil.)	4.3%	32.6	27.1	(78.1)	55.7	38.5
Market value ($ mil.)	8.0%	483.1	357.7	86.0	381.8	656.8
Employees	(11.9%)	265	291	290	143	160

INTELLABRIDGE TECHNOLOGY CORP
NBB: KASH F

2060 Broadway Suite B1
Boulder, CO 80302
Phone: 303 578-3578
Fax: 604 682-4768
Web: www.intellabridge.com

CEO: John Eagleton
CFO: Maria Eagleton
HR: –
FYE: December 31
Type: Public

Afrasia Mineral Fields doesn't have mining operations in Africa or Asia but it does do business in Canada. The company is looking to acquire or partner with other mineral exploration businesses in its sector. It found something it liked in 2010 when it agreed to buy a copper project in Arizona for about $12.5 million. Afrasia Mineral Fields is managed and administered by venture capital firm Varshney Capital. Praveen Varshney CEO of Afrasia Mineral Fields also heads up Varshney Capital.

	Annual Growth	05/17*	12/17	12/18	12/19	12/20
Sales ($ mil.)	(72.6%)	–	–	1.1	0.6	0.1
Net income ($ mil.)	–	–	(0.2)	(7.0)	(0.7)	(0.4)
Market value ($ mil.)	143.2%	–	–	1.2	0.5	7.1
Employees	–	–	–	–	–	18

*Fiscal year change

INTELLICHECK INC
NMS: IDN

200 Broadhollow Road, Suite 207
Melville, NY 11747
Phone: 516 992-1900
Fax: –
Web: www.icmobil.com

CEO: Bryan Lewis
CFO: Bill White
HR: –
FYE: December 31
Type: Public

IntelliCheck Mobilisa will need to see some ID. The company provides handheld electronic card readers and related software for the commercial government and military markets. Used to secure military and federal government locations its Defense ID System can read barcodes magnetic stripes optical character recognition (OCR) and radio frequency identification (RFID) codes. Its ID-Check systems are designed to verify the age and identity of customers who swipe a driver's license military ID or other magnetically encoded ID card. The company has installed systems in airports bars casinos convenience stores hotels and stadiums.

	Annual Growth	12/16	12/17	12/18	12/19	12/20
Sales ($ mil.)	29.3%	3.8	3.6	4.4	7.7	10.7
Net income ($ mil.)	–	(5.7)	(6.0)	(4.0)	(2.5)	0.6
Market value ($ mil.)	42.7%	50.6	47.1	39.4	137.9	210.0
Employees	11.4%	24	29	34	34	37

INTELLICORP INC.

2900 Lakeside Dr. Ste. 221
Santa Clara CA 95054
Phone: 408-454-3500
Fax: 408-454-3529
Web: www.intellicorp.com

CEO: –
CFO: –
HR: –
FYE: June 30
Type: Private

IntelliCorp isn't a sap when it comes to good software. The company provides software and services that enable businesses to integrate enterprise customer relationship management (CRM) software made by SAP with back-office functions such as logistics accounting and order processing. Its products include applications for business process management (LivdModel) efficiency monitoring (LiveCompare) and data management (DataWorks). Intellicorp also offers consulting related to software integration and legacy CRM systems migration. Intellicorp has offices in the US and the UK. It sells directly and through systems integrators and other distributors. Customers have included Boeing and General Motors.

INTELLIDYNE L.L.C.

5203 LEESBURG PIKE # 400
FALLS CHURCH, VA 22041-3401
Phone: 703-575-9715
Fax: –
Web: www.intellidynellc.com

CEO: Robert Grey
CFO: Joseph W Kuhn
HR: –
FYE: December 31
Type: Private

IntelliDyne likes to think it takes a smarter approach to solving IT problems. The company consults with US government and commercial customers to help them plan design install lease and manage information technology systems and services. Its areas of expertise include network security cloud computing custom software development business process management and data center consolidation. IntelliDyne primarily serves defense homeland security law enforcement and civilian agencies. The US Department of Defense its largest client uses its services primarily to support medical centers and hospitals. The company was established in 1999 by president Robert Grey.

	Annual Growth	12/01	12/02	12/04	12/05	12/10
Sales ($ mil.)	18.0%	–	14.1	18.7	26.3	53.0
Net income ($ mil.)	17.1%	–	1.4	6.0	1.2	4.9
Market value ($ mil.)	–	–	–	–	–	–
Employees	–	–	–	–	–	275

INTELLIGENT SOFTWARE SOLUTIONS INC.

5450 TECH CENTER DR # 400   CEO: Pete Cannito
COLORADO SPRINGS, CO 809192339   CFO: Scott Crane
Phone: 719-452-7000   HR: –
Fax: –   FYE: December 31
Web: www.issinc.com   Type: Private

Intelligent Software Solutions is no dummy when it comes to software development and IT systems analysis. The privately-held company develops and integrates custom software used for such applications as data visualization and analysis pattern detection and mission planning for the aerospace defense and maritime industries. It also provides on-site product and development support and training. As a government contractor it serves a range of public sector agencies within the US Department of Defense US Department of Homeland Security and US Air Force. Intelligent Software Solutions corporate clients have included Lockheed Martin Northrop Grumman and Leidos.

	Annual Growth	12/07	12/08	12/09	12/10	12/11
Sales ($ mil.)	39.1%	–	–	86.5	121.3	167.3
Net income ($ mil.)	30647.7%	–	–	0.0	7.5	12.6
Market value ($ mil.)	–	–	–	–	–	–
Employees	–	–	–	–	–	650

INTER PARFUMS, INC.   NMS: IPAR

551 Fifth Avenue   CEO: Jean Madar
New York, NY 10176   CFO: Russell Greenberg
Phone: 212 983-2640   HR: –
Fax: 212 983-4197   FYE: December 31
Web: www.interparfumsinc.com   Type: Public

Inter Parfums manufactures markets and distributes a wide array of prestige fragrance and fragrance related products. Most of the fragrance developer and manufacturer's revenue is generated by sales of its prestige fragrance brands including Karl Lagerfeld Jimmy Choo Lanvin Montblanc Repetto S.T. Dupont and Van Cleef & Arpels among others. (The company owns the Lanvin and Jean Philippe brand names.) Customers include specialty shops and department stores mass merchandisers and perfumeries. Its fragrances are sold in more than 120 countries. Europe generates nearly 80% of Inter Parfums net sales. Inter Parfums was founded in 1982.

	Annual Growth	12/16	12/17	12/18	12/19	12/20
Sales ($ mil.)	0.8%	521.1	591.3	675.6	713.5	539.0
Net income ($ mil.)	3.5%	33.3	41.6	53.8	60.2	38.2
Market value ($ mil.)	16.6%	1,035.2	1,373.4	2,072.6	2,298.3	1,912.0
Employees	3.4%	347	355	313	402	396

INTER-AMERICAN DEVELOPMENT BANK

1300 New York Ave. NW   CEO: –
Washington DC 20577   CFO: Gustavo De Rosa
Phone: 202-623-1000   HR: –
Fax: 202-623-3096   FYE: December 31
Web: www.iadb.org   Type: Private - Member-Own

Inter-American Development Bank is like a mutual aid society that packs an economic punch. The institution was founded in 1959 to aid in the social and economic development of Latin America and the Caribbean. It provides grants and loans to help fund public and private projects promote sustainable growth modernize public institutions foster free trade and fight poverty and injustice. The bank is also involved in cross-border issues such as infrastructure and energy. Governments government organizations (such as state banks and universities) civil societies and private-sector companies are all eligible to receive Inter-American Development Bank loans.

INTERACTIVE BROKERS GROUP INC   NMS: IBKR

One Pickwick Plaza   CEO: Milan Galik
Greenwich, CT 06830   CFO: Paul Brody
Phone: 203 618-5800   HR: –
Fax: –   FYE: December 31
Web: www.interactivebrokers.com   Type: Public

Global electronic broker Interactive Brokers Group performs low-cost trade order management execution and portfolio management services through its Interactive Brokers subsidiaries. Catering to institutional and experienced individual investors the company offers access to more than 135 electronic exchanges and trading centers worldwide processing trades in stocks options futures foreign exchange instruments bonds and mutual funds. The company also licenses its trading interface to large banks and brokerages through white branding agreements. Interactive Brokers operates worldwide but generates about 70% of its revenue in the US.

	Annual Growth	12/16	12/17	12/18	12/19	12/20
Sales ($ mil.)	12.3%	1,396.0	1,702.0	1,903.0	1,937.0	2,218.0
Net income ($ mil.)	23.4%	84.0	76.0	169.0	161.0	195.0
Market value ($ mil.)	13.7%	3,314.1	5,374.7	5,063.3	4,231.8	5,529.9
Employees	14.0%	1,204	1,228	1,413	1,643	2,033

INTERACTIVE INTELLIGENCE GROUP INC.   NMS: ININ

7601 Interactive Way   CEO: –
Indianapolis, IN 46278   CFO: –
Phone: 317 872-3000   HR: –
Fax: –   FYE: December 31
Web: www.inin.com   Type: Public

Interactive Intelligence knows legacy PBX telephone systems are going the way of the telegraph. The company's software manages call center operations for both inbound and outbound applications. Its Customer Interaction Center software can process thousands of interactions per hour across various media channels: telephone calls emails faxes voice mail Internet chat sessions IP telephony calls text messages and social media. Products are available in two dozen languages and have been installed in more than 100 different countries. The company's technology handles the automated call center operations for more than 6000 customers including CarMax IKEA and Walgreens.

	Annual Growth	12/10	12/11	12/12	12/13	12/14
Sales ($ mil.)	19.7%	166.3	209.5	237.4	318.2	341.3
Net income ($ mil.)	–	14.9	14.8	0.9	9.5	(41.4)
Market value ($ mil.)	16.3%	556.7	487.7	713.7	1,433.3	1,019.3
Employees	25.7%	849	1,106	1,437	1,848	2,122

INTERACTIVE INTELLIGENCE INC.   NASDAQ: ININ

7601 Interactive Way   CEO: –
Indianapolis IN 46278   CFO: –
Phone: 317-872-3000   HR: –
Fax: +972-3-976-4040   FYE: December 31
Web: www.audiocodes.com   Type: Public

Interactive Intelligence is hoping legacy PBX telephone systems go the way of the telegraph. The company's software helps integrate a wide array of communication systems via VoIP technology from phone calls voice mail and e-mail to faxes and Web-based communications. Its applications integrate with enterprise messaging platforms such as Microsoft Exchange and Lotus Notes and provide tools for connecting mobile and home-based workers to enterprise information systems. The company's technology handles the call center operations for more than 3500 customers including Ceridian InfoCision Vizio and Walgreens. Chairman and CEO Donald Brown founded Interactive Intelligence in 1994; he owns 26% of its stock.

INTERBOND CORPORATION OF AMERICA

3200 SW 42ND ST
HOLLYWOOD, FL 33020
Phone: 954-797-4000
Fax: –
Web: www.brandsmartusa.com

CEO: Michael Perlman
CFO: Eric Beazley
HR: –
FYE: September 24
Type: Private

Interbond Corporation of America (doing business as BrandsMart USA) boasts more than 500 brand names across its nearly 50000 electronics and entertainment products. It sells them in the US and internationally. It offers low-priced appliances computers TVs car stereos mobile phones personal care gadgets movie music games and more. The retailer runs about 10 electronics stores under the BrandsMart USA banner in the South Florida and Atlanta metropolitan areas. Each stocks more than $8 million in merchandise. BrandsMart USA also sells products online providing shipping for orders placed throughout the US Latin America and the Caribbean. Chairman Robert Perlman founded the company in 1977.

	Annual Growth	09/06	09/07	09/08	09/10	09/11
Sales ($ mil.)	(7.4%)	–	–	936.5	800.0	743.7
Net income ($ mil.)	(43.3%)	–	–	19.7	7.2	3.6
Market value ($ mil.)	–	–	–	–	–	–
Employees	–	–	–	–	–	2,400

INTERCEPT PHARMACEUTICALS INC NMS: ICPT

10 Hudson Yards, 37th Floor
New York, NY 10001
Phone: 646 747-1000
Fax: –
Web: www.interceptpharma.com

CEO: Jerome Durso
CFO: Andrew Saik
HR: –
FYE: December 31
Type: Public

Intercept Pharmaceuticals looks to cut liver disease off at the pass. A biopharmaceutical company Intercept Pharmaceuticals is developing and seeking to commercialize therapies to treat chronic liver disease. Its lead product candidate obeticholic acid (OCA) is being developed to treat primary biliary cirrhosis an autoimmune liver disease that can lead to liver failure and death. OCA is currently in late-stage clinical development. Intercept also has other candidates in its pipeline in earlier stages of development including treatments for other forms of cirrhosis portal hypertension (pressure in a key vein leading to the liver) fibrosis and Type 2 diabetes. Intercept went public in 2012.

	Annual Growth	12/16	12/17	12/18	12/19	12/20
Sales ($ mil.)	88.2%	25.0	131.0	179.8	252.0	312.7
Net income ($ mil.)	–	(412.8)	(360.4)	(309.2)	(344.7)	(274.9)
Market value ($ mil.)	(30.9%)	3,587.1	1,928.8	3,327.6	4,091.3	815.5
Employees	2.2%	456	507	483	583	498

INTERCLOUD SYSTEMS INC NBB: ICLD

1030 Broad Street, Suite 102
Shrewsbury, NJ 07702
Phone: 561 988-1988
Fax: –
Web: www.intercloudsys.com

CEO: Mark Munro
CFO: Timothy A Larkin
HR: –
FYE: December 31
Type: Public

It took a lot of storms to form InterCloud Systems. Formerly real estate firm Genesis Group Holdings the company changed its name to InterCloud Systems in 2013 and now oversees a group of subsidiaries that serve the telecom industry. It owns ADEX Corporation which provides engineering and installation services; structured cabling and DAS installers TNS and Tropical Communications; engineering firm Rives-Monteiro Engineering and equipment provider Rives-Monteiro Leasing; and AW Solutions which provides network systems design and engineering services. Customers include wireless and wireline telcos (Sprint) cable broadband multiple system operators (Verizon) and original equipment manufacturers (Ericsson).

	Annual Growth	12/13	12/14	12/15	12/16	12/17
Sales ($ mil.)	(9.5%)	51.4	76.2	74.9	78.0	34.5
Net income ($ mil.)	–	(24.4)	(18.8)	(65.8)	(26.5)	(44.3)
Market value ($ mil.)	–	54.6	54.6	54.6	0.3	0.0
Employees	7.3%	354	483	529	422	469

INTERCONTINENTAL EXCHANGE INC NYS: ICE

5660 New Northside Drive
Atlanta, GA 30328
Phone: 770 857-4700
Fax: 770 937-0020
Web: www.theice.com

CEO: Jeffrey Sprecher
CFO: Warren Gardiner
HR: –
FYE: December 31
Type: Public

Intercontinental Exchange (ICE) is a leading provider of regulated marketplaces and clearing services for global commodity trading primarily of electricity and agricultural commodities metals interest rates equities exchange traded funds or ETFs credit derivatives digital assets bonds and currencies and also offer mortgage and technology services. It manages a handful of global over-the-counter (OTC) markets and regulated futures exchanges. The firm also owns ICE Futures Europe a leading European energy futures and options platform as well as NYSE Holdings (including the New York Stock Exchange). The company serves clients in over 150 countries. ICE's largest geographical market is the US with nearly 65% of the company's revenue.

	Annual Growth	12/17	12/18	12/19	12/20	12/21
Sales ($ mil.)	12.0%	5,834.0	6,276.0	6,547.0	8,244.0	9,168.0
Net income ($ mil.)	12.7%	2,514.0	1,988.0	1,933.0	2,089.0	4,058.0
Market value ($ mil.)	18.0%	39,584.2	42,260.1	51,920.6	64,677.7	76,728.0
Employees	15.6%	4,952	5,161	5,989	8,890	8,858

INTERCONTINENTALEXCHANGE INC. NYS: ICE

5660 New Northside Drive
Atlanta, GA 30328
Phone: 770 857-4700
Fax: 770 937-0020
Web: www.theice.com

CEO: Jeffrey C Sprecher
CFO: –
HR: –
FYE: December 31
Type: Public

If there were money to be made in ice futures Intercontinental Exchange (ICE) would probably trade that as well. The firm is a leading provider of online marketplaces and clearing services for global commodity trading primarily of electricity natural gas crude oil refined petroleum products precious metals and weather and emission credits. It manages a handful of global OTC markets and regulated futures exchanges. The firm owns the ICE Futures Europe a leading European energy futures and options platform. ICE Data provides real-time daily and historical market data reports. ICE serves clients in more than 120 countries globally. It acquired NYSE Holdings in late 2013.

	Annual Growth	12/10	12/11	12/12	12/13	12/14
Sales ($ mil.)	28.1%	1,149.9	1,327.5	1,363.0	1,674.0	3,092.0
Net income ($ mil.)	25.3%	398.3	509.7	551.6	254.0	981.0
Market value ($ mil.)	16.5%	13,464.0	13,622.2	13,990.5	25,416.0	24,779.8
Employees	32.8%	933	1,013	1,077	4,232	2,902

INTERDIGITAL INC (PA) NMS: IDCC

200 Bellevue Parkway, Suite 300
Wilmington, DE 19809-3727
Phone: 302 281-3600
Fax: –
Web: www.interdigital.com

CEO: Lawrence Chen
CFO: Richard Brezski
HR: –
FYE: December 31
Type: Public

Interdigital Inc. is one of the world's largest pure research innovation and licensing companies after uniting the two main communication technologies ? wireless communication and video communication. It is also a leader in 5G research and beyond a thought leader in the industry with its engineers designing and developing a wide range of advanced technologies that are used in digital cellular and wireless products and networks including 2G 3G 4G and IEEE 802-related products and networks. In addition it solves many of the industry's most critical and complex technical challenges inventing solutions for more efficient broadband networks better video delivery and richer multimedia experiences years ahead of market deployment. The company started in 1986 by Sherwin Seligsohn.

	Annual Growth	12/17	12/18	12/19	12/20	12/21
Sales ($ mil.)	(5.5%)	532.9	307.4	318.9	359.0	425.4
Net income ($ mil.)	(24.9%)	174.3	63.9	20.9	44.8	55.3
Market value ($ mil.)	(1.5%)	2,337.0	2,038.7	1,672.2	1,862.2	2,198.3
Employees	9.9%	350	390	487	514	510

INTERFACE INC.

NMS: TILE

1280 West Peachtree Street
Atlanta, GA 30309
Phone: 770 437-6800
Fax: –
Web: www.interface.com

CEO: Daniel Hendrix
CFO: Bruce Hausmann
HR: –
FYE: January 03
Type: Public

Interface provides a soft place to land. The company is a leading global producer and seller of modular carpet also known as carpet tile. The tiles and rolls used in offices and many institutional facilities are sold under brand names Interface Glas-Bac and FLOR. Interface's other offerings include an antimicrobial chemical Intersept which it blends in its carpet as well as licenses for use in air filters and the TacTiles carpet tile installation system. Core markets are the Americas Europe and the Asia/Pacific region; the Americas represent more than 55% of sales.

	Annual Growth	01/17*	12/17	12/18	12/19*	01/21
Sales ($ mil.)	3.6%	958.6	996.4	1,179.6	1,343.0	1,103.3
Net income ($ mil.)	–	54.2	53.2	50.3	79.2	(71.9)
Market value ($ mil.)	(13.3%)	1,088.2	1,475.4	834.2	970.3	616.0
Employees	2.0%	3,561	3,319	4,509	4,335	3,858

*Fiscal year change

INTERFACE SECURITY SYSTEMS L.L.C.

3773 Corporate Center Dr.
Earth City MO 63045
Phone: 314-595-0100
Fax: 314-595-0376
Web: www.interfacesys.com

CEO: –
CFO: Ken Obermeyer
HR: –
FYE: July 31
Type: Private

Interface Security Systems is a leading provider of security systems and monitoring services for businesses and residential customers. It installs and monitors alarm systems for access control fire and life safety and intrusion detection. The company also offers video monitoring and alarm verification remote managed access monitoring and support and Internet-based alarm monitoring. Interface Security Systems has offices in about a dozen states mostly in the South and Southwest. The company was founded in 1981.

INTERGROUP CORP. (THE)

NAS: INTG

1516 S. Bundy Drive, Suite 200
Los Angeles, CA 90025
Phone: 310 889-2500
Fax: –
Web: www.intgla.com

CEO: John Winfield
CFO: Danfeng Xu
HR: –
FYE: June 30
Type: Public

InterGroup buys develops and manages affordable housing and other projects with an eye toward social responsibility. The company owns around 20 apartment complexes two commercial real estate properties two single-family residences and through subsidiary Santa Fe Financial majority interest in a San Francisco hotel. Its holdings are primarily concentrated in California and Texas. InterGroup also invests in securities and in real estate portfolios. It holds a stake in Comstock Mining a precious metals producing company. Chairman and CEO John Winfield controls about 62% of the company. Winfield is also CEO of Santa Fe Financial and its subsidiary Portsmouth Square.

	Annual Growth	06/17	06/18	06/19	06/20	06/21
Sales ($ mil.)	(19.7%)	69.0	71.6	74.8	58.0	28.7
Net income ($ mil.)	–	(1.7)	4.1	1.5	(3.8)	10.4
Market value ($ mil.)	14.1%	56.5	59.4	68.2	58.9	95.6
Employees	(44.6%)	286	33	28	30	27

INTERIM HEALTHCARE INC.

1601 SWGRS CORP PKWY # 220
SUNRISE, FL 333232883
Phone: 800-338-7786
Fax: –
Web: www.interimhealthcare.com

CEO: Jennifer Sheets
CFO: David Waltzer
HR: Krista Kocha
FYE: December 31
Type: Private

Interim HealthCare places health care staff where they are needed whether in a hospital or in a patient's home. Its home health care business marketed as Interim HomeStyle Services provides nurses therapists and personal care aides to patients in their houses. The company also provides health care personnel to hospitals long-term care facilities and other home health care providers. Interim HealthCare has about 300 franchised locations in the US and Puerto Rico and serves some 50000 patients daily. Investment firm Sentinel Capital Partners owns the company which was founded in 1966 as Medical Personnel Pool.

	Annual Growth	12/12	12/13	12/14	12/15	12/16
Assets ($ mil.)	4.1%	–	–	–	19.3	20.1
Net income ($ mil.)	1.5%	–	–	–	8.8	9.0
Market value ($ mil.)	–	–	–	–	–	–
Employees	–	–	–	–	–	2,689

INTERLEUKIN GENETICS INC

NBB: ILIU

135 Beaver Street
Waltham, MA 02452
Phone: 781 398-0700
Fax: 781 398-0720
Web: www.ilgenetics.com

CEO: –
CFO: –
HR: –
FYE: December 31
Type: Public

Interleukin Genetics counts on the high failure rate of crystal balls. The genetics-based personalized health company develops genetic tests for use in the emerging personalized health market to identify individuals' chances of developing certain diseases. Its PerioPredict product tests for gum disease and is available in the US and Europe. The company also offers predictive tests for heart disease and general nutrition through its partnership with Alticor. Interleukin Genetics has also teamed with Alticor to develop nutritional and skin care products.

	Annual Growth	12/11	12/12	12/13	12/14	12/15
Sales ($ mil.)	(15.7%)	2.9	2.2	2.4	1.8	1.4
Net income ($ mil.)	–	(5.0)	(5.1)	(7.1)	(6.3)	(7.9)
Market value ($ mil.)	(26.0%)	33.7	53.6	60.5	24.2	10.1
Employees	–	–	–	–	–	–

INTERLINE BRANDS INC.

NYSE: IBI

801 W. Bay St.
Jacksonville FL 32204
Phone: 904-421-1400
Fax: 904-358-2486
Web: www.interlinebrands.com

CEO: –
CFO: –
HR: –
FYE: December 31
Type: Private

When something breaks bursts or drips you can call Interline Brands a national distributor and direct marketer of repair and maintenance products. The company sells about 100000 plumbing hardware electrical janitorial and related products under private labels such as AmSan CleanSource Hardware Express Maintenance USA Sexauer U.S. Lock and Wilmar. Interline Brands operates 55 regional distribution centers and more than 25 showrooms that serve professional contractors throughout North America. Interline Brands which went public in 2004 was formed in 2000 through the merger of the Wilmar Barnett and Sexauer companies. Two private equity firms acquired the company in 2012.

INTERLINK ELECTRONICS INC   NAS: LINK

1 Jenner, Suite 200
Irvine, CA 92618
Phone: 805 484-8855
Fax: 805 484-9457
Web: www.interlinkelectronics.com

CEO: Steven N Bronson
CFO: Ryan J Hoffman
HR: –
FYE: December 31
Type: Public

Interlink Electronics designs electronic signature capture devices and specialty interface products. The company's signature capture products include its ePad line of hardware devices and IntegriSign software. Its sensor interface components enable menu navigation cursor control and character input in devices such as computer mice and mobile phones. Interlink's patented force-sensing technology enables smaller more touch-sensitive input devices. The company also provides design and integration services. Special Situations Technology Fund owns about 40% of the company.

	Annual Growth	12/16	12/17	12/18	12/19	12/20
Sales ($ mil.)	(12.8%)	11.9	11.2	8.9	7.3	6.9
Net income ($ mil.)	(55.5%)	2.9	1.3	0.6	(0.5)	0.1
Market value ($ mil.)	6.4%	46.3	34.5	13.9	31.4	59.4
Employees	(6.2%)	111	97	85	–	86

INTERMATIC INCORPORATED

1950 INNOVATION WAY # 300
LIBERTYVILLE, IL 600482079
Phone: 815-675-7000
Fax: –
Web: www.shop.intermatic.com

CEO: G Richard Boutilier Jr
CFO: –
HR: Penny Brichta
FYE: December 31
Type: Private

Intermatic offers an extensive catalog of lighting and energy controls surge protection devices weatherproof covers and Wi-Fi enabled solutions as it continues to evolve and push the industry forward. Its product portfolio broadened to include industrial- and commercial-grade controls and would soon expand with a variety of progressive energy-saving solutions. The company manufactures home timers that include pool and spa controls timer controls and in-wall controls. It also offers photocontrols that include fixed mount electronic locking type electronic fixed mount thermal and locking type thermal photocontrols. Other products include occupancy/vacancy sensors photo controls LED and HID lighting industrial surge protectors weatherproof covers for electrical outlets and enclosures.

	Annual Growth	12/0-1	12/00	12/03	12/04	12/17
Sales ($ mil.)	(5.3%)	–	317.5	330.0	380.0	124.7
Net income ($ mil.)	(4.9%)	–	16.6	63.2	240.8	7.0
Market value ($ mil.)	–	–	–	–	–	–
Employees	–	–	–	–	–	746

INTERMETRO COMMUNICATIONS, INC. (NV)   NBB: IMTO

2685 Park Center Drive, Building A
Simi Valley, CA 93065
Phone: 805 433-8000
Fax: –
Web: www.intermetrocomm.net

CEO: Charles Rice
CFO: James Winter
HR: Lynne Gilbert
FYE: December 31
Type: Public

InterMetro Communications hopes to take over the VoIP market city by city. The company's national private voice-over Internet Protocol (VoIP) network delivers long-distance phone service to telecoms providers and calling card users. InterMetro's more than 200 customers include traditional long-distance carriers broadband companies VoIP service providers and wireless providers. Its VoIP network utilizes proprietary software switching equipment and fiber-optic lines to deliver carrier-quality VoIP services which are typically more cost efficient than circuit-based technologies used in traditional long-distance networks. Chairman and CEO Charles Rice owns almost 40% of the company.

	Annual Growth	12/09	12/10	12/11	12/12	12/13
Sales ($ mil.)	(15.1%)	22.3	28.0	21.3	20.1	11.6
Net income ($ mil.)	–	(4.9)	3.2	3.6	0.7	(2.5)
Market value ($ mil.)	50.5%	0.8	5.0	4.1	8.3	4.1
Employees	(2.9%)	27	29	23	30	24

INTERMOLECULAR INC   NMS: IMI

3011 N. First Street
San Jose, CA 95134
Phone: 408 582-5700
Fax: –
Web: www.intermolecular.com

CEO: Chris Kramer
CFO: C Richard Neely
HR: Kendra Newby
FYE: December 31
Type: Public

Intermolecular sees R&D as a service that can be sold to semiconductor and clean energy customers. Through multi-year collaborative development programs (CDPs) customers pay the company service fees to help them develop proprietary technology and intellectual property (IP) so that they can quickly move new devices materials and processes into high-volume production. Intermolecular uses its High Productivity Combinatorial (HPC) platform to reduce the time needed to experiment with and prototype devices. Smaller portions of revenues are made from the sale of its Tempus HPC hardware and software platform and royalty fees from licensing out its IP. Founded in 2004 Intermolecular went public in 2011.

	Annual Growth	12/13	12/14	12/15	12/16	12/17
Sales ($ mil.)	(13.8%)	67.4	47.7	45.3	47.3	37.2
Net income ($ mil.)	–	(8.8)	(21.8)	(21.0)	(15.4)	(10.4)
Market value ($ mil.)	(27.4%)	243.9	95.7	115.0	47.0	67.9
Employees	(19.7%)	253	166	175	145	105

INTERMOUNTAIN HEALTH CARE INC

36 S STATE ST STE 1600
SALT LAKE CITY, UT 841111633
Phone: 801-442-2000
Fax: –
Web: www.intermountainhealthcare.org

CEO: Marc Harrison
CFO: –
HR: –
FYE: December 31
Type: Private

Intermountain Healthcare is a team of 41000 caregivers that serve the healthcare needs of people across the Intermountain West primarily in Utah Idaho and Nevada. In addition a not-for-profit health system based in Salt Lake City Utah with clinics a medical group affiliate networks hospitals homecare telehealth health insurance plans and subsidiaries such as SelectHealth Saltzer Health and Intermountain Healthcare. It has about 2400 physicians advanced practice providers 3800 affiliated physicians. In addition the not-for-profit health system operates 24 hospitals (includes virtual hospital) telehealth services practice providers a six-state area and some 215 clinics. Intermountain also has an insurance arm named SelectHealth covering around 900000 people in three states.

	Annual Growth	12/16	12/17	12/18	12/19	12/20
Sales ($ mil.)	13.3%	–	6,940.0	7,724.2	8,812.0	10,082.0
Net income ($ mil.)	14.0%	–	1,061.7	420.9	1,212.0	1,571.0
Market value ($ mil.)	–	–	–	–	–	–
Employees	–	–	–	–	–	35,000

INTERMUNE INC.   NMS: ITMN

3280 Bayshore Boulevard
Brisbane, CA 94005
Phone: 415 466-2200
Fax: –
Web: www.intermune.com

CEO: Daniel G Welch
CFO: John C Hodgman
HR: –
FYE: December 31
Type: Public

InterMune develops and sells drugs that interfere with pulmonary and immune system functions. The company's lead candidate Esbriet (pirfenidone) is a treatment for idiopathic pulmonary fibrosis (IPF) that was approved for sale in Europe in 2011. To focus on the development of Esbriet for additional markets InterMune divested its other primary commercial product rare congenital disorder treatment Actimmune (interferon gamma-1b) in 2012. Additional research programs aim to discover treatments for additional pulmonary and fibrotic conditions.

	Annual Growth	12/08	12/09	12/10	12/11	12/12
Sales ($ mil.)	(14.1%)	48.2	48.7	259.3	25.6	26.2
Net income ($ mil.)	–	(97.7)	(116.0)	122.4	(154.8)	(150.1)
Market value ($ mil.)	(2.2%)	698.8	861.3	2,404.2	832.2	640.0
Employees	(1.6%)	130	121	105	201	122

INTERNAP CORP
NBB: INAP Q

12120 Sunset Hills Road, Suite 330
Reston, VA 20190
Phone: 404 302-9700
Fax: –
Web: www.internap.com

CEO: Michael Sicoli
CFO: Lisa Mayr
HR: Jackie Coats
FYE: December 31
Type: Public

Internap (INAP) is a hybrid infrastructure company that partners with IT leaders to design and operate high-performance hybrid infrastructure. It identifies the right environments for customers' apps and data resulting in purpose-built expertly managed deployments that simplifies their cloud journey and accelerates innovation. INAP's robust global network includes around 45 data centers in over 90 points of presence with more than 2000 fiber miles. Its managed services include managed cloud with INAP intelligent monitoring which offers comprehensive in-depth monitoring alert remediation powered by Smart Workflow system fully manages infrastructure and OS support and includes feature-rich infrastructure management toolkit.

	Annual Growth	12/15	12/16	12/17	12/18	12/19
Sales ($ mil.)	(2.2%)	318.3	298.3	280.7	317.4	291.5
Net income ($ mil.)	–	(48.4)	(124.7)	(45.3)	(62.5)	(138.3)
Market value ($ mil.)	(35.6%)	170.0	40.9	417.2	110.2	29.2
Employees	(4.5%)	650	530	503	640	540

INTERNAP HOLDING LLC

12120 SUNSET HILLS RD # 3
RESTON, VA 201905853
Phone: 404-302-9700
Fax: –
Web: www.inap.com

CEO: Michael Sicoli
CFO: Lisa Mayr
HR: Jackie Coats
FYE: December 31
Type: Private

Internap (INAP) is a hybrid infrastructure company that partners with IT leaders to design and operate high-performance hybrid infrastructure. It identifies the right environments for customers' apps and data resulting in purpose-built expertly managed deployments that simplifies their cloud journey and accelerates innovation. INAP's robust global network includes around 45 data centers in over 90 points of presence with more than 2000 fiber miles. Its managed services include managed cloud with INAP intelligent monitoring which offers comprehensive in-depth monitoring alert remediation powered by Smart Workflow system fully manages infrastructure and OS support and includes feature-rich infrastructure management toolkit.

	Annual Growth	12/15	12/16	12/17	12/18	12/19
Sales ($ mil.)	(0.8%)	–	298.3	280.7	317.4	291.5
Net income ($ mil.)	–	–	(124.7)	(45.3)	(62.4)	(138.2)
Market value ($ mil.)	–	–	–	–	–	–
Employees	–	–	–	–	–	503

INTERNATIONAL ASSOCIATION OF AMUSEMENT PARKS & ATTRACTIONS INC

1448 DUKE ST
ALEXANDRIA, VA 223143403
Phone: 703-836-3677
Fax: –
Web: www.iaapa.org

CEO: Hal McEvoy
CFO: –
HR: –
FYE: July 31
Type: Private

Work is just a walk in the park for this group. The International Association of Amusement Parks and Attractions (IAAPA) is the world's largest trade organization for the amusement and theme park industry with 5000 members in 80 countries. The not-for-profit group develops services training products and networking opportunities for its members which include zoo museum arcade and family fun center operators. It holds annual trade shows publishes FUNWORLD magazine offers management and customer service advice sets safety standards and lobbies government on behalf of the industry. IAAPA was founded in 1918.

	Annual Growth	07/03	07/04	07/05*	06/06*	07/08
Sales ($ mil.)	(72.1%)	–	–	599.7	0.0	13.0
Net income ($ mil.)	241.5%	–	–	0.0	(0.0)	0.7
Market value ($ mil.)	–	–	–	–	–	–
Employees	–	–	–	–	–	33

*Fiscal year change

INTERNATIONAL BALER CORP
NBB: IBAL

5400 Rio Grande Avenue
Jacksonville, FL 32254
Phone: 904 358-3812
Fax: –
Web: www.intl-baler.com

CEO: D. Roger Griffin
CFO: William Nielsen
HR: –
FYE: October 31
Type: Public

No need to bail on International Baler. This holding company formerly known as Waste Technology banks on its business being in the dumps. International Baler manufactures about 50 different types of waste baling equipment. It also sells replacement parts for waste haulers. In addition International Baler produces accessories such as conveyor belts and "rufflers" which break down refuse for better compaction. Customers include rubber and polymer makers solid-waste recycling facilities power generating facilities textile and paper mills cotton gins and supermarkets. International Baler makes about three-quarters of its sales in the US.

	Annual Growth	10/17	10/18	10/19	10/20	10/21
Sales ($ mil.)	(1.2%)	10.5	11.1	9.5	9.0	10.0
Net income ($ mil.)	–	0.1	0.3	(0.3)	(0.4)	(0.1)
Market value ($ mil.)	(1.2%)	10.4	9.6	7.5	6.5	9.9
Employees	(6.5%)	59	57	50	49	45

INTERNATIONAL BANCSHARES CORP.
NMS: IBOC

1200 San Bernardo Avenue
Laredo, TX 78042-1359
Phone: 956 722-7611
Fax: –
Web: www.ibc.com

CEO: Dennis Nixon
CFO: –
HR: –
FYE: December 31
Type: Public

International Bancshares is leading post-NAFTA banking in South Texas. One of the state's largest bank holding companies it does business through nearly 200 locations of International Bank of Commerce (IBC) IBC-Oklahoma Commerce Bank IBC Zapata and IBC Brownsville. The company facilitates trade between the US and Mexico and serves Texas' growing Hispanic population; about 30% of its deposits come from south of the border. In addition to commercial and international banking services for small and midsized businesses International Bancshares provides retail deposit services insurance and investment products mortgages and consumer loans. The bulk of the company's portfolio is made up of commercial financial and agricultural loans and real estate loans for construction.

	Annual Growth	12/16	12/17	12/18	12/19	12/20
Assets ($ mil.)	4.4%	11,804.0	12,184.7	11,872.0	12,112.9	14,029.5
Net income ($ mil.)	5.7%	133.9	157.4	215.9	205.1	167.3
Market value ($ mil.)	(2.1%)	2,581.8	2,512.2	2,176.8	2,725.5	2,369.2
Employees	(6.5%)	3,216	3,273	3,390	3,314	2,456

INTERNATIONAL BROTHERHOOD OF ELECTRICAL WORKERS

900 7TH ST NW BSMT 1
WASHINGTON, DC 200014089
Phone: 202-833-7000
Fax: –
Web: www.ibew.org

CEO: –
CFO: –
HR: –
FYE: June 30
Type: Private

These brothers are held together with wire steel girders fiber optic cable and conveyor belts. The International Brotherhood of Electrical Workers (IBEW) is about a 725000-member labor union for workers in such industries as utilities construction telecommunications and manufacturing in the US and Canada. The union lobbies government on behalf of its members provides training and scholarships maintains an electronic job board and helps members secure higher wages better health care and safer working conditions. The union was formally organized in 1891 at a convention in St. Louis run by the original American Federation of Labor a predecessor to the AFL-CIO with which the union is affiliated.

	Annual Growth	06/14	06/15	06/16	06/19	06/20
Sales ($ mil.)	1.5%	–	160.0	161.1	181.7	172.2
Net income ($ mil.)	(39.9%)	–	15.5	13.2	27.9	1.2
Market value ($ mil.)	–	–	–	–	–	–
Employees	–	–	–	–	–	970

INTERNATIONAL BROTHERHOOD OF TEAMSTERS

25 LOUISIANA AVE NW
WASHINGTON, DC 200012130
Phone: 202-624-6800
Fax: –
Web: www.teamster.org

CEO: –
CFO: –
HR: –
FYE: December 31
Type: Private

One of the largest and best-known labor unions in the US the International Brotherhood of Teamsters has 1.4 million members. The Teamsters represents workers in nearly 25 industry sectors including airlines freight parcel delivery industrial trades and public service. Most of the union's members are employees of package delivery giant United Parcel Service. Besides negotiating labor contracts with employers on behalf of its members the union oversees pension funds and serves as an advocate in legislative and regulatory arenas. The union and its affiliates have about 1900 local chapters in the US. Puerto Rico and Canada including about 360 Teamsters locals. The Teamsters union was founded in 1903.

	Annual Growth	12/05	12/06	12/07	12/08	12/09
Sales ($ mil.)	–	–	–	(91.4)	155.7	172.8
Net income ($ mil.)	353635.6%	–	–	0.0	(22.3)	12.5
Market value ($ mil.)	–	–	–	–	–	–
Employees	–	–	–	–	–	649

INTERNATIONAL BUILDING TECHNOLOGIES GROUP INC.   OTC: INBG

17800 Castleton St. Ste. 638
City of Industry CA 91748
Phone: 626-581-8500
Fax: 626-626-7603
Web: www.ibtgi.com

CEO: Kenneth Yeung
CFO: Kenneth Yeung
HR: –
FYE: December 31
Type: Public

International Building Technologies Group (INBG) has raced from business to business. Formerly a card game developer for casinos and a seller of racing and motorsports accessories and apparel the company changed lanes in 2007. That's when it began a new life as a manufacturer of a specialty panel-based technology that helps buildings withstand earthquakes and hurricane-force winds. INBG also offers other services including site planning engineering contractor services training and supervision. In 2011 a a merger plan between INBG and Chinese petroleum storage company FHH Sino New Energies was terminated. The deal would have allowed INBG to move into yet another line of business — the energy sector.

INTERNATIONAL BUSINESS MACHINES CORP   NYS: IBM

One New Orchard Road
Armonk, NY 10504
Phone: 914 499-1900
Fax: 914 765-4190
Web: www.ibm.com

CEO: Arvind Krishna
CFO: James J Kavanaugh
HR: –
FYE: December 31
Type: Public

International Business Machines (IBM) provides integrated solutions and products that leverage data information technology deep expertise in industries and business processes. The company is investing in what it calls cognitive computing systems led by the Watson artificial intelligence platform that help customers analyze massive amounts of data to make better decisions. Among other areas the company is betting on for growth are artificial intelligence security cloud systems quantum computing and more. IBM's information technology business services and software units are among the largest in the world. While IBM has placed less emphasis on hardware the company maintains enterprise server and data storage product lines that are among industry leaders. The company generates about 35% of sales from the US.

	Annual Growth	12/17	12/18	12/19	12/20	12/21
Sales ($ mil.)	(7.7%)	79,139.0	79,591.0	77,147.0	73,620.0	57,350.0
Net income ($ mil.)	(0.0%)	5,753.0	8,728.0	9,431.0	5,590.0	5,743.0
Market value ($ mil.)	(3.4%)	137,781.7	102,083.5	120,377.1	113,048.9	120,035.8
Employees	(4.3%)	366,600	350,600	383,800	375,300	307,600

INTERNATIONAL CARD ESTABLISHMENT INC.   OTC: ICRD

555 Airport Way Ste. A
Camarillo CA 93010
Phone: 209-946-2344
Fax: 212-261-4286
Web: www.dentsuamerica.com

CEO: –
CFO: –
HR: –
FYE: December 31
Type: Public

International Card Establishment (ICE) believes that it's cool for every merchant big or small to have the ability to swipe your credit card. More and more customers are using electronic payments to purchase items and ICE is there to provide businesses with the ability to accept transactions. ICE targets small businesses as its core customer base and offers a variety of credit card servicing offerings including processing systems processing services software and loyalty management programs. ICE has used acquisitions to transition away from its previous business of providing Web-based event management software and services.

INTERNATIONAL CREATIVE MANAGEMENT INC.

10250 Constellation Blvd.
Los Angeles CA 90067
Phone: 310-550-4000
Fax: 310-550-4100
Web: www.icmtalent.com

CEO: –
CFO: –
HR: –
FYE: July 30
Type: Private

If anyone can manage creativity internationally it's International Creative Management (ICM). The agency represents film and television actors and directors as well as artists in theater music publishing and new media. A major "tenpercentery" (along with CAA and William Morris Endeavor) ICM represents such A-list clients as Susan Sarandon Al Pacino Robert Duvall Beyonce Knowles Chris Rock and Jay Leno as well as emerging performers. It has offices in Los Angeles New York and London. ICM was formed in 1975 by the merger of Creative Management Associates and The International Famous Agency. Private equity firm Traverse Rizvi Management and Merrill Lynch hold controlling stakes in the agency.

INTERNATIONAL FINANCE CORP. (WORLD CORPORATIONS GOV'T)

2121 Pennsylvania Avenue, N.W.
Washington, DC 20433
Phone: 202 473-3800
Fax: 202 974-4384
Web: www.ifc.org

CEO: Philippe Le Houerou
CFO: –
HR: Jeannie Crist
FYE: June 30
Type: Public

International Finance Corporation (IFC) is the lender known 'round the world. IFC promotes economic development worldwide by providing loans and equity financing for private-sector investment. Boasting $90 billion in assets the IFC typically focuses on small and mid-sized businesses financing projects in several industries including manufacturing agribusiness services infrastructure natural resources financial markets telecom media & technology and venture investing. Established in 1956 the IFC is the private sector arm of the World Bank group. Although it often acts in concert with the World Bank the IFC is legally and financially autonomous. It is owned by some 185 member countries.

	Annual Growth	06/10	06/11	06/12	06/13	06/14
Sales ($ mil.)	0.2%	3,383.0	3,178.0	3,120.0	2,514.0	3,415.0
Net income ($ mil.)	(4.0%)	1,746.0	1,579.0	1,328.0	1,018.0	1,483.0
Market value ($ mil.)	–	–	–	–	–	–
Employees	–	–	–	–	–	–

INTERNATIONAL FINANCE CORPORATION

2121 Pennsylvania Ave. NW
Washington DC 20433
Phone: 202-473-3800
Fax: 202-974-4384
Web: www.ifc.org

CEO: Philippe Le Houerou
CFO: –
HR: Jeannie Crist
FYE: June 30
Type: Private - Member-Own

International Finance Corporation (IFC) is the lender known 'round the world. IFC promotes economic development worldwide by providing loans and equity financing for private-sector investment. The IFC typically focuses on small and midsized businesses financing projects in all types of industries including manufacturing infrastructure tourism health education and financial services. Established in 1956 the IFC is the private sector arm of the World Bank group. Although it often acts in concert with the World Bank the IFC is legally and financially autonomous. It is owned by some 180 member countries.

INTERNATIONAL FLAVORS & FRAGRANCES INC. NYS: IFF

521 West 57th Street
New York, NY 19803-2907
Phone: 212 765-5500
Fax: –
Web: www.iff.com

CEO: Frank Clyburn
CFO: Glenn Richter
HR: –
FYE: December 31
Type: Public

International Flavors & Fragrances (IFF) is one of the leading innovators of sensory food and beverage pharmaceutical health and wellness home and personal care integrated solutions and ingredients around the world. As a leading creator of flavor offerings the company helps its customers deliver on the promise of delicious and healthy foods and drinks. It also creates natural-focused compounds and ingredients for niche markets. In early 2021 IFF completed the approximately $26.2 billion merger with DuPont's Nutrition & Biosciences business. About 75% of its sales comes from outside North America.

	Annual Growth	12/16	12/17	12/18	12/19	12/20
Sales ($ mil.)	13.0%	3,116.4	3,398.7	3,977.5	5,140.1	5,084.2
Net income ($ mil.)	(2.7%)	405.0	295.7	337.3	455.9	363.2
Market value ($ mil.)	(2.0%)	12,600.5	16,319.8	14,358.6	13,797.1	11,639.1
Employees	18.7%	6,900	7,300	13,000	13,600	13,700

INTERNATIONAL FLEET SALES INC.

476 MCCORMICK ST
SAN LEANDRO, CA 945771106
Phone: 510-569-9770
Fax: –
Web: www.internationalfleetsales.com

CEO: Michael Libasci
CFO: Peggy King
HR: –
FYE: December 31
Type: Private

By air land or sea International Fleet Sales (IFS) can ship North American cars to international buyers. IFS is an authorized export distributor of General Motors vehicles (including Cadillac Chevrolet and GMC) as well as parts and service. It is also an export distributor of Blue Bird Bus and Volvo Trucks North America parts. Customers include auto retailers and distributors governments individual buyers and humanitarian aid agencies. The company's US office handles sales in Central and South America Asia Africa and the Middle East while its Netherlands office supports sales in Europe. IFS was founded in 1999 by president and CEO Mike Libasci.

	Annual Growth	12/05	12/06	12/07	12/08	12/09
Sales ($ mil.)	–	–	–	(593.2)	37.5	63.4
Net income ($ mil.)	1645.5%	–	–	0.0	2.0	5.0
Market value ($ mil.)	–	–	–	–	–	–
Employees	–	–	–	–	–	15

INTERNATIONAL ISOTOPES INC NBB: INIS

4137 Commerce Circle
Idaho Falls, ID 83401
Phone: 208 524-5300
Fax: –
Web: www.internationalisotopes.com

CEO: Steve Laflin
CFO: Matthew Cox
HR: –
FYE: December 31
Type: Public

Despite its name International Isotopes is confined to a single US state. The firm operates primarily through subsidiary International Isotopes Idaho where it makes calibration and measurement equipment used with nuclear imaging cameras. Most of its nuclear imaging products including dose measurement devices and testing equipment are made under contract with RadQual a privately held firm that markets the devices; International Isotopes owns a minority stake in RadQual. The company partnered with RadQual in late 2010 to acquire Technology Imaging Services. The joint venture called TI Services LLC distributes products and services for nuclear medicine nuclear cardiology and PET imaging.

	Annual Growth	12/16	12/17	12/18	12/19	12/20
Sales ($ mil.)	9.3%	6.6	7.4	10.4	9.0	9.4
Net income ($ mil.)	–	(1.9)	(3.8)	(0.8)	(1.5)	2.2
Market value ($ mil.)	(18.8%)	49.8	33.9	27.2	22.1	21.6
Employees	3.4%	28	30	32	37	32

INTERNATIONAL LEASE FINANCE CORP. NYS: AIG 09

10250 Constellation Blvd., Suite 3400
Los Angeles, CA 90067
Phone: 310 788-1999
Fax: –
Web: www.ilfc.com

CEO: Henri Courpron
CFO: Elias Habayeb
HR: –
FYE: December 31
Type: Public

John Travolta bought his own Boeing; if your company's cash flow is more limited International Lease Finance Corporation (ILFC) will lease you one. The company which leases the entire range of Boeing and Airbus commercial aircraft is the world's second-largest lessor of new aircraft and widebody carriers. It boasts of owning the world's most valuable fleet of leasable aircraft — about 930 planes. ILFC's airplane-parts management business maintains the aging aircraft in its fleet. Commercial airlines outside the US generate more than 95% of revenue; ILFC counts most of the world's airlines as customers. Parent AIG (American International Group) spun off ILFC's holding company ILFC Holdings as an IPO in 2011.

	Annual Growth	12/09	12/10	12/11	12/12	12/13
Sales ($ mil.)	(4.5%)	5,321.7	4,798.9	4,526.7	4,504.2	4,417.4
Net income ($ mil.)	–	895.6	(383.8)	(723.9)	410.3	(517.1)
Market value ($ mil.)	–	–	–	–	–	–
Employees	36.9%	180	194	497	564	632

INTERNATIONAL LOTTERY & TOTALIZATOR SYSTEMS, INC. NBB: ITSI

2310 Cousteau Court
Vista, CA 92081-8346
Phone: 760 598-1655
Fax: –
Web: www.ilts.com

CEO: –
CFO: –
HR: –
FYE: April 30
Type: Public

Designing systems for gambling and the ballot booth maybe this company should be called Tote & Vote. International Lottery & Totalizator Systems (ILTS) is a leading manufacturer of computerized wagering systems used by pari-mutuel racing operators off-track betting centers and lottery operators. It also provides consulting and training services along with its software and hardware. In addition to wagering ILTS markets electronic voting systems through its Unisyn Voting Solutions subsidiary. Berjaya Lottery Management a subsidiary of Malaysia-based Berjaya Group owns more than 70% of ILTS.

	Annual Growth	04/09	04/10	04/11	04/12	04/13
Sales ($ mil.)	12.9%	6.5	7.1	5.9	12.1	10.6
Net income ($ mil.)	–	(0.9)	(0.6)	(1.0)	1.2	3.1
Market value ($ mil.)	50.9%	2.7	3.1	3.4	7.8	14.0
Employees	(0.7%)	36	36	32	36	35

INTERNATIONAL MINERALS CORPORATION
TORONTO: IMZ

7950 E. Acoma Dr. Ste. 211
Scottsdale AZ 85260
Phone: 480-483-9932
Fax: 480-483-9926
Web: www.intlminerals.com

CEO: -
CFO: -
HR: -
FYE: June 30
Type: Public

International Minerals is working to develop gold and silver properties in South America. The company's primary projects include the Rio Blanco Gaby and Ca?icapa properties in Ecuador and the Antabamba and Pallancata properties in Peru. Through a 2010 purchase of Ventura Gold International Minerals owns a 51% interest in the Peruvian Inmaculada gold/silver project. Hochschild Mining owns the remaining stake. It also bought Metallic Ventures that same year winning a bidding contest with Solitario Exploration to add to its Goldmine and Converse operations in Nevada. The company continues to look to acquire low-cost gold and silver mining operations in the Americas.

INTERNATIONAL MONETARY SYSTEMS LTD
NBB: ITNM

16901 West Glendale Drive
New Berlin, WI 53151
Phone: 262 780-3640
Fax: -
Web: www.imsbarter.com

CEO: John Strabley
CFO: David Powell
HR: Jennifer Weber
FYE: December 31
Type: Public

Who says the barter system is dead? Not International Monetary Systems (IMS). IMS runs one of the world's largest trade exchanges or barter networks allowing businesses and professionals to convert excess inventory into goods and services. Its IMS Barter Network serves approximately 17000 clients in major markets in the US and Canada. Users swap excess goods or services electronically with trade dollars IMS' electronic currency. Founded in 1985 the company has expanded by acquiring other trade exchanges.

	Annual Growth	12/16	12/17	12/18	12/19	12/20
Sales ($ mil.)	(4.6%)	11.7	11.4	11.4	11.7	9.7
Net income ($ mil.)	-	(0.0)	0.1	0.4	0.4	0.9
Market value ($ mil.)	(0.9%)	2.7	2.9	2.9	2.4	2.6
Employees	-	-	-	-	-	-

INTERNATIONAL PAPER CO
NYS: IP

6400 Poplar Avenue
Memphis, TN 38197
Phone: 901 419-9000
Fax: -
Web: www.internationalpaper.com

CEO: Mark Sutton
CFO: Timothy Nicholls
HR: Thomas Plath
FYE: December 31
Type: Public

International Paper (IP) is a global producer of renewable fiber-based packaging and pulp products. Products include uncoated paper used in printers and market pulp for tissue and paper products. In the US IP is #1 in containerboard production where some 80% of materials are converted to industrial corrugated boxes. Most of its over 240 mills converting and packaging plants and recycling facilities are in the US. It also runs a pulp and paper business in Russia via a 50/50 joint venture with Ilim S.A. More than 75% of IP's revenue is generated in the US.

	Annual Growth	12/17	12/18	12/19	12/20	12/21
Sales ($ mil.)	(2.9%)	21,743.0	23,306.0	22,376.0	20,580.0	19,363.0
Net income ($ mil.)	(4.9%)	2,144.0	2,012.0	1,225.0	482.0	1,752.0
Market value ($ mil.)	(5.1%)	21,933.4	15,278.4	17,432.4	18,821.7	17,784.5
Employees	(9.1%)	56,000	53,000	51,000	49,300	38,200

INTERNATIONAL RECTIFIER CORP.
NYS: IRF

101 N. Sepulveda Blvd.
El Segundo, CA 90245
Phone: 310 726-8000
Fax: 310 322-3332
Web: www.irf.com

CEO: Oleg Khaykin
CFO: Ilan Daskal
HR: -
FYE: June 30
Type: Public

International Rectifier (IR) is a top maker of power management semiconductors which refine the electricity flowing into a device from a battery or a power grid enabling more efficient operation. Its products — including MOSFETs (metal oxide semiconductor field-effect transistors) diodes relays and rectifiers — are used in appliances automobiles computers communication devices lighting and displays gaming consoles industrial motors and military equipment. IR sells its products through distributors OEMs and contract manufacturers. Most of the global company's sales come from Asian customers.

	Annual Growth	06/09	06/10	06/11	06/12	06/13
Sales ($ mil.)	7.2%	740.4	895.3	1,176.6	1,050.6	977.0
Net income ($ mil.)	-	(247.4)	80.8	166.5	(55.1)	(88.8)
Market value ($ mil.)	9.3%	1,034.2	1,419.9	1,836.7	1,403.8	1,474.2
Employees	1.4%	3,939	4,534	4,920	4,911	4,162

INTERNATIONAL SHIPHOLDING CORP
NBB: ISHC Q

11 North Water St., Suite 18290
Mobile, AL 36602
Phone: 251 243-9100
Fax: -
Web: www.intship.com

CEO: Erik L Johnsen
CFO: Manuel G Estrada
HR: -
FYE: December 31
Type: Public

International Shipholding helps put the "car" in cargo. Most of the company's sales come from its time-charter vessels including car and truck carriers ships with strengthened hulls (used in polar regions) and coal and sulfur carriers. Its fleet consists of some nearly 40 US and international-flag vessels. International Shipholding's primary subsidiaries include Central Gulf Lines Waterman Steamship Corp. LCI Shipholdings CG Railway and East Gulf Shipholding. The company has offices in Mobile Alabama; New York City; Singapore; and Shanghai. Customers have included such big names as Toyota Hyundai Motor International Paper and the US Navy's Military Sealift Command.

	Annual Growth	12/11	12/12	12/13	12/14	12/15
Sales ($ mil.)	(0.4%)	263.2	243.5	310.2	294.8	259.5
Net income ($ mil.)	-	31.5	22.0	18.2	(54.7)	(179.7)
Market value ($ mil.)	(47.3%)	137.1	120.9	216.3	109.3	10.6
Employees	1.9%	424	561	625	593	458

INTERNATIONAL SPEEDWAY CORP
NMS: ISCA

One Daytona Boulevard
Daytona Beach, FL 32114
Phone: 386 254-2700
Fax: -
Web: www.internationalspeedwaycorporation.com

CEO: Lesa France Kennedy
CFO: Gregory S Motto
HR: -
FYE: November 30
Type: Public

International Speedway Corporation (ISC) doesn't believe in slow and steady. The company is the top motorsports operator in the US with more than a dozen racetracks hosting more than 100 events annually. Its race facilities include Daytona International Speedway (home of the Daytona 500) Talladega Superspeedway and Michigan International Speedway. In addition ISC operates the Daytona 500 EXperience theme park and museum and it owns 50% of motorsports merchandiser Motorsports Authentics with rival Speedway Motorsports. Former CEO James France and his family own about 70% control of the company. Events sanctioned by NASCAR also controlled by the France family account for about 90% of sales.

	Annual Growth	11/14	11/15	11/16	11/17	11/18
Sales ($ mil.)	0.9%	651.9	645.4	661.0	671.4	675.0
Net income ($ mil.)	35.2%	67.4	56.6	76.3	110.8	225.3
Market value ($ mil.)	7.9%	1,346.7	1,532.3	1,584.4	1,775.9	1,822.9
Employees	0.1%	845	807	792	820	850

INTERNATIONAL TEXTILE GROUP, INC. NBB: ITXN

804 Green Valley Road, Suite 300
Greensboro, NC 27408
Phone: 336 379-6299
Fax: -
Web: www.itg-global.com

CEO: Per-Olof Loof
CFO: Gail A Kuczkowski
HR: Arturo Bahena
FYE: December 31
Type: Public

The totally material group — International Textile (ITG) — asks dress uniform or jeans? ITG makes a range of apparel and technical fabrics military garb as well as specialty textiles and less so auto safety fabrics. It stands as the world's #1 producer of better denim fabrics including premium brand Cone Denim used in retail goods. Other business units include Burlington Safety Components Narricot and Carlisle Finishing. ITG is also one of North America's top manufacturers of worsted wool and commission printers and finishers. The US and Mexico are its largest markets.

	Annual Growth	12/10	12/11	12/12	12/13	12/14
Sales ($ mil.)	(0.9%)	616.1	694.4	619.1	624.2	595.4
Net income ($ mil.)	-	(37.6)	(59.1)	(64.7)	23.3	0.4
Market value ($ mil.)	38.8%	0.7	0.5	0.1	2.1	2.6
Employees	(14.5%)	8,700	7,800	4,800	4,800	4,650

INTERNATIONAL WIRE GROUP, INC.

12 MASONIC AVE
CAMDEN, NY 133161202
Phone: 315-245-2000
Fax: -
Web: www.internationalwiregroup.com

CEO: -
CFO: Glenn J Holler
HR: -
FYE: December 31
Type: Private

International Wire Group (IWG) bares it all in the wire business. Through three divisions — Bare Wire Products Engineered Products - Europe and High Performance Conductors — IWG makes multi-gauge bare silver- nickel- and tin-plated copper wire as well as engineered wire products and performance conductors. The company's customers (General Cable is one of its largest) include suppliers and OEMs. IWG's wire products are used in industrial/energy consumer electronics aerospace and defense medical electronics automotive and appliance applications.

	Annual Growth	12/04	12/05	12/06	12/07	12/08
Sales ($ mil.)	-	-	-	(1,789.4)	730.8	736.4
Net income ($ mil.)	13597.3%	-	-	0.0	15.9	6.5
Market value ($ mil.)	-	-	-	-	-	-
Employees	-	-	-	-	-	1,600

INTERNET AMERICA INC. NBB: GEEK

6210 Rothway Street, Suite 100
Houston, TX 77064
Phone: 713 968-2500
Fax: -
Web: www.internetamerica.com

CEO: William E Ladin Jr
CFO: -
HR: Victor Joseph
FYE: June 30
Type: Public

Internet America is changing its "lines" of business. Traditionally a provider of dial-up Internet access and to a lesser degree of wire-line DSL broadband Internet access to rural and suburban markets in Texas the company is battling dwindling subscriber numbers by expanding its wireless broadband Internet business. Total subscribers number more than 30000 with about one quarter of those connecting wirelessly. Internet America also provides installation and maintenance services from its three Texas operational centers in Corsicana San Antonio and Stafford (near Houston). The ISP founded in 1995 is known regionally for its 1-800-BE-A-GEEK sign-up number.

	Annual Growth	06/10	06/11	06/12	06/13	06/14
Sales ($ mil.)	2.2%	7.4	7.0	7.3	7.8	8.1
Net income ($ mil.)	-	(1.0)	(0.3)	0.6	4.5	5.9
Market value ($ mil.)	31.6%	4.2	4.2	4.9	6.7	12.6
Employees	7.5%	39	35	44	48	52

INTERNET CORPORATION FOR ASSIGNED NAMES AND NUMBERS

12025 WATERFRONT DR # 300
LOS ANGELES, CA 900943220
Phone: 310-823-9358
Fax: -
Web: www.icann.org

CEO: -
CFO: -
HR: -
FYE: June 30
Type: Private

Can anyone manage the Internet? This group says "ICANN." The Internet Corporation for Assigned Names and Numbers (ICANN) is a not-for-profit organization responsible for the management of the Internet's domain name system (DNS) allocation of Internet protocol (IP) addresses and assignment of protocol parameters. The DNS allows people to type in an address like "www.hoovers.com" rather than the string of numbers that represents the underlying IP address. Internet users register some 20 domain names ending in .com . org .info and .net among others through ICANN-accredited DNS registrars. The group is also managing the application process for a slew of new generic top-level domains (gTLDs).

	Annual Growth	06/13	06/14	06/15	06/19	06/20
Sales ($ mil.)	2.7%	-	127.8	219.6	161.2	149.6
Net income ($ mil.)	23.2%	-	3.5	87.9	11.1	12.4
Market value ($ mil.)	-	-	-	-	-	-
Employees	-	-	-	-	-	160

INTERPACE BIOSCIENCES INC NBB: IDXG

Morris Corporate Center 1, Building C, 300 Interpace Parkway
Parsippany, NJ 07054
Phone: 855 776-6419
Fax: -
Web: www.interpacediagnostics.com

CEO: Thomas W Burnell
CFO: Thomas Freeburg
HR: -
FYE: December 31
Type: Public

PDI handles sales and marketing for pharmaceutical companies that would rather focus on product development. As a contract sales organization (CSO) the company provides sales teams dedicated to a single client and teams that represent multiple non-competing brands. Sales teams typically are assigned to geographic territories on a client's behalf. Each year contract sales services account for about 90% of PDI's revenue. The company's marketing and strategic consulting services operations are represented by its Pharmakon Interactive Healthcare Communications unit. PDI was established in 1987.

	Annual Growth	12/16	12/17	12/18	12/19	12/20
Sales ($ mil.)	25.4%	13.1	15.9	21.9	24.1	32.4
Net income ($ mil.)	-	(8.3)	(12.2)	(12.2)	(26.7)	(26.5)
Market value ($ mil.)	(8.1%)	17.8	4.1	3.2	2.0	12.7
Employees	25.6%	61	75	89	178	152

INTERPORE SPINE LTD.

181 Technology Dr.
Irvine CA 92618-2402
Phone: 949-453-3200
Fax: 949-453-3225
Web: www.interpore.com

CEO: -
CFO: Greg Hartman
HR: -
FYE: May 31
Type: Subsidiary

Interpore Spine has biomaterials deep in its bones. The company which operates as Interpore Cross makes synthetic tissue bone products and implant systems for spinal and orthopedic procedures. Interpore also makes biological grafting products that encourage bone growth. Interpore Spine also manufactures minimally invasive surgery systems used by orthopedic surgeons and neurologists. Brands include Pro Osteon InterGro and BioPlex. The company is a subsidiary of Biomet; other sister company products include dental implants sports medicine devices and bracing equipment.

INTERPUBLIC GROUP OF COMPANIES INC. — NYS: IPG

909 Third Avenue
New York, NY 10022
Phone: 212 704-1200
Fax: –
Web: www.interpublic.com

CEO: Amy Armstrong
CFO: Ellen Johnson
HR: –
FYE: December 31
Type: Public

The Interpublic Group of Companies (IPG) is one of the world's largest advertising and marketing services companies. The company has offices in more than 100 countries from which it operates three global networks that provide integrated large-scale advertising and marketing services: McCann Worldgroup; Foote Cone & Belding (FCB); and MullenLowe Group. IPG Mediabrands is the global media and data arm of IPG and includes the UM and Initiative agencies. The firm also has agencies that specialize in certain practice areas such as Octagon (sports entertainment and lifestyle marketing) and MRM//McCann (digital services). The US is IPG's largest market accounting for about 65% of sales.

	Annual Growth	12/17	12/18	12/19	12/20	12/21
Sales ($ mil.)	6.8%	7,882.4	9,714.4	10,221.3	9,061.0	10,240.7
Net income ($ mil.)	13.3%	579.0	618.9	656.0	351.1	952.8
Market value ($ mil.)	16.7%	7,949.1	8,134.4	9,108.3	9,273.9	14,766.5
Employees	2.6%	50,200	54,000	54,300	50,200	55,600

INTERSECTIONS INC — NMS: INTX

3901 Stonecroft Boulevard
Chantilly, VA 20151
Phone: 703 488-6100
Fax: –
Web: www.intersections.com

CEO: Hari Ravichandran
CFO: Ronald L Barden
HR: Renee Waxman
FYE: December 31
Type: Public

Robert Johnson went to the crossroads to get the blues; consumers can go to Intersections to make sure they don't. Intersections provides credit management and identity theft protection to subscribers in North America. Its offerings include credit reports and ongoing record monitoring through major reporting agencies Equifax Experian and TransUnion. Its Intersections Insurance Services unit offers customers discounts on insurance products. Bank of America is the firm's #1 client accounting for more than 40% of its revenue. Amid declining sales and profits Intersections has exited the bail bonds and market intelligence businesses to focus on its core consumer protection services business.

	Annual Growth	12/12	12/13	12/14	12/15	12/16
Sales ($ mil.)	(15.8%)	349.2	310.3	246.6	203.8	175.7
Net income ($ mil.)	–	19.7	2.4	(30.7)	(44.5)	(30.5)
Market value ($ mil.)	(19.5%)	225.0	184.9	92.8	68.1	94.7
Employees	(15.2%)	817	644	478	448	422

INTERSTATE POWER & LIGHT CO — NMS: IPLD P

Alliant Energy Tower
Cedar Rapids, IA 52401
Phone: 319 786-4411
Fax: –
Web: www.alliantenergy.com

CEO: –
CFO: –
HR: –
FYE: December 31
Type: Public

Interstate Power and Light (IP&L) got the bright idea of providing electricity and has hit the road to make it happen. The company provides energy in a tri-state area of the Midwest (portions of Minnesota Iowa and Wisconsin). The Alliant Energy utility subsidiary serves more than 528355 electricity customers and more than 234560 natural gas customers in more than 700 communities. In addition IP&L has 2409 MW of generating capacity from fossil-fueled and nuclear power plants; it provides steam to two customers in Cedar Rapids; and it offers other energy-related services across its service area.

	Annual Growth	12/16	12/17	12/18	12/19	12/20
Sales ($ mil.)	1.7%	1,820.4	1,870.3	2,042.3	2,089.6	1,947.0
Net income ($ mil.)	10.3%	225.8	227.0	274.2	294.3	334.0
Market value ($ mil.)	2.1%	325.6	340.6	320.9	343.0	353.7
Employees	(8.5%)	1,679	1,670	1,628	1,418	1,176

INTERSYSTEMS CORPORATION

1 Memorial Dr.
Cambridge MA 02142
Phone: 617-621-0600
Fax: 617-494-1631
Web: www.intersystems.com

CEO: –
CFO: –
HR: –
FYE: December 31
Type: Private

InterSystems serves healthcare firms and other corporate and government clients with its flagship database software and associated products. Cache is an object database designed for high-performance handling of large volumes of transactional data. The company also offers an embeddable business intelligence product (DeepSee) for use with Cache as well as an integration platform (Ensemble). Its two healthcare-specific offerings include HealthShare which enables the creation of electronic health records and TrakCare a unified healthcare information system for use outside the US. The company which was founded in 1978 serves clients worldwide from offices in about two dozen countries.

INTERVEST BANCSHARES CORP. — NMS: IBCA

One Rockefeller Plaza, Suite 400
New York, NY 10020-2002
Phone: 212 218-2800
Fax: –
Web: www.intervestnatbank.com

CEO: –
CFO: –
HR: –
FYE: December 31
Type: Public

Intervest Bancshares is the holding company for Intervest National Bank which operates one branch in New York City and six other branches in Pinellas County Florida. Most of the company's lending activities are real estate-related: Commercial mortgages make up more than half of its loan portfolio while multifamily residential mortgages account for another 40%. Some of the company's lending has historically been carried out by its Intervest Mortgage Corporation arm. However the subsidiary drastically scaled back its lending practices as market conditions deteriorated in 2008. The family of chairman and CEO Lowell Dansker controls Intervest Bancshares.

	Annual Growth	12/08	12/09	12/10	12/11	12/12
Assets ($ mil.)	(7.5%)	2,271.8	2,401.2	2,070.9	1,969.5	1,665.8
Net income ($ mil.)	13.9%	7.3	3.1	(53.3)	11.2	12.2
Market value ($ mil.)	(0.6%)	86.1	70.8	63.3	57.2	84.0
Employees	2.3%	72	72	73	75	79

INTEST CORP. — ASE: INTT

804 East Gate Drive, Suite 200
Mt. Laurel, NJ 08054
Phone: 856 505-8800
Fax: 856 505-8801
Web: www.intest.com

CEO: Richard Grant
CFO: Duncan Gilmour
HR: Gina Floyd
FYE: December 31
Type: Public

When semiconductor makers are testing their chips inTEST handles the trickiest chores. The semiconductor test equipment supplier offers test head manipulators docking hardware and systems for managing temperatures during integrated circuit (IC) production and testing. inTEST's products facilitate testing procedures by quickly moving and connecting IC components to handling and testing equipment. The company's clients include Analog Devices Freescale Semiconductor Intel Sony STMicroelectronics and Texas Instruments (14% of sales). inTEST built up its product line through a series of acquisitions. The company gets most of its sales in the US.

	Annual Growth	12/16	12/17	12/18	12/19	12/20
Sales ($ mil.)	7.6%	40.2	66.8	78.6	60.7	53.8
Net income ($ mil.)	–	2.7	1.0	3.0	2.3	(0.9)
Market value ($ mil.)	9.0%	48.4	91.1	64.5	62.6	68.3
Employees	15.9%	113	199	209	198	204

INTEVAC, INC.

NMS: IVAC

3560 Bassett Street
Santa Clara, CA 95054
Phone: 408 986-9888
Fax: –
Web: www.intevac.com

CEO: Nigel Hunton
CFO: James Moniz
HR: Kimberly Burk
FYE: January 01
Type: Public

The more film deposits Intevac's equipment makes the more bank deposits the company can make. Its Equipment division makes machines ? called sputtering systems ? that deposit magnetic films non-magnetic films and protective carbon-based overcoats. The films magnetize the drives enabling them to record information. The Equipment division also makes disk lubrication systems used in disk drive manufacturing and processing equipment used to manufacture solar cells. Intevac's Photonics division develops electro-optical devices used in night vision and materials identification applications. Top customers include Seagate Technology US Government Jolywood (Hongkong) Industrial Holdings Co. Limited which collectively account for majority of sales. It generates most of its sales internationally.

	Annual Growth	12/17	12/18	12/19*	01/21	01/22
Sales ($ mil.)	(19.3%)	112.8	95.1	108.9	97.8	38.5
Net income ($ mil.)	45.2%	4.1	3.6	1.1	1.1	26.6
Market value ($ mil.)	(7.2%)	168.8	125.9	165.3	177.6	116.0
Employees	(12.7%)	298	257	272	269	151

*Fiscal year change

INTRALINKS HOLDINGS INC

NYS: IL

150 East 42nd Street, 8th Floor
New York, NY 10017
Phone: 212 543-7700
Fax: –
Web: www.intralinks.com

CEO: Leif Oleary
CFO: Shay Gonen
HR: –
FYE: December 31
Type: Public

IntraLinks can keep a secret. The company provides hosted software known as virtual data rooms. The IntraLinks platform is used by businesses to create secure collaborative online digital workspaces for conducting financial transactions managing mergers and acquisitions exchanging documents and collaborating with advisers customers and suppliers. While it has a strong position within the banking industry IntraLinks has branched out into other fields and tailors industry-specific versions of its products for use in markets such as life sciences legal private equity investing media and real estate. Customers have included Citigroup KPMG and Pfizer.

	Annual Growth	12/10	12/11	12/12	12/13	12/14
Sales ($ mil.)	8.5%	184.3	213.5	216.7	234.5	255.8
Net income ($ mil.)	–	(12.4)	(1.2)	(17.4)	(15.3)	(26.5)
Market value ($ mil.)	(10.7%)	1,068.0	356.2	352.2	691.3	679.3
Employees	15.6%	454	601	635	666	810

INTRAWEST RESORTS HOLDINGS INC

NYS: SNOW

1621 18th Street, Suite 300
Denver, CO 80202
Phone: 303 749-8200
Fax: –
Web: www.intrawest.com

CEO: Rusty Gregory
CFO: Adam Knox
HR: –
FYE: June 30
Type: Public

Intrawest Resorts Holdings wants to snow you a good time. The company owns six North American ski mountain resorts including well-known spots Mammoth Mountain Snowshoe Steamboat and Winter Park. Instrawest also runs a real estate business and an adventure travel business. Its mountain resorts offer activities combining outdoor adventure and fitness with services and amenities such as retail equipment rental dining lodging ski school spa services golf mountain biking and other summer activities. All told the company's six resort areas offer a total of about 8000 skiable acres and more than 1100 acres of land available for real estate development. In early 2014 Instrawest went public.

	Annual Growth	06/12	06/13	06/14	06/15	06/16
Sales ($ mil.)	2.7%	513.4	524.4	527.1	587.6	570.9
Net income ($ mil.)	–	(336.1)	(296.0)	(188.6)	(6.9)	40.9
Market value ($ mil.)	6.4%	–	–	455.4	461.7	515.8
Employees	15.7%	–	–	4,000	5,400	5,350

INTREPID POTASH INC

NYS: IPI

1001 17th Street, Suite 1050
Denver, CO 80202
Phone: 303 296-3006
Fax: –
Web: www.intrepidpotash.com

CEO: Robert Jornayvaz
CFO: Matthew Preston
HR: Katie Sweet
FYE: December 31
Type: Public

Hungry plants turn to Intrepid Potash for their food supply. The mining company produces two potassium-containing minerals potash or potassium chloride that are essential ingredients in plant and crop fertilizer. Intrepid culls these minerals from a handful mines in New Mexico and Utah where it also operates production facilities. The company has the capacity to annually produce about 390000 tons of potash and 400000 tons of Trio and sells its products primarily in the US to the agricultural industrial and feed markets. Intrepid Potash is the largest producer of muriate of potash (potassium chloride) in the US the second-largest consuming country of potash.

	Annual Growth	12/16	12/17	12/18	12/19	12/20
Sales ($ mil.)	(1.7%)	210.9	157.6	208.3	220.1	197.0
Net income ($ mil.)	–	(66.6)	(22.9)	11.8	13.6	(27.2)
Market value ($ mil.)	84.7%	27.1	62.1	33.9	35.4	315.2
Employees	(2.9%)	494	454	429	445	440

INTRICON CORP

NMS: IIN

1260 Red Fox Road
Arden Hills, MN 55112
Phone: 651 636-9770
Fax: 651 636-9503
Web: www.intricon.com

CEO: Scott Longval
CFO: Annalee Lutgen
HR: –
FYE: December 31
Type: Public

IntriCon hears its future calling and that future is in precision microminiature components and molded plastic parts such as volume controls and switches primarily used in hearing aids. IntriCon's components are also used in professional audio equipment such as headsets and microphones and in biotelemetry devices for such uses as diagnostic monitoring and drug delivery. The company has concentrated its product portfolio on what it terms "body-worn devices" through a series of acquisitions and divestitures including the 2010 sale of its RTI Electronics business line to Shackleton Equity Partners.

	Annual Growth	12/16	12/17	12/18	12/19	12/20
Sales ($ mil.)	10.9%	68.0	88.3	116.5	113.5	102.8
Net income ($ mil.)	–	(4.6)	1.8	5.5	(3.8)	(2.5)
Market value ($ mil.)	27.2%	61.8	177.2	236.1	161.1	162.0
Employees	4.3%	644	670	810	780	762

INTRUSION INC

NAS: INTZ

101 East Park Blvd, Suite 1300
Plano, TX 75074
Phone: 972 234-6400
Fax: –
Web: www.intrusion.com

CEO: Anthony Scott
CFO: B. Franklin Byrd
HR: –
FYE: December 31
Type: Public

Think of Intrusion as a virtual police force protecting and serving your network. The security specialist sells network intrusion detection and security monitoring systems. Its products include software and stand-alone security appliances that guard against misuse of classified or private information and aid law enforcement agencies in battling cyber crimes. Intrusion also provides consulting design installation and technical support services. The company sells its products directly and through distributors and resellers. Intrusion markets its products to government agencies as well as businesses ranging from health care providers to telecommunications service operators.

	Annual Growth	12/16	12/17	12/18	12/19	12/20
Sales ($ mil.)	2.1%	6.1	6.9	10.3	13.6	6.6
Net income ($ mil.)	–	(1.6)	(0.0)	2.3	4.5	(6.5)
Market value ($ mil.)	184.3%	4.7	4.7	4.7	4.7	306.9
Employees	18.5%	32	31	31	32	63

INTRUST FINANCIAL CORPORATION

105 N. Main St.
Wichita KS 67202
Phone: 316-383-1111
Fax: 316-383-5765
Web: www.intrustbank.com

CEO: Charles Q Chandler III
CFO: Jay L Smith
HR: –
FYE: December 31
Type: Private

INTRUST Financial wants to be entrusted with your cash. The holding company owns INTRUST Bank which is the largest bank headquartered in Kansas. The bank operates about 40 branches in the Sunflower State in addition to a handful of locations in Oklahoma and Arkansas. Serving consumers and small businesses the bank offers a range of financial products including savings checking and retirement accounts; CDs; credit cards; and loans and mortgages. INTRUST Bank was founded in 1876 as the Farmers and Merchants Bank. It has been run by the Chandler family for more than a century.

INTUIT INC   NMS: INTU

2700 Coast Avenue
Mountain View, CA 94043
Phone: 650 944-6000
Fax: –
Web: www.intuit.com

CEO: Sasan Goodarzi
CFO: Michelle Clatterbuck
HR: –
FYE: July 31
Type: Public

Intuit is a leading developer of software used for small business accounting (QuickBooks) and consumer tax preparation (TurboTax). Mint the online service helps manage personal finances and budgeting. Professional accountants boot up Intuit's Lacerte ProSeries and ProConnect Tax Online products. About 80% of revenue comes from products hosted on Intuit's servers what the company calls connected services. Intuit claims more than 100 million users for its products and services. The company perform its operation on its offices in the US Canada and the UK.

	Annual Growth	07/17	07/18	07/19	07/20	07/21
Sales ($ mil.)	16.8%	5,177.0	5,964.0	6,784.0	7,679.0	9,633.0
Net income ($ mil.)	20.7%	971.0	1,211.0	1,557.0	1,826.0	2,062.0
Market value ($ mil.)	40.2%	37,490.6	55,805.5	75,770.8	83,711.0	144,806.4
Employees	13.3%	8,200	8,900	9,400	10,600	13,500

INTUITIVE SURGICAL INC   NMS: ISRG

1020 Kifer Road
Sunnyvale, CA 94086
Phone: 408 523-2100
Fax: –
Web: www.intuitive.com

CEO: Gary Guthart
CFO: Marshall L Mohr
HR: –
FYE: December 31
Type: Public

Intuitive Surgical is one of the pioneers of robotic-assisted surgery. The company develops the da Vinci Surgical System a combination of software hardware and optics that allows doctors to perform robotically aided surgery from a remote console. The da Vinci system reproduces the doctor's hand movements during minimally invasive surgery in real time performed by tiny electromechanical arms and instruments. The company manufactures its systems and relies upon contract manufacturers to supply the instruments and accessories used with the systems. The US accounts for about 70% of the company's revenue.

	Annual Growth	12/17	12/18	12/19	12/20	12/21
Sales ($ mil.)	16.2%	3,128.9	3,724.2	4,478.5	4,358.4	5,710.1
Net income ($ mil.)	26.8%	660.0	1,127.9	1,379.3	1,060.6	1,704.6
Market value ($ mil.)	(0.4%)	130,539.0	171,309.7	211,454.4	292,634.4	128,521.6
Employees	21.8%	4,444	5,527	7,326	8,031	9,793

INUVO INC   ASE: INUV

500 President Clinton Ave., Suite 300
Little Rock, AR 72201
Phone: 501 205-8508
Fax: –
Web: www.inuvo.com

CEO: Richard Howe
CFO: Wallace D Ruiz
HR: Melanie Clayton
FYE: December 31
Type: Public

Inuvo provides online marketing and advertising services through its Exchange segment which includes technology and analytics and its Direct segment which consists of websites designed to drive traffic to advertisers. Included in the Exchange segment is the Inuvo Platform which offers affiliate marketing search engine marketing and lead generation services helping customers drive Web traffic and convert that traffic into sales. Its Inuvo Search platform acts as a pay-per-click marketplace. Inuvo's Direct segment websites include BabytoBee (pregnancy advice) and Kowabunga (daily deals). In 2018 e-commerce tech company ConversionPoint Technologies agreed to acquire Inuvo.

	Annual Growth	12/16	12/17	12/18	12/19	12/20
Sales ($ mil.)	(11.1%)	71.5	79.6	73.3	61.5	44.6
Net income ($ mil.)	–	(0.8)	(3.1)	(5.9)	(4.5)	(7.3)
Market value ($ mil.)	(27.8%)	163.7	79.4	104.9	29.0	44.4
Employees	3.9%	61	80	60	64	71

INVACARE CORP   NYS: IVC

One Invacare Way
Elyria, OH 44035
Phone: 440 329-6000
Fax: –
Web: www.invacare.com

CEO: Matthew Monaghan
CFO: Kathleen Leneghan
HR: –
FYE: December 31
Type: Public

The company is a leading maker of wheelchairs including manual powered custom-made and performance chairs used by athletes. It also makes other medical equipment including recreational products recreational adaptive sports products non-acute bed systems patient transfer and bathing equipment and supplementary respiratory therapy devices. The company sells its products to health care providers consumers and medical equipment dealers in North America Europe and the Asia Pacific region. Most of the Ohio-based company's revenue comes from international markets.

	Annual Growth	12/16	12/17	12/18	12/19	12/20
Sales ($ mil.)	(5.1%)	1,047.5	966.5	972.3	928.0	850.7
Net income ($ mil.)	–	(42.9)	(76.5)	(43.9)	(53.3)	(28.3)
Market value ($ mil.)	(9.0%)	504.0	650.7	166.1	348.3	345.6
Employees	(7.3%)	4,600	4,200	4,200	3,900	3,400

INVENSENSE INC   NYS: INVN

1745 Technology Drive, Suite 200
San Jose, CA 95110
Phone: 408 501-2200
Fax: –
Web: www.invensense.com

CEO: Behrooz Abdi
CFO: Mark Dentinger
HR: Nick Caminada
FYE: April 03
Type: Public

InvenSense is ready to move technology beyond point and click. The semiconductor manufacturer offers motion sound and directional interface sensors used to detect track and assess a user's position and other physical characteristics. Its MotionTracking sensors which include MEMS (microelectromechanical systems) gyroscopes and motion measurement processing units are used in consumer devices such as smartphones tablets wearables gaming consoles and smart TVs to provide a more immersive user interface. InvenSense outsources manufacturing to contractors. It generates the majority of sales in Asia. In 2016 InvenSense agreed to be bought by TDK for $1.3 billion. The deal is expected to close in 2017.

	Annual Growth	04/12*	03/13	03/14	03/15*	04/16
Sales ($ mil.)	28.6%	153.0	208.6	252.5	372.0	418.4
Net income ($ mil.)	–	36.9	51.7	6.1	(1.1)	(21.2)
Market value ($ mil.)	(17.3%)	1,683.5	993.3	2,111.3	1,419.3	785.9
Employees	24.5%	263	326	476	644	632

*Fiscal year change

INVENTERGY GLOBAL INC   NBB: INVT

19925 Stevens Creek Blvd., #142
Cupertino, CA 95014
Phone: 408 389-3510
Fax: –
Web: www.inventergy.com

CEO: Joseph Beyers
CFO: John G Niedermaier
HR: –
FYE: December 31
Type: Public

eOn Communications knows it's been ages since you've had a good customer service experience. The company's products integrate voice and Internet communications for large call centers and e-commerce customer contact centers. eOn's communications servers feature automatic call distribution e-mail queuing and customer identification. It also sells the Millennium voice switching hardware platform a private branch exchange (PBX) system with computer telephony integration. Customers include Lillian Vernon and Rockhurst University. eOn gets more than 90% of sales from the US. Chairman David Lee owns about 27% of the company.

	Annual Growth	07/12	07/13*	12/14	12/15	12/16
Sales ($ mil.)	(47.0%)	22.5	20.6	0.7	4.9	1.8
Net income ($ mil.)	–	0.5	0.1	(20.1)	(11.7)	(7.7)
Market value ($ mil.)	(4.2%)	10.2	10.3	8.1	18.6	8.6
Employees	(56.3%)	82	75	15	8	3

*Fiscal year change

INVENTURE FOODS INC.   NMS: SNAK

5415 East High Street, Suite #350
Phoenix, AZ 85054
Phone: 623 932-6200
Fax: –
Web: www.inventurefoods.com

CEO: Dylan B Lissette
CFO: John W Thompson
HR: –
FYE: December 26
Type: Public

Inventure Foods caters to avid snackers and the more health conscious alike. The company's Rader Farms business grows and processes berries and produces frozen fruits vegetables and beverages for sale primarily to grocery and club stores and mass merchandisers. The snack business makes potato and other snack chips pretzels and more under Bob's Texas Style Braids Poore Brothers Boulder Canyon Natural Foods to name a few. Inventure Foods also makes salted snacks branded with the T.G.I. Friday's and Nathan's Famous names and manufactures private label snacks for food stores in the US. Costco is the company's #1 customer. With roots in salty snacks Inventure is now focused on healthier fare.

	Annual Growth	12/11	12/12	12/13	12/14	12/15
Sales ($ mil.)	14.9%	162.2	185.2	215.6	285.7	282.6
Net income ($ mil.)	–	2.8	7.4	6.6	10.6	(20.8)
Market value ($ mil.)	17.7%	73.3	123.7	264.2	241.6	140.8
Employees	25.2%	448	497	785	821	1,100

INVESCO LTD.   NYSE: IVZ

1555 Peachtree St. NE Ste. 1800
Atlanta GA 30309
Phone: 404-479-1095
Fax: 510-492-1098
Web: www.esstech.com

CEO: Martin Flanagan
CFO: L. Allison Dukes
HR: –
FYE: December 31
Type: Public

Invesco offers a range of investment products and services including mutual funds exchange-traded funds separately managed accounts and savings plans. Invesco serves retail and institutional clients in more than 20 countries in North America Europe the Middle East and the Asia/Pacific region. It operates under the Invesco Invesco Perpetual and Powershares brands (it dropped the AIM brand in 2010). Subsidiary Atlantic Trust offers private wealth management services. Invesco and its subsidiaries have more than $660 billion of assets under management. The company also owns turnaround firm WL Ross.

INVESCO MORTGAGE CAPITAL INC   NYS: IVR

1555 Peachtree Street N.E., Suite 1800
Atlanta, GA 30309
Phone: 404 892-0896
Fax: –
Web: www.invescomortgagecapital.com

CEO: John Anzalone
CFO: Richard Phegley
HR: –
FYE: December 31
Type: Public

Invesco Mortgage Capital is ready to roll now that the mortgage industry has finally reversed its course. Invesco Mortgage is a real estate investment trust (REIT) that finances and manages residential and commercial mortgage-backed securities and mortgage loans. It purchases agency-backed mortgages secured by the likes of Fannie Mae and Freddie Mac and is managed and advised by sibling Invesco Institutional a subsidiary of Invesco Ltd. The firm's mortgage-backed securities portfolio is concentrated within the four populous states of California Florida Texas and New York.

	Annual Growth	12/17	12/18	12/19	12/20	12/21
Assets ($ mil.)	(18.0%)	18,657.3	17,813.5	22,346.5	8,632.9	8,443.8
Net income ($ mil.)	–	348.6	(70.8)	364.1	(1,674.4)	(90.0)
Market value ($ mil.)	(37.2%)	5,881.7	4,776.6	5,492.4	1,115.0	917.1
Employees	–	–	–	–	–	–

INVESTMENT TECHNOLOGY GROUP INC.   NYS: ITG

165 Broadway
New York, NY 10006
Phone: 212 588-4000
Fax: –
Web: www.itginc.com

CEO: Douglas Cifu
CFO: –
HR: –
FYE: December 31
Type: Public

Investment Technology Group (ITG) provides automated equity option and derivative trading products and services related to order and execution management; it is involved throughout the trading process from analysis before the trade to post-transaction processing and evaluation. The company also offers tools to assist in portfolio modeling and construction compliance monitoring and asset valuation. ITG serves institutional investors brokerages alternative investment funds and asset managers in more than 50 countries in North America Europe and the Asia/Pacific region; international operations account for roughly 55% of sales. It is being acquired by financial services firm Virtu Financial.

	Annual Growth	12/13	12/14	12/15	12/16	12/17
Sales ($ mil.)	(2.3%)	530.8	559.8	634.8	469.1	483.7
Net income ($ mil.)	–	31.1	50.9	91.6	(25.9)	(39.4)
Market value ($ mil.)	(1.6%)	670.3	678.8	554.9	643.5	627.6
Employees	(1.7%)	1,001	1,087	1,037	956	934

INVESTORS BANCORP INC (NEW)   NMS: ISBC

101 JFK Parkway
Short Hills, NJ 07078
Phone: 973 924-5100
Fax: –
Web: www.investorsbank.com

CEO: –
CFO: –
HR: –
FYE: December 31
Type: Public

Investors Bancorp is the holding company for Investors Savings Bank which serves New Jersey and New York from more than 130 branch offices. Founded in 1926 the bank offers such standard deposit products as savings and checking accounts CDs money market accounts and IRAs. Nearly 40% of the bank's loan portfolio is made up of residential mortgages while multi-family loans and commercial real estate loans make up more than 50% combined. The bank also originates business industrial and consumer loans. Founded in 1926 Investors Bancorp's assets now exceed $20 billion.

	Annual Growth	12/16	12/17	12/18	12/19	12/20
Assets ($ mil.)	2.9%	23,174.7	25,129.2	26,229.0	26,698.8	26,023.2
Net income ($ mil.)	3.6%	192.1	126.7	202.6	195.5	221.6
Market value ($ mil.)	(6.7%)	3,458.6	3,441.3	2,578.5	2,954.1	2,618.1
Employees	0.6%	1,829	1,959	1,962	1,793	1,874

INVESTORS CAPITAL HOLDINGS, LTD.   ASE: ICH

Six Kimball Lane, Suite 150 — CEO: –
Lynnfield, MA 01940 — CFO: –
Phone: 781 593-8565 — HR: –
Fax: – — FYE: March 31
Web: www.investorscapital.com — Type: Public

The name pretty much says it all. Investors Capital Holdings offers brokerage and investment advisory services to clients across the US through more than 500 registered independent advisors. The company provides marketing technology and compliance support as well as approved investment products to its representatives in exchange for a negotiated percentage of commissions. Its Investors Capital Corporation (ICC) broker-dealer subsidiary provides securities trading research online brokerage and other services. Subsidiary ICC Insurance Agency sells variable life insurance and annuities. The company's Investors Capital Advisory business surpassed $1 billion in assets under management in 2010

	Annual Growth	03/09	03/10	03/11	03/12	03/13
Sales ($ mil.)	1.0%	81.6	79.2	85.3	81.0	84.9
Net income ($ mil.)	–	(1.8)	0.3	(0.9)	(2.3)	0.4
Market value ($ mil.)	28.7%	9.7	10.4	43.4	28.3	26.6
Employees	(3.8%)	69	81	83	57	59

INVESTORS HERITAGE CAPITAL CORP.   NBB: IHRC

200 Capital Avenue — CEO: –
Frankfort, KY 40602 — CFO: Larry J Johnson II
Phone: 502 223-2361 — HR: –
Fax: – — FYE: December 31
Web: www.investorsheritage.com — Type: Public

Investors Heritage Capital puts its money into insurance. The company (formerly Kentucky Investors) operates through primary subsidiary Investors Heritage Life Insurance which provides group and individual life insurance burial insurance credit insurance and similar products which are sold through independent agents and through funeral homes in about 30 states. Investors Heritage Life Insurance does most of its business in the East Midwest and Southeast. Investors Heritage Capital also owns non-insurance subsidiaries which offer commercial printing investment holding services and funeral lending services.

	Annual Growth	12/12	12/13	12/14	12/15	12/16
Assets ($ mil.)	0.1%	576.0	563.6	585.2	570.0	579.4
Net income ($ mil.)	6.1%	2.1	1.8	1.3	1.0	2.7
Market value ($ mil.)	(2.4%)	19.5	22.9	23.7	21.0	17.7
Employees	(54.6%)	1,905	2,058	1,936	1,541	81

INVESTORS TITLE CO.   NMS: ITIC

121 North Columbia Street — CEO: James Fine
Chapel Hill, NC 27514 — CFO: James A Fine Jr
Phone: 919 968-2200 — HR: –
Fax: – — FYE: December 31
Web: www.invtitle.com — Type: Public

Investors Title insures you in case your land is well not completely yours. It's the holding company for Investors Title Insurance and Northeast Investors Title Insurance which underwrite land title insurance and sell reinsurance to other title companies. (Title insurance protects those who invest in real property against loss resulting from defective titles.) Investors Title Insurance serves customers from about 30 offices in North Carolina South Carolina Michigan and Nebraska and through branches or agents in 20 additional states. Northeast Investors Title operates through an agency office in New York. Founder and CEO J. Allen Fine and his family own more than 20% of Investors Title.

	Annual Growth	12/16	12/17	12/18	12/19	12/20
Assets ($ mil.)	5.4%	228.9	248.9	244.3	263.9	282.9
Net income ($ mil.)	19.2%	19.5	25.7	21.9	31.5	39.4
Market value ($ mil.)	(0.8%)	299.5	375.3	334.3	301.2	289.5
Employees	9.3%	320	383	385	402	456

ION GEOPHYSICAL CORP   NYS: IO

2105 CityWest Blvd., Suite 100 — CEO: Christopher Usher
Houston, TX 77042-2855 — CFO: Michael Morrison
Phone: 281 933-3339 — HR: –
Fax: 281 879-3626 — FYE: December 31
Web: www.iongeo.com — Type: Public

There's a whole lotta shakin' goin' on at ION Geophysical. The seismic data-acquisition imaging and software systems company helps worldwide petroleum exploration contractors identify and measure subsurface geological structures that could contain oil and gas. Its data acquisition products are capable of processing 3-D 4-D and multi-component 3-C seismic data for land marine and transition areas (such as swamps shoreline marsh and jungle). ION Geophysical also makes other products such as geophysical software digital sensors cables and telemetry systems. Its marine positioning systems map the geography of the ocean's floor. Nearly 75% of total revenue accounts outside North America.

	Annual Growth	12/16	12/17	12/18	12/19	12/20
Sales ($ mil.)	(8.2%)	172.8	197.6	180.0	174.7	122.7
Net income ($ mil.)	–	(65.1)	(30.2)	(71.2)	(48.2)	(37.2)
Market value ($ mil.)	(20.2%)	86.0	283.1	74.2	124.4	34.8
Employees	(2.8%)	480	478	496	519	428

IONIS PHARMACEUTICALS INC   NMS: IONS

2855 Gazelle Court — CEO: Brett P Monia
Carlsbad, CA 92010 — CFO: Elizabeth L Hougen
Phone: 760 931-9200 — HR: –
Fax: – — FYE: December 31
Web: www.ionispharma.com — Type: Public

Ionis Pharmaceuticals develops biotech drugs to target neurological disorders and other conditions. Products are based on its antisense technology in which drugs attach themselves to strands of RNA to prevent them from producing disease-causing proteins; the hoped-for result is a therapy that fights disease without harming healthy cells. Commercial medicines approved in major global markets include SPINRAZA for spinal muscular atrophy and TEGSEDI for polyneuropathy caused by hereditary TTR amyloidosis (marketed by Akcea). Ionis has more than 40 pipeline drugs under development in therapeutic areas such as neurodegenerative diseases cardiometabolic diseases cancer and others.

	Annual Growth	12/16	12/17	12/18	12/19	12/20
Sales ($ mil.)	20.4%	346.6	507.7	599.7	1,122.6	729.3
Net income ($ mil.)	–	(86.6)	(6.0)	273.7	294.1	(451.3)
Market value ($ mil.)	4.3%	6,713.7	7,060.4	7,588.2	8,479.5	7,936.3
Employees	14.9%	435	547	737	817	757

IOWA HEALTH SYSTEM

1776 WEST LAKES PKWY # 400 — CEO: Sue Thompson
WEST DES MOINES, IA 502668377 — CFO: Mark Johnson
Phone: 515-241-6161 — HR: –
Fax: – — FYE: December 31
Web: www.unitypoint.org — Type: Private

Iowa Health System (IHS) which does business as UnityPoint is an integrated health care system that operates more than 20 acute care hospitals in large communities throughout Iowa as well as parts of western Illinois and Madison Wisconsin. UnityPoint also supports more than 15 rural hospitals and it manages about 300 physician clinics located in rural and suburban areas. The system's hospitals provide general medical-surgical care as well as care in a number of medical specialties such as cardiovascular disease mental health and home health services.

	Annual Growth	12/13	12/14	12/15	12/16	12/17
Sales ($ mil.)	2.5%	–	–	–	4,054.8	4,157.2
Net income ($ mil.)	54.4%	–	–	–	148.7	229.5
Market value ($ mil.)	–	–	–	–	–	–
Employees	–	–	–	–	–	18,923

IOWA STATE UNIVERSITY OF SCIENCE AND TECHNOLOGY

515 MORRILL RD
AMES, IA 500112105
Phone: 515-294-6162
Fax: -
Web: www.iastate.edu

CEO: -
CFO: -
HR: -
FYE: June 30
Type: Private

Home to the Cyclones athletics teams Iowa State University of Science and Technology (ISU) can be a whirlwind experience for some. ISU is a public land-grant institution offering higher education courses and programs with an emphasis on science technology and related areas. ISU's eight colleges offer more than 100 undergraduate degrees and nearly 200 fields of study leading to graduate and professional degrees. The university has an enrollment of more than 31000 students and charges more than $7720 in tuition and fees for resident students for two semesters.

	Annual Growth	06/16	06/17	06/18	06/19	06/20
Sales ($ mil.)	0.6%	-	920.8	948.4	952.0	937.0
Net income ($ mil.)	(17.8%)	-	77.6	58.9	97.3	43.2
Market value ($ mil.)	-	-	-	-	-	-
Employees	-	-	-	-	-	5,800

IPASS INC   NAS: IPAS

3800 Bridge Parkway
Redwood Shores, CA 94065
Phone: 650 232-4100
Fax: -
Web: www.ipass.com

CEO: -
CFO: Darin R Vickery
HR: -
FYE: December 31
Type: Public

On the information superhighway iPass is in the passing lane. The company provides mobile employees with remote access to their company's internal networks and data. Through agreements with telecom carriers ISPs and other network service providers its mobile offerings create a virtual network in more than 120 countries. The network includes dial-up Ethernet and Wi-Fi access points. The cloud-based Open Mobile platform lets users connect from mobile devices over a wide range of carrier-independent networks. iPass also offers managed network services that allow enterprises to offer in-store and in-office Wi-Fi for employees and customers. It generates more than half of its sales in the US.

	Annual Growth	12/13	12/14	12/15	12/16	12/17
Sales ($ mil.)	(16.4%)	111.1	69.8	62.6	63.2	54.4
Net income ($ mil.)	-	(12.3)	7.0	(15.5)	(7.8)	(20.6)
Market value ($ mil.)	(24.2%)	10.9	9.5	6.9	11.4	3.6
Employees	(18.0%)	350	250	205	163	158

IPAYMENT INC.

40 Burton Hills Blvd. Ste. 415
Nashville TN 37215
Phone: 615-665-1858
Fax: 847-391-2253
Web: www.uop.com

CEO: -
CFO: Mark C Monaco
HR: -
FYE: December 31
Type: Private

iPayment doesn't want small businesses to pay an arm and a leg for credit and debit card processing. The company's approximately 133000 clients are mostly small US merchants firms taking money over the phone or Internet and those that previously may have accepted only cash or checks as payment. iPayment markets through independent sales organizations and has grown by consolidating its niche buying a dozen competitors and merchant portfolios since 2003. A typical iPayment merchant generates less than $185000 of charge volume per year with an average transaction value of about $70. Company co-founder Greg Daily sold his two-thirds' stake and stepped down as CEO in 2011.

IPC HEALTHCARE, INC.   NMS: IPCM

4605 Lankershim Boulevard, Suite 617
North Hollywood, CA 91602
Phone: 888 447-2362
Fax: -

CEO: Adam D Singer
CFO: Richard H Kline III
HR: -
FYE: December 31
Type: Public

IPC The Hospitalist Company (IPC) is on the leading edge of a growing US trend toward hospitalist specialization. The staffing firm provides 1800 hospitalists to more than 400 hospitals and 1200 post-acute care facilities facilities in about 30 states. Hospitalists are health care providers (physicians nurses and physicians assistants) who oversee all of a patient's treatment from the beginning to the end of their stay. They answer questions and coordinate treatment programs to improve the quality of care and reduce the length of a patient's hospital stay. In addition to providing staff IPC offers training data management billing and risk management services for its medical professionals and clients.

	Annual Growth	12/09	12/10	12/11	12/12	12/13
Sales ($ mil.)	18.4%	310.5	363.4	457.5	523.5	609.5
Net income ($ mil.)	22.1%	18.6	24.3	29.3	32.6	41.4
Market value ($ mil.)	15.6%	565.8	663.8	778.0	675.7	1,010.6
Employees	17.5%	1,451	1,792	2,030	2,381	2,769

IPC SYSTEMS INC.

Harborside Financial Center 1500 Plaza 10 15th Fl.
Jersey City NJ 07311
Phone: 201-253-2000
Fax: 201-253-2361
Web: www.ipc.com

CEO: Robert Santella
CFO: Noah Asher
HR: -
FYE: September 30
Type: Private

IPC Systems makes and services "turret" communications systems also called dealerboards that combine PBX data switching computer telephony voice recording and multimedia capabilities. Its products are used by financial institutions for voice and data transmission and routing in their trading environments. These products are designed to integrate with products from technology vendors such as Avaya and Cisco. With more than 115000 dealerboards worldwide IPC's financial extranet includes some 4000 locations in more than 700 cities. Its offerings also include enhanced voice services business continuity and support. IPC Systems is owned by Silver Lake Partners.

IPG PHOTONICS CORP   NMS: IPGP

50 Old Webster Road
Oxford, MA 01540
Phone: 508 373-1100
Fax: -
Web: www.ipgphotonics.com

CEO: Eugene Shcherbakov
CFO: Timothy Mammen
HR: -
FYE: December 31
Type: Public

IPG Photonics develops manufactures and sells fiber lasers and amplifiers and diode lasers which are primarily used in materials processing applications (some 90% of sales) such as welding cutting marking and engraving. Its fiber lasers are also used in additive manufacturing such as 3D printing and ablation. The company's largest customer is Han's Laser ehich account for nearly 10% of sales. Deriving about 80% of its sales outside North America IPG Photonics operates sales offices in the US Germany and Russia.

	Annual Growth	12/17	12/18	12/19	12/20	12/21
Sales ($ mil.)	0.9%	1,408.9	1,459.9	1,314.6	1,200.7	1,460.9
Net income ($ mil.)	(5.4%)	347.6	404.0	180.2	159.6	278.4
Market value ($ mil.)	(5.3%)	11,351.1	6,005.5	7,682.2	11,863.2	9,125.2
Employees	5.1%	5,390	6,465	5,960	6,060	6,580

IQVIA HOLDINGS INC
NYS: IQV

4820 Emperor Blvd.
Durham, NC 27703
Phone: 919 998-2000
Fax: –
Web: www.quintiles.com

CEO: Ari Bousbib
CFO: Ronald Bruehlman
HR: –
FYE: December 31
Type: Public

IQVIA Holdings provides advanced analytics technology solution and clinical research services to the life sciences industry. It also offers the IQVIA Connected Intelligence which delivers powerful insights that enable customers to accelerate clinical development and commercialization of medical treatments. It also boasts one of the largest and most comprehensive health information collections in the world which includes patient records prescription and promotional data medical claims genomic social media and many more. It has a diversified base of over 10000 clients including pharmaceutical companies biotechnology companies device and diagnostic companies and consumer health companies in over 100 countries. IQVIA gets about 35% of its revenue in the US.

	Annual Growth	12/17	12/18	12/19	12/20	12/21
Sales ($ mil.)	9.3%	9,739.0	10,412.0	11,088.0	11,359.0	13,874.0
Net income ($ mil.)	(7.3%)	1,309.0	259.0	191.0	279.0	966.0
Market value ($ mil.)	30.3%	18,659.7	22,142.0	29,449.6	34,149.8	53,775.9
Employees	9.5%	55,000	58,000	67,000	70,000	79,000

IRC RETAIL CENTERS LLC

814 COMMERCE DR STE 300
OAK BROOK, IL 605238823
Phone: 877-206-5656
Fax: –
Web: www.pinetree.com

CEO: Mark E Zalatoris
CFO: Brett A Brown
HR: –
FYE: December 31
Type: Private

IRC Retail Centers (formerly Inland Real Estate Corporation) buys leases and operates retail properties mainly in the Midwest with a concentration in the Chicago and Minneapolis/St. Paul metropolitan markets. The self-managed real estate investment trust (REIT) owns about 150 properties most of which are strip shopping centers anchored by a grocery or big-box store. It also invests in single-tenant retail properties and develops properties usually through joint ventures. The REIT's portfolio totals about 14 million sq. ft. of leasable space in a dozen states. IRC Retail Centers was acquired by DRA Advisors in early 2015.

	Annual Growth	12/10	12/11	12/12	12/13	12/14
Assets ($ mil.)	12.5%	–	–	1,243.4	1,529.9	1,573.0
Net income ($ mil.)	48.7%	–	–	17.7	111.7	39.1
Market value ($ mil.)	–	–	–	–	–	–
Employees	–	–	–	–	–	129

IRIDEX CORP.
NMS: IRIX

1212 Terra Bella Avenue
Mountain View, CA 94043-1824
Phone: 650 940-4700
Fax: –
Web: www.iridex.com

CEO: David Bruce
CFO: Fuad Ahmad
HR: –
FYE: January 02
Type: Public

A meeting with IRIDEX can be an eye-opening experience. The company makes laser systems and peripheral devices used to treat serious eye conditions including the three major causes of blindness: macular degeneration glaucoma and diabetic retinopathy. The company markets its products under such brands as IQ and OcuLight through a direct sales staff in the US and through distributors in more than 100 countries worldwide. Its ophthalmic systems including laser consoles delivery devices and disposable probes are used by ophthalmologists in hospitals surgery centers and physician practice centers. IRIDEX exited its aesthetics business (lasers for dermatology and plastic surgery procedures) in 2012.

	Annual Growth	12/16	12/17	12/18	12/19*	01/21
Sales ($ mil.)	(4.7%)	46.2	41.6	42.6	43.4	36.3
Net income ($ mil.)	–	(11.7)	(12.9)	(12.8)	(8.8)	(6.3)
Market value ($ mil.)	(29.1%)	195.4	105.9	61.9	32.7	34.9
Employees	(3.6%)	154	154	152	132	128

*Fiscal year change

IRIDIUM COMMUNICATIONS INC
NMS: IRDM

1750 Tysons Boulevard, Suite 1400
McLean, VA 22102
Phone: 703 287-7400
Fax: –
Web: www.iridium.com

CEO: Matthew J Desch
CFO: Thomas J Fitzpatrick
HR: –
FYE: December 31
Type: Public

If you want to make a phone call from the North Pole you want Iridium Communications (formerly Iridium Satellite). The company offers mobile voice data and Internet services worldwide targeting companies that operate in remote areas. While Iridium focuses on such commercial industries as energy defense maritime and mining its main customer is the US government. Boeing primarily operates and maintains the Iridium satellite system which consists of more than 65 operational satellites with in-orbit and ground spares and related ground infrastructure. The mobile satellite communications company has operations center in Virginia and generates almost 55% of sales in the US.

	Annual Growth	12/17	12/18	12/19	12/20	12/21
Sales ($ mil.)	8.2%	448.0	523.0	560.4	583.4	614.5
Net income ($ mil.)	–	233.9	(13.4)	(162.0)	(56.1)	(9.3)
Market value ($ mil.)	36.8%	1,549.8	2,423.3	3,236.3	5,165.0	5,423.1
Employees	6.6%	420	475	512	522	543

IRIDIUM COMMUNICATIONS INC.
NASDAQ: IRDM

1750 Tysons Blvd. Ste. 400
McLean VA 22102
Phone: 703-287-7400
Fax: 703-287-7450
Web: www.iridium.com

CEO: Matthew J Desch
CFO: –
HR: –
FYE: December 31
Type: Public

If you want to make a phone call from the North Pole you want Iridium Communications (formerly Iridium Satellite). The company offers mobile voice data and Internet services worldwide targeting companies that operate in remote areas. While Iridium focuses on such commercial industries as energy defense maritime and mining its main customer is the US Department of Defense. Boeing primarily operates and maintains the Iridium satellite system which consists of 66 low-earth-orbit satellites linked to ground stations (the world's largest commercial satellite operation). The company has operations centers in Arizona and Virginia.

IRIS INTERNATIONAL INC.
NASDAQ: IRIS

9172 Eton Ave.
Chatsworth CA 91311-5874
Phone: 818-709-1244
Fax: 818-700-9661
Web: www.proiris.com

CEO: Cesar M Garcia
CFO: Amin I Khalifa
HR: –
FYE: December 31
Type: Public

To really know a person IRIS International doesn't look deep into their eyes. Instead the company manufactures automated in-vitro diagnostic systems that analyze bodily fluids. Beginning with urinalysis technology the company has expanded to include blood (hematology) and other fluids. Its Iris Diagnostics division develops the iQ family of automated imaging systems used in urinalysis and microscopic analysis as well as related consumables (reagents and test strips) and services. The Iris Sample Processing division markets centrifuges small instruments and laboratory supplies for specimen processing. The company was acquired by industrial and medical conglomerate Danaher in October 2012.

IROBOT CORP
NMS: IRBT

8 Crosby Drive
Bedford, MA 01730
Phone: 781 430-3000
Fax: –
Web: www.irobot.com

CEO: Colin Angle
CFO: Julie Zeiler
HR: Russell Campanello
FYE: January 01
Type: Public

iRobot is a leading consumer robot company that designs and builds robots that empower people to do more around the globe. Models range from basic sweepers to higher-end devices that can be programed for specific houses. iRobot has also introduced robotic mops and is developing a robotic lawn mower. The company sells its home products worldwide through retailers and distributors. It operates worldwide but generates just more than half its revenue in the US. Since its founding iRobot has sold more than 30 million robots.

	Annual Growth	12/17	12/18	12/19*	01/21	01/22
Sales ($ mil.)	12.1%	883.9	1,092.6	1,214.0	1,430.4	1,565.0
Net income ($ mil.)	(9.8%)	51.0	88.0	85.3	147.1	30.4
Market value ($ mil.)	(3.0%)	2,071.4	2,196.1	1,409.7	2,168.3	1,779.2
Employees	8.3%	920	1,032	1,128	1,209	1,372

*Fiscal year change

IRON MOUNTAIN INC (NEW)
NYS: IRM

One Federal Street
Boston, MA 02110
Phone: 617 535-4766
Fax: –
Web: www.ironmountain.com

CEO: William Meaney
CFO: Barry Hytinen
HR: –
FYE: December 31
Type: Public

Iron Mountain is one of the world's largest records storage and information management companies. The firm stores lot of paper as well as microfilm and microfiche audio and video files film and X-rays. It also provides records filing database management disaster recovery and information disposal services. The company also operates data centers across the US. It serves about 225000 corporate clients in North America Europe Latin America the Middle East and the Asia/Pacific region. Iron Mountain generates most of its sales in the US.

	Annual Growth	12/16	12/17	12/18	12/19	12/20
Sales ($ mil.)	4.2%	3,511.5	3,845.6	4,225.8	4,262.6	4,147.3
Net income ($ mil.)	34.5%	104.8	183.8	363.4	267.4	342.7
Market value ($ mil.)	(2.4%)	9,363.1	10,876.5	9,342.9	9,187.3	8,498.3
Employees	0.0%	24,000	24,000	26,000	25,000	24,000

IRONPLANET INC.

4695 Chabot Dr. Ste. 102
Pleasanton CA 94588-2756
Phone: 925-225-8800
Fax: 925-225-8610
Web: www.ironplanet.com

CEO: Gregory J Owens
CFO: –
HR: –
FYE: December 31
Type: Private

Need to auction off heavy equipment but don't feel like sweating it out in an auction house? An online marketplace operator IronPlanet provides virtual auctions through which customers buy and sell a variety of heavy construction mining and agricultural equipment including bulldozers dump trucks excavators tractors and harvesters. The company which operates on a consignment basis offers weekly public auctions as well as private and daily auctions; it also provides equipment inspection services. It serves customers — from sole proprietors to large corporations — in North America and to a lesser extent the Asia-Pacific region. Founded in 1999 IronPlanet withdrew its initial public offering in 2012.

IRONWOOD PHARMACEUTICALS INC
NMS: IRWD

100 Summer Street, Suite 2300
Boston, MA 02110
Phone: 617 621-7722
Fax: –
Web: www.ironwoodpharma.com

CEO: Thomas McCourt
CFO: Sravan Emany
HR: –
FYE: December 31
Type: Public

Ironwood Pharmaceuticals takes a stand against gastrointestinal ailments and other medical conditions. The firm develops internally discovered gastrointestinal drugs; its first commercial product Linzess (or linaclotide) a treatment for irritable bowel syndrome (IBS) and chronic constipation is sold in the US and in Canada under the brand name Constella. To support the development and commercialization of linaclotide worldwide it partnered with pharmaceutical companies including with Allergan in the US AstraZeneca in China and Astellas in Japan. The company is also advancing its MD-7246 a delayed release formulation of linaclotide as an oral intestinal non-opioid pain-relieving agent for patients with abdominal pain associated with certain GI diseases. MD-7246 is designed to have the pain-relieving effect of linaclotide with minimal impact on bowel function.

	Annual Growth	12/17	12/18	12/19	12/20	12/21
Sales ($ mil.)	8.5%	298.3	346.6	428.4	389.5	413.8
Net income ($ mil.)	–	(116.9)	(282.4)	21.5	106.2	528.4
Market value ($ mil.)	(6.1%)	2,428.9	1,678.7	2,156.7	1,845.6	1,889.3
Employees	(26.0%)	730	515	317	232	219

ISC8 INC
NBB: ISCI

151 Kalmus Drive, Suite A-203
Costa Mesa, CA 92626
Phone: 714 444-8753
Fax: –
Web: www.isc8.com

CEO: –
CFO: –
HR: –
FYE: September 30
Type: Public

Irvine Sensors puts its hopes in big returns from tiny products. Much of the company's sales come from research and development contracts related to its minute solid-state microcircuitry technology in which circuits are assembled in 3-D stacks (rather than flat layouts) to lower weight and boost performance. Irvine Sensors also develops and manufactures miniaturized infrared and electro-optical cameras and image processors as well as products incorporating the components primarily for defense and security applications. The US government and its contractors account for nearly all of the company's sales. Leading customers include the US Air Force US Army and Optics 1 a defense contractor.

	Annual Growth	09/09*	10/10	10/11*	09/12	09/13
Sales ($ mil.)	(54.3%)	11.5	11.7	14.1	4.2	0.5
Net income ($ mil.)	–	0.9	(11.2)	(15.8)	(19.7)	(28.0)
Market value ($ mil.)	(43.4%)	100.7	25.5	19.5	22.6	10.3
Employees	(17.2%)	85	81	150	89	40

*Fiscal year change

ISG TECHNOLOGY LLC

127 N 7TH ST
SALINA, KS 674012603
Phone: 785-823-1555
Fax: –
Web: www.isgtech.com

CEO: Ben Foster
CFO: –
HR: –
FYE: March 31
Type: Private

ISG Technology hopes to help you capitalize on all of your technology operations. The company which does business as Integrated Solutions Group provides information technology (IT) and telecommunications services primarily to small and midsized businesses in the midwestern US. ISG services include network design hardware and software procurement web development and hosting and training. Clients come from fields such as financial services manufacturing telecommunications and health care. The company has seven locations in the Midwest including offices in Kansas Missouri and Oklahoma.

	Annual Growth	03/04	03/05	03/06	03/07	03/08
Sales ($ mil.)	(75.9%)	–	–	954.3	44.4	55.3
Net income ($ mil.)	77119.0%	–	–	0.0	0.2	12.5
Market value ($ mil.)	–	–	–	–	–	–
Employees	–	–	–	–	–	118

ISIGN SOLUTIONS INC

NBB: ISGN

2033 Gateway Place, Suite 659
San Jose, CA 95110
Phone: 650 802-7888
Fax: –
Web: www.isignnow.com

CEO: Philip Sassower
CFO: Michael Engmann
HR: –
FYE: December 31
Type: Public

If your intelligent communication involves hunting and pecking try Communication Intelligence Corp. (CIC). The company's handwriting recognition software including its SignatureOne Sign-it and iSign products recognizes character strokes of words from English Chinese and Western European languages and converts them to digital text. Industries served by CIC include banking insurance and financial services which often require electronic signatures for legal documents. Customers have included Charles Schwab and Wells Fargo. CIC was founded in 1981 in conjunction with Stanford University's Research Institute. Phoenix Ventures is the company's largest shareholder with a 37% stake.

	Annual Growth	12/16	12/17	12/18	12/19	12/20
Sales ($ mil.)	(2.4%)	1.1	1.0	0.9	0.8	1.0
Net income ($ mil.)	–	(3.5)	(1.9)	(1.0)	(1.1)	(0.5)
Market value ($ mil.)	(15.3%)	3.5	2.0	4.0	2.6	1.8
Employees	0.0%	14	16	7	14	14

ISLE OF CAPRI CASINOS INC

NMS: ISLE

600 Emerson Road, Suite 300
Saint Louis, MO 63141
Phone: 314 813-9200
Fax: –
Web: www.isleofcapricasinos.com

CEO: Eric L Hausler
CFO: Michael A Hart
HR: –
FYE: April 24
Type: Public

Rollin' on the river takes on new meaning when you're talking about Isle of Capri Casinos. The company owns and operates about 15 dockside riverboat and land-based casinos in Colorado Iowa Louisiana Mississippi Missouri and Pennsylvania. In addition the company has a pari-mutuel harness racetrack and casino in Pompano Beach Florida. Most of the company's casinos have hotels and feature restaurants live entertainment and private lounges for high-rollers. Altogether Isle of Capri's properties feature approximately 12000 slot machines and 300 table games (including some 80 poker tables) as well as more than 2200 hotel rooms and 40 restaurants.

	Annual Growth	04/12	04/13	04/14	04/15	04/16
Sales ($ mil.)	0.0%	977.4	965.2	954.6	996.3	978.6
Net income ($ mil.)	–	(129.8)	(47.6)	(127.7)	5.2	46.2
Market value ($ mil.)	23.5%	262.1	287.4	275.2	605.4	610.3
Employees	(3.8%)	7,700	7,500	7,000	7,100	6,600

ISO NEW ENGLAND INC.

1 SULLIVAN RD
HOLYOKE, MA 010402841
Phone: 413-535-4000
Fax: –
Web: www.iso-ne.com

CEO: Gordon Van Welie
CFO: Robert Ludlow
HR: Janice S Dickstein
FYE: December 31
Type: Private

The transmission lines in the Northeast power grid keep humming because of ISO New England. The not-for-profit corporation is responsible for electricity generation and transmission throughout Connecticut Maine Massachusetts New Hampshire Rhode Island and Vermont. The independent systems operator (ISO) runs about 31000 MW generating capacity grid that is owned by utilities of the New England Power Pool and manages the wholesale electric market. The power grid is made up of hundreds of generating units (about 350 under direct ISO New England control) connected by some 9000 miles of high-voltage transmission lines. It provides power to more than 7.2 million households and businesses.

	Annual Growth	12/15	12/16	12/17	12/18	12/19
Sales ($ mil.)	2.3%	–	181.6	184.4	193.0	194.3
Net income ($ mil.)	–	–	0.0	0.0	0.0	0.0
Market value ($ mil.)	–	–	–	–	–	–
Employees	–	–	–	–	–	610

ISOLA GROUP LTD.

3100 W. Ray Rd. Ste. 301
Chandler AZ 85226
Phone: 480-893-6527
Fax: 480-893-1409
Web: www.isola-group.com

CEO: Travis Kelly
CFO: Troy Ruhrer
HR: –
FYE: December 31
Type: Private

Isola puts the "board" in printed circuit board (PCB). The company manufactures base materials used to make PCBs at more than a dozen facilities around the globe. Its manufacturing processes for laminates and other materials such as glass cellulose and epoxy use state-of-the-art technologies (closed-loop feed-forward and feed-back cure and thickness control systems) to ensure composite integrity. Other technical innovations ensure tight dielectric thickness control. End users include customers in the automotive computer medical military and wireless communications markets. Nearly 80% of sales come from outside the US. Investment firm TPG Capital owns Isola which filed to go public in late 2011.

ISOMET CORP.

NBB: IOMT

5263 Port Royal Road
Springfield, VA 22151
Phone: 703 321-8301
Fax: 703 321-8546
Web: www.isomet.com

CEO: –
CFO: Jerry Rayburn
HR: –
FYE: December 31
Type: Public

Isomet never met a laser beam it couldn't control. The company makes acousto-optic systems that manipulate interactions between light and sound to control laser beams especially in color image reproduction applications such as laser printing and phototypesetting. Isomet had long made graphic arts systems of its own — including digital scanners and graphics plotters — but has been winding down that business as it expands its production of birefringent materials (such as lead molybdate) used in fiber-optic applications. The company also offers components such as athermal filters anti-reflection coatings tunable filters and optical switches.

	Annual Growth	12/15	12/16	12/17	12/18	12/19
Sales ($ mil.)	(2.1%)	4.0	2.8	3.4	3.9	3.6
Net income ($ mil.)	–	0.1	(0.3)	(0.1)	0.1	(0.2)
Market value ($ mil.)	–	0.0	0.0	0.0	0.1	0.1
Employees	–	–	–	–	–	–

ISORAY, INC.

ASE: ISR

350 Hills St., Suite 106
Richland, WA 99354
Phone: 509 375-1202
Fax: –
Web: www.isoray.com

CEO: Lori Woods
CFO: Jonathan Hunt
HR: Jennifer Streeter
FYE: June 30
Type: Public

IsoRay hopes its medical device is a seed of change for cancer patients. Through subsidiary IsoRay Medical the company produces and sells FDA-approved Proxcelan Cs-131 brachytherapy seeds which are mainly used in the treatment of prostate cancer. Brachytherapy is a procedure that implants anywhere from eight to 125 small seed devices containing therapeutic radiation as close as possible to a cancerous tumor. The seeds can be used alone or in combination with external beam radiation surgery or other therapies. Proxcelan Cs-131's application is also expanding to other areas of the body with US approval for use in the treatment of head and neck tumors as well as eye lung colorectal and chest wall cancers.

	Annual Growth	06/17	06/18	06/19	06/20	06/21
Sales ($ mil.)	20.5%	4.8	5.9	7.3	9.7	10.1
Net income ($ mil.)	–	(6.2)	(6.7)	(5.1)	(3.4)	(3.4)
Market value ($ mil.)	6.3%	88.7	63.9	58.2	78.8	113.2
Employees	16.8%	36	38	43	53	67

ISRAEL DISCOUNT BANK OF NEW YORK

511 5th Ave.
New York NY 10017
Phone: 212-551-8500
Fax: 212-551-8540
Web: www.idbny.com

CEO: Ziv Biron
CFO: Scott Graham
HR: –
FYE: December 31
Type: Subsidiary

Israel Discount Bank of New York (IDB Bank) is all over the map. The institution offers personal commercial and private banking services in the US and abroad. Focusing on middle-market businesses the bank provides lending services such as working capital commercial real estate loans construction and land development loans asset-based lending and factoring. It specializes in serving accounting law and professional services firms and not-for-profit organizations. International services include import financing letters of credit and foreign exchange. A subsidiary of Israel Discount Bank Limited IDB Bank has about 10 locations in the US Israel and South America.

ISRAMCO, INC.

1001 West Loop South, Suite 750
Houston, TX 77027
Phone: 713 621-5946
Fax: –
Web: www.isramcousa.com

NAS: ISRL
CEO: Haim Tsuff
CFO: Edy Francis
HR: –
FYE: December 31
Type: Public

There may be milk and honey on the other side of the River Jordan but to date not much oil. Because of that Isramco focuses on growing its US operations and is engaged (through subsidiaries) in oil and gas exploration primarily in Colorado Louisiana Oklahoma New Mexico Texas Utah and Wyoming. It also has oil and gas assets in offshore Israel. In 2015 Isramco reported proved reserves of 36.2 million barrels of oil equivalent. Its 2015 production average was 3.8 million barrels of oil per day. It also operates a well service company serving oil companies and independent oil and natural gas production firms active in the US. Chairman and CEO Haim Tsuff owns 71% of Isramco.

	Annual Growth	12/13	12/14	12/15	12/16	12/17
Sales ($ mil.)	(1.0%)	68.7	93.9	74.5	54.9	65.9
Net income ($ mil.)	–	(6.7)	5.2	(17.3)	6.7	(24.3)
Market value ($ mil.)	(4.7%)	345.3	375.0	242.7	337.8	284.4
Employees	(4.1%)	228	263	224	170	193

ISTA PHARMACEUTICALS INC.

50 Technology Dr.
Irvine CA 92618
Phone: 949-788-6000
Fax: 949-788-6010
Web: www.istavision.com

NASDAQ: ISTA
CEO: –
CFO: –
HR: –
FYE: December 31
Type: Public

ISTA Pharmaceuticals has set its sights on treating eye diseases. The pharmaceutical company has products in development and on the market. ISTA's marketed products include Bepreve (for itchy eyes associated with allergic conjunctivitis) Istalol (a glaucoma treatment) and Bromday (used for pain and inflammation following cataract surgery) in the US. Its drug Vitrase is a spreading agent that promotes absorption of injected drugs. The drug candidates in the company's pipeline include treatments for dry eye syndrome ocular pain and inflammation. The company has additional ocular and allergy treatments in research and development stages. ISTA was acquired by global eye health company Bausch & Lomb in 2012.

ISTAR INC

1114 Avenue of the Americas, 39th Floor
New York, NY 10036
Phone: 212 930-9400
Fax: –
Web: www.istar.com

NYS: STAR
CEO: Jay Sugarman
CFO: Jeremy Fox-geen
HR: –
FYE: December 31
Type: Public

iStar Financial is a real estate investment trust (REIT) that finances invests in and develops real estate and real estate related projects as part of its fully-integrated investment platform. Its financing activities include first mortgages senior and mezzanine real estate debt and corporate capital net lease financing and equity investments. Its operating properties represent a pool of assets across a broad range of geographies and property types including industrial hotel multifamily retail condominium entertainment/leisure and office properties. Office properties make up of some 20% of its secured assets while land makes up another about 10%

	Annual Growth	12/16	12/17	12/18	12/19	12/20
Sales ($ mil.)	2.7%	477.0	679.2	798.1	479.5	530.9
Net income ($ mil.)	–	95.3	175.7	(32.3)	324.0	(42.4)
Market value ($ mil.)	4.7%	915.0	835.8	678.3	1,073.3	1,098.4
Employees	(7.2%)	193	186	166	155	143

ITA GROUP, INC

4600 WESTOWN PKWY STE 100
WEST DES MOINES, IA 502661047
Phone: 515-326-3400
Fax: –
Web: www.itagroup.com

CEO: Thomas J Mahoney
CFO: Brent V Waal
HR: –
FYE: August 31
Type: Private

ITA Group (doing business as ITAGroup) bets it can make your company better. Specializing in performance marketing ITAGroup (standing for "Ideas to Action") builds and manages programs that help clients increase sales and customer satisfaction through incentives and training. The company's services include research and program design administration fulfillment and measurement for employee recognition and rewards programs business-to-business loyalty programs and sales incentive programs. ITAGroup also provides business meeting and event planning services.

	Annual Growth	08/08	08/09	08/10	08/11	08/12
Sales ($ mil.)	–	–	–	0.0	233.1	288.3
Net income ($ mil.)	–	–	–	0.0	0.0	0.0
Market value ($ mil.)	–	–	–	–	–	–
Employees	–	–	–	–	–	590

ITC HOLDINGS CORP

27175 Energy Way
Novi, MI 48377
Phone: 248 946-3000
Fax: –
Web: www.itc-holdings.com

NYS: ITC
CEO: Linda Blair
CFO: Gretchen Holloway
HR: –
FYE: December 31
Type: Public

ITC Holdings (ITC) owns and operates 15000 circuit miles of power transmission lines. Through its subsidiaries ITC Transmission Michigan Electric Transmission Company (METC) ITC Great Plains and ITC Midwest ITC operates regulated high-voltage transmission systems in Michigan's Lower Peninsula and portions of Illinois Iowa Kansas Minnesota Missouri and Oklahoma serving a combined peak load of more than 26000 MW. ITC is a member of the Midwest ISO (MISO) a regional transmission organization. The company also operates as ITC Grid Development which invests in transmission infrastructure development. In 2016 Fortis agreed to buy the company for $11.3 billion.

	Annual Growth	12/10	12/11	12/12	12/13	12/14
Sales ($ mil.)	10.1%	696.8	757.4	830.5	941.3	1,023.0
Net income ($ mil.)	13.8%	145.7	171.7	187.9	233.5	244.1
Market value ($ mil.)	(10.1%)	9,615.6	11,772.1	11,931.9	14,865.6	6,272.3
Employees	7.9%	433	452	503	539	587

ITC^DELTACOM INC.

7037 Old Madison Pike
Huntsville AL 35806
Phone: 256-382-5900
Fax: 256-264-9924
Web: www.deltacom.com

CEO: –
CFO: –
HR: –
FYE: December 31
Type: Subsidiary

ITC^DeltaCom keeps businesses in the Southeast connected. Doing business as Deltacom the competitive local-exchange carrier (CLEC) operates in eight states — Alabama Florida Georgia Louisiana Mississippi North Carolina South Carolina and Tennessee — offering integrated voice and data communications including local and long-distance phone service and DSL Internet access mainly to business customers. Deltacom also wholesales transmission capacity to other carriers on its fiber-optic network which spans more than 16000 miles from New York to Florida and as far west as Texas. Deltacom was acquired by ISP EarthLink for $524 million in late 2010 and folded into the company's EarthLink Business segment.

ITERIS INC
NAS: ITI

1250 S. Capital of Texas Hwy., Building 1, Suite 330
Austin, TX 78746
Phone: 512 716-0808
Fax: –
Web: www.iteris.com

CEO: J. Bergera
CFO: Douglas Groves
HR: –
FYE: March 31
Type: Public

Thanks to the technology and services Iteris provides for traffic management motorcycle cops might have to start using their ticket pads for scribbling shopping lists. The company's roadway sensors business segment includes video vehicle detection systems installed at intersections to help manage traffic flow and traffic data collection; product brands include Vantage SmartCycle and VersiCam. In 2020 the company sold its Agriculture and Weather Analytics segment.

	Annual Growth	03/17	03/18	03/19	03/20	03/21
Sales ($ mil.)	5.1%	96.0	103.7	99.1	114.1	117.1
Net income ($ mil.)	–	(4.8)	(3.5)	(7.8)	(5.6)	10.1
Market value ($ mil.)	3.2%	226.8	206.8	173.8	133.4	257.2
Employees	0.4%	432	447	393	440	439

ITEX CORP
NBB: ITEX

15900 SE Eastgate Way, Suite 100
Bellevue, WA 98008
Phone: 425 463-4000
Fax: 425 463-4040
Web: www.itex.com

CEO: Steven White
CFO: John Wade
HR: Mike Ryan
FYE: July 31
Type: Public

ITEX provides a business-to-business payment system for corporate members through a licensed broker network across the US and Canada. In lieu of cash some 24000 member businesses of the company's ITEX Marketplace barter time-sensitive slow-moving or surplus goods and services valued in ITEX dollars. Members represent a variety of industries including advertising construction dining health care hospitality media printing and professional services. ITEX administers the trade exchange; it (or any of its 95 franchisees or licensed brokers) also acts as a record keeper for member transactions.

	Annual Growth	07/16	07/17	07/18	07/19	07/20
Sales ($ mil.)	(8.2%)	11.1	10.2	9.7	8.9	7.9
Net income ($ mil.)	–	(1.5)	0.6	0.6	0.8	0.8
Market value ($ mil.)	(0.8%)	6.3	5.9	6.6	6.9	6.1
Employees	–	–	13	–	–	–

ITRON INC
NMS: ITRI

2111 N Molter Road
Liberty Lake, WA 99019
Phone: 509 924-9900
Fax: –
Web: www.itron.com

CEO: Thomas L Deitrich
CFO: Joan S Hooper
HR: –
FYE: December 31
Type: Public

Itron is a leader in the Industrial Internet of Things (IIoT) enabling utilities and cities to safely securely and reliably deliver critical infrastructure solutions for electric natural gas and water utilities. Its proven platform enables smart networks software services devices and sensors to help customers better manage their operations in the energy water and smart city spaces. It also offers end-to-end device solutions networked solutions and outcomes-based products and services to the utility and municipal sectors. Its systems are installed in some 100 countries. The company also provides consulting licensing hardware technology and technical support services. Around 65% of Itron's total sales comes from US and Canada.

	Annual Growth	12/16	12/17	12/18	12/19	12/20
Sales ($ mil.)	1.9%	2,013.2	2,018.2	2,376.1	2,502.5	2,173.4
Net income ($ mil.)	–	31.8	57.3	(99.3)	49.0	(58.0)
Market value ($ mil.)	11.1%	2,541.9	2,758.3	1,912.6	3,395.3	3,878.6
Employees	(1.9%)	7,300	7,800	8,000	7,900	6,749

ITT EDUCATIONAL SERVICES INC
NBB: ESIN Q

13000 North Meridian Street
Carmel, IN 46032-1404
Phone: 317 706-9200
Fax: –
Web: www.ittesi.com

CEO: –
CFO: –
HR: –
FYE: December 31
Type: Public

ITT Educational Services operates Daniel Webster College a single-campus institution located in Nashua New Hampshire. Daniel Webster offers undergraduate and graduate programs in arts and sciences aviation sciences business and management and engineering and computer sciences. It has some 650 students and about 80 faculty members. In 2016 ITT Educational Services shut down its namesake ITT Technical Institutes which provided technology-focused degrees in such areas as computer-aided design (CAD) engineering technology and information technology after the US government barred the schools from using federal financial aid to enroll new students. There were some 140 ITT Technical Institutes throughout the US.

	Annual Growth	12/11	12/12	12/13	12/14	12/15
Sales ($ mil.)	(13.2%)	1,499.9	1,287.2	1,072.3	961.8	849.8
Net income ($ mil.)	(47.5%)	307.8	140.5	(27.0)	29.3	23.3
Market value ($ mil.)	(49.4%)	1,346.8	409.8	795.0	227.5	88.3
Employees	(4.3%)	10,000	9,800	9,500	8,900	8,400

ITT INC
NYS: ITT

1133 Westchester Avenue
White Plains, NY 10604
Phone: 914 641-2000
Fax: –
Web: www.itt.com

CEO: Denise L Ramos
CFO: Thomas M Scalera
HR: Jason Greenwood
FYE: December 31
Type: Public

ITT Corporation hopes its customers are pumped moved and energized about its products. A diversified manufacturer ITT makes a range of industrial products through four operating segments: industrial process (pumping systems though Goulds Pumps valves and services for oil and gas and chemical companies); motion technologies (brake pads and friction materials for transportation markets); interconnect solutions (ICS connectors for fiber optic RF power and other electronic products); and control technologies (hydraulic valves actuators and switches for aerospace companies).

	Annual Growth	12/17	12/18	12/19	12/20	12/21
Sales ($ mil.)	1.7%	2,585.3	2,745.1	2,846.4	2,477.8	2,765.0
Net income ($ mil.)	29.2%	113.5	333.7	325.1	72.5	316.3
Market value ($ mil.)	17.6%	4,563.1	4,127.1	6,319.3	6,585.2	8,737.2
Employees	(0.3%)	10,000	10,000	10,500	9,700	9,900

IVCI, LLC

601 OLD WILLETS PATH # 100
HAUPPAUGE, NY 117884111
Phone: 631-273-5800
Fax: –
Web: www.ivci.com

CEO: Robert Swing
CFO: –
HR: –
FYE: December 31
Type: Private

IVCi screens its calls. The company resells and installs cameras video servers speaker phones and other equipment used for video audio and Web conferences. It supplies and supports equipment made by such industry leaders as Cisco and Polycom. In addition to installation IVCi's Audio/Visual Division offers conference room design consulting project management on-site technical assistance maintenance and training services. Its private video communications network enables 24-hour access to a secure managed conferencing environment. It serves customers in the education to health care industries as well legal and federal and state government clients. IVCi was founded in 1995 by CEO Robert Swing.

	Annual Growth	06/13	06/14*	12/14	12/15	12/16
Sales ($ mil.)	58.9%	–	32.3	65.6	69.4	81.5
Net income ($ mil.)	121.1%	–	0.5	1.0	0.7	2.5
Market value ($ mil.)	–	–	–	–	–	–
Employees	–	–	–	–	–	180

*Fiscal year change

IVEY MECHANICAL COMPANY, LLC

134 W WASHINGTON ST
KOSCIUSKO, MS 390903633
Phone: 662-289-3646
Fax: –
Web: www.iveymechanical.com

CEO: –
CFO: Randy Dew
HR: –
FYE: December 31
Type: Private

More blue-collar than Ivy League Ivey Mechanical Company gets an "A" for its slate of mechanical services. The specialty contractor designs fabricates and manufactures sheet metal work as well as air conditioning/heating and medical gas and plumbing/piping systems. It also provides system repairs maintenance and emergency services. With projects covering 30 states Ivey Mechanical drives preconstruction and construction and prefabrication work for commercial and industrial facilities correctional health care and government contracts. The company operates through service offices dotting the Southeast US. It is owned by CEO Larry Terrell along with members of Ivey Mechanical's management team.

	Annual Growth	12/13	12/14	12/15	12/16	12/17
Sales ($ mil.)	10.0%	–	125.2	129.6	168.0	166.6
Net income ($ mil.)	–	–	0.0	0.0	0.0	0.0
Market value ($ mil.)	–	–	–	–	–	–
Employees	–	–	–	–	–	790

IWATT INC.

675 Campbell Technology Pkwy. Ste. 150
Campbell CA 95008
Phone: 408-374-4200
Fax: 408-341-0455
Web: www.iwatt.com

CEO: Ronald Edgerton
CFO: James McCanna
HR: –
FYE: December 31
Type: Private

iWatt makes watts behave inside electronic gear. The fabless semiconductor company designs power management chips used in flat panel displays notebook computers digital cameras and other portable devices. Its chips are designed into high-density low-cost AC/DC and DC/DC power supplies that make more efficient use of electricity saving on operating costs and helping equipment run cooler. iWatt also makes custom power converter modules for computer servers and workstations. Founded in 2000 iWatt has offices in China Hong Kong Japan South Korea Taiwan and the US. Investors include VantagePoint Venture Partners (39% of shares) and Sigma Partners (31%). The company filed for an IPO in 2012.

IXIA

26601 West Agoura Road
Calabasas, CA 91302
Phone: 818 871-1800
Fax: 818 871-1805
Web: www.ixiacom.com

NMS: XXIA
CEO: –
CFO: Jason Kary
HR: –
FYE: December 31
Type: Public

Ixia nixes network glitches. The company designs network validation testing hardware and software that provides visibility into traffic performance and also addresses the network applications. Hardware consists of optical and electrical interface cards and the chassis to hold them. Its software tests the functionality of video voice conformance and security across ethernet wi-fi and 3G/LTE equipment and networks. Ixia primarily serves network equipment manufacturers (Cisco) service providers (AT&T) corporate customers (Bloomberg) the federal government (US Army) and its contractors (General Dynamics). Geographically sales are about evenly divided between the US and international customers.

	Annual Growth	12/11	12/12	12/13	12/14	12/15
Sales ($ mil.)	13.8%	308.4	413.4	467.3	464.5	516.9
Net income ($ mil.)	(29.3%)	23.8	45.5	11.9	(41.6)	6.0
Market value ($ mil.)	4.3%	849.3	1,372.1	1,075.5	909.1	1,004.4
Employees	7.4%	1,300	1,710	1,846	1,755	1,727

IXYS CORP.

1590 Buckeye Drive
Milpitas, CA 95035-7418
Phone: 408 457-9000
Fax: –
Web: www.ixys.com

NMS: IXYS
CEO: Nathan Zommer
CFO: Uzi Sasson
HR: –
FYE: March 31
Type: Public

The US Constitution does a pretty good job with transfer of power. So does IXYS in a different context. IXYS (pronounced ike-sys) makes a variety of power semiconductors (including transistors and rectifiers) and power modules which convert and control electric power in electronic gear. They are used in such equipment as power supplies and medical electronics. IXYS also sells microcontroller chips display drivers power management integrated circuits (ICs) gallium arsenide field-effect transistors and proprietary direct copper bond substrate technology. The company's 2500-plus customers include ABB Boston Scientific Emerson Medtronic Schneider Electric and Siemens. Three quarters of the company's sales come from customers outside the US.

	Annual Growth	03/12	03/13	03/14	03/15	03/16
Sales ($ mil.)	(3.6%)	368.0	280.0	336.3	338.8	317.2
Net income ($ mil.)	(16.5%)	30.3	7.6	6.0	23.7	14.7
Market value ($ mil.)	(4.0%)	414.2	300.9	356.1	386.5	352.0
Employees	(4.1%)	1,173	1,010	1,016	958	992

J & D PRODUCE, INC.

7310 N EXPRESSWAY 281
EDINBURG, TX 785421232
Phone: 956-380-0353
Fax: –
Web: www.littlebearproduce.com

CEO: –
CFO: –
HR: Eddie Escovar
FYE: December 31
Type: Private

J & D Produce is a leading vegetable and melon grower in the Rio Grande Valley of Texas. Marketing its produce under the Little Bear brand the company harvests packs and ships such items as asparagus carrots and lettuce along with cabbage limes and a variety of melons. It supplies fresh produce primarily to supermarkets grocery stores and other food retailers. J & D Produce was founded in the early 1980s by Jimmy Bassetti and his wife Diane.

	Annual Growth	12/07	12/08	12/12	12/13	12/14
Sales ($ mil.)	(2.2%)	–	121.1	0.0	106.0	105.8
Net income ($ mil.)	(14.4%)	–	3.2	0.0	1.3	1.2
Market value ($ mil.)	–	–	–	–	–	–
Employees	–	–	–	–	–	420

J M SMITH CORPORATION

101 W SAINT JOHN ST # 305
SPARTANBURG, SC 293065150
Phone: 864-542-9419
Fax: –
Web: www.jmsmith.com

CEO: Paula Harper Bethea
CFO: Philip Ryan
HR: –
FYE: February 28
Type: Private

J M Smith Corporation is the third-largest privately-held company in South Carolina operating industry-leading healthcare and technology business units including Smith Drug Company which provides purchasing and distribution services in more than 30 US states and RxMedic Systems a pharmacy automation manufacturer. Founded in 1925 by James M. Smith Sr. as a single community pharmacy in Asheville North Carolina the company supplies services and technology to organizations across the US.

	Annual Growth	02/11	02/12	02/13	02/14	02/15
Sales ($ mil.)	4.2%	–	–	2,362.8	2,370.0	2,566.2
Net income ($ mil.)	33.8%	–	–	26.3	38.4	47.1
Market value ($ mil.)	–	–	–	–	–	–
Employees	–	–	–	–	–	235

J&J SNACK FOODS CORP.

NMS: JJSF

6000 Central Highway
Pennsauken, NJ 08109
Phone: 856 665-9533
Fax: –
Web: www.jjsnack.com

CEO: Daniel Fachner
CFO: Ken Plunk
HR: –
FYE: September 25
Type: Public

J & J Snack Foods manufactures snack foods and distributes frozen beverages which it markets nationally to the food service and retail supermarket industries. The company offers an assortment of brands including SUPERPRETZEL ICEE frozen drinks Whole Fruit juice treats Tio Pepe's churros and Funnel Cake Factory funnel cakes. J & J also sells snacks such as Auntie Anne's pretzels Sour Patch Kids sticks and Minute Maid's frozen lemonade and juice bars. The company's customer base comprises small and large foodservice operators including snack bars and food stands and supermarket chains. It also has approximately 119000 company-owned and customer-owned frozen beverage dispensing machines. Products are manufactured in facilities in more than a dozen US states and reach customers via 160 warehouse and distribution facilities in the US as well as Canada and Mexico.

	Annual Growth	09/17	09/18	09/19	09/20	09/21
Sales ($ mil.)	1.4%	1,084.2	1,138.3	1,186.5	1,022.0	1,144.6
Net income ($ mil.)	(8.5%)	79.2	103.6	94.8	18.3	55.6
Market value ($ mil.)	4.0%	2,505.7	2,879.6	3,652.7	2,459.7	2,932.3
Employees	0.6%	4,200	4,500	4,600	4,100	4,300

J. CREW GROUP INC.

770 Broadway
New York NY 10003
Phone: 212-209-2500
Fax: 212-209-2666
Web: www.jcrew.com

CEO: Jan Singer
CFO: Vincent Zanna
HR: –
FYE: January 31
Type: Private

The crews appearing in the polished catalogs of the J. Crew Group are far from motley. The retailer is known for its preppy fashions including jeans khakis and other basic (but pricey) items sold to young professionals through its catalogs websites and more than 360 retail and factory stores in the US (and now Canada) under the J. Crew crewcuts (for kids) and Madewell banners. Madewell is a women's-only collection of hip casual clothes. CEO Millard "Mickey" Drexler recruited from The Gap to revive J. Crew's ailing fortunes has led a renaissance at the firm capped by a public offering in 2006. In 2011 the company was taken private by TPG Capitaland Leonard Green & Partners.

J. D. STREETT & COMPANY, INC.

144 WELDON PKWY
MARYLAND HEIGHTS, MO 630433100
Phone: 314-432-6600
Fax: –
Web: www.jdstreett.com

CEO: Newell A Baker Jr
CFO: James A Schuering
HR: Kristy Pedroli
FYE: December 31
Type: Private

Word on the street is that J. D. Streett tries to stay streets ahead of its rivals as it supplies its customers with a wide range of fuels oxygenates lubricants transmission fluids and antifreezes. The company operates more than 20 retail locations (convenience stores and gas stations) under its own ZX label and/or BP brand in Missouri and Illinois. J. D. Streett also serves more than 10 international markets. In addition the company offers terminalling services for distillate ethanol and oil products and owns and operates a chain of discount cigarette shops (most that also sell beer) across Missouri.

	Annual Growth	12/16	12/17	12/18	12/19	12/20
Sales ($ mil.)	(5.3%)	–	184.4	204.4	189.0	156.8
Net income ($ mil.)	21.8%	–	3.4	2.1	2.5	6.2
Market value ($ mil.)	–	–	–	–	–	–
Employees	–	–	–	–	–	240

J. F. WHITE CONTRACTING COMPANY

10 BURR ST
FRAMINGHAM, MA 01701-4692
Phone: 508-879-4700
Fax: –
Web: www.jfwhite.com

CEO: –
CFO: –
HR: –
FYE: September 30
Type: Private

From excavating the foundation for the Harvard Business School to working on Boston's Big Dig project J.F. White Contracting has been a key player in heavy civil construction in New England for over 80 years. The group has civil design/build mechanical electrical and fiber optic/telecom divisions to provide a large range of engineering construction infrastructure and equipment and wiring installation services. J.F. White also has a diving division (marine construction) to complement its heavy civil construction operations. The company was founded in 1924 by Joseph F. White Sr.

	Annual Growth	09/07	09/08	09/09	09/11	09/12
Sales ($ mil.)	–	–	0.0	251.8	374.5	271.3
Net income ($ mil.)	–	–	0.0	0.0	0.0	0.0
Market value ($ mil.)	–	–	–	–	–	–
Employees	–	–	–	–	–	400

J. H. FINDORFF & SON, INC.

300 S BEDFORD ST
MADISON, WI 537033622
Phone: 608-257-5321
Fax: –
Web: www.findorff.com

CEO: –
CFO: Daniel L Petersen
HR: –
FYE: September 30
Type: Private

J.H. Findorff & Son has been building its resume since the 19th century. The company constructs commercial and institutional projects in the US Midwest. It provides general contracting design/build and construction management services. Projects include schools government buildings health care centers hotels condos offices and shopping complexes. Findorff also self-performs trade work including carpentry concrete masonry drywall and steel erection. Among its projects is Madison Wisconsin's Children's Museum and the Overture Center for the Arts. It also built the Wisconsin Institutes for Discovery at The University of Wisconsin-Madison. John Findorff founded the company as J.H. Findorff in 1890.

	Annual Growth	09/05	09/06	09/08	09/11	09/12
Sales ($ mil.)	7.4%	–	209.1	322.0	209.2	320.9
Net income ($ mil.)	(14.0%)	–	10.2	3.8	0.3	4.1
Market value ($ mil.)	–	–	–	–	–	–
Employees	–	–	–	–	–	500

J.D. ABRAMS, L.P.

5811 TRADE CENTER DR #1
AUSTIN, TX 787441309
Phone: 512-322-4000
Fax: –
Web: www.jdabrams.com

CEO: –
CFO: –
HR: –
FYE: December 31
Type: Private

J.D. Abrams builds the infrastructure that helps travelers drive across Texas. While highway and bridge construction projects from the Texas Department of Transportation make up the bulk of its construction work the civil engineering and construction firm also works on flood control dams reservoirs waterways railroad test track airport taxiways and other infrastructure projects in Texas and elsewhere in the Sun Belt. J.D. Abrams also operates two subsidiaries Transmountain Equipment and Austin Prestress which runs a concrete casting plant. Founded in 1966 the company operates from four Texas-based offices in Austin Dallas El Paso and Houston.

	Annual Growth	12/06	12/07	12/08	12/09	12/12
Sales ($ mil.)	42.4%	–	–	42.9	307.8	176.6
Net income ($ mil.)	–	–	–	1.2	15.0	(2.3)
Market value ($ mil.)	–	–	–	–	–	–
Employees	–	–	–	–	–	750

J.E. DUNN CONSTRUCTION COMPANY

1001 LOCUST ST
KANSAS CITY, MO 641061904
Phone: 816-474-8600
Fax: –
Web: www.jedunn.com

CEO: Gordon E Landsford III
CFO: Beth A Soukup
HR: –
FYE: December 31
Type: Private

From first building designs to the last brick J.E. Dunn Construction helps make building plans a done deal. The contractor offers general construction services construction management and design/build services nationwide. It's known for its work on campus health care and commercial projects including the BayCare Health System CHI Health - Creighton University Medical Center - Bergan Mercy Seaton Hall/Regnier Hall Decatur High School and Ron Clark Academy. Founded in 1924 the company is one of Kansas City's top commercial construction firms and has been listed as one of the nation's top 20 general building companies. It operates as a subsidiary of J.E. Dunn Construction Group.

	Annual Growth	12/13	12/14	12/15	12/16	12/17
Sales ($ mil.)	9.5%	–	2,242.7	2,909.4	2,909.4	2,945.8
Net income ($ mil.)	–	–	0.0	0.0	0.0	0.0
Market value ($ mil.)	–	–	–	–	–	–
Employees	–	–	–	–	–	1,635

J.E. DUNN CONSTRUCTION GROUP, INC.

1001 LOCUST ST
KANSAS CITY, MO 641061904
Phone: 816-474-8600
Fax: –
Web: www.jedunn.com

CEO: Gordon Lansford III
CFO: Beth Soukup
HR: –
FYE: December 31
Type: Private

Owned by descendants of founder John Ernest Dunn J.E. Dunn Construction Group operates as the holding company for a group of construction firms and JE Dunn Capital Partners its real estate investment subsidiary. Founded in 1924 it builds institutional commercial and industrial structures nationwide. It also provides construction and program management and design/build services. J.E. Dunn Construction which is among the largest US general builders was one of the first contractors to offer the construction management delivery method. Some of its major projects have included an IRS facility and the world headquarters for H&R Block both located in Kansas City Missouri.

	Annual Growth	12/12	12/13	12/14	12/15	12/19
Sales ($ mil.)	11.6%	–	2,243.7	2,243.7	2,910.6	4,329.2
Net income ($ mil.)	–	–	0.0	0.0	0.0	0.0
Market value ($ mil.)	–	–	–	–	–	–
Employees	–	–	–	–	–	2,080

J.M. HUBER CORPORATION

499 Thornall St. 8th Fl.
Edison NJ 08837-2267
Phone: 732-549-8600
Fax: 732-549-7256
Web: www.huber.com

CEO: Michael Marberry
CFO: Jeffrey Prosinski
HR: Eddie Cartee
FYE: December 31
Type: Private

As great as toothpaste paint and tires may be J.M. Huber claims to make them even better. The company makes specialty additives and minerals used to thicken and improve the cleaning properties of toothpaste the brightness and gloss of paper the strength and durability of rubber and the flame-retardant properties of wire and cable. The diverse company also makes oriented strand board (a plywood substitute) explores for and produces oil and gas and provides technical and financial services. Huber also makes hydrocolloids (thickeners for gums) among other products through subsidiary CP Kelco.

J.R. SIMPLOT COMPANY

999 Main St. Ste. 1300
Boise ID 83702
Phone: 208-336-2110
Fax: 510-271-6493
Web: www.kaiserpermanente.org

CEO: –
CFO: Annette Elg
HR: –
FYE: August 31
Type: Private

J.R. Simplot hopes you'll have fries with that. Potato potentate J. R. "Jack" Simplot simply shook hands with McDonald's pioneer Ray Kroc in the mid-1960s and his company's french fry sales have sizzled ever since. Simplot still remains the major french fry supplier for McDonald's and supplies Burger King and Wendy's as well. Along with potatoes J.R. Simplot produces fruits and vegetables under the RoastWorks and Simplot Classic labels. It owns and operates more than 82000 acres on some 40 farms located primarily in Idaho and Washington. It produces more than 3 billion pounds of frozen french fries and formed potatoes annually making it one of the world's largest processors of frozen potatoes.

JABIL INC

10800 Roosevelt Boulevard North
St. Petersburg, FL 33716
Phone: 727 577-9749
Fax: –
Web: www.jabil.com

NYS: JBL
CEO: Mark Mondello
CFO: Michael Dastoor
HR: –
FYE: August 31
Type: Public

Jabil Inc. is one of the leading providers of worldwide manufacturing services and solutions. Some of its services include comprehensive electronics design production and product management services to companies in various industries and end markets. The company distributes its products and has facilities globally including China Hungary Malaysia Mexico Singapore and the US where it gets about 10% of its revenue. Its segments typically serve customers in the 5G wireless and cloud digital print and retail industrial and semi-cap and networking and storage industries as well.

	Annual Growth	08/17	08/18	08/19	08/20	08/21
Sales ($ mil.)	11.3%	19,063.1	22,095.4	25,282.3	27,266.4	29,285.0
Net income ($ mil.)	52.4%	129.1	86.3	287.1	53.9	696.0
Market value ($ mil.)	18.5%	4,530.0	4,271.3	4,162.9	4,934.5	8,927.0
Employees	13.3%	170,000	199,000	200,000	240,000	280,000

JACK HENRY & ASSOCIATES, INC.

NMS: JKHY

663 Highway 60, P.O. Box 807
Monett, MO 65708
Phone: 417 235-6652
Fax: -
Web: www.jackhenry.com

CEO: David Foss
CFO: Kevin Williams
HR: -
FYE: June 30
Type: Public

Jack Henry & Associates (JKHY) provides an extensive array of products and services that includes processing transactions automating business processes and managing information for nearly 8400 financial institutions and diverse corporate entities. Products include core processing systems electronic funds transfer (EFT) systems automated teller machine networking products digital check and document imaging systems Internet banking and electronic payment solutions. The company's three primary brands include Jack Henry Banking Symitar and ProfitStars. JHA also provides bills payment services through iPay and Banno. It primarily serves commercial banks and savings institutions with up to $50 billion in assets. The company sold select products and services primarily in Latin America the Caribbean and Canada.

	Annual Growth	06/17	06/18	06/19	06/20	06/21
Sales ($ mil.)	5.3%	1,431.1	1,536.6	1,552.7	1,697.1	1,758.2
Net income ($ mil.)	6.1%	245.8	376.7	271.9	296.7	311.5
Market value ($ mil.)	12.0%	7,686.6	9,646.9	9,910.4	13,618.6	12,100.1
Employees	3.0%	5,972	6,327	6,402	6,717	6,714

JACK IN THE BOX, INC.

NMS: JACK

9357 Spectrum Center Blvd.
San Diego, CA 92123
Phone: 858 571-2121
Fax: -
Web: www.jackinthebox.com

CEO: Darin Harris
CFO: Timothy Mullany
HR: -
FYE: October 03
Type: Public

Jack in the Box is one of the nation's largest hamburger chains. The company operates and franchises about 2220 Jack in the Box quick-service restaurants primarily in the western and southern US including one in Guam. Jack in the Box offers such standard fast-food fare as burgers fries and ice cream as well as salads tacos curly fries egg rolls and breakfast items. About 165 locations are company-owned while the rest are franchised. Opened in 1951 the company allows its guests to customize their meals to their tastes and order any product when they want it including breakfast items any time of day or night.

	Annual Growth	10/17*	09/18	09/19	09/20*	10/21
Sales ($ mil.)	(7.4%)	1,553.9	869.7	950.1	1,021.5	1,143.7
Net income ($ mil.)	5.2%	135.3	121.4	94.4	89.8	165.8
Market value ($ mil.)	(0.6%)	2,141.6	1,761.5	1,900.6	1,686.0	2,091.0
Employees	(24.8%)	16,600	5,200	5,200	5,200	5,300

*Fiscal year change

JACKSON COUNTY MEMORIAL HOSPITAL AUTHORITY

1200 E PECAN ST
ALTUS, OK 735216141
Phone: 580-482-4781
Fax: -
Web: www.jcmh.com

CEO: Steve Hartgraves
CFO: Nancy Davidson
HR: Anqi Xu
FYE: June 30
Type: Private

If you happen to get hobbled in Hollis get the gout in Gould get tripped up in Tipton or are ailing in Altus chances are your best bet for care is at Jackson County Memorial Hospital Trust Authority (JCMHTA). JCMHTA provides medical care to residents of Southwest Oklahoma and North Texas through its 150-bed Jackson County Memorial Hospital and 55-bed Tamarack Assisted Living Center an assisted-living facility. More than 20 specialized services include home health and hospice care emergency medicine pediatrics and orthopedics. The hospital also offers an outpatient same-day surgery unit a women's center a cancer center and an intensive care unit.

	Annual Growth	06/06	06/07	06/08	06/09	06/12
Sales ($ mil.)	(51.3%)	-	-	1,375.0	70.5	77.2
Net income ($ mil.)	-	-	-	0.0	1.8	(1.5)
Market value ($ mil.)	-	-	-	-	-	-
Employees	-	-	-	-	-	800

JACKSON ELECTRIC MEMBERSHIP CORPORATION

850 COMMERCE RD
JEFFERSON, GA 305493329
Phone: 706-367-5281
Fax: -
Web: www.jacksonemc.com

CEO: Randall Pugh
CFO: Greg Keith
HR: -
FYE: May 31
Type: Private

Jackson EMC distributes electricity to more than 197800 individual customers (more than 210200 meters) in 10 counties around Atlanta and in northeastern Georgia. The majority of customers are residential with commercial and industrial customers accounting for 42% of fiscal year 2013 revenues. One of the largest non-profit power cooperatives in the US and the largest electric cooperative in Georgia Jackson EMC is owned by its members. The cooperative's generation and transmission partners include Oglethorpe Power Corp. Georgia Systems Operation and Georgia Transmission Corp.

	Annual Growth	05/17	05/18	05/19	05/20	05/21
Sales ($ mil.)	2.7%	-	548.3	571.4	585.6	593.1
Net income ($ mil.)	(0.8%)	-	37.5	29.3	37.3	36.6
Market value ($ mil.)	-	-	-	-	-	-
Employees	-	-	-	-	-	445

JACKSON ENERGY AUTHORITY

119 E COLLEGE ST
JACKSON, TN 383016201
Phone: 731-422-7500
Fax: -
Web: www.jaxenergy.com

CEO: Danny Wheeler
CFO: -
HR: Stacy Scoggins
FYE: June 30
Type: Private

Jackson Energy Authority has the power and the authority to provide for all of Jackson Tennessee's energy needs. The municipal utility distributes electricity natural gas and water and provides wastewater services to about 40000 residential commercial and industrial customers in Jackson and surrounding areas. Jackson Energy also sells propane and offers broadband telecommunications services (cable Internet and telephone). Other services provided by Jackson Energy Authority include the sale of outdoor security lights surge protection systems gas grills and decorative lights.

	Annual Growth	06/17	06/18	06/19	06/20	06/21
Sales ($ mil.)	(1.3%)	-	-	254.3	243.6	247.9
Net income ($ mil.)	(19.9%)	-	-	40.2	23.3	25.8
Market value ($ mil.)	-	-	-	-	-	-
Employees	-	-	-	-	-	425

JACKSON HEALTHCARE, LLC

2655 NORTHWINDS PKWY
ALPHARETTA, GA 300092280
Phone: 770-643-5500
Fax: -
Web: www.jacksonhealthcare.com

CEO: Richard L Jackson
CFO: Douglas B Kline
HR: -
FYE: December 31
Type: Private

Jackson Healthcare can help find physicians to work at hospitals and help keep track of patients as they enter and leave hospitals. Its staffing businesses offer job search recruiting and placement services for physicians and other health care professionals; provide anesthesiologists; and coordinate the work of traveling nurses. Jackson Healthcare's physician job boards attract thousands of visitors per month giving it a reputation for filling openings quickly. Subsidiary Patient Placement Systems manages patient flow through the medical system and Care Logistics provides patient tracking software. Richard Jackson formed the company in 1978.

	Annual Growth	12/06	12/07	12/15	12/16	12/17
Sales ($ mil.)	9.5%	-	385.0	696.9	838.1	949.8
Net income ($ mil.)	18.4%	-	18.3	70.8	93.0	99.3
Market value ($ mil.)	-	-	-	-	-	-
Employees	-	-	-	-	-	949

JACKSON HEWITT TAX SERVICE INC.

3 Sylvan Way
Parsippany NJ 07054
Phone: 973-630-1040
Fax: 973-496-2785
Web: www.jacksonhewitt.com

CEO: Alan D Ferber
CFO: Daniel P O'Brien
HR: –
FYE: April 30
Type: Private

For Jackson Hewitt there's no season like tax season. The tax preparer ranked #2 in the US behind H&R Block prepares tax returns for primarily low- and middle-income customers. Jackson Hewitt provides full-service individual federal and state income tax preparation through more than 6500 primarily franchised offices including 2800 locations within Wal-Mart Stores and mall kiosks. The firm's tax preparers which use its proprietary ProFiler decision-tree software filed more than 2 million tax returns in the fiscal year ended April 2010. Beset by heavy debt that followed aggressive expansion Jackson Hewitt filed for Chapter 11 bankruptcy protection in 2011 but emerged later that year.

JACKSON HOSPITAL & CLINIC, INC

1725 PINE ST
MONTGOMERY, AL 361061117
Phone: 334-293-8000
Fax: –
Web: www.jackson.org

CEO: Joe B Riley
CFO: Paul Peiffer
HR: –
FYE: December 31
Type: Private

Jackson Hospital & Clinic looks after the health and well being of a large number of residents of Montgomery and central Alabama. The privately held not-for-profit medical institution has about 345 acute care beds. Specialized services include cardiac care emergency medicine neurology orthopedics oncology and women's and infant's health care. The medical center also provides family medicine primary care and diagnostic services through its outpatient clinic facilities and it offers medical laboratory services for other regional health care providers.

	Annual Growth	12/16	12/17	12/18	12/19	12/20
Sales ($ mil.)	7.7%	–	216.4	244.1	268.1	270.5
Net income ($ mil.)	–	–	(10.4)	3.1	3.2	10.7
Market value ($ mil.)	–	–	–	–	–	–
Employees	–	–	–	–	–	1,400

JACKSON STATE UNIVERSITY

1400 J R LYNCH ST STE 206
JACKSON, MS 392170001
Phone: 601-979-2121
Fax: –
Web: www.jsums.edu

CEO: –
CFO: –
HR: –
FYE: June 30
Type: Private

Jackson State University (JSU) is a public coeducational institution that offers more than 90 undergraduate and graduate degrees. It offers programs through five academic colleges covering business; education and human development; liberal arts; public service; and science technology and engineering. The historically black school now serves a diverse 9000-strong student body. JSU also operates the Mississippi Urban Research Center which analyzes and distributes information relating to public policies and activities that affect urban life. The school was founded as Natchez Seminary in 1877; after multiple name changes it became JSU in 1974 after achieving university status.

	Annual Growth	06/06	06/07	06/17	06/18	06/19
Sales ($ mil.)	2.6%	–	112.2	251.3	104.1	153.5
Net income ($ mil.)	–	–	0.7	5.1	(14.9)	(10.9)
Market value ($ mil.)	–	–	–	–	–	–
Employees	–	–	–	–	–	2,000

JACKSONVILLE BANCORP INC (FL)   NAS: JAXB

100 North Laura Street, Suite 1000
Jacksonville, FL 32202
Phone: 904 421-3040
Fax: –
Web: www.jaxbank.com

CEO: –
CFO: –
HR: –
FYE: December 31
Type: Public

Need to stow some greenbacks in Jax? Check out Jacksonville Bancorp the holding company for Jacksonville Bank which has about 10 branches in and around Jacksonville Florida. The community bank offers standard deposit products including checking and savings accounts money market accounts CDs and IRAs. Commercial mortgages make up more than half of the bank's loan portfolio; residential mortgages account for most of the rest. Subsidiary Fountain Financial sells insurance and investment products. Ameris Bancorp agreed to buy the company in late 2015.

	Annual Growth	12/10	12/11	12/12	12/13	12/14
Assets ($ mil.)	(7.0%)	651.8	561.4	565.1	507.3	488.6
Net income ($ mil.)	–	–	(11.4)	(24.1)	(43.0)	(1.0)	1.9
Market value ($ mil.)	13.6%	42.8	18.3	4.6	73.0	71.2
Employees	(28.5%)	283	106	100	103	74

JACKSONVILLE BANCORP INC (MD)   NAS: JXSB

1211 West Morton Avenue
Jacksonville, IL 62650
Phone: 217 245-4111
Fax: –
Web: www.jacksonvillesavings.com

CEO: –
CFO: –
HR: –
FYE: December 31
Type: Public

Jacksonville Bancorp (unaffiliated with the Florida corporation of the same name) is the holding company for Jacksonville Savings Bank which serves consumers and businesses in western Illinois through eight branches including its Chapin State Bank First Midwest Savings Bank and Litchfield Community Savings divisions. The bank is mainly a real estate lender with residential commercial and agricultural mortgages accounting for more than half of its loan portfolio. Subsidiary Financial Resources Group offers investment and trust services. Ameris Bancorp purchased Jacksonville Bancorp and its eight branches in March 2016.

	Annual Growth	12/12	12/13	12/14	12/15	12/16
Assets ($ mil.)	(0.2%)	321.4	318.4	311.9	308.6	319.3
Net income ($ mil.)	(3.9%)	3.6	3.2	3.0	3.0	3.0
Market value ($ mil.)	14.7%	31.2	35.2	41.4	47.3	54.0
Employees	(2.8%)	112	106	102	101	100

JACKSONVILLE ELECTRIC AUTHORITY

21 W CHURCH ST FL 1
JACKSONVILLE, FL 322023152
Phone: 904-665-6000
Fax: –
Web: www.jea.com

CEO: Jay Stowe
CFO: Melissa Dykes
HR: –
FYE: September 30
Type: Private

As long as sparks are flying in Jacksonville everything is A-OK with JEA. The community-owned not-for-profit utility provides electricity to 438000 customers in Jacksonville and surrounding areas in northeastern Florida. Managing an electric system that dates back to 1895 JEA has a net generating capacity of 3747 MW. It owns an electric system with five primarily fossil-fueled generating plants. JEA also gets 12.8 MW of generating capacity from two methane-fueled landfill plants. The company resells electricity to other utilities including NextEra Energy. JEA also provides water and wastewater services; it serves 321600 water customers and 247500 wastewater customers.

	Annual Growth	06/08	06/09*	09/16	09/17	09/18
Sales ($ mil.)	3.4%	–	1,319.9	1,782.1	1,875.2	1,790.0
Net income ($ mil.)	6.5%	–	71.9	210.0	254.6	126.5
Market value ($ mil.)	–	–	–	–	–	–
Employees	–	–	–	–	–	2,356

*Fiscal year change

JACLYN INC.

PINK SHEETS: JCLY

197 W. Spring Valley Ave.
Maywood NJ 07607
Phone: 201-909-6000
Fax: 626-568-7144
Web: www.jacobs.com

CEO: Robert Chestnov
CFO: Anthony Christon
HR: –
FYE: February 28
Type: Public

Jaclyn has Jack and Jill covered. The company designs markets and distributes private-label children's wear and women's and some men's apparel. Jaclyn's apparel includes sleepwear loungewear and robes and infants' and children's play clothing marketed under the Jaclyn Apparel and Topsville labels. The company also supplies backpacks handbags cosmetic bags sport bags and travel bags some of which is used in creating promotional products for toiletries through its Premium Incentive and Bonnie Int'l divisions. The apparel and handbags made by outside contractors in Asia are sold in the US through mass merchandise department and specialty stores. Wal-Mart represents more than 40% of Jaclyn's sales.

JACO OIL COMPANY

3101 STATE RD
BAKERSFIELD, CA 933084931
Phone: 661-393-7000
Fax: –
Web: www.jaco.host

CEO: T J Jamieson
CFO: Brian Busacca
HR: –
FYE: December 31
Type: Private

Jaco Oil Company is jockeying for its piece of the convenience store pie. The company's Fastrip Food Stores subsidiary operates more than 50 convenience stores and gas stations primarily in and around Bakersfield California but also in Arizona. Besides offering customers traditional convenience-store fare which includes coffee milk beer snacks tobacco and the like the Fastrip chain stocks a full range of grocery items and provides in-store financial service centers. Financial services include check cashing payday loans wire transfer services via The Western Union Company refund anticipation loans and other services at many locations. Jaco Oil Company was founded in 1970.

	Annual Growth	12/16	12/17	12/18	12/19	12/20
Sales ($ mil.)	3.1%	–	506.6	636.7	657.9	555.9
Net income ($ mil.)	14.9%	–	13.5	19.5	25.9	20.4
Market value ($ mil.)	–	–	–	–	–	–
Employees	–	–	–	–	–	350

JACOBS ENGINEERING GROUP, INC.

NYS: J

1999 Bryan Street, Suite 1200
Dallas, TX 75201
Phone: 214 583-8500
Fax: –
Web: www.jacobs.com

CEO: Steven Demetriou
CFO: Kevin Berryman
HR: –
FYE: October 01
Type: Public

Jacobs Engineering Group provides a full spectrum of professional services including consulting technical scientific and project delivery for government and private sector throughout the world. Jacobs handles project design architectural and engineering construction and construction management services operations and maintenance services and process scientific and systems consulting services. Around 70% of revenue comes from the US while the rest originates in other countries primarily in Europe. PA consulting serves as the company's third segment at the moment.

	Annual Growth	09/17	09/18	09/19*	10/20	10/21
Sales ($ mil.)	8.9%	10,022.8	14,984.6	12,737.9	13,567.0	14,092.6
Net income ($ mil.)	12.9%	293.7	163.4	848.0	491.8	477.0
Market value ($ mil.)	23.3%	7,510.6	9,860.3	11,689.3	12,146.8	17,356.7
Employees	0.1%	54,700	80,800	52,000	55,000	55,000

*Fiscal year change

JACOBS FINANCIAL GROUP INC

NL:

179 Summers Street, Suite 307
Charleston, WV 25301
Phone: 304 343-8171
Fax: –
Web: www.thejacobsfinancialgroup.com

CEO: John M Jacobs
CFO: John M Jacobs
HR: –
FYE: May 31
Type: Public

If Jacob needed to bond his ladder Jacobs Financial Group could provide the surety. Through subsidiaries Jacobs Financial provides surety and insurance as well as investment advisory services. The company's FS Investments (FSI) is a holding company that develops surety business by creating companies engaged in the issuance of surety bonds (bonds collateralized by accounts managed by Jacobs & Co.). FSI's wholly owned subsidiary Triangle Surety Agency specializes in placing surety bonds with insurance companies with an emphasis on clients in industries such as coal oil and gas. Jacobs Financial whose background is in energy has been expanding its insurance and surety operations through acquisitions.

	Annual Growth	05/13	05/14	05/15	05/16	05/17
Sales ($ mil.)	20.9%	1.3	1.3	1.6	1.3	2.9
Net income ($ mil.)	–	(2.0)	(1.8)	(1.6)	(0.0)	(1.3)
Market value ($ mil.)	(25.2%)	3.2	2.3	1.1	1.0	1.0
Employees	10.7%	6	9	9	9	9

JACOBS, MALCOLM & BURTT

18 CROW CANYON CT STE 210
SAN RAMON, CA 945831786
Phone: 415-285-0400
Fax: –
Web: www.jmb-produce.com

CEO: –
CFO: –
HR: –
FYE: December 31
Type: Private

Jacobs Malcolm & Burtt may sound like a law office but the only argument this company would make is to eat your vegetables. The firm is a California-based wholesaler and distributor of fruits and vegetables such as asparagus oranges and berries. Jacobs and Malcolm founded the company in 1888 and Burtt joined the name in 1969. Leo Rolandelli owns 50% of the capital stock the Wilson Family Trust owns 31% and the rest is controlled by the other officers.

	Annual Growth	12/12	12/13	12/14	12/15	12/17
Sales ($ mil.)	7.7%	–	56.1	54.9	59.0	75.5
Net income ($ mil.)	34.4%	–	0.2	0.4	0.5	0.8
Market value ($ mil.)	–	–	–	–	–	–
Employees	–	–	–	–	–	31

JACUZZI BRANDS CORP.

13925 City Center Dr. Ste. 200
Chino Hills CA 91709
Phone: 909-247-2920
Fax: 408-746-5060
Web: solutions.us.fujitsu.com

CEO: Robert Rowen
CFO: Jeffrey B Park
HR: –
FYE: September 30
Type: Private

If hot tubs really were time machines Jacuzzi would be the name brand of hydrotherapeutic time travel. For more than 50 years Jacuzzi Brands has made the eponymous jetted baths spas and showers that soothe the aches and pains of residential and commercial customers around the world. Besides hot tubs baths and showers Jacuzzi also offers luxury mattresses bedding and accessories. The company's bath division also makes toilets sinks and accessories such as bath pillows towel warmers and radiant floor heating systems. Investment firm Apollo Management owns Jacuzzi Brands.

JAGGED PEAK INC.

OTC: JGPK

3000 Bayport Dr. Ste. 250
Tampa FL 33607
Phone: 813-637-6900
Fax: 800-749-4998
Web: www.jaggedpeak.com

CEO: -
CFO: -
HR: -
FYE: December 31
Type: Public

Jagged Peak rises up to help customers reach the peak of supply chain management. The company's E-Business Dynamic Global Engine (EDGE) software is a ready-to-use Web-based application that captures processes and distributes orders from multiple sources sending them in real-time to warehouses. With automated purchases and orders companies can streamline their supply chain processes to improve delivery reduce costs and integrate inventory information. Jagged Peak took its present form in 2005 when publicly traded Absolute Glass Protection acquired the private company and adopted its name officers and operations.

JAKKS PACIFIC INC

NMS: JAKK

2951 28th Street
Santa Monica, CA 90405
Phone: 424 268-9444
Fax: -
Web: www.jakks.com

CEO: -
CFO: John L Kimble
HR: -
FYE: December 31
Type: Public

JAKKS Pacific is one of the US's top toy companies. It makes and sells action figures (including licenses for Harry Potter and Nintendo) die-cast and plastic cars electronic products dolls (such as Disney Princess and Fancy Nancy) Halloween costumes and dress-up products and a host of other playthings. Its products are sold to US mass merchandisers such as Target and Wal-Mart which together account for a hefty 50% of sales; the company sells its products through e-commerce sites including Walmart.com Target.com and Amazon.com. The US is the company's largest market by far.

	Annual Growth	12/16	12/17	12/18	12/19	12/20
Sales ($ mil.)	(7.6%)	706.6	613.1	567.8	598.6	515.9
Net income ($ mil.)	-	1.2	(83.1)	(42.4)	(55.5)	(14.3)
Market value ($ mil.)	(0.8%)	29.3	13.4	8.4	5.9	28.4
Employees	(6.9%)	832	751	626	477	626

JAMBA INC

NMS: JMBA

3001 Dallas Parkway, Suite 140
Frisco, TX 75034
Phone: 469 294-9800
Fax: -
Web: www.jambajuice.com

CEO: -
CFO: Michael J Dixon
HR: -
FYE: January 03
Type: Public

This company is blending up business with its fruit-filled drinks. Jamba operates the Jamba Juice chain the leading outlet for blended fruit drinks with about 875 smoothie stands throughout the US and in a handful of other countries. Its menu includes more than 30 varieties of custom smoothies (including Aloha Pineapple Mango-a-go-go and Strawberry Surf Rider) and Jamba Boosts (smoothies made with vitamin and protein supplements) along with other fruit juices and food items. Jamba Juice locations include freestanding units as well as on-site kiosks in high traffic areas including college campuses gyms and airports.

	Annual Growth	01/13*	12/13	12/14	12/15*	01/17
Sales ($ mil.)	(23.2%)	228.8	229.2	218.0	161.7	79.6
Net income ($ mil.)	-	0.3	2.1	(3.6)	9.4	(22.4)
Market value ($ mil.)	46.4%	34.5	191.5	225.4	212.7	158.6
Employees	(27.7%)	4,300	4,000	4,200	1,313	1,177

*Fiscal year change

JAMES MADISON UNIVERSITY

800 S MAIN ST
HARRISONBURG, VA 228070002
Phone: 540-568-6211
Fax: -
Web: www.jmu.edu

CEO: -
CFO: John Knight
HR: -
FYE: June 30
Type: Private

James Madison is known as the Father of the Constitution and America's fourth president but he also has a public institution of higher education named after him. James Madison University (JMU) offers some 70 undergraduate and 40 graduate degrees through more than a half-dozen colleges including arts and letters business education visual and performing arts and science and mathematics. The university enrolls about 20000 students mostly undergrads with a faculty of 1200 teachers and a student-to-faculty ratio of 16:1. JMU also has extensive men's and women's athletic programs. JMU was established in 1908 in Harrisonburg Virginia.

	Annual Growth	06/06	06/07	06/08	06/11	06/13
Sales ($ mil.)	6.2%	-	-	270.4	323.3	365.0
Net income ($ mil.)	0.7%	-	-	69.2	56.5	71.7
Market value ($ mil.)	-	-	-	-	-	-
Employees	-	-	-	-	-	1,700

JAMES RIVER COAL CO

NMS: JRCC

901 E. Byrd Street, Suite 1600
Richmond, VA 23219
Phone: 804 780-3000
Fax: -
Web: www.jamesrivercoal.com

CEO: Peter T Socha
CFO: -
HR: -
FYE: December 31
Type: Public

James River keeps the coal flowing. The company operates about 40 mines in Kentucky and West Virginia (in the Central Appalachian Basin) and Indiana (in the Illinois Basin) that produce more than 10 million tons of coal annually. Though a small percentage of the coal it sells comes from independent operators and third-party producers the vast majority of James River's coal is produced from company-operated mines. It controls approximately 362.8 million tons of proved and probable reserves (92% in Appalachia). The company sell its coal to power station in the southern US and to steel producers around the world.

	Annual Growth	12/08	12/09	12/10	12/11	12/12
Sales ($ mil.)	17.9%	568.5	681.6	701.1	1,177.7	1,099.6
Net income ($ mil.)	-	(96.0)	51.0	78.2	(39.1)	(138.9)
Market value ($ mil.)	(32.4%)	549.8	663.2	908.5	248.2	115.1
Employees	4.9%	1,751	1,736	1,746	2,405	2,124

JANEL CORP

NBB: JANL

80 Eighth Avenue
New York, NY 10011
Phone: 212 373-5895
Fax: 718 527-1689
Web: www.janelcorp.com

CEO: Dominique Schulte
CFO: Vincent A Verde
HR: -
FYE: September 30
Type: Public

Janel Corporation is a holding company with subsidiaries in three business segments: Global Logistics Services Manufacturing and Life Sciences. Janel and its consolidated subsidiaries employ about 175 full-time people in the US. It provides cargo transportation logistics management services including freight forwarding via air- ocean- and land-based carriers customs brokerage services warehousing and distribution services and other logistics services. The company offers logistics services and also antibodies Aves IgG and Phospo. Through a combined portfolio of approximately 1200 products and a range of custom services the Life Sciences segment provides the scientific community with high quality tools to support critical research efforts.

	Annual Growth	09/17	09/18	09/19	09/20	09/21
Sales ($ mil.)	17.1%	77.8	67.5	84.4	82.4	146.4
Net income ($ mil.)	78.2%	0.5	0.2	0.6	(1.7)	5.2
Market value ($ mil.)	27.9%	8.1	7.7	8.5	8.5	21.7
Employees	27.2%	121	176	174	173	317

JANONE INC

325 E. Warm Springs Road, Suite 102
Las Vegas, NV 89119
Phone: 702 997-5968
Fax: –
Web: www.janone.com

NAS: JAN
CEO: Tony Isaac
CFO: Virland A Johnson
HR: –
FYE: January 02
Type: Public

Appliance Recycling Centers of America (ARCA) retrieves recycles repairs and resells household appliances. The company's retail business operates 20 ApplianceSmart Factory Outlet stores in Minnesota Georgia Ohio and Texas that sell new reconditioned and "special-buy" appliances from manufacturers such as Electrolux GE and Whirlpool. ARCA provides recycling and replacement services for appliance makers electric utilities and energy-efficiency programs in North America. The firm also cashes in on byproducts collecting fees for appliance disposal and selling scrap metal and reclaimed chlorofluorocarbon refrigerants from processed appliances. ARCA was founded in 1976 as a used appliance retailer.

	Annual Growth	12/16	12/17	12/18	12/19*	01/21
Sales ($ mil.)	(20.0%)	103.6	41.5	36.8	35.1	33.9
Net income ($ mil.)	–	(1.5)	0.1	(5.6)	(12.0)	(8.5)
Market value ($ mil.)	34.8%	2.0	1.9	0.9	5.4	8.9
Employees	(16.7%)	445	165	159	208	179

*Fiscal year change

JANUS CAPITAL GROUP INC

151 Detroit Street
Denver, CO 80206
Phone: 303 333-3863
Fax: –
Web: www.janus.com

NYS: JNS
CEO: Richard M Weil
CFO: Jennifer J McPeek
HR: –
FYE: December 31
Type: Public

Named after the Roman god with two faces Janus Capital Group provides investment management and advisory services for institutional and individual customers. Known for its intensive equities research the company manages dozens of mutual funds including its flagship Janus Fund (formed in 1969) as well as separate accounts and sub-advised portfolios. Subsidiary INTECH manages institutional portfolios by utilizing investment strategies based on mathematical analysis of the stock market while Perkins Investment Management focuses on long-term value investments. All told Janus Capital and its subsidiaries have $183 billion of assets under management. Janus is merging with UK-based asset manager Henderson Group.

	Annual Growth	12/12	12/13	12/14	12/15	12/16
Sales ($ mil.)	4.4%	850.0	873.9	953.2	1,076.2	1,010.7
Net income ($ mil.)	9.3%	102.3	114.7	154.4	155.8	146.1
Market value ($ mil.)	11.7%	1,556.4	2,259.6	2,946.5	2,573.8	2,424.0
Employees	2.5%	1,156	1,194	1,209	1,272	1,277

JAVELIN MORTGAGE INVESTMENT CORP

3001 Ocean Drive, Suite 201
Vero Beach, FL 32963
Phone: 772 617-4340
Fax: –

NYS: JMI
CEO: Scott J Ulm
CFO: James R Mountain
HR: –
FYE: December 31
Type: Public

JAVELIN Mortgage Investment is looking to spearhead a new effort in mortgage-related investments. The company formed in June 2012 as a real estate investment trust (REIT) with plans to invest in mortgage securities backed by government-supported enterprises such as Fannie Mae Freddie Mac and Ginnie Mae as well as other mortgage securities. As a REIT JAVELIN Mortgage Investment will be exempt from paying federal income tax as long as it makes a quarterly distribution to shareholders. It will be externally managed by ARMOUR Residential Management LLC the same external manager of sister company ARMOUR Residential REIT Inc. The company went public in 2012.

	Annual Growth	12/10	12/11	12/12	12/13	12/14
Sales ($ mil.)	–	0.0	0.0	8.4	(31.0)	(8.0)
Net income ($ mil.)	–	0.0	0.0	6.1	(43.8)	(21.8)
Market value ($ mil.)	–	0.0	0.0	228.8	167.0	124.3
Employees	–	–	–	–	–	–

JAYCO INC.

903 S. Main St.
Middlebury IN 46540
Phone: 574-825-5861
Fax: 574-825-6062
Web: www.jayco.com

CEO: Derald Bontrager
CFO: –
HR: –
FYE: August 31
Type: Private

Jayco's motto could be "have trailer will travel." The company develops and manufactures its line of camping trailers light-weight trailers park and travel trailers fifth-wheels toy haulers and motor homes and markets them through a network of about 300 authorized dealers in the US and Canada. It also makes and distributes aftermarket parts. Product brand names include Eagle Greyhawk Jay Feather Jay Flight Jay Series Sport and Octane ZX. The company also offers roadside assistance through membership to its Customer First program. Chairman and CEO Wilbur Bontrager and his family own Jayco. His father the late Lloyd Bontrager founded the company in 1968 in two chicken houses and a barn.

JDA SOFTWARE GROUP INC.

14400 N. 87th St.
Scottsdale AZ 85260-3649
Phone: 480-308-3000
Fax: 480-308-3001
Web: www.jda.com

NASDAQ: JDAS
CEO: Girish Rishi
CFO: –
HR: –
FYE: December 31
Type: Private

JDA Software Group makes software that helps companies manage their supply chains. It offers integrated supply chain planning and execution software as well as a comprehensive set of services to help companies manage everything from raw materials to delivery of finished products. Its services include cloud consulting education and support. JDA Software Group serves a wide variety of industries and companies of all sizes with a particular focus on retail companies like Dr Pepper Snapple Group Kraft Foods and OfficeMax. Manufacturers distributors and logistics service providers are also among its customer base. In December 2012 JDA Software Group was acquired by RedPrairie in a $1.9 billion deal.

JEFFERIES FINANCIAL GROUP INC

520 Madison Avenue
New York, NY 10022
Phone: 212 460-1900
Fax: 212 598-4869
Web: www.jefferies.com

NYS: JEF
CEO: Richard Handler
CFO: Teresa Gendron
HR: –
FYE: November 30
Type: Public

Jefferies Financial Group is a financial services company engaged in investment banking and capital markets asset management and direct investing. The company's industry coverage groups include retail energy Institutions healthcare industrials media real estate financial sponsors and public finance. Jefferies offers advisory equity underwriting and debt underwriting which include both mergers and acquisitions and restructuring and recapitalization expertise. Some of its holdings include Idaho Timber Vitesse Energy Finance JETX Energy LLC and HomeFed. It also has interests in a gold and silver mining company and a telecommunications business in Italy. About 85% of revenues comes from US customers.

	Annual Growth	12/17*	11/18	11/19	11/20	11/21
Sales ($ mil.)	(8.0%)	11,436.4	3,764.0	3,893.0	6,010.9	8,185.3
Net income ($ mil.)	76.7%	171.7	1,026.8	964.7	775.2	1,674.4
Market value ($ mil.)	9.1%	6,451.4	5,321.4	5,090.0	5,535.7	9,152.3
Employees	(37.6%)	36,700	4,700	4,800	4,945	5,556

*Fiscal year change

JEFFERSON BANCSHARES INC (TN)   NMS: JFBI

120 Evans Avenue
Morristown, TN 37814
Phone: 423 586-8421
Fax: –
Web: www.jeffersonfederal.com

CEO: –
CFO: –
HR: –
FYE: June 30
Type: Public

Here's a Tennessee bank that will definitely volunteer its services. Jefferson Bancshares is the holding company for Jefferson Federal Bank which has about a dozen locations in eastern parts of the Volunteer State. Founded in 1963 the bank serves individuals and businesses in Hamblen Knox Sullivan and Washington counties offering standard services such as checking and savings accounts CDs and IRAs. Lending activities primarily consist of commercial real estate loans and one- to four-family residential mortgages which together account for a majority of the company's loan portfolio. In 2008 Jefferson Bancshares acquired State of Franklin Bancshares a community bank hurt by the national mortgage crisis.

	Annual Growth	06/09	06/10	06/11	06/12	06/13
Assets ($ mil.)	(6.7%)	662.7	630.8	561.2	522.9	503.0
Net income ($ mil.)	(11.8%)	2.6	(24.0)	0.0	(4.0)	1.6
Market value ($ mil.)	(1.9%)	40.2	26.3	21.4	16.2	37.3
Employees	(4.9%)	175	155	146	142	143

JEFFERSON HOMEBUILDERS, INC.

501 N MAIN ST
CULPEPER, VA 227012607
Phone: 540-825-5898
Fax: –
Web: www.jeffersonhomebuilders.com

CEO: –
CFO: –
HR: –
FYE: September 30
Type: Private

Culpeper Wood Preservers may sound like the name of an environmental nonprofit but this Virginia-based building materials supplier has more commercial interests in mind. Jefferson Homebuilders which does business as Culpeper Wood Preservers manufactures and distributes pressure-treated lumber from plants located in the midwestern and northeastern US (pressure treating protects wood from damage by moisture and insects). Products include standard dimensional lumber plywood and timbers. The company also makes such specialty products as deck accessories lattice fencing and landscaping items. It has ten plants in Virginia Indiana Maryland North and South Carolina.

	Annual Growth	09/03	09/04	09/05	09/06	09/07
Sales ($ mil.)	(10.3%)	–	–	195.5	166.0	157.2
Net income ($ mil.)	(32.1%)	–	–	6.9	5.1	3.2
Market value ($ mil.)	–	–	–	–	–	–
Employees	–	–	–	–	–	177

JEFFERSON HOSPITAL ASSOCIATION, INC.

1600 W 40TH AVE
PINE BLUFF, AR 716036301
Phone: 870-541-7100
Fax: –
Web: www.jrmc.org

CEO: –
CFO: Nathan Van Genderan
HR: –
FYE: June 30
Type: Private

Jefferson Regional Medical Center (JRMC) provides acute care and other health services to residents of Pine Bluff and an 11-county area of southern Arkansas. The not-for-profit community-owned hospital has about 470 acute care beds and offers general medical and surgical care as well as services in a range of specialties including urology orthopedics cardiology and oncology. It also has a 25-bed skilled nursing unit that cares for patients transitioning to long-term care or home care. A network of clinics offers outpatient surgery diagnostic imaging wound care and other ambulatory health services. Additionally the health system operates a nursing school and home health and hospice agencies.

	Annual Growth	06/14	06/15	06/16	06/19	06/20
Sales ($ mil.)	4.3%	–	170.8	164.4	187.7	210.6
Net income ($ mil.)	–	–	13.1	10.6	(4.7)	(10.4)
Market value ($ mil.)	–	–	–	–	–	–
Employees	–	–	–	–	–	1,700

JEFFERSON REGIONAL MEDICAL CENTER

565 COAL VALLEY RD
CLAIRTON, PA 15025-3703
Phone: 412-469-5000
Fax: –
Web: www.jeffersonregional.com

CEO: John J Dempster
CFO: –
HR: Paulette Skillman
FYE: June 30
Type: Private

Jefferson Regional Medical Center serves the South Hills area of Pittsburgh. The hospital has about 370 beds. In addition to primary care Jefferson Regional Medical Center offers such specialized services as a heart institute for treating cardiovascular conditions and a physical rehabilitation and sports medicine center. Its emergency department treats more than 55000 patients each year. Jefferson Regional Medical Center also provides home health care and emergency helicopter transportation services and it operates nearby outpatient clinics and physician offices.

	Annual Growth	06/05	06/06	06/07	06/08	06/09
Sales ($ mil.)	(65.7%)	–	–	1,737.0	216.5	204.8
Net income ($ mil.)	–	–	–	0.0	(19.6)	(19.2)
Market value ($ mil.)	–	–	–	–	–	–
Employees	–	–	–	–	–	2,000

JEFFERSONVILLE BANCORP   NBB: JFBC

4866 State Route 52, P.O. Box 398
Jeffersonville, NY 12748
Phone: 845 482-4000
Fax: –
Web: www.jeffbank.com

CEO: George Kinne
CFO: John Russell
HR: –
FYE: December 31
Type: Public

Jeffersonville Bancorp is the holding company for The First National Bank of Jeffersonville. The bank serves businesses and consumers through about 10 locations in southeastern New York's Sullivan County. First National Bank of Jeffersonville offers such standard retail services as demand deposit savings and money market accounts; NOW accounts; CDs; and IRAs to fund a variety of loans. Nearly 40% of the bank's loan portfolio consists of residential mortgages while commercial mortgages account for another 35%. The bank also provides home equity business consumer construction and agricultural loans.

	Annual Growth	12/16	12/17	12/18	12/19	12/20
Assets ($ mil.)	6.3%	483.8	502.1	506.7	511.6	616.6
Net income ($ mil.)	(1.5%)	5.1	4.3	6.2	6.5	4.8
Market value ($ mil.)	0.8%	69.8	69.4	76.9	76.3	72.2
Employees	–	–	–	–	–	–

JENNIFER CONVERTIBLES INC.   PINK SHEETS: JENNQ

419 Crossways Park Dr.
Woodbury NY 11797
Phone: 516-496-1900
Fax: 516-496-0008
Web: www.jenniferfurniture.com

CEO: –
CFO: Rami Abada
HR: –
FYE: August 31
Type: Public

Houseguests are likely to get a good night's sleep thanks to Jennifer Convertibles. The company owns and operates about 80 namesake stores and some 10 Jennifer Leather stores that sell sofa beds loveseats recliners and chairs. The furniture firm also is among one of the top dealers of Sealy sofa beds in the US. Besides its network of Jennifer-branded stores the retailer also boasts half a dozen licensed Ashley Furniture HomeStores. Jennifer Convertibles sells name-brand products as well as the company's private-label: the Bellissimo Collection. In early 2011 Jennifer Convertibles emerged from Chapter 11 bankruptcy protection under new ownership and a new CEO.

JERRY BIGGERS CHEVROLET INC.

1385 E CHICAGO ST
ELGIN, IL 601204715
Phone: 847-742-9000
Fax: –
Web: www.biggerschevy.com

CEO: –
CFO: –
HR: –
FYE: December 31
Type: Private

Jerry Biggers Chevrolet (dba Biggers Chevy Heaven) certainly enjoys its size. The company which has been in business for more than 40 years sells Chevy Camaros Corvettes Impalas and Yukons along with Isuzu Rodeos Ascenders and Amigos at a dealership in Elgin Illinois. It also offers a variety of used car models. In addition to cars Biggers Chevrolet sells aftermarket accessories like DVD players and truck bed liners and offers parts service and fleet sales. Its Web site allows customers to apply for financing search new and used inventory and schedule service. Help is available in English Spanish and Polish. The big dog at Biggers is owner Jim Leichter.

	Annual Growth	12/03	12/04	12/05	12/06	12/08
Sales ($ mil.)	(8.0%)	–	80.5	51.5	67.8	57.6
Net income ($ mil.)	–	–	–	(0.3)	0.0	(0.6)
Market value ($ mil.)	–	–	–	–	–	–
Employees	–	–	–	–	–	105

JERSEY CENTRAL POWER & LIGHT COMPANY

76 S MAIN ST
AKRON, OH 443081812
Phone: 800-736-3402
Fax: –
Web: www.firstenergycorp.com

CEO: Donald M Lynch
CFO: Marlene A Barwood
HR: –
FYE: December 31
Type: Private

New Jersey native son Bruce Springsteen may be The Boss but Jersey Central Power & Light (JCP&L) electrifies more fans than he does every day. The company a subsidiary of multi-utility holding company FirstEnergy transmits and distributes electricity to 1.1 million homes and businesses in 13 counties in central and northern New Jersey. JCP&L operates 22670 miles of distribution lines; its 2550-mile transmission system is overseen by regional transmission organization (RTO) PJM Interconnection. The utility also has some power plant interests.

	Annual Growth	12/09	12/10	12/11	12/16	12/17
Sales ($ mil.)	(7.1%)	–	3,027.1	2,495.0	1,787.4	1,801.1
Net income ($ mil.)	(7.1%)	–	192.1	144.0	80.6	115.1
Market value ($ mil.)	–	–	–	–	–	–
Employees	–	–	–	–	–	1,413

JERSEY CITY MEDICAL CENTER, INC.

355 GRAND ST
JERSEY CITY, NJ 073024321
Phone: 201-915-2000
Fax: –
Web: www.rwjbh.org

CEO: Joe Scott
CFO: –
HR: –
FYE: December 31
Type: Private

With roots extending back to 1882 Jersey City Medical Center (JCMC) may have history but it's not stuck in the past. The 350-bed acute-care hospital serves residents of New Jersey's Hudson County area. Operated by Liberty Healthcare the hospital includes a trauma center a perinatal center and a heart institute. JCMC also offers pediatric women's health rehabilitation and ambulatory care and it is a teaching affiliate for the Mount Sinai School of Medicine. JCMC's modern incarnation came about in the Great Depression when it was constructed by a political ally of Franklin Roosevelt.

	Annual Growth	12/15	12/16	12/17	12/18	12/19
Sales ($ mil.)	4.1%	–	354.6	385.1	402.5	399.9
Net income ($ mil.)	–	–	(2.7)	26.3	13.3	(40.8)
Market value ($ mil.)	–	–	–	–	–	–
Employees	–	–	–	–	–	1,942

JETBLUE AIRWAYS CORP

27-01 Queens Plaza North
Long Island City, NY 11101
Phone: 718 286-7900
Fax: –
Web: www.jetblue.com

NMS: JBLU
CEO: Robin Hayes
CFO: Steve Priest
HR: –
FYE: December 31
Type: Public

JetBlue Airways' network served about a hundred BlueCities in approximately 30 US states the District of Columbia Puerto Rico and twenty-three countries in the Caribbean and Latin America. Domestic flights represent its largest market accounting for about 65% of total company sales. Most of its flights arrive or depart from Boston New York Orlando Fort Lauderdale Los Angeles and San Juan Puerto Rico. JetBlue's fleet of more than 265 aircraft consists mainly of Airbus A220 Airbus A320s and A321s but also includes Embraer E190s. Dubbed "New York's Hometown Airline" about half of JetBlue's flights are to and from the New York metropolitan area. It was founded in 1999.

	Annual Growth	12/17	12/18	12/19	12/20	12/21
Sales ($ mil.)	(3.7%)	7,015.0	7,658.0	8,094.0	2,957.0	6,037.0
Net income ($ mil.)	–	1,147.0	188.0	569.0	(1,354.0)	(182.0)
Market value ($ mil.)	(10.6%)	7,148.8	5,139.2	5,990.4	4,652.8	4,556.8
Employees	(0.6%)	19,978	20,892	21,569	20,742	19,466

JEWEL-OSCO

150 Pierce Rd.
Itasca IL 60143
Phone: 630-948-6895
Fax: 630-948-6959
Web: www.jewelosco.com

CEO: –
CFO: –
HR: –
FYE: February 28
Type: Business Segment

Jewel-Osco operates about 180 combination food-and-drug stores mostly in Illinois but also in Indiana and Iowa. The regional chain is the #1 seller of groceries in Chicago with more than 30 stores there and about 31% of the market (triple that of its nearest competitor Safeway-owned Dominick's). Jewel-Osco trails rival Walgreen in pharmacy sales in the Windy City. The company also runs about 30 fuel centers. Started as the Jewel Tea Company in 1899 Jewel-Osco is the largest traditional supermarket chain owned by grocery retailer and wholesaler SUPERVALU. Long accustomed to being #1 in a two-company market Jewel-Osco is fighting to stay on top of an increasingly crowded Chicago grocery scene.

JEWETT-CAMERON TRADING CO. LTD.

32275 N.W. Hillcrest
North Plains, OR 97133
Phone: 503 647-0110
Fax: 503 647-2272
Web: www.jewettcameron.com

NAS: JCTC F
CEO: Chad Summers
CFO: Mitch Van Domelen
HR: –
FYE: August 31
Type: Public

Jewett-Cameron Trading Company (JCTC) puts the lumber in lumberyards the air in pneumatic tools and greenhouses in the garden. Its JC USA subsidiary supplies wood and other building materials to home improvement chains in the western US from distribution centers in Oregon. The MSI-PRO subsidiary imports pneumatic air tools and industrial clamps from Asia. Jewett-Cameron Seed Company processes and distributes agricultural seed. Other brands are involved in supplying greenhouses dog kennels modular garages and gate and fencing products. JCTC was incorporated in 1953.

	Annual Growth	08/17	08/18	08/19	08/20	08/21
Sales ($ mil.)	4.8%	47.7	53.9	45.4	44.9	57.5
Net income ($ mil.)	6.1%	2.7	2.9	2.1	3.0	3.5
Market value ($ mil.)	(6.6%)	48.7	30.3	28.0	26.3	37.0
Employees	5.8%	59	57	58	63	74

JFK HEALTH SYSTEM, INC.

80 JAMES ST
EDISON, NJ 088203938
Phone: 732-321-7000
Fax: –
Web: www.jfkhealthsystem.org

CEO: Raymond Fredericks
CFO: –
HR: –
FYE: December 31
Type: Private

JFK Health System provides medical services in a tri-county area in central New Jersey through flagship facility JFK Medical Center. The hospital has about 500 acute care beds and is one of the Garden State's major health care facilities. Included in the medical center complex are JFK Johnson Rehabilitation Institute JFK New Jersey Neuroscience Institute and a number of outpatient care and imaging centers. Other JFK Health System facilities provide primary and specialty services as well as senior living home health and hospice care. In 2017 JFK Health agreed to merge with Hackensack Meridian; the combined system will operate 15 hospitals in New Jersey.

	Annual Growth	12/13	12/14	12/15	12/17	12/18
Sales ($ mil.)	–	–	–	0.0	0.0	0.0	591.8
Net income ($ mil.)	–	–	–	0.0	0.0	(0.0)	128.7
Market value ($ mil.)	–	–	–	–	–	–	–
Employees	–	–	–	–	–	–	6,735

JIVE SOFTWARE INC   NMS: JIVE

325 Lytton Avenue,, Suite 200
Palo Alto, CA 94301
Phone: 650 319-1920
Fax: –

CEO: Elisa A Steele
CFO: Bryan J Leblanc
HR: –
FYE: December 31
Type: Public

Jive Software brings social networking into the workplace. The company offers its flagship Jive Social Business Platform that allows businesses to communicate collaborate and create and share content through internal social networks for employees and external communities for customers and partners to engage with each other and the business. The core platform can be expanded with optional modules such as analytics ideation (prioritizing ideas) mobile and video. The platform also accommodates cloud and customer-built applications through the Jive Apps Market. Customers include HP SAP and Starbucks. Jive Software was founded in 2001.

	Annual Growth	12/11	12/12	12/13	12/14	12/15
Sales ($ mil.)	26.2%	77.3	113.7	145.8	178.7	195.8
Net income ($ mil.)	–	(50.8)	(47.4)	(75.4)	(56.2)	(34.9)
Market value ($ mil.)	(28.9%)	1,222.3	1,110.0	859.4	460.7	311.7
Employees	13.8%	430	527	673	658	721

JLG INDUSTRIES INC.

13224 Fountain Head Plaza
Hagerstown MD 21742
Phone: 240-420-2661
Fax: 240-420-8719
Web: www.jlg.com

CEO: –
CFO: –
HR: –
FYE: July 31
Type: Subsidiary

Need a boost? JLG Industries' lift equipment can provide that extra reach. Since 1969 when founder John L. Grove invented the first self-propelled boom lift the company has been providing such products as aerial work platforms telescopic material handlers stock pickers (to access high shelving) and power deck trailers for ground-level loading of everything from heavy construction equipment to vending machines. Products are sold under such names as JLG SkyTrak and Lull. The company supplies customers in the government equipment leasing construction contracting agricultural and military markets. Equipment manufacturer Oshkosh Corp. has owned JLG since 2007.

JLM COUTURE INC.   NBB: JLMC

525 Seventh Avenue, Suite 1703
New York, NY 10018
Phone: 212 221-8203
Fax: –
Web: www.jlmcouture.com

CEO: Joseph Murphy
CFO: –
HR: –
FYE: October 31
Type: Public

Here comes the bride and she might be wearing a gown from JLM Couture. The company designs manufactures and markets bridal and bridesmaid gowns veils and related items in the US and the UK. Its bridal gowns which boast price tags of several thousand dollars are made under the Alvina Valenta Jim Hjelm Couture Jim Hjelm Visions Tara Keely and Lazaro names. JLM Couture markets its gowns through bridal magazines trunk shows and catalogs. The company's bridesmaid and flower girl collections are produced under the Jim Hjelm Occasions and Lazaro Bridesmaids labels; they're peddled through bridal boutiques and bridal departments in clothing stores. Its Party by JLM is a collection of evening wear.

	Annual Growth	10/16	10/17	10/18	10/19	10/20
Sales ($ mil.)	(10.5%)	28.5	31.8	30.2	24.9	18.3
Net income ($ mil.)	–	(0.8)	1.2	0.9	(1.0)	(0.8)
Market value ($ mil.)	(7.5%)	4.5	5.1	15.1	9.7	3.3
Employees	–	–	–	–	–	–

JM FAMILY ENTERPRISES INC.

100 Jim Moran Blvd.
Deerfield Beach FL 33442
Phone: 954-429-2000
Fax: 954-429-2300
Web: www.jmfamily.com

CEO: Brent Burns
CFO: Eric Gebhard
HR: Carmen Johnson
FYE: December 31
Type: Private

JM Family Enterprises is a family affair. Owned by the family of founder James Moran JMFE is a holding company (Florida's second-largest private company in fact after Publix Super Markets) with about a dozen automotive-related businesses including the world's largest-volume Lexus retailer JM Lexus in Margate Florida. JMFE's major subsidiary Southeast Toyota Distributors is the nation's largest independent Toyota and Scion distribution franchise delivering vehicles to 170-plus dealers across Alabama Florida Georgia Texas and the Carolinas. As part of its business JMFE also offers financial services insurance inspections dealer IT products and marketing services. It was established in 1968.

JMP GROUP LLC   NYS: JMP

600 Montgomery Street, Suite 1100
San Francisco, CA 94111
Phone: 415 835-8900
Fax: –
Web: www.jmpg.com

CEO: Joseph A Jolson
CFO: Raymond S Jackson
HR: –
FYE: December 31
Type: Public

JMP Group wants to get the jump on the competition. Positioning itself as an alternative to bulge-bracket firms the company provides investment banking services such as strategic advice corporate finance and equity underwriting sales trading and research to small and midsized growth companies. It focuses on the technology health care financial services and real estate sectors. Its research department covers more than 300 small- and mid-cap public companies. JMP Group's Heartland Capital Strategies (HCS) subsidiary manages alternative investments such as equity hedge funds middle-market corporate loans and private equity for institutional and high-net-worth investors.

	Annual Growth	12/15	12/16	12/17	12/18	12/19
Sales ($ mil.)	(9.1%)	172.1	169.4	154.6	193.9	117.4
Net income ($ mil.)	–	(0.2)	2.9	(15.9)	(2.2)	(6.5)
Market value ($ mil.)	(12.3%)	106.5	119.8	109.3	76.1	63.0
Employees	(4.1%)	247	228	230	226	209

JOHN BEAN TECHNOLOGIES CORP   NYS: JBT

70 West Madison Street, Suite 4400 — CEO: Brian Deck
Chicago, IL 60602 — CFO: Matthew Meister
Phone: 312 861-5900 — HR: Jason Clayton
Fax: – — FYE: December 31
Web: www.jbtcorporation.com — Type: Public

John Bean Technologies Corporation (JBT) is a leading global technology solutions and service provider to high-value segments of the industrial food beverage and aviation support industry. JBT manufactures industrial equipment for the food processing and air transportation industries. Its JBT FoodTech segment provides comprehensive solutions throughout the food production value chain. JBT AeroTech markets its solutions and services to domestic and international airport authorities passenger airlines airfreight and ground handling companies military forces and defense contractors. Approximately 60% of JBT's revenue is generated in the US.

	Annual Growth	12/16	12/17	12/18	12/19	12/20
Sales ($ mil.)	6.4%	1,350.5	1,635.1	1,919.7	1,945.7	1,727.8
Net income ($ mil.)	12.6%	67.6	80.5	104.1	129.0	108.8
Market value ($ mil.)	7.3%	2,727.2	3,515.7	2,278.5	3,574.7	3,613.1
Employees	5.5%	5,000	5,800	5,800	6,400	6,200

JOHN C. LINCOLN HEALTH NETWORK

2500 E DUNLAP AVE — CEO: –
PHOENIX, AZ 85020 — CFO: –
Phone: 602-870-6060 — HR: –
Fax: – — FYE: December 31
— Type: Private

John C. Lincoln Health Network takes care of the health of John Q. Public in Arizona. The not-for-profit health care network serves the northern Phoenix area and is home to two hospitals: John C. Lincoln Deer Valley Hospital with more than 200 beds and John C. Lincoln North Mountain Hospital with roughly 260 beds (the Valley's first Magnet nursing hospital an accredited Chest Pain Center and the host of a Level 1 Trauma Center). The system also features a children's care facility various physician and dental clinics a food bank and assisted living facilities for the elderly all operating under the Desert Mission moniker. John C. Lincoln Health Network is part of the Scottsdale Lincoln Health Network along with Scottsdale Healthcare.

	Annual Growth	12/09	12/10	12/11	12/12	12/13
Sales ($ mil.)	2.0%	–	551.2	486.8	509.2	584.5
Net income ($ mil.)	31.3%	–	19.5	17.5	32.7	44.1
Market value ($ mil.)	–	–	–	–	–	–
Employees	–	–	–	–	–	3,500

JOHN CARROLL UNIVERSITY

1 JOHN CARROLL BLVD — CEO: –
UNIVERSITY HEIGHTS, OH 441184581 — CFO: –
Phone: 216-397-1886 — HR: –
Fax: – — FYE: May 31
Web: www.jcu.edu — Type: Private

John Carroll University (JCU) is a Roman Catholic school that offers degree programs in more than 40 fields of the liberal arts social sciences natural sciences business and interdisciplinary studies at the undergraduate level and in selected areas at the master's level. Operated by the Society of Jesus — the Jesuits — it provides instruction to about 3600 students (including 2950 undergraduates). The school is one of 28 Jesuit universities in the US and has been listed in U.S. News & World Report magazine's top 10 rankings of Midwest regional universities for more than 20 consecutive years.

	Annual Growth	05/13	05/14	05/15	05/16	05/20
Sales ($ mil.)	10.1%	–	91.5	96.1	155.8	162.6
Net income ($ mil.)	–	–	14.7	3.7	(2.8)	(7.6)
Market value ($ mil.)	–	–	–	–	–	–
Employees	–	–	–	–	–	2,343

JOHN D AND CATHERINE T MACARTHUR FOUNDATION

140 S DEARBORN ST — CEO: –
CHICAGO, IL 606035202 — CFO: –
Phone: 312-332-0101 — HR: Keith Krellwitz
Fax: – — FYE: December 31
Web: www.macfound.org — Type: Private

Granted The John D. and Catherine T. MacArthur Foundation gives away a lot of money. With some $5.3 billion in assets the private foundation issues more than $250 million in grants annually to groups and individuals working to improve the human condition. Its two primary programs are Human and Community Development (affordable housing education reform mental health) and Global Security and Sustainability (world peace population reduction conservation human rights). The foundation also funds special initiatives and awards $500000 MacArthur Fellowships to a variety of individuals. Since making its first grant in 1978 The John D. and Catherine T. MacArthur Foundation has distributed about $4 billion.

	Annual Growth	12/02	12/03	12/04	12/05	12/13
Sales ($ mil.)	(6.0%)	–	–	–	705.8	430.1
Net income ($ mil.)	–	–	–	–	0.0	144.1
Market value ($ mil.)	–	–	–	–	–	–
Employees	–	–	–	–	–	150

JOHN D. OIL AND GAS COMPANY   OTC: JDOG

8500 Station St. Ste. 345 — CEO: Richard M Osborne
Mentor OH 44060 — CFO: Carolyn Coatoam
Phone: 440-255-6325 — HR: –
Fax: 440-205-8680 — FYE: December 31
Web: www.johndoilandgas.com — Type: Public

John D. Oil and Gas (formerly Liberty Self-Stor) has shed its storage sheds in favor of oil and natural gas extraction in northeastern Ohio and the Appalachian Basin. In 2008 John D. Oil and Gas reported proved reserves of 2.1 billion cu. ft. of natural gas and 17500 barrels of oil. That year it had 49 net productive wells. The company also owns and manages Kykuit Resources LLC which leases natural gas and oil rights to more than 203840 acres in the Montana Breaks region in Montana. Chairman and CEO Richard Osborne owns 46% of John D. Oil and Gas.

JOHN F KENNEDY CENTER FOR THE PERFORMING ARTS

2700 F ST NW — CEO: –
WASHINGTON, DC 205660001 — CFO: Lynne Pratt
Phone: 202-416-8000 — HR: –
Fax: – — FYE: September 30
Web: www.kennedy-center.org — Type: Private

The John F. Kennedy Center for the Performing Arts also known as The Kennedy Center traces its roots to 1958 when president Dwight Eisenhower signed the National Cultural Center Act calling for a privately funded venture featuring a variety of classic and contemporary programming with an educational focus. The center was a pet project and fund raiser beneficiary of president Kennedy; it was named as a living memorial to him after his death. Located on 17 acres overlooking the Potomac River in Washington D.C. the center opened in 1971 and presents some 2000 events a year including musicals dance performances and jazz and orchestral concerts. It also produces TV programming workshops and lectures.

	Annual Growth	09/09	09/10	09/15	09/16	09/19
Sales ($ mil.)	6.7%	–	182.8	239.1	236.2	326.5
Net income ($ mil.)	14.1%	–	21.8	30.0	13.7	71.6
Market value ($ mil.)	–	–	–	–	–	–
Employees	–	–	–	–	–	1,144

JOHN HINE PONTIAC

1545 CAMINO DEL RIO S
SAN DIEGO, CA 921083575
Phone: 619-297-4251
Fax: –
Web: www.johnhine.com

CEO: –
CFO: –
HR: –
FYE: December 31
Type: Private

John Hine Mazda (formerly John Hine Pontiac) sells new and used Mazda brand vehicles to customers in the San Diego area. The dealership also offers parts service and collision repair through its John Hine Auto Body Center. Visitors to its Web site can check new and used inventory get a quote on a vehicle schedule service order parts and apply for financing. The company is a founding member of the California Sales Training Academy a private training program that has become an associates degree program at a local community college. The company was established in 1957. Prior to the discontinuation of the Pontiac brand the dealership sold Dodge and Pontiac vehicles in addition to Mazdas.

	Annual Growth	12/05	12/06	12/07	12/08	12/09
Sales ($ mil.)	(11.6%)	–	69.0	0.0	58.7	47.7
Net income ($ mil.)	–	–	–	0.0	(0.4)	(0.1)
Market value ($ mil.)	–	–	–	–	–	–
Employees	–	–	–	–	–	201

JOHN MORRELL & CO.

805 E. Kemper Rd.
Cincinnati OH 45246-2515
Phone: 513-346-3540
Fax: 513-346-7556
Web: www.johnmorrell.com

CEO: –
CFO: –
HR: Annette Bushelman
FYE: April 30
Type: Subsidiary

Here's one of the top names in meat. John Morrell & Co. is a leading producer of processed-meat and fresh-pork products. It makes bacon fresh pork hams and sausage as well as cold cuts and lunch meats hot dogs and deli meats. The company's brands include E-Z-Cut Farmers Hickory and its flagship John Morrell banner. Most of its products are sold through supermarkets and other retail grocers. John Morrell also sells pork products to convenience stores foodservice suppliers restaurants and other customers in the hospitality industry. Tracing its roots to the UK where it was founded in 1827 John Morrell is a subsidiary of top US pork producer Smithfield Foods.

JOHN MUIR HEALTH

1601 YGNACIO VALLEY RD
WALNUT CREEK, CA 945983122
Phone: 925-947-4449
Fax: –
Web: www.johnmuirhealth.com

CEO: Calvin Knight
CFO: –
HR: –
FYE: December 31
Type: Private

John Muir Health provides health care throughout the scenic San Francisco Bay area. The John Muir Health Walnut Creek Medical Center has about 555 beds and that serves as Contra Costa County's only designated trauma center. The John Muir Health Concord Medical Center has about 245 beds. Both are recognized as the finest centers for neurosciences orthopedics cancer care cardiovascular care and high-risk obstetrics. The John Muir Behavioral Health Center is a nearly 75-bed psychiatric hospital. John Muir Health also offers home health rehabilitation and wellness programs.

	Annual Growth	12/14	12/15	12/16	12/17	12/20
Sales ($ mil.)	5.0%	–	–	1,734.5	1,831.6	2,106.0
Net income ($ mil.)	13.5%	–	–	107.2	92.3	178.2
Market value ($ mil.)	–	–	–	–	–	–
Employees	–	–	–	–	–	2,200

JOHN T. MATHER MEMORIAL HOSPITAL OF PORT JEFFERSON, NEW YORK, INC.

75 N COUNTRY RD
PORT JEFFERSON, NY 117772119
Phone: 631-476-2738
Fax: –
Web: www.matherhospital.org

CEO: –
CFO: –
HR: –
FYE: December 31
Type: Private

Shipbuilder John T. Mather envisioned a legacy that would keep his community of Port Jefferson in good health and John T. Mather Memorial Hospital came to fruition in 1929 one year after it's namesake's death. The not-for-profit hospital has some 250 beds and provides a variety of health care services to the residents of Port Jefferson New York and surrounding areas of Suffolk County. Services include emergency care occupational therapy psychiatry and radiology. Mather Hospital is a member of Long Island Health Network an association of about a dozen affiliated hospitals all serving Long Island. It is also Magnet® recognized hospital by the American Nurses Credentialing Center.

	Annual Growth	12/14	12/15	12/16	12/17	12/18
Sales ($ mil.)	4.2%	–	279.4	306.0	320.1	315.7
Net income ($ mil.)	–	–	(1.1)	2.5	0.4	5.5
Market value ($ mil.)	–	–	–	–	–	–
Employees	–	–	–	–	–	2,568

JOHN WIELAND HOMES AND NEIGHBORHOODS INC.

1950 Sullivan Rd.
Atlanta GA 30337
Phone: 770-996-1400
Fax: 770-907-3485
Web: www.jwhomes.com

CEO: –
CFO: –
HR: –
FYE: September 30
Type: Private

John Wieland Homes and Neighborhoods develops land and builds cluster homes townhomes and upscale single-family houses in the southeastern US. Target markets include Atlanta Charlotte Charleston Nashville and Raleigh with home prices ranging from around $200000 to more than $1 million. The company also operates New Home Design Studios that provide customizable interior and exterior design services. WFS Mortgage a joint venture with Wells Fargo Home Mortgage offers lending to John Wieland Homes' customers and others. John Wieland also has a commercial division which develops office retail and mixed-use properties. Chairman John Wieland owns his namesake firm which he founded in 1970.

JOHNS HOPKINS ALL CHILDREN'S HOSPITAL, INC.

501 6TH AVE S
SAINT PETERSBURG, FL 337014634
Phone: 727-898-7451
Fax: –
Web: www.hopkinsallchildrens.org

CEO: Jonathan Ellen
CFO: Douglas Myers
HR: –
FYE: June 30
Type: Private

Johns Hopkins All Children's Hospital has about 260 beds all dedicated to the health of west-central Florida's children. With roughly 200 pediatric physician specialists on board the hospital offers its young patients (infants children and teens) a variety of services including a Neonatal Intensive Care Unit for premature and "at-risk" infants. Its heart bone marrow and kidney transplant programs are nationally renowned. The teaching hospital is also affiliated with the University of South Florida College of Medicine. All Children's Hospital is a member of the Johns Hopkins Medicine network.

	Annual Growth	06/13	06/14	06/15	06/16	06/21
Sales ($ mil.)	4.8%	–	–	408.1	400.7	540.7
Net income ($ mil.)	–	–	–	(1.5)	21.7	144.9
Market value ($ mil.)	–	–	–	–	–	–
Employees	–	–	–	–	–	2,325

JOHNS HOPKINS BAYVIEW MEDICAL CENTER, INC.

4940 EASTERN AVE
BALTIMORE, MD 212242735
Phone: 410-550-0100
Fax: –
Web: www.hopkinsmedicine.org

CEO: –
CFO: –
HR: –
FYE: June 30
Type: Private

If you've just been pulled from the bay like an old empty crab trap Johns Hopkins Bayview might be the first place you're taken. One of five member institutions in the Johns Hopkins Health System Johns Hopkins Bayview Medical Center is a community teaching hospital. Its Baltimore-based operations include a neonatal intensive care unit as well as centers devoted to trauma geriatrics sleep disorders and weight management. It also features the state's only regional burn center. The facility includes a meditation labyrinth for patients families and staff to walk. Established in 1773 the medical center has more than 560 beds.

	Annual Growth	06/17	06/18	06/19	06/20	06/21
Sales ($ mil.)	4.5%	–	628.5	648.1	669.1	716.9
Net income ($ mil.)	96.1%	–	12.1	(39.1)	(41.0)	91.2
Market value ($ mil.)	–	–	–	–	–	–
Employees	–	–	–	–	–	3,300

JOHNS HOPKINS MEDICINE INTERNATIONAL L.L.C.

600 N. Wolfe St.
Baltimore MD 21287
Phone: 410-955-5000
Fax: 410-442-1082
Web: www.bshsi.org

CEO: Harris Benny
CFO: –
HR: –
FYE: June 30
Type: Private - Not-for-Pr

Johns Hopkins Medicine has a sterling reputation for health care in Baltimore and beyond. Consisting of Johns Hopkins University School of Medicine and the Johns Hopkins Health System Johns Hopkins Medicine oversees six area hospitals (with a combined total of almost 2680 beds) in addition to the academic offerings of the medical school and and a nursing program. It also operates a pediatric facility in Florida. Other facilities and programs include community clinics a home health care provider and its own managed care plan. The system has educational patient care and management partnerships with neighboring medical centers including Greater Baltimore Medical Center and Anne Arundel Medical Center.

JOHNS HOPKINS UNIVERSITY

3400 N CHARLES ST
BALTIMORE, MD 212182680
Phone: 410-516-8000
Fax: –
Web: www.jhu.edu

CEO: –
CFO: –
HR: –
FYE: June 30
Type: Private

Founded in 1876 The Johns Hopkins University has established its reputation by molding itself in the image of a European research institution. While renowned for its School of Medicine the private university offers more than 400 academic programs spanning fields of study including arts and sciences business engineering and international studies. The university enrolls more than 29000 full- and part-time students throughout nine academic divisions. Johns Hopkins has about a half-dozen campuses in Maryland and Washington DC as well as facilities in China and Italy. The student-teacher ratio is 10:1. The affiliated Johns Hopkins Health System treats more than 3920 patients from approximately 145 countries in its facilities based in the US.

	Annual Growth	06/17	06/18	06/19	06/20	06/21
Sales ($ mil.)	3.4%	–	6,021.0	6,410.1	6,470.6	6,659.0
Net income ($ mil.)	69.4%	–	705.4	2,017.6	903.8	3,427.4
Market value ($ mil.)	–	–	–	–	–	–
Employees	–	–	–	–	–	37,600

JOHNSON & JOHNSON

One Johnson & Johnson Plaza
New Brunswick, NJ 08933
Phone: 732 524-0400
Fax: 732 214-0332
Web: www.jnj.com

NYS: JNJ
CEO: Joaquin Duato
CFO: Joseph Wolk
HR: –
FYE: January 02
Type: Public

Johnson & Johnson (J&J) is engaged in the research and development manufacture and sale of a broad range of products in the health care field. Its Pharmaceuticals division is focused on manufacturing medicines for immunology infectious diseases neuroscience cardiovascular metabolism pulmonary hypertension and oncology ailments. Top sellers are psoriasis drugs Remicade and Stelara. J&J's Medical Devices division offers surgical equipment orthopedic products and contact lenses among other items. Finally J&J's Consumer business makes over-the-counter (OTC) drugs and products for baby skin oral women's and first-aid care. The company operates worldwide but makes about half of revenue in the US.

	Annual Growth	12/17	12/18	12/19*	01/21	01/22
Sales ($ mil.)	4.2%	76,450.0	81,581.0	82,059.0	82,584.0	93,775.0
Net income ($ mil.)	74.2%	1,300.0	15,297.0	15,119.0	14,714.0	20,878.0
Market value ($ mil.)	–	0.0	0.0	0.0	0.0	0.0
Employees	1.5%	134,000	135,100	133,200	136,400	144,300

*Fiscal year change

JOHNSON & WALES UNIVERSITY INC

8 ABBOTT PARK PL
PROVIDENCE, RI 029033775
Phone: 401-598-1000
Fax: –
Web: www.jwu.edu

CEO: –
CFO: Joseph J Greene Jr
HR: –
FYE: June 30
Type: Private

Things are a little upside-down at Johnson & Wales University and that's just the way the school likes it. The private not-for-profit accredited institution provides what it calls an upside-down curriculum allowing students to take courses in their major during the first year so they learn right away if their career choice is right for them. At the end of two years of study students earn an associate's degree and the opportunity to go on to earn a bachelor's degree. Founded in 1914 the school enrolls more than 12000 graduate undergraduate and online students across its four campuses in Colorado Florida North Carolina and Rhode Island.

	Annual Growth	06/17	06/18	06/19	06/20	06/21
Sales ($ mil.)	(12.6%)	–	330.4	301.5	289.3	220.3
Net income ($ mil.)	6.0%	–	13.4	(11.2)	(31.3)	16.0
Market value ($ mil.)	–	–	–	–	–	–
Employees	–	–	–	–	–	1,400

JOHNSON CITY ENERGY AUTHORITY

2600 BOONES CREEK RD
JOHNSON CITY, TN 376154448
Phone: 423-952-5000
Fax: –
Web: www.brightridge.com

CEO: –
CFO: Brian Bolling
HR: Connie Crouch
FYE: June 30
Type: Private

Board members have real power (to dispense) on the Johnson City Power Board. Based in Johnson City Tennessee the Johnson City Power Board provides electricity and related programs services and products to approximately 68000 residential and business customers in Washington County as well as parts of Carter Greene and Sullivan Counties. The company is one of 158 power companies throughout Alabama Georgia Kentucky and Tennessee which purchase electricity from the Tennessee Valley Authority. Johnson City Power Board teams with cities towns governments economic development and Chambers of Commerce to promote business and industry in its service area.

	Annual Growth	06/15	06/16	06/17	06/18	06/19
Sales ($ mil.)	1.3%	–	–	199.0	201.5	204.2
Net income ($ mil.)	(4.0%)	–	–	12.4	13.0	11.5
Market value ($ mil.)	–	–	–	–	–	–
Employees	–	–	–	–	–	174

JOHNSON CONTROLS FIRE PROTECTION LP

6600 CONGRESS AVE
BOCA RATON, FL 334871213
Phone: 561-988-7200
Fax: -
Web: www.tycosimplexgrinnell.com

CEO: George R Oliver
CFO: -
HR: -
FYE: September 30
Type: Private

SimplexGrinnell handles emergencies well. The company provides integrated security alarm fire suppression healthcare communications and emergency lighting systems. SimplexGrinnell reaches some 1 million customers in the US and Canada through more than 150 district offices located in the Americas Europe Asia and other regions. In addition to providing security and fire related products Simplex-Grinnell operates a service division devoted to test and inspection preventive maintenance central station monitoring and emergency services. The company's clients include members of local state and federal government agencies corporations oil and gas companies hospitals and educational facilities.

	Annual Growth	09/06	09/07	09/08	09/09	09/16
Sales ($ mil.)	1.0%	-	-	-	1,750.5	1,871.4
Net income ($ mil.)	-	-	-	-	0.0	182.5
Market value ($ mil.)	-	-	-	-	-	-
Employees	-	-	-	-	-	9,500

JOHNSON CONTROLS, INC.

5757 N GREEN BAY AVE
GLENDALE, WI 532094408
Phone: 800-382-2804
Fax: -
Web: www.johnsoncontrols.com

CEO: George Oliver
CFO: Brian Stief
HR: Eric Niemi
FYE: September 30
Type: Private

Climate control for offices Johnson Controls manufactures installs and services energy-efficient heating ventilation and air conditioning (HVAC) systems. Its products cover everything needed to make a place of work comfortable and safe to be in extending to fire detection and suppression and security measures such as electronic card site access. Originally an American company Johnson Controls completed a reverse merger with Cork-based Tyco International and is now domiciled in Ireland (although the US remains its largest market by far). The company sold its car battery manufacturing operations in 2018 to Brookfield Business Partners.

	Annual Growth	09/11	09/12	09/13	09/14	09/15
Sales ($ mil.)	(6.7%)	-	-	42,730.0	42,828.0	37,179.0
Net income ($ mil.)	13.8%	-	-	1,297.0	1,335.0	1,679.0
Market value ($ mil.)	-	-	-	-	-	-
Employees	-	-	-	-	-	105,000

JOHNSON MATTHEY INC.

435 Devon Park Dr. Ste. 600
Wayne PA 19087
Phone: 610-971-3000
Fax: 610-971-3191
Web: www.jmusa.com

CEO: -
CFO: -
HR: -
FYE: March 31
Type: Subsidiary

According to Johnson Matthey's math it adds up to serve the precious metals catalysts coatings and pharmaceutical industries in the US. The company also provides contract research and development for the pharmaceutical industry. Its Emission Control Technologies segment makes catalytic systems and emission controls for a range of industries including automotive manufacturing. The Precious Metals segment is engaged in supplying fabricated precious metal alloys chemicals and catalysts as well as medical device components and colors and coatings. The company is the North American unit of UK chemicals and catalysts maker Johnson Matthey plc.

JOHNSON OUTDOORS INC

NMS: JOUT

555 Main Street
Racine, WI 53403
Phone: 262 631-6600
Fax: -
Web: www.johnsonoutdoors.com

CEO: Helen Johnson-Leipold
CFO: David Johnson
HR: -
FYE: October 01
Type: Public

Founded in 1987 Johnson Outdoors keeps sports buffs from staying indoors. The company makes markets and sells camping and outdoor equipment (such as Jetboil cooking systems and Eureka! tents and backpacks). It also focuses on supplying equipment for water activities with its diving gear (Scubapro and Uwatec masks fins snorkels and tanks) trolling motors (Minn Kota) fish finders (Humminbird) and watercraft (Old Town canoes). With GPS technologies and electric boat motors The Johnson family including CEO Helen Johnson-Leipold controls the company. Most of the company's sales come from the US.

	Annual Growth	09/17	09/18	09/19*	10/20	10/21
Sales ($ mil.)	11.3%	490.6	544.3	562.4	594.2	751.7
Net income ($ mil.)	24.1%	35.2	40.7	51.4	55.2	83.4
Market value ($ mil.)	10.6%	742.1	941.7	593.8	872.8	1,110.7
Employees	6.2%	1,100	1,200	1,200	1,200	1,400

*Fiscal year change

JOHNSON SUPPLY AND EQUIPMENT CORPORATION

10151 STELLA LINK RD
HOUSTON, TX 770255398
Phone: 713-830-2300
Fax: -
Web: www.johnsonsupply.com

CEO: Carl I Johnson
CFO: Donald K Wile
HR: -
FYE: March 31
Type: Private

Global warming? Bring it on! Keeping Texas and Louisiana residents cool is no easy task but Johnson Supply does what it can. Through about two dozen locations in hot spots like Houston and Lake Charles Louisiana Johnson Supply distributes air-conditioning and refrigeration equipment controls parts and supplies from more than 200 manufacturers. Since those places also get cold relatively speaking the company sells heating and ventilation equipment as well. Its 200 suppliers include names like York Friedrich Warren Mueller and Johnson Controls. The company was founded in 1953 by Carl I. Johnson Sr.

	Annual Growth	03/02	03/03	03/04	03/05	03/08
Sales ($ mil.)	1.2%	-	97.9	105.8	110.3	103.9
Net income ($ mil.)	137.8%	-	0.3	22.4	80.0	24.9
Market value ($ mil.)	-	-	-	-	-	-
Employees	-	-	-	-	-	210

JOHNSONVILLE SAUSAGE LLC

N6928 Johnsonville Way
Sheboygan Falls WI 53085
Phone: 920-453-6900
Fax: 920-459-7824
Web: www.johnsonville.com

CEO: Nick Meriggioli
CFO: -
HR: -
FYE: December 31
Type: Private

Johnsonville Sausage has found the missing link to family meals. The company makes a variety of top-selling fresh pre-cooked and smoked sausage products. Its products portfolio includes bratwurst breakfast links and bulk rolls chorizo and smoked and Italian sausage. Outside mealtime the company offers snack sausages and deli bites. Sold under the Johnsonville and Table for Two brand names the company's more than 50 link and bulk sausage meats are sold primarily through grocery stores and food service operators. Johnsonville's sausage is available in some 30 countries worldwide. Its products are on the menu at more than 4000 US McDonald's restaurants. The privately-owned company was founded in 1945.

JOHNSTON ENTERPRISES, INC.

411 W CHESTNUT AVE
ENID, OK 737012057
Phone: 580-249-4449
Fax: –

CEO: Lew Meibergen
CFO: Gary Tucker
HR: –
FYE: April 30
Type: Private

Johnston Enterprises serves the harvesters of America's amber waves of grain. The company offers farmers in Oklahoma and other Midwestern states grain-processing and storage facilities and inland water transportation services through its Johnston Grain and Johnston Port Terminals divisions. Its Johnston Seed subsidiary sells wildflower and turf wild forage and native grass seed and wildlife feed. The company was founded in 1893 by W. B. Johnston and is owned and operated by the founder's descendants president Lew Meibergen and COO Butch Meibergen.

	Annual Growth	04/08	04/09	04/10	04/11	04/12
Sales ($ mil.)	45.7%	–	–	140.2	289.9	297.8
Net income ($ mil.)	147.4%	–	–	0.3	1.4	1.6
Market value ($ mil.)	–	–	–	–	–	–
Employees	–	–	–	–	–	335

JOIE DE VIVRE HOSPITALITY INC.

530 Bush St. Ste. 501
San Francisco CA 94108
Phone: 415-835-0300
Fax: 415-835-0317
Web: www.jdvhotels.com

CEO: Stephen T Conley Jr
CFO: –
HR: –
FYE: December 31
Type: Private

You might say this company has a zest for hotel life. Joie de Vivre Hospitality operates boutique hotels with more than 30 properties in California many of which are in the San Francisco Bay area. Hotels include Hotel Rex featuring a book-lined lounge inspired by 1930s literary salons and Phoenix Hotel a funky San Francisco landmark that is frequented by entertainers and celebrities. (So much so that it is known as the "rock 'n roll hotel.") Some properties feature spa facilities and upscale restaurants. Chip Conley founded Joie de Vivre in 1987. John Pritzker son of Hyatt Hotels Corporation founder Jay Pritzker owns a majority of the firm. The company is joining Thompson Hotels to form JT Hospitality.

JONES GROUP INC   NYS: JNY

1411 Broadway
New York, NY 10018
Phone: 212 642-3860
Fax: –
Web: www.jonesgroupinc.com

CEO: –
CFO: –
HR: –
FYE: December 31
Type: Public

While some are busy keeping up with the Joneses The Jones Group (formerly Jones Apparel Group) is too busy taking stock in its own brand portfolio to take notice. The company provides a wide range of clothing shoes and accessories for men women and juniors. Its brands include Anne Klein Jones New York Gloria Vanderbilt Nine West Evan-Picone and l.e.i. among some 30 others. Through licensing agreements Jones also supplies Givenchy jewelry Rachel Roy designer apparel and Dockers footwear. It is active in both the retail and wholesale sectors. The Jones Group operates about 950 outlet and specialty stores in the US and internationally as well as branded e-commerce sites.

	Annual Growth	12/08	12/09	12/10	12/11	12/12
Sales ($ mil.)	1.2%	3,616.4	3,327.4	3,642.7	3,785.3	3,798.1
Net income ($ mil.)	–	(765.4)	(86.6)	53.8	50.7	(56.1)
Market value ($ mil.)	17.2%	464.1	1,272.0	1,230.8	835.6	876.0
Employees	(1.9%)	12,710	11,535	10,940	12,060	11,790

JONES LANG LASALLE INC   NYS: JLL

200 East Randolph Drive
Chicago, IL 60601
Phone: 312 782-5800
Fax: 312 782-4339
Web: www.jll.com

CEO: Richard Bloxam
CFO: Karen Brennan
HR: –
FYE: December 31
Type: Public

Jones Lang LaSalle (JLL) provides real estate without borders. Its services include commercial leasing real estate brokerage management advisory and financing through more than 350 corporate offices around the world. The company's LaSalle Investment Management arm is a diversified real estate management firm with more than $68.9 billion in assets under management. JLL has commercial real estate expertise across office retail health care industrial and multifamily residential properties. It manages approximately 5.4 billion sq. ft. worldwide. JLL was formed through the 1999 merger of Jones Lang Wootton (founded in England in 1783) and LaSalle Partners (founded in the US in 1968).

	Annual Growth	12/16	12/17	12/18	12/19	12/20
Sales ($ mil.)	25.0%	6,803.8	7,932.4	16,318.4	17,983.2	16,589.9
Net income ($ mil.)	6.1%	318.2	254.2	484.5	535.3	402.5
Market value ($ mil.)	10.1%	5,163.7	7,611.1	6,469.9	8,896.9	7,582.5
Employees	4.1%	77,300	81,900	90,000	93,400	90,800

JONES SODA CO.   NBB: JSDA

66 South Hanford Street, Suite 150
Seattle, WA 98134
Phone: 206 624-3357
Fax: 206 624-6857
Web: www.jonessoda.com

CEO: Mark Murray
CFO: Joe Culp
HR: –
FYE: December 31
Type: Public

Keeping up with the Joneses at Jones Soda requires an adventurous palate. The beverage company makes markets and sells brightly colored sodas with wacky names and flavors like Fufu Berry and Blue Bubblegum. Seasonal offerings include Turkey and Gravy for Thanksgiving and Chocolate Fudge for Valentine's Day. To keep things interesting it regularly discontinues flavors and introduces new ones; labels also can be customized with photos submitted by customers. Jones Soda also sells Jones Zilch (zero calories) and the WhoopAss Energy Drink an energy beverage that's available with or without sugar. Jones Soda's beverages are distributed throughout North America as well as in Australia the UK and Ireland.

	Annual Growth	12/16	12/17	12/18	12/19	12/20
Sales ($ mil.)	(6.7%)	15.7	13.3	12.6	11.5	11.9
Net income ($ mil.)	–	(0.2)	(1.3)	(2.1)	(2.8)	(3.0)
Market value ($ mil.)	(15.4%)	27.9	22.6	14.6	18.0	14.3
Employees	(4.3%)	25	25	24	29	21

JORDAN CF INVESTMENTS LLP

7700 CF JORDAN DR
EL PASO, TX 799128808
Phone: 915-877-3333
Fax: –
Web: www.jordanfosterconstruction.com

CEO: –
CFO: –
HR: –
FYE: December 31
Type: Private

A high-flier in construction services C.F. Jordan is a top building contractor that offers preconstruction design/build development and project management services. The company has traditionally built hotels and resorts but has diversified into military residential highway and school construction. Its contracts include projects for the Immigration and Naturalization Service for border patrol stations health care centers and detention centers. Other works have included Sea World in San Antonio the Insights Science Museum in El Paso and the Pearl Harbor Commissary and Exchange in Hawaii. Chairman Charles "Paco" Jordan started the Texas-based firm in 1988.

	Annual Growth	12/03	12/04	12/05	12/08	12/09
Sales ($ mil.)	6.8%	–	–	260.0	337.9	337.9
Net income ($ mil.)	11.3%	–	–	2.5	3.9	3.9
Market value ($ mil.)	–	–	–	–	–	–
Employees	–	–	–	–	–	500

JOS. A. BANK CLOTHIERS, INC.   NMS: JOSB

500 Hanover Pike
Hampstead, MD 21074-2095
Phone: 410 239-2700
Fax: –
Web: www.josbank.com

CEO: R Neal Black
CFO: David E Ullman
HR: –
FYE: February 02
Type: Public

When casual Fridays put a wrinkle in the starched selling philosophy of Jos. A. Bank Clothiers the company dressed down. Although it is still best known for making tailored clothing for the professional man including suits sport coats dress shirts and pants it has added casual wear suitable for those dress-down Fridays and weekends. It also launched the David Leadbetter line of golf wear. The company sells its Jos. A. Bank clothes and a few shoe brands through its catalogs website and some 625 company-owned or franchised stores in 40-plus states and the District of Columbia. For corporate customers it offers a credit card that provides users with discounts. Most of its stores house a tailoring shop.

	Annual Growth	01/09	01/10	01/11	01/12*	02/13
Sales ($ mil.)	17.7%	546.4	770.3	858.1	979.9	1,049.3
Net income ($ mil.)	16.5%	43.2	71.2	85.8	97.5	79.7
Market value ($ mil.)	10.5%	767.8	1,171.9	1,173.0	1,343.9	1,144.5
Employees	11.9%	4,040	4,318	4,998	5,883	6,342

*Fiscal year change

JOURNAL COMMUNICATIONS INC   NYS: JRN

333 West State Street
Milwaukee, WI 53203
Phone: 414 224-2000
Fax: –
Web: www.journalcommunications.com

CEO: –
CFO: –
HR: –
FYE: December 29
Type: Public

You might say this company chronicles the news in Milwaukee. Journal Communications is a diversified media company with operations in publishing radio and TV broadcasting and interactive media. Its publishing business is anchored by its flagship paper the Milwaukee Journal Sentinel a leading daily newspaper in Milwaukee with a circulation of about 185000. Its Journal Community Publishing Group also runs about 50 community newspapers and shoppers serving markets in Wisconsin and Florida. Journal Communications owns and operates about 35 radio stations and 15 TV stations in a dozen states through its Journal Broadcast unit. It also operates several websites in conjunction with its media properties.

	Annual Growth	12/09	12/10	12/11	12/12	12/13
Sales ($ mil.)	(2.2%)	433.6	376.8	356.8	400.0	397.3
Net income ($ mil.)	57.0%	4.3	34.4	22.2	33.3	26.2
Market value ($ mil.)	23.4%	200.2	259.1	234.7	262.7	464.3
Employees	(4.2%)	3,200	2,600	2,500	2,500	2,700

JOY GLOBAL INC   NYS: JOY

100 East Wisconsin Avenue, Suite 2780
Milwaukee, WI 53202
Phone: 414 319-8500
Fax: –
Web: www.joyglobal.com

CEO: Edward L Doheny II
CFO: James M Sullivan
HR: –
FYE: October 28
Type: Public

Joy Global makes heavy equipment for the mining industry through two subsidiaries. Its Joy Global Underground Machinery subsidiary makes underground coal-mining equipment that includes armored face conveyors roof supports longwall shearers and shuttle cars. Other operations make electric mining shovels rotary blasthole drills and other equipment used in surface open-pit mining; it also provides parts and service through its P&H MinePro Services network. Joy Global in mid-2016 agreed to be acquired by Komatsu America a subsidiary of construction equipment maker behemoth Komatsu.

	Annual Growth	10/12	10/13	10/14	10/15	10/16
Sales ($ mil.)	(19.5%)	5,660.9	5,012.7	3,778.3	3,172.1	2,371.4
Net income ($ mil.)	–	762.0	533.7	331.0	(1,178.0)	(58.4)
Market value ($ mil.)	(18.0%)	6,051.7	5,711.5	5,174.7	1,689.2	2,740.2
Employees	(7.7%)	18,019	16,600	15,400	13,400	13,100

JOYCE LESLIE INC

401 TOWNE CENTRE DR
HILLSBOROUGH, NJ 088444698
Phone: 201-804-7800
Fax: –
Web: www.rainbowshops.com

CEO: Celia Clancy
CFO: Peter Left
HR: Donna Finch
FYE: January 30
Type: Private

Club-hoppers (and high schoolers) hoping to look like Paris Hilton without spending like her do their shopping at Joyce Leslie. The northeastern retail chain specializes in trendy and inexpensive women's and junior's clothing aimed primarily at teens and tweens. It operates about 50 shops filled with high-fashion knockoffs in Connecticut New Jersey New York and Pennsylvania. Joyce Leslie named after the daughter of the company's founder Julius Gewirtz was established in Brooklyn in 1945 and originally sold women's dresses. In February 2016 after struggling to find a business strategic partner to save the business the company announced it would be closing its stores for good.

	Annual Growth	01/06	01/07	01/08	01/09	01/10
Sales ($ mil.)	3.1%	–	–	95.0	100.9	101.0
Net income ($ mil.)	2.4%	–	–	1.2	1.2	1.3
Market value ($ mil.)	–	–	–	–	–	–
Employees	–	–	–	–	–	900

JPMORGAN CHASE & CO   NYS: JPM

383 Madison Avenue
New York, NY 10179
Phone: 212 270-6000
Fax: –
Web: www.jpmorganchase.com

CEO: Jamie Dimon
CFO: Jeremy Barnum
HR: Robin Leopold
FYE: December 31
Type: Public

Boasting some $3.4 trillion in assets JPMorgan Chase is the largest bank holding company in the US and a leader in investment banking financial services for consumers and small businesses commercial banking financial transaction processing and asset management. The company operates through nearly 5000 branches in about 40 states and Washington D.C. Its principal bank subsidiary is JPMorgan Chase Bank National Association a national banking association; while its principal non-bank subsidiary is J.P. Morgan Securities LLC a US broker-dealer. Both of its subsidiaries operate nationally and overseas through branches representative office and subsidiary foreign banks.

	Annual Growth	12/17	12/18	12/19	12/20	12/21
Assets ($ mil.)	10.3%	2,533,600.0	2,622,532.0	2,687,379.0	3,386,071.0	3,743,567.0
Net income ($ mil.)	18.6%	24,441.0	32,474.0	36,431.0	29,131.0	48,334.0
Market value ($ mil.)	–	0.0	0.0	0.0	0.0	0.0
Employees	1.8%	252,539	256,105	256,981	255,351	271,025

JPS INDUSTRIES INC.   NBB: JPST

55 Beattie Place, Suite 1510
Greenville, SC 29601
Phone: 864 239-3900
Fax: –

CEO: Mikel H Williams
CFO: Charles R Tutterow
HR: –
FYE: November 02
Type: Public

JPS Industries' glass and plastic products can be found surfing the waves and saving lives. Its JPS Composite Materials arm makes high-strength fiberglass and synthetic fabrics for the aerospace military electrical construction and other industries. The products are used in myriad applications including body armor insulation circuit boards and even surfboards. JPS Industries also operates as JPS Elastomerics which includes Stevens Urethane a maker of polyurethane film sheet and tubing used to make an array of goods such as athletic shoes medical devices and scuba equipment. JPS Elastomerics' traces back to the 1863 founding of predecessor Easthampton Rubber Thread.

	Annual Growth	10/09	10/10	10/11	10/12*	11/13
Sales ($ mil.)	1.4%	191.3	186.7	190.3	158.3	202.0
Net income ($ mil.)	38.7%	0.6	3.2	(0.9)	1.3	2.0
Market value ($ mil.)	15.0%	28.8	41.7	69.5	72.0	50.4
Employees	–	–	–	–	–	–

*Fiscal year change

JTH HOLDING INC.

1716 Corporate Landing Pkwy.
Virginia Beach VA 23454
Phone: 757-493-8855
Fax: 800-880-6432
Web: www.libertytax.com

CEO: -
CFO: Mark F Baumgartner
HR: -
FYE: April 30
Type: Private

JTH Holding wants to free you from those tax preparation shackles. Doing business as Liberty Tax Service it is the third-largest income tax preparation chain (behind H&R Block and Jackson Hewitt). Liberty Tax Service provides computerized tax preparation services through about 4200 offices throughout the US and in Canada. More than 98% of the offices are operated by franchises and are easily recognized by the costumed Uncle Sams or Lady Liberties waving out front. The company's eSmart Tax product allows customers to file their taxes online. Liberty Tax also offers tax-preparation courses refund loans audit assistance and related programs and services. CEO John Hewitt founded the company in 1997.

JTH TAX INC.

1716 CORPORATE LANDING PA
VIRGINIA BEACH, VA 23454-5681
Phone: 757-493-8855
Fax: -
Web: www.libertytax.com

CEO: -
CFO: Mark F Baumgartner
HR: -
FYE: April 30
Type: Private

JTH Holding wants to free you from those tax preparation shackles. Doing business as Liberty Tax Service it is the third-largest income tax preparation chain (behind H&R Block and Jackson Hewitt). Liberty Tax Service provides computerized tax preparation services through about 4200 offices throughout the US and in Canada. More than 98% of the offices are operated by franchises and are easily recognized by the costumed Uncle Sams or Lady Liberties waving out front. The company's eSmart Tax product allows customers to file their taxes online. Liberty Tax also offers tax-preparation courses refund loans audit assistance and related programs and services. CEO John Hewitt founded the company in 1997.

	Annual Growth	04/05	04/06	04/07	04/08	04/09
Sales ($ mil.)	7.6%	-	66.2	75.1	87.6	82.4
Net income ($ mil.)	13.5%	-	8.3	15.7	16.9	12.1
Market value ($ mil.)	-	-	-	-	-	-
Employees	-	-	-	-	-	280

JTM PROVISIONS COMPANY INC.

200 Sales Dr.
Harrison OH 45030
Phone: 513-367-4900
Fax: 513-367-1132
Web: www.jtmfoodgroup.com

CEO: Anthony A Maas
CFO: -
HR: -
FYE: December 31
Type: Private

The lunch lady makes a mean meal with help from JTM Provisions. The company produces some 600 fully cooked meals from traditional to ethic dishes for the food-service industry. Its mainstay offerings are marketed in North America under name brands including Cecilia's Italian Favorites Cocina Tejada Mexican Favorites Soaring Dragon Asian Sauces and Main Street Cafe American Fare. JTM Provisions also supplies bakery items such as hoagie rolls and prepared meats including meatloaf. It caters to food distributors and institutional buyers for schools restaurants and delis military commissaries and some convenience/grocery stores. The family-owned company has been in business for more than half a century.

JUDLAU CONTRACTING, INC.

2615 ULMER ST
FLUSHING, NY 113541144
Phone: 718-554-2309
Fax: -
Web: www.judlau.com

CEO: Ashok Patel
CFO: Martin Saitzyk
HR: -
FYE: December 31
Type: Private

Judlau Contracting takes on hefty jobs that help keep New York City hustling and bustling. One of eight firms under The Judlau Companies group banner Judlau Contracting specializes in heavy construction and large public works projects primarily around the New York metropolitan area and northeastern US. It builds bridges mass transit tunnels roads underground utility stations and wastewater treatment plants. The general contractor also has expertise in electrical work and environmental remediation. Major clients have included Consolidated Edison New York State Department of Transportation and Verizon. Spanish construction group OHL acquired a majority of Judlau in late 2010.

	Annual Growth	12/09	12/10	12/11	12/12	12/14
Sales ($ mil.)	52.6%	-	-	-	134.6	313.4
Net income ($ mil.)	77.1%	-	-	-	4.2	13.2
Market value ($ mil.)	-	-	-	-	-	-
Employees	-	-	-	-	-	140

JUJAMCYN THEATERS LLC

246 W. 44th St.
New York NY 10036
Phone: 212-840-8181
Fax: 212-944-0708
Web: www.jujamcyn.com

CEO: -
CFO: -
HR: Ashley Earick
FYE: June 30
Type: Private

Jujamcyn Theaters screws in a lot of the light bulbs on the Great White Way. The company owns and operates five theaters in New York City that house plays and musicals such as Tony award winner The Producers and Pulitzer Prize winner Angels in America. Its theaters include the St. James and the August Wilson Theatre (formerly the Virginia). Jujamcyn — along with The Shubert Organization and the Nederlander Producing Company — controls most Broadway productions. Jujamcyn was founded in 1956 by James Binger. It's named after his children Ju[dith] Jam[es] and Cyn[thia]. Former president and producer Rocco Landesman bought Jujamcyn in 2005 for about $30 million but left the company in 2009 to head the NEA.

JUNIATA COLLEGE

1700 MOORE ST
HUNTINGDON, PA 16652-2196
Phone: 814-641-3000
Fax: -
Web: www.juniata.edu

CEO: -
CFO: -
HR: -
FYE: May 31
Type: Private

Brothers and sisters are welcome at Juniata College an independent co-educational school affiliated with the Church of the Brethren. The college offers bachelor of arts (BA) and bachelor of science (BS) degrees in about 100 fields at its two dozen academic departments. Students are encouraged to design their own majors or "programs of emphasis" (POEs); nearly half do just that. Its most popular POEs include biology pre-health accounting business education environmental science psychology chemistry and sociology. Founded in 1876 Juniata College enrolls about 1600 students.

	Annual Growth	05/09	05/10	05/10	05/12	05/13
Sales ($ mil.)	11.3%	-	46.4	61.6	49.9	63.9
Net income ($ mil.)	-	-	(1.6)	11.9	(1.6)	12.9
Market value ($ mil.)	-	-	-	-	-	-
Employees	-	-	-	-	-	500

JUNIATA VALLEY FINANCIAL CORP
NBB: JUVF

Bridge and Main Streets
Mifflintown, PA 17059
Phone: 855 582-5101
Fax: –
Web: www.jvbonline.com

CEO: Marcie Barber
CFO: JoAnn Mcminn
HR: –
FYE: December 31
Type: Public

Juniata Valley Financial is the holding company for Juniata Valley Bank which serves central Pennsylvania from some 15 locations. The bank offers standard products such as checking and savings accounts money market accounts certificates of deposit individual retirement accounts and credit cards. Residential estate mortgages account for about half the company's loan portfolio which also includes commercial construction home equity municipal and personal loans. The bank offers trust and investment services as well. Juniata Valley Bank was established in 1867.

	Annual Growth	12/16	12/17	12/18	12/19	12/20
Assets ($ mil.)	8.1%	580.4	591.9	625.2	670.6	793.7
Net income ($ mil.)	2.1%	5.2	4.5	5.9	5.8	5.6
Market value ($ mil.)	(0.7%)	91.7	100.5	106.8	97.2	89.0
Employees	(0.1%)	168	165	178	177	167

JUNIPER GROUP INC.
OTC: JUNP

20283 State Rd. 7 Ste. 300
Boca Raton FL 33498
Phone: 561-807-8990
Fax: 516-829-4691
Web: www.junipergroup.com

CEO: –
CFO: –
HR: –
FYE: December 31
Type: Public

The Juniper Group is hoping to turn over a new leaf. The company primarily provides broadband installation and wireless infrastructure construction services through its Tower West Communications subsidiary including tower erection and construction site installation and surveying and antenna installation. Its clients include national providers of wireless voice messaging and data services. Juniper also is involved in film distribution acquiring motion picture rights from independent producers; that business line accounted for less than 2% of revenues in fiscal 2008.

JUNIPER NETWORKS INC
NYS: JNPR

1133 Innovation Way
Sunnyvale, CA 94089
Phone: 408 745-2000
Fax: 408 745-2100
Web: www.juniper.net

CEO: Rami Rahim
CFO: Kenneth Miller
HR: –
FYE: December 31
Type: Public

Juniper Networks makes high-performance network offerings that are designed to meet the performance reliability and security requirements of the world's most demanding enterprises such as financial services; national federal state and local government; as well as research and educational institutions. Its routers switches and security technologies are high-performance networks that enable customers to build scalable reliable secure and cost-effective networks for their businesses while achieving agility and improved operating efficiency through automation. Juniper sells directly and through resellers and distributors including Ingram Micro and Hitachi. Approximately half of the company's sales are made to customers based in the US. The company was founded in 1996.

	Annual Growth	12/17	12/18	12/19	12/20	12/21
Sales ($ mil.)	(1.5%)	5,027.2	4,647.5	4,445.4	4,445.1	4,735.4
Net income ($ mil.)	(4.7%)	306.2	566.9	345.0	257.8	252.7
Market value ($ mil.)	5.8%	9,165.6	8,654.3	7,921.0	7,239.2	11,484.3
Employees	2.1%	9,381	9,283	9,419	2,880	10,191

JUNIPER PHARMACEUTICALS INC
NMS: JNP

33 Arch Street
Boston, MA 02110
Phone: 617 639-1500
Fax: –
Web: www.columbialabs.com

CEO: –
CFO: –
HR: –
FYE: December 31
Type: Public

Columbia Laboratories knows the power hormones have over us. The company develops manufactures and markets hormone therapies. Its products in development include a progesterone product delivered through a propriety bioadhesive technology to reduce the risk of preterm births. Columbia Laboratories already developed two such products PROCHIEVE and CRINONE and is now working on a new generation in agreement with Watson Pharmaceuticals. The company relies upon third-party manufacturers to produce its products.

	Annual Growth	12/12	12/13	12/14	12/15	12/16
Sales ($ mil.)	20.6%	25.8	29.2	32.5	37.6	54.6
Net income ($ mil.)	(12.0%)	9.9	6.7	3.4	(2.1)	6.0
Market value ($ mil.)	72.2%	6.9	71.7	60.7	111.7	60.7
Employees	88.5%	11	77	85	105	139

JUPITER MEDICAL CENTER, INC.

1210 S OLD DIXIE HWY
JUPITER, FL 334587205
Phone: 561-747-2234
Fax: –
Web: www.jupitermed.com

CEO: Donald McKenna
CFO: –
HR: –
FYE: September 30
Type: Private

Nope this hospital is not on the fifth planet from the Sun but by Jupiter it delivers great health care to a number of Floridians. Located in Palm Beach County and the Treasure Coast region Jupiter Medical Center provides specialty services that include orthopedics and spine care; cancer care and oncology; cardiac and vascular care; neuroscience and stroke care; women's and children's services; urgent care; and other key areas. The not-for-profit medical center has about 240 beds and some 665 physicians. Jupiter Medical Center was built and opened its doors in 1979.

	Annual Growth	09/15	09/16	09/17	09/18	09/19
Sales ($ mil.)	16.3%	–	203.1	228.3	236.9	319.6
Net income ($ mil.)	50.1%	–	9.3	(3.1)	2.3	31.4
Market value ($ mil.)	–	–	–	–	–	–
Employees	–	–	–	–	–	1,780

K&G MEN'S COMPANY INC

1225 Chattahoochee Ave. NW
Atlanta GA 30318-3648
Phone: 404-351-7987
Fax: 404-351-8038
Web: www.kgmens.com

CEO: –
CFO: Jon W Kimmins
HR: –
FYE: January 31
Type: Subsidiary

The feminization of K&G Men's Company is well underway. The retailer operates about 100 deep-discount career apparel superstores in nearly 30 states. Its stores feature brand-name and private-label tailored and casual clothing footwear and accessories for men women and children. The bargain warehouse-type stores average about 23000 sq. ft. and offer first-run merchandise at prices 30%-60% lower than department stores. Founded in 1989 K&G is a subsidiary of The Men's Wearhouse and accounts for about 18% of its parent company's sales. After purchasing K&G Men's Wearhouse converted most of its outlets to the K&G Fashion Superstores banner and began adding women's and kids' apparel to the racks.

K-SEA TRANSPORTATION PARTNERS L.P.

1 Tower Center Blvd. 17th Fl.
East Brunswick NJ 08816
Phone: 732-339-6100
Fax: 732-339-6140
Web: www.k-sea.com

CEO: –
CFO: Terrence P Gill
HR: –
FYE: June 30
Type: Subsidiary

Not to be confused with the KC & the Sunshine Band tour bus K-Sea Transportation hauls refined petroleum products via its fleet of about 130 tank barges and tugboats. The company's barges have a carrying capacity of more than 4 million barrels. From locations in New York Philadelphia Seattle Honolulu and Norfolk Virginia K-Sea serves major oil companies and refiners along the US east and west coasts and up into coastal Canada and Alaska. Most of its business comes from contracts with customers such as BP ConocoPhillips Exxon Mobil and Tesoro. Kirby Corp. took over K-Sea in a deal valued at approximately $604 million in 2011 from unit holders and general partner K-Sea GP Holdings LP.

K-TRON INTERNATIONAL INC.

Rtes. 55 and 553
Pitman NJ 08071
Phone: 856-589-0500
Fax: 856-589-8113
Web: www.ktron.com

CEO: Edward B Cloues II
CFO: Robert E Wisniewski
HR: –
FYE: September 30
Type: Subsidiary

K-Tron International helps manufacturers watch their weight. Operating via subsidiary companies K-Tron makes feeders that let manufacturers control the flow (by weight or volume) of bulk solids and liquids during manufacturing processes. The group's expertise lies in the building of pneumatic conveying systems that use vacuum and pressure to precisely control the flow of ingredients to make pharmaceutical food chemical and plastic products. These pneumatic conveying systems are branded under the Colormax Limited Premier Pneumatics and Pneumatic Conveying Systems Limited product lines. K-Tron is owned by casket maker Hillenbrand.

K-VA-T FOOD STORES INC.

201 Trigg St.
Abingdon VA 24210
Phone: 276-628-5503
Fax: 276-623-5440
Web: www.foodcity.com

CEO: Steven C Smith
CFO: Michael T Lockard
HR: Joe Greene
FYE: December 31
Type: Private

What do you call a chain of supermarkets in Kentucky Virginia and Tennessee? How about K-VA-T Food Stores? K-VA-T is one of the largest grocery chains in the region with more than 100 supermarkets under the Food City and Super Dollar Discount Foods banners. Originally a Piggly Wiggly franchise with three stores K-VA-T was founded in 1955. It has grown by acquiring stores from other regional food retailers opening new stores and adding services such as about 75 pharmacies 55 Gas'N Go gasoline outlets and banking. Its Food City Distribution Center provides warehousing and distribution services. The founding Smith family owns a majority of K-VA-T; employees own about 14% of the company.

KADANT INC

One Technology Park Drive
Westford, MA 01886
Phone: 978 776-2000
Fax: –
Web: www.kadant.com

NYS: KAI
CEO: Jeffrey Powell
CFO: Michael Mckenney
HR: –
FYE: January 02
Type: Public

Kadant is a global supplier of high-value critical components and engineered systems used in process industries. It develops and manufactures a range of products and equipment used in process industries such as paper packaging and tissue; wood products; mining; metals; food processing; and recycling and waste management among others. Kadant's diverse customer base includes global and regional industrial manufacturers and distributors who participate in the broader resource transformation sector. Its major product brands many of which are sold under the Kadant name through its subsidiaries include well-known industry names such as AES Black Clawson (stock preparation) Carmanah Goslin Johnson Lamort Link-Belt Lodding Nicholson Manufacturing Noss PAAL Syntron Unaflex Valon Kone and Vickery. Most of Kadant's revenues are generated outside the US.

	Annual Growth	12/16	12/17	12/18	12/19*	01/21
Sales ($ mil.)	8.9%	414.1	515.0	633.8	704.6	635.0
Net income ($ mil.)	11.5%	32.1	31.1	60.4	52.1	55.2
Market value ($ mil.)	18.2%	706.4	1,158.8	936.3	1,220.7	1,627.2
Employees	5.4%	2,000	2,400	2,500	2,800	2,600

*Fiscal year change

KADLEC REGIONAL MEDICAL CENTER

888 SWIFT BLVD
RICHLAND, WA 993523514
Phone: 509-946-4611
Fax: –
Web: www.kadlec.org

CEO: Lane Savitch
CFO: Julie Meek
HR: –
FYE: December 31
Type: Private

Kadlec Regional Medical Center is an acute care hospital facility serving southeastern Washington and northeastern Oregon. In addition to providing comprehensive medical surgical and emergency services the hospital provides neonatal intensive care cardiopulmonary rehabilitation interventional cardiology neurology cancer care and other specialist services. Not-for-profit Kadlec Regional has some 270 inpatient beds including pediatric intensive intermediate and critical care capacity. It also operates outpatient physician offices and clinics in surrounding areas.

	Annual Growth	12/14	12/15	12/16	12/17	12/18
Sales ($ mil.)	8.3%	–	504.6	534.2	595.8	640.4
Net income ($ mil.)	–	–	(7.2)	9.9	87.3	51.1
Market value ($ mil.)	–	–	–	–	–	–
Employees	–	–	–	–	–	2,668

KAISER ALUMINUM CORP.

27422 Portola Parkway, Suite 200
Foothill Ranch, CA 92610-2831
Phone: 949 614-1740
Fax: –
Web: www.kaiseraluminum.com

NMS: KALU
CEO: Keith Harvey
CFO: Neal West
HR: Mark Krouse
FYE: December 31
Type: Public

Kaiser Aluminum manufactures and sells semi-fabricated specialty aluminum mill products. It operates more than 10 fabricated product plants in the US and one in Canada. Also known as Kaiser it manufactures rolled extruded and drawn aluminum products to serve customers in the aerospace automotive and general engineering. The company purchases primary aluminum and recycled and scrap aluminum from third-party suppliers to make its fabricated products. Some of its facilities supply billet log and other intermediate materials to its other plants for use in production. Serving more than 680 customers majority of its revenue comes from the US.

	Annual Growth	12/16	12/17	12/18	12/19	12/20
Sales ($ mil.)	(3.1%)	1,330.6	1,397.5	1,585.9	1,514.1	1,172.7
Net income ($ mil.)	(25.1%)	91.7	45.4	91.7	62.0	28.8
Market value ($ mil.)	6.2%	1,228.4	1,689.5	1,411.9	1,753.4	1,563.8
Employees	(1.7%)	2,760	2,770	2,860	2,820	2,575

KAISER FOUNDATION HOSPITALS INC

1 KAISER PLZ
OAKLAND, CA 946123610
Phone: 510-271-6611
Fax: –
Web: www.kaisercenter.com

CEO: Gregory A Adams
CFO: Kathy Lancaster
HR: –
FYE: December 31
Type: Private

Kaiser Foundation Hospitals is on a roll. The hospital group operates nearly 40 acute care hospitals and 680 medical offices in eight states (California Colorado Georgia Hawaii Maryland Oregon Virginia and Washington) and Washington D.C. The company's largest presence is in California where the majority of its hospitals are located. Kaiser Foundation Hospitals employs more than 21000 physicians representing all medical specialties. Kaiser Foundation Hospital's doctors group is controlled by Permanente Medical Groups and its HMO is offered through Kaiser Foundation Health Plan. Altogether the group provides care for about 11.7 million members.

	Annual Growth	12/03	12/04	12/05	12/08	12/09
Sales ($ mil.)	10.7%	–	–	9,852.0	0.2	14,795.3
Net income ($ mil.)	(13.7%)	–	–	774.0	0.2	429.5
Market value ($ mil.)	–	–	–	–	–	–
Employees	–	–	–	–	–	175,668

KAISER-FRANCIS OIL COMPANY

6733 S. Yale Ave.
Tulsa OK 74136-3302
Phone: 918-494-0000
Fax: 918-491-4694
Web: www.kfoc.net

CEO: George B Kaiser
CFO: Don Millican
HR: –
FYE: June 30
Type: Private

King of the Tulsa oil patch oil and gas exploration and production independent Kaiser-Francis Oil Company buys sells and develops oil and gas properties primarily in Arkansas Colorado Kansas Nebraska New Mexico North Dakota Oklahoma Oregon Texas West Virginia and Wyoming. The company teamed up with fellow Tulsa-based energy firm SemGas LP to help build the Wyckoff Gas Storage facility (6 billion cu. ft. of working gas storage) in Steuben County New York. Local billionaire George Kaiser owns and manages Kaiser-Francis Oil. In 2009 Forbes pegged George Kaiser's estimated wealth at $9.5 billion.

KALEIDA HEALTH

726 EXCHANGE ST
BUFFALO, NY 142101484
Phone: 716-859-5600
Fax: –
Web: www.kaleidahealth.org

CEO: Robert Nesselbush
CFO: Robert J Nesselbush
HR: Jerry Venable
FYE: December 31
Type: Private

Kaleida Health provides a kaleidoscope of services to residents of western New York. The health system operates five acute care hospitals including Buffalo General Hospital and Gates Vascular Institute (combined with about 550 beds) The Women & Children's Hospital of Buffalo (200) DeGraff Memorial Hospital (70) and Millard Fillmore Suburban Hospital (260). Community health needs are met through a network of some 80 medical clinics. Kaleida Health also operates skilled nursing care facilities and provides home health care through its Visiting Nursing Association. To help train future medical professionals Buffalo General Hospital is a teaching affiliate of the State University of New York.

	Annual Growth	12/07	12/08	12/09	12/13	12/17
Sales ($ mil.)	1.8%	–	–	1,155.7	1,139.2	1,331.2
Net income ($ mil.)	(2.7%)	–	–	75.4	(14.3)	60.4
Market value ($ mil.)	–	–	–	–	–	–
Employees	–	–	–	–	–	9,000

KALOBIOS PHARMACEUTICALS INC.   NASDAQ: KBIO

260 E. Grand Ave.
South San Francisco CA 94080
Phone: 650-243-3100
Fax: 650-243-3260
Web: www.kalobios.com

CEO: Cameron Durrant
CFO: Timothy Morris
HR: –
FYE: December 31
Type: Private

KaloBios Pharmaceuticals seeks the "good life" (its meaning from the Greek) for patients afflicted with serious medical conditions especially respiratory diseases and certain cancers. It is developing drugs containing antibodies produced via its own technology. The most advanced is in clinical trials and is engineered to fight common bacteria found even in hospitals that cause pneumonia in patients treated by mechanical ventilation. KaloBios has partnered with Sanofi Pasteur to further develop manufacture and market the drug. It also is working on antibodies to treat severe cases of asthma and blood disease. In early 2012 the company went public with an offering valued at $70.6 million.

KAMAN CORP.   NYS: KAMN

1332 Blue Hills Avenue
Bloomfield, CT 06002
Phone: 860 243-7100
Fax: –
Web: www.kaman.com

CEO: Ian Walsh
CFO: James Coogan
HR: Megan Morgan
FYE: December 31
Type: Public

Kaman makes aircraft components for the aerospace medical and industrial distribution markets. The company manufactures Kaman-branded aircraft bearings and components in addition to metallic/composite aerostructures for commercial military and general aviation (fixed and rotary wing) aircraft. It also makes safety and arming solutions for missile and bomb systems for the US and its allies; restores modifies and supports its SH-2G Super Seasprite maritime helicopters; and manufactures and supports its K-MAX manned and unmanned medium-to-heavy lift helicopters. Customers have included such notable names as Airbus Bell and Boeing. While it generates sales from most continents the company's sales from North America make up most of its revenue.

	Annual Growth	12/16	12/17	12/18	12/19	12/20
Sales ($ mil.)	(18.8%)	1,808.4	1,805.9	1,875.4	761.6	784.5
Net income ($ mil.)	–	58.9	49.8	54.2	209.8	(69.7)
Market value ($ mil.)	3.9%	1,356.5	1,631.2	1,555.0	1,827.5	1,583.8
Employees	(11.8%)	5,265	5,300	5,100	2,935	3,193

KANA SOFTWARE INC.

840 W. California Ave Ste. 100
Sunnyvale CA 94086
Phone: 650-614-8300
Fax: 408-736-7613
Web: www.kana.com

CEO: Mark Duffell
CFO: Jeff Wylie
HR: –
FYE: December 31
Type: Private

KANA Software knows that a good customer experience can be just a click away. The company's customer relationship management (CRM) software is used by call centers and businesses with e-commerce websites. Its capabilities include customer service interaction through live chat e-mail phone and customer self-service portals. It also offers applications used to assist agents in their conversations with customers. KANA serves companies in the communications financial services retail health care and technology industries as well as government clients in such cities as Boston Brisbane San Francisco Sheffield Toronto and Vancouver.

KANSAS CITY BOARD OF PUBLIC UTILITIES

540 MINNESOTA AVE
KANSAS CITY, KS 661012930
Phone: 913-573-9000
Fax: –
Web: www.bpu.com

CEO: –
CFO: –
HR: –
FYE: September 30
Type: Private

Goin' to ... Kansas City? The Board of Public Utilities of Kansas City Kansas (known as the Kansas City Board of Public Utilities) will help light the way. The utility provides electric transmission and distribution services to 63000 customers and water distribution services to 50000 customers in the Kansas City metropolitan area (in Wyandotte and Johnson counties). Most electric customers are residential but commercial and industrial customers account for the bulk of the utility's power revenues. The Kansas City Board of Public Utilities also has interests in coal gas and oil-fired power generation facilities. The utility is owned by the Unified Government of Wyandotte County and Kansas City.

	Annual Growth	03/16	03/17*	06/17	06/18*	09/18
Sales ($ mil.)	265.4%	–	74.0	147.7	169.4	270.4
Net income ($ mil.)	2131.5%	–	1.8	0.8	17.2	39.2
Market value ($ mil.)	–	–	–	–	–	–
Employees	–	–	–	–	–	545

*Fiscal year change

KANSAS CITY CHIEFS FOOTBALL CLUB INC.

1 Arrowhead Dr.
Kansas City MO 64129
Phone: 816-920-9300
Fax: 816-923-4719
Web: www.kcchiefs.com

CEO: Daniel L Crumb
CFO: –
HR: –
FYE: January 31
Type: Private

These chiefs are trying to lead a tribe of football fans to the Super Bowl. The Kansas City Chiefs Football Club was founded by oilman and sports impresario Lamar Hunt as the Dallas Texans in 1959 a charter member of the American Football League. (Hunt also helped start the AFL and served as its first president.) The franchise moved to Kansas City Missouri in 1963 and was renamed the Chiefs. After winning three league titles and one Super Bowl the franchise joined the National Football League when the rival associations merged in 1970. The Chiefs play host at Kansas City's Arrowhead Stadium. Hunt's family led by his son Clark Hunt continues to own the football franchise.

KANSAS CITY LIFE INSURANCE CO (KANSAS CITY, MO) — NBB: KCLI

3520 Broadway
Kansas City, MO 64111-2565
Phone: 816 753-7000
Fax: 816 753-4902
Web: www.kclife.com

CEO: R. Philip Bixby
CFO: –
HR: –
FYE: December 31
Type: Public

Kansas City Life Insurance and its subsidiaries provide insurance products throughout the US to individuals (life and disability coverage and annuities) and to groups (life dental vision and disability insurance). Subsidiary Grange Life sells traditional life insurance universal life products and fixed annuities. The insurance companies sell through independent agents and agencies. Kansas City Life Insurance was established in 1895 and is based in Kansas City Missouri. Chairman and CEO R. Philip Bixby and his family control the company.

	Annual Growth	12/16	12/17	12/18	12/19	12/20
Assets ($ mil.)	5.3%	4,449.4	4,530.7	4,971.5	5,219.9	5,463.0
Net income ($ mil.)	(9.2%)	22.3	51.5	15.7	24.4	15.2
Market value ($ mil.)	(5.4%)	460.0	438.2	358.3	324.9	368.0
Employees	–	–	–	–	–	–

KANSAS CITY SOUTHERN — NYS: KSU

427 West 12th Street
Kansas City, MO 64105
Phone: 816 983-1303
Fax: 816 556-0297
Web: www.kcsouthern.com

CEO: Patrick Ottensmeyer
CFO: Michael Upchurch
HR: Lora Cheatum
FYE: December 31
Type: Public

Kansas City Southern (KCS) operates trains on a 6700-mile network that stretches from Missouri to Mexico. The company's Kansas City Southern Railway (KCSR) owns and operates about 3400 miles of track in the Midwestern and southeast US. KCS offers rail freight service in Mexico through Kansas City Southern de M©xico which maintains more than 3300 miles of track and serves three major ports. Another KCS unit Texas Mexican Railway connects the KCSR and KCSM systems. The KCS railroads transport such freight as industrial and consumer products agricultural and mineral products and chemical and petroleum products. The US represents slightly more than 50% of the company's total sales and Mexico the rest.

	Annual Growth	12/16	12/17	12/18	12/19	12/20
Sales ($ mil.)	3.1%	2,334.2	2,582.9	2,714.0	2,866.0	2,632.6
Net income ($ mil.)	6.6%	478.1	962.0	627.4	538.9	617.0
Market value ($ mil.)	24.5%	7,725.3	9,580.0	8,690.4	13,944.8	18,585.4
Employees	(1.1%)	6,820	7,130	7,200	7,040	6,522

KANSAS DEPARTMENT OF TRANSPORTATION

700 SW HARRISON ST # 500
TOPEKA, KS 666033964
Phone: 785-296-3501
Fax: –
Web: www.ksdot.org

CEO: –
CFO: –
HR: –
FYE: June 30
Type: Private

The Kansas Department of Transportation (KDOT) helps connect the dots with residents who love to travel the 140000-plus miles across the Sunflower State. The agency focuses on providing a transportation system for citizens in the state by offering a wide range of services such as maintaining roads and bridges transportation planning and designing construction projects. The department also provides federal fund program administration as well as administrative support travel information and programs in traffic safety. KDOT traces its roots to the organization of interstate travel in 1917.

	Annual Growth	06/17	06/18	06/19	06/20	06/21
Sales ($ mil.)	3.3%	–	1,476.1	1,583.0	1,540.2	1,624.9
Net income ($ mil.)	(56.9%)	–	265.6	312.1	104.5	21.2
Market value ($ mil.)	–	–	–	–	–	–
Employees	–	–	–	–	–	3,000

KANSAS ELECTRIC POWER COOPERATIVE, INC.

600 SW CORPORATE VW
TOPEKA, KS 666151233
Phone: 785-273-7010
Fax: –
Web: www.kepco.org

CEO: Suzanne Lain
CFO: –
HR: –
FYE: December 31
Type: Private

If Dorothy lived in rural Kansas today she'd probably hear that tornado warning and reach safety thanks to the power supplied by Kansas Electric Power Cooperative (KEPCo). KEPCo operates power plants and purchases additional energy for its 19 member distribution cooperatives which serve more than 110000 rural customers. The generation and transmission utility's assets include a 6% stake in Wolf Creek Nuclear Operating Corporation which operates Kansas' Wolf Creek Generating Station. Subsidiary KSI Engineering provides utility construction and infrastructure services. KEPCo which was formed in 1975 is part of the alliance of Touchstone Energy Cooperatives.

	Annual Growth	12/13	12/14	12/16	12/17	12/18
Sales ($ mil.)	(1.4%)	–	174.2	161.8	155.2	164.6
Net income ($ mil.)	(6.1%)	–	3.5	1.9	2.4	2.7
Market value ($ mil.)	–	–	–	–	–	–
Employees	–	–	–	–	–	24

KANSAS STATE UNIVERSITY

ANDERSON HALL 110 1301 MI
MANHATTAN, KS 66506
Phone: 785-532-6011
Fax: –
Web: www.k-state.edu

CEO: –
CFO: –
HR: –
FYE: June 30
Type: Private

K-State is a big deal in the Little Apple. Located in Manhattan Kansas (aka the Little Apple) Kansas State University (K-State) is a land grant institution that has an enrollment of some 24000 students. It offers more than 250 undergraduate majors 65 master's degrees 45 doctoral degrees and more than 20 graduate certificate programs. Major fields of study include agriculture technology and veterinary medicine. Notable alumni include former White House press secretary Marlin Fitzwater and actor Gordon Jump. Along with the University of Kansas and other universities technical schools and community colleges in the state K-State is governed by The Kansas Board of Regents.

	Annual Growth	06/07	06/08	06/09	06/10	06/17
Sales ($ mil.)	5.0%	–	–	420.6	459.8	620.2
Net income ($ mil.)	21.4%	–	–	10.7	50.5	50.8
Market value ($ mil.)	–	–	–	–	–	–
Employees	–	–	–	–	–	5,168

KAPSTONE PAPER & PACKAGING CORP — NYS: KS

1101 Skokie Blvd., Suite 300
Northbrook, IL 60062
Phone: 847 239-8800
Fax: 847 205-7551
Web: www.kapstonepaper.com

CEO: Steve C Voorhees
CFO: Ward H Dickson
HR: –
FYE: December 31
Type: Public

KapStone Paper and Packaging keeps things under wraps. The company manufactures linerboard a type of paperboard that is converted into laminated tier sheets and wrapping material. It also produces kraft paper (industry-speak for strong wrapping paper) for multiwall bags; saturating kraft (sold under the Durasorb brand) to produce mainly high pressure laminates for furniture construction materials and electronics; and unbleached folding carton board (Kraftpak) which is converted into packaging for consumer goods.

	Annual Growth	12/12	12/13	12/14	12/15	12/16
Sales ($ mil.)	26.1%	1,216.6	1,748.2	2,300.9	2,789.3	3,077.3
Net income ($ mil.)	8.4%	62.5	127.3	171.9	106.4	86.3
Market value ($ mil.)	(0.2%)	2,144.4	5,398.3	2,832.5	2,183.1	2,130.9
Employees	23.4%	2,760	4,601	4,628	6,400	6,400

KAR AUCTION SERVICES INC. — NYS: KAR

11299 N. Illinois Street
Carmel, IN 46032
Phone: 800 923-3725
Fax: –
Web: www.karauctionservices.com

CEO: Peter Kelly
CFO: Eric Loughmiller
HR: –
FYE: December 31
Type: Public

KAR Auction Services is a leading provider of used vehicle auctions and related vehicle remarketing services in North America and Europe. KAR is a holding company for ADESA the second-largest wholesaler of used vehicles at auction in North America; and Automotive Finance Corporation a capital funding business that serves used car dealers. In addition to around 75 physical auction located throughout North America KAR also hosts online auctions. The company makes money through auction fees extended to vehicle buyers and sellers and by providing add-on services such as inspections storage transportation reconditioning salvage recovery and titling and financing. About 80% of its revenue comes from its US customers.

	Annual Growth	12/16	12/17	12/18	12/19	12/20
Sales ($ mil.)	(8.7%)	3,150.1	3,458.0	3,769.6	2,781.9	2,187.7
Net income ($ mil.)	(78.2%)	222.4	362.0	328.0	188.5	0.5
Market value ($ mil.)	(18.7%)	5,527.8	6,551.2	6,189.3	2,826.2	2,413.7
Employees	(12.9%)	17,400	17,500	18,400	15,300	10,000

KARYOPHARM THERAPEUTICS INC — NMS: KPTI

85 Wells Avenue, 2nd Floor
Newton, MA 02459
Phone: 617 658-0600
Fax: –
Web: www.karyopharm.com

CEO: Richard Paulson
CFO: Michael Mason
HR: –
FYE: December 31
Type: Public

Karyopharm Therapeutics is a commercial-stage pharmaceutical company that focuses on the treatment of cancer and other diseases. Its lead product Xpovio (selinexor) is the first Selective Inhibitor of Nuclear Export (SINE) compound to receive FDA approval and is being marketed for use in adult patients with relapsed or refractory multiple myeloma. The company also has a number of other products lined up for approval namely Eltanexor Verdinexor and KPT-9274. The company caters to specialty distributors and specialty pharmacies that resell Karyopharm's products. The company was founded in 2008 and has operation in Massachusetts.

	Annual Growth	12/16	12/17	12/18	12/19	12/20
Sales ($ mil.)	414.7%	0.2	1.6	30.3	40.9	108.1
Net income ($ mil.)	–	(109.6)	(129.0)	(178.4)	(199.6)	(196.3)
Market value ($ mil.)	13.3%	694.9	709.7	692.7	1,417.1	1,144.3
Employees	41.4%	108	154	332	347	432

KASPIEN HOLDINGS INC — NAS: KSPN

2818 N. Sullivan Rd. Ste. 30
Spokane, WA 99216
Phone: 855 300-2710
Fax: –
Web: www.kaspien.com

CEO: Kunal Chopra
CFO: Edwin Sapienza
HR: –
FYE: January 30
Type: Public

Just an F.Y.I. but Trans World Entertainment operates F.Y.E. and a handful of other retail ventures. F.Y.E. (aka For Your Entertainment) stores sell CDs DVDs video games software and related products at about 390 locations throughout the US Puerto Rico and the Virgin Islands. Trans World's other bricks-and-mortar operations include about 15 video stores under the Saturday Matinee and Suncoast Motion Pictures banners. Most of the firm's retail outlets are located in shopping malls. Trans World also sells entertainment products via its e-commerce sites (including fye.com secondspin.com and wherehouse.com). Chairman and CEO Bob Higgins founded the company in 1972.

	Annual Growth	01/17*	02/18	02/19	02/20*	01/21
Sales ($ mil.)	(18.2%)	353.5	442.9	418.2	325.9	158.3
Net income ($ mil.)	–	3.2	(42.6)	(97.4)	(58.7)	(3.9)
Market value ($ mil.)	90.9%	5.6	3.1	1.1	6.7	74.3
Employees	(53.9%)	3,000	2,600	2,200	155	136

*Fiscal year change

KATE SPADE LLC

48 W. 25th St.
New York NY 10010-2708
Phone: 212-739-6550
Fax: 212-739-6544
Web: www.katespade.com

CEO: Anna Bakst
CFO: –
HR: –
FYE: December 31
Type: Subsidiary

kate spade's story is one of simplicity like the bags it sells and expansion. The company begun in 1993 by designer Kate Spade and her husband Andy to make kate spade handbags has since lent its uncomplicated design for the manufacture of stationery various functional bags (think diaper bags) and licensed products — with lines of homewares (sheets tabletop items and wallpaper) as well as beauty items eyewear and shoes. Women's items are sold under the kate spade name; men's products carry the jack spade moniker. Owned by Fifth & Pacific the firm distributes products in Asia and sells them through more than 70 company-owned specialty and outlet stores upscale US department stores and its website.

KATY INDUSTRIES, INC.   NBB: KATY

11840 Westline Industrial Dr, Suite 200   CEO: –
St. Louis, MO 63146   CFO: –
Phone: 314 656-4321   HR: –
Fax: –   FYE: December 31
Web: www.katyindustries.com   Type: Public

Katy Industries gives janitors the tools and supplies to clean up the acts of others. The firm makes and markets commercial cleaning products as well as plastic home storage items. Its Continental Commercial Products (CCP) subsidiary operates multiple divisions including: Container Contico Continental and Wilen. Products are sold under the Continental Kleen Aire Huskee KingKan Unibody SuperKan and Tilt-N-Wheel brands. CCP has operations in Missouri and California as well as Canada. Its customers include janitorial/sanitary and food service distributors that supply restaurants hotels schools and other facilities. Founded in 1967 Katy is restructuring to return to profitability.

	Annual Growth	12/11	12/12	12/13	12/14	12/15
Sales ($ mil.)	(1.3%)	120.3	100.5	78.3	99.7	114.0
Net income ($ mil.)	–	4.8	(15.1)	(1.5)	2.5	(8.0)
Market value ($ mil.)	57.5%	1.3	1.4	3.3	11.1	8.0
Employees	(13.3%)	533	407	263	341	301

KAZ INC.

1775 Broadway Ste. 2405   CEO: –
New York NY 10019   CFO: –
Phone: 212-586-1630   HR: –
Fax: 212-265-9248   FYE: February 28
Web: www.kaz.com   Type: Subsidiary

Kaz allows customers to blow off a little steam. The company makes humidifiers vaporizers air purifiers and filters thermometers heating pads and portable heaters as well as electronic mosquito traps. Its products made under the Kaz Braun Enviracare Honeywell and Vicks brand names are sold worldwide through drugstore chains and mass merchandisers such as CVS Kmart Target and Wal-Mart and some medical distributors and home improvement stores. Vicks and Braun brands are licensed from Procter & Gamble (P&G) and the Honeywell label from Honeywell International. The company operates as the healthcare/home environment segment of personal care products giant Helen of Troy which acquired Kaz in 2011.

KB HOME   NYS: KBH

10990 Wilshire Boulevard   CEO: Jeffrey Mezger
Los Angeles, CA 90024   CFO: Jeff Kaminski
Phone: 310 231-4000   HR: –
Fax: 310 231-4222   FYE: November 30
Web: www.kbhome.com   Type: Public

KB Home is one of the largest house builders in the US. The company constructs single-family (attached and detached) houses townhouses and condominiums suited mainly for first-time move-up and active adult buyers in nine states on the West Coast and in the Southwest Central US and Southeast. Its Built-to-Order brand allows buyers to customize their houses by choosing a floor plan as well as exterior and interior features. KB Home's average selling price for a house is in the range of $400000 to $422000. To help with the buying process KB Home also offers mortgage banking title services and insurance. KB has built more than 655000 homes since it was founded in 1957.

	Annual Growth	11/17	11/18	11/19	11/20	11/21
Sales ($ mil.)	7.0%	4,368.5	4,547.0	4,552.7	4,183.2	5,724.9
Net income ($ mil.)	33.0%	180.6	170.4	268.8	296.2	564.7
Market value ($ mil.)	6.3%	2,976.9	2,003.9	3,282.5	3,341.4	3,796.1
Employees	4.0%	1,915	2,005	2,140	1,776	2,244

KBR INC   NYS: KBR

601 Jefferson Street, Suite 3400   CEO: Stuart Bradie
Houston, TX 77002   CFO: Mark Sopp
Phone: 713 753-2000   HR: –
Fax: –   FYE: December 31
Web: www.kbr.com   Type: Public

KBR is a global provider of differentiated professional services and technologies to US government and hydrocarbon industries. The company's business involves planning design program management construction and construction management and operations and maintenance at various project sites throughout the world including oil field and related energy infrastructure construction services in and around sensitive environmental areas such as rivers lakes and wetlands. KBR provides these and other support services to a diverse customer base including domestic and foreign governments international and national integrated energy and industrial companies such as scientific research defense systems engineering operational support information operations and technology. Operations outside the US account for more than half of KBR's revenue.

	Annual Growth	12/16	12/17	12/18	12/19	12/20
Sales ($ mil.)	7.8%	4,268.0	4,171.0	4,913.0	5,639.0	5,767.0
Net income ($ mil.)	–	(61.0)	434.0	281.0	202.0	(72.0)
Market value ($ mil.)	16.7%	2,349.4	2,791.4	2,136.8	4,293.4	4,353.9
Employees	1.3%	27,500	20,000	25,000	28,000	29,000

KBR WYLE SERVICES, LLC

7701 GREENBELT RD STE 400   CEO: –
GREENBELT, MD 207706521   CFO: Joseph Morway
Phone: 301-614-8600   HR: –
Fax: –   FYE: September 30
Web: www.kbr.com   Type: Private

Like its acronym name suggests SGT (aka Stinger Ghaffarian Technologies) is used to taking military orders; in this case very specific technical ones. An engineering services firm SGT provides aerospace engineering project management IT systems development and related services to NASA the US Navy the US Air Force and other primarily military-related government entities through contracts. The company also offers science-related services such as earth climate and planetary modeling and analysis. SGT's facilities are located near airfields and other military facilities.

	Annual Growth	09/07	09/08	09/12	09/13	09/15
Sales ($ mil.)	10.0%	–	293.0	374.7	416.5	570.8
Net income ($ mil.)	16.3%	–	8.3	9.0	15.5	23.9
Market value ($ mil.)	–	–	–	–	–	–
Employees	–	–	–	–	–	2,300

KBS, INC.

8050 KIMWAY DR   CEO: –
RICHMOND, VA 232282831   CFO: James Lipscombe
Phone: 804-262-0100   HR: –
Fax: –   FYE: September 30
Web: www.kbsgc.com   Type: Private

You would hit the nail right on the head if you were to call KBS a "regional contractor." The company provides design/build planning general contracting and construction management services for commercial and multifamily residential projects in Virginia. Its projects include office buildings apartment complexes shopping centers hotels schools jails warehouses and senior living facilities. Some 60% of the company's business comes in the form of repeat customers. Clients have included Cousins Properties Forest City Enterprises Ukrop's Best Buy Wal-Mart and Virginia Commonwealth University. President Bill Paulette founded KBS in a sheet metal shop in 1975.

	Annual Growth	09/14	09/15	09/16	09/17	09/19
Sales ($ mil.)	11.2%	–	180.7	200.4	244.8	276.7
Net income ($ mil.)	21.9%	–	4.9	4.9	8.5	10.9
Market value ($ mil.)	–	–	–	–	–	–
Employees	–	–	–	–	–	130

KECK GRADUATE INSTITUTE

535 WATSON DR
CLAREMONT, CA 917114817
Phone: 909-621-8000
Fax: –
Web: www.kgi.edu

CEO: –
CFO: Robert W Caragher
HR: –
FYE: June 30
Type: Private

Those who attend Keck Graduate Institute (KGI) know good things come in small packages. The institute which enrolls 82 students (and has 21 faculty members for a ratio of approximately 1-to-4) specializes in applied life sciences and is a member of The Claremont Colleges maintained by the Claremont University Consortium. KGI offers a two-year graduate program that culminates in a Master of Bioscience (MBS) degree. Those who earn their MBS may put in an additional three years for a Ph.D. in Applied Life Sciences. Curriculum is designed to prepare students for careers in the biotech medical device and pharmaceutical industries. KGI was founded in 1997 with a $50 million grant from the W.M. Keck Foundation.

	Annual Growth	06/09	06/10	06/11	06/12	06/13
Sales ($ mil.)	5.1%	–	12.3	9.0	16.5	14.3
Net income ($ mil.)	–	–	–	2.7	(0.0)	(2.8)
Market value ($ mil.)	–	–	–	–	–	–
Employees	–	–	–	–	–	65

KEENAN, HOPKINS, SCHMIDT AND STOWELL CONTRACTORS, INC.

5422 BAY CENTER DR # 200
TAMPA, FL 336093437
Phone: 813-628-9330
Fax: –
Web: www.khss.com

CEO: Michael R Cannon
CFO: Lynda Licht
HR: –
FYE: December 31
Type: Private

Business is always looking up for KHS&S Contractors which specializes in wall and ceiling construction including interior exterior acoustical and insulation work. KHS&S is one of the largest theme park contractors in the US completing more than 5.5 million square feet of thematic finishes and providing water feature and rockwork technology and concrete/tilt-up construction. The specialty contractor has worked on projects for Busch Gardens Cheetah Hunt and Walt Disney Parks & Resorts. KHS&S also works on casinos convention centers health care facilities office buildings laboratories and other commercial projects. Founded in 1984 the company is owned by its employees.

	Annual Growth	12/15	12/16	12/17	12/18	12/19
Sales ($ mil.)	27.0%	–	71.6	116.8	140.8	146.7
Net income ($ mil.)	93.6%	–	2.2	5.0	10.1	15.6
Market value ($ mil.)	–	–	–	–	–	–
Employees	–	–	–	–	–	350

KEHE DISTRIBUTORS LLC

900 N. Schmidt Rd.
Romeoville IL 60446-4056
Phone: 630-343-0000
Fax: 815-886-1111
Web: www.kehefood.com

CEO: Brandon Barnholt
CFO: Christopher Meyers
HR: –
FYE: April 30
Type: Private

KeHE Distributors plays a key role in getting specialty foods on to grocery store shelves. It is a wholesale supplier of ethnic and gourmet foods serving more than 33000 food retailers across the US Canada Mexico and the Caribbean. It distributes more than 60000 items from 3500 vendors and offers African-American Asian Latin American Mediterranean and kosher food products as well as a wide variety of organic and natural food items. The company's KeHE Direct unit provides online ordering services for its customers. Arthur Kehe founded the employee-owned company in 1952 in the basement of his home.

KEITHLEY INSTRUMENTS INC.

28775 Aurora Rd.
Solon OH 44139
Phone: 440-248-0400
Fax: 440-248-6168
Web: www.keithley.com

CEO: Joseph P Keithley
CFO: Mark J Plush
HR: –
FYE: September 30
Type: Subsidiary

Keithley Instruments wants to be instrumental to the success of engineers scientists and technicians. The company makes some 500 different products used to control measure and trace signals whether they take the form of electrical current light or radio waves. Its offerings include digital multimeters semiconductor parametric test and device characterization systems signal analyzers and generators and plug-in boards that enable PCs to be used for data acquisition. Keithley primarily sells to the precision electronics research and education semiconductor and wireless markets. In 2010 Danaher acquired Keithley in a deal valued at around $300 million.

KELLOGG CO

One Kellogg Square, P.O. Box 3599
Battle Creek, MI 49016-3599
Phone: 269 961-2000
Fax: –
Web: www.kelloggcompany.com

NYS: K
CEO: Steven Cahillane
CFO: Amit Banati
HR: –
FYE: January 01
Type: Public

From the company's home base in Battle Creek Michigan Kellogg Company battles with rival General Mills for the #1 spot in the US cereal market. Kellogg founded in 1906 boasts many familiar cereal brands including Kellogg's Corn Flakes Frosted Flakes Froot Loops Special K and Rice Krispies. While the company works to fill the world's cereal bowls it actually makes more money these days from its snacks and convenience brands such as Kashi Pringles and Cheez-It Eggo waffles and Nutri-Grain and Bear Naked cereal bars. Though its products are sold worldwide the company generates over 55% of its revenue domestically.

	Annual Growth	12/17	12/18	12/19*	01/21	01/22
Sales ($ mil.)	1.9%	12,923.0	13,547.0	13,578.0	13,770.0	14,181.0
Net income ($ mil.)	3.2%	1,269.0	1,336.0	960.0	1,251.0	1,488.0
Market value ($ mil.)	(1.1%)	23,206.8	19,543.8	23,609.6	21,243.9	21,991.5
Employees	(1.2%)	33,000	34,000	31,000	31,000	31,000

*Fiscal year change

KELLSTROM AEROSPACE, LLC

14400 NW 77TH CT STE 306
MIAMI LAKES, FL 330161592
Phone: 847-233-5800
Fax: –

CEO: –
CFO: –
HR: –
FYE: December 31
Type: Private

Does the spell-check at aircraft parts inventory service Kellstrom Aerospace correct "enginuity"? Using its ingenuity to specialize in engines made by CFM International General Electric Pratt & Whitney and Rolls-Royce the company supplies new and overhauled products for military and commercial aircraft. Kellstrom doing business as Kellstrom Industries also provides maintenance for military and commercial aircraft components. Customers include commercial airlines US and foreign military forces and maintenance repair and overhaul facilities. Kellstrom Aerospace was established in 1990 and has been privately owned since 2002.

	Annual Growth	12/07	12/08	12/09	12/10	12/11
Sales ($ mil.)	(2.4%)	–	–	163.2	149.4	155.5
Net income ($ mil.)	(24.5%)	–	–	1.7	2.7	1.0
Market value ($ mil.)	–	–	–	–	–	–
Employees	–	–	–	–	–	83

KELLWOOD COMPANY

600 Kellwood Pkwy.
Chesterfield MO 63017
Phone: 314-576-3100
Fax: 314-576-3460
Web: www.kellwood.com

CEO: David Falwell
CFO: Adrian Kowalewski
HR: –
FYE: January 31
Type: Private

Who would be one of the leading US apparel makers? Kellwood would. The firm generates most of its sales from women's wear including the Rebecca Taylor David Meister and Sag Harbor lines. It also makes and designs juniors and girls clothes and accessories. Its portfolio of about 20 brands also includes My Michelle Baby Phat Phat Farm Rewind Vince and XOXO. The company is a major supplier to department stores as well as mass retailers specialty boutiques and catalogs. Kellwood also operates Vince Lamb & Flag and Rebecca Taylor brand outlet stores across the US. Kellwood has been adding contemporary brands while shedding mainstream brands such as Koret. The company is owned by Sun Capital Partners.

KELLY SERVICES, INC.

999 West Big Beaver Road
Troy, MI 48084
Phone: 248 362-4444
Fax: –
Web: www.kellyservices.com

NMS: KELY A
CEO: Peter Quigley
CFO: Olivier Thirot
HR: –
FYE: January 02
Type: Public

One of the biggest staffing firms in the US Kelly Services provides temporary employees to companies operating in the light industrial technical and professional sectors including information technology specialists marketers and accountants. It also places engineers scientists substitute teachers and government personnel. Overall Kelly Services assign approximately 370000 temporary employees around the world. Over 70% of revenue is generated in the US. Kelly Services was founded in 1946 by William Russell Kelly.

	Annual Growth	12/17	12/18	12/19*	01/21	01/22
Sales ($ mil.)	(1.8%)	5,374.4	5,513.9	5,355.6	4,516.0	4,909.7
Net income ($ mil.)	16.9%	71.6	22.9	112.4	(72.0)	156.1
Market value ($ mil.)	(9.3%)	1,071.7	796.2	872.9	808.4	659.1
Employees	(6.9%)	507,800	506,800	446,700	374,300	354,500

*Fiscal year change

KEMET CORP.

KEMET Tower, One East Broward Blvd
Fort Lauderdale, FL 33301
Phone: 954 766-2800
Fax: –
Web: www.kemet.com

NYS: KEM
CEO: William Lowe
CFO: Gregory Thompson
HR: Stefano Vetralla
FYE: March 31
Type: Public

KEMET is one of the world's largest makers of tantalum and multilayer ceramic capacitors — devices that store filter and regulate electrical energy and that are used in virtually all electronic devices. KEMET makes about 35 billion capacitors a year; its focus is on surface-mount capacitors including specialized units for aerospace automotive communications systems computers and military equipment. The company also makes solid aluminum capacitors for high-frequency applications. More than 70% of its sales come from outside the US.

	Annual Growth	03/15	03/16	03/17	03/18	03/19
Sales ($ mil.)	13.8%	823.2	734.8	757.8	1,199.9	1,382.8
Net income ($ mil.)	–	(14.1)	(53.6)	48.0	254.5	206.6
Market value ($ mil.)	42.3%	239.4	111.6	693.9	1,048.3	981.2
Employees	11.7%	9,225	8,800	9,100	14,850	14,350

KEMIRA CHEMICALS INC.

1950 Vaughn Rd.
Kennesaw GA 30144
Phone: 770-436-1542
Fax: 770-436-3432
Web: www.kemirachemicals.com

CEO: Tarjei Johansen
CFO: Paul Kimberling
HR: –
FYE: December 31
Type: Subsidiary

Kemira Chemicals brings a Nordic approach to the chemical industry in the New World. The company is the North American subsidiary of Finnish international specialty chemical maker Kemira Oyj. It manufactures specialty and process chemicals for the pulp and paper water treatment mineral slurries and chemical industries. Products include biocides colloidal silica de-foamers dispersants hazardous waste stabilizers polishing slurries sodium aluminate and water treatment polymers. It also produces bleaching agents for detergents and titanium dioxide as well as organic acids salts and blends.

KEMPER CORP (DE)

200 E. Randolph Street, Suite 3300
Chicago, IL 60601
Phone: 312 661-4600
Fax: –
Web: www.kemper.com

NYS: KMPR
CEO: Joseph P Lacher Jr
CFO: James J McKinney
HR: –
FYE: December 31
Type: Public

Kemper is a diversified insurance holding company with subsidiaries that provide automobile homeowners life health and other insurance products to individuals and businesses. The Kemper family of companies is one of the nation's leading specialized insurers. With nearly $14.9 billion in assets Kemper is improving the world of insurance by providing affordable and easy-to-use personalized solutions to individuals families and businesses through its auto personal insurance life and health brands. Kemper serves more than 6.5 million policyholders and is represented by more than 35400 agents and brokers.

	Annual Growth	12/17	12/18	12/19	12/20	12/21
Assets ($ mil.)	15.5%	8,376.2	11,544.9	12,989.1	14,341.9	14,916.5
Net income ($ mil.)	–	120.9	190.1	531.1	409.9	(120.5)
Market value ($ mil.)	(3.9%)	4,387.9	4,227.4	4,935.6	4,892.9	3,744.0
Employees	(20.2%)	5,550	8,100	8,900	2,100	2,250

KEN'S FOODS INC.

1 D'angelo Dr.
Marlborough MA 01752-3066
Phone: 508-485-7540
Fax: 570-473-4303
Web: www.keystoneinsgrp.com

CEO: Frank A Crowley III
CFO: James Sutherby
HR: –
FYE: April 30
Type: Private

Having some leafy greens with that steak? Ask Ken's Foods for some dressing. The condiments company manufactures and markets more than 400 varieties of bottled salad dressings marinades and sauces under the Ken's Steak House brand name. Its products are distributed to retail food companies such as Albertsons Wal-Mart Hy-Vee Kroger Meijer HEB and others and to foodservice operators throughout most of the US. As part of its business Ken's Foods which is family owned and operated also offers production labeling and packaging services for other food manufacturers. The dressings manufacturer owns and operates production facilities in Massachusetts Georgia and Nevada.

KENERGY CORP.

6402 OLD CORYDON RD
HENDERSON, KY 424209392
Phone: 270-926-4141
Fax: –
Web: www.kenergycorp.com

CEO: Stanford Noveick
CFO: –
HR: –
FYE: December 31
Type: Private

Kenergy kens energy as the Scots might say. Electric distribution cooperative Kenergy serves about 55000 customers in 14 counties (Breckinridge Caldwell Crittenden Daviess Hancock Henderson Hopkins Livingston Lyon McLean Muhlenberg Ohio Union and Webster) in Western Kentucky. Kenergy serves its customer base of households commercial enterprises and industries via more than 6700 miles of power lines. The customer-owned company is part of Touchstone Energy Cooperatives a national alliance of more than 600 local consumer-owned electric utility cooperatives.

	Annual Growth	12/11	12/12	12/13	12/14	12/15
Sales ($ mil.)	(8.8%)	–	496.0	506.9	474.8	375.7
Net income ($ mil.)	(0.0%)	–	0.1	0.1	0.1	0.1
Market value ($ mil.)	–	–	–	–	–	–
Employees	–	–	–	–	–	155

KENEXA CORPORATION   NASDAQ: KNXA

650 E. Swedesford Rd. 2nd Fl.
Wayne PA 19087
Phone: 610-971-9171
Fax: 610-971-9181
Web: www.kenexa.com

CEO: Nooruddin S Karsan
CFO: Donald F Volk
HR: –
FYE: December 31
Type: Public

Kenexa can execute on HR functions. The company develops integrated and Web-based or cloud applications that automate human resources activities such as recruitment skills testing and employee development tracking. Kenexa also offers outsourcing options to clients taking over part or all of the recruitment and hiring process. In addition the company conducts employee surveys for its customers. It sells its services and software products mostly on a subscription basis to about 9000 large and midsized corporations such as Eli Lilly and KPMG. In 2012 Kenexa agreed to be acquired by IBM in a cash transaction valued at around $1.3 billion.

KENNAMETAL INC.   NYS: KMT

525 William Penn Place, Suite 3300
Pittsburgh, PA 15219
Phone: 412 248-8000
Fax: –
Web: www.kennametal.com

CEO: Christopher Rossi
CFO: Damon Audia
HR: –
FYE: June 30
Type: Public

Kennametal offers a host of metal-cutting tools and tooling supplies for machining steel equipment for mining and highway construction and engineering services for production processes. Its lines include cutting milling and drilling tools used in metalworking; earth cutting tools and systems used in mining; and construction. The company which sells its products globally serves customers in the aerospace defense transportation engineering energy and mining sectors. Some 40% of sales come from outside of the US.

	Annual Growth	06/17	06/18	06/19	06/20	06/21
Sales ($ mil.)	(2.7%)	2,058.4	2,367.9	2,375.2	1,885.3	1,841.4
Net income ($ mil.)	2.6%	49.1	200.2	241.9	(5.7)	54.4
Market value ($ mil.)	(1.0%)	3,128.8	3,001.7	3,092.9	2,400.6	3,003.4
Employees	(5.2%)	10,700	10,500	10,400	9,000	8,635

KENNEDY HEALTH SYSTEM, INC.

1099 WHITE HORSE RD
VOORHEES, NJ 080434405
Phone: 856-566-5200
Fax: –
Web: –

CEO: –
CFO: –
HR: –
FYE: September 30
Type: Private

Like its namesake The Kennedy Health System is all about service to the public. The system operates three acute care hospitals with more than 600 beds in southern interior New Jersey. Its operations include several outpatient centers and wellness programs cancer care dialysis centers primary care facilities and a nursing home. Its outpatient services are vast and varied ranging from behavioral and occupational health centers to balance centers (to treat dizziness and balance problems) and sleep centers. Affiliated with the Rowan University School of Osteopathic Medicine Kennedy Health System was founded in 1965 as John F. Kennedy Hospital. It plans to merge with Thomas Jefferson University Hospitals.

	Annual Growth	12/05	12/06	12/07	12/08*	09/09
Sales ($ mil.)	–	–	–	0.0	455.8	355.3
Net income ($ mil.)	–	–	–	0.0	(15.1)	11.0
Market value ($ mil.)	–	–	–	–	–	–
Employees	–	–	–	–	–	4,000

*Fiscal year change

KENNEDY KRIEGER INSTITUTE, INC.

707 N BROADWAY
BALTIMORE, MD 212051888
Phone: 443-923-9200
Fax: –
Web: www.kennedykrieger.org

CEO: –
CFO: Michael Neuman
HR: –
FYE: June 30
Type: Private

Kennedy Krieger Institute is dedicated to the research education and treatment of children with disorders of the brain spinal cord and musculoskeletal systems. It operates more than 55 outpatient clinics that provide services in behavioral psychology neuropsychology family support occupational and physical therapies and speech pathology among others. Altogether the institute serves more than 25000 individuals each year. Its 70-bed inpatient pediatric hospital caters to children who suffer from feeding problems and severe behaviors such as self-injury and aggression. Kennedy Krieger also runs schools for special-education students ages five to 21 that focuses on the development of academic social emotional and behavioral skills in an environment that recognizes and capitalizes on the individual strengths of each child.

	Annual Growth	06/07	06/08	06/09	06/13	06/19
Sales ($ mil.)	2.9%	–	–	200.4	213.5	267.3
Net income ($ mil.)	–	–	–	(23.6)	13.9	(9.7)
Market value ($ mil.)	–	–	–	–	–	–
Employees	–	–	–	–	–	2,500

KENNEDY-WILSON HOLDINGS INC   NYS: KW

151 S El Camino Drive
Beverly Hills, CA 90212
Phone: 310 887-6400
Fax: –
Web: www.kennedywilson.com

CEO: William Mcmorrow
CFO: Justin Enbody
HR: –
FYE: December 31
Type: Public

International real estate company Kennedy-Wilson Holdings invests in and leases mostly commercial properties in the US UK Ireland and Spain. In addition to office space the company's KW Investments unit acquires and manages portfolios of multifamily residences and office properties. With about $1 billion in assets under management its KW Investment Management and Real Estate Services (IMRES) division provides property and investment management auction and residential sales and brokerage services to financial institutions institutional investors insurance companies government entities and builders. Kennedy Wilson has ownership interests in about 50 million sq. ft. of property. Most of its sales came from Europe.

	Annual Growth	12/16	12/17	12/18	12/19	12/20
Sales ($ mil.)	(10.5%)	703.4	810.6	773.5	569.7	450.9
Net income ($ mil.)	110.6%	5.6	100.5	150.0	226.7	110.1
Market value ($ mil.)	(3.3%)	2,898.0	2,452.7	2,568.6	3,152.4	2,529.0
Employees	(20.3%)	500	498	375	318	202

KENNESAW STATE UNIVERSITY

1000 CHASTAIN RD NW
KENNESAW, GA 301445591
Phone: 770-423-6000
Fax: –
Web: www.kennesaw.edu

CEO: –
CFO: –
HR: –
FYE: June 30
Type: Private

Kennesaw State University (KSU) is a stomping ground for higher education students in northwest Georgia. The college offers nearly 165 undergraduate and graduate degree programs including bachelor's master's and doctorate programs in the core areas of nursing business and education as well as such subjects as public administration information technology and social work. KSU enrolls nearly 41000 students at its two campuses in the Atlanta metropolitan area. The university is the third largest member of the University System of Georgia after University of Georgia and Georgia State.

	Annual Growth	06/06	06/07	06/08	06/09	06/19
Sales ($ mil.)	10.2%	–	99.6	113.9	116.5	321.0
Net income ($ mil.)	(10.6%)	–	10.2	10.8	(0.7)	2.7
Market value ($ mil.)	–	–	–	–	–	–
Employees	–	–	–	–	–	3,000

KENNESTONE HOSPITAL AT WINDY HILL, INC.

677 CHURCH ST NE
MARIETTA, GA 300601101
Phone: 770-793-5000
Fax: –
Web: www.wellstar.org

CEO: Thomas E Hill
CFO: Dick Stovall
HR: –
FYE: June 30
Type: Private

Kennestone cures kidney stones and other ailments for residents of Cobb County Georgia. WellStar Kennestone Hospital has more than 630 beds and a full range of specialty services. The hospital's physicians provide cardiac care inpatient and outpatient surgery and rehabilitation trauma diabetes care oncology dialysis and home health care. The hospital also operates centers specializing in women's health senior living facilities diagnostic clinics and a wellness and fitness center. WellStar Kennestone Hospital is part of the not-for-profit WellStar Health System which operates hospitals and other medical facilities throughout Georgia.

	Annual Growth	06/02	06/03	06/04	06/05	06/15
Sales ($ mil.)	0.3%	–	792.4	878.0	481.8	821.3
Net income ($ mil.)	12.9%	–	24.8	50.2	54.2	106.2
Market value ($ mil.)	–	–	–	–	–	–
Employees	–	–	–	–	–	2,950

KENNETH COLE PRODUCTIONS INC.

NYSE: KCP

603 W. 50th St.
New York NY 10019
Phone: 212-265-1500
Fax: 866-741-5753
Web: www.kennethcole.com

CEO: Marc Schneider
CFO: David P Edelman
HR: –
FYE: December 31
Type: Private

Kenneth Cole is a trendy old sole. Known for its shoes Kenneth Cole Productions makes stylish apparel and accessories under the Kenneth Cole New York Kenneth Cole Reaction Unlisted and Gentle Souls names. Kenneth Cole licenses its name for hosiery luggage watches and eyewear. It continues to expand adding new lines for women and children as well as fragrances. About 4700 department and specialty stores carry its products. Kenneth Cole operates about 100 retail and outlet stores and sells through catalogs and websites. Chairman Kenneth Cole who effective September 2012 owns the namesake company took Kenneth Cole Productions private through a merger with his KCP Holdco Inc.

KENSEY NASH CORPORATION

NASDAQ: KNSY

735 Pennsylvania Dr.
Exton PA 19341
Phone: 484-713-2100
Fax: 484-713-2900
Web: www.kenseynash.com

CEO: Joseph W Kaufmann
CFO: Michael Celano
HR: –
FYE: June 30
Type: Public

Kensey Nash takes heart in its surgical sucesses. The firm developed the Angio-Seal a bio-absorbable material to seal arterial punctures which can occur during cardiovascular procedures. St. Jude Medical has licensed the rights to manufacture and market Angio-Seal worldwide. Kensey Nash manufactures biomaterial components for the Angio-Seal system including collagen plugs and polymer anchors. The company also makes other biomaterial products including tissue and bone grafting material and fixation devices for orthopedic surgeries collagen-based burn treatments and wound dressings and dental surgery aids. In 2012 Kensey Nash was acquired by global life sciences and materials sciences company Royal DSM.

KENSINGTON PUBLISHING CORP.

119 W 40TH ST FL 21
NEW YORK, NY 100182522
Phone: 212-407-1500
Fax: –
Web: www.kensingtonbooks.com

CEO: Steven Zacharius
CFO: Michael Rosamilia
HR: –
FYE: September 30
Type: Private

Kensington Publishing holds court with readers. The independent publisher sells hardcover trade and mass market fiction and non-fiction books through its Kensington Zebra Pinnacle and Citadel imprints. The company publishes about 600 titles a year and has a backlist of more than 3000. Romance and women's fiction account for more than half of its titles published each year. Other niche topics covered include wicca gambling gay & lesbian and military history. Readers can turn to the company's Rebel Base Books Web site to order titles such as I Hope They Serve Beer in Hell by Tucker Max which sold more than 70000 copies its first year and made the New York Times Bestseller list in 2006 2007 and 2008.

	Annual Growth	09/03	09/04	09/05	09/06	09/11
Sales ($ mil.)	(36.4%)	–	–	980.9	57.0	64.7
Net income ($ mil.)	544.4%	–	–	0.0	1.9	3.2
Market value ($ mil.)	–	–	–	–	–	–
Employees	–	–	–	–	–	81

KENT COUNTY MEMORIAL HOSPITAL

455 TOLL GATE RD
WARWICK, RI 028862770
Phone: 401-737-7000
Fax: –
Web: www.kentri.org

CEO: –
CFO: –
HR: –
FYE: September 30
Type: Private

As one of Rhode Island's largest hospitals Kent County Memorial Hospital offers Ocean Staters a sea of medical care options. The healthcare facility provides inpatient acute care as well as outpatient services (such as diagnostic imaging) and primary care. It also offers a range of specialties including cardiology orthopedics oncology surgery pediatrics and women's health. A member of the Care New England Health System Kent Hospital opened in 1951 with 90 beds; today the hospital has about 360 beds and a staff of some 600 doctors.

	Annual Growth	09/13	09/14	09/15	09/19	09/20
Sales ($ mil.)	1.7%	–	323.6	318.3	372.8	357.3
Net income ($ mil.)	–	–	4.6	14.8	1.1	(16.7)
Market value ($ mil.)	–	–	–	–	–	–
Employees	–	–	–	–	–	1,850

KENT FINANCIAL SERVICES INC.   NASDAQ: KENT

10911 Raven Ridge Rd. Ste. 103-45 — CEO: Bryan P Healey
Raleigh NC 27614 — CFO: Sue Ann Merrill
Phone: 919-847-8710 — HR: –
Fax: 201-791-8015 — FYE: December 31
Web: www.kreisler-ind.com — Type: Public

Kent Financial Services (once known as Texas American Energy) has moved from the oil patch to the financial services field. The firm holds a majority stake in publicly traded Kent International Holdings (formerly Cortech) which scrapped its pharmaceutical research and is seeking new business opportunities in the US and China. The company in 2010 also scrapped subsidiary Kent Educational Services which controlled The Academy for Teaching and Leadership a provider of educational programs for school administrators and teachers. Chairman and CEO Paul Koether owns approximately 60% of Kent Financial Services.

KENT STATE UNIVERSITY

1500 HORNING RD — CEO: –
KENT, OH 442420001 — CFO: –
Phone: 330-672-3000 — HR: –
Fax: – — FYE: June 30
Web: www.kent.edu — Type: Private

Kent State University (KSU) knows all about learning from history. The school offers some 300 degrees in art business management technology medicine biology psychology and other fields. Through eight campuses located in northeastern Ohio KSU educates some 43000 students making it Ohio's second-largest public university (behind Ohio State). Its campuses include more than 24 residence halls and the university encourages on-campus living. The school has a student-teacher ratio of about 20:1 and it offers both graduate and undergraduate degrees. KSU was founded in 1910 for teacher training and is one of the state's oldest universities.

	Annual Growth	06/07	06/08	06/09	06/11	06/13
Sales ($ mil.)	6.4%	–	–	358.8	420.3	460.1
Net income ($ mil.)	–	–	–	(63.5)	107.3	54.9
Market value ($ mil.)	–	–	–	–	–	–
Employees	–	–	–	–	–	5,466

KENTUCKY FIRST FEDERAL BANCORP   NMS: KFFB

655 Main Street — CEO: Don Jennings
Hazard, KY 41702 — CFO: R. Clay Hulette
Phone: 502 223-1638 — HR: –
Fax: – — FYE: June 30
Web: www.ffsbky.bank — Type: Public

Kentucky First Federal wants to be second to none for banking in the Bluegrass State. Formed in 2005 to be the holding company for First Federal Savings and Loan of Hazard and First Federal Savings Bank of Frankfort which operate three branches in the state's capital and one in the town of Hazard. The banks offer traditional deposit products such as checking and savings accounts NOW and money market accounts and CDs. Lending is focused on residential mortgages but the banks also offer loans secured by churches and commercial real estate as well as consumer and construction loans. Kentucky First Federal which has received final regulatory approval is merging with CKF Bancorp.

	Annual Growth	06/17	06/18	06/19	06/20	06/21
Assets ($ mil.)	2.3%	308.5	318.4	330.8	321.1	338.1
Net income ($ mil.)	18.1%	0.9	1.3	0.8	(12.5)	1.8
Market value ($ mil.)	(6.1%)	77.7	69.5	64.6	55.5	60.5
Employees	(3.3%)	71	70	64	63	62

KENTUCKY MEDICAL SERVICES FOUNDATION, INC.

2333 ALUMNI PARK PLZ # 200 — CEO: –
LEXINGTON, KY 405174012 — CFO: –
Phone: 859-257-7910 — HR: Cindy Gillespie
Fax: – — FYE: June 30
Web: www.kmsf.com — Type: Private

Does the mailbox at your old Kentucky home contain doctors' bills? They might be from Kentucky Medical Services Foundation. The physician's practice group provides billing and other administrative services for the more than 600 physicians and other health care providers affiliated with the University of Kentucky's health system UK HealthCare. The network provides more than 80 specialty services offers educational programs and operates acute medical centers including Chandler Hospital Good Samaritan Hospital and Kentucky Children's Hospital.

	Annual Growth	06/09	06/10	06/13	06/14	06/15
Sales ($ mil.)	9.3%	–	196.6	225.1	236.2	306.7
Net income ($ mil.)	–	–	(4.6)	(0.4)	1.7	11.0
Market value ($ mil.)	–	–	–	–	–	–
Employees	–	–	–	–	–	150

KENTUCKY POWER COMPANY

1 Riverside Plaza — CEO: –
Columbus OH 43215-2372 — CFO: Holly K Koeppel
Phone: 614-716-1000 — HR: –
Fax: 614-716-1823 — FYE: December 31
Web: www.kentuckypower.com — Type: Subsidiary

The sun may shine bright on old Kentucky homes but Kentucky Power provides light regardless of the sun's hue. Organized in 1919 the utility distributes electricity to about 175000 homes and businesses across 20 counties in eastern Kentucky. An operating unit of holding company American Electric Power (AEP) Kentucky Power also sells electricity to wholesale customers and has coal-fired power plant interests that combined have a generating capacity of more than 1060 MW. The company operates more than 11040 miles of overhead transmission and distribution power lines.

KENYON COLLEGE

1 KENYON COLLEGE — CEO: –
GAMBIER, OH 430229623 — CFO: –
Phone: 740-427-5000 — HR: –
Fax: – — FYE: June 30
Web: www.kenyon.edu — Type: Private

Kenyon College is a small liberal arts school located approximately 45 miles northeast of Columbus Ohio. With an enrollment of some 1600 students the school offers bachelor's degrees in more than 30 majors in fields such as fine arts humanities natural sciences and social sciences. Notable alumni include actor Paul Newman and poet Robert Lowell. The college also produces renowned literary journal The Kenyon Review. The oldest private institution of higher education in Ohio Kenyon College was founded in 1824 by Philander Chase an Episcopal bishop.

	Annual Growth	06/05	06/06	06/08	06/16	06/17
Sales ($ mil.)	(0.5%)	–	131.9	123.7	116.6	124.3
Net income ($ mil.)	(2.1%)	–	58.6	24.6	(9.2)	46.3
Market value ($ mil.)	–	–	–	–	–	–
Employees	–	–	–	–	–	450

KERYX BIOPHARMACEUTICALS INC.   NAS: KERX

One Marina Park Drive, 12th Floor
Boston, MA 02210
Phone: 617 466-3500
Fax: –
Web: www.keryx.com
CEO: Jodie P Morrison
CFO: Scott A Holmes
HR: –
FYE: December 31
Type: Public

Drugs are a life-or-death business for Keryx Biopharmaceuticals. The company specializes in developing treatments for life-threatening ailments such as cancer and kidney disease. Its lead candidates are Zerenex a compound that may reduce high phosphate levels in patients with end-stage renal disease. The drug has been approved for sale in Japan under the name Riona to treat elevated phosphate levels in patients with chronic kidney disease. Marketing rights there have been granted to partner Japan Tobacco. Keryx is also testing Zerenx as a treatment for elevated phosphorous levels and iron deficiency in patients with kidney disease.

	Annual Growth	12/12	12/13	12/14	12/15	12/16
Sales ($ mil.)	65.9%	–	7.0	10.8	13.7	32.0
Net income ($ mil.)	–	(22.7)	(46.7)	(111.5)	(123.1)	(161.1)
Market value ($ mil.)	22.3%	277.3	1,370.6	1,497.7	534.5	620.2
Employees	66.7%	25	41	155	184	193

KETTERING ADVENTIST HEALTHCARE

3535 SOUTHERN BLVD
DAYTON, OH 454291221
Phone: 937-298-4331
Fax: –
Web: www.ketteringhealth.org
CEO: –
CFO: –
HR: –
FYE: December 31
Type: Private

Kettering Adventist Healthcare dba Kettering Health Network and named for famed inventor Charles F. Kettering is an Ohio-based health care system. It comprises about 120 outpatient facilities including seven acute care hospitals: Kettering Medical Center Grandview Medical Center Sycamore Medical Center Southview Medical Center Fort Hamilton Hospital Greene Memorial Hospital and Soin Medical Center. Other facilities include Kettering Behavioral Hospital and multiple outpatient diagnostic senior care and urgent care clinics. Among its specialized services are heart care rehabilitation orthopedics women's health and emergency medicine.

	Annual Growth	12/14	12/15	12/16	12/17	12/18
Sales ($ mil.)	8.7%	–	–	1,577.6	1,753.8	1,863.2
Net income ($ mil.)	(15.4%)	–	–	98.1	171.3	70.2
Market value ($ mil.)	–	–	–	–	–	–
Employees	–	–	–	–	–	6,800

KETTERING UNIVERSITY

1700 UNIVERSITY AVE
FLINT, MI 485044898
Phone: 810-762-9500
Fax: –
Web: www.kettering.edu
CEO: –
CFO: –
HR: –
FYE: June 30
Type: Private

Sometimes referred to as the "West Point of Industry" Kettering University specializes in engineering science and mathematics programs. Other academic fields include business pre-law pre-med and computer gaming. The private school offers about 15 undergraduate degrees and five graduate degrees to a small student body of more than 1680. As part of its cooperative educational framework the school provides academic credit for structured job experience. Kettering's students work with employers in aerospace accounting government law medical and not-for-profits and research firms in addition to companies in the manufacturing sector. Its student/faculty ratio is 13:1.

	Annual Growth	06/13	06/14	06/15	06/16	06/17
Sales ($ mil.)	4.3%	–	57.3	64.8	59.2	65.0
Net income ($ mil.)	(5.9%)	–	13.3	8.9	(2.2)	11.1
Market value ($ mil.)	–	–	–	–	–	–
Employees	–	–	–	–	–	425

KEURIG DR PEPPER INC   NMS: KDP

53 South Avenue
Burlington, MA 01803
Phone: 781 418-7000
Fax: –
Web: www.keurig.com
CEO: Robert Gamgort
CFO: Ozan Dokmecioglu
HR: –
FYE: December 31
Type: Public

Whether you like your caffeine hot or cold Keurig Dr Pepper (KDP) has you covered. The company formerly Dr Pepper Snapple Group is one of North America's largest beverage companies with more than 125 owned licensed and partner brands. It owns the top single-serve coffee system in the US (Keurig) and one of the US's leading soft drinks (Dr Pepper) as well as Green Mountain coffee Canada Dry A&W root beer Snapple tea and juice and Mott's fruit juice among many other products. KDP operates facilities across North America. The company serves major retailers in the U.S. Canada and Mexico. Their largest retailer was Walmart representing approximately 15% of sales in 2020. Majority of the company's sales were generated in the US.

	Annual Growth	12/16	12/17	12/18	12/19	12/20
Sales ($ mil.)	15.9%	6,440.0	6,690.0	7,442.0	11,120.0	11,618.0
Net income ($ mil.)	11.8%	847.0	1,076.0	586.0	1,254.0	1,325.0
Market value ($ mil.)	(22.9%)	127,596.3	136,588.7	36,082.2	40,740.2	45,032.3
Employees	7.8%	20,000	21,000	25,500	25,500	27,000

KEURIG GREEN MOUNTAIN INC   NMS: GMCR

33 Coffee Lane
Waterbury, VT 05676
Phone: 802 244-5621
Fax: –
Web: www.gmcr.com
CEO: Robert Gamgort
CFO: Peter Leemputt
HR: –
FYE: September 26
Type: Public

Keurig Green Mountain's business amounts to far more than a hill of beans. The company (formerly Green Mountain Coffee Roasters) is a leader in the specialty coffee and coffeemaker business in North America. Its Keurig subsidiary makes single-cup brewing systems for home and office use and roasts coffee for its K-Cups and Vue portion packs. Green Mountain also roasts and packages whole bean and ground coffee and supplies apple cider teas cocoa and other beverages wholesale to food stores resorts and office-delivery services. The company markets coffee under the Newman's Own Organics Tully's and Green Mountain Coffee labels. In Canada it owns the Van Houtte gourmet coffee and coffee-service business.

	Annual Growth	09/11	09/12	09/13	09/14	09/15
Sales ($ mil.)	14.3%	2,650.9	3,859.2	4,358.1	4,707.7	4,520.0
Net income ($ mil.)	25.7%	199.5	362.6	483.2	596.5	498.3
Market value ($ mil.)	(14.6%)	15,973.6	3,637.2	11,472.3	20,013.7	8,506.2
Employees	1.7%	5,600	5,800	6,300	6,600	6,000

KEWAUNEE SCIENTIFIC CORPORATION   NMS: KEQU

2700 West Front Street
Statesville, NC 28677-2927
Phone: 704 873-7202
Fax: 704 873-5160
Web: www.kewaunee.com
CEO: Thomas Hull
CFO: Donald Gardner
HR: Elizabeth Phillips
FYE: April 30
Type: Public

The nutty professor once wreaked havoc on furniture like that made by Kewaunee Scientific. The company makes furniture for laboratories including wood and steel cabinets fume hoods and work surfaces. It also makes technical workstations workbenches and computer enclosures for local area networking applications. Kewaunee's primary customers are schools health care institutions and labs (pharmaceutical biotech industrial chemical and commercial research). The company's products are sold through VWR International a school and lab products supplier as well as through designated Kewaunee dealers. Kewaunee's subsidiaries in Singapore and India handle sales in the Asian and Middle Eastern markets.

	Annual Growth	04/17	04/18	04/19	04/20	04/21
Sales ($ mil.)	1.6%	138.6	158.1	146.6	147.5	147.5
Net income ($ mil.)	–	–	4.5	5.2	1.5	(4.7)	(3.7)
Market value ($ mil.)	(14.9%)	63.3	96.6	62.5	28.3	33.2
Employees	3.0%	745	820	856	912	838

KEY CITY FURNITURE COMPANY INC

1804 RIVER ST
WILKESBORO, NC 286977633
Phone: 336-838-4191
Fax: –

CEO: –
CFO: –
HR: –
FYE: January 01
Type: Private

Family-owned and -operated since 1927 Key City Furniture has a lock on handcrafting furniture. The company operates facilities in Wilkesboro and North Wilkesboro North Carolina. More than 400 types of furniture are made to order including sleeper sofas sectionals rockers and ottomans. The company offers its customers some 1200 different fabrics and leathers. Key City Furniture founded by James E. Caudill is run by his grandsons F.D. Forester III and James Caudill Forester.

	Annual Growth	12/05	12/06	12/07*	01/09	01/10
Sales ($ mil.)	(70.8%)	–	–	384.0	13.1	9.5
Net income ($ mil.)	–	–	–	0.0	(2.2)	(0.8)
Market value ($ mil.)	–	–	–	–	–	–
Employees	–	–	–	–	–	105

*Fiscal year change

KEY ENERGY SERVICES INC (DE)   NBB: KEGX

1301 McKinney Street, Suite 1800
Houston, TX 77010
Phone: 713 651-4300
Fax: –
Web: www.keyenergy.com

CEO: J Marshall Dodson
CFO: Nelson Haight
HR: –
FYE: December 31
Type: Public

Energy is the key to growth for Key Energy Services one of the US's largest well-servicing and workover companies. The company provides maintenance workover and recompletion of wells primarily for onshore drilling. It provides services such as contract drilling well completion oilfield fluid transportation production testing and storage and disposal services to major and independent oil companies. Key Energy Services has a technology development and control systems business based in Canada. The company filed for Chapter 11 bankruptcy protection in 2016.

	Annual Growth	12/16	12/16	12/17	12/18	12/19
Sales ($ mil.)	1.2%	399.4	17.8	436.2	521.7	413.9
Net income ($ mil.)	–	(131.7)	(10.2)	(120.6)	(88.8)	(97.4)
Market value ($ mil.)	–	–	13.1	4.8	0.9	0.0
Employees	(14.7%)	–	3,225	3,000	2,600	2,000

KEY FOOD STORES CO-OPERATIVE, INC.

100 MATAWAN RD STE 100 # 100
MATAWAN, NJ 077473913
Phone: 718-370-4200
Fax: –
Web: www.keyfood.com

CEO: Dean Janeway
CFO: –
HR: –
FYE: April 25
Type: Private

Key Food Stores Co-Operative is a friend to independent New York area grocers. The co-op provides retail support and other services to 150 independently owned food retailers in the New York City area. Key Food's member-owners run stores mainly in Brooklyn and Queens but also in the other boroughs and surrounding counties. It operates stores primarily under the Key Food banner but it also has Key Food Marketplace locations that feature expanded meat deli and produce departments. In addition the co-op supplies Key Foods-branded products to member stores. Among its members are Pick Quick Foods Dan's Supreme Super Markets Gemstone Supermarkets and Queens Supe rmarkets. Key Foods was founded in 1937.

	Annual Growth	04/09	04/10	04/11	04/14	04/15
Sales ($ mil.)	–	–	0.0	537.7	753.4	893.2
Net income ($ mil.)	–	–	0.0	(0.0)	0.0	(0.7)
Market value ($ mil.)	–	–	–	–	–	–
Employees	–	–	–	–	–	84

KEY TECHNOLOGY INC   NMS: KTEC

150 Avery Street
Walla Walla, WA 99362
Phone: 509 529-2161
Fax: 509 522-3378
Web: www.key.net

CEO: Michael J Kachmer
CFO: Craig Reuther
HR: –
FYE: September 30
Type: Public

When good french fries go bad Key Technology can sort out the problem. The company makes food and material processing automation equipment under brand names such as Manta Tegra and Optyx. Its electro-optical automated inspection sorting and product preparation systems can be used to evaluate fresh fruits and vegetables beans potato chips and other snacks. Items can be sorted by color size and shape to identify defective or inconsistent products for removal. The company also makes conveyor and sorting systems for the tobacco pharmaceutical nutraceutical and coffee industries.

	Annual Growth	09/13	09/14	09/15	09/16	09/17
Sales ($ mil.)	0.6%	136.8	118.3	102.9	120.0	139.9
Net income ($ mil.)	0.1%	4.0	(5.4)	(5.0)	(0.7)	4.0
Market value ($ mil.)	8.2%	89.5	85.9	76.3	71.4	122.6
Employees	2.1%	602	559	555	587	653

KEY TRONIC CORP   NMS: KTCC

4424 North Sullivan Road
Spokane Valley, WA 99216
Phone: 509 928-8000
Fax: –
Web: www.keytronic.com

CEO: Craig Gates
CFO: Brett Larsen
HR: –
FYE: July 03
Type: Public

Key Tronic unlocks the door to electronic systems manufacturing for its contract customers. The company which does business as KeyTronicEMS to highlight its focus on electronics manufacturing services provides printed circuit board (PCB) assembly integrated electronic and mechanical engineering precision plastic molding sheet metal fabrication and complete product assembly services. In addition Key Tronic offers product design engineering materials management and in-house testing services. The company began as a maker of computer keyboards and it still makes customized and standard keyboards for PCs terminals and workstations. Customers in the US generate about 75% of revenue.

	Annual Growth	07/17*	06/18	06/19	06/20*	07/21
Sales ($ mil.)	2.6%	467.8	446.3	464.0	449.5	518.7
Net income ($ mil.)	(6.2%)	5.6	(1.3)	(8.0)	4.8	4.3
Market value ($ mil.)	(2.0%)	76.3	81.6	53.6	56.6	70.5
Employees	2.0%	5,038	4,701	4,067	5,741	5,450

*Fiscal year change

KEYCORP   NYS: KEY

127 Public Square
Cleveland, OH 44114-1306
Phone: 216 689-3000
Fax: –
Web: www.key.com

CEO: Christopher Gorman
CFO: Donald Kimble
HR: Brian Fishel
FYE: December 31
Type: Public

With a focus on retail operations KeyBank a subsidiary of KeyCorp operates about 1075 branches and around 1385 ATMs in some 15 states across the US. Its operations are divided into two groups: Consumer Bank offers traditional services such as deposits loans credit cards securities lending personal financial and planning services access to mutual funds treasury services and international banking services. Commercial Bank community development financing securities underwriting investment banking and capital markets products and brokerage. KeyCorp is also one of the largest bank-based financial services companies providing deposit lending cash management and investment services to individuals and small and medium-sized businesses.

	Annual Growth	12/17	12/18	12/19	12/20	12/21
Assets ($ mil.)	7.9%	137,698.0	139,613.0	144,988.0	170,336.0	186,346.0
Net income ($ mil.)	19.3%	1,296.0	1,866.0	1,717.0	1,343.0	2,625.0
Market value ($ mil.)	3.5%	18,734.9	13,728.4	18,799.9	15,242.4	21,484.3
Employees	(1.0%)	18,415	18,180	17,045	16,826	17,654

KEYW HOLDING CORP

NMS: KEYW

7740 Milestone Parkway, Suite 400
Hanover, MD 21076
Phone: 443 733-1600
Fax: –
Web: www.keywcorp.com

CEO: William J Weber
CFO: Michael J Alber
HR: –
FYE: December 31
Type: Public

KeyW is a key player in US cybersecurity with its eyes focused on the intelligence community. Operating through contractor KeyW Corp. and its subsidiaries including Sotera Defense the company is an IT contractor to the federal government. Its capabilities include cyber operations and training; geospatial intelligence; cloud and data analytics; engineering; and intelligence analysis and operations. Customers include US government intelligence and defense agencies like the National Security Agency and the FBI and agencies in US Department of Defense. Some 95% of the company's revenue comes from the US government.

	Annual Growth	12/13	12/14	12/15	12/16	12/17
Sales ($ mil.)	10.3%	298.7	290.5	311.8	288.0	441.6
Net income ($ mil.)	–	(10.6)	(12.9)	(58.6)	(25.7)	(11.0)
Market value ($ mil.)	(18.7%)	670.3	517.7	300.3	588.0	292.8
Employees	16.2%	1,068	1,087	1,173	1,058	1,949

KFORCE INC.

NMS: KFRC

1001 East Palm Avenue
Tampa, FL 33605
Phone: 813 552-5000
Fax: –
Web: www.kforce.com

CEO: Joseph Liberatore
CFO: David Kelly
HR: –
FYE: December 31
Type: Public

Kforce is a US-based placement firm that matches skilled technology and finance workers with the companies that need them. The specialty staffing firm provides temporary staffing services (and to a lesser extent permanent placement) primarily in information technology finance and accounting. Among Kforce's clients are FORTUNE 1000 corporations (including 70% of the Fortune 100) small and midsize firms nationwide. The K in Kforce stands for Knowledge. A majority of its revenue comes from US operations.

	Annual Growth	12/16	12/17	12/18	12/19	12/20
Sales ($ mil.)	1.4%	1,319.7	1,357.9	1,418.4	1,347.4	1,397.7
Net income ($ mil.)	14.4%	32.8	33.3	58.0	130.9	56.0
Market value ($ mil.)	16.2%	512.2	559.9	685.6	880.3	933.3
Employees	(1.2%)	14,600	14,600	13,800	12,900	13,900

KGBO HOLDINGS, INC

4289 IVY POINTE BLVD
CINCINNATI, OH 452450002
Phone: 513-831-2600
Fax: –

CEO: –
CFO: –
HR: –
FYE: December 30
Type: Private

Total Quality Logistics sets a high standard for moving merchandise. The third-party logistics (non-asset based) provider specializes in arranging freight transportation using reefers (refrigerated trucks) vans and flatbeds — moving in excess of 500000 loads each year. The trucking brokerage company serves more than 7000 clients across the US Canada and Mexico ranging from small businesses to Fortune 500 organizations. Founded in 1997 by company president Ken Oaks Total Quality Logistics (TQL) has contracts with carriers that include single owner operators and large fleets. Customers have included Kroger Dole Food and Laura's Lean Beef.

	Annual Growth	12/08	12/09	12/10	12/11	12/12
Sales ($ mil.)	34.9%	–	–	762.1	1,046.7	1,387.4
Net income ($ mil.)	–	–	–	0.0	0.0	0.0
Market value ($ mil.)	–	–	–	–	–	–
Employees	–	–	–	–	–	4,077

KID BRANDS, INC.

NBB: KIDB Q

301 Route 17 North, 6th Floor
Rutherford, NJ 07070
Phone: 201 405-2400
Fax: 204 405-7355
Web: www.kidbrands.com

CEO: –
CFO: –
HR: –
FYE: December 31
Type: Public

Kid Brands sells products for brand-new people: newborns to 3-year-olds. Through its subsidiaries the company designs imports and markets infant and juvenile bedding and furniture as well as related nursery accessories. It also peddles infant-development toys and teething feeding and bath and baby care products. Kid Brands' principal subsidiaries include Sassy Kids Line LaJobi and CoCaLo. The company also makes juvenile products under license from Carters Disney Graco and Serta. Founded in 1963 by the late Russell Berrie the company (formerly Russ Berrie and Co.) changed its name to Kid Brands in 2009 to underscore its shift to infant and juvenile products.

	Annual Growth	12/09	12/10	12/11	12/12	12/13
Sales ($ mil.)	(6.3%)	243.9	275.8	252.6	229.5	188.2
Net income ($ mil.)	–	11.7	34.7	(38.6)	(54.1)	(28.8)
Market value ($ mil.)	(30.5%)	96.7	188.8	69.8	34.2	22.5
Employees	(3.1%)	340	304	320	300	300

KILLBUCK BANCSHARES, INC.

NBB: KLIB

165 North Main Street, P.O. Box 407
Killbuck, OH 44637
Phone: 330 276-2771
Fax: 330 276-0216
Web: www.killbuckbank.com

CEO: Craig Lawhead
CFO: Lawrence M Cardinal Jr
HR: –
FYE: December 31
Type: Public

Interestingly enough if you want to save a buck you can take your doe to Killbuck. Killbuck Bancshares is the holding company for The Killbuck Savings Bank which operates about 10 branches in northeast Ohio. It offers traditional retail products to individuals and small to midsized businesses including checking and savings accounts credit cards and IRAs. Residential and commercial mortgages make up about two-thirds of its loan portfolio which also includes business loans and consumer loans. Killbuck Bancshares is the #1 financial institution in Holmes County where most of its offices are located. It also has branches in Knox and Tuscarawas counties.

	Annual Growth	12/11	12/12	12/13	12/14	12/15
Assets ($ mil.)	3.1%	436.5	460.4	461.8	479.8	492.3
Net income ($ mil.)	12.3%	2.9	3.3	3.6	4.1	4.6
Market value ($ mil.)	0.4%	65.4	65.2	61.9	67.0	66.4
Employees	–	121	–	–	–	–

KILROY REALTY CORP

NYS: KRC

12200 W. Olympic Boulevard, Suite 200
Los Angeles, CA 90064
Phone: 310 481-8400
Fax: –
Web: www.kilroyrealty.com

CEO: John Kilroy
CFO: Michelle Ngo
HR: –
FYE: December 31
Type: Public

Kilroy is a self-administered real estate investment trust (REIT) which operates in premier office and mixed-use submarkets along the West Coast. Kilroy Realty owns manages and develops Class A office space mostly in suburban Southern California's Orange County San Diego and Los Angeles but it has since expanded to the San Francisco Bay and greater Seattle area. Its portfolio includes about 120 office properties encompassing about 15 million square feet of leasable space. In addition the company also boasts five future development sites which accounts for more than 60 gross acres of undeveloped land. A majority of Kilroy Realty's some 450-plus tenants are involved in technology media healthcare and entertainment.

	Annual Growth	12/17	12/18	12/19	12/20	12/21
Sales ($ mil.)	7.4%	719.0	747.3	837.5	898.4	955.0
Net income ($ mil.)	39.8%	164.6	258.4	195.4	187.1	628.1
Market value ($ mil.)	(2.9%)	8,694.1	7,323.3	9,771.3	6,685.0	7,740.2
Employees	(0.7%)	251	276	267	252	244

KIMBALL ELECTRONICS GROUP INC.

1600 Royal St. GO-149
Jasper IN 47549
Phone: 812-634-4200
Fax: 812-634-4600
Web: www.kegroup.com

CEO: –
CFO: Michael K Sergesketter
HR: Judith Brosseau
FYE: June 30
Type: Subsidiary

Kimball Electronics Group (a subsidiary of Kimball International) makes printed circuit boards and electronic assemblies along with offering such services as design engineering prototyping testing and packaging. The company was established in 1961 to build electronic organs for its parent firm then transitioned into the contract electronics manufacturing services business in 1985. Customers have included FLIR Systems Johnson Controls TRW Automotive Holdings and Xhale Innovations. Kimball Electronics has facilities in China Mexico Poland Thailand and the US.

KIMBALL INTERNATIONAL, INC. NMS: KBAL

1600 Royal Street
Jasper, IN 47546-2256
Phone: 812 482-1600
Fax: –
Web: www.kimballinternational.com

CEO: Kristine Juster
CFO: Timothy Wolfe
HR: –
FYE: June 30
Type: Public

Kimball International is a leading omnichannel commercial furnishings company with deep expertise in the workplace health and hospitality markets. The Kimball and National brands provide furniture designed for collaborative and open workspace areas conference rooms training rooms and private rooms. Kimball Hospitality provides furniture designed for hotel properties and mixed use developments including commercial and residential. In addition Kimball International designs products specifically for the healthcare market such as patient/exam room and lounge seating and case goods. Founded in 1857 Kimball International has a long and storied history that includes being the world's largest piano maker. The company generates almost all of its revenue in the US.

	Annual Growth	06/17	06/18	06/19	06/20	06/21
Sales ($ mil.)	(4.0%)	669.9	685.6	768.1	727.9	569.0
Net income ($ mil.)	(33.3%)	37.5	34.4	39.3	41.1	7.4
Market value ($ mil.)	(5.8%)	615.4	595.9	642.5	426.3	484.9
Employees	(8.2%)	3,089	3,074	3,127	2,808	2,196

KIMBALL MEDICAL CENTER INC.

600 RIVER AVE
LAKEWOOD, NJ 087015281
Phone: 732-363-1900
Fax: –
Web: www.saintbarnabas.com

CEO: –
CFO: –
HR: –
FYE: December 31
Type: Private

Kimball Medical Center knows that life on the Jersey Shore isn't always as beachy as it's cracked up to be. Kimball Medical Center is a 350-bed acute care hospital and part of the Saint Barnabas Health Care System. Located in Lakewood the medical center serves the southern Monmouth and Ocean counties of New Jersey. Services include cancer treatment rehabilitation emergency care maternity and pediatrics and occupational medicine. The hospital also offers wellness and health education programs and support groups at its Center For Healthy Living.

	Annual Growth	12/07	12/08	12/12	12/15	12/16
Sales ($ mil.)	(4.1%)	–	147.9	141.8	108.9	106.0
Net income ($ mil.)	–	–	(18.0)	(3.3)	9.7	5.2
Market value ($ mil.)	–	–	–	–	–	–
Employees	–	–	–	–	–	1,500

KIMBERLY-CLARK CORP. NYS: KMB

P.O. Box 619100
Dallas, TX 75261-9100
Phone: 972 281-1200
Fax: –
Web: www.kimberly-clark.com

CEO: Michael Hsu
CFO: Maria Henry
HR: –
FYE: December 31
Type: Public

One of the world's largest makers of personal paper products Kimberly-Clark operates through three business segments: Personal Care Consumer Tissue and K-C Professional. Kimberly-Clark's largest unit Personal Care makes products such as diapers (Huggies Pull-Ups) feminine care items (Kotex) and incontinence care products (Poise Depend). Through its Consumer Tissue segment the manufacturer offers facial and bathroom tissues paper towels and other household items under the names Cottonelle Kleenex Viva and Scott (plus the Scott Naturals line). Kimberly-Clark's K-C Professional unit makes WypAll commercial wipes among other items. The US accounts for about 50% of Kimberly-Clark's sales.

	Annual Growth	12/17	12/18	12/19	12/20	12/21
Sales ($ mil.)	1.6%	18,259.0	18,486.0	18,450.0	19,140.0	19,440.0
Net income ($ mil.)	(5.5%)	2,278.0	1,410.0	2,157.0	2,352.0	1,814.0
Market value ($ mil.)	4.3%	40,642.5	38,379.0	46,331.7	45,415.5	48,140.5
Employees	1.7%	42,000	41,000	40,000	46,000	45,000

KIMCO REALTY CORP NYS: KIM

500 North Broadway, Suite 201
Jericho, NY 11753
Phone: 516 869-9000
Fax: –
Web: www.kimcorealty.com

CEO: Conor Flynn
CFO: Glenn Cohen
HR: –
FYE: December 31
Type: Public

Kimco Realty is a self-managed and self-administered real estate investment trust (REIT) owns or has interests in about 400 community shopping centers with about 70 million sq. ft. of leasable space in metropolitan areas in more than 25 states and Puerto Rico. In addition the company had more than 120 other property interests primarily through the company's preferred equity investments and other real estate investments totaling 5.4 million square feet of GLA. Kimco properties are usually anchored by a grocery store off-price retailer discounter or service-oriented tenant. Home Depot Ahold Delhaize TJX Albertsons and Petsmart are its largest tenants. Through subsidiaries the company also develops shopping centers and provides real estate management and disposition services to retailers.

	Annual Growth	12/16	12/17	12/18	12/19	12/20
Sales ($ mil.)	(2.5%)	1,170.8	1,200.8	1,164.8	1,158.9	1,057.9
Net income ($ mil.)	27.5%	378.9	426.1	497.8	410.6	1,000.8
Market value ($ mil.)	(12.1%)	10,882.2	7,850.2	6,336.4	8,957.5	6,492.1
Employees	(3.2%)	551	546	–	502	484

KIMPTON HOTEL & RESTAURANT GROUP LLC

222 Kearney St. Ste. 200
San Francisco CA 94108
Phone: 415-397-5572
Fax: 415-296-8031
Web: www.kimptonhotels.com

CEO: Mike Depatie
CFO: Ben Rowe
HR: –
FYE: December 31
Type: Private

Kimpton Hotel & Restaurant Group hopes a little style can help it stand out in the crowded leisure industry. The company owns some 12 boutique hotels and manages about 40 others in more than 20 markets across the US. Kimpton buys older buildings in urban areas and transforms them into four-star hotels hotels that feature mostly smaller European-style accommodations. Upscale Kimpton Restaurants are located next to most hotels. The company's management services include strategic planning sales and marketing human resources and administration support. Investment banker and founder Bill Kimpton opened the company's first hotel the Clarion Bedford in San Francisco in 1981.

KINDER MORGAN ENERGY PARTNERS, L.P.   NYS: KMP

1001 Louisiana Street, Suite 1000
Houston, TX 77002
Phone: 713 369-9000
Fax: –
Web: www.kindermorgan.com

CEO: Richard D Kinder
CFO: Kimberly A Dang
HR: –
FYE: December 31
Type: Public

Kinder Morgan Energy Partners (KMP) keeps energy on the move throughout the North America. The company holds stakes in more than 37000 miles of natural gas and petroleum product pipelines and owns 180 bulk terminals and rail transloading facilities with 200 millions barrels of storage capacity that handle 100 million tons of coal petroleum coke and bulk products annually. KMP transports refined petroleum products (gasoline diesel and jet fuel) through 8400 miles of pipelines and stores the products in 60 terminals in the US. Through its CO2 subsidiary KMP transports carbon dioxide. Kinder Morgan owns about 13% of KMP and through its Kinder Morgan Management unit acts as general partner.

	Annual Growth	12/08	12/09	12/10	12/11	12/12
Sales ($ mil.)	(7.4%)	11,740.3	7,003.4	8,077.7	8,211.2	8,642.0
Net income ($ mil.)	0.6%	1,304.8	1,267.5	1,316.3	1,257.8	1,339.0
Market value ($ mil.)	14.9%	17,073.4	22,757.0	26,220.2	31,702.3	29,776.7
Employees	31.6%	–	–	–	8,120	10,685

KINDER MORGAN INC.   NYS: KMI

1001 Louisiana Street, Suite 1000
Houston, TX 77002
Phone: 713 369-9000
Fax: –
Web: www.kindermorgan.com

CEO: Steven Kean
CFO: David Michels
HR: –
FYE: December 31
Type: Public

Kinder Morgan Inc. (KMI) is one of the largest energy infrastructure companies in North America. It operates approximately 83000 miles of pipelines and some 145 terminals that transport natural gas refined petroleum products crude oil condensate CO2 and other products to its customers across America. Its terminals store and handle various commodities including gasoline diesel fuel chemicals ethanol metals and petroleum coke. KMI owns and operates 50% of Natural Gas Pipeline Company of America (NGPL). It generates most of its sales in the US.

	Annual Growth	12/17	12/18	12/19	12/20	12/21
Sales ($ mil.)	4.9%	13,705.0	14,144.0	13,209.0	11,700.0	16,610.0
Net income ($ mil.)	76.7%	183.0	1,609.0	2,190.0	119.0	1,784.0
Market value ($ mil.)	–	0.0	0.0	0.0	0.0	0.0
Employees	(0.9%)	10,897	11,012	954	10,524	10,529

KINDRED BIOSCIENCES INC   NAS: KIN

1555 Bayshore Highway, Suite 200
Burlingame, CA 94010
Phone: 650 701-7901
Fax: –
Web: www.kindredbio.com

CEO: –
CFO: Wendy Wee
HR: –
FYE: December 31
Type: Public

Kindred Biosciences has big plans to apply human medicine to our kindred spirits our pet dogs. The company is creating pharmaceuticals that were originally developed for human use and reformulating them for animals. It has three product candidates in development - CereKin for osteoarthritis pain and inflammation in dogs; AtoKin for atopic dermatitis in dogs; and SentiKin for post-operative pain in dogs. (It hopes to have these pharmaceuticals approved in 2015.) In addition the company has seven other early-stage drugs in development that would treat various ailments in dogs cats and horses. Founded in 2012 by CEO Richard Chin Kindred Biosciences went public in 2013 raising $52 million in its IPO.

	Annual Growth	12/15	12/16	12/17	12/18	12/19
Sales ($ mil.)	116.5%	–	–	–	2.0	4.3
Net income ($ mil.)	–	(27.1)	(22.5)	(30.9)	(49.7)	(61.4)
Market value ($ mil.)	25.7%	133.3	166.6	370.5	429.3	332.4
Employees	41.4%	39	41	63	146	156

KINDRED HEALTHCARE INC   NYS: KND

680 South Fourth Street
Louisville, KY 40202-2412
Phone: 502 596-7300
Fax: –
Web: www.kindredhealthcare.com

CEO: Benjamin A Breier
CFO: –
HR: –
FYE: December 31
Type: Public

Families unable to provide 24-hour care to their kin can at least turn to Kindred Healthcare. As a leading provider of long-term health care Kindred operates about more than 80 transitional care hospitals about 20 inpatient rehabilitation hospitals 20 sub-acute units and 615 home health hospice and non-medical home care centers throughout the US. Its Kindred's RehabCare business provides contract rehabilitation therapy services at more than 1700 facilities. Its facilities have a combined capacity of about 19000 beds and span 45 states. A consortium of investors is taking Kindred private in a $4.1 billion transaction.

	Annual Growth	12/12	12/13	12/14	12/15	12/16
Sales ($ mil.)	4.0%	6,181.3	4,900.5	5,027.6	7,054.9	7,219.5
Net income ($ mil.)	–	(40.4)	(168.5)	(79.8)	(93.4)	(664.2)
Market value ($ mil.)	(7.7%)	921.5	1,681.2	1,548.3	1,014.3	668.6
Employees	6.4%	78,000	63,300	61,500	102,000	100,100

KINECTA FEDERAL CREDIT UNION

1440 Rosecrans Ave.
Manhattan Beach CA 90266
Phone: 310-643-5458
Fax: 310-643-8350
Web: www.kinecta.org

CEO: Keith Sultemeier
CFO: –
HR: –
FYE: December 31
Type: Private - Not-for-Pr

Kinecta Federal Credit Union provides retail financial services to more than 225000 member-owners in Southern California where it operates about two dozen branches. Members also have access to more than 4000 branches worldwide through a network of affiliated credit unions. Kinecta's offerings include checking and savings accounts IRAs savings bonds and credit cards. The credit union with about $3.5 billion in assets originates residential mortgages in some 25 states. Other lending activities include automobile and home equity loans. Retirement investment and insurance products are offered through subsidiaries Kinecta Financial & Insurance Services and Apollo Insurance Services.

KINETIC CONCEPTS INC.

8023 Vantage Dr.
San Antonio TX 78230-4726
Phone: 210-524-9000
Fax: 210-255-6998
Web: www.kci1.com

CEO: –
CFO: Robert Hureau
HR: –
FYE: December 31
Type: Private

Kinetic Concepts Inc. (KCI) exudes positive energy for wound-healing purposes. The company's active healing solutions (AHS) business makes vacuum-assisted wound care systems (including the V.A.C. Via system) which use KCI's negative pressure technology to speed patient recovery from complex wounds. The unit also makes negative pressure systems to aid in the healing of surgical incisions. Its LifeCell business develops tissue regeneration products used in reconstructive surgical procedures. The firm is selling its therapeutic support systems (TSS) business which makes hospital beds specialized mattresses and patient mobility assistance devices. KCI is owned by a consortium of private-investors.

KINETIC SYSTEMS, INC.

3083 INDEPENDENCE DR CEO: –
LIVERMORE, CA 945517707 CFO: –
Phone: 510-683-6000 HR: –
Fax: – FYE: December 31
Web: www.prestonscientific.com Type: Private

Kinetic Systems stays in motion. The company (known as Kinetics) provides process and mechanical systems primarily to the microelectronics solar energy and biopharmaceutical industries in the Americas Asia and Europe. It installs gas chemical water and utility systems as well as fabricated steel pipe HVAC and plumbing systems. While most of its work is done designing and constructing laboratories and manufacturing facilities Kinetics also installs systems for data centers condominiums schools and water treatment plants. Kinetics has served clients including AMD Merck and Pepsi. Founded in 1973 the firm is controlled by Ares Management.

	Annual Growth	12/15	12/16	12/17	12/18	12/19
Sales ($ mil.)	42.4%	–	–	112.4	172.0	227.9
Net income ($ mil.)	150.8%	–	–	0.6	1.5	4.1
Market value ($ mil.)	–	–	–	–	–	–
Employees	–	–	–	–	–	500

KING KULLEN GROCERY CO. INC.

185 Central Ave. CEO: Ronald Conklin
Bethpage NY 11714 CFO: –
Phone: 516-733-7100 HR: –
Fax: 516-827-6325 FYE: September 30
Web: www.kingkullen.com Type: Private

How's this for a crowning achievement? King Kullen Grocery claims to have been the originator of the supermarket format. Heralding itself as "America's first supermarket" the firm operates some 40 grocery stores on Long Island New York. King Kullen also owns four Wild By Nature natural foods stores and offers a line of vitamins and supplements under the same name in some King Kullen stores. Most outlets average about 35000 sq. ft. but it has a 62000-sq.-ft. upscale market with features such as ethnic fare catering and a Wild By Nature section. Started in a Queens New York warehouse in 1930 by Michael Cullen the firm is owned and operated by Cullen's descendants.

KING'S COLLEGE

133 N RIVER ST CEO: –
WILKES BARRE, PA 187110801 CFO: –
Phone: 570-208-5900 HR: –
Fax: – FYE: June 30
Web: www.kings.edu Type: Private

King's College emphasizes intelligence over royalty. The school is a Catholic university offering more than 35 majors in allied health business education natural science and humanities and social sciences. King's enrolls about 2700 undergraduate and graduate students. The school also offers about a dozen pre-professional programs as well as special concentration programs in ethics forensic studies and other fields. Founded in 1946 by the Holy Cross congregation from the University of Notre Dame the school is part of a national network of Holy Cross colleges and universities.

	Annual Growth	06/11	06/12	06/13	06/15	06/16
Sales ($ mil.)	2.3%	–	83.1	83.5	82.5	91.1
Net income ($ mil.)	51.0%	–	1.6	4.3	2.1	8.2
Market value ($ mil.)	–	–	–	–	–	–
Employees	–	–	–	–	–	500

KINGSBROOK JEWISH MEDICAL CENTER INC

585 SCHENECTADY AVE STE 2 CEO: Linda Brady
BROOKLYN, NY 112031809 CFO: John Schmitt
Phone: 718-604-5000 HR: –
Fax: – FYE: December 31
Web: www.kingsbrook.org Type: Private

Kingsbrook Jewish Medical Center (KJMC) cares for the health needs of all Brooklyn residents. Founded in 1925 to serve the area's Jewish community the campus includes an acute care hospital with about 320 inpatient beds and an adult and pediatric long-term care facility with 540 beds. KJMC provides emergency surgical cardiology gastroenterology pulmonary wound care and diagnostic imaging services as well as skilled nursing services. The hospital also serves as a training facility for medical dental and pharmacy residents. It also operates a primary and specialty care outpatient center and a rehabilitation institute.

	Annual Growth	12/13	12/14	12/15	12/16	12/17
Sales ($ mil.)	4.5%	–	211.6	218.4	215.7	241.3
Net income ($ mil.)	28.7%	–	12.8	(1.1)	15.0	27.3
Market value ($ mil.)	–	–	–	–	–	–
Employees	–	–	–	–	–	2,100

KINGSTONE COMPANIES INC   NAS: KINS

15 Joys Lane CEO: Barry Goldstein
Kingston, NY 12401 CFO: –
Phone: 845 802-7900 HR: –
Fax: – FYE: December 31
Web: www.kingstonecompanies.com Type: Public

Kingstone Companies (formerly DCAP Group) keeps things covered. While the company has transformed itself from a broker into an underwriter its main business is still insurance. Its Kingstone Insurance Company (formerly Commercial Mutual Insurance Company) provides property/casualty insurance policies for individuals and businesses in New York State. Its products including auto business and homeowners' policies are sold through independent agents. The company has divested its former insurance brokerage business which offered life and property/casualty policies through owned and franchised retail locations in New York and eastern Pennsylvania.

	Annual Growth	12/16	12/17	12/18	12/19	12/20
Sales ($ mil.)	14.1%	77.4	92.8	113.8	145.6	131.4
Net income ($ mil.)	(42.5%)	8.9	10.0	3.1	(6.0)	1.0
Market value ($ mil.)	(16.6%)	146.0	199.6	187.8	82.3	70.6
Employees	2.1%	80	97	101	97	87

KINGSWAY FINANCIAL SERVICES INC (DE)   NYS: KFS

150 E. Pierce Road CEO: John Fitzgerald
Itasca, IL 60143 CFO: Kent Hansen
Phone: 847 871-6408 HR: –
Fax: – FYE: December 31
Web: www.kingsway-financial.com Type: Public

Kingsway Financial Services is an investment firm with an eye on the royal prize. Its portfolio has focused on insurance and warranty companies which it typically holds for 15 - 30 years. Its current holdings include non-standard auto insurance (coverage for high-risk drivers) underwriter Mendota as well as three extended warranty firms — Trinity IWS Acquisition and Professional Warranty Service. All are active in the US. Its Kingsway America holding provides non-standard (coverage of high-risk drivers) personal auto coverage in the US. However Kingsway has decided to sell that business to focus on its other holdings.

	Annual Growth	12/16	12/17	12/18	12/19	12/20
Assets ($ mil.)	(2.5%)	501.0	484.6	378.2	399.6	452.5
Net income ($ mil.)	–	0.8	(15.5)	(30.1)	(5.9)	(6.7)
Market value ($ mil.)	(6.9%)	138.8	112.2	63.7	41.3	104.4
Employees	(5.4%)	299	316	123	172	239

KIOR, INC.

13001 Bay Park Road
Pasadena, TX 77507
Phone: 281 694-8700
Fax: –
Web: www.kior.com

NBB: KIOR Q
CEO: –
CFO: –
HR: –
FYE: December 31
Type: Public

Renewable crude oil. Wait - what? KiOR makes actual crude oil using renewable non-food biomass like wood chips and switch grass. It also makes gasoline and diesel as well as blends for standard gasoline from its crude. Refined in standard petrochemical refinery equipment the development stage company's products can be transported using existing oil and gas transportation infrastructure. Unlike ethanol and biodiesel KiOR's fuel is completely interchangeable with fossil fuels and can be "dropped in" to engines. The company claims it can produce a gallon of gas for $1.80 with an 80% reduction in greenhouse gas emissions compared to standard gasoline.

	Annual Growth	12/09	12/10	12/11	12/12	12/13
Sales ($ mil.)	1997.7%	–	–	–	0.1	1.8
Net income ($ mil.)	–	(14.1)	(45.9)	(64.1)	(96.4)	(347.5)
Market value ($ mil.)	(59.4%)	–	–	1,121.8	706.4	185.1
Employees	19.6%	–	107	163	212	183

KIPS BAY MEDICAL INC.

3405 Annapolis Lane North, Suite 200
Minneapolis, MN 55447
Phone: 763 235-3540
Fax: –
Web: www.kipsbaymedical.com

NBB: KIPS
CEO: Scott Kellen
CFO: –
HR: –
FYE: December 31
Type: Public

Kips Bay Medical makes medical devices that help veins do their jobs in patients with coronary artery disease. The company is focused on developing and commercializing a vein support device called eSVS MESH a mesh sleeve implanted by surgeons in coronary artery bypass grafting (CABG) that when placed over a patient's vein graft improves the graft's structure and long-term performance. It is designed to mimic the artery's job of constricting the vein and preventing harmful vessel expansion. The company began selling the eSVS MESH in Europe and other international markets in 2010 and it plans to seek marketing approval in the US as well. Kips Bay Medical completed an IPO in 2011.

	Annual Growth	12/09	12/10	12/11	12/12	12/13
Sales ($ mil.)	(16.5%)	–	0.2	0.3	0.2	0.1
Net income ($ mil.)	–	(3.3)	(10.9)	(4.3)	(5.5)	(6.1)
Market value ($ mil.)	(26.8%)	–	–	36.2	16.9	19.4
Employees	1.9%	13	13	15	13	14

KIRBY CORP.

55 Waugh Drive, Suite 1000
Houston, TX 77007
Phone: 713 435-1000
Fax: 713 435-1010
Web: www.kirbycorp.com

NYS: KEX
CEO: David Grzebinski
CFO: Raj Kumar
HR: –
FYE: December 31
Type: Public

Kirby Corporation is one of the largest inland tank barge operators in the US. Its fleet operated by subsidiary Kirby Inland Marine consists of almost 1100 barges with transportation capacity of about 24.1 million barrels and about 250 inland towboats. The vessels are used to transport liquid bulk cargo petrochemicals crude and refined petroleum products and agricultural chemicals. Its coastal operations are conducted through wholly owned subsidiaries Kirby Offshore Marine and Kirby Ocean Transport. Kirby also offers diesel engine repair and overhaul services and parts for marine oilfield and power generation customers and manufactures oilfield service equipment.

	Annual Growth	12/17	12/18	12/19	12/20	12/21
Sales ($ mil.)	0.4%	2,214.4	2,970.7	2,838.4	2,171.4	2,246.7
Net income ($ mil.)	–	313.2	78.5	142.3	(272.5)	(247.0)
Market value ($ mil.)	(2.9%)	4,015.4	4,049.1	5,381.7	3,115.6	3,571.8
Employees	(2.9%)	5,775	5,650	3,350	5,400	5,125

KIRBY RISK CORPORATION

1815 SAGAMORE PKWY N
LAFAYETTE, IN 479041765
Phone: 765-448-4567
Fax: –
Web: www.kirbyrisk.com

CEO: James K Risk III
CFO: Jason J Bricker
HR: –
FYE: December 31
Type: Private

Kirby Risk named after one of its co-founders is a full-service distributor of electrical automation products lighting enterprise and power distribution products and solutions. The company operates through four business units comprising Electrical Supply Service Center Mechanical Solutions and Service and Precision Machining. The Electrical Supply distribution unit handles more than 90000 products from over 2000 manufacturers. Other operations include ARCO Electric Products (phase converters). CEO James Risk III owns the company that was founded in 1926.

	Annual Growth	12/10	12/11	12/12	12/13	12/14
Sales ($ mil.)	3.4%	–	377.9	398.4	401.3	417.9
Net income ($ mil.)	–	–	0.0	0.0	0.0	0.0
Market value ($ mil.)	–	–	–	–	–	–
Employees	–	–	–	–	–	950

KIRKLAND & ELLIS LLP

300 N. LaSalle St.
Chicago IL 60654
Phone: 312-862-2000
Fax: 312-862-2200
Web: www.kirkland.com

CEO: –
CFO: –
HR: –
FYE: January 31
Type: Private - Partnershi

Known for its work in cases that go to trial law firm Kirkland & Ellis maintains a variety of practices aimed mainly at corporate clients. Besides litigation the firm's core practice areas include corporate transactions intellectual property restructuring and tax. Kirkland & Ellis represents public and private companies from a wide range of industries as well as individuals and government agencies. Over the years its clients have included companies such as Bank of America General Motors McDonald's and Siemens. The firm was founded in 1908.

KIRKLAND'S INC

5310 Maryland Way
Brentwood, TN 37027
Phone: 615 872-4800
Fax: –
Web: www.kirklands.com

NMS: KIRK
CEO: Steve Woodward
CFO: Nicole Strain
HR: –
FYE: January 30
Type: Public

Kirkland's hopes you'll explore its stores for affordable home d ©cor. The company sells more than 14000 products through over 430 stores in more than 35 US states and through its kirklands.com website. It is known for stocking decorative home accessories and gifts including holiday d ©cor furniture wall d ©cor art textiles mirrors fragrances lamps and other home decorating items The majority of its stores are located in strip malls. Kirkland's also adds seasonal holiday items to its merchandise mix. Headquartered in the Nashville Tennessee Kirkland's was founded in 1966 by Carl Kirkland.

	Annual Growth	01/17*	02/18	02/19	02/20*	01/21
Sales ($ mil.)	(2.2%)	594.3	634.1	647.1	603.9	543.5
Net income ($ mil.)	10.8%	11.0	5.3	3.8	(53.3)	16.6
Market value ($ mil.)	16.9%	195.1	155.8	145.9	16.4	363.9
Employees	(12.2%)	7,900	7,500	7,300	6,800	4,700

*Fiscal year change

KISH BANCORP INC.

NBB: KISB

4255 East Main Street
Belleville, PA 17004
Phone: 844 554-4748
Fax: –
Web: www.kishbank.com

CEO: William P Hayes
CFO: Sangeeta Kishore
HR: –
FYE: December 31
Type: Public

Get your banking needs sealed with a Kish. Kish Bancorp is the holding company for Kishacoquillas Valley National Bank commonly referred to as Kish Bank. The bank serves individual and business customers through about 10 offices in Centre Huntingdon and Mifflin counties in central Pennsylvania. It offers checking and savings accounts IRAs CDs and other retail products and uses funds from deposits to write primarily real estate loans (commercial and residential mortgages each account for about one-third of its loan portfolio). Other subsidiaries of Kish Bancorp provide insurance investment management financial planning and travel services.

	Annual Growth	12/16	12/17	12/18	12/19	12/20
Assets ($ mil.)	11.1%	725.1	811.2	850.5	918.3	1,106.6
Net income ($ mil.)	14.9%	4.6	4.1	6.0	7.0	8.0
Market value ($ mil.)	(11.3%)	119.7	151.0	83.3	80.0	74.2
Employees	–	–	–	–	–	–

KISSIMMEE UTILITY AUTHORITY (INC)

1701 W CARROLL ST
KISSIMMEE, FL 347416804
Phone: 407-933-7777
Fax: –
Web: www.kua.com

CEO: –
CFO: –
HR: –
FYE: September 30
Type: Private

Kissimmee Utility Authority (KUA) is committed to redoubling efforts to serve this Florida city with three double letters in its name. KUA operates the municipal power distribution system serving 58000 commercial and industrial and residential customers in Kissimmee and surrounding areas. It also offers its customers internet telephone and security services. In addition the community-owned utility has stakes in and handful of power plants and has a total generating capacity of 410 MW. The venerable company is used to managing operations in a hurricane-prone area and is equipped to mobilize maintenance crews to quickly restore power in the wake of infrastructure damage caused by severe storms.

	Annual Growth	09/08	09/09	09/10	09/11	09/18
Sales ($ mil.)	(14.6%)	–	881.6	196.4	174.3	213.9
Net income ($ mil.)	256.0%	–	0.0	9.1	3.4	44.5
Market value ($ mil.)	–	–	–	–	–	–
Employees	–	–	–	–	–	300

KITCHELL CORPORATION

1707 E HIGHLAND AVE # 100
PHOENIX, AZ 850164668
Phone: 602-264-4411
Fax: –
Web: www.kitchell.com

CEO: –
CFO: –
HR: –
FYE: December 31
Type: Private

From the first structure design sketch to the last brick laid Kitchell builds the whole kit and caboodle. The employee-owned company which operates through half a dozen subsidiaries offers general contracting project and construction management engineering and architectural services and environmental services. Its projects run the gamut of public- and private-sector work and include bioscience labs casinos student housing hotels jails custom homes and performing arts centers. Kitchell is also active in facility and project management and real estate development as well as fleet management and air conditioning equipment wholesale supply. While the western US is its primary area of focus Kitchell boasts projects in about two dozen US states.

	Annual Growth	12/06	12/07	12/08	12/09	12/10
Sales ($ mil.)	(31.6%)	–	–	1,027.8	677.8	480.8
Net income ($ mil.)	–	–	–	0.0	0.0	0.0
Market value ($ mil.)	–	–	–	–	–	–
Employees	–	–	–	–	–	946

KITE REALTY GROUP TRUST

NYS: KRG

30 S. Meridian Street, Suite 1100
Indianapolis, IN 46204
Phone: 317 577-5600
Fax: –
Web: www.kiterealty.com

CEO: John Kite
CFO: Heath Fear
HR: –
FYE: December 31
Type: Public

Kite Realty Group Trust is a publicly-held real estate investment trust which through its majority-owned subsidiary Kite Realty Group L.P. owns interests in various operating subsidiaries and joint ventures engaged in the ownership and operation acquisition development and redevelopment of high-quality neighborhood and community shopping centers in select markets in the US. It owns interests in 90 operating and redevelopment properties totaling approximately 17.3 million square feet. It also owned two development projects under construction. The REIT derives its revenue primarily from activities associated with the collection of contractual rents and reimbursement payments from tenants at its properties. Its largest tenants include Publix Super Markets The TJX Companies PetSmart and Ross Stores.

	Annual Growth	12/16	12/17	12/18	12/19	12/20
Sales ($ mil.)	(6.8%)	354.1	358.8	354.2	315.2	266.6
Net income ($ mil.)	–	1.2	11.9	(46.6)	(0.5)	(16.2)
Market value ($ mil.)	(10.7%)	1,976.7	1,650.1	1,186.2	1,644.2	1,259.5
Employees	(7.3%)	153	147	144	133	113

KIWANIS INTERNATIONAL

3636 Woodview Trace
Indianapolis IN 46268-3196
Phone: 317-875-8755
Fax: 317-879-0204
Web: www.kiwanis.org

CEO: Stan Soderstrom
CFO: Bob Broderick
HR: –
FYE: September 30
Type: Private - Not-for-Pr

Kiwanians focus on kids. Kiwanis International unites local clubs that serve children and young adults through various service projects. These projects are targeted to address one or more of the club's six permanent "Objects of Kiwanis" which include fostering spiritual values and higher social standards developing a more aggressive citizenship and increasing patriotism and goodwill. Kiwanis' Circle K is its collegiate club Key Club is for high schoolers Builders Club serves junior high and middle school students K-Kids is for elementary kids and Aktion Club helps adults with disabilities do service projects. Founded in 1915 Kiwanis International operates more than 8000 clubs in about 95 countries.

KIWIBOX.COM, INC.

NBB: KIWB

330 West 42nd Street, Suite 3210
New York, NY 10036
Phone: 347 836-4727
Fax: –
Web: www.kiwibox.com

CEO: Andre Scholz
CFO: –
HR: –
FYE: December 31
Type: Public

Kiwibox.com (formerly Magnitude Information Systems) offered a line of ergonomic software tools that helped employees avoid repetitive stress injuries in their use of computers. In 2007 Magnitude acquired Kiwibox Media which operates a social networking site for teenagers. In late 2009 the company changed its name to Kiwibox.com as part of a shifting strategy to focus on its social networking operations. With social media only getting stronger in 2012 it completed its purchase of European social network site KWICK! based near Stuttgart Germany for about ?6.4 million ($8.3 million). KWICK! reports more than 10 million registered users and 1 million active users.

	Annual Growth	12/12	12/13	12/14	12/15	12/16
Sales ($ mil.)	(70.1%)	1.5	0.9	0.0	0.0	0.0
Net income ($ mil.)	–	(14.0)	(7.0)	(4.7)	(4.4)	(4.9)
Market value ($ mil.)	(39.9%)	4.6	3.1	0.8	0.7	0.6
Employees	(30.7%)	13	3	4	3	3

KKR & CO. L.P.

9 W. 57th St. Ste. 4200
New York NY 10019
Phone: 212-750-8300
Fax: 212-750-0003
Web: www.kkr.com

CEO: Joseph Bae
CFO: Robert Lewin
HR: –
FYE: December 31
Type: Public

Have the barbarians at the gate become civilized? KKR & Co. the master of the leveraged buyout has ditched its hostile takeover image for a kinder gentler buy-and-build strategy. The global investment firm has some $59 billion in assets under management including significant stakes in such companies as Del Monte Foods Samson Investment and Go Daddy. An active owner it often supervises or installs new management and revamps strategy and corporate structure selling underperforming units or adding new ones. KKR tends to hold onto its investments for the long term. The company has offices in major business centers in Asia Australia Europe and the US. KKR went public via a nearly $2 billion IPO in 2010.

KMART CORPORATION

3333 Beverly Rd.
Hoffman Estates IL 60179
Phone: 847-286-2500
Fax: 847-286-5500
Web: www.kmart.com

CEO: –
CFO: –
HR: –
FYE: January 31
Type: Subsidiary

Attention Kmart shoppers: Kmart is the #3 discount retailer in the US behind Wal-Mart and Target. It sells name-brand and private-label goods (including its Joe Boxer and Jaclyn Smith labels) mostly to low- and mid-income families. It runs about 1300 off-mall stores (including 30 Supercenters) in 49 US states Puerto Rico Guam and the US Virgin Islands. About 270 Kmart stores sell home appliances (including Sears' Kenmore brand) and some 980 locations house in-store pharmacies. Poor sales have forced its parent Sears Holdings Corp. to close 100 to 120 Kmart and sister subsidiary Sears Roebuck stores. Kmart also operates the kmart.com website which includes merchandise from Sears.

KKR FINANCIAL HOLDINGS LLC   NYS: KFN

555 California Street, 50th Floor
San Francisco, CA 94104
Phone: 415 315-3620
Fax: 415 391-3077
Web: www.ir.kkr.com/kfn_ir/kfn_overview.cfm

CEO: William J Janetschek
CFO: Thomas N Murphy
HR: –
FYE: December 31
Type: Public

KKR Financial Holdings is a specialty finance company that invests in a variety of financial products primarily below-investment-grade corporate debt as well as public and private equity. Its portfolio which weighs in at more than $8 billion includes syndicated bank loans mezzanine loans high-yield corporate bonds asset-backed securities commercial real estate and debt and equity securities. KKR Financial Holdings is externally managed by KKR Financial Advisors; both firms are affiliates of private equity and leveraged buyout giant KKR & Co.

	Annual Growth	12/08	12/09	12/10	12/11	12/12
Assets ($ mil.)	(9.6%)	12,515.1	10,300.0	8,418.4	8,647.2	8,358.9
Net income ($ mil.)	–	(1,075.0)	76.9	371.1	318.1	348.2
Market value ($ mil.)	60.8%	281.9	1,034.9	1,659.5	1,557.8	1,884.3
Employees	–	–	–	–	–	–

KMG CHEMICALS, INC.   NYS: KMG

300 Throckmorton Street
Fort Worth, TX 76102
Phone: 817 761-6100
Fax: –
Web: www.kmgchemicals.com

CEO: Christopher Fraser
CFO: –
HR: –
FYE: July 31
Type: Public

KMG Chemicals protects wood helps make chips and keeps the engines of industry humming. Its electronic chemicals are used in the manufacture of semiconductors. KMG's largest customer is silicon chip kingpin Intel which regularly accounts for about 10% of total sales. Its wood preservatives are pentachlorophenol (penta) and sodium penta. KMG sells penta in the US primarily to the railroad construction and utility industries. Sodium penta is sold in Latin America. In the industrial lubricants area KMG makes and distributes industrial sealants lubricants and related equipment.

	Annual Growth	07/13	07/14	07/15	07/16	07/17
Sales ($ mil.)	6.1%	263.3	353.4	320.5	298.0	333.4
Net income ($ mil.)	26.1%	9.3	(1.0)	12.1	18.7	23.6
Market value ($ mil.)	22.4%	268.5	199.4	259.6	326.8	601.9
Employees	0.4%	740	733	657	626	751

KLA CORP   NMS: KLAC

One Technology Drive
Milpitas, CA 95035
Phone: 408 875-3000
Fax: –
Web: www.kla.com

CEO: Richard Wallace
CFO: Bren Higgins
HR: –
FYE: June 30
Type: Public

KLA Corp. (formerly KLA-Tencor; also known as KLA) is a supplier of process control equipment and data analytics products for a broad range of industries including semiconductors printed circuit boards (PCB) and displays. It provides solutions for manufacturing and testing wafers and reticles integrated circuits (IC or chip) packaging light-emitting diodes (LED) power devices compound semiconductor devices microelectromechanical systems (MEMS) data storage PCBs flat and flexible panel displays and general materials research as well as providing contracted and comprehensive installation and maintenance services across its installed base. Customers in international markets account for about 90% of the company's revenue.

	Annual Growth	06/17	06/18	06/19	06/20	06/21
Sales ($ mil.)	18.7%	3,480.0	4,036.7	4,568.9	5,806.4	6,918.7
Net income ($ mil.)	22.4%	926.1	802.3	1,175.6	1,216.8	2,078.3
Market value ($ mil.)	37.2%	13,980.5	15,664.1	18,058.1	29,711.9	49,531.5
Employees	17.8%	5,990	6,550	10,020	10,600	11,550

KNAPE & VOGT MANUFACTURING COMPANY

2700 Oak Industrial Dr. NE
Grand Rapids MI 49505
Phone: 616-459-3311
Fax: 616-459-3467
Web: www.knapeandvogt.com

CEO: Peter Martin
CFO: Rick McQuigg
HR: –
FYE: June 30
Type: Private

Knape & Vogt Manufacturing (KV) believes in easy access to your drawers — and all your stuff — whether it's at home or the office. The company makes drawer slides shelving systems closet rods and other storage-related hardware items. It also offers kitchen and bath storage products from its Real Solutions for Real Life brand and ergonomic office products from its idea@WORK brand. KV sells mostly to original equipment manufacturers office furniture retailers hardware chains and specialty distributors in the US and Canada but it also sells directly to consumers and government agencies. The company is owned by private equity firm Wind Point Partners.

KNIGHT TRANSPORTATION INC.   NYS: KNX

20002 North 19th Avenue
Phoenix, AZ 85027
Phone: 602 269-2000
Fax: –
Web: www.knighttrans.com

CEO: David A Jackson
CFO: Adam W Miller
HR: –
FYE: December 31
Type: Public

Knight Transportation drivers don't drive long hours into the night. The truckload carrier instead focuses on short- to medium-haul trips averaging about 500 miles. From some 35 regional operations centers mainly in the southern midwestern and western US Knight carries such cargo as consumer goods food and beverages and paper products. It has a fleet of more than 4100 tractors and 9700 trailers including nearly 900 refrigerated trailers. Besides for-hire hauling Knight provides dedicated contract carriage in which drivers and equipment are assigned to a customer long-term. It also offers freight brokerage services.

	Annual Growth	12/11	12/12	12/13	12/14	12/15
Sales ($ mil.)	8.1%	866.2	936.0	969.2	1,102.3	1,183.0
Net income ($ mil.)	18.0%	60.2	64.1	69.3	102.9	116.7
Market value ($ mil.)	11.6%	1,266.3	1,184.5	1,484.9	2,725.3	1,961.8
Employees	7.3%	4,682	5,176	5,177	5,485	6,196

KNIGHTS OF COLUMBUS

1 COLUMBUS PLZ STE 1700
NEW HAVEN, CT 065103326
Phone: 203-752-4000
Fax: –
Web: www.kofc.org

CEO: –
CFO: –
HR: –
FYE: December 31
Type: Private

Good Knight! The Knights of Columbus is a men who lead serve protect and defend whether it is are giving out Coats for Kids lending a hand in disaster relief efforts supporting local pregnancy centers by donating ultrasound machines or providing top-quality financial products.. The fraternal organization is also a force to be reckoned with in the insurance world providing life insurance annuities and long-term care insurance to its members and their families. In addition the group manages the Knights of Columbus Museum in New Haven Connecticut. The group was founded in 1882 by Father Michael J. McGivney.

	Annual Growth	12/09	12/10	12/11	12/12	12/13
Assets ($ mil.)	6.8%	–	16,862.0	18,026.6	19,401.7	20,534.4
Net income ($ mil.)	9.5%	–	86.5	81.0	127.7	113.7
Market value ($ mil.)	–	–	–	–	–	–
Employees	–	–	–	–	–	2,300

KNOLL INC   NYS: KNL

1235 Water Street
East Greenville, PA 18041
Phone: 215 679-7991
Fax: –
Web: www.knoll.com

CEO: Andrew B Cogan
CFO: Charles W Rayfield
HR: –
FYE: December 31
Type: Public

From the Bauhaus style to business chic Knoll has designs on the furniture market. One of the leading global manufacturers of commercial and residential furniture the company makes a variety of distinctively designed curvilinear office furniture and related accessories including office systems (aka cubicles). Its products are sold under such names as AutoStrada Generation Knoll-Studio Holly Hunt Muuto KnollTextiles and Spinneyback. Other items include ergonomic seating tables and desks and filing systems. Founded in 1938 it offers an upscale line of designed furniture (KnollStudio) computer and desk accessories (KnollExtra) and fabric and leather upholstery (KnollTextiles). The company markets its products directly and through a network of independent dealers distribution partners and showrooms in North America Canada and Europe. Most of its sales comes from the US.

	Annual Growth	12/15	12/16	12/17	12/18	12/19
Sales ($ mil.)	6.6%	1,104.4	1,164.3	1,132.9	1,302.3	1,428.1
Net income ($ mil.)	0.6%	66.0	82.1	80.2	73.2	67.5
Market value ($ mil.)	7.7%	935.8	1,390.2	1,146.8	820.3	1,257.3
Employees	2.5%	3,386	3,471	3,402	3,541	3,734

KNOUSE FOODS COOPERATIVE, INC.

800 PACH GLEN IDAVILLE RD
PEACH GLEN, PA 173750001
Phone: 717-677-8181
Fax: –
Web: www.knouse.com

CEO: Lawrence Martin
CFO: Craig Hinkle
HR: –
FYE: June 30
Type: Private

Is there a Knouse in the house? Might be. With retail brand names such as Apple Time Lucky Leaf Musselman's Lincoln and Speas Farm Knouse Foods Cooperative's apple products are in many a pantry. The company is a growers' co-op made up of some 150 Appalachian Mountain and Midwestern grower/members. It processes its members' apples for sale as canned and bottled applesauce juice cider vinegar apple butter pie fillings and snack packs all of which are available nationwide. In addition to stocking supermarket shelves Knouse founded in 1949 supplies foodservice operators and industrial-ingredient companies with bulk apple and other fruit products. It also offers private-label and co-packing services.

	Annual Growth	06/13	06/14	06/15	06/16	06/17
Sales ($ mil.)	(5.1%)	–	–	–	297.0	281.7
Net income ($ mil.)	(72.5%)	–	–	–	2.0	0.6
Market value ($ mil.)	–	–	–	–	–	–
Employees	–	–	–	–	–	1,099

KNOWLES CORP   NYS: KN

1151 Maplewood Drive
Itasca, IL 60143
Phone: 630 250-5100
Fax: 630 250-0575
Web: www.knowles.com

CEO: Jeffrey Niew
CFO: John Anderson
HR: Raymond Cabrera
FYE: December 31
Type: Public

Knowles is a market leader and global provider of advanced micro- acoustic audio processing and precision device solutions serving the mobile consumer electronics communications medtech defense electric vehicle and industrial markets. It is also a leader in acoustic components high-end capacitors and mmWave radio frequency (RF) solutions for a diverse set of markets. Knowles founded in 1946 has facilities located in roughly 15 countries around the world. Although based in US Knowles generates about three-fourth of revenue in Asia region.

	Annual Growth	12/17	12/18	12/19	12/20	12/21
Sales ($ mil.)	3.9%	744.2	826.9	854.8	764.3	868.1
Net income ($ mil.)	21.8%	68.3	67.7	49.1	6.6	150.4
Market value ($ mil.)	12.3%	1,347.2	1,223.1	1,943.6	1,693.6	2,145.7
Employees	(3.0%)	7,900	8,000	8,500	7,000	7,000

KNOXVILLE UTILITIES BOARD

445 S GAY ST
KNOXVILLE, TN 379021125
Phone: 865-594-7531
Fax: –
Web: www.kub.org

CEO: Mintha Roach
CFO: –
HR: –
FYE: June 30
Type: Private

Providing utility services to residential and business customers has proven to be an excellent idea for Knoxville Utilities Board (KUB) an independent agency that serves the city of Knoxville and surrounding areas. The multi-utility provides services to 196500 electric 96920 gas 77600 water and 68740 wastewater customers. The company accesses electric power from the Tennessee Valley Authority. KUB's natural gas supply comes from the East Tennessee Natural Gas pipeline. It also maintains five treatment plants which provide water and wastewater services.

	Annual Growth	06/17	06/18	06/19	06/20	06/21
Sales ($ mil.)	0.3%	–	815.5	815.4	803.8	822.3
Net income ($ mil.)	5.9%	–	63.6	65.3	78.0	75.5
Market value ($ mil.)	–	–	–	–	–	–
Employees	–	–	–	–	–	500

KOCH ENTERPRISES INC.

14 S 11TH AVE
EVANSVILLE, IN 47712-5020
Phone: 812-465-9800
Fax: –
Web: www.kochenterprises.com

CEO: –
CFO: Susan E Parsons
HR: Glen Muehlbauer
FYE: December 31
Type: Private

Koch gets straight A's for diversification; it's a private holding company active in automobile parts manufacturing metals recycling wholesale distribution and equipment design and construction. Subsidiaries include Audubon Metals (processes aluminum) George Koch Sons (engineers installs and services auto finishing systems) Koch Air (distributes Carrier HVAC equipment) Gibbs Die Casting (parts for making cars lighter) Brake Supply (repairs brakes and hydraulic systems for auto and mining equipment) and Uniseal (makes structural adhesives thermoplastics and sealant systems for industrial and auto markets). George Koch founded the company in 1873.

	Annual Growth	12/08	12/09	12/10	12/11	12/12
Sales ($ mil.)	4.3%	–	830.9	851.1	915.6	942.6
Net income ($ mil.)	–	–	0.0	22.7	0.0	0.0
Market value ($ mil.)	–	–	–	–	–	–
Employees	–	–	–	–	–	2,482

KOCH FOODS INCORPORATED

1300 W. Higgins Rd.
Park Ridge IL 60068
Phone: 847-384-5940
Fax: 847-384-5961
Web: www.kochfoods.com

CEO: Joseph Grendys
CFO: –
HR: –
FYE: December 31
Type: Private

Why did the chicken cross the road? To escape "America's Chicken Specialist" Koch Foods no doubt. The vertically-integrated poultry processor makes commodity and value-added fresh and frozen chicken products such as chicken tenderloins tenders strips boneless breasts and wings along with diced and pulled white and dark meat and whole and whole cut-up chickens. Koch's customers include companies in the retail food and foodservice sectors throughout the US as well as overseas. The company sells its value-added poultry products under the Antioch and Cravers retail brands. Koch Foods began as a one-room chicken de-boning and cutting operation in 1985.

KOCH INDUSTRIES INC.

4111 E. 37th St. North
Wichita KS 67220-3203
Phone: 316-828-5500
Fax: 316-828-5739
Web: www.kochind.com

CEO: Charles Koch
CFO: –
HR: –
FYE: December 31
Type: Private

Koch (pronounced "coke") Industries is the real thing one of the largest (if not the largest) private companies in the US. Koch's operations are diverse including refining and chemicals process and pollution control equipment and technologies; fibers and polymers; commodity and financial trading; and forest and consumer products (led by Georgia-Pacific). Its Flint Hills Resources subsidiary owns three refineries that together process more than 800000 barrels of crude oil daily. Koch operates crude gathering systems and pipelines across North America as well as cattle ranches with more than 15000 head of cattle in Kansas Montana and Texas. Brothers Charles and David Koch control the company.

KODIAK OIL & GAS CORP.
NYSE AMEX: KOG

1625 Broadway Ste. 330
Denver CO 80202
Phone: 303-592-8075
Fax: 303-592-8071
Web: www.kodiakog.com

CEO: James J Volker
CFO: Michael J Stevens
HR: –
FYE: December 31
Type: Public

Kodiak Oil & Gas bears the responsibility for exploration development and production of oil and natural gas in the Rockies. The company which focuses on assets in the Vermillion Basin of the Green River Basin and the Williston Basin (located in Montana and North Dakota) has proved reserves of 1.2 billion cu. ft. of natural gas and 344000 barrels of oil. Kodiak Oil & Gas has 99434 net acres of land holdings. In the Green River Basin it is exploring for unconventional gas through the exploitation of coalbed methane over-pressured shales and tight-gas-sands. In recent years the company has increased its holdings in the Williston Basin to 110000 acres through deals worth $345 million.

KOHL'S CORP.
NYS: KSS

N56 W17000 Ridgewood Drive
Menomonee Falls, WI 53051
Phone: 262 703-7000
Fax: 262 703-6373
Web: www.kohls.com

CEO: Michelle Gass
CFO: Jill Timm
HR: –
FYE: January 30
Type: Public

Clothing retailer Kohl's operates over 1160 namesake department stores across the US as well as more than 10 FILA outlets. Competing with discount and mid-level department stores the company sells moderately priced name-brand and private-label apparel shoes accessories and housewares. Its private-label brands include Apt. 9 Croft & Barrow SO Sonoma Goods for Life and Jumping Beans; Kohl's also sells exclusive brands through agreements with Lauren Conrad Vera Wang and the Food Network among others. About 80% of the company's stores are in strip centers with the rest are freestanding and located in malls.

	Annual Growth	01/17*	02/18	02/19	02/20*	01/21
Sales ($ mil.)	(3.9%)	18,686.0	19,095.0	20,229.0	19,974.0	15,955.0
Net income ($ mil.)	–	556.0	859.0	801.0	691.0	(163.0)
Market value ($ mil.)	3.1%	6,162.0	10,028.3	10,537.0	6,754.5	6,961.5
Employees	(5.5%)	138,000	137,000	129,000	122,000	110,000

*Fiscal year change

KOHLBERG CAPITAL CORPORATION
NASDAQ: KCAP

295 Madison Ave. 6th Fl.
New York NY 10017
Phone: 212-455-8300
Fax: 212-983-7654
Web: www.kohlbergcapital.com

CEO: Ted Goldthorpe
CFO: Jason Roos
HR: –
FYE: December 31
Type: Public

Kohlberg Capital acts as the middleman for companies in need of a loan. The internally managed investment firm provides loans to middle market companies earning between $10 million to $50 million with debt of $25 million to $150 million. It originates junior and senior secured term loans mezzanine debt and equity securities. Its Katonah Debt Advisors which has more than $2 billion of assets under management manages collateralized loan obligation funds that invest in syndicated loans and high-yield bonds. Organized as a business development company Kohlberg Capital pays 4% in income tax as long as it distributes 90% of its profits back to shareholders. The company was spun off from Kohlberg & Co. in 2006.

KOHN PEDERSEN FOX ASSOCIATES, PC

11 W 42ND ST STE 8A
NEW YORK, NY 100368002
Phone: 212-977-6500
Fax: –
Web: www.kpf.com

CEO: –
CFO: Peter Catalano
HR: –
FYE: December 31
Type: Private

Kohn Pedersen Fox Associates (KPF) puts its stamp on buildings around the world. One of the top 10 architectural and planning firms in the US the company offers services such as master planning urban design space planning programming building analysis graphic and product and interior design. It specializes in such projects as corporate headquarters government offices health care facilities hotels and educational facilities. KPF's structures range from small pavilions to entire cities. The firm operates from offices in New York London and Shanghai. Architects A. Eugene Kohn William Pedersen and Sheldon Fox founded the firm in 1976.

	Annual Growth	12/02	12/03	12/04	12/05	12/07
Sales ($ mil.)	5.3%	–	–	62.4	64.1	72.8
Net income ($ mil.)	142.4%	–	–	0.4	22.2	6.3
Market value ($ mil.)	–	–	–	–	–	–
Employees	–	–	–	–	–	350

KOHR BROTHERS INC.

2151 RICHMOND RD STE 200
CHARLOTTESVILLE, VA 229113636
Phone: 434-975-1500
Fax: –
Web: www.kohrbros.com

CEO: –
CFO: –
HR: –
FYE: October 31
Type: Private

Kohr Brothers operates and franchises more than 30 Kohr Bros. Frozen Custard outlets in about 10 states a majority of which are in New Jersey. Most of its shops are in high traffic areas such as shopping malls airports and sports arenas. School teacher Archie Kohr started the chain with his brothers in 1919 in order to sell more cream from the family's dairy business. The brothers began with a single ice cream shop on Coney Island's boardwalk.

	Annual Growth	10/10	10/11	10/12	10/13	10/14
Sales ($ mil.)	4.5%	–	10.9	11.3	11.3	12.4
Net income ($ mil.)	5.4%	–	–	0.6	0.5	0.6
Market value ($ mil.)	–	–	–	–	–	–
Employees	–	–	–	–	–	250

KONA GRILL INC

NBB: KONA Q

15059 North Scottsdale Road, Suite 300
Scottsdale, AZ 85254
Phone: 480 922-8100
Fax: –
Web: www.konagrill.com

CEO: Christi Hing
CFO: Christi Hing
HR: –
FYE: December 31
Type: Public

This company is pinning its hopes on the flavor of the Big Island to draw a few mainlanders into its restaurants. Kona Grill operates about 40 upscale casual-dining restaurants offering both seafood and American dishes with an island twist. The restaurants serve both lunch and diner menus and they offer a wide selection of sushi. In addition to dining each location typically has a bar area for happy hour with margaritas and martinis. The restaurants are typically found near upscale shopping areas in Arizona Texas and more than 16 other states in addition to Puerto Rico.

	Annual Growth	12/14	12/15	12/16	12/17	12/18
Sales ($ mil.)	7.1%	119.1	143.0	169.5	179.1	156.9
Net income ($ mil.)	–	0.7	(4.5)	(21.6)	(23.4)	(32.0)
Market value ($ mil.)	(53.8%)	306.3	210.4	166.5	23.2	13.9
Employees	2.0%	2,743	4,067	4,066	3,638	2,968

KOPIN CORP.

NAS: KOPN

125 North Drive
Westborough, MA 01581-3335
Phone: 508 870-5959
Fax: –
Web: www.kopin.com

CEO: John Fan
CFO: Richard Sneider
HR: –
FYE: December 26
Type: Public

A pioneer of wearable technology Kopin Corp. makes headset computers for hands-free mobile computing based on its proprietary Golden-i technology. The company's newest GEN 3.8D headset enables wearers — typically workers in light industry — to control the devices with their voices and movements. The company's other wearable technology products are based on CyberDisplay transmissive LCDs that use high-quality single-crystal silicon transistors. Kopin's display devices used in consumer electronics eyewear and military products. Kopin was founded in 1984 by engineers from the Massachusetts Institute of Technology's Electronic Materials Group including co-founder and CEO John Fan. More than half of company's revenue comes from Americas.

	Annual Growth	12/16	12/17	12/18	12/19	12/20
Sales ($ mil.)	15.4%	22.6	27.8	24.5	29.5	40.1
Net income ($ mil.)	–	(23.4)	(25.2)	(35.9)	(29.5)	(4.4)
Market value ($ mil.)	(0.7%)	242.7	273.4	94.0	35.9	235.8
Employees	(2.1%)	174	175	180	153	160

KOPPERS HOLDINGS INC

NYS: KOP

436 Seventh Avenue
Pittsburgh, PA 15219
Phone: 412 227-2001
Fax: –
Web: www.koppers.com.

CEO: Leroy Ball
CFO: Jimmi Sue Smith
HR: –
FYE: December 31
Type: Public

Koppers Holdings makes carbon compounds and treated-wood products for the chemical railroad aluminum utility residential lumber construction and steel industries around the world. Its carbon materials and chemicals unit makes materials for producing of polyester resins plasticizers and alkyd paints. The railroad and utility products unit supplies treated crossties and utility poles and treats wood for vineyard construction and other uses. The US generates about 70% of the company's total sales. Koppers was established in December 1988 and went public 2006.

	Annual Growth	12/16	12/17	12/18	12/19	12/20
Sales ($ mil.)	4.2%	1,416.2	1,475.5	1,710.2	1,772.8	1,669.1
Net income ($ mil.)	42.8%	29.3	29.1	23.4	66.6	122.0
Market value ($ mil.)	(6.2%)	850.3	1,073.9	359.5	806.4	657.4
Employees	2.7%	1,853	1,800	2,229	2,120	2,061

KORN FERRY

NYS: KFY

1900 Avenue of the Stars, Suite 2600
Los Angeles, CA 90067
Phone: 310 552-1834
Fax: –
Web: www.kornferry.com

CEO: Gary Burnison
CFO: Robert Rozek
HR: –
FYE: April 30
Type: Public

Korn Ferry is a global organizational consulting firm helping private public middle market and emerging growth companies as well as government and not-for-profit clients organize their strategies and talent to drive superior business performance such as leadership and professional development and rewards and benefits. At the core of the company's approach is deep IP and research that informs smarter more data-driven outcomes for clients which are house inside its Talent Hub and conducts research and analytics through its Korn Ferry Institute. The company also serves consumers through Korn Ferry Advance which helps people looking to make their next career move and provides career services to employees within organizations. Korn Ferry operates in about 100 offices in nearly 55 countries.

	Annual Growth	04/17	04/18	04/19	04/20	04/21
Sales ($ mil.)	2.9%	1,621.7	1,819.5	1,973.9	1,977.3	1,819.9
Net income ($ mil.)	8.0%	84.2	133.8	102.7	104.9	114.5
Market value ($ mil.)	20.3%	1,749.9	2,887.3	2,539.5	1,557.1	3,666.6
Employees	2.2%	7,232	7,643	8,678	8,198	7,889

KORN/FERRY INTERNATIONAL FUTURESTEP INC.

1900 Avenue of the Stars Ste. 2600
Los Angeles CA 90067
Phone: 310-552-1834
Fax: 310-553-6452
Web: www.futurestep.com

CEO: –
CFO: –
HR: –
FYE: April 30
Type: Subsidiary

Futurestep connects mid-level managers with jobs. A subsidiary of executive search giant Korn/Ferry the company combines traditional search techniques with Internet-based recruiting to provide a range of opportunities globally. The company maintains a database of more than one million pre-screened candidates in order to quickly match up jobs with employees. In addition to middle management recruiting Futurestep offers specialized talent consulting services project-based recruitment recruitment outsourcing and recruitment for interim positions. Founded in 1998 the company has nearly 40 locations in 17 countries and is headquartered in Los Angeles.

KOSS CORP

NAS: KOSS

4129 North Port Washington Avenue
Milwaukee, WI 53212
Phone: 414 964-5000
Fax: –
Web: www.koss.com

CEO: Michael J Koss
CFO: David D Smith
HR: –
FYE: June 30
Type: Public

Koss makes sure you can turn up the volume without disturbing the neighbors. The company makes stereo headphones or "stereophones" and related accessories for consumers and audio professionals. Its lineup includes full-size noise-cancellation portable earbud and wireless headphones. Products are sold through more than 17000 US retail outlets including specialty audio stores discount stores and mass merchandisers as well as by catalogs and online merchants. The company also produces classical music recordings through its Koss Classics subsidiary. In addition to its US operations Koss has an international sales office in Switzerland. Founded by John Koss the firm has roots reaching back to the 1950s.

	Annual Growth	06/17	06/18	06/19	06/20	06/21
Sales ($ mil.)	(5.1%)	24.1	23.5	21.8	18.3	19.5
Net income ($ mil.)	–	(1.0)	(3.4)	0.4	(0.5)	0.5
Market value ($ mil.)	89.2%	15.6	20.2	17.2	11.7	199.9
Employees	(2.7%)	39	34	34	34	35

KORTE CONSTRUCTION COMPANY

5700 OAKLAND AVE STE 275
SAINT LOUIS, MO 631101375
Phone: 314-231-3700
Fax: –
Web: www.korteco.com

CEO: Brent Korte
CFO: –
HR: –
FYE: December 31
Type: Private

The Korte Company provides design/build design/build/furnish construction management and interior design services for a variety of commercial and industrial construction projects. The group works on projects that include warehouse/distribution centers recreational centers schools office complexes churches and facilities for local state and federal government agencies including Department of Defense. The Korte Company which was founded in 1958 operates from offices in Las Vegas St. Louis and Highland Illinois.

KPMG L.L.P.

3 Chestnut Ridge Rd.
Montvale NJ 07645-0435
Phone: 201-307-7000
Fax: 201-930-8617
Web: www.us.kpmg.com

CEO: –
CFO: –
HR: –
FYE: September 30
Type: Private - Partnershi

KPMG L.L.P. is the US member firm of KPMG International a global network of accountancies with a 300-year history. Today parent KPMG is one of the industry's Big Four (alongside Deloitte Touche Tohmatsu Ernst & Young and PricewaterhouseCoopers). The US-centric business of KPMG provides audit tax and advisory services through approximately 90 offices located nationwide. As part of its business focus KPMG L.L.P. targets several industries such as financial services media and entertainment consumer products chemicals and healthcare and pharmaceuticals. KPMG L.L.P. is part of KPMG's Americas division which accounts for about a third of the group's global revenues.

	Annual Growth	12/14	12/15	12/16	12/17	12/18
Sales ($ mil.)	23.6%	–	119.9	268.5	341.2	226.3
Net income ($ mil.)	–	–	(2.5)	0.8	(3.9)	(0.3)
Market value ($ mil.)	–	–	–	–	–	–
Employees	–	–	–	–	–	170

KOSMOS ENERGY LTD (DE)

NYS: KOS

8176 Park Lane
Dallas, TX 75231
Phone: 214 445-9600
Fax: –
Web: www.kosmosenergy.com

CEO: –
CFO: –
HR: –
FYE: December 31
Type: Public

Searching the cosmos for energy? No searching Africa for oil and gas. Kosmos Energy is a US-based oil and gas exploration firm with about 30 producing wells off the coast of Ghana. The company also has leases on oil fields off the coasts of Cameroon and Morocco. It looks for underdeveloped or "misunderstood" energy assets off west Africa. Kosmos Energy owns about 31% and 18% of its two producing units off Ghana and 75% each in the other assets. The company was formed in 2003 by management before it was acquired by Hess Corporation. Kosmos went public in 2011. In 2016 BP agreed to acquire stakes in exploration blocks in Mauritania and Senegal from Kosmos for $916 million.

KRAFT FOODS GROUP INC

NMS: KRFT

Three Lakes Drive
Northfield, IL 60093-2753
Phone: 847 646-2000
Fax: –
Web: www.kraftfoodsgroup.com

CEO: –
CFO: –
HR: –
FYE: December 28
Type: Public

What's old is new again at Kraft Foods Group. The newly-independent company was spun off by Mondelez International (formerly Kraft Foods Inc.) separating the North American grocery from the global snacks business in 2012. Kraft Foods Group is one of the largest consumer packaged food and beverage companies in North America. Its familiar brands include Kraft natural/processed cheeses beverages (Maxwell House coffee Kool-Aid drinks) convenient meals (Oscar Mayer meats and Kraft mac 'n cheese) grocery fare (Cool Whip topping Shake N' Bake coatings) and nuts (Planters). While globetrotting Mondelez is focused on growth overseas Kraft Foods Group is looking to revive its business in North America.

	Annual Growth	12/16	12/17	12/18	12/19	12/20
Sales ($ mil.)	23.5%	385.4	636.8	902.4	1,509.9	896.2
Net income ($ mil.)	–	(283.8)	(222.8)	(94.0)	(55.8)	(411.6)
Market value ($ mil.)	(23.9%)	2,842.2	2,777.4	1,650.2	2,311.1	952.8
Employees	(1.7%)	270	280	380	360	252

	Annual Growth	12/09	12/10	12/11	12/12	12/13
Sales ($ mil.)	1.3%	17,278.0	17,797.0	18,655.0	18,339.0	18,218.0
Net income ($ mil.)	5.8%	2,170.0	3,531.0	1,839.0	1,642.0	2,715.0
Market value ($ mil.)	20.9%	–	–	–	26,478.8	32,020.8
Employees	(2.2%)	–	–	23,500	23,000	22,500

KRAFT HEINZ CO (THE)   NMS: KHC

One PPG Place
Pittsburgh, PA 15222
Phone: 412 456-5700
Fax: –
Web: www.kraftheinzcompany.com

CEO: Miguel Patricio
CFO: Paulo Basilio
HR: –
FYE: December 25
Type: Public

The Kraft Heinz Company is one of the largest food and beverage companies in the world. In addition to its two namesakes the company's portfolio of iconic brands include such names as Oscar Mayer Capri Sun Ore-Ida Kool-Aid Jell-O Philadelphia Lunchables Maxwell House and Velveeta. Kraft Heinz which generates more than 45% sales from condiments and sauces and cheese and dairy products offers its goods through e-commerce platforms retailers and foodservice distributors. It manages its sales portfolio through six consumer-driven product platforms. The US accounts for nearly 70% of the company's total sales.

	Annual Growth	12/17	12/18	12/19	12/20	12/21
Sales ($ mil.)	(0.2%)	26,232.0	26,268.0	24,977.0	26,185.0	26,042.0
Net income ($ mil.)	(44.9%)	10,999.0	(10,192.0)	1,935.0	356.0	1,012.0
Market value ($ mil.)	(17.9%)	95,178.2	53,329.7	38,702.9	42,815.5	43,146.0
Employees	(2.0%)	39,000	38,000	37,000	38,000	36,000

KRATON CORP   NYS: KRA

15710 John F. Kennedy Blvd., Suite 300
Houston, TX 77032
Phone: 281 504-4700
Fax: –
Web: www.kraton.com

CEO: Kevin Fogarty
CFO: Atanas Atanasov
HR: –
FYE: December 31
Type: Public

Kraton Corporation makes hydrogenated and unhydrogenated styrenic block copolymers (SBCs). SBCs are used in a wide range of products including adhesives coatings consumer and personal care products sealants lubricants medical packaging automotive paving and roofing and footwear products and other applications. They impart qualities such as temperature cracking and impact resistance; water dispersion; so-feel; and stretchiness. Polymer segment accounts for about 55% of sales. Under its Cariflex brand it sells isoprene rubber latex products such as medical products personal care adhesives tackifiers paints and coatings. Chemicals segment makes products derived from pine wood pulping co-products. SBCs were invented and commercialized by Kraton more than 50 years ago. The company generates more than 35% of revenue from US.

	Annual Growth	12/16	12/17	12/18	12/19	12/20
Sales ($ mil.)	(2.7%)	1,744.1	1,960.4	2,011.7	1,804.4	1,563.2
Net income ($ mil.)	–	107.3	97.5	67.0	51.3	(225.6)
Market value ($ mil.)	(0.6%)	907.7	1,535.3	696.1	807.0	885.8
Employees	(2.1%)	1,971	1,931	1,918	1,944	1,808

KRATOS DEFENSE & SECURITY SOLUTIONS, INC.   NMS: KTOS

1 Chisholm Trail, Suite 3200
Round Rock, TX 78681
Phone: 512 238-9840
Fax: –
Web: www.kratosdefense.com

CEO: Eric DeMarco
CFO: Deanna Lund
HR: –
FYE: December 27
Type: Public

Kratos Defense & Security Solutions is a government contractor that designs and implements information technology systems and provides engineering and other technical services to federal intelligence military and international commercial customers as well as state and local agencies. The company's primary focus areas are unmanned systems space and satellite communications microwave electronics cybersecurity/warfare rocket hypersonic and missile defense systems turbine technologies Command Control Communication Computing Combat Intelligence Surveillance and Reconnaissance (C5ISR) Systems and training systems. The US Navy US Air Force and US Army are its key customers. Kratos was founded in 1995 and initially focused on commercial clients.

	Annual Growth	12/16	12/17	12/18	12/19	12/20
Sales ($ mil.)	2.8%	668.7	751.9	618.0	717.5	747.7
Net income ($ mil.)	–	(60.5)	(42.7)	(3.5)	12.5	79.6
Market value ($ mil.)	36.9%	924.1	1,303.1	1,691.9	2,186.5	3,248.4
Employees	2.5%	2,900	2,900	2,600	3,000	3,200

KREHER STEEL COMPANY, LLC

1550 N 25TH AVE
MELROSE PARK, IL 601601801
Phone: 708-345-8180
Fax: –
Web: www.kreher.com

CEO: –
CFO: –
HR: –
FYE: September 30
Type: Private

Kreher Steel is a nationwide distributor of alloy carbon stainless and tool steel. It also offers sawing and turning services. A pioneer in just-in-time delivery Kreher Steel operates warehouses throughout the US to serve automotive manufacturers steel processors aerospace companies and other customers. It also owns Kreher Wire which makes fasteners and industrial products from its facility in Michigan. A joint venture between specialty metals distributors A. M. Castle & Co. and European steel trader Duferco owns two-thirds of Kreher Steel; chairman Thomas Kreher owns the rest. Kreher Steel was founded in 1978.

	Annual Growth	12/02	12/03	12/05	12/06*	09/19
Sales ($ mil.)	1.1%	–	95.8	130.9	131.0	114.1
Net income ($ mil.)	(8.1%)	–	6.4	8.6	8.6	1.7
Market value ($ mil.)	–	–	–	–	–	–
Employees	–	–	–	–	–	50

*Fiscal year change

KREISLER MANFACTURING CORP.   NBB: KRSL

180 Van Riper Avenue
Elmwood Park, NJ 07407
Phone: 201 791-0700
Fax: –
Web: www.kreislermfg.com

CEO: Michael D Stern
CFO: Edward A Stern
HR: –
FYE: June 30
Type: Public

Your Chrysler might have a hemi under the hood but this Kreisler focuses on bigger engines. Kreisler Manufacturing through subsidiary Kreisler Industrial makes precision metal components for commercial and military aircraft engines and industrial gas turbines. Tube assemblies — used to transfer fuel for combustion hydraulic fluid for thrust reversers and oil for lubrication — account for most of the company's sales. A second subsidiary Kreisler Polska supplies machined components to Kreisler Industrial from a manufacturing plant in Krakow Poland.

	Annual Growth	06/11	06/12	06/13	06/14	06/15
Sales ($ mil.)	2.7%	27.4	37.5	30.4	30.6	30.5
Net income ($ mil.)	–	(0.8)	(2.3)	1.8	2.7	1.0
Market value ($ mil.)	32.4%	6.6	10.4	15.8	24.4	20.3
Employees	–	–	–	–	–	–

KRISPY KREME DOUGHNUTS INC   NYS: KKD

370 Knollwood Street
Winston-Salem, NC 27103
Phone: 336 725-2981
Fax: 336 733-3794
Web: www.krispykreme.com

CEO: Michael J Tattersfield
CFO: G Price Cooper
HR: Marla Wiedmann
FYE: February 01
Type: Public

You might say these sweet treats are wholly delicious. Krispy Kreme Doughnuts operates a leading chain of doughnut outlets with more than 1000 locations throughout the US and in about 25 other countries. The shops are popular for their glazed doughnuts that are served fresh and hot out of the fryer. In addition to its original glazed variety Krispy Kreme serves cake and filled doughnuts crullers and fritters as well as hot coffee and other beverages. The company owns and operates 114 locations and franchises the rest. Krispy Kreme also markets its doughnuts through grocery stores and supermarkets.

	Annual Growth	01/11	01/12*	02/13	02/14	02/15
Sales ($ mil.)	7.9%	362.0	403.2	435.8	460.3	490.3
Net income ($ mil.)	41.0%	7.6	166.3	20.8	34.3	30.1
Market value ($ mil.)	32.1%	414.9	496.7	842.7	1,120.0	1,264.1
Employees	10.4%	3,370	3,800	4,300	4,300	5,000

*Fiscal year change

KROGER CO (THE)   NYS: KR

1014 Vine Street
Cincinnati, OH 45202
Phone: 513 762-4000
Fax: 513 762-1400
Web: www.thekrogerco.com

CEO: William McMullen
CFO: Gary Millerchip
HR: Timothy Massa
FYE: January 30
Type: Public

Kroger is one of the world's largest traditional grocer despite Wal-Mart overtaking the chain as the world's largest seller of groceries years ago. It operates more than 2740 supermarkets in 35 states under variety of local banners; approximately 2255 locations have pharmacies and about 1595 have fuel centers. The company offers Pickup and Harris Teeter ExpressLane ? personalized order online pick up at the store services ? at about 2225 of its supermarkets and provide home delivery service to substantially all of Kroger households. It also has 35 food processing plants in the US mostly bakeries and dairies.

	Annual Growth	01/17*	02/18	02/19	02/20*	01/21
Sales ($ mil.)	3.5%	115,337.0	122,662.0	121,162.0	122,286.0	132,498.0
Net income ($ mil.)	7.0%	1,975.0	1,907.0	3,110.0	1,659.0	2,585.0
Market value ($ mil.)	0.8%	25,286.9	22,239.7	21,277.1	20,359.9	26,151.0
Employees	1.2%	443,000	449,000	453,000	435,000	465,000

*Fiscal year change

KRONES, INC.

9600 S 58TH ST
FRANKLIN, WI 531329107
Phone: 414-409-4000
Fax: –
Web: www.krones.com

CEO: Holger Beckmann
CFO: –
HR: –
FYE: December 31
Type: Private

Krones is in the business of keeping things all bottled up. The company develops manufactures and installs packaging machinery and systems that design clean rinse and fill bottles cans and plastic containers. Its offerings include labeling and sealing machines inspection and monitoring systems and mixing and carbonating systems. Krones caters to companies in North and Central America and the Caribbean in the food and beverage beer wine and spirits health and cosmetic pharmaceutical and household goods industries. Krones is a subsidiary of KRONES which is owned largely by the founding Kronseder family.

	Annual Growth	12/04	12/05	12/06	12/07	12/08
Sales ($ mil.)	(1.7%)	–	383.1	364.4	359.7	363.9
Net income ($ mil.)	58.2%	–	1.5	2.3	6.8	6.0
Market value ($ mil.)	–	–	–	–	–	–
Employees	–	–	–	–	–	570

KRONOS INCORPORATED

297 Billerica Rd.
Chelmsford MA 01824
Phone: 978-250-9800
Fax: 978-367-5900
Web: www.kronos.com

CEO: Aron J AIN
CFO: John A Butler
HR: –
FYE: September 30
Type: Private

Kronos knows time is money for its customers. The company makes and implements workforce management software particularly for organizations with large complex workforces. With a goal of controlling labor costs and improving employee productivity its software products automatically collect time and attendance data manage scheduling and absence oversee administrative HR payroll and hiring processes and provide data analytics on cost and performance problems. Serving more than half of the Fortune 1000 it focuses on the education health care hospitality manufacturing retail and government markets among others. Kronos is owned by an investment group led by private equity firm Hellman & Friedman.

KRONOS WORLDWIDE INC   NYS: KRO

5430 LBJ Freeway, Suite 1700
Dallas, TX 75240-2620
Phone: 972 233-1700
Fax: –
Web: www.kronostio2.com

CEO: Robert Graham
CFO: Tim Hafer
HR: Patricia Kropp
FYE: December 31
Type: Public

Kronos Worldwide produces pigments that impart whiteness brightness and opacity to everything from plastics paper and coatings to inks food and cosmetics. Controlled by Valhi Kronos is a leading manufacturer of a commercially used base white inorganic pigment known as titanium dioxide (TiO2). TiO2 is designed based on specific end-use applications. Kronos makes and sell over 40 different TiO2 grades; the company and its distributors and agents also provide technical services for its products to approximately 4000 customers in some 100 countries mainly in Europe North America Asia Pacific region. The US generates about 35% of the company's total sales.

	Annual Growth	12/16	12/17	12/18	12/19	12/20
Sales ($ mil.)	4.7%	1,364.3	1,729.0	1,661.9	1,731.1	1,638.8
Net income ($ mil.)	10.2%	43.3	354.5	205.0	87.1	63.9
Market value ($ mil.)	5.7%	1,379.1	2,976.4	1,330.6	1,547.7	1,722.1
Employees	(0.2%)	2,260	2,245	2,195	2,200	2,242

KRUEGER INTERNATIONAL, INC.

1330 BELLEVUE ST
GREEN BAY, WI 543022197
Phone: 920-468-8100
Fax: –
Web: www.ki.com

CEO: Brian Krenke
CFO: Nick Guerrieri
HR: –
FYE: December 31
Type: Private

Krueger International is one of the world's leading contract furniture manufacturers in the industry. The company which does business as KI makes ergonomic seating cabinets sleepers occasional tables and other furniture used by businesses healthcare organizations government agencies and educational institutions. It offers everything from benches and beds to desks and tables not to mention shelving filing systems and movable walls. KI markets its products through sales representatives furniture dealers architects and interior designers worldwide. Founded in 1941 KI is 100% employee-owned.

	Annual Growth	12/08	12/09	12/10	12/11	12/15
Sales ($ mil.)	–	–	–	(40.1)	649.7	617.3
Net income ($ mil.)	1047.2%	–	–	0.0	56.9	53.3
Market value ($ mil.)	–	–	–	–	–	–
Employees	–	–	–	–	–	2,300

KSW INC.   NASDAQ: KSW

37-16 23rd St.
Long Island City NY 11101
Phone: 718-361-6500
Fax: 718-784-1943
Web: www.kswmechanical.com

CEO: –
CFO: Richard Lucas
HR: –
FYE: December 31
Type: Public

KSW may have a need to vent on occasion but the company still knows how to keep its cool. Its KSW Mechanical Services subsidiary installs HVAC and process piping systems for large-scale industrial commercial institutional public and residential projects. The company also provides mechanical trade management services and engineering assistance. KSW primarily works in the New York metropolitan area but hopes to expand in the Northeast. Much of KSW's business comes from repeat customers; the company is an authorized bidder for agencies including the New York City Transit Authority and the Port Authority of New York and New Jersey. Real estate developer Related Companies is buying KSW in a $32 million deal.

KUAKINI HEALTH SYSTEM

347 N KUAKINI ST
HONOLULU, HI 968172382
Phone: 808-547-9148
Fax: –
Web: www.kuakinifcu.com

CEO: –
CFO: Quin Ogawa
HR: –
FYE: June 30
Type: Private

Say aloha to better health! Kuakini Health System operates the non-profit Kuakini Medical Center a 250-bed acute care hospital that provides specialty services including cancer treatment cardiac care and orthopedic surgery. The hospital serves as a teaching center for the University of Hawaii's John A. Burns School of Medicine. Kuakini Health System also operates the 234-bed Kuakini Geriatric Care facility which offers nursing home and adult day care for Honolulu's senior citizens. The system also maintains two medical office buildings. The Kuakini Health System was founded by Japanese immigrants in 1900. It is a member of the Premier group purchasing alliance.

	Annual Growth	06/13	06/14	06/15	06/16	06/20
Sales ($ mil.)	(0.6%)	–	–	–	148.3	144.9
Net income ($ mil.)	–	–	–	–	(23.8)	(14.4)
Market value ($ mil.)	–	–	–	–	–	–
Employees	–	–	–	–	–	1,400

KURT MANUFACTURING COMPANY INC.

5280 MAIN ST NE
MINNEAPOLIS, MN 554211594
Phone: 763-572-1500
Fax: –
Web: www.kurt.com

CEO: Paul Lillyblad
CFO: Paul Lillyblad
HR: –
FYE: October 31
Type: Private

Kurt Manufacturing helps you provide decisions on precision when it comes to the manufacturing process. It makes precision-machined parts and components on a contract basis for the aerospace automotive oil and defense markets. Kurt operates through divisions including Hydraulics Engineered Systems Kinetic and Workholding. These divisions make gauging systems hydraulic coupling and hoses vises and other workholding tools to a list of clients that have included such big names as ATK Deere & Co. General Dynamics General Electric General Motors Honeywell IBM and Lockheed Martin. Kurt is an employee owned company.

	Annual Growth	10/05	10/06	10/07*	11/08*	10/09
Sales ($ mil.)	(79.6%)	–	–	1,623.2	108.9	67.8
Net income ($ mil.)	–	–	–	0.0	3.3	(1.3)
Market value ($ mil.)	–	–	–	–	–	–
Employees	–	–	–	–	–	410

*Fiscal year change

KVH INDUSTRIES, INC.

NMS: KVHI

50 Enterprise Center
Middletown, RI 02842
Phone: 401 847-3327
Fax: –
Web: www.kvh.com

CEO: Martin Kits van Heyningen
CFO: Roger Kuebel
HR: –
FYE: December 31
Type: Public

KVH Industries' mobile satellite communications products include antennas and compasses for yachts and commercial ships and mobile satellite TVs telephones and high-speed Internet antennas (TracVision and TracPhone) for automobiles boats small planes and RVs. It sells to retailers and distributors as well as boat and other vehicle manufacturers. KVH's inertial navigation products — sold mainly to US and allied governments and defense contractors — include digital compasses fiber optic gyros for tactical navigation and guidance systems for torpedoes and unmanned aerial vehicles. About 65% of the company's revenue is from international customers.

	Annual Growth	12/16	12/17	12/18	12/19	12/20
Sales ($ mil.)	(2.6%)	176.1	160.1	170.8	157.9	158.7
Net income ($ mil.)	–	(7.5)	(11.0)	(8.2)	33.3	(21.9)
Market value ($ mil.)	(1.0%)	217.5	190.7	189.6	205.1	209.2
Employees	0.2%	635	604	715	604	639

KWIK TRIP, INC.

1626 OAK ST
LA CROSSE, WI 546032308
Phone: 608-781-8988
Fax: –
Web: www.kwiktrip.com

CEO: –
CFO: –
HR: Tom Reinhart
FYE: September 27
Type: Private

Midwesterners who need to make a quick trip to get gas or groceries cigarettes or donuts race on over to Kwik Trip stores. Kwik Trip owns and operates more than 600 Kwik Trip and Kwik Star convenience stores in Iowa Minnesota and Wisconsin. Kwik Trip owns in-house dairy and bakery operations and makes many of its products in-house; popular products include Glazers donuts and Karuba Coffee. All Kwik Trip stores built since 1990 are owned by Convenience Store Investments a separate firm which leases the land and stores to Kwik Trip. Kwik Trip which opened its first store in 1965 in Eau Claire Wisconsin is owned by the family of CEO Don Zietlow.

	Annual Growth	09/01	09/02	09/03	09/04	09/08
Sales ($ mil.)	17.1%	–	–	1,651.1	1,887.1	3,640.4
Net income ($ mil.)	(0.2%)	–	–	24.1	24.7	23.9
Market value ($ mil.)	–	–	–	–	–	–
Employees	–	–	–	–	–	10,500

L & S ELECTRIC, INC.

5101 MESKER ST
SCHOFIELD, WI 544763056
Phone: 715-359-3155
Fax: –
Web: www.lselectric.com

CEO: –
CFO: David Krause
HR: –
FYE: December 31
Type: Private

L&S Electric isn't a run of the mill distributor even if its products run the mill. The company specializes in selling motors controls drives and integrated systems used in power generation railway pulp and paper mill mining and other industrial applications. It also offers engineering and repair services worldwide through an engineering division and its L&S Electric of Canada subsidiary. L&S Electric has about eight locations in Wisconsin Minnesota and Michigan. The company was formed in the 1983 merger of Leverence Electric and Snapp Electric two motor repair shops that dated back to the 1930s. L&S Electric is owned by the Lewitzke family.

	Annual Growth	12/12	12/13	12/14	12/15	12/16
Sales ($ mil.)	(1.6%)	–	84.0	81.4	85.5	80.1
Net income ($ mil.)	–	–	5.8	2.6	1.6	(0.4)
Market value ($ mil.)	–	–	–	–	–	–
Employees	–	–	–	–	–	350

L&L ENERGY INC

NBB: LLEN

130 Andover Park East, Suite 200
Seattle, WA 98188
Phone: 206 264-8065
Fax: 206 838-0488
Web: www.llenergyinc.com

CEO: –
CFO: –
HR: –
FYE: April 30
Type: Public

You'll excuse L & L Energy (formerly L & L International) if it's a bit jet lagged. Incorporated in Nevada with headquarters in Seattle the company mines coal in China. Granted a license by the government to extract a set amount of coal in exchange for up-front fees L & L owns mines in China's Yunnan and Guizhou provinces. The company currently extracts more than 630000 tons of coal per year from the mines. It also processes coal to produce coke used in steel production medium coal used for heating and coal slurries used as a lower quality fuel. L & L is swapping a stake in a coking mine with Singapore-based Union Energy to acquire a 50% stake in the LuoZhou coal mine.

	Annual Growth	04/09	04/10	04/11	04/12	04/13
Sales ($ mil.)	48.5%	40.9	109.2	223.9	143.6	199.0
Net income ($ mil.)	40.1%	10.0	32.9	36.8	14.2	38.4
Market value ($ mil.)	21.1%	68.6	411.5	264.8	85.7	147.4
Employees	3.3%	1,200	1,400	1,600	1,330	1,364

L. & R. DISTRIBUTORS INC.

9301 AVENUE D
BROOKLYN, NY 11236-1899
Phone: 718-272-2100
Fax: –
Web: www.lrdist.com

CEO: Marc J Bodner
CFO: Craig Zumbo
HR: –
FYE: December 31
Type: Private

Stocking shelves? L&R Distributors (formerly Allied Supply) is a wholesale distributor of a wide variety of household and personal care products stationery items toys and sundries to supermarkets independent pharmacies and discount and stationery stores. Its offerings have ranged from ACE bandages to Zippo lighters and from Wiffle balls to baby wipes. The company operates throughout the US; among its key partners have been pharmaceutical distributors such as McKesson and Cardinal Health. L&R Distributors has been assembled via a string of transactions dating to the 1950s including the 1986 merger of E&N Sales Corp. and Ortner Drug Co.

	Annual Growth	12/00	12/01	12/02	12/06	12/10
Sales ($ mil.)	14.0%	–	44.6	43.3	76.5	145.1
Net income ($ mil.)	17.5%	–	0.3	0.7	0.8	1.4
Market value ($ mil.)	–	–	–	–	–	–
Employees	–	–	–	–	–	550

L3HARRIS TECHNOLOGIES INC

NYS: LHX

1025 West NASA Boulevard
Melbourne, FL 32919
Phone: 321 727-9100
Fax: –
Web: www.l3harris.com

CEO: Bill Brown
CFO: Michelle Turner
HR: –
FYE: January 01
Type: Public

L3Harris Technologies (formerly Harris Corp. and L3 Technologies) is an agile global aerospace and defense technology innovator delivering end-to-end solutions that meet customers' mission-critical needs that provide advance defense and commercial technologies across air land sea space and cyber domains for government and commercial customers in approximately 130 countries. It makes tactical communications and other integrated vision solutions; air traffic management; and intelligence surveillance and reconnaissance systems. Although about three-quarters of L3Harris' revenue comes from US government agencies particularly the Department of Defense it also has customers in the commercial sector. In 2019 the former Harris Corp. and L3 Technologies combined to form L3Harris Technologies the sixth largest defense contractor in the US.

	Annual Growth	06/17	06/18	06/19*	01/20	01/21
Sales ($ mil.)	32.5%	5,900.0	6,182.0	6,801.0	9,263.0	18,194.0
Net income ($ mil.)	19.3%	553.0	718.0	949.0	822.0	1,119.0
Market value ($ mil.)	14.7%	22,713.8	30,097.6	39,382.6	43,826.2	39,359.7
Employees	29.6%	17,000	17,500	18,200	50,000	48,000

*Fiscal year change

LA FRANCE CORP.

1 LAFRANCE WAY
CONCORDVILLE, PA 19331
Phone: 610-361-4300
Fax: –
Web: www.lafrancecorp.com

CEO: –
CFO: Thomas Sheehan
HR: –
FYE: December 31
Type: Private

LaFrance Corp. also known as LaFrance makes nameplates functional components and other products through several divisions. It offers an array of alternatives for its customer's decorative or functional component. Its comprehensive product offering of metals and plastics can be combined to create unique emblems logos trim and functional pieces. It uses electroform metal letters stainless steel and more to create its products. Starting out in the jewelry business in 1946 Joseph A. Teti Jr. the founder recognized a match between LaFrance's precision manufacturing capabilities and a market need for high-quality product branding.

	Annual Growth	12/09	12/10	12/11	12/12	12/13
Sales ($ mil.)	14.1%	–	–	–	115.1	131.4
Net income ($ mil.)	(5.8%)	–	–	–	10.9	10.3
Market value ($ mil.)	–	–	–	–	–	–
Employees	–	–	–	–	–	2,400

LA JOLLA PHARMACEUTICAL CO.

NAS: LJPC

201 Jones Road, Suite 400
Waltham, MA 02451
Phone: 617 715-3600
Fax: –
Web: www.ljpc.com

CEO: Larry Edwards
CFO: Michael Hearne
HR: –
FYE: December 31
Type: Public

La Jolla Pharmaceutical Company is dedicated to the development and commercialization of innovative therapies that improve outcomes in patients suffering from life-threatening diseases. GIAPREZA (angiotensin II) is approved by the US Food and Drug Administration (FDA) as a vasoconstrictor indicated to increase blood pressure in adults with septic or other distributive shock. XERAVA (eravacycline) is approved by the US FDA for the treatment of complicated intra-abdominal infections. In 2020 La Jolla completed its acquisition of Tetraphase a biopharmaceutical company focused on commercializing its novel tetracycline XERAVA to treat serious and life-threatening infections.

	Annual Growth	12/16	12/17	12/18	12/19	12/20
Sales ($ mil.)	171.4%	0.6	–	10.1	23.1	33.4
Net income ($ mil.)	–	(78.2)	(114.8)	(199.5)	(116.5)	(39.4)
Market value ($ mil.)	(31.4%)	480.4	881.8	258.4	107.7	106.3
Employees	(13.4%)	105	309	169	91	59

LA MADELEINE OF TEXAS INC.

12201 Merit Dr. Ste. 900
Dallas TX 75251
Phone: 214-696-6962
Fax: 214-696-0485
Web: www.lamadeleine.com

CEO: –
CFO: –
HR: –
FYE: June 30
Type: Private

This company hopes its creme brulee croissants and quiche prove as memorable as Proust's famous teacake. La Madeleine operates 60 la Madeleine Bakery Cafe & Bistro casual dining locations mostly in Texas Georgia and Louisiana offering French country cuisine for breakfast lunch and dinner. The restaurants which welcome patrons with such interior appointments as a stone hearth and handcrafted wood tables use a cafeteria-style serving line and limited table service. Each location also sells a variety of fresh baked goods. French native Patrick Leon Esquerre started the business in 1983. La Madeleine is owned by a group of investors including restaurant operator Groupe Le Duff.

LA-Z-BOY INC.

NYS: LZB

One La-Z-Boy Drive
Monroe, MI 48162-5138
Phone: 734 242-1444
Fax: –
Web: www.la-z-boy.com

CEO: Kurt Darrow
CFO: Melinda Whittington
HR: –
FYE: April 24
Type: Public

La-Z-Boy is a top US maker of upholstered and wood furniture. It sells its ubiquitous recliners as well as chairs sofas tables bedroom and dining room sets and modular seating units. Its brands include La-Z-Boy England Hammary American Drew and Kincaid. La-Z-Boy sells its products through about 160 company-owned stores and more than 900 independent locations under the La-Z-Boy Furniture Galleries and La-Z-Boy Comfort Studio names. It also sells furniture to retailers across the US Canada and some 65 other countries. The US is the company's largest market.

	Annual Growth	04/17	04/18	04/19	04/20	04/21
Sales ($ mil.)	3.4%	1,520.1	1,583.9	1,745.0	1,704.0	1,734.2
Net income ($ mil.)	5.5%	85.9	80.9	68.6	77.5	106.5
Market value ($ mil.)	11.6%	1,265.6	1,329.1	1,472.0	955.8	1,960.5
Employees	6.5%	8,950	9,000	9,700	9,500	11,500

LABORATORY CORPORATION OF AMERICA HOLDINGS   NYS: LH

358 South Main Street   CEO: Adam Schechter
Burlington, NC 27215   CFO: Glenn Eisenberg
Phone: 336 229-1127   HR: –
Fax: –   FYE: December 31
Web: www.labcorp.com   Type: Public

Laboratory Corporation of America (LabCorp) is a leading global life sciences company that provides vital information to help doctors hospitals pharmaceutical companies researchers and patients make clear and confident decisions. Labcorp serves a broad range of customers including MCOs biopharmaceutical medical device and diagnostics companies governmental agencies physicians and other healthcare providers hospitals and health systems employers patients and consumers contract research organizations (CROs) and independent clinical laboratories. Services range from routine urinalyses HIV tests and Pap smears to specialty testing for diagnostic genetics disease monitoring forensics identity clinical drug trials and allergies. Majority of the company's sales were generated from the North America.

	Annual Growth	12/16	12/17	12/18	12/19	12/20
Sales ($ mil.)	9.7%	9,641.8	10,441.4	11,333.4	11,554.8	13,978.5
Net income ($ mil.)	20.7%	732.1	1,268.2	883.7	823.8	1,556.1
Market value ($ mil.)	12.2%	12,517.1	15,552.2	12,320.1	16,494.1	19,846.1
Employees	8.6%	52,000	60,000	61,000	65,000	72,400

LACKS ENTERPRISES INC.

5460 Cascade Rd. SE   CEO: –
Grand Rapids MI 49546   CFO: –
Phone: 616-949-6570   HR: –
Fax: 616-285-2367   FYE: July 31
Web: www.lacksenterprises.com   Type: Private

It's not "hipp" if your car lacks a wheel cover or has a rusty grille. Lacks Enterprises makes high-impact plated plastic (HIPP) alternatives to die-cast and stainless steel automotive products such as wheel covers and grilles. The company's HIPP parts plated with copper nickel chrome are lighter and cheaper than all-metal alternatives as well as resistant to dents and rust. Other products include molding rocker panels and trim. Automotive OEM customers have included Ford General Motors Honda Nissan and Toyota. Its Plastic-Plate subsidiary makes items such as cell phone face plates for manufacturers of consumer electronics and telecommunications equipment. The Lacks family owns Lacks Enterprises.

LACROSSE FOOTWEAR INC.   NASDAQ: BOOT

17634 NE Airport Way   CEO: Joseph P Schneider
Portland OR 97230   CFO: David P Carlson
Phone: 503-262-0110   HR: –
Fax: 503-262-0115   FYE: December 31
Web: www.lacrossefootwear.com/   Type: Public

If customers are wearing its protective boots LaCrosse Footwear doesn't care who steps on their toes. The company offers sturdy footwear for outdoor pursuits (hunting snowmobiling) and occupations such as farming general utility and construction. LaCrosse makes rubber vinyl and leather footwear as well as rainwear and protective clothing for adults and children. Its brands include LaCrosse Danner Burly Camohide and Iceman among other names. LaCrosse's products are sold throughout North America to catalog and online merchants retailers wholesalers and the US government as well as through company websites and outlet stores. The company's Danish subsidiary supplies retailers in Asia and Europe.

LADDER CAPITAL CORP   NYS: LADR

345 Park Avenue   CEO: Brian Harris
New York, NY 10154   CFO: Paul Miceli
Phone: 212 715-3170   HR: –
Fax: –   FYE: December 31
Web: www.laddercapital.com   Type: Public

This specialty finance firm is looking to climb to the top of the commercial real-estate lending business. Ladder Capital Corp. is a non-bank operating company engaged in three major lines of business: commercial mortgage lending mortgage backed securities and real-estate assets. Its loans typically range from $5 million to $100 million. More than 50% of its loans originate in the Northeast. Hotel retail and office properties account for about three-quarters of Ladder's loan portfolio. Since its founding in 2008 the commercial real estate finance firm has originated $5.4 billion in conduit loans. Ladder Capital went public in 2014 with an offering valued at $225 million.

	Annual Growth	12/17	12/18	12/19	12/20	12/21
Assets ($ mil.)	(0.7%)	6,025.6	6,272.9	6,669.2	5,881.2	5,851.3
Net income ($ mil.)	(12.2%)	95.3	180.0	122.6	(14.4)	56.5
Market value ($ mil.)	(3.2%)	1,709.9	1,940.8	2,263.2	1,226.9	1,504.2
Employees	(2.5%)	72	74	76	58	65

LADENBURG THALMANN FINANCIAL SERVICES INC   NBB: LTSA

4400 Biscayne Boulevard, 12th Floor   CEO: Jamie Price
Miami, FL 33137   CFO: Brett Kaufman
Phone: 305 572-4100   HR: –
Fax: –   FYE: December 31
Web: www.ladenburg.com   Type: Public

Ladenburg Thalmann Financial Services is a wholly-owned subsidiary of Advisor Group Holdings Inc. which is owned by private investment funds sponsored by Reverence Capital Partners LLC. Ladenburg's subsidiaries include industry-leading independent advisory and brokerage (IAB) firms Securities America Triad Advisors Securities Service Network Investacorp and KMS Financial Services as well as Premier Trust Ladenburg Thalmann Asset Management Highland Capital Brokerage a leading independent life insurance brokerage company and full-service annuity processing and marketing company and Ladenburg Thalmann & Co. Inc. an investment bank.

	Annual Growth	12/15	12/16	12/17	12/18	12/19
Sales ($ mil.)	6.3%	1,152.1	1,107.0	1,268.2	1,391.1	1,469.3
Net income ($ mil.)	–	(11.2)	(22.3)	7.7	33.8	22.8
Market value ($ mil.)	0.3%	3,694.0	3,574.5	3,779.2	3,535.7	3,744.7
Employees	3.7%	1,307	1,299	1,379	1,512	1,510

LADENBURG THALMANN FINANCIAL SERVICES INC.

4400 BISCAYNE BLVD FL 12   CEO: Jamie Price
MIAMI, FL 331373212   CFO: Brett Kaufman
Phone: 305-572-4100   HR: –
Fax: –   FYE: December 31
Web: www.ladenburg.com   Type: Private

Ladenburg Thalmann Financial Services is a wholly-owned subsidiary of Advisor Group Holdings Inc. which is owned by private investment funds sponsored by Reverence Capital Partners LLC. Ladenburg's subsidiaries include industry-leading independent advisory and brokerage (IAB) firms Securities America Triad Advisors Securities Service Network Investacorp and KMS Financial Services as well as Premier Trust Ladenburg Thalmann Asset Management Highland Capital Brokerage a leading independent life insurance brokerage company and full-service annuity processing and marketing company and Ladenburg Thalmann & Co. Inc. an investment bank.

	Annual Growth	12/15	12/16	12/17	12/18	12/19
Sales ($ mil.)	9.9%	–	1,107.0	1,268.2	1,391.1	1,469.3
Net income ($ mil.)	–	–	(22.3)	7.7	33.8	22.7
Market value ($ mil.)	–	–	–	–	–	–
Employees	–	–	–	–	–	1,512

LADIES PROFESSIONAL GOLF ASSOCIATION

100 INTERNATIONAL GOLF DR
DAYTONA BEACH, FL 321241082
Phone: 386-274-6200
Fax: -
Web: www.lpga.com

CEO: -
CFO: -
HR: Wendy Caves
FYE: December 31
Type: Private

This organization has chipped out a place for itself in the male-dominated sports world. The Ladies Professional Golf Association (LPGA) is the organizing body for women's golf overseeing development and promotion of the game and its star players. It operates the LPGA Tour consisting of about 30 events a year. In addition to its high-profile golf tournaments the organization runs the LPGA Teaching & Club Professional Division which is the golf education and development subsidiary for its 1200 members. The LPGA was founded in 1950 making it one of the oldest women's sports organizations in the world.

	Annual Growth	12/07	12/08	12/09	12/12	12/13
Sales ($ mil.)	5.7%	-	-	82.5	89.1	102.9
Net income ($ mil.)	-	-	-	(3.2)	0.2	1.2
Market value ($ mil.)	-	-	-	-	-	-
Employees	-	-	-	-	-	85

LAFAYETTE COLLEGE

730 SULLIVAN RD
EASTON, PA 180421760
Phone: 610-330-5000
Fax: -
Web: www.lafayette.edu

CEO: -
CFO: -
HR: -
FYE: June 30
Type: Private

Lafayette College has a revolutionary background. Named after the French hero of the American Revolution the school offers bachelor's degrees in 37 areas of study in engineering sciences and the arts. Some 2450 students — all undergraduates — are enrolled on the campus located about 70 miles west of New York City and 60 miles north of Philadelphia. Students come from 46 US states and territories and from 48 other countries. Lafayette is a member of the Lehigh Valley Association of Independent Colleges which also includes Cedar Crest College DeSales University Lehigh University Moravian College and Muhlenberg College.

	Annual Growth	06/12	06/13	06/14	06/15	06/20
Sales ($ mil.)	7.0%	-	142.1	145.6	265.7	228.5
Net income ($ mil.)	-	-	-	69.6	97.8	73.3	(0.1)
Market value ($ mil.)	-	-	-	-	-	-
Employees	-	-	-	-	-	675

LAFAYETTE GENERAL MEDICAL CENTER, INC.

1214 COOLIDGE BLVD
LAFAYETTE, LA 705032621
Phone: 337-289-7991
Fax: -
Web: www.ochsnerlg.org

CEO: -
CFO: -
HR: -
FYE: September 30
Type: Private

Serving the people of Acadiana (southern Louisiana) Lafayette General Medical Center (LGMC) provides general inpatient medical and surgical care as well as specialized trauma care and neonatal intensive care. The nonprofit hospital which has 365 beds also offers a cancer center home health services outpatient care occupational medicine and mental health care. As part of umbrella group Lafayette Health LGMC is affiliated with Lafayette General Surgical Hospital Lafayette General Southwest St. Martin Hospital Acadia General Hospital University Hospital and Clinics and Abrom Kaplan Memorial Hospital. It's also a teaching hospital for LSU. Non-profit foundation Lafayette General Foundation supports and governs Lafayette Health.

	Annual Growth	09/15	09/16	09/17	09/18	09/19
Sales ($ mil.)	7.1%	-	454.8	465.0	480.3	559.0
Net income ($ mil.)	(4.4%)	-	50.9	44.2	45.1	44.5
Market value ($ mil.)	-	-	-	-	-	-
Employees	-	-	-	-	-	1,626

LAIRD TECHNOLOGIES INC.

3481 Rider Trail South
Earth City MO 63045
Phone: 636-898-6000
Fax: 636-898-6100
Web: www.lairdtech.com

CEO: John Zheng
CFO: -
HR: -
FYE: December 31
Type: Subsidiary

Laird Technologies feels that the shield is mightier than the sword. The company manufactures electromagnetic interference (EMI) shielding materials such as custom metal stampings signal integrity components thermal management products wireless antennas and radio frequency modules. It also produces metalized fabric and conductive tape and offers product engineering and testing services. Laird Technologies has two divisions: Performance Materials (handset metals) which includes EMI shields signal integrity products and thermal management products; and Wireless Systems such as telematics and satellite radio antennas handset antennas and other wireless systems. Laird Technologies is an operating unit of Laird PLC.

LAKE AREA CORN PROCESSORS CO-OPERATIVE

46269 SD HIGHWAY 34
WENTWORTH, SD 570756934
Phone: 605-483-2676
Fax: -
Web: www.dakotaethanol.com

CEO: -
CFO: -
HR: -
FYE: December 31
Type: Private

Lake Area Corn Processors produces ethanol and its byproduct distillers grains which are used in livestock feed. Through its Dakota Ethanol unit the company produces about 48 million gallons of ethanol per year. Dakota Ethanol had worked in tandem with Broin Companies a manufacturer of ethanol processing plants until Lake Area Corn Processors bought out Broin's minority stake in Dakota Ethanol in 2006. The following year the company acquired a stake in its ethanol distributor Renewable Products Marketing Group. Lake Area Corn Processors is owned by its 1000 members.

	Annual Growth	12/04	12/05	12/06	12/07	12/10
Sales ($ mil.)	3.8%	-	80.0	103.9	103.7	96.4
Net income ($ mil.)	(8.3%)	-	10.9	46.0	18.0	7.0
Market value ($ mil.)	-	-	-	-	-	-
Employees	-	-	-	-	-	40

LAKE FOREST COLLEGE

555 N SHERIDAN RD
LAKE FOREST, IL 600452338
Phone: 847-234-3100
Fax: -
Web: www.lakeforest.edu

CEO: -
CFO: -
HR: -
FYE: May 31
Type: Private

Living up to its name Lake Forest College is a liberal arts school near the shores of Lake Michigan just north of Chicago. The school sits on about a 100 acre campus 30 miles north of downtown Chicago and offers undergraduate and graduate programs to its approximately 1500 students. With nearly 20 departmental and about 10 interdisciplinary majors its subjects include economics international studies neuroscience and pre-law. The College's Center for Chicago Programs facilitates research and internships at Chicago institutions as well as brings Chicago-based artists and artisans alike to the campus for lectures and performances.

	Annual Growth	05/13	05/14	05/15	05/17	05/18
Sales ($ mil.)	(12.5%)	-	108.0	104.5	63.9	63.2
Net income ($ mil.)	(26.4%)	-	18.9	12.2	10.4	5.5
Market value ($ mil.)	-	-	-	-	-	-
Employees	-	-	-	-	-	385

LAKE HOSPITAL SYSTEM, INC.

7590 AUBURN RD
CONCORD TOWNSHIP, OH 440779176
Phone: 440-375-8100
Fax: –
Web: www.lakehealth.org

CEO: Cynthia Moore-Hardy
CFO: –
HR: –
FYE: December 31
Type: Private

Lake Health serves eight counties in Ohio. The not-for-profit health system comprises three main hospital campuses (Beachwood Medical Center TriPoint Medical Center and West Medical Center) which provides patient- and family-centered care with a 24/7 Emergency Department surgery center labor and delivery suites lab imaging physical therapy retail pharmacy and physician offices. The system's Lake Health Physician Group includes physicians ranging from family practitioners to vascular surgeons. Lake Health was founded in 1959.

	Annual Growth	12/13	12/14	12/16	12/17	12/18
Sales ($ mil.)	4.5%	–	313.8	334.2	356.9	373.9
Net income ($ mil.)	–	–	(3.3)	(13.2)	33.3	(7.4)
Market value ($ mil.)	–	–	–	–	–	–
Employees	–	–	–	–	–	2,700

LAKE SHORE BANCORP INC

NMS: LSBK

31 East Fourth Street
Dunkirk, NY 14048
Phone: 716 366-4070
Fax: –
Web: www.lakeshoresavings.com

CEO: Daniel Reininga
CFO: Rachel Foley
HR: –
FYE: December 31
Type: Public

Money washes up along this shore. Lake Shore Bancorp is the holding company for Lake Shore Savings Bank which serves consumers and businesses through 11 branches in Chautauqua and Erie counties in western New York near Lake Erie. Founded in 1891 the community oriented savings bank focuses on residential real estate lending with one- to four-family mortgages accounting for a majority of its loan portfolio. Lake Shore Savings Bank also offers home equity loans and commercial and consumer loans as well as checking and savings accounts CDs and IRAs. Mutual holding company Lake Shore MHC owns about 60% of Lake Shore Bancorp.

	Annual Growth	12/16	12/17	12/18	12/19	12/20
Assets ($ mil.)	8.8%	489.2	519.0	545.7	610.9	686.2
Net income ($ mil.)	6.7%	3.5	3.4	4.0	4.1	4.6
Market value ($ mil.)	(5.4%)	94.7	99.9	87.7	89.1	75.7
Employees	1.5%	111	114	115	116	118

LAKE SUNAPEE BANK GROUP

NMS: LSBG

9 Main Street, P.O. Box 9
Newport, NH 03773
Phone: 603 863-0886
Fax: –
Web: www.nhthrift.com

CEO: –
CFO: –
HR: –
FYE: December 31
Type: Public

New Hampshire Thrift Bancshares is the holding company for Lake Sunapee Bank which operates nearly 30 branches in western and central New Hampshire and western Vermont. Targeting individuals and local businesses the bank mainly uses funds from deposits to originate a variety of loans mainly residential and commercial mortgages. It also offers investment insurance and trust services. New Hampshire Thrift Bancshares expanded into Vermont with the 2007 acquisition of First Brandon National Bank which now operates as a division of Lake Sunapee Bank. The company bought insurance agency McCrillis & Eldredge in 2011. It now plans to buy the single-branch Nashua Bank.

	Annual Growth	12/10	12/11	12/12	12/13	12/14
Assets ($ mil.)	10.9%	995.1	1,041.8	1,270.5	1,423.9	1,503.8
Net income ($ mil.)	6.0%	7.9	7.7	7.8	8.4	10.0
Market value ($ mil.)	5.6%	103.6	93.3	104.9	125.9	129.0
Employees	11.3%	249	274	304	382	382

LAKELAND BANCORP, INC.

NMS: LBAI

250 Oak Ridge Road
Oak Ridge, NJ 07438
Phone: 973 697-2000
Fax: –
Web: www.lakelandbank.com

CEO: Thomas Shara
CFO: Thomas Splaine
HR: –
FYE: December 31
Type: Public

Lakeland Bancorp is the holding company for Lakeland Bank which serves northern and central New Jersey from around 50 branch offices. Targeting individuals and small to midsized businesses the bank offers standard retail products such as checking and savings accounts money market and NOW accounts and CDs. It also offers financial planning and advisory services for consumers. The bank's lending activities primarily consist of commercial loans and mortgages (around three-quarters of the company's loan portfolio) and residential mortgages. Lakeland also offers commercial lease financing for commercial equipment.

	Annual Growth	12/16	12/17	12/18	12/19	12/20
Assets ($ mil.)	10.8%	5,093.1	5,405.6	5,806.1	6,711.2	7,664.3
Net income ($ mil.)	8.5%	41.5	52.6	63.4	70.7	57.5
Market value ($ mil.)	(10.2%)	984.4	971.7	747.6	877.3	641.1
Employees	4.7%	592	621	652	692	711

LAKELAND FINANCIAL CORP

NMS: LKFN

202 East Center Street
Warsaw, IN 46580
Phone: 574 267-6144
Fax: –
Web: www.lakecitybank.com

CEO: David Findlay
CFO: Lisa O'Neill
HR: –
FYE: December 31
Type: Public

Lakeland Financial is the holding company for Lake City Bank which serves area business customers and individuals through around 50 branches scattered across about 15 northern and central Indiana counties. With $4.8 billion in assets the community bank offers such standard retail services as checking and savings accounts money market accounts and CDs. Commercial loans including agricultural loans and mortgages make up about 90% of the bank's loan portfolio. Lake City Bank also offers investment products and services such as corporate and personal trust brokerage and estate planning.

	Annual Growth	12/16	12/17	12/18	12/19	12/20
Assets ($ mil.)	8.0%	4,290.0	4,683.0	4,875.3	4,946.7	5,830.4
Net income ($ mil.)	12.8%	52.1	57.3	80.4	87.0	84.3
Market value ($ mil.)	3.1%	1,195.4	1,223.9	1,013.6	1,235.0	1,352.3
Employees	2.8%	524	539	553	568	585

LAKELAND INDUSTRIES, INC.

NMS: LAKE

1525 Perimeter Parkway, Suite 325
Huntsville, AL 35806
Phone: 256 350-3873
Fax: 256 350-0773
Web: www.lakeland.com

CEO: Charles Roberson
CFO: Allen E Dillard
HR: –
FYE: January 31
Type: Public

The wrong clothing can be hazardous to your health — not based on style but by OSHA and EPA standards. Lakeland makes protective clothing for on-the-job hazards. It uses DuPont specialty fabrics such as Kevlar TyChem and Tyvek as well as its own fabrics to make industrial disposable garments toxic-waste cleanup suits fire- and heat-resistant apparel (including Fyrepel gear for firefighters) industrial work gloves high-visibility garments and industrial/medical garments. Lakeland manufactures its products in Brazil China India Mexico and the US. Customers — nearly 65% are outside of the US — include high tech electronics manufacturers construction companies hospitals and laboratories.

	Annual Growth	01/17	01/18	01/19	01/20	01/21
Sales ($ mil.)	16.5%	86.2	96.0	99.0	107.8	159.0
Net income ($ mil.)	73.3%	3.9	0.4	1.5	3.3	35.1
Market value ($ mil.)	26.5%	86.6	112.6	88.8	111.3	222.0
Employees	19.1%	993	1,072	1,632	1,829	2,000

LAKELAND REGIONAL MEDICAL CENTER, INC.

1324 LAKELAND HILLS BLVD
LAKELAND, FL 338054500
Phone: 863-687-1100
Fax: –
Web: www.mylrh.org

CEO: Elaine C Thompson
CFO: –
HR: –
FYE: September 30
Type: Private

Lakeland Regional Medical Center (LRMC) serves Florida's Polk County (roughly between Kissimmee and Tampa) through an acute care hospital with approximately 850 beds. Among its specialty services are cardiac care cancer treatment senior care urology emergency medicine orthopedics women's and children's health care and surgery. LRMC also operates general care and specialty outpatient clinics. Additionally the hospital provides medical training programs for radiology specialists. Its LRMC Foundation offers financial support for indigent patients facing ongoing treatment.

	Annual Growth	09/13	09/14	09/15	09/16	09/19
Sales ($ mil.)	7.9%	–	618.3	674.5	790.3	905.4
Net income ($ mil.)	(0.3%)	–	66.9	68.5	84.5	65.7
Market value ($ mil.)	–	–	–	–	–	–
Employees	–	–	–	–	–	3,100

LAKESIDE FOODS INC.

808 Hamilton St.
Manitowoc WI 54220
Phone: 920-684-3356
Fax: 920-686-4033
Web: www.lakesidefoods.com

CEO: –
CFO: –
HR: –
FYE: April 30
Type: Private

Lakeside Foods is full of beans — green wax lima and more. The company specializes in the production of private-label canned and frozen vegetables and beans. Lakeside's customers are retail food industry companies including Roundy's and IGA located in the Midwest. The food manufacturer and marketer also offers other food items such as canned meat and stews; jams jellies and preserves; frozen and shelf-stable meals; salsa and other sauces; and whipped toppings. The food maker operates more than a dozen plants and about 10 distribution centers in both Minnesota and Wisconsin. Lakeside exports its food products to nearly 15 countries overseas.

LAKESIDE INDUSTRIES, INC.

6505 226TH PL SE STE 200
ISSAQUAH, WA 980278905
Phone: 425-313-2600
Fax: –
Web: www.lakesideindustries.com

CEO: Timothy Lee Jr
CFO: Hank Waggoner
HR: –
FYE: November 30
Type: Private

Lakeside Industries is one of the largest highway contractors in the Pacific Northwest. A leading asphalt paving contractor and manufacturer the company works on municipal commercial and industrial sites as well as residential projects. It also sells hot-mix and cold asphalt to other paving contractors. It has about a dozen offices in western Washington northwestern Oregon and central Idaho. Owned by the founding Lee family Lakeside Industries was established when the family combined their mining sand and gravel asphalt and trucking businesses in 1972.

	Annual Growth	11/02	11/03	11/04	11/05	11/07
Sales ($ mil.)	10.9%	–	136.1	0.0	147.5	206.0
Net income ($ mil.)	–	–	0.0	0.0	6.0	0.0
Market value ($ mil.)	–	–	–	–	–	–
Employees	–	–	–	–	–	750

LAM RESEARCH CORP

NMS: LRCX

4650 Cushing Parkway
Fremont, CA 94538
Phone: 510 572-0200
Fax: 510 572-6454
Web: www.lamresearch.com

CEO: Timothy Archer
CFO: Douglas Bettinger
HR: –
FYE: June 27
Type: Public

Lam Research is a leading manufacturer of the equipment used to make semiconductors. Its plasma etch machines are used to create tiny circuitry patterns on silicon wafers. The company also makes cleaning equipment that keeps unwanted particles from contaminating processed wafers. Lam also provides products and services to maximize equipment performance. Lam's customers include some of the world's largest chip makers such as Micron Technology and Samsung Electronics. Customers in four Asian countries account for nearly 85% of Lam's revenue. The company traces its historical roots back to 1980.

	Annual Growth	06/17	06/18	06/19	06/20	06/21
Sales ($ mil.)	16.2%	8,013.6	11,077.0	9,653.6	10,044.7	14,626.2
Net income ($ mil.)	23.2%	1,697.8	2,380.7	2,191.4	2,251.8	3,908.5
Market value ($ mil.)	42.8%	21,628.8	24,894.9	26,767.4	43,109.4	89,838.3
Employees	10.7%	9,400	10,900	10,700	11,300	14,100

LAMAR ADVERTISING CO (NEW)

NMS: LAMR

5321 Corporate Blvd.
Baton Rouge, LA 70808
Phone: 225 926-1000
Fax: –
Web: www.lamar.com

CEO: Sean Reilly
CFO: Jay Johnson
HR: –
FYE: December 31
Type: Public

Lamar Advertising is one of the largest billboard operators in the US along with Outfront Media and Clear Channel Outdoor. The company maintains approximately 153200 billboards in about 45 states plus Canada. It also operates more than 137100 logo sign advertising displays over 47700 transit advertising displays and more than 3600 digital billboard advertising displays as well. In addition Lamar Advertising offers generally large illuminated and generally smaller advertising structures that are located on major highways and streets and target vehicular and pedestrian traffic. Chairman Kevin Reilly Jr. together with members of his family controls about 65% voting stake in the company. The company was established in 1902.

	Annual Growth	12/16	12/17	12/18	12/19	12/20
Sales ($ mil.)	1.1%	1,500.3	1,541.3	1,627.2	1,753.6	1,568.9
Net income ($ mil.)	(5.0%)	298.8	317.7	305.2	372.1	243.4
Market value ($ mil.)	5.5%	6,785.3	7,491.7	6,981.1	9,007.4	8,397.9
Employees	0.0%	3,300	3,400	3,600	3,600	3,300

LAMB WESTON HOLDINGS INC

NYS: LW

599 S. Rivershore Lane
Eagle, ID 83616
Phone: 208 938-1047
Fax: –
Web: www.lambweston.com

CEO: Thomas Werner
CFO: Bernadette M Madarieta
HR: –
FYE: May 30
Type: Public

Lamb Weston Holdings Inc. (Lamb Weston) is the largest supplier of frozen potatoes in North America producing a variety of French fries as well as appetizers such as baked potato skins mozzarella sticks and breaded mushrooms. The company markets its products under Lamb Weston LW Private Reserve Stealth Fries and Sweet Things brand names. It distributes its products to restaurants grocery stores specialty retailers food service distributors and educational institutions. The Idaho-based company has customers across the globe but gets most of its custom from the North American market.

	Annual Growth	05/17	05/18	05/19	05/20	05/21
Sales ($ mil.)	3.8%	3,168.0	3,423.7	3,756.5	3,792.4	3,670.9
Net income ($ mil.)	(0.7%)	326.9	416.8	478.6	365.9	317.8
Market value ($ mil.)	15.9%	6,675.1	9,565.3	9,082.9	8,780.3	12,059.4
Employees	4.7%	6,500	7,200	7,600	7,700	7,800

LANCASTER COLONY CORP   NMS: LANC

380 Polaris Parkway, Suite 400 — CEO: David Ciesinski
Westerville, OH 43082 — CFO: Thomas Pigott
Phone: 614 224-7141 — HR: –
Fax: 614 469-8219 — FYE: June 30
Web: www.lancastercolony.com — Type: Public

Lancaster Colony is a US-based food wholesaler serving three categories of retail products Frozen Breads Refrigerated Dressings and Dips and Shelf-Stable Dressings and Croutons. Specific products include garlic bread salad dressings pizza bases and croutons sold under brands such as New York Brand Bakery Sister Schubert's Marzetti and Flatout. Lancaster Colony is dependent on a small number of large customers with the top five customers accounting for approximately 55% of sales. It also partners with third-parties including Olive Garden Chick-fil-A and Buffalo Wild Wings to produce branded products for retail. Lancaster has 10 main factories and seven warehouses. Lancaster was founded as a holding company in 1961.

	Annual Growth	06/17	06/18	06/19	06/20	06/21
Sales ($ mil.)	5.1%	1,201.8	1,222.9	1,307.8	1,334.4	1,467.1
Net income ($ mil.)	5.4%	115.3	135.3	150.5	137.0	142.3
Market value ($ mil.)	12.1%	3,375.9	3,810.8	4,091.1	4,267.0	5,327.5
Employees	3.4%	2,800	2,900	3,200	3,200	3,200

LAND O' LAKES INC

4001 Lexington Avenue North — CEO: –
Arden Hills, MN 55126 — CFO: –
Phone: 651 481-2222 — HR: –
Fax: – — FYE: December 31
Web: www.landolakesinc.com — Type: Public

Best known for its #1 US butter brand Land O'Lakes looks to butter everyone's bread to boost its bottom line. One of the largest dairy co-ops in the nation it's owned by 4331 dairy farmer/members and some 900 member associations. It markets dairy-based consumer food service and food ingredient items. The co-op makes more than 300 dairy products from the 12 billion pounds of milk that members supply annually. Land O'Lakes produces animal feed through Land O'Lakes Purina Feed. The co-op also offers members seed and crop protection products animal feed and agricultural assistance. It operates dairy facilities in the US and does business in all 50 states and 60-plus countries.

	Annual Growth	12/11	12/12	12/13	12/14	12/15
Sales ($ mil.)	0.3%	12,849.3	14,116.2	14,236.4	14,965.5	13,007.7
Net income ($ mil.)	14.0%	182.2	240.4	306.0	266.5	307.6
Market value ($ mil.)	–	–	–	–	–	–
Employees	4.2%	–	–	9,600	10,000	–

LANDAUER, INC.   NYS: LDR

2 Science Road — CEO: Mike Kaminski
Glenwood, IL 60425 — CFO: –
Phone: 708 755-7000 — HR: –
Fax: – — FYE: September 30
Web: www.landauer.com — Type: Public

If your employees are glowing — and not with joy — Landauer can tell you why. Through its subsidiaries Landauer manufactures and markets dosimeters (radiation detection monitors) used in nuclear plants hospitals and university and government laboratories. Landauer's services include distribution and collection of radiation monitors and exposure reporting. Its HomeBuyer's Preferred subsidiary provides residential radon monitoring services. Landauer also offers medical physics services to hospitals and radiation therapy centers through its GPS subsidiary.

	Annual Growth	09/12	09/13	09/14	09/15	09/16
Sales ($ mil.)	(0.5%)	152.4	150.2	155.1	151.3	149.2
Net income ($ mil.)	(2.0%)	19.3	4.8	(25.2)	14.5	17.8
Market value ($ mil.)	(7.1%)	580.9	498.5	321.1	359.8	432.7
Employees	(2.4%)	660	650	600	600	600

LANDEC CORP.   NMS: LNDC

2811 Airpark Drive — CEO: Albert Bolles
Santa Maria, CA 93455 — CFO: John Morberg
Phone: 650 306-1650 — HR: –
Fax: 650 368-9818 — FYE: May 30
Web: www.landec.com — Type: Public

Landec designs develops manufactures and sells differentiated products for food and biomaterials markets and license technology applications to partners. Its natural food company Curation Foods Inc. focuses on innovating and distributing plant-based foods with 100% clean ingredients to retail club and foodservice channels. Curation Foods can maximize product freshness through its geographically dispersed family of growers refrigerated supply chain and patented BreatheWay packaging technology. Its biomedical company Lifecore Biomedical Inc. offers highly differentiated capabilities in the development fill and finish of sterile injectable pharmaceutical products in syringes and vials including injectable grade Hyaluronic Acid. The company's top customers include Costco Corporation and Walmart.

	Annual Growth	05/17	05/18	05/19	05/20	05/21
Sales ($ mil.)	0.6%	532.3	524.2	557.6	590.4	544.2
Net income ($ mil.)	–	10.6	24.8	0.4	(38.2)	(32.7)
Market value ($ mil.)	(3.2%)	400.4	412.1	276.3	313.0	351.1
Employees	7.8%	670	710	736	796	905

LANDMARK BANCORP INC   NMS: LARK

701 Poyntz Avenue — CEO: Michael Scheopner
Manhattan, KS 66502 — CFO: Mark Herpich
Phone: 785 565-2000 — HR: –
Fax: – — FYE: December 31
Web: www.landmarkbancorpinc.com — Type: Public

Landmark Bancorp is a tourist attraction for Kansas money. It is the holding company for Landmark National Bank which has about 15 branches in communities in central eastern and southwestern Kansas. The bank provides standard commercial banking products including checking savings and money market accounts as well as CDs and credit and debit cards. It primarily uses funds from deposits to write residential and commercial mortgages and business loans. Landmark National Bank offers non-deposit investment services through its affiliation with Investment Planners.

	Annual Growth	12/16	12/17	12/18	12/19	12/20
Assets ($ mil.)	6.9%	911.4	929.5	985.8	998.5	1,188.0
Net income ($ mil.)	21.4%	9.0	4.4	10.4	10.7	19.5
Market value ($ mil.)	(5.0%)	139.8	144.6	115.7	125.0	114.0
Employees	0.0%	292	286	291	289	292

LANDRY'S INC.

1510 W. Loop South — CEO: Tilman J Fertitta
Houston TX 77027 — CFO: Richard H Liem
Phone: 713-850-1010 — HR: –
Fax: 713-850-7205 — FYE: December 31
Web: www.landrysinc.com — Type: Private

Landry's Restaurants is a leading full-service restaurant operator with more than 275 locations throughout the US. The company's estate of eateries is anchored by its flagship Landry's Seafood House chain; other concepts include Rainforest Cafe McCormick & Schmick's Saltgrass Steak House and Bubba Gump Shrimp. Through an agreement with an affiliate Landry's manages the Claim Jumper chain of about 35 restaurants. The company also owns and operates the iconic Golden Nugget Hotel & Casino in Las Vegas along with a number of other entertainment properties including aquariums hotels and other tourist attractions. CEO Tilman Fertitta led a buyout of Landry's in 2010 taking the company private.

LANDSTAR SYSTEM, INC.

NMS: LSTR

13410 Sutton Park Drive South
Jacksonville, FL 32224
Phone: 904 398-9400
Fax: –
Web: www.landstar.com

CEO: James Gattoni
CFO: Federico Pensotti
HR: –
FYE: December 25
Type: Public

Landstar System is a US truckload freight carrier with a fleet of around 17000 third-party trailers (including flatbed step decks drop decks low boys refrigerated and standard dry vans). Its fleet is primarily operated by independent contractors under exclusive contracts and its services are marketed by sales agents. Landstar's freight carrier units transport general commodities and goods such as automotive products building materials chemicals electronics metals foodstuffs and machinery retail as well as military equipment. Customers include third-party logistics providers and government agencies such as the US Department of Defense. In addition to truckload transportation Landstar offers logistics and customs brokerage services.

	Annual Growth	12/17	12/18	12/19	12/20	12/21
Sales ($ mil.)	15.7%	3,648.9	4,619.0	4,089.6	4,136.4	6,540.4
Net income ($ mil.)	21.2%	177.1	255.3	227.7	192.1	381.5
Market value ($ mil.)	13.4%	3,923.9	3,588.4	4,266.2	5,102.2	6,492.4
Employees	2.4%	1,273	1,306	1,333	1,320	1,399

LANE BRYANT INC.

3344 Morse Crossing
Columbus OH 43219
Phone: 614-463-5200
Fax: 614-463-5240
Web: www.lanebryant.com

CEO: –
CFO: –
HR: –
FYE: January 31
Type: Subsidiary

Lane Bryant is a big name in women's plus-size fashion. The nation's #1 plus-size clothing chain operates some 800 full-line and outlet stores in about 45 states that sell moderately-priced private label and select name brand career and casual apparel (in sizes 12 to 32) accessories hosiery and intimate apparel for women ages 35 to 55. Lane Bryant stores are found in malls and strip shopping centers and average about 5500 square feet. Women can also shop online at lanebryant.com. Founded in 1904 by Lena Bryant (she misspelled her name on a bank loan) Lane Bryant is owned by Ascena Retail Group.

LANE POWELL PC

1420 5TH AVE STE 4200
SEATTLE, WA 981012375
Phone: 206-223-7000
Fax: –
Web: www.lanepowell.com

CEO: –
CFO: –
HR: –
FYE: December 31
Type: Private

Lane Powell PC brings the power of attorney to the Pacific Northwest. Operating out of offices in Washington Oregon Alaska and internationally in London the law firm specializes in a range of legal services including corporate finance intellectual property regulation and taxation real estate labor relations and commercial litigation. Lane Powell employs more than 200 attorneys and around 300 support personnel handling local national and international clientele. The law firm traces its roots back to 1889 when it was named Strudwick Peters & Collins. (John Powell arrived that same year while W. Byron Lane joined the firm in 1929.)

	Annual Growth	12/12	12/13	12/14	12/16	12/17
Sales ($ mil.)	0.0%	–	94.3	91.5	99.5	94.4
Net income ($ mil.)	–	–	0.2	(0.2)	1.2	(0.6)
Market value ($ mil.)	–	–	–	–	–	–
Employees	–	–	–	–	–	420

LANGSTON SNYDER L P

17962 COWAN
IRVINE, CA 926146026
Phone: 949-863-9200
Fax: –
Web: www.snyder-langston.com

CEO: John Rochford
CFO: Gary Campanaro
HR: –
FYE: December 31
Type: Private

No Snyder Langston isn't the name of a "wacky neighbor" sitcom character but it might have built the property next door. Snyder Langston develops and builds commercial industrial and multifamily residential properties. Serving business clients ranging from start-ups to Fortune 500 firms the company provides a range of services such as planning design financing government relations general contracting and construction management. Properties that Snyder Langston has developed include business parks retail centers office buildings manufacturing facilities parking garages car dealerships condominiums churches schools and hotels. The firm was founded in 1959 by Donald Snyder and William Langston.

	Annual Growth	12/05	12/06	12/07	12/09	12/10
Sales ($ mil.)	(38.3%)	–	–	238.6	78.9	56.0
Net income ($ mil.)	–	–	–	0.0	(1.5)	(1.7)
Market value ($ mil.)	–	–	–	–	–	–
Employees	–	–	–	–	–	91

LANIER PARKING HOLDINGS INC.

233 PEACHTREE ST
ATLANTA, GA 30303
Phone: 404-523-0864
Fax: –
Web: www.lanierparking.com

CEO: Bijan Eghtedari
CFO: Brian Dubay
HR: –
FYE: December 31
Type: Private

Lanier Parking offers more than just a spot to park your car. It offers a full array of parking and transportation services from shuttle and valet to design/build and financial consulting at more than 300 locations throughout the Southeast. In addition to providing traditional parking management and facility operations the company touts its planning capabilities at sites where there is likely to be insufficient space or heavy congestion such as hospitals hotels municipalities sports and entertainment venues and universities. Its consulting services include feasibility site selection and master planning. The company was founded by J. Michael Robison in 1989.

	Annual Growth	12/07	12/08	12/09	12/10	12/12
Sales ($ mil.)	9.3%	–	59.1	59.6	61.3	84.3
Net income ($ mil.)	19.1%	–	–	2.3	2.1	3.9
Market value ($ mil.)	–	–	–	–	–	–
Employees	–	–	–	–	–	2,000

LANNETT CO., INC.

NYS: LCI

1150 Northbrook Drive, Suite 155
Trevose, PA 19053
Phone: 215 333-9000
Fax: –
Web: www.lannett.com

CEO: Timothy Crew
CFO: John Kozlowski
HR: –
FYE: June 30
Type: Public

Lannett develops manufactures packages markets and distributes generic prescription drugs in the US including Fluphenazine tablets for the management of psychotic disorders Verapamil SR tablets for the treatment of high blood pressure and Methylphenidate CD for the treatment of Attention Deficit Hyperactivity Disorder (ADHD). The company sells its pharmaceutical products to generic pharmaceutical distributors drug wholesalers chain drug retailers private label distributors mail-order pharmacies other pharmaceutical companies and health maintenance organizations. Lannett maintains two facilities in Philadelphia Pennsylvania. It markets more than 100 products mainly tablet capsule or liquid oral generic medications across multiple therapeutic categories.

	Annual Growth	06/17	06/18	06/19	06/20	06/21
Sales ($ mil.)	(6.8%)	633.3	684.6	655.4	545.7	478.8
Net income ($ mil.)	–	(0.6)	28.7	(272.1)	(33.4)	(363.5)
Market value ($ mil.)	(30.8%)	807.4	538.2	239.8	287.3	184.8
Employees	(7.9%)	1,126	1,251	1,020	954	810

LANSING BOARD OF WATER AND LIGHT

1110 S PENNSYLVANIA AVE
LANSING, MI 489121635
Phone: 517-702-6714
Fax: –
Web: www.lbwl.com

CEO: Dick Peffley
CFO: Heather Shawa
HR: –
FYE: June 30
Type: Private

Letting off a little steam is a good thing for Lansing Board of Water and Light which provides electricity to 95000 residential commercial and industrial customers and water to about 55000 customers in Lansing Michigan. The city-owned utility also produces and distributes steam to 162 customers along 14 miles of steam line. Lansing Board of Water and Light can chill out too. Its chilled water system delivers up to 10000 tons of chilled water capacity to 16 customers to cool the interior of buildings in the downtown area. Lansing Board of Water and Light is the largest municipally owned utility in the state. It is also a major employer in the Lansing area.

	Annual Growth	06/14	06/15	06/16	06/17	06/18
Sales ($ mil.)	(4.9%)	–	–	–	371.4	353.1
Net income ($ mil.)	226.1%	–	–	–	4.3	14.1
Market value ($ mil.)	–	–	–	–	–	–
Employees	–	–	–	–	–	740

LANTRONIX INC.

7535 Irvine Center Drive, Suite 100
Irvine, CA 92618
Phone: 949 453-3990
Fax: 949 453-3995
Web: www.lantronix.com

NAS: LTRX
CEO: Paul Pickle
CFO: Jeremy Whitaker
HR: –
FYE: June 30
Type: Public

Lantronix is a provider of software as a service ("SaaS") engineering services and hardware for Edge Computing the Internet of Things ("IoT") and Remote Environment Management ("REM"). Lantronix enables its customers to provide reliable and secure solutions while accelerating their time to market. Lantronix's products and services dramatically simplify operations through the creation development deployment and management of customer projects at scale while providing quality reliability and security. Lantronix which outsources its manufacturing sells primarily through OEMs resellers system integrators and distributors. Its products are geared at a wide range of global markets from energy agriculture environmental infrastructure to government. Ingram Micro and Arrow are its largest customers. The company's largest market is the Americas which accounts for more than 55% of sales.

	Annual Growth	06/17	06/18	06/19	06/20	06/21
Sales ($ mil.)	12.4%	44.7	45.6	46.9	59.9	71.5
Net income ($ mil.)	–	(0.3)	0.7	(0.4)	(10.7)	(4.0)
Market value ($ mil.)	20.7%	70.7	82.6	96.9	107.9	150.1
Employees	24.2%	131	147	210	242	312

LAPOLLA INDUSTRIES INC

Intercontinental Business Park, 15402 Vantage Parkway East, Suite 322
Houston, TX 77032
Phone: 281 219-4700
Fax: –
Web: www.lapolla.com

NBB: LPAD
CEO: Douglas J Kramer
CFO: Jomarc C Marukot
HR: –
FYE: December 31
Type: Public

LaPolla Industries would hate for its customers to have leaky roofs over their heads or insufficiently protected exterior walls. The company makes foam products used to protect roofs and the "building envelope" which is the separation of the exterior and interior parts of a building. It also makes coatings for weatherproofing concrete and metal roofing and other materials. The company changed its name in 2005 when it absorbed subsidiary LaPolla Industries a provider of roof coatings and polyurethane foam construction systems. The former IFT Corp. which had previously been called Urecoats acquired LaPolla in 2005. Chairman Richard Kurtz owns 57% of LaPolla.

	Annual Growth	12/11	12/12	12/13	12/14	12/15
Sales ($ mil.)	(2.3%)	86.2	70.4	71.2	72.1	78.6
Net income ($ mil.)	–	(3.5)	(4.4)	(2.0)	(3.7)	(0.6)
Market value ($ mil.)	(17.2%)	61.1	22.0	91.6	50.1	28.7
Employees	(4.9%)	88	71	73	62	72

LAREDO PETROLEUM HOLDINGS INC.

15 W. Sixth St. Ste. 1800
Tulsa OK 74119
Phone: 918-513-4570
Fax: 918-513-4571
Web: www.laredopetro.com

NYSE: LPI
CEO: Randy A Foutch
CFO: –
HR: –
FYE: December 31
Type: Public

Only in Oklahoma would a company named Laredo Petroleum be based in Tulsa. Laredo Petroleum drills for oil and natural gas across 338000 net acres in the abundant Wolfberry plan in the Permian Basin in West Texas and Granite Wash in the Anadarko Basin located along the Texas Panhandle and into western Oklahoma. The company reported proved reserves of 137000 million barrels of oil equivalent for the first six months of 2011 and has interests in about 1000 gross producing wells. It generated 52% of sales from oil and 47% from gas in 2010. Laredo Petroleum is owned by investment firm Warburg Pincus. It filed an initial public offering in August 2011 and went public ($298 million in proceeds) in December.

LARKIN COMMUNITY HOSPITAL, INC.

7031 SW 62ND AVE
SOUTH MIAMI, FL 331434701
Phone: 305-757-5707
Fax: –
Web: www.larkinhospital.com

CEO: –
CFO: Mark Early
HR: –
FYE: December 31
Type: Private

Larkin Community Hospital may be small but it doesn't skimp on its array of health care services. The 110-bed hospital provides general medical and surgical services to the sun-drenched residents of the Miami-Dade County area of Florida. Larkin Community Hospital offers more than 40 specialties including diagnostic radiology intensive care arthritis services an inpatient psychiatric ward surgery cardiovascular care and rehabilitation (including physical occupational and speech therapy). President and CEO Jack Michel owns the health care facility.

	Annual Growth	12/03	12/04	12/12	12/14	12/16
Sales ($ mil.)	8.9%	–	37.3	74.4	101.5	103.7
Net income ($ mil.)	(9.3%)	–	2.5	2.3	4.7	0.8
Market value ($ mil.)	–	–	–	–	–	–
Employees	–	–	–	–	–	1,225

LAS VEGAS SANDS CORP

3355 Las Vegas Boulevard South
Las Vegas, NV 89109
Phone: 702 923-9000
Fax: –
Web: www.sands.com

NYS: LVS
CEO: Robert Goldstein
CFO: Randy Hyzak
HR: –
FYE: December 31
Type: Public

Las Vegas Sands Corp. (LVSC) is a Fortune 500 company and the leading global developer of destination projects that feature premium accommodations world-class gaming entertainment and retail malls convention and exhibition facilities celebrity chef restaurants and other amenities. Through its majority-owned Sands China subsidiary the company operates The Venetian Macao on the Cotai Strip (the Chinese equivalent of the Las Vegas Strip) as well as four other properties in Macao the only place in China where gambling is legal. LVSC's portfolio also includes the Marina Bay Sands in Singapore and The Venetian Resort and the Sands Expo and Convention Center in Las Vegas. Approximately 80% of the company's revenue is generated outside the US.

	Annual Growth	12/17	12/18	12/19	12/20	12/21
Sales ($ mil.)	(24.3%)	12,882.0	13,729.0	13,739.0	3,612.0	4,234.0
Net income ($ mil.)	–	2,806.0	2,413.0	2,698.0	(1,685.0)	(961.0)
Market value ($ mil.)	(14.2%)	53,089.6	39,765.7	52,745.9	45,533.8	28,756.6
Employees	(3.0%)	50,500	51,500	50,000	46,000	44,700

LAS VEGAS VALLEY WATER DISTRICT

1001 S VALLEY VIEW BLVD
LAS VEGAS, NV 891074447
Phone: 702-870-2011
Fax: –
Web: www.lvvwd.com

CEO: –
CFO: –
HR: –
FYE: June 30
Type: Private

If casinos can bloom in the desert why can't water flow? It can thanks to the Las Vegas Valley Water District (LVVWD) which provides water to some one million residents living in one of the driest places in the US. In addition to Las Vegas the LVVWD serves residents of Blue Diamond Coyote Springs Jean Kyle Canyon Laughlin Searchlight and other parts of Clark County in Southern Nevada. The district delivers water to customers through some 4500 miles of water transmission pipeline connected to 59 pumping stations 104 wells and 94 reservoirs and tanks. (Its tanks and reservoirs have the capacity to store more than 900 million gallons.) The LVVWD sources 90% of its water to the Colorado River.

	Annual Growth	06/06	06/07	06/18	06/20	06/21
Sales ($ mil.)	0.4%	–	377.5	372.3	373.7	397.9
Net income ($ mil.)	9.3%	–	30.0	43.9	54.2	104.6
Market value ($ mil.)	–	–	–	–	–	–
Employees	–	–	–	–	–	1,200

LASALLE HOTEL PROPERTIES

7550 Wisconsin Avenue, 10th Floor
Bethesda, MD 20814
Phone: 301 941-1500
Fax: 301 941-1553
Web: www.lasallehotels.com

NYS: LHO
CEO: –
CFO: –
HR: –
FYE: December 31
Type: Public

LaSalle Hotel Properties is a self-administered and self-managed real estate investment trust (REIT) that invests in renovates and leases full-service luxury hotels in the US. It owns more than 45 properties in 10 states and the District of Columbia. LaSalle Hotel Properties' holdings which altogether boast more than 12000 rooms are typically located in major urban markets near convention centers business districts and resorts. The properties are managed by outside hotel companies that operate under such names as Marriott Sheraton Hilton and Hyatt. LaSalle Hotel Properties became self-managing in 2001 after three years under the wing of Jones Lang LaSalle.

	Annual Growth	12/12	12/13	12/14	12/15	12/16
Sales ($ mil.)	9.1%	867.1	977.3	1,109.8	1,216.6	1,227.6
Net income ($ mil.)	37.2%	71.3	89.9	212.8	135.6	252.8
Market value ($ mil.)	4.7%	2,871.3	3,489.9	4,576.7	2,845.3	3,445.8
Employees	1.5%	33	36	35	35	35

LASALLE UNIVERSITY

1900 W OLNEY AVE
PHILADELPHIA, PA 191411199
Phone: 215-951-1000
Fax: –
Web: www.lasalle.edu

CEO: –
CFO: –
HR: Susan Rohanna
FYE: May 31
Type: Private

La Salle University is an independent Catholic institution of higher learning with an enrollment of more than 7000 students. It offers about 40 undergraduate majors and 15 minors as well as 15 graduate programs (including a doctoral program in Clinical Psychology) and about 40 certificate programs. The liberal arts university consists of three schools: arts and sciences business and nursing and health sciences plus a College of Professional and Continuing Studies. Nursing psychology education accounting and communications are among the school's most popular undergraduate areas of study.

	Annual Growth	05/16	05/17	05/18	05/19	05/20
Sales ($ mil.)	10.0%	–	117.4	114.7	162.2	156.1
Net income ($ mil.)	–	–	5.0	2.2	(0.8)	(1.9)
Market value ($ mil.)	–	–	–	–	–	–
Employees	–	–	–	–	–	900

LASERLOCK TECHNOLOGIES INC.

837 Lindy Ln.
Bala Cynwyd PA 19004
Phone: 610-668-1952
Fax: 610-668-2771
Web: www.laserlocktech.com

OTC: LLTI
CEO: Patrick White
CFO: Margaret Gezerlis
HR: –
FYE: December 31
Type: Public

Willy Wonka could have used LaserLock Technologies to help ensure that each Golden Ticket was the genuine article. A development-stage company LaserLock plans to license an invisible ink to third parties that can be used to authenticate documents. The company's system is targeted to the gambling industry where uses could include verification of cashless tickets from slot machines and detection of counterfeit cards chips or dice. LaserLock has plans to raise additional capital and/or enter into strategic alliances or partnerships with other companies in order to do business.

LASTAR INC.

3555 KETTERING BLVD
MORAINE, OH 45439-2014
Phone: 937-224-8646
Fax: –
Web: www.cablestogo.com

CEO: –
CFO: –
HR: –
FYE: December 31
Type: Private

Lastar is the parent company of two main operating units Cables To Go and Quiktron that provide cabling and connectivity products and services to computer audio/video electrical and industrial distributors.

	Annual Growth	12/03	12/04	12/05	12/06	12/07
Sales ($ mil.)	42.0%	–	32.0	53.3	68.4	91.6
Net income ($ mil.)	42.9%	–	2.0	21.0	3.8	5.9
Market value ($ mil.)	–	–	–	–	–	–
Employees	–	–	–	–	–	420

LATHAM & WATKINS LLP

355 S. Grand Ave.
Los Angeles CA 90071-1560
Phone: 213-485-1234
Fax: 213-891-8763
Web: www.lw.com

CEO: –
CFO: –
HR: –
FYE: December 31
Type: Private - Partnershi

Latham & Watkins' founders Dana Latham and Paul Watkins flipped a coin in 1934 to determine which of their names would go first on the law firm's shingle. From that coin toss the firm has grown into one of the largest in the US and boasts more than 2000 lawyers in about 30 offices around the world from Europe to Asia. Latham & Watkins organizes its practices into five main areas: corporate; environment land and resources; finance; litigation; and tax. The firm has counted companies such as Amgen Time Warner Inc. and Morgan Stanley among its clients.

LATTICE INC
NBB: LTTC

7150 N. Park Drive, Suite 500
Pennsauken, NJ 08109
Phone: 856 910-1166
Fax: 856 910-1811
Web: www.latticeincorporated.com

CEO: Paul Burgess
CFO: Joseph Noto
HR: –
FYE: December 31
Type: Public

Government IT contractor Lattice has constructed a diverse product framework. The company provides data management applications Internet server technology and information systems for federal agencies. Deriving the majority of its revenue from Dept. of Defense it develops applications related to business management geographic information systems (GIS) Web services and geospatial systems. In addition the company's Nexus Call Control System provides technology that allows correctional facilities to monitor and control inmate collect-only phone calls. Lattice which began in the 1970s as a telephone services company also offers direct telecom services to correctional facilities.

	Annual Growth	12/11	12/12	12/13	12/14	12/15
Sales ($ mil.)	(9.8%)	11.4	10.8	8.3	8.9	7.6
Net income ($ mil.)	–	(6.1)	(0.6)	(1.0)	(1.8)	(5.5)
Market value ($ mil.)	(22.1%)	11.4	7.6	15.6	9.5	4.2
Employees	(11.5%)	44	37	26	23	27

LATTICE SEMICONDUCTOR CORP
NMS: LSCC

5555 NE Moore Court
Hillsboro, OR 97124
Phone: 503 268-8000
Fax: –

CEO: James Anderson
CFO: Sherri Luther
HR: –
FYE: January 02
Type: Public

Lattice Semiconductor is a developer of technologies that it monetize through different programmable logic semiconductor products system solutions design services and licenses. Lattice also low programmable leader that solves customer problems across the network from Edge to the Cloud in growing communications computing industrial consumer and automotive applications. Its field-programmable gate arrays (FPGAs) devices enable us to provide its customers with a strong growing base of control connect and compute technologies. The majority of sales come from Asia.

	Annual Growth	12/16	12/17	12/18	12/19*	01/21
Sales ($ mil.)	(0.9%)	427.1	386.0	398.8	404.1	408.1
Net income ($ mil.)	–	(54.1)	(70.6)	(26.3)	43.5	47.4
Market value ($ mil.)	44.2%	1,002.7	787.4	927.8	2,619.8	6,242.3
Employees	(5.4%)	986	834	754	747	746

*Fiscal year change

LAUREN ENGINEERS & CONSTRUCTORS, INC.

901 S 1ST ST
ABILENE, TX 796021502
Phone: 325-670-9660
Fax: –
Web: www.laurenec.com

CEO: –
CFO: –
HR: –
FYE: December 31
Type: Private

Lauren Engineers & Constructors is a contractor that targets the power chemical and polymer oil and gas and refining industries. In addition to its core engineering procurement and construction capabilities the company offers fabrication project management and mechanical and electrical maintenance services. With offices in the southern US Lauren Engineers & Constructors serves about 25 states. It also operates in Canada centered from its presence in Calgary. Some of its power and chemical customers include Flying J Florida Power & Light General Electric Company and Procter & Gamble. The company was originally established in 1984 as a subsidiary of Comstock Mechanical.

	Annual Growth	12/12	12/13	12/14	12/15	12/16
Sales ($ mil.)	14.7%	–	163.3	237.4	582.6	246.2
Net income ($ mil.)	–	–	(3.4)	3.9	14.2	7.3
Market value ($ mil.)	–	–	–	–	–	–
Employees	–	–	–	–	–	1,100

LAWNWOOD MEDICAL CENTER, INC.

1700 S 23RD ST
FORT PIERCE, FL 349504899
Phone: 772-461-4000
Fax: –
Web: www.lawnwoodmed.com

CEO: Eric Goldman
CFO: Robert Dunwoody Jr
HR: –
FYE: September 30
Type: Private

Lawnwood Regional Medical Center & Heart Institute part of the HCA system of health care providers is a 340-bed acute-care hospital that serves Florida's Treasure Coast area. Its Heart Institute is a specialty cardiac facility. The hospital's 35-bed Lawnwood Pavilion facility provides inpatient mental health and physical rehabilitation services. The hospital also provides specialty services in the areas of women's and children's health heart and prostate surgery diagnostic imaging and medical laboratory services. Lawnwood Regional is part of HCA's East Florida division.

	Annual Growth	03/07	03/08	03/09*	09/14	09/15
Sales ($ mil.)	347.5%	–	–	0.0	283.9	300.1
Net income ($ mil.)	658.3%	–	–	0.0	59.3	54.2
Market value ($ mil.)	–	–	–	–	–	–
Employees	–	–	–	–	–	1,200

*Fiscal year change

LAWRENCE + MEMORIAL HOSPITAL, INC.

365 MONTAUK AVE
NEW LONDON, CT 063204769
Phone: 860-442-0711
Fax: –
Web: www.lmhospital.org

CEO: Bruce D Cummings
CFO: –
HR: –
FYE: September 30
Type: Private

Lawrence & Memorial Hospital (L + M) connects residents of Connecticut with health care whether they're near the Rhode Island border or enjoying the Connecticut River. The not-for-profit hospital founded in 1912 provides services to a 10-town region on the Connecticut shoreline and neighboring areas in the Northeast. L + M has roughly 280 beds and provides general acute care including medical surgical rehabilitative pediatric psychiatric and obstetrical services. The hospital also runs about a dozen community physician practices and specialty clinics.L + M is owned by Yale New Haven Health Services.

	Annual Growth	09/11	09/12	09/13	09/14	09/15
Sales ($ mil.)	3.7%	–	–	315.4	337.1	339.3
Net income ($ mil.)	16.6%	–	–	10.8	6.0	14.6
Market value ($ mil.)	–	–	–	–	–	–
Employees	–	–	–	–	–	2,200

LAWSON PRODUCTS, INC.
NMS: LAWS

8770 W. Bryn Mawr Avenue, Suite 900
Chicago, IL 60631
Phone: 773 304-5050
Fax: –
Web: www.lawsonproducts.com

CEO: Michael Decata
CFO: Ronald Knutson
HR: –
FYE: December 31
Type: Public

Lawson Products offers more than 357000 different industrial supply products from about 3100 suppliers. Major product types include fasteners cutting tools and abrasives fluid power products aftermarket automotive supplies and safety equipment. Lawson serves industrial commercial institutional and government maintenance repair and operations (MRO) markets. The company primarily operates by buying in bulk and redistributing products to customers. Sales are generated mainly in the US via about 1100 sales representatives who also provide inventory management services. In addition Lawson's Bolt business serves customers in Western Canada.

	Annual Growth	12/16	12/17	12/18	12/19	12/20
Sales ($ mil.)	6.2%	276.6	305.9	349.6	370.8	351.6
Net income ($ mil.)	–	(1.6)	29.7	6.2	7.2	15.1
Market value ($ mil.)	20.9%	215.7	224.3	286.3	472.1	461.3
Employees	4.7%	1,590	1,720	1,740	1,770	1,910

LAYNE CHRISTENSEN CO
NMS: LAYN

1800 Hughes Landing Boulevard Ste 800
The Woodlands, TX 77380
Phone: 281 475-2600
Fax: 281 475-2733
Web: www.layne.com

CEO: Michael J Caliel
CFO: J Michael Anderson
HR: Tracey Waheed
FYE: January 31
Type: Public

Layne Christensen aims to christen new water and mineral sources around the world. The company provides drilling and construction services related to water sourcing and delivery wastewater treatment and mineral exploration. Its clients include public and private water utilities industrial companies and mining firms. Layne Christensen's contract work and services on water and wastewater operations account for around 80% of its revenue while its mineral exploration operations comprise most of the rest. Layne Christensen has 85 sales and operations offices worldwide throughout North America and in Africa Australia Europe and Brazil.

	Annual Growth	01/13	01/14	01/15	01/16	01/17
Sales ($ mil.)	(13.5%)	1,075.6	859.3	797.6	683.0	602.0
Net income ($ mil.)	–	(36.7)	(128.6)	(110.2)	(44.8)	(52.2)
Market value ($ mil.)	(17.6%)	449.0	335.9	160.2	101.4	206.6
Employees	(14.2%)	4,600	4,100	3,380	2,680	2,491

LCA-VISION INC.
NMS: LCAV

7840 Montgomery Road
Cincinnati, OH 45236
Phone: 513 792-9292
Fax: 513 792-5620
Web: www.lca-vision.com

CEO: Craig Joffe
CFO: –
HR: –
FYE: December 31
Type: Public

LCA-Vision thinks its services are a sight better than glasses. The company provides laser vision correction procedures at about 55 Lasik"Plus" freestanding facilities. LCA-Vision's facilities treat nearsightedness farsightedness and astigmatism primarily using laser-assisted in situ keratomileusis (LASIK) which reshapes the cornea with a computer-guided excimer laser. Additionally the company's centers offer photorefractive keratectomy (PRK) and other corrective procedures. LCA-Vision operates through centers located in major cities across North America.

	Annual Growth	12/08	12/09	12/10	12/11	12/12
Sales ($ mil.)	(16.1%)	205.2	129.2	99.8	103.0	101.5
Net income ($ mil.)	–	(6.6)	(33.2)	(20.6)	(6.2)	(8.5)
Market value ($ mil.)	(8.7%)	78.3	97.5	109.5	55.2	54.3
Employees	(9.5%)	568	450	365	380	381

LCI INDUSTRIES
NYS: LCII

3501 County Road 6 East
Elkhart, IN 46514
Phone: 574 535-1125
Fax: –
Web: www.lci1.com

CEO: Jason Lippert
CFO: Brian Hall
HR: –
FYE: December 31
Type: Public

LCI Industries makes components for recreational vehicle (RVs) and other original equipment manufacturers. Through its primary operating subsidiary Lippert Components the company makes windows and doors chassis furniture and slide-out walls for travel trailers and fifth-wheel RVs. The company also serves adjacent markets including manufactured home buses trailers used to haul boats livestock equipment and other cargo trucks modular housing and trains. LCI's aftermarket segment sells to RV and trailer dealers distributors and service centers. Over 90% of the company's sales came from its customers from its US customers.

	Annual Growth	12/16	12/17	12/18	12/19	12/20
Sales ($ mil.)	13.6%	1,678.9	2,147.8	2,475.8	2,371.5	2,796.2
Net income ($ mil.)	5.1%	129.7	132.9	148.6	146.5	158.4
Market value ($ mil.)	4.7%	2,710.6	3,270.3	1,680.4	2,695.0	3,262.2
Employees	12.8%	7,654	9,852	10,260	10,500	12,400

LCNB CORP
NAS: LCNB

2 North Broadway
Lebanon, OH 45036
Phone: 513 932-1414
Fax: –
Web: www.lcnb.com

CEO: Eric Meilstrup
CFO: Robert Haines
HR: –
FYE: December 31
Type: Public

It just makes cents that LCNB counts bucks in the Buckeye State. The firm is the holding company for LCNB National Bank which operates some 36 offices across southwestern Ohio. The bank serves about 10 Ohio counties offering personal and commercial banking services. such as checking and savings accounts money markets IRAs and CDs. Residential mortgages account for nearly half of the company's loan book. Other offerings include commercial mortgages consumer loans including credit cards and business loans. It also provides trust services. LCNB's subsidiary Dakin Insurance Agency sells commercial and personal property/casualty insurance.

	Annual Growth	12/16	12/17	12/18	12/19	12/20
Assets ($ mil.)	7.5%	1,306.8	1,295.6	1,636.9	1,639.3	1,745.9
Net income ($ mil.)	12.6%	12.5	13.0	14.8	18.9	20.1
Market value ($ mil.)	(10.8%)	299.0	263.0	194.8	248.2	188.9
Employees	4.1%	282	310	325	332	331

LDR HOLDING CORP
NMS: LDRH

13785 Research Boulevard, Suite 200
Austin, TX 78750
Phone: 512 344-3333
Fax: –
Web: www.ldrholding.com

CEO: Christophe Lavigne
CFO: Robert McNamara
HR: –
FYE: December 31
Type: Public

LDR Holdings is at the spinal frontier of medical devices. The company makes cervical disc replacements used in spinal implant surgeries. Its VerteBRIDGE fusion device is affixed to discs without using screws and its Mobi-C non-fusion device is the only FDA approved implant for one- and two-level cervical disc surgeries. Mobi-C received FDA approval in 2013. LDR Holdings also makes and sells traditional fusion products under the brands C-Plate Easyspine MC+ ROI and SpineTune. Its products are sold in more than 25 countries but the US accounts for about 70% of sales. Founded in France in 2000 LDR Holdings went public in 2013 raising $75 million in its IPO which it will use to launch Mobi-C in the US.

	Annual Growth	12/10	12/11	12/12	12/13	12/14
Sales ($ mil.)	–	0.0	78.0	90.9	111.6	141.3
Net income ($ mil.)	–	0.0	(1.8)	(9.7)	(27.9)	(11.0)
Market value ($ mil.)	–	0.0	–	–	624.4	867.3
Employees	24.8%	–	–	290	323	452

LE MOYNE COLLEGE

1419 SALT SPRINGS RD
SYRACUSE, NY 132141301
Phone: 315-445-4100
Fax: –
Web: www.lemoyne.edu

CEO: –
CFO: –
HR: –
FYE: May 31
Type: Private

Le Moyne College offers more than 700 courses leading to Bachelor of Arts or Bachelor of Science degrees in 24 different majors. A Jesuit Catholic school Le Moyne has approximately 2200 undergraduate students and 700 students in the graduate program which offers degrees in business administration and education. It has a 13-1 ratio of students to faculty. Le Moyne was founded in 1946.

	Annual Growth	05/13	05/14	05/15	05/17	05/18
Sales ($ mil.)	(6.7%)	–	116.4	123.2	88.3	88.3
Net income ($ mil.)	22.1%	–	8.0	7.9	17.8	17.8
Market value ($ mil.)	–	–	–	–	–	–
Employees	–	–	–	–	–	500

LEAF GROUP LTD   NYS: LEAF

1655 26th Street
Santa Monica, CA 90404
Phone: 310 656-6253
Fax: -
Web: www.leafgroup.com

CEO: Sean Moriarty
CFO: Brian Gephart
HR: -
FYE: December 31
Type: Public

Leaf Group is a diversified consumer internet company that builds enduring digital-first brands that reach passionate audiences in large and growing lifestyle categories including fitness and wellness and art and design. Leaf Group's Marketplaces segment serve a global community of approximately 475000 independent artists that empower artists to reach a global audience. It also include made-to-order marketplace business site Society6.com and SaatchiArt.com an online art gallery. Its media properties that educate and inform consumers on a broad range of topics reached more than 69 million unique visitors each month in the US. Around 85% of total revenue comes from domestic market.

	Annual Growth	12/15	12/16	12/17	12/18	12/19
Sales ($ mil.)	5.3%	126.0	113.5	129.0	155.0	155.0
Net income ($ mil.)	-	(43.5)	(2.0)	(31.1)	(23.2)	(26.8)
Market value ($ mil.)	(7.7%)	144.6	172.2	260.2	180.0	105.1
Employees	(0.6%)	350	265	286	346	341

LEAP WIRELESS INTERNATIONAL INC   NMS: LEAP

5887 Copley Drive
San Diego, CA 92111
Phone: 858 882-6000
Fax: -
Web: www.leapwireless.com

CEO: S Douglas Hutcheson
CFO: R Perley McBride
HR: -
FYE: December 31
Type: Public

Leap Wireless wants to hurdle the competition. Through its Cricket Communications subsidiary the company provides wireless voice and data services to some 5.3 million customers (down from 6 million in 2012) in 48 US states and the District of Columbia. It primarily targets the youth and minority markets with no-contract flexible payment plans that are a key component of its marketing message. Leap's service features unlimited flat-rate local calling a prepaid roaming option multimedia music and wireless data as well as mobile Web access through its Cricket Broadband service. The company makes sales through its chain of 195 retail locations via partnerships with distributors and resellers and on the Internet. It is being acquired by AT&T.

	Annual Growth	12/08	12/09	12/10	12/11	12/12
Sales ($ mil.)	12.5%	1,958.9	2,383.2	2,697.2	3,071.1	3,142.3
Net income ($ mil.)	-	(147.8)	(238.0)	(785.1)	(317.7)	(187.3)
Market value ($ mil.)	(29.5%)	2,129.5	1,389.9	970.9	735.7	526.6
Employees	(1.0%)	3,423	4,202	4,362	3,891	3,292

LEAPFROG ENTERPRISES INC   NYS: LF

6401 Hollis Street, Suite 100
Emeryville, CA 94608-1463
Phone: 510 420-5000
Fax: -
Web: www.leapfroginvestor.com

CEO: Nick Delany
CFO: Alec Anderson
HR: -
FYE: March 31
Type: Public

If putting pen to interactive paper helps your little Einstein learn LeapFrog Enterprises wants to spend some time with your pint-sized genius. The toy maker develops interactive reading systems educational games books and learning toys in five languages covering subjects from math to music. Its bestselling brands include LeapPad Leapster LeapBand Learning Path and Tag. Products are sold to retailers distributors and schools worldwide as well as to consumers via the company's website. LeapFrog's target market is infants and children through age nine. Former vice chairman and CEO Michael Wood founded LeapFrog in 1995 because he felt the toy market offered nothing to help his 3-year-old learn phonics. Vtech Holdings agreed to buy LeapFrog in February 2016 for $72 million.

	Annual Growth	12/11	12/12	12/13*	03/14	03/15
Sales ($ mil.)	(7.1%)	455.1	581.3	553.6	56.9	339.1
Net income ($ mil.)	-	19.9	86.5	84.0	(11.8)	(218.8)
Market value ($ mil.)	(21.0%)	394.0	608.2	559.6	528.6	153.6
Employees	1.5%	494	552	579	-	524

*Fiscal year change

LEAR CORP.   NYS: LEA

21557 Telegraph Road
Southfield, MI 48033
Phone: 248 447-1500
Fax: 248 447-5250
Web: www.lear.com

CEO: Raymond Scott
CFO: Jason Cardew
HR: -
FYE: December 31
Type: Public

Lear Corporation is a leading manufacturer of seating and related components for automobiles. In addition to seating the company's E-Systems business produces automotive electronics and manufactures wire harnesses junction boxes terminals and connectors and body control modules. The company operates from about 255 facilities in about 40 countries. It generates over 75% of revenue outside the US. Its largest customers are General Motors Ford Daimler Volkswagen and Stellantis. Lear traces its history back to 1917 when it was founded in Detroit as American Metal Products.

	Annual Growth	12/17	12/18	12/19	12/20	12/21
Sales ($ mil.)	(1.5%)	20,467.0	21,148.5	19,810.3	17,045.5	19,263.1
Net income ($ mil.)	(27.0%)	1,313.4	1,149.8	753.6	158.5	373.9
Market value ($ mil.)	0.9%	10,534.3	7,326.2	8,181.3	9,483.0	10,909.4
Employees	(0.8%)	165,000	169,000	164,100	174,600	160,100

LEARJET INC.

1 Learjet Way
Wichita KS 67209
Phone: 316-946-2000
Fax: 316-946-2200
Web: www.learjet.com

CEO: -
CFO: -
HR: -
FYE: January 31
Type: Subsidiary

A pioneer in the aerospace industry Learjet Inc. builds high-performance business jets — the limos of the sky. The company has produced more than 2000 aircraft at its Wichita Kansas plant since its first jet rolled off the assembly line in 1964. Current Learjet models — light business aircraft including the 40 XR 45 XR 60 XR and 85 — tout superior cruise velocities the highest operating ceilings ascent rates and operating maximums and competitive operating costs. In addition to private businesses Learjet occasionally wins work with the US Air Force. The company has operated as a subsidiary of Canada's Bombardier since 1990.

LEARNING TREE INTERNATIONAL INC   NBB: LTRE

13650 Dulles Technology Drive, Suite 400
Herndon, VA 20171
Phone: 703 709-9119
Fax: -
Web: www.learningtree.com

CEO: Richard A Spires
CFO: Igor Lima
HR: -
FYE: September 28
Type: Public

This tree of knowledge won't trick you into eating evil apples. It will however further your knowledge of information. Information technology that is. The Learning Tree offers more than 180 courses including professional certification programs to IT managers in corporations and government agencies. The bulk of the company's course library focuses on IT topics such as Web development programming languages network security and operating systems. Learning Tree has a growing list of management training offerings as well with courses in business skills leadership development and project management. It offers its classes in Japan Europe and North America and online.

	Annual Growth	10/14	10/15*	09/16	09/17	09/18
Sales ($ mil.)	(14.1%)	118.2	94.9	81.6	70.7	64.3
Net income ($ mil.)	-	0.0	(12.6)	(12.7)	(2.1)	(2.1)
Market value ($ mil.)	(15.3%)	30.9	16.7	24.2	39.7	15.9
Employees	(5.4%)	1,006	948	288	257	806

*Fiscal year change

LEE COUNTY ELECTRIC COOPERATIVE, INC.

4980 BAYLINE DR
FORT MYERS, FL 339173998
Phone: 800-599-2356
Fax: -
Web: www.lcec.net

CEO: Dennie Hamilton
CFO: Donald Schleicher
HR: -
FYE: December 31
Type: Private

If you are a Floridian who is a really early riser or a night owl Lee County Electric Cooperative (LCEC) may help light your way. The electric cooperative provides power to more than 198880 residential and commercial customers across five counties in southwestern Florida (Lee County and parts of Collier Hendry Charlotte and Broward counties. The member-owned non-profit electric utility operates more than 8000 miles of transmission and distribution lines and more than 20 substations. Tampa-based Seminole Electric Cooperative serves as LCEC's wholesale power supplier.

	Annual Growth	12/09	12/10	12/11	12/12	12/15
Sales ($ mil.)	0.8%	-	-	-	404.5	413.8
Net income ($ mil.)	-	-	-	-	2.5	(0.3)
Market value ($ mil.)	-	-	-	-	-	-
Employees	-	-	-	-	-	400

LEE ENTERPRISES, INC.

4600 E. 53rd Street
Davenport, IA 52807
Phone: 563 383-2100
Fax: -

NMS: LEE
CEO: Kevin Mowbray
CFO: Timothy Millage
HR: Astrid Garcia
FYE: September 26
Type: Public

Lee Enterprises is a trusted local news provider and an innovative digitally focused marketing solutions company operating in more than 75 mid-sized markets across some 25 states. Its local media operations range from large daily newspapers and the associated digital products such as the St. Louis Post-Dispatch and The Buffalo News to non-daily newspapers with news websites and digital platforms serving smaller communities. Lee also offers services including a full service digital marketing agency in Amplified Digital Agency as well as one of the largest web-hosting and content management services providers in North America through their majority-owned subsidiary TownNews. The company's printed newspapers reach almost 1.2 million households daily.

	Annual Growth	09/17	09/18	09/19	09/20	09/21
Sales ($ mil.)	8.8%	566.9	544.0	509.9	618.0	794.6
Net income ($ mil.)	(4.6%)	27.5	45.8	14.3	(3.1)	22.8
Market value ($ mil.)	83.2%	12.4	15.6	11.8	4.8	139.8
Employees	9.6%	3,555	3,241	2,954	5,613	5,130

LEE LEWIS CONSTRUCTION, INC.

7810 ORLANDO AVE
LUBBOCK, TX 794231942
Phone: 806-797-8400
Fax: -
Web: www.leelewis.com

CEO: -
CFO: -
HR: -
FYE: June 30
Type: Private

General builder Lee Lewis Construction has waltzed across Texas and beyond to keep in step with the top US contractors. The company provides construction-related services and construction management for commercial institutional and industrial projects. Among its projects is the Garland ISD Special Events Center in Garland Texas; it also worked on the Grand Floridian Resort at Walt Disney World. The company earns much of its revenue from projects for Texas school systems. Projects for hometown neighbor Texas Tech University have generated a significant portion of the company's business. CEO Lee Lewis founded the company in 1976.

	Annual Growth	06/03	06/04	06/05	06/06	06/09
Sales ($ mil.)	10.6%	-	138.8	176.5	245.1	229.5
Net income ($ mil.)	47.7%	-	0.9	2.3	4.3	6.3
Market value ($ mil.)	-	-	-	-	-	-
Employees	-	-	-	-	-	200

LEE MEMORIAL HEALTH SYSTEM FOUNDATION, INC.

2776 CLEVELAND AVE
FORT MYERS, FL 339015864
Phone: 239-343-2000
Fax: -
Web: www.leehealth.org

CEO: James R Nathan
CFO: -
HR: -
FYE: September 30
Type: Private

Not feeling so bright in the Sunshine State? Lee Memorial Health System can help. Serving residents of Fort Myers and surrounding areas in Southwestern Florida's Lee County the community-owned not-for-profit health care system is home to four acute care hospitals (with a total of more than 1400 beds) a home health agency a 112-bed nursing home and numerous outpatient treatment and diagnostic centers. The flagship Lee Memorial Hospital also houses a 60-bed inpatient rehabilitation hospital and the HealthPark Medical Center location includes a dedicated 100-bed children's hospital. Lee Memorial Health Systems' corporate services include pre-employment screenings drug screens and wellness programs.

	Annual Growth	09/01	09/02	09/03	09/04	09/18
Sales ($ mil.)	8.6%	-	477.3	522.6	585.3	1,790.0
Net income ($ mil.)	17.4%	-	7.7	51.0	46.8	101.0
Market value ($ mil.)	-	-	-	-	-	-
Employees	-	-	-	-	-	7,870

LEE UNIVERSITY

1120 N OCOEE ST STE 102
CLEVELAND, TN 373114475
Phone: 423-614-8000
Fax: -
Web: www.leeuniversity.edu

CEO: -
CFO: -
HR: -
FYE: June 30
Type: Private

Lee University is a Christian liberal arts college located in southeastern Tennessee. Boasting an enrollment of more than 4250 students the university offers academic programs at both baccalaureate and master's levels. Religion courses are a requirement of each student. Lee University is owned and operated by the Church of God. It was founded in 1918.

	Annual Growth	06/07	06/08	06/09	06/10	06/11
Sales ($ mil.)	-	-	-	0.0	74.8	75.2
Net income ($ mil.)	-	-	-	0.0	9.7	4.6
Market value ($ mil.)	-	-	-	-	-	-
Employees	-	-	-	-	-	635

LEGACY EMANUEL HOSPITAL & HEALTH CENTER

2801 N GANTENBEIN AVE
PORTLAND, OR 972271623
Phone: 503-413-2200
Fax: -
Web: www.legacyhealth.org

CEO: George J Brown
CFO: -
HR: -
FYE: March 31
Type: Private

Legacy Emanuel Hospital and Health Center part of the Legacy Health System provides acute and specialized health care to residents of Portland Oregon and surrounding communities. The 420-bed teaching hospital's operations include centers devoted to trauma treatment burn care oncology birthing neurosurgery orthopedics and cardiology. It also houses a pediatric hospital and operates the region's Life Flight Network service which is owned by a consortium of local hospitals. Legacy Emanuel's emergency department handles more than 15600 visits every year.

	Annual Growth	03/13	03/14	03/15	03/17	03/20
Sales ($ mil.)	7.0%	-	649.8	705.0	778.2	977.4
Net income ($ mil.)	-	-	31.0	29.5	(12.1)	(49.2)
Market value ($ mil.)	-	-	-	-	-	-
Employees	-	-	-	-	-	3,619

LEGACY FARMERS COOPERATIVE

6566 COUNTY ROAD 236　　　　　　　　　　　　　　　　CEO: –
FINDLAY, OH 458409769　　　　　　　　　　　　　　　CFO: –
Phone: 419-423-2611　　　　　　　　　　　　　　　　 HR: –
Fax: –　　　　　　　　　　　　　　　　　　　　FYE: February 28
Web: www.legacyfarmers.com　　　　　　　　　　　　Type: Private

Supporting local farmers gives Blanchard Valley Farmers Cooperative (BVFC) roots and reach. Founded in 1989 BVFC has about 1700 area members. The co-op owns more than a dozen locations including four agronomy stations two seasonal grain facilities a farm and garden store and two petroleum sites. Member-farmers benefit from the co-op's array of products and services including seed feed fertilizer grain crop storage crop applications and farming equipment sales and rental. The feed store also sells mulch birdseed and pet supplies as well as conducts soil testing and arranges seeding and fertilizer programs. BVFC's petroleum locations offer gasoline and home-heating oil among several products.

	Annual Growth	02/14	02/15	02/19	02/20	02/21
Sales ($ mil.)	(3.2%)	–	278.5	236.1	153.0	229.0
Net income ($ mil.)	(4.1%)	–	4.6	2.7	(3.7)	3.6
Market value ($ mil.)	–	–	–	–	–	–
Employees	–	–	–	–	–	122

LEGACY HEALTH

1919 NW LOVEJOY ST　　　　　　　　　　　　　　CEO: George J Brown
PORTLAND, OR 972091503　　　　　　　　　　　　　　CFO: –
Phone: 503-415-5600　　　　　　　　　　　　　　　　HR: –
Fax: –　　　　　　　　　　　　　　　　　　　　　FYE: March 31
Web: www.legacyhealth.org　　　　　　　　　　　　　Type: Private

Legacy Health is a locally owned nonprofit health system that offers a unique blend of health services across the Portland/Vancouver metro area and mid-Willamette Valley. Its services range from wellness and urgent care to dedicated children's services and advanced medical centers for patients of all ages. It operates half a dozen hospitals including Legacy Emanuel Medical Center and Legacy Good Samaritan Medical Center as well as the Randall Children's Hospital at Legacy Emanuel. Legacy Health has more than 70 primary care specialty and urgent care clinics and its facilities provide such services as acute and critical care behavioral health and outpatient and health education programs. It also operates labs research and hospice.

	Annual Growth	03/17	03/18	03/19	03/20	03/21
Sales ($ mil.)	2.3%	–	2,117.9	2,219.4	2,336.5	2,266.0
Net income ($ mil.)	53.6%	–	100.2	84.1	(42.1)	363.3
Market value ($ mil.)	–	–	–	–	–	–
Employees	–	–	–	–	–	10,675

LEGACY RESERVES INC　　　　　　　　　　　　　　NMS: LGCY

303 W. Wall, Suite 1800　　　　　　　　　　　　CEO: James Westcott
Midland, TX 79701　　　　　　　　　　　　　　　CFO: Robert Norris
Phone: 432 689-5200　　　　　　　　　　　　　　　HR: –
Fax: –　　　　　　　　　　　　　　　　　　　　FYE: December 31
Web: www.legacylp.com　　　　　　　　　　　　　　Type: Public

Legacy Reserves has its sights set on creating its very own prosperous legacy. The independent oil and gas company explores for oil and gas deposits in the Permian Basin of West Texas and southeast New Mexico and exploits those resources. In 2013 Legacy Reserves had proved reserves of 87.6 million barrels of oil equivalent (70% oil and natural gas liquids; 85% proved developed). The company owns interests in producing oil and natural gas properties in 664 fields in the Permian Basin Texas Panhandle Wyoming North Dakota Montana Oklahoma and several other states. In 2013 it had 664 fields and 8071 gross productive wells of which 3734 were operated and 4337 non-operated.

	Annual Growth	12/13	12/14	12/15	12/16	12/17
Sales ($ mil.)	(2.6%)	485.5	532.3	338.8	314.4	436.3
Net income ($ mil.)	–	(35.3)	(283.6)	(701.5)	(55.8)	(53.9)
Market value ($ mil.)	(51.1%)	2,047.1	830.9	127.2	154.1	117.0
Employees	6.8%	254	300	147	328	331

LEGACYTEXAS FINANCIAL GROUP INC　　　　　　　NMS: LTXB

5851 Legacy Circle　　　　　　　　　　　　　　　　CEO: –
Plano, TX 75024　　　　　　　　　　　　　　　　　CFO: –
Phone: 972 578-5000　　　　　　　　　　　　　　　HR: –
Fax: –　　　　　　　　　　　　　　　　　　　　　FYE: December 31
Web: www.legacytexasfinancialgroup.com　　　　　　Type: Public

With its eye on the Lone Star State LegacyTexas Financial (formerly ViewPoint Financial) provides retail and commercial banking through its LegacyTexas Bank subsidiary which operates about 50 branches located mostly in the Dallas/Fort Worth area. LegacyTexas offers standard deposit products such as checking and savings accounts and CDs and uses deposit funds to originate primarily real estate loans: Commercial Real Estate loans account for nearly 50% of its lending portfolio while consumer real estate loans make up another nearly 20%. Non-real estate commercial loans make up almost 30% of its loan portfolio.

	Annual Growth	12/13	12/14	12/15	12/16	12/17
Assets ($ mil.)	26.7%	3,525.2	4,164.1	7,691.9	8,362.3	9,086.2
Net income ($ mil.)	29.6%	31.7	31.3	70.9	97.8	89.5
Market value ($ mil.)	11.4%	1,320.8	1,147.6	1,203.9	2,071.9	2,031.0
Employees	10.8%	576	530	856	896	869

LEGAL SERVICES CORPORATION

3333 K ST NW STE 1　　　　　　　　　　　　　　　CEO: –
WASHINGTON, DC 200073522　　　　　　　　　　　　CFO: –
Phone: 202-295-1500　　　　　　　　　　　　　　　HR: –
Fax: –　　　　　　　　　　　　　　　　　　　　　FYE: September 30
Web: www.lsc.gov　　　　　　　　　　　　　　　　Type: Private

Legal Services Corporation (LSC) works to deliver Francis Bellamy's pledge "with liberty and justice for all." A private not-for-profit entity established by Congress and President Richard Nixon in 1974 LSC helps poor Americans gain equal access to the judicial system. It doesn't provide legal services directly but instead grants funds to independent local programs throughout the country. It makes grants to more than 130 programs and is the nation's single-largest funder of civil legal aid for the poor (with 811 offices across the US). LSC-funded programs handle about 1.8 million cases each year. About 64 million US citizens are eligible to receive assistance from the organization.

	Annual Growth	09/13	09/14	09/15	09/16	09/18
Sales ($ mil.)	3.7%	–	370.6	377.8	387.9	428.3
Net income ($ mil.)	150.4%	–	0.6	0.9	(0.3)	23.6
Market value ($ mil.)	–	–	–	–	–	–
Employees	–	–	–	–	–	130

LEGALSHIELD　　　　　　　　　　　　　　　　　　NYSE: PPD

1 Pre-Paid Way　　　　　　　　　　　　　　　　　CEO: –
Ada OK 74820　　　　　　　　　　　　　　　　　　CFO: –
Phone: 580-436-1234　　　　　　　　　　　　　　　HR: –
Fax: 580-421-6305　　　　　　　　　　　　　　　　FYE: December 31
Web: www.legalshield.com　　　　　　　　　　　　Type: Private

LegalShield (formerly Pre-Paid Legal Services) wants to help see that justice is done. The company's membership plans which are similar to insurance give participants access to an independent network of attorneys and other legal professionals at provider law firms for a monthly fee. Covered services include IRS audit protection traffic violation defense and will preparation. LegalShieldhas about 1.5 million members mainly in the US but also in Canada. Private equity company MidOcean Partners acquired the company in 2011 and took it private.

LEGALZOOM.COM INC.

101 N. Brand Blvd. 11th Fl.
Glendale CA 91203
Phone: 323-962-8600
Fax: 323-962-8300
Web: www.legalzoom.com

CEO: Daniel Wernikoff
CFO: Noel Watson
HR: –
FYE: December 31
Type: Private

Where there's a will (or a trust or business entity) LegalZoom.com looks to find a virtual way. A provider of online legal services in the US LegalZoom.com offers small businesses and consumers access to a portfolio of self-help interactive legal documents which can be purchased on a transactional basis. Business clients use the company's services to set up legal entities (e.g. LLC Inc.) and apply for trademarks while consumers may set up wills living trusts powers of attorney and even file for divorce. For customers in need of legal advice the company offers access to a network of independent attorneys via subscription. Formed in 1999 LegalZoom filed to go public in mid-2012.

LEGEND OIL & GAS LTD

555 North Point Center East, Suite 410
Alpharetta, GA 30022
Phone: 678 366-4587
Fax: –
Web: www.legendoilandgas.com

NBB: LOGL
CEO: –
CFO: –
HR: –
FYE: December 31
Type: Public

SIN Holdings owns and operates Senior-Inet.com (The Senior Information Network) a Web portal for senior citizens throughout the US seeking information about support services for senior citizens in ten cities in Colorado as well as for the City of Houston. Information categories include health housing senior centers travel services rehabilitation Alzheimer's hospice and adult day care and funeral services. James Vandeberg an attorney from Seattle acquired controlling interest in SIN Holdings from founder and former company president Steve Sinohui.

	Annual Growth	12/12	12/13	12/14	12/15	12/16
Sales ($ mil.)	11.8%	2.5	2.0	0.7	4.7	3.9
Net income ($ mil.)	–	(9.3)	(12.3)	(2.4)	(15.0)	(6.2)
Market value ($ mil.)	(60.3%)	56.5	33.1	1.8	2.8	1.4
Employees	37.7%	5	4	–	17	18

LEGG MASON, INC.

100 International Drive
Baltimore, MD 21202
Phone: 410 539-0000
Fax: –
Web: www.leggmason.com

NYS: LM
CEO: Joseph A Sullivan
CFO: Peter H Nachtwey
HR: –
FYE: March 31
Type: Public

Legg Mason specializes in wealth management and mutual fund management. The financial services firm has several subsidiaries that offer asset management trust services and annuities to retail and institutional investors. Managing around $755 billion in assets across some 130 mutual funds under the Legg Mason and Royce Funds banners the firm also manages around 30 closed-end funds and separately managed accounts. Legg Mason distributes its products through its own offices retirement plans and financial intermediaries as well as through an agreement with Morgan Stanley Smith Barney. The company mostly has offices in North America and the UK but also has a presence in 18 other countries.

	Annual Growth	03/15	03/16	03/17	03/18	03/19
Sales ($ mil.)	0.7%	2,819.1	2,660.8	2,886.9	3,140.3	2,903.3
Net income ($ mil.)	–	237.1	(25.0)	227.3	285.1	(28.5)
Market value ($ mil.)	(16.1%)	4,722.7	2,967.1	3,089.4	3,477.9	2,341.7
Employees	2.1%	2,982	3,066	3,338	3,275	3,246

LEGGETT & PLATT, INC.

No. 1 Leggett Road
Carthage, MO 64836
Phone: 417 358-8131
Fax: –
Web: www.leggett.com

NYS: LEG
CEO: Jack Dolloff
CFO: Jeffrey Tate
HR: –
FYE: December 31
Type: Public

Leggett & Platt (L&P) is a diversified manufacturer serving an array of industries including bedding automotive aerospace office furniture and home furniture. Bedding-related products include steel coils used in mattress innersprings specialty foam used in bedding and furniture and mattresses. L&P also makes machinery for sewing mattress quilting and other industrial sewing and finishing machines. Other products include automotive seating components (wire seat suspensions and motors and actuators for vehicle power systems) and tubing used in aerospace fluid conveyance systems. The US accounts for more than 65% of sales.

	Annual Growth	12/17	12/18	12/19	12/20	12/21
Sales ($ mil.)	6.5%	3,943.8	4,269.5	4,752.5	4,280.2	5,072.6
Net income ($ mil.)	8.3%	292.6	305.9	333.8	247.6	402.4
Market value ($ mil.)	(3.6%)	6,367.2	4,781.1	6,780.7	5,909.6	5,490.7
Employees	(2.2%)	22,200	22,000	22,000	20,400	20,300

LEHIGH UNIVERSITY

27 MEMORIAL DR W UNIT 8
BETHLEHEM, PA 180153005
Phone: 610-758-3000
Fax: –
Web: www.lehigh.edu

CEO: –
CFO: –
HR: –
FYE: June 30
Type: Private

Lehigh University (LU) nestled in eastern Pennsylvania's Lehigh Valley offers about 90 undergraduate programs and majors at colleges of arts and sciences business and economics engineering and applied sciences and education. It also offers more than 40 masters and doctoral degree programs as well as certificate programs. Tuition is more than $40000 per year; more than half of students receive financial aid. LU has an enrollment of nearly 7000 undergraduate and graduate students. The university was founded in 1865 by entrepreneur and philanthropist Asa Packer.

	Annual Growth	06/13	06/14	06/17	06/18	06/21
Sales ($ mil.)	0.9%	–	367.3	396.6	416.3	390.7
Net income ($ mil.)	18.1%	–	156.4	171.6	110.1	499.8
Market value ($ mil.)	–	–	–	–	–	–
Employees	–	–	–	–	–	1,693

LEHIGH VALLEY HEALTH NETWORK, INC.

1247 S CEDAR CREST BLVD # 105
ALLENTOWN, PA 181036298
Phone: 610-402-8000
Fax: –
Web: www.lvhn.org

CEO: Elliot J Sussman
CFO: –
HR: –
FYE: June 30
Type: Private

Lehigh Valley Health Network (LVHN) is a not-for-profit health care provider operates through nine full-service hospital campuses. LVHN serves as a regional referral center for trauma and burn care and organ transplantation as well as specialty care such as cardiology women's health and pediatric surgery. LVHN also boasts a network of physician practices and community health centers as well as home health and hospice units. Through Lehigh Valley Physician Group LVHN has more than 2000 primary care and specialty physicians as well as more than 800 advanced practice clinicians. HNL Lab Medicine provides an extensive range of laboratory tests from the most critical medical applications to simple pre-employment drug screenings.

	Annual Growth	06/17	06/18	06/19	06/20	06/21
Sales ($ mil.)	7.8%	–	2,739.8	2,978.2	3,129.7	3,437.0
Net income ($ mil.)	87.2%	–	106.7	118.5	2.1	700.2
Market value ($ mil.)	–	–	–	–	–	–
Employees	–	–	–	–	–	12,000

LEHMAN TRIKES USA INC. TSX VENTURE: LHT

125 Industrial Dr.
Spearfish SD 57783
Phone: 605-642-2111
Fax: 605-642-1184
Web: www.lehmantrikes.com

CEO: –
CFO: –
HR: –
FYE: November 30
Type: Private

Lehman Trikes proudly proclaims that it is the "leader of the three-world." Through its US subsidiary the company builds motorized tricycles by converting heavy-cruiser motorcycles manufactured by Honda Victory and Suzuki. In 2010 Lehman Trikes ended its supply agreement with Harley-Davidson a customer that represented approximately 80% of the tricycle maker's sales. The company also produces and wholesales the kits for do-it-yourselfers to convert traditional two-wheelers into motor trikes. In addition the company offers a line of accessories including custom wheels lights racks and running boards. The company's products are sold in the US and Canada through a dealer network located in the US.

LEMAITRE VASCULAR INC NMS: LMAT

63 Second Avenue
Burlington, MA 01803
Phone: 781 221-2266
Fax: –
Web: www.lemaitre.com

CEO: –
CFO: Joseph Pellegrino
HR: Daniel Mumford
FYE: December 31
Type: Public

LeMaitre Vascular makes both disposable and implanted surgical vascular devices including catheters and stents under such brands as AnastoClip and Pruitt-Inahara. Originally founded by a vascular surgeon to develop a valvulotome to prepare veins for arterial bypass surgery the company has since expanded its offerings to include a device to create dialysis access sites and another to treat aortic aneurysms. Le Maitre sells about 15 product lines most of which are used in open vascular surgery and some of which are used in endovascular procedures. Its US operation accounts for the highest geographic market.

	Annual Growth	12/16	12/17	12/18	12/19	12/20
Sales ($ mil.)	9.8%	89.2	100.9	105.6	117.2	129.4
Net income ($ mil.)	19.0%	10.6	17.2	22.9	17.9	21.2
Market value ($ mil.)	12.4%	520.1	653.5	485.2	737.8	831.2
Employees	0.4%	397	423	483	479	403

LEIDOS HOLDINGS INC NYS: LDOS

1750 Presidents Street
Reston, VA 20190
Phone: 571 526-6000
Fax: –
Web: www.leidos.com

CEO: Roger Krone
CFO: Christopher Cage
HR: –
FYE: December 31
Type: Public

Leidos Holdings provides cybersecurity information technology and analytics services to government agencies and companies in the defense intelligence homeland security civil and health markets. The company's areas of expertise include operations and logistics; sensors; software development; and systems engineering. It also operates one of the country's largest health system integrators. Most of the company's revenue (over 85%) comes from the US government.

	Annual Growth	12/17	12/18*	01/20	01/21*	12/21
Sales ($ mil.)	7.8%	10,170.0	10,194.0	11,094.0	12,297.0	13,737.0
Net income ($ mil.)	19.8%	366.0	581.0	667.0	628.0	753.0
Market value ($ mil.)	8.3%	9,039.8	7,336.0	13,927.2	14,716.8	12,446.0
Employees	8.5%	31,000	32,000	34,000	39,000	43,000

*Fiscal year change

LENDINGTREE INC (NEW) NMS: TREE

1415 Vantage Park Dr., Suite 700
Charlotte, NC 28203
Phone: 704 541-5351
Fax: –
Web: www.lendingtree.com

CEO: Douglas Lebda
CFO: Trent Ziegler
HR: –
FYE: December 31
Type: Public

LendingTree is the nation's leading online marketplace. Through multiple branded marketplaces LendingTree empowers consumers to shop for financial services the same way they would shop for airline tickets or hotel stays comparing multiple offers from a nationwide network of over 800 partners (refer to as Network Partners). Services include mortgage loans mortgage refinances auto loans personal loans business loans student refinances credit cards insurance and more. In addition it offer tools and resources including free credit scores that facilitate comparison shopping for loans deposit products insurance and other offerings. Through the My LendingTree platform consumers receive free credit scores credit monitoring and recommendations to improve credit health.

	Annual Growth	12/16	12/17	12/18	12/19	12/20
Sales ($ mil.)	24.0%	384.4	617.7	764.9	1,106.6	910.0
Net income ($ mil.)	–	27.5	15.6	96.5	17.8	(48.3)
Market value ($ mil.)	28.2%	1,330.2	4,468.4	2,881.8	3,982.6	3,593.5
Employees	34.4%	399	535	909	1,107	1,303

LELAND STANFORD JUNIOR UNIVERSITY

450 JANE STANFORD WAY
STANFORD, CA 943052004
Phone: 650-723-2300
Fax: –
Web: www.stanford.edu

CEO: –
CFO: Randall S Livingston
HR: –
FYE: August 31
Type: Private

The Leland Stanford Junior University better known as simply Stanford University is one of the top universities in the US. It boasts respected programs across seven schools and about 20 interdisciplinary institutes such as business engineering law and medicine among others. Stanford serves about 17245 students (taught by nearly 2280 faculty members) from all 50 US states and approximately 55 other countries. Its student-teacher ratio sits at about 5:1. A private institution Stanford is supported through an endowment of some $28.9 billion one of the largest in the US. The university was established in 1885 by Leland Stanford Sr. It was named after his son Leland Stanford Jr.

LENNAR CORP NYS: LEN

700 Northwest 107th Avenue
Miami, FL 33172
Phone: 305 559-4000
Fax: –
Web: www.lennar.com

CEO: Richard Beckwitt
CFO: Diane Bessette
HR: –
FYE: November 30
Type: Public

Lennar is one of the largest homebuilding land-owning loan-making leviathans in the US. The company builds single-family attached and detached homes and multi-family rental properties in about 20 states under brand names including Lennar and CalAtlantic Group. Lennar targets first-time move-up active adult and luxury homebuyers and markets its homes as "everything included". The company delivered more about 59800 homes in 2021 at an average price of around $424000. Lennar traces its roots back to 1954 as a local Miami homebuilder and went public in 1971.

	Annual Growth	08/16	08/17	08/18	08/19	08/20
Sales ($ mil.)	30.5%	–	5,604.6	11,311.4	12,262.0	12,455.4
Net income ($ mil.)	(12.6%)	–	2,972.0	2,653.4	1,961.4	1,983.9
Market value ($ mil.)	–	–	–	–	–	–
Employees	–	–	–	–	–	15,000

	Annual Growth	11/17	11/18	11/19	11/20	11/21
Sales ($ mil.)	21.0%	12,646.4	20,571.6	22,259.6	22,488.9	27,130.7
Net income ($ mil.)	52.9%	810.5	1,695.8	1,849.1	2,465.0	4,430.1
Market value ($ mil.)	13.7%	18,798.5	12,794.8	17,861.3	22,715.1	31,455.6
Employees	4.2%	9,111	11,626	10,106	9,495	10,753

LENNOX INTERNATIONAL INC

NYS: LII

2140 Lake Park Blvd.
Richardson, TX 75080
Phone: 972 497-5000
Fax: –
Web: www.lennoxinternational.com

CEO: Todd Bluedorn
CFO: Joseph Reitmeier
HR: –
FYE: December 31
Type: Public

Lennox International makes sure the temperature is just right. The company makes climate control equipment such as heating ventilation air conditioning and refrigeration (HVACR) units for residential commercial and Industrial uses. Its Residential Heating & Cooling segment sells furnaces heat pumps packaged heating and cooling systems indoor air quality equipment comfort control products air conditioners replacement parts and supplies under such brands as Lennox Dave Lennox Signature Collection Armstrong Air Ducane and Lennox Stores among others. Lennox's largest single market is the US which accounts for more than 85% of total sales. Named after inventor Dave Lennox the company was founded in 1895.

	Annual Growth	12/17	12/18	12/19	12/20	12/21
Sales ($ mil.)	2.2%	3,839.6	3,883.9	3,807.2	3,634.1	4,194.1
Net income ($ mil.)	11.0%	305.7	359.0	408.7	356.3	464.0
Market value ($ mil.)	11.7%	7,629.4	8,017.7	8,937.6	10,036.6	11,882.6
Employees	(1.0%)	11,450	11,350	11,200	10,300	11,000

LENOX CORPORATION

1414 RADCLIFFE ST FL 1
BRISTOL, PA 190075418
Phone: 267-525-7800
Fax: –
Web: www.lenox.com

CEO: Bob Burbank
CFO: –
HR: Regina Snedeker
FYE: April 02
Type: Private

Lenox makes and markets tabletop and giftware items under the Lenox and Reed and Barton names. It offers dinnerware flatware kitchenware drinkware accessories and home decors. Lenox's legacy begins in a small art studio to appearances at the White House. Under licensing agreements Lenox makes products under the additional name such as Kate Spade New York. Lenox was founded in 1889 by Walter Scott Lenox as the Ceramic Art Company. It brings a rich history of craftsmanship to modern day life; where families and friends gather to celebrate using pieces that are versatile and timeless.

	Annual Growth	03/12	03/13	03/14	03/15*	04/16
Sales ($ mil.)	8.1%	–	–	–	224.1	242.4
Net income ($ mil.)	(3.1%)	–	–	–	5.8	5.6
Market value ($ mil.)	–	–	–	–	–	–
Employees	–	–	–	–	–	1,030

*Fiscal year change

LEO A. DALY COMPANY

8600 INDIAN HILLS DR
OMAHA, NE 681144039
Phone: 808-521-8889
Fax: –
Web: www.leoadaly.com

CEO: Leo A Daly III
CFO: –
HR: –
FYE: February 28
Type: Private

Firmly ensconced among the lions of design Leo A Daly takes great pride in its work. The company provides architecture engineering design and program management services for commercial industrial and public projects in more than 85 countries. Its project portfolio includes the award-winning First National Tower in its home state of Nebraska and the Lockheed Martin Center for Leadership Excellence in Maryland. Leo A Daly also owns engineering group Lockwood Andrews & Newnam which specializes in infrastructure management and consulting. Leo A Daly and its subsidiaries have more than 30 offices worldwide. Established in 1915 by Leo A. Daly Sr. the company is now led by his grandson Leo A. Daly III.

	Annual Growth	02/14	02/15	02/16	02/17	02/18
Sales ($ mil.)	(6.6%)	–	139.4	162.3	107.1	113.6
Net income ($ mil.)	–	–	(2.0)	3.2	(1.9)	0.8
Market value ($ mil.)	–	–	–	–	–	–
Employees	–	–	–	–	–	750

LESCARDEN INC

NBB: LCAR

420 Lexington Avenue, Ste 212
New York, NY 10170
Phone: 212 687-1050
Fax: 212 687-1051
Web: www.lescarden.com

CEO: William Luther
CFO: William E Luther
HR: –
FYE: May 31
Type: Public

Lescarden lessens scarring when it can. The company develops clinical dermatological osteoarthritis and wound care products. Lescarden focuses on developing natural therapies. Many of its products utilize bovine cartilage which is said to possess beneficial healing qualities. Its lead product the bovine-based and FDA-approved Catrix is sold as a dressing for non-healing wounds such as diabetic ulcers. Lescarden also markets a line of Catrix-based skin care products targeting the plastic surgery dermatology and medical spa markets. Other products include Poly-Nag an anti-arthritic compound made from chitin a material found in the shells of invertebrates and BIO-CARTILAGE a nutritional supplement.

	Annual Growth	05/12	05/13	05/14	05/15	05/16
Sales ($ mil.)	(26.9%)	0.4	0.4	0.4	0.3	0.1
Net income ($ mil.)	–	(0.2)	(0.3)	(0.2)	(0.2)	(0.1)
Market value ($ mil.)	(7.7%)	1.1	1.9	1.7	1.6	0.8
Employees	0.0%	1	1	1	1	1

LESTER E. COX MEDICAL CENTERS

1423 N JEFFERSON AVE
SPRINGFIELD, MO 658021917
Phone: 417-269-3000
Fax: –
Web: www.coxhealth.com

CEO: Steven D Edwards
CFO: Jake McWay
HR: –
FYE: September 30
Type: Private

Lester E. Cox Medical Centers (dba CoxHealth) is the area leader in health care and community involvement. CoxHealth's network includes six acute care hospitals (with nearly 1015 licensed beds) five ERs and more than 80 physician clinics. Centers for cardiac care cancer treatment orthopedics and women's health are among CoxHealth's specialized care options. In addition to a wide range of treatments and services CoxHealth contributes millions each year to community outreach medical education and research foundation grants donations and other contributions to the community. The organization was named after its primary fundraiser in the 1940s.

	Annual Growth	09/10	09/11	09/12	09/13	09/14
Sales ($ mil.)	3.2%	–	–	843.2	858.3	898.4
Net income ($ mil.)	(13.0%)	–	–	66.9	106.0	50.6
Market value ($ mil.)	–	–	–	–	–	–
Employees	–	–	–	–	–	11,170

LEVEL 3 COMMUNICATIONS, INC.

NYS: LVLT

1025 Eldorado Blvd.
Broomfield, CO 80021-8869
Phone: 720 888-1000
Fax: –
Web: www.level3.com

CEO: Jeff K Storey
CFO: Sunit S Patel
HR: –
FYE: December 31
Type: Public

Level 3 Communications makes valuable connections through its networking efforts — and without a name tag. Operator of one of the world's largest fiber-optic communications networks the firm connects customers in 60 countries. Its services include broadband Internet access wholesale voice origination and termination enterprise voice content distribution broadband transport and colocation services. Wholesale customers include ISPs telecom carriers cable-TV operators wireless providers and the US government. The company markets its products and services directly to businesses government agencies and schools. Its content delivery unit targets video distributors Web portals online gaming and software companies and social networking sites.

	Annual Growth	12/11	12/12	12/13	12/14	12/15
Sales ($ mil.)	17.4%	4,333.0	6,376.0	6,313.0	6,777.0	8,229.0
Net income ($ mil.)	–	(756.0)	(422.0)	(109.0)	314.0	3,433.0
Market value ($ mil.)	33.7%	6,054.8	8,235.8	11,820.9	17,597.8	19,372.5
Employees	3.5%	10,900	10,800	10,000	13,500	12,500

LEVI STRAUSS & CO.
NYS: LEVI

1155 Battery Street
San Francisco, CA 94111
Phone: 415 501-6000
Fax: –
Web: www.levistrauss.com

CEO: Charles Bergh
CFO: Harmit Singh
HR: –
FYE: November 28
Type: Public

Levi Strauss & Co. (LS&CO) is a global manufacturer of brand-name clothing LS&CO sells jeans and sportswear under the Levi's Dockers Signature by Levi Strauss and Denizen labels in more than 110 countries. The company distributes its brand products through approximately 50000 retail stores worldwide which includes 3100 brand-dedicated stores and shop-in-shops. It designs markets and sells ? directly or through third parties and licensees ? products that include jeans pants tops shorts skirts dresses jackets footwear and related accessories for men women and children. About 45% of the company total revenue comes from US operation. Founded In 1853 Levi Strauss opened a wholesale dry goods business in San Francisco that became known as Levi Strauss & Co.

	Annual Growth	11/17	11/18	11/19	11/20	11/21
Sales ($ mil.)	4.1%	4,904.0	5,575.4	5,763.1	4,452.6	5,763.9
Net income ($ mil.)	18.4%	281.4	283.1	394.6	(127.1)	553.5
Market value ($ mil.)	26.5%	–	–	6,792.2	7,659.7	10,873.9
Employees	4.7%	13,800	15,100	15,800	14,800	16,600

LEVI STRAUSS & CO.

1155 BATTERY ST
SAN FRANCISCO, CA 941111264
Phone: 415-501-6000
Fax: –
Web: www.levistrauss.com

CEO: Charles Bergh
CFO: Harmit Singh
HR: –
FYE: November 25
Type: Private

Levi Strauss & Co. (LS&CO) is a global manufacturer of brand-name clothing LS&CO sells jeans and sportswear under the Levi's Dockers Signature by Levi Strauss and Denizen labels in more than 110 countries. The company distributes its brand products through approximately 50000 retail stores worldwide which includes 3100 brand-dedicated stores and shop-in-shops. It designs markets and sells ? directly or through third parties and licensees ? products that include jeans pants tops shorts skirts dresses jackets footwear and related accessories for men women and children. About 45% of the company total revenue comes from US operation. Founded In 1853 Levi Strauss opened a wholesale dry goods business in San Francisco that became known as Levi Strauss & Co.

	Annual Growth	11/14	11/15	11/16	11/17	11/18
Sales ($ mil.)	7.4%	–	4,494.5	4,552.7	4,904.0	5,575.4
Net income ($ mil.)	10.8%	–	209.9	291.2	284.6	285.2
Market value ($ mil.)	–	–	–	–	–	–
Employees	–	–	–	–	–	14,800

LEVINDALE HEBREW GERIATRIC CENTER AND HOSPITAL, INC.

2434 W BELVEDERE AVE # 1
BALTIMORE, MD 212155267
Phone: 410-601-2400
Fax: –
Web: www.levindale.com

CEO: Ronald Rothstein
CFO: –
HR: –
FYE: June 30
Type: Private

Levindale Hebrew Geriatric Center and Hospital is a Jewish-sponsored nursing home that also operates a specialty hospital. In addition to traditional skilled nursing services the hospital provides subacute (short-term) medical care inpatient and outpatient mental health care and adult day-care services. Founded in 1890 the medical center has more than 290 beds. Among its specialized services are rehabilitation pain management and wound care as well as hospice care. Levindale Hebrew is part of the LifeBridge Health network of facilities in the Baltimore area and is sponsored by the Jewish Community Federation of Baltimore.

	Annual Growth	06/13	06/14	06/15	06/16	06/17
Sales ($ mil.)	(2.5%)	–	84.7	76.3	77.5	78.4
Net income ($ mil.)	(0.6%)	–	7.2	0.8	3.9	7.1
Market value ($ mil.)	–	–	–	–	–	–
Employees	–	–	–	–	–	461

LEWIS & CLARK COLLEGE

615 S PALATINE HILL RD
PORTLAND, OR 972198091
Phone: 503-768-7933
Fax: –
Web: www.lclark.edu

CEO: –
CFO: Andrea Dooley
HR: –
FYE: May 31
Type: Private

Lewis & Clark College sends students on an expedition to higher learning. The private university offers bachelor's degrees in more than two dozen majors through its College of Arts and Sciences. Fields of study include the humanities art history communications psychology natural sciences and mathematics. The school also offers master's and doctoral degrees at its Graduate School of Education and Counseling and its School of Law. Lewis & Clark has an enrollment of more than 3700 students. Founded as Albany Collegiate Institute in 1867 the college changed its name to Lewis & Clark when it moved to Portland Oregon in 1942.

	Annual Growth	05/17	05/18	05/19	05/20	05/21
Sales ($ mil.)	(0.9%)	–	124.7	125.7	124.9	121.3
Net income ($ mil.)	62.5%	–	17.3	9.3	(2.2)	74.4
Market value ($ mil.)	–	–	–	–	–	–
Employees	–	–	–	–	–	800

LEXICON PHARMACEUTICALS, INC.
NMS: LXRX

2445 Technology Forest Blvd., 11th Floor
The Woodlands, TX 77381
Phone: 281 863-3000
Fax: –
Web: www.lexpharma.com

CEO: Lonnel Coats
CFO: Jeffrey Wade
HR: Rocio Harrelson
FYE: December 31
Type: Public

Lexicon Pharmaceuticals is focused on a handful of potential medicines in clinical and pre-clinical research stages. Its first FDA-approved drug is XERMELO an oral treatment for carcinoid syndrome diarrhea used in combination with somatostatin; it was launched in the US in 2017. XERMELO is also approved in Japan and Canada. Lexicon's development candidates have been identified by its gene knock-out technology and aim to treat conditions such as diabetes irritable bowel syndrome and carcinoid syndrome.

	Annual Growth	12/16	12/17	12/18	12/19	12/20
Sales ($ mil.)	(26.7%)	83.3	90.3	63.2	322.1	24.0
Net income ($ mil.)	–	(141.4)	(129.1)	(120.5)	130.1	(58.6)
Market value ($ mil.)	(29.5%)	1,956.9	1,398.0	939.5	587.2	483.9
Employees	(17.5%)	168	174	202	184	78

LEXINGTON MEDICAL CENTER

2720 SUNSET BLVD
WEST COLUMBIA, SC 291694810
Phone: 803-791-2000
Fax: –
Web: www.lexmed.com

CEO: Tod Augsburger
CFO: Melinda Kruzner
HR: –
FYE: September 30
Type: Private

Lexington Medical Center is a not-for-profit health care organization serving the residents of South Carolina's Lexington County. Established in 1971 the medical center has some 415 beds and provides general emergency surgical and diagnostic services. Specialty services include cancer treatment cardiovascular care women's health and rehabilitation. Lexington Medical Center also operates a skilled nursing center as well as a network of affiliated community health centers urgent care clinics and affiliated physician practices. The hospital is managed by the Lexington County Health Service District.

	Annual Growth	09/13	09/14	09/15	09/16	09/17
Sales ($ mil.)	6.8%	–	781.7	863.9	906.1	953.5
Net income ($ mil.)	–	–	95.6	86.5	21.2	(9.2)
Market value ($ mil.)	–	–	–	–	–	–
Employees	–	–	–	–	–	5,616

LEXMARK INTERNATIONAL, INC.
NYS: LXK

One Lexmark Centre Drive, 740 West New Circle Road
Lexington, KY 40550
Phone: 859 232-2000
Fax: –
Web: www.lexmark.com

CEO: Allen Waugerman
CFO: Chuck Butler
HR: –
FYE: December 31
Type: Public

Increasingly Lexmark is about what ends up on a printed page than it is about the printing. Still a leading maker of printers and related supplies the company has been adding software for capturing and managing data and images to its business. Its printer business Imaging Solutions and Services (ISS) offers laser and dot matrix printers multifunction devices and related products. Through its Perceptive Software segment the company offers content document output and business process management services. Lexmark expects to double the size of its software business with its $1 billion acquisition of Kofax. The company markets worldwide to individual consumers as well as large organizations in the financial services government health care manufacturing and retail sectors.

	Annual Growth	12/10	12/11	12/12	12/13	12/14
Sales ($ mil.)	(3.0%)	4,199.7	4,173.0	3,797.6	3,667.6	3,710.5
Net income ($ mil.)	(30.5%)	340.0	320.9	106.3	261.8	79.1
Market value ($ mil.)	4.3%	2,134.5	2,027.2	1,421.5	2,177.4	2,529.9
Employees	(1.0%)	13,200	13,300	12,200	12,000	12,700

LGI HOMES, INC.
NMS: LGIH

1450 Lake Robbins Drive, Suite 430
The Woodlands, TX 77380
Phone: 281 362-8998
Fax: –
Web: www.lgihomes.com

CEO: Eric Lipar
CFO: Charles Merdian
HR: –
FYE: December 31
Type: Public

LGI Homes is engaged in the design construction and sale of new homes in markets in West Northwest Central Midwest Florida Southeast and Mid-Atlantic. Its product offerings include entry-level homes including both detached and attached homes and move-up homes which are sold under its LGI Homes brand and its luxury series homes which are sold under its Terrata Homes brand. Its homes were priced between $140000 and $700000 and ranged from 1000 to 4500 sq. ft. The builder's higher-quality Terrata Homes started at average sales price of $418000 home. LGI Homes has constructed and closed over 45000 homes since its founding in 2003.

	Annual Growth	12/17	12/18	12/19	12/20	12/21
Sales ($ mil.)	24.8%	1,258.0	1,504.4	1,838.2	2,367.9	3,050.1
Net income ($ mil.)	39.5%	113.3	155.3	178.6	323.9	429.6
Market value ($ mil.)	19.8%	1,794.5	1,081.5	1,689.8	2,531.7	3,694.8
Employees	7.0%	726	857	953	938	952

LGL GROUP INC (THE)
ASE: LGL

2525 Shader Road
Orlando, FL 32804
Phone: 407 298-2000
Fax: –
Web: www.lglgroup.com

CEO: Michael Ferrantino
CFO: James Tivy
HR: –
FYE: December 31
Type: Public

The LGL Group is hoping that one isn't the loneliest number. Previously made up of two separate businesses the company has a sole remaining line of business: its MtronPTI subsidiary. The subsidiary produces frequency control devices such as crystals and oscillators used primarily in communications equipment. MtronPTI was formed in the 2004 merger of M-tron Industries and Piezo Technology Inc. In 2007 The LGL Group sold certain assets of its unprofitable Lynch Systems subsidiary for about $3 million. The company's sales are roughly split between the US and other countries.

	Annual Growth	12/16	12/17	12/18	12/19	12/20
Sales ($ mil.)	10.5%	20.9	22.4	24.9	31.9	31.2
Net income ($ mil.)	59.9%	0.1	0.1	1.4	7.0	1.0
Market value ($ mil.)	25.7%	26.5	29.6	32.2	79.1	66.1
Employees	22.5%	142	276	308	353	320

LHC GROUP INC
NMS: LHCG

901 Hugh Wallis Road South
Lafayette, LA 70508
Phone: 337 233-1307
Fax: 337 235-8037
Web: www.lhcgroup.com

CEO: Keith Myers
CFO: Dale Mackel
HR: –
FYE: December 31
Type: Public

LHC Group administers post-acute health care services through more than 825 home nursing agencies hospices and long-term acute care hospitals (LTACH) in about 35 US states and the District of Columbia ? reaching 60% of the US population aged 65 and older. LHC's home health nursing agencies provide care to Medicare beneficiaries offering such services as private duty nursing physical therapy and medically-oriented social services. Its hospices provide palliative care for terminal patients while its LTACHs serve patients who no longer need intensive care but still require complex care in a hospital setting.

	Annual Growth	12/16	12/17	12/18	12/19	12/20
Sales ($ mil.)	22.5%	914.8	1,072.1	1,810.0	2,080.2	2,063.2
Net income ($ mil.)	32.2%	36.6	50.1	63.6	95.7	111.6
Market value ($ mil.)	47.0%	1,423.1	1,907.3	2,923.4	4,289.8	6,642.8
Employees	24.6%	11,598	14,554	30,985	30,399	27,959

LHH CORPORATION

100 E 77TH ST
NEW YORK, NY 100751850
Phone: 212-434-2000
Fax: –
Web: www.lenoxhill.northwell.edu

CEO: –
CFO: –
HR: –
FYE: December 31
Type: Private

When Manhattanites are looking for health care many of them head for the hill: Lenox Hill Hospital to be exact. The 650-bed facility provides care to patients on Manhattan's Upper East Side — about 45% of its patient base is from Manhattan the rest from surrounding boroughs. Services include cardiac care high-risk obstetrics pediatrics and orthopedics and sports medicine. Lenox Hill serves as a teaching affiliate for NYU Medical Center and also owns Manhattan Eye Ear and Throat Hospital a provider of specialty care for vision hearing and speech disorders. Today it's part of North Shore-Long Island Jewish Health System.

	Annual Growth	12/12	12/13	12/14	12/16	12/18
Sales ($ mil.)	7.7%	–	–	790.5	960.6	1,064.5
Net income ($ mil.)	119.1%	–	–	3.2	21.8	73.9
Market value ($ mil.)	–	–	–	–	–	–
Employees	–	–	–	–	–	2,955

LIBBEY INC.
ASE: LBY

300 Madison Avenue
Toledo, OH 43604
Phone: 419 325-2100
Fax: 419 727-2473
Web: www.libbey.com

CEO: Michael P Bauer
CFO: Juan Amezquita
HR: –
FYE: December 31
Type: Public

The sound of breaking glass is music to Libbey's ears. It signals potential sales for the company which is a leading maker and seller of glassware tableware and flatware to the foodservice industry retailers (Bed Bath & Beyond Target Wal-Mart) and business-to-business channels in the US and Canada. Libbey's products are made in five countries including the US Mexico and China and are sold in more than 100 others. It generates about 60% of sales from North America. The company's brands include Libbey Crisa and Royal Leerdam among others. Libbey's roots reach back to 1888 when The W.L. Libbey & Son Company was founded.

	Annual Growth	12/14	12/15	12/16	12/17	12/18
Sales ($ mil.)	(1.6%)	855.9	825.2	796.2	785.2	801.1
Net income ($ mil.)	–	–	5.0	66.3	10.1	(93.4)	(8.0)
Market value ($ mil.)	(40.7%)	696.6	472.4	431.2	166.6	86.0
Employees	(1.8%)	6,553	6,543	6,237	6,230	6,083

LIBERTY BANCORP INC (MO)
NBB: LBCP

16 West Franklin Street
Liberty, MO 64068
Phone: 816 781-4822
Fax: –
Web: www.banklibertykc.com

CEO: Brent M Giles
CFO: Marc J Weishaar
HR: –
FYE: December 31
Type: Public

Liberty Bancorp was formed in 2006 to be the holding company for BankLiberty (formerly Liberty Savings Bank) which operates about 10 branches in the Kansas City area. It offers traditional deposit services such as checking and savings accounts CDs and IRAs in addition to newfangled offerings like Internet banking bill payment and cash management services. Commercial real estate loans account for the largest portion of the company's loan portfolio (around 40%) followed by construction loans mainly to custom homebuilders. However citing depressed market conditions the bank has decreased its volume of construction loans. It also offers business residential real estate and consumer loans.

	Annual Growth	12/13	12/14	12/15	12/16	12/17
Assets ($ mil.)	(2.7%)	510.1	457.3	435.9	438.8	458.0
Net income ($ mil.)	8.1%	3.1	4.1	4.5	5.0	4.2
Market value ($ mil.)	0.0%	17.3	17.3	17.3	17.3	17.3
Employees	–	–	–	–	–	–

LIBERTY DIVERSIFIED INTERNATIONAL INC.

5600 N. Hwy. 169
New Hope MN 55428-3096
Phone: 763-536-6600
Fax: 763-536-6685
Web: www.libertydiversified.com

CEO: Michael Fiterman
CFO: Mike Vanyo
HR: –
FYE: May 31
Type: Private

Give me Liberty or give me Diversity — Liberty Diversified International (LDI; formerly Liberty Diversified Industries) gives you both. Its companies provide products and services for key markets including health care (Ergolet); precision machining (Milltronics and Takumi); paper packaging and recycling (Presentation Packaging Liberty Carton and Liberty Paper); building and construction (Diversi-Plast); office products and furniture (Safco); and hauling (LDI Transport). It also manufactures corrugated and plastic pallets for the shipping industry material handling products and graphic arts products. Family-owned LDI is led by its founder's grandson CEO Mike Fiterman.

LIBERTY HOMES INC

1101 EISENHOWER DR N
GOSHEN, IN 465265309
Phone: 574-533-0438
Fax: –
Web: www.libertyhomesinc.com

CEO: –
CFO: Marc A Dosmann
HR: –
FYE: December 31
Type: Private

Liberty Homes gives home buyers the freedom to move about the land. The company builds modular homes for the US and Canada from seven manufacturing facilities. The company's floor plans range from two to five bedrooms and cost from $35000 to about $125000. Options include kitchen islands utility rooms and front porches. The company builds homes under the Liberty Homes Waverlee Homes and Badger Built Homes brand names. Independent dealers and company-owned retail centers sell the company's products. CEO Edward Hussey and his family control Liberty Homes.

	Annual Growth	12/04	12/05	12/06	12/07	12/08
Sales ($ mil.)	(79.3%)	–	–	1,908.9	80.9	81.7
Net income ($ mil.)	–	–	–	0.0	(3.5)	(6.3)
Market value ($ mil.)	–	–	–	–	–	–
Employees	–	–	–	–	–	100

LIBERTY MUTUAL HOLDING COMPANY INC.

175 Berkeley St.
Boston MA 02116
Phone: 617-357-9500
Fax: 617-350-7648
Web: www.libertymutual.com

CEO: David H Long
CFO: Christopher L Peirce
HR: –
FYE: December 31
Type: Private - Mutual Com

Liberty Mutual Holding defends our freedom to buy car insurance. As the parent company of Liberty Mutual Group and its operating subsidiaries Liberty Mutual is one of the top property/casualty insurers in the US and among the top 10 providers of automobile insurance. The company also offers homeowners' insurance workers compensation general liability group disability fire and surety and commercial lines for small to large companies. Liberty Mutual operates through four business divisions: Liberty Mutual Agency Corporation (LMAC) International Personal Markets and Commercial Markets. It distributes its products through a diversified blend of independent and exclusive agents brokers and direct sales.

LIBERTY ORCHARDS COMPANY INC.

117 MISSION AVE
CASHMERE, WA 988151007
Phone: 509-782-4088
Fax: –
Web: www.libertyorchards.com

CEO: –
CFO: –
HR: –
FYE: December 31
Type: Private

Liberty Orchards exercises its freedom to manufacture candies and baked goods. The company's signature products are aplets and cotlets — jellied fruit candies made from apples and apricots. It also makes and sells chocolates and fruity breads and cookies. Liberty Orchards products are sold online and by major chain retail stores. The candy maker was founded in 1919 as a fruit dehydration and canning enterprise by Armenian immigrants Mark Balaban and Armen Tertsagian.

	Annual Growth	12/02	12/03	12/05	12/06	12/07
Sales ($ mil.)	1.2%	–	13.5	15.4	14.4	14.2
Net income ($ mil.)	16.2%	–	–	0.1	0.2	0.2
Market value ($ mil.)	–	–	–	–	–	–
Employees	–	–	–	–	–	80

LIBERTY PROPERTY TRUST
NYS: LPT

650 East Swedesford Road
Wayne, PA 19087
Phone: 610 648-1700
Fax: –
Web: www.libertyproperty.com

CEO: William P Hankowsky
CFO: Christopher J Papa
HR: –
FYE: December 31
Type: Public

There's the "Land of the Free" but no such thing as "free land" to Liberty Property Trust. The self-managed real estate investment trust (REIT) owns leases manages and has interests in nearly 500 industrial properties including distribution warehouse light manufacturing and research and development facilities and some 180 office buildings. The company's properties encompass some 96 million sq. ft. of space mainly in the mid-Atlantic southeastern and Midwestern regions of the US as well as the UK. The REIT also owns nearly 1500 acres of developable land. Liberty Property has some 1200 tenants; The Vanguard Group and GlaxoSmithKline are the two largest.

	Annual Growth	12/13	12/14	12/15	12/16	12/17
Sales ($ mil.)	2.7%	645.9	792.6	808.7	746.7	719.8
Net income ($ mil.)	7.7%	209.7	217.9	238.0	356.8	282.3
Market value ($ mil.)	6.2%	4,994.2	5,548.6	4,578.3	5,824.3	6,341.9
Employees	(11.0%)	471	449	384	301	295

LICKING MEMORIAL HEALTH SYSTEMS

1320 W MAIN ST
NEWARK, OH 430551822
Phone: 220-564-4000
Fax: –
Web: www.lmhealth.org

CEO: Robert Montagnese
CFO: Rob Montagnese
HR: –
FYE: December 31
Type: Private

Here to help Buckeye Staters lick disease is Licking Memorial Health Systems. The the not-for-profit health care provider operates the 230-bed Licking Memorial Hospital. Specialty services at the hospital include cancer care home health occupational health cardiology rehabilitation and obstetrics. Licking Memorial Hospital administers behavioral health care (including substance abuse treatments) through its Shepherd Hill department. The health system also includes area outpatient medical practices largely through the multi-specialty physician group Licking Memorial Health Professionals which has 100-plus physicians in various practices.

	Annual Growth	12/08	12/09	12/10	12/11	12/13
Sales ($ mil.)	1.8%	–	–	199.0	184.2	209.7
Net income ($ mil.)	108.7%	–	–	4.4	(7.7)	39.7
Market value ($ mil.)	–	–	–	–	–	–
Employees	–	–	–	–	–	1,900

LICT CORP

NBB: LICT

401 Theodore Fremd Avenue
Rye, NY 10580-1430
Phone: 914 921-8821
Fax: 914 921-6410
Web: www.lictcorp.com

CEO: Mario Gabelli
CFO: Daniel E Hopkins
HR: –
FYE: December 31
Type: Public

LICT (formerly Lynch Interactive) is a holding company that operates through 12 small (mostly rural) local-exchange phone companies located primarily in the Midwestern and Western US; it also has a limited presence in the Northeast. The company provides local telephone service over nearly 60000 access lines while dial-up and broadband Internet service lines number about 50000. Subsidiaries include JBN Telephone Haviland Telephone and Giant Communications in Kansas; Centra-Com Interactive in Utah; and Bretton Woods Telephone in New Hampshire. Chairman Mario Gabelli owns 24% of LICT.

	Annual Growth	12/16	12/17	12/18	12/19	12/20
Sales ($ mil.)	8.2%	90.7	106.7	115.8	118.0	124.2
Net income ($ mil.)	50.5%	7.3	22.4	25.8	26.2	37.3
Market value ($ mil.)	31.5%	110.3	215.9	267.8	333.6	329.9
Employees	4.0%	293	206	315	338	343

LIEBERT CORPORATION

1050 Dearborn Dr.
Columbus OH 43085
Phone: 614-841-6700
Fax: 614-841-6022
Web: www.emersonnetworkpower.com/en-us/brands/liebe

CEO: Rob Johnson
CFO: David Fallon
HR: –
FYE: September 30
Type: Subsidiary

Liebert keeps its cool in the face of a power meltdown. The company designs makes and markets surge suppressors uninterruptable power supply (UPS) units precision cooling equipment enclosures and monitoring equipment that helps protect and support IT environments. Its products are used by companies in the communications government industrial and utilities sectors. Liebert which also provides support services sells directly and through independent and factory-direct representatives distributors and resellers. Customers have included BayCare Health System Terminix and Hess Corporation. Founded in 1965 Liebert is part of Emerson Network Power a business segment of Emerson Electric.

LIFE CARE CENTERS OF AMERICA INC.

3570 KEITH ST NW
CLEVELAND, TN 373124309
Phone: 423-472-9585
Fax: –
Web: www.lcca.com

CEO: –
CFO: –
HR: –
FYE: September 30
Type: Private

If you or a loved one has reached the Golden Age of retirement there's a good chance Life Care Centers of America offers a service you can use. The company is a privately owned operator of more than 260 retirement and health care centers in 28 states across the US. Its offerings include retirement communities assisted-living facilities and nursing homes (and even some campuses that provide all three in a continuum of care). In addition Life Care operates centers specifically for people with Alzheimer's disease or related dementia. Some of Life Care's specialized services include home health care adult day care hospice and wound care.

	Annual Growth	12/01	12/02*	09/05	09/06	09/08
Sales ($ mil.)	–	–	0.0	0.0	40.8	82.9
Net income ($ mil.)	–	–	–	0.0	6.2	3.2
Market value ($ mil.)	–	–	–	–	–	–
Employees	–	–	–	–	–	29,000

*Fiscal year change

LIFE PARTNERS HOLDINGS INC

NBB: LPHI Q

204 Woodhew Drive
Waco, TX 76712
Phone: 254 751-7797
Fax: –
Web: www.lphi.com

CEO: Colette C Pieper
CFO: –
HR: –
FYE: February 28
Type: Public

Life Partners Holdings parent company of Life Partners Inc. makes its bucks by helping its customers make a buck. The company facilitates viatical and life settlement transactions in which an institution or wealthy investor purchases individual life insurance policies (at a discount) and becomes the beneficiary of those policies when they mature. Viatical settlements involve terminally ill policyholders with only a couple of years to live; life settlement transactions involve sellers with longer life expectancies. Life Partners makes its money from fees earned by facilitating viatical and life settlements. Nearly all of the company's business is done through life settlement brokers. It filed for Chapter 11 bankruptcy in early 2015.

	Annual Growth	02/10	02/11	02/12	02/13	02/14
Sales ($ mil.)	(39.0%)	113.0	101.6	32.9	18.9	15.7
Net income ($ mil.)	–	29.4	23.4	(3.1)	(2.9)	(2.5)
Market value ($ mil.)	(41.5%)	383.8	154.0	79.3	74.2	44.9
Employees	(26.9%)	6,454	1,885	1,806	1,823	1,844

LIFE STORAGE INC

NYS: LSI

6467 Main Street
Williamsville, NY 14221
Phone: 716 633-1850
Fax: 716 633-1860
Web: www.lifestorage.com

CEO: Joseph Saffire
CFO: Andrew Gregoire
HR: Alyssa Harlach
FYE: December 31
Type: Public

Life Storage Inc. is a fully integrated self-administered and self-managed real estate investment trust (REIT) that acquires and manages self-storage properties throughout the US. Headquartered in Buffalo New York the company operates approximately 925 self-storage facilities encompassing over 67 million square feet in about 35 states. Life Storage Inc. currently operates under the brand name Life Storage and is one of the largest self-storage companies in the world. Founded in 1982 the company was originally a financial planning firm but opened its first self-storage facility in Florida in 1985.

	Annual Growth	12/16	12/17	12/18	12/19	12/20
Sales ($ mil.)	7.5%	462.6	529.8	550.9	574.7	616.8
Net income ($ mil.)	15.5%	85.2	96.4	206.6	258.7	151.6
Market value ($ mil.)	8.8%	6,327.3	6,610.1	6,901.0	8,035.7	8,860.2
Employees	7.8%	1,537	1,792	1,953	1,943	2,078

LIFE-TIME FITNESS INC
NYS: LTM

2902 Corporate Place
Chanhassen, MN 55317
Phone: 952 947-0000
Fax: –
Web: www.lifetimefitness.com

CEO: Bahram Akradi
CFO: Eric J Buss
HR: –
FYE: December 31
Type: Public

Life Time Fitness wants to help you keep your New Year's resolutions. The company operates more than 100 exercise and recreation centers. Life Time Fitness facilities offer swimming pools basketball and racquet courts child care centers spas dining services and climbing walls in addition to some 400 pieces of exercise equipment. Most facilities are open 24 hours a day seven days a week and average around 100000 sq. ft. in size. They target a membership of about 7500 to 11000 and are designed to serve as an all-in-one sports and athletic club professional fitness facility family recreation center and spa and resort.

	Annual Growth	12/09	12/10	12/11	12/12	12/13
Sales ($ mil.)	9.6%	837.0	912.8	1,013.7	1,126.9	1,205.9
Net income ($ mil.)	13.9%	72.4	80.7	92.6	111.5	121.7
Market value ($ mil.)	17.2%	1,049.9	1,726.3	1,968.9	2,072.5	1,979.4
Employees	6.6%	17,400	19,000	20,000	21,700	22,500

LIFEBRIDGE HEALTH, INC.

2401 W BELVEDERE AVE
BALTIMORE, MD 212155216
Phone: 410-601-5653
Fax: –
Web: www.lifebridgehealth.org

CEO: Neil M Meltzer
CFO: David Krajewski
HR: –
FYE: June 30
Type: Private

LifeBridge Health links patients to healthcare. Serving the Baltimore region the not-for-profit company operates two general hospitals — Sinai Hospital of Baltimore and Northwest Hospital — with specialties including oncology neurology pediatrics and sports medicine. The LifeBridge Health network also provides long-term care at the Levindale Hebrew Geriatric Center and Hospital (nursing subacute and adult day care services) and the Courtland Gardens Nursing & Rehabilitation Center. Altogether the health system boasts some 1190 beds. LifeBridge's Health Wellness division includes a health and fitness program and community fitness center.

	Annual Growth	06/14	06/15	06/17	06/19	06/20
Sales ($ mil.)	62.8%	–	145.3	1,527.1	1,610.4	1,662.2
Net income ($ mil.)	134.1%	–	0.8	111.0	65.5	54.5
Market value ($ mil.)	–	–	–	–	–	–
Employees	–	–	–	–	–	6,000

LIFECORE BIOMEDICAL INC.

3515 Lyman Blvd.
Chaska MN 55318-3051
Phone: 952-368-4300
Fax: 952-368-3411
Web: www.lifecore.com

CEO: Kipling Thacker
CFO: Scott Collins
HR: –
FYE: May 31
Type: Subsidiary

Lifecore Biomedical aims to help bodies plump up smooth out and keep moving. Lifecore manufactures hyaluronan a natural lubricating compound found in animal and human connective tissues. The hyaluronan is then turned into products used in ophthalmic surgeries during bone grafting as pain treatments for osteoarthritis and in veterinary orthopedics. Hyaluronan might eventually be used in cosmetic procedures as a dermal filler (to smooth out wrinkles). Lifecore has supply agreements with Alcon to use its hyaluronan solution in cataract surgery products. Landec Corporation acquired Lifecore in 2010.

LIFELOCK INC
NYS: LOCK

60 East Rio Salado Parkway, Suite 400
Tempe, AZ 85281
Phone: 480 682-5100
Fax: –
Web: www.lifelock.com

CEO: Hilary A Schneider
CFO: Chris Power
HR: –
FYE: December 31
Type: Public

LifeLock is trying to put a choke hold on identity theft. One of the fastest growing privately-held companies in the US and a leader in the security industry LifeLock serves consumers and businesses in the US Puerto Rico and the Virgin Islands with its identity theft protection and detection services. Members pay annual or monthly subscription fees to receive alerts about potentially fraudulent credit applications made in their names. Its eRecon and TrueAddress services search the Web for illegal selling and trading of personal information as well as fraudulent address change attempts. LifeLock was founded in 2005 and went public through a 2012 IPO.

	Annual Growth	12/10	12/11	12/12	12/13	12/14
Sales ($ mil.)	30.9%	162.3	193.9	276.4	369.7	476.0
Net income ($ mil.)	–	(15.4)	(4.3)	23.5	52.5	2.5
Market value ($ mil.)	50.9%	–	–	763.4	1,540.9	1,738.1
Employees	2.8%	–	616	644	675	669

LIFELOCK INC.
NYSE: LOCK

60 E. Rio Salado Pkwy. Ste. 400
Tempe AZ 85281
Phone: 480-682-5100
Fax: 888-244-9823
Web: www.lifelock.com

CEO: Hilary A Schneider
CFO: Chris Power
HR: –
FYE: December 31
Type: Private

LifeLock is trying to put a choke hold on identity theft. One of the fastest growing privately-held companies in the US and a leader in the security industry LifeLock serves consumers and businesses in the US Puerto Rico and the Virgin Islands with its identity theft protection and detection services. Members pay annual or monthly subscription fees to receive alerts about potentially fraudulent credit applications made in their names. Its eRecon and TrueAddress services search the Web for illegal selling and trading of personal information as well as fraudulent address change attempts. The company was founded in 2005 and went public through a 2012 IPO.

LIFEPOINT HEALTH INC
NMS: LPNT

330 Seven Springs Way
Brentwood, TN 37027
Phone: 615 920-7000
Fax: –
Web: www.lifepointhospitals.com

CEO: David M Dill
CFO: Michael S Coggin
HR: –
FYE: December 31
Type: Public

LifePoint Health helps folks who get sick in the country get well. The company operates more than 70 hospitals located in non-urban areas. In most cases the hospitals (which combined house more than 9400 beds) are the only available acute care facilities in the region. LifePoint operates its hospitals in 22 states through its subsidiaries with a concentration in the southeastern US. In many markets LifePoint also operates outpatient clinics that provide family care diagnostic surgical and therapeutic services.

	Annual Growth	12/12	12/13	12/14	12/15	12/16
Sales ($ mil.)	17.0%	3,391.8	3,678.3	4,483.1	5,214.3	6,364.0
Net income ($ mil.)	(5.4%)	151.9	128.2	126.1	181.9	121.9
Market value ($ mil.)	10.8%	1,507.8	2,110.6	2,872.3	2,931.8	2,268.8
Employees	13.8%	28,000	31,000	38,000	40,000	47,000

LIFEQUEST WORLD CORP
NBB: LQWC

100 Challenger Road, 8th Floor
Ridgefield Park, NJ 07660
Phone: 646 201-5242
Fax: –
Web: www.lifequestcorp.com

CEO: Anthony Jurak
CFO: –
HR: –
FYE: May 31
Type: Public

Tired? Run-down? Listless? Do you poop out at parties? Time to call Tonicman! LifeQuest World uses its Tonicman radio shows to help get the word out about its Jurak Classic Whole Body Tonic but its main distribution is through multilevel marketing. The company's primary product is a liquid herbal formula created in 1943 by Carl Jurak father of CEO Anthony Jurak (who owns 41% of the company). LifeQuest has acquired ImmunXT for about $2 million and since has invested heavily in marketing the immune stimulating dietary supplement (even hiring actor and body builder Peter Lupus as its spokesman). The company expects ImmunXT — which is an algae-based botanical complex — to become its flagship product.

	Annual Growth	05/17	05/18	05/19	05/20	05/21
Sales ($ mil.)	166.0%	–	0.0	0.0	0.4	0.5
Net income ($ mil.)	–	(0.0)	(0.2)	(8.3)	(0.1)	(0.5)
Market value ($ mil.)	214.2%	0.2	67.3	67.3	37.0	19.5
Employees	–	–	–	–	–	–

LIFESPAN CORPORATION

10 DAVOL SQ STE 300
PROVIDENCE, RI 029034754
Phone: 401-421-4000
Fax: –
Web: www.lifespan.org

CEO: Timothy J Babineau
CFO: –
HR: Suehaiti Rivera
FYE: September 30
Type: Private

Founded in 1994 Rhode Island's first health system Lifespan is a not-for-profit comprehensive integrated academic health system with The Warren Alpert Medical School of Brown University. The multi-hospital health system includes the state's largest acute care facility Rhode Island Hospital. The flagship hospital has 719 beds and provides general and advanced medical-surgical care in a wide range of specialties including cardiology diabetes oncology surgery and orthopedics. Rhode Island Hospital and its sister facility the 247-bed Miriam Hospital serve as teaching facilities for Warren Alpert Medical School of Brown University.

	Annual Growth	09/12	09/13	09/14	09/15	09/19
Sales ($ mil.)	9.0%	–	143.5	156.7	187.2	240.4
Net income ($ mil.)	–	–	(2.0)	6.1	1.4	1.9
Market value ($ mil.)	–	–	–	–	–	–
Employees	–	–	–	–	–	8,000

LIFESTORE FINANCIAL GROUP
PINK SHEETS: LSFG

21 E. Ashe St.
West Jefferson NC 28694
Phone: 336-246-4344
Fax: 336-246-3966
Web: www.golifestore.com

CEO: Robert Washburn
CFO: Melanie Miller
HR: –
FYE: June 30
Type: Public

LifeStore helps you prepeare for whatever life has in store. Formerly AF Financial Group LifeStore Financial Group provides good ol' traditional banking and insurance services through subsidiaries LifeStore Bank and LifeStore Insurance Services. The bank operates seven offices in northwestern North Carolina's Alleghany Ashe and Watauga counties. It provides standard deposit products such as checking and savings accounts and CDs. Residential mortgages make up about half of its loan portfolio. The bank also offers investment products and services through a pact with a third-party provider. LifeStore Insurance Services sells bonds and auto homeowners health and life insurance.

LIFETIME BRANDS INC
NMS: LCUT

1000 Stewart Avenue
Garden City, NY 11530
Phone: 516 683-6000
Fax: –
Web: www.lifetimebrands.com

CEO: Robert Kay
CFO: Laurence Winoker
HR: –
FYE: December 31
Type: Public

Lifetime Brands designs and distributes kitchenware tableware and functional home products including cutlery scales thermometers baking trays food storage and other products for the home. Its top brands (both owned and licensed) include Farberware KitchenAid Taylor Mikasa Pfaltzgraff Rabbit Kamenstein and Built NY. The company sells its varied lines in the US Canada Mexico Central and South America Europe and Asia through high-end retailers supermarkets department stores and discount chains (including Bed Bath & Beyond Wal-Mart and Target) as well as online. About 85% of the company's total sales is generated from the US.

	Annual Growth	12/16	12/17	12/18	12/19	12/20
Sales ($ mil.)	6.7%	592.6	579.5	704.5	734.9	769.2
Net income ($ mil.)	–	15.7	2.2	(1.7)	(44.4)	(3.0)
Market value ($ mil.)	(3.8%)	386.2	359.0	218.2	151.2	330.7
Employees	(1.2%)	1,416	1,403	1,500	1,400	1,350

LIFEWAY CHRISTIAN RESOURCES OF THE SOUTHERN BAPTIST CONVENTION

1 LIFEWAY PLZ
NASHVILLE, TN 372341001
Phone: 615-251-2000
Fax: –
Web: www.lifeway.com

CEO: –
CFO: –
HR: –
FYE: September 30
Type: Private

LifeWay Christian Resources of the Southern Baptist Convention helps to spread the teachings of Jesus. The company is a not-for-profit Christian publisher. It also sells Bibles audio video gifts and other supplies. The retailer sells products online and through authorized dealers. LifeWay was founded in 1891 by Dr. J.M. Frost.

	Annual Growth	09/15	09/16	09/17	09/19	09/20
Sales ($ mil.)	(19.9%)	–	503.0	476.2	266.5	206.6
Net income ($ mil.)	–	–	8.2	43.7	(82.7)	(109.0)
Market value ($ mil.)	–	–	–	–	–	–
Employees	–	–	–	–	–	5,000

LIFEWAY FOODS, INC.
NMS: LWAY

6431 West Oakton
Morton Grove, IL 60053
Phone: 847 967-1010
Fax: –
Web: www.lifewayfoods.com

CEO: Julie Smolyansky
CFO: Eric Hanson
HR: –
FYE: December 31
Type: Public

Kefir is not milk with a pedigree but it is cultured and it's the lifeblood of Lifeway Foods. In addition to the yogurt-like dairy beverage called Kefir (sold under the Tuscan Lassi and BasicsPlus brands) the company's products include farmer and cream cheeses Sweet Kiss (a sweetened cheese spread) and a vegetable-based seasoning called Golden Zesta. Its ProBugs offering a flavored drink with live kefir cultures packaged in pouches is aimed at children. A longtime staple in the dairy cases of health-food stores Lifeway's products are available throughout the US as well as internationally. The dairy products company has been expanding its menu of products with additional children's items.

	Annual Growth	12/16	12/17	12/18	12/19	12/20
Sales ($ mil.)	(4.7%)	123.9	118.9	103.4	93.7	102.0
Net income ($ mil.)	(1.8%)	3.5	(0.3)	(3.1)	0.5	3.2
Market value ($ mil.)	(17.2%)	179.6	124.8	29.3	31.1	84.4
Employees	(0.3%)	320	340	322	307	316

LIGAND PHARMACEUTICALS INC
NMS: LGND

5980 Horton Street, Suite 405
Emeryville, CA 94608
Phone: 858 550-7500
Fax: –
Web: www.ligand.com

CEO: John Higgins
CFO: Matthew Korenberg
HR: –
FYE: December 31
Type: Public

Biopharmaceutical firm Ligand Pharmaceuticals seeks to discover disease-curing molecules. The drug development company works with gene transcription technology to address assorted illnesses. Its research and development projects include treatments for osteoporosis cardiovascular disease cancer and diabetes. Ligand conducts many of its programs through partnerships with other drug makers including Sanofi Pfizer and Lilly. The company is focused on expanding its development pipeline through additional partnerships and technology licensing agreements as well as via acquisitions.

	Annual Growth	12/16	12/17	12/18	12/19	12/20
Sales ($ mil.)	14.4%	109.0	141.1	251.5	120.3	186.4
Net income ($ mil.)	–	(1.6)	12.6	143.3	629.3	(3.0)
Market value ($ mil.)	(0.5%)	1,633.9	2,201.8	2,182.0	1,677.0	1,599.1
Employees	62.9%	22	39	116	115	155

LIGHTBRIDGE CORP
NAS: LTBR

11710 Plaza America Drive, Suite 2000
Reston, VA 20190
Phone: 571 730-1200
Fax: –
Web: www.ltbridge.com

CEO: Seth Grae
CFO: Lawrence Goldman
HR: –
FYE: December 31
Type: Public

Lightbridge is ready to illuminate the wonders of using thorium as a possible nuclear fuel. The development-stage company has been working on a new kind of nuclear fuel that uses thorium a less radioactive element than uranium to power nuclear reactors. Thorium's lessened radioactivity also means it doesn't produce enough plutonium to make nuclear weapons unlike uranium. The company's ideas for thorium were developed by the late nuclear engineer Dr. Alvin Radkowsky who co-founded Lightbridge's predecessor Thorium Power in 1992. While Lightbridge's plans for thorium power plants are not ready for commercialization the company has earned some revenue as a nuclear energy consultant.

	Annual Growth	12/13	12/14	12/15	12/16	12/17
Sales ($ mil.)	(44.9%)	1.9	1.3	0.9	0.8	0.2
Net income ($ mil.)	–	(4.9)	(4.8)	(4.3)	(6.3)	(7.1)
Market value ($ mil.)	(4.3%)	18.5	19.7	12.7	14.5	15.5
Employees	(12.6%)	12	12	9	8	7

LIGHTHOUSE COMPUTER SERVICES, INC.

6 BLACKSTONE VALLEY PL # 205
LINCOLN, RI 028651112
Phone: 401-334-0799
Fax: –
Web: www.lighthousecs.com

CEO: Thomas Mrva
CFO: –
HR: –
FYE: December 31
Type: Private

Lighthouse Computer Services shines a light on companies' IT needs. The firm provides IT services to businesses primarily FORTUNE 1000 and midsized companies in the New England region. Lighthouse's services include customization implementation data migration network design and systems administration. It also refurbishes and sells computer equipment from IBM and other vendors. The company's consultants employ products from a variety of software and hardware partners including Cisco Systems Microsoft NetApp STORServer Symantec and VMware. CEO Tom Mrva controls Lighthouse Computer Services which he founded in 1995.

	Annual Growth	12/02	12/03	12/04	12/06	12/07
Sales ($ mil.)	17.8%	–	62.1	51.8	97.5	119.7
Net income ($ mil.)	42.5%	–	0.7	0.1	2.6	2.7
Market value ($ mil.)	–	–	–	–	–	–
Employees	–	–	–	–	–	105

LIGHTING SCIENCE GROUP CORP
NBB: LSCG D

1350 Division Road, Suite 204
West Warwick, RI 02893
Phone: 321 779-5520
Fax: –
Web: www.lsgc.com

CEO: Edward Bednarcik
CFO: David Quigley
HR: –
FYE: December 31
Type: Public

Going green turns on Lighting Science (LSGC). The company designs manufactures and markets eco-friendly light-emitting diode (LED) technologies that conserve energy and eliminate the use of hazardous materials. It products use LED chips to integrate power sources with thermal management optic and control systems. The company sells optimized digital lighting (ODL) and LED replacement lamps fixtures and bulbs for streets garages stages and retail displays. While most of its customers are in retail commercial industrial and public sectors LSGC also customizes ambiance and lighting systems for entertainment venues and nightclubs.

	Annual Growth	12/12	12/13	12/14	12/15	12/16
Sales ($ mil.)	(19.8%)	127.1	83.2	91.3	79.7	52.7
Net income ($ mil.)	–	(111.3)	(89.8)	(65.6)	(27.1)	(20.2)
Market value ($ mil.)	(48.3%)	122.0	67.5	20.0	17.4	8.7
Employees	(34.8%)	377	177	94	78	68

LIGHTPATH TECHNOLOGIES, INC.
NAS: LPTH

2603 Challenger Tech Court, Suite 100
Orlando, FL 32826
Phone: 407 382-4003
Fax: 407 382-4007
Web: www.lightpath.com

CEO: Shmuel Rubin
CFO: Albert Miranda
HR: –
FYE: June 30
Type: Public

LightPath Technologies is lighting the optical networking way. The company which has traditionally used its patented GRADIUM glass to make distortion-reducing lenses for inspection equipment is developing new applications for its technologies in the optoelectronics and fiber-optic communications fields. Its optoelectronics products include collimators (optical network components) and optical isolators (filters that prevent light waves from reflecting backwards). LightPath serves such customers as CyOptics Intel Santur ThorLabs and T-Networks. The company targets aerospace telecommunications health care instrumentation and the military. LightPath gets about two-thirds of its sales in the US.

	Annual Growth	06/17	06/18	06/19	06/20	06/21
Sales ($ mil.)	7.9%	28.4	32.5	33.7	35.0	38.5
Net income ($ mil.)	–	7.7	1.1	(2.7)	0.9	(3.2)
Market value ($ mil.)	(1.5%)	72.9	62.1	24.6	90.1	68.5
Employees	3.0%	321	342	350	372	361

LILLY (ELI) & CO
NYS: LLY

Lilly Corporate Center
Indianapolis, IN 46285
Phone: 317 276-2000
Fax: –
Web: www.lilly.com

CEO: David Ricks
CFO: Anat Ashkenazi
HR: Stephen Fry
FYE: December 31
Type: Public

Eli Lilly is a leading pharmaceutical company that develops diabetes oncology immunology and neuroscience medicines. Its top-selling drugs include Trulicity (treatment of type 2 diabetes and reducing the risk of adverse cardiovascular events in patients with type 2 diabetes and cardiovascular risk factors); Humalog (an injectable human insulin analog); Alimta (treatment for various cancers); Taltz (treatment for moderated-to-severe plaque psoriasis); Humulin (injectable human insulin); and Jardiance (treatment for type 2 diabetes and reducing the risk of cardiovascular death with patients with type 2 diabetes and heart diseases) among others. The company generates most of its revenue in the US.

	Annual Growth	12/17	12/18	12/19	12/20	12/21
Sales ($ mil.)	5.5%	22,871.3	24,555.7	22,319.5	24,539.8	28,318.4
Net income ($ mil.)	–	(204.1)	3,232.0	8,318.4	6,193.7	5,581.7
Market value ($ mil.)	34.5%	80,545.5	110,356.7	125,338.6	161,014.8	263,418.0
Employees	(3.7%)	40,655	38,680	33,625	35,000	35,000

LIME ENERGY CO
NBB: LIME D

4 Gateway Center,, 100 Mulberry Street
Newark, NJ 07102
Phone: 201 416-2559
Fax: –
Web: www.lime-energy.com

CEO: C Adam Procell
CFO: Bruce D Torkelson
HR: –
FYE: December 31
Type: Public

Being green is easy with help from Lime Energy. The company designs and installs programs for small businesses mostly utility companies that analyze energy use and develop a plan to reduce energy consumption and maintenance costs. Lime Energy helps its customers identify multiple energy-consuming points of a building and redesigns lighting systems to help them cost save and also reduce harmful emissions of carbon dioxide sulfur dioxide and nitric dioxide. The company works on all types of buildings including factories high rises retail data centers banks government facilities schools and hospitals.

	Annual Growth	12/11	12/12	12/13	12/14	12/15
Sales ($ mil.)	(1.6%)	120.1	43.4	51.6	58.8	112.6
Net income ($ mil.)	–	(11.6)	(31.8)	(15.6)	(2.6)	(3.2)
Market value ($ mil.)	–	–	–	–	–	–
Employees	(5.7%)	342	167	125	164	270

LIMELIGHT NETWORKS INC
NMS: LLNW

2220 W. 14th Street
Tempe, AZ 85281
Phone: 602 850-5000
Fax: –
Web: www.limelight.com

CEO: Bob Lyons
CFO: Daniel Boncel
HR: –
FYE: December 31
Type: Public

Limelight Networks provides industry-leading content delivery and edge services to many of the biggest brands worldwide. The company provides edge services platform that includes a globally distributed high-performance private network intelligent software and support services and a wide variety of connected devices. Services include content delivery website personalization web content management online video publishing mobile device delivery and cloud storage. Limelight's global network infrastructure includes more than 100 points-of-presence and is also directly interconnected with over 1000 major Internet service providers. It serves more than 525 active customers worldwide and its biggest geographic market is the Americas.

	Annual Growth	12/17	12/18	12/19	12/20	12/21
Sales ($ mil.)	4.2%	184.4	195.7	200.6	230.2	217.6
Net income ($ mil.)	–	(7.6)	9.8	(16.0)	(19.3)	(54.8)
Market value ($ mil.)	(6.1%)	592.4	314.3	548.1	536.0	460.8
Employees	0.9%	533	563	610	618	552

LIMESTONE BANCORP INC
NAS: LMST

2500 Eastpoint Parkway
Louisville, KY 40223
Phone: 502 499-4800
Fax: –
Web: www.limestonebank.com

CEO: John Taylor
CFO: Phillip Barnhouse
HR: –
FYE: December 31
Type: Public

Porter Bancorp could be a stout evaluator of what "ales" your finances. It is the holding company for PBI Bank which serves local residents and businesses through about 20 offices in Louisville and other portions of central Kentucky. The company also operates Ascencia a nationwide online banking platform. PBI Bank offers standard financial services such as checking savings and money market accounts certificates of deposit and trust services. Loans collateralized by real estate such as commercial mortgages (more than 35% of the company's loan portfolio) residential mortgages (more than 25%) and construction loans (approximately 20%) comprise the lion's share of the company's loan portfolio.

	Annual Growth	12/16	12/17	12/18	12/19	12/20
Assets ($ mil.)	8.6%	945.2	970.8	1,069.7	1,245.8	1,312.3
Net income ($ mil.)	–	(2.8)	38.5	8.8	10.5	9.0
Market value ($ mil.)	0.5%	92.4	107.4	103.2	135.0	94.2
Employees	(1.3%)	238	217	214	251	226

LIMETREE BAY TERMINALS LLC

1 ESTATE HOPE
CHRISTIANSTED, VI 00820
Phone: 340-692-3000
Fax: –

CEO: –
CFO: –
HR: –
FYE: December 31
Type: Private

HOVENSA brings together US and Latin American know-how and operations to handle oil products in the US Virgin Islands. HOVENSA is a joint venture of Hess and Venezuelan oil giant PDVSA (its major crude oil supplier). Once the largest private employer in the US Virgin Islands the company operated a 500000-barrels-per-day crude oil refinery on St. Croix along with two specialized oil processing complexes a 150000-barrels-per-day fluid catalytic cracking unit and a 58000-barrels-per-day delayed coker unit. However the St. Croix refinery had run up losses for years; it was shut down in 2012 and was put up for sale in 2013.

	Annual Growth	12/05	12/06	12/07	12/08	12/09
Sales ($ mil.)	(42.5%)	–	–	–	17,479.7	10,048.3
Net income ($ mil.)	–	–	–	–	95.0	(451.2)
Market value ($ mil.)	–	–	–	–	–	–
Employees	–	–	–	–	–	1,300

LIMONEIRA CO
NMS: LMNR

1141 Cummings Road
Santa Paula, CA 93060
Phone: 805 525-5541
Fax: 805 525-8211
Web: www.limoneira.com

CEO: Harold Edwards
CFO: Mark Palamountain
HR: Debra Walker
FYE: October 31
Type: Public

Limoneira is an agribusiness company founded and based in Santa Paula California committed to responsibly using and managing its approximately 15400 acres of land water resources and other assets to maximize long-term stockholder value. Their current operations consist of fruit production sales and marketing rental operations real estate and capital investment activities. In addition to growing lemons and avocados Limoneira grows oranges and a variety of specialty citrus and other crops. Limoneira packs its own lemons and those of other growers.

	Annual Growth	10/17	10/18	10/19	10/20	10/21
Sales ($ mil.)	8.2%	121.3	129.4	171.4	164.6	166.0
Net income ($ mil.)	–	6.6	20.2	(5.9)	(16.4)	(3.4)
Market value ($ mil.)	(8.8%)	413.0	435.9	334.6	244.6	285.3
Employees	(1.4%)	284	286	319	299	268

LINC LOGISTICS COMPANY

11355 Stephens Rd.
Warren MI 48089
Phone: 586-467-1500
Fax: 704-499-9301
Web: www.portraitinnovations.com

CEO: –
CFO: –
HR: –
FYE: December 31
Type: Private

LINC Logistics is a not-so-missing link between car manufacturers and car buyers. A third-party logistics company LINC provides a variety of supply chain and freight transportation services including material handling and packaging warehousing freight delivery and international freight forwarding services (where companies purchase transportation capacity from carriers and resell it to customers). It serves primarily auto manufacturers including the "Big Three" — Ford GM and Chrysler as well as industrial technology and aerospace companies. LINC in late 2012 was acquired by Universal Truckload Services for about $350 million which included the assumption of debt.

LINCARE HOLDINGS INC.
NASDAQ: LNCR

19387 US 19 North
Clearwater FL 33764
Phone: 727-530-7700
Fax: 727-532-9692
Web: www.lincare.com

CEO: Crispin Teufel
CFO: Tracy Veillette
HR: –
FYE: December 31
Type: Public

There are some things you shouldn't have to leave the house to get Lincare Holdings believes oxygen therapy is one of them. The company helps some 800000 patients with chronic obstructive pulmonary diseases (including emphysema and severe asthma) by providing oxygen therapy services through a network of offices. Lincare's local service centers deliver oxygen equipment to patients in their homes trains them and monitors use of the equipment. Lincare offers positive airway pressure (PAP) machines for sleep apnea as well as other home medical equipment. It also provides home infusion such as chemotherapy pain therapy and parenteral nutrition. Global gases firm Linde owns Lincare.

LINCOLN INDUSTRIES

600 W. E St.
Lincoln NE 68522
Phone: 402-475-3671
Fax: 402-475-9565
Web: www.lincolnindustries.com

CEO: Marc Edward Lebaron
CFO: Andrew Hunzeker
HR: –
FYE: September 30
Type: Private

Two score and fifteen years ago Lincoln Industries brought forth on this continent a metal finishing company; its capabilities include anodizing chromate conversion coating and nickel plating. The company specializes in the functional and decorative finishing of steel aluminum and brass operating more than 20 automated and manual lines capable of more than 40 finishing processes. Lincoln's integrated finishing services include sourcing materials management manufacturing and assembly polishing packaging inventory management and design and engineering support.

LINCOLN EDUCATIONAL SERVICES CORP
NMS: LINC

14 Sylvan Way, Suite A
Parsippany, NJ 07054
Phone: 973 736-9340
Fax: –
Web: www.lincolnedu.com

CEO: Scott Shaw
CFO: Brian Meyers
HR: –
FYE: December 31
Type: Public

Lincoln hopes its graduates are better " Abe -l" to get a career. Lincoln Educational Services provides vocational programs from schools including Lincoln Technical Institute and Nashville Auto-Diesel College. It offers programs in automotive technology and skilled trades (including HVAC and electronics). Some 14000 students are enrolled at more than 30 campuses and five training sites more than 15 states throughout the US. Lincoln tends to grow by buying smaller schools and by opening campuses in new markets. It also expands its campus facilities to accommodate higher enrollment numbers. The company announced plans to divest its health care and other professions business in 2015.

	Annual Growth	12/16	12/17	12/18	12/19	12/20
Sales ($ mil.)	10.5%	196.9	261.9	263.2	273.3	293.1
Net income ($ mil.)	–	(28.3)	(11.5)	(6.5)	2.0	48.6
Market value ($ mil.)	35.7%	50.8	53.5	84.7	71.5	172.1
Employees	(3.1%)	2,197	1,980	1,884	1,922	1,933

LINCOLN NATIONAL CORP.
NYS: LNC

150 N. Radnor Chester Road, Suite A305
Radnor, PA 19087
Phone: 484 583-1400
Fax: –
Web: www.lfg.com

CEO: Dennis Glass
CFO: Randal Freitag
HR: –
FYE: December 31
Type: Public

Lincoln National which operates as Lincoln Financial Group is a holding company which operates multiple insurance and retirement businesses through subsidiary companies. It also offers group non-medical insurance products and services including short- and long-term disability statutory disability and paid family medical leave administration and absence management services term life dental vision and accident and critical illness benefits and services to the employer marketplace through various forms of employee-paid and employer-paid plans. The company does business through such subsidiaries as Lincoln National Life Insurance Lincoln Life & Annuity Company of New York and First Penn-Pacific Life Insurance Company.

	Annual Growth	12/17	12/18	12/19	12/20	12/21
Assets ($ mil.)	8.3%	281,763.0	298,147.0	334,761.0	365,948.0	387,301.0
Net income ($ mil.)	(9.3%)	2,079.0	1,641.0	886.0	499.0	1,405.0
Market value ($ mil.)	(2.9%)	13,620.9	9,091.8	10,456.2	8,914.6	12,095.2
Employees	1.6%	10,194	11,034	11,357	10,966	10,848

LINCOLN ELECTRIC HOLDINGS, INC.
NMS: LECO

22801 St. Clair Avenue
Cleveland, OH 44117
Phone: 216 481-8100
Fax: 216 486-1751
Web: www.lincolnelectric.com

CEO: Christopher Mapes
CFO: Gabriel Bruno
HR: Michele Kuhrt
FYE: December 31
Type: Public

Lincoln Electric is a global manufacturer of welding cutting and brazing products including arc welding power sources consumable electrodes plasma cutters fluxes fume extraction equipment robotic welding systems and wire feeders. Other products include computer numeric controlled (CNC) plasma and oxy-fuel cutting systems and regulators and torches used in plasma cutting and brazing. The company also offers a line of brazing and soldering alloys. The US accounts for around 55% of sales.

LINCOLN PROVISION INC.

824 W. 38th Place
Chicago IL 60609
Phone: 773-254-2400
Fax: 773-254-2405
Web: www.chigourmetsteaks.com

CEO: Rob Brown
CFO: Niteen Joshi
HR: –
FYE: December 31
Type: Private

Chicago has a loop around some of the best steer in the herd. Chicago Gourmet Steaks offers a plateful of the best cuts of beef including chateaubriand filet mignon and porterhouse steaks to hungry eaters. It sells its premium flash-frozen packed-in-ice meats through its website or by telephone or fax. The company also supplies foodservice establishments mainly high-end restaurants. CEO James Stevens acquired the company in 1990 from the late Walter Mander a longtime fixture in the Chicago meatpacking industry. Mander's Lincoln Meat Company which closed that same year was one of the last surviving slaughterhouses in the city.

	Annual Growth	12/17	12/18	12/19	12/20	12/21
Sales ($ mil.)	5.4%	2,624.4	3,028.7	3,003.3	2,655.4	3,234.2
Net income ($ mil.)	2.8%	247.5	287.1	293.1	206.1	276.5
Market value ($ mil.)	11.1%	5,383.7	4,635.3	5,686.4	6,834.0	8,199.0
Employees	0.0%	11,000	11,000	11,000	10,700	11,000

LINDSAY CORP
NYS: LNN

18135 Burke Street, Suite 100
Omaha, NE 68022
Phone: 402 829-6800
Fax: 402 829-6834
Web: www.lindsay.com

CEO: Randy Wood
CFO: Brian Ketcham
HR: –
FYE: August 31
Type: Public

Lindsay designs and manufactures irrigation systems primarily for farmers. The Zimmatic brand irrigation system a self-propelled center-pivot and lateral-move lineup is designed to use water energy and labor more efficiently than traditional flood or surface irrigation equipment. Touting better-to-bumper crop yields a dealer network sells to farmers in key markets worldwide. The US represents approximately 55% of sales. Lindsay offers chemical injection systems water pumping stations as well as replacement parts. An infrastructure division supplies movable barriers for traffic control and crash cushions for road safety.

	Annual Growth	08/17	08/18	08/19	08/20	08/21
Sales ($ mil.)	2.3%	518.0	547.7	444.1	474.7	567.6
Net income ($ mil.)	16.4%	23.2	20.3	2.2	38.6	42.6
Market value ($ mil.)	17.5%	944.3	1,044.7	962.7	1,090.0	1,797.1
Employees	(3.3%)	1,410	1,412	1,069	1,125	1,235

LINEAGE CELL THERAPEUTICS INC
ASE: LCTX

2173 Salk Avenue, Suite 200
Carlsbad, CA 92008
Phone: 442 287-8990
Fax: –
Web: www.lineagecell.com

CEO: Brian Culley
CFO: Kevin Cook
HR: –
FYE: December 31
Type: Public

Lineage Cell Therapeutics (formerly BioTime) is a clinical-stage biotechnology company developing novel cell therapies for unmet medical needs. Lineage Cell Therapeutics develops therapies for degenerative retinal diseases neurological conditions associated with demyelination and aiding the body in detecting and combating cancer. Its programs are based on proprietary cell-based therapy platform and associated development and manufacturing capabilities. Top three allogeneic cell therapy programs in clinical development include OpRegen (retinal pigment epithelium) OPC1 (oligodendrocyte progenitor) and VAC2 (cancer immunotherapy). Majority of its revenue comes from the US market.

	Annual Growth	12/16	12/17	12/18	12/19	12/20
Sales ($ mil.)	(25.5%)	5.9	3.5	5.0	3.5	1.8
Net income ($ mil.)	–	33.6	(20.0)	(46.0)	(11.7)	(20.6)
Market value ($ mil.)	(16.4%)	552.7	329.2	139.8	136.3	269.4
Employees	(14.3%)	102	95	79	55	55

LINEAGE POWER CORPORATION

601 Shiloh Rd.
Plano TX 75149-7507
Phone: 972-244-9288
Fax: 703-273-7011
Web: www.spacequest.com

CEO: –
CFO: –
HR: –
FYE: December 31
Type: Subsidiary

Lineage Power has a tradition of serving those in power. The company makes power converters filter modules inverters power bays and cabinets power supplies and rectifiers for electrical power conversion equipment. Customers have included telecommunications network operator Verizon Communications. Lineage sells directly and through distributors resellers and systems intgrators. The company also offers a range of services including systems engineering installation facility design project management and energy auditing. Lineage was acquired by GE in 2011 for about $520 million. GE used the deal to expand its high-efficiency energy products for telecom and data center applications to keep pace with demand.

LINEAR TECHNOLOGY CORP
NMS: LLTC

1630 McCarthy Boulevard
Milpitas, CA 95035
Phone: 408 432-1900
Fax: 408 434-0507
Web: www.linear.com

CEO: Lothar Maier
CFO: Donald P Zerio
HR: Sandy Ellyson
FYE: July 03
Type: Public

Linear Technology's high performance linear integrated circuits (ICs) create a connection from the analog world to the digital one. Its chips convert temperature pressure sound speed and other information into a digital form that can be read by digital devices. Linear Technology also makes linear devices that control power and regulate voltage in electronic systems. The company's products are used in a myriad of equipment from PCs to radar systems satellites and industrial instrumentation. It caters largely to communications and industrial markets as well as to the computer consumer goods aerospace and automotive markets. Linear agreed to sell to Analog Devices for $14.8 billion in July 2016.

	Annual Growth	07/12*	06/13	06/14	06/15*	07/16
Sales ($ mil.)	3.0%	1,266.6	1,282.2	1,388.4	1,475.1	1,423.9
Net income ($ mil.)	5.6%	398.1	406.9	460.0	521.0	494.3
Market value ($ mil.)	10.2%	7,508.4	8,828.9	11,187.0	10,873.1	11,076.8
Employees	3.1%	4,365	4,306	4,661	4,868	4,923

*Fiscal year change

LINKEDIN CORP
NYS: LNKD

2029 Stierlin Court
Mountain View, CA 94043
Phone: 650 687-3600
Fax: –
Web: www.linkedin.com

CEO: –
CFO: Steve Sordello
HR: –
FYE: December 31
Type: Public

Feeling a bit disconnected to the business world? LinkedIn wants to help. The firm operates an online professional network designed to help members find jobs connect with other professionals and locate business opportunities. The site has grown to reach more than 340 million users in some 200 countries since its launch in 2003. LinkedIn is free to join; it offers a paid premium membership with additional tools and sells advertising. It additionally earns revenue through its job listing service which allows companies to post job openings and search for candidates on LinkedIn.

	Annual Growth	12/11	12/12	12/13	12/14	12/15
Sales ($ mil.)	54.7%	522.2	972.3	1,528.5	2,218.8	2,990.9
Net income ($ mil.)	–	11.9	21.6	26.8	(15.3)	(164.8)
Market value ($ mil.)	37.5%	8,320.4	15,161.9	28,632.2	30,333.0	29,721.6
Employees	45.1%	2,116	3,458	5,045	6,897	9,372

LINKSHARE CORPORATION

215 Park Ave. South 9th Fl.
New York NY 10003
Phone: 646-943-8200
Fax: 646-943-8204
Web: www.linkshare.com

CEO: Stuart Simms
CFO: Bodie Gavnon
HR: –
FYE: June 30
Type: Subsidiary

Turning clicks into commerce has been LinkShare's plan since 1996. The company doing business as Rakuten LinkShare operates a performance-based affiliate marketing network. Clients which have included retailers Dell and Land's End market their products through promotional links placed on affiliate websites. Rakuten LinkShare charges clients based on volume of traffic and purchases made. The firm also offers tools that help clients manage track and analyze affiliate search and e-mail marketing campaigns. It has offices throughout the US as well as in the UK and Japan. LinkShare was founded in 1996 by brother and sister Stephen and Heidi Messer. Today it is part of Japanese online retailer Rakuten.

LINNCO LLC
NASDAQ: LNCO
600 Travis Ste. 5100
Houston TX 77002
Phone: 281-840-4000
Fax: 303-625-2710
Web: www.globeimmune.com
CEO: Mark E Ellis
CFO: David B Rottino
HR: -
FYE: December 31
Type: Private

LinnCo. LLC knows the drill on how to raise money. The company formed in April 2012 in order to buy shares of stock in Linn Energy LLC an oil and natural gas concern focused on production in the Mid-Continent California and the Permian Basin. LinnCo. LLC filed a $1 billion initial public offering in June 2012 with plans to buy stock in Linn Energy and become a major shareholder. (Linn Energy completed its IPO in January 2006 and doesn't have any significant shareholders.) While LinnCo. LLC doesn't have any operations or assets of its own as an investment vehicle its IPO (which took place in October 2012) helped raise additional equity capital for Linn Energy.

LINUX FOUNDATION
1 LETTERMAN DR D4700
SAN FRANCISCO, CA 941291494
Phone: 415-723-9709
Fax: -
Web: www.linuxfoundation.org
CEO: Jim Zemlin
CFO: Lisbeth McNabb
HR: -
FYE: December 31
Type: Private

The Linux Foundation is dedicated to promoting the use of the Linux computer operating system in academia the corporate world and government. The company was formed in 2007 by the merger of Open Source Development Labs with the Free Standards Group. The Linux Foundation promotes and standardizes the Linux operating system by providing resources and services needed for open source development including offering intellectual property protection for developers. The foundation operates the Linux.com Web site to provide information on Linux. Linux serves as an alternative to Microsoft's Windows operating system on which most of the PCs in the world are based and is derived from the UNIX operating system.

	Annual Growth	12/08	12/09	12/13	12/15	12/16
Sales ($ mil.)	36.6%	-	6.9	23.1	39.3	61.1
Net income ($ mil.)	49.3%	-	0.6	3.5	3.7	9.4
Market value ($ mil.)	-	-	-	-	-	-
Employees	-	-	-	-	-	9

LIONBRIDGE TECHNOLOGIES INC.
NMS: LIOX
1050 Winter Street
Waltham, MA 02451
Phone: 781 434-6000
Fax: -
Web: www.lionbridge.com
CEO: John Fennelly
CFO: Marc Litz
HR: -
FYE: December 31
Type: Public

Lionbridge Technologies wants to be king of the jungle at bridging the language gap. The company offers translation (or localization) of software user manuals Web content and other content. It prepares materials for international use by tailoring them to individual languages and cultures. The firm sells subscriptions to access its branded Web-based translation software; it also supplies human interpreters to government agencies and businesses. Additionally Lionbridge provides testing services under its VeriTest brand through which it checks websites software and hardware to ensure their quality. Among its more than 400 clients include Microsoft Google Adobe Systems and Samsung Group.

	Annual Growth	12/11	12/12	12/13	12/14	12/15
Sales ($ mil.)	7.0%	427.9	457.2	489.2	490.6	560.0
Net income ($ mil.)	69.4%	1.7	11.3	11.6	8.1	14.2
Market value ($ mil.)	21.0%	145.8	255.9	379.4	366.0	312.5
Employees	7.5%	4,500	5,000	4,800	5,500	6,000

LIPSCOMB UNIVERSITY
1 UNIVERSITY PARK DR
NASHVILLE, TN 372043956
Phone: 615-966-1000
Fax: -
Web: www.lipscomb.edu
CEO: -
CFO: Danny Taylor
HR: -
FYE: May 31
Type: Private

Lipscomb University was founded in 1891 as the Nashville Bible School by David Lipscomb and James A. Harding; it was renamed in Lipscomb's honor in 1918. The coeducational Christian school offers more than 150 programs of study in about 80 majors leading to bachelor's degrees about eight of them at colleges of arts and humanities Bible and ministry business education engineering pharmacy and health sciences and professional studies. It also offers graduate degrees in areas such as theology accountancy business administration conflict management counseling and education in addition to a doctorate degree in pharmacy. Lipscomb has an annual enrollment of approximately 4500 students.

	Annual Growth	05/14	05/15	05/17	05/18	05/19
Sales ($ mil.)	(2.3%)	-	167.2	143.3	146.4	152.2
Net income ($ mil.)	-	-	5.5	14.6	19.2	(5.3)
Market value ($ mil.)	-	-	-	-	-	-
Employees	-	-	-	-	-	550

LIQUEFIED NATURAL GAS LTD
NBB: LNGL Y
1001 McKinney, Suite 600
Houston, TX 77002
Phone: 713 815-6900
Fax: 713 815-6905
Web: www.lnglimited.com.au
CEO: -
CFO: -
HR: -
FYE: June 30
Type: Public

When the founders of Liquefied Natural Gas (LNG) created the company's name they went straight to the point. As a producer and distributor of liquefied natural gas LNG turns coalbed methane gas supplied by third-party companies into liquid form for more efficient transport. It operates more than 30 liquefaction plants around the world and targets energy users in developing markets that have little or no existing natural gas resources. Distributing its liquid gas products by land and sea the company operates a fleet of more than 260 carriers as well as 60 reception terminals located around the world. LNG was established as a public company in 2004.

	Annual Growth	06/15	06/16	06/17	06/18	06/19
Sales ($ mil.)	(2.2%)	0.5	0.4	0.3	0.2	0.5
Net income ($ mil.)	-	(66.3)	(85.6)	(22.5)	(16.8)	(23.5)
Market value ($ mil.)	-	-	-	-	-	-
Employees	(15.4%)	43	39	32	29	22

LIQUID INVESTMENTS, INC.
3840 VIA DE LA VALLE # 300
DEL MAR, CA 920144268
Phone: 858-509-8510
Fax: -
Web: www.nextsolutions.us
CEO: Ron L Fowler
CFO: -
HR: -
FYE: December 31
Type: Private

Liquid Investments has nothing to do with your bank accounts your retirement fund or your broker. The company supplies beer malt beverages soda energy drinks and water to customers in parts of California and Colorado. It owns the Mesa Beverage Co. in Santa Rosa California which handles over 1500 accounts in Sonoma and Marin counties. It also serves 475 accounts in the western slope area of Colorado through Colorado Beverage Distribution which has locations in Grand Junction and Montrose Colorado. Liquid distributes imported domestic and craft beers. It also offers regional and local beers along with soda and bottled water. Its latest addition to its craft labels is Victoria lagers.

	Annual Growth	12/07	12/08	12/09	12/10	12/11
Sales ($ mil.)	(0.5%)	-	95.3	93.2	91.8	93.8
Net income ($ mil.)	(79.0%)	-	128.0	0.4	(0.1)	1.2
Market value ($ mil.)	-	-	-	-	-	-
Employees	-	-	-	-	-	629

LIQUIDITY SERVICES INC
NMS: LQDT

6931 Arlington Road, Suite 200
Bethesda, MD 20814
Phone: 202 467-6868
Fax: –
Web: www.liquidityservices.com

CEO: William Angrick
CFO: Jorge Celaya
HR: –
FYE: September 30
Type: Public

Liquidity Services (LSI) is an online auction firm. LSI provides manufacturers retailers corporations and governments with an electronic marketplace to dispose of liquidate and track goods in the reverse supply chain. More than 4 million professional buyers are registered on the firm's online marketplaces through which professional buyers can bid for wholesale surplus and salvage items like retail customer returns overstock products and end-of-life goods. LSI founded in 1999 also offers services which include program management valuation asset management reconciliation refurbishment and recycling fulfillment marketing and sales warehousing and transportation buyer support among others. The US generates majority of the company's total revenue.

	Annual Growth	09/17	09/18	09/19	09/20	09/21
Sales ($ mil.)	(1.2%)	270.0	224.5	226.5	205.9	257.5
Net income ($ mil.)	–	(39.2)	(11.6)	(19.3)	(3.8)	50.9
Market value ($ mil.)	38.3%	196.1	211.0	245.9	247.9	718.2
Employees	(10.2%)	946	669	687	574	614

LIQUIDMETAL TECHNOLOGIES INC
NBB: LQMT

20321 Valencia Circle
Lake Forest, CA 92630
Phone: 949 635-2100
Fax: –
Web: www.liquidmetal.com

CEO: Tony Chung
CFO: –
HR: –
FYE: December 31
Type: Public

It's not liquid it's not metal — well OK it is metal. Still Liquidmetal Technologies has built on research done at the California Institute of Technology by company officers William Johnson and Atakan Peker to sell amorphous metal alloys. Those products include an alloy that's lighter than titanium but twice as strong as conventional titanium alloys. The company's products are sold as bulk alloys coatings composites and powders. Applications include casings for cell phones defense products (armor-piercing ammunition) industrial coatings and sporting goods (baseball bats tennis rackets). Electronics giant Samsung is among the company's largest customers.

	Annual Growth	12/16	12/17	12/18	12/19	12/20
Sales ($ mil.)	19.8%	0.5	0.3	0.5	1.4	1.0
Net income ($ mil.)	–	(18.7)	(8.7)	(7.4)	(7.4)	(2.6)
Market value ($ mil.)	(20.5%)	190.2	212.2	102.4	94.2	76.1
Employees	(25.5%)	26	28	25	9	8

LIRO PROGRAM AND CONSTRUCTION MANAGEMENT P.C.

3 AERIAL WAY
SYOSSET, NY 11791-5501
Phone: 516-938-5476
Fax: –
Web: www.liro.com

CEO: Luis Tormenta
CFO: Lawrence Roberts
HR: –
FYE: December 31
Type: Private

The LiRo Group does construction with a New York accent. Through its operating companies LiRo provides engineering architectural and construction management services to mostly public sector clients in New York New Jersey and Connecticut. It offers a wide range of engineering and inspection services including civil structural mechanical electrical traffic and environmental. Its projects have included renovation of municipal buildings such as schools correctional facilities fire stations and court houses as well as reconstruction of highways bridges and subways and capital improvements at professional sports facilities like Yankee Stadium. LiRo was co-founded in 1983 by owner Rocco L. Trotta.

	Annual Growth	12/0-1	12/00	12/01	12/02	12/10
Sales ($ mil.)	20.5%	–	11.7	14.7	12.9	75.6
Net income ($ mil.)	17.2%	–	1.6	2.5	2.9	7.8
Market value ($ mil.)	–	–	–	–	–	–
Employees	–	–	–	–	–	200

LITEHOUSE, INC.

100 LITEHOUSE DR
SANDPOINT, ID 838640528
Phone: 208-920-2000
Fax: –
Web: www.litehousefoods.com

CEO: –
CFO: –
HR: Charmaine Cook
FYE: December 28
Type: Private

This company shines its light on salads. Litehouse is a leading maker of salad dressings sauces and vegetable dips under the Litehouse label. It produces a variety of dressings including blue cheese ranch and vinaigrette along with low fat and organic products. The company also makes fruit dips glazes and cheese crumbles as well as apple cider marinades and freeze-dried herbs. With manufacturing facilities in Idaho Utah and Michigan Litehouse products are sold through supermarkets and warehouse clubs in the US and Canada. Litehouse also supplies dressings and other products to food service distributors and restaurants. Founded by Edward Hawkins in 1963 Litehouse is run by the Hawkins family.

	Annual Growth	01/15	01/16*	12/17	12/18	12/19
Sales ($ mil.)	14.0%	–	214.5	254.0	316.2	317.9
Net income ($ mil.)	18.8%	–	12.7	8.7	11.3	21.3
Market value ($ mil.)	–	–	–	–	–	–
Employees	–	–	–	–	–	1,146

*Fiscal year change

LITHIA MOTORS INC
NYS: LAD

150 N. Bartlett Street
Medford, OR 97501
Phone: 541 776-6401
Fax: –
Web: www.lithiainvestorrelations.com

CEO: Bryan DeBoer
CFO: Tina Miller
HR: –
FYE: December 31
Type: Public

Lithia Motors is a leading provider of personal transportation solutions reaching 100% of the United States within 400 miles. The auto dealer specializes in famed US auto brands such as Chrysler General Motors and Ford and operates nearly 210 locations representing over 30 brands in more than 20 states. The company offers a wide array of products and services fulfilling the entire vehicle ownership lifecycle including new and used vehicles finance and insurance products and automotive repair and maintenance. Chairman Sidney DeBoer controls Lithia Motors through Lithia Holding Co.

	Annual Growth	12/17	12/18	12/19	12/20	12/21
Sales ($ mil.)	22.7%	10,086.5	11,821.4	12,672.7	13,124.3	22,831.7
Net income ($ mil.)	44.2%	245.2	265.7	271.5	470.3	1,060.1
Market value ($ mil.)	27.2%	3,350.9	2,251.7	4,336.5	8,633.8	8,760.0
Employees	13.2%	12,899	13,643	14,320	14,538	21,150

LITTELFUSE INC
NMS: LFUS

8755 West Higgins Road, Suite 500
Chicago, IL 60631
Phone: 773 628-1000
Fax: –
Web: www.littelfuse.com

CEO: David Heinzmann
CFO: Meenal Sethna
HR: Maggie Chu
FYE: January 01
Type: Public

Littelfuse is big on circuit protection. The company is one of the world's largest fuse makers. In addition to its fuses Littelfuse's other circuit protection devices include positive temperature coefficient devices that limit current when too much is being supplied and electrostatic discharge suppressors that redirect transient high voltage. The company's thyristors protect telecommunications circuits from transient voltage caused by lightning strikes. It also supplies fuses for HVAC systems elevators and machine tools. Littelfuse's 7000 customers include distributors electronics manufacturers automakers and the automotive aftermarket.

	Annual Growth	12/17	12/18	12/19	12/20*	01/22
Sales ($ mil.)	11.2%	1,221.5	1,718.5	1,503.9	1,445.7	2,079.9
Net income ($ mil.)	18.9%	119.5	164.6	139.1	130.0	283.8
Market value ($ mil.)	9.7%	4,883.4	4,148.0	4,740.2	6,212.5	7,768.2
Employees	9.7%	10,700	12,300	11,300	12,200	17,000

*Fiscal year change

LITTLE LADY FOODS INC.

2323 Pratt Blvd.
Elk Grove Village IL 60007
Phone: 847-806-1440
Fax: 847-806-0026
Web: www.littleladyfoods.com

CEO: Rick Anderson
CFO: James Sharwarko
HR: –
FYE: December 31
Type: Private

This Little Lady serves up man-sized portions of frozen food. Little Lady Foods is a leading supplier of frozen food products for the foodservice and retail food industries. With facilities in the greater Chicago area the company makes stone-fired and kid-sized pizzas and a line of sandwiches that includes breakfast sandwiches paninis and wrap-style sandwiches on tortillas and flatbreads. The company markets its sandwiches for restaurants lunch stands and retail operators worldwide. It also offers sweet goods including an apple pancake muffins and turnovers. Little Lady Foods founded in 1961 provides custom product design creation and marketing services for private-label customers.

LITTLE SIOUX CORN PROCESSORS LLC

4808 F AVE
MARCUS, IA 510357070
Phone: 712-376-2800
Fax: –
Web: www.littlesiouxcornprocessors.com

CEO: Steve Roe
CFO: Gary Grotjohn
HR: –
FYE: September 30
Type: Private

Pursuing the corny American Heartland dream of profitable renewable energy Little Sioux Corn Processors operates an ethanol plant in northwest Iowa. (It actually owns a 60% interest in the limited partnership that owns the ethanol facility.) The company converts bushels of corn into ethanol distiller grains (used as feed for the dairy and beef industries) and corn oil. Ethanol is used as an additive to gasoline as well as a fuel enhancer for high-octane motors and it burns more cleanly than normal gasoline thereby reducing carbon monoxide emissions. Little Sioux's production capacity is about 90 million gallons of ethanol annually more than double its orginal capacity after successive expansions.

	Annual Growth	09/02	09/03	09/10	09/11	09/13
Sales ($ mil.)	27.0%	–	31.8	–	329.7	346.7
Net income ($ mil.)	1.3%	–	4.1	–	9.5	4.6
Market value ($ mil.)	–	–	–	–	–	–
Employees	–	–	–	–	–	48

LITTLER MENDELSON P.C.

650 California St. 20th Fl.
San Francisco CA 94108-2693
Phone: 415-433-1940
Fax: 415-399-8490
Web: www.littler.com

CEO: –
CFO: –
HR: –
FYE: December 31
Type: Private - Partnershi

Most national law firms aim to be full-service shops but Littler Mendelson concentrates on the law of the workplace. With about 800 lawyers Littler Mendelson is one of the largest employment law firms in the US. Its specialty is representing management in all types of labor disputes and employee lawsuits. Practice areas include appellate work business restructuring employment litigation unfair competition and workplace safety. Littler Mendelson has more than 50 offices spanning cities from New York to Seattle. The firm was founded in San Francisco in 1942; it began expanding beyond California in the 1990s.

LIVE NATION ENTERTAINMENT INC

9348 Civic Center Drive
Beverly Hills, CA 90210
Phone: 310 867-7000
Fax: –
Web: www.livenationentertainment.com

NYS: LYV
CEO: Michael Rapino
CFO: Joe Berchtold
HR: –
FYE: December 31
Type: Public

Live Nation Entertainment is the world's largest ticket seller and promoter of live entertainment. All total the company connects over 580 million fans across all of our concerts and ticketing platforms in about 45 countries. Through Ticketmaster it sells more than 485 million tickets annually for events at arenas stadiums theaters festival sites clubs and other venues across the world. Live Nation owns operates has exclusive booking rights for or has an interest in about 290 venues including the House of Blues clubs. Also a leading artist management firm the company has nearly 110 managers providing services to more than 500 artists. Live Nation generates about 65% of its revenue in the US.

	Annual Growth	12/17	12/18	12/19	12/20	12/21
Sales ($ mil.)	(11.8%)	10,337.4	10,787.8	11,548.0	1,861.2	6,268.4
Net income ($ mil.)	–	(6.0)	60.2	69.9	(1,724.5)	(650.9)
Market value ($ mil.)	29.5%	9,564.4	11,065.2	16,057.5	16,509.1	26,891.3
Employees	3.8%	8,800	9,500	10,500	8,200	10,200

LIVE VENTURES INC

325 E. Warm Springs Road, Suite 102
Las Vegas, NV 89119
Phone: 702 997-5968
Fax: –
Web: www.liveventures.com

NAS: LIVE
CEO: Jon Isaac
CFO: Virland A Johnson
HR: –
FYE: September 30
Type: Public

LiveDeal (formerly YP Corp.) is an Internet yellow pages and local online classifieds provider. The company offers goods and services listed for sale through its online classified marketplace at classifieds.livedeal.com; LiveDeal also publishes about 17 million business listings via its business directory at yellowpages.livedeal.com. Sources of revenue include advertising sales a pay-per-lead program with major auto dealers and optional listing upgrade and e-commerce/fraud prevention fees. The company changed its name from YP Corp. after its 2007 purchase of online local classifieds marketplace LiveDeal.

	Annual Growth	09/17	09/18	09/19	09/20	09/21
Sales ($ mil.)	15.8%	152.1	199.6	193.3	191.7	273.0
Net income ($ mil.)	48.0%	6.5	5.9	(4.0)	10.9	31.2
Market value ($ mil.)	31.4%	19.6	14.2	13.6	14.1	58.5
Employees	0.9%	1,211	1,155	1,000	1,150	1,253

LIVEPERSON INC

530 7th Avenue, Floor M1
New York, NY 10018
Phone: 212 609-4200
Fax: –
Web: www.liveperson.com

NMS: LPSN
CEO: Robert LoCascio
CFO: John Collins
HR: –
FYE: December 31
Type: Public

LivePerson makes life easier for people and brands everywhere through trusted Conversational AI. Conversational AI allows humans and machines to interact using natural language including speech or text. The Conversational Cloud its enterprise-class cloud-based platform enables businesses to become conversational by securely deploying AI-powered messaging at scale for brands with tens of millions of customers and many thousands of agents. It powers conversations across each of a brand's primary digital channels including mobile apps mobile and desktop web browsers short message service (SMS) social media and third-party consumer messaging platforms. Customers in the US make up about 65% of sales. The company was founded by Robert LoCascio back in 1995.

	Annual Growth	12/16	12/17	12/18	12/19	12/20
Sales ($ mil.)	13.3%	222.8	218.9	249.8	291.6	366.6
Net income ($ mil.)	–	(25.9)	(18.2)	(25.0)	(96.1)	(107.6)
Market value ($ mil.)	69.4%	510.0	776.9	1,274.1	2,499.5	4,203.9
Employees	5.1%	985	981	1,106	1,341	1,201

LIVERAMP HOLDINGS INC
NYS: RAMP

225 Bush Street, Seventeenth Floor
San Francisco, CA 94104
Phone: 866 352-3267
Fax: –
Web: www.liveramp.com

CEO: –
CFO: –
HR: –
FYE: March 31
Type: Public

Acxiom a provider of data and software used for direct marketing and customer relationship management (CRM) collects and maintains a storehouse of consumer information covering nearly every household in the US. Acxiom helps companies manage customer data and integrate that information into marketing systems. It draws clients from various sectors including automotive financial services packaged goods health care and telecommunications. The company has operations in China Europe and the US. Acxiom is part of The Interpublic Group of Companies.

	Annual Growth	03/17	03/18	03/19	03/20	03/21
Sales ($ mil.)	(15.8%)	880.2	917.4	285.6	380.6	443.0
Net income ($ mil.)	–	4.1	23.5	1,028.5	(124.5)	(90.3)
Market value ($ mil.)	16.2%	1,942.5	1,549.5	3,723.3	2,246.1	3,539.7
Employees	(22.1%)	3,260	3,380	950	1,150	1,200

LIVEWORLD, INC.
NBB: LVWD

2105 South Bascom Ave., Suite 159
Campbell, CA 95008
Phone: 800 301-9507
Fax: –
Web: www.liveworld.com

CEO: Peter Friedman
CFO: David Houston
HR: Christina Gazzano
FYE: December 31
Type: Public

LiveWorld hopes that online collaboration is the key to its livelihood. Promoting itself as a "social brand flow" manager the company designs websites and offers applications that can be added to a customers' existing site. It also offers customized pages on popular social media sites including Twitter and Facebook as well as moderators and community managers on these sites to keep the discussion headed in the right direction. LiveWorld has created online communities for prominent companies including HSBC Johnson & Johnson The Campbell Soup Company and Warner Brothers. Chairman and CEO Peter Friedman and EVP Jenna Woodul founded LiveWorld in 1996 from remnants of Apple's now-defunct eWorld online service.

	Annual Growth	12/16	12/17	12/18	12/19	12/20
Sales ($ mil.)	(3.2%)	9.7	9.9	7.7	7.4	8.6
Net income ($ mil.)	–	(1.3)	(1.3)	(0.6)	(0.4)	0.4
Market value ($ mil.)	8.1%	2.2	1.9	0.4	0.6	3.0
Employees		–	–	–	–	–

LKQ CORP
NMS: LKQ

500 West Madison Street, Suite 2800
Chicago, IL 60661
Phone: 312 621-1950
Fax: –
Web: www.lkqcorp.com

CEO: Dominick Zarcone
CFO: Varun Laroyia
HR: –
FYE: December 31
Type: Public

LKQ distributes replacement parts and components needed to repair passenger cars and trucks. It's one of the leading aftermarket parts suppliers in the US through subsidiary Keystone Automotive. LKQ also offers reconditioned remanufactured and refurbished parts including wheels bumpers covers and light and remanufactured engines and transmissions as well as recycled parts that are reclaimed from salvage vehicles. Customers include collision repair and mechanical repair shops. LKQ which generates just some half its sales in the US was formed in 1998.

	Annual Growth	12/16	12/17	12/18	12/19	12/20
Sales ($ mil.)	7.9%	8,584.0	9,736.9	11,876.7	12,506.1	11,628.8
Net income ($ mil.)	8.3%	464.0	533.7	480.1	541.3	638.4
Market value ($ mil.)	3.6%	9,303.9	12,345.5	7,203.3	10,836.8	10,697.2
Employees	0.9%	42,500	43,000	51,000	51,000	44,000

LL FLOORING HOLDINGS INC
NYS: LL

4901 Bakers Mill Lane
Richmond, VA 23230
Phone: 800 366-4204
Fax: –
Web: www.lumberliquidators.com

CEO: Charles Tyson
CFO: Nancy Walsh
HR: –
FYE: December 31
Type: Public

Known for its low prices Lumber Liquidators Holdings is one of the nation's largest retailers of hardwood flooring. It sells extensive assortment of domestic and exotic species of hardwoods from approximately 410 Lumber Liquidators stores in more than 45 states and Canada online by catalog and from its Virginia call center. The company also offers laminate flooring moldings underlayments adhesives tools and installation products. Its brands include Bellawood Builder's Pride and Virginia Mill Works. Lumber Liquidators primarily sells to homeowners or to contractors on behalf of homeowners as well as to commercial (Pro) customers. The company was founded in 1994 by chairman Tom Sullivan.

	Annual Growth	12/16	12/17	12/18	12/19	12/20
Sales ($ mil.)	3.4%	960.6	1,028.9	1,084.6	1,092.6	1,097.7
Net income ($ mil.)	–	(68.6)	(37.8)	(54.4)	9.7	61.4
Market value ($ mil.)	18.2%	455.1	907.5	275.2	282.5	888.7
Employees	1.5%	2,100	2,100	2,200	2,200	2,230

LMI AEROSPACE, INC.
NMS: LMIA

411 Fountain Lakes Blvd.
St. Charles, MO 63301
Phone: 636 946-6525
Fax: –
Web: www.lmiaerospace.com

CEO: Cliff Stebe
CFO: Clifford C Stebe Jr
HR: –
FYE: December 31
Type: Public

LMI Aerospace doesn't have to "just wing it." The company makes key airplane structures such as cockpit window frames fuselage skins and interior components. Its aerostructures segment fabricates machines finishes and integrates more than 40000 aluminum and specialty alloy components for commercial corporate and military aircraft. The engineering services unit (D3 Technologies) provides design engineering and program management services for aircraft. The Intec division designs and tests composites for production parts. The company also makes components for laser equipment used by semiconductor makers and reusable containers with industrial and military applications.

	Annual Growth	12/11	12/12	12/13	12/14	12/15
Sales ($ mil.)	10.2%	254.0	278.6	412.6	387.8	375.1
Net income ($ mil.)	–	16.4	16.5	(58.5)	(29.0)	(2.2)
Market value ($ mil.)	(13.0%)	232.5	256.2	195.3	186.8	133.4
Employees	7.1%	1,480	2,420	2,330	1,970	1,945

LNB BANCORP, INC.
NMS: LNBB

457 Broadway
Lorain, OH 44052-1769
Phone: 440 244-6000
Fax: 440 244-4815
Web: www.4lnb.com

CEO: –
CFO: –
HR: –
FYE: December 31
Type: Public

LNB Bancorp is the holding company for The Lorain National Bank which operates more than 20 branches in Ohio's Cuyahoga Erie Lorain and Summit counties. The bank serves local businesses and individuals offering such deposit products as checking and savings accounts money market accounts CDs and IRAs. It also offers trust services and credit cards. The bank's lending activities primarily consist of commercial loans (approximately 60% of its portfolio) and real estate mortgages as well as installment and home equity loans. The Lorain National Bank offers brokerage and investment services to customers through an agreement with Investment Centers of America.

	Annual Growth	12/09	12/10	12/11	12/12	12/13
Assets ($ mil.)	1.7%	1,149.5	1,152.5	1,168.4	1,178.3	1,230.3
Net income ($ mil.)	–	(2.0)	5.4	5.0	6.1	6.2
Market value ($ mil.)	23.5%	41.7	48.1	45.5	57.1	97.0
Employees	(0.5%)	272	272	260	262	267

LOCAL CORP
NBB: LOCM Q

7555 Irvine Center Drive
Irvine, CA 92618
Phone: 949 784-0800
Fax: 949 784-0880
Web: www.localcorporation.com

CEO: Frederick Thiel
CFO: Kenneth Cragun
HR: –
FYE: December 31
Type: Public

Local.com traffics in keywords. Specializing in paid-search advertising the company connects businesses to consumers online. It attracts more than 30 million visitors per month through its Local.com search site its network of more than 1000 regional media websites and ones that distribute its advertising feeds to third-party sites. It makes money from direct advertisers who bid for placement (based on keywords) and pay per click and from indirect advertising subscribers that gain inclusion on the network through paid-search firms including Yahoo! and SuperMedia. Local.com also offers search engine optimization and other advertising support services.

	Annual Growth	12/10	12/11	12/12	12/13	12/14
Sales ($ mil.)	(0.3%)	84.1	78.8	97.8	94.4	83.1
Net income ($ mil.)	–	4.2	(14.6)	(24.2)	(10.4)	(5.5)
Market value ($ mil.)	(36.7%)	151.2	49.4	47.8	36.8	24.2
Employees	(11.9%)	116	227	146	88	70

LOEB & LOEB LLP

10100 Santa Monica Blvd. Ste. 2200
Los Angeles CA 90067
Phone: 310-282-2000
Fax: 310-282-2200
Web: www.loeb.com

CEO: –
CFO: –
HR: –
FYE: January 31
Type: Private - Partnershi

Law firm Loeb & Loeb offers counsel in areas such as commercial finance entertainment intellectual property litigation real estate and tax. The firm has five US offices and international offices in Beijing and Hong Kong. Loeb & Loeb has more than 300 lawyers overall including former California governor Gray Davis. Clients have included classic rock 'n' roll band The Grateful Dead the estate of late actress Marilyn Monroe and the Motion Picture Association as well as corporate titans such as Bertelsmann Merrill Lynch and Prudential Securities.

LOEBER MOTORS, INC.

4255 W TOUHY AVE
LINCOLNWOOD, IL 607121933
Phone: 847-675-1000
Fax: –
Web: www.loebermotors.com

CEO: –
CFO: –
HR: –
FYE: December 31
Type: Private

Want to buy a car from a son of a son of a salesman? Go to Loeber Motors family-owned and -operated for three generations. The company sells Mercedes-Benz Porsche and smart cars vans and trucks from its dealerships in Lincolnwood Illinois. Loeber Motors also sells used cars and maintains parts and service departments. Loeber's Web site allows visitors to get quick quotes on new cars schedule service appointments order parts apply for finance and search for used vehicles. The site also provides a forum for owners to chat about their cars. Martin Loeber founded Loeber Motors in 1938.

	Annual Growth	12/14	12/15	12/16	12/17	12/18
Sales ($ mil.)	0.2%	–	315.0	330.2	268.2	316.7
Net income ($ mil.)	0.4%	–	3.8	4.6	1.8	3.9
Market value ($ mil.)	–	–	–	–	–	–
Employees	–	–	–	–	–	110

LOEHMANN'S HOLDINGS INC.

2500 Halsey St.
Bronx NY 10461
Phone: 718-409-2000
Fax: 718-518-2766
Web: www.loehmanns.com

CEO: –
CFO: –
HR: –
FYE: January 31
Type: Private

Humorist Erma Bombeck claimed that "All I Know About Animal Behavior I Learned in Loehmann's Dressing Room" — and if you've ever tussled over the last discounted Donna Karan blouse at one of this retailer's stores you know what she was talking about. With some 40 Loehmann's stores in about a dozen states and the District of Columbia Loehmann's stores sells designer and brand-name women's and men's apparel accessories intimate apparel fragrances shoes and gifts at deep discounts. But caution to the shy: Loehmann's is famous for its communal dressing rooms. Founded in Brooklyn in 1921 by Frieda Loehmann the company was acquired by Dubai-based Istithmar PJSC in 2006. It emerged from Chapter 11 in 2011.

LOEWS CORP.
NYS: L

667 Madison Avenue
New York, NY 10065-8087
Phone: 212 521-2000
Fax: –
Web: www.loews.com

CEO: James Tisch
CFO: David Edelson
HR: –
FYE: December 31
Type: Public

Loews is a diversified company with businesses in the insurance energy hospitality and packaging industries. The multi-industry holding company's main interest is insurance through publicly traded subsidiary CNA Financial which offers commercial property casualty coverage. It also owns hotels in the US and Canada through its Loews Hotels subsidiary. The company's Boardwalk Pipelines is engaged in interstate natural gas transmission pipeline systems while Altium Packaging is a packaging solutions provider and manufacturer in North America. Loews is controlled and run by the Tisch family including co-chairmen and cousins Andrew and Jonathan.

	Annual Growth	12/17	12/18	12/19	12/20	12/21
Assets ($ mil.)	0.6%	79,586.0	78,316.0	82,243.0	80,236.0	81,626.0
Net income ($ mil.)	7.9%	1,164.0	636.0	932.0	(931.0)	1,578.0
Market value ($ mil.)	3.7%	12,428.3	11,307.9	13,039.4	11,183.7	14,348.6
Employees	(13.1%)	18,100	17,900	18,605	12,200	10,340

LOGANSPORT FINANCIAL CORP.
NBB: LOGN

723 East Broadway
Logansport, IN 46947
Phone: 574 722-3855
Fax: 574 722-3857
Web: www.logansportsavings.com

CEO: Chad Higgins
CFO: Dottye Robeson
HR: –
FYE: December 31
Type: Public

Community banking is the main sport at Logansport. Logansport Financial is the holding company for Logansport Savings Bank which serves customers in Cass County Indiana. From a single office in Logansport the bank offers individuals and businesses a variety of financial services including such deposit products as checking savings and NOW accounts as well as IRAs and certificates of deposit. Logansport Savings Bank uses funds from deposits to originate residential mortgages which account for almost half of its loan portfolio. The bank originally chartered in 1925 also offers home equity home improvement commercial real estate business and consumer loans.

	Annual Growth	12/05	12/06	12/07	12/13	12/14
Assets ($ mil.)	0.1%	157.8	159.9	156.8	166.0	159.7
Net income ($ mil.)	5.7%	1.1	1.0	0.8	1.7	1.8
Market value ($ mil.)	5.6%	11.4	10.9	10.2	16.4	18.6
Employees	–	–	–	–	–	–

LOGIC DEVICES INCORPORATED   PINK SHEETS: LOGC

1375 Geneva Dr.
Sunnyvale CA 94089
Phone: 408-542-5400
Fax: 408-542-0080
Web: www.logicdevices.com

CEO: Bill Volz
CFO: Kimiko Milheim
HR: –
FYE: September 30
Type: Public

LOGIC Devices doesn't produce philosophical machines. Rather LOGIC specializes in high-end digital signal processor (DSP) chips used in applications including medical imaging instrumentation telecommunications and military weapons systems. The company outsources production of its chips to Asian foundries primarily Taiwan Semiconductor Manufacturing. LOGIC works with sales representatives and international distributors and also sells directly to OEMs including Lockheed Martin QUALCOMM Raytheon Sony Teradyne and Texas Instruments.

LOGICALIS, INC.

1 PENN PLZ STE 5130
NEW YORK, NY 101195160
Phone: 212-596-7160
Fax: –
Web: www.logicalis.com

CEO: Vince Deluca
CFO: Sally Brandtneris
HR: –
FYE: February 28
Type: Private

Logicalis believes enterprise technology should operate in a straightforward fashion. The company provides a variety of IT services such as consulting implementation systems integration staffing network design and training. Logicalis also offers managed services for tasks such as network security IT infrastructure management and monitoring and application management. Customers come from a variety of fields including manufacturing financial services and health care. In the US Logicalis operates from more than 30 offices. It is a subsidiary of UK-based Logicalis Group. Both are owned by South Africa-based Datatec Limited.

	Annual Growth	02/11	02/12	02/13	02/14	02/15
Sales ($ mil.)	0.2%	–	384.3	422.3	386.0	386.3
Net income ($ mil.)	7.5%	–	4.3	6.6	5.2	5.3
Market value ($ mil.)	–	–	–	–	–	–
Employees	–	–	–	–	–	700

LOGICQUEST TECHNOLOGY INC   NBB: LOGQ

410 Park Avenue, 15th Floor #31,
New York, NY 10022
Phone: 212 231-0033
Fax: –
Web: www.bluegate.com

CEO: –
CFO: Yew Cheng
HR: –
FYE: December 31
Type: Public

Bluegate holds the keys to the gates of medical information. The company provides information technology (IT) services to the health care industry. It specializes in medical-grade network and managed services that meet HIPAA compliance regulations. It serves hospitals medical practices and other centralized health care providers. The company operates a leading Medical Grade Network dedicated to health care-related security and privacy concerns; Bluegate markets it as the only such network in the US. Memorial Hermann Health Net Providers a subsidiary of the Memorial Hermann Healthcare System is a client; Bluegate also provides services to the Texas-based Renaissance Healthcare Systems.

	Annual Growth	12/10	12/11	12/12	12/13	12/14
Sales ($ mil.)	(40.0%)	0.3	0.2	0.1	0.1	0.0
Net income ($ mil.)	–	(0.2)	(0.5)	(0.5)	(0.6)	(0.5)
Market value ($ mil.)	–	0.0	0.0	0.0	0.0	0.0
Employees	–	–	–	–	–	–

LOGISTICS MANAGEMENT SOLUTIONS L.C.

1 CITYPLACE DR STE 415
SAINT LOUIS, MO 63141-7066
Phone: 314-692-8886
Fax: –
Web: www.lmslogistics.com

CEO: Dennis Schoemehl
CFO: Scott Hunt
HR: –
FYE: December 31
Type: Private

Logistics Management Solutions (LMS) ensures a speedy delivery. The company provides a variety of third-party logistics and supply chain management services from process optimization consulting to shipment execution and transportation management. LMS also offers TOTAL a Web-based software package designed to work with customers' enterprise resource planning (ERP) systems. The company operates through a network of independent shippers to safely efficiently and cost-effectively manage the transportation of freight for manufacturers as well as wholesalers and retailers. Its roster of customers has included Monsanto (former parent) BASF Sara Lee Honeywell and American Railcar.

	Annual Growth	12/05	12/06	12/07	12/08	12/09
Sales ($ mil.)	–	–	–	(371.3)	108.4	97.5
Net income ($ mil.)	1353.8%	–	–	0.0	2.6	3.5
Market value ($ mil.)	–	–	–	–	–	–
Employees	–	–	–	–	–	146

LOGMEIN INC   NMS: LOGM

320 Summer Street
Boston, MA 02210
Phone: 781 638-9050
Fax: 781 437-1803
Web: www.logmein.com

CEO: Mike Kohlsdorf
CFO: Edward K Herdiech
HR: Jo Deal
FYE: December 31
Type: Public

LogMeIn wants to help you stay productive even on the go. The company provides Web-based remote access software and services to consumers small and midsized businesses and IT service providers. Its user access and remote collaboration offerings serve consumers and business users while businesses and IT service providers use LogMeIn's technology to provide remote management and support. LogMeIn offers both free and subscription-based services. Its paid services add advanced features such as file transfer remote printing and drive mapping. Corporate customers include 3M AMD and IBM. About two-thirds of LogMeIn's sales come from US clients. In 2017 LogMeIn merged with GoToBusiness in a $1.8 billion transaction.

	Annual Growth	12/14	12/15	12/16	12/17	12/18
Sales ($ mil.)	52.6%	222.0	271.6	336.1	989.8	1,204.0
Net income ($ mil.)	74.9%	8.0	14.6	2.6	99.5	74.4
Market value ($ mil.)	13.4%	2,501.1	3,401.4	4,894.3	5,804.2	4,134.9
Employees	44.6%	804	1,006	1,124	2,760	3,515

LOJACK CORPORATION

2400 N GLNVLLE DR STE 225
RICHARDSON, TX 75082
Phone: 781-302-4200
Fax: –
Web: www.lojack.com

CEO: Randy Ortiz
CFO: Kenneth Dumas
HR: –
FYE: December 31
Type: Private

LoJack's signature product helps police recover stolen vehicles — a chilling thought for those driving hot cars. When a car equipped with a LoJack transmitter is stolen its signal is activated and tracked by police. The company rents tracking computers to law enforcement agencies then markets transponders to dealers and operators in 28 states and the District of Columbia and roughly 30 countries internationally. It also sells products for tracking people personal electronics cargo data and commercial equipment. LoJack provides installation and maintenance of its units which are manufactured by third parties.

	Annual Growth	12/11	12/12	12/13	12/14	12/15
Sales ($ mil.)	(3.0%)	–	–	–	133.6	129.6
Net income ($ mil.)	–	–	–	–	(18.0)	3.3
Market value ($ mil.)	–	–	–	–	–	–
Employees	–	–	–	–	–	490

LOMA LINDA UNIVERSITY

11060 ANDERSON ST
LOMA LINDA, CA 923501736
Phone: 909-558-4540
Fax: –
Web: www.home.llu.edu

CEO: –
CFO: –
HR: –
FYE: June 30
Type: Private

Loma Linda University (LLU) is a Seventh-day Adventist institution that focuses on health sciences. The university offers more than 50 degree (bachelor's master's and doctorate) and certificate programs in the fields of allied health behavioral health dentistry medicine nursing pharmacy public health and religion. It has an enrollment of approximately 5000 students. LLU is an affiliate of the Loma Linda University Adventist Health Sciences Center where physicians and other health-care professionals provide medical care at the Loma Linda University Medical Center campuses. The school was founded in 1905 and is one of 15 Seventh-day Adventist universities.

	Annual Growth	06/16	06/17	06/18	06/19	06/20
Sales ($ mil.)	(1.9%)	–	301.4	269.1	268.4	284.6
Net income ($ mil.)	–	–	42.3	(28.3)	(27.9)	(85.8)
Market value ($ mil.)	–	–	–	–	–	–
Employees	–	–	–	–	–	7,000

LONG BEACH MEDICAL CENTER

2801 ATLANTIC AVE FL 2
LONG BEACH, CA 908061701
Phone: 562-933-2000
Fax: –
Web: www.memorialcare.org

CEO: John Bishop
CFO: Wendy Dorchester
HR: –
FYE: June 30
Type: Private

Long Beach Medical Center (LBMC) is an old-timer in the Long Beach health care market. A subsidiary of Memorial Care LBMC provides a full range of health services to residents of the Long Beach California area. Services include primary emergency diagnostic surgical therapeutic and rehabilitative care. The hospital is home to centers for treatment of cancer heart stroke and women's and children's health concerns. It also provides home and hospice care programs as well as occupational health services. Through Outpatient Wound Healing Center LBMC provides full-services wound care for adults and children in Los Angeles County and Orange County.

	Annual Growth	06/10	06/11	06/15	06/16	06/18
Sales ($ mil.)	(7.4%)	–	1,083.1	624.1	618.8	633.6
Net income ($ mil.)	0.1%	–	63.5	93.9	88.8	63.8
Market value ($ mil.)	–	–	–	–	–	–
Employees	–	–	–	–	–	6,000

LONG ISLAND JEWISH MEDICAL CENTER

27005 76TH AVE
NEW HYDE PARK, NY 110401496
Phone: 516-465-2600
Fax: –
Web: www.lijed.com

CEO: Michael J Dowling
CFO: –
HR: –
FYE: December 31
Type: Private

Long Island Jewish Medical Center serves the western edge of Long Island and the eastern edge of the greater metropolitan New York area. The medical center campus includes Long Island Jewish Hospital a general acute care hospital; Cohen Children's Medical Center of New York Hospital which provides a full range of pediatric care services; and The Zucker Hillside Hospital a psychiatric hospital for patients of all ages. The medical center's staff includes 1200 physicians. Long Island Jewish Medical Center is the primary clinical and medical training facility of Northwell Health.

	Annual Growth	12/14	12/15	12/16	12/17	12/18
Sales ($ mil.)	17.1%	–	1,524.8	2,093.9	2,222.7	2,448.9
Net income ($ mil.)	7.6%	–	44.9	162.8	154.3	56.1
Market value ($ mil.)	–	–	–	–	–	–
Employees	–	–	–	–	–	1,214

LONG ISLAND POWER AUTHORITY

333 EARLE OVINGTON BLVD # 403
UNIONDALE, NY 115533606
Phone: 516-222-7700
Fax: –
Web: www.lipower.org

CEO: Matthew Cohen
CFO: Herbert L Hogue
HR: –
FYE: December 31
Type: Private

The long and short of it is that Long Island Power Authority (LIPA) owns the electric transmission and distribution system on Long Island that delivers power to more than 1.1 million retail customers. The company's network which is managed and operated by the National Grid USA consists of nearly 14000 miles of overhead and underground lines. LIPA offers energy conservation products and services as well as incentive programs to encourage customers to purchase energy from "green" (environmentally friendly) power generation sources. LIPA is a municipally owned not-for-profit utility company.

	Annual Growth	12/15	12/16	12/18	12/19	12/20
Sales ($ mil.)	3.5%	–	3,399.1	3,576.3	3,516.4	3,900.7
Net income ($ mil.)	–	–	(26.4)	22.7	24.0	18.8
Market value ($ mil.)	–	–	–	–	–	–
Employees	–	–	–	–	–	100

LONG ISLAND UNIVERSITY WESTCHESTER & ROCKLAND ALUMNI ASSOCIATION LTD.

700 NORTHERN BLVD
GREENVALE, NY 115481319
Phone: 516-299-2535
Fax: –
Web: www.liu.edu

CEO: –
CFO: Robert Altholz
HR: –
FYE: August 31
Type: Private

Long Island University (LIU) helps students see a long future in professional fields including medicine and business. LIU has an enrollment of more than 24000 students at multiple locations in New York State. The university employs more than 600 full-time faculty members and has a 12:1 student-to-teacher ratio. LIU offers 575 degree programs and certificates in fields including pharmacy nursing health sciences education liberal arts sciences business and information studies. The school traces its roots to 1886 when the Brooklyn College of Pharmacy was founded.

	Annual Growth	08/09	08/10	08/11	08/14	08/15
Sales ($ mil.)	(4.1%)	–	–	468.6	501.7	396.8
Net income ($ mil.)	91.8%	–	–	2.5	41.4	33.7
Market value ($ mil.)	–	–	–	–	–	–
Employees	–	–	–	–	–	3,300

LOOKSMART LTD.

NAS: LOOK

50 California Street, 16th Floor
San Francisco, CA 94108
Phone: 415 348-7000
Fax: –
Web: www.looksmart.com

CEO: –
CFO: –
HR: –
FYE: December 31
Type: Public

It's hard to find anything online without looking unless you're talking about ads. LookSmart helps publishers advertisers and consumers see what they want when it comes to online advertising. The company earns most of its revenue through its Advertiser Networks offering (AdCenter) which provides advertisers with targeted pay-per-click search advertising contextual advertising and banner products. It also offers Publisher Solutions that help content publishers maintain advertiser relationships online. LookSmart completed its transition to a full-on provider of advertising and publishing services after a couple of years spent divesting its non-core consumer website assets.

	Annual Growth	12/09	12/10	12/11	12/12	12/13
Sales ($ mil.)	(40.1%)	51.8	47.5	27.6	15.7	6.7
Net income ($ mil.)	–	(6.2)	1.0	(2.5)	(11.0)	(5.4)
Market value ($ mil.)	18.9%	5.9	12.2	7.4	5.1	11.8
Employees	(20.5%)	65	52	50	38	26

LOOP LLC

137 NORTHPARK BLVD
COVINGTON, LA 704335071
Phone: 985-276-6100
Fax: –
Web: www.loopllc.com

CEO: –
CFO: –
HR: –
FYE: December 31
Type: Private

LOOP (Louisiana Offshore Oil Port) offloads crude oil from tankers stores it and routes it to pipelines and refineries along the Gulf Coast and the Midwest. It is also the storage and terminalling facility for the MARS pipeline system and its supply of offshore Gulf of Mexico crude oil. Oil is stored in eight underground caverns leached out of a naturally occurring salt dome. These caverns are capable of storing about 50 million barrels of crude oil. The company is owned by Marathon Ashland Pipe Line Murphy Oil and Shell Oil. In addition to other services LOOP has an above-ground tank farm made up of six 600000 barrel tanks.

	Annual Growth	12/05	12/06	12/08	12/09	12/16
Sales ($ mil.)	1.7%	–	235.8	265.3	243.6	279.9
Net income ($ mil.)	1.9%	–	104.3	79.2	87.3	125.9
Market value ($ mil.)	–	–	–	–	–	–
Employees		–	–	–	–	128

LOOPNET INC.

NASDAQ: LOOP

185 Berry St. Ste. 4000
San Francisco CA 94107
Phone: 415-243-4200
Fax: 415-764-1622
Web: www.loopnet.com

CEO: Richard J Boyle Jr
CFO: Brent Stumme
HR: –
FYE: December 31
Type: Subsidiary

Feeling out of the loop when it comes to commercial real estate? LoopNet provides information services to the commercial real estate market through LoopNet.com. Its flagship LoopNet Marketplace includes some 788000 property listings; it offers a free basic membership as well as a subscription-based premium membership. LoopNet has more than 4 million registered members and about 68000 premium members. The firm also offers LoopLink which helps real estate brokers integrate LoopNet listings into their own websites; BizBuySell and BizQuest online marketplaces for businesses that are for sale; and commercial real estate network CityFeet.com. Real estate data firm CoStar Group owns LoopNet.

LORILLARD, INC.

NYS: LO

714 Green Valley Road
Greensboro, NC 27408-7018
Phone: 336 335-7000
Fax: –
Web: www.lorillard.com

CEO: –
CFO: –
HR: –
FYE: December 31
Type: Public

Money smells of menthol at Lorillard the #3 cigarette maker in the US (behind Philip Morris and Reynolds American). Flagship brand Newport is its best-selling menthol cigarette and #2-top selling cigarette name in the US accounting for about 85% of sales. Other brands include the premium and discount lines of Kent Old Gold True and Maverick as well as the blu e-cigarette. The company sells its lineup to wholesale distributors (who supply retail and chain stores and government agencies). Lorillard was known as the Carolina Group until 2008 when it split from former parent Loews. Founded in 1760 by French immigrant Pierre Lorillard it is the nation's oldest continuously operating tobacco business.

	Annual Growth	12/10	12/11	12/12	12/13	12/14
Sales ($ mil.)	4.2%	5,932.0	6,466.0	6,623.0	6,950.0	6,990.0
Net income ($ mil.)	3.6%	1,029.0	1,116.0	1,099.0	1,180.0	1,187.0
Market value ($ mil.)	(6.4%)	29,541.6	41,040.0	42,001.2	18,244.8	22,658.4
Employees	1.8%	2,700	2,800	2,900	2,900	2,900

LOS ANGELES COUNTY DEPARTMENT OF HEALTH SERVICES

313 N. Figueroa St.
Los Angeles CA 90012
Phone: 213-240-8101
Fax: 213-250-4013
Web: www.ladhs.org

CEO: –
CFO: –
HR: Marlon Manalo
FYE: June 30
Type: Government Agency

Los Angeles County Department of Health Services is one of the US's largest publicly supported health systems. The department includes three general acute care hospitals a rehabilitation hospital (Rancho Los Amigos National Rehabilitation Center which has some 400 beds) two ambulatory care centers and several community health clinics. The system is the main provider of health care for the area's poor and uninsured. It provides general medical and surgical care and is affiliated with the medical school at USC. The system also manages the Emergency Medical Services (EMS) Agency and the Community Health Plan HMO a low-cost managed care plan for members of Medicaid and other state-funded programs.

LOS ANGELES COUNTY METROPOLITAN TRANSPORTATION AUTHORITY

1 Gateway Plaza
Los Angeles CA 90012-2952
Phone: 213-922-6000
Fax: 213-922-2704
Web: www.metro.net

CEO: Stephanie Wiggins
CFO: Nalini Ahuja
HR: –
FYE: June 30
Type: Government-owned

In the City of Angels it takes more than wings to get around. Thanks to the bus and rail systems of the Los Angeles County Metropolitan Transportation Authority (LACMTA or Metro) millions of passengers are carried through one of the most populous counties in the US via Metro Bus Metrolink (commuter rail) and Metro Rail (subway and light rail). Together they cover an extensive freeway network four airports and various ports. LACTMA operates these systems and it serves as a transportation planner designer and builder. A 14-member board consisting of elected officials (including the mayor) and appointees secures the budget (approximately $4 billion) and selects the projects for Metro.

LOS ANGELES DEPARTMENT OF WATER AND POWER

111 N HOPE ST
LOS ANGELES, CA 900122607
Phone: 213-367-1320
Fax: –
Web: www.ladwp.com

CEO: –
CFO: Ann M Santilli
HR: –
FYE: June 30
Type: Private

The Los Angeles Department of Water and Power (LADWP) keeps the movie cameras running and the swimming pools full. The largest municipally owned utility in the US LADWP provides electricity to approximately 1.4 million residential and business customers and water to some 681000 customers. The company has net dependable capacity of about 8010 MW from a diverse mix of energy resources; it also buys and sells wholesale power. As a revenue-producing proprietary department the LADWP transfers a portion of its annual estimated electric revenues to the City of Los Angeles general fund.

	Annual Growth	06/08	06/09	06/10	06/11	06/17
Sales ($ mil.)	4.7%	–	–	812.4	3,126.0	1,118.5
Net income ($ mil.)	11.1%	–	–	67.3	57.6	140.5
Market value ($ mil.)	–	–	–	–	–	–
Employees		–	–	–	–	9,500

LOS ANGELES PHILHARMONIC ASSOCIATION

151 S GRAND AVE
LOS ANGELES, CA 900123034
Phone: 213-972-7300
Fax: –
Web: www.laphil.com

CEO: Chad Smith
CFO: Karen Sturges
HR: –
FYE: September 30
Type: Private

The Los Angeles Philharmonic Association promotes its orchestra which is one of Southern California's leading performing arts institutions. The orchestra often known simply as the LA Phil performs orchestral and chamber music jazz world music and holiday concerts at the Walt Disney Concert Hall (in winter) and the Hollywood Bowl (in summer). The orchestra that would become the Los Angeles Philharmonic was originally founded and financed back in 1919 by copper baron and music enthusiast William Andrews Clark Jr. The Association was officially formed in 1976 but traces its roots to the beginning of the orchestra.

	Annual Growth	09/07	09/08	09/13	09/14	09/19
Sales ($ mil.)	(13.0%)	–	864.5	124.8	145.5	187.2
Net income ($ mil.)	318.9%	–	0.0	14.5	27.7	20.9
Market value ($ mil.)	–	–	–	–	–	–
Employees	–	–	–	–	–	2,000

LOUIS VUITTON NORTH AMERICA INC.

19 E. 57th St.
New York NY 10022
Phone: 212-931-2000
Fax: 212-931-2730
Web: www.lvmh.com

CEO: Antonio Belloni
CFO: Patrice Pfistner
HR: –
FYE: December 31
Type: Subsidiary

Louis Vuitton North America knows fashion and leather retailing. The company is the North American operating subsidiary of French luxury goods giant LVMH Moet Hennessy Louis Vuitton which boasts more than 60 luxury brands including Clicquot Dom Perignon Moet & Chandon Christian Dior Givenchy Donna Karan (DKI) Sephora and TAG Heuer. Louis Vuitton North America runs the Louis Vuitton fashion and leather goods business in the US. The company also dabbles in duty free shopping. Louis Vuitton North America operates more than 530 US stores including a four-story emporium on New York's Fifth Avenue. The North American arm of the Maison contributed about 20% of its parent company's 2012 sales.

LOUISIANA BANCORP INC

NMS: LABC

1600 Veterans Memorial Boulevard
Metairie, LA 70005
Phone: 504 834-1190
Fax: –
Web: www.bankofneworleans.com

CEO: –
CFO: –
HR: –
FYE: December 31
Type: Public

Louisiana Bancorp's vault isn't filled with Mardi Gras doubloons ch re. The holding company owns the Bank of New Orleans which offers standard retail banking products to individuals and small businesses including deposit accounts loans and mortgages and credit cards. Residential mortgages represent about half of the bank's loan portfolio; commercial mortgages and land loans make up most of the rest. Bank of New Orleans operates three locations and a loan office in the Crescent City; a fourth branch has been closed since being damaged by Hurricane Katrina in 2005. The bank was founded in 1909 as Greater New Orleans Homestead.

	Annual Growth	12/09	12/10	12/11	12/12	12/13
Assets ($ mil.)	(1.0%)	329.8	320.9	313.1	311.9	316.7
Net income ($ mil.)	1.7%	2.5	2.6	2.1	2.5	2.7
Market value ($ mil.)	5.9%	41.9	42.1	45.8	49.0	52.6
Employees	0.7%	68	65	64	72	70

LOUISIANA TECH UNIVERSITY

1100 HULL AVE
RUSTON, LA 712705551
Phone: 318-257-3267
Fax: –
Web: www.latech.edu

CEO: –
CFO: –
HR: Lauryn Brooks
FYE: June 30
Type: Private

Louisiana Tech University founded in 1894 has an annual enrollment of approximately 11000 students. The public research university offers bachelor's master's and doctoral degrees through more than 80 undergraduate and more than 40 graduate academic programs at colleges of applied and natural sciences business education engineering and science and liberal arts. It also confers associate degrees and post-bachelor's certificates. The university's research centers focus on education and government technology and commercialization and economic development and community support. Louisiana Tech's student-athletes compete in more than 15 varsity sports.

	Annual Growth	06/04	06/05	06/18	06/19	06/20
Sales ($ mil.)	2.4%	–	82.0	115.0	120.2	116.1
Net income ($ mil.)	6.5%	–	5.6	18.0	16.0	14.6
Market value ($ mil.)	–	–	–	–	–	–
Employees	–	–	–	–	–	1,230

LOUISIANA-PACIFIC CORP

NYS: LPX

414 Union Street, Suite 2000
Nashville, TN 37219
Phone: 615 986-5600
Fax: –

CEO: William Southern
CFO: Alan Haughie
HR: Robin Everhart
FYE: December 31
Type: Public

Specializing in floors walls and roofs Louisiana-Pacific (LP) might just have you surrounded. The building materials company makes specialized wood products such as oriented strand board (a lower-cost version of plywood) siding and laminated lumber and related products. Its offerings are used in new home construction repair and remodeling and outdoor structures markets. The company sells its products to a variety of specialized and broad-line wholesale distributors and dealers focused primarily on the supply of products for use by professional builders and contractors. It has production facilities throughout North and South America but generates most of its revenue in US.

	Annual Growth	12/17	12/18	12/19	12/20	12/21
Sales ($ mil.)	13.6%	2,733.9	2,828.0	2,310.0	2,788.0	4,553.0
Net income ($ mil.)	37.1%	389.8	394.6	(5.0)	499.0	1,377.0
Market value ($ mil.)	31.4%	2,248.8	1,902.8	2,540.8	3,183.1	6,709.6
Employees	(1.0%)	5,000	4,900	4,800	4,500	4,800

LOUISVILLE-JEFFERSON COUNTY METRO GOVERNMENT

527 W JEFFERSON ST # 400
LOUISVILLE, KY 402022814
Phone: 502-574-2003
Fax: –
Web: www.jeffersoncountyclerk.org

CEO: –
CFO: Daniel Frockt
HR: –
FYE: June 30
Type: Private

Louisville is so much more than bourbon baseball bats and horse races. The largest city in Kentucky Louisville counts about 600000 people in the urban area which has the same parameters as Jefferson County. Louisville is home to liquor company Brown-Forman; Hillerich & Bradsby maker of Louisville Slugger baseball bats; and Churchill Downs where the Kentucky Derby is held. In addition Louisville has a few Fortune 500 companies in the city - fast food operator YUM! Brands and health care companies Humana and Kindred.

	Annual Growth	06/16	06/17	06/18	06/19	06/20
Sales ($ mil.)	2.6%	–	797.3	825.9	873.6	860.2
Net income ($ mil.)	30.8%	–	11.8	14.7	(38.4)	26.5
Market value ($ mil.)	–	–	–	–	–	–
Employees	–	–	–	–	–	6,500

LOVE'S TRAVEL STOPS & COUNTRY STORES INC.

10601 N. Pennsylvania Ave.
Oklahoma City OK 73120
Phone: 405-751-9000
Fax: 405-749-9110
Web: www.loves.com

CEO: Tom E Love
CFO: Doug Stussi
HR: –
FYE: December 31
Type: Private

If you're a trucker or RVer on the road all you need is Love's. Love's Travel Stops & Country Stores operates more than 290 travel stop locations and 150 truck tire care centers throughout a swath of about 40 states from California to Virginia including convenience stores in Colorado Kansas New Mexico Oklahoma and Texas. Each travel stop includes a convenience store; a fast-food restaurant such as Taco Bell or Subway; and gas outlets for cars trucks and RVs. The travel stops also provide shower rooms laundry facilities game rooms and mail drops. Love's Travel Stops & Country Stores is owned by the family of CEO Tom Love who founded the company in 1964.

LOWE'S FOOD STORES INC.

1381 Old Mill Circle Ste. 200
Winston-Salem NC 27114
Phone: 336-659-0180
Fax: 336-768-4702
Web: www.lowesfoods.com

CEO: –
CFO: –
HR: Bobby Long
FYE: September 30
Type: Subsidiary

Lowe's Food Stores operates a chain of more than 100 supermarkets in North Carolina South Carolina and Virginia. The stores offer traditional supermarket fare including fresh meat seafood deli and bakery departments in addition to natural foods and supplements. The regional grocery chain's Lowe's-Foods-to-Go program lets customers shop online and either pick up their groceries at their local Lowe's Food store or have them delivered. The company's Just$ave division operates more than 15 discount food stores in North Carolina as well as more than half a dozen fuel stations. Founded in 1954 Lowe's Food Stores is owned by food wholesaler Alex Lee.

LOW TEMP INDUSTRIES INC.

9192 TARA BLVD
JONESBORO, GA 302364913
Phone: 678-379-0913
Fax: –
Web: www.lowtempind.com

CEO: William E Casey
CFO: Mike Moody
HR: –
FYE: October 31
Type: Private

Bam! Cooks kick it up a notch on Low Temp Industries' commercial chef's counters and dish tables. Constructed of stainless steel the tables and counters outfit the kitchens of restaurants hospitals schools and cafeterias. The chef's counter can be custom built for the customer to include a variety of food warmers shelves self-contained sandwich units cutting boards and a sink. Low Temp also manufactures custom serving counters for dining areas and automatic dish conveyors with washing systems. Low Temp's Colorpoint division builds mobile fiberglass serving line equipment while its Visions division designs and builds specialty counters booths window treatments signage and menu boards.

	Annual Growth	10/02	10/03	10/04	10/06	10/07
Sales ($ mil.)	4.7%	–	19.6	20.3	24.4	23.5
Net income ($ mil.)	–	–	–	0.0	0.0	0.0
Market value ($ mil.)	–	–	–	–	–	–
Employees	–	–	–	–	–	150

LOWELL, CITY OF (INC)

375 MERRIMACK ST RM 27
LOWELL, MA 018525939
Phone: 978-970-4200
Fax: –
Web: www.lowellma.gov

CEO: –
CFO: Thomas Moses
HR: –
FYE: June 30
Type: Private

The City of Lowell is the fourth-largest city in Massachusetts with a population of more than 100000. The mayor and seven city council members (elected for two-year terms) govern the city by setting policies as well as appointing heads of departments boards and commissions. The City of Lowell operates through nearly 30 departments and programs including emergency management recycling and veterans' services. Located about 30 miles northwest of Boston Lowell was established in 1826 as a planned industrial city. CVS and the Market Basket grocery store chain were both founded in Lowell.

	Annual Growth	06/05	06/06	06/15	06/16	06/18
Sales ($ mil.)	–	–	0.0	371.8	385.5	422.5
Net income ($ mil.)	–	–	0.0	10.0	(1.5)	(0.7)
Market value ($ mil.)	–	–	–	–	–	–
Employees	–	–	–	–	–	3,000

LOWE'S COMPANIES INC

NYS: LOW

1000 Lowes Blvd.
Mooresville, NC 28117
Phone: 704 758-1000
Fax: –
Web: www.lowes.com

CEO: Marvin Ellison
CFO: David Denton
HR: Janice Dupre
FYE: January 29
Type: Public

Lowe's Companies is a Fortune 50 company and the world's second largest home improvement retailer. Its stores offer approximately 40000 products for repair and improvement projects (such as lumber paint plumbing and electrical supplies and tools) gardening and outdoor living and home furnishing and decorating. It targets homeowners renters and professional customers with national brand-name merchandise as well as its own private labels including Kobalt (tools) Harbor Breeze (ceiling fans) Sta-Green (lawn and garden products) Moxie (cleaning products) and Style Selection (home décor products) among other. The company only operates in North America with the vast majority of sales generated in the US.

	Annual Growth	02/17	02/18	02/19*	01/20	01/21
Sales ($ mil.)	8.3%	65,017.0	68,619.0	71,309.0	72,148.0	89,597.0
Net income ($ mil.)	17.2%	3,093.0	3,447.0	2,314.0	4,281.0	5,835.0
Market value ($ mil.)	22.8%	53,575.0	74,196.5	70,987.4	84,971.4	121,967.4
Employees	4.1%	290,000	310,000	300,000	320,000	340,000

*Fiscal year change

LOWER COLORADO RIVER AUTHORITY

3700 LAKE AUSTIN BLVD
AUSTIN, TX 787033504
Phone: 512-473-3200
Fax: –
Web: www.lcra.org

CEO: –
CFO: Richard Williams
HR: –
FYE: June 30
Type: Private

The Lower Colorado River Authority serves customers and communities throughout Texas by managing the lower Colorado River; generating and transmitting electric power; providing a clean reliable water supply; and offering outdoor adventures at more than 40 parks along the Colorado River from the Texas Hill Country to the Gulf Coast. LCRA and its employees are committed to fulfilling its mission to enhance the quality of life of the Texans it serves through water stewardship energy and community service. LCRA was created by the Texas Legislature in 1934 and receives no state appropriations.

	Annual Growth	06/09	06/10	06/11	06/12	06/15
Sales ($ mil.)	(3.9%)	–	1,244.4	1,185.8	1,261.7	1,021.3
Net income ($ mil.)	(32.5%)	–	110.6	48.9	101.4	15.5
Market value ($ mil.)	–	–	–	–	–	–
Employees	–	–	–	–	–	1,800

LOYOLA MARYMOUNT UNIVERSITY

1 LMU DR UHALL STE 4900
LOS ANGELES, CA 90045
Phone: 310-338-2700
Fax: -
Web: www.lmu.edu

CEO: Thomas O Fleming
CFO: Aimee Uen
HR: -
FYE: May 31
Type: Private

Loyola Marymount University (LMU) in Los Angeles is a Jesuit (Catholic) institution with an enrollment of more than 9500 students. It offers more than 115 graduate and undergraduate programs through four colleges: Bellarmine College of Liberal Arts College of Business Administration College of Communication and Fine Arts and Seaver College of Science and Engineering. There is also the School of Education and School of Film and Television. Other programs include the Graduate Division Continuing Education Program and Loyola Law School. LMU has an 11:1 student-to-faculty ratio. The university was formed in 1973 by the merger of Loyola College (founded in 1911) and Marymount Junior College.

	Annual Growth	05/17	05/18	05/19	05/20	05/21
Sales ($ mil.)	(1.5%)	-	393.3	415.6	411.5	375.4
Net income ($ mil.)	50.2%	-	51.6	20.1	8.7	174.9
Market value ($ mil.)	-	-	-	-	-	-
Employees	-	-	-	-	-	1,449

LOYOLA UNIVERSITY MARYLAND, INC.

5000 YORK RD STE 200
BALTIMORE, MD 212124437
Phone: 410-617-2000
Fax: -
Web: www.loyola.edu

CEO: -
CFO: -
HR: -
FYE: May 31
Type: Private

Loyola University in Maryland is a Jesuit Catholic university that offers studies in liberal arts and sciences. In addition to its undergraduate programs Loyola has graduate degree programs in education speech pathology finance psychology modern studies pastoral counseling and engineering science. The university annually enrolls about 3500 undergraduate and some 2600 graduate students. The school has more than 300 full-time faculty and a student-teacher ratio of about 12:1. Loyola was founded in 1852 by Father John Early and eight other Jesuits.

	Annual Growth	05/10	05/11	05/12	05/13	05/14
Sales ($ mil.)	24.2%	-	-	185.2	263.0	285.6
Net income ($ mil.)	-	-	-	(2.3)	19.5	27.7
Market value ($ mil.)	-	-	-	-	-	-
Employees	-	-	-	-	-	2,066

LOYOLA UNIVERSITY NEW ORLEANS INC

6363 SAINT CHARLES AVE
NEW ORLEANS, LA 701186195
Phone: 504-865-2011
Fax: -
Web: www.loyno.edu

CEO: -
CFO: -
HR: -
FYE: July 31
Type: Private

Loyola University New Orleans provides law nursing and fine arts education programs in the Big Easy. The university is part of US network of Jesuit universities and enrolls nearly 4550 students. The liberal arts university offers some 110 undergraduate and about 35 graduate and professional degree programs through five colleges: Business Arts and Sciences Nursing & Health Law Music and Media as well as online studies. Loyola University New Orleans has a student-to-teacher ratio of 12:1. It is one of a network of 28 Jesuit colleges and universities across the US.

	Annual Growth	07/11	07/12	07/13	07/14	07/20
Sales ($ mil.)	4.5%	-	126.7	154.3	135.0	180.7
Net income ($ mil.)	-	-	(16.0)	26.3	3.2	(0.2)
Market value ($ mil.)	-	-	-	-	-	-
Employees	-	-	-	-	-	1,000

LOYOLA UNIVERSITY OF CHICAGO INC

1032 W SHERIDAN RD
CHICAGO, IL 606601537
Phone: 773-274-3000
Fax: -
Web: www.luc.edu

CEO: -
CFO: -
HR: -
FYE: June 30
Type: Private

Loyola University is a Jesuit Catholic university with a reach that extends far beyond the Windy City. In addition to its three Chicago-area campuses the university also maintains an undergraduate campus in Italy and a study center in Beijing China. Loyola University's nearly 14765 students can choose from more than 80 undergraduate nearly 100 master's a dozen doctoral and more than 140 graduate professional and certificate programs. With nearly 1390 full-time faculty and staff members the not-for-profit school has a 15:1 student-teacher ratio. Notable alumni include actor Bob Newhart and writer Sandra Cisneros. Established in 1870 by a group of Jesuit priests the university turned its medical center into a separate subsidiary in 1995.

	Annual Growth	06/17	06/18	06/19	06/20	06/21
Sales ($ mil.)	(2.3%)	-	594.8	614.2	611.4	554.1
Net income ($ mil.)	40.2%	-	109.5	78.7	23.4	302.0
Market value ($ mil.)	-	-	-	-	-	-
Employees	-	-	-	-	-	10,500

LOZIER CORPORATION

6336 JOHN J PERSHING DR
OMAHA, NE 681101122
Phone: 402-457-8000
Fax: -
Web: www.lozier.com

CEO: Andy Lozier
CFO: Matt Simon
HR: -
FYE: December 26
Type: Private

Lozier is a leader in the manufacturing store fixtures industry. The company makes retail store fixtures including gondolas display shelving and freestanding displays for pharmacy groceries food service convenience store and hardware. It has manufacturing facilities and a distribution center in Alabama Indiana Missouri Nebraska and Pennsylvania. Lozier distributes fixtures across the US as well as internationally. The company maintains a sales and service network for its international retailers. In addition to selling fixtures Lozier also offers installation services. To expedite parcel pickup and simplify the order fulfillment process the company offers Buy Online Pick up In Store (BOPIS) products and solutions.

	Annual Growth	12/16	12/17	12/18	12/19	12/20
Sales ($ mil.)	(9.6%)	-	-	552.5	525.2	451.4
Net income ($ mil.)	-	-	-	0.0	0.0	0.0
Market value ($ mil.)	-	-	-	-	-	-
Employees	-	-	-	-	-	2,210

LPL FINANCIAL HOLDINGS INC.

NMS: LPLA

4707 Executive Drive
San Diego, CA 92121
Phone: 800 877-7210
Fax: -
Web: www.lpl.com

CEO: Dan Arnold
CFO: Matthew Audette
HR: -
FYE: December 31
Type: Public

LPL Financial is a leader in the retail financial advice market and the nation's largest independent broker-dealer. It provides technology research clearing and compliance services and practice management to some 17300 independent financial advisors financial institutions (such as credit unions) across the country. LPL also supports some 3000 advisors affiliated with insurance companies that use LPL's clearing and advisory platforms. LPL was formed in 1989 by the merger of Linsco and Private Ledger.

	Annual Growth	12/16	12/17	12/18	12/19	12/20
Sales ($ mil.)	9.7%	4,049.4	4,281.5	5,188.4	5,624.9	5,871.6
Net income ($ mil.)	25.3%	191.9	238.9	439.5	559.9	472.6
Market value ($ mil.)	31.2%	2,798.2	4,541.0	4,854.1	7,331.2	8,282.4
Employees	9.7%	3,288	3,736	4,229	4,343	4,756

LRI HOLDINGS INC.

3011 Armory Dr. Ste. 300
Nashville TN 37204
Phone: 615-885-9056
Fax: 615-885-9057
Web: www.logansroadhouse.com

CEO: Samuel Borgese
CFO: Edmund J Schwartz
HR: Michael Martin
FYE: July 31
Type: Private

LRI Holdings earns a lot of peanuts even though it gives them away for free. The company operates Logan's Roadhouse a chain of casual restaurants that serve generous-sized plates of grilled steaks chicken barbecued ribs and hamburgers. The chain prides itself on its affordable prices (the average bill is less than $15) while also offering free all-you-can-eat buckets of shelled peanuts and rolls. LRI Holdings has 185 company-owned locations of Logan's Roadhouse across 20 states and 26 franchises in four states. LRI Holdings was formed in 2006 by a private investor group. The company agreed to be acquired by private equity firm Kelso & Co. in 2010.

LRR ENERGY, L.P.   NYS: LRE

Heritage Plaza, 1111 Bagby, Suite 4600
Houston, TX 77002
Phone: 713 292-9510
Fax: –

CEO: –
CFO: Richard A Robert
HR: –
FYE: December 31
Type: Public

What do Texas Oklahoma and New Mexico have in common? Oil gas and LRR Energy. An oil and natural gas producer LRR Energy owns assets in the Permian Basin in West Texas and southern New Mexico the Mid-Continent region in Oklahoma and East Texas and along the Gulf Coast in Texas. The company's properties have proved reserves of more than 30 million barrels of oil equivalent. It operates more than 850 oil or gas-producing wells. Formed in April 2011 from assets held by investment fund Lime Rock Resources LRR Energy and went public in November 2011.

	Annual Growth	12/09	12/10	12/11	12/12	12/13
Sales ($ mil.)	–	0.0	0.0	21.8	105.5	115.1
Net income ($ mil.)	–	0.0	0.0	12.2	(0.0)	(48.7)
Market value ($ mil.)	–	0.0	0.0	515.8	452.1	447.9
Employees	–	–	–	–	–	–

LSB FINANCIAL CORP.   NMS: LSBI

101 Main Street
Lafayette, IN 47901
Phone: 765 742-1064
Fax: –
Web: www.lsbank.com

CEO: Randolph F Williams
CFO: Mary Jo David
HR: –
FYE: December 31
Type: Public

There's nothing psychedelic about LSB. Straight-laced LSB Financial is the holding company for Lafayette Savings Bank which has been serving northern Indiana since 1869. Today the bank has a handful of branches in the communities of Lafayette and West Lafayette offering checking savings and money market accounts NOW accounts and CDs. It primarily writes real estate loans with residential mortgages making up about half of the company's loan portfolio. It also writes commercial and multifamily residential mortgages real estate construction loans and land development loans.

	Annual Growth	12/08	12/09	12/10	12/11	12/12
Assets ($ mil.)	(0.6%)	373.0	371.1	371.8	364.3	364.6
Net income ($ mil.)	11.2%	1.7	0.5	2.1	0.5	2.7
Market value ($ mil.)	18.6%	15.5	15.2	21.1	21.0	30.7
Employees	1.3%	91	97	93	100	96

LSB INDUSTRIES, INC.   NYS: LXU

3503 N.W. 63rd Street, Suite 500
Oklahoma City, OK 73116
Phone: 405 235-4546
Fax: –
Web: www.lsbindustries.com

CEO: Mark Behrman
CFO: Cheryl Maguire
HR: –
FYE: December 31
Type: Public

LSB Industries makes and markets a wide variety of chemicals (including nitric acid). Its chemical business makes grade ammonium nitrate fertilizers urea ammonia nitrate and nitric acids for agricultural mining and industrial markets. LSB Industries products are sold through distributors and directly to end customers throughout the US and parts of Mexico and Canada. It produces ammonia at its El Dorado Cherokee and Pryor Facilities. Founded in 1968 the company's agricultural products account for about 50% of the company revenues.

	Annual Growth	12/16	12/17	12/18	12/19	12/20
Sales ($ mil.)	(1.6%)	374.6	427.5	378.2	365.1	351.3
Net income ($ mil.)	–	112.2	(29.2)	(72.2)	(63.4)	(61.9)
Market value ($ mil.)	(20.3%)	319.7	332.6	209.6	159.5	128.7
Employees	(1.6%)	610	569	576	593	573

LSI CORP   NMS: LSI

1320 Ridder Park Drive
San Jose, CA 95131
Phone: 408 433-8000
Fax: –
Web: www.lsi.com

CEO: Hock E Tan
CFO: –
HR: –
FYE: December 31
Type: Public

LSI can show you around the circuit. The fabless semiconductor developer provides standard integrated circuits (ICs) and custom-designed application-specific ICs (ASICs) focusing on broadband and wireless communications data storage personal computer and networking markets. LSI (an acronym for large-scale integration) was a pioneer of system-on-a-chip (SoC) devices which combine elements of an electronic system — essentially a microprocessor memory and logic — onto a single chip. LSI also provides hardware and software for storage area networks. Customers located in the Asia/Pacific region account for most of the company's sales. LSI has agreed to be acquired by Avago Technologies for $6.6 billion.

	Annual Growth	12/08	12/09	12/10	12/11	12/12
Sales ($ mil.)	(1.6%)	2,677.1	2,219.2	2,570.0	2,044.0	2,506.1
Net income ($ mil.)	–	(622.3)	(47.7)	40.0	331.5	196.2
Market value ($ mil.)	21.1%	1,812.4	3,310.9	3,299.9	3,277.8	3,894.8
Employees	(1.9%)	5,488	5,397	5,718	4,588	5,080

LSI INDUSTRIES INC.   NMS: LYTS

10000 Alliance Road
Cincinnati, OH 45242
Phone: 513 793-3200
Fax: –
Web: www.lsicorp.com

CEO: James Clark
CFO: James Galeese
HR: Thomas Caneris
FYE: June 30
Type: Public

LSI Industries makes lighting graphics and menu boards for various commercial markets primarily in the US and Canada. LSI operates via several business segments. Its lighting unit makes LED light fixtures for outdoor/indoor/landscape use such as convenience and chain store lighting. A graphics arm produces indoor/outdoor graphics lighting and menu boards including digital signage canopy graphics and shelf talkers. It products are sold primarily throughout US but also in Canada Mexico Australia and Latin America (outside of US generates some 5% of total revenue). Founded in 1976 LSI went public in 1985.

	Annual Growth	06/17	06/18	06/19	06/20	06/21
Sales ($ mil.)	(1.2%)	331.4	342.0	328.9	305.6	315.6
Net income ($ mil.)	18.3%	3.0	(19.5)	(16.3)	9.6	5.9
Market value ($ mil.)	(3.0%)	240.0	141.6	96.8	171.6	212.4
Employees	(0.2%)	1,345	1,346	1,246	1,101	1,335

LTC PROPERTIES, INC.

2829 Townsgate Road, Suite 350
Westlake Village, CA 91361
Phone: 805 981-8655
Fax: –
Web: www.ltcreit.com

CEO: Wendy Simpson
CFO: Pamela Shelley-Kessler
HR: –
FYE: December 31
Type: Public

NYS: LTC

Specializing in TLC LTC Properties sees long-term care real estate as a healthy investment. The self-administered real estate investment trust (REIT) mostly invests in health care and long-term care facilities. Its portfolio includes about 200 assisted living skilled-nursing and other healthcare properties with more than 15000 living units across about 30 states with its largest markets being in Texas Florida Colorado and Arizona. Its top tenant operators include Brookdale Senior Living Carespring Senior Care Centers and Senior Lifestyle Corporation which in aggregate contribute around 45% to its total rental income. The REIT also invests in mortgage loans tied to long-term care properties.

	Annual Growth	12/17	12/18	12/19	12/20	12/21
Sales ($ mil.)	(2.0%)	168.1	168.6	185.3	159.3	155.3
Net income ($ mil.)	(10.6%)	87.3	155.0	80.5	95.3	55.9
Market value ($ mil.)	(5.9%)	1,714.7	1,641.1	1,762.8	1,532.0	1,344.2
Employees	5.7%	20	21	22	24	25

LUBY'S, INC.

13111 Northwest Freeway, Suite 600
Houston, TX 77040
Phone: 713 329-6800
Fax: 210 654-3211
Web: www.lubysinc.com

CEO: John Garilli
CFO: Eric Montague
HR: –
FYE: August 26
Type: Public

NYS: LUB

This company has a spot in the cafeteria line and behind the burger grill. Luby's is a multi-branded company in the restaurant industry and in the contract food services with two flagship brands: Luby's and Fuddruckers. Its namesake chain includes about 85 restaurants found almost entirely in Texas that offer a large variety of different entrees salads and desserts. Its menu is heavy on such comfort foods as fried fish macaroni and cheese and Chicken Tetrazzini. Luby's also operates and franchises about 70 Fuddruckers locations in the US that serves the World's Greatest Hamburgers. In addition the company owns several smaller chains and provides contract foodservices for organizations that offer on-site food service such as healthcare facilities colleges and universities sports stadiums businesses and institutions as well as sales through retail grocery outlets.

	Annual Growth	08/16	08/17	08/18	08/19	08/20
Sales ($ mil.)	(14.6%)	402.6	376.0	365.2	323.5	214.0
Net income ($ mil.)	–	(10.3)	(23.3)	(33.6)	(15.2)	(29.5)
Market value ($ mil.)	(29.7%)	137.8	80.9	62.5	45.3	33.7
Employees	(21.2%)	7,988	7,320	6,589	6,133	3,074

LUCASFILM ENTERTAINMENT COMPANY LTD.

1110 Gorgas Ave.
San Francisco CA 94129
Phone: 415-746-8000
Fax: +82-2-3773-2292
Web: www.lg.co.kr

CEO: –
CFO: –
HR: –
FYE: April 30
Type: Subsidiary

Not so long ago in a galaxy not so far away filmmaker George Lucas founded a software company to entertain audiences with something other than movies. Lucasfilm Entertainment (which does business as LucasArts) produces games for computers and home video game consoles. Much of that source material is of course the "Star Wars" films created by Lucas. LucasArts has more "Star Wars" games than you can shake a lightsaber at and it also produces games based on Lucasfilm's successful trilogy of "Indiana Jones" films as well as other titles such as the popular and acclaimed Monkey Island series. LucasArts' products are distributed in about 60 countries worldwide through its own distribution efforts and those of partners.

LUCID INC.

2320 Brighton Henrietta Town Line Rd.
Rochester NY 14623
Phone: 585-239-9800
Fax: 585-239-9806
Web: www.lucid-tech.com

CEO: L Michael Hone
CFO: John Sprague
HR: –
FYE: December 31
Type: Private

Lucid Inc. hopes to have a clear understanding of skin cancer. The company's medical imaging device the VivaScope cuts down on the ouch factor for skin biopsies. The VivaScope takes a microscopic-resolution picture of a skin lesion a less painful alternative to the traditional method of cutting out a portion of the lesion to ship off to the lab. Lucid Inc. has also developed a complementary network called VivaNet that allows immediate transfer of the images over the Internet for pathologists to diagnose melanoma and give patients same-day results. The VivaScope is cleared for sale and use in Australia China the European Union and the US. Lucid Inc. filed a modest $28.75 million IPO in April 2011.

LUCKEY FARMERS, INC.

1200 W MAIN ST
WOODVILLE, OH 434699701
Phone: 419-849-2711
Fax: –
Web: www.luckeyfarmers.com

CEO: Daniel Walski
CFO: –
HR: –
FYE: January 31
Type: Private

You don't have to be lucky to be a grain farmer in northwestern Ohio but the members of Luckey Farmers agricultural cooperative might feel fortunate just the same. The co-op offers services such as grain storage and marketing for the corn soybean and wheat crops of its member-farmers. It supplies its members with grain marketing and agronomy services and information feed and seed processing facilities gas stations and fuel-delivery services. Luckey Farmers which has approximately 2000 member/farmers was established in 1919.

	Annual Growth	01/03	01/04	01/05	01/06	01/07
Sales ($ mil.)	(7.7%)	–	–	95.6	72.3	81.4
Net income ($ mil.)	7019.8%	–	–	0.0	0.9	0.7
Market value ($ mil.)	–	–	–	–	–	–
Employees	–	–	–	–	–	115

LUCY WEBB HAYES NATIONAL TRAINING SCHOOL FOR DEACONESSES AND MISSIONARIES

5255 LOUGHBORO RD NW
WASHINGTON, DC 200162633
Phone: 202-537-4257
Fax: –
Web: www.hopkinsmedicine.org

CEO: –
CFO: –
HR: –
FYE: June 30
Type: Private

The Lucy Webb Hayes National Training School for Deaconesses and Missionaries commonly known as Sibley Memorial Hospital provides medical surgical therapeutic assisted living and home care services in Washington DC. Sibley Memorial is a not-for-profit acute-care community facility with some 320 beds. Sibley Memorial specializes in obstetrics neurology and thoracic care among other medical areas. Lucy Webb Hayes was the wife of Rutherford B. Hayes the 19th president of the United States. Troops commanded by her husband during the Civil War referred to Lucy Webb Hayes as as "Mother Lucy" for her tending of the wounded and dying. Sibley Memorial was acquired by Johns Hopkins Medicine in 2010.

	Annual Growth	06/13	06/14	06/15	06/16	06/19
Sales ($ mil.)	13.4%	–	–	252.7	267.9	418.3
Net income ($ mil.)	105.4%	–	–	7.4	6.1	131.1
Market value ($ mil.)	–	–	–	–	–	–
Employees	–	–	–	–	–	2,000

LUMEN TECHNOLOGIES INC
NYS: LUMN

100 CenturyLink Drive
Monroe, LA 71203
Phone: 318 388-9000
Fax: 318 789-8656
Web: www.lumen.com

CEO: Jeffrey Storey
CFO: Indraneel Dev
HR: Scott Trezise
FYE: December 31
Type: Public

Lumen (formerly CenturyLink) provides cyber links throughout the country on one of the longest fiber networks in the US. Historically a regional wireline local and long-distance telephone provider it is connecting with the times by transforming into a broadband and network services provider for business residential wholesale and government clients. The company is the one of the largest US wireline telecom companies with about 450000 route miles of fiber optic cable globally. Serving more than 60 countries most of its revenue comes from the US.

	Annual Growth	12/16	12/17	12/18	12/19	12/20
Sales ($ mil.)	4.3%	17,470.0	17,656.0	23,443.0	22,401.0	20,712.0
Net income ($ mil.)	–	626.0	1,389.0	(1,733.0)	(5,269.0)	(1,232.0)
Market value ($ mil.)	(20.0%)	26,084.8	18,296.6	16,618.4	14,490.3	10,695.0
Employees	(0.6%)	40,000	51,000	45,000	42,500	39,000

LUMINEX CORP
NMS: LMNX

12212 Technology Blvd.
Austin, TX 78727
Phone: 512 219-8020
Fax: –
Web: www.luminexcorp.com

CEO: Nachum Shamir
CFO: –
HR: –
FYE: December 31
Type: Public

William Blake could "see a world in a grain of sand" and Luminex can reveal hundreds of secrets in a drop of fluid. Its xMAP (Multi-Analyte Profiling) technology allows simultaneous analysis of up to 500 bioassays or tests from a single drop of fluid. xMAP consists of instruments software and disposable microspheres (microscopic polystyrene beads on which tests are performed). Luminex also uses Multi-Code real-time polymerase chain reaction and xTAG technology. Luminex's systems are used by clinical and research laboratories and are distributed through strategic partnerships with other life sciences firms. Luminex also develops testing assays and disposable testing supplies for the clinical diagnostics market.

	Annual Growth	12/15	12/16	12/17	12/18	12/19
Sales ($ mil.)	8.9%	237.7	270.6	306.6	315.8	334.6
Net income ($ mil.)	–	36.9	13.8	29.4	18.5	(3.8)
Market value ($ mil.)	2.0%	948.1	896.7	873.2	1,024.4	1,026.6
Employees	12.1%	797	936	896	988	1,257

LUMINIS HEALTH ANNE ARUNDEL MEDICAL CENTER, INC

2001 MEDICAL PKWY
ANNAPOLIS, MD 214013773
Phone: 443-481-1000
Fax: –
Web: www.aahs.org

CEO: –
CFO: –
HR: –
FYE: June 30
Type: Private

The ill and infirm get the royal treatment at Anne Arundel Medical Center. The full-service acute-care hospital serves the residents of Anne Arundel Calvert Prince George's and Queen Anne counties in Maryland. With about 425 beds the hospital administers care for women's health oncology pediatrics (it has a level III neonatal intensive care unit) neurology orthopedics and cardiovascular care. The medical center also has weight loss sleep disorder and rehabilitation centers. Anne Arundel which opened its doors in 1902 and is part of the Anne Arundel Health System has expanded its service offerings through various affiliations with regional specialty and primary care clinics. It also has a partnership with Johns Hopkins Medicine.

	Annual Growth	06/12	06/13	06/14	06/15	06/19
Sales ($ mil.)	2.7%	–	493.1	492.2	526.0	579.4
Net income ($ mil.)	0.3%	–	16.8	20.2	40.0	17.1
Market value ($ mil.)	–	–	–	–	–	–
Employees	–	–	–	–	–	1,890

LUMOS NETWORKS CORP
NMS: LMOS

One Lumos Plaza
Waynesboro, VA 22980
Phone: 540 946-2000
Fax: –
Web: www.lumosnetworks.com

CEO: Timothy G Biltz
CFO: Johan G Broekhuysen
HR: –
FYE: December 31
Type: Public

Lumos Networks hopes your every telephone conversation is illuminating. The company spun off from wireless operator NTELOS in 2011 comprises NTELOS' wireline business. Lumos Networks provides data voice and IP service to carrier business government and residential customers over a 7800-mile fiber network in the Mid-Atlantic region (Virginia West Virginia and portions of Kentucky Maryland Ohio and Pennsylvania). Its network allows it to offer bundled cable internet and phone service. It also operates as a rural local-exchange carrier (RLEC) in the rural Virginia cities of Waynesboro and Covington and portions of Alleghany Augusta and Botetourt counties. The company was acquired by EQT Partners in 2017.

	Annual Growth	12/11	12/12	12/13	12/14	12/15
Sales ($ mil.)	(0.4%)	207.4	206.9	207.5	201.5	204.3
Net income ($ mil.)	–	(43.9)	16.3	17.8	21.5	10.0
Market value ($ mil.)	(7.6%)	352.7	230.4	482.8	386.7	257.5
Employees	3.1%	524	602	579	604	593

LUMOS PHARMA INC
NMS: LUMO

4200 Marathon Blvd #200
Austin, TX 78756
Phone: 512 215-2630
Fax: –
Web: www.newlinkgenetics.com

CEO: Richard Hawkins
CFO: Lori Lawley
HR: –
FYE: December 31
Type: Public

Lumos Pharma is hoping to give a boost to the immune systems of cancer patients. A biopharmaceutical company focused on discovering cancer treatments Lumos Pharma develops and commercializes small-molecule immunotherapy therapies that stimulate patients' immune systems. The company's leading small-molecule product candidates currently in clinical development target the indoleamine-2 3-dioxygenase (IDO) pathway which is one of the key pathways for cancer immune escape. In 2020 Newlink Genetics merged with Lumos Pharma and took its name.

	Annual Growth	12/16	12/17	12/18	12/19	12/20
Sales ($ mil.)	(73.8%)	35.8	28.7	12.5	0.9	0.2
Net income ($ mil.)	–	(85.2)	(72.0)	(53.6)	(43.0)	(5.7)
Market value ($ mil.)	36.5%	85.4	67.4	12.6	21.0	296.6
Employees	(28.4%)	122	76	55	21	32

LUNA INNOVATIONS INC
NAS: LUNA

301 First Street SW, Suite 200
Roanoke, VA 24011
Phone: 540 769-8400
Fax: –
Web: www.lunainc.com

CEO: Scott Graeff
CFO: Eugene Nestro
HR: –
FYE: December 31
Type: Public

Luna Innovations is a research and development firm. The company makes practical use of cutting-edge technologies in the areas of molecular technology and sensing. Its molecular technology efforts focus on materials (including polymers reagents and nanomaterials) with enhanced performance characteristics; Luna has developed contrast agents for MRI testing nanomaterials used in solar cells and protective coatings. It has also created sensing technologies used in medical monitoring equipment as well as wireless and fiber-optic monitoring systems for defense and industrial instrumentation. In mid-2015 Luna Innovations merged with Advanced Photonix.

	Annual Growth	12/16	12/17	12/18	12/19	12/20
Sales ($ mil.)	8.7%	59.2	46.2	42.9	70.5	82.7
Net income ($ mil.)	–	(2.4)	14.6	11.0	5.3	3.3
Market value ($ mil.)	61.0%	45.6	75.4	103.9	226.2	306.5
Employees	14.8%	245	198	196	267	426

LUTHER COLLEGE

700 COLLEGE DR
DECORAH, IA 521011041
Phone: 563-387-1372
Fax: –
Web: www.luther.edu

CEO: –
CFO: –
HR: –
FYE: May 31
Type: Private

Luther College is an independent liberal arts school offering undergraduate and graduate programs to about 2500 students from about 35 states and 40 countries. The college provides more than 60 majors and professional certificate programs. The Luther student body has more than 110 student-run clubs and organizations 19 athletic teams and 15 student music ensembles. Courses are conducted by 181 full-time teaching faculty members 89% with Ph.D. or equivalent. The ratio of students to faculty is 12:1. Luther College is affiliated with the Evangelical Lutheran Church in America.

	Annual Growth	05/14	05/15	05/16	05/17	05/18
Sales ($ mil.)	(1.9%)	–	80.2	78.5	78.8	75.7
Net income ($ mil.)	–	–	(1.0)	(2.7)	9.6	5.7
Market value ($ mil.)	–	–	–	–	–	–
Employees	–	–	–	–	–	550

LUTHERAN MEDICAL CENTER

150 55th St.
Brooklyn NY 11220
Phone: 718-630-7000
Fax: 317-848-0713
Web: www.deltafaucet.com

CEO: –
CFO: –
HR: –
FYE: December 31
Type: Private - Not-for-Pr

Unlike the Dodgers Lutheran Medical Center isn't leaving Brooklyn. The health care system serves patients in the New York City borough through a network that includes its primary Lutheran Medical Center (LMC) as well as the 240-bed skilled nursing facility Lutheran Augustana Center for Extended Care and Rehabilitation and several neighborhood clinics and nursing homes. LMC is a 470-bed tertiary care teaching hospital affiliated with the State University of New York Health Science Center at Brooklyn and other university medical programs. Lutheran Medical Center also operates a home health program under the Community Care Organization name. It's a social ministry of the Evangelical Lutheran Church in America.

LXP INDUSTRIAL TRUST

One Penn Plaza, Suite 4015
New York, NY 10119-4015
Phone: 212 692-7200
Fax: –
Web: www.lxp.com

NYS: LXP
CEO: T. Wilson Eglin
CFO: Beth Boulerice
HR: Sara Klein
FYE: December 31
Type: Public

Lexington Realty Trust is a self-managed real estate investment trust (REIT) that owns and manages approximately 130 consolidated real estate properties in about 30 states and containing an aggregate of more than 52 million sq. ft. of rentable space. The trust also provides financing for mortgage and loans. Most properties are subject to net or similar leases in which tenants are responsible for expenses such as real estate taxes and repairs. Its property occupancy rate is more than 95%. Prominent tenants include Dow Nissan and Dana.

	Annual Growth	12/16	12/17	12/18	12/19	12/20
Sales ($ mil.)	(6.3%)	429.5	391.6	395.3	326.0	330.4
Net income ($ mil.)	17.7%	95.6	85.6	227.4	279.9	183.3
Market value ($ mil.)	(0.4%)	2,993.2	2,674.5	2,275.4	2,943.4	2,943.4
Employees	(1.3%)	59	59	60	57	56

LYDALL, INC.

One Colonial Road
Manchester, CT 06042
Phone: 860 646-1233
Fax: 860 646-4917
Web: www.lydall.com

NYS: LDL
CEO: John Dandolph
CFO: –
HR: –
FYE: December 31
Type: Public

Lydall's products help to beat the heat nix the noise and filter the rest. The company makes specialty engineered nonwoven filtration media industrial thermal insulating solutions and thermal and acoustical barriers for filtration/separation and heat abatement and sound dampening applications. Lydall's products are sold to original equipment manufacturers (OEMs) and tier-one suppliers. Its brands are Fiberlox Checkstatic Microfelt and Pleatlox. One of its customers is Ford Motor Company. The company was founded in 1869 and generates more than half of its sales in its home country the US.

	Annual Growth	12/15	12/16	12/17	12/18	12/19
Sales ($ mil.)	12.4%	524.5	566.9	698.4	785.9	837.4
Net income ($ mil.)	–	46.3	37.2	49.3	34.9	(70.5)
Market value ($ mil.)	(12.8%)	625.2	1,089.9	894.3	357.9	361.6
Employees	11.5%	2,100	2,700	2,600	3,300	3,250

LYNTEGAR ELECTRIC COOPERATIVE, INC.

1701 US HWY 87 W ACCSS RD
TAHOKA, TX 79373
Phone: 806-561-4588
Fax: –
Web: www.lyntegar.coop

CEO: Greg Henley
CFO: –
HR: Jana Bishop
FYE: December 31
Type: Private

Lyntegar Electric Cooperative is based in the agricultural heart of the Texas Panhandle where the summer heat sizzles and the winter ice storms freeze. The rural power cooperative provides electric utility services to customers in Borden Dawson Gaines Garza Hockley Lynn Martin Terry and Yoakum counties. The cooperative also sells electric grills and provides internet and television services. In addition Lyntegar Electric Cooperative produces Typically Texas Cookbooks which share collections of recipes used by cooperative member-consumers.

	Annual Growth	12/13	12/14	12/15	12/16	12/17
Sales ($ mil.)	(2.4%)	–	76.3	58.1	63.2	70.9
Net income ($ mil.)	5.1%	–	6.2	3.1	3.7	7.2
Market value ($ mil.)	–	–	–	–	–	–
Employees	–	–	–	–	–	117

LYNUXWORKS INC.

855 Embedded Way
San Jose CA 95138-1018
Phone: 408-979-3900
Fax: 408-979-3920
Web: www.lynuxworks.com

CEO: Gurjot Singh
CFO: –
HR: –
FYE: April 30
Type: Private

LynxWorks works hard to make Linux work for its clients. The company's LynxOS and BlueCat operating systems power miniaturized computers known as embedded systems that are built into hardware for airplanes cellular phone switches copiers and other products. LynxWorks caters to embedded systems developers working with Linux the open-source operating system that has found some favor over Microsoft operating systems for speed and flexibility. The company also provides consulting technical training and support services as well as its LynxSecure technology which is used for securely running multiple operating systems simultaneously.